HARRAP'S POCKET

English-French
DICTIONARY

DICTIONNAIRE
Français-Anglais

Editor/Rédacteur
Michael Janes

Consultant Editors
Avec la collaboration de
Fabrice Antoine
Isabelle Elkaim

HARRAP

First published in Great Britain 1988
by Harrap Books Ltd
43-45 Annandale Street, Edinburgh EH7 4AZ, UK

© Chambers Harrap Publishers Ltd 1995

ISBN 0 245 60575 4

(Also available, in PVC,
as Harrap's *Pocket Plus Dictionary*,
0 245 60523 1)

Typeset by Morton Word Processing Ltd
Printed in Great Britain by Mackays of Chatham PLC

Contents/Table des matières

Trademarks

Marques Déposées

Preface

This dictionary, based on the text of Harrap's *Pocket French-English Dictionary*, is a new publication offering a wide-ranging selection of the most useful words and expressions of French and English. A large amount of new material has been incorporated as well as extensive examples of usage and a great deal of helpful grammatical and context information. A handy, reliable and up-to-date work of reference, the dictionary aims to provide a high level of understanding of the French and English languages of today for students and general users alike.

The text is presented in a clear and attractive form with grammatical categories and sense divisions in longer entries starting on a new line. In order to save space, some derived words are included within the entry of the main headword. All such forms are written in full and highlighted by means of the symbol ● to make them easy to find.

Dictionary entries consist of headwords followed by pronunciation and part of speech. When there is more than one translation, context words in brackets are supplied to help the user make the correct choice. Further guidance in the understanding of translations is provided by the use of labels to indicate the level of style (eg *Fam* for 'familiar' or colloquial) or to define a particular usage or field (eg *Am* for 'American' or *Comptr* for 'computing'). Context words and labels are also given when considered helpful for the understanding of single translations (eg **article** *n* (*object, clause, in newspaper*) & *Grammar* article *m*, or **putty** *n* mastic *m* (*pour vitres*)). The user is also helped by having context indicators and labels in French in the French section and in English in the English section of the dictionary.

Style and field labels follow bracketed indicators (eg **corn** *n* (*wheat*) *Br* blé *m*, or **bidule** *nm* (*chose*) *Fam* whatsit). In the event of more than one translation within a grammatical category being qualified by the same style or field label, the label may then precede (see **trucker** where *Am* covers both senses given).

The user will find in the text important abbreviated words in English (eg **BA, HIV**) and in French (eg **BCBG, OVNI**), useful geographical information such as names of countries, and a wide coverage of American words and usage (eg **diaper, pinkie**). The vocabulary includes French and English colloquialisms and slang, and important technical and business terms. Comparatives and superlatives of English adjectives are also indicated.

An oblique stroke within an entry is a useful space-saving device to separate non-interchangeable parts of a phrase or expression matched exactly in French and English (eg **to be able to swim/drive** savoir nager/conduire is to be understood as: **to be able to swim** savoir nager and **to be able to drive** savoir conduire).

In common with other Harrap dictionaries, when a headword appears in an example in the same form, it is represented by its initial letter (eg **at h.** stands for **at home** in headword **home**). This applies whether the headword starts a new line or appears within an entry (eg ● **household** *a* . . . **h. name** . . .).

The pronunciation of both English and French is shown using the latest symbols of the International Phonetic Alphabet. Pronunciation is given for headwords at the start of an entry, and, as an additional help to the user, for those words within the entry where the correct pronunciation may be difficult to derive (eg ● **aristocratie** [-asi] not [-ati]; ● **rabid** ['ræbɪd] not ['reɪbɪd]).

Stress in English is indicated for headwords and for derived words in which stress differs from that of a headword (eg **miracle** ['mɪrək(ə)l] and ● **mi'raculous**). American English pronunciation is listed wherever it is considered to show a marked difference from that of British English (eg **tomato** [tə'mɑːtəʊ, *Am* tə'meɪtəʊ]). American spelling is also supplied if sufficiently different from British (eg **tire** and **tyre, plow** and **plough**).

A major feature of this dictionary is its semantic approach to the order and arrangement of entries: the meaning of words determines the structure of entries. Important semantic categories have been indicated by bold Arabic numerals within an entry (eg **1, 2, 3, 4**) (see **bolt, tail, général**) or have been entered as separate headwords (see **bug**[1] and **bug**[2], **draw**[1] and **draw**[2], **start**[1] and **start**[2]). The different grammatical divisions of separate headwords are easily identified by means of the symbol **|**. The symbol **|** is used in lists of English phrasal verbs (eg **| to move along** or **| to move away**) to mark the start of each new phrasal.

Words may be entered under the headword from which they are considered to derive (eg ● **astronomer** follows **astronomy**, and ● **planétaire** follows **planète**). Present and past participles are, in most cases, entered within an entry immediately after the infinitive, any other derived words there may be following in alphabetical order (eg **accuse** *vt* ... ●**accused** *n* ... ● **accusing** *a* ... **accusation** *n*; **exagérer** *vt* ... ● **exagéré, –ée** *a* ... ● **exagération** *nf*).

The author wishes to express his gratitude to Stuart Fortey and Hazel Curties for their substantial contributions to the first edition of this dictionary, and to his wife, Susan, for her help with Americanisms.

M. Janes
London 1994

Préface

Cet ouvrage, établi à partir du Harrap's *Pocket Dictionnaire Français-Anglais*, est un dictionnaire nouveau: on y trouvera un large échantillon du vocabulaire français et anglais le plus courant et le plus utile. On y a fait figurer quantité de termes jusqu'alors absents, ainsi que de très nombreux exemples d'emploi et un grand nombre d'indications précieuses sur le contexte et le fonctionnement grammatical. C'est un outil moderne, fiable et maniable qui permettra à l'étudiant comme à l'utilisateur occasionnel de comprendre très aisément le français et l'anglais d'aujourd'hui.

Ce dictionnaire se présente sous la forme la plus claire et la plus agréable possible: les catégories grammaticales et sémantiques des articles longs sont présentées en paragraphes distincts. Par souci de concision, on a fait figurer certains dérivés au sein de l'article principal; dans ce cas, ces mots apparaissent en toutes lettres et sont repérés par le symbole ● qui permet de les localiser aisément.

Chaque article de ce dictionnaire présente le mot d'entrée suivi de sa prononciation, puis de la catégorie grammaticale à laquelle il appartient. Lorsque plusieurs traductions sont apportées, des indications de contexte sont données entre parenthèses pour guider l'utilisateur vers la traduction adéquate. Le sens des différentes traductions est éclairé encore davantage par les indications de niveau de langue (par exemple: *Fam* pour 'familier') ou de domaines d'utilisation (par exemple: *Am* pour 'américain' ou *Ordinat* pour 'informatique') données sous forme abrégée. Les mêmes indications, de contexte, de niveau de langue ou de domaine d'utilisation, accompagnent également une traduction unique d'un mot d'entrée lorsque celle-ci peut être ambiguë (par exemple: **article** *n* (*object, clause, in newspaper*) & *Grammar* article *m*, ou **putty** *n* mastic *m* (*pour vitres*)). L'accès à l'ouvrage est également facilité par l'utilisation d'indications en français dans la partie français-anglais et en anglais dans la partie anglais-français.

Les indications de niveau de langue et de domaine d'utilisation viennent à la suite de celles entre parenthèses (par exemple: **corn** *n* (*wheat*) *Br* blé *m*, ou **bidule** *nm* (*chose*) *Fam* whatsit) Lorsque plusieurs traductions dans la même catégorie grammaticale sont définies par la même indication, celle-ci peut venir en tête (voir **trucker** où l'indication *Am* concerne les deux sens envisagés).

L'utilisateur trouvera dans cet ouvrage des abréviations courantes, tant anglaises (par exemple: **BA, HIV**) que françaises (par exemple: **BCBG, OVNI**), de précieux éléments de géographie tels que des noms de pays, ainsi qu'une large sélection d'américanismes (par exemple: **diaper, pinkie**). Le lexique retenu comprend des mots et expressions familiers et argotiques, tant en français qu'en anglais, et les termes essentiels de la langue technique et des affaires. De plus, les comparatifs et superlatifs des adjectifs anglais sont indiqués.

Préface

Par souci de concision, on utilise dans le corps d'un article une barre oblique pour mettre en parallèle des expressions sans répéter un élément qui ne varie pas (par exemple: **to be able to swim/drive** savoir nager/conduire se lira: **to be able to swim** savoir nager, **to be able to drive** savoir conduire).

Comme il est d'usage dans les autres dictionnaires Harrap, lorsqu'un mot d'entrée est repris sans modification dans un exemple, il est remplacé par sa première lettre. Cela est le cas aussi bien lorsque le mot figure au début d'un article (par exemple: **at h.** se lira **at home** dans l'article **home**) ou apparaît dans le corps d'un article (par exemple: ● **household** *a* . . . **h. name** . . .).

La prononciation de l'anglais comme du français est fournie; elle utilise la notation la plus moderne de l'Alphabet Phonétique International. On donne la prononciation des mots d'entrée en début d'article, et, par souci de clarté, pour tout mot au sein de l'article dont il pourrait être difficile de déduire la prononciation (par exemple: ●**aristocratie** [-asi] et non [-ati]; ● **rabid** ['ræbɪd] et non ['reɪbɪd]).

L'accent tonique est indiqué pour les mots d'entrée anglais et pour les dérivés chaque fois que l'accentuation diffère de celle du mot principal (par exemple: **miracle** ['mɪrək(ə)l] et ● **mi'raculous**). Les prononciations américaines sont indiquées chaque fois qu'elles diffèrent nettement de celles de l'anglais britannique (par exemple: **tomato** [tə'mɑːtəʊ, *Am* tə'meɪtəʊ]). On a également fait figurer l'orthographe américaine lorsqu'elle est notablement différente de celle de l'anglais britannique (par exemple: **tire** et **tyre**, **plow** et **plough**).

Une des caractéristiques essentielles de ce dictionnaire est son approche sémantique du classement et de l'organisation des articles: c'est le sens des mots qui détermine l'organisation des articles. Les catégories sémantiques importantes sont indiquées par des chiffres arabes en gras (voir **bolt**, **tail**, **général**) ou donnent lieu à des articles séparés (voir **bug**¹ et **bug**², **draw**¹ et **draw**², **start**¹ et **start**²). Au sein d'un article, les différentes catégories grammaticales sont repérables aisément grâce au symbole ● qui les précède. Le symbole ▌ sert à repérer les verbes à particule anglais (par exemple: ▌**to move along** ou ▌**to move away**) dans une série de tels verbes.

Les mots apparaissent, dans certains cas, sous les mots d'entrée dont ils sont dérivés (par exemple: ●**astronomer** suit **astronomy**, et ● **planétaire** suit **planète**). Les participes présents et passés sont, dans la plupart des cas, placés à la suite de l'infinitif dont ils sont dérivés; tous les autres dérivés éventuels apparaissent ensuite par ordre alphabétique (par exemple: **accuse** *vt* . . . ●**accused** *n* . . . ● **accusin** *a* . . . **accusation** *n*; **exagérer** *vt* . . . ● **exagéré, –ée** *a* . . . ● **exagération** *nf*).

L'auteur tient à exprimer sa gratitude à Stuart Fortey et Hazel Curties pour leur importante contribution à la première édition du présent dictionnaire, et à son épouse, Susan, pour ses conseils et suggestions concernant les américanismes.

M. Janes
Londres 1994

Grammar Notes

In French, the feminine of an adjective is formed, when regular, by adding e to the masculine form (eg compétent, compétente; carré, carrée; fin, fine). If the masculine already ends in e, the feminine is the same as the masculine (eg utile). Both regular and irregular feminine forms of adjectives (eg généreux, généreuse; léger, légère; doux, douce) are given on the French-English side of the dictionary. They are listed in the following way: compétent, -ente; carré, -ée; fin, fine; généreux, -euse; léger, -ère; doux, douce. On the English-French side, French adjectives are shown in the masculine but highly irregular feminine forms (eg frais, fraîche; faux, fausse) have been included as an additional help to the user.

To form the plural of a French noun or adjective s is usually added to the singular (eg arbre, arbres; taxi, taxis; petit, petits). The plural form of a noun ending in s, x or z (eg pois, croix, nez) is the same as that of the singular. Plurals of nouns and adjectives which do not follow these general rules are listed in the French section, including the plurals of French compounds where the formation of the plural involves a change *other than* the addition of final s (eg chou-fleur, choux-fleurs; arc-en-ciel, arcs-en-ciel). The plurals of compounds which are formed simply by adding s (eg tire-bouchon) are not given.

The irregular plurals of French nouns (and irregular masculine plurals of French adjectives) ending in al, eau, eu, au, ail and ou are listed on the English-French side (eg cerveau, -x; général, -aux). Included on the English-French side, as an additional help to the user, are the plurals of French nouns (and adjectives) ending in al, eu and au where s, and not the usual x, forms the plural (eg pneu, pneus; naval, navals) and of those nouns in ail and ou where the plural is formed with x, and not the usual s (eg vitrail, vitraux; chou, choux).

In English also, s is added to form the plural of a noun (eg cat, cats; taxi, taxis) but a noun ending in ch, s, sh, x or z forms its plural by the addition of es, pronounced [-ɪz] (eg glass, glasses; match, matches). (Note that when ch is pronounced [k], the plural is in s, eg monarch, monarchs.) When a noun ends in y preceded by a consonant, y is changed to ies to form the plural (eg army, armies). English plurals not following these general rules are given on the English-French side, including the plurals of English compounds where the formation of the plural involves a change other than the addition of final s (eg brother-in-law, brothers-in-law). Common English irregular plurals involving a change of vowel (eg tooth, teeth) are given, for convenience, at both singular and plural headword positions.

Most French verbs have regular conjugations though some display spelling anomalies (see French Verb Conjugations on p (i)). In the French section an asterisk is used to mark an irregular verb, and refers the user to the table of irregular verbs on p (ii).

Most English verbs form their past tense and past participle by adding ed to the infinitive (eg look, looked) or d to an infinitive already ending in e (eg love, loved). When a verb ends in y preceded by a consonant, y becomes ied (eg satisfy, satisfied). To form the third person singular of a verb in the present tense s is added to the infinitive (eg know, knows) but an infinitive in ch, s, sh, x or z forms its third person singular by the addition of es, pronounced [-ɪz] (eg dash, dashes). When an infinitive ends in y preceded by a consonant, y is changed to ies to form the third person singular (eg satisfy, satisfies).

The English present participle is formed by the addition of ing to the infinitive (eg look, looking) but final e is omitted when an infinitive ends in e (eg love, loving). When the infinitive ends in a single consonant preceded by a vowel (eg tug), the final consonant is usually doubled in the past tense, past and present participles (eg tug, tugged, tugging). The doubling of consonants in English verbs is indicated in the text in the following way: **tug** ... *vt* (**-gg-**).

Irregular English verb conjugations are given in the English headword list, and a summary of the most important irregular verbs may also be found on p (ix).

Notes sur la grammaire

En français, le féminin d'un adjectif se forme régulièrement en ajoutant **e** au masculin (par exemple: compétent, -ente; carré, carrée; fin, fine). Lorsque le masculin se termine déjà par **e**, le féminin est identique (par exemple: utile). Les féminins de tous les adjectifs, réguliers et irréguliers, (par exemple: généreux, généreuse; léger, légère; doux, douce) sont donnés dans la partie français-anglais où ils sont notés comme suit: compétent, -ente; carré, -ée; fin, fine; généreux, -euse; léger, -ère; doux, douce. Dans la partie anglais-français, on ne donne que le masculin des adjectifs, mais, par souci de fournir une information complémentaire utile, on indique les féminins irréguliers remarquables (par exemple: frais, fraîche; faux, fausse).

On forme en général le pluriel d'un nom ou d'un adjectif français en ajoutant **s** au singulier (par exemple: arbre, arbres; taxi, taxis; petit, petits). Le pluriel d'un nom se terminant par **s**, **x** ou **z** (par exemple: pois, croix, nez) est identique au singulier. Les pluriels des noms et adjectifs qui font exception à ces règles générales sont signalés dans la partie français-anglais, de même que les pluriels des mots composés français dont le passage au pluriel appelle une modification *autre que* le simple ajout d'un **s** final (par exemple: chou-fleur, choux-fleurs; arc-en-ciel, arcs-en-ciel). Les pluriels des mots composés ne sont pas donnés lorsqu'ils se forment par simple ajout d'un **s** (par exemple: tire-bouchon).

Les pluriels irréguliers des noms français, de même que ceux des adjectifs masculins, qui se terminent par **al**, **eau**, **eu**, **au**, **ail** et **ou** sont indiqués dans la partie français-anglais (par exemple: cerveau, -x; général, -aux). Un complément d'information est fourni, dans la partie anglais-français, par la mention des pluriels des noms et adjectifs français qui se terminent par **al**, **eu** et **au** et forment leur pluriel en **s** au lieu de **x** (par exemple: pneu, pneus; naval, navals); il en va de même pour ceux qui se terminent par **ail** et **ou** et qui forment leur pluriel en **x**, au lieu de **s** (par exemple: vitrail, vitraux; chou, choux).

De la même façon, en anglais, on forme le pluriel des noms en ajoutant **s** (par exemple: cat, cats; taxi, taxis) mais on ajoutera **es**, prononcé [-ɪz], aux noms qui se terminent par **ch**, **s**, **sh**, **x** ou **z** (par exemple: glass, glasses; match, matches). (Noter cependant que lorsque **ch** se prononce [k], le pluriel est en **s**, comme dans monarch, monarchs.) Lorsqu'un nom se termine par un **y** précédé d'une consonne, ce **y** devient **ies** au pluriel (par exemple: army, armies). Les pluriels des noms anglais qui font exception à ces règles générales sont signalés dans la partie anglais-français, de même que les pluriels des mots composés anglais dont le passage au pluriel entraîne une modification autre que le simple ajout d'un **s** final (par exemple: brother-in-law, brothers-in-law).

La plupart des verbes français ont des conjugaisons régulières; cependant, certains subissent des variations orthographiques (voir: Conjugaisons des verbes français à la page (i)). Dans la partie français-anglais, un astérisque signale un verbe irrégulier et renvoie à la table des verbes irréguliers donnée en page (ii).

En anglais, le passé et le participe passé des verbes se forment dans la plupart des cas en ajoutant **ed** à l'infinitif (par exemple: look, looked) ou seulement **d** lorsque l'infinitif se termine par un **e** (par exemple: love, loved). Lorsqu'un verbe se termine par un **y** précédé d'une consonne, ce **y** devient **ied** (par exemple: satisfy, satisfied). La troisième personne du singulier du présent se forme en ajoutant **s** à l'infinitif (par exemple: know, knows), mais on ajoutera **es**, prononcé [-ɪz], aux infinitifs qui se terminent par **ch**, **s**, **sh**, **x** ou **z** (par exemple: dash, dashes). Enfin, lorsqu'un verbe se termine par un **y** précédé d'une consonne, ce **y** devient **ies** à la troisième personne du singulier (par exemple: satisfy, satisfies).

Le participe présent en anglais se forme en ajoutant la désinence **ing** à l'infinitif (par exemple: look, looking); lorsqu'un infinitif comporte un **e** final, celui-ci disparaît (par exemple: love, loving). Lorsque l'infinitif se termine par une seule consonne précédée d'une voyelle (par exemple: tug), la consonne finale est le plus souvent doublée au passé et aux participes passé et présent (par exemple: tug, tugged, tugging). Le doublement des consonnes dans les verbes anglais est signalé comme suit: **tug** ... *vt* (**-gg-**).

Abbreviations

Abréviations

adjective	*a*	adjectif
abbreviation	*abbr, abrév*	abréviation
adverb	*adv*	adverbe
agriculture	*Agr*	agriculture
American	*Am*	américain
anatomy	*Anat*	anatomie
architecture	*Archit*	architecture
slang	*Arg*	argot
article	*art*	article
cars, motoring	*Aut*	automobile
auxiliary	*aux*	auxiliaire
aviation, aircraft	*Av*	aviation
biology	*Biol*	biologie
botany	*Bot*	botanique
British	*Br*	britannique
Canadian	*Can*	canadien
carpentry	*Carp*	menuiserie
chemistry	*Ch*	chimie
commerce	*Com*	commerce
computing	*Comptr*	informatique
conjunction	*conj*	conjonction
cookery	*Culin*	cuisine
definite	*def, déf*	défini
demonstrative	*dem, dém*	démonstratif
economics	*Econ, Écon*	économie
electricity	*El, Él*	électricité
et cetera	*etc*	et cetera
feminine	*f*	féminin
familiar	*Fam*	familier
figurative	*Fig*	figuré
finance	*Fin*	finance
feminine plural	*fpl*	féminin pluriel
French	*Fr*	français
geography	*Geog, Géog*	géographie
geology	*Geol, Géol*	géologie
geometry	*Geom, Géom*	géométrie
history	*Hist*	histoire
humorous	*Hum*	humoristique
indefinite	*indef, indéf*	indéfini
indicative	*indic*	indicatif
infinitive	*inf*	infinitif
interjection	*int*	interjection
invariable	*inv*	invariable
ironic	*Iron*	ironique
legal, law	*Jur*	juridique
linguistics	*Ling*	linguistique
literary	*Lit, Litt*	littéraire
literature	*Liter, Littér*	littérature
masculine	*m*	masculin
mathematics	*Math*	mathématiques
medicine	*Med, Méd*	médecine
carpentry	*Menuis*	menuiserie
meteorology	*Met, Mét*	météorologie

military	*Mil*	militaire
masculine plural	*mpl*	masculin pluriel
music	*Mus*	musique
noun	*n*	nom
nautical	*Nau*	nautique
noun feminine	*nf*	nom féminin
noun masculine	*nm*	nom masculin
noun masculine and feminine	*nmf*	nom masculin et féminin
computing	*Ordinat*	informatique
pejorative	*Pej, Péj*	péjoratif
philosophy	*Phil*	philosophie
photography	*Phot*	photographie
physics	*Phys*	physique
plural	*pl*	pluriel
politics	*Pol*	politique
possessive	*poss*	possessif
past participle	*pp*	participe passé
prefix	*pref, préf*	préfixe
preposition	*prep, prép*	préposition
present participle	*pres p, p prés*	participe présent
present tense	*pres t*	temps présent
pronoun	*pron*	pronom
psychology	*Psy*	psychologie
past tense	*pt*	prétérit
	qch	quelque chose
	qn	quelqu'un
registered trademark	®	marque déposée
railway, *Am* railroad	*Rail*	chemin de fer
relative	*rel*	relatif
religion	*Rel*	religion
school	*Sch, Scol*	école
singular	*sing*	singulier
slang	*Sl*	argot
someone	*s.o.*	
something	*sth*	
subjunctive	*sub*	subjonctif
suffix	*suff*	suffixe
technical	*Tech*	technique
telephone	*Tel, Tél*	téléphone
textiles	*Tex*	industrie textile
television	*TV*	télévision
typography, printing	*Typ*	typographie
university	*Univ*	université
United States	*US*	États-Unis
auxiliary verb	*v aux*	verbe auxiliaire
intransitive verb	*vi*	verbe intransitif
impersonal verb	*v imp*	verbe impersonnel
pronominal verb	*vpr*	verbe pronominal
transitive verb	*vt*	verbe transitif
transitive and intransitive verb	*vti*	verbe transitif et intransitif
vulgar	*Vulg*	vulgaire

Pronunciation of French

Table of Phonetic Symbols

Vowels

[i]	vite, cygne, sortie	[y]	cru, sûr, rue
[e]	été, donner	[ɸ]	feu, meule, nœud
[ɛ]	elle, mais, père	[œ]	œuf, jeune
[a]	chat, fameux	[ə]	le, refaire, entre
[ɑ]	pas, âgé	[ɛ̃]	vin, plein, faim, saint
[ɔ]	donne, fort, album	[ɑ̃]	enfant, temps, paon
[o]	dos, chaud, peau	[ɔ̃]	mon, nombre
[u]	tout, cour, roue	[œ̃]	lundi, humble

Consonants

[p]	pain, absolu, frapper	[n]	né, canne
[b]	beau, abbé	[ɲ]	campagne
[t]	table, nette	[ŋ]	jogging
[d]	donner, sud	[']	This symbol is placed before
[k]	camp, képi, qui		the phonetics of a word
[g]	garde, guerre, second		beginning with **h** to show that
[f]	feu, phrase		there is no elision or liaison:
[v]	voir, wagon		the preceding word must not
[s]	sou, cire, nation		be abbreviated (eg la hache
[z]	cousin, zéro		and not l'hache), and the final
[ʃ]	chose, schéma		consonant of the preceding
[ʒ]	gilet, jeter		word must not be pronounced
[l]	lait, facile, elle		(eg les haches: [leaʃ] and not
[r]	rare, rhume, barreau		[lezaʃ]).
[m]	mon, flamme		

Semi-consonants

[j]	piano, voyage, fille
[w]	ouest, noir, tramway
[ɥ]	muet, lui

Prononciation de l'anglais

Tableau des Signes Phonétiques

Voyelles et diphtongues

[iː]	bee, police		[ɒ]	lot, what
[ɪə]	beer, real		[ɔː]	all, saw
[ɪ]	bit, added		[ɔɪ]	boil, toy
[e]	bet, said		[əʊ]	low, soap
[eɪ]	date, nail		[ʊ]	put, wool
[eə]	bear, air		[uː]	shoe, too
[æ]	bat, plan		[ʊə]	poor, sure
[aɪ]	fly, life		[ʌ]	cut, some
[ɑː]	ar , ask		[ɜː]	burn, learn
[aʊ]	fowl, house		[ə]	china, annoy
			[(ə)]	relation

Consonnes

[p]	pat, top		[ð]	that, breathe
[b]	but, tab		[h]	hat, rehearse
[t]	tap, patter		[l]	lad, all
[d]	dab, ladder		[r]	red, sorry
[k]	cat, kite		[r]	better, here (*représente un r*
[g]	go, rogue			*final qui se prononce en*
[f]	fat, phrase			*liaison devant une voyelle,*
[v]	veal, rave			*par exemple* 'here is' [hɪərɪz])
[s]	sat, ace		[m]	mat, hammer
[z]	zero, houses		[n]	no, banner
[ʃ]	dish, pressure		[ŋ]	singing, link
[ʒ]	pleasure		[j]	yet, onion
[tʃ]	charm, rich		[w]	wall, quite
[dʒ]	judge, rage		[']	*marque l'accent tonique;*
[θ]	thank, breath			*précède la syllabe accentuée*

A

A, a [eɪ] *n* A, a *m*; **5A** (*number*) 5 bis; **A1** (*dinner etc*) *Fam* super, superbe; **to go from A to B** aller du point A au point B.

a [ə, *stressed* eɪ] (*before vowel or mute h* **an** [ən, *stressed* æn]) *indef art* **1** un, une; **a man** un homme; **an apple** une pomme.

2 (= *def art in Fr*) **sixty pence a kilo** soixante pence le kilo; **50 km an hour** 50 km à l'heure; **I have a broken arm** j'ai le bras cassé.

3 (*art omitted in Fr*) **he's a doctor** il est médecin; **Caen, a town in Normandy** Caen, ville de Normandie; **what a man!** quel homme!; **a hundred** cent; **a thousand** mille.

4 (*a certain*) **a Mr Smith** un certain M. Smith.

5 (*time*) **twice a month** deux fois par mois.

6 (*some*) **to make a noise/a fuss** faire du bruit/des histoires.

aback [ə'bæk] *adv* **taken a.** déconcerté.

abandon [ə'bændən] **1** *vt* abandonner. **2** *n* (*freedom of manner*) laisser-aller *m*, abandon *m*. ● **abandonment** *n* abandon *m*.

abashed [ə'bæʃt] *a* confus, gêné.

abate [ə'beɪt] *vi* (*of storm, pain*) se calmer; (*of flood*) baisser **∎** *vt* diminuer, réduire. ● **abatement** *n* diminution *f*, réduction *f*.

abbey [ˈæbɪ] *n* abbaye *f*.

abbot [ˈæbət] *n* abbé *m*. ● **abbess** *n* abbesse *f*.

abbreviate [əˈbriːvɪeɪt] *vt* abréger. ● **abbreviation** [-ˈeɪʃ(ə)n] *n* abréviation *f*.

abdicate [ˈæbdɪkeɪt] *vti* abdiquer. ● **abdication** [-ˈkeɪʃ(ə)n] *n* abdication *f*.

abdomen [ˈæbdəmən] *n* abdomen *m*. ● **ab'dominal** *a* abdominal.

abduct [æbˈdʌkt] *vt* (*kidnap*) enlever. ● **abduction** *n* enlèvement *m*, rapt *m*.

aberration [æbəˈreɪʃ(ə)n] *n* (*folly, lapse*) aberration *f*.

abet [əˈbet] *vt* (**-tt-**) **to aid and a. s.o.** *Jur* être le complice de qn.

abeyance [əˈbeɪəns] *n* **in a.** (*matter*) en suspens.

abhor [əbˈhɔːr] *vt* (**-rr-**) avoir horreur de, exécrer. ● **abhorrent** [əbˈhɒrənt] *a* exécrable. ● **abhorrence** *n* horreur *f*.

abide [əˈbaɪd] **1** *vi* **to a. by** (*promise etc*) rester fidèle à. **2** *vt* supporter; **I can't a. him** je ne peux pas le supporter.

ability [əˈbɪlətɪ] *n* capacité *f* (**to do** pour faire), aptitude *f* (**to do** à faire); **to the best of my a.** de mon mieux.

abject [ˈæbdʒekt] *a* abject; **a. poverty** la misère.

ablaze [əˈbleɪz] *a* en feu; **a. with** (*light*) re-

splendissant de; (*anger*) enflammé de.

able [ˈeɪb(ə)l] *a* (**-er, -est**) capable, compétent; **to be a. to do** être capable de faire, pouvoir faire; **to be a. to swim/drive** savoir nager/conduire. ● **able-'bodied** *a* robuste. ● **ably** *adv* habilement.

ablutions [əˈbluːʃ(ə)nz] *npl* ablutions *fpl*.

abnormal [æbˈnɔːm(ə)l] *a* anormal. ● **abnor'mality** *n* anomalie *f*; (*of body*) difformité *f*. ● **abnormally** *adv* (*more than usually*) exceptionnellement.

aboard [əˈbɔːd] *adv* (*on ship*) à bord; **all a.** (*on train*) en voiture **∎** *prep* **a. the ship** à bord du navire; **a. the train** dans le train.

abode [əˈbəʊd] *n* (*house*) *Lit* demeure *f*; *Jur* domicile *m*.

abolish [əˈbɒlɪʃ] *vt* supprimer, abolir. ● **abo'lition** *n* suppression *f*, abolition *f*.

abominable [əˈbɒmɪnəb(ə)l] *a* abominable. ● **abomination** [-ˈneɪʃ(ə)n] *n* abomination *f*.

aboriginal [æbəˈrɪdʒ(ə)nɪl] *a* & *n* aborigène (*m*). ● **aborigines** [æbəˈrɪdʒɪniz] *npl* aborigènes *mpl*.

abort [əˈbɔːt] *vt* (*space flight, computer program*) abandonner; (*fetus*) provoquer l'avortement de. ● **abortion** [-ʃ(ə)n] *n* avortement *m*; **to have an a.** se faire avorter. ● **abortive** *a* (*plan etc*) manqué, avorté.

abound [əˈbaʊnd] *vi* abonder (**in, with** en).

about [əˈbaʊt] *adv* **1** (*approximately*) à peu près, environ; (**at**) **a. two o'clock** vers deux heures.

2 (*here and there*) çà et là, ici et là; (*ideas, flu*) *Fig* dans l'air; **there's a rumour...a.** (**that**) il y a une rumeur qui circule (selon laquelle); **to look a.** regarder autour de soi; **to follow a.** suivre partout; **to bustle a.** s'affairer; **there are lots a.** il y en a beaucoup *or* plein; (**out and**) **a.** (*after illness*) sur pied, guéri; (**up and**) **a.** (*out of bed*) levé, debout; **a. turn, a. face** *Mil* demi-tour *m*; *Fig* volte-face *f*.

∎ *prep* **1** (*around*) **a. the garden** autour du jardin; **a. the streets** par *or* dans les rues.

2 (*near to*) **a. here** par ici.

3 (*concerning*) au sujet de; **to talk a.** parler de; **a book a.** un livre sur; **what's it (all) a.?** de quoi s'agit-il?; **while you're a. it** pendant que vous y êtes; **what** *or* **how a. me?** et moi alors?; **what** *or* **how a. a drink?** que dirais-tu de prendre un verre?, et si on prenait un verre?

4 (+ *inf*) **a. to do** sur le point de faire; **I was a. to say** j'étais sur le point de dire, j'allais dire.

above [əˈbʌv] *adv* au-dessus; (*in book*) ci-

dessus; **from a.** d'en haut; **floor a.** étage *m* supérieur *or* du dessus.
❚ *prep* au-dessus de; **a. all** par-dessus tout, surtout; **a. the bridge** (*on river*) en amont du pont; **he's a. me** (*in rank*) c'est mon supérieur; **she's not a. lying** elle n'est pas incapable de mentir; **he's not a. asking** il n'est pas trop fier pour demander. ●**above-'mentioned** *a* susmentionné.

aboveboard [əbʌv'bɔːd] *a* ouvert, honnête ❚ *adv* sans tricherie, cartes sur table.

abrasion [ə'breɪʒ(ə)n] *n* frottement *m*; (*wound*) écorchure *f*. ●**abrasive** *a* (*substance*) abrasif; (*rough*) *Fig* rude, dur; (*irritating*) agaçant ❚ *n* abrasif *m*.

abreast [ə'brest] *adv* côte à côte, de front; **four a.** par rangs de quatre; **to keep a. of** *or* **with** se tenir au courant de.

abridge [ə'brɪdʒ] *vt* (*book etc*) abréger. ●**abridg(e)ment** *n* abrégement *m* (**of** de); (*abridged version*) abrégé *m*.

abroad [ə'brɔːd] *adv* **1** (*in or to a foreign country*) à l'étranger; **from a.** de l'étranger. **2** (*over a wide area*) de tous côtés; **rumour a.** bruit *m* qui court.

abrogate ['æbrəgeɪt] *vt* abroger.

abrupt [ə'brʌpt] *a* (*sudden*) brusque; (*person*) brusque, abrupt; (*slope, style*) abrupt. ●**abruptly** *adv* (*suddenly*) brusquement; (*rudely*) avec brusquerie.

abscess ['æbses] *n* abcès *m*.

abscond [əb'skɒnd] *vi* (*run off*) s'enfuir.

absence ['æbsəns] *n* absence *f*; **in the a. of sth** à défaut de qch, faute de qch; **a. of mind** distraction *f*.

absent ['æbsənt] *a* absent (**from** de); (*look*) distrait ❚ [æb'sent] *vt* **to a. oneself** s'absenter. ●**absent-'minded** *a* distrait. ●**absent-'mindedness** *n* distraction *f*.

absentee [æbsən'tiː] *n* absent, -ente *mf*. ●**absenteeism** *n* absentéisme *m*.

absolute ['æbsəluːt] *a* absolu; (*proof etc*) indiscutable; (*coward etc*) parfait, véritable. ●**absolutely** *adv* absolument; (*forbidden*) formellement.

absolve [əb'zɒlv] *vt* (*sinner, accused*) absoudre; **to a. from** (*vow*) libérer de. ●**absolution** [æbsə'luːʃ(ə)n] *n* absolution *f*.

absorb [əb'zɔːb] *vt* (*liquid etc*) absorber; (*shock*) amortir; **to become absorbed in** (*work*) s'absorber dans; **absorbed in** (*one's thoughts*) plongé dans. ●**absorbing** *a* (*work*) absorbant; (*book, film*) prenant. ●**absorption** [-ʃ(ə)n] *n* absorption *f*.

absorbent [əb'zɔːbənt] *a* absorbant; **a. cotton** *Am* coton *m* hydrophile, ouate *f*.

absorber [əb'zɔːbər] *n* **shock a.** (*in vehicle*) amortisseur *m*.

abstain [əb'steɪn] *vi* (*refuse to vote*) s'abstenir; **to a. from sth/from doing** s'abstenir de qch/de faire. ●**abstention** [-'stenʃ(ə)n] *n* abstention *f*.

abstemious [əb'stiːmɪəs] *a* sobre, frugal.

abstinence ['æbstɪnəns] *n* abstinence *f*.

abstract ['æbstrækt] **1** *a* & *n* abstrait (*m*). **2**
n (*summary*) résumé *m*. **3** [əb'strækt] *vt* (*remove*) retirer; (*notion*) abstraire. ●**ab'straction** *n* (*idea*) abstraction *f*; (*absent-mindedness*) distraction *f*.

abstruse [əb'struːs] *a* obscur.

absurd [əb'sɜːd] *a* absurde, ridicule. ●**absurdity** *n* absurdité *f*. ●**absurdly** *adv* absurdement.

abundant [ə'bʌndənt] *a* abondant. ●**abundance** *n* abondance *f*. ●**abundantly** *adv* **a. clear** tout à fait clair.

abuse [ə'bjuːs] *n* (*abusing*) abus *m* (**of** de); (*of child etc*) mauvais traitements *mpl*; (*insults*) injures *fpl* ❚ [ə'bjuːz] *vt* (*use badly or wrongly*) abuser de; (*ill-treat*) maltraiter; (*speak ill of*) dire du mal de; (*insult*) injurier. ●**abusive** [ə'bjuːsɪv] *a* (*person*) grossier; (*words*) injurieux.

abysmal [ə'bɪzm(ə)l] *a* (*bad*) *Fam* désastreux, exécrable.

abyss [ə'bɪs] *n* abîme *m*.

acacia [ə'keɪʃə] *n* (*tree*) acacia *m*.

academic [ækə'demɪk] *a* (*year, diploma etc*) universitaire; (*scholarly*) érudit, intellectuel; (*issue etc*) *Pej* théorique; (*style, art*) académique ❚ *n* (*teacher*) universitaire *mf*.

academy [ə'kædəmɪ] *n* (*society*) académie *f*; (*military*) école *f*; (*of music*) conservatoire *m*. ●**acade'mician** *n* académicien, -ienne *mf*.

accede [ək'siːd] *vi* **to a. to** (*request, throne, position*) accéder à.

accelerate [ək'seləreɪt] *vt* accélérer ❚ *vi* s'accélérer; (*of vehicle, driver*) accélérer. ●**acceleration** [-'reɪʃ(ə)n] *n* accélération *f*. ●**accelerator** *n* (*pedal, device*) accélérateur *m*.

accent ['æksənt] *n* accent *m* ❚ [æk'sent] *vt* accentuer. ●**accentuate** [æk'sentʃʊeɪt] *vt* accentuer.

accept [ək'sept] *vt* accepter. ●**accepted** *a* (*opinion, custom*) reçu; (*fact*) reconnu. ●**acceptable** *a* (*worth accepting, tolerable*) acceptable. ●**acceptance** *n* acceptation *f*; (*approval, favour*) accueil *m* favorable.

access ['ækses] *n* accès *m* (**to sth** à qch, **to s.o.** auprès de qn). ●**ac'cessible** *a* accessible.

accession [æk'seʃ(ə)n] *n* accession *f* (**to** à); (*increase*) augmentation *f*; (*sth added*) nouvelle acquisition *f*.

accessories [ək'sesərɪz] *npl* (*objects*) accessoires *mpl*.

accessory [ək'sesərɪ] *n* (*accomplice*) *Jur* complice *mf*.

accident ['æksɪdənt] *n* accident *m*; **by a.** (*by chance*) par accident; (*unintentionally*) accidentellement, sans le vouloir. ●**accident-prone** *a* qui attire les accidents.

accidental [æksɪ'dent(ə)l] *a* accidentel, fortuit. ●**acci'dentally** *adv* accidentellement, par mégarde; (*by chance*) par accident.

acclaim [ə'kleɪm] *vt* (*cheer*) acclamer; (*praise*) faire l'éloge de; **to a. king** proclamer roi ❚ *n* (*critical*) **a.** éloges *mpl* (de la critique); **the film enjoys critical a.** le film a reçu un accueil élogieux de la critique.

acclimate ['æklımeıt] *vti Am* = acclimatize. ● **a'cclimatize** *vt Br* █ *vi* s'acclimater. ● **accli'mation** *n Am or* **acclima'tization** *Br* acclimatisation *f*.

accolade ['ækəleıd] *n* (*praise*) louange *f*.

accommodate [ə'kɒmədeıt] *vt* (*of house*) loger, recevoir; (*have room for*) avoir de la place pour (mettre); (*adapt*) adapter (**to** à); (*supply*) fournir (**s.o. with sth** qch à qn); (*oblige*) rendre service à; (*reconcile*) concilier; **to a. oneself to** se faire à. ● **accommodating** *a* accommodant, obligeant.

accommodation [əkɒmə'deıʃ(ə)n] *n* **1** (*lodging*) logement *m*; (*rented room or rooms*) chambre(s) *f(pl)*; **accommodations** (*in hotel*) *Am* chambre(s) *f(pl)*. **2** (*compromise*) compromis *m*, accommodement *m*.

accompany [ə'kʌmpənı] *vt* accompagner. ● **accompaniment** *n* accompagnement *m*. ● **accompanist** *n* (*musician*) accompagnateur, -trice *mf*.

accomplice [ə'kʌmplıs] *n* complice *mf*.

accomplish [ə'kʌmplıʃ] *vt* (*task*, *duty*) accomplir; (*aim*) réaliser. ● **accomplished** *a* accompli. ● **accomplishment** *n* (*of task*, *duty*) accomplissement *m*; (*thing achieved*) réalisation *f*; **accomplishments** (*skills*) talents *mpl*; **writing a novel is a great a.** écrire un roman, c'est vraiment quelque chose.

accord [ə'kɔːd] **1** *n* accord *m*; **of my own a.** volontairement, de mon plein gré █ *vi* concorder. **2** *vt* (*grant*) accorder. ● **accordance** *n* **in a. with** conformément à.

according to [ə'kɔːdıŋtuː] *prep* selon, d'après, suivant. ● **accordingly** *adv* en conséquence.

accordion [ə'kɔːdıən] *n* accordéon *m*.

accost [ə'kɒst] *vt* accoster, aborder.

account [ə'kaʊnt] **1** *n* (*with bank or firm*) compte *m*; **accounts department** comptabilité *f*; **ten pounds on a.** un acompte de dix livres. **2** *n* (*report*) compte rendu *m*, récit *m*; (*explanation*) explication *f*; **by all accounts** au dire de tous; **to give a good a. of oneself** s'en tirer à son avantage █ *vi* **to a. for** (*explain*) expliquer; (*give reckoning of*) rendre compte de; (*represent*) représenter. **3** (*expressions*) **on a. of** à cause de; **on no a.** en aucun cas; **of some a.** d'une certaine importance; **to take into a.** tenir compte de. **4** *vt* **to a. oneself lucky/etc** (*consider*) se considérer heureux/etc. ● **accountable** *a* responsable (**for** de, **to** devant); (*explainable*) explicable.

accountant [ə'kaʊntənt] *n* comptable *mf*. ● **accountancy** *n* comptabilité *f*.

accoutrements [ə'kuːtrəmənts] (*Am* **accouterments** [ə'kuːtəmənts]) *npl* équipement *m*.

accredit [ə'kredıt] *vt* (*ambassador*) accréditer; **to a. s.o. with sth** attribuer qch à qn.

accrue [ə'kruː] *vi* (*of interest*) *Fin* s'accumuler; **to a. to** (*of advantage*) revenir à.

accumulate [ə'kjuːmjʊleıt] *vt* accumuler, amasser █ *vi* s'accumuler. ● **accumulation** [-'leıʃ(ə)n] *n* accumulation *f*; (*mass*) amas *m*.

accurate ['ækjʊrət] *a* exact, précis. ● **accuracy** *n* exactitude *f*, précision *f*. ● **accurately** *adv* avec précision.

accursed [ə'kɜːsıd] *a* maudit, exécrable.

accuse [ə'kjuːz] *vt* accuser (**of** de). ● **accused** *n* (*the*). *Jur* l'inculpé, -ée *mf*, l'accusé, -ée *mf*. ● **accusing** *a* accusateur. ● **accusation** [ækjuː'zeıʃ(ə)n] *n* accusation *f*.

accustom [ə'kʌstəm] *vt* habituer, accoutumer. ● **accustomed** *a* habitué (**to sth** à qch, **to doing** à faire); **to get a. to** s'habituer à, s'accoutumer à.

ace [eıs] *n* (*card*, *person*) as *m*.

acetate ['æsıteıt] *n* acétate *m*.

acetic [ə'siːtık] *a* acétique.

ache [eık] *n* douleur *f*, mal *m*; **to have an a. in one's arm** avoir mal au bras █ *vi* faire mal; **my head aches** la tête me fait mal; **I'm aching all over** j'ai mal partout; **it makes my heart a.** cela me serre le cœur; **to be aching to do sth/etc** brûler de faire. ● **aching** *a* douloureux. ● **achy** ['eıkı] *a* **to be a.** avoir mal partout.

achieve [ə'tʃiːv] *vt* (*success*, *result*) obtenir; (*aim*) atteindre; (*ambition*, *feat*) réaliser; (*victory*) remporter; **he can never a. anything** il n'arrive jamais à faire quoi que ce soit. ● **achievement** *n* (*success*) réussite *f*; (*of ambition*) réalisation *f*; **writing a novel is quite an a.** écrire un roman, c'est vraiment quelque chose.

acid ['æsıd] *a & n* acide (*m*); **a. rain** pluies *fpl* acides. ● **a'cidity** *n* acidité *f*.

acknowledge [ək'nɒlıdʒ] *vt* reconnaître (**as** pour); (*greeting*) répondre à; **to a.** (**receipt of**) accuser réception de; **to a. defeat** s'avouer vaincu. ● **acknowledg(e)ment** *n* (*of letter*) accusé *m* de réception; (*receipt*) reçu *m*; (*confession*) aveu *m* (**of** de); **in a. of** en reconnaissance de.

acme ['ækmı] *n* sommet *m*, comble *m*.

acne ['æknı] *n* acné *f*.

acorn ['eıkɔːn] *n* gland *m* (*de chêne*).

acoustic [ə'kuːstık] *a* acoustique. ● **acoustics** *npl* acoustique *f*.

acquaint [ə'kweınt] *vt* **to a. s.o. with sth** informer qn de qch; **to be acquainted with** (*person*) connaître; (*fact*) savoir; **we are acquainted** on se connaît. ● **acquaintance** *n* (*person*, *knowledge*) connaissance *f*.

acquiesce [ækwı'es] *vi* acquiescer (**in** à). ● **acquiescence** *n* acquiescement *m*.

acquire [ə'kwaıər] *vt* acquérir; (*taste*) prendre (**for** à); (*friends*) se faire; **acquired taste** goût *m* qui s'acquiert. ● **acqui'sition** *n* acquisition *f*. ● **acquisitive** *a* avide, cupide.

acquit [ə'kwıt] *vt* (-tt-) **to a. s.o.** (*of a crime*) acquitter qn. ● **acquittal** *n* acquittement *m*.

acre ['eıkər] *n* acre *f* (= 0,4 hectare). ● **acreage** *n* superficie *f*.

acrid ['ækrıd] *a* (*smell*, *taste*) âcre; (*manner*) acerbe.

acrimonious [ækrı'məʊnıəs] *a* acerbe.

acrobat ['ækrəbæt] *n* acrobate *mf*. ● **acro'batic** *a* acrobatique; **a. movement** *or* **feat** acrobatie *f*. ● **acro'batics** *npl* acrobaties *fpl.*

acronym ['ækrənɪm] *n* sigle *m.*

across [ə'krɒs] *adv & prep (from side to side (of))* d'un côté à l'autre (de); *(on the other side (of))* de l'autre côté (de); *(crossways)* en travers (de); **to be a kilometre**/*etc* **a.** *(wide)* avoir un kilomètre/*etc* de large; **to walk** *or* **go a.** *(street etc)* traverser; **to come a.** *(person)* rencontrer (par hasard), tomber sur; *(lost object)* trouver (par hasard); *(reference etc)* tomber sur, trouver (par hasard); **to get sth a. to s.o.** faire comprendre qch à qn.

acrostic [ə'krɒstɪk] *n* acrostiche *m.*

acrylic [ə'krɪlɪk] *n* acrylique *m* ▌ *a (paint)* acrylique; **a. socks**/*etc* chaussettes *fpl*/*etc* en acrylique.

act [ækt] **1** *n (deed)* acte *m;* **a. (of parliament)** loi *f;* **caught in the a.** pris sur le fait; **a. of walking** action *f* de marcher; **an a. of folly** une folie.
2 *n (part of play) Theatre* acte *m;* *(in circus, cabaret etc)* numéro *m;* **in on the a.** *Fam* dans le coup; **to put on an a.** *Fam* jouer la comédie ▌ *vt (part in play or film)* jouer; **to a. the fool** faire l'idiot ▌ *vi (in play or film)* jouer; *(pretend)* jouer la comédie.
3 *vi (do sth, behave)* agir; *(function)* fonctionner; **to a. as** *(secretary etc)* faire office de; *(of object)* servir de; **to a. (up)on** *(affect)* agir sur; *(advice)* suivre; **to a. on behalf of** représenter; **to a. up** *(of person, machine) Fam* faire des siennes. ● **acting 1** *a (manager etc)* intérimaire. **2** *n (of play)* représentation *f;* *(actor's art)* jeu *m;* *(career)* théâtre *m.*

action ['ækʃ(ə)n] *n* action *f;* *(military)* combat *m;* *(legal)* procès *m,* action *f;* **to take a.** prendre les mesures; **to put into a.** *(plan)* exécuter; **out of a.** hors d'usage, hors (de) service; *(person)* hors de combat; **killed in a.** mort au champ d'honneur; **to take industrial a.** *Br* se mettre en grève.

activate ['æktɪveɪt] *vt Ch* activer; *(mechanism)* actionner.

active ['æktɪv] *a* actif; *(interest, dislike)* vif; *(volcano)* en activité ▌ *n Grammar* actif *m.*
● **ac'tivity** *n* activité *f;* *(in street)* animation *f.*

activist ['æktɪvɪst] *n* activiste *mf.*

actor ['æktər] *n* acteur *m.* ● **actress** *n* actrice *f.*

actual ['æktʃʊəl] *a* réel, véritable; *(example)* concret; **the a. book** le livre même; **in a. fact** en réalité, effectivement. ● **actually** *adv (truly)* réellement; *(in fact)* en réalité, en fait.

actuary ['æktʃʊərɪ] *n* actuaire *mf.*

actuate ['æktʃʊeɪt] *vt (machine)* actionner.

acumen [*Br* 'ækjumən, *Am* ə'kju:mən] *n* perspicacité *f,* finesse *f;* **to have business a.** avoir le sens des affaires.

acupuncture ['ækjʊpʌŋktʃər] *n* acupuncture *f.*

acute [ə'kju:t] *a (pain, angle etc)* aigu *(f -uë);* *(anxiety, emotion)* vif, profond; *(mind,*

observer) perspicace; *(shortage)* grave.
● **acutely** *adv (to suffer, feel)* vivement, profondément. ● **acuteness** *n* acuité *f;* *(of mind)* perspicacité *f.*

ad [æd] *n Fam* pub *f;* *(private, in newspaper)* annonce *f;* **small ad** *Br* want ad *Am* petite annonce.

AD [eɪ'di:] *abbr (anno Domini)* après Jésus-Christ.

adage ['ædɪdʒ] *n* adage *m.*

Adam ['ædəm] *n* A.'s apple pomme *f* d'Adam.

adamant ['ædəmənt] *a* inflexible; **to be a. that** maintenir que.

adapt [ə'dæpt] *vt* adapter (**to** à); **to a. (oneself)** s'adapter. ● **adaptable** *a (person)* souple, capable de s'adapter. ● **adaptation** [ædæp'teɪʃ(ə)n] *n* adaptation *f.* ● **adaptor** *n (device)* adaptateur *m;* *(plug)* prise *f* multiple.

add [æd] *vt* ajouter (**to** à, **that** que); **to a. (up** *or* **together)** *(numbers)* additionner; **to a. in** inclure ▌ *vi* **to a. to** *(increase)* augmenter; **to a. up to** *(total)* s'élever à; *(mean)* signifier; *(represent)* constituer; **it all adds up** *Fam* ça s'explique. ● **a'ddendum,** *pl* **-da** *n* supplément *m.* ● **adding machine** *n* machine *f* à calculer.

adder ['ædər] *n* vipère *f.*

addict ['ædɪkt] *n (drugs, alcohol etc)* intoxiqué, -ée *mf;* jazz/TV/*etc* **a.** fana(tique) *mf* du jazz/de la télé/*etc;* **drug a.** drogué, -ée *mf.*
● **a'ddicted** *a* **to be a. to** *(music, sport)* se passionner pour, être un fana de; *(work)* être un fou de; *(study)* s'adonner à; **to be a. to doing sth** *(have the habit of)* avoir la manie de faire qch; **a. to drink** alcoolique; **a. to cigarettes** accroché à la cigarette.

addiction [ə'dɪkʃ(ə)n] *n (habit)* manie *f;* *(dependency)* dépendance *f;* **drug a.** toxicomanie *f.* ● **addictive** *a (drug, TV etc)* qui crée une dépendance.

addition [ə'dɪʃ(ə)n] *n* addition *f;* *(increase)* augmentation *f;* **in a.** de plus; **in a. to** en plus de. ● **additional** *a* supplémentaire. ● **additionally** *adv* de plus.

additive ['ædɪtɪv] *n* additif *m.*

address [*Br* ə'dres, *Am* 'ædres] *n (on letter etc)* adresse *f;* *(speech)* allocution *f;* **form of a.** formule *f* de politesse ▌ [ə'dres] *vt (person)* s'adresser à; *(audience)* parler devant; *(words, speech)* adresser (**to** à); *(letter)* mettre l'adresse sur. ● **addressee** [ædre'si:] *n* destinataire *mf.*

adenoids ['ædɪnɔɪdz] *npl* végétations *fpl* (adénoïdes).

adept [ə'dept] *a* expert (**in, at** à).

adequate ['ædɪkwət] *a (quantity etc)* suffisant; *(acceptable)* convenable; *(person)* compétent; *(performance)* acceptable. ● **adequacy** *n (of person)* compétence *f;* **to doubt the a. of sth** douter que qch soit suffisant.
● **adequately** *adv (sufficiently)* suffisamment; *(acceptably)* convenablement.

adhere [əd'hɪər] *vi* **to a. to** adhérer à; *(deci-*

sion, *rule*) s'en tenir à. ● **adherence** *n* (*support*) adhésion *f*. ● **adhesion** [-'hiːʒ(ə)n] *n* (*grip*) adhérence *f*. ● **adhesive** *a* & *n* adhésif (*m*).

ad infinitum [ædɪnfɪ'naɪtəm] *adv* à l'infini.

adjacent [ə'dʒeɪsənt] *a* (*house*, *angle etc*) adjacent (to à).

adjective ['ædʒɪktɪv] *n* adjectif *m*.

adjoin [ə'dʒɔɪn] *vt* avoisiner. ● **adjoining** *a* voisin, avoisinant.

adjourn [ə'dʒɜːn] *vt* (*postpone*) ajourner; (*session*) lever, suspendre ▮ *vi* lever la séance; **to a. to** (*go*) passer à. ● **adjournment** *n* ajournement *m*; (*of session*) suspension *f* (de séance), levée *f* de séance.

adjudicate [ə'dʒuːdɪkeɪt] *vti* juger. ● **adjudication** [-'keɪʃ(ə)n] *n* jugement *m*. ● **adjudicator** *n* juge *m*, arbitre *m*.

adjust [ə'dʒʌst] *vt* (*machine*) régler; (*machine part*) ajuster, régler; (*salaries*, *prices*) (r)ajuster; (*arrange*) arranger; **to a.** (**oneself**) **to** s'adapter à. ● **adjustable** *a* (*seat etc*) réglable. ● **adjustment** *n* Tech réglage *m*; (*of person*) adaptation *f*; (*of salaries*, *prices*) (r)ajustement *m*.

ad-lib [æd'lɪb] *vi* (**-bb-**) improviser ▮ *a* (*joke etc*) improvisé.

administer [əd'mɪnɪstər] *vt* (*manage*, *dispense*) administrer (**to** à). ● **admini'stration** *n* administration *f*; (*government*) gouvernement *m*. ● **administrative** *a* administratif. ● **administrator** *n* administrateur, -trice *mf*.

admirable ['ædmərəb(ə)l] *a* admirable. ● **admiration** [-'reɪʃ(ə)n] *n* admiration *f*.

admiral ['ædmərəl] *n* amiral *m*.

admire [əd'maɪər] *vt* admirer (**for sth** pour qch, **for doing** de faire). ● **admiring** *a* admiratif. ● **admirer** *n* admirateur, -trice *mf*.

admit [əd'mɪt] *vt* (**-tt-**) (*let in*) laisser entrer, admettre; (*acknowledge*) reconnaître, admettre (**that** que) ▮ *vi* **to a. to sth** (*confess*) avouer qch; **to a. of** permettre. ● **admissible** *a* admissible. ● **admission** [-ʃ(ə)n] *n* (*entry to theatre etc*) entrée *f* (**to** à, de); (*to club*, *school*) admission *f*; (*acknowledgment*) aveu *m*; **a.** (**charge**) (prix *m* d')entrée *f*. ● **admittance** *n* entrée *f*; '**no a.**' 'entrée interdite'. ● **admittedly** [-ɪdlɪ] *adv* c'est vrai (que).

admonish [əd'mɒnɪʃ] *vt* (*rebuke*) réprimander; (*warn*) avertir.

ado [ə'duː] *n* **without further a.** sans (faire) plus de façons.

adolescent [ædə'lesənt] *n* adolescent, -ente *mf*. ● **adolescence** *n* adolescence *f*.

adopt [ə'dɒpt] *vt* (*child*, *method*, *attitude etc*) adopter; (*candidate*) Pol choisir. ● **adopted** *a* (*child*) adoptif; (*country*) d'adoption. ● **adoption** [-ʃ(ə)n] *n* adoption *f*. ● **adoptive** *a* (*parent*) adoptif.

adore [ə'dɔːr] *vt* adorer (**doing** faire); **he adores being flattered** il adore qu'on le flatte. ● **adorable** *a* adorable. ● **adoration** [ædə'reɪʃ(ə)n] *n* adoration *f*.

adorn [ə'dɔːn] *vt* (*room*, *book*) orner; (*person*, *dress*) parer. ● **adornment** *n* orne-

ment *m*; (*finery*) parure *f*.

adrenalin(e) [ə'drenəlɪn] *n* adrénaline *f*.

Adriatic [eɪdrɪ'ætɪk] *n* **the A.** l'Adriatique *f*.

adrift [ə'drɪft] *a* & *adv* (*boat*) à la dérive; **to come a.** (*of rope*, *collar etc*) se détacher; **to turn s.o. a.** Fig abandonner qn à son sort.

adroit [ə'drɔɪt] *a* adroit, habile.

adulation [ædjʊ'leɪʃ(ə)n] *n* adulation *f*.

adult ['ædʌlt, ə'dʌlt] *n* adulte *mf* ▮ *a* (*animal etc*) adulte; **a. class/film/etc** classe *f*/film *m*/etc pour adultes. ● **adulthood** *n* âge *m* adulte.

adulterate [ə'dʌltəreɪt] *vt* (*food*) altérer.

adultery [ə'dʌltərɪ] *n* adultère *m*; **to commit a.** commettre l'adultère. ● **adulterous** *a* adultère.

advance [əd'vɑːns] *n* (*movement*, *money*) avance *f*; (*of science*) progrès *mpl*; **advances** (*of love*, *friendship*) avances *fpl*; **in a.** à l'avance, d'avance; (*to arrive*) en avance; **in a. of s.o.** avant qn.
▮ *a* (*payment*) anticipé; **a. booking** réservation *f*; **a. guard** avant-garde *f*.
▮ *vt* (*put forward*, *lend*) avancer; (*science*, *one's work*) faire avancer.
▮ *vi* (*go forward*, *progress*) avancer; **to a. towards s.o.** s'avancer *or* avancer vers qn.
● **advanced** *a* avancé; (*studies*, *level*) supérieur; (*course*) de niveau supérieur; **a. in years** âgé. ● **advancement** *n* (*progress*, *promotion*) avancement *m*.

advantage [əd'vɑːntɪdʒ] *n* avantage *m* (**over** sur); **to take a. of** (*situation etc*) profiter de; (*person*) tromper, exploiter; (*woman*) séduire; **to show** (**off**) **to a.** faire valoir. ● **advan'tageous** *a* avantageux (**to**, pour), profitable.

advent ['ædvent] *n* arrivée *f*, avènement *m*; **A.** Rel l'Avent *m*.

adventure [əd'ventʃər] *n* aventure *f* ▮ *a* (*film etc*) d'aventures. ● **adventurer** *n* aventurier, -ière *m*. ● **adventurous** *a* aventureux.

adverb ['ædvɜːb] *n* adverbe *m*.

adversary ['ædvəsərɪ] *n* adversaire *mf*.

adverse ['ædvɜːs] *a* hostile, défavorable. ● **ad'versity** *n* adversité *f*.

advert ['ædvɜːt] *n* Br Fam pub *f*; (*private*, *in newspaper*) annonce *f*.

advertise ['ædvətaɪz] *vt* (*commercially*) faire de la publicité pour; (*privately*) passer une annonce pour vendre; (*make known*) annoncer ▮ *vi* faire de la publicité; (*privately*) passer une annonce (**for** pour trouver). ● **advertising** *n* publicité *f*; **a. agency** agence *f* de publicité. ● **advertiser** *n* annonceur *m*.

advertisement [Br əd'vɜːtɪsmənt, Am ædvə'taɪzmənt] *n* publicité *f*; (*private or classified in newspaper*) annonce *f*; (*poster*) affiche *f*; **classified a.** petite annonce; **the advertisements** TV la publicité.

advice [əd'vaɪs] *n* conseil(s) *m*(*pl*); (*notification*) Com avis *m*; **a piece of a.** un conseil.

advise [əd'vaɪz] *vt* (*counsel*) conseiller; (*recommend*) recommander; (*notify*) informer; **to a. s.o. to do** conseiller à qn de faire; **to a.**

against déconseiller; **he would be well advised to leave** il ferait bien de partir. ● **advisable** a (action) à conseiller; **it's a. to wait/etc** il est plus prudent d'attendre/etc. ● **advisedly** [-ɪdlɪ] adv après réflexion. ● **adviser** or **advisor** n conseiller, -ère mf. ● **advisory** a consultatif; **in an a. capacity** à titre consultatif.

advocate 1 ['ædvəkət] n (of cause) défenseur m, avocat, -ate mf; (lawyer) avocat m. **2** ['ædvəkeɪt] vt préconiser, recommander.

aegis ['iːdʒɪs] n **under the a. of** sous l'égide de.

aeon ['iːən] n éternité f.

aerial ['eərɪəl] n Br antenne f ▌a (photo etc) aérien.

aerobatics [eərə'bætɪks] npl acrobatie f aérienne. ● **ae'robics** npl aérobic f. ● **'aerodrome** n aérodrome m. ● **aero-dy'namic** a aérodynamique. ● **aero'nautics** npl aéronautique f. ● **'aeroplane** n Br avion m. ● **'aerosol** n aérosol m. ● **'aerospace** a (industry) aérospatial.

aesthetic [Br iːs'θetɪk, Am es'θetɪk] a esthétique.

afar [ə'fɑːr] adv **from a.** de loin.

affable ['æfəb(ə)l] a affable, aimable.

affair ['əfeər] n (matter, concern) affaire f; (love) **a.** liaison f; **state of affairs** situation f.

affect [ə'fekt] vt (concern, move) toucher, affecter; (harm) nuire à; (influence) influer sur; (pretend to have) affecter. ● **affected** a (manner) affecté; (by disease) atteint. ● **affectation** [æfek'teɪʃ(ə)n] n affectation f.

affection [ə'fekʃ(ə)n] n affection f (**for** pour). ● **affectionate** a affectueux, aimant. ● **affectionately** adv affectueusement.

affiliate [ə'fɪlɪeɪt] vt affilier; **to be affiliated** s'affilier (**to** à); **affiliated company** filiale f. ● **affiliation** [-'eɪʃ(ə)n] n affiliation f; **affiliations** (political) attaches fpl.

affinity [ə'fɪnɪtɪ] n affinité f.

affirm [ə'fɜːm] vt affirmer. ● **affirmation** [æfə'meɪʃ(ə)n] n affirmation f. ● **affirmative** a affirmatif ▌n affirmative f; **to answer in the a.** répondre par l'affirmative.

affix [ə'fɪks] vt (stamp, signature) apposer.

afflict [ə'flɪkt] vt affliger (**with** de). ● **affliction** n (misery) affliction f; (disability) infirmité f.

affluent ['æfluənt] a riche; **a. society** société f d'abondance. ● **affluence** n richesse f.

afford [ə'fɔːd] vt **1** (pay for) avoir les moyens d'acheter, pouvoir se payer; **he can't a. the time (to read it)** il n'a pas le temps (de le lire); **I can a. to wait** je peux me permettre d'attendre. **2** (provide) fournir, donner; **to a. s.o. sth** fournir qch à qn. ● **affordable** a (price etc) abordable.

affray [ə'freɪ] n Jur rixe f, bagarre f.

affront [ə'frʌnt] n affront m ▌vt faire un affront à.

Afghanistan [æf'gænɪstɑːn] n Afghanistan m.

afield [ə'fiːld] adv **further a.** plus loin; **too far a.** trop loin.

afloat [ə'fləʊt] adv (ship, swimmer, business) à flot; (awash) submergé; **life a.** la vie sur l'eau; **to stay a.** (of ship) rester à flot; (of businessman) surnager.

afoot [ə'fʊt] adv **there's something a.** il se trame quelque chose; **there's a plan a. to...** on prépare un projet pour...

aforementioned [ə'fɔːmenʃənd] a susmentionné.

afraid [ə'freɪd] a **to be a.** avoir peur (**of s.o./ sth** de qn/qch); **to be a. to do** or **of doing** avoir peur de faire; **to make s.o. afraid** faire peur à qn; **I'm a. (that) he'll fall** j'ai peur qu'il (ne) tombe; **he's a. (that) she may be ill** il a peur qu'elle (ne) soit malade; **I'm a. he's out** (I regret to say) je regrette, il est sorti.

afresh [ə'freʃ] adv de nouveau.

Africa ['æfrɪkə] n Afrique f. ● **African** a africain ▌n Africain, -aine mf.

after ['ɑːftər] adv après; **the month a.** le mois suivant, le mois d'après ▌prep après; **a. all** après tout; **a. eating** après avoir mangé; **day a. day** jour après jour; **page a. page** page sur page; **time a. time** bien des fois; **a. you!** je vous en prie!; **ten a. four** Am quatre heures dix; **to be a. sth/s.o.** (seek) chercher qch/qn ▌conj après que; **a. he saw you** après qu'il t'a vu.

aftercare ['ɑːftəkeər] n Med soins mpl post-opératoires; Jur surveillance f. ● **aftereffects** npl suites fpl, séquelles fpl. ● **afterlife** n vie f future. ● **aftermath** [-mɑːθ, -mæθ] n suites fpl. ● **aftersales service** n service m après-vente. ● **aftershave (lotion)** n lotion f après-rasage, aftershave m. ● **aftertaste** n arrière-goût m. ● **afterthought** n réflexion f après coup; **to add/say/etc sth as an a.** ajouter/dire/etc qch après coup. ● **afterward(s)** adv après, plus tard.

afternoon [ɑːftə'nuːn] n après-midi m or f inv; **in the a.** l'après-midi; **at three in the a.** à trois heures de l'après-midi; **every Monday a.** tous les lundis après-midi; **good a.!** (hello) bonjour!; (goodbye) au revoir! ● **after'noons** adv Am l'après-midi.

afters ['ɑːftəz] npl Br Fam dessert m.

again [ə'gen, ə'geɪn] adv de nouveau, encore une fois; (furthermore) en outre; **to do a. re-faire; to go down/up a.** redescendre/remonter; **she won't do it a.** elle ne le fera plus; **never a.** plus jamais; **half as much a.** moitié plus; **a. and a., time and (time) a.** bien des fois, maintes fois; **what's his name a.?** comment s'appelle-t-il déjà?

against [ə'genst, ə'geɪnst] prep contre; **to go** or **be a.** s'opposer à; **a. the law** illégal; **a law a. drinking** une loi qui interdit de boire; **his age is a. him** son âge lui est défavorable; **a. a background of** sur (un) fond de; **a. the light** à contre-jour; **a. the rules** Br, **a. the rule** Am interdit, contraire aux règlements.

age [eɪdʒ] n âge m; (old) **a.** vieillesse f; **the Middle Ages** le moyen âge; **what a. are you?, what's your a.?** quel âge as-tu?; **five years of a.** âgé de cinq ans; **to be of a.** être majeur; **to come of a.** atteindre sa majorité; **under a.** trop jeune, mineur; **to wait (for) ages** *Fam* attendre une éternité; **a. gap** différence *f* d'âge; **a. group** tranche *f* d'âge; **a. limit** limite *f* d'âge.

❚ *vti* (*pres p* ag(e)ing) vieillir. ●**age-old** *a* séculaire. ●**aged** *a* [eɪdʒd] **a. ten** âgé de dix ans; ['eɪdʒɪd] vieux, âgé; **the a.** les personnes *fpl* âgées. ●**ageless** *a* toujours jeune.

agenda [ə'dʒendə] *n* ordre *m* du jour.

agent ['eɪdʒənt] *n* agent *m*; (*dealer selling cars etc*) concessionnaire *mf*. ●**agency** *n* **1** (*office*) agence *f*. **2 through the a. of s.o.** par l'intermédiaire de qn.

aggravate ['ægrəveɪt] *vt* (*make worse*) aggraver; **to a. s.o.** *Fam* exaspérer qn. ●**aggravation** [-'veɪʃ(ə)n] *n* aggravation *f*; *Fam* exaspération *f*; (*bother*) ennui(s) *m(pl)*.

aggregate ['ægrɪgət] *a* global ❚ *n* (*total*) ensemble *m*.

aggression [ə'greʃ(ə)n] *n* agression *f*. ●**aggressive** *a* agressif. ●**aggressiveness** *n* agressivité *f*. ●**aggressor** *n* agresseur *m*.

aggrieved [ə'gri:vd] *a* (*offended*) blessé, froissé; (*tone*) peiné.

aggro ['ægrəʊ] *n inv* (*bother*) *Br Fam* embêtements *mpl*.

aghast [ə'gɑːst] *a* consterné, horrifié.

agile [*Br* 'ædʒaɪl, *Am* 'ædʒ(ə)l] *a* agile. ●**a'gility** *n* agilité *f*.

agitate ['ædʒɪteɪt] *vt* (*worry*) agiter; **to be agitated** être agité ❚ *vi* **to a. for** (*political cause*) faire campagne pour. ●**agitation** [-'teɪʃ(ə)n] *n* (*anxiety, unrest*) agitation *f*. ●**agitator** *n* (*political*) agitateur, -trice *mf*.

aglow [ə'gləʊ] *a* **to be a.** briller (**with** de).

agnostic [æg'nɒstɪk] *a* & *n* agnostique (*mf*).

ago [ə'gəʊ] *adv* **a year a.** il y a un an; **how long a.?** il y a combien de temps (de cela)?; **long a.** autrefois; **as long a. as 1800** (déjà) en 1800.

agog [ə'gɒg] *a* (*excited*) en émoi; (*eager*) impatient.

agonize ['ægənaɪz] *vi* se faire beaucoup de souci. ●**agonized** *a* (*look*) angoissé; (*cry*) de douleur. ●**agonizing** *a* (*pain*) atroce; (*situation*) angoissant.

agony ['ægənɪ] *n* (*pain*) douleur *f* atroce; (*anguish*) angoisse *f*; **to be in a.** souffrir horriblement; **a. column** (*in newspaper*) courrier *m* du cœur.

agree [ə'gri:] *vi* (*come to an agreement*) se mettre d'accord, s'accorder; (*be in agreement*) être d'accord, s'accorder (**with** avec); (*of facts, dates etc*) concorder; (*of verb etc*) s'accorder; **to a. (up)on** (*decide*) convenir de; **to a. to sth/to doing** consentir à qch/à faire; **it doesn't a. with me** (*food, climate*) ça ne me réussit pas.

❚ *vt* (*figures, sums*) faire concorder; (*approve*) approuver (*comptabilité etc*); **to a. to do** accepter de faire; **to a. that** (*admit*) admettre que. ●**agreed** *a* (*time, place*) convenu; **we are a.** nous sommes d'accord; **a.!** entendu! ●**agreement** *n* accord *m* (**with** avec); **to be in a. with/on** être d'accord avec/sur.

agreeable [ə'gri:əb(ə)l] *a* **1** (*pleasant*) agréable. **2 to be a.** (*agree*) être d'accord; **to be a. to sth** consentir à qch.

agriculture ['ægrɪkʌltʃər] *n* agriculture *f*. ●**agri'cultural** *a* agricole.

aground [ə'graʊnd] *adv* **to run a.** (*of ship*) (s')échouer.

ah! [ɑː] *int* ah!

ahead [ə'hed] *adv* (*in space*) en avant; (*leading*) en tête; (*in the future*) dans l'avenir; **a.** (*of time or of schedule*) en avance (sur l'horaire); **one hour/etc a.** une heure/*etc* d'avance (**of** sur); **a. of** (*space*) devant; (*time, progress*) en avance sur; **to go a.** (*advance*) avancer; (*continue*) continuer; (*start*) commencer; **go a.!** allez-y!; **to go a. with** (*task*) poursuivre; **to get a.** prendre de l'avance; (*succeed*) réussir; **to think a.** penser à l'avenir; **straight a.** (*to walk*) tout droit; (*to look*) droit devant soi.

aid [eɪd] *n* (*help*) aide *f*; (*device*) accessoire *m*; (*visual etc*) moyen *m*, support *m*; **with the a. of** (*a stick etc*) à l'aide de; **in a. of** (*charity etc*) au profit de; **what's (all) this in a. of?** *Fam* quel est le but de tout ça?, ça sert à quoi? ❚ *vt* aider (**s.o. to do** qn à faire).

aide [eɪd] *n* (*to politician etc*) collaborateur, -trice *mf*.

AIDS [eɪdz] *n abbr* (*acquired immune deficiency syndrome*) SIDA *m*; **A. victim/virus** malade *mf*/virus *m* du SIDA.

ail [eɪl] *vt* **what ails you?** de quoi souffrez-vous? ●**ailing** *a* (*ill*) souffrant; (*company*) en difficulté. ●**ailment** *n* (*petit*) ennui *m* de santé.

aim [eɪm] *n* but *m*; **to take a.** viser; **with the a. of** dans le but de ❚ *vt* (*gun*) braquer, diriger (**at** sur); (*stone*) lancer (**at** à, vers); (*blow, remark*) décocher (**at** à); **aimed at children/etc** (*product*) destiné aux enfants/*etc* ❚ *vi* viser; **to a. at s.o.** viser qn; **to a. to do** *or* **at doing** avoir l'intention de faire. ●**aimless** *a*, **aimlessly** *adv* sans but.

air [eər] **1** *n* air *m*; **in the open a.** en plein air; **by a.** (*to travel*) en *or* par avion; (*to send letter or goods*) par avion; **to be** *or* **go on the a.** (*of person*) passer à l'antenne; (*of programme*) être diffusé; **to throw (up) in(to) the a.** jeter en l'air; **(up) in the a.** (*plan*) incertain, en l'air; **there's something in the a.** *Fig* il se prépare quelque chose.

❚ *a* (*raid, base etc*) aérien; **a. fare** prix *m* du billet d'avion; **a. force** armée *f* de l'air; **a. hostess** *Br* hôtesse *f* de l'air; **a. terminal** aérogare *f*.

❚ *vt* (*room*) aérer; (*views*) exposer; **airing cupboard** *Br* armoire *f* sèche-linge.

2 *n* (*appearance, tune*) air *m*; **to put on airs** se donner des airs; **with an a. of sadness/etc** d'un air triste/*etc*.

airborne ['eəbɔːn] *a* en (cours de) vol;

airy (*troops*) aéroporté; **to become a.** (*of aircraft*) décoller. ●**airbridge** *n* pont *m* aérien. ●**air-conditioned** *a* climatisé. ●**air-conditioner** *n* climatiseur *m*. ●**air-conditioning** *n* climatisation *f*. ●**aircraft** *n inv* avion(s) *m(pl)*; **a. carrier** porte-avions *m inv*. ●**aircrew** *n* équipage *m* (*d'un avion*). ●**airfield** *n* terrain *m* d'aviation. ●**airgun** *n* carabine *f* à air comprimé. ●**airletter** *n* aérogramme *m*. ●**airlift** *n* pont *m* aérien ‖ *vt* transporter par avion. ●**airline** *n* ligne *f* aérienne; **a. ticket** billet *m* d'avion. ●**airliner** *n* avion *m* de ligne. ●**airlock** *n* (*chamber in submarine, spacecraft etc*) sas *m*; (*in pipe*) bouchon *m*. ●**airmail** *n* poste *f* aérienne; **by a.** par avion. ●**airman** *n* (*pl* -**men**) aviateur *m*. ●**airplane** *n Am* avion *m*. ●**airpocket** *n* trou *m* d'air. ●**airport** *n* aéroport *m*. ●**air-raid shelter** *n* abri *m* antiaérien. ●**airship** *n* dirigeable *m*. ●**airsick** **a to be a.** avoir le mal de l'air. ●**airsickness** *n* mal *m* de l'air. ●**airstrip** *n* terrain *m* d'atterrissage. ●**airtight** *a* hermétique. ●**air traffic controller** *n* contrôleur *m* aérien, aiguilleur *m* du ciel. ●**airway** *n* (*route*) couloir *m* aérien. ●**airworthy** *a* en état de navigation.

airy ['eərɪ] *a* (-**ier**, -**iest**) (*room*) bien aéré; (*promise*) *Fig* vain; (*step*) léger. ●**airy-fairy** *a Fam* farfelu. ●**airily** *adv* (*not seriously*) d'un ton léger.

aisle [aɪl] *n* (*in plane, supermarket, cinema etc*) allée *f*; (*in church*) (*on side*) nef *f* latérale; (*central*) allée *f* centrale.

aitch [eɪtʃ] *n* (*letter*) h *m*.

ajar [ə'dʒɑːr] *a* & *adv* (*door*) entrouvert.

akin [ə'kɪn] *a* **a.** (**to**) apparenté (à).

alabaster ['æləbɑːstər] *n* albâtre *m*.

alacrity [ə'lækrɪtɪ] *n* empressement *m*.

à la mode [ælæ'məʊd] *a* (*dessert*) *Am* avec de la crème glacée.

alarm [ə'lɑːm] *n* (*warning, fear, device in house or car*) alarme *f*; (*mechanism*) sonnerie *f* (*d'alarme*); **false a.** fausse alerte *f*; **a.** (**clock**) réveil *m*, réveille-matin *m inv* ‖ *vt* (*frighten*) alarmer; (*worry*) inquiéter; **to be alarmed** s'inquiéter (**at what's happening/***etc*) de ce qui se passe/*etc*); **I'm alarmed at that** ça m'inquiète. ●**alarmist** *n* alarmiste *mf*.

alas! [ə'læs] *int* hélas!

Albania [æl'beɪnɪə] *n* Albanie *f*. ●**Albanian** *a* Albanais, -aise *mf*. ‖ *n* Albanais, -aise *mf*.

albatross ['ælbətrɒs] *n* albatros *m*.

albeit [ɔːl'biːɪt] *conj Lit* quoique (+ *sub*).

albino [*Br* æl'biːnəʊ, *Am* æl'baɪnəʊ] *n* (*pl* -**os**) albinos *mf*.

album ['ælbəm] *n* (*book, record*) album *m*; **stamp a.** album à timbres; (*with stamps in*) album de timbres.

alchemy ['ælkəmɪ] *n* alchimie *f*. ●**alchemist** *n* alchimiste *m*.

alcohol ['ælkəhɒl] *n* alcool *m*. ●**alco'holic** *a* (*person*) alcoolique; **a. drink** boisson *f* alcoolisée ‖ *n* (*person*) alcoolique *mf*. ●**alcoholism** *n* alcoolisme *m*.

alcove ['ælkəʊv] *n* alcôve *f*.

ale [eɪl] *n* bière *f*.

alert [ə'lɜːt] *a* (*paying attention*) vigilant; (*sharp, awake*) (*mind, baby etc*) éveillé ‖ *n* alerte *f*; **on the a.** sur le qui-vive ‖ *vt* alerter. ●**alertness** *n* vigilance *f*; (*of mind, baby*) vivacité *f*.

A level ['eɪlev(ə)l] *n* (*exam*) *Br* = épreuve *f* de bac.

alfalfa [æl'fælfə] *n Am* luzerne *f*.

algebra ['ældʒɪbrə] *n* algèbre *f*. ●**alge'braic** *a* algébrique.

Algeria [æl'dʒɪərɪə] *n* Algérie *f*. ●**Algerian** *a* algérien ‖ *n* Algérien, -ienne *mf*.

alias ['eɪlɪəs] *adv* alias ‖ *n* nom *m* d'emprunt.

alibi ['ælɪbaɪ] *n* alibi *m*.

alien ['eɪlɪən] *a* étranger (**to** à) ‖ *n* étranger, -ère *mf*. ●**alienate** *vt* aliéner; **to a. s.o.** (*make unfriendly*) se mettre qn à dos; **to feel alienated** se sentir exclu.

alight [ə'laɪt] 1 *a* (*fire*) allumé; (*building*) en feu; (*face*) éclairé; **to set a.** mettre le feu à. 2 *vi* (*of passenger etc*) descendre (**from** de); (*of bird*) se poser (**sur** on).

align [ə'laɪn] *vt* aligner; **to a. oneself with** (*politically*) s'aligner sur. ●**alignment** *n* alignement *m*.

alike [ə'laɪk] 1 *a* (*people, things*) semblables, pareils; **to look** *or* **be a.** se ressembler. 2 *adv* de la même manière; **summer and winter a.** été comme hiver.

alimony [*Br* 'ælɪmənɪ, *Am* 'ælɪməʊnɪ] *n Jur* pension *f* alimentaire.

alive [ə'laɪv] *a* vivant, en vie; **a. to** conscient de; **a. with worms/***etc* (*crawling*) grouillant de vers/*etc*; **burnt a.** brûlé vif; **anyone a. will tell you** n'importe qui vous le dira; **to keep a.** (*custom, memory*) entretenir, perpétuer; **a. and kicking** *Fam* plein de vie; **look a.!** *Fam* active-toi!

all [ɔːl] *a* tout, toute, *pl* tous, toutes; **a. day** toute la journée; **a. (the) men** tous les hommes; **with a. speed** à toute vitesse; **for a. his wealth** malgré toute sa fortune.

‖ *pron* tous *mpl*, toutes *fpl*; (*everything*) tout; **a. will die** tous mourront; **my sisters are a.** here toutes mes sœurs sont ici; **he ate it a., he ate a. of it** il a tout mangé; **take a. of it** prends (le) tout; **a. (that)** he has tout ce qu'il a; **a. of us** nous tous; **a. in a.** à tout prendre; **in a., a. told** en tout; **a. but impossible/***etc* (*almost*) presque impossible/*etc*; **anything at a.** quoi que ce soit; **if he comes at a.** s'il vient effectivement; **if there's any wind at a.** s'il y a le moindre vent; **nothing at a.** rien du tout; **not at a.** pas du tout; (*after 'thank you'*) il n'y a pas de quoi.

‖ *adv* tout; **a. alone** tout seul; **a. bad** *etc* entièrement mauvais; **a. over** (*everywhere*) partout; (*finished*) fini; **a. too soon** bien trop tôt; **six a.** *Football* six buts partout; **a. there** *Fam* éveillé, intelligent; **not a. there** *Fam* simple d'esprit; **a. in** *Br Fam* épuisé; **a.-in price** *Br* prix global.

‖ *n* my a. *Lit* tout ce que j'ai. ●**all-'clear** *n Mil* fin *f* d'alerte. ●**all-night** *a* (*party*) qui dure toute la nuit; (*shop*) ouvert toute la nuit. ●all-out *a* (*effort*) énergique; (*war, strike*) tous azimuts. ●all-'powerful *a* tout-puissant. ●all-purpose *a* (*tool*) universel. ●all-round *a* (*knowledge etc*) approfondi; (*athlete etc*) complet. ●all-'rounder *n* personne *f* qui est forte en tout. ●all-time *a* (*record*) jamais atteint; **to reach an a.-time low/high** arriver au point le plus bas/le plus haut.

allay [ə'leɪ] *vt* (*fears etc*) calmer, apaiser.

allegation [ælɪ'geɪʃ(ə)n] *n* accusation *f*.

allege [ə'ledʒ] *vt* prétendre (**that** que). ●alleged *a* (*so-called*) (*crime, fact etc*) prétendu; (*author, culprit*) présumé; he is a. **to be** on prétend qu'il est. ●allegedly [-ɪdlɪ] *adv* d'après ce qu'on dit.

allegiance [ə'li:dʒəns] *n* fidélité *f* (**to** à).

allegory [*Br* 'æligəri, *Am* 'ælǝgɔ:ri] *n* allégorie *f*. ●alle'gorical *a* allégorique.

allergy ['ælədʒɪ] *n* allergie *f*. ●allergic [ə'lɜ:dʒɪk] *a* allergique (**to** à).

alleviate [ə'li:vɪeɪt] *vt* (*pain, suffering*) soulager; (*burden, task*) alléger; (*problem*) remédier à.

alley ['ælɪ] *n* ruelle *f*; (*in park*) allée *f*; **blind a.** impasse *f*; **that's (right) up my a.** *Fam* c'est mon truc. ●alleyway *n* ruelle *f*.

alliance [ə'laɪəns] *n* alliance *f*.

allied ['ælaɪd] *a* (*country*) allié; (*matters*) liés.

alligator ['ælɪgeɪtər] *n* alligator *m*.

allocate ['æləkeɪt] *vt* (*assign*) attribuer, allouer (**to** à); (*distribute*) répartir. ●allocation [-'keɪʃ(ə)n] *n* attribution *f*.

allot [ə'lɒt] *vt* (**-tt-**) (*assign*) attribuer; (*distribute*) répartir. ●allotment *n* **1** (*action*) attribution *f*; (*share*) partage *m*. **2** (*land*) *Br* lopin *m* de terre (*loué pour la culture*).

allow [ə'laʊ] **1** *vt* permettre (**s.o. sth** qch à qn); (*give, grant*) accorder (**s.o. sth** qch à qn); (*a request*) accéder à; **to a. a discount** accorder *or* consentir une réduction; **to a. s.o. to do** permettre à qn de faire, autoriser qn à faire; **to a. an hour/a metre/etc** (*estimated period or quantity*) prévoir une heure/un mètre/*etc*; **a. me!** permettez(-moi)!; **it's not allowed** c'est interdit; **you're not allowed to go** on vous interdit de partir.
2 *vi* **to a. for sth** tenir compte de qch. ●allowable *a* (*acceptable*) admissible; (*expense*) déductible.

allowance [ə'laʊəns] *n* allocation *f*; (*for travel, housing, food*) indemnité *f*; (*for duty-free goods*) tolérance *f*; (*tax-free amount*) abattement *m*; **to make allowance(s) or (an) a. for** (*person*) être indulgent envers; (*thing*) tenir compte de.

alloy ['ælɔɪ] *n* alliage *m*.

all right [ɔ:l'raɪt] *a* (*satisfactory*) bien *inv*; (*unharmed*) sain et sauf; (*undamaged*) intact; (*without worries*) tranquille; **it's all r.** ça va; **I'm all r.** (*healthy*) je vais bien; **the TV is all r. now** (*fixed*) la télé marche maintenant; **he's all r.** (*trustworthy etc*) c'est quelqu'un de bien.

▮ *adv* (*well*) bien; **all r.!** (*agreement*) d'accord!; **I received your letter all r.** (*emphatic*) j'ai bien reçu votre lettre.

allude [ə'lu:d] *vi* **to a. to** faire allusion à. ●allusion [-ʒ(ə)n] *n* allusion *f*.

allure [ə'lʊər] *vt* attirer.

ally ['ælaɪ] *n* allié, -ée *mf* ▮ [ə'laɪ] *vt* (*country, person*) allier.

almanac ['ɔ:lmənæk] *n* almanach *m*.

almighty [ɔ:l'maɪtɪ] **1** *a* tout-puissant ▮ **the A.** le Tout-Puissant. **2** *a* (*enormous*) *Fam* terrible, formidable.

almond ['ɑ:mənd] *n* amande *f*.

almost ['ɔ:lməʊst] *adv* presque; **he a. fell**/*etc* il a failli tomber/*etc*.

alms [ɑ:mz] *npl* aumône *f*.

aloft [ə'lɒft] *adv* *Lit* en haut.

alone [ə'ləʊn] *a* & *adv* seul; **an expert a. can...** seul un expert peut...; **I did it (all) a.** je l'ai fait à moi tout seul, je l'ai fait (tout) seul; **to leave** *or* **let a.** (*person*) laisser tranquille *or* en paix; (*thing*) ne pas toucher à; **they can't dance, let a. sing** ils ne savent pas danser, et encore moins chanter.

along [ə'lɒŋ] *prep* (**all**) **a.** (tout) le long de; **to go** *or* **walk a.** (*street*) passer par; **a. here** par ici; **a.** with avec.
▮ *adv* **all a.** (*all the time*) dès le début; (*all the way*) d'un bout à l'autre; **to move a.** avancer; **to hobble/plod a.** avancer en boitant/péniblement; **I'll be** *or* **come a. shortly** je viendrai tout à l'heure; **come a.!** venez donc!

alongside [əlɒŋ'saɪd] *prep* & *adv* à côté (de); **to come a.** (*of ship*) accoster; **a. the kerb** le long du trottoir.

aloof [ə'lu:f] *a* distant ▮ *adv* à distance; **to keep a.** garder ses distances (**from** par rapport à). ●aloofness *n* réserve *f*.

aloud [ə'laʊd] *adv* à haute voix.

alphabet ['ælfəbet] *n* alphabet *m*. ●alpha'betical *a* alphabétique.

Alps [ælps] *npl* **the A.** les Alpes *fpl*. ●alpine *a* (*club, range etc*) alpin; (*scenery*) alpestre.

already [ɔ:l'redɪ] *adv* déjà.

alright [ɔ:l'raɪt] *adv* *Fam* = **all right.**

Alsatian [æl'seɪʃ(ə)n] *n* (*dog*) berger *m* allemand, chien-loup *m*.

also ['ɔ:lsəʊ] *adv* aussi, également; (*moreover*) de plus. ●also-ran *n* (*person*) perdant, -ante *mf*.

altar ['ɔ:ltər] *n* autel *m*.

alter ['ɔ:ltər] *vt* changer, modifier; (*clothing*) retoucher ▮ *vi* changer. ●alteration [-'reɪʃ(ə)n] *n* changement *m*, modification *f*; (*of clothing*) retouche *f*; **alterations** (*to building*) travaux *mpl*.

altercation [ɔ:ltə'keɪʃ(ə)n] *n* altercation *f*.

alternate [ɔ:l'tɜ:nət] *a* alterné; **on a. days** tous les deux jours; **a. laughter and tears** des rires et des larmes qui se succèdent ▮ ['ɔ:ltəneɪt] *vi* alterner (**with** avec); **alternating current** *El* courant *m* alternatif ▮ *vt* faire alterner. ●alternately *adv* alternativement. ●alternation [-'neɪʃ(ə)n] *n* alternance *f*.

alternative [ɔːlˈtɜːnətɪv] *a (other)* autre, *pl* d'autres; **an a. way**/*etc* une autre façon/*etc*; **a. answers**/*etc* d'autres réponses/*etc* (différentes) **‖** *n (choice)* alternative *f*. ● **alternatively** *adv* (or) **a.** *(or else)* ou alors, ou bien.

although [ɔːlˈðəʊ] *adv* bien que, quoique (+ *sub*).

altitude [ˈæltɪtjuːd] *n* altitude *f*.

altogether [ɔːltəˈgeðər] *adv (completely)* tout à fait; *(on the whole)* somme toute; **how much a.?** combien en tout?

aluminium [*Br* æljʊˈmɪnjəm] (*Am* **aluminum** [əˈluːmɪnəm]) *n* aluminium *m*.

alumnus, *pl* **-ni** [əˈlʌmnəs, -naɪ] *n Am* ancien(ne) élève *mf*, ancien(ne) étudiant, -ante *mf*.

always [ˈɔːlweɪz] *adv* toujours; **he's a. criticizing** il est toujours à critiquer; **as a.** comme toujours.

am [æm, *unstressed* əm] *see* be.

a.m. [ˈeɪˈem] *adv* du matin.

amalgam [əˈmælgəm] *n (mix)* amalgame *m*.

amalgamate [əˈmælgəmeɪt] *vt (organizations, clubs etc)* fusionner **‖** *vi (of organizations etc)* fusionner.

amass [əˈmæs] *vt (riches, a fortune etc)* amasser.

amateur [ˈæmətər] *n* amateur *m*; **a. painter/actress**/*etc* peintre *m*/actrice *f*/*etc* amateur **‖** *a (interest, sports)* d'amateur. ● **amateurish** *a (work) Pej* d'amateur; *(person) Pej* maladroit, malhabile. ● **amateurism** *n* amateurisme *m*.

amaze [əˈmeɪz] *vt* stupéfier, étonner. ● **amazed** *a* stupéfait **(at sth de)**, étonné **(at sth** par *or* de qch); *(filled with wonder)* émerveillé; **a. at seeing**/*etc* stupéfait *or* étonné de voir/*etc*. ● **amazing** *a* stupéfiant; *(incredible)* extraordinaire. ● **amazingly** *adv* extraordinairement; *(miraculously)* par miracle.

amazement [əˈmeɪzmənt] *n* stupéfaction *f*; *(sense of wonder)* émerveillement *m*; **to my a.** à ma (grande) stupéfaction.

ambassador [æmˈbæsədər] *n* ambassadeur *m*; *(woman)* ambassadrice *f*.

amber [ˈæmbər] *n* ambre *m*; **a. (light)** *(of traffic signal)* (feu *m*) orange *m*; **the lights are at a.** le feu est à l'orange.

ambidextrous [æmbɪˈdekstrəs] *a* ambidextre.

ambiguous [æmˈbɪgjʊəs] *a* ambigu (*f* -uë). ● **ambiguously** *adv* de façon ambiguë. ● **ambi'guity** *n* ambiguïté *f*.

ambition [æmˈbɪʃ(ə)n] *n* ambition *f*. ● **ambitious** *a* ambitieux.

ambivalent [æmˈbɪvələnt] *a* ambigu (*f* -uë), équivoque.

amble [ˈæmb(ə)l] *vi* marcher d'un pas tranquille.

ambulance [ˈæmbjʊləns] *n* ambulance *f*; **a. driver** ambulancier, -ière *mf*.

ambush [ˈæmbʊʃ] *n* embuscade *f*, guet-apens *m* **‖** *vt* prendre en embuscade; **to be ambushed** tomber dans une embuscade.

amen [*Br* ɑːˈmen, *Am* eɪˈmen] *int* amen.

amenable [əˈmiːnəb(ə)l] *a* docile; **a. to** *(responsive to)* sensible à; **a. to reason** raisonnable.

amend [əˈmend] *vt (text)* modifier; *(law etc) Pol* amender; *(conduct)* corriger. ● **amendment** *n (to law, rule)* Pol amendement *m*.

amends [əˈmendz] *npl* **to make a. for** réparer; **to make a.** réparer son erreur.

amenities [*Br* əˈmiːnɪtɪz, *Am* əˈmenɪtɪz] *npl* *(pleasant things)* agréments *mpl*; *(of sports club etc)* équipement *m*; *(of town)* aménagements *mpl*.

America [əˈmerɪkə] *n* Amérique *f*; **North/South A.** Amérique du Nord/du Sud. ● **American** *a* américain **‖** *n* Américain, -aine *mf*. ● **Americanism** *n* américanisme *m*.

amethyst [ˈæməθɪst] *n* améthyste *f*.

amiable [ˈeɪmɪəb(ə)l] *a* aimable.

amicable [ˈæmɪkəb(ə)l] *a* amical. ● **amicably** *adv (to part etc)* amicalement; *(to settle a dispute etc)* Jur à l'amiable.

amid(st) [əˈmɪd(st)] *prep* au milieu de, parmi.

amiss [əˈmɪs] *adv & a* mal (à propos); **something is a.** *(wrong)* quelque chose ne va pas; **that wouldn't come a.** ça ne ferait pas de mal; **to take sth a.** prendre qch en mauvaise part.

ammonia [əˈməʊnjə] *n (gas)* ammoniac *m*; *(liquid)* ammoniaque *f*.

ammunition [æmjʊˈnɪʃ(ə)n] *n* munitions *fpl*.

amnesia [æmˈniːzjə] *n* amnésie *f*.

amnesty [ˈæmnəstɪ] *n* amnistie *f*.

amniocentesis [æmnɪəʊsenˈtiːsɪs] *n* amniocentèse *f*.

amok [əˈmɒk] *adv* **to run 'a.** *(of crowd)* se déchaîner; *(of person, animal)* devenir fou furieux.

among(st) [əˈmʌŋ(st)] *prep (amidst)* parmi; *(between)* entre; **a. the crowd/books/others/**/*etc* parmi la foule/les livres/les autres/*etc*; **a. themselves/friends** entre eux/amis; **a. the French**/*etc (group)* chez les Français/*etc*; **a. other things** entre autres (choses).

amoral [eɪˈmɒrəl] *a* amoral.

amorous [ˈæmərəs] *a (look, words)* polisson; *(person)* d'humeur polissonne; *(adventure etc)* amoureux.

amount [əˈmaʊnt] **1** *n* quantité *f*; *(sum of money)* somme *f*; *(total figure of invoice, debt etc)* montant *m*; *(scope, size)* importance *f*. **2** *vi* **to a. to** s'élever à; *(mean) Fig* signifier; *(represent)* représenter; **it amounts to the same thing** ça revient au même.

amp [æmp] *n (unit of electricity)* ampère *m*; **3-a. plug** *Br* prise *f* avec fusible de 3 ampères.

amphibian [æmˈfɪbɪən] *n & a* amphibie *(m)*. ● **amphibious** *a* amphibie.

amphitheatre [ˈæmfɪθɪətər] *n (Greek, Roman)* amphithéâtre *m*.

ample [ˈæmp(ə)l] *a (enough)* largement assez de *(livres, argent etc)*; *(roomy)* ample;

11 annuity

(*reasons, means*) solides; **you have a. time** tu
as largement le temps; **that's (quite) a.** c'est
largement suffisant. ●**amply** *adv* largement,
amplement.
amplify ['æmplɪfaɪ] *vt* (*sound*) amplifier.
●**amplifier** *n* amplificateur *m*.
amputate ['æmpjuteɪt] *vt* amputer; **to a.
s.o.'s hand**/etc amputer qn de la main/etc.
●**amputation** [-'teɪʃ(ə)n] *n* amputation *f*.
amuck [ə'mʌk] *adv see* **amok**.
amuse [ə'mjuːz] *vt* amuser, divertir; **to keep
s.o. amused** amuser qn. ●**amusing** *a* amusant. ●**amusement** *n* amusement *m*, divertissement *m*; (*pastime*) distraction *f*;
amusements (*at fairground*) attractions *fpl*;
(*gambling machines*) machines *fpl* à sous; **a.
arcade** salle *f* de jeux; **a. park** parc *m*
d'attractions.
an [æn, *unstressed* ən] *see* **a**.
anachronism [ə'nækrənɪz(ə)m] *n* anachronisme *m*.
an(a)emia [ə'niːmɪə] *n* anémie *f*. ●**an(a)emic**
a anémique; **to become a.** faire de l'anémie.
an(a)esthesia [ænɪs'θiːzɪə] *n* anesthésie *f*.
●**an(a)esthetic** [ænɪs'θetɪk] *n* anesthésie *f*;
(*substance*) anesthésique *m*; **under the a.**
sous anesthésie; **general/local a.** anesthésie *f*
générale/locale. ●**an(a)esthetize** [ə'niːsθɪtaɪz]
vt anesthésier.
anagram ['ænəgræm] *n* anagramme *f*.
anal ['eɪnəl] *a* anal.
analogy [ə'nælədʒɪ] *n* analogie *f* (**with** avec).
●**analogous** *a* analogue (**to** à).
analyse ['ænəlaɪz] *vt* analyser. ●**analysis,** *pl*
-yses [ə'nælɪsɪs, -ɪsiːz] *n* analyse *f*. ●**analyst**
n analyste *mf*. ●**ana'lytical** *a* analytique.
anarchy ['ænəkɪ] *n* anarchie *f*. ●**a'narchic** *a*
anarchique. ●**anarchist** *n* anarchiste *mf*.
anathema [ə'næθəmə] *n Rel* anathème *m*; **it
is (an) a. to me** j'ai une sainte horreur de
cela.
anatomy [ə'nætəmɪ] *n* anatomie *f*.
●**ana'tomical** *a* anatomique.
ancestor ['ænsestər] *n* ancêtre *m*.
●**an'cestral** *a* ancestral; **a. home** demeure *f*
ancestrale. ●**ancestry** *n* (*lineage*) ascendance
f; (*ancestors*) ancêtres *mpl*.
anchor ['æŋkər] *n* ancre *f*; **to weigh a.** lever
l'ancre ▌ *vt* (*ship*) mettre à l'ancre ▌ *vi* jeter
l'ancre, mouiller. ●**anchored** *a* ancré, à
l'ancre. ●**anchorage** *n* mouillage *m*.
anchovy [*Br* 'æntʃəvɪ, *Am* æn'tʃəʊvɪ] *n*
anchois *m*.
ancient ['eɪnʃənt] *a* ancien; (*pre-medieval*)
antique; (*person*) *Hum* d'un grand âge.
ancillary [æn'sɪlərɪ] *a* auxiliaire.
and [ænd, *unstressed* ən(d)] *conj* et; **a knife
a. fork** un couteau et une fourchette; **two
hundred a. two** deux cent deux; **four a. three
quarters** quatre trois quarts; **better a. better**
de mieux en mieux; **go a. see** va voir; **I
knocked a. knocked** j'ai frappé bien des fois.
anecdote ['ænɪkdəʊt] *n* anecdote *f*.
anemone [ə'nemənɪ] *n* anémone *f*.
anew [ə'njuː] *adv Lit* de *or* à nouveau.

angel ['eɪndʒəl] *n* ange *m*. ●**an'gelic** *a* angélique.
anger ['æŋgər] *n* colère *f*; **in a., out of a.**
sous le coup de la colère ▌ *vt* mettre en colère, fâcher.
angina [æn'dʒaɪnə] *n* angine *f* de poitrine.
angle¹ ['æŋg(ə)l] *n* angle *m*; **at an a.** en biais.
angle² ['æŋg(ə)l] *vi* (*to fish*) pêcher à la
ligne; **to a. for** (*compliments etc*) *Fig* quêter.
●**angling** *n* pêche *f* à la ligne. ●**angler** *n*
pêcheur, -euse *mf* à la ligne.
Anglican ['æŋglɪkən] *a & n* anglican, -ane
(*mf*).
anglicism ['æŋglɪsɪz(ə)m] *n* anglicisme *m*.
Anglo- ['æŋgləʊ] *pref* anglo-. ●**Anglo-'Saxon**
a & n anglo-saxon, -onne (*mf*).
angora [æn'gɔːrə] *n* (*wool*) angora *m*; **a.
sweater**/etc pull *m*/etc en angora.
angry ['æŋgrɪ] *a* (**-ier, -iest**) (*person*) en colère, fâché; (*look*) fâché; **an a. letter** une
lettre indignée; **a. words** des paroles in-
dignées; **to get a.** se fâcher, se mettre en colère (**with** contre). ●**angrily** *adv* (*to leave*) en
colère; (*to speak*) avec colère.
anguish ['æŋgwɪʃ] *n* angoisse *f*. ●**anguished**
a (*look, voice etc*) angoissé.
angular ['æŋgjʊlər] *a* (*face*) anguleux.
animal ['ænɪməl] *a* (*kingdom, fat etc*) animal
▌ *n* animal *m*, bête *f*.
animate ['ænɪmeɪt] *vt* animer ▌ ['ænɪmət] *a*
(*alive*) animé. ●**animated** *a* (*lively*) animé;
to become a. s'animer. ●**animation** [-'meɪʃ(ə)n]
n (*liveliness*) & *Cinema* animation *f*.
animosity [ænɪ'mɒsɪtɪ] *n* animosité *f*.
aniseed ['ænɪsiːd] *n* (*as flavouring*) anis *m*;
a. drink/etc boisson *f*/etc à l'anis.
ankle ['æŋk(ə)l] *n* cheville *f*; **a. sock** so-
quette *f*.
annals ['æn(ə)lz] *npl* annales *fpl*.
annex [ə'neks] *vt* annexer. ●**annexation**
[ænek'seɪʃ(ə)n] *n* annexion *f*.
annex, *Br* **annexe** ['æneks] *n* (*building*)
annexe *f*.
annihilate [ə'naɪəleɪt] *vt* anéantir, annihiler.
●**annihilation** [-'leɪʃ(ə)n] *n* anéantissement *m*.
anniversary [ænɪ'vɜːsərɪ] *n* (*of event*) anniversaire *m*, commémoration *f*.
annotate ['ænəteɪt] *vt* annoter. ●**annotation**
[-'teɪʃ(ə)n] *n* annotation *f*.
announce [ə'naʊns] *vt* annoncer; (*birth,
marriage*) faire part de. ●**announcement** *n*
(*statement*) annonce *f*; (*notice of birth,
marriage, death*) avis *m*; (*private letter*)
faire-part *m inv*. ●**announcer** *n* (*on TV*)
speaker *m*, speakerine *f*.
annoy [ə'nɔɪ] *vt* (*inconvenience*) ennuyer,
gêner; (*irritate*) agacer, contrarier.
●**annoyed** *a* contrarié, fâché; **to get a.** se
fâcher (**with** contre). ●**annoying** *a* ennuyeux,
contrariant. ●**annoyance** *n* contrariété *f*, ennui *m*.
annual ['ænjʊəl] *a* annuel ▌ *n* (*yearbook*)
annuaire *m*; (*children's*) album *m*. ●**annually**
adv annuellement.
annuity [ə'njuːɪtɪ] *n* (*of retired person*) pen-

sion f viagère.

annul [ə'nʌl] vt (**-ll-**) (contract, marriage etc) annuler. ● **annulment** n annulation f.

anoint [ə'nɔɪnt] vt oindre (**with** de). ● **anointed** a oint.

anomalous [ə'nɒmələs] a anormal. ● **anomaly** n anomalie f.

anon [ə'nɒn] adv Hum tout à l'heure.

anonymous [ə'nɒnɪməs] a anonyme; **to remain a.** garder l'anonymat. ● **ano'nymity** n anonymat m.

anorak ['ænəræk] n anorak m.

anorexia [ænə'reksɪə] n anorexie f. ● **anorexic** a & n anorexique (mf).

another [ə'nʌðər] a & pron un(e) autre; **a. man** (different) un autre homme; **a. month** (additional) encore un mois, un autre mois; **a. ten** encore dix; **one a.** l'un(e) l'autre; **they** les un(e)s les autres; **they love one a.** ils s'aiment (l'un l'autre).

answer ['ɑːnsər] n réponse f; (to problem, riddle) & Math solution f (to de); (reason) explication f; **in a. to your letter** en réponse à votre lettre.

❙ vt (person, question, letter, phone etc) répondre à; (prayer, wish) exaucer; **he answered 'yes'** il a répondu 'oui'; **to a. the bell** or **the door** ouvrir la porte; **to a. s.o. back** (be rude to) répondre à qn.

❙ vi répondre; **to a. back** (rudely) répondre, répliquer; **to a. for s.o./sth** (be responsible for) répondre de qn/qch; **to a. (to) a description** (of police suspect) répondre à un signalement. ● **answering machine** n répondeur m.

answerable ['ɑːnsərəb(ə)l] a responsable (**for sth** de qch, **to s.o.** devant qn).

ant [ænt] n fourmi f. ● **anthill** n fourmilière f.

antagonism [æn'tægənɪz(ə)m] n (hostility) hostilité f. ● **antagonist** n adversaire mf. ● **antagonize** vt provoquer (l'hostilité de).

Antarctic [æn'tɑːktɪk] a antarctique ❙ n the A. l'Antarctique m.

antecedent [æntɪ'siːd(ə)nt] n antécédent m.

antechamber ['æntɪtʃeɪmbər] n antichambre f.

antedate ['æntɪdeɪt] vt (letter) antidater.

antelope ['æntɪləup] n antilope f.

antenatal [æntɪ'neɪt(ə)l] a Br prénatal; **a. clinic** service m de gynécologie-obstétrique ❙ n Br examen m prénatal.

antenna¹, pl **-ae** [æn'tenə, -iː] n (of insect etc) antenne f.

antenna² [æn'tenə] n (pl **-as**) (for TV, radio) Am antenne f.

anteroom ['æntɪrum] n antichambre f.

anthem ['ænθəm] n national a. hymne m national.

anthill ['ænθɪl] n see ant.

anthology [æn'θɒlədʒɪ] n recueil m, anthologie f.

anthropology [ænθrə'pɒlədʒɪ] n anthropologie f.

anti- [Br 'æntɪ, Am 'æntaɪ] pref anti-; **to be a. sth** Fam être contre qch. ● **anti'aircraft** a

antiaérien. ● **antibi'otic** a & n antibiotique (m). ● **antibody** n anticorps m. ● **anti'climax** n chute f dans l'ordinaire; (letdown) déception f. ● **anti'clockwise** adv Br dans le sens inverse des aiguilles d'une montre. ● **anti'cyclone** n anticyclone m. ● **antidote** n antidote m. ● **antifreeze** n (for vehicle) antigel m. ● **anti'histamine** n (drug) antihistaminique m. ● **anti'perspirant** n antisudoral m. ● **anti-Se'mitic** a antisémite. ● **anti-'Semitism** n antisémitisme m. ● **anti'septic** a & n antiseptique (m). ● **anti'social** a (misfit) asocial; (measure, principles) antisocial; (unsociable) peu sociable.

anticipate [æn'tɪsɪpeɪt] vt (foresee) prévoir; (expect) s'attendre à; (forestall) devancer; (the future) anticiper sur. ● **antici'pation** n (expectation) attente f; (foresight) prévision f; **in a. of** dans l'attente de, en prévision de; **in a.** (to thank s.o., pay etc) d'avance.

antics ['æntɪks] npl singeries fpl.

antipathy [æn'tɪpəθɪ] n antipathie f.

antipodes [æn'tɪpədiːz] npl antipodes mpl.

antiquarian [æntɪ'kweərɪən] a. **bookseller** libraire mf spécialisé(e) dans le livre ancien.

antiquated ['æntɪkweɪtɪd] a (expression, custom etc) vieilli; (person) vieux jeu inv; (object, machine) antédiluvien.

antique [æn'tiːk] a (furniture etc) ancien; (of Greek or Roman antiquity) antique; **a. dealer** antiquaire mf; **a. shop** magasin m d'antiquités ❙ n antiquité f, objet m ancien or d'époque. ● **antiquity** n (period etc) antiquité f.

antithesis, pl **-eses** [æn'tɪθəsɪs, -ɪsiːz] n antithèse f.

antler ['æntlər] n (of deer) andouiller m; **the antlers** les bois mpl.

antonym ['æntənɪm] n antonyme m.

Antwerp ['æntwɜːp] n Anvers m or f.

anus ['eɪnəs] n anus m.

anvil ['ænvɪl] n enclume f.

anxiety [æŋ'zaɪətɪ] n (worry) inquiétude f (about au sujet de); (fear) anxiété f; (eagerness) impatience f (to do de faire, for sth de qch).

anxious ['æŋkʃəs] a (worried) inquiet (about de, pour); (troubled) anxieux; (causing worry) inquiétant; (eager) impatient (to do de faire); **I'm a. (that) he should leave** je tiens beaucoup à ce qu'il parte. ● **anxiously** adv avec inquiétude; (to wait, await etc) impatiemment.

any ['enɪ] a **1** (in questions) du, de la, des; **have you a. milk/tickets?** avez-vous du lait/des billets?; **is there a. man (at all) who...?** y a-t-il un homme (quelconque) qui...?

2 (negative) de; (not the slightest) aucun; **he hasn't got a. milk/tickets/etc** il n'a pas de lait/de billets/etc; **there isn't a. proof/doubt/problem** il n'y a aucune preuve/aucun doute/aucun problème.

3 (no matter which) n'importe quel; **ask a. doctor** demande à n'importe quel médecin.

4 (every) tout; **at a. moment** à tout moment;

in a. case, at a. rate de toute façon.

▌ *pron* 1 (*no matter which one*) n'importe lequel; (*somebody*) quelqu'un; **if a. of you** si l'un d'entre vous, si quelqu'un parmi vous; **more than a.** plus qu'aucun. 2 (*quantity*) en; **have you got a.?** en as-tu?; **I don't see a.** je n'en vois pas.

▌ *adv* **not a.** further/happier/*etc* pas plus loin/plus heureux/*etc*; **I don't see him a.** more je ne le vois plus; **a. more tea?** (*a little*) encore du thé?, encore un peu de thé?; **a. better?** (un peu) mieux?

anybody ['enɪbɒdɪ] *pron* 1 (*somebody*) quelqu'un; **do you see a.?** vois-tu quelqu'un?; **more than a.** plus que tout autre. 2 (*negative*) personne; **he doesn't know a.** il ne connaît personne. 3 (*no matter who*) n'importe qui; **a. would think that...** on croirait que....

anyhow ['enɪhaʊ] *adv* (*at any rate*) de toute façon; (*badly*) n'importe comment; **to leave sth a.** (*in confusion*) laisser qch sens dessus dessous.

anyone ['enɪwʌn] *pron* = **anybody**.

anyplace ['enɪpleɪs] *adv Am* = **anywhere**.

anything ['enɪθɪŋ] *pron* 1 (*something*) quelque chose; **can you see a.?** voyez-vous quelque chose? 2 (*negative*) rien; **he doesn't do a.** il ne fait rien; **without a.** sans rien. 3 (*everything*) tout; **a. you like** (tout) ce que tu veux; **like a.** (*to work etc*) *Fam* comme un fou. 4 (*no matter what*) **a. (at all)** n'importe quoi.

anyway ['enɪweɪ] *adv* (*at any rate*) de toute façon.

anywhere ['enɪweər] *adv* 1 (*no matter where*) n'importe où. 2 (*everywhere*) partout; **a. you go** où que vous alliez, partout où vous allez; **a. you like** (là) où tu veux. 3 (*somewhere*) quelque part; **is he going a.?** va-t-il quelque part? 4 (*negative*) nulle part; **he doesn't go a.** il ne va nulle part; **without a.** to put it sans un endroit où le mettre.

apace [ə'peɪs] *adv* rapidement.

apart [ə'pɑːt] *adv* 1 (*separated, separate*) **we kept them a.** nous les tenions séparés; **with legs (wide) a.** les jambes écartées; **they are a metre a.** ils se trouvent à un mètre l'un de l'autre; **to come a.** (*of two objects*) se séparer; (*of knot etc*) se défaire; **to tell two things/people a.** distinguer deux choses/personnes (l'une de l'autre); **worlds a.** (*very different*) diamétralement opposé. 2 (*to pieces*) **to tear a.** mettre en pièces; **to take a.** démonter. 3 (*to one side*) à part; **joking a.** plaisanterie à part; **a. from** (*except for*) à part.

apartheid [ə'pɑːteɪt] *n* apartheid *m*.

apartment [ə'pɑːtmənt] *n* (*flat*) *Am* appartement *m*; (*room*) chambre *f*; **a. house** *Am* immeuble *m* (d'habitation).

apathy ['æpəθɪ] *n* apathie *f*. ● **apa'thetic** *a* apathique.

ape [eɪp] *n* singe *m* ▌ *vt* (*imitate*) singer.

aperitif [ə'perətiːf] *n* apéritif *m*.

aperture ['æpətʃʊər] *n* ouverture *f*.

apex ['eɪpeks] *n* (*of triangle etc*) & *Fig* sommet *m*.

aphorism ['æfərɪz(ə)m] *n* aphorisme *m*.

aphrodisiac [æfrə'dɪzɪæk] *a* & *n* aphrodisiaque (*m*).

apiece [ə'piːs] *adv* chacun; **a pound a.** une livre (la) pièce *or* chacun.

apish ['eɪpɪʃ] *a* simiesque; (*imitative*) imitateur.

apocalypse [ə'pɒkəlɪps] *n* apocalypse *f*. ● **apoca'lyptic** *a* apocalyptique.

apocryphal [ə'pɒkrɪfəl] *a* apocryphe.

apogee ['æpədʒiː] *n* apogée *m*.

apologetic [əpɒlə'dʒetɪk] *a* (*letter*) plein d'excuses; **a. smile** sourire *m* d'excuse; **to be a. (about)** s'excuser (de). ● **apologetically** *adv* en s'excusant.

apology [ə'pɒlədʒɪ] *n* excuses *fpl*; **an a. for a dinner** *Fam Pej* un dîner minable. ● **apologist** *n* apologiste *mf*. ● **apologize** *vi* s'excuser (for de); **to a. to s.o.** faire ses excuses à qn (for pour).

apoplexy ['æpəpleksɪ] *n* apoplexie *f*. ● **apo'plectic** *a* & *n* apoplectique (*mf*).

apostle [ə'pɒs(ə)l] *n* apôtre *m*.

apostrophe [ə'pɒstrəfɪ] *n* apostrophe *f*.

appal [ə'pɔːl] (*Am* **appall**) *vt* (-ll-) consterner; **to be appalled (at)** être horrifié (de). ● **appalling** *a* épouvantable.

apparatus [*Br* æpə'reɪtəs, *Am* -'rætəs] *n* (*equipment, organization*) appareil *m*; (*in gym*) *Br* agrès *mpl*.

apparel [ə'pærəl] *n Lit* habit *m*; **an article of a.** un habit.

apparent [ə'pærənt] *a* (*obvious, seeming*) apparent; **it's a. that** il est évident que. ● **apparently** *adv* apparemment.

apparition [æpə'rɪʃ(ə)n] *n* (*phantom*) apparition *f*.

appeal [ə'piːl] *n* (*charm*) attrait *m*; (*interest*) intérêt *m*; (*call*) appel *m*; (*pleading*) supplication *f*; (*to a court*) appel *m*.

▌ *vt* **to a. to** (*s.o., s.o.'s kindness*) faire appel à; **to a. to s.o.** (*attract*) plaire à qn, séduire qn; (*interest*) intéresser qn; **to a. to s.o. for sth** demander qch à qn; **to a. to s.o. to do** supplier qn de faire.

▌ *vi* (*in court*) faire appel. ● **appealing** *a* (*attractive*) (*offer, job etc*) séduisant; (*begging*) (*look*) suppliant.

appear [ə'pɪər] *vi* (*become visible*) apparaître; (*present oneself*) se présenter; (*seem, be published*) paraître; (*on stage, in film*) jouer; (*in court*) comparaître; **it appears that** (*it seems*) il semble que (+ *sub or indic*); (*it is rumoured*) il paraîtrait que (+ *indic*). ● **appearance** *n* (*act*) apparition *f*; (*look*) apparence *f*, aspect *m*; (*of book*) parution *f*; **to put in an a.** faire acte de présence; **to keep up appearances** sauver les apparences.

appease [ə'piːz] *vt* (*soothe*) apaiser; (*curiosity*) satisfaire.

append [ə'pend] *vt* joindre, ajouter (to à). ● **appendage** *n Anat* appendice *m*.

appendix, pl **-ixes** or **-ices** [ə'pendɪks, -ɪksɪz, -ɪsiːz] n (in book, body) appendice m; **to have one's a. out** se faire opérer de l'appendicite. ● **appendicitis** [əpendɪ'saɪtɪs] n appendicite f.

appertain [æpə'teɪn] vi **to a. to** se rapporter à.

appetite ['æpɪtaɪt] n appétit m; **to take away s.o.'s a.** couper l'appétit à qn. ● **appetizer** n (drink) apéritif m; (food) amuse-gueule m inv. ● **appetizing** a (food) appétissant.

applaud [ə'plɔːd] vt (clap) applaudir; (approve of) approuver, applaudir à ∎ vi applaudir. ● **applause** n applaudissements mpl.

apple ['æp(ə)l] n pomme f; Br **stewed apples,** Am **a. sauce** compote f de pommes; **cooking a.** pomme f à cuire; **eating a.** pomme à manger crue; **a. pie** tarte f aux pommes; **a. core** trognon m de pomme; **a. tree** pommier m.

appliance [ə'plaɪəns] n appareil m.

applicable [ə'plɪkəb(ə)l] a (rule etc) applicable (**to** à); (relevant) pertinent.

applicant ['æplɪkənt] n candidat, -ate mf (for à).

application [æplɪ'keɪʃ(ə)n] n **1** (request) demande f (for de); (for job) candidature f; (for membership) demande f d'adhésion or d'inscription; **a. (form)** (for job) formulaire m de candidature; (for club) formulaire m d'inscription or d'adhésion. **2** (diligence) application f.

apply [ə'plaɪ] vt **1** (put on, carry out etc) appliquer; (brake of vehicle) appuyer sur; **to a. oneself to** s'appliquer à. **2** vi (be relevant) s'appliquer (**to** à); **to a. for** (job) poser sa candidature à, postuler; **to a. to s.o.** (ask) s'adresser à qn (**for** pour). ● **applied** a Math Ling etc appliqué.

appoint [ə'pɔɪnt] vt (person) nommer (**to a post** à un poste, **to do** pour faire); (director, minister etc) nommer; (secretary, clerk etc) engager; (time, place etc) fixer; **at the appointed time** à l'heure dite; **well-appointed** (kitchen etc) bien équipé. ● **appointment** n nomination f; (meeting) rendez-vous m inv; (post) situation f, place f; **to make an a. with** prendre rendez-vous avec.

apportion [ə'pɔːʃ(ə)n] vt répartir; **to a. blame** dégager les responsabilités.

apposite ['æpəzɪt] a juste, à propos.

appraise [ə'preɪz] vt évaluer. ● **appraisal** n évaluation f.

appreciable [ə'priːʃəb(ə)l] a appréciable, sensible.

appreciate [ə'priːʃɪeɪt] **1** vt (enjoy, value, assess) apprécier; (understand) comprendre; (be grateful for) être reconnaissant de. **2** vi prendre de la valeur. ● **appreciation** [-'eɪʃ(ə)n] n **1** (gratitude) reconnaissance f; (judgment) appréciation f. **2** (rise in value) augmentation f (de la valeur). ● **appreciative** a (grateful) reconnaissant (**of** de); (favourable) élogieux; **to be a. of** (enjoy) apprécier.

apprehend [æprɪ'hend] vt (seize, arrest) appréhender.

apprehension [æprɪ'henʃ(ə)n] n (fear) appréhension f. ● **apprehensive** a inquiet (**about** de, au sujet de); **to be a.** redouter, appréhender.

apprentice [ə'prentɪs] n apprenti, -ie mf ∎ vt mettre (qn) en apprentissage (**to** chez). ● **apprenticeship** n apprentissage m.

approach [ə'prəʊtʃ] vt (draw near to) s'approcher de (qn, feu, porte etc); (age, result, town) approcher de; (subject) aborder; (accost) aborder (qn); **to a. s.o. about** parler à qn de.
∎ vi (of person, vehicle) s'approcher; (of date etc) approcher.
∎ n (method) façon f de s'y prendre; (path, route) (voie f d')accès m; (of winter, vehicle) approche f; **at the a. of** à l'approche de; **a. to** (question) manière f d'aborder; **to make approaches to** faire des avances à. ● **approachable** a (person) abordable; (place) accessible **by road**/etc que la route/etc.

appropriate 1 [ə'prəʊprɪət] a (place, clothes, means etc) qui convient, indiqué; (remark, time etc) qui convient, opportun; **a. to** or **for** qui convient à; **it is a. to do** il est indiqué de faire. **2** [ə'prəʊprɪeɪt] vt (steal) s'approprier; (set aside) affecter (**for** à). ● **appropriately** adv convenablement.

approval [ə'pruːvəl] n approbation f; **on a.** (goods) à l'essai.

approve [ə'pruːv] vt approuver; **to a. of** (conduct, decision, idea etc) approuver; **I don't a. of him** il ne me plaît pas, je ne l'apprécie pas; **I a. of his going** je trouve bon qu'il y aille; **I a. of his accepting** or **having accepted** je l'approuve d'avoir accepté. ● **approving** a (look etc) approbateur.

approximate 1 [ə'prɒksɪmət] a approximatif ∎ [ə'prɒksɪmeɪt] vi **to a. to** se rapprocher de. ● **approximately** adv à peu près, approximativement. ● **approximation** [-'meɪʃ(ə)n] n approximation f.

apricot ['eɪprɪkɒt] n abricot m.

April ['eɪprəl] n avril m; **to make an A. fool of s.o.** faire un poisson d'avril à qn; **A. fool!** poisson d'avril!

apron ['eɪprən] n (garment) tablier m.

apse [æps] n (of church) abside f.

apt [æpt] a (remark, reply, means etc) qui convient; (word, name) bien choisi; (student) doué, intelligent; **she/it is a. to fall**/etc (likely) (in general) elle/ça a tendance à tomber/etc; (on a particular occasion) elle/ça pourrait bien tomber/etc; **a. at sth** (manual work) habile à qch; (intellectual) doué pour qch. ● **aptly** adv convenablement; **a. named** qui porte bien son nom.

aptitude ['æptɪtjuːd] n aptitude f (**for** à, pour); (of student) don m (**for French**/etc pour le français/etc).

aqualung ['ækwəlʌŋ] n scaphandre m autonome.

aquarium [ə'kweərɪəm] n aquarium m.

Aquarius [ə'kweərɪəs] n (sign) le Verseau.

aquatic [ə'kwætɪk] a (plant etc) aquatique;

(sport) nautique.

aqueduct ['ækwɪdʌkt] *n* aqueduc *m*.

aquiline ['ækwɪlaɪn] *a (nose, profile)* aquilin.

Arab ['ærəb] *a* arabe ∎ *n* Arabe *mf*. ● **Arabian** [ə'reɪbɪən] *a* arabe. ● **Arabic** *a & n (language)* arabe *(m)*; **A. numerals** chiffres *mpl* arabes.

arabesque [ærə'besk] *n (decoration)* arabesque *f*.

arable ['ærəb(ə)l] *a (land)* arable.

arbiter ['ɑːbɪtər] *n* arbitre *m*.

arbitrary ['ɑːbɪtrərɪ] *a (decision, arrest etc)* arbitraire.

arbitrate ['ɑːbɪtreɪt] *vti* arbitrer. ● **arbitration** [-'treɪʃ(ə)n] *n* arbitrage *m*; **to go to a.** soumettre la question à l'arbitrage. ● **arbitrator** *n (in dispute)* médiateur, -trice *mf*.

arbour ['ɑːbər] *n* tonnelle *f*, charmille *f*.

arc [ɑːk] *n (of circle)* arc *m*.

arcade [ɑː'keɪd] *n (for shops) (small)* passage *m* couvert; *(large)* galerie *f* marchande.

arch [ɑːtʃ] *n (of bridge)* arche *f*; *(of building)* voûte *f*, arc *m*; *(of foot)* cambrure *f* ∎ *vt (one's back etc)* arquer, courber. ● **archway** *n* passage *m* voûté, voûte *f*.

arch- [ɑːtʃ] *pref (villain, hypocrite etc)* achevé, fini; **a.-enemy** ennemi *m* numéro un.

arch(a)eology [ɑːkɪ'ɒlədʒɪ] *n* archéologie *f*. ● **arch(a)eologist** *n* archéologue *mf*.

archaic [ɑː'keɪɪk] *a* archaïque.

archangel [ɑːkeɪndʒəl] *n* archange *m*.

archbishop [ɑːtʃ'bɪʃəp] *n* archevêque *m*.

archer ['ɑːtʃər] *n* archer *m*. ● **archery** *n* tir *m* à l'arc.

archetype ['ɑːkɪtaɪp] *n* archétype *m*.

archipelago [ɑːkɪ'peləgəʊ] *n (pl -oes or -os)* archipel *m*.

architect ['ɑːkɪtekt] *n* architecte *mf*. ● **architecture** *n* architecture *f*.

archives ['ɑːkaɪvz] *npl* archives *fpl*. ● **archivist** ['ɑːkɪvɪst] *n* archiviste *mf*.

arctic ['ɑːktɪk] *a* arctique; *(weather)* polaire, glacial ∎ *n* **the A.** l'Arctique *m*.

ardent ['ɑːdənt] *a (supporter etc)* ardent, chaud. ● **ardently** *adv* ardemment. ● **ardour** *n* ardeur *f*.

arduous ['ɑːdjʊəs] *a* pénible, ardu. ● **arduously** *adv* péniblement, ardument.

are [ɑːr] *see* be.

area ['eərɪə] *n (of country)* région *f*; *(of town)* quartier *m*; Mil zone *f*; Geom superficie *f*; *(domain of knowledge)* Fig domaine *m*, secteur *m*, terrain *m*; **built-up a.** agglomération *f*; **parking a.** aire *f* de stationnement; **dining a.** coin-repas *m*; **kitchen a.** coin-cuisine *m*; **play a.** *(in house)* coin-jeux *m*; *(outdoors)* aire *f* de jeux; **a. code** *(phone number)* Am indicatif *m*; **a. office** agence *f* régionale.

arena [ə'riːnə] *n (for sports)* & Fig arène *f*.

aren't [ɑːnt] = **are not**.

Argentina [ɑːdʒən'tiːnə] *n* Argentine *f*.

Argentine ['ɑːdʒəntaɪn] *n* **the A.** l'Argentine *f*. ● **Argen'tinian** *a* argentin ∎ *n* Argentin,

-ine *mf*.

arguable ['ɑːgʊəb(ə)l] *a* discutable. ● **arguably** *adv* on pourrait soutenir que.

argue ['ɑːgjuː] *vi (quarrel)* se disputer **(with** avec, **about** au sujet de); *(reason)* raisonner **(with** avec, **about** sur); **to a. in favour of** plaider pour ∎ *vt (matter)* discuter; **to a. that** *(maintain)* soutenir que.

argument ['ɑːgjʊmənt] *n (quarrel)* dispute *f*; *(reasoning)* argument *m*; *(debate)* discussion *f*; **to have an a.** se disputer **(with** avec). ● **argu'mentative** *a* querelleur.

aria ['ɑːrɪə] *n* Mus air *m* (d'opéra).

arid ['ærɪd] *a* aride.

Aries ['eəriːz] *n (sign)* le Bélier.

arise [ə'raɪz] *vi (pt arose, pp arisen) (of problem, opportunity etc)* se présenter; *(of cry, objection)* s'élever; *(result)* résulter **(from** de); *(get up)* Lit se lever.

aristocracy [ærɪ'stɒkrəsɪ] *n* aristocratie *f*. ● **aristocrat** [Br 'ærɪstəkræt, Am ə'rɪstəkræt] *n* aristocrate *mf*. ● **aristo'cratic** *a* aristocratique.

arithmetic [ə'rɪθmətɪk] *n* arithmétique *f*.

ark [ɑːk] *n* **Noah's a.** l'arche *f* de Noé.

arm¹ [ɑːm] *n* bras *m*; **a. in a.** bras dessus bras dessous; **with open arms** à bras ouverts. ● **armband** *n* brassard *m*; *(for swimming)* manchon *m*. ● **armchair** *n* fauteuil *m*. ● **armful** *n* brassée *f*. ● **armhole** *n* emmanchure *f*. ● **armpit** *n* aisselle *f*. ● **armrest** *n* accoudoir *m*.

arm² [ɑːm] *vt (with weapon)* armer **(with** de). ● **armaments** *npl* armements *mpl*.

armadillo [ɑːmə'dɪləʊ] *n (pl -os)* tatou *m*.

armistice ['ɑːmɪstɪs] *n* armistice *m*.

armour ['ɑːmər] *n (of knight etc)* armure *f*; *(of tank etc)* blindage *m*. ● **armoured** or **armour-plated** *a (car etc)* blindé. ● **armoury** *n* arsenal *m*.

arms [ɑːmz] *npl (weapons)* armes *fpl*; **the a. race** la course aux armements.

army ['ɑːmɪ] *n* armée *f*; **to join the a.** s'engager; **the regular a.** l'armée active ∎ *a (uniform etc)* militaire.

aroma [ə'rəʊmə] *n* arôme *m*. ● **aro'matic** *a* aromatique. ● **aroma'therapy** *n* aromathérapie *f*.

arose [ə'rəʊz] *see* arise.

around [ə'raʊnd] *prep* autour de; *(approximately)* environ, autour de; **to go a. the world** faire le tour du monde.

∎ *adv* autour; **all a.** tout autour; **to follow s.o. a.** suivre qn partout; **to rush a.** courir çà et là; **a. here** par ici; **he's still a.** il est encore là; **there's a lot of flu a.** il y a pas mal de grippe en ce moment; **up and a.** *(after illness)* Am sur pied, guéri.

arouse [ə'raʊz] *vt (suspicion, anger, curiosity etc)* éveiller, susciter; *(sexually)* exciter *(qn)*; **to a. s.o. from sleep** tirer qn du sommeil.

arrange [ə'reɪndʒ] *vt* arranger; *(time, meeting)* fixer; **it was arranged that** il était convenu que; **to a. to do** s'arranger pour faire. ● **arrangement** *n (layout, agreement)*

---

arrangement *m*; **arrangements** (*preparations*) préparatifs *mpl*; (*plans*) projets *mpl*; **to make arrangements to do** s'arranger pour faire.

array [əˈreɪ] *n* (*display*) étalage *m*. ●**arrayed** *a* (*dressed*) *Lit* (re)vêtu (**in** de).

arrears [əˈrɪəz] *npl* (*payment*) arriéré *m*; **to be in a.** avoir du retard dans ses paiements; **to be three months in a.** avoir trois mois de retard dans ses paiements.

arrest [əˈrest] *vt* (*criminal, progress etc*) arrêter **I** *n* (*of criminal*) arrestation *f*; **under a.** en état d'arrestation; **cardiac a.** arrêt *m* du cœur. ●**arresting** *a* (*striking*) *Fig* frappant.

arrive [əˈraɪv] *vi* arriver; **to a. at** (*conclusion, decision*) arriver à, parvenir à. ●**arrival** *n* arrivée *f*; **on my a.** à mon arrivée; **new a.** nouveau venu *m*, nouvelle venue *f*; (*baby*) nouveau-né, -ée *mf*.

arrogant [ˈærəgənt] *a* arrogant. ●**arrogance** *n* arrogance *f*. ●**arrogantly** *adv* avec arrogance.

arrow [ˈærəʊ] *n* flèche *f*.

arsenal [ˈɑːsən(ə)l] *n* arsenal *m*.

arsenic [ˈɑːsnɪk] *n* arsenic *m*.

arson [ˈɑːs(ə)n] *n* incendie *m* volontaire. ●**arsonist** *n* incendiaire *mf*, pyromane *mf*.

art [ɑːt] *n* art *m*; (*cunning*) artifice *m*; **work of a.** œuvre *f* d'art; **fine arts** beaux-arts *mpl*; **faculty of arts, arts faculty** faculté *f* des lettres; **arts degree** licence *f* ès lettres; **a. exhibition** exposition *f* d'œuvres d'art; **a. school** école *f* des beaux-arts.

artefact [ˈɑːtɪfækt] *n* objet *m* fabriqué.

artery [ˈɑːtərɪ] *n* (*in body, main route*) artère *f*. ●**arterial** [ɑːˈtɪərɪəl] *a* (*blood*) artériel; **a. road** *Br* route *f* principale.

artful [ˈɑːtfəl] *a* rusé, astucieux. ●**artfully** *adv* astucieusement.

arthritis [ɑːˈθraɪtɪs] *n* arthrite *f*.

artichoke [ˈɑːtɪtʃəʊk] *n* (*globe*) **a.** artichaut *m*; **Jerusalem a.** topinambour *m*.

article [ˈɑːtɪk(ə)l] *n* (*object, clause, in newspaper*) & *Grammar* article *m*; **a. of clothing** vêtement *m*; **articles of value** objets *mpl* de valeur; **leading a.** (*in newspaper*) éditorial *m*; **articles** (*of lawyer*) *Br* contrat *m* de stage.

articulate [ɑːˈtɪkjʊlət] *a* (*person*) qui s'exprime clairement; (*speech*) net (*f* nette), distinct **I** [ɑːˈtɪkjʊleɪt] *vti* (*speak*) articuler. ●**articulated lorry** *n* *Br* semi-remorque *m*. ●**articulation** [-ˈleɪʃ(ə)n] *n* articulation *f*.

artifact [ˈɑːtɪfækt] *n* objet *m* fabriqué.

artifice [ˈɑːtɪfɪs] *n* artifice *m*.

artificial [ɑːtɪˈfɪʃ(ə)l] *a* artificiel. ●**artificiˈality** *n* caractère *m* artificiel. ●**artificially** *adv* artificiellement.

artillery [ɑːˈtɪlərɪ] *n* artillerie *f*.

artisan [ˈɑːtɪzæn] *n* artisan *m*.

artist [ˈɑːtɪst] *n* (*painter, actor etc*) artiste *mf*. ●**artiste** [ɑːˈtiːst] *n* (*singer, dancer*) artiste *m*. ●**arˈtistic** *a* (*pattern, treasure etc*) artistique; (*person*) artiste. ●**artistry** *n* art *m*.

artless [ˈɑːtləs] *a* naturel, naïf.

arty [ˈɑːtɪ] *a* *Pej* du genre artiste.

as [æz, *unstressed* əz] *adv* & *conj* **1** (*manner*

etc) comme; **as you like** comme tu veux; **such as** comme; **as I like** comme tu veux; **dressed up as a clown/king/etc** déguisé en clown/roi/etc; **as much *or* as hard as I can** (au)tant que je peux; **as it is** (*this being the case*) les choses étant ainsi; **to leave sth as it is** laisser qch comme ça *or* tel quel; **it's late as it is** il est déjà tard; **as if, as though** comme si; **you look as if *or* as though you're tired** tu as l'air fatigué.

2 (*comparison*) **as tall as you** aussi grand que vous; **is he as tall as you?** est-il aussi *or* si grand que vous?; **as white as a sheet** blanc comme un linge; **as much *or* as hard as you** autant que vous; **the same as** le même que; **twice as big as** deux fois plus grand que.

3 (*though*) **(as) clever as he is** si *or* aussi intelligent qu'il soit.

4 (*capacity*) **as a teacher** comme professeur, en tant que *or* en qualité de professeur; **to act as a father** agir en père.

5 (*reason*) puisque, comme; **as it's late** puisqu'il est tard, comme il est tard.

6 (*time*) **as I was leaving, as I left** comme je partais; **as one grows older** à mesure que l'on vieillit; **as he slept** pendant qu'il dormait; **one day as...** un jour que...; **as from, as of** (*time*) à partir de.

7 (*concerning*) **as for that, as to that** quant à cela.

8 (+ *inf*) **so as to** de manière à; **so stupid as to** assez bête pour.

asap [eɪeseɪˈpiː] *abbr* (*as soon as possible*) le plus tôt possible.

asbestos [æsˈbestəs] *n* amiante *f*.

ascend [əˈsend] *vi* monter **I** *vt* (*throne*) monter sur; (*stairs*) monter; (*mountain*) faire l'ascension de. ●**ascent** *n* ascension *f* (**of** de); (*slope*) côte *f*.

ascertain [æsəˈteɪn] *vt* (*discover*) établir; (*truth*) découvrir; (*check*) s'assurer de; **to a. that** s'assurer que.

ascetic [əˈsetɪk] *a* ascétique **I** *n* ascète *mf*.

ascribe [əˈskraɪb] *vt* attribuer (**to** à).

ash [æʃ] *n* **1** (*of cigarette, fire etc*) cendre *f*; **A. Wednesday** mercredi *m* des Cendres. **2** (*tree*) frêne *m*. ●**ashtray** *n* cendrier *m*.

ashamed [əˈʃeɪmd] *a* **to be/feel a.** avoir honte (**of s.o./sth** de qn/qch); **to be a. of oneself** avoir honte; **to make s.o. a.** faire honte à qn.

ashen [ˈæʃ(ə)n] *a* (*pale grey*) cendré; (*face*) pâle.

ashore [əˈʃɔːr] *adv* **to go a.** débarquer; **to put s.o. a.** débarquer qn.

Asia [ˈeɪʃə, ˈeɪʒə] *n* Asie *f*. ●**Asian** *a* asiatique; (*from India*) *Br* indien **I** *n* Asiatique *mf*; (*Indian*) *Br* Indien, -ienne *mf*.

aside [əˈsaɪd] **1** *adv* de côté; **to draw a.** (*curtain*) écarter; **to take *or* draw s.o. a.** prendre qn à part; **to step a.** s'écarter; **a. from** *Am* en dehors de. **2** *n* (*in play, film*) aparté *m*.

asinine [ˈæsɪnaɪn] *a* stupide, idiot.

ask [ɑːsk] *vt* (*request, inquire*) demander; (*in-*

vite) inviter (**to sth** à qch); **to a. (s.o.) a question** poser une question (à qn); **to a. s.o. the way/the reason/***etc* demander le chemin/la raison/*etc* à qn; **to a. s.o. for sth** demander qch à qn; **to a. s.o. to do** (*request*) demander à qn de faire; (*invite*) inviter qn à faire; **to a. to leave/***etc* demander à partir/*etc*. **‖** *vi* demander; **to a. for sth/s.o.** demander qch/qn; **to a. for sth back** redemander qch; **to a. about sth** se renseigner sur qch; **to a. after** *or* **about s.o.** demander des nouvelles de qn; **to a. s.o. about sth/s.o.** interroger qn sur qch/qn; **the asking price** le prix demandé.

askance [əˈskɑːns] *adv* **to look a. at** regarder avec méfiance.

askew [əˈskjuː] *adv* de biais, de travers.

aslant [əˈslɑːnt] *adv* de travers.

asleep [əˈsliːp] *a* endormi; (*arm, leg*) engourdi; **to be a.** dormir; **to fall a.** s'endormir.

asp [æsp] *n* (*snake*) aspic *m*.

asparagus [əˈspærəgəs] *n* (*plant*) asperge *f*; (*shoots for cooking*) asperges *fpl*.

aspect [ˈæspekt] *n* aspect *m*; (*of house*) orientation *f*.

aspersions [Br əˈspɜːʃ(ə)nz, Am -ʒ(ə)nz] *npl* **to cast a. on** dénigrer.

asphalt [Br ˈæsfælt, Am ˈæsfɔːlt] *n* asphalte *m* **‖** *vt* asphalter.

asphyxia [əsˈfɪksɪə] *n* asphyxie *f*. ● **asphyxiate** *vt* asphyxier. ● **asphyxiation** [æsfɪksɪˈeɪʃ(ə)n] *n* asphyxie *f*.

aspire [əˈspaɪər] *vi* **to a. to** aspirer à. ● **aspiration** [æspəˈreɪʃ(ə)n] *n* aspiration *f*.

aspirin [ˈæsprɪn] *n* aspirine *f*.

ass [æs] *n* (*animal*) âne *m*; (*person*) *Fam* imbécile *mf*, âne *m*; **she-a.** ânesse *f*.

assail [əˈseɪl] *vt* assaillir (**with** de). ● **assailant** *n* agresseur *m*.

assassin [əˈsæsɪn] *n* assassin *m*. ● **assassinate** *vt* (*politician, king etc*) assassiner. ● **assassination** [-ˈneɪʃ(ə)n] *n* assassinat *m*.

assault [əˈsɔːlt] *n* (*military*) assaut *m*; (*crime*) agression *f* **‖** *vt* (*attack*) agresser; (*woman*) violenter.

assemble [əˈsemb(ə)l] *vt* (*objects, ideas*) assembler; (*people*) rassembler; (*machine*) monter **‖** *vi* se rassembler. ● **assembly** *n* (*meeting*) assemblée *f*; (*of machine*) montage *m*, assemblage *m*; (*in school*) rassemblement *m*; **a. line** (*in factory*) chaîne *f* de montage.

assent [əˈsent] *n* assentiment *m* **‖** *vi* consentir (**to** à).

assert [əˈsɜːt] *vt* affirmer (**that** que); (*rights*) revendiquer; **to a. oneself** s'affirmer. ● **assertion** [-ʃ(ə)n] *n* (*statement*) affirmation *f*; (*of rights*) revendication *f*.

assertive [əˈsɜːtɪv] *a* (*forceful*) (*tone person etc*) affirmatif; (*authoritarian*) autoritaire.

assess [əˈses] *vt* (*estimate, evaluate*) évaluer; (*decide amount of*) fixer le montant de; (*person*) juger. ● **assessment** *n* évaluation *f*; (*of person*) jugement *m*. ● **assessor** *n* (*valuer*) expert *m*.

asset [ˈæset] *n* (*advantage*) atout *m*, avantage *m*; **assets** (*of business*) biens *mpl*, avoir *m*.

assiduous [əˈsɪdjʊəs] *a* assidu, appliqué. ● **assiduously** *adv* avec application.

assign [əˈsaɪn] *vt* (*give*) attribuer; (*day, time etc*) fixer; (*appoint*) nommer; (*send, move*) affecter (**to** à); **he was assigned as director** il a été nommé directeur. ● **assignment** *n* (*task*) mission *f*; (*for student*) devoir *m*.

assimilate [əˈsɪmɪleɪt] *vt* (*absorb*) assimiler **‖** *vi* (*of immigrants etc*) s'assimiler. ● **assimilation** [-ˈleɪʃ(ə)n] *n* assimilation *f*.

assist [əˈsɪst] *vti* aider (**in doing, to do** à faire). ● **assistance** *n* aide *f*; **to be of a. to s.o.** aider qn. ● **assistant** *n* assistant, -ante *mf*; (*in shop*) *Br* vendeur, -euse *mf* **‖** *a* adjoint.

assizes [əˈsaɪzɪz] *npl* (*court meetings*) *Br* assises *fpl*.

associate [əˈsəʊʃɪeɪt] *vt* associer (**with sth** à *or* avec qch, **with s.o.** à qn **‖** *vi* **to a. with s.o.** (*mix socially*) fréquenter qn; **to a. (oneself) with s.o.** (*in business venture*) s'associer à *or* avec qn **‖** [əˈsəʊʃɪət] *n & a* associé, -ée (*mf*). ● **association** [-ˈeɪʃ(ə)n] *n* association *f*; **associations** (*memories*) souvenirs *mpl*.

assorted [əˈsɔːtɪd] *a* (*different*) variés; (*foods*) assortis; **a well-a. couple/***etc* un couple/*etc* bien assorti. ● **assortment** *n* (*of cheeses etc*) assortiment *m*; **an a. of people** des gens de toutes sortes.

assuage [əˈsweɪdʒ] *vt* *Lit* apaiser, adoucir.

assume [əˈsjuːm] *vt* 1 (*suppose*) supposer, présumer (**that** que); **let us a. that...** supposons que... (+ *sub*). 2 (*take on*) prendre; (*responsibility, role*) assumer; (*attitude, name*) adopter. ● **assumed** *a* (*feigned*) faux (*f* fausse); **a. name** nom *m* d'emprunt. ● **assumption** [əˈsʌmpʃ(ə)n] *n* (*supposition*) supposition *f*; **on the a. that** en supposant que (+ *sub*).

assurance [əˈʃʊərəns] *n* (*confidence, certainty*) assurance *f*; (*promise*) engagement *m*, assurance *f*.

assure [əˈʃʊər] *vt* assurer (**s.o. that** à qn que, **s.o. of sth** qn de qch). ● **assuredly** [-ɪdlɪ] *adv* assurément.

asterisk [ˈæstərɪsk] *n* astérisque *m*.

astern [əˈstɜːn] *adv* (*in ship*) à l'arrière.

asthma [Br ˈæsmə, Am ˈæzmə] *n* asthme *m*. ● **asth'matic** *a & n* asthmatique (*mf*).

astir [əˈstɜːr] *a* (*excited*) *Lit* en émoi; (*out of bed*) *Lit* debout.

astonish [əˈstɒnɪʃ] *vt* étonner; **to be astonished** s'étonner (**at sth** de qch). ● **astonishing** *a* étonnant. ● **astonishingly** *adv* étonnamment. ● **astonishment** *n* étonnement *m*.

astound [əˈstaʊnd] *vt* stupéfier, étonner. ● **astounding** *a* stupéfiant.

astray [əˈstreɪ] *adv* **to go a.** s'égarer; **to lead a.** égarer.

astride [əˈstraɪd] *adv* à califourchon **‖** *prep* à cheval sur.

astringent [əˈstrɪndʒənt] *a* (*harsh*) sévère.

astrology [əˈstrɒlədʒɪ] *n* astrologie *f*. ● **astro-**

astronaut

18

loger n astrologue mf.
astronaut ['æstrənɔːt] n astronaute mf.
astronomy [ə'strɒnəmɪ] n astronomie f.
●**astronomer** n astronome m.
●**astro'nomical** a astronomique.
astute [ə'stjuːt] a (crafty) rusé; (clever) astucieux.
asunder [ə'sʌndər] adv to tear a. (to pieces) mettre en pièces; to break a. (in two) casser en deux.
asylum [ə'saɪləm] n asile m; lunatic a. Pej maison f de fous, asile m d'aliénés.
at [æt, unstressed ət] prep 1 à; at the end à la fin; at school à l'école; at work au travail; at six (o'clock) à six heures; at Easter à Pâques; to drive at ten miles an hour rouler à quinze kilomètres à l'heure; to buy/sell at ten francs a kilo acheter/vendre (à) dix francs le kilo.
2 chez; at the doctor's chez le médecin; at home chez soi, à la maison.
3 en; at sea en mer; at war en guerre; good at (geography etc) fort en.
4 contre; angry at fâché contre.
5 sur; to shoot at tirer sur; at my request sur ma demande.
6 de; to laugh at rire de; surprised at surpris de.
7 (au)près de; at the window (au)près de la fenêtre.
8 par; to come in at the door entrer par la porte; six at a time six par six.
9 (phrases) at night la nuit; to look at regarder; not at all pas du tout; (after 'thank you') il n'y a pas de quoi!; nothing at all rien du tout (see also all); to be (hard) at it travailler dur; he's always (on) at me Br Fam il est toujours après moi.
ate [Br et, Am eɪt] see eat.
atheism ['eɪθɪɪz(ə)m] n athéisme m. ●**atheist** n athée mf.
Athens ['æθɪnz] n Athènes m or f.
athlete ['æθliːt] n athlète mf; a.'s foot (disease) mycose f. ●**ath'letic** a athlétique; a. meeting Br réunion f d'athlétisme; Am réunion f sportive. ●**ath'letics** npl Br athlétisme m; Am sport m.
atishoo! [ə'tɪʃuː] (Am atchoo [ə'tʃuː]) int atchoum!
Atlantic [ət'læntɪk] a (coast, ocean) atlantique ∎ n the A. l'Atlantique m.
atlas ['ætləs] n atlas m.
atmosphere ['ætməsfɪər] n atmosphère f. ●**atmospheric** [-'ferɪk] a atmosphérique.
atom ['ætəm] n atome m; a. bomb bombe f atomique. ●**a'tomic** a (bomb etc) atomique. ●**atomizer** n atomiseur m.
atone [ə'təʊn] vi to a. for (one's sins) expier. ●**atonement** n expiation f (for de).
atrocious [ə'trəʊʃəs] a atroce. ●**atrocity** n (cruel action) atrocité f.
atrophy ['ætrəfɪ] vi (of muscle etc) s'atrophier.
attach [ə'tætʃ] vt attacher (to à); (document) joindre (to à); attached to s.o. (fond of) attaché à qn.

attaché [ə'tæʃeɪ] n 1 (in embassy) attaché, -ée mf. 2 a. case attaché-case m.
attachment [ə'tætʃmənt] n (affection) attachement m (to s.o. à qn); (tool) accessoire m; (fastener) attache f.
attack [ə'tæk] 1 n (military etc) attaque f (on contre); (on s.o.'s life) attentat m ∎ vt attaquer; (problem, plan) s'attaquer à ∎ vi attaquer. 2 n (of illness) crise f; (of fever) accès m; an a. of migraine une migraine; heart a. crise f cardiaque. ●**attacker** n agresseur m.
attain [ə'teɪn] vt (aim) parvenir à, atteindre; (ambition) réaliser; (rank) parvenir à. ●**attainable** a (aim) accessible; (ambition, result) réalisable. ●**attainment** n (of ambition) réalisation f (of de); attainments (skills) talents mpl.
attempt [ə'tempt] n tentative f; to make an a. to do essayer or tenter de faire; to make an a. on (record) faire une tentative pour battre; a. on s.o.'s life attentat m contre qn ∎ vt tenter; (task) entreprendre; to a. to do essayer or tenter de faire; attempted murder tentative f de meurtre.
attend [ə'tend] vt (meeting etc) assister à; (course) suivre; (school, church) aller à; (patient) soigner; (wait on, serve) servir; (escort) accompagner; well-attended course cours m très suivi; the meeting was well attended il y avait du monde à la réunion ∎ vi assister; to a. to (take care of) s'occuper de (travail, client etc); (pay attention to) Lit prêter attention à.
attendance [ə'tendəns] n présence f (at à); (people) assistance f; (school) a. scolarité f; in a. de service.
attendant [ə'tendənt] 1 n employé, -ée mf; (in service station) pompiste mf; (in museum) Br gardien, -ienne mf; attendants (of prince, king etc) suite f. 2 a (fact) concomitant.
attention [ə'tenʃ(ə)n] n attention f; to pay a. faire or prêter attention (to à); for the a. of à l'attention de; to stand at a./to a. (of soldier etc) être/se mettre au garde-à-vous; a.! garde-à vous!; a. to detail minutie f.
attentive [ə'tentɪv] a (heedful) attentif (to à); (thoughtful) attentionné (to pour). ●**attentively** adv avec attention, attentivement.
attenuate [ə'tenjʊeɪt] vt atténuer.
attest [ə'test] vt (certify, confirm) confirmer ∎ vi to a. to témoigner de.
attic ['ætɪk] n grenier m.
attire [ə'taɪər] n Lit vêtements mpl.
attitude ['ætɪtjuːd] n attitude f.
attorney [ə'tɜːnɪ] n (lawyer) Am avocat m; district a. Am = procureur m (de la République).
attract [ə'trækt] vt attirer.
attraction [ə'trækʃ(ə)n] n (charm, appeal) attrait m; (place, person etc that attracts) attraction f; (between people) attirance f; (magnetic etc) attraction f; attractions (at fun fair) attractions fpl.
attractive [ə'træktɪv] a (house, room, car

etc) beau (*f* belle); (*price, offer etc*) intéressant; (*landscape*) attrayant; **a. girl** belle fille *f*; **a. boy** beau garçon *m*.

attribute 1 ['ætrıbju:t] *n* (*quality*) attribut *m*. **2** [ə'trıbju:t] *vt* (*ascribe*) attribuer (**to** à). ● **attributable** *a* attribuable (**to** à).

attrition [ə'trıʃ(ə)n] *n* **war of a.** guerre *f* d'usure.

attuned [ə'tju:nd] *a* **a. to** (*of ideas, trends etc*) en accord avec; (*used to*) habitué à.

atypical [eɪ'tıpık(ə)l] *a* peu typique.

aubergine ['əʊbəʒi:n] *n Br* aubergine *f*.

auburn ['ɔ:bən] *a* (*hair*) châtain roux.

auction ['ɔ:kʃən] *n* vente *f* (aux enchères) ▮ *vt* **to a.** (**off**) vendre (aux enchères). ● **auctio'neer** *n* commissaire-priseur *m*, adjudicateur, -trice *mf*.

audacious [ɔ:'deɪʃəs] *a* audacieux. ● **audacity** *n* audace *f*.

audible ['ɔ:dıb(ə)l] *a* (*sound, words etc*) perceptible, audible. ● **audibly** *adv* distinctement.

audience ['ɔ:dıəns] *n* **1** (*of speaker, musician*) auditoire *m*, public *m*; (*in theatre, cinema*) spectateurs *mpl*, public *m*; (*of writer*) public *m*; (*of radio broadcast*) auditeurs *mpl*; **TV a.** téléspectateurs *mpl*. **2** (*interview*) audience *f* (**with s.o.** avec qn).

audio ['ɔ:dıəʊ] *a* (*cassette, system etc*) audio *inv*; **a. tape** cassette *f* audio. ● **audiotypist** *n* dactylo *f* au magnétophone, audiotypiste *mf*. ● **audio-'visual** *a* audio-visuel.

audit ['ɔ:dıt] *vt* (*accounts*) vérifier ▮ *n* vérification *f* (des comptes). ● **auditor** *n* commissaire *m* aux comptes.

audition [ɔ:'dıʃ(ə)n] *n* audition *f* ▮ *vti* auditionner.

auditorium [ɔ:dı'tɔ:rıəm] *n* salle *f* (*de spectacle, concert etc*).

augment [ɔ:g'ment] *vt* augmenter (**with, by** de).

augur ['ɔ:gər] *vi* **to a. well** être de bon augure ▮ *vt* présager.

august [ɔ:'gʌst] *a* auguste.

August ['ɔ:gəst] *n* août *m*.

aunt [ɑ:nt] *n* tante *f*. ● **auntie** *or* **aunty** *n Fam* tata *f*.

au pair [əʊ'peər] *adv* au pair ▮ *n* **au p.** (**girl**) jeune fille *f* au pair.

aura ['ɔ:rə] *n* (*of place*) atmosphère *f*; (*of person*) aura *f*.

auspices ['ɔ:spısız] *npl* **under the a. of** sous les auspices de.

auspicious [ɔ:'spıʃəs] *a* favorable.

austere [ɔ:'stıər] *a* austère. ● **austerity** *n* austérité *f*.

Australia [ɒ'streılıə] *n* Australie *f*. ● **Australian** *a* australien ▮ *n* Australien, -ienne *mf*.

Austria ['ɒstrıə] *n* Autriche *f*. ● **Austrian** *a* autrichien ▮ *n* Autrichien, -ienne *mf*.

authentic [ɔ:'θentık] *a* authentique. ● **authenticate** *vt* authentifier. ● **authen'ticity** *n* authenticité *f*.

author ['ɔ:θər] *n* auteur *m*. ● **authoress** *n* femme *f* auteur. ● **authorship** *n* (*of book etc*)

paternité *f*.

authoritarian [ɔ:θɒrı'teərıən] *a* & *n* autoritaire (*mf*).

authoritative [ɔ:'θɒrıtətıv] *a* (*report, book etc*) qui fait autorité; (*tone, person*) autoritaire.

authority [ɔ:'θɒrıtı] *n* autorité *f*; (*permission*) autorisation *f* (**to do** de faire); **to be in a.** (*in charge*) être responsable; **to be an a.** on faire autorité en ce qui concerne.

authorize ['ɔ:θəraız] *vt* autoriser (**to do** à faire). ● **authorization** [-'zeıʃ(ə)n] *n* autorisation *f* (**to do** de faire).

autistic [ɔ:'tıstık] *a* autiste.

auto ['ɔ:təʊ] *n* (*pl* **-os**) *Am* auto *f*, voiture *f*.

autobiography [ɔ:təʊbaı'ɒgrəfı] *n* autobiographie *f*. ● **autobio'graphical** *a* autobiographique.

autocrat ['ɔ:təkræt] *n* autocrate *m*. ● **auto'cratic** *a* autocratique.

autograph ['ɔ:təgrɑ:f] *n* autographe *m*; **a. book** album *m* d'autographes ▮ *vt* dédicacer (**for s.o.** à qn).

automate ['ɔ:təmeıt] *vt* automatiser. ● **automation** [-'meıʃ(ə)n] *n* automatisation *f*.

automatic [ɔ:tə'mætık] *a* automatique. ● **automatically** *adv* automatiquement.

automaton [ɔ:'tɒmətən] *n* automate *m*.

automobile ['ɔ:təməbi:l] *n Am* auto(mobile) *f*.

autonomous [ɔ:'tɒnəməs] *a* autonome. ● **autonomy** *n* autonomie *f*.

autopsy ['ɔ:tɒpsı] *n* autopsie *f*.

autumn ['ɔ:təm] *n* automne *m*; **in a.** en automne. ● **autumnal** [ɔ:'tʌmnəl] *a* (*weather, day etc*) d'automne, automnal.

auxiliary [ɔ:g'zılıərı] *a* & *n* auxiliaire (*mf*); **a.** (**verb**) (verbe *m*) auxiliaire *m*.

avail [ə'veıl] **1** *vt* **to a. oneself of** profiter de, tirer avantage de. **2** *n* **to no a.** en vain; **of no a.** inutile.

available [ə'veıləb(ə)l] *a* (*object, means, details etc*) disponible; (*person*) libre, disponible; **a. to all** (*education, goal etc*) accessible à tous. ● **availa'bility** *n* (*of object etc*) disponibilité *f*; (*of education etc*) accessibilité *f*.

avalanche ['ævəlɑ:nʃ] *n* avalanche *f*.

avarice ['ævərıs] *n* avarice *f*. ● **ava'ricious** *a* avare.

Ave *abbr* = **avenue**.

avenge [ə'vendʒ] *vt* venger; **to a. oneself** se venger (**on** de).

avenue ['ævənju:] *n* avenue *f*; (*way to a result*) *Fig* voie *f*.

average ['ævərıdʒ] *n* moyenne *f*; **on a.** en moyenne; **above/below a.** au-dessus/au-dessous de la moyenne ▮ *a* moyen ▮ *vt* (*do*) faire en moyenne; (*reach*) atteindre la moyenne de; (*figures*) faire la moyenne de.

averse [ə'vɜ:s] *a* **to be a. to doing** répugner à faire. ● **aversion** [*Br* -ʃ(ə)n, *Am* -ʒ(ə)n] *n* (*dislike*) aversion *f*, répugnance *f*; **to have an a. to sth/to doing** avoir de la répugnance pour qch/à faire.

avert [ə'vɜ:t] *vt* (*prevent*) éviter; **to a. one's**

eyes (*turn away*) détourner les yeux (**from** de).

aviary ['eɪvɪərɪ] *n* volière *f*.

aviation [eɪvɪ'eɪʃ(ə)n] *n* aviation *f*. ● **'aviator** *n* aviateur, -trice *mf*.

avid ['ævɪd] *a* avide (**for** de). ● **avidly** *adv* avidement.

avocado [ævə'kɑːdəʊ] *n* (*pl* -os) **a. (pear)** avocat *m*.

avoid [ə'vɔɪd] *vt* éviter; **to a.** doing éviter de faire; **I can't a. doing it** je ne peux pas ne pas le faire. ● **avoidable** *a* évitable. ● **avoidance** *n* his a. of danger/*etc* son désir *m* d'éviter le danger/*etc*; **tax a.** évasion *f* fiscale.

avowed [ə'vaʊd] *a* (*enemy*) déclaré, avoué.

await [ə'weɪt] *vt* attendre.

awake [ə'weɪk] *vi* (*pt* awoke, *pp* awoken) se réveiller █ *vt* (*person*) réveiller; (*old memories etc*) *Lit* éveiller, réveiller █ *a* réveillé, éveillé; (**wide-)a.** (*not feeling sleepy*) éveillé; **to keep s.o. a.** empêcher qn de dormir, tenir qn éveillé; **he's (still) a.** il ne dort pas (encore); **to lie a.** être incapable de dormir; **a. to** (*conscious of*) conscient de. ● **awaken 1** *vti* = awake. **2** *vt* **to a. s.o. to sth** faire prendre conscience de qch à qn. ● **awakening** *n* réveil *m*; **a rude a.** (*shock*) un réveil brutal.

award [ə'wɔːd] *vt* (*money*) attribuer; (*prize*) décerner, attribuer; **to a. damages** (*of judge*) accorder des dommages-intérêts █ *n* (*prize*) prix *m*, récompense *f*; (*scholarship*) bourse *f*.

aware [ə'weər] *a* **to be a. of** (*conscious*) être conscient de; (*informed*) être au courant de; (*realize*) se rendre compte de; **to become a. of/that** se rendre compte de/que; **to be a. that** se rendre compte que. ● **awareness** *n* conscience *f*.

awash [ə'wɒʃ] *a* inondé (**with** de).

away [ə'weɪ] *adv* **1** (*distant*) loin; **far a.** au loin, très loin; **5 km a.** à 5 km (de distance). **2** (*in time*) **ten days a.** dans dix jours. **3** (*absent, gone*) parti, absent; **a. with you!** va-t-en!; **to drive a.** partir (en voiture); **to fade/melt a.** disparaître/fondre complètement.

4 (*to one side*) **to look** *or* **turn a.** détourner les yeux.

5 (*continuously*) **to work/talk/**etc **a.** travailler/parler/*etc* sans arrêt.

6 to play a. (*of team*) *Br* jouer à l'extérieur.

awe [ɔː] *n* crainte *f* (*mêlée de respect*); **to be in a. of s.o.** éprouver de la crainte envers qn. ● **awe-inspiring** *a* (*impressive*) imposant. ● **awesome** *a* (*impressive*) imposant; (*frightening*) effrayant; (*marvellous*) *Fam* super.

awful ['ɔːfəl] *a* affreux; (*terrifying*) épouvantable; (*ill*) malade; **an a. lot of** *Fam* un nombre incroyable de; **I feel a. (about it)** j'ai vraiment honte. ● **awfully** *adv* (*to suffer etc*) affreusement; (*very*) (*good, pretty etc*) extrêmement, vraiment; (*bad, late etc*) affreusement; **thanks a.** merci infiniment.

awhile [ə'waɪl] *adv* quelque temps; (*to stay, wait*) un peu.

awkward ['ɔːkwəd] *a* **1** (*clumsy*) (*person, gesture etc*) maladroit. **2** (*difficult*) difficile; (*cumbersome*) gênant; (*tool*) peu commode; (*time*) mal choisi; (*silence*) gêné; **the a. age** l'âge ingrat. ● **awkwardly** *adv* (*to walk etc*) maladroitement; (*to speak*) d'un ton gêné; (*placed, situated*) à un endroit peu pratique. ● **awkwardness** *n* maladresse *f*; (*difficulty*) difficulté *f*; (*discomfort*) gêne *f*.

awl [ɔːl] *n* poinçon *m*.

awning ['ɔːnɪŋ] *n* (*of tent*) auvent *m*; (*over shop, window*) store *m*; (*canvas or glass canopy*) marquise *f* (*d'hôtel etc*).

awoke(n) [ə'wəʊk(ən)] *see* awake.

awry [ə'raɪ] *adv* **to go a.** (*of plan etc*) mal tourner.

axe [æks] (*Am* ax) *n* hache *f*; (*reduction*) *Fig* coupe *f* sombre; **to get the a.** (*of project etc*) être abandonné; (*of worker etc*) être mis à la porte █ *vt* réduire; (*job etc*) supprimer; (*project etc*) abandonner.

axiom ['æksɪəm] *n* axiome *m*.

axis, *pl* **axes** ['æksɪs, 'æksiːz] *n Geom etc* axe *m*.

axle ['æks(ə)l] *n* essieu *m*.

ay(e) [aɪ] **1** *adv* oui. **2** *n* **the ayes** (*votes*) les voix *fpl* pour.

azalea [ə'zeɪlɪə] *n* (*plant*) azalée *f*.

B

B, b [biː] n B, b m; **2B** (number) 2 ter.
BA abbr = **Bachelor of Arts.**
babble ['bæb(ə)l] vi (mumble) bredouiller; (of baby, stream) gazouiller ▌ vt to b. (out) (words) bredouiller ▌ n inv (of voices) rumeur f; (of baby, stream) gazouillement m, gazouillis m.
babe [beɪb] n **1** petit(e) enfant mf, bébé m. **2** (girl) Sl pépée f.
baboon [bə'buːn] n babouin m.
baby ['beɪbɪ] **1** n bébé m; **b. boy** petit garçon m; **b. girl** petite fille f; **b. tiger/etc** bébé-tigre/etc m; **b. clothes/toys/etc** vêtements mpl/jouets mpl/etc de bébé; **b. carriage** Am voiture f d'enfant; **b. sling** kangourou® m, porte-bébé m; **b. face** visage m poupin.
2 n Sl (girl) pépée f; (girlfriend) copine f.
3 n Fam dorloter. ●**baby-batterer** n bourreau m d'enfants. ●**baby-minder** n Br gardien, -ienne mf d'enfants. ●**baby-sit** vi (pt & pp -sat, pres p -sitting) garder les enfants, faire du baby-sitting. ●**baby-sitter** n babysitter mf. ●**baby-snatching** n rapt m d'enfant. ●**baby-walker** n trotteur m, youpala® m.
babyish ['beɪbɪɪʃ] a de bébé; (puerile) bébé inv, puéril; that's too b. ça fait trop bébé.
bachelor ['bætʃələr] n **1** célibataire m; **b. flat** Br garçonnière f. **2** B. of Arts/of Science licencié, -ée m/f ès lettres/ès sciences.
back¹ [bæk] n (of person, animal) dos m; (of chair) dossier m; (of hand) revers m; (of house) arrière m, derrière m; (of vehicle, train, head) arrière m; (of room) fond m; (of page) verso m; (of fabric) envers m; Football arrière m; **at the b. of the book** à la fin du livre; **in** or **at the b. of the car** à l'arrière de la voiture; **at the b. of one's mind** derrière la tête; **b. to front** devant derrière, à l'envers; **to get off s.o.'s b.** Fam ficher la paix à qn; **to get s.o.'s b. up** Fam irriter qn; **in b. of** Am derrière.
back² [bæk] a (wheel, seat) arrière inv; **b. door** porte f de derrière; **b. end** (of bus) arrière m; **b. number** (of magazine etc) vieux numéro m; **b. pay** rappel m de salaire; **b. payments** arriéré m; **b. room** pièce f du fond; **b. street** rue f écartée; **b. taxes** arriéré m d'impôts; **b. tooth** molaire f.
back³ [bæk] adv (behind) en arrière; **far b., a long way b.** loin derrière; **a long way b. in the past** à une époque reculée; **a month b.** il y a un mois; **to stand b.** (of house) être en retrait (**from the road** par rapport à la route); **to go b. and forth** aller et venir; **to come b.** revenir; **he's b.** il est de retour, il est rentré or revenu; **the trip there and b.** le

voyage aller et retour.
back⁴ [bæk] vt (with money) financer; (horse etc) parier sur, jouer; (vehicle) faire reculer; **to be backed with** (of curtain, picture etc) être renforcé de; **to b. s.o (up)** (support) appuyer qn; **to b. up** Comptr sauvegarder.
▌ vi (move backwards) reculer; **to b. down** se dégonfler; **to b. out** (withdraw) se retirer; (of vehicle) sortir en marche arrière; **to b. on to** (of house etc) donner par derrière sur; **to b. up** (of vehicle) faire marche arrière.
backache [bæk] n mal m de dos or aux reins. ●**back'bencher** n Br Pol membre m sans portefeuille. ●**backbiting** n médisance f. ●**backbone** n see below. ●**backbreaking** a éreintant. ●**backchat** n Br impertinence f. ●**backcloth** n toile f de fond. ●**back'date** vt (Br cheque, Am check) antidater; **backdated (salary) increase** augmentation f (de salaire) avec effet rétroactif. ●**back'fire** vi see below. ●**background** n see below. ●**back'handed** a (compliment) équivoque. ●**backhander** n (stroke) revers m; (bribe) Br Fam pot-de-vin m. ●**backpack** n sac m à dos. ●**backrest** n dossier m. ●**backside** n (buttocks) Fam derrière m. ●**back'stage** adv dans les coulisses. ●**backstroke** n (in swimming) dos m crawlé. ●**backtrack** vi rebrousser chemin. ●**backup** n appui m; (tailback) Am embouteillage m; Comptr sauvegarde f; **b. lights** (of vehicle) Am feux mpl de recul. ●**backwater** n (place) trou m perdu. ●**backwoods** npl forêt(s) f(pl) vierge(s); **to live in the b.** Fig habiter dans le bled. ●**back'yard** n Br arrière-cour f; Am jardin m (à l'arrière d'une maison).
backbone ['bækbəʊn] n colonne f vertébrale; (of fish) grande arête f; (main support) Fig pivot m.
backer ['bækər] n (supporter) partisan m; (on horses etc) parieur, -euse mf; (financial) bailleur m de fonds.
backfire [bæk'faɪər] vi **1** (of vehicle) pétarader. **2** (of plot etc) échouer.
backgammon ['bækgæmən] n trictrac m.
background ['bækgraʊnd] n fond m, arrière-plan m; (events) Fig antécédents mpl; (education) formation f; (environment) milieu m; (social, political etc conditions) contexte m; **to keep s.o. in the b.** tenir qn à l'écart; **b. music/noise** musique f/bruit m de fond.
backing ['bækɪŋ] n (aid) soutien m; (material) support m, renfort m.
backlash ['bæklæʃ] n choc m en retour, retour m de flamme.

backlog ['bæklɒg] n b. of work travail m en retard.

backward ['bækwəd] a (person, country etc) arriéré; (glance etc) en arrière ▌ adv = backwards. ● backwardness n (of person, country etc) retard m. ● backwards adv en arrière; (to walk) à reculons; (to fall) à la renverse; to go or move b. reculer; to go b. and forwards aller et venir.

bacon ['beɪkən] n lard m; (in rashers) bacon m; b. and eggs œufs mpl au bacon.

bacteria [bæk'tɪərɪə] npl bactéries fpl.

bad [bæd] a (worse, worst) mauvais; (wicked) méchant; (sad) triste; (accident, wound etc) grave; (tooth) carié; (arm, leg) malade; (pain) violent; (air) vicié; b. language gros mots mpl; it's b. to think that... ce n'est pas bien de penser que...; to feel b. (ill) se sentir mal; to feel b. about sth s'en vouloir de qch; things are b. ça va mal; that's not b.! ce n'est pas mal!; to go b. (of fruit, meat) se gâter; (of milk) tourner; in a b. way mal en point; (ill) très mal; (in trouble) dans le pétrin; too b.! tant pis! ● bad-'mannered a mal élevé. ● bad-'tempered a grincheux.

badge [bædʒ] n (of plastic, bearing slogan or joke) badge m; (of metal, bearing logo) pin's m; (of postman, policeman etc) plaque f; (on school uniform) insigne m.

badger ['bædʒər] 1 n (animal) blaireau m. 2 vt importuner.

badly ['bædlɪ] adv mal; (hurt) grièvement; b. affected/shaken très touché/bouleversé; to be b. mistaken se tromper lourdement; to be b. off dans la gêne; to be b. off for manquer de; to want b. avoir grande envie de.

badminton ['bædmɪntən] n badminton m.

baffle ['bæf(ə)l] vt (person) déconcerter, dérouter.

bag¹ [bæg] n sac m; bags (luggage) valises fpl, bagages mpl; (under the eyes) poches fpl; bags of Fam (lots of) beaucoup de; an old b. une vieille taupe; in the b. Fam dans la poche f; b. lady Fam clocharde f. ● bagful n (plein) sac m.

bag² [bæg] vt (-gg-) (take, steal) Fam piquer, s'adjuger; (hunted animal) tuer.

baggage ['bægɪdʒ] n bagages mpl; (of soldier) équipement m; b. car Am fourgon m; b. handler (in airport) bagagiste m; b. room Am consigne f.

baggy ['bægɪ] a (-ier, -iest) (Br trousers, Am pants) faisant des poches; (suit) trop ample.

bagpipes ['bægpaɪps] npl cornemuse f.

Bahamas [bə'hɑːməz] npl the B. les Bahamas fpl.

bail [beɪl] 1 n Jur caution f; on b. en liberté provisoire ▌ vt to b. (out) fournir une caution pour; to b. out (ship) écoper; (person, company) venir en aide à. 2 vi to b. out (from aircraft) Am sauter (en parachute).

bailiff ['beɪlɪf] n (law officer) huissier m; (of landowner) Br régisseur m.

bait [beɪt] 1 n amorce f, appât m ▌ vt (fishing hook) amorcer. 2 vt (annoy) asticoter,

tourmenter.

baize [beɪz] n green b. (on card table etc) tapis m vert.

bake [beɪk] vt (faire) cuire (au four) ▌ vi (cook) faire de la pâtisserie or du pain; (of cake etc) cuire (au four); we're or it's baking (hot) Fam on cuit. ● baked a (potatoes, apples) au four; b. beans haricots mpl blancs (à la tomate). ● baking n cuisson f; b. tin moule m à pâtisserie; b. powder levure f (chimique).

baker ['beɪkər] n boulanger, -ère mf. ● bakery n boulangerie f.

balaclava [bælə'klɑːvə] n b. (helmet) Br passe-montagne m.

balance ['bæləns] n (equilibrium) équilibre m; (of account) solde m; (remainder) reste m; (scales) & Econ Pol balance f; to lose one's b. perdre l'équilibre; to strike a b. trouver le juste milieu; sense of b. sens m de la mesure; in the b. incertain; on b. à tout prendre; b. of payments balance f des paiements; b. sheet bilan m.
▌ vt tenir or mettre en équilibre (on sur); (budget, account) équilibrer; (compare) mettre en balance, peser; to b. (out) (compensate for) compenser; well balanced (person, diet) bien équilibré.
▌ vi (of person) se tenir en équilibre; (of accounts) être en équilibre, s'équilibrer; to b. (out) (even out) s'équilibrer.

balcony ['bælkənɪ] n balcon m.

bald [bɔːld] a (-er, -est) chauve; (statement) brutal; (Br tyre, Am tire) lisse; b. patch or spot tonsure f. ● bald-'headed a chauve. ● balding a to be b. perdre ses cheveux. ● baldness n calvitie f.

balderdash ['bɔːldədæʃ] n Lit balivernes fpl.

bale [beɪl] 1 n (of cotton etc) balle f. 2 vi to b. out (from aircraft) sauter (en parachute).

baleful ['beɪlfəl] a Lit sinistre, funeste.

balk [bɔːk] vi reculer (at devant), regimber (at contre).

Balkans ['bɔːlkənz] npl the B. les Balkans mpl.

ball¹ [bɔːl] n balle f; (inflated, for football, rugby etc) ballon m; Billiards bille f; (of string, wool) pelote f; (sphere) boule f; (of meat or fish) boulette f; on the b. (alert) Fam éveillé; he's on the b. (efficient, knowledgeable) Fam il connaît son affaire, il est au point; b. bearing roulement m à billes; b. game Am partie f de baseball; it's a whole new b. game or a different b. game Am Fig c'est une tout autre affaire.

ball² [bɔːl] n (dance) bal m (pl bals).

ballad ['bæləd] n (poem) ballade f; (song) romance f.

ballast ['bæləst] n lest m ▌ vt lester.

ballcock ['bɔːlkɒk] n Br robinet m à flotteur.

ballerina [bælə'riːnə] n ballerine f.

ballet ['bæleɪ] n ballet m.

ballistic [bə'lɪstɪk] a b. missile engin m balistique.

balloon [bə'luːn] *n* (*toy, airship*) ballon *m*; (*in cartoon*) bulle *f*; (**weather**) **b.** ballon-sonde *m*.

ballot ['bælət] *n* (*voting*) scrutin *m*; **b.** (**paper**) bulletin *m* de vote; **b. box** urne ▎ *vt* (*members*) consulter (par un scrutin).

ballpoint (pen) ['bɔːlpɔɪnt(pen)] *n* stylo *m* à bille.

ballroom ['bɔːlruːm] *n* salle *f* de danse; **b. dancing** danse *f* de salon.

ballyhoo [bælɪ'huː] *n Fam* battage *m* (publicitaire).

balm [bɑːm] *n* (*oil, comfort*) baume *m*. ● **balmy** *a* (**-ier, -iest**) **1** (*air*) *Lit* embaumé. **2** (*crazy*) *Br Fam* dingue, timbré.

baloney [bə'ləʊnɪ] *n* (*nonsense*) *Sl* foutaises *fpl*.

Baltic ['bɔːltɪk] *n* **the B.** la Baltique.

balustrade ['bæləstreɪd] *n* balustrade *f*.

bamboo [bæm'buː] *n* bambou *m*; **b. shoots** pousses *fpl* de bambou.

bamboozle [bæm'buːz(ə)l] *vt* (*cheat*) *Fam* embobiner.

ban [bæn] *n* interdiction *f* ▎ *vt* (**-nn-**) interdire; **to ban s.o. from doing** interdire à qn de faire; **to b. s.o. from** (*club etc*) exclure qn de.

banal [*Br* bə'nɑːl, *Am* 'beɪn(ə)l] *a* banal (*mpl* **-als**). ● **ba'nality** *n* banalité *f*.

banana [bə'nɑːnə] *n* banane *f*; **b. skin** peau *f* de banane.

band [bænd] *n* **1** (*strip*) bande *f*; (*of hat*) ruban *m*; **rubber** *or* **elastic b.** élastique *m*. **2** *n* (*group of people*) bande *f*; (*of musicians*) (petit) orchestre *m*; (*pop group*) groupe *m*; (**brass**) fanfare *f* ▎ *vi* **to b. together se** (re)grouper.

bandage ['bændɪdʒ] *n* (*strip*) bande *f*; (*dressing*) bandage *m* ▎ *vt* **to b.** (**up**) (*arm, leg*) bander; (*wound*) mettre un bandage sur.

Band-Aid® ['bændeɪd] *n* pansement *m* adhésif.

B and B [biːən'biː] *n Br abbr* **bed and breakfast**.

bandit ['bændɪt] *n* bandit *m*. ● **banditry** *n* banditisme *m*.

bandstand ['bændstænd] *n* kiosque *m* à musique.

bandwagon ['bændwægən] *n* **to jump on the b.** *Fig* suivre le mouvement.

bandy¹ ['bændɪ] *a* (**-ier, -iest**) (*person*) bancal (*mpl* **-als**); **to have b. legs** avoir les jambes arquées. ● **bandy-'legged** *a* bancal.

bandy² ['bændɪ] *vt* **to b. about** (*story, rumour etc*) faire circuler.

bane [beɪn] *n Lit* fléau *m*. ● **baneful** *a Lit* funeste.

bang¹ [bæŋ] *n* (*hit, noise*) coup *m* (violent); (*of gun etc*) détonation *f*; (*of door*) claquement *m*.

▎ *vt* cogner, frapper; (*door*) (faire) claquer; **to b. one's head** se cogner la tête; **to b. down** (*lid*) rabattre (violemment).

▎ *vi* cogner, frapper; (*of door*) claquer; (*of gun*) détoner; (*of firework*) éclater; **to b. into**

sth/s.o. heurter qch/qn.

▎ *int* vlan!, pan!; **to go** (**off**) **b.** éclater.

bang² [bæŋ] *adv Br Fam* (*exactly*) exactement; **b. in the middle** en plein milieu; **b. on six** à six heures tapantes.

banger ['bæŋər] *n Br* **1** (*sausage*) *Fam* saucisse *f*. **2** (*firecracker*) pétard *m*. **3 old b.** (*car*) *Fam* tacot *m*, guimbarde *f*.

Bangladesh [bæŋglə'deʃ] *n* Bangladesh *m*. ● **Bangladeshi** *a* du Bangladesh ▎ *n* habitant, -ante *mf* du Bangladesh.

bangle ['bæŋg(ə)l] *n* bracelet *m* (rigide).

bangs [bæŋz] *npl* (*of hair*) *Am* frange *f*.

banish ['bænɪʃ] *vt* bannir.

banister ['bænɪstər] *n* **banister(s)** rampe *f* (d'escalier).

banjo ['bændʒəʊ] *n* (*pl* **-os** *or* **-oes**) banjo *m*.

bank [bæŋk] **1** *n* (*of river*) bord *m*, rive *f*; (*raised*) berge *f*; (*of earth*) talus *m*; (*of sand*) banc *m*; **the Left B.** (*in Paris*) la Rive gauche ▎ *vt* **to b.** (**up**) (*earth etc*) amonceler; (*fire*) couvrir.

2 *n* (*for money*) banque *f*; **b. account** compte *m* en banque; **b. card** carte *f* d'identité bancaire; **b. holiday** *Br* jour *m* férié; **b. note** *Br* billet *m* de banque; **b. rate** taux *m* d'escompte ▎ *vt* (*money*) mettre en banque ▎ *vi* avoir un compte en banque (**with** à).

3 *vi* (*of aircraft*) virer.

4 *vi* **to b. on s.o./sth** (*rely on*) compter sur qn/qch. ● **banking** *a* (*transaction etc*) bancaire ▎ *n* (*activity, profession*) la banque.

banker ['bæŋkər] *n* banquier *m*; **b.'s card** *Br* = **bank card**.

bankrupt ['bæŋkrʌpt] *a* **to go b.** faire faillite; **b. of** (*ideas*) *Fig* dénué de; **morally b.** qui n'a plus de valeurs ▎ *vt* mettre en faillite. ● **bankruptcy** *n* faillite *f*.

banner ['bænər] *n* (*across street, at rallies etc, on two poles*) banderole *f*; (*military flag*) & *Fig* bannière *f*.

banns [bænz] *npl* bans *mpl* (*de mariage*); **to put up the b.** publier les bans.

banquet ['bæŋkwɪt] *n* banquet *m*.

banter ['bæntər] *vi* plaisanter ▎ *n* plaisanterie *f*. ● **bantering** *a* (*tone, air*) plaisantin.

baptism ['bæptɪzəm] *n* baptême *m*. ● **Baptist** *n* & *a* baptiste (*mf*).

baptize [bæp'taɪz] *vt* baptiser.

bar [bɑːr] **1** *n* (*of metal etc*) barre *f*; (*of gold*) lingot *m*; (*of chocolate*) tablette *f*; (*on window*) barreau *m*; **b. of soap** savonnette *f*; **behind bars** (*criminal*) sous les verrous; **to be a b. to** faire obstacle à; **the B.** *Jur* le barreau; **b. code** (*on product*) code *m* à barres, code-barres *m*.

2 *n* (*pub*) bar *m*; (*counter*) bar *m*, comptoir *m*.

3 *n* (*group of musical notes*) mesure *f*.

4 *vt* (**-rr-**) **to b. s.o.'s way** bloquer *or* barrer le passage à qn; **barred window** fenêtre *f* grillagée.

5 *vt* (*prohibit*) interdire (**s.o. from doing** à qn de faire); (*exclude*) exclure (**from** à).

6 *prep* (*except*) sauf; **b. none** sans exception. ●**barmaid** *n* serveuse *f* de bar. ●**barman** *n* barman *m*. ●**bartender** *n* *Am* barman *m*.

Barbados [bɑːˈbeɪdɒs] *n* Barbade *f*.

barbarian [bɑːˈbeərɪən] *n* barbare *mf*. ●**barbaric** *a* barbare. ●**barbarity** *n* barbarie *f*.

barbecue [ˈbɑːbɪkjuː] *n* barbecue *m* ▌ *vt* griller (au barbecue).

barbed wire [bɑːbdˈwaɪər] *n* fil *m* de fer barbelé; (*fence*) barbelés *mpl*.

barber [ˈbɑːbər] *n* coiffeur *m* (*pour hommes*).

Barbie® [ˈbɑːbɪ] *n* **B. doll** poupée *f* Barbie®.

barbiturate [bɑːˈbɪtjʊrət] *n* barbiturique *m*.

bare [beər] *a* (**-er, -est**) nu; (*tree, hill etc*) dénudé; (*room, Br cupboard, Am closet*) vide; (*mere*) simple; **the b. necessities** le strict nécessaire; **with his b. hands** à mains nues ▌ *vt* (*arm, wire etc*) dénuder; **to b. one's head** se découvrir. ●**bareness** *n* (*of room etc*) dépouillement *m*.

bareback [ˈbeəbæk] *adv* **to ride b.** monter à cru. ●**barefaced** *a* (*lie*) éhonté. ●**barefoot** *adv* nu-pieds ▌ *a* aux pieds nus. ●**bare'headed** *a & adv* nu-tête *inv*.

barely [ˈbeəlɪ] *adv* (*scarcely*) à peine, tout juste.

bargain [ˈbɑːgɪn] *n* (*deal*) marché *m*, affaire *f*; **a b.** (*cheap buy*) une occasion, une bonne affaire; **a real b.** une véritable occasion *or* affaire; **it's a b.!** (*agreed*) c'est entendu!; **to make a b.** faire un marché (**with s.o.** avec qn); **into the b.** (*in addition*) par-dessus le marché; **b. price** prix *m* exceptionnel; **b. counter** rayon *m* des soldes.

▌ *vi* (*negotiate*) négocier; (*haggle*) marchander; **to b. for** *or* **on sth** (*expect*) s'attendre à qch. ●**bargaining** *n* négociations *fpl*; (*haggling*) marchandage *m*.

barge [bɑːdʒ] *n* chaland *m*, péniche *f*. **2** *vi* **to b. in** (*enter a room*) faire irruption; (*interrupt s.o.*) interrompre; **to b. into** (*hit*) se cogner contre.

baritone [ˈbærɪtəʊn] *n* (*voice, singer*) baryton *m*.

bark [bɑːk] **1** *n* (*of tree*) écorce *f*. **2** *vi* (*of dog etc*) aboyer ▌ *n* aboiement *m*. ●**barking** *n* aboiements *mpl*.

barley [ˈbɑːlɪ] *n* orge *f*; **b. sugar** sucre *m* d'orge.

barmy [ˈbɑːmɪ] *a* (**-ier, -iest**) (*crazy*) *Br Fam* dingue, timbré.

barn [bɑːn] *n* (*for crops etc*) grange *f*; (*for horses*) écurie *f*; (*for cattle*) étable *f*. ●**barnyard** *n* basse-cour *f*.

barometer [bəˈrɒmɪtər] *n* baromètre *m*.

baron [ˈbærən] *n* baron *m*; (*industrialist*) *Fig* magnat *m*; **press/oil b.** magnat de la presse/du pétrole. ●**baroness** *n* baronne *f*.

baroque [*Br* bəˈrɒk, *Am* bəˈrəʊk] *a & n* (*style etc*) *Archit Mus etc* baroque (*m*).

barracks [ˈbærəks] *npl* caserne *f*.

barrage [*Br* ˈbærɑːʒ, *Am* bəˈrɑːʒ] *n* (*barrier across river*) barrage *m*; **a b. of questions**/*etc*

un feu roulant de questions/*etc*.

barrel [ˈbærəl] *n* **1** (*cask*) tonneau *m*; (*of oil*) baril *m*. **2** (*of gun*) canon *m*. **3 b. organ** orgue *m* de Barbarie.

barren [ˈbærən] *a* (*land, woman, ideas*) stérile; (*style*) aride.

barrette [bəˈret] *n* (*hair slide*) *Am* barrette *f*.

barricade [ˈbærɪkeɪd] *n* barricade *f* ▌ *vt* barricader; **to b. oneself (in)** se barricader.

barrier [ˈbærɪər] *n* barrière *f*; *Fig* obstacle *m*, barrière *f*; (*ticket*) **b.** *Br Rail* portillon *m*; **sound b.** mur *m* du son.

barring [ˈbɑːrɪŋ] *prep* sauf, excepté.

barrister [ˈbærɪstər] *n* *Br* avocat *m*.

barrow [ˈbærəʊ] *n* (*wheelbarrow*) brouette *f*; (*cart*) charrette *f* *or* voiture *f* à bras.

barter [ˈbɑːtər] *vt* troquer, échanger (**for** contre) ▌ *n* troc *m*, échange *m*.

base [beɪs] **1** *n* (*bottom, main ingredient*) base *f*; (*of tree, lamp*) pied *m*; **b. rate** (*of bank*) taux *m* de base.

2 *n* (*military*) base *f*.

3 *vt* baser, fonder (**on** sur); **based in London** (*person, company etc*) basé à Londres.

4 *a* (*dishonourable*) bas (*f* basse), ignoble.

5 *a* **b. metal** métal *m* vil. ●**baseless** *a* sans fondement. ●**baseness** *n* bassesse *f*.

baseball [ˈbeɪsbɔːl] *n* base-ball *m*.

baseboard [ˈbeɪsbɔːd] *n* *Am* plinthe *f*.

basement [ˈbeɪsmənt] *n* sous-sol *m*.

bash [bæʃ] *n* (*bang*) coup *m*; **to have a b.** (*try*) *Br Fam* essayer un coup ▌ *vt* (*hit*) cogner; **to b. (about)** (*ill-treat*) malmener; **b. s.o. up** tabasser qn; **to b. in** *or* **down** (*door, fence etc*) défoncer. ●**bashing** *n* (*thrashing*) *Fam* raclée *f*; **to get a b.** prendre une raclée.

bashful [ˈbæʃfəl] *a* timide.

basic [ˈbeɪsɪk] *a* essentiel, de base; (*elementary*) élémentaire; (*pay, food*) de base; (*room, house, meal*) tout simple ▌ *n* **the basics** *Fam* l'essentiel *m*. ●**basically** [-klɪ] *adv* au fond.

basil [ˈbæz(ə)l] *n* (*herb*) basilic *m*.

basilica [bəˈzɪlɪkə] *n* basilique *f*.

basin [ˈbeɪs(ə)n] *n* bassine *f*; (*for soup, food*) (grand) bol *m*; (*of river*) bassin *m*; (*portable washbasin*) cuvette *f*; (*sink*) lavabo *m*.

basis, *pl* **-ses** [ˈbeɪsɪs, -siːz] *n* (*of agreement etc*) bases *fpl*; **on the b. of** d'après; **on that b.** dans ces conditions; **on a weekly**/*etc* **basis** chaque semaine/*etc*.

bask [bɑːsk] *vi* (*in the sun*) se chauffer.

basket [ˈbɑːskɪt] *n* panier *m*; (*for bread, laundry, litter*) corbeille *f*. ●**basketball** *n* basket(-ball) *m*.

Basque [bæsk] *a & n* basque (*mf*).

bass¹ [beɪs] *n* *Mus* basse *f* ▌ *a* (*note, voice, flute etc*) bas (*f* basse).

bass² [bæs] *n* (*sea fish*) bar *m*; (*fresh-water*) perche *f*.

bassinet [bæsɪˈnet] *n* (*cradle*) *Am* couffin *m*.

bassoon [bəˈsuːn] *n* basson *m*.

bastard [ˈbɑːstəd] *n* **1** *a & n* (*a child*) bâtard, -arde (*mf*). **2** *n* (*unpleasant person*) *Sl* salaud *m*, salope *f*.

baste [beɪst] vt **1** (fabric) bâtir. **2** (meat) arroser.

bastion ['bæstɪən] n bastion m.

bat [bæt] **1** n (animal) chauve-souris f. **2** n Cricket Baseball batte f; Table Tennis raquette f; **off my own b.** de ma propre initiative ∎ vt (-tt-) (ball) frapper. **3** vt **she didn't b. an eyelid** elle n'a pas sourcillé.

batch [bætʃ] n (of people) groupe m; (of letters) paquet m; (of books) lot m; (of loaves) fournée f; (of papers) liasse f.

bated ['beɪtɪd] a **with b. breath** en retenant son souffle.

bath [bɑːθ] n (pl -s [bɑːðz]) bain m; (tub) baignoire f; **to have** or **take a b.** prendre un bain; **b. towel** serviette f de bain; **swimming baths** Br piscine f ∎ vt Br baigner ∎ vi Br prendre un bain. ●**bathrobe** n Br peignoir m (de bain); Am robe f de chambre. ●**bathroom** n salle f de bain(s); (toilet) Am toilettes fpl. ●**bathtub** n baignoire f.

bathe [beɪð] vt baigner; (wound) laver ∎ vi se baigner; Am prendre un bain ∎ n bain m (de mer), baignade f; **to go for a b.** se baigner. ●**bathing** n baignade(s) f(pl); **b. suit,** Br **b. costume** maillot m de bain.

baton [Br 'bætən, Am bə'tɒn] n (of conductor) baguette f; (of policeman) matraque f; (of soldier, drum majorette) bâton m.

battalion [bə'tæljən] n bataillon m.

batter ['bætər] **1** n pâte f à frire. **2** vt (strike) rouer (qn) de coups; frapper (qch) à coups redoublés; (baby, child) martyriser; (town etc with shells) pilonner; **to b. down** (door) défoncer. ●**battered** a (car, hat) cabossé; (house) délabré; (face) meurtri; **b. baby** or **child** enfant m martyr; **b. wife** femme f battue. ●**battering** n **to take a b.** souffrir beaucoup.

battery ['bætərɪ] n (in vehicle, of guns, for hens) batterie f; (in radio, appliance etc) pile f; **b. hen** poule f de batterie.

battle ['bæt(ə)l] n bataille f; (struggle) lutte f; **that's half the b.** Fam on etc a déjà fait la moitié du chemin; **b. dress** tenue f de campagne ∎ vi se battre, lutter. ●**battlefield** n champ m de bataille. ●**battleship** n cuirassé m.

battlements ['bæt(ə)lmənts] npl (indentations) créneaux mpl; (wall) remparts mpl.

batty ['bætɪ] a (-ier, -iest) (crazy) Br Sl dingue, toqué.

baulk [bɔːk] vi reculer (at devant), regimber (at contre).

bawdy ['bɔːdɪ] a (-ier, -iest) paillard, grossier.

bawl [bɔːl] vti **to b. (out)** beugler, brailler; **to b. s.o. out** Am Sl engueuler qn.

bay [beɪ] **1** n (part of coastline) baie f. **2** n (in room) renfoncement m; **b. window** bow-window m, oriel m. **3** n (tree) laurier m; **b. leaf** feuille f de laurier. **4** n (for loading) Br aire f. **5** n (of dog) aboiement m; **at b.** (animal, criminal) aux abois; **to keep** or **hold at b.** (enemy, wild dog etc) tenir en respect;

(disease) juguler ∎ vi aboyer. **6** a (horse) bai.

bayonet ['beɪənɪt] n baïonnette f.

bazaar [bə'zɑːr] n (market, shop) bazar m; (charity sale) vente f de charité.

bazooka [bə'zuːkə] n bazooka m.

BC [biː'siː] abbr (before Christ) avant Jésus-Christ.

be [biː] vi (pres t am, are, is; pt was, were; pp been; pres p being) **1** être; **it is green/small**/etc c'est vert/petit/etc; **he's a doctor** il est médecin; **he's an Englishman** c'est un Anglais; **it's him** c'est lui; **it's them** ce sont eux, c'est eux; **it's 3 (o'clock)** il est trois heures; **it's the sixth of May,** Am **it's May sixth** c'est or nous sommes le six mai.

2 avoir; **to be hot/right/lucky** avoir chaud/raison/de la chance; **my feet are cold** j'ai froid aux pieds; **he's 20** (age) il a 20 ans; **to be 2 metres high** avoir 2 mètres de haut; **to be 6 feet tall** mesurer 1,80 m.

3 (health) aller; **how are you?** comment vas-tu?; **I'm well/not well** je vais bien/mal.

4 (place, situation) se trouver, être; **she's in York** elle se trouve or elle est à York.

5 (exist) être; **the best painter there is** le meilleur peintre qui soit; **leave me be** laissez-moi (tranquille); **that may be** cela se peut.

6 (go, come) **I've been to see her** je suis allé or j'ai été la voir; **he's (already) been** il est (déjà) venu.

7 (weather, calculations) faire; **it's fine** il fait beau; **it's foggy** il y a du brouillard; **2 and 2 are 4** 2 et 2 font 4.

8 (cost) coûter, faire; **it's 20 pence** ça coûte 20 pence; **how much is it?** ça fait combien?, c'est combien?

9 (auxiliary) **I am/was doing** je fais/faisais; **I'll be staying** je resterai, je vais rester; **I'm listening to the radio** (in the process of) je suis en train d'écouter la radio; **what has she been doing?** qu'est-ce qu'elle a fait?; **she's been there some time** elle est là depuis longtemps; **he was killed** il a été tué, on l'a tué; **I've been waiting (for) two hours** j'attends depuis deux heures; **it is said** on dit; **she's to be pitied** elle est à plaindre.

10 (in questions and answers) **isn't it?, aren't you?** etc n'est-ce pas?, non?; **she's ill, is she?** (surprise) alors, comme ça, elle est malade?; **I am!, he is!** etc oui!

11 (+ inf) **he is to come at once** (must) il doit venir tout de suite; **he's shortly to go** (intends to) il va bientôt partir.

12 **there is** or **are** il y a; (pointing) voilà; **here is** or **are** voici; **there she is** la voilà; **here they are** les voici.

beach [biːtʃ] n plage f. ●**beachcomber** n (person) ramasseur, -euse mf d'épaves.

beacon ['biːkən] n (for ship, aircraft) balise f; (lighthouse) phare m.

bead [biːd] n (small sphere) perle f; (of rosary) grain m; (of sweat) goutte f, gouttelette f; (string of) **beads** collier m.

beak [biːk] n bec m.

beaker ['biːkər] *n* gobelet *m*.

beam [biːm] **1** *n* (*of wood*) poutre *f*. **2** *n* (*of light, sunlight*) rayon *m*; (*of headlight, flashlight*) faisceau *m* (lumineux) **I** *vi* (*of light*) rayonner; (*of face, person*) rayonner (**with joy** de joie); (*smile broadly*) sourire largement. **3** *vt* (*signals, radio or TV programme etc*) transmettre (**to** à). ● **beaming** *a* (*face, person, smile*) radieux, rayonnant.

bean [biːn] *n* haricot *m*; (*of coffee*) grain *m*; (*broad*) **b.** fève *f*; **to be full of beans** *Fam* déborder d'entrain. ● **beanshoots** *or* **beansprouts** *npl* germes *mpl* de soja.

bear¹ [beər] *n* (*animal*) ours *m*; **b. cub** ourson *m*.

bear² [beər] *vt* (*pt* **bore**, *pp* **borne**) (*carry, show*) porter; (*endure*) supporter; (*resemblance*) offrir; (*comparison*) soutenir; (*responsibility*) assumer; (*child*) donner naissance à; **I can't b. him/it** je ne peux pas le supporter/supporter ça; **to b. in mind** tenir compte de; **to b. out** corroborer.
I *vi* **to b. left/right** (*turn*) tourner à gauche/droite; **to b. north/etc** (*go*) aller en direction du nord/etc; **to b. (up)on** (*relate to*) se rapporter à; **to b. heavily on s.o.** (*of burden*) *Fig* peser sur qn; **to b. with s.o.** être indulgent envers qn, être patient avec qn; **to bring one's energies to b. on a task/etc** consacrer toute son énergie à un travail/etc; **to bring pressure to b. on s.o.** faire pression sur qn (**to do** pour faire); **to b. up** ne pas se décourager, tenir le coup; **b. up!** courage!

bearable ['beərəb(ə)l] *a* supportable.

beard [biəd] *n* barbe *f*; **to have a b.** porter la barbe. ● **bearded** *a* barbu.

bearer ['beərər] *n* porteur, -euse *mf*.

bearing ['beəriŋ] *n* (*relationship, relevance*) relation *f* (**on** avec); (*posture, conduct*) maintien *m*; (*of ship, aircraft*) position *f*; **to get one's bearings** s'orienter; **I've lost my bearings** je ne sais plus où j'en suis.

beast [biːst] *n* bête *f*, animal *m*; (*cruel person*) brute *f*.

beastly ['biːstlɪ] *a Br Fam* (*bad*) vilain, infect; (*spiteful*) méchant; **a b. trick** un sale tour **I** *adv Br Fam* terriblement.

beat [biːt] *n* (*of heart, drum*) battement *m*; (*of policeman*) ronde *f*; (*in music*) mesure *f*, rythme *m*.
I *vt* (*pt* **beat**, *pp* **beaten**) battre; (*defeat*) vaincre, battre; **to b. a drum** battre du tambour; **that beats me** *Fam* ça me dépasse; **to b. s.o. to it** devancer qn; **b. it!** *Fam* fichez le camp!; **to b. back** *or* **off** repousser; **to b. down** (*price*) faire baisser; **to b. down** *or* **in** (*door*) défoncer; **to b. out** (*rhythm*) marquer; (*tune*) jouer; **to b. s.o. up** tabasser qn.
I *vi* battre; (*at door*) frapper (**at** à); **to b. about** *or* **around the bush** *Fam* tourner autour du pot; **to b. down** (*of rain*) tomber à verse; (*of sun*) taper. ● **beating** *n* (*blows, defeat*) raclée *f*; (*of heart, drums*) battement *m*; **to take a b.** souffrir beaucoup.

beater ['biːtər] *n* (*for eggs*) batteur *m*.

beautician [bjuːˈtɪʃ(ə)n] *n* esthéticienne *f*.

beautiful ['bjuːtɪf(ə)l] *a* (très) beau (*f* belle); (*superb*) merveilleux. ● **beautifully** *adv* (*after verb*) à merveille; (*before adjective*) merveilleusement.

beauty ['bjuːtɪ] *n* (*quality, woman*) beauté *f*; **it's a b.!** (*car, house etc*) c'est une merveille!; **the b. of it is (that)...** le plus beau, c'est que...; **b. parlour** *or* **salon** institut *m* de beauté; **b. spot** (*on skin*) grain *m* de beauté; (*in countryside*) *Br* endroit *m* or site *m* pittoresque.

beaver ['biːvər] *n* castor *m* **I** *vi* **to b. away** travailler dur (**at sth** à qch).

because [bɪˈkɒz] *conj* parce que; **b. of** à cause de.

beck [bek] *n* **at s.o.'s b. and call** aux ordres de qn.

beckon ['bekən] *vti* **to b. (to) s.o.** faire signe à qn (**to do** de faire).

become [bɪˈkʌm] **1** *vi* (*pt* **became**, *pp* **become**) devenir; **to b. a painter** devenir peintre; **to b. thin** maigrir; **to b. worried** commencer à s'inquiéter; **what has b. of her?** qu'est-elle devenue?
2 *vt* **that hat becomes her** ce chapeau lui sied *or* lui va. ● **becoming** *a* (*clothes*) seyant; (*modesty*) bienséant.

bed [bed] *n* lit *m*; (*flower bed*) parterre *m*; (*of vegetables*) carré *m*; (*of sea*) fond *m*; (*of river*) lit *m*; (*of rock etc*) couche *f*; **to go to b.** (aller) se coucher; **to put to b.** coucher (*un enfant etc*); **in b.** couché; **to get out of b.** se lever; **to make the b.** faire le lit; **b. and breakfast** (*in hotel etc*) chambre *f* avec petit déjeuner; **b. settee** *Br* (canapé *m*) convertible *m*; **air b.** matelas *m* pneumatique.
I *vt* (**-dd-**) **to b. (out)** (*plant*) repiquer.
I *vi* **to b. down** se coucher.

bedbug ['bedbʌg] *n* punaise *f*. ● **bedclothes** *npl* couvertures *fpl* et draps *mpl*. ● **bedding** *n* literie *f*. ● **bedpan** *n* bassin *m* (hygiénique). ● **bedridden** *a* alité. ● **bedroom** *n* chambre *f* à coucher. ● **bedside** *n* chevet *m*; **b. lamp/book/table** lampe *f*/livre *m*/table *f* de chevet. ● **bed'sitter** *n* *or* **bedsit** *n Br* chambre *f* meublée. ● **bedspread** *n* dessus-de-lit *m inv*. ● **bedtime** *n* heure *f* du coucher.

bedeck [bɪˈdek] *vt* orner (**with** de).

bedevil [bɪˈdev(ə)l] *vt* (*Br* **-ll-**, *Am* **-l-**) (*plague*) tourmenter; (*confuse*) embrouiller; **bedevilled by** (*problems etc*) perturbé par, empoisonné par.

bedlam ['bedləm] *n* (*noise*) *Fam* chahut *m*.

bedraggled [bɪˈdræg(ə)ld] *a* (*clothes, person*) débraillé (et tout trempé).

bee [biː] *n* abeille *f*. ● **beehive** *n* ruche *f*.

beech [biːtʃ] *n* (*tree, wood*) hêtre *m*.

beef [biːf] **1** *n* bœuf *m*. **2** *vi* (*complain*) *Sl* rouspéter. ● **beefburger** *n* hamburger *m*. ● **beefy** *a* (**-ier, -iest**) *Fam* musclé, costaud.

beekeeper ['biːkiːpər] *n* apiculteur, -trice *mf*. ● **beekeeping** *n* apiculture *f*.

beeline ['biːlaɪn] *n* **to make a b. for** aller

droit vers.
been [biːn] *pp of* be.
beer [bɪər] *n* bière *f*; **bottle of b.** bouteille *f* de bière; (*small*) cannette *f*; **b. glass** chope *f*. ●**beery** *a* (*room, person*) qui sent la bière.
beet [biːt] *n* betterave *f* (à sucre); *Am* = beetroot. ●**beetroot** *n* betterave *f* (potagère).
beetle ['biːt(ə)l] **1** *n* scarabée *m*; (*any beetle-shaped insect*) bestiole *f*. **2** *vi* **to b. off** (*run off*) *Br Fam* se sauver.
befall [bɪ'fɔːl] *vt* (*pt* befell, *pp* befallen) arriver à.
befit [bɪ'fɪt] *vt* (-tt-) convenir à.
before [bɪ'fɔːr] *adv* avant; (*already*) déjà; (*in front*) devant; **the month b.** le mois d'avant *or* précédent; **the day b.** la veille; **I've never done it b.** je ne l'ai (encore) jamais fait. ▮ *prep* (*time*) avant; (*place*) devant; **the year b.** l'an d'avant; **b. last** il y a deux ans. ▮ *conj* avant que (+ ne + *sub*), avant de (+ *inf*); **b. he goes** avant qu'il (ne) parte; **b. going** avant de partir. ●**beforehand** *adv* à l'avance, avant.
befriend [bɪ'frend] *vt* offrir son amitié à.
befuddled [bɪ'fʌd(ə)ld] *a* (*drunk*) ivre.
beg [beg] *vt* (-gg-) **to b. (for)** (*favour, help etc*) sollicitér, demander; (*bread, money*) mendier; **to b. s.o. to do sth** supplier qn de faire qch; **I b. to differ** permettez-moi de ne pas être d'accord; **to b. the question** esquiver la question. ▮ *vi* (*in street etc*) mendier; (*ask earnestly*) supplier; **to go begging** (*of food, articles*) ne pas trouver d'amateurs.
beget [bɪ'get] *vt* (*pt* begot, *pp* begotten, *pres p* begetting) engendrer.
beggar ['begər] *n* mendiant, -ante *mf*; (*person*) *Br Fam* type *m*; **lucky b.** veinard, -arde *mf*. ●**beggarly** *a* misérable.
begin [bɪ'gɪn] *vt* (*pt* began, *pp* begun, *pres p* beginning) commencer; (*fashion, campaign*) lancer; (*bottle, sandwich*) entamer, commencer; (*conversation*) engager; **to b. doing** *or* **to do** commencer *or* se mettre à faire. ▮ *vi* commencer (**with** par, **by doing** par faire); **to b. on sth** commencer qch; **beginning from** à partir de; **to b. with** (*first of all*) d'abord.
beginner [bɪ'gɪnər] *n* débutant, -ante *mf*.
beginning [bɪ'gɪnɪŋ] *n* commencement *m*, début *m*.
begrudge [bɪ'grʌdʒ] *vt* (*envy*) envier (s.o. sth qch à qn); (*reproach*) reprocher (s.o. sth qch à qn); (*give unwillingly*) donner à contrecœur; **to b. doing sth** faire qch à contre-cœur.
behalf [bɪ'hɑːf] *n* **on b. of** (*representing*) pour, au nom de, de la part de; (*in the interests of*) en faveur de, pour.
behave [bɪ'heɪv] *vi* se conduire; (*of machine*) fonctionner; **to b. (oneself)** se tenir bien; (*of child*) être sage.
behaviour [bɪ'heɪvjər] (*Am* **behavior**) *n* conduite *f*, comportement *m*; **to be on one's best**

b. se conduire de son mieux.
behead [bɪ'hed] *vt* décapiter.
behest [bɪ'hest] *n* **at the b. of** *Lit* sur l'ordre de.
behind [bɪ'haɪnd] **1** *prep* derrière; (*in terms of progress*) en retard sur ▮ *adv* derrière; (*late*) en retard (**with** *or* **in one's work/payments**/*etc*) dans son travail/ses paiements/ *etc*). **2** *n* (*buttocks*) *Fam* derrière *m*. ●**behindhand** *adv* en retard (**with, in** dans).
beholden [bɪ'həʊldən] *a* redevable (**to** à, **for** de).
beige [beɪʒ] *a & n* beige (*m*).
Beijing [beɪ'dʒɪn] *n* Beijing *m or f*.
being ['biːɪŋ] *n* (*person, soul*) être *m*; **to come into b.** naître, être créé; **with all my b.** de tout mon être.
belated [bɪ'leɪtɪd] *a* tardif.
belch [beltʃ] **1** *vi* (*of person*) faire un renvoi, éructer ▮ *n* renvoi *m*. **2** *vt* **to b. (out)** (*smoke*) vomir.
beleaguered [bɪ'liːgəd] *a* (*besieged*) assiégé.
belfry ['belfrɪ] *n* beffroi *m*, clocher *m*.
Belgium ['beldʒəm] *n* Belgique *f*. ●**Belgian** ['beldʒən] *a* belge ▮ *n* Belge *mf*.
belie [bɪ'laɪ] *vt* démentir.
belief [bɪ'liːf] *n* (*believing, thing believed*) croyance *f* (**in s.o.** en qn, **in sth** à *or* en qch); (*trust*) confiance *f*, foi *f* (**in** en); (*religious faith*) foi *f*; **to the best of my b.** pour autant que je sache.
believe [bɪ'liːv] *vti* croire (**in sth** à qch, **in God/s.o.** en Dieu/qn); **I b. so/not** je crois que oui/que non; **I b. I'm right** je crois avoir raison, je crois que j'ai raison; **to b. in doing** croire qu'il faut faire; **he doesn't b. in smoking** il désapprouve que l'on fume. ●**believable** *a* croyable. ●**believer** *n* (*religious*) croyant, -ante *mf*; **to be a b. in** = believe in.
Belisha beacon [bəlɪːʃə'biːkən] *n* *Br* signal *m* lumineux orange (*marquant un passage pour piétons*).
belittle [bɪ'lɪt(ə)l] *vt* dénigrer.
bell [bel] *n* (*large*) (*of church etc*) cloche *f*; (*small*) clochette *f*; (*in phone, mechanism, alarm*) sonnerie *f*; (*on door, bicycle*) sonnette *f*; (*on tambourine, dog*) grelot *m*; **b. tower** clocher *m*. ●**bellboy** *or* **bellhop** *n* *Am* groom *m*.
belle [bel] *n* (*woman*) beauté *f*, belle *f*.
belligerent [bɪ'lɪdʒərənt] *a & n* belligérant, -ante *mf*.
bellow ['beləʊ] *vi* beugler, mugir.
bellows ['beləʊz] *npl* (*pair of*) **b.** soufflet *m*.
belly ['belɪ] *n* ventre *m*; **b. button** *Fam* nombril *m*. ●**bellyache** *n* *Fam* mal *m* au ventre ▮ *vi* *Sl* (*complain*) rouspéter. ●**bellyful** *n* **to have had a b.** *Sl* en avoir plein le dos.
belong [bɪ'lɒŋ] *vi* appartenir (**to** à); **to b. to a club**/*etc* être membre d'un club/*etc*; **the cup belongs here** la tasse se range ici; **he doesn't b.** il n'est pas à sa place. ●**belongings** *npl* affaires *fpl*.
beloved [bɪ'lʌvɪd] *a & n* bien-aimé, -ée (*mf*).

below [bɪ'ləʊ] *prep* (*lower than*) au-dessous de; (*under*) sous, au-dessous de; (*unworthy of*) *Fig* indigne de ▮ *adv* en dessous; **see b.** (*in book etc*) voir ci-dessous.

belt [belt] **1** *n* ceinture *f*; (*in machine*) courroie *f* ▮ *vi* **to b. up** (*fasten seat belt*) attacher sa ceinture. **2** *n* (*area*) zone *f*, région *f*. **3** *vt* (*hit*) *Sl* rosser. **4** *vi* **to b. (along)** (*rush*) *Br Sl* filer à toute allure; **b. up!** (*shut up*) *Br Sl* boucle-la!

bemoan [bɪ'məʊn] *vt* déplorer.

bemused [bɪ'mjuːzd] *a* perplexe.

bench [bentʃ] *n* (*seat*) banc *m*; (*work table*) établi *m*, banc *m*; **the B.** *Jur* la magistrature (assise); (*court*) le tribunal.

bend [bend] *n* courbe *f*; (*in river, pipe*) coude *m*; (*in road*) virage *m*; (*of arm, knee*) pli *m*; **double b.** (*on road*) *Br* virage *m* en S, double virage *m*; **round the b.** (*mad*) *Fam* cinglé.
▮ *vt* (*pt & pp* **bent**) courber; (*leg, arm*) plier; **to b. one's head** baisser la tête; **to b. the rules** faire une entorse au règlement.
▮ *vi* (*of branch*) plier; (*of road*) tourner; **to b. (down)** (*stoop*) se baisser, se courber; **to b. (over or forward)** se pencher; **to b. over backwards to do** *Fig* se mettre en quatre pour faire; **to b. to s.o.'s will/etc** se soumettre à la volonté de qn/etc.

bendy ['bendɪ] *a* (**-ier, -iest**) (*road*) *Br Fam* plein de virages; **b. straw** paille *f* flexible.

beneath [bɪ'niːθ] *prep* au-dessous de, sous; (*unworthy of*) au-dessous de, indigne de ▮ *adv* (au-)dessous.

benediction [benɪ'dɪkʃ(ə)n] *n* bénédiction *f*.

benefactor ['benɪfæktər] *n* bienfaiteur *m*.
● **benefactress** *n* bienfaitrice *f*.

beneficial [benɪ'fɪʃəl] *a* bénéfique.

beneficiary [benɪ'fɪʃərɪ] *n* bénéficiaire *mf*.

benefit ['benɪfɪt] *n* (*advantage*) avantage *m*; (*money*) allocation *f*; **benefits** (*of science, education*) bienfaits *mpl*; **child b.** *Br* allocations *fpl* familiales; **to s.o.'s b.** dans l'intérêt de qn; **for your (own) b.** pour vous, pour votre bien; **to be of b.** faire du bien (**to s.o.** à qn); **to give s.o. the b. of the doubt** accorder à qn le bénéfice du doute; **b. concert/etc** concert*m*/etc de bienfaisance.
▮ *vt* faire du bien à; (*be useful to*) profiter à.
▮ *vi* **you'll b. from the rest/etc** le repos/etc vous fera du bien; **to b. from doing** gagner à faire.

Benelux ['benɪlʌks] *n* Bénélux *m*.

benevolent [bɪ'nevələnt] *a* bienveillant.
● **benevolence** *n* bienveillance *f*.

benign [bɪ'naɪn] *a* (*kind*) bienveillant; (*climate*) doux (*f* douce); **b. tumour** tumeur *f* bénigne.

bent [bent] **1** *a* (*nail, mind*) tordu; (*dishonest*) *Fam* corrompu; **b. on doing** résolu à faire. **2** *n* (*talent*) aptitude *f* (**for** pour); (*inclination, liking*) penchant *m*, goût *m* (**for** pour).

bequeath [bɪ'kwiːð] *vt* léguer (**to** à). ● **bequest** *n* legs *m*.

bereaved [bɪ'riːvd] *a* endeuillé ▮ *n* **the b.** la famille (*or* la femme, le mari *etc*) du défunt *or* de la défunte. ● **bereavement** *n* deuil *m*.

bereft [bɪ'reft] *a* **b. of** dénué de.

beret [*Br* 'bereɪ, *Am* bə'reɪ] *n* béret *m*.

berk [bɜːk] *n Br Sl* imbécile *mf*.

Bermuda [bə'mjuːdə] *n* Bermudes *fpl*.

berry ['berɪ] *n* baie *f*.

berserk [bə'zɜːk] *a* **to go b.** devenir fou, se déchaîner.

berth [bɜːθ] **1** *n* (*in ship, train*) couchette *f*. **2** *n* (*anchorage*) mouillage *m* ▮ *vi* (*of ship*) mouiller. **3** *n* **to give a place/person a wide b.** éviter un endroit/une personne comme la peste.

beseech [bɪ'siːtʃ] *vt* (*pt & pp* **besought** *or* **beseeched**) *Lit* implorer (**to do** de faire).

beset [bɪ'set] *vt* (*pt & pp* **beset,** *pres p* **besetting**) assaillir (*qn*); **b. with obstacles/etc** semé *or* hérissé d'obstacles/etc.

beside [bɪ'saɪd] *prep* à côté de; **that's b. the point** ça n'a rien à voir; **b. oneself** (*angry*) hors de soi.

besides [bɪ'saɪdz] *prep* (*in addition to*) en plus de; (*except*) excepté; **there are ten of us b. Paul** nous sommes dix sans compter Paul ▮ *adv* (*in addition*) de plus; (*moreover*) d'ailleurs; **there are more b.** il y en a d'autres encore.

besiege [bɪ'siːdʒ] *vt* (*of soldiers, crowd*) assiéger; (*annoy*) *Fig* assaillir (*qn*) (**with questions/etc** de questions/etc).

besotted [bɪ'sɒtɪd] *a* (*drunk*) abruti; **b. with** (*infatuated*) entiché de.

bespatter [bɪ'spætər] *vt* éclabousser (**with** de).

bespectacled [bɪ'spektɪk(ə)ld] *a* à lunettes.

bespoke [bɪ'spəʊk] *a* (*tailor*) à façon.

best [best] *a* meilleur; **the b. page in the book** la meilleure page du livre; **the b. part of** (*most*) la plus grande partie de; **that's the b. thing** c'est le mieux; **the b. thing is to accept** le mieux c'est d'accepter; **'b. before'** (*on product*) 'à consommer avant'; **b. man** (*at wedding*) témoin *m*, garçon *m* d'honneur.
▮ *n* **the b.** (*one*) le meilleur, la meilleure; **it's for the b.** c'est pour le mieux; **at b.** au mieux; **to do one's b.** faire de son mieux; **to look one's b.,** be at one's b. être à son avantage; **to the b. of my knowledge** autant que je sache; **to make the b. of** (*accept*) s'accommoder de (*situation etc*); **to get the b. of** it avoir le dessus; **in one's Sunday b.** endimanché; **all the (very) b.!** (*when leaving s.o.*) portez-vous bien!; (*in letter*) amicalement.
▮ *adv* (**the) b.** (*to play, sing etc*) le mieux; **to like** *or* **love sth/s.o. (the) b.** aimer qch/qn le plus; **the b. loved** le plus aimé; **to think it b. to wait/etc** juger prudent d'attendre/etc. ● **best-'seller** *n* (*book*) best-seller *m*.

bestow [bɪ'stəʊ] *vt* accorder, conférer (**on** à).

bet [bet] *n* pari *m* ▮ *vti* (*pt & pp* **bet** *or* **betted,** *pres p* **betting**) parier (**on** sur, **that** que); **you b.!** *Fam* (*of course*) tu parles!

betoken [bɪ'təʊkən] vt Lit annoncer.
betray [bɪ'treɪ] vt (person, secret etc) trahir; **to b. to s.o.** (give away to) livrer à qn. ● **betrayal** n (disloyalty) trahison f; (disclosure) (of secret etc) révélation f.
better ['betər] a meilleur (than que); **I need a b. car** j'ai besoin d'une meilleure voiture; **she's (much) b.** (in health) elle va (bien) mieux; **he's b. than you** (at sports) il joue mieux que vous; (in French, history etc) il est plus fort que vous; **that's b.** c'est mieux; **to get b.** (recover) se remettre; (improve) s'améliorer; **it's b. to go** il vaut mieux partir; **the b. part of** (most) la plus grande partie de.
▮ adv mieux (than que); **b. dressed/known/etc** mieux habillé/connu/etc; **I had b. go** il vaut mieux que je parte; **so much the b., all the b.** tant mieux (for pour).
▮ n **to get the b. of s.o.** l'emporter sur qn; **change for the b.** amélioration f; **one's betters** ses supérieurs mpl.
▮ vt (improve) améliorer; (do better than) dépasser; **to b. oneself** améliorer sa condition; **to b. s.o.'s results/etc** (do better than) dépasser les résultats/etc de qn. ● **betterment** n amélioration f.
betting ['betɪŋ] n pari(s) m(pl); **b. shop** or **office** Br bureau m du pari mutuel.
between [bɪ'twi:n] prep entre; **we did it b. (the two of) us** nous l'avons fait à nous deux; **b. you and me** entre nous; **in b.** entre ▮ adv **in b.** (space) au milieu, entre les deux; (time) dans l'intervalle.
bevel ['bevəl] n (edge) biseau m. ● **bevelled** a (Am **beveled**) **b. edge** biseau m.
beverage ['bevərɪdʒ] n boisson f.
bevy ['bevɪ] n **a b. of** (girls, reporters etc) un essaim or une bande de.
beware [bɪ'weər] vi **to b. of** (s.o., sth) se méfier de, prendre garde à; **b.!** méfiez-vous!, prenez garde!; **b. of falling/etc** prenez garde de (ne pas) tomber/etc; **'b. of the trains!'** 'attention aux trains!'; **'b. of the dog!'** 'attention, chien méchant!'; **'danger b.!'** 'attention! danger!'
bewilder [bɪ'wɪldər] vt dérouter, rendre perplexe. ● **bewildering** a déroutant. ● **bewilderment** n confusion f.
bewitch [bɪ'wɪtʃ] vt enchanter. ● **bewitching** a enchanteur.
beyond [bɪ'jɒnd] **1** prep (further than) au-delà de; **b. a year/etc** (longer than) plus d'un an/etc; **b. reach/doubt** hors de portée/de doute; **b. belief** incroyable; **b. my/his/our/etc means** au-dessus de mes/ses/nos/etc moyens; **it's b. me** ça me dépasse ▮ adv (further) au-delà. **2** prep (except) sauf.
bias ['baɪəs] **1** n penchant m (towards pour); (prejudice) préjugé m, parti pris m ▮ vt (-ss- or -s-) influencer. **2** n cut on the b. (fabric) coupé dans le biais. ● **bias(s)ed** a partial; **to be b. against** avoir des préjugés contre.
bib [bɪb] n (baby's) bavoir m.
bible ['baɪb(ə)l] n bible f; **the B.** la Bible.

● **biblical** ['bɪblɪk(ə)l] a biblique.
bibliography [bɪblɪ'ɒɡrəfɪ] n bibliographie f.
bicarbonate [baɪ'kɑ:bənət] n **b. of soda** bicarbonate m de soude.
bicentenary [baɪsen'ti:nərɪ] or **bicentennial** n bicentenaire m.
biceps ['baɪseps] n inv (muscle) biceps m.
bicker ['bɪkər] vi se chamailler. ● **bickering** n chamailleries fpl.
bicycle ['baɪsɪk(ə)l] n bicyclette f; **by b.** à bicyclette ▮ vi **to b. to** (travel) aller à bicyclette à.
bid¹ [bɪd] **1** vt (pt & pp bid, pres p bidding) (sum of money) offrir, faire une offre de ▮ vi faire une offre (for pour); (for doing a job) faire une soumission (for pour) ▮ n (at auction) offre f, enchère f (for pour); (for doing a job) soumission f (for pour).
2 n (attempt) tentative f; **a b. for attention/love** une tentative pour attirer l'attention/se faire aimer; **to make a b. for power** tenter d'accéder au pouvoir ▮ vi **to b. for** = **to make a b. for.** ● **bidding¹** n (at auction) enchères fpl. ● **bidder** n (at auction) enchérisseur m; (tenderer) soumissionnaire mf; **to the highest b.** au plus offrant.
bid² [bɪd] vt (pt bade [bæd], pp bidden or bid, pres p bidding) (command) commander (s.o. to do à qn de faire); (say) dire, souhaiter; **to b. s.o. good day** dire bonjour à qn, souhaiter le bonjour à qn. ● **bidding²** n **at s.o.'s b.** sur les ordres de qn.
bide [baɪd] vt **to b. one's time** attendre le bon moment.
bier [bɪər] n (for coffin) brancards mpl.
bifocals [baɪ'fəʊkəlz] npl verres mpl à double foyer.
big [bɪɡ] a (bigger, biggest) grand, gros (f grosse); (in age, generous) grand; (in bulk, amount) gros; **b. deal!** Fam (bon) et alors!; **b. mouth** Fam grande gueule f; **b. toe** gros orteil m; **it's the b. time** Fam c'est mon, ton etc heure.
▮ adv **to do things b.** Fam faire les choses en grand; **to look b.** Fam faire l'important; **to talk b.** Fam fanfaronner. ● **bighead** n or **big'headed** a Fam (conceited) prétentieux, -euse (mf); (boasting) vantard, -arde (mf). ● **big-'hearted** a généreux. ● **bigshot** or **bigwig** n Fam gros bonnet m. ● **big-time** a (criminal etc) Fam de grande envergure.
bigamy ['bɪɡəmɪ] n bigamie f. ● **bigamist** n bigame mf. ● **bigamous** a bigame.
bigot ['bɪɡət] n sectaire mf, fanatique mf; (religious) bigot, -ote mf. ● **bigoted** a sectaire, fanatique; (religious) bigot. ● **bigotry** n sectarisme m, fanatisme m; bigoterie f.
bike [baɪk] n Fam vélo m; (motorbike) moto f ▮ vi **to b. to** (travel) Fam aller à vélo or à moto à.
bikini [bɪ'ki:nɪ] n deux-pièces m inv; **b. briefs** mini-slip m.
bilberry ['bɪlbərɪ] n myrtille f.
bile [baɪl] n bile f. ● **bilious** ['bɪlɪəs] a bilieux; **b. attack** Br crise f de foie.

bilingual [baɪˈlɪŋgwəl] *a* bilingue.

bill¹ [bɪl] **1** *n* (*invoice*) facture *f*, note *f*; (*in restaurant*) addition *f*; (*in hotel*) note *f*; (*banknote*) *Am* billet *m*; (*bank draft*) effet *m*; **b. of sale** acte *m* de vente █ *vt* **to b. s.o.** envoyer la facture à qn. **2** *n* (*proposed law*) projet *m* de loi; **b. of rights** déclaration *f* des droits. **3** *n* (*of play, concert etc*) affiche *f* █ *vt* mettre à l'affiche, annoncer. **4** *n* (*list*) **b. of fare** menu *m*. ●**billboard** *n Am* panneau *m* d'affichage. ●**billfold** *n* (*wallet*) *Am* porte-feuille *m*.

bill² [bɪl] *n* (*of bird*) bec *m*.

billet [ˈbɪlɪt] *vt Mil* cantonner █ *n* cantonnement *m*.

billiard [ˈbɪljəd] *a* (*table etc*) de billard. ●**billiards** *n* (jeu *m* de) billard *m*.

billion [ˈbɪljən] *n* milliard *m*. ●**billio'naire** *n* milliardaire *mf*.

billow [ˈbɪləʊ] *n* (*of smoke*) (épaisse) volute *f* █ *vi* (*of smoke*) tourbillonner; (*of sea*) se soulever; (*of sail*) se gonfler; **billowing smoke** des tourbillons *mpl* de fumée.

billy goat [ˈbɪlɪgəʊt] *n* bouc *m*.

bimbo [ˈbɪmbəʊ] *n* (*pl* -os) *Fam Pej* minette *f*.

bimonthly [baɪˈmʌnθlɪ] *a* (*every two weeks*) bimensuel; (*every two months*) bimestriel.

bin [bɪn] *n* boîte *f*; (*for bread*) *Br* huche *f*, boîte *f*; (*for litter*) poubelle *f*, boîte *f* à ordures.

binary [ˈbaɪnərɪ] *a* binaire.

bind [baɪnd] **1** *vt* (*pt* & *pp* **bound**) (*fasten*) attacher, lier; (*book*) relier; (*fabric, hem*) border; (*unite*) lier (*qn*); **to b. s.o. (hand and foot)** ligoter qn; **to b. s.o. to do** (*oblige*) obliger *or* astreindre qn à faire. **2** *n* (*bore*) *Fam* plaie *f*. ●**binding 1** *n* (*of book*) reliure *f*. **2** *a* (*contract*) irrévocable; **to be b. on s.o.** (*legally*) lier qn.

binder [ˈbaɪndər] *n* (*for papers*) classeur *m*.

binge [bɪndʒ] *n* **to go on a b.** *Fam* (*merry-making, drinking etc*) faire la bringue; (*eating*) se gaver.

bingo [ˈbɪŋgəʊ] *n* loto *m*.

binoculars [bɪˈnɒkjʊləz] *npl* jumelles *fpl*.

biochemistry [baɪəʊˈkemɪstrɪ] *n* biochimie *f*. ●**biochemical** *a* biochimique.

biodegradable [baɪəʊdɪˈgreɪdəb(ə)l] *a* biodégradable.

biography [baɪˈɒgrəfɪ] *n* biographie *f*. ●**bio'graphical** *a* biographique. ●**biographer** *n* biographe *m*.

biology [baɪˈɒlədʒɪ] *n* biologie *f*. ●**bio'logical** *a* biologique. ●**biologist** *n* biologiste *mf*.

biped [ˈbaɪped] *n* bipède *m*.

birch [bɜːtʃ] *n* **1** (*silver*) **b.** (*tree*) bouleau *m*. **2** (*whip*) verge *f* █ *vt* fouetter.

bird [bɜːd] *n* oiseau *m*; (*fowl*) volaille *f*; (*girl*) *Br Old-fashioned Sl* poulette *f*, nana *f*; **b.'s-eye view** perspective *f* à vol d'oiseau; (*of plan etc*) *Fig* vue *f* d'ensemble. ●**birdseed** *n* grains *mpl* de millet.

biro® [ˈbaɪərəʊ] *n* (*pl* -os) *Br* stylo *m* à bille, bic® *m*.

birth [bɜːθ] *n* naissance *f*; **to give b. to** donner naissance à; **from b.** de naissance; **b. certificate** acte *m* de naissance; **b. control** limitation *f* des naissances.

birthday [ˈbɜːθdeɪ] *n* anniversaire *m*; **happy b.!** bon anniversaire! **b. party** fête *f* d'anniversaire. ●**birthmark** *n* tache *f* de vin. ●**birthplace** *n* lieu *m* de naissance; (*house*) maison *f* natale. ●**birthrate** *n* (taux *m* de) natalité *f*. ●**birthright** *n* droit *m* (*qu'on a dès sa naissance*), patrimoine *m*.

biscuit [ˈbɪskɪt] *n Br* biscuit *m*, gâteau *m* sec; *Am* petit pain *m* au lait.

bishop [ˈbɪʃəp] *n* évêque *m*; (*in chess*) fou *m*.

bison [ˈbaɪs(ə)n] *n inv* bison *m*.

bit¹ [bɪt] *n* **1** morceau *m*; (*of string, time*) bout *m*; **a b.** (*a little*) un peu; **a tiny b.** un tout petit peu; **quite a b.** (*very*) très; (*a lot*) beaucoup; **not a b.** pas du tout; **a b. of luck** une chance; **b. by b.** petit à petit; **in bits (and pieces)** en morceaux; **to come to bits** se démonter; **to do one's b.** y mettre du sien. **2** (*coin*) pièce *f*. **3** (*of horse*) mors *m*. **4** (*of drill*) mèche *f*. **5** (*computer information*) bit *m*.

bit² [bɪt] *see* **bite**.

bitch [bɪtʃ] **1** *n* chienne *f*; (*unpleasant woman*) *Fam* garce *f*. **2** *vi* (*complain*) *Fam* râler. ●**bitchy** *a* (-ier, -iest) (*remark, behaviour etc*) *Fam* vache.

bite [baɪt] *n* (*wound*) morsure *f*; (*from insect*) piqûre *f*; *Fishing* touche *f*; (*mouthful*) bouchée *f*; (*of style, text etc*) *Fig* mordant *m*; **a b. to eat** un morceau à manger █ *vti* (*pt* **bit**, *pp* **bitten**) (*of insect*) piquer; mordre; **to b. one's nails** se ronger les ongles; **to b. on sth** mordre qch; **to b. sth off** arracher qch d'un coup de dent(s); **to b. off a piece of apple** mordre dans la pomme. ●**biting** *a* (*cold*) mordant; (*wind*) cinglant; (*irony etc*) *Fig* mordant.

bitter [ˈbɪtər] **1** *a* (*person, taste, irony etc*) amer; (*cold, wind*) glacial, âpre; (*criticism*) acerbe; (*shock, fate*) cruel; (*conflict*) violent; **to feel b. (about sth)** être plein d'amertume (à cause de qch).

2 *n* (*beer*) *Br* bière *f* (pression). ●**bitterly** *adv* **to cry/regret b.** pleurer/regretter amèrement; **b. disappointed** cruellement déçu; **it's b. cold** il fait un froid glacial. ●**bitterness** *n* amertume *f*; (*of the cold etc*) âpreté *f*; (*of conflict*) violence *f*. ●**bittersweet** *a* aigre-doux (*f* -douce); **b. chocolate** *Am* chocolat *m* à croquer.

bivouac [ˈbɪvʊæk] *n Mil* bivouac *m* █ *vi* (-ck-) bivouaquer.

bizarre [bɪˈzɑːr] *a* bizarre.

blab [blæb] *vi* (-bb-) jaser. ●**blabber** *vi* jaser. ●**blabbermouth** *n* jaseur, -euse *mf*.

black [blæk] *a* (-er, -est) noir; **b. eye** œil *m* poché *or* au beurre noir; **to give s.o. a b. eye** pocher l'œil à qn; **b. and blue** (*bruised*) couvert de bleus; **b. sheep** *Fig* brebis *f* galeuse;

b. ice Br verglas m; Br **b. pudding** boudin m.
∎ n (colour) noir m; (person) Noir, -e mf.
∎ vt noircir; (refuse to deal with) boycotter.
∎ vi **to b. out** (faint) s'évanouir. ● **blacken** vti
noircir. ● **blackish** a noirâtre. ● **blackness** n
noirceur f; (of night) obscurité f.
blackberry [Br 'blækbərɪ, Am -berɪ] n mûre
f. ● **blackbird** n merle m. ● **blackboard** n tableau m (noir); **on the b.** au tableau.
● **black'currant** n cassis m. ● **blackleg** n
(strike breaker) Br jaune m. ● **blacklist** n
liste f noire ∎ vt mettre sur la liste noire.
● **blackmail** n chantage m ∎ vt faire chanter;
to b. s.o. into doing faire chanter qn pour
qu'il fasse. ● **blackmailer** n maître chanteur
m. ● **blackout** n panne f d'électricité; (during
war) black-out m; (fainting fit) syncope f;
(news) **b.** black-out m. ● **blacksmith** n forgeron m.
blackguard ['blægɑ:d, -gəd] n Old-fashioned
canaille f.
bladder ['blædər] n vessie f.
blade [bleɪd] n lame f; (of Br windscreen or
Am windshield wiper) caoutchouc m; **b. of
grass** brin m d'herbe.
blame [bleɪm] vt accuser; (criticize) blâmer;
to b. sth on(to) s.o. or s.o. for sth rejeter la
responsabilité de qch sur qn; **to b. s.o. for
sth** (reproach) reprocher qch à qn; **you're to
b. c'est ta faute; ∎ b. you for doing that** je
considère que c'est toi qui es responsable de
cela.
∎ n responsabilité f; (criticism) blâme m; **to
lay the b. (for sth) on s.o.** rejeter la responsabilité (de qch) sur qn. ● **blameless** a
irréprochable.
blanch [blɑ:ntʃ] vt (vegetables) blanchir ∎ vi
(turn pale with fear etc) blêmir.
blancmange [blə'mɒnʒ] n Br blanc-manger
m.
bland [blænd] a (-er, -est) (food) (mild) sans
saveur particulière; (insipid) fade, insipide;
(remark, joke) quelconque, fade.
blank [blæŋk] a (paper, page) blanc (f
blanche), vierge; (Br cheque, Am check) en
blanc; (look, mind) vide; (puzzled) ébahi;
(refusal) absolu; **to leave b.** (on form) laisser
en blanc; **b. tape** cassette f vierge.
∎ a & n. (space) blanc m; **b. (cartridge)**
cartouche f à blanc; **my mind's a b.** j'ai la
tête vide. ● **blankly** adv **to look at b.** regarder, le visage inexpressif; (without understanding) regarder sans comprendre.
blanket ['blæŋkɪt] ∎ n (on bed) couverture f;
(of snow, leaves etc) couche f ∎ vt (cover) Fig
recouvrir. 2 a (term, remark etc) général. ● **blanketing** n (blankets) couvertures
fpl.
blare [bleər] n (noise) beuglement m; (of
trumpet) sonnerie f ∎ vi **to b. (out)** (of radio)
beugler; (of music, car horn) retentir.
blarney ['blɑ:nɪ] n Fam boniment(s) m(pl).
blasé ['blɑ:zeɪ] a blasé.
blaspheme [blæs'fi:m] vti blasphémer.
● **blasphemous** ['blæsfəməs] a (text etc)

blasphématoire; (person) blasphémateur.
● **blasphemy** ['blæsfəmɪ] n blasphème m.
blast [blɑ:st] 1 n explosion f; (air from explosion) souffle m; (of wind) rafale f, coup m;
(of trumpet) sonnerie f; **(at) full b.** (loud) à
plein volume; (fast) à pleine vitesse; **b.
furnace** haut fourneau m ∎ vt (blow up) faire
sauter; (hopes) Fig détruire; **to b. s.o.** Fam
réprimander qn.
2 int Br Fam zut!, merde! **b. you!** tu
m'enquiquines! ● **blasted** a Br Fam fichu.
● **blast-off** n (of spacecraft) mise f à feu.
blatant ['bleɪtənt] a (obvious) flagrant,
criant; (shameless) éhonté.
blaze [bleɪz] 1 n (flame) flamme f, (fire) feu
m; (large) incendie m; (splendour) Fig éclat
m; **a b. of colour** une explosion de couleurs;
b. of light torrent m de lumière ∎ vi (fire)
flamber; (of sun, colour, eyes) flamboyer. 2
vt **to b. a trail** marquer la voie. ● **blazing** a
(burning) en feu; (sun) brûlant; (argument)
Fig violent.
blazer ['bleɪzər] n blazer m.
bleach [bli:tʃ] n (household) eau f de Javel;
(for hair) décolorant m ∎ vt (hair) décolorer,
oxygéner; (linen) blanchir.
bleachers ['bli:tʃəz] npl (at athletic stadium)
Am gradins mpl.
bleak [bli:k] a (-er, -est) (appearance etc)
morne; (future, situation etc) sombre; (countryside) désolé.
bleary ['blɪərɪ] a (eyes) troubles, voilés.
bleat [bli:t] vi bêler.
bleed [bli:d] vti (pt & pp bled) saigner; **to b.
to death** perdre tout son sang. ● **bleeding** a 1
(wound) saignant. 2 a **b. idiot**/etc (bloody)
Br Sl un foutu crétin/etc.
bleep [bli:p] n bip m ∎ vt appeler au bip.
● **bleeper** n (portable pager) bip m.
blemish ['blemɪʃ] n (fault) défaut m; (on
fruit, reputation) tache f ∎ vt (reputation)
ternir.
blend [blend] n mélange m ∎ vt mélanger
(**with** à) ∎ vi se mélanger; (go together) (of
styles, colours etc) se marier (**with** avec);
everything blends (in) (decor of room etc)
tout est assorti. ● **blender** n (for food) mixer
m.
bless [bles] vt bénir; **to be blessed with good
health**/**with children** avoir le bonheur d'être
en bonne santé/d'avoir des enfants; **b. you!**
(sneezing) à vos souhaits! ● **blessed** [-ɪd] a 1
saint, béni; (happy) Rel bienheureux. 2
(blasted) Fam fichu, sacré. ● **blessing** n
bénédiction f; (divine favour) grâce f,
(benefit) bienfait m; **what a b. that...** quelle
chance que....
blew [blu:] see blow[2].
blight [blaɪt] n (on plants) rouille f; (scourge)
Fig fléau m; **to be or cast a b. on** avoir une
influence néfaste sur; **urban b.** (area)
quartier m délabré; (condition) délabrement
m (de quartier).
blighter ['blaɪtər] n (person) Br Fam type m.
blimey! ['blaɪmɪ] int Br Fam zut!, mince!

blimp [blɪmp] n dirigeable m.

blind [blaɪnd] 1 a aveugle; **b. person** aveugle mf; **b. in one eye** borgne; **he's b. to her faults**/etc il ne voit pas ses défauts/etc; **to turn a b. eye to** fermer les yeux sur; **b. alley** impasse f ■ n **the b.** les aveugles mpl ■ vt (dazzle, make blind) aveugler.
2 n (on window) Br store m.
3 adv **b. drunk** complètement ivre. ● **blindly** adv aveuglément. ● **blindness** n cécité f.

blinders ['blaɪndəz] npl Am œillères fpl.

blindfold ['blaɪndfəʊld] n bandeau m ■ vt bander les yeux à ■ adv les yeux bandés.

blink [blɪŋk] vi (of person) cligner des yeux; (of eyes) cligner; (of light) clignoter ■ vt **to b. one's eyes** cligner des yeux ■ n clignement m; **on the b.** (machine) Fam détraqué. ● **blinking** a (bloody) Br Fam sacré, fichu.

blinkers ['blɪŋkəz] npl (of horse) Br œillères fpl; (indicators of vehicle) clignotants mpl.

bliss [blɪs] n félicité f. ● **blissful** a (wonderful) merveilleux; (very happy) (person) ravi, aux anges. ● **blissfully** adv (happy, unaware) parfaitement.

blister ['blɪstər] n (on skin) ampoule f ■ vi se couvrir d'ampoules.

blithe [blaɪð] a joyeux.

blitz [blɪts] n (air attack) raid m éclair; (bombing) bombardement m aérien; (onslaught) Fam offensive f ■ vt bombarder.

blizzard ['blɪzəd] n tempête f de neige.

bloated ['bləʊtɪd] a (swollen, full after eating) gonflé.

blob [blɒb] n (of water) (grosse) goutte f; (of ink, colour) tache f.

bloc [blɒk] n (political group) bloc m.

block [blɒk] 1 n (of stone etc) bloc m; (of buildings) pâté m (de maisons); (in pipe) obstruction f; (mental) blocage m; **b. of flats** immeuble m; **a b. away** Am une rue plus loin; **school b.** groupe m scolaire; **b. capitals** or **letters** majuscules fpl.
2 vt (obstruct) boucher; (pipe) boucher, bloquer; (s.o.'s view) boucher; **to b. off** (road) barrer; (light) intercepter; **to b. up** (pipe, hole) bloquer. ● **blockage** n obstruction f.

blockade [blɒ'keɪd] n blocus m ■ vt bloquer.

blockbuster ['blɒkbʌstər] n (film) film m à grand spectacle, superproduction f.

blockhead ['blɒkhed] n Fam imbécile mf.

bloke [bləʊk] n Br Fam type m.

blond [blɒnd] a & n blond (m). ● **blonde** a & n blonde (f).

blood [blʌd] n sang m ■ a (group, transfusion etc) sanguin; **b. bank** banque f du sang; **b. bath** bain m de sang; **b. donor** donneur, -euse mf de sang; **b. poisoning** empoisonnement m du sang; **b. pressure** tension f (artérielle); **high b. pressure** (hyper)tension f; **to have high b. pressure** avoir de la tension; **b. test** analyse f de sang; **b. sausage** Am boudin m.

bloodcurdling ['blʌdkɜːdlɪŋ] a à vous tourner le sang. ● **bloodhound** n (dog, detective) limier m. ● **bloodletting** n saignée f. ● **bloodshed** n effusion f de sang. ● **blood-shot** a (eye) injecté de sang. ● **bloodstained** a taché de sang. ● **bloodstream** n système m sanguin. ● **bloodsucker** n (insect, person) sangsue f. ● **bloodthirsty** a sanguinaire.

bloody ['blʌdɪ] 1 a (-ier, -iest) sanglant. 2 a Br Fam **b. weather**/etc (awful) saleté f de temps/etc, sale temps/etc; **a b. liar**/etc un sale menteur/etc ■ adv (very, completely) Br Fam vachement. ● **bloody-'minded** a hargneux, pas commode.

bloom [bluːm] n fleur f; **in b.** en fleur(s) ■ vi (of tree, flower) fleurir; (of person) Fig s'épanouir. ● **blooming** a 1 (in bloom) en fleur(s); (thriving) florissant; (person) resplendissant. 2 (bloody) Br Fam sacré, fichu.

bloomer ['bluːmər] n Br Fam (mistake) gaffe f.

blossom ['blɒsəm] n fleur(s) f(pl) ■ vi fleurir; **to b. (out)** (of person) s'épanouir; **to b. (out) into** (a real beauty etc) devenir.

blot [blɒt] n tache f ■ vt (-tt-) (stain) tacher; (dry) sécher; **to b. out** (obliterate) effacer. ● **blotter** n buvard m. ● **blotting paper** n (papier m) buvard m.

blotch [blɒtʃ] n tache f. ● **blotchy** a (-ier, -iest) couvert de taches; (face, skin) marbré.

blouse [Br blauz, Am blaus] n chemisier m.

blow¹ [bləʊ] n (with fist, tool etc) coup m; **to come to blows** en venir aux mains.

blow² [bləʊ] vt (pt blew, pp blown) (of wind) pousser (un navire etc), chasser (la pluie etc); (of person) (smoke, glass) souffler; (bubbles) faire; (trumpet) souffler dans; (kiss) envoyer (to à); (money) Br Fam claquer; **to b. a fuse** faire sauter un plomb or un fusible; **to b. one's nose** se moucher; **to b. a whistle** siffler.
■ vi (of wind, person) souffler; (of fuse) sauter; (of papers etc) (in wind) s'éparpiller; **b.!** Br Fam zut!

blow away vt (of wind) emporter (qch) ■ vi (of hat etc) s'envoler ■ **to blow down** vt (chimney etc) faire tomber ■ vi (fall) tomber ■ **to blow off** vt (hat etc) emporter; (arm) arracher ■ **to blow out** vt (candle) souffler; (cheeks) gonfler ■ vi (of light) s'éteindre. ● **blowout** n (of Br tyre, Am tire) éclatement m; (meal) Br Sl gueuleton m. ■ **to blow over** 1 vti = blow down. 2 vi (of quarrel etc) passer, se tasser ■ **to blow up** vt (building etc) faire sauter; (pump up) gonfler; (photo) agrandir ■ vi (explode) exploser. ● **blow-up** n (of photo) agrandissement m.

blow-dry ['bləʊdraɪ] n brushing m ■ vt **to b.-dry s.o.'s hair** faire un brushing à qn.

blowlamp ['bləʊlæmp] n Br (Am blowtorch) chalumeau m.

blowy ['bləʊɪ] a **it's b.** Fam il y a du vent.

blowzy ['blaʊzɪ] a **b. woman** (slovenly) Fam femme f débraillée.

blubber ['blʌbər] n graisse f (de baleine).

bludgeon ['blʌdʒən] n gourdin m ■ vt matraquer.

blue [bluː] a (bluer, bluest) bleu (mpl bleus); **to feel b.** Fam avoir le cafard; **b. film** Fam film *m* porno ▮ *n* bleu *m* (*pl* bleus); **the blues** (*depression*) *Fam* le cafard; (*music*) le blues; **out of the b.** (*unexpectedly*) de manière inattendue, sans crier gare.

bluebell ['blu:bel] *n* jacinthe *f* des bois. ● **blueberry** *n* airelle *f*. ● **bluebottle** *n* mouche *f* à viande. ● **blueprint** *n* *Fig* plan *m* (de travail).

bluff [blʌf] **1** *a* (*person*) brusque, direct. **2** *vti* bluffer ▮ *n* bluff *m*.

blunder ['blʌndər] **1** *n* (*mistake*) gaffe *f*, bévue *f* ▮ *vi* faire une gaffe *or* une bévue. **2** *vi* (*move awkwardly*) avancer à tâtons. ● **blundering** *a* (*clumsy*) maladroit ▮ *n* maladresse *f*.

blunt [blʌnt] *a* (**-er, -est**) (*edge*) émoussé; (*pencil*) mal taillé; (*person, speech*) franc (*f* franche), brusque ▮ *vt* (*blade etc*) émousser; (*pencil*) user la mine de. ● **bluntly** *adv* (*to say etc*) carrément. ● **bluntness** *n* (*of person*) brusquerie *f*; (*of speech*) franchise *f*.

blur [blɜ:r] *n* tache *f* floue, contour *m* imprécis ▮ *vt* (**-rr-**) (*outline, etc*) estomper, rendre flou, brouiller. ● **blurred** *a* (*image, outline*)) flou, estompé.

blurb [blɜ:b] *n* *Fam* résumé *m* publicitaire, laïus *m*.

blurt [blɜ:t] *vt* **to b. (out)** (*secret*) laisser échapper; (*excuse*) bredouiller.

blush [blʌʃ] *vi* rougir (**with** de) ▮ *n* rougeur *f*; **with a b.** en rougissant.

bluster ['blʌstər] *vi* (*of person*) tempêter; (*of wind*) faire rage. ● **blustery** *a* (*weather*) de grand vent, à bourrasques.

BO [bi:'əʊ] *n* *abbr* (*body odour*) **to have BO** sentir la transpiration, sentir mauvais.

boa ['bəʊə] *n* (*snake*) boa *m*.

boar [bɔ:r] *n* (*wild*) **b.** sanglier *m*.

board¹ [bɔ:d] **1** *n* (*piece of wood*) planche *f*; (*for notices etc*) tableau *m*; (*for games*) plateau *m*; (*cardboard*) carton *m*; **on b.** (*ship, aircraft*) à bord (de); **to go on b.** (**a** **ship/etc**) monter à bord (d'un navire/etc); **to go by the b.** (*of plan*) être abandonné. **2** *vt* (*ship, aircraft*) monter à bord de; (*bus, train*) monter dans; **to b. up** (*door*) boucher ▮ *vi* *Nau Av etc* monter (à bord). ● **boarding** *n* (*of passengers*) embarquement *m*; **b. pass** carte *f* d'embarquement. ● **boardwalk** *n* *Am* promenade *f*.

board² [bɔ:d] *n* (*committee*) conseil *m*, commission *f*; **b. (of directors)** conseil *m* d'administration; **b. (of examiners)** jury *m* (d'examen); **B. of Trade** *Br Pol* ministère *m* du Commerce; **across the b.** (*pay increase, measures etc*) général; **b. room** salle *f* du conseil.

board³ [bɔ:d] *n* (*food*) pension *f*; **full b.** *Br* pension *f* complète; **half b.** *Br* demi-pension *f*; **b. and lodging, bed and b.** (chambre *f* avec) pension *f* ▮ *vi* (*lodge*) être en pension (**with** chez); **boarding house** pension *f* (de famille); **boarding school** pensionnat *m*. ● **boarder** *n* pensionnaire *mf*.

boast [bəʊst] *vi* se vanter (**about, of** de) ▮ *vt*

se glorifier de; **to b. that one can do sth** se vanter de (pouvoir) faire qch ▮ *n* vantardise *f*. ● **boasting** *n* vantardise *f*.

boastful ['bəʊstfəl] *a* vantard. ● **boastfully** *adv* en se vantant.

boat [bəʊt] *n* bateau *m*; (*small*) barque *f*, canot *m*; (*liner*) paquebot *m*; **by b.** en bateau; **in the same b.** *Fig* logé à la même enseigne; **b. race** course *f* d'aviron. ● **boating** *n* canotage *m*; **b. trip** excursion *f* en bateau.

boatswain ['bəʊs(ə)n] *n* maître *m* d'équipage.

bob [bɒb] *vi* (**-bb-**) **to b. (up and down)** (*on water*) danser sur l'eau.

bobbin ['bɒbɪn] *n* bobine *f*.

bobby ['bɒbɪ] *n* **1** (*policeman*) *Br Fam* flic *m*, agent *m*. **2 b. pin** *Am* pince *f* à cheveux.

bode [bəʊd] *vi* **to b. well/ill** être de bon/ mauvais augure.

bodice ['bɒdɪs] *n* corsage *m*.

bodily ['bɒdɪlɪ] *a* (*need*) physique ▮ *adv* (*to lift, seize*) à bras-le-corps; (*to carry*) dans ses bras; (*as a whole*) tout entier.

body ['bɒdɪ] *n* corps *m*; (*of vehicle*) carrosserie *f*; (*quantity*) masse *f*; (*institution*) organisme *m*; **dead b.** cadavre *m*; **the main b. of the audience** le gros de l'assistance; **b. building** culturisme *m*. ● **bodyguard** *n* garde *m* du corps, *Fam* gorille *m*. ● **body warmer** *n* gilet *m* matelassé. ● **bodywork** *n* carrosserie *f*.

boffin ['bɒfɪn] *n* *Br Fam* chercheur, -euse *mf* scientifique.

bog [bɒg] *n* (*swamp*) marécage *m* ▮ *vt* **to get bogged down** (*in mud, in one's work etc*) s'enliser. ● **boggy** *a* (**-ier, -iest**) marécageux.

bogey ['bəʊgɪ] *n* (*of war etc*) spectre *m*. ● **bogeyman** *n* croque-mitaine *m*.

boggle ['bɒg(ə)l] *vi* **the mind boggles** cela confond l'imagination.

boggy ['bɒgɪ] *see* bog.

bogus ['bəʊgəs] *a* (*accent, doctor etc*) faux (*f* fausse).

bohemian [bəʊ'hi:mɪən] *a* & *n* (*artist etc*) bohème (*mf*).

boil¹ [bɔɪl] *n* (*pimple*) furoncle *m*, clou *m*.

boil² [bɔɪl] *vi* bouillir; **to b. away** (*until dry*) s'évaporer; (*on and on*) bouillir sans arrêt; **to b. down to** (*of situation, question etc*) *Fig* se ramener à; **to b. over** (*of milk, Fig emotions etc*) déborder.

▮ *vt* **to b. (up)** faire bouillir.

▮ *n* **to be on the b., come to the b.** bouillir; **to bring to the b.** amener à ébullition. ● **boiled** *a* (*beef*) bouilli; (*potato*) à l'anglaise; (*with skin*) (cuit) à l'eau; **b. egg** œuf *m* à la coque. ● **boiling** *n* ébullition *f*; **to be at b. point** (*of liquid*) bouillir ▮ *a* **a b. (hot)** bouillant; **it's b. (hot)** (*weather*) il fait une chaleur infernale.

boiler ['bɔɪlər] *n* chaudière *f*; **b. suit** *Br* bleus *mpl* (de travail).

boisterous ['bɔɪstərəs] *a* (*noisy*) tapageur, chahuteur; (*child*) turbulent; (*meeting*) houleux.

bold [bəʊld] *a* (**-er, -est**) hardi; **in b. type** en

(caractères) gras. ● **boldness** n hardiesse f.
Bolivia [bə'lɪvɪə] n Bolivie f. ● **Bolivian** a bolivien ▮ n Bolivien, -ienne mf.
bollard ['bɒləd, 'bɒlɑːd] n (for traffic) Br
borne f.
boloney [bə'ləʊnɪ] n (nonsense) Sl foutaises
fpl.
bolster ['bəʊlstər] 1 n (pillow) traversin m,
polochon m. 2 vt to b. (up) (support) soutenir.
bolt [bəʊlt] 1 n (on door etc) verrou m; (for
nut) boulon m ▮ vt (door) fermer au verrou,
verrouiller.
2 n (dash) fuite f, ruée f; **to make a b. for
the door/etc** se précipiter vers la porte/etc ▮
vi (dash) se précipiter; (run away) détaler;
(of horse) s'emballer.
3 n b. (of lightning) éclair m.
4 vt (food) engloutir.
5 adv b. upright tout droit.
bomb [bɒm] n bombe f; **letter b.** lettre f piégée; **b. disposal** désamorçage m; **b. disposal
unit** équipe f de déminage ▮ vt (from the air)
bombarder; (of terrorist) faire sauter une
bombe dans or à. ● **bombing** n bombardement m; (terrorist act) attentat m à la
bombe. ● **bomber** n (aircraft) bombardier m;
(terrorist) plastiqueur m. ● **bombshell** n to
come as a b. tomber comme une bombe.
● **bombsite** n terrain m vague, lieu m
bombardé.
bombard [bɒm'bɑːd] vt (with bombs, questions etc) bombarder (with de). ● **bombard-
ment** n bombardement m.
bona fide [Br bəʊnə'faɪdɪ, Am -'faɪd] a sérieux, de bonne foi.
bonanza [bə'nænzə] n Fig mine f d'or.
bond [bɒnd] 1 n (link) lien m; (investment
certificate) bon m, obligation f; (agreement,
promise) engagement m; (adhesion) adhérence f. 2 vt (of glue etc) coller (to à). 3 n
bonded warehouse entrepôt m en douane.
bondage ['bɒndɪdʒ] n esclavage m.
bone [bəʊn] 1 n os m; (of fish) arête f; **b. of
contention** pomme f de discorde; **b. china**
porcelaine f tendre ▮ vt (meat etc) désosser.
2 vi to **b. up on** (subject) Am Fam bûcher.
● **bony** a (-ier, -iest) (thin) osseux, maigre;
(fish) plein d'arêtes.
bone-dry [bəʊn'draɪ] a tout à fait sec (f
sèche). ● **bone-idle** a Br paresseux comme
une couleuvre.
bonfire ['bɒnfaɪər] n (for celebration) feu m
de joie; (for dead leaves) Br feu m (de
jardin).
bonkers ['bɒŋkəz] a (crazy) Br Fam dingue.
bonnet ['bɒnɪt] n (hat) bonnet m; (of vehicle) Br capot m.
bonus ['bəʊnəs] n prime f; **no claims b.** (of
car driver) bonus m.
bony ['bəʊnɪ] a see **bone**.
boo [buː] 1 int (to frighten s.o.) hou! 2 vti
siffler, huer ▮ n boos sifflets mpl, huées fpl.
boob [buːb] 1 Br Fam n (mistake) gaffe f ▮ vi
gaffer. 2 n boobs (breasts) Fam nénés mpl.

booby-trap ['buːbɪtræp] n engin m piégé ▮ vt
(-pp-) piéger.
book¹ [bʊk] n livre m; (of tickets) carnet m;
(record) registre m; (exercise) b. cahier m;
(bank) b. livret m (de banque); **books**
(accounts) comptes mpl; **b. club** club m du
livre.
book² [bʊk] vt to b. (up) (seat etc) réserver,
retenir; **to b. s.o.** (for speeding etc) Br
donner un procès-verbal à qn; **to b. (down)**
(write down) inscrire; **(fully) booked (up)**
(hotel, concert) complet; (person) pris ▮ vi to
b. (up) réserver des places; **to b. in** (in hotel)
signer le registre; **to b. into** (a hotel) prendre
une chambre dans, descendre à. ● **booking**
n réservation f; **b. clerk** guichetier, -ière mf;
b. office bureau m de location, guichet m.
bookable ['bʊkəb(ə)l] a (seat) qu'on peut réserver.
bookbinding ['bʊkbaɪndɪŋ] n reliure f.
● **bookcase** n bibliothèque f. ● **bookend** n
serre-livres m inv. ● **bookie** n Fam bookmaker m. ● **bookkeeper** n comptable mf.
● **bookkeeping** n comptabilité f. ● **booklet** n
brochure f. ● **book-lover** n bibliophile mf.
● **bookmaker** n bookmaker m. ● **bookmark** n
marque f, marque-page m. ● **bookseller** n libraire mf. ● **bookshelf** n rayon m. ● **bookshop** Br or **bookstore** Am n librairie f.
● **bookstall** n kiosque m (à journaux).
● **bookworm** n rat m de bibliothèque.
bookish ['bʊkɪʃ] a (word, theory) livresque;
(person) studieux.
boom [buːm] 1 vi (of thunder, gun etc)
gronder ▮ n (noise) grondement m; **sonic b.**
bang m. 2 n (economic) expansion f, essor
m, boom m.
boomerang ['buːməræŋ] n boomerang m.
boon [buːn] n avantage m.
boor [bʊər] n rustre m. ● **boorish** a rustre.
boost [buːst] vt (increase) augmenter; (product) faire de la réclame pour; (economy)
stimuler; (s.o.'s morale) remonter; **to b. s.o.
(up)** (push upwards) soulever qn ▮ n to give a
b. to = to boost. ● **booster** n b. (injection)
(piqûre f de) rappel m.
boot¹ [buːt] 1 n (shoe) botte f; (ankle) b.
bottillon m; (knee) b. bottine f; **to get the b.**
Fam être mis à la porte; **b. polish** cirage m ▮
vt (kick) donner un coup or des coups de
pied à; **to b. s.o. out** mettre qn à la porte. 2
n (of vehicle) Br coffre m. 3 n to b. (in addition) en plus. ● **bootblack** n cireur m.
● **bootee** n (of baby) chausson m. ● **bootlace**
n lacet m.
boot² [buːt] Comptr vt amorcer ▮ vi
s'amorcer.
booth [buːθ, buːð] n (for phone, in language
lab) cabine f; (at fair) baraque f; (for voting)
isoloir m.
booty ['buːtɪ] n (stolen goods) butin m.
booze [buːz] n Fam alcool m, boisson(s)
f(pl) ▮ vi Fam boire (beaucoup). ● **boozer** n
Fam (person) buveur, -euse mf; (place) Br
bistrot m. ● **booze-up** n (drinking bout) Br

Fam beuverie *f*.

border ['bɔːdər] *n* (*of country*) & *Fig* frontière *f*; (*edge*) bord *m*; (*of garden etc*) bordure *f* ▐ *a* (*town*) frontière *inv*; (*incident*) de frontière ▐ *vt* (*street*) border; to b. (on) (*country*) toucher à; to b. (up)on (*resemble, verge on*) être voisin de. ● **borderland** *n* pays *m* frontière. ● **borderline** *n* frontière *f*; b. case cas *m* limite.

bore[1] [bɔːr] 1 *vt* (*weary*) ennuyer; to be bored s'ennuyer; I'm bored with that job/teacher/*etc* ce travail/ce professeur/*etc* m'ennuie ▐ *n* (*person*) raseur, -euse *mf*; it's a b. c'est ennuyeux *or* rasoir. 2 *vt* (*hole*) percer; (*rock, well*) forer, creuser ▐ *vi* to b. for forer. 3 *n* (*of gun*) calibre *m*. ● **boring** *a* ennuyeux.

bore[2] [bɔːr] *pt of* bear[2].

boredom ['bɔːdəm] *n* ennui *m*.

born [bɔːn] *a* né; to be b. naître; he was b. in Paris/in 1953/*etc* il est né à Paris/en 1953/*etc*.

borne [bɔːn] *pp of* bear[2].

borough ['bʌrə] *n* (*town*) municipalité *f*; (*part of town*) arrondissement *m*.

borrow ['bɒrəʊ] *vt* emprunter (**from** à). ● **borrowing** *n* emprunt *m*.

Borstal ['bɔːst(ə)l] *n Br* maison *f* d'éducation surveillée.

Bosnia ['bɒznɪə] *n* Bosnie *f*.

bosom ['buzəm] *n* (*chest, breasts*) poitrine *f*, seins *mpl*; (*breast*) sein *m*; (*heart, soul*) *Fig* sein *m*; b. friend ami, -ie *mf* intime.

boss [bɒs] *n* patron, -onne *mf*, chef *m* ▐ *vt* to b. s.o. around *or* about commander qn, régenter qn. ● **bossy** *a* (-ier, -iest) *Fam* autoritaire.

boss-eyed ['bɒsaɪd] *a* to be b.-eyed loucher.

bosun ['bəʊs(ə)n] *n* maître *m* d'équipage.

botany ['bɒtənɪ] *n* botanique *f*. ● **bo'tanical** *a* botanique. ● **botanist** *n* botaniste *mf*.

botch [bɒtʃ] *vt* to b. (up) (*spoil*) bâcler; (*repair badly*) rafistoler.

both [bəʊθ] *a* les deux ▐ *pron* tous *or* toutes (les) deux, l'un(e) et l'autre; b. of the boys les deux garçons, l'un et l'autre des garçons; b. of us nous deux ▐ *adv* (*at the same time*) à la fois; b. you and I know that... vous et moi, nous savons que....

bother ['bɒðər] *vt* (*annoy, worry*) ennuyer; (*disturb*) déranger; (*pester*) importuner; (*hurt, itch etc*) (*of foot, eye etc*) gêner; to b. doing *or* to do se donner la peine de faire; I can't be bothered! je n'en ai pas envie!, ça m'embête!

▐ *vi* to b. about (*worry about*) se préoccuper de; (*deal with*) s'occuper de.

▐ *n* (*trouble*) ennui *m*; (*effort*) peine *f*; (*inconvenience*) dérangement *m*; (oh) b.! *Br* zut alors!

bottle ['bɒt(ə)l] *n* bouteille *f*; (*small*) flacon *m*; (*wide-mouthed*) bocal *m*; (*for baby*) biberon *m*; (hot-water) b. bouillotte *f*; b. opener ouvre-bouteilles *m inv*; b. bank conteneur *m* pour verre usagé.

▐ *vt* (*milk, wine etc*) mettre en bouteilles; to b. up (*feeling*) contenir. ● **bottle-feed** *vt* (*pt*

& *pp* -fed) nourrir au biberon. ● **bottleneck** *n* (*in road*) goulot *m* d'étranglement; (*traffic holdup*) bouchon *m*.

bottom ['bɒtəm] *n* (*of sea, box etc*) fond *m*; (*of page, hill etc*) bas *m*; (*buttocks*) *Fam* derrière *m*; (*of table*) bout *m*; to be (at the) b. of the class être le dernier de la classe ▐ *a* (*shelf*) inférieur, du bas; b. floor rez-de-chaussée *m*; b. gear première vitesse *f*; b. part *or* half partie *f* inférieure; that's the b. line *Fig* c'est la seule chose qui compte. ● **bottomless** *a* (*funds*) inépuisable; b. pit abîme *m* sans fond; b. coffee *Am* du café à volonté.

bough [baʊ] *n Lit* rameau *m*.

bought [bɔːt] *pt* & *pp of* buy.

boulder ['bəʊldər] *n* rocher *m*.

boulevard ['buːləvɑːd] *n* boulevard *m*.

bounce [baʊns] 1 *vi* (*of ball*) rebondir; (*of person*) faire des bonds; to b. into the hole/etc (*of ball*) rebondir et atterrir dans le trou/etc ▐ *vt* (*ball*) faire rebondir ▐ *n* (re)bond *m*. 2 *vi* (*of Br cheque, Am check*) *Fam* être sans provision, être en bois. ● **bouncing baby** *n* beau bébé *m*.

bouncer ['baʊnsər] *n* (*at club etc*) *Fam* videur *m*.

bound[1] [baʊnd] *pt* & *pp of* bind. 1 *a* b. to do (*obliged*) obligé de faire; (*certain*) sûr de faire; it's b. to happen/snow/*etc* ça arrivera/il neigera/*etc* sûrement; to be b. for (*of person, ship*) être en route pour; (*of train, plane*) être à destination de. 2 *a* b. up with (*connected*) lié à.

bound[2] [baʊnd] *n* (*leap*) bond *m* ▐ *vi* bondir.

boundary ['baʊnd(ə)rɪ] *n* limite *f*.

bounded ['baʊndɪd] *a* b. by limité par. ● **boundless** *a* sans bornes.

bounds [baʊndz] *npl* limites *fpl*; out of b. (*place*) interdit.

bountiful ['baʊntɪfʊl] *a* généreux.

bounty ['baʊntɪ] *n* (*reward*) prime *f*.

bouquet [bəʊ'keɪ] *n* (*of flowers, wine*) bouquet *m*.

bourbon ['bɜːbən] *n* (*whisky*) *Am* bourbon *m*.

bout [baʊt] *n* (*of fever, coughing, violence etc*) accès *m*; (*of asthma, malaria etc*) crise *f*; *Boxing* combat *m*; (*session*) séance *f*; (*period*) période *f*; a b. of flu une grippe.

boutique [buː'tiːk] *n* boutique *f* (de mode).

bow[1] [bəʊ] *n* (*weapon*) arc *m*; (*of violin etc*) archet *m*; (*knot*) nœud *m*; b. tie nœud *m* papillon. ● **bow-'legged** *a* aux jambes arquées.

bow[2] [baʊ] 1 *n* (*with knees bent*) révérence *f*, (*nod*) salut *m*; to take a b. (*of actor*) saluer ▐ *vt* (*one's head*) incliner, courber ▐ *vi* s'incliner (**to** devant); (*nod*) incliner la tête (**to** devant); to b. down (*submit*) s'incliner (**to** devant). 2 *n* (*of ship*) proue *f*.

bowels ['baʊəlz] *npl* intestins *mpl*; in the b. of the earth *Lit* dans les entrailles de la terre.

bowl [bəʊl] 1 *n* (*for food*) bol *m*; (*basin, of lavatory etc*) cuvette *f*; (*for sugar*) sucrier *m*; (*for salad*) saladier *m*; (*for fruit*) (*of glass*, *plastic*) coupe *f*; (*wicker*) corbeille *f*. **2** *vi* Cricket lancer la balle; **to b. along** (*in car etc*) rouler vite ▮ *vt* (*ball*) Cricket servir; **to b. s.o. over** (*astound*) bouleverser qn; (*knock down*) renverser qn. ●**bowler¹** *n* Cricket lanceur, -euse *mf*.

bowler² ['bəʊlər] *n* **b.** (**hat**) *Br* (chapeau *m*) melon *m*.

bowling ['bəʊlɪŋ] *n* (**tenpin**) **b.** bowling *m*; **b. alley** bowling *m*; **b. green** terrain *m* de boules.

bowls [bəʊlz] *npl* (*game*) boules *fpl*.

box [bɒks] **1** *n* boîte *f*; (*large*) caisse *f*; (*of cardboard*) carton *m*; (*in theatre*) loge *f*; (*for horse, in stable*) box *m*; (*television*) *Br Fam* télé *f*; *Br* **witness b.** barre *f* or banc *m* des témoins; **b. number** (*at post office*) numéro *m* de boîte postale; (*at newspaper*) référence *f* (*de petite annonce*); **b. office** bureau *m* de location, guichet *m*; **b. room** *Br* (*lumber room*) débarras *m*; (*bedroom*) petite chambre *f* (carrée) ▮ *vt* **to b.** (**up**) mettre en boîte; **to b. in** (*enclose*) enfermer.

2 *vi* Boxing boxer; **to b. against s.o.** boxer contre qn.

3 *vt* **to b. s.o.'s ears** gifler qn. ●**boxing** *n* **1** boxe *f*; **b. gloves/match** gants *mpl*/combat *m* de boxe; **b. ring** ring *m*. **2 B. Day** *Br* le lendemain de Noël.

boxcar ['bɒkskɑːr] *n* Rail *Am* wagon *m* couvert.

boxer ['bɒksər] *n* boxeur *m*.

boxwood ['bɒkswʊd] *n* buis *m*.

boy [bɔɪ] *n* garçon *m*; **English b.** jeune Anglais *m*; **old b.** (*former pupil*) *Br* ancien élève *m*; **yes, old b.!** *Br* oui, mon vieux!; **the boys** (*pals*) *Fam* les copains *mpl*; **my dear b.** mon cher ami; **oh b.!** mon Dieu! ●**boyfriend** *n* (petit) ami *m*. ●**boyhood** *n* enfance *f*. ●**boyish** *a* de garçon; *Pej* puéril.

boycott ['bɔɪkɒt] *vt* boycotter ▮ *n* boycottage *m*.

bra [brɑː] *n* soutien-gorge *m*.

brace [breɪs] *n* (*dental*) appareil *m*; (*on leg, arm*) appareil *m* orthopédique; (*for fastening*) attache *f*; **braces** (*trouser straps*) *Br* bretelles *fpl* ▮ *vt* (*fix*) attacher; (*press*) appuyer; **to b. oneself for** (*news, shock*) se préparer à. ●**bracing** *a* (*air etc*) fortifiant.

bracelet ['breɪslɪt] *n* bracelet *m*.

bracken ['brækən] *n* fougère *f*.

bracket ['brækɪt] *n* (*for shelf etc*) équerre *f*; (*round sign*) parenthèse *f*; (*square sign*) crochet *m*; (*group*) *Fig* groupe *m*, tranche *f* ▮ *vt* mettre entre parenthèses or crochets; **to b. together** *Fig* mettre dans la même groupe.

brag [bræg] *vi* (**-gg-**) se vanter (**about** or **of** sth **of** qch, **about doing** or **doing** de faire). ●**bragging** *n* vantardise *f*. ●**braggart** *n* vantard, -arde *mf*.

braid [breɪd] *vt* (*hair*) tresser; (*trim*) galonner ▮ *n* tresse *f*; (*trimming*) galon *m*.

Braille [breɪl] *n* braille *m*; **in B.** en braille.

brain [breɪn] *n* cerveau *m*; (*of animal, bird*) & *Pej* cervelle *f*; **to have brains** (*sense*) avoir

de l'intelligence; **use your brain(s)!** *Hum* utilise ta cervelle!

▮ *a* (*operation, disease*) cérébral; **b. death** mort *f* cérébrale; **b. drain** fuite *f* des cerveaux.

▮ *vt* (*hit*) *Fam* assommer.

brainchild ['breɪntʃaɪld] *n* invention *f* personnelle. ●**brainstorm** *n* *Am* idée *f* géniale; *Br Psy* aberration *f*. ●**brainwash** *vt* faire un lavage de cerveau à. ●**brainwashing** *n* lavage *m* de cerveau. ●**brainwave** *n* idée *f* géniale.

brainy ['breɪnɪ] *a* (**-ier, -iest**) *Fam* intelligent.

braise [breɪz] *vt* (*meat etc*) braiser.

brake [breɪk] *n* frein *m*; **b. light** (*on vehicle*) stop *m*; **b. fluid** liquide *m* de freins ▮ *vi* freiner. ●**braking** *n* freinage *m*.

bramble ['bræmb(ə)l] *n* (*bush*) ronce *f*.

bran [bræn] *n* (*of wheat*) son *m*.

branch [brɑːntʃ] *n* branche *f*; (*of road*) embranchement *m*; (*of store, office etc*) succursale *f*; **b. office** succursale *f* ▮ *vi* **to b. off** (*of road*) bifurquer; **to b. out** (*of firm, person*) étendre ses activités; (*of family, tree*) se ramifier.

brand [brænd] *n* (*trademark, & on cattle*) marque *f*; (*variety*) type *m*, style *m*; **b. name** marque *f* ▮ *vt* (*mark*) marquer; (*stigmatize*) flétrir; **to be branded as a liar/etc** avoir une réputation de menteur/*etc*.

brandish ['brændɪʃ] *vt* brandir.

brand-new [brænd'njuː] *a* tout neuf (*f* toute neuve), flambant neuf (*f* flambant neuve).

brandy ['brændɪ] *n* cognac *m*; (*made with pears etc*) eau-de-vie *f*.

brash [bræʃ] *a* effronté.

brass [brɑːs] *n* cuivre *m*; (*instruments in orchestra*) cuivres *mpl*; **the top b.** (*officers, executives*) *Fam* les huiles *fpl*; **b. band** fanfare *f*.

brassiere [*Br* 'bræzɪər, *Am* brə'zɪər] *n* soutien-gorge *m*.

brat [bræt] *n* (*child*) *Pej* môme *mf*, gosse *mf*; (*badly behaved*) sale gosse *mf*.

bravado [brə'vɑːdəʊ] *n* bravade *f*.

brave [breɪv] *a* (**-er, -est**) courageux, brave ▮ *n* (*Red Indian*) guerrier *m* (indien), brave *m* ▮ *vt* (*danger etc*) braver, affronter; **to b. the elements** braver or affronter les éléments. ●**bravely** *adv* courageusement. ●**bravery** *n* courage *m*.

bravo! ['brɑːvəʊ] *int* bravo!

brawl [brɔːl] *n* (*fight*) bagarre *f* ▮ *vi* se bagarrer. ●**brawling** *a* bagarreur ▮ *n* bagarres *fpl*.

brawn [brɔːn] *n* muscles *mpl*. ●**brawny** *a* (**-ier, -iest**) musclé.

bray [breɪ] *vi* (*of ass*) braire.

brazen ['breɪz(ə)n] *a* (*shameless*) effronté ▮ *vt* **to b. it out** payer d'audace, faire front.

Brazil [brə'zɪl] *n* Brésil *m*. ●**Brazilian** *a* brésilien ▮ *n* Brésilien, -ienne *mf*.

breach [briːtʃ] **1** *n* violation *f*, infraction *f* (**of** de); **b. of contract** rupture *f* de contrat; **b. of trust** abus *m* de confiance ▮ *vt* (*law, code*) violer. **2** n (*gap*) brèche f ∎ vt (*wall etc*) ouvrir une brèche dans.

bread [bred] n inv pain m; (*money*) Sl blé m, fric m; **loaf of b.** pain m; **brown b.** pain bis; (*slice or piece of*) **b. and butter** tartine f; **it's my b. and butter** (*job*) c'est mon gagne-pain m; **b. knife** couteau m à pain. ●**breadbin** Br or **breadbox** Am n boîte f à pain. ●**bread-board** n planche f à pain. ●**breadcrumb** n miette f (de pain); **breadcrumbs** (*in cooking*) chapelure f. ●**breaded** a pané. ●**breadline** n **on the b.** indigent. ●**breadwinner** n soutien m de famille.

breadth [bretθ] n largeur f.

break [breɪk] vt (*pt* **broke**, *pp* **broken**) casser; (*into pieces, with force*) briser; (*silence, spell, vow etc*) rompre; (*strike, heart, will, ice etc*) briser; (*agreement, treaty*) violer, rompre; (*sports record*) battre; (*law*) violer; (*one's promise, an appointment*) manquer à; (*journey*) interrompre; (*sound barrier*) franchir; (*a fall*) amortir; (*news*) annoncer (**to à**); **to b.** (**oneself of**) (*habit*) se débarrasser de; **to b. open** (*safe*) percer; **to b. new ground** innover.

∎ vi (se) casser; (*into pieces, of heart etc*) se briser; (*of spell*) se rompre; (*of voice*) s'altérer; (*of boy's voice*) muer; (*of weather*) se gâter; (*of news*) éclater; (*of day*) se lever; (*of wave*) déferler; (*stop work*) faire la pause; **to b. free** se libérer; **to b. loose** s'échapper; **to b. with s.o.** rompre avec qn.

∎ n cassure f; (*in bone*) fracture f; (*with person, group & in continuity*) rupture f; (*in journey*) interruption f; (*rest*) repos m; (*in activity, for tea*) pause f; (*in school*) récréation f; (*change in weather*) changement m; **a lucky b.** Fam une chance. ●**breakable** a fragile. ●**breakage** n casse f; **breakages** (*things broken*) la casse. ●**breaker** n (*wave*) brisant m; (*dealer in old cars*) Br casseur m. ●**breaking point** n **at b. point** (*patience*) à bout; (*person*) sur le point de craquer, à bout.

break away vi se détacher ∎ vt détacher. ●**breakaway** a (*group*) dissident. ∎ **to break down** vt (*door*) enfoncer; (*resistance*) briser; (*analyse*) analyser ∎ vi (*of vehicle, machine*) tomber en panne; (*of talks, negotiations*) échouer; (*collapse*) (*of person*) s'effondrer; (*have nervous breakdown*) craquer; (*start crying*) éclater en sanglots. ●**breakdown** n panne f; (*of figures etc*) analyse f; (*in talks*) rupture f; (*nervous*) dépression f, **b. lorry** or **van** Br dépanneuse f; **b. service** Br service m de dépannage. ∎ **to break in** vi (*of burglar*) entrer par effraction; (*interrupt*) interrompre ∎ vt (*door*) enfoncer; (*horse*) dresser; (*vehicle*) Am roder. ●**break-in** n cambriolage m. ∎ **to break into** vt (*house etc*) cambrioler; (*safe*) forcer; (*start*) entamer (*explication etc*) ∎ **to break off** vt (*piece of chocolate etc*) détacher; (*relations*) rompre ∎ vi se détacher; (*stop*) s'arrêter; **to b. off with s.o.** rompre avec qn ∎ **to break out** vi (*of war, fire*) écla-

ter; (*escape*) s'échapper; **to b. out in a rash** faire une éruption de boutons ∎ **to break through** vi (*of sun, army*) percer ∎ vt (*defences*) percer. ●**breakthrough** n (*discovery*) percée f, découverte f. ∎ **to break up** vt mettre en morceaux; (*marriage*) briser; (*fight*) mettre fin à ∎ vi (*end*) prendre fin; (*of group*) se disperser; (*of marriage*) se briser; (*from school*) partir en vacances. ●**break-up** n fin f; (*in marriage, friendship*) rupture f.

breakfast ['brekfəst] n petit déjeuner m; **to have b.** prendre le petit déjeuner; **b. TV** émissions fpl télévisées du matin.

breakwater ['breɪkwɔːtər] n brise-lames m inv.

breast [brest] n sein m; (*chest*) poitrine f; (*of chicken*) blanc m. ●**breastfeed** vt (*pt & pp* **-fed**) allaiter. ●**breaststroke** n (*in swimming*) brasse f.

breath [breθ] n haleine f, souffle m; (*of air*) souffle m; **out of b.** (*tout*) essoufflé, à bout de souffle; **to get a b. of air** prendre l'air; **to take a deep b.** respirer profondément; **under one's b.** tout bas; **one's last b.** son dernier soupir. ●**breathalyser**® n alcootest® m. ●**breathless** a haletant. ●**breathtaking** a sensationnel.

breathe [briːð] vti respirer; **to b. in** aspirer; **to b. out** expirer; **to b. air into sth** souffler dans qch ∎ vt (*utter*) pousser (*soupir*); **she didn't b. a word (about it)** elle n'en a pas soufflé mot. ●**breathing** n respiration f; **b. space** moment m de repos.

breather ['briːðər] n Fam moment m de repos; **to go for a b.** sortir prendre l'air.

bred [bred] pt & pp of **breed 1** ∎ a **well-b.** bien élevé.

breeches ['brɪtʃɪz] npl culotte f.

breed [briːd] **1** vt (*pt & pp* **bred**) (*animals*) élever; (*cause*) Fig engendrer (*la haine, la violence etc*) ∎ vi (*of animals*) se reproduire. **2** n race f, espèce f. ●**breeding** n élevage m; (*procreation*) reproduction f; (*good manners*) Fig éducation f. ●**breeder** n éleveur, -euse mf.

breeze [briːz] n brise f. ●**breezy** a (**-ier**, **-iest**) **1** (*weather, day*) frais, venteux. **2** (*cheerful*) jovial; (*relaxed*) décontracté.

breezeblock ['briːzblɒk] n parpaing m.

brevity ['brevɪtɪ] n brièveté f.

brew [bruː] vt (*beer*) brasser; (*trouble, plot*) préparer; **to b. tea** préparer du thé; (*infuse*) (*faire*) infuser du thé ∎ vi (*of beer*) fermenter; (*of tea*) infuser; (*of storm*) se préparer; **something is brewing** il se prépare quelque chose ∎ n (*drink*) breuvage m; (*of tea*) infusion f. ●**brewer** n brasseur m. ●**brewery** n brasserie f.

bribe [braɪb] n pot-de-vin m ∎ vt acheter, soudoyer (*qn*); **to b. s.o. into doing sth** soudoyer qn pour qu'il fasse qch. ●**bribery** n corruption f.

brick [brɪk] n brique f; (*child's*) cube m; **to drop a b.** Br Fam faire une gaffe ∎ vt **to b.**

up (*gap, door*) murer. ●**bricklayer** n maçon m. ●**brickwork** n (*bricks*) briques *fpl*; (*construction*) ouvrage m en briques.

bridal ['braɪd(ə)l] a (*ceremony, bed etc*) nuptial; **b. gown** robe f de mariée; **b. suite** (*in hotel*) suite f nuptiale.

bride [braɪd] n mariée f; **the b. and groom** les mariés *mpl*. ●**bridegroom** n marié m. ●**bridesmaid** n demoiselle f d'honneur.

bridge [brɪdʒ] **1** n pont m; (*on ship*) passerelle f; (*of nose*) arête f; (*false tooth*) bridge m ▮ vt **to b. a gap** combler une lacune. **2** n Cards bridge m.

bridle ['braɪd(ə)l] n (*for horse*) bride f; **b. path** allée f cavalière ▮ vt (*horse*) brider.

brief[1] [briːf] a (-er, -est) bref (f brève); **in b.** en résumé. ●**briefly** adv (*quickly*) en vitesse; (*to say*) brièvement.

brief[2] [briːf] n (*military etc instructions*) instructions *fpl*; (*legal*) dossier m; (*task*) Fig tâche f, fonctions *fpl* ▮ vt donner des instructions à; (*inform*) mettre au courant (**on** de). ●**briefing** n instructions *fpl*; (*to pilot etc*) briefing m.

briefcase ['briːfkeɪs] n serviette f.

briefs [briːfs] npl (*underpants*) slip m.

brigade [brɪ'geɪd] n brigade f. ●**brigadier** [brɪgə'dɪər] n général m de brigade.

bright [braɪt] a (-er, -est) (*star, eyes, situation etc*) brillant; (*light, colour*) vif; (*weather, room*) clair; (*clever*) intelligent; (*happy*) joyeux; (*future*) brillant, prometteur; (*idea*) génial; **b. interval** (*sunny period*) éclaircie f ▮ adv **b. and early** (*to get up*) de bonne heure. ●**brightly** adv avec éclat. ●**brightness** n éclat m; (*of person*) intelligence f.

brighten ['braɪtən] vt **to b. (up)** (*room*) égayer ▮ vi **to b. (up)** (*of weather*) s'éclaircir; (*of face*) s'éclairer.

brilliant ['brɪljənt] a (*light*) éclatant; (*very clever*) (*person, idea etc*) brillant; (*fantastic*) Br Fam super. ●**brilliance** n éclat m; (*of person*) grande intelligence f.

brim [brɪm] n (*of hat, cup etc*) bord m ▮ vi (-mm-) **to b. over** déborder (**with** de).

brine [braɪn] n (*for preserving food*) saumure f.

bring [brɪŋ] vt (pt & pp **brought**) (*person, vehicle etc*) amener; (*object*) apporter; (*to cause*) amener; **to b. a (legal) action against s.o.** intenter un procès contre or à qn; **to b. sth to** (*perfection, a peak etc*) porter qch à; **to b. to an end** mettre fin à; **to b. to mind** rappeler; **to b. sth on oneself** s'attirer qch; **I can't b. myself to do it** je ne peux pas me résoudre à le faire.

bring about vt provoquer, amener ▮ **to bring along** vt (*object*) apporter; (*person*) amener ▮ **to bring back** vt (*person*) ramener; (*object*) rapporter; (*memories*) rappeler ▮ **to bring down** vt (*object*) descendre; (*overthrow*) faire tomber; (*reduce*) réduire; (*shoot down*) abattre (*avion*) ▮ **to bring forward** vt (*in time or space*) avancer; (*witness*) produire ▮ **to bring in** vt (*object*) rentrer; (*person*) faire

entrer or venir; (*introduce*) introduire; (*income*) rapporter ▮ **to bring off** vt (*task*) mener à bien ▮ **to bring out** vt (*object*) sortir; (*person*) faire sortir; (*meaning*) faire ressortir; (*book*) publier; (*product*) lancer ▮ **to bring over** vt **to b. s.o. over to** (*convert*) convertir qn à ▮ **to bring round** vt ranimer (qn); (*convert*) convertir (qn) (**to** à) ▮ **to bring to** vt **to b. s.o. to** ranimer qn ▮ **to bring together** vt (*friends, members*) réunir; (*reconcile*) réconcilier; (*put in touch*) mettre en contact ▮ **to bring up** vt (*object*) monter; (*child etc*) élever; (*question*) soulever; (*subject*) mentionner; (*food*) rendre.

brink [brɪŋk] n bord m; **on the b. of sth** au bord de qch.

brisk [brɪsk] a (-er, -est) (*lively*) vif; **at a b. pace** vite, d'un bon pas; **trading is b.** le marché est actif; **business is b.** les affaires marchent bien. ●**briskly** adv vivement; (*to walk*) vite, d'un bon pas. ●**briskness** n vivacité f.

bristle ['brɪs(ə)l] n poil m ▮ vi se hérisser; **bristling with difficulties/etc** hérissé de difficultés/etc.

Britain ['brɪt(ə)n] n Grande-Bretagne f. ●**British** a britannique; **the B. Isles** les îles *fpl* Britanniques ▮ n **the B.** les Britanniques *mpl*. ●**Briton** n Britannique *mf*.

Brittany ['brɪtəni] n Bretagne f.

brittle ['brɪt(ə)l] a fragile, cassant.

broach [brəʊtʃ] vt (*topic*) entamer.

broad[1] [brɔːd] a (-er, -est) (*wide*) large; (*accent*) prononcé; **in b. daylight** en plein jour; **the b. outline of** (*plan etc*) les grandes lignes de; **b. bean** fève f; **b. jump** Sport Am saut m en longueur. ●**broad-'minded** a (*person*) à l'esprit large; **b.-minded views** des idées *fpl* larges (**on** sur). ●**broad-'shouldered** a large d'épaules.

broad[2] [brɔːd] n (*woman*) Am Sl nana f.

broadcast ['brɔːdkɑːst] vt (pt & pp **broadcast**) diffuser, retransmettre; **b. account** (*of event*) reportage m (radio or télévisé) ▮ vi (*of station*) émettre; (*of person*) parler à la radio or à la télévision ▮ n émission f. ●**broadcasting** n radiodiffusion f; TV télévision f. ●**broadcaster** n journaliste *mf* de radio or de télévision.

broaden ['brɔːd(ə)n] vt élargir ▮ vi s'élargir.

broadly ['brɔːdlɪ] adv **b. (speaking)** en gros, grosso modo.

broccoli ['brɒkəlɪ] n inv (*plant*) brocoli m; (*food*) brocolis *mpl*.

brochure ['brəʊʃər] n brochure f, dépliant m.

brogue [brəʊg] n (*Irish*) accent m irlandais.

broil [brɔɪl] vti griller. ●**broiler** n poulet m (à-rôtir); (*apparatus*) gril m.

broke [brəʊk] **1** pt of **break**. **2** a (*penniless*) fauché. ●**broken** pp of **break** ▮ a (*man, voice, line*) brisé; (*ground*) accidenté; (*spirit*) abattu; **in b. English** en mauvais anglais m; **b. home** foyer m brisé. ●**broken-'down** a (*machine etc*) (tout) déglingué, détraqué.

broker ['brəʊkər] n courtier, -ière mf.
brolly ['brɒlɪ] n (umbrella) Br Fam pépin m.
bronchitis [brɒŋ'kaɪtɪs] n bronchite f.
bronze [brɒnz] n bronze m; **b. statue**/etc statue f/etc en bronze.
brooch [brəʊtʃ] n (ornament) broche f.
brood [bruːd] **1** n couvée f, nichée f ‖ vi (of bird) couver. **2** vi méditer tristement (over, on sur); **to b. over** (a plan) ruminer.
● **broody** a (-ier, -iest) (person) (sulky) maussade; (dreamy) rêveur; (woman) Br Fam en mal d'enfant.
brook [brʊk] **1** n ruisseau m. **2** vt (tolerate) souffrir, tolérer.
broom [bruːm] n **1** (for sweeping) balai m. **2** (wild shrub) genêt m. ● **broomstick** n manche m à balai.
Bros abbr (Brothers) Frères mpl.
broth [brɒθ] n bouillon m.
brothel ['brɒθ(ə)l] n maison f close, bordel m.
brother ['brʌðər] n frère m. ● **brother-in-law** n (pl **brothers-in-law**) beau-frère m. ● **brotherhood** n fraternité f. ● **brotherly** a fraternel.
brought [brɔːt] pt & pp of **bring**.
brow [braʊ] n **1** (forehead) front m. **2** (of hill) sommet m.
browbeat ['braʊbiːt] vt (pt -beat, pp -beaten) intimider; **to b. s.o. into doing sth** faire faire qch à qn à force d'intimidation.
brown [braʊn] a (-er, -est) brun; (reddish) marron; (hair) châtain; (tanned) bronzé ‖ n brun m; (reddish) marron m ‖ vt (of sun) bronzer, brunir (la peau); (food) faire dorer; **to be browned off** Br Fam en avoir marre. ● **brownish** a brunâtre.
brownie ['braʊnɪ] n (cake) Am petit gâteau m au chocolat.
Brownie ['braʊnɪ] n (girl scout) jeannette f.
browse [braʊz] vi **1** (in bookshop) feuilleter des livres; (in shop, supermarket) regarder; **to b. through** (book) feuilleter. **2** (of animal) brouter.
bruise [bruːz] vt **to b. one's knee/hand**/etc se faire un bleu au genou/à la main/etc; **to b. a fruit** taler un fruit ‖ n bleu m, contusion f; (on fruit) meurtrissure f. ● **bruised** a (covered in bruises) couvert de bleus. ● **bruising** n (bruises) bleus mpl.
brunch [brʌntʃ] n brunch m (petit déjeuner pris comme déjeuner).
brunette [bruː'net] n brunette f.
brunt [brʌnt] n **to bear the b. of** (attack, anger etc) subir or essuyer le plus gros de; (expense) assumer la plus grosse part de.
brush [brʌʃ] n brosse f; (for shaving) blaireau m; (for sweeping, cleaning car etc) balayette f; (action) coup m de brosse; (fight) accrochage m.
‖ vt (teeth, hair etc) brosser; (clothes) donner un coup de brosse à; **to b. aside** écarter; **to b. away** or **off** enlever; **to b. up (on) one's French**/etc se remettre au français/etc.
‖ vi **to b. against** effleurer. ● **brush-off** n Fam

to give s.o. the b.-off envoyer promener qn. ● **brush-up** n coup m de brosse.
brushwood ['brʌʃwʊd] n broussailles fpl.
brusque [bruːsk] a brusque.
Brussels ['brʌs(ə)lz] n Bruxelles m or f; **B. sprouts** choux mpl de Bruxelles.
brutal ['bruːt(ə)l] a brutal. ● **bru'tality** n brutalité f.
brute [bruːt] n (animal, person) brute f ‖ a **by b. force** par la force.
BSc, Am **BS** abbr = **Bachelor of Science**.
bubble ['bʌb(ə)l] n (of air, soap etc, in boiling liquid) bulle f; Br **b. and squeak** Fam friture f de purée et de viande réchauffées; **b. bath** bain m moussant; **b. gum** bubble-gum m ‖ vi (of liquid) bouillonner; **to b. over** déborder (with de). ● **bubbly** a Hum Fam champagne m.
buck [bʌk] **1** n Am Fam dollar m. **2** n (animal) mâle m (de lapin, lièvre etc). **3** n **to pass the b. to s.o.** Fam se décharger de ses responsabilités sur qn. **4** vt **to b. up** remonter le moral à (qn) ‖ vi **to b. up** (become livelier) reprendre du poil de la bête; (hurry) se grouiller.
bucket ['bʌkɪt] n seau m.
buckle ['bʌk(ə)l] **1** n boucle f ‖ vt boucler. **2** vti (warp) voiler, gauchir. **3** vi **to b. down to a task**/etc s'atteler à un travail/etc.
buckshot ['bʌkʃɒt] n inv du gros plomb m.
bucktooth [bʌk'tuːθ] n (pl -teeth) dent f saillante.
bud [bʌd] n (on tree) bourgeon m; (on flower) bouton m ‖ vi (-dd-) bourgeonner; (of flower) pousser des boutons. ● **budding** a (talent) naissant; (doctor etc) en herbe.
Buddhist ['bʊdɪst] a & n bouddhiste (mf).
buddy ['bʌdɪ] n Am Fam copain m, pote m.
budge [bʌdʒ] vi bouger ‖ vt faire bouger.
budgerigar ['bʌdʒərɪgɑːr] n Br perruche f.
budget ['bʌdʒɪt] n budget m ‖ vi dresser un budget; **to b. for** inscrire au budget. ● **budgetary** a budgétaire.
budgie ['bʌdʒɪ] n Br Fam perruche f.
buff [bʌf] **1** a **b.(-coloured)** chamois inv. **2** n jazz/film/etc **b.** Fam fana(tique) mf de jazz/ de cinéma/etc. **3** n **in the b.** Fam tout nu.
buffalo ['bʌfələʊ] n (pl -oes or -o) buffle m; (American) b. bison m.
buffer ['bʌfər] n (on train) tampon m; (at end of track) butoir m; (safeguard) Fig protection f (against contre); **b. state** état m tampon.
buffet¹ ['bʊfeɪ] n (table, meal, Br café) buffet m; **cold b.** viandes fpl froides; **b. car** (on train) Br voiture-bar f.
buffet² ['bʌfɪt] vt (of waves) battre (navire etc); (of wind, rain) cingler (qn).
buffoon [bə'fuːn] n bouffon m.
bug¹ [bʌg] **1** n punaise f; (any insect) bestiole f; (germ) Fam microbe m, virus m; **the travel b.** (urge) le désir de voyager; **the skiing b.** le virus du ski. **2** n (in machine) défaut m; (in computer program) erreur f. **3** n (listening device) micro m (clandestin) ‖ vt (-gg-)

(*room*) installer des micros dans.
bug² [bʌg] *vt* (**-gg-**) (*annoy*) *Fam* embêter.
bugbear ['bʌgbeər] *n* (*worry*) cauchemar *m*.
buggy ['bʌgɪ] *n* (*baby*) **b.** (*folding pushchair*) *Br* poussette-canne *f*; (*pram*) *Am* landau *m* (*pl* -aus).
bugle ['bjuːg(ə)l] *n* clairon *m*. ● **bugler** *n* (*person*) clairon *m*.
build¹ [bɪld] *n* (*of person*) carrure *f*.
build² [bɪld] **1** *vt* (*pt & pp* **built**) construire; (*house, town*) construire, bâtir; **to b. sth into a wall** encastrer qch dans un mur ▐ *vi* (*build houses etc*) bâtir, construire. **2 to build up** *vt* (*increase*) augmenter; (*collection*) constituer; (*business*) monter; (*speed, one's strength*) prendre; (*reputation*) bâtir ▐ *vi* (*of tension, pressure*) augmenter, monter; (*of dust, snow*) s'accumuler; (*of traffic*) devenir dense; (*of interest in account*) s'accumuler.
builder ['bɪldər] *n* (*of houses etc*) (*skilled workman*) maçon *m*; (*contractor*) entrepreneur *m*; (*unskilled worker*) ouvrier *m*.
building ['bɪldɪŋ] *n* bâtiment *m*; (*flats, offices*) immeuble *m*; (*action*) construction *f*; **b. society** *Br* = société *f* de crédit immobilier.
build-up ['bɪldʌp] *n* (*increase*) augmentation *f*; (*of dust etc*) accumulation *f*; (*of troops*) concentration *f*; (*for author, book*) publicité *f*.
built-in [bɪlt'ɪn] *a* (*Br cupboard, Am closet*) encastré; (*part of machine etc*) incorporé; (*innate*) *Fig* inné.
built-up ['bɪltʌp] *a* urbanisé; **b.-up area** agglomération *f*.
bulb [bʌlb] *n* (*of plant*) oignon *m*, bulbe *m*; (*of lamp*) ampoule *f*.
bulbous ['bʌlbəs] *a* (*shape, nose etc*) gros et rond; (*table leg*) renflé.
Bulgaria [bʌl'geərɪə] *n* Bulgarie *f*. ● **Bulgarian** *a* bulgare ▐ *n* Bulgare *mf*.
bulge [bʌldʒ] *vi* **to b.** (**out**) se renfler, bomber; (*of eyes*) sortir de la tête ▐ *n* renflement *m*; (*increase*) *Fam* augmentation *f*. ● **bulging** *a* renflé, bombé; (*eyes*) protubérant; **to be b.** (*of bag, pocket etc*) être plein à craquer, être gonflé (**with** de).
bulimia [buː'lɪmɪə] *n* (*illness*) boulimie *f*.
bulk [bʌlk] *n inv* (*of building, parcel etc*) volume *m*; (*of person*) grosseur *f*; **the b. of** (*most*) la majeure partie de; **in b.** (*to buy, sell*) en gros. ● **bulky** *a* (-**ier**, -**iest**) gros (*f* grosse), volumineux.
bull [bʊl] *n* **1** (*animal*) taureau *m*. **2** (*nonsense*) *Fam* foutaises *fpl*. ● **bullfight** *n* corrida *f*. ● **bullfighter** *n* matador *m*. ● **bullring** *n* arène *f*.
bulldog ['bʊldɒg] *n* bouledogue *m*; **b. clip** pince *f* (à dessin).
bulldoze ['bʊldəʊz] *vt* (*site*) passer au bulldozer; (*building*) raser (au bulldozer). ● **bulldozer** *n* bulldozer *m*, bouteur *m*.
bullet ['bʊlɪt] *n* balle *f* (*de revolver etc*). ● **bulletproof** *a* (*car etc*) blindé; **b. jacket** *Br*, **b. vest** *Am* gilet *m* pare-balles *inv*; **it's b. glass** c'est une vitre blindée.

bulletin ['bʊlətɪn] *n* bulletin *m*; **b. board** *Am* tableau *m* d'affichage.
bullfight ['bʊlfaɪt] *n see* **bull**.
bullion ['bʊljən] *n* or *m or* argent *m* en lingots.
bullock ['bʊlək] *n* bœuf *m*.
bullring ['bʊlrɪŋ] *n see* **bull**.
bull's-eye ['bʊlzaɪ] *n* (*of target*) centre *m*; **to hit the b.-eye** faire mouche.
bully ['bʊlɪ] *n* (*grosse*) brute *f* ▐ *vt* (*ill-treat*) brutaliser; **to b. into doing** forcer à faire. ● **bullying** *n* (*in school*) brutalités *fpl*.
bulwark ['bʊlwək] *n* rempart *m*.
bum [bʌm] **1** *n Fam* (*loafer*) clochard, -arde *mf*; (*good-for-nothing*) propre *mf* à rien ▐ *vi* (**-mm-**) **to b.** (**around**) se balader. **2** *vt* (**-mm-**) **to b. sth off s.o.** (*cadge*) *Am Fam* taper qn de qch. **3** *n* (*buttocks*) *Br Fam* derrière *m*; **b. bag** banane *f*.
bumblebee ['bʌmb(ə)lbiː] *n* bourdon *m*.
bumf [bʌmf] *n* (*documents etc*) *Br Sl* paperasses *fpl*.
bump [bʌmp] *vt* (*of car etc*) heurter; **to b. one's head/knee/etc** se cogner la tête/le genou/etc; **to b. into** se cogner contre; (*of car*) rentrer dans; (*meet*) tomber sur; **to b. off** (*kill*) *Sl* liquider; **to b. up** (*price etc*) *Fam* augmenter.
▐ *vi* **to b. along** (*on rough road*) (*in car etc*) cahoter.
▐ *n* (*impact*) choc *m*; (*jerk*) cahot *m*; (*on road, body*) bosse *f*. ● **bumper** *n* (*of car etc*) pare-chocs *m inv* ▐ *a* (*crop, year etc*) exceptionnel; **b. cars** autos *fpl* tamponneuses.
bumpkin ['bʌmpkɪn] *n* (*country*) **b.** rustre *m*.
bumptious ['bʌmpʃəs] *a* prétentieux.
bumpy ['bʌmpɪ] *a* (-**ier**, -**iest**) (*road, ride*) cahoteux; **we had a b. flight** on a eu beaucoup de trous d'air pendant le vol.
bun [bʌn] *n* **1** (*cake*) petit pain *m* au lait. **2** (*of hair*) chignon *m*.
bunch [bʌntʃ] *n* (*of flowers*) bouquet *m*; (*of keys*) trousseau *m*; (*of bananas*) régime *m*; (*of people*) bande *f*; **b. of grapes** grappe *f* de raisin; **a b. of books/ideas/etc** (*mass*) *Fam* un tas de livres/d'idées/etc.
bundle ['bʌnd(ə)l] **1** *n* paquet *m*; (*of papers*) liasse *f*; (*of firewood*) fagot *m*. **2** *vt* (*put*) fourrer; (*push*) pousser (**into** dans); **to b. up** (*newspapers, letters*) mettre en paquet; **to b. s.o. off** (*to school etc*) expédier qn ▐ *vi* **to b.** (**oneself**) **up** se couvrir (bien).
bung [bʌŋ] **1** *n* (*stopper*) bonde *f* ▐ *vt* **to b. up** (*stop up*) boucher. **2** *vt* (*toss*) *Br Fam* balancer, jeter.
bungalow ['bʌŋgələʊ] *n* bungalow *m*.
bungle ['bʌŋg(ə)l] *vt* gâcher ▐ *vi* travailler mal. ● **bungling** *n* gâchis *m* ▐ *a* (*clumsy*) maladroit. ● **bungler** *n* **to be a b.** faire du mauvais travail.
bunion ['bʌnjən] *n* (*on toe*) oignon *m*.
bunk [bʌŋk] *n* **1** (*in ship, train*) couchette *f*; **b. beds** lits *mpl* superposés. **2** *Sl* = **bunkum**. ● **bunkum** *n* (*nonsense*) *Sl* foutaises *fpl*.

bunker ['bʌŋkər] n Mil Golf bunker m; (coalstore in garden) coffre m.

bunny ['bʌnɪ] n b. (rabbit) Fam Jeannot m lapin.

bunting ['bʌntɪŋ] n (flags) guirlande f de drapeaux.

buoy [bɔɪ] n bouée f ▮ vt to b. up (support) Fig soutenir.

buoyant ['bɔɪənt] a (cheerful) gai, optimiste; (successful economy) florissant; **the market is b.** Fin le marché est florissant.

burden ['bɜːd(ə)n] n fardeau m; **the tax b.** le poids des impôts ▮ vt charger, accabler (s.o. with qn de).

bureau, pl **-eaux** ['bjʊərəʊ, -əʊz] n (office) bureau m; (desk) Br secrétaire m; (chest of drawers) Am commode f.

bureaucracy [bjʊə'rɒkrəsɪ] n bureaucratie f. ● **bureaucrat** ['bjʊərəkræt] n bureaucrate mf.

burger ['bɜːgər] n hamburger m.

burglar ['bɜːglər] n cambrioleur, -euse mf; **b. alarm** alarme f antivol. ● **burglarize** vt Am cambrioler. ● **burglary** n cambriolage m. ● **burgle** vt Br cambrioler.

burial ['berɪəl] n enterrement m ▮ a (service) funèbre; **b. ground** cimetière m.

burlap ['bɜːlæp] n (sacking) Am toile f à sac.

burlesque [bɜː'lesk] n (parody) parodie f.

burly ['bɜːlɪ] a (-ier, -iest) costaud.

Burma ['bɜːmə] n Birmanie f. ● **Bur'mese** a birman ▮ n Birman, -ane mf.

burn [bɜːn] n brûlure f.
▮ vt (pt & pp **burned** or **burnt**) brûler; **burnt alive** brûlé vif; **to b. down** (house etc) détruire par le feu; **to b. off** (paint etc) décaper au chalumeau; **to b. up** (consume) brûler (du carburant etc).
▮ vi brûler; **to b. down** (of house) brûler (complètement), être réduit en cendres; **to b. out** (of fire) s'éteindre; (of fuse) sauter. ● **burning** a en feu; (fire) allumé; (topic, fever etc) Fig brûlant ▮ n smell of b. odeur f de brûlé.

burner ['bɜːnər] n (on stove) brûleur m; **to put sth on the back b.** Fig remettre qch à plus tard.

burp [bɜːp] n Fam rot m ▮ vi Fam roter.

burrow ['bʌrəʊ] n (hole) terrier m ▮ vti creuser.

bursar ['bɜːsər] n (in school) intendant, -ante mf.

bursary ['bɜːsərɪ] n (scholarship) bourse f.

burst [bɜːst] n éclatement m, explosion f; (of laughter) éclat m; (of applause) salve f; (of thunder) coup m; (explosion) éclatement m; (surge) élan m; (fit) accès m; (burst water pipe) Fam tuyau m crevé.
▮ vi (pt & pp **burst**) (of bubble, balloon, boil, tyre, cloud etc) crever; (with force) (of shell, boiler etc) éclater; **to b. into a room/etc** faire irruption dans une pièce/etc; **to b. into tears** fondre en larmes; **to b. into flames** prendre feu, s'embraser; **to b. open** (of door etc) s'ouvrir avec force; **to b. out laughing** éclater de rire.

▮ vt (bubble, balloon, boil etc) crever; (with force) faire éclater; **to b. a blood vessel** se rompre une veine; **to b. open** (door etc) ouvrir avec force. ● **bursting** a (full) (pockets etc) plein à craquer (with de); **b. with joy/etc** débordant de joie/etc; **to be b. to do** mourir d'envie de faire.

bury ['berɪ] vt (dead person) enterrer; (hide) enfouir; (plunge) plonger (in dans); **buried in one's work/etc** plongé dans son travail/etc.

bus [bʌs] n (auto)bus m; (long-distance) (auto)car m; **b. driver/ticket/etc** conducteur m/billet m/etc d'autobus or d'autocar; **b. shelter** Abribus® m; **b. station** gare f routière; **b. stop** arrêt m d'autobus ▮ vt (-ss-) (children) transporter (en bus) à l'école. ● **bussing** n (of schoolchildren) ramassage m scolaire.

bush [bʊʃ] n buisson m; **the b.** (land) la brousse; **a b. of hair** une tignasse. ● **bushy** a (-ier, -iest) (hair, tail etc) broussailleux.

bushed [bʊʃt] a (tired) Fam crevé.

busily ['bɪzɪlɪ] adv (actively) activement.

business ['bɪznɪs] n affaires fpl, commerce m; (shop) commerce m; (task, concern, matter) affaire f; **the textile/construction b.** l'industrie f du textile/de la construction; **the travel b.** le tourisme; **big b.** les grosses entreprises fpl commerciales; **on b.** (to travel) pour affaires; **to go out of b.** (stop trading) fermer boutique; **it's quite a b.** c'est toute une affaire; **it's your b. to...** c'est à vous de...; **you have no b. to...** vous n'avez pas le droit de...; **that's none of your b.!, mind your own b.!** ça ne vous regarde pas!; **to mean b.** Fam ne pas plaisanter.
▮ a commercial; (meeting, trip, lunch) d'affaires; **b. card** carte f de visite; **b. hours** (office) heures fpl de travail; (shop) heures fpl d'ouverture. ● **businesslike** a sérieux, pratique. ● **businessman** n (pl -men) homme m d'affaires. ● **businesswoman** n (pl -women) femme f d'affaires.

busker ['bʌskər] n Br musicien, -ienne mf des rues.

bust [bʌst] 1 n (sculpture) buste m; (woman's breasts) poitrine f. 2 a (broken) Fam fichu; **to go b.** (bankrupt) faire faillite ▮ vti (pt & pp **bust** or **busted**) Fam = **to burst** & **to break.** ● **bust-up** n Fam (quarrel) engueulade f; (breakup) rupture f.

bustle ['bʌs(ə)l] vi **to b. (about)** s'affairer ▮ n activité f, branle-bas m. ● **bustling** a (street) bruyant.

busy ['bɪzɪ] a (-ier, -iest) occupé (**doing** à faire); (active) actif; (day) chargé; (street) animé; (phone, line) Am occupé; **to be b. doing** (in the process of) être en train de faire; **b. signal** Am sonnerie f 'occupé' ▮ vt **to b. oneself** s'occuper (**with** sth à qch, **doing** à faire). ● **busybody** n to be a b. faire la mouche du coche.

but [bʌt, unstressed bət] 1 conj mais. 2 prep (except) sauf; **b. for that** sans cela; **b. for him** sans lui; **no one b. you** personne d'autre que toi. **3** *adv* (*only*) ne...que, seulement; he's b. a boy ce n'est qu'un garçon; **one can b. try** on ne peut qu'essayer.

butane ['bjuːteɪn] *n* **b.** (gas) (gaz *m*) butane *m*.

butcher ['butʃər] *n* boucher *m*; **b.'s** (shop) boucherie *f* ∎ *vt* (*people*) massacrer; (*animal*) abattre. ● **butchery** *n* massacre *m* (of de).

butler ['bʌtlər] *n* maître *m* d'hôtel.

butt [bʌt] **1** *n* (*of cigarette*) mégot *m*; (*of gun*) crosse *f*; (*buttocks*) *Am Fam* derrière *m*; **b. for** ridicule objet *m* de risée. **2** *vi* **to b. in** interrompre, intervenir. **3** *vt* (*with one's head*) donner un coup de tête à.

butter ['bʌtər] *n* beurre *m*; **b. bean** *Br* haricot *m* blanc; **b. dish** beurrier *m* ∎ *vt* beurrer; **to b. s.o. up** *Fam* flatter qn. ● **butterfingers** *n* maladroit, -oite *mf*. ● **buttermilk** *n* lait *m* de beurre. ● **butterscotch** *n* caramel *m* (dur) au beurre.

buttercup ['bʌtəkʌp] *n* bouton-d'or *m*.

butterfly ['bʌtəflaɪ] *n* papillon *m*; **to have butterflies** *Fam* avoir le trac; **b. stroke** (*in swimming*) brasse *f* papillon.

buttock ['bʌtək] *n* fesse *f*.

button ['bʌtən] *n* bouton *m*; (*of phone*) touche *f*; (*badge*) *Am* badge *m* ∎ *vt* **to b. (up)** boutonner ∎ *vi* **to b. (up)** (*of garment*) se boutonner. ● **buttonhole 1** *n* boutonnière *f*; (*flower*) fleur *f*. **2** *vt* (*person*) *Fam* accrocher.

buttress ['bʌtrɪs] *n* (*for wall*) *Archit* contrefort *m*; *Fig* soutien *m*; **flying b.** arc-boutant *m* ∎ *vt* (*support*) *Archit* & *Fig* soutenir.

buxom ['bʌksəm] *a* (*woman*) bien en chair.

buy [baɪ] **1** *vt* (*pt & pp* **bought**) acheter (**from s.o.** à qn, **for s.o.** à or pour qn); **to b.** back racheter; **to b. over** (*bribe*) corrompre; **to b. up** acheter en bloc ∎ *n* **a good b.** une bonne affaire.

2 *vt* (*accept, believe*) *Am Fam* croire, avaler (*histoire etc*); **I'll b. that!** je veux bien le croire! ● **buyer** *n* acheteur, -euse *mf*.

buzz [bʌz] **1** *vi* bourdonner; **to b. off** *Fam* décamper ∎ *n* bourdonnement *m*. **2** *vt* (*of aircraft*) raser (*bâtiment, ville*). **3** *vt* **to b. s.o.** (*using buzzer*) appeler qn ∎ *n* (*phone call*) **to give s.o. a b.** *Fam* passer un coup *m* de fil à qn. ● **buzzer** *n* (*internal phone*) interphone

m; (*of bell, clock*) sonnerie *f*.

by [baɪ] *prep* **1** (*agent*) par; de; **hit/chosen/etc by** frappé/choisi/*etc* par; **surrounded/ followed/etc by** entouré/suivi/*etc* de; **a book/ painting by...** un livre/tableau de....

2 (*manner, means*) par; en; à; de; **by sea** par mer; **by mistake** par erreur; **by car** en voiture; **by bicycle** à bicyclette; **by moonlight** au clair de lune; **by doing** en faisant; **one by one** un à un; **day by day** de jour en jour; **by sight/day/far** de vue/jour/loin; **by the door** (*through*) par la porte; (**all**) **by oneself** tout seul.

3 (*next to*) à côté de; (*near*) près de; **by the lake/sea** au bord du lac/de la mer; **to go or pass by the bank/school/etc** passer devant la banque/l'école/*etc*.

4 (*before in time*) avant; **by Monday** avant lundi, d'ici lundi; **by now** à cette heure-ci, déjà; **by yesterday** (dès) hier.

5 (*amount, measurement*) à; **by the kilo** au kilo; **taller by a metre** plus grand d'un mètre; **paid by the hour** payé à l'heure.

6 (*according to*) à, d'après; **by my watch** à or d'après ma montre; **it's fine** or **OK** or **all right by me** si vous voulez.

∎ *adv* **close by** tout près; **to go by, pass by** passer; **to put by** mettre de côté; **by and by** bientôt; **by and large** en gros. ● **by-election** *n* élection *f* partielle. ● **by-law** *n* arrêté *m* (municipal); (*of organization*) *Am* statut *m*. ● **by-product** *n* sous-produit *m*. ● **by-road** *n* chemin *m* de traverse.

bye(-bye)! [baɪ('baɪ)] *int Fam* salut!, au revoir!

bygone ['baɪɡɒn] *a* **in b. days** jadis ∎ *npl* **let bygones be bygones** oublions le passé.

bypass ['baɪpɑːs] *n* déviation *f* (routière), voie *f* de contournement; (**heart**) **b. operation** pontage *m* ∎ *vt* (*town etc*) contourner; (*ignore*) *Fig* éviter de passer par (*qn*).

bystander ['baɪstændər] *n* (*at scene of accident etc*) spectateur, -trice *mf*; (*at street scene*) badaud, -aude *mf*.

byte [baɪt] *n Comptr* octet *m*.

byword ['baɪwɜːd] *n* **a b. for** *Pej* un synonyme de.

C

C, c [siː] *n* C, c *m*.

c *abbr* = **cent**.

cab [kæb] *n* taxi *m*; (*of train driver etc*) cabine *f*; (*horse-drawn*) *Hist* fiacre *m*.

cabaret ['kæbəreɪ] *n* (*show*) spectacle *m*; (*place*) cabaret *m*.

cabbage ['kæbɪdʒ] *n* chou *m* (*pl* choux).

cabbie *or* **cabby** ['kæbɪ] *n Fam* chauffeur *m* de taxi.

cabin ['kæbɪn] *n* (*on ship, aircraft*) cabine *f*; (*hut*) cabane *f*, case *f*; **c. class** *Av* = deuxième classe *f*; **c. crew** *Av* équipage *m*.

cabinet[1] ['kæbɪnɪt] *n* (*Br cupboard, Am closet*) armoire *f*; (*for display*) vitrine *f*; (*filing*) **c.** classeur *m* (de bureau). ● **cabinet-maker** *n* ébéniste *m*.

cabinet[2] ['kæbɪnɪt] *n* (*government ministers*) gouvernement *m*; **c. meeting** conseil *m* des ministres; **c. minister** ministre *m*.

cable ['keɪb(ə)l] *n* câble *m*; **c. car** (*with overhead cable*) téléphérique *m*; (*on tracks*) funiculaire *m*; **c. television** la télévision par câble; **to have c.** *Fam* avoir le câble ‖ *vt* (*message etc*) câbler (**to** à).

caboose [kəˈbuːs] *n* (*on train*) *Am* fourgon *m* (de queue).

cache [kæʃ] *n* (*place*) cachette *f*; **an arms' c.** une cache d'armes.

cachet ['kæʃeɪ] *n* (*mark, character etc*) cachet *m*.

cackle ['kæk(ə)l] *vi* (*of hen*) caqueter; (*laugh*) glousser ‖ *n* caquet *m*; (*laughter*) gloussement *m*.

cacophony [kəˈkɒfənɪ] *n* cacophonie *f*.

cactus, *pl* **-ti** *or* **-tuses** ['kæktəs, -taɪ, -təsɪz] *n* cactus *m*.

cad [kæd] *n Old-fashioned Pej* goujat *m*.

cadaverous [kəˈdævərəs] *a* cadavérique.

caddie ['kædɪ] *n Golf* caddie *m*.

caddy ['kædɪ] *n* (*tea*) c. boîte *f* à thé.

cadence ['keɪdəns] *n* (*rhythm*) & *Mus* cadence *f*.

cadet [kəˈdet] *n* élève *mf* d'une école militaire; **officer c.** élève officier; **police c.** *Br* élève *mf* d'une école de police.

cadge [kædʒ] *vi* (*beg*) quémander ‖ *vt* (*meal*) se faire payer (**off s.o.** par qn); **to c. money from** *or* **off s.o.** taper qn.

Caesarean [sɪˈzeərɪən] *n* **c. (section)** (*operation*) césarienne *f*.

café ['kæfeɪ] *n* café(-restaurant) *m*.

cafeteria [kæfɪˈtɪərɪə] *n* cafétéria *f*.

caffeine ['kæfiːn] *n* caféine *f*.

cage [keɪdʒ] *n* cage *f* ‖ *vt* **to c. (up)** mettre en cage.

cagey ['keɪdʒɪ] *a Fam* peu communicatif (**about** à l'égard de).

cahoots [kəˈhuːts] *n* **in c.** *Sl* de mèche, en cheville (**with s.o.** avec qn).

Cairo ['kaɪərəʊ] *n* Le Caire *m*.

cajole [kəˈdʒəʊl] *vt* amadouer, enjôler.

cake[1] [keɪk] *n* gâteau *m*; (*small*) pâtisserie *f*; **c. shop** pâtisserie *f*; **c. of soap** savonnette *f*.

cake[2] [keɪk] *vt* **caked with blood/mud** couvert de sang/boue séché(e); **caked blood/mud** sang *m*/boue *f* séché(e).

calamine ['kæləmaɪn] *n* **c. (lotion)** lotion *f* apaisante (à la calamine).

calamity [kəˈlæmɪtɪ] *n* calamité *f*. ● **calamitous** *a* désastreux.

calcium ['kælsɪəm] *n* calcium *m*.

calculate ['kælkjʊleɪt] *vti* calculer; **to c. that** (*estimate*) calculer que; *Fam* supposer que; **to c. on** (*rely on*) compter sur. ● **calculated** *a* (*deliberate*) délibéré; **a c. risk** un risque calculé. ● **calculating** *a* (*shrewd*) calculateur. ● **calculation** [-ˈleɪʃ(ə)n] *n* calcul *m*.

calculator ['kælkjʊleɪtər] *n* (*desk computer*) calculatrice *f*; (*pocket*) **c.** calculatrice (de poche).

calculus ['kælkjʊləs] *n Math Med* calcul *m*.

calendar ['kælɪndər] *n* calendrier *m*; (*directory*) annuaire *m*; (*for engagements*) *Am* agenda *m*; **c. month/year** mois *m*/année *f* civil(e).

calf [kɑːf] *n* (*pl* **calves**) **1** (*animal*) veau *m*. **2** (*part of leg*) mollet *m*.

calibre ['kælɪbər] (*Am* **caliber**) *n* calibre *m*. ● **calibrate** *vt* calibrer.

calico ['kælɪkəʊ] *n* (*pl* **-oes** *or* **-os**) (*fabric*) calicot *m*; (*printed*) *Am* indienne *f*.

call [kɔːl] *n* appel *m*; (*shout*) cri *m*; (*vocation*) vocation *f*; (*visit*) visite *f*; (**telephone**) **c.** communication *f*, appel *m* téléphonique; **to make a c.** (*phone*) téléphoner (**to** à); **on c.** (*doctor etc*) de garde; **there's no c. to do that** il n'y a aucune raison de faire cela; **there's no c. for that** article cet article n'est pas très demandé; **c. box** *Br* cabine *f* (téléphonique); **c. girl** call-girl *f*.

‖ *vt* appeler; (*shout*) crier; (*wake up*) réveiller; (*person to meeting*) convoquer (**to** à); (*attention*) attirer (**to** sur); (*truce*) demander; (*consider*) considérer; **he's called David** il s'appelle David; **to c. a meeting** convoquer une assemblée; **to c. s.o. a liar/etc** traiter *or* qualifier qn de menteur/etc; **she calls herself an expert** elle se dit expert; **to c. into question** mettre en question; **let's c. it a day** *Fam* on va s'arrêter là, ça suffit.

‖ *vi* appeler; (*cry out*) crier; (*visit*) passer.

call back *vti* rappeler ‖ **to call by** *vi* (*visit*) passer ▮ **to call for** vt (require) demander; (summon) appeler; (collect) passer prendre ▮ **to call in** vt (into room etc) faire venir ou entrer; (police) appeler; (recall) rappeler, faire rentrer (appareil défectueux) ▮ vi **to c. in** (on s.o.) (visit) passer (chez qn); **c.-in programme** (on radio) émission f à ligne ouverte. ▮ **to call off** vt (cancel) annuler; (dog) rappeler ▮ **to call on** vi (visit) passer voir, passer chez; (invoke) invoquer (Dieu etc); **to c. (up)on s.o. to do** inviter qn à faire; (urge) sommer qn de faire. ▮ **to call out** vt (shout) crier; (doctor) appeler; (workers) donner une consigne de grève à ▮ vi (shout) crier; **to c. out to s.o.** interpeller qn; **to c. out for** demander à haute voix ▮ **to call over** vi (visit) passer. ▮ **to call round** vi (visit) passer. ▮ **to call up** vt (phone) appeler; (recruits) Mil appeler, mobiliser; (memories) évoquer. ●**call-up** n (of recruits) appel m, mobilisation f.

caller ['kɔːlər] n visiteur, -euse mf; (on phone) correspondant, -ante mf.

calligraphy [kə'lɪɡrəfɪ] n calligraphie f.

calling ['kɔːlɪŋ] n vocation f; **c. card** Am carte f de visite.

callous ['kæləs] a 1 (cruel) cruel, insensible. 2 (skin) calleux.

callow ['kæləʊ] a **c. youth** blanc-bec m.

callus ['kæləs] n durillon m, cal m.

calm [kɑːm] a (-er, -est) calme, tranquille; **keep c.!** (don't panic) du calme! ▮ n calme m ▮ vt **to c. (down)** calmer ▮ vi **to c. down** se calmer. ●**calmly** adv calmement. ●**calmness** n calme m.

Calor gas ['kæləɡæs] n Br butagaz® m; **C. gas stove** camping-gaz® m.

calorie ['kælərɪ] n calorie f.

calumny ['kæləmnɪ] n calomnie f.

calve [kɑːv] vi (of cow) vêler.

camber ['kæmbər] n (in road) bombement m.

camcorder ['kæmkɔːdər] n caméscope m.

came [keɪm] pt of come.

camel ['kæməl] n chameau m.

camellia [kə'miːlɪə] n (plant) camélia m.

cameo ['kæmɪəʊ] n (gem) camée m; **c. role** Cinema petit rôle m.

camera ['kæmrə] n appareil (photo) m; (TV or film) **c.** caméra f. ●**cameraman** n (pl -men) cameraman m, cadreur m.

camomile ['kæməmaɪl] n (plant) camomille f.

camouflage ['kæməflɑːʒ] n camouflage m ▮ vt camoufler.

camp¹ [kæmp] n camp m, campement m; **c. bed** lit m de camp ▮ vi **to c. (out)** camper. ●**camping** n camping m; **c. site** (terrain m de) camping m. ●**camper** n (person) campeur, -euse mf; (vehicle) camping-car m. ●**campfire** n feu m de camp. ●**campsite** n camping m.

camp² [kæmp] a (affected) affecté, exagéré (et risible).

campaign [kæm'peɪn] n (political, military etc) campagne f; **press/publicity c.** campagne f de presse/publicité ▮ vi faire campagne (for pour, against contre). ●**campaigner** n militant, -ante mf (for pour).

campus ['kæmpəs] n (of university) campus m.

can¹ [kæn, unstressed kən] v aux (pres t can, pt could) (be able to) pouvoir; (know how to) savoir; **he couldn't help me** il ne pouvait pas m'aider; **if I c.** si je peux; **she c. swim** elle sait nager; **if I could swim** si je savais nager; **he could do it tomorrow** il pourrait le faire demain; **he could have done it** il aurait pu le faire; **you could be wrong** (possibility) tu as peut-être tort; **he can't be dead** (probability) il ne peut pas être mort; **that can't be right!** (disbelief) ce n'est pas possible!; **c. I come in?** (permission) puis-je entrer?; **yes, you c.!** oui!; **you can't or c. not or cannot come** tu ne peux pas venir; **I c. see** je vois; **as happy/etc as c. be** aussi heureux/etc que possible.

can² [kæn] n (for water etc) bidon m; (for food, beer) boîte f ▮ vt (-nn-) mettre en boîte. ●**canned** a en boîte, en conserve; **c. beer** bière f en boîte; **c. food** conserves fpl. ●**can-opener** n ouvre-boîtes m inv.

Canada ['kænədə] n Canada m. ●**Canadian** [kə'neɪdɪən] a canadien ▮ n Canadien, -ienne mf.

canal [kə'næl] n canal m.

canary [kə'neərɪ] n canari m, serin m.

cancan ['kænkæn] n french-cancan m.

cancel ['kænsəl] vt (Br -ll-, Am -l-) (flight, appointment etc) annuler; (goods, taxi) décommander; (train) supprimer; (word, paragraph etc) biffer; (stamp) oblitérer; **to c. a ticket** (punch) (with date) composter un billet; (with hole) poinçonner un billet; **to c. each other out** s'annuler. ●**cancellation** [-'leɪʃ(ə)n] n annulation f; (of train) suppression f; (of stamp) oblitération f.

cancer ['kænsər] n cancer m; **C.** (sign) le Cancer; **stomach/etc c.** cancer de l'estomac/etc; **c. patient** cancéreux, -euse mf; **c. specialist** cancérologue mf. ●**cancerous** a cancéreux.

candelabra [kændɪ'lɑːbrə] n candélabre m.

candid ['kændɪd] a franc (f franche), sincère. ●**candour** (Am candor) n franchise f, sincérité f.

candidate ['kændɪdeɪt] n candidat, -ate mf. ●**candidacy** or **candidature** n candidature f.

candle ['kænd(ə)l] n (wax) bougie f; (tallow) chandelle f; (in church) cierge m; **c. grease** suif m. ●**candlelight** n **by c.** à la (lueur d'une) bougie; **to have dinner by c.** dîner aux chandelles. ●**candlestick** n bougeoir m; (tall) chandelier m.

candy ['kændɪ] n Am bonbon(s) m(pl); (sugar) **c.** sucre m candi; **c. store** Am confiserie f. ●**candied** a (fruit) confit. ●**candyfloss** n Br barbe f à papa.

cane [keɪn] n (stick) canne f; (for basket) rotin m; (for punishing s.o.) baguette f ▮ vt (*punish*) fouetter (*élève*).

canine ['keɪnaɪn] **1** *a* (*tooth, race etc*) canin. **2** *n* (*tooth*) canine *f*.

canister ['kænɪstər] *n* boîte *f* (*en métal*).

canker ['kæŋkər] *n* (*evil*) chancre *m*.

cannabis ['kænəbɪs] *n* (*drug*) haschisch *m*, cannabis *m*; (*plant*) chanvre *m* indien.

cannibal ['kænɪbəl] *n* cannibale *mf*. ● **canniba'listic** *a* (*habits etc*) cannibale.

cannon ['kænən] *n* (*pl* -*s or inv*) canon *m*. ● **cannonball** *n* boulet *m* (de canon).

cannot ['kænɒt] = **can not**.

canny ['kænɪ] *a* (-ier, -iest) rusé, malin (*f* -igne).

canoe [kə'nuː] *n* canoë *m*, kayak *m*; (*dugout*) pirogue *f* **1** *vi* faire du canoë-kayak. ● **canoeing** *n* **to go c.** faire du canoë-kayak. ● **canoeist** *n* canoéiste *mf*.

canon ['kænən] *n* (*law*) canon *m*; (*clergyman*) chanoine *m*. ● **canonize** *vt* Rel canoniser.

canopy ['kænəpɪ] *n* (*hood of Br pram or Am baby carriage*) capote *f*; (*awning*) auvent *m*; (*over bed, altar etc*) dais *m*; (*made of glass*) marquise *f*; (*of leaves*) Fig voûte *f*.

cant [kænt] *n* (*jargon*) jargon *m*.

can't [kɑːnt] = **can not**.

cantaloup(e) [Br 'kæntəluːp, Am -ləʊp] *n* (*melon*) cantaloup *m*.

cantankerous [kæn'tæŋkərəs] *a* (*old man etc*) grincheux, acariâtre.

cantata [kæn'tɑːtə] *n* Mus cantate *f*.

canteen [kæn'tiːn] *n* (*in school, factory etc*) cantine *f*; (*flask*) gourde *f*; **c. of cutlery** Br ménagère *f*.

canter ['kæntər] *n* petit galop *m* **1** *vi* aller au petit galop.

cantor ['kæntər] *n* (*singer*) Rel chantre *m*, maître *m* de chapelle.

canvas ['kænvəs] *n* (grosse) toile *f*; (*for embroidery*) canevas *m*; **under c.** (*in a tent*) sous la tente.

canvass ['kænvəs] *vt* (*an area*) faire du démarchage dans; (*opinions*) sonder; **to c. s.o.** (*seek votes*) solliciter des voix de qn; (*seek orders*) solliciter des commandes de qn. ● **canvassing** *n* (*for orders*) démarchage *m*, prospection *f*; (*for votes*) démarchage *m* (électoral). ● **canvasser** *n* Pol agent *m* électoral, démarcheur, -euse *mf* (électoral(e)); Com démarcheur, -euse *mf*.

canyon ['kænjən] *n* cañon *m*, canyon *m*.

cap¹ [kæp] *n* **1** (*hat*) casquette *f*; (*for shower, of sailor*) bonnet *m*; (*of soldier*) képi *m*. **2** (*of bottle, tube, valve*) bouchon *m*; (*of milk or beer bottle*) capsule *f*; (*of pen*) capuchon *m*. **3** (*of child's gun*) amorce *f*. **4** (**Dutch**) **c.** (*contraceptive*) diaphragme *m*.

cap² [kæp] *vt* (-pp-) **1** (*outdo*) surpasser; **to c. it all** pour comble. **2** (*expenses*) Br limiter. **3** (*cover*) **capped with** surmonté de; **capped with snow** coiffé de neige.

CAP [siːr'piː] *n abbr* (*common agricultural policy*) PAC *f*.

capable ['keɪpəb(ə)l] *a* (*person*) capable (of

sth de qch, **of doing** de faire); compétent; **c. of** (*situation, text etc*) susceptible de. ● **capa'bility** *n* capacité *f*. ● **capably** *adv* avec compétence.

capacity [kə'pæsɪtɪ] *n* (*of container*) capacité *f*, contenance *f*; (*ability*) aptitude *f*, capacité *f* (**for sth** pour qch, **for doing** à faire); (*output*) rendement *m*; **in my c. as a doctor/etc** en ma qualité de médecin/etc; **in an advisory/etc c.** à titre consultatif/etc; **filled to c.** (*concert hall etc*) absolument plein, comble; **c. audience** salle *f* comble.

cape [keɪp] *n* **1** (*cloak*) cape *f*; (*of cyclist*) pèlerine *f*. **2** (*of coast*) cap *m*; **C. Town** Le Cap.

caper ['keɪpər] **1** *vi* (*jump about*) gambader. **2** *n* (*activity*) Sl affaire *f*; (*prank*) Fam farce *f*; (*trip*) Fam virée *f*. **3** *n* (*for seasoning*) câpre *f*.

capital ['kæpɪtəl] **1** *a* (*letter, importance*) capital; **c. punishment** peine *f* capitale **1** *n* **c.** (**city**) capitale *f*; **c.** (**letter**) majuscule *f*, capitale *f*. **2** *n* (*money*) capital *m*, capitaux *mpl*. ● **capitalism** *n* capitalisme *m*. ● **capitalist** *a* & *n* capitaliste (*mf*). ● **capitalize** *vi* **to c. on** tirer parti de.

capitulate [kə'pɪtʃʊleɪt] *vi* capituler. ● **capitulation** [-'leɪʃ(ə)n] *n* capitulation *f*.

cappuccino [kæpu'tʃiːnəʊ] *n* (*pl* -os) cappuccino *m*.

caprice [kə'priːs] *n* caprice *m*. ● **capricious** [kə'prɪʃəs] *a* capricieux.

Capricorn ['kæprɪkɔːn] *n* (*sign*) le Capricorne.

capsicum ['kæpsɪkəm] *n* poivron *m*.

capsize [kæp'saɪz] *vi* (*of boat*) chavirer **1** *vt* (faire) chavirer.

capsule [Br 'kæpsjuːl, Am 'kæpsəl] *n* (*medicine, of spaceship etc*) capsule *f*.

captain ['kæptɪn] *n* capitaine *m* **1** *vt* (*ship*) commander; (*team*) être le capitaine de.

caption ['kæpʃ(ə)n] *n* (*under illustration*) légende *f*; (*of film, heading of article*) sous-titre *m*.

captivate ['kæptɪveɪt] *vt* captiver. ● **captivating** *a* captivant.

captive ['kæptɪv] *n* prisonnier, -ière *mf*, captif, -ive *mf*. ● **cap'tivity** *n* **in c.** en captivité.

capture ['kæptʃər] *vt* (*person, animal, ship*) capturer, prendre; (*escaped prisoner or animal*) reprendre; (*town*) prendre; (*attention*) capter; (*represent in words, on film etc*) rendre, reproduire **1** *n* capture *f*.

car [kɑːr] *n* voiture *f*, auto(mobile) *f*; (*train carriage*) wagon *m*, voiture *f*; **c. insurance/industry** assurance *f*/industrie *f* automobile; **the c. door/etc** la porte/etc de la voiture; **c. boot sale** Br (*sorte de*) braderie *f*; **c. chase** poursuite *f* en voiture; **c. ferry** ferry-boat *m*; **c. hire** Br, **c. rental** Am location *f* de voitures; **c. park** Br parking *m*; **c. phone** téléphone *m* de voiture; **c. radio** autoradio *m*; **c. wash** (*machine*) lave-auto *m*; (*action*) lavage *m* automatique. ● **carfare** *n* Am frais *mpl* de voyage. ● **carport** *n* auvent *m* (pour voiture. ●**carsick** a to be c. être malade en voiture.

carafe [kə'ræf] n carafe f.

caramel ['kærəməl] n (flavouring, Br sweet, Am candy) caramel m.

carat ['kærət] n carat m; **18 c.** gold or m à 18 carats.

caravan ['kærəvæn] n (vehicle) Br caravane f; (horse-drawn) roulotte f; (in desert) caravane f; **c. site** camping m pour caravanes.

caraway ['kærəweɪ] n (plant) cumin m, carvi m; **c. seeds** graines fpl de carvi or de cumin.

carbohydrates [kɑːbəʊ'haɪdreɪts] npl (in diet) féculents mpl.

carbon ['kɑːbən] n carbone m; **c. copy** double m (au carbone); (of crime etc) Fig double m; **c. paper** (papier m) carbone m.

carbuncle ['kɑːbʌŋk(ə)l] n (swelling) furoncle m, clou m.

carburettor [kɑːbjʊ'retər] (Am **carburetor** ['kɑːbəreɪtər]) n carburateur m.

carcass ['kɑːkəs] n carcasse f.

carcinogenic [kɑːsɪnə'dʒenɪk] a cancérigène.

card [kɑːd] n carte f; (cardboard) carton m; (index) c. fiche f; **c. index** fichier m; **c. game** (type of game) jeu m de cartes; (game of cards) partie f de cartes; **c. table** table f de jeu; **to play cards** jouer aux cartes; Br **on** or Am **in the cards** Fam très vraisemblable. ●**cardphone** n téléphone m or publiphone m à carte. ●**cardsharp** n tricheur, -euse mf.

cardboard ['kɑːdbɔːd] n carton m; **c. box** boîte f en carton, carton m.

cardiac ['kɑːdɪæk] a cardiaque.

cardigan ['kɑːdɪgən] n gilet m.

cardinal ['kɑːdɪn(ə)l] **1** a (number, point etc) cardinal. **2** n (priest) cardinal m.

care [keər] **1** vi to c. about (feel concern about) se soucier de, s'intéresser à; I don't c. ça m'est égal; I couldn't c. less Fam je m'en fiche; who cares? qu'est-ce que ça fait?

2 vi (like) aimer, vouloir; would you c. to try? voulez-vous essayer?, aimeriez-vous essayer?; I don't c. for it (much) (opera, tennis etc) je n'aime pas tellement ça; to c. for a drink/a change/etc avoir envie d'un verre/d'un changement/etc; to c. about or for s.o. (be fond of) avoir de la sympathie pour qn; to c. for s.o. (look after) s'occuper de qn; (sick person) soigner qn.

3 n (attention) soin(s) m(pl), attention f; (protection) garde f, soin m; (anxiety) souci m; to take c. not to do faire attention à ne pas faire; to take c. to do veiller à faire; to take c. of s'occuper de (qch, qn); (sick person) prendre soin de; to take c. of oneself (manage) se débrouiller; (keep healthy) faire bien attention à soi; that will take c. of itself ça s'arrangera; **c. of** (on envelope) 'chez'.

career [kə'rɪər] **1** n carrière f; to make a c. in faire carrière dans. **2** a (diplomat etc) de carrière; the job has c. prospects cet emploi offre des perspectives de carrière. **2** vi to c.

along aller à toute vitesse.

carefree ['keəfriː] a insouciant.

careful ['keəf(ə)l] a (exact, thorough) soigneux (about de); (work) soigné; (cautious) prudent; **c.** (about or with money) regardant; to be c. of or with faire attention à; to be c. not to be careless il ne pas faire; to be c. to do veiller à faire; be c. she doesn't see you! (fais) attention qu'elle ne te voie pas! ●**carefully** adv avec soin; (cautiously) prudemment.

careless ['keələs] a négligent; (absent-minded) étourdi; (work) peu soigné; **c. about** one's work/appearance/etc peu soigneux de son travail/de sa personne/etc. ●**carelessness** n négligence f, manque m de soin.

carer ['keərər] n (professional) c. travailleur m social.

caress [kə'res] n caresse f ▮ vt (stroke) caresser; (kiss) embrasser.

caretaker ['keəteɪkər] n gardien, -ienne mf, concierge mf.

cargo ['kɑːgəʊ] n (pl Br -oes, Am -os) cargaison f; **c. boat** cargo m.

Caribbean [Br kærɪ'biːən, Am kə'rɪbɪən] a caraïbe ▮ n the C. (Islands) les Antilles fpl.

caricature ['kærɪkətʃʊər] n caricature f ▮ vt caricaturer.

caring ['keərɪŋ] a (loving) aimant; (understanding) très humain ▮ n affection f.

carnage ['kɑːnɪdʒ] n carnage m.

carnal ['kɑːnəl] a charnel, sexuel.

carnation [kɑː'neɪʃən] n œillet m.

carnival ['kɑːnɪvəl] n carnaval m (pl -als).

carnivore ['kɑːnɪvɔːr] n carnivore m. ●**car'nivorous** a carnivore.

carol ['kærəl] n chant m (de Noël).

carouse [kə'raʊz] vi faire la fête.

carp [kɑːp] **1** n (fish) carpe f. **2** vi critiquer; to c. at critiquer.

carpenter ['kɑːpɪntər] n (for house building) charpentier m; (for light woodwork) menuisier m. ●**carpentry** n charpenterie f; (for light woodwork) menuiserie f.

carpet ['kɑːpɪt] n tapis m; (Br fitted, Am wall-to-wall) moquette f; **c. sweeper** balai m mécanique ▮ vt recouvrir d'un tapis or d'une moquette; (of snow etc) Fig tapisser. ●**carpeting** n (carpets) tapis mpl; (wall-to-wall) c. Am moquette f.

carriage ['kærɪdʒ] n (of train) Br voiture f; (horse-drawn) voiture f, équipage m; (transport of goods) Br transport m; (of typewriter) chariot m; **c. paid** Br port payé.

carriageway ['kærɪdʒweɪ] n Br chaussée f.

carrier ['kærɪər] n (of illness) porteur, -euse mf; (company) entreprise f de transports; (airline) transporteur m aérien; **c. (bag)** Br sac m (en plastique); **c. pigeon** pigeon m voyageur.

carrot ['kærət] n carotte f.

carry ['kærɪ] vt porter; (goods) transporter; (by wind) emporter; (motion) Pol faire passer, voter; (sound) conduire; (sell) sto-

cker; (*in calculation*) *Math* retenir; **to c.
water**/*etc* **to** (*of pipe etc*) amener de l'eau/*etc*
à; **to c. responsibility** (*of job*) comporter des
responsabilités; **to c. sth too far** pousser qch
trop loin; **to c. oneself** se comporter.
▮ *vi* (*of sound*) porter.
carryall ['kærɪɔːl] *n* (*bag*) *Am* fourre-tout *m
inv*. ●**carrycot** *n Br* (nacelle *f*) porte-bébé
m.
carry away *vt* emporter; (*of idea etc*) *Fig*
transporter; **to be** *or* **get carried away**
(*excited*) s'emballer ▮ **to carry back** *vt* (*thing*)
rapporter; (*person*) ramener; (*in thought*) reporter ▮ **to carry forward** (*in bookkeeping*)
reporter ▮ **to c. off** *vt* emporter; (*kidnap*) enlever; (*prize*) remporter; **to c. it off** réussir ▮
to carry on *vt* continuer (doing à faire); (*negotiations*) diriger, mener; (*conversation*)
soutenir ▮ *vi* continuer; (*behave*) *Pej* se conduire (mal); (*complain*) se plaindre; **to c. on
with sth** continuer qch; **to c. on about** (*talk*)
causer de. ●**carryings-'on** *npl Pej* activités
fpl louches; (*behaviour*) façons *fpl*. ▮ **to
carry out** *vt* (*plan, order, promise etc*) exécuter, réaliser; (*repair, reform*) effectuer;
(*duty*) accomplir; (*meal*) *Am* emporter ▮ **to
carry through** *vt* (*plan etc*) mener à bonne
fin.
cart [kɑːt] **1** *n* (*horse-drawn*) charrette *f*;
(*handcart*) voiture *f* à bras; (*in supermarket*)
Am caddie® *m*; (**serving**) **c.** *Am* table *f* roulante. **2** *vt* (*goods, people*) transporter; **to c.
(around)** *Fam* trimbal(l)er; **to c. away**
emporter. ●**carthorse** *n* cheval *m* de trait.
cartel [kɑː'tel] *n* (*of businesses*) cartel *m*.
cartilage ['kɑːtɪlɪdʒ] *n* cartilage *m*.
carton ['kɑːtən] *n* (*box*) carton *m*; (*of milk,
fruit juice etc*) brique *f*; (*of cigarettes*)
cartouche *f*; (*of cream*) pot *m*.
cartoon [kɑː'tuːn] *n* (*in newspaper etc*)
dessin *m* (humoristique); (*film*) dessin *m*
animé; (**strip**) *vt* bande *f* dessinée. ●**cartoonist** *n* dessinateur, -trice *mf* (humoristique).
cartridge ['kɑːtrɪdʒ] *n* (*of firearm, pen, camera, tape deck*) cartouche *f*; (*of record player*) cellule *f*; **c. belt** cartouchière *f*.
cartwheel ['kɑːtwiːl] *n* **to do a c.** (*in gymnastics*) faire la roue.
carve [kɑːv] *vt* (*cut*) tailler (**out of** dans); (*initials etc*) graver; (*sculpt*) sculpter; **to c. (up)**
(*meat*) découper; **to c. up** (*country*) dépecer,
morceler; **to c. out a career for oneself** se
tailler une carrière. ●**carving** *a* **c. knife** couteau *m* à découper ▮ *n* (*wood*) **c.** sculpture *f*
(sur bois).
cascade [kæs'keɪd] *n* (*of rocks*) chute *f*; (*of
blows*) déluge *m*; (*of lace*) flot *m* ▮ *vi* (*fall*)
tomber; (*hang*) pendre.
case[1] [keɪs] *n* (*instance, in hospital*) cas *m*;
(*in court*) affaire *f*; (*arguments*) arguments
mpl; **in any c.** en tout cas; **in c. it rains** pour
le cas où il pleuvrait; **in c. of** en cas de;
(**just**) **in c.** à tout hasard.
case[2] [keɪs] *n* (*bag*) valise *f*; (*crate*) caisse *f*;
(*for pen, glasses, camera, violin, cigarettes*)

étui *m*; (*for jewels*) coffret *m*.
cash [kæʃ] *n* argent *m*; **to pay (in) c.** (*not by
Br cheque or Am check*) payer en espèces *or*
en liquide; **to pay c. (down)** (*not on credit*)
payer comptant; **c. price** prix *m* (au)
comptant; **c. box** caisse *f*; **c. desk** *Br* caisse *f*;
c. dispenser *or* **machine** distributeur *m* de
billets; **he has c. flow problems** il a des
problèmes d'argent; **c. register** caisse *f* enregistreuse.
▮ *vt* **to c. a** *Br* **cheque** *or* **Am check** (*of
person*) encaisser un chèque; (*of bank*)
payer un chèque; **to c. in on** (*situation*) *Fam*
profiter de.
cashew ['kæʃuː] *n* (*nut*) noix *f* de cajou.
cashier [kæ'ʃɪər] **1** *n* caissier, -ière *mf*. **2** *vt*
(*dismiss*) casser (*officier*).
cashmere ['kæʃmɪər] *n* cachemire *m*.
casing ['keɪsɪŋ] *n* (*covering*) enveloppe *f*.
casino [kə'siːnəʊ] *n* (*pl* -os) casino *m*.
cask [kɑːsk] *n* fût *m*, tonneau *m*. ●**casket** *n*
(*box*) coffret *m*; (*coffin*) cercueil *m*.
casserole ['kæsərəʊl] *n* (*covered dish*) cocotte *f*; (*stew*) ragoût *m* en cocotte.
cassette [kə'set] *n* (*audio, video*) cassette *f*;
(*for camera*) cartouche *f*; **c. player** lecteur *m*
de cassettes; **c. recorder** magnétophone *m* à
cassettes.
cassock ['kæsək] *n* soutane *f*.
cast [kɑːst] **1** *n* (*actors*) acteurs *mpl*; (*list of
actors*) distribution *f*; (*mould*) moulage *m*;
(*of dice*) coup *m*; (*for broken bone*) plâtre
m; (*squint*) léger strabisme *m*; **in a c.** *Med*
dans le plâtre; **c. of mind** tournure *f* d'esprit.
2 *vt* (*pt & pp* **cast**) (*throw*) jeter; (*light, shadow*) projeter; (*blame*) rejeter; (*glance*) jeter
(**at**, **sur**); (*metal*) couler; (*theatrical role*)
distribuer; (*actor*) donner un rôle à; **to c.
doubt on sth** jeter le doute sur qch; **to c. a
spell on s.o.** jeter un sort sur qn, envoûter
qn; **to c. one's mind back** se reporter en
arrière; **to c. a vote** voter; **to c. aside** rejeter;
to c. off (*chains etc*) se libérer de; (*person*)
Fig abandonner; **to c. off its skin** (*of animal*)
muer, se dépouiller.
3 *vi* **to c. off** (*of ship*) appareiller.
4 *n* **c. iron** fonte *f*. ●**cast-'iron** *a* (*pan etc*) en
fonte; (*will*) *Fig* de fer, solide; (*alibi, excuse*)
Fig en béton.
castaway ['kɑːstəweɪ] *n* naufragé, -ée *mf*.
caste [kɑːst] *n* caste *f*.
caster ['kɑːstər] *n* (*wheel*) roulette *f*; **c. sugar**
Br sucre *m* en poudre, sucre semoule.
castle ['kɑːs(ə)l] *n* château *m*; *Chess* tour *f*.
castoffs ['kɑːstɒfs] *npl* vieux vêtements *mpl*.
castor ['kɑːstər] *n* (*wheel*) roulette *f*; **c. oil**
huile *f* de ricin; **c. sugar** *Br* sucre *m* en
poudre, sucre semoule.
castrate [kæ'streɪt] *vt* châtrer. ●**castration**
[-ʃ(ə)n] *n* castration *f*.
casual ['kæʒʊəl] *a* (*remark*) fait en passant;
(*stroll*) sans but; (*meeting*) fortuit; (*offhand*)
désinvolte, insouciant; (*worker*) temporaire;
(*work*) irrégulier; **c. clothes** vêtements *mpl*
sport; **she's a c. acquaintance** c'est quelqu'un

que je connaîs un peu. ● **casually** adv (*informally*) avec désinvolture; (*to remark*) en passant.

casualty ['kæʒjʊəltɪ] n (*dead*) mort m, morte f; (*wounded*) blessé, -ée mf; (*accident victim*) accidenté, -ée mf; **casualties** morts et blessés mpl; **c.** (**department**) (*in hospital*) Br (*service m des*) urgences fpl.

cat [kæt] n chat m; (*female*) chatte f; **c. food** pâtée f; **c. burglar** monte-en-l'air m inv; **c.'s eyes**® Br cataphotes® mpl.

cataclysm ['kætəklɪzəm] n cataclysme m.

catalogue ['kætəlɒg] (*Am* **catalog**) n catalogue m ▮ vt cataloguer.

catalyst ['kætəlɪst] n Ch & Fig catalyseur m.

catapult ['kætəpʌlt] n (*toy*) lance-pierres m inv; (*on aircraft carrier*) catapulte f ▮ vt catapulter.

cataract ['kætərækt] n (*of eye*) cataracte f.

catarrh [kə'tɑːr] n Br gros rhume m.

catastrophe [kə'tæstrəfɪ] n catastrophe f. ● **cata'strophic** a catastrophique.

catcall ['kætkɔːl] n sifflet m, huée f.

catch [kætʃ] vt (*pt & pp* **caught**) (*ball, thief, illness etc*) attraper; (*grab*) prendre, saisir; (*surprise*) (sur)prendre; (*understand*) saisir; (*train, bus etc*) attraper; (*réussir à*) prendre; (*garment on nail etc*) accrocher (**on** à); **to c. one's finger/etc** se prendre le doigt/etc dans; **to c. s.o.'s eye** or **attention** attirer l'attention de qn; **to c. sight of** apercevoir; **to c. fire** prendre feu; **to c. s.o. (in)** Fam trouver qn (chez soi); **to c. one's breath** (*rest a while*) reprendre haleine; (*stop breathing*) retenir son souffle; **I didn't c. the train/etc** j'ai manqué le train/etc; **to c. s.o. doing** surprendre or prendre qn à faire; **to c. s.o. out** prendre qn en défaut; **to c. s.o. up** rattraper qn.

▮ vi (*of fire*) prendre; **her skirt (got) caught in the door** sa jupe s'est prise or coincée dans la porte; **to c. on** (*become popular*) prendre, devenir populaire; (*understand*) saisir; **to c. up** se rattraper; **to c. up with s.o.** rattraper qn.

▮ n (*captured animal*) capture f, prise f; (*fish*) prise f; (*many fish*) pêche f; (*trick, snare*) piège m; (*on door*) loquet m; **there's a c.** (*hidden difficulty etc*) ça cache quelque chose. ● **catching** a (*illness*) contagieux. ● **catchphrase** or **catchword** n slogan m.

catchy ['kætʃɪ] a (-**ier**, -**iest**) (*tune*) Fam facile à retenir.

catechism ['kætɪkɪzəm] n Rel catéchisme m.

category ['kætɪgərɪ] n catégorie f. ● **cate'gorical** a catégorique. ● **categorize** vt classer (par catégorie).

cater ['keɪtər] vi (*prepare food and drink*) s'occuper des repas (**for** pour); **to c. to**, Br **c. for** (*need, taste*) satisfaire; (*of book, newspaper*) s'adresser à (*enfants, étudiants etc*). ● **catering** n restauration f; **to do the c.** s'occuper des repas. ● **caterer** n traiteur m.

caterpillar ['kætəpɪlər] n chenille f; **c. track**® chenille f.

catgut ['kætgʌt] n (*cord*) boyau m.

cathedral [kə'θiːdrəl] n cathédrale f.

catholic ['kæθlɪk] **1** a & n C. catholique (*mf*). **2** a (*taste*) universel; (*view*) libéral. ● **Ca'tholicism** n catholicisme m.

cattle ['kæt(ə)l] npl bétail m, bestiaux mpl.

catty ['kætɪ] a (-**ier**, -**iest**) (*spiteful*) Fam rosse, méchant.

catwalk ['kætwɔːk] n (*in fashion show*) Br podium m.

caucus ['kɔːkəs] n (*to choose candidates*) Pol Am comité m électoral.

caught [kɔːt] see **catch**.

cauldron ['kɔːldrən] n chaudron m.

cauliflower ['kɒlɪflaʊər] n chou-fleur m; **c. cheese** Br chou-fleur au gratin.

cause [kɔːz] n (*origin, ideal, aim*) & Jur cause f; (*reason*) cause f, raison f (**of** de); **c. for complaint/dispute** sujet m de plainte/ dispute; **to have no c. to worry/etc** n'avoir aucune raison de s'inquiéter/etc; **to have c. for complaint** avoir à se plaindre.

▮ vt causer, occasionner; **to c. trouble for s.o.** créer ou causer des ennuis à qn; **to c. sth/ s.o. to fall/etc** faire tomber/etc qch/qn.

causeway ['kɔːzweɪ] n chaussée f (*chemin surélevé*).

caustic ['kɔːstɪk] a (*remark, substance*) caustique; **c. soda** soude f caustique.

cauterize ['kɔːtəraɪz] vt (*wound*) cautériser.

caution ['kɔːʃ(ə)n] n (*care*) prudence f, précaution f; (*warning*) avertissement m ▮ vt (*warn*) avertir; **to c. s.o. against sth** mettre qn en garde contre qch.

cautionary ['kɔːʃən(ə)rɪ] a **c. tale** conte m moral.

cautious ['kɔːʃəs] a prudent, circonspect. ● **cautiously** adv prudemment.

cavalier [kævə'lɪər] **1** a (*selfish*) cavalier. **2** n (*horseman, knight*) Hist cavalier m.

cavalry ['kævəlrɪ] n cavalerie f.

cave [keɪv] **1** n caverne f, grotte f. **2** vi **to c. in** (*fall in*) (*of ceiling etc*) s'effondrer. ● **caveman** n (*pl* -**men**) homme m des cavernes.

cavern ['kævən] n caverne f.

caviar(e) ['kævɪɑːr] n caviar m.

cavity ['kævɪtɪ] n cavité f.

cavort [kə'vɔːt] vi Fam cabrioler; **to c. naked/etc** se balader tout nu/etc.

CD [siː'diː] abbr (*compact* Br *disc* or Am *disk*) CD m.

cease [siːs] vti cesser (**doing** de faire). ● **cease-fire** n cessez-le-feu m inv. ● **ceaseless** a incessant. ● **ceaselessly** adv sans cesse.

cedar ['siːdər] n (*tree, wood*) cèdre m.

cedilla [sɪ'dɪlə] n Grammar cédille f.

ceiling ['siːlɪŋ] n (*of room*, Fig *on wages etc*) plafond m.

celebrate ['selɪbreɪt] vt (*event*) fêter; (*mass, s.o.'s merits etc*) célébrer ▮ vi faire la fête; **we should c. (that)!** il faut fêter ça! ● **celebrated** a célèbre. ● **celebration** [-'breɪʃ(ə)n] n (*event*) fête f; **the celebrations** les festivités fpl; **the c. of** (*marriage etc*) la célébration de.

celebrity [sə'lebrətɪ] n (person) célébrité f.

celery ['selərɪ] n céleri m; **stick of c.** côte f de céleri.

celibate ['selɪbət] a (abstaining from sex) chaste, célibataire; (monk, priest etc) abstinent. ●**celibacy** n (of young person etc) chasteté f, célibat m; (of monk etc) abstinence f.

cell [sel] n cellule f; El élément m.

cellar ['selər] n cave f.

cello ['tʃeləʊ] n (pl -os) violoncelle m. ●**cellist** n violoncelliste mf.

cellophane® ['seləfeɪn] n cellophane® f.

cellular ['seljʊlər] a cellulaire; **c. blanket** couverture f en cellular; **c. phone** téléphone m cellulaire.

celluloid ['seljʊlɔɪd] n celluloïd m.

cellulose ['seljʊləʊs] n cellulose f.

Celsius ['selsɪəs] a Celsius inv.

Celt [kelt] n Celte mf. ●**Celtic** a celtique, celte.

cement [sɪ'ment] n ciment m; **c. mixer** bétonnière f ▌ vt cimenter.

cemetery [Br 'semətrɪ, Am 'semətərɪ] n cimetière m.

cenotaph ['senətɑːf] n cénotaphe m.

censor ['sensər] n censeur m ▌ vt (film etc) censurer. ●**censorship** n censure f.

censure ['senʃər] vt (criticize) blâmer; (government, party etc) censurer ▌ n blâme m; **c. motion, vote of c.** motion f de censure.

census ['sensəs] n recensement m.

cent [sent] n (coin) cent m; **not a c.** Fam pas un sou.

centenary [Br sen'tiːnərɪ, Am sen'tenərɪ] n centenaire m.

center ['sentər] n Am = centre.

centigrade ['sentɪɡreɪd] a centigrade.

centimetre ['sentɪmiːtər] n centimètre m.

centipede ['sentɪpiːd] n mille-pattes m inv.

central ['sentrəl] a central. ●**centralize** vt centraliser.

centre ['sentər] (Am **center**) n centre m; **c. forward** Football avant-centre m ▌ vt (object, discussion etc) centrer (**on** sur); (photo) cadrer ▌ vi **to c. on** (of thoughts) se concentrer sur; (of question) tourner autour de.

centrifugal [sen'trɪfjʊɡəl] a centrifuge.

century ['sentʃərɪ] n siècle m; (score) Cricket cent points mpl; **in the twenty-first c.** au vingt-et-unième siècle.

ceramic [sə'ræmɪk] a (tile etc) de or en céramique. ●**ceramics** npl (objects) céramiques fpl; (art) céramique f.

cereal ['sɪərɪəl] n céréale f; (breakfast) **c.** céréales fpl (pour petit déjeuner).

cerebral [Br 'serɪbrəl, Am sə'riːbrəl] a cérébral.

ceremony ['serɪmənɪ] n (event) cérémonie f; **to stand on c.** faire des cérémonies or des façons. ●**cere'monial** a c. dress/etc tenue f/etc de cérémonie ▌ n cérémonial m. ●**cere'monious** a cérémonieux.

certain ['sɜːtən] a 1 (sure) certain, sûr (that que); **she's c. to come, she'll come for c.**

c'est certain or sûr qu'elle viendra; **I'm not c. what to do** je ne sais pas très bien ce qu'il faut faire; **to be c. of sth/that** être certain de qch/que; **for c.** (to say, know) avec certitude; **be c. to go!** vas-y sans faute!; **to make c. of** (fact) s'assurer de; (seat, s.o.'s safety etc) s'assurer.

2 (particular, some) certain; **a c. person** une certaine personne; **c. people** certaines personnes. ●**certainly** adv (undoubtedly) certainement; (yes) bien sûr; (without fail) sans faute. ●**certainty** n certitude f.

certificate [sə'tɪfɪkɪt] n certificat m; (from university) diplôme m.

certify ['sɜːtɪfaɪ] vt (document, signature etc) certifier; **to c. s.o.** (insane) déclarer qn dément; **certified public accountant** Am expert-comptable m; **certified letter** Am = lettre f recommandée ▌ vi **to c. to sth** attester qch.

cervix ['sɜːvɪks] n col m de l'utérus.

cesspool ['sespuːl] n fosse f d'aisances; (of corruption etc) Fig cloaque m.

chafe [tʃeɪf] vt (skin) Lit frotter.

chaff [tʃæf] vt (tease) taquiner.

chaffinch ['tʃæfɪntʃ] n (bird) pinson m.

chagrin [Br 'ʃæɡrɪn, Am ʃə'ɡrɪn] n contrariété f ▌ vt contrarier.

chain [tʃeɪn] n (of rings, mountains) chaîne f; (of ideas, events) enchaînement m, suite f; (of lavatory) chasse f d'eau; **c. reaction** réaction f en chaîne; **to be a c.-smoker** fumer cigarette sur cigarette, fumer comme un pompier; **c. saw** tronçonneuse f; **c. store** magasin m à succursales multiples.

▌ vt **to c. (down)** enchaîner; **to c. (up)** (dog) mettre à l'attache. ●**chain-smoke** vi fumer comme un pompier.

chair [tʃeər] n chaise f; (armchair) fauteuil m; (of university professor) chaire f; **the c.** (office of chairperson) la présidence; **c. lift** télésiège m ▌ vt (meeting) présider. ●**chairman** (pl -men) or **chairperson** n président, -ente m ●**chairmanship** n présidence f.

chalet ['ʃæleɪ] n chalet m.

chalk [tʃɔːk] n craie f; **not by a long c.** loin de là, tant s'en faut ▌ vt écrire or marquer à la craie; **to c. up** (success) Fig remporter. ●**chalky** a (-ier, -iest) crayeux.

challenge ['tʃælɪndʒ] n défi m; (task) challenge m, gageure f; (order from soldier) sommation f ▌ a **c. for sth** (bid) une tentative d'obtenir qch ▌ vt défier (s.o. to do qn de faire); (question, dispute) contester; **to c. s.o. to a game** inviter qn à jouer; **to c. s.o. to a duel** provoquer qn en duel. ●**challenging** a (job) exigeant; (book) stimulant. ●**challenger** n (in sports) challenger m.

chamber ['tʃeɪmbər] n (room, assembly, hollow of gun etc) chambre f; **chambers** (of judge) Br cabinet m; **c. of commerce** chambre f de commerce; **c. music/orchestra** musique f/orchestre m de chambre; **c. pot** pot m de chambre. ●**chambermaid** n femme f de chambre.

chameleon [kəˈmiːliən] n caméléon m.

chamois [ˈʃæmi] n c. **(leather)** peau f de chamois.

champagne [ʃæmˈpeɪn] n champagne m.

champion [ˈtʃæmpiən] n champion, -onne mf; **c. skier, skiing c.** champion, -onne de ski ▮ vt (support) se faire le champion de (cause, personne etc). ●**championship** n championnat m.

chance [tʃɑːns] n (luck) hasard m; (possibility) chances fpl, possibilité f; (opportunity) occasion f; (risk) risque m; **by c.** par hasard; **by any c.** (possibly) par hasard; **to have the c. to do sth** or **of doing sth** avoir l'occasion de faire qch; **to give s.o.** (another) **c.** donner à qn une deuxième chance; **to take a c.** tenter le coup; **on the off c. (that) you could help me** au cas où tu pourrais m'aider. ▮ a (remark) fait au hasard; **c. meeting** rencontre f fortuite; **c. occurrence** événement m accidentel. ▮ vt **to c. doing** prendre le risque de faire; **to c. to find**/etc trouver/etc par hasard; **to c. it** risquer le coup ▮ v imp **it chanced that** (happened) il s'est trouvé que (+ indic).

chancel [ˈtʃɑːnsəl] n (in church) chœur m.

chancellor [ˈtʃɑːnsələr] n Pol etc chancelier m. ●**chancellery** n chancellerie f.

chandelier [ʃændəˈliər] n lustre m.

change [tʃeɪndʒ] n changement m; (money) monnaie f; **for a c.** pour changer; **it makes a c. from** ça change de; **to have a c. of heart** changer d'avis; **a c. of clothes** des vêtements de rechange. ▮ vt (modify) changer; (exchange) échanger (for contre); (money, wheel) changer; (transform) changer, transformer (qn, qch) (into en); **to c. trains/one's skirt**/etc changer de train/de jupe/etc; **to c. gear** (in vehicle) changer de vitesse; **to c. colour** changer de couleur; **to c. the subject** changer de sujet. ▮ vi (alter) changer; (change clothes) se changer; **to c. into** (be transformed) changer or se transformer en; **she changed into a dress** elle a mis une robe; **to c. over** passer (from de, to à). ●**changing** n the c. of the guard Br la relève de la garde; **c. room** vestiaire m.

changeable [ˈtʃeɪndʒəb(ə)l] a (weather, mood etc) changeant, variable.

changeover [ˈtʃeɪndʒəʊvər] n passage m (from de, to à).

channel [ˈtʃæn(ə)l] n (on television) chaîne f, canal m; (for irrigation) rigole f; (route for boats) chenal m; (groove) rainure f; (of inquiry etc) Fig voie f; **through the c. of** par le canal de; **to go through the usual channels** passer par la voie normale; **the C.** Geog la Manche; **the C. Tunnel** le tunnel sous la Manche; **the C. Islands** les îles anglo-normandes ▮ vt (Br **-ll-**, Am **-l-**) (energies, crowd, money etc) canaliser (into vers).

chant [tʃɑːnt] n (of demonstrators) chant m scandé; (religious) psalmodie f ▮ vt (slogan)

scander ▮ vi (of demonstrators) scander des slogans.

chaos [ˈkeɪɒs] n chaos m. ●**chaotic** a (room etc) sens dessus dessous; (situation, scene) chaotique.

chap [tʃæp] **1** n (fellow) Br Fam type m; **old c.!** mon vieux! **2** n (on skin) gerçure f ▮ vi (-pp-) se gercer ▮ vt gercer; **chapped hands/lips**/etc des mains/lèvres/etc gercées.

chapel [ˈtʃæp(ə)l] n chapelle f; (nonconformist church) temple m.

chaperon(e) [ˈʃæpərəʊn] n chaperon m ▮ vt chaperonner.

chaplain [ˈtʃæplɪn] n aumônier m.

chapter [ˈtʃæptər] n chapitre m.

char [tʃɑːr] **1** vt see **charred**. **2** n (cleaning woman) Br Fam femme f de ménage ▮ vi **to go charring** Br Fam faire des ménages. **3** n (tea) Br Sl thé m.

character [ˈkærɪktər] n **1** (of person, place etc) caractère m; (in book, film) personnage m; (strange person) numéro m; **c. actor** acteur m de genre. **2** (typographical) caractère m; **in bold characters** en caractères gras.

characteristic [kærɪktəˈrɪstɪk] a & n caractéristique (f). ●**characteristically** adv typiquement.

characterize [ˈkærɪktəraɪz] vt caractériser.

charade [Br ʃəˈrɑːd, Am ʃəˈreɪd] n (game) charade f (mimée); (travesty) parodie f, comédie f.

charcoal [ˈtʃɑːkəʊl] n charbon m (de bois); (crayon) fusain m, charbon m.

charge¹ [tʃɑːdʒ] n (in battle) charge f; (in court) accusation f; (responsibility) responsabilité f, charge f; (care) garde f; **to take c. of** prendre en charge; **to be in c. of** (child etc) avoir la garde de; (office etc) être responsable de; **the person in c.** le or la responsable; **who's in c. here?** qui commande ici?; **the battery is on c.** la batterie est en charge. ▮ vt (battery, soldiers) charger; (accuse) Jur accuser, inculper (with de). ▮ vi (rush) se précipiter; **c.!** Mil chargez! ●**charger** n (for battery) chargeur m.

charge² [tʃɑːdʒ] n (cost) prix m; **charges** (expenses) frais mpl; **there's a c. (for it)** c'est payant; **to make a c. for sth** faire payer qch; **free of c.** gratuit; **extra c.** supplément m; **c. card** carte f de clientèle ▮ vt (amount) demander (for pour); **to c. s.o.** faire payer qn; **to c. sth (up) to s.o.** mettre qch sur le compte de qn; **how much do you c.?** combien demandez-vous? ●**chargeable** a **c. to s.o.** aux frais de qn.

chariot [ˈtʃærɪət] n (Roman etc) char m.

charisma [kəˈrɪzmə] n charisme m.

charity [ˈtʃærɪtɪ] n (kindness, alms) charité f; (society) fondation f or œuvre f charitable; **to give to c.** faire la charité. ●**charitable** a charitable.

charlady [ˈtʃɑːleɪdɪ] n Br femme f de ménage.

charlatan [ˈʃɑːlətən] n charlatan m.

charm [tʃɑːm] n (*attractiveness, spell*) charme m; (*trinket*) breloque f ▌ vt charmer. ●**charming** a charmant. ●**charmingly** adv d'une façon charmante.

charred [tʃɑːd] a (*burnt until black*) carbonisé; (*scorched*) brûlé légèrement.

chart [tʃɑːt] n (*map*) carte f; (*table*) tableau m; (*graph*) graphique m; **temperature c.** courbe f or feuille f de température; (*pop*) **charts** hit-parade m ▌ vt (*route*) porter sur la carte; (*make a graph of*) faire le graphique de (*chiffres etc*); (*of graph*) montrer; (*observe*) suivre (attentivement) (*une évolution etc*).

charter [ˈtʃɑːtər] **1** n (*aircraft*) charter m; **the c. of** (*hiring*) l'affrètement m de; **c. flight** (vol m) charter m ▌ vt (*aircraft etc*) affréter. **2** n (*document*) charte f. ●**chartered accountant** n Br expert-comptable m.

charwoman [ˈtʃɑːwʊmən] n (*pl* -women) Br femme f de ménage.

chary [ˈtʃeərɪ] a (-ier, -iest) (*cautious*) prudent; **to be c. of doing** hésiter à faire.

chase [tʃeɪs] n poursuite f, chasse f; **to give c.** se lancer à la poursuite (**to** de) ▌ vt poursuivre; **to c. s.o. away** *or* **off** chasser qn; **to c. sth up** *Fam* essayer d'obtenir qch, rechercher qch ▌ vi **to c. after s.o./sth** courir après qn/qch.

chasm [ˈkæzəm] n abîme m, gouffre m.

chassis [*Br* ˈʃæsɪ, *Am* ˈtʃæsɪ] n (*of vehicle*) châssis m.

chaste [tʃeɪst] a chaste. ●**chastity** n chasteté f.

chasten [ˈtʃeɪs(ə)n] vt *Lit* (*punish*) châtier; (*cause to improve*) faire se corriger, assagir. ●**chastening** a (*experience*) instructif.

chastise [tʃæˈstaɪz] vt punir.

chat [tʃæt] n petite conversation f; **to have a c.** bavarder (**with** avec) ▌ vi (-tt-) causer, bavarder (**with** avec) ▌ vt **to c. s.o. up** *Br Fam* baratiner qn, draguer qn.

chatter [ˈtʃætər] vi (*of person*) bavarder; (*of birds, monkeys*) jacasser; **his teeth are chattering** il claque des dents ▌ n bavardage m; (*of birds etc*) jacassement m. ●**chatterbox** n bavard, -arde mf.

chatty [ˈtʃætɪ] a (-ier, -iest) (*person*) bavard; (*style*) familier; (*text*) plein de bavardages.

chauffeur [ˈʃəʊfər] n chauffeur m (de maître).

chauvinist [ˈʃəʊvɪnɪst] n & a chauvin, -ine (mf); (*male*) **c.** *Pej* macho m, phallocrate m.

cheap [tʃiːp] a (-er, -est) bon marché *inv*, pas cher; (*rate, fare*) réduit; (*worthless*) (*goods etc*) sans valeur; (*superficial*) (*emotion, remark*) facile; (*mean, petty*) mesquin; **cheaper** moins cher, meilleur marché; **to feel c.** (*humiliated*) se sentir humilié; (*ashamed*) avoir honte ▌ adv (*to buy*) (à) bon marché, au rabais ▌ n **on the c.** (à) bon marché. ●**cheaply** adv (à) bon marché. ●**cheapness** n bas prix m; (*meanness*) Fig mesquinerie f.

cheapen [ˈtʃiːpən] vt (*degrade*) avilir; (*disparage*) déprécier.

cheat [tʃiːt] vt (*deceive*) tromper; (*defraud*) frauder; **to c. s.o. out of sth** escroquer qch à qn; **to c. on** (*wife, husband*) faire une infidélité *or* des infidélités à ▌ vi (*at games etc*) tricher; (*defraud*) frauder ▌ n (*at games etc*) tricheur, -euse mf; (*crook*) escroc m. ●**cheating** n (*at games etc*) tricherie f; (*deceit*) tromperie f. ●**cheater** n *Am* = **cheat**.

check¹ [tʃek] a (*dress etc*) à carreaux ▌ n **c.** (*pattern*) carreaux mpl. ●**checked** a (*patterned*) à carreaux.

check² [tʃek] vt (*examine*) vérifier; (*inspect*) contrôler; (*mark off, Br tick*) cocher, pointer; (*stop*) arrêter, enrayer; (*restrain*) contenir, maîtriser; (*rebuke*) réprimander; (*baggage*) Am mettre à la consigne. ▌ vi vérifier; **to c. on sth** vérifier qch. ▌ n vérification f; (*inspection*) contrôle m; (*halt*) arrêt m; *Chess* échec m; (*curb*) frein m (**on** à); (*tick*) Am = croix f; (*receipt*) Am reçu m; (*bill in restaurant etc*) Am addition f; (*cheque*) Am chèque m; **to keep a c. on sth** contrôler qch; **to keep s.o. in c.** tenir qn en échec; **to put a c. on sth** mettre un frein à qch.

checkbook [ˈtʃekbʊk] n Am carnet m de chèques. ●**checking account** n compte m courant. ●**checklist** n liste f de contrôle. ●**checkmate** n *Chess* échec et mat m. ●**checkpoint** n contrôle m. ●**checkroom** n Am vestiaire m; (*left-luggage office*) Am consigne f.

checkered [ˈtʃekəd] a Am = **chequered**.

checkers [ˈtʃekəz] npl Am jeu m de dames. ●**checkerboard** n Am damier m.

check in vt (*luggage*) enregistrer ▌ vi (*at hotel*); (*arrive*) arriver; (*sign in*) signer le registre; (*at airport*) se présenter (à l'enregistrement), enregistrer ses bagages. ●**check-in** n (*at airport*) enregistrement m (des bagages). ▌ **to check off** vt (*names on list etc*) cocher ▌ **to check out** vt (*confirm*) confirmer ▌ vi (*at hotel*) régler sa note. ●**checkout** n (*in supermarket*) caisse f. ▌ **check up** vi vérifier, se renseigner. ●**check-up** n (*medical*) bilan m de santé; **to have a c.** passer un bilan de santé.

cheddar [ˈtʃedər] n (*cheese*) cheddar m.

cheek [tʃiːk] n joue f; (*impudence*) *Br Fig* culot m. ●**cheekbone** n pommette f. ●**cheeky** a (-ier, -iest) (*person, reply etc*) *Br* insolent, effronté.

cheep [tʃiːp] vi (*of bird*) piauler.

cheer¹ [tʃɪər] n **cheers** (*shouts*) acclamations fpl; **cheers!** *Fam* à votre santé! ▌ vt (*applaud*) acclamer; **to c. on** encourager; **to c. (up)** (*comfort*) donner du courage à (qn); (*amuse*) égayer (qn). ▌ vi applaudir; **to c. up** prendre courage; (*be amused*) s'égayer; **c. up!** (*du*) courage! ●**cheering** n (*shouts*) acclamations fpl ▌ a (*encouraging*) réjouissant.

cheer² [tʃɪər] n (*gaiety*) joie f; **good c.** (*food*) la bonne chère.

cheerful [ˈtʃɪəfəl] a gai. ●**cheerfully** adv

gaiement. ●**cheerless** a morne.
cheerio! [tʃɪəriˈəʊ] int Br salut!, au revoir!
cheese [tʃiːz] n fromage m; **c. board** plateau
m de fromages. ●**cheeseburger** n cheeseburger m. ●**cheesecake** n tarte f au fromage
blanc.
cheesed [tʃiːzd] a **to be c. (off)** Fam en avoir
marre (**with** de).
cheesy ['tʃiːzɪ] a (-ier, -iest) (shabby, bad)
Am Fam miteux.
cheetah ['tʃiːtə] n guépard m.
chef [ʃef] n (cook) chef m.
chemical a chimique ∎ n produit m chimique.
chemist ['kemɪst] n (pharmacist) Br pharmacien, -ienne mf; (scientist) chimiste mf; **c.'s
shop** Br pharmacie f. ●**chemistry** n chimie f.
chemotherapy [kiːməʊ'θerəpɪ] n chimiothérapie f; **to have a c.** faire de la chimiothérapie.
cheque [tʃek] n Br chèque m; **c. card** carte f
d'identité bancaire. ●**chequebook** n Br
carnet m de chèques.
chequered ['tʃekəd] a Br (pattern) à
carreaux; (career) qui connaît des hauts et
des bas; **c. flag** Sport drapeau m à damier.
cherish ['tʃerɪʃ] vt (hope) nourrir, caresser;
(person) chérir.
cherry ['tʃerɪ] n cerise f; **c. brandy** cherry m
∎ a **c.(-red)** cerise inv.
chess [tʃes] n échecs mpl. ●**chessboard** n
échiquier m.
chest [tʃest] n **1** (part of body) poitrine f. **2**
(box) coffre m; **c. of drawers** commode f.
chestnut ['tʃesnʌt] n châtaigne f; (cooked)
châtaigne f, marron m ∎ a **c. hair** cheveux
mpl châtains; **c. tree** châtaignier m.
chew [tʃuː] vt **to c. (up)** mâcher; **to c. over**
(plan, problem etc) Fig ruminer ∎ vi mastiquer; **chewing gum** chewing-gum m.
chick [tʃɪk] n poussin m; (girl) Am Fam
nana f.
chicken ['tʃɪkɪn] n **1** poulet m; **it's c. feed**
Fam c'est deux fois rien, c'est une bagatelle.
2 a (cowardly) Fam froussard ∎ vi **to c. out**
(avoid doing sth) Fam se dégonfler. ●**chick-
enpox** n varicelle f.
chickpea ['tʃɪkpiː] n pois m chiche.
chicory ['tʃɪkərɪ] n inv (for salad) endive f;
(in coffee etc) chicorée f.
chide [tʃaɪd] vt gronder.
chief [tʃiːf] n (boss) Fam patron m,
chef m; **commander/editor in c.** commandant
m/rédacteur m en chef ∎ a (main, highest in
rank) principal. ●**chiefly** adv principalement,
surtout. ●**chieftain** [-tən] n (of clan) chef m.
chilblain ['tʃɪlbleɪn] n engelure f.
child pl **children** [tʃaɪld, 'tʃɪldrən] n enfant
mf; **c. care** (for working parents) crèches fpl
et garderies fpl; **c. minder** Br nourrice f,
assistante f maternelle; **it's child's play**
(easy) c'est un jeu d'enfant.
childbearing ['tʃaɪldbeərɪŋ] n (motherhood)
maternité f; **of c. age** en âge de procréer.
●**childbirth** n accouchement m, couches fpl.

●**childhood** n enfance f. ●**childish** a puéril,
enfantin. ●**childishness** n puérilité f. ●**childlike** a naïf, innocent. ●**childproof** a (lock etc)
qui ne peut pas être ouvert par les enfants.
Chile ['tʃɪlɪ] n Chili m.
chill [tʃɪl] n froid m; (coldness in feelings)
froideur f; (illness) refroidissement m; **to
catch a c.** prendre froid ∎ vt (wine, melon)
faire rafraîchir; (meat) réfrigérer; **to c. s.o.**
(with fear, cold etc) faire frissonner qn (**with**
de); **to be chilled to the bone** être transi;
chilled wine vin m frais or frappé; **chilled
dessert** dessert m frais. ●**chilling** a (report,
thought etc) qui fait froid dans le dos.
chilli ['tʃɪlɪ] n (pl -ies) piment m (de
Cayenne).
chilly ['tʃɪlɪ] a (-ier, -iest) froid; (sensitive to
cold) frileux; **it's c.** il fait (un peu) froid.
chime [tʃaɪm] vi (of bell) carillonner; (of
clock) sonner; **to c. in** (interrupt) interrompre ∎ n carillon m; (of clock) sonnerie f.
chimney ['tʃɪmnɪ] n cheminée f. ●**chimney-
pot** n Br tuyau m de cheminée.
●**chimneysweep** n ramoneur m.
chimpanzee [tʃɪmpæn'ziː] n chimpanzé m.
chin [tʃɪn] n menton m.
china ['tʃaɪnə] n inv porcelaine f ∎ a en
porcelaine. ●**chinaware** n (objects) porcelaine f.
China ['tʃaɪnə] n Chine f. ●**Chi'nese** a chinois; **c. leaves** Br, **c. cabbage** Am chou m
chinois ∎ n inv (person) chinois, -oise mf;
(language) chinois m; (meal) Fam repas m
chinois; **to eat c.** Fam manger chinois.
chink [tʃɪŋk] n **1** (slit) fente f. **2** vi (of glasses
etc) tinter ∎ vt faire tinter ∎ n tintement m.
chip [tʃɪp] vt (-pp-) (cup, blade etc) ébrécher;
(table) abîmer; (paint) écailler; (cut) tailler
(pierre, marbre etc).
∎ vi **to c. in** Fam (contribute) contribuer;
(interrupt) mettre son grain de sel.
∎ n (splinter) éclat m; (break) ébréchure f;
(microchip) puce f; (counter) jeton m; **chips**
(French fries) Br frites fpl; (crisps) Am chips
fpl. ●**chipboard** n (bois m) aggloméré m.
●**chippings** npl **road** or **loose c.** gravillons
mpl.
chiropodist [kɪ'rɒpədɪst] n Br pédicure mf.
●**chiropody** n Br soins mpl du pied.
chirp [tʃɜːp] vi (of bird) pépier ∎ n pépiement m.
chirpy ['tʃɜːpɪ] a (-ier, -iest) gai, plein
d'entrain.
chisel ['tʃɪz(ə)l] n ciseau m ∎ vt (Br -ll-, Am
-l-) ciseler.
chit [tʃɪt] n (paper) note f, billet m.
chitchat ['tʃɪttʃæt] n bavardage m.
chivalry ['ʃɪvəlrɪ] n (courtesy) galanterie f;
(of medieval knights) chevalerie f. ●**chivalrous** a (man) galant.
chives [tʃaɪvz] npl ciboulette f.
chlorine ['klɔːriːn] n chlore m. ●**chlorinate** vt
chlorer; **chlorinated water** eau f chlorée.
chloroform ['klɒrəfɔːm] n chloroforme m.
choc-ice ['tʃɒkaɪs] n (ice cream) Br esqui-

mau m.

chock [tʃɒk] n (wedge) cale f ▌ vt caler.

chock-a-block [tʃɒkə'blɒk] Br or **chock-'full** a (room etc) Fam archiplein.

chocolate ['tʃɒklɪt] n chocolat m; **milk c.** chocolat au lait; Br **plain** or Am **bittersweet c.** chocolat à croquer; **drinking c.** chocolat m en poudre ▌ a (cake) au chocolat; (colour) chocolat inv; **c. egg** œuf m en chocolat. ● **chocolate-coated** a enrobé de chocolat.

choice [tʃɔɪs] n choix m; **from c., out of c.** de son propre choix; **I had no c.** je n'ai pas eu le choix ▌ a (goods) de choix.

choir ['kwaɪər] n chœur m. ● **choirboy** n jeune choriste m.

choke [tʃəʊk] **1** vt (person) étrangler, étouffer; (clog) boucher, engorger (tuyau); **to c. back** (sobs, tears etc) étouffer ▌ vi s'étrangler, étouffer; **to c. on** (fish bone etc) s'étrangler avec. **2** n (in vehicle) starter m. ● **choker** n (necklace) collier m (de chien).

cholera ['kɒlərə] n choléra m.

cholesterol [kə'lestərɒl] n cholestérol m; **c. level** taux m de cholestérol.

choose [tʃuːz] vt (pt **chose**, pp **chosen**) choisir; **to c. to do** (make a firm choice) choisir de faire; (decide) juger bon de faire ▌ vi choisir; **as I/you/etc c.** comme il me/vous/etc plaît.

choos(e)y ['tʃuːzɪ] a (-sier, -siest) difficile (about sur).

chop [tʃɒp] **1** n (of lamb, pork) côtelette f; **to lick one's chops** Fig s'en lécher les babines; **to get the c.** Br Sl être flanqué à la porte.
2 vt (-pp-) couper (à la hache); (food) hacher; **to c. down** (tree) abattre; **to c. off** (branch, finger etc) couper; **to c. up** couper en morceaux.
3 vi (-pp-) **to c. and change** changer constamment d'idées, de projets etc. ● **chopper** n hachoir m; (helicopter) Sl hélico m.

choppy ['tʃɒpɪ] a (sea, river) agité.

chopsticks ['tʃɒpstɪks] npl baguettes fpl (pour manger).

choral ['kɔːrəl] a choral; **c. society** chorale f. ● **chorister** ['kɒrɪstər] n choriste mf.

chord [kɔːd] n (in music) accord m.

chore [tʃɔːr] n travail m (routinier); (unpleasant) corvée f; (household) chores (travaux mpl du) ménage m; **to do the chores** faire le ménage.

choreographer [kɒrɪ'ɒgrəfər] n chorégraphe mf.

chortle ['tʃɔːt(ə)l] vi (laugh) glousser ▌ n gloussement m.

chorus ['kɔːrəs] n (part of song) refrain m; (singers) chœur m; (dancers) troupe f; **c. girl** girl f.

chose, chosen [tʃəʊz, 'tʃəʊz(ə)n] see **choose.**

chowder ['tʃaʊdər] n Am soupe f aux poissons or aux fruits de mer.

Christ [kraɪst] n Christ m. ● **Christian** ['krɪstʃən] a & n chrétien, -ienne (mf); **C. name** prénom m. ● **Christi'anity** n christia-

nisme m.

christen ['krɪs(ə)n] vt (baptize) baptiser (qn); (name) Fig baptiser (navire etc). ● **christening** n baptême m.

Christmas ['krɪsməs] n Noël m; **at C.** (time) à (la) Noël; **Merry** or **Happy C.** Joyeux Noël; **Father C.** le père Noël ▌ a (tree, card, day, party etc) de Noël; **C. box** Br étrennes fpl; **C. Eve** la veille de Noël.

chrome [krəʊm] or **chromium** n chrome m.

chromosome ['krəʊməsəʊm] n chromosome m.

chronic ['krɒnɪk] a (disease, state etc) chronique; (bad) Sl atroce.

chronicle ['krɒnɪk(ə)l] n chronique f ▌ vt faire la chronique de.

chronology [krə'nɒlədʒɪ] n chronologie f. ● **chrono'logical** a chronologique; **in c. order** par ordre chronologique.

chronometer [krə'nɒmɪtər] n chronomètre m.

chrysanthemum [krɪ'sænθəməm] n chrysanthème m.

chubby ['tʃʌbɪ] a (-ier, -iest) (person, hands etc) potelé; (cheeks) rebondi. ● **chubby-'cheeked** a joufflu.

chuck [tʃʌk] vt (throw) Fam jeter, lancer; **to c. (in)** or **(up)** (give up) Br Fam laisser tomber (travail etc); **to c. away** Fam (old clothes etc) balancer; (money) gaspiller; **to c. out** (old clothes, person etc) Fam balancer.

chuckle ['tʃʌk(ə)l] vi glousser, rire ▌ n gloussement m.

chuffed [tʃʌft] a Br Sl super content; (displeased) Iron pas heureux.

chug [tʃʌg] vi (-gg-) **to c. along** (of vehicle) avancer lentement (en faisant teuf-teuf).

chum [tʃʌm] n Fam copain m. ● **chummy** a (-ier, -iest) Fam amical; **c. with** copain avec.

chump [tʃʌmp] n (fool) crétin, -ine mf.

chunk [tʃʌŋk] n (gros) morceau m. ● **chunky** a (-ier, -iest) (person) Fam trapu; (coat, sweater, material etc) de grosse laine.

church [tʃɜːtʃ] n église f; (service) office m; (Catholic) messe f; **to go to c.** aller à l'église or à l'office; (of Catholic) aller à la messe; **in c.** à l'église; **c. hall** salle f paroissiale. ● **churchgoer** n pratiquant, -ante mf. ● **churchyard** n cimetière m.

churlish ['tʃɜːlɪʃ] a (rude) grossier; (bad-tempered) hargneux.

churn [tʃɜːn] **1** n (for making butter) baratte f; (milk can) bidon m. **2** vt **to c. out** Pej (cars, books etc) produire (en série).

chute [ʃuːt] n (in pool, playground) Br toboggan m; (for Br rubbish, Am garbage) vide-ordures m inv.

chutney ['tʃʌtnɪ] n condiment m épicé (à base de fruits).

CID [siːaɪ'diː] abbr (Criminal Investigation Department) Br = PJ f.

cider ['saɪdər] n cidre m.

cigar [sɪ'gɑːr] n cigare m.

cigarette [sɪgə'ret] n cigarette f; **c. end** mégot m; **c. holder** fume-cigarette m inv; **c.**

lighter briquet *m*.
cinch [sɪntʃ] *n* **it's a c.** *Fam* (*easy*) c'est facile; (*sure*) c'est (sûr et) certain.
cinder ['sɪndər] *n* cendre *f*; **burnt to a c.** (*meat etc*) carbonisé; **c. track** (*for running*) *Br* cendrée *f*.
Cinderella [sɪndə'relə] *n* Cendrillon *f*; *Fig* parent *m* pauvre.
cine-camera ['sɪnɪkæmrə] *n Br* caméra *f*.
cinema ['sɪnəmə] *n* (*art*) cinéma *m*; (*place*) *Br* cinéma *m*. ●**cinemagoer** *Br n* cinéphile *mf*. ●**cinemascope** *n* cinémascope *m*.
cinnamon ['sɪnəmən] *n* (*spice*) cannelle *f*.
cipher ['saɪfər] *n* (*code, number*) chiffre *m*; (*zero, person*) *Fig* zéro *m*.
circle ['sɜːk(ə)l] *n* (*shape, group, range etc*) cercle *m*; (*around eyes*) cerne *m*; *Theatre* balcon *m*; **circles** (*political etc*) milieux *mpl* ▮ *vt* (*move round*) faire le tour de; (*word etc*) encadrer ▮ *vi* (*of aircraft, bird*) décrire des cercles.
circuit ['sɜːkɪt] *n* (*electrical path, in sport, journey*) circuit *m*; (*of entertainers, Br judge*) tournée *f*; **c. breaker** *El* disjoncteur *m*. ●**circuitous** [sɜː'kjuːɪtəs] *a* (*route, means*) indirect. ●**circuitry** *n El* circuits *mpl*.
circular ['sɜːkjʊlər] *a* circulaire ▮ *n* (*letter*) circulaire *f*; (*advertisement*) prospectus *m*.
circulate ['sɜːkjʊleɪt] *vi* circuler ▮ *vt* faire circuler. ●**circulation** [-'leɪʃ(ə)n] *n* circulation *f*; (*of newspaper etc*) tirage *m*; **to be in c.** (*person*) *Fam* être dans le circuit.
circumcised ['sɜːkəmsaɪzd] *a* circoncis. ●**circumcision** [-'sɪʒ(ə)n] *n* circoncision *f*.
circumference [sɜː'kʌmfərəns] *n* circonférence *f*.
circumflex ['sɜːkəmfleks] *n & a* **c.** (*accent*) accent *m* circonflexe.
circumscribe ['sɜːkəmskraɪb] *vt* circonscrire.
circumspect ['sɜːkəmspekt] *a* circonspect.
circumstance ['sɜːkəmstæns] *n* circonstance *f*; **circumstances** (*financial*) situation *f* financière; **in or under no circumstances** en aucun cas. ●**circum'stantial** *a* **c. evidence** (*in court*) preuves *fpl* indirectes; **on c. evidence** (*to convict s.o.*) sur la base de preuves indirectes.
circumvent [sɜːkəm'vent] *vt* (*rule, law, difficulty etc*) contourner.
circus ['sɜːkəs] *n* cirque *m*.
cirrhosis [sɪ'rəʊsɪs] *n* (*disease*) cirrhose *f*.
CIS *abbr* (*Commonwealth of Independent States*) CEI *f*.
cistern ['sɪstən] *n* (*in house*) réservoir *m* (d'eau); (*for lavatory*) réservoir *m* (de la chasse d'eau).
citadel ['sɪtəd(ə)l] *n* citadelle *f*.
cite [saɪt] *vt* (*quote, commend*) citer. ●**citation** [saɪ'teɪʃ(ə)n] *n* citation *f*.
citizen ['sɪtɪz(ə)n] *n* citoyen, -enne *mf*; (*of town*) habitant, -ante *mf*; **Citizens' Band** (*Radio*) la CB. ●**citizenship** *n* citoyenneté *f*.
citrus ['sɪtrəs] *a* **c. fruit(s)** agrumes *mpl*.
city ['sɪtɪ] *n* (grande) ville *f*, cité *f*; **c. dweller**

citadin, -ine *mf*; **c. centre** centre-ville *m*; **c. hall** *Am* hôtel *m* de ville; **c. page** (*in newspaper*) *Br* rubrique *f* financière.
civic ['sɪvɪk] *a* (*duty*) civique; (*centre*) administratif; (*authorities*) municipal. ●**civics** *npl* (*social science*) instruction *f* civique.
civil ['sɪv(ə)l] *a* **1** (*rights, war, marriage etc*) civil; **c. defence** défense *f* passive; **c. servant** fonctionnaire *mf*; **c. service** fonction *f* publique. **2** (*polite*) civil. ●**ci'vility** *n* civilité *f*.
civilian [sɪ'vɪljən] *n & a* civil, -ile (*mf*).
civilize ['sɪvɪlaɪz] *vt* civiliser. ●**civilization** [-'zeɪʃ(ə)n] *n* civilisation *f*.
civvies ['sɪvɪz] *npl* **in c.** *Fam* (habillé) en civil.
clad [klæd] *a Lit* vêtu (**in** de).
claim [kleɪm] *vt* (*one's due etc*) réclamer, revendiquer; (*payment, benefit, reduction etc*) demander à bénéficier de; **to c. s.o.'s attention** demander l'attention de qn; **to c. that** (*assert*) prétendre que.
▮ *n* (*demand*) revendication *f*; (*statement*) affirmation *f*; (*complaint*) réclamation *f*; (*right*) droit *m* (**to** à); (*land claimed*) concession *f*; (*insurance*) c. demande *f* d'indemnité; **to lay c. to** prétendre à. ●**claimant** *n* (*entitled to social benefits*) *Br* demandeur, -euse *mf*, allocataire *mf*.
clairvoyant [kleə'vɔɪənt] *n* voyant, -ante *mf*.
clam [klæm] **1** *n* (*shellfish*) palourde *f*. **2** *vi* **to c. up** (*stop talking*) *Fam* se taire.
clamber ['klæmbər] *vi* **to c. (up)** grimper; **to c. up** (*stairs*) grimper; (*hill*) gravir.
clammy ['klæmɪ] *a* (*hands etc*) moite. (et froid).
clamour ['klæmər] (*Am* **clamor**) *n* clameur *f* ▮ *vi* **to c. for** demander à grands cris.
clamp [klæmp] *n* (*clip-like*) pince *f*; (*large, iron*) crampon *m*; (*in carpentry*) serre-joint(s) *m*; (*wheel*) **c.** (*for vehicle*) sabot *m* (de Denver) ▮ *vt* serrer; (*vehicle*) mettre un sabot à ▮ *vi* **to c. down** *Fam* sévir (**on** contre). ●**clampdown** *n Fam* coup *m* d'arrêt, restriction *f* (**on** à).
clan [klæn] *n* clan *m*.
clandestine [klæn'destɪn] *a* clandestin.
clang [klæŋ] *n* son *m* métallique.
clanger ['klæŋər] *n Br Sl* gaffe *f*; **to drop a c.** faire une gaffe.
clap [klæp] **1** *vti* (**-pp-**) (*applaud*) applaudir; **to c.** (*one's hands*) battre des mains ▮ *n* battement *m* (des mains); (*on back*) tape *f*; (*of thunder*) coup *m*. **2** *vt* (**-pp-**) (*put*) *Fam* fourrer. ●**clapped-'out** *a* (*car, person*) *Br Fam* HS *inv*. ●**clapping** *n* applaudissements *mpl*.
claptrap ['klæptræp] *n* (*nonsense*) *Fam* boniment(s) *m(pl)*; **to talk c.** raconter des boniments.
claret ['klærət] *n* (*wine*) bordeaux *m* rouge.
clarify ['klærɪfaɪ] *vt* clarifier. ●**clarification** [-ɪ'keɪʃ(ə)n] *n* clarification *f*.
clarinet [klærɪ'net] *n* clarinette *f*.
clarity ['klærətɪ] *n* (*of expression, argument etc*) clarté *f*; (*of sound*) pureté *f*; (*of water*)

transparence f.

clash [klæʃ] vi (of plates, pans) s'entrechoquer; (of interests, armies) se heurter; (of colours) jurer (with avec); (of people) se bagarrer; (coincide) tomber en même temps (with que) ∎ n (noise) choc m, heurt m; (of interests) conflit m; (of events) coïncidence f.

clasp [klɑːsp] vt (hold) serrer; to c. one's hands joindre les mains ∎ n (fastener) fermoir m; (of belt) boucle f.

class [klɑːs] n classe f; (lesson) cours m; (university grade) Br mention f; the c. of 1993 Am la promotion de 1993; to have c. avoir de la classe ∎ vt classer (as comme). • **classmate** n camarade mf de classe. • **classroom** n (salle f de) classe f.

classic ['klæsɪk] a classique ∎ n (writer, work etc) classique m; to study classics étudier les humanités fpl. • **classical** a classique. • **classicism** n classicisme m.

classify ['klæsɪfaɪ] vt classer, classifier. • **classified** a (information, document) secret; c. advertisement petite annonce f. • **classification** [-ɪ'keɪʃ(ə)n] n classification f.

classy ['klɑːsɪ] a (-ier, -iest) Fam chic inv.

clatter ['klætər] n bruit m, fracas m.

clause [klɔːz] n (in sentence) proposition f; (in legal document) clause f.

claustrophobia [klɔːstrə'fəʊbɪə] n claustrophobie f. • **claustrophobic** a (person) claustrophobe; (room, atmosphere) oppressant, qui rend claustrophobe.

claw [klɔː] n (of lobster) pince f; (of cat, sparrow etc) griffe f; (of eagle) serre f ∎ vt (scratch) griffer; to c. back (money etc) Pej Fam repiquer, récupérer.

clay [kleɪ] n argile f.

clean [kliːn] a (-er, -est) propre; (clear-cut) net (f nette); (joke) pour toutes les oreilles; (fair) (game of football etc) loyal; c. living vie f saine; a c. record (of suspect) un casier judiciaire vierge; to make a c. breast of it, come c. tout avouer.
∎ adv (utterly) complètement, carrément; to break c. (se) casser net; to cut c. couper net. ∎ n to give sth a c. nettoyer qch.
∎ vt nettoyer; (wash) laver; (wipe) essuyer; to c. one's teeth se brosser or se laver les dents; to c. out (room etc) nettoyer; (empty) vider (coffre, compte bancaire etc); to c. up (room etc) nettoyer; (reform) Fig épurer.
∎ vi to c. (up) faire le nettoyage. • **cleaning** n nettoyage m; (housework) ménage m; c. woman femme f de ménage. • **cleaner** n (in home) femme f de ménage; (dry) c. teinturier, -ière mf. • **cleanly** adv (to break, cut) net. • **cleanness** n propreté f.

clean-cut [kliːn'kʌt] a net (f nette). • **clean-'living** a honnête, chaste. • **clean-'shaven** a (with no beard or moustache) glabre; (closely shaven) rasé (de près). • **clean-up** n Fig purge f, coup m de balai.

cleanliness ['klenlɪnɪs] n propreté f.

cleanse [klenz] vt nettoyer; (soul, person etc) Fig purifier (of de); **cleansing cream** crème f démaquillante. • **cleanser** n (cream or lotion for skin) démaquillant m.

clear [klɪər] a (-er, -est) (sky, water, sound, thought etc) clair; (glass) transparent; (outline, photo) net (f nette), clair; (road) libre, dégagé; (majority) net (f nette); (mind) lucide; (obvious) évident, clair; (certain) certain; c. profit bénéfices mpl nets; to be c. of (free of) être libre de; (out of) être hors de; to make oneself (completely or abundantly) c. se faire (bien) comprendre; it is c. that il est évident or clair que; c. conscience conscience f nette or tranquille; two c. weeks (complete) deux semaines entières.
∎ adv to get c. away disparaître complètement; c. of (away from) à l'écart de; to keep or steer c. of se tenir à l'écart de; to get c. of (away from) s'éloigner de.
∎ vt (path, road, table) débarrasser, dégager; (land) défricher; (fence) franchir (sans toucher); (obstacle) éviter; (accused person) disculper; (Br cheque, Am check) faire passer (sur un compte); (debts, goods) liquider; (through customs) dédouaner; (for security) autoriser; to c. s.o. of suspicion laver qn de tout soupçon; to c. one's throat s'éclaircir la gorge.
∎ vi (of weather) s'éclaircir; (of fog) se dissiper. • **clearing** n (in woods) clairière f. • **clearly** adv clairement; (to understand) bien, clairement; (obviously) évidemment. • **clearness** n (of sound) clarté f, netteté f; (of mind) lucidité f.

clearance ['klɪərəns] n (sale) soldes mpl; (space) dégagement m; (permission) autorisation f; (of Br cheque, Am check) compensation f.

clear away vt (remove) enlever ∎ vi (of fog) se dissiper ∎ **to clear off** vi (leave) Fam filer ∎ vt (table) débarrasser ∎ **to clear out** vt (empty) vider; (clean) nettoyer; (remove) enlever ∎ **to clear up** vt (mystery etc) éclaircir; (tidy) ranger (pièce etc) ∎ vi (of weather) s'éclaircir; (of fog) se dissiper; (tidy a room etc) ranger.

clear-cut [klɪə'kʌt] a net (f nette). • **clear-'headed** a lucide.

clearway ['klɪəweɪ] n Br route f à stationnement interdit.

cleavage ['kliːvɪdʒ] n (split) clivage m; (of woman) Fam naissance f des seins.

clef [klef] n Mus clef f.

cleft [kleft] a c. palate palais m fendu ∎ n fissure f.

clement ['klemənt] a (person, weather etc) clément. • **clemency** n clémence f.

clementine ['kleməntaɪn] n clémentine f.

clench [klentʃ] vt to c. one's fist/teeth serrer le poing/les dents.

clergy ['klɜːdʒɪ] n clergé m. • **clergyman** n (pl -men) ecclésiastique m.

cleric ['klerɪk] n Rel clerc m. • **clerical** a (job) d'employé; (work) de bureau; (error) d'écriture; Rel clérical.

clerk [*Br* klɔːk, *Am* klɜːk] *n* employé, -ée *mf* (de bureau); (*in store*) *Am* vendeur, -euse *mf*; **solicitor's c.** *Br* clerc *m* de notaire; **c. of the court** greffier *m*.

clever ['klevər] *a* (**-er, -est**) intelligent; (*smart, shrewd*) astucieux; (*skilful*) habile (**at sth** à qch, **at doing** à faire); (*ingenious*) (*machine, plan etc*) ingénieux; (*gifted*) doué; **c. at English**/*etc* fort en anglais/*etc*; **c. with one's hands** habile or adroit de ses mains. ●**cleverly** *adv* intelligemment; (*ingeniously*) astucieusement; (*skilfully*) habilement. ●**cleverness** *n* intelligence *f*; (*ingenuity*) astuce *f*; (*skill*) habileté *f*.

cliché ['kliːʃeɪ] *n* (*idea*) cliché *m*.

click [klɪk] **1** *n* déclic *m*, bruit *m* sec ▌ *vi* faire un déclic; (*of lovers etc*) *Fam* se plaire du premier coup; **it suddenly clicked** (*I realized*) *Fam* j'ai compris tout à coup. **2** *vt* to **c. one's heels** (*of soldier*) claquer des talons; **to c. one's tongue** faire claquer sa langue.

client ['klaɪənt] *n* client, -ente *mf*. ●**clientele** [kliːən'tel] *n* clientèle *f*.

cliff [klɪf] *n* falaise *f*.

climate ['klaɪmɪt] *n* (*weather, Fig conditions*) climat *m*; **c. of opinion** opinion *f* générale. ●**cli'matic** *a* (*changes etc*) climatique.

climax ['klaɪmæks] *n* point *m* culminant; (*sexual*) orgasme *m* ▌ *vi* atteindre son point culminant; (*sexually*) atteindre l'orgasme.

climb [klaɪm] *vt* to **c. (up)** (*steps*) monter, gravir; (*hill, mountain*) gravir, faire l'ascension de; (*tree, ladder*) monter à, grimper à; **to c. (over)** (*wall*) escalader; **to c. down (from)** (*wall, tree, hill etc*) descendre de.

▌ *vi* (*of plant*) grimper; to **c. (up)** (*up steps, tree etc*) monter; (*up hill etc*) gravir; to **c. down** descendre; (*back down*) *Fig* en rabattre.

▌ *n* montée *f*. ●**climbing** *n* montée *f*; (**mountain**) **c.** alpinisme *m*; (**rock-**)**c.** varappe *f*. ●**climber** *n* grimpeur, -euse *mf*; (*mountaineer*) alpiniste *mf*; (*on rocks*) varappeur, -euse *mf*; (*plant*) plante *f* grimpante; **social c.** arriviste *mf*.

climb-down ['klaɪmdaʊn] *n* reculade *f*.

clinch [klɪntʃ] *vt* (*deal, bargain*) conclure; (*argument*) consolider.

cling [klɪŋ] *vt* (*pt & pp* **clung**) se cramponner, s'accrocher (**to** à); (*stick*) adhérer (**to** à). ●**clinging** *a* (*clothes*) collant.

clingfilm ['klɪŋfɪlm] *n Br* film *m* plastique.

clinic ['klɪnɪk] *n* (*private*) *Br* clinique *f*; (*health centre*) centre *m* médical. ●**clinical** *a Med* clinique; (*attitude etc*) *Fig* scientifique, objectif.

clink [klɪŋk] *vi* tinter ▌ *vt* faire tinter ▌ *n* tintement *m*.

clip [klɪp] **1** *vt* (**-pp-**) (*cut*) couper; (*hedge*) tailler; (*ticket*) poinçonner; (*sheep*) tondre; **to c. sth out of** (*newspaper etc*) découper qch dans.

2 *n* (*for paper*) trombone *m*; (*fastener*) attache *f*; (*of brooch, of cyclist, for hair*)

pince *f* ▌ *vt* (**-pp-**) **to c. (on)** (*attach*) attacher (**to** à); **to c. together** attacher.

3 *n* (*of film*) extrait *m*; (*blow*) *Br Fam* taloche *f*. ●**clipping** *n* (*newspaper article*) *Am* coupure *f*. ●**clippers** *npl* (*for hair*) tondeuse *f*; (*for finger nails*) coupe-ongles *m inv*.

clique [kliːk] *n Pej* clique *f*. ●**cliquey** *a Pej* (*group of people etc*) très fermé.

cloak [kləʊk] *n* (*grande*) cape *f*; (*of night*) *Fig* manteau *m*; **c. and dagger** (*film etc*) d'espionnage. ●**cloakroom** *n* vestiaire *m*; (*lavatory*) *Br* toilettes *fpl*.

clobber ['klɒbər] **1** *vt* (*hit*) *Sl* tabasser. **2** *n* (*clothes*) *Br Sl* affaires *fpl*.

clock [klɒk] *n* (*large*) horloge *f*; (*small*) pendule *f*; (*in vehicle*) *Br* compteur *m*; (**alarm**) **c.** réveil *m*; **a race against the c.** une course contre la montre; **round the c.** vingt-quatre heures sur vingt-quatre; **c. radio** radio-réveil *m*; **c. tower** clocher *m*.

▌ *vt* (*athlete etc*) chronométrer; **to c. up** (*miles*) (*in car*) *Fam* faire.

▌ *vi* **to c. in** or **out** (*of worker*) pointer. ●**clockwise** *adv* dans le sens des aiguilles d'une montre.

clockwork ['klɒkwɜːk] *a* (*toy etc*) mécanique ▌ *n* **to go like c.** aller or marcher comme sur des roulettes.

clod [klɒd] *n* **1** (*of earth*) motte *f*. **2** (*oaf*) *Fam* balourd *m*, -ourde *mf*.

clog [klɒg] **1** *n* (*shoe*) sabot *m*. **2** *vt* (**-gg-**) **to c. (up)** (*obstruct*) boucher (*tuyau etc*).

cloister ['klɔɪstər] *n* cloître *m* ▌ *vt* cloîtrer.

close¹ [kləʊs] *a* (**-er, -est**) (*place, relative etc*) proche; (*collaboration, resemblance, connection*) étroit; (*friend*) intime; (*contest*) serré; (*study*) rigoureux; **the weather is c., it's c.** *Br* il fait lourd; **it's c. in this room** cette pièce est mal aérée; **c. vowel** *Ling* voyelle *f* fermée; **c. to** (*near*) près de, proche de; **c. to tears** au bord des larmes; **I'm not very c. to her** (*friendly with*) je ne suis pas très proche d'elle; **to have a c. shave** or **call** l'échapper belle.

▌ *adv* **c. (by), c. at hand** (*tout*) près; **c. to** près de; **c. behind** juste derrière; **c. on** (*almost*) *Fam* pas loin de; **we stood/sat c. together** nous étions debout/assis serrés les uns contre les autres; **to follow c.** suivre de près; **to hold s.o. c.** tenir qn contre soi. ●**close-'cropped** *a* (*hair*) (*coupé*) ras. ●**close-fitting** *a* (*clothes*) ajusté. ●**close-'knit** *a* (*group, family etc*) très uni. ●**close-up** *n* gros plan *m*.

close² [kləʊz] *n* (*end*) fin *f*, conclusion *f*; **to bring to a c.** mettre fin à; **to draw to a c.** tirer à sa fin.

▌ *vt* (*door, shop etc*) fermer; (*discussion*) clore, terminer; (*opening*) boucher; (*road*) barrer; (*gap*) réduire; (*deal*) conclure; (*bank account*) clore, fermer; **to c. the meeting** lever la séance; **to c. ranks** serrer les rangs.

▌ *vi* se fermer; (*end*) se terminer; (*of shop*) fermer; (*of wound*) se refermer.

closed [kləʊzd] *a* (*door, shop etc*) fermé; **c.-**

circuit television télévision *f* en circuit fermé.
close down *vti* (*close for good*) fermer (définitivement) ▮ *vi* (*of TV station*) terminer les émissions. ●**close-down** *n* fermeture *f* (définitive); *TV* fin *f* (des émissions). ▮ **to close in** *vt* (*enclose*) enfermer ▮ *vi* (*approach*) approcher; **to c. in on s.o.** se rapprocher de qn ▮ **to close up** *vt* fermer ▮ *vi* (*of shop-keeper*) fermer; (*of wound*) se refermer; (*of line of people*) se resserrer.

closely ['kləʊslɪ] *adv* (*to follow, guard*) de près; (*to listen*) attentivement; **c. linked** étroitement lié (**to** à); **c. contested** très disputé; **to hold s.o. c.** tenir qn contre soi. ●**closeness** *n* proximité *f*; (*of collaboration etc*) étroitesse *f*; (*of friendship*) intimité *f*; (*of weather*) *Br* lourdeur *f*.

closet ['klɒzɪt] *n* *Am* (*cupboard*) placard *m*; (*wardrobe*) penderie *f*.

closing ['kləʊzɪŋ] *n* fermeture *f*; (*of session*) clôture *f* ▮ *a* (*words, remarks*) dernier; **c. speech** discours *m* de clôture; **c. date** (*for application etc*) date *f* limite; **c. time** heure *f* de fermeture.

closure ['kləʊʒər] *n* fermeture *f*.

clot [klɒt] **1** *n* (*of blood*) caillot *m* ▮ *vt* (-tt-) (*blood*) coaguler ▮ *vi* (*of blood*) se coaguler. **2** *n* (*person*) *Br* *Fam* imbécile *mf*.

cloth [klɒθ] *n* tissu *m*, étoffe *f*; (*of linen*) toile *f*; (*of wool*) drap *m*; (*for dusting*) chiffon *m*; (*for dishes*) torchon *m*; (*table-cloth*) nappe *f*.

clothe [kləʊð] *vt* habiller, vêtir (**in** de). ●**clothing** *n* (*clothes*) vêtements *mpl*; **an article of c.** un vêtement.

clothes [kləʊðz] *npl* vêtements *mpl*; **to put one's c. on** s'habiller; **to take one's c. off** se déshabiller; **c. shop** magasin *m* d'habillement; **c. brush** brosse *f* à habits; **c. peg** *Br*, **c. pin** *Am* pince *f* à linge; **c. line** corde *f* à linge.

cloud [klaʊd] *n* nuage *m*; (*of arrows, insects*) *Fig* nuée *f* ▮ *vt* (*mind*) obscurcir; (*window*) embuer; **to c. the issue** embrouiller la question ▮ *vi* **to c.** (**over**) (*of sky*) se couvrir. ●**cloudburst** *n* averse *f*. ●**cloudy** *a* (-ier, -iest) (*weather, sky*) couvert, nuageux; (*liquid*) trouble; **it's c., it's a c. day** le temps est couvert.

clout [klaʊt] **1** *n* (*blow*) *Fam* taloche *f* ▮ *vt* *Fam* flanquer une taloche à, talocher. **2** *n* (*influence*) *Fam* influence *f*, pouvoir *m*, poids *m*; **to have** (**plenty of**) **c.** avoir du poids.

clove [kləʊv] *n* clou *m* de girofle; **c. of garlic** gousse *f* d'ail.

clover ['kləʊvər] *n* trèfle *m*.

clown [klaʊn] *n* clown *m* ▮ *vi* **to c.** (**around** *or* **about**) faire le clown.

cloying ['klɔɪɪŋ] *a* (*smell, sentiments*) écœurant.

club [klʌb] **1** *n* (*weapon*) matraque *f*, massue *f*; (*golf*) **c.** (*stick*) club *m* ▮ *vt* (-bb-) matraquer. **2** *n* (*society*) club *m*, cercle *m* ▮ *vi* (-bb-) **to c. together** *Br* se cotiser (**to buy sth**

pour acheter qch). **3** *n* **club(s)** *Cards* trèfle *m*. ●**clubhouse** *n* pavillon *m*. ●**club soda** *n* *Am* eau *f* gazeuse.

clubfoot ['klʌbfʊt] *n* pied *m* bot. ●**club'footed** *a* pied-bot *inv*.

cluck [klʌk] *vi* (*of hen*) glousser.

clue [kluː] *n* indice *m*; (*of crossword*) définition *f*; (*to mystery*) clef *f*; **I don't have a c.** *Fam* je n'en ai pas la moindre idée. ●**clueless** *a* *Br* *Fam* stupide, nul (*f* nulle).

clump [klʌmp] *n* (*of flowers, trees*) massif *m*.

clumsy ['klʌmzɪ] *a* (-ier, -iest) maladroit; (*shape*) lourd; (*tool*) peu commode. ●**clumsily** *adv* maladroitement. ●**clumsiness** *n* maladresse *f*.

clung [klʌŋ] *see* cling.

cluster ['klʌstər] *n* groupe *m*; (*of flowers*) grappe *f*; (*of stars*) amas *m* ▮ *vi* se grouper.

clutch [klʌtʃ] **1** *vt* (*hold tight*) serrer, étreindre; (*cling to*) se cramponner à; (*grasp*) saisir ▮ *vi* **to c.** at essayer de saisir ▮ *n* **to fall into/escape from s.o.'s clutches** tomber dans les griffes/s'échapper des griffes de qn. **2** *n* (*in vehicle*) embrayage *m*; (*pedal*) pédale *f* d'embrayage; **to let in/out the c.** embrayer/débrayer.

clutter ['klʌtər] *n* (*objects*) fouillis *m*, désordre *m* ▮ *vt* **to c.** (**up**) (*room, table etc*) encombrer (**with** de).

cm *abbr* (*centimetre*) cm.

co- [kəʊ] *pref* co-.

c/o *abbr* (*care of*) (*on envelope*) chez.

Co *abbr* (*company*) Cie.

coach [kəʊtʃ] **1** *n* (*train carriage*) *Br* voiture *f*, wagon *m*; (*bus*) *Br* autocar *m*; (*horse-drawn*) carrosse *m*. **2** *n* (*private tutor*) répétiteur, -trice *mf*; (*for sports*) entraîneur, -euse *mf* ▮ *vt* (*pupil*) donner des leçons (particulières) à; (*sportsman etc*) entraîner; **to c. s.o. for** (*exam*) préparer qn à. ●**coachman** *n* (*pl* -men) cocher *m*.

coagulate [kəʊˈægjʊleɪt] *vi* (*of blood*) se coaguler ▮ *vt* coaguler.

coal [kəʊl] *n* charbon *m*; (*for industrial purposes*) houille *f* ▮ *a* (*merchant, fire*) de charbon; (*cellar, bucket*) à charbon; **c. industry** industrie *f* houillère. ●**coalfield** *n* bassin *m* houiller. ●**coalmine** *n* mine *f* de charbon. ●**coalminer** *n* mineur *m*.

coalition [kəʊəˈlɪʃ(ə)n] *n* coalition *f*.

coarse [kɔːs] *a* (-er, -est) (*person, manners*) grossier, vulgaire; (*surface*) rude; (*fabric*) grossier; (*accent*) commun, vulgaire; **c. salt** gros sel *m*. ●**coarsely** *adv* grossièrement. ●**coarseness** *n* grossièreté *f*; (*of accent*) vulgarité *f*.

coast [kəʊst] **1** *n* côte *f*; **the c. is clear** la voie est libre. **2** *vi* (*down or along*) (*of vehicle, bicycle*) descendre en roue libre. ●**coastal** *a* côtier. ●**coastguard** *n* (*person*) garde *m* maritime, garde-côte *m*. ●**coastline** *n* littoral *m*.

coaster ['kəʊstər] *n* (*for glass etc*) dessous *m* de verre, rond *m*; (*ship*) caboteur *m*.

coat [kəʊt] *n* manteau *m*; (*overcoat*)

pardessus *m*; (*jacket*) veste *f*; (*of animal*) pelage *m*; (*of paint*) couche *f*; (*of arms* armoiries *fpl*, blason *m* ▌ *vt* couvrir, enduire (**with** de); (*with chocolate etc*) enrober (**with** de); **to have a coated tongue** avoir la langue chargée. ● **coating** *n* couche *f*.

coathanger ['kəʊthæŋər] *n* cintre *m*.

coax [kəʊks] *vt* amadouer, cajoler; **to c. s.o. to do** *or* **into doing** amadouer qn pour qu'il fasse; **she needed coaxing** elle s'est bien fait tirer l'oreille. ● **coaxing** *n* cajoleries *fpl*.

cob [kɒb] *n* **corn on the c.** épi *m* de maïs.

cobble ['kɒb(ə)l] *n* pavé *m* ▌ *vt* **to c. together** (*text, compromise etc*) *Fam* bricoler. ● **cobbled** *a* pavé. ● **cobblestone** *n* pavé *m*.

cobbler ['kɒblər] *n* cordonnier *m*.

cobra ['kəʊbrə] *n* (*snake*) cobra *m*.

cobweb ['kɒbweb] *n* toile *f* d'araignée.

Coca-Cola® [kəʊkə'kəʊlə] *n* Coca-Cola® *m*.

cocaine [kəʊ'keɪn] *n* cocaïne *f*.

cock [kɒk] **1** *n* (*rooster*) coq *m*; (*male bird*) (*oiseau m*) mâle *m*. **2** *vt* (*gun*) armer; **to c. (up) one's ears** (*listen carefully*) dresser l'oreille. ● **cock-a-doodle-'doo** *n & int* cocorico (*m*). ● **cock-and-bull story** *n* histoire *f* à dormir debout.

cockatoo [kɒkə'tuː] *n* (*bird*) cacatoès *m*.

cocker ['kɒkər] *n* **c. (spaniel)** cocker *m*.

cockerel ['kɒkərəl] *n* coquelet *m*, jeune coq *m*.

cock-eyed [kɒk'aɪd] *a Fam* **1** (*cross-eyed*) bigleux. **2** (*crooked*) (*picture etc*) de travers. **3** (*crazy*) (*plan, idea etc*) absurde, stupide.

cockle ['kɒk(ə)l] *n* (*shellfish*) coque *f*.

cockney ['kɒknɪ] *a & n* cockney (*mf*) (*natif des quartiers est de Londres*).

cockpit ['kɒkpɪt] *n* (*of aircraft*) poste *m* de pilotage.

cockroach ['kɒkrəʊtʃ] *n* (*beetle*) cafard *m*.

cocksure [kɒk'ʃʊər] *a Fam* trop sûr de soi.

cocktail ['kɒkteɪl] *n* (*drink*) cocktail *m*; (*fruit*) **c.** macédoine *f* (de fruits); **c. party** cocktail *m*; **prawn c.** crevettes *fpl* à la mayonnaise.

cocky ['kɒkɪ] *a* (**-ier, -iest**) *Fam* trop sûr de soi, arrogant.

cocoa ['kəʊkəʊ] *n* cacao *m*.

coconut ['kəʊkənʌt] *n* noix *f* de coco; **c. palm** cocotier *m*.

cocoon [kə'kuːn] *n* cocon *m*.

cod [kɒd] *n* morue *f*; (*bought fresh*) cabillaud *m*. ● **cod-liver 'oil** *n* huile *f* de foie de morue.

COD [siːəʊ'diː] *Br abbr* (*cash on delivery*) contre remboursement.

coddle ['kɒd(ə)l] *vt* dorloter.

code [kəʊd] *n* code *m*; **in c.** (*letter, message etc*) codé; **c. word** code *m* ▌ *vt* coder. ● **coding** *n* codage *m*.

codeine ['kəʊdiːn] *n* codéine *f*.

codify ['kəʊdɪfaɪ] *vt* codifier.

co-educational [kəʊedjuː'keɪʃən(ə)l] *a* (*school, teaching*) mixte.

coefficient [kəʊɪ'fɪʃənt] *n* (*number*) *Math* coefficient *m*.

coerce [kəʊ'ɜːs] *vt* contraindre (**s.o. into doing** qn à faire). ● **coercion** [-ʃ(ə)n] *n* contrainte *f*.

coexist [kəʊɪg'zɪst] *vi* coexister. ● **coexistence** *n* coexistence *f*.

coffee ['kɒfɪ] *n* café *m*; **white c.** *Br*, **c. with milk** *Am* café *m* au lait; (*ordered in restaurant etc*) (café *m*) crème *m*; **black c.** café *m* noir, café nature; **c. bar** *Br*, **c. house** café *m*, cafétéria *f*; **c. break** pause-café *f*; **c. cup** tasse *f* à café; **c. table** table *f* basse ▌ *a* **c.(-coloured)** café au lait *inv*. ● **coffeepot** *n* cafetière *f*.

coffers ['kɒfəz] *npl* (*funds*) coffres *mpl*.

coffin ['kɒfɪn] *n* cercueil *m*.

cog [kɒg] *n* (*tooth of wheel*) dent *f*; (*person*) *Fig* rouage *m*.

cogent ['kəʊdʒənt] *a* (*reason, argument*) puissant, convaincant.

cogitate ['kɒdʒɪteɪt] *vi Iron* cogiter.

cognac ['kɒnjæk] *n* cognac *m*.

cohabit [kəʊ'hæbɪt] *vi* (*of unmarried people*) vivre en concubinage.

coherent [kəʊ'hɪərənt] *a* (*logical*) (*idea etc*) cohérent; (*way of speaking*) compréhensible, intelligible; **you're not very c.** tu n'es pas très clair. ● **cohesion** [-ʒ(ə)n] *n* cohésion *f*. ● **cohesive** *a* cohésif.

cohort ['kəʊhɔːt] *n* (*group*) cohorte *f*.

coil [kɔɪl] *n* (*of wire, rope etc*) rouleau *m*; (*single loop*) (*of hair*) boucle *f*; (*of snake*) anneau *m*; (*electrical*) bobine *f*; (*contraceptive*) stérilet *m* ▌ *vt* (*rope, hair, hose*) enrouler ▌ *vi* (*of snake etc*) s'enrouler (**around** autour de).

coin [kɔɪn] *n* pièce *f* (de monnaie); (*currency*) monnaie *f*; **c. bank** *Am* tirelire *f* ▌ *vt* (*money*) frapper; (*word*) *Fig* inventer, forger; **to c. a phrase** pour ainsi dire. ● **coinage** *n* (*coins*) monnaie *f*; *Fig* invention *f*; **a recent c.** (*word*) un mot de formation récente. ● **coin-operated** *a* (*washing machine etc*) automatique, à pièces.

coincide [kəʊɪn'saɪd] *vi* coïncider (**with** avec). ● **co'incidence** *n* coïncidence *f*. ● **coinci'dental** *a* (*resemblance etc*) fortuit; **it's c.** c'est une coïncidence.

coke [kəʊk] *n* **1** (*fuel*) coke *m*. **2** (*Coca-Cola®*) coca *m*.

colander ['kʌləndər] *n* (*for vegetables etc*) passoire *f*.

cold¹ [kəʊld] *n* froid *m*; **to catch c.** prendre froid; **to be out in the c.** être dehors dans le froid; **to be left out in the c.** *Fig* être abandonné *or* en carafe.
▌ *a* (**-er, -est**) froid; **to be** *or* **feel c.** (*of person*) avoir froid; **my hands are c.** j'ai froid aux mains; **it's c.** (*of weather*) il fait froid; **to get c.** (*of weather*) se refroidir; (*of food*) refroidir; **I'm getting c.** je commence à avoir froid; **to get c. feet** *Fam* se dégonfler; **in c. blood** de sang-froid; **c. cream** crème *f* de beauté; **c. meats** *Br*, **c. cuts** *Am* assiette *f* anglaise; **c. sore** bouton *m* de fièvre. ● **coldly** *adv* avec froideur. ● **coldness** *n* froideur *f*.

cold² [kəʊld] n (illness) rhume m; **a bad** or **nasty c.** un gros rhume; **to have a c.** être enrhumé; **to catch a c.** attraper un rhume; **to get a c.** s'enrhumer.

cold-blooded ['kəʊldblʌdɪd] a (person) cruel, insensible; (murder) (commis) de sang-froid.

cold-shoulder [kəʊld'ʃəʊldər] vt snober.

coleslaw ['kəʊlslɔ:] n salade f de chou cru.

colic ['kɒlɪk] n (illness) coliques fpl.

collaborate [kə'læbəreɪt] vi collaborer (on à). ●**collaboration** [-'reɪʃ(ə)n] n collaboration f. ●**collaborator** n collaborateur, -trice mf.

collage ['kɒlɑ:ʒ] n (picture) collage m.

collapse [kə'læps] vi (of person, building) s'effondrer, s'écrouler; (of government) tomber; (faint) se trouver mal █ n effondrement m, écroulement m; (of government) chute f. ●**collapsible** a (chair etc) pliant.

collar ['kɒlər] n (on garment) col m; (of dog) collier m; **to seize s.o. by the c.** saisir qn au collet █ vt Fam (seize) saisir (qn) au collet; (buttonhole) retenir (qn); (take, steal) piquer (qch). ●**collarbone** n clavicule f.

collate [kə'leɪt] vt (documents etc) (gather) rassembler; (compare) collationner, confronter; (pages) collationner.

colleague ['kɒli:g] n collègue mf, confrère m.

collect [kə'lekt] vt (pick up) ramasser; (gather) rassembler, recueillir; (taxes) percevoir; (rent) encaisser; (stamps etc as hobby) collectionner; (call for) (passer) prendre; **to c. money** (in street, church etc) quêter.
█ vi (of dust) s'accumuler; (of people) se rassembler; (in street, church) quêter (for pour).
█ adv **to call** or **phone c.** Am téléphoner en PCV.

collection [kə'lekʃ(ə)n] n (of objects, stamps) collection f; (of poems etc) recueil m; (of money in church etc) quête f; (of mail) levée f; (of taxes) perception f; (of twigs, Br rubbish or Am garbage etc) ramassage m.

collective [kə'lektɪv] a collectif. ●**collectively** adv collectivement.

collector [kə'lektər] n (of stamps etc) collectionneur, -euse mf.

college ['kɒlɪdʒ] n (university) université f; (within university) collège m; Pol Rel collège m; **c. of music** conservatoire m de musique; **c. of education, teachers' training e.** Br = institut m de formation des maîtres; **art c.** école f des beaux-arts; **agricultural c.** institut m d'agronomie, lycée m agricole; **technical c.** Br = lycée m technique.

collide [kə'laɪd] vi entrer en collision (with avec), se heurter (with à). ●**collision** [-'lɪʒ(ə)n] n (crash) collision f; (clash) Fig conflit m, collision f.

colliery ['kɒlɪərɪ] n Br houillère f.

colloquial [kə'ləʊkwɪəl] a (word etc) familier. ●**colloquialism** n expression f familière.

collusion [kə'lu:ʒ(ə)n] n collusion f; **to be in c. with** être de collusion avec.

collywobbles ['kɒlɪwɒb(ə)lz] npl **to have the c.** (feel nervous) Fam avoir la frousse.

cologne [kə'ləʊn] n eau f de Cologne.

colon ['kəʊlən] n **1** (punctuation mark) deux-points m inv. **2** (intestine) côlon m.

colonel ['kɜ:n(ə)l] n colonel m.

colonial [kə'ləʊnɪəl] a colonial.

colonize ['kɒlənaɪz] vt coloniser. ●**colonization** [-'zeɪʃ(ə)n] n colonisation f.

colony ['kɒlənɪ] n colonie f.

colossal [kə'lɒs(ə)l] a colosse.

colour ['kʌlər] (Am **color**) n couleur f █ a (photo, television) en couleurs; (television set) couleur inv, en couleurs; (problem) racial; **c. supplement** (of newspaper) supplément m illustré; **off c.** (not well) Br mal fichu; (improper) (joke etc) Am déplacé, scabreux █ vt colorer; **to c. (in)** (drawing) colorier. ●**coloured** a (person, pencil) de couleur; (glass, water) coloré. ●**colouring** n (in food) colorant m; (complexion) teint m; (with crayons) coloriage m; (shade, effect) coloris m; (blend of colours) couleurs fpl; **c. book** album m de coloriages.

colour-blind ['kʌləblaɪnd] a daltonien. ●**colour-blindness** n daltonisme m.

colourfast ['kʌləfɑ:st] a grand teint inv.

colourful ['kʌləf(ə)l] a (crowd, story) coloré; (person) pittoresque.

colt [kəʊlt] n (horse) poulain m.

column ['kɒləm] n colonne f; (newspaper feature) chronique f. ●**columnist** n (in newspaper) chroniqueur m; **gossip c.** échotier, -ière mf.

coma ['kəʊmə] n coma m; **in a c.** dans le coma.

comb [kəʊm] n peigne m █ vt (hair) peigner; (search) Fig ratisser (ville etc); **to c. one's hair** se peigner.

combat ['kɒmbæt] n combat m █ vti combattre (for pour). ●**combatant** n combattant, -ante mf.

combine¹ [kəm'baɪn] vt (activities, qualities, features, elements, sounds etc) combiner; (efforts) joindre, unir; **our combined efforts have produced a result** en joignant nos efforts nous avons obtenu un résultat; **combined wealth/etc** (put together) richesses/ etc fpl réunies; **combined forces** Mil forces fpl alliées.
█ vi (of teams, groups etc) s'unir; (of elements) se combiner; (of gases etc) s'associer; **everything combined to...** tout s'est ligué pour.... ●**combination** [-'neɪʃ(ə)n] n combinaison f; (of qualities) réunion f; (of events) concours m; **in c. with** en association avec; **c. lock** serrure f à combinaison.

combine² ['kɒmbaɪn] n **1** (commercial) association f; (cartel) cartel m. **2** **c. harvester** (machine) moissonneuse-batteuse f.

combustion [kəm'bʌstʃ(ə)n] n combustion f.

come [kʌm] *vi* (*pt* came, *pp* come) venir (**from** de, **to** à); **to c. first** (*in race*) arriver premier; (*in exam*) être le premier; **c. and see me** viens me voir; **I've just c. from** j'arrive de; **to c. home** rentrer; **coming!** j'arrive!; **c. now!** voyons!; **to c. as a surprise (to)** surprendre; **to c. near** *or* **close to doing** faillir faire; **to c. on page 2** se trouver à la page 2; **nothing came of it** ça n'a abouti à rien; **to c. true** se réaliser; **c. May/etc** *Fam* en mai/etc; **the life to c.** la vie future; **how c. that...?** *Fam* comment se fait-il que...?; **c. what may** quoi qu'il arrive.

come about *vi* (*happen*) se faire, arriver ▮ **to come across** *vi* (*of speech*) faire de l'effet; (*of feelings*) se montrer ▮ *vt* (*person*) rencontrer (par hasard), tomber sur; (*lost object*) trouver (par hasard); (*reference etc*) tomber sur, trouver (par hasard) ▮ **to come along** *vi* venir (**with** avec); (*progress*) (*of work, student etc*) avancer; **c. along!** allons! ▮ **to come apart** *vi* (*of two objects*) se séparer ▮ **to come at** *vt* (*attack*) attaquer ▮ **to come away** *vi* (*leave, come off*) partir (**from** de); **to c. away from** (*step or move back from*) s'éloigner de, s'écarter de ▮ **to come back** *vi* revenir; (*return home*) rentrer. ● **comeback** *n* (*into fashion*) retour *m* (en vogue); (*of actor, politician etc*) retour *m*. ▮ **to come by** *vt* (*obtain*) obtenir; (*find*) trouver ▮ **to come down** *vi* descendre; (*of rain, price*) tomber; (*of building*) être démoli ▮ *vt* (*stairs, hill etc*) descendre ▮ **to come down with** (*illness*) attraper. ● **comedown** *n* *Fam* humiliation *f*. ▮ **to come for** *vt* venir chercher (*qch, qn*) ▮ **to come forward** *vi* (*make oneself known, volunteer*) se présenter ▮ **to come forward with** *vt* offrir, suggérer ▮ **to come in** *vi* (*enter*) entrer; (*of tide*) monter; (*of train, athlete*) arriver; (*of politician*) arriver au pouvoir; (*of clothes*) devenir à la mode, se faire beaucoup; (*of money*) rentrer ▮ **to come in for** *vt* (*criticism*) essuyer ▮ **to come into** *vt* (*room etc*) entrer dans; (*money*) hériter de ▮ **to come off** *vi* (*of button etc*) se détacher, partir; (*succeed*) réussir; (*happen*) avoir lieu; (*get along, manage*) s'en tirer ▮ *vt* (*fall from*) tomber de; (*get down from*) descendre de ▮ **to come on** *vi* (*follow*) suivre; (*progress*) (*of work, student etc*) avancer; (*start*) commencer; (*arrive*) arriver; (*of play*) être joué; **c. on!** allez! ▮ **to come out** *vi* sortir; (*of sun, book*) paraître; (*of stain*) s'enlever, partir; (*of secret*) être révélé; (*of photo*) réussir; **to c. out on strike** se mettre en grève ▮ **to come over** *vi* (*visit*) venir, passer (**to** chez); **to c. over to** (*approach*) s'approcher de; **to c. over funny** *or* **peculiar** se trouver mal; **I don't know what came over me** je ne sais pas ce qui m'a pris ▮ *vt* (*take hold of*) (*of feeling*) saisir (*qn*), prendre (*qn*) ▮ **to come round** *vi* (*visit*) venir, passer (**to** chez); (*of date*) revenir; (*regain consciousness*) revenir à soi ▮ **to come through** *vi* (*survive*) s'en tirer ▮ *vt* (*crisis etc*) se tirer indemne de

▮ **to come to** *vi* (*regain consciousness*) revenir à soi ▮ *vt* (*amount to*) revenir à, faire; (*a decision*) parvenir à; **to c. to an end** toucher à sa fin; **to c. to understand/etc** en venir à comprendre/etc; **when it comes to buying a car** quand il s'agit d'acheter une voiture ▮ **to come under** *vt* (*heading etc*) être classé sous; (*s.o.'s influence*) tomber sous ▮ **to come up** *vi* (*rise*) monter; (*of plant*) sortir; (*of question, job*) se présenter ▮ *vt* (*stairs etc*) monter ▮ **to come up against** (*wall, problem*) se heurter à ▮ **to come up to** *vt* (*reach*) arriver jusqu'à; (*approach*) s'approcher de; (*one's hopes*) *Fig* répondre à ▮ **to come up with** *vt* (*idea, money*) trouver ▮ **to come upon** *vt* (*book, reference etc*) tomber sur.

comedy ['kɒmɪdɪ] *n* comédie *f*. ● **co'median** *n* (*actor m*) comique *m*, actrice *f* comique.

comet ['kɒmɪt] *n* comète *f*.

comeuppance [kʌm'ʌpəns] *n* **he got his c.** *Pej Fam* il n'a eu que ce qu'il mérite.

comfort ['kʌmfət] *n* confort *m*; (*consolation*) réconfort *m*, consolation *f*; **to be a c. to s.o.** être d'un grand réconfort à qn; **to like one's comforts** aimer ses aises *fpl*; **too close/etc for c.** trop près/etc à mon, son etc goût; **c. station** *Am* toilettes *fpl* ▮ *vt* consoler; (*cheer*) réconforter.

comfortable ['kʌmfətəb(ə)l] *a* (*chair, house etc*) confortable; (*rich*) aisé; **he's c.** (*in chair etc*) il est à l'aise, il est bien; **make yourself c.** mets-toi à l'aise. ● **comforting** *a* (*reassuring*) (*words, situation etc*) réconfortant. ● **comfortably** *adv* (*to sit*) confortablement; **to live c.** vivre à l'aise; **c. off** (*rich*) à l'aise.

comforter ['kʌmfətər] *n* (*quilt*) *Am* édredon *m*; (*for baby*) sucette *f*.

comfy ['kʌmfɪ] *a* (**-ier, -iest**) (*chair etc*) *Fam* confortable; **I'm c.** je suis bien.

comic ['kɒmɪk] *a* comique ▮ *n* (*actor*) comique *m*; (*actress*) actrice *f* comique; (*magazine*) *Br* illustré *m*; **c. strip** bande *f* dessinée. ● **comical** *a* comique, drôle.

coming ['kʌmɪŋ] *a* (*future*) (*years etc*) à venir; **the c. month/days/etc** le mois/les jours/etc prochain(s) ▮ *n* (*of Messiah etc*) avènement *m*; **comings and goings** allées *fpl* et venues.

comma ['kɒmə] *n* virgule *f*.

command [kə'mɑːnd] *vt* (*order*) commander (**s.o. to do** à qn de faire); (*control*) commander (*régiment, navire etc*); (*dominate*) (*of building etc*) dominer, commander (*vallée etc*); (*be able to use*) disposer de (*crédits etc*); (*respect*) imposer (**from** à); (*require*) exiger.
▮ *vi* (*of captain etc*) commander.
▮ *n* (*order*) ordre *m*; (*authority*) commandement *m*; (*troops*) troupes *fpl*; (*mastery*) maîtrise *f* (**of** qch); *Comptr* commande *f*; **at one's c.** (*disposal*) à sa disposition; **to be in c. (of)** (*ship, army etc*) commander; (*situation*) être maître de; **to take c. of** (*ship etc*) prendre le commandement de; **under the c. of** sous le

commandement de. ●**commanding** a (authoritative) imposant; (position) dominant; **c. officer** commandant m.

commandant ['kɒmandænt] n (army officer) commandant m (d'un camp etc).

commandeer [kɒmən'dɪər] vt réquisitionner.

commander [kə'mɑːndər] n (military) commandant m; **c. in chief** commandant m en chef.

commandment [kə'mɑːndmənt] n (religious) commandement m.

commando [kə'mɑːndəʊ] n (pl -os or -oes) (soldiers) commando m.

commemorate [kə'meməreɪt] vt commémorer. ●**commemoration** [-'reɪʃ(ə)n] n commémoration f. ●**commemorative** a commémoratif.

commence [kə'mens] vti commencer (**doing** à faire). ●**commencement** n commencement m; (university ceremony) Am remise f des diplômes.

commend [kə'mend] vt (praise) louer; (recommend) recommander; (entrust) Lit confier (**to** à). ●**commendable** a louable. ●**commendation** [-'deɪʃ(ə)n] n (praise) éloge m.

commensurate [kə'menʃərət] a proportionné (**to**, with à).

comment ['kɒment] n commentaire m, remarque f; **'no c!'** (je n'ai) rien à dire! ▮ vi faire des commentaires or des remarques (**on** sur); **I won't c.** je n'ai rien à dire; **to c. on** (text, event, news item) commenter; **to c. that** remarquer que. ●**commentary** n commentaire m; (live) **c.** (on TV or radio) reportage m (en direct). ●**commentate** vi (on event, on TV or radio) faire un reportage (**on** sur). ●**commentator** n (on TV or radio) commentateur, -trice mf (**on** de).

commerce ['kɒmɜːs] n commerce m. ●**co'mmercial** 1 a commercial; **c. break** plage f de publicité; **c. district** quartier m commerçant; **c. traveller** Br voyageur m or représentant m de commerce. 2 n (advertisement) (on TV) publicité f; **the commercials** (on TV) la publicité.

commercialize [kə'mɜːʃəlaɪz] vt (event) Pej transformer en une affaire de gros sous. ●**commercialized** a (district etc) devenu or rendu (trop) commercial.

commiserate [kə'mɪzəreɪt] vi **to c. with s.o.** s'apitoyer sur (le sort de) qn. ●**commiseration** [-'reɪʃ(ə)n] n commisération f.

commission [kə'mɪʃ(ə)n] n (fee, group) commission f; (order for work) commande f; **out of c.** (machine) hors service; **to get one's c.** (of soldier) être nommé officier. ▮ vt (artist) passer une commande à; (book) commander; **to c. s.o. to do** charger qn de faire; **to be commissioned** (in the army) être nommé officier; **commissioned officer** officier m.

commissionaire [kəmɪʃə'neər] n (in hotel etc) Br chasseur m. ●**commissioner** n Pol

etc commissaire m; (**police**) **c.** Br préfet m (de police).

commit [kə'mɪt] vt (-tt-) (crime) commettre; (bind) engager (qn); (devote) consacrer (des efforts etc) (**to** à); **to c. sth to s.o.'s care** confier qch à (la garde de) qn; **to c. suicide** se suicider; **to c. sth to memory** apprendre qch par cœur; **to c. s.o. to prison** incarcérer qn; **to c. oneself** (make a promise) s'engager (**to** à); (compromise oneself) se compromettre. ●**commitment** n (duty, responsibility) obligation f; (promise) engagement m; (devotion) dévouement m (**to** à).

committee [kə'mɪtɪ] n comité m; (parliamentary) commission f.

commodity [kə'mɒdɪtɪ] n produit m, article m.

common ['kɒmən] 1 a (-er, -est) (shared, vulgar) commun; (frequent) courant, fréquent, commun; **the c. man** l'homme m du commun; **in c.** (shared) en commun (**with** avec); **to have nothing in c.** n'avoir rien de commun (**with** avec); **in c. with** (like) comme; **c. law** droit m coutumier; **c.-law wife** concubine f; **C. Market** Marché m commun; **c. room** (for students) salle f commune; (for teachers) salle f des professeurs; **c. or garden** ordinaire.
2 n (land) terrain m communal; **House of Commons** Br Can etc Chambre f des Communes; **the Commons** Br Can etc les Communes fpl.

commoner ['kɒmənər] n roturier, -ière mf. ●**commonly** adv (generally) en général; (vulgarly) d'une façon commune. ●**commonness** n fréquence f; (vulgarity) vulgarité f.

commonplace ['kɒmənpleɪs] a banal (mpl -als) ▮ n banalité f.

commonsense [kɒmən'sens] n sens m commun, bon sens m ▮ a (sensible) sensé.

Commonwealth ['kɒmənwelθ] n **the C.** Br le Commonwealth.

commotion [kə'məʊʃ(ə)n] n agitation f.

communal [kə'mjuːn(ə)l] a (shared) (bathroom, kitchen etc) commun; (of the community) communautaire; ●**communally** adv (to own) en commun; (to live) en communauté.

commune 1 ['kɒmjuːn] n (district) commune f; (group) communauté f. 2 [kə'mjuːn] vi **to c. with nature/God** être en communion avec la nature/Dieu. ●**co'mmunion** n communion f (**with** avec); (**Holy**) **C.** communion f.

communicate [kə'mjuːnɪkeɪt] vt communiquer; (illness) transmettre (**to** à) ▮ vi (of person, rooms etc) communiquer (**with** avec). ●**communication** [-'keɪʃ(ə)n] n communication f; **c. cord** (on train) Br signal m d'alarme.

communicative [kə'mjuːnɪkətɪv] a communicatif.

communiqué [kə'mjuːnɪkeɪ] n (announcement) communiqué m.

communism ['kɒmjunɪz(ə)m] n communisme m. ●**communist** a & n communiste *(mf)*.

community [kə'mjuːnɪtɪ] *n* communauté *f*; **the student c.** les étudiants *mpl* **l** *a* (*rights, life, spirit*) communautaire; **c. centre** *m* socio-culturel; **c. worker** animateur, -trice *mf* socio-culturel(le).

commute [kə'mjuːt] **1** *vi* (*travel*) faire la navette (**to work** pour se rendre à son travail) **l** *n* (*journey*) trajet *m*. **2** *vt* (*of judge*) commuer (*une sentence*) (**to** en). **●commuting** *n* (*journeys*) trajets *mpl* journaliers. **●commuter** *n* banlieusard, -arde *mf*; **c. train** train *m* de banlieue.

compact[1] [kəm'pækt] *a* (*car, crowd, substance*) compact; (*style*) condensé; **c. disc** Br, **c. disk** Am ['kɒmpækt] disque *m* compact.

compact[2] ['kɒmpækt] *n* (*for face powder*) poudrier *m*.

companion [kəm'pænjən] *n* (*person*) compagnon *m*, compagne *f*; (*handbook*) manuel *m*. **●companionship** *n* camaraderie *f*.

company ['kʌmpənɪ] *n* (*companionship*) compagnie *f*; (*guests*) invités, -ées *mfpl*; (*people present*) assemblée *f*; (*business*) société *f*, compagnie *f*; **(theatre) c.** compagnie *f* (théâtrale); **to keep s.o. c.** tenir compagnie à qn; **in s.o.'s c.** avec qn, en compagnie de qn; **to keep good c.** avoir de bonnes fréquentations; **he's good c.** c'est un bon compagnon; **c. car** voiture *f* de société.

comparable ['kɒmpərəb(ə)l] *a* comparable (**with, to** à).

comparative [kəm'pærətɪv] *a* (*method etc*) comparatif; (*law, literature etc*) comparé; (*relative*) (*costs etc*) relatif **l** *n* Grammar comparatif *m*. **●comparatively** *adv* relativement.

compare [kəm'peər] *vt* comparer (**with, to** à); **compared to** *or* **with** en comparaison de **l** *vi* être comparable, se comparer (**with** à). **●comparison** *n* comparaison *f* (**between** entre, **with** avec); **in c. with** en comparaison avec; **by** *or* **in c.** en comparaison.

compartment [kəm'pɑːtmənt] *n* compartiment *m*. **●compart'mentalize** *vt* compartimenter.

compass ['kʌmpəs] *n* **1** (*for finding direction*) boussole *f*; (*on ship*) compas *m*; (*range*) Fig portée *f*. **2** (*for drawing, measuring etc*) Am compas *m*; **(pair of) compasses** compas *m*.

compassion [kəm'pæʃ(ə)n] *n* compassion *f*. **●compassionate** *a* compatissant; **on c. grounds** pour raisons de famille.

compatible [kəm'pætɪb(ə)l] *a* compatible. **●compati'bility** *n* compatibilité *f*.

compatriot [kəm'pætrɪət, kəm'peɪtrɪət] *n* compatriote *mf*.

compel [kəm'pel] *vt* (**-ll-**) forcer, contraindre (**to do** à faire); (*respect, obedience etc*) forcer (**from s.o.** chez qn); **compelled to do** forcé *or* contraint de faire. **●compelling** *a* (*film, argument etc*) irrésistible.

compendium [kəm'pendɪəm] *n* abrégé *m*.

compensate ['kɒmpənseɪt] *vt* **to c. s.o.** (*with payment, reward*) dédommager qn (**for de**) **l** *vi* compenser; **to c. for sth** (*make up for*) compenser qch. **●compensation** *n* [-'seɪʃ(ə)n] *n* (*financial*) dédommagement *m*; (*consolation*) compensation *f*; **in c. for** en compensation de.

compère ['kɒmpeər] *n* (*on TV or radio*) Br animateur, -trice *mf*, présentateur, -trice *mf* **l** *vt* (*a show*) Br animer, présenter.

compete [kəm'piːt] *vi* (*take part in race etc*) concourir (**in** à); **to c.** (**with s.o.**) rivaliser (avec qn); (*in business*) faire concurrence (à qn); **to c. for sth** se disputer qch; **to c. in a race/rally** courir dans une course/un rallye.

competent ['kɒmpɪtənt] *a* (*capable*) compétent (**to do** pour faire); (*sufficient*) (*knowledge etc*) suffisant. **●competently** *adv* avec compétence. **●competence** *n* compétence *f*.

competition [kɒmpə'tɪʃ(ə)n] *n* (*rivalry*) compétition *f*, concurrence *f*; **a c.** (*contest*) un concours; (*in sport*) une compétition.

competitive [kəm'petɪtɪv] *a* (*price, market*) compétitif; (*selection*) par concours; (*person*) aimant la compétition; **c. examination** concours *m*. **●competitor** *n* concurrent, -ente *mf*.

compile [kəm'paɪl] *vt* (*dictionary*) rédiger; (*list, catalogue*) dresser; (*documents*) compiler. **●compiler** *n* (*of dictionary*) rédacteur, -trice *mf*.

complacent [kəm'pleɪsənt] *a* content de soi. **●complacence** *or* **complacency** *n* autosatisfaction *f*; **there is no room for c.** ce n'est pas le moment de faire de l'autosatisfaction.

complain [kəm'pleɪn] *vi* se plaindre (**to s.o.** à qn; **of** *or* **about sth/s.o.** de qch/qn; **that** que); **to c. of** *or* **about being tired/etc** se plaindre d'être fatigué/etc. **●complaint** *n* plainte *f*; (*in shop etc*) réclamation *f*; (*illness*) maladie *f*; (*cause for*) **c.** sujet *m* de plainte; **to have cause for c.** avoir à se plaindre.

complement ['kɒmplɪmənt] *n* complément *m* **l** ['kɒmplɪment] *vt* compléter. **●comple'mentary** *a* complémentaire.

complete [kəm'pliːt] *a* (*total*) complet; (*finished*) achevé; **a c. idiot/etc** (*downright*) un parfait imbécile/etc **l** *vt* (*add sth missing to*) compléter; (*finish*) achever; (*a form*) remplir. **●completely** *adv* complètement. **●completion** *n* [-ʃ(ə)n] *n* achèvement *m*, réalisation *f*; (*of contract, sale*) exécution *f*.

complex ['kɒmpleks] **1** *a* complexe. **2** *n* (*feeling, buildings*) complexe *m*; **housing c.** grand ensemble *m*. **●com'plexity** *n* complexité *f*.

complexion [kəm'plekʃ(ə)n] *n* (*of the face*) teint *m*; Fig caractère *m*, nature *f* (**of** de).

compliance [kəm'plaɪəns] *n* (*agreement*) conformité *f* (**with** avec).

complicate ['kɒmplɪkeɪt] *vt* compliquer (**with** de). **●complicated** *a* compliqué. **●complication** *n* [-'keɪʃ(ə)n] *n* complication *f*.

complicity [kəm'plɪsɪtɪ] *n* complicité *f*.

63   **conciliate**

compliment ['kɒmplɪmənt] n compliment m;
compliments (of author) hommages mpl; to
pay s.o. a c. faire un compliment à qn; compliments of the season meilleurs vœux pour
Noël et la nouvelle année ▮ ['kɒmplɪment] vt
complimenter, faire des compliments à.
● compli'mentary a 1 (flattering) flatteur. 2
(free) (seat, copy of book etc) (offert) à titre
gracieux; c. ticket billet m de faveur.

comply [kəm'plaɪ] vi (obey) obéir; to c. with
(order, rule) obéir à; (request) accéder à.

component [kəm'pəʊnənt] n (of structure,
self-assembly furniture, problem etc) élément
m; (of machine) pièce f, élément m; (chemical, electronic) composant m ▮ a c. part
partie f constituante.

compose [kəm'pəʊz] vt composer; to c. oneself se calmer. ●composed a calme.
● composer n (of music) compositeur, -trice
mf. ● composition [kɒmpə'zɪʃ(ə)n] n (in music, art, chemistry etc) composition f; (school
essay) rédaction f.

compost [Br 'kɒmpɒst, Am 'kɒmpəʊst] n
compost m.

composure [kəm'pəʊʒər] n calme m, sang-
froid m.

compound 1 ['kɒmpaʊnd] n (substance,
word) composé m; (area) enclos m ▮ a (substance, word, interest) composé; (sentence,
number) complexe. 2 [kəm'paʊnd] vt (make
worse) aggraver (problème etc).

comprehend [kɒmprɪ'hend] vt comprendre.
● comprehensible a compréhensible. ●com-
prehension [-ʃ(ə)n] n compréhension f.

comprehensive [kɒmprɪ'hensɪv] a complet;
(knowledge) étendu; (view, measure)
d'ensemble; (insurance) tous risques inv ▮ a
& n c. (school) Br = collège m d'enseignement secondaire.

compress [kəm'pres] vt (gas, air etc) comprimer; (ideas, facts etc) Fig condenser ▮
['kɒmpres] n (to relieve pain) compresse f.
● compression [-ʃ(ə)n] n compression f; Fig
condensation f.

comprise [kəm'praɪz] vt (consist of) comprendre, inclure; (make up) constituer; to be
comprised of comprendre, inclure.

compromise ['kɒmprəmaɪz] vt compromettre ▮ vi accepter un compromis ▮ n compromis m; c. solution/etc solution f/etc de
compromis.

compulsion [kəm'pʌlʃ(ə)n] n contrainte f.
● compulsive a (behaviour) compulsif; (smoker, gambler) invétéré; c. liar mythomane
mf, menteur, -euse mf invétéré(e); c. eater
boulimique mf.

compulsory [kəm'pʌlsərɪ] a obligatoire.

compunction [kəm'pʌŋkʃ(ə)n] n scrupule m
(about doing à faire).

compute [kəm'pjuːt] vt calculer. ●compu-
ting n informatique f.

computer [kəm'pjuːtər] n ordinateur m ▮ a
(program, system, network) informatique;
(course, firm) d'informatique; c. game jeu m
électronique; c. language langage m de pro-

grammation; c. operator opérateur, -trice mf
sur ordinateur; c. science informatique f; c.
scientist informaticien, -ienne mf. ●compu-
terization [-'zeɪʃ(ə)n] n informatisation f.
● computerized a informatisé.

comrade ['kɒmreɪd] n camarade mf.
● comradeship n camaraderie f.

con [kɒn] vt (-nn-) Sl rouler, escroquer; to be
conned se faire avoir or rouler ▮ n Sl escroquerie f; c. man escroc m.

concave ['kɒnkeɪv] a concave.

conceal [kən'siːl] vt (hide) dissimuler (object) (from s.o. à qn); (plan, news etc) cacher
(from s.o. à qn). ●concealment n dissimulation f.

concede [kən'siːd] vt concéder (to à, that
que) ▮ vi céder.

conceit [kən'siːt] n vanité f. ●conceited a
vaniteux. ●conceitedly adv avec vanité.

conceive [kən'siːv] vt (idea, child etc) concevoir; (believe) voir, envisager ▮ vi (of woman) concevoir; to c. of concevoir. ●con-
ceivable a concevable, envisageable; it's c.
that il est concevable or envisageable que +
sub. ●conceivably adv yes, c. oui, c'est concevable.

concentrate ['kɒnsəntreɪt] 1 vt concentrer
(on sur) ▮ vi (mentally) se concentrer (on sth
sur qch); to c. on doing s'appliquer à faire;
to c. on one's exams/work/etc se consacrer
particulièrement à ses examens/son travail/
etc. 2 vi (converge) se concentrer (on sur).
● concentration [-'treɪʃ(ə)n] n concentration
f; c. camp camp m de concentration.

concentric [kən'sentrɪk] a concentrique.

concept ['kɒnsept] n concept m. ●concep-
tion [-'sepʃ(ə)n] n (idea, fertilization) conception f.

concern [kən'sɜːn] vt concerner; to c. oneself
with, be concerned with (be busy) s'occuper
de; to be concerned about (be worried)
s'inquiéter de; as far as I'm concerned en ce
qui me concerne ▮ n (matter) affaire f;
(anxiety) inquiétude f; (business) c. entreprise f; his c. for son souci de; that's not my
c. cela ne me regarde pas. ●concerned a
(anxious) inquiet (about, at au sujet de); the
department c. (correct, relevant) le service
compétent; the main person c. le principal
intéressé or concerné. ●concerning prep en
ce qui concerne.

concert ['kɒnsət] n concert m; in c. (together) de concert (with avec); c. hall salle f
de concert. ●concert-goer n habitué, -ée m
des concerts.

concerted [kən'sɜːtɪd] a (effort) concerté.

concertina [kɒnsə'tiːnə] n concertina m; c.
crash (of vehicles) carambolage m.

concerto [kən'tʃɜːtəʊ] n (pl -os) concerto m.

concession [kən'seʃ(ə)n] n concession f (to
à). ●concessionary a (rate, price) réduit.

conciliate [kən'sɪlɪeɪt] vt to c. s.o. (win over)
se concilier qn; (soothe) apaiser qn. ●conci-
liation [-'eɪʃ(ə)n] n conciliation f; (soothing)
apaisement m. ●conciliatory [kən'sɪlɪətərɪ,

Am -tɔːrɪ] a (tone, person etc) conciliant.
concise [kən'saɪs] a concis. ●**concisely** adv
avec concision. ●**conciseness** or **concision**
[-ʒ(ə)n] n concision f.
conclude [kən'kluːd] vt (end, settle) conclure; **to c. that** (infer) conclure que **I** vi (of
event etc) se terminer (with par); (of speaker) conclure. ●**concluding** a (remarks,
speech etc) final (mpl finals). ●**conclusion**
[-ʒ(ə)n] n conclusion f; **in c.** pour conclure;
to come to the c. that arriver à la conclusion
que.
conclusive [kən'kluːsɪv] a concluant. ●**con-
clusively** adv de manière concluante.
concoct [kən'kɒkt] vt (dish) Pej concocter,
confectionner; (scheme) Pej combiner.
●**concoction** [-ʃ(ə)n] n (substance) Pej
mixture f; (of dish) confection f.
concord ['kɒŋkɔːd] n concorde f.
concourse ['kɒŋkɔːs] n (hall) Am hall m;
(at train station) hall m, salle f des pas
perdus.
concrete ['kɒŋkriːt] **1** n béton m; **c. wall**/etc
mur m/etc en béton; **c. mixer** bétonnière f. **2**
a (real, positive) (ideas, example etc) concret.
concur [kən'kɜːr] vi (-rr-) **1** (agree) être
d'accord (with avec). **2** (happen together)
coïncider; **to c. to** (contribute) concourir à.
concurrent [kən'kʌrənt] a simultané. ●**con-
currently** adv simultanément.
concussion [kən'kʌʃ(ə)n] n (injury)
commotion f (cérébrale).
condemn [kən'dem] vt condamner (qn) (to
à); (building) déclarer inhabitable; **condemned man** condamné m à mort. ●**condemnation** [kɒndem'neɪʃ(ə)n] n condamnation f.
condense [kən'dens] vt condenser **I** vi se
condenser. ●**condensation** [kɒndən'seɪʃ(ə)n]
n condensation f (of de); (mist) buée f.
condescend [kɒndɪ'send] vi condescendre
(to do à faire). ●**condescension** [-ʃ(ə)n] n
condescendance f.
condiment ['kɒndɪmənt] n condiment m.
condition [kən'dɪʃ(ə)n] n **1** (stipulation,
circumstance, rank) condition f; (state) état
m, condition f; **on c. that one does** à condition de faire, à condition que l'on fasse; **in
good c.** en bon état; **in/out of c.** en bonne/
mauvaise forme.
2 vt (action, behaviour etc) déterminer, conditionner; **to c. s.o.** (train) conditionner qn
(to do à faire). ●**conditional** a conditionnel;
to be c. upon dépendre de **I** n Grammar
conditionnel m.
conditioner [kən'dɪʃənər] n (hair) c. après-
shampooing m.
condo ['kɒndəʊ] n (pl -os) abbr Am =
condominium.
condolences [kən'dəʊlənsɪz] npl condoléances fpl; **condolence card** carte f de condoléances.
condom ['kɒndəm, -dɒm] n préservatif m.
condominium [kɒndə'mɪnɪəm] n Am (build-

ing) (immeuble m en) copropriété f; (apartment) appartement m dans une copropriété.
condone [kən'dəʊn] vt (overlook) fermer les
yeux sur; (forgive) excuser.
conducive [kən'djuːsɪv] a **to be c. to** être favorable à, inciter à; **not to be c. to** ne pas inciter à.
conduct ['kɒndʌkt] n (behaviour, directing)
conduite f **I** [kən'dʌkt] vt (lead) conduire,
mener (touristes, enquête etc); (orchestra)
diriger; (electricity, heat) conduire; **to c.
one's business** diriger ses affaires; **to c. oneself** se conduire; **conducted visit** or **tour** (of
building etc) visite f guidée; **conducted tour**
(around region) excursion f accompagnée.
conductor [kən'dʌktər] n (of orchestra) chef
m d'orchestre; (on bus) Br receveur m; (on
train) Am chef m de train; (metal, cable etc)
conducteur m. ●**conductress** n (on bus) Br
receveuse f.
cone [kəʊn] n cône m; (of ice cream) cornet
m; (paper) c. cornet m (de papier); **traffic c.**
Br cône m de chantier; **pine** or **fir c.** pomme
f de pin.
confectioner [kən'fekʃənər] n (of Br sweets,
Am candy) confiseur, -euse mf; (of cakes)
pâtissier, -ière mf. ●**confectionery** n (Br
sweets, Am candy) confiserie f; (cakes) pâtisserie f.
confederate [kən'fedərət] a confédéré **I** n
(accomplice) complice mf, acolyte m. ●**con-
federacy** or **confederation** [-'reɪʃ(ə)n] n
confédération f.
confer [kən'fɜːr] **1** vt (-rr-) (grant) conférer
(on à); (university degrees) délivrer; **to c. a
degree on s.o.** remettre un diplôme à qn. **2**
vi (-rr-) (talk together) conférer, se consulter
(on, about sur); **to c. with s.o.** consulter qn.
conference ['kɒnfərəns] n conférence f;
(scientific, academic etc) congrès m; **press** or
news c. conférence f de presse; **in c. (with)**
en conférence (avec).
confess [kən'fes] **1** vt avouer, confesser
(that que, to s.o. à qn) **I** vi avouer; **to c. to**
(crime etc) avouer, confesser. **2** vt (sins etc)
confesser **I** vi (to priest etc) se confesser.
●**confession** [-ʃ(ə)n] n aveu(x) m(pl), confession f; (religious) confession f; **to go to c.**
aller à confesse. ●**confessional** n Rel confessionnal m.
confetti [kən'fetɪ] n confettis mpl.
confidant, -ante ['kɒnfɪdænt] n confident,
-ente mf.
confide [kən'faɪd] vt confier (to à, that que)
I vi **to c. in** (talk to) se confier à.
confidence ['kɒnfɪdəns] n (trust) confiance
f; (secret) confidence f; (self-)c. confiance f
en soi; **in c.** (adv) en confidence; (a) confidentiel; **in strict c.** (adv) tout à fait con-
fidentiellement; (a) tout à fait confidentiel;
motion of no c. Pol motion f de censure; **c.
trick** escroquerie f; **c. trickster** escroc m.
●**confident** a sûr, assuré; (self-)c. sûr de soi.
●**confidently** adv avec confiance.
confidential [kɒnfɪ'denʃəl] a confidentiel;

(*secretary*) particulier. ● **confidentially** *adv* en confidence.

configuration [kənfɪgjʊ'reɪʃ(ə)n] *n* configuration *f*.

confine [kən'faɪn] *vt* 1 (*limit*) limiter (**to** à); **to c. oneself to doing** se limiter à faire. 2 (*keep prisoner*) enfermer, confiner (**to, in** dans). ● **confined** *a* (*atmosphere*) confiné; (*space*) réduit; **c. to bed** cloué au lit, obligé de garder le lit; **c. to the house/one's room** obligé de rester chez soi/de garder la chambre. ● **confinement** *n* (*of pregnant woman*) couches *fpl*; (*of prisoner etc*) emprisonnement *m*.

confines ['kɒnfaɪnz] *npl* limites *fpl*, confins *mpl*.

confirm [kən'fɜːm] *vt* confirmer (**that** que); (*strengthen*) raffermir (*autorité, résolution etc*); **to be confirmed** (*religious ceremony*) recevoir la confirmation. ● **confirmed** *a* (*bachelor*) endurci; (*smoker, habit*) invétéré. ● **confirmation** [kɒnfə'meɪʃ(ə)n] *n* confirmation *f*; **it's subject to c.** c'est à confirmer.

confiscate ['kɒnfɪskeɪt] *vt* confisquer (**from s.o.** à qn). ● **confiscation** [-'keɪʃ(ə)n] *n* confiscation *f*.

conflagration [kɒnflə'greɪʃ(ə)n] *n* (grand) incendie *m*, brasier *m*.

conflict ['kɒnflɪkt] *n* conflit *m* ▌ [kən'flɪkt] *vi* (*of statement etc*) être en contradiction (**with** avec); (*of dates, events, TV programmes*) tomber en même temps (**with** que). ● **conflicting** *a* (*views, theories etc*) contradictoires; (*dates*) incompatibles.

confluence ['kɒnflʊəns] *n* (*of rivers*) confluent *m*.

conform [kən'fɔːm] *vi* (*of person*) se conformer (**to, with** à); (*of ideas, actions etc*) être en conformité (**to** with). ● **conformist** *a* & *n* conformiste (*mf*). ● **conformity** *n* (*likeness*) conformité *f*; (*behaviour etc*) *Pej* conformisme *m*.

confound [kən'faʊnd] *vt* (*surprise, puzzle*) confondre; **c. him!** que le diable l'emporte!; **c. it!** quelle barbe!, flûte! ● **confounded** *a* (*damned*) *Fam* sacré.

confront [kən'frʌnt] *vt* (*danger*) affronter; (*problems*) faire face à; **to c. s.o.** (*be face to face with*) se trouver en face de qn; (*oppose*) s'opposer à qn; **to c. s.o. with s.o.** confronter qn avec qn; **to c. s.o. with sth** mettre qn en face de qch. ● **confrontation** [kɒnfrən'teɪʃ(ə)n] *n* confrontation *f*.

confuse [kən'fjuːz] *vt* (*make unsure*) embrouiller (*qn*); **to c. s.o./s.o.** with (*mistake for*) confondre qch/qn avec; **to c. matters** *or* **the issue** embrouiller la question. ● **confused** *a* (*situation, noises, idea etc*) confus; **to be c.** (*of person*) s'y perdre; **I'm (all** *or* **quite) c. (about it)** je m'y perds; **she's (always) c.** elle a (toujours) les idées embrouillées; **to get c.** s'embrouiller. ● **confusing** *a* déroutant, difficile à comprendre. ● **confusion** [-ʒ(ə)n] *n* confusion *f*; **in (a state of) c.** en désordre.

congeal [kən'dʒiːl] *vi* (*of blood*) se coagular.

● **congealed** *a* **c. blood** sang *m* coagulé.

congenial [kən'dʒiːnɪəl] *a* sympathique.

congenital [kən'dʒenɪtəl] *a* congénital.

congested [kən'dʒestɪd] *a* (*street*) embouteillé, encombré; (*district, town*) surpeuplé; (*nose*) bouché, pris; (*lungs*) congestionné. ● **congestion** [-tʃ(ə)n] *n* (*obstruction*) encombrement *m*; (*traffic*) encombrements *mpl*; (*overcrowding*) surpeuplement *m*; (*in lungs etc*) congestion *f*.

Congo ['kɒŋgəʊ] *n* Congo *m*.

congratulate [kən'grætʃʊleɪt] *vt* féliciter (**s.o. on sth** qn de qch, **s.o. on doing sth** qn d'avoir fait qch). ● **congratulations** [-'leɪʃ(ə)nz] *npl* félicitations *fpl* (**on** pour). ● **congratu'latory** *a* (*telegram etc*) de félicitations.

congregate ['kɒŋgrɪgeɪt] *vi* se rassembler. ● **congregation** [kɒŋgrɪ'geɪʃ(ə)n] *n* (*worshippers*) fidèles *mfpl*, assemblée *f*.

congress ['kɒŋgres] *n* congrès *m*; **C.** (*political body*) *Am* le Congrès. ● **Congressman** *n* (*pl* -**men**) *Am* membre *m* du Congrès. ● **Con'gressional** *a* (*committee etc*) *Am* du Congrès.

conical ['kɒnɪk(ə)l] *a* conique.

conifer ['kɒnɪfər] *n* (*tree*) conifère *m*.

conjecture [kən'dʒektʃər] *n* conjecture *f* ▌ *vt* conjecturer ▌ *vi* faire des conjectures. ● **conjectural** *a* conjectural.

conjugal ['kɒndʒʊgəl] *a* conjugal.

conjugate ['kɒndʒʊgeɪt] *vt* (*verb*) conjuguer. ● **conjugation** [-'geɪʃ(ə)n] *n* conjugaison *f*.

conjunction [kən'dʒʌŋkʃ(ə)n] *n* *Grammar* conjonction *f*; **in c. with** conjointement avec.

conjunctivitis [kəndʒʌŋktɪ'vaɪtɪs] *n* conjonctivite *f*; **to have c.** avoir *or* faire de la conjonctivite.

conjure ['kʌndʒər] *vt* **to c. (up)** (*by magic*) faire apparaître (*objet, fantôme etc*); **to c. up** (*memories, images etc*) *Fig* évoquer; **conjuring trick** tour *m* de prestidigitation. ● **conjurer** *n* prestidigitateur, -trice *mf*.

conk [kɒŋk] 1 *vi* **to c. out** (*break down*) (*of TV set etc*) *Fam* tomber en panne *or* en rade. 2 *n* (*nose*) *Br Sl* pif *m*. 3 *n* (*blow*) *Sl* gnon *m*.

conker ['kɒŋkər] *n* (*horse-chestnut fruit*) *Br Fam* marron *m* (d'Inde).

connect [kə'nekt] *vt* relier (**with, to** à); (*telephone, washing machine etc*) brancher; **to c. s.o. with** (*on phone*) mettre qn en communication avec; **to c. sth/s.o. with** (*in memory*) associer qch/qn avec.

▌ *vi* (*be connected*) être relié; (*of rooms*) communiquer; (*of roads*) se rejoindre; **to c. with** (*of train, bus*) assurer la correspondance avec. ● **connected** *a* (*facts, events etc*) liés; (*speech*) suivi; **to be c. with** (*have dealings with*) être lié à; (*have to do with, relate to*) avoir rapport à, être lié à; (*by marriage*) être allié à.

connection [kə'nekʃ(ə)n] *n* (*link*) rapport *m*, relation *f* (**with** avec); (*train, bus etc*) correspondance *f*; (*phone call*) communication f; (*between electrical wires*) contact m; (*between pipes*) raccord m; **connections** (*contacts*) relations fpl; **to have no c. with** n'avoir aucun rapport avec; **in c. with** à propos de; **in this** *or* **that c.** à ce propos; **there's a loose c.** (*in electrical appliance*) il y a un faux contact.

connive [kə'naɪv] vi **to c. at** fermer les yeux sur; **to c. to do** se mettre de connivence pour faire (**with s.o.** avec qn); **to c. together** agir en complicité. ● **connivance** n connivence f.

connoisseur [kɒnə'sɜːr] n connaisseur m.

connotation [kɒnə'teɪʃ(ə)n] n connotation f.

conquer ['kɒŋkər] vt (*country, freedom etc*) conquérir; (*enemy, habit*) vaincre. ● **conquering** a victorieux. ● **conqueror** n conquérant, -ante mf, vainqueur m. ● **conquest** n conquête f.

cons [kɒnz] npl **the pros and (the) c.** le pour et le contre.

conscience ['kɒnʃəns] n conscience f. ● **conscience-stricken** a pris de remords.

conscientious [kɒnʃɪ'enʃəs] a consciencieux; **c. objector** objecteur m de conscience. ● **conscientiousness** n application f, sérieux m.

conscious ['kɒnʃəs] a (*awake*) conscient; (*intentional*) (*effort, decision etc*) délibéré; **c. of sth** (*aware*) conscient de qch; **c. that** conscient que; **to be c. of doing** avoir conscience de faire. ● **consciously** adv (*knowingly*) consciemment. ● **consciousness** n conscience f (**of** de); **to lose/regain c.** perdre/reprendre connaissance.

conscript ['kɒnskrɪpt] n (*soldier*) conscrit m ▮ [kən'skrɪpt] vt enrôler (par conscription). ● **conscription** [kən'skrɪpʃ(ə)n] n conscription f.

consecrate ['kɒnsɪkreɪt] vt (*church, temple, place, bishop*) consacrer. ● **consecration** [-'kreɪʃ(ə)n] n consécration f.

consecutive [kən'sekjʊtɪv] a consécutif. ● **consecutively** adv consécutivement.

consensus [kən'sensəs] n consensus m, accord m (général).

consent [kən'sent] vi consentir (**to** à) ▮ n consentement m; **by common c.** de l'aveu de tous; **by mutual c.** d'un commun accord.

consequence ['kɒnsɪkwəns] n (*result*) conséquence f; (*importance*) importance f, conséquence f. ● **consequently** adv par conséquent.

conservative [kən'sɜːvətɪv] 1 a (*estimate*) modeste; (*view, attitude etc*) traditionnel; (*person*) traditionaliste. 2 a & n **C.** Br Pol conservateur, -trice (mf). ● **conservatism** n (*in behaviour*) & Br Pol conservatisme m.

conservatoire [kən'sɜːvətwɑːr] n conservatoire m (*de musique*).

conservatory [kən'sɜːvətrɪ] n (*room next to house*) Br véranda f.

conserve [kən'sɜːv] vt (*energy, water, electricity etc*) économiser, faire des économies de; (*preserve unchanged*) préserver (*des privilèges, la faune etc*); **to c. one's strength** éco-

nomiser *or* ménager ses forces. ● **conservation** [kɒnsə'veɪʃ(ə)n] n (*energy-saving*) économies fpl d'énergie; (*of nature*) protection f de l'environnement; **c. area** zone f naturelle protégée. ● **conservationist** n défenseur m de l'environnement.

consider [kən'sɪdər] vt considérer; (*take into account*) tenir compte de; **I'll c. it** j'y réfléchirai; **to c. doing** envisager de faire; **to c. that** estimer *or* considérer que; **he's** *or* **she's being considered for the job** sa candidature est à l'étude; **all things considered** tout compte fait.

considerable [kən'sɪdərəb(ə)l] a (*large*) considérable; (*much*) beaucoup de. ● **considerably** adv beaucoup, considérablement.

considerate [kən'sɪdərət] a plein d'égards (**to** pour), attentionné (**to** à l'égard de).

consideration [kənsɪdə'reɪʃ(ə)n] n (*thought, thoughtfulness, reason*) considération f; **under c.** à l'étude; **out of c. for** par égard pour; **to take sth into c.** prendre qch en considération.

considering [kən'sɪdərɪŋ] prep compte tenu de, étant donné; **c. that** étant donné que, vu que ▮ adv Fam **the result was good c.** Fam le résultat était bon, après tout.

consign [kən'saɪn] vt (*send*) expédier (*marchandises*); (*give, entrust*) confier (**to** à). ● **consignment** n (*goods arriving*) arrivage m, envoi m; (*goods sent off*) envoi m; (*sending*) expédition f.

consist [kən'sɪst] vi consister (**of** en, **in** dans, **in doing** à faire).

consistent [kən'sɪstənt] a (*unchanging*) (*loyalty etc*) constant; (*friend*) fidèle; (*coherent*) (*ideas, argument etc*) cohérent, logique; **to be c. with** (*of statement etc*) concorder avec, cadrer avec. ● **consistency** n 1 (*of liquid etc*) consistance f. 2 (*of ideas etc*) cohérence f. ● **consistently** adv (*always*) constamment; (*regularly*) régulièrement; (*logically*) avec logique.

console¹ [kən'səʊl] vt consoler. ● **consolation** [kɒnsə'leɪʃ(ə)n] n consolation f; **c. prize** lot m de consolation.

console² ['kɒnsəʊl] n (*control desk*) console f.

consolidate [kən'sɒlɪdeɪt] vt consolider ▮ vi se consolider. ● **consolidation** [-'deɪʃ(ə)n] n consolidation f.

consonant ['kɒnsənənt] n consonne f.

consort 1 ['kɒnsɔːt] n époux m, épouse f; **prince c.** prince m consort. **2** [kən'sɔːt] vi **to c. with** (*criminals, addicts etc*) fréquenter.

consortium [kən'sɔːtɪəm] n (*of companies etc*) consortium m.

conspicuous [kən'spɪkjʊəs] a (*noticeable*) visible, en évidence; (*striking*) remarquable, manifeste; (*showy*) voyant; **to be c. by one's absence** briller par son absence; **in a c. position** (bien) en évidence; **to make oneself c.** se faire remarquer, se mettre en évidence. ● **conspicuously** adv visiblement.

conspire [kən'spaɪər] 1 vi (*plot*) conspirer

(against contre); **to c. to do** comploter de faire. **2** vt **to c. to do** (of events) conspirer or concourir à faire. ● **conspiracy** [-'spırəsı] n conspiration f.

constable ['kʌnstəb(ə)l] n (police) c. Br agent m (de police); **chief c.** Br = préfet m de police. ● **con'stabulary** n Br la police.

constant ['kɒnstənt] a (frequent) incessant; (unchanging) constant; (faithful) fidèle. ● **constancy** n constance f. ● **constantly** adv constamment, sans cesse.

constellation [kɒnstə'leıʃ(ə)n] n constellation f.

consternation [kɒnstə'neıʃ(ə)n] n consternation f.

constipate ['kɒnstıpeıt] vt constiper. ● **constipated** a constipé. ● **constipation** [-'peıʃ(ə)n] n constipation f.

constituent [kən'stıtjuənt] **1** n (part) élément m constituant ∎ a (element, part) constituant, constitutif. **2** n (voter) électeur, -trice mf (d'une circonscription). ● **constituency** n circonscription f électorale; (voters) électeurs mpl.

constitute ['kɒnstıtjuːt] vt constituer. ● **constitution** [-'tjuːʃ(ə)n] n (of person, country, committee etc) constitution f. ● **consti'tutional** a Pol constitutionnel.

constrain [kən'streın] vt **1** contraindre (s.o. to do qn à faire); **constrained to do** contraint de faire. **2** (of clothing etc) gêner (qn). ● **constraint** n contrainte f.

constrict [kən'strıkt] vt (tighten, narrow) resserrer; (movement) gêner. ● **constriction** [-'strıkʃ(ə)n] n resserrement m.

construct [kən'strʌkt] vt construire. ● **construction** [-ʃ(ə)n] n (building, structure) & Grammar construction f; **under c.** en construction. ● **constructive** a constructif.

construe [kən'struː] vt interpréter, comprendre.

consul ['kɒnsəl] n consul m. ● **consular** a consulaire. ● **consulate** n consulat m.

consult [kən'sʌlt] vt consulter ∎ vi **to c. with** discuter avec, conférer avec; **consulting room** (of doctor) Br cabinet m de consultation. ● **consultation** [kɒnsəl'teıʃ(ə)n] n consultation f; **in c. with** en consultation avec.

consultancy [kən'sʌltənsı] n c. (firm) cabinet m d'experts-conseils. **c. fee** honoraires mpl de conseils. ● **consultant** n (doctor) Br spécialiste mf; (adviser) conseiller, -ère mf; (financial, legal) conseil m, expert-conseil m ∎ a (engineer etc) consultant. ● **consultative** a (committee, role) consultatif.

consume [kən'sjuːm] vt (food, supplies etc) consommer; (of fire) consumer (bâtiment etc); (of grief, hate etc) dévorer (qn); **to be consumed by** or **with** (jealousy etc) être dévoré de; **consuming ambition/passion** ambition f/passion f dévorante. ● **consumer** n consommateur, -trice mf; **gas/electricity c.** abonné, -ée mf au gaz/à l'électricité; **c. goods/society** biens mpl/société f de consommation; **c. magazine** magazine m de dé-

fense du consommateur; **c. protection** défense f du consommateur. ● **consumerism** n consumérisme m. ● **consumption** [-'sʌmpʃ(ə)n] n consommation f (of de).

consummate ['kɒnsəmət] a (perfect) (artist etc) consommé, parfait; (liar etc) fini, parfait.

contact ['kɒntækt] n contact m; (person) contact m, relation f; **in c. with** en contact avec; **c. lenses** lentilles fpl or verres mpl de contact ∎ vt contacter, se mettre en contact avec.

contagious [kən'teıdʒəs] a contagieux.

contain [kən'teın] vt (enclose, hold back) contenir; **to c. oneself** se contenir. ● **container** n (box, jar etc) récipient m; (for transporting goods) conteneur m, container m.

contaminate [kən'tæmıneıt] vt contaminer. ● **contamination** [-'neıʃ(ə)n] n contamination f.

contemplate ['kɒntəmpleıt] vt (look at) contempler; (consider) envisager (**doing** de faire). ● **contemplation** [-'pleıʃ(ə)n] n contemplation f; **deep in c.** en pleine contemplation.

contemporary [kən'tempərərı] a contemporain (**with** de); (pattern, colour, style etc) moderne ∎ n (person) contemporain, -aine mf.

contempt [kən'tempt] n mépris m; **to hold s.o./sth in c.** mépriser qn/qch. ● **contemptible** a méprisable. ● **contemptuous** a dédaigneux (**of** de).

contend [kən'tend] **1** vi **to c. with** (problem, difficulty) faire face à; **to c. with s.o.** (deal with) avoir affaire à qn; (compete with) rivaliser avec qn; (struggle with) se battre avec qn. **2** vt **to c. that** (claim) soutenir que. ● **contender** n concurrent, -ente mf.

content[1] [kən'tent] a satisfait (**with** de); **he's c. to do** il ne demande pas mieux que de faire. ● **contented** a satisfait. ● **contentment** n contentement m.

content[2] ['kɒntent] n (of book, text, film etc) (subject matter) contenu m; **contents** (of container, letter, book etc) (total contained within) contenu m; (table of) **contents** (of book) table f des matières; **alcoholic/iron/etc c.** teneur f en alcool/fer/etc.

contention [kən'tenʃ(ə)n] n **1** (claim, belief) affirmation f. **2** (disagreement) désaccord m.

contentious [kən'tenʃəs] a (issue) litigieux.

contest [kən'test] vt (dispute) contester; (fight for) disputer ∎ ['kɒntest] n (competition) concours m; (fight) lutte f; Boxing combat m. ● **con'testant** n concurrent, -ente mf; (in fight) adversaire mf.

context ['kɒntekst] n contexte m; **in/out of c.** (word) dans/hors de son contexte.

continent ['kɒntınənt] n continent m; **the C.** l'Europe f (continentale); **on the c.** en Europe. ● **conti'nental** a (of Europe) européen; (of other continents) continental; **c. breakfast** petit déjeuner m à la française

▮ *n* Européen, -enne *mf* (continental(e)).

contingent [kən'tɪndʒənt] **1** *a* to **be c. upon** dépendre de. **2** *nm* (*group of people, soldiers*) contingent *m*. ●**contingency** *n* éventualité *f*; **c. plan** plan *m* d'urgence.

continual [kən'tɪnjʊəl] *a* continuel. ●**continually** *adv* continuellement.

continue [kən'tɪnjuː] *vt* continuer (**to do or doing** à *or* de faire); **to c. (with)** (*work, speech etc*) poursuivre, continuer; (*resume*) reprendre ▮ *vi* continuer; (*resume*) reprendre; **to c. in one's job** garder son emploi; **to c. with s.o.** (*in job*) garder qn. ●**continued** *a* (*interest, attention etc*) soutenu, assidu; (*presence*) continu(el); **to be c.** (*of story*) à suivre. ●**continuance** *n* continuation *f*. ●**continuation** [-'eɪʃ(ə)n] *n* continuation *f*; (*resumption*) reprise *f*; (*new episode*) suite *f*.

continuity [kɒntɪ'njuːɪtɪ] *n* continuité *f*.

continuous [kən'tɪnjʊəs] *a* continu; **c. film programme, c. performance** cinéma *m* permanent. ●**continuously** *adv* sans interruption.

contort [kən'tɔːt] *vt* (*twist*) tordre; **to c. oneself** se contorsionner. ●**contortion** [-ʃ(ə)n] *n* contorsion *f*. ●**contortionist** *n* (*acrobat*) contorsionniste *m*.

contour ['kɒntʊər] *n* contour *m*; **c. (line)** (*on map*) courbe *f* de niveau.

contraband ['kɒntrəbænd] *n* contrebande *f*.

contraception [kɒntrə'sepʃ(ə)n] *n* contraception *f*. ●**contraceptive** *a & n* contraceptif (*m*); **c. device** contraceptif *m*.

contract¹ ['kɒntrækt] *n* contrat *m*; **c. work** travail *m* en sous-traitance ▮ *vt* **to c. to do** s'engager (par un contrat) à faire ▮ *vi* **to c. out of** (*agreement etc*) se dégager de. ●**con'tractor** *n* entrepreneur *m*.

contract² [kən'trækt] *vt* (*illness, habit, debt, muscle etc*) contracter ▮ *vi* (*of heart, market etc*) se contracter. ●**contraction** [-ʃ(ə)n] *n* (*of muscle etc, word*) contraction *f*.

contradict [kɒntrə'dɪkt] *vt* (*person, statement etc*) contredire; (*belief*) démentir; **to c. each other** se contredire. ●**contradiction** [-ʃ(ə)n] *n* contradiction *f*. ●**contradictory** *a* contradictoire.

contralto [kən'træltəʊ] *n* (*pl* **-os**) contralto *m*.

contraption [kən'træpʃ(ə)n] *n Fam* engin *m*, machin *m*.

contrary 1 ['kɒntrərɪ] *a* (*opposite*) contraire (**to** à) ▮ *adv* **c. to** contrairement à ▮ *n* contraire *m*; **on the c.** au contraire; **unless you, I** *etc* **hear to the c.** sauf avis contraire; **she said nothing to the c.** elle n'a rien dit contre. **2** [kən'treərɪ] *a* (*obstinate*) entêté, difficile.

contrast 1 ['kɒntrɑːst] *n* contraste *m*; **in c. to** par opposition à. **2** [kən'trɑːst] *vi* contraster (**with** avec) ▮ *vt* mettre en contraste, faire contraster. ●**contrasting** *a* (*colours, opinions etc*) opposés.

contravene [kɒntrə'viːn] *vt* (*law*) enfreindre. ●**contravention** [-'venʃ(ə)n] *n* **in c. of** en contravention de.

contribute [kən'trɪbjuːt] *vt* donner, fournir (**to** à); (*article*) écrire (**to** pour); **to c. money to** contribuer à, verser de l'argent à. ▮ *vi* **to c. to** contribuer à; (*publication*) collaborer à; (*discussion, debate*) participer à. ●**contribution** [kɒntrɪ'bjuːʃ(ə)n] *n* contribution *f*; (*to pension fund etc*) cotisation(s) *f(pl)*; (*newspaper article*) article *m*. ●**contributor** *n* (*to newspaper etc*) collaborateur, -trice *mf*; (*of money*) donateur, -trice *mf*. ●**contributory** *a* **a c. factor** un facteur qui a contribué (**in** à).

contrite [kən'traɪt] *a* contrit. ●**contrition** [-ʃ(ə)n] *n* contrition *f*.

contrivance [kən'traɪvəns] *n* (*device*) dispositif *m*; (*scheme*) invention *f*.

contrive [kən'traɪv] *vt* **to c. to do** trouver moyen de faire.

contrived [kən'traɪvd] *a* (*meeting, incident*) arrangé; (*plot, ending*) artificiel.

control [kən'trəʊl] *vt* (**-ll-**) (*business, organization*) diriger; (*traffic*) régler; (*prices, quality*) contrôler; (*emotion, reaction*) maîtriser, contrôler; (*disease*) enrayer; (*situation*) être maître de, contrôler; **to c. oneself** se contrôler.

▮ *n* (*authority*) autorité *f* (**over** sur); (*over prices, quality*) contrôle *m*; (*over one's emotions*) maîtrise *f*; **the controls** (*of train etc*) les commandes *fpl*; (*knobs of TV set, radio etc*) les boutons *mpl*; (**self-)c.** le contrôle de soi-même, la maîtrise (de soi); **to keep s.o. under c.** tenir qn; **the situation** *or* **everything is under c.** je contrôle la situation; **everything is under c.** (*OK*) tout est en ordre, tout va bien; **to bring** *or* **get a fire/inflation under c.** maîtriser un incendie/l'inflation; **to take** *or* **assume c. of** (*country, business etc*) prendre le contrôle de; **to be in c. of** (*situation, vehicle*) être maître de; **I'm in c.** (*of situation*) j'ai la situation en main; **to lose c. of** (*situation, vehicle*) perdre le contrôle de; **out of c.** (*situation, crowd*) difficilement maîtrisable; **c. key** *Comptr* touche *f* de contrôle; **c. room** (*in space station*) salle *f* de contrôle; **c. tower** (*at airport*) tour *f* de contrôle.

controller [kən'trəʊlər] *n* **air traffic c.** contrôleur *m* aérien, aiguilleur *m* du ciel.

controversy ['kɒntrəvɜːsɪ] *n* controverse *f*. ●**controversial** [-'vɜːʃəl] *a* (*book, author*) contesté, discuté; (*doubtful*) discutable.

conundrum [kə'nʌndrəm] *n* devinette *f*, énigme *f*; (*mystery*) énigme *f*.

conurbation [kɒnɜː'beɪʃ(ə)n] *n* conurbation *f*.

convalesce [kɒnvə'les] *vi* (*rest*) être en convalescence; **to c. from** (*recover*) se remettre de. ●**convalescence** *n* convalescence *f*. ●**convalescent** *n* convalescent, -ente *mf*; **c. home** maison *f* de convalescence.

convector [kən'vektər] *n* **c. (heater)** convecteur *m*, radiateur *m* à convection.

convene [kən'viːn] *vt* (*meeting*) convoquer ▮ *vi* (*meet*) se réunir.

convenience [kən'viːnɪəns] *n* commodité *f*;

(*comfort*) confort *m*, commodité *f*; (*advantage*) avantage *m*; (*closeness*) proximité *f* (*des magasins, écoles etc*); **come at your (own) c.** venez quand vous voudrez; **all modern conveniences** tout le confort moderne; (**public**) **conveniences** *Br* toilettes *fpl*; **c. food(s)** plats *mpl* tout préparés; **c. store** magasin *m* de proximité.

convenient [kən'vi:nɪənt] *a* commode, pratique; (*well-situated*) bien situé (**for the shops/** *etc* par rapport aux magasins/*etc*); (*moment*), convenable, opportun; **to be c. (for)** (*suit*) convenir (à). ● **conveniently** *adv* (*to arrive, say sth etc*) à propos; **c. situated** bien situé.

convent ['kɒnvənt] *n* couvent *m*; **c. school** couvent *m*.

convention [kən'venʃ(ə)n] *n* (*custom*) usage *m*, convention *f*; (*agreement*) convention *f*; (*meeting*) assemblée *f*; (*political*) *Am* convention *f*. ● **conventional** *a* conventionnel; **c. weapons** armes *fpl* classiques.

converge [kən'vɜːdʒ] *vi* converger (**on** sur). ● **converging** *a* convergent. ● **convergence** *n* convergence *f*.

conversant [kən'vɜːsənt] *a* **to be c. with** (*custom, book, author etc*) connaître; (*fact*) savoir; (*cars, painting etc*) s'y connaître en.

conversation [kɒnvə'seɪʃ(ə)n] *n* conversation *f* (**with** avec). ● **conversational** *a* (*tone*) de la conversation; (*person*) loquace; **to study c. French** étudier le français parlé. ● **conversationalist** *n* causeur, -euse *mf*; **to be a (good) c.** avoir de la conversation.

converse 1 [kən'vɜːs] *vi* s'entretenir (**with** avec). **2** ['kɒnvɜːs] *a* & *n* inverse (*m*). ● **con'versely** *adv* inversement.

convert [kən'vɜːt] **1** *vt* (*change*) convertir (**into, to** en); (*building*) aménager (**into, to** en). **2** *vt* **to c. s.o.** (*to another religion*) convertir qn (**to** à) ▌ *vi* (*change religion*) se convertir; **to c. into a bed** (*of sofa*) se transformer en lit ▌ ['kɒnvɜːt] *n* converti, -ie *mf*. ● **conversion** [*Br* -ʃ(ə)n, *Am* -ʒ(ə)n] *n* conversion *f*; (*of building*) aménagement *m*.

convertible [kən'vɜːtəb(ə)l] *a* (*car*) (voiture *f*) décapotable *f* ▌ *a* **c. currency/sofa/***etc* monnaie *f*/canapé *m*/*etc* convertible.

convex ['kɒnveks] *a* convexe.

convey [kən'veɪ] *vt* (*goods, people*) transporter; (*sound, message, order*) transmettre; (*idea*) communiquer (**to** à); (*evoke*) évoquer; (*water etc through pipes*) amener. ● **conveyance** *n* transport *m*; (*vehicle*) véhicule *m*. ● **conveyor belt** *n* tapis *m* roulant.

convict ['kɒnvɪkt] *n* forçat *m* ▌ [kən'vɪkt] *vt* reconnaître *or* déclarer coupable (**of murder/***etc* de meurtre/*etc*). ● **con'viction** [-ʃ(ə)n] *n* (*for crime*) condamnation *f*; (*belief*) conviction *f* (**that** que); **to carry c.** (*of argument etc*) être convaincant.

convince [kən'vɪns] *vt* convaincre, persuader (**of sth** de qch, **to do sth** qn de faire qch). ● **convincing** *a* (*argument, person*) convaincant. ● **convincingly** *adv* (*to argue etc*)

de façon convaincante.

convivial [kən'vɪvɪəl] *a* (*event etc*) joyeux, gai; (*person*) bon vivant.

convoke [kən'vəʊk] *vt* (*meeting etc*) convoquer.

convoluted [kɒnvə'luːtɪd] *a* (*argument, style*) compliqué, tarabiscoté.

convolvulus [kən'vɒlvjʊləs] *n* liseron *m*.

convoy ['kɒnvɔɪ] *n* (*ships, cars etc*) convoi *m*.

convulse [kən'vʌls] *vt* (*shake*) bouleverser, ébranler; (*face*) convulser; **to be convulsed with pain** se tordre de douleur. ● **convulsion** [-ʃ(ə)n] *n* convulsion *f*. ● **convulsive** *a* convulsif.

coo [kuː] *vi* (*of dove*) roucouler.

cook [kʊk] *vt* (faire) cuire; **to c. the accounts** *or* **books** *Fam* truquer les comptes; **to c. up** *Fam* inventer (*excuse etc*).

▌ *vi* (*of food*) cuire; (*of person*) faire la cuisine; **what's cooking?** *Fam* qu'est-ce qui se passe?

▌ *n* (*person*) cuisinier, -ière *mf*. ● **cooking** *n* (*activity, food*) cuisine *f*; **to do the c.** faire la cuisine; **c. apple** pomme *f* à cuire. ● **cooker** *n* *Br* (*stove*) cuisinière *f*; (*apple*) pomme *f* à cuire.

cookbook ['kʊkbʊk] *n* livre *m* de cuisine. ● **cookery** *n* cuisine *f*; **c. book** *Br* livre *m* de cuisine.

cookie ['kʊkɪ] *n* *Am* biscuit *m*, gâteau *m* sec.

cool [kuːl] *a* (-**er**, -**est**) (*weather, place etc*) frais (*f* fraîche); (*having cooled down*) (*tea, soup etc*) qui n'est plus très chaud; (*clothes*) léger; (*calm*) (*manner, person*) calme; (*unfriendly*) (*reception etc*) froid; (*impertinent*) *Fam* effronté; (*excellent*) *Fam* super *inv*; (*acceptable*) *Fam* cool *inv*; **I feel c.** (*too cold*) j'ai (un peu) froid; (*no longer too hot*) j'ai moins chaud; **a (nice) c. drink** une boisson (bien) fraîche; **a c. 50 pounds** la coquette somme de 50 livres; **the weather is c., it's c.** il fait frais; **to keep sth c.** tenir qch au frais.

▌ *n* (*of evening*) fraîcheur *f*; **to keep sth in the c.** tenir qch au frais; **to keep/lose one's c.** garder/perdre son sang-froid.

▌ *vt* **to c. (down)** refroidir, rafraîchir.

▌ *vi* **to c. (down or off)** (*of hot liquid*) refroidir; (*of enthusiasm*) se refroidir; (*of anger, angry person*) se calmer; **to c. off** (*refresh oneself by drinking, swimming etc*) se rafraîchir; **to c. off towards s.o.** se refroidir en vers qn. ● **cooler** *n* (*for food*) glacière *f*. ● **coolly** *adv* (*calmly*) calmement; (*to welcome*) froidement; (*boldly*) effrontément. ● **coolness** *n* fraîcheur *f*; (*unfriendliness*) froideur *f*.

cool-headed [kuːl'hedɪd] *a* calme.

coop [kuːp] **1** *n* (*for chickens*) poulailler *m*. **2** *vt* **to c. up** (*person, animal*) enfermer; **I've been cooped up** je suis resté enfermé.

co-op ['kəʊɒp] *n* *Am* appartement *m* en copropriété.

co-operate [kəʊ'ɒpəreɪt] *vi* coopérer (**in** à, **with** avec). ●**co-operation** [-'reɪʃ(ə)n] *n* coopération *f*.

co-operative [kəʊ'ɒpərətɪv] *a* coopératif ▮ *n* coopérative *f*.

co-opt [kəʊ'ɒpt] *vt* coopter (**on to** à).

co-ordinate [kəʊ'ɔːdɪneɪt] *vt* coordonner. ●**co-ordination** [-'neɪʃ(ə)n] *n* coordination *f*. ●**co-ordinator** *n* (*of project*) coordinateur, -trice *mf*.

co-ordinates [kəʊ'ɔːdɪnəts] *npl* Math coordonnées *fpl*; (*clothes*) coordonnés *mpl*.

co-owner [kəʊ'əʊnər] *n* copropriétaire *mf*.

cop [kɒp] **1** *n* (*policeman*) Fam flic *m*. **2** *vt* (**-pp-**) (*catch*) Br Sl piquer. **3** *vi* (**-pp-**) to c. out Sl se défiler, éviter ses responsabilités.

cope [kəʊp] *vi* to c. with s'occuper de; (*problem*) faire face à; (**to be able**) **to c.** (*savoir*) se débrouiller; **I** (**just**) **can't c.** je n'y arrive plus.

copier ['kɒpɪər] *n* (*photocopying machine*) photocopieuse *f*.

co-pilot ['kəʊpaɪlət] *n* copilote *m*.

copious ['kəʊpɪəs] *a* (*meal*) copieux; (*sunshine, amount*) abondant.

copper ['kɒpər] *n* **1** (*metal*) cuivre *m*; **coppers** (*coins*) Br petite monnaie *f*. **2** (*policeman*) Br Fam flic *m*.

coppice ['kɒpɪs] *or* **copse** [kɒps] *n* (*trees, bushes*) bosquet *m*.

copulate ['kɒpjuleɪt] *vi* s'accoupler. ●**copulation** [-'leɪʃ(ə)n] *n* copulation *f*.

copy ['kɒpɪ] *n* copie *f*; (*of book, magazine etc*) exemplaire *m*; (*of photo*) épreuve *f* ▮ *vt* copier; **to c. out** *or* **down** (*text, letter etc*) (re)copier ▮ *vi* copier. ●**copyright** *n* copyright *m*.

coral ['kɒrəl] *n* corail *m*; **c. reef** récif *m* de corail.

cord [kɔːd] *n* **1** (*heavy string*) (*of curtain, bell, Br pyjamas, Am pajamas*) cordon *m*; (*electrical*) cordon *m* électrique; **vocal cords** cordes *fpl* vocales. **2 cords** (*corduroy Br trousers or Am pants*) Fam velours *m*, pantalon *m* en velours (côtelé).

cordial ['kɔːdɪəl] **1** *a* (*friendly*) cordial. **2** *n* (*fruit*) **c.** Br sirop *m*.

cordless ['kɔːdləs] *a* **c. phone** téléphone *m* sans fil.

cordon ['kɔːdən] *n* cordon *m* ▮ *vt* **to c. off** (*of police*) interdire l'accès de, boucler (*lieu*).

corduroy ['kɔːdərɔɪ] *n* (*fabric*) velours *m* côtelé; **corduroys** (*Br trousers, Am pants*) pantalon *m* en velours (côtelé), velours *m*.

core [kɔːr] *n* (*of apple etc*) trognon *m*; (*of problem*) cœur *m*; (*group of people*) & Geol noyau *m*; **rotten to the c.** corrompu jusqu'à la moelle; **c. vocabulary** vocabulaire *m* de base ▮ *vt* (*apple*) vider. ●**corer** *n* (*apple*) **c.** vide-pomme *m*.

cork [kɔːk] *n* (*material*) liège *m*; (*for bottle*) bouchon *m* ▮ *vt* **to c.** (**up**) (*bottle*) boucher. ●**corkscrew** *n* tire-bouchon *m*.

corn [kɔːn] *n* **1** (*wheat*) Br blé *m*; (*maize*) Am maïs *m*; (*seed*) grain *m*; **c. on the cob**

épi *m* de maïs. **2** (*hard skin on foot*) cor *m*.

corned beef [kɔːnd'biːf] *n* corned-beef *m*.

cornea ['kɔːnɪə] *n* (*of eye*) cornée *f*.

corner ['kɔːnər] **1** *n* coin *m*; (*of street, room*) coin *m*, angle *m*; (*bend in road*) virage *m*; Football corner *m*; **in a (tight) c.** dans une situation difficile; **around the c.** (*shops, school etc*) à deux pas; (*help, spring etc*) tout proche; **c. shop** magasin *m* du coin. **2** *vt* (*trap so as to speak to, capture etc*) coincer, accrocher (*qn*); (*animal*) acculer; **to c. the market** monopoliser le marché. **3** *vi* (*of vehicle*) prendre un virage. ●**cornerstone** *n* pierre *f* angulaire.

cornet ['kɔːnɪt] *n* (*of ice cream etc*) Br cornet *m*; (*instrument*) cornet *m* (à pistons).

cornflakes ['kɔːnfleɪks] *npl* céréales *fpl*, corn flakes *mpl*.

cornflour ['kɔːnflaʊər] *n* farine *f* de maïs, maïzena® *f*.

cornflower ['kɔːnflaʊər] *n* bleuet *m*.

cornstarch ['kɔːnstɑːtʃ] *n* Am = **cornflour**.

Cornwall ['kɔːnwəl] *n* Cornouailles *f*. ●**Cornish** *a* de Cornouailles.

corny ['kɔːnɪ] *a* (**-ier, -iest**) (*joke etc*) rebattu.

corollary [Br kə'rɒlərɪ, Am 'kɒrələrɪ] *n* corollaire *m*.

coronary ['kɒrənərɪ] *n* (*heart attack*) infarctus *m*.

coronation [kɒrə'neɪʃ(ə)n] *n* couronnement *m*, sacre *m*.

coroner ['kɒrənər] *n* coroner *m* (*officier de police judiciaire qui enquête en cas de mort suspecte*).

corporal ['kɔːpərəl] **1** *n* (*in army*) caporal (-chef) *m*. **2** *a* **c. punishment** châtiment *m* corporel.

corporate ['kɔːpərət] *a* (*decision etc*) collectif; (*action etc*) en commun; (*budget, image etc*) de l'entreprise; **c. body** Jur corps *m* constitué.

corporation [kɔːpə'reɪʃ(ə)n] *n* (*business*) société *f* commerciale; (*of town*) Br conseil *m* municipal.

corps [kɔːr, *pl* kɔːz] *n* Mil Pol etc corps *m*; **the press c.** les journalistes *mpl*.

corpse [kɔːps] *n* cadavre *m*.

corpulent ['kɔːpjulənt] *a* corpulent. ●**corpulence** *n* corpulence *f*.

corpus ['kɔːpəs] *n* (*texts, words*) corpus *m*.

corpuscle ['kɔːpʌs(ə)l] *n* (*blood cell*) globule *m*.

corral [kə'ræl] *n* Am corral *m* (*pl* -als).

correct [kə'rekt] *a* (*right, accurate*) (*answer etc*) exact, correct; (*proper*) correct; **he's c.** il a raison; **the c. time** l'heure exacte ▮ *vt* corriger. ●**correctly** *adv* correctement. ●**correctness** *n* (*accuracy, propriety*) correction *f*.

correction [kə'rekʃ(ə)n] *n* correction *f*; **c. fluid** liquide *m* correcteur.

corrective [kə'rektɪv] *a* (*act, measure*) rectificatif.

correlate ['kɒrəleɪt] *vi* correspondre (**with** à) ▮ *vt* faire correspondre. ●**correlation**

[-'leɪʃ(ə)n] n corrélation f (between entre).

correspond [kɒrɪ'spɒnd] vi 1 (agree, be similar) correspondre (to, with à). 2 (by letter) correspondre (with avec). ● **corresponding** a (matching) correspondant; (similar) semblable.

correspondence [kɒrɪ'spɒndəns] n correspondance f; c. course cours m par correspondance. ● **correspondent** n (journalist) envoyé, -ée mf; (letter writer) correspondant, -ante mf.

corridor ['kɒrɪdɔːr] n couloir m, corridor m; air c. couloir m aérien.

corroborate [kə'rɒbəreɪt] vt corroborer.

corrode [kə'rəʊd] vt ronger, corroder ▮ vi se corroder; (rust) rouiller f. ● **corroded** a (rusty) rouillé. ● **corrosion** [-ʒ(ə)n] n corrosion f; (rust) rouille f. ● **corrosive** a corrosif.

corrugated ['kɒrəgeɪtɪd] a c. iron tôle f ondulée; c. cardboard carton m ondulé.

corrupt [kə'rʌpt] vt corrompre ▮ a corrompu. ● **corruption** [-ʃ(ə)n] n corruption f.

corset ['kɔːsɪt] n (boned) corset m; (elasticated) gaine f.

Corsica ['kɔːsɪkə] n Corse f. ● **Corsican** a corse ▮ n Corse mf.

cos [kɒs] n c. (lettuce) Br (laitue f) romaine f.

cosh [kɒʃ] n Br matraque f ▮ vt Br matraquer.

cosiness ['kəʊzɪnəs] n intimité f, confort m.

cosmetic [kɒz'metɪk] n produit m de beauté ▮ a (surgery) esthétique; (change etc) Fig superficiel.

cosmopolitan [kɒzmə'pɒlɪtən] a & n cosmopolite (mf).

cosmos ['kɒzmɒs] n cosmos m. ● **cosmic** a cosmique. ● **cosmonaut** n cosmonaute mf.

Cossack ['kɒsæk] n cosaque m.

cosset ['kɒsɪt] vt choyer.

cost [kɒst] vti (pt & pp cost) coûter; how much does it c.? ça coûte or ça vaut combien?; to c. the earth Fam coûter les yeux de la tête.
▮ n prix m, coût m; the c. of living le coût de la vie; at great c. à grands frais; to my c. à mes dépens; at any c., at all costs à tout prix; at c. price Br au prix coûtant. ● **cost-effective** a rentable. ● **costly** a (-ier, -iest) (expensive) (car, trip etc) coûteux; (valuable) (jewel, antique etc) de (grande) valeur; c. error erreur f qui coûte cher.

co-star ['kəʊstɑːr] n (in film, play) partenaire mf.

Costa Rica [kɒstə'riːkə] n Costa Rica m.

costume ['kɒstjuːm] n costume m; (woman's suit) tailleur m; (swimming) c. Br maillot m (de bain); c. jewellery Br, c. jewelry Am bijoux mpl de fantaisie.

cosy ['kəʊzɪ] 1 a (-ier, -iest) (house etc) Br douillet; (atmosphere etc) intime; make yourself (nice and) c. mets-toi à l'aise; we're c. on est bien ici. 2 n (tea) c. couvre-théière m.

cot [kɒt] n (for baby) Br lit m (d'enfant);

(camp bed) Am lit m de camp; c. death Br mort f subite du nourrisson.

cottage ['kɒtɪdʒ] n petite maison f de campagne; (thatched) c. chaumière f; c. cheese fromage m blanc (maigre); c. industry travail m à domicile (activité artisanale); c. pie Br hachis m Parmentier.

cotton ['kɒtən] n coton m; (yarn) fil m (de coton); absorbent c. Am, c. wool Br coton m hydrophile, ouate f; c. shirt/etc chemise f/etc de or en coton; c. candy Am barbe f à papa. 2 vi to c. on (to) (realize) Sl piger.

couch [kaʊtʃ] 1 n (sofa) canapé m; (for doctor's patient) lit m. 2 vt (express) formuler.

couchette [kuː'ʃet] n (on train) Br couchette f.

cough [kɒf] 1 n toux f; c. syrup or medicine, Br c. mixture sirop m contre la toux ▮ vi tousser ▮ vt to c. up (blood) cracher. 2 vt to c. up (money) Sl cracher ▮ vi to c. up Sl casquer.

could [kʊd, unstressed kəd] see can¹.

couldn't ['kʊd(ə)nt] = could not.

council ['kaʊns(ə)l] n conseil m; (town or city) c. conseil m municipal; Security C. Conseil m de Sécurité; c. flat/house Br appartement m/maison f loué(e) à la municipalité, = HLM m or f; c. offices bureaux mpl de la municipalité. ● **councillor** n conseiller, -ère mf; (town) c. conseiller m municipal.

counsel ['kaʊnsəl] n inv (advice) conseil m; (lawyer) avocat, -ate mf ▮ vt (Br -ll-, Am -l-) conseiller (s.o. to do à qn de faire). ● **counselling** (Am **counseling**) n (advice) conseils mpl; (psychiatric etc) assistance f. ● **counsellor** (Am **counselor**) n conseiller, -ère mf.

count¹ [kaʊnt] vt (find number of, include) compter; (deem) considérer; not counting Paul sans compter Paul; to c. in (include) inclure; to c. out (exclude) exclure; (money) compter.
▮ vi (calculate, be important) compter; to c. against s.o. être un désavantage pour qn, jouer contre qn; to c. on s.o./sth (rely on) compter sur qn/qch; to c. on doing compter faire.
▮ n compte m; (charge) Jur chef m (d'accusation); he's lost c. of or he can't keep c. of the books he has il ne sait plus combien il a de livres; to keep (a) c. (of) tenir le compte (de). ● **countdown** n compte m à rebours.

count² [kaʊnt] n (title) comte m.

countenance ['kaʊntɪnəns] 1 n (face) Lit mine f, expression f. 2 vt (allow) tolérer; (approve) approuver.

counter ['kaʊntər] 1 n (in shop, bar etc) comptoir m; (in bank etc) guichet m; the food c. (in store) le rayon alimentation; under the c. Fig clandestinement, au marché noir; over the c. (to obtain medicine) sans ordonnance.

2 *n* (*in games*) jeton *m*.
3 *n* Tech compteur *m*.
4 *adv* **c. to** à l'encontre de.
5 *vt* (*threat*) répondre à; (*decision*) s'opposer à; (*effects*) neutraliser; (*plan*) contrarier; (*insult*) riposter à; (*blow*) parer ▮ *vi* riposter (**with** par).

counter- ['kaʊntər] *pref* contre-.
counteract [kaʊntə'rækt] *vt* (*influence, effects etc*) neutraliser.
counterattack ['kaʊntərətæk] *n* contre-attaque *f* ▮ *vti* contre-attaquer.
counterbalance ['kaʊntəbæləns] *n* contre-poids *m* ▮ *vt* contrebalancer.
counterclockwise [kaʊntə'klɒkwaɪz] *a* & *adv* Am dans le sens inverse des aiguilles d'une montre.
counterfeit ['kaʊntəfɪt] *a* faux (*f* fausse) ▮ *n* contrefaçon *f*, faux *m* ▮ *vt* contrefaire.
counterfoil ['kaʊntəfɔɪl] *n* souche *f*.
counterpart ['kaʊntəpɑːt] *n* (*thing*) équivalent *m*; (*person*) homologue *mf*.
counterpoint ['kaʊntəpɔɪnt] *n* (*musical*) contrepoint *m*.
counterproductive [kaʊntəprə'dʌktɪv] *a* (*action*) inefficace, qui produit l'effet contraire.
countersign ['kaʊntəsaɪn] *vt* contresigner.
countess ['kaʊntɪs] *n* comtesse *f*.
countless ['kaʊntləs] *a* innombrable.
countrified ['kʌntrɪfaɪd] *a* rustique.
country ['kʌntrɪ] *n* pays *m*; (*regarded with affection*) patrie *f*; (*region*) région *f*, pays *m*; (*opposed to town*) campagne *f*; **in the c.** à la campagne ▮ *a* (*house, road etc*) de campagne; **c. dancing** la danse folklorique. ● **countryman** *n* (*pl* **-men**) (*fellow*) *n*. compatriote *m*. ● **countryside** *n* campagne *f*; **in the c.** à la campagne.
county ['kaʊntɪ] *n* comté *m*; **c. seat** Am, **c. town** Br chef-lieu *m*.
coup [kuː], *pl* kuːz] *n* Pol coup *m* d'état.
coupé ['kuːpeɪ] *n* (*car*) coupé *m*.
couple ['kʌp(ə)l] **1** *n* (*of people*) couple *m*; **a c. of** deux ou trois; (*a few*) quelques. **2** *vt* (*connect*) accoupler. **3** *vi* (*mate*) s'accoupler.
coupon ['kuːpɒn] *n* (*voucher for gift, meal etc*) bon *m*; (*ticket*) coupon *m*.
courage ['kʌrɪdʒ] *n* courage *m*. ● **courageous** [kə'reɪdʒəs] *a* courageux.
courgette [kʊə'ʒet] *n* Br courgette *f*.
courier ['kʊrɪər] *n* (*for tourists*) guide *m*; (*messenger*) messager *m*; **c. service** service *m* de messagerie.
course [kɔːs] **1** *n* (*duration, movement*) cours *m*; (*of ship*) route *f*; (*of river*) cours *m*; (*way*) Fig route *f*, chemin *m*; (*means*) moyen *m*; **c.** (*of action*) ligne *f* de conduite; (*option*) parti *m*; **your best c. is to...** le mieux c'est de...; **as a matter of c.** normalement; **in the c. of** au cours de; **in** (**the**) **c. of time** avec le temps, à la longue; **in due c.** en temps utile. **2** *n* (*lessons*) cours *m*; **c. of lectures** série *f* de conférences.
3 *n* **c.** (*of treatment*) traitement *m*.

4 *n* (*of meal*) plat *m*; **first c.** entrée *f*; **main c.** plat *m* principal *or* de résistance.
5 *n* (*racecourse*) champ *m* de courses; (*golf*) **c.** terrain *m* (de golf).
6 *adv* **of c.!** bien sûr!, mais oui!; **of c. not!** bien sûr que non!

court[1] [kɔːt] *n* (*of king etc*) cour *f*; (*for trials*) cour *f*, tribunal *m*; (**tennis**) **c.** court *m* (de tennis); **c. of inquiry** commission *f* d'enquête; **high c.** cour *f* suprême; **to take s.o. to c.** poursuivre qn en justice; **c. shoe** Br escarpin *m*. ● **courthouse** *n* palais *m* de justice. ● **courtroom** *n* salle *f* du tribunal. ● **courtyard** *n* cour *f*.
court[2] [kɔːt] *vt* (*woman*) faire la cour à; (*danger*) aller au-devant de; (*s.o.'s support*) rechercher ▮ *vi* **they are courting** ils sortent ensemble; **a courting couple** un couple d'amoureux. ● **courtship** *n* (*act, period of time*) cour *f*.
courteous ['kɜːtɪəs] *a* poli, courtois. ● **courtesy** *n* politesse *f*, courtoisie *f*.
courtier ['kɔːtɪər] *n* Hist courtisan *m*.
court-martial [kɔːt'mɑːʃəl] *n* conseil *m* de guerre ▮ *vt* (Br **-ll-**, Am **-l-**) faire passer en conseil de guerre.
cousin ['kʌz(ə)n] *n* cousin, -ine *mf*.
cove [kəʊv] *n* (*bay*) anse *f*.
covenant ['kʌvənənt] *n* (*legal*) convention *f*; (*religious*) alliance *f*.
Coventry ['kɒvəntrɪ] *n* **to send s.o. to C.** (*punish*) Br mettre qn en quarantaine.
cover ['kʌvər] *n* (*lid*) couvercle *m*; (*of book*) couverture *f*; (*for furniture, typewriter*) housse *f*; (*bedspread*) dessus-de-lit *m*; **the covers** (*on bed*) les couvertures *fpl* et les draps *mpl*; **to take c.** se mettre à l'abri; **under c.** (*sheltered*) à l'abri; **c. charge** (*in restaurant*) couvert *m*; **c. note** (*insurance*) Br certificat *m* provisoire d'assurance; **under separate c.** (*letter*) sous pli séparé.
▮ *vt* couvrir (**with** de); (*protect*) protéger, couvrir; (*distance*) parcourir; (*pay for*) couvrir; (*include*) englober, recouvrir; (*treat*) traiter (sujet); (*event*) (*in newspaper, on TV etc*) couvrir, faire le reportage de; (*aim gun at*) tenir en joue; (*insure*) assurer (**against** contre); **to c. over** (*floor, saucepan etc*) recouvrir; **to c. up** recouvrir; (*truth, tracks*) dissimuler; (*scandal*) étouffer, camoufler.
▮ *vi* **to c.** (**oneself**) **up** (*wrap up*) se couvrir; **to c. up for s.o.** couvrir qn. ● **cover-up** *n* tentative *f* pour étouffer *or* camoufler une affaire.
coverage ['kʌvərɪdʒ] *n* (*of event on TV etc*) reportage *m* (**of** sur).
coveralls ['kʌvərɔːlz] *npl* Am bleus *mpl* de travail.
covering ['kʌvərɪŋ] *n* (*wrapping*) enveloppe *f*; (*layer*) couche *f*; **c. letter** lettre *f* jointe (à *un document*).
covert ['kəʊvət, 'kʌvət] *a* secret.
covet ['kʌvɪt] *vt* convoiter. ● **covetous** *a* avide.

cow¹ [kaʊ] n vache f; (nasty woman) Fam chameau m; **c. elephant/etc** éléphant m/etc femelle. ●**cowboy** n cow-boy m. ●**cowhand** n vacher, -ère mf. ●**cowshed** n étable f.

cow² [kaʊ] vt to be cowed (frightened) être intimidé (by par).

coward ['kaʊəd] n lâche mf. ●**cowardice** n lâcheté f. ●**cowardly** a lâche.

cower ['kaʊər] vi (crouch) se tapir; (with fear) trembler; (move back) reculer (par peur).

cowslip ['kaʊslɪp] n (plant) coucou m.

cox [kɒks] vt (boat) barrer ▌ n barreur, -euse mf.

coy [kɔɪ] a (-er, -est) qui fait son or sa timide. ●**coyness** n timidité f feinte.

coyote [kaɪ'əʊtɪ] n (wolf) Am coyote m.

cozy ['kəʊzɪ] Am = **cosy.**

CPA [siːpiː'eɪ] n abbr (certified public accountant) Am expert-comptable m.

crab [kræb] **1** n crabe m. **2** n c. apple pomme f sauvage. **3** vi (-bb-) (complain) Fam rouspéter (about à cause de).

crabby ['kræbɪ] a (-ier, -iest) (person) grincheux.

crack¹ [kræk] n (split) fente f; (in glass, china, bone etc) fêlure f; (in skin) crevasse f; (snapping noise) craquement m; (of whip) claquement m; (blow) coup m; (joke) Fam plaisanterie f (at aux dépens de); to have a **c. at doing** Fam essayer de faire; **at the c. of dawn** au point du jour.

▌ vt (glass, ice) fêler; (nut) casser; (ground, skin) crevasser; (whip) faire claquer; (joke) lancer; (problem) résoudre; (code) déchiffrer; (safe) percer; **it's not as hard as it's cracked up to be** ce n'est pas aussi dur qu'on le dit.

▌ vi se fêler; (of skin) se crevasser; (of branch, wood) craquer; **to get cracking** (get to work) Fam s'y mettre; (hurry) Fam se grouiller; **to c. down on** sévir contre; **to c. up** (mentally) Fam craquer. ●**crack-up** n Fam dépression f nerveuse; (crash) Am Fam accident m.

crack² [kræk] a (first-rate) (driver, skier etc) de premier ordre; **c. shot** tireur m d'élite.

crack³ [kræk] n (drug) crack m.

cracked [krækt] a (crazy) Fam cinglé.

cracker ['krækər] n **1** (biscuit) biscuit m (salé). **2** (firework) pétard m; **Christmas c.** diablotin m. **3 she's a c.** Br Fam elle est sensationnelle. ●**crackers** a (mad) Sl cinglé.

crackle ['kræk(ə)l] vi (of fire) crépiter; (of sth frying) grésiller; (of radio) crachoter ▌ n crépitement m; grésillement m; crachotement m.

crackpot ['krækpɒt] n Fam cinglé, -ée mf.

cradle ['kreɪd(ə)l] n berceau m ▌ vt bercer.

craft [krɑːft] **1** n (skill) art m; (job) métier m (artisanal) ▌ vt façonner. **2** n (cunning) ruse f. **3** n inv (boat) bateau m. ●**craftsman** n (pl -men) artisan m. ●**craftsmanship** n (skill) art m; **a fine piece of c.** un beau travail, une belle pièce.

crafty ['krɑːftɪ] a (-ier, -iest) astucieux; Pej rusé.

crag [kræg] n rocher m à pic. ●**craggy** a (rock) à pic; (face) rude.

cram [kræm] vt (-mm-) to c. sth into (force) fourrer qch dans; **to c. with** (fill) bourrer de ▌ vi to c. into (of people) s'entasser dans; **to c. (for an exam)** bachoter.

cramp [kræmp] n (muscle pain) crampe f (in à).

cramped [kræmpt] a (in a room or one's clothes) à l'étroit; **in c. conditions** à l'étroit.

cranberry ['krænbərɪ] n canneberge f.

crane [kreɪn] **1** n (machine, bird) grue f. **2** vt to c. one's neck tendre le cou.

crank [kræŋk] **1** n (person) Fam excentrique mf; (fanatic) fanatique mf. **2** n (handle) manivelle f ▌ vt to c. (up) (vehicle) faire démarrer à la manivelle. ●**cranky** a (-ier, -iest) excentrique; (bad-tempered) Am grincheux.

crannies ['krænɪz] npl **nooks and c.** coins et recoins mpl.

craps [kræps] n **to shoot c.** Am jouer aux dés.

crash [kræʃ] n (accident) accident m; (collapse of firm) faillite f; (noise) fracas m; (of thunder) coup m; **c. course/diet** cours m/ régime m intensif; **c. barrier** (on road) glissière f de sécurité; **c. helmet** casque m (anti-choc); **c. landing** atterrissage m en catastrophe.

▌ int (of fallen object) patatras!

▌ vt (car) avoir un accident avec; **to c. one's car into** faire rentrer sa voiture dans.

▌ vi (of car, plane) s'écraser; **to c. into** rentrer dans; **the cars crashed (into each other)** les voitures se sont percutées or rentrées dedans; **to c. (down)** (fall) tomber; (break) se casser; (of roof) s'effondrer. ●**crash-land** vi atterrir en catastrophe.

crass [kræs] a grossier; (stupidity) crasse.

crate [kreɪt] n (large) caisse f; (small) cageot m; (for bottles) casier m.

crater ['kreɪtər] n cratère m; (bomb) c. entonnoir m.

cravat [krə'væt] n foulard m (autour du cou).

crave [kreɪv] vt to c. (for) éprouver un grand besoin de; (mercy) implorer. ●**craving** n désir m, grand besoin m (for de).

craven ['kreɪvən] a (cowardly) Lit lâche.

crawl [krɔːl] vi (of snake, animal) ramper; (of child) marcher à quatre pattes; (of vehicle) avancer au pas; **to be crawling with** grouiller de ▌ n (swimming stroke) crawl m; **to do the c.** nager le crawl; **to move at a c.** (in vehicle) avancer au pas.

crayfish ['kreɪfɪʃ] n inv (freshwater) écrevisse f.

crayon ['kreɪən] n crayon m de couleur (en cire).

craze [kreɪz] n manie f (for de), engouement m (for pour). ●**crazed** a affolé.

crazy ['kreɪzɪ] a (-ier, -iest) fou (f folle); **to go c.** devenir fou; **c. about sth** fana de qch; **c. about s.o.** fou de qn; **c. paving** dallage m irrégulier. ●**craziness** n folie f.

creak [kriːk] vi (of hinge) grincer; (of floorboard, timber) craquer. ●**creaky** a grinçant; (floorboard etc) qui craque.

cream [kriːm] n crème f; (élite) Fig crème f, gratin m; **c.(-coloured)** crème inv; **c. cake** gâteau m à la crème; **c. cheese** fromage m blanc ▮ vt (milk) écrémer; **to c. off** (best students etc) Fig écrémer. ●**creamy** a (-ier, -iest) crémeux.

crease [kriːs] vt froisser, plisser ▮ vi se froisser ▮ n pli m; (accidental) (faux) pli m. ●**crease-resistant** a infroissable.

create [kriːˈeɪt] vt créer; (impression, noise) faire. ●**creation** [-ʃ(ə)n] n création f. ●**creator** n créateur, -trice mf.

creative [kriːˈeɪtɪv] a (person, activity) créatif. ●**creativeness** or **crea'tivity** n créativité f.

creature [ˈkriːtʃər] n animal m, bête f; (person) créature f; **one's c. comforts** ses aises fpl.

crèche [kreʃ] n (nursery) Br crèche f; (nativity scene) Am crèche f.

credence [ˈkriːdəns] n **to give** or **lend c. to** ajouter foi à.

credentials [krɪˈdenʃəlz] npl références fpl; (identity) pièces fpl d'identité; (of diplomat) lettres fpl de créance.

credible [ˈkredɪb(ə)l] a (believable) croyable; (politician, information) crédible. ●**credi'bility** n crédibilité f.

credit [ˈkredɪt] n (financial) crédit m; (merit) mérite m; (influence, prestige) crédit m; (from university) unité f de valeur; **credits** (of film) générique m; **to give c. to** (person) Fin faire crédit à; Fig reconnaître le mérite de; (statement) ajouter foi à; **to be a c. to** faire honneur à; **on c.** à crédit; **to be in c.** (of account) être créditeur; (of person) avoir un solde positif; **to one's c.** Fig à son actif; **c. balance** solde m créditeur; **c. card** carte f de crédit; **c. facilities** facilités fpl de paiement. ▮ vt (of bank) créditer (s.o. with sth qn de qch); (believe) croire (qch); **to c. s.o./sth with** (qualities) attribuer à qn/qch. ●**creditable** a honorable. ●**creditor** n créancier, -ière mf. ●**creditworthy** a solvable.

credulous [ˈkredjʊləs] a crédule.

creed [kriːd] n credo m.

creek [kriːk] n (stream) Am ruisseau m; (bay) Br crique f; **up the c.** (in trouble) Br Sl dans le pétrin.

creep [kriːp] **1** vi (pt & pp crept) ramper; (silently) se glisser (furtivement); (slowly) avancer lentement; **it makes my flesh c.** ça me donne la chair de poule.

2 n (person) Sl salaud m; **it gives me the creeps** Fam ça me fait froid dans le dos. ●**creepy** a (-ier, -iest) Fam (scary) terrifiant; (nasty) vilain. ●**creepy-'crawly** Br Fam or **creepy-'crawler** Am Fam n bestiole f.

cremate [krɪˈmeɪt] vt incinérer. ●**cremation** [-ʃ(ə)n] n crémation f.

crematorium [kreməˈtɔːrɪəm] (Am **crematory** [ˈkriːmətɔːrɪ]) n crématorium m.

Creole [ˈkriːəʊl] n Am créole mf; (language) créole m.

creosote [ˈkrɪəsəʊt] n créosote f.

crêpe [kreɪp] n (fabric) crêpe m; **c. (rubber)** crêpe m; **c. bandage** bande f Velpeau®; **c. paper** papier m crêpon.

crept [krept] pt & pp of creep **1**.

crescendo [krɪˈʃendəʊ] n (pl -os) crescendo m inv.

crescent [ˈkres(ə)nt] n croissant m; (street) Br Fig rue f (en demi-lune).

cress [kres] n cresson m.

crest [krest] n (of wave, mountain, bird) crête f; (of hill) sommet m; (on seal, letters etc) armoiries fpl.

Crete [kriːt] n Crète f.

cretin [Br ˈkretɪn, Am ˈkriːt(ə)n] n crétin, -ine mf. ●**cretinous** a crétin.

crevasse [krɪˈvæs] n (in ice) crevasse f.

crevice [ˈkrevɪs] n (crack) crevasse f, fente f.

crew [kruː] n (of ship, plane) équipage m; (gang) équipe f; **c. cut** (coupe f en) brosse f. ●**crew-neck(ed)** a à col ras.

crib [krɪb] **1** n (cot) Am lit m d'enfant; (cradle) berceau m; (nativity scene) crèche f; **c. death** Am mort f subite du nourrisson. **2** n (list of answers) Br pompe f, antisèche f; (copy) plagiat m ▮ vti (-bb-) copier.

crick [krɪk] n **c. in the neck** torticolis m; **c. in the back** tour m de reins.

cricket [ˈkrɪkɪt] n **1** (game) cricket m. **2** (insect) grillon m. ●**cricketer** n joueur, -euse mf de cricket.

crikey! [ˈkraɪkɪ] int Br Sl zut (alors)!

crime [kraɪm] n crime m; (not serious) délit m; (criminal practice) criminalité f; **c. wave** vague f de criminalité.

criminal [ˈkrɪmɪnəl] n criminel, -elle mf ▮ a criminel; **c. offence** (minor) délit m; (serious) crime m; **c. record** casier m judiciaire.

crimson [ˈkrɪmz(ə)n] a & n cramoisi (m).

cringe [krɪndʒ] vi reculer (from devant); (be humble) faire des courbettes (to, before à). ●**cringing** a (attitude etc) servile.

crinkle [ˈkrɪŋk(ə)l] vt (crumple) froisser; (fold) froncer ▮ vi se froisser ▮ n fronce f. ●**crinkly** a (crumpled) froissé; (folded) froncé; (hair) frisé.

cripple [ˈkrɪpəl] n (lame) estropié, -ée mf; (disabled) infirme mf ▮ vt (disable) rendre infirme, estropier; (nation etc) Fig paralyser; **crippling taxes** impôts mpl écrasants; **crippling strike** grève f paralysante. ●**crippled** a infirme, estropié; (ship) désemparé; **c. with rheumatism/pain** perclus de rhumatismes/ douleurs.

crisis, pl **-ses** [ˈkraɪsɪs, -siːz] n crise f.

crisp [krɪsp] **1** a (-er, -est) (biscuit) croustillant; (apple, vegetables etc) croquant; (snow) craquant; (air, style) vif. **2** npl (potato) **crisps** Br (pommes fpl) chips fpl; **packet of crisps** sachet m de chips. ●**crispbread** n pain m suédois.

criss-cross [ˈkrɪskrɒs] a (lines) entrecroisés; (muddled) enchevêtrés ▮ vi s'entrecroiser ▮ vt sillonner (en tous sens).

criterion [kraɪˈtɪərɪən], pl **-ia** [kraɪˈtɪərɪən, -ɪə] n critère m.

critic [ˈkrɪtɪk] n critique m. ●**critical** a critique. ●**critically** adv (to examine etc) en critique; (harshly) sévèrement; **c. ill** gravement malade. ●**criticism** n critique f. ●**criticize** vti critiquer. ●**critique** [krɪˈtiːk] n (essay etc) critique f.

croak [krəʊk] vi (of frog) croasser; (of person) parler d'une voix enrouée ‖ n croassement m.

Croatia [krəʊˈeɪʃə] n Croatie f.

crochet [ˈkrəʊʃeɪ] vt faire au crochet ‖ vi faire du crochet ‖ n (travail m au) crochet m; **c. hook** crochet m.

crock [krɒk] n **a c., an (old) c.** Fam (person) un croulant; (car) un tacot.

crockery [ˈkrɒkərɪ] n (cups etc) vaisselle f.

crocodile [ˈkrɒkədaɪl] n crocodile m.

crocus [ˈkrəʊkəs] n crocus m.

croft [krɒft] n Br petite ferme f.

crony [ˈkrəʊnɪ] n Pej Fam copain m, copine f.

crook [krʊk] n **1** (thief) escroc m. **2** (shepherd's stick) houlette f.

crooked [ˈkrʊkɪd] a (stick) courbé; (path) tortueux; (hat, picture) de travers; (deal, person) malhonnête ‖ adv de travers. ●**crookedly** adv de travers.

croon [kruːn] vti chanter (à voix basse).

crop [krɒp] **1** n (harvest) récolte f; (produce) culture f; (of questions etc) Fig série f; (of people) groupe m. **2** vt (-pp-) (hair) couper (ras) ‖ n **c. of hair** chevelure f. **3** vi (-pp-) **to c. up** se présenter, survenir. ●**cropper** n **to come a c.** Br Sl (fall) ramasser une pelle; (fail) échouer.

croquet [ˈkrəʊkeɪ] n (game) croquet m.

croquette [krəʊˈket] n (mashed potato etc) croquette f.

cross¹ [krɒs] n croix f; **a c. between** (animal) un croisement entre or de; **it's a c. between a car and a van** Fig c'est un compromis entre une voiture et une camionette; **c. street/** etc rue f/etc transversale.

cross² [krɒs] vt (street, room etc) traverser; (barrier, threshold) franchir; (legs, animals) croiser; (thwart) contrecarrer; (cheque, Am check) barrer; **to c. off or out** (word, name etc) rayer; **to c. over** (road etc) traverser; **it never crossed my mind that...** il ne m'est pas venu à l'esprit que...; **crossed lines** (of telephone) lignes fpl embrouillées.

‖ vi (of paths) se croiser; **to c. over** traverser.

cross³ [krɒs] a (angry) fâché (with contre); **to get c.** se fâcher (with contre). ●**crossly** adv d'un air fâché.

crossbow [ˈkrɒsbəʊ] n arbalète f.

crosscheck [krɒsˈtʃek] n contre-épreuve f ‖ vt vérifier.

cross-country [krɒsˈkʌntrɪ] a (walk etc) à travers champs; **c.-country race** cross m. ●**cross-examination** [-ɪɡˈzæmɪ-] n contre-interrogatoire m. ●**cross-e'xamine** vt interroger. ●**cross-eyed** a qui louche. ●**cross-**

'legged a & adv les jambes croisées. ●**cross-'purposes** npl **to be at c.-purposes** se comprendre mal. ●**cross-'reference** n renvoi m. ●**cross-section** [-ˈʃ(ə)n] n coupe f transversale; (sample) échantillon m.

crossfire [ˈkrɒsfaɪər] n feux mpl croisés.

crossing [ˈkrɒsɪŋ] n (by ship) traversée f; (pedestrian) c. Br passage m protégé or clouté.

crossroads [ˈkrɒsrəʊdz] n carrefour m.

crosswalk [ˈkrɒswɔːk] n Am passage m protégé or clouté.

crosswind [ˈkrɒswɪnd] n vent m de travers.

crossword [ˈkrɒswɜːd] n **c. (puzzle)** mots mpl croisés.

crotch [krɒtʃ] n (of garment, person) entre-jambe f.

crotchet [ˈkrɒtʃɪt] n (musical note) noire f.

crotchety [ˈkrɒtʃɪtɪ] a grincheux.

crouch [kraʊtʃ] vi **to c. (down)** s'accroupir, se tapir. ●**crouching** a accroupi, tapi.

croupier [ˈkruːpɪər] n (in casino) croupier m.

crow [krəʊ] **1** n corbeau m, corneille f; **as the c. flies** à vol d'oiseau; **c.'s nest** (on ship) nid m de pie. **2** vi (of cock) chanter; (boast) Fig se vanter (about de).

crowbar [ˈkrəʊbɑːr] n levier m, pince f à levier.

crowd [kraʊd] n foule f; (particular group) bande f; (of things) Fam masse f; **quite a c.** beaucoup de monde.

‖ vi **to c. into** (of people) s'entasser dans; **to c. round s.o./sth** se presser autour de qn/qch; **to c. together** se serrer.

‖ vt (fill) remplir; **to c. people/objects into** entasser des gens/des objets dans; **don't c. me!** Fam ne me bousculez pas! ●**crowded** a plein (with de); (train, room etc) bondé, plein; (city) encombré; **it's very c.!** il y a beaucoup de monde!

crown [kraʊn] n (of king etc) couronne f; (of head, hill) sommet m; **c. court** Br cour f d'assises; **C. jewels** Br joyaux mpl de la Couronne; **c. prince** prince m héritier ‖ vt couronner. ●**crowning** a (glory etc) suprême; **c. achievement** (of career) couronnement m.

crucial [ˈkruːʃəl] a crucial.

crucify [ˈkruːsɪfaɪ] vt crucifier. ●**crucifix** [ˈkruːsɪfɪks] n crucifix m. ●**cruci'fixion** [-ˈfɪk(ʃ)ə)n] n crucifixion f.

crude [kruːd] a (-er, -est) (manners, person, language) grossier; (painting, work) rudimentaire; (fact) brut; **c. oil** pétrole m brut. ●**crudely** adv (to say, order etc) crûment; (to build, paint etc) grossièrement. ●**crudeness** n (of manners etc) grossièreté f; (of painting etc) état m rudimentaire.

cruel [kruəl] a (crueller, cruellest) cruel. ●**cruelty** n cruauté f; **an act of c.** une cruauté.

cruet [ˈkruːɪt] n **c. (stand)** Br salière f, poivrière f et huilier m.

cruise [kruːz] n croisière f ‖ vi (of ship) croiser; (of vehicle) rouler; (of plane) voler; (of taxi) marauder; (of tourists) faire une croisière; **cruising speed** (*of ship, plane*) vitesse *f* de croisière. ● **cruiser** *n* (*ship*) croiseur *m*; **cabin c.** cruiser *m*, yacht *m* de croisière.

crumb [krʌm] *n* miette *f*; (*of comfort*) Fig brin *m*; **crumbs!** Br Hum Fam zut!

crumble ['krʌmb(ə)l] *vt* (*bread*) émietter ▮ *vi* (*of bread*) s'émietter; (*collapse*) (*of resistance etc*) s'effondrer; **to c. (away)** (*in small pieces*) s'effriter; (*become ruined*) (*of building etc*) tomber en ruine. ● **crumbly** *a* (*pastry etc*) friable.

crummy ['krʌmɪ] *a* (-ier, -iest) Fam moche, minable.

crumpet ['krʌmpɪt] *n* Br petite crêpe *f* grillée (*servie beurrée*).

crumple ['krʌmp(ə)l] *vt* froisser ▮ *vi* se froisser.

crunch [krʌntʃ] **1** *vt* (*food*) croquer ▮ *vi* (*of snow*) craquer. **2** *n* **when it comes to the c.** Fam au moment critique. ● **crunchy** *a* (-ier, -iest) (*apple, vegetables etc*) croquant; (*bread, Br biscuit, Am cookie*) croustillant.

crusade [kruːˈseɪd] *n* Hist & Fig croisade *f* ▮ *vi* faire une croisade. ● **crusader** *n* Hist croisé *m*; Fig militant, -ante *mf*.

crush [krʌʃ] **1** *n* (*crowd*) cohue *f*; (*rush*) bousculade *f*; **to have a c. on s.o.** Fam en pincer pour qn. **2** *vt* écraser; (*hope*) détruire; (*clothes*) froisser; (*cram*) entasser (**into** dans). ● **crushing** *a* (*defeat*) écrasant. ● **crush-resistant** *a* infroissable.

crust [krʌst] *n* croûte *f*. ● **crusty** *a* (-ier, -iest) (*bread*) croustillant.

crutch [krʌtʃ] *n* **1** (*of invalid*) béquille *f*. **2** (*crotch*) entre-jambe *m*.

crux [krʌks] *n* **the c. of the matter/problem** le nœud de l'affaire/du problème.

cry [kraɪ] *n* (*shout*) cri *m*; **to have a c.** Fam pleurer.
▮ *vi* (*weep*) pleurer; **to c. (out)** pousser un cri, crier; (*exclaim*) s'écrier; **to c. (out) for** (*of person*) demander (à grands cris); **to be crying out for** (*of thing*) avoir grand besoin de; **to c. off** (*withdraw*) abandonner; **to c. off** (**sth**) se désintéresser (de qch); **to c. over sth/s.o.** pleurer qch/qn.
▮ *vt* **to c. (out)** (*shout*) crier. ● **crying** *a* (*need*) très grand; **a c. shame** une véritable honte ▮ *n* (*shouts*) cris *mpl*; (*weeping*) pleurs *mpl*.

crypt [krɪpt] *n* crypte *f*.

cryptic ['krɪptɪk] *a* secret, énigmatique.

crystal ['krɪst(ə)l] *n* cristal *m*; **c. ball** boule *f* de cristal. ● **crystal-clear** *a* (*water, sound*) cristallin; (*explanation etc*) clair comme le jour *or* l'eau de roche.

crystallize ['krɪstəlaɪz] *vt* cristalliser ▮ *vi* (se) cristalliser.

cub [kʌb] *n* **1** (*of animal*) petit *m*, petite *f*. **2** (*scout*) louveteau *m*.

Cuba ['kjuːbə] *n* Cuba *m*. ● **Cuban** *a* cubain ▮ *n* Cubain, -aine *mf*.

cubbyhole ['kʌbɪhəʊl] *n* cagibi *m*.

cube [kjuːb] *n* cube *m*; (*of meat etc*) dé *m*. ● **cubic** *a* (*shape*) cubique; **c. metre/etc** mètre

m/etc cube; **c. capacity** volume *m*; (*of engine of car etc*) cylindrée *f*.

cubicle ['kjuːbɪk(ə)l] *n* (*for changing clothes*) cabine *f*; (*in hospital, dormitory*) box *m*.

cuckoo [Br 'kʊkuː, Am 'kuːkuː] **1** *n* (*bird*) coucou *m*; **c. clock** coucou *m*. **2** *a* (*stupid*) Sl cinglé.

cucumber ['kjuːkʌmbər] *n* concombre *m*.

cuddle ['kʌd(ə)l] *vt* (*hug*) serrer (dans ses bras); (*caress*) câliner ▮ *vi* (*of lovers etc*) se serrer; **to (kiss and) c.** s'embrasser; **to c. up to s.o.** (*huddle*) se serrer *or* se blottir contre qn ▮ *n* caresse *f*. ● **cuddly** *a* (-ier, -iest) (*person*) câlin, caressant; (*toy*) doux (*f* douce), en peluche.

cudgel ['kʌdʒəl] *n* trique *f*, gourdin *m*.

cue [kjuː] *n* **1** (*in theatre*) réplique *f*; (*signal*) signal *m*. **2** (*billiard*) c. queue *f* (de billard).

cuff [kʌf] *n* **1** (*of shirt etc*) poignet *m*, manchette *f*; (*of trousers*) Am revers *m*; **off the c.** (*remark etc*) impromptu; **c. link** bouton *m* de manchette. **2** *vt* (*strike*) gifler.

cul-de-sac ['kʌldəsæk] *n* Br impasse *f*, cul-de-sac *m*.

culinary ['kʌlɪnərɪ] *a* culinaire.

cull [kʌl] *vt* choisir (**from** dans); (*animals*) abattre sélectivement.

culminate ['kʌlmɪneɪt] *vi* **to c. in** finir par. ● **culmination** [-ˈneɪʃ(ə)n] *n* point *m* culminant.

culprit ['kʌlprɪt] *n* coupable *mf*.

cult [kʌlt] *n* culte *m*.

cultivate ['kʌltɪveɪt] *vt* (*land, mind etc*) cultiver. ● **cultivated** *a* cultivé. ● **cultivation** [-ˈveɪʃ(ə)n] *n* culture *f*; **land** *or* **fields under c.** cultures *fpl*.

culture ['kʌltʃər] *n* culture *f*. ● **cultural** *a* culturel. ● **cultured** *a* (*person, mind etc*) cultivé.

cumbersome ['kʌmbəsəm] *a* encombrant.

cumulative ['kjuːmjʊlətɪv] *a* cumulatif; **c. effect** (*long-term*) effet *m* *or* résultat *m* à long terme.

cunning ['kʌnɪŋ] *a* (*ingenious*) astucieux; (*devious*) rusé ▮ *n* astuce *f*; Pej ruse *f*. ● **cunningly** *adv* avec astuce; Pej avec ruse.

cup [kʌp] *n* tasse *f*; (*goblet, prize*) coupe *f*; **that's not my c. of tea** Fam ce n'est pas mon truc; **c. final** Football finale *f* de la coupe. ● **cupful** *n* tasse *f*.

cupboard ['kʌbəd] *n* Br armoire *f*; (*built into wall*) placard *m*.

Cupid ['kjuːpɪd] *n* Cupidon *m*.

cupola ['kjuːpələ] *n* (*dome*) coupole *f*.

cuppa ['kʌpə] *n* Br Fam tasse *f* de thé.

cup-tie [kʌpˈtaɪ] *n* Football match *m* éliminatoire.

curate ['kjʊərɪt] *n* vicaire *m*.

curator [kjʊəˈreɪtər] *n* (*of museum*) conservateur *m*.

curb [kɜːb] **1** *n* (*kerb*) Am bord *m* du trottoir. **2** *vt* (*feelings*) refréner, freiner; (*ambitions*) modérer; (*expenses*) limiter ▮ *n* frein *m*; **to put a c. on** mettre un frein à.

curdle ['kɜːd(ə)l] *vt* cailler ▮ *vi* se cailler; **my**

blood curdled *Fig* mon sang s'est figé.
curds [kɜːdz] *npl* lait *m* caillé. ●**curd cheese**
n fromage *m* blanc (maigre).
cure [kjʊər] **1** *vt* (*person, illness*) guérir;
(*poverty etc*) *Fig* éliminer; **to c. s.o. of** guérir
qn de **I** *n* remède *m* (**for** contre); (*recovery*)
guérison *f*; **rest c.** cure *f* de repos. **2** *vt*
(*meat, fish*) (*smoke*) fumer; (*salt*) saler; (*dry*)
sécher. ●**curable** *a* guérissable, curable.
●**curative** *a* curatif.
curfew [kɜːfjuː] *n* couvre-feu *m*.
curio [kjʊərɪəʊ] *n* (*pl* -os) bibelot *m*.
curious [kjʊərɪəs] *a* (*odd*) curieux; (*inquisitive*) curieux (**about** de); **to be c. to know/**
see/etc être curieux de savoir/voir/etc. ●**curiously** *adv* (*oddly*) curieusement; (*inquisitively*) avec curiosité.
curiosity [kjʊərɪˈɒsɪtɪ] *n* curiosité *f* (**about**
de).
curl [kɜːl] **1** *vti* (*hair*) boucler; (*with small*
tight curls) friser **I** *n* (*in hair*) boucle *f*; (*of*
smoke) *Fig* spirale *f*. **2** *vi* **to c. up** (*shrivel*) se
racornir; **to c. (oneself) up** (*into a ball*) se pelotonner. ●**curler** *n* bigoudi *m*. ●**curly** *a*
(**-ier, -iest**) bouclé; (*having many tight curls*)
frisé.
currant [kʌrənt] *n* (*dried grape*) raisin *m* de
Corinthe; (*fruit*) groseille *f*.
currency [kʌrənsɪ] *n* **1** (*money*) monnaie *f*;
(*foreign*) devises *fpl* (étrangères). **2 to gain**
c. (*of ideas etc*) se répandre.
current [kʌrənt] **1** *a* (*fashion, trend etc*)
actuel; (*opinion, use, phrase*) courant; (*year,*
month) en cours, courant; **c. account** (*in*
bank) compte *m* courant; **c. affairs** questions
fpl d'actualité; **c. events** actualité *f*; **the c.**
issue (*of magazine etc*) le dernier numéro. **2**
n (*of river, air, electricity*) courant *m*.
●**currently** *adv* actuellement, à présent.
curriculum, *pl* -la [kəˈrɪkjʊləm, -lə] *n* programme *m* (scolaire); **c. vitae** *Br* curriculum
vitae *m inv*.
curry [kʌrɪ] **1** *n* (*dish*) curry *m*, cari *m*. **2** *vt*
to c. favour with s'insinuer dans les bonnes
grâces de.
curse [kɜːs] *n* malédiction *f*; (*swearword*)
juron *m*; (*scourge*) fléau *m* (**of** terrorism/*etc*
du terrorisme/etc) **I** *vt* maudire; **cursed with**
(*blindness etc*) affligé de **I** *vi* (*swear*) jurer.
●**cursed** [-ɪd] *a Fam* maudit.
cursor [kɜːsər] *n* (*on computer screen*)
curseur *m*.
cursory [kɜːsərɪ] *a* (*trop*) rapide, superficiel.
curt [kɜːt] *a* brusque. ●**curtly** *adv* d'un ton
brusque. ●**curtness** *n* brusquerie *f*.
curtail [kɜːˈteɪl] *vt* (*visit etc*) écourter,
raccourcir; (*expenses*) réduire. ●**curtailment**
n raccourcissement *m*; (*of expenses*) réduction *f*.
curtain [kɜːt(ə)n] *n* rideau *m*; **to draw the**
curtains (*close*) tirer les rideaux; **c. call** (*in*
theatre) rappel *m*.
curts(e)y [kɜːtsɪ] *n* révérence *f* **I** *vi* faire une
révérence (**to** à).

vt courber **I** *vi* se courber; (*of road*) tourner,
faire une courbe.
cushion [kʊʃən] *n* coussin *m* **I** *vt* (*shock*)
Fig amortir. ●**cushioned** *a* (*seat*) rembourré;
c. against *Fig* protégé contre.
cushy [kʊʃɪ] *a* (**-ier, -iest**) (*job, life*) *Fam*
pépère, facile.
custard [kʌstəd] *n* crème *f* anglaise; (*when*
set) crème *f* renversée.
custodian [kʌˈstəʊdɪən] *n* (*of traditions etc*)
gardien, -ienne *mf*.
custody [kʌstədɪ] *n* (*care*) garde *f* (*d'un en-*
fant etc); (*imprisonment*) garde à vue de; **to**
take s.o. into c. mettre qn en détention préventive. ●**cu'stodial** *a* **c. sentence** peine *f* de
prison.
custom [kʌstəm] *n* coutume *f*; (*of individ-*
ual) habitude *f*; (*customers*) clientèle *f*.
●**custom-built** *or* **customized** *a* (*car etc*)
(fait) sur commande. ●**custom-made** *a* (*shirt*
etc) (fait) sur mesure.
customary [kʌstəmərɪ] *a* habituel, coutumier; **it is c. to** il est d'usage de.
customer [kʌstəmər] *n* client, -ente *mf*; (*in-*
dividual) *Pej* individu *m*.
customs [kʌstəmz] *n & npl* (**the**) **c.** la
douane; **c.** (**duties**) droits *mpl* de douane; **c.**
officer douanier *m*; **c. union** union *f* douanière.
cut [kʌt] *n* (*mark*) coupure *f*; (*stroke*) coup
m; (*of clothes, hair*) coupe *f*; (*in salary,*
prices etc) réduction *f*; (*of meat*) morceau *m*.
I *vt* (*pt & pp* **cut**, *pres p* **cutting**) couper;
(*meat, chicken*) découper; (*glass, diamond,*
tree) tailler; (*hay*) faucher; (*salary, prices,*
profits etc) réduire; **to c. a corner** (*in vehicle*)
prendre un virage à la corde; **to c. a tooth**
(*of child*) percer une dent; **to get one's hair**
c. se faire couper les cheveux; **to c. open**
ouvrir (*au couteau etc*); **to c. short** (*visit*)
abréger.
I *vi* (*of person, scissors*) couper; **this cloth**
cuts easily ce tissu se coupe facilement.
to cut away *vt* (*remove*) enlever **I to cut back**
(**on**) *vti* réduire. ●**cutback** *n* réduction *f*. **I to**
cut down *vt* (*tree*) abattre, couper **I to cut**
down (on) *vti* réduire **I to cut in** *vi* (*inter-*
rupt) interrompre; (*in vehicle*) faire une
queue de poisson (**on s.o.** à qn) **I to cut into**
(*cake, bread etc*) entamer **I to cut off** *vt*
(*piece, limb, hair etc*) couper; (*isolate*) isoler
I to cut out *vi* (*of car engine*) caler **I** *vt*
(*article*) découper; (*garment*) tailler; (*re-*
move) enlever; (*eliminate*) supprimer; **to c.**
out drinking (*stop*) s'arrêter de boire; **c. it**
out! *Fam* ça suffit!; **c. out to be a doctor/etc**
fait pour être médecin/etc. ●**cutout** *n*
(*picture*) découpage *m*; (*electrical*) coupe-
circuit *m inv*. **I to cut up** *vt* couper (en
morceaux); (*meat, chicken*) découper; **to be**
c. up about (*upset*) être très affecté par; (*de-*
moralized) être démoralisé par.
cute [kjuːt] *a* (**-er, -est**) *Fam* (*pretty*) mignon
(*f* mignonne); (*shrewd*) astucieux.
cuticle [kjuːtɪk(ə)l] *n* petites peaux *fpl* (*de*

l'ongle), envies *fpl*.
cutlery ['kʌtləri] *n* couverts *mpl*.
cutlet ['kʌtlɪt] *n* (*of veal etc*) côtelette *f*.
cut-price [kʌt'praɪs] *a* à prix réduit.
cutthroat ['kʌtθrəʊt] *n* assassin *m* ▮ *a*
(*competition*) impitoyable.
cutting ['kʌtɪŋ] *n* coupe *f*; (*of glass, diamond
etc*) taille *f*; (*newspaper article*) *Br* coupure *f*;
(*plant*) bouture *f*; (*of film*) montage *m*; (*for
train*) tranchée *f* ▮ *a* (*remark, tone*) cinglant,
mordant; **c. edge** tranchant *m*.
cuttlefish ['kʌt(ə)lfɪʃ] *n* seiche *f*.
CV [siː'viː] *n abbr Br* curriculum (vitae) *m
inv*.
cwt *abbr* = **hundredweight**.
cyanide ['saɪənaɪd] *n* cyanure *m*.
cybernetics [saɪbə'netɪks] *n* cybernétique *f*.
cycle[1] ['saɪk(ə)l] *n* (*bicycle*) bicyclette *f*, vélo
m; **c. shed** abri *m* à bicyclettes; **c. path** *or*
track piste *f* cyclable; **c. race** course *f*
cycliste ▮ *vi* aller à bicyclette (**to** à); (*as activity*) faire de la bicyclette. ●**cycling** *n* cyclisme *m*; **c. champion** champion *m* cycliste.

●**cyclist** *n* cycliste *mf*.
cycle[2] ['saɪk(ə)l] *n* (*series, period*) cycle *m*.
●**cyclical** ['sɪklɪk(ə)l] *a* cyclique.
cyclone ['saɪkləʊn] *n* cyclone *m*.
cylinder ['sɪlɪndər] *n* cylindre *m*; **c. head** (*in
car engine*) culasse *f*. ●**cy'lindrical** *a* cylindrique.
cymbal ['sɪmb(ə)l] *n* cymbale *f*.
cynic ['sɪnɪk] *n* cynique *mf*. ●**cynical** *a* cynique. ●**cynicism** *n* cynisme *m*.
cypress ['saɪprəs] *n* (*tree*) cyprès *m*.
Cyprus ['saɪprəs] *n* Chypre *f*. ●**Cypriot**
['sɪprɪət] *a* cypriote ▮ *n* Cypriote *mf*.
cyst [sɪst] *n* (*growth*) kyste *m*.
cystitis [sɪ'staɪtəs] *n* cystite *f*.
czar [zɑːr] *n* tsar *m*.
Czech [tʃek] *a* tchèque; **the C. Republic** la
République tchèque ▮ *n* (*language*) tchèque
m; (*person*) Tchèque *mf*. ●**Czecho'slovak** *a*
tchécoslovaque ▮ *n* Tchécoslovaque *mf*.
●**Czechoslo'vakia** *n* (*former State*) Tchécoslovaquie *f*. ●**Czechoslo'vakian** *a* tsché-
coslovaque ▮ *n* Tchécoslovaque *mf*.

D

D, d [di:] n D, d m. ● **D.-day** n le jour J.
dab [dæb] n a d. of un petit peu de ▮ vt
(-bb-) (*wound, brow etc*) tamponner; **to d.**
sth on sth appliquer qch (à petits coups) sur
qch.
dabble ['dæb(ə)l] vi **to d. in** s'occuper *or* se
mêler un peu de.
Dacron® ['dækrɒn] n Am tergal® m.
dad [dæd] n Fam papa m. ● **daddy** n Fam
papa m; **d. longlegs** (*cranefly*) Br tipule f;
(*spider*) Am faucheur m.
daffodil ['dæfədɪl] n jonquille f.
daft [dɑːft] a (-er, -est) Fam idiot, bête.
dagger ['dægər] n poignard m; **at daggers**
drawn à couteaux tirés (**with** avec).
dahlia [Br 'deɪljə, Am 'dæljə] n dahlia m.
daily ['deɪlɪ] a quotidien, journalier; (*wage*)
journalier ▮ adv chaque jour, quotidiennement; **three times d.** trois fois par jour ▮ n **d.**
(paper) quotidien m; **d. (help)** (*cleaning woman*) Br femme f de ménage.
dainty ['deɪntɪ] a (-ier, -iest) (*delicate*) délicat; (*pretty*) mignon; (*small, slender*) menu;
(*tasteful*) élégant. ● **daintily** adv (*to eat etc*)
délicatement; (*to dress etc*) élégamment.
dairy ['deərɪ] n (*on farm*) laiterie f; (*shop*)
crémerie f ▮ a laitier; **d. farm/cow** ferme f/
vache f laitière; **d. product** produit m laitier;
d. produce produits mpl laitiers. ● **dairyman**
n (*pl* -men) employé m de laiterie. ● **dairy-**
woman n (*pl* -women) employée f de laiterie.
daisy ['deɪzɪ] n pâquerette f.
dale [deɪl] n (*valley*) Lit vallée f.
dally ['dælɪ] vi musarder, lanterner.
dam [dæm] n (*wall*) barrage m ▮ vt (-mm-)
(*river*) barrer.
damage ['dæmɪdʒ] n dégâts mpl, dommages
mpl; (*harm*) préjudice m; **damages** (*in court*)
dommages-intérêts mpl ▮ vt (*object*) endommager, abîmer; (*health*) abîmer, nuire à;
(*eyesight*) abîmer; (*plans, reputation etc*)
compromettre. ● **damaging** a (*harmful*) préjudiciable (**to** à).
dame [deɪm] n Lit dame f; Am Sl nana f,
fille f
damn [dæm] vt (*condemn, doom*) condamner; (*of God*) damner; (*curse*) maudire;
d. him! Fam qu'il aille se faire voir!
▮ int **d. (it)!** Fam merde!
▮ n **he doesn't care** *or* **give a d.** Fam il s'en
fiche pas mal.
▮ a (*awful*) Fam fichu, sacré; **your d. car** ta
fichue *or* sacrée bagnole.
▮ adv (*very*) Fam vachement; **d. all** Br rien
de rien. ● **damned 1** a (*soul*) damné. **2** Fam

= **damn** a & adv. ● **damning** a (*evidence etc*)
accablant.
damnation [dæm'neɪʃ(ə)n] n damnation f ▮
int Hum Fam merde!
damp [dæmp] a (-er, -est) humide; (*skin*)
moite ▮ n humidité f. ● **damp(en)** vt humecter; **to d. (down)** (*enthusiasm, zeal*) refroidir; (*ambition*) étouffer; **to d. s.o.'s spir-**
its décourager qn. ● **dampness** n humidité f.
damper ['dæmpər] n **to put a d. on** jeter un
froid sur.
damsel ['dæmzəl] n Lit & Hum demoiselle f.
damson ['dæmzən] n prune f de Damas.
dance [dɑːns] n danse f; (*social event*) bal m
(*pl* bals); **d. hall** dancing m, salle f de danse
▮ vi danser; **to d. for joy** sauter de joie ▮ vt
(*waltz, polka etc*) danser. ● **dancing** n danse
f; **d. partner** cavalier, -ière mf. ● **dancer** n
danseur, -euse mf.
dandelion ['dændɪlaɪən] n pissenlit m.
dandruff ['dændrʌf] n pellicules fpl.
dandy ['dændɪ] **1** n dandy m. **2** a (*very good*)
Am Fam formidable, super inv.
Dane [deɪn] n Danois, -oise mf.
danger ['deɪndʒər] n (*peril*) danger m (**to**
pour); **in d.** en danger; **out of d.** hors de
danger; **in d. of** (*threatened by*) menacé de
(*guerre nucléaire etc*); **to be in d. of falling/**
etc risquer de tomber/etc; **on the d. list**
(*hospital patient*) dans un état critique; **'d. of**
fire' 'risque d'incendie'; **d. signal** (*on train*
etc) signal m d'alarme; **d. zone** zone f
dangereuse. ● **dangerous** a (*place, illness,*
person etc) dangereux (**to** pour). ● **danger-**
ously adv dangereusement; **d. ill** gravement
malade.
dangle ['dæŋg(ə)l] vt (*keys etc*) balancer;
(*prospect*) Fig faire miroiter (**before s.o.** aux
yeux de qn) ▮ vi (*hang*) pendre; (*swing*) se
balancer.
Danish ['deɪnɪʃ] a danois ▮ n (*language*) danois m.
dank [dæŋk] a (-er, -est) humide (et froid).
dapper ['dæpər] a pimpant, fringant.
dappled ['dæp(ə)ld] a pommelé, tacheté.
dare [deər] vt oser (do faire); **she d. not come**
elle n'ose pas venir; **he doesn't d. (to) go** il
n'ose pas y aller; **if you d. (to)** si tu l'oses, si
tu oses le faire; **I d. say he tried** il a sans
doute essayé, je suppose qu'il a essayé; **to d.**
s.o. to do défier qn de faire.
daredevil ['deədev(ə)l] n casse-cou m inv,
risque-tout m inv.
daring ['deərɪŋ] a audacieux ▮ n audace f.
dark [dɑːk] a (-er, -est) (*room, night etc*) obscur, noir, sombre; (*colour*) foncé, sombre;

(*skin*) brun, foncé; (*eyes*) foncé; (*gloomy*) sombre; **d. hair** cheveux *mpl* bruns *or* foncés; (*black*) cheveux noirs; **it's d.** il fait nuit *or* noir; **to keep sth d.** tenir qch secret; **d. glasses** lunettes *fpl* noires. ∎ *n* noir *m*, obscurité *f*; **after d.** après la tombée de la nuit; **to keep s.o. in the d.** laisser qn dans l'ignorance (**about** de). ●**dark-'haired** *a* aux cheveux bruns; (*black*) aux cheveux noirs. ●**dark-'skinned** *a* (*person*) brun, à peau brune.

darken ['dɑːk(ə)n] *vt* assombrir, obscurcir; (*colour*) foncer ∎ *vi* s'assombrir; (*of colour*) foncer.

darkness ['dɑːknəs] *n* obscurité *f*, noir *m*.

darkroom ['dɑːkruːm] *n* (*for photography*) chambre *f* noire.

darling ['dɑːlɪŋ] *n* (*favourite*) chouchou, -oute *mf*; (**my) d.** (*mon*) chéri, (*ma*) chérie; **he's a d.** c'est un amour; **be a d.!** sois un ange! ∎ *a* chéri; (*delightful*) *Fam* adorable.

darn [dɑːn] **1** *vt* (*socks*) repriser. **2** *int* **d. it!** bon sang! ●**darning** *n* reprise *f* ∎ *a* (*needle, wool*) à repriser.

dart [dɑːt] **1** *vi* (*dash*) se précipiter, s'élancer (**for** vers) ∎ *n* **to make a d.** se précipiter (**for** vers). **2** *n* (*in game*) fléchette *f*; **darts** (*game*) fléchettes *fpl*. ●**dartboard** *n* cible *f*.

dash [dæʃ] **1** *n* (*run, rush*) ruée *f*; **to make a d.** se précipiter (**for** vers) ∎ *vi* se précipiter; (*of waves*) se briser (**against** contre); **to d. off** *or* **away** partir *or* filer en vitesse ∎ *vt* (*throw*) jeter (avec force); (*shatter*) *Fig* briser (*espérances, rêves etc*); **d. (it)!** *Br Fam* zut!; **to d. off** (*letter*) faire en vitesse. **2** *n* **a. of** (*a petit*) peu de; **a d. of milk** une goutte *or* un nuage de lait. **3** *n* (*handwritten stroke*) trait *m*; (*punctuation sign*) tiret *m*.

dashboard ['dæʃbɔːd] *n* (*of vehicle*) tableau *m* de bord.

dashing ['dæʃɪŋ] *a* (*person*) pimpant, fringant.

data ['deɪtə] *npl* données *fpl*. **d. bank/base** *Comptr* banque *f*/base *f* de données; **d. capture** saisie *f* de données; **d. processing** informatique *f*.

date[1] [deɪt] *n* date *f*; (*meeting*) *Fam* rendez-vous *m inv*; (*person*) *Fam* copain, -ine *mf* (*avec qui on a un rendez-vous*); **up to d.** moderne; (*information*) à jour; (*well-informed*) au courant (**on** de); **out of d.** (*old-fashioned*) démodé; (*expired*) périmé; **to d.** à ce jour, jusqu'ici; **d. stamp** (*object*) (*tampon m*) dateur *m*; (*mark*) cachet *m*. ∎ *vt* (*letter etc*) dater; (*girl, boy*) *Fam* sortir avec. ∎ *vi* (*become out of date*) dater; **to d. back to, d. from** dater de.

date[2] [deɪt] *n* (*fruit*) datte *f*.

datebook ['deɪtbʊk] *n Am* agenda *m*.

dated ['deɪtɪd] *a* démodé.

dative ['deɪtɪv] *n Grammar* datif *m*.

daub [dɔːb] *vt* barbouiller (**with** de).

daughter ['dɔːtər] *n* fille *f*. ●**daughter-in-law**

n (*pl* **daughters-in-law**) belle-fille *f*, bru *f*.

daunt [dɔːnt] *vt* décourager, rebuter. ●**dauntless** *a* intrépide.

dawdle ['dɔːd(ə)l] *vi* traîner, lambiner. ●**dawdler** *n* traînard, -arde *mf*.

dawn [dɔːn] *n* aube *f*, aurore *f*; **at d.** à l'aube ∎ *vi* (*of day*) se lever, poindre; (*of new era, idea*) naître, voir le jour; **it dawned upon him that...** il lui est venu à l'esprit que....

day [deɪ] *n* jour *m*; (*working period, whole day long*) journée *f*; **days** (*period*) époque *f*, temps *mpl*; **all d. (long)** toute la journée; **what d. is it?** quel jour sommes-nous?; **the following** *or* **next d.** le lendemain; **the d. before** la veille; **the d. before yesterday** *or* before **last** avant-hier; **the d. after tomorrow** après-demain; **to the d.** jour pour jour; **d. boarder** *Br* demi-pensionnaire *mf*; **d. nursery** *Br* crèche *f*; **d. return** (*on train*) *Br* aller et retour *m* (*pour une journée*); **d. tripper** *Br* excursionniste *mf*.

daybreak ['deɪbreɪk] *n* point *m* du jour. ●**daycare** *n* **d. (facilities)** (*for children*) service *m* de garderie. ●**daydream** *n* rêverie *f* ∎ *vi* rêvasser. ●**daylight** *n* (*lumière f du*) jour *m*; (*dawn*) point *m* du jour; **it's d.** il fait jour. ●**daytime** *n* journée *f*, jour *m*.

day-to-day [deɪtə'deɪ] *a* quotidien, journalier; **on a d.-to-d. basis** (*every day*) journellement.

daze [deɪz] *vt* (*by blow*) étourdir; (*of drug etc*) hébéter ∎ *n* **in a d.** étourdi; (*because of drugs*) hébété; (*astonished*) ahuri.

dazzle ['dæz(ə)l] *vt* éblouir ∎ *n* éblouissement *m*.

deacon ['diːkən] *n* (*clergyman*) diacre *m*.

dead [ded] *a* mort; (*numb*) (*arm etc*) engourdi; (*party etc*) qui manque de vie, mortel; (*telephone*) sans tonalité; **in (the) d. centre** au beau milieu; **to be a d. loss** (*of person*) *Fam* être bon à rien; **it's a d. loss** *Fam* ça ne vaut rien; **d. silence** un silence de mort; **a d. stop** un arrêt complet; **d. end** (*street*) & *Fig* impasse *f*; **a d.-end job** un travail sans avenir. ∎ *adv* (*completely*) absolument; (*very*) très; **d. beat** *Br Fam* éreinté; **d. drunk** *Fam* ivre mort; **to stop d.** s'arrêter net. ∎ *n* **the d.** les morts *mpl*; **in the d. of night/winter**/*etc* au cœur de la nuit/l'hiver/*etc*.

deadbeat ['dedbiːt] *n* (*sponger*) *Am Fam* parasite *m*. ●**deadline** *n* date *f* limite; (*hour*) heure *f* limite. ●**deadlock** *n Fig* impasse *f*. ●**deadpan** *a* (*face*) figé, impassible.

deaden ['ded(ə)n] *vt* (*shock*) amortir; (*pain*) calmer; (*feeling*) émousser.

deadly ['dedlɪ] *a* (**-ier, -iest**) (*enemy, silence*) mortel; (*paleness*) mortel, de mort; (*boring*) (*evening etc*) *Fam* mortel; **d. weapon** arme *f* meurtrière; **d. sins** péchés *mpl* capitaux ∎ *adv* (*pale, boring*) mortellement.

deaf [def] *a* sourd; **d. and dumb** sourd-muet; **d. in one ear** sourd d'une oreille; **d. to s.o.'s requests**/*etc* sourd aux prières/*etc* de qn ∎ *n* **the d.** les sourds *mpl*. ●**deaf-aid** *n Br* audio-

decibel   82

decibel [ˈdesɪbel] *n* décibel *m*.
decide [dɪˈsaɪd] *vt* (*question, matter etc*) décider, régler; (*s.o.'s career, fate etc*) décider
de; **to d. to do** décider de faire; **to d. that**
décider que; **to d. s.o. to do** décider qn à
faire.
 I *vi* (*make decisions*) décider; (*make up
one's mind*) se décider (**on doing** à faire); **to
d. on sth** décider de qch, se décider à qch;
(*choose*) se décider pour qch; **the deciding
factor** le facteur décisif. ●**decided** *a* (*firm*)
décidé, résolu; (*clear*) net. ●**decidedly** [-ɪdlɪ]
adv (*firmly*) résolument; (*clearly*) nettement.
decimal [ˈdesɪməl] *a* décimal; **d. point**
virgule *f* **I** *n* décimale *f*. ●**decimalization**
[-aɪˈzeɪʃ(ə)n] *n* décimalisation *f*.
decimate [ˈdesɪmeɪt] *vt* décimer.
decipher [dɪˈsaɪfər] *vt* déchiffrer.
decision [dɪˈsɪʒ(ə)n] *n* décision *f*.
decisive [dɪˈsaɪsɪv] *a* (*defeat, tone etc*) décisif; (*victory*) net (*f* nette), incontestable.
 ●**decisively** *adv* (*to state*) avec décision; (*to
win*) nettement, incontestablement.
deck [dek] **1** *n* (*of ship*) pont *m*; **top d.** (*of
bus*) impériale *f*. **2** *n* **d. of cards** jeu *m* de
cartes. **3** *n* (*of record player*) platine *f*. **4** *vt*
to d. (out) (*adorn*) orner. ●**deckchair** *n*
chaise *f* longue.
declare [dɪˈkleər] *vt* déclarer (**that** que);
(*verdict, result*) proclamer. ●**declaration**
[dekləˈreɪʃ(ə)n] *n* déclaration *f*; (*of verdict
etc*) proclamation *f*.
decline [dɪˈklaɪn] **1** *vi* (*become less*) (*of
popularity, birthrate etc*) être en baisse; (*deteriorate*) (*of health, strength etc*) décliner; **to
d. in importance** perdre de l'importance;
one's declining years ses dernières années **I** *n*
déclin *m*; (*fall*) baisse *f*. **2** *vt* (*offer etc*) refuser, décliner; **to d. to do** refuser de faire.
declutch [dɪˈklʌtʃ] *vi* Aut Br débrayer.
decode [diːˈkəʊd] *vt* (*message*) décoder.
 ●**decoder** *n* Comptr TV décodeur *m*.
decompose [diːkəmˈpəʊz] *vi* (*rot*) se décomposer **I** *vt* (*chemical compound etc*) décomposer. ●**decomposition** [-kɒmpəˈzɪʃ(ə)n]
n décomposition *f*.
decompression [diːkəmˈpreʃ(ə)n] *n* décompression *f*; **d. chamber** sas *m* de décompression.
decontaminate [diːkənˈtæmɪneɪt] *vt* décontaminer.
decor [ˈdeɪkɔːr] *n* décor *m*.
decorate [ˈdekəreɪt] *vt* (*cake, house, soldier*)
décorer (**with** de); (*hat, skirt etc*) orner (**with**
de); (*paint, wallpaper etc*) peindre (et tapisser) (*pièce, maison etc*). ●**decorating** *n*
interior d. décoration *f* d'intérieurs. ●**decoration** [-ˈreɪʃ(ə)n] *n* décoration *f*. ●**decorative** *a* décoratif. ●**decorator** *n* (*house
painter etc*) Br peintre *m* décorateur; (*interior*) **d.** décorateur, -trice *mf*, ensemblier *m*.
decorum [dɪˈkɔːrəm] *n* bienséances *fpl*.
decoy [ˈdiːkɔɪ] *n* (*artificial bird*) appeau *m*;
(*police*) **d.** policier *m* en civil.
decrease [dɪˈkriːs] *vti* diminuer **I** [ˈdiːkriːs] *n*

diminution *f* (**in** de). ●**decreasing** *a* (*number
etc*) décroissant. ●**decreasingly** *adv* de
moins en moins.
decree [dɪˈkriː] *n* (*by king etc*) décret *m*; (*by
court*) jugement *m*; (*municipal*) arrêté *m* **I** *vt*
(*pt & pp* **decreed**) décréter (**that** que).
decrepit [dɪˈkrepɪt] *a* (*building*) en ruine;
(*person*) décrépit.
decry [dɪˈkraɪ] *vt* décrier.
dedicate [ˈdedɪkeɪt] *vt* (*devote*) consacrer (**to**
à); (*book*) dédier (**to** à); **to d. oneself to** se
consacrer à. ●**dedicated** *a* (*teacher etc*) consciencieux. ●**dedication** [-ˈkeɪʃ(ə)n] *n* (*in
book*) dédicace *f*; (*devotion*) dévouement *m*.
deduce [dɪˈdjuːs] *vt* (*conclude*) déduire
(**from** de, **that** que).
deduct [dɪˈdʌkt] *vt* (*subtract*) déduire, retrancher (**from** de); (*from wage, account*)
prélever (**from** sur). ●**deductible** *a* (*from invoice etc*) à déduire (**from** de); (*from income*) (*expenses etc*) déductible. ●**deduction**
[-ʃ(ə)n] *n* (*subtraction, conclusion*) déduction *f*.
deed [diːd] *n* action *f*, acte *m*; (*feat*) exploit
m; (*legal document*) acte *m* (notarié).
deem [diːm] *vt* juger, estimer.
deep [diːp] *a* (*-er, -est*) profond; (*snow*)
épais (*f* épaisse); (*voice*) grave; (*musical
note*) bas (*f* basse); (*person*) (*difficult to
understand*) insondable; **to be six metres/etc
d.** avoir six mètres/etc de profondeur; **d. in
thought** absorbé *or* plongé dans ses pensées;
the d. end (*in swimming pool*) le grand bain;
d. red rouge foncé.
 I *adv* (*to breathe*) profondément; **she went in
d.** (*into water*) elle alla (jusqu')où elle
n'avait pas pied; **d. into the night** tard dans
la nuit.
 I *n* **the d.** l'océan *m*. ●**deeply** *adv* (*grateful,
to breathe, regret etc*) profondément.
deepen [ˈdiːpən] *vt* (*increase*) augmenter;
(*canal, knowledge*) approfondir **I** *vi* devenir
plus profond; (*of mystery*) s'épaissir. ●**deepening** *a* (*gap etc*) grandissant; **the d.
recession/crisis** l'aggravation *f* de la
récession/crise.
deep-freeze [diːpˈfriːz] *vt* surgeler **I** *n* congélateur *m*. ●**deep-fryer** *n* friteuse *f*. ●**deep-
rooted** *or* **deep-seated** *a* bien ancré, profond. ●**deep-sea** ʹ**diving** *n* plongée *f* sous-
marine (en haute mer). ●**deep-set** *a* (*eyes*)
enfoncés.
deer [dɪər] *n inv* cerf *m*.
deface [dɪˈfeɪs] *vt* (*damage*) dégrader; (*daub*)
barbouiller.
defamation [defəˈmeɪʃ(ə)n] *n* diffamation *f*.
 ●**deʹfamatory** *a* diffamatoire.
default [dɪˈfɔːlt] *n* **by d.** Comptr par défaut;
to win by d. gagner par forfait **I** *vi* (*fail to
appear in court*) être défaillant; **to d. on
one's payments** être en rupture de paiement.
defeat [dɪˈfiːt] *vt* (*opponent, army etc*) battre,
vaincre; (*plan, effort*) faire échouer; **that de-
feats the purpose** *or* **object** ça va à l'encontre
de ce qu'on veut faire. **I** *n* défaite *f*. ●**de-

phone *m*, prothèse *f* auditive. ●**deafen** *vt* assourdir. ●**deafness** *n* surdité *f*.

deal[1] [di:l] *n* a good *or* great d. (*a lot*) beaucoup (**of** de).

deal[2] [di:l] *n* **1** (*in business*) marché *m*, affaire *f*; *Cards* donne *f*; **to make** *or* **do a d. (with s.o.)** conclure *or* faire un marché *or* une affaire (avec qn); **to give s.o. a fair d.** traiter qn équitablement; **to get a fair d. from s.o.** être traité équitablement par qn; **it's a d.!** d'accord!; **big d.!** *Iron* la belle affaire!
2 *vt* (*pt & pp* **dealt** [delt]) **to d. s.o. a blow** porter un coup à qn; **to d. (out)** (*cards*) donner; (*money*) distribuer.
3 *vi* (*trade*) traiter (**with** avec qn); **to d. in** faire le commerce de; **to d. with** (*take care of*) s'occuper de; (*concern*) (*of book etc*) traiter de, parler de; **I can d. with him** (*handle*) je sais m'y prendre avec lui.

deal[3] [di:l] *n* (*wood*) sapin *m*.

dealer ['di:lər] *n* marchand, -ande *mf* (**in** de); (*agent*) dépositaire *mf*; (*for cars*) concessionnaire *mf*; (*in drugs*) revendeur, -euse *mf* (de drogues); *Cards* donneur, -euse *mf*.

dealings ['di:lɪŋz] *npl* relations *fpl* (**with** avec); (*in business*) transactions *fpl*.

dean [di:n] *n* (*in church, Br university*) doyen *m*; (*in secondary school*) *Am* CPE *mf*, conseiller, -ère *mf* principal(e) d'éducation.

dear [dɪər] *a* (**-er, -est**) (*loved, precious, expensive*) cher; (*price*) élevé; **D. Sir** (*in letter*) Monsieur; **D. Sirs** Messieurs; **D. Uncle** (mon) cher oncle; **oh d.!** oh là là!, oh mon Dieu!
❚ *n* (**my**) **d.** (*darling*) (mon) chéri, (ma) chérie; (*friend*) mon cher, ma chère; **she's a d.** c'est un amour; **be a d.!** sois un ange!
❚ *adv* (*to cost, pay*) cher. ●**dearly** *adv* (*to love*) tendrement; (*very much*) beaucoup; **to pay d.** for sth payer qch cher.

dearth [dɜ:θ] *n* manque *m*, pénurie *f*.

death [deθ] *n* mort *f*; **to put s.o. to d.** mettre qn à mort; **to be bored to d.** s'ennuyer à mourir; **to be burnt to d.** mourir carbonisé; **to be sick to d.** en avoir vraiment marre (**of** de); **there were many deaths** (*people killed*) il y a eu de nombreux morts *mpl*. ●**d. certificate** acte *m* de décès; **d. duty** *or* **duties** *Br*, **d. taxes** *Am* droits *mpl* de succession; **d. march** marche *f* funèbre; **d. mask** masque *m* mortuaire; **d. penalty** peine *f* de mort; **d. rate** (taux *m* de) mortalité *f*; **d. sentence** condamnation *f* à mort; **it's a d. trap** il y a danger de mort; **d. wish** désir *m* de mort. ●**deathbed** *n* lit *m* de mort. ●**deathblow** *n* coup *m* mortel. ●**deathly** *a* (*silence, paleness*) de mort, mortel ❚ *adv* **d. pale** d'une pâleur mortelle.

debar [dɪ'bɑ:r] *vt* (**-rr-**) exclure (**from sth** de qch); **to d. s.o. from doing** interdire à qn de faire.

debase [dɪ'beɪs] *vt* (*person*) avilir; (*reputation, talents*) galvauder; (*coinage*) altérer.

debate [dɪ'beɪt] *vti* discuter; **to d. (with oneself) whether to leave/etc** se demander si on doit partir/etc ❚ *n* débat *m*, discussion *f*. ●**debatable** *a* discutable, contestable; **it's d. whether she will succeed** il est difficile de dire si elle réussira.

debauch [dɪ'bɔ:tʃ] *vt* corrompre, débaucher. ●**debauchery** *n* débauche *f*.

debilitate [dɪ'bɪlɪteɪt] *vt* débiliter. ●**debility** *n* faiblesse *f*, débilité *f*.

debit ['debɪt] *n* débit *m*; **in d.** (*account*) débiteur; **d. balance** solde *m* débiteur ❚ *vt* débiter (**s.o. with sth** qn de qch).

debonair [debə'neər] *a* (*cheerful*) jovial; (*charming*) charmant; (*polite*) poli.

debrief [di:'bri:f] *vt* **to be debriefed** (*of soldier*) rendre compte (**by** à).

debris ['debri] *n* débris *mpl*.

debt [det] *n* dette *f*; **to be in d.** avoir des dettes; **to be 50 dollars in d.** devoir 50 dollars; **to run** *or* **get into d.** faire des dettes. ●**debtor** *n* débiteur, -trice *mf*.

debug [di:'bʌg] *vt* (*computer program*) éliminer les erreurs de.

debunk [di:'bʌŋk] *vt* (*idea etc*) *Fam* démystifier.

debut ['debju:] *n* (*on stage*) début *m*.

decade ['dekeɪd] *n* décennie *f*.

decadent ['dekədənt] *a* décadent. ●**decadence** *n* décadence *f*.

decaffeinated [di:'kæfɪneɪtɪd] *a* décaféiné.

decal ['di:kæl] *n* (*transfer*) *Am* décalcomanie *f*.

decant [dɪ'kænt] *vt* (*wine*) décanter. ●**decanter** *n* carafe *f*.

decapitate [dɪ'kæpɪteɪt] *vt* décapiter.

decathlon [dɪ'kæθlɒn] *n* *Sport* décathlon *m*.

decay [dɪ'keɪ] *vi* (*go bad*) se gâter; (*rot*) pourrir; (*of tooth*) se carier, se gâter; (*of building*) tomber en ruine; (*decline*) (*of nation etc*) *Fig* décliner ❚ *n* (*rot*) pourriture *f*; (*of building*) délabrement *m*; (*of tooth*) carie(s) *f(pl)*; (*of nation*) décadence *f*; **to fall into d.** (*of building*) tomber en ruine. ●**decaying** *a* (*meat, fruit etc*) pourrissant; (*nation*) décadent.

deceased [dɪ'si:st] *a* décédé, défunt ❚ *n* **the d.** le défunt, la défunte; *pl* les défunt(e)s.

deceit [dɪ'si:t] *n* tromperie *f*. ●**deceitful** *a* trompeur. ●**deceitfully** *adv* avec duplicité.

deceive [dɪ'si:v] *vti* tromper; **to d. oneself** se faire des illusions.

December [dɪ'sembər] *n* décembre *m*.

decent ['di:sənt] *a* (*respectable*) convenable, décent; (*good*) bon; (*kind*) gentil; **that was d. (of you)** c'était chic de ta part. ●**decency** *n* décence *f*; (*kindness*) gentillesse *f*. ●**decently** *adv* décemment.

decentralize [di:'sentrəlaɪz] *vt* décentraliser. ●**decentralization** [-'zeɪʃ(ə)n] *n* décentralisation *f*.

deception [dɪ'sepʃ(ə)n] *n* tromperie *f*. ●**deceptive** *a* trompeur. ●**deceptively** *adv* **it looks d. straightforward** ça a l'air simple mais il ne faut pas s'y fier.

featism n défaitisme m. ● **defeatist** a & n défaitiste (mf).

defect¹ ['di:fekt] n défaut m.

defect² [dɪ'fekt] vi (of party member, soldier etc) déserter, faire défection; **to d. to** (the enemy etc) passer à. ● **defection** [-ʃ(ə)n] n défection f. ● **defector** n transfuge mf.

defective [dɪ'fektɪv] a (machine, brakes etc) défectueux.

defence [dɪ'fens] (Am **defense**) n défense f; **the body's defences** la défense de l'organisme (**against** contre); **to speak in d. of s.o.** prendre la défense de qn; **in his d.** à sa décharge, pour le défendre. ● **defenceless** a sans défense.

defend [dɪ'fend] vt défendre. ● **defendant** n (accused) prévenu, -ue mf. ● **defender** n défenseur m; (of sports title) détenteur, -trice mf.

defense [dɪ'fens] n Am = **defence**.

defensible [dɪ'fensəb(ə)l] a défendable.

defensive [dɪ'fensɪv] a défensif ▮ n **on the d.** sur la défensive.

defer [dɪ'fɜː] **1** vt (-rr-) (postpone) différer, reporter. **2** vi (-rr-) **to d. to s.o.** (yield) déférer à qn. ● **deferment** n (postponement) report m.

deference ['defərəns] n déférence f. ● **deferential** [-'renʃ(ə)l] a déférent, plein de déférence.

defiant [dɪ'faɪənt] a (tone etc) de défi; (person) rebelle. ● **defiance** n (resistance) défi m (**of** à); **in d. of** (contempt) au mépris de. ● **defiantly** adv d'un air de défi.

deficient [dɪ'fɪʃənt] a (not adequate) insuffisant; (faulty) défectueux; **to be d. in** manquer de. ● **deficiency** n (shortage) manque m; (in vitamins, calcium etc) carence f (**in** de); (flaw) défaut m.

deficit ['defɪsɪt] n déficit m.

defile [dɪ'faɪl] vt (make dirty) souiller, salir.

define [dɪ'faɪn] vt définir.

definite ['defɪnɪt] a (exact) (date, plan) précis, déterminé; (clear) (reply, improvement) net (f nette); (firm) (offer, order) ferme; (certain, sure) certain; **d. article** Grammar article m défini; **it's d. that** il est certain que (+ indic); **I was quite d.** j'ai été tout à fait formel. ● **definitely** adv certainement; (considerably) nettement; (to say) catégoriquement.

definition [defɪ'nɪʃ(ə)n] n définition f.

definitive [dɪ'fɪnɪtɪv] a définitif.

deflate [dɪ'fleɪt] vt (Br tyre, Am tire) dégonfler. ● **deflation** [-ʃ(ə)n] n dégonflement m; (economic) déflation f.

deflect [dɪ'flekt] vt (bullet etc) faire dévier; **to d. s.o. from a plan/aim** détourner qn d'un projet/objectif ▮ vi (of bullet etc) dévier.

deform [dɪ'fɔːm] vt déformer. ● **deformed** a (body) difforme. ● **deformity** n difformité f.

defraud [dɪ'frɔːd] vt (customs, State etc) frauder; **to d. s.o. of sth** escroquer qch à qn.

defray [dɪ'freɪ] vt (expenses) payer.

defrost [diː'frɒst] vt (fridge) dégivrer; (food)

décongeler.

deft [deft] a adroit (**with** de). ● **deftness** n adresse f.

defunct [dɪ'fʌŋkt] a défunt.

defuse [diː'fjuːz] vt (bomb, conflict) désamorcer.

defy [dɪ'faɪ] vt (person, death etc) défier; (efforts) résister à; **to d. s.o. to do** défier qn de faire; **it defies description** cela défie toute description.

degenerate [dɪ'dʒenəreɪt] vi dégénérer (**into** en) ▮ [dɪ'dʒenərət] a & n dégénéré, -ée (mf). ● **degeneration** [-'reɪʃ(ə)n] n dégénérescence f.

degrade [dɪ'greɪd] vt dégrader. ● **degrading** a dégradant. ● **degradation** [degrə'deɪʃ(ə)n] n Mil Ch dégradation f; (of person) déchéance f.

degree [dɪ'griː] n **1** (angle, temperature, extent etc) degré m; **by degrees** par degrés; **it's 20 degrees** il fait 20 degrés; **not in the slightest d.** pas du tout; **to some d., to a certain d.** jusqu'à un certain point; **to such a d.** à tel point (**that** que). **2** (from university) diplôme m; (Bachelor's) licence f; (Master's) maîtrise f; (PhD) doctorat m.

dehumanize [diː'hjuːmənaɪz] vt déshumaniser.

dehydrated [diːhaɪ'dreɪtɪd] a déshydraté; **to get d.** se déshydrater.

de-ice [diː'aɪs] vt (car window etc) dégivrer.

deign [deɪn] vt daigner (**to do** faire).

deity ['diːɪtɪ] n dieu m.

dejected [dɪ'dʒektɪd] a abattu, découragé. ● **dejection** [-ʃ(ə)n] n abattement m.

dekko ['dekəʊ] n Br Sl coup m d'œil.

delay [dɪ'leɪ] vt retarder; (payment) différer; **to d. doing sth** tarder à faire; **to be delayed** avoir du retard, être retardé ▮ vi (be slow) tarder (**in doing** à faire); (linger) s'attarder ▮ n (lateness) retard m; (waiting period) délai m; **without d.** sans tarder. ● **delayed-'action** a (bomb, fuse) à retardement. ● **delaying** a **d. tactics** or **actions** moyens mpl dilatoires.

delectable [dɪ'lektəb(ə)l] a délectable.

delegate 1 ['delɪgeɪt] vt déléguer (**to** à). **2** ['delɪgət] n délégué, -ée mf. ● **delegation** [delɪ'geɪʃ(ə)n] n délégation f.

delete [dɪ'liːt] vt rayer, supprimer. ● **deletion** [-ʃ(ə)n] n (thing deleted) rature f; (act) suppression f.

deleterious [delɪ'tɪərɪəs] a (effect etc) néfaste.

deliberate¹ [dɪ'lɪbərət] a (intentional) délibéré; (cautious) réfléchi; (slow) mesuré. ● **deliberately** adv (intentionally) exprès, délibérément; (to walk) avec mesure.

deliberate² [dɪ'lɪbəreɪt] vi délibérer (**on** sur) ▮ vt (discuss) délibérer sur. ● **deliberation** [-'reɪʃ(ə)n] n (discussion) délibération f.

delicate ['delɪkət] a délicat. ● **delicacy** n délicatesse f; (food) mets m délicat, gourmandise f. ● **delicately** adv délicatement.

delicatessen [delɪkə'tesən] n traiteur m et

delicious

84

épicerie *f* fine.
delicious [dɪ'lɪʃəs] *a* délicieux.
delight [dɪ'laɪt] *n* (*pleasure*) délice *m*, (grand) plaisir *m*, joie *f*; (*delicious food etc*) délice *m*; **delights** (*pleasures, things*) délices *fpl*; **to my (great) d.** à mon grand plaisir, à ma grande joie; **to be the d. of** faire les délices de; **to take d. in sth/in doing** se délecter de qch/à faire ▮ *vt* réjouir ▮ *vi* **to d. in doing** se délecter à faire. ●**delighted** *a* ravi, enchanté (**with sth** de qch, **to do** de faire, **that** que).
delightful [dɪ'laɪtfəl] *a* charmant; (*meal, perfume, sensation*) délicieux. ●**delightfully** *adv* (*with charm*) avec beaucoup de charme; (*wonderfully*) merveilleusement.
delineate [dɪ'lɪnɪeɪt] *vt* (*outline*) esquisser; (*portray*) décrire.
delinquent [dɪ'lɪŋkwənt] *a & n* délinquant, -ante (*mf*). ●**delinquency** *n* délinquance *f*.
delirious [dɪ'lɪərɪəs] *a* délirant; **to be d.** avoir le délire, délirer. ●**delirium** *n* (*illness*) délire *m*.
deliver [dɪ'lɪvər] *vt* **1** (*goods, milk etc*) livrer; (*letters*) distribuer; (*hand over*) remettre (**to** à). **2** (*rescue*) délivrer (*qn*) (**from** de). **3** (*give birth to*) mettre au monde, accoucher de; **to d. a woman's baby** accoucher une femme. **4** (*speech*) prononcer; (*warning, ultimatum*) lancer; (*blow*) porter. ●**deliveryman** *n* (*pl* **-men**) livreur *m*.
deliverance [dɪ'lɪvərəns] *n* délivrance *f* (**from** de).
delivery [dɪ'lɪvərɪ] *n* **1** livraison *f*; (*of letters*) distribution *f*; (*handing over*) remise *f*. **2** (*birth*) accouchement *m*. **3** (*speaking*) débit *m*. ●**deliveryman** *n* (*pl* **-men**) livreur *m*.
delta ['deltə] *n* (*of river*) delta *m*.
delude [dɪ'luːd] *vt* tromper; **to d. oneself** se faire des illusions. ●**delusion** [-ʒ(ə)n] *n* illusion *f*; (*in mental illness*) aberration *f* mentale.
deluge ['deljuːdʒ] *n* (*of water, Fig questions etc*) déluge *m* ▮ *vt* inonder (**with** de).
de luxe [dɪ'lʌks] *a* de luxe.
delve [delv] *vi* **to d. into** (*question, past*) fouiller; (*books*) fouiller dans.
demagogue ['deməɡɒɡ] *n* démagogue *mf*.
demand [dɪ'mɑːnd] *vt* exiger (**sth from s.o.** qch de qn), réclamer (**sth from s.o.** qch à qn); (*rights, more pay*) revendiquer; **to d. that** exiger que; **to d. to know** insister pour savoir.
▮ *n* exigence *f*; (*claim*) revendication *f*, réclamation *f*; (*for goods*) demande *f* (**for** pour); **demands** (*of terrorists etc*) exigences *fpl*; **to be in (great) d.** être très demandé; **to make demands on s.o.** exiger beaucoup de qn. ●**demanding** *a* exigeant.
demarcation [diːmɑː'keɪʃ(ə)n] *n* démarcation *f*; **d. line** ligne *f* de démarcation.
demean [dɪ'miːn] *vt* **to d. oneself** s'abaisser, s'avilir. ●**demeaning** *a* dégradant.
demeanour [dɪ'miːnər] (*Am* **demeanor**) *n* (*behaviour*) comportement *m*.
demented [dɪ'mentɪd] *a* dément.

demerara [demə'reərə] *n* **d. (sugar)** *Br* sucre *m* roux, cassonade *f*.
demise [dɪ'maɪz] *n* (*death*) décès *m*; (*of newspaper, custom etc*) *Fig* disparition *f*.
demister [diː'mɪstər] *n* (*for vehicle*) *Br* dispositif *m* de désembuage.
demo ['deməʊ] *n* (*pl* **-os**) (*demonstration*) *Fam* manif *f*.
demobilize [diː'məʊbɪlaɪz] *vt* démobiliser.
democracy [dɪ'mɒkrəsɪ] *n* démocratie *f*. ●**democrat** ['deməkræt] *n* démocrate *mf*. ●**demo'cratic** *a* démocratique; (*person*) démocrate. ●**demo'cratically** *adv* démocratiquement.
demography [dɪ'mɒɡrəfɪ] *n* démographie *f*.
demolish [dɪ'mɒlɪʃ] *vt* démolir. ●**demolition** [demə'lɪʃ(ə)n] *n* démolition *f*.
demon ['diːmən] *n* démon *m*.
demonstrate ['demənstreɪt] *vt* démontrer; (*machine*) faire une démonstration de; **to d. how to do** montrer comment faire ▮ *vi* (*protest*) manifester. ●**demonstration** [-'streɪʃ(ə)n] *n* démonstration *f*; (*protest*) manifestation *f*; **to hold *or* stage a d.** manifester. ●**demonstrator** *n* (*protester*) manifestant, -ante *mf*; (*in shop etc*) démonstrateur, -trice *mf*.
demonstrative [dɪ'mɒnstrətɪv] **1** *a* (*person, attitude*) démonstratif. **2** *a & n Grammar* démonstratif (*m*).
demoralize [dɪ'mɒrəlaɪz] *vt* démoraliser.
demote [dɪ'məʊt] *vt* rétrograder.
demure [dɪ'mjʊər] *a* sage, réservé.
den [den] *n* (*of lion, Fig person*) tanière *f*, antre *m*.
denationalize [diː'næʃ(ə)nəlaɪz] *vt* dénationaliser.
denial [dɪ'naɪəl] *n* (*of rumour, allegation*) démenti *m*; (*of the truth of sth*) dénégation *f*; **to issue a d.** publier un démenti.
denigrate ['denɪɡreɪt] *vt* dénigrer.
denim ['denɪm] *n* (*toile f de*) coton *m*; **denims** (*jeans*) (blue-)jean *m*.
denizen ['denɪz(ə)n] *n* habitant, -ante *mf*.
Denmark ['denmɑːk] *n* Danemark *m*.
denomination [dɪnɒmɪ'neɪʃ(ə)n] *n* (*religion*) confession *f*, religion *f*; (*sect*) secte *f*; (*of coin, banknote*) valeur *f*; (*of weights etc*) unité *f*. ●**denominational** *a* (*school*) confessionnel, religieux.
denominator [dɪ'nɒmɪneɪtər] *n Math & Fig* dénominateur *m*.
denote [dɪ'nəʊt] *vt* dénoter.
denounce [dɪ'naʊns] *vt* (*person, injustice etc*) dénoncer (**to** à); **to d. s.o. as a spy/etc** accuser qn publiquement d'être un espion/etc.
dense [dens] *a* (**-er, -est**) dense; (*stupid*) *Fam* lourd, bête. ●**densely** *adv* **d. populated/etc** très peuplé/etc. ●**density** *n* densité *f*.
dent [dent] *n* (*in car, metal etc*) bosse *f*, *Fam* gnon *m*; **full of dents** (*car etc*) cabossé; **to make a d. in** cabosser; **to make a d. in one's savings** (*of purchase*) écorner ses économies

▌ vt cabosser, bosseler.

dental ['dent(ə)l] a dentaire; **d. appointment** rendez-vous m chez le dentiste; **d. surgeon** chirurgien m dentiste.

dentist ['dentɪst] n dentiste mf; **to go to the d.('s)** aller chez le dentiste. ● **dentistry** n médecine f dentaire; **school of d.** école f dentaire.

dentures ['dentʃəz] npl dentier m.

denunciation [dɪnʌnsɪ'eɪʃ(ə)n] n dénonciation f; (public) accusation f publique.

deny [dɪ'naɪ] vt nier (**doing avoir fait, that** que); (rumour) démentir; (authority) rejeter; (disown) renier; **to d. s.o. sth** refuser qch à qn.

deodorant [diː'əʊdərənt] n déodorant m.

depart [dɪ'pɑːt] vi partir; (deviate) s'écarter (**from** de) ▌ vt **to d. this world** Lit quitter ce monde. ● **departed** a (dead) défunt ▌ n **the d.** le défunt, la défunte.

department [dɪ'pɑːtmənt] n département m; (in office) service m; (in shop) rayon m; (in university) section f, département m; **that's your d.** (sphere) c'est ton rayon; **d. store** grand magasin m. ● **depart'mental** a **d. manager** (in office) chef m de service; (in shop) chef m de rayon.

departure [dɪ'pɑːtʃər] n départ m; **a d. from** (custom, rule) un écart par rapport à, une entorse à; **to be a new d. for** constituer une nouvelle voie pour; **d. lounge** (in airport) salle f de départ.

depend [dɪ'pend] vi dépendre (**on, upon** de); **to d. (up)on** (rely on) compter sur (**for sth** pour qch); **you can d. on it!** tu peux en être sûr! ● **dependable** a (person, information etc) sûr; (machine) fiable, sûr. ● **dependant** n personne m à charge. ● **dependence** n dépendance f (**on** de). ● **dependency** n (country) dépendance f. ● **dependent** a dépendant (**on, upon** de); (relative, child) à charge; **to be d. (up)on** dépendre de.

depict [dɪ'pɪkt] vt (describe) dépeindre; (in pictures) représenter. ● **depiction** [-ʃ(ə)n] n peinture f; (in picture form) représentation f.

deplete [dɪ'pliːt] vt (use up) épuiser; (reduce) réduire. ● **depletion** [-ʃ(ə)n] n épuisement m; (reduction) réduction f.

deplore [dɪ'plɔːr] vt déplorer. ● **deplorable** a déplorable. ● **deplorably** adv déplorablement.

deploy [dɪ'plɔɪ] vt (troops etc) déployer.

depopulate [diː'pɒpjuleɪt] vt dépeupler. ● **depopulation** [-'leɪʃ(ə)n] n dépeuplement m.

deport [dɪ'pɔːt] vt (foreigner, criminal etc) expulser; (to concentration camp etc) Hist déporter. ● **deportation** [diːpɔː'teɪʃ(ə)n] n expulsion f; Hist déportation f.

deportment [dɪ'pɔːtmənt] n maintien m.

depose [dɪ'pəʊz] vt (king, ruler etc) déposer.

deposit [dɪ'pɒzɪt] **1** vt (object, money etc) déposer ▌ n (of money in bank) dépôt m; (part payment) acompte m; (against damage) caution f; (on bottle) consigne f; **d. account**

compte m d'épargne. **2** n (sediment in liquid etc) dépôt m; (of gold, oil etc) gisement m. ● **depositor** n déposant, -ante mf, épargnant, -ante mf.

depot [Br 'depəʊ, Am 'diːpəʊ] n (for goods etc) dépôt m; (railroad station) Am gare f; (bus) Am gare f routière.

deprave [dɪ'preɪv] vt dépraver. ● **depraved** a dépravé. ● **depravity** n dépravation f.

deprecate ['deprɪkeɪt] vt désapprouver.

depreciate [dɪ'priːʃɪeɪt] vt (reduce in value) déprécier ▌ vi (fall in value) se déprécier. ● **depreciation** [-'eɪʃ(ə)n] n dépréciation f.

depress [dɪ'pres] vt (discourage) déprimer; (push down) appuyer sur. ● **depressed** a (person, market) déprimé; (industry) (in decline) en déclin; (in crisis) en crise; **to get d.** se décourager. ● **depression** [-ʃ(ə)n] n dépression f.

deprive [dɪ'praɪv] vt priver (**of** de). ● **deprived** a (child etc) déshérité. ● **deprivation** [deprə'veɪʃ(ə)n] n (hardship) privation f; (loss) perte f.

depth [depθ] n profondeur f; (of snow) épaisseur f; (of interest) intensité f; **in the depths of** (forest, despair) au plus profond de; (winter) au cœur de; **to get out of one's d.** (be unable to cope) perdre pied, nager; **in d.** en profondeur.

deputation [depjʊ'teɪʃ(ə)n] n députation f.

deputize ['depjʊtaɪz] vi assurer l'intérim (**for s.o.** de qn) ▌ vt députer (**s.o. to do** qn pour faire).

deputy ['depjʊtɪ] n (replacement) remplaçant, -ante mf; (assistant) adjoint, -ointe mf; **d. (sheriff)** Am shérif m adjoint; **d. chairman** vice-président, -ente mf.

derailed [dɪ'reɪld] a **to be d.** (of train) dérailler. ● **derailment** n déraillement m.

deranged [dɪ'reɪndʒd] a **he's (mentally) d., his mind is d.** il a le cerveau dérangé.

derby ['dɑːbɪ] n (bowler hat) Am (chapeau m) melon m.

derelict ['derɪlɪkt] a (building etc) abandonné.

deride [dɪ'raɪd] vt tourner en dérision. ● **derision** [-ʒ(ə)n] n dérision f. ● **derisive** a (laughter etc) moqueur; (amount etc) dérisoire. ● **derisory** [dɪ'raɪsərɪ] a (amount etc) dérisoire.

derive [dɪ'raɪv] vt **to d. from sth** (pleasure, profit etc) tirer de qch; (word, meaning etc) dériver de qch; **to be derived from** (of word etc) dériver de, provenir de ▌ vi **to d. from** dériver de. ● **derivation** [derɪ'veɪʃ(ə)n] n Ling dérivation f. ● **derivative** [dɪ'rɪvətɪv] a & n Ling Ch dérivé (m).

dermatitis [dɜːmə'taɪtɪs] n dermatite f.

dermatology [dɜːmə'tɒlədʒɪ] n dermatologie f ● **dermatologist** n dermatologue mf.

derogatory [dɪ'rɒgət(ə)rɪ] a (word) péjoratif; (remark) désobligeant (**to** pour).

derrick ['derɪk] n (over oil well) derrick m.

derv [dɜːv] n Br gazole m, gas-oil m.

descend [dɪ'send] vi descendre (**from** de);

(of rain) tomber; **to d. upon** *(of tourists)* envahir; *(attack)* faire une descente sur, tomber sur; **in descending order** en ordre décroissant **▌** *vt (stairs)* descendre; **to be descended from** descendre de.

descendant [dɪ'sendənt] *n* descendant, -ante *mf*.

descent [dɪ'sent] *n* **1** *(of aircraft etc)* descente *f*; **his d. into crime** sa chute dans le crime. **2** *(ancestry)* origine *f*, souche *f*.

describe [dɪ'skraɪb] *vt* décrire. ● **description** [-ʃ(ə)n] *n* description *f*; *(on passport)* signalement *m*; **of every d.** de toutes sortes. ● **descriptive** *a* descriptif.

desecrate ['desɪkreɪt] *vt* profaner. ● **desecration** [-'kreɪʃ(ə)n] *n* profanation *f*.

desegregate [diː'segrɪgeɪt] *vt (school etc)* supprimer la ségrégation raciale dans. ● **desegregation** [-'geɪʃ(ə)n] *n* déségrégation *f*.

desert[1] ['dezət] *n* désert *m*; **d. climate/plant/** *etc* climat *m*/plante *f*/*etc* désertique *or* du désert; **d. animal** animal *m* du désert; **d. island** île *f* déserte.

desert[2] [dɪ'zɜːt] *vt (person)* abandonner; *(place, cause etc)* déserter; **to d. s.o.** *(of luck etc)* abandonner qn **▌** *vi (of soldier)* déserter. ● **deserted** *a (place)* désert. ● **deserter** *n (soldier)* déserteur *m*.

desertion [dɪ'zɜːʃ(ə)n] *n (by soldier)* désertion *f*; *(by spouse)* abandon *m* (du domicile conjugal).

deserts [dɪ'zɜːts] *n* **to get one's just d.** recevoir ce qu'on mérite.

deserve [dɪ'zɜːv] *vt* mériter **(to do de faire).** ● **deserving** *a (person)* méritant; *(action, cause)* louable, méritoire; **to be d. of** *(praise, s.o.'s love etc)* être digne de. ● **deservedly** [-ɪdlɪ] *adv* à juste titre.

desiccated ['desɪkeɪtɪd] *a* (des)séché.

design [dɪ'zaɪn] **1** *vt (car, furniture etc)* dessiner; *(dress)* créer, dessiner; *(devise)* concevoir *(projet, moyen etc)*; **designed to do/for s.o.** conçu pour faire/pour qn; **well designed** bien conçu.
▌ *n (pattern)* motif *m*, dessin *m*; *(sketch)* plan *m*, dessin *m*; *(type of dress or car)* modèle *m*; *(planning)* conception *f*, création *f*; **industrial d.** dessin *m* industriel; **to study d.** étudier le dessin *or* le design.
2 *n (aim)* dessein *m*, intention *f*; **by d.** intentionnellement; **to have designs on** avoir des desseins sur. ● **designer** *n (artistic)* dessinateur, -trice *mf*; *(industrial)* (concepteur-) dessinateur *m*; *(of clothes)* styliste *mf*; *(well-known)* couturier *m*; **d. clothes** vêtements *mpl* griffés.

designate ['dezɪgneɪt] *vt* désigner. ● **designation** [-'neɪʃ(ə)n] *n* désignation *f*.

desire [dɪ'zaɪər] *n* désir *m*; **I've got no d. to do that** je n'ai aucune envie de faire cela **▌** *vt* désirer **(to do de faire).** ● **desirable** *a* désirable; **d. property/etc** *(in advertising)* (très) belle propriété/*etc*.

desk [desk] *n (in school)* table *f*; *(in office)* bureau *m*; *(in shop)* Br caisse *f*; **(reception**

d. *(in hotel etc)* réception *f*; **the news d.** le service des informations; **d. job** travail *m* de bureau; **d. clerk** *(in hotel)* Am réceptionniste *mf*.

desktop ['desktɒp] *n* **d. computer** ordinateur *m* de bureau; **d. publishing** microédition *f*, publication *f* assistée par ordinateur.

desolate ['desələt] *a (deserted)* désolé; *(in ruins)* dévasté; *(dreary, bleak)* morne, triste; *(person)* affligé. ● **desolation** [-'leɪʃ(ə)n] *n (ruin)* dévastation *f*; *(emptiness)* solitude *f*.

despair [dɪ'speər] *n* désespoir *m*; **to drive s.o. to d.** désespérer qn; **to be in d.** être au désespoir **▌** *vi* désespérer **(of s.o.** de qn, **of doing** de faire). ● **despairing** *a* désespéré. ● **despairingly** *adv* avec désespoir.

despatch [dɪ'spætʃ] *see* **dispatch.**

desperado [despə'rɑːdəʊ] *n (pl* **-oes** *or* **-os)** criminel *m*.

desperate ['despərət] *a* désespéré; *(criminal)* capable de tout; *(serious)* grave; **to be d. for** *(money, love etc)* avoir désespérément besoin de; *(a cigarette, baby etc)* mourir d'envie d'avoir. ● **desperately** *adv (ill)* gravement; *(in love)* éperdument.

desperation [despə'reɪʃ(ə)n] *n* désespoir *m*; **in d.** *(as a last resort)* en désespoir de cause.

despicable [dɪ'spɪkəb(ə)l] *a* méprisable.

despise [dɪ'spaɪz] *vt* mépriser.

despite [dɪ'spaɪt] *prep* malgré.

despondent [dɪ'spɒndənt] *a* découragé. ● **despondency** *n* découragement *m*.

despot ['despɒt] *n* despote *m*. ● **despotism** *n* despotisme *m*.

dessert [dɪ'zɜːt] *n* dessert *m*. ● **dessertspoon** *n Br* cuillère *f* à dessert.

destabilize [diː'steɪbəlaɪz] *vt* déstabiliser.

destination [destɪ'neɪʃ(ə)n] *n* destination *f*.

destine ['destɪn] *vt* destiner **(for à, to do à faire); it was destined to happen** ça devait arriver.

destiny ['destɪnɪ] *n* destin *m*; *(fate of individual)* destinée *f*.

destitute ['destɪtjuːt] *a (poor)* indigent; **d. of** *(lacking in)* dénué de. ● **destitution** [-'tjuːʃ(ə)n] *n* dénuement *m*.

destroy [dɪ'strɔɪ] *vt* détruire; *(horse, monkey etc)* abattre; *(cat, dog)* faire piquer. ● **destroyer** *n (ship)* contre-torpilleur *m*, *(person)* destructeur, -trice *mf*.

destruction [dɪ'strʌkʃ(ə)n] *n* destruction *f*. ● **destructive** *a (person, war)* destructeur; *(power)* destructif; **d. child** enfant *mf* qui casse tout, brise-fer *m*.

detach [dɪ'tætʃ] *vt* détacher **(from** de). ● **detached** *a (indifferent) (person, manner)* détaché; *(without bias) (view)* désintéressé; **d. house** *Br* maison *f* individuelle.

detachable [dɪ'tætʃəb(ə)l] *a (lining etc)* amovible.

detachment [dɪ'tætʃmənt] *n (attitude, group of soldiers)* détachement *m*; **the d. of** *(action)* la séparation de.

detail [*Br* 'diːteɪl, *Am* dɪ'teɪl] **1** *n* détail *m*; **in d.** en détail **▌** *vt* raconter *or* exposer en détail *or* par le menu, détailler. **2** *vt Mil* détacher (*qn*) **(to do pour faire)** ▌ *n* (*group of soldiers*) détachement *m*. ●**detailed** *a* (*account etc*) détaillé.

detain [dɪ'teɪn] *vt* retenir; (*prisoner*) détenir; (*in hospital*) garder, hospitaliser. ●**detai'nee** *n Pol Jur* détenu, -ue *mf*. ●**detention** [dɪ'tenʃ(ə)n] *n* (*school punishment*) retenue *f*; (*in prison*) détention *f*.

detect [dɪ'tekt] *vt* (*discover*) découvrir; (*see, hear*) distinguer; (*identify*) identifier; (*mine*) détecter; (*illness*) dépister. ●**detection** [-ʃ(ə)n] *n* découverte *f*; (*identification*) identification *f*; (*of mine*) détection *f*; (*of illness*) dépistage *m*.

detective [dɪ'tektɪv] *n* inspecteur *m* de police, policier *m* (en civil); (*private*) détective *m* (privé); **d. film/novel** *or* **story** film *m*/ roman *m* policier.

detector [dɪ'tektər] *n* détecteur *m*; **smoke d.** détecteur *m* de fumée.

deter [dɪ'tɜːr] *vt* (**-rr-**) **to d. s.o.** dissuader *or* décourager qn **(from doing** de faire, **from sth** de qch).

detergent [dɪ'tɜːdʒənt] *n* détergent *m*.

deteriorate [dɪ'tɪərɪəreɪt] *vi* se détériorer; (*of morals*) dégénérer. ●**deterioration** [-'reɪʃ(ə)n] *n* détérioration *f*; (*of morals*) dégénérescence *f*.

determine [dɪ'tɜːmɪn] *vt* déterminer; (*price*) fixer; **to d. s.o. to do** décider qn à faire; **to d. that** décider que; **to d. to do** se déterminer à faire. ●**determined** *a* (*look, person, quantity*) déterminé; **to be d. to do** *or* **on doing** être décidé à faire; **I'm d. she'll succeed** je suis bien décidé à ce qu'elle réussisse.

deterrent [*Br* dɪ'terənt, *Am* dɪ'tɜːrənt] *n* (*military*) force *f* de dissuasion; **to be a d., act as a d.** *Fig* être dissuasif.

detest [dɪ'test] *vt* détester **(doing** faire). ●**detestable** *a* détestable.

detonate ['detəneɪt] *vt* faire exploser *or* détoner ▌ *vi* exploser, détoner. ●**detonation** [-'neɪʃ(ə)n] *n* détonation *f*. ●**detonator** *n* détonateur *m*.

detour ['diːtʊər] *n* détour *m*; **to make a d.** faire un détour.

detract [dɪ'trækt] *vi* **to d. from** (*make less*) diminuer. ●**detractor** *n* détracteur, -trice *mf*.

detriment ['detrɪmənt] *n* **to the d. of** au détriment de. ●**detri'mental** *a* préjudiciable **(to** à).

devalue [diː'væljuː] *vt* (*money*) dévaluer; (*person, s.o.'s worth etc*) dévaloriser. ●**devaluation** [-'eɪʃ(ə)n] *n* dévaluation *f*.

devastate ['devəsteɪt] *vt* (*lay waste, wreck*) dévaster; (*opponent*) anéantir; (*upset, shock*) *Fig* foudroyer (*qn*). ●**devastating** *a* (*storm etc*) dévastateur; (*overwhelming*) (*news, results etc*) confondant, accablant; (*shock*) terrible; (*charm*) irrésistible.

develop [dɪ'veləp] *vt* développer; (*area, land*) mettre en valeur; (*habit, illness*) contracter; (*talent*) manifester; (*photo*) développer; **to d. a liking for** prendre goût à.

vi se développer; (*of event, argument, crisis*) se produire; (*of talent, illness*) se manifester; **to d. into** devenir. ●**developing** *a* **d. country** pays *m* en voie de développement ▌ *n* (*of photos*) développement *m*.

developer [dɪ'veləpər] *n* **(property) d.** promoteur *m* (de construction).

development [dɪ'veləpmənt] *n* développement *m*; (*of land*) mise *f* en valeur; (*housing*) **d.** lotissement *m*; (*large*) grand ensemble *m*; **a (new) d.** (*in situation*) un fait nouveau.

deviate ['diːvɪeɪt] *vi* dévier **(from** de); **to d. from the norm** s'écarter de la norme. ●**deviant** *a* (*behaviour etc*) anormal. ●**deviation** [-'eɪʃ(ə)n] *n* déviation *f*.

device [dɪ'vaɪs] *n* (*instrument, gadget etc*) dispositif *m*, engin *m*; (*scheme*) procédé *m*; **explosive/nuclear d.** engin *m* explosif/ nucléaire; **safety d.** dispositif *m* de sécurité; **left to one's own devices** livré à soi-même.

devil ['dev(ə)l] *n* diable *m*; **a** *or* **the d. of a problem** *Fam* un problème d'enfer; **a** *or* **the d. of a noise** *Fam* un bruit infernal; **I had a** *or* **the d. of a job** *Fam* j'ai eu un mal fou **(doing, to do** à faire); **what/where/why the d.?** *Fam* que/où/pourquoi diable?; **to run/etc like the d.** courir/*etc* comme un fou. ●**devilish** *a* diabolique. ●**devilry** *n* (*mischief*) diablerie *f*.

devious ['diːvɪəs] *a* (*mind, behaviour*) tortueux; **he's d.** il a l'esprit tortueux. ●**deviousness** *n* (*of person*) esprit *m* tortueux.

devise [dɪ'vaɪz] *vt* (*a plan*) combiner; (*a plot*) tramer; (*invent*) inventer.

devitalize [diː'vaɪtəlaɪz] *vt* rendre exsangue.

devoid [dɪ'vɔɪd] *a* **d. of** dénué *or* dépourvu de; (*guilt*) exempt de.

devolution [diːvə'luːʃ(ə)n] *n Pol* décentralisation *f*; **the d. of** (*power*) la délégation de.

devolve [dɪ'vɒlv] *vi* **to d. upon** incomber à.

devote [dɪ'vəʊt] *vt* consacrer **(to** à). ●**devoted** *a* dévoué; (*admirer*) fervent. ●**devotedly** [-ɪdlɪ] *adv* avec dévouement.

devotee [dɪvəʊ'tiː] *n* (*of music, tennis etc*) passionné, -ée *mf* (**of** de).

devotion [dɪ'vəʊʃ(ə)n] *n* dévouement *m* (**to s.o.** à qn); (*religious*) dévotion *f*; **devotions** (*prayers*) dévotions *fpl*.

devour [dɪ'vaʊər] *vt* (*eat, engulf, read etc*) dévorer.

devout [dɪ'vaʊt] *a* dévot, pieux, (*supporter, prayer*) fervent.

dew [djuː] *n* rosée *f*. ●**dewdrop** *n* goutte *f* de rosée.

dext(e)rous ['dekst(ə)rəs] *a* adroit, habile. ●**dex'terity** *n* adresse *f*, dextérité *f*.

diabetes [daɪə'biːtiːz] *n* (*illness*) diabète *m*. ●**diabetic** [-'betɪk] *n* diabétique *mf* ▌ *a* diabétique; **d. jam/etc** confiture *f*/etc pour diabétiques.

diabolical [daɪə'bɒlɪk(ə)l] *a* diabolique; (*bad*) (*behaviour, weather etc*) épouvantable.

diadem ['daɪədem] *n* diadème *m*.

diagnose [*Br* 'daɪəgnəʊz, *Am* -'nəʊs] *vt* diagnostiquer. ● **diagnosis**, *pl* **-oses** [daɪəgˈnəʊsɪs, -əʊsiːz] *n* diagnostic *m*.

diagonal [daɪˈægən(ə)l] *a* diagonal ▌ *n d.* **(line)** diagonale *f*. ● **diagonally** *adv* en diagonale.

diagram [ˈdaɪəgræm] *n* schéma *m*, diagramme *m*; *(geometrical)* figure *f*. ● **diagrammatic** *a* schématique.

dial [ˈdaɪəl] *n* cadran *m* ▌ *vt* (*Br* **-ll-**, *Am* **-l-**) *(phone number)* faire, composer; *(person)* appeler; **to d. s.o. direct** appeler qn à l'automatique. ● **dialling code** *n Br* indicatif *m*. ● **dialling tone** *n Br* tonalité *f*. ● **dial tone** *n Am* tonalité *f*.

dialect [ˈdaɪəlekt] *n* *(regional)* dialecte *m*; *(rural)* patois *m*.

dialogue [ˈdaɪəlɒg] *(Am* **dialog)** *n* dialogue *m*.

dialysis, *pl* **-yses** [daɪˈælɪsɪs, -ɪsiːz] *n* *(medical process)* dialyse *f*; **to be in d.**, **be having d.** être sous dialyse.

diameter [daɪˈæmɪtər] *n* diamètre *m*. ● **diametrically** *adv* **d. opposed** *(opinion etc)* diamétralement opposé.

diamond [ˈdaɪəmənd] *n* **1** *(stone)* diamant *m*; *(shape)* losange *m*; *(baseball)* **d.** *Am* terrain *m* (de baseball); **d. necklace/etc** rivière *f/etc* de diamants. **2 diamond(s)** *Cards* carreau *m*.

diaper [ˈdaɪəpər] *n* *(for baby)* *Am* couche *f*.

diaphragm [ˈdaɪəfræm] *n* diaphragme *m*.

diarrh(o)ea [daɪəˈriːə] *n* diarrhée *f*; **to have d.** avoir la diarrhée.

diary [ˈdaɪərɪ] *n* *(calendar)* *Br* agenda *m*; *(private)* journal *m* (intime).

dice [daɪs] *n inv* dé *m* (à jouer) ▌ *vt (food)* couper en dés.

dicey [ˈdaɪsɪ] *a* **(-ier, -iest)** *Fam* risqué.

dichotomy [daɪˈkɒtəmɪ] *n* dichotomie *f*.

dickens [ˈdɪkɪnz] *n* **where/why/what the d.?** *Fam* où/pourquoi/que diable?

dictaphone® [ˈdɪktəfəʊn] *n* dictaphone® *m*.

dictate [dɪkˈteɪt] *vt (letter, conditions etc)* dicter **(to à)** ▌ *vi* dicter; **to d. to s.o.** *(order around)* faire la loi à qn, régenter qn. ● **dictation** *n* -ʃ(ə)n] dictée *f*.

dictates [ˈdɪkteɪts] *npl* préceptes *mpl*; **the d. of conscience** la voix de la conscience.

dictator [dɪkˈteɪtər] *n* dictateur *m*. ● **dictatorial** *a* dictatorial. ● **dictatorship** *n* dictature *f*.

diction [ˈdɪkʃ(ə)n] *n* langage *m*; *(way of speaking)* diction *f*.

dictionary [ˈdɪkʃənərɪ] *n* dictionnaire *m*; **English d.** dictionnaire *m* d'anglais.

dictum [ˈdɪktəm] *n* dicton *m*.

did [dɪd] *pt of* **do**.

diddle [ˈdɪd(ə)l] *vt (cheat)* *Br Sl* rouler; **to d. s.o. out of sth** carotter qch à qn; **to get diddled out of sth** se faire refaire de qch.

die¹ [daɪ] *vi (pt & pp* **died**, *pres p* **dying)** mourir *(of, from* de); **to be dying to do** mourir d'envie de faire; **to be dying for sth** avoir une envie folle de qch; **to d. away** *(of noise)* mourir; **to d. down** *(of fire)* mourir; *(of storm)* se calmer; **to d. off** mourir (les

uns après les autres); **to d. out** *(of custom)* mourir.

die² [daɪ] *n (mould)* matrice *f*; *(in engraving)* coin *m*; **the d. is cast** *Fig* les dés sont jetés.

diehard [ˈdaɪhɑːd] *n* réactionnaire *mf*.

diesel [ˈdiːzəl] *a* **(engine)** *(motor m)* diesel *m*; **d. (oil)** gazole *m*.

diet [ˈdaɪət] *n* *(for losing weight)* régime *m*; *(usual food)* alimentation *f*; **to go on a d.** faire un régime ▌ *vi* suivre un régime. ● **dietary** *a* diététique; **d. fibre** fibre(s) *f(pl)* alimentaire(s). ● **dietician** [-ˈtɪʃ(ə)n] *n* diététicien, -ienne *mf*.

differ [ˈdɪfər] *vi* différer **(from** de); *(disagree)* ne pas être d'accord **(from** avec).

difference [ˈdɪf(ə)rəns] *n* différence *f* (**in** de); *(in age, weight etc)* écart *m*, différence *f*; **d. (of opinion)** différend *m*; **it makes no d.** ça n'a pas d'importance; **it makes no d. to me** ça m'est égal; **that will make a (big) d.** ça changera pas mal de choses.

different [ˈdɪf(ə)rənt] *a* différent **(from, to** de); *(another)* autre; *(various)* divers, différents. ● **differently** *adv* autrement **(from, to que)**, différemment **(from, to** de).

differential [dɪfəˈrenʃəl] *a* différentiel ▌ **differentials** *(in pay)* écarts *mpl* salariaux.

differentiate [dɪfəˈrenʃɪeɪt] *vt* différencier **(from** de) ▌ *vti* **d. (between)** faire la différence entre.

difficult [ˈdɪfɪkəlt] *a* difficile **(to do** à faire); **it's d. for us to...** il nous est difficile de...; **the d. thing is to...** le plus difficile est de....

difficulty [ˈdɪfɪkəltɪ] *n* difficulté *f*; **to have d. doing** avoir du mal à faire; **to be in d.** avoir des difficultés; **to have d. or difficulties with sth/s.o.** *(problems)* avoir des ennuis avec qch/qn.

diffident [ˈdɪfɪdənt] *a* *(person)* qui manque d'assurance; *(smile, tone)* mal assuré. ● **diffidence** *n* manque *m* d'assurance.

diffuse [dɪˈfjuːz] *vt (spread)* diffuser ▌ [dɪˈfjuːs] *a* *(spread out, wordy)* diffus. ● **diffusion** [-ʒ(ə)n] *n* diffusion *f*.

dig [dɪg] *vt (pt & pp* **dug**, *pres p* **digging)** *(ground, garden)* bêcher; *(hole, grave etc)* creuser; *(understand)* *Sl* piger; *(appreciate)* *Sl* aimer; **to d. sth into sth** *(push)* planter *or* enfoncer qch dans qch; **to d. out** *(animal etc from ground)* déterrer; *(accident victim)* dégager; *(find)* *Fam* dénicher; **to d. up** *(from ground)* déterrer; *(weed)* arracher; *(earth)* retourner; *(street)* piocher.

▌ *vi (dig a hole)* creuser; *(of pig)* fouiller; **to d. (oneself) in** *(of soldier)* se retrancher; **to d. in** *(eat)* *Fam* manger; **to d. into** *(s.o.'s past)* fouiller dans; *(meal)* *Fam* attaquer; **to d. into one's savings** puiser dans ses économies.

▌ *n (with spade)* coup *m* de bêche; *(archeological)* fouilles *fpl*; *(with elbow)* coup *m* de coude; *(with fist)* coup *m* de poing; *(remark)* *Fam* coup *m* de griffe.

digest [daɪˈdʒest] *vti* digérer ▌ [ˈdaɪdʒest] *n* *(summary of texts)* condensé *m*. ● **digestible**

a digeste. ●**digestion** [-tʃ(ə)n] *n* digestion *f*. ●**digestive** *a* digestif.

digger ['dɪgər] *n* (*machine*) pelleteuse *f*.

digit ['dɪdʒɪt] *n* (*number*) chiffre *m*. ●**digital** *a* (*watch*) numérique; (*tape, recording*) audionumérique.

dignified ['dɪgnɪfaɪd] *a* digne, qui a de la dignité. ●**dignify** *vt* donner de la dignité à; **to d. with the name of** honorer du nom de. ●**dignitary** *n* dignitaire *m*. ●**dignity** *n* dignité *f*.

digress [daɪ'gres] *vi* faire une digression; **to d. from** s'écarter de. ●**digression** [-ʃ(ə)n] *n* digression *f*.

digs [dɪgz] *npl Br Fam* chambre *f* (meublée); **to be in d.** avoir une chambre en ville.

dike [daɪk] *n* = dyke.

dilapidated [dɪ'læpɪdeɪtɪd] *a* (*house*) délabré. ●**dilapidation** [-'deɪʃ(ə)n] *n* délabrement *m*.

dilate [daɪ'leɪt] *vt* dilater ▮ *vi* se dilater. ●**dilation** -ʃ(ə)n] *n* dilatation *f*.

dilemma [daɪ'lemə] *n* dilemme *m*.

dilettante [dɪlɪ'tæntɪ] *n* dilettante *mf*.

diligent ['dɪlɪdʒənt] *a* assidu, appliqué; **to be d. in doing sth** faire qch avec zèle. ●**diligence** *n* zèle *m*, assiduité *f*.

dilly-dally [dɪlɪ'dælɪ] *vi Fam* (*dawdle*) lambiner, lanterner; (*hesitate*) tergiverser.

dilute [daɪ'luːt] *vt* diluer ▮ *a* (*liquid etc*) dilué.

dim [dɪm] *a* (**dimmer, dimmest**) (*light*) faible; (*colour*) terne; (*room*) sombre; (*memory, outline*) vague; (*person*) stupide. ▮ *vt* (**-mm-**) (*light*) baisser, réduire; (*glory*) ternir; (*memory*) estomper; **to d. one's headlights** *Am* se mettre en code. ●**dimly** *adv* (*to shine*) faiblement; (*vaguely*) vaguement; **d. lit** mal éclairé. ●**dimness** *n* faiblesse *f*; (*of memory etc*) vague *m*; (*of room*) pénombre *f*.

dime [daɪm] *n* (*US & Can coin*) (pièce *f* de) dix cents *mpl*; **a d. store** = un Prisunic®, un Monoprix®.

dimension [daɪ'menʃ(ə)n] *n* dimension *f*; **the dimension(s) of the problem/etc** (*extent*) l'étendue *f* du problème/etc. ●**dimensional** *a* **two-d.** à deux dimensions.

diminish [dɪ'mɪnɪʃ] *vti* diminuer. ●**diminishing** *a* qui diminue.

diminutive [dɪ'mɪnjʊtɪv] **1** *a* (*tiny*) minuscule. **2** *a* & *n Grammar* diminutif (*m*).

dimmer ['dɪmər] *n* **d.** (**switch**) variateur *m* (de lumière).

dimmers ['dɪməz] *npl* (*low beams of vehicle*) *Am* phares *mpl* code *inv*, codes *mpl*.

dimple ['dɪmp(ə)l] *n* fossette *f*. ●**dimpled** *a* (*chin, cheek*) à fossettes.

dimwit ['dɪmwɪt] *n* idiot, -ote *mf*. ●**dimwitted** *a* idiot.

din [dɪn] **1** *n* (*noise*) vacarme *m*. **2** *vt* (**-nn-**) **to d. into s.o. that** rabâcher à qn que.

dine [daɪn] *vi* dîner (**on, off** de); **to d. out** dîner en ville. ●**diner** *n* (*person*) dîneur, -euse *mf*; (*train carriage*) wagon-restaurant *m*; (*short-order restaurant*) *Am* petit restaurant

m. ●**dining car** *n* (*on train*) wagon-restaurant *m*. ●**dining room** *n* salle *f* à manger.

ding(dong)! ['dɪŋ(dɒŋ)] *int* (*sound of bell*) dring!, ding (dong)!

dinghy ['dɪŋgɪ] *n* petit canot *m*, youyou *m*; (*rubber*) canot *m* pneumatique.

dingy ['dɪndʒɪ] *a* (**-ier, -iest**) (*room etc*) minable; (*colour*) terne. ●**dinginess** *n* malpropreté *f*.

dinner ['dɪnər] *n* (*evening meal*) dîner *m*; (*lunch*) déjeuner *m*; (*for dog, cat*) pâtée *f*; **to have d.** dîner; **to have s.o. to d.** avoir qn à dîner; **d. dance** dîner-dansant *m*; **d. jacket** smoking *m*; **d. party** dîner *m* (à la maison); **d. plate** grande assiette *f*; **d. service, d. set** service *m* de table; **it's d. time** c'est l'heure de dîner; (*lunch*) c'est l'heure de déjeuner.

dinosaur ['daɪnəsɔːr] *n* dinosaure *m*.

dint [dɪnt] *n* **by d. of sth/of doing** à force de qch/de faire.

diocese ['daɪəsɪs] *n* (*of bishop*) diocèse *m*.

dip [dɪp] *vt* (**-pp-**) plonger; (*into liquid*) tremper, plonger; **to d. one's headlights** *Br* se mettre en code ▮ *vi* (*of road*) plonger; (*of sun etc*) baisser; **to d. into** (*pocket, savings*) puiser dans; (*book*) feuilleter ▮ *n* (*in road*) petit creux *m*; **to go for a d.** (*swim*) faire trempette.

diphtheria [dɪp'θɪərɪə] *n* diphtérie *f*.

diphthong ['dɪfθɒŋ] *n* (*vowel*) diphtongue *f*.

diploma [dɪ'pləʊmə] *n* diplôme *m*.

diplomacy [dɪ'pləʊməsɪ] *n* (*tact*) & *Pol* diplomatie *f*.

diplomat ['dɪpləmæt] *n* diplomate *mf*. ●**diplo'matic** *a* diplomatique; **to be d.** (*tactful*) être diplomate.

dipper ['dɪpər] *n* **the big d.** (*at fairground*) *Br* les montagnes *fpl* russes.

dipstick ['dɪpstɪk] *n* jauge *f* (de niveau) d'huile.

dire ['daɪər] *a* (*situation etc*) affreux; (*poverty, need*) extrême.

direct¹ [daɪ'rekt] *a* (*result, flight, person etc*) direct; (*danger*) immédiat; **d. debit** *Br* prélèvement *m* automatique ▮ *adv* directement. ●**directness** *n* (*of person, reply*) franchise *f*.

direct² [daɪ'rekt] *vt* (*work, one's steps, one's attention*) diriger; (*letter, remark*) adresser (**to** à); (*efforts*) orienter (**to, towards** vers); (*film*) réaliser; (*play*) mettre en scène; **to d. s.o. to** (*place*) adresser à qn le chemin de; **to d. s.o. to do** charger qn de faire.

direction [daɪ'rekʃ(ə)n] *n* direction *f*, sens *m*; (*management*) direction *f*; (*of film*) réalisation *f*; (*of play*) mise *f* en scène; **directions** (*orders*) indications *fpl*; **directions** (**for use**) mode *m* d'emploi; **in the opposite d.** en sens inverse.

directive [dɪ'rektɪv] *n* directive *f*.

directly [daɪ'rektlɪ] *adv* (*without detour*) directement; (*exactly*) juste; (*at once*) tout de suite; (*to speak*) franchement; **d. in front/behind** juste devant/derrière ▮ *conj* (*as soon as*) *Br Fam* aussitôt que (+ *indic*).

director [daɪ'rektər] n directeur, -trice mf; (of film) réalisateur, -trice mf; (of play) metteur m en scène; (board member in firm) administrateur, -trice mf. ●**directorship** n poste m de directeur; (as board member) poste m d'administrateur.

directory [daɪ'rektərɪ] n (phone book) annuaire m; (of streets) guide m; (of addresses) & Comptr répertoire m; **telephone d.** annuaire m du téléphone; **d. inquiries** Br renseignements mpl.

dirge [dɜːdʒ] n chant m funèbre.

dirt [dɜːt] n saleté f; (filth) ordure f; (mud) boue f; (earth) terre f; (talk) Fig obscénité(s) f(pl); **d. cheap** Fam très bon marché; **d. road** chemin m de terre; **d. track** Sport cendrée f.

dirty ['dɜːtɪ] a (-ier, -iest) sale; (job) salissant; (obscene, unpleasant) sale; (word) grossier, obscène; **to get d.** se salir; **to get with d.** salir qch; **a d. joke** une histoire cochonne; **a d. trick** un sale tour; **a d. old man** un vieux cochon ‖ adv (to fight) déloyalement ‖ vt (machine) encrasser ‖ vi se salir; **it dirties easily** ça se salit facilement.

dis- [dɪs] pref dé-, dés-.

disability [dɪsə'bɪlɪtɪ] n (injury) infirmité f; (condition) invalidité f; Fig désavantage m.

disable [dɪ'seɪb(ə)l] vt rendre infirme; (maim) mutiler. ●**disabled** a infirme, handicapé; (maimed) mutilé ‖ n **the d.** les infirmes mpl, les handicapés mpl.

disadvantage [dɪsəd'vɑːntɪdʒ] n désavantage m ‖ vt désavantager.

disaffected [dɪsə'fektɪd] a mécontent. ●**disaffection** [-ʃ(ə)n] n désaffection f (for pour).

disagree [dɪsə'griː] vi ne pas être d'accord, être en désaccord (with avec); (of figures) ne pas concorder; **to d. with s.o.** (of food etc) ne pas réussir à qn. ●**disagreement** n désaccord m; (quarrel) différend m.

disagreeable [dɪsə'griːəb(ə)l] a désagréable.

disallow [dɪsə'laʊ] vt rejeter.

disappear [dɪsə'pɪər] vi disparaître. ●**disappearance** n disparition f.

disappoint [dɪsə'pɔɪnt] vt décevoir; **I'm disappointed with it** ça m'a déçu. ●**disappointing** a décevant. ●**disappointment** n déception f.

disapproval [dɪsə'pruːv(ə)l] n désapprobation f.

disapprove [dɪsə'pruːv] vi **to d. of s.o./sth** désapprouver qn/qch; **I d.** je suis contre. ●**disapproving** a (look etc) désapprobateur.

disarm [dɪs'ɑːm] vti désarmer. ●**disarmament** n désarmement m.

disarray [dɪsə'reɪ] n (distress) désarroi m; (disorder) désordre m; **in d.** (army, political party) en plein désarroi; (clothes, hair) en désordre.

disaster [dɪ'zɑːstər] n désastre m, catastrophe f; **d. area** région f sinistrée. ●**disaster-stricken** a sinistré. ●**disastrous** a désastreux.

disband [dɪs'bænd] vt disperser ‖ vi se disperser.

disbelief [dɪsbə'liːf] n incrédulité f.

disc [dɪsk] (Am **disk**) n disque m; **identity d.** plaque f d'identité; **d. jockey** disc-jockey m.

discard [dɪs'kɑːd] vt (get rid of) se débarrasser de; (plan, hope etc) Fig abandonner.

discern [dɪ'sɜːn] vt discerner. ●**discerning** a (person) averti, sagace.

discernible [dɪ'sɜːnəb(ə)l] a perceptible.

discernment [dɪ'sɜːnmənt] n discernement m.

discharge [dɪs'tʃɑːdʒ] vt (patient, employee) renvoyer; (soldier) libérer; (unfit soldier) réformer; (gun, accused person) décharger; (liquid) déverser; (one's duty) accomplir. ‖ vi (of wound) suppurer.

‖ ['dɪstʃɑːdʒ] n (of gun, electrical) décharge f; (of pus, liquid) écoulement m; (dismissal) renvoi m; (freeing) libération f; (of unfit soldier) réforme f.

disciple [dɪ'saɪp(ə)l] n disciple m.

disciplinarian [dɪsɪplɪ'neərɪən] n partisan m de la discipline; **to be a (strict) d.** être très à cheval sur la discipline.

disciplinary [dɪsɪ'plɪnərɪ] a (measure etc) disciplinaire.

discipline ['dɪsɪplɪn] n (behaviour, subject) discipline f ‖ vt (control) discipliner; (punish) punir.

disclaim [dɪs'kleɪm] vt (responsibility) (dé)nier; (knowledge) désavouer.

disclose [dɪs'kləʊz] vt révéler, divulguer. ●**disclosure** [-ʒər] n révélation f.

disco ['dɪskəʊ] n (pl -os) Fam discothèque f.

discolour [dɪs'kʌlər] (Am **discolor**) vt décolorer; (teeth) jaunir ‖ vi se décolorer; (of teeth) jaunir. ●**discolo(u)ration** [-'reɪʃ(ə)n] n décoloration f; (of teeth) jaunissement m.

discomfort [dɪs'kʌmfət] n (physical) douleur f; (mental) malaise m; (hardship) inconvénient m; **I get d. from my wrist** mon poignet me gêne.

disconcert [dɪskən'sɜːt] vt déconcerter.

disconnect [dɪskə'nekt] vt (unfasten etc) détacher; (unplug) débrancher; (wires) déconnecter; (gas, telephone) couper. ●**disconnected** a (speech, words) décousu.

discontent [dɪskən'tent] n mécontentement m. ●**discontented** a mécontent.

discontinue [dɪskən'tɪnjuː] vt cesser, interrompre. ●**discontinued** a (article) qui ne se fait plus.

discord ['dɪskɔːd] n (disagreement) discorde f; (musical notes) dissonance f.

discotheque ['dɪskətek] n (club) discothèque f.

discount 1 ['dɪskaʊnt] n (on article) remise f, réduction f; (on account paid early) escompte m; **at a d.** (to buy, sell) à prix réduit, au rabais; **d. store** solderie f. **2** [dɪs'kaʊnt] vt (story etc) ne pas tenir compte de.

discourage [dɪs'kʌrɪdʒ] vt décourager (s.o. from doing qn de faire); **to get discouraged** se décourager. ●**discouragement** n découragement *m*.

discourse ['dɪskɔːs] *n* discours *m*.

discourteous [dɪs'kɜːtɪəs] *a* discourtois, impoli (**towards** envers). ●**discourtesy** *n* manque *m* de courtoisie, impolitesse *f*.

discover [dɪs'kʌvər] *vt* découvrir (**that** que). ●**discovery** *n* découverte *f*.

discredit [dɪs'kredɪt] *vt* (*cast slur on*) discréditer; (*refuse to believe*) ne pas croire ▮ *n* discrédit *m*. ●**discreditable** *a* indigne.

discreet [dɪ'skriːt] *a* (*unassuming, reserved etc*) discret; (*careful, cautious*) prudent, avisé.

discrepancy [dɪ'skrepənsɪ] *n* divergence *f*, contradiction *f* (**between** entre).

discretion [dɪ'skreʃ(ə)n] *n* (*tact, discernment*) discrétion *f*; (*caution*) prudence *f*; **I'll use my own d.** je ferai comme bon me semblera. ●**discretionary** *a* discrétionnaire.

discriminate [dɪ'skrɪmɪneɪt] *vi* **to d. against** faire de la discrimination contre; **to d. between** distinguer entre. ●**discriminating** *a* (*person*) averti, sagace; (*ear*) fin. ●**discrimination** [-'neɪʃ(ə)n] *n* (*against s.o.*) discrimination *f*; (*judgment*) discernement *m*; (*distinction*) distinction *f*. ●**discriminatory** [-ətərɪ] *a* discriminatoire.

discus ['dɪskəs] *n Sport* disque *m*.

discuss [dɪ'skʌs] *vt* (*talk about*) discuter de (*politique, personne etc*); (*examine in detail*) discuter (*projet, question, prix etc*). ●**discussion** [-ʃ(ə)n] *n* discussion *f*; **under d.** (*matter etc*) en question, en discussion.

disdain [dɪs'deɪn] *n* dédain *m* ▮ *vt* dédaigner (**to do** de faire). ●**disdainful** *a* dédaigneux; **to be d. of** dédaigner.

disease [dɪ'ziːz] *n* maladie *f*. ●**diseased** *a* malade.

disembark [dɪsɪm'bɑːk] *vti* débarquer. ●**disembarkation** [dɪsembɑː'keɪʃ(ə)n] *n* débarquement *m*.

disembodied [dɪsɪm'bɒdɪd] *a* désincarné.

disembowel [dɪsɪm'baʊəl] *vt* (*Br* **-ll-**, *Am* **-l-**) éventrer.

disenchant [dɪsɪn'tʃɑːnt] *vt* désenchanter. ●**disenchantment** *n* désenchantement *m*.

disengage [dɪsɪn'geɪdʒ] *vt* (*object*) dégager (**from** de); (*troops*) désengager; **to d. the clutch** *Br* débrayer.

disentangle [dɪsɪn'tæŋg(ə)l] *vt* (*string etc*) démêler; **to d. oneself from** se dégager de.

disfavour [dɪs'feɪvər] (*Am* **disfavor**) *n* défaveur *f*.

disfigure [dɪs'fɪgər] *vt* défigurer. ●**disfigured** *a* (*face etc*) défiguré. ●**disfigurement** *n* défigurement *m*.

disgorge [dɪs'gɔːdʒ] *vt* (*water, Fig passengers*) dégorger; (*food*) vomir.

disgrace [dɪs'greɪs] *n* (*shame*) honte *f* (**to** à); (*disfavour*) disgrâce *f* ▮ *vt* déshonorer, faire honte à. ●**disgraced** *a* (*politician etc*) disgracié.

disgraceful [dɪs'greɪsfəl] *a* honteux (**of s.o.** de la part de qn). ●**disgracefully** *adv* honteusement.

disgruntled [dɪs'grʌnt(ə)ld] *a* mécontent.

disguise [dɪs'gaɪz] *vt* déguiser (**as en**) ▮ *n* déguisement *m*; **in d.** déguisé.

disgust [dɪs'gʌst] *n* dégoût *m* (**for, at, with** de); **in d.** dégoûté ▮ *vt* dégoûter, écœurer. ●**disgusted** *a* (**at, by, with** de); **to be d. with s.o.** (*annoyed*) être fâché contre qn; **I was d. to hear that...** j'étais indigné d'apprendre que.... ●**disgusting** *a* dégoûtant, écœurant. ●**disgustingly** *adv* d'une façon dégoûtante.

dish [dɪʃ] **1** *n* (*container*) plat *m*; (*food*) mets *m*, plat *m*; **the dishes** la vaisselle; **to do the dishes** faire la vaisselle. **2** *vt* **to d. out** *Fam* distribuer; **to d. out** *or* **up** (*food*) servir.

disharmony [dɪs'hɑːmənɪ] *n* désaccord *m*; (*in music*) dissonance *f*.

dishcloth ['dɪʃklɒθ] *n* (*for washing*) lavette *f*; (*for drying*) torchon *m*.

dishearten [dɪs'hɑːt(ə)n] *vt* décourager.

dishevelled [dɪ'ʃevəld] *a* (*Am* **disheveled**) (*person, hair*) hirsute, ébouriffé.

dishonest [dɪs'ɒnɪst] *a* malhonnête; (*insincere*) de mauvaise foi. ●**dishonesty** *n* malhonnêteté *f*; (*lack of sincerity*) mauvaise foi *f*.

dishonour [dɪs'ɒnər] (*Am* **dishonor**) *n* déshonneur *m* ▮ *vt* déshonorer; (*Br cheque, Am check*) refuser d'honorer. ●**dishonourable** *a* peu honorable. ●**dishonourably** *adv* avec déshonneur.

dishpan ['dɪʃpæn] *n Am* bassine *f* (à vaisselle). ●**dishtowel** *n* torchon *m* (à vaisselle). ●**dishwasher** *n* lave-vaisselle *m inv*.

dishy ['dɪʃɪ] *a* (**-ier, -iest**) (*woman, man*) *Fam* sexy, qui a du chien.

disillusion [dɪsɪ'luːʒ(ə)n] *vt* décevoir; **to be disillusioned (with)** être déçu (de) ▮ *n* désillusion *f*. ●**disillusionment** *n* désillusion *f*.

disincentive [dɪsɪn'sentɪv] *n* mesure *f* dissuasive; **to be a d.** to s.o. décourager qn; **it's a d. to work/invest/etc** cela n'encourage pas à travailler/investir/*etc*.

disinclined [dɪsɪn'klaɪnd] *a* peu disposé (**to do** à faire). ●**disinclination** [-'neɪʃ(ə)n] *n* répugnance *f* (**to do** à faire).

disinfect [dɪsɪn'fekt] *vt* désinfecter. ●**disinfectant** *a & n* désinfectant (*m*). ●**disinfection** [-ʃ(ə)n] *n* désinfection *f*.

disinherit [dɪsɪn'herɪt] *vt* déshériter.

disintegrate [dɪs'ɪntɪgreɪt] *vi* se désintégrer ▮ *vt* désintégrer. ●**disintegration** [-'greɪʃ(ə)n] *n* désintégration *f*.

disinterested [dɪs'ɪntrɪstɪd] *a* (*impartial*) désintéressé; (*uninterested*) *Fam* indifférent (**in** à).

disjointed [dɪs'dʒɔɪntɪd] *a* (*words, style etc*) décousu.

disk [dɪsk] *n* **1** *Am* = **disc. 2** (*of computer*) disque *m*; **hard d.** disque *m* dur; **on d.** sur disque; **d. drive** lecteur *m* de disquettes *or* de disques. ●**diskette** [dɪs'ket] *n* disquette *f*.

dislike [dɪs'laɪk] *vt* ne pas aimer (**doing** faire); **he doesn't d. it** ça ne lui déplaît pas ▮

n aversion *f* (**for, of** pour); **to take a d. to s.o./sth** prendre qn/qch en grippe; **our likes and dislikes** nos goûts et dégoûts *mpl*.

dislocate ['dısləkeıt] *vt* (*limb*) démettre; (*disrupt*) *Fig* désorganiser; **to d. one's shoulder/etc** se démettre l'épaule/*etc*. ● **dislocation** [-'keıʃ(ə)n] *n* dislocation *f*.

dislodge [dıs'lɒdʒ] *vt* faire bouger, déplacer; (*enemy*) déloger.

disloyal [dıs'lɔıəl] *a* déloyal. ● **disloyally** *adv* (*to act etc*) déloyalement. ● **disloyalty** *n* déloyauté *f*.

dismal ['dızməl] *a* morne, triste. ● **dismally** *adv* (*to fail, behave*) lamentablement.

dismantle [dıs'mænt(ə)l] *vt* (*machine etc*) démonter; (*organization*) démanteler.

dismay [dıs'meı] *vt* consterner ∎ *n* consternation *f*.

dismember [dıs'membər] *vt* (*country etc*) démembrer.

dismiss [dıs'mıs] *vt* (*from job*) renvoyer, congédier (**from** de); (*official*) destituer; (*thought, suggestion etc from one's mind*) écarter; **to d. an appeal** (*in court*) rejeter un appel; **to d. a case** (*of judge*) rendre une fin de non-recevoir; **d.!** (*to soldiers*) rompez!; (*to class*) vous pouvez partir. ● **dismissal** *n* renvoi *m*; (*of official*) destitution *f*.

dismount [dıs'maunt] *vi* (*of person*) descendre (**from** de) ∎ *vt* (*of horse*) démonter, désarçonner (*cavalier*).

disobedience [dısə'biːdıəns] *n* désobéissance *f*. ● **disobedient** *a* désobéissant.

disobey [dısə'beı] *vt* désobéir à ∎ *vi* désobéir.

disorder [dıs'ɔːdər] *n* (*confusion*) désordre *m*; (*illness*) troubles *mpl*; (*riots*) désordres *mpl*. ● **disorderly** *a* (*behaviour, person, room*) désordonné; (*meeting, crowd*) houleux.

disorganize [dıs'ɔːgənaız] *vt* désorganiser; **to be disorganized** être désorganisé.

disorientate [dıs'ɔːrıənteıt] (*Am* **disorient** [dıs'ɔːrıent]) *vt* désorienter.

disown [dıs'əun] *vt* désavouer, renier.

disparage [dıs'pærıdʒ] *vt* dénigrer. ● **disparaging** *a* (*remark etc*) peu flatteur, désobligeant.

disparate ['dıspərət] *a* disparate. ● **dis'parity** *n* écart *m*, disparité *f* (**between** entre).

dispassionate [dıs'pæʃənət] *a* (*unemotional*) calme; (*not biased*) impartial.

dispatch [dıs'pætʃ] *vt* (*send*) expédier (*lettre, paquet etc*); (*troops, messenger*) envoyer; (*finish off*) expédier (*travail etc*) ∎ *n* (*sending*) expédition *f* (**of** de); (*report by journalist or army officer*) dépêche *f*; **d. rider** (*on motorcycle*) messager *m*, estafette *f*, courrier *m*.

dispel [dıs'pel] *vt* (**-ll-**) dissiper.

dispensary [dıs'pensərı] *n* (*in hospital*) pharmacie *f*; (*in chemist's shop*) officine *f*.

dispense [dıs'pens] **1** *vt* (*give out*) distribuer; (*justice*) administrer; (*medicine*) préparer; **dispensing chemist** *Br* pharmacien, -ienne *mf* diplômé(e); (*shop*) pharmacie *f*.

2 *vi* **to d. with** (*do without*) se passer de; **that dispenses with the need for...** cela rend superflu.... ● **dispensation** [-'seıʃ(ə)n] *n* distribution *f*; **special d.** (*exemption*) dérogation *f*. ● **dispenser** *n* (*device*) distributeur *m*; **cash d.** distributeur *m* de billets.

disperse [dıs'pɜːs] *vt* disperser ∎ *vi* se disperser. ● **dispersal** *or* **dispersion** [*Br* -ʃ(ə)n, *Am* -ʒ(ə)n] *n* dispersion *f*.

dispirited [dı'spırıtıd] *a* découragé.

displace [dıs'pleıs] *vt* (*refugees, furniture, bone*) déplacer; (*replace*) supplanter; **displaced person** personne *f* déplacée.

display [dı'spleı] *vt* montrer; (*notice, electronic data etc*) afficher; (*painting, goods*) exposer; (*courage etc*) faire preuve de ∎ *n* (*in shop*) étalage *m*; (*of electronic data*) affichage *m*; (*of force*) déploiement *m*; (*of anger etc*) manifestation *f*; (*of paintings*) exposition *f*; (*of luxury*) étalage *m*; **d.** (*unit*) (*of computer*) moniteur *m*; **on d.** exposé; **air d.** fête *f* aéronautique.

displease [dıs'pliːz] *vt* déplaire à. ● **displeased** *a* mécontent (**with** de). ● **displeasing** *a* désagréable.

displeasure [dıs'pleʒər] *n* mécontentement *m*.

disposable [dı'spəuzəb(ə)l] *a* (*plate, Br nappy, Am diaper etc*) à jeter, jetable; (*income*) disponible.

disposal [dı'spəuzəl] *n* (*sale*) vente *f*; (*of waste*) évacuation *f*; **at the d. of** à la disposition de.

dispose[1] [dı'spəuz] *vi* **to d. of** (*get rid of*) se débarrasser de; (*throw away*) jeter (*papier etc*); (*take away*) enlever (*ordures etc*); (*one's time, money*) disposer de; (*sell*) vendre; (*matter, problem*) expédier, liquider; (*kill*) liquider.

dispose[2] [dı'spəuz] *vt* **to d. s.o. to do** (*make willing*) disposer qn à faire; **to be disposed to do** être disposé à faire; **well-disposed towards** bien disposé envers.

disposition [dıspəzıʃ(ə)n] *n* (*placing*) disposition *f*; (*character*) naturel *m*; (*readiness*) inclination *f*.

dispossess [dıspə'zes] *vt* déposséder (**of** de).

disproportion [dısprə'pɔːʃ(ə)n] *n* disproportion *f*. ● **disproportionate** *a* disproportionné.

disprove [dıs'pruːv] *vt* réfuter.

dispute [dı'spjuːt] *n* (*quarrel*) dispute *f*; (*debate*) discussion *f*; (*industrial*) conflit *m*; (*legal*) litige *m*; **beyond d.** incontestable; **in d.** (*matter*) débattu; (*facts, territory etc*) contesté; (*competence etc*) en question ∎ *vt* (*claim, will etc*) contester.

disqualify [dıs'kwolıfaı] *vt* (*make unfit*) rendre inapte (**from** à); *Sport* disqualifier; **to d. s.o. from driving** retirer son permis à qn. ● **disqualification** [-'keıʃ(ə)n] *n* *Sport* disqualification *f*; **his d. from driving** le retrait de son permis de conduire.

disquiet [dıs'kwaıət] *n* inquiétude *f* ∎ *vt* inquiéter. ● **disquieting** *a* inquiétant.

disregard [dɪsrɪ'gɑːd] *vt* ne tenir aucun compte de ∎ *n* indifférence *f* (**for** à); (*for the law*) désobéissance *f* (**for** à).

disrepair [dɪsrɪ'peər] *n* **in (a state of)** d. en mauvais état.

disreputable [dɪs'repjutəb(ə)l] *a* peu recommandable; (*behaviour*) honteux.

disrepute [dɪsrɪ'pjuːt] *n* discrédit *m*; **to bring sth into d.** jeter le discrédit sur qch.

disrespect [dɪsrɪ'spekt] *n* manque *m* de respect. ● **disrespectful** *a* irrespectueux (**to** envers).

disrupt [dɪs'rʌpt] *vt* (*traffic, class etc*) perturber; (*communications*) interrompre; (*plan, s.o.'s books etc*) déranger. ● **disruption** [-ʃ(ə)n] *n* perturbation *f*; (*of communications*) interruption *f*; (*of plan etc*) dérangement *m*.

disruptive [dɪs'rʌptɪv] *a* (*child*) turbulent; (*element*) perturbateur.

dissatisfied [dɪ'sætɪsfaɪd] *a* mécontent (**with** de). ● **dissatisfaction** [-'fækʃ(ə)n] *n* mécontentement *m* (**with** devant).

dissect [daɪ'sekt] *vt* disséquer. ● **dissection** [-ʃ(ə)n] *n* dissection *f*.

disseminate [dɪ'semɪneɪt] *vt* disséminer.

dissension [dɪ'senʃ(ə)n] *n* dissension *f*.

dissent [dɪ'sent] *vi* différer (d'opinion) (**from** sth à l'égard de qch) ∎ *n* dissentiment *m*. ● **dissenting** *a* (*voice*) dissident.

dissertation [dɪsə'teɪʃ(ə)n] *n* (*essay*) mémoire *m*.

disservice [dɪ'sɜːvɪs] *n* **to do s.o. a d.** rendre un mauvais service à qn.

dissident ['dɪsɪdənt] *a & n* dissident, -ente (*mf*). ● **dissidence** *n* dissidence *f*.

dissimilar [dɪ'sɪmɪlər] *a* différent (**to** de), dissemblable (**to** à).

dissipate ['dɪsɪpeɪt] *vt* (*clouds, fog, fears etc*) dissiper; (*energy, fortune*) gaspiller. ● **dissipation** [-'peɪʃ(ə)n] *n* dissipation *f*; (*of energy etc*) gaspillage *m*.

dissociate [dɪ'səʊʃɪeɪt] *vt* dissocier (**from** de).

dissolute ['dɪsəluːt] *a* (*life, person*) dissolu.

dissolve [dɪ'zɒlv] *vt* dissoudre ∎ *vi* se dissoudre. ● **dissolution** [dɪsə'luːʃ(ə)n] *n* dissolution *f*.

dissuade [dɪ'sweɪd] *vt* dissuader (**from doing** de faire); **to d. s.o. from sth** détourner qn de qch. ● **dissuasion** [-ʒ(ə)n] *n* dissuasion *f*.

distance ['dɪstəns] *n* distance *f*; **in the d.** au loin; **from a d.** de loin; **at a d.** à quelque distance; **it's within walking d.** on peut y aller à pied; **to keep one's d.** garder ses distances.

distant ['dɪstənt] *a* éloigné, lointain; (*relative*) éloigné; (*reserved*) distant; **5 km d. from** à (une distance de) 5 km de. ● **distantly** *adv* **we're d. related** nous sommes parents éloignés.

distaste [dɪs'teɪst] *n* aversion *f* (**for** pour). ● **distasteful** *a* désagréable, déplaisant.

distemper [dɪs'tempər] **1** *n* (*paint*) badigeon *m* ∎ *vt* badigeonner. **2** *n* (*in dogs*) la maladie.

distend [dɪs'tend] *vt* distendre; **distended sto-**mach ventre *m* ballonné ∎ *vi* se distendre.

distil [dɪ'stɪl] *vt* (**-ll-**) distiller; **distilled water** (*for car battery, iron*) eau *f* déminéralisée. ● **distillation** [-'leɪʃ(ə)n] *n* distillation *f*. ● **distillery** *n* distillerie *f*.

distinct [dɪ'stɪŋkt] *a* **1** (*clear*) (*voice, light etc*) distinct; (*definite, marked*) (*difference, improvement etc*) net (*f* nette), marqué; (*promise*) formel. **2** (*different*) distinct (**from** de). ● **distinctly** *adv* (*to see etc*) distinctement; (*to forbid, stipulate*) formellement; (*definitely*) sensiblement; (*really*) vraiment; **d. possible** tout à fait possible.

distinction [dɪ'stɪŋkʃ(ə)n] *n* distinction *f*; (*in university examination*) mention *f* très bien; **singer/writer/etc of d.** chanteur, -euse *mf*/écrivain *m*/etc de marque.

distinctive [dɪ'stɪŋktɪv] *a* distinctif.

distinguish [dɪ'stɪŋgwɪʃ] *vti* distinguer (**from** de, **between** entre); **to d. oneself** se distinguer (**as** en tant que); **distinguishing mark** signe *m* particulier. ● **distinguished** *a* distingué.

distinguishable [dɪ'stɪŋgwɪʃəb(ə)l] *a* qu'on peut distinguer; (*discernible*) (*sound, glow etc*) perceptible.

distort [dɪ'stɔːt] *vt* déformer. ● **distorted** *a* (*false*) (*idea etc*) faux (*f* fausse). ● **distortion** [-ʃ(ə)n] *n* (*of features, sound etc*) distorsion *f*; (*of truth*) déformation *f*.

distract [dɪ'strækt] *vt* distraire (**from** de). ● **distracted** *a* (*troubled*) préoccupé; (*mad with worry*) éperdu. ● **distracting** *a* (*noise etc*) gênant.

distraction [dɪ'strækʃ(ə)n] *n* (*lack of attention, amusement*) distraction *f*; **to drive s.o. to d.** rendre qn fou.

distraught [dɪ'strɔːt] *a* éperdu, affolé.

distress [dɪ'stres] *n* (*pain*) douleur *f*; (*anguish, misfortune, danger*) détresse *f*; **in d.** (*ship, soul*) en détresse; **in (great) d.** (*poverty*) dans la détresse ∎ *vt* affliger, peiner. ● **distressing** *a* affligeant, pénible.

distribute [dɪ'strɪbjuːt] *vt* (*goods, prizes, leaflets etc*) distribuer; (*spread evenly*) répartir (*poids etc*). ● **distribution** [-'bjuːʃ(ə)n] *n* distribution *f*; (*even spread*) répartition *f*. ● **distributor** *n* (*in car, of films etc*) distributeur *m*; (*commercial dealer*) concessionnaire *mf*.

district ['dɪstrɪkt] *n* région *f*; (*of town*) quartier *m*; (*administrative*) district *m*, - arrondissement *m*; postal d. division *f* postale; **d. attorney** *Am* = procureur *m* (de la République); **d. nurse** *Br* infirmière *f* visiteuse.

distrust [dɪs'trʌst] *vt* se méfier de ∎ *n* méfiance *f* (**of** de). ● **distrustful** *a* méfiant; **to be d. of** se méfier de.

disturb [dɪ'stɜːb] *vt* (*sleep, water*) troubler; (*papers, belongings*) déranger; **to d. s.o.** (*bother*) déranger qn; (*worry, alarm*) troubler qn. ● **disturbed** *a* (*person*) (*worried, mentally unbalanced*) perturbé, troublé. ● **disturbing** *a* (*worrying*) inquiétant; (*annoy-*

ing, irksome) gênant.

disturbance [dɪ'stɜːbəns] *n* (*noise*) tapage *m*; **disturbances** (*riots*) troubles *mpl*.

disunity [dɪs'juːnɪtɪ] *n* désunion *f*.

disuse [dɪs'juːs] *n* **to fall into d.** tomber en désuétude. ● **disused** [-'juːzd] *a* (*building*) désaffecté.

ditch [dɪtʃ] **1** *n* fossé *m*. **2** *vt* (*dump*) *Fam* se débarrasser de.

dither ['dɪðər] *vi Fam* hésiter, tergiverser; **to d.** (**around**) (*waste time*) tourner en rond.

ditto ['dɪtəʊ] *adv* idem.

divan [dɪ'væn] *n* divan *m*.

dive [daɪv] **1** *vi* (*pt* **dived**, *Am* **dove** [dəʊv]) plonger; (*rush*) se précipiter, se jeter; **to d. for pearls** pêcher des perles ▌ *n* (*of swimmer, goalkeeper*) plongeon *m*; (*of submarine*) plongée *f*; (*of aircraft*) piqué *m*. **2** *n* (*bar, club*) *Pej* boui-boui *m*. ● **diving** *n* (*underwater*) plongée *f* sous-marine; **d. suit** combinaison *f* de plongée, scaphandre *m*; **d. board** plongeoir *m*. ● **diver** *n* plongeur, -euse *mf*; (*in suit*) scaphandrier *m*.

diverge [daɪ'vɜːdʒ] *vi* diverger (**from** de). ● **divergence** *n* divergence *f*. ● **divergent** *a* divergent.

diverse [daɪ'vɜːs] *a* divers. ● **diversify** *vt* diversifier ▌ *vi* (*of firm etc*) se diversifier. ● **diversity** *n* diversité *f*.

diversion [*Br* daɪ'vɜːʃ(ə)n, *Am* -ʒ(ə)n] *n* (*on road*) *Br* déviation *f*; (*distraction*) & *Mil* diversion *f*.

divert [daɪ'vɜːt] *vt* (*attention, suspicions, river etc*) détourner; (*traffic*) *Br* dévier; (*aircraft*) dérouter; (*amuse*) divertir (*qn*); **to d. s.o. from** détourner qn de.

divest [daɪ'vest] *vt* **to d. of** (*power, rights*) priver de.

divide [dɪ'vaɪd] *vt* diviser (**into** en); **to d. sth** (**off**) séparer qch (**from sth** de qch); **to d. sth up** (*share out*) partager qch; **to d. one's time between** partager son temps entre ▌ *vi* (*of group, road etc*) se diviser (**into** en); **dividing line** ligne *f* de démarcation. ● **divided** *a* (*family, group etc*) divisé; **opinions are d.** les avis sont partagés (**on** sur).

dividend ['dɪvɪdend] *n* (*money*) dividende *m*.

divine [dɪ'vaɪn] *a* divin. ● **divinity** *n* (*quality, god*) divinité *f*; (*study*) théologie *f*.

division [dɪ'vɪʒ(ə)n] *n* division *f*; (*dividing object*) séparation *f*. ● **divisible** *a* divisible. ● **divisive** [-'vaɪsɪv] *a* (*policy etc*) qui cause des dissensions.

divorce [dɪ'vɔːs] *n* divorce *m* ▌ *vt* (*husband, wife*) divorcer d'avec; (*idea etc*) *Fig* séparer ▌ *vi* divorcer. ● **divorced** *a* divorcé (**from** d'avec); **to get d.** divorcer. ● **divorcee** [*Br* dɪvɔː'siː, *Am* dɪvɔː'seɪ] *n* divorcé, -ée *mf*.

divulge [dɪ'vʌldʒ] *vt* divulguer.

DIY [diːaɪ'waɪ] *n abbr* (*do-it-yourself*) *Br* bricolage *m*.

dizzy ['dɪzɪ] *a* (**-ier, -iest**) (*heights, speeds*) vertigineux; **to be** *or* **feel d.** avoir le vertige; **to make s.o.** (**feel**) **d.** donner le vertige à qn.

● **dizziness** *n* vertige *m*.

DJ [diː'dʒeɪ] *abbr* = disc jockey.

do [duː] **1** *v aux* (*3rd person sing pres t* **does**; *pt* **did**; *pp* **done**; *pres p* **doing**) **do you know?** savez-vous?, est-ce que vous savez?; **I do not** *or* **don't see** je ne vois pas; **he did say so** (*emphasis*) il l'a bien dit; **do stay** reste donc; **you know him, don't you?** tu le connais, n'est-ce pas?; **better than I do** mieux que je ne le fais; **neither do I** moi non plus; **so do I** moi aussi; **oh, does he?** (*surprise*) ah oui?; **don't!** non!

2 *vt* faire; **to do nothing but sleep** ne faire que dormir; **what does she do?** (*in general*), **what is she doing?** (*now*) qu'est-ce qu'elle fait?, que fait-elle?; **what have you done** (**with...**)**?** qu'as-tu fait (de)...?; **well done** (*congratulations*) bravo!; (*steak etc*) bien cuit; **it's over and done** (**with**) c'est fini; **that'll do me** (*suit*) ça fera mon affaire; **I've been done** (*cheated*) *Br Fam* je me suis fait avoir; **I'll do you!** *Fam* je t'aurai!; **to do s.o. out of sth** escroquer qch à qn; **he's hard done by** on le traite durement; **I'm done (in)** (*tired*) *Sl* je suis claqué *or* vanné; **he's done for** *Fam* il est fichu; **to do in** (*kill*) *Sl* supprimer; **to do out** (*clean*) nettoyer; **to do over** (*redecorate*) refaire; **to do up** (*coat, button*) boutonner; (*Br* zip, *Am* zipper) fermer; (*house*) refaire; (*goods*) emballer; **do yourself up** (**well**)**!** (*wrap up*) couvre-toi (bien)!

3 *vi* (*get along*) aller, marcher; (*suit, be suitable*) faire l'affaire, convenir; (*be enough*) suffire; (*finish*) finir; **that will do** (*be OK*) ça fera l'affaire, ça ira; (*be enough*) ça suffit; **have you done?** vous avez fini?; **business is doing well** les affaires marchent *or* vont bien; **how do you do?** (*introduction*) enchanté; (*greeting*) bonjour; **he did well** *or* **right to leave** il a bien fait de partir; **do as I do** fais comme moi; **to make do** se débrouiller; **to do away with sth/s.o.** supprimer qch/qn; **I could do with a coffee/some luck/etc** (*need, want*) j'aimerais bien (prendre) un café/avoir un peu de chance/*etc*; **to do without sth/s.o.** se passer de qch/qn; **it has to do with...** (*relates to*) cela a à voir avec...; (*concerns*) cela concerne...; **anything doing?** *Fam* est-ce qu'il se passe quelque chose?

4 *n* (*pl* dos *or* do's) (*party*) *Br Fam* soirée *f*, fête *f*; **the do's and don'ts** ce qu'il faut faire ou ne pas faire.

docile ['dəʊsaɪl] *a* docile.

dock [dɒk] **1** *n* (*for ship*) dock *m* ▌ *vi* (*of ship*) (*at quayside*) se mettre à quai; (*in port*) relâcher; (*of spacecraft*) s'arrimer. **2** *n* (*in court*) banc *m* des accusés. **3** *vt* (*wages*) rogner; **to d. sth from** (*wages*) retenir qch sur. **4** *vt* (*animal's tail*) couper. ● **docker** *n* docker *m*. ● **dockyard** *n* chantier *m* naval.

docket ['dɒkɪt] *n* fiche *f*, bordereau *f*.

doctor ['dɒktər] **1** *n* (*medical*) médecin *m*, docteur *m*; (*having doctor's degree*) docteur *m*. **2** *vt* (*text, food*) altérer; (*cat*) *Fam* châtrer. ●**doctorate** n doctorat m (**in ès, en**).

doctrine ['dɒktrɪn] n doctrine f. ●**doctri'naire** a & n Pej doctrinaire (mf).

document ['dɒkjumənt] n document m ▮ ['dɒkjument] vt (inform) documenter; (report in detail) (of film, action etc) rendre compte de (la vie de qn etc); **well documented** (person) bien renseigné; (book) bien documenté. ●**docu'mentary** a documentaire ▮ n (film) documentaire m.

doddering ['dɒdərɪŋ] a (senile) gâteux; (shaky) branlant.

doddle ['dɒd(ə)l] n **it's a d.** Br Fam c'est simple comme bonjour.

dodge [dɒdʒ] vt (question, acquaintance etc) esquiver; (pursuer) échapper à; (tax) éviter de payer ▮ vi (to one side) faire un saut (de côté); **to d. out of sight** s'esquiver; **to d. through** (crowd) se faufiler dans ▮ n (to one side) mouvement m de côté; (trick) Fig truc m, tour m.

dodgems ['dɒdʒəmz] npl autos fpl tamponneuses.

dodgy ['dɒdʒɪ] a (-ier, -iest) Fam (tricky) délicat; (dubious) douteux; (unreliable) peu sûr.

doe [dəʊ] n (deer) biche f.

doer ['duːər] n Fam personne f dynamique.

does [dʌz] see do. ●**doesn't** ['dʌz(ə)nt] = **does not**.

dog¹ [dɒg] n chien m; (female) chienne f; **dirty d.** (person) Pej sale type m; **d. biscuit** biscuit m or croquette f pour chien; **d. food** pâtée f; **d. collar** collier m de chien; (of clergyman) Fam col m de pasteur; **d. days** canicule f. ●**dog-eared** a (page etc) écorné. ●**dog-'tired** a Fam claqué, crevé.

dog² [dɒg] vt (-gg-) (follow) poursuivre.

dogged ['dɒgɪd] a obstiné. ●**doggedly** adv obstinément.

doggy ['dɒgɪ] n Fam toutou m; **d. bag** (in restaurant) petit sac m pour emporter les restes.

doghouse ['dɒghaʊs] n (kennel) Am niche f; **you're in the d.!** Fam je suis fâché contre toi!

dogma ['dɒgmə] n dogme m. ●**dog'matic** a dogmatique. ●**dogmatism** n dogmatisme m.

dogsbody ['dɒgzbɒdɪ] n Pej bonne f à tout faire, factotum m, sous-fifre m.

doily ['dɔɪlɪ] n napperon m.

doing ['duːɪŋ] n **that's your d.** c'est toi qui as fait ça; **doings** (activities) Fam activités fpl.

do-it-yourself [duːɪtjə'self] n Br bricolage m; **do-it-yourself store/book/**etc magasin m/livre m/etc de bricolage.

doldrums ['dɒldrəmz] npl **to be in the d.** (of person) avoir le cafard; (of business) être en plein marasme.

dole [dəʊl] **1** n Br **d.** (money) allocation f de chômage; **to go on the d.** s'inscrire au chômage. **2** vt **to d. out** distribuer au compte-gouttes.

doleful ['dəʊlfəl] a morne, triste.

doll [dɒl] **1** n poupée f; **doll's house** Br, **doll-**

house Am maison f de poupée. **2** vt **to d. oneself up** Fam se bichonner.

dollar ['dɒlər] n dollar m.

dollop ['dɒləp] n (of food) gros morceau m.

dolly ['dɒlɪ] n (doll) Fam poupée f.

dolphin ['dɒlfɪn] n (sea animal) dauphin m.

domain [dəʊ'meɪn] n (land, sphere) domaine m.

dome [dəʊm] n dôme m, coupole f.

domestic [də'mestɪk] a familial, domestique; (animal) domestique; (trade, flight) intérieur; (product) national; **d. science** arts mpl ménagers; **d. servant** domestique mf. ●**domesticated** a habitué à la vie du foyer; (animal) domestique.

domicile ['dɒmɪsaɪl] n domicile m.

dominant ['dɒmɪnənt] a dominant; (person) dominateur. ●**dominance** n prédominance f.

dominate ['dɒmɪneɪt] vti dominer. ●**domination** [-'neɪʃ(ə)n] n domination f.

domineering [dɒmɪ'nɪərɪŋ] a (person, character etc) dominateur.

dominion [də'mɪnjən] n domination f (over sur); (land) territoire m.

domino ['dɒmɪnəʊ] n (pl -oes) domino m; **dominoes** (game) dominos mpl.

don [dɒn] **1** n (in university) Br professeur m. **2** vt (-nn-) (coat etc) Lit revêtir.

donate [dəʊ'neɪt] vt faire don de; (blood) donner ▮ vi donner. ●**donation** [-ʃ(ə)n] n don m.

done [dʌn] pp of **do**.

donkey ['dɒŋkɪ] n âne m; **I haven't seen him for d.'s years** Br Fam je ne l'ai pas vu depuis belle lurette or depuis un siècle; **d. work** travail m ingrat.

donor ['dəʊnər] n (of blood, organ) donneur, -euse mf.

don't [dəʊnt] = **do not**.

doodle ['duːd(ə)l] vi griffonner.

doom [duːm] n ruine f; (fate) destin m; (gloom) Fam tristesse f ▮ vt condamner, destiner (**to** à); **to be doomed (to failure)** être voué à l'échec.

door [dɔːr] n porte f; (of vehicle, train) portière f, porte f; **out of doors** dehors; **d.-to-d. salesman** démarcheur m. ●**doorbell** n sonnette f. ●**door handle** n poignée f de porte. ●**doorknob** n bouton m or poignée f de porte. ●**doorknocker** n marteau m. ●**doorman** n (pl -men) (of hotel etc) portier m, concierge m. ●**doormat** n paillasson m. ●**doorstep** n seuil m. ●**doorstop(per)** n butoir m (de porte). ●**doorway** n **in the d.** dans l'encadrement de la porte.

dope [dəʊp] **1** n (drugs) Fam drogue f; (for horse, athlete) dopant m ▮ vt doper. **2** n (information) Fam tuyaux mpl. **3** n (idiot) Fam imbécile mf.

dopey ['dəʊpɪ] a (-ier, -iest) Fam (stupid) abruti; (sleepy) endormi; (drugged) drogué, camé.

dorm [dɔːm] n abbr Fam = **dormitory**.

dormant ['dɔːmənt] a (volcano, matter) en sommeil; (passion) endormi.

dormer ['dɔːmər] n d. (window) lucarne f.

dormitory [Br 'dɔːmɪtrɪ, Am 'dɔːmɪtɔːrɪ] n dortoir m; (university residence) Am résidence f (universitaire).

dormouse, pl **-mice** ['dɔːmaʊs, -maɪs] n loir m.

dose [dəʊs] n dose f; (of hard work) Fig période f; (of illness) attaque f; a d. of flu une grippe ▮ vt to d. oneself (up) se bourrer de médicaments. ●**dosage** n (amount) dose f.

doss [dɒs] vi to d. down Br Sl se pieuter.

dosshouse ['dɒshaʊs] n Br Sl asile m (de nuit).

dossier ['dɒsɪeɪ] n (papers) dossier m.

dot [dɒt] n point m; polka d. pois m; on the d. Fam à l'heure pile ▮ vt (-tt-) (an i) mettre un point sur; (dress) parsemer de; dotted with parsemé de; dotted line pointillé m. ●**dot matrix printer** n Comptr imprimante f matricielle.

dote [dəʊt] vt to d. on être gaga de. ●**doting** a affectueux; her d. husband/father son mari/père qui lui passe tout.

dotty ['dɒtɪ] a (-ier, -iest) Br Fam cinglé.

double ['dʌb(ə)l] a double; a d. bed un grand lit; a d. room une chambre pour deux personnes; d. 's' deux 's'; d. six deux fois six; d. three four two (phone number) trente-trois quarante-deux. ▮ adv (twice) deux fois, le double; (to fold) en deux; he earns d. what I earn il gagne le double de moi ou deux fois plus que moi; to see d. voir double. ▮ n double m; (person) double m, sosie m; (stand-in in film) doublure f; on or at the d. au pas de course. ▮ vt doubler; (fold) replier qch; to be doubled over in pain être plié (en deux) de douleur. ▮ vi doubler; to d. back (of person) revenir en arrière; to d. up with pain/laughter être plié (en deux) de douleur/rire.

double-barrelled [dʌb(ə)l'bærəld] a (gun) à deux canons; (name) à rallonges. ●**double-'bass** n (instrument) Br contrebasse f. ●**double-'breasted** a (jacket) croisé. ●**double-'check** vti revérifier. ●**double-'cross** vt tromper. ●**double-'dealing** n double jeu m. ●**double-'decker (bus)** n autobus m à impériale. ●**double-'door(s)** n porte f à deux battants. ●**double-'dutch** n Fam baragouin m. ●**double-'glazing** n (window) double vitrage m. ●**double-'jointed** a désarticulé. ●**double-'parking** n stationnement m en double file. ●**double-'quick** adv en vitesse. ●**double-sided 'disk** n (for computer) disque m (à) double face.

doubly ['dʌblɪ] adv doublement.

doubt [daʊt] n doute m; to be in d. about sth avoir des doutes sur qch; I have no d. about it je n'en doute pas; no d. (probably) sans doute; in d. (result, career etc) dans la balance ▮ vt douter de; to d. whether or that or if douter que (+ sub).

doubtful ['daʊtfəl] a (person, future, success etc) incertain; (dubious) (quality etc) douteux; to be d. (about sth) avoir des doutes (sur qch); it's d. whether or that or if ce n'est pas certain que (+ sub). ●**doubtless** adv sans doute.

dough [dəʊ] n pâte f; (money) Fam fric m, blé m.

doughnut ['dəʊnʌt] n beignet m (rond).

dour ['dʊər] a austère.

douse [daʊs] vt arroser, tremper; (light) Fam éteindre.

dove¹ [dʌv] n colombe f. ●**dovecote** [-kɒt] n colombier m.

dove² [dəʊv] Am pt of dive 1.

Dover ['dəʊvər] n Douvres m or f.

dovetail ['dʌvteɪl] **1** n (wood joint) queue f d'aronde. **2** vi (fit) Fig concorder.

dowdy ['daʊdɪ] a (-ier, -iest) peu élégant, sans chic.

down¹ [daʊn] adv en bas; (to the ground) par terre, à terre; (from upstairs) descendu; (of sun) couché; (of curtain, temperature) baissé; (of Br tyre, Am tire) dégonflé; d. (in writing) inscrit; (lie) d.! (to dog) couché!; to come or go d. descendre; to come d. from (place) arriver de; to fall d. tomber (par terre); d. there or here en bas; d. with traitors/etc! à bas les traîtres/etc!; d. with (the) flu grippé; to feel d. (depressed) Fam avoir le cafard; d. to (in series, numbers, dates etc) jusqu'à; d. payment acompte m; d. under aux antipodes, en Australie; d. at heel Br, d. at the heels Am miteux. ▮ prep (at bottom of) en bas de; (from top to bottom of) du haut en bas de; (along) le long de; to go d. (hill, street, stairs) descendre; to live d. the street habiter plus loin dans la rue. ▮ vt (shoot down) abattre; (knock down) terrasser; to d. a drink vider un verre.

down² [daʊn] n (on bird, person etc) duvet m. ●**downy** a (-ier, -iest) (skin) duveté.

down-and-out ['daʊnənaʊt] a sur le pavé ▮ n clochard, -arde mf. ●**downbeat** a (gloomy) Fam pessimiste. ●**downcast** a découragé. ●**downfall** n chute f. ●**downgrade** vt (job etc) déclasser; (person) rétrograder. ●**down'hearted** a découragé. ●**down'hill** adv en pente; to go d. descendre (of sick person, business) aller de plus en plus mal. ●**downmarket** a Br (car, furniture etc) bas de gamme; (neighbourhood, accent) populaire; (person, crowd) ordinaire. ●**downpour** n averse f, pluie f torrentielle. ●**downright** a (rogue etc) véritable; (refusal etc) catégorique; a d. nerve or Br cheek un sacré culot ▮ adv (rude, disagreeable etc) franchement. ●**downscale** a Am = downmarket. ●**downstairs** ['daʊnsteəz] a (room, neighbours) (below) d'en bas; (on the Br ground or Am first floor) du rez-de-chaussée ▮ [daʊn'steəz] adv en bas; au rez-de-chaussée; to come or go d. descendre l'escalier. ●**down'stream** adv en aval. ●**down-to-'earth** a terre-à-terre inv. ●**down'town** adv en ville; d. Chicago/etc le centre de Chicago/*etc.* ●**downtrodden** *a* opprimé. ●**downward** *a* vers le bas; (*path*) qui descend; (*trend*) à la baisse. ●**downward(s)** *adv* vers le bas.

downs [daʊnz] *npl* (*hills*) *Br* collines *fpl*.

Down's [daʊnz] *a* **D. syndrome** mongolisme *m*, trisomie *f*; **a D. baby** un bébé mongolien *or* trisomique.

dowry ['daʊərɪ] *n* dot *f*.

doz *abbr* = **dozen**.

doze [dəʊz] *n* petit somme *m* ▮ *vi* sommeiller; **to d. off** s'assoupir. ●**dozy** *a* (**-ier, -iest**) somnolent; (*silly*) *Br Fam* bête, gourde.

dozen ['dʌz(ə)n] *n* douzaine *f*; **a d. books/ eggs/***etc* une douzaine de livres/d'œufs/*etc*; **dozens of** *Fig* des dizaines de.

Dr *abbr* (*Doctor*) Docteur.

drab [dræb] *a* terne; (*weather*) gris. ●**drabness** *n* caractère *m* terne; (*of weather*) grisaille *f*.

draconian [drə'kəʊnɪən] *a* (*measures etc*) draconien.

draft [drɑːft] **1** *n* (*outline*) ébauche *f*; (*of letter etc*) brouillon *m*; (*commercial document*) traite *f* ▮ *vt* **to d.** (**out**) (*sketch out*) faire le brouillon de; (*write out*) rédiger. **2** *n* (*military*) *Am* conscription *f*; (*men*) contingent *m*; **d. dodger** réfractaire *m* ▮ *vt* (*conscript*) appeler (sous les drapeaux). **3** *n Am* = **draught**.

draftsman ['drɑːftsmən] *n* (*pl* **-men**) *Am* = **draughtsman**.

drafty ['drɑːftɪ] *a* (**-ier, -iest**) *Am* = **draughty**.

drag [dræg] *vt* (**-gg-**) traîner, tirer; (*river*) draguer; **to d. sth from s.o.** (*confession, promise etc*) *Fig* arracher qch à qn; **to d. s.o./sth along** (en)traîner qn/qch; **to d. s.o. away from** arracher qn à; **to d. s.o. into** entraîner qn dans. ▮ *vi* traîner; **to d. on** *or* **out** (*last a long time*) se prolonger. ▮ *n Fam* (*boring task*) corvée *f*; (*boring person*) raseur, -euse *mf*; (*on cigarette*) bouffée *f* (**on** de); **it's a d.!** c'est la barbe!; **in d.** (*clothing*) en travesti; **the main d.** *Am* la rue principale.

dragon ['drægən] *n* dragon *m*.

dragonfly ['drægənflaɪ] *n* libellule *f*.

drain [dreɪn] *n* (*sewer*) égout *m*; (*pipe, channel*) canal *m*; (*outside house*) puisard *m*; (*in street*) bouche *f* d'égout; **it's down the d.** (*wasted efforts, hopes etc*) *Fam* c'est fichu; **to be a d. on** (*resources, patience*) épuiser. ▮ *vt* (*glass, tank*) vider; (*vegetables*) égoutter; (*land*) drainer; (*resources*) épuiser; **to d.** (**off**) (*liquid*) faire écouler; **to d. sth/s.o. of** (*deprive of*) priver qch/qn de. ▮ *vi* **to d.** (**off**) (*of liquid*) s'écouler; **to d. away** (*of strength*) s'épuiser; **draining board** paillasse *f*. ●**drainage** *n* (*sewers*) système *m* d'égouts; (*draining of land*) drainage *m*. ●**drainer** *n* (*board*) paillasse *f*; (*rack, basket*) égouttoir *m*.

drainboard ['dreɪnbɔːd] *n Am* paillasse *f*.

drainpipe ['dreɪnpaɪp] *n* tuyau *m* d'évacuation.

drake [dreɪk] *n* canard *m* (mâle).

dram [dræm] *n* (*drink*) *Fam* goutte *f*.

drama ['drɑːmə] *n* (*event*) drame *m*; (*dramatic art*) théâtre *m*; **d. critic** critique *m* dramatique.

dramatic [drə'mætɪk] *a* dramatique; (*very great, striking*) spectaculaire. ●**dramatically** *adv* (*to change, drop etc*) de façon spectaculaire. ●**dramatics** *n* théâtre *m*.

dramatist ['dræmətɪst] *n* dramaturge *m*.

dramatize ['dræmətaɪz] *vt* (*exaggerate*) dramatiser; (*novel etc*) adapter (pour la scène *or* l'écran).

drank [dræŋk] *pt of* **drink**.

drape [dreɪp] *vt* (*person, shoulders etc*) draper (**with** de); (*wall*) tapisser (de tentures). ●**draper** *n Br* marchand, -ande *mf* de tissus. ●**drapes** *npl* (*hangings*) *Br* tentures *fpl*; (*heavy curtains*) *Am* rideaux *mpl*.

drastic ['dræstɪk] *a* (*change, measure etc*) radical; (*remedy*) puissant; **d. reductions** (*in shop*) soldes *mpl* monstres. ●**drastically** *adv* radicalement; **d. reduced prices** prix *mpl* cassés.

draught [drɑːft] (*Am* **draft**) *n* **1** (*wind*) courant *m* d'air; (*for fire*) tirage *m*; **d. excluder** bourrelet *m* (*de porte, de fenêtre*). **2** **draughts** (*game*) *Br* dames *fpl*. ●**draught 'beer** *n* bière *f* (à la) pression. ●**draughtboard** *n Br* damier *m*. ●**draught horse** *n* cheval *m* de trait.

draughtsman ['drɑːftsmən] (*Am* **draftsman**) *n* (*pl* **-men**) dessinateur, -trice *mf* (industriel(le) or civil).

draughty ['drɑːftɪ] (*Am* **drafty**) *a* (**-ier, -iest**) (*room*) plein de courants d'air.

draw¹ [drɔː] *n Sport* match *m* nul; (*of lottery*) tirage *m* au sort; (*attraction*) attraction *f*. ▮ *vt* (*pt* **drew**, *pp* **drawn**) (*pull*) tirer; (*pass, move*) passer (**over** sur, **into** dans); (*prize*) gagner; (*applause*) provoquer; (*money from bank*) retirer (**from, out of** de); (*salary*) toucher; (*attract*) attirer; (*water from well, Fig comfort*) puiser (**from** dans); **to d. a smile** faire sourire (**from** s.o. qn); **to d. a bath** faire couler un bain; **to d. sth to a close** mettre fin à qch; **to d. a match** *Sport* faire match nul; **to d. in** (*claws*) rentrer; **to d. out** (*money from bank*) retirer; (*prolong*) faire traîner (*réunion, repas etc*) en longueur; **to d. up** (*chair*) approcher; (*contract, list, plan*) dresser, rédiger; **to d. (up)on** (*savings*) puiser dans. ▮ *vi Sport* faire match nul; **to d. near (to)** s'approcher (de); (*of time*) approcher (de); **to d. to a close** tirer à sa fin; **to d. aside** (*step aside*) s'écarter; **to d. away** (*go away*) s'éloigner; **to d. back** (*go backwards*) reculer; **to d. in** (*of days*) diminuer; (*of train*) arriver (en gare); **to d. into the station** (*of train*) entrer en gare; **to d. on** (*of time*) s'avancer; **to d. up** (*of vehicle*) s'arrêter.

draw² [drɔ:] vt (pt **drew**, pp **drawn**) (picture) dessiner; (circle) tracer; (parallel, distinction) Fig faire (**between** entre) ▮ vi (as artist) dessiner.

drawback ['drɔ:bæk] n inconvénient m.

drawbridge ['drɔ:brɪdʒ] n pont-levis m.

drawer [drɔ:r] n (in furniture) tiroir m.

drawing ['drɔ:ɪŋ] n dessin m; **d. board** planche f à dessin; **d. pin** Br punaise f; **d. room** salon m.

drawl [drɔ:l] vi parler d'une voix traînante ▮ n voix f traînante.

drawn [drɔ:n] pp of **drawn**[1,2] ▮ a (face) tiré, crispé; **d. match** or **game** match m nul.

dread [dred] vt (exam etc) appréhender; **to d. doing** appréhender de faire ▮ n crainte f, terreur f.

dreadful ['dredfəl] a épouvantable; (child) insupportable; (ill) malade; **I feel d. about it** j'ai vraiment honte. ● **dreadfully** adv terriblement; **to be** or **feel d. sorry** regretter infiniment.

dream [dri:m] vi (pt & pp **dreamed** or **dreamt** [dremt]) rêver; (of or about s.o./sth de qn/qch, of or about doing de faire); **I wouldn't d. of it!** (il n'en est pas question!) ▮ vt rêver (that que); **I never dreamt that...** (imagined) je n'ai jamais imaginé or songé que...; **to d. sth up** imaginer qch. ▮ n rêve m; (wonderful thing or person) Fam merveille f; **to have a d.** faire un rêve (about de); **to have dreams of** rêver de; **a d. house/ etc** une maison/etc de rêve; **a d. world** un monde imaginaire. ● **dreamer** n rêveur, -euse mf. ● **dreamy** a (-ier, -iest) rêveur.

dreary ['drɪərɪ] a (-ier, -iest) (gloomy) morne; (monotonous) monotone; (boring) ennuyeux.

dredge [dredʒ] vt (river etc) draguer ▮ n drague f. ● **dredger** n (ship) dragueur m.

dregs [dregz] npl **the d.** (in liquid, Fig of society) la lie.

drench [drentʃ] vt tremper; **to get drenched** se faire tremper (jusqu'aux os).

dress [dres] 1 n (woman's garment) robe f; (style of dressing) tenue f; **d. circle** (in theatre) Br (premier) balcon m; **d. designer** styliste mf, dessinateur, -trice mf de mode; (well-known) couturier m; **d. rehearsal** (in theatre) (répétition f) générale f; **d. shirt** chemise f de soirée.
2 vt (person) habiller; (wound) panser; (salad) assaisonner; (chicken) préparer; **to get dressed** s'habiller; **dressed for tennis/etc** en tenue de tennis/etc.
▮ vi s'habiller; **to d. up** (smartly) bien s'habiller; (in disguise) se déguiser (**as** en).

dresser ['dresər] n 1 (furniture) Br vaisselier m; (dressing table) Am coiffeuse f. 2 **she's a good d.** elle s'habille toujours bien.

dressing ['dresɪŋ] n (for wound) pansement m; (seasoning) assaisonnement m; **to give s.o. a d.-down** passer un savon à qn; **d. gown** Br robe f de chambre; (of boxer) peignoir m; **d. room** (in theatre) loge f; (in store) cabine f d'essayage; **d. table** coiffeuse f.

dressmaker ['dresmeɪkər] n couturière f. ● **dressmaking** n couture f.

dressy ['dresɪ] a (-ier, -iest) (smart) chic inv; (too) **d.** trop habillé.

drew [dru:] pt of **draw**[1,2].

dribble ['drɪb(ə)l] 1 vi (of baby) baver; (of liquid) tomber goutte à goutte ▮ vt laisser tomber goutte à goutte. 2 vi (of footballer) dribbler ▮ vt (ball) dribbler.

dribs [drɪbz] npl **in d. and drabs** par petites quantités; (to arrive) par petits groupes.

dried [draɪd] a (fruit) sec (f sèche); (milk, eggs) en poudre; (flowers) séché.

drier ['draɪər] n = **dryer**.

drift [drɪft] vi (through air, on water) être emporté par le vent or le courant; (of ship) dériver; (of person, nation etc) Fig aller à la dérive; (of snow) s'amonceler; **to d. about** (aimlessly) (walk around) se promener sans but, traînailler; **to d. apart** (of husband and wife) devenir des étrangers l'un pour l'autre; **to d. into crime/etc** sombrer dans le crime/ etc; **to d. towards disaster/etc** s'acheminer vers la catastrophe/etc.
▮ n (movement) mouvement m; (direction) sens m; (of events) cours m; (of snow) congère f; (meaning) sens m général. ● **drifter** n (aimless person) paumé, -ée mf. ● **driftwood** n bois m flotté.

drill [drɪl] 1 n (tool) perceuse f; (bit) mèche f; (pneumatic) marteau m piqueur; (dentist's) roulette f, fraise f; (for rock) foreuse f ▮ vt (wood etc) percer; (tooth) fraiser; (oil well) forer ▮ vi **to d. for oil** faire de la recherche pétrolière.
2 n (training exercise in army, school etc) exercice(s) m(pl); (correct procedure) marche f à suivre ▮ vi faire l'exercice ▮ vt faire faire l'exercice à (qn).

drily ['draɪlɪ] adv (to remark etc) sèchement, d'un ton sec.

drink [drɪŋk] n boisson f; (glass of sth alcoholic) verre m; **to give s.o. a d.** donner (quelque chose) à boire à qn; **to have a d.** boire quelque chose; (alcoholic) prendre or boire un verre ▮ vt (pt **drank**, pp **drunk**) boire; **to d. oneself to death** se tuer à force de boire; **to d. sth down** or **up** boire qch.
▮ vi boire (**out of** dans); **to d. up** finir son verre; **to d. to s.o.** boire à la santé de qn; **drinking bout** beuverie f; **drinking chocolate** chocolat m en poudre; **drinking fountain** fontaine f publique, borne-fontaine f; **drinking song** chanson f à boire; **drinking trough** abreuvoir m; **drinking water** eau f potable.

drinkable ['drɪŋkəb(ə)l] a (fit for drinking) potable; (not unpleasant) buvable.

drip [drɪp] vi (-pp-) (of water, rain etc) dégouliner, goutter; (of washing, vegetables) s'égoutter; (of Br tap, Am faucet) goutter ▮ vt (paint etc) laisser couler ▮ n (drop) goutte f; (sound) bruit m de goutte; (for hospital patient) goutte-à-goutte m inv; (fool) Fam nouille f. ● **drip-dry** a (shirt etc) sans repassage.

dripping ['drɪpɪŋ] **1** n (Am **drippings**) (fat)
graisse f (de rôti). **2** a & adv d. (wet) dégou-
linant.

drive [draɪv] n (in car) promenade f en
voiture; (energy) énergie f; (campaign)
campagne f; (road to private house) allée f;
(for disks or diskettes) Comptr lecteur m,
drive m; **an hour's d.** une heure de voiture;
left-hand d. (vehicle) (véhicule m à) conduite
f à gauche; **front-wheel d.** (vehicle) traction f
avant; **the sex d.** la pulsion sexuelle.
▌ vt (pt **drove**, pp **driven**) (vehicle, train,
passenger) conduire (**to** à); (machine)
actionner; (chase away) chasser; **to d. s.o. to
do** pousser qn à faire; **to d. s.o. to despair**
réduire qn au désespoir; **to d. s.o. mad or
crazy** rendre qn fou; **to d. the rain/smoke
against** (of wind) rabattre la pluie/fumée
contre; **to d. s.o. hard** surmener qn; **he
drives a Ford** il a une Ford.
▌ vi (drive a car) conduire; (go by car) rouler; **to d. on the left** rouler à gauche; **to d. to
Paris/etc** aller (en voiture) à Paris/etc; **what
are you driving at?** Fig où veux-tu en venir?
drive along (in car) rouler ▌ **to drive
away** vt (chase away) chasser ▌ vi (in car)
partir (en voiture) ▌ **to drive back** vt
(passenger) ramener (en voiture); (enemy
etc) repousser ▌ vi (in car) revenir (en
voiture) ▌ **to drive in** vt (nail, knife etc) enfoncer ▌ **to drive off** vi (in car) partir (en
voiture) ▌ **to drive on** vi (in car) continuer ▌
to drive out vt (chase away) chasser (qn,
qch) ▌ **to drive over** vt (crush) écraser (qch)
▌ **to drive up** vi (in car) arriver (en voiture).
drive-in ['draɪvɪn] a Am accessible en
voiture; **d.-in** (movie theater) drive-in m; **d.-
in** (restaurant) restaurant m où l'on est servi
dans sa voiture.

drivel ['drɪv(ə)l] vi (Br **-ll-**, Am **-l-**) (talk
nonsense) radoter ▌ n idioties fpl.

driver ['draɪvər] n (of car) conducteur, -trice
mf; (of taxi, Br lorry, Am truck) chauffeur
m, conducteur, -trice mf; (train or engine) d.
mécanicien m; **she's a good d.** elle conduit
bien; **d.'s license** Am permis m de conduire.

driveway ['draɪvweɪ] n (road to house) allée
f.

driving ['draɪvɪŋ] **1** n (in car etc) conduite f;
d. lesson leçon f de conduite; **d. licence** Br,
d. test permis m de conduire; **d. school**
auto-école f. **2** a (forceful) **d. force** force f
agissante; **d. rain** pluie f battante.

drizzle ['drɪz(ə)l] n bruine f, crachin m ▌ vi
bruiner. ● **drizzly** a it's d., the weather is d.
il bruine.

droll [drəʊl] a drôle, comique.

dromedary [Br 'drɒmədərɪ, Am 'drɒmɪderɪ]
n dromadaire m.

drone [drəʊn] **1** n (hum) bourdonnement m;
(purr) ronronnement m; (of person) Fig débit m monotone ▌ vi (of engine) ronronner;
(of bee) bourdonner; **to d. (on)** (of person)
Fig parler d'une voix monotone. **2** n (bee)

abeille f mâle.

drool [druːl] vi (slaver) baver; (talk nonsense)
Fig radoter; **to d. over** Fig s'extasier devant.

droop [druːp] vi (of flower) se faner; (of
head) pencher; (of eyelids, shoulders)
tomber.

drop [drɒp] **1** n (of liquid) goutte f; **eye/nose
drops** gouttes fpl pour les yeux/le nez.
2 n (fall) baisse f, chute f (**in** de); (distance
of fall) hauteur f (de chute); (slope)
descente f; (jump from aircraft) saut m; (of
supplies from aircraft) parachutage m.
▌ vt (**-pp-**) laisser tomber; (price, voice)
baisser; (bomb) larguer; (passenger, goods
from vehicle) déposer; (from boat) débarquer; (put) mettre; (leave out) faire sauter, omettre; (remark) laisser échapper; (get
rid of) supprimer; (habit) abandonner; (team
member) écarter; **to d. s.o. off** (from vehicle)
déposer qn; **to d. a line/postcard** écrire un
petit mot/une carte postale à; **to d. a hint**
faire une allusion; **to d. a hint that** laisser
entendre que; **to d. one's h's** ne pas prononcer les h; **to d. a word in s.o.'s ear** glisser un
mot à l'oreille de qn.
▌ vi (fall) tomber; (of person) (se laisser)
tomber; (of price) baisser; **he's ready to d.**
Fam il tombe de fatigue; **let it d.!** Fam laisse
tomber!; **to d. away** (diminish) diminuer; **to
d. back or behind** rester en arrière, se laisser
distancer; **to d. by or in** (visit s.o.) passer
(chez qn); **to d. off** (fall asleep) s'endormir;
(fall off) tomber; (of interest, sales etc) diminuer; **to d. out** (fall out) tomber; (withdraw)
se retirer; (socially) se mettre en marge de
la société; (of student) laisser tomber ses
études; **to d. over or round** (visit s.o.) passer
(chez qn).

drop-out ['drɒpaʊt] n marginal, -ale mf;
(student) étudiant, -ante mf qui abandonne
ses études.

dropper ['drɒpər] n (for eye drops etc)
compte-gouttes m inv.

droppings ['drɒpɪŋz] npl (of animal) crottes
fpl; (of bird) fiente f.

dross [drɒs] n déchets mpl.

drought [draʊt] n sécheresse f.

drove [drəʊv] pt of **drive**.

droves [drəʊvz] npl (of people) foules fpl; **in
d.** en foule.

drown [draʊn] vi se noyer ▌ vt noyer; **to d.
oneself, be drowned** se noyer. ● **drowning** a
(man, woman etc) qui se noie ▌ n (death)
noyade f.

drowse [draʊz] vi somnoler.

drowsy ['draʊzɪ] a (-ier, -iest) somnolent; **to
be or feel d.** avoir sommeil; **to make s.o.
(feel) d.** assoupir qn. ● **drowsily** adv d'un air
somnolent. ● **drowsiness** n somnolence f.

drubbing ['drʌbɪŋ] n (beating) raclée f; **to
take a d.** (be defeated) se faire écraser.

drudge [drʌdʒ] n bête f de somme, esclave
mf du travail ▌ vi trimer. ● **drudgery** n
corvée(s) f(pl), travail m ingrat.

drug [drʌg] n (against illness) médicament m,

drogue f; (narcotic) stupéfiant m, drogue f; (activity, hobby etc) Fig drogue f; **drugs** (narcotics in general) la drogue; **to be on drugs, take drugs** se droguer; **d. addict** drogué, -ée mf; **d. addiction** toxicomanie f; **d. taking** usage m de la drogue **‖** vt (-gg-) droguer (qn); (drink) mêler un somnifère à.

druggist ['drʌgɪst] n Am pharmacien, -ienne mf, droguiste mf.

drugstore ['drʌgstɔ:r] n Am drugstore m.

drum [drʌm] n Mus tambour m; (for oil) bidon m; **the big or bass d.** Mus la grosse caisse; **the drums** (of orchestra etc) la batterie.

‖ vi (-mm-) battre du tambour; (with fingers) tambouriner.

‖ vt I tried to d. it into him j'ai essayé de le lui faire rentrer dans le crâne; **to d. up** (support, interest) susciter; **to d. up business or custom** attirer les clients. **●drummer** n (joueur, -euse mf de) tambour m; (in pop or jazz group) batteur m. **●drumstick** n (for drum) baguette f de tambour; (of chicken) pilon m.

drunk [drʌŋk] pp of **drink ‖** a ivre; **to get d.** s'enivrer; **d. with power/success** Fig enivré or grisé par le pouvoir/le succès **‖** n ivrogne mf, pochard, -arde mf. **●drunkard** n ivrogne mf. **●drunken** a (person) (regularly) ivrogne; (driver) ivre; (quarrel, brawl) d'ivrogne; **d. driving** conduite f en état d'ivresse. **●drunkenness** n (state) ivresse f; (habit) ivrognerie f.

dry [draɪ] a (drier, driest) sec (f sèche); (well, river) à sec; (day) sans pluie; (toast) sans beurre; (wit) caustique; (subject, book) aride; **on d. land** sur la terre ferme; **to keep sth d.** tenir qch au sec; **to wipe sth d.** essuyer qch; **to run d.** se tarir; **to feel or be d.** (thirsty) avoir soif; **d. dock** cale f sèche; **d. goods store** Am magasin m de nouveautés.

‖ vt sécher; (clothes in tumble dryer etc) faire sécher; (by wiping) essuyer; **to d. the dishes** essuyer la vaisselle; **to d. sth off or up** sécher qch.

‖ vi sécher; **to d. off** sécher; **to d. up** sécher; (dry the dishes) essuyer la vaisselle; (run dry) (of stream etc) se tarir; **d. up!** Fam tais-toi! **●dryer** n (for hair, clothes) séchoir m; (helmet-style for hair) casque m. **●dryness** n sécheresse f; (of wit) causticité f; (of book etc) aridité f.

dry-clean [draɪ'kli:n] vt nettoyer à sec. **●dry-cleaner** n teinturier, -ière mf; **the d.-cleaner's** (shop) le pressing, la teinturerie.

DSS [di:es'es] n abbr Br **Department of Social Security** (see social).

dual ['dju:əl] a double; **d. carriageway** Br route f à deux voies (séparées). **●du'ality** n dualité f.

dub [dʌb] vt (-bb-) **1** (film) doubler. **2** (nickname) surnommer. **●dubbing** n (of film) doublage m.

dubious ['dju:bɪəs] a (offer, person etc) dou-

teux; **I'm d. about going** or **about whether to go** je me demande si je dois y aller; **to be d. about sth** douter de qch.

duchess ['dʌtʃɪs] n duchesse f. **●duchy** n duché m.

duck [dʌk] **1** n canard m. **2** vi se baisser (vivement) **‖** vt (head) baisser; **to d. s.o.** plonger qn dans l'eau. **●ducking** n bain m forcé. **●duckling** n caneton m.

duct [dʌkt] n (tube in body, pipe) conduit m.

dud [dʌd] a Fam (coin) faux (f fausse); (Br cheque, Am check) en bois; (watch etc) qui ne marche pas; (bomb) non éclaté **‖** n (person) zéro m, type m nul.

dude [du:d] n Am Fam dandy m; **d. ranch** ranch(-hôtel) m.

due[1] [dju:] a (money, sum) dû (to à); (rent, bill) à payer; (respect) qu'on doit (to à); (fitting, proper) qui convient; **to fall d.** échoir; **she's d. for** (salary increase etc) elle doit or devrait recevoir; **he's d. (to arrive)** (is awaited) il doit arriver, il est attendu; **I'm d. there** je dois être là-bas; **in d. course** (at proper time) en temps utile; (finally) à la longue; **d. to** (caused by) dû à; (because of) à cause de; (thanks to) grâce à.

‖ n dû m; **dues** (of club) cotisation f; (official charges) droits mpl; **to give s.o. his d.** admettre que qn a raison.

due[2] [dju:] adv **d. north/south/etc** plein nord/sud/etc, droit vers le nord/sud/etc.

duel ['dju:əl] n duel m **‖** vi (-ll-, Am -l-) se battre en duel.

duet [dju:'et] n duo m.

duffel, duffle ['dʌf(ə)l] a **d. bag** sac m de marin; **d. coat** duffel-coat m.

dug [dʌg] pt & pp of **dig. ●dugout** n **1** (canoe) pirogue f. **2** (soldier's shelter) abri m souterrain.

duke [dju:k] n duc m.

dull [dʌl] a (-er, -est) (boring) ennuyeux; (colour, character) terne; (weather) maussade; (sound, ache) sourd; (mind) lourd, borné; (edge, blade) émoussé; (hearing, sight) faible.

‖ vt (sound, pain) amortir; (senses) émousser; (mind) engourdir; (colour) ternir. **●dullness** n (of life, town) monotonie f; (of colour) manque m d'éclat; (of mind) lourdeur f d'esprit.

duly ['dju:lɪ] adv (properly) comme il convient (convenait etc); (in fact) en effet; (in due time) en temps utile.

dumb [dʌm] a (-er, -est) muet (f muette); (stupid) idiot, bête; **d. animals** les bêtes fpl. **●dumbness** n mutisme m; (stupidity) bêtise f.

dumbbell ['dʌmbel] n (weight) haltère m.

dumbfound [dʌm'faund] vt sidérer, ahurir.

dumbwaiter [dʌm'weɪtər] n (lift for food) monte-plats m inv.

dummy ['dʌmɪ] **1** n (of baby) Br sucette f; (for displaying clothes) mannequin m; (of ventriloquist) pantin m; (of book) maquette f; (fool) Fam idiot, -ote mf. **2** a factice, faux (f fausse); **d. run** (in car etc) essai m.

dump [dʌmp] vt (Br rubbish, Am garbage) déposer; (bricks etc) décharger; (data) Comptr transférer; **to d. (down)** déposer; **to d. s.o.** (ditch) Fam plaquer qn.
▮ n (for ammunition) dépôt m; (dirty or dull town) Fam trou m; (house) Fam baraque f; (Br rubbish or Am garbage) **d.** tas m d'ordures; (place) dépôt m d'ordures, décharge f; (untidy room) dépotoir m; **to be (down) in the dumps** Fam avoir le cafard; **d. truck = dumper.** ●**dumper** n **d. (truck)** Br camion m à benne basculante.

dumpling ['dʌmplɪŋ] n (food) boulette f (de pâte).

Dumpster® ['dʌmpstər] n Am benne f à ordures.

dumpy ['dʌmpɪ] a (-ier, -iest) (person) boulot (f -otte), gros (f grosse) et court.

dunce [dʌns] n cancre m, âne m.

dune [djuːn] n (sand) **d.** dune f.

dung [dʌŋ] n (of horse) crotte f; (of cattle) bouse f; (manure) fumier m.

dungarees [dʌŋgə'riːz] npl (of child, workman) salopette f; (jeans) Am jean m.

dungeon ['dʌndʒən] n cachot m.

dunk [dʌŋk] vt (bread, Br biscuit, Am cookie) tremper.

dupe [djuːp] vt duper ▮ n dupe f.

duplex ['duːpleks] n (apartment) Am duplex m.

duplicate ['djuːplɪkeɪt] vt (key, map etc) faire un double de; (on machine) polycopier ▮ ['djuːplɪkət] n double m; **in d.** en deux exemplaires; **a d. copy**/etc une copie/etc en double; **a d. key** un double de la clef. ●**duplication** [-'keɪʃ(ə)n] n (on machine) polycopie f; (of effort) répétition f. ●**duplicator** n duplicateur m.

duplicity [djuː'plɪsɪtɪ] n duplicité f.

durable ['djuərəb(ə)l] a (material, shoes etc) résistant; (friendship, love) durable. ●**dura'bility** n résistance f; (of friendship etc) durabilité f.

duration [djuə'reɪʃ(ə)n] n durée f.

duress [djuˈres] n **under d.** sous la contrainte.

during ['djuərɪŋ] prep pendant, durant.

dusk [dʌsk] n (twilight) crépuscule m.

dusky ['dʌskɪ] a (-ier, -iest) (complexion) foncé.

dust [dʌst] **1** n poussière f; **d. cloth** Am chiffon m; **d. cover** or **sheet** (for furniture) housse f; **d. cover** or **jacket** (for book) jaquette f.
▮ vt (furniture etc) essuyer (la poussière de).

▮ vi faire la poussière. **2** vt (sprinkle) saupoudrer (**with** de). ●**dustbin** n Br poubelle f. ●**dustcart** n Br camion-benne m. ●**dustman** n (pl -men) Br éboueur m, boueux m. ●**dustpan** n petite pelle f (à poussière).

duster ['dʌstər] n Br chiffon m.

dusty ['dʌstɪ] a (-ier, -iest) (room, road etc) poussiéreux.

Dutch [dʌtʃ] a hollandais, néerlandais; **D. cheese** hollande m; **to go D.** partager les frais (**with** avec) ▮ n (language) hollandais m; **the D.** (people) les Hollandais mpl. ●**Dutchman** n (pl -men) Hollandais m. ●**Dutchwoman** n (pl -women) Hollandaise f.

dutiful ['djuːtɪf(ə)l] a (son, child etc) respectueux, obéissant; (worker) consciencieux.

duty ['djuːtɪ] n devoir m; (tax) droit m; **duties** (responsibilities) fonctions fpl; **on d.** (policeman, soldier, teacher etc) de service; (doctor, pharmacist etc) de garde; (in office) de permanence; **off d.** libre. ●**duty-'free** a (goods, shop) hors-taxe inv.

duvet ['duːveɪ] n Br couette f.

dwarf [dwɔːf] n nain m, naine f ▮ vt (of building, trees etc) écraser, rapetisser; (of person) faire paraître tout petit.

dwell [dwel] vi (pt & pp dwelt) demeurer; **to d. (up)on** (think about) penser sans cesse à; (speak about) parler sans cesse de, s'étendre sur; (insist on) appuyer sur.

dwelling ['dwelɪŋ] n habitation f. ●**dweller** n habitant, -ante mf.

dwindle ['dwɪnd(ə)l] vi diminuer (peu à peu). ●**dwindling** a (interest, resources etc) décroissant; (supplies) qui s'épuisent.

dye [daɪ] n teinture f ▮ vt teindre; **to d. green**/etc teindre en vert/etc. ●**dyeing** n teinture f; (industry) teinturerie f. ●**dyer** n teinturier, -ière mf.

dying ['daɪɪŋ] see **die**[1] a (person, animal) mourant; (custom) qui se perd; (wish, words) dernier; **to my d. day** jusqu'à ma mort ▮ n (death) mort f.

dyke [daɪk] n (wall) digue f; (ditch) Br fossé m.

dynamic [daɪ'næmɪk] a dynamique. ●'**dynamism** n dynamisme m.

dynamite ['daɪnəmaɪt] n dynamite f ▮ vt dynamiter.

dynamo ['daɪnəməʊ] n (pl -os) dynamo f.

dynasty [Br 'dɪnəstɪ, Am 'daɪnəstɪ] n dynastie f.

dysentery ['dɪsəntrɪ] n (illness) dysenterie f.

dyslexia [dɪs'leksɪə] n dyslexie f. ●**dyslexic** [dɪs'leksɪk] a & n dyslexique (mf).

E

E, e [iː] *n* E, e *m*.

each [iːtʃ] *a* chaque; **e. one** chacun, -une ‖ *pron* chacun, -une; **e. other** l'un(e) l'autre, *pl* les un(e)s les autres; **to see/greet/etc other** se voir/se saluer/*etc* (l'un(e) l'autre); **separated from e. other** séparés l'un de l'autre; **e. of us** chacun, -une d'entre nous.

eager ['iːgər] *a* impatient (**to do** de faire); (*enthusiastic*) plein d'enthousiasme; **to be e. for sth** désirer qch vivement; **e. for money** avide d'argent; **to be e. to do** (*want*) tenir (beaucoup) à faire; **e. to help** empressé (à aider). ● **eagerly** *adv* (*to work etc*) avec enthousiasme; (*to await*) avec impatience. ● **eagerness** *n* impatience *f* (**to do** de faire); (*zeal*) enthousiasme *m* (**for sth** pour qch).

eagle ['iːg(ə)l] *n* aigle *m*. ● **eagle-'eyed** *a* au regard d'aigle.

ear¹ [ɪər] *n* oreille *f*; **to be all ears** *Fam* être tout ouïe; **up to one's ears in work** débordé de travail; **to play it by e.** *Fam* agir selon la situation; **to give s.o. a thick e.** *Fam* donner une gifle à qn. ● **earache** *n* mal *m* à l'oreille. ● **eardrum** *n* tympan *m*.

ear² [ɪər] *n* (*of corn*) épi *m*.

earl [ɜːl] *n* comte *m*.

early ['ɜːlɪ] *a* (**-ier, -iest**) (*first*) premier; (*fruit, season*) précoce; (*death*) prématuré; (*age*) jeune; (*painting, work*) de jeunesse; (*reply*) rapide; (*return, retirement*) anticipé; (*ancient*) ancien; **it's e.** (*on clock*) il est tôt; (*referring to meeting, appointment etc*) c'est tôt; **it's too e. to get up/etc** il est trop tôt pour se lever/*etc*; **to be e.** (*ahead of time*) être en avance, arriver de bonne heure *or* tôt; (*in getting up*) être matinal; **to have an e. meal/night** manger/se coucher de bonne heure; **in e. times** jadis; **in e. summer** au début de l'été; **to be in one's e. fifties** avoir à peine plus que la cinquantaine; **one's e. life** sa jeunesse.
‖ *adv* tôt, de bonne heure; (*ahead of time*) en avance; (*to book a ticket etc*) à l'avance; (*to die*) prématurément; **as e. as possible** le plus tôt possible; **earlier (on)** plus tôt; **at the earliest** au plus tôt; **as e. as yesterday** déjà hier. ● **early-'warning system** *n* dispositif *m* de première alerte.

earmark ['ɪəmɑːk] *vt* (*funds*) assigner (**for** à).

earmuffs ['ɪəmʌfs] *npl* protège-oreilles *m inv*.

earn [ɜːn] *vt* gagner; (*interest*) rapporter. ● **earnings** *npl* (*wages*) rémunérations *fpl*; (*profits*) bénéfices *mpl*.

earnest ['ɜːnɪst] *a* (*serious*) sérieux; (*sincere*) sincère ‖ *n* **in e.** sérieusement; **it's raining in e.** il pleut pour de bon; **he's in e.** il est sérieux. ● **earnestness** *n* sérieux *m*; (*sincerity*) sincérité *f*.

earphones ['ɪəfəʊnz] *npl* casque *m*. ● **earpiece** *n* écouteur *m*. ● **earplug** *n* (*to keep out noise etc*) boule *f* Quiès®. ● **earring** *n* boucle *f* d'oreille. ● **earshot** *n* **within e.** à portée de voix. ● **ear-splitting** *a* (*noise*) assourdissant.

earth [ɜːθ] *n* (*world, ground*) terre *f*; (*electrical wire*) *Br* terre *f*, masse *f*; **to fall to e.** tomber à *or* par terre; **nothing/nobody on e.** rien/personne au monde; **where/what on e.?** où/que diable?

earthenware ['ɜːθənweər] *n* faïence *f*; **e. plate/etc** assiette *f/etc* en faïence.

earthly ['ɜːθlɪ] *a* (*possessions etc*) terrestre; **not an e. chance** *Fam* pas la moindre chance; **for no e. reason** *Fam* sans la moindre raison.

earthquake ['ɜːθkweɪk] *n* tremblement *m* de terre. ● **earthworks** *npl* (*excavations*) terrassements *mpl*. ● **earthworm** *n* ver *m* de terre.

earthy ['ɜːθɪ] *a* (**-ier, -iest**) (*taste, smell etc*) de terre, terreux; (*person*) *Fig* terre-à-terre *inv*.

earwig ['ɪəwɪg] *n* (*insect*) perce-oreille *m*.

ease [iːz] **1** *n* (*facility*) facilité *f*; (*physical*) bien-être *m*; (*mental*) tranquillité *f*; **with e.** facilement; (*ill*) **at e.** (*in situation*) (mal) à l'aise; **my mind is at e.** j'ai l'esprit tranquille; (*stand*) **at e.!** (*to soldier*) repos!
2 *vt* (*pain*) soulager; (*mind*) calmer; (*tension*) diminuer; (*loosen*) relâcher; **to e. sth off/along** enlever/déplacer qch doucement; **to e. oneself through** se glisser par.
‖ *vi* **to e.** (**off** *or* **up**) (*become less*) (*of pressure*) diminuer; (*of demand*) baisser; (*of pain*) se calmer; (*not work so hard*) se relâcher; **the situation is easing** la situation se détend.

easel ['iːz(ə)l] *n* chevalet *m*.

easily ['iːzɪlɪ] *adv* facilement; **e. the best/etc** de loin le meilleur/*etc*; **that could e. be the case** ça pourrait bien être le cas. ● **easiness** *n* aisance *f*.

east [iːst] *n* est *m*; (**to the**) **e. of** à l'est de; **the E.** (*Eastern Europe*) l'Est *m*; (*the Orient*) l'Orient *m*; **Middle/Far E.** Moyen-/Extrême-Orient *m*.
‖ *a* (*coast*) est *inv*; (*wind*) d'est; **E. Africa** Afrique *f* orientale.
‖ *adv* à l'est, vers l'est. ● **eastbound** *a* (*traffic*) en direction de l'est; (*carriageway*) *Br* est *inv*. ● **easterly** *a* (*point*) est *inv*; (*direction*) de l'est; (*wind*) d'est. ● **eastern** *a* (*coast*) est *inv*; **E. France** l'Est *m* de la

France; **E. Europe** Europe *f* de l'Est. ● **easterner** *n* habitant, -ante *mf* de l'Est. ● **eastward(s)** *a* & *adv* vers l'est.

Easter ['iːstər] *n* Pâques *m sing or fpl*; **Happy E.!** joyeuses Pâques!; **E. egg** œuf *m* de Pâques; **E. week** semaine *f* pascale.

easy ['iːzɪ] *a* (**-ier, -iest**) (*not difficult*) facile; (*pace*) modéré; (*manners*) naturel; (*style*) aisé; **an e. life** une vie tranquille; **it's e. to do** c'est facile à faire; **it's e. for them to do it** il leur est facile de faire ça; **to feel e. in one's mind** être tranquille; **to be e. first** (*in race etc*) être bon premier; **I'm e.** *Br Fam* ça m'est égal; **e. chair** fauteuil *m* (rembourré).
▌ *adv* doucement; **go e. on** (*sugar, salt etc*) vas-y doucement ou mollo avec; (*person*) ne sois pas trop dur avec *ou* envers; **take it e.** (*rest*) repose-toi; (*work less*) ne te fatigue pas; (*calm down*) calme-toi; (*go slow*) ne te presse pas. ● **easy'going** *a* (*carefree*) insouciant; (*easy to get along with*) facile à vivre.

eat [iːt] *vt* (*pt* **ate** [*Br* et, *Am* eɪt], *pp* **eaten** ['iːt(ə)n]) manger; (*meal*) prendre; **to e. breakfast** déjeuner, prendre le petit déjeuner; **to e. one's words** *Fig* ravaler ses paroles; **what's eating you?** *Sl* qu'est-ce qui te tracasse?; **to e. sth up** (*finish*) finir qch; **eaten up with jealousy** dévoré de jalousie.
▌ *vi* manger; **to e. into sth** (*of acid*) ronger qch; **to e. into one's savings** entamer ses économies; **to e. out** manger dehors; **eating place** restaurant *m*. ● **eatable** *a* mangeable. ● **eater** *n* **big e.** gros mangeur *m*, grosse mangeuse *f*.

eau de Cologne [əʊdəkə'ləʊn] *n* eau *f* de Cologne.

eaves [iːvz] *npl* avant-toit *m*. ● **eavesdrop** *vti* (**-pp-**) **to e. (on)** écouter (de façon indiscrète). ● **eavesdropper** *n* oreille *f* indiscrète.

ebb [eb] *n* reflux *m*; **e. and flow** le flux et le reflux; **e. tide** marée *f* descendante; **to be at a low e.** (*patient, spirits*) *Fig* être très bas ▌ *vi* refluer; **to e. (away)** (*of strength etc*) *Fig* décliner.

ebony ['ebənɪ] *n* (*wood*) ébène *f*.

ebullient [ɪ'bʌlɪənt] *a* exubérant.

EC [iː'siː] *n abbr* (*European Community*) CEE *f*.

eccentric [ɪk'sentrɪk] *a* & *n* excentrique (*mf*). ● **eccen'tricity** *n* excentricité *f*.

ecclesiastic [ɪkliːzɪ'æstɪk] *a* & *n* ecclésiastique (*m*). ● **ecclesiastical** *a* ecclésiastique.

echelon ['eʃəlɒn] *n* (*of organization, government etc*) échelon *m*.

echo ['ekəʊ] *n* (*pl* **-oes**) écho *m* ▌ *vt* (*sound*) répercuter; (*repeat*) *Fig* répéter ▌ *vi* **the explosion/etc echoed** l'écho de l'explosion/*etc* se répercuta; **the room/etc echoes** la pièce/*etc* est très sonore; **to e. with the sound of** (*of building etc*) résonner de l'écho de.

éclair [eɪ'kleər] *n* (*cake*) éclair *m*.

eclectic [ɪ'klektɪk] *a* éclectique.

eclipse [ɪ'klɪps] *n* (*of sun, moon*) éclipse *f*; (*loss of fame, overshadowing*) *Fig* éclipse *f* ▌

vt éclipser.

ecology [ɪ'kɒlədʒɪ] *n* écologie *f*. ● **eco'logical** *a* écologique.

economic [iːkə'nɒmɪk] *a* économique; (*profitable*) rentable. ● **economical** *a* économique; (*thrifty*) économe. ● **economically** *adv* économiquement. ● **economics** *n* science *f* économique, économie *f*; (*profitability*) (*of a business etc*) aspect *m* financier.

economist [ɪ'kɒnəmɪst] *n* économiste *mf*.

economize [ɪ'kɒnəmaɪz] *vti* économiser (**on** sur).

economy [ɪ'kɒnəmɪ] *n* (*saving, system, thrift*) économie *f*; **e. class** (*on aircraft*) classe *f* touriste.

ecstasy ['ekstəsɪ] *n* extase *f*. ● **ec'static** *a* extasié; **to be e. about** s'extasier sur. ● **ec'statically** *adv* avec extase.

ECU [eɪ'kjuː] *n abbr* (*European Currency Unit*) ECU *m inv*.

Ecuador ['ekwədɔːr] *n* Équateur *m*.

ecumenical [iːkjuː'menɪk(ə)l] *a* œcuménique.

eczema ['eksɪmə] *n Med* eczéma *m*.

eddy ['edɪ] *n* tourbillon *m*, remous *m*.

edge [edʒ] *n* bord *m*; (*of forest*) lisière *f*; (*of town*) abords *mpl*; (*of page*) marge *f*; (*of knife, blade etc*) tranchant *m*, fil *m*; **to be on e.** (*of person*) être énervé; (*of nerves*) être tendus; **to set s.o.'s teeth on e.** (*irritate s.o.*) crisper qn, faire grincer les dents à qn; **to have the e.** *or* **a slight e.** *Fig* être légèrement supérieur (**over, on** à).
▌ *vt* (*clothing etc*) border (**with** de).
▌ *vti* **to e. (oneself) into** (*move*) se glisser dans; **to e. (oneself) forward** avancer doucement. ● **edging** *n* (*border*) bordure *f*.

edgeways ['edʒweɪz] *adv Br*, **edgewise** ['edʒwaɪz] *adv Am* de côté; **I can't get a word in e.** *Fam* je n'arrive pas à placer un mot.

edgy ['edʒɪ] *a* (**-ier, -iest**) énervé. ● **edginess** *n* nervosité *f*.

edible ['edɪb(ə)l] *a* (*mushroom, berry etc*) comestible; (*not unpleasant*) (*meal, food*) mangeable.

edict ['iːdɪkt] *n* décret *m*; *Fr Hist* édit *m*.

edifice ['edɪfɪs] *n* (*building, organization*) édifice *m*.

edify ['edɪfaɪ] *vt* (*improve the mind of*) édifier.

Edinburgh ['edɪnb(ə)rə] *n* Édimbourg *m or f*.

edit ['edɪt] *vt* (*newspaper etc*) diriger; (*article etc*) mettre au point; (*film*) monter; (*annotate*) éditer (*texte*); (*compile*) rédiger (*dictionnaire etc*); **to e. (out)** (*cut out*) couper.

edition [ɪ'dɪʃ(ə)n] *n* édition *f*.

editor ['edɪtər] *n* (*in charge of newspaper*) rédacteur, -trice *mf* en chef; (*in charge of magazine*) directeur, -trice *mf*; (*compiler of dictionary etc*) rédacteur, -trice *mf*; (*annotator of text*) éditeur, -trice *mf*; (*proofreader*) correcteur, -trice *mf*; (*of TV or radio broadcast*) réalisateur, -trice *mf*; **sports e.** (*in* *newspaper*) rédacteur *m* sportif, rédactrice *f* sportive; **the e. in chief** (*of newspaper*) le rédacteur *or* la rédactrice en chef. ●**edi'torial** *a* de la rédaction; **e. staff** rédaction *f* ▮ *n* éditorial *m*.

educate ['edjʊkeɪt] *vt* (*bring up*) éduquer (*enfant, famille*); (*in school*) instruire (*élève*); (*train*) former, éduquer (*l'esprit*); **to be educated at** faire ses études à. ●**educated** *a* (*voice*) cultivé; (**well-**)**e.** (*person*) instruit.

education [edjʊ'keɪʃ(ə)n] *n* éducation *f*; (*teaching*) instruction *f*, enseignement *m*; (*training*) formation *f*; (*university subject*) pédagogie *f*; **the e. system** le système éducatif. ●**educational** *a* (*establishment*) d'enseignement; (*method, theory, content*) pédagogique; (*game, film*) éducatif; (*supplies*) scolaire; (*experience*) instructif; **e. qualifications** diplômes *mpl*. ●**educationally** *adv* du point de vue de l'éducation.

educator ['edjʊkeɪtər] *n* éducateur, -trice *mf*.

EEC [iːiː'siː] *n abbr* (*European Economic Community*) CEE *f*.

eel [iːl] *n* anguille *f*.

eerie ['ɪərɪ] *a* (*-ier, -iest*) sinistre, étrange.

efface [ɪ'feɪs] *vt* effacer.

effect [ɪ'fekt] **1** *n* (*result, impression*) effet *m* (**on** sur); **effects** (*goods*) biens *mpl*; **to no e.** en vain; **in e.** en fait; **to put into e.** mettre en application, faire entrer en vigueur; **to come into e., take e.** (*of law, rule etc*) entrer en vigueur; **to take e.** (*of drug, medicine etc*) agir; **to have an e.** (*of medicine etc*) faire de l'effet; **to have no e.** rester sans effet; **to this e.** (*with this meaning or result in mind*) dans ce sens; **to write a letter to the e. that** (*saying that*) écrire une lettre comme quoi.
2 *vt* (*carry out*) effectuer, réaliser.

effective [ɪ'fektɪv] *a* (*efficient*) efficace; (*striking*) frappant; (*actual*) effectif; **to become e.** (*of law*) prendre effet. ●**effectively** *adv* efficacement; (*in fact*) effectivement. ●**effectiveness** *n* efficacité *f*; (*quality*) effet *m* frappant.

effeminate [ɪ'femɪnɪt] *a* efféminé.

effervescent [efə'ves(ə)nt] *a* (*drink*) gazeux; (*mixture, liquid, youth*) effervescent. ●**effervesce** [efə'ves] *vi* (*of drink*) pétiller. ●**effervescence** *n* (*excitement, bubbling*) effervescence *f*; (*of drink*) pétillement *m*.

effete [ɪ'fiːt] *a* (*feeble*) mou (*f* molle), faible; (*decadent*) décadent.

efficient [ɪ'fɪʃ(ə)nt] *a* (*method, treatment etc*) efficace; (*person*) compétent, efficace; (*organization*) efficace, performant; (*machine*) performant, à haut rendement. ●**efficiency** *n* efficacité *f*; (*of person*) compétence *f*; (*of machine*) performances *fpl*. ●**efficiently** *adv* efficacement; (*competently*) avec compétence; **to work e.** (*of machine*) bien fonctionner.

effigy ['efɪdʒɪ] *n* effigie *f*.

effort ['efət] *n* effort *m*; **to make an e.** faire un effort (**to** pour); **it isn't worth the e.** ça

ne *or* n'en vaut pas la peine; **his** *or* **her latest e.** (*attempt*) *Fam* sa dernière tentative. ●**effortless** *a* (*victory, progress etc*) facile; **with e. ease** sans effort. ●**effortlessly** *adv* facilement, sans effort.

effrontery [ɪ'frʌntərɪ] *n* effronterie *f*.

effusive [ɪ'fjuːsɪv] *a* (*person*) expansif; (*thanks, excuses*) sans fin. ●**effusively** *adv* avec effusion.

e.g. [iː'dʒiː] *abbr* (*exempli gratia*) par exemple.

egalitarian [ɪgælɪ'teərɪən] *a* (*society etc*) égalitaire.

egg[1] [eg] *n* œuf *m*; **e. timer** sablier *m*; **e. whisk** fouet *m* (à œufs). ●**eggcup** *n* coquetier *m*. ●**egghead** *n Pej* intellectuel, -elle *mf*. ●**eggplant** *n Am* aubergine *f*. ●**eggshell** *n* coquille *f* (d'œuf).

egg[2] [eg] *vt* **to e. s.o. on** (*encourage*) inciter qn (**to do** à faire).

ego ['iːgəʊ] *n* (*pl* **-os**) **the e.** l'ego *m*; (*in psychoanalysis*) le moi, l'ego *m*; **one's e.** (*self-image*) son image *f* de soi; (*self-esteem*) son amour-propre *m*; **to have an enormous e.** avoir très haute opinion de soi. ●**ego'centric** *a* égocentrique.

egoism ['egəʊɪz(ə)m] *n* égoïsme *m*. ●**egoist** *n* égoïste *mf*. ●**ego'istic(al)** *a* égoïste.

egotism ['egəʊtɪz(ə)m] *n* égotisme *m*. ●**egotist** *n* égotiste *mf*.

Egypt ['iːdʒɪpt] *n* Égypte *f*. ●**Egyptian** [ɪ'dʒɪpʃən] *a* égyptien ▮ *n* Égyptien, -ienne *mf*.

eh? [eɪ] *int Fam* hein?

eiderdown ['aɪdədaʊn] *n* édredon *m*.

eight [eɪt] *a & n* huit (*m*). ●**eighth** *a & n* huitième (*mf*); **an e.** un huitième.

eighteen [eɪ'tiːn] *a & n* dix-huit (*m*). ●**eighteenth** *a & n* dix-huitième (*mf*).

eighty ['eɪtɪ] *a & n* quatre-vingts (*m*); **e.-one** quatre-vingt-un. ●**eightieth** *a & n* quatre-vingtième (*mf*).

Eire ['eərə] *n* Eire *f*, République *f* d'Irlande.

either ['aɪðər] **1** *a & pron* (*one or other*) l'un(e) ou l'autre; (*with negative*) ni l'un(e) ni l'autre; (*each*) chaque; **on e. side** de chaque côté, des deux côtés; **I don't know e. man** *or* **e. of the men** je ne connais ni l'un ni l'autre de ces hommes.
2 *adv* **she can't swim e.** elle ne sait pas nager non plus; **I don't e.** (ni) moi non plus; **and it's not so far off e.** (*moreover*) et ce n'est pas si loin d'ailleurs.
3 *conj* **e.... or** ou ou (bien)... ou (bien), soit... soit; (*with negative*) ni... ni; **it isn't e. green or red** ce n'est ni vert ni rouge.

eject [ɪ'dʒekt] *vt* (*from hall etc*) expulser (*qn*) (**from** de); (*from aircraft, machine*) éjecter ▮ *vi* (*of pilot*) s'éjecter. ●**ejector** *a* **e. seat** (*in aircraft*) siège *m* éjectable.

eke [iːk] *vt* **to e. out** faire durer; **to e. out a living** gagner (difficilement) sa vie.

elaborate[1] [ɪ'læbərət] *a* compliqué, détaillé; (*preparation*) minutieux; (*style*) recherché; (*meal*) raffiné. ●**elaborately** *adv* (**to** plan) minutieusement; (*to decorate*) avec recherche.

elaborate² [ɪˈlæbəreɪt] *vt* (*theory etc*) élaborer ▮ *vi* entrer dans les détails (**on** de). ●**elaboration** [-ˈreɪʃ(ə)n] *n* élaboration *f*.

elapse [ɪˈlæps] *vi* (*of period of time*) s'écouler.

elastic [ɪˈlæstɪk] *a* (*object, Fig character*) élastique; **e. band** *Br* élastique *m* ▮ *n* (*fabric*) élastique *m*. ●**ela'sticity** *n* élasticité *f*.

elated [ɪˈleɪtɪd] *a* transporté de joie. ●**elation** [-ʃ(ə)n] *n* exaltation *f*.

elbow [ˈelbəʊ] *n* coude *m*; **e. grease** *Fam* huile *f* de coude; **to have enough e. room** avoir assez de place ▮ *vt* **to e. one's way** se frayer un chemin (à coups de coude) (**through** à travers).

elder¹ [ˈeldər] *a* & *n* (*of two people*) aîné, -ée (*mf*). ●**eldest** *a* & *n* aîné, -ée (*mf*); **his** or **her e. brother** l'aîné de ses frères.

elder² [ˈeldər] *n* (*tree*) sureau *m*.

elderly [ˈeldəlɪ] *a* assez âgé, entre deux âges ▮ *n* **the e.** les personnes *fpl* âgées.

elect [ɪˈlekt] *vt* (*by voting*) élire (*qn*) (**to** à); **to e. to do** choisir de faire ▮ *a* **the president/** *etc* **e.** le président/*etc* désigné.

election [ɪˈlekʃ(ə)n] *n* élection *f*; **general e.** élections *fpl* législatives ▮ *a* (*campaign*) électoral; (*day, results*) du scrutin, des élections. ●**electio'neering** *n* campagne *f* électorale.

elective [ɪˈlektɪv] *a* (*course*) *Am* facultatif.

electoral [ɪˈlektər(ə)l] *a* électoral. ●**electorate** *n* électorat *m*.

electric [ɪˈlektrɪk] *a* électrique; **e. blanket** couverture *f* chauffante; **e. fire** *Br* radiateur *m* électrique; **e. shock** décharge *f* électrique; **e. shock treatment** électrochoc *m*. ●**electrical** *a* électrique; **e. engineer** ingénieur *m* électricien.

electrician [ɪlekˈtrɪʃən] *n* électricien *m*.

electricity [ɪlekˈtrɪsɪtɪ] *n* électricité *f*; **to switch off the e.** couper le courant *or* l'électricité.

electrify [ɪˈlektrɪfaɪ] *vt* (*Br railway or Am railroad line*) électrifier; (*excite*) *Fig* électriser.

electrocute [ɪˈlektrəkjuːt] *vt* électrocuter.

electrode [ɪˈlektrəʊd] *n* électrode *f*.

electron [ɪˈlektrɒn] *n* électron *m*; **e. microscope** microscope *m* électronique.

electronic [ɪlekˈtrɒnɪk] *a* électronique; **e. mail** *Comptr* messagerie *f or* courrier *m* électronique. ●**electronics** *n* électronique *f*.

elegant [ˈelɪgənt] *a* élégant. ●**elegance** *n* élégance *f*. ●**elegantly** *adv* avec élégance, élégamment.

elegy [ˈelədʒɪ] *n* élégie *f*.

element [ˈelɪmənt] *n* (*component, chemical, person etc*) élément *m*; (*of heater, kettle etc*) résistance *f*; **an e. of truth** un grain *or* une part de vérité; **the human/chance e.** le facteur humain/chance; **the elements** (*bad weather*) les éléments *mpl*; **in one's e.** dans son élément. ●**ele'mental** *a Lit* élémentaire.

elementary [elɪˈment(ə)rɪ] *a* élémentaire; (*school*) *Am* primaire; **e. courtesy** la courtoisie la plus élémentaire.

elephant [ˈelɪfənt] *n* éléphant *m*. ●**elephantine** [elɪˈfæntaɪn] *a* (*large*) éléphantesque; (*clumsy*) gauche.

elevate [ˈelɪveɪt] *vt* élever (**to** à). ●**elevation** [-ˈveɪʃ(ə)n] *n* élévation *f* (**of** de); (*height*) altitude *f*; (*promotion in job or rank*) avancement *m*.

elevator [ˈelɪveɪtər] *n Am* ascenseur *m*.

eleven [ɪˈlev(ə)n] *a* & *n* onze (*m*). ●**elevenses** [ɪˈlev(ə)nzɪz] *n Br Fam* pause-café *f* (*vers onze heures du matin*). ●**eleventh** *a* & *n* onzième (*m*).

elf [elf] *n* (*pl* **elves**) lutin *m*.

elicit [ɪˈlɪsɪt] *vt* tirer, obtenir (**from** de).

elide [ɪˈlaɪd] *vt* (*vowel*) élider. ●**elision** [ɪˈlɪʒ(ə)n] *n* élision *f*.

eligible [ˈelɪdʒəb(ə)l] *a* (*for post etc*) admissible (**for** à); (*for political office*) éligible (**for** à); **to be e. for sth** (*entitled to*) avoir droit à qch; **an e. young man** (*suitable as husband*) un beau parti. ●**eligi'bility** *n* admissibilité *f*; *Pol* éligibilité *f*.

eliminate [ɪˈlɪmɪneɪt] *vt* supprimer (**from** de); (*applicant, possibility, suspect*) éliminer. ●**elimination** [-ˈneɪʃ(ə)n] *n* suppression *f*; (*of applicant etc*) élimination *f*.

elite [eɪˈliːt] *n* élite *f* (**of** de).

elk [elk] *n* (*animal*) élan *m*.

ellipse [ɪˈlɪps] *n* (*shape*) ellipse *f*. ●**elliptical** *a* elliptique.

elm [elm] *n* (*tree, wood*) orme *m*.

elocution [eləˈkjuːʃ(ə)n] *n* élocution *f*.

elongate [ˈiːlɒŋgeɪt] *vt* allonger. ●**elongated** *a* allongé.

elope [ɪˈləʊp] *vi* (*of lovers*) s'enfuir (**with** avec). ●**elopement** *n* fugue *f* (amoureuse).

eloquent [ˈeləkwənt] *a* éloquent. ●**eloquence** *n* éloquence *f*. ●**eloquently** *adv* avec éloquence.

El Salvador [elˈsælvədɔːr] *n* Le Salvador.

else [els] *adv* d'autre; **somebody/anybody e.** quelqu'un/n'importe qui d'autre; **everybody e.** tous les autres, tout le monde à part moi, vous *etc*; **nobody/nothing e.** personne/rien d'autre; **something e.** autre chose; **anything e.?** (*in shop etc*) autre chose?; **anything e. to add?** encore quelque chose à ajouter?; **somewhere e.**, *Am* **someplace e.** ailleurs, autre part; **anywhere/nowhere e.** n'importe où/ nulle part ailleurs; **anywhere e.?** ailleurs?; **who e.?** qui d'autre?, qui encore?; **how e.?** de quelle autre façon?; **or e.** ou bien, sinon. ●**elsewhere** *adv* ailleurs; **e. in the town** dans une autre partie de la ville.

elucidate [ɪˈluːsɪdeɪt] *vt* élucider.

elude [ɪˈluːd] *vt* (*of word, name*) échapper à (*qn*); (*question*) éluder; (*obligation*) se dérober à; (*blow*) esquiver. ●**elusive** *a* (*enemy, aims, quality*) insaisissable; (*reply*) évasif.

emaciated [ɪˈmeɪsɪeɪtɪd] *a* émacié.

emanate [ˈe

 məneɪt] *vi* émaner (**from** de).

emancipate [ɪˈmænsɪpeɪt] *vt* (*women etc*)

émanciper. ●**emancipation** [-'peɪʃ(ə)n] *n* émancipation *f*.

embalm [ɪm'bɑːm] *vt* (*dead body*) embaumer.

embankment [ɪm'bæŋkmənt] *n* (*of path etc*) talus *m*; (*of river*) berge *f*.

embargo [ɪm'bɑːgəʊ] *n* (*pl* -**oes**) embargo *m*; **to impose an e. on** mettre l'embargo sur.

embark [ɪm'bɑːk] *vi* (s')embarquer; **to e. on** (*start*) commencer (*voyage, travail etc*); (*launch into*) se lancer dans, s'embarquer dans (*aventure, carrière etc*) **▮** *vt* (*passengers, goods*) embarquer. ●**embarkation** [embaː'keɪʃ(ə)n] *n* embarquement *m*.

embarrass [ɪm'bærəs] *vt* embarrasser, gêner. ●**embarrassing** *a* (*question, situation etc*) embarrassant. ●**embarrassment** *n* embarras *m*, gêne *f*; (*financial*) embarras *mpl*.

embassy ['embəsɪ] *n* ambassade *f*.

embattled [ɪm'bæt(ə)ld] *a* (*political party, person etc*) assiégé de toutes parts.

embedded [ɪm'bedɪd] *a* (*stick, bullet etc*) enfoncé (**in** dans); (*jewel*) enchâssé; (*in s.o.'s memory*) gravé; (*in stone*) scellé.

embellish [ɪm'belɪʃ] *vt* embellir. ●**embellishment** *n* embellissement *m*.

embers ['embəz] *npl* braise(s) *f*(*pl*), charbons *mpl* ardents.

embezzle [ɪm'bez(ə)l] *vt* (*money*) détourner. ●**embezzlement** *n* détournement *m* de fonds. ●**embezzler** *n* escroc *m*, voleur *m*.

embitter [ɪm'bɪtər] *vt* (*person*) aigrir; (*relations, situation*) envenimer. ●**embittered** *a* (*person*) aigri.

emblem ['embləm] *n* emblème *m*.

embody [ɪm'bɒdɪ] *vt* (*express*) exprimer; (*represent*) incarner; (*include*) réunir. ●**embodiment** *n* incarnation *f* (**of** de).

emboss [ɪm'bɒs] *vt* (*paper*) gaufrer; (*metal*) emboutir, bosseler. ●**embossed** *a* (*pattern, characters etc*) en relief; **e. paper** papier *m* gaufré.

embrace [ɪm'breɪs] *vt* prendre dans ses bras, étreindre, embrasser; (*include, adopt*) embrasser **▮** *vi* s'étreindre, s'embrasser **▮** *n* étreinte *f*.

embroider [ɪm'brɔɪdər] *vt* (*cloth*) broder; (*story, facts*) Fig enjoliver. ●**embroidery** *n* broderie *f*.

embroil [ɪm'brɔɪl] *vt* **to e. s.o. in** mêler qn à.

embryo ['embrɪəʊ] *n* (*pl* -**os**) embryon *m*. ●**embry'onic** *a* (*plan, state etc*) embryonnaire.

emcee [em'siː] *n* *Am* présentateur, -trice *mf*.

emend [ɪ'mend] *vt* (*text*) corriger.

emerald ['emərəld] *n* émeraude *f*.

emerge [ɪ'mɜːdʒ] *vi* apparaître (**from** de); (*from hole etc*) sortir; (*of truth, from water*) émerger; (*of nation*) naître; **it emerges that** il apparaît que. ●**emergence** *n* apparition *f*.

emergency [ɪ'mɜːdʒənsɪ] *n* (*situation, case*) urgence *f*; (*contingency*) éventualité *f*; **in an e.** en cas d'urgence; **this is an e.** (*speaking on telephone*) j'appelle pour une urgence **▮** *a*

(*measure, operation etc*) d'urgence; **e. exit**/**brake** sortie *f*/frein *m* de secours; **e. ward** *Br*, **e. room** *Am* salle *f* des urgences; **e. landing** atterrissage *m* forcé; **e. powers** (*of government etc*) pouvoirs *mpl* extraordinaires; **e. services** services *mpl* d'urgence.

emery ['emərɪ] *a* **e. board** lime *f* à ongles en carton; **e. cloth** toile *f* (d')émeri.

emigrant ['emɪgrənt] *n* émigrant, -ante *mf*. ●**emigrate** *vi* émigrer. ●**emigration** [-'greɪʃ(ə)n] *n* émigration *f*.

eminent ['emɪnənt] *a* éminent. ●**eminence** *n* distinction *f*; **your E.** (*to cardinal*) votre Éminence. ●**eminently** *adv* hautement, remarquablement.

emir [e'mɪər] *n* émir *m*. ●**emirate** ['emɪrət] *n* émirat *m*.

emissary ['emɪsərɪ] *n* émissaire *m*.

emission [ɪ'mɪʃ(ə)n] *n* (*of pollutant*) émission *f*.

emit [ɪ'mɪt] *vt* (-**tt**-) (*light, heat etc*) émettre; (*smell*) dégager.

emotion [ɪ'məʊʃ(ə)n] *n* (*strength of feeling*) émotion *f*; (*joy, love etc*) sentiment *m*.

emotional [ɪ'məʊʃ(ə)n(ə)l] *a* (*person, reaction*) émotif; (*story, speech, plea*) émouvant; (*moment*) d'intense émotion; **an e. state** *Psy* un état émotionnel. ●**emotionally** *adv* (*to say*) avec émotion; **to be e. unstable** avoir des troubles émotifs.

emotive [ɪ'məʊtɪv] *a* (*word*) affectif; (*person*) émotif; **an e. issue** une question sensible.

empathy ['empəθɪ] *n* (*sympathy*) compassion *f*.

emperor ['empərər] *n* empereur *m*.

emphasis ['emfəsɪs] *n* (*in word or phrase*) accent *m*; (*insistence*) insistance *f*; **to lay or put e. on** mettre l'accent sur.

emphasize ['emfəsaɪz] *vt* (*importance of sth etc*) souligner; (*word, fact*) appuyer sur, insister sur, souligner; (*vowel, syllable*) appuyer sur, insister sur; **to e. that** souligner que.

emphatic [ɪm'fætɪk] *a* (*denial, refusal etc*) (*clear*) catégorique; (*forceful*) énergique; **to be e. about sth** insister sur qch; **she was e.** elle a été catégorique. ●**emphatically** *adv* (*to refuse etc*) catégoriquement; (*forcefully*) énergiquement; **e. no!** absolument pas!

empire ['empaɪər] *n* empire *m*.

empirical [em'pɪrɪk(ə)l] *a* empirique. ●**empiricism** *n* empirisme *m*.

employ [ɪm'plɔɪ] *vt* (*person, means*) employer **▮** *n* **in the e. of** employé par. ●**employee** [ɪm'plɔɪiː, emplɔɪ'iː] *n* employé, -ée *mf*. ●**employer** *n* patron, -onne *mf*. ●**employment** *n* emploi *m*; **place of e.** lieu *m* de travail; **to be in the e. of** être employé par; **e. agency** bureau *m* de placement.

empower [ɪm'paʊər] *vt* autoriser (qn) (**to do** à faire).

empress ['empris] *n* impératrice *f*.

empty ['emptɪ] *a* (-**ier**, -**iest**) vide; (*stomach*) creux, vide; (*threat, promise etc*) vain; **on an**

e. stomach à jeun; **to return/etc e.-handed**
revenir/etc les mains vides.

▌ *n* **empties** (*bottles*) bouteilles *fpl* vides.

▌ *vt* **to e. (out)** (*box, pocket, liquid etc*) vider;
(*vehicle*) décharger; (*objects in box etc*)
sortir (**from, out of** de).

▌ *vi* (*of building, tank etc*) se vider; **to e. into**
(*of river*) se jeter dans. ● **emptiness** *n* (*in
s.o.'s life etc*) vide *m*; **I was surprised by the
e. of the theatre** j'ai été surpris de trouver le
théâtre vide.

emulate ['emjʊleɪt] *vt* imiter. ● **emulation**
[-'leɪʃ(ə)n] *n* émulation *f*.

emulsion [ɪ'mʌlʃ(ə)n] *n* (*paint*) peinture *f*
acrylique (mate); *Phot* émulsion *f*.

enable [ɪ'neɪb(ə)l] *vt* **to e. s.o. to do**
permettre à qn de faire.

enact [ɪn'ækt] *vt* (*law*) promulguer; (*play,
part in play*) jouer.

enamel [ɪ'næm(ə)l] *n* émail *m* (*pl* émaux) ▌ *a*
en émail ▌ *vt* (*Br* -ll-, *Am* -l-) émailler.

enamoured [ɪn'æməd] *a* **e. of** (*thing*) séduit
par; (*person*) amoureux de.

encamp [ɪn'kæmp] *vi* camper. ● **encampment** *n* campement *m*.

encapsulate [ɪn'kæpsjʊleɪt] *vt* (*ideas, views
etc*) résumer.

encase [ɪn'keɪs] *vt* (*cover*) recouvrir (**in** de),
envelopper (**in** dans).

enchant [ɪn'tʃɑːnt] *vt* enchanter. ● **enchanting** *a* enchanteur. ● **enchantment** *n* enchantement *m*.

encircle [ɪn'sɜːk(ə)l] *vt* entourer; (*of army,
police*) encercler.

encl *abbr* (*enclosure(s)*) pièce(s) *f(pl)*
jointe(s), PJ.

enclave ['enkleɪv] *n* enclave *f*.

enclose [ɪn'kləʊz] *vt* (*send with letter*)
joindre (**in, with** à); (*fence off*) clôturer; **to
e. sth with a wall**/etc entourer qch d'un mur/
etc. ● **enclosed** *a* (*receipt, document etc*) ci-
joint; (*market*) couvert; **e. space** espace *m*
clos; **please find e.** veuillez trouver ci-joint.

enclosure [ɪn'kləʊʒər] *n* (*in letter*) pièce *f*
jointe; (*place, fence*) enceinte *f*.

encompass [ɪn'kʌmpəs] *vt* (*include*) inclure;
(*surround*) entourer.

encore ['ɒŋkɔːr] *int* & *n* bis (*m*) ▌ *vt* bisser.

encounter [ɪn'kaʊntər] *vt* (*person, resistance
etc*) rencontrer ▌ *n* rencontre *f*.

encourage [ɪn'kʌrɪdʒ] *vt* encourager (**to do**
à faire). ● **encouragement** *n* encouragement
m.

encroach [ɪn'krəʊtʃ] *vi* empiéter (**on, upon**
sur); **to e. on the land** (*of sea*) gagner du
terrain. ● **encroachment** *n* empiétement *m*.

encumber [ɪn'kʌmbər] *vt* encombrer (**with**
de). ● **encumbrance** *n* embarras *m*.

encyclical [ɪn'sɪklɪk(ə)l] *n* (*sent by Pope*)
encyclique *f*.

encyclop(a)edia [ɪnsaɪklə'piːdɪə] *n* encyclopédie *f*. ● **encyclop(a)edic** *a* encyclopédique.

end [end] *n* (*of street, box etc*) bout *m*, extrémité *f*; (*of month, meeting, book etc*) fin *f*;
(*purpose*) fin *f*, but *m*; **at an e.** (*discussion,*

war etc) fini, terminé; (*period of time*)
écoulé; **my patience is at an e.** ma patience
est à bout; **in the e.** à la fin; **to come to an e.**
prendre fin; **to put an e. to sth, bring sth to
an e.** mettre fin à qch; **there's no e. to it** ça
n'en finit plus; **no e. of** *Fam* beaucoup de;
six days on e. six jours d'affilée; **for days on
e.** pendant des jours et des jours; **to stand a
box**/etc **on e.** mettre une boîte/etc debout.

▌ *a* (*row, house etc*) dernier; **e. product** (*industrial*) produit *m* fini; *Fig* résultat *m*
(final).

▌ *vt* finir, terminer, achever (**with** par); (*rumour, speculation etc*) mettre fin à.

▌ *vi* finir, se terminer, s'achever; **to e. in failure** se solder par un échec; **to e. in a point**
finir en pointe; **to e. up doing** finir par faire;
to e. up in London/etc se retrouver à
Londres/etc; **he ended up in prison/a doctor**
il a fini en prison/médecin.

endanger [ɪn'deɪndʒər] *vt* mettre en danger;
endangered species espèce *f* menacée *or* en
voie de disparition.

endear [ɪn'dɪər] *vt* faire aimer *or* apprécier
(**qn**) (**to** de); **that's what endears him to me**
c'est cela qui me plaît en lui. ● **endearing** *a*
(*person*) attachant, sympathique; (*quality*)
qui inspire la sympathie. ● **endearment** *n*
parole *f* tendre; **term of e.** terme *m*
d'affection.

endeavour [ɪn'devər] (*Am* **endeavor**) *vi*
s'efforcer (**to do** de faire) ▌ *n* effort *m* (**to do**
pour faire).

ending ['endɪŋ] *n* fin *f*; (*of word*) terminaison *f*; **a happy e.** (*in story etc*) un heureux
dénouement, un happy end.

endive [*Br* 'endɪv, *Am* 'endaɪv] *n* (*curly*) chicorée *f*; (*smooth*) endive *f*.

endless ['endləs] *a* (*speech, series etc*) interminable; (*patience*) infini; (*countless*) innombrable. ● **endlessly** *adv* interminable-
ment.

endorse [ɪn'dɔːs] *vt* (*Br cheque, Am check*)
endosser; (*action, plan*) approuver; (*claim,
application*) appuyer. ● **endorsement** *n* (*on
driving licence*) *Br* = point/etc enlevé(s) sur
le permis de conduire.

endow [ɪn'daʊ] *vt* (*institution*) doter (**with**
de); (*university chair, hospital bed etc*)
fonder; **to be endowed with** (*of person*) être
doté de. ● **endowment** *n* dotation *f*; (*of university chair etc*) fondation *f*.

endurance [ɪn'djʊərəns] *n* endurance *f*, résistance *f*; **e. test** épreuve *f* d'endurance.

endure [ɪn'djʊər] **1** *vt* (*bear*) supporter
(**doing** de faire). **2** *vi* (*last*) durer. ● **enduring**
a durable.

enemy ['enəmɪ] *n* ennemi, -ie *mf* ▌ *a* (*army,
tank etc*) ennemi.

energetic [enə'dʒetɪk] *a* énergique; **to feel e.**
se sentir en pleine forme. ● **energetically** *adv*
énergiquement.

energy ['enədʒɪ] *n* énergie *f* ▌ *a* (*crisis, resources etc*) énergétique.

enforce [ɪn'fɔːs] *vt* (*law*) faire respecter;

(*discipline*) imposer (**on** à). ●**enforced** *a* (*rest, silence etc*) forcé.

engage [ɪnˈɡeɪdʒ] *vt* (*take on*) engager, prendre; **to e. s.o. in conversation** engager la conversation avec qn; **to e. the clutch** (*in vehicle*) *Br* embrayer ▌ *vi* **to e. in** (*launch into*) se lancer dans; (*be involved in*) être mêlé à.

engaged [ɪnˈɡeɪdʒd] *a* **1** (*occupied*) (*person, toilet, phone*) *Br* occupé; **to be e. in business/etc** être dans les affaires/etc. **2** **e.** (**to be married**) fiancé; **to get e.** se fiancer.

engagement [ɪnˈɡeɪdʒmənt] *n* (*agreement to marry*) fiançailles *fpl*; (*meeting*) rendez-vous *m inv*; (*undertaking*) engagement *m*; **to have a prior e.** (*be busy*) être déjà pris, ne pas être libre; **e. ring** bague *f* de fiançailles.

engaging [ɪnˈɡeɪdʒɪŋ] *a* (*smile*) engageant.

engender [ɪnˈdʒendər] *vt* (*produce*) engendrer.

engine [ˈendʒɪn] *n* (*of vehicle, aircraft*) moteur *m*; (*of train*) locomotive *f*; (*of ship*) machine *f*; **e. driver** (*of train*) *Br* mécanicien *m*.

engineer [endʒɪˈnɪər] **1** *n* ingénieur *m*; (*repairer*) *Br* dépanneur, -euse *mf*; (*train driver*) *Am* mécanicien *m*; (*on ship*) mécanicien *m*; **civil e.** ingénieur *m* des travaux publics; **mechanical e.** ingénieur *m* mécanicien.
2 *vt* (*arrange secretly*) combiner, manigancer (*plan etc*). ●**engineering** *n* ingénierie *f*; (**civil**) **e.** génie *m* civil, travaux *mpl* publics; (**mechanical**) **e.** mécanique *f*; **e. factory** atelier *m* de construction mécanique.

England [ˈɪŋɡlənd] *n* Angleterre *f*.

English [ˈɪŋɡlɪʃ] *a* anglais; **E. teacher** professeur *m* d'anglais; **the E. Channel** la Manche ▌ *n* (*language*) anglais *m*; **the E.** (*people*) les Anglais *mpl*. ●**Englishman** *n* (*pl* **-men**) Anglais *m*. ●**English-speaking** *a* (*person, country etc*) anglophone. ●**Englishwoman** *n* (*pl* **-women**) Anglaise *f*.

engrave [ɪnˈɡreɪv] *vt* graver. ●**engraving** *n* gravure *f*. ●**engraver** *n* graveur *m*.

engrossed [ɪnˈɡrəʊst] *a* **e. in one's work** absorbé par son travail; **e. in one's book** absorbé dans sa lecture.

engulf [ɪnˈɡʌlf] *vt* engloutir.

enhance [ɪnˈhɑːns] *vt* (*beauty, prestige etc*) rehausser; (*value*) augmenter.

enigma [ɪˈnɪɡmə] *n* énigme *f*. ●**enig'matic** *a* énigmatique.

enjoy [ɪnˈdʒɔɪ] *vt* aimer (**doing faire**); (*meal*) apprécier; (*good health, standard of living etc*) jouir de; **to e. the evening** passer une bonne soirée; **to e. oneself** s'amuser; **to e. being in London/etc** se plaire à Londres/etc. ●**enjoyable** *a* agréable; (*meal*) excellent. ●**enjoyably** *adv* agréablement. ●**enjoyment** *n* plaisir *m*.

enlarge [ɪnˈlɑːdʒ] *vt* agrandir ▌ *vi* s'agrandir; **to e.** (**up**)**on** (*say more about*) s'étendre sur. ●**enlargement** *n* (*increase*) & *Phot* agrandissement *m*.

enlighten [ɪnˈlaɪt(ə)n] *vt* éclairer (**s.o. on** *or*

about sth qn sur qch). ●**enlightening** *a* instructif. ●**enlightenment** *n* (*explanations*) éclaircissements *mpl*; **an age of e.** une époque éclairée.

enlist [ɪnˈlɪst] *vi* (*in the army etc*) s'engager ▌ *vt* (*recruit*) engager; (*supporter*) recruter; (*support*) obtenir. ●**enlistment** *n* engagement *m*; (*of supporter*) recrutement *m*.

enliven [ɪnˈlaɪv(ə)n] *vt* (*meeting etc*) animer; (*people*) égayer.

enmesh [ɪnˈmeʃt] *vt* empêtrer (**in** dans).

enmity [ˈenmɪtɪ] *n* inimitié *f* (**between** entre).

enormous [ɪˈnɔːməs] *a* énorme; (*explosion, blow*) terrible; (*patience, gratitude*) immense; **an e. success** un succès fou *or* immense. ●**enormity** *n* (*vastness, extent*) énormité *f*; (*atrocity*) atrocité *f*. ●**enormously** *adv* (*very much*) énormément; (*very*) extrêmement.

enough [ɪˈnʌf] *a* & *n* assez (de); **e. time/ cups/etc** assez de temps/de tasses/etc; **to have e. to live on** avoir de quoi vivre; **to have e. to drink** avoir assez à boire; **to have had e. of s.o./sth** (*be fed up with*) en avoir assez de qn/qch; **it's e. for me to see that...** il me suffit de voir que...; **that's e.** ça suffit, c'est assez.
▌ *adv* (*to work, sleep etc*) assez, suffisamment; **big/good/etc e.** assez *or* suffisamment grand/bon/etc (**to** pour); **strangely e., he left** chose curieuse, il est parti.

enquire [ɪnˈkwaɪər] *v* = **inquire**.

enquiry [ɪnˈkwaɪərɪ] *n* = **inquiry**.

enrage [ɪnˈreɪdʒ] *vt* mettre en rage.

enrapture [ɪnˈræptʃər] *vt* ravir.

enrich [ɪnˈrɪtʃ] *vt* enrichir; (*soil*) fertiliser. ●**enrichment** *n* enrichissement *m*.

enrol [ɪnˈrəʊl] (*Am* **enroll**) *vi* (**-ll-**) s'inscrire (**in, for** à) ▌ *vt* inscrire. ●**enrolment** (*Am* **enrollment**) *n* inscription *f*; (*people enrolled*) effectif *m*.

ensconced [ɪnˈskɒnst] *a* bien installé (**in** dans).

ensemble [ɒnˈsɒmb(ə)l] *n* (*musicians, clothes*) ensemble *m*.

ensign [ˈensən, ˈensaɪn] *n* (*flag*) pavillon *m*; (*naval rank*) *Am* enseigne *m* de vaisseau.

enslave [ɪnˈsleɪv] *vt* asservir.

ensue [ɪnˈsjuː] *vi* s'ensuivre. ●**ensuing** *a* (*day, year etc*) suivant; (*event*) qui s'ensuit.

ensure [ɪnˈʃʊər] *vt* assurer; **to e. that** (*make sure*) s'assurer que.

entail [ɪnˈteɪl] *vt* (*imply, involve*) supposer, impliquer.

entangle [ɪnˈtæŋɡ(ə)l] *vt* emmêler, enchevêtrer; **to get entangled in** (*seaweed, explanations etc*) s'empêtrer dans. ●**entanglement** *n* enchevêtrement *m*; **to have an e. with** (*police*) avoir des démêlés *mpl* avec.

enter [ˈentər] *vt* (*room, vehicle, army etc*) entrer dans; (*road*) s'engager dans; (*university*) s'inscrire à; (*write down*) (*on list etc*) inscrire (**in** dans, **on** sur); (*in accounts book*) porter (**in** sur); (*computer data*) entrer, introduire; **to e. s.o. for** (*exam*) présenter *or* inscrire qn à; **to e. a painting/etc in** (*competition*) présenter un tableau/*etc* à; **it didn't e. my head** *or* **mind** ça ne m'est pas venu à l'esprit (*that* que).

▮ *vi* entrer; **to e. for** (*race, exam*) s'inscrire pour, se présenter à; **to e. into** (*relations*) entrer en; (*explanation*) entamer; (*contract*) passer (**with** avec); **to e. into a conversation with s.o.** entamer *or* engager la conversation avec qn; **you don't e. into it** tu n'y es pour rien; **to e. into** *or* **upon** (*career*) entrer dans; (*negotiations*) entamer; (*agreement*) conclure.

enterprise ['entəpraız] *n* (*undertaking, firm*) entreprise *f*; (*spirit, initiative*) initiative *f*. ● **enterprising** *a* (*a person*) plein d'initiative; (*attempt*) hardi.

entertain [entə'teın] *vt* amuser, distraire; (*guest*) recevoir; (*idea, possibility*) envisager; (*doubt, hope*) nourrir; **to e. s.o. to a meal** recevoir qn à dîner **▮** *vi* (*receive guests*) recevoir. ● **entertaining** *a* amusant. ● **entertainer** *n* artiste *mf*. ● **entertainment** *n* amusement *m*, distraction *f*; (*show*) spectacle *m*.

enthral(l) [ın'θrɔːl] *vt* (**-ll-**) (*delight*) captiver.

enthuse [ın'θjuːz] *vi* **to e. over** *Fam* s'emballer pour.

enthusiasm [ın'θjuːzıæz(ə)m] *n* enthousiasme *m*. ● **enthusiast** *n* enthousiaste *mf*; **jazz**/*etc* **e.** passionné, -ée *mf* de jazz/*etc*.

enthusiastic [ınθjuːzı'æstık] *a* enthousiaste; (*golfer, photographer etc*) passionné; **to be e. about** (*hobby*) être passionné de; **he was e. about** *or* **over** (*gift, idea etc*) il a été emballé par; **to get e.** s'emballer (**about** pour). ● **enthusiastically** *adv* avec enthousiasme.

entice [ın'taıs] *vt* attirer (par la ruse) (**into** dans); **to e. s.o. to do** entraîner qn (par la ruse) à faire. ● **enticing** *a* séduisant, alléchant. ● **enticement** *n* (*bait*) attrait *m*.

entire [ın'taıər] *a* entier. ● **entirely** *adv* tout à fait, entièrement.

entirety [ın'taıərətı] *n* intégralité *f*; **in its e.** en entier.

entitle [ın'taıt(ə)l] *vt* **to e. s.o. to do** donner à qn le droit de faire; **to e. s.o. to sth** donner à qn (le) droit à qch; **that entitles me to believe that...** ça m'autorise à croire que.... ● **entitled** *a* **1 to be e.** to do avoir le droit de faire; **to be e. to sth** avoir droit à qch. **2 a book e....** un livre intitulé.... ● **entitlement** *n* **one's e.** son dû.

entity ['entıtı] *n* entité *f*.

entourage ['ɒntʊrɑːʒ] *n* entourage *m*.

entrails ['entreılz] *npl* entrailles *fpl*.

entrance 1 ['entrəns] *n* entrée *f* (**to** de); (*to university, school etc*) admission *f* (**to** à); **e. examination** examen *m* d'entrée. **2** [ın'trɑːns] *vt* (*captivate*) transporter, ravir (*qn*).

entrant ['entrənt] *n* (*in race*) concurrent, -ente *mf*; (*for exam*) candidat, -ate *mf*.

entreat [ın'triːt] *vt* supplier, implorer (**to do** de faire). ● **entreaty** *n* supplication *f*.

entrée ['ɒntreı] *n Br Culin* entrée *f*; (*main dish*) *Am* plat *m* principal.

entrench [ın'trentʃ] *vt* **to e. oneself** (*of* soldier*) & *Fig* se retrancher.

entrepreneur [ɒntrəprə'nɜːr] *n* entrepreneur *m*.

entrust [ın'trʌst] *vt* confier (**to** à); **to e. s.o. with sth** confier qch à qn.

entry ['entrı] *n* (*way in, action*) entrée *f*; (*bookkeeping item*) écriture *f*; (*term in dictionary, logbook etc*) entrée *f*; (*competitor in race etc*) concurrent, -ente *mf*; (*thing to be judged in competition*) objet *m* (*or* œuvre *f or* projet *m*) soumis au jury; **e. form** feuille *f* d'inscription; '**no e.**' (*on door etc*) 'entrée interdite'; (*road sign*) 'sens interdit'.

entwine [ın'twaın] *vt* entrelacer.

enumerate [ı'njuːməreıt] *vt* énumérer. ● **enumeration** [-'reıʃ(ə)n] *n* énumération *f*.

enunciate [ı'nʌnsıeıt] *vt* (*word*) articuler; (*theory*) énoncer. ● **enunciation** [-'eıʃ(ə)n] *n* articulation *f*; (*of theory*) énonciation *f*.

envelop [ın'veləp] *vt* envelopper (**in fog/mystery**/*etc* de brouillard/mystère/*etc*).

envelope ['envələʊp] *n* enveloppe *f*.

enviable ['envıəb(ə)l] *a* enviable.

envious ['envıəs] *a* envieux (**of sth** de qch); **e. of s.o.** jaloux de qn. ● **enviously** *adv* avec envie.

environment [ın'vaıərənmənt] *n* (*social, moral etc*) milieu *m*; **the e.** (*natural*) l'environnement *m*; **e.-friendly product**/*etc* produit *m*/*etc* qui ne nuit pas à l'environnement. ● **environ'mental** *a* du milieu; (*natural*) de l'environnement, écologique. ● **environ'mentalist** *n* écologiste *mf*.

envisage [ın'vızıdʒ] *vt* (*imagine*) envisager; (*foresee*) prévoir; **to e. doing** envisager de faire.

envision [ın'vıʒ(ə)n] *vt Am* = **envisage**.

envoy ['envɔı] *n* (*messenger*) envoyé, -ée *mf*; (*diplomat*) ministre *m* plénipotentiaire.

envy ['envı] *n* envie *f* **▮** *vt* envier (**s.o. sth** qch à qn).

ephemeral [ı'femərəl] *a* éphémère.

epic ['epık] *a* épique **▮** *n* épopée *f*; (**screen**) **e.** film *m* à grand spectacle.

epidemic [epı'demık] *n* épidémie *f*; **to reach e. proportions** prendre des allures d'épidémie.

epidural [epı'djʊərəl] *n* (*anaesthetic*) (anesthésie *f*) péridurale *f*.

epilepsy ['epılepsı] *n* épilepsie *f*. ● **epi'leptic** *a* & *n* épileptique (*mf*).

epilogue ['epılɒg] *n* épilogue *m*.

episode ['epısəʊd] *n* épisode *m*. ● **episodic** [epı'sɒdık] *a* épisodique.

epistle [ı'pıs(ə)l] *n* épître *f*.

epitaph ['epıtɑːf] *n* épitaphe *f*.

epithet ['epıθet] *n* épithète *f*.

epitome [ı'pıtəmı] *n* **the e. of** l'exemple même de, l'incarnation de. ● **epitomize** *vt* incarner.

epoch ['iːpɒk] *n* époque *f*. ● **epoch-making** *a* (*event*) qui fait date.

equal ['iːkwəl] *a* égal (**to** à); **with e. hostility/ respect**/*etc* avec la même hostilité/le même respect/*etc*; **on an e. footing** sur un pied d'égalité (**with** avec); **to be e. to** (*in number, quantity*) égaler; **she's e. to** (*task, situation*) elle est à la hauteur de.

█ *n* (*person*) égal, -ale *mf*; **to treat s.o. as an e.** traiter qn en égal *or* d'égal à égal; **he doesn't have his e.** il n'a pas son pareil.

equality [ɪˈkwɒlɪtɪ] *n* égalité *f*.

equalize [ˈiːkwəlaɪz] *vi* (*score in football etc*) égaliser █ *vt* égaliser.

equally [ˈiːkwəlɪ] *adv* (*to an equal degree, also*) également; (*to divide*) en parts égales; **he's e. stupid** (*just as*) il est tout aussi bête.

equanimity [ekwəˈnɪmɪtɪ] *n* égalité *f* d'humeur.

equate [ɪˈkweɪt] *vt* mettre sur le même pied (**with** que), assimiler (**with** à).

equation [ɪˈkweɪʒ(ə)n] *n* (*mathematical*) équation *f*.

equator [ɪˈkweɪtər] *n* équateur *m*; **at** *or* **on the e.** sous l'équateur. ● equatorial [ekwəˈtɔːrɪəl] *a* équatorial.

equestrian [ɪˈkwestrɪən] *a* équestre.

equilibrium [iːkwɪˈlɪbrɪəm] *n* équilibre *m*.

equinox [ˈiːkwɪnɒks, ˈek-] *n* équinoxe *m*.

equip [ɪˈkwɪp] *vt* (**-pp-**) équiper (**with** de); (**well-**)**equipped with** pourvu de; **to be (well-)equipped to do** être compétent pour faire. ● equipment *n* équipement *m*, matériel *m*.

equity [ˈekwɪtɪ] *n* **1** (*fairness*) équité *f*. **2** *Com* (*investment*) participation *f* (financière); **equities** (*shares*) actions *fpl* (ordinaires). ● equitable *a* équitable *a*.

equivalent [ɪˈkwɪvələnt] *a* & *n* équivalent (*m*). ● equivalence *n* équivalence *f*.

equivocal [ɪˈkwɪvək(ə)l] *a* équivoque.

era [*Br* ˈɪərə, *Am* ˈerə] *n* époque *f*; (*historical, geological*) ère *f*.

eradicate [ɪˈrædɪkeɪt] *vt* supprimer; (*evil, prejudice*) extirper.

erase [*Br* ɪˈreɪz, *Am* ɪˈreɪs] *vt* effacer. ● eraser *n* (*rubber for pencil marks*) gomme *f*. ● erasure [ɪˈreɪʒər] *n* rature *f*.

erect [ɪˈrekt] *a* **1** (*upright*) (bien) droit. **2** *vt* (*build*) construire; (*statue, monument*) ériger; (*scaffolding*) monter; (*tent*) dresser, monter. ● erection [-ʃ(ə)n] *n* construction *f*; (*of statue etc*) érection *f*; (*of scaffolding etc*) montage *m*.

ERM [iːɑːˈrem] *n abbr* (*Exchange Rate Mechanism*) = SME *m*.

ermine [ˈɜːmɪn] *n* (*animal, fur*) hermine *f*.

erode [ɪˈrəʊd] *vt* (*of sea etc*) éroder; (*confidence etc*) *Fig* miner, ronger. ● erosion [-ʒ(ə)n] *n* érosion *f*.

erotic [ɪˈrɒtɪk] *a* érotique. ● eroticism *n* érotisme *m*.

err [ɜːr] *vi* (*be wrong*) se tromper; (*sin*) pécher.

errand [ˈerənd] *n* commission *f*, course *f*; **e. boy** garçon *m* de courses.

erratic [ɪˈrætɪk] *a* (*unpredictable*) (*service, machine etc*) capricieux, fantaisiste; (*person, behaviour*) lunatique; (*irregular*) (*perfor-*

mance, results etc) irrégulier.

erroneous [ɪˈrəʊnɪəs] *a* erroné.

error [ˈerər] *n* (*mistake*) erreur *f*; **to do sth in e.** faire qch par erreur; **typing/printing e.** faute *f* de frappe/d'impression.

erudite [*Br* ˈeruːdaɪt, *Am* ˈerjudaɪt] *a* érudit, savant. ● erudition [-ˈdɪʃ(ə)n] *n* érudition *f*.

erupt [ɪˈrʌpt] *vi* (*of volcano*) entrer en éruption; (*of pimples*) apparaître; (*of war, violence*) éclater. ● eruption [-ʃ(ə)n] *n* (*of volcano, pimples, anger*) éruption *f* (**of** de); (*of violence*) flambée *f*.

escalate [ˈeskəleɪt] *vi* (*of war, violence*) s'intensifier; (*of prices*) monter en flèche █ *vt* intensifier. ● escalation [-ˈleɪʃ(ə)n] *n* escalade *f*.

escalator [ˈeskəleɪtər] *n* escalier *m* roulant.

escapade [ˈeskəpeɪd] *n* (*prank*) frasque *f*.

escape [ɪˈskeɪp] *vi* (*of gas, animal etc*) s'échapper; (*of prisoner*) s'évader, s'échapper; **to e. from** (*person*) échapper à; (*place, cage*) s'échapper de; **escaped prisoner** évadé, -ée *mf*.

█ *vt* (*death*) échapper à; (*punishment*) éviter; **that name escapes me** ce nom m'échappe; **to e. notice** passer inaperçu.

█ *n* (*of gas, liquid*) fuite *f*; (*of person*) évasion *f*, fuite *f*; **to have a lucky** *or* **narrow e.** l'échapper belle.

escapism [ɪˈskeɪpɪz(ə)m] *n* évasion *f* (hors de la réalité). ● escapist *a* (*film, novel etc*) d'évasion.

escort [ˈeskɔːt] *n* (*soldiers, ships etc*) escorte *f*; (*of woman to social event*) cavalier *m*; **it's dangerous — she needs an e.** c'est dangereux — elle a besoin de quelqu'un pour l'accompagner █ [ɪˈskɔːt] *vt* escorter.

Eskimo [ˈeskɪməʊ] *n* (*pl* **-os**) Esquimau, -aude *mf* █ *a* esquimau (*inv or f* -aude).

esoteric [esəʊˈterɪk] *a* obscur, ésotérique.

especial [ɪˈspeʃəl] *a* (tout) spécial; (*care, attention*) (tout) particulier. ● especially *adv* (*in particular*) spécialement, particulièrement; (*for particular purpose*) (tout) spécialement; **e. as** d'autant plus que.

espionage [ˈespɪənɑːʒ] *n* espionnage *m*.

esplanade [ˈespləneɪd] *n* esplanade *f*.

espouse [ɪˈspaʊz] *vt* (*a cause*) épouser.

espresso [eˈspresəʊ] *n* (*pl* **-os**) (*café m*) express *m*.

Esq [ɪˈskwaɪər] *Br abbr* (*esquire*) **J.** Smith Esq (*on envelope*) Monsieur J. Smith.

essay [ˈeseɪ] *n* (*in school*) rédaction *f*; (*in university*) dissertation *f*; (*literary*) essai *m* (**on** sur).

essence [ˈesəns] *n* (*distinctive quality*) essence *f*; (*of food*) extrait *m*, essence *f*; **the e. of** (*main point*) l'essentiel *m* de; **in e.** essentiellement.

essential [ɪˈsenʃ(ə)l] *a* (*principal*) essentiel; (*necessary*) indispensable, essentiel; **it's e. that** il est indispensable que (+ *sub*) █ *npl* **the essentials** l'essentiel *m* (**of** de); (*of grammar*) les éléments *mpl*. ● essentially *adv* essentiellement.

establish [ɪ'stæblɪʃ] vt établir; (state, society, business company) fonder; (post) créer. ●**established** a (well-)e. (business company) solide; (fact) reconnu; (reputation) établi; **she's (well-)e.** (well-known) elle a une réputation établie. ●**establishment** n (institution, business company) établissement m; **the e. of** (action) l'établissement de; (state etc) la fondation de; (post) la création de; **the E.** (dominant group) les classes fpl dirigeantes.

estate [ɪ'steɪt] n (land) terre(s) f(pl), propriété f; (possessions) biens mpl; (property after death) succession f; **housing e.** Br lotissement m; (workers') cité f (ouvrière); **industrial e.** Br zone f industrielle; **e. agency** Br agence f immobilière; **e. agent** Br agent m immobilier; **e. car** Br break m; **e. duty** Br, **e. tax** Am droits mpl de succession.

esteem [ɪ'stiːm] vt estimer; **highly esteemed** très estimé ▌ n estime f.

esthetic [es'θetɪk] a Am esthétique.

estimate ['estɪmeɪt] vt (value) estimer, évaluer; (consider) estimer (that que) ▌ ['estɪmət] n (assessment) évaluation f, estimation f; (judgment) évaluation f; (price for work to be done) devis m; **rough e.** chiffre m approximatif. ●**estimation** [-'meɪʃ(ə)n] n jugement m; (esteem) estime f; (calculation) estimation f; **in my e.** à mon avis.

estranged [ɪ'streɪndʒd] a **to become e.** (of married couple) se séparer.

estuary ['estjʊərɪ] n estuaire m.

etc [et'setərə] adv etc.

etch [etʃ] vti graver à l'eau forte. ●**etching** n (picture) eau-forte f.

eternal [ɪ'tɜːn(ə)l] a éternel. ●**eternally** adv éternellement. ●**eternity** n éternité f.

ether ['iːθər] n éther m.

ethic ['eθɪk] n éthique f. ●**ethics** n (moral standards) moralité f; (philosophical study) éthique f. ●**ethical** a moral, éthique.

Ethiopia [iːθɪ'əʊpɪə] n Éthiopie f. ●**Ethiopian** a éthiopien ▌ n Éthiopien, -ienne mf.

ethnic ['eθnɪk] a ethnique; **e. minority** minorité f ethnique; **e. music/dancing/etc** musique f/danses fpl traditionnelle(s) (d'Afrique, d'Orient etc); **e. cleansing** purification f ethnique.

ethos ['iːθɒs] n génie m.

etiquette ['etɪket] n (rules) bienséances fpl; (diplomatic) e. protocole m, étiquette f; **professional e.** déontologie f.

etymology [etɪ'mɒlədʒɪ] n étymologie f.

eucalyptus [juːkə'lɪptəs] n eucalyptus m.

eulogy ['juːlədʒɪ] n panégyrique m, éloge m.

euphemism ['juːfəmɪz(ə)m] n euphémisme m.

euphoria [juː'fɔːrɪə] n euphorie f. ●**euphoric** a euphorique.

Euro- ['jʊərəʊ] pref euro-; **Euro-MP** membre m du parlement européen.

Eurocheque ['jʊərəʊtʃek] n eurochèque m.

Eurocrat ['jʊərəʊkræt] n eurocrate mf.

Europe ['jʊərəp] n Europe f. ●**European**

[jʊərə'piːən] a européen ▌ n Européen, -enne mf.

euthanasia [juːθə'neɪzɪə] n euthanasie f.

evacuate [ɪ'vækjʊeɪt] vt évacuer. ●**evacuation** [-'eɪʃ(ə)n] n évacuation f.

evade [ɪ'veɪd] vt éviter, esquiver; (pursuer, tax) échapper à; (law, question) éluder.

evaluate [ɪ'væljʊeɪt] vt évaluer (at à). ●**evaluation** [-'eɪʃ(ə)n] n évaluation f.

evangelical [iːvæn'dʒelɪk(ə)l] a évangélique. ●**evangelist** [ɪ'vændʒəlɪst] n évangéliste m.

evaporate [ɪ'væpəreɪt] vi (of liquid) s'évaporer; (of hopes) s'évanouir; **evaporated milk** lait m concentré. ●**evaporation** [-'reɪʃ(ə)n] n évaporation f.

evasion [ɪ'veɪʒ(ə)n] n **e. of** (pursuer etc) fuite f devant; (question) esquive f de; **tax e.** évasion f fiscale.

evasive [ɪ'veɪsɪv] a évasif.

eve [iːv] n **on the e. of** à la veille de.

even ['iːv(ə)n] 1 a (flat) uni, égal; (equal) égal; (regular) régulier; (number) pair; **to get e. with s.o.** se venger de qn; **I'll get e. with him (for that)** je lui revaudrai ça; **we're e.** (not owing anything to each other) nous sommes quittes; (in score) nous sommes à égalité; **to break e.** (financially) s'y retrouver ▌ vt **to e. sth (out or up)** égaliser qch.

2 adv même; (with comparative) better/more encore mieux/plus; **e. if or though** même si; **e. so** quand même. ●**evenly** adv de manière égale; (regularly) régulièrement. ●**evenness** n (of surface, temper) égalité f; (of movement etc) régularité f. ●**even-'tempered** a de caractère égal.

evening ['iːvnɪŋ] n soir m; (whole evening, event) soirée f; **in the e.,** Am **evenings** le soir; **at seven in the e.** à sept heures du soir; **every Tuesday e.** tous les mardis soir; **all e. (long)** toute la soirée; **e. meal/newspaper/etc** repas m/journal m/etc du soir; **e. class** cours m du soir; **e. dress** (of man) tenue f de soirée; (of woman) robe f du soir or de soirée; **e. performance** (in theatre) soirée f.

event [ɪ'vent] n événement m; Sport épreuve f; **in the e. of death** en cas de décès; **in any e.** en tout cas; **after the e.** après coup.

eventful [ɪ'ventfəl] a (journey, life etc) mouvementé; (occasion) mémorable.

eventual [ɪ'ventʃʊəl] a (final) final, définitif; (possible) éventuel. ●**eventu'ality** n éventualité f. ●**eventually** adv finalement, à la fin, (some day or other) un jour ou l'autre.

ever ['evər] adv jamais; **has he e. seen it?** l'a-t-il jamais vu?; **more than e.** plus que jamais; **nothing e.** jamais rien; **hardly e.** presque jamais; **e. ready** toujours prêt; **the first e.** le tout premier; **e. since** (that event etc) depuis; **e. since then** depuis lors, dès lors; **for e.** (for always) pour toujours; (continually) sans cesse; **the best son e.** le meilleur fils du monde; **e. so sorry/happy/etc** vraiment désolé/heureux/etc; **thank you e. so much** Br merci mille fois; **it's e. such a pity** Br c'est vraiment dommage; **why e. not?** mais pourquoi pas?

evergreen ['evəgriːn] n arbre m à feuilles persistantes.

everlasting [evə'lɑːstɪŋ] a éternel.

evermore [evə'mɔːr] adv for e. à (tout) jamais.

every ['evrɪ] a chaque; **e. child** chaque enfant, tous les enfants; **e. time** chaque fois (that que); **e. one** chacun; **e. single one** tous (sans exception); **e. second** or **other day** tous les deux jours; **her e. gesture** ses moindres gestes; **e. bit as big** tout aussi grand (as que); **e. so often**, **e. now and then** de temps en temps; **to have e. confidence in** avoir pleine confiance en.

everybody ['evrɪbɒdɪ] pron tout le monde; **e. in turn** chacun à son tour. ● **everyday** a (happening, life etc) de tous les jours; (ordinary) banal; **in e. use** d'usage courant. ● **everyone** pron = everybody. ● **everyplace** adv Am = everywhere. ● **everything** pron tout; **e. I have** tout ce que j'ai. ● **everywhere** adv partout; **e. she goes** où qu'elle aille, partout où elle va.

evict [ɪ'vɪkt] vt expulser (from de). ● **eviction** [-ʃ(ə)n] n expulsion f.

evidence ['evɪdəns] n (proof) preuve(s) f(pl); (testimony) témoignage m; **to give e.** témoigner (against contre); **to accept the e.** se rendre à l'évidence; **e. of** (wear etc) des signes mpl de; **in e.** (noticeable) (bien) en vue.

evident ['evɪdənt] a évident (that que); **it is e. from...** il apparaît de... (that que). ● **evidently** adv (obviously) évidemment; (apparently) apparemment.

evil ['iːv(ə)l] a (spell, influence, person etc) malfaisant; (deed, advice, system) mauvais; (consequence) funeste ∎ n mal m; **to speak e.** dire du mal (about, of de).

evince [ɪ'vɪns] vt manifester.

evocative [ɪ'vɒkətɪv] a évocateur.

evoke [ɪ'vəʊk] vt (recall, conjure up) évoquer; (admiration) susciter.

evolution [iːvə'luːʃ(ə)n] n évolution f.

evolve [ɪ'vɒlv] vi (of society, idea etc) évoluer; (of plan) se développer ∎ vt (system etc) développer.

ewe [juː] n brebis f.

ex [eks] n (former spouse) Fam ex mf.

ex- [eks] pref ex-; **ex-wife** ex-femme f.

exacerbate [ɪk'sæsəbeɪt] vt (situation) empirer; (pain) exacerber.

exact [ɪg'zækt] **1** a (accurate, precise etc) exact; **to be (more) e. about sth** préciser qch. **2** vt (demand) exiger (from de); (money) extorquer (from à). ● **exactly** adv exactement; **it's e. 5 o'clock** il est 5 heures juste, il est exactement 5 heures. ● **exactness** n exactitude f.

exacting [ɪg'zæktɪŋ] a (demanding) exigeant.

exaggerate [ɪg'zædʒəreɪt] vt exagérer; **to e. sth** (in one's own mind) s'exagérer qch ∎ vi exagérer. ● **exaggeration** [-'reɪʃ(ə)n] n exagération f.

exalt [ɪg'zɔːlt] vt (praise) exalter. ● **exalted** a (position, rank) élevé. ● **exaltation** [-'teɪʃ(ə)n] n exaltation f.

exam [ɪg'zæm] n abbr (examination) examen m.

examine [ɪg'zæmɪn] vt examiner; (accounts, luggage) vérifier; (passport) contrôler; (question) interroger (élève, témoin). ● **examination** [-'neɪʃ(ə)n] n (in school etc) examen m; (inspection) examen m; (of accounts etc) vérification f; (of passport) contrôle m; **class e.** devoir m surveillé or sur table; **medical e.** examen m médical. ● **examiner** n (for school exam) examinateur, -trice mf.

example [ɪg'zɑːmp(ə)l] n exemple m; **for e.** par exemple; **to set an e.** or **a good e.** donner l'exemple or le bon exemple (to à); **to set a bad e.** donner le mauvais exemple (to à); **to make an e. of s.o.** punir qn pour l'exemple.

exasperate [ɪg'zɑːspəreɪt] vt exaspérer; **to get exasperated** s'exaspérer (at de). ● **exasperation** [-'reɪʃ(ə)n] n exaspération f.

excavate ['ekskəveɪt] vt (dig) creuser; (for relics etc) fouiller; (uncover) déterrer. ● **excavation** [-'veɪʃ(ə)n] n (digging) creusement m; (archeological) fouille(s) f(pl).

exceed [ɪk'siːd] vt dépasser; (one's powers) excéder.

exceedingly [ɪk'siːdɪŋlɪ] adv extrêmement.

excel [ɪk'sel] vi (-ll-) **to e. in** or **at sth** être excellent en qch, exceller en qch; **to e. at** or **in doing sth** exceller à faire qch ∎ vt (be better than) surpasser.

Excellency [eksələnsɪ] n (title) Excellence f.

excellent ['eksələnt] a excellent. ● **excellence** n excellence f. ● **excellently** adv parfaitement, admirablement.

except [ɪk'sept] prep sauf, excepté; **e. for** à part; **e. that** sauf que, à part le fait que; **e. if** sauf si; **to do nothing e. wait** ne rien faire sinon attendre ∎ vt excepter.

exception [ɪk'sepʃ(ə)n] n exception f; **with the e. of** à l'exception de; **to take e. to** (object to) désapprouver; (be hurt by) s'offenser de.

exceptional [ɪk'sepʃən(ə)l] a exceptionnel. ● **exceptionally** adv exceptionnellement.

excerpt ['eksɜːpt] n (from film, book etc) extrait m.

excess ['ekses] n excès m; (surplus) excédent m; **one's excesses** ses excès mpl; **to eat/ drink/etc to e.** manger/boire/etc à l'excès; **a sum/etc in e. of...** une somme/etc qui dépasse...; **e. calories/etc** des calories fpl/etc en trop; **e. fare** supplément m (de billet); **e. luggage** excédent m de bagages; **e. weight** kilos mpl en trop.

excessive [ɪk'sesɪv] a excessif. ● **excessively** adv (too, too much) excessivement; (very) extrêmement.

exchange [ɪks'tʃeɪndʒ] vt (addresses, blows etc) échanger (for contre) ∎ n échange m; (of foreign currencies) change m; (telephone) e. central m (téléphonique); **in e.** en échange (for de); **e. rate** taux m de change.

Exchequer [ɪks'tʃekər] n **Chancellor of the E.** Br = ministre m des Finances.

excise ['eksaɪz] n taxe f (**on** sur).

excitable [ɪk'saɪtəb(ə)l] a excitable.

excite [ɪk'saɪt] vt (enthuse) passionner, exciter; (agitate, provoke, stimulate) exciter. ●**excited** a (happy) surexcité; (nervous) énervé; **to get e.** (nervous, angry, enthusiastic) s'exciter; **to be e. about** (new car, news etc) se réjouir de; **to be e. about the** Br **holidays** or Am **vacation** être surexcité à l'idée de partir en vacances. ●**excitedly** [-ɪdlɪ] adv avec agitation; (to wait, jump about) dans un état de surexcitation. ●**exciting** a (book, adventure etc) passionnant.

excitement [ɪk'saɪtmənt] n agitation f, excitation f, fièvre f; (emotion) vive émotion f; (adventure) aventure f; **great e.** surexcitation f.

exclaim [ɪk'skleɪm] vti s'exclamer, s'écrier (**that** que). ●**exclamation** [eksklə'meɪʃ(ə)n] n exclamation f; **e. mark** Br, **e. point** Am point m d'exclamation.

exclude [ɪks'klu:d] vt exclure (**from** de); (name from list) écarter (**from** de). ●**exclusion** [-ʒ(ə)n] n exclusion f.

exclusive [ɪks'klu:sɪv] a (right, interest, design) exclusif; (club, group) fermé; (interview, news item) en exclusivité; **e. of** wine/etc vin/etc non compris. ●**exclusively** adv exclusivement.

excommunicate [ekskə'mju:nɪkeɪt] vt excommunier. ●**excommunication** [-'keɪʃ(ə)n] n excommunication f.

excrement ['ekskrəmənt] n excrément(s) m(pl).

excruciating [ɪk'skru:ʃɪeɪtɪŋ] a insupportable, atroce.

excursion [ɪk'skɜ:ʃ(ə)n] n excursion f.

excuse [ɪk'skju:z] vt (forgive, justify) excuser (**s.o. for doing** qn d'avoir fait, qn de faire); (exempt) dispenser (**from** de); **e. me for asking** permettez-moi de demander; **e. me!** excusez-moi!, pardon!; **you're excused** (you may go) tu peux t'en aller or sortir ▮ [ɪk'skju:s] n excuse f; **to make an e.**, **make excuses** se trouver une excuse; **it was an e. for a party/etc** cela a servi de prétexte à une petite sauterie/etc.

ex-directory [eksdaɪ'rektərɪ] a (telephone number) Br sur la liste rouge; **to go ex-d**, demander à être sur la liste rouge.

execute ['eksɪkju:t] vt (criminal, order, plan etc) exécuter. ●**execution** [-'kju:ʃ(ə)n] n exécution f. ●**exe'cutioner** n bourreau m.

executive [ɪg'zekjutɪv] a (job) de cadre; (car, plane) de direction; (power, committee) exécutif; **e. model** (of car) version f grand luxe ▮ n (person) cadre m; (board, committee) bureau m; **the e.** (part of government) l'exécutif m; **(senior) e.** cadre m supérieur; **junior e.** jeune cadre m; **sales e.** cadre m commercial.

exemplary [ɪg'zemplərɪ] a exemplaire.

exemplify [ɪg'zemplɪfaɪ] vt (show) illustrer;

(serve as an example of) servir d'exemple de.

exempt [ɪg'zempt] a (person) dispensé (**from** de) ▮ vt dispenser (**from sth** de qch, **from doing** de faire). ●**exemption** [-ʃ(ə)n] n dispense f.

exercise ['eksəsaɪz] n (training, activity, task etc) exercice m; **the e. of** (power) l'exercice m de; **exercises** (in university) Am cérémonies fpl; **e. book** cahier m; **e. bike** vélo m d'appartement. ▮ vt exercer; (troops) faire faire l'exercice à; (dog, horse etc) promener; (tact, judgment, restraint etc) faire preuve de; (rights) faire valoir, exercer. ▮ vi (take exercise) faire de l'exercice.

exert [ɪg'zɜ:t] vt exercer; (force) employer; **to e. oneself** (physically) se dépenser; **don't e. yourself!** ne te fatigue pas!; **to e. oneself to do** (try hard) s'efforcer de faire. ●**exertion** [-ʃ(ə)n] n effort m; (of force) emploi m.

ex gratia [eks'greɪʃə] a (payment) exceptionnel, non prévu au contrat.

exhale [eks'heɪl] vt (breathe out) expirer; (give off) exhaler ▮ vi expirer.

exhaust [ɪg'zɔ:st] **1** vt (use up, tire) épuiser; **to become exhausted** s'épuiser. **2** n **e.** (pipe) (of vehicle) tuyau m d'échappement; **e.** (fumes) gaz mpl d'échappement. ●**exhausted** a (person, supplies etc) épuisé. ●**exhausting** a épuisant.

exhaustion [ɪg'zɔ:stʃ(ə)n] n épuisement m.

exhaustive [ɪg'zɔ:stɪv] a (study, analysis etc) complet, exhaustif; (research) approfondi.

exhibit [ɪg'zɪbɪt] vt (put on display) exposer; (ticket, courage etc) montrer ▮ n objet m exposé; (in court) pièce f à conviction.

exhibition [egzɪ'bɪʃ(ə)n] n exposition f; **an e. of** (skill, arrogance etc) une démonstration de; **to make an e. of oneself** se donner en spectacle. ●**exhibitionist** n exhibitionniste mf.

exhibitor [ɪg'zɪbɪtər] n exposant, -ante mf.

exhilarate [ɪg'zɪləreɪt] vt stimuler; (of air, breeze) vivifier; (make happy) rendre fou de joie. ●**exhilarating** a (experience etc) grisant; (air etc) vivifiant. ●**exhilaration** [-'reɪʃ(ə)n] n joie f, liesse f.

exhort [ɪg'zɔ:t] vt exhorter (**to do** à faire, **to sth** à qch).

exhume [eks'hju:m] vt exhumer.

exile ['egzaɪl] vt exiler ▮ n (absence) exil m; (person) exilé, -ée mf.

exist [ɪg'zɪst] vi exister; (live) vivre (**on** de); **the notion exists that...** il existe une notion selon laquelle...; **some doubt (still) exists** le doute subsiste. ●**existing** a (situation, circumstances) actuel; (law) existant.

existence [ɪg'zɪstəns] n existence f; **to come into e.** être créé; **to be in e.** exister.

exit ['eksɪt, 'egzɪt] n (action) sortie f; (door, window) sortie f, issue f ▮ vi (of actor) sortir.

exodus ['eksədəs] n inv exode m.

exonerate [ɪg'zɒnəreɪt] vt (from blame) disculper (**from** de).

exorbitant [ɪg'zɔ:bɪtənt] a exorbitant.

●**exorbitantly** adv démesurément.
exorcize [ˈeksɔːsaɪz] vt exorciser. ●**exorcism**
n exorcisme m.
exotic [ɪgˈzɒtɪk] a exotique.
expand [ɪkˈspænd] vt (one's knowledge, influence, fortune etc) étendre; (trade, idea)
développer; (production) augmenter; (gas,
metal) dilater; **to e. a range of products**
élargir une gamme de produits ▌ vi
s'étendre; (of trade etc) se développer; (of
production) augmenter; (of gas etc) se dilater; **to e. on** développer ses idées sur; (fast
or rapidly) **expanding sector**/etc secteur m/etc
en (pleine) expansion.
expanse [ɪkˈspæns] n étendue f.
expansion [ɪkˈspænʃ(ə)n] n (economic, colonial etc) expansion f; (of trade etc) développement m; (of production) augmentation
f; (of gas, metal) expansion f. ●**expansion-
ism** n expansionnisme m.
expansive [ɪkˈspænsɪv] a expansif. ●**expan-
sively** adv avec effusion.
expatriate [Br eksˈpætrɪət, Am eksˈpeɪtrɪət]
a & n expatrié, -ée (mf).
expect [ɪkˈspekt] vt (anticipate) s'attendre à,
escompter; (think) penser (that que);
(suppose) supposer (that que); (await)
attendre (qn); **to e. sth from s.o./sth** attendre
qch de qn/qch; **to e. to do** compter faire; **to
e. that** (anticipate) s'attendre à ce que (+
sub); **I e. you to come** (want) je compte que
vous viendrez; **it was expected** c'était prévu
(that que); **as expected** comme prévu; **she's
expecting** (a baby) elle attend un bébé.
expectancy [ɪkˈspektənsɪ] n attente f; **life e.**
espérance f de vie.
expectant [ɪkˈspektənt] a (crowd) qui
attend; **e. mother** future mère f.
expectation [ekspekˈteɪʃ(ə)n] n attente f; **to
come up to s.o.'s expectations** répondre à
l'attente de qn.
expedient [ɪksˈpiːdɪənt] a avantageux; (suitable) opportun ▌ n (action, plan) expédient
m.
expedite [ˈekspədaɪt] vt (hasten) accélérer;
(task) expédier.
expedition [ekspɪˈdɪʃ(ə)n] n expédition f.
expel [ɪkˈspel] vt (-ll-) (from school) renvoyer; (foreigner, demonstrator etc) expulser
(from de); (enemy) chasser.
expend [ɪkˈspend] vt (energy, money) dépenser; (resources) épuiser. ●**expendable** a
(object) remplaçable; (soldiers) sacrifiable.
expenditure [ɪkˈspendɪtʃər] n (money spent)
dépenses fpl; **an e. of time/money** une dépense de temps/d'argent.
expense [ɪkˈspens] n frais mpl, dépense f;
expenses frais mpl; **business/travelling
expenses** frais mpl généraux/de déplacement;
to go to some e. faire des frais; **at the e. of
s.o./sth** (causing harm) aux dépens de qn/
qch; **to laugh at s.o.'s e.** rire aux dépens de
qn; **an e. account** une note de frais (pro-
fessionnels).
expensive [ɪkˈspensɪv] a (goods, hotel etc)

cher; (tastes) de luxe, dispendieux; **to be e.**
coûter or être cher; **an e. mistake** une faute
qui coûte cher. ●**expensively** adv e.
dressed/furnished/etc habillé/meublé/etc
luxueusement; **to do sth e.** faire qch à grands
frais.
experience [ɪkˈspɪərɪəns] n (knowledge,
skill, event) expérience f; **from** or **by e.** par
expérience; **he has had e. of this work**/of
grief il a déjà fait ce travail/éprouvé le chagrin; **I've had e. of driving** j'ai déjà conduit;
practical e. pratique f; **previous e.** (in job)
expérience f antérieure; **terrible experiences**
(hardship) de rudes épreuves fpl; **unforgettable e.** moment m inoubliable.
▌ vt (undergo) connaître, subir; (difficulty,
remorse) éprouver; (joy) ressentir. ●**experienced** a (person) expérimenté; (eye, ear)
exercé; **to be e. in photography**/etc s'y connaître en (matière de) photographie/etc.
experiment [ɪkˈsperɪmənt] n expérience f ▌
[ɪkˈsperɪment] vi faire une expérience or des
expériences; **to e. with sth** (scientifically)
expérimenter qch; **to e. with drugs** toucher à
la drogue. ●**experi'mental** a expérimental; **e.
period** période f d'expérimentation.
expert [ˈekspɜːt] n expert m (**on, in** en),
spécialiste mf (**on, in** de) ▌ a expert (**in sth**
en qch, **in** or **at doing** à faire); **e. advice** le
conseil d'un expert; **e. eye** l'œil m d'un connaisseur; **e. touch** doigté m, grande habileté
f. ●**expertise** [-'tiːz] n compétence f (**in** en).
●**expertly** adv habilement.
expiate [ˈekspɪeɪt] vt (sins) expier.
expire [ɪkˈspaɪər] vi expirer. ●**expired** a
(ticket, passport etc) périmé.
expiry [ɪkˈspaɪərɪ] (Am **expiration** [ekspə-
ˈreɪʃ(ə)n] n expiration f; **e. date** (on ticket
etc) date f d'expiration; (on product) date f
limite d'utilisation.
explain [ɪkˈspleɪn] vt expliquer (**to** à, **that**
que); (reasons) exposer; (mystery) éclaircir;
e. yourself! explique-toi!; **to e. sth away**
justifier qch. ●**explainable** a explicable.
explanation [ekspləˈneɪʃ(ə)n] n explication
f.
explanatory [ɪkˈsplænət(ə)rɪ] a explicatif.
expletive [Br ɪkˈspliːtɪv, Am ˈeksplətɪv] n
(oath) juron m.
explicit [ɪkˈsplɪsɪt] a explicite. ●**explicitly** adv
explicitement.
explode [ɪkˈspləʊd] vi (of bomb etc) exploser; **to e. with laughter** Fig éclater de rire ▌
vt (bomb etc) faire exploser; (theory) Fig discréditer.
exploit 1 [ɪkˈsplɔɪt] vt (person, land etc)
exploiter. **2** [ˈeksplɔɪt] n (feat) exploit m.
●**exploitation** [eksplɔɪˈteɪʃ(ə)n] n exploitation f.
exploratory [ɪkˈsplɒrət(ə)rɪ] a (journey etc)
d'exploration; (talks, step etc) préliminaire,
exploratoire; **e. operation** (by surgeon) sondage m.
explore [ɪkˈsplɔːr] vt explorer; (causes, possibilities etc) examiner. ●**exploration** [eksplə-

'reɪʃ(ə)n] *n* exploration *f*.

explorer [ɪk'splɔːrər] *n* explorateur, -trice *mf*.

explosion [ɪk'spləʊʒ(ə)n] *n* explosion *f*.

explosive [ɪk'spləʊsɪv] *a* (*weapon, situation, question*) explosif; (*mixture, gas*) détonant; **e. device** engin *m* explosif █ *n* explosif *m*.

exponent [ɪk'spəʊnənt] *n* (*of opinion, theory etc*) interprète *m* (**of** dc).

export ['ekspɔːt] *n* exportation *f*; **e. goods/permit/***etc* marchandises *fpl*/permis *m* d'exportation █ [ɪk'spɔːt] *vt* exporter (**to** vers, **from** de). ●**ex'porter** *n* exportateur, -trice *mf*; (*country*) pays *m* exportateur.

expose [ɪk'spəʊz] *vt* (*leave uncovered etc*) exposer; (*wire*) dénuder; (*photographic film*) exposer; (*plot, scandal etc*) révéler, dévoiler; (*crook etc*) démasquer; **to e. s.o. to** (*subject to*) exposer qn à; **to e. oneself** (*in public place*) commettre un attentat à la pudeur; **exposed film/position** pellicule *f*/position *f* exposée; **to be in an exposed position** *Fig* être (très) exposé. ●**exposition** [ekspə-'zɪʃ(ə)n] *n* exposition *f*.

exposure [ɪk'spəʊʒər] *n* exposition *f* (**to** à); (*of plot etc*) révélation *f*; (*of building*) exposition *f*; (*in photography*) pose *f*; **to die of e.** mourir de froid.

expound [ɪk'spaʊnd] *vt* (*theory etc*) exposer.

express¹ [ɪk'spres] *vt* exprimer; (*proposition*) énoncer; **to e. oneself** s'exprimer.

express² [ɪk'spres] *a* (*letter, delivery*) exprès *inv*; (*train*) rapide, express *inv*; (*order*) exprès, formel; (*intention*) explicite; **with the e. purpose of doing** dans le seul but de faire █ *adv* (*to send*) par exprès █ *n* (*train*) rapide *m*, express *m inv*. ●**expressly** *adv* (*to forbid etc*) expressément.

expression [ɪk'spreʃ(ə)n] *n* (*phrase, look etc*) expression *f*; **an e. of** (*gratitude, affection etc*) un témoignage de.

expressive [ɪk'spresɪv] *a* expressif.

expressway [ɪk'spresweɪ] *n Am* autoroute *f*.

expulsion [ɪk'spʌlʃ(ə)n] *n* expulsion *f*; (*from school*) renvoi *m*.

expurgate ['ekspəgeɪt] *vt* expurger.

exquisite [ɪk'skwɪzɪt] *a* exquis. ●**exquisitely** *adv* d'une façon exquise.

ex-serviceman [eks'sɜːvɪsmən] *n* (*pl* **-men**) *Br* ancien combattant *m*.

extant ['ekstənt, ek'stænt] *a* existant.

extend [ɪk'stend] *vt* (*arm, business*) étendre; (*line, visit, meeting*) prolonger (**by** de); (*hand*) tendre (**to s.o.** à qn); (*house*) agrandir; (*knowledge*) élargir; (*time limit*) reculer; (*help, thanks*) offrir (**to** à); **to e. an invitation to** faire une invitation à █ *vi* (*of wall, plain etc*) s'étendre (**to** jusqu'à); (*in time*) se prolonger; **great joy extended to everyone** l'allégresse gagna tout le monde.

extension [ɪk'stenʃ(ə)n] *n* (*for table*) rallonge *f*; (*to building*) agrandissement(s) *m(pl)*; (*of telephone*) appareil *m* supplémentaire; (*of office telephone*) poste *m*; (*in time*) prolongation *f*; (*in space*) prolongement *m*; (*of meaning, powers, strike*) exten-

sion *f*; **an e.** (**of time**) (*extra time*) un délai.

extensive [ɪk'stensɪv] *a* (*powers, forests etc*) étendu, vaste; (*repairs, damage etc*) important; **it's in e. use** (*machine etc*) c'est très couramment utilisé. ●**extensively** *adv* (*very much*) énormément, considérablement; **e. used** (*method*) répandu; (*procedure*) courant.

extent [ɪk'stent] *n* (*scope*) étendue *f*; (*size*) importance *f*; (*degree*) mesure *f*; **to a large** *or* **great e.** dans une large mesure; **to some e.** *or* **a certain e.** dans une certaine mesure; **to such an e. that** à tel point que.

extenuating [ɪk'stenjʊeɪtɪŋ] *a* **e. circumstances** circonstances *fpl* atténuantes.

exterior [ɪks'tɪərɪər] *a* & *n* extérieur (*m*).

exterminate [ɪk'stɜːmɪneɪt] *vt* (*people, animals*) exterminer; (*evil*) extirper. ●**extermination** [-'neɪʃ(ə)n] *n* extermination *f*.

external [ek'stɜːn(ə)l] *a* (*wall, influence, trade etc*) extérieur; **for e. use** (*medicine*) à usage externe; **e. affairs** *Pol* affaires *fpl* étrangères. ●**externally** *adv* extérieurement.

extinct [ɪk'stɪŋkt] *a* (*volcano*) éteint; (*species, animal*) disparu. ●**extinction** [-ʃ(ə)n] *n* extinction *f*; (*of species*) disparition *f*.

extinguish [ɪk'stɪŋgwɪʃ] *vt* éteindre. ●**extinguisher** *n* (*fire*) e. extincteur *m*.

extol [ɪk'stəʊl] *vt* (**-ll-**) exalter, louer.

extort [ɪk'stɔːt] *vt* (*money*) extorquer (**from** à); (*consent*) arracher (**from** à). ●**extortion** [-ʃ(ə)n] *n* (*crime*) extorsion *f* de fonds; **it's** (**sheer**) **e.!** c'est du vol!

extortionate [ɪk'stɔːʃənət] *a* (*price etc*) exorbitant.

extra ['ekstrə] *a* (*additional*) supplémentaire; **one e. glass** un verre de *or* en plus, encore un verre; (**any**) **e. bread?** encore du pain?; **to be e.** (*spare*) être en trop; (*cost more*) être en supplément; **postage is e.** les frais d'envoi sont en plus *or* en sus; **e. care** un soin tout particulier; **e. charge** *or* **portion** supplément *m*; **e. time** *Football* prolongation *f*.
█ *adv* **to pay e.** payer un supplément; **wine costs** *or* **is 3 francs e.** il y a un supplément de 3F pour le vin; **e. big/***etc* plus grand/*etc* que d'habitude.
█ *n* (*perk*) à-côté *m*; (*actor in film etc*) figurant, -ante *mf*; **extras** (*expenses*) frais *mpl* supplémentaires; **an optional e.** (*for car etc*) un accessoire en option.

extra- ['ekstrə] *pref* extra-. ●**extra-'dry** *a* (*champagne*) brut. ●**extra-'fine** *a* extra-fin. ●**extra-'strong** *a* extra-fort.

extract [ɪk'strækt] *vt* extraire (**from** de); (*tooth*) arracher, extraire; (*promise*) arracher, soutirer (**from s.o.** à qn); (*money*) soutirer (**from s.o.** à qn) █ ['ekstrækt] *n* (*of book, poem etc*) extrait *m*; (*chemical or food substance*) extrait *m*; **beef e.** extrait *m* de viande. ●**extraction** [-ʃ(ə)n] *n* **1** extraction *f*; (*of tooth, promise*) arrachement *m*. **2** (*descent*) origine *f*.

extra-curricular [ekstrəkə'rɪkjʊlər] *a* (*activities etc*) extrascolaire, en dehors des heures de cours.

extradite ['ekstrədaɪt] vt extrader. ●**extradition** [-'dɪʃ(ə)n] n extradition f.

extramarital [ekstrə'mærɪt(ə)l] a en dehors du mariage, extra-conjugal.

extramural [ekstrə'mjʊərəl] a (studies) Br hors faculté.

extraneous [ɪk'streɪnɪəs] a (detail etc) accessoire.

extraordinary [ɪk'strɔːd(ə)nrɪ] a (strange, exceptional) extraordinaire. ●**extraordinarily** adv extraordinairement.

extra-special [ekstrə'speʃəl] a (occasion) très spécial; (care) tout particulier.

extraterrestrial [ekstrətə'restrɪəl] a & n extraterrestre (mf).

extravagant [ɪk'strævəgənt] a (behaviour, idea etc) extravagant; (claim) exagéré; (wasteful with money) dépensier, prodigue. ●**extravagance** n (of behaviour etc) extravagance f; (wastefulness) prodigalité f; (thing bought) folle dépense f; (wasteful expenses) prodigalités fpl.

extravaganza [ɪkstrævə'gænzə] n (musical etc entertainment) spectacle m somptueux.

extreme [ɪk'striːm] a (exceptional, furthest) extrême; (danger, poverty, importance) très grand; (praise) outré; **at the e. end** à l'extrémité; **of e. importance** de première importance ▮ n (furthest degree) extrême m; **to carry** or **take sth to extremes** pousser qch à l'extrême; **extremes of temperature** températures fpl extrêmes; **extremes of climate** excès mpl du climat. ●**extremely** adv extrêmement.

extremist [ɪk'striːmɪst] a & n extrémiste (mf). ●**extremism** n extrémisme m.

extremity [ɪk'stremɪtɪ] n extrémité f.

extricate ['ekstrɪkeɪt] vt (free) dégager (qch, qn) (from de); **to e. oneself from a difficulty/a danger** se tirer d'une situation difficile/d'un danger.

extrovert ['ekstrəvɜːt] n extraverti, -ie mf.

exuberant [ɪg'z(j)uːbərənt] a exubérant. ●**exuberance** n exubérance f.

exude [ɪg'zjuːd] vt (charm, honesty etc) respirer.

exultation [egzʌl'teɪʃ(ə)n] n exultation f.

eye¹ [aɪ] n œil m (pl yeux); **before my very eyes** sous mes yeux; **to be all eyes** être tout yeux; **as far as the e. can see** à perte de vue; **up to one's eyes in debt** endetté jusqu'au cou; **up to one's eyes in work** débordé de travail; **to have one's e. on** (house, car etc) avoir en vue; **to keep an e. on** surveiller; **to make eyes at** Fam faire de l'œil à; **to lay** or **set eyes on** voir; **to take one's eyes off s.o./sth** quitter qn/qch des yeux; **to catch s.o.'s e.** attirer l'attention de qn; **keep your eyes open!, keep an e. out!** ouvre l'œil!, sois vigilant!; **we don't see e. to e.** nous ne voyons pas les choses du même œil; **to be an e.-opener for s.o.** Fam être une révélation pour qn.

eye² [aɪ] vt (look at) regarder; (with envy) dévorer des yeux; (with lust) reluquer.

eyeball ['aɪbɔːl] n globe m oculaire. ●**eyebrow** n sourcil m. ●**eyecatching** a (title etc) accrocheur. ●**eyeglass** n monocle m. ●**eyeglasses** npl (spectacles) Am lunettes fpl. ●**eyelash** n cil m. ●**eyelid** n paupière f. ●**eyeliner** n eye-liner m. ●**eyepiece** n (of telescope etc) oculaire m. ●**eye shadow** n ombre f or fard m à paupières. ●**eyesight** n vue f. ●**eyesore** n (building etc) horreur f. ●**eyestrain** n **to have e.** avoir les yeux qui tirent. ●**eyewash** n (nonsense) Fam sottises fpl. ●**eyewitness** n témoin m oculaire.

F

F, f [ef] *n* F, f *m*.
fable ['feɪb(ə)l] *n* fable *f*.
fabric ['fæbrɪk] *n* (*cloth*) tissu *m*, étoffe *f*; (*of building*) structure *f*; **the f. of society** le tissu social.
fabricate ['fæbrɪkeɪt] *vt* (*invent, make*) fabriquer. ●**fabrication** [-'keɪʃ(ə)n] *n* fabrication *f*.
fabulous ['fæbjʊləs] *a* (*wonderful*) *Fam* formidable; (*incredible, legendary*) fabuleux.
façade [fə'sɑːd] *n* (*of building & false appearance*) façade *f*.
face [feɪs] *n* (*of person*) visage *m*, figure *f*; (*expression*) mine *f*; (*of clock*) cadran *m*; (*of building*) façade *f*; (*of cube, mountain*) face *f*; (*of cliff*) paroi *f*; **the f. of the earth** la surface de la terre; **she laughed in my f.** elle m'a ri au nez; **to show one's f.** se montrer; **f. down(wards)** (*person*) face contre terre; (*thing*) tourné à l'envers; **f. to f.** face à face; **in the f. of** devant; (*despite*) en dépit de; **to save/lose f.** sauver/perdre la face; **to make** *or* **pull faces** faire des grimaces; **to tell s.o. sth to his f.** dire qch à qn en face; **f. powder** poudre *f*; **f. value** (*of stamp, coin etc*) valeur *f*; **to take sth at f. value** prendre qch au pied de la lettre.
█ *vt* (*danger, enemy, problem etc*) faire face à; (*accept*) accepter; (*look in the face*) regarder (*qn*) bien en face; **to f., be facing** (*be opposite*) être en face de; (*of window, door, room etc*) donner sur (*le jardin, la mer etc*); **faced with** (*prospect, problem*) confronté à, face à; (*defeat*) menacé par; (*bill*) contraint à payer; **he can't f. leaving** il n'a pas le courage de partir.
█ *vi* (*of house*) être orienté (**north**/*etc* au nord/*etc*); (*of person*) (*turn*) se tourner; (*of person, object*) (*be turned*) être tourné (**towards** vers); **to f. up to** (*danger, problem*) faire face à; (*fact*) accepter; **about f.!** *Am Mil* demi-tour!
facecloth ['feɪsklɒθ] *n Br* gant *m* de toilette.
faceless ['feɪsləs] *a* anonyme.
facelift ['feɪslɪft] *n* (*by surgeon*) lifting *m*; (*of building*) ravalement *m*.
facet ['fæsɪt] *n* (*of problem, diamond etc*) facette *f*.
facetious [fə'siːʃəs] *a* (*person*) facétieux; (*remark*) plaisant; **don't be f.!** ne plaisante pas!
facial ['feɪʃ(ə)l] *a* (*expression*) du visage █ *n* soin *m* du visage.
facile [*Br* 'fæsaɪl, *Am* 'fæs(ə)l] *a* facile, superficiel.
facilitate [fə'sɪlɪteɪt] *vt* faciliter.
facility [fə'sɪlɪtɪ] *n* (*ease*) facilité *f*; (*service*

service *m*; (*device*) dispositif *m*; (*in computer*) fonction *f*. ●**facilities** *npl* (*for sports, cooking etc*) équipements *mpl*; (*in harbour, airport etc*) installations *fpl*; (*possibilities*) facilités *fpl*; (*means*) moyens *mpl*, ressources *fpl*; **special f.** (*conditions*) conditions *fpl* spéciales (**for** pour); **credit f.** facilités *fpl* de paiement.
facing ['feɪsɪŋ] *n* (*of dress, jacket etc*) parement *m*.
fact [fækt] *n* fait *m*; **as a matter of f., in f.** en fait; **the facts of life** les choses *fpl* de la vie; **is that a f.?** c'est vrai?; **f. and fiction** le réel et l'imaginaire.
faction ['fækʃ(ə)n] *n* (*group*) faction *f*.
factor ['fæktər] *n* (*element*) facteur *m*.
factory ['fækt(ə)rɪ] *n* (*large*) usine *f*; (*small*) fabrique *f*; **arms/porcelain f.** manufacture *f* d'armes/de porcelaine.
factual ['fæktʃʊəl] *a* objectif, basé sur les faits, factuel; (*error*) de fait.
faculty ['fækəltɪ] *n* (*aptitude, section of university*) faculté *f*.
fad [fæd] *n* (*fashion*) folie *f*, mode *f* (**for** de); (*personal habit*) marotte *f*.
fade [feɪd] *vi* (*of flower*) se faner; (*of light*) baisser; (*of colour*) passer; (*of fabric*) se décolorer; **to f.** (**away**) (*of memory, smile*) s'effacer; (*of sound*) s'affaiblir; (*of person*) dépérir █ *vt* (*fabric*) décolorer.
fag [fæg] *n* **1** (*cigarette*) *Br Fam* clope *m* or *f*; **f. end** mégot *m*. **2** (*male homosexual*) *Am Sl Pej* pédé *m*.
fagged [fægd] *a* **f.** (**out**) (*tired*) *Br Sl* claqué.
faggot ['fægət] *n* **1** (*meatball*) *Br* boulette *f* (de viande). **2** (*male homosexual*) *Am Sl Pej* pédé *m*.
fail [feɪl] *vi* (*of person, plan etc*) échouer; (*of business*) faire faillite; (*of health, sight, light*) baisser; (*of memory, strength*) défaillir; (*of car brakes*) lâcher; (*run short*) (*of supplies*) manquer; (*of gas, electricity*) être coupé; (*of engine*) tomber en panne; **to f. in an exam** échouer à un examen; **to f. in one's duty** manquer à son devoir.
█ *vt* (*exam*) rater, échouer à; (*candidate*) refuser, recaler; **to f. s.o.** (*let down*) laisser tomber qn, décevoir qn; **words f. me** les mots me manquent; **to f. to do** (*forget*) manquer de faire; (*not be able*) ne pas arriver à faire; **I f. to see the reason** je ne vois pas la raison.
█ *n* **without f.** à coup sûr, sans faute. ●**failed** *a* (*attempt, poet*) manqué. ●**failing** *n* (*fault*) défaut *m* █ *prep* à défaut de; **f. this, f. that** à défaut.

failure ['feɪljər] n échec m; (of business) faillite f; (of engine, machine) panne f; (of gas etc) coupure f, panne f; (person) raté, -ée mf; **f. to do** (inability) incapacité f de faire; **her f. to leave** le fait qu'elle n'est pas partie; **to end in f.** se solder par un échec; **heart f.** arrêt m du cœur.

faint [feɪnt] 1 a (-er, -est) (weak) (voice, trace, breeze, hope etc) faible; (colour) pâle; (idea) vague; **I haven't got the faintest idea** je n'en ai pas la moindre idée. 2 a **to feel f.** se trouver mal, défaillir; **f. with hunger/etc** défaillant de faim/etc ▮ vi s'évanouir (with fear/from fatigue/etc de peur/fatigue/etc); **she fainted with hunger** elle s'est trouvée mal tellement elle a eu faim; **fainting fit** évanouissement m. ●**faintly** adv (weakly) faiblement; (slightly) légèrement. ●**faintness** n (of voice etc) faiblesse f.

faint-hearted [feɪnt'hɑːtɪd] a timoré, timide.

fair[1] [feər] n foire f; (for charity) fête f; (funfair) Br fête f foraine; (larger) parc m d'attractions. ●**fairground** n champ m de foire.

fair[2] [feər] 1 a (-er, -est) (just) juste, équitable; (game, fight) loyal; **she's f. to him** elle est juste envers lui; **that's f. to him** c'est juste pour lui; **f. (and square)** honnête(ment); **f. play** fair-play m inv; **that's not f. play!** ce n'est pas du jeu!; **f. enough!** très bien! ▮ adv (to play, fight) loyalement. 2 a (rather good) passable, assez bon; (price, amount, warning) raisonnable; **a f. amount (of)** (a lot) pas mal (de); **f. copy** copie f au propre. 3 a (wind) favorable; (weather) beau. ●**fairly** adv 1 (to treat) équitablement; (to act, play, fight, get) loyalement. 2 (rather) assez, plutôt; **f. sure** presque sûr. ●**fairness**[1] n justice f; (of person) impartialité f; (of decision) équité f; **in all f.** en toute justice. ●**fair-'minded** a impartial. ●**fair-'sized** a assez grand.

fair[3] [feər] a (hair, person) blond; (complexion, skin) clair. ●**fairness**[2] n (of hair) blond m; (of skin) blancheur f. ●**fair-'haired** a blond. ●**fair-'skinned** a à la peau claire.

fairy ['feərɪ] n fée f; **f. tale** or **story** conte m de fées; **f. lights** Br guirlande f multicolore.

faith [feɪθ] n foi f; **to have f. in s.o.** avoir confiance en qn; **to put one's f. in** (justice, medicine etc) se fier à; **in good/bad f.** (to act etc) de bonne/mauvaise foi; **f. healer** guérisseur, -euse mf.

faithful ['feɪθfəl] a fidèle. ●**faithfully** adv fidèlement; **yours f.** (in letter) Br veuillez agréer l'expression de mes salutations distinguées. ●**faithfulness** n fidélité f.

faithless ['feɪθləs] a déloyal, infidèle.

fake [feɪk] n (painting, document etc) faux m; (person) imposteur m ▮ vt (document, signature etc) falsifier, maquiller; (election) truquer; **to f. death** faire semblant d'être mort ▮ vi (pretend) faire semblant ▮ a faux (f fausse); (elections) truqué.

falcon ['fɔːlkən] n faucon m.

fall [fɔːl] n chute f; (in price, demand etc) baisse f; **falls** (waterfall) chutes fpl (d'eau); **the f.** (season) Am l'automne m.

▮ vi (pt fell, pp fallen) tomber; (of price, temperature etc) baisser, tomber; **the dollar is falling** le dollar est en baisse; (of building) s'effondrer; **her face fell** son visage se rembrunit; **to f. into** (hole, trap etc) tomber dans; (habit) prendre; **to f. off a bicycle/etc** tomber d'une bicyclette/etc; **to f. off or down a ladder** tomber (en bas) d'une échelle; **the onus falls on you** la responsabilité vous incombe; **to f. on a Monday/etc** (of event) tomber un lundi/etc; **to f. out of a window/etc** tomber d'une fenêtre/etc; **to f. over sth** (chair etc) tomber en butant contre qch; (balcony etc) tomber de qch; **to f. short of s.o.'s expectations** ne pas répondre à l'attente de qn; **to f. short of being** être loin d'être; **to f. victim** devenir victime (to de); **to f. asleep** s'endormir; **to f. ill** tomber malade; **to f. due** échoir.

fall apart vi (of machine) tomber en morceaux; (of group) se désagréger ▮ **to fall away** vi (come off) se détacher, tomber; (of numbers) diminuer ▮ **to fall back on** vt (as last resort) se rabattre sur ▮ **to fall behind** vi (stay behind) rester en arrière; (in work, payments) prendre du retard ▮ **to fall down** vi tomber; (of building) s'effondrer ▮ **to fall for** vt (person) tomber amoureux de; (trick) se laisser prendre à ▮ **to fall in** vi (collapse) s'écrouler ▮ **to fall in with** vt (tally with) cadrer avec; (agree to) accepter ▮ **to fall off** vi (come off) se détacher, tomber; (of numbers) diminuer ▮ **to fall out** vi (quarrel) se brouiller (with avec) ▮ **to fall over** vi tomber; (of table, vase) se renverser ▮ **to fall through** vi (of plan) tomber à l'eau, échouer.

fallacious [fə'leɪʃəs] a faux (f fausse). ●**fallacy** ['fæləsɪ] n erreur f; (in argument) faux raisonnement m.

fallen ['fɔːlən] a tombé; (angel, woman) déchu; **f. leaf** feuille f morte.

fallible ['fæləb(ə)l] a faillible.

falling-off [fɔːlɪŋ'ɒf] n (of interest etc) diminution f.

fallout ['fɔːlaʊt] n (radioactive) retombées fpl; **f. shelter** abri m antiatomique.

fallow ['fæləʊ] a (land, fields) en jachère.

false [fɔːls] a faux (f fausse); **f. teeth** fausses dents fpl; **a f. bottom** un double fond. ●**falsehood** n mensonge m; **truth and f.** le vrai et le faux. ●**falseness** n fausseté f.

falsify ['fɔːlsɪfaɪ] vt falsifier.

falter ['fɔːltər] vi (of step, resolution) chanceler; (of voice, speaker) hésiter; (of courage) vaciller.

fame [feɪm] n renommée f; (glory) gloire f. ●**famed** a renommé.

familiar [fə'mɪljər] a (task, person, face, atmosphere, word etc) familier; (event) habituel; **to be f. with s.o.** (too friendly) être familier avec qn; **to be f. with s.o./sth** (know) connaître qn/qch; **I'm f. with her voice** je connais bien sa voix, sa voix m'est familière; **to make oneself f. with** se familiariser avec; **he looks f. (to me)** je l'ai déjà vu (quelque part).

familiarity [fəmɪlɪ'ærətɪ] n familiarité f (**with** avec); (of event, sight etc) caractère m familier.

familiarize [fə'mɪljəraɪz] vt familiariser (**with** avec); **to f. oneself with** se familiariser avec.

family ['fæmɪlɪ] n famille f ▪ a (name, doctor, jewels etc) de famille; (planning, problems) familial; **f. friend** ami m de la famille; **f. man** père m de famille; **f. tree** arbre m généalogique.

famine ['fæmɪn] n famine f.

famished ['fæmɪʃt] a affamé.

famous ['feɪməs] a célèbre (**for** pour, par) ▪ n the f. les célébrités fpl. ●**famously** adv (very well) Fam rudement bien.

fan¹ [fæn] n (held in hand) éventail m; (mechanical) ventilateur m; **f. belt** (of vehicle) courroie f de ventilateur; **f. heater** radiateur m soufflant ▪ vt (-nn-) (person etc) éventer; (fire, quarrel) attiser ▪ vi **to f. out** se déployer (en éventail).

fan² [fæn] n (of person) fan mf, admirateur, -trice mf; (of sportsman, team etc) supporter m; **to be a jazz/sports f.** être passionné or mordu de jazz/de sport; **f. mail** courrier m des admirateurs.

fanatic [fə'nætɪk] n fanatique mf. ●**fanatical** a fanatique. ●**fanaticism** n fanatisme m.

fancier ['fænsɪər] n horse/etc f. amateur m de chevaux/etc.

fanciful ['fænsɪfəl] a fantaisiste.

fancy ['fænsɪ] 1 n (whim, imagination) fantaisie f; (liking) goût m; **to take a f. to s.o.** se prendre d'affection pour qn; **I took a f. to it, it took my f.** j'en ai eu envie; **when the f. takes me** quand ça me chante.
▪ a (hat, button etc) fantaisie inv; (car) de luxe; (house, restaurant) chic; (idea) fantaisiste; (price) exorbitant; **f. dress** (costume) Br travesti m; **f.-dress ball** Br bal m masqué. 2 vt (want) Br avoir envie de; (like) Br aimer; **to f. that** (imagine) se figurer que; (think) croire que; **f. that!** tiens (donc)!; **he fancies her** Dr Fam elle lui plaît; **to f. oneself as** Br Fam se prendre pour; **she fancies herself!** Br Fam elle se prend pour qn!

fanfare ['fænfeər] n (of trumpets) fanfare f.

fang [fæŋ] n (of dog, wolf etc) croc m; (of snake) crochet m.

fanny ['fænɪ] n (buttocks) Am Fam derrière m; **f. pack** banane f.

fantastic [fæn'tæstɪk] a fantastique; **a f. idea** (absurd, unlikely) une idée aberrante.

fantasy ['fæntəsɪ] n (imagination) fantaisie f; (dream) rêve m; (fanciful, sexual) fantasme m. ●**fantasize** vi (dream) rêver (**about** de); (fancifully, sexually) fantasmer (**about** sur).

far [fɑːr] adv (farther or further, farthest or furthest) (distance) loin; **f. bigger/more expensive/etc** (much) beaucoup plus grand/

plus cher/etc (**than** que); **f. more/better** beaucoup plus/mieux; **f. advanced** très avancé; **how f. is it to...?** combien y a-t-il d'ici à...?; **is it f. to...?** sommes-nous, suis-je etc loin de...?; **how f. are you going?** jusqu'où vas-tu?; **how f. has he got with?** (his plans, work etc) où en est-il de?; **so f.** (time) jusqu'ici; (place) jusque-là; **as f.** (place) jusqu'à; **as f. or so f. as I know** autant que je sache; **as f. or so f. as I'm concerned** en ce qui me concerne; **as f. back as 1820** dès 1820; **f. from doing** loin de faire; **f. from it!** loin de là!; **f. away or off** au loin; **to be f. away** être loin (**from** de); **f. and wide** partout; **by f.** de loin; **f. into the night** très avant dans la nuit.
▪ a (other) the f. side/end l'autre côté/bout; **it's a f. cry from** on est loin de; **the F. East** l'Extrême-Orient.

faraway [fɑːrə'weɪ] a (country) lointain; (look) distrait, dans le vague. ●**far-'fetched** a forcé, exagéré. ●**far-'flung** a (widespread) vaste. ●**far-'off** a lointain. ●**far-'reaching** a de grande portée. ●**far-'sighted** a clairvoyant.

farce [fɑːs] n farce f. ●**farcical** a grotesque, ridicule.

fare [feər] 1 n (price of journey) (in train, bus etc) prix m du billet; (in taxi) prix m de la course; (taxi passenger) client, -ente mf. 2 n (food) chère f, nourriture f; **prison f.** régime m de prison; **bill of f.** menu m. 3 vi (manage) se débrouiller; **how did she f.?** comment ça s'est passé (pour elle)?

farewell [feə'wel] n & int adieu (m) ▪ a (party, speech etc) d'adieu.

farm [fɑːm] n ferme f; **to work on a f.** travailler dans une ferme ▪ a (worker, produce etc) agricole; **f. land** terres fpl cultivées ▪ vt cultiver ▪ vi être agriculteur. ●**farming** n agriculture f; (breeding) élevage m; **dairy f.** industrie f laitière. ●**farmer** n fermier, -ière mf, agriculteur m.

farmhand ['fɑːmhænd] n ouvrier, -ière mf agricole. ●**farmhouse** n ferme f. ●**farm worker** n = farmhand. ●**farmyard** n basse-cour f.

fart [fɑːt] vi Vulgar Sl péter.

farther ['fɑːðər] adv plus loin; **nothing is f. from** (my mind, the truth etc) rien n'est plus éloigné de; **f. forward** plus avancé; **to get f. away** s'éloigner ▪ a **at the f. end of** à l'autre bout de. ●**farthest** a le plus éloigné ▪ adv le plus loin.

fascinate ['fæsɪneɪt] vt fasciner. ●**fascination** [fæsɪ'neɪ(ə)n] n fascination f.

fascism ['fæʃɪz(ə)m] n fascisme m. ●**fascist** a & n fasciste (mf).

fashion ['fæʃ(ə)n] 1 n (style in clothes etc) mode f; **in f.** à la mode; **out of f.** démodé; **f. designer** (grand) couturier m; **f. house** maison f de couture; **f. show** présentation f de collections. 2 n (manner) façon f; (custom) habitude f; **after a f.** tant bien que mal, plus au moins. 3 vt (make) façonner. ●**fashionable** a à la mode; (place) chic inv; **it's f. to**

do that il est de bon ton de faire cela.
● **fashionably** adv (dressed etc) à la mode.

fast¹ [fɑːst] 1 a (-er, -est) rapide; **to be f.** (of clock) avancer (**by** de); **f. colour** couleur f grand teint inv; **f. food** restauration f rapide; **f. food restaurant** fast-food m; **f. living** vie f dissolue ‖ adv (quickly) vite; **how f.?** à quelle vitesse? 2 adv **f. asleep** profondément endormi. 3 adv (firmly) **stuck f.** (drawer etc) bien coincé; (in mind) bien pris; **to hold f.** (of person) tenir ferme.

fast² [fɑːst] vi (go without food) jeûner ‖ n jeûne m.

fasten ['fɑːs(ə)n] vt attacher (**to** à); (door, window) fermer (bien); **to f. sth down** or **up** attacher qch ‖ vi (of dress etc) s'attacher; (of door, window) se fermer. ●**fastener** or **fastening** n (clip) attache f; (of garment) fermeture f; (of bag) fermoir m; (hook) agrafe f.

fastidious [fæ'stɪdɪəs] a difficile (à contenter), exigeant.

fat [fæt] 1 n graisse f; (on meat) gras m; **vegetable f.** huile f végétale. 2 a (fatter, fattest) gras (f grasse); (cheeks, salary, book) gros (f grosse); **to get f.** grossir; **that's a f. lot of good** or **use!** Iron Fam ça va vraiment servir (à quelque chose!) ●**fathead** n imbécile mf.

fatal ['feɪt(ə)l] a mortel; (mistake, blow etc) Fig fatal. ●**fatally** adv **f. wounded** mortellement blessé.

fatality [fə'tælɪtɪ] n 1 (person killed) victime f. 2 (of event) fatalité f.

fate [feɪt] n destin m, sort m; **one's f.** son sort. ●**fated** a **to be f. to do** être destiné à faire; **our meeting/his death/etc was f.** notre rencontre/sa mort/etc devait arriver. ●**fateful** a (important) fatal, décisif; (prophetic) fatidique; (disastrous) néfaste.

father ['fɑːðər] n père m; **F. Martin** (in monastic order, priest) le Père Martin; **yes, F.** (to priest) oui, mon père ‖ vt (child) engendrer. ●**father-in-law** n (pl fathers-in-law) beau-père m.

fatherhood ['fɑːðəhʊd] n paternité f.

fatherland ['fɑːðəlænd] n patrie f.

fatherly ['fɑːðəlɪ] a paternel.

fathom ['fæðəm] 1 n (nautical measurement) brasse f (= 1,8 m). 2 vt **to f. (out)** (understand) comprendre.

fatigue [fə'tiːg] 1 n fatigue f ‖ vt fatiguer. 2 n **f.** (duty) (of soldier) corvée f.

fatness ['fætnɪs] n corpulence f.

fatten ['fæt(ə)n] vt engraisser. ●**fattening** a (food) qui fait grossir.

fatty ['fætɪ] a (-ier, -iest) (food) gras (f grasse); **f. tissue** (in body) tissu m adipeux ‖ n (person) Fam gros lard m.

fatuous ['fætjʊəs] a stupide.

faucet ['fɔːsɪt] n (tap) Am robinet m.

fault [fɔːlt] n (blame) faute f; (defect, failing) défaut m; (mistake) erreur f; Geol faille f; **to find f.** (with) critiquer; **it's your f.** c'est ta faute; **he's at f.** il est fautif, c'est sa faute; **his** or **her memory is at f.** sa mémoire lui fait

défaut ‖ vt **to f. s.o./sth** trouver des défauts chez qn/à qch. ●**fault-finding** a critique, chicanier.

faultless ['fɔːltləs] a irréprochable.

faulty ['fɔːltɪ] a (-ier, -iest) défectueux.

fauna ['fɔːnə] n (animals) faune f.

faux pas [fəʊ'pɑː] n inv gaffe f.

favour ['feɪvər] (Am favor) n (act of kindness) service m; (approval) faveur f; **to do s.o. a f.** rendre service à qn; **in f.** (fashion) en vogue; **in f. (with s.o.)** bien vu (de qn); **it's in her f. to do that** elle a intérêt à faire cela; **in f. of** (for the sake of) au profit de, en faveur de; **to be in f. of** (support) être pour, être partisan de; (prefer) préférer. ‖ vt (encourage) favoriser; (prefer) préférer; (support) être partisan de; **he favoured me with a visit** il a eu la gentillesse de me rendre visite. ●**favourable** a favorable (**to** à).

favourite ['feɪv(ə)rɪt] (Am favorite) a favori, préféré ‖ n favori, -ite mf. ●**favouritism** n favoritisme m.

fawn [fɔːn] 1 n (deer) faon m ‖ a & n (colour) fauve (m). 2 vi **to f. (up)on** flatter bassement.

fax [fæks] n (message) télécopie f, fax m; (machine) télécopieur m, fax m; **f. number** numéro m de fax or de télécopie ‖ vt (message) faxer; **to f. s.o.** envoyer une télécopie or un fax à qn.

fear [fɪər] n crainte f, peur f; **for f. of doing** de peur de faire; **for f. that** de peur que (+ ne + sub); **there's no f. of his going** il ne risque pas d'y aller; **there are fears (that) he might leave** on craint qu'il ne parte ‖ vt craindre; **I f. (that) he might leave** je crains qu'il ne parte; **to f. for one's life/career/etc** craindre pour sa vie/carrière/etc.

fearful ['fɪəfəl] a (timid) (person) peureux; (frightful, awful) (noise etc) affreux. ●**fearless** a intrépide. ●**fearlessness** n intrépidité f. ●**fearsome** a redoutable.

feasible ['fiːzəb(ə)l] a (practicable) faisable; (theory, explanation etc) plausible. ●**feasi'bility** n possibilité f (of doing de faire); (of theory etc) plausibilité f; **f. study** étude f de faisabilité.

feast [fiːst] n festin m, banquet m; (religious) fête f ‖ vi banqueter; **to f. on cakes/etc** se régaler de gâteaux/etc.

feat [fiːt] n exploit m, tour m de force; **f. of skill** tour m d'adresse.

feather ['feðər] 1 n plume f; **f. duster** plumeau m. 2 vt **to f. one's nest** (enrich oneself) faire son beurre or sa pelote.

feature ['fiːtʃər] 1 n (of face, person) trait m; (of thing, place, machine) caractéristique f; **f. (article)** article m de fond; **f. (film)** grand film m; **to be a regular f.** (in newspaper) paraître régulièrement. 2 vt (of newspaper, book, film etc) (present) présenter; (portray) représenter; (news item) mettre en avant; **a film featuring Chaplin** un film avec Charlot en vedette ‖ vi (appear) figurer (**in** dans).

February ['februərɪ] n février m.

fed [fed] *pt & pp of* feed ▌ *a* to be f. up *Fam* en avoir marre *or* ras le bol (with de).

federal ['fedərəl] *a* fédéral. ●**federate** *vt* fédérer. ●**federation** [-'reɪʃ(ə)n] *n* fédération *f.*

fedora [fə'dɔːrə] *n Am* chapeau *m* mou.

fee [fiː] *n* (*price*) prix *m*; **fee(s)** (*professional*) (*of doctor, lawyer etc*) honoraires *mpl*; (*of artist*) cachet *m*; (*for registration, examination*) droits *mpl*; **to charge a f. (for a job)** se faire payer (pour un travail); **for a small f.** pour une petite somme; **school** *or* **tuition fees** frais *mpl* de scolarité; **entrance f.** prix *m or* droit *m* d'entrée; **membership fee(s)** cotisation *f*; **f.-paying school** école *f* privée.

feeble ['fiːb(ə)l] *a* (**-er, -est**) faible; (*excuse, smile*) pauvre; (*joke, attempt*) pitoyable. ●**feeble-'minded** *a* imbécile.

feed [fiːd] *n* (*food for animal*) aliments *mpl*; (*baby's breast feed*) tétée *f*; (*baby's bottle feed*) biberon *m.*
▌ *vt* (*pt & pp* fed) donner à manger à, nourrir; (*breastfeed*) allaiter (*un bébé*); (*bottlefeed*) donner le biberon à (*un bébé*); (*machine*) *Fig* alimenter; **to f. s.o.** faire manger qch à qn; **to f. sth into** (*machine*) introduire qch dans; (*computer*) entrer qch dans.
▌ *vi* (*eat*) manger; **to f. on sth** se nourrir de qch. ●**feeding** *n* alimentation *f.*

feedback ['fiːdbæk] *n* réaction(s) *f(pl).*

feel [fiːl] *n* (*touch*) toucher *m*; (*feeling*) sensation *f.*
▌ *vt* (*pt & pp* felt) (*be aware of*) sentir; (*experience*) éprouver, ressentir; (*touch*) tâter, palper; **to f. that** (*think*) avoir l'impression que; **to f. one's way** avancer à tâtons.
▌ *vi* **to f. (about)** (*grope*) tâtonner; (*in pocket etc*) fouiller (**for sth** pour trouver qch); **it feels hard** c'est dur (au toucher); **to f. tired/old/ill/***etc* se sentir fatigué/vieux/malade/*etc*; **I f. hot/sleepy/hungry/***etc* j'ai chaud/sommeil/faim/*etc*; **she feels better** elle va mieux; **he doesn't f. well** il ne se sent pas bien; **to f. like sth** (*want*) avoir envie de qch; **it feels like cotton** on dirait du coton; **to f. as if** avoir l'impression que; **what do you f. about...?** que pensez-vous de...?; **I f. bad about it** ça m'ennuie, ça me fait de la peine; **what does it f. like?** quelle impression ça fait?; **to f. for s.o.** (*pity*) éprouver de la pitié pour qn; **to f. up to doing** être (assez) en forme pour faire.

feeler ['fiːlər] *n* (*of snail etc*) antenne *f*; **to put out a f.** *or* **feelers** *Fig* lancer un ballon d'essai.

feeling ['fiːlɪŋ] *n* (*emotion, impression*) sentiment *m*; (*physical*) sensation *f*; **a f. for** (*person*) de la sympathie pour; (*music, painting etc*) une appréciation de; **bad f.** animosité *f.*

feet [fiːt] *see* foot¹.

feign [feɪn] *vt* feindre, simuler.

feint [feɪnt] *n Boxing etc* feinte *f.*

feisty ['faɪstɪ] *a* (**-ier, -iest**) (*lively*) *Am Fam*

felicitous [fə'lɪsɪtəs] *a* heureux.

feline ['fiːlaɪn] *a* félin.

fell [fel] **1** *pt of* fall. **2** *vt* (*tree, giant etc*) abattre.

fellow ['feləʊ] *n* **1** (*man, boy*) type *m*, gars *m*; **an old f.** un vieux; **poor f.!** pauvre malheureux! **2** (*companion*) **f. being** semblable *m*; **f. countryman, f. countrywoman** compatriote *mf*; **f. passenger/worker/***etc* compagnon *m* de voyage/travail/*etc*, compagne *f* de voyage/travail/*etc*. **3** (*of society*) membre *m.*

fellowship ['feləʊʃɪp] *n* (*feeling*) camaraderie *f*; (*group*) association *f*; (*membership*) qualité *f* de membre; (*scholarship*) bourse *f* universitaire.

felony ['felənɪ] *n* crime *m.*

felt¹ [felt] *pt & pp of* feel.

felt² [felt] *n* feutre *m.* ●**felt-tip (pen)** *n* crayon *m* feutre.

female ['fiːmeɪl] *a* (*name, voice, quality etc*) féminin; (*animal*) femelle; **the f. vote** le vote des femmes; **f. student** étudiante *f* ▌ *n* (*woman*) femme *f*; (*girl*) fille *f*; (*animal*) femelle *f.*

feminine ['femɪnɪn] *a* féminin ▌ *n Grammar* féminin *m.* ●**femi'ninity** *n* féminité *f.* ●**feminist** *a & n* féministe (*mf*).

fence [fens] **1** *n* barrière *f*, clôture *f*; (*in race*) obstacle *m* ▌ *vt* **to f. (in)** (*land*) clôturer. **2** *vi* (*with sword*) faire de l'escrime. **3** *n* (*criminal*) *Fam* receleur, -euse *mf*. ●**fencing** *n Sport* escrime *f.*

fend [fend] **1** *vi* **to f. for oneself** se débrouiller. **2** *vt* **to f. off** (*blow etc*) parer.

fender ['fendər] *n* **1** (*of car*) *Am* aile *f.* **2** (*for fire*) garde-feu *m inv.*

fennel ['fen(ə)l] *n* (*plant, herb*) fenouil *m.*

ferment ['fɜːment] *n* (*substance*) ferment *m*; (*excitement*) *Fig* effervescence *f* ▌ [fə'ment] *vi* fermenter. ●**fermentation** [-'teɪʃ(ə)n] *n* fermentation *f.*

fern [fɜːn] *n* fougère *f.*

ferocious [fə'rəʊʃəs] *a* féroce. ●**ferocity** [fə'rɒsɪtɪ] *n* férocité *f.*

ferret ['ferɪt] *n* (*animal*) furet *m* ▌ *vi* **to f. about** (*pry*) fureter ▌ *vt* **to f. out** (*person, information*) dénicher.

Ferris wheel ['ferɪswiːl] *n* (*in fairground*) grande roue *f.*

ferry ['ferɪ] *n* ferry-boat *m*; (*small, for river*) bac *m* ▌ *vt* transporter.

fertile [*Br* 'fɜːtaɪl, *Am* 'fɜːt(ə)l] *a* (*land, imagination*) fertile; (*person, animal*) fécond. ●**fer'tility** *n* fertilité *f*; **f. drug** médicament *m* de traitement de la stérilité.

fertilize ['fɜːtəlaɪz] *vt* (*land*) fertiliser; (*egg, animal etc*) féconder. ●**fertilizer** *n* engrais *m.*

fervent ['fɜːv(ə)nt] *a* fervent. ●**fervour** (*Am* **fervor**) *n* ferveur *f.*

fester ['festər] *vi* (*of wound*) suppurer; (*of anger etc*) *Fig* couver.

festival ['festɪv(ə)l] *n* (*of music, film etc*) festival *m* (*pl* -als); (*religious*) fête *f.*

festive ['festɪv] *a* (*atmosphere, clothes*) de

fête; (*mood*) joyeux; **the f. season** la période des fêtes. ● **fe'stivities** *npl* festivités *fpl*, réjouissances *fpl*.

festoon [fe'stu:n] *vt* **to f. with** orner de.

fetch [fetʃ] *vt* **1** (*bring*) amener (*qn*); (*object*) apporter; **to (go and) f.** aller chercher; **to f. sth in** rentrer qch; **to f. sth out** sortir qch. **2** (*be sold for*) rapporter (**ten pounds/***etc* dix livres/*etc*); **it fetched a high price** cela a atteint un prix élevé. ● **fetching** *a* (*smile etc*) charmant, séduisant.

fête [feɪt] *n Br* fête *f* ▮ *vt* (*person etc*) fêter.

fetid ['fetɪd] *a* fétide.

fetish ['fetɪʃ] *n* (*obsession*) manie *f*, obsession *f*; **to make a f. of sth** être obsédé par qch.

fetter ['fetər] *vt* (*hinder*) entraver.

fettle ['fet(ə)l] *n* **in fine f.** en pleine forme.

fetus ['fi:təs] *n Am* fœtus *m*.

feud [fju:d] *n* querelle *f*, dissension *f*.

feudal ['fju:d(ə)l] *a* féodal.

fever ['fi:vər] *n* fièvre *f*; **to have a f.** (*temperature*) avoir de la fièvre; **a high f.** une forte *or* grosse fièvre. ● **feverish** *a* (*person, activity*) fiévreux.

few [fju:] *a & pron* peu (de); **f. towns/***etc* peu de villes/*etc*; **a f. towns/***etc* quelques villes/*etc*; **f. of them** peu d'entre eux; **a f.** quelques-un(e)s (of de); **a f. of us** quelques-uns d'entre nous; **one of the f. books** l'un des rares livres; **quite a f., a good f.** bon nombre (de); **a f. more books/***etc* encore quelques livres/*etc*; **f. and far between** rares (et espacés); **f. came** peu sont venus; **the examples are f.** les exemples sont peu nombreux; **every f. days** tous les trois ou quatre jours.

fewer ['fju:ər] *a & pron* moins (de) (**than** que); **f. houses/***etc* moins de maisons/*etc* (**than** que); **to be f.** être moins nombreux (**than** que); **no f. than** pas moins de. ● **fewest** ['fju:ɪst] *a & pron* le moins (de).

fiancé(e) [fɪ'ɒnseɪ] *n* fiancé, -ée *mf*.

fiasco [fɪ'æskəʊ] *n* (*pl* -os, *Am* -oes) fiasco *m*.

fib [fɪb] *n Fam* blague *f*, bobard *m* ▮ *vi* (-bb-) *Fam* raconter des blagues. ● **fibber** *n Fam* blagueur, -euse *mf*.

fibre ['faɪbər] (*Am* **fiber**) *n* fibre *f*; (*in diet*) fibre(s) *f(pl)*; **high-f. diet** alimentation *f* riche en fibres. ● **fibreglass** *n* fibre *f* de verre.

fickle ['fɪk(ə)l] *a* inconstant.

fiction ['fɪkʃ(ə)n] *n* (*imagination*) fiction *f*; (**works of**) **f.** romans *mpl*; **that's pure f.** ce sont des histoires. ● **fictional** *a* (*character etc*) fictif.

fictitious [fɪk'tɪʃəs] *a* (*false, imaginary*) fictif.

fiddle ['fɪd(ə)l] **1** *n* (*violin*) *Fam* violon *m* ▮ *vi Fam* jouer du violon.

2 *vi* **to f. about** (*waste time*) traînailler, perdre son temps; **to f. (about) with** (*watch, pen etc*) tripoter; (*cars etc*) bricoler.

3 *n* (*dishonest act*) *Br Fam* combine *f*, magouille *f*, fraude *f* ▮ *vi* (*swindle*) *Br Fam* magouiller ▮ *vt* (*accounts etc*) *Br Fam* falsifier.

● **fiddler** *n* **1** (*violin player*) *Fam* joueur, -euse *mf* de violon. **2** (*swindler*) *Br Fam* combinard, -arde *mf*.

fiddling ['fɪdlɪŋ] *a* (*petty*) insignifiant.

fiddly ['fɪdlɪ] *a* (-ier, -iest) (*task*) délicat.

fidelity [fɪ'delɪtɪ] *n* fidélité *f* (**to** à).

fidget ['fɪdʒɪt] *vi* **to f. (about)** gigoter, se trémousser; **to f. (about) with** tripoter ▮ *n* personne *f* qui ne tient pas en place. ● **fidgety** *a* agité, remuant.

field [fi:ld] *n* champ *m*; (*for sports*) terrain *m*; (*sphere*) domaine *m*; **to have a f. day** (*a good day*) s'en donner à cœur joie; **f. glasses** jumelles *fpl*; **f. marshal** maréchal *m*.

fiend [fi:nd] *n* démon *m*; **a jazz/***etc* **f.** *Fam* un(e) fana de jazz/*etc*; (**sex**) **f.** *Fam* satyre *m*; **fresh-air f.** maniaque *mf* du grand air. ● **fiendish** *a* (*cruel*) diabolique; (*difficult, awful*) abominable.

fierce [fɪəs] *a* (-er, -est) (*animal, warrior, tone etc*) féroce; (*attack, wind*) furieux. ● **fierceness** *n* férocité *f*; (*of attack etc*) fureur *f*.

fiery ['faɪərɪ] *a* (-ier, -iest) (*person, speech*) fougueux; (*sun, eyes*) ardent.

fiesta [fɪ'estə] *n* fiesta *f*.

fifteen [fɪf'ti:n] *a & n* quinze (*m*). ● **fifteenth** *a & n* quinzième (*mf*).

fifth [fɪfθ] *a & n* cinquième (*mf*); **a f.** un cinquième.

fifty ['fɪftɪ] *a & n* cinquante (*m*); **a f.-fifty chance** une chance sur deux; **to split the profits f.-fifty** partager les bénéfices moitié-moitié. ● **fiftieth** *a & n* cinquantième (*mf*).

fig [fɪg] *n* figue *f*; **f. tree** figuier *m*.

fight [faɪt] *n* (*brawl between people*) bagarre *f*; (*between boxers, soldiers etc*) combat *m*; (*struggle*) lutte *f* (*against* contre); (*quarrel*) dispute *f*; **to put up a (good) f.** bien se défendre.

▮ *vi* (*pt & pp* **fought**) se battre (**against** contre); (*of soldiers*) se battre, combattre; (*struggle*) lutter; (*quarrel*) se disputer; **to f. back** (*in self-defence*) se défendre; **to f. over sth** se disputer qch; **to f. against an illness/for a cause** lutter contre une maladie/pour une cause.

▮ *vt* se battre avec (*qn*); (*evil*) lutter contre, combattre; **to f. a battle** livrer bataille; **to f. an election** (*of candidate for parliament*) se présenter à une élection; **to f. back** (*tears*) refouler; **to f. off** (*attacker, attack*) repousser; (*illness*) lutter contre; **to f. it out** se bagarrer.

fighter ['faɪtər] *n* (*determined person*) battant, -ante *mf*; (*in brawl, battle*) combattant, -ante *mf*; (*boxer*) boxeur *m*; (*aircraft*) chasseur *m*.

fighting ['faɪtɪŋ] *n* (*between soldiers*) combat(s) *m(pl)*; (*brawling*) bagarres *fpl*; **f. spirit** combativité *f*; **f. troops** troupes *fpl* de combat.

figment ['fɪgmənt] *n* **a f. of one's imagination** une création de son esprit.

figurative ['fɪgjʊrətɪv] *a* (*meaning*) figuré;

(*art*) figuratif. ● **figuratively** *adv* au figuré.

figure¹ [*Br* 'figər, *Am* 'figjər] *n* **1** (*numeral*) chiffre *m*; (*price*) prix *m*; **figures** (*arithmetic*) calcul *m*.

2 (*shape*) forme *f*; (*outline*) silhouette *f*; (*of woman*) ligne *f*; **she has a nice f.** elle est bien faite.

3 (*diagram*) figure *f*; **f. of eight** *Br*, **f. eight** *Am* huit *m*; **f. skating** patinage *m* artistique.

4 (*expression, word*) **a f. of speech** (*figurative usage*) une façon de parler; (*in literature*) une figure de rhétorique.

5 (*important person*) figure *f*, personnage *m*.

figure² [*Br* 'figər, *Am* 'figjər] **1** *vt* **to f. that** (*guess*) penser que; (*imagine*) (s')imaginer que; **to f. out** (*person, motive*) arriver à comprendre; (*problem*) résoudre; (*answer*) trouver; (*price*) calculer; (*plan*) élaborer ● *vi* **that figures** (*makes sense*) ça s'explique; **to f. on doing** compter faire.

2 *vi* (*appear*) figurer (**on** sur).

figurehead ['figəhed] *n* (*of organization*) potiche *f*; (*of ship*) figure *f* de proue.

filament ['filəmənt] *n* filament *m*.

filch [filtʃ] *vt* (*steal*) voler (**from** s.o. à qn).

file [fail] **1** *n* (*tool*) lime *f* ● *vt* **to f. (down)** limer.

2 *n* (*folder, information*) dossier *m* (**on** sur); (*loose-leaf*) classeur *m*; (*for card index, computer data*) fichier *m*; **to be on f.** figurer au dossier ● *vt* (*complaint, claim, application etc*) déposer; **to f. (away)** (*document*) classer.

3 *n* **in single f.** en file ● *vi* **to f. in/out** entrer/sortir à la queue leu leu; **to f. past** (*general, coffin etc*) défiler devant. ● **filing** *a* **f. clerk** documentaliste *mf*; **f. cabinet** classeur *m* (*meuble*). ● **filings** *npl* (*particles*) limaille *f*.

Filipino [filɪˈpiːnəʊ] *n* (*pl* **-os**) Philippin, -ine *mf*.

fill [fil] *vt* remplir (**with** de); (*tooth*) plomber; **to f. a need** répondre à un besoin; **to f. in** (*form*) *Br* remplir; (*hole*) remplir, combler; (*door, window*) condamner; **to f. s.o. in on sth** mettre qn au courant de qch; **to f. out** (*form*) remplir; **to f. up** (*container, form*) remplir.

● *vi* **to f. (up)** se remplir; **to f. in for s.o.** remplacer qn; **to f. out** (*get fatter*) grossir, se remplumer; **to f. up** (*with Br petrol or Am gas*) faire le plein.

● *n* **to eat one's f.** manger à sa faim; **to have had one's f. of s.o./sth** en avoir assez de.

filler ['filər] *n* (*for cracks in wood*) mastic *m*.

fillet [*Br* 'filit, *Am* fiˈlei] *n* (*of fish, meat*) filet *m* ● *vt* (*pt & pp Am* [filˈleid]) (*fish*) découper en filets; (*meat*) désosser.

filling ['filiŋ] *a* (*meal etc*) nourrissant, substantiel ● *n* (*in tooth*) plombage *m*; (*in food*) garniture *f*; **f. station** poste *m* d'essence.

fillip ['filip] *n* (*stimulus*) coup *m* de fouet.

filly ['fili] *n* (*horse*) pouliche *f*.

film [film] *n* film *m*; (*for camera*) pellicule *f*; (*layer of dust etc*) fine couche *f*, pellicule *f*; (*for wrapping food*) film *m* plastique.

● *a* (*studio, technician, critic*) de cinéma; **f.**

club ciné-club *m*; **f. fan** *or* **buff** cinéphile *mf*; **f. festival** festival *m* du film; **f. library** cinémathèque *f*; **f. maker** cinéaste *m*; **f. star** vedette *f* (de cinéma).

● *vt* filmer.

● *vi* (*of film maker, actor*) tourner.

Filofax® ['failəʊfæks] *n* (*agenda m*) organiseur *m*.

filter ['filtər] *n* filtre *m*; (*traffic sign*) *Br* flèche *f*; **f. lane** *Br Aut* couloir *m* (pour tourner); **f. tip** (*bout m*) filtre *m*; **f.-tipped cigarette** cigarette *f* (à bout) filtre ● *vt* filtrer ● *vi* filtrer (**through** sth à travers qch); **to f. through** filtrer.

filth [filθ] *n* saleté *f*; (*obscenities*) *Fig* saletés *fpl*. ● **filthy** *a* (**-ier, -iest**) (*hands, shoes etc*) sale; (*language*) obscène; (*habit*) dégoûtant; **f. weather** *Br Fam* un temps infect, un sale temps.

fin [fin] *n* (*of fish, seal*) nageoire *f*; (*of shark*) aileron *m*; (*of swimmer*) *Am* palme *f*.

final ['fain(ə)l] *a* (*last*) dernier; (*definite*) (*decision, answer etc*) définitif ● *n Sport* finale *f*; **finals** (*university exams*) *Br* examens *mpl* de dernière année. ● **finalist** *n Sport* finaliste *mf*. ● **finalize** *vt* (*plan*) mettre au point; (*date*) fixer (définitivement). ● **finally** *adv* (*lastly*) enfin, en dernier lieu; (*eventually*) finalement, enfin; (*once and for all*) définitivement.

finale [fiˈnɑːli] *n* (*musical*) finale *m*.

finance ['fainæns] *n* finance *f*; **finances** (*of person*) finances *fpl*; (*of company*) situation *f* financière; **f. company** établissement *m* de crédit ● *vt* financer.

financial [faiˈnænʃəl] *a* financier; **f. year** année *f* budgétaire. ● **financially** *adv* financièrement.

financier [faiˈnænsiər] *n* (*grand*) financier *m*.

find [faind] *n* (*discovery*) trouvaille *f* ● *vt* (*pt & pp* **found**) trouver; (*sth or s.o. lost*) retrouver; **I f. that** je trouve que; **to f. difficulty doing sth** éprouver de la difficulté à faire qch; **£20 all found** 20 livres logé et nourri; **to f. s.o. guilty** (*in court*) déclarer qn coupable; **to f. one's feet** (*settle in*) s'adapter; **to f. oneself** (*to be*) se trouver.

find out *vt* (*secret, information etc*) découvrir; (*person*) démasquer ● *vi* (*inquire*) se renseigner (**about** s.o./sth sur qn/qch); **to f. out about sth** (*discover*) découvrir qch.

findings ['faindiŋz] *npl* conclusions *fpl*.

fine¹ [fain] *n* (*money*) amende *f*; (*for driving offence*) contravention *f* ● *vt* **to f. s.o. (£10/ etc)** infliger une amende (de dix livres/*etc*) à qn.

fine² [fain] **1** *a* (**-er, -est**) (*thin, not coarse*) (*hair, needle etc*) fin; (*gold, metal*) pur; (*feeling*) délicat; (*distinction*) subtil ● *adv* (*to cut, write*) menu.

2 *a* (**-er, -est**) (*very good*) excellent; (*beautiful*) (*weather, statue etc*) beau (*f* belle); **it's f.** (*weather*) il fait beau; **he's f.** (*healthy*) il va bien ● *adv* (*very well*) très bien; **f.!** très bien!

● **finely** *adv* (*dressed*) magnifiquement; (*em-*

broidered, ground) finement; (*painted, expressed*) délicatement; **f. chopped** haché menu.

finery ['faɪnərɪ] *n* (*clothes*) parure *f*, belle toilette *f*.

finesse [fɪ'nes] *n* (*skill, tact*) doigté *m*; (*refinement*) finesse *f*.

finger ['fɪŋgər] *n* doigt *m*; **to keep one's fingers crossed** croiser les doigts; **little f.** petit doigt *m*, auriculaire *m*; **middle f.** majeur *m*; **f. mark** trace *f* de doigt ▌ *vt* toucher (des doigts), palper. ●**fingering** *n Mus* doigté *m*. ●**fingernail** *n* ongle *m*. ●**fingerprint** *n* empreinte *f* (digitale). ●**fingerstall** *n* doigtier *m*. ●**fingertip** *n* bout *m* du doigt.

finicky ['fɪnɪkɪ] *a* (*precise*) méticuleux; (*difficult*) difficile (**about** sur).

finish ['fɪnɪʃ] *n* (*end*) fin *f*; (*of race*) arrivée *f*; (*of article, car etc*) finition *f*; **paint with a matt f.** peinture *f* mate.
▌ *vt* **to f.** (**off** *or* **up**) finir, terminer; **to f. eating**/*etc* finir de manger/*etc*; **to f. s.o. off** (*kill*) achever qn.
▌ *vi* (*of meeting, event etc*) finir, se terminer; (*of person*) finir, terminer; **to f. first** terminer premier; (*in race*) arriver premier; **to have finished with** (*object*) ne plus avoir besoin de; (*situation, person*) en avoir fini avec; **to f. off** *or* **up** (*of person*) finir, terminer; **to f. up** (*in end up in*) se retrouver à; **to f. up doing** finir par faire; **finishing line** (*of race*) ligne *f* d'arrivée; **finishing school** institution *f* pour jeunes filles; **to put the finishing touch(es) to sth** mettre la dernière main *or* la touche finale à qch. ●**finished** *a* (*ended, complete, ruined etc*) fini.

finite ['faɪnaɪt] *a* fini.

Finland ['fɪnlənd] *n* Finlande *f*. ●**Finn** *n* Finlandais, -aise *mf*, Finnois, -oise *mf*. ●**Finnish** *a* finlandais, finnois ▌ *n* (*language*) finnois *m*.

fir [fɜːr] *n* (*tree, wood*) sapin *m*.

fire¹ ['faɪər] *n* feu *m*; (*accidental*) incendie *m*; (*electric heater*) *Br* radiateur *m*; **to light** *or* **make a f.** faire du feu; **to set f. to** mettre le feu à; **to catch f.** prendre feu; **on f.** en feu; **(there's a) f.!** au feu!; **f.!** (*to soldiers*) feu!; **to open f.** ouvrir le feu; **f. alarm** alarme *f* d'incendie; **f. brigade** *Br*, **f. department** *Am* pompiers *mpl*; **f. engine** (*vehicle*) voiture *f* de pompiers; (*machine*) pompe *f* à incendie; **f. escape** escalier *m* de secours; **f. exit** sortie *f* de secours; **f. station** caserne *f* de pompiers.

fire² ['faɪər] *vt* (*cannon*) tirer; (*pottery*) cuire; (*imagination*) *Fig* enflammer; **to f. a gun** tirer un coup de fusil *or* de pistolet; **to f. questions at s.o.** bombarder qn de questions; **to f. s.o.** (*dismiss*) renvoyer qn ▌ *vi* tirer (**at** sur); **f. away!** (*start speaking*) *Fam* vas-y, parle!; **firing squad** peloton *m* d'exécution; *Br* **in** *or* *Am* **on the firing line** en butte aux attaques.

firearm ['faɪərɑːm] *n* arme *f* à feu. ●**firebug** *n* pyromane *mf*. ●**firecracker** *n Am* pétard

m. ●**fireguard** *n* garde-feu *m inv*. ●**fireman** *n* (*pl* **-men**) (sapeur-)pompier *m*. ●**fireplace** *n* cheminée *f*. ●**fireproof** *a* (*door*) ignifugé, coupe-feu *inv*. ●**fireside** *n* **by the f.** au coin du feu; **f. chair** fauteuil *m*. ●**firewood** *n* bois *m* de chauffage. ●**firework** *n* fusée *f*; (*firecracker*) pétard *m*; **f. display** *Br* feu *m* d'artifice.

firm¹ [fɜːm] *n* (*company*) entreprise *f*, maison *f*, firme *f*.

firm² [fɜːm] *a* (**-er, -est**) (*earth, decision etc*) ferme; (*faith*) solide; (*character*) résolu; **to be f. with s.o.** être ferme avec qn ▌ *adv* **to stand f.** tenir bon *or* ferme. ●**firmly** *adv* (*to shut, believe etc*) fermement; (*to speak*) d'une voix ferme. ●**firmness** *n* fermeté *f*; (*of faith*) solidité *f*.

first [fɜːst] *a* premier; **I'll do it f. thing in the morning** je le ferai dès le matin, sans faute; **f. cousin** cousin, -ine *mf* germain(e).
▌ *adv* d'abord, premièrement; (*for the first time*) pour la première fois; **f. of all** tout d'abord; **at f.** d'abord; **to come f.** (*in race*) arriver premier; (*in exam*) être premier.
▌ *n* (*person, thing*) premier, -ière *mf*; (*British university degree*) = licence *f* avec mention très bien; **from the f.** dès le début; **f. aid** premiers secours *mpl or* soins *mpl*; **f. (gear)** (*of vehicle*) première *f*.

first-class [fɜːst'klɑːs] *a* excellent; (*ticket etc*) de première (classe); (*mail*) ordinaire ▌ *adv* (*to travel*) en première. ●**first-hand** *a* (*news etc*) de première main; **to have (had) f.-hand experience of** avoir fait l'expérience personnelle de ▌ *adv* (*to hear news etc*) de première main. ●**first-'rate** *a* excellent.

firstly ['fɜːstlɪ] *adv* premièrement.

fiscal ['fɪsk(ə)l] *a* fiscal.

fish [fɪʃ] *n* (*pl inv or* **-es** [-ɪz]) poisson *m*; **f. market** marché *m* aux poissons; **f. bone** arête *f*; **f. bowl** bocal *m*; **f. fingers** *Br*, **f. sticks** *Am* bâtonnets *mpl* de poisson; **f. shop** poissonnerie *f*; **f.-and-chip shop** *Br* boutique *f* de fritures.
▌ *vi* pêcher; **to f. for** (*salmon etc*) pêcher; (*compliment etc*) *Fig* chercher.
▌ *vt* **to f. out** (*from water*) repêcher; (*from pocket, drawer etc*) sortir. ●**fishing** *n* pêche *f*; **to go f.** aller à la pêche; **f. boat/line**/*etc* bateau *m*/ligne *f*/*etc* de pêche; **f. net** (*of fisherman*) filet *m* (de pêche); (*of angler*) épuisette *f*; **f. pole** *Am* canne *f* à pêche; **f. rod** canne *f* à pêche.

fisherman ['fɪʃəmən] *n* (*pl* **-men**) pêcheur *m*.

fishmonger ['fɪʃmʌŋgər] *n* poissonnier, -ière *mf*.

fishy ['fɪʃɪ] *a* (**-ier, -iest**) (*smell, taste*) de poisson; (*story, business etc*) *Fig* louche.

fission ['fɪʃ(ə)n] *n* **nuclear f.** fission *f* nucléaire.

fissure ['fɪʃər] *n* (*crack*) fissure *f*.

fist [fɪst] *n* poing *m*. ●**fistful** *n* poignée *f* (**of** de).

fit¹ [fɪt] **1** *a* (**fitter, fittest**) (*healthy*) en bonne santé; (*in good shape*) en forme; (*suitable*) propre (**for** à, **to do** à faire); (*worthy*) digne (**for** de, **to do** de faire); (*able*) apte (**for** à, **to do** à faire); **f. to eat** *or* **for eating** bon à manger, mangeable; **to see f. to do** juger à propos de faire; **as you see f.** comme bon vous semble; **I was f. to drop** *Fam* je ne tenais plus debout; **to keep f.** se maintenir en forme.

2 *vt* (**-tt-**) (*of clothes etc*) aller (bien) à (*qn*), être à la taille de (*qn*); (*match*) répondre à, correspondre à (*description, besoin etc*); (*equal*) égaler; (*put in*) poser (*fenêtre, moquette etc*); **to f. sth on s.o.** (*garment*) ajuster qch à qn; **to f. sth** (**on**) **to sth** (*put*) poser qch sur qch; (*adjust*) adapter qch à qch; (*fix*) fixer qch à qch; **to f.** (**out** *or* **up**) **with sth** (*house, ship etc*) équiper de qch; **to f. in** (*install*) poser (*fenêtre etc*); (*insert*) faire entrer (*qch*); **to f. in a customer/etc** (*find time to see*) prendre un client/etc; **to f.** (**in**) **sth** (*go in*) (*of key etc*) aller dans qch; **to f.** (**on**) **sth** (*go on*) (*of lid etc*) aller sur qch.

❚ *vi* (*of clothes*) aller (bien) (**à** qn); **this shirt fits** (*fits me*) cette chemise me va (bien); **to f.** (**in**) (*go in*) entrer, aller; (*of facts, plans*) s'accorder, cadrer (**with** avec); **he doesn't f. in** il ne peut pas s'intégrer.

❚ *n* **a good f.** (*clothes*) à la bonne taille; **a close** *or* **tight f.** (*clothes*) ajusté.

fit² [fɪt] *n* (*attack of illness, anger etc*) accès *m*, crise *f*; **a f. of crying** une crise de larmes; **a f. of enthusiasm** un accès d'enthousiasme; **in fits and starts** par à-coups.

fitful [ˈfɪtfəl] *a* (*sleep*) agité.

fitment [ˈfɪtmənt] *n* (*furniture*) *Br* meuble *m* encastré; (*machine accessory*) accessoire *m*.

fitness [ˈfɪtnɪs] *n* (*health*) santé *f*; (*of remark etc*) à-propos *m*; (*for job*) aptitudes *fpl* (**for** pour).

fitted [ˈfɪtɪd] *a* *Br* (*cupboard*) encastré; (*garment*) ajusté; **f. carpet** moquette *f*; **f. kitchen** cuisine *f* aménagée; **f.** (**kitchen**) **units** éléments *mpl* de cuisine.

fitter [ˈfɪtər] *n* (*of machinery*) *Br* monteur, -euse *mf*.

fitting [ˈfɪtɪŋ] **1** *a* (*suitable*) convenable. **2** *n* (*of clothes*) essayage *m*; **f. room** (*booth in store*) cabine *f* d'essayage. ● **fittings** *npl* (*in house etc*) installations *fpl*.

five [faɪv] *a* & *n* cinq *m*. ● **fiver** *n* *Br Fam* billet *m* de cinq livres.

fix [fɪks] **1** *vt* (*make firm, decide*) fixer; (*tie with rope*) attacher; (*mend*) réparer; (*deal with*) arranger; (*prepare, cook*) préparer, faire; (*rig*) *Fam* truquer (*élections etc*); (*bribe*) acheter (*qn*); **to f. one's hopes on s.o./sth** mettre ses espoirs en qn/qch; **to f. the blame on s.o.** rejeter la responsabilité sur qn; **to f. s.o.** (*punish*) *Fam* régler son compte à qn; **it's fixed in my mind** c'est gravé dans mon esprit; **to f.** (**on**) (*lid etc*) mettre en place; **to f. up** (*trip etc*) arranger; **to f. s.o. up with a job/etc** procurer un travail/etc à qn.

2 *n* (*of plane, ship*) position *f*; (*injection*) *Sl* piqûre *f*; **in a f.** *Fam* dans le pétrin.

fixation [fɪkˈseɪʃ(ə)n] *n* fixation *f*.

fixed [fɪkst] *a* (*idea, price etc*) fixe; (*resolution*) inébranlable; **how's he f. for cash?** *Fam* a-t-il assez d'argent?; **how are you f. for tomorrow?** *Fam* qu'est-ce que tu fais pour demain?

fixer [ˈfɪksər] *n* (*schemer*) *Fam* combinard, -arde *mf*.

fixings [ˈfɪksɪŋz] *npl* *Culin Am* garniture *f*.

fixture [ˈfɪkstʃər] *n* **1** *Sport* rencontre *f* (prévue). **2 fixtures** (*in house*) installations *fpl*.

fizz [fɪz] *vi* (*of champagne*) pétiller; (*of gas*) siffler. ● **fizzy** *a* (**-ier, -iest**) pétillant.

fizzle [ˈfɪz(ə)l] *vi* (*hiss*) siffler; (*of liquid*) pétiller; **to f. out** (*of firework*) rater, faire long feu; (*of plan*) *Fig* tomber à l'eau; (*of custom*) disparaître.

flabbergasted [ˈflæbəgɑːstɪd] *a Fam* sidéré.

flabby [ˈflæbɪ] *a* (**-ier, -iest**) (*skin, character, person*) mou (*f* molle), flasque.

flag [flæg] **1** *n* drapeau *m*; (*on ship*) pavillon *m*; (*for charity*) insigne *m*; **f. stop** *Am* arrêt *m* facultatif ❚ *vt* (**-gg-**) **to f. down** (*taxi*) faire signe à. **2** *vi* (**-gg-**) (*of conversation*) languir; (*of worker*) fléchir; (*of plant*) dépérir. ● **flagpole** *n* mât *m*.

flagrant [ˈfleɪɡrənt] *a* flagrant.

flagstone [ˈflæɡstəʊn] *n* dalle *f*.

flair [fleər] *n* (*intuition*) flair *m*; **to have a f. for** (*natural talent*) avoir un don pour.

flak [flæk] *n* **to get a lot of f.** (*criticism*) *Fam* se faire rentrer dedans.

flake [fleɪk] *n* (*of snow etc*) flocon *m*; (*of soap, metal*) paillette *f* ❚ *vi* **to f.** (**off**) (*of paint*) s'écailler. ● **flaky** *a* **f. pastry** *Br* pâte *f* feuilletée.

flamboyant [flæmˈbɔɪənt] *a* (*person, manner*) extravagant.

flame [fleɪm] *n* flamme *f*; **to burst into flame(s)**, **go up in flames** prendre feu, s'enflammer; **in flames** en flammes ❚ *vi* **to f.** (**up**) (*of fire, house*) flamber. ● **flaming** *a* **1** (*sun*) flamboyant. **2** (*damn*) *Br Fam* **f. idiot/etc** fichu imbécile m/etc.

flamingo [fləˈmɪŋɡəʊ] *n* (*pl* **-os** *or* **-oes**) (*bird*) flamant *m*.

flammable [ˈflæməb(ə)l] *a* inflammable.

flan [flæn] *n* tarte *f*.

flank [flæŋk] *n* flanc *m* ❚ *vt* flanquer; **flanked by** flanqué de.

flannel [ˈflænəl] *n* (*cloth*) flanelle *f*; (*face*) **f.** *Br* gant *m* de toilette, carré-éponge *m*; **flannels** (*trousers*) *Br* pantalon *m* de flanelle. ● **flanne'lette** *n* pilou *m*, finette *f*; **f. sheet** drap *m* en flanelle.

flap [flæp] **1** *vi* (**-pp-**) (*of wings, sail, shutter etc*) battre ❚ *vt* **to f. its wings** (*of bird*) battre des ailes ❚ *n* (*flapping noise*) battement *m*. **2** *n* (*of pocket, envelope*) rabat *m*; (*of table*) abattant *m*; (*of door*) battant *m*.

flare [fleər] *n* (*distress signal*) fusée *f* éclairante; (*runway light*) balise *f*; (*sudden blaze*) flambée *f*; (*sudden light*) éclat *m* ❚ *vi* (*blaze*) flamber; (*shine*) briller; **to f. up** (*of fire*) prendre; (*of violence, war*) éclater; (*of region in revolt*) s'embraser; (*get angry*) s'emporter. ●**flare-up** *n* (*of violence, fire*) flambée *f*; (*of region*) embrasement *m*.

flared [fleəd] *a* (*skirt*) évasé; (*Br trousers, Am pants*) (à) pattes d'éléphant.

flash [flæʃ] *n* (*of light*) éclat *m*; (*of genius, anger*) éclair *m*; (*for camera*) flash *m*; **f. of lightning** éclair *m*; **news f.** flash *m*; **in a f.** in un clin d'œil.

▮ *vi* (*shine*) briller; (*on and off*) clignoter; **to f. past** *or* **by** (*rush*) passer comme un éclair; **flashing lights** clignotants *mpl*.

▮ *vt* (*a light*) projeter; (*aim*) diriger (**on, at** sur); (*a glance*) jeter; **to f. sth** (**around**) (*flaunt*) étaler qch; **to f. one's** (**head**)**lights** faire un appel de phares. ●**flashback** *n* retour *m* en arrière. ●**flashlight** *n* (*torch*) *Br* lampe *f* de poche, lampe *f* électrique; (*for camera*) flash *m*.

flashy ['flæʃɪ] *a* (**-ier, -iest**) *a* voyant, tape-à-l'œil *inv*.

flask [flɑːsk] *n* thermos® *m* *or* *f* *inv*; (*for brandy, medicine*) flacon *m*; (*phial*) fiole *f*.

flat¹ [flæt] *a* (**flatter, flattest**) plat; (*Br tyre or Am tire, battery*) à plat; (*beer*) éventé; (*refusal*) net (*f* nette); (*rate, fare*) fixe; (*razed to the ground*) rasé; **f. nose** nez *m* aplati; **f. fee** prix *m* unique; **to put sth** (**down**) **f.** mettre qch à plat; **to be f.-footed** avoir les pieds plats.

▮ *adv* **to sing f.** chanter trop bas; **I told him f.** je le lui ai dit carrément; **to fall f. on one's face** tomber à plat ventre; **to fall f.** (*of joke, play etc*) tomber à plat; **to fold f.** (*of ironing board etc*) se (re)plier; **f. broke** *Fam* complètement fauché; **in two minutes f.** en deux minutes pile; **f. out** (*to work*) d'arrache-pied; (*to run*) à toute vitesse; **to be lying f. out** être étendu de tout son long.

▮ *n* (*puncture*) crevaison *f*; (*of hand*) plat *m*; (*in music*) bémol *m*. ●**flatly** *adv* (*to deny, refuse etc*) catégoriquement. ●**flatness** *n* (*of surface*) égalité *f*.

flat² [flæt] *n* (*rooms*) *Br* appartement *m*.

flatmate ['flætmeɪt] *n* **my f.** *Br* la personne avec qui je partage mon appartement.

flatten ['flætən] *vt* (*crops*) coucher; (*town, buildings*) raser; **to f.** (**out**) (*metal etc*) aplatir.

flatter ['flætər] *vt* flatter; (*of clothes*) avantager (*qn*). ●**flattering** *a* (*remark, words etc*) flatteur; **it's a f. hat, the hat is f. on you** ce chapeau vous avantage. ●**flatterer** *n* flatteur, -euse *mf*.

flattery ['flætərɪ] *n* flatterie *f*.

flatulence ['flætjʊləns] *n* **to have f.** avoir des gaz.

flaunt [flɔːnt] *vt* (*show off*) faire étalage de; (*defy, treat with scorn*) *Am* narguer, défier.

flautist ['flɔːtɪst] *n* *Br* flûtiste *mf*.

flavour ['fleɪvər] (*Am* **flavor**) *n* (*taste*) goût *m*, saveur *f*; (*of ice cream, Br sweet or Am candy etc*) parfum *m* ▮ *vt* (*food*) assaisonner;

(*sauce*) relever; (*ice cream etc*) parfumer (**with** à); **lemon/etc-flavoured** (parfumé) au citron/*etc.*
●**flavouring** *n* (*seasoning*) assaisonnement *m*; (*in cake, ice cream etc*) parfum *m*.

flaw [flɔː] *n* défaut *m*. ●**flawed** *a* imparfait.
●**flawless** *a* parfait.

flax [flæks] *n* lin *m*. ●**flaxen** *a* de lin.

flay [fleɪ] *vt* (*animal*) écorcher; (*criticize*) *Fig* éreinter.

flea [fliː] *n* puce *f*; **f. market** marché *m* aux puces. ●**fleapit** *n* *Br Fam* cinéma *m* miteux.

fleck [flek] *n* (*mark*) petite tache *f*.

fledgling ['fledʒlɪŋ] *n* (*novice*) blanc-bec *m*.

flee [fliː] *vi* (*pt & pp* **fled**) s'enfuir, fuir, se sauver ▮ *vt* (*place*) s'enfuir de; (*danger, temptation etc*) fuir.

fleece [fliːs] **1** *n* (*sheep's coat*) toison *f*. **2** *vt* (*rob*) *Fam* voler (*qn*). ●**fleecy** *a* (**-ier, -iest**) (*gloves etc*) molletonné.

fleet [fliːt] *n* (*of ships*) flotte *f*; **a f. of buses/etc** (*belonging to company*) un parc d'autobus/*etc*; (*providing shuttle service*) une noria d'autobus/*etc*; **a f. of vehicles** (*of company*) un parc automobile.

fleeting ['fliːtɪŋ] *a* (*visit, moment*) bref (*f* brève); (*beauty*) éphémère. ●**fleetingly** *adv* fugitivement, un bref instant.

Flemish ['flemɪʃ] *a* flamand ▮ *n* (*language*) flamand *m*; **the F.** (*people*) les Flamands *mpl*.

flesh [fleʃ] *n* chair *f*; **in the f.** en chair et en os; **he's your** (**own**) **f. and blood** (*child*) c'est la chair de ta chair; (*brother, father etc*) il est de ton sang; **f. wound** blessure *f* superficielle. ●**fleshy** *a* (**-ier, -iest**) charnu.

flew [fluː] *see* **fly²**.

flex [fleks] **1** *vt* (*limb*) fléchir; (*muscle*) faire jouer, bander. **2** *n* (*wire*) fil *m* (souple); (*for telephone*) cordon *m*.

flexible ['fleksɪb(ə)l] *a* (*person, wire, plans*) souple, flexible. ●**flexi'bility** *n* flexibilité *f*.

flick [flɪk] *vt* (*with whip etc*) donner un petit coup à; **to f. sth off** (*remove*) enlever qch (d'une chiquenaude); **to f. a switch** pousser un bouton; **to f. on/off the light** allumer/éteindre ▮ *vi* **to f. over** *or* **through** (*pages*) feuilleter ▮ *n* (*with finger*) chiquenaude *f*; (*with whip etc*) petit coup *m*; **f. knife** *Br* couteau *m* à cran d'arrêt.

flicker ['flɪkər] *vi* (*of flame, light*) vaciller; (*of needle*) osciller ▮ *n* vacillement *m*; **f. of light** lueur *f*.

flier ['flaɪər] *n* **1** (*leaflet*) *Am* prospectus *m*; (*political*) tract *m*. **2** (*person*) aviateur, -trice *mf*; **high f.** (*ambitious person*) jeune loup *m*.

flies [flaɪz] *npl* (*on Br trousers or Am pants*) braguette *f*.

flight [flaɪt] *n* **1** (*of bird, aircraft etc*) vol *m*; (*of bullet*) trajectoire *f*; (*of imagination*) *Fig* élan *m*; **f. to/from** vol *m* à destination de/en provenance de; **she had a good f.** elle a fait bon voyage; **f. attendant** (*man*) steward *m*; (*woman*) hôtesse *f* de l'air; **f. deck** cabine *f* de pilotage; **f. path** (*of aircraft*) trajectoire *f* de vol. **2** (*floor, Br storey, Am story*) étage *m*; **f. of stairs** escalier *m*. **3** (*escape*) fuite *f* (**from** de); **to take f.** prendre la fuite.

flighty ['flaɪtɪ] *a* (**-ier, -iest**) inconstant, volage.

flimsy ['flɪmzɪ] *a* (**-ier, -iest**) (*cloth, structure etc*) (*light*) (trop) léger; (*thin*) (trop) mince; (*excuse, reason*) mince, frivole.

flinch [flɪntʃ] *vi* (*with pain*) tressaillir; **to f. from** (*duty etc*) se dérober à; **without flinching** (*complaining*) sans broncher.

fling [flɪŋ] **1** *vt* (*pt & pp* **flung**) lancer, jeter; **to f. open** (*door etc*) ouvrir brutalement. **2** *n* **to have one's** *or* **a f.** (*indulge oneself*) s'en donner à cœur joie.

flint [flɪnt] *n* (*stone*) silex *m*; (*for cigarette lighter*) pierre *f*.

flip [flɪp] **1** *vt* (**-pp-**) (*with finger*) donner une chiquenaude à; **to f. a switch** pousser un bouton; **to f. sth over** retourner qch ▮ *vi* **to f. through** (*book etc*) feuilleter ▮ *n* chiquenaude *f*; **the f. side** (*of record*) la face deux. **2** *a* (*impudent*) *Am Fam* effronté.

flip-flops ['flɪpflɒps] *npl* (*rubber sandals*) tongs *fpl*.

flippant ['flɪpənt] *a* irrévérencieux; (*offhand*) désinvolte.

flipper ['flɪpər] *n* (*of swimmer*) palme *f*; (*of seal*) nageoire *f*.

flipping ['flɪpɪŋ] *Br Fam a* (*idiot, rain etc*) sacré ▮ *adv* sacrément, bougrement.

flirt [flɜːt] *vi* flirter (**with** avec) ▮ *n* flirteur, -euse *mf*. ●**flirtation** [-'teɪʃ(ə)n] *n* flirt *m*.

flit [flɪt] *vi* (**-tt-**) (*fly*) voltiger; **to f. in and out** (*of person*) *Fig* entrer et sortir (rapidement).

float [fləʊt] *n* *Fishing* flotteur *m*; (*in parade*) char *m* ▮ *vi* flotter (**on** sur); **to f. down the river** descendre la rivière ▮ *vt* (*boat, wood*) faire flotter; (*idea, rumour*) lancer; **to f. a currency** laisser flotter une monnaie; **to f. a loan** émettre un emprunt. ●**floating** *a* (*wood, debt etc*) flottant; (*population*) instable; **f. voters** électeurs *mpl* indécis.

flock [flɒk] *n* (*of sheep etc*) troupeau *m*; (*of birds*) volée *f*; (*religious congregation*) *Hum* ouailles *fpl*; (*of tourists etc*) foule *f* ▮ *vi* venir en foule (**to the coast/***etc* à la côte/*etc*); **to f. round s.o.** s'attrouper autour de qn.

floe [fləʊ] *n* (**ice**) **f.** banquise *f*.

flog [flɒg] *vt* (**-gg-**) **1** (*beat*) flageller. **2** (*sell*) *Br Sl* bazarder. ●**flogging** *n* flagellation *f*.

flood [flʌd] *n* inondation *f*; (*of letters, tears, insults etc*) *Fig* flot *m*, déluge *m*, torrent *m* ▮ *vt* (*field etc*) inonder (**with** de); (*river*) faire déborder; **to f. (out)** (*house*) inonder ▮ *vi* (*of river*) déborder; (*of building*) être inondé; **to f. in** (*of people, money*) affluer; **to f. into** (*of tourists etc*) envahir (*un pays etc*). ●**flooding** *n* (*of field etc*) inondation *f*; (*floods*) inondations *fpl*.

floodgate ['flʌdgeɪt] *n* (*in water*) & *Fig* vanne *f*.

floodlight ['flʌdlaɪt] *n* projecteur *m* ▮ *vt* (*pt & pp* **floodlit**) illuminer; **floodlit match** *or Am* **game** (match *m* en) nocturne *f*.

floor [flɔːr] **1** *n* (*ground*) sol *m*; (*wooden etc*

in building) plancher *m*; (*Br storey, Am story*) étage *m*; (*dance*) **f.** piste *f* (de danse); **on the f.** par terre; **on the first f.** *Br* au premier étage; (*ground floor*) *Am* au rez-de-chaussée; **f. polish** cire *f*, encaustique *f*; **f. show** spectacle *m* (de cabaret). **2** *vt* (*knock down*) terrasser; (*puzzle*) stupéfier.

floorboard ['flɔːbɔːd] *n* planche *f*.

flop [flɒp] **1** *vi* (**-pp-**) **to f. down** (*collapse*) s'effondrer; **to f. about** s'agiter mollement. **2** *vi* (**-pp-**) *Fam* (*fail*) (*of business, efforts etc*) échouer; (*of play, film etc*) faire un four ▮ *n Fam* échec *m*, fiasco *m*; (*play etc*) four *m*.

floppy ['flɒpɪ] *a* (**-ier, -iest**) (*soft*) mou (*f* molle); (*clothes*) (trop) large; (*ears*) pendant; **f. disk** (*of computer*) disquette *f*.

flora ['flɔːrə] *n* (*plants*) flore *f*. ●**floral** *a* (*material, pattern*) à fleurs; (*art, exhibition*) floral.

florid ['flɒrɪd] *a* (*style*) fleuri; (*complexion*) rougeaud, fleuri.

florist ['flɒrɪst] *n* fleuriste *mf*.

floss [flɒs] *n* (**dental**) **f.** fil *m* (de soie) dentaire.

flotilla [flə'tɪlə] *n* (*of ships*) flottille *f*.

flounce [flaʊns] *n* (*frill on dress, tablecloth etc*) volant *m*.

flounder ['flaʊndər] **1** *vi* (*in water etc*) patauger (avec effort), se débattre; (*in speech*) hésiter, patauger. **2** *n* (*fish*) carrelet *m*.

flour ['flaʊər] *n* farine *f*.

flourish ['flʌrɪʃ] **1** *vi* (*of person, business, plant etc*) prospérer; (*of the arts*) fleurir. **2** *vt* (*wave*) brandir (*bâton, épée etc*) ▮ *n* (*gesture*) grand geste *m*; (*decoration*) fioriture *f*; (*trumpet music*) fanfare *f*. ●**flourishing** *a* prospère, florissant.

flout [flaʊt] *vt* narguer, braver.

flow [fləʊ] *vi* couler; (*of electric current, information*) circuler; (*of hair, clothes*) flotter; (*of traffic*) s'écouler; **to f. back** (*of liquid*) refluer; **to f. in** (*of people, money*) affluer; **to f. into the sea** (*of river*) se jeter dans la mer. ▮ *n* (*of river*) courant *m*; (*of tide*) flux *m*; (*of current, information, blood*) circulation *f*; (*of traffic, liquid*) écoulement *m*; **a f. of visitors/words** un flot de visiteurs/paroles; **f. chart** organigramme *m*. ●**flowing** *a* (*movement*) gracieux; (*style*) coulant, aisé; (*beard*) flottant.

flower ['flaʊər] *n* fleur *f*; **in f.** en fleur(s); **f. bed** parterre *m*; **f. pot** pot *m* de fleurs; **f. shop** (boutique *f* de) fleuriste *mf*; **f. show** floralies *fpl* ▮ *vi* fleurir. ●**flowered** *a* (*dress*) à fleurs. ●**flowering** *n* floraison *f* ▮ *a* (*in bloom*) en fleurs; (*producing flowers*) (*shrub etc*) à fleurs.

flowery ['flaʊərɪ] *a* (*style etc*) fleuri; (*material*) à fleurs.

flown [fləʊn] *pp of* **fly²**.

flu [fluː] *n* (*influenza*) *Fam* grippe *f*.

fluctuate ['flʌktʃʊeɪt] *vi* varier. ●**fluctuation(s)** [-'eɪʃ(ə)n(z)] *n(pl)* (*in prices etc*) fluctuations *fpl* (**in** de).

flue [fluː] *n* (*of chimney*) conduit *m*.

fluent ['fluːənt] a (style) aisé; **he's f. in Russian, his Russian is f.** il parle couramment le russe; **to be a f. speaker** s'exprimer avec facilité. ●**fluency** n facilité f. ●**fluently** adv (to write, express oneself) avec facilité; **to speak French/etc f.** parler couramment le français/etc.

fluff [flʌf] 1 n (of material) Br peluche(s) f(pl); (on floor) Br moutons mpl; (down on bird etc) duvet m. 2 vt (bungle) Fam rater. ●**fluffy** a (-ier, -iest) (bird etc) duveteux; (material) pelucheux; (toy) en peluche; (hair) bouffant; **f. kitten** chaton m tout doux; **light and f.** (cake etc) très léger.

fluid ['fluːɪd] a fluide; (plans) flexible, non arrêté ▮ n fluide m, liquide m.

fluke [fluːk] n Fam coup m de chance; **by a f.** par raccroc.

flummox ['flʌməks] vt Br Fam désorienter.

flung [flʌŋ] pt & pp of **fling** 1.

flunk [flʌŋk] vi (in exam) Am Fam être collé ▮ vt Am Fam (exam) être collé à; (pupil) coller; (school) laisser tomber.

flunk(e)y ['flʌŋkɪ] n Pej larbin m.

fluorescent [fluəˈres(ə)nt] a fluorescent.

fluoride ['fluəraɪd] n (in water etc) fluor m; **f. toothpaste** dentifrice m au fluor.

flurry ['flʌrɪ] n 1 (of activity) poussée f. 2 (of snow) rafale f.

flush [flʌʃ] 1 n (blush) rougeur f; (of youth, beauty) éclat m; **hot flushes** bouffées fpl de chaleur; **the f. of victory** l'ivresse f de la victoire ▮ vi (blush) rougir.

2 vt wash (out) (clean) nettoyer qch à grande eau; **to f. the pan** or **toilet** tirer la chasse d'eau; **to f. sth down the pan** or **toilet** faire disparaître qch dans les toilettes; **to f. s.o. out** (chase away) faire sortir qn (from de) ▮ n (of toilet) chasse f d'eau.

3 a (level) de niveau (**with** de); **f. (with money)** Fam bourré de fric. ●**flushed** a (cheeks etc) rouge; **f. with success/etc** ivre de succès/etc.

fluster ['flʌstər] vt énerver; **to get flustered** s'énerver.

flute [fluːt] n flûte f. ●**flutist** n Am flûtiste mf.

flutter ['flʌtər] 1 vi (of bird, butterfly) voltiger; (of wing) battre; (of flag) flotter (mollement); (of heart) palpiter; **to f. about** (of person) papillonner ▮ vt **to f. its wings** (of bird) battre des ailes. 2 n **to have a f.** (bet) Br Fam jouer une petite somme (**on the horses/etc** aux courses/etc).

flux [flʌks] n **in a state of f.** en changement constant.

fly¹ [flaɪ] n (insect) mouche f; **f. swatter** (instrument) tapette f. ●**flypaper** n papier m tue-mouches.

fly² [flaɪ] vi (pt **flew**, pp **flown**) (of bird, aircraft etc) voler; (of passenger) aller en avion; (of time) passer vite; (of flag) flotter; (flee) Lit fuir; **to f. away** or **off** s'envoler; **to f. out** (of passenger) partir en avion; **to f. out of a room** sortir d'une pièce à toute vitesse; **I**

must f.! il faut que je file!; **to f. at s.o.** (attack) sauter sur qn; **the door flew open** la porte s'ouvrit brusquement.

▮ vt (aircraft) piloter; (passengers) transporter (par avion); (airline) voyager par; (flag) arborer; (kite) faire voler; **to f. the French flag** battre pavillon français; **to f. the Atlantic** traverser l'Atlantique en avion; **to f. across** or **over** (country, city) survoler.

fly³ [flaɪ] n (on trousers) Br braguette f.

flyby ['flaɪbaɪ] n (by plane) Am défilé m aérien. ●**fly-by-night** a (firm) véreux. ●**flyover** n (bridge) Br toboggan m. ●**flypast** n (by plane) Br défilé m aérien.

flyer ['flaɪər] n = flier.

flying ['flaɪɪŋ] n (flight) vol m; (air travel) (as pilot) aviation f; (as passenger) l'avion m ▮ a (doctor, personnel etc) volant; **to succeed with f. colours** réussir haut la main; **to get off to a f. start** prendre un très bon départ; **f. saucer** soucoupe f volante; **f. visit** visite f éclair inv; **f. time** (length of plane trip) durée f du vol; **ten hours'/etc f. time** dix heures/etc de vol.

FM [efˈem] n abbr (frequency modulation) modulation f de fréquence.

foal [fəʊl] n poulain m.

foam [fəʊm] n (on sea, mouth) écume f; (on beer) mousse f; **f. rubber** caoutchouc m mousse; **f. (rubber) mattress/etc** matelas m/etc mousse; **f. bath** bain m moussant ▮ vi (of sea, mouth) écumer; (of beer, soap) mousser.

fob [fob] vt (-bb-) **to f. s.o. off** with sth (object, excuse etc) se débarrasser de qn en lui donnant or lui racontant qch; **to f. off sth on (to) s.o.** refiler qch à qn.

focal ['fəʊk(ə)l] a focal; **f. point** point m central.

focus ['fəʊkəs] n (of attention, interest) centre m; (optical, geometrical) foyer m; **the photo is in f./out of f.** la photo est nette/floue.

▮ vt (image, camera) mettre au point; (light) faire converger; (efforts) concentrer (**on** sur).

▮ vi (converge) (of light) converger (**on** sur); **to f. on s.o./sth** (with camera) mettre au point sur qn/qch.

▮ vti **to f.** (one's eyes) **on** fixer les yeux sur; **to f. (one's attention) on** se tourner vers.

fodder ['fodər] n fourrage m.

foe [fəʊ] n ennemi, -ie mf.

foetus ['fiːtəs] n Br fœtus m.

fog [fog] n brouillard m, brume f ▮ vt (-gg-) **to f. the issue** embrouiller la question. ●**fogbound** a bloqué par le brouillard. ●**foghorn** n corne f de brume; (harsh voice) voix f tonifruante. ●**foglamp** or **foglight** n (on vehicle) (phare m) anti-brouillard m.

fog(e)y ['fəʊgɪ] n old f. vieille baderne f.

foggy ['fogɪ] a (-ier, -iest) **it's f.** il y a du brouillard; **f. weather** brouillard m; **on a f. day** par un jour de brouillard; **she hasn't got the foggiest (idea)** Fam elle n'en a pas la moindre idée.

foible ['fɔɪb(ə)l] *n* petit défaut *m*.

foil [fɔɪl] **1** *n* (*for cooking*) papier *m* alu(minium); (*metal sheet*) feuille *f* de métal. **2** *n* (*contrasting person*) repoussoir *m*. **3** *vt* (*plans etc*) déjouer. **4** *n* (*sword for fencing*) fleuret *m*.

foist [fɔɪst] *vt* to f. sth (off) on s.o. (*fob off*) refiler qch à qn; **to f. oneself on s.o.** s'imposer à qn.

fold[1] [fəʊld] *n* (*in paper, cloth etc*) pli *m* **▌** *vt* plier; (*wrap*) envelopper (**in** dans); **to f. away** *or* **down** *or* **up** (*chair etc*) plier; **to f. back** *or* **over** (*blanket etc*) replier; **to f. one's arms** (se) croiser les bras.

▌ *vi* (*of chair etc*) se plier; (*of business*) *Fam* s'écrouler; **to f. away** *or* **down** *or* **up** (*of chair etc*) se plier; **to f. back** *or* **over** (*of blanket etc*) se replier. ●**folding** *a* (*chair, bed etc*) pliant.

fold[2] [fəʊld] *n* (*for sheep*) parc *m* à moutons; **to return to the f.** *Fig* rentrer au bercail.

-fold [fəʊld] *suff* **tenfold** *a* par dix **▌** *adv* dix fois; **he earns tenfold what I earn** il gagne dix fois plus que moi.

folder ['fəʊldər] *n* (*file holder*) chemise *f*; (*for drawings*) carton *m* à dessins; (*pamphlet*) dépliant *m*.

foliage ['fəʊlɪdʒ] *n* feuillage *m*.

folk [fəʊk] **1** *npl* (*Am* **folks**) gens *mpl or fpl*; **my folks** (*parents*) *Fam* mes parents *mpl*; **hello folks!** *Fam* salut tout le monde!; **old f.** *Br* les vieux *mpl*. **2** *a* (*dance, costume etc*) folklorique; **f. music** (*contemporary*) (musique *f*) folk *m*.

folklore ['fəʊklɔːr] *n* folklore *m*.

follow ['fɒləʊ] *vt* suivre; (*career*) poursuivre; **followed by** suivi de; **to f. suit** (*do the same*) en faire autant; **to f. s.o. around** suivre qn partout; **to f. through** (*plan, idea etc*) poursuivre jusqu'au bout; **to f. up** (*idea, story*) creuser; (*clue, suggestion, case*) suivre; (*letter*) donner suite à; (*remark*) faire suivre (**with** de); (*advantage*) exploiter.

▌ *vi* (*of person, event etc*) suivre; **it follows that** il s'ensuit que; **that doesn't f.** ce n'est pas logique; **to f. on** (*come after*) suivre. ●**follow-up** *n* suite *f* (**to** de); (*letter*) rappel *m*; **f.-up visit** (*by doctor*) visite *f* de contrôle; **f.-up treatment** traitement *m* complémentaire.

follower ['fɒləʊər] *n* (*supporter*) partisan *m*.

following ['fɒləʊɪŋ] **1** *a* suivant **▌** *prep* à la suite de. **2** *n* (*supporters*) partisans *mpl*; **to have a large f.** avoir de nombreux partisans; (*of TV programme, fashion etc*) être très suivi.

folly ['fɒlɪ] *n* folie *f*, sottise *f*; **an act of f.** une folie.

foment [fəʊ'ment] *vt* (*revolt etc*) fomenter.

fond [fɒnd] *a* (**-er, -est**) (*loving*) tendre, affectueux; (*doting*) indulgent; (*memory, thought*) doux (*f* douce); **to be (very) f. of sth/s.o.** aimer beaucoup qch/qn; **with f. regards** (*in letter*) bien amicalement. ●**fondly** *adv* tendrement. ●**fondness** *n* prédilection *f*

(**for sth** pour qch); (*affection*) affection *f* (**for s.o.** pour qn).

fondle ['fɒnd(ə)l] *vt* caresser.

font [fɒnt] *n* **1** (*in church*) fonts *mpl* baptismaux. **2** *Typ Ordinat* police *f* de caractères.

food [fuːd] *n* nourriture *f*; (*particular substance*) aliment *m*; (*cooking*) cuisine *f*; (*for cats, dogs, pigs etc*) pâtée *f*; (*for plants*) engrais *m*; **foods** (*foodstuffs*) aliments *mpl*; **fast f.** restauration *f* rapide **▌** *a* (*needs, industry etc*) alimentaire; **f. poisoning** intoxication *f* alimentaire; **f. value** valeur *f* nutritive.

foodstuffs ['fuːdstʌfs] *npl* denrées *fpl or* produits *mpl* alimentaires.

fool [fuːl] *n* imbécile *mf*, idiot, -ote *mf*; **(you) silly f.!** espèce d'imbécile!; **to make a f. of s.o.** (*ridicule*) ridiculiser qn; (*trick*) rouler qn; **to be f. enough to do sth** être assez stupide pour faire qch; **to play the f.** faire l'imbécile.

▌ *vt* (*trick*) duper, rouler.

▌ *vi* **to f. (about** *or* **around)** faire l'imbécile; (*waste time*) perdre son temps; **to f. around** (*make love*) *Fam* faire l'amour (**with** avec).

foolhardy ['fuːlhɑːdɪ] *a* (*rash*) téméraire. ●**foolhardiness** *n* témérité *f*.

foolish ['fuːlɪʃ] *a* bête, idiot. ●**foolishly** *adv* bêtement. ●**foolishness** *n* bêtise *f*, sottise *f*.

foolproof ['fuːlpruːf] *a* (*scheme etc*) infaillible.

foot[1], *pl* **feet** [fʊt, fiːt] *n* pied *m*; (*of animal*) patte *f*; (*measure*) pied *m* (= 30,48 *cm*); **at the f. of** (*page, stairs*) au bas de; (*table*) au bout de; **on f.** à pied; **to be on one's feet** (*standing*) être sur pied; (*recovered from illness*) être sur pied; **f. brake** (*of vehicle*) frein *m* au plancher; **f.-and-mouth disease** fièvre *f* aphteuse.

foot[2] [fʊt] *vt* (*bill*) payer.

footage ['fʊtɪdʒ] *n* (*part of film*) séquences *fpl* (**on** sur).

football ['fʊtbɔːl] *n* *Br* (*game*) football *m*; (*ball*) ballon *m*. ●**footballer** *n* *Br* joueur, -euse *mf* de football. ●**footbridge** *n* passerelle *f*. ●**foothills** *npl* contreforts *mpl*. ●**foothold** *n* prise *f* (de pied); *Fig* position *f*; **to gain a f.** (*of person*) prendre pied (**in** dans). ●**footlights** *npl* (*in theatre*) rampe *f*. ●**footloose** *a* libre de toute attache. ●**footman** *n* (*pl* **-men**) valet *m* de pied. ●**footmark** *n* empreinte *f* (de pied). ●**footnote** *n* note *f* au bas de la page; (*extra comment*) *Fig* post-scriptum *m*. ●**footpath** *n* sentier *m*; (*ur roadside*) chemin *m* (piétonnier). ●**footstep** *n* pas *m*; **to follow in s.o.'s footsteps** suivre les traces de qn. ●**footstool** *n* petit tabouret *m*. ●**footwear** *n* chaussures *fpl*.

footing ['fʊtɪŋ] *n* prise *f* (de pied); *Fig* position *f*; **on a war f.** sur le pied de guerre; **on an equal f.** sur un pied d'égalité.

for [fɔr, *unstressed* fər] **1** *prep* pour; (*for a distance or period of*) pendant; (*in spite of*) malgré; **f. you/me/etc** pour toi/moi/*etc*; **it's f. tomorrow/f. this reason/f. eating** c'est pour demain/pour cette raison/pour manger;

what's it f.? ça sert à quoi?; **I did it f. love/
pleasure** je l'ai fait par amour/par plaisir; **to
swim/rush f.** (*towards*) nager/se précipiter
vers; **a train f.** un train à destination de *or*
en direction de, un train pour; **the road f.
London** la route (en direction) de Londres;
it's time f. breakfast/etc c'est l'heure du petit
déjeuner/etc; **to come f. dinner** venir dîner;
to sell sth f. seven dollars vendre qch sept
dollars; **what's the Russian f. 'book'?** comment dit-on 'livre' en russe?; **she walked f. a
kilometre** elle a marché pendant un kilomètre; **he was away f. a month** il a été
absent pendant un mois; **he won't be back f.
a month** il ne sera pas de retour avant un
mois; **he's been here f. a month** (*he's still
here*) il est ici depuis un mois; **I haven't seen
him f. ten years** voilà dix ans que je ne l'ai
vu, je ne l'ai pas vu depuis dix ans; **it's
easy/possible/etc f. her to do it** il lui est
facile/possible/etc de le faire; **it's f. you to
say** c'est à toi de dire; **f. that to be done**
pour que ça soit fait.
2 *conj* (*because*) car.

forage ['fɒrɪdʒ] *vt* **to f.** (*about*) fourrager (**for**
pour trouver).

foray ['fɒreɪ] *n* incursion *f*.

forbearance [fɔːˈbeərəns] *n* patience *f*.

forbid [fəˈbɪd] *vt* (*pt* forbad(e), *pp* forbidden,
pres p forbidding) interdire, défendre (**s.o.
to do** à qn de faire); **to f. s.o. sth** interdire *or*
défendre qch à qn. ●**forbidden** *a* (*fruit, region, palace etc*) défendu; **she is f. to leave** il
lui est interdit de partir. ●**forbidding** *a*
(*look, landscape etc*) menaçant, sinistre.

force [fɔːs] *n* force *f*; **the (armed) forces** les
forces armées; **by (sheer) f.** de force; **in f.**
(*rule*) en vigueur; (*in great numbers*) en
grand nombre, en force.
 I *vt* forcer, contraindre (**to do** à faire);
(*impose*) imposer (**on** à); (*door, lock*) forcer;
(*confession*) arracher (**from** à); **to f. one's
way into** entrer de force dans; **to f. back** (*enemy, demonstrators etc*) faire reculer; (*repress*) refouler (*larmes, sanglots*); **to f. down**
(*aircraft*) forcer à atterrir; **to f. sth into sth**
faire entrer qch de force dans qch; **to f. sth
out** faire sortir qch de force. ●**forced** *a* **f. to
do** obligé *or* forcé de faire; **a f. smile** un
sourire forcé. ●**force-feed** *vt* (*pt & pp* **f.-
fed**) nourrir de force.

forceful ['fɔːsfəl] *a* énergique, puissant.
 ●**forcefully** *adv* avec force, énergiquement.

forceps ['fɔːseps] *n* forceps *m*.

forcible ['fɔːsəb(ə)l] *a* (*treatment etc*) de
force; (*forceful*) énergique. ●**forcibly** *adv*
(*by force*) de force; (*to argue, express etc*)
avec force.

ford [fɔːd] *n* gué *m* **I** *vt* (*river etc*) passer à
gué.

fore [fɔːr] *n* **to come to the f.** (*of question,
preoccupation etc*) passer au premier plan.

forearm ['fɔːrɑːm] *n* avant-bras *m inv*.

forebode [fɔːˈbəʊd] *vt* (*be a warning of*) présager. ●**foreboding** *n* (*feeling*) pressentiment
m.

forecast ['fɔːkɑːst] *vt* (*pt & pp* **forecast**) prévoir **I** *n* prévision *f*; (*of weather*) prévisions
fpl; (*in racing*) pronostic *m*.

forecourt ['fɔːkɔːt] *n* (*of hotel etc*) avant-
cour *f*; (*of Br petrol or Am gas station*) aire *f*
(de service), devant *m*.

forefathers ['fɔːfɑːðəz] *npl* aïeux *mpl*.

forefinger ['fɔːfɪŋgər] *n* index *m*.

forefront ['fɔːfrʌnt] *n* **in the f. of** au premier
rang de.

forego [fɔːˈgəʊ] *vt* (*pp* **foregone**) renoncer à;
it's a foregone conclusion c'est couru
d'avance.

foregoing [fɔːˈgəʊɪŋ] *a* précédent.

foreground ['fɔːgraʊnd] *n* premier plan *m*.

forehead ['fɒrɪd, 'fɔːhed] *n* (*brow*) front *m*.

foreign ['fɒrən] *a* (*language, person, country
etc*) étranger; (*trade*) extérieur; (*travel,
correspondent*) à l'étranger; (*produce*) de
l'étranger; **f. body** (*in eye etc*) corps *m*
étranger; **F. Minister**, *Br* **F. Secretary** ministre *m* des Affaires étrangères; **the f. service**
Am le service diplomatique. ●**foreigner** *n*
étranger, -ère *mf*.

foreman ['fɔːmən] *n* (*pl* -**men**) (*worker*) contremaître *m*; (*of jury*) président *m*.

foremost ['fɔːməʊst] **1** *a* principal. **2** *adv* **first
and f.** tout d'abord.

forensic [fəˈrensɪk] *a* **f. medicine** médecine *f*
légale; **f. laboratory/department** laboratoire
m/service *m* médico-légal.

forerunner ['fɔːrʌnər] *n* précurseur *m*.

foresee [fɔːˈsiː] *vt* (*pt* foresaw, *pp* foreseen)
prévoir. ●**foreseeable** *a* prévisible.

foreshadow [fɔːˈʃædəʊ] *vt* présager.

foresight ['fɔːsaɪt] *n* prévoyance *f*.

forest ['fɒrɪst] *n* forêt *f*. ●**forester** *n* (*garde
m*) forestier *m*.

forestall [fɔːˈstɔːl] *vt* devancer.

foretaste ['fɔːteɪst] *n* avant-goût *m* (**of** de).

foretell [fɔːˈtel] *vt* (*pt & pp* foretold) prédire.

forethought ['fɔːθɔːt] *n* prévoyance *f*.

forever [fəˈrevər] *adv* (*for always*) pour toujours; (*continually*) sans cesse.

forewarn [fɔːˈwɔːn] *vt* avertir.

foreword ['fɔːwɜːd] *n* avant-propos *m inv*.

forfeit ['fɔːfɪt] *vt* (*lose*) perdre **I** *n* (*penalty*)
peine *f*; (*in game*) gage *m*.

forge [fɔːdʒ] **1** *vt* (*signature, money*) contrefaire; (*document*) falsifier. **2** *vt* (*friendship,
bond*) forger. **3** *vi* **to f. ahead** (*progress*) aller
de l'avant. **4** *vt* (*metal, iron*) forger **I** *n* forge
f. ●**forged** *a* (*passport etc*) faux (*f* fausse);
f. money fausse monnaie *f*. ●**forger** *n* (*of documents, money etc*) faussaire *m*.

forgery ['fɔːdʒərɪ] *n* faux *m*, contrefaçon *f*.

forget [fəˈget] *vt* (*pt* forgot, *pp* forgotten,
pres p forgetting) oublier (**to do** de faire); **f.
it!** *Fam* (*when thanked*) pas de quoi!; (*it
doesn't matter*) peu importe!; **to f. oneself**
s'oublier **I** *vi* oublier; **to f. about** oublier.
 ●**forget-me-not** *n* (*plant*) myosotis *m*.

forgetful [fəˈgetfəl] *a* **he's f.** il n'a pas de
mémoire; **to be f. of** oublier, être oublieux

de. ●**forgetfulness** n manque m de mémoire; (carelessness) négligence f; **in a moment of f.** dans un moment d'oubli.

forgive [fə'gɪv] vt (pt **forgave**, pp **forgiven**) pardonner (s.o. sth qch à qn). ●**forgiving** a indulgent. ●**forgiveness** n pardon m; (compassion) clémence f.

forgo [fɔː'gəʊ] vt (pp **forgone**) renoncer à.

fork [fɔːk] **1** n (for eating) fourchette f; (for garden etc) fourche f. **2** vi (of road) bifurquer; **to f. left** (in vehicle) prendre à gauche [f. in road] bifurcation f, fourche f. **3** vt **to f. out** (money) Fam allonger ■ vi **to f. out** (pay) Fam casquer (on pour). ●**forked** a (branch etc) fourchu. ●**forklift truck** n chariot m élévateur.

forlorn [fə'lɔːn] a (forsaken) abandonné; (unhappy) triste, affligé.

form [fɔːm] n (shape, type, style) forme f; (document) formulaire m; (in school) Br classe f; **it's good f.** c'est ce qui se fait; **in the f. of** en forme de; **a f. of speech** une façon de parler; **on f., in good** or **top f.** en (pleine) forme.
■ vt (group, basis, character etc) former; (clay) façonner; (habit) contracter; (constitute) constituer, former (gouvernement, alliance etc); **to f. part of** faire partie de; **to f. an opinion/impression (of)** se faire une opinion/impression (of de).
■ vi (appear) se former.

formal ['fɔːm(ə)l] a (person, tone etc) cérémonieux; (stuffy) compassé; (official) (announcement, dinner etc) officiel; (in due form) (agreement etc) en bonne et due forme; (denial, structure, logic) formel; (resemblance) extérieur; **f. dress** tenue f or habit m de cérémonie; **f. education** éducation f scolaire; **f. language** langue f soignée. ●**for'mality** n (requirement) formalité f; (of occasion etc) cérémonie f. ●**formally** adv (to declare etc) officiellement; **f. dressed** en tenue de cérémonie.

format ['fɔːmæt] n (layout) présentation f; (size) format m ■ vt (computer diskette etc) formater.

formation [fɔː'meɪʃ(ə)n] n formation f.

formative ['fɔːmətɪv] a formateur.

former ['fɔːmər] **1** a (previous) (president, teacher, job, house etc) ancien; (situation, life) antérieur; **my f. colleague** mon ancien collègue; **her f. husband** son ex-mari m; **in f. days** autrefois. **2** a (of two) premier ■ pron **the f.** celui-ci, celle-là, le premier, la première. ●**formerly** adv autrefois.

formidable ['fɔːmɪdəb(ə)l] a effroyable, terrible.

formula ['fɔːmjʊlə] n **1** (pl **-as** or **-ae** [-iː]) (rule, symbols etc) formule f. **2** (pl **-as**) (baby food) lait m maternisé (en poudre). ●**formulate** vt formuler. ●**formulation** [-'leɪʃ(ə)n] n formulation f.

forsake [fə'seɪk] vt (pt **forsook**, pp **forsaken**) abandonner.

fort [fɔːt] n (building) Mil fort m; **to hold the**

f. (look after shop, office in s.o.'s absence) Fam garder la boutique.

forte [Br 'fɔːteɪ, Am fɔːt] n (strong point) fort m; **that's not my f.** ce n'est pas mon fort.

forth [fɔːθ] adv en avant; **from this day f.** désormais; **and so f.** et ainsi de suite; **to go back and f.** aller et venir.

forthcoming [fɔːθ'kʌmɪŋ] a **1** (event) à venir; (book, film) qui va sortir; **my f. book** mon prochain livre. **2** (available) disponible. **3** (open, frank) (person) communicatif, franc (f franche); (helpful) serviable.

forthright ['fɔːθraɪt] a direct, franc (f franche).

forthwith [fɔːθ'wɪð] adv sur-le-champ.

fortieth ['fɔːtɪəθ] a & n quarantième (mf).

fortify ['fɔːtɪfaɪ] vt (strengthen) fortifier; **to f. s.o.** (of food, drink) réconforter qn, remonter qn. ●**fortification** [-'keɪʃ(ə)n] n fortification f.

fortitude ['fɔːtɪtjuːd] n courage m (moral).

fortnight ['fɔːtnaɪt] n Br quinze jours mpl, quinzaine f (de jours). ●**fortnightly** a Br bimensuel ■ adv tous les quinze jours.

fortress ['fɔːtrɪs] n forteresse f.

fortuitous [fɔː'tjuːɪtəs] a fortuit.

fortunate ['fɔːtʃənɪt] a (choice, event etc) heureux; **to be f.** (of person) avoir de la chance; **to be f. enough to...** avoir la chance de...; **it's f. (for her) that** c'est heureux (pour elle) que (+ sub). ●**fortunately** adv heureusement.

fortune ['fɔːtʃuːn] n (wealth) fortune f; (luck) chance f; (chance) sort m, hasard m, fortune f; **to have the good f. to do** avoir la chance or le bonheur de faire; **to tell s.o.'s f.** dire la bonne aventure à qn; **to make one's f.** faire fortune; **to cost a f.** coûter une (petite) fortune. ●**fortune-teller** n diseur, -euse mf de bonne aventure.

forty ['fɔːtɪ] a & n quarante (m).

forum ['fɔːrəm] n forum m.

forward ['fɔːwəd] adv **forward(s)** en avant; **to go f.** avancer; **from this time f.** désormais ■ a (movement) en avant; (child) Fig précoce; (impudent) effronté; **the f. gears** (in vehicle) les vitesses fpl avant ■ n Football avant m ■ vt (letter) faire suivre; (goods) expédier; **forwarding address** nouvelle adresse f (pour faire suivre le courrier). ●**forward-looking** a tourné vers l'avenir. ●**forwardness** n (of child) précocité f; (impudence) effronterie f.

fossil ['fɒs(ə)l] n fossile m ■ a (animal, plant) fossile.

foster ['fɒstər] **1** vt (music, art etc) encourager. **2** vt (child) élever en famille d'accueil ■ a (child, parents) adoptif; **f. home** or **family** famille f d'accueil.

fought [fɔːt] pt & pp of fight.

foul [faʊl] **1** a (-er, -est) (smell, taste, weather, person etc) infect; (air) vicié; (breath) fétide; (language) grossier; (action, place) immonde; **to be f.-mouthed** avoir un langage grossier.

2 n Sport coup m irrégulier; Football faute f
∎ a f. play Sport jeu m irrégulier; (violence)
Jur acte m criminel.
3 vt to f. (up) (get dirty) salir; (air) vicier;
(pipe, drain) encrasser; to f. up (plans, s.o.'s
life) Fam gâcher; to f. the pavement (of dog)
Br salir le trottoir. ●**foul-up** n (disorder) cafouillage m; (in system) Fam raté m.
found¹ [faʊnd] pt & pp of **find**.
found² [faʊnd] vt (town, political party etc)
fonder; (opinion, suspicions etc) fonder,
baser (on sur). ●**founder¹** n fondateur, -trice
mf.
foundation [faʊn'deɪʃ(ə)n] n fondation f;
(basis of agreement etc) bases fpl, fonde-
ment(s) m(pl); **the foundations** (of building)
les fondations fpl; **without f.** sans fondement; **f. cream** fond m de teint.
founder² ['faʊndər] vi (of ship) sombrer.
foundry ['faʊndrɪ] n fonderie f.
fountain ['faʊntɪn] n fontaine f; **f. pen**
stylo(-plume) m.
four [fɔːr] a & n quatre (m); **on all fours** à
quatre pattes; **f.-letter word** = mot m de
cinq lettres. ●**fourth** a & n quatrième (mf).
fourfold ['fɔːfəʊld] a quadruple ∎ adv au
quadruple.
foursome ['fɔːsəm] n (two couples) deux
couples mpl; **to go out as a f.** sortir à deux
couples.
fourteen [fɔː'tiːn] a & n quatorze (m).
●**fourteenth** a & n quatorzième (mf).
fowl [faʊl] n (hens etc for breeding) la volaille; **a f.** une volaille.
fox [fɒks] **1** n renard m. **2** vt (puzzle) mystifier; (trick) tromper. ●**foxy** a (sly) rusé, futé.
foxglove ['fɒksglʌv] n (plant) digitale f.
foyer [Br 'fɔɪeɪ, Am 'fɔɪər] n (in theatre)
foyer m; (in hotel) hall m.
fraction ['frækʃ(ə)n] n fraction f. ●**fraction-
ally** adv un tout petit peu.
fractious ['frækʃəs] a grincheux.
fracture ['fræktʃər] n fracture f ∎ vt fracturer;
to f. one's leg/etc se fracturer la jambe/etc ∎
vi se fracturer.
fragile [Br 'frædʒaɪl, Am 'frædʒ(ə)l] a fragile. ●**fragility** [frə'dʒɪlətɪ] n fragilité f.
fragment ['frægmənt] n fragment m,
morceau m. ●**frag'mented** or **fragmentary** a
fragmentaire.
fragrant ['freɪgrənt] a parfumé. ●**fragrance** n
parfum m.
frail [freɪl] a (-er, -est) (person) fragile, frêle;
(hope, health) fragile. ●**frailty** n fragilité f.
frame [freɪm] **1** n (of building, person)
charpente f; (of picture, bicycle) cadre m;
(of window, car) châssis m; (of spectacles)
monture f; **f. of mind** humeur f ∎ vt (picture)
encadrer; (proposals, ideas etc) Fig formuler.
2 vt **to f. s.o.** Fam monter un coup contre
qn. ●**frame-up** n Fam coup m monté.
●**framework** n structure f; **(with)in the f. of**
(context) dans le cadre de.
franc [fræŋk] n franc m.
France [frɑːns] n France f.

franchise ['fræntʃaɪz] n **1** (right to vote)
droit m de vote. **2** (right to sell product)
franchise f.
Franco- ['fræŋkəʊ] pref franco-.
frank¹ [fræŋk] a (-er, -est) (honest) franc (f
franche). ●**frankly** adv franchement. ●**frankness** n franchise f.
frank² [fræŋk] **1** vt (letter) affranchir; **frank-
ing machine** machine f à affranchir. **2** n Am
Fam = **frankfurter**.
frankfurter ['fræŋkfɜːtər] n saucisse f de
Francfort.
frantic ['fræntɪk] a (activity, shouts) frénétique; (rush, efforts, desire) effréné; (person)
hors de soi; **f. with joy** fou de joie. ●**frantically** adv (to run, search etc) comme un fou.
fraternal [frə'tɜːn(ə)l] a fraternel. ●**fraternity**
n (bond of friendship) fraternité f; (in American university) association f de camarades
de classe; **the publishing**/etc **f.** la grande famille de l'édition/etc. ●**fraternize**
['frætənaɪz] vi fraterniser (**with** avec).
fraud [frɔːd] n **1** (crime) fraude f; **to obtain
sth by f.** obtenir qch frauduleusement. **2**
(person) imposteur m. ●**fraudulent** a frauduleux.
fraught [frɔːt] a **f. with** plein de, chargé de;
to be f. (of situation, person) être tendu.
fray [freɪ] **1** vi (of garment) s'effilocher; (of
rope) s'user ∎ vt (garment) effilocher; (rope)
user; **my nerves are frayed** j'ai les nerfs à
vif; **tempers were frayed** on s'énervait. **2** n
(fight) rixe f.
freak [friːk] n (person) phénomène m, monstre m; **a jazz**/etc **f.** Fam un(e) fana de jazz/
etc ∎ a (result, weather etc) anormal; **a f.
accident** un accident très rare. ●**freakish** a
anormal.
freckle ['frek(ə)l] n tache f de rousseur.
●**freckled** a couvert de taches de rousseur.
free [friː] a (**freer**, **freest**) (at liberty, not
occupied) libre; (without cost) gratuit; (lavish) généreux (**with** de); **to get f.** se libérer;
f. to do libre de faire; **to let s.o. go f.** relâcher qn; **f. of charge** gratuit; **f. of pain**/
s.o./etc (rid of) débarrassé d'une douleur/de
qn/etc; **to have a f. hand** Fig avoir carte
blanche (**to do** pour faire); **f. and easy** décontracté; **f. gift** prime f; **f. kick** Football
coup m franc; **f.-range egg** Br œuf m de
ferme; **f. speech** liberté f d'expression; **f.
trade** libre-échange m.
∎ adv **f. (of charge)** gratuitement.
∎ vt (pt & pp **freed**) (prisoner, country etc)
libérer; (trapped person) dégager; (person
trapped in car wreckage) désincarcérer; (untie) détacher.
freebie ['friːbiː] n Fam petit cadeau m,
prime f.
freedom ['friːdəm] n liberté f; **f. of speech**
liberté f d'expression; **f. from worry**/
responsibility/etc absence f de souci/de
responsabilité/etc; **f. fighter** guérillero m.
Freefone® ['friːfəʊn] n (phone number) Br =
numéro m vert. ●**free-for-'all** n mêlée f gé-

nérale. ●**freehold** *n* propriété *f* foncière
libre. ●**freelance** *a* indépendant ▌ *n* collaborateur, -trice *mf* indépendant(e). ●**freeloader**
n (*sponger*) parasite *m*. ●**Freemason** *n*
franc-maçon *m*. ●**Freemasonry** *n* franc-maçonnerie *f*. ●**Freepost**® *n Br* Libre Réponse *f*. ●**freestyle** *n Swimming* nage *f* libre.
●**free'thinker** *n* libre penseur, -euse *mf*.
●**freeway** *n Am* autoroute *f*. ●**free'wheel** *vi*
(*in vehicle*) rouler en roue libre.

freely ['friːli] *adv* (*to speak, act, circulate etc*)
librement; (*to give*) libéralement.

freeze [friːz] *vi* (*pt* **froze**, *pp* **frozen**) geler;
(*of smile*) *Fig* se figer; (*of person*) (*stop
dead*) s'arrêter net; **f.!** *Am* ne bougez plus!;
to f. to death mourir de froid; **to f. easily/
well** (*of food*) se congeler facilement/bien; **to
f. up** *or* **over** (*of lake etc*) geler; (*of window*)
se givrer.
▌ *vt* (*food*) congeler, surgeler; (*credits, river*)
geler; (*prices, wages*) bloquer; **frozen food**
surgelés *mpl*.
▌ *n* (*freezing weather*) gel *m*; (*of prices etc*)
blocage *m*. ●**freeze-dry** *vt* (*food*) lyophiliser.

freezer ['friːzər] *n* (*deep-freeze*) congélateur
m; (*in fridge*) freezer *m*.

freezing ['friːzɪŋ] *a* (*weather etc*) glacial;
(*hands, person*) gelé; **it's f.** on gèle ▌ *adv* **f.
cold** très froid; **I'm f. cold** j'ai très froid ▌ *n*
it's 5 degrees below f. il fait 5 degrés au-dessous de zéro.

freight [freɪt] *n* (*goods, price for transport*)
fret *m*; (*transport*) transport *m*; **f. train** *Am*
train *m* de marchandises ▌ *vt* (*ship*) affréter.
●**freighter** *n* (*ship*) cargo *m*.

French [frentʃ] *a* français; (*teacher*) de
français; (*embassy*) de France; **F. fries** *Am*
frites *fpl* ▌ *n* (*language*) français *m*; **the F.**
(*people*) les Français *mpl*. ●**Frenchman** *n* (*pl*
-men) Français *m*. ●**French-speaking** *a* (*person, country etc*) francophone. ●**Frenchwoman** *n* (*pl* **-women**) Française *f*.

frenzy ['frenzi] *n* frénésie *f*. ●**frenzied** *a*
(*shouts etc*) frénétique; (*person*) effréné;
(*attack*) violent.

frequency ['friːkwənsi] *n* fréquence *f*.

frequent *a* ['friːkwənt] *a* fréquent; **f. visitor**
habitué, -ée *mf* (**to** de) ▌ *vt* [frɪ'kwent] *vt* fréquenter. ●**frequently** *adv* fréquemment.

fresco ['freskəʊ] *n* (*pl* **-oes** *or* **-os**) fresque *f*.

fresh [freʃ] **1** *a* (**-er, -est**) frais (*f* fraîche);
(*new*) nouveau (*f* nouvelle); (*impudent*) *Fam*
culotté; **to get some f. air** prendre l'air; **f.-
water** fish poisson *m* d'eau douce. **2** *adv* **to
be f. from** (*city, country*) arriver tout juste
de; (*school, university*) sortir tout juste de.
●**freshly** *adv* (*arrived, picked etc*) fraîchement. ●**freshness** *n* fraîcheur *f*. (*impudence*)
Fam culot *m*.

freshen ['freʃən] **1** *vi* (*of wind*) fraîchir. **2** *vi*
to f. up (*have a wash*) faire un brin de toilette ▌ *vt* **to f. up** (*house etc*) retaper; **to f.
s.o. up** (*of bath, shower*) rafraîchir qn.
●**freshener** *n* **air f.** désodorisant *m*.

fresher ['freʃər] *n Br* étudiant, -ante *mf* de

première année.

freshman ['freʃmən] *n* (*pl* **-men**) *Am* étudiant, -ante *mf* de première année.

fret [fret] *vi* (**-tt-**) (*worry*) se faire du souci,
s'en faire; (*of baby*) pleurer. ●**fretful** *a*
(*baby, child*) grognon (*f* -onne).

friar ['fraɪər] *n* frère *m*, moine *m*.

friction ['frɪkʃ(ə)n] *n* friction *f*.

Friday [*Br* 'fraɪdɪ, *Am* -deɪ] *n* vendredi *m*;
Good F. Vendredi Saint.

fridge [frɪdʒ] *n* frigo *m*.

fried [fraɪd] *pt* & *pp* of **fry** ▌ *a* (*fish etc*) frit;
f. egg œuf *m* sur le plat. ●**frier** *n* (*pan*) friteuse *f*.

friend [frend] *n* ami, -ie *mf*; (*from school,
work*) camarade *mf*; **to be friends with s.o.**
être ami avec qn; **to make friends with s.o.**
se lier avec qn. ●**friendly** *a* (**-ier, -iest**) aimable, gentil (**to** avec); (*child, animal*)
gentil, affectueux; (*attitude, smile*) amical;
some f. advice un conseil d'ami; **to be on f.
terms with s.o.** être en bons termes avec qn;
to be f. with s.o. être en bons termes avec
qn; (*friends*) être ami avec qn. ●**friendship** *n*
amitié *f*.

frieze [friːz] *n* (*on building*) frise *f*.

frigate ['frɪgət] *n* (*ship*) frégate *f*.

fright [fraɪt] *n* peur *f*; **to have a f.** avoir peur;
to give s.o. a f. faire peur à qn; **you look a
f.!** *Fam* tu te verrais (— tu es grotesque!)

frighten ['fraɪtən] *vt* effrayer, faire peur à; **to
f. away** *or* **off** (*animal, person*) faire fuir.
●**frightened** *a* effrayé; **to be f.** avoir peur (**of**
de). ●**frightening** *a* effrayant.

frightful ['fraɪtfəl] *a* affreux. ●**frightfully** *adv*
(*ugly, late*) affreusement; (*kind, glad*)
terriblement; **f. sorry** absolument désolé.

frigid ['frɪdʒɪd] *a* (*greeting, manner etc*) froid;
(*woman*) frigide.

frill [frɪl] *n* **1** (*on dress, curtain etc*) volant *m*.
2 frills (*useless embellishments*) fioritures *fpl*,
superflu *m*; **no frills** (*machine, Br holiday,
Am vacation etc*) sans rien de superflu; **we
had a no frills meal** nous avons fait un repas
des plus simples.

fringe [frɪndʒ] **1** *n* (*of hair*) *Br* frange *f*; (*on
clothes, curtains etc*) frange *f*. **2** *n* (*of forest*)
lisière *f*; **on the fringe(s) of society** en marge
de la société; **f. group/lifestyle/etc** groupe *m*/
mode *m* de vie/etc marginal; **f. benefits** (*in
job*) avantages *mpl* divers; **f. theatre** *Br*
théâtre *m* expérimental.

Frisbee® ['frɪzbiː] *n* Frisbee® *m*.

frisk [frɪsk] **1** *vt* (*search*) fouiller (au corps). **2**
vi **to f.** (**about**) gambader.

frisky ['frɪskɪ] *a* (**-ier, -iest**) (*lively*) vif.

fritter ['frɪtər] **1** *vt* **to f. away** (*waste*) gaspiller
(*son temps etc*). **2** *n* (*fried food*) beignet *m*.

frivolous ['frɪvələs] *a* frivole. ●**fri'volity** *n*
frivolité *f*.

frizzy ['frɪzɪ] *a* (*hair*) crépu.

fro [frəʊ] *adv* **to go to and f.** aller et venir.

frock [frɒk] *n* (*dress*) robe *f*; (*of monk*) froc
m.

frog [frɒg] *n* grenouille *f*; **to have a f. in one's**

throat *Fam* avoir un chat dans la gorge.
●**frogman** *n* (*pl* **-men**) homme-grenouille *m*.

frolic ['frolik] *vi* (*pt* & *pp* **frolicked**) to f.
(about) gambader. ●**frolics** *npl* (*playing*)
gambades *fpl*; (*pranks*) gamineries *fpl*.

from [from, *unstressed* frəm] *prep* **1** de; a
letter f. une lettre de; to suffer f. souffrir de;
where are you f.? d'où êtes-vous?; a train f.
un train en provenance de; to be ten metres
(away) f. the house être à dix mètres de la
maison.

2 (*time onwards*) à partir de, dès, depuis; f.
today (on), as f. today à partir d'aujourd'hui,
dès aujourd'hui; f. her childhood dès *or* depuis son enfance.

3 (*numbers, prices, time onwards*) à partir
de; f. five francs à partir de cinq francs; f.
tomorrow (on *or* onwards) à partir de demain.

4 (*away from*) à; to take/hide/borrow f.
prendre/cacher/emprunter à.

5 (*out of*) dans; sur; to take f. (*box*) prendre
dans; (*table*) prendre sur; to drink f. a cup/
etc boire dans une tasse/*etc*; to drink
(straight) f. the bottle boire à (même) la
bouteille.

6 (*according to*) d'après; f. what I saw
d'après ce que j'ai vu; f. a poem by...
d'après un poème de....

7 (*cause*) par; f. conviction/habit/*etc* par
conviction/habitude/*etc*.

8 (*on the part of, on behalf of*) de la part de;
tell her f. me dis-lui de ma part.

front [frʌnt] *n* (*of garment, building*) devant
m; (*of boat, car*) avant *m*; (*of crowd*) premier rang *m*; (*of book*) début *m*; *Mil Pol
Met* front *m*; on the (sea) f. (*beach*) *Br* sur le
front de mer; it's just a f. (*appearance*) *Fig*
ce n'est qu'une façade; in f. of s.o./sth devant qn/qch; in f. devant; (*further ahead*) en
avant; (*in race*) en tête; in the f. (*of vehicle*)
à l'avant; (*of house*) devant.
▮ *a* (*tooth, garden etc*) de devant; (*part,
wheel, car seat*) avant *inv*; (*row, page*) premier; f. view (*not side view*) vue *f* de face; f.
door porte *f* d'entrée; f. line *Mil* front *m*; f.
room (*lounge*) *Br* salon *m*; f. runner *Fig* favori, -ite *mf*; f.-wheel drive (*on vehicle*) traction *f* avant.
▮ *vi* to f. on to (*of windows etc*) donner sur.

frontage ['frʌntidʒ] *n* façade *f*.

frontal ['frʌntəl] *a* (*attack*) de front.

frontier ['frʌntiər] *n* frontière *f*; f. town/post
ville *f*/poste *m* frontière *inv*.

frost [frost] *n* gel *m*, gelée *f*; (*frozen drops
on window, grass etc*) givre *m*, gelée *f*
blanche ▮ *vi* to f. up (*of window etc*) se
givrer.

frostbite ['frostbait] *n* gelure *f*. ●**frostbitten**
a gelé.

frosted ['frostid] *a* **1** (*glass*) dépoli. **2** (*cake*)
Am glacé.

frosting ['frostiŋ] *n* (*icing on cake*) *Am* glaçage *m*.

frosty ['frosti] *a* (**-ier, -iest**) (*air, night,*

weather, *Fig* welcome *etc*) glacial; (*window*)
givré; it's f. il gèle.

froth [froθ] *n* mousse *f* ▮ *vi* mousser. ●**frothy**
a (**-ier, -iest**) (*beer etc*) mousseux.

frown [fraun] *n* froncement *m* de sourcils ▮ *vi*
froncer les sourcils; to f. (up)on *Fig* désapprouver.

froze, frozen [frəuz, 'frəuz(ə)n] *pt* & *pp* of
freeze.

frugal ['fruːg(ə)l] *a* (*meal, life, person*) frugal. ●**frugally** *adv* frugalement.

fruit [fruːt] *n* fruit *m*; (*some*) f. (*one item*) un
fruit; (*more than one*) des fruits; to like f. aimer les fruits; f. basket/bowl corbeille *f*/
coupe *f* à fruits; f. drink boisson *f* aux fruits;
f. juice jus *m* de fruit; f. salad salade *f* de
fruits; f. tree arbre *m* fruitier; f. machine
(*for gambling*) *Br* machine *f* à sous.
●**fruitcake** *n* cake *m*. ●**fruiterer** *n* *Br* fruitier,
-ière *mf*.

fruitful ['fruːtfəl] *a* (*meeting, career etc*)
fructueux, fécond. ●**fruitless** *a* (*efforts etc*)
stérile.

fruition [fruːˈɪʃ(ə)n] *n* to come to f. (*of plan
etc*) se réaliser.

fruity ['fruːti] *a* (**-ier, -iest**) (*taste, smell*) de
fruit; (*joke*) *Br Fam* corsé.

frumpish ['frʌmpiʃ] *or* **frumpy** ['frʌmpi] *a*
Fam (*woman*) (mal) fagotée.

frustrate [frʌˈstreit] *vt* (*person*) frustrer;
(*plans*) faire échouer; (*hopes, ambitions*) décevoir. ●**frustrated** *a* (*mentally, sexually*)
frustré; (*effort*) vain. ●**frustrating** *a* irritant.
●**frustration** [-ˈstreiʃ(ə)n] *n* frustration *f*;
(*disappointment*) déception *f*.

fry¹ [frai] *vt* (*pt* & *pp* **fried**) faire frire ▮ *vi*
frire. ●**frying** *n* friture *f*; f. pan poêle *f* (à
frire). ●**fryer** *n* (*deep pan*) friteuse *f*.

fry² [frai] *n* small f. (*people*) menu fretin *m*;
it's small f. (*project, affair etc*) ce n'est pas
grand-chose.

fry-up ['fraiʌp] *n* *Br Fam* = pommes de
terre, bacon, saucisses *etc* frits ensemble.

ft *abbr* (*measure*) = foot, feet.

fuddled ['fʌd(ə)ld] *a* (*drunk*) gris; (*confused*)
embrouillé.

fuddy-duddy ['fʌdidʌdi] *n* he's an old f.-
duddy *Fam* c'est un vieux schnoque.

fudge [fʌdʒ] **1** *n* (*Br sweet, Am candy*) caramel *m* mou. **2** *vt* to f. the issue refuser
d'aborder le problème.

fuel [fjuəl] *n* combustible *m*; (*for vehicle*)
carburant *m*; f. (oil) mazout *m*; f. tank (*in
vehicle*) réservoir *m* ▮ *vt* (*Br* **-ll-**, *Am* **-l-**)
(*stove*) alimenter; (*vehicle, plane, ship*) ravitailler (en combustible); (*s.o.'s anger, hatred
etc*) attiser; to be fuelled by diesel/*etc* (*of
engine*) marcher au gazole/*etc*.

fugitive ['fjuːdʒitiv] *n* fugitif, -ive *mf*.

fugue [fjuːg] *n* *Mus* fugue *f*.

fulfil, *Am* **fulfill** [fulˈfil] *vt* (**-ll-**) (*ambition,
dream, wish*) réaliser; (*condition, duty, pro-
mise*) remplir; (*desire*) satisfaire; (*order*)
exécuter; to f. oneself s'épanouir. ●**fulfilling**
a satisfaisant. ●**fulfilment** *or* *Am* **fulfillment** *n*

(*of ambition etc*) réalisation *f* (**of** de); (*feeling*) satisfaction *f*.

full [ful] *a* (**-er, -est**) plein (**of** de); (*bus, theatre, meal*) complet; (*life, day, programme*) (bien) rempli; (*skirt*) ample; **to be f. (up)** (*of person*) n'avoir plus faim; (*of hotel*) être complet; **f. information/examination** des renseignements/un examen complet(s); **a f. member** un membre à part entière; **to wait a f. hour** attendre une heure entière; **the f. price** le prix fort; **to pay (the) f. fare** payer plein tarif; **the f. facts** tous les faits; **at f. speed** à toute vitesse; **f. name** (*on form*) nom et prénom; **f. stop** *Grammar Br* point *m*.

▎ *adv* **to know f. well** savoir fort bien; **f. in the face** (*to hit etc*) en pleine figure.

▎ *n* **in f.** (*to read sth, publish sth*) en entier, intégralement; (*to write one's name*) en toutes lettres; **the text in f.** le texte intégral; **to pay in f.** tout payer, payer en totalité; **to the f.** (*completely*) tout à fait.

full-back ['fulbæk] *n Football* arrière *m*. **●full-'grown** *a* (*person, animal etc*) adulte; (*foetus*) arrivé à terme. **●full-'length** *a* (*film*) de long métrage; (*portrait*) en pied; (*dress*) long. **●full-'scale** *a* (*model, drawing etc*) grandeur nature *inv*; (*operation, attack etc*) de grande envergure. **●full-'sized** *a* (*model, drawing etc*) grandeur nature *inv*. **●full-'time** *a* & *adv* (*work etc*) à plein temps.

fullness ['fulnɪs] *n* (*of details*) abondance *f*; (*of dress*) ampleur *f*.

fully ['fulɪ] *adv* (*completely*) entièrement; (*thoroughly*) à fond; (*at least*) au moins.

fully-fledged, *Am* **full-fledged** [ful(ɪ)'fledʒd] *a* (*engineer, teacher etc*) diplômé; (*member*) à part entière. **●fully-formed** *a* (*baby etc*) formé. **●fully-grown** *a* = **full-grown.**

fulsome ['fulsəm] *a* (*praise etc*) excessif; **a f. apology** de plates excuses.

fumble ['fʌmb(ə)l] *vi* **to f.** (**about**) (*grope*) (*in the dark etc*) tâtonner; (*search*) (*in drawer etc*) fouiller (**for** pour trouver); **to f.** (**about**) **with** tripoter.

fume [fjuːm] 1 *vi* (*of person*) rager. 2 *vi* (*give off fumes*) fumer **▎** *npl* **fumes** vapeurs *fpl*; (*from car exhaust*) gaz *mpl*.

fumigate ['fjuːmɪgeɪt] *vt* désinfecter (par fumigation).

fun [fʌn] *n* amusement *m*; **to be** (*good or great*) **f.** être (très) amusant; **to have (some) f.** s'amuser; **to make f. of, poke f. at** se moquer de; **for f., for the f. of it** pour le plaisir; **to spoil s.o.'s f.** empêcher qn de s'amuser.

function ['fʌŋkʃ(ə)n] 1 *n* (*role, duty*) & *Math Comptr* fonction *f*; (*party*) réception *f*; (*meeting*) réunion *f*; (*public ceremony*) cérémonie *f* (publique). 2 *vi* (*work*) (*of machine etc*) fonctionner. **●functional** *a* fonctionnel.

fund [fʌnd] *n* (*for pension, emergency etc*) caisse *f*, fonds *m*; (*of knowledge etc*) *Fig* fond *m*; **funds** (*money resources*) fonds *mpl*; (*for special purpose*) crédits *mpl*; **f. manager** gestionnaire *mf* de fonds **▎** *vt* (*with money*) fournir des fonds *or* des crédits à.

fundamental [fʌndə'ment(ə)l] *a* fondamental **▎** *npl* **fundamentals** principes *mpl* essentiels.

funeral ['fjuːnərəl] *n* enterrement *m*; (*grandiose*) funérailles *fpl*; **f. service/march/etc** service *m*/marche *fletc* funèbre; **f. parlour** *Br*, **f. home** *Am* entreprise *f* de pompes funèbres; (*chapel*) chapelle *f* ardente.

funfair ['fʌnfeər] *n Br* fête *f* foraine; (*larger*) parc *m* d'attractions.

fungus, *pl* **-gi** ['fʌŋgəs, -gaɪ] *n* (*plant*) champignon *m*; (*Br mould, Am mold*) moisissure *f*.

funicular [fju'nɪkjulər] *n* funiculaire *m*.

funk [fʌŋk] *n* **to be in a f.** (*afraid*) *Fam* avoir la frousse; (*depressed, sulking*) *Am Fam* faire la gueule.

funnel ['fʌn(ə)l] *n* 1 (*of ship*) cheminée *f*. 2 (*tube for pouring*) entonnoir *m*.

funny ['fʌnɪ] *a* (**-ier, -iest**) (*amusing*) drôle; (*strange*) bizarre; **a f. idea** une drôle d'idée; **there's some f. business going on** il y a quelque chose de louche; **to feel f.** ne pas se sentir très bien. **●funnily** *adv* (*amusingly*) drôlement; (*strangely*) bizarrement; **f. enough, I was just about to...** chose bizarre, j'étais sur le point de....

fur [fɜːr] 1 *n* (*of animal, for wearing*) fourrure *f*; (*of dog, cat*) pelage *m*, poil *m*; **f. coat** manteau *m* de fourrure. 2 *n* (*in kettle, boiler etc*) *Br* dépôt *m* (de tartre) **▎** *vi* (**-rr-**) **to f.** (**up**) (*of kettle etc*) *Br* s'entartrer.

furious ['fjuərɪəs] *a* (*violent, angry*) furieux (**with, at** contre); (*efforts, struggle*) acharné; **at a f. speed** à une allure folle. **●furiously** *adv* furieusement; (*to struggle*) avec acharnement; (*to drive, rush*) à une allure folle.

furlong ['fɜːlɒŋ] *n* (*measurement*) = 201 mètres.

furnace ['fɜːnɪs] *n* (*forge*) fourneau *m*; (*hot room etc*) *Fig* fournaise *f*.

furnish ['fɜːnɪʃ] *vt* 1 (*room*) meubler. 2 (*supply*) fournir (**s.o. with sth** qch à qn). **●furnishings** *npl* ameublement *m*.

furniture ['fɜːnɪtʃər] *n* meubles *mpl*; **a piece of f.** un meuble; **f. shop** magasin *m* d'ameublement.

furrier ['fʌrɪər] *n* fourreur *m*.

furrow ['fʌrəu] *n* (*on brow, in earth*) sillon *m*.

furry ['fɜːrɪ] *a* (*animal*) à poil, (*toy*) en peluche.

further ['fɜːðər] 1 *adv* & *a* = **farther.** 2 *adv* (*more*) davantage, plus; (*besides*) en outre; **f. to my letter** suite à ma lettre **▎** *a* (*additional*) supplémentaire; **f. details** de plus amples détails; **a f. case/etc** (*another*) un autre cas/etc; **without f. delay** sans plus attendre; **f. education** enseignement *m* postscolaire. 3 *vt* (*cause, research, interests etc*) promouvoir.

furthermore ['fɜːðəmɔːr] *adv* en outre. **●furthest** *a* & *adv* = **farthest.**

furtive ['fɜːtɪv] *a* (*action, smile etc*) furtif; (*person*) sournois.

fury ['fjʊərɪ] n (*violence, anger*) fureur f.

fuse [fju:z] **1** vt **to f. the lights**/*etc* faire sauter les plombs **▌** vi **the lights**/*etc* **have fused** les plombs ont sauté **▌** n (*wire*) fusible m, plomb m. **2** n (*of bomb*) amorce f. **3** vt (*metal*) fondre; (*join together*) réunir par fusion (*pièces de métal*); (*merge*) *Fig* fusionner (*deux partis etc*) **▌** vi (*of metals*) fondre.

fused [fju:zd] a **a f. plug** *Br* fiche f avec fusible incorporé.

fuselage ['fju:zəlɑ:ʒ] n (*of aircraft*) fuselage m.

fusion ['fju:ʒən] n (*union*) & *Phys Biol* fusion f.

fuss [fʌs] n chichis mpl, façons fpl, histoires fpl; (*noise, bustle*) agitation f; **what a (lot of) f.!** quelle histoire!; **to make a f.**, *Br* **kick up a f.** faire des histoires; **to make a f. of s.o.** être aux petits soins pour qn.
▌ vi faire des chichis; (*worry*) se tracasser (**about** pour); (*rush about*) s'agiter; **to f. over s.o.** être aux petits soins pour qn. **●fusspot**

or *Am* **fussbudget** n *Fam* enquiquineur, -euse mf. **●fussy** a (-ier, -iest) tatillon, méticuleux; (*difficult*) difficile (**about** sur); **I'm not f.** (*I don't mind*) ça m'est égal.

fusty ['fʌstɪ] a (-ier, -iest) (*smell*) de renfermé.

futile [*Br* 'fju:taɪl, *Am* 'fju:t(ə)l] a futile, vain. **●fu'tility** n futilité f.

future ['fju:tʃər] n avenir m; *Grammar* futur m; **in f.** (*from now on*) à l'avenir; **in the f.** (*one day*) un jour (futur) **▌** a futur; **my f. wife** ma future épouse; **the f. tense** le futur; **at a** or **some f. date** à une date ultérieure.

fuze [fju:z] n, vt & vi *Am* = **fuse 1 & 2.**

fuzz [fʌz] n **1** (*down on face, legs etc*) *Fam* duvet m; (*of material*) *Am* peluche(s) f(pl); -(*on floor*) *Am* moutons mpl. **2 the f.** (*police*) *Sl* les flics mpl.

fuzzy ['fʌzɪ] a (-ier, -iest) **1** (*unclear*) (*picture, idea*) flou. **2** (*fleecy*) (*material, coat*) *Am* velouté. **3 f. hair** cheveux mpl crépus.

G

G, g [dʒiː] *n* G, g *m*. ●**G-string** *n* (*cloth*) cache-sexe *m inv*.

gab [gæb] *n* **to have the gift of the g.** *Fam* avoir du bagou(t).

gabardine [gæbə'diːn] *n* (*material, coat*) gabardine *f*.

gabble ['gæb(ə)l] *vi* (*chatter*) jacasser; (*indistinctly*) bredouiller ▮ *n* baragouin *m*.

gable ['geɪb(ə)l] *n* (*of building*) pignon *m*.

gad [gæd] *vi* (**-dd-**) **to g. about** *or* **around** vadrouiller, se balader.

gadget ['gædʒɪt] *n* gadget *m*.

Gaelic ['geɪlɪk, 'gælɪk] *a* & *n* gaélique (*m*).

gaffe [gæf] *n* (*blunder*) gaffe *f*, bévue *f*.

gag [gæg] **1** *n* (*over mouth*) bâillon *m* ▮ *vt* (**-gg-**) (*victim, Fig press etc*) bâillonner. **2** *n* (*joke*) plaisanterie *f*; (*of actor*) gag *m*. **3** *vi* (**-gg-**) (*choke*) s'étouffer (**on** avec); (*retch*) avoir des haut-le-cœur.

gaggle ['gæg(ə)l] *n* (*of geese*) troupeau *m*.

gaiety ['geɪtɪ] *n* (*cheerfulness etc*) gaieté *f*; (*brightness of colour*) éclat *m*. ●**gaily** *adv* gaiement.

gain [geɪn] *vt* (*obtain, win*) gagner; (*experience, reputation*) acquérir; (*objective*) atteindre; **to g. speed/weight** prendre de la vitesse/du poids; **to g. popularity** gagner en popularité; **to g. support** (*of person, idea, plan etc*) recueillir de plus en plus d'opinions favorables.

▮ *vi* (*of watch, clock*) avancer; **my watch gains 5 minutes a day** ma montre avance de *or* prend 5 minutes par jour; **to g. in strength** gagner en force; **to g. on s.o.** (*catch up with*) rattraper qn.

▮ *n* (*increase*) augmentation *f* (**in** de); (*profit*) bénéfice *m*, gain *m*; *Fig* avantage *m*.

gainful ['geɪnfəl] *a* profitable; **g. employment** emploi *m* rémunéré.

gainsay [geɪn'seɪ] *vt* (*pt* & *pp* **gainsaid** [-sed]) (*person*) contredire; (*facts*) nier.

gait [geɪt] *n* (*walk*) démarche *f*.

gala [*Br* 'gɑːlə, *Am* 'geɪlə] *n* gala *m*; **swimming g.** *Br* concours *m* de natation.

galaxy ['gæləksɪ] *n* galaxie *f*.

gale [geɪl] *n* grand vent *m*, rafale *f* (de vent).

gall [gɔːl] **1** *n* (*bitterness*) *Lit* fiel *m*; (*impudence*) *Fam* effronterie *f*. **2 g. bladder** vésicule *f* biliaire. **3** *vt* (*annoy*) irriter.

gallant ['gælənt] *a* (*chivalrous*) galant; (*brave*) courageux; (*splendid*) *Lit* magnifique. ●**gallantry** *n* (*bravery*) courage *m*.

galleon ['gælɪən] *n* (*ship*) *Hist* galion *m*.

gallery ['gælərɪ] *n* (*room etc*) galerie *f*; (*for public, press*) tribune *f*; **the g.** (*in theatre*) les troisièmes galeries *fpl*; **art g.** (*private*) galerie *f* d'art; (*public*) musée *m* d'art.

galley ['gælɪ] *n* (*ship*) *Hist* galère *f*; (*kitchen in ship, on aircraft*) office *m*.

Gallic ['gælɪk] *a* (*French*) français. ●**gallicism** *n* (*word etc*) gallicisme *m*.

galling ['gɔːlɪŋ] *a* irritant.

gallivant ['gælɪvænt] *vi* **to g. (about)** *Fam* vadrouiller, courir.

gallon ['gælən] *n* gallon *m* (*Br* = 4,5 litres, *Am* = 3,8 litres).

gallop ['gæləp] *n* galop *m* ▮ *vi* galoper; **to g. away** (*rush off*) partir au galop *or* en vitesse; **galloping inflation** l'inflation *f* galopante.

gallows ['gæləʊz] *npl* potence *f*.

gallstone ['gɔːlstəʊn] *n* *Med* calcul *m* biliaire.

galore [gə'lɔːr] *adv* à gogo, en abondance.

galoshes [gə'lɒʃɪz] *npl* (*shoes*) caoutchoucs *mpl*.

galvanize ['gælvənaɪz] *vt* (*metal, Fig person*) galvaniser.

Gambia ['gæmbɪə] *n* **The G.** la Gambie *f*.

gambit ['gæmbɪt] *n* **opening g.** (*ploy*) manœuvre *f* stratégique.

gamble ['gæmb(ə)l] *vi* jouer (**on** sur, **with** avec); **to g. on sth** (*count on*) miser sur qch ▮ *vt* (*bet*) parier, jouer (**ten dollars/***etc* dix dollars/*etc*); **to g. (away)** (*lose*) perdre (au jeu) ▮ *n* (*risk*) coup *m* risqué. ●**gambling** *n* jeu *m*. ●**gambler** *n* joueur, -euse *mf*.

game¹ [geɪm] **1** *n* jeu *m*; (*of football, cricket etc*) match *m*; (*of tennis, chess, cards*) partie *f*; **to have a g. of** (*football etc*) jouer un match de; (*tennis etc*) faire une partie de; **games** (*in school*) *Br* le sport; **games teacher** *Br* professeur *m* d'éducation physique. **2** *n* (*animals, birds*) gibier *m*; **big g.** le gros gibier; **to be fair g. for** *Fig* être une proie idéale pour.

game² [geɪm] *a* **1** (*brave*) courageux; **g. for sth** (*willing to do*) prêt à qch; **I'm g.** je suis partant. **2** (*leg*) estropié; **to have a g. leg** être boiteux.

gamekeeper ['geɪmkiːpər] *n* garde-chasse *m*.

gammon ['gæmən] *n* (*ham*) *Br* jambon *m* fumé.

gammy ['gæmɪ] *a* *Fam* = **game²** 2.

gamut ['gæmət] *n* *Mus* & *Fig* gamme *f*.

gang [gæŋ] *n* (*of children, friends etc*) bande *f*; (*of workers*) équipe *f*; (*of criminals*) bande *f*, gang *m* ▮ *vi* **to g. up on** *or* **against** se mettre à plusieurs contre.

Ganges ['gændʒiːz] *n* **the G.** le Gange.

gangling ['gæŋglɪŋ] *a* dégingandé.

gangrene ['gæŋgriːn] *n* gangrène *f*.

gangster ['gæŋstər] n gangster m.

gangway ['gæŋweɪ] n **1** Br passage m; (in train) couloir m; (in bus, cinema, theatre) allée f. **2** (footbridge to ship or aircraft) passerelle f; **g.!** dégagez!

gaol [dʒeɪl] n & vt = **jail.**

gap [gæp] n (empty space) trou m, vide m (between entre); (in wall, fence etc) trou m; (in time) intervalle m; (in knowledge) lacune f; **the g. between** (difference) l'écart m entre.

gape [geɪp] vi (stare) rester or être bouche bée; **to g.** at regarder bouche bée. ● **gaping** a (hole, wound, chasm) béant.

garage [Br 'gærɑː(d)ʒ, 'gærɪdʒ, Am gə'rɑːʒ] n garage m ▮ vt mettre au garage.

garb [gɑːb] n (clothes) costume m.

garbage ['gɑːbɪdʒ] n Am ordures fpl; **g. can** poubelle f; **g. man** or **collector** éboueur m; **g. truck** camion-benne m.

garble ['gɑːb(ə)l] vt (words etc) rendre confus or incompréhensible; **garbled message** message m incompréhensible.

garden ['gɑːd(ə)n] n jardin m; **gardens** (park) parc m; (public) jardin m public, parc m; **g. centre** (store) jardinerie f; **g. party** garden-party f; **g. produce** produits mpl maraîchers ▮ vi jardiner, faire du jardinage. ● **gardening** n jardinage m. ● **gardener** n jardinier, -ière m f.

gargle ['gɑːg(ə)l] vi se gargariser ▮ n gargarisme m.

gargoyle ['gɑːgɔɪl] n Archit gargouille f.

garish [Br 'geərɪʃ, Am 'gærɪʃ] a (clothes etc) voyant, criard; **g. light** lumière f crue.

garland ['gɑːlənd] n guirlande f.

garlic ['gɑːlɪk] n ail m; **g. sausage** saucisson m à l'ail.

garment ['gɑːmənt] n vêtement m.

garnish ['gɑːnɪʃ] vt garnir (**with** de) ▮ n garniture f.

garret ['gærət] n (room) mansarde f.

garrison ['gærɪsən] n (soldiers) garnison f.

garrulous ['gærələs] a (talkative) loquace.

garter ['gɑːtər] n (round leg) jarretière f; (attached to belt) Am jarretelle f; (for men) fixe-chaussette m.

gas [gæs] **1** n gaz m inv; (gasoline) Am essence f; (for operation) Med anesthésie f au masque; **g. mask/meter/chamber/etc** masque m/compteur m/chambre f/etc à gaz; **g. cooker** Br cuisinière f à gaz; **g. heater**, Br **g. fire** appareil m de chauffage à gaz; **g. heating** chauffage m au gaz; **g. industry** industrie f du gaz; **g. pipe** tuyau m de gaz; **g. ring** (burner) brûleur m; **g. station** Am station-service f; **g. stove** (large) cuisinière f à gaz; (portable) réchaud m à gaz; **g. tank** Am réservoir m à essence ▮ vt (-ss-) (poison) asphyxier (qn); Mil gazer (qn).
2 vi (-ss-) (talk) bavarder ▮ n **for a g.** (fun) Am Fam pour rire.

gasbag ['gæsbæg] n Fam commère f.

gash [gæʃ] n entaille f ▮ vt (skin) entailler; **to g. one's knee/etc** se faire une blessure profonde au genou/etc.

gasket ['gæskɪt] n (in car engine) joint m de culasse.

gasman ['gæsmæn] n (pl -men) employé m du gaz.

gasoline ['gæsəliːn] n Am essence f.

gasp [gɑːsp] **1** vi (for breath) haleter ▮ n halètement m. **2** vi **to g. with** or **in surprise/etc** avoir le souffle coupé de surprise/etc ▮ vt (say gasping) dire d'une voix entrecoupée ▮ n **a g. of surprise/etc** un hoquet de surprise/etc.

gassy ['gæsɪ] a (-ier, -iest) (drink) gazeux.

gastric ['gæstrɪk] a (juices, ulcer etc) gastrique; **g. flu** grippe f gastro-intestinale.

gastronomy [gæ'strɒnəmɪ] n gastronomie f.

gasworks ['gæswɜːks] n Br usine f à gaz.

gate [geɪt] n (of level crossing, field etc) barrière f; (metal, of garden) grille f; (of castle, building, in airport etc) porte f; (at stadium) entrée f; (in Paris Metro) portillon m; **gate(s)** (of park) grilles fpl.

gâteau, pl **-eaux** ['gætəʊ, -əʊz] n (cake) Br gros gâteau m à la crème.

gatecrash ['geɪtkræʃ] vt **to g. a party** s'inviter (de force) à une réception ▮ vi s'inviter (de force).

gateway ['geɪtweɪ] n **the g. to success/etc** le chemin du succès/etc.

gather ['gæðər] **1** vt (people, objects) rassembler; (pick up) ramasser; (flowers) cueillir; (information) recueillir; **to g. speed** prendre de la vitesse; **to g. in** (crops, harvest) rentrer; (exam papers) ramasser; **to g. (up) one's strength** rassembler ses forces; **to g. up** (pick up) ramasser (papiers etc).
▮ vi (of people) se rassembler, s'assembler, s'amasser; (of clouds) se former; (of dust) s'accumuler; **to g. round** (come closer) s'approcher; **to g. round s.o.** entourer qn.
2 vt (understand) comprendre; **I g. that...** je crois comprendre que....
3 vt (sew pleats in) froncer (jupe etc).

gathering ['gæðərɪŋ] n (group) rassemblement m.

gaudy ['gɔːdɪ] a (-ier, -iest) voyant, criard.

gauge [geɪdʒ] n (instrument) jauge f, indicateur m; Rail écartement m; **to be a g. of sth** Fig permettre de jauger qch ▮ vt (estimate) évaluer, jauger; (measure) mesurer.

gaunt [gɔːnt] a (thin) décharné.

gauntlet ['gɔːntlɪt] n gant m; **to run the g. of** (endure) essuyer (le feu de).

gauze [gɔːz] n (fabric) gaze f.

gave [geɪv] pt of **give.**

gawk [gɔːk] vi **to g. (at)** regarder bouche bée.

gawp [gɔːp] vi = **gawk.**

gay [geɪ] a (-er, -est) **1** a & n homosexuel (m), homo (m inv), gay (m). **2** a (cheerful) gai, joyeux; (colour) vif, gai.

gaze [geɪz] n regard m (fixe) ▮ vi regarder; **to g. at** regarder (fixement).

gazelle [gə'zel] n (animal) gazelle f.

gazette [gə'zet] n journal m officiel.

gazetteer [gæzə'tɪər] n répertoire m géographique.

gazump [gə'zʌmp] *vt* **to be gazumped** *Br* se retrouver avec une promesse de vente annulée (par le vendeur).

GB [dʒiː'biː] *abbr* (*Great Britain*) Grande-Bretagne *f.*

GCE [dʒiːsiː'iː] *n abbr Br* (*General Certificate of Education*) = épreuve *f* de bac.

GCSE [dʒiːsiːes'iː] *n abbr Br* (*General Certificate of Secondary Education*) = épreuve *f* de brevet.

GDP [dʒiːdiː'piː] *n abbr Br* (*gross domestic product*) PIB *m.*

gear [gɪər] **1** *n* équipement *m*, matériel *m*; (*belongings*) affaires *fpl*; (*clothes*) *Fam* vêtements *mpl*; (*speed in vehicle*) vitesse *f*; (*toothed wheels in machine*) engrenage *m*; **in g.** (*vehicle etc*) en prise; **not in g.** au point mort; **g. lever** *Br*, **g. shift** *Am* levier *m* de (changement de) vitesse.

2 *vt* (*adapt*) adapter (*qch*) (**to** à); **to be geared (up) to do** être prêt à faire; **to g. oneself up for** se préparer pour.

gearbox ['gɪəbɒks] *n* boîte *f* de vitesses.

gee! [dʒiː] *int Am Fam* ça alors!

geese [giːs] *see* **goose**.

geezer ['giːzər] *n* (*man*) *Br Sl* type *m.*

Geiger counter ['gaɪgəkaʊntər] *n* compteur *m* Geiger.

gel [dʒel] *n* (*substance*) gel *m.*

gelatin(e) [*Br* 'dʒelətiːn, *Am* -tən] *n* gélatine *f.*

gelignite ['dʒelɪgnaɪt] *n* dynamite *f* (au nitrate de soude).

gem [dʒem] *n* (*stone*) pierre *f* précieuse; (*person of value*) *Fig* perle *f*; (*thing of value*) *Fig* bijou *m* (*pl* -oux); (*error*) *Iron* perle *f.*

Gemini ['dʒemɪnaɪ] *n* (*sign*) les Gémeaux *mpl.*

gen [dʒen] *n* (*information*) *Br Fam* tuyaux *mpl* **ɪ** *vi* (-nn-) **to g. up on sth/s.o.** *Br Fam* se rancarder sur qch/qn.

gender ['dʒendər] *n* *Grammar* genre *m*; (*of person*) sexe *m.*

gene [dʒiːn] *n* (*part of cell*) gène *m.*

genealogy [dʒiːnɪ'ælədʒɪ] *n* généalogie *f.*

general ['dʒenərəl] **1** *a* général; **in g.** en général; **the g. public** le (grand) public; **for g. use** à l'usage du public; **a g. favourite** aimé *or* apprécié de tous; **g. delivery** *Am* poste *f* restante; **to be g.** (*widespread*) être très répandu; **g.-purpose tool**/*etc* outil *m*/*etc* universel. **2** *n* (*army officer*) général *m.*

generality [dʒenə'rælətɪ] *n* généralité *f.*

generalize ['dʒen(ə)rəlaɪz] *vti* généraliser.
● **generalization** [-'zeɪʃ(ə)n] *n* généralisation *f.*

generally ['dʒen(ə)rəlɪ] *adv* généralement; **g. speaking** en général, généralement parlant.

generate ['dʒenəreɪt] *vt* (*fear, hope, unemployment, ideas etc*) & *Ling* engendrer; (*heat, electricity*) produire; (*jobs*) susciter la création de.

generation [dʒenə'reɪʃ(ə)n] *n* génération *f*; **the g. of** (*heat etc*) la production de; **g. gap** conflit *m* des générations.

generator ['dʒenəreɪtər] *n* groupe *m* électrogène, génératrice *f.*

generous ['dʒenərəs] *a* généreux (**with** de); (*helping, meal etc*) copieux. ● **gene'rosity** *n* générosité *f.* ● **generously** *adv* généreusement; (*to serve s.o. with food*) copieusement.

genesis ['dʒenəsɪs] *n* (*of idea etc*) genèse *f.*

genetic [dʒɪ'netɪk] *a* génétique; **g. engineering** génie *m or* ingénierie *f* génétique. ● **genetics** *n* génétique *f.*

Geneva [dʒɪ'niːvə] *n* Genève *m or f.*

genial ['dʒiːnɪəl] *a* (*kind*) affable; (*cheerful*) jovial.

genie ['dʒiːnɪ] *n* (*goblin*) génie *m.*

genital ['dʒenɪt(ə)l] *a* génital. ● **genitals** *npl* organes *mpl* génitaux.

genius ['dʒiːnɪəs] *n* (*ability, person*) génie *m*; **to have a g. for doing/for sth** avoir le génie pour faire/de qch.

genocide ['dʒenəsaɪd] *n* génocide *m.*

gent [dʒent] *n Br Fam* monsieur *m*; **gents' shoes** *Br* chaussures *fpl* pour hommes; **the gents** *Br* les toilettes *fpl* (pour hommes).

genteel [dʒen'tiːl] *a Iron* distingué.

gentle ['dʒent(ə)l] *a* (-er, -est) (*person, sound, slope etc*) doux (*f* douce); (*hint, reminder*) discret; (*exercise, speed, progress*) modéré; **g. breeze** légère brise *f*; **g. pace** allure *f* modérée; **to have a g. touch** (*of pianist etc*) avoir un toucher léger; **to be g. to s.o.** traiter qn avec douceur; **be g. with your sister!** ne sois pas brutal avec ta sœur!; **of g. birth** noble, bien né. ● **gentleness** *n* douceur *f.* ● **gently** *adv* doucement; (*to remind*) discrètement; (*smoothly*) (*to land in aircraft etc*) en douceur.

gentleman ['dʒent(ə)lmən] *n* (*pl* -men) monsieur *m*; (*well-bred*) gentleman *m*, monsieur *m* bien élevé. ● **gentlemanly** *a* distingué, bien élevé.

gentrified ['dʒentrɪfaɪd] *a* (*houses, street*) devenu de plus grand standing.

genuine ['dʒenjuɪn] *a* (*authentic*) (*leather, diamond etc*) véritable; (*signature, work of art etc*) authentique; (*sincere*) sincère, vrai. ● **genuinely** *adv* (*surprised etc*) véritablement; (*to think etc*) sincèrement. ● **genuineness** *n* authenticité *f*; (*sincerity*) sincérité *f.*

geography [dʒɪ'ɒgrəfɪ] *n* géographie *f.* ● **geo'graphical** *a* géographique.

geology [dʒɪ'ɒlədʒɪ] *n* géologie *f.* ● **geo'logical** *a* géologique. ● **geologist** *n* géologue *mf.*

geometry [dʒɪ'ɒmɪtrɪ] *n* géométrie *f.* ● **geo'metric(al)** *a* géométrique.

geostationary [dʒiːəʊ'steɪʃən(ə)rɪ] *a* géostationnaire.

geranium [dʒɪ'reɪnɪəm] *n* (*plant*) géranium *m.*

geriatric [dʒerɪ'ætrɪk] *a* (*hospital*) gériatrique; **g. ward** service *m* de gériatrie.

germ [dʒɜːm] *n* (*in body, food etc*) microbe *m*; (*seed of plant, idea etc*) germe *m*; **g. war-**

fare guerre *f* bactériologique.

German ['dʒɜːmən] *a* allemand; **G. measles** rubéole *f*; **G. shepherd** (*dog*) *Am* berger *m* allemand ∎ *n* (*person*) Allemand, -ande *mf*; (*language*) allemand *m*. ●**Ger'manic** *a* germanique.

Germany ['dʒɜːmənɪ] *n* Allemagne *f*.

germinate ['dʒɜːmɪneɪt] *vi* (*of seed, Fig idea etc*) germer.

gerund ['dʒerənd] *n Grammar* gérondif *m*.

gestation [dʒe'steɪʃ(ə)n] *n* gestation *f*.

gesticulate [dʒes'tɪkjʊleɪt] *vi* gesticuler.

gesture ['dʒestʃər] *n* geste *m* ∎ *vi* **to g. to s.o. to do** faire signe à qn de faire.

get [get] *vt* (*pt & pp* **got**, *pp Am* **gotten**, *pres p* **getting**) (*obtain*) obtenir, avoir; (*find*) trouver; (*buy*) acheter; (*receive*) recevoir, avoir; (*catch*) attraper; (*bus, train*) prendre; (*seize*) prendre, saisir; (*fetch*) aller chercher (*qn, qch*); (*put*) mettre; (*derive*) tirer (**from** de); (*understand*) comprendre, saisir; (*prepare*) préparer; (*lead*) mener; (*hit with fist, stick etc*) atteindre, avoir; (*reputation*) se faire; (*annoy*) *Fam* ennuyer; **I have got,** *Am* **I have gotten** j'ai; **to g. s.o. to do sth** faire faire qch à qn; **to g. sth built/etc** faire construire/etc qch; **to g. things going** *or* **started** faire démarrer les choses; **to g. sth to s.o.** (*send*) faire parvenir qch à qn; **to g. s.o. to the station/etc** (*bring*) amener qn à la gare/etc.

2 *vi* (*go*) aller (**to** à); (*arrive*) arriver (**to** à); (*become*) (*tired, old etc*) devenir; **to g. caught/run over/etc** se faire prendre/écraser/ etc; **to g. married** se marier; **to g. dressed/ washed** s'habiller/se laver; **to g. paid** être payé; **where have you got** *or Am* **gotten to?** où en es-tu?; **you've got to stay** (*must*) tu dois rester; **to g. to do** (*succeed in doing*) parvenir à faire; **I'm getting to understand** (*starting*) je commence à comprendre; **to g. working** (*start*) se mettre à travailler.

get about *or* **(a)round** *vi* se déplacer; (*of news*) circuler ∎ **to get across** *vt* (*road*) traverser; (*message*) communiquer; **to g. s.o. across** faire traverser qn ∎ *vi* traverser; (*of speaker*) se faire comprendre (**to** de); **to g. across to s.o. that** faire comprendre à qn que ∎ **to get along** *vi* (*manage*) se débrouiller; (*progress*) avancer; (*be on good terms*) s'entendre (**with** avec); (*leave*) se sauver ∎ **to get at** *vt* (*reach*) parvenir à, atteindre; (*taunt*) s'en prendre à; **what is he getting at?** où veut-il en venir? ∎ **to get away** *vi* (*leave*) partir, s'en aller; (*escape*) s'échapper; **to g. away with a fine** s'en tirer avec une amende; **he got away with that crime** il n'a pas été inquiété pour ce crime; **there's no getting away from it** il faut le reconnaître, c'est comme ça. ●**getaway** *n* (*escape*) fuite *f*. ∎ **to get back** *vt* (*recover*) récupérer; (*replace*) remettre ∎ *vi* (*return*) revenir, retourner; (*move back*) reculer; **to g. back at, g. one's own back at** (*punish*) se venger de ∎ **to get by** *vi* (*pass*) passer; (*manage*) se débrouiller

∎ **to get down** *vi* (*go down*) descendre (**from** de); **to g. down to** (*task, work*) se mettre à ∎ *vt* (*bring down*) descendre (**from** de); (*write down*) noter; **to g. s.o. down** (*depress*) *Fam* déprimer qn; **to g. down the stairs/a ladder** descendre l'escalier/d'une échelle ∎ **to get into** *vt* entrer dans; (*vehicle, train*) monter dans; (*habit*) prendre; **to g. into bed/a rage** se mettre au lit/en colère ∎ **to get off** *vi* (*leave*) partir; (*from vehicle or train*) descendre (**from** de); (*escape*) s'en tirer; (*finish work*) sortir; (*be acquitted in court*) être acquitté ∎ *vt* (*remove*) enlever; (*send*) expédier; (*in court*) faire acquitter (*qn*); **to g. off a chair** se lever d'une chaise; **to g. off a bus** descendre d'un bus; **to g. off doing** *Fam* se dispenser de faire ∎ **to get on** *vt* (*shoes, clothes*) mettre; (*bus, train*) monter dans ∎ *vi* (*progress*) marcher, avancer; (*manage*) se débrouiller; (*succeed*) réussir; (*enter bus or train*) monter; (*be on good terms*) s'entendre (**with** avec); **how are you getting on?** comment ça va?; **to g. on to s.o.** (*on phone*) contacter qn, toucher qn; **to g. on with** (*task*) continuer ∎ **to get out** *vi* sortir; (*from vehicle or train*) descendre (**of,** **from** de); **to g. out of** (*obligation*) échapper à; (*danger*) se tirer de; (*habit*) perdre ∎ *vt* (*remove*) enlever; (*bring out*) sortir (*qch*), faire sortir (*qn*) ∎ **to get over** *vt* (*road*) traverser; (*obstacle*) surmonter; (*fence*) franchir; (*illness*) se remettre de; (*surprise*) revenir de; (*ideas*) communiquer; **let's g. it over with** *vi* (*cross*) traverser; (*visit*) passer ∎ **to get round** *vt* (*obstacle*) contourner; (*person, by persuasion etc*) entortiller ∎ *vi* (*visit*) passer; **to g. round to doing** en venir à faire ∎ **to get through** *vi* (*pass*) passer; (*finish*) finir; (*pass exam*) être reçu; ∎ *vt* (*hole etc*) passer par; (*task, meal*) venir à bout de; (*exam*) être reçu à; **g. me through to your boss** (*on the phone*) passe-moi ton patron ∎ **to get together** *vi* (*of people*) se rassembler. ●**get-together** *n* réunion *f*. ∎ **to get up** *vi* (*rise, stand up*) se lever (**from** de); **to g. up to** (*in book*) en arriver à; **to g. up to something** *or* **to mischief** faire des bêtises ∎ *vt* (*ladder, stairs etc*) monter; (*party, group*) organiser; **to g. sth up** (*bring up*) monter qch. ●**get-up** *n* (*clothes*) *Fam* accoutrement *m*.

geyser ['giːzər] *n* **1** (*water heater*) *Br* chauffe-eau *m inv* (à gaz). **2** (*underground spring*) geyser *m*.

Ghana ['gɑːnə] *n* Ghana *m*.

ghastly ['gɑːstlɪ] *a* (**-ier, -iest**) (*horrible*) affreux; (*pale*) blême, pâle.

gherkin ['gɜːkɪn] *n* cornichon *m*.

ghetto ['getəʊ] *n* (*pl* -os) ghetto *m*; **g. blaster** *Fam* mini-stéréo *f* portable.

ghost [gəʊst] *n* fantôme *m*; **not the g. of a chance** pas l'ombre d'une chance; **g. story** histoire *f* de fantômes; **g. ship** vaisseau *m* fantôme; **g. town** ville *f* fantôme. ●**ghostly** *a* spectral.

ghoul [guːl] *n* goule *f*.

ghoulish ['guːlɪʃ] *a* morbide.

giant ['dʒaɪənt] *n* géant *m* ▮ *a* (*tree, packet etc*) géant; (*struggle, efforts etc*) gigantesque; **with g. steps** à pas de géant.

gibberish ['dʒɪbərɪʃ] *n* baragouin *m*.

gibe [dʒaɪb] *vi* railler; **to g. at** railler ▮ *n* raillerie *f*.

giblets ['dʒɪblɪts] *npl* (*of fowl*) abats *mpl*.

giddy ['gɪdɪ] *a* (-ier, -iest) (*a. heights* hauteurs *fpl* vertigineuses; **to be** *or* **feel g.** (*at great height*) avoir le vertige; (*in room etc*) avoir un *or* des vertige(s); **to make s.o. g.** donner le vertige à qn. ●**giddiness** *n* vertige *m*.

gift [gɪft] *n* cadeau *m*; (*talent, donation*) don *m*; **g. voucher** *or* **token** chèque-cadeau *m*. ●**gifted** *a* doué (**with** de, **for** pour); **g. child** (*with genius-level IQ*) enfant *mf* surdoué(e).

giftwrapped ['gɪftræpt] *a* en paquet-cadeau. ●**giftwrapping** *n* emballage-cadeau *m*.

gig [gɪg] *n* (*by pop musicians*) *Fam* engagement *m*, séance *f*.

gigantic [dʒaɪ'gæntɪk] *a* gigantesque.

giggle ['gɪg(ə)l] *vi* rire (bêtement) ▮ *n* petit rire *m* bête; **to have the giggles** avoir le fou rire.

gild [gɪld] *vt* dorer. ●**gilt** *a* doré ▮ *n* dorure *f*.

gills [gɪlz] *npl* (*of fish*) ouïes *fpl*.

gimmick ['gɪmɪk] *n* (*trick, object*) truc *m*.

gin [dʒɪn] *n* (*drink*) gin *m*.

ginger ['dʒɪndʒər] **1** *a* (*hair*) roux (*f* rousse). **2** *n* (*plant, spice*) gingembre *m*; **g. beer** boisson *f* gazeuse au gingembre. ●**gingerbread** *n* pain *m* d'épice.

gingerly ['dʒɪndʒəlɪ] *adv* avec précaution.

gipsy ['dʒɪpsɪ] *n* bohémien, -ienne *mf*; (*Central European*) Tsigane *mf*; (*Spanish*) gitan, -ane *mf*; **g. music** musique *f* tsigane; (*Spanish*) musique *f* gitane.

giraffe [dʒɪ'ræf, *Br* dʒɪ'rɑːf] *n* girafe *f*.

girder ['gɜːdər] *n* (*metal beam*) poutre *f*.

girdle ['gɜːd(ə)l] *n* (*belt*) ceinture *f*; (*corset*) gaine *f*.

girl [gɜːl] *n* (*child*) (petite) fille *f*, fillette *f*; (*young woman*) jeune fille *f*; (*daughter*) fille *f*; (*sweetheart*) *Fam* petite amie *f*; **English g.** jeune Anglaise *f*; **g. guide** éclaireuse *f*. ●**girlfriend** *n* (*of girl*) amie *f*; (*of boy*) petite amie *f*. ●**girlish** *a* de (jeune) fille. ●**girlhood** *n* (première) jeunesse *f*.

giro ['dʒaɪrəʊ] *n* (*pl* -os) *Br* **bank g.** virement *m* bancaire; **g. (cheque)** (*welfare payment*) chèque *m* (de paiement) d'indemnités (maladie *or* chômage); **g. account** compte *m* courant postal, CCP *m*.

girth [gɜːθ] *n* (*measure*) circonférence *f*; (*of waist*) tour *m*.

gist [dʒɪst] *n* **to get the g. of** comprendre l'essentiel de.

give [gɪv] *vt* (*pt* gave, *pp* given) donner (**to** à); (*one's support*) apporter; (*a smile, a gesture, pleasure*) faire; (*a sigh*) pousser; (*a look*) jeter; (*a blow*) porter; **g. me York 234** (*phone number*) passez-moi le 234 à York; **she doesn't g. a damn** *Fam* elle s'en fiche pas mal; **to g. way** .(*yield, break*) (*of branch, person etc*) céder (**to** à); (*collapse*) (*of roof etc*) s'effondrer; (*in vehicle*) céder la priorité (**to** à) ▮ *n* (*in fabric etc*) élasticité *f*.

give away *vt* (*prize*) distribuer; (*money*) donner; (*facts*) révéler; (*betray*) trahir (*qn*) ▮ **to give back** *vt* (*return*) rendre ▮ **to give in** *vi* (*surrender*) céder (**to** à) ▮ *vt* (*hand in*) remettre ▮ **to give off** *vt* (*smell, heat*) dégager ▮ **to give out** *vt* (*hand out*) distribuer (*livres etc*); (*make known*) annoncer (*nouvelle etc*) ▮ *vi* (*of supplies, patience*) s'épuiser; (*of engine*) rendre l'âme ▮ **to give over** *vt* (*devote*) consacrer (**to** à); **to g. oneself over to** (*despair, bad habit etc*) s'abandonner à ▮ *vi* **g. over!** (*stop*) *Br Fam* arrête! ▮ **to give up** *vi* abandonner, renoncer ▮ *vt* abandonner, renoncer à; (*seat*) céder (**to** à); (*prisoner*) livrer (**to** à); (*patient*) condamner; **to g. up smoking** cesser de fumer.

given ['gɪv(ə)n] *a* (*fixed*) donné; **at a g. time** à un moment donné; **to be g. to doing** (*prone to do*) avoir l'habitude de faire; **g. your age** (*in view of this*) étant donné votre âge; **g. that** étant donné que.

giver ['gɪvər] *n* donateur, -trice *mf*.

glacier [*Br* 'glæsɪər, *Am* 'gleɪʃər] *n* glacier *m*.

glad [glæd] *a* (*person*) content (**of, about** de; **that** que + *sub*); **I'm g. to know/hear/**etc **that...** je suis content de savoir/d'apprendre/*etc* que...; **she's only too g. to help you** elle ne demande pas mieux que de vous aider. ●**gladden** *vt* *Lit* réjouir. ●**gladly** *adv* (*willingly*) volontiers.

glade [gleɪd] *n* clairière *f*.

gladiolus, *pl* -i [glædɪ'əʊləs, -aɪ] *n* (*plant*) glaïeul *m*.

glamorize ['glæməraɪz] *vt* montrer sous un jour séduisant. ●**glamorous** *a* (*person, dress, life etc*) séduisant; (*career, job*) prestigieux.

glamour ['glæmər] *n* (*charm*) enchantement *m*; (*splendour*) éclat *m*; (*of career etc*) prestige *m*.

glance [glɑːns] **1** *n* coup *m* d'œil ▮ *vi* jeter un coup d'œil (**at** à, sur). **2** *vt* **to g. off sth** (*of bullet*) ricocher sur qch.

gland [glænd] *n* glande *f*. ●**glandular fever** *n Br* mononucléose *f* infectieuse.

glare [gleər] **1** *vi* **to g. at s.o.** foudroyer qn (du regard) ▮ *n* regard *m* furieux. **2** *vi* (*of sun*) briller d'un éclat aveuglant ▮ *n* éclat *m* aveuglant. ●**glaring** *a* (*light*) éblouissant; (*sun*) aveuglant; (*eyes*) furieux; (*injustice*) flagrant; **a g. mistake** une faute grossière.

glass [glɑːs] *n* verre *m*; (*mirror*) miroir *m*, glace *f*; **a pane of g.** une vitre, un carreau ▮ *a* (*bottle etc*) de verre; **g. door** porte *f* vitrée; **g. industry** industrie *f* du verre. ●**glassful** *n* (plein) verre *m*. ●**glassware** *n* objets *mpl* de or en verre.

glasses ['glɑːsɪz] *npl* (*spectacles*) lunettes *fpl*.

glaze [gleɪz] *vt* (*door*) vitrer; (*pottery*) vernisser; (*paper*) glacer ▮ *n* (*on pottery*) vernis *m*; (*on paper*) glacé *m*. ●**glazier** *n* vitrier *m*.

gleam [gliːm] *n* lueur *f* ▮ *vi* (re)luire.

glean [gliːn] *vt* (*information, grain etc*) glaner.

glee [gliː] *n* joie *f*. ●**gleeful** *a* joyeux.

glen [glen] *n* vallon *m*.

glib [glɪb] *a* (*a person*) qui a la parole facile; (*speech*) facile, peu sincère. ●**glibly** *adv* (*to say*) peu sincèrement.

glide [glaɪd] *vi* glisser; (*of aircraft, bird*) planer; (*of vehicle*) avancer silencieusement. ●**gliding** *n* (*sport*) vol *m* à voile. ●**glider** *n* (*aircraft*) planeur *m*.

glimmer ['glɪmər] *vi* luire (faiblement) ▮ *n* (*light, of hope etc*) (faible) lueur *f*.

glimpse [glɪmps] *n* aperçu *m*; **to catch** or **get** or **have a g. of** entrevoir ▮ *vt* = **to catch a g. of.**

glint [glɪnt] *vi* (*shine with flashes*) briller ▮ *n* éclair *m*; (*in eye*) étincelle *f*.

glisten ['glɪs(ə)n] *vi* (*of wet surface*) briller; (*of water*) miroiter.

glitch [glɪtʃ] *n* Comptr *etc* Fam problème *m* (technique).

glitter ['glɪtər] *vi* scintiller, briller ▮ *n* scintillement *m*. ●**glittering** *a* (*prize, career*) extraordinaire.

gloat [gləʊt] *vi* jubiler (**over** à l'idée de).

global ['gləʊb(ə)l] *a* (*universal*) (*influence etc*) mondial, universel; (*comprehensive*) (*amount, view etc*) global; **g. warming** réchauffement *m* de la planète.

globe [gləʊb] *n* globe *m*.

gloom [gluːm] *n* (*sadness*) tristesse *f*; (*darkness*) obscurité *f*. ●**gloomy** *a* (**-ier, -iest**) (*sad*) triste; (*pessimistic*) pessimiste; (*dark, dismal*) sombre, triste.

glorify ['glɔːrɪfaɪ] *vt* (*praise*) glorifier; **it's a glorified barn**/*etc* Br ce n'est guère plus qu'une grange/*etc*.

glorious ['glɔːrɪəs] *a* (*splendid*) magnifique; (*full of glory*) glorieux.

glory ['glɔːrɪ] *n* gloire *f*; (*great beauty*) splendeur *f*; **to be in one's g.** (*very happy*) Fam être à son affaire ▮ *vi* **to g. in** se glorifier de.

gloss [glɒs] **1** *n* (*shine*) brillant *m*; **g. paint** peinture *f* brillante; **g. finish** brillant *m*. **2** *n* (*note*) glose *f*, commentaire *m*. **3** *vt* **to g. over** (*minimize, make light of*) glisser sur; (*conceal*) dissimuler. ●**glossy** *a* (**-ier, -iest**) brillant; (*photo*) glacé; (*magazine*) de luxe.

glossary ['glɒsərɪ] *n* glossaire *m*.

glove [glʌv] *n* gant *m*; **g. compartment** (*in car*) (*shelf*) vide-poches *m inv*; (*enclosed*) boîte *f* à gants. ●**gloved** *a* **a g. hand** une

main gantée.

glow [gləʊ] *vi* (*of sky, fire, embers*) rougeoyer; (*of lamp*) luire; (*of eyes, person*) Fig rayonner (**with** de) ▮ *n* rougeoiement *m*; (*of lamp*) lueur *f*; (*of complexion*) éclat *m*. ●**glowing** *a* (*account, terms, reference etc*) très favorable, enthousiaste. ●**glow-worm** *n* ver *m* luisant.

glucose ['gluːkəʊs] *n* glucose *m*.

glue [gluː] *n* colle *f* ▮ *vt* coller (**to, on** à); **with one's eyes glued to** Fam les yeux fixés or rivés sur; **to be glued to the television** Fam être cloué devant la télévision. ●**glue-sniffing** *n* inhalation *f* de la colle.

glum [glʌm] *a* (**glummer, glummest**) triste.

glut [glʌt] *vt* **the market is glutted** le marché est encombré or saturé (**with** de) ▮ *n* (*of goods, oil etc*) surplus *m* (**of** de).

glutton ['glʌt(ə)n] *n* glouton, -onne *mf*; **g. for work** bourreau *m* de travail; **g. for punishment** masochiste *mf*. ●**gluttony** *n* gloutonnerie *f*.

glycerin(e) ['glɪsəriːn] *n* glycérine *f*.

GMT [dʒiːemˈtiː] *abbr* (*Greenwich Mean Time*) GMT.

gnarled [nɑːld] *a* noueux.

gnash [næʃ] *vt* **to g. one's teeth** grincer des dents.

gnat [næt] *n* (petit) moustique *m*.

gnaw [nɔː] *vti* **to g. (at)** ronger.

gnome [nəʊm] *n* (*little man*) gnome *m*; **garden g.** nain *m* or lutin *m* de jardin.

GNP [dʒiːenˈpiː] *n abbr* (*gross national product*) PNB *m*.

go [gəʊ] **1** *vi* (*3rd person sing pres t* **goes**; *pt* **went**; *pp* **gone**; *pres p* **going**) aller (**to** à, **from** de); (*depart*) partir, s'en aller; (*disappear*) disparaître, partir; (*be sold*) se vendre; (*function*) marcher, fonctionner; (*progress*) aller, marcher; (*become*) devenir; (*of time*) passer; (*of hearing, strength*) baisser; (*of fuse*) sauter; (*of bulb*) griller; (*of material*) s'user; (*of rope*) céder; **to go well/badly** (*of event*) se passer bien/mal; **she's going to do** (*is about to, intends to*) elle va faire; **it's all gone** (*finished*) il n'y en a plus; **to go and get** (*fetch*) aller chercher; **to go and see** aller voir; **to go riding/sailing/on a trip**/*etc* faire du cheval/de la voile/un voyage/*etc*; **to let go of** lâcher; **to go to a doctor/lawyer**/*etc* aller voir un médecin/un avocat/*etc*; **to get things going** faire démarrer les choses; **let's get going** allons-y; **is there any beer going?** (*available*) y a-t-il de la bière?; **it goes to show that...** ça montre que...; **two hours**/*etc* **to go** (*still left*) encore deux heures/*etc*.

2 *n* (*pl* **goes**) (*attempt*) coup *m*; (*energy*) dynamisme *m*; **to have a go at** (**doing**) **sth** essayer (de faire) qch; **at one go** d'un seul coup; **on the go** en mouvement, actif; **to make a go of sth** (*make a success of*) réussir qch.

go about or **(a)round** *vi* se déplacer; (*of news, rumour*) circuler ▮ **to go about** *vt* (*one's duties etc*) s'occuper de; **to know how**

to go **about it** savoir s'y prendre ∎ to go **across** vt traverser ∎ vi (cross) traverser; (go) aller (to à); to go **across** to s.o.('s) faire un saut chez qn ∎ to go **after** vt (chase) poursuivre; (seek) (re)chercher; (job) essayer d'obtenir ∎ to go **against** vt (of result) être défavorable à; (s.o.'s wishes) aller contre; (harm) nuire à ∎ to go **ahead** vi avancer; (continue) continuer; (start) commencer; go ahead! allez-y!; to go **ahead** with (plan, idea etc) poursuivre. ∎ to go **along** vi aller; (move forward, progress) avancer; to go **along** with s.o./sth (agree) être d'accord avec qn/qch ∎ to go **away** vi partir, s'en aller ∎ to go **back** vi retourner; (in time) remonter; (step back, retreat) reculer; to go **back** on one's promise or word revenir sur sa promesse ∎ to go **by** vi passer ∎ vt (act according to) se fonder sur; (judge from) juger d'après; (instruction) suivre ∎ to go **down** vi descendre; (fall down) tomber; (of ship) couler; (of sun) se coucher; (of storm) s'apaiser; (of temperature, price etc) baisser; (of Br tyre or Am tire) se dégonfler; to go **down** well (of speech etc) être bien reçu; to go **down** with an illness attraper une maladie ∎ to go **down** the stairs/street descendre l'escalier/la rue ∎ to go **for** vt (fetch) aller chercher; (attack) attaquer, sauter sur; (like) Fam aimer beaucoup ∎ to go **forward(s)** vi avancer ∎ to go **in** vi (r)entrer; (of sun) se cacher; to go **in for** Br (exam) se présenter à; (hobby, sport) faire; (career) entrer dans; (like) Fam aimer beaucoup ∎ vt to go **in** a room/etc entrer dans une pièce/etc ∎ to go **into** vt (room etc) entrer dans; (question) examiner ∎ to go **off** vi (leave) partir; (go bad) se gâter; (of alarm) se déclencher; (of gun) partir; (of bomb) exploser; (of event) se passer; (of effect) passer ∎ vt (one's food) perdre le goût de ∎ to go **on** vi continuer (doing à faire); (travel) poursuivre sa route; (happen) se passer; (last) durer; (of time) passer; to go **on at** s.o. (nag) Fam s'en prendre à qn; to go **on about** sth/s.o. Fam parler sans cesse de qch/qn ∎ to go **out** vi sortir; (of light, fire) s'éteindre; (of tide) descendre; (of newspaper, product) être distribué (to à); (depart) partir; to go **out** to work travailler (au dehors) ∎ to go **over** vi (go) aller (to à); (cross over) traverser; (to enemy) passer (to à); to go **over** to s.o.('s) faire un saut chez qn, passer chez qn ∎ vt examiner; (in one's mind) repasser; (speech) revoir; (touch up) retoucher; (overhaul) réviser (véhicule, montre) ∎ to go **round** vi (turn) tourner; (make a detour) faire le tour; (be sufficient) suffire; to go **round** to s.o.('s) faire un saut chez qn, passer chez qn; enough to go **round** assez pour tout le monde ∎ to go **round** a corner tourner un coin; to go **round** the world faire le tour du monde ∎ to go **through** vi (of deal) être conclu ∎ vt (suffer, undergo) subir; (examine) examiner; (search) fouiller; (spend) dépenser; (wear out) user; (perform)

accomplir; to go **through** with (carry out) aller jusqu'au bout de, réaliser ∎ to go **under** vi (of ship, person, firm) couler ∎ to go **up** vi monter; (explode) sauter ∎ vt to go **up** the stairs/street monter l'escalier/la rue ∎ to go **up** without vi se passer de.

goad [gəud] vt to g. s.o. (on) aiguillonner qn.

go-ahead ['gəuəhed] a dynamique ∎ n to get the g. avoir le feu vert; to give s.o. the g. donner le feu vert à qn.

goal [gəul] n but m. ●**goalie** n Football Br Fam goal m. ●**goalkeeper** n Football gardien m de but, goal m. ●**goalpost** n Football poteau m de but.

goat [gəut] n chèvre f; to get s.o.'s g. Fam énerver qn.

goatee [gəu'ti:] n (beard) barbiche f.

gobble ['gɒb(ə)l] vt to g. (up or down) (food) engloutir, engouffrer.

go-between ['gəubitwi:n] n intermédiaire mf.

goblet ['gɒblit] n verre m à pied.

goblin ['gɒblin] n (evil spirit) lutin m.

god [gɒd] n dieu m; G. Dieu m; the gods (in theatre) Fam le poulailler. ●**god-fearing** a croyant. ●**god-forsaken** a (place) perdu.

godchild ['gɒdtʃaild] n (pl -children) filleul, -eule mf. ●**goddaughter** n filleule f. ●**godfather** n parrain m. ●**godmother** n marraine f. ●**godson** n filleul m.

goddam(n) ['gɒdæm] a Am Fam foutu.

goddess ['gɒdis] n déesse f.

godly ['gɒdli] a dévot.

godsend ['gɒdsend] n to be a (real) g. (of thing, person) être un don du ciel.

goes [gəuz] see go 1.

gofer ['gəufər] n (messenger) Am Fam coursier, -ière mf, garçon m de courses.

goggle ['gɒg(ə)l] vi to g. at regarder en roulant de gros yeux. ●**goggles** npl (spectacles) lunettes fpl (de protection, de plongée). ●**goggle-eyed** a to be g.-eyed Fam avoir les yeux saillants; (with surprise) avoir les yeux ronds.

going ['gəuiŋ] 1 n (conditions) conditions fpl; it's hard or heavy g. c'est difficile. 2 a the g. price le prix pratiqué (for pour); the g. rate le tarif en vigueur; the g. salary le salaire habituel; a g. concern une entreprise qui marche bien. ●**goings-'on** npl Pej activités fpl.

go-kart ['gəuka:t] n (for racing) kart m.

gold [gəuld] n or m ∎ a (watch etc) en or, (coin, dust) d'or; g. medal Sport médaille f d'or. ●**golden** a (of gold colour) (hair etc) doré; g. rule règle f d'or; it's a g. opportunity c'est une occasion en or. ●**goldmine** n mine f d'or. ●**gold-'plated** a plaqué or. ●**goldsmith** n orfèvre m.

goldfinch ['gəuldfintʃ] n (bird) chardonneret m.

goldfish ['gəuldfiʃ] n poisson m rouge.

golf [gɒlf] n golf m. ●**golfer** n golfeur, -euse mf. ●**golfing** n to go g. faire du golf.

golly ['gɒli] int (by) g.! Old-fashioned Fam

mince (alors)!

gondola ['gɒndələ] n (boat) gondole f.
●**gondolier** [-'lɪər] n gondolier m.

gone [gɒn] pp of go 1 ∎ a it's g. two Br Fam
il est plus de deux heures. ●**goner** n to be a
g. Sl être fichu.

gong [gɒŋ] n gong m.

goo [guː] n Fam truc m collant or visqueux.

good [gʊd] a (better, best) bon (f bonne);
(kind) gentil; (well-behaved) sage; to have g.
weather avoir du beau temps; would you be
g. enough to...? auriez-vous la gentillesse
de...?; my g. friend mon cher ami; a g.
fellow or guy or Br chap or Br bloke un
brave type; g. and strong bien fort; a g.
(long) walk une bonne promenade; g.! bon!,
bien!; very g.! (all right) très bien!; that's g.
of you c'est gentil de ta part; to feel g. se
sentir bien; that isn't g. enough (bad) ça ne
va pas; (not sufficient) ça ne suffit pas; it's g.
for us ça nous fait du bien; to be g. at
French/etc (at school) être bon or fort en
français/etc; to be g. at swimming/telling
jokes/etc savoir bien nager/raconter des
blagues/etc; to be g. with children/etc savoir
s'y prendre avec les enfants/etc; it's a g.
thing (that)... heureusement que...; a g.
many, a g. deal (of) beaucoup (de); as g. as
(almost) pratiquement; g. afternoon, g.
morning bonjour; (on leaving someone) au
revoir; g. evening bonsoir; g. night bonsoir;
(before going to bed) bonne nuit.
∎ n (advantage, virtue) bien m; for her (own)
g. pour son bien; for the g. of your family/
career/etc pour ta famille/carrière/etc; it will
do you (some) g. ça te fera du bien; there's
some g. in him il a du bon; it's no g. crying/
shouting/etc ça ne sert à rien de pleurer/
crier/etc; that's no g. (worthless) ça ne vaut
rien; (not all right, bad) ça ne va pas; what's
the g.? à quoi bon?; what's the g. of crying/
etc? à quoi bon pleurer/etc?; for g. (to leave,
give up etc) pour de bon. ●**good-for-nothing**
a & n propre à rien (mf). ●**good-'humoured**
a de bonne humeur. ●**good-'looking** a
beau (f belle). ●**good-'natured** a (person)
d'humeur toujours égale.

goodbye [gʊd'baɪ] int & n au revoir (m inv).

goodly ['gʊdlɪ] a (size, number) grand.

goodness ['gʊdnɪs] n bonté f; my g.! mon
Dieu!

goods [gʊdz] npl marchandises fpl; (articles
for sale) articles mpl; g. train Br train m de
marchandises.

goodwill [gʊd'wɪl] n (kindness) bonne volonté f; (zeal) zèle m.

gooey ['guːɪ] a Fam gluant, poisseux.

goof [guːf] vi to g. (up) (blunder) Am faire
une gaffe.

goon [guːn] n Fam idiot, -ote mf.

goose, pl **geese** [guːs, giːs] n oie f; g.
pimples or bumps chair f de poule. ●**gooseflesh** n chair f de poule.

gooseberry [Br 'gʊzbərɪ, Am 'guːsbərɪ] n
groseille f à maquereau.

gorge [gɔːdʒ] 1 n (ravine) gorge f. 2 vt
(food) engloutir; to g. oneself se gaver (on
de).

gorgeous ['gɔːdʒəs] a magnifique.

gorilla [gə'rɪlə] n gorille m.

gormless ['gɔːmləs] a Br Fam stupide.

gorse [gɔːs] n inv ajonc(s) m(pl).

gory ['gɔːrɪ] a (-ier, -iest) (bloody) sanglant;
(details) Fig horrible.

gosh! [gɒʃ] int Fam mince (alors)!

gosling ['gɒzlɪŋ] n oison m.

go-slow [gəʊ'sləʊ] n (strike) Br grève f
perlée.

gospel ['gɒspəl] n évangile m; G. Évangile
m.

gossip ['gɒsɪp] n (talk) bavardage(s) m(pl);
(malicious) cancan(s) m(pl); (person)
commère f; g. column (in newspaper) échos
mpl ∎ vi bavarder; (maliciously) cancaner.
●**gossiping** or **gossipy** a bavard; (maliciously) cancanier.

got [gɒt] pt & Br pp of get.

Gothic ['gɒθɪk] a & n gothique (m).

gotten ['gɒt(ə)n] Am pp of get.

gouge [gaʊdʒ] vt to g. out (eye) crever.

goulash ['guːlæʃ] n (dish) goulasch f.

gourmet ['gʊəmeɪ] n gourmet m; g. cook
cordon-bleu m; g. restaurant restaurant m
gastronomique.

gout [gaʊt] n (illness) goutte f.

govern ['gʌvən] vt (rule) gouverner; (city,
province) administrer; (emotion) maîtriser;
(influence) déterminer ∎ vi (rule)
gouverner; **governing body** conseil m
d'administration.

governess ['gʌvənɪs] n gouvernante f.

government ['gʌvənmənt] n gouvernement
m; local g. administration f locale ∎ a (decision, policy etc) gouvernemental, du gouvernement; g. loan emprunt m d'État. ●**govern'mental** a gouvernemental.

governor ['gʌv(ə)nər] n gouverneur m; (of
school) administrateur, -trice mf; (of prison)
directeur, -trice mf.

gown [gaʊn] n (woman's dress) robe f; (of
judge, lecturer) Br toge f.

GP [dʒiː'piː] n abbr (general practitioner)
(médecin m) généraliste m.

grab [græb] vt (-bb-) to g. (hold of) saisir,
agripper; to g. sth from s.o. arracher qch à
qn.

grace [greɪs] 1 n (charm, goodwill, religious
mercy etc) grâce f; to say g. (before meals)
dire le bénédicité; g. (period) (extension of
time) délai m de grâce; 10 days' grace 10
jours de grâce. 2 vt (adorn) orner; (honour)
honorer (with de).

graceful ['greɪsfəl] a (movement, person etc)
gracieux. ●**gracefully** adv (to dance etc) avec
grâce; to accept g. accepter de bonne grâce.

gracious ['greɪʃəs] a (kind) aimable, gracieux (to envers); (elegant) élégant; good g.!
Fam bonté divine! ●**graciously** adv (to
accept) de bonne grâce.

gradation [Br grə'deɪʃ(ə)n, Am greɪ'deɪʃ(ə)n] n gradation f.

grade [greɪd] n catégorie f; (of soldier) grade m; (of product) qualité f; (of eggs, fruit) calibre m; (level) niveau m; (mark in exam etc) note f; (class in school) Am classe f; **g. school** Am école f primaire; **g. crossing** Am passage m à niveau ∎ vt (classify) classer; (colours, exercises etc) graduer; (school or college paper) noter.

gradient ['greɪdɪənt] n (slope) inclinaison f.

gradual ['grædʒʊəl] a progressif, graduel; (slope) doux (f douce). ●**gradually** adv progressivement, peu à peu.

graduate¹ ['grædʒʊeɪt] vi (from university) obtenir son diplôme; (from school) Am obtenir son baccalauréat; **to g. from** sortir de ∎ vt **to be graduated** (from university, school) Am = **to graduate** vi ∎ ['grædʒʊət] n diplômé, -ée mf, licencié, -ée mf. ●**graduation** [-'eɪʃ(ə)n] n Univ remise f des diplômes.

graduate² ['grædʒʊeɪt] vt (mark with degrees) graduer. ●**graduated** a (tube etc) gradué.

graffiti [grə'fiːtɪ] npl graffiti mpl.

graft [grɑːft] 1 n (of skin, on plant) greffe f ∎ vt greffer (**on to** à). 2 n (bribery) Am Fam pots-de-vin mpl. 3 n hard g. Br Fam boulot m.

grain [greɪn] n (seed, particle) grain m; (seeds) grain(s) m(pl); (cereals) céréales fpl; (in cloth) fil m; (in wood) fibre f; (in leather, paper) grain m; **a g. of truth/commonsense** Fig une once de vérité/de bon sens.

gram(me) [græm] n gramme m.

grammar ['græmər] n grammaire f; **g. (book)** grammaire f; **g. school** Br lycée m; US école f primaire. ●**gra'mmatical** a grammatical.

gramophone ['græməfəʊn] n phonographe m.

granary ['grænərɪ] n (farm building) grenier m; **g. loaf** Br pain m complet.

grand [grænd] 1 a (-er, -est) (splendid) magnifique, grand; (style) grandiose; (wonderful) Fam magnifique; **with a g. gesture** d'un geste majestueux; **g. duke** grand duc m; **g. piano** piano m à queue; **g. total** somme f totale; **the g. tour** (of town, museum etc) la visite complète; (of house) le tour du propriétaire. 2 n inv Am Sl mille dollars mpl; Br Sl mille livres fpl.

grandchild ['græntʃaɪld] n (pl -children) petit(e)-enfant mf. ●**grand(d)ad** n Fam papi m, pépé m. ●**granddaughter** n petite-fille f. ●**grandfather** n grand-père m. ●**grandma** [-mɑː] n Fam mamie f. ●**grandmother** n grand-mère f. ●**grandpa** [-pɑː] n Fam papi m, pépé m. ●**grandparents** npl grands-parents mpl. ●**grandson** n petit-fils m.

grandeur ['grændʒər] n magnificence f; (of person, country) grandeur f.

grandstand ['grændstænd] n (at sports ground) tribune f.

grange [greɪndʒ] n (house) manoir m.

granite ['grænɪt] n granit(e) m.

granny ['grænɪ] n Fam mamie f.

grant [grɑːnt] 1 vt accorder (**to** à); (request) accéder à; (prayer, wish) exaucer; (admit) admettre (**that** que); **to take sth for granted** considérer qch comme acquis; **to take s.o. for granted** considérer qn comme faisant partie du décor; **I take it for granted that...** je présume que.... 2 n subvention f, allocation f; (for study at university etc) bourse f.

granule ['grænjuːl] n granule m. ●**granulated sugar** n sucre m cristallisé.

grape [greɪp] n grain m de raisin; **grapes** le raisin, les raisins mpl; **to eat (some) grapes** manger du raisin or des raisins; **g. harvest** vendange f; **g. juice** jus m de raisin.

grapefruit ['greɪpfruːt] n pamplemousse m.

grapevine ['greɪpvaɪn] n **on** or **through the g.** Fig par le téléphone arabe.

graph [græf, grɑːf] n courbe f, graphique m; **g. paper** papier m millimétré.

graphic ['græfɪk] a (description) explicite, vivant; (art etc) graphique; **g. design** (drawing etc) arts mpl graphiques. ●**graphically** adv (to describe) explicitement. ●**graphics** npl (computer) graphiques mpl.

grapple ['græp(ə)l] vi **to g. with** (person, problem etc) se colleter avec.

grasp [grɑːsp] vt (seize, understand) saisir ∎ n (firm hold) prise f; (understanding) compréhension f; (knowledge) connaissance f; **to have a strong g.** (strength of hand) avoir de la poigne; **within s.o.'s g.** (reach) à la portée de qn. ●**grasping** a (greedy) rapace.

grass [grɑːs] n herbe f; (lawn) gazon m; **the g. roots** (of organization) la base. ●**grasshopper** n sauterelle f. ●**grassland** n prairie f. ●**grassy** a herbeux.

grate [greɪt] 1 n (for fireplace) grille f de foyer. 2 vt (cheese, carrot etc) râper. 3 vi (of sound) grincer (**on sth** sur qch); **to g. on the ears** écorcher les oreilles; **to g. on s.o.'s nerves** taper sur les nerfs de qn. ●**grating 1** a (sound) grinçant; Fig irritant. **2** n (bars) grille f. ●**grater** n (for cheese etc) râpe f.

grateful ['greɪtfəl] a reconnaissant (**to** à, **for** de); (words, letter) de remerciement; (attitude, friend) plein de reconnaissance; **I'm g. (to you) for your help** je vous suis reconnaissant de votre aide; **I'd be g. if you'd be quieter** j'aimerais mieux que tu fasses moins de bruit; **g. thanks** mes sincères remerciements. ●**gratefully** adv avec reconnaissance.

gratify ['grætɪfaɪ] vt (whim) satisfaire; **to g. s.o.** faire plaisir à qn. ●**gratified** a (pleased) très content (**by** or **with sth** de qch, **to do sth** de faire). ●**gratifying** a très satisfaisant or agréable; **it's g. to know that...** ça fait plaisir de savoir que.... ●**gratification** [-'keɪʃ(ə)n] n satisfaction f.

gratis ['grætɪs, 'greɪtɪs] adv gratis.

gratitude ['grætɪtjuːd] n reconnaissance f, gratitude f (**for** de).

gratuitous [grə'tjuːɪtəs] a (act etc) gratuit.

gratuity [grə'tjuːɪtɪ] n (tip) pourboire m.

grave¹ [greɪv] n tombe f; **g. digger** fossoyeur

m. ●**gravestone** n pierre f tombale. ●**graveyard** n cimetière m; **auto g.** Am Fam cimetière m de voitures.

grave² [greɪv] a (-er, -est) (serious) grave. ●**gravely** adv (ill, to say etc) gravement; **g. concerned/displeased** extrêmement inquiet/mécontent.

gravel ['græv(ə)l] n gravier m; **g. path** allée f de gravier.

gravitate ['græviteit] vi to **g. towards** (be drawn towards) être attiré vers; (move towards) se diriger vers. ●**gravitation** [-'teɪʃ(ə)n] n gravitation f.

gravity ['grævɪtɪ] n 1 (force) Phys pesanteur f. 2 (seriousness) gravité f.

gravy ['greɪvɪ] n jus m de viande.

gray [greɪ] Am = grey.

graze [greɪz] 1 vt (scrape) écorcher; (touch lightly) frôler, effleurer ▮ n (wound) écorchure f. 2 vi (of cattle) paître.

grease [griːs] n graisse f ▮ vt graisser. ●**greaseproof (paper)** a & n Br papier m sulfurisé. ●**greasy** a (-ier, -iest) plein de graisse; (hair, ointment) gras (f grasse); (surface, road) glissant.

great [greɪt] a (-er, -est) grand; (effort, heat, parcel) gros (f grosse); grand; (excellent) Fam magnifique, merveilleux; **to be g. at tennis/etc** être très doué pour le tennis/etc; **a g. deal or number (of), a g. many** beaucoup (de); **a g. opinion of** une haute opinion de; **a very g. age** un âge très avancé; **the greatest team/etc** (best) la meilleure équipe/etc; **Greater London** le grand Londres. ●**great-'grandfather** n arrière-grand-père m. ●**great-'grandmother** n arrière-grand-mère m.

Great Britain [greɪt'brɪt(ə)n] n Grande-Bretagne f.

greatly ['greɪtlɪ] adv (much) beaucoup; (very) très, bien; **I g. prefer** je préfère beaucoup.

greatness ['greɪtnɪs] n (in size, importance) grandeur f; (in degree) intensité f.

Greece [griːs] n Grèce f.

greed [griːd] n avidité f (for de); (for food) gourmandise f.

greedy ['griːdɪ] a (-ier, -iest) avide (for de); (for food) glouton, gourmand. ●**greedily** adv avidement; (to eat) gloutonnement. ●**greediness** n = greed.

Greek [griːk] a grec (f grecque) ▮ n Grec m, Grecque f; (language) grec m.

green [griːn] a (-er, -est) vert; (pale) blême, vert; (immature) Fig inexpérimenté, naïf; Pol vert, écologiste; **to turn or go g.** (of mixture etc) devenir vert; (of garden, tree etc) verdir; **the g. belt** (land) Br la ceinture verte; **g. card** US permis m de travail; **to get the g. light** avoir le (feu) vert; **to have** Br **g. fingers** or Am **a g. thumb** avoir la main verte; **g. with envy** Fig vert de jalousie.
▮ n (colour) vert m; (lawn) pelouse f; (village square) place f gazonnée; (bowling) **g.** terrain m pour jeu de boules; **greens** (vegetables) légumes mpl verts; **the Greens** Pol les Verts mpl.

greenery ['griːnərɪ] n (plants, leaves) verdure f. ●**greenfly** n puceron m (des plantes). ●**greengage** n (plum) reine-claude f. ●**greengrocer** n Br marchand, -ande mf de légumes. ●**greenhouse** n serre f; **the g. effect** (in atmosphere) l'effet m de serre. ●**greenish** a verdâtre. ●**greenness** n (colour) vert m; (greenery) verdure f.

Greenland ['griːnlənd] n Groenland m.

greet [griːt] vt (with a nod, a hello etc) saluer (qn); (welcome) accueillir (qn, qch); (receive) accueillir (nouvelle etc); **to g. s.o.** (of sight) s'offrir aux regards de qn. ●**greeting** n salutation f; (welcome) accueil m; **greetings** (for birthday, festival) vœux mpl; **send my greetings to...** envoie mon bon souvenir à...; **greeting(s) card** carte f de vœux.

gregarious [grɪ'geərɪəs] a (person) sociable; (instinct, animal) grégaire.

gremlin ['gremlɪn] n petit diable m.

grenade [grə'neɪd] n (bomb) grenade f; **to throw a g.** lancer une grenade.

grew [gruː] pt of grow.

grey [greɪ] Br a (-er, -est) gris; (pale) (complexion) blême; **the outlook is g.** les perspectives sont sombres; **to be going g.** grisonner ▮ vi **to be greying** être grisonnant. ●**grey-'haired** a Br aux cheveux gris. ●**greyhound** n lévrier m. ●**greyish** a Br grisâtre.

grid [grɪd] n (grating, lines on map) grille f; **the (national) g.** Br le réseau électrique national.

griddle ['grɪd(ə)l] n (on stove) plaque f à griller.

grief [griːf] n chagrin m, douleur f; **to come to g.** (have problems) avoir des ennuis; (of driver, pilot etc) avoir un accident; (of plan) échouer; **good g.!** (surprise etc) ciel!, bon sang!

grievance ['griːvəns] n grief m; **grievances** (complaints) doléances fpl; **to have a g. against s.o.** avoir à se plaindre de qn.

grieve [griːv] vi s'affliger (over sth de qch); **to g. for s.o.** pleurer qn; **she's still grieving** elle pleure toujours sa perte ▮ vt peiner, affliger.

grievous ['griːvəs] a (serious) très grave; **g. bodily harm** Br Jur coups mpl et blessures fpl.

grill [grɪl] n 1 (utensil) gril m; (dish) grillade f ▮ vti griller. 2 vt (question) Fam cuisiner (qn).

grille [grɪl] n (metal bars) grille f; (radiator) **g.** (of vehicle) calandre f.

grim [grɪm] a (grimmer, grimmest) (stern) (face etc) sombre, sévère; (bleak) (future etc) sombre; (horrifying) sinistre; (bad) Fam affreux; **a g. determination** une volonté inflexible; **the g. truth** la triste vérité. ●**grimly** adv (to look at) sévèrement.

grimace ['grɪməs] n grimace f ▮ vi grimacer.

grime [graɪm] n crasse f. ●**grimy** a (-ier, -iest) crasseux.

grin [grɪn] vi (-nn-) avoir un large sourire ▮ n

large sourire *m*.

grind [graɪnd] **1** *vt* (*pt & pp* **ground**) (*coffee, pepper etc*) moudre; (*meat*) *Am* hacher; (*blade, tool*) aiguiser; (*oppress*) *Fig* écraser; **to g. one's teeth** grincer des dents ▮ *vi* **to g. to a halt** s'arrêter (progressivement); **grinding poverty** la misère noire. **2** *n* (*work, routine*) *Fam* corvée *f*, travail *m* long et monotone; **the daily g.** le boulot quotidien. ●**grinder** *n* coffee **g.** moulin *m* à café.

grip [grɪp] *vt* (-pp-) (*seize*) saisir; (*hold*) tenir serré; (*of story*) *Fig* empoigner (*qn*); **to g. the road** (*of Br* tyre, *Am* tire) adhérer à la route.
▮ *vi* (*of brakes, screw*) mordre; (*of Br* tyre, *Am* tire) adhérer.
▮ *n* (*hold*) prise *f*; (*on situation*) contrôle *m* (**on** de); (*of subject*) *Fam* connaissance *f*; (*hand clasp*) poigne *f*; (*of Br* tyre, *Am* tire) adhérence *f*; (*handle*) poignée *f*; **to lose one's g.** *Fig* ne plus être à la hauteur, baisser; **get a g. on yourself!** secoue-toi!; **to come** *or* **get to grips with** (*problem, subject*) s'attaquer à; **in the g. of** (*despair etc*) en proie à. ●**gripping** *a* (*book, film etc*) passionnant.

gripe [graɪp] *vi* (*complain*) *Sl* rouspéter.

grisly ['grɪzlɪ] *a* (*gruesome*) horrible.

gristle ['grɪs(ə)l] *n* (*in meat*) cartilage *m*.

grit [grɪt] **1** *n* (*sand*) sable *m*; (*gravel*) gravillon *m* ▮ *vt* (-tt-) (*road*) sabler. **2** *n* (*courage*) *Fam* cran *m*. **3** *vt* (-tt-) **to g. one's teeth** serrer les dents.

grizzle ['grɪz(ə)l] *vi* *Fam* pleurnicher. ●**grizzly** *a* **1** (*child*) *Fam* pleurnicheur. **2** **g. bear** grizzli *m*.

groan [grəʊn] *vi* (*with pain*) gémir; (*complain*) grogner, gémir ▮ *n* (*of pain*) gémissement *m*; (*of dissatisfaction*) grognement *m*.

grocer ['grəʊsər] *n* épicier, -ière *mf*; **g.'s shop** épicerie *f*. ●**grocery** *n* (*shop*) *Am* épicerie *f*; **groceries** (*food*) provisions *fpl*.

grog [grɒg] *n* (*drink*) grog *m*.

groggy ['grɒgɪ] *a* (-ier, -iest) (*shaky on one's feet*) pas solide sur les jambes; (*weak*) faible; (*from a blow*) groggy.

groin [grɔɪn] *n* aine *f*; (*genitals*) bas-ventre *m*.

groom [gruːm] **1** *n* (*bridegroom*) marié *m*. **2** *n* (*for horses*) lad *m* ▮ *vt* (*horse*) panser; **to g. s.o. for a job/etc** préparer qn pour un poste/ *etc*; **well groomed** (*person*) très soigné.

groove [gruːv] *n* (*slot for sliding door etc*) rainure *f*; (*in record*) sillon *m*.

grope [grəʊp] *vi* **to g. (about)** tâtonner; **to g. for** chercher à tâtons.

gross [grəʊs] **1** *a* (*total*) (*weight, income, output etc*) brut; **g. domestic product** produit *m* intérieur brut; **g. national product** produit national brut ▮ *vt* faire une recette brute de. **2** *a* (-er, -est) (*coarse*) grossier; **g. error** grosse erreur *f*, erreur *f* grossière; **g. injustice** injustice *f* flagrante. **3** *n* (*number*) grosse *f*. ●**grossly** *adv* (*very*) extrêmement; (*bluntly, coarsely*) grossièrement.

grotesque [grəʊ'tesk] *a* (*ludicrous, strange*)

grotesque; (*frightening*) monstrueux.

grotto ['grɒtəʊ] *n* (*pl* -oes *or* -os) grotte *f*.

grotty ['grɒtɪ] *a* (-ier, -iest) *Br Fam* (*ugly*) moche; (*of poor quality*) nul.

ground¹ [graʊnd] **1** *n* terre *f*, sol *m*; (*area for camping, football etc*) terrain *m*; (*estate*) terres *fpl*; (*electrical wire*) *Am* terre *f*, masse *f*; (*background*) fond *m*; **grounds** (*reasons*) raisons *fpl*, motifs *mpl*; (*gardens*) parc *m*; **on the g.** (*lying, sitting etc*) par terre; **to gain/ lose g.** gagner/perdre du terrain; **g. crew** (*at airport*) personnel *m* au sol; **g. floor** *Br* rez-de-chaussée *m inv*; **g. frost** gelée *f* blanche.
2 *vt* (*aircraft*) bloquer *or* retenir au sol. ●**grounding** *n* connaissances *fpl* (de fond) (**in** en). ●**groundless** *a* sans fondement.

ground² [graʊnd] *pt & pp of* **grind** ▮ *a* (*coffee*) moulu; **g. meat** *Am* viande *f* hachée ▮ *npl* (*coffee*) **grounds** marc *m* (de café).

groundnut ['graʊndnʌt] *n* arachide *f*. ●**groundsheet** *n* tapis *m* de sol. ●**groundswell** *n* lame *f* de fond. ●**groundwork** *n* préparation *f*.

group [gruːp] *n* groupe *m* ▮ *vt* **to g. (together)** grouper ▮ *vi* se grouper. ●**grouping** *n* (*group*) groupe *m*.

grouse [graʊs] **1** *n inv* (*bird*) coq *m* de bruyère. **2** *vi* (*complain*) *Fam* rouspéter.

grove [grəʊv] *n* bocage *m*.

grovel ['grɒv(ə)l] *vi* (*Br* -ll-, *Am* -l-) (*be humble*) ramper, s'aplatir (**to s.o.** devant qn).

grow [grəʊ] *vi* (*pt* grew, *pp* grown) (*of person*) grandir; (*of plant, hair*) pousser; (*increase*) augmenter, grandir, croître; (*of firm, town*) se développer; (*of gap, family*) s'agrandir; **to g. fat(ter)** grossir; **to g. to like** finir par aimer; **to g. into** devenir; **to g. on s.o.** (*of book, music etc*) plaire progressivement à qn; **to g. out of** (*one's clothes*) devenir trop grand pour; (*a habit*) perdre; **to g. up** devenir adulte; **when I g. up** quand je serai grand.
▮ *vt* (*plant, crops*) cultiver, faire pousser; (*beard, hair*) laisser pousser. ●**growing** *a* (*child*) qui grandit; (*number, discontent etc*) grandissant. ●**grower** *n* (*person*) cultivateur, -trice *mf* (of de).

growl [graʊl] *vi* grogner (**at** contre) ▮ *n* grognement *m*.

grown [grəʊn] *a* (*man, woman*) adulte. ●**grown-up** *n* grande personne *f*, adulte *mf* ▮ *a* (*ideas, behaviour etc*) d'adulte.

growth [grəʊθ] *n* croissance *f*; (*increase*) augmentation *f* (**in** de); (*lump*) tumeur *f* (**on** à); **a week's g. of beard** une barbe de huit jours.

grub [grʌb] *n* **1** (*food*) *Fam* bouffe *f*. **2** (*insect*) larve *f*.

grubby ['grʌbɪ] *a* (-ier, -iest) sale.

grudge [grʌdʒ] **1** *n* rancune *f*; **to have a g. against s.o.** garder rancune à qn. **2** *vt* **to g. s.o. sth** (*give*) donner qch à qn à contre-cœur; (*reproach*) reprocher qch à qn; **to g. doing sth** faire qch à contrecœur. ●**grudging**

a peu généreux. ●**grudgingly** *adv (to give etc)* à contrecœur.

gruelling, *Am* **grueling** ['grʊəlɪŋ] *a (day, detail etc)* éprouvant, atroce.

gruesome ['gru:səm] *a* horrible.

gruff [grʌf] *a* (-er, -est) *(voice, person)* bourru.

grumble ['grʌmb(ə)l] *vi (complain)* râler, grogner **(about, at** contre).

grumpy ['grʌmpɪ] *a* (-ier, -iest) grincheux.

grunt [grʌnt] *vti* grogner ▮ *n* grognement *m.*

guarantee [gærən'ti:] *n* garantie *f* ▮ *vt* garantir **(against** contre); *(vouch for)* se porter garant de; **to g. s.o. that** garantir *or* certifier à qn que. ●**guarantor** *n* garant, -ante *mf.*

guard [gɑ:d] *n (vigilance, group of soldiers etc)* garde *f*; *(individual person)* garde *m*; *(on train)* chef *m* de train; **to keep a g. on** surveiller; **under g.** sous surveillance; **on one's g.** sur ses gardes; **to catch s.o. off his g.** prendre qn au dépourvu; **on g. (duty)** de garde; **to stand g.** monter la garde.
▮ *vt (protect)* protéger **(against** contre); *(watch over)* surveiller, garder.
▮ *vi* **to g. against** *(protect oneself)* se prémunir contre; *(prevent)* empêcher; **to g. against doing/being** se garder de faire/d'être. ●**guarded** *a (cautious)* prudent.

guardian ['gɑ:dɪən] *n (of child) Jur* tuteur, -trice *mf*; *(protector)* gardien, -ienne *mf*; **g. angel** ange *m* gardien.

Guatemala [gwætɪ'mɑ:lə] *n* Guatemala *m.*

Guernsey ['gɜ:nzɪ] *n* Guernesey *m or f.*

guerrilla [gə'rɪlə] *n (person)* guérillero *m*; **g. warfare** guérilla *f.*

guess [ges] *n* conjecture *f*; *(intuition)* intuition *f*; *(estimate)* estimation *f*; **to make** *or* **take a g.** (essayer de) deviner; **an educated** *or* **informed g.** une conjecture fondée; **at a g.** à vue de nez, au jugé.
▮ *vt* deviner **(that** que); *(length, number etc)* estimer; **to g. that** *(suppose) Am* supposer que; *(think) Am* croire que.
▮ *vi* deviner; **to g. right** deviner juste; **you guessed wrong** tu n'as pas deviné *or* trouvé; **I g. (so)** *Am* je suppose; *(I think so)* je crois. ●**guesswork** *n* hypothèse *f*; **by g.** à vue de nez, au jugé.

guest [gest] *n* invité, -ée *mf*; *(in hotel)* client, -ente *mf*; *(at meal)* convive *mf*; **our g. speaker/singer/**etc le conférencier/chanteur/etc qui est notre invité. ●**guesthouse** *n* pension *f* de famille. ●**guestroom** *n* chambre *f* d'ami.

guffaw [gə'fɔ:] *vi* rire bruyamment.

guidance ['gaɪdəns] *n (advice)* conseils *mpl.*

guide [gaɪd] *n (person)* guide *m*; *(indication)* indication *f*; **(book)** guide *m*; *(girl) Br* éclaireuse *f*; **g. dog** chien *m* d'aveugle ▮ *vt (lead)* guider; **guiding principle** principe *m* directeur. ●**guided** *a (missile, rocket)* guidé; **g. tour** visite *f* guidée. ●**guidelines** *npl* indications *fpl* (à suivre), lignes *fpl* directrices.

guild [gɪld] *n* association *f*; *Hist* corporation *f.*

guile [gaɪl] *n (deceit)* ruse *f.*

guillotine ['gɪləti:n] *n (for execution)* guillotine *f*; *(for paper) Br* massicot *m.*

guilt [gɪlt] *n* culpabilité *f.* ●**guilty** *a* (-ier, -iest) coupable; **g. person** coupable *mf*; **to find s.o. g./not g.** déclarer qn coupable/non coupable.

guinea pig ['gɪnɪpɪg] *n (animal)* & *Fig* cobaye *m.*

guise [gaɪz] *n* **under the g. of** sous l'apparence de.

guitar [gɪ'tɑ:r] *n* guitare *f.* ●**guitarist** *n* guitariste *mf.*

gulf [gʌlf] *n (in sea)* golfe *m*; *(chasm)* gouffre *m*; **a g. between** *(gap)* un abîme entre.

gull [gʌl] *n (bird)* mouette *f.*

gullet ['gʌlɪt] *n* gosier *m.*

gullible ['gʌlɪb(ə)l] *a* crédule.

gully ['gʌlɪ] *n (valley)* ravine *f*; *(drain)* rigole *f.*

gulp [gʌlp] **1** *vt* **to g. (down)** avaler (vite) ▮ *n (of drink)* gorgée *f*, lampée *f*; **in** *or* **at one g.** d'une seule gorgée. **2** *vi (with emotion)* avoir la gorge serrée ▮ *n* serrement *m* de gorge.

gum¹ [gʌm] *n (around teeth)* gencive *f.* ●**gumboil** *n* abcès *m* (dentaire).

gum² [gʌm] **1** *n (glue)* colle *f*; *(substance from tree)* gomme *f* ▮ *vt* (-mm-) coller. **2** *n (for chewing)* chewing-gum *m.*

gumption ['gʌmpʃ(ə)n] *n Fam (courage)* initiative *f*; *(commonsense)* jugeote *f.*

gun [gʌn] *n* pistolet *m*, revolver *m*; *(rifle)* fusil *m*; *(firing shells)* canon *m* ▮ *vt* (-nn-) to **g. down** abattre. ●**gunfight** *n* échange *m* de coups de feu. ●**gunfire** *n* coups *mpl* de feu; *(in battle)* tir *m* d'artillerie. ●**gunman** *n* (*pl* -men) bandit *m* armé. ●**gunner** *n (in army etc)* artilleur *m.* ●**gunpoint** *n* **to hold s.o. at g.** tenir qn sous la menace d'un pistolet *or* d'un fusil *or* d'une arme. ●**gunpowder** *n* poudre *f* à canon. ●**gunshot** *n* coup *m* de feu; **g. wound** blessure *f* par balle.

gunge [gʌndʒ] *n Br Fam* magma *m.*

gung-ho [gʌŋ'həʊ] *a* **g.-ho about sth** très enthousiaste à l'idée de qch.

gurgle ['gɜ:g(ə)l] *vi (of water)* glouglouter; *(of baby)* gazouiller ▮ *n* glouglou *m*; *(of baby)* gazouillis *m.*

guru ['gʊru:] *n (leader) Fam* gourou *m.*

gush [gʌʃ] *vi* **to g. (out)** jaillir **(of** de) ▮ *n* jaillissement *m.*

gust [gʌst] *n (of smoke)* bouffée *f*; **g. (of wind)** rafale *f* (de vent) ▮ *vi (of wind)* souffler eu rafales. ●**gusty** *a* (-ier, -iest) *(weather)* venteux; *(day)* de vent.

gusto ['gʌstəʊ] *n* **with g.** avec entrain.

gut [gʌt] *n (inside body)* intestin *m*; *(catgut)* boyau *m*; **guts** *Fam (insides)* ventre *m*, tripes *fpl*; *(courage)* cran *m*, tripes *fpl*; **he hates your guts** *Fam* il ne peut pas te sentir. **2** *vt* (-tt-) *(of fire)* ne laisser que les quatre murs de *(maison etc).*

gutter ['gʌtər] *n (on roof)* gouttière *f*; *(in street)* caniveau *m.* ●**guttering** *n* gouttières *fpl.*

guttural ['gʌtərəl] *a* guttural.
guy [gaɪ] *n (fellow)* *Fam* type *m*.
guzzle ['gʌz(ə)l] *vi (eat)* bâfrer ▮ *vt (eat)* engloutir *(gâteau etc)*; *(drink)* siffler *(vin etc)*.
gym [dʒɪm] *n* gym(nastique) *f*; *(gymnasium)* gymnase *m*; **g. shoes** tennis *fpl or mpl*. ● **gymnasium** [-'neɪzɪəm] *n* gymnase *m*.

● **gymnast** *n* gymnaste *mf*. ● **gym'nastics** *n* gymnastique *f*.
gynaecology, *Am* **gynecology** [gaɪnɪ'kɒlədʒɪ] *n* gynécologie *f*. ● **gynaecologist,** *Am* **gynecologist** *n* gynécologue *mf*.
gypsy ['dʒɪpsɪ] = gipsy.
gyrate [dʒaɪ'reɪt] *vi* tournoyer.

H

H, h [eɪtʃ] *n* H, h *m*; **H bomb** bombe *f* H.

haberdasher ['hæbədæʃər] *n* (*selling sewing items*) *Br* mercier, -ière *mf*; (*men's outfitter*) *Am* chemisier *m*. ● **haberdashery** *n* mercerie *f*; *Am* chemiserie *f*.

habit ['hæbɪt] *n* **1** habitude *f*; **to be in/get into the h. of doing** avoir/prendre l'habitude de faire; **to make a h. of doing** avoir pour habitude de faire. **2** (*addiction*) accoutumance *f*; **a h.-forming drug** une drogue qui crée une accoutumance. **3** (*costume of monk or nun*) habit *m*.

habitable ['hæbɪtəb(ə)l] *a* habitable. ● **habitat** *n* (*of animal, plant*) habitat *m*. ● **habitation** [-'teɪʃ(ə)n] *n* habitation *f*; **fit for (human) h.** habitable.

habitual [hə'bɪtʃʊəl] *a* habituel; (*smoker, drinker etc*) invétéré. ● **habitually** *adv* habituellement.

hack [hæk] **1** *vt* (*cut*) tailler. **2** *n* (*old horse*) rosse *f*; (*hired horse*) cheval *m* de louage; **h.** (*writer*) *Pej* écrivaillon *m*; **h. work** (*drudgery*) tâches *fpl* ingrates.

hacker ['hækər] *n Comptr* pirate *m* (informatique).

hackneyed ['hæknɪd] *a* (*saying*) rebattu, banal (*mpl* -als).

had [hæd] *pt & pp of* **have**.

haddock ['hædək] *n* (*fish*) aiglefin *m*; **smoked h.** haddock *m*.

haemorrhage ['hemərɪdʒ] *n* (*bleeding*) hémorragie *f*.

haemorrhoids ['hemərɔɪdz] *npl* hémorroïdes *fpl*.

hag [hæg] *n* (*old*) **h.** (vieille) sorcière *f*.

haggard ['hægəd] *a* (*person, face*) hâve, émacié.

haggle ['hæg(ə)l] *vi* marchander; **to h. over** (*article*) marchander; **to h. over the price** discuter le prix. ● **haggling** *n* marchandage *m*.

Hague (The) [ðə'heɪg] *n* La Haye.

ha-ha! [hɑː'hɑː] *int* (*laughter*) ha, ha!

hail¹ [heɪl] *n* grêle *f*; **a h. of bullets/etc** *Fig* une grêle de balles/*etc* ▮ *v imp* grêler; **it's hailing** il grêle. ● **hailstone** *n* grêlon *m*.

hail² [heɪl] **1** *vt* (*greet*) saluer; (*taxi*) héler. **2** *vi* **to h. from** (*of person*) être originaire de; (*of ship, train etc*) être en provenance de.

hair [heər] *n* (*on head*) cheveux *mpl*; (*on body, of animal*) poils *mpl*; **a h.** (*on head*) un cheveu; (*on body, of animal*) un poil; **by a h.'s breadth** de justesse; **h. cream** brillantine *f*; **h. dryer** sèche-cheveux *m inv*; **h. spray** (*bombe f de*) laque *f*.

hairbrush ['heəbrʌʃ] *n* brosse *f* à cheveux. ● **haircut** *n* coupe *f* de cheveux; **to have a h.**

se faire couper les cheveux. ● **hairdo** *n* (*pl* -dos) *Fam* coiffure *f*. ● **hairdresser** *n* coiffeur, -euse *mf*. ● **hairgrip** *n* pince *f* à cheveux. ● **hairnet** *n* résille *f*. ● **hairpiece** *n* postiche *m*. ● **hairpin** *n* épingle *f* à cheveux; **h. bend** (*in road*) virage *m* en épingle à cheveux. ● **hair-raising** *a* effrayant, à faire dresser les cheveux sur la tête. ● **hairsplitting** *n* ergotage *m*. ● **hairstyle** *n* coiffure *f*.

-haired [heəd] *suff* **long-/red-/etc h.** aux cheveux longs/roux/*etc*.

hairy ['heərɪ] *a* (**-ier, -iest**) (*person, animal, body*) poilu; (*frightening*) *Fam* effrayant.

hake [heɪk] *n* (*fish*) colin *m*.

hale [heɪl] *a* **h. and hearty** vigoureux.

half [hɑːf] *n* (*pl* **halves**) moitié *f*, demi, -ie *mf*; (*part of match*) mi-temps *f*; (*half fare*) *Br* demi-tarif *m*; **h. (of) the apple/etc** la moitié de la pomme/*etc*; **ten and a h.** dix et demi; **ten and a h. weeks** dix semaines et demie; **to cut in h.** couper en deux; **to go halves with** partager les frais avec.

▮ *a* demi; **h. a day, a h.-day** une demi-journée; **h. a dozen, a h.-dozen** une demi-douzaine; **h. fare** demi-tarif *m*; **at h. price** à moitié prix; **h. man h. beast** mi-homme mi-bête; **h. sleeves** manches *fpl* mi-longues.

▮ *adv* (*dressed, full etc*) à moitié, à demi; (*almost*) presque; **h. asleep** à moitié endormi; **h. past one** une heure et demie; **he isn't h. lazy/etc** *Br Fam* il est drôlement *or* rudement paresseux/*etc*; **h. as much as** moitié moins que; **h. as much again** moitié plus.

half-back ['hɑːfbæk] *n Football* demi *m*. ● **half-'baked** *a* (*idea*) *Fam* à la manque, à la noix. ● **half-caste** *n* métis, -isse *mf*. ● **half-'dozen** *n* demi-douzaine *f*. ● **half-'hearted** *a* (*person, manner*) peu enthousiaste; (*effort*) timide. ● **half-'hour** *n* demi-heure *f*. ● **half-light** *n* pénombre *f*, demi-jour *m*. ● **half-'mast** *n* **at h.-mast** (*flag*) en berne. ● **half-'open** *a* entrouvert. ● **half-'price** *a & adv* à moitié prix. ● **half-'term** *n* (*in British school*) petites vacances *fpl*, congé *m* de demi-trimestre. ● **half-'time** *n* (*in game*) mi-temps *f*. ● **half'way** *adv* (*between places*) à mi-chemin (*between* entre); **to fill/etc h.** remplir/*etc* à moitié; **to be h. through a book/etc** être (arrivé) à la moitié d'un livre/*etc*. ● **half-wit** *n or* **half-'witted** *a* imbécile (*mf*).

halibut ['hælɪbət] *n* (*fish*) flétan *m*.

hall [hɔːl] *n* (*room*) salle *f*; (*house entrance*) entrée *f*, vestibule *m*; (*of hotel*) hall *m*; (*mansion*) manoir *m*; (*for meals, in British* *university*) réfectoire *m*; **h. of residence** *Br* résidence *f* universitaire; **halls of residence** *Br* cité *f* universitaire; **lecture h.** amphithéâtre *m*.

hallelujah [hælɪ'luːjə] *n & int* alléluia (*m*).

hallmark ['hɔːlmɑːk] *n* (*on silver or gold*) poinçon *m*; (*of genius, talent*) *Fig* sceau *m*.

hallo! [hə'ləʊ] *int* (*greeting*) bonjour!; (*answering phone*) allô!; (*surprise*) tiens!

hallow ['hæləʊ] *vt* sanctifier.

Hallowe'en [hæləʊ'iːn] *n* la veille de la Toussaint.

hallstand ['hɔːlstænd] *n Br* portemanteau *m*.

hallucination [həluːsɪ'neɪʃ(ə)n] *n* hallucination *f*.

hallway ['hɔːlweɪ] *n* entrée *f*, vestibule *m*.

halo ['heɪləʊ] *n* (*pl* -oes *or* -os) (*round angel etc*) auréole *f*; (*round person, thing*) *Fig* auréole *f*, halo *m*.

halogen ['hælədʒən] *n* **h. lamp** lampe *f* halogène.

halt [hɔːlt] *n* halte *f*; **to call a h.** to mettre fin à; **to come to a h.** s'arrêter ▮ *vi* (*of soldiers etc*) faire halte; (*of production etc*) s'arrêter ▮ *vt* (*stop*) arrêter ▮ *int* (*to soldiers*) halte! ● **halting** *a* (*voice*) hésitant.

halve [hɑːv] *vt* (*time, expense*) réduire de moitié; (*number, cake etc*) diviser en deux.

ham [hæm] *n* **1** jambon *m*; **h. and eggs** œufs *mpl* au jambon; **h. sandwich** sandwich *m* au jambon. **2** (*actor*) *Pej* cabotin, -ine *mf*.

hamburger ['hæmbɜːgər] *n* hamburger *m*.

ham-fisted [hæm'fɪstɪd] *a Fam* maladroit.

hamlet ['hæmlɪt] *n* hameau *m*.

hammer ['hæmər] *n* marteau *m* ▮ *vt* (*nail*) enfoncer (**into** dans); (*metal*) marteler; (*defeat*) *Fam* battre à plate(s) couture(s); (*criticize*) *Fam* démolir; **to h. out** (*agreement, plan*) mettre au point ▮ *vi* frapper (**au marteau**); **to h. on the door** frapper à la porte à coups redoublés. ● **hammering** *n* (*defeat*) *Fam* raclée *f*, défaite *f*.

hammock ['hæmək] *n* hamac *m*.

hamper ['hæmpər] **1** *vt* (*hinder*) gêner. **2** *n* (*basket*) *Br* panier *m* (*à provisions, à pique-nique*); (*laundry basket*) *Am* panier *m* à linge.

hamster ['hæmstər] *n* hamster *m*.

hand¹ [hænd] **1** *n* main *f*; **to hold in one's h.** tenir à la main; **by h.** (*to make, sew etc*) à la main; **to deliver sth by h.** remettre qch en mains propres; **at** *or* **to h.** (*within reach*) sous la main, à portée de la main; (*close*) at h. (*person etc*) tout près; (*day etc*) proche; **the situation is in h.** la situation est bien en main; **the matter in h.** l'affaire *f* en question; **to have money in h.** avoir de l'argent disponible; **work in h.** travail *m* en cours; **on h.** (*ready for use*) disponible; **to have s.o. on one's hands** *Fig* avoir qn sur les bras; **on the right h.** du côté droit (**of** de); **on the one h....** d'une part...; **on the other h....** d'autre part...; **hands up!** (*in attack*) haut les mains!; (*to schoolchildren*) levez la main!; **hands off!** pas touche!, bas les pattes!; **my hands are** full *Fig* je suis très occupé; **to give s.o. a (helping) h.** donner un coup de main à qn; **to get out of h.** (*of child etc*) devenir impossible; (*of situation*) devenir incontrôlable; **h. in h.** la main dans la main; **it goes h. in h. with** (*together with*) *Fig* cela va de pair avec; **at first h.** de première main; **to win hands down** gagner haut la main ▮ *a* (*luggage, grenade etc*) à main; (*cream, lotion*) pour les mains.

2 *n* (*worker*) ouvrier, -ière *mf*; (*of clock*) aiguille *f*; *Cards* jeu *m*; (*style of writing*) écriture *f*.

hand² [hænd] *vt* (*give*) donner (**to** à); **to h. down** (*bring down*) descendre; (*knowledge, heirloom*) transmettre (**to** à); **to h. in** remettre; **to h. out** distribuer; **to h. over** remettre; (*power*) transmettre; **to h. round** (*cakes, photos etc*) passer.

handbag ['hændbæg] *n* sac *m* à main. ● **handball** *n Sport* hand-ball *m*. ● **handbill** *n* prospectus *m*. ● **handbook** *n* (*manual*) manuel *m*; (*guide*) guide *m*. ● **handbrake** *n* frein *m* à main. ● **handbrush** *n* balayette *f*. ● **handcuff** *vt* passer les menottes à; **to be handcuffed** avoir les menottes aux poignets. ● **handcuffs** *npl* menottes *fpl*. ● **hand'made** *a* fait à la main. ● **hand'picked** *a* (*team member etc*) trié sur le volet. ● **handrail** *n* (*on stairs*) rampe *f*. ● **handshake** *n* poignée *f* de main. ● **hands-on** *a* (*experience etc*) pratique, direct. ● **handwriting** *n* écriture *f*. ● **hand'written** *a* écrit à la main.

handful ['hændfʊl] *n* (*bunch, group*) poignée *f*; **she's (quite) a h.** elle est difficile.

handicap ['hændɪkæp] *n* (*disadvantage*) & *Sport* handicap *m* ▮ *vt* (-pp-) handicaper; **to be handicapped** (*after an accident*) rester handicapé. ● **handicapped** *a* (*disabled*) handicapé.

handicraft ['hændɪkrɑːft] *n* artisanat *m* d'art. ● **handiwork** *n* artisanat *m* d'art; (*action, work achieved*) ouvrage *m*.

handkerchief ['hæŋkətʃɪf] *n* (*pl* -fs) mouchoir *m*.

handle ['hænd(ə)l] **1** *n* (*of door*) poignée *f*; (*of knife*) manche *m*; (*of bucket*) anse *f*; (*of saucepan*) queue *f*; (*of pump*) bras *m*. **2** *vt* (*manipulate*) manier; (*touch*) toucher à; (*vehicle, ship*) manœuvrer; (*deal with*) s'occuper de; (*difficult child etc*) s'y prendre avec ▮ *vi* **to h. well** (*of machine*) être facile à manier.

handlebars ['hænd(ə)lbɑːz] *npl* guidon *m*.

handout ['hændaʊt] *n* (*leaflet*) prospectus *m*; (*money*) aumône *f*.

handsome ['hænsəm] *a* (*person, building etc*) beau (*f* belle); (*profit, sum*) considérable; (*gift*) généreux. ● **handsomely** *adv* (*generously*) généreusement.

handy ['hændɪ] *a* (-ier, -iest) (*convenient, practical*) commode, pratique; (*skilful*) habile (**at doing** à faire); (*useful*) utile; (*within reach*) sous la main; (*place*) accessible; **to come in h.** se révéler utile; **to keep sth h.** avoir qch sous la main. ● **handyman** *n* (*pl*

-men) (*DIY enthusiast*) bricoleur *m*; (*work-man*) homme *m* à tout faire.

hang¹ [hæŋ] **1** *vt* (*pt* & *pp* hung) suspendre (on, from à); (*on hook*) accrocher (on, from à), suspendre; (*wallpaper*) poser; (*let dangle*) laisser pendre (from, out of de); to h. sth with sth (*decorate with*) orner qch de qch.
■ *vi* (*dangle*) pendre; (*of threat*) planer; (*of fog, smoke*) flotter.
2 *n* to get the h. of sth *Fam* arriver à comprendre qch; to get the h. of doing sth *Fam* trouver le truc pour faire qch. ●**hanging¹** *a* suspendu (from à); (*leg, arm*) pendant; h. on the wall accroché au mur.

hang² [hæŋ] *vt* (*pt* & *pp* hanged) (*criminal*) pendre (for murder/*etc* pour meurtre/*etc*) ■ *vi* (*of criminal*) être pendu. ●**hanging²** *n* (*execution*) pendaison *f*. ●**hangman** *n* (*pl* -men) bourreau *m*.

hang about *or* **around** *vi* (*loiter*) traîner, rôder; (*wait*) *Fam* attendre ■ **to hang down** *vi* (*dangle*) pendre; (*of hair*) tomber ■ **to hang on** *vi* (*hold out*) résister; (*wait*) *Fam* attendre; to h. on to (*cling to*) ne pas lâcher; (*keep*) garder ■ **to hang out** *vt* (*washing*) étendre; (*flag*) arborer ■ *vi* (*of tongue, shirt*) pendre; (*live*) *Sl* crécher ■ **to hang together** *vi* (*of facts*) se tenir; (*of plan*) tenir debout ■ **to hang up** *vt* (*picture etc*) accrocher ■ *vi* (*on phone*) raccrocher.

hangar ['hæŋər] *n* (*for aircraft*) hangar *m*.
hanger ['hæŋər] *n* (*coat*) h. cintre *m*.
●**hanger-'on** *n* (*pl* hangers-on) (*unwanted follower*) parasite *m*.
hang-glider ['hæŋglaɪdər] *n* delta-plane® *m*. ●**hang-gliding** *n* vol *m* libre.
hangnail ['hæŋneɪl] *n* petites peaux *fpl*.
hangover ['hæŋəʊvər] *n* (*after drinking*) *Fam* gueule *f* de bois.
hangup ['hæŋʌp] *n Fam* complexe *m*.
hanker ['hæŋkər] *vi* to h. after *or* for avoir envie de. ●**hankering** *n* (forte) envie *f*.
hankie, hanky ['hæŋkɪ] *n Fam* mouchoir *m*.
hanky-panky [hæŋkɪ'pæŋkɪ] *n inv Fam* (*sexual behaviour*) galipettes *fpl*, papouilles *fpl*, pelotage *m*; (*deceit*) manigances *fpl*, magouilles *fpl*.
haphazard [hæp'hæzəd] *a* (fait) au hasard, (fait) au petit bonheur; (*selection, arrangement*) aléatoire. ●**haphazardly** *adv* au hasard.
hapless ['hæplɪs] *a Lit* infortuné.
happen ['hæpən] *vi* arriver, se passer, se produire; to h. to s.o./sth arriver à qn/qch; I h. to know, it (so) happens that I know il se trouve que je le sais; do you h. to have...? est-ce que par hasard vous avez...?; whatever happens quoi qu'il arrive. ●**happening** *n* événement *m*.
happily ['hæpɪlɪ] *adv* joyeusement; (*contentedly*) tranquillement; (*fortunately*) heureusement; h. married couple couple *m* heureux.
happiness ['hæpɪnɪs] *n* bonheur *m*.
happy ['hæpɪ] *a* (-ier, -iest) heureux (to do de faire, about sth de qch); I'm not (too *or*

very) h. about (doing) it ça ne me plaît pas beaucoup (de le faire); H. New Year! bonne année!; H. Christmas! Joyeux Noël! ●**happy-go-'lucky** *a* insouciant.
harass [*Br* 'hærəs, *Am* hə'ræs] *vt* harceler. ●**harassment** *n* harcèlement *m*; sexual h. harcèlement *m* sexuel.
harbour ['hɑːbər] (*Am* harbor) **1** *n* port *m*. **2** *vt* (*shelter*) cacher, abriter (*assassin, fugitif*). **3** *vt* (*have*) nourrir (*crainte, secret*); to h. a grudge against garder rancune contre.
hard [hɑːd] *a* (-er, -est) (*not soft, severe*) dur; (*difficult*) difficile, dur; (*study*) assidu; (*drink*) (fortement) alcoolisé; (*water*) calcaire; to be h. on *or* to s.o. être dur avec qn; to find it h. to sleep/*etc* avoir du mal à dormir/*etc*; no h. feelings! sans rancune!; h. of hearing dur d'oreille; h. cash espèces *fpl*; h. core (*group*) noyau *m* dur, élite *f*; h. disk (*of computer*) disque *m* dur; h. drinker/worker gros buveur *m*/travailleur *m*; h. evidence preuves *fpl* tangibles; the h. facts les faits bruts; h. frost une forte gelée; h. labour travaux *mpl* forcés; h. up (*broke*) *Fam* fauché; to be h. up for sth manquer de qch.
■ *adv* (-er, -est) (*to work*) dur; (*to pull*) fort; (*to hit, freeze*) dur, fort; (*to study*) assidûment; (*to rain*) à verse; (*badly*) mal; to look h. at regarder fixement; (*examine*) regarder de près; to look h. (*seek*) chercher bien; to think h. réfléchir bien; h. at work en plein travail; h. by tout près; to be h. done by être traité injustement.
hard-and-fast [hɑːdən(d)'fɑːst] *a* (*rule*) strict. ●**'hardback** *n* livre *m* relié. ●**'hardboard** *n* Isorel® *m*. ●**hard-'boiled** *a* (egg) dur. ●**hard-'core** *a* (*supporter etc*) inconditionnel. ●**'hard-earned** *a* (*money*) péniblement gagné; (*rest etc*) bien mérité. ●**hard'headed** *a* réaliste. ●**hard'wearing** *a* résistant. ●**hardwood** *n* bois *m* de feuillu. ●**hard-'working** *a* travailleur.
harden ['hɑːd(ə)n] *vti* durcir; to become hardened to s'endurcir à. ●**hardened** *a* (*criminal*) endurci.
hardly ['hɑːdlɪ] *adv* à peine; he h. talks il parle à peine, il ne parle guère; h. anyone/anything presque personne/rien; h. ever presque jamais.
hardness ['hɑːdnɪs] *n* dureté *f*.
hardship ['hɑːdʃɪp] *n* (*ordeal*) épreuve(s) *f(pl)*; (*deprivation*) privation(s) *f(pl)*.
hardware ['hɑːdweər] *n inv* quincaillerie *f*; (*of computer*) & *Mil* matériel *m*; h. shop quincaillerie *f*.
hardy ['hɑːdɪ] *a* (-ier, -iest) (*person, plant*) résistant.
hare [heər] *n* lièvre *m*. ●**hare-brained** *a* (*person*) écervelé; (*scheme*) insensé.
harem ['hɑːriːm] *n* harem *m*.
hark [hɑːk] *vi Lit* écouter; to h. back to (*subject etc*) *Fam* revenir sur.
harm [hɑːm] *n* (*hurt*) mal *m*; (*wrong*) tort *m*; he means (us) no h. il ne nous veut pas de mal; she'll come to no h. il ne lui arrivera

rien; **out of h.'s way** à l'abri du danger ▌ *vt* (*hurt*) faire du mal à (*qn*); (*health, interests, cause etc*) nuire à, faire du tort à; (*object*) endommager, abîmer. ●**harmful** *a* nuisible. ●**harmless** *a* (*person, treatment*) inoffensif; (*hobby, act*) innocent; (*gas, fumes etc*) qui n'est pas nuisible, inoffensif.

harmonic [haːˈmɒnɪk] *a & n Mus* harmonique (*m*).

harmonica [haːˈmɒnɪkə] *n* harmonica *m*.

harmonious [haːˈməʊnɪəs] *a* harmonieux.

harmonium [haːˈməʊnɪəm] *n* (*musical instrument*) harmonium *m*.

harmonize [ˈhaːmənaɪz] *vt* harmoniser ▌ *vi* s'harmoniser.

harmony [ˈhaːmənɪ] *n* harmonie *f*.

harness [ˈhaːnɪs] *n* (*for horse, baby*) harnais *m* ▌ *vt* (*horse*) harnacher; (*energy etc*) *Fig* exploiter.

harp [haːp] 1 *n* harpe *f*. 2 *vt* **to h. on about sth** *Fam* ne pas s'arrêter de parler de qch. ●**harpist** *n* harpiste *mf*.

harpoon [haːˈpuːn] *n* harpon *m* ▌ *vt* (*whale*) harponner.

harpsichord [ˈhaːpsɪkɔːd] *n* (*musical instrument*) clavecin *m*.

harrowing [ˈhærəʊɪŋ] *a* (*story, memory*) poignant; (*experience*) très éprouvant; (*cry, sight*) déchirant.

harsh [haːʃ] *a* (**-er, -est**) (*severe*) dur, sévère; (*winter, climate*) rude, rigoureux; (*sound*) discordant; (*voice*) rauque; (*taste*) âpre; (*surface*) rugueux; (*fabric*) rêche; **h. light** lumière *f* crue; **to be h. with s.o.** être dur *or* sévère envers qn. ●**harshly** *adv* durement, sévèrement. ●**harshness** *n* dureté *f*, sévérité *f*; (*of winter etc*) rigueur *f*; (*of sound*) discordance *f*; (*of taste*) âpreté *f*; (*of surface*) rugosité *f*.

harvest [ˈhaːvɪst] *n* moisson *f*; (*of fruit*) récolte *f* ▌ *vt* moissonner; (*fruit*) récolter.

has [hæz] *see* **have**. ●**has-been** *n Fam* personne *f* finie.

hash [hæʃ] 1 *n* (*food*) hachis *m* ▌ *vt* **to h. (up)** hacher. 2 *n* (*mess*) *Fam* gâchis *m*; **to make a h. of sth** faire un beau gâchis de qch. 3 *n* (*hashish*) *Fam* hasch *m*, H *m*.

hashish [ˈhæʃiːʃ] *n* haschisch *m*.

hassle [ˈhæs(ə)l] *n Fam* (*trouble*) histoires *fpl*; (*bother*) mal *m*, peine *f*.

haste [heɪst] *n* hâte *f*; **in h.** à la hâte; **to make h.** se hâter.

hasten [ˈheɪs(ə)n] *vi* se hâter (**to do** de faire) ▌ *vt* hâter.

hasty [ˈheɪstɪ] *a* (**-ier, -iest**) (*sudden*) précipité; (*visit*) rapide; (*decision, work*) hâtif. ●**hastily** *adv* (*quickly*) à la hâte; (*too quickly*) hâtivement.

hat [hæt] *n* chapeau *m*; (*of child*) bonnet *m*; (*cap*) casquette *f*; **that's old h.** *Fam* (*old-fashioned*) c'est vieux jeu; (*stale*) c'est vieux comme les rues; **to score** *or* **get a h. trick** *Sport* réussir trois coups consécutifs.

hatch [hætʃ] 1 *vi* (*of chick, egg*) éclore ▌ *vt* faire éclore; (*plot*) *Fig* tramer. 2 *n* (*in kitchen wall*) *Br* passe-plats *m inv*; (*on ship*) écoutille *f*.

hatchback [ˈhætʃbæk] *n* (*car*) trois-portes *m inv*, cinq-portes *f inv*; (*door*) hayon *m*.

hatchet [ˈhætʃɪt] *n* hachette *f*.

hate [heɪt] *vt* détester, haïr; **to h. doing** *or* **to do** détester faire; **I h. to say it** ça me gêne de le dire ▌ *n* haine *f*; **pet h.** *Br Fam* bête *f* noire. ●**hateful** *a* haïssable. ●**hatred** [ˈheɪtrɪd] *n* haine *f*.

hatstand [ˈhætstænd] *n* portemanteau *m*.

haughty [ˈhɔːtɪ] *a* (**-ier, -iest**) hautain. ●**haughtily** *adv* avec hauteur.

haul [hɔːl] 1 *vt* (*pull*) tirer, traîner; (*goods*) camionner. 2 *n* (*fish caught*) prise *f*; (*of thief*) butin *m*; **a long h.** (*trip*) un long voyage. ●**haulage** *n* camionnage *m*. ●**hauler** *Am or* **haulier** *Br n* transporteur *m* routier.

haunt [hɔːnt] 1 *vt* hanter. 2 *n* (*place*) endroit *m* favori; (*of criminal*) repaire *m*. ●**haunted** *a* (*house etc*) hanté. ●**haunting** *a* (*music, memory*) obsédant.

have [hæv] 1 (*3rd person sing pres t* **has**; *pt & pp* **had**; *pres p* **having**) *vt* avoir; (*get*) recevoir, avoir; (*meal, shower, lesson etc*) prendre; **he has got, he has** il a; **to h. a walk/dream/etc** faire une promenade/un rêve/etc; **to h. a drink** prendre *or* boire un verre; **to h. a wash** se laver; **to h. a pleasant** *Br* **holiday** *or Am* **vacation** (*spend*) passer d'agréables vacances; **let's h. a party** *or* **celebration** on va fêter ça; **will you h....?** (*a cake, some tea etc*) est-ce que tu veux...?; **to let s.o. h. sth** donner qch à qn; **to h. it from s.o. that** tenir de qn que; **he had me by the hair** il me tenait par les cheveux; **I won't h. this** (*allow*) je ne tolérerai pas ça; **you've had it!** *Fam* tu es fichu!; **I've been had** (*cheated*) *Fam* je me suis fait avoir; **to h. gloves/a dress/etc on** porter des gants/une robe/etc; **to h. something on** (*be busy*) être pris; **to h. s.o. over** *or* **round** inviter qn chez soi.

2 *v aux* avoir; (*with* entrer, monter *etc* & *pronominal verbs*) être; **to h. decided** avoir décidé; **to h. gone** être allé; **to h. cut oneself** s'être coupé; **she has been punished** elle a été punie, on l'a punie; **I've just done it** je viens de le faire; **to h. to do** (*must*) devoir faire; **I've got to go, I h. to go** je dois partir, je suis obligé de partir, il faut que je parte; **I don't h. to go** je ne suis pas obligé de partir; **to h. sth done** (*get sth done*) faire faire qch; **he's had his suitcase brought up** il a fait monter sa valise; **she's had her hair cut** elle s'est fait couper les cheveux; **I've had my car stolen** on m'a volé mon auto; **I've been doing it for months** je le fais depuis des mois; **haven't I?, hasn't she?** *etc* n'est-ce pas?; **no I haven't!** non!; **yes I h.!** si!; **after he had eaten** *or* **after having eaten, he left** après avoir mangé, il partit.

3 *npl* **the haves and (the) have-nots** les riches *mpl* et les pauvres *mpl*.

haven [ˈheɪv(ə)n] *n* refuge *m*, havre *m*.

haven't ['hævənt] = have not.

haversack ['hævəsæk] *n* (*shoulder bag*) musette *f*.

havoc ['hævək] *n* ravages *mpl*; **to wreak** *or* **cause h.** causer des ravages.

hawk [hɔːk] **1** *n* (*bird*) & *Pol* faucon *m*. **2** *vt* (*goods*) colporter. **●hawker** *n* colporteur, -euse *mf*.

hawthorn ['hɔːθɔːn] *n* aubépine *f*.

hay [her] *n* foin *m*; **h. fever** rhume *m* des foins. **●haystack** *n* meule *f* de foin.

haywire ['herwarər] *a* **to go h.** (*of machine*) se détraquer; (*of scheme, plan*) mal tourner.

hazard ['hæzəd] *n* risque *m*; **health h.** risque *m* pour la santé; **it's a fire h.** ça risque de provoquer un incendie; **h. (warning) lights** (*on vehicle*) *Br* feux *mpl* de détresse ▮ *vt* (*guess, remark etc*) hasarder, risquer. **●hazardous** *a* hasardeux.

haze [herz] **1** *n* brume *f*; **in a h.** (*person*) (*confused*) dans le brouillard. **2** *vt* (*student*) *Am* bizuter. **●hazing** *n* *Am* bizutage *m*.

hazel ['herz(ə)l] *n* (*bush*) noisetier *m* ▮ *a* **to have h. eyes** avoir les yeux noisette. **●hazelnut** *n* noisette *f*.

hazy ['herzi] *a* (-ier, -iest) (*weather*) brumeux; (*photo, idea*) flou; **h. sunshine** soleil *m* voilé; **I'm h. about my plans** je ne suis pas sûr de mes projets.

he [hiː] *pron* il; (*stressed*) lui; **he wants it** il veut; **he's a happy man** c'est un homme heureux; **if I were he** si j'étais lui; **he and I** lui et moi ▮ *n* (*male*) *Fam* mâle *m*; **he-bear** ours *m* mâle; **it's a he** (*baby*) *Fam* c'est un garçon.

head [hed] **1** *n* (*of person, hammer etc*) tête *f*; (*leader*) chef *m*; (*headmaster*) *Br* directeur *m*; (*headmistress*) *Br* directrice *f*; (*of bed*) chevet *m*, tête *f*; (*of arrow*) pointe *f*; (*subject heading*) rubrique *f*; (*tape*) **h.** (*of tape recorder, VCR*) tête *f* magnétique; **h. of hair** chevelure *f*; **h. first** la tête la première; **this beer has a (good) h.** cette bière a de la mousse *or* un faux-col; **it didn't enter my h.** ça ne m'est pas venu à l'esprit (**that** que); **to take it into one's h. to do** se mettre en tête de faire; **to shout one's h. off** *Fam* crier à tue-tête; **to have a good h. for business** avoir le sens des affaires; **at the h. of** (*in charge of*) à la tête de; **at the h. of the table** au haut bout de la table; **at the h. of the list** en tête de liste; **at the h. of the page** en haut de (la) page; **it's above my h.** ça me dépasse; **to keep one's h.** garder son sang-froid; **to lose one's h.** perdre la tête; **to go off one's h.** devenir fou; **it's coming to a h.** (*of situation*) ça devient critique; **heads or tails?** pile ou face?; **per h., a h.** (*each*) par personne; **h. cold** rhume *m* de cerveau.
2 *a* (*salesperson etc*) principal; **h. gardener** jardinier *m* en chef; **h. waiter** maître *m* d'hôtel; **to have a h. start** avoir une grosse avance (**over** sur).
3 *vt* (*group, firm*) être à la tête de; (*list, poll*) être en tête de; (*vehicle*) diriger (**to-**

wards vers); **to h. the ball** *Football* faire une tête; **to h. off** (*person*) détourner de son chemin; (*prevent*) empêcher (*qch*); **to be headed for** *Am* = **to h. for.**
4 *vi* **to h. for, be heading for** (*place*) se diriger vers; (*ruin etc*) *Fig* aller à.

headache ['hederk] *n* mal *m* de tête; (*difficulty, person*) *Fig* problème *m*, (*véritable*) casse-tête *m inv*; **to have a h.** avoir mal à la tête. **●headdress** *n* (*ornamental*) coiffe *f*. **●headlamp** *Br* or **headlight** *n* (*of vehicle*) phare *m*. **●headline** *n* (*of newspaper*) manchette *f*; **the headlines** les (gros) titres *mpl*; (*on radio, TV*) les (grands) titres *mpl*. **●headlong** *adv* (*to fall*) la tête la première; **to rush** *or* **run h.** courir tête baissée. **●head'master** *n* (*of school*) *Br* directeur *m*; (*of lycée*) proviseur *m*. **●head'mistress** *n* (*of school*) *Br* directrice *f*; (*of lycée*) proviseur *m*. **●head·'on** *adv* & *a* (*to collide, collision*) de plein fouet. **●headphones** *npl* casque *m* (à écouteurs). **●headquarters** *npl* (*of company, political party*) siège *m* (central); (*of army, police*) quartier *m* général, QG *m*. **●headrest** *n* appuie-tête *m inv*. **●headscarf** *n* (*pl* -scarves) foulard *m*. **●headstrong** *a* têtu. **●headway** *n* progrès *mpl*; **to make h.** faire des progrès.

headed ['hedrd] *a* **h. (note)paper** *Br* papier *m* (à lettres) en-tête.

-headed ['hedrd] *suff* **two-h.** (*monster etc*) à deux têtes; **curly-h.** aux cheveux frisés.

header ['hedər] *n* *Football* (coup *m* de) tête *f*.

heading ['hedrŋ] *n* (*of chapter, page etc*) titre *m*; (*of subject*) rubrique *f*; (*printed on letter etc*) en-tête *m*.

heady ['hedi] *a* (-ier, -iest) (*wine etc*) capiteux; (*action, speech*) impétueux.

heal [hiːl] *vi* **to h. (up)** (*of wound*) se cicatriser; (*of bruise*) disparaître; (*of bone*) se ressouder ▮ *vt* (*wound*) cicatriser, guérir; (*bruise*) faire disparaître; (*bone*) ressouder; (*person, Fig sorrow*) guérir. **●healer** *n* guérisseur, -euse *mf*.

health [helθ] *n* santé *f*; **in good/bad h.** en bonne/mauvaise santé; **h. food** aliment *m* naturel; **h. food** *Br* **shop** *or* *Am* **store** magasin *m* de produits diététiques; **h. food restaurant** restaurant *m* diététique; **h. resort** station *f* climatique; **the (National) H. Service** *Br* = la Sécurité Sociale. **●healthful** *a* sain.

healthy ['helθi] *a* (-ier, -iest) (*person*) en bonne santé, sain; (*food, attitude etc*) sain; (*appetite*) bon, robuste.

heap [hiːp] *n* tas *m*; **heaps of** (*money, people*) *Fam* des tas de; **to have heaps of time** *Fam* avoir largement le temps ▮ *vt* entasser, empiler; **to h. on s.o.** (*praise, gifts*) couvrir qn de; (*insults, work*) accabler qn de; **a heaped spoonful** *Br*, **a heaping spoonful** *Am* une grosse cuillerée.

hear [hɪər] *vt* (*pt & pp* **heard** [hɜːd]) entendre; (*listen to*) écouter; (*learn*) apprendre (**that** que); **I heard him come** *or* **coming** je l'ai entendu venir; **to h. it said that** entendre dire que; **have you heard the news?** connais-tu la nouvelle?; **I've heard that...** on m'a dit que..., j'ai appris que...; **to h. s.o. out** écouter qn jusqu'au bout; **h., h.!** bravo!

▌ *vi* entendre; (*get news*) recevoir *or* avoir des nouvelles (**from** de); **I've heard of** *or* **about him** j'ai entendu parler de lui; **she wouldn't h. of it** elle ne voulait pas en entendre parler; **I wouldn't h. of it!** pas question! ●**hearing** *n* **1** (*sense*) ouïe *f*; **hard of h.** dur d'oreille; **h. aid** appareil *m* auditif. **2** (*of committee etc*) séance *f*; **the h.'s content** tout son saoul *or* content; **at h.** au fond; **his h. is set on it** il veut à tout prix, il y tient; **his h. is set on doing it** il veut le faire à tout prix, il tient à le faire; **h. attack** crise *f* cardiaque; **h. disease** maladie *f* de cœur.

heartache ['hɑːteɪk] *n* chagrin *m*. ●**heartbeat** *n* battement *m* de cœur. ●**heartbreaking** *a* navrant, déchirant. ●**heartbroken** *a* inconsolable, désespéré. ●**heartburn** *n* (*indigestion*) brûlures *fpl* d'estomac. ●**heartfelt** *a* (très) sincère. ●**heartland** *n* (*of country*) cœur *m*, centre *m*. ●**heartthrob** *n* (*male singer etc*) *Fam* idole *f*.

hearten ['hɑːt(ə)n] *vt* encourager. ●**heartening** *a* encourageant.

hearth [hɑːθ] *n* foyer *m*; **h. rug** devant *m* de foyer.

hearty ['hɑːtɪ] *a* (**-ier, -iest**) (*appetite, meal*) gros. ●**heartily** *adv* (*to eat*) avec appétit; (*to laugh, detest*) de tout son cœur; (*absolutely*) (*to approve, agree*) absolument.

heat [hiːt] **1** *n* chaleur *f*; (*heating*) chauffage *m*; (*of oven*) température *f*; **in the h. of the argument** dans le feu de la discussion; **in the h. of the day** au plus chaud de la journée; **at low h., on a low h.** (*to cook food*) à feu doux; **h. wave** vague *f* de chaleur ▌ *vti* **to h.** (**up**) chauffer.

2 *n* (*in race, competition*) éliminatoire *f*; **it was a dead h.** ils sont arrivés ex æquo. ●**heated** *a* (*swimming pool*) chauffé; (*argument*) passionné; **the house is centrally h.** la maison a le chauffage central. ●**heatedly** *adv* avec passion. ●**heating** *n* chauffage *m*; **central h.** chauffage *m* central.

heater ['hiːtər] *n* appareil *m* de chauffage, radiateur *m*; **water h.** chauffe-eau *m inv*.

heath [hiːθ] *n* (*land, place*) lande *f*.

heathen ['hiːð(ə)n] *a & n* païen, -enne (*mf*).

heather ['heðər] *n* (*plant*) bruyère *f*.

heave [hiːv] *vt* (*lift*) soulever; (*pull*) tirer; (*drag*) traîner; (*throw*) *Fam* lancer; **to h. a sigh** pousser un soupir ▌ *vi* (*of stomach,*

chest) se soulever; (*feel sick*) *Fam* avoir des haut-le-cœur ▌ *n* (*effort*) effort *m* (*pour soulever etc*).

heaven ['hev(ə)n] *n* ciel *m*, paradis *m*; **h. knows when** *Fam* Dieu sait quand; **good heavens!** *Fam* mon Dieu!; **it was h.** *Fam* c'était divin. ●**heavenly** *a* (*pleasing*) *Fam* divin; (*of heaven*) (*body etc*) céleste.

heavily ['hevɪlɪ] *adv* (*to walk, tax etc*) lourdement; (*to breathe*) péniblement; (*to smoke, drink*) beaucoup; **to rain h.** pleuvoir à verse; **to snow h.** neiger beaucoup *or* fort; **h. involved in** lourdement impliqué dans; **to depend h. on** dépendre beaucoup *or* largement de; **h. underlined** fortement souligné; **h. in debt** lourdement endetté.

heavy ['hevɪ] *a* (**-ier, -iest**) lourd; (*work, cold etc*) gros (*f* grosse); (*blow*) violent; (*rain, concentration*) fort; (*traffic*) dense; (*smoker, drinker*) grand; (*film, text*) difficile; (*timetable, schedule*) chargé; **a h. day** une journée chargée; **h. casualties** de nombreuses victimes; **h. snow** d'abondantes *or* de fortes chutes de neige; **to be h. on** *Br* **petrol** *or* *Am* **gas** (*of vehicle*) consommer beaucoup; **it's h. going** c'est difficile; **h. goods vehicle** *Br* poids lourd. ●**heaviness** *n* pesanteur *f*, lourdeur *f*. ●**heavyweight** *n Boxing* poids *m* lourd; *Fig* personnage *m* important.

Hebrew ['hiːbruː] *n* (*language*) hébreu *m* ▌ *a* hébreu (*m only*), hébraïque.

Hebrides ['hebrɪdiːz] *n* **the H.** les Hébrides *fpl*.

heck [hek] *int Fam* zut! ▌ *n* = **hell** *in expressions.*

heckle ['hek(ə)l] *vt* interpeller, interrompre. ●**heckling** *n* interpellations *fpl*. ●**heckler** *n* interpellateur, -trice *mf*.

hectic ['hektɪk] *a* (*activity*) fiévreux; (*period*) très agité; (*trip*) mouvementé; **h. life** vie *f* trépidante.

he'd [hiːd] = **he had** & **he would.**

hedge [hedʒ] **1** *n* (*bushes*) haie *f*. **2** *vi* (*answer evasively*) ne pas se mouiller, éviter de se compromettre.

hedgehog ['hedʒhɒg] *n* (*animal*) hérisson *m*.

hedgerow ['hedʒrəʊ] *n* (*bushes*) *Br* haie *f*.

heed [hiːd] *vt* faire attention à ▌ *n* **to pay h. to, take h.** of faire attention à. ●**heedless** *a* **h. of the danger/etc** inattentif au danger/*etc*.

heel [hiːl] *n* **1** (*of foot, shoe etc*) talon *m*; **down at h.** *Br*, **down at the heels** *Am* (*shabby*) miteux; **h. bar** cordonnerie *f* express; (*on sign*) 'talon minute'. **2** (*person*) *Am Fam* salaud *m*.

hefty ['heftɪ] *a* (**-ier, -iest**) (*large, heavy*) gros (*f* grosse); (*person*) costaud.

heifer ['hefər] *n* (*cow*) génisse *f*.

height [haɪt] *n* hauteur *f*; (*of person*) taille *f*; (*of mountain, aircraft*) altitude *f*; **the h. of** (*success, fame, glory*) le sommet de, l'apogée *m* de; (*folly, pain*) le comble de; **at the h. of** (*summer, storm*) au cœur de; **it's the h. of fashion** c'est la dernière mode.

heighten ['haɪt(ə)n] *vt* (*tension, interest etc*)

augmenter.

heinous ['heɪnəs] a (crime etc) atroce.

heir [eər] n héritier m. ●**heiress** n héritière f. ●**heirloom** n héritage m, bijou m or meuble m de famille.

heist [haɪst] n (holdup) Am Sl braquage m.

held [held] pt & pp of **hold**.

helicopter ['helɪkɒptər] n hélicoptère m. ●**heliport** n héliport m.

hell [hel] n enfer m; **a h. of a lot** (to work, suffer etc) Fam énormément, vachement; **a h. of a lot of** (very many, very much) Fam énormément de, un paquet de; **a h. of a nice guy** Fam un type super; **what the h. are you doing?** Fam qu'est-ce que tu fous?; **to h. with him** Fam qu'il aille se faire voir; **h.!** Fam zut!; **to be h.-bent** Br on doing or Am to do Fam être acharné à faire. ●**hellish** a diabolique.

he'll [hiːl] = he will.

hello! [hə'ləʊ] int bonjour!; (answering phone) allô!; (surprise) tiens!

helm [helm] n (of boat) barre f.

helmet ['helmɪt] n casque m.

help [help] n aide f, secours m; (cleaning woman) Br femme f de ménage; (office or shop workers) employés, -ées mfpl; **with the h. of a stick/etc** à l'aide d'un bâton/etc; **to cry or shout for h.** crier au secours, appeler à l'aide; **h.!** au secours! ▮ vt aider; **to h. s.o. do** or **to do** aider qn à faire; **to h. s.o. to soup/etc** (serve) servir du potage/etc à qn; **h. yourself** servez-vous (to de); **to h. s.o. out** aider qn; (of trouble, predicament) dépanner qn; **to h. s.o. up** aider qn à monter; **I can't h. laughing/etc** je ne peux (pas) m'empêcher de rire/etc; **he can't h. being blind/etc** ce n'est pas sa faute s'il est aveugle/etc; **it can't be helped** on n'y peut rien.
▮ vi aider; **to h. out** aider, donner un coup de main. ●**helping** n (serving) portion f. ●**helper** n assistant, -ante mf.

helpful ['helpfəl] a (useful) utile; (obliging) (person) serviable.

helpless ['helpləs] a (powerless) impuissant; (baby) désarmé; (disabled) impotent. ●**helplessly** adv (to struggle) en vain.

helpline ['helpplaɪn] n Tel ligne f d'assistance.

helter-skelter [heltə'skeltər] **1** n (slide) toboggan m. **2** adv à la débandade.

hem [hem] n ourlet m ▮ vt (-mm-) (garment) ourler; **to be hemmed in** (surrounded) être cerné (by de); (unable to move) être coincé.

he-man ['hiːmæn] n Fam mâle m.

hemisphere ['hemɪsfɪər] n hémisphère m.

hemorrhage ['hemərɪdʒ] n (bleeding) hémorragie f.

hemorrhoids ['hemərɔɪdz] npl hémorroïdes fpl.

hemp [hemp] n chanvre m.

hen [hen] n poule f; **h. bird** oiseau m femelle.

hence [hens] adv **1** (therefore) d'où. **2** (from now) **ten years/etc h.** d'ici dix ans/etc.

●**henceforth** adv désormais.

henchman ['hentʃmən] n (pl -men) Pej acolyte m.

henpecked ['henpekt] a (husband) harcelé or dominé par sa femme.

hepatitis [hepə'taɪtɪs] n hépatite f.

her [hɜːr] **1** pron la, l'; (after prep, 'than', 'it is') elle; (to) h. (indirect) lui; **I see h.** je la vois; **I saw h.** je l'ai vue; **I give (to) h.** je lui donne; **with h.** avec elle. **2** poss a son, sa, pl ses.

herald ['herəld] vt annoncer.

heraldry ['herəldrɪ] n héraldique f.

herb [Br hɜːb, Am ɜːb] n herbe f; **herbs** (in cooking) fines herbes fpl; **h. tea** Br = herbal tea. ●**herbal** a h. tea infusion f (d'herbes); **h. medicine** phytothérapie f.

Hercules ['hɜːkjʊliːz] n (strong man) hercule m.

herd [hɜːd] n troupeau m ▮ vti **to h. together** (se) rassembler (en troupeau).

here [hɪər] **1** adv ici; **h. is, h. are** voici; **h. she is** la voici; **h. we are** nous voici; **h. comes the teacher** voici le professeur (qui arrive); **this man is h.** cet homme-ci; **I won't be h. tomorrow** je ne serai pas là demain; **summer is h.** l'été est là, c'est l'été; **h. and there** çà et là; **h. you are!** (take this) tenez!; **h.'s to you!** (toast) à la tienne!
2 int **h.!** (calling s.o.'s attention) holà!, écoutez!; (giving s.o. sth) tenez! ●**herea'bouts** adv par ici. ●**here'after** adv après; (in book) ci-après. ●**here'by** adv (to declare etc) par le présent acte; (in writing) par la présente. ●**here'with** adv (with letter) ci-joint.

heredity [hɪ'redɪtɪ] n hérédité f. ●**hereditary** a héréditaire.

heresy ['herəsɪ] n hérésie f. ●**heretic** n hérétique mf. ●**he'retical** a hérétique.

heritage ['herɪtɪdʒ] n héritage m.

hermetic [hɜː'metɪk] a hermétique. ●**hermetically** adv h. sealed fermé hermétiquement.

hermit ['hɜːmɪt] n solitaire mf, ermite m.

hernia ['hɜːnɪə] n hernie f.

hero ['hɪərəʊ] n (pl -oes) héros m. ●**heroic** [hɪ'rəʊɪk] a héroïque. ●**he'roics** npl (action) héroïsme m inutile; (words) grandiloquence f. ●**heroine** ['herəʊɪn] n héroïne f. ●**heroism** ['herəʊɪz(ə)m] n héroïsme m.

heroin ['herəʊɪn] n (drug) héroïne f.

heron ['herən] n (bird) héron m.

herring ['herɪŋ] n hareng m; **a red h.** Fig une diversion.

hers [hɜːz] poss pron le sien, la sienne, pl les sien(ne)s; **this hat is h.** ce chapeau est à elle or est le sien; **a friend of h.** une amie à elle.

herself [hɜː'self] pron elle-même; (reflexive) se, s'; (after prep) elle; **she did it h.** elle l'a fait elle-même; **she cut h.** elle s'est coupée; **she thinks of h.** elle pense à elle.

hesitant ['hezɪtənt] a hésitant. ●**hesitantly** adv avec hésitation.

hesitate ['hezɪteɪt] vi hésiter (over, about sur) ▮ vt **to h. to do sth** hésiter à faire qch.

● **hesitation** [-'teɪʃ(ə)n] n hésitation f.

hessian ['hesɪən] n toile f de jute.

heterogeneous [het(ə)rəʊ'dʒiːnɪəs] a hétérogène.

heterosexual [hetərəʊ'seksjʊəl] a hétérosexuel(le) (mf).

het up [het'ʌp] a Fam énervé.

hew [hjuː] vt (pp hewn or hewed) tailler.

hexagon ['heksəgən] n hexagone m. ● **hex'agonal** a hexagonal.

hey! [heɪ] int (calling s.o.) hé!, ohé!; (expressing surprise, annoyance) ho!

heyday ['heɪdeɪ] n (of thing) âge m d'or; (of person) apogée m; **in its h.** à son âge d'or; **in my h.** à l'apogée de ma vie or de ma carrière.

hi! [haɪ] int Fam salut!

hiatus [haɪ'eɪtəs] n (gap) hiatus m.

hibernate ['haɪbəneɪt] vi hiberner. ● **hibernation** [-'neɪʃ(ə)n] n hibernation f.

hiccup, hiccough ['hɪkʌp] n hoquet m; Fig (petit) problème m, anicroche f; **to have (the) hiccups** or **(the) hiccoughs** avoir le hoquet ▌ vi hoqueter.

hick [hɪk] n (peasant) Am Fam Pej plouc mf.

hide¹ [haɪd] vt (pt hid, pp hidden) cacher, dissimuler (**from** à) ▌ vi **to h.** (away or out) se cacher (**from** de). ● **hide-and-'seek** n cache-cache m inv; **to play h.-and-seek** jouer à cache-cache.

hide² [haɪd] n (skin) peau f.

hideaway ['haɪdəweɪ] n refuge m.

hideous ['hɪdɪəs] a (weather, experience, task, crime etc) horrible; (person, sight) horrible, hideux. ● **hideously** adv (badly, very) horriblement.

hideout ['haɪdaʊt] n cachette f.

hiding ['haɪdɪŋ] n **1 to go into h.** se cacher; **h. place** cachette f. **2 a good h.** (thrashing) Fam une bonne raclée or volée.

hierarchy ['haɪərɑːkɪ] n hiérarchie f.

hi-fi ['haɪfaɪ] n (system, equipment) chaîne f hi-fi; (sound reproduction) hi-fi f inv ▌ a hi-fi inv.

high [haɪ] a (-er, -est) haut; (speed) grand; (price) élevé; (number, ideal) grand, élevé; (colour) vif; (complexion) rougeaud; (meat, game) faisandé; (on drugs) Fam défoncé; **to be five metres h.** avoir or faire cinq mètres de haut, être haut de cinq mètres; **it is h. time that** il est grand temps que (+ sub); **h. and mighty** arrogant; **to leave s.o. h. and dry** Fam laisser qn en plan; **h. fever** torte or grosse fièvre f; **h. jump** Sport saut m en hauteur; **h. noon** plein midi m; **h. priest** grand prêtre m; **h. school** = lycée m; **h. school diploma** Am diplôme m de fin d'études secondaires; **h. spirits** entrain m; **h. spot** (of visit, day) point m culminant; (of show) clou m; **h. street** Br grand-rue f; **h. summer** le cœur de l'été; **h. table** table f d'honneur; **h. voice** voix f aiguë; **h. winds** des vents mpl violents. ▌ adv **h.** (up) (to fly, throw etc) haut; **to aim h.** viser haut.

▌ n **a new h., an all-time h.** (peak) un nouveau record; **on h.** Rel & Fig en haut.

highbrow ['haɪbraʊ] a & n intellectuel, -elle (mf).

high-chair ['haɪtʃeər] n chaise f haute. ● **high-'class** a (service) de premier ordre; (building) de luxe; (person) raffiné. ● **high-'flown** a (language) ampoulé. ● **high-'handed** a tyrannique. ● **high-'minded** a à l'âme noble. ● **high-'pitched** a (sound) aigu (f -uë). ● **high-'powered** a (person) très dynamique. ● **high-rise** a **h.-rise flats** Br tour f. ● **high-'speed** a ultra-rapide; **h.-speed train** train m à grande vitesse. ● **high-'strung** a Am nerveux. ● **high-'up** a (person) Fam haut placé.

higher ['haɪər] a (number, speed, quality etc) supérieur (**than** à); **h. education** enseignement m supérieur ▌ adv (to fly, aim etc) plus haut (**than** que).

highlands ['haɪləndz] npl régions fpl montagneuses.

highlight ['haɪlaɪt] n (of visit, day) point m culminant; (of show) clou m; (in hair) reflet m ▌ vt souligner; (with marker) surligner. ● **highlighter** n (marker) surligneur m.

highly ['haɪlɪ] adv hautement, fortement; (interesting, amusing, pleased) très; (to recommend) chaudement; **h. paid** très bien payé; **to speak h. of** dire beaucoup de bien de; **h. strung** Br nerveux.

Highness ['haɪnɪs] n (title) Altesse f.

highroad ['haɪrəʊd] n Br grand-route f.

highway ['haɪweɪ] n Am autoroute f; **public h.** Br voie f publique; **H. Code** Br Code m de la route.

hijack ['haɪdʒæk] vt (aircraft, vehicle) détourner ▌ n détournement m. ● **hijacking** n (air piracy) piraterie f aérienne; (hijack) détournement m. ● **hijacker** n (of aircraft) pirate m de l'air.

hike [haɪk] **1** n excursion f à pied ▌ vi marcher à pied. **2** vt (price etc) Fam augmenter ▌ n (increase) Fam hausse f. ● **hiker** n excursionniste mf.

hilarious [hɪ'leərɪəs] a (funny) désopilant.

hill [hɪl] n colline f; (small) coteau m; (slope) pente f; (in road) côte f. ● **hillbilly** n Am Fam péquenaud, -aude mf. ● **hillside** n **on the h.** à flanc de colline or de coteau. ● **hilly** a (-ier, -iest) accidenté.

hilt [hɪlt] n (of sword) poignée f; **to the h.** Fig au maximum.

him [hɪm] pron le, l'; (after prep, 'than', 'it is') lui; (indirect) lui; **I see h.** je le vois; **I saw h.** je l'ai vu; **I give (to) h.** je lui donne; **with h.** avec lui.

himself [hɪm'self] pron lui-même; (reflexive) se, s'; (after prep) lui; **he did it h.** il l'a fait lui-même; **he cut h.** il s'est coupé; **he thinks of h.** il pense à lui.

hind [haɪnd] a **h. legs** pattes fpl de derrière or postérieures. ● **hindquarters** npl arrière-train m.

hinder ['hɪndər] vt (obstruct) gêner; (prevent) empêcher (**from doing** de faire). ● **hindrance**

n gêne *f*.

hindsight ['haɪndsaɪt] *n* **with h.** rétrospectivement.

Hindu ['hɪndu:] *a & n* hindou, -oue (*mf*).

hinge [hɪndʒ] **1** *n* (*of box, stamp*) charnière *f*; (*of door*) gond *m*, charnière *f*. **2** *vi* **to h. on** (*depend on*) dépendre de. ● **hinged** *a* (*lid etc*) à charnière(s).

hint [hɪnt] *n* (*insinuation*) allusion *f*; (*sign*) indication *f*; (*trace*) trace *f*; **hints** (*advice*) conseils *mpl*; **to drop a h.** faire une allusion ▮ *vt* laisser entendre (*that que*) ▮ *vi* **to h. at** sth/s.o. faire allusion à qch/qn.

hip [hɪp] *n* hanche *f*.

hippie ['hɪpɪ] *n* hippie *mf*.

hippopotamus [hɪpə'pɒtəməs] *n* hippopotame *m*.

hire ['haɪər] *vt* (*vehicle etc*) louer; (*worker*) engager; **to h. out** donner en location, louer ▮ *n* location *f*; **for h.** à louer; (*sign on taxi*) *Br* 'libre'; **on h.** en location. **h. purchase** *Br* vente *f* or achat *m* à crédit, location-vente *f*; **on h. purchase** *Br* à crédit.

his [hɪz] **1** *poss a* son, sa, *pl* ses. **2** *poss pron* le sien, la sienne, *pl* les sien(ne)s; **this hat is h.** ce chapeau est à lui or est le sien; **a friend of h.** un ami à lui.

Hispanic [hɪs'pænɪk] *a Am* hispano-américain *m* Hispano-Américain, -aine *mf*.

hiss [hɪs] *vti* siffler ▮ *n* sifflement *m*; **hisses** (*booing*) sifflets *mpl*. ● **hissing** *n* sifflement(s) *m(pl)*.

history ['hɪstərɪ] *n* (*study, events*) histoire *f*; **it will make h.** or **go down in h.** ça va faire date; **your medical h.** vos antécédents médicaux. ● **historian** [hɪs'tɔːrɪən] *n* historien, -ienne *mf*. ● **hi'storic(al)** *a* historique.

histrionic [hɪstrɪ'ɒnɪk] *a Pej* théâtral ▮ *npl* **histrionics** attitudes *fpl* théâtrales.

hit [hɪt] *vt* (*pt & pp* **hit**, *pres p* **hitting**) (*beat etc*) frapper; (*bump into*) heurter; (*reach*) atteindre; (*affect*) toucher, affecter; (*find*) trouver; (*problem, difficulty*) rencontrer; **to h. the headlines** *Fam* faire les gros titres; **to h. it off** *Fam* s'entendre bien (*with s.o.* avec qn).

▮ *vi* frapper; **to h. back** rendre coup pour coup; (*answer criticism, counterattack*) riposter; **to h. out (at)** *Fam* attaquer; **to h. (up)on** (*find*) tomber sur.

▮ *n* (*blow*) coup *m*; (*success*) coup *m* réussi; (*play, film, book*) succès *m*; **h.** (*song*) chanson *f* à succès; **to make a h. with** (*book etc*) *Fam* avoir un succès avec. ● **hit-and-run driver** *n* chauffard *m* (*qui prend la fuite*). ● **hit-or-'miss** *a* (*chancy, random*) aléatoire.

hitch [hɪtʃ] **1** *n* (*snag*) problème *m*, anicroche *f*. **2** *vt* (*fasten*) accrocher (*to* à). **3** *vti* **to h. (a ride)**, *Br* **h. a lift** *Fam* faire du stop (*to* jusqu'à).

hitchhike ['hɪtʃhaɪk] *vi* faire de l'auto-stop (*to* jusqu'à). ● **hitchhiking** *n* auto-stop *m*. ● **hitchhiker** *n* auto-stoppeur, -euse *mf*.

hi-tech ['haɪtek] *a* **hi-tech industry** industrie *f* de pointe.

hitherto [hɪðə'tu:] *adv* jusqu'ici.

HIV [eɪtʃaɪ'vi:] *n* (*virus*) VIH *m*; **HIV positive/negative** séropositif/séronégatif.

hive [haɪv] **1** *n* ruche *f*. **2** *vt* **to h. off** (*industry*) dénationaliser.

HMS [eɪtʃe'mes] *n abbr Br* Her or His Majesty's Ship.

hoard [hɔːd] *n* réserve *f*; (*of money*) trésor *m* ▮ *vt* amasser.

hoarding ['hɔːdɪŋ] *n* (*for advertising*) *Br* panneau *m* d'affichage.

hoarfrost ['hɔːfrɒst] *n* givre *m*.

hoarse [hɔːs] *a* (**-er, -est**) (*person, voice*) enroué. ● **hoarseness** *n* enrouement *m*.

hoax [həʊks] *n* canular *m* ▮ *vt* faire un canular à, mystifier.

hob [hɒb] *n* (*on stove*) plaque *f* chauffante.

hobble ['hɒb(ə)l] *vi* (*walk*) boitiller.

hobby ['hɒbɪ] *n* passe-temps *m inv*; **my h.** mon passe-temps favori. ● **hobbyhorse** *n* (*favourite subject*) dada *m*.

hobnob ['hɒbnɒb] *vi* (**-bb-**) **to h. with** frayer avec.

hobo ['həʊbəʊ] *n* (*pl* **-oes** or **-os**) *Am* vagabond, -onde *mf*.

hock [hɒk] *vt* (*pawn*) *Fam* mettre au clou ▮ *n* **in h.** *Fam* au clou.

hockey ['hɒkɪ] *n* hockey *m*; **ice h.** hockey *m* sur glace.

hocus-pocus [həʊkəs'pəʊkəs] *n* (*talk*) charabia *m*; (*deception*) tromperie *f*.

hodgepodge ['hɒdʒpɒdʒ] *n* fatras *m*.

hoe [həʊ] *n* binette *f*, houe *f* ▮ *vt* biner.

hog [hɒg] **1** *n* (*pig*) cochon *m*, porc *m*; **road h.** (*bad driver*) chauffard *m*. **2** *n* **to go the whole h.** *Fam* aller jusqu'au bout. **3** *vt* (**-gg-**) *Fam* monopoliser, garder pour soi.

hoist [hɔɪst] *vt* hisser ▮ *n* (*machine*) palan *m*.

hold [həʊld] *n* (*grip*) prise *f*; (*of ship*) cale *f*; (*of aircraft*) soute *f*; **to get h. of** (*grab*) saisir; (*contact*) joindre; (*find*) trouver; **to get a h. of oneself** se maîtriser.

▮ *vt* (*pt & pp* **held**) tenir; (*breath, interest, heat, attention*) retenir; (*a post*) occuper; (*a record*) détenir; (*weight*) supporter; (*party, bazaar, exhibition etc*) organiser; (*ceremony, mass*) célébrer; (*possess*) posséder; (*contain*) contenir; (*keep*) garder; **I h. that...** (*believe*) je maintiens que...; **to h. hands** se tenir par la main; **to h. one's own** se débrouiller; (*of sick person*) se maintenir; **h. the line!** (*on phone*) ne quittez pas!; **h. it!** (*stay still*) ne bouge pas!; **to be held** (*of event*) avoir lieu.

▮ *vi* (*of nail, rope*) tenir; (*of weather*) se maintenir; **to h. (good)** (*of argument*) valoir (*for* pour).

holdall ['həʊldɔːl] *n* (*bag*) *Br* fourre-tout *m inv*.

hold back *vt* (*crowd, tears*) contenir; (*hide*) cacher (*from s.o.* à qn) ▮ **to hold down** *vt* (*price*) maintenir bas; (*person on ground*) maintenir au sol; **to h. down a job** (*keep*) garder un emploi (*occupy*) avoir un emploi ▮ **to hold forth** *vi* (*talk*) *Pej* disserter ▮ **to hold in** *vt* **to h. one's stomach in** rentrer son ventre ▮ **to hold off** *vt* (*enemy*) tenir à distance ▮ *vi* **if the rain holds off** s'il ne pleut pas ▮ **to hold on** *vt* (*keep in place*) tenir en place (*son chapeau etc*) ▮ *vi* (*wait*) attendre; (*stand firm*) tenir bon; **h. on!** (*on phone*) ne quittez pas!; **h. on (tight)!** tenez bon! ▮ **to hold onto** *vt* (*cling to*) tenir bien; (*keep*) garder ▮ **to hold out** *vt* (*offer*) offrir; (*arm*) étendre ▮ *vi* (*resist*) résister; (*last*) durer ▮ **to hold over** *vt* (*postpone*) remettre ▮ **to hold together** *vt* (*nation, group*) assurer l'union de ▮ **to hold up** *vt* (*raise*) lever; (*support*) soutenir; (*delay*) retarder; (*bank*) attaquer (à main armée).

holder ['həʊldər] *n* (*of passport, post*) titulaire *mf*; (*of record, card, ticket*) détenteur, -trice *mf*; (*container*) support *m*.

holdings ['həʊldɪŋz] *npl Fin* possessions *fpl*.

holdup ['həʊldʌp] *n* (*attack*) hold-up *m inv*; (*traffic jam*) *Br* bouchon *m*; (*delay*) retard *m*.

hole [həʊl] *n* trou *m*; (*town, village etc*) *Fam* bled *m*, trou *m*; (*room*) *Fam* baraque *f* ▮ *vt* trouer ▮ *vi* **to h. up** (*hide*) *Fam* se terrer.

holiday ['hɒlɪdeɪ] *n Br* **holiday(s)** (*from work, school etc*) vacances *fpl*; **a h.** (*day off*) un congé; **a** (**public** *or* **bank**) **h.** *Br*, **a legal h.** *Am* un jour férié; **a** (**religious**) **h.** une fête; **on h.** en vacances; **holidays with pay** congés *mpl* payés ▮ *a* (*camp, clothes etc*) de vacances; **the h. season** la période des vacances; **in h. mood** d'humeur folâtre. ●**holidaymaker** *n Br* vacancier, -ière *mf*.

holiness ['həʊlɪnəs] *n* sainteté *f*.

Holland ['hɒlənd] *n* Hollande *f*.

hollow ['hɒləʊ] *a* creux; (*victory*) faux (*f* fausse); (*promise*) vain ▮ *n* creux *m* ▮ *vt* **to h. out** creuser.

holly ['hɒlɪ] *n* houx *m*.

holocaust ['hɒləkɔːst] *n* (*massacre*) holocauste *m*.

hologram ['hɒləgræm] *n* hologramme *m*.

holster ['həʊlstər] *n* étui *m* de revolver.

holy ['həʊlɪ] *a* (**-ier, -iest**) saint; (*bread, water*) bénit; (*ground*) sacré.

homage ['hɒmɪdʒ] *n* hommage *m*; **to pay h. to** rendre hommage à.

home¹ [həʊm] *n* maison *f*; (*country*) pays *m* (natal); (*for old soldiers, sailors etc*) foyer *m*; (*old people's*) **h.** maison *f* de retraite; **at h.** à la maison, chez soi; **to feel at h.** se sentir à l'aise; **to make oneself at h.** se mettre à l'aise; **to play at h.** (*of football team*) jouer à domicile; **far from h.** loin de chez soi; **a broken h.** un foyer désuni; **a good h.** une bonne famille; **to make one's h. in** s'installer à *or* en; **my h. is here** j'habite ici.

▮ *adv* à la maison, chez soi; **to go** *or* **come (back) h.** rentrer; **to be h.** être rentré; **to drive h.** ramener (*qn*) (en voiture); (*nail*) enfoncer; **to bring sth h. to s.o.** *Fig* faire voir qch à qn.

▮ *a* (*life, pleasures, atmosphere*) de famille, familial; (*visit, match*) à domicile; (*product,*

market etc) national; **h. computer** ordinateur *m* domestique; **h. economics** économie *f* domestique; **h. help** *Br* aide *f* ménagère; **h. loan** prêt *m* immobilier; **H. Office** *Br* = ministère *m* de l'Intérieur; **h. owner** propriétaire *mf* (de son logement); **h. rule** autonomie *f*; **H. Secretary** *Br* = ministre *m* de l'Intérieur; **h. team** équipe *f* qui reçoit; **h. town** (*birth place*) ville *f* natale.

home² [həʊm] *vi* **to h. in on** se diriger automatiquement sur.

homecoming ['həʊmkʌmɪŋ] *n* retour *m* au foyer. ●**home'grown** *a* (*fruit, vegetables*) du jardin; (*not grown abroad*) du pays. ●**homeland** *n* patrie *f*. ●**homeloving** *a* casanier. ●**home'made** *a* (fait à la) maison *inv*.

homeless ['həʊmlɪs] *a* sans abri ▮ *n* **the h.** les sans-abri *m inv*.

homely ['həʊmlɪ] *a* (**-ier, -iest**) (*simple*) simple; (*comfortable*) accueillant; (*ugly*) *Am* laid.

homeopathic [həʊmɪəʊ'pæθɪk] *a* (*medicine*) homéopathique.

homesick ['həʊmsɪk] *a* **to be h.** avoir envie de rentrer chez soi; (*for one's country*) avoir le mal du pays. ●**homesickness** *n* envie *f* de rentrer chez soi; (*for country*) nostalgie *f*, mal *m* du pays.

homeward ['həʊmwəd] *a* (*trip*) de retour ▮ *adv* **h. bound** sur le chemin de retour.

homework ['həʊmwɜːk] *n* (*taken home from school*) devoir(s) *m(pl)*.

homey ['həʊmɪ] *a* (**-ier, -iest**) *Am Fam* accueillant.

homicide ['hɒmɪsaɪd] *n* (*murder*) homicide *m*; **two homicides** *Am* deux meurtres *mpl*.

homily ['hɒmɪlɪ] *n* homélie *f*.

homogeneous [həʊmə'dʒiːnɪəs] *a* homogène.

homosexual [həʊmə'seksjʊəl] *a & n* homosexuel, -elle (*mf*). ●**homosexu'ality** *n* homosexualité *f*.

Honduras [hɒn'djʊərəs] *n* Honduras *m*.

honest ['ɒnɪst] *a* honnête; (*frank*) franc (*f* franche) (**with** avec); (*profit, money*) honnêtement gagné; **the h. truth** la pure vérité; **to be (quite) h....** pour être franc.... ●**honestly** *adv* (*to act etc*) honnêtement; (*frankly*) franchement; **h.!** (*showing annoyance*) vraiment! ●**honesty** *n* honnêteté *f*; (*frankness*) franchise *f*; (*of report, text*) exactitude *f*.

honey ['hʌnɪ] *n* miel *m*; (*person*) *Fam* chéri, -ie *mf*. ●**honeycomb** *n* rayon *m* de miel; (*for eating*) *Br* gâteau *m* de miel. ●**honeymoon** *n* lune *f* de miel; **to be on one's h.** être en voyage *m* de noces. ●**honeysuckle** *n* (*plant*) chèvrefeuille *f*.

Hong Kong [hɒŋ'kɒŋ] *n* Hong Kong *f*.

honk [hɒŋk] *vi* (*in vehicle*) klaxonner ▮ *n* coup *m* de klaxon®.

honorary ['ɒnərərɪ] *a* (*member*) honoraire; (*title*) honorifique.

honour ['ɒnər] (*Am* **honor**) *n* honneur *m*; **in h. of** en l'honneur de; **the h. of doing** *or* **to do** l'honneur de faire; **honours degree** (*in*

British university) = licence *f* **‖** *vt* honorer (with de).

honourable ['ɒnərəb(ə)l] *a* honorable.

hood [hud] *n* **1** capuchon *m*; (*mask of robber*) cagoule *f*; (*soft car roof, roof of Br pram or Am baby carriage*) capote *f*; (*car bonnet*) *Am* capot *m*; (*above stove*) hotte *f*. **2** (*hoodlum*) *Am Sl* gangster *m*. ●**hooded** *a* (*person*) encapuchonné; (*coat*) à capuchon.

hoodlum ['huːdləm] *n Fam* (*gangster*) gangster *m*; (*hooligan*) voyou *m*.

hoodwink ['hudwɪŋk] *vt* tromper, duper.

hoof, *pl* **-fs** *or* **-ves** [huːf, -fs, -vz] (*Am* [huf, -fs, huːvz]) *n* sabot *m*.

hoo-ha ['huːhɑː] *n Fam* tumulte *m*.

hook [huk] *n* crochet *m*; (*on clothes*) agrafe *f*; *Fishing* hameçon *m*; **off the h.** (*phone*) décroché; **to let** *or* **get s.o. off the h.** tirer qn d'affaire **‖** *vt* **to h.** (*on or up*) accrocher (to à). ●**hooked** *a* (*nose, beak*) recourbé, crochu; (*end, object*) recourbé; **to be h. on** **chess/etc** *Fam* être enragé d'échecs/etc, être accro des échecs/etc; **to be h. on s.o.** (*infatuated with*) *Fam* être entiché de qn; **to be h.** (**on drugs**) *Fam* être accro.

hooker ['hukər] *n Fam* prostituée *f*.

hook(e)y ['hukɪ] *n* **to play h.** *Am Fam* sécher (la classe).

hooligan ['huːlɪɡən] *n* vandale *m*, voyou *m*. ●**hooliganism** *n* vandalisme *m*.

hoop [huːp] *n* cerceau *m*; (*of barrel*) cercle *m*.

hoot [huːt] **1** *vi* (*of vehicle*) *Br* klaxonner; (*of train*) siffler; (*of owl*) hululer **‖** *n* (*of vehicle*) *Br* coup *m* de klaxon®. **2** *vti* (*jeer*) huer **‖** *n* huée *f*. ●**hooter** *n* (*of vehicle*) *Br* klaxon® *m*; (*of factory*) sirène *f*.

hoover® ['huːvər] *n Br* aspirateur *m* **‖** *vt Br* (*room*) passer l'aspirateur dans; (*carpet*) passer l'aspirateur sur; **to h.** (**up**) (*dust*) enlever à l'aspirateur.

hop [hɒp] *vi* (**-pp-**) (*of person*) sauter (à cloche-pied); (*of kangaroo etc*) sauter; (*of bird*) sautiller; **h. in!** (*in car*) montez!; **to h. on a bus** monter dans un autobus; **to h. on a plane** attraper un vol **‖** *vt* **h. it!** *Fam* fiche le camp! **‖** *n* (*leap*) saut *m*; (*plane journey*) *Fam* étape *f*.

hope [həup] *n* espoir *m*, espérance *f* **‖** *vi* espérer; **to h. for** (*wish for*) espérer; (*expect*) attendre; **I h. so/not** j'espère que oui/non **‖** *vt* **to h. to do sth** espérer faire qch; **to h. that** espérer que.

hopeful ['həupfəl] *a* (*person*) optimiste, plein d'espoir; (*promising*) prometteur; (*encouraging*) encourageant; **to be h. that** avoir bon espoir que. ●**hopefully** *adv* avec optimisme; (*one hopes*) on espère (que).

hopeless ['həupləs] *a* désespéré, sans espoir; (*useless, bad*) nul; (*liar*) invétéré. ●**hopelessly** *adv* (*extremely*) (*lost, out of date*) complètement; (*in love*) éperdument; (*to live, act*) sans espoir.

hops [hɒps] *npl* (*for beer*) houblon *m*.

hopscotch ['hɒpskɒtʃ] *n* (*game*) marelle *f*.

horde [hɔːd] *n* horde *f*, foule *f*.

horizon [həˈraɪz(ə)n] *n* horizon *m*; **on the h.** à l'horizon.

horizontal [hɒrɪˈzɒnt(ə)l] *a* horizontal. ●**horizontally** *adv* horizontalement.

hormone ['hɔːməun] *n* hormone *f*.

horn [hɔːn] *n* **1** (*of animal*) corne *f*; (*on vehicle*) klaxon® *m*; (*musical instrument*) cor *m*. **2** *vi* **to h. in** *Am Fam* mêler son grain de sel (**on a conversation** à une conversation); (*interrupt*) interrompre.

hornet ['hɔːnɪt] *n* (*insect*) frelon *m*.

horny ['hɔːnɪ] *a* (**-ier, -iest**) (*aroused*) *Fam* excité.

horoscope ['hɒrəskəup] *n* horoscope *m*.

horrendous [hɒˈrendəs] *a* horrible.

horrible ['hɒrəb(ə)l] *a* horrible, affreux. ●**horribly** *adv* horriblement.

horrid ['hɒrɪd] *a* horrible; (*child*) épouvantable, méchant.

horrific [hɒˈrɪfɪk] *a* horrible, horrifiant.

horrify ['hɒrɪfaɪ] *vt* horrifier.

horror ['hɒrər] *n* horreur *f*; (**little**) **h.** (*child*) *Fam* petit monstre *m*; **h. film/story** film *m*/ histoire *f* d'épouvante *or* d'horreur.

hors-d'œuvre [ɔːˈdɜːv] *n* hors-d'œuvre *m inv*.

horse [hɔːs] *n* **1** cheval *m*; **to go h. riding** faire du cheval; **h. show** concours *m* hippique. **2** *Fam* **h. chestnut** marron *m* (d'Inde). ●**horseback** *n* **on h.** à cheval; **to go h. riding** *Am* faire du cheval. ●**horseman** *n* (*pl* **-men**) cavalier *m*. ●**horseplay** *n* jeux *mpl* brutaux. ●**horsepower** *n* cheval *m* (vapeur). ●**horseracing** *n* courses *fpl*. ●**horseradish** *n* radis *m* noir, raifort *m*. ●**horseshoe** *n* fer *m* à cheval. ●**horsewoman** *n* (*pl* **-women**) cavalière *f*.

horticulture ['hɔːtɪkʌltʃər] *n* horticulture *f*. ●**horti'cultural** *a* horticole.

hose [həuz] *n* (*tube*) tuyau *m*; **garden h.** tuyau *m* d'arrosage **‖** *vt* (*garden etc*) arroser; **to h. down** (*car etc*) laver au jet. ●**hosepipe** *n Br* = **hose**.

hosiery [*Br* 'həuzɪərɪ, *Am* 'həuʒərɪ] *n* bonneterie *f*.

hospice ['hɒspɪs] *n* (*for dying people*) hospice *m* (pour incurables).

hospitable [hɒˈspɪtəb(ə)l] *a* accueillant, hospitalier (**to s.o.** envers qn). ●**hospitably** *adv* avec hospitalité. ●**hospi'tality** *n* hospitalité *f*.

hospital ['hɒspɪt(ə)l] *n* hôpital *m*; **in h.** *Br*, **in the h.** *Am* à l'hôpital; **h. bed/food** lit *m*/ nourriture *f* d'hôpital; **h. staff/services** personnel *m*/services *mpl* hospitalier(s). ●**hospitalize** *vt* hospitaliser.

host [həust] *n* **1** (*man who receives guests*) hôte *m*; (*on TV or radio show*) présentateur, -trice *m* *f* (*programme*) présenter. **2 a h. of** (*many*) une foule de. **3** *Rel* hostie *f*.

hostage ['hɒstɪdʒ] *n* otage *m*; **to take s.o. h.** prendre qn en otage; **to be held h.** être retenu en otage.

hostel ['hɒst(ə)l] *n* foyer *m*; **youth h.** auberge *f* de jeunesse.

hostess ['həustıs] *n* (*in house, nightclub*) hôtesse *f*; (**air**) **h.** hôtesse *f* (de l'air).

hostile [*Br* 'həstaıl, *Am* 'həst(ə)l] *a* hostile (**to, towards** à). ●**ho'stility** *n* hostilité *f* (**to, towards** envers); **hostilities** (*in battle*) hostilités *fpl*.

hot¹ [hət] *a* (**hotter, hottest**) chaud; (*spice*) fort; (*temperament*) passionné; (*news*) *Fam* dernier; **to be** *or* **feel h.** avoir chaud; **it's h.** il fait chaud; **not so h. at Spanish/***etc* (*good at*) *Fam* pas très calé en espagnol/*etc*; **not so h.** (*bad*) *Fam* pas fameux; **h. dog** (*sausage*) hot-dog *m*; **h. favourite** *Sport* grand(e) favori(te) *mf*.

hot² [hət] *vi* (**-tt-**) **to h. up** (*increase*) s'intensifier; (*become dangerous or excited*) chauffer.

hotbed ['hətbed] *n Pej* foyer *m* (**of** de). ●**hot-'blooded** *a* ardent. ●**hotcake** *n* (*pancake*) *Am* crêpe *f*. ●**hothead** *n* tête *f* brûlée. ●**hot'headed** *a* impétueux. ●**hothouse** *n* serre *f* (chaude). ●**hotplate** *n* chauffe-plats *m inv*; (*on stove*) plaque *f* chauffante. ●**hot-'tempered** *a* emporté. ●**hot-'water bottle** *n* bouillotte *f*.

hotchpotch ['hətʃpətʃ] *n* fatras *m*.

hotel [həʊ'tel] *n* hôtel *m*; **h. room/bed/***etc* chambre *f*/lit *m*/*etc* d'hôtel; **h. prices** le prix des hôtels; **the h. industry** l'industrie *f* hôtelière. ●**hotelier** [həʊ'telɪeɪ] *n* hôtelier, -ière *mf*.

hotly ['hətlɪ] *adv* passionnément.

hound [haʊnd] **1** *vt* (*pursue*) traquer, poursuivre avec acharnement; (*bother, worry*) harceler; **to h. out** chasser. **2** *n* (*dog*) chien *m* courant.

hour ['aʊər] *n* heure *f*; **half an h., a half-h.** une demi-heure; **a quarter of an h.** un quart d'heure; **paid fifty francs an h.** payé cinquante francs (de) l'heure; **ten miles an h.** dix miles à l'heure; **open all hours** ouvert à toute heure; **h. hand** (*of watch, clock*) petite aiguille *f*.

hourly ['aʊəlɪ] *a* (*rate, pay*) horaire; **an h. bus/train/***etc* un bus/train/*etc* toutes les heures ∎ *adv* toutes les heures; **h. paid, paid h.** payé à l'heure.

house¹, *pl* **-ses** [haʊs, -zɪz] *n* maison *f*; (*audience in theatre*) salle *f*, auditoire *m*; (*performance of play*) séance *f*; **the H.** *Pol* la Chambre; **the Houses of Parliament** le Parlement; **at** *or* **to my h.** chez moi; **on the h.** (*free of charge*) aux frais de la maison; **h. doctor** *Br* = **houseman**; **h. guest** invité, -ée *mf*; **h. prices** prix *mpl* immobiliers.

house² [haʊz] *vt* loger; (*of building*) abriter; **it is housed in** (*kept*) on le garde dans. ●**housing** *n* logement *m*; (*houses*) logements *mpl*; **h. crisis/***etc* crise *f*/*etc* du logement.

houseboat ['haʊsbəʊt] *n* péniche *f* (aménagée). ●**housebound** *a* confiné chez soi. ●**housebreaking** *n* (*crime*) cambriolage *m*. ●**housebroken** *a* (*dog etc*) *Am* propre. ●**housecoat** *n* robe *f* d'intérieur. ●**housefly**

n mouche *f* (domestique). ●**household** *n* famille *f*, ménage *m*, maison *f*; **h. duties** soins *mpl* du ménage; **a h. name** un nom très connu. ●**householder** *n* (*owner*) propriétaire *mf*; (*family head*) chef *m* de famille. ●**househusband** *n* homme *m* au foyer. ●**housekeeper** *n* (*employee*) gouvernante *f*; (*housewife*) ménagère *f*. ●**housekeeping** *n* ménage *m*. ●**houseman** *n* (*pl* **-men**) *Br* interne *mf* (des hôpitaux). ●**houseproud** *a* qui s'occupe méticuleusement de sa maison. ●**housetrained** *a* (*dog etc*) *Br* propre. ●**housewarming** *n* & *a* **to have a h.-warming** (*party*) pendre la crémaillère. ●**housewife** *n* (*pl* **-wives**) ménagère *f*. ●**housework** *n* (travaux *mpl* du) ménage *m*.

hovel ['hɒv(ə)l] *n* (*slum*) taudis *m*.

hover ['hɒvər] *vi* (*of bird, aircraft, Fig danger etc*) planer; **to h.** (**around**) (*of person*) rôder, traîner.

hovercraft ['hɒvəkrɑ:ft] *n* aéroglisseur *m*.

how [haʊ] *adv* comment; **h.'s that?, h. so?, h. come?** *Fam* comment ça?; **h. kind!** comme c'est gentil!; **h. do you do?** (*greeting*) bonjour; **h. long/high is...?** quelle est la longueur/hauteur de...?; **h. much?, h. many?** combien?; **h. many apples/***etc?* combien de pommes/*etc*?; **h. about a walk?** si on faisait une promenade?; **h. about some coffee?** (si on prenait) du café?; **h. about me?** et moi?

howdy! ['haʊdɪ] *int Am Fam* salut!

however [haʊ'evər] **1** *adv* **h. big he may be** si *or* quelque grand qu'il soit; **h. she may do it, h. she does it** de quelque manière qu'elle le fasse; **h. that may be** quoi qu'il en soit. **2** *conj* cependant.

howl [haʊl] *vi* hurler; (*of baby*) brailler; (*of wind*) mugir ∎ *n* hurlement *m*; (*of baby*) braillement *m*; (*of wind*) mugissement *m*; **h. of laughter** éclat *m* de rire.

howler ['haʊlər] *n* (*mistake*) *Fam* gaffe *f*.

HP [eɪtʃ'pi:] *Br abbr* = **hire purchase**.

hp *abbr* (*horsepower*) CV.

HQ [eɪtʃ'kju:] *abbr* = **headquarters**.

hub [hʌb] *n* (*of wheel*) moyeu *m*; *Fig* centre *m*. ●**hubcap** *n* (*of car*) enjoliveur *m*.

hubbub ['hʌbʌb] *n* vacarme *m*.

huckleberry ['hʌk(ə)lbərɪ] *n Am* myrtille *f*.

huddle ['hʌd(ə)l] *vi* **to h.** (**together**) se blottir (les uns contre les autres).

hue [hju:] *n* **1** (*colour*) teinte *f*, couleur *f*. **2** **h. and cry** hourra tollé *m*.

huff [hʌf] *n* **in a h.** (*offended*) *Fam* fâché.

hug [hʌg] *vt* (**-gg-**) (*person*) serrer (dans ses bras), étreindre; **to h. the kerb/coast** (*stay near*) serrer le trottoir/la côte ∎ *n* **to give s.o. a h.** serrer qn (dans ses bras).

huge [hju:dʒ] *a* énorme. ●**hugely** *adv* énormément. ●**hugeness** *n* énormité *f*.

hulk [hʌlk] *n* (*person*) lourdaud, -aude *mf*.

hull [hʌl] *n* (*of ship*) coque *f*.

hullabaloo [hʌləbə'lu:] *n Fam* (*noise*) vacarme *m*; (*fuss*) histoire(s) *f(pl)*.

hullo! [hʌ'ləʊ] *int Br* bonjour!; *(answering phone)* allô!; *(surprise)* tiens!

hum [hʌm] *vi* (-mm-) *(of insect)* bourdonner; *(of person)* fredonner; *(of spinning top, radio)* ronfler; *(of engine)* vrombir ∎ *vt (tune)* fredonner ∎ *n (of insect)* bourdonnement *m*.

human ['hjuːmən] *a* humain; **h. being** être *m* humain ∎ *npl* **humans** humains *mpl*. ●**humanly** *adv* **h. possible** humainement possible.

humane [hjuː'meɪn] *a (kind)* humain. ●**humanely** *adv* humainement.

humanitarian [hjuːmænɪ'teərɪən] *a & n* humanitaire *(mf)*.

humanity [hjuː'mænətɪ] *n (human beings, kindness)* humanité *f*.

humble ['hʌmb(ə)l] *a* humble ∎ *vt* humilier. ●**humbly** *adv* humblement.

humbug ['hʌmbʌg] *n (talk)* fumisterie *f*; *(person)* fumiste *mf*.

humdrum ['hʌmdrʌm] *a* monotone.

humid ['hjuːmɪd] *a* humide. ●**hu'midify** *vt* humidifier. ●**hu'midity** *n* humidité *f*.

humiliate [hjuː'mɪlɪeɪt] *vt* humilier. ●**humiliation** [-'eɪʃ(ə)n] *n* humiliation *f*.

humility [hjuː'mɪlətɪ] *n* humilité *f*.

humorist ['hjuːmərɪst] *n* humoriste *mf*.

humorous ['hjuːmərəs] *a (book etc)* humoristique; *(person)* plein d'humour. ●**humorously** *adv* avec humour.

humour ['hjuːmər] *(Am* **humor)** **1** *n (fun)* humour *m*; *(temper)* humeur *f*; **to have a sense of h.** avoir le sens de l'humour; **in a good h.** de bonne humeur. **2** *vt* **to h. s.o.** faire plaisir à qn, ménager qn.

hump [hʌmp] **1** *n (lump, mound in road)* bosse *f* ∎ *vt (one's back)* voûter. **2** *n* **to have the h.** *Br Fam (depression)* avoir le cafard; *(bad temper)* être en rogne. ●**humpback(ed) bridge** *n Br* pont *m* en dos d'âne.

hunch [hʌntʃ] **1** *n (idea) Fam* intuition *f*, idée *f*. **2** *vt (one's shoulders)* voûter. ●**hunchback** *n* bossu, -ue *mf*.

hundred ['hʌndrəd] *a & n* cent *(m)*; **a h. pages** cent pages; **two h. pages** deux cents pages; **hundreds of** des centaines de. ●**hundredfold** *a* centuple ∎ *adv* au centuple. ●**hundredth** *a & n* centième *(mf)*. ●**hundredweight** *n Br* 112 livres (= *50,8 kg)*; *Am* 100 livres (= *45,3 kg)*.

hung [hʌŋ] *pt & pp of* **hang¹**.

Hungary ['hʌŋgərɪ] *n* Hongrie *f*. ●**Hun'garian** [hʌŋ'geərɪən] *a* hongrois ∎ *n (language)* hongrois *m*; *(person)* Hongrois, -oise *mf*.

hunger ['hʌŋgər] *n* faim *f*; **h. strike** grève *f* de la faim. ●**hungry** *a* (-ier, -iest) **to be or feel h.** avoir faim; **to go hungry** souffrir de la faim; **to make s.o. h.** donner faim à qn; **h. for** *(news etc)* avide de. ●**hungrily** *adv* avidement.

hunk [hʌŋk] *n (gros)* morceau *m*.

hunt [hʌnt] *n (search)* recherche *f* **(for** de); *(for animals)* chasse *f* ∎ *vt (animals)* chasser; *(pursue)* poursuivre; *(seek)* chercher; **to h. down** *(fugitive etc)* traquer; **to h. out** *(in-*

formation etc) dénicher ∎ *vi (kill animals)* chasser; **to h. for sth** (re)chercher qch. ●**hunting** *n* chasse *f*. ●**hunter** *n (person)* chasseur *m*.

hurdle ['hɜːd(ə)l] *n (fence in race)* haie *f*; *(problem) Fig* obstacle *m*.

hurl [hɜːl] *vt (throw)* jeter, lancer **(at** à); **to h. oneself at s.o.** se ruer sur qn; **to h. insults** *or* **abuse at s.o.** lancer des insultes à qn.

hurly-burly ['hɜːlɪbɜːlɪ] *n* tumulte *m*.

hurray! [hʊ'reɪ] *int* hourra!

hurricane [*Br* 'hʌrɪkən, *Am* 'hʌrɪkeɪn] *n* ouragan *m*.

hurry ['hʌrɪ] *n* hâte *f*; **in a h.** à la hâte; **to be in a h.** être pressé; **to be in a h. to do sth** avoir hâte de faire qch; **there's no h.** rien ne presse.
∎ *vi* se dépêcher, se presser **(to do** de faire); **to h. along** *or* **up** se dépêcher; **to h. back** se dépêcher de revenir; **to h. out** sortir à la hâte; **to h. towards** se précipiter vers.
∎ *vt (person)* bousculer, presser; *(pace)* presser; **to h. one's meal** manger à toute vitesse; **to h. one's work** se précipiter dans son travail, faire son travail à la hâte; **to h. s.o. out** faire sortir qn à la hâte. ●**hurried** *a (steps, decision etc)* précipité; *(work)* fait à la hâte; *(visit)* éclair *inv*; **to be h.** *(in a hurry)* être pressé.

hurt [hɜːt] *vt (pt & pp* **hurt)** *(physically)* faire du mal à; *(causing a wound)* blesser; *(emotionally)* faire de la peine à; *(offend)* blesser; *(prejudice, damage)* nuire à *(réputation etc)*; **to h. s.o.'s feelings** blesser qn; **his arm hurts (him)** son bras lui fait mal ∎ *vi* faire mal ∎ *n* mal *m* ∎ *a (wounded, offended)* blessé. ●**hurtful** *a (remark)* blessant.

hurtle ['hɜːt(ə)l] *vi* **to h. along** aller à toute vitesse; **to h. down** dégringoler.

husband ['hʌzbənd] *n* mari *m*.

hush [hʌʃ] *n* silence *m* ∎ *int* chut! ∎ *vt (person)* faire taire; *(baby)* calmer; **to h. up** *(scandal)* étouffer. ●**hushed** *a (voice)* étouffé; *(silence)* profond. ●**hush-hush** *a Fam* ultra-secret.

husk [hʌsk] *n (of rice, grain)* enveloppe *f*.

husky ['hʌskɪ] *a* (-ier, -iest) *(voice)* enroué, voilé.

hussy ['hʌsɪ] *n Pej* friponne *f*, coquine *f*.

hustings ['hʌstɪŋz] *npl Br* campagne *f* électorale, élections *fpl*.

hustle ['hʌs(ə)l] **1** *vt (shove, rush)* bousculer *(qn)* ∎ *vi (work busily) Am* se démener **(to get sth** pour avoir qch). **2** *n* **h. and bustle** tourbillon *m*, agitation *f*.

hut [hʌt] *n* cabane *f*, hutte *f*.

hutch [hʌtʃ] *n (for rabbit)* clapier *m*.

hyacinth ['haɪəsɪnθ] *n* jacinthe *f*.

hybrid ['haɪbrɪd] *a & n* hybride *(m)*.

hydrangea [haɪ'dreɪndʒə] *n (shrub)* hortensia *m*.

hydrant ['haɪdrənt] *n (fire)* **h.** bouche *f* d'incendie.

hydraulic [haɪ'drɔːlɪk] *a* hydraulique.

hydrocarbon [haɪdrəʊ'kɑːbən] *n* hydrocarbure *m*.

hydroelectric [haɪdrəʊɪ'lektrɪk] *a* hydro-électrique.

hydrogen ['haɪdrədʒən] *n* (*gas*) hydrogène *m*.

hyena [haɪ'iːnə] *n* (*animal*) hyène *f*.

hygiene ['haɪdʒiːn] *n* hygiène *f*. ● **hy'gienic** *a* hygiénique. ● **hy'gienist** *n* (*dental*) **h**. spécialiste *mf* de l'hygiène dentaire.

hymn [hɪm] *n* cantique *m*, hymne *m*.

hype [haɪp] *n* (*publicity*) *Fam* grand battage *m* publicitaire.

hyper- ['haɪpər] *pref* hyper-.

hypermarket ['haɪpəmɑːkɪt] *n* hypermarché *m*.

hyphen ['haɪf(ə)n] *n* trait *m* d'union. ● **hyphenate** *vt* mettre un trait d'union à. ● **hyphenated** *a* (*word*) à trait d'union.

hypnosis [hɪp'nəʊsɪs] *n* hypnose *f*. ● **hypnotic** *a* hypnotique. ● **'hypnotism** *n* hypnotisme *m*. ● **'hypnotist** *n* hypnotiseur *m*. ● **'hypnotize** *vt* hypnotiser.

hypoallergenic [haɪpəʊælə'dʒenɪk] *a* hypoal-lergénique.

hypochondriac [haɪpə'kɒndrɪæk] *n* malade *mf* imaginaire.

hypocrisy [hɪ'pɒkrɪsɪ] *n* hypocrisie *f*. ● **hypocrite** ['hɪpəkrɪt] *n* hypocrite *mf*. ● **hypo'critical** *a* hypocrite.

hypodermic [haɪpə'dɜːmɪk] *a* hypodermique.

hypothermia [haɪpə'θɜːmɪə] *n* *Med* hypothermie *f*.

hypothesis, *pl* **-eses** [haɪ'pɒθɪsɪs, -ɪsiːz] *n* hypothèse *f*. ● **hypo'thetical** *a* hypothétique.

hysteria [hɪ'stɪərɪə] *n* hystérie *f*. ● **hysterical** [hɪ'sterɪk(ə)l] *a* (*very upset*) qui a une crise de nerfs; (*funny*) *Fam* désopilant; **he became h.** il a eu une crise de nerfs. ● **hysterically** *adv* (*to cry*) sans pouvoir s'arrêter; **to laugh h.** rire aux larmes. ● **hysterics** *npl* (*tears etc*) crise *f* de nerfs; (*laughter*) crise *f* de rire; **to be in h.** avoir une crise de nerfs; (*with laughter*) être écroulé de rire; **he had us in h.** il nous a fait tordre de rire.

I

I, i [aɪ] n I, i m.

I [aɪ] pron je, j'; (stressed) moi; **I want** je veux; **she and I** elle et moi.

ice¹ [aɪs] n glace f; (on road) verglas m; **black i.** (on road) Br verglas m ▌ vi **to i.** (over or up) (of lake) geler; (of window) se givrer.•**iced** a (tea, coffee) glacé.

ice² [aɪs] vt (cake) Br glacer. •**icing** n (on cake etc) Br glaçage m.

iceberg ['aɪsbɜːg] n iceberg m •**icebox** n Am réfrigérateur m; (for storing food) glacière f. •**ice-'cold** a glacial; (drink) glacé. •**ice cream** n glace f. •**ice cube** n glaçon m. •**ice-skating** n patinage m (sur glace).

Iceland ['aɪslənd] n Islande f. •**Ice'landic** a islandais.

icicle ['aɪsɪk(ə)l] n glaçon m (naturel).

icon ['aɪkɒn] n Rel icône f.

icy ['aɪsɪ] a (-ier, -iest) (water, hands, room) glacé; (weather, manner, welcome) glacial; (road etc) verglacé.

ID [aɪ'diː] n pièce f d'identité.

I'd [aɪd] = I had & I would.

idea [aɪ'dɪə] n idée f; **I have an i. that...** j'ai l'impression que...; **that's my i. of rest** c'est ce que j'appelle du repos; **that's the i.!** Fam c'est ça!; **not the slightest** or **foggiest i.** pas la moindre idée.

ideal [aɪ'dɪəl] a idéal (mpl -aux or -als) ▌ n idéal m (pl -aux or -als). •**idealism** [aɪ'dɪəlɪz(ə)m] n idéalisme m. •**idealist** n idéaliste mf. •**idea'listic** a idéaliste. •**idealize** vt idéaliser.

ideally [aɪ'dɪəlɪ] adv idéalement; **i. we should stay** l'idéal, ce serait de rester or que nous restions.

identical [aɪ'dentɪk(ə)l] a identique (to, with à).

identify [aɪ'dentɪfaɪ] vt identifier; **to i. (oneself) with** s'identifier avec. •**identification** [-'keɪʃ(ə)n] n identification f; **to have (some) i.** (document) avoir une pièce d'identité.

identikit [aɪ'dentɪkɪt] n portrait-robot m.

identity [aɪ'dentɪtɪ] n identité f; **i. card** carte f d'identité.

ideology [aɪdɪ'ɒlədʒɪ] n idéologie f. •**ideo'logical** a idéologique.

idiocy ['ɪdɪəsɪ] n idiotie f.

idiom ['ɪdɪəm] n (phrase) expression f idiomatique; (language) idiome m; (style) style m. •**idio'matic** a idiomatique.

idiosyncrasy [ɪdɪə'sɪŋkrəsɪ] n particularité f.

idiot ['ɪdɪət] n idiot, -ote mf. •**idi'otic** a idiot, bête. •**idi'otically** adv idiotement.

idle ['aɪd(ə)l] a (unoccupied) inactif, désœuvré; (lazy) paresseux; (unemployed) au chômage; (promise) vain; (pleasure, question) futile, vain; (rumour) sans fondement; **to lie i.** (of machine) être au repos; **an i. moment** un moment de loisir ▌ vi (of engine, machine) tourner au ralenti; (laze about) paresser ▌ vt **to i. away** the or one's time gaspiller son temps. •**idleness** n oisiveté f; (laziness) paresse f. •**idler** n paresseux, -euse mf. •**idly** adv (lazily) paresseusement; (to suggest, say) négligemment.

idol ['aɪd(ə)l] n idole f. •**idolize** vt (adore) traiter comme une idole.

idyllic [aɪ'dɪlɪk] a idyllique.

i.e. [aɪ'iː] abbr (id est) c'est-à-dire.

if [ɪf] conj si; **if he comes** s'il vient; **even if** même si; **if so** dans ce cas, si c'est le cas; **if not** sinon; **if only I were rich** si seulement j'étais riche; **if only to look** ne serait-ce que pour regarder; **as if** comme si; **as if nothing had happened** comme si de rien n'était; **as if to say** comme pour dire; **if necessary** s'il le faut.

igloo ['ɪgluː] n igloo m.

ignite [ɪg'naɪt] vt mettre le feu à ▌ vi prendre feu. •**ignition** [-'nɪʃ(ə)n] n (in vehicle) allumage m; **to switch on/off the i.** mettre/ couper le contact; **i. key** clef f de contact.

ignominious [ɪgnə'mɪnɪəs] a déshonorant, ignominieux.

ignoramus [ɪgnə'reɪməs] n ignare mf.

ignorance ['ɪgnərəns] n ignorance f (of de). •**ignorant** a ignorant (of de). •**ignorantly** adv par ignorance.

ignore [ɪg'nɔːr] vt ne prêter aucune attention à, ne tenir aucun compte de (qch); (duty) méconnaître; (pretend not to recognize) faire semblant de ne pas reconnaître (qn).

iguana [ɪg'wɑːnə] n (lizard) iguane m.

ilk [ɪlk] n of that i. (kind) de cet acabit.

ill [ɪl] a (sick) malade; (bad) mauvais; **i. will** malveillance f ▌ npl ills (misfortunes) maux mpl, malheurs mpl ▌ adv mal; **to speak i. of** dire du mal de.

I'll [aɪl] = I will or I shall.

ill-advised [ɪləd'vaɪzd] a peu judicieux, malavisé. •**ill-'fated** a malheureux. •**ill-'gotten** a **i.-gotten gains** biens mpl mal acquis. •**ill-in'formed** a mal renseigné. •**ill-'mannered** a mal élevé. •**ill-'natured** a (mean, unkind) désagréable. •**ill-'timed** a inopportun. •**ill-'treat** vt maltraiter. •**ill-'treatment** n mauvais traitements mpl.

illegal [ɪ'liːg(ə)l] a illégal. •**ille'gality** n illégalité f.

illegible [ɪ'ledʒəb(ə)l] a illisible.

illegitimate [ɪlɪ'dʒɪtɪmət] a (child, action,

claim) illégitime. ● **illegitimacy** *n* illégitimité *f*.

illicit [ɪ'lɪsɪt] *a* illicite.

illiterate [ɪ'lɪtərət] *a & n* illettré, -ée (*mf*), analphabète (*mf*). ● **illiteracy** *n* analphabétisme *m*.

illness ['ɪlnɪs] *n* maladie *f*.

illogical [ɪ'lɒdʒɪk(ə)l] *a* illogique.

illuminate [ɪ'lu:mɪneɪt] *vt* (*street, Fig question etc*) éclairer; (*monument etc for special occasion*) illuminer. ● **illumination** [-'neɪʃ(ə)n] *n* (*of street etc*) éclairage *m*; (*of monument etc*) illumination *f*; **the illuminations** (*decorative lights*) *Br* les illuminations *fpl*.

illusion [ɪ'lu:ʒ(ə)n] *n* illusion *f* (*about* sur); **to have the i. that** avoir l'illusion que; **I'm not under any i. about** je ne me fais aucune illusion sur. ● **illusive** *or* **illusory** *a* illusoire.

illustrate ['ɪləstreɪt] *vt* (*with pictures, examples*) illustrer (**with** de). ● **illustration** [-'streɪʃ(ə)n] *n* illustration *f*. ● **illustrative** [ɪ'lʌstrətɪv] *a* (*example*) explicatif.

illustrious [ɪ'lʌstrɪəs] *a* illustre.

image ['ɪmɪdʒ] *n* image *f*; (*public*) **i.** (*of company etc*) image *f* de marque; **he's the** (**living** *or* **spitting** *or* **very**) **i. of his brother** c'est tout le portrait de son frère. ● **imagery** *n* images *fpl*.

imaginable [ɪ'mædʒɪnəb(ə)l] *a* imaginable; **the worst thing i.** le pire que l'on puisse imaginer.

imaginary [ɪ'mædʒɪn(ə)rɪ] *a* imaginaire.

imagination [ɪmædʒɪ'neɪʃ(ə)n] *n* imagination *f*.

imaginative [ɪ'mædʒɪnətɪv] *a* (*plan, novel etc*) plein d'imagination; (*person*) imaginatif, plein d'imagination.

imagine [ɪ'mædʒɪn] *vt* (*picture to oneself*) (s')imaginer, se figurer (**that** que); (*suppose*) imaginer (**that** que); **i. that...** imaginez que...; **you're imagining (things)!** tu te fais des illusions! ● **imaginings** *npl* (*dreams*) imaginations *fpl*.

imbalance [ɪm'bæləns] *n* déséquilibre *m*.

imbecile [*Br* 'ɪmbəsi:l, *Br* -saɪl, *Am* 'ɪmbəs(ə)l] *a & n* imbécile (*mf*). ● **imbe'cility** *n* imbécillité *f*.

imbibe [ɪm'baɪb] *vt* absorber.

imbued [ɪm'bju:d] *a* **i. with** (*ideas*) imprégné de; (*feelings*) pénétré de, imbu de.

imitate ['ɪmɪteɪt] *vt* imiter. ● **imitation** [-'teɪʃ(ə)n] *n* imitation *f*; **i. jewellery** *Br*, **i. jewelry** *Am* bijoux *mpl* fantaisie; **i. leather** similicuir *m*.

imitative ['ɪmɪtətɪv] *a* (*sound etc*) imitatif; (*person*) imitateur.

imitator ['ɪmɪteɪtə] *n* imitateur, -trice *mf*.

immaculate [ɪ'mækjʊlət] *a* (*person, appearance, shirt etc*) impeccable.

immaterial [ɪmə'tɪərɪəl] *a* peu important (**to** pour).

immature [ɪmə'tʃʊər] *a* (*person*) qui manque de maturité; (*animal*) jeune; (*fruit*) vert.

immeasurable [ɪ'meʒərəb(ə)l] *a* in-

commensurable.

immediate [ɪ'mi:dɪət] *a* immédiat. ● **immediacy** *n* caractère *m* immédiat. ● **immediately** *adv* (*at once*) tout de suite, immédiatement; (*to concern, affect*) directement; **it's i. above/below** c'est juste au-dessus/en dessous ▌*conj* (*as soon as*) *Br* dès que.

immense [ɪ'mens] *a* immense. ● **immensely** *adv* (*rich etc*) extraordinairement; **to enjoy oneself i.** s'amuser énormément *or* extraordinairement. ● **immensity** *n* immensité *f*.

immerse [ɪ'mɜ:s] *vt* (*in liquid*) plonger, immerger; **immersed in work** plongé dans le travail. ● **immersion** [-ʃ(ə)n] *n* immersion *f*; **i. heater** *Br* chauffe-eau *m inv* électrique.

immigrate ['ɪmɪgreɪt] *vi* immigrer. ● **immigrant** *n* (*established*) immigré, -ée *mf*; (*in the process of immigrating*) immigrant, -ante *mf* ▌*a* (*family etc*) immigré. ● **immigration** [-'greɪʃ(ə)n] *n* immigration *f*.

imminent ['ɪmɪnənt] *a* imminent. ● **imminence** *n* imminence *f*.

immobile [*Br* ɪ'məʊbaɪl, *Am* ɪ'məʊb(ə)l] *a* immobile. ● **immo'bility** *n* immobilité *f*. ● **immobilize** *vt* immobiliser.

immoderate [ɪ'mɒdərət] *a* immodéré.

immodest [ɪ'mɒdɪst] *a* impudique.

immoral [ɪ'mɒrəl] *a* immoral. ● **immo'rality** *n* immoralité *f*.

immortal [ɪ'mɔ:t(ə)l] *a* immortel. ● **immor'tality** *n* immortalité *f*. ● **immortalize** *vt* immortaliser.

immune [ɪ'mju:n] *a* (*naturally*) immunisé (**to** contre); (*vaccinated*) vacciné; **i. system** système *m* immunitaire; **i. to danger/criticism** *Fig* à l'abri du danger/de la critique. ● **immunity** *n* immunité *f*. ● **'immunize** *vt* vacciner, immuniser (**against** contre).

immutable [ɪ'mju:təb(ə)l] *a* immuable.

imp [ɪmp] *n* diablotin *m*, lutin *m*; (**you**) **little i.!** (*to child*) petit coquin!

impact ['ɪmpækt] *n* (*shock*) impact *m*; (*effect*) effet *m*, impact *m* (**on** sur).

impair [ɪm'peər] *vt* détériorer; (*hearing, health*) abîmer.

impale [ɪm'peɪl] *vt* empaler.

impart [ɪm'pɑ:t] *vt* communiquer (**to** à).

impartial [ɪm'pɑ:ʃ(ə)l] *a* impartial. ● **imparti'ality** *n* impartialité *f*.

impassable [ɪm'pɑ:səb(ə)l] *a* (*road*) impraticable; (*river*) infranchissable.

impasse [*Br* 'æmpɑ:s, *Am* 'ɪmpæs] *n* (*situation*) impasse *f*.

impassioned [ɪm'pæʃ(ə)nd] *a* (*speech, request etc*) enflammé, passionné.

impassive [ɪm'pæsɪv] *a* impassible, imperturbable. ● **impassively** *adv* imperturbablement. ● **impassiveness** *n* impassibilité *f*.

impatient [ɪm'peɪʃ(ə)nt] *a* impatient (**to do** de faire); **i. with s.o.** intolérant à l'égard de qn; **to get i. with s.o.** s'impatienter contre qn. ● **impatience** *n* impatience *f*. ● **impatiently** *adv* avec impatience, impatiemment.

impeccable [ɪm'pekəb(ə)l] *a* (*manners,*

person etc) impeccable. ● **impeccably** *adv* impeccablement.

impecunious [ımpı'kju:nıəs] *a* sans le sou.

impede [ım'pi:d] *vt* (*hamper*) gêner; **to i. s.o. from doing** (*prevent*) empêcher qn de faire.

impediment [ım'pedımənt] *n* obstacle *m*; (*speech*) i. défaut *m* d'élocution.

impel [ım'pel] *vt* (**-ll-**) (*drive*) pousser; (*force*) obliger (**to do** à faire).

impending [ım'pendıŋ] *a* imminent.

impenetrable [ım'penıtrəb(ə)l] *a* (*forest, mystery etc*) impénétrable.

imperative [ım'perətıv] *a* (*need, tone*) impérieux; (*necessary*) essentiel, indispensable; **it is i. that** il faut absolument *or* il est indispensable que (+ *sub*) ▌ *n* Grammar impératif *m*.

imperceptible [ımpə'septəb(ə)l] *a* imperceptible (**to** à).

imperfect [ım'pɜ:fıkt] **1** *a* imparfait; (*goods*) défectueux. **2** *a* & *n* **i.** (*tense*) Grammar imparfait *m*. ● **imperfection** [-'fekʃ(ə)n] *n* imperfection *f*.

imperial [ım'pıərıəl] *a* impérial; (*majestic*) majestueux; **i. measure** Br mesure *f* légale (anglo-saxonne). ● **imperialism** *n* impérialisme *m*.

imperil [ım'perıl] *vt* (*Br* **-ll-**, *Am* **-l-**) mettre en péril.

imperious [ım'pıərıəs] *a* impérieux.

impersonal [ım'pɜ:sən(ə)l] *a* impersonnel.

impersonate [ım'pɜ:səneıt] *vt* (*pretend to be*) se faire passer pour; (*on TV etc*) imiter. ● **impersonation** [-'neıʃ(ə)n] *n* imitation *f*. ● **impersonator** *n* (*on TV etc*) imitateur, -trice *mf*.

impertinent [ım'pɜ:tınənt] *a* impertinent (**to** envers). ● **impertinence** *n* impertinence *f*. ● **impertinently** *adv* avec impertinence.

impervious [ım'pɜ:vıəs] *a* imperméable (**to** à).

impetuous [ım'petjʊəs] *a* impétueux. ● **impetu'osity** *n* impétuosité *f*.

impetus ['ımpıtəs] *n* impulsion *f*.

impinge [ım'pındʒ] *vi* **to i. on** (*affect*) affecter; (*encroach on*) empiéter sur.

impish ['ımpıʃ] *a* (*naughty*) espiègle.

implacable [ım'plækəb(ə)l] *a* implacable.

implant [ım'plɑ:nt] *vt* (*surgically*) implanter (**in** dans); (*ideas*) inculquer (**in** à) ▌ ['ımplɑ:nt] *n* (*in body*) implant *m*.

implement[1] ['ımplımənt] *n* (*tool*) instrument *m*; (*utensil*) ustensile *m*; **farm implements** matériel *m* agricole.

implement[2] ['ımplıment] *vt* (*carry out*) mettre en œuvre, exécuter. ● **implementation** [-'teıʃ(ə)n] *n* mise *f* en œuvre, exécution *f*.

implicate ['ımplıkeıt] *vt* impliquer (**in** dans). ● **implication** [-'keıʃ(ə)n] *n* (*consequence*) conséquence *f*; (*involvement*) implication *f*; (*innuendo*) insinuation *f*; (*impact*) portée *f*; **by i.** implicitement.

implicit [ım'plısıt] *a* (*implied*) implicite; (*belief, obedience etc*) absolu. ● **implicitly** *adv* implicitement.

implore [ım'plɔ:r] *vt* implorer (**s.o. to do** qn de faire).

imply [ım'plaı] *vt* (*suggest*) laisser entendre (**that** que); (*assume*) impliquer, supposer (**that** que); (*insinuate*) insinuer (**that** que). ● **implied** *a* implicite.

impolite [ımpə'laıt] *a* impoli. ● **impoliteness** *n* impolitesse *f*.

import 1 [ım'pɔ:t] *vt* (*goods etc*) importer (**from** de) ▌ ['ımpɔ:t] *n* (*imported product*) importation *f*. **2** ['ımpɔ:t] *n* (*meaning*) sens *m*. ● **im'porter** *n* importateur, -trice *mf*.

importance [ım'pɔ:təns] *n* importance *f*; **to be of i.** avoir de l'importance; **of no i.** sans importance.

important [ım'pɔ:tənt] *a* important (**to** à, **for** pour); **it's i. that** il est important que (+ *sub*). ● **importantly** *adv* **more i.** ce qui est plus important.

impose [ım'pəʊz] *vt* (*conditions, silence etc*) imposer (**on** à); (*fine, punishment*) infliger (**on s.o.** à qn) ▌ *vi* (*cause trouble*) déranger; **to i. on s.o.** déranger qn. ● **imposition** [-'zıʃ(ə)n] *n* imposition *f* (**of** de); (*inconvenience*) dérangement *m*.

imposing [ım'pəʊzıŋ] *a* (*building, height etc*) impressionnant.

impossible [ım'pɒsəb(ə)l] *a* impossible (**to do** à faire); **it is i.** (**for us**) **to do il** (nous) est impossible de faire; **it is i. that** il est impossible que (+ *sub*); **to make it i. for s.o. to do sth** mettre qn dans l'impossibilité de faire qch ▌ *n* **to do the i.** faire l'impossible. ● **impossi'bility** *n* impossibilité *f*. ● **impossibly** *adv* (*late, hard etc*) incroyablement.

impostor [ım'pɒstər] *n* imposteur *m*.

impotent ['ımpətənt] *a* (*powerless & sexually*) impuissant. ● **impotence** *n* impuissance *f*.

impound [ım'paʊnd] *vt* (*of police*) saisir, confisquer; (*vehicle*) emmener à la fourrière.

impoverish [ım'pɒvərıʃ] *vt* appauvrir. ● **impoverished** *a* appauvri, pauvre.

impracticable [ım'præktıkəb(ə)l] *a* impraticable, irréalisable.

impractical [ım'præktık(ə)l] *a* peu réaliste.

imprecise [ımprı'saıs] *a* imprécis.

impregnable [ım'pregnəb(ə)l] *a* (*fortress etc*) imprenable; (*argument*) Fig inattaquable.

impregnate ['ımpregneıt] *vt* (*imbue*) imprégner (**with** de); (*fertilize*) féconder.

impresario [ımprı'sɑ:rıəʊ] *n* (*pl* **-os**) impresario *m*.

impress [ım'pres] *vt* impressionner (*qn*); (*imprint*) imprimer (*marque etc*) (**on** sur, **in** dans); **to i. sth on s.o.** faire comprendre qch à qn.

impression [ım'preʃ(ə)n] *n* impression *f*; **to be under** *or* **have the i. that** avoir l'impression que; **to make a good i. on s.o.** faire une bonne impression à qn. ● **impressionable** *a* (*person*) impressionnable; (*age*) où l'on est impressionnable.

impressionist [ım'preʃənıst] *n* (*entertainer*) imitateur, -trice *mf*; (*artist*) impressionniste *mf.*

impressive [ɪm'presɪv] *a* impressionnant.

imprint [ɪm'prɪnt] *vt* imprimer ▌ ['ɪmprɪnt] *n* empreinte *f*; **publisher's i.** nom *m* de l'éditeur.

imprison [ɪm'prɪz(ə)n] *vt* emprisonner. ●**imprisonment** *n* emprisonnement *m*; **life i.** la prison à vie.

improbable [ɪm'prɒbəb(ə)l] *a* improbable; (*story, excuse*) invraisemblable. ●**improba'bility** *n* improbabilité *f*; (*of story etc*) invraisemblance *f*.

impromptu [ɪm'prɒmptjuː] *a & adv* impromptu.

improper [ɪm'prɒpər] *a* (*indecent*) indécent, inconvenant; (*wrong*) (*use, sense etc*) incorrect. ●**impropriety** [ɪmprə'praɪətɪ] *n* (*in behaviour, language etc*) inconvenance *f*; (*wrong use of word etc*) impropriété *f*.

improve [ɪm'pruːv] *vt* améliorer; (*mind*) cultiver, développer; **to i. one's English** se perfectionner en anglais; (*of mind*) développer; (*progress*) progrès *m(pl)*; **there has been some** *or* **an i.** il y a du mieux; **to be an i. on sth** (*be better than*) être supérieur à qch *or* meilleur que qch.

improvise ['ɪmprəvaɪz] *vti* improviser. ●**improvisation** [-'zeɪʃ(ə)n] *n* improvisation *f*.

impudent ['ɪmpjudənt] *a* impudent. ●**impudence** *n* impudence *f*.

impulse ['ɪmpʌls] *n* impulsion *f*; **on i.** sur un coup de tête. ●**im'pulsive** *a* (*person, act*) impulsif, irréfléchi; (*remark*) irréfléchi. ●**im'pulsively** *adv* (*to act etc*) de manière impulsive.

impunity [ɪm'pjuːnɪtɪ] *n* **with i.** impunément.

impure [ɪm'pjuər] *a* impur. ●**impurity** *n* impureté *f*.

in [ɪn] *prep* **1** dans; **in the box/the school/***etc* dans la boîte/l'école/*etc*; **in an hour('s time)** dans une heure; **in the garden** dans le jardin, au jardin; **in luxury** dans le luxe; **in so far as** dans la mesure où.

2 à; **in school** à l'école; **in Paris** à Paris; **in the USA** aux USA; **in Portugal** au Portugal; **in fashion** à la mode; **in pencil** au crayon; **in ink** à l'encre; **in my opinion** à mon avis; **in spring** au printemps; **the woman in the red dress** la femme à la robe rouge.

3 en; **in summer/secret/French** en été/secret/français; **in Spain** en Espagne; **in May** en mai, au mois de mai; **in season** (*fruit etc*) de saison; **in fashion** en vogue; **in an hour** (*during the period of an hour*) en une heure; **in doing** en faisant; **dressed in black** habillé en noir; **in all** en tout.

4 de; **in a soft voice** d'une voix douce; **the best in the class** le meilleur de la classe; **an increase in salary** une augmentation de sa-

laire; **at six in the evening** à six heures du soir.

5 chez; **in children/adults/animals** chez les enfants/les adultes/les animaux; **in Shakespeare** chez Shakespeare.

6 in the rain sous la pluie; **in the morning** le matin; **he hasn't done it in months/years** ça fait des mois/années qu'il ne l'a pas fait; **in an hour** (*at the end of an hour*) au bout d'une heure; **one in ten** un sur dix; **in tens** dix par dix; **in hundreds/thousands** par centaines/milliers; **in here** ici; **in there** là-dedans.

7 *adv* **to be in** (*home*) être là, être à la maison; (*of train*) être arrivé; (*in fashion*) être en vogue; (*in season*) (*fruit etc*) être de saison; (*in power*) être au pouvoir; **day in day out** jour après jour; **in on a secret** au courant d'un secret; **we're in for some rain/trouble/***etc* on va avoir de la pluie/des ennuis/*etc*; **it's the in thing** *Fam* c'est dans le vent.

8 *npl* **the ins and outs of** les moindres détails de.

in- [ɪn] *pref* in-.

inability [ɪnə'bɪlɪtɪ] *n* incapacité *f* (**to do** de faire).

inaccessible [ɪnək'sesəb(ə)l] *a* inaccessible.

inaccurate [ɪn'ækjurət] *a* inexact. ●**inaccuracy** *n* inexactitude *f*; **an i.** (*error*) une inexactitude.

inaction [ɪn'ækʃ(ə)n] *n* inaction *f*.

inactive [ɪn'æktɪv] *a* inactif; (*mind*) inerte. ●**inac'tivity** *n* inactivité *f*, inaction *f*.

inadequate [ɪn'ædɪkwət] *a* (*quantity*) insuffisant; (*person*) pas à la hauteur, insuffisant; (*work*) médiocre. ●**inadequacy** *n* insuffisance *f*. ●**inadequately** *adv* insuffisamment.

inadmissible [ɪnəd'mɪsəb(ə)l] *a* inadmissible.

inadvertently [ɪnəd'vɜːtəntlɪ] *adv* par inadvertance.

inadvisable [ɪnəd'vaɪzəb(ə)l] *a* (*action*) à déconseiller; **it is i. to go out alone/***etc* il est déconseillé de sortir seul/*etc*.

inane [ɪ'neɪn] *a* (*absurd*) inepte.

inanimate [ɪn'ænɪmət] *a* inanimé.

inappropriate [ɪnə'prəuprɪət] *a* (*unsuitable*) (*place, clothes etc*) qui ne convient pas; (*remark, moment*) qui ne convient pas, inopportun.

inarticulate [ɪnɑː'tɪkjulət] *a* (*person*) incapable de s'exprimer; (*sound*) inarticulé.

inasmuch as [ɪnəz'mʌtʃəz] *adv* (*because*) vu que; (*to the extent that*) en ce sens que.

inattentive [ɪnə'tentɪv] *a* inattentif (**to** à).

inaudible [ɪn'ɔːdəb(ə)] *a* inaudible.

inaugural [ɪ'nɔːgjurəl] *a* (*speech, meeting*) inaugural.

inaugurate [ɪ'nɔːgjureɪt] *vt* (*building, policy*) inaugurer; (*official*) installer (dans ses fonctions). ●**inauguration** [-'reɪʃ(ə)n] *n* inauguration *f*; (*of official*) investiture *f*.

inauspicious [ɪnɔː'spɪʃəs] *a* peu propice.

inborn [ɪn'bɔːn] *a* inné.

inbred [ɪn'bred] *a* (*quality etc*) inné.

Inc *abbr* (*Incorporated*) *Am* Com SA, SARL.

incalculable [ɪn'kælkjʊləb(ə)l] *a* incalculable.

incandescent [ɪnkæn'des(ə)nt] *a* incandescent.

incapable [ɪn'keɪpəb(ə)l] *a* incapable (**of doing** de faire); **i. of pity/***etc* inaccessible à la pitié/*etc*.

incapacitate [ɪnkə'pæsɪteɪt] *vt* (*for work*) rendre (*qn*) incapable (de travailler); (*of alcohol, drugs etc*) rendre (*qn*) incapable de faire quoi que ce soit. ● **incapacity** *n* (*inability*) incapacité *f.*

incarcerate [ɪn'kɑːsəreɪt] *vt* incarcérer. ● **incarceration** [-'reɪʃ(ə)n] *n* incarcération *f.*

incarnate [ɪn'kɑːnət] *a* incarné ▮ [ɪn'kɑːneɪt] *vt* incarner. ● **incarnation** [-'neɪʃ(ə)n] *n* incarnation *f.*

incendiary [ɪn'sendɪərɪ] *a* **i. device** *or* **bomb** bombe *f* incendiaire.

incense **1** [ɪn'sens] *vt* mettre en colère. **2** ['ɪnsens] *n* (*substance*) encens *m.*

incentive [ɪn'sentɪv] *n* encouragement *m*, motivation *f*; **to give s.o. an i. to work/***etc* encourager qn à travailler/*etc*.

inception [ɪn'sepʃ(ə)n] *n* début *m.*

incessant [ɪn'ses(ə)nt] *a* incessant. ● **incessantly** *adv* sans cesse.

incest ['ɪnsest] *n* inceste *m.* ● **in'cestuous** *a* incestueux.

inch [ɪntʃ] *n* pouce *m* (= *2,54 cm*); **a few inches** (*loosely*) quelques centimètres; **within an i. of** (*success, death*) à deux doigts de; **i. by i.** petit à petit ▮ *vti* **to i.** (**one's way**) **forward** avancer petit à petit.

incidence ['ɪnsɪdəns] *n* fréquence *f.*

incident ['ɪnsɪdənt] *n* incident *m*; (*in book, film etc*) épisode *m.*

incidental [ɪnsɪ'dent(ə)l] *a* (*additional*) accessoire, secondaire; **i. music** musique *f* de fond; **i. expenses** frais *mpl* accessoires; **it's i. to the main plot** c'est secondaire par rapport à l'intrigue principale. ● **incidentally** *adv* (*by the way*) à propos; (*additionally*) accessoirement.

incinerate [ɪn'sɪnəreɪt] *vt* (*refuse, leaves etc*) incinérer. ● **incinerator** *n* incinérateur *m.*

incipient [ɪn'sɪpɪənt] *a* naissant.

incision [ɪn'sɪʒ(ə)n] *n* incision *f.*

incisive [ɪn'saɪsɪv] *a* incisif.

incisor [ɪn'saɪzər] *n* (*tooth*) incisive *f.*

incite [ɪn'saɪt] *vt* inciter (**to do** à faire). ● **incitement** *n* incitation *f* (**to do** à faire).

inclination [ɪnklɪ'neɪʃ(ə)n] *n* (*tendency*) inclination *f*; (*desire*) envie *f* (**to do** de faire); **to have no i. to do** n'avoir aucune envie de faire.

incline **1** [ɪn'klaɪn] *vt* (*bend, tilt*) incliner; **to be inclined to do** (*feel a wish to*) avoir bien envie de faire; (*tend to*) avoir tendance à faire; **to be inclined towards** (*indulgence etc*) incliner à; (*opinion etc*) pencher pour; **to i. s.o. to do** incliner qn à faire ▮ *vi* **to i. to sth** = **to be inclined towards sth.** **2** ['ɪnklaɪn] *n* (*slope*) inclinaison *f.*

include [ɪn'kluːd] *vt* (*contain*) comprendre, englober, inclure; **my invitation includes you** mon invitation s'adresse aussi à vous; **to be included** être compris; (*on list*) être inclus. ● **including** *prep* y compris; **i. service** service *m* compris.

inclusion [ɪn'kluːʒ(ə)n] *n* inclusion *f.*

inclusive [ɪn'kluːsɪv] *a* inclus; **from the fourth to the tenth of May i.** du quatre jusqu'au dix mai inclus(ivement); **to be i. of** comprendre; **i. of tax** toutes taxes comprises; **i. charge** *or* **price** prix *m* global.

incognito [ɪnkɒg'niːtəʊ] *adv* incognito.

incoherent [ɪnkəʊ'hɪərənt] *a* incohérent. ● **incoherently** *adv* (*to speak, act etc*) de façon incohérente.

income ['ɪŋkʌm] *n* revenu *m* (**from** de); **private i.** rentes *fpl*; **i. tax** impôt *m* sur le revenu.

incoming ['ɪnkʌmɪŋ] *a* (*tenant, president etc*) nouveau (*f* nouvelle); **i. calls** (*on telephone*) appels *mpl* de l'extérieur; **i. mail** courrier *m* à l'arrivée; **i. tide** marée *f* montante.

incommunicado [ɪnkəmjuː'kɑːdəʊ] *a* (*tenu*) au secret.

incomparable [ɪn'kɒmpərəb(ə)l] *a* incomparable.

incompatible [ɪnkəm'pætəb(ə)l] *a* incompatible (**with** avec). ● **incompati'bility** *n* incompatibilité *f.*

incompetent [ɪn'kɒmpɪtənt] *a* incompétent. ● **incompetence** *n* incompétence *f.*

incomplete [ɪnkəm'pliːt] *a* incomplet.

incomprehensible [ɪnkɒmprɪ'hensəb(ə)l] *a* incompréhensible.

inconceivable [ɪnkən'siːvəb(ə)l] *a* inconcevable.

inconclusive [ɪnkən'kluːsɪv] *a* peu concluant.

incongruous [ɪn'kɒŋgrʊəs] *a* (*building, colours*) qui jure(nt) (**with** avec); (*remark, attitude*) incongru; (*absurd*) absurde.

inconsequential [ɪnkɒnsɪ'kwenʃ(ə)l] *a* sans importance.

inconsiderate [ɪnkən'sɪdərət] *a* (*action, remark*) irréfléchi, inconsidéré; **to be i.** (*of person*) ne pas être très gentil, manquer d'égards (**towards** avec, envers).

inconsistent [ɪnkən'sɪstənt] *a* (*reports etc at variance*) en contradiction (**with** avec); (*person, behaviour etc*) inconsistant, incohérent. ● **inconsistency** *n* (*of person etc*) inconséquence *f*, incohérence *f*; **an i.** une incohérence.

inconsolable [ɪnkən'səʊləb(ə)l] *a* inconsolable.

inconspicuous [ɪnkən'spɪkjʊəs] *a* peu en évidence, qui passe inaperçu. ● **inconspicuously** *adv* discrètement.

incontinent [ɪn'kɒntɪnənt] *a* incontinent.

inconvenience [ɪnkən'viːnɪəns] *n* (*bother*) dérangement *m*; (*disadvantage*) inconvénient *m* ▮ *vt* déranger, gêner.

inconvenient [ɪnkən'viːnɪənt] *a* (*moment, si-*

tuation etc) gênant; (*house, school etc*) mal situé; **it's i.** (**for me**) **to...** ça me dérange de...; **that's very i.** c'est très gênant. ●**inconveniently** *adv* (*to arrive, happen*) à un moment gênant; **i. situated** mal situé.

incorporate [ɪn'kɔːpəreɪt] *vt* (*contain*) contenir; (*introduce*) incorporer (**into** dans); **incorporated society** *Am* société *f* anonyme, société *f* à responsabilité limitée.

incorrect [ɪnkə'rekt] *a* (*answer etc*) inexact; (*behaviour etc*) incorrect; **you're i.** vous avez tort.

incorrigible [ɪn'kɒrɪdʒəb(ə)l] *a* incorrigible.

incorruptible [ɪnkə'rʌptəb(ə)l] *a* incorruptible. ·

increase [ɪn'kriːs] *vi* augmenter; (*of effort, noise*) s'intensifier; **to i. in weight** prendre du poids ▮ *vt* augmenter; (*effort etc*) intensifier ▮ ['ɪnkriːs] *n* augmentation *f* (**in, of** de); (*of effort etc*) intensification *f* (**in, of** de); **on the i.** en hausse. ●**increasing** *a* (*amount etc*) croissant. ●**increasingly** *adv* de plus en plus.

incredible [ɪn'kredəb(ə)l] *a* incroyable. ●**incredibly** *adv* incroyablement.

incredulous [ɪn'kredjʊləs] *a* incrédule. ●**incre'dulity** *n* incrédulité *f*.

increment ['ɪŋkrəmənt] *n* augmentation *f*.

incriminate [ɪn'krɪmɪneɪt] *vt* incriminer. ●**incriminating** *a* compromettant.

incubate ['ɪŋkjʊbeɪt] *vt* (*eggs*) couver ▮ *vi* (*of illness*) être en période d'incubation. ●**incubation** [-'beɪʃ(ə)n] *n* incubation *f*. ●**incubator** *n* (*for baby, eggs*) couveuse *f*.

inculcate ['ɪnkʌlkeɪt] *vt* inculquer (**in** à).

incumbent [ɪn'kʌmbənt] *a* **it is i. upon him** or **her to...** il lui incombe de... ▮ *n* (*holder of office*) titulaire *mf*.

incur [ɪn'kɜːr] *vt* (**-rr-**) (*expenses*) faire; (*loss*) subir; (*debt*) contracter; (*criticism, danger*) s'attirer.

incurable [ɪn'kjʊərəb(ə)l] *a* incurable.

incursion [*Br* ɪn'kɜːʃ(ə)n, *Am* -ʒ(ə)n] *n* incursion *f* (**into** dans).

indebted [ɪn'detɪd] *a* **i. to s.o. for sth/for doing sth** redevable à qn de qch/d'avoir fait qch. ●**indebtedness** *n* dette *f*.

indecent [ɪn'diːs(ə)nt] *a* (*obscene*) indécent; (*improper*) peu approprié; **i. assault** *Br* attentat *m* à la pudeur. ●**indecency** *n* indécence *f*, (*crime*) *Br* outrage *m* à la pudeur. ●**indecently** *adv* indécemment.

indecisive [ɪndɪ'saɪsɪv] *a* (*person, answer*) indécis. ●**indecision** [-ʒ(ə)n] *n*, ●**indecisiveness** *n* indécision *f*.

indeed [ɪn'diːd] *adv* en effet; **very good/etc i.** vraiment très bon/*etc*; **yes i.!** bien sûr!; **thank you very much i.!** merci infiniment!, merci mille fois!

indefensible [ɪndɪ'fensəb(ə)l] *a* indéfendable.

indefinable [ɪndɪ'faɪnəb(ə)l] *a* indéfinissable.

indefinite [ɪn'defɪnət] *a* (*feeling, duration etc*) indéfini; (*plan*) mal déterminé. ●**indefinitely** *adv* indéfiniment.

indelible [ɪn'deləb(ə)l] *a* (*ink, memory*) in-

délébile; **i. pen** stylo *m* à encre indélébile.

indelicate [ɪn'delɪkət] *a* (*coarse*) indélicat.

indemnify [ɪn'demnɪfaɪ] *vt* indemniser (**for** de). ●**indemnity** *n* (*compensation*) indemnité *f*; **an i. against** (*protection*) une garantie contre.

indented [ɪn'dentɪd] *a* (*edge*) dentelé, découpé; (*line of print*) renfoncé. ●**indentation** [-'teɪʃ(ə)n] *n* dentelure *f*, découpure *f*; *Typ* renfoncement *m*.

independence [ɪndɪ'pendəns] *n* indépendance *f*.

independent [ɪndɪ'pendənt] *a* indépendant (**of** de); (*opinions, reports*) de sources différentes. ●**independently** *adv* de façon indépendante; **i. of** indépendamment de.

indescribable [ɪndɪ'skraɪbəb(ə)l] *a* indescriptible.

indestructible [ɪndɪ'strʌktəb(ə)l] *a* indestructible.

indeterminate [ɪndɪ'tɜːmɪnət] *a* indéterminé.

index ['ɪndeks] *n* (*in book etc*) index *m*; (*in library*) catalogue *m*; (*number, sign*) indice *m*; **cost of living i.** indice *m* du coût de la vie; **i. card** fiche *f*; **i. finger** index *m* ▮ *vt* (*classify*) classer. ●**index-'linked** *a* (*wages etc*) indexé (**sur**).

India ['ɪndɪə] *n* Inde *f*. ●**Indian** *a* indien ▮ *n* Indien, -ienne *mf*.

indicate ['ɪndɪkeɪt] *vt* indiquer (**that** que); **I was indicating right** (*in vehicle*) j'avais mis mon clignotant droit. ●**indication** [-'keɪʃ(ə)n] *n* (*sign*) indice *m*, indication *f*; (*idea*) idée *f*.

indicative [ɪn'dɪkətɪv] *a* **to be i. of** (*symptomatic*) être symptomatique de, renseigner sur ▮ *n* *Grammar* indicatif *m*.

indicator ['ɪndɪkeɪtər] *n* (*instrument*) indicateur *m*; (*sign*) indication *f* (**of** de); (*in vehicle*) clignotant *m*; (*display board*) tableau *m* (indicateur).

indict [ɪn'daɪt] *vt* inculper (**for** de). ●**indictment** *n* inculpation *f*.

Indies ['ɪndɪz] *npl* **the West I.** les Antilles *fpl*.

indifferent [ɪn'dɪf(ə)rənt] *a* indifférent (**to** à); (*mediocre*) médiocre. ●**indifference** *n* indifférence *f* (**to** à). ●**indifferently** *adv* indifféremment.

indigenous [ɪn'dɪdʒɪnəs] *a* indigène.

indigestion [ɪndɪ'dʒestʃ(ə)n] *n* problèmes *mpl* de digestion; (**an attack of**) **i.** une indigestion. ●**indigestible** *a* indigeste.

indignant [ɪn'dɪgnənt] *a* indigné (**at** de, **with** contre); **to become i.** s'indigner. ●**indignantly** *adv* avec indignation. ●**indignation** [-'neɪʃ(ə)n] *n* indignation *f*.

indignity [ɪn'dɪgnɪtɪ] *n* indignité *f*.

indigo ['ɪndɪgəʊ] *n* & *a* (*colour*) indigo *m* & *a inv*.

indirect [ɪndaɪ'rekt] *a* indirect. ●**indirectly** *adv* indirectement.

indiscreet [ɪndɪ'skriːt] *a* indiscret. ●**indiscretion** [-'kreʃ(ə)n] *n* indiscrétion *f*.

indiscriminate [ɪndɪ'skrɪmɪnət] a (random) fait, donné etc au hasard; (person) qui manque de discernement. ● **indiscriminately** adv (at random) au hasard; (without discrimination) sans discernement.

indispensable [ɪndɪ'spensəb(ə)l] a indispensable (to à).

indisposed [ɪndɪ'spəʊzd] a (unwell) indisposé. ● **indisposition** [-pə'zɪʃ(ə)n] n (illness) indisposition f.

indisputable [ɪndɪ'spjuːtəb(ə)l] a incontestable.

indistinct [ɪndɪ'stɪŋkt] a indistinct.

indistinguishable [ɪndɪ'stɪŋgwɪʃəb(ə)l] a indifférenciable (from de).

individual [ɪndɪ'vɪdʒʊəl] a (separate, personal) (responsibility, fact etc) individuel; (specific) particulier ▌ n (person) individu m. ● **individu'ality** n (distinctiveness) individualité f. ● **individually** adv (separately) individuellement; (unusually) de façon (très) personnelle.

individualist [ɪndɪ'vɪdʒʊəlɪst] n individualiste mf. ● **individua'listic** a individualiste.

indivisible [ɪndɪ'vɪzəb(ə)l] a indivisible.

Indo-China [ɪndəʊ'tʃaɪnə] n Indochine f.

indoctrinate [ɪn'dɒktrɪneɪt] vt endoctriner. ● **indoctrination** [-'neɪʃ(ə)n] n endoctrinement m.

indolent ['ɪndələnt] a indolent. ● **indolence** n indolence f.

indomitable [ɪn'dɒmɪtəb(ə)l] a (will, energy) indomptable.

Indonesia [ɪndəʊ'niːzə] n Indonésie f.

indoor ['ɪndɔːr] a (games, shoes etc) d'intérieur; (swimming pool etc) couvert. ● **in'doors** adv à l'intérieur; to go or come i. rentrer.

induce [ɪn'djuːs] vt (persuade) persuader (qn) (to do de faire); (cause) provoquer; to i. labour (in pregnant woman) déclencher le travail. ● **inducement** n encouragement m (to do à faire); (bribe) pot-de-vin m.

indulge [ɪn'dʌldʒ] vt (s.o.'s wishes) satisfaire; (child etc) gâter, tout passer à; to i. oneself se gâter ▌ vi to i. in (ice cream, cigar etc) se permettre; (hobby, vice etc) s'adonner à. ● **indulgence** n indulgence f. ● **indulgent** a indulgent (to envers).

industrial [ɪn'dʌstrɪəl] a industriel; (conflict, legislation) du travail; i. action Br mouvement m revendicatif; to take i. action Br se mettre en grève; i. estate Br, i. park Am zone f industrielle; i. relations relations fpl patronat-salariés. ● **industrialist** n industriel m. ● **industrialized** a industrialisé.

industrious [ɪn'dʌstrɪəs] a travailleur.

industry ['ɪndəstrɪ] n industrie f; (hard work) application f.

inebriated [ɪn'iːbrɪeɪtɪd] a ivre.

inedible [ɪn'edɪb(ə)l] a immangeable.

ineffective [ɪnɪ'fektɪv] a (measure etc) inefficace, sans effet; (person) incapable. ● **ineffectiveness** n inefficacité f.

ineffectual [ɪnɪ'fektʃʊəl] a (measure etc) in-

efficace; (person) incompétent.

inefficient [ɪnɪ'fɪʃ(ə)nt] a (person, measure etc) inefficace; (machine) peu performant. ● **inefficiency** n inefficacité f.

ineligible [ɪn'elɪdʒəb(ə)l] a (candidate) inéligible; to be i. for (scholarship etc) ne pas avoir droit à.

inept [ɪ'nept] a (unskilled) peu habile (at sth à qch); (incompetent) incapable, inapte; (foolish) inepte. ● **ineptitude** n (incapacity) inaptitude f.

inequality [ɪnɪ'kwɒlɪtɪ] n inégalité f.

inert [ɪ'nɜːt] a inerte. ● **inertia** [ɪ'nɜːʃə] n inertie f.

inescapable [ɪnɪ'skeɪpəb(ə)l] a inéluctable.

inevitable [ɪn'evɪtəb(ə)l] a inévitable. ● **inevitably** adv inévitablement.

inexcusable [ɪnɪk'skjuːzəb(ə)l] a inexcusable.

inexhaustible [ɪnɪg'zɔːstəb(ə)l] a inépuisable.

inexorable [ɪn'eksərəb(ə)l] a inexorable.

inexpensive [ɪnɪk'spensɪv] a bon marché inv.

inexperience [ɪnɪk'spɪərɪəns] n inexpérience f. ● **inexperienced** a inexpérimenté.

inexplicable [ɪnɪk'splɪkəb(ə)l] a inexplicable.

inexpressible [ɪnɪk'spresəb(ə)l] a inexprimable.

inextricable [ɪnɪk'strɪkəb(ə)l] ā inextricable.

infallible [ɪn'fæləb(ə)l] a infaillible. ● **infalli'bility** n infaillibilité f.

infamous ['ɪnfəməs] a (evil) infâme. ● **infamy** n infamie f.

infancy ['ɪnfənsɪ] n petite enfance f; to be in its i. (of art, technique etc) en être à ses premiers balbutiements.

infant ['ɪnfənt] n (child) petit(e) enfant mf; (baby) nourrisson m; i. school Br classes fpl préparatoires.

infantile ['ɪnfəntaɪl] a (illness, reaction etc) infantile.

infantry ['ɪnfəntrɪ] n infanterie f.

infatuated [ɪn'fætʃʊeɪtɪd] a amoureux; i. with (person) amoureux de, engoué de; (sport, hobby etc) engoué de. ● **infatuation** [-'eɪʃ(ə)n] n engouement m (for, with pour).

infect [ɪn'fekt] vt (wound, person etc) infecter; to get or become infected s'infecter; to i. s.o. with sth communiquer qch à qn. ● **infection** [-ʃ(ə)n] n infection f.

infectious [ɪn'fekʃəs] a (disease) contagieux, infectieux; (person, laughter etc) contagieux.

infer [ɪn'fɜːr] vt (-rr-) déduire (from de, that que). ● **inference** n déduction f; by i. par déduction; to draw an i. from tirer une conclusion de.

inferior [ɪn'fɪərɪər] a inférieur (to à); (goods, work) de qualité inférieure ▌ n (person) inférieur, -eure mf. ● **inferi'ority** n infériorité f; i. complex complexe m d'infériorité.

infernal [ɪn'fɜːn(ə)l] a infernal. ● **infernally** adv Fam épouvantablement.

inferno [ɪn'fɜːnəʊ] n (pl -os) (blaze) brasier

m, incendie m; (hell) enfer m.

infertile [Br ɪnˈfɜːtaɪl, Am ɪnˈfɜːt(ə)l] a (person, land) stérile.

infest [ɪnˈfest] vt infester (with de); **rat-/ shark-infested** infesté de rats/requins.

infidelity [ɪnfɪˈdelɪtɪ] n infidélité f.

infighting [ˈɪnfaɪtɪŋ] n (within group, office etc) luttes fpl intestines.

infiltrate [ˈɪnfɪltreɪt] vi s'infiltrer (into dans) ▮ vt (group etc in order to disrupt) s'infiltrer dans, noyauter. ● **infiltration** [-ˈtreɪʃ(ə)n] n infiltration f; Pol noyautage m.

infinite [ˈɪnfɪnɪt] a & n infini (m). ● **infinitely** adv infiniment. ● **inˈfinity** n Math Phot infini m; **to i.** Math à l'infini.

infinitive [ɪnˈfɪnɪtɪv] n Grammar infinitif m.

infirm [ɪnˈfɜːm] a infirme.

infirmary [ɪnˈfɜːmərɪ] n (hospital) hôpital m; (sickbay) infirmerie f.

infirmity [ɪnˈfɜːmɪtɪ] n (disability) infirmité f.

inflame [ɪnˈfleɪm] vt enflammer. ● **inflamed** a (throat, wound etc) enflammé.

inflammable [ɪnˈflæməb(ə)l] a inflammable. ● **inflammation** [ɪnfləˈmeɪʃ(ə)n] n inflammation f. ● **inflammatory** a (remark, speech etc) incendiaire.

inflate [ɪnˈfleɪt] vt (balloon, prices etc) gonfler. ● **inflatable** a gonflable.

inflation [ɪnˈfleɪʃ(ə)n] n (rising prices) inflation f. ● **inflationary** a inflationniste.

inflection [ɪnˈflekʃ(ə)n] n Grammar flexion f; (of voice) inflexion f.

inflexible [ɪnˈfleksəb(ə)l] a inflexible.

inflexion [ɪnˈflekʃ(ə)n] n = **inflection**.

inflict [ɪnˈflɪkt] vt (a wound) occasionner (on s.o. à qn); (punishment, torture) infliger (on s.o. à qn); **to i. pain on s.o.** faire souffrir qn.

influence [ˈɪnflʊəns] n influence f; **under the i. of** (anger, drugs) sous l'effet de; **under the i. of drink** or **alcohol** en état d'ébriété ▮ vt influencer. ● **influential** [-ˈenʃəl] a **to be i.** avoir une grande influence, être influent.

influenza [ɪnflʊˈenzə] n grippe f.

influx [ˈɪnflʌks] n (of tourists, refugees etc) afflux m (of de).

info [ˈɪnfəʊ] n Fam tuyaux mpl, renseignements mpl (on sur).

inform [ɪnˈfɔːm] vt informer (of de, that que) ▮ vi **to i. on s.o.** dénoncer qn. ● **informed** a (person, public etc) informé; **to keep s.o. i. of sth** tenir qn au courant de qch.

informal [ɪnˈfɔːm(ə)l] a (manner, attitude, person etc) simple, décontracté; (occasion) dénué de formalité; (tone, expression) familier; (announcement) officieux; (meeting) non-officiel. ● **inforˈmality** n simplicité f; (of tone etc) familiarité f. ● **informally** adv (without fuss) sans cérémonie; (to dress) simplement; (to discuss) à titre non-officiel; (to meet) officieusement.

informant [ɪnˈfɔːmənt] n informateur, -trice mf.

information [ɪnfəˈmeɪʃ(ə)n] n (facts) renseignements mpl (about, on sur); (knowledge) & Comptr information f; **a piece of i.**

un renseignement, une information; **to get some i.** se renseigner; **i. technology** informatique f.

informative [ɪnˈfɔːmətɪv] a instructif.

informer [ɪnˈfɔːmər] n (police) i. indicateur, -trice mf.

infrared [ɪnfrəˈred] a infrarouge.

infrequent [ɪnˈfriːkwənt] a peu fréquent. ● **infrequently** adv rarement.

infringe [ɪnˈfrɪndʒ] vt (rule) contrevenir à ▮ vi **i. upon** (encroach on) empiéter sur. ● **infringement** n infraction f (of à).

infuriate [ɪnˈfjʊərɪeɪt] vt exaspérer. ● **infuriating** a exaspérant.

infuse [ɪnˈfjuːz] vt (tea) (faire) infuser. ● **infusion** [-ʒ(ə)n] n infusion f.

ingenious [ɪnˈdʒiːnɪəs] a ingénieux. ● **ingenuity** [ɪndʒɪˈnuːɪtɪ] n ingéniosité f.

ingot [ˈɪŋgət] n lingot m.

ingrained [ɪnˈgreɪnd] a (prejudice, attitude etc) enraciné; **i. dirt** crasse f.

ingratiate [ɪnˈgreɪʃɪeɪt] vt **to i. oneself with s.o.** s'insinuer dans les bonnes grâces de qn. ● **ingratiating** a (person, smile) insinuant.

ingratitude [ɪnˈgrætɪtjuːd] n ingratitude f.

ingredient [ɪnˈgriːdɪənt] n ingrédient m.

ingrowing [ˈɪngrəʊɪŋ] (Am **ingrown** [ˈɪngrəʊn]) a (toenail) incarné.

inhabit [ɪnˈhæbɪt] vt habiter. ● **inhabitable** a habitable. ● **inhabitant** n habitant, -ante mf.

inhale [ɪnˈheɪl] vt (smell etc) aspirer; (smoke, fumes) respirer; **to i. the smoke** (of smoker) avaler la fumée. ● **inhalation** [ɪnhəˈleɪʃ(ə)n] n inhalation f. ● **inhaler** n (for medication) inhalateur m.

inherent [ɪnˈhɪərənt] a inhérent (in à). ● **inherently** adv intrinsèquement, en soi.

inherit [ɪnˈherɪt] vt hériter (de); (title) succéder à. ● **inheritance** n héritage m; (legal process) succession f; (cultural) patrimoine m.

inhibit [ɪnˈhɪbɪt] vt (hinder) gêner; (control) maîtriser (impulsion etc); **to i. s.o. from doing sth** empêcher qn de faire qch; **to be inhibited** être inhibé, avoir des inhibitions. ● **inhibition** [-ˈbɪʃ(ə)n] n inhibition f.

inhospitable [ɪnhɒˈspɪtəb(ə)l] a peu accueillant, inhospitalier.

inhuman [ɪnˈhjuːmən] a (not human, cruel) inhumain. ● **inhuˈmane** a (not kind) inhumain. ● **inhuˈmanity** n brutalité f, cruauté f.

inimitable [ɪˈnɪmɪtəb(ə)l] a inimitable.

iniquitous [ɪˈnɪkwɪtəs] a inique. ● **iniquity** n iniquité f.

initial [ɪˈnɪʃ(ə)l] a premier, initial ▮ npl **initials** (letters) initiales fpl; (signature) paraphe' m ▮ vt (Br **-ll-**, Am **-l-**) parapher. ● **initially** adv au début, initialement.

initiate [ɪˈnɪʃɪeɪt] vt (reform, negotiations) amorcer; (attack, fashion) lancer; (policy, period) inaugurer; **to i. s.o. into** initier qn à; **to i. proceedings against s.o.** engager des poursuites contre qn ▮ **the initiated** les initiés mpl. ● **initiation** [-ˈeɪʃ(ə)n] n amorce f; (of attack) lancement m; (of policy) inauguration f; (of person) initiation f. ●**initiator** n (of idea etc) initiateur, -trice mf.

initiative [ɪ'nɪʃətɪv] n initiative f.

inject [ɪn'dʒekt] vt injecter (**into sth** dans qch); (new life etc) Fig insuffler (**into** à); **to i. sth into s.o., i. s.o. with sth** faire une piqûre de qch à qn, injecter qch à qn. ●**injection** [-ʃ(ə)n] n injection f, piqûre f.

injunction [ɪn'dʒʌŋkʃ(ə)n] n (court order) ordonnance f.

injure ['ɪndʒər] vt (physically) blesser, faire du mal à; (damage) nuire à, compromettre (réputation etc); **to i. one's foot/etc** se blesser au pied/etc; **to i. s.o.'s feelings** offenser qn. ●**injured** a blessé ❚ **n the i.** les blessés mpl.

injurious [ɪn'dʒʊərɪəs] a préjudiciable (**to** à).

injury ['ɪndʒərɪ] n (to flesh) blessure f; (fracture) fracture f; (sprain) foulure f; (bruise) contusion f; (wrong) Fig préjudice m.

injustice [ɪn'dʒʌstɪs] n injustice f.

ink [ɪŋk] n encre f; **Indian i.** encre f de Chine. ●**inkpot** or **inkwell** n encrier m. ●**inky** a couvert d'encre.

inkling ['ɪŋklɪŋ] n (petite) idée f; **to have some** or **an i. of sth** soupçonner qch, avoir une (petite) idée de qch.

inlaid [ɪn'leɪd] a (marble etc) incrusté (**with** de); (wood) marqueté.

inland ['ɪnlənd, 'ɪnlænd] a intérieur; **the I. Revenue** Br le fisc, le service des impôts ❚ [ɪn'lænd] adv à l'intérieur (des terres).

in-laws ['ɪnlɔːz] npl belle-famille f.

inlet ['ɪnlet] n (of sea) crique f; **i. pipe** tuyau m d'arrivée.

inmate ['ɪnmeɪt] n (of prison) détenu, -ue mf; (of asylum) interné, -ée mf; (of hospice, home) pensionnaire mf.

inmost ['ɪnməʊst] a le plus profond.

inn [ɪn] n auberge f.

innards ['ɪnədz] npl Fam entrailles fpl.

innate [ɪ'neɪt] a inné.

inner ['ɪnər] a intérieur; (feelings) intime, profond; (ear) interne; **an i. circle** (group of people) un cercle restreint; **the i. circle** le saint des saints; **the i. city** les quartiers du centre-ville; **i. tube** (of Br tyre, Am tire) chambre f à air. ●**innermost** a le plus profond.

inning ['ɪnɪŋ] n Baseball tour m de batte. ●**innings** n inv Cricket tour m de batte; **a good i.** Fig une vie longue.

innkeeper ['ɪnkiːpər] n aubergiste mf.

innocent ['ɪnəs(ə)nt] a innocent. ●**innocence** n innocence f. ●**innocently** adv innocemment.

innocuous [ɪ'nɒkjʊəs] a inoffensif.

innovate ['ɪnəveɪt] vi innover. ●**innovation** [-'veɪʃ(ə)n] n innovation f. ●**innovator** n innovateur, -trice mf.

innuendo [ɪnjʊ'endəʊ] n (pl -oes or -os) insinuation f.

innumerable [ɪ'njuːmərəb(ə)l] a innombrable.

inoculate ['ɪnɒkjʊleɪt] vt vacciner (**against** contre). ●**inoculation** [-'leɪʃ(ə)n] n vaccination f, inoculation f.

inoffensive [ɪnə'fensɪv] a inoffensif.

inoperative [ɪn'ɒpərətɪv] a (machine) qui ne fonctionne pas; (rule) inopérant.

inopportune [ɪn'ɒpətjuːn] a inopportun.

inordinate [ɪ'nɔːdɪnət] a excessif. ●**inordinately** adv excessivement.

in-patient ['ɪnpeɪʃ(ə)nt] n Br malade mf hospitalisé(e).

input ['ɪnpʊt] n (computer operation) entrée f; (data) données fpl; (electrical current) énergie f; (resources) ressources fpl; (contribution) apport m ❚ vt (into computer) entrer (données).

inquest ['ɪnkwest] n enquête f.

inquire [ɪn'kwaɪər] vi se renseigner (**about** sur); **to i. after s.o.** demander des nouvelles de qn; **to i. into** faire une enquête sur, examiner ❚ vt demander; **to i. how to get to** demander le chemin de. ●**inquiring** a (mind, look) curieux.

inquiry [ɪn'kwaɪərɪ] n (request for information) demande f de renseignements; (investigation) enquête f; **'inquiries'** (sign) 'renseignements'; **to make inquiries** demander des renseignements; (of police) enquêter.

inquisitive [ɪn'kwɪzɪtɪv] a curieux. ●**inquisitively** adv avec curiosité. ●**inquisition** [-'zɪʃ(ə)n] n (inquiry) & Rel inquisition f.

inroads ['ɪnrəʊdz] npl (attacks) incursions fpl (**into** dans); **to make i. into** (start on) entamer.

insane [ɪn'seɪn] a fou (f folle), dément. ●**insanely** adv comme un fou. ●**insanity** n folie f, démence f.

insanitary [ɪn'sænɪt(ə)rɪ] a insalubre.

insatiable [ɪn'seɪʃəb(ə)l] a insatiable.

inscribe [ɪn'skraɪb] vt inscrire; (book) dédicacer (**to** à). ●**inscription** [-'skrɪpʃ(ə)n] n inscription f; (in book) dédicace f.

inscrutable [ɪn'skruːtəb(ə)l] a impénétrable.

insect ['ɪnsekt] n insecte m; **i. powder/spray** poudre f/bombe f insecticide; **i. repellent** crème f anti-insecte. ●**in'secticide** n insecticide m.

insecure [ɪnsɪ'kjʊər] a (not securely fixed) mal fixé; (furniture, ladder) branlant, bancal; (window) mal fermé; (uncertain) incertain; (unsafe) peu sûr; (person) qui manque d'assurance. ●**insecurity** n (of person, situation) insécurité f.

insemination [ɪnsemɪ'neɪʃ(ə)n] n **artificial i.** insémination artificielle.

insensible [ɪn'sensəb(ə)l] a (unconscious) inconscient.

insensitive [ɪn'sensɪtɪv] a insensible (**to** à). ●**insensi'tivity** n insensibilité f.

inseparable [ɪn'sep(ə)rəb(ə)l] a inséparable (**from** de).

insert [ɪn'sɜːt] vt insérer (**in, into** dans). ●**insertion** [-ʃ(ə)n] n insertion f.

inshore ['ɪnʃɔːr] a côtier ❚ adv (to fish etc) près de la côte.

inside [ɪn'saɪd] adv dedans, à l'intérieur;

come i.! entrez!
I *prep* à l'intérieur de, dans; (*time*) en moins de.
I *n* dedans *m*, intérieur *m*; **insides** (*stomach*) *Fam* ventre *m*; **on the i.** à l'intérieur (**of** de); **i. out** (*coat, socks etc*) à l'envers; (*to know, study etc*) à fond; **to turn everything i. out** *Fig* tout chambouler.
I *a* intérieur; (*information*) obtenu à la source; **the i. lane** *Br* la voie de gauche, *Am* la voie de droite.
insider [ɪnˈsaɪdər] *n* initié, -ée *mf*; **i. dealing** *or* **trading** (*on Stock Exchange*) délit *m* d'initié.
insidious [ɪnˈsɪdɪəs] *a* insidieux.
insight [ˈɪnsaɪt] *n* perspicacité *f*; (*into question etc*) aperçu *m*; **to give s.o. an i. into** (*s.o.'s character*) permettre à qn de comprendre; (*question etc*) donner à qn un aperçu de.
insignia [ɪnˈsɪɡnɪə] *npl* (*of important person*) insignes *mpl*.
insignificant [ɪnsɪɡˈnɪfɪkənt] *a* insignifiant. ●**insignificance** *n* insignifiance *f*.
insincere [ɪnsɪnˈsɪər] *a* peu sincère. ●**insincerity** *n* manque *m* de sincérité.
insinuate [ɪnˈsɪnjʊeɪt] *vt* 1 (*suggest*) insinuer (**that** que). 2 **to i. oneself into** s'insinuer dans. ●**insinuation** [-ˈeɪʃ(ə)n] *n* insinuation *f*.
insipid [ɪnˈsɪpɪd] *a* insipide.
insist [ɪnˈsɪst] *vi* insister (**on doing** pour faire); **to i. on sth** (*demand*) exiger qch; (*assert*) affirmer qch I *vt* (*order*) insister (**that** pour que + *sub*); (*declare firmly*) affirmer (**that** que); **I i. that you come** *or* **on your coming** j'insiste pour que tu viennes.
insistence [ɪnˈsɪstəns] *n* insistance *f*; **her i. on seeing me** l'insistance qu'elle met à vouloir me voir.
insistent [ɪnˈsɪstənt] *a* (*person, request*) insistant; **to be i. (that)** insister (**pour que** + *sub*); **I was i. about it** j'ai été pressant. ●**insistently** *adv* avec insistance.
insolent [ˈɪnsələnt] *a* insolent. ●**insolence** *n* insolence *f*. ●**insolently** *adv* insolemment.
insoluble [ɪnˈsɒljʊb(ə)l] *a* insoluble.
insolvent [ɪnˈsɒlvənt] *a* (*financially*) insolvable.
insomnia [ɪnˈsɒmnɪə] *n* insomnie *f*. ●**insomniac** *n* insomniaque *mf*.
insomuch as [ɪnsəʊˈmʌtʃəz] *adv* = **inasmuch as**.
inspect [ɪnˈspekt] *vt* inspecter; (*tickets*) contrôler; (*troops*) passer en revue. ●**inspection** [-ʃ(ə)n] *n* inspection *f*; (*of tickets*) contrôle *m*; (*of troops*) revue *f*. ●**inspector** *n* inspecteur, -trice *mf*; (*on train*) contrôleur, -euse *mf*.
inspire [ɪnˈspaɪər] *vt* inspirer (**s.o. with sth** qch à qn); **to be inspired to do** avoir l'inspiration de faire. ●**inspired** *a* inspiré. ●**inspiring** *a* (*example etc*) inspirant, qui inspire. ●**inspiration** [-spəˈreɪʃ(ə)n] *n* inspiration *f*; (*person*) source *f* d'inspiration.

instability [ɪnstəˈbɪlɪtɪ] *n* instabilité *f*.
install [ɪnˈstɔːl] (*Am* **instal**) *vt* installer. ●**installation** [-stəˈleɪʃ(ə)n] *n* installation *f*.
instalment [ɪnˈstɔːlmənt] (*Am* **installment**) *n* (*of money*) acompte *m*, versement *m* (*partiel*); (*of serial, story*) épisode *m*; (*of publication*) fascicule *m*; **to buy on the i. plan** *Am* acheter à crédit.
instance [ˈɪnstəns] *n* (*example*) exemple *m*; (*case*) cas *m*; **for i.** par exemple; **in this i.** dans le cas présent; **in the first i.** en premier lieu.
instant [ˈɪnstənt] *a* immédiat; **i. coffee** café *m* instantané *or* soluble, nescafé® *m*; **i. camera** appareil (photo) *m* à développement instantané; **of the 3rd i.** (*in commercial letter*) *Br* du 3 courant I *n* (*moment*) instant *m*; **this (very) i.** (*at once*) à l'instant; **the i. that** (*as soon as*) dès que. ●**instantly** *adv* immédiatement.
instantaneous [ɪnstənˈteɪnɪəs] *a* instantané.
instead [ɪnˈsted] *adv* (*as alternative*) plutôt, au lieu de cela; **i. of sth** au lieu de qch; **i. of doing sth** au lieu de faire qch; **i. of s.o.** à la place de qn; (*of him or her*) à sa place.
instep [ˈɪnstep] *n* (*of foot*) cou-de-pied *m*; (*of shoe*) cambrure *f*.
instigate [ˈɪnstɪɡeɪt] *vt* provoquer. ●**instigation** [-ˈɡeɪʃ(ə)n] *n* instigation *f*. ●**instigator** *n* instigateur, -trice *mf*.
instil [ɪnˈstɪl] (*Am* **instill**) *vt* (**-ll-**) (*idea*) inculquer (**into** à); (*courage*) insuffler (**into** à).
instinct [ˈɪnstɪŋkt] *n* instinct *m*; **by i.** d'instinct. ●**instinctive** *a* instinctif. ●**instinctively** *adv* instinctivement.
institute [ˈɪnstɪtjuːt] *n* institut *m* I *vt* (*rule, practice*) instituer; (*inquiry*) entamer, intenter; **to i. proceedings against s.o.** engager *or* intenter des poursuites contre qn.
institution [ɪnstɪˈtjuːʃ(ə)n] *n* (*private organization, custom etc*) institution *f*; (*financial, religious, psychiatric*) établissement *m*; **educational i.** établissement *m* scolaire. ●**institutional** *a* institutionnel.
instruct [ɪnˈstrʌkt] *vt* (*teach*) enseigner (**s.o. in sth** qch à qn); **to i. s.o. about sth** (*inform*) instruire qn de qch; **to i. s.o. to do** (*order*) charger qn de faire.
instruction [ɪnˈstrʌkʃ(ə)n] *n* (*teaching*) instruction *f*; **instructions** (*orders*) instructions *fpl*; **instructions (for use)** mode *m* d'emploi.
instructive [ɪnˈstrʌktɪv] *a* instructif.
instructor [ɪnˈstrʌktər] *n* (*for judo, dance etc*) professeur *m*; (*for skiing, swimming etc*) moniteur, -trice *mf*; (*military*) instructeur *m*; (*in American university*) maître-assistant, -ante *mf*; **driving i.** moniteur, -trice *mf* d'auto-école.
instrument [ˈɪnstrəmənt] *n* instrument *m*.
instrumental [ɪnstrəˈment(ə)l] *a* (*music*) instrumental; **to be i. in sth/in doing sth** contribuer à qch/à faire qch. ●**instrumentalist** *n* (*performer*) instrumentaliste *mf*.
instrumentation [ɪnstrəmənˈteɪʃ(ə)n] *n Mus* orchestration *f*.

insubordinate [ɪnsə'bɔːdɪnət] *a* indiscipliné.
● **insubordination** [-'neɪʃ(ə)n] *n* indiscipline
f.

insubstantial [ɪnsəb'stænʃ(ə)l] *a* (*argument,
evidence*) peu solide.

insufferable [ɪn'sʌfərəb(ə)l] *a* intolérable.

insufficient [ɪnsə'fɪʃənt] *a* insuffisant. ● **in-
sufficiently** *adv* insuffisamment.

insular ['ɪnsjʊlər] *a* (*climate*) insulaire;
(*views*) étroit, borné.

insulate ['ɪnsjʊleɪt] *vt* (*against cold etc, and
electrically*) isoler; (*against sound*) insonoriser; **to i. s.o. from** *Fig* protéger qn de; **insulating tape** chatterton *m*. ● **insulation**
[-'leɪʃ(ə)n] *n* isolation *f*; (*against sound*) insonorisation *f*; (*material*) isolant *m*.

insulin ['ɪnsjʊlɪn] *n* insuline *f*.

insult [ɪn'sʌlt] *vt* insulter ▮ ['ɪnsʌlt] *n* insulte *f*
(**to** à). ● **insulting** *a* (*words, offer etc*) insultant.

insuperable [ɪn'suːpərəb(ə)l] *a* insurmontable.

insure [ɪn'ʃʊər] *vt* **1** (*house, car, goods etc*)
assurer (**against** contre). **2** *Am* = **ensure**.
● **insurance** *n* assurance *f*; **i. company**
compagnie *f* d'assurances; **i. policy** police *f*
d'assurance.

insurgent [ɪn'sɜːdʒənt] *n* insurgé, -ée *mf*.

insurmountable [ɪnsə'maʊntəb(ə)l] *a* insurmontable.

insurrection [ɪnsə'rekʃ(ə)n] *n* insurrection *f*.

intact [ɪn'tækt] *a* intact.

intake ['ɪnteɪk] *n* (*of food*) consommation *f*;
(*of students, schoolchildren*) admissions *fpl*;
(*of recruits*) contingent *m*; (*of gas, air etc*)
Tech admission *f*.

intangible [ɪn'tændʒəb(ə)l] *a* intangible.

integral ['ɪntɪɡrəl] *a* intégral; **to be an i. part
of** faire partie intégrante de.

integrate ['ɪntɪɡreɪt] *vt* intégrer (**into** dans);
integrated school/*etc* école *f*/*etc* où se pratique la déségrégation raciale ▮ *vi* s'intégrer
(**into** dans); ● **integration** [-'ɡreɪʃ(ə)n] *n* intégration *f*; (**racial**) **i. déségrégation** *f* raciale.

integrity [ɪn'teɡrɪtɪ] *n* intégrité *f*.

intellect ['ɪntɪlekt] *n* (*faculty*) intelligence *f*,
intellect *m*; (*cleverness, person*) intelligence
f. ● **inte'llectual** *a* & *n* intellectuel, -elle
(*mf*).

intelligence [ɪn'telɪdʒəns] *n* intelligence *f*;
(*information about enemy*) renseignements
mpl.

intelligent [ɪn'telɪdʒənt] *a* intelligent. ● **intelligently** *adv* intelligemment.

intelligentsia [ɪntelɪ'dʒentsɪə] *n* intelligentsia *f*.

intelligible [ɪn'telɪdʒəb(ə)l] *a* compréhensible, intelligible. ● **intelligi'bility** *n* intelligibilité *f*.

intemperance [ɪn'tempərəns] *n* intempérance *f*.

intend [ɪn'tend] *vt* (*gift, remark etc*) destiner
(**for** à); **to be intended for s.o.** être destiné à
qn; **to be intended to do/be** être destiné à
faire/être; **to i. to do** avoir l'intention de

faire; **I i. you to stay** mon intention est que
vous restiez. ● **intended** *a* (*deliberate*) voulu,
intentionnel; (*planned*) projeté.

intense [ɪn'tens] *a* intense; (*interest*) vif;
(*person*) passionné. ● **intensely** *adv* (*to look
etc*) intensément; (*very*) *Fig* extrêmement.

intensify [ɪn'tensɪfaɪ] *vt* intensifier ▮ *vi*
s'intensifier. ● **intensification** [-'keɪʃ(ə)n] *n*
intensification *f*.

intensity [ɪn'tensətɪ] *n* intensité *f*.

intensive [ɪn'tensɪv] *a* intensif; **in i. care** en
réanimation; **i. care unit** service *m* de réanimation.

intent [ɪn'tent] **1** *a* (*look*) attentif; **i. on doing**
résolu à faire; **i. on one's task**/*etc* absorbé
par son travail/*etc*. **2** *n* intention *f*; **to all in-
tents and purposes** en fait, essentiellement.

intention [ɪn'tenʃ(ə)n] *n* intention *f* (**of doing**
de faire).

intentional [ɪn'tenʃ(ə)n(ə)l] *a* intentionnel; **it
wasn't i.** ce n'était pas fait exprès. ● **intentionally** *adv* exprès, intentionnellement.

inter [ɪn'tɜːr] *vt* (**-rr-**) enterrer.

inter- ['ɪntə(r)] *pref* inter-.

interact [ɪntə'rækt] *vi* (*of people*) agir conjointement; (*of ideas etc*) être interdé-
pendants; (*of chemicals*) interagir. ● **interaction** [-ʃ(ə)n] *n* interaction *f*. ● **interactive** *a*
Comptr interactif.

intercede [ɪntə'siːd] *vi* intercéder (**with**
auprès de).

intercept [ɪntə'sept] *vt* intercepter. ● **interception** [-ʃ(ə)n] *n* interception *f*.

interchange ['ɪntətʃeɪndʒ] *n* (*on road*) *Br*
échangeur *m*.

interchangeable [ɪntə'tʃeɪndʒəb(ə)l] *a*
interchangeable.

inter-city [ɪntə'sɪtɪ] *a* **i.-city train** *Br* train *m*
de grandes lignes; **i.-city service** *Br* (service
m) grandes lignes *fpl*.

intercom ['ɪntəkɒm] *n* interphone *m*.

interconnected [ɪntəkə'nektɪd] *a* (*facts etc*)
liés. ● **interconnecting** *a* **i. rooms** pièces *fpl*
communicantes.

intercontinental [ɪntəkɒntɪ'nent(ə)l] *a* intercontinental.

intercourse ['ɪntəkɔːs] *n* (*sexual*) rapports
mpl (sexuels).

interdependent [ɪntədɪ'pendənt] *a* interdépendant; (*parts of machine*) solidaire.

interest ['ɪnt(ə)rɪst, 'ɪntrest] *n* intérêt *m*;
(*money*) intérêts *mpl*; **an i. in a company**
(*stake*) une participation or des intérêts dans
une société; **his or her i. is** (*hobby etc*) ce
qui l'intéresse c'est; **to take an i. in sth/s.o.**
s'intéresser à qch/qn; **to lose i. in sth/s.o.** se
désintéresser de qch/qn; **to be of i. to s.o.**
intéresser qn.
▮ *vt* intéresser. ● **interested** *a* (*motive,
person*) intéressé; **i. party** partie *f* intéressée;
to seem i. sembler intéressé (**in par**); **to be
in sth/s.o.** s'intéresser à qch/qn; **I'm i. in
doing that** ça m'intéresse de faire ça; **are you
i.?** ça vous intéresse? ● **interesting** *a* intéressant. ● **interestingly** *adv* **i. (enough), she...**

curieusement, elle….

interface ['ɪntəfeɪs] n Comptr & Fig interface f.

interfere [ɪntə'fɪər] vi se mêler des affaires des autres; **to i. in** s'ingérer dans; **to i. with** (upset) déranger (projet etc); (touch) toucher (à). ●**interfering** a (person) qui se mêle de tout.

interference [ɪntə'fɪərəns] n ingérence f; (on radio) parasites mpl.

interim ['ɪntərɪm] **n in the i.** entre-temps ▮ a (measure etc) provisoire; (post) intérimaire.

interior [ɪn'tɪərɪər] a intérieur ▮ n intérieur m; **Department of the I.** Am ministère m de l'Intérieur.

interjection [ɪntə'dʒekʃ(ə)n] n Grammar interjection f.

interlock [ɪntə'lɒk] vi (of machine parts etc) s'emboîter.

interloper ['ɪntələʊpər] n intrus, -use mf.

interlude ['ɪntəluːd] n (on TV) interlude m; (in theatre) entracte m; (period of time) intervalle m.

intermarry [ɪntə'mærɪ] vi se marier (entre eux). ●**intermarriage** n mariage m (entre personnes de races etc différentes).

intermediary [ɪntə'miːdɪərɪ] a & n intermédiaire (mf).

intermediate [ɪntə'miːdɪət] a (stage etc) intermédiaire; (course, group) de niveau moyen.

interminable [ɪn'tɜːmɪnəb(ə)l] a interminable.

intermingle [ɪntə'mɪŋg(ə)l] vi se mélanger.

intermission [ɪntə'mɪʃ(ə)n] n Cinema Theatre entracte m.

intermittent [ɪntə'mɪtənt] a intermittent. ●**intermittently** adv par intermittence.

intern 1 [ɪn'tɜːn] vt (imprison) interner. **2** ['ɪntɜːn] n (doctor) Am interne mf (des hôpitaux). ●**inter'nee** n interné, -ée mf. ●**in'ternment** n Pol internement m.

internal [ɪn'tɜːn(ə)l] a interne; (flight, policy) intérieur; **i. combustion engine** moteur m à explosion; **the I. Revenue Service** Am le fisc, le service des impôts. ●**internally** adv intérieurement; 'not to be taken i.' (medicine) 'à usage externe'.

international [ɪntə'næʃ(ə)nəl] a international ▮ n (match) rencontre f internationale; (player) international m. ●**internationally** adv i, famous mondialement connu; **i. recognized** reconnu dans le monde entier.

interplanetary [ɪntə'plænɪt(ə)rɪ] a interplanétaire.

interplay ['ɪntəpleɪ] n interaction f, jeu m.

interpolate [ɪn'tɜːpəleɪt] vt interpoler.

interpret [ɪn'tɜːprɪt] vt interpréter ▮ vi (translate for people) faire l'interprète. ●**interpretation** [-'teɪʃ(ə)n] n interprétation f. ●**interpreter** n interprète mf.

interrelated [ɪntərɪ'leɪtɪd] a en corrélation. ●**interrelation** [-ʃ(ə)n] n corrélation f.

interrogate [ɪn'terəgeɪt] vt (question closely) interroger. ●**interrogation** [-'geɪʃ(ə)n] n interrogation f; (by police) interrogatoire m. ●**interrogator** n (questioner) interrogateur, -trice mf.

interrogative [ɪntə'rɒgətɪv] a & n Grammar interrogatif (m).

interrupt [ɪntə'rʌpt] vt interrompre. ●**interruption** [-ʃ(ə)n] n interruption f.

intersect [ɪntə'sekt] vt couper ▮ vi (of roads, lines etc) se couper, s'entrecouper. ●**intersection** [-ʃ(ə)n] n (crossroads) croisement m, intersection f; (of lines etc) intersection f.

interspersed [ɪntə'spɜːst] a i. with (quotations, flowers etc) parsemé de; **weeks of work i. with visits to the theatre** des semaines de travail entrecoupées de sorties au théâtre.

intertwine [ɪntə'twaɪn] vt entrelacer.

interval ['ɪntəv(ə)l] n intervalle m; (in theatre, cinema) Br entracte m; **at intervals** (time) de temps à autre; (space) par intervalles; **at five-minute intervals** toutes les cinq minutes; **bright** or **sunny intervals** éclaircies fpl.

intervene [ɪntə'viːn] vi (of person) intervenir; (of event) survenir; **ten years intervened** dix années s'écoulèrent; **if nothing intervenes** s'il n'arrive rien entre-temps. ●**intervention** [-'venʃ(ə)n] n intervention f.

interview ['ɪntəvjuː] n entrevue f, entretien m (with avec); (on TV etc) interview f; **to call s.o. for** or **to an i.** convoquer qn ▮ vt avoir une entrevue avec; (on TV etc) interviewer [-vjuve]. ●**interviewer** n (on TV etc) interviewer [-vjuvœr] m; (for research, in canvassing) enquêteur, -euse mf.

intestine [ɪn'testɪn] n intestin m.

intimate¹ ['ɪntɪmət] a intime; (friendship) profond; (knowledge, analysis) approfondi. ●**intimacy** n intimité f. ●**intimately** adv intimement.

intimate² ['ɪntɪmeɪt] vt (hint) suggérer (that que). ●**intimation** [-'meɪʃ(ə)n] n (announcement) annonce f; (hint) suggestion f; (sign) indication f.

intimidate [ɪn'tɪmɪdeɪt] vt intimider. ●**intimidation** [-'deɪʃ(ə)n] n intimidation f.

into ['ɪntuː, unstressed 'ɪntə] prep **1** dans; **to put i.** mettre dans; **to go i.** (room, detail) entrer dans.

2 en; **to translate i.** traduire en; **to change s.o. i.** transformer or changer qn en; **to go i. town** aller en ville; **to break i. pieces** briser en morceaux.

3 Math **three i. six goes two** six divisé par trois fait deux.

4 to be i. yoga/etc Fam être à fond dans le yoga/etc.

intolerable [ɪn'tɒlərəb(ə)l] a intolérable (that que + sub). ●**intolerably** adv insupportablement.

intolerance [ɪn'tɒlərəns] n intolérance f. ●**intolerant** a intolérant (of de). ●**intolerantly** adv avec intolérance.

intonation [ɪntə'neɪʃ(ə)n] n (of voice) intonation f.

intoxicate [ɪn'tɒksɪkeɪt] vt enivrer. ●**intoxi-**

cated a ivre. ● **intoxication** [-'keɪʃ(ə)n] n
ivresse f.

intra- ['ɪntrə] pref intra-.

intractable [ɪn'træktəb(ə)l] a (person) intraitable; (problem) épineux.

intransigent [ɪn'trænsɪdʒənt] a intransigeant. ● **intransigence** n intransigeance f.

intransitive [ɪn'trænsɪtɪv] a Grammar intransitif.

intravenous [ɪntrə'viːnəs] a Med intraveineux.

in-tray ['ɪntreɪ] n (in office) corbeille f (du
courrier) 'arrivée'.

intrepid [ɪn'trepɪd] a intrépide.

intricate ['ɪntrɪkət] a complexe, compliqué.
● **intricacy** n complexité f. ● **intricately** adv
de façon complexe.

intrigue 1 [ɪn'triːg] vt (interest) intriguer; **I'm
intrigued to know...** je suis curieux de savoir.... **2** ['ɪntriːg] n (plot) intrigue f. ● **intriguing** a (news, attitude etc) curieux.

intrinsic [ɪn'trɪnsɪk] a intrinsèque. ● **intrinsically** adv intrinsèquement.

introduce [ɪntrə'djuːs] vt (bring in, insert) introduire (into dans); (programme, subject)
présenter; **to i. s.o. (to s.o.)** présenter qn (à
qn); **to i. oneself (to s.o.)** se présenter (à qn);
to i. s.o. to Dickens/geography/etc faire découvrir Dickens/la géographie/etc à qn.

introduction [ɪntrə'dʌkʃ(ə)n] n introduction
f; (of person to person) présentation f; (book
title) initiation f; **her i. to** (life abroad etc)
son premier contact avec; **letter of i.** lettre f
de recommandation (to s.o. auprès de qn).

introductory [ɪntrə'dʌktərɪ] a (words)
d'introduction; (speech) de présentation;
(course) d'initiation; **i. price** prix m de lancement.

introspective [ɪntrə'spektɪv] a introspectif.
● **introspection** [-ʃ(ə)n] n introspection f.

introvert ['ɪntrəvɜːt] n introverti, -ie mf.

intrude [ɪn'truːd] vi (of person) déranger (on
s.o. qn), s'imposer (on s.o. à qn); **to i. on
s.o.'s time** abuser du temps de qn; **to i. on
s.o.'s privacy** porter atteinte à la vie privée
de qn. ● **intruder** n intrus, -use mf. ● **intrusion** [-ʒ(ə)n] n (bother) dérangement m;
(interference) intrusion f (into dans); **forgive
my i.** pardonnez-moi de vous avoir dérangé.

intuition [ɪntjuː'ɪʃ(ə)n] n intuition f.
● **in'tuitive** a intuitif.

Inuit ['ɪnjuːɪt] n Inuit m inv ▌ a inuit inv.

inundate ['ɪnʌndeɪt] vt inonder (with de); inundated with work/letters/etc submergé de
travail/lettres/etc. ● **inundation** [-'deɪʃ(ə)n] n
inondation f.

invade [ɪn'veɪd] vt envahir; **to i. s.o.'s privacy** violer la vie privée de qn. ● **invader** n
envahisseur, -euse mf.

invalid¹ ['ɪnvəlɪd] a & n malade (mf);
(through injury) infirme (mf); **i. car** Br
voiture f d'infirme.

invalid² [ɪn'vælɪd] a (ticket etc) non valable.
● **invalidate** vt (ticket etc) annuler; (election,
law etc) invalider.

invaluable [ɪn'væljʊəb(ə)l] a (help etc)
inestimable.

invariable [ɪn'veərɪəb(ə)l] a invariable. ● **invariably** adv (always) toujours.

invasion [ɪn'veɪʒ(ə)n] n invasion f; **i. of
s.o.'s privacy** atteinte f à la vie privée de qn.

invective [ɪn'vektɪv] n invective f.

inveigh [ɪn'veɪ] vi **to i. against** invectiver
contre.

inveigle [ɪn'veɪg(ə)l] vt **to i. s.o. into doing
sth** amener qn à faire qch par la ruse.

invent [ɪn'vent] vt inventer. ● **invention**
[-ʃ(ə)n] n invention f. ● **inventive** a inventif.
● **inventiveness** n esprit m d'invention. ● **inventor** n inventeur, -trice mf.

inventory ['ɪnvənt(ə)rɪ] n inventaire m.

inverse [ɪn'vɜːs] a inverse; **in i. proportion to**
inversement proportionnel à.

invert [ɪn'vɜːt] vt (order etc) intervertir; (object) retourner; **inverted commas** Br guillemets mpl. ● **inversion** [-ʃ(ə)n] n interversion
f; Grammar Anat etc inversion f.

invest [ɪn'vest] vt (money) placer, investir (in
dans); (funds) investir (in dans); (time,
effort) consacrer (in à); **to i. s.o. with** (endow) investir qn de ▌ vi **to i. in** (project) placer son argent dans; (company) investir
dans; (new house, radio etc) Fig se payer.

investigate [ɪn'vestɪgeɪt] vt (examine) examiner, étudier; (crime) enquêter sur ▌ vi **to go
and i.** Fam aller voir ce qui se passe. ● **investigation** [-'geɪʃ(ə)n] n examen m, étude f;
(inquiry by journalist, police etc) enquête f
(of, into sur). ● **investigator** n (detective) enquêteur, -euse mf; (private) détective m.

investiture [ɪn'vestɪtʃ(ə)r] n (of bishop etc)
investiture f.

investment [ɪn'vestmənt] n investissement
m, placement m. ● **investor** n (in shares)
actionnaire mf; (saver) épargnant, -ante mf.

inveterate [ɪn'vetərət] a invétéré.

invidious [ɪn'vɪdɪəs] a qui suscite la jalousie;
(hurtful) blessant; (odious) odieux.

invigilate [ɪn'vɪdʒɪlet] vi (in school etc) Br
être de surveillance (à un examen). ● **invigilator** n Br surveillant, -ante mf.

invigorate [ɪn'vɪgəreɪt] vt revigorer. ● **invigorating** a stimulant.

invincible [ɪn'vɪnsəb(ə)l] a invincible.

invisible [ɪn'vɪzəb(ə)l] a invisible; **i. ink** encre f sympathique.

invite [ɪn'vaɪt] vt inviter (to do à faire); (ask
for) demander; (give occasion for) provoquer (critiques, doutes etc); **you're inviting
trouble** tu cherches des ennuis; **to i. s.o. out**
inviter qn (à sortir); **to i. s.o. over** inviter qn
(à venir) ▌ ['ɪnvaɪt] n Fam invitation f. ● **inviting** a (prospect etc) engageant, séduisant;
(food) appétissant. ● **invitation** [-'teɪʃ(ə)n] n
invitation f.

invoice ['ɪnvɔɪs] n facture f ▌ vt facturer.

invoke [ɪn'vəʊk] vt invoquer.

involuntary [ɪn'vɒləntərɪ] a involontaire.
● **involuntarily** adv involontairement.

involve [ɪn'vɒlv] vt (include) mêler (qn) (in

à), impliquer (*qn*) (**in** dans); (*associate*) associer (*qn*) (**in** à); (*entail*) entraîner; **to i. oneself, get involved** (*commit oneself*) s'engager (**in** dans); **to i. s.o. in expense** entraîner qn à des dépenses; **the job involves going abroad** le poste nécessite des déplacements à l'étranger.

involved [ɪn'vɒlvd] *a* (*concerned*) concerné; (*committed*) engagé (**in** dans); (*complicated*) compliqué; **the factors/etc i.** (*at stake*) les facteurs/etc en jeu; **the person i.** la personne en question; **i. with s.o.** mêlé aux affaires de qn; **personally i.** (*directement*) concerné; **emotionally i. with s.o.** amoureux de qn; **to become i.** (*of police*) intervenir.

involvement [ɪn'vɒlvmənt] *n* participation *f* (**in** à), implication *f* (**in** dans); (*commitment*) engagement *m* (**in** dans); **emotional i.** liaison *f*.

invulnerable [ɪn'vʌln(ə)rəb(ə)l] *a* invulnérable.

inward ['ɪnwəd] *a & adv* (*movement, to move*) vers l'intérieur ▌ *a* (*inner*) (*happiness etc*) intérieur; (*thoughts etc*) intime. ●**inward-looking** *a* replié sur soi. ●**inwardly** *adv* (*to laugh, curse etc*) intérieurement; (*inside*) à l'intérieur. ●**inwards** [-wədz] *adv* vers l'intérieur.

iodine [*Br* 'aɪədiːn, *Am* 'aɪədaɪn] *n* (*antiseptic*) teinture *f* d'iode.

iota [aɪ'əʊtə] *n* (*of truth, guilt etc*) brin *m*, once *f*.

IOU [aɪəʊ'juː] *n abbr* (*I owe you*) reconnaissance *f* de dette.

IQ [aɪ'kjuː] *n abbr* (*intelligence quotient*) QI *m inv*.

Iran [ɪ'rɑːn, ɪ'ræn] *n* Iran *m*. ●**Iranian** [ɪ'reɪnɪən, *Am* ɪ'rɑːnɪən] *a* iranien ▌ *n* Iranien, -ienne *mf*.

Iraq [ɪ'rɑːk] *n* Irak *m*. ●**Iraqi** *a* irakien ▌ *n* Irakien, -ienne *mf*.

irascible [ɪ'ræsəb(ə)l] *a* irascible.

ire [aɪər] *n Lit* courroux *m*. ●**irate** [aɪ'reɪt] *a* furieux.

Ireland ['aɪələnd] *n* Irlande *f*. ●**Irish** *a* irlandais ▌ *n* (*language*) irlandais *m*; **the I.** (*people*) les Irlandais *mpl*. ●**Irishman** *n* (*pl -men*) Irlandais *m*. ●**Irishwoman** *n* (*pl -women*) Irlandaise *f*.

iris ['aɪərɪs] *n* (*plant, of eye*) iris *m*.

irk [ɜːk] *vt* ennuyer. ●**irksome** [ˈsɔm] *a* ennuyeux.

iron ['aɪən] *n* fer *m*; (*for clothes*) fer *m* (à repasser); **old i., scrap i.** *Br* ferraille *f*; **i. and steel industry** sidérurgie *f* ▌ *vt* (*clothes*) repasser; **to i. out** (*difficulties*) aplanir. ●**ironing** *n* repassage *m*; **i. board** planche *f* à repasser.

ironmonger ['aɪənmʌŋgər] *n* quincaillier, -ière *mf*; **i.'s shop** quincaillerie *f*. ●**ironmongery** *n* quincaillerie *f*.

ironwork ['aɪənwɜːk] *n* ferronnerie *f*.

irony ['aɪərənɪ] *n* ironie *f*. ●**i'ronic(al)** *a* ironique.

irradiate [ɪ'reɪdɪeɪt] *vt* (*subject to radiation*) irradier; **irradiated food** aliments *mpl* irradiés.

irrational [ɪ'ræʃən(ə)l] *a* (*person*) peu rationnel, illogique; (*act*) irrationnel; (*fear*) irraisonné.

irreconcilable [ɪrekən'saɪləb(ə)l] *a* (*people*) irréconciliable, inconciliable; (*views, laws etc*) inconciliable.

irrefutable [ɪrɪ'fjuːtəb(ə)l] *a* (*evidence etc*) irréfutable.

irregular [ɪ'regjʊlər] *a* irrégulier. ●**irre-gu'larity** *n* irrégularité *f*.

irrelevant [ɪ'reləvənt] *a* sans rapport (**to** avec); (*remark*) non pertinent; (*useless*) (*activity, course*) peu utile; **that's i.** ça n'a rien à voir. ●**irrelevance** *n* manque *m* de rapport.

irreparable [ɪ'rep(ə)rəb(ə)l] *a* (*harm, loss*) irréparable.

irreplaceable [ɪrɪ'pleɪsəb(ə)l] *a* irremplaçable.

irrepressible [ɪrɪ'presəb(ə)l] *a* (*laughter etc*) irrépressible.

irreproachable [ɪrɪ'prəʊtʃəb(ə)l] *a* irréprochable.

irresistible [ɪrɪ'zɪstəb(ə)l] *a* (*person, charm etc*) irrésistible.

irresolute [ɪ'rezəluːt] *a* irrésolu, indécis.

irrespective of [ɪrɪ'spektɪvəv] *prep* sans tenir compte de.

irresponsible [ɪrɪ'sponsəb(ə)l] *a* (*act*) irréfléchi; (*person*) irresponsable. ●**irresponsibly** *adv* (*to behave*) de façon irresponsable.

irretrievable [ɪrɪ'triːvəb(ə)l] *a* irréparable.

irreverent [ɪ'revərənt] *a* irrévérencieux.

irreversible [ɪrɪ'vɜːsəb(ə)l] *a* (*process*) irréversible; (*decision*) irrévocable.

irrevocable [ɪ'revəkəb(ə)l] *a* irrévocable.

irrigate ['ɪrɪgeɪt] *vt* irriguer. ●**irrigation** [-'geɪʃ(ə)n] *n* irrigation *f*.

irritable ['ɪrɪtəb(ə)l] *a* (*easily annoyed*) irritable.

irritant ['ɪrɪtənt] *n* irritant *m*.

irritate ['ɪrɪteɪt] *vt* (*annoy, inflame*) irriter. ●**irritating** *a* irritant.

irritation [ɪrɪ'teɪʃ(ə)n] *n* (*anger, inflammation*) irritation *f*.

IRS [aɪɑːr'es] *n abbr Am* = **Internal Revenue Service.**

is [ɪz] *see* **be.**

Islam ['ɪzlɑːm] *n* islam *m*. ●**Islamic** [ɪz'læmɪk] *a* islamique.

island ['aɪlənd] *n* île *f*; (*traffic*) **i.** refuge *m* (*pour piétons*). ●**islander** *n* insulaire *mf*.

isle [aɪl] *n* île *f*; **the British Isles** les îles Britanniques.

isn't ['ɪz(ə)nt] = **is not.**

isolate ['aɪsəleɪt] *vt* isoler (**from** de). ●**isolated** *a* (*remote, unique*) isolé. ●**isolation** [-'leɪʃ(ə)n] *n* isolement *m*; **in i.** isolément.

Israel ['ɪzreɪl] *n* Israël *m*. ●**Is'raeli** *a* israélien ▌ *n* Israélien, -ienne *mf*.

issue ['ɪʃuː] *vt* (*book etc*) publier; (*tickets*) distribuer; (*passport*) délivrer; (*an order*) donner; (*warning*) lancer; (*stamps, bank-*

notes) émettre; (*supply*) fournir (**with** de, **to à**). ▌ *vi* **to i. from** (*of smell*) se dégager de; (*stem from*) provenir de.

▌ *n* (*of newspaper, magazine*) numéro *m*; (*matter*) question *f*; (*problem*) problème *m*; (*outcome*) résultat *m*; (*of text*) publication *f*; (*of stamps etc*) émission *f*; **at i.** (*at stake*) en cause; **to make an i. or a big i. of sth** faire toute une affaire de qch; **to take i. with s.o.** être en désaccord avec qn.

isthmus ['ɪsməs] *n Geog* isthme *m*.

it [ɪt] *pron* **1** (*subject*) il, elle; (*object*) le, la, l'; (*to*) **it** (*indirect object*) lui; **it bites** (*dog etc*) il mord; **I've done it** je l'ai fait.

2 (*impersonal*) il; **it's snowing** il neige; **it's hot** il fait chaud.

3 (*non specific*) ce, cela, ça; **it's good** c'est bon; **it was pleasant** c'était agréable; **who is it?** qui est-ce?; **that's it!** (*I agree*) c'est ça!; (*it's done*) ça y est!; **to consider it wise to do sth** juger prudent de faire qch; **it was Paul who...** c'est Paul qui...; **she's got it in her to succeed** elle est capable de réussir; **to have it in for s.o.** en vouloir à qn.

4 of it, from it, about it en; **in it, to it, at it** y; **on it** dessus; **under it** dessous.

italic [ɪ'tælɪk] *a* (*character etc*) italique. ●**italics** *npl* italique *m*; **in i.** en italique.

Italy ['ɪtəlɪ] *n* Italie *f*. ●**I'talian** *a* italien ▌ *n* (*language*) italien *m*; (*person*) Italien, -ienne *mf*.

itch [ɪtʃ] *n* démangeaison(s) *f(pl)*; **to have an i. to do** avoir une envie folle de faire ▌ *vi* (*of leg etc*) démanger; (*of person*) avoir des démangeaisons; **his arm itches** son bras le *or* lui démange; **I'm itching to do** ça me démange de faire. ●**itching** *n* démangeaison(s) *f(pl)*. ●**itchy** *a* **I have an i. hand** j'ai une main qui me démange; **I'm (all) i.** j'ai des démangeaisons.

item ['aɪtəm] *n* (*object for sale, on list, in newspaper etc*) article *m*; (*matter*) question *f*; (*on entertainment programme*) numéro *m*; **i. of clothing** vêtement *m*; **news i.** information *f*. ●**itemize** *vt* (*invoice etc*) détailler.

itinerant [aɪ'tɪnərənt] *a* (*musician, actor*) ambulant; (*judge, preacher*) itinérant.

itinerary [aɪ'tɪnərərɪ] *n* itinéraire *m*.

its [ɪts] *poss a* son, sa, *pl* ses. ●**it'self** *pron* lui-même, elle-même; (*reflexive*) se, s'; **goodness i.** la bonté même; **by i.** tout seul.

IUD [aɪjuː'diː] *n abbr* (*intrauterine device*) stérilet *m*.

ivory ['aɪvərɪ] *n* ivoire *m*; **i. statuette/etc** statuette *f/etc* en ivoire.

ivy ['aɪvɪ] *n* lierre *m*.

J

J, j [dʒeɪ] n J, j m.

jab [dʒæb] vt (-bb-) (knife, stick etc) enfoncer (into dans); (prick) piquer (qn) (with sth du bout de qch) ▮ n coup m (sec); (injection) Br Fam piqûre f.

jabber ['dʒæbər] vi bavarder, jaser ▮ vt to j. out (excuse etc) bredouiller. ●jabbering n bavardage m.

jack [dʒæk] 1 n (for vehicle) cric m ▮ vt to j. up (vehicle) soulever (avec un cric); (price) Fig augmenter. 2 n Cards valet m. 3 vt to j. (in) (job etc) Br Fam plaquer. 4 n j. of all trades homme m à tout faire. ●jack-in-the-box n diable m (à ressort).

jackal ['dʒæk(ə)l] n (animal) chacal m.

jackass ['dʒækæs] n (fool) idiot, -ote mf.

jackdaw ['dʒækdɔː] n (bird) choucas m.

jacket ['dʒækɪt] n (short coat) veste f; (of man's suit) veston m; (of woman) veste f, jaquette f; (bulletproof) Br gilet m; (dust) j. (of book) jaquette f; **j. potato,** potato in its **j.** Br pomme f de terre en robe des champs.

jack-knife ['dʒæknaɪf] 1 n couteau m de poche. 2 vi (of truck, Br lorry) se mettre en travers de la route.

jackpot ['dʒækpɒt] n gros lot m.

jacks [dʒæks] npl (jeu m d')osselets mpl.

jacuzzi [dʒə'kuːzɪ] n (bath, pool) jacuzzi m.

jade [dʒeɪd] n 1 (stone) jade m. 2 (horse) rosse f, canasson m.

jaded ['dʒeɪdɪd] a blasé.

jagged ['dʒægɪd] a déchiqueté.

jaguar [Br 'dʒægjuər, Am -wɑːr] n (animal) jaguar m.

jail [dʒeɪl] n prison f ▮ vt emprisonner (for theft/etc pour vol/etc); **to j. s.o. for ten years** condamner qn à dix ans de prison; **to j. s.o. for life** condamner qn à perpétuité. ●jailer n gardien, -ienne mf de prison.

jalopy [dʒə'lɒpɪ] n (car) Fam vieux tacot m.

jam¹ [dʒæm] n (preserve) confiture f; **strawberry/etc j.** confiture f de fraises/etc. ●jamjar n pot m à confiture.

jam² [dʒæm] n (traffic) **j.** embouteillage m; **in a j.** (trouble) Fam dans le pétrin.
2 vt (-mm-) (squeeze, make stuck) coincer, bloquer; (gun) enrayer; (street, corridor etc) encombrer; (building) envahir; (broadcast, radio station) brouiller; **to j. sth into** (pack, cram) (en)tasser qch dans; **to j. people into** (en)tasser des gens dans; **to j. a stick/etc into** (poke, thrust) enfoncer un bâton/etc dans; **to j. on** (brakes) bloquer.
▮ vi (get stuck) se coincer, se bloquer; (of gun) s'enrayer; **to j. into** (of crowd) s'entasser dans. ●jammed a (machine etc)

coincé, bloqué; (street etc) encombré. ●jam-'packed a (hall, train etc) bourré de monde.

Jamaica [dʒə'meɪkə] n Jamaïque f.

jangle ['dʒæŋg(ə)l] vi cliqueter ▮ n cliquetis m. ●jangling a (noise) discordant.

janitor ['dʒænɪtər] n (caretaker) Am concierge m.

January ['dʒænjuərɪ] n janvier m.

Japan [dʒə'pæn] n Japon m. ●Japa'nese a japonais ▮ n (language) japonais m ▮ n inv (person) Japonais, -aise mf.

jar [dʒɑːr] 1 n (container) pot m; (large, glass) bocal m. 2 n (jolt) choc m ▮ vt (-rr-) (shake) ébranler. 3 vi (-rr-) (of noise) grincer; (of musical note) détonner; (of colours, words) jurer (with avec); **it jars on my nerves** cela me tape sur les nerfs; **it jars on my ears** cela m'écorche les oreilles. ●jarring a (noise, voice) discordant.

jargon ['dʒɑːgən] n jargon m.

jasmine ['dʒæzmɪn] n (shrub) jasmin m.

jaundice ['dʒɔːndɪs] n (illness) jaunisse f. ●jaundiced a (bitter) aigri; **to take a j. view of sth** voir qch d'un mauvais œil.

jaunt [dʒɔːnt] n (journey) balade f.

jaunty ['dʒɔːntɪ] a (-ier, -iest) (carefree) insouciant; (cheerful, lively) allègre; (hat etc) coquet, chic. ●jauntily adv avec insouciance; (cheerfully) allègrement.

javelin ['dʒævlɪn] n javelot m.

jaw [dʒɔː] 1 n Anat mâchoire f. 2 vi (talk) Pej Fam papoter ▮ n **to have a j.** Pej Fam tailler une bavette.

jay [dʒeɪ] n (bird) geai m.

jaywalker ['dʒeɪwɔːkər] n piéton m imprudent. ●jaywalking n imprudence f (de piéton).

jazz [dʒæz] n jazz m ▮ vt **to j. up** Fam (enliven) animer; (clothes, room) égayer; (music) jazzifier.

JCB® [dʒeɪsiː'biː] n Br tractopelle m or f.

jealous ['dʒeləs] a jaloux (f -ouse) (of de). ●jealousy n jalousie f.

jeans [dʒiːnz] npl (pair of) **j.** jean m.

jeep® [dʒiːp] n jeep® f.

jeer [dʒɪər] vti **to j. (at)** (mock) railler; (boo) huer ▮ n raillerie f; **jeers** (boos) huées fpl. ●jeering a railleur ▮ n (mocking) railleries fpl; (of crowd) huées fpl.

jell [dʒel] vi (of ideas etc) Fam prendre tournure.

jello® ['dʒeləʊ] n inv (dessert) Am gelée f. ●jellied a (eel etc) Br en gelée. ●jelly n (preserve, Br dessert) gelée f. ●jellyfish n méduse f.

jeopardy ['dʒepədɪ] n danger m, péril m.

● **jeopardize** *vt* mettre en danger *or* en péril.

jerk [dʒɜːk] **1** *vt* donner une secousse à (*pour tirer, pousser etc*) ▮ *n* secousse *f*, saccade *f*. **2** *n* (*person*) (**stupid**) j. *Fam* crétin, -ine *mf*, abruti, -ie *mf*.

jerky ['dʒɜːkɪ] *a* (**-ier, -iest**) **1** (*movement, voice etc*) saccadé. **2** (*stupid*) *Am Fam* stupide, bête. ● **jerkily** *adv* par saccades.

jersey ['dʒɜːzɪ] *n* (*garment*) tricot *m* (de laine); *Football* maillot *m*; (*cloth*) jersey *m*.

Jersey ['dʒɜːzɪ] *n* Jersey *f*.

jest [dʒest] *n* plaisanterie *f*; **in j.** pour rire ▮ *vi* plaisanter. ● **jester** *n* (*court*) j. *Hist* bouffon *m* (du roi).

Jesus ['dʒiːzəs] *n* Jésus *m*; **J. Christ** Jésus-Christ *m*.

jet [dʒet] **1** *n* (*plane*) avion *m* à réaction; **j. engine** réacteur *m*, moteur *m* à réaction; **j. lag** fatigue *f* (due au décalage horaire) ▮ *vi* **to j. off** *Fam* s'envoler (to pour). **2** *n* (*steam, liquid etc*) jet *m*.

jet-black [dʒet'blæk] *a* (noir) de jais, noir comme (du) jais.

jetfoil ['dʒetfɔɪl] *n* hydroglisseur *m*.

jet-lagged ['dʒetlægd] *a Fam* qui souffre du décalage horaire.

jettison ['dʒetɪs(ə)n] *vt* (*cargo from ship*) jeter à la mer; (*fuel from plane*) larguer; *Fig* abandonner.

jetty ['dʒetɪ] *n* jetée *f*; (*landing place*) embarcadère *m*.

Jew [dʒuː] *n* (*man*) Juif *m*; (*woman*) Juive *f*. ● **Jewess** *n* Juive *f*. ● **Jewish** *a* juif.

jewel ['dʒuːəl] *n* bijou *m* (*pl* **-oux**); (*in watch*) rubis *m*. ● **jewelled** *or Am* **jeweled** *a* orné de bijoux. ● **jeweller** *or Am* **jeweler** *n* bijoutier, -ière *mf*. ● **jewellery** *or Am* **jewelry** *n* bijoux *mpl*.

jib [dʒɪb] *vi* (**-bb-**) regimber (at devant); **to j. at doing** se refuser à faire.

jibe [dʒaɪb] *vi & n* = gibe.

jiffy ['dʒɪfɪ] *n Fam* instant *m*.

Jiffy bag® ['dʒɪfɪbæg] *n* enveloppe *f* matelassée.

jig [dʒɪg] *n* (*dance, music*) gigue *f*.

jigsaw ['dʒɪgsɔː] *n* **j. (puzzle)** puzzle *m*.

jilt [dʒɪlt] *vt* (*lover*) laisser tomber.

jingle ['dʒɪŋg(ə)l] **1** *vi* (*of keys, bell etc*) tinter ▮ *vt* faire tinter ▮ *n* tintement *m*. **2** *n* (*in TV etc advertisement*) sonal *m*, jingle *m*.

jinx [dʒɪŋks] *n* (*person, object*) porte-malheur *m inv*; (*spell, curse*) (mauvais) sort *m*, poisse *f*.

jitters ['dʒɪtəz] *npl* **to have the j.** *Fam* avoir la frousse. ● **jittery** *a* **to be j.** *Fam* avoir la frousse.

job [dʒɒb] *n* (*task, work*) travail *m*; (*employment, post*) poste *m*, emploi *m*, situation *f*; (*crime*) *Fam* coup *m*; **to have a (hard) j. doing** *or* **to do** (*much trouble*) *Fam* avoir du mal à faire; **to have the j. of doing** (*unpleasant task*) être obligé de faire; (*for a living etc*) être chargé de faire; **it's a good j. (that)** *Br Fam* heureusement que (+ *indic*); **that's just the j.** *Fam* c'est juste ce qu'il faut; **out of a j.** au chômage.

jobcentre ['dʒɒbsentər] *n Br* = agence *f* nationale pour l'emploi.

jobless ['dʒɒbləs] *a* au chômage, sans travail.

jock [dʒɒk] *n* (*sportsman*) *Am Fam* sportif *m*.

jockey ['dʒɒkɪ] **1** *n* jockey *m*. **2** *vi* **to j. for** (*position, job*) manœuvrer pour obtenir.

jockstrap ['dʒɒkstræp] *n* slip *m* à coquille.

ocular ['dʒɒkjʊlər] *a* jovial, amusant.

joey ['dʒəʊɪ] *n Fam* petit kangourou *m*.

jog [dʒɒg] **1** *n* (*shake, jolt*) secousse *f*; (*nudge*) coup *m* de coude ▮ *vt* (**-gg-**) (*shake*) secouer; (*push*) pousser (d'un coup sec); (*memory*) *Fig* rafraîchir. **2** *vi* (**-gg-**) **to j. along** (*of vehicle*) cahoter; (*of work*) aller tant bien que mal; (*of person*) faire son petit bonhomme de chemin. **3** *vi* (**-gg-**) *Sport* faire du jogging. ● **jogging** *n Sport* jogging *m*.

john [dʒɒn] *n* **the j.** (*lavatory*) *Am Fam* le petit coin.

join [dʒɔɪn] **1** *vt* (*put together*) joindre, réunir; (*wires, pipes*) raccorder; (*words, towns*) relier; **to j. sth to sth** joindre qch à qch; (*link*) relier qch à qch; **to j. s.o.** (*catch up with, meet*) rejoindre qn; (*associate oneself with, go with*) se joindre à qn (in doing pour faire); **to j. the sea** (*of river*) rejoindre la mer; **to j. hands** se donner la main; **to j. together** *or* **up** (*objects*) joindre.

▮ *vi* (*of roads, rivers etc*) se rejoindre; **to j. (together** *or* **up)** (*of objects*) se joindre (**with** à); **to j. in** prendre part, participer; **to j. in a game/etc** prendre part à un jeu/*etc*.

▮ *n* raccord *m*, joint *m*.

2 *vt* (*become a member of*) s'inscrire à (*club, parti*); (*army, police, company, group*) entrer dans; **to j. the** *Br* **queue** *or Am* **line** prendre la queue.

▮ *vi* (*become a member*) devenir membre; **to j. up** (*join the army etc*) s'engager.

joiner ['dʒɔɪnər] *n Br* menuisier *m*.

joint [dʒɔɪnt] **1** *n* (*in body*) articulation *f*; (*meat*) *Br* rôti *m*; *Tech* joint *m*; (*in carpentry*) assemblage *m*; **out of j.** (*shoulder etc*) déboîté. **2** *n* (*nightclub etc*) *Fam* boîte *f*. **3** *n* (*cannabis cigarette*) *Fam* joint *m*. **4** *a* (*decision etc*) commun; **j. account** compte *m* joint; **j. author** coauteur *m*; **j. efforts** efforts *mpl* conjugués. ● **jointly** *adv* conjointement.

joist [dʒɔɪst] *n* solive *f*.

joke [dʒəʊk] *n* plaisanterie *f*; (*trick*) tour *m*; **it's no j.** (*it's unpleasant*) ce n'est pas drôle (**doing** de faire) ▮ *vi* plaisanter (**about** sur). ● **joker** *n* plaisantin *m*; (*fellow*) *Fam* type *m*; *Cards* joker *m*. ● **jokingly** *adv* (*to say*) en plaisantant.

jolly[1] ['dʒɒlɪ] *a* (**-ier, -iest**) (*happy*) gai; (*drunk*) *Fam* éméché. ● **jollification** [-'keɪʃ(ə)n] *n* (*merry-making*) réjouissances *fpl*. ● **jollity** *n* jovialité *f*; (*merry-making*) réjouissances *fpl*.

jolly[2] ['dʒɒlɪ] *adv* (*very*) *Br Fam* rudement; **j. good!** très bien!

jolt [dʒəʊlt] vt (shake) secouer; **to j. s.o.** (of vehicle) cahoter or secouer qn; (shock, surprise) secouer qn ▌ vi to j. (along) (of vehicle) cahoter ▌ n cahot m, secousse f; (shock) secousse f.

Jordan ['dʒɔːd(ə)n] n Jordanie f.

jostle ['dʒɒs(ə)l] vti (push) bousculer; **don't j.!** ne bousculez pas! ▌ vi (push each other) se bousculer (**for sth** pour obtenir qch).

jot [dʒɒt] vt (-tt-) **to j. down** noter. ●**jotter** n (notepad) bloc-notes m.

journal ['dʒɜːn(ə)l] n (periodical) revue f. ●**journa'lese** n jargon m journalistique.

journalism ['dʒɜːnəlɪz(ə)m] n journalisme m. ●**journalist** n journaliste mf.

journey ['dʒɜːnɪ] n (trip) voyage m; (distance) trajet m; **to go on a j.** partir en voyage ▌ vi voyager.

jovial ['dʒəʊvɪəl] a jovial.

joy [dʒɔɪ] n joie f; **the joys of** (countryside, motherhood etc) les plaisirs mpl de. ●**joyful** or **joyous** a joyeux.

joyride ['dʒɔɪraɪd] n équipée f en voiture volée, rodéo m. ●**joyrider** n petit(e) voleur, -euse mf de voitures.

joystick ['dʒɔɪstɪk] n (of aircraft, computer) manche m à balai.

JP [dʒeɪ'piː] Br abbr = **Justice of the Peace.**

jubilant ['dʒuːbɪlənt] a **to be j.** jubiler. ●**jubilation** [-'leɪʃ(ə)n] n jubilation f.

jubilee ['dʒuːbɪliː] n (golden) j. jubilé m.

Judaism ['dʒuːdeɪɪz(ə)m] n judaïsme m.

judder ['dʒʌdər] vi (shake) vibrer ▌ n vibration f.

judge [dʒʌdʒ] n juge m ▌ vti juger; **judging by** à en juger par. ●**judg(e)ment** n jugement m.

judicial [dʒuː'dɪʃ(ə)l] a judiciaire.

judiciary [dʒuː'dɪʃ(ə)rɪ] n magistrature f.

judicious [dʒuː'dɪʃ(ə)s] a judicieux.

judo ['dʒuːdəʊ] n judo m.

jug [dʒʌg] n cruche f; (for milk) pot m.

juggernaut ['dʒʌgənɔːt] n (truck) Br poids m lourd, mastodonte m.

juggle ['dʒʌg(ə)l] vi jongler (**with** avec) ▌ vt jongler avec. ●**juggler** n jongleur, -euse mf.

juice [dʒuːs] n jus m; (in stomach) suc m. ●**juicy** a (-ier, -iest) (fruit) juteux; (meat) succulent; (story) Fig savoureux.

jukebox ['dʒuːkbɒks] n juke-box m.

July [dʒuː'laɪ] n juillet m.

jumble ['dʒʌmb(ə)l] vt to j. (up) (objects, facts etc) mélanger, brouiller ▌ n (disorder) fouillis m, pagaïe f; (unwanted articles) Br bric-à-brac m inv; **j. sale** Br (used clothes etc) vente f de charité; (for school etc) vente f (au profit de l'école etc).

jumbo ['dʒʌmbəʊ] a (packet etc) géant ▌ a & n (pl -os) (j. (jet) avion m géant, gros-porteur m, jumbo-jet m.

jump [dʒʌmp] n (leap) saut m, bond m; (start) sursaut m; (increase) hausse f; **j. leads** Br câbles mpl de démarrage; **j. rope** Am corde f à sauter.
▌ vi sauter (**at** sur); (start) sursauter; (of

price, heart) faire un bond; **to j. about** sautiller; **to j. across sth** traverser qch d'un bond; **to j. to conclusions** tirer des conclusions hâtives; **to j. in** or **on** (train, vehicle, bus) sauter or monter dans; **j. in** or **on!** montez!; **to j. off** or **out** sauter (from bus etc) descendre; **to j. off sth, j. out of sth** sauter de qch; **to j. out of the window** sauter par la fenêtre; **to j. up** se lever d'un bond.
▌ vt (ditch etc) sauter; **to j. the lights** (in vehicle) griller un feu rouge; **to j. the rails** (of train) dérailler; **to j. the queue** Br passer avant son tour, resquiller; **to j. rope** Am sauter à la corde.

jumper ['dʒʌmpər] n Br pull(-over) m; (dress) Am robe f chasuble; **j. cables** Am câbles mpl de démarrage.

jumpy ['dʒʌmpɪ] a (-ier, -iest) nerveux.

junction ['dʒʌŋkʃ(ə)n] n (crossroads) carrefour m; (joining) jonction f; **j. 23** (on motorway) Br (exit) la sortie 23; (entrance) l'entrée f 23.

juncture ['dʒʌŋktʃər] n **at this j.** (critical point in time) en ce moment même.

June [dʒuːn] n juin m.

jungle ['dʒʌŋg(ə)l] n jungle f.

junior ['dʒuːnɪər] a (younger) plus jeune (in rank, status etc) subalterne; (teacher, doctor) jeune; **to be s.o.'s j., be j. to s.o.** être plus jeune que qn; (in rank, status) être au-dessous de qn; **Smith J.** Smith fils or junior; **j. school** Br école f primaire (entre 7 et 11 ans); **j. high school** Am = collège m d'enseignement secondaire.
▌ n cadet, -ette mf; (in school) petit, -ite mf, petit(e) élève mf; Sport junior mf, cadet, -ette mf.

junk¹ [dʒʌŋk] 1 n (unwanted objects) bric-à-brac m inv; (metal) ferraille f; (inferior goods) camelote f; (waste) ordures fpl; (bad film, book etc) navet m; (nonsense) idioties fpl; **j. food** aliment m peu nutritif; **j. mail** courrier m publicitaire; **j. shop** (boutique f de) brocanteur m. ●**junkyard** n dépôt m de ferrailleur.

junk² [dʒʌŋk] vt (get rid of) Am Fam balancer.

junkie ['dʒʌŋkɪ] n Fam drogué, -ée mf.

junta [Br 'dʒʌntə, Am 'hʊntə] n Mil Pol junte f.

jurisdiction [dʒʊərɪs'dɪkʃ(ə)n] n juridiction f; **to be within the j.** of tomber sous la juridiction de.

jury ['dʒʊərɪ] n (in, competition, court) jury m. ●**juror** n (in court) juré m.

just [dʒʌst] 1 adv (exactly, slightly) juste; (only) juste, seulement; (simply) (tout) simplement; **j. before/after** juste avant/après; **it's j. as I thought** c'est bien ce que je pensais; **j. at that time** à cet instant même; **she has/had j. left** elle vient/venait de partir; **I've j. come from** j'arrive de; **I'm j. coming!** j'arrive!; **he'll (only) j. catch the bus** il aura son bus de justesse; **he j. missed it** il l'a manqué de peu; **j. as big/light/**etc tout aussi grand/léger/

etc (as que); **j. listen!** écoute donc!; **j. a moment!** un instant!; **j. over ten** un peu plus de dix; **j. one** un(e) seul(e) **(of** de); **j. about** *(approximately)* à peu près; *(almost)* presque; **to be j. about to do** être sur le point de faire.

2 *a (fair)* juste **(to** envers). ● **justly** *adv* avec justice, à juste titre. ● **justness** *n (of cause etc)* justice *f*.

justice ['dʒʌstɪs] *n* justice *f*; *(judge)* juge *m*; **to do j. to** *(meal)* faire honneur à; **it doesn't do you j.** *(hat, photo)* cela ne vous avantage pas; *(attitude)* cela ne vous fait pas honneur; **J. of the Peace** juge *m* de paix.

justify ['dʒʌstɪfaɪ] *vt* justifier; **to be justified in doing** *(have right)* être en droit de faire; *(have reason)* être fondé à faire. ● **justi'fiable** *a* justifiable. ● **justi'fiably** *adv* légitimement. ● **justification** [-'keɪʃ(ə)n] *n* justification *f*.

jut [dʒʌt] *vi* (**-tt-**) **to j. out** faire saillie; **to j. out over sth** *(overhang)* surplomber qch.

jute [dʒuːt] *n (fibre)* jute *m*.

juvenile ['dʒuːvənaɪl, *Am* -ən(ə)l] *n* adolescent, -ente *mf* ▌ *a (court, book etc)* pour enfants; *(behaviour)* puéril; **j. delinquent** jeune délinquant, -ante *mf*.

juxtapose [dʒʌkstə'pəuz] *vt* juxtaposer. ● **juxtaposition** [-pə'zɪʃ(ə)n] *n* juxtaposition *f*.

K

K, k [keɪ] *n* K, k *m*.
kaleidoscope [kə'laɪdəskəʊp] *n* kaléido-scope *m*.
kangaroo [kæŋgə'ruː] *n* kangourou *m*.
kaput [kə'pʊt] *a* (*broken, ruined*) *Sl* fichu.
karate [kə'rɑːtɪ] *n Sport* karaté *m*.
kebab [kə'bæb] *n* brochette *f*.
keel [kiːl] *n* (*of boat*) quille *f* ▌ *vi* to k. over (*of boat*) chavirer.
keen [kiːn] *a* **1** *Br* (*eager, enthusiastic*) plein d'enthousiasme; **he's a k. sportsman** c'est un passionné de sport; **to be k. to do** *or* **on doing** (*want*) tenir (beaucoup) à faire; **to be k. on doing** (*like*) aimer (beaucoup) faire; **to be k. on** (*music, sport etc*) être passionné de; **he is k. on her/the idea** elle/l'idée lui plaît beaucoup.
2 (*edge, appetite*) aiguisé; (*interest, feeling*) vif; (*mind*) pénétrant; (*wind*) coupant, piquant; **to have k. eyesight** avoir la vue perçante. ●**keenly** *adv* (*to work/etc*) *Br* avec enthousiasme; (*to feel, interest*) vivement. ●**keenness** *n Br* enthousiasme *m*; (*of mind*) pénétration *f*; (*of interest*) intensité *f*; **k. to do** *Br* empressement *m* à faire.
keep[1] [kiːp] *vt* (*pt & pp* **kept**) garder, (*shop, car*) avoir; (*diary, promise*) tenir; (*family*) entretenir; (*rule*) respecter, observer; (*feast day*) célébrer; (*birthday*) fêter; (*delay, detain*) retenir; (*put*) mettre; **to k. doing** (*continue*) continuer à faire; **to k. sth clean** tenir *or* garder qch propre; **to k. sth from s.o.** (*hide*) cacher qch à qn; **to k. s.o. from doing** (*prevent*) empêcher qn de faire; **to k. s.o. waiting/working** faire attendre/travailler qn; **to k. sth going** (*engine, machine*) laisser qch en marche; **to k. s.o. in whisky/etc** fournir qn en whisky/etc; **to k. an appointment** se rendre à un rendez-vous.
▌ *vi* (*remain*) rester; (*continue*) continuer; (*of food*) se garder, se conserver; (*wait*) attendre; **how is he keeping?** comment va-t-il?; **to k. still** rester *or* se tenir tranquille; **to k. left** tenir sa gauche; **to k. from doing** (*refrain*) s'abstenir de faire; **to k. going** (*continue*) continuer; **to k. at it** (*keep doing it*) continuer à le faire.
▌ *n* (*food*) nourriture *f*, subsistance *f*; **to have one's k.** être logé et nourri; **for keeps** *Fam* pour toujours.
keep[2] [kiːp] *n* (*tower*) *Hist* donjon *m*.
keep away *vt* (*person*) éloigner (**from** de) ▌ *vi* ne pas s'approcher (**from** de) ▌ **to keep back** *vt* (*crowd*) contenir; (*delay, withhold*) retenir; (*hide*) cacher (**from** à) ▌ *vi* ne pas s'approcher (**from** de) ▌ **to keep down** *vt* (*re-*

strict) limiter; (*control*) maîtriser; (*price, costs*) maintenir bas ▌ **to keep in** *vt* empêcher (*qn*) de sortir; (*as punishment in school*) mettre en retenue, consigner (*élève*) ▌ **to keep off** *vt* (*person*) éloigner; **'k. off the grass'** 'ne pas marcher sur les pelouses'; **k. your hands off!** n'y touche(z) pas! ▌ *vi* (*not go near*) ne pas s'approcher; **if the rain keeps off** s'il ne pleut pas ▌ **to keep on** *vt* (*hat, employee*) garder; **to k. on doing** continuer à faire ▌ *vi* **to k. on at s.o.** harceler qn ▌ **to keep out** *vt* empêcher (*qn*) d'entrer ▌ *vi* rester en dehors (**of** de) ▌ **to keep to** *vt* (*subject, path*) ne pas s'écarter de; (*room*) garder; **to k. sth to oneself** garder qch pour soi ▌ *vi* **to the left** tenir la gauche; **to k. to oneself** se tenir à l'écart. ▌ **to keep up** *vt* (*continue, maintain*) continuer (**doing sth** à faire qch); (*road, building*) entretenir ▌ *vi* (*continue*) continuer; (*follow*) suivre; **to k. up with s.o.** (*follow*) suivre qn; (*in quality of work etc*) se maintenir à la hauteur de qn.
keeper ['kiːpər] *n* (*in park, zoo*) gardien, -ienne *mf*.
keeping ['kiːpɪŋ] *n* **in k. with** en rapport avec; **to have sth in one's k.** avoir qch sous sa garde.
keepsake ['kiːpseɪk] *n* souvenir *m* (*objet*).
keg [keg] *n* tonnelet *m*.
kennel ['ken(ə)l] *n Br* niche *f*; (*for boarding dogs*) chenil *m*; **kennels** *Br* chenil *m*.
Kenya ['kenjə, 'kiːnjə] *n* Kenya *m*.
kept [kept] *pt & pp of* **keep**[1] *a* **well** *or* **nicely k.** (*house etc*) bien tenu.
kerb [kɜːb] *n Br* bord *m* du trottoir.
kernel ['kɜːn(ə)l] *n* (*of nut*) amande *f*.
kerosene ['kerəsiːn] *n* (*paraffin*) *Am* pétrole *m* (lampant); (*aviation fuel*) kérosène *m*.
ketchup ['ketʃəp] *n* (*sauce*) ketchup *m*.
kettle ['ket(ə)l] *n* bouilloire *f*; **the k. is boiling** l'eau bout; **to put on the k.** mettre l'eau à chauffer (*pour le thé etc*).
key [kiː] *n* clef *f*, clé *f*; (*of piano, typewriter, computer*) touche *f* ▌ *a* (*industry, post etc*) clef (*f inv*), clé (*f inv*); **k. person** pivot *m*; **k. ring** porte-clefs *m inv* ▌ *vt* **to k. in** (*computer data*) saisir, faire la saisie de.
keyboard ['kiːbɔːd] *n* (*of piano, computer etc*) clavier *m*; **k. operator** opérateur, -trice *mf* de saisie ▌ *vt* (*data*) faire la saisie de. ●**keyhole** *n* trou *m* (la) serrure. ●**keynote** *n* (*of speech*) note *f* dominante. ●**keystone** *n* (*of policy etc*) & *Archit* clef *f* de voûte.
keyed [kiːd] *a* **to be k. up** avoir les nerfs tendus.
khaki ['kɑːkɪ] *a & n* kaki *a inv & m*.

kibbutz [kɪ'buts] n kibboutz m.

kick [kɪk] n coup m de pied; (of horse) ruade f; **to get a k. out of doing** (thrill) Fam prendre un malin plaisir à faire; **for kicks** Fam pour le plaisir ▮ vt donner un coup de pied à; (of horse) lancer une ruade à ▮ vi donner des coups de pied; (of horse) ruer.

kick back vt (ball) renvoyer (du pied) ▮ **to kick down** or **in** vt (door etc) démolir à coups de pied ▮ **to kick off** vi Football donner le coup d'envoi; (start) démarrer. ● **kick-off** n Football coup m d'envoi. ▮ **to kick out** vt (throw out) Fam flanquer dehors ▮ **to kick up** vt **to k. up a fuss/row** Br Fam faire des histoires/du vacarme.

kickback ['kɪkbæk] n (bribe) pot-de-vin m.

kid [kɪd] **1** n (child) Fam gosse mf; **my k. brother** Am Fam mon petit frère. **2** n (goat) chevreau m. **3** vti (-dd-) (joke, tease) Fam blaguer; **to k. oneself** se faire des illusions.

kidnap ['kɪdnæp] vt (-pp-) kidnapper. ● **kidnapping** n enlèvement m. ● **kidnapper** n ravisseur, -euse mf.

kidney ['kɪdnɪ] n rein m; (as food) rognon m; **on a k. machine** sous rein artificiel; **k. bean** haricot m rouge.

kill [kɪl] vt (person, animal, plant etc) tuer; (rumour) Fig étouffer; (story) Fam supprimer; (engine) Fam arrêter; **to k. oneself** se tuer; **my feet are killing me** Fam je ne sens plus mes pieds, j'ai les pieds en compote; **to k. off** (bacteria etc) & Fig détruire. ▮ vi tuer. ▮ n mise f à mort; (prey) animaux mpl tués. ● **killing 1** n (of person) meurtre m; (of group) massacre m; (of animal) mise f à mort; **to make a k.** (financially) réussir un beau coup. **2** a (tiring) Fam tuant; (amusing) Fam crevant. ● **killer** n tueur, -euse mf.

killjoy ['kɪldʒɔɪ] n rabat-joie m inv.

kiln [kɪln] n (for pottery) four m.

kilo ['ki:ləʊ] n (pl -os) kilo m. ● **kilogram(me)** ['kɪləʊgræm] n kilogramme m.

kilobyte ['kɪləbaɪt] n Comptr kilo-octet m, k.-o m.

kilometre [kɪ'lɒmɪtər] (Am **kilometer**) n kilomètre m.

kilowatt ['kɪləʊwɒt] n kilowatt m.

kilt [kɪlt] n kilt m.

kimono [kɪ'məʊnəʊ] n (pl -os) kimono m.

kin [kɪn] n (relatives) parents mpl; **one's next of k.** son plus proche parent.

kind¹ [kaɪnd] n (sort, type) sorte f, genre m, espèce f (of de); **to pay in k.** payer en nature; **what k. of drink/etc is it?** qu'est-ce que c'est comme boisson/etc?; **that's the k. of man he is** il est comme ça; **nothing of the k.!** absolument pas!; **k. of worried/sad/etc** (somewhat) plutôt inquiet/triste/etc; **in a k. of way** d'une certaine façon; **it's the only one of its k.**, it's one of a k. c'est unique en son genre; **we are two of a k.** nous nous ressemblons.

kind² [kaɪnd] a (-er, -est) (helpful, pleasant) gentil (to avec, pour), bon (f bonne) (to

pour); **that's k. of you** c'est gentil or aimable à vous. ● **kind-'hearted** a qui a bon cœur.

kindergarten ['kɪndəgɑːt(ə)n] n jardin m d'enfants.

kindle ['kɪnd(ə)l] vt allumer ▮ vi s'allumer.

kindly ['kaɪndlɪ] adv avec bonté; **k. wait/etc** ayez la bonté d'attendre/etc; **not to take k. to sth** ne pas apprécier qch ▮ a (person) bienveillant.

kindness ['kaɪndnɪs] n gentillesse f, bonté f.

kindred ['kɪndrɪd] n (relationship) parenté f; (relatives) parents mpl; **k. spirit** semblable mf, âme f sœur.

king [kɪŋ] n roi m. ● **king-size(d)** a géant; (cigarette) long.

kingdom ['kɪŋdəm] n royaume m; **animal/plant k.** règne m animal/végétal.

kingfisher ['kɪŋfɪʃər] n (bird) martin-pêcheur m.

kingly ['kɪŋlɪ] a royal.

kink [kɪŋk] n (in rope) entortillement m.

kinky ['kɪŋkɪ] a (-ier, -iest) (person) qui a des goûts bizarres; (clothes, tastes etc) bizarre.

kinship ['kɪnʃɪp] n parenté f.

kiosk ['ki:ɒsk] n kiosque m; (telephone) k. Br cabine f (téléphonique).

kip [kɪp] vi (-pp-) (sleep) Br Sl roupiller.

kipper ['kɪpər] n (herring) kipper m.

kiss [kɪs] n baiser m, bise f; **the k. of life** (in first aid) le bouche-à-bouche ▮ vt (person) embrasser; **to k. s.o.'s hand** baiser la main de qn ▮ vi s'embrasser.

kit [kɪt] n équipement m, matériel m; (set of articles) trousse f; (belongings) Br affaires fpl; **gym/tennis/etc k.** Br affaires fpl de gym/ de tennis/etc; **first-aid k.** trousse f de pharmacie; **tool k.** trousse f à outils; (do-it-yourself) k. kit m; **model aircraft k.** maquette f d'avion à assembler; **in k. form** en kit; **k. bag** sac m (de soldat etc) ▮ vt (-tt-) **to k. s.o. out** Br équiper qn (with de).

kitchen ['kɪtʃɪn] n cuisine f; **k. cabinet** buffet m de cuisine; **k. garden** jardin m potager; **k. sink** évier m; **k. units** éléments mpl de cuisine. ● **kitche'nette** n coin-cuisine m, kitchenette f. ● **kitchenware** n ustensiles mpl de cuisine; (dishes) vaisselle f de cuisine.

kite [kaɪt] n (toy) cerf-volant m.

kith [kɪθ] n **k. and kin** amis mpl et parents mpl.

kitten ['kɪt(ə)n] n chaton m, petit chat m.

kitty ['kɪtɪ] n (fund) cagnotte f.

kiwi ['ki:wi:] n (bird, fruit) kiwi m.

km abbr (kilometre) km.

knack [næk] n (skill) coup m (de main), truc m (of doing pour faire); **to have a** or **the k. of doing** (aptitude, tendency) avoir le don de faire.

knackered ['nækəd] a (tired) Br Sl vanné.

knapsack ['næpsæk] n sac m à dos.

knead [ni:d] vt (dough) pétrir.

knee [ni:] n genou m; **to go down on one's knees** se mettre à genoux; **k. pad** Sport genouillère f. ● **kneecap** n (bone) rotule f.

●**knee-deep** *a* (*in water etc*) jusqu'aux genoux. ●**knees-up** *n* (*party*) *Br Fam* soirée *f* dansante, sauterie *f*.

kneel [niːl] *vi* (*pt & pp* knelt *or* kneeled) to k. (**down**) s'agenouiller; **to be kneeling** (**down**) être à genoux.

knell [nel] *n* glas *m*.

knew [n(j)uː] *pt of* **know**.

knickers ['nɪkəz] *npl* (*woman's undergarment*) *Br* slip *m*; (*longer*) culotte *f*.

knick-knack ['nɪknæk] *n* babiole *f*.

knife [naɪf] *n* (*pl* knives) couteau *m*; (*penknife*) canif *m* ▌ *vt* poignarder.

knight [naɪt] *n Hist & Br* chevalier *m*; *Chess* cavalier *m* ▌ *vt* **to be knighted** *Br* être fait chevalier. ●**knighthood** *n Br* titre *m* de chevalier.

knit [nɪt] *vt* (-tt-) tricoter; **to k. one's brow** froncer les sourcils ▌ *vi* tricoter; **to k.** (**together**) (*of bones*) se souder. ●**knitting** *n* (*activity, material*) tricot *m*; **k. needle** aiguille *f* à tricoter. ●**knitwear** *n* tricots *mpl*.

knob [nɒb] *n* (*on door etc*) bouton *m*; (*on walking stick*) pommeau *m*; **k. of butter** noix *f* de beurre.

knock [nɒk] *vt* (*strike*) frapper; (*collide with*) heurter; (*criticize*) *Fam* critiquer; **to k. one's head on sth** se cogner la tête contre qch; **to k. s.o. senseless** assommer qn; **to k. to the ground** jeter à terre.
▌ *vi* (*strike*) frapper; **to k. against** *or* **into** (*bump into*) heurter.
▌ *n* (*blow*) coup *m*; (*collision*) heurt *m*; **there's a k. at the door** quelqu'un frappe; **I heard a k.** j'ai entendu frapper.

knock about *vt* (*ill-treat*) malmener ▌ *vi* (*travel*) *Fam* bourlinguer; (*lie around, stand around*) *Fam* traîner ▌ **to knock back** (*drink, glass*) *Br Fam* s'envoyer (derrière la cravate), siffler ▌ **to knock down** *vt* (*vase, pedestrian etc*) renverser; (*house, tree, wall etc*) abattre; (*price*) baisser, casser ▌ **to knock in** *vt* (*nail*) enfoncer ▌ **to knock off** *vt* (*person, object*) faire tomber (**from** de); (*do quickly*) *Fam* expédier; (*steal*) *Br Fam* piquer; **to k. £5 off** (**the price**) baisser le prix de cinq livres, faire cinq livres sur le prix ▌ *vi* (*stop work*) *Fam* s'arrêter de travailler ▌ **to knock out** *vt* (*make unconscious*) assommer; *Boxing* mettre k.-o.; (*beat in competition*) éliminer; **to k. oneself out** (*tire*) *Fam* s'esquinter (**doing** à faire) ▌ **to knock over** *vt* (*pedestrian, vase etc*) renverser ▌ **to knock up** *vt* (*meal*) *Br Fam* préparer à la hâte.

knockdown ['nɒkdaʊn] *a* **k. price** *Br* prix *m* imbattable. ●**knock-'kneed** *a* cagneux. ●**knock-out** *n Boxing* knock-out *m*; **to be a k.-out** (*of person, film etc*) *Fam* être formi-

dable.

knocker ['nɒkər] *n* (*for door*) marteau *m*.

knot [nɒt] **1** *n* (*in rope etc*) nœud *m* ▌ *vt* (-tt-) nouer. **2** *n* (*unit of speed at sea*) nœud *m*. ●**knotty** *a* (-ier, -iest) (*wood etc*) noueux; (*problem*) *Fig* épineux.

know [nəʊ] *vt* (*pt* knew, *pp* known) (*facts, language etc*) savoir; (*person, place etc*) connaître; (*recognize*) reconnaître (**by** à); **to k. that** savoir que; **to k. how to do** savoir faire; **for all I k.** (*autant*) que je sache; **I'll let you k.** je vous le ferai savoir; **I'll have you k. that...** sachez que...; **to k.** (**a lot**) **about** (*person, event*) en savoir long sur; **to k.** (**a lot**) **about cars/sewing/etc** s'y connaître en voitures/couture/etc; **I've never known him to complain** je ne l'ai jamais vu se plaindre; **to get to k.** (**about**) **sth** apprendre qch; **to get to k. s.o.** (*meet*) faire la connaissance de qn.
▌ *vi* savoir; **I k.** je (le) sais; **I wouldn't k., I k. nothing about it** je n'en sais rien; **I k. about that** je suis au courant, je sais ça; **to k. of** (*have heard of*) avoir entendu parler de; **do you k. of a good dentist/etc?** connais-tu un bon dentiste/etc?; **you** (**should**) **k. better than to do that** tu es trop intelligent pour faire ça; **you should have known better** tu aurais dû réfléchir.
▌ *n* **in the k.** *Fam* au courant. ●**knowing** *a* (*smile, look*) entendu. ●**knowingly** *adv* (*consciously*) sciemment. ●**known** *a* connu; **a k. expert** un expert reconnu; **well k.** (**bien**) connu (**that** que); **she is k. to be...** on sait qu'elle est....

know-all ['nəʊɔːl] *n* (*Am* **know-it-all**) *Pej* je-sais-tout *mf inv*. ●**know-how** *n* (*skill*) savoir-faire *m inv*, compétence *f*.

knowledge ['nɒlɪdʒ] *n* connaissance *f* (**of** de); (*learning*) connaissances *fpl*, savoir *m*; **to** (**the best of**) **my k.** à ma connaissance; **without s.o.'s k.** à l'insu de qn; **to have no k. of sth** ignorer qch; **general k.** culture *f* générale. ●**knowledgeable** *a* bien informé (**about** sur).

knuckle ['nʌk(ə)l] **1** *n* articulation *f* (du doigt). **2** *vi* **to k. down to** (*task*) *Fam* s'atteler à; **to k. under** céder.

Koran [kə'rɑːn] *n* the **K.** le Coran.

Korea [kə'rɪə] *n* Corée *f*. ●**Korean** *a* coréen ▌ *n* (*language*) coréen *m*; (*person*) Coréen, -enne *mf*.

kosher ['kəʊʃər] *a* (*food*) kascher *inv*.

kowtow [kaʊ'taʊ] *vi* se prosterner (**to s.o.** devant qn).

kudos ['kjuːdɒs] *n* (*glory*) gloire *f*; (*prestige*) prestige *m*.

Kuwait [kjuː'weɪt] *n* Koweït *m*. ●**Kuwaiti** *a* koweïtien ▌ *n* Koweïtien, -ienne *mf*.

L

L, l [el] *n* L, l *m*.

lab [læb] *n Fam* labo *m*. ● **laboratory** [*Br* ləˈbɒrət(ə)rɪ, *Am* ˈlæbrətərɪ] *n* laboratoire *m*; **language l.** laboratoire *m* de langues.

label [ˈleɪb(ə)l] *n* étiquette *f* ❚ *vt* (*Br* **-ll-**, *Am* **-l-**) (*with price*) étiqueter; (*for identification*) mettre une étiquette sur; **to l. s.o.** (**as**) étiqueter qn (comme).

laborious [ləˈbɔːrɪəs] *a* laborieux.

labour [ˈleɪbər] (*Am* **labor**) *n* (*work*) travail *m*; (*workers*) main-d'œuvre *f*; **L.** (*political party*) *Br* les travaillistes *mpl*; **in l.** (*woman*) en train d'accoucher.

❚ *a* (*market, situation*) du travail; (*relations*) ouvriers-patronat *inv*; **l. dispute** conflit *m* ouvrier; **l. force** main-d'œuvre *f*; **l. union** *Am* syndicat *m*; **l. unrest** agitation *f* ouvrière.

❚ *vi* (*toil*) peiner.

❚ *vt* **to l. a point** insister sur un point. ● **laboured** *a* (*style*) laborieux. ● **labourer** *n* (*on roads etc*) manœuvre *m*; (*on farm*) ouvrier *m* agricole.

laburnum [ləˈbɜːnəm] *n* (*tree*) cytise *f*.

labyrinth [ˈlæbɪrɪnθ] *n* labyrinthe *m*.

lace [leɪs] **1** *n* (*cloth*) dentelle *f*. **2** *n* (*of shoe etc*) lacet *m* ❚ *vt* **to l.** (**up**) (*tie up*) lacer (*chaussure etc*). **3** *vt* (*drink*) additionner, arroser (**with** de).

lacerate [ˈlæsəreɪt] *vt* (*flesh etc*) lacérer. ● **laceration** [-ˈreɪʃ(ə)n] *n* (*cut on skin*) entaille *f*.

lack [læk] *n* manque *m*; **for l. of** à défaut de ❚ *vt* manquer de ❚ *vi* **to be lacking** manquer (**in** de); **they l. for nothing** ils ne manquent de rien.

lackey [ˈlækɪ] *n Pej* laquais *m*.

laconic [ləˈkɒnɪk] *a* laconique.

lacquer [ˈlækər] *n* (*for wood, hair*) laque *f* ❚ *vt* (*wood*) laquer; (*hair*) mettre de la laque sur.

lad [læd] *n* gamin *m*, gosse *m*, garçon *m*; **when I was a l.** quand j'étais gosse *or* gamin.

ladder [ˈlædər] *n* échelle *f*; (*in stocking*) *Br* maille *f* filée ❚ *vti* (*stocking*) *Br* filer.

laden [ˈleɪd(ə)n] *a* chargé (**with** de).

ladle [ˈleɪd(ə)l] *n* louche *f*.

lady [ˈleɪdɪ] *n* dame *f*; **a young l.** une jeune fille; (*married*) une jeune femme; **the l. of the house** la maîtresse de maison; **Ladies and Gentlemen!** Mesdames, Mesdemoiselles, Messieurs!; **l. doctor** femme *f* médecin; **l. friend** amie *f*; **the ladies' room**, *Br* **the ladies** les toilettes *fpl* pour dames. ● **lady-in-'waiting** *n* (*pl* ladies-in-waiting) dame *f* d'honneur.

ladybird [ˈleɪdɪbɜːd] *or Am* **ladybug** [ˈleɪdɪbʌg] *n* coccinelle *f*.

ladylike [ˈleɪdɪlaɪk] *a* (*manner*) distingué; **she's (very) l.** elle est très grande dame.

lag [læg] **1** *vi* (**-gg-**) **to l. behind** (*in progress, work*) avoir du retard; (*dawdle*) traîner; **to l. behind s.o.** avoir du retard sur qn ❚ *n* **time l.** (*between events*) décalage *m*; (*between countries*) décalage *m* horaire. **2** *vt* (**-gg-**) (*pipe*) calorifuger.

lager [ˈlɑːgər] *n Br* bière *f* blonde.

lagoon [ləˈguːn] *n* lagune *f*; (*small, coral*) lagon *m*.

laid [leɪd] *pt & pp of* lay². ● **laid-'back** *a Fam* relax.

lain [leɪn] *pp of* lie¹.

lair [leər] *n* tanière *f*.

laity [ˈleɪɪtɪ] *n* **the l.** les laïcs *mpl*.

lake [leɪk] *n* lac *m*.

lamb [læm] *n* agneau *m*. ● **lambswool** *n* laine *f* d'agneau, lambswool *m*; **l. sweater** pull *m* en lambswool.

lame [leɪm] *a* (**-er, -est**) (*person, argument*) boiteux; (*excuse*) piètre; **to be l.** boiter. ● **lameness** *n Med* claudication *f*; (*of excuse*) *Fig* faiblesse *f*.

lament [ləˈment] *n* lamentation *f* ❚ *vt* **to l.** (**over**) se lamenter sur. ● **lamentable** *a* lamentable. ● **lamentation** [læmenˈteɪʃ(ə)n] *n* lamentation *f*.

laminated [ˈlæmɪneɪtɪd] *a* (*glass*) feuilleté; (*metal*) laminé.

lamp [læmp] *n* lampe *f*; (*bulb*) ampoule *f*, lampe *f*; (*on vehicle*) feu *m*. ● **lamppost** *n* lampadaire *m* (*de rue*). ● **lampshade** *n* abat-jour *m inv*.

lanai [ləˈnaɪ] *n* (*verandah*) *Am* véranda *f*.

lance [lɑːns] **1** *n* (*weapon*) lance *f*. **2** *vt* (*abscess*) inciser.

land¹ [lænd] *n* terre *f*; (*country*) pays *m*; (*plot of*) **l.** terrain *m*; **on dry l.** sur la terre ferme; **no man's l.** (*between armies etc, wasteland*) no man's land *m inv*; **to travel by l.** voyager par voie terrestre ❚ *a* (*transport, flora etc*) terrestre; (*reform, law*) agraire; (*tax*) foncier.

land² [lænd] *vi* (*of aircraft*) atterrir, se poser; (*of ship*) mouiller, relâcher; (*of passengers*) débarquer; (*of bomb, missile etc*) (re)tomber; **to l. up** (*in a ditch, in jail etc*) se retrouver.

❚ *vt* (*passengers, cargo*) débarquer; (*aircraft*) poser; (*blow*) flanquer (**on** à); (*job, prize etc*) *Fam* décrocher; **to l. s.o. in trouble** *Fam* mettre qn dans le pétrin; **to be landed with** *Fam* (*person*) avoir sur les bras; (*fine*) ramasser, écoper de. ● **landing** *n* **1** (*of aircraft*) atterrissage *m*; (*of ship*) débarquement *m*; **forced l.** atterrissage *m* forcé; **l. stage** débarcadère *m*. **2** (*at top of stairs*) palier *m*. **landed** ['lændɪd] *a* (*owning land*) terrien. **landlady** ['lændleɪdɪ] *n* propriétaire *f*, logeuse *f*; (*of pub*) patronne *f*. ●**landlocked** *a* sans accès à la mer. ●**landlord** *n* propriétaire *m*; (*of pub*) patron *m*. ●**landmark** *n* point *m* de repère. ●**landowner** *n* propriétaire *m* foncier. ●**landslide** *n* (*falling rocks*) éboulement *m*, glissement *m* de terrain; (*election victory*) raz-de-marée *m inv* électoral.

landscape ['lændskeɪp] *n* paysage *m*.

lane [leɪn] *n* (*in country*) chemin *m*; (*in town*) ruelle *f*; (*division of road*) voie *f*; (*line of traffic*) file *f*; (*for aircraft, shipping, runner*) couloir *m*; 'get in l.' (*traffic sign*) 'prenez votre file'; **bus l.** Br couloir *m* (*réservé aux autobus*).

language ['læŋgwɪdʒ] *n* (*English, French etc*) langue *f*; (*faculty, style*) langage *m*; **computer l.** langage *m* machine ● *a* (*laboratory*) de langues; (*teacher, studies*) de langue(s).

languid ['læŋgwɪd] *a* languissant. ●**languish** *vi* languir (**for, after** après).

lank [læŋk] *a* (*hair*) plat et terne.

lanky ['læŋkɪ] *a* (-**ier, -iest**) dégingandé.

lantern ['læntən] *n* lanterne *f*; **Chinese l.** lampion *m*.

lap [læp] **1** *n* (*of person*) genoux *mpl*; **in the l. of luxury** dans le plus grand luxe. **2** *n* (*in race*) tour *m* (*de piste*). **3** *vt* (-**pp**-) **to l. up** (*drink*) laper; (*like very much*) Fam adorer; (*believe*) Fam gober ● *vi* (*of waves*) clapoter. **4** *vi* (-**pp**-) **to l. over** (*overlap*) se chevaucher.

lapel [lə'pel] *n* (*of jacket etc*) revers *m*.

lapse [læps] **1** *n* (*fault*) faute *f*; (*weakness*) défaillance *f*; **a l. of memory** un trou de mémoire; **a l. in behaviour** un écart de conduite ● *vi* (*err*) commettre une faute; **to l. into** (*bad habits etc*) retomber dans. **2** *n* (*interval*) intervalle *m*; **a l. of time** un intervalle (**between** entre). **3** *vi* (*expire*) (*of ticket, passport etc*) se périmer, expirer; (*of subscription*) prendre fin; (*of insurance policy*) cesser d'être valable.

laptop ['læptop] *a & n* **l.** (**computer**) (ordinateur *m*) portable *m*.

larceny ['lɑːsənɪ] *n* vol *m* simple.

lard [lɑːd] *n* saindoux *m*.

larder ['lɑːdər] *n* (*cupboard*) garde-manger *m inv*.

large [lɑːdʒ] *a* (-**er, -est**) (*in size or extent*) grand; (*in volume, bulkiness*) gros (*f* grosse); (*quantity*) grand, important; **to become or grow or get l.** grossir, grandir; **to a l. extent** en grande mesure; **at l.** (*of prisoner, animal*) en liberté; (*as a whole*) en général; **by and l.** dans l'ensemble, généralement. ●**large-scale** *a* (*operation, reform etc*) de grande envergure.

largely ['lɑːdʒlɪ] *adv* (*to a great extent*) en grande mesure.

largeness ['lɑːdʒnəs] *n* grandeur *f*; (*bulkiness*) grosseur *f*.

largesse [lɑː'ʒes] *n* largesse *f*.

lark [lɑːk] **1** *n* (*bird*) alouette *f*. **2** *n* (*joke*) Fam rigolade *f*, blague *f* ● *vi* **to l. about** Br Fam s'amuser.

larva, pl -vae ['lɑːvə, -viː] *n* (*of insect*) larve *f*.

larynx ['lærɪŋks] *n* larynx *m*. ●**laryngitis** [-'dʒaɪtəs] *n* (*infection*) laryngite *f*.

lasagna [lə'zænjə] *n* lasagne *f*.

lascivious [lə'sɪvɪəs] *a* lascif.

laser ['leɪzər] *n* laser *m*; **l. beam/printer/etc** rayon *m*/imprimante *f*/etc laser.

lash[1] [læʃ] *n* (*with whip*) coup *m* de fouet ● *vt* (*strike*) fouetter; (*tie*) attacher (**to** à); **the dog lashed its tail** le chien donna un coup de queue ● *vi* **to l. out** (*spend wildly*) Fam claquer son argent; **to l. out at** (*hit*) envoyer des coups à; (*insult*) Fig invectiver; (*criticize*) Fig fustiger.

lash[2] [læʃ] *n* (*eyelash*) cil *m*.

lashings ['læʃɪŋz] *npl* **l. of** (*cream, jam etc*) Br Fam une montagne de.

lass [læs] *n* Br jeune fille *f*.

lassitude ['læsɪtjuːd] *n* lassitude *f*.

lasso [Br læ'suː, Am 'læsəʊ] *n* (*pl* -**os**) lasso *m* ● *vt* attraper au lasso.

last[1] [lɑːst] *a* dernier; **the l. ten lines** les dix dernières lignes; **l. but one** avant-dernier; **l. night** (*evening*) hier soir; (*night*) la nuit dernière ● *adv* (*lastly*) en dernier lieu, enfin; (*on the last occasion*) (pour) la dernière fois; **to leave l.** sortir en dernier or le dernier. ● *n* (*person, object*) dernier, -ière *mf*; (*end*) fin *f*; **the l. of the beer/etc** (*remainder*) le reste de la bière/etc; **the day before l.** avant-hier; **at** (**long**) **l.** enfin. ●**last-minute** *a* (*decision etc*) de dernière minute.

last[2] [lɑːst] *vi* durer; **to l.** (**out**) (*endure, resist*) tenir; (*of money, supplies*) durer; **it lasted me ten years** ça m'a duré or fait dix ans. ●**lasting** *a* (*impression, peace etc*) durable.

lastly ['lɑːstlɪ] *adv* en dernier lieu, enfin.

latch [lætʃ] **1** *n* loquet *m*; **the door is on the l.** la porte n'est pas fermée à clef. **2** *vi* **to l. on to** Fam (*adopt*) adopter (*idée etc*); (*understand*) saisir (*idée etc*); (*grab*) s'accrocher à (*qn*). ●**latchkey** *n* clef *f* de maison.

late[1] [leɪt] *a* (-**er, -est**) (*not on time*) en retard (**for** à); (*meal, fruit, season, hour*) tardif; (*stage*) avancé, (*edition*) dernier; **to be l.** (*of person, train etc*) être en retard, avoir du retard; **he's an hour l.** il a une heure de retard; **to make s.o. l.** mettre qn en retard; **it's l.** il est tard; **Easter/etc is l.** Pâques/etc est tard; **in l. June/etc** fin juin/etc; **to be in one's l. forties/etc** approcher de la cinquantaine/etc; **the l. Prime Minister/etc** (*former*) l'ancien Premier ministre/etc; **a later edition/etc** (*more recent*) une édition/etc plus récente; **the latest edition/etc** (*last*) la dernière édition/etc; **in later life** plus tard dans la vie; **to take a later train** prendre un train plus tard; **at a later**

date à une date ultérieure; **the latest date** la date limite; **at the latest** au plus tard; **of l.** dernièrement.
l adv (in the day, season etc) tard; (not on time) en retard; **it's getting l.** il se fait tard; **later (on)** plus tard; **not** or **no later than** pas plus tard que. *

late² [leɪt] a **the l.** Mr Smith/etc (deceased) feu Monsieur Smith/etc; **our l. friend** notre regretté ami.

latecomer ['leɪtkʌmər] n retardataire mf.

lately ['leɪtlɪ] adv dernièrement.

lateness ['leɪtnəs] n (of person, train etc) retard m; **constant l.** des retards continuels; **the l. of the hour** l'heure tardive.

latent ['leɪtənt] a latent.

lateral ['lætərəl] a latéral.

lathe [leɪð] n (machine) tour m.

lather ['lɑːðər] n mousse f (de savon) **l** vt savonner **l** vi mousser.

Latin ['lætɪn] a latin; **L. America** Amérique f latine **l** n (person) Latin, -ine mf; (language) latin m. **● Latin American** a d'Amérique latine **l** n Latino-Américain, -aine mf.

latitude ['lætɪtjuːd] n (on map, Fig freedom) latitude f.

latrines [lə'triːnz] npl latrines fpl.

latter ['lætər] a (later, last-named) dernier; (second) deuxième **l** n **the l.** ce or le dernier, cette or la dernière; (of two) le second, la seconde. **● latterly** adv (recently) récemment, dernièrement.

lattice ['lætɪs] n treillis m.

laudable ['lɔːdəb(ə)l] a louable.

laugh [lɑːf] n rire m; **to have a good l.** bien rire **l** vi rire (at, about de); **to l. to oneself** rire en soi-même **l** vt **to l. sth off** tourner qch en plaisanterie. **● laughing** a riant; **it's no l. matter** il n'y a pas de quoi rire; **to be the l. stock of** être la risée de.

laughable ['lɑːfəb(ə)l] a ridicule.

laughter ['lɑːftər] n rire(s) m(pl); **to roar with l.** rire aux éclats.

launch [lɔːntʃ] **1** n (motor boat) vedette f; (pleasure boat) bateau m de plaisance. **2** vt (rocket, boat, fashion etc) lancer **l** vi **to l. (out) into** (begin) se lancer dans **l** n lancement m; **l. pad** aire f de lancement. **● launching** n lancement m; **l. pad** aire f de lancement.

launder ['lɔːndər] vt (clothes) blanchir; (money from drugs etc) Fig blanchir. **● laundering** n blanchissage m.

launderette [lɔːndə'ret] or Am **Laundromat®** ['lɔːndrəmæt] n laverie f automatique.

laundry ['lɔːndrɪ] n (place) blanchisserie f; (clothes) linge m.

laurel ['lɒrəl] n (tree) laurier m.

lava ['lɑːvə] n lave f.

lavatory ['lævətrɪ] n cabinets mpl.

lavender ['lævɪndər] n lavande f.

lavish ['lævɪʃ] a prodigue (with de); (helping, meal) généreux; (decor, house etc) somptueux; (expenditure) excessif **l** vt prodiguer (sth on s.o. qch à qn). **● lavishly** adv (to

give) généreusement; (to furnish) somptueusement.

law [lɔː] n (rule, rules) loi f; (study, profession, system) droit m; **against the l.** illégal; **court of l., l. court** cour f de justice; **l. and order** l'ordre m public; **l. school** Am faculté f de droit; **l. student** étudiant, -ante mf en droit. **● law-abiding** a respectueux des lois.

lawful ['lɔːfəl] a (action, age etc) légal; (child, wife, claim etc) légitime. **● lawfully** adv légalement.

lawless ['lɔːləs] a (country) anarchique. **● lawlessness** n anarchie f.

lawn [lɔːn] n pelouse f, gazon m; **l. mower** tondeuse f (à gazon); **l. tennis** tennis m (sur gazon).

lawsuit ['lɔːsuːt] n procès m.

lawyer ['lɔːjər] n (in court) avocat m; (for wills, sales) notaire m; (legal expert, author) juriste m.

lax [læks] a (person) négligent; (discipline, behaviour) relâché; **to be l. in doing sth** négliger de faire qch. **● laxity** or **laxness** n négligence f; (of discipline) relâchement m.

laxative ['læksətɪv] n & a laxatif (m).

lay¹ [leɪ] a (non-religious) laïque; (non-specialized) (opinion etc) d'un profane; **l. person** profane mf; **● layman** n (pl -men) (non-specialist) profane mf.

lay² [leɪ] (pt & pp laid) **1** vt (put down, place) poser; (blanket) étendre (over sur); (trap) tendre; (money) miser (on sur); (accusation) porter; (ghost) exorciser; **to l. the table** Br mettre la table or le couvert; **to l. bare** mettre à nu; **to l. waste** ravager; **to l. s.o. open to** exposer qn à; **to l. one's hands on** mettre la main sur; **to l. a hand** or **a finger on s.o.** lever la main sur qn. **2** vt (egg) pondre **l** vi (of bird) pondre.

lay³ [leɪ] pt of **lie¹**.

layabout ['leɪəbaʊt] n Fam fainéant, -ante mf. **● lay-by** n (pl -bys) (for vehicles) Br aire f de stationnement or de repos. **● lay-off** n (of worker) licenciement m. **● layout** n disposition f; (of text) mise f en pages. **● lay-over** n Am halte f.

lay down vt (put down) poser; (arms) déposer; (condition) (im)poser; **to l. down one's life** sacrifier sa vie (for pour); **to l. down the law** faire la loi (to à) **l to lay into** vt Fam attaquer **l to lay off** vt **to l. s.o. off** (worker) licencier qn **l** vi (stop) Fam arrêter; **to l. off s.o.** (leave alone) Fam laisser qn tranquille; **l. off!** (don't touch) Fam pas touche! **l to lay on** vt (install) Br mettre, installer; (supply) fournir; **to l. it on (thick)** Fam y aller un peu fort **l to lay out** vt (garden) dessiner; (house) concevoir; (prepare) préparer; (display) disposer; (money) Fam mettre (on dans); **to l. s.o. out** (flat) (knock unconscious) coucher qn sur le carreau **l** vi (spend money) Fam claquer de l'argent **l to be laid up** (in bed) être obligé de garder le lit, être alité.

layer ['leɪər] n couche f.

layman ['leɪmən] n see **lay¹**.

laze [leɪz] *vi* **to l. (about** *or* **around)** paresser.

lazy ['leɪzɪ] *a* **(-ier, -iest)** *(person etc)* paresseux; *(afternoon etc)* passé à ne rien faire. ● **lazy-bones** *n Fam* paresseux, -euse *mf*.

lb *abbr (libra)* = **pound** *(weight)*.

lead¹ [liːd] *vt (pt & pp* **led)** *(guide, conduct take)* mener, conduire **(to** à); *(team, government etc)* diriger; *(expedition, attack)* mener, commander; *(be at the head of)* être en tête de *(cortège etc)*; **to l. a happy/etc life** mener une vie heureuse/*etc*; **to l. s.o. in/out/etc** faire entrer/sortir/*etc* qn; **to l. s.o. to do** *(cause, induce)* amener qn à faire; **to l. the way** montrer le chemin; **to l. the world** tenir le premier rang mondial; **easily led** influençable.

❙ *vi (of street, door etc)* mener, conduire **(to** à); *(in race)* être en tête; *(in match)* être en tête; *(go ahead)* aller devant; **to l. to** *(result in)* aboutir à; *(cause)* causer, amener; **to l. up to** *(of street etc)* conduire à, mener à; *(precede)* précéder; *(approach gradually)* en venir à.

❙ *n (distance or time ahead)* avance *f* **(over** sur); *(example)* exemple *m*, initiative *f*; *(clue)* piste *f*, indice *m*; *(star part in film etc)* rôle *m* principal; *(for dog) Br* laisse *f*; *(electric wire)* fil *m*; **to take the l.** *(in race)* prendre la tête; **to be in the l.** *(in race)* être en tête; *(in match)* mener; **l. singer** *(in pop group)* chanteur, -euse *mf* vedette.

lead² [led] *n (metal)* plomb *m*; *(of pencil)* mine *f*; **l. pencil** crayon *m* à mine de plomb. ● **leaded** *a (Br petrol, Am gas)* au plomb. ● **leaden** *a* **l. sky** ciel *m* de plomb. ● **lead-free** *a (Br petrol, Am gas)* sans plomb.

lead away *vt* emmener *(qn)* ❙ **to lead back** *vt* ramener *(qn)* ❙ **to lead off** *vt* emmener *(qn)* ❙ **to lead on** *vt (tease)* faire marcher *(qn)*.

leader ['liːdər] *n* **1** chef *m*; *(of country, party)* dirigeant, -ante *mf*; *(of strike, riot)* meneur, -euse *mf*; *(guide)* guide *m*; **to be the l.** *(in race)* être en tête. **2** *(newspaper article) Br* éditorial *m*. ● **leadership** *n* direction *f*; *(qualities)* qualités *fpl* de chef; *(leaders)* dirigeants *mpl*.

leading ['liːdɪŋ] *a (main)* principal; *(important)* important; **the l. car/etc** *(in front)* la voiture/*etc* de tête; **the l. author** l'auteur principal *or* le plus important; **a l. figure,** **a l. light** un personnage marquant; **the l. lady** *(in film etc)* la vedette féminine; **l. article** *(in newspaper) Br* éditorial *m*.

leaf [liːf] **1** *n (pl* **leaves)** feuille *f*; *(of book)* feuillet *m*; *(of table)* rallonge *f*. **2** *vi* **to l. through** *(book)* feuilleter. ● **leafy** *a* **(-ier, -iest)** *(tree)* feuillu.

leaflet ['liːflɪt] *n* prospectus *m*; ¶*containing instructions)* notice *f*.

league [liːg] *n* **1** *(alliance)* ligue *f*; *Sport* championnat *m*; **in l. with** *Pej* de connivence avec. **2** *(measure) Hist* lieue *f*.

leak [liːk] *n (in pipe, information etc)* fuite *f*; *(in boat)* voie *f* d'eau ❙ *vi (of liquid, pipe, Br tap, Am faucet etc)* fuir; *(of ship)* faire eau; **to l. out** *(of information) Fig* être divulgué ❙

vt (liquid) répandre; *(information) Fig* divulguer. ● **leakage** *n* fuite *f*; *(amount lost)* perte *f*. ● **leaky** *a* **(-ier, -iest)** *(kettle etc)* qui fuit.

lean¹ [liːn] *a* **(-er, -est)** *(thin)* maigre; *(year)* difficile. ● **leanness** *n* maigreur *f*.

lean² [liːn] *vi (pt & pp* **leaned** *or* **leant** [lent]) *(of object)* pencher; *(of person)* se pencher; **to l. against/on sth** *(of person)* s'appuyer contre/sur qch; **to l. back against** s'adosser à; **to l. on s.o.** *(influence) Fam* faire pression sur qn **(to do** pour faire); **to l. forward** *(of person)* se pencher (en avant); **to l. over** *(of person)* se pencher; *(of object)* pencher.

❙ *vt* appuyer *(qch)* **(against** contre); **to l. one's head on/out of sth** pencher la tête sur/par qch. ● **leaning** *a* penché; **l. against** *(resting)* appuyé contre. ● **leanings** *npl* tendances *fpl* **(towards** à). ● **lean-to** *n Br (pl* **-tos)** *(building)* appentis *m*.

leap [liːp] *n (jump)* bond *m*, saut *m*; *(change, increase etc) Fig* bond *m*; **l. year** année *f* bissextile; **in leaps and bounds** à pas de géant.

❙ *vi (pt & pp* **leaped** *or* **leapt** [lept]) bondir, sauter; *(of flames)* jaillir; *(of profits)* faire un bond; **to l. to one's feet, l. up** se lever d'un bond.

leapfrog ['liːpfrɒg] *n* saute-mouton *m inv*; **to play l.** jouer à saute-mouton.

learn [lɜːn] *vt (pt & pp* **learned** *or* **learnt)** apprendre **(that** que); **to l. (how) to do** apprendre à faire ❙ *vi* apprendre; **to l. about** *(study)* étudier; *(hear about)* apprendre. ● **learned** [-ɪd] *a* savant. ● **learning** *n (of language)* apprentissage *m* **(of** de); *(knowledge)* érudition *f*, savoir *m*. ● **learner** *n* débutant, -ante *mf*.

lease [liːs] *n* bail *m*; **a new l.** *Br* **of life** *or* *Am* **on life** un regain de vie, une nouvelle vie ❙ *vt (house etc)* louer à bail. ● **leasehold** *n* propriété *f* louée à bail.

leash [liːʃ] *n (of dog)* laisse *f*; **on a l.** en laisse.

least [liːst] *a* **the l.** *(smallest amount of)* le moins de; *(slightest)* le *or* la moindre; **he has (the) l. talent** il a le moins de talent **(of all** de tous); **the l. effort/noise/etc** le moindre effort/bruit/*etc*.

❙ *n* **the l.** le moins; **at l.** du moins; *(with quantity)* au moins; **at l. that's what she says** du moins c'est ce qu'elle dit; **not in the l.** pas du tout.

❙ *adv (to work, eat etc)* le moins; *(with adjective)* le *or* la moins; **l. of all** *(especially not)* surtout pas.

leather ['leðər] *n* cuir *m*; *(wash)* **l.** peau *f* de chamois. ● **leatherette** *n* Skaï ® *m*.

leave [liːv] **1** *n (Br holiday, Am vacation)* congé *m*; *(of soldier from army)* permission *f*; *(consent)* permission *f*; **to be on l.** être en congé; **l. of absence** congé *m* exceptionnel; **to take (one's) l. of s.o.** prendre congé de qn.

2 *vt (pt & pp* **left)** *(allow to remain, forget)*

laisser; (*go away from*) quitter; (*room*) sortir de, quitter; **to l. the table** sortir de table; **to l. s.o. in charge of s.o./sth** laisser à qn la garde de qn/qch; **to l. sth with s.o.** (*entrust, give*) laisser qch à qn; **to be left** (*over*) rester; **there's no hope/bread/etc left** il ne reste plus d'espoir/de pain/etc; **l. it to me!** laisse-moi faire!; **I'll l. it** (up) **to you** je m'en remets à toi; **to l. go** (of) (*release*) lâcher; **to l. behind** (*not take*) laisser; (*surpass*) dépasser; (*in race, at school*) distancer; **to l. off** (*lid*) ne pas (re)mettre; **to l. off doing** (*stop*) *Fam* arrêter de faire; **to l. on** (*hat, gloves*) garder; **to l. out** (*forget to put*) oublier (de mettre) (*accent etc*); (*word, line*) sauter; (*exclude*) exclure.
▮ *vi* (*go away*) partir (**from** de, **for** pour); **to l. off** (*stop*) *Fam* s'arrêter. ●**leavings** *npl* restes *mpl*.

Lebanon ['lebənən] *n* Liban *m*. ●**Leba'nese** *a* libanais ▮ *n* Libanais, -aise *mf*.

lecher ['letʃər] *n* débauché *m*. ●**lecherous** *a* lubrique, luxurieux.

lectern ['lektən] *n* (*for giving speeches*) pupitre *m*; (*in church*) lutrin *m*.

lecture ['lektʃər] **1** *n* (*public speech*) conférence *f*; (*as part of series at university*) cours *m* (magistral) ▮ *vi* faire une conférence *or* un cours; **she lectures in chemistry** elle est professeur de chimie.
2 *vt* (*scold*) faire la morale à, sermonner ▮ *n* (*scolding*) sermon *m*. ●**lecturer** *n* conférencier, -ière *mf*; (*at university*) *Br* professeur *m*. ●**lectureship** *n Br* poste *m* à l'université.

led [led] *pt* & *pp* of **lead**[1].

ledge [ledʒ] *n* (*on wall, window*) rebord *m*; (*on mountain*) saillie *f*.

ledger ['ledʒər] *n* (*in bookkeeping*) grand livre *m*.

leech [liːtʃ] *n* (*worm, person*) sangsue *f*.

leek [liːk] *n* poireau *m*.

leer [lɪər] *vi* lorgner; **to l. at s.o.** lorgner qn ▮ *n* regard *m* sournois *or* polisson.

leeway ['liːweɪ] *n* (*freedom*) liberté *f* d'action; (*safety margin*) marge *f* de sécurité.

left[1] [left] *pt* & *pp* of **leave 2**. ●**left luggage office** *n Br* consigne *f*.

left[2] [left] *a* (*side, hand etc*) gauche ▮ *adv* à gauche ▮ *n* gauche *f*; **on** *or* **to the l.** à gauche (**of** de). ●**left-hand** *a* or de gauche; **on the l.-hand side** à gauche (**of** de). ●**left-'handed** *a* (*person*) gaucher. ●**left-wing** *a* (*views, government etc*) de gauche.

leftist ['leftɪst] *n* & *a Pol* gauchiste (*mf*).

leftovers ['leftəʊvəz] *npl* restes *mpl*.

leg [leg] *n* jambe *f*; (*of dog, bird etc*) patte *f*; (*of table*) pied *m*; (*of journey*) étape *f*; **l.** (**of chicken**) cuisse *f* de poulet; **l. of lamb** gigot *m* d'agneau; **to pull s.o.'s l.** (*make fun of*) mettre qn en boîte; **on its last legs** (*machine, car etc*) *Fam* prêt à claquer; **to be on one's last legs** *Fam* avoir un pied dans la tombe. ●**leg-room** *n* (*in vehicle etc*) place *f* pour les jambes.

legacy ['legəsɪ] *n* (*bequest*) & *Fig* legs *m*.

legal ['liːg(ə)l] *a* (*lawful*) légal; (*affairs, adviser, mind*) juridique; (*error*) judiciaire; **l. aid** *Br* assistance *f* judiciaire; **l. expert** juriste *m*; **l. proceedings** procès *m*. ●**le'gality** *n* légalité *f*. ●**legalize** *vt* légaliser. ●**legally** *adv* légalement.

legation [lɪ'geɪʃ(ə)n] *n Pol* légation *f*.

legend ['ledʒənd] *n* (*story, inscription etc*) légende *f*. ●**legendary** *a* légendaire.

leggings ['legɪŋz] *npl* jambières *fpl*.

leggy ['legɪ] *a* (*-ier, -iest*) (*person*) aux longues jambes, tout en jambes.

legible ['ledʒəb(ə)l] *a* lisible. ●**legi'bility** *n* lisibilité *f*. ●**legibly** *adv* lisiblement.

legion ['liːdʒən] *n* (*of soldiers, Fig of people*) légion *f*.

legislate ['ledʒɪsleɪt] *vi* légiférer. ●**legislation** [-'leɪʃ(ə)n] *n* (*laws*) législation *f*; (*action*) élaboration *f* des lois; (*piece of*) **l.** loi *f*.

legislative ['ledʒɪslətɪv] *a* législatif.

legitimate [lɪ'dʒɪtɪmət] *a* (*reason, child etc*) légitime. ●**legitimacy** *n* légitimité *f*.

legless ['legləs] *a* (*drunk*) *Br* saoul (complètement) bourré.

leg-room ['legruːm] *n see* **leg**.

leisure [*Br* 'leʒər, *Am* 'liːʒər] *n* **l.** (**time**) loisirs *mpl*; **l. activities** loisirs *mpl*; **l. centre** *or* **complex** centre *m* de loisirs; **moment of l.** moment *m* de loisir; **at** (**one's**) **l.** à tête reposée. ●**leisurely** *a* (*walk, occupation*) peu fatigant; (*meal, life*) calme; **at a l. pace, in a l. way** sans se presser.

lemon ['lemən] *n* citron *m*; **l. drink, Br l. squash** citronnade *f*; **l. tea** thé *m* au citron. ●**lemo'nade** *n* (*fizzy*) *Br* limonade *f*; (*still*) *Am* citronnade *f*.

lend [lend] *vt* (*pt* & *pp* **lent**) prêter (**to** à); (*charm, colour etc*) *Fig* donner (**to** à); **to l. credence to** ajouter foi à. ●**lending** *n* prêt *m*; **l. library** bibliothèque *f* de prêt. ●**lender** *n* prêteur, -euse *mf*.

length [leŋθ] *n* longueur *f*; (*section of pipe etc*) morceau *m*; (*of road*) tronçon *m*; (*of cloth*) métrage *m*; (*in horseracing, swimming etc*) longueur *f*; (*duration*) durée *f*; **l. of time** temps *m*; **at l.** (*at last*) enfin; **at** (**great**) **l.** (*in detail*) (*to explain etc*) dans le détail; (*for a long time*) (*to speak etc*) longuement; **to go to great lengths** se donner beaucoup de mal (**to do** pour faire).

lengthen ['leŋθən] *vt* allonger; (*in time*) prolonger. ●**lengthwise** *adv* dans le sens de la longueur. ●**lengthy** *a* (*-ier, -iest*) long.

lenient ['liːnɪənt] *a* indulgent (**to** envers). ●**leniency** *n* indulgence *f*. ●**leniently** *adv* avec indulgence.

lens [lenz] *n* lentille *f*; (*in spectacles*) verre *m*; (*of camera*) objectif *m*.

Lent [lent] *n Rel* Carême *m*.

lentil ['lent(ə)l] *n* (*seed, plant*) lentille *f*.

Leo ['liːəʊ] *n* (*sign*) le Lion *m*.

leopard ['lepəd] *n* léopard *m*.

leotard ['liːətɑːd] *n* collant *m* (*de danse*).

leper ['lepər] *n* lépreux, -euse *mf*. ●**leprosy** *n* lèpre *f*.

lesbian ['lezbɪən] *n* & *a* lesbienne (*f*).

lesion ['liːʒ(ə)n] *n* (*injury*) *Med* lésion *f*.

less [les] *a* & *adv* moins (de) (**than** que); **l. time**/*etc* moins de temps/*etc*; **she has l.** (**than you**) elle en a moins (que toi); **l. than a kilo/ten**/*etc* (*with quantity, number*) moins d'un kilo/de dix/*etc*; **l.** (*to sleep, know etc*) moins (**than** que); **l.** (*often*) moins souvent; **l. and l.** de moins en moins; **one l.** un(e) de moins.

▮ *prep* moins; **l. six francs** moins six francs.

-less [ləs] *suff* sans; **childless** sans enfants.

lessen ['les(ə)n] *vti* diminuer. ●**lessening** *n* diminution *f*.

lesser ['lesər] *a* moindre **▮** *n* **the l.** of le *or* la moindre de.

lesson ['les(ə)n] *n* leçon *f*; **an English l.** une leçon *or* un cours d'anglais; **I have lessons now** j'ai cours maintenant.

lest [lest] *conj Lit* de peur que (+ ne + *sub*).

let¹ [let] **1** *vt* (*pt* & *pp* **let**, *pres p* **letting**) (*allow*) laisser (**s.o. do** qn faire); **to l. s.o. have sth** donner qch à qn.

2 *v aux* **l. us eat/go**/*etc*, **l.'s eat/go**/*etc* mangeons/partons/*etc*; **l.'s go for a stroll** allons nous promener; **l. him come** qu'il vienne.

let² [let] *vt* (*pt* & *pp* **let**, *pres p* **letting**) **to l.** (**off** *or* **out**) (*house, room etc*) louer. ●**letting** *n* (*renting*) location *f*.

let away *vt* (*allow to leave*) laisser partir **▮ to let down** *vt* (*lower*) baisser; (*hair*) dénouer; (*dress*) rallonger; (*plane down*) (*Br tyre, Am tire*) dégonfler; **to l. s.o. down** (*disappoint*) décevoir qn; **don't l. me down** je compte sur toi; **the car l. me down** la voiture est tombée en panne. ●**letdown** *n* déception *f*. **▮ to let in** *vt* (*person, dog*) faire entrer; (*noise, light*) laisser entrer; **to l. in the clutch** (*in vehicle*) *Br* embrayer; **to l. s.o. in on sth** mettre qn au courant de qch; **to l. oneself in for a lot of expense** se laisser entraîner à des dépenses; **to l. oneself in for trouble** s'attirer des ennuis **▮ to let off** *vt* (*firework, gun*) faire partir; (*bomb*) faire éclater; **to l. s.o. off** (*allow to leave*) laisser partir qn; (*not punish*) ne pas punir qn; (*clear of crime*) disculper qn; **to l. s.o. off with a fine**/*etc* s'en tirer avec une amende/*etc*; **to l. s.o. off doing** dispenser qn de faire **▮ to let on** *vi* **not to l. on** *Fam* ne rien dire, garder la bouche cousue; **to l. on that** *Fam* (*admit*) avouer que; (*reveal*) dire que **▮ to let out** *vt* (*allow to leave*) faire *or* laisser sortir; (*prisoner*) relâcher; (*cry, secret*) laisser échapper; (*skirt*) élargir; **to l. s.o. out** (*of the house*) ouvrir la porte à qn; **to l. out the clutch** (*in vehicle*) *Br* débrayer **▮ to let up** *vi* (*of rain, person etc*) s'arrêter. ●**letup** *n* arrêt *m*, répit *m*.

letdown ['letdaʊn] *see* **let away**.

lethal ['liːθ(ə)l] *a* (*blow, dose etc*) mortel; (*weapon*) meurtrier.

lethargy ['leθədʒɪ] *n* léthargie *f*. ●**le'thargic**

a léthargique.

letter ['letər] *n* (*message, part of word*) lettre *f*; **man of letters** homme *m* de lettres; **l. bomb** lettre *f* piégée; **l. opener** coupe-papiers *m inv*; **l. writer** correspondant, -ante *mf*.

letterbox ['letəbɒks] *n Br* boîte *f* aux *or* à lettres. ●**letterhead** *n* en-tête *m*. ●**letterheaded** *a* **l. paper** papier *m* à en-tête. ●**lettering** *n* (*letters*) lettres *fpl*; (*on tomb*) inscription *f*.

lettuce ['letɪs] *n* laitue *f*, salade *f*.

letup ['letʌp] *n see* **let away**.

leuk(a)emia [luːˈkiːmɪə] *n* leucémie *f*.

level ['lev(ə)l] **1** *n* niveau *m*; (*rate*) taux *m*; **speed on the l.** vitesse *f* en palier.

▮ *a* (*surface*) plat, uni; (*object on surface*) d'aplomb; (*equal in score*) à égalité (**with** avec); (*in height*) au même niveau, à la même hauteur (**with** que); **l. spoonful** cuillerée *f* rase; **l. crossing** (*for train*) *Br* passage *m* à niveau.

▮ *vt* (*Br* **-ll-**, *Am* **-l-**) (*surface, differences*) aplanir, niveler; (*plane down*) raboter; (*building*) raser; (*gun*) braquer (**at** sur); (*accusation*) lancer (**at** contre).

▮ *vi* **to l. off** *or* **out** (*stabilize*) (*of prices etc*) se stabiliser.

2 *n* **on the l.** *Fam* (*honest*) honnête, franc (*f* franche); (*frankly*) honnêtement, franchement.

▮ *vi* (*Br* **-ll-**, *Am* **-l-**) **to l. with s.o.** *Fam* être franc avec qn. ●**level-headed** *a* équilibré.

lever [*Br* 'liːvər, *Am* 'levər] *n* levier *m*. ●**leverage** *n* (*power*) influence *f*.

levity ['levɪtɪ] *n* légèreté *f*.

levy ['levɪ] *vt* (*tax, troops*) lever **▮** *n* (*tax*) impôt *m*.

lewd [luːd] *a* (**-er**, **-est**) obscène.

liability [laɪəˈbɪlɪtɪ] *n* responsabilité *f* (**for** de); (*disadvantage*) handicap *m*; **liabilities** (*debts*) dettes *fpl*.

liable ['laɪəb(ə)l] *a* **l. to** (*dizziness etc*) sujet à; (*fine, tax*) passible de; **he's l. to do it** est susceptible de faire, il pourrait faire; **l. for** (*responsible*) responsable de.

liaise [lɪˈeɪz] *vi* travailler en liaison (**with s.o.** avec qn). ●**liaison** [liːˈeɪzɒn] *n* (*contact, love affair*) & *Mil* liaison *f*.

liar ['laɪər] *n* menteur, -euse *mf*.

libel ['laɪb(ə)l] *vt* (*Br* **-ll-**, *Am* **-l-**) diffamer (*par écrit*) **▮** *n* diffamation *f*.

liberal ['lɪbərəl] *a* (*open-minded*) & *Pol* libéral; (*generous*) généreux (**with** de) **▮** *n Pol* libéral, -ale *mf*. ●**liberalism** *n* libéralisme *m*.

liberate ['lɪbəreɪt] *vt* libérer. ●**liberation** [-ˈreɪʃ(ə)n] *n* libération *f*. ●**liberator** *n* libérateur, -trice *mf*.

liberty ['lɪbətɪ] *n* liberté *f*; **to be at l. to do** être libre de faire; **what a l.!** (*impudence*) *Fam* quel culot!; **to take liberties with s.o.** se permettre des familiarités avec qn.

Libra ['liːbrə] *n* (*sign*) la Balance.

library ['laɪbrərɪ] *n* bibliothèque *f*. ●**li'brarian** *n* bibliothécaire *mf*.

libretto [lɪ'bretəʊ] n (pl -os) livret m (d'opéra etc).

Libya ['lɪbjə] n Libye f. ●**Libyan** a libyen ▮ n Libyen, -enne mf.

lice [laɪs] see louse.

licence, Am **license** ['laɪsəns] n 1 permis m, autorisation f; (for driving) permis m; (for trading etc) licence f; pilot's l. brevet m de pilote; l. fee (for television, radio) redevance f; l. plate/number (of vehicle) plaque f/ numéro m d'immatriculation. 2 (freedom) licence f.

license ['laɪsəns] vt accorder un permis or une licence or un brevet à; (permit) autoriser (s.o. to do qn à faire); licensed premises Br établissement m qui a une licence de débit de boissons ▮ n Am = licence.

licit ['lɪsɪt] a licite.

lick [lɪk] vt lécher; (defeat) Fam écraser; (beat physically) Fam rosser; to be licked (by problem etc) Fam être dépassé; to l. one's lips s'en lécher les babines ▮ n coup m de langue; a l. of paint un coup de peinture. ●**licking** n Fam (defeat) déculottée f; (beating) rossée f.

licorice ['lɪkərɪʃ, -rɪs] n Am réglisse f.

lid [lɪd] n 1 (of box etc) couvercle m. 2 (of eye) paupière f.

lido ['liːdəʊ] n (pl -os) Br piscine f (découverte).

lie¹ [laɪ] vi (pt lay, pp lain, pres p lying) (in flat position) s'allonger, s'étendre; (remain) rester; (be) être; (in grave) reposer; to be lying (on the grass etc) être allongé or étendu; he lay asleep il dormait; here lies (on tomb) ci-gît; the problem lies in le problème réside dans; it's lying heavy on my stomach (of meal) cela me pèse sur l'estomac; to l. low (hide) se cacher; (be inconspicuous) se faire tout petit.

lie² [laɪ] vi (pt & pp lied, pres p lying) (tell lies) mentir ▮ n mensonge m; to give the l. to sth (show as untrue) démentir qch.

lie about or **around** vi (of objects, person) traîner ▮ **to lie down** vi s'allonger, se coucher; **lying down** (resting) allongé, couché. ●**lie-down** n Br to have a l.-down = to lie down ▮ **to lie in** vi Br Fam faire la grasse matinée. ●**lie-in** n Br to have a l.-in = to lie in.

lieu [luː] n in l. of au lieu de.

lieutenant [Br lef'tenənt, Am luː'tenənt] n lieutenant m.

life [laɪf] n (pl lives) vie f; (of battery, machine) durée f (de vie); to come to l. (of party, street etc) s'animer; at your time of l. à ton âge; loss of l. perte f en vies humaines; true to l. conforme à la réalité; to take one's (own) l. se donner la mort; bird l. les oiseaux mpl; l. annuity rente f viagère; l. blood Fig âme f; l. force force f vitale; l. insurance assurance-vie f; l. jacket gilet m de sauvetage; l. peer Br pair m à vie; l. preserver Am ceinture f de sauvetage; l. raft radeau m de sauvetage; l. span durée f de vie;

l. style style m de vie.

lifebelt ['laɪfbelt] n ceinture f de sauvetage. ●**lifeboat** n canot m de sauvetage. ●**lifebuoy** n bouée f de sauvetage. ●**lifeguard** n maître nageur m (sauveteur). ●**lifeless** a sans vie. ●**lifelike** a qui semble vivant. ●**lifeline** n to be s.o.'s l. être essentiel à la survie de qn. ●**lifelong** a de toute sa vie; (friend) de toujours. ●**lifesaving** n sauvetage m. ●**life-size(d)** a grandeur nature inv. ●**life-support system** n respirateur m artificiel. ●**lifetime** n vie f; Fig éternité f; in my l. de mon vivant; a once-in-a-l. experience/etc l'expérience f/etc de votre vie.

lift [lɪft] vt lever; (sth heavy) (sou)lever; (ban, siege) Fig lever; (idea etc) Fig voler, prendre (from à) ▮ vi (of fog) se lever ▮ n (elevator) Br ascenseur m; to give s.o. a l. emmener or accompagner qn (en voiture) (to à).

lift down vt (take down) descendre (from de) ▮ **to lift off** vt (take down) descendre (from de) ▮ vi (of space vehicle) décoller. ●**lift-off** n (of space vehicle) décollage m ▮ **to lift out** vt (take out) sortir ▮ **to lift up** vt (arm, object, eyes) lever; (heavy object) (sou)lever.

ligament ['lɪgəmənt] n ligament m.

light¹ [laɪt] n lumière f; (daylight) jour m, lumière f; (on vehicle) feu m; (vehicle headlight) phare m; by the l. of à la lumière de; in the l. of (considering) à la lumière de; in that l. Fig sous ce jour or cet éclairage; against the l. à contre-jour; to bring sth to l. mettre qch en lumière; to come to l. être découvert; to throw l. on (matter) éclaircir; do you have a l.? (for cigarette) est-ce que vous avez du feu?; to set l. to mettre le feu à; l. bulb ampoule f (électrique).

▮ vt (pt & pp lit or lighted) (fire, candle, gas etc) allumer; (match) allumer, gratter; to l. (up) (room) éclairer; (cigarette) allumer.

▮ vi to l. up (of window) s'allumer. ●**lighting** n (lights) éclairage m; the l. of (candle etc) l'allumage m de. ●**light-year** n année-lumière f.

light² [laɪt] a (bright, not dark) clair; a l. green jacket une veste vert clair.

light³ [laɪt] a (in weight, quantity, strength etc) léger; (task) facile; (low-fat) allégé; (low-calorie) pauvre en calories; l. rain pluie f fine; to travel l. voyager avec peu de bagages. ●**light-'fingered** a chapardeur. ●**light-'headed** a (giddy, foolish) étourdi. ●**light-'hearted** a gai.

light⁴ [laɪt] vi (pt & pp lit or lighted) to l. upon Lit trouver par hasard.

lighten ['laɪt(ə)n] 1 vt (colour, hair) éclaircir; (light up) éclairer (visage etc). 2 vt to l. a weight or a load diminuer un poids. 3 vi to l. up (become less gloomy) se dérider.

lighter ['laɪtər] n (for cigarettes) briquet m; (for Br cooker, Am stove) allume-gaz m inv.

lighthouse, pl -ses ['laɪthaʊs, -zɪz] n phare m.

lightly ['laɪtlɪ] adv légèrement; l. boiled egg

œuf *m* à la coque; **to get off l.** s'en tirer à bon compte.

lightness ['laɪtnəs] *n* **1** (*brightness*) clarté *f*. **2** (*in weight*) légèreté *f*.

lightning ['laɪtnɪŋ] *n* (*flashes of light*) éclairs *mpl*; (*charge*) la foudre; (**flash of**) l. éclair *m* ▮ *a* (*speed*) foudroyant; (*visit*) éclair *inv*; **l. conductor** *Br*, **l. rod** *Am* paratonnerre *m*.

lightweight ['laɪtweɪt] *a* (*shoes, cloth etc*) léger; (*not serious*) (*politician etc*) pas sérieux, léger ▮ *n Boxing* poids *m* léger.

like¹ [laɪk] *prep* comme; **l. this** comme ça; **what's he l.?** (*physically, as character*) comment est-il?; **to be** *or* **look l.** ressembler à; **what was the book l.?** comment as-tu trouvé le livre?; **what does it smell l.?** cela sent quoi?; **I have one l. it** j'en ai un pareil.

▮ *adv* **nothing l. as big/*etc*** loin d'être aussi grand/*etc*.

▮ *conj* (*as*) *Fam* comme; **it's l. I say** c'est comme je vous le dis; **do l. I do** fais comme moi.

▮ *n* ...and the l. ...et ainsi de suite; **the l. of which we shall never see again** comme on n'en reverra plus; **the likes of you** des gens de ton acabit.

like² [laɪk] *vt* aimer (bien) (**to do, doing** faire); **I l. him** je l'aime bien, il me plaît; **she likes it here** elle se plaît ici; **to l. sth/s.o. best** aimer mieux qch/qn, aimer qch/qn le plus, préférer qch/qn; **I'd l. to come** (*want*) je voudrais (bien) *or* j'aimerais (bien) venir; **I'd l. a kilo of apples** je voudrais un kilo de pommes; **would you l. an apple?** voulez-vous une pomme?; **if you l.** si vous voulez; **how would you l. to come?** ça te plairait *or* te dirait de venir?

▮ *npl* **one's likes and dislikes** nos préférences *fpl*. ●**liking** *n* **a l. for** (*person*) de la sympathie pour; (*thing*) du goût pour; **to my l.** à mon goût.

likeable ['laɪkəb(ə)l] *a* sympathique.

likely ['laɪklɪ] *a* (**-ier, -iest**) (*result, event etc*) probable; (*excuse*) vraisemblable; (*place*) propice; (*candidate*) prometteur; **a l. excuse!** *Iron* belle excuse!; **it's l. (that) she'll come** il est probable qu'elle viendra; **he's l. to come** il viendra probablement; **he's not l. to come** il ne risque pas de venir.

▮ *adv* **very l.** très probablement; **not l.!** pas question! ●**likelihood** *n* probabilité *f*; **there isn't much l. that** il y a peu de chances que (+ *sub*).

liken ['laɪkən] *vt* comparer (**to** à).

likeness ['laɪknɪs] *n* ressemblance *f*; **a family l.** un air de famille; **it's a good l.** c'est très ressemblant.

likewise ['laɪkwaɪz] *adv* (*similarly*) de même, pareillement.

liking ['laɪkɪŋ] *n see* **like²**.

lilac ['laɪlək] *n* lilas *m* ▮ *a* (*colour*) lilas *inv*.

Lilo® ['laɪləʊ] *n* (*pl* **-os**) *Br* matelas *m* pneumatique.

lilt [lɪlt] *n* (*in song, voice*) cadence *f*.

lily ['lɪlɪ] *n* lis *m*, lys *m*; **l. of the valley** mu-

guet *m*.

limb [lɪm] *n* (*of body*) membre *m*; **to be out on a l.** (*in dangerous position*) être sur la corde raide.

limber ['lɪmbər] *vi* **to l. up** faire des exercices d'assouplissement.

limbo (in) [ɪn'lɪmbəʊ] *adv* (*uncertain, waiting*) dans l'expectative.

lime [laɪm] *n* **1** (*fruit*) lime *f*, citron *m* vert; **l. juice** jus *m* de citron vert. **2** (*tree*) tilleul *m*. **3** (*substance*) chaux *f*.

limelight ['laɪmlaɪt] *n* **in the l.** (*glare of publicity*) en vedette.

limerick ['lɪmərɪk] *n* = poème *m* humoristique de cinq vers.

limit ['lɪmɪt] *n* limite *f*; (*restriction*) limitation *f* (**on** de); **that's the l.!** *Fam* c'est le comble!; **within limits** dans une certaine limite.

▮ *vt* limiter (**to** à); **to l. oneself to doing** se borner à faire. ●**limited** *a* (*restricted*) limité; (*edition*) à tirage limité; (*mind*) borné; **l. company** société *f* à responsabilité limitée; **(public) l. company** (*with shareholders*) *Br* société *f* anonyme; **to a l. degree** jusqu'à un certain point. ●**limitation** [-'teɪʃ(ə)n] *n* limitation *f*. ●**limitless** *a* illimité.

limousine [lɪmə'ziːn] *n* (*airport etc shuttle*) *Am* voiture-navette *f*; (*car*) limousine *f*.

limp [lɪmp] **1** *vi* (*of person*) boiter; **to l. along** (*of vehicle, ship etc*) *Fig* avancer tant bien que mal ▮ *n* **to have a l.** boiter. **2** *a* (**-er, -est**) (*soft*) mou (*f* molle); (*flabby*) (*skin etc*) flasque; (*person, hat*) avachi.

limpid ['lɪmpɪd] *a* (*liquid*) *Lit* limpide.

linchpin ['lɪntʃpɪn] *n* (*person*) pivot *m*.

linctus ['lɪŋktəs] *n* (*cough medicine*) *Br* sirop *m* (contre la toux).

line¹ [laɪn] *n* ligne *f*; (*stroke*) trait *m*, ligne *f*; (*of poem*) vers *m*; (*wrinkle*) ride *f*; (*track*) voie *f*; (*rope*) corde *f*; (*row*) rangée *f*, ligne *f*; (*of vehicles*) file *f*; (*queue of people*) *Am* file *f*, queue *f*; (*family*) lignée *f*; (*business*) métier *m*, rayon *m*; (*of products for sale*) ligne *f* (*de produits*); **one's lines** (*of actor*) son texte *m*; **to be on the l.** (*at other end of phone line*) être au bout du fil; (*at risk*) (*of job etc*) être menacé; **hold the l.!** (*remain on the phone*) ne quittez pas!; **the hot l.** le téléphone rouge; **to stand in l.** *Am* faire la queue; **to step** *or* **get out of l.** *Fig* refuser de se conformer; (*misbehave*) faire une incartade; **out of l. with** (*s.o.'s ideas etc*) en désaccord avec; **in l. with** conforme à; **he's in l. for promotion** il doit obtenir de l'avancement; **to take a hard l.** adopter une attitude ferme; **along the same lines** (*to work, think, act etc*) de la même façon; **something along those lines** quelque chose dans ce genre-là; **to drop a l.** (*send a letter*) *Fam* envoyer un mot (**to** à); **where do we draw the l.?** où fixer les limites?

▮ *vt* **to l. the street** (*of trees*) border la rue; (*of people*) faire la haie le long de la rue; **to l. up** (*children, objects*) aligner; (*arrange*) organiser; (*get ready*) préparer; **to have**

something lined up (*in mind*) avoir quelque chose en vue; **lined face** visage *m* ridé; **lined paper** papier *m* réglé.
I *vi* to **l. up** s'aligner; (*queue up*) *Am* faire la queue; **to l. up in twos**/*etc* se mettre en rangs par deux/*etc*. ● **line-up** *n* (*row of people etc*) file *f*; (*of countries etc*) *Pol* front *m*; (*of programmes*) *TV* programme *m*; (*of guests*) *TV* invités *mpl*.

line² [laɪn] *vt* (*clothes*) doubler; **to l. one's pockets** *Fig* se remplir les poches. ● **lining** *n* (*of clothes*) doublure *f*; **brake l.** garniture *f* de frein.

lineage ['lɪnɪɪdʒ] *n* lignée *f*.

linear ['lɪnɪər] *a* linéaire.

linen ['lɪnɪn] *n* (*sheets etc*) linge *m*; (*material*) (toile *f* de) lin *m*, fil *m*; **l. basket** *Br* panier *m* à linge; **l. cupboard** *Br*, **l. closet** *Am* armoire *f* à linge; **l. sheet** drap *m* de lin.

liner ['laɪnər] *n* **1** (*ocean*) **l.** paquebot *m*. **2** **(dust)bin l.** *Br*, **garbage can l.** *Am* sac *m* poubelle.

linesman ['laɪnzmən] *n* (*pl* -men) *Football etc* juge *m* de touche.

linger ['lɪŋgər] *vi* to **l. (on)** (*of person*) s'attarder; (*of smell, memory*) persister; (*of doubt*) subsister; **a lingering death** une mort lente.

lingo ['lɪŋgəʊ] *n* (*pl* -oes) *Fam* jargon *m*.

linguist ['lɪŋgwɪst] *n* (*specialist*) linguiste *mf*; **to be a good l.** être doué pour les langues. ● **lin'guistic** *a* linguistique. ● **lin'guistics** *n* linguistique *f*.

liniment ['lɪnɪmənt] *n* onguent *m*, pommade *f*.

link [lɪŋk] *vt* (*connect*) relier (**to** à); (*relate, associate*) lier (**to** à); **to l. up** relier; (*computer*) connecter **I** *vi* to **l. up** (*of companies, countries etc*) s'associer; (*of computers*) se connecter; (*of roads*) se rejoindre **I** *n* (*connection*) lien *m*; (*of chain*) maillon *m*; (*by road, rail*) liaison *f*. ● **link-up** *n* (*of spacecraft*) jonction *f*; (*between TV stations etc*) liaison *f*.

lino ['laɪnəʊ] *n* (*pl* -os) *Br* lino *m*. ● **linoleum** [lɪ'nəʊlɪəm] *n* linoléum *m*.

linseed ['lɪnsiːd] *n* **l. oil** huile *f* de lin.

lint [lɪnt] *n* (*bandage*) tissu *m* ouaté; (*fluff*) peluche(s) *f(pl)*.

lion ['laɪən] *n* lion *m*; **l. cub** lionceau *m*; **l. tamer** dompteur, -euse *mf* de lions. ● **lioness** *n* lionne *f*.

lip [lɪp] *n* (*of person*, *Fig wound*) lèvre *f*; (*rim*) (*of cup etc*) bord *m*; (*impudence*) *Sl* culot *m*; **to pay l. service to sth** se déclarer en faveur de qch pour la forme seulement. ● **lip-read** *vi* (*pt* & *pp* -read [red]) lire sur les lèvres. ● **lipstick** *n* (*substance*) rouge *m* à lèvres; (*stick*) bâton *m* ou tube *m* de rouge.

liquefy ['lɪkwɪfaɪ] *vt* liquéfier **I** *vi* se liquéfier.

liqueur [Br lɪ'kjʊər, Am lɪ'kɜːr] *n* liqueur *f*.

liquid ['lɪkwɪd] *n* & *a* liquide (*m*).

liquidate ['lɪkwɪdeɪt] *vt* (*debt*) liquider; (*kill*) *Fam* liquider (*qn*). ● **liquidation** [-'deɪʃ(ə)n] *n* liquidation *f*.

liquidizer ['lɪkwɪdaɪzər] *n* (*for fruit juices, purées etc*) *Br* mixer *m*. ● **liquidize** *vt* *Br* passer au mixer.

liquor ['lɪkər] *n* alcool *m*, spiritueux *m*; **l. store** *Am* magasin *m* de vins et de spiritueux.

liquorice ['lɪkərɪʃ, -rɪs] *n* *Br* réglisse *f*.

lira *pl* **lire** ['lɪərə, 'lɪərɪ] *n* (*currency*) lire *f*.

lisp [lɪsp] *vi* zézayer **I** *n* to have a **l.** zézayer.

list [lɪst] **1** *n* liste *f* **I** *vt* (*one's possessions etc*) faire la liste de; (*name one by one*) énumérer; (*catalogue*) cataloguer; **listed building** *Br* monument *m* classé. **2** *vi* (*of ship*) gîter.

listen ['lɪs(ə)n] *vi* écouter; **to l. to** écouter; **to l. (out) for** (*telephone, person etc*) guetter (le bruit *or* les cris *etc* de); **to l. in (to)** *Radio* écouter. ● **listening** *n* écoute *f* (**to** de). ● **listener** *n* (*to radio*) auditeur, -trice *mf*; **to be a good l.** (*pay attention*) savoir écouter.

listeria [lɪ'stɪərɪə] *n* (*illness*) listériose *f*.

listless ['lɪstləs] *a* apathique, indolent. ● **listlessness** *n* apathie *f*.

lit [lɪt] *pt* & *pp* of **light** (*see* **light¹**).

litany ['lɪtənɪ] *n* (*prayers*) litanies *fpl*.

liter ['liːtər] *n* *Am* litre *m*.

literal ['lɪtərəl] *a* littéral; (*not exaggerated*) réel. ● **literally** *adv* littéralement; (*really*) réellement; **he took it l.** il l'a pris au pied de la lettre.

literary ['lɪtərərɪ] *a* littéraire.

literate ['lɪtərət] *a* qui sait lire et écrire; **highly l.** (*person*) très instruit. ● **literacy** *n* (*of country*) degré *m* d'alphabétisation; (*of person*) capacité *f* de lire et d'écrire.

literature ['lɪt(ə)rɪtʃər] *n* littérature *f*; (*pamphlets etc*) documentation *f*.

lithe [laɪð] *a* agile, souple.

litigation [lɪtɪ'geɪʃ(ə)n] *n* (*in court of law*) litige *m*.

litre ['liːtər] (*Am* **liter**) *n* litre *m*.

litter ['lɪtər] **1** *n* (*Br rubbish, Am garbage*) détritus *m*; (*papers*) papiers *mpl*; (*bedding for animals*) litière *f*; (*jumble, confusion*) *Fig* fouillis *m*; **l. basket** *or* **bin** *Br* boîte *f* à ordures.
I *vt* to **l. (with papers** *or* *Br* **rubbish** *or* *Am* **garbage**) (*street etc*) laisser traîner des papiers *or* des détritus dans; **a street littered with** une rue jonchée de.
2 *n* (*young animals*) portée *f*. ● **litterbug** *n* personne *f* qui jette des détritus n'importe où.

little¹ ['lɪt(ə)l] *a* (*small*) petit; **the l. ones** les petits; **a l. bit** un (petit) peu.

little² ['lɪt(ə)l] **1** *a* & *n* (*not much*) peu (de); **l. time/money**/*etc* peu de temps/d'argent/*etc*; **I've l. left** il m'en reste peu; **she eats l.** elle mange peu; **to have l. to say** avoir peu de chose à dire; **as l. as possible** le moins possible. **2** *a* & *n* **a l.** (*some*) un peu (de); **a l. money/time**/*etc* un peu d'argent/de temps/*etc*; **I have a l.** j'en ai un peu; **the l. that I have** le peu que j'ai.
I *adv* (*somewhat, rather*) peu; **a l. heavy**/*etc*

un peu lourd/*etc*; **to work**/*etc* **a l.** travailler/*etc* un peu; **it's a l. better** c'est un peu mieux; **it's l. better** (*not much*) ce n'est guère mieux; **l. by l.** peu à peu.

liturgy ['lɪtədʒɪ] *n* liturgie *f*.

live[1] [lɪv] *vi* vivre; (*reside*) habiter, vivre; **where do you l.?** où habitez-vous?; **to l. in Paris** habiter (à) Paris ∎ *vt* (*life*) mener, vivre; (*one's faith etc*) vivre pleinement; **to l. it up** *Fam* mener la grande vie.

live[2] [laɪv] **1** *a* (*electric wire*) sous tension; (*switch*) mal isolé; (*plugged in*) (*appliance*) branché; (*alive*) (*animal etc*) vivant; (*ammunition*) réel, de combat; (*bomb*) non explosé; (*coal*) ardent; **a real l. king**/*etc* un roi/*etc* en chair et en os.
2 *a & adv Rad TV* en direct; **a l. broadcast** une émission en direct; **a l. audience** le *or* un public; **a l. recording** un enregistrement public.

live down *vt* faire oublier (avec le temps) ∎ **to live off** *or* **on** *vt* (*eat*) vivre de; (*sponge on*) vivre aux crochets *or* aux dépens de (*qn*) ∎ **to live on** *vi* (*of memory etc*) survivre, se perpétuer ∎ **to live through** *vt* (*experience*) vivre (guerre, événement); (*survive*) survivre à (guerre *etc*); **l. through the winter** passer l'hiver ∎ **to live up to** *vt* (*one's principles*) vivre selon; (*s.o.'s expectations*) se montrer à la hauteur de.

livelihood ['laɪvlɪhʊd] *n* moyens *mpl* de subsistance; **my l.** mon gagne-pain; **to earn one's** *or* **a l.** gagner sa vie.

lively ['laɪvlɪ] *a* (**-ier, -iest**) (*person*, *style*) vif, vivant; (*street*, *story*) vivant; (*interest*, *mind*, *colour*) vif; (*day*) mouvementé; (*discussion*, *conversation*) animé; (*forceful*) (*protest*, *campaign*) vigoureux. ● **liveliness** *n* vivacité *f*.

liven ['laɪv(ə)n] *vt* **to l. up** (*person*) égayer; (*party*) animer ∎ *vi* **to l. up** (*of person*, *party*) s'animer.

liver ['lɪvər] *n* foie *m*.

livery ['lɪvərɪ] *n* (*uniform*) livrée *f*; **in l.** en livrée.

livestock ['laɪvstɒk] *n* bétail *m*.

livid ['lɪvɪd] *a* (*angry*) furieux; (*blue-grey*) (*complexion*) livide; **l. with cold** blême de froid.

living ['lɪvɪŋ] **1** *a* (*alive*) vivant; **not a l. soul** (*nobody*) personne, pas âme qui vive; **within l. memory** de mémoire d'homme; **l. or dead** mort ou vif; **the l.** les vivants *mpl*.
2 *n* (*livelihood*) vie *f*; **to make** *or* **earn a** *or* **one's l.** gagner sa vie; **to work for a l.** travailler pour vivre; **the cost of l.** le coût de la vie; **l. conditions** conditions *fpl* de vie; **a l. wage** un salaire qui permet de vivre. ● **living room** *n* salle *f* de séjour.

lizard ['lɪzəd] *n* lézard *m*.

llama ['lɑːmə] *n* (*animal*) lama *m*.

load [ləʊd] *n* (*object carried*, *burden*) charge *f*; (*freight*) chargement *m*, charge *f*; (*strain*, *weight*) poids *m*; **a l. of**, **loads of** (*people*, *money etc*) *Fam* un tas de, énormément de;

to take a l. off s.o.'s mind ôter un grand poids à qn.
∎ *vt* (*truck*, *gun etc*) charger (**with** de); **to l. s.o. down with** (*presents etc*) charger qn de; **to l. up** (*car*, *ship etc*) charger (**with** de).
∎ *vi* **to l.** (**up**) charger la voiture, le navire *etc*.

loaded ['ləʊdɪd] *a* (*gun*, *vehicle etc*) chargé; (*rich*) *Fam* plein aux as; **a l. question** une question piège; **the dice are l.** les dés sont pipés; **l.** (**down**) **with** (*debts*) accablé de.

loaf [ləʊf] **1** *n* (*pl* **loaves**) pain *m*; **French l.** baguette *f*. **2** *vi* **to l.** (**about**) fainéanter. ● **loafer** *n* fainéant, -ante *mf*.

loam [ləʊm] *n* (*soil*) terreau *m*.

loan [ləʊn] *n* (*money lent*) prêt *m*; (*money borrowed*) emprunt *m*; **on l. from** prêté par; (**out**) **on l.** (*book*) sorti; **may I have the l. of...?** puis-je emprunter...? ∎ *vt* (*lend*) prêter (**to** à).

loath [ləʊθ] *a* **l. to do** *Lit* peu disposé à faire.

loathe [ləʊð] *vt* détester (**doing** faire). ● **loathing** *n* dégoût *m*. ● **loathsome** *a* détestable.

lobby ['lɒbɪ] **1** *n* (*of hotel*) hall *m*, vestibule *m*; (*of theatre*) foyer *m*. **2** *n* (*in politics*) groupe *m* de pression, lobby *m* ∎ *vt* faire pression sur (*qn*) ∎ *vi* **to l. for sth** faire pression pour obtenir qch.

lobe [ləʊb] *n* (*of ear etc*) lobe *m*.

lobster ['lɒbstər] *n* homard *m*; (*spiny*) langouste *f*.

local ['ləʊk(ə)l] *a* local; (*regional*) régional; (*of the neighbourhood*) du *or* de quartier; (*of the region*) de la région; **are you l.?** êtes-vous du coin *or* d'ici?; **the doctor is l.** le médecin est tout près d'ici; **a l. phone call** (*within town*) une communication urbaine.
∎ *n* (*pub*) *Br Fam* bistrot *m* du coin, pub *m*; **she's a l.** elle est du coin; **the locals** (*people*) les gens du coin.

locality [ləʊ'kælətɪ] *n* (*neighbourhood*) environs *mpl*; (*region*) région *f*; (*place*) lieu *m*; (*site*) emplacement *m*.

localize ['ləʊkəlaɪz] *vt* (*confine*) localiser.

locally *adv* dans le coin, dans les environs; (*around here*) par ici; (*in precise place*) localement.

locate [ləʊ'keɪt] *vt* (*find*) trouver, repérer; (*pain*, *noise*, *leak*) localiser; (*situate*) situer; (*build*) construire; **to be located in Paris**/*etc* être situé à Paris/*etc*. ● **location** [-ʃ(ə)n] *n* (*site*) emplacement *m*; (*act*) repérage *m*; (*of pain etc*) localisation *f*; **on l.** (*to shoot a film*) en extérieur.

lock [lɒk] **1** *vt* (*door*, *car etc*) fermer à clef; **to l. the wheels** (*of vehicle*) bloquer les roues ∎ *vi* fermer à clef ∎ *n* (*on door*, *chest etc*) serrure *f*; (*of gun*) cran *m* de sûreté; (*turning circle of vehicle*) rayon *m* de braquage; (**anti-theft**) **l.** (*on vehicle*) antivol *m*; **under l. and key** sous clef.
2 *n* (*on canal*) écluse *f*.
3 *n* (*of hair*) mèche *f*.

lock away *vt* (*prisoner*) enfermer; (*jewels*

etc) mettre sous clef, enfermer ▮ **to lock in** *vt* (*person*) enfermer; **to l. s.o. in sth** enfermer qn dans qch ▮ **to lock out** *vt* (*person*) (*accidentally*) enfermer dehors ▮ **to lock up** *vt* (*house, car etc*) fermer à clef; (*prisoner*) enfermer; (*jewels etc*) mettre sous clef, enfermer ▮ *vi* fermer à clef.

locker ['lɒkər] *n* (*in school etc*) casier *m*; (*for luggage*) (*at station, airport etc*) casier *m* de consigne automatique; (*for clothes*) vestiaire *m* (métallique); **l. room** *Sport Am* vestiaire *m*.

locket ['lɒkɪt] *n* (*jewel*) médaillon *m*.

lockout ['lɒkaʊt] *n* (*industrial*) lock-out *m inv*.

locksmith ['lɒksmɪθ] *n* serrurier *m*.

lockup ['lɒkʌp] *a & n* **l.** (*garage*) *Br* box *m*.

loco ['ləʊkəʊ] *a* (*crazy*) *Sl* cinglé, fou (*f* folle).

locomotion [ləʊkə'məʊʃ(ə)n] *n* locomotion *f*.

locomotive [ləʊkə'məʊtɪv] *n* locomotive *f*.

locum ['ləʊkəm] *n* (*doctor*) *Br* remplaçant, -ante *mf*.

locust ['ləʊkəst] *n* criquet *m*, sauterelle *f*.

lodge [lɒdʒ] **1** *vt* (*person*) loger; (*valuables*) déposer (*with chez*); **to l. a complaint** porter plainte ▮ *vi* (*of bullet*) se loger (**in** dans); **to be lodging** (*accommodated*) être logé (**with** chez). **2** *n* (*house*) pavillon *m* de gardien or de chasse; (*of porter*) loge *f*.

lodger ['lɒdʒər] *n* (*room and meals*) pensionnaire *mf*; (*room only*) locataire *mf*.

lodging ['lɒdʒɪŋ] *n* (*accommodation*) logement *m*; **lodgings** (*Br flat, Am apartment*) logement *m*; (*room*) chambre *f*; **in lodgings** en meublé.

loft [lɒft] *n* (*attic*) grenier *m*.

lofty ['lɒftɪ] *a* (*-ier, -iest*) (*high, noble*) élevé; (*haughty, superior*) hautain. ●**loftiness** *n* hauteur *f*.

log [lɒg] **1** *n* (*tree trunk*) tronc *m* d'arbre; (*for fire*) bûche *f*; **l. fire** feu *m* de bois. **2** *vt* (*-gg-*) (*facts*) noter; **to l. (up)** (*distance*) faire, couvrir. **3** *vi Comptr* **to l. in/out** entrer/sortir. ●**logbook** *n* (*on ship*) journal *m* de bord; (*on aircraft*) carnet *m* de vol; (*of vehicle*) *Br* = carte *f* grise.

loggerheads (at) [æt'lɒgəhedz] *adv* en désaccord (**with** avec).

logic ['lɒdʒɪk] *n* logique *f*. ●**logical** *a* logique. ●**logically** *adv* logiquement.

logistics [lə'dʒɪstɪks] *n* logistique *f*.

logo ['ləʊgəʊ] *n* (*pl -os*) logo *m*.

loin [lɔɪn] *n* (*meat*) filet *m* (*de veau etc*); **l. chop** côte *f* première.

loincloth ['lɔɪnklɒθ] *n* pagne *m*.

loins [lɔɪnz] *npl* (*lower back, genitals*) reins *mpl*.

loiter ['lɔɪtər] *vi* traîner.

loll [lɒl] *vi* (*in armchair etc*) se prélasser.

lollipop ['lɒlɪpɒp] *n* (*Br sweet or Am candy on stick*) sucette *f*; (*ice on stick*) esquimau *m*; **l. man/lady** *Br* gardien *m*/gardienne *f* de passage pour piétons. ●**lolly** *n* **1** *Fam* sucette

f; (**ice**) **l.** esquimau *m*. **2** (*money*) *Sl* fric *m*.

London ['lʌndən] *n* Londres *m* or *f* ▮ *a* (*taxi etc*) londonien. ●**Londoner** *n* Londonien, -ienne *mf*.

lone [ləʊn] *a* solitaire; **l. wolf** *Fig* solitaire *mf*.

loneliness ['ləʊnlɪnəs] *n* solitude *f*. ●**lonely** *a* (*-ier, -iest*) (*road, house, life etc*) solitaire; (*person*) seul, solitaire.

loner ['ləʊnər] *n* solitaire *mf*.

lonesome ['ləʊnsəm] *a* solitaire.

long[1] [lɒŋ] **1** *a* (*-er, -est*) long (*f* longue); **to be ten metres l.** avoir dix mètres de long, être long de dix mètres; **to be six weeks l.** durer six semaines; **how l. is...?** quelle est la longueur de...?; (*time*) quelle est la durée de...?; **a l. time** longtemps; **in the l. run** à la longue; **a l. face** une grimace; **a l. memory** une bonne mémoire; **l. jump** *Sport* saut *m* en longueur.

2 *adv* (*a long time*) longtemps; **l. before/after** longtemps avant/après; **has he been here l.?** il y a longtemps qu'il est ici?, il est ici depuis longtemps?; **how l.?** (*how much time*) combien de temps?; **how l. ago?** il y a combien de temps?; **not l.** peu de temps; **before l.** sous *or* avant peu; **no longer** ne plus; **she no longer swims** elle ne nage plus; **a bit longer** (*to wait etc*) encore un peu; **I won't be l.** je n'en ai pas pour longtemps; **don't be l.** dépêche-toi (de revenir), ne traîne pas; **at the longest** (*tout*) au plus; **all summer/winter l.** tout l'été/l'hiver; **l. live the queen/***etc* vive la reine/*etc*; **as l. as, so l. as** (*provided that*) pourvu que (+ *sub*); **as l. as I live** tant que je vivrai.

long[2] [lɒŋ] *vi* **to l. for sth** avoir très envie de qch; **to l. for s.o.** languir après qn; **to l. to do** avoir très envie de faire. ●**longing** *n* désir *m*, envie *f*.

long-awaited [lɒŋə'weɪtɪd] *a* tant attendu. ●**long-distance** *a* (*race*) de fond; (*phone call*) interurbain; (*flight*) long-courrier. ●**long-drawn-'out** *a* interminable. ●**long-'haired** *a* aux cheveux longs. ●**'longhand** *n* écriture *f* normale. ●**'long-life** *a* (*battery*) longue durée *inv*; (*milk*) longue conservation. ●**long-'playing** *a* **l.-playing record** 33 tours *m inv*. ●**long-'range** *a* (*forecast*) à long terme. ●**long'sighted** *a* (*person*) presbyte. ●**long'standing** *a* de longue date. ●**long'suffering** *a* très patient. ●**long-'term** *a* à long terme. ●**long-'winded** *a* (*speech, speaker*) verbeux.

longevity [lɒn'dʒevɪtɪ] *n* longévité *f*.

longitude ['lɒndʒɪtjuːd] *n* longitude *f*.

longways ['lɒŋweɪz] *adv* en longueur.

loo [luː] *n* **the l.** (*toilet*) *Br Fam* le petit coin.

look [lʊk] *n* regard *m*; (*appearance*) air *m*, allure *f*; (**good**) **looks** un beau physique, la beauté; **to have a l. (at)** jeter un coup d'œil (à), regarder; **to have a l. (for)** chercher; **to have a l. (a)round** regarder; (*walk*) faire un tour; **let me have a l.** fais voir; **I like the l. of him** il me fait bonne impression, il me plaît.

▌ *vti* regarder; **to l. s.o. in the face** regarder qn dans les yeux; **to l. tired/happy/***etc* (*seem*) sembler *or* avoir l'air fatigué/heureux/*etc*; **to l. pretty/ugly** (*be*) être joli/laid; **to l. one's age** faire son âge; **l. here!** dites donc!; **you l. like *or* as if *or* as though you're tired** tu as l'air fatigué, on dirait que tu es fatigué; **it looks like *or* as if *or* as though she won't leave** elle n'a pas l'air de vouloir partir; **it looks like it** c'est probable; **to l. like a child** avoir l'air d'un enfant; **to l. like an apple** avoir l'air d'être une pomme; **you l. like my brother** (*resemble*) tu ressembles à mon frère; **it looks like rain (to me)** il me semble *or* on dirait qu'il va pleuvoir; **what does he l. like?** (*describe him*) comment est-il?; **to l. well *or* good** (*of person*) avoir bonne mine; **you l. good in that hat/***etc* ce chapeau/*etc* te va très bien; **that looks bad** (*action etc*) ça fait mauvais effet.

look after *vt* (*deal with*) s'occuper de (*qch, qn*); (*sick person, hair*) soigner; (*keep safely*) garder (**for s.o.** pour qn); **to l. after oneself** (*keep healthy*) faire bien attention à soi; (*manage, cope*) se débrouiller ▌ **to look around** *vt* (*visit*) visiter ▌ *vi* (*have a look*) regarder; (*walk round*) faire un tour ▌ **to look at** *vt* regarder; (*consider*) considérer, voir; (*check*) vérifier ▌ **to look away** *vi* détourner les yeux ▌ **to look back** *vi* regarder derrière soi; (*in time*) regarder en arrière ▌ **to look down** *vi* baisser les yeux; (*from a height*) regarder en bas; (*consider scornfully*) mépriser, regarder de haut ▌ **to look for** *vt* (*seek*) chercher ▌ **to look forward to** *vt* (*event*) attendre avec impatience; **to l. forward to doing** avoir hâte de faire ▌ **to look in** *vi* regarder (à l'intérieur); **to l. in on s.o.** passer voir qn ▌ **to look into** *vt* (*examine*) examiner; (*find out about*) se renseigner sur ▌ **to look on** *vi* (*watch*) regarder ▌ *vt* (*consider*) considérer (**as** comme) ▌ **to look out** *vi* (*be careful*) faire attention (**for** à); **to l. out for** (*seek*) chercher; (*watch*) guetter; **to l. (out) on to** (*of window, house etc*) donner sur ▌ **to look over** *vt* (*examine fully*) examiner, regarder de près; (*briefly*) parcourir; (*region, town*) parcourir, visiter ▌ **to look round** *vt* (*visit*) visiter ▌ *vi* (*have a look*) regarder; (*walk round*) faire un tour; (*look back*) se retourner; **to l. round for** (*seek*) chercher ▌ **to look through** *vt* = **to look over** ▌ **to look up** *vi* (*of person*) lever les yeux; (*into the air or sky*) regarder en l'air; (*improve*) (*of situation etc*) s'améliorer; **to l. up to s.o.** *Fig* respecter qn ▌ *vt* (*word*) chercher (*dans le dictionnaire etc*); **to l. s.o. up** (*visit*) passer voir qn.

-looking ['lʊkɪŋ] *suff* **pleasant-/tired-/***etc* **l.** à l'air agréable/fatigué/*etc*.

looking-glass ['lʊkɪŋglɑːs] *n* glace *f*, miroir *m*.

lookout ['lʊkaʊt] *n* (*soldier*) guetteur *m*; (*sailor*) vigie *f*; **l. (post)** observatoire *m*; (*on ship*) vigie *f*; **to be on the l.** faire le guet; **to**

be on the l. for guetter; **that's your l.!** c'est ton problème!

loom [luːm] **1** *vi* **to l. (up)** (*of mountain etc*) apparaître indistinctement; (*of event etc*) paraître imminent. **2** *n* (*weaving machine*) métier *m* à tisser.

loony ['luːnɪ] *n & a Sl* imbécile (*mf*).

loop [luːp] *n* (*in river etc, aircraft manœuvre*) boucle *f*; (*contraceptive device*) stérilet *m* ▌ *vt* **to l. the loop** (*in aircraft*) boucler la boucle.

loophole ['luːphəʊl] *n* (*in rules*) point *m* faible, lacune *f*; (*way out*) échappatoire *f*.

loose [luːs] *a* (**-er, -est**) (*screw, belt, knot*) desserré; (*tooth, stone*) branlant; (*page*) détaché; (*clothes*) flottant; (*hair*) dénoué; (*flesh*) flasque; (*wording, translation*) approximatif, vague; (*link*) vague; (*discipline*) relâché; (*articles for sale*) en vrac; (*cheese, tea etc*) *Br* au poids; (*woman*) *Fig* facile; **there's an animal/prisoner l.** (*having escaped*) il y a un animal échappé/un prisonnier évadé; **l. change** petite monnaie *f*; **l. covers** *Br* housses *fpl*; **l. living** vie *f* dissolue; **to come *or* get l.** (*of knot, screw etc*) se desserrer; (*of page*) se détacher; (*of tooth*) se mettre à bouger; **to get l.** (*of dog*) se détacher; **to set *or* turn l.** (*dog etc*) lâcher, libérer; **he's at a l. end** *Br*, **he's at l. ends** *Am* il ne sait pas trop quoi faire.

▌ *n* **on the l.** (*prisoner etc*) évadé; (*animal*) échappé.

▌ *vt* (*animal*) lâcher.

loosely ['luːslɪ] *adv* (*to hang*) lâchement; (*to hold, tie*) sans serrer; (*to translate*) librement; (*to link*) vaguement.

loosen ['luːs(ə)n] *vt* (*knot, belt, screw*) desserrer; (*rope*) détendre; **to l. ᴗ.ᴗ's grip** relâcher son étreinte ▌ *vi* **to l. up** *Sport* faire des exercices d'assouplissement.

looseness ['luːsnəs] *n* (*of screw, machine parts*) jeu *m*.

loot [luːt] *n* butin *m*; (*money*) *Sl* fric *m* ▌ *vt* piller. ●**looting** *n* pillage *m*. ●**looter** *n* pillard, -arde *mf*.

lop [lɒp] *vt* (**-pp-**) **to l. (off)** couper.

lop-sided [lɒp'saɪdɪd] *a* (*crooked*) de travers; **to walk l.-sided** (*limp*) se déhancher.

loquacious [ləʊ'kweɪʃəs] *a* loquace.

lord [lɔːd] *n* seigneur *m*; (*British title*) lord *m*; **the L.** (*God*) le Seigneur; **L. knows if...** Dieu sait si...; **good L.!** *Fam* bon sang!; **oh L.!** *Fam* mince!; **my l.** (*to judge*) *Br* Monsieur le juge; **the House of Lords** *Br Pol* la Chambre des Lords ▌ *vt* **to l. it over s.o.** *Fam* dominer qn.

lordly ['lɔːdlɪ] *a* digne d'un grand seigneur; (*arrogant*) hautain.

lordship ['lɔːdʃɪp] *n* **Your L.** (*to judge*) *Br* Monsieur le juge.

lore [lɔːr] *n* traditions *fpl*.

lorry ['lɒrɪ] *n Br* camion *m*; (*heavy*) poids *m* lourd; **l. driver** camionneur *m*; **long-distance l. driver** routier *m*.

lose [luːz] *vt* (*pt & pp* **lost**) perdre; **to get lost** (*of person*) se perdre; **the ticket/***etc* **got lost**

on a perdu le billet/*etc*; **that lost us the war/ our jobs** cela nous a fait perdre la guerre/ notre travail; **get lost!** *Fam* fiche le camp!; **I've lost my bearings** je suis désorienté; **the clock loses six minutes a day** la pendule retarde de six minutes par jour; **to l. one's life** trouver la mort (in dans).

▮ *vi* perdre; **to l. out** être perdant; **to l. to s.o.** (*in contest etc*) être battu par qn. ●**losing** *a* (*number, team, horse*) perdant; **a l. battle** une bataille perdue d'avance. ●**loser** *n* (*in contest etc*) perdant, -ante *mf*; (*failure in life*) *Fam* paumé, -ée *mf*; **to be a good l.** être bon *or* beau joueur.

loss [lɒs] *n* perte *f*; **at a l.** (*confused*) perplexe; **to sell sth at a l.** vendre qch à perte; **at a l. to do sth** (*unable*) incapable de faire qch; **to be at a l. (to know) what to say** ne savoir que dire.

lost [lɒst] *pt & pp of* lose ▮ *a* perdu; **l. property** *Br*, **l. and found** *Am* objets *mpl* trouvés.

lot¹ [lɒt] *n* (*destiny*) sort *m*; (*batch, plot of land*) lot *m*; **to draw lots** tirer au sort; **parking l.** *Am* parking *m*; **a bad l.** (*person*) *Br Fam* un mauvais sujet.

lot² [lɒt] *n* **the l.** (*everything*) (le) tout; **the l. of you** vous tous; **a l. of, lots of** beaucoup de; **a l.** beaucoup; **quite a l.** pas mal (of de); **such a l.** tellement, tant (of de); **what a l. of flowers/water/**etc! regarde toutes ces fleurs/toute cette eau/*etc*!, que de fleurs/ d'eau/*etc*!; **what a l.!** quelle quantité!; **what a l. of flowers/**etc **you have!** (ce) que vous avez (beaucoup) de fleurs/*etc*!

lotion ['ləʊʃ(ə)n] *n* lotion *f*.

lottery ['lɒtərɪ] *n* loterie *f*; **l. ticket** billet *m* de loterie.

lotto ['lɒtəʊ] *n* (*game*) loto *m*.

loud [laʊd] *a* (-er, -est) (*voice, music*) fort; (*noise, cry*) grand; (*laugh*) bruyant, grand; (*gaudy*) voyant; **the radio is too l.** le son (de la radio) est trop fort ▮ *adv* (*to shout etc*) fort; **out l.** tout haut. ●**loudly** *adv* (*to speak, laugh etc*) bruyamment, fort; (*to shout*) fort. ●**loudness** *n* (*of voice etc*) force *f*; (*noise*) bruit *m*.

loudhailer [laʊd'heɪlər] *n Br* mégaphone *m*. ●**loudmouth** *n* (*person*) *Fam* grande gueule *f*. ●**loud'speaker** *n* haut-parleur *m*; (*for speaking to crowd*) porte-voix *m inv*; (*of stereo system*) enceinte *f*.

lounge [laʊndʒ] **1** *n* (*in house, hotel*) salon *m*; **airport l.** salle *f* d'aéroport; **departure l.** (*in airport*) salle *f* d'embarquement; **l. suit** *Br* complet *m* veston. **2** *vi* (*loll in armchair etc*) se prélasser; **to l. about** (*idle*) paresser; (*stroll*) flâner.

louse, *pl* **lice** [laʊs, laɪs] **1** *n* (*insect*) pou *m*. **2** *n* (*person*) *Pej Sl* salaud *m*. **3** *vt* **to l. up** (*mess up*) *Sl* gâcher (*situation, projet etc*).

lousy ['laʊzɪ] *a* (-ier, -iest) (*bad*) (*food, weather etc*) *Fam* infect; **l. with** (*crammed, loaded*) *Sl* bourré de.

lout [laʊt] *n* rustre *m*. ●**loutish** *a* (*attitude*) de rustre.

lovable ['lʌvəb(ə)l] *a* adorable.

love [lʌv] **1** *n* amour *m*; **in l.** amoureux (**with** de); **they're in l.** ils s'aiment; **art is their l.** l'art est leur passion; **yes, my l.** oui mon amour; **yes, l.!** *Sl* = oui monsieur *ou* madame!

▮ *vt* aimer; (*like very much*) aimer (beaucoup), adorer (**to do, doing** faire); **give him or her my l.** (*greeting*) dis-lui bien des choses de ma part; **l. affair** liaison *f* (amoureuse); **l. life** vie *f* sentimentale.

2 *n Tennis* rien *m*, zéro *m*; **15 l.** 15 à rien, 15 zéro. ●**loving** *a* affectueux, aimant.

lovely ['lʌvlɪ] *a* (-ier, -iest) (*pleasing*) agréable, bon (*f* bonne); (*excellent*) excellent; (*pretty*) joli; (*charming*) charmant; (*kind*) gentil; **the weather's l.** il fait beau; **l. to see you!** je suis ravi de te voir!; **l. and warm/ dry/**etc bien chaud/sec/*etc*.

lover ['lʌvər] *n* (*man*) amant *m*; (*woman*) maîtresse *f*; **a l. of music/art/**etc un amateur de musique/d'art/*etc*; **a nature l.** un amoureux de la nature.

lovesick ['lʌvsɪk] *a* amoureux.

low¹ [ləʊ] *a* (-er, -est) bas (*f* basse); (*speed, income, intelligence*) faible; (*opinion, quality*) mauvais; **she's l. on** (*money etc*) elle n'a plus beaucoup de; **to feel l.** (*depressed*) être déprimé; **in a l. voice** à voix basse; **lower inférieur**; **the lower middle class** la petite bourgeoisie.

▮ *adv* (-er, -est) bas; **to turn (down) l.** mettre plus bas; **to run l.** (*of supplies*) s'épuiser.

n Met dépression *f*; **to reach a new l.** *or* **an all-time l.** (*of prices etc*) atteindre leur niveau le plus bas.

low² [ləʊ] *vi* (*of cattle*) meugler.

low beams [ləʊ'biːmz] *npl* (*of vehicle*) *Am* codes *mpl*. ●**low-'calorie** *a* (*diet*) (à) basses calories. ●**low-'cost** *a* bon marché *inv*. ●**low-cut** *a* décolleté. ●**low-down** *a* méprisable. ●**lowdown** *n* (*facts*) *Fam* tuyaux *mpl*. ●**low-'fat** *a* (*milk*) écrémé; (*cheese*) allégé. ●**low-'key** *a* (*discreet*) discret. ●**'lowland(s)** *n* plaine *f*. ●**low-'level** *a* bas (*f* basse). ●**low-'loader** *n* camion *m* à plateforme surbaissée. ●**low-'lying** *a* (*region etc*) bas (*f* basse). ●**low-paid** *a* mal payé. ●**low-'salt** *a* (*food*) à faible teneur en sel.

lower ['ləʊər] *vt* baisser; **to l. s.o./sth** (*by rope*) descendre qn/qch; **to l. oneself** *Fig* s'abaisser. ●**lowering** *n* (*drop*) baisse *f*.

lowly ['ləʊlɪ] *a* (-ier, -iest) humble.

lox [lɒks] *n Am* saumon *m* fumé.

loyal ['lɔɪəl] *a* fidèle (**to** à), loyal (**to** envers). ●**loyalty** *n* fidélité *f*, loyauté *f*.

lozenge ['lɒzɪndʒ] *n* (*tablet*) pastille *f*; (*shape*) losange *m*.

LP [el'piː] *abbr* (*long-playing record*) 33 tours - *m inv*.

L-plates ['elpleɪts] *npl* (*for vehicle*) *Br* plaques *fpl* d'apprenti conducteur.

Ltd *abbr* (*Limited*) *Br Com* SARL.

lubricate ['luːbrɪkeɪt] *vt* lubrifier; (*machine,*

car wheels etc) graisser. ●**lubricant** *n* lubrifiant *m*. ●**lubrication** [-'keɪʃ(ə)n] *n* (*of machine etc*) graissage *m*.

lucid ['luːsɪd] *a* lucide. ●**lu'cidity** *n* lucidité *f*.

luck [lʌk] *n* (*chance*) chance *f*; (*good fortune*) (bonne) chance *f*, bonheur *m*; (*fate*) hasard *m*, fortune *f*; **bad l.** malchance *f*, malheur *m*; **hard l.!, tough l.!** pas de chance!; **worse l.** (*unfortunately*) malheureusement; **to be in l./out of l.** avoir/ne pas avoir de la chance.

luckily ['lʌkɪlɪ] *adv* heureusement.

lucky ['lʌkɪ] *a* (**-ier, -iest**) (*person*) chanceux, heureux; (*guess, event*) heureux; **to be l.** (*of person*) avoir de la chance; **it's l. that** c'est une chance que (+ *sub*); **I've had a l. day** j'ai eu de la chance aujourd'hui; **l. charm** porte-bonheur *m inv*; **l. number/***etc* chiffre *m*/*etc* porte-bonheur; **l. dog** veinard, -arde *mf*; **how l.!** quelle chance!

lucrative ['luːkrətɪv] *a* lucratif.

ludicrous ['luːdɪkrəs] *a* ridicule.

ludo ['luːdəʊ] *n* (*game*) *Br* jeu *m* des petits chevaux.

lug [lʌg] *vt* (**-gg-**) (*pull*) traîner; **to l. sth around** trimbaler qch.

luggage ['lʌgɪdʒ] *n* bagages *mpl*; **a piece of l.** un bagage; **hand l.** bagages *mpl* à main; **l. compartment** compartiment *m* à bagages; **l. van** (*on train*) *Br* fourgon *m*.

lugubrious [luː'guːbrɪəs] *a* lugubre.

lukewarm ['luːkwɔːm] *a* tiède.

lull [lʌl] **1** *n* arrêt *m*; (*in storm*) accalmie *f*. **2** *vt* (**-ll-**) apaiser; **to l. s.o. to sleep** endormir qn; **to be lulled into a false sense of security** s'endormir dans un sentiment de sécurité trompeur.

lullaby ['lʌləbaɪ] *n* berceuse *f*.

lumbago [lʌm'beɪgəʊ] *n* lumbago *m*.

lumber¹ ['lʌmbər] *n* (*timber*) bois *m* de charpente; (*junk*) *Br* bric-à-brac *m inv*. ●**lumberjack** *n* *Am Can* bûcheron *m*. ●**lumberjacket** *n* blouson *m*. ●**lumber-room** *n* *Br* débarras *m*.

lumber² ['lʌmbər] *vt* *Br Fam* **to l. s.o. with sth/s.o.** coller qch/qn à qn; **he got lumbered with the chore** il s'est appuyé la corvée.

luminous ['luːmɪnəs] *a* (*colour, paper, ink etc*) fluo *inv*; (*dial, clock*) lumineux.

lump [lʌmp] *n* morceau *m*; (*in soup*) grumeau *m*; (*bump*) bosse *f*; (*swelling*) grosseur *f*; **l. sum** somme *f* forfaitaire ▮ *vt* **to l. together** réunir; *Fig Pej* mettre dans le même sac. ●**lumpy** *a* (**-ier, -iest**) (*soup etc*) grumeleux; (*surface*) bosselé; (*mattress*) rembourré avec des noyaux de pêche.

lunacy ['luːnəsɪ] *n* folie *f*, démence *f*; **it's**

(*sheer*) **l.** c'est de la folie *or* de la démence.

lunar ['luːnər] *a* lunaire; **l. module** module *m* lunaire.

lunatic ['luːnətɪk] *a* fou (*f* folle), dément ▮ *n* fou *m*, folle *f*.

lunch [lʌntʃ] *n* déjeuner *m*; **to have l.** déjeuner; **l. break, l. hour, l. time** heure *f* du déjeuner ▮ *vi* déjeuner (**on, off** de). ●**lunchbox** *n* boîte *f* à sandwichs *or* à casse-croûte.

luncheon ['lʌnʃ(ə)n] *n* déjeuner *m*; **l. meat** mortadelle *f*, saucisson *m*; **l. voucher** *Br* chèque-déjeuner *m*.

lung [lʌŋ] *n* poumon *m*; **l. cancer** cancer *m* du poumon.

lunge [lʌndʒ] *n* coup *m* en avant ▮ *vi* **to l. at s.o.** se ruer sur qn.

lurch [lɜːtʃ] **1** *vi* (*of person*) tituber; (*of ship*) faire une embardée. **2** *n* **to leave s.o. in the l.** *Fam* laisser qn en plan, laisser tomber qn.

lure [lʊər] *vt* attirer (par la ruse) (**into** dans) ▮ *n* (*attraction*) attrait *m*.

lurid ['lʊərɪd] *a* (*horrifying*) horrible, affreux; (*sensational*) à sensation; (*gaudy*) voyant; (*colour, sunset*) sanglant.

lurk [lɜːk] *vi* (*hide*) se cacher (**in** dans); (*prowl*) rôder; (*of suspicion, fear etc*) persister.

luscious ['lʌʃəs] *a* (*food etc*) appétissant.

lush [lʌʃ] **1** *a* (*vegetation*) luxuriant; (*wealthy*) (*surroundings etc*) opulent. **2** *n* (*drunkard*) *Am Sl* poivrot, -ote *mf*.

lust [lʌst] *n* (*for person, object*) convoitise *f* (**for** de); (*for power, knowledge*) soif *f* (**for** de) ▮ *vi* **to l. after** (*object, person*) convoiter; (*power, knowledge*) avoir soif de.

lustre ['lʌstər] (*Am* **luster**) *n* (*gloss*) lustre *m*.

lusty ['lʌstɪ] *a* (**-ier, -iest**) vigoureux.

lute [luːt] *n* (*musical instrument*) luth *m*.

Luxembourg ['lʌksəmbɜːg] *n* Luxembourg *m*.

luxuriant [lʌg'zʊərɪənt] *a* luxuriant.

luxuriate [lʌg'zʊərɪeɪt] *vi* (*laze about*) paresser (**in bed**/*etc* au lit/*etc*).

luxury ['lʌkʃərɪ] *n* luxe *m* ▮ *a* (*goods, car, home etc*) de luxe. ●**luxurious** [lʌg'zʊərɪəs] *a* luxueux.

lychee [laɪ'tʃiː] *n* (*fruit*) litchi *m*.

lying ['laɪɪŋ] *pres p of* **lie¹,²** ▮ *n* le mensonge ▮ *a* (*journalist etc*) menteur.

lynch [lɪntʃ] *vt* lyncher. ●**lynching** *n* lynchage *m*.

lynx [lɪŋks] *n* (*animal*) lynx *m*.

lyre ['laɪər] *n* (*musical instrument*) *Hist* lyre *f*.

lyric ['lɪrɪk] *a* lyrique. ●**lyrics** *npl* (*of song*) paroles *fpl*. ●**lyrical** *a* (*person*) (*effusive etc*) lyrique. ●**lyricism** *n* lyrisme *m*.

M

M, m [em] n M, m m.
m abbr **1** (metre) mètre m. **2** (mile) mile m.
MA abbr = Master of Arts.
ma'am [mæm] n madame f.
mac [mæk] n (raincoat) Br Fam imper m.
macabre [mə'kɑːbrə] a macabre.
macaroni [mækə'rəʊni] n macaroni(s) m(pl);
m. cheese Br macaroni(s) au gratin.
macaroon [mækə'ruːn] n (cake) macaron m.
mace [meis] n (staff, rod) masse f.
Machiavellian [mækɪə'veliən] a machiavélique.
machination [mækɪ'neiʃ(ə)n] n machination f.
machine [mə'ʃiːn] n (apparatus, car, system etc) machine f; **change/cash m.** distributeur m de monnaie/billets; **m. code** (for computer) code m machine.
machinegun [mə'ʃiːngʌn] n (heavy) mitrailleuse f; (portable) mitraillette f ▮ vt (-nn-) mitrailler.
machinery [mə'ʃiːnəri] n (machines) machines fpl; (works) mécanisme m; (of organization etc) Fig rouages mpl.
machinist [mə'ʃiːnist] n (on sewing machine) Br piqueur, -euse mf.
macho ['mætʃəʊ] n (pl -os) macho m ▮ a (attitude etc) macho (f inv).
mackerel ['mækrəl] n (fish) maquereau m.
mackintosh ['mækintɒʃ] n Br imperméable m.
macro ['mækrəʊ] n (pl -os) Comptr macro-instruction f.
mad [mæd] a (madder, maddest) fou (f folle); (angry) furieux (contre qn); **to be m. about** or Br **m. (keen) on** Fam (person) être fou de; (films etc) être passionné de, se passionner or s'emballer pour; **to drive s.o. m.** rendre qn fou; (irritate) énerver qn; **he drove me m. to go** Fam il m'a cassé les pieds pour que j'y aille; **to run/work/etc like m.** courir/travailler/etc comme un fou or une folle; **m. dog** chien m enragé; **m. bull** taureau m furieux.
Madagascar [mædə'gæskər] n Madagascar f.
madam ['mædəm] n (married) madame f; (unmarried) mademoiselle f.
maddening ['mæd(ə)nɪŋ] a exaspérant.
made [meɪd] pt & pp of **make**. ●**made-to-measure** a (suit etc) Br (fait) sur mesure.
Madeira [mə'dɪərə] n (island) Madère f; (wine) madère m.
madhouse ['mædhaʊs] n Fam maison f de fous. ●**madly** adv (in love, to spend money etc) follement; (desperately) désespérément. ●**madman** n (pl -men) fou m. ●**madness** n

folie f. ●**madwoman** n (pl -women) folle f.
madonna [mə'dɒnə] n Rel madone f.
maestro ['maistrəʊ] n (pl -os) (skilled musician) maestro m.
Mafia ['mæfɪə] n maf(f)ia f.
magazine [mægə'ziːn] n (periodical) magazine m, revue f; (TV or radio broadcast) magazine m; (of gun, slide projector) magasin m.
maggot ['mægət] n ver m, asticot m. ●**maggoty** a véreux.
magic ['mædʒɪk] n magie f ▮ a (wand etc) magique; **m. spell** sort m; **the m. word** la formule magique. ●**magical** a (atmosphere, evening etc) magique. ●**magician** [mə'dʒɪʃən] n magicien, -ienne mf.
magistrate ['mædʒɪstreɪt] n magistrat m.
magnanimous [mæg'nænɪməs] a magnanime.
magnate ['mægneɪt] n (tycoon) magnat m.
magnesium [mæg'niːzɪəm] n magnésium m.
magnet ['mægnɪt] n aimant m. ●**mag'netic** a magnétique. ●**magnetism** n magnétisme m. ●**magnetize** vt magnétiser.
magnificent [mæg'nɪfɪsənt] a magnifique. ●**magnificence** n magnificence f. ●**magnificently** adv magnifiquement.
magnify ['mægnɪfaɪ] vt (image) grossir; (sound) amplifier; (exaggerate) Fig grossir; **magnifying glass** loupe f. ●**magnification** [-'keɪʃ(ə)n] n grossissement m; (of sound) amplification f.
magnitude ['mægnɪtuːd] n (of disaster etc) ampleur f.
magnolia [mæg'nəʊlɪə] n (tree) magnolia m.
magpie ['mægpaɪ] n (bird) pie f.
mahogany [mə'hɒgənɪ] n acajou m.
maid [meɪd] n (servant) bonne f; **old m.** Pej vieille fille f; **m. of honor** (at wedding) Am première demoiselle d'honneur.
maiden ['meɪd(ə)n] n Old-fashioned jeune fille f ▮ a (speech, flight, voyage) inaugural; **m. name** nom m de jeune fille. ●**maidenly** a Old-fashioned virginal.
mail [meɪl] n (system) poste f; (letters) courrier m ▮ a (bag etc) postal; **m. order** vente f par correspondance; **m. van** Br (vehicle) camion m des postes; (in train) fourgon m postal ▮ vt (letter) poster, mettre à la poste; **mailing list** liste f d'adresses. ●**mailbox** n Am boîte f aux or à lettres. ●**mailman** n (pl -men) Am facteur m.
maim [meɪm] vt mutiler, estropier.
main[1] [meɪn] a principal; **the m. thing is to...** l'essentiel est de...; **m. line** Rail grande ligne f; **m. road** grand-route f; **in the m.** (mostly)

en gros, dans l'ensemble.

main² [meɪn] *n* water/gas m. conduite *f* d'eau/de gaz; **the mains** (*electricity*) le secteur; **a mains radio** une radio secteur.

mainframe ['meɪnfreɪm] *n* **m.** (*computer*) ordinateur *m* central. ● **mainland** *n* continent *m*.

mainly ['meɪnlɪ] *adv* surtout, principalement.

mainstay ['meɪnsteɪ] *n* (*of family etc*) soutien *m*; (*of organization, policy*) pilier *m*. ● **mainstream** *n* tendance *f* dominante.

maintain [meɪn'teɪn] *vt* (*continue*) maintenir (*tradition, candidature etc*); (*vehicle, family etc*) entretenir; (*silence*) garder; **to m. law and order** faire respecter l'ordre public; **to m. that** (*assert*) affirmer *or* maintenir que. ● **maintenance** *n* (*of vehicle, road etc*) entretien *m*; (*of tradition, prices, position etc*) maintien *m*; (*alimony*) pension *f* alimentaire.

maisonette [meɪzə'net] *n* Br duplex *m*.

maître d' [meɪtrə'diː] *n* (*in restaurant*) Am maître *m* d'hôtel.

maize [meɪz] *n* (*cereal*) Br maïs *m*.

majesty ['mædʒəstɪ] *n* majesté *f*; **Your M.** (*title*) Votre Majesté. ● **ma'jestic** *a* majestueux.

major ['meɪdʒər] **1** *a* (*main, great*) & Mus majeur; **a m. road** une grande route. **2** *n* (*officer*) commandant *m*. **3** *n* (*subject of study in university*) Am dominante *f* ▮ *vi* **to m. in** se spécialiser en.

Majorca [mə'jɔːkə] *n* Majorque *f*.

majorette [meɪdʒə'ret] *n* (*drum*) **m.** majorette *f*.

majority [mə'dʒɒrɪtɪ] *n* majorité *f* (**of** de); **to be in the** *or* **a m.** être en majorité *or* majoritaire; **the m. of people** la plupart des gens ▮ *a* (*vote etc*) majoritaire.

make [meɪk] *vt* (*pt & pp* made) faire; (*tool, vehicle etc*) fabriquer; (*decision*) prendre; (*friends, salary*) se faire; (*destination*) arriver à; **to m. s.o. happy/tired/etc** rendre qn heureux/fatigué/etc; **he made ten francs on it** (*as profit*) ça lui a rapporté dix francs; **she made the train** (*did not miss*) elle a eu le train; **to m. s.o. do sth** faire faire qch à qn, obliger qn à faire qch; **to m. oneself heard** se faire entendre; **to m. oneself at home** se mettre à l'aise; **to m. sth ready** préparer qch; **to m. sth yellow** jaunir qch; **she made him her husband** elle en a fait son mari; **to m. do** (*manage*) se débrouiller (with avec); **to m. do with sth/s.o.** (*be satisfied with*) se contenter de qch/qn; **to m. it** (*arrive*) arriver; (*succeed*) réussir; **I m. it five o'clock** j'ai cinq heures; **what do you m. of it?** qu'en pensestu?; **I can't m. anything of it** je n'y comprends rien; **you're made (for life)** ton avenir est assuré; **to m. as if to** (*appear to*) faire mine de; **to m. believe** (*pretend*) faire semblant; **to m. believe that one is...** faire semblant d'être...; **to m. good** réussir; **to m. good a loss** compenser une perte; **to m. good the damage** réparer les dégâts; **to m. light of sth** prendre qch à la légère.

▮ *n* (*brand*) marque *f*; **of French/etc m.** de fabrication française/*etc*.

make-believe ['meɪkbəliːv] *n* **it's m.-believe** (*story etc*) c'est (de la) pure invention; **to live in a world of m.-believe** se bercer d'illusions.

make for *vi* (*go towards*) aller vers ▮ **to make off** *vi* (*run away*) se sauver ▮ **to make out** *vt* (*see*) distinguer; (*understand*) comprendre; (*decipher*) déchiffrer; (*write*) faire (*chèque, liste*); (*claim*) prétendre (that que); **you made me out to be stupid** tu m'as fait passer pour un idiot ▮ *vi* (*manage*) Fam se débrouiller ▮ **to make over** *vt* (*transfer*) céder; (*change, convert*) transformer (into en) ▮ **to make up** *vt* (*story*) inventer; (*put together*) faire (*collection, liste, lit etc*); (*prepare*) préparer; (*form*) former, composer; (*loss*) compenser; (*quantity*) compléter; (*quarrel*) régler; (*one's face*) maquiller ▮ *vti* **to m. (it) up** (*of friends*) se réconcilier; **to m. up for** (*loss, damage, fault*) compenser; (*lost time, mistake*) rattraper. ● **make-up** *n* (*for face*) maquillage *m*; (*of object etc*) constitution *f*; (*of person*) caractère *m*; **to wear m.-up** se maquiller; **m.-up bag** trousse *f* de maquillage.

maker ['meɪkər] *n* (*of product*) fabricant, -ante *mf*.

makeshift ['meɪkʃɪft] *n* expédient *m* ▮ *a* (*arrangement, building etc*) de fortune, provisoire.

making ['meɪkɪŋ] *n* (*manufacture*) fabrication *f*; (*of dress*) confection *f*; **history in the m.** l'histoire en train de se faire; **the makings of** les éléments *mpl* (essentiels) de; **to have the makings of a pianist/etc** avoir l'étoffe d'un pianiste/*etc*.

maladjusted [mælə'dʒʌstɪd] *a* inadapté.

malaise [mæ'leɪz] *n* malaise *m*.

malaria [mə'leərɪə] *n* malaria *f*.

Malaysia [mə'leɪzɪə] *n* Malaisie *f*.

male [meɪl] *a* (*child, animal, hormone etc*) mâle; (*clothes, sex*) masculin ▮ *n* mâle *m*.

malevolent [mə'levələnt] *a* malveillant. ● **malevolence** *n* malveillance *f*.

malfunction [mæl'fʌŋkʃ(ə)n] *n* mauvais fonctionnement *m* ▮ *vi* fonctionner mal.

malice ['mælɪs] *n* méchanceté *f*; **to bear s.o. m.** vouloir du mal à qn. ● **malicious** [mə'lɪʃəs] *a* malveillant; **m. damage** Jur dommage *m* causé avec intention de nuire. ● **ma'liciously** *adv* avec malveillance.

malign [mə'laɪn] *vt* (*slander*) dénigrer, médire de; **much maligned** très dénigré.

malignant [mə'lɪgnənt] *a* (*person etc*) malfaisant; **m. tumour** *or* **growth** tumeur *f* maligne. ● **malignancy** *n* Med malignité *f*.

malingerer [mə'lɪŋgərər] *n* (*pretending illness*) simulateur, -trice *mf*.

mall [mɔːl] *n* (*shopping*) **m.** (*covered, Am streets with shops*) centre *m* commercial.

malleable ['mælɪəb(ə)l] *a* malléable.

mallet ['mælɪt] *n* (*tool*) maillet *m*.

malnutrition [mælnjuː'trɪʃ(ə)n] *n* malnutri-

tion *f*, sous-alimentation *f*.
malpractice [mæl'præktɪs] *n* (*of doctor, lawyer*) faute *f* professionnelle.
malt [mɔːlt] *n* malt *m*.
Malta ['mɔːltə] *n* Malte *f*. ● **Mal'tese** *a* maltais ▮ *n* Maltais, -aise *mf*.
mammal ['mæm(ə)l] *n* mammifère *m*.
mammoth ['mæməθ] *a* (*large*) monstre, immense ▮ *n* (*extinct animal*) mammouth *m*.
man [mæn] *n* (*pl* **men** [men]) homme *m*; (*player in sports team*) joueur *m*; (*chess piece*) pièce *f*; **a golf m.** (*enthusiast*) un amateur de golf; **he's a Bristol m.** (*by birth*) il est de Bristol; **to be m. and wife** être mari et femme; **my old m.** *Fam* (*father*) mon père; (*husband*) mon homme; **yes old m.!** *Br Fam* oui mon vieux!; **the m. in the street** l'homme de la rue.
▮ *vt* (**-nn-**) (*be on duty at*) être de service à; (*ship*) pourvoir d'un équipage; (*fortress*) armer; (*guns*) servir; **manned spacecraft** engin *m* spatial habité. ● **manfully** *adv* vaillamment. ● **manhood** *n* (*period*) âge *m* d'homme. ● **manhunt** *n* chasse *f* à l'homme. ● **man'kind** *n* (*humanity*) le genre humain. ● **manlike** *a* (*quality*) d'homme viril. ● **manly** *a* (**-ier, -iest**) viril. ● **man-'made** *a* artificiel; (*fibre*) synthétique. ● **manservant** *n* (*pl* **menservants**) domestique *m*. ● **man-to-'man** *a* & *adv* (*discussion, to discuss*) d'homme à homme.
manacle ['mænɪk(ə)l] *n* menotte *f*.
manage ['mænɪdʒ] *vt* (*run*) diriger (*équipe, projet etc*); (*business, hotel etc*) gérer, diriger; (*handle*) manier; (*take*) *Fam* prendre; (*eat*) *Fam* manger; (*contribute*) *Fam* donner; **to m. to do** (*succeed*) réussir *or* arriver à faire; (*by being smart*) se débrouiller pour faire; **I'll m. it** j'y arriverai.
▮ *vi* (*succeed*) y arriver; (*make do*) se débrouiller (**with** avec); **to m. without sth** se passer de qch; **managing director** directeur *m* général; **the managing director** *Br* le PDG. ● **manageable** *a* (*parcel, person, car etc*) maniable; (*hair*) souple; (*feasible*) (*task, etc*) faisable. ● **management** *n* (*running, managers*) direction *f*; (*of property etc*) gestion *f*; (*executive staff*) cadres *mpl*.
manager ['mænɪdʒər] *n* directeur *m*; (*of shop, café*) gérant *m*; (*business*) **m.** (*of actor, boxer etc*) manager *m*. ● **manage'ress** *n* directrice *f*; (*of shop, café*) gérante *f*.
managerial [mænə'dʒɪərɪəl] *a* directorial; **m. job** poste *m* de direction; **the m. staff** les cadres *mpl*.
mandarin ['mændərɪn] **1** *a* & *n m.* (*orange*) mandarine *f*. **2** *n* *Br* (*high-ranking official*) haut fonctionnaire *m*; (*in political party*) bonze *m*; (*in university*) *Pej* mandarin *m*.
mandate ['mændeɪt] *n* (*authority*) mandat *m*.
mandatory ['mændətərɪ] *a* obligatoire.
mane [meɪn] *n* crinière *f*.
maneuver [mə'nuːvər] *n* & *vti* *Am* = **manoeuvre**.
mangle ['mæŋɡ(ə)l] **1** *vt* (*damage*) mutiler. **2**

n (*for wringing clothes*) essoreuse *f*.
mango ['mæŋɡəʊ] *n* (*pl* **-oes** *or* **-os**) (*fruit*) mangue *f*.
mangy ['meɪndʒɪ] *a* (*animal*) galeux.
manhandle [mæn'hænd(ə)l] *vt* maltraiter.
manhole ['mænhəʊl] *n* trou *m* d'homme; **m. cover** plaque *f* d'égout.
mania ['meɪnɪə] *n* manie *f*.
maniac ['meɪnɪæk] *n* fou *m*, folle *f*; **sex m.** obsédé *m* sexuel.
manicure ['mænɪkjʊər] *n* soin *m* des mains ▮ *vt* (*person*) manucurer; (*s.o.'s nails*) faire. ● **manicurist** *n* manucure *mf*.
manifest ['mænɪfest] **1** *a* (*plain*) manifeste. **2** *vt* (*show*) manifester.
manifesto [mænɪ'festəʊ] *n* (*pl* **-os** *or* **-oes**) (*of political party*) manifeste *m*.
manifold ['mænɪfəʊld] *a* multiple.
manipulate [mə'nɪpjʊleɪt] *vt* manœuvrer; (*facts, electors etc*) *Pej* manipuler. ● **manipulation** [-'leɪʃ(ə)n] *n* manœuvre *f*; (*of facts etc*) *Pej* manipulation *f* (**of** de).
mankind [mæn'kaɪnd] *n* (*humanity*) le genre humain.
manner ['mænər] *n* (*way*) manière *f*; (*behaviour*) attitude *f*, comportement *m*; **manners** (*social habits*) manières *fpl*; **in this m.** (*like this*) de cette manière; **all m. of** toutes sortes de; **to have good/bad manners** être bien/mal élevé.
mannered ['mænəd] *a* (*affected*) maniéré; **well-/bad-m.** bien/mal élevé.
mannerism ['mænərɪz(ə)m] *n* *Pej* tic *m*.
manoeuvre [mə'nuːvər] (*Am* **maneuver**) *n* manœuvre *f* ▮ *vti* manœuvrer. ● **manoeuvra'bility** *n* (*of vehicle etc*) maniabilité *f*.
manor ['mænər] *n* **m. (house)** *Br* manoir *m*.
manpower ['mænpaʊər] *n* (*labour*) main-d'œuvre *f*; (*soldiers etc*) effectifs *mpl*; (*effort*) force *f*.
mansion ['mænʃ(ə)n] *n* (*in town*) hôtel *m* particulier; (*in country*) manoir *m*.
manslaughter ['mænslɔːtər] *n* *Jur* homicide *m* involontaire.
mantelpiece ['mænt(ə)lpiːs] *n* (*shelf*) cheminée *f*.
mantle ['mænt(ə)l] *n* (*cloak*) cape *f*.
manual ['mænjʊəl] **1** *a* (*work etc*) manuel. **2** *n* (*book*) manuel *m*.
manufacture [mænjʊ'fæktʃər] *vt* fabriquer ▮ *n* fabrication *f*. ● **manufacturer** *n* fabricant, -ante *mf*.
manure [mə'njʊər] *n* fumier *m*, engrais *m*.
manuscript ['mænjʊskrɪpt] *n* manuscrit *m*.
many ['menɪ] *a* & *n* beaucoup (de); **m. things** beaucoup de choses; **m. came** beaucoup sont venus; **very m., a good** *or* **great m.** un très grand nombre (de); **(a good** *or* **great) m. of** (*very*) **m. of** un (très) grand nombre de; **m. of them** un grand nombre d'entre eux; **m. times, m. a time** bien des fois; **m. kinds** toutes sortes (of de); **how m.?** combien (de)?; **too m.** trop (de); **one too m.** un de trop; **there are too m. of them** ils sont

trop nombreux; **so m.** tant (de); **as m. books**/*etc* as autant de livres/*etc* que; **as m. as fifty**/*etc* (*up to*) jusqu'à cinquante/*etc*.

map [mæp] *n* (*of country, region etc*) carte *f*; (*plan of town, bus or train network etc*) plan *m* ▌*vt* (**-pp-**) (*country, town etc*) faire la carte *or* le plan de; **to m. out** (*road*) faire le tracé de; (*one's day, career etc*) *Fig* organiser.

maple ['meɪp(ə)l] *n* (*tree, wood*) érable *m*.

mar [mɑːr] *vt* (**-rr-**) gâter.

marathon ['mærəθən] *n* marathon *m*.

maraud [mə'rɔːd] *vi* piller. ●**marauding** *a* pillard. ●**marauder** *n* pillard, -arde *mf*.

marble ['mɑːb(ə)l] *n* (*substance*) marbre *m*; (*toy ball*) bille *f*.

march [mɑːtʃ] *n* marche *f* (*militaire*) ▌*vi* (*of soldiers, demonstrators*) défiler; (*walk in step*) marcher (au pas); **to m. in/out/***etc* *Fig* entrer/sortir/*etc* d'un pas décidé; **to m. past** défiler; **to m. past s.o.** défiler devant qn ▌*vt* **to m. s.o. off** *or* **away** emmener qn. ●**march-past** *n* *Br* défilé *m*.

March [mɑːtʃ] *n* mars *m*.

marchioness ['mɑːʃənes] *n* (*title*) marquise *f*.

mare [meər] *n* jument *f*.

margarine [mɑːdʒə'riːn] *n* margarine *f*.

marge [mɑːdʒ] *n* *Br Fam* margarine *f*.

margin ['mɑːdʒɪn] *n* (*of page etc*) marge *f*; **by a narrow m.** (*to win*) de justesse. ●**marginal** *a* marginal; (*unimportant*) négligeable; **m. seat** *Br Pol* siège *m* disputé. ●**marginally** *adv* très légèrement.

marguerite [mɑːgə'riːt] *n* (*daisy*) marguerite *f*.

marigold ['mærɪgəʊld] *n* (*flower*) souci *m*.

marijuana [mærɪ'wɑːnə] *n* marijuana *f*.

marina [mə'riːnə] *n* (*for pleasure boats*) marina *f*.

marinate ['mærɪneɪt] *vti* Culin mariner.

marine [mə'riːn] **1** *a* (*life, flora etc*) marin. **2** *n* (*soldier*) fusilier *m* marin, *Am* marine *m*.

marionette [mærɪə'net] *n* marionnette *f*.

marital ['mærɪt(ə)l] *a* matrimonial; (*relations*) conjugal; **m. status** situation *f* de famille.

maritime ['mærɪtaɪm] *a* (*climate, province etc*) maritime.

marjoram ['mɑːdʒərəm] *n* (*spice*) marjolaine *f*.

mark¹ [mɑːk] *n* (*symbol*) marque *f*; (*stain, trace*) trace *f*, tache *f*, marque *f*; (*token, sign*) signe *m*; (*for school exercise etc*) note *f*; (*target*) but *m*; (*model of machine, aircraft etc*) série *f*; **to make one's m.** *Fig* s'imposer; **up to the m.** (*person, work*) à la hauteur.

▌*vt* marquer; (*exam etc*) corriger, noter; (*pay attention to*) faire attention à; **to m. time** (*of soldier etc*) marquer le pas; (*wait*) *Fig* piétiner; **m. you...!** *Br* remarquez que...; **to m. down** (*price*) baisser; **to m. off** (*separate*) séparer; (*on list*) cocher; (*area*) délimiter; **to m. out** (*area*) délimiter; **to m. s.o. out for** désigner qn pour; **to m. up** (*price*) augmenter.

mark² [mɑːk] *n* (*currency*) mark *m*.

marked [mɑːkt] *a* (*noticeable*) marqué. ●**markedly** [-ɪdlɪ] *adv* visiblement.

marker ['mɑːkər] *n* (*pen*) marqueur *m*; (*flag etc*) marque *f*; (*bookmark*) signet *m*.

market ['mɑːkɪt] *n* marché *m*; **on the open m.** en vente libre; **on the black m.** au marché noir; **the Common M.** le Marché commun; **m. value** valeur *f* marchande; **m. price** prix *m* courant; **m. garden** *Br* jardin *m* maraîcher; **m. gardener** *Br* maraîcher, -ère *mf*.

▌*vt* (*sell*) vendre; (*launch*) commercialiser. ●**marketing** *n* marketing *m*, vente *f*.

marketable ['mɑːkɪtəb(ə)l] *a* vendable.

marking(s) ['mɑːkɪŋz] *n(pl)* (*on animal etc*) marques *fpl*; (*on road*) signalisation *f* horizontale.

marksman ['mɑːksmən] *n* (*pl* **-men**) tireur *m* d'élite.

marmalade ['mɑːməleɪd] *n* confiture *f* d'oranges.

maroon [mə'ruːn] *a* (*colour*) bordeaux *inv*.

marooned [mə'ruːnd] *a* abandonné; (*in snowstorm etc*) bloqué (by par).

marquee [mɑː'kiː] *n* (*for concerts etc*) chapiteau *m*; (*awning*) *Am* marquise *f*.

marquis ['mɑːkwɪs] *n* marquis *m*.

marriage ['mærɪdʒ] *n* mariage *m*; **to be related by m. to s.o.** être parent par alliance de qn; **m. bond** lien *m* conjugal; **m. bureau** agence *f* matrimoniale; **m. certificate** extrait *m* d'acte de mariage. ●**marriageable** *a* en état de se marier.

marrow ['mærəʊ] *n* **1** (*of bone*) moelle *f*. **2** (*vegetable*) *Br* courge *f*.

marry ['mærɪ] *vt* épouser, se marier avec; **to m. s.o. (off)** (*of priest etc*) marier qn ▌*vi* se marier. ●**married** *a* marié; (*life, state*) conjugal; **m. name** nom *m* de femme mariée; **to get m.** se marier.

marsh [mɑːʃ] *n* marais *m*, marécage *m*. ●**marshland** *n* marécages *mpl*.

marshal ['mɑːʃ(ə)l] **1** *n* (*in army*) maréchal *m*; (*in airforce*) général *m*; (*at public event*) *Br* membre *m* du service d'ordre; (*police officer*) *Am* shérif *m*. **2** *vt* (*Br* **-ll-**, *Am* **-l-**) (*gather*) rassembler (*faits, troupes*); (*lead*) mener cérémonieusement.

marshmallow [mɑːʃ'mæləʊ] *n* (*sweet food*) (pâte *f* de) guimauve *f*.

martial ['mɑːʃ(ə)l] *a* (*art, bearing etc*) martial; **m. law** loi *f* martiale.

Martian ['mɑːʃ(ə)n] *n & a* martien, -ienne (*mf*).

martyr ['mɑːtər] *n* martyr, -yre *mf* ▌*vt* martyriser. ●**martyrdom** *n* martyre *m*.

marvel ['mɑːv(ə)l] *n* (*wonder*) merveille *f*; (*miracle*) miracle *m* ▌*vi* (*Br* **-ll-**, *Am* **-l-**) s'émerveiller (at de) ▌*vt* **to m. that** s'étonner de ce que (+ *sub or indic*).

marvellous ['mɑːv(ə)ləs] (*Am* **marvelous**) *a* merveilleux.

Marxism ['mɑːksɪz(ə)m] *n* marxisme *m*. ●**Marxist** *a & n* marxiste (*mf*).

marzipan ['mɑːzɪpæn] *n* pâte *f* d'amandes.
mascara [mæ'skɑːrə] *n* mascara *m*.
mascot ['mæskɒt] *n* mascotte *f*.
masculine ['mæskjʊlɪn] *a* masculin.
● **mascu'linity** *n* masculinité *f*.
mash [mæʃ] *n* (*potatoes*) *Br* purée *f* (de pommes de terre); (*for poultry, pigs etc*) pâtée *f* ▮ *vt* **to m. (up)** (*crush*) écraser (en purée); **mashed potatoes** purée *f* de pommes de terre.
mask [mɑːsk] *n* masque *m* ▮ *vt* (*cover, hide*) masquer (**from** à).
masochism ['mæsəkɪz(ə)m] *n* masochisme *m*. ● **masochist** *n* masochiste *mf*. ● **maso'chistic** *a* masochiste.
mason ['meɪs(ə)n] *n* (*stonemason, Freemason*) maçon *m*. ● **masonry** *n* maçonnerie *f*.
masquerade [mɑːskə'reɪd] *vi* **to m. as** se faire passer pour ▮ *n* (*gathering, disguise*) mascarade *f*.
mass¹ [mæs] **1** *n* masse *f*; **a m. of** (*many*) une multitude de; (*pile*) un tas de, une masse de; **to be a m. of bruises** *Fam* être couvert de bleus; **masses of** des masses de; **the masses** (*people*) les masses *fpl*.
▮ *a* (*education*) des masses; (*demonstration, culture*) de masse; (*protests, departure*) en masse; (*unemployment, destruction*) massif; (*hysteria*) collectif; **m. grave** fosse *f* commune; **m. media** mass media *mpl*; **m. murderer** boucher *m*; **m. production** production *f* en série.
2 *vi* (*of troops, people*) se masser. ● **mass-pro'duce** *vt* fabriquer en série.
mass² [mæs] *n* (*church service*) messe *f*.
massacre ['mæsəkər] *n* massacre *m* ▮ *vt* massacrer.
massage ['mæsɑːʒ] *n* massage *m* ▮ *vt* masser; **to m. the figures** *Fig* manipuler les chiffres. ● **ma'sseur** *n* masseur *m*. ● **ma'sseuse** *n* masseuse *f*.
massive ['mæsɪv] *a* (*huge*) énorme, considérable; (*dose, vote*) massif; (*solid*) (*building etc*) massif. ● **massively** *adv* (*to increase, reduce etc*) considérablement, énormément.
mast [mɑːst] *n* (*of ship*) mât *m*; (*for TV, radio*) pylône *m*.
master ['mɑːstər] *n* maître *m*; (*teacher in secondary school*) *Br* professeur *m*; (*in primary school*) *Br* instituteur *m*, maître *m*; **a m.'s degree** une maîtrise (**in** de); **M. of Arts/Science** (*person*) Maître *m* ès lettres/sciences; **m. of ceremonies** (*presenter*) *Am* animateur, -trice *mf*; **m. card** carte *f* maîtresse; **m. copy** original *m*; **m. key** passe-partout *m inv*; **m. plan** plan *m* d'action; **m. stroke** coup *m* de maître; **old m.** (*painting*) tableau *m* de maître; **I'm my own m.** je ne dépends que de moi.
▮ *vt* (*control*) maîtriser; (*subject, situation*) dominer; **she has mastered Latin/English/etc** elle possède le latin/l'anglais/etc.
masterly ['mɑːstəlɪ] *a* magistral.
mastermind ['mɑːstəmaɪnd] *n* (*person*) cerveau *m* (**behind** derrière) ▮ *vt* organiser.

masterpiece ['mɑːstəpiːs] *n* chef-d'œuvre *m*.
mastery ['mɑːstərɪ] *n* maîtrise *f* (**of** de).
mastic ['mæstɪk] *n* (*for window frames etc*) mastic *m* (silicone).
masturbate ['mæstəbeɪt] *vi* se masturber. ● **masturbation** [-'beɪʃ(ə)n] *n* masturbation *f*.
mat¹ [mæt] *n* tapis *m*; (*of straw*) natte *f*; (*at door*) paillasson *m*; (*for table*) (*of fabric*) napperon *m*; (*hard*) dessous-de-plat *m inv*; (**place**) **m. set** *m* (de table).
mat² [mæt] *a* (*paint, paper*) mat (*f* mate).
match¹ [mætʃ] *n* (*stick*) allumette *f*; **book of matches** pochette *f* d'allumettes. ● **matchbox** *n* boîte *f* d'allumettes. ● **matchstick** *n* allumette *f*.
match² [mætʃ] *n* (*game*) match *m*; **tennis m.** partie *f* de tennis.
match³ [mætʃ] *n* (*equal*) égal, -ale *mf*; (*marriage*) mariage *m*; **to be a good m.** (*of colours, people etc*) être bien assortis; **he's a good m.** (*man to marry*) c'est un bon parti.
▮ *vt* (*of clothes, colour etc*) aller (bien) avec; (*plates etc*) assortir; (*equal*) égaler; **to m. up** (*plates etc*) assortir; **to m. up (to)** (*equal*) égaler; (*s.o.'s hopes or expectations*) répondre à; **to be well-matched** (*of colours, people etc*) être (bien) assortis, aller (bien) ensemble.
▮ *vi* (*go with each other*) être assortis, aller (bien) ensemble. ● **matching** *a* (*dress, shirt etc*) assorti.
mate [meɪt] **1** *n* (*friend*) *Br* camarade *mf*; (*of animal*) mâle *m*, femelle *f*; **builder's/electrician's/etc m.** *Br* aide-maçon/-électricien/etc m. **2** *vi* (*of animals*) s'accoupler (**with** avec). **3** *n* *Chess* mat *m* ▮ *vt* faire ou mettre mat.
material [mə'tɪərɪəl] **1** *a* (*needs, world etc*) matériel; (*important*) important; (*fact, evidence*) *Jur* pertinent. **2** *n* (*substance*) matière *f*; (*cloth*) tissu *m*; (*for book*) matériaux *mpl*; **material(s)** (*equipment*) matériel *m*; **building materials** matériaux *mpl* de construction.
materialism [mə'tɪərɪəlɪz(ə)m] *n* matérialisme *m*. ● **materialist** *n* matérialiste *mf*. ● **materia'listic** *a* matérialiste.
materialize [mə'tɪərɪəlaɪz] *vi* se matérialiser.
materially [mə'tɪərɪəlɪ] *adv* matériellement; (*well-off etc*) sur le plan matériel.
maternal [mə'tɜːn(ə)l] *a* maternel.
maternity [mə'tɜːnɪtɪ] *n* maternité *f*; **m. allowance** *or Br* **benefit** allocation *f* de maternité; **m. clothes** vêtements *mpl* de grossesse; **m. hospital, m. unit** maternité *f*; **m. leave** congé *m* de maternité.
mathematical [mæθə'mætɪk(ə)l] *a* mathématique; **to have a m. brain** être doué pour les maths.
mathematician [mæθəmə'tɪʃ(ə)n] *n* mathématicien, -ienne *mf*.
mathematics [mæθə'mætɪks] *n* mathématiques *fpl*. ● **maths** *or Am* **math** *n Fam* maths *fpl*.
matinée ['mætɪneɪ] *n* (*in theatre etc*) matinée *f*.

matriculation [mətrıkjʊ'leıʃ(ə)n] *n Univ* inscription *f*.

matrimony ['mætrımənı] *n* mariage *m*. ● **matri'monial** *a* matrimonial.

matrix, *pl* **-ices** ['meıtrıks, -ısi:z] *n Math etc* matrice *f*.

matron ['meıtrən] *n* (*nurse*) *Br* infirmière *f* (en) chef; (*in boarding school*) *Br* infirmière *f*; (*middle-aged woman*) *Lit* mère *f* de famille, dame *f* âgée. ● **matronly** *a* (*air etc*) de mère de famille; (*mature*) mûr; (*stout*) corpulent.

matt [mæt] *a* (*paint, paper*) mat (*f* mate).

matted ['mætıd] *a* **m. hair** cheveux *mpl* emmêlés.

matter¹ ['mætər] *n* matière *f*; (*subject, affair*) affaire *f*, question *f*; **no m.!** peu importe!; **no m. what she does** quoi qu'elle fasse!; **no m. where you go** où que tu ailles; **no m. who you are** qui que vous soyez; **no m. when** quel que soit le moment; **what's the m.?** qu'est-ce qu'il y a?; **what's the m. with you?** qu'est-ce que tu as?; **there's something the m.** il y a quelque chose qui ne va pas; **there's something the m. with my leg** j'ai quelque chose à la jambe; **there's nothing the m. with him** il n'a rien.

▮ *vi* (*be important*) importer (**to s.o.** à qn); **it doesn't m. if/when/who/***etc* peu importe si/quand/qui/*etc*; **it doesn't m.!** ça ne fait rien!, peu importe!

matter² ['mætər] *n* (*pus*) pus *m*.

matter-of-fact ['mætərəv'fækt] *a* (*person, manner*) terre à terre; (*voice*) neutre.

matting ['mætıŋ] *n* (*material*) nattage *m*; **a piece of m., some m.** une natte.

mattress ['mætrəs] *n* matelas *m*.

mature [mə'tʃʊər] *a* mûr; (*cheese*) fait ▮ *vt* (*person, plan*) (faire) mûrir ▮ *vi* mûrir; (*of cheese*) se faire. ● **maturity** *n* maturité *f*.

maul [mɔ:l] *vt* (*of animal*) mutiler; (*of person*) *Fig* malmener.

Mauritius [mɔ'rıʃəs] *n* l'île *f* Maurice.

mausoleum [mɔ:sə'lıəm] *n* mausolée *m*.

mauve [məʊv] *a* & *n* (*colour*) mauve (*m*).

maverick ['mævərık] *n* & *a Pol etc* dissident, -ente (*mf*).

mawkish ['mɔ:kıʃ] *a* d'une sensiblerie excessive, mièvre.

maxim ['mæksım] *n* maxime *f*.

maximize ['mæksımaız] *vt* porter au maximum.

maximum [‚mæksıməm] *n* (*pl* **-ima** [-ımə] or **-imums**) maximum *m* ▮ *a* maximum (*f inv*), maximal.

may [meı] *v aux* (*pt* **might**) **1** (*possibility*) **he m. come** il peut arriver; **he might come** il pourrait arriver; **I m.** *or* **might be wrong** il se peut que je me trompe, je me trompe peut-être; **you m.** *or* **might have** tu aurais pu; **I m.** *or* **might have forgotten it** je l'ai peut-être oublié; **we m.** *or* **might as well go** nous ferions aussi bien de partir; **she's afraid I m.** *or* **might get lost** elle a peur que je ne me perde.

2 (*permission*) **m. I stay?** puis-je rester?; **m. I?** vous permettez?; **you m. go** tu peux partir.

3 (*wish*) **m. you be happy** (que tu) sois heureux.

May [meı] *n* mai *m*; **M. Day** le premier mai.

maybe ['meıbi:] *adv* peut-être.

mayday ['meıdeı] *n* (*distress signal*) mayday *m*, SOS *m*.

mayhem ['meıhem] *n* (*chaos*) pagaïe *f*; (*havoc*) ravages *mpl*.

mayonnaise [meıə'neız] *n* mayonnaise *f*.

mayor [meər] *n* (*man, woman*) maire *m*. ● **mayoress** *n* femme *f* du maire.

maze [meız] *n* labyrinthe *m*.

MC [em'si:] *abbr* = master of ceremonies.

MD [em'di:] *n abbr* **1** (*managing director*) *Br* PDG *m*. **2** (*Doctor of Medicine*) docteur *m* en médecine.

me [mi:] *pron* me, m'; (*after prep, 'than', 'it is' etc*) moi; **(to) me** (*indirect*) me, m'; **she knows me** elle me connaît; **he helps me** il m'aide; **he gives (to) me** il me donne; **with me** avec moi.

meadow ['medəʊ] *n* pré *m*, prairie *f*.

meagre ['mi:gər] (*Am* **meager**) *a* maigre.

meal [mi:l] *n* **1** (*food*) repas *m*. **2** (*flour*) farine *f*.

mealy-mouthed [mi:lı'maʊðd] *a* mielleux.

mean¹ [mi:n] *vt* (*pt* & *pp* **meant** [ment]) (*signify*) vouloir dire, signifier; (*intend*) destiner (**for** à); (*result in*) entraîner; (*represent*) représenter; (*refer to*) faire allusion à; **to m. to do** (*intend*) avoir l'intention de faire, vouloir faire; **I m. it, I m. what I say** je suis sérieux; **to m. something to s.o.** (*matter*) avoir de l'importance pour qn; **it means sth to me** (*name, face*) ça me dit qch; **I didn't m. to!** je ne l'ai pas fait exprès!; **you were meant to come** vous étiez censé venir.

mean² [mi:n] *a* (**-er, -est**) (*stingy with money etc*) avare, mesquin; (*petty*) mesquin; (*nasty*) méchant; (*inferior*) misérable; **she's no m. dancer/***etc* c'est une excellente danseuse/*etc*. ● **meanness** *n* (*greed*) avarice *f*; (*nastiness*) méchanceté *f*.

mean³ [mi:n] *a* (*average*) (*distance, temperature etc*) moyen ▮ *n* (*middle position*) milieu *m*; (*average, mid-point*) *Math* moyenne *f*; **the happy m.** le juste milieu.

meander [mı'ændər] *vi* (*of river*) faire des méandres.

meaning ['mi:nıŋ] *n* sens *m*, signification *f*. ● **meaningful** *a* significatif. ● **meaningless** *a* qui n'a pas de sens; (*absurd*) *Fig* insensé.

means [mi:nz] *n*(*pl*) (*method*) moyen(s) *m*(*pl*) (**to do, of doing** de faire); (*wealth*) moyens *mpl*; **by m. of a stick/***etc* au moyen d'un bâton/*etc*; **by m. of hard work/of concentration/***etc* à force de travail/de concentration/*etc*; **by all m.!** très certainement!; **by no m.** nullement; **to have independent** *or* **private m.** disposer de *or* avoir une fortune personnelle.

meant [ment] *pt* & *pp* of **mean¹**.

meantime ['miːntaɪm] *adv* & *n* (**in the**) **m.** entre-temps.

meanwhile ['miːnwaɪl] *adv* entre-temps.

measles ['miːz(ə)lz] *n* rougeole *f*.

measly ['miːzlɪ] *a* (*contemptible*) *Fam* minable.

measure ['meʒər] *n* mesure *f*; (*ruler*) règle *f*; **made to m.** *Br* fait sur mesure ▮ *vt* mesurer; (*adjust, adapt*) adapter (**to** à); **to m. out** (*ingredient*) mesurer; **to m. up** (*plank etc*) mesurer ▮ *vi* **to m. up to** (*task etc*) être à la hauteur de. ●**measured** *a* (*careful*) mesuré.

measurement ['meʒəmənt] *n* (*of chest, waist etc*) tour *m*; **measurements** (*dimensions*) mesures *fpl*; **your hip/waist/etc measurement(s)** votre tour de hanches/de taille/ etc.

meat [miːt] *n* viande *f*; (*of crab, lobster etc*) chair *f*; *Fig* substance *f*; **m. diet** régime *m* carné. ●**meatball** *n* boulette *f* (de viande). ●**meaty** *a* (**-ier, -iest**) (*fleshy*) charnu; (*flavour*) de viande; (*book etc*) *Fig* substantiel.

Mecca ['mekə] *n* la Mecque.

mechanic [mɪˈkænɪk] *n* mécanicien, -ienne *mf*. ●**mechanical** *a* mécanique; (*reply, gesture etc*) *Fig* machinal. ●**mechanics** *n* (*science*) mécanique *f*; **the mechanics** (*working parts*) le mécanisme.

mechanism ['mekənɪz(ə)m] *n* mécanisme *m*.

mechanize ['mekənaɪz] *vt* mécaniser.

medal ['med(ə)l] *n* médaille *f*.

medallion [məˈdæljən] *n* (*ornament, jewel*) médaillon *m*.

medallist ['medəlɪst] (*Am* **medalist**) *n* médaillé, -ée *mf*; **to be a gold/silver m.** *Sport* être médaille d'or/d'argent.

meddle ['med(ə)l] *vi* (*interfere*) se mêler (**in** de); (*tamper*) toucher (**with** à). ●**meddlesome** *a* qui se mêle de tout.

media ['miːdɪə] *npl* **1** **the** (**mass**) **m.** les médias *mpl*; **m. event** événement *m* médiatique. **2** *see* **medium 2**.

mediaeval [medɪˈiːv(ə)l] *a* médiéval.

median ['miːdɪən] *a* & *n* **m.** (**strip**) (*on highway*) *Am* bande *f* médiane.

mediate ['miːdɪeɪt] *vi* servir d'intermédiaire (**between** entre). ●**mediation** [-ˈeɪʃ(ə)n] *n* médiation *f*. ●**mediator** *n* médiateur, -trice *mf*.

Medicaid ['medɪkeɪd] *n* *Am* = assistance *f* médicale aux défavorisés.

medical ['medɪk(ə)l] *a* médical; (*school, studies*) de médecine; (*student*) en médecine; **m. insurance** assurance *f* maladie ▮ *n* (*in school, army*) visite *f* médicale; (*private*) examen *m* médical.

Medicare ['medɪkeər] *n* *Am* = assistance *f* médicale aux personnes âgées.

medicated ['medɪkeɪtɪd] *a* **m. shampoo** shampooing *m* médical.

medication [medɪˈkeɪʃ(ə)n] *n* médicaments *mpl*.

medicine ['medəsən] *n* (*substance*) médicament *m*; (*science*) médecine *f*; **alternative m.**

la médecine douce; **m. cabinet**, **m. chest** (armoire *f* à) pharmacie *f*. ●**me'dicinal** *a* médicinal.

medieval [medɪˈiːv(ə)l] *a* médiéval.

mediocre [miːdɪˈəʊkər] *a* médiocre. ●**mediocrity** *n* médiocrité *f*.

meditate ['medɪteɪt] *vi* méditer (**on** sur). ●**meditation** [-ˈteɪʃ(ə)n] *n* méditation *f*. ●**meditative** *a* méditatif.

Mediterranean [medɪtəˈreɪnɪən] *a* méditerranéen ▮ *n* **the M.** la Méditerranée.

medium ['miːdɪəm] **1** *a* (*average, middle*) moyen. **2** *n* (*pl* **media** ['miːdɪə]) (*of thought etc*) véhicule *m*; *Biol* milieu *m*; (*for conveying data or publicity*) support *m*; **through the m. of s.o./sth** par l'intermédiaire de qn/qch; **to find a happy m.** trouver le juste milieu. **3** *n* (*person*) (*in spiritualism*) médium *m*. ●**medium-sized** *a* moyen, de taille moyenne.

medley ['medlɪ] *n* mélange *m*; (*of songs, tunes*) pot-pourri *m*.

meek [miːk] *a* (**-er, -est**) doux (*f* douce).

meet [miːt] *vt* (*pt* & *pp* **met**) (*person, team etc*) rencontrer; (*person by arrangement*) retrouver; (*pass in street, road etc*) croiser; (*fetch*) (aller *ou* venir) chercher; (*wait for*) attendre; (*debt, enemy, danger*) faire face à; (*need*) combler; (*be introduced to*) faire la connaissance de; **to arrange to m. s.o.** donner rendez-vous à qn.
▮ *vi* (*of people, teams, rivers, looks*) se rencontrer; (*of people by arrangement*) se retrouver; (*be introduced*) se connaître; (*of club, society*) se réunir; (*of trains, vehicles*) se croiser.
▮ *n* *Sport Am* réunion *f*; **to make a m. with s.o.** *Fam* donner rendez-vous à qn.

meeting ['miːtɪŋ] *n* réunion *f*; (*large*) assemblée *f*; (*by chance between two people*) rencontre *f*; (*prearranged between two people*) rendez-vous *m inv*; **to be in a m.** être en conférence; **m. place** lieu *m* de réunion.

meet up *vi* (*of people*) se rencontrer; (*by arrangement*) se retrouver; **to m. up with s.o.** rencontrer qn; (*by arrangement*) retrouver qn ▮ **to meet with** *vt* (*accident, problem*) avoir; (*refusal, loss*) essuyer; (*obstacle, difficulty*) rencontrer; **to m. with s.o.** *Am* rencontrer qn; (*as arranged*) retrouver qn.

mega- ['megə] *pref* méga-.

megabyte ['megəbaɪt] *n* *Comptr* méga-octet *m*.

megalomania [megələʊˈmeɪnɪə] *n* mégalomanie *f*. ●**megalomaniac** *n* mégalomane *mf*.

megaphone ['megəfəʊn] *n* porte-voix *m inv*.

megastar ['megəstɑːr] *n* mégastar *f*.

melancholy ['melənkəlɪ] *n* mélancolie *f* ▮ *a* mélancolique.

mellow ['meləʊ] *a* (**-er, -est**) (*fruit*) mûr; (*colour, voice, wine*) moelleux; (*character*) mûri par l'expérience ▮ *vi* (*of person*) s'adoucir.

melodrama ['melədrɑːmə] *n* mélodrame *m*. ●**melodra'matic** *a* mélodramatique.

melody ['melədɪ] n mélodie f. ● me'lodic a mélodique. ● **melodious** [mə'ləʊdɪəs] a mélodieux.

melon ['melən] n melon m.

melt [melt] vi fondre; **to m. away** (of snow etc) fondre complètement; **to m. into** (merge into) (of colour etc) se fondre dans ▮ vt (faire) fondre; **to m. down** (metal object) fondre; **melting point** point m de fusion; **melting pot** Fig creuset m. ● **meltdown** n (of core of nuclear reactor) fusion f.

member ['membər] n membre m; **M. of Parliament** Br, **M. of Congress** Am = député m; **she's a m. of the family** elle fait partie de la famille. ● **membership** n adhésion f (of à); (number) nombre m de(s) membres; (members) membres mpl; **m. (fee)** cotisation f.

membrane ['membreɪn] n membrane f.

memento [mə'mentəʊ] n (pl -os or -oes) (object) souvenir m.

memo ['meməʊ] n (pl -os) note f; **m. pad** bloc-notes m. ● **memorandum** [memə-'rændəm] n (in office etc) note f; Pol Com mémorandum m.

memoirs ['memwɑːz] npl (essays) mémoires mpl.

memorable ['memərəb(ə)l] a mémorable.

memorial [mə'mɔːrɪəl] a (plaque etc) commémoratif ▮ n mémorial m, monument m.

memorize ['meməraɪz] vt apprendre par cœur.

memory ['memərɪ] n mémoire f; (recollection) souvenir m; **to the** or **in m. of** à la mémoire de.

men [men] npl see **man**; **the men's room** les toilettes fpl pour hommes. ● **menfolk** n Old-fashioned hommes mpl.

menace ['menɪs] n danger m; (threat) menace f; (nuisance) Fam plaie f ▮ vt (threaten) menacer. ● **menacing** a (tone etc) menaçant. ● **menacingly** adv (to say) d'un ton menaçant; (to do) d'une manière menaçante.

menagerie [mɪ'nædʒərɪ] n ménagerie f.

mend [mend] vt (repair) réparer; (clothes) raccommoder; **to m. one's ways** se corriger, s'amender ▮ n (in clothes) raccommodage m; **to be on the m.** (after illness) aller mieux.

menial ['miːnɪəl] a (work etc) inférieur.

meningitis [menɪn'dʒaɪtɪs] n méningite f.

menopause ['menəpɔːz] n ménopause f.

menstruate ['menstrʊeɪt] vi avoir ses règles. ● **menstruation** [ˌmenstrʊ'eɪʃ(ə)n] n menstruation f.

menswear ['menzweər] n vêtements mpl pour hommes.

mental ['ment(ə)l] a mental; (mad) Br Sl fou (f folle); **m. block** blocage m; **m. hospital** hôpital m psychiatrique; **m. strain** tension f nerveuse. ● **mentally** adv mentalement; **he's m. handicapped** c'est un handicapé mental; **she's m. ill** c'est une malade mentale.

mentality [men'tælətɪ] n mentalité f.

mention ['menʃ(ə)n] vt mentionner, faire mention de; **not to m....** sans parler de..., sans compter...; **don't m. it!** il n'y a pas de quoi!; **she has no savings/etc worth mentioning** elle n'a pratiquement pas d'économies/etc ▮ n mention f.

mentor ['mentɔːr] n (adviser) mentor m.

menu ['menjuː] n (in restaurant) (for set meal) menu m; (list) carte f; Comptr menu m.

MEP [emiː'piː] n abbr (Member of the European Parliament) membre m du Parlement européen.

mercantile ['mɜːkəntaɪl] a (activity, law etc) commercial; (nation) commerçant.

mercenary ['mɜːsɪnərɪ] a (bassement) intéressé ▮ n (soldier) mercenaire m.

merchandise ['mɜːtʃəndaɪz] n (articles) marchandises fpl; (total stock) marchandise f.

merchant ['mɜːtʃ(ə)nt] n (trader) négociant, -ante mf; (Br shopkeeper, Am storekeeper) commerçant, -ante mf; **retail m.** commerçant, -ante mf en détail; **wine m.** négociant, -ante mf en vins; (retail) marchand m de vins ▮ a (Br navy, Am marine) marchand; (seaman) de la marine marchande; **m. bank** Br banque f de commerce; **m. vessel** navire m marchand.

mercury ['mɜːkjʊrɪ] n mercure m.

merciful ['mɜːsɪfəl] a miséricordieux (to pour). ● **mercifully** adv (fortunately) Fam heureusement.

merciless ['mɜːsɪləs] a impitoyable.

mercy ['mɜːsɪ] n pitié f; (of God) miséricorde f; **to beg for m.** demander grâce; **at the m. of** à la merci de; **it's a m. that...** (stroke of luck) c'est une chance que...; **m. killing** euthanasie f.

mere [mɪər] a simple; (only) ne... que; **she's a m. child** ce n'est qu'une enfant; **it's a m. kilometre** ça ne fait qu'un kilomètre; **by m. chance** par pur hasard; **the m. sight of them** leur seule vue. ● **merely** adv (tout) simplement.

merge [mɜːdʒ] vi (blend) se mêler (with à); (of roads) se (re)joindre; (of companies, banks etc) fusionner ▮ vt (unify) unifier (partis, systèmes etc); (companies etc) & Comptr fusionner. ● **merger** n Com fusion f.

meridian [mə'rɪdɪən] n méridien m.

meringue [mə'ræŋ] n (cake) meringue f.

merit ['merɪt] n mérite m; **on its merits** (to consider sth etc) objectivement ▮ vt mériter.

mermaid ['mɜːmeɪd] n (woman) sirène f

merrily ['merɪlɪ] adv gaiement. ● **merriment** n gaieté f, rires mpl.

merry ['merɪ] a (-ier, -iest) gai; (drunk) éméché; **M. Christmas** Joyeux Noël. ● **merry-go-round** n (at funfair etc) manège m. ● **merry-making** n réjouissances fpl.

mesh [meʃ] n (of net etc) maille f; (fabric) tissu m à mailles; (of intrigue etc) Fig réseau m; (of circumstances) Fig engrenage m; **wire m.** grillage m.

mesmerize ['mezməraɪz] vt hypnotiser.

mess¹ [mes] **1** n (confusion) désordre m, pagaïe f; (muddle) gâchis m; (dirt) saleté f; **in**

a m. sens dessus dessous, en désordre; (*trouble*) dans le pétrin; (*sorry state*) dans un triste état; **to make a m. of sth** (*spoil*) gâcher qch.

2 *vt* **to m. s.o. about** (*bother, treat badly*) *Br Fam* déranger qn, embêter qn; **to m. up** (*spoil*) gâcher; (*dirty*) salir; (*room*) mettre sens dessus dessous or en désordre.

❚ *vi* **to m. about** *or* **around** (*have fun, waste time*) s'amuser; (*play the fool*) faire l'idiot; **to m. about** *or* **around with sth** (*fiddle with*) s'amuser avec qch. ●**mess-up** *n Br Fam* (*disorder*) gâchis *m*; (*mix-up*) confusion *f*.

mess² [mes] *n* (*room*) *Mil* mess *m inv*.

message ['mesɪdʒ] *n* message *m*.

messenger ['mesɪndʒər] *n* messager, -ère *mf*; (*in office, hotel*) coursier, -ière *mf*.

Messiah [mɪ'saɪə] *n* Messie *m*.

Messrs ['mesəz] *npl* **M. Brown** Messieurs *or* MM Brown.

messy ['mesɪ] *a* (**-ier, -iest**) (*untidy*) en désordre; (*dirty*) sale; (*confused*) (*situation, solution etc*) *Fig* embrouillé, confus.

met [met] *pt & pp of* **meet**.

metal ['met(ə)l] *n* métal *m*; **m. ladder/***etc* échelle *f/etc* métallique. ●**metallic** [mə'tælɪk] *a* (*sound etc*) métallique; (*paint*) métallisé; **a m. green car** une voiture vert métallisé. ●**metalwork** *n* (*study, craft*) travail *m* des métaux; (*objects*) ferronnerie *f*.

metamorphosis, *pl* **-oses** [metə'mɔːfəsɪs, -əsiːz] *n* métamorphose *f*.

metaphor ['metəfər] *n* métaphore *f*. ●**meta-'phorical** *a* métaphorique.

metaphysical [metə'fɪzɪk(ə)l] *a* métaphysique.

mete [miːt] *vt* **to m. out** (*punishment*) infliger (**to** à); **to m. out justice** rendre la justice.

meteor ['miːtɪər] *n* météore *m*. ●**mete'oric** *a* **m. rise** (*of politician, film star etc*) ascension *f* fulgurante. ●**meteorite** *n* météorite *m* or *f*.

meteorology [miːtɪə'rɒlədʒɪ] *n* météorologie *f*. ●**meteoro'logical** *a* météorologique.

meter¹ ['miːtər] *n* (*device*) compteur *m*; (*parking*) **m.** parcmètre *m*; **m. maid** (*for traffic*) *Br Fam & Am* contractuelle *f*; **m. man** *Am* contractuel *m*.

meter² ['miːtər] *n* (*measurement*) *Am* mètre *m*.

method ['meθəd] *n* méthode *f*. ●**me'thodical** *a* méthodique.

Methodist ['meθədɪst] *a & n Rel* méthodiste (*mf*).

methylated ['meθɪleɪtɪd] *a* **m. spirit(s)** *Br* alcool *m* à brûler. ●**meths** *n Br Fam* = **methylated spirits.**

meticulous [mɪ'tɪkjʊləs] *a* méticuleux. ●**meticulousness** *n* soin *m* méticuleux.

Met Office ['metɒfɪs] *n Br* = Météo *f* France.

metre ['miːtər] *n* (*Am* **meter**) *n* mètre *m*. ●**metric** ['metrɪk] *a* métrique.

metropolis [mə'trɒpəlɪs] *n* (*chief city*) métropole *f*. ●**metro'politan** *a* métropolitain; **the M. Police** la police de Londres.

mettle ['met(ə)l] *n* courage *m*; (*spirit*) fougue *f*.

mew [mjuː] *vi* (*of cat*) miauler.

mews [mjuːz] *n* (*street*) ruelle *f*; **m. flat** *Br* appartement *m* chic (*aménagé dans une ancienne écurie*).

Mexico ['meksɪkəʊ] *n* Mexique *m*. ●**Mexican** *a* mexicain ❚ *n* Mexicain, -aine *mf*.

mezzanine ['mezəniːn] *n* **m. (floor)** entresol *m*.

miaow [miːˈaʊ] *vi* (*of cat*) miauler ❚ *n* miaulement *m* ❚ *int* miaou.

mice [maɪs] *see* **mouse**.

mickey ['mɪkɪ] *n* **to take the m. out of s.o.** *Br Fam* charrier qn.

micro- ['maɪkrəʊ] *pref* micro-.

microbe ['maɪkrəʊb] *n* microbe *m*.

microchip ['maɪkrəʊtʃɪp] *n Comptr* puce *f*.

microcosm ['maɪkrəʊkɒz(ə)m] *n* microcosme *m*.

microfilm ['maɪkrəʊfɪlm] *n* microfilm *m*.

microlight ['maɪkrəʊlaɪt] *n* (*plane*) ULM *m*.

microphone ['maɪkrəfəʊn] *n* micro *m*.

microprocessor ['maɪkrəʊ'prəʊsesər] *n* microprocesseur *m*.

microscope ['maɪkrəskəʊp] *n* microscope *m*. ●**micro'scopic** *a* microscopique.

microwave ['maɪkrəʊweɪv] *n* micro-onde *f*; **m. (oven)** four *m* à micro-ondes.

mid [mɪd] *a* (**in**) **m.-June** (à) la mi-juin; (**in**) **m. morning** au milieu de la matinée; **in m. air** en plein ciel; **to be in one's m.-twenties** avoir environ vingt-cinq ans.

midday [mɪd'deɪ] *n* midi *m*; **at m.** à midi ❚ *a* (*sun, meal etc*) de midi.

middle ['mɪd(ə)l] *n* milieu *m*; (*waist*) *Fam* taille *f*; (**right**) **in the m. of** au (beau) milieu de; **in the m. of work** en plein travail; **in the m. of saying/working/***etc* en train de dire/travailler/*etc*.

❚ *a* (*central*) du milieu; **the M. Ages** le moyen âge; **in m. age** vers la cinquantaine; **the m. class(es)** les classes moyennes; **the m. ear** l'oreille moyenne; **the M. East** le Moyen-Orient; **m. name** deuxième nom. ●**middle-'aged** *a* d'un certain âge. ●**middle-'class** *a* bourgeois. ●**middle-of-the-'road** *a* (*politics, views*) modéré; (*music, tastes*) sage.

middling ['mɪdlɪŋ] *a* moyen, passable.

midge [mɪdʒ] *n* (*fly*) moucheron *m*.

midget ['mɪdʒɪt] *n* nain *m*, naine *f* ❚ *a* (*tiny*) minuscule.

Midlands ['mɪdləndz] *npl* **the M.** les comtés *mpl* du centre de l'Angleterre.

midnight ['mɪdnaɪt] *n* minuit *f*.

midpoint ['mɪdpɔɪnt] *n* milieu *m*.

midriff ['mɪdrɪf] *n Anat* diaphragme *m*; (*belly*) *Fam* ventre *m*.

midst [mɪdst] *n* **in the m. of** (*middle*) au milieu de; **in our/their m.** parmi nous/eux.

midsummer [mɪd'sʌmər] *n* milieu *m* de l'été; (*solstice*) solstice *m* d'été.

midterm ['mɪdtɜːm] *a* **m. holidays** (*in schools*) *Br* petites vacances *fpl*.

midway [mɪd'weɪ] *a & adv* à mi-chemin.

midweek [mɪd'wiːk] n milieu m de la semaine.

Midwest [mɪd'west] n the M. Am le Middle West (américain).

midwife ['mɪdwaɪf] n (pl -wives) sage-femme f.

midwinter [mɪd'wɪntər] n milieu m de l'hiver; (solstice) solstice m d'hiver.

miffed [mɪft] a (offended) Fam vexé (by de).

might[1] [maɪt] see may.

might[2] [maɪt] n (strength) force f. ● **mighty** a (-ier, -iest) puissant; (ocean) vaste; (very great) Fam sacré; **high and m.** arrogant ▮ adv (very) Am Fam rudement.

migraine ['miːgreɪn, 'maɪgreɪn] n migraine f.

migrate [maɪ'greɪt] vi (of people) émigrer, migrer; (of birds) migrer. ● **migrant** ['maɪgrənt] a & n m. (worker) migrant, -ante (mf). ● **migration** [-ʃ(ə)n] n migration f.

mike [maɪk] n abbr (microphone) Fam micro m.

mild [maɪld] a (-er, -est) (weather, taste, behaviour etc) doux (f douce); (beer, punishment) léger; (medicine, illness) bénin (f bénigne); (exercise) modéré. ● **mildly** adv doucement; (slightly) légèrement; **to put it m.** pour ne pas dire plus. ● **mildness** n (of weather etc) douceur f; (of beer etc) légèreté f; (of illness etc) caractère m bénin.

mildew ['mɪldjuː] n (on cheese etc) moisissure f.

mile [maɪl] n mile m, mille m (= 1,6 km); **miles** (loosely) = kilomètres mpl; **to walk for miles** marcher pendant des kilomètres; **miles better** (much) Fam bien mieux. ● **mileage** n (distance) = kilométrage m; m. (per gallon) = consommation f aux cent kilomètres. ● **mileometer** n Br = **milometer**. ● **milestone** n = borne f kilométrique; (in history, one's life etc) Fig jalon m.

militant ['mɪlɪtənt] a & n militant, -ante (mf).

military ['mɪlɪt(ə)rɪ] a militaire ▮ n the m. les militaires mpl; (army) l'armée f.

militate ['mɪlɪteɪt] vi (of arguments etc) militer (against contre, in favour of pour).

militia [mə'lɪʃə] n milice f. ● **militiaman** n (pl -men) milicien m.

milk [mɪlk] n lait m; **evaporated m.** lait m concentré; **m. bottle/can** bouteille f/boîte f à lait; **m. chocolate** chocolat m au lait; **m. diet** régime m lacté; **m. float** Br voiture f de laitier; **m. round** Br tournée f du laitier; **m. produce** produits mpl laitiers; **m. shake** milk-shake m.

▮ vt (cow) traire; (exploit) Fig exploiter; **to m. s.o. of sth** Fig soutirer qch à qn. ● **milking** n traite f.

milkman ['mɪlkmən] n (pl -men) laitier m.

milky ['mɪlkɪ] a (-ier, -iest) (diet) lacté; (coffee, tea) au lait; (colour) laiteux; **the M. Way** la Voie lactée.

mill [mɪl] 1 n moulin m; (factory) usine f; **cotton m.** filature f de coton; **paper m.** papeterie f; **steel m.** aciérie f ▮ vt (grind) moudre.

2 vi **to m. around** (of crowd) grouiller. ● **miller** n meunier, -ière mf.

millennium, pl **-nia** [mɪ'lenɪəm, -nɪə] n millénaire m.

millet ['mɪlɪt] n (plant) millet m.

milli- [mɪlɪ] pref milli-.

millimetre ['mɪlɪmiːtər] (Am **millimeter**) n millimètre m.

million ['mɪljən] n million m; **a m. men/etc** un million d'hommes/etc; **two m.** deux millions. ● **millio'naire** n millionnaire mf. ● **millionth** a & n millionième (mf).

millstone ['mɪlstəʊn] n **it's a m. around my neck** (burden) c'est un boulet que je traîne.

milometer [maɪ'lɒmɪtər] n Br = compteur m (kilométrique).

mime [maɪm] n (actor) mime mf; (art) mime m ▮ vti mimer.

mimeograph® ['mɪmɪəgræf] vt polycopier.

mimic ['mɪmɪk] vt (-ck-) imiter ▮ n imitateur, -trice mf. ● **mimicking** or **mimicry** n imitation f.

mimosa [mɪ'məʊzə] n (tree) mimosa m.

minaret [mɪnə'ret] n (of mosque) minaret m.

mince [mɪns] n (meat) Br viande f hachée, hachis m (de viande); (dried fruit) Am mélange m de fruits secs; **m. pie** Br tartelette f fourrée au mincemeat ▮ vt hacher; **not to m. matters** or **one's words** ne pas mâcher ses mots. ● **mincemeat** n (dried fruit) mélange m de fruits secs; (meat) Br viande f hachée, hachis m (de viande). ● **mincer** n (machine) hachoir m.

mind[1] [maɪnd] n esprit m; (sanity) raison f; (memory) mémoire f; (head) tête f; **to change one's m.** changer d'avis; **to my m.** Br à mon avis; **to be in two minds** (undecided) Br être irrésolu; **to make up one's m.** se décider; **it's on my m.** (worries me) cela me préoccupe; **to be out of one's m.** (mad) être fou; **to bring sth to m.** (recall) rappeler qch; **to bear** or **keep sth in m.** (remember) se souvenir de qch; **to have s.o./sth in m.** avoir qn/qch en vue; **to have a good m. to do sth** Br avoir bien envie de faire qch.

mind[2] [maɪnd] vti (pay attention to) Br faire attention à; (look after) garder, s'occuper de; (noise, dirt etc) être gêné par; (one's language) surveiller; **m. you don't fall** Br (beware) prends garde or fais attention de ne pas tomber; **m. you do it** Br n'oublie pas de le faire; **do you m. if?** (I smoke etc) ça vous gêne si?; (I leave, help etc) ça ne vous fait rien si?; **I don't m. the sun** ne me gêne pas, je ne suis pas gêné par le soleil; **I don't m.** (care) ça m'est égal; **I wouldn't m. a cup of tea** (would like) j'aimerais bien une tasse de thé; **I m. that...** ça me gêne or m'ennuie que...; **never m.!** (it doesn't matter) ça ne fait rien!, tant pis!; (don't worry) ne vous en faites pas!; **m. (out)!** (watch out) Br attention!; **m. you...** Br remarquez, ...; **m. your own business!**, never **you m.!** ça ne vous regarde pas!, mêlez-vous de ce qui vous regarde!

mind-boggling ['maɪndbɒglɪŋ] *a* stupéfiant, qui confond l'imagination.

-minded ['maɪndɪd] *suff* **fair-m.** impartial; **like-m.** de même opinion.

minder ['maɪndər] *n Br* (*for children*) nourrice *f*; (*bodyguard*) *Fam* gorille *m*; **child m.** nourrice *f*.

mindful ['maɪndfəl] *a* **m. of sth/doing** attentif à qch/à faire.

mindless ['maɪndləs] *a* (*job, destruction etc*) stupide.

mine¹ [maɪn] *poss pron* le mien, la mienne, *pl* les mien(ne)s; **this hat is m.** ce chapeau est à moi *or* est le mien; **a friend of m.** un ami à moi, un de mes amis.

mine² [maɪn] **1** *n* (*for coal, gold etc*) & *Fig* mine *f* ∎ *vti* **to m. (for)** (*coal etc*) extraire. **2** *n* (*explosive*) mine *f* ∎ *vt* (*beach, bridge etc*) miner. ●**mining** *n* exploitation *f* minière ∎ *a* (*industry, region etc*) minier. ●**miner** *n* mineur *m*.

mineral ['mɪnərəl] *a & n* minéral (*m*); **m. water** eau *f* minérale.

minestrone [mɪnɪ'strəʊnɪ] *n* minestrone *m*.

mingle ['mɪŋg(ə)l] *vi* se mêler (**with** à); **to m. with** (*socially*) fréquenter.

mingy ['mɪndʒɪ] *a* (**-ier, -iest**) (*mean*) *Br Fam* radin.

mini ['mɪnɪ] *pref* mini-.

miniature ['mɪnɪtʃər] *a* (*tiny*) minuscule; (*train, model etc*) miniature *inv* ∎ *n* miniature *f*; **in m.** en miniature.

minibus ['mɪnɪbʌs] *n* minibus *m*. ●**minicab** *n Br* (radio-)taxi *m*.

minim ['mɪnɪm] *n* (*musical note*) *Br* blanche *f*.

minimal ['mɪnɪməl] *a* minimal.

minimize ['mɪnɪmaɪz] *vt* minimiser.

minimum ['mɪnɪməm] *n* (*pl* **-ima** [-ɪmə] *or* **-imums**) minimum. *m* ∎ *a* minimum (*f inv*), minimal.

mining ['maɪnɪŋ] *n see* **mine²**.

minister¹ ['mɪnɪstər] *n* (*politician*) *Br* ministre *m*; (*of religion*) pasteur *m*. ●**mini'sterial** *a Br Pol* ministériel. ●**ministry** *n Br Pol* ministère *m*; **to enter** *or* **join the m.** *Rel* devenir pasteur.

minister² ['mɪnɪstər] *vi* **to m. to s.o.'s needs** subvenir aux besoins de qn.

mink [mɪŋk] *n* (*animal, fur*) vison *m*.

minor ['maɪnər] *a* (*small*) (*detail, operation, repair etc*) petit; *Mus Rel Phil etc* mineur ∎ *n* (*child*) *Jur* mineur, -eure *mf*; **to be a m.** être mineur(e).

Minorca [mɪ'nɔːkə] *n* Minorque *f*.

minority [maɪ'nɒrɪtɪ] *n* minorité *f*; **to be in the** *or* **a m.** être en minorité *or* minoritaire ∎ *a* minoritaire.

mint [mɪnt] **1** *n* (*place*) Hôtel *m* de la Monnaie; **to make a m.** (*of money*) *Fig* faire une petite fortune ∎ *vt* (*money*) frapper ∎ *a* **stamp** timbre *m* neuf; **in m. condition** à l'état neuf. **2** *n* (*herb*) menthe *f*; (*Br sweet, Am candy*) bonbon *m* à la menthe; **m. tea/sauce/** *etc* thé *m*/sauce *f*/etc à la menthe.

minus ['maɪnəs] *prep* (*with numbers*) moins; (*without*) *Fam* sans; **it's m. ten** (*degrees*) il fait moins dix (degrés) ∎ *n* **m. (sign)** (signe *m*) moins *m*.

minute¹ ['mɪnɪt] *n* minute *f*; **this** (*very*) **m.** (*now*) tout de suite; **any m.** (*now*) d'une minute à l'autre; **m. hand** (*of clock*) grande aiguille *f*. ●**minutes** *npl* (*of meeting*) procès-verbal *m*.

minute² [maɪ'njuːt] *a* (*tiny*) minuscule; (*careful, exact*) (*examination etc*) minutieux.

minx [mɪŋks] *n* (*girl*) *Pej* diablesse *f*, chipie *f*.

miracle ['mɪrək(ə)l] *n* miracle *m*; **by some m.** par miracle. ●**mi'raculous** *a* miraculeux.

mirage ['mɪrɑːʒ] *n* mirage *m*.

mire [maɪər] *n Lit* fange *f*; (*difficult situation*) bourbier *m*.

mirror ['mɪrər] *n* miroir *m*, glace *f*; (*representation*) *Fig* miroir *m*; (*rear view*) **m.** (*of vehicle*) rétroviseur *m* ∎ *vt* (*reflect*) refléter.

mirth [mɜːθ] *n Lit* gaieté *f*, hilarité *f*.

misadventure [mɪsəd'ventʃər] *n* (*mishap*) mésaventure *f*; **death by m.** *Jur* mort *f* accidentelle.

misanthropist [mɪ'zænθrəpɪst] *n* misanthrope *mf*.

misapprehension [mɪsæprɪ'henʃ(ə)n] *n* malentendu *m*; **to be under a m.** ne pas avoir bien compris.

misappropriate [mɪsə'prəʊprɪeɪt] *vt* (*money*) détourner.

misbehave [mɪsbɪ'heɪv] *vi* se conduire mal; (*of child*) faire des sottises.

miscalculate [mɪs'kælkjʊleɪt] *vt* mal calculer ∎ *vi* (*make a mistake*) se tromper. ●**miscalculation** [-'leɪʃ(ə)n] *n* erreur *f* de calcul.

miscarriage [mɪs'kærɪdʒ] *n* **to have a m.** (*of woman*) faire une fausse couche; **m. of justice** erreur *f* judiciaire. ●**miscarry** *vi* (*of woman*) faire une fausse couche; (*of plan*) *Fig* échouer.

miscellaneous [mɪsɪ'leɪnɪəs] *a* divers.

mischief ['mɪstʃɪf] *n* espièglerie *f*; (*malice*) méchanceté *f*; **to get into m.** faire des bêtises; **full of m.** = mischievous; **to make m. for s.o.** (*trouble*) créer des ennuis à qn; **to do s.o. a m.** (*harm*) *Br* faire mal à qn; **a little m.** (*child*) *Br* un petit démon.

mischievous ['mɪstʃɪvəs] *a* (*naughty, playful*) espiègle, malicieux; (*malicious*) méchant.

misconception [mɪskən'sepʃ(ə)n] *n* idée *f* fausse.

misconduct [mɪs'kɒndʌkt] *n* (*bad behaviour*) mauvaise conduite *f*; (*bad management*) *Com* mauvaise gestion *f*.

misconstrue [mɪskən'struː] *vt* mal interpréter.

misdeed [mɪs'diːd] *n* méfait *m*.

misdemeanour [mɪsdɪ'miːnər] (*Am* **misdemeanor**) *n* écart *m* de conduite; *Am Jur* délit *m*.

misdirect [mɪsdɪ'rekt, -daɪ'rekt] *vt* (*letter*) mal adresser; (*person*) mal renseigner; (*one's energies*) mal diriger.

miser ['maɪzər] *n* avare *mf*. ●**miserly** *a* avare.

miserable ['mɪzərəb(ə)l] *a* (*wretched*) misérable; (*unhappy*) malheureux; (*awful*) affreux; (*derisory*) (*salary etc*) dérisoire. ●**miserably** *adv* (*wretchedly*) misérablement; (*to fail*) lamentablement.

misery ['mɪzəri] *n* (*suffering*) souffrances *fpl*; (*sadness*) tristesse *f*; (*sad person*) *Fam* grincheux, -euse *mf*; **miseries** (*misfortunes*) misères *fpl*; **his life is a m.** il est malheureux.

misfire [mɪs'faɪər] *vi* (*of plan*) rater; (*of engine*) avoir des ratés.

misfit ['mɪsfɪt] *n* (*person*) *Pej* inadapté, -ée *mf*.

misfortune [mɪs'fɔːtʃuːn] *n* malheur *m*.

misgivings [mɪs'gɪvɪŋz] *npl* (*doubts*) doutes *mpl* (**about** sur); (*fears*) craintes *fpl* (**about** à propos de).

misguided [mɪs'gaɪdɪd] *a* (*action etc*) imprudent; **to be m.** (*of person*) se tromper.

mishandle [mɪs'hænd(ə)l] *vt* (*affair, situation*) traiter avec maladresse; (*person*) s'y prendre mal avec.

mishap ['mɪshæp] *n* (*hitch*) contretemps *m*; (*accident*) mésaventure *f*.

misinform [mɪsɪn'fɔːm] *vt* mal renseigner.

misinterpret [mɪsɪn'tɜːprɪt] *vt* mal interpréter.

misjudge [mɪs'dʒʌdʒ] *vt* (*person, distance etc*) mal juger.

mislay [mɪs'leɪ] *vt* (*pt & pp* **mislaid**) égarer.

mislead [mɪs'liːd] *vt* (*pt & pp* **misled**) tromper. ●**misleading** *a* trompeur.

mismanage [mɪs'mænɪdʒ] *vt* mal administrer. ●**mismanagement** *n* mauvaise administration *f*.

misnomer [mɪs'nəʊmər] *n* (*name*) nom *m* or terme *m* impropre.

misogynist [mɪ'sɒdʒɪnɪst] *n* misogyne *mf*.

misplace [mɪs'pleɪs] *vt* (*lose*) égarer; (*trust etc*) mal placer. ●**misplaced** *a* (*remark etc*) déplacé; **m. accent** accent *m* mal placé.

misprint ['mɪsprɪnt] *n* faute *f* d'impression, coquille *f*.

mispronounce [mɪsprə'naʊns] *vt* mal prononcer.

misquote [mɪs'kwəʊt] *vt* citer inexactement.

misrepresent [mɪsreprɪ'zent] *vt* présenter sous un faux jour.

miss¹ [mɪs] *vt* (*train, target, opportunity etc*) manquer, rater; (*not see*) ne pas voir; (*not understand*) ne pas comprendre; (*one's youth, deceased person etc*) regretter; (*sth just lost*) remarquer l'absence de; **he misses Paris/her** Paris/elle lui manque; **I m. you** tu me manques; **I'm missing my wallet!** je n'ai plus mon portefeuille!; **we'll be missed** on remarquera notre absence; **don't m. seeing this play** (*don't fail to*) ne manque pas de voir cette pièce; **to m. sth out** (*leave out*) sauter qch.

▮ *vi* manquer, rater; **to m. out** (*lose a chance*) rater l'occasion; **to m. out on** (*opportunity etc*) rater, laisser passer.

▮ *n* coup *m* manqué; **that was** or **we had a near m.** on l'a échappé belle; **I'll give it a m.** *Fam* (*not go*) je n'y irai pas; (*not take or drink or eat*) je n'en prendrai pas.

miss² [mɪs] *n* (*woman*) mademoiselle *f*; **Miss Brown** Mademoiselle or Mlle Brown.

misshapen [mɪs'ʃeɪp(ə)n] *a* difforme.

missile [*Br* 'mɪsaɪl, *Am* 'mɪs(ə)l] *n* (*rocket*) missile *m*; (*object thrown*) projectile *m*.

missing ['mɪsɪŋ] *a* (*absent*) absent; (*in war, after disaster*) disparu; (*object*) manquant; **there are two cups/students m.** il manque deux tasses/deux étudiants; **the m. cups** les tasses qui manquent; **nothing is m.** rien ne manque; **to go m.** disparaître.

mission ['mɪʃ(ə)n] *n* mission *f*.

missionary ['mɪʃənərɪ] *n* missionnaire *m*.

missive ['mɪsɪv] *n* (*letter*) missive *f*.

misspell [mɪs'spel] *vt* (*pt & pp* **-ed** *or* **misspelt**) mal écrire.

mist [mɪst] *n* (*fog*) brume *f*; (*on glass*) buée *f*
▮ *vi* **to m. over** *or* **up** s'embuer.

mistake [mɪ'steɪk] *n* erreur *f*, faute *f*; **to make a m.** se tromper, faire (une) erreur; **by m.** par erreur.

▮ *vt* (*pt* **mistook**, *pp* **mistaken**) (*meaning, intention etc*) se tromper sur; **to m. the date/place/etc** se tromper de date/de lieu/*etc*; **you can't m.** or **there's no mistaking his face/my car/etc** il est impossible de ne pas reconnaître son visage/ma voiture/*etc*; **to m. s.o./sth for** prendre qn/qch pour. ●**mistaken** *a* (*idea, opinion etc*) erroné; **to be m.** (*of person*) se tromper (**about** sur). ●**mistakenly** *adv* par erreur.

mister ['mɪstər] *n Fam* monsieur *m*.

mistletoe ['mɪs(ə)ltəʊ] *n* (*shrub*) gui *m*.

mistreat [mɪs'triːt] *vt* maltraiter.

mistress ['mɪstrɪs] *n* maîtresse *f*; (*in secondary school*) *Br* professeur *m*; (*in primary school*) *Br* institutrice *f*; **the French m.** le professeur de français.

mistrust [mɪs'trʌst] *n* méfiance *f* **▮** *vt* se méfier de. ●**mistrustful** *a* méfiant.

misty ['mɪstɪ] *a* (**-ier, -iest**) (*foggy*) brumeux; (*glass*) embué.

misunderstand [mɪsʌndə'stænd] *vti* (*pt & pp* **-stood**) mal comprendre. ●**misunderstanding** *n* (*disagreement, mistake*) malentendu *m*. ●**misunderstood** *a* (*person*) incompris.

misuse [mɪs'juːz] *vt* (*word, tool*) mal employer; (*power etc*) abuser de **▮** [mɪs'juːs] *n* (*of word*) emploi *m* abusif; (*of tool*) usage *m* abusif; (*of power etc*) abus *m*.

mite [maɪt] *n* **1** (*insect*) mite *f*. **2** (**poor**) **m.** (*child*) (pauvre) petit, -ite *mf*. **3 a m.** (*bigger etc*) (*somewhat*) *Fam* un petit peu.

mitigate ['mɪtɪgeɪt] *vt* atténuer.

mitt(en) [mɪt, 'mɪt(ə)n] *n* (*glove*) moufle *f*.

mix [mɪks] *vt* mélanger, mêler; (*cement, cake*) préparer; (*salad*) remuer; **to m. up** (*drinks, papers etc*) mélanger; (*make confused*) embrouiller (*qn*); (*mistake*) confondre (*qch, qn*) (**with** avec); **to be mixed up with**

s.o. (*involved*) être mêlé aux affaires de qn; **to m.** s.o. **up in** (*involve*) mêler qn à. ▮ *vi* se mêler; (*of colours*) s'allier; **to m. with** s.o. (*socially*) fréquenter qn; **she doesn't m.** (**in**) elle n'est pas sociable. ▮ *n* (*mixture*) mélange *m*.

mixed [mɪkst] *a* (*school, marriage etc*) mixte; (*results*) divers; (*nuts, chocolates etc*) assortis; **m. grill** assortiment *m* de grillades; **m. feelings** sentiments *mpl* mitigés; **I have m. feelings about that** je suis partagé au sujet de cela; **to be (all) m. up** (*of person*) être désorienté; (*of facts, account etc*) être embrouillé; **in m. company** en présence de personnes des deux sexes.

mixer ['mɪksər] *n* (*electric, for food*) mixe(u)r *m*; **to be a good m.** (*of person*) être sociable; **m. tap** *Br* (robinet *m*) mélangeur *m*.

mixture ['mɪkstʃər] *n* mélange *m*; (*for cough*) sirop *m*.

mix-up ['mɪksʌp] *n* confusion *f*.

mm *abbr* (*millimetre*) mm.

moan [məʊn] *vi* (*groan*) gémir; (*complain*) se plaindre (**to** à, **about** de, **that** que) ▮ *n* gémissement *m*; (*complaint*) plainte *f*.

moat [məʊt] *n* douve(s) *f(pl)*.

mob [mɒb] *n* (*crowd*) foule *f*, cohue *f*; (*gang, group*) bande *f*; **the m.** (*masses*) la populace; (*Mafia*) *Am Sl* la mafia ▮ *vt* (**-bb-**) (*film star, store etc*) assiéger. ●**mobster** *n Am Sl* gangster *m*.

mobile [*Br* 'məʊbaɪl, *Am* 'məʊb(ə)l] *a* mobile; (*having a car etc*) *Fam* motorisé; **m. home** mobil-home *m*; **m. library** bibliobus *m*; **m. phone** téléphone *m* portatif ▮ *n* (*Am* ['məʊbi:l]) (*ornament*) mobile *m*. ●**mo'bility** *n* mobilité *f*.

mobilize ['məʊbɪlaɪz] *vti* mobiliser. ●**mobilization** [-'zeɪʃ(ə)n] *n* mobilisation *f*.

moccasin ['mɒkəsɪn] *n* (*shoe*) mocassin *m*.

mocha [*Br* 'mɒkə, *Am* 'məʊkə] *n* moka *m*.

mock [mɒk] **1** *vt* se moquer de; (*mimic*) singer ▮ *vi* se moquer (**at de**). **2** *a* (*false*) simulé; **m. exam** examen *m* blanc. ●**mocking** *n* moquerie *f* ▮ *a* moqueur.

mockery ['mɒkərɪ] *n* (*act*) moquerie *f*; (*farce, parody*) parodie *f*; **to make a m. of sth** tourner qch en ridicule.

mock-up ['mɒkʌp] *n* (*model*) maquette *f*.

mod cons [mɒd'kɒnz] *abbr Fam* = **modern conveniences.**

mode [məʊd] *n* (*manner, way*) & *Comptr* mode *m*; (*fashion, vogue*) mode *f*.

model ['mɒd(ə)l] *n* (*example, representation etc*) modèle *m*; (*person posing for artist etc*) modèle *m*; (**fashion**) **m.** mannequin *m*; (**scale**) **m.** modèle *m* (réduit). ▮ *a* (*behaviour, factory, student etc*) modèle; (*car, plane etc*) modèle réduit *inv*; **m. railway** *Br*, **m. railroad** *Am* train *m* miniature. ▮ *vt* (*Br* **-ll-**, *Am* **-l-**) (*clay etc*) modeler; (*hats, dresses etc*) présenter (les modèles de); **to m. sth on** modeler qch sur; **to m. oneself on** se modeler sur.

▮ *vi* (*for fashion*) être mannequin; (*pose for artist*) poser. ●**modelling** (*Am* **modeling**) *n* (*of statues, in clay etc*) modelage *m*.

modem ['məʊdəm] *n Comptr* modem *m*.

moderate[1] ['mɒdərət] *a* (*opinion, amount success etc*) modéré; (*in speech*) mesuré ▮ *n Pol* modéré, -ée *mf*. ●**moderately** *adv* (*in moderation*) modérément; (*averagely*) moyennement.

moderate[2] ['mɒdəreɪt] *vt* (*diminish, tone down*) modérer ▮ *vi* (*of wind*) se calmer. ●**moderation** [-'reɪʃ(ə)n] *n* modération *f*; **in m.** avec modération.

modern ['mɒd(ə)n] *a* moderne; **m. languages** langues *fpl* vivantes; **m. conveniences** tout le confort moderne. ●**modernism** *n* modernisme *m*.

modernize ['mɒdənaɪz] *vt* moderniser ▮ *vi* se moderniser. ●**modernization** [-'zeɪʃ(ə)n] *n* modernisation *f*.

modest ['mɒdɪst] *a* (*person, salary, success etc*) modeste. ●**modesty** *n* (*of person*) modestie *f*; (*of request*) modération *f*; (*of salary*) modicité *f*.

modicum ['mɒdɪkəm] *n* **a m. of** un soupçon de, un petit peu de.

modify ['mɒdɪfaɪ] *vt* (*alter*) modifier; (*tone down*) modérer. ●**modification** [-'keɪʃ(ə)n] *n* modification *f* (**to** à).

modulate ['mɒdjʊleɪt] *vt* moduler. ●**modulation** [-'leɪʃ(ə)n] *n* modulation *f*.

module ['mɒdju:l] *n* module *m*.

moggie ['mɒgɪ] *n* (*cat*) *Br Fam* minou *m*.

mogul ['məʊg(ə)l] *n* magnat *m*, manitou *m*.

mohair ['məʊheər] *n* mohair *m*; **m. sweater** pull *m* en mohair.

moist [mɔɪst] *a* (**-er, -est**) humide; (*clammy, sticky*) moite. ●**moisten** ['mɔɪs(ə)n] *vt* humecter.

moisture ['mɔɪstʃər] *n* humidité *f*; (*on glass*) buée *f*.

moisturize ['mɔɪstʃəraɪz] *vt* (*skin*) hydrater. ●**moisturizer** *n* (*cream*) crème *f* hydratante.

molar ['məʊlər] *n* (*tooth*) molaire *f*.

molasses [mə'læsɪz] *n* (*treacle*) *Am* mélasse *f*.

mold [məʊld] *n & vt Am* = **mould.**

mole [məʊl] *n* **1** (*on skin*) grain *m* de beauté. **2** (*animal, spy*) taupe *f*.

molecule ['mɒlɪkju:l] *n* molécule *f*.

molest [mə'lest] *vt* (*annoy*) importuner; (*child, woman*) *Jur* attenter à la pudeur de.

mollusc ['mɒləsk] *n* mollusque *m*.

mollycoddle ['mɒlɪkɒd(ə)l] *vt* dorloter.

molt [məʊlt] *vi Am* = **moult.**

molten ['məʊlt(ə)n] *a* (*metal, rock*) en fusion.

mom [mɒm] *n Am Fam* maman *f*.

moment ['məʊmənt] *n* moment *m*, instant *m*; **this** (**very**) **m.** (*now*) à l'instant; **the m. she leaves** dès qu'elle partira; **any m.** (**now**) d'un moment *or* d'un instant à l'autre.

momentary ['məʊməntərɪ] *a* momentané. ●**momentarily** (*Am* [məʊmən'terɪlɪ]) *adv* (*temporarily*) momentanément; (*soon*) *Am* tout à l'heure.

momentous [məu'mentəs] a important.

momentum [məu'mentəm] n (speed) élan m; **to gather** or **gain m.** (of ideas etc) gagner du terrain; (of project) prendre un bon rythme.

mommy ['mɒmɪ] n Am Fam maman f.

Monaco ['mɒnəkəu] n Monaco f.

monarch ['mɒnək] n monarque m. ●**monarchy** n monarchie f.

monastery ['mɒnəst(ə)rɪ] n monastère m.

Monday [Br 'mʌndɪ, Am -deɪ] n lundi m.

monetary ['mʌnɪt(ə)rɪ] a monétaire.

money ['mʌnɪ] n argent m; **paper m.** papier-monnaie m, billets mpl; **to get one's m.'s worth** en avoir pour son argent; **he gets** or **earns good m.** il gagne bien (sa vie); **to be in the m.** Fam rouler sur l'or; **m. order** mandat m.

moneybags ['mʌnɪbægz] n Pej Fam richard, -arde mf. ●**moneybox** n tirelire f. ●**moneychanger** n changeur m. ●**moneylender** n prêteur, -euse mf sur gages. ●**moneymaking** a lucratif. ●**money-spinner** n (source of wealth) Fam mine f d'or.

mongol ['mɒŋg(ə)l] n & a Med Pej mongolien, -ienne (mf).

mongrel ['mʌŋgrəl] n (dog) bâtard m.

monitor ['mɒnɪtər] **1** n (screen, device) Comptr TV Tech etc moniteur m. **2** n (pupil) Br chef m de classe. **3** vt (radio broadcast) écouter; (check) contrôler.

monk [mʌŋk] n moine m, religieux m.

monkey ['mʌŋkɪ] n singe m; **little m.** (child) Fam polisson, -onne mf; **m. business** Fam singeries fpl; **m. nut** Br Fam cacah(o)uète f; **m. wrench** clef f anglaise ∎ vi **to m. about** or **around** Fam faire l'idiot.

mono ['mɒnəu] a (record etc) mono inv ∎ n **in m.** en monophonie.

mono- ['mɒnəu] pref mono-.

monocle ['mɒnək(ə)l] n monocle m.

monogram ['mɒnəgræm] n monogramme m.

monologue ['mɒnəlɒg] n monologue m.

mononucleosis [mɒnəunju:klɪ'əusɪs] n Am mononucléose f, infectieuse.

monopoly [mə'nɒpəlɪ] n monopole m. ●**monopolize** vt monopoliser.

monosyllable ['mɒnəsɪləb(ə)l] n monosyllabe m. ●**monosyllabic** a monosyllabique.

monotone ['mɒnətəun] n **in a m.** sur un ton monocorde.

monotony [mə'nɒtənɪ] n monotonie f. ●**monotonous** a monotone.

monsoon [mɒn'su:n] n (wind, rain) mousson f.

monster ['mɒnstər] n monstre m.

monstrosity [mɒn'strɒsətɪ] n (horror) monstruosité f.

monstrous ['mɒnstrəs] a (terrible, enormous) monstrueux.

month [mʌnθ] n mois m.

monthly ['mʌnθlɪ] a mensuel; **m. payment** mensualité f ∎ n (periodical) mensuel m ∎ adv (every month) mensuellement.

Montreal [mɒntrɪ'ɔ:l] n Montréal m or f.

monument ['mɒnjumənt] n monument m.

monumental [mɒnju'ment(ə)l] a (error, stupidity etc) monumental; **m. mason** marbrier m.

moo [mu:] vi meugler ∎ n meuglement m.

mooch [mu:tʃ] **1** vi **to m. around** Fam flâner. **2** vt **to m. sth off s.o.** (cadge) Am Sl taper qch à qn.

mood [mu:d] n (of person) humeur f; (of country) état m d'esprit; Grammar mode m; **in a good/bad m.** de bonne/mauvaise humeur; **to be in the m. to do** or **for doing** être d'humeur à faire, avoir envie de faire.

moody ['mu:dɪ] a (-ier, -iest) (bad-tempered) de mauvaise humeur; (changeable) d'humeur changeante.

moon [mu:n] n lune f; **full m.** pleine lune; **once in a blue m.** (rarely) Fam tous les trente-six du mois; **over the m.** (delighted) Br Fam ravi (about de). ●**moonlight 1** n clair m de lune; **by m.** au clair de lune. **2** vi Fam travailler au noir. ●**moonlit** a (landscape etc) éclairé par la lune.

moonshine ['mu:nʃaɪn] n (foolish talk) Fam balivernes fpl.

moor [muər] **1** vt (ship) amarrer ∎ vi (of ship) mouiller. **2** n (open land) lande f. ●**moorings** npl Nau (ropes etc) amarres fpl; (place) mouillage m.

moose [mu:s] n inv (animal) élan m; (Canadian) original m.

moot [mu:t] a **it's a m. point** c'est discutable.

mop [mɒp] n balai m (à laver), balai m éponge; **dish m.** lavette f; **m. of hair** tignasse f ∎ vt (-pp-) **to m.** (up) (floor etc) essuyer; **to m. up** (liquid) éponger; **to m. one's brow** s'essuyer le front.

mope [məup] vi **to m. about** errer or traîner comme une âme en peine.

moped ['məuped] n mobylette® f, cyclomoteur m.

moral ['mɒrəl] a moral ∎ n (of story etc) morale f; **morals** (standards) moralité f, morale f. ●**morale** [Br mə'ra:l, Am mə'ræl] n moral m. ●**moralist** n moraliste mf. ●**mo'rality** n (morals) moralité f. ●**moralize** vi moraliser. ●**morally** adv moralement; **m. wrong** immoral.

morass [mə'ræs] n (mess, situation) bourbier m; (land) marais m.

moratorium [mɒrə'tɔ:rɪəm] n moratoire m.

morbid ['mɔ:bɪd] a morbide. ●**morbidly** adv (obsessed etc) morbidement.

more [mɔ:r] a & n plus (de) (than que); (other) d'autres; **m. cars/etc** plus de voitures/etc; **he has m.** (than you) il en a plus (que toi); **a few m. months** encore quelques mois, quelques mois de plus; (some) **m. tea/etc** encore du thé/etc; (some) **m. details** d'autres détails; **m. than a kilo/ten/etc** (with quantity, number) plus d'un kilo/de dix/etc.
∎ adv (tired, rapidly etc) plus (than que); **m. and m.** de plus en plus; **m. or less** plus ou moins; **the m. he shouts the m. hoarse he gets** plus il crie plus il s'enroue; **she doesn't**

have any m. elle n'en a plus.
moreish ['mɔ:rɪʃ] a Br Fam qui a un goût de
revenez-y.
moreover [mɔ:'rəʊvər] adv de plus.
mores ['mɔ:reɪz] npl mœurs fpl.
morgue [mɔ:g] n (mortuary) morgue f.
moribund ['mɒrɪbʌnd] a moribond.
morning ['mɔ:nɪŋ] n matin m; (duration of
morning) matinée f; **in the m.** le matin;
(during the course of the morning) pendant
la matinée; (tomorrow) demain matin; **at
seven in the m.** à sept heures du matin;
every Tuesday m. tous les mardis matin; **in
the early m.** au petit matin █ a (newspaper
etc) du matin; **m. sickness** (of pregnant woman) nausées fpl matinales. ●**mornings** adv
Am le matin.
Morocco [mə'rɒkəʊ] n Maroc m. ●**Moroccan** a marocain █ n Marocain, -aine mf.
moron ['mɔ:rɒn] n crétin, -ine mf.
morose [mə'rəʊs] a morose.
morphine ['mɔ:fi:n] n morphine f.
Morse [mɔ:s] n & a **M. (code)** morse m.
morsel ['mɔ:s(ə)l] n (food) petite bouchée f.
mortal ['mɔ:t(ə)l] a & n mortel, -elle (mf).
●**mor'tality** n (death rate) mortalité f.
mortar ['mɔ:tər] n mortier m.
mortgage ['mɔ:gɪdʒ] n prêt-logement m; **to
take out a m.** obtenir un prêt-logement █ vt
(house, future) hypothéquer.
mortician [mɔ:'tɪʃ(ə)n] n Am entrepreneur
m de pompes funèbres.
mortify ['mɔ:tɪfaɪ] vt mortifier.
mortuary ['mɔ:tʃʊərɪ] n morgue f.
mosaic [məʊ'zeɪɪk] n mosaïque f.
Moscow [Br 'mɒskəʊ, Am 'mɒskaʊ] n
Moscou m or f.
Moses ['məʊzɪz] a **M. basket** couffin m.
Moslem ['mɒzlɪm] a & n musulman, -ane
(mf).
mosque [mɒsk] n mosquée f.
mosquito [mɒ'ski:təʊ] n (pl -oes) moustique
m; **m. net** moustiquaire f.
moss [mɒs] n mousse f (plante). ●**mossy** a
moussu.
most [məʊst] a & n **the m.** (greatest in
amount etc) le plus (de); **I have (the) m.
books** j'ai le plus de livres; **I have (the) m.**
j'en ai le plus; **m. (of the) books/etc** la plupart des livres/etc; **m. of the cake/etc** la plus
grande partie du gâteau/etc; **m. of them** la
plupart d'entre eux; **m. of it** la plus grande
partie; **at (the very) m.** tout au plus; **to make
the m. of sth** profiter (au maximum) de qch.
█ adv (le) plus; (very) très, fort; **the m. beautiful** le plus beau, la plus belle (in, de); **to
talk (the) m.** parler le plus; **m. unhappy/
grateful/etc** très malheureux/reconnaissant/
etc; **m. of all** (especially) surtout. ●**mostly**
adv surtout, pour la plupart.
MOT [eməʊ'ti:] n abbr (Ministry of
Transport) Br = contrôle m obligatoire des
véhicules de plus de trois ans.
motel [məʊ'tel] n motel m.
moth [mɒθ] n papillon m de nuit; (clothes)

m. mite f. ●**moth-eaten** a mité. ●**mothball**
n boule f de naphtaline.
mother ['mʌðər] n mère f; **M.'s Day** la fête
des Mères; **m. tongue** langue f maternelle █
vt (care for) materner. ●**motherhood** n maternité f. ●**motherly** a maternel.
mother-in-law ['mʌðərɪnlɔ:] n (pl mothers-
in-law) belle-mère f. ●**mother-of-pearl** n
(substance) nacre f. ●**mother-to-'be** n (pl
mothers-to-be) future mère f.
motion ['məʊʃ(ə)n] n (of arm etc) mouvement m; (in meeting etc) motion f; **to set sth
in m.** mettre qch en mouvement; **m. picture**
film m █ vti **to m.** (to) s.o. to do faire signe à
qn de faire. ●**motionless** a immobile.
motivate ['məʊtɪveɪt] vt (person, decision
etc) motiver. ●**motivated** a motivé. ●**motivation** [-'veɪʃ(ə)n] n motivation f; (incentive)
encouragement m.
motive ['məʊtɪv] n motif m (for de); Jur mobile m (for de).
motley ['mɒtlɪ] a (collection) hétéroclite;
(coloured) bigarré.
motor ['məʊtər] n (engine) moteur m; (car)
Br Fam auto f █ a (industry, vehicle etc)
automobile; (accident) d'auto; **m. boat** canot
m automobile; **m. mechanic** Br mécanicien-
auto m; **m. mower** tondeuse f à moteur █ vi
(drive) Br rouler en auto. ●**motoring** n Br
automobilisme m, tourisme m automobile;
school of m. Br auto-école f.
motorbike ['məʊtəbaɪk] n Fam moto f.
●**motorcade** n cortège m (officiel) (de
voitures). ●**motorcar** n Br automobile f.
●**motorcycle** n moto f, motocyclette f.
●**motorcyclist** n motocycliste mf. ●**motorist**
n Br automobiliste mf. ●**motorized** a (regiment etc) motorisé. ●**motorway** n Br autoroute f.
mottled ['mɒt(ə)ld] a tacheté.
motto ['mɒtəʊ] n (pl -oes ou -os) devise f.
mould [məʊld] (Am mold) **1** n (shape) moule
m █ vt (clay etc) mouler; (statue, Fig character) modeler. **2** n (growth, mildew) moisissure f. ●**mouldy** (Am moldy) a (-ier, -iest)
moisi; **to go m.** moisir.
moult [məʊlt] (Am molt) vi muer. ●**moulting**
(Am molting) n mue f.
mound [maʊnd] n (of earth) tertre m; (untidy pile) Fig monceau m.
mount [maʊnt] **1** n (frame for photo or slide)
cadre m; (stamp hinge) charnière f; (horse)
monture f █ vt (horse, hill, jewel, photo, demonstration etc) monter; (ladder, tree etc)
monter sur, grimper à; (stamp) coller (dans
un album) █ vi **to m. up.** (up) (on horse) se
mettre en selle.
2 vi (increase, rise) monter; **to m. up** (add
up) chiffrer (to à); (accumulate) (of debts,
bills etc) s'accumuler.
Mount [maʊnt] n (= mountain in place
names) mont m.
mountain ['maʊntɪn] n montagne f █ a
(plant, shoes etc) de montagne; **m. bike** vélo
m tout terrain; **m. people** peuple m mon-

tagnard.

mountaineer [maʊntɪˈnɪər] *n* alpiniste *mf*. ● **mountaineering** *n* alpinisme *m*.

mountainous [ˈmaʊntɪnəs] *a* montagneux.

mourn [mɔːn] *vti* to m. (for) s.o., m. the loss of s.o. pleurer (la perte de) qn; she's mourning elle en est en deuil. ● **mourning** *n* deuil *m*; in m. en deuil. ● **mourner** *n* parent, -ente *mf* or ami, -ie *mf* du défunt *or* de la défunte.

mournful [ˈmɔːnfəl] *a* triste.

mouse, *pl* **mice** [maʊs, maɪs] *n* (*animal*) & Comptr souris *f*. ● **mousetrap** *n* souricière *f*.

mousse [muːs] *n* mousse *f* (*dessert*); (*for hair*) mousse *f* (coiffante).

moustache [Br məˈstɑːʃ, Am ˈmʌstæʃ] *n* moustache *f*.

mousy [ˈmaʊsɪ] *a* (-ier, -iest) (*hair*) Br Pej châtain terne; (*shy*) Fig timide.

mouth [maʊθ] *n* (*pl* -s [maʊðz]) bouche *f*; (*of dog, lion etc*) gueule *f*; (*of river*) embouchure *f*; (*of cave, harbour*) entrée *f* ▮ [maʊð] *vt* Pej dire.

mouthful [ˈmaʊθfəl] *n* (*of food*) bouchée *f*; (*of liquid*) gorgée *f*. ● **mouthorgan** *n* harmonica *m*. ● **mouthpiece** *n* (*of musical instrument*) embouchure *f*; (*spokesperson*) porte-parole *m inv*. ● **mouthwash** *n* bain *m* de bouche. ● **mouth-watering** *a* appétissant.

movable [ˈmuːvəb(ə)l] *a* mobile.

move [muːv] *n* mouvement *m*; (*change of house etc*) déménagement *m*; (*change of job*) changement *m* d'emploi; (*transfer of employee*) mutation *f*; (*in game*) coup *m*; (*one's turn*) tour *m*; (*act*) démarche *f*; (*step*) pas *m*; (*attempt*) tentative *f*; to make a m. (*leave*) se préparer à partir; (*act*) passer à l'action; to get a m. on *Fam* se dépêcher; on the m. en marche.
▮ *vt* déplacer, remuer, bouger; (*arm, leg*) remuer; (*crowd*) faire partir; (*put*) mettre; (*transport*) transporter; (*piece in game*) jouer; (*propose in debate etc*) proposer (that que); to m. s.o. (*emotionally*) émouvoir qn; (*transfer in job*) muter qn; (*incite*) pousser qn (to do à faire); to m. house déménager.
▮ *vi* bouger, remuer; (*go*) aller (to à); (*pass*) passer (to à); (*leave*) partir; (*change seats*) changer de place; (*progress*) avancer; (*act*) agir; (*play*) jouer; (*out of house etc*) déménager; to m. to a new house/Paris/etc aller habiter une nouvelle maison/Paris/etc; to m. into a house/etc emménager dans une maison/etc.

moveable [ˈmuːvəb(ə)l] *a* mobile.

move about *or* **around** *vi* se déplacer; (*fidget*) remuer ▮ **to move along** *vi* avancer ▮ **to move away** *vi* (*go away*) s'éloigner; (*move house etc*) déménager ▮ **to move back** *vt* (*chair etc*) reculer; (*to its position*) remettre ▮ *vi* (*withdraw*) reculer; (*return*) retourner ▮ **to move down** *vt* (*take down*) descendre (qch) ▮ *vi* (*come down*) descendre ▮ **to move forward** *vti* avancer ▮ **to move in** *vi* (*into house etc*) emménager ▮ **to move off** *vi* (*go away*) s'éloigner; (*of vehicle*) démarrer ▮ **to move**

out *vi* (*out of house etc*) déménager ▮ **to move over** *vt* pousser ▮ *vi* (*make room*) se pousser ▮ **to move up** *vi* (*on seats etc*) se pousser.

movement [ˈmuːvmənt] *n* (*action, group, part of symphony etc*) mouvement *m*.

movie [ˈmuːvɪ] *n* film *m*; the movies (*cinema*) le cinéma; m. camera caméra *f*; m. star vedette *f* (*de cinéma*); m. theater *Am* cinéma *m*. ● **moviegoer** *n* cinéphile *mf*.

moving [ˈmuːvɪŋ] *a* en mouvement; (*vehicle*) en marche; (*touching*) émouvant; m. part (*of machine*) pièce *f* mobile; m. stairs escalier *m* mécanique.

mow [məʊ] *vt* (*pp* mown *or* mowed) (*field, wheat etc*) faucher; to m. the lawn tondre le gazon; to m. down (*kill etc*) Fig faucher. ● **mower** *n* (lawn) m. tondeuse *f* (à gazon).

Mozambique [məʊzæmˈbiːk] *n* Mozambique *m*.

MP [emˈpiː] *n abbr* (*Member of Parliament*) député *m*.

mph [empiːˈeɪtʃ] *abbr* (*miles per hour*) = km/h.

Mr [ˈmɪstər] *n* Mr Brown Monsieur *or* M. Brown.

Mrs [ˈmɪsɪz] *n* (*married woman*) Mrs Brown Madame *or* Mme Brown.

Ms [mɪz] *n* (*married or unmarried woman*) Ms Brown Madame *or* Mme Brown.

MSc, *Am* **MS** *abbr* = Master of Science.

much [mʌtʃ] *a* & *n* beaucoup (de); not m. time/money/etc pas beaucoup de temps/d'argent/etc; not m. pas beaucoup; m. of sth (*a good deal of*) une bonne partie de qch; as m. as (*to do, know, have etc*) autant que; as m. wine/etc as autant de vin/etc que; as m. as you like autant que tu veux; twice as m. deux fois plus (de); twice as m. as deux fois plus que; how m.? combien (de)?; too m. trop (de); so m. tant (de), tellement (de); I know/I shall do this m. je sais/je ferai ceci (du moins); this m. wine ça de vin; it's not m. of a garden ce n'est pas merveilleux comme jardin; the same presque le même.
▮ *adv* very m. beaucoup; not (very) m. pas beaucoup; she doesn't say very m. elle ne dit pas grand-chose.

muck [mʌk] **1** *n* (*manure*) fumier *m*; (*filth*) Fig saleté *f*.
2 *vi* to m. about *or* around *Br Fam* (*have fun, waste time*) s'amuser; (*play the fool*) faire l'idiot; to m. about *or* around with *Br Fam* (*fiddle with*) s'amuser avec (qch); (*alter*) changer (*texte etc*); to m. in (*join in*) *Br Fam* participer, contribuer.
▮ *vt* to m. s.o. about *Br Fam* embêter qn, déranger qn; to m. sth up (*spoil*) *Br Fam* gâcher qch. ● **muck-up** *n Br Fam* gâchis *m*. ● **mucky** *a* (-ier, -iest) sale.

mucus [ˈmjuːkəs] *n* mucosités *fpl*.

mud [mʌd] *n* boue *f*. ● **muddy** *a* (-ier, -iest) (*water, road*) boueux; (*hands etc*) couvert de boue. ● **mudguard** *n* garde-boue *m inv*.

muddle 216

muddle ['mʌd(ə)l] n (mix-up) confusion f; (mess) désordre m; **in a m.** (person) désorienté; (bread roll) Br petit pain m au lait.
I vt (person, facts etc) embrouiller; (papers) mélanger.
I vi **to m. through** Fam se débrouiller tant bien que mal.
muff [mʌf] n (for hands) manchon m.
muffin ['mʌfin] n (cake) sorte de petite brioche; (bread roll) Br petit pain m au lait.
muffle ['mʌf(ə)l] vt (noise) assourdir. ●**muffled** a (noise) sourd. ●**muffler** n (on vehicle) Am silencieux m.
mug¹ [mʌg] n 1 (for tea, coffee etc) grande tasse f; (beer) m. chope f. 2 (face) Fam gueule f; m. shot Sl photo f (d'identité). 3 (fool) Br Fam niais, -aise mf.
mug² [mʌg] vt (-gg-) (attack in street etc) agresser, attaquer. ●**mugging** n agression f. ●**mugger** n agresseur m.
muggy ['mʌgi] a (-ier, -iest) (weather) lourd.
mulberry ['mʌlbəri] n (fruit) mûre f.
mule [mjuːl] n (male) mulet m; (female) mule f.
mull [mʌl] 1 vt (wine) chauffer. 2 vi **to m. over** (think over) ruminer.
mullet ['mʌlit] n (fish) mulet m; (red) m. rouget m.
multi- ['mʌlti] pref multi-.
multicoloured ['mʌltikʌləd] a multicolore.
multifarious [mʌlti'feəriəs] a divers.
multimillionaire [mʌltimiljə'neər] n milliardaire mf.
multinational [mʌlti'næʃ(ə)nəl] n & a m. (company) multinationale f.
multiple ['mʌltip(ə)l] a multiple; m. sclerosis (illness) sclérose f en plaques **I** n (number) Math multiple m.
multiplicity [mʌlti'plisiti] n multiplicité f.
multiply ['mʌltiplai] vt multiplier **I** vi (of animals, insects) se multiplier. ●**multiplication** [-'keiʃ(ə)n] n multiplication f.
multiracial [mʌlti'reiʃ(ə)l] a multiracial.
multistorey [mʌlti'stɔːri] (Am **multistoried**) a (car park etc) à étages.
multitude ['mʌltitjuːd] n multitude f.
mum [mʌm] 1 n Br Fam maman f. 2 a **to keep m.** garder le silence.
mumble ['mʌmb(ə)l] vti marmotter.
mumbo-jumbo [mʌmbəʊ'dʒʌmbəʊ] n (gibberish) charabia m.
mummy ['mʌmi] n 1 (mother) Br Fam maman f. 2 (embalmed body) momie f.
mumps [mʌmps] n oreillons mpl.
munch [mʌntʃ] vti (chew) mastiquer; **to m. (on)** (eat) Fam manger or croquer à belles dents.
mundane [mʌn'dein] a banal (mpl -als).
municipal [mjuː'nisip(ə)l] a municipal. ●**munici'pality** n municipalité f.
munitions [mjuː'niʃ(ə)nz] npl munitions fpl.
mural ['mjʊərəl] n fresque f, peinture f murale **I** a mural.
murder ['mɜːdər] n meurtre m, assassinat m;

it's m. (dreadful) Fam c'est affreux **I** vt (kill) assassiner; (spoil) Fig massacrer. ●**murderer** n meurtrier, -ière mf, assassin m. ●**murderous** a meurtrier.
murky ['mɜːki] a (-ier, -iest) obscur; (water, business, past) trouble; (weather) nuageux.
murmur ['mɜːmər] n murmure m; (of traffic) bourdonnement m; (heart) m. souffle m (au cœur). **I** vti murmurer.
muscle ['mʌs(ə)l] n muscle m **I** vi **to m.** in on (group, meeting) Sl s'introduire par la force dans or à. ●**muscular** a (brawny) (arm etc) musclé; (tissue etc) musculaire.
muse [mjuːz] vi méditer (on sur).
museum [mjuː'ziəm] n musée m.
mush [mʌʃ] n (soft mass of food etc) bouillie f; Fig sentimentalité f. ●**mushy** a (-ier, -iest) (food etc) en bouillie; (sentimental) Fig à l'eau de rose.
mushroom ['mʌʃrʊm] n champignon m **I** vi (grow) (of buildings, towns etc) pousser comme des champignons; (spread) (of problems etc) se multiplier.
music ['mjuːzik] n musique f; m. centre chaîne f stéréo compacte; m. critic critique m musical; m. hall music-hall m; m. lover mélomane mf; canned or piped m. musique f (de fond) enregistrée. ●**musical** a musical; m. instrument instrument m de musique; **to be (very) m.** être (très) musicien **I** n (film, play) comédie f musicale. ●**musician** [-'ziʃ(ə)n] n musicien, -ienne mf.
musk [mʌsk] n (scent) musc m.
Muslim ['mʊzlim] a & n musulman, -ane (mf).
muslin ['mʌzlin] n (cotton) mousseline f.
mussel ['mʌs(ə)l] n (shellfish) moule f.
must [mʌst] v aux 1 (necessity) you m. obey tu dois obéir, il faut que tu obéisses. 2 (certainty) she m. be clever elle doit être intelligente; I m. have seen it j'ai dû le voir; m. you be so silly? qu'est-ce que tu peux être bête! **I** n this is a m. ceci est (absolument) indispensable.
mustache ['mʌstæʃ] n Am moustache f.
mustard ['mʌstəd] n moutarde f.
muster ['mʌstər] vt (gather) rassembler (troupes, courage, forces etc); (sum) réunir **I** vi se rassembler.
mustn't ['mʌs(ə)nt] = must not.
musty ['mʌsti] a (-ier, -iest) (smell, taste) de moisi; it smells m., it's m. ça sent le moisi.
mutant ['mjuːtənt] n Biol mutant m. ●**mutation** [-'teiʃ(ə)n] n Biol mutation f.
mute [mjuːt] a (silent) & Ling muet (f muette) **I** vt (sound, colour) assourdir. ●**muted** a (criticism) voilé; (colour) sourd.
mutilate ['mjuːtileit] vt mutiler. ●**mutilation** [-'leiʃ(ə)n] n mutilation f.
mutiny ['mjuːtini] n mutinerie f **I** vi se mutiner. ●**mutinous** a (troops) mutiné.
mutter ['mʌtər] vti marmonner.
mutton ['mʌt(ə)n] n (meat) mouton m; leg of m. gigot m.
mutual ['mjuːtʃʊəl] a (help, love etc) mutuel,

réciproque; (*common*, *shared*) (*friend etc*) commun; **m. fund** (*investment*) *Am* fonds *m* commun de placement. ● **mutually** *adv* mutuellement.

muzzle ['mʌz(ə)l] *n* (*device for dog etc*) muselière *f*; (*snout*) museau *m*; (*of gun*) gueule *f* ▮ *vt* (*animal*, *Fig the press etc*) museler.

muzzy ['mʌzɪ] *a* (**-ier**, **-iest**) (*confused*) (*person*) aux idées confuses; (*ideas etc*) confus; (*blurred*) (*outline etc*) flou.

my [maɪ] *poss a* mon, ma, *pl* mes.

myself [maɪ'self] *pron* moi-même; (*reflexive*) me, m'; (*after prep*) moi; **I wash m.** je me lave; **I think of m.** je pense à moi.

mystery ['mɪstərɪ] *n* mystère *m*. ● **my'sterious** *a* mystérieux.

mystic ['mɪstɪk] *a* & *n* mystique (*mf*). ● **mystical** *a* mystique. ● **mysticism** *n* mysticisme *m*. ● **mystique** [mɪ'stiːk] *n* (*mystery*, *power*) mystique *f* (**of** de).

mystify ['mɪstɪfaɪ] *vt* (*bewilder*) laisser perplexe; (*fool*) mystifier. ● **mystification** [-'keɪʃ(ə)n] *n* (*bewilderment*) perplexité *f*.

myth [mɪθ] *n* mythe *m*. ● **mythical** *a* mythique. ● **mytho'logical** *a* mythologique. ● **my'thology** *n* mythologie *f*.

N

N, n [en] *n* N, n *m*; **the nth time** la énième fois.

nab [næb] *vt* (**-bb-**) (*catch*, *arrest*) *Fam* épingler, coffrer.

naff [næf] *a Br Fam* (*stupid*) bête; (*unfashionable*) ringard.

nag [næg] *vti* (**-gg-**) **to n.** (**at**) s.o. (*pester*) harceler *or* embêter qn (**to do** pour qu'il fasse); (*find fault with*) critiquer qn. ● **nagging** *a* (*doubt*, *headache*) qui subsiste ▌ *n* critiques *fpl*.

nail [neɪl] **1** *n* (*of finger*, *toe*) ongle *m*; **n. brush** brosse *f* à ongles; **n. file** lime *f* à ongles; **n. polish**, *Br* **n. varnish** vernis *m* à ongles. **2** *n* (*metal*) clou *m* ▌ *vt* clouer; **to n.** s.o. (*nab*) *Fam* épingler qn; **to n. down** (*lid etc*) clouer.

naïve [naɪˈiːv] *a* naïf. ● **naïveté** [naɪˈiːvteɪ] *n* naïveté *f*.

naked [ˈneɪkɪd] *a* (*person*) (tout) nu; **to see sth with the n. eye** voir qch à l'œil nu; **n. flame** flamme *f* nue. ● **nakedness** *n* nudité *f*.

name [neɪm] *n* nom *m*; (*reputation*) réputation *f*; **my n. is...** je m'appelle...; **in the n. of** au nom de; **to put one's n. down for** (*school*, *course*) s'inscrire à; (*job*, *house*) demander, faire une demande pour avoir; **to call s.o. names** injurier qn; **first n.**, **given n.** prénom *m*; **last n.** nom *m* de famille; **a good/bad n.** *Fig* une bonne/mauvaise réputation; **n. plate** plaque *f*.
▌ *vt* nommer; (*ship*, *street*) baptiser; (*date*, *price*) fixer; **to n. s.o. to do sth** nommer qn pour faire qch; **he was named** *Br* **after** *or Am* **for...** il a reçu le nom de.... ● **nameless** *a* sans nom, anonyme.

namely [ˈneɪmlɪ] *adv* (*that is*) à savoir.

namesake [ˈneɪmseɪk] *n* (*person*) homonyme *m*.

nanny [ˈnænɪ] *n* nurse *f*, bonne *f* d'enfants; (*grandmother*) *Fam* mamie *f*.

nanny-goat [ˈnænɪɡəʊt] *n* chèvre *f*.

nap [næp] *n* (*sleep*) petit somme *m*; **to have** *or* **take a n.** faire un petit somme; (*after lunch*) faire la sieste ▌ *vi* (**-pp-**) sommeiller; **to catch s.o. napping** *Fig* prendre qn au dépourvu.

nape [neɪp] *n* **n. (of the neck)** nuque *f*.

napkin [ˈnæpkɪn] *n* (*at table*) serviette *f*; (*for baby*) *Old-fashioned Br* couche *f*. ● **nappy** *n* (*for baby*) *Br* couche *f*; **to have n. rash** avoir des rougeurs aux fesses (*dues aux couches*). ● **nappy-liner** *n Br* protège-couche *m*.

narcotic [nɑːˈkɒtɪk] *a* & *n* narcotique (*m*).

narrate [nəˈreɪt] *vt* raconter. ● **narrative** [ˈnærətɪv] *n* (*story*) récit *m*, narration *f*; (*art*, *act*) narration *f*. ● **narrator** *n* narrateur, -trice *mf*.

narrow [ˈnærəʊ] *a* (**-er**, **-est**) étroit; (*majority*) faible, petit ▌ *vi* (*of path*) se rétrécir; **to n. down** (*of choice etc*) se limiter (**to** à) ▌ *vt* **to n. (down)** (*choice*, *meaning etc*) limiter. ● **narrowly** *adv* (*to miss etc*) de justesse; (*strictly*) strictement; **he n. escaped** *or* **missed being killed/etc** il a failli être tué/etc. ● **narrowness** *n* étroitesse *f*.

narrow-minded [nærəʊˈmaɪndɪd] *a* borné. ● **narrow-mindedness** *n* étroitesse *f* (d'esprit).

nasal [ˈneɪz(ə)l] *a* nasal; (*voice*) nasillard.

nasty [ˈnɑːstɪ] *a* (**-ier**, **-iest**) (*bad*) mauvais, vilain; (*spiteful*) méchant, désagréable (**to**, **towards** avec); **a n. mess** *or* **muddle** un gâchis. ● **nastily** *adv* (*to behave*) méchamment; (*to rain*) horriblement. ● **nastiness** *n* (*malice*) méchanceté *f*; **the n. of the weather/taste/etc** le mauvais temps/goût/etc.

nation [ˈneɪʃ(ə)n] *n* nation *f*; **United Nations** (Organisation *f* des) Nations unies.

national [ˈnæʃən(ə)l] *a* national; **n. anthem** hymne *m* national; **N. Health Service** *Br* = Sécurité *f* Sociale; **n. insurance** *Br* = assurances *fpl* sociales ▌ *n* (*citizen*) ressortissant, -ante *mf*.

nationalist [ˈnæʃənəlɪst] *n* nationaliste *mf*. ● **nationa'listic** *a Pej* nationaliste.

nationality [næʃəˈnælətɪ] *n* nationalité *f*.

nationalize [ˈnæʃənəlaɪz] *vt* nationaliser.

nationally [ˈnæʃənəlɪ] *adv* (*to travel*, *be known etc*) dans le pays (tout) entier.

nationwide [ˈneɪʃənwaɪd] *a* & *adv* dans le pays (tout) entier.

native [ˈneɪtɪv] *a* (*country*) natal (*mpl* **-als**); (*habits*, *costume*) du pays; (*tribe*, *plant*) indigène; (*charm*, *ability*) inné; **n. language** langue *f* maternelle; **to be an English n. speaker** parler l'anglais comme langue maternelle ▌ *n* (*formerly*, *non-European in colony*) indigène *mf*; **to be a n. of** être originaire *or* natif de.

Nativity [nəˈtɪvɪtɪ] *n Rel* Nativité *f*.

NATO [ˈneɪtəʊ] *n abbr* (*North Atlantic Treaty Organization*) OTAN *f*.

natter [ˈnætər] *vi Br Fam* bavarder ▌ *n Br Fam* **to have a n.** bavarder.

natural [ˈnætʃ(ə)rəl] *a* naturel; (*actor*, *gardener etc*) né ▌ *n* **to be a n. for** (*job etc*) *Fam* être celui qu'il faut pour, être fait pour; **he's a n.** (*as actor*) *Fam* c'est un acteur-né. ● **naturalist** *n* naturaliste *mf*. ● **naturally** *adv* (*as normal*, *of course*) naturellement; (*by nature*) de nature; (*with naturalness*) (*to behave etc*) avec naturel. ● **naturalness** *n* naturel *m*.

naturalize ['nætʃ(ə)rəlaɪz] vt (person) naturaliser; **to become naturalized** se faire naturaliser. ●**naturalization** [-'zeɪʃ(ə)n] n naturalisation f.

nature ['neɪtʃər] n (natural world, character) nature f; (person's disposition) naturel m; **by n.** de nature; **n. study** sciences fpl naturelles.

naturist ['neɪtʃərɪst] n naturiste mf.

naught [nɔːt] n 1 Br Math zéro m. 2 (nothing) Lit rien m.

naughty ['nɔːtɪ] a (-ier, -iest) (child) vilain, malicieux; (joke, story) osé, grivois. ●**naughtily** adv (to behave) mal; (to say) avec malice. ●**naughtiness** n mauvaise conduite f.

nausea ['nɔːzɪə] n nausée f. ●**nauseate** vt écœurer. ●**nauseating** a (disgusting) écœurant. ●**nauseous** [Br 'nɔːzɪəs, Am 'nɔːʃəs] a (smell etc) nauséabond; **to feel n.** Am (sick) avoir envie de vomir; (disgusted) être écœuré.

nautical ['nɔːtɪk(ə)l] a nautique.

naval ['neɪv(ə)l] a naval; (hospital, power) maritime; (officer) de marine.

nave [neɪv] n (of church) nef f.

navel ['neɪv(ə)l] n nombril m.

navigate ['nævɪgeɪt] vi naviguer ▮ vt (boat) diriger, piloter; (river) naviguer sur. ●**navigable** a (river) navigable; (seaworthy) (boat etc) en état de naviguer. ●**navigation** [-'geɪʃ(ə)n] n navigation f. ●**navigator** n (on aircraft, boat etc) navigateur m.

navvy ['nævɪ] n (labourer) Br terrassier m.

navy ['neɪvɪ] n marine f ▮ a n. (blue) bleu marine inv.

Nazi ['nɑːtsɪ] a & n Pol Hist nazi, -ie (mf).

NB [en'biː] abbr (nota bene) NB.

near [nɪər] adv (-er, -est) près; **quite n., n. at hand** tout près; **to draw n.** (s')approcher (**to** de); (of date) approcher; **n. to** près de; **to come n. to being killed**/etc faillir être tué/etc; **n. enough** (more or less) plus ou moins. ▮ prep (-er, -est) n. (to) près de; **n. the bed** près du lit; **to be n.** (to) victory/death frôler la victoire/la mort; **n.** (to) **the end** vers la fin; **to come n. s.o.** s'approcher de qn. ▮ a (-er, -est) proche; **the nearest hospital** l'hôpital le plus proche; **the nearest way** la route la plus directe; **in the n. future** dans un avenir proche; **to the nearest franc** (to calculate) à un franc près; (to round up or down) au franc supérieur or inférieur; **n. side** Aut côté m gauche, Am côté m droit. ▮ vt (approach) approcher de; **nearing completion** près d'être achevé. ●**nearness** n (in space, time) proximité f.

nearby [nɪə'baɪ] adv tout près ▮ ['nɪəbaɪ] a proche.

nearly ['nɪəlɪ] adv presque; **she (very) n. fell** elle a failli tomber; **not n. as clever**/etc **as** loin d'être aussi intelligent/etc que.

near-sighted [nɪə'saɪtɪd] a myope.

neat [niːt] a (-er, -est) (clothes, work) soigné, propre, net (f nette); (room) bien rangé, ordonné; (style) élégant; (pretty) Fam joli, beau (f belle); (pleasant) Fam agréable; (good) Fam super; **to drink one's whisky**/etc **n.** prendre son whisky/etc sec. ●**neatly** adv avec soin; (skilfully) habilement. ●**neatness** n netteté f; (of room) ordre m.

nebulous ['nebjʊləs] a (idea etc) flou.

necessary ['nesɪs(ə)rɪ] a nécessaire; **it's n. to do** il est nécessaire de faire, il faut faire; **to make it n. for s.o. to do** mettre qn dans la nécessité de faire; **to do what's n.** faire le nécessaire (**for pour**) ▮ n **to do the n.** Fam faire le nécessaire; **the necessaries** (food etc) l'indispensable m. ●**nece'ssarily** adv **not n.** pas forcément.

necessitate [nɪ'sesɪteɪt] vt nécessiter.

necessity [nɪ'sesɪtɪ] n (obligation, need) nécessité f; (poverty) indigence f; **there's no n. for you to do that** tu n'es pas obligé de faire cela; **of n.** nécessairement; **to be a n.** être indispensable; **the (bare) necessities** le (strict) nécessaire.

neck¹ [nek] n cou m; (of dress, horse) encolure f; (of bottle) col m; **low n.** (of dress) décolleté m; **n. and n.** (in race etc) à égalité. ●**necklace** n collier m. ●**neckline** n encolure f. ●**necktie** n cravate f.

neck² [nek] vi (kiss etc) Fam se peloter.

nectarine ['nektərɪn] n (fruit) nectarine f, brugnon m.

née [neɪ] adv **n. Dupont** née Dupont.

need [niːd] n 1 (necessity, want, poverty) besoin m; **in n.** dans le besoin; **to be in n. of** avoir besoin de; **there's no n.** (for you) to do that tu n'as pas besoin de faire cela; **if n. be** si besoin est, s'il le faut. ▮ vt avoir besoin de; **you n. it** tu en as besoin, il te le faut; **it needs an army** or **an army is needed to do that** il faut une armée pour faire cela; **this sport needs patience** ce sport demande de la patience; **her hair needs cutting** il faut qu'elle se fasse couper les cheveux. 2 v aux **n. he wait?** est-il obligé d'attendre?, a-t-il besoin d'attendre?; **I needn't have rushed** ce n'était pas la peine de me presser; **I n. hardly say that...** je n'ai guère besoin de dire que.... ●**needy** a (-ier, -iest) nécessiteux.

needle ['niːd(ə)l] 1 n aiguille f; (of record player) saphir m. 2 vt (irritate) Fam agacer. ●**needlepoint** n tapisserie f (à l'aiguille). ●**needlework** n couture f, travaux mpl d'aiguille; (object) ouvrage m.

needless ['niːdləs] a inutile. ●**needlessly** adv inutilement.

negate [nɪ'geɪt] vt (nullify) annuler; (deny) nier. ●**negation** [-'geɪʃ(ə)n] n (denial) & Grammar négation f.

negative ['negətɪv] a négatif ▮ n (of photo) négatif m; (word, word group) négation f; (grammatical form) forme f négative; **to answer in the n.** répondre par la négative.

neglect [nɪ'glekt] vt (person, health, work etc) négliger; (garden, car etc) ne pas s'occuper de; (duty) négliger, manquer à;

(*rule*) désobéir à, méconnaître; **to n. to do** négliger de faire. ● *n* (*of person*) manque *m* de soins (**of** envers); (*of rule*) désobéissance *f* (**of** à); (*of duty*) manquement *m* (**of** à); (*carelessness*) négligence *f*; **in a state of n.** (*garden, house etc*) mal tenu. ●**neglected** *a* (*appearance, person*) négligé; (*garden, house etc*) mal tenu; **to feel n.** sentir qu'on vous néglige. ●**neglectful** *a* négligent; **to be n. of** négliger.

negligent ['negl ɪdʒ ənt] *a* négligent. ●**negligence** *n* négligence *f*. ●**negligently** *adv* négligemment.

negligible ['negl ɪdʒ əb(ə)l] *a* négligeable.

negotiate [n ɪ'ɡəʊʃ ɪeɪt] **1** *vti* (*discuss*) négocier. **2** *vt* (*fence, obstacle*) franchir; (*bend*) (*in vehicle*) négocier. ●**negotiable** *a* Fin négociable. ●**negotiation** [-'eɪʃ(ə)n] *n* négociation *f*; **in n. with** en pourparlers avec. ●**negotiator** *n* négociateur, -trice *mf*.

Negro ['niːɡrəʊ] *n* (*pl* -oes) *often Pej* (*man*) Noir *m*; (*woman*) Noire *f* ● *a* noir; (*art, sculpture etc*) nègre.

neigh [neɪ] *vi* (*of horse*) hennir ● *n* hennissement *m*.

neighbour ['neɪbər] (*Am* neighbor) *n* voisin, -ine *mf*. ●**neighbourhood** (*Am* neighborhood) *n* (*district*) quartier *m*, voisinage *m*; (*neighbours*) voisinage *m*; **in the n. of ten dollars/kilos** dans les dix dollars/kilos. ●**neighbouring** (*Am* neighboring) *a* voisin. ●**neighbourly** (*Am* neighborly) *a* (*feeling etc*) amical, de bon voisinage; **they're n.** (*people*) ils sont bons voisins.

neither [*Br* 'naɪðər, *Am* 'niːðər] *adv* ni; **n....nor ni...ni; n. you nor me** ni toi ni moi; **he n. sings nor dances** il ne chante ni ne danse. ● *conj* (*not either*) (ne)...non plus; **n. will I go** je n'y irai pas non plus; **n. do I, n. can I** *etc* (ni) moi non plus. ● *a* **n. boy** (**came**) aucun des deux garçons (n'est venu); **on n. side** ni d'un côté ni de l'autre. ● *pron* **n.** (**of them**) ni l'un(e) ni l'autre, aucun(e) (des deux).

neo- ['niːəʊ] *pref* néo-.

neon ['niːɒn] *n* (*gas*) néon *m*; **n. lighting/ sign/etc** éclairage *m*/enseigne *f* au néon.

nephew ['nevjuː, 'nefjuː] *n* neveu *m*.

nepotism ['nepət ɪz(ə)m] *n* népotisme *m*.

nerd [n ɜːd] *n* (*stupid person*) *Sl* nullard, -arde *mf*, ducon *m*.

nerve [n ɜːv] *n* nerf *m*; (*courage*) courage *m* (**to do** de faire); (*confidence*) assurance *f*; (*calm*) sang-froid *m*; (*impudence*) *Fam* culot *m* (**to do** de faire); **you get on my nerves** *Fam* tu me tapes sur les nerfs; **to have an attack of nerves** (*fear, anxiety*) avoir le trac; **she's a bundle** *or* **mass** *or* **bag of nerves** *Fam* c'est un paquet de nerfs; **to have bad nerves** être nerveux; **n. cell** cellule *f* nerveuse; **n. centre** centre *m* nerveux. ●**nerve-racking** *a* éprouvant pour les nerfs.

nervous ['n ɜːvəs] *a* (*person*) (*tense*) nerveux; (*worried*) inquiet (**about** de); (*uneasy*) mal à l'aise; (*illness etc*) nerveux; **to be** *or* **feel n.** (*before exam, performance etc*) avoir le trac; **to have a n. breakdown** faire une dépression nerveuse. ●**nervously** *adv* nerveusement; (*worriedly*) avec inquiétude. ●**nervousness** *n* nervosité *f*; (*fear*) trac *m*.

nervy ['n ɜːvɪ] *a* (-ier, -iest) *Fam* (*anxious*) nerveux; (*brash*) *Am* culotté.

nest [nest] *n* nid *m*; **n. egg** (*money saved*) pécule *m*; **n. of tables** table *f* gigogne ● *vi* (*of bird*) (se) nicher.

nestle ['nes(ə)l] *vi* se pelotonner (**up to** contre); **a village nestling in** (*forest, valley etc*) un village niché dans.

net [net] *n* filet *m*; **n. curtain** voilage *m* ● *vt* (-tt-) (*fish*) prendre au filet. **2** *a* (*profit, weight, value etc*) net (*f* nette) ● *vt* (-tt-) (*of person, company etc*) gagner net; **this venture netted them...** cette entreprise leur a rapporté.... ●**netting** *n* (*nets*) filets *mpl*; (*mesh*) mailles *fpl*; (*fabric*) voile *m*; (*wire*) **n.** grillage *m*.

Netherlands (the) [ðə'neðələndz] *npl* les Pays-Bas *mpl*.

nettle ['net(ə)l] *n* ortie *f*.

network ['netw ɜːk] *n* réseau *m*.

neuro- ['njʊərəʊ] *pref* neuro-.

neurosis, *pl* -oses [njʊ'rəʊs ɪs, -əʊsiːz] *n* névrose *f*. ●**neurotic** [-'rɒt ɪk] *a* & *n* névrosé, -ée (*mf*).

neuter ['njuːtər] **1** *a* & *n* *Grammar* neutre (*m*). **2** *vt* (*cat etc*) châtrer.

neutral ['njuːtrəl] *a* neutre; (*policy*) de neutralité ● *n* (*electrical wire*) neutre *m*; **in n.** (*gear*) (*vehicle*) au point mort. ●**neu'trality** *n* neutralité *f*. ●**neutralize** *vt* neutraliser.

never ['nevər] *adv* **1** (*not ever*) (ne...) jamais; **she n. lies** elle ne ment jamais; **n. in** (**all**) **my life** jamais de ma vie; **n. again** plus jamais. **2** (*not*) *Fam* **I n. did it** je ne l'ai pas fait. ●**never-'ending** *a* interminable.

nevertheless [nevəðə'les] *adv* néanmoins, quand même.

new [njuː] *a* **1** (-er, -est) nouveau (*f* nouvelle); (*brand-new*) neuf (*f* neuve); **to be n. to** (*job*) être nouveau dans; (*city*) être un nouveau-venu dans, être fraîchement installé dans; **a n. boy** (*in school*) un nouveau; **a n. girl** une nouvelle; **what's n.?** *Fam* quoi de neuf?; **to break n. ground** innover; **n. look** (*of person*) nouveau look *m*; (*of company etc*) nouvelle image *f*; **it's as good as n.** c'est comme neuf; **a n.-born baby** un nouveau-né, une nouveau-née; **a n.-laid egg** *Br* un œuf du jour. **2** (*different*) **a n. glass/pen/etc** un autre verre/stylo/etc.

newcomer ['njuːkʌmər] *n* nouveau-venu *m*, nouvelle-venue *f*. ●**new'fangled** *a* (*trop*) moderne. ●**new-found** *a* nouveau (*f* nouvelle). ●**newly** *adv* (*recently*) nouvellement, fraîchement; **the n.-weds** les nouveaux mariés. ●**newness** *n* (*condition*) état *m* neuf; (*novelty*) nouveauté *f*.

news [njuːz] *n* nouvelle(s) *f(pl)*; (*in the*

media) informations *fpl*, actualités *fpl*; **sports**/*etc* n. (*newspaper column*) chronique *f* or rubrique *f* sportive/*etc*; **a piece of n.**, some n. une nouvelle; (*in the media*) une information; **n. agency** agence *f* de presse; **n. flash** flash *m*; **n. headlines** titres *mpl* de l'actualité; **n. stand** kiosque *m* à journaux.

newsagent ['njuːzeɪdʒənt] *n* Br marchand, -ande *mf* de journaux. ● **newsboy** *n* vendeur *m* de journaux. ● **newscaster** *n* présentateur, -trice *mf*. ● **newsdealer** *n* Am = newsagent. ● **newsletter** *n* (*of club, group etc*) bulletin *m*. ● **newspaper** *n* journal *m*. ● **newspaperman** *n* (*pl* -men) journaliste *m*. ● **newsprint** *n* papier *m* (de) journal. ● **newsreader** *n* Br présentateur, -trice *mf*. ● **newsreel** *n* Cinema actualités *fpl*. ● **newsworthy** *a* digne de faire l'objet d'un reportage. ● **newsy** *a* (*-ier, -iest*) (*letter etc*) Fam plein de nouvelles.

newt [njuːt] *n* (*animal*) triton *m*.

New Zealand [njuːˈziːlənd] *n* Nouvelle-Zélande *f* ▮ *a* néo-zélandais. ● **New Zealander** *n* Néo-Zélandais, -aise *mf*.

next [nekst] *a* prochain; (*room, house*) d'à-côté, voisin; (*following*) suivant; **n. month** (*in the future*) le mois prochain; **he returned the n. month** (*in the past*) il revint le mois suivant; **the n. day** le lendemain; **the n. morning** le lendemain matin; **within the n. ten days** d'ici (à) dix jours, dans un délai de dix jours; (**by**) **this time n. week** d'ici (à) la semaine prochaine; **from one year to the n.** d'une année à l'autre; **you're n.** c'est ton tour; **n. (please)!** (au) suivant!; **the n. thing to do is...** ce qu'il faut faire ensuite c'est...; **the n. size (up)** la taille au-dessus; **to live**/*etc* **n. door** habiter/*etc* à côté (to de); **n.-door neighbour/room** voisin *m*/pièce *f* d'à-côté.

▮ *n* (*in series etc*) suivant, -ante *mf*.

▮ *adv* (*afterwards*) ensuite, après; (*now*) maintenant; **when you come n.** la prochaine fois que tu viendras; **the n. best solution** la seconde solution.

▮ *prep* **n. to** (*beside*) à côté de; **n. to nothing** presque rien.

NHS [eneɪtʃˈes] *n abbr* (*National Health Service*) Br = Sécurité *f* Sociale.

nib [nɪb] *n* (*of pen*) plume *f*, bec *m*.

nibble ['nɪb(ə)l] *vti* (*eat*) grignoter; (*bite*) mordiller.

Nicaragua [nɪkəˈrægjʊə] *n* Nicaragua *m*.

nice [naɪs] *a* (*-er, -est*) (*pleasant*) agréable; (*charming*) charmant, gentil (*f* gentille); (*good*) bon (*f* bonne); (*fine*) beau (*f* belle); (*pretty*) joli; (*kind*) gentil (**to** avec); (*respectable*) bien *inv*; (*subtle*) délicat; **it's n. here** c'est bien ici; **n. and easy/warm**/*etc* (*very*) bien facile/chaud/*etc*. ● **nice-looking** *a* beau (*f* belle), joli. ● **nicely** *adv* agréablement; (*kindly*) gentiment; (*well*) bien.

niceties ['naɪsətɪz] *npl* (*pleasant things*) agréments *mpl*; (*subtleties*) subtilités *fpl*.

niche [niːʃ, nɪtʃ] *n* **1** (*recess*) niche *f*. **2** (*job*) (bonne) situation *f*; (*direction*) voie *f*; **to make a n. for oneself** faire son trou;

(**market**) n. créneau *m*.

nick [nɪk] *n* **1** (*on skin, wood*) entaille *f*; (*in blade, crockery*) brèche *f*. **2** *n* (*prison*) Br Sl taule *f* ▮ *vt* (*steal, arrest*) Br Sl piquer. **3** *n* **in the n. of time** juste à temps; **in good n.** Br Sl en bon état.

nickel ['nɪk(ə)l] *n* (*metal*) nickel *m*; (*coin*) Am pièce *f* de cinq cents.

nickname ['nɪkneɪm] *n* (*informal name*) surnom *m*; (*short form*) diminutif *m* ▮ *vt* surnommer.

nicotine ['nɪkətiːn] *n* nicotine *f*.

niece [niːs] *n* nièce *f*.

nifty ['nɪftɪ] *a* (*-ier, -iest*) (*stylish*) chic *inv*; (*skilful*) habile; (*fast*) rapide.

Nigeria [naɪˈdʒɪərɪə] *n* Nigéria *m*. ● **Nigerian** *a* nigérian ▮ *n* Nigérian, -ane *mf*.

niggardly ['nɪgədlɪ] *a* (*person*) avare; (*amount*) mesquin.

niggling ['nɪglɪŋ] *a* (*trifling*) insignifiant; (*irksome*) irritant; (*doubt*) persistant.

night [naɪt] *n* (*evening*) soir *m*; **at n.** la nuit; **by n.** de nuit; **last n.** (*evening*) hier soir; (*night*) cette nuit, la nuit dernière; **to have an early/late n.** se coucher tôt/tard; **to have a good n.('s sleep)** bien dormir; **first n.** (*of play*) première *f*; **the last n.** (*of play*) la dernière.

▮ *a* (*work, flight etc*) de nuit; **n. life** vie *f* nocturne; **n. school** cours *mpl* du soir; **n. shift** poste *m* de nuit; (*workers*) équipe *f* de nuit; **n. watchman** veilleur *m* de nuit.

nightcap ['naɪtkæp] *n* (*drink*) boisson *f* (*alcoolisée ou chaude prise avant de se coucher*). ● **nightclub** *n* boîte *f* de nuit. ● **nightdress** *or* **nightgown** *or* Fam **nightie** *n* (*woman's*) chemise *f* de nuit. ● **nightfall** *n* **at n.** à la tombée de la nuit. ● **nightlight** *n* veilleuse *f*. ● **nighttime** *n* nuit *f*.

nightingale ['naɪtɪŋgeɪl] *n* rossignol *m*.

nightly ['naɪtlɪ] *adv* chaque nuit *or* soir ▮ *a* de chaque nuit *or* soir.

nightmare ['naɪtmeər] *n* cauchemar *m*.

nil [nɪl] *n* (*nothing*) & Br Sport zéro *m*; **the risk/result**/*etc* **is n.** le risque/résultat/*etc* est nul.

Nile [naɪl] *n* **the N.** le Nil.

nimble ['nɪmb(ə)l] *a* (*-er, -est*) agile.

nincompoop ['nɪŋkəmpuːp] *n* Fam imbécile *mf*.

nine [naɪn] *a & n* neuf (*m*).

nineteen [naɪnˈtiːn] *a & n* dix-neuf (*m*). ● **nineteenth** *a & n* dix-neuvième (*mf*).

ninety ['naɪntɪ] *a & n* quatre-vingt-dix (*m*). ● **ninetieth** *a & n* quatre-vingt-dixième (*mf*).

ninth ['naɪnθ] *a & n* neuvième (*mf*); **a n.** un neuvième.

nip [nɪp] **1** *vt* (**-pp-**) (*pinch, bite*) pincer; **to n. sth in the bud** Fig étouffer qch dans l'œuf ▮ *n* pinçon *m*; **there's a n. in the air** ça pince. **2** *vi* (**-pp-**) **to n. round to s.o.** Br Fam faire un saut chez qn, courir chez qn; **to n. in/out** (*dash*) Br Fam entrer/sortir un instant.

nipper ['nɪpər] *n* (*child*) Br Fam gosse *mf*.

nipple ['nɪp(ə)l] *n* bout *m* de sein, mamelon

m; (*on baby's bottle*) Am tétine *f*.

nippy ['nɪpɪ] *a* **1** (**-ier, -iest**) (*chilly*) (*wind etc*) frais (*f* fraîche); **it's n.** (*weather*) *Fam* ça pince. **2 to be n.** (**about it**) (*quick*) *Br Fam* faire vite.

nit [nɪt] *n* **1** (*fool*) *Br Fam* idiot, -ote *mf*. **2** (*of louse*) lente *f*.

nitrogen ['naɪtrədʒən] *n* azote *m*.

nitty-gritty [nɪtɪ'grɪtɪ] *n* **to get down to the n.-gritty** *Fam* en venir au fond du problème.

nitwit ['nɪtwɪt] *n* (*fool*) *Fam* idiot, -ote *mf*.

no [nəʊ] *adv* & *n* non (*m inv*); **no!** non!; **no more than ten/a kilo**/*etc* pas plus de dix/d'un kilo/*etc*; **no less than ten**/*etc* pas moins de dix/*etc*; **no more time**/*etc* plus de temps/*etc*; **I have no more time** je n'ai plus de temps; **no more/less than you** pas plus/moins que vous; **you can do no better** tu ne peux pas faire mieux; **the noes** (*in voting*) les non. **I** *a* aucun(e); pas de; **I've got** *or* **I have no idea** je n'ai aucune idée; **no child came** aucun enfant n'est venu; **I've got** *or* **I have no money/time**/*etc* je n'ai pas d'argent/de temps/*etc*; **I have no time to play**/*etc* je n'ai pas le temps de jouer/*etc*; **of no importance/value**/*etc* sans importance/valeur/*etc*; **with no gloves/hat**/*etc* **on** sans gants/chapeau/*etc*; **there's no knowing...** impossible de savoir...; **'no smoking'** 'défense de fumer'; **no way!** *Fam* pas question!; **no one = nobody.**

noble ['nəʊb(ə)l] *a* (**-er, -est**) noble; (*building*) majestueux. ●**no'bility** *n* (*character, class*) noblesse *f*. ●**nobleman** *n* (*pl* **-men**) noble *m*. ●**noblewoman** *n* (*pl* **-women**) noble *f*.

nobody ['nəʊbɒdɪ] *pron* (ne...) personne; **n. came** personne n'est venu; **he knows n.** il ne connaît personne; **n.!** personne! **I** *n* **a n.** une nullité.

nocturnal [nɒk'tɜːn(ə)l] *a* nocturne.

nod [nɒd] **1** *vti* (**-dd-**) **to n.** (**one's head**) faire un signe de tête, incliner la tête **I** *n* signe *m* *or* inclination *f* de tête. **2** *vi* (**-dd-**) **to n. off** (*go to sleep*) s'assoupir.

noise [nɔɪz] *n* bruit *m*; (*of bell, drum*) son *m*; **to make a n.** faire du bruit.

noisy ['nɔɪzɪ] *a* (**-ier, -iest**) (*person, street etc*) bruyant. ●**noisily** *adv* bruyamment.

nomad ['nəʊmæd] *n* nomade *mf*. ●**no'madic** *a* nomade.

nominal ['nɒmɪn(ə)l] *a* (*value, fee etc*) nominal; (*rent, salary*) symbolique; (*ruler*) de nom.

nominate ['nɒmɪneɪt] *vt* (*appoint*) nommer, désigner; (*as candidate*) proposer (**for** comme candidat à). ●**nomination** [-'neɪʃ(ə)n] *n* (*appointment*) nomination *f*; (*as candidate*) proposition *f* de candidat. ●**nomi'nee** *n* (*candidate*) candidat *m*.

non- [nɒn] *pref* non-.

non-aligned [nɒnə'laɪnd] *a* (*country*) non-aligné.

nonchalant ['nɒnʃələnt] *a* nonchalant.

noncommissioned [nɒnkə'mɪʃ(ə)nd] *a* **n. officer** *Mil* sous-officier *m*.

non-committal [nɒnkə'mɪt(ə)l] *a* (*answer, person*) évasif.

nonconformist [nɒnkən'fɔːmɪst] *a* & *n* non-conformiste (*mf*).

nondescript ['nɒndɪskrɪpt] *a* quelconque, très ordinaire.

none [nʌn] *pron* aucun(e) *mf*; (*in filling out a form*) néant; **n. of them** aucun d'eux; **she has n.** (**at all**) elle n'en a pas (du tout); **n.** (**at all**) **came** pas un(e) seul(e) n'est venu(e); **n. can tell** personne ne peut le dire; **n. of the cake**/*etc* pas une seule partie du gâteau/*etc*; **n. of the trees**/*etc* aucun des arbres/*etc*, aucun arbre/*etc*; **n. of it** *or* **this** rien (de ceci). **I** *adv* **n. too hot**/*etc* pas tellement chaud/*etc*; **he's n. the happier/wiser**/*etc* (**for it**) il n'en est pas plus heureux/sage/*etc*; **n. the less** néanmoins. ●**nonethe'less** *adv* néanmoins.

nonentity [nɒ'nentɪtɪ] *n* (*person*) nullité *f*.

non-existent [nɒnɪg'zɪstənt] *a* inexistant.

non-fiction [nɒn'fɪkʃ(ə)n] *n* littérature *f* non-romanesque; (*in library*) ouvrages *mpl* généraux.

non-flammable [nɒn'flæməb(ə)l] *a* ininflammable.

non-iron [nɒn'aɪən] *a* (*shirt etc*) qui ne se repasse pas.

nonplus [nɒn'plʌs] *vt* (**-ss-**) dérouter.

non-political [nɒnpə'lɪtɪk(ə)l] *a* apolitique.

non-profit-making [nɒn'prɒfɪtmeɪkɪŋ] (*Am* **non-profit**) *a* sans but lucratif.

nonsense ['nɒnsəns] *n* absurdités *fpl*; **that's n.** c'est absurde. ●**non'sensical** *a* absurde.

non-smoker [nɒn'sməʊkər] *n* (*person*) non-fumeur, -euse *mf*; (*compartment on train*) compartiment *m* non-fumeurs.

non-stick [nɒn'stɪk] *a* (*pan*) anti-adhésif, qui n'attache pas.

non-stop [nɒn'stɒp] *a* sans arrêt; (*train, flight*) direct **I** *adv* (*to work etc*) sans arrêt; (*to fly*) sans escale.

noodles ['nuːd(ə)lz] *npl* nouilles *fpl*; (*in soup*) vermicelle(s) *m*(*pl*).

nook [nʊk] *n* coin *m*; **in every n. and cranny** dans tous les coins (et recoins).

noon [nuːn] *n* midi *m*; **at n.** à midi **I** *a* (*sun etc*) de midi.

no-one ['nəʊwʌn] *pron* = **nobody.**

noose [nuːs] *n* (*loop*) nœud *m* coulant; (*of hangman*) corde *f*.

nor [nɔːr] *conj* ni; **neither you n. me** ni toi ni moi; **she neither drinks n. smokes** elle ne fume ni ne boit; **n. do I, n. can I** *etc* (ni) moi non plus; **n. will I** (**go**) je n'y irai pas non plus.

norm [nɔːm] *n* norme *f*.

normal ['nɔːm(ə)l] *a* normal **I** *n* **above/below n.** au-dessus/au-dessous de la normale. ●**nor'mality** *n* normalité *f*. ●**normalize** *vt* normaliser. ●**normally** *adv* normalement.

Norman ['nɔːmən] *a* normand. ●**Normandy** *n* Normandie *f*.

north [nɔːθ] *n* nord *m*; (**to the**) **n. of** au nord de. **I** *a* (*coast*) nord *inv*; (*wind*) du nord; **N.**

America/Africa Amérique *f*/Afrique *f* du Nord; **N. American** (*a*) nord-américain; (*n*) Nord-Américain, -aine *mf*.

▌ *adv* au nord, vers le nord. ●**northbound** *a* (*traffic*) en direction du nord; (*carriageway*) *Br* nord *inv*. ●**north-'east** *n* & *a* nord-est *m* & *a inv*. ●**northerly** ['nɔːðəlɪ] *a* (*point*) nord *inv*; (*direction, wind*) du nord. ●**northern** ['nɔːðən] *a* (*coast*) nord *inv*; (*town*) du nord; **N. France** le Nord de la France; **N. Europe** Europe *f* du Nord; **N. Ireland** Irlande *f* du Nord. ●**northerner** *n* habitant, -ante *mf* du Nord. ●**northward(s)** *a* & *adv* vers le nord. ●**north-'west** *n* & *a* nord-ouest *m* & *a inv*.

Norway ['nɔːweɪ] *n* Norvège *f*. ●**Nor'wegian** [nɔː'wiːdʒən] *a* norvégien ▌ *n* (*language*) norvégien *m*; (*person*) Norvégien, -ienne *mf*.

nose [nəʊz] *n* nez *m*; **her n. is bleeding** elle saigne du nez; **to turn one's n. up** *Fig* faire le dégoûté (**at** devant) ▌ *vi* **n. about** (*pry*) *Fam* fouiner. ●**nosebleed** *n* saignement *m* de nez. ●**nosedive** *n* (*of aircraft*) piqué *m*; (*in prices*) chute *f*.

nosey ['nəʊzɪ] *a* (-**ier**, -**iest**) indiscret, fouineur; **n. parker** *Br* fouineur, -euse *mf*.

nosh [nɒʃ] *vi Fam* (*have a light meal*) grignoter (entre les repas); (*eat*) *Br* bouffer ▌ *n Fam* (*light meal*) (petit) en-cas *m*; (*food*) *Br* bouffe *f*.

nostalgia [nɒ'stældʒɪə] *n* nostalgie *f*. ●**nostalgic** *a* nostalgique.

nostril ['nɒstr(ə)l] *n* (*of person*) narine *f*; (*of horse*) naseau *m*.

nosy ['nəʊzɪ] *a* = **nosey**.

not [nɒt] *adv* **1** (ne...) pas; **he's n. there, he isn't there** il n'est pas là; **n. yet** pas encore; **why n.?** pourquoi pas?; **n.one reply/etc** pas une seule réponse/*etc*; **n. at all** pas du tout; (*after 'thank you'*) je vous en prie.
2 non; **I think/hope n.** je pense/j'espère que non; **n. guilty** non coupable; **isn't she?, don't you?** *etc* non?

notable ['nəʊtəb(ə)l] *a* (*remarkable*) notable ▌ *n* (*person*) notable *m*. ●**notably** *adv* (*noticeably*) notablement; (*particularly*) notamment.

notary ['nəʊtərɪ] *n* notaire *m*.

notation [nəʊ'teɪʃ(ə)n] *n* notation *f*.

notch [nɒtʃ] **1** *n* (*in wood etc*) encoche *f*, entaille *f*; (*in belt, wheel*) cran *m*. **2** *vt* **to n. up** (*a score*) marquer; (*a victory*) enregistrer.

note [nəʊt] *n* (*written comment, tone, musical etc*) note *f*; (*summary preface*) notice *f*; (*banknote*) *Br* billet *m*; (*piano key*) touche *f*; (*message, letter*) petit mot *m*; **to take (a) n. of, make a n. of** prendre note de; **actor/etc of n.** acteur *m*/etc éminent.
▌ *vt* (*take note of*) noter; (*notice*) remarquer, noter; **to n. down** (*word, remark etc*) noter. ●**notebook** *n* carnet *m*; (*for school*) cahier *m*; (*pad*) bloc-notes *m*. ●**notepad** *n* bloc-notes *m*. ●**notepaper** *n* papier *m* à lettres.

noted ['nəʊtɪd] *a* (*author, actor etc*) éminent; **to be n. for one's charm/its beauty/etc** être

connu pour son charme/sa beauté/*etc*.

noteworthy ['nəʊtwɜːðɪ] *a* notable.

nothing ['nʌθɪŋ] *pron* (ne...) rien; **he knows n.** il ne sait rien; **n. at all** rien du tout; **n. to do/eat/etc** rien à faire/manger/*etc*; **n. big/etc** rien de grand/*etc*; **n. much** pas grand-chose; **n. but problems/etc** rien que des problèmes/*etc*; **I've got n. to do with it** je n'y suis pour rien; **I can do n. (about it)** je n'y peux rien; **to come to n.** (*of efforts etc*) ne rien donner; **there's n. like it** il n'y a rien de tel; **for n.** (*in vain, free of charge*) pour rien; **to have n. on** être tout nu.
▌ *adv* **to look n. like s.o.** ne ressembler nullement à qn; **n. like as large/etc** loin d'être aussi grand/*etc*.
▌ *n* **a** (**mere**) **n.** (*person*) une nullité; (*thing*) un rien. ●**nothingness** *n* (*void*) néant *m*.

notice ['nəʊtɪs] *n* (*notification*) avis *m*; (*in newspaper*) annonce *f*; (*sign*) pancarte *f*, écriteau *m*; (*poster*) affiche *f*; (*review of film etc*) critique *f*; (*attention*) attention *f*; **(advance) n.** (*of departure etc*) préavis *m*; **to give s.o. (advance) n.** (*inform*) avertir qn (**of** de); **n. (to quit), n. (of dismissal)** congé *m*; **to give (in) one's n.** (*resignation*) donner sa démission; **to take n.** faire attention (**of** à); **to bring sth to s.o.'s n.** porter qch à la connaissance de qn; **until further n.** jusqu'à nouvel ordre; **at short n.** au dernier moment; **n. board** *Br* tableau *m* d'affichage.
▌ *vt* (*become aware of*) remarquer (qn); (*fact, trick, danger etc*) s'apercevoir de, remarquer; **I n. that** je m'aperçois que, je remarque que.
▌ *vi* remarquer.

noticeable ['nəʊtɪsəb(ə)l] *a* visible, perceptible; **that's n.** ça se voit; **she's n.** elle se fait remarquer.

notify ['nəʊtɪfaɪ] *vt* (*inform*) avertir (**s.o. of sth** qn de qch); (*announce*) notifier (**to** à). ●**notification** [-'keɪʃ(ə)n] *n* avis *m*, annonce *f*.

notion ['nəʊʃ(ə)n] *n* (*thought*) idée *f*; (*awareness*) notion *f*; **to have some n. of** (*knowledge*) avoir quelques notions de. ●**notions** *npl* (*sewing articles*) *Am* mercerie *f*.

notorious [nəʊ'tɔːrɪəs] *a* (*event, person etc*) tristement célèbre; (*stupidity, criminal*) notoire. ●**notoriety** [nəʊtə'raɪətɪ] *n* (triste) notoriété *f*.

notwithstanding [nɒtwɪð'stændɪŋ] *prep* malgré ▌ *adv* tout de même.

nougat [*Br* 'nuːgɑː, 'nʌgət] *n* nougat *m*.

nought [nɔːt] *n Br Math* zéro *m*; **noughts and crosses** (*game*) *Br* = morpion *m*.

noun [naʊn] *n Grammar* nom *m*.

nourish ['nʌrɪʃ] *vt* nourrir. ●**nourishing** *a* nourrissant. ●**nourishment** *n* nourriture *f*.

novel ['nɒv(ə)l] **1** *n* roman *m*. **2** *a* (*new*) nouveau (*f* nouvelle), original. ●**novelist** *n* romancier, -ière *mf*. ●**novelty** *n* (*newness, object, idea*) nouveauté *f*.

November [nəʊ'vembər] *n* novembre *m*.

novice ['nɒvɪs] *n* novice *mf* (**at** en).

now [naʊ] *adv* maintenant; **just n., right n.** en ce moment; **I saw her just n.** je l'ai vue à l'instant; **for n.** pour le moment; **even n.** encore maintenant; **from n. on** désormais, à partir de maintenant; **until n., up to n.** jusqu'ici, jusqu'à maintenant; **before n.** avant; **n. and then** de temps à autre; **n. hot, n. cold** tantôt chaud, tantôt froid; **n. (then)!** bon!, alors!; *(telling s.o. off)* allons!; **n. it happened that…** or il advint que…. ▮ *conj* **n. (that)** maintenant que.

nowadays ['naʊədeɪz] *adv* aujourd'hui, de nos jours.

noway ['nəʊweɪ] *adv Am* nullement.

nowhere ['nəʊweər] *adv* nulle part; **n. else** nulle part ailleurs; **it's n.** I know ce n'est pas un endroit que je connais; **n. near the house** loin de la maison; **n. near enough** loin d'être assez.

nozzle ['nɒz(ə)l] *n (of hose)* jet *m*, lance *f* (à eau); *(of syringe, tube)* embout *m*.

nth [enθ] *a* nième.

nuance ['njuːɑːns] *n (of meaning, colour etc)* nuance *f*.

nub [nʌb] *n (of problem)* cœur *m*.

nuclear ['njuːklɪər] *a* nucléaire; **n. scientist** spécialiste *mf* du nucléaire, atomiste *mf*.

nucleus, *pl* **-clei** ['njuːklɪəs, -klɪaɪ] *n* noyau *m (pl* noyaux).

nude [njuːd] *a* nu ▮ *n (female or male figure)* nu *m*; **in the n.** (tout) nu.

nudge [nʌdʒ] *vt (with elbow)* pousser du coude ▮ *n* coup *m* de coude.

nudism ['njuːdɪz(ə)m] *n* nudisme *m*, naturisme *m*. ●**nudist** *n* nudiste *mf*, naturiste *mf* ▮ *a (camp)* de nudistes, de naturistes.

nudity ['njuːdɪtɪ] *n* nudité *f*.

nugget ['nʌgɪt] *n (of gold etc)* pépite *f*.

nuisance ['njuːs(ə)ns] *n (annoyance)* embêtement *m*; *(person)* peste *f*; **that's a n.** c'est embêtant; **he's being a n., he's making a n. of himself** il nous embête, il m'embête *etc*.

null [nʌl] *a* **n. (and void)** nul (et non avenu). ●**nullify** *vt* infirmer.

numb [nʌm] *a (stiff) (hand etc)* engourdi; *Fig (with fear)* paralysé; *(with shock, horror)* hébété; **n. with cold** engourdi par le froid ▮ *vt* engourdir; *Fig (of fear)* paralyser; *(of shock etc)* hébéter. ●**numbness** *n (of hand etc)* engourdissement *m*.

number ['nʌmbər] *n* nombre *m*; *(of page, house, telephone etc)* numéro *m*; **a dance/ song n.** un numéro de danse/de chant; **a/any n. of** un certain/grand nombre de; **n. plate** *(of vehicle) Br* plaque *f* d'immatriculation. ▮ *vt (page etc)* numéroter; *(include, count, amount to)* compter; **they n. eight** ils sont au nombre de huit. ●**numbering** *n* numérotage *m*.

numeral ['njuːm(ə)rəl] *n* chiffre *m* ▮ *a* numéral.

numerate ['njuːm(ə)rət] *a (person)* qui sait compter.

numerical [njuːˈmerɪk(ə)l] *a* numérique.

numerous ['njuːmərəs] *a* nombreux.

nun [nʌn] *n* religieuse *f*.

nurse [nɜːs] **1** *n* infirmière *f*; *(for children in household)* nurse *f*; **(male) n.** infirmier *m*. **2** *vt (look after)* soigner; *(suckle)* nourrir, allaiter; *(cradle)* bercer; *(a grudge etc) Fig* nourrir; *(support, encourage) Fig* épauler *(qn)*. ●**nursing** *a* **n. mother** mère *f* qui allaite; **the n. staff** le personnel infirmier ▮ *n (care)* soins *mpl*; *(job)* profession *f* d'infirmière *or* d'infirmier; **n. home** *Br* clinique *f*.

nursemaid ['nɜːsmeɪd] *n* bonne *f* d'enfants.

nursery ['nɜːsərɪ] *n (children's room)* chambre *f* d'enfants; *(for plants, trees)* pépinière *f*; **(day) n.** *(school etc)* crèche *f*, garderie *f*; **n. education** *Br* enseignement *m* de la maternelle; **n. nurse** *Br* puéricultrice *f*; **n. rhyme** chanson *f* enfantine; **n. school** école *f* maternelle.

nurture ['nɜːtʃər] *vt (educate)* éduquer.

nut¹ [nʌt] *n (fruit)* fruit *m* à coque; *(walnut)* noix *f*; *(hazelnut)* noisette *f*; *(peanut)* cacah(o)uète *f*; **Brazil/cashew n.** noix *f* du Brésil/de cajou. ●**nutcracker(s)** *n(pl)* casse-noix *m inv*. ●**nutshell** *n* coquille *f* de noix; **in a n.** *Fig* en un mot.

nut² [nʌt] *n* **1** *(for bolt)* écrou *m*. **2** *(head) Sl* caboche *f*.

nut³ [nʌt] *n (crazy person) Sl* cinglé, -ée *mf*. ●**nutcase** *n Sl* cinglé, -ée *mf*. ●**nuts** *a (crazy) Sl* cinglé **(about** de). ●**nutty** *a* **(-ier, -iest)** *Sl* cinglé.

nutmeg ['nʌtmeg] *n* muscade *f*.

nutrient ['njuːtrɪənt] *n* élément *m* nutritif.

nutrition [njuːˈtrɪʃ(ə)n] *n* nutrition *f*. ●**nutritional** *a (value etc)* nutritionnel.

nutritious [njuːˈtrɪʃəs] *a (meal, food)* nutritif.

nylon ['naɪlɒn] *n* nylon *m*; **nylons** *(stockings)* bas *mpl* nylon; **n. shirt/etc** chemise *f/etc* en nylon.

nymph [nɪmf] *n* nymphe *f*. ●**nymphoˈmaniac** *n Pej* nymphomane *f*.

O

O, o [əʊ] *n* O, o *m*.

oaf [əʊf] *n* balourd, -ourde *mf*. ●**oafish** *a* (*manners etc*) de balourd; **he's rather o.** il est un peu balourd.

oak [əʊk] *n* (*tree, wood*) chêne *m*; **o. table/etc** table *f*/etc de ou en chêne.

OAP [əʊeɪ'piː] *n abbr* (*old age pensioner*) *Br* retraité, -ée *mf*.

oar [ɔːr] *n* aviron *m*, rame *f*.

oasis, *pl* **oases** [əʊ'eɪsɪs, əʊ'eɪsiːz] *n* oasis *f*.

oath [əʊθ] *n* (*pl* -s [əʊðz]) (*promise*) serment *m*; (*profanity*) juron *m*; **to take an o. to do** faire le serment de faire.

oatmeal ['əʊtmiːl] *n* farine *f* d'avoine; **o. biscuits** *Br*, **o. cookies** biscuits *mpl* à la farine d'avoine.

oats [əʊts] *npl* avoine *f*; (*porridge*) **o.** flocons *mpl* d'avoine.

obedient [ə'biːdɪənt] *a* obéissant. ●**obedience** *n* obéissance *f* (**to** à). ●**obediently** *adv* docilement.

obelisk ['ɒbəlɪsk] *n* (*monument*) obélisque *m*.

obese [əʊ'biːs] *a* obèse. ●**obesity** *n* obésité *f*.

obey [ə'beɪ] *vt* (*person, order, instructions etc*) obéir à; **to be obeyed** être obéi ▮ *vi* obéir.

obituary [ə'bɪtʃʊərɪ] *n* nécrologie *f*.

object¹ ['ɒbdʒɪkt] *n* (*thing*) objet *m*; (*aim*) but *m*, objet *m*; *Grammar* complément *m* (d'objet); **with the o. of** dans le but de; **that's no o.** (*no problem*) ça ne pose pas de problème; **price no o.** prix *m* indifférent.

object² [əb'dʒekt] *vi* **to o. to sth/s.o.** désapprouver qch/qn; **I o. to you(r) doing that** ça me gêne que tu fasses ça; **I o.!** je proteste!; **she didn't o. when...** elle n'a fait aucune objection quand... ▮ *vt* **to o. that** objecter que.

objection [əb'dʒekʃ(ə)n] *n* objection *f*; **I've got no o.** ça ne me gêne pas, je n'y vois pas d'objection *ou* d'inconvénient.

objectionable [əb'dʒekʃ(ə)nəb(ə)l] *a* très désagréable.

objective [əb'dʒektɪv] **1** *n* (*aim, target*) objectif *m*. **2** *a* (*opinion etc*) objectif. ●**objectively** *adv* objectivement. ●**objec'tivity** *n* objectivité *f*.

objector [əb'dʒektər] *n* opposant, -ante *mf* (**to** à); **conscientious o.** objecteur *m* de conscience.

obligate ['ɒblɪgeɪt] *vt* contraindre (**to do** à faire). ●**obligation** [-'geɪʃ(ə)n] *n* obligation *f*; (*debt*) dette *f*; **under an o. to do** dans l'obligation de faire; **under an o. to s.o.** redevable à qn (**for** de).

obligatory [ə'blɪgət(ə)rɪ] *a* (*compulsory*) obligatoire; (*imposed by custom*) de rigueur.

oblige [ə'blaɪdʒ] *vt* **1** (*compel*) contraindre, obliger (**s.o. to do** qn à faire); **obliged to do** contraint à faire, obligé de faire. **2** (*help*) rendre service à, faire plaisir à (*qn*); **obliged to s.o.** reconnaissant à qn (**for** de); **much obliged!** merci infiniment! ●**obliging** *a* (*kind*) serviable, obligeant. ●**obligingly** *adv* obligeamment.

oblique [ə'bliːk] *a* (*line, angle, look etc*) oblique; (*reference, route*) indirect.

obliterate [ə'blɪtəreɪt] *vt* effacer. ●**obliteration** [-'reɪʃ(ə)n] *n* effacement *m*.

oblivion [ə'blɪvɪən] *n* oubli *m*.

oblivious [ə'blɪvɪəs] *a* inconscient (**to, of** de).

oblong ['ɒblɒŋ] *a* (*elongated*) oblong (*f* oblongue); (*rectangular*) rectangulaire ▮ *n* rectangle *m*.

obnoxious [əb'nɒkʃəs] *a* (*person, behaviour etc*) odieux; (*smell*) nauséabond.

oboe ['əʊbəʊ] *n* (*musical instrument*) hautbois *m*.

obscene [əb'siːn] *a* obscène. ●**obscenity** [əb'senətɪ] *n* obscénité *f*; **obscenities** (*rude words*) obscénités *fpl*.

obscure [əb'skjʊər] *a* (*word, reason, actor, life etc*) obscur ▮ *vt* (*hide*) cacher; (*confuse*) embrouiller, obscurcir. ●**obscurely** *adv* obscurément. ●**obscurity** *n* obscurité *f*.

obsequious [əb'siːkwɪəs] *a* obséquieux.

observance [əb'zɜːvəns] *n* (*of rule etc*) observation *f*.

observant [əb'zɜːvənt] *a* (*child etc*) observateur.

observation [ɒbzə'veɪʃ(ə)n] *n* (*observing, remark*) observation *f*; (*by police etc*) surveillance *f*; **under o.** (*hospital patient*) en observation.

observatory [əb'zɜːvət(ə)rɪ] *n* observatoire *m*.

observe [əb'zɜːv] *vt* (*notice, watch, respect*) observer; (*say*) (faire) remarquer (**that** que); **to o. the speed limit** respecter la limitation de vitesse. ●**observer** *n* observateur, -trice *mf*.

obsess [əb'ses] *vt* obséder. ●**obsession** [-ʃ(ə)n] *n* obsession *f*; **to have an o. with** *or* **about sth** avoir l'obsession de qch; **to have an o. with s.o.** être obsédé par qn. ●**obsessive** *a* (*memory, idea*) obsédant; (*fear*) obsessif; (*neurotic*) obsessionnel; **to be o. about sth** avoir l'obsession de qch.

obsolescent [ɒbsə'lesənt] *a* quelque peu désuet; (*word*) vieilli. ●**obsolescence** *n* built-in o. (of car, appliance etc) obsolescence f programmée.

obsolete [ˈɒbsəliːt] a (out of date, superseded) dépassé, désuet; (ticket) périmé; (machinery) archaïque.

obstacle [ˈɒbstək(ə)l] n obstacle m.

obstetrician [ɒbstəˈtrɪʃ(ə)n] n médecin m accoucheur.

obstetrics [əbˈstetrɪks] n Med obstétrique f.

obstinate [ˈɒbstɪnət] a (person, resistance etc) obstiné, opiniâtre; (disease, pain) rebelle, opiniâtre. ●**obstinacy** n obstination f. ●**obstinately** adv obstinément.

obstreperous [əbˈstrepərəs] a turbulent.

obstruct [əbˈstrʌkt] vt (block) boucher; (hinder) gêner, entraver; (traffic) gêner, entraver, bloquer. ●**obstruction** [-ʃ(ə)n] n (act, state) & Med Pol Sport obstruction f; (obstacle) obstacle m; (in pipe) bouchon m; (traffic jam) embouteillage m. ●**obstructive** a to be o. faire de l'obstruction.

obtain [əbˈteɪn] 1 vt obtenir. 2 vi (of practice etc) Lit avoir cours. ●**obtainable** a (available) disponible; (on sale) en vente.

obtrusive [əbˈtruːsɪv] a (person) importun; (building etc) trop en évidence.

obtuse [əbˈtjuːs] a (angle, mind) obtus.

obviate [ˈɒbvɪeɪt] vt to o. the necessity or need to do sth éviter d'avoir à faire qch.

obvious [ˈɒbvɪəs] a évident (that que); he's the o. man to see c'est évidemment l'homme qu'il faut voir. ●**obviously** adv (evidently, of course) évidemment; (conspicuously) visiblement.

occasion [əˈkeɪʒ(ə)n] 1 n (time, opportunity) occasion f; (event, ceremony) événement m; on the o. of à l'occasion de; on o. à l'occasion; on several occasions à plusieurs reprises or occasions. 2 n (cause) raison f, occasion f ‖ vt occasionner.

occasional [əˈkeɪʒənəl] a (infrequent) qu'on fait, voit etc de temps en temps; (event) qui a lieu de temps en temps; (rain, showers) intermittent; she drinks the o. whisky elle boit un whisky de temps en temps. ●**occasionally** adv de temps en temps; very o. très peu souvent, rarement.

occult [əˈkʌlt] a occulte ‖ n the o. le surnaturel.

occupant [ˈɒkjʊpənt] n (inhabitant) occupant, -ante mf.

occupation [ɒkjʊˈpeɪʃ(ə)n] n (activity) occupation f; (job) emploi m; (trade) métier m; (profession) profession f; the o. of (action) l'occupation f de; fit for o. (house) habitable. ●**occupational** a o. hazard (in job) risque m du métier; o. disease maladie f du travail; o. therapy ergothérapie f.

occupier [ˈɒkjʊpaɪər] n (of house etc) occupant, -ante mf; (of country etc) occupant m.

occupy [ˈɒkjʊpaɪ] vt (house, time, space, post, country etc) occuper; to keep oneself occupied s'occuper (doing à faire).

occur [əˈkɜːr] vi (-rr-) (happen) avoir lieu; (be found) se rencontrer; (arise) se pré-

senter; it occurs to me that... il me vient à l'esprit que...; the idea occurred to her to... l'idée lui est venue de....

occurrence [əˈkʌrəns] n (event) événement m; (existence) existence f; (of word etc) Ling occurrence f.

ocean [ˈəʊʃ(ə)n] n océan m. ●**oceanic** [əʊʃɪˈænɪk] a (climate etc) océanique.

o'clock [əˈklɒk] adv (it's) three o'c./etc (il est) trois heures/etc.

octagon [ˈɒktəgən] n octogone m. ●**oc'tagonal** a octogonal.

octave [ˈɒktɪv, ˈɒkteɪv] n Mus octave f.

October [ɒkˈtəʊbər] n octobre m.

octogenarian [ɒktəʊˈdʒɪneərɪən] n octogénaire mf.

octopus [ˈɒktəpəs] n pieuvre f.

OD [əʊˈdiː] vi to OD on heroin/etc prendre une overdose d'héroïne/etc.

odd [ɒd] a 1 (strange) bizarre, curieux; an o. size une taille peu courante.
2 (number) impair.
3 (left over) I have an o. penny il me reste un penny; a few o. stamps quelques timbres (qui restent); the o. man out, the o. one out l'exception f; sixty o. soixante et quelques; an o. glove/sock/etc un gant/une chaussette/ etc dépareillé(e).
4 (occasional) qu'on fait, voit etc de temps en temps; to find the o. mistake trouver de temps en temps une (petite) erreur; at o. moments de temps en temps; o. jobs (around house) menus travaux mpl; o. job man Br homme m à tout faire. ●**oddly** adv bizarrement; o. enough, he was elected chose curieuse, il a été élu. ●**oddness** n bizarrerie f.

oddity [ˈɒdɪtɪ] n (person) personne f bizarre; (object) curiosité f; **oddities** (of language, situation) bizarreries fpl.

oddment [ˈɒdmənt] n Br Com fin f de série.

odds [ɒdz] npl 1 (in betting) cote f; (chances) chances fpl; we have heavy o. against us nous avons très peu de chances de réussir. 2 it makes no o. (no difference) Fam ça ne fait rien. 3 at o. (in disagreement) en désaccord (with avec). 4 o. and ends des petites choses.

ode [əʊd] n (poem) ode f.

odious [ˈəʊdɪəs] a détestable, odieux.

odometer [əʊˈdɒmɪtər] n Am compteur m (kilométrique).

odour [ˈəʊdər] n (Am odor) n odeur f. ●**odourless** (Am odorless) a inodore.

of [əv, stressed ɒv] prep de, d' (de + le = du, de + les = des); of the table de la table; of the boy du garçon; of the boys des garçons; of a book d'un livre; of wood/ paper/etc de or en bois/papier/etc; of it, of them en; she has a lot of it or of them elle en a beaucoup; I have ten of them j'en ai dix; there are ten of us nous sommes dix; a friend of his un ami à lui, un de ses amis; that's nice of you c'est gentil de ta part; of no value/interest/etc sans valeur/intérêt/etc; of late dernièrement, ces derniers temps; a man of fifty un homme de cinquante ans; the fifth

of June *Br* le cinq juin.

off [ɒf] **1** *adv* (*gone away*) parti; (*light, gas, radio etc*) éteint, fermé; (*Br tap, Am faucet*) fermé; (*switched off at mains*) coupé; (*detached*) détaché; (*removed*) enlevé; (*cancelled*) annulé; (*not fit to eat or drink*) mauvais; (*milk, meat*) tourné; **it's 2 km o.** c'est à 2 km (d'ici or de là); **to be** *or* **go o.** (*leave*) partir; **where are you o. to?** où vas-tu?; **he has his hat o.** il a enlevé son chapeau; **with his, my** *etc* **gloves o.** sans gants; **a day o.** (*holiday*) un jour de congé; **time o.** du temps libre; **I'm o. today, I have today o.** j'ai congé aujourd'hui; **the strike's o.** il n'y aura pas de grève, la grève est annulée; **5% o.** une réduction de 5%; **hands o.!** pas touche!; **on and o., o. and on** (*sometimes*) de temps à autre; **to be better o.** (*wealthier, in a better position*) être mieux.

2 *prep* (*from*) de; (*distant*) éloigné de; **to fall/etc o. the wall/ladder/etc** tomber/etc du mur/de l'échelle/etc; **to get o. the bus/etc** descendre du bus/etc; **to take sth o. the table/etc** prendre qch sur la table/etc; **to eat o. a plate** manger dans une assiette; **to keep** *or* **stay o. the grass** ne pas marcher sur les pelouses; **she's o. her food** elle ne mange plus rien; **o. Dover/etc** (*ship etc*) au large de Douvres/etc; **it's o. limits** c'est interdit; **the o. side** (*of vehicle*) le côté droit, *Am* le côté gauche. ● **off-'beat** *a* excentrique. ● **off-'colour** (*Am* **off-'color**) *a* (*ill*) *Br* patraque; (*indecent*) scabreux. ● **off-'hand** *a* (*abrupt*) brusque, impoli ▌ *adv* (*to say, know etc*) comme ça. ● **off-'handedness** *n* désinvolture *f.* ● **off-licence** *n Br* magasin *m* de vins et de spiritueux. ● **off-'line** *a* (*computer*) autonome; (*printer*) déconnecté. ● **off-'load** *vt* (*vehicle etc*) décharger; **to o.-load sth onto s.o.** (*task etc*) décharger de qch sur qn. ● **off-'peak** *a* (*traffic, crowds*) aux heures creuses; (*rate, price*) heures creuses *inv*; **o.-peak hours** heures *fpl* creuses. ● **off-'putting** *a Br Fam* rebutant. ● **off-'side** *a* **to be o.** *Football* être hors jeu. ● **off-'stage** *a & adv* dans les coulisses. ● **off-the-'peg** (*Am* **off-the-'rack**) *a* (*clothes*) de confection. ● **off-the-'wall** *a* (*crazy*) (*demands etc*) *Am* dément, démentiel. ● **off-'white** *a* blanc cassé *inv.*

offal ['ɒf(ə)l] *n* (*meat*) abats *mpl.*

offence [ə'fens] (*Am* **offense**) *n* (*crime*) délit *m*; **to take o.** s'offenser (**at** de); **to give o. (to s.o.)** offenser (qn).

offend [ə'fend] *vt* froisser, offenser (*qn*); **to o. the eye/ear** choquer la vue/l'oreille; **to be offended (at)** se froisser (des), s'offenser (de). ● **offending** *a* (*object, remark*) incriminé. ● **offender** *n* (*criminal*) délinquant, -ante *mf*; (*habitual*) récidiviste *mf.*

offense [ə'fens] *n Am* = **offence.**

offensive [ə'fensɪv] **1** *a* (*unpleasant*) choquant, repoussant; (*insulting*) (*words etc*) insultant, offensant (**to s.o.** pour qn); **o. weapon** *Jur* arme *f* offensive; **to be o.** **to s.o.** (*of person*) être insultant avec qn. **2** *n* (*attack*) *Mil & Fig* offensive *f*; **to be on the o.** être

passé à l'offensive.

offer ['ɒfər] *n* offre *f*; **on (special) o.** (*in shop*) en promotion, en réclame; **o. of marriage** demande *f* en mariage ▌ *vt* offrir; (*opinion, remark*) proposer; **to o. to do** offrir or proposer de faire. ● **offering** *n* (*gift*) offrande *f*; (*act*) offre *f*; **peace o.** cadeau *m* de réconciliation.

office ['ɒfɪs] *n* **1** (*room*) bureau *m*; (*of doctor*) *Am* cabinet *m*; (*of lawyer*) étude *f*; **head o.** siège *m* central; **o. block** *Br*, **o. building** immeuble *m* de bureaux; **o. boy** garçon *m* de bureau; **o. worker** employé, -ée *mf* de bureau. **2** (*post*) fonction *f*; (*duty*) fonctions *fpl*; **to be in o.** (*of political party etc*) être au pouvoir. **3** **one's good offices** (*help*) ses bons offices *mpl.*

officer ['ɒfɪsər] *n* (*in the army, navy etc*) officier *m*; (*in company, firm*) responsable *mf*, directeur, -trice *mf*; (*police*) o. agent *m* (de police).

official [ə'fɪʃ(ə)l] **1** *a* officiel; (*uniform*) réglementaire. **2** *n* (*person of authority*) responsable *mf*, officiel *m*; (*civil servant*) fonctionnaire *mf*; (*employee*) employé, -ée *mf.* ● **officialdom** *n* bureaucratie *f.* ● **officially** *adv* officiellement.

officiate [ə'fɪʃɪeɪt] *vi* (*preside*) présider; (*of priest etc*) officier; **to o. at a wedding** célébrer un mariage.

officious [ə'fɪʃəs] *a Pej* empressé.

offing ['ɒfɪŋ] *n* **in the o.** en perspective.

offset ['ɒfset, ɒf'set] *vt* (*pt & pp* **offset**, *pres p* **offsetting**) (*compensate for*) compenser; (*s.o.'s beauty etc by contrast*) faire ressortir.

offshoot ['ɒfʃuːt] *n* (*of organization, group etc*) ramification *f*; (*consequence*) conséquence *f.*

offshore [ɒf'ʃɔːr] *a* (*waters*) proche du littoral; **o. oil terminal** terminal *m* pétrolier en mer.

offspring ['ɒfsprɪŋ] *n* progéniture *f.*

often ['ɒf(t)ən] *adv* souvent; **how o.?** combien de fois?; **how o. do they run?** (*trains, buses etc*) il y en a tous les combien?; **once too o.** une fois de trop; **every so o.** de temps en temps.

ogle ['əʊg(ə)l] *vt Pej* reluquer.

ogre ['əʊgər] *n* ogre *m.*

oh! [əʊ] *int* oh!, ah!; (*pain*) aïe!; **oh yes!** mais oui!; **oh yes?** ah oui?, ah bon?

oik [ɔɪk] *n Br Fam* prolo *mf.*

oil [ɔɪl] *n* (*for machine, in cooking etc*) huile *f*; (*extracted from ground*) pétrole *m*; (*fuel*) mazout *m*; **to paint in oils** faire de la peinture à l'huile ▌ *a* (*industry, product*) pétrolier; (*painting, paint*) à l'huile; **o. change** (*in vehicle*) vidange *f*; **o. lamp** lampe *f* à pétrole *or* à huile; **o. refinery** raffinerie *f* de pétrole ▌ *vt* (*machine*) graisser, huiler.

oilcan ['ɔɪlkæn] *n* burette *f.* ● **oilfield** *n* gisement *m* de pétrole. ● **oilfired** *a* (*central heating*) au mazout. ● **oilskin(s)** *n*(*pl*) (*garment*) ciré *m.* ● **oily** *a* (*-ier, -iest*) (*substance, skin*) huileux; (*hands*) graisseux; (*food*) gras (*f* grasse).

ointment ['ɔɪntmənt] n pommade f.

OK, okay [əʊ'keɪ] a & adv see **all right** ▮ vt (pt & pp OKed, okayed, pres p OKing, okaying) approuver.

old [əʊld] a (-er, -est) vieux (f vieille); (former) ancien; **how o. is he?** quel âge a-t-il?; **he's ten years o.** il a dix ans, il est âgé de dix ans; **he's older than me** il est plus âgé que moi; **an older son** un fils aîné; **the oldest son** le fils aîné; **o. enough to** do assez grand pour faire; **o. enough to marry/vote** en âge de se marier/de voter; **to get** or **grow old(er)** vieillir; **o. age** vieillesse f; **o. man** vieillard m, vieil homme m; **o. woman** vieille femme f; **the O. Testament** l'Ancien Testament; **the O. World** l'Ancien Monde; **any o. how** Fam n'importe comment.
▮ **n the o.** (people) les vieux mpl.

olden ['əʊld(ə)n] a **in o. days** jadis.

old-fashioned [əʊld'fæʃənd] a (out-of-date) démodé; (person) rétro inv; (from former times) (customs etc) d'autrefois.

old-timer [əʊld'taɪmər] n (old man) Fam vieillard m.

olive ['ɒlɪv] n (fruit) olive f ▮ a **o. (green)** (vert) olive inv; **o. oil** huile f d'olive; **o. tree** olivier m.

Olympic [ə'lɪmpɪk] a (games etc) olympique.

ombudsman ['ɒmbʊdzmən] n (pl -men) (government official) médiateur m.

omelet(te) ['ɒmlɪt] n omelette f; **cheese/etc o.** omelette au fromage/etc.

omen ['əʊmən] n augure m.

ominous ['ɒmɪnəs] a de mauvais augure; (tone) menaçant; (noise) sinistre.

omit [əʊ'mɪt] vt (-tt-) omettre (to do or faire). ●**omission** [-ʃ(ə)n] n omission f.

omni- ['ɒmnɪ] pref omni-. ●**omnipotent** [ɒm'nɪpətənt] a omnipotent.

on [ɒn] prep **1** (position) sur; **on the chair** sur la chaise; **to put on (to)** mettre sur; **to look out on to** donner sur.
2 (concerning, about) sur; **an article on** un article sur; **to speak** or **talk on Dickens/etc** parler sur Dickens/etc.
3 (manner, means) **on foot** à pied; **on the blackboard** au tableau; **on the radio** à la radio; **on the train/plane/etc** dans le train/l'avion/etc; **on holiday** Br, **on vacation** Am en vacances; **to be on** (course) suivre; (project) travailler à; (salary) toucher; (team, committee) être membre de, faire partie de; **to keep** or **stay on** (road, path etc) suivre; **it's on me!** (I'll pay) Fam c'est moi qui paie!
4 (time) **on Monday** lundi; **on Mondays** le lundi; **on May 3rd** le 3 mai; **on the evening of May 3rd** le 3 mai au soir; **on my arrival** à mon arrivée.
5 (+ present participle) en; **on learning that...** en apprenant que...; **on seeing this** en voyant ceci.
▮ adv (ahead) en avant; (in progress) en cours; (started) commencé; (lid, brake) mis; (light, radio) allumé; (gas, Br tap, Am fau-

cet) ouvert; (machine) en marche; **on (and on)** sans cesse; **to play/etc on** continuer à jouer/etc; **she has her hat on** elle a mis or elle porte son chapeau; **he has something/nothing on** il est habillé/tout nu; **I've got something on** (I'm busy) je suis pris; **the strike is on** la grève aura lieu; **what's on?** (television) qu'y a-t-il à la télé?; (in theatre, Br cinema, Am movie theater) qu'est-ce qu'on joue?; **there's a film on** on passe un film; **that's (just) not on!** Fam (unacceptable) c'est inadmissible; (impossible) ce n'est pas possible; **to be on at s.o.** (pester) Fam être après qn; **I've been on to him** (on phone) je l'ai eu au bout du fil; **to be on to s.o.** (of police etc) être sur la piste de qn; **from then on** à partir de là. ●**on-coming** a (vehicle) qui vient en sens inverse. ●**on-going** a (project, discussions etc) en cours. ●**on-'line** a (computer) en ligne.

once [wʌns] adv (on one occasion) une fois; (formerly) autrefois; **o. a month/etc** une fois par mois/etc; **o. again, o. more** encore une fois; **at o.** (immediately) tout de suite; **all at o.** (suddenly) tout à coup; (at the same time) à la fois; **o. and for all** une fois pour toutes; **o. upon a time** (in story) il était une fois.
▮ conj une fois que. ●**once-over** n **to give sth the o.-over** (quick look) Fam jeter un coup d'œil à qch.

one [wʌn] a **1** un, une; **o. man** un homme; **o. woman** une femme; **page o.** la page un; **twenty-o.** vingt-et-un.
2 (only) seul; **my o. (and only) aim** mon seul (et unique) but.
3 (same) même; **in the o. bus** dans le même bus.
▮ pron **1** un, une; **do you want o.?** en veux-tu (un)?; **he's o. of us** il est des nôtres; **o. of them** l'un d'eux, l'une d'elles; **a big/small/etc o.** un grand/petit/etc; **this book is o. that I've read** ce livre est parmi ceux que j'ai lus; **she's o.** (a teacher, gardener etc) elle l'est; **I'm a teacher and she's o. too** je suis professeur et elle aussi; **this o.** celui-ci, celle-ci; **that o.** celui-là, celle-là; **the o. who** or **which** celui or celle qui; **it's Paul's o.** Br Fam c'est celui de Paul; **it's my o.** Br Fam c'est à moi; **another o.** un(e) autre; **I for o.** pour ma part.
2 (impersonal) on; **o. knows** on sait; **it helps o.** ça nous or vous aide; **o.'s family** sa famille.

one-'armed [wʌn'ɑːmd] a (person) manchot. ●**one-'eyed** a borgne. ●**one-legged** [-'legɪd] a **o.-legged man** or **woman** unijambiste mf. ●**one-'liner** n (joke) bon mot m. ●**one-man** a (business, office) dirigé par un seul homme. ●**one-'off** or Am **one-of-a-'kind** a Fam unique, exceptionnel. ●**one-parent family** n famille f monoparentale. ●**one-'sided** a (judgment etc) partial; (contest) inégal; (decision) unilatéral. ●**one-time** a (former) ancien. ●**one-to-'one** a (discussion) en tête-à-tête. ●**one-track 'mind** n **to have a o.-track**

mind ne penser qu'à une chose. ●**one-'upmanship** n l'art m de se montrer supérieur aux autres. ●**one-'way** a (*street*) à sens unique; (*traffic*) en sens unique; **o.-way ticket** billet m simple.

onerous ['əʊnərəs] a (*task etc*) difficile; (*taxes etc*) lourd.

oneself [wʌn'self] pron soi-même; (*reflexive*) se, s'; **to cut o.** se couper.

onion ['ʌnjən] n oignon m.

onlooker ['ɒnlʊkər] n spectateur, -trice mf.

only ['əʊnlɪ] a seul; **the o. house/etc** la seule maison/etc; **the o.** one le seul, la seule; **an o. son** un fils unique.

▌ adv seulement, ne...que; **I o. have ten, I have ten o.** je n'en ai que dix, j'en ai dix seulement; **if o.** si seulement; **not o.** non seulement; **I have o. just seen it** je viens tout juste de le voir; **he knows** lui seul le sait.

▌ conj (*but*) Fam seulement; **o. I can't** seulement je ne peux pas.

onset ['ɒnset] n (*of disease, winter etc*) début m; (*of old age*) approche f.

onslaught ['ɒnslɔːt] n attaque f.

onto ['ɒntu, *unstressed* 'ɒntə] prep = **on to.**

onus ['əʊnəs] n inv **the o. is on you/etc** c'est votre/etc responsabilité (**to do de** faire).

onward(s) ['ɒnwəd(z)] adv en avant; **from that time o.** à partir de là.

onyx ['ɒnɪks] n (*precious stone*) onyx m.

ooze [uːz] vi **to o. (out)** suinter ▌ vt (*blood etc*) laisser couler.

opal ['əʊp(ə)l] n (*precious stone*) opale f.

opaque [əʊ'peɪk] a opaque; (*unclear*) Fig obscur.

open ['əʊpən] a ouvert; (*site, view, road*) dégagé; (*car*) décapoté, découvert; (*meeting*) public (f -ique); (*competition*) ouvert à tous; (*post, job*) vacant; (*attempt, envy*) manifeste; (*question*) non résolu; (*result*) indécis; (*airline ticket*) open inv; **wide o.** grand ouvert; **in the o. air** en plein air; **in (the) o. country** en rase campagne; **the o. spaces** les grands espaces; **it's o. to doubt** c'est douteux; **o. to** (*criticism, attack*) exposé à; (*ideas, suggestions*) ouvert à; **I've got an o. mind on it** je n'ai pas d'opinion arrêtée là-dessus; **to leave o.** (*date*) ne pas préciser.

▌ n (*out*) **in the o.** (*outside*) en plein air; **to sleep (out) in the o.** dormir à la belle étoile; **to bring (out) into the o.** (*reveal*) divulguer qch.

▌ vt ouvrir; (*conversation*) entamer; (*legs*) écarter; **to o. out** (*newspaper etc*) ouvrir; **to o. up** (*door etc*) ouvrir.

▌ vi (*of flower, door, eyes etc*) s'ouvrir; (*of shop, office, person*) ouvrir; (*of play*) débuter; (*of film*) sortir; **the door opens** (*is opened by s.o.*) la porte s'ouvre; (*can open*) la porte ouvre; **to o. on to** (*of window etc*) donner sur; **to o. out** (*of flower etc*) s'ouvrir; (*widen*) s'élargir; **to o. up** (*of door, opportunity etc*) s'ouvrir; (*open the door*) ouvrir.

open-air [əʊpən'eər] a (*pool etc*) en plein air. ●**open-'heart** a (*operation*) à cœur ouvert. ●**open-'minded** a à l'esprit ouvert. ●**open-'necked** a (*shirt*) sans cravate. ●**open-'plan** a (*office etc*) sans cloisons.

opening ['əʊpənɪŋ] n ouverture f; (*of flower*) éclosion f; (*career prospect, trade outlet*) débouché m; **late(-night)** o. nocturne f ▌ a (*time, speech*) d'ouverture; **o. night** (*of play, musical etc*) première f.

openly ['əʊpənlɪ] adv (*not secretly, frankly*) ouvertement; (*publicly*) publiquement. ●**openness** n (*frankness*) franchise f; **o. of mind** ouverture f d'esprit.

opera ['ɒprə] n opéra m; **o. glasses** jumelles fpl de théâtre. ●**ope'ratic** a d'opéra. ●**ope'retta** n opérette f.

operate ['ɒpəreɪt] 1 vi (*of surgeon*) opérer (**on s.o.** qn, **for de**). 2 vi (*of machine etc*) fonctionner; (*proceed*) opérer ▌ vt faire fonctionner; (*business*) gérer. ●**operating** a **o. costs** frais mpl d'exploitation; **o. theatre**, Br, **o. room** Am salle f d'opération; **o. wing** bloc m opératoire.

operation [ɒpə'reɪʃ(ə)n] n Med Mil Math etc opération f; (*working*) fonctionnement m; **in o.** (*machine*) en service; (*plan etc*) en vigueur; **to have an o.** se faire opérer. ●**operational** a opérationnel.

operative ['ɒpərətɪv] a (*scheme, measure, law etc*) en vigueur; Med opératoire ▌ n (*worker*) ouvrier, -ière mf.

operator ['ɒpəreɪtər] n (*on phone*) standardiste mf; (*on machine*) opérateur, -trice mf; (*criminal*) escroc m; **tour o.** organisateur, -trice mf de voyages, voyagiste m.

opinion [ə'pɪnjən] n opinion f, avis m; **in my o.** à mon avis. ●**opinionated** a dogmatique.

opium ['əʊpɪəm] n opium m.

opponent [ə'pəʊnənt] n adversaire mf.

opportune ['ɒpətjuːn] a opportun.

opportunism ['ɒpətjuːnɪz(ə)m, -'tjuːnɪz(ə)m] n opportunisme m.

opportunity [ɒpə'tjuːnɪtɪ] n occasion f (**to do, of doing de** faire); **opportunities** (*prospects*) perspectives fpl; **equal opportunities** des chances fpl égales; **to take the o. to do sth** profiter de l'occasion pour faire qch.

oppose [ə'pəʊz] vt (*person, measure etc*) s'opposer à; (*motion, decision etc*) Pol vt faire opposition à. ●**opposed** a opposé (**to** à); **as o. to** par opposition à. ●**opposing** a (*team, interests etc*) opposé.

opposite ['ɒpəzɪt] a (*side etc*) opposé; (*house*) en face; **one's o. number** (*counterpart*) son homologue m ▌ adv (*to sit etc*) en face ▌ prep **o. (to)** en face de ▌ n **the o.** le contraire, l'opposé m.

opposition [ɒpə'zɪʃ(ə)n] n opposition f (**to** à); **the o.** (*rival camp*) l'adversaire m; (*in business*) la concurrence; **he put up no/considerable o.** il n'a opposé aucune résistance/a fait preuve d'une résistance acharnée.

oppress [ə'pres] vt (*treat cruelly*) opprimer; (*of heat, anguish*) oppresser ▌ n **the op-**

pressed les opprimés *mpl*. ● **oppression**
[-ʃ(ə)n] *n* oppression *f*. ● **oppressive** *a* (*heat*)
accablant, étouffant; (*weather*) étouffant;
(*ruler etc*) oppressif; (*régime*) tyrannique.
● **oppressor** *n* oppresseur *m*.

opt [ɒpt] *vi* to o. for sth décider pour qch,
opter pour qch; to o. to do choisir de faire;
to o. out refuser de participer (of à).

optical ['ɒptɪk(ə)l] *a* (*instrument, illusion etc*)
d'optique; (*lens, fibre, disk etc*) optique; o.
character reader *Comptr* lecteur *m* optique.

optician [ɒp'tɪʃ(ə)n] *n* opticien, -ienne *mf*.

optimism ['ɒptɪmɪz(ə)m] *n* optimisme *m*.
● **optimist** *n* optimiste *mf*; to be an o. être
optimiste, être un optimiste. ● **opti'mistic** *a*
optimiste. ● **opti'mistically** *adv* avec optimisme.

optimum ['ɒptɪməm] *a* & *n* optimum (*m*);
the o. temperature la température optimum.
● **optimal** *a* optimal.

option ['ɒpʃ(ə)n] *n* (*choice*) choix *m*; (*school
subject*) matière *f* à option; she has no o. elle
n'a pas le choix. ● **optional** *a* facultatif; o.
extra (*on car etc*) option *f*, accessoire *m* en
option.

opulent ['ɒpjʊlənt] *a* opulent. ● **opulence** *n*
opulence *f*.

or [ɔːr] *conj* ou; one or two un ou deux; he
doesn't drink or smoke il ne boit ni ne fume;
ten or so environ dix.

oracle ['ɒrək(ə)l] *n* oracle *m*.

oral ['ɔːrəl] *a* oral ▮ *n* (*exam*) oral *m*. ● **orally**
adv oralement; *Med* par voie orale.

orange ['ɒrɪndʒ] 1 *n* (*fruit*) orange *f*; o.
drink boisson *f* à l'orange; o. juice jus *m*
d'orange; o. tree oranger *m*. 2 *a* & *n*
(*colour*) orange *a* & *m inv*. ● **orangeade** *n*
orangeade *f*.

orang-outang [ɔːræŋuː'tæŋ] *n* orang-
outan(g) *m*.

oration [ɔː'reɪʃ(ə)n] *n* funeral o. oraison *f* funèbre.

orator ['ɒrətər] *n* (*speaker*) orateur *m*. ● **ora-
tory** *n* (*words*) rhétorique *f*.

orbit ['ɔːbɪt] *n* (*of planet etc*) orbite *f*; (*sphere
of influence*) *Fig* orbite *f* ▮ *vt* (*sun etc*) graviter autour de.

orchard ['ɔːtʃəd] *n* verger *m*.

orchestra ['ɔːkɪstrə] *n* orchestre *m*; the o.
(*seats in theater*) *Am* l'orchestre *m*.
● **or'chestral** *a* (*music*) orchestral; (*concert*)
symphonique. ● **orchestrate** *vt* (*organize*) &
Mus orchestrer.

orchid ['ɔːkɪd] *n* orchidée *f*.

ordain [ɔː'deɪn] *vt* (*priest*) ordonner; to o.
that décréter que.

ordeal [ɔː'diːl] *n* épreuve *f*, supplice *m*.

order ['ɔːdər] *n* (*command, arrangement etc*)
ordre *m*; (*purchase*) commande *f*; in o.
(*passport etc*) en règle; (*drawer, room etc*)
en ordre; in (numerical) o. dans l'ordre
numérique; in working o. en état de marche;
in o. of age par ordre d'âge; in o. to do pour
faire; in o. that pour que (+ *sub*); it's in o.
to smoke/etc (*allowed*) il est permis de

fumer/etc; out of o. (*machine*) en panne;
(*telephone*) en dérangement; to make or
place an o. (*purchase*) passer une
commande; on o. (*goods*) commandé; money
o. mandat *m*; postal o. *Br* mandat *m* postal.
▮ *vt* (*command*) ordonner (s.o. to do à qn de
faire); (*meal, goods etc*) commander; (*taxi*)
appeler; to o. s.o. around commander qn,
régenter qn.
▮ *vi* (*in café etc*) commander.

orderly ['ɔːdəlɪ] 1 *a* (*tidy*) (*room, life etc*)
ordonné; (*mind*) méthodique; (*crowd*) discipliné. 2 *n* (*soldier*) planton *m*; (*in hospital*) garçon *m* de salle.

ordinal ['ɔːdɪnəl] *a* (*number*) ordinal.

ordinary ['ɔːd(ə)nrɪ] *a* (*usual*) ordinaire;
(*average*) moyen; (*mediocre*) médiocre, ordinaire; an o. individual un simple particulier;
in o. use d'usage courant; in the o. course of
events en temps normal; in the o. way
normalement; it's out of the o. ça sort de
l'ordinaire.

ordination [ɔːdɪ'neɪʃ(ə)n] *n* (*of priest*) ordination *f*.

ordnance ['ɔːdnəns] *n* (*guns*) *Mil* artillerie *f*.

ore [ɔːr] *n* minerai *m*.

organ ['ɔːgən] *n* 1 (*in body*) organe *m*;
(*newspaper*) *Fig* organe *m*. 2 (*musical instrument*) orgue *m*, orgues *fpl*; barrel o. orgue
m de Barbarie. ● **organist** *n* organiste *mf*.

organic [ɔː'gænɪk] *a* organique; (*vegetables
etc*) biologique.

organism ['ɔːgənɪz(ə)m] *n* organisme *m*.

organization [ɔːgənaɪ'zeɪʃ(ə)n] *n* (*arrangement, association*) organisation *f*.

organize ['ɔːgənaɪz] *vt* organiser. ● **organized** *a* (*mind, group etc*) organisé. ● **organizer** *n* (*person*) organisateur, -trice *mf*;
(**personal) o.** (*for papers etc*) (agenda *m*)
organiseur *m*.

orgasm ['ɔːgæz(ə)m] *n* orgasme *m*.

orgy ['ɔːdʒɪ] *n* orgie *f*.

orient ['ɔːrɪənt] *vt Am* = **orientate**. ● **orientate** *vt Br* orienter.

Orient ['ɔːrɪənt] *n* the O. l'Orient *m*.
● **ori'ental** *a* oriental ▮ *n* Oriental, -ale *mf*.

orifice ['ɒrɪfɪs] *n* orifice *m*.

origin ['ɒrɪdʒɪn] *n* origine *f*.

original [ə'rɪdʒɪn(ə)l] *a* (*novel, unusual*)
(*idea, artist etc*) original; (*first*) premier, originel, primitif; (*copy, version*) original; (*sin*)
originel ▮ *n* (*document etc*) original *m*. ● **ori-
gi'nality** *n* originalité *f*. ● **originally** *adv* (*at
first*) au départ, à l'origine; (*in a novel way*)
originalement; she comes o. from elle est originaire de.

originate [ə'rɪdʒɪneɪt] *vi* (*begin*) prendre
naissance (in dans); to o. from (*of idea etc*)
émaner de; (*of person*) être originaire de ▮
vt être l'auteur de. ● **originator** *n* auteur *m*
(of de).

Orkneys (The) [ðiː'ɔːknɪz] *npl* les Orcades
fpl.

ornament ['ɔːnəmənt] *n* (*decoration on dress
etc*) ornement *m*; (*vase etc*) bibelot *m*.

● **orna'mental** *a* décoratif, ornemental. ● **ornamentation** [-'teɪʃ(ə)n] *n* ornementation *f*.

ornate [ɔː'neɪt] *a* (*style, decor etc*) (très) orné. ● **ornately** *adv* (*decorated etc*) de façon surchargée, à outrance.

orphan ['ɔːf(ə)n] *n* orphelin, -ine *mf* ▍ *a* orphelin. ● **orphaned** *a* orphelin; **he was o. by the accident** l'accident l'a rendu orphelin. ● **orphanage** *n* orphelinat *m*.

orthodox ['ɔːθədɒks] *a* orthodoxe. ● **orthodoxy** *n* orthodoxie *f*.

orthop(a)edic [ɔːθə'piːdɪk] *a* orthopédique. ● **orthop(a)edics** *n* orthopédie *f*.

Oscar ['ɒskər] *n* Cinema oscar *m*.

oscillate ['ɒsɪleɪt] *vi* osciller.

ostensibly [ɒ'stensɪblɪ] *adv* apparemment.

ostentation [ɒsten'teɪʃ(ə)n] *n* ostentation *f*. ● **ostentatious** *a* prétentieux, plein d'ostentation.

osteopath ['ɒstɪəpæθ] *n* ostéopathe *mf*.

ostracism ['ɒstrəsɪz(ə)m] *n* ostracisme *m*. ● **ostracize** *vt* proscrire, frapper d'ostracisme.

ostrich ['ɒstrɪtʃ] *n* autruche *f*.

other ['ʌðər] *a* autre; **o. doctors** d'autres médecins; **o. people** d'autres; **the o. one** l'autre *mf*; **I have no o. gloves than these** je n'ai pas d'autres gants que ceux-ci.
▍ *pron* **the o.** l'autre *mf*; (**some**) **others** d'autres; **some do, others don't** les uns le font, les autres ne le font pas; **none o. than**, **no o. than** nul autre que.
▍ *adv* **o. than** autrement que. ● **otherwise** *adv & conj* autrement ▍ *a* (*different*) (tout) autre.

OTT [əʊtiː'tiː] *a abbr* (*over the top*) (*exaggerated*) *Fam* outrancier.

otter ['ɒtər] *n* loutre *f*.

ouch! [aʊtʃ] *int* aïe!, ouille!

ought [ɔːt] *v aux* **1** (*obligation, desirability*) **you o. to leave** tu devrais partir; **I o. to have done it** j'aurais dû le faire; **he said he o. to stay** il a dit qu'il devrait rester. **2** (*probability*) **it o. to be ready** ça devrait être prêt.

ounce [aʊns] *n* (*measure*) once *f* (= 28,35 g); (*bit*) *Fig* once *f* (**of** de).

our [aʊər] *poss a* notre, *pl* nos. ● **ours** *pron* le nôtre, la nôtre, *pl* les nôtres; **this book is o.** ce livre est à nous *or* est le nôtre; **a friend of o.** un ami à nous, un de nos amis. ● **our'selves** *pron* nous-mêmes; (*reflexive & after prep*) nous; **we wash o.** nous nous lavons.

oust [aʊst] *vt* évincer (**from** de).

out [aʊt] *adv* (*outside*) dehors; (*not at home etc*) sorti; (*light, fire*) éteint; (*news, secret*) connu, révélé; (*flower*) ouvert; (*book*) publié, sorti; (*finished*) fini; **to be o. or go o. a lot** sortir beaucoup; **he's o. in Italy** il est (parti) en Italie; **to have a day o.** sortir pour la journée; **5 km o.** (*from the shore*) à 5 km du rivage; **the sun's o.** il fait (du) soleil; **the tide's o.** la marée est basse; **you're o.** (*wrong*) tu t'es trompé; (*in game etc*) tu es éliminé (**of** de); **the trip** *or* **journey o.** l'aller *m*; **o. there** là-bas; **to be o. to win** être résolu à gagner.
▍ *prep* **o. of** (*outside*) en dehors de; (*danger, reach, water*) hors de; (*without*) sans; **o. of pity/love/etc** par pitié/amour/*etc*; **to look/jump/etc o. of the window** regarder/sauter/*etc* par la fenêtre; **to drink/take/copy o. of sth** boire/prendre/copier dans qch; **made o. of wood/etc** fait en bois/*etc*; **to make sth o. of a box/rag/etc** faire qch avec une boîte/un chiffon/*etc*; **a page o. of** une page de; **she's o. of town** elle n'est pas en ville; **5 km o.** (*away from*) à 5 km de; **four o. of five** quatre sur cinq; **o. of the blue** de manière inattendue; **to feel o. of place** ne pas se sentir intégré; **to feel o. of it** *or* **of things** se sentir hors du coup.

out-and-out ['aʊtənaʊt] *a* (*cheat, liar etc*) achevé; (*believer*) à tout crin. ● **out-of-'date** *a* (*expired*) périmé; (*old-fashioned*) démodé. ● **out-of-'doors** *adv* dehors. ● **out-of-the-'way** *a* (*place*) écarté.

outbid [aʊt'bɪd] *vt* (*pt & pp* **outbid**, *pres p* **outbidding**) **to o. s.o.** (*sur*)enchérir sur qn.

outboard ['aʊtbɔːd] *a* **o. motor** (*of boat*) moteur *m* hors-bord *inv*.

outbreak ['aʊtbreɪk] *n* (*of war, epidemic*) début *m*; (*of violence, pimples*) éruption *f*; (*of fever*) accès *m*; (*of hostilities*) ouverture *f*.

outbuilding ['aʊtbɪldɪŋ] *n* (*of mansion, farm*) dépendance *f*.

outburst ['aʊtbɜːst] *n* (*of anger, joy*) explosion *f*; (*of violence*) flambée *f*; (*of laughter*) éclat *m*.

outcast ['aʊtkɑːst] *n* (*social*) **o.** paria *m*.

outcome ['aʊtkʌm] *n* résultat *m*, issue *f*.

outcry ['aʊtkraɪ] *n* tollé *m*.

outdated [aʊt'deɪtɪd] *a* démodé.

outdistance [aʊt'dɪstəns] *vt* distancer.

outdo [aʊt'duː] *vt* (*pt* **outdid**, *pp* **outdone**) surpasser (**in** en).

outdoor ['aʊtdɔːr] *a* (*pool, market, life*) en plein air; (*game*) de plein air; **o. clothes** tenue *f* pour sortir. ● **out'doors** *adv* dehors.

outer ['aʊtər] *a* extérieur; **o. space** l'espace *m* (cosmique); **the o. suburbs** la grande banlieue.

outfit ['aʊtfɪt] *n* (*clothes*) costume *m*; (*for woman*) toilette *f*; (*toy*) panoplie *f* (*de pompier, cow-boy etc*); (*equipment*) équipement *m*; (*kit*) trousse *f*; (*group, gang*) *Fam* bande *f*; (*commercial company*) *Fam* boîte *f*; **sports/ski o.** tenue *f* de sport/de ski. ● **outfitter** *n Br* chemisier *m*.

outgoing ['aʊtgəʊɪŋ] *a* **1** (*minister etc*) sortant; (*mail, ship*) en partance; **o. calls** (*on phone*) appels *mpl* vers l'extérieur. **2** (*sociable*) liant, ouvert. ● **outgoings** *npl* (*expenses*) dépenses *fpl*.

outgrow [aʊt'grəʊ] *vt* (*pt* **outgrew**, *pp* **outgrown**) (*clothes*) devenir trop grand pour; (*habit*) perdre (en grandissant); **to o. s.o.** (*grow more than*) grandir plus vite que qn.

outhouse ['authaus] n (of mansion, farm) Br dépendance f; (lavatory) Am cabinets mpl extérieurs.

outing ['autɪŋ] n sortie f, excursion f.

outlandish [aut'lændɪʃ] a (weird) bizarre; (barbaric) barbare.

outlast [aut'lɑːst] vt durer plus longtemps que; (survive) survivre à.

outlaw ['autlɔː] n hors-la-loi m inv ▮ vt (ban) proscrire.

outlay ['autleɪ] n (expense) dépense(s) f(pl).

outlet ['autlet] n (market for goods) débouché m; (for liquid, of tunnel etc) sortie f; (electrical) prise f de courant; (for feelings, energy) exutoire m, moyen m d'expression; **retail** o. point m de vente, magasin m; **factory** o. magasin m d'usine.

outline ['autlaɪn] n (shape) contour m, profil m; (rough) o. (of article, plan etc) esquisse f; **the broad** or **general** or **main outline(s)** (chief features) les grandes lignes ▮ vt (plan, situation) esquisser, décrire à grands traits; (book, speech) résumer; **to be outlined against** (of tree etc) se profiler sur.

outlive [aut'lɪv] vt survivre à.

outlook ['autluk] n inv (for future) perspective(s) f(pl); (point of view) perspective f (on sur), attitude f (on à l'égard de); (weather forecast) prévisions fpl.

outlying ['autlaɪɪŋ] a (remote) isolé; (neighbourhood) périphérique.

outmoded [aut'məudɪd] a démodé.

outnumber [aut'nʌmbər] vt être plus nombreux que.

outpatient ['autpeɪʃ(ə)nt] n Br malade mf en consultation externe.

outpost ['autpəust] n avant-poste m.

output ['autput] n rendement m, production f; (computer data) données fpl de sortie; (computer process) sortie f.

outrage ['autreɪdʒ] n (scandal) scandale m; (anger) indignation f; (crime) atrocité f; (indignity) indignité f; **bomb** o. attentat m à la bombe ▮ vt (morals) outrager; **outraged by sth** indigné de qch.

outrageous [aut'reɪdʒəs] a (shocking) scandaleux; (atrocious) atroce; (dress, hat etc) grotesque.

outright [aut'raɪt] adv (to say, tell) franchement; (completely) complètement; (to be killed) sur le coup; **to buy** o. (for cash) acheter au comptant ▮ ['autraɪt] a (complete) complet; (lie, folly) pur; (refusal, rejection etc) catégorique, net (f nette); (winner) incontesté.

outset ['autset] n **at the** o. au début; **from the** o. dès le départ.

outside [aut'saɪd] adv (au) dehors, à l'extérieur; **to go** o. sortir.
▮ prep à l'extérieur de, en dehors de; (beyond) Fig en dehors de; o. **my room** or **door** à la porte de ma chambre.
▮ n extérieur m, dehors m.
▮ ['autsaɪd] a extérieur; (bus or train seat etc) côté couloir inv; (maximum) Fig maximum;

the o. **lane** (on road) Br la voie de droite, Am la voie de gauche; **an** o. **chance** une faible chance.

outsider [aut'saɪdər] n (stranger) étranger, -ère mf; (horse etc in race) outsider m.

outsize ['autsaɪz] a (clothes) grande taille inv.

outskirts ['autskɜːts] npl banlieue f.

outsmart [aut'smɑːt] vt être plus malin que.

outspoken [aut'spəuk(ə)n] a (frank) franc (f franche).

outstanding [aut'stændɪŋ] a remarquable, exceptionnel; (problem, business) non réglé, en suspens; (debt) impayé; **work** o. travail m à faire.

outstay [aut'steɪ] vt **to** o. **one's welcome** abuser de l'hospitalité de son hôte, s'incruster.

outstretched [aut'stretʃt] a (arm) tendu; (wings) déployé.

outstrip [aut'strɪp] vt (-pp-) devancer.

out-tray ['auttreɪ] n (in office) corbeille f (du courrier) 'départ'.

outward ['autwəd] a (sign, appearance) extérieur; (movement, look) vers l'extérieur; o. **journey** or **trip** aller m. ● **outward(s)** adv vers l'extérieur.

outweigh [aut'weɪ] vt (be more important than) l'emporter sur.

outwit [aut'wɪt] vt (-tt-) être plus malin que.

oval ['əuv(ə)l] a & n ovale (m).

ovary ['əuvərɪ] n (reproductive organ) ovaire m.

ovation [əu'veɪʃ(ə)n] n (standing) o. ovation f.

oven ['ʌv(ə)n] n four m; (hot place) Fig fournaise f; o. **glove** gant m isolant.

over ['əuvər] prep (on) sur; (above) au-dessus de; (on the other side of) de l'autre côté de; **bridge** o. **the river** pont m sur le fleuve; **to jump/look/etc** o. **sth** sauter/regarder/etc par-dessus qch; **to fall** o. **the balcony/etc** tomber du balcon/etc; **she fell** o. **it** elle en est tombée; o. **it** (on) dessus; (above) au-dessus; **to jump** o. **it** sauter par-dessus; **to criticize/etc** o. **sth** (about) critiquer/etc à propos de qch; **an advantage** o. un avantage sur or par rapport à; o. **the radio** (on) à la radio; o. **the phone** au téléphone; o. **the holidays** (during) Br pendant les vacances; o. **ten days** (more than) plus de dix jours; **men** o. **sixty** les hommes de plus de soixante ans; o. **and above** en plus de; **he's** o. **his flu** (recovered from) il est remis de sa grippe; **all** o. **Spain** (everywhere in) dans toute l'Espagne, partout en Espagne; **all** o. **the carpet** (everywhere on) partout sur le tapis.
▮ adv (above) (par-)dessus; (finished) fini; (danger) passé; (again) encore; (too) trop; **jump** o.! sautez par-dessus!; o. **here** ici; o. **there** là-bas; **to come** or **go** or **be** o. (visit) passer; **to ask s.o.** o. inviter qn (à venir); **he's** o. **in Italy** il est (parti) en Italie; **she's** o. **from Paris** elle est venue de Paris; **all** o. (everywhere) partout; **wet all** o. tout mouillé;

it's all o.! (*finished*) c'est fini!; she's o. (on the ground) (*fallen*) elle est tombée; a kilo or o. (*more*) un kilo ou plus; I have ten o. (*left*) il m'en reste dix; there's some bread o. il reste du pain; o. and o. (*again*) (*often*) à plusieurs reprises; to start all o. (*again*) recommencer à zéro; o. pleased/*etc* trop content/*etc*.

over-abundant [əuvərəˈbʌndənt] *a* surabondant. ●**over-deˈveloped** *a* trop développé. ●**over-faˈmiliar** *a* trop familier. ●**over-inˈdulge** *vt* (*one's desires, whims etc*) céder trop facilement à; (*person*) trop gâter. ●**over-subˈscribed** *a* (*course*) ayant trop d'inscrits.

overall 1 [əuvərˈɔːl] *a* (*measurement, length, etc*) total; (*result, effort etc*) global ▮ *adv* globalement, dans l'ensemble. **2** [ˈəuvərɔːl] *n Br* blouse *f* (de travail); *Am* = **overalls**; **overalls** (*of workman*) *Br* bleus *mpl* de travail.

overawe [əuvərˈɔː] *vt* intimider.

overbalance [əuvəˈbæləns] *vi* basculer.

overbearing [əuvəˈbeərɪŋ] *a* autoritaire.

overboard [ˈəuvəbɔːd] *adv* à la mer.

overbook [əuvəˈbuk] *vt* (*flight*) surréserver, surbooker; (*hotel*) surréserver.

overburden [əuvəˈbɜːd(ə)n] *vt* surcharger.

overcast [ˈəuvəkɑːst] *a* (*sky*) couvert.

overcharge [əuvəˈtʃɑːdʒ] *vt* to o. s.o. for sth faire payer qch trop cher à qn.

overcoat [ˈəuvəkəut] *n* pardessus *m*.

overcome [əuvəˈkʌm] *vt* (*pt* **overcame**, *pp* **overcome**) (*problem, disgust*) surmonter; (*shyness, enemy etc*) vaincre; to be o. by (*fatigue, grief*) être accablé par; (*fumes, temptation*) succomber à; he was o. by emotion l'émotion eut raison de lui.

overcook [əuvəˈkuk] *vt* faire cuire trop.

overcrowded [əuvəˈkraudɪd] *a* (*house, country*) surpeuplé; (*bus, train*) bondé. ●**overcrowding** *n* surpeuplement *m*.

overdo [əuvəˈduː] *vt* (*pt* **overdid**, *pp* **overdone**) exagérer; (*overcook*) faire cuire trop; to o. it ne pas y aller doucement; don't o. it! vas-y doucement!

overdose [ˈəuvədəus] *n* overdose *f*, dose *f* excessive (*de barbituriques etc*).

overdraft [ˈəuvədrɑːft] *n* (*with bank*) découvert *m*. ●**over·draw** *vt* (*pt* **overdrew**, *pp* **overdrawn**) (*account*) mettre à découvert; **overdrawn account** compte *m* à découvert.

overdress [əuvəˈdres] *vi* s'habiller avec trop de recherche.

overdue [əuvəˈdjuː] *a* (*train, bus etc*) en retard; (*debt*) arriéré; (*apology, thanks*) tardif.

overeat [əuvərˈiːt] *vi* manger trop.

overestimate [əuvərˈestɪmeɪt] *vt* surestimer.

overexcited [əuvərɪkˈsaɪtɪd] *a* surexcité.

overfeed [əuvəˈfiːd] *vt* (*pt & pp* **overfed**) (*person, animal*) suralimenter.

overflow 1 [əuvəˈfləu] *vi* (*of river, bath etc*) déborder (**with** de); to be overflowing with (*of town, shop, house etc*) regorger de (*visiteurs, livres etc*). **2** [ˈəuvəfləu] *n* (*outlet*)

trop-plein *m*; (*of people, objects*) *Fig* excédent *m*.

overgrown [əuvəˈgrəun] *a* envahi par la végétation; **o. with weeds**/*etc* envahi par les mauvaises herbes/*etc*; **you're an o. schoolgirl** *Fig Pej* tu as la mentalité d'une écolière.

overhang [əuvəˈhæŋ] *vi* (*pt & pp* **overhung**) faire saillie ▮ *vt* surplomber.

overhaul [əuvəˈhɔːl] *vt* (*vehicle, schedule, text etc*) réviser ▮ [ˈəuvəhɔːl] *n* révision *f*.

overhead [əuvəˈhed] *adv* au-dessus ▮ [ˈəuvəhed] **1** *a* (*cable, Br railway, Am railroad etc*) aérien. **2** *n Am* = **overheads**. ●**overheads** [ˈəuvəhedz] *npl* (*expenses*) frais *mpl* généraux.

overhear [əuvəˈhɪər] *vt* (*pt & pp* **overheard**) surprendre, entendre.

overheat [əuvəˈhiːt] *vt* surchauffer ▮ *vi* (*of engine*) chauffer.

overjoyed [əuvəˈdʒɔɪd] *a* fou (*f* folle) de joie.

overland [ˈəuvəlænd] *a & adv* par voie de terre.

overlap [əuvəˈlæp] *vi* (**-pp-**) se chevaucher ▮ *vt* chevaucher ▮ [ˈəuvəlæp] *n* chevauchement *m*.

overleaf [əuvəˈliːf] *adv* au verso.

overload [əuvəˈləud] *vt* surcharger.

overlook [əuvəˈluk] *vt* **1** (*not notice*) ne pas remarquer; (*forget*) oublier; (*disregard, ignore*) passer sur. **2** (*of window, house etc*) donner sur (*parc etc*); (*of tower, fort*) dominer (*vallée, ville etc*).

overly [ˈəuvəlɪ] *adv* excessivement.

overmanning [əuvəˈmænɪŋ] *n* sureffectifs *mpl*.

overmuch [əuvəˈmʌtʃ] *adv* trop, excessivement.

overnight [əuvəˈnaɪt] *adv* (*during the night*) (pendant) la nuit; (*suddenly*) *Fig* du jour au lendemain; to stay o. passer la nuit ▮ [ˈəuvənaɪt] *a* (*train, flight*) de nuit; (*stay*) d'une nuit; (*clothes*) pour une nuit; o. bag (petit) sac *m* de voyage; o. stop arrêt *m* pour la nuit.

overpass [ˈəuvəpɑːs, *Am* -pæs] *n* (*bridge*) *Am* toboggan *m*.

overpopulated [əuvəˈpɒpjuleɪtɪd] *a* surpeuplé.

overpower [əuvəˈpauər] *vt* (*physically*) maîtriser; (*defeat*) vaincre; (*overwhelm*) *Fig* accabler. ●**overpowering** *a* (*heat, smell etc*) accablant; (*charm etc*) irrésistible.

overpriced [əuvəˈpraɪst] *a* (bien) trop cher.

overrate [əuvəˈreɪt] *vt* surestimer. ●**over-rated** *a* (*book, film etc*) surfait.

overreach [əuvəˈriːtʃ] *vt* to o. oneself trop entreprendre.

overreact [əuvərɪˈækt] *vi* réagir excessivement.

override [əuvəˈraɪd] *vt* (*pt* **overrode**, *pp* **overridden**) (*be more important than*) l'emporter sur; (*invalidate*) annuler; (*take no notice of*) passer outre à. ●**overriding** *a* (*importance*) primordial; (*passion*) prédominant; my o.

consideration (*priority*) ma priorité.

overrule [əʊvə'ruːl] *vt* (*decision etc*) annuler; (*argument, objection*) repousser, rejeter.

overrun [əʊvə'rʌn] *vt* (*pt* **overran**, *pp* **overrun**, *pres p* **overrunning**) **1** (*invade*) envahir. **2** (*go beyond*) aller au-delà de.

overseas [əʊvə'siːz] *adv* (*Africa, Japan etc*) outre-mer; (*abroad*) à l'étranger ▮ ['əʊvəsiːz] *a* (*visitor, market etc*) d'outre-mer; étranger; (*trade*) extérieur.

oversee [əʊvə'siː] *vt* (*pt* **oversaw**, *pp* **overseen**) (*work etc*) superviser, surveiller. • **overseer** ['əʊvəsiːər] *n* (*foreman*) contremaître *m*.

overshadow [əʊvə'ʃædəʊ] *vt* (*make less important*) éclipser; (*make gloomy*) assombrir.

overshoot [əʊvə'ʃuːt] *vt* (*pt & pp* **overshot**) (*of aircraft, vehicle, train etc*) dépasser.

oversight ['əʊvəsaɪt] *n* oubli *m*, omission *f*; (*mistake*) erreur *f*.

oversimplify [əʊvə'sɪmplɪfaɪ] *vti* trop simplifier.

oversize(d) ['əʊvəsaɪz(d)] *a* trop grand.

oversleep [əʊvə'sliːp] *vi* (*pt & pp* **overslept**) dormir trop longtemps, oublier de se réveiller.

overspend [əʊvə'spend] *vi* dépenser trop.

overstaffed [əʊvə'stɑːft] *a* au personnel pléthorique.

overstate [əʊvə'steɪt] *vt* exagérer.

overstay [əʊvə'steɪ] *vt* **to o. one's welcome** abuser de l'hospitalité de son hôte, s'incruster.

overstep [əʊvə'step] *vt* (**-pp-**) (*limit etc*) dépasser; **to o. one's authority** outrepasser ses pouvoirs; **to o. the mark** dépasser les bornes.

overt ['əʊvɜːt] *a* manifeste.

overtake [əʊvə'teɪk] *vt* (*pt* **overtook**, *pp* **overtaken**) dépasser; (*vehicle*) *Br* doubler, dépasser; **overtaken by nightfall/etc** surpris par la nuit/*etc* ▮ *vi* (*in vehicle*) *Br* doubler, dépasser.

overtax [əʊvə'tæks] *vt* **1** **to o. one's brain** se fatiguer la cervelle; **to o. one's strength** abuser de ses forces. **2** (*taxpayer*) surimposer.

overthrow [əʊvə'θrəʊ] *vt* (*pt* **overthrew**, *pp* **overthrown**) (*dictator, government etc*) renverser ▮ ['əʊvəθrəʊ] *n* renversement *m*.

overtime ['əʊvətaɪm] *n* heures *fpl* supplémentaires ▮ *adv* **to work o.** faire des heures supplémentaires.

overtones ['əʊvətəʊnz] *npl* (*traces, hint*) note *f*, nuance *f* (**of** de).

overture ['əʊvətjʊər] *n* (*music, gesture*) ouverture *f*.

overturn [əʊvə'tɜːn] *vi* (*of car, boat*) se retourner ▮ *vt* (*chair, table etc*) renverser; (*car, boat*) retourner; (*decision etc*) *Fig* annuler.

overweight [əʊvə'weɪt] *a* **to be o.** (*of person*) avoir des kilos en trop; (*of suitcase etc*) peser trop.

overwhelm [əʊvə'welm] *vt* (*of feelings, heat etc*) accabler; (*defeat*) écraser; (*amaze*) bouleverser. • **overwhelmed** *a* (*overjoyed*) ravi (**by, with** de); **o. with** (*work, offers*) submergé de; **o. with** grief accablé par le chagrin; **o. by** (*kindness, gift etc*) vivement touché par. • **overwhelming** *a* (*heat, grief etc*) accablant; (*majority, defeat*) écrasant; (*desire*) irrésistible; (*impression*) dominant; **the o. majority of people** l'écrasante majorité des gens. • **overwhelmingly** *adv* (*to vote, reject etc*) en masse; (*utterly*) carrément.

overwork [əʊvə'wɜːk] *n* surmenage *m* ▮ *vi* se surmener ▮ *vt* surmener.

overwrought [əʊvə'rɔːt] *a* (*tense*) tendu.

owe [əʊ] *vt* (*money, respect, apology etc*) devoir (**to** à); **I'll o. it to you, I'll o. you (for) it** (*money*) je te le devrai; **to o. it to oneself to do** se devoir de faire. • **owing 1** *a* (*money etc*) dû, qu'on doit. **2** *prep* **o. to** à cause de.

owl [aʊl] *n* hibou *m* (*pl* hiboux).

own [əʊn] **1** *a* propre; **my o. house** ma propre maison ▮ *pron* **it's my (very) o.** c'est à moi (tout seul); **a house of his o.** sa propre maison, sa maison à lui; (**all**) **on one's o.** (*alone*) tout seul; **to get one's o. back** se venger (**on s.o.** de qn, **for sth** de qch), prendre sa revanche (**on s.o.** sur qn, **for sth** de qch); **to come into one's o.** (*fulfil oneself*) s'épanouir. **2** *vt* (*possess*) posséder; **who owns this ball/ etc?** à qui appartient cette balle/*etc*?

3 *vi* **to o. up** (*confess*) avouer; **to o. up to sth** avouer qch.

owner ['əʊnər] *n* propriétaire *mf*. • **ownership** *n* possession *f*; **home o.** accession *f* à la propriété; **public o.** *Econ* nationalisation *f*.

ox, *pl* **oxen** [ɒks, 'ɒks(ə)n] *n* bœuf *m*.

oxide ['ɒksaɪd] *n Ch* oxide *m*. • **oxidize** ['ɒksɪdaɪz] *vi* s'oxyder ▮ *vt* oxyder.

oxygen ['ɒksɪdʒ(ə)n] *n* oxygène *m*; **o. mask/ tent** masque *m*/tente *f* à oxygène.

oyster ['ɔɪstər] *n* huître *f*.

oz *abbr* (*ounce*) once *f*.

ozone ['əʊzəʊn] *n Ch* ozone *m*; **o. friendly** (*product*) qui préserve la couche d'ozone; **o. layer** couche *f* d'ozone.

P

P, p [piː] *n* P, p *m*.

p [piː] *abbr Br* = **penny, pence.**

pa [pɑː] *n* (*father*) *Fam* papa *m*.

PA [piːˈeɪ] *n abbr* = **personal assistant.**

pace [peɪs] *n* (*speed*) pas *m*, allure *f*; (*step, measure*) pas *m*; **to keep p. with s.o.** (*follow*) suivre qn; (*in quality of work etc*) se maintenir à la hauteur de qn ∎ *vi* **to p. up and down** faire les cent pas ∎ *vt* (*room etc*) arpenter.

pacemaker [ˈpeɪsmeɪkər] *n* (*for heart*) stimulateur *m* cardiaque.

Pacific [pəˈsɪfɪk] *a* (*coast etc*) pacifique ∎ *n* **the P.** le Pacifique.

pacifier [ˈpæsɪfaɪər] *n* (*of baby*) *Am* sucette *f*, tétine *f*.

pacifist [ˈpæsɪfɪst] *n & a* pacifiste (*mf*).

pacify [ˈpæsɪfaɪ] *vt* (*country etc*) pacifier; (*crowd, angry person, critic*) calmer; (*nervous person, fears*) apaiser.

pack¹ [pæk] *n* (*bundle, packet*) paquet *m*; (*rucksack*) sac m (à dos); (*of animal*) charge *f*; (*of soldier*) paquetage *m*; (*of hounds, wolves*) meute *f*; (*of runners*) peloton *m*; (*of thieves*) bande *f*; (*of cards*) jeu *m*; (*of lies*) tissu *m*.

pack² [pæk] *vt* (*fill*) remplir (**with** de); (*excessively*) bourrer; (*suitcase*) faire; (*object into box etc*) emballer; (*object into suitcase*) mettre dans sa valise; (*make into package*) empaqueter; (*crush, compress*) tasser. ∎ *vi* (*fill one's bags*) faire ses valises.

package [ˈpækɪdʒ] *n* paquet *m*; (*computer programs*) progiciel *m*; **p. deal** *Com* contrat *m* global, train *m* de propositions; **p. holiday** *Br* vacances *fpl* organisées; **p. tour** *Br* voyage *m* organisé ∎ *vt* emballer, empaqueter. ●**packaging** *n* (*material, action*) emballage *m*.

pack away *vt* (*tidy away*) ranger ∎ **to pack down** *vt* (*crush, compress*) tasser ∎ **to pack in** *vt Br Fam* (*stop*) arrêter; (*give up*) laisser tomber (*métier, activité etc*); **p. it in!** laisse tomber! ∎ **to pack into** *vt* (*cram*) entasser dans; (*put*) mettre dans ∎ *vi* (*crowd into*) s'entasser dans ∎ **to pack off** *vt* (*person*) *Fam* expédier ∎ **to pack up** *vt* (*put into box*) emballer; (*put into suitcase*) mettre dans sa valise; (*give up*) *Fam* laisser tomber ∎ *vi Fam* (*stop*) s'arrêter; (*of machine, vehicle*) tomber en rade *or* en panne.

packed [pækt] *a* (*bus, room etc*) bourré; **p. lunch** *Br* panier-repas *m*; **p. out** (*crowded*) *Br Fam* bourré.

packet [ˈpækɪt] *n* paquet *m*; (*of Br sweets, Am candies*) sachet *m*, paquet *m*; **to make/ cost a p.** *Fam* faire/coûter beaucoup d'argent.

packing [ˈpækɪŋ] *n* (*material, action*) emballage *m*; **p. case** caisse *f* d'emballage.

pact [pækt] *n* pacte *m*.

pad [pæd] *n* (*wad or plug of cloth etc*) tampon *m*; (*for writing, notes etc*) bloc *m*; (*on knee*) *Sport* genouillère *f*; (*on leg*) jambière *f*; (*room*) *Sl* piaule *f*; **launch(ing) p.** aire *f* de lancement; **ink(ing) p.** tampon *m* encreur ∎ *vt* (**-dd-**) (*stuff*) rembourrer (*fauteuil etc*); matelasser (*vêtement*); **to p. out** (*speech, text*) délayer. ●**padded** *a* (*armchair etc*) rembourré; (*jacket etc*) matelassé. ●**padding** *n* (*material*) rembourrage *m*; (*of speech, text*) délayage *m*.

paddle [ˈpæd(ə)l] *1 vi* (*dip one's feet*) se mouiller les pieds; (*splash about*) barboter ∎ *n* **to have a (little) p.** se mouiller les pieds. *2 n* (*pole*) pagaie *f*; **p. boat, p. steamer** bateau *m* à roues ∎ *vt* **to p. a canoe** pagayer. ●**paddling pool** *n* (*small, inflatable*) piscine *f* gonflable; (*large, purpose-built*) pataugeoire *f*.

paddock [ˈpædək] *n* enclos *m*; (*at racecourse*) paddock *m*.

paddy [ˈpædɪ] *n* **p.** (**field**) rizière *f*.

padlock [ˈpædlɒk] *n* (*on door etc*) cadenas *m*; (*on bicycle, moped*) antivol *m* ∎ *vt* (*door etc*) cadenasser.

p(a)ediatrician [piːdɪəˈtrɪʃ(ə)n] *n* (*doctor*) pédiatre *mf*. ●**p(a)ediatrics** *n* pédiatrie *f*.

pagan [ˈpeɪgən] *a & n* païen, -enne (*mf*). ●**paganism** *n* paganisme *m*.

page [peɪdʒ] *1 n* (*of book etc*) page *f*. *2 n* **p.** (**boy**) (*in hotel etc*) groom *m*; (*at court*) *Hist* page *m*; (*at wedding*) garçon *m* d'honneur ∎ *vt* **to p. s.o.** faire appeler qn. ●**pager** *n* récepteur *m* d'appel.

pageant [ˈpædʒənt] *n* grand spectacle *m* historique. ●**pageantry** *n* pompe *f*, apparat *m*.

pagoda [pəˈgəʊdə] *n* pagode *f*.

paid [peɪd] *pt & pp of* **pay** ∎ *a* (*assassin etc*) à gages; **to put p. to** (*hopes, plans*) *Br* anéantir; **to put p. to s.o.** (*ruin*) *Br* couler qn.

pail [peɪl] *n* seau *m*.

pain [peɪn] *n* (*physical*) douleur *f*; (*grief*) peine *f*; **pains** (*efforts*) efforts *mpl*; **to have a p. in one's arm** avoir mal *or* une douleur au bras; **to be in p.** souffrir; **to go to *or* take (great) pains to do** (*exert oneself*) se donner du mal à faire; **to go to *or* take (great) pains not to do** (*be careful*) prendre bien soin de ne pas faire; **to be a p. (in the neck)** (*of person*) *Fam* être casse-pieds.

▌ *vt* (*grieve*) peiner.
painful ['peɪnfəl] *a* (*illness, operation*) douloureux; (*arm, leg*) qui fait mal, douloureux; (*distressing*) douloureux, pénible; (*difficult*) pénible; (*bad*) *Fam* affreux. ● **painfully** *adv* douloureusement; (*with difficulty*) péniblement; (*very*) *Fam* affreusement.
painkiller ['peɪnkɪlər] *n* calmant *m*; **on painkillers** sous calmants.
painless ['peɪnləs] *a* sans douleur; (*illness, operation*) indolore; (*easy*) *Fam* facile. ● **painlessly** *adv* sans douleur; (*easily*) sans effort.
painstaking ['peɪnzteɪkɪŋ] *a* (*person*) soigneux; (*work*) soigné. ● **painstakingly** *adv* avec soin.
paint [peɪnt] *n* peinture *f*; **paints** (*in box, tube*) couleurs *fpl*; **p. stripper** décapant *m* ▌ *vt* (*colour, describe*) peindre; **to p. blue**/*etc* peindre en bleu/*etc* ▌ *vi* peindre. ● **painting** *n* (*activity*) peinture *f*; (*picture*) tableau *m*, peinture *f*. ● **painter** *n* peintre *m*; **p. and decorator** *Br*, (*house*) **p.** *Am* peintre *m* décorateur.
paintbrush ['peɪntbrʌʃ] *n* pinceau *m*.
paintwork ['peɪntwɜːk] *n* (*of building, vehicle*) peinture(s) *f(pl)*.
pair [peər] *n* (*two*) paire *f*; (*man and woman*) couple *m*; **a p. of shorts** un short; **the p. of you** *Fam* vous deux ▌ *vi* **to p. off** (*of people*) former un couple.
pajama(s) [pəˈdʒɑːmə(z)] *a & npl Am* = **pyjama(s)**.
Pakistan [pɑːkɪˈstɑːn] *n* Pakistan *m*. ● **Pakistani** *a* pakistanais ▌ *n* Pakistanais, -aise *mf*.
pal [pæl] *n* *Fam* copain *m*, copine *f* ▌ *vi* (-ll-) *Br Fam* **to p. up** devenir copains; **to p. up with s.o.** devenir copain avec qn.
palace ['pælɪs] *n* (*building*) palais *m*. ● **palatial** [pəˈleɪʃ(ə)l] *a* comme un palais.
palatable ['pælətəb(ə)l] *a* (*food*) agréable; (*idea, fact etc*) acceptable.
palate ['pælɪt] *n* (*in mouth*) palais *m*.
palaver [pəˈlɑːvər] *n* *Fam* (*fuss*) *Br* histoire(s) *f(pl)*; (*talk*) palabres *mpl*.
pale [peɪl] *a* (-er, -est) (*face, colour etc*) pâle; **p. ale** *Br* bière *f* blonde ▌ *vi* pâlir. ● **paleness** *n* pâleur *f*.
Palestine ['pæləstaɪn] *n* Palestine *f*. ● **Pale'stinian** *a* palestinien ▌ *n* Palestinien, -ienne *mf*.
palette ['pælɪt] *n* (*of artist*) palette *f*.
paling ['peɪlɪŋ] *n* (*fence*) palissade *f*.
pall [pɔːl] 1 *vi* devenir insipide *or* ennuyeux (*on pour*). 2 *n* (*of smoke*) voile *m*.
pallbearer ['pɔːlbeərər] *n* personne *f* qui aide à porter un cercueil.
pallid ['pælɪd] *a* pâle. ● **palior** *n* pâleur *f*.
pally ['pælɪ] *a* (-ier, -iest) *Fam* copain *am*, copine *af* (**with** avec).
palm [pɑːm] 1 *n* (*of hand*) paume *f*. 2 *n* (*symbol*) palme *f*; **p.** (*tree*) palmier *m*; **p.** (*leaf*) palme *f*; **P. Sunday** les Rameaux *mpl*. 3 *vt* *Fam* **to p. sth off** (*pass off*) refiler qch

(**on s.o.** à qn), coller qch (**on s.o.** à qn); **to p. s.o. off** **on s.o.** coller qn à qn.
palmist ['pɑːmɪst] *n* chiromancien, -ienne *mf*. ● **palmistry** *n* chiromancie *f*.
palpable ['pælpəb(ə)l] *a* (*obvious*) manifeste.
palpitate ['pælpɪteɪt] *vi* (*of heart*) palpiter. ● **palpitation** [-ˈteɪʃ(ə)n] *n* palpitation *f*; **to have** *or* **get palpitations** avoir des palpitations.
paltry ['pɔːltrɪ] *a* (-ier, -iest) (*trifling*) (*sum etc*) dérisoire; **a p. excuse/painter** (*bad*) une piètre excuse/un piètre peintre.
pamper ['pæmpər] *vt* dorloter.
pamphlet ['pæmflɪt] *n* brochure *f*.
pan [pæn] 1 *n* casserole *f*; (*for frying*) poêle *f* (à frire); (*of lavatory*) *Br* cuvette *f*. 2 *vt* (-nn-) (*criticize*) *Fam* éreinter. 3 *vi* (-nn-) **to p. out** (*succeed*) aboutir.
Pan- [pæn] *pref* pan-.
panacea [pænəˈsɪə] *n* panacée *f*.
panache [pəˈnæʃ] *n* (*showy manner*) panache *m*.
Panama ['pænəmɑː] *n* Panama *m*.
pancake ['pænkeɪk] *n* crêpe *f*.
pancreas ['pæŋkrɪəs] *n* *Anat* pancréas *m*.
panda ['pændə] *n* (*animal*) panda *m*; **P. car** *Br* = voiture *f* pie *inv* (de la police).
pandemonium [pændɪˈməʊnɪəm] *n* chaos *m*; (*uproar*) tumulte *m*; (*place*) bazar *m*.
pander ['pændər] *vi* **to p. to** (*fashion, tastes etc*) sacrifier à; **to p. to s.o.** *or* **to s.o.'s desires** se plier aux désirs de qn.
pane [peɪn] *n* vitre *f*, carreau *m*.
panel ['pæn(ə)l] *n* 1 (*of door etc*) panneau *m*; (*control*) **p.** console *f*; (*instrument*) **p.** (*in aircraft, vehicle*) tableau *m* de bord. 2 (*of judges*) jury *m*; (*of experts*) groupe *m*; (*of candidates*) équipe *f*; **a p. of guests** des invités; **a p. game** (*on TV etc*) un jeu par équipes.
panelled ['pæn(ə)ld] (*Am* **paneled**) *a* (*room etc*) lambrissé. ● **panelling** (*Am* **paneling**) *n* lambris *m*.
panellist ['pænəlɪst] *n* (*on TV etc*) (*guest*) invité, -ée *mf*; (*expert*) expert *m*; (*candidate*) candidat, -ate *mf*.
pangs [pæŋz] *npl* **p. of conscience** remords *mpl* (de conscience); **p. of hunger** tiraillements *mpl* d'estomac; **p. of death/jealousy** les affres *fpl* de la mort/de la jalousie.
panic ['pænɪk] *n* panique *f*; **to get into a p.** paniquer ▌ *vi* (-ck-) s'affoler, paniquer. ● **panic-stricken** *a* affolé. ● **panicky** (*person*) *a* *Fam* qui s'affole facilement; **to get p.** s'affoler.
panorama [pænəˈrɑːmə] *n* panorama *m*. ● **panoramic** *a* panoramique.
pansy ['pænzɪ] *n* 1 (*plant*) pensée *f*. 2 (*homosexual*) *Pej* tante *f*, tapette *f*.
pant [pænt] *vi* (*gasp*) haleter.
panther ['pænθər] *n* (*animal*) panthère *f*.
panties ['pæntɪz] *npl* (*female underwear*) slip *m*; (*longer*) culotte *f*.
pantomime ['pæntəmaɪm] *n* (*show*) *Br* spectacle *m* de Noël.

pantry ['pæntrɪ] n (larder) garde-manger m inv; (storeroom in hotel, ship) office m or f.

pants [pænts] npl (male underwear) slip m; (long, loose) caleçon m; (female underwear) slip m; (long) culotte f; (trousers) Am pantalon m.

pantyhose ['pæntɪhəʊz] n (tights) Am collant(s) m(pl).

papacy ['peɪpəsɪ] n papauté f. ●**papal** a papal.

paper ['peɪpər] n papier m; (newspaper) journal m; (wallpaper) papier m peint; (exam) épreuve f (écrite); (student's exercise) copie f; (learned article) communication f, exposé m; **brown p.** papier m d'emballage; **to put sth down on p.** mettre qch par écrit. ▮ a (bag etc) en papier; (cup, plate) en carton; **p. clip** trombone m; **p. knife** coupe-papier m inv; **p. mill** papeterie f; **p. round** (newspaper delivery) tournée f; **p. shop** Br marchand m de journaux. ▮ vt (room, wall) tapisser.

paperback ['peɪpəbæk] n (book) livre m de poche. ●**paperboy** n livreur m de journaux. ●**paperweight** n presse-papiers m inv. ●**paperwork** n (in office etc) écritures fpl; (red tape) Pej paperasserie f.

paprika ['pæprɪkə] n paprika m.

par [pɑːr] n Golf par m; **on a p.** au même niveau (with que); **below p.** (unwell) Fam pas en forme.

para- ['pærə] pref para-.

parable ['pærəb(ə)l] n (story) parabole f.

paracetamol [pærə'siːtəmɒl] n paracétamol m; (tablet) comprimé m de paracétamol.

parachute ['pærəʃuːt] n parachute m; **to drop by p.** (men, supplies) parachuter ▮ vi descendre en parachute ▮ vt parachuter. ●**parachutist** n parachutiste m.

parade [pə'reɪd] 1 n (procession) défilé m; (military ceremony) parade f; **fashion p.** défilé m de mode or de mannequins; **p. ground** (for soldiers) terrain m de manœuvres ▮ vi (of soldiers, demonstrators etc) défiler; **to p. about** (walk about) se balader. 2 n (display, show) **to make a p. of** (one's wealth etc) faire étalage de ▮ vt faire étalage de. 3 n (street) Br avenue f.

paradise ['pærədaɪs] n paradis m.

paradox ['pærədɒks] n paradoxe m. ●**para'doxically** adv paradoxalement.

paraffin ['pærəfɪn] n Br pétrole m (lampant); (wax) Am paraffine f; **p. lamp** Br lampe f à pétrole.

paragon ['pærəg(ə)n] n **p. of virtue** modèle m de vertu.

paragraph ['pærəgrɑːf] n paragraphe m; **'new p.'** 'à la ligne'.

Paraguay ['pærəgwaɪ] n Paraguay m.

parakeet ['pærəkiːt] n (bird) perruche f.

parallel ['pærəlel] a (line, road etc) parallèle (with, to à); (comparable) parallèle, semblable (with, to à); **to run p. to or** with être parallèle à ▮ n (comparison) & Geog parallèle m; (line) Math parallèle f ▮ vt être

semblable à.

paralysis [pə'ræləsɪs] n paralysie f. ●**paralyse** ['pærəlaɪz] vt (Am **-lyze**) paralyser. ●**para'lytic** a & n paralytique (mf).

paramedic [pærə'medɪk] n auxiliaire mf médical(e).

parameter [pə'ræmɪtər] n paramètre m.

paramount ['pærəmaʊnt] a **of p. importance** de la plus haute importance.

paranoia [pærə'nɔɪə] n paranoïa f. ●**'paranoid** a & n paranoïaque (mf).

parapet ['pærəpɪt] n parapet m.

paraphernalia [pærəfə'neɪlɪə] n attirail m.

paraphrase ['pærəfreɪz] n paraphrase f ▮ vt paraphraser.

paraplegic [pærə'pliːdʒɪk] n paraplégique mf.

parasite ['pærəsaɪt] n (person, organism) parasite m.

parasol ['pærəsɒl] n (over table, on beach) parasol m; (lady's) ombrelle f.

paratrooper ['pærətruːpər] n (soldier) parachutiste m. ●**paratroops** npl parachutistes mpl.

parboil [pɑː'bɔɪl] vt (vegetables etc) faire bouillir à demi.

parcel ['pɑːs(ə)l] 1 n colis m, paquet m; **to be part and p. of** faire partie intégrante de. 2 vt (Br **-ll-**, Am **-l-**) **to p. out** (divide) partager; **to p. up** faire un paquet de.

parch [pɑːtʃ] vt dessécher; **to be parched** (thirsty) être assoiffé; **to make s.o. parched** (thirsty) donner très soif à qn.

parchment ['pɑːtʃmənt] n parchemin m.

pardon ['pɑːd(ə)n] n (by king, president etc) grâce f; (forgiveness) pardon m; **general p.** amnistie f; **I beg your p.** (apologize) je vous prie de m'excuser; (not hearing) vous dites? **p.?** (not hearing) comment? **p. (me)!** (sorry) pardon! ▮ vt pardonner (s.o. for sth qch à qn); **to p. s.o.** pardonner (à) qn; (of king etc) gracier qn.

pare [peər] vt (trim) rogner; (peel) éplucher; **to p. down** Fig réduire, rogner.

parent ['peərənt] n père m, mère f; **one's parents** ses parents mpl, son père et sa mère; **p. company,** Br **p. firm** maison f mère. ●**parentage** n (origin) origine f. ●**par'ental** [pə'rent(ə)l] a (responsibility etc) des parents, parental. ●**parenthood** n paternité f, maternité f.

parenthesis, pl **-eses** [pə'renθəsɪs, -əsiːz] n parenthèse f.

Paris ['pærɪs] n Paris m or f. ●**Parisian** [Br pə'rɪzɪən, Am pə'riːʒən] a parisien ▮ n Parisien, -ienne mf.

parish ['pærɪʃ] n (religious) paroisse f; (civil) commune f ▮ a (church, register, hall etc) paroissial; **p. council** conseil m municipal. ●**pa'rishioner** n paroissien, -ienne mf.

parity ['pærɪtɪ] n parité f (with avec, between entre).

park¹ [pɑːk] n (garden) parc m; **p. keeper** gardien, -ienne mf de parc.

park² [pɑːk] vt (vehicle) garer; (put) Fam
mettre, poser ▌ vi (of vehicle) se garer; (remain parked) stationner. ●**parking** n stationnement m; 'no p.' 'défense de stationner'; p. bay or area aire f de stationnement; p. light Br veilleuse f; p. lot Am parking m; p. meter parcmètre m; p. place or space place f de parking; p. ticket contravention f.

parka ['pɑːkə] n (coat) parka f or m.

parkway ['pɑːkweɪ] n Am avenue f.

parliament ['pɑːləmənt] n parlement m; P. Br Parlement m. ●**parlia'mentary** a parlementaire. ●**parliamen'tarian** n parlementaire mf (expérimenté(e)).

parlour ['pɑːlər] (Am parlor) n (in mansion) (petit) salon m; ice-cream p. Am salon m de glaces; p. game jeu m de société.

parochial ['pɑːrəʊkɪəl] a (mentality, quarrel) Pej de clocher; (person) Pej provincial, borné; Rel paroissial; p. school Am école f catholique.

parody ['pærədɪ] n parodie f ▌ vt parodier.

parole [pə'rəʊl] n on p. (prisoner) en liberté conditionnelle.

parquet ['pɑːkeɪ] n p. (floor) parquet m.

parrot ['pærət] n perroquet m; p. fashion Pej comme un perroquet.

parry ['pærɪ] vt (blow) parer; (question) éluder ▌ n (in fencing, boxing) parade f.

parsimonious [pɑːsɪ'məʊnɪəs] a parcimonieux. ●**parsimoniously** adv avec parcimonie.

parsley ['pɑːslɪ] n persil m.

parsnip ['pɑːsnɪp] n panais m.

parson ['pɑːs(ə)n] n (Protestant priest) pasteur m; the p.'s nose (of chicken) Br le croupion.

part¹ [pɑːt] n partie f; (of machine) pièce f; (of periodical) fascicule m; (of serial) épisode m; (role in play, film etc) rôle m; (quantity in mixture) mesure f; (in hair) Am raie f; to take p. participer (in à); to take s.o.'s p. (side) prendre parti pour qn; in p. en partie; for the most p. dans l'ensemble; to be a p. of faire partie de; on the p. of (on behalf of) de la part de; for my p. pour ma part; in these parts dans ces parages; p. exchange reprise f; to take in p. exchange reprendre ▌ n in p. exchange en p.; p. owner copropriétaire mf; p. payment paiement m partiel.
▌ adv (partly) en partie; p. American en partie américain.

part² [pɑːt] vt (separate) séparer; (crowd) écarter; to p. one's hair se faire une raie; to p. company with s.o. (leave) quitter qn ▌ vi (of friends etc) se quitter; (of married couple) se séparer; to p. with sth (get rid of) se séparer de qch.

partake [pɑː'teɪk] vi (pt partook, pp partaken) to p. in participer à; to p. of (meal, food) prendre, manger.

partial ['pɑːʃəl] a (not total) partiel; (biased) partial (towards envers); to be p. to sth (fond of) avoir un faible pour qch.

● **parti'ality** n (bias) partialité f; (liking) prédilection f.

participate [pɑː'tɪsɪpeɪt] vi participer (in à). ●**participant** n participant, -ante mf. ●**parti-ci'pation** [-'peɪʃ(ə)n] n participation f.

participle ['pɑːtɪsɪp(ə)l] n Grammar participe m.

particle ['pɑːtɪk(ə)l] n (of atom, dust, name) particule f; (of truth) grain m.

particular [pə'tɪkjʊlər] a (specific, special) particulier; (fussy, fastidious) difficile (about sur); (showing care) méticuleux; this p. book ce livre-ci en particulier; in p. en particulier; to be p. about (one's work etc) faire très attention à. ●**particulars** npl (details) détails mpl; (information) renseignements mpl; s.o.'s p. (address etc) les coordonnées fpl de qn, le nom et l'adresse de qn. ●**particularly** adv particulièrement.

parting ['pɑːtɪŋ] 1 n (in hair) Br raie f. 2 n (separation) séparation f ▌ a (gift, words etc) d'adieu.

partisan [Br pɑːtɪ'zæn, Am 'pɑːtɪz(ə)n] n partisan m.

partition [pɑː'tɪʃ(ə)n] 1 n (of room) cloison f ▌ vt to p. off cloisonner. 2 Pol n (of country) partition f, partage m ▌ vt (country) partager.

partly ['pɑːtlɪ] adv en partie; p. English p. French moitié anglais moitié français.

partner ['pɑːtnər] n (in business) associé, -ée mf; (lover, spouse) & Sport Pol partenaire mf; (of racing driver etc) coéquipier, -ière mf; (dancing) p. cavalier, -ière mf. ●**partnership** n association f; to take s.o. into p. prendre qn comme associé(e); in p. with en association avec.

partridge ['pɑːtrɪdʒ] n perdrix f.

part-time [pɑːt'taɪm] a & adv à temps partiel; (half-time) à mi-temps.

party ['pɑːtɪ] n 1 (gathering) (formal) réception f; (with friends) soirée f; (for birthday) fête f; (with dancing, for young people) boum f; cocktail p. cocktail m; dinner p. dîner m; tea p. thé m.
2 (group) groupe m; (political) parti m; (in contract, lawsuit) partie f; (telephone caller) correspondant, -ante mf; rescue p. équipe f de secours or de sauveteurs; third p. (in insurance etc) tiers m; innocent p. innocent, -ente mf; to be (a) p. to (crime) être complice de; p. line (telephone line) ligne f partagée; Pol ligne f du parti; p. ticket Br billet m collectif.

pass¹ [pɑːs] n (entry permit) laissez-passer m inv; (free theatre, concert etc ticket) billet m de faveur; (season ticket) carte f d'abonnement; (over mountains) col m; Football etc passe f; to get a p. (in exam) Br être reçu (in French/etc en français/etc); to make a p. at s.o. faire des avances à qn; p. key passe-partout m inv; p. mark (in exam) moyenne f, barre f d'admissibilité.

pass² [pɑːs] vi (go, come, disappear) passer (to à, through par); (overtake in vehicle) dé-

pathology

passer; (in exam) être reçu (**in French**/etc en français/etc); **that'll p.** (be acceptable) ça ira; **he can p. for thirty** on lui donnerait trente ans.

▮ vt (move, spend, give etc) passer (**to** à); (go past) passer devant (immeuble etc); (vehicle) dépasser; (exam) être reçu à; (candidate) recevoir; (opinion, judgment) prononcer (**on** sur); (remark) faire; (allow) autoriser; (bill, law) (of parliament) voter; **to p. s.o.** (in street) croiser qn.

passable ['pɑːsəb(ə)l] a (not bad) passable; (road) praticable; (river) franchissable.

passage ['pæsɪdʒ] n (of text, speech etc) passage m; (act of passing, way through) passage m; (of time) écoulement m; (corridor) couloir m; (by boat) traversée f, passage m. **●passageway** n (corridor) couloir m; (alleyway, way through) passage m.

pass along vi passer **▮ to pass away** vi (die) mourir **▮ to pass by** vi passer (à côté) **▮** vt (building etc) passer devant; **to p. by s.o.** (in street) croiser qn **▮ to pass off** vi (happen) se passer **▮** vt **p. oneself off as** se faire passer pour; **to p. sth off on s.o.** (fob off) refiler qch à qn **▮ to pass on** vt (message, illness, title etc) transmettre (**to** à) **▮** vi **to p. on to** (move on to) passer à **▮ to pass out** vi (faint) s'évanouir **▮** vt (hand out) distribuer (tracts etc) **▮ to pass over** vt (ignore) passer sur (qch) **▮ to pass round** vt (cakes, document etc) faire passer; (hand out) distribuer (tracts etc) **▮ to pass through** vi passer **▮ to pass up** vt (chance etc) laisser passer.

passbook ['pɑːsbʊk] n livret m de caisse d'épargne.

passenger ['pæsɪndʒər] n passager, -ère mf; (on train) voyageur, -euse mf.

passer-by [pɑːsə'baɪ] n (pl **passers-by**) passant, -ante mf.

passing ['pɑːsɪŋ] a (vehicle etc) qui passe; (beauty) passager; **p. place** aire f de croisement **▮** n (of vehicle, visitor etc) passage m; (of time) écoulement m; (death) disparition f; **in p.** en passant.

passion ['pæʃ(ə)n] n passion f; **to have a p. for** (cars etc) avoir la passion de, adorer. **●passionate** a passionné. **●passionately** adv passionnément.

passive ['pæsɪv] a (not active) passif; **p. smoking** tabagisme m passif; **the p. voice** Grammar la voix passive **▮** n Grammar passif m; **in the p.** au passif. **●passiveness** n passivité f.

Passover ['pɑːsəʊvər] n (Jewish festival) Pâque f.

passport ['pɑːspɔːt] n passeport m; **p. control** le contrôle des passeports.

password ['pɑːswɜːd] n mot m de passe.

past 1 n (time, history) passé m; **in the p.** (formerly) dans le temps; **it's a thing of the p.** ça n'existe plus.

▮ a (gone by) passé; (former) ancien; **these p. months** ces derniers mois; **that's all p.** c'est du passé; **in the p. tense** Grammar au

passé.

2 prep (in front of) devant; (after) après; (further than) plus loin que; (too old for) trop vieux pour; **p. four o'clock** quatre heures passées, plus de quatre heures; **to be p. fifty** avoir cinquante ans passés; **it's p. belief** c'est incroyable; **I wouldn't put it p. him** ça ne m'étonnerait pas de lui, il en est bien capable.

▮ adv devant; **to go p.** passer (devant); **to run p.** passer en courant.

pasta ['pæstə] n (food) pâtes fpl.

paste [peɪst] 1 n (mixture) pâte f; (of meat) pâté m; (of fish) beurre m; (dough) pâte f; **puff p.** Am pâte f feuilletée. **2** n (glue) colle f (blanche) **▮** vt coller; **to p. up** (notice etc) coller, afficher.

pastel [Br 'pæstəl, Am pæ'stel] n pastel m **▮** a (drawing) au pastel; **p. shade** teinte f pastel inv.

pasteurized ['pæstəraɪzd] a (milk) pasteurisé.

pastiche [pæ'stiːʃ] n pastiche m.

pastille [Br 'pæstɪl, Am pæ'stiːl] n pastille f.

pastime ['pɑːstaɪm] n passe-temps m inv.

pastor ['pɑːstər] n Rel pasteur m. **●pastoral** a pastoral; **p. duties** charges fpl pastorales.

pastry ['peɪstrɪ] n (dough) pâte f; (cake) pâtisserie f; **puff p.** Br pâte f feuilletée. **●pastrycook** n pâtissier, -ière mf.

pasture ['pɑːstʃər] n pâturage m.

pasty 1 ['pæstɪ] n (pie) petit pâté m (en croûte). **2** ['peɪstɪ] a (-ier, -iest) (complexion) terreux.

pat [pæt] 1 vt (-tt-) (cheek, table etc) tapoter; (animal) caresser **▮** n petite tape; (of animal) caresse f. **2** adv **to answer p.** avoir la réponse toute prête; **to know sth off p.** savoir qch sur le bout du doigt.

patch [pætʃ] n (for clothes) pièce f; (over eye) bandeau m; (for bicycle Br tyre or Am tire) rustine® f; (of colour) tache f; (of sky) morceau m; (of fog) nappe f; (of ice) plaque f; **a cabbage**/etc **p.** un carré de choux/etc; **bad p.** Fig mauvaise période f; **not to be a p. on** (not as good as) Fam (of person) ne pas arriver à la cheville de; (of thing) n'être rien à côté de.

▮ vt **to p. (up)** (clothing) rapiécer; **to p. up** (quarrel) régler; (marriage) replâtrer.

patchwork ['pætʃwɜːk] n patchwork m.

patchy ['pætʃɪ] a (-ier, -iest) inégal.

patent 1 ['peɪtənt] a patent, manifeste; **p. leather** cuir m verni. **2** ['peɪtənt, 'pætənt] n brevet m (d'invention) **▮** vt (faire) breveter. **●patently** adv manifestement; **it's p. obvious** c'est absolument évident.

paternal [pə'tɜːn(ə)l] a paternel. **●paternity** n paternité f.

path [pɑːθ] n (pl **-s** [pɑːðz]) sentier m, chemin m; (in park) allée f; (of river) cours m; (of bullet, planet) trajectoire f.

pathetic [pə'θetɪk] a pitoyable.

pathology [pə'θɒlədʒɪ] n pathologie f. **●pathological** a pathologique.

pathos ['peɪθɒs] n pathétique m.

pathway ['pɑːθweɪ] n sentier m, chemin m.

patience ['peɪʃəns] n 1 patience f; **to have p.** prendre patience; **to lose p.** perdre patience (**with s.o.** avec qn); **I have no p. with him** il m'impatiente. 2 (card game) Br réussite f; **to play p.** faire des réussites.

patient[1] ['peɪʃ(ə)nt] a patient; **be p.!** sois patient! ● **patiently** adv patiemment.

patient[2] ['peɪʃənt] n (in hospital) malade mf, patient, -ente mf; (on doctor's or dentist's list) patient, -ente mf.

patio ['pætɪəʊ] n (pl -os) (terrace) terrasse f; **p. doors** Br porte-fenêtre f.

patriarch ['peɪtrɪɑːk] n patriarche m.

patriot ['pætrɪət, 'peɪtrɪət] n patriote mf. ● **patri'otic** a (views, speech etc) patriotique; (person) patriote. ● **patriotism** n patriotisme m.

patrol [pə'trəʊl] n patrouille f; **p. boat** patrouilleur m; **police p. car** voiture f de police; **p. wagon** Am fourgon cellulaire ▮ vi (-ll-) patrouiller ▮ vt patrouiller dans. ● **patrolman** n (pl -men) (policeman) Am agent m de police; (repair man employed by motorists' association) Br dépanneur m.

patron ['peɪtrən] n (of artist) protecteur, -trice mf; (customer) client, -ente mf; (of theatre etc) habitué, -ée mf; **patrons** (of shop etc) clientèle f; (of theatre etc) public m; **p. saint** patron, -onne mf.

patronage ['peɪtrənɪdʒ] n (support) patronage m; (of the arts) protection f; (custom) clientèle f.

patronize [Br 'pætrənaɪz, Am 'peɪtrənaɪz] vt 1 (be condescending towards) traiter (qn) avec condescendance. 2 (store, hotel etc) accorder sa clientèle à. ● **patronizing** a condescendant.

patter ['pætər] n 1 (of footsteps) petit bruit m; (of rain, hail) crépitement m ▮ vi (of rain, hail) crépiter, tambouriner. 2 n (talk) baratin m.

pattern ['pæt(ə)n] n dessin m, motif m; (paper model for garment) patron m; (fabric sample) échantillon m; Fig modèle m; (plan) plan m; (tendency) tendance f; (method) formule f; (of a crime) scénario m. ● **patterned** a (dress, cloth etc) à motifs.

paucity ['pɔːsɪtɪ] n pénurie f.

paunch [pɔːntʃ] n panse f, bedon m. ● **paunchy** a (-ier, -iest) bedonnant.

pauper ['pɔːpər] n pauvre mf, indigent, -ente mf.

pause [pɔːz] n pause f; (in conversation) silence m ▮ vi (stop) faire une pause; (hesitate) hésiter.

pave [peɪv] vt paver; **to p. the way for** Fig ouvrir la voie à. ● **paved** a pavé. ● **paving** n (surface) pavage m, dallage m; **p. stone** pavé m.

pavement ['peɪvmənt] n Br trottoir m; (roadway) Am chaussée f; (stone) pavé m.

pavilion [pə'vɪljən] n (building) pavillon m.

paw [pɔː] 1 n patte f ▮ vt (of animal) donner des coups de patte à. 2 vt (touch improperly) tripoter (qn).

pawn [pɔːn] 1 n Chess pion m. 2 vt mettre en gage ▮ n in p. en gage. ● **pawnbroker** n prêteur, -euse mf sur gages. ● **pawnshop** n bureau m de prêteur sur gages.

pay [peɪ] n salaire m; (of workman) paie f, salaire m; (of soldier) solde f, paie f; **p. cheque** Br chèque m de règlement de salaire; **p. day** jour m de paie; **p. packet** enveloppe f de paie; (pay) Fig paie f; **p. phone** téléphone m public; **p. slip** Br, **p. stub** Am bulletin m or fiche f de paie.

▮ vt (pt & pp paid) (person, sum) payer; (deposit) verser; (yield) (of investment) rapporter; (compliment, visit) faire (to à); **to p. s.o. to do** or **for doing** payer qn pour faire; **to p. s.o. for sth** payer qch à qn; **to p. money into one's account** or **the bank** verser de l'argent sur son compte; **it pays (one) to be cautious** on a intérêt à être prudent; **to p. attention** faire or prêter attention (**to** à); **to p. homage** or **tribute** to rendre hommage à. ▮ vi payer; **to p. a lot** payer cher.

payable ['peɪəb(ə)l] a (due) payable; **a** Br **cheque** or Am **check p. to** un chèque à l'ordre de.

pay back vt (person, loan etc) rembourser; **I'll p. you back for this!** je te revaudrai ça! ▮ **to pay for** vt payer (qch) ▮ **to pay in** vt (Br cheque, Am check) verser (**to one's account** sur son compte) ▮ **to pay off** vt (debt, person etc) rembourser; (in instalments) rembourser par acomptes; (staff, worker) licencier; **to p. off an old score** or **a grudge** régler un vieux compte ▮ vi (be successful) être payant ▮ **to pay out** vt (spend) dépenser ▮ **to pay up** vti payer.

paycheck ['peɪtʃek] n Am chèque m de règlement de salaire. ● **payoff** n Fam (reward) récompense f; (bribe) pot-de-vin m; (settling of accounts) règlement m de comptes. ● **payphone** n téléphone m public. ● **payroll** n **to be on the p. of** (company, factory) être employé par; **to have twenty workers on the p.** employer vingt ouvriers.

paying ['peɪɪŋ] a (guest) payant; (profitable) rentable.

payment ['peɪmənt] n paiement m; (of deposit) versement m; (reward) récompense f; **on p. of 20 francs** moyennant 20 francs.

PC [piː'siː] n abbr = personal computer.

PE [piː'iː] n abbr (physical education) EPS f.

pea [piː] n pois m; **peas**, Br garden or green **peas** petits pois mpl; **p. soup** soupe f aux pois.

peace [piːs] n paix f; **p. of mind** tranquillité f d'esprit; **in p.** en paix; **at p.** en paix (**with** avec); **to have (some) p. and quiet** avoir la paix; **to disturb the p.** troubler l'ordre public; **to hold one's p.** garder le silence. ● **peace-keeping** a (force) de maintien de la paix; (measure) de pacification. ● **peace-loving** a pacifique.

peaceable ['piːsəb(ə)l] a paisible, pacifique.

peaceful ['piːsfəl] a paisible, calme; (demonstration, coexistence, purpose) pacifique. ● **peacefully** adv paisiblement. ● **peacefulness** n paix f.

peach [piːtʃ] n (fruit) pêche f; **p. (tree)** pêcher m ▮ a (colour) pêche inv.

peacock ['piːkɒk] n paon m.

peak [piːk] n (mountain top) sommet m; (mountain) pic m; (of cap) visière f; (of fame etc) Fig sommet m, apogée m; **the traffic has reached** or **is at its p.** la circulation est à son maximum ▮ a (hours, period) de pointe; (demand, production) maximum ▮ vi (of sales etc) atteindre son maximum.

peaked [piːkt] a **p. cap** casquette f.

peaky ['piːki] a (-ier, -iest) Br Fam (ill) patraque; (pale) pâlot.

peal [piːl] 1 n (of laughter) éclat m; (of thunder) roulement m. 2 n p. **of bells** carillon m ▮ vi to p. (out) (of bells) carillonner.

peanut ['piːnʌt] n cacah(o)uète f; (plant) arachide f; **p. butter** beurre m de cacah(o)uètes; **to earn peanuts** (little money) Fam gagner des clopinettes; **it's worth peanuts** ça vaut des clopinettes.

pear [peər] n poire f; **p. tree** poirier m.

pearl [pɜːl] n perle f; (mother-of-pearl) nacre f; **p. necklace** collier m de perles. ● **pearly** a (-ier, -iest) (colour) nacré.

peasant ['pezənt] n & a paysan, -anne (mf).

peashooter ['piːʃuːtər] n sarbacane f.

peat [piːt] n tourbe f.

pebble ['peb(ə)l] n (stone) caillou m (pl -oux); (on beach) galet m. ● **pebbly** a (beach) (couvert) de galets.

pecan ['piːkæn] n (nut) Am noix f de pécan.

peck [pek] vti to p. (at) (of bird) picorer (du pain etc); donner un coup de bec à (qn); to **p. at one's food** (of person) picorer, manger du bout des dents; **the pecking order** Fig la hiérarchie ▮ n coup m de bec; (kiss) Fam bécot m.

peckish ['pekiʃ] a to be **p.** (hungry) Br Fam avoir un petit creux.

peculiar [pɪ'kjuːliər] a (strange) bizarre; (special, characteristic) particulier (to à). ● **pecul'iarity** n (feature) particularité f; (oddity) bizarrerie f. ● **peculiarly** adv bizarrement; (specially) particulièrement.

pedal ['ped(ə)l] n pédale f; **p. boat** pédalo m ▮ vi (Br -ll-, Am -l-) pédaler ▮ vt to p. a **bicycle** faire marcher un vélo; (ride) rouler en vélo. ● **pedalbin** n poubelle f à pédale.

pedant ['pedənt] n pédant, -ante mf. ● **pe'dantic** a pédant. ● **pedantry** n pédantisme m.

peddle ['ped(ə)l] vt colporter; (drugs) faire le trafic de ▮ vi faire du colportage. ● **peddler** n (door-to-door) colporteur, -euse mf; (in street) camelot m; **drug p.** revendeur, -euse mf de drogues.

pedestal ['pedɪst(ə)l] n (of statue etc) piédestal m; **to put s.o. on a p.** Fig mettre qn sur un piédestal.

pedestrian [pə'destriən] 1 n piéton m; **p.**

crossing Br passage m pour piétons; **p. precinct** Br zone f piétonnière. 2 a (speech, style) prosaïque. ● **pedestrianize** vt (street etc) rendre piétonnier; **pedestrianized street/** etc rue f/etc piétonne or piétonnière.

pediatrician [piːdɪə'trɪʃ(ə)n] n (doctor) pédiatre mf.

pedigree ['pedɪɡriː] n (of dog, horse etc) pedigree m; (of person) ascendance f ▮ a (dog, horse etc) de race.

pedlar ['pedlər] n (door-to-door) colporteur, -euse mf; (in street) camelot m.

pee [piː] n to go for a **p.** Fam faire pipi.

peek [piːk] n to have a **p.** = to peek ▮ vi jeter un petit coup d'œil (at à).

peel [piːl] n (of vegetable, fruit) épluchure(s) f(pl), pelure(s) f(pl); (orange skin) écorce f; (in food, drink) zeste m; **a piece of p., some p.** une épluchure, une pelure ▮ vt (apple, potato etc) éplucher, peler; **to keep one's eyes peeled** Fam être vigilant; **to p. off** (label etc) décoller ▮ vi (of sunburnt skin) peler; (of paint) s'écailler; **to p. easily** (of fruit) se peler facilement. ● **peelings** npl épluchures fpl, pelures fpl. ● **peeler** n (potato) p. (knife) éplucheur m, couteau m à éplucher.

peep [piːp] 1 n to have a **p.** = to peep ▮ vi jeter un petit coup d'œil (at à); **to p. out** se montrer; **peeping Tom** voyeur, -euse mf. 2 vi (of bird) pépier. ● **peephole** n judas m.

peer [pɪər] 1 n (equal) pair m, égal, -ale mf; (noble) pair m. 2 vi to p. (at) regarder attentivement (comme pour mieux voir); **to p. into the darkness** scruter l'obscurité. ● **peerage** n (rank) Br pairie f.

peeved [piːvd] a Fam irrité.

peevish ['piːvɪʃ] a grincheux, irritable.

peg [peɡ] 1 n (for coat, hat etc) patère f; (for clothes) pince f (à linge); (for tent) piquet m; (wooden) cheville f; (metal) fiche f; **to buy sth off the p.** Br acheter qch en prêt-à-porter. 2 vt (-gg-) (prices) stabiliser.

pejorative [pɪ'dʒɒrətɪv] a péjoratif.

Peking [piː'kɪŋ] n Pékin m or f.

pekin(g)ese [piːkɪ'niːz] n (dog) pékinois m.

pelican ['pelɪk(ə)n] n (bird) pélican m; **p. crossing** Br passage m pour piétons (avec feux à déclenchement manuel).

pellet ['pelɪt] n (of paper etc) boulette f; (for gun) (grain m de) plomb m.

pelmet ['pelmɪt] n (fabric, wood) cantonnière f.

pelt [pelt] 1 vi it's **pelting (down)** (raining) il pleut à verse. 2 vt to p. s.o. with (stones etc) bombarder qn de. 3 vi to p. along (run, dash) Fam foncer, courir. 4 n (skin) peau f; (fur) fourrure f.

pelvis ['pelvɪs] n Anat bassin m.

pen [pen] 1 n (fountain pen) stylo m (à plume or à encre); (ballpoint) stylo m (à bille), stylo(-)bille m; (dipped in ink) porteplume m inv; **to live by one's p.** Fig vivre de sa plume; **p. friend** Br, **p. pal** correspondant, -ante mf; **p. name** pseudonyme m; **p. nib** (bec m de) plume f; **p. pusher** Pej gratte-papier *m inv* ▌ *vt* (**-nn-**) (*write*) écrire. **2** *n* (*enclosure for baby, sheep, cattle*) parc *m*.

penal ['pi:n(ə)l] *a* (*code, law etc*) pénal; (*colony*) pénitentiaire. ●**penalize** *vt* (*punish*) & *Sport* pénaliser (**for** pour); (*handicap*) désavantager.

penalty ['pen(ə)ltɪ] *n* (*prison sentence*) peine *f*; (*fine*) amende *f*; *Sport* pénalisation *f*; *Football* penalty *m*; *Rugby* pénalité *f*; **to pay the p.** *Fig* subir les conséquences.

penance ['penəns] *n* pénitence *f*.

pence [pens] *npl see* **penny.**

pencil ['pens(ə)l] *n* crayon *m*; **in p.** au crayon; **p. box** plumier *m*; **p. case** trousse *f*; **p. sharpener** taille-crayon(s) *m inv* ▌ *vt* (*Br* **-ll-**, *Am* **-l-**) crayonner; **to p. in** (*note down*) *Fig* noter provisoirement.

pendant ['pendənt] *n* (*around neck*) pendentif *m*; (*on earring, chandelier*) pendeloque *f*.

pending ['pendɪŋ] **1** *a* (*matter, business*) en suspens. **2** *prep* (*until*) en attendant.

pendulum ['pendjʊləm] *n* (*of clock*) balancier *m*, pendule *m*.

penetrate ['penɪtreɪt] *vt* (*substance*) pénétrer; (*secret, plan etc*) découvrir; (*mystery*) percer ▌ *vti* **to p.** (**into**) (*forest, group etc*) pénétrer dans. ●**penetrating** *a* (*mind, cold etc*) pénétrant. ●**penetration** [-'treɪʃ(ə)n] *n* pénétration *f*.

penguin ['peŋgwɪn] *n* manchot *m*, pingouin *m*.

penicillin [penɪ'sɪlɪn] *n* pénicilline *f*; **to be on p.** prendre la pénicilline.

peninsula [pə'nɪnsjʊlə] *n* presqu'île *f*, péninsule *f*. ●**peninsular** *a* péninsulaire.

penis ['pi:nɪs] *n* pénis *m*.

penitent ['penɪtənt] *a* repentant, pénitent. ●**penitence** *n* pénitence *f*.

penitentiary [penɪ'tenʃərɪ] *n Am* prison *f* (centrale).

penknife ['pennaɪf] *n* (*pl* **-knives**) canif *m*.

pennant ['penənt] *n* (*flag on bicycle, boat etc*) fanion *m*.

penniless ['penɪləs] *a* sans le sou.

penny ['penɪ] *n* **1** (*pl* **pennies**) (*coin*) *Br* penny *m*; *Am Can* cent *m*; **I don't have a p.** *Fig* je n'ai pas le or un sou; **you won't get a p.** tu n'auras pas un sou. **2** (*pl* **pence** [pens]) (*value, currency*) *Br* penny *m*. ●**penny-pinching** *a* (*miserly*) *Fam* avare.

pension ['penʃ(ə)n] *n* pension *f*; (*retirement*) **p.** retraite *f*; **old-age p.** *Br* pension *f* de vieillesse; **to retire on a p.** toucher une retraite; **p. fund** fonds *m* de retraite; **p. scheme** *Br* régime *m* de retraite ▌ *vt* **to p. s.o. off** mettre qn à la retraite. ●**pensionable** *a* (*age*) de la retraite; (*job*) qui donne droit à une retraite. ●**pensioner** *n* pensionné, -ée *mf*; (*on retirement pension*) retraité, -ée *mf*; **old age p.** *Br* retraité, -ée *mf*.

pensive ['pensɪv] *a* pensif.

Pentagon ['pentəgən] *n* **the P.** *Am Pol* le Pentagone.

pentathlon [pen'tæθlən] *n Sport* pentathlon *m*.

Pentecost ['pentɪkɒst] *n* (*Whitsun*) *Am* Pentecôte *f*.

penthouse ['penthaʊs] *n* appartement *m* de luxe (*construit sur le toit d'un immeuble*).

pent-up [pent'ʌp] *a* (*feelings*) refoulé.

penultimate [pɪ'nʌltɪmət] *a* avant-dernier.

peony ['pɪənɪ] *n* (*plant*) pivoine *f*.

people ['pi:p(ə)l] *npl* (*in general*) gens *mpl or fpl*; (*specific persons*) personnes *fpl*; (*of region, town*) habitants *mpl*, gens *mpl or fpl*; **the p.** (*citizens*) le peuple; **old p.** les personnes *fpl* âgées; **old people's home** hospice *m* de vieillards; (*private*) maison *f* de retraite; **two p.** deux personnes; **English p.** les Anglais *mpl*; **a lot of p.** beaucoup de monde or de gens; **p. think that...** on pense que.... ▌ *n* (*nation*) peuple *m*. ▌ *vt* (*populate*) peupler (**with** de).

pep [pep] *n Fam* dynamisme *m*; **p. talk** petit laïus *m* d'encouragement ▌ *vt* (**-pp-**) **to p. s.o. up** (*perk up*) ragaillardir qn.

pepper ['pepər] *n* poivre *m*; (*vegetable*) poivron *m* ▌ *vt* poivrer. ●**peppercorn** *n* grain *m* de poivre. ●**pepperpot** *n* poivrière *f*. ●**peppery** *a* poivré.

peppermint ['pepəmɪnt] *n* (*flavour*) menthe *f*; (*Br sweet, Am candy*) bonbon *m* à la menthe.

per [pɜːr] *prep* par; **p. annum** par an; **p. head, p. person** par personne; **p. cent** pour cent; **50 pence p. kilo** 50 pence le kilo; **40 km p. hour** 40 km à l'heure.

perceive [pə'siːv] *vt* (*see, hear*) percevoir; (*notice*) remarquer (**that** que).

percentage [pə'sentɪdʒ] *n* pourcentage *m*.

perceptible [pə'septəb(ə)l] *a* perceptible. ●**perception** [-ʃ(ə)n] *n* perception *f* (**of** de); (*intuition*) intuition *f*. ●**perceptive** *a* (*person*) perspicace; (*study, remark*) pénétrant.

perch [pɜːtʃ] **1** *n* (*for bird*) perchoir *m* ▌ *vi* (*of bird*) se percher, percher (**on** sur); (*of person*) *Fig* se percher, se jucher ▌ *vt* (*put*) percher. **2** *n* (*fish*) perche *f*.

percolate ['pɜːkəleɪt] *vi* (*of liquid*) filtrer, passer (**through** par) ▌ *vt* (*coffee*) faire dans une cafetière; **percolated coffee** du vrai café. ●**percolator** *n* cafetière *f*; (*in café or restaurant*) percolateur *m*.

percussion [pə'kʌʃ(ə)n] *n Mus* percussion *f*.

peremptory [pə'remptərɪ] *a* (*tone etc*) péremptoire.

perennial [pə'renɪəl] *a* (*complaint, subject etc*) perpétuel. **2** *a* (*plant*) vivace ▌ *n* plante *f* vivace.

perfect ['pɜːfɪkt] *a* parfait ▌ *a* & *n*. **p.** (**tense**) *Grammar* parfait *m* ▌ [pə'fekt] *vt* (*book, knowledge etc*) parachever, parfaire; (*technique, process*) mettre au point; (*one's French etc*) parfaire ses connaissances. ●**perfectly** *adv* parfaitement.

perfection [pə'fekʃ(ə)n] *n* perfection *f*; (*of technique etc*) mise *f* au point (**of** de); **to p. à** la perfection. ●**perfectionist** *n* perfectionnis-

te *mf.*
perfidious [pəˈfɪdɪəs] *a Lit* perfide.
perforate [ˈpɜːfəreɪt] *vt* perforer. ●**perforation** [-ˈreɪʃ(ə)n] *n* perforation *f.*
perform [pəˈfɔːm] *vt* (*task, miracle*) accomplir; (*one's duty, a function*) remplir; (*rite*) célébrer; (*surgical operation*) pratiquer (**on** sur); (*a play, piece of music*) jouer; (*sonata*) interpréter.
❚ *vi* (*act, play*) jouer; (*sing*) chanter; (*dance*) danser; (*of circus animal*) faire un numéro; (*of machine, vehicle*) (*function*) fonctionner; (*behave*) se comporter; (*in one's job*) réussir; **you performed very well!** tu as très bien fait!
●**performing** *a* (*dog, seal etc*) savant.
performance [pəˈfɔːməns] *n* **1** (*show*) (*in theatre*) représentation *f*, séance *f*; (*in concert hall, Br cinema, Am movie theater*) séance *f*. **2** (*of actor, musician etc*) interprétation *f*; (*of athlete, machine etc*) performance *f*; (*in job, of company, firm*) performances *fpl*; (*circus act*) numéro *m*; (*fuss*) *Fam* histoire(s) *f(pl)*; **the p. of one's duties** l'exercice *m* de ses fonctions.
performer [pəˈfɔːmər] *n* (*entertainer*) artiste *mf*; (*in play, of music*) interprète *mf* (**of** de).
perfume [ˈpɜːfjuːm] *n* parfum *m* ❚ [pəˈfjuːm] *vt* parfumer.
perfunctory [pəˈfʌŋktərɪ] *a* (*action*) superficiel; (*smile etc*) de commande.
perhaps [pəˈhæps] *adv* peut-être; **p. not/so** peut-être que non/que oui; **p. you will help me** peut-être que tu m'aideras.
peril [ˈperɪl] *n* péril *m*, danger *m*; **at your p.** à vos risques et péril. ●**perilous** *a* périlleux.
perimeter [pəˈrɪmɪtər] *n* périmètre *m.*
period [ˈpɪərɪəd] **1** *n* (*length of time, moment in time*) période *f*; (*historical*) époque *f*; (*time limit*) délai *m*; (*school lesson*) leçon *f*; (*full stop*) *Am Grammar* point *m*; **in the p. of a month** en l'espace d'un mois; **I refuse, p.!** *Am* je refuse, un point c'est tout! ❚ *a* (*furniture etc*) d'époque; (*costume*) de l'époque. **2** *n* (*monthly*) **period(s)** (*of woman*) règles *fpl*.
periodic [pɪərɪˈɒdɪk] *a* périodique. ●**periodical** *n* (*magazine*) périodique *m.* ●**periodically** *adv* périodiquement.
periphery [pəˈrɪfərɪ] *n* périphérie *f.* ●**peripheral** *a* (*question*) sans rapport direct (**to** avec); (*interest*) accessoire; (*neighbourhood etc*) & *Comptr* périphérique. ●**peripherals** *npl Comptr* périphériques *mpl.*
periscope [ˈperɪskəʊp] *n* périscope *m.*
perish [ˈperɪʃ] *vi* (*die*) périr; (*of food, substance*) se détériorer; **to be perished** *or* **perishing** (*of person*) *Fam* être frigorifié. ●**perishing** *a* (*cold, weather*) *Fam* glacial.
perishable [ˈperɪʃəb(ə)l] *a* (*food*) périssable. ●**perishables** *npl* denrées *fpl* périssables.
perjure [ˈpɜːdʒər] *vt* **to p. oneself** se parjurer. ●**perjurer** *n* (*person*) parjure *mf.* ●**perjury** *n* parjure *m*; **to commit p.** se parjurer.
perk [pɜːk] **1** *vi* **to p. up** (*become livelier*) reprendre du poil de la bête ❚ *vt* **to p. s.o. up**

remonter qn, ragaillardir qn. **2** *n* (*in job*) *Br* avantage *m* en nature. ●**perky** *a* (**-ier, -iest**) (*cheerful*) guilleret (*f* **-ette**), plein d'entrain.
perm [pɜːm] *n* (*of hair*) permanente *f* ❚ *vt* **to have one's hair permed** se faire faire une permanente.
permanent [ˈpɜːmənənt] *a* permanent; (*address*) fixe; **she's p. here** (*of office worker etc*) elle est ici à titre permanent. ●**permanence** *n* permanence *f.* ●**permanently** *adv* à titre permanent.
permeable [ˈpɜːmɪəb(ə)l] *a* perméable.
permeate [ˈpɜːmɪeɪt] *vt* (*of ideas etc*) se répandre dans; **to p. (through) sth** (*of liquid etc*) pénétrer qch.
permissible [pəˈmɪsəb(ə)l] *a* permis.
permission [pəˈmɪʃ(ə)n] *n* permission *f*, autorisation *f* (**to do** de faire); **to ask (for) p.** demander la permission; **to give s.o. p.** donner la permission à qn.
permissive [pəˈmɪsɪv] *a* (*trop*) tolérant, laxiste. ●**permissiveness** *n* laxisme *m.*
permit [pəˈmɪt] *vt* (**-tt-**) permettre (**s.o. to do** à qn de faire); **weather permitting** si le temps le permet ❚ [ˈpɜːmɪt] *n* (*authorization*) permis *m*; (*entrance pass*) laissez-passer *m inv.*
permutation [pɜːmjuˈteɪʃ(ə)n] *n* permutation *f.*
pernicious [pəˈnɪʃəs] *a* (*harmful*) & *Med* pernicieux.
pernickety [pəˈnɪkətɪ] *a Br Fam* (*precise*) pointilleux; (*demanding*) difficile (**about** sur).
peroxide [pəˈrɒksaɪd] *n* (*bleach*) eau *f* oxygénée ❚ *a* (*hair, blond*) oxygéné.
perpendicular [pɜːpənˈdɪkjʊlər] *a* & *n* perpendiculaire (*f*).
perpetrate [ˈpɜːpɪtreɪt] *vt* (*crime*) commettre, perpétrer. ●**perpetrator** *n* auteur *m.*
perpetual [pəˈpetʃʊəl] *a* perpétuel. ●**perpetually** *adv* perpétuellement. ●**perpetuate** *vt* perpétuer. ●**perpetuity** [pɜːpɪˈtjuːɪtɪ] *n* perpétuité *f.*
perplex [pəˈpleks] *vt* rendre perplexe, dérouter. ●**perplexed** *a* perplexe. ●**perplexing** *a* déroutant. ●**perplexity** *n* perplexité *f*; (*complexity*) complexité *f.*
persecute [ˈpɜːsɪkjuːt] *vt* persécuter. ●**persecution** [-ˈkjuːʃ(ə)n] *n* persécution *f.*
persevere [pɜːsɪˈvɪər] *vi* persévérer (**in** dans). ●**persevering** *a* (*persistent*) persévérant. ●**perseverance** *n* persévérance *f.*
Persian [ˈpɜːʃ(ə)n, ˈpɜːʒ(ə)n] *a* (*language, cat etc*) persan; **P. carpet** tapis *m* de Perse; **the P. Gulf** le golfe Persique ❚ *n* (*language*) persan *m.*
persist [pəˈsɪst] *vi* persister (**in doing** à faire, **in sth** dans qch). ●**persistence** *n* persistance *f.* ●**persistent** *a* (*person*) obstiné; (*fever, smell etc*) persistant; (*noise, attempts etc*) continuel. ●**persistently** *adv* (*stubbornly*) obstinément; (*continually*) continuellement.
person [ˈpɜːs(ə)n] *n* personne *f*; **in p.** en personne; **a p. to p. call** (*on telephone*) une communication avec préavis.

personable [ˈpɜːsənəb(ə)] *a* avenant, qui présente bien.

personal [ˈpɜːsən(ə)l] *a* personnel; *(application)* en personne; *(friend, hygiene)* intime; *(life)* privé; *(indiscreet)* indiscret; **p. assistant, p. secretary** secrétaire *m* particulier, secrétaire *f* particulière; **the p. column, the p. ads** les annonces *fpl* personnelles; **p. computer** ordinateur *m* personnel; **p. organizer** agenda *m* organiseur; **p. stereo** baladeur *m*.

personality [pɜːsəˈnælətɪ] *n (character, famous person)* personnalité *f*; **a television p.** une vedette de la télévision.

personalize [ˈpɜːsənəlaɪz] *vt* personnaliser.

personally [ˈpɜːsənəlɪ] *adv* personnellement; *(in person)* en personne; **don't take it p.** n'y voyez rien de personnel.

personify [pəˈsɒnɪfaɪ] *vt* personnifier. ● **personification** [-ˈkeɪʃ(ə)n] *n* personnification *f*.

personnel [pɜːsəˈnel] *n (staff)* personnel *m*; *(department)* service *m* du personnel.

perspective [pəˈspektɪv] *n (artistic & viewpoint)* perspective *f*; **in (its true) p.** *Fig* sous son vrai jour.

Perspex® [ˈpɜːspeks] *n Br* Plexiglas® *m*.

perspire [pəˈspaɪər] *vi* transpirer. ● **perspiration** [pɜːspəˈreɪʃ(ə)n] *n* transpiration *f*, sueur *f*.

persuade [pəˈsweɪd] *vt* persuader **(s.o. to do** qn de faire). ● **persuasion** [-ʒ(ə)n] *n* persuasion *f*; *(creed)* religion *f*. ● **persuasive** *a (person, argument etc)* persuasif. ● **persuasively** *adv* de façon persuasive.

pert [pɜːt] *a (impertinent)* impertinent; *(lively)* plein d'entrain, gai; *(hat etc)* coquet, chic. ● **pertly** *adv* avec impertinence.

pertain [pəˈteɪn] *vi* **to p. to** *(relate)* se rapporter à; *(belong)* appartenir à.

pertinent [ˈpɜːtɪnənt] *a* pertinent. ● **pertinently** *adv* pertinemment.

perturb [pəˈtɜːb] *vt* troubler, perturber.

Peru [pəˈruː] *n* Pérou *m*. ● **Peruvian** *a* péruvien **❚** *n* Péruvien, -ienne *mf*.

peruse [pəˈruːz] *vt* lire *(attentivement)*; *(skim through)* parcourir. ● **perusal** *n* lecture *f*.

pervade [pəˈveɪd] *vt* se répandre dans. ● **pervasive** *a* qui se répand partout, envahissant.

perverse [pəˈvɜːs] *a (awkward)* contrariant; *(obstinate)* entêté; *(wicked)* pervers. ● **perversion** [*Br* -ʃ(ə)n, *Am* -ʒ(ə)n] *n* perversion *f*; *(of justice, truth)* travestissement *m*. ● **perversity** *n* esprit *m* de contradiction; *(obstinacy)* entêtement *m*; *(wickedness)* perversité *f*.

pervert [pəˈvɜːt] *vt* pervertir; *(mind)* corrompre; *(truth, justice)* travestir **❚** [ˈpɜːvɜːt] *n (sexual)* détraqué, -ée *mf*, pervers, -erse *mf*.

pesky [ˈpeskɪ] *a (-ier, -iest) (troublesome) Am Fam* embêtant.

pessimism [ˈpesɪmɪz(ə)m] *n* pessimisme *m*.

● **pessimist** *n* pessimiste *mf*. ● **pessi'mistic** *a* pessimiste. ● **pessi'mistically** *adv* avec pessimisme.

pest [pest] *n* animal *m* or insecte *m* nuisible; *(person)* casse-pieds *mf inv*, peste *f*.

pester [ˈpestər] *vt (harass)* harceler **(with questions de questions); to p. s.o. to do sth/for sth** harceler *or* tarabuster qn pour qu'il fasse qch/jusqu'à ce qu'il donne qch.

pesticide [ˈpestɪsaɪd] *n* pesticide *m*.

pet [pet] **1** *n* animal *m* (domestique); *(favourite person)* chouchou, -oute *mf*; **yes (my) p.** *Fam* oui mon chou; **to have** *or* **keep a p.** avoir un animal chez soi.

❚ *a (dog, cat etc)* domestique; *(tiger etc)* apprivoisé; *(favourite)* favori *(f* -ite*)*; **p. shop** magasin *m* d'animaux; **p. hate** *Br* bête *f* noire; **p. name** petit nom *m* (d'amitié); **p. subject** dada *m*.

2 *vt* (**-tt-**) *(fondle)* caresser; *(sexually) Fam* peloter **❚** *vi Fam* se peloter.

petal [ˈpet(ə)l] *n* pétale *m*.

peter [ˈpiːtər] *vi* **to p. out** *(dry up)* tarir; *(die out)* mourir; *(run out)* s'épuiser; *(disappear)* disparaître.

petite [pəˈtiːt] *a (woman)* menue, petite et mince.

petition [pəˈtɪʃ(ə)n] *n (signatures)* pétition *f*; *(request to court of law)* requête *f*; **p. for divorce** demande *f* en divorce **❚** *vt* adresser une pétition *or* une requête à **(for sth** pour demander qch).

petrify [ˈpetrɪfaɪ] *vt (frighten)* pétrifier de terreur; **to be petrified** être pétrifié de terreur.

petrol [ˈpetrəl] *n Br* essence *f*; **I've run out of p.** je suis tombé en panne d'essence; **p. can** bidon *m* d'essence; **p. engine** moteur *m* à essence; **p. station** station-service *f*, poste *m* d'essence; **p. tank** réservoir *m* (d'essence).

petroleum [pəˈtrəʊlɪəm] *n* pétrole *m*.

petticoat [ˈpetɪkəʊt] *n* jupon *m*.

petty [ˈpetɪ] *a (-ier, -iest) (small) (trivial)* insignifiant, menu, petit; *(mean)* mesquin; **p. cash** *(in office etc)* petite caisse *f*, menue monnaie *f*; **p. criminal** petit délinquant *m*, petit malfaiteur *m*; **p. officer** *(on ship)* second maître *m*. ● **pettiness** *n* petitesse *f*; *(triviality)* insignifiance *f*; *(meanness)* mesquinerie *f*.

petulant [ˈpetjʊlənt] *a* irritable. ● **petulance** *n* irritabilité *f*.

petunia [pɪˈtjuːnɪə] *n (plant))* pétunia *m*.

pew [pjuː] *n* banc *m* d'église; **take a p.!** *Hum* assieds-toi!

pewter [ˈpjuːtər] *n* étain *m*.

phallic [ˈfælɪk] *a* phallique.

phantom [ˈfæntəm] *n* fantôme *m*.

pharmacy [ˈfɑːməsɪ] *n* pharmacie *f*. ● **pharmaceutical** [-ˈsjuːtɪk(ə)l] *a* pharmaceutique. ● **pharmacist** *n* pharmacien, -ienne *mf*.

pharynx [ˈfærɪŋks] *n Anat* pharynx *m*. ● **pharyn'gitis** *n (illness)* pharyngite *f*.

phase [feɪz] *n (stage)* phase *f* **❚** *vt* **to p. sth**

in/out introduire/supprimer qch progressivement. ●**phased** a (changes etc) progressif.

PhD [piːeɪtʃˈdiː] n abbr (Doctor of Philosophy) (university degree) doctorat m.

pheasant ['fezənt] n (bird) faisan m.

phenomenon, pl **-ena** [fɪˈnɒmɪnən, -ɪnə] n phénomène m. ●**phenomenal** a phénoménal.

phew! [fjuː] int (relief) ouf!

philanderer [fɪˈlændərər] n coureur m de jupons.

philanthropist [fɪˈlænθrəpɪst] n philanthrope mf. ●**philan'thropic** a philanthropique.

philately [fɪˈlætəlɪ] n philatélie f. ●**phila'telic** a philatélique. ●**philatelist** n philatéliste mf.

philharmonic [fɪlɑːˈmɒnɪk] a (orchestra) philharmonique.

Philippines ['fɪlɪpiːnz] npl **the P.** les Philippines fpl.

philistine ['fɪlɪstaɪn] n béotien, -ienne mf, philistin m.

philosophy [fɪˈlɒsəfɪ] n philosophie f. ●**philosopher** n philosophe mf. ●**philo'sophical** a philosophique; (stoical, resigned) Fig philosophe. ●**philo'sophically** adv (to say etc) avec philosophie. ●**philosophize** vi philosopher (on sur).

phlegm [flem] n (in throat) glaires fpl; (calmness) Fig flegme m. ●**phleg'matic** a flegmatique.

phobia ['fəʊbɪə] n phobie f.

phone [fəʊn] n téléphone m; **on the p.** (speaking here) au téléphone; (at other end) au bout du fil; **to be on the p.** (as subscriber) avoir le téléphone; **p. call** coup m de fil or de téléphone; **to make a p. call** téléphoner (**to** à); **p. book** annuaire m; **p. box** Br, p. **booth** cabine f téléphonique; **p. number** numéro m de téléphone.
∎ vt (message) téléphoner (**to** à); **to p. s.o.** (**up**) téléphoner à qn; **to p. s.o. back** rappeler qn.
∎ vi **to p.** (**up**) téléphoner; **to p. back** rappeler. ●**phonecard** n Br télécarte f. ●**phone-in** n émission f à ligne ouverte.

phonetic [fəˈnetɪk] a phonétique. ●**phonetics** n (science) phonétique f; (words) transcription f phonétique.

phoney ['fəʊnɪ] a (-ier, -iest) Fam (jewels, writer etc) faux (f fausse); (company, excuse) bidon inv; (attitude) de faux-jeton ∎ n Fam (impostor) imposteur m; (insincere person) faux-jeton m; **it's a p.** (jewel, coin etc) c'est du faux.

phonograph ['fəʊnəgræf] n Am électrophone m.

phosphate ['fɒsfeɪt] n Ch phosphate m.

phosphorus ['fɒsfərəs] n Ch phosphore m.

photo ['fəʊtəʊ] n (pl **-os**) photo f; **to take a p. of** prendre une photo de; **to have one's p. taken** se faire prendre en photo.

photocopy ['fəʊtəʊkɒpɪ] n photocopie f ∎ vt photocopier. ●**photocopier** n (machine) photocopieuse f.

photogenic [fəʊtəʊˈdʒenɪk] a photogénique.

photograph ['fəʊtəgræf] n photographie f ∎

vt photographier ∎ vi **to p. well** être photogénique. ●**photographer** [fəˈtɒgrəfər] n photographe mf. ●**photo'graphic** a photographique. ●**photography** [fəˈtɒgrəfɪ] n (activity) photographie f.

photostat® ['fəʊtəʊstæt] n = photocopy.

phrase [freɪz] n (saying) expression f; (idiom) & Grammar locution f ∎ vt (express) exprimer; (letter) rédiger. ●**phrasing** n (wording) termes mpl. ●**phrasebook** n (for tourists) manuel m de conversation.

Phys Ed [fɪzˈed] n abbr (physical education) Am EPS f.

physical ['fɪzɪk(ə)l] a physique; (object, world) matériel; **p. examination** examen m médical; **p. education, p. training** éducation f physique. ●**physically** adv physiquement; **p. impossible** matériellement impossible.

physician [fɪˈzɪʃ(ə)n] n médecin m.

physics ['fɪzɪks] n (science) physique f. ●**physicist** n physicien, -ienne mf.

physiology [fɪzɪˈɒlədʒɪ] n physiologie f. ●**physio'logical** a physiologique.

physiotherapy [fɪzɪəʊˈθerəpɪ] n kinésithérapie f. ●**physiotherapist** n kinésithérapeute mf.

physique [fɪˈziːk] n (appearance) physique m; (constitution) constitution f.

piano [pɪˈænəʊ] n (pl **-os**) piano m. ●**pianist** ['pɪənɪst] n pianiste mf.

piazza [pɪˈætsə] n (square) place f; (covered) passage m couvert.

picayune [pɪkəˈjuːn] a (petty) Am Fam mesquin.

pick [pɪk] n (choice) choix m; **to take one's p.** faire son choix, choisir; **the p. of** (best) le meilleur de; **the p. of the bunch** le dessus du panier.
∎ vt (choose) choisir; (flower, fruit etc) cueillir; (hole) faire (**in** dans); (pimple etc) gratter; (lock) crocheter; **to p. one's nose** se mettre les doigts dans le nez; **to p. one's teeth** se curer les dents; **to p. a fight** chercher la bagarre (**with** avec); **to p. holes in** Fig relever les défauts de.
∎ vi **to p. and choose** prendre son temps pour choisir.

pick at vt **to p. at one's food** picorer ∎ **to pick off** vt (remove) enlever ∎ **to pick on** vt (nag, blame) s'en prendre à (qn) ∎ **to pick out** vt (choose) choisir; (identify) reconnaître, distinguer ∎ **to pick up** vt (sth dropped) ramasser; (fallen person or chair) relever; (person into air, weight) soulever; (a cold) attraper; (habit, accent, speed) prendre; (fetch, collect) (passer) prendre; (find) trouver; (baby) prendre dans ses bras; (radio programme) capter; (survivor) recueillir; (arrest) arrêter, ramasser; (learn) apprendre ∎ vi (improve) s'améliorer; (of business, trade) reprendre; (of patient) aller mieux; (resume) continuer.

pick(axe) (Am **-ax**) ['pɪk(æks)] n (tool) pioche f; **ice pick** pic m à glace.

picket ['pɪkɪt] **1** n (striker) gréviste mf; **p.**

(line) piquet *m* (de grève) **|** *vt* (*factory*) installer des piquets de grève aux portes de. **2** *n* (*stake*) piquet *m*.

pickings ['pɪkɪŋz] *npl* (*leftovers*) restes *mpl*; (*profits*) profits *mpl*; **rich p.** jolis profits *mpl*.

pickle ['pɪk(ə)l] **1** *n* (*brine*) saumure *f*; (*vinegar*) vinaigre *m*; **pickles** (*vegetables*) *Br* pickles *mpl*; *Am* concombres *mpl*, cornichons *mpl* **|** *vt* mariner; **pickled onion/** *etc* oignon *m*/etc au vinaigre. **2 n in a p.** (*trouble*) *Fam* dans le pétrin.

pick-me-up ['pɪkmiːʌp] *n* (*drink*) *Fam* remontant *m*.

pickpocket ['pɪkpɒkɪt] *n* (*thief*) pickpocket *m*.

pick-up ['pɪkʌp] *n* (*person*) *Pej Fam* partenaire *mf* de rencontre; **p.-up** (*truck*) pick-up *m*; **p.-up point** (*for bus passengers*) point *m* de ramassage.

picky ['pɪkɪ] *a* (**-ier, -iest**) (*choosy*) *Am* difficile.

picnic ['pɪknɪk] *n* pique-nique *m*; **p. basket**, *Br* **p. hamper** panier *m* à pique-nique **|** *vi* (**-ck-**) pique-niquer.

pictorial [pɪk'tɔːrɪəl] *a* (*in pictures*) en images; (*periodical*) illustré.

picture ['pɪktʃər] **1** *n* image *f*; (*painting*) tableau *m*, peinture *f*; (*drawing*) dessin *m*; (*photo*) photo *f*; (*film*) film *m*; (*scene*) *Fig* tableau *m*; **the pictures** (*movies*) *Br Fam* le cinéma; **to put s.o. in the p.** *Fig* mettre qn au courant; **p. frame** cadre *m*. **2** *vt* (*imagine*) s'imaginer (**that** que); (*remember*) revoir; (*depict*) décrire.

picturesque [pɪktʃə'resk] *a* pittoresque.

piddling ['pɪdlɪŋ] *a Pej* dérisoire.

pidgin ['pɪdʒɪn] *n* **p. (English)** pidgin *m*.

pie [paɪ] *n* (*open*) tarte *f*; (*with pastry on top*) tourte *f*; **meat p.** pâté *m* en croûte; **cottage p.** *Br* hachis *m* Parmentier.

piebald ['paɪbɔːld] *a* (*pony etc*) pie *inv*.

piece [piːs] *n* morceau *m*; (*of bread, paper, chocolate etc*) bout *m*, morceau *m*; (*of fabric, machine, artillery, in game*) pièce *f*; (*coin*) pièce *f*; **bits and pieces** des petites choses; **in pieces** en morceaux, en pièces; **to smash to pieces** briser en morceaux; **to take to pieces** (*machine etc*) démonter; **to come to pieces** se démonter; **to go to pieces** (*of person*) *Fig* craquer; **a p. of news/advice/ luck/**etc une nouvelle/un conseil/une chance/ etc; **in one p.** (*object*) intact; (*person*) indemne.

| *vt* **to p. together** (*facts*) reconstituer; (*one's life*) refaire.

piecemeal ['piːsmiːl] *adv* petit à petit **|** *a* (*unsystematic*) peu méthodique.

piecework ['piːswɜːk] *n* travail *m* à la tâche *or* à la pièce.

pier [pɪər] *n* (*for walking, with entertainments*) jetée *f*; (*for landing*) appontement *m*.

pierce [pɪəs] *vt* percer (*qch*); (*of cold, bullet, sword etc*) transpercer (*qn*); **to have one's ears pierced** se faire percer les oreilles.
●**piercing** *a* (*voice, look etc*) perçant; (*wind*

etc) glacial.

piety ['paɪətɪ] *n* piété *f*.

piffling ['pɪflɪŋ] *a Fam* insignifiant.

pig [pɪg] *n* cochon *m*, porc *m*; (*glutton*) goinfre *m*; (*evil person*) cochon *m* **|** *vi* **to p. out** (*overeat*) *Am Fam* se goinfrer (**on** de).
●**piggish** *a* (*dirty*) sale; (*greedy*) goinfre.
●**piggy** *a* (*greedy*) *Fam* goinfre.

pigeon ['pɪdʒɪn] *n* pigeon *m*.

pigeonhole ['pɪdʒɪnhəʊl] *n* casier *m* **|** *vt* (*classify, label*) classer; (*shelve*) mettre en suspens.

piggyback ['pɪgɪbæk] *n* **to give s.o. a p.** porter qn sur le dos.

piggybank ['pɪgɪbæŋk] *n* tirelire *f* (*en forme de cochon*).

pigheaded [pɪg'hedɪd] *a* obstiné.

pigment ['pɪgmənt] *n* pigment *m*.
●**pigmentation** [-'teɪʃ(ə)n] *n* pigmentation *f*.

pigsty ['pɪgstaɪ] *n* porcherie *f*.

pigtail ['pɪgteɪl] *n* (*hair*) natte *f*.

pike [paɪk] *n* **1** (*fish*) brochet *m*. **2** (*weapon*) *Hist* pique *f*.

pilchard ['pɪltʃəd] *n* pilchard *m* (*grosse sardine*).

pile¹ [paɪl] *n* tas *m*; (*neatly arranged*) pile *f*; (*fortune*) *Fam* fortune *f*; **piles of, a p. of** *Fam* beaucoup de, un tas de **|** *vt* entasser; (*neatly*) empiler.

pile² [paɪl] *n* (*of carpet*) poils *mpl*.

pile into *vi* (*crowd into*) s'entasser dans **|** **to pile up** *vt* entasser; (*neatly*) empiler **|** *vi* (*accumulate*) s'accumuler.

piles [paɪlz] *npl* (*illness*) hémorroïdes *fpl*.

pile-up ['paɪlʌp] *n* (*on road*) carambolage *m*, collision *f* en chaîne.

pilfer ['pɪlfər] *vt* (*steal*) chaparder (**from s.o.** à qn).
●**pilfering** *or* **pilferage** *n* chapardage *m*.

pilgrim ['pɪlgrɪm] *n* pèlerin *m*.
●**pilgrimage** *n* pèlerinage *m*.

pill [pɪl] *n* pilule *f*; **to be on the p.** (*of woman*) prendre la pilule; **to go on/off the p.** se mettre à/arrêter la pilule.

pillage ['pɪlɪdʒ] *vti* piller **|** *n* pillage *m*.

pillar ['pɪlər] *n* pilier *m*; (*of smoke*) *Fig* colonne *f*.

pillar-box ['pɪləbɒks] *n Br* boîte *f* aux *or* à lettres (*située sur le trottoir*).

pillion ['pɪljən] *adv* **to ride p.** (*on motorbike*) monter derrière.

pillory ['pɪlərɪ] *vt* (*ridicule, scorn*) mettre au pilori.

pillow ['pɪləʊ] *n* oreiller *m*. ●**pillowcase** *or* **pillowslip** *n* taie *f* d'oreiller.

pilot ['paɪlət] **1** *n* (*of aircraft, ship*) pilote *m* **|** *vt* piloter **|** *a* **p. light** (*on appliance*) voyant *m*; (*on gas Br cooker or Am stove*) veilleuse *f*. **2** *a* (*experimental*) (-)pilote; **p. scheme** projet(-)pilote *m*.

pimento [pɪ'mentəʊ] *n* (*pl* **-os**) piment *m*.

pimp [pɪmp] *n* souteneur *m*.

pimple ['pɪmp(ə)l] *n* bouton *m*. ●**pimply** *a* (-**ier, -iest**) boutonneux.

pin [pɪn] *n* épingle *f*; (*drawing pin*) *Br* punaise *f*; (*in machine etc*) goupille *f*; **to have**

pins and needles *Fam* avoir des fourmis (**in** dans); **p. money** argent *m* de poche.

▮ *vt* (**-nn-**) **to p. (on)** (*attach*) épingler (**to** sur, à); (*to wall*) punaiser (**to, on** à); **to p. one's hopes on sth/s.o.** mettre tous ses espoirs dans qch/qn; **to p. a crime/etc on (to) s.o.** accuser qn d'un crime/etc; **to p. down** (*immobilize*) immobiliser; (*fix*) fixer; (*enemy*) clouer; **to p. s.o. down** *Fig* forcer qn à préciser ses idées; **to p. up** (*notice*) punaiser, afficher.

PIN [pɪn] *n abbr* (*personal identification number*) **P. number** *Br* code *m* confidentiel.

pinafore ['pɪnəfɔːr] *n* (*apron*) *Br* tablier *m*; (*dress*) robe *f* chasuble.

pinball ['pɪnbɔːl] *n* flipper *m*; **p. machine** flipper *m*.

pincers ['pɪnsəz] *npl* (*tool*) tenailles *fpl*.

pinch [pɪntʃ] **1** *n* (*mark*) pinçon *m*; (*of salt*) pincée *f*; **to give s.o. a p.** pincer qn; **at a p.** *Br*, **in a p.** *Am* (*if necessary*) au besoin; **to feel the p.** *Fig* souffrir (*du manque d'argent etc*) **▮** *vt* pincer **▮** *vi* (*of shoes*) faire mal. **2** *vt Br Fam* (*steal*) piquer (**from** à); (*arrest*) pincer.

pincushion ['pɪnkʊʃ(ə)n] *n* pelote *f* (à épingles).

pine [paɪn] **1** *n* (*tree, wood*) pin *m*; **p. forest** pinède *f*. **2** *vi* **to p. for** désirer vivement (retrouver), languir après; **to p. away** dépérir.

pineapple ['paɪnæp(ə)l] *n* ananas *m*.

ping [pɪŋ] *n* bruit *m* métallique. **●pinger** *n* (*on appliance*) signal *m* sonore.

ping-pong ['pɪŋpɒŋ] *n* ping-pong *m*.

pinhead ['pɪnhed] *n* tête *f* d'épingle; **it's the size of a p.** c'est gros comme une tête d'épingle.

pink [pɪŋk] *a* & *n* (*colour*) rose (*m*).

pinkie ['pɪŋkɪ] *n Am* petit doigt *m*.

pinnacle ['pɪnək(ə)l] *n* (*highest point*) *Fig* apogée *m*.

pinpoint ['pɪnpɔɪnt] *vt* (*locate*) repérer; (*define*) définir.

pinstripe ['pɪnstraɪp] *a* (*suit*) rayé.

pint [paɪnt] *n* pinte *f* (*Br* = 0,57 litre, *Am* = 0,47 litre); **a p. of beer** = un demi.

pinta ['paɪntə] *n Br Fam* demi-litre *m* de lait.

pinup ['pɪnʌp] *n* (*girl*) pin-up *f inv*.

pioneer [paɪə'nɪər] *n* pionnier, -ière *mf* **▮** *vt* (*research, study*) entreprendre pour la première fois.

pious ['paɪəs] *a* (*person, deed*) pieux.

pip [pɪp] **1** *n* (*of fruit*) *Br* pépin *m*. **2** *n* (*on military uniform*) *Br* galon *m*, *Fam* sardine *f*. **3** *npl* **the pips** (*sound on radio etc*) *Br* le top.

pipe [paɪp] **1** *n* tuyau *m*; (*of smoker*) pipe *f*; (*musical instrument*) pipeau *m*; **the pipes** (*bagpipes*) la cornemuse; (*peace*) **p.** calumet *m* de la paix; **to smoke a p.** fumer la pipe; **p. cleaner** cure-pipe *m*; **p. dream** chimère *f*.

▮ *vt* (*water etc*) transporter par tuyaux or par canalisation; **piped music** musique *f* (de fond) enregistrée.

2 *vi* **to p. down** (*shut up*) *Fam* la boucler, se taire. **●piping** *n* (*system of pipes*) canalisa-

tions *fpl*, tuyaux *mpl*; **length of p.** tuyau *m* **▮** *adv* **it's p. hot** (*soup etc*) c'est très chaud.

pipeline ['paɪplaɪn] *n* pipeline *m*; **it's in the p.** *Fig* c'est en route.

pique [piːk] *n* dépit *m*.

pirate ['paɪərət] *n* pirate *m* **▮** *a* (*radio, ship*) pirate. **●piracy** *n* piraterie *f*. **●pirated** *a* (*book, record, CD etc*) pirate.

Pisces ['paɪsiːz] *npl* (*sign*) les Poissons *mpl*.

pissed [pɪst] *a* (*drunk*) *Sl* rond, beurré.

pistachio [pɪ'stæʃɪəʊ] *n* (*pl* **-os**) (*fruit, flavour*) pistache *f*.

pistol ['pɪstəl] *n* pistolet *m*.

piston ['pɪst(ə)n] *n* (*of engine*) piston *m*.

pit [pɪt] **1** *n* (*hole*) trou *m*; (*mine*) mine *f*; (*quarry*) carrière *f*; (*of stomach*) creux *m*; (*in theatre*) *Br* orchestre *m*; (*in motor racing*) stand *m* de ravitaillement; **it's the pits** *Fam* c'est complètement nul. **2** *vt* (**-tt-**) **to p. oneself** or **one's wits against** se mesurer à. **3** *n* (*stone of fruit*) *Am* noyau *m* (*pl* noyaux); (*smaller*) pépin *m*.

pitch¹ [pɪtʃ] **1** *n Football etc* terrain *m*; (*in market*) place *f*. **2** *n* (*degree*) degré *m*; (*of voice*) hauteur *f*; (*musical*) ton *m*. **3** *vt* (*tent*) dresser; (*camp*) établir; (*ball*) lancer; **a pitched battle** (*between armies*) une bataille rangée; *Fig* une belle bagarre. **4** *vi* (*of ship*) tanguer. **5** *vi* **to p. in** (*cooperate*) *Fam* se mettre de la partie; **to p. into s.o.** attaquer qn.

pitch² [pɪtʃ] *n* (*tar*) poix *f*. **●pitch-'black** or **pitch-'dark** *a* noir comme dans un four.

pitcher ['pɪtʃər] *n* cruche *f*, broc *m*.

pitchfork ['pɪtʃfɔːk] *n* fourche *f* (à foin).

pitfall ['pɪtfɔːl] *n* (*trap*) piège *m*.

pith [pɪθ] *n* (*of orange*) peau *f* blanche; (*essence*) *Fig* moelle *f*. **●pithy** *a* (**-ier, -iest**) (*remark etc*) piquant et concis.

pitiful ['pɪtɪfəl] *a* pitoyable. **●pitiless** *a* impitoyable.

pitta ['piːtə] *a* & *n* **p.** (*bread*) pita *m*.

pittance ['pɪtəns] *n* (*income*) revenu *m* or salaire *m* misérable; (*sum*) somme *f* dérisoire.

pitted ['pɪtɪd] *a* **1** (*face*) grêlé; **p. with rust** piqué de rouille. **2** (*fruit*) *Am* dénoyauté.

pitter-patter ['pɪtəpætər] *n* = **patter 1**.

pity ['pɪtɪ] *n* pitié *f*; (**what) a p.!** (quel) dommage!; **it's a p.** c'est or il est dommage (**that** que (+ *sub*), **to do** de faire); **to take** or **have p. on s.o.** avoir pitié de qn **▮** *vt* plaindre.

pivot ['pɪvət] *n* pivot *m* **▮** *vi* pivoter.

pixie ['pɪksɪ] *n* (*fairy*) lutin *m*.

pizza ['piːtsə] *n* pizza *f*; **p. parlour** pizzeria *f*. **●pizzeria** [piːtsə'rɪə] *n* pizzeria *f*.

placard ['plækɑːd] *n* (*notice*) affiche *f*.

placate [*Br* plə'keɪt, *Am* 'pleɪkeɪt] *vt* calmer.

place [pleɪs] *n* endroit *m*, lieu *m*; (*house*) maison *f*; (*premises*) locaux *mpl*; (*seat, position, rank*) place *f*; **in the first p.** (*firstly*) en premier lieu; **to take p.** (*happen*) avoir lieu; **at my p., to my p.** *Fam* chez moi; **some p.** (*somewhere*) *Am* quelque part; **no p.** (*no-*

where) *Am* nulle part; **all over the p.** partout; **to lose one's p.** perdre sa place; (*in book etc*) perdre sa page; **to take the p. of** remplacer; **to change** *or* **swap** *or* **trade places** changer de place; **in p. of** à la place de; **out of p.** (*remark*) déplacé; (*object*) pas à sa place; **to feel out of p.** ne pas se sentir intégré; **p. of work** lieu *m* de travail; **market p.** (*square*) place *f* du marché; *Fin* marché *m*; **in the market p.** *Fin* sur le marché; **p. mat** set *m* (de table); **p. setting** couvert *m*; **to set** *or Br* **lay three places** (*at the table*) mettre trois couverts.

‖ *vt* (*put, situate, invest*) & *Sport* placer; (*an order*) *Com* passer (**with s.o.** à qn); **to p. s.o.** (*remember, identify*) remettre qn; **I can't p. him** je ne le remets pas. ●**placing** *n* (*of money*) placement *m*.

placid ['plæsɪd] *a* placide.

plagiarize ['pleɪdʒəraɪz] *vt* plagier. ●**plagiarism** [-ɪzəm] *n* plagiat *m*.

plague [pleɪg] **1** *n* (*disease*) peste *f*; (*nuisance*) *Fam* plaie *f*. **2** *vt* (*pester, harass*) harceler (**with** de).

plaice [pleɪs] *n* (*fish*) carrelet *m*, plie *f*.

plaid [plæd] *n* (*fabric*) tissu *m* écossais.

plain[1] [pleɪn] *a* (**-er, -est**) (*clear, obvious*) clair; (*simple*) simple; (*outspoken*) franc (*f* franche); (*sheer*) (*madness etc*) pur; (*without a pattern*) uni; (*woman, man*) sans beauté; **in p. clothes** en civil; **to make it p. to s.o. that** faire comprendre à qn que; **p. speaking** franc-parler *m* **‖** *adv* (*tired etc*) tout bonnement. ●**plainly** *adv* clairement; (*frankly*) franchement. ●**plainness** *n* clarté *f*; (*simplicity*) simplicité *f*; (*of woman, man*) manque *m* de beauté.

plain[2] [pleɪn] *n* (*land*) plaine *f*.

plaintiff ['pleɪntɪf] *n* (*in court of law*) plaignant, -ante *mf*.

plaintive ['pleɪntɪv] *a* (*tone etc*) plaintif.

plait [plæt] *n* tresse *f*, natte *f* **‖** *vt* tresser, natter.

plan [plæn] *n* projet *m*; (*elaborate*) plan *m*; (*economic, political, of house, book etc*) plan *m*; **the best p. would be to...** le mieux serait de...; **according to p.** comme prévu; **to have no plans** (*be free*) n'avoir rien de prévu; **to change one's plans** (*decide differently*) changer d'idée; **master p.** stratégie *f* d'ensemble; **pension p.** régime *m* de retraite.

‖ *vt* (**-nn-**) (*envisage, decide on*) prévoir, projeter; (*organize*) organiser; (*prepare*) préparer; (*design*) concevoir; *Econ* planifier; **to p. to do** *or* **on doing** (*intend*) avoir l'intention de faire; **as planned** comme prévu.

‖ *vi* faire des projets; **to p. for** (*rain, disaster*) prévoir.

plane [pleɪn] **1** *n* (*aircraft*) avion *m*. **2** *n* (*tool*) rabot *m* **‖** *vt* raboter. **3** *n* **p.** (*tree*) platane *m*. **4** *n* (*level, surface*) & *Fig* plan *m*; **on the economic p.** sur le plan économique.

planet ['plænɪt] *n* planète *f*. ●**plane'tarium** *n* planétarium *m*. ●**planetary** *a* planétaire.

plank [plæŋk] *n* planche *f*.

planner ['plænər] *n* (*economic*) planificateur, -trice *m*; (*town*) **p.** urbaniste *mf*.

planning ['plænɪŋ] *n* (*economic*) planification *f*; (*industrial, commercial*) planning *m*, planification *f*; (*organization*) organisation *f*; **family p.** planning *m* familial; **town p.** urbanisme *m*; **p. permission** permis *m* de construire.

plant [plɑːnt] **1** *n* plante *f*; **house p.** plante *f* verte **‖** *vt* (*flower etc*) planter; (*field etc*) planter (**with** en, de); (*bomb*) *Fig* (dé)poser; **to p. sth on s.o.** (*hide*) cacher qch sur qn. **2** *n* (*factory*) usine *f*; (*machinery*) matériel *m*; (*fixtures*) installation *f*. ●**plantation** [-'teɪʃ(ə)n] *n* (*trees, land etc*) plantation *f*.

plaque [plæk] *n* **1** (*commemorative plate*) plaque *f*. **2** (*on teeth*) plaque *f* dentaire.

plasma ['plæzmə] *n* (*in blood*) plasma *m*.

plaster ['plɑːstər] *n* (*substance*) plâtre *m*; (*sticking*) **p.** *Br* sparadrap *m*; **p. of Paris** plâtre *m* à mouler; **in p.** (*arm etc*) dans le plâtre; **p. cast** (*for broken arm etc*) plâtre *m* **‖** *vt* plâtrer; **to p. down** (*hair*) plaquer; **to p. with** (*cover*) couvrir de. ●**plastered** *a* (*drunk*) *Fam* bourré. ●**plasterer** *n* plâtrier *m*.

plastic ['plæstɪk] *a* (*object*) en plastique; (*substance, art*) plastique; **p. bag** sac *m* en plastique; **p. explosive** plastic *m*; **p. surgery** chirurgie *f* esthétique **‖** *n* plastique *m*, matière *f* plastique.

plasticine® ['plæstɪsiːn] *n Br* pâte *f* à modeler.

plate [pleɪt] *n* (*dish*) assiette *f*; (*metal sheet on door, on vehicle etc*) plaque *f*; (*book illustration*) gravure *f*; (*dental*) dentier *m*; **gold/silver p.** vaisselle *f* d'or/d'argent; **to have a lot on one's p.** (*work etc*) avoir du pain sur la planche; (*worries*) avoir largement son lot de soucis; **p. glass** verre *m* à vitre **‖** *vt* (*jewels, metal*) plaquer (**with** de). ●**plateful** *n* assiettée *f*, assiette *f*.

plateau ['plætəʊ] *n* (*pl* **-s** *or* **-x**) (*flat land*) plateau *m*.

platform ['plætfɔːm] *n* (*at train station*) quai *m*; (*on bus etc*) plate-forme *f*; (*for speaker etc*) estrade *f*; **p. shoes** chaussures *fpl* à semelles compensées.

platinum ['plætɪnəm] *n* (*metal*) platine *m* **‖** *a* **p.** *or* **p.-blond(e) hair** cheveux *mpl* platinés.

platitude ['plætɪtjuːd] *n* platitude *f*.

platonic [plə'tɒnɪk] *a* (*love, relationship etc*) platonique.

platoon [plə'tuːn] *n* (*of soldiers*) section *f*.

platter ['plætər] *n* (*dish*) plat *m*.

plaudits ['plɔːdɪts] *npl* (*commendation*) *Lit* applaudissements *mpl*.

plausible ['plɔːzəb(ə)l] *a* (*argument etc*) plausible; (*speaker etc*) convaincant.

play [pleɪ] *n* (*in theatre*) pièce *f* (de théâtre); (*amusement, looseness*) jeu *m*; **a p. on words** un jeu de mots; **to come into p.** entrer en jeu; **to call into p.** faire entrer en jeu.

‖ *vt* (*part, tune, card etc*) jouer; (*game*) jouer à; (*instrument*) jouer de; (*match*) disputer (**with** avec); (*team, opponent*) jouer contre;

(*record*, *compact disc*) passer; (*radio*, *tape recorder*) faire marcher; **to p. the fool** faire l'idiot; **to p. a part in doing/in sth** contribuer à faire/à qch; **to p. ball with** *Fig* coopérer avec; **to p. it cool** *Fam* garder son sang-froid. ▪ *vi* jouer (**with** avec, **at** à); (*of record player, tape recorder*) marcher; **what are you playing at?** *Fam* qu'est-ce que tu fais?

play about *or* **around** *vi* jouer, s'amuser ▪ **to play back** *vt* (*tape*) réécouter ▪ **to play down** *vt* (*reduce the importance of*) minimiser ▪ **to play on** *vt* (*piano etc*) jouer de; (*s.o.'s emotions etc*) jouer sur ▪ **to play out** *vt* (*scene, fantasy etc*) jouer; **to be played out** *Fam* (*of idea, method etc*) être périmé *or* vieux jeu *inv* ▪ **to play up** *vi* (*of child, machine etc*) *Fam* faire des siennes; **to p. up to s.o.** *Fam* faire de la lèche à qn ▪ *vt* **to p. s.o. up** (*of child etc*) *Fam* faire enrager qn; (*of bad back etc*) tracasser qn.

play-act ['pleɪækt] *vi* jouer la comédie. ● **playboy** *n* playboy *m*. ● **playgoer** *n* amateur *m* de théâtre. ● **playground** *n* (*in school*) *Br* cour *f* de récréation; (*with swings etc*) terrain *m* de jeux. ● **playgroup** *n* = **playschool**. ● **playmate** *n* camarade *mf*. ● **playpen** *n* parc *m* (pour enfants). ● **playroom** *n* (*in house*) salle *f* de jeux. ● **playschool** *n* garderie *f* (d'enfants). ● **plaything** *n* (*toy, Fig person*) jouet *m*. ● **playtime** *n* (*in school*) récréation *f*. ● **playwright** *n* dramaturge *mf*.

player ['pleɪər] *n* (*in game, of instrument*) joueur, -euse *mf*; (*in theatre*) acteur *m*, actrice *f*; **clarinet/etc** p. joueur, -euse *mf* de clarinette/etc; **cassette/CD** p. lecteur *m* de cassettes/de CD.

playful ['pleɪfəl] *a* enjoué; (*child*) joueur. ● **playfully** *adv* (*to say*) en badinant. ● **playfulness** *n* enjouement *m*.

playing ['pleɪɪŋ] *n* jeu *m*; **p. card** carte *f* à jouer; **p. field** terrain *m* de jeu.

plc [pi:el'si:] *abbr* (*public limited company*) *Br* SA.

plea [pli:] *n* (*request*) appel *m*; (*excuse*) excuse *f*; **to make a p. of guilty** plaider coupable.

plead [pli:d] *vi* (*in court*) plaider; **to p. with s.o. to do** implorer qn de faire; **to p. for** (*help etc*) implorer ▪ *vt* (*argue*) plaider; (*as excuse*) alléguer. ● **pleading** *n* (*requests*) prières *fpl*.

pleasant ['plezənt] *a* agréable; (*polite*) aimable, agréable (**to** avec). ● **pleasantly** *adv* agréablement. ● **pleasantness** *n* (*charm*) charme *m*; (*of person*) amabilité *f*.

pleasantries ['plezəntrɪz] *npl* (*polite remarks*) civilités *fpl*; (*jokes*) plaisanteries *fpl*.

please [pli:z] *adv* s'il vous plaît, s'il te plaît; **p. sit down** asseyez-vous, je vous prie, veuillez vous asseoir; **p. do!** bien sûr!, je vous en prie!; **'no smoking p.'** 'prière de ne pas fumer'.

▪ *vt* **to p. s.o.** plaire à qn; (*satisfy*) contenter qn; **hard to p.** difficile (à contenter), exigeant; **p. yourself!** comme tu veux!

▪ *vi* plaire; **do as you p.** fais comme tu veux; **as much** *or* **as many as you p.** autant qu'il vous plaira. ● **pleased** *a* content (**with** de, **that** que (+ *sub*), **to do** de faire); **p. to meet you!** enchanté!; **I'd be p. to!** avec plaisir! ● **pleasing** *a* agréable, plaisant.

pleasure ['pleʒər] *n* plaisir *m*; **p. boat** bateau *m* de plaisance. ● **pleasurable** *a* très agréable.

pleat [pli:t] *n* (*fold in skirt etc*) pli *m* ▪ *vt* plisser. ● **pleated** *a* (*skirt etc*) plissé.

plebiscite [*Br* 'plebɪsɪt, *Am* -saɪt] *n* plébiscite *m*.

pledge [pledʒ] **1** *n* (*promise*) promesse *f*, engagement *m* (**to do** de faire) ▪ *vt* promettre (**to do** de faire). **2** *n* (*token, object*) gage *m* ▪ *vt* (*as security, pawn*) engager.

plenty ['plentɪ] *n* abondance *f*; **in p.** en abondance; **p. of** beaucoup de; **that's p.** (*enough*) c'est assez, ça suffit. ● **plentiful** *a* abondant.

plethora ['pleθərə] *n* (*amount*) pléthore *f*.

pleurisy ['plʊərɪsɪ] *n* (*illness*) pleurésie *f*.

pliable ['plaɪəb(ə)l] *a* souple.

pliers ['plaɪəz] *npl* (*tool*) pince(s) *f(pl)*.

plight [plaɪt] *n* (*crisis*) situation *f* critique; (*sorry*) p. triste situation *f*.

plimsoll ['plɪmsəʊl] *n* *Br* chaussure *f* de tennis, tennis *m*.

plinth [plɪnθ] *n* socle *m*.

plod [plɒd] *vi* (**-dd-**) **to p.** (**along**) (*walk etc*) avancer laborieusement; (*work*) travailler laborieusement; **to p. through** (*book*) lire laborieusement. ● **plodding** *a* (*slow*) lent; (*step*) pesant. ● **plodder** *n* (*steady worker*) bûcheur, -euse *mf*.

plonk [plɒŋk] **1** *int* (*thud*) vlan!; (*splash*) plouf! **2** *vt* **to p. sth** (**down**) (*drop*) *Fam* poser qch (bruyamment). **3** *n* (*wine*) *Br Sl* pinard *m*.

plot [plɒt] **1** *n* (*conspiracy*) complot *m* (**against** contre); (*story of novel, film etc*) intrigue *f* ▪ *vti* (**-tt-**) comploter (**to do** de faire). **2** *n* **p.** (**of land**) terrain *m*; (*patch in garden*) carré *m* de terre; **building p.** terrain *m* à bâtir. **3** *vt* (**-tt-**) **to p.** (**out**) (*route etc*) déterminer; (*diagram, graph*) tracer; (*one's position*) relever. ● **plotting** *n* (*conspiracies*) complots *mpl*.

plough [plaʊ] (*Am* **plow**) *n* charrue *f* ▪ *vt* (*field etc*) labourer; **to p. money into sth** mettre *or* investir beaucoup d'argent dans qch; **to p. money back into sth** réinvestir de l'argent dans qch ▪ *vi* labourer; **to p. into** (*crash into*) percuter; **to p. through** (*snow etc*) avancer péniblement dans; (*fence, wall*) défoncer. ● **ploughman** *n* (*pl* **-men**) laboureur *m*; **p.'s lunch** (*snack*) *Br* assiette *f* composée (*de crudités et fromage*).

plow [plaʊ] *n & vti Am* = **plough**.

ploy [plɔɪ] *n* stratagème *m*.

pluck [plʌk] **1** *vt* (*fowl*) plumer; (*flower*) cueillir; (*eyebrows*) épiler; (*string of guitar etc*) pincer. **2** *n* courage *m* ▪ *vt* **to p. up courage** s'armer de courage. ● **plucky** *a* (**-ier,**

-iest) courageux.

plug [plʌg] **1** n (of Br cotton wool, Am absorbent cotton, wood etc) tampon m; (for sink or bath drainage) bonde f; (wall) p. (for screw) cheville f ▮ vt (-gg-) **to p. (up)** (stop up) boucher.

2 n (electrical) fiche f, prise f (mâle); (socket) prise f de courant ▮ vt (-gg-) **to p. in** (appliance etc) brancher.

3 n (in vehicle engine) bougie f.

4 n (publicity) Fam battage m publicitaire ▮ vt (-gg-) Fam faire du battage publicitaire pour.

5 vi (-gg-) **to p. away** (work) Fam bosser (at à). ●**plughole** n trou m (du lavabo etc), vidange f.

plum [plʌm] n prune f; **a p. job** Fam un travail en or, un bon fromage.

plumage ['plu:mɪdʒ] n plumage m.

plumb [plʌm] **1** vt **to p. in** (washing machine) raccorder, installer. **2** vt **to p. the depths** (of despair) toucher le fond. **3** vt (probe, understand) Lit sonder. **4** adv (crazy etc) Am Fam complètement; **p. in the middle** en plein milieu.

plumber ['plʌmər] n plombier m. ●**plumbing** n plomberie f.

plume [plu:m] n (feather) plume f; (on hat etc) plumet m; **a p. of smoke** un panache de fumée.

plummet ['plʌmɪt] vi (of prices) dégringoler; (of aircraft etc) plonger.

plump [plʌmp] **1** a (-er, -est) (person, arm etc) potelé; (chicken) dodu; (cushion, cheek) rebondi. **2** vi **to p. for** (choose) se décider pour, choisir. ●**plumpness** n rondeur f.

plunder ['plʌndər] vt piller ▮ n (act) pillage m; (goods) butin m.

plunge [plʌndʒ] vt (thrust) plonger (qch) (into dans) ▮ vi (dive) plonger (into dans); (fall) tomber (from de); (rush) se lancer ▮ n (dive) plongeon m; (fall) chute f; **to take the p.** (take on a difficult task) sauter le pas, se jeter à l'eau; (get married) se marier. ●**plunger** n ventouse f (pour déboucher un tuyau), débouchoir m. ●**plunging neckline** n décolleté m plongeant.

plural ['pluərəl] a (form) pluriel; (noun) au pluriel ▮ n pluriel m; **in the p.** au pluriel.

plus [plʌs] prep plus; (as well as) en plus de; **two p. two** deux plus deux ▮ a (factor, quantity etc) & El positif; **twenty p.** vingt et quelques ▮ n p. (sign) (signe m) plus m; **that's a p.** c'est un plus.

plush [plʌʃ] a (-er, -est) (splendid) somptueux.

plutonium [plu:'təʊnɪəm] n plutonium m.

ply [plaɪ] **1** vt (trade) exercer; (oar, tool) Lit manier. **2** vi **to p. between** (travel) faire la navette entre. **3** vt **to p. s.o. with** (whisky etc) faire boire continuellement à qn; (questions) bombarder qn de.

plywood ['plaɪwʊd] n contre-plaqué m.

p.m. [pi:'em] adv (afternoon) de l'après-midi; (evening) du soir.

PM [pi:'em] n abbr (Prime Minister) Premier ministre m.

pneumatic [nju:'mætɪk] a **p. drill** marteau-piqueur m, marteau m pneumatique.

pneumonia [nju:'məʊnɪə] n pneumonie f.

poach [pəʊtʃ] **1** vt (egg) pocher. **2** vi (hunt, steal) braconner ▮ vt (employee from rival company) débaucher, piquer. ●**poaching** n braconnage m. ●**poacher** n **1** (person) braconnier m. **2** (egg) pocheuse f.

PO Box [pi:əʊ'bɒks] abbr (Post Office Box) boîte f postale, BP f.

pocket ['pɒkɪt] n poche f; (small area) Fig petite zone f; (of resistance) poche f, îlot m; **i'm 50 francs out of p.** j'ai perdu 50 francs; **p. money/handkerchief/etc** argent m/mouchoir m/etc de poche; **p. calculator** calculatrice f de poche ▮ vt (gain, steal) empocher. ●**pocketbook** n (notebook) carnet m; (woman's handbag) Am sac m à main. ●**pocketful** n **a p. of** une pleine poche de.

pockmarked ['pɒkmɑ:kt] a (face) grêlé.

pod [pɒd] n cosse f.

podgy ['pɒdʒɪ] a (-ier, -iest) (person) rondelet (f -ette); (arm etc) dodu.

podiatrist [pə'daɪətrɪst] n Am pédicure mf.

podium ['pəʊdɪəm] n podium m.

poem ['pəʊɪm] n poème m. ●**poet** n poète m. ●**po'etic** a poétique. ●**poetry** n poésie f.

po-faced ['pəʊfeɪst] a (expression, person) Pej Fam pincé.

poignant ['pɔɪnjənt] a poignant.

point [pɔɪnt] **1** n (of knife etc) pointe f; **points** (for train) Br aiguillage m; (power) p. Br prise f (de courant).

2 n (dot, position, score, degree, question etc) point m; (decimal) virgule f; (meaning) sens m; (importance) intérêt m; (remark) remarque f; **p. of view** point m de vue; **at this p. (in time)** en ce moment; **on the p. of doing** sur le point de faire; **what's the p.?** à quoi bon? (of waiting/etc attendre/etc); **there's no p. (in) staying/etc** ça ne sert à rien de rester/etc; **that's not the p.** il ne s'agit pas de ça; **that's beside the p.** c'est à côté de la question; **to the p.** (relevant) pertinent; **get to the p.!** au fait!; **to make a p. of doing** prendre garde de faire; **his good points** ses qualités fpl; **his bad points** ses défauts mpl.

3 vt (aim) pointer (at sur); (vehicle) tourner (towards vers); **to p. the way** indiquer le chemin (to à); Fig montrer la voie (to à); **to p. one's finger** at montrer du doigt; **to p. out** (show) indiquer; (mention) signaler (to à, that que) ▮ vi (of person) montrer du doigt; **to p. at** or **to s.o./sth** (with finger) montrer qn/qch; **to p. to,** be **pointing to** (indicate) indiquer; **everything points to success** tout indique qu'il réussira, que nous réussirons etc; **to p. east** indiquer l'est; **to be pointing at** (of gun) être braqué sur; **to be pointing towards** (of vehicle) être tourné vers.

point-blank [pɔɪnt'blæŋk] adv & a (to shoot, a shot) à bout portant; (to refuse, a refusal) Fig (tout) net; (to request, a request) de but en blanc.

pointed ['pɔɪntɪd] a pointu; (beard) en pointe; (remark, criticism) Fig pertinent; (incisive) mordant. ●**pointedly** adv (to the point) avec pertinence; (incisively) d'un ton mordant.

pointer ['pɔɪntər] n (on dial etc) index m; (advice) conseil m; (clue) indice m; to be a p. to (possible solution etc) laisser entrevoir.

pointless ['pɔɪntləs] a inutile, futile. ●**pointlessly** adv inutilement.

poise [pɔɪz] n (confidence) assurance f; (composure) calme m; (grace) grâce f; (bearing) port m; (balance) équilibre m ▮ vt tenir en équilibre. ●**poised** a (composed) calme; (hanging) suspendu; (balanced) en équilibre; p. to attack/etc (ready) prêt à attaquer/etc.

poison ['pɔɪz(ə)n] n poison m; (of snake) venin m; p. gas gaz m toxique ▮ vt empoisonner; to p. s.o.'s mind corrompre qn. ●**poisoning** n empoisonnement m.

poisonous ['pɔɪzənəs] a (fumes, substance) toxique; (snake) venimeux; (plant) vénéneux.

poke [pəʊk] vt (push) pousser (du doigt, avec un bâton etc); (touch) toucher; (fire) tisonner; to p. sth into sth (put, thrust) fourrer or enfoncer qch dans qch; to p. one's finger at s.o. pointer son doigt vers qn; to p. one's nose into sth fourrer le nez dans qch; to p. a hole in sth faire un trou dans qch; to p. one's head out of the window passer la tête par la fenêtre; to p. out s.o.'s eye crever un œil à qn.
▮ vi pousser; to p. about or around in (drawer etc) fouiner dans.
▮ n (jab) (petit) coup m; (shove) poussée f, coup m.

poker ['pəʊkər] n 1 (for fire) tisonnier m. 2 Cards poker m.

poky ['pəʊkɪ] a (-ier, -iest) (small) (house, room etc) Br exigu (f -guë) et misérable; (slow) Am lent.

Poland ['pəʊlənd] n Pologne f. ●**Pole** n Polonais, -aise mf.

polarize ['pəʊləraɪz] vt polariser.

Polaroid ['pəʊlərɔɪd] n (camera) Polaroïd m.

pole [pəʊl] n 1 (rod) perche f; (fixed) poteau m; (for flag) mât m; p. vaulting Sport saut m à la perche. 2 Geog pôle m; North/South P. pôle Nord/Sud. ●**polar** a polaire; p. bear ours m blanc.

polemic [pə'lemɪk] n polémique f. ●**polemical** a polémique.

police [pə'liːs] n police f; more or extra p. des renforts mpl de police ▮ a (inquiry, dog, State etc) policier; (protection, intervention) de la police; p. cadet Br agent m de police stagiaire; p. car voiture f de police; p. chief, chief of p. Am commissaire m de police; the p. department Am la police; p. force police f; p. station commissariat m de police; p. van Br fourgon m cellulaire.
▮ vt (city etc) maintenir l'ordre or la paix dans; (frontier) contrôler. ●**policeman** n (pl

-men) agent m de police. ●**policewoman** n (pl -women) femme-agent f.

policy ['pɒlɪsɪ] n 1 (of government, organization etc) politique f; (individual course of action) règle f, façon f d'agir; policies (ways of governing) politique f; it's a matter of p. c'est une question de principe. 2 (insurance) p. police f (d'assurance); p. holder assuré, -ée mf.

polio ['pəʊlɪəʊ] n polio f; p. victim polio mf. ●**poliomyelitis** [-maɪə'laɪtɪs] n poliomyélite f.

polish ['pɒlɪʃ] vt (floor, table, shoes etc) cirer; (metal) astiquer; (rough surface) polir; (manners) Fig raffiner; (style) Fig polir; to p. off (food, work etc) Fam liquider, finir (en vitesse); to p. up one's French/etc travailler son français/etc.
▮ n (for shoes) cirage m; (for floor, furniture) cire f; (shine) vernis m; Fig raffinement m; (nail) p. vernis m (à ongles); to give sth a p. faire briller qch.

Polish ['pəʊlɪʃ] a polonais ▮ n (language) polonais m.

polite [pə'laɪt] a (-er, -est) poli (to, with avec); in p. society dans la bonne société. ●**politely** adv poliment. ●**politeness** n politesse f.

politic ['pɒlɪtɪk] a (tactful) habile, avisé.

political [pə'lɪtɪk(ə)l] a politique. ●**politicize** vt politiser.

politician [pɒlɪ'tɪʃ(ə)n] n homme m or femme f politique.

politics ['pɒlɪtɪks] n politique f.

polka [Br 'pɒlkə, Am 'pəʊlkə] n (dance) polka f; p. dot pois m.

poll [pəʊl] n (voting) scrutin m, élection f; (vote) vote m; (turnout) participation f électorale; (list) liste f électorale; to go to the polls aller aux urnes; (opinion) p. sondage m (d'opinion); 50% of the p. 50% des votants.
▮ vt (votes) obtenir; (people) sonder l'opinion de. ●**polling** n (election) élections fpl; p. booth isoloir m; p. station Br, p. place Am bureau m de vote.

pollen ['pɒlən] n pollen m.

pollute [pə'luːt] vt polluer. ●**pollutant** n polluant m. ●**pollution** [-ʃ(ə)n] n pollution f; noise p. pollution f sonore.

polo ['pəʊləʊ] n Sport polo m; p. neck (sweater, neckline) col m roulé.

polyester [pɒlɪ'estər] n polyester m; p. shirt/etc chemise f/etc en polyester.

Polynesia [pɒlɪ'niːʒə] n Polynésie f.

polyp ['pɒlɪp] n (growth) polype m.

polystyrene [pɒlɪ'staɪriːn] n polystyrène m.

polytechnic [pɒlɪ'teknɪk] n Br institut m universitaire de technologie, IUT m.

polythene ['pɒlɪθiːn] n Br polyéthylène m; p. bag sac m en plastique.

polyunsaturated [pɒlɪʌn'sætʃʊreɪtɪd] a (oil etc) polyinsaturé.

pomegranate ['pɒmɪgrænɪt] n (fruit) grenade f.

pomp [pɒmp] n pompe f, faste m.

pompon ['pɒmpɒn] n (ornament) pompon m.

pompous ['pɒmpəs] a pompeux. ● **pom'posity** n emphase f, solennité f.

poncho ['pɒntʃəʊ] n (pl -os) poncho m.

pond [pɒnd] n étang m; (stagnant) mare f; (artificial) bassin m.

ponder ['pɒndər] vt to p. (over) sth réfléchir à qch ▮ vi réfléchir.

ponderous ['pɒndərəs] a (heavy, slow) pesant.

pong [pɒŋ] n (stink) Br Sl mauvaise odeur f ▮ vi Br Sl schlinguer, puer.

pontificate [pɒn'tɪfɪkeɪt] vi (speak pompously) pontifier (about sur).

pony ['pəʊnɪ] n poney m. ● **ponytail** n (hair) queue f de cheval.

poodle ['puːd(ə)l] n caniche m.

poof [pʊf] n (homosexual) Br Pej Sl pédé m.

pooh [puː] int bah!; (bad smell) ça pue!

pooh-pooh [puː'puː] vt (scorn) dédaigner; (dismiss) se moquer de.

pool [puːl] 1 n (puddle) flaque f; (of blood) mare f; (for swimming) piscine f; (pond) étang m.
2 n (of experience, talent) réservoir m; (of advisers etc) équipe f; (of typists) pool m; (kitty in games) cagnotte f; (football) **pools** Br pronostics mpl (sur les matchs de football) ▮ vt (share) mettre en commun; (combine) unir.
3 n (billiards) billard m américain.

pooped [puːpt] a (exhausted) Am Fam vanné, crevé.

poor [pʊər] a (-er, -est) (not rich, deserving pity) pauvre; (bad) mauvais; (inferior) médiocre; (meagre) maigre; (weak) faible; **p. thing!** le or la pauvre! ▮ n the p. les pauvres mpl. ● **poorly** 1 adv (badly) mal; (clothed, furnished) pauvrement. 2 a (ill) Br malade.

pop¹ [pɒp] 1 int pan! ▮ n (noise) bruit m sec; **to go p.** faire pan; (of champagne bottle) faire pop ▮ vt (-pp-) (balloon etc) crever; (bottle top, button) faire sauter ▮ vi (burst) crever; (come off) sauter; (of ears) se déboucher.
2 vt (put) Fam mettre ▮ vi Br Fam (go) **to p. in** entrer (un instant); **to p. off** partir; **to p. out** sortir (un instant); **to p. over** or **round** faire un saut (to chez); **to p. up** (of person) surgir, réapparaître; (of question etc) surgir.

pop² [pɒp] 1 n (music) pop m ▮ a (concert, singer etc) pop inv. 2 n (father) Am Fam papa m. 3 n (soda) **p.** (drink) Am soda m.

popcorn ['pɒpkɔːn] n pop-corn m.

pope [pəʊp] n pape m.

pop-eyed ['pɒp'aɪd] a aux yeux écarquillés.

poplar ['pɒplər] n (tree, wood) peuplier m.

popper ['pɒpər] n (on clothes, bags etc) Br pression f.

poppy ['pɒpɪ] n (red, wild) coquelicot m; (cultivated) pavot m.

popsicle® ['pɒpsɪk(ə)l] n (ice lolly) Am = esquimau m.

popular ['pɒpjʊlər] a (person, song, vote, science etc) populaire; (fashionable) à la mode; **to be p. with** plaire beaucoup à. ● **popu'larity** n popularité f (with auprès de). ● **popularize** vt populariser; (science, knowledge) vulgariser. ● **popularly** adv communément.

populate ['pɒpjʊleɪt] vt peupler; **highly/sparsely/etc populated** très/peu/etc peuplé; **populated by** or **with** peuplé de.

population [pɒpjʊ'leɪʃ(ə)n] n population f.

populous ['pɒpjʊləs] a (crowded) populeux.

pop-up book ['pɒpʌpbʊk] n livre m en relief.

porcelain ['pɔːsəlɪn] n porcelaine f.

porch [pɔːtʃ] n porche m; (veranda) Am véranda f.

porcupine ['pɔːkjʊpaɪn] n porc-épic m.

pore [pɔːr] 1 n (of skin) pore m. 2 vi **to p. over** (book, question etc) étudier de près. ● **porous** a poreux.

pork [pɔːk] n (meat) porc m; **p. butcher** charcutier, -ière m; **p. pie** pâté m (de porc) en croûte.

pornography [pɔː'nɒgrəfɪ] n (Fam **porn**) pornographie f. ● **porno'graphic** a pornographique, porno (f inv).

porpoise ['pɔːpəs] n (sea animal) marsouin m.

porridge ['pɒrɪdʒ] n porridge m (bouillie de flocons d'avoine); **p. oats** flocons mpl d'avoine.

port [pɔːt] 1 n (harbour) port m; **p. of call** escale f ▮ a (authorities, installations etc) portuaire. 2 n **p. (side)** (left in ship or aircraft) bâbord m ▮ a de bâbord. 3 n (wine) porto m.

portable ['pɔːtəb(ə)l] a portable, portatif.

portal ['pɔːt(ə)l] n portail m.

porter ['pɔːtər] n 1 (for luggage) porteur m. 2 Br (doorman) (of hotel) portier m; (caretaker) concierge m; (of public building) gardien, -ienne mf.

portfolio [pɔːt'fəʊlɪəʊ] n (pl -os) (for documents) serviette f; (of shares etc) & Pol portefeuille m.

porthole ['pɔːthəʊl] n (in ship, aircraft) hublot m.

portico ['pɔːtɪkəʊ] n (pl -oes or -os) (with pillars) portique m; (of house) porche m.

portion ['pɔːʃ(ə)n] n (share, helping) portion f; (of train, book etc) partie f ▮ vt **to p. out** répartir.

portly ['pɔːtlɪ] a (-ier, -iest) corpulent.

portrait ['pɔːtreɪt, 'pɔːtrɪt] n portrait m; **p. painter** portraitiste mf.

portray [pɔː'treɪ] vt (describe) représenter. ● **portrayal** n représentation f, portrait m.

Portugal ['pɔːtjʊg(ə)l] n Portugal m. ● **Portu'guese** a portugais ▮ n (language) portugais m ▮ n inv (person) Portugais, -aise mf.

pose [pəʊz] 1 n (of model etc in art or photography) & Fig pose f ▮ vi (of model etc) poser (for pour); **to p. as a lawyer/etc** se faire passer pour un avocat/etc. 2 vt (question) poser. ●**poser** n 1 (*question*) *Fam* colle f. 2 = poseur. ●**poseur** [-'zɜːr] n (*show-off*) poseur, -euse mf.

posh [pɒʃ] a *Fam* (*smart*) chic inv; (*snobbish*) snob (f inv).

position [pə'zɪʃ(ə)n] n (*place, posture, opinion etc*) position f; (*of building, town*) emplacement m, position f; (*job, circumstances*) situation f; (*customer window in bank etc*) guichet m; **in a p. to do sth** en mesure or en position de faire qch; **in a good p.** to do sth bien placé pour faire qch; **in p.** en place, en position ▮ vt (*camera, machine etc*) mettre en position; (*put*) placer.

positive ['pɒzɪtɪv] a positif; (*progress, change*) réel; (*order*) catégorique; (*tone*) assuré; (*sure*) sûr, certain (**of** de, **that** que); **p. reply** (*saying yes*) réponse f affirmative; **a p. genius** *Fam* un vrai génie. ●**positively** adv (*for certain*) positivement; (*undeniably*) indéniablement; (*completely*) complètement; (*categorically*) catégoriquement; **to reply p.** (*saying yes*) répondre par l'affirmative.

possess [pə'zes] vt posséder. ●**possession** [-ʃ(ə)n] n (*ownership*) possession f; **possessions** (*belongings*) biens mpl; **in p. of** en possession de; **to take p. of** prendre possession de. ●**possessor** n possesseur m.

possessive [pə'zesɪv] 1 a (*person, attitude etc*) possessif. 2 a & n *Grammar* possessif m.

possibility [pɒsɪ'bɪlɪtɪ] n possibilité f; **there is some p. of** il y a quelques chances de; **there's some p. that** il est (tout juste) possible que (+ *sub*); **she has possibilities** elle promet; **it's a distinct p.** c'est bien possible.

possible ['pɒsəb(ə)l] a possible; **it is p.** (**for us**) **to do it** il (nous) est possible de le faire; **it is p. that** il est possible que (+ *sub*); **as far as p.** autant que possible; **if p.** si possible; **as much** or **as many as p.** le plus possible ▮ n (*person, object*) *Fam* choix m possible.

possibly ['pɒsɪblɪ] adv 1 (*perhaps*) peut-être. 2 (*with can, could etc*) **if you p. can** si cela t'est possible; **to do all one p. can** faire tout son possible (**to do** pour faire); **he cannot p. stay** il ne peut absolument pas rester.

post¹ [pəʊst] n *Br* (*postal system*) poste f; (*letters*) courrier m; **by p.** par la poste; **to catch/miss the p.** avoir/manquer la levée; **p. office** (*bureau m de*) poste f; **the P. Office** (*administration*) les postes fpl, le service des postes ▮ vt (*put in postbox*) poster, mettre à la poste; (*send*) envoyer; **to keep s.o. posted** (*informed*) tenir qn au courant.

post² [pəʊst] n (*job, place*) poste m; (*of soldier, sailor etc*) poste m ▮ vt (*sentry, guard*) poster; (*employee*) *Br* affecter (**to** à). ●**posting** n (*appointment*) *Br* affectation f.

post³ [pəʊst] n (*pole*) poteau m; (*of door, bed*) montant m; **finishing** or **winning p.** (*in race*) poteau m d'arrivée ▮ vt **to p.** (**up**) (*notice etc*) afficher, coller.

post- [pəʊst] pref post-; **p.-1800** après 1800.

postage ['pəʊstɪdʒ] n tarif m (postal), tarifs mpl (postaux) (**to** pour); **p. stamp** timbre-poste m.

postal ['pəʊstəl] a (*services, district etc*) postal; (*inquiries*) par la poste; (*vote*) par correspondance; **p. worker** employé, -ée mf des postes; **p. van** *Br* camion m des postes.

postbag ['pəʊstbæg] n *Br* sac m postal. ●**postbox** n *Br* boîte f aux or à lettres. ●**postcard** n carte f postale. ●**postcode** n *Br* code m postal. ●**post-'free** *Br* or **post'paid** adv franco.

postdate [pəʊst'deɪt] vt postdater.

poster ['pəʊstər] n affiche f; (*for decoration*) poster m.

posterior [pɒ'stɪərɪər] n (*buttocks*) *Hum* postérieur m.

posterity [pɒ'sterɪtɪ] n postérité f.

postgraduate [pəʊst'grædʒʊət] n étudiant, -ante mf de troisième cycle ▮ a (*studies etc*) de troisième cycle.

posthumous ['pɒstjʊməs] a (*publication etc*) posthume; **to receive a p. award/etc** recevoir un prix/etc à titre posthume. ●**posthumously** adv à titre posthume.

postman ['pəʊstmən] n (pl -men) facteur m. ●**postmark** n cachet m de la poste ▮ vt litérer. ●**postmaster** n *Br* receveur m (des postes). ●**postmistress** n *Br* receveuse f (des postes).

post-mortem [pəʊst'mɔːtəm] n **p.-mortem** (*examination*) autopsie f (**on** de).

postnatal ['pəʊstneɪt(ə)l] a (*checkup etc*) postnatal (mpl -als); **p. depression** dépression f d'après l'accouchement.

postpone [pə'spəʊn] vt remettre (**for** de, **until** à), renvoyer (à plus tard). ●**postponement** n remise f, renvoi m.

postscript ['pəʊstskrɪpt] n post-scriptum m inv.

postulate ['pɒstjʊleɪt] vt postuler.

posture ['pɒstʃər] n (*of body*) posture f; *Fig* attitude f ▮ vi (*for effect*) *Pej* poser.

postwar ['pəʊstwɔːr] a d'après-guerre.

posy ['pəʊzɪ] n petit bouquet m (de fleurs).

pot [pɒt] 1 n pot m; (*for cooking*) marmite f; **pots and pans** casseroles fpl; **jam p.** pot m à confiture; **to take p. luck** tenter sa chance; (*with food*) manger à la fortune du pot; **to go to p.** *Fam* aller à la ruine; **gone to p.** (*person, plans etc*) *Fam* fichu ▮ vt (-tt-) mettre en pot. 2 n (*drug*) *Fam* hasch m.

potato [pə'teɪtəʊ] n (pl -oes) pomme f de terre; **p. peeler** (*knife*) éplucheur m, couteau m à éplucher; **p. crisps** *Br*, **p. chips** *Am* pommes fpl chips.

potbelly ['pɒtbelɪ] n bedaine f. ●**potbellied** a ventru.

potent ['pəʊtənt] a (*drug, remedy etc*) puissant; (*drink*) fort; (*man*) viril. ●**potency** n puissance f; (*of man*) virilité f.

potential [pə'tenʃ(ə)l] a (*client, sales*) éventuel; (*danger, resources*) potentiel; (*leader, hero etc*) en puissance ▮ n potentiel

pothole 254

m; (*future promise*) *Fig* (perspectives *fpl* d')avenir m; **to have p.** (*of person, company etc*) avoir de l'avenir. ● **potenti'ality** n potentialité f; **potentialities** *Fig* (perspectives *fpl* d')avenir m. ● **potentially** adv potentiellement.

pothole ['pɒthəʊl] n (*in road*) nid m de poules; (*in rock*) gouffre m; (*cave*) caverne f. ● **potholer** n *Br* spéléologue mf. ● **potholing** n *Br* spéléologie f.

potion ['pəʊʃ(ə)n] n breuvage m magique; (*medicine*) potion f.

potshot ['pɒtʃɒt] n **to take a p.** faire un carton (**at** sur).

potted ['pɒtɪd] a 1 (*plant*) en pot; (*jam, meat*) en bocaux. 2 (*version etc*) *Br* abrégé, condensé.

potter ['pɒtər] 1 n (*person*) potier m. 2 vi to **p.** (*about*) *Br* bricoler. ● **pottery** n (*art*) poterie f; (*objects*) poteries *fpl*; **a piece of p.** une poterie.

potty ['pɒtɪ] 1 n pot m (de bébé). 2 a (-ier, -iest) (*mad*) *Br Fam* toqué.

pouch [paʊtʃ] n petit sac m; (*of kangaroo, under eyes*) poche f; (*for tobacco*) blague f.

pouf(fe) [puːf] n (*seat*) pouf m.

poultice ['pəʊltɪs] n (*dressing*) cataplasme m.

poultry ['pəʊltrɪ] n volaille f. ● **poulterer** n volailler m.

pounce [paʊns] vi (*leap*) sauter, bondir (**on** sur); **to p. on** (*idea*) *Fig* sauter sur; (*mistake*) se précipiter sur ● n bond m.

pound [paʊnd] 1 n (*weight*) livre f (= 453,6 grammes); **p. (sterling)** livre f (sterling). 2 n (*for cars, dogs*) fourrière f.
3 vt (*spices, nuts etc*) piler; (*meat*) attendrir; (*bombard with shells etc*) pilonner (*ville etc*); **to p. (on)** (*thump*) tambouriner sur, marteler (*table*); tambouriner à, marteler (*porte*); taper sur (*piano*); (*of sea*) battre (*bateau, falaise etc*) ● vi (*of heart*) battre à tout rompre; (*walk heavily*) marcher à pas pesants.

pour [pɔːr] vt (*liquid*) verser; (*wax*) couler; **to p. money into sth** investir beaucoup d'argent dans qch ● vi **it's pouring** il pleut à verse; **the pouring rain** la pluie torrentielle.

pour away vt (*liquid*) vider ● **to pour down** vi **it's pouring down** il pleut à verse ● **to pour in** vt (*liquid*) verser ● vi (*of water, rain, sunshine*) entrer à flots; (*of people, money*) affluer ● **to pour off** vt (*liquid*) vider ● **to pour out** vt (*liquid*) verser; (*cup etc*) vider; (*one's love, heart*) *Fig* épancher ● vi (*of liquid*) couler or sortir à flots; (*of people*) sortir en masse (**from** de); (*of smoke*) s'échapper (**from** de).

pout [paʊt] vti **to p. (one's lips)** faire la moue ● n moue f.

poverty ['pɒvətɪ] n pauvreté f; (**extreme**) **p.** la misère. ● **poverty-stricken** a (*person*) indigent; (*neighbourhood, conditions*) misérable.

powder ['paʊdər] n poudre f; **p. keg** (*dangerous place*) poudrière f; **p. puff** houppette f; **p. room** toilettes *fpl* (*pour dames*) ● vt (*body, skin*) poudrer; **to p. one's face** or

nose se poudrer. ● **powdered** a (*milk, eggs*) en poudre. ● **powdery** a (*snow*) poudreux; (*face*) couvert de poudre.

power ['paʊər] n (*ability, authority*) pouvoir m; (*strength, nation*) & *Math Tech* puissance f; (*energy*) énergie f; (*electric current*) courant m; **he's a (real) p. within the company** c'est un homme de poids au sein de l'entreprise; **in p.** (*political party etc*) au pouvoir; **in one's p.** en son pouvoir; **the p.** of **speech** la faculté de la parole; **p. failure** or *Br* **cut** coupure f de courant; **p. station** *Br*, **p. plant** *Am* centrale f (électrique).
● vt **to be powered by** être actionné or propulsé par; (*gas, oil etc*) fonctionner à.
powerboat ['paʊəbəʊt] n offshore m.
powerful ['paʊəfəl] a puissant. ● **powerfully** adv puissamment. ● **powerless** a impuissant (**to do** à faire).

PR [piː'ɑːr] n abbr = **public relations.**

practicable ['præktɪkəb(ə)l] a (*project, road etc*) praticable.

practical ['præktɪk(ə)l] a (*tool, knowledge, person etc*) pratique; **p. joke** farce f. ● **practi'cality** n (*of person*) sens m pratique; **the practicalities** (*of situation, scheme etc*) l'aspect m pratique; (*details*) les détails *mpl* pratiques.

practically ['præktɪk(ə)lɪ] adv (*almost*) pratiquement.

practice ['præktɪs] n (*exercise, way of proceeding*) pratique f; (*habit*) habitude f; (*training*) entraînement m; (*rehearsal*) répétition f; (*of profession*) exercice m (**of** de); (*clients*) clientèle f; **to be out of p.** manquer d'entraînement; **to put sth into p.** mettre qch en pratique; **in p.** (*in reality*) en pratique; **to be in p.** (*of doctor, lawyer*) exercer; (*in one's skill*) être bien entraîné; **to be in general p.** (*of doctor*) faire de la médecine générale.

practise ['præktɪs] (*Am* **practice**) vt (*sport, art etc*) pratiquer; (*medicine, law etc*) exercer; (*flute, piano etc*) s'exercer à; (*language*) (s'exercer à) parler (**on** avec); (*work at*) travailler (*ses maths, un discours etc*) ● vi (*of musician, sportsman etc*) s'exercer; (*of doctor, lawyer*) exercer. ● **practised** a (*experienced*) chevronné; (*ear, eye*) exercé. ● **practising** a (*Catholic etc*) pratiquant; (*doctor, lawyer*) exerçant.

practitioner [præk'tɪʃ(ə)nər] n praticien, -ienne mf; **general p.** (médecin m) généraliste m.

pragmatic [præg'mætɪk] a pragmatique.

prairie(s) ['preərɪ(z)] n(pl) (*in North America*) Prairies *fpl*.

praise [preɪz] vt louer (qn) (**for sth** de qch); **to p. s.o. for doing** or **having done** louer qn d'avoir fait ● n louange(s) f(pl), éloge(s) m(pl); **in p. of** à la louange de. ● **praiseworthy** a digne d'éloges.

pram [præm] n *Br* landau m (pl -aus).

prance [prɑːns] vi **to p. about** (*of dancer etc*) caracoler; (*strut*) se pavaner; (*go about*) *Fam* se balader.

prank [præŋk] *n* (*trick*) farce *f*, tour *m*; (*escapade*) frasque *f*.

prat [præt] *n* (*idiot*) *Br Offensive Sl* ducon *m*.

prattle ['præt(ə)l] *vi* jacasser.

prawn [prɔːn] *n* crevette *f* (rose), bouquet *m*.

pray [preɪ] *vi* prier; **to p. for good weather/a miracle** prier pour avoir du beau temps/pour un miracle **l** *vt* **to p. that** prier pour que (+ *sub*); **to p. s.o. to do sth** *Lit* prier qn de faire qch.

prayer [preər] *n* prière *f*.

pre- [priː] *pref* **p.-1800** avant 1800.

preach [priːtʃ] *vti* prêcher; **to p. to s.o.** (*of priest*) & *Fig* prêcher qn; **to p. a sermon** faire un sermon. ●**preaching** *n* prédication *f*. ●**preacher** *n* prédicateur *m*.

preamble [priːˈæmb(ə)l] *n* préambule *m*.

prearrange [priːəˈreɪndʒ] *vt* arranger à l'avance.

precarious [prɪˈkeərɪəs] *a* précaire.

precaution [prɪˈkɔːʃ(ə)n] *n* précaution *f* (**of doing** de faire); **as a p.** par précaution.

precede [prɪˈsiːd] *vti* précéder; **to p. sth by sth** faire précéder qch de qch. ●**preceding** *a* précédent.

precedence ['presɪdəns] *n* (*priority*) priorité *f*; (*in rank*) préséance *f*; **to take p. over** avoir la priorité sur; (*in rank*) avoir la préséance sur.

precedent ['presɪdənt] *n* précédent *m*; **to create** *or* **set a p.** créer un précédent.

precept ['priːsept] *n* précept *m*.

precinct ['priːsɪŋkt] *n* (*of convent, palace etc*) enceinte *f*; (*boundary*) limite *f*; (*electoral district*) *Am* circonscription *f*; (*police district*) *Am* secteur *m*; (*for shopping*) *Br* zone *f* piétonnière; **p. station** (*police station*) *Am* commissariat *m* de quartier.

precious ['preʃəs] **1** *a* précieux; **her p. little bike** *Iron* son cher petit vélo. **2** *adv* **p. few**, **p. little** *Fam* très peu (de).

precipice ['presɪpɪs] *n* (*sheer face of mountain etc*) à-pic *m inv*; (*chasm*) *Fig* précipice *m*.

precipitate [prɪˈsɪpɪteɪt] *vt* (*hasten, throw*) & *Ch* précipiter; (*reaction, trouble etc*) provoquer, déclencher. ●**precipitation** [-ˈteɪʃ(ə)n] *n* (*haste*) & *Ch* précipitation *f*; (*rainfall*) précipitations *fpl*.

précis ['preɪsiː, *pl* 'preɪsiːz] *n inv* précis *m*.

precise [prɪˈsaɪs] *a* précis; (*person*) minutieux. ●**precisely** *adv* (*accurately, exactly*) précisément; **at 3 o'clock p.** à 3 heures précises; **p. nothing** absolument rien. ●**precision** [-ʒ(ə)n] *n* précision *f*.

preclude [prɪˈkluːd] *vt* (*prevent*) empêcher (**from doing** de faire); (*possibility*) exclure.

precocious [prɪˈkəʊʃəs] *a* (*child etc*) précoce. ●**precociousness** *n* précocité *f*.

preconceived [priːkənˈsiːvd] *a* préconçu. ●**preconception** [-ˈsepʃ(ə)n] *n* préconception *f*.

precondition [priːkənˈdɪʃ(ə)n] *n* préalable *m*.

precursor [priːˈkɜːsər] *n* précurseur *m*.

predate [priːˈdeɪt] *vt* (*precede*) précéder; (*document, Br cheque, Am check etc*) antidater.

predator ['predətər] *n* (*animal*) prédateur *m*. ●**predatory** *a* (*animal, person*) rapace.

predecessor ['priːdɪsesər] *n* prédécesseur *m*.

predicament [prɪˈdɪkəmənt] *n* situation *f* fâcheuse.

predicate ['predɪkət] *n* *Grammar* prédicat *m*.

predict [prɪˈdɪkt] *vt* prédire. ●**predictable** *a* prévisible. ●**prediction** [-ʃ(ə)n] *n* prédiction *f*.

predispose [priːdɪˈspəʊz] *vt* prédisposer (**to do** à faire). ●**predisposition** [-pəˈzɪʃ(ə)n] *n* prédisposition *f*.

predominant [prɪˈdɒmɪnənt] *a* prédominant. ●**predominance** *n* prédominance *f*. ●**predominantly** *adv* (*almost all*) pour la plupart, en majorité.

predominate [prɪˈdɒmɪneɪt] *vi* prédominer (**over** sur).

pre-eminent [priːˈemɪnənt] *a* prééminent. ●**pre-eminently** *adv* suprêmement.

pre-empt [priːˈempt] *vt* (*decision, plans etc*) devancer.

preen [priːn] *vt* (*feathers*) lisser; **to p. itself** (*of bird*) se lisser les plumes; **she's preening herself** (*grooming herself*) elle se bichonne.

prefab ['priːfæb] *n* *Br Fam* maison *f* préfabriquée. ●**pre'fabricate** *vt* préfabriquer.

preface ['prefɪs] *n* préface *f* **l** *vt* (*speech etc*) faire précéder (**with** de).

prefect ['priːfekt] *n* (*in school*) *Br* élève *mf* chargé(e) de la discipline; (*French official*) préfet *m*.

prefer [prɪˈfɜːr] *vt* (**-rr-**) **1** préférer (**to** à), aimer mieux (**to que**); **to p. to do** préférer faire, aimer mieux faire. **2 to p. charges** (*in court of law*) porter plainte (**against** contre).

preferable ['prefərəb(ə)l] *a* préférable (**to** à). ●**preferably** *adv* de préférence.

preference ['prefərəns] *n* préférence *f* (**for** pour); **in p. to** de préférence à. ●**pre'ferential** *a* (*terms, price etc*) préférentiel; **p. treatment** traitement *m* de faveur.

prefix ['priːfɪks] *n* *Grammar* préfixe *m*.

pregnant ['pregnənt] *a* (*woman*) enceinte; (*animal*) pleine; **five months p.** enceinte de cinq mois. ●**pregnancy** *n* (*of woman*) grossesse *f*; **p. test** test *m* de grossesse.

prehistoric [priːhɪˈstɒrɪk] *a* préhistorique.

prejudge [priːˈdʒʌdʒ] *vt* (*question*) préjuger de; (*person*) juger d'avance.

prejudice ['predʒədɪs] *n* (*personal bias*) préjugé *m*, parti *m* pris; (*people's attitude*) préjugés *mpl*; (*harm*) *Jur* préjudice *m*; **to be full of p.** être plein de préjugés.

l *vt* (*person*) prévenir (**against** contre); (*success, chances etc*) porter préjudice à, nuire à. ●**prejudiced** *a* (*idea*) partial; **she's p.** elle a des préjugés *or* un préjugé (**against** contre); (*on a particular issue*) elle est de parti pris. ●**preju'dicial** a (harmful) Jur préjudiciable.

preliminary [prɪ'lɪmɪnərɪ] a (speech, inquiry, exam etc) préliminaire. ●**preliminaries** npl préliminaires mpl.

prelude ['prelju:d] n prélude m (**to** à) ❙ vt préluder à.

premarital [pri:'mærɪt(ə)l] a avant le mariage.

premature [Br 'premətʃʊər, Am pri:mə'tʊər] a prématuré. ●**prematurely** adv prématurément; (born) avant terme.

premeditate [pri:'medɪteɪt] vt préméditer. ●**premeditation** [-'teɪʃ(ə)n] n préméditation f.

premier [Br 'premɪər, Am prɪ'mɪər] 1 n Premier ministre m. 2 a (foremost) (tout) premier.

première [Br 'premɪeər, Am prɪ'mjeər] n (of play, film) première f.

premise ['premɪs] n Phil prémisse f.

premises ['premɪsɪz] npl locaux mpl; **on the p.** sur les lieux; **off the p.** hors des lieux.

premium ['pri:mɪəm] n (bonus) Fin prime f; (insurance) p. prime f (d'assurance); **to be at a p.** (rare) être (une) denrée rare; **p. bond** Br bon m à lots.

premonition [Br premə'nɪʃ(ə)n, Am pri:mə'nɪʃ(ə)n] n pressentiment m, prémonition f.

prenatal [pri:'neɪt(ə)l] a Am prénatal (mpl -als).

preoccupy [pri:'ɒkjʊpaɪ] vt (worry) préoccuper; **to be preoccupied** être préoccupé (**with** de). ●**preoccupation** [-'peɪʃ(ə)n] n préoccupation f; **a p. with money/success/**etc une obsession de l'argent/de la réussite/etc.

prep [prep] a **p. school** Br école f primaire privée; Am école f secondaire privée ❙ n (school homework) devoirs mpl.

pre-packed [pri:'pækt] a (meat, vegetables etc) pré-emballé.

prepaid [pri:'peɪd] a (reply) payé.

preparation [prepə'reɪʃ(ə)n] n préparation f; **preparations** préparatifs mpl (**for** de).

preparatory [prə'pærət(ə)rɪ] a préparatoire; **p. school = prep school**.

prepare [prɪ'peər] vt préparer (**sth for** qch pour, **s.o. for** qn à); **to p. to do** se préparer à faire ❙ vi **to p. for** (journey, occasion) faire des préparatifs pour; (get dressed up for) se préparer pour; (exam) préparer. ●**prepared** a (ready) prêt, disposé (**to do** à faire); **to be p. for sth** (expect) s'attendre à qch.

preposition [prepə'zɪʃ(ə)n] n préposition f.

prepossessing [pri:pə'zesɪŋ] a avenant, sympathique.

preposterous [prɪ'pɒstərəs] a absurde.

prep school ['prepsku:l] n see prep.

prerecorded [pri:rɪ'kɔ:dɪd] a (message etc) enregistré à l'avance; **p. broadcast** (on radio or television) émission f en différé.

prerequisite [pri:'rekwɪzɪt] n (condition f) préalable m.

prerogative [prɪ'rɒgətɪv] n prérogative f.

Presbyterian [prezbɪ'tɪərɪən] a & n Rel presbytérien, -ienne (mf).

preschool ['pri:sku:l] a (age, activities etc) préscolaire.

prescribe [prɪ'skraɪb] vt (of doctor) prescrire. ●**prescribed** a (textbook) (inscrit) au programme. ●**prescription** [-ʃ(ə)n] n (for medicine) ordonnance f; (order) prescription f; **on p.** sur ordonnance.

presence ['prezəns] n présence f; **in the p. of** en présence de; **p. of mind** présence f d'esprit.

present¹ ['prezənt] 1 a (not absent) présent (**at** à, **in** dans); **those p.** les personnes présentes. 2 a (year, state etc) actuel, présent; (being considered) (matter, request etc) présent; (job, house etc) actuel; **the p. tense** le présent ❙ n **the p.** (time, tense) le présent; **for the p.** pour le moment; **at p.** à présent. 3 n (gift) cadeau m. ●**presently** adv (soon) tout à l'heure; (now) à présent. ●**present-'day** a actuel.

present² [prɪ'zent] vt (show, introduce, compère etc) présenter (**to** à); (concert, film etc) donner; (proof) fournir; **to p. s.o. with** (gift) offrir à qn; (prize) remettre à qn. ●**presentable** a (person, appearance etc) présentable. ●**presenter** n présentateur, -trice mf.

presentation [prezən'teɪʃ(ə)n] n présentation f; (of prize) remise f.

preservation [prezə'veɪʃ(ə)n] n conservation f.

preservative [prɪ'zɜ:vətɪv] n (in food) agent m de conservation.

preserve [prɪ'zɜ:v] 1 vt (keep, maintain) conserver; (fruit etc) mettre en conserve; **to p. from** (protect) préserver de. 2 n **preserve(s)** (jam) confiture f. 3 n (sphere) domaine m.

preserver [prɪ'zɜ:vər] n **life p.** Am gilet m de sauvetage.

preside [prɪ'zaɪd] vi présider; **to p. over** or **at a meeting** présider une réunion.

presidency ['prezɪdənsɪ] n présidence f.

president ['prezɪdənt] n président, -ente mf. ●**presi'dential** [prezɪ'denʃ(ə)l] a présidentiel.

press¹ [pres] n 1 (newspapers) presse f; (printing company) imprimerie f; (printing) **p.** presse f; **p. conference/campaign/**etc conférence f/campagne f/etc de presse. 2 (machine for pressing trousers, gluing etc) presse f; (for making wine) pressoir m.

press² [pres] vt (button, doorbell etc) appuyer sur; (tube, lemon) presser; (hand) serrer; (clothes) repasser; (demand, insist on) insister sur; **to p. a claim** renouveler une réclamation; **to p. s.o. to do sth** (urge) presser qn de faire qch; **to p. charges** (in court of law) engager des poursuites (**against** contre).

❙ vi (with finger) appuyer (**on** sur); (of weight) faire pression (**on** sur); **time presses** le temps presse. ·

❙ n **to give sth a p.** (Br trousers, Am pants etc) repasser qch.

press down vt (button etc) appuyer sur ❙ to

press for vt (demand) insister pour obtenir (qch) ■ **to press on** vi (carry on) continuer (with sth qch).

pressed [prest] a (busy) débordé; **to be hard p.** (in difficulties) être en difficultés; (busy) être débordé; **to be p. for time/money** être à court d'argent/de temps.

pressgang ['presɡæŋ] vt **to p. s.o.** faire pression sur qn (**into doing** pour qu'il fasse). ● **press-stud** n Br bouton-pression m. ● **press-up** n (exercise) pompe f.

pressing ['presɪŋ] 1 a (urgent) pressant. 2 n (ironing) repassage m.

pressure ['preʃər] n pression f; **the p. of work** le surmenage; **p. cooker** cocotte-minute f; **p. gauge** (for Br tyres, Am tires) manomètre m; **p. group** groupe m de pression; **under p.** (to confess etc) sous la contrainte; (worker, to work) sous pression ■ vt **to p. s.o.** faire pression sur qn (**to do, into doing** pour qu'il fasse).

pressurize ['preʃəraɪz] vt (aircraft etc) pressuriser; **pressurized cabin** cabine f pressurisée; **to p. s.o.** faire pression sur qn (**to do, into doing** pour qu'il fasse).

prestige [pre'sti:ʒ] n prestige m. ● **prestigious** [Br pre'stɪdʒəs, Am -'sti:dʒəs] a prestigieux.

presume [prɪ'zju:m] vt (suppose) présumer (**that** que); **to p. to do** (venture) Lit se permettre de faire. ● **presumably** adv (you'll come etc) je présume que. ● **presumption** [-'zʌmpʃ(ə)n] n (supposition, bold attitude) présomption f.

presumptuous [prɪ'zʌmptʃuəs] a présomptueux.

presuppose [pri:sə'pəuz] vt présupposer (**that** que).

pretence [prɪ'tens] (Am **pretense**) n (sham) feinte f; (claim, affectation) prétention f; (pretext) prétexte m; **to make a p. of sth/of doing sth** feindre qch/de faire qch; **on** or **under false pretences** sous des prétextes fallacieux.

pretend [prɪ'tend] vt (make believe) faire semblant (**to do** de faire, **that** que); (claim, maintain) prétendre (**to do** faire, **that** que) ■ vi faire semblant; **to p. to** (throne, title) Lit prétendre à.

pretension [prɪ'tenʃ(ə)n] n (claim, vanity) prétention f.

pretentious [prɪ'tenʃəs] a prétentieux.

pretext ['pri:tekst] n prétexte m; **on the p. of/that** sous prétexte de/que.

pretty ['prɪtɪ] 1 a (-ier, -iest) joli. 2 adv Fam (rather, quite) assez; **p. well, p. much, p. nearly** (almost) pratiquement, à peu de chose près.

prevail [prɪ'veɪl] vi (be prevalent) prédominer; (win) prévaloir (**against** contre); **to p. (up)on s.o.** (persuade) persuader qn (**to do** de faire). ● **prevailing** a (most common) courant; (most important) prédominant; (situation) actuel; (wind) dominant.

prevalent ['prevələnt] a courant, répandu.

● **prevalence** n fréquence f; (predominance) prédominance f.

prevaricate [prɪ'værɪkeɪt] vi user de faux-fuyants.

prevent [prɪ'vent] vt empêcher (**from doing** de faire). ● **preventable** a évitable. ● **prevention** [-ʃ(ə)n] n prévention f. ● **preventive** a préventif.

preview ['pri:vju:] n (of film, painting) avant-première f; (overall view) Fig aperçu m.

previous ['pri:vɪəs] a précédent; **to have p. experience** avoir une expérience préalable; **she's had a p. job** elle a déjà eu un emploi ■ adv **p. to** avant. ● **previously** adv avant, précédemment.

prewar ['pri:wɔ:r] a d'avant-guerre.

prey [preɪ] n proie f; **to be (a) p. to** être en proie à; **bird of p.** rapace m, oiseau m de proie ■ vi **to p. on** (of animal) faire sa proie de; (of person) abuser de; **to p. on s.o.'s mind** (worry) tracasser qn.

price [praɪs] n (of object, success etc) prix m; **to pay a high p. for sth** payer cher qch; Fig payer chèrement qch; **he wouldn't do it at any p.** il ne le ferait à aucun prix ■ a (control, war, rise etc) des prix; **p. list** tarif m ■ vt mettre un prix à; **it's priced at £5** ça coûte cinq livres.

priceless ['praɪsləs] a (jewel, help etc) inestimable; (amusing) (joke etc) Fam impayable.

pricey ['praɪsɪ] a (-ier, -iest) Fam cher, hors de prix.

prick [prɪk] vt (jab) piquer (**with** avec); (burst) crever; **to p. up one's ears** dresser l'oreille ■ n (act, mark, pain) piqûre f.

prickle ['prɪk(ə)l] n (of animal) piquant m; (of plant) piquant m, épine f. ● **prickly** a (-ier, -iest) (plant) piquant, épineux; (beard) piquant; (animal) hérissé; (subject) Fig épineux; (person) Fig irritable.

pride [praɪd] n (satisfaction) fierté f; (exaggerated) orgueil m; (self-respect) amour-propre m, orgueil m; **to take p. in** (person, work etc) être fier de; (look after) prendre soin de; **to take p. in doing sth** mettre (toute) sa fierté à faire qch; **to be s.o.'s p. and joy** être la fierté de qn; **to have p. of place** avoir la place d'honneur ■ vt **to p. oneself on sth/on doing** s'enorgueillir de qch/de faire.

priest [pri:st] n prêtre m. ● **priesthood** n (function) sacerdoce m; **to enter the p.** se faire prêtre. ● **priestly** a sacerdotal.

prig [prɪɡ] n hypocrite mf, pharisien, -ienne mf. ● **priggish** a suffisant.

prim [prɪm] a (primmer, primmest) **p. (and proper)** (affected) bégueule, guindé; (seemly) convenable; (neat) impeccable.

primacy ['praɪməsɪ] n primauté f.

primarily [Br 'praɪmərəlɪ, Am praɪ'merɪlɪ] adv essentiellement.

primary ['praɪmərɪ] a (main, basic) principal, premier; Pol Geol etc primaire; **of p.**

importance de première importance; **p. education** enseignement *m* primaire; **p. school** *Br* école *f* primaire ∎ *n* (*election*) *Am* primaire *f*.

primate ['praɪmeɪt] *n* (*mammal*) primate *m*.

prime [praɪm] **1** *a* (*reason etc*) principal; (*quality*) premier; (*example, condition*) excellent, parfait; (*meat*) de premier choix; **of p. importance** de première importance; **P. Minister** Premier ministre *m*; **p. number** nombre *m* premier. **2 n in the p. of life** dans la force de l'âge. **3** *vt* (*gun, pump*) amorcer; (*surface*) apprêter. ● **primer** *n* **1** (*book*) premier livre *m*. **2** (*paint*) apprêt *m*.

primeval [praɪ'miːv(ə)l] *a* primitif.

primitive ['prɪmɪtɪv] *a* (*society, conditions, art etc*) primitif. ● **primitively** *adv* (*to live*) dans des conditions primitives.

primrose ['prɪmrəʊz] *n* (*plant*) primevère *f* (jaune).

prince [prɪns] *n* prince *m*. ● **princely** *a* princier. ● **prin'cess** *n* princesse *f*.

principal ['prɪnsɪp(ə)l] **1** *a* (*main*) principal. **2** *n* (*of school*) directeur, -trice *mf*; (*of university*) président, -ente *mf*. ● **principally** *adv* principalement.

principality [prɪnsɪ'pælɪtɪ] *n* principauté *f*.

principle ['prɪnsɪp(ə)l] *n* principe *m*; **in p.** en principe; **on p.** par principe.

print [prɪnt] *n* (*of finger, foot etc*) empreinte *f*; (*letters*) caractères *mpl*; (*engraving*) gravure *f*, estampe *f*; (*fabric, textile design*) imprimé *m*; (*photo*) épreuve *f*; (*ink*) encre *m*; **in p.** (*book*) disponible (en librairie); **out of p.** (*book*) épuisé. ∎ *vt* (*book etc*) imprimer; (*photo*) tirer; (*write*) écrire en caractères d'imprimerie; **to p. 100 copies of a book/etc** tirer un livre/etc à 100 exemplaires; **to have a book printed** publier un livre; **to p. out** (*of computer*) imprimer. ● **printed** *a* imprimé; **p. matter or papers** imprimés *mpl*. ● **printing** *n* (*action*) impression *f*; (*technique, art*) imprimerie *f*; (*of photo*) tirage *m*; **p. press** presse *f*.

printable ['prɪntəb(ə)l] *a* **not p.** (*word etc*) *Fig* obscène.

printer ['prɪntər] *n* (*of computer*) imprimante *f*; (*person*) imprimeur *m*. ● **print-out** *n* (*of computer*) sortie *f* sur imprimante.

prior ['praɪər] *a* précédent, antérieur; (*experience*) préalable ∎ *adv* **p. to sth** avant qch; **p. to doing sth** avant de faire qch.

priority [praɪ'ɒrɪtɪ] *n* priorité *f* (**over** sur).

priory ['praɪərɪ] *n Rel* prieuré *m*.

prise [praɪz] *vt* **to p. open/off** (*box, lid*) *Br* ouvrir/enlever (en faisant levier).

prism ['prɪz(ə)m] *n* prisme *m*.

prison ['prɪz(ə)n] *n* prison *f*; **in p.** en prison ∎ *a* (*life, system etc*) pénitentiaire; (*camp*) de prisonniers; **p. officer** gardien, -ienne *mf* de prison. ● **prisoner** *n* prisonnier, -ière *mf*; **to take s.o. p.** faire qn prisonnier.

prissy ['prɪsɪ] *a* (**-ier, -iest**) bégueule.

pristine ['prɪstiːn] *a* (*condition*) parfait; (*primitive*) primitif.

privacy ['praɪvəsɪ, *Br* 'prɪvəsɪ] *n* intimité *f*; (*solitude*) solitude *f*; (*quiet place*) coin *m* retiré; (*secrecy*) secret *m*; **to give s.o. some p.** laisser qn seul.

private ['praɪvɪt] **1** *a* privé; (*lesson, car etc*) particulier; (*report, letter*) confidentiel; (*personal*) personnel; (*dinner, wedding etc*) intime; **a p. citizen** un simple particulier; **p. detective, p. investigator,** *Fam* **p. eye** détective *m* privé; **p. parts** parties *fpl* génitales; **p. place** coin *m* retiré; **p. secretary** secrétaire *m* particulier, secrétaire *f* particulière; **p. tutor** professeur *m* particulier, précepteur *m*; **to be a very p. person** aimer la solitude.
∎ *n* **in p.** (*not publicly*) en privé; (*to have dinner, get married etc*) dans l'intimité.
2 *n* (*soldier*) (simple) soldat *m*.

privately ['praɪvɪtlɪ] *adv* (*in private*) en privé; (*in one's heart of hearts*) intérieurement, en son for intérieur; (*personally*) à titre personnel; (*to have dinner, get married etc*) dans l'intimité; **p. owned** (*company, house etc*) appartenant à un particulier; **to be p. educated** (*go to private school*) aller dans le privé; **to be treated p.** = se faire soigner par un médecin non conventionné.

privatize ['praɪvətaɪz] *vt* privatiser. ● **privatization** [-'zeɪʃ(ə)n] *n* privatisation *f*.

privet ['prɪvɪt] *n* (*bush*) troène *m*.

privilege ['prɪvɪlɪdʒ] *n* privilège *m*. ● **privileged** *a* privilégié; **to be p. to do sth** avoir le privilège de faire qch.

privy ['prɪvɪ] *a* **to be p. to sth** avoir connaissance de qch.

prize¹ [praɪz] *n* prix *m*; (*in lottery*) lot *m*; **the first p.** (*in lottery*) le gros lot ∎ *a* (*essay, animal etc*) primé; **a p. fool/etc** *Hum* un parfait idiot/etc. ● **prize-giving** *n* distribution *f* des prix. ● **prize-winner** *n* lauréat, -ate *mf*; (*in lottery*) gagnant, -ante *mf*. ● **prize-winning** *a* (*essay, animal etc*) primé; (*ticket*) gagnant.

prize² [praɪz] *vt* (*value*) priser; **this is my most prized possession** c'est mon bien le plus précieux.

prize³ [praɪz] *vt Br* = **prise**.

pro [prəʊ] *n* (*professional*) *Fam* pro *mf*.

pro- [prəʊ] *pref* pro-.

probable ['prɒbəb(ə)l] *a* probable (**that** que); (*convincing*) vraisemblable. ● **proba'bility** *n* probabilité *f*; **in all p.** selon toute probabilité. ● **probably** *adv* probablement, vraisemblablement.

probation [prə'beɪʃ(ə)n] *n* **on p.** (*criminal*) en liberté surveillée, sous contrôle judiciaire; (*employee in job*) à l'essai; **p. officer** responsable *mf* des délinquants mis en liberté surveillée. ● **probationary** *a* (*period*) (*in job etc*) d'essai; (*of criminal*) de liberté surveillée.

probe [prəʊb] *n* (*inquiry*) enquête *f* (**into** dans); (*device*) sonde *f* ∎ *vt* (*investigate*) sonder (*conscience, plaie etc*); (*examine*) examiner (*situation, causes etc*) ∎ *vi* (*investigate*) faire des recherches; (*poke one's nose*) fouiner; **to p. into** (*origins, s.o.'s past etc*)

sonder. ● **probing** a (*question etc*) pénétrant.
problem ['prɒbləm] n problème m; **he's got a drug/a drink p.** c'est un drogué/un alcoolique; **you've got a smoking p.** tu fumes beaucoup trop; **no p.!** Am Fam pas de problème!; **to have a p. doing** avoir du mal à faire; **p. child** enfant mf difficile or caractériel(le); **p. family** famille f à problèmes.
problematic [prɒblə'mætɪk] a problématique; **it's p. whether** il est douteux que (+ sub).
procedure [prə'siːdʒər] n procédure f.
proceed [prə'siːd] vi (*go*) avancer, aller; (*act*) procéder; (*continue*) continuer; (*of debate*) se poursuivre; **to p. to** (*next question etc*) passer à; **to p. with** (*task etc*) continuer; **to p. to do** (*start*) se mettre à faire.
proceedings [prə'siːdɪŋz] npl (*events*) événements mpl; (*meeting*) séance f; (*discussions*) débats mpl; (*minutes of meeting*) actes mpl; **to take (legal) proceedings** intenter un procès (**against** contre).
proceeds ['prəʊsiːdz] npl (*profits from sale etc*) produit m, bénéfices mpl.
process ['prəʊses] 1 n (*method*) procédé m (**for** or **of doing** pour faire); (*chemical, scientific, economic, political etc*) processus m; **in p.** (*work etc*) en cours; **in the p. of doing sth** en train de faire qch. 2 vt (*food, data etc*) traiter; (*examine*) examiner; (*photo*) développer; **processed cheese =** fromage m fondu. ● **processing** n traitement m; (*of photo*) développement m; **data** or **information p.** informatique f.
procession [prə'seʃ(ə)n] n cortège m, défilé m.
processor ['prəʊsesər] n (*in computer*) processeur m; **food p.** robot m (*ménager*); **word p.** machine f à or de traitement de texte.
proclaim [prə'kleɪm] vt proclamer (**that** que); **to p. s.o. king** proclamer qn roi. ● **proclamation** [prɒklə'meɪʃ(ə)n] n proclamation f.
procrastinate [prə'kræstɪneɪt] vi tergiverser, temporiser. ● **procrastination** [-'neɪʃ(ə)n] n tergiversations fpl.
procreate ['prəʊkrɪeɪt] vt procréer. ● **procreation** [-'eɪʃ(ə)n] n procréation f.
procure [prə'kjʊər] vt obtenir; **to p. sth (for oneself)** se procurer qch; **to p. sth for s.o.** procurer qch à qn.
prod [prɒd] vti (**-dd-**) **to p. (at)** pousser (*du coude, avec un bâton etc*); **to p. s.o. into doing sth** Fig pousser qn à faire qch ▮ n (*petit*) coup m; (*shove*) poussée f.
prodigal ['prɒdɪg(ə)l] a (*son etc*) prodigue.
prodigious [prə'dɪdʒəs] a prodigieux.
prodigy ['prɒdɪdʒɪ] n prodige m; **child p., infant p.** enfant mf prodige.
produce¹ [prə'djuːs] vt (*manufacture, yield etc*) produire; (*bring out, show*) sortir (*pistolet, mouchoir etc*); (*passport, proof*) présenter; (*profit*) rapporter; (*cause*) provoquer, produire; (*publish*) publier; (*film*) produire; (*theatre or television play*) mettre en scène;

(*radio programme*) réaliser; (*baby*) donner naissance à; **oil-producing country** pays m producteur de pétrole.
▮ vi (*of factory etc*) produire. ● **producer** n (*of goods, film*) producteur, -trice m f; Theatre TV metteur m en scène; Radio réalisateur, -trice mf.
produce² [Br 'prɒdjuːs, Am 'prəʊduːs] n (*agricultural etc*) produits mpl.
product ['prɒdʌkt] n (*article, creation etc*) & Math produit m.
production [prə'dʌkʃ(ə)n] n production f; (*of play*) mise f en scène; Radio réalisation f; **to work on the p. line** travailler à la chaîne.
productive [prə'dʌktɪv] a (*land, meeting, efforts etc*) productif. ● **produc'tivity** n productivité f.
profane [prə'feɪn] a (*sacrilegious*) sacrilège; (*secular*) profane ▮ vt (*dishonour*) profaner.
profanities [prə'fænɪtɪz] npl (*swear words*) grossièretés fpl; (*blasphemies*) blasphèmes mpl.
profess [prə'fes] vt (*opinion, disgust etc*) professer; **to p. to be** prétendre être. ● **professed** a (*anarchist etc*) déclaré.
profession [prə'feʃ(ə)n] n profession f; **by p.** de profession.
professional [prə'feʃən(ə)l] a professionnel; (*man, woman*) qui exerce une profession libérale; (*army*) de métier; (*diplomat*) de carrière; (*piece of work*) de professionnel ▮ n professionnel, -elle mf; (*lawyer, doctor etc*) membre m des professions libérales. ● **professionalism** n professionnalisme m. ● **professionally** adv professionnellement; (*to perform, play*) en professionnel; (*to meet s.o.*) dans le cadre de son travail.
professor [prə'fesər] n Br professeur m (d'université); Am enseignant, -ante mf d'université. ● **profe'ssorial** a professoral.
proffer ['prɒfər] vt offrir.
proficient [prə'fɪʃ(ə)nt] a compétent (**in** en). ● **proficiency** n compétence f.
profile ['prəʊfaɪl] n (*of person, object*) profil m; **in p.** de profil; **to keep a low p.** Fig garder un profil bas. ● **profiled** a **to be p. against** se profiler sur.
profit ['prɒfɪt] n profit m, bénéfice m; **to sell at a p.** vendre à profit; **p. margin** marge f bénéficiaire; **p. motive** recherche f du profit ▮ vi **to p. by** or **from sth** tirer profit de qch. ● **profit-making** a à but lucratif; **non** or **not p.-making** sans but lucratif.
profitable ['prɒfɪtəb(ə)l] a (*commercially*) rentable; (*worthwhile*) Fig rentable, profitable. ● **profita'bility** n rentabilité f. ● **profitably** adv avec profit.
profiteer [prɒfɪ'tɪər] n Pej profiteur, -euse mf ▮ vi Pej faire des profits malhonnêtes.
profound [prə'faʊnd] a (*silence, remark etc*) profond. ● **profoundly** adv profondément. ● **profundity** n profondeur f.
profuse [prə'fjuːs] a abondant; **p. in praise/compliments/etc** prodigue d'éloges/de

compliments/etc. ●**profusely** adv (to bleed) abondamment; (to flow, grow) à profusion: (to thank) avec effusion; to **apologize p.** se répandre en excuses. ●**profusion** f. -ʒ(ə)n] n profusion f; **in p.** à profusion.

progeny [ˈprɒdʒɪnɪ] n progéniture f.

program¹ [ˈprəʊɡræm] n (of computer) programme m; **computer p.** programme m informatique ▮ vt (-mm-) (computer) programmer. ●**programming** n (computer) p. programmation f. ●**programmer** n (computer) p. programmeur, -euse mf.

programme, Am **program²** [ˈprəʊɡræm] n programme m; (broadcast) émission f ▮ vt (machine, Br video, Am VCR etc) programmer (**to do** pour faire); (person) Fig conditionner.

progress [ˈprəʊɡres] n progrès m(pl); **to make (good) p.** faire des progrès; (when driving, walking etc) bien avancer; **in p.** en cours ▮ [prəˈɡres] vi (advance, improve) progresser; (of story, meeting) se dérouler.

progression [prəˈɡreʃ(ə)n] n progression f.

progressive [prəˈɡresɪv] a (gradual) progressif; (company, ideas, political party) progressiste. ●**progressively** adv progressivement.

prohibit [prəˈhɪbɪt] vt interdire (**s.o. from doing** à qn de faire); **we're prohibited from leaving/etc** il nous est interdit de partir/etc. ●**prohibition** [prəʊɪˈbɪʃ(ə)n] n prohibition f.

prohibitive [prəˈhɪbɪtɪv] a (price, measure etc) prohibitif.

project¹ [ˈprɒdʒekt] n (plan) projet m (**for sth** pour qch; **to do, for doing** pour faire); (undertaking) entreprise f; (at school) étude f; (housing) **p.** (for workers) Am cité f (ouvrière). ●**projected** a (planned) prévu.

project² [prəˈdʒekt] vt (throw, show etc) projeter ▮ vi (jut out) faire saillie.

projection [prəˈdʒekʃ(ə)n] n projection f; (projecting object) saillie f. ●**projectionist** n projectionniste mf. ●**projector** n (for films or slides) projecteur m.

proletarian [prəʊləˈteərɪən] n prolétaire mf ▮ a (class) prolétarien; (outlook) de prolétaire. ●**proletariat** n prolétariat m.

proliferate [prəˈlɪfəreɪt] vi proliférer. ●**proliferation** [-ˈreɪʃ(ə)n] n prolifération f.

prolific [prəˈlɪfɪk] a (author etc) prolifique.

prologue [ˈprəʊlɒɡ] n prologue m (**to** de, à).

prolong [prəˈlɒŋ] vt prolonger.

prom [prɒm] n abbr (promenade) **1** (at seaside) Br promenade f. **2** (dance) Am bal m d'étudiants. ●**proms** npl abbr (promenade concerts) Br concerts-promenade mpl.

promenade [prɒməˈnɑːd] n (at seaside & leisurely stroll) promenade f; (gallery in theatre) promenoir m.

prominent [ˈprɒmɪnənt] a (person) important, marquant; (nose) proéminent; (chin, tooth) saillant; (role) majeur, important; (striking) frappant, remarquable; (conspicuous) (bien) en vue. ●**prominence** n (importance) importance f. ●**prominently**

adv (displayed, placed etc) bien en vue.

promiscuous [prəˈmɪskjʊəs] a (person) qui mène une vie très libre; (behaviour) immoral. ●**promiscuity** [prɒmɪsˈkjuːɪtɪ] n liberté f de mœurs; (of behaviour) immoralité f.

promise [ˈprɒmɪs] n promesse f; **to show (great) p., be full of p.** (hope) être très prometteur ▮ vt promettre (**s.o. sth, sth to s.o.** qch à qn; **to do** de faire; **that** que) ▮ vi **I p.!** je te le promets!; **p.?** promis? ●**promising** a (situation etc) prometteur (f -euse); (person) qui promet; **that looks p.** ça s'annonce bien.

promote [prəˈməʊt] vt (product, research, idea etc) promouvoir; (good health, awareness) favoriser; **to p. s.o.** (in job) donner de l'avancement à qn, promouvoir qn; **promoted (to) manager/general/etc** promu directeur/général/etc. ●**promoter** n Sport organisateur, -trice mf; (instigator) promoteur, -trice mf; **sales p.** promoteur, -trice mf de ventes. ●**promotion** [-ʃ(ə)n] n (of person) avancement m, promotion f; (of sales, research etc) promotion f.

prompt¹ [prɒmpt] a (speedy) rapide; (punctual) à l'heure, ponctuel; **p. to act** prompt à agir ▮ adv **at 8 o'clock p.** à 8 heures pile. ●**promptly** adv rapidement; (punctually) ponctuellement; **to pay p.** payer sans tarder. ●**promptness** n rapidité f; (readiness to act) promptitude f; (punctuality) ponctualité f.

prompt² [prɒmpt] **1** vt (urge) inciter, pousser (qn) (**to do** à faire); (cause) provoquer. **2** vt (actor) souffler (son rôle) à. **3** n (message) Comptr message-guide m. ●**prompting** n (urging) incitation f. ●**prompter** n (in theatre) souffleur, -euse mf.

prone [prəʊn] a **1 p. to** (illnesses, accidents etc) prédisposé à; **to be p. to do sth** avoir tendance à faire qch. **2** (lying flat) sur le ventre.

prong [prɒŋ] n (of fork) dent f.

pronoun [ˈprəʊnaʊn] n Grammar pronom m. ●**pro'nominal** a pronominal.

pronounce [prəˈnaʊns] vt (say, articulate, declare) prononcer ▮ vi (articulate) prononcer; (give judgment) se prononcer (**on** sur). ●**pronouncement** n déclaration f. ●**pronunciation** [prənʌnsɪˈeɪʃ(ə)n] n prononciation f.

pronto [ˈprɒntəʊ] adv (at once) Fam illico.

proof [pruːf] **1** n (evidence) preuve(s) f(pl); (of food, photo) épreuve f; (of drink) teneur f en alcool. **2** a **p. against** (material) à l'épreuve de (feu, acide etc); (person) Lit à l'abri de (tentation, attentat etc). ●**proofreader** n correcteur, -trice mf (d'épreuves).

prop [prɒp] **1** n (for wall, tunnel etc) étai m; (for clothes line) perche f; (person) Fig soutien m ▮ vt (-pp-) **to p. up** (ladder etc) appuyer (**against** contre); (one's head) caler; (wall) étayer; (help) Fig soutenir (qn). **2** n prop(s) (in theatre) accessoire(s) m(pl).

propaganda [prɒpəˈɡændə] n propagande f. ●**propagandist** n propagandiste mf.

propagate [ˈprɒpəɡeɪt] vt propager ▮ vi se

propager.
propel [prə'pel] *vt* (**-ll-**) (*drive, hurl*) propulser. ●**propeller** *n* (*of aircraft, ship etc*) hélice *f*.
propensity [prə'pensɪtɪ] *n* propension *f* (**for** sth à qch, **to do** à faire).
proper ['prɒpər] *a* (*suitable, respectable*) convenable; (*correct*) (*behaviour, dress*) correct, convenable; (*right*) bon (*f* bonne); (*downright*) *Br* véritable; (*noun, meaning*) propre; **the p. address/method/***etc* (*right*) la bonne adresse/méthode/*etc*; **in the p. way** comme il faut; **the village/***etc* **p.** le village/*etc* proprement dit. ●**properly** *adv* comme il faut, convenablement, correctement; (*completely*) *Fam* vraiment; **very p.** (*rightly*) à juste titre.
property ['prɒpətɪ] **1** *n* (*building etc*) propriété *f*; (*possessions, land*) biens *mpl*, propriété *f* ▮ *a* (*market, crisis, speculator etc*) immobilier; (*tax*) foncier; **p. company** société *f* immobilière; **p. owner** propriétaire *m* foncier. **2** *n* (*of substance etc*) propriété *f*. ●**propertied** *a* **p. class** classe *f* possédante; **p. people** les possédants *mpl*.
prophecy ['prɒfɪsɪ] *n* prophétie *f*. ●**prophesy** [-ɪsaɪ] *vti* prophétiser; **to p. that** prédire que.
prophet ['prɒfɪt] *n* prophète *m*.
prophetic [prə'fetɪk] *a* prophétique.
proponent [prə'pəʊnənt] *n* (*of cause etc*) défenseur *m*, partisan *n*.
proportion [prə'pɔːʃ(ə)n] *n* (*ratio*) proportion *f*; (*portion*) partie *f*; (*amount*) pourcentage *m*; **proportions** (*size*) dimensions *fpl*, proportions *fpl*; **in p.** en proportion (**to** de); **out of p.** hors de proportion (**to** avec) ▮ *vt* proportionner (**to** à); **well** *or* **nicely proportioned** bien proportionné. ●**proportional** *or* **proportionate** *a* proportionnel (**to** à).
proposal [prə'pəʊz(ə)l] *n* proposition *f*; (*of marriage*) demande *f* (en mariage). ●**proposition** [prɒpə'zɪʃ(ə)n] *n* (*offer, suggestion etc*) proposition *f*; (*matter*) affaire *f*.
propose [prə'pəʊz] *vt* (*suggest*) proposer (**to** à, **that** que (+ *sub*)); **to p. to do, p. doing** (*intend*) se proposer de faire ▮ *vi* faire une demande (en mariage) (**to** à).
propound [prə'paʊnd] *vt* (*theory, idea etc*) proposer.
proprietor [prə'praɪətər] *n* propriétaire *mf*. ●**proprietary** *a* (*article, goods*) de marque déposée; **p. name** marque *f* déposée.
propriety [prə'praɪətɪ] *n* (*behaviour*) bienséance *f*; (*of conduct, remark*) justesse *f*; **to observe the proprieties** observer les bienséances.
propulsion [prə'pʌlʃ(ə)n] *n* propulsion *f*.
pros [prəʊz] *npl* **the p. and cons** le pour et le contre.
prosaic [prəʊ'zeɪɪk] *a* prosaïque.
proscribe [prəʊ'skraɪb] *vt* proscrire.
prose [prəʊz] *n* prose *f*; (*translation*) *Br* thème *m*; **French p.** (*translation*) thème *m* français.
prosecute ['prɒsɪkjuːt] *vt* poursuivre (en

justice) (**for stealing/***etc* pour vol/*etc*). ●**prosecution** [-'kjuːʃ(ə)n] *n* (*in court*) poursuites *fpl*; **the p.** (*lawyers*) = le ministère public. ●**prosecutor** *n* (**public**) **p.** *Jur* procureur *m*.
prospect[1] ['prɒspekt] *n* (*idea, outlook*) perspective *f* (**of doing** de faire); (*possibility*) possibilité *f*, perspective *f* (**of** sth de qch); (*future*) **prospects** perspectives *fpl* d'avenir; **it has prospects** c'est prometteur; **she has prospects** elle a de l'avenir. ●**pro'spective** *a* (*possible*) éventuel; (*future*) futur.
prospect[2] [prə'spekt] *vi* **to p. for** (*gold, oil etc*) chercher ▮ *vt* (*land*) prospecter. ●**prospecting** *n* prospection *f*. ●**prospector** *n* prospecteur, -trice *mf*.
prospectus [prə'spektəs] *n* (*publicity leaflet*) prospectus *m*; (*for university*) *Br* guide *m* (de l'étudiant).
prosper ['prɒspər] *vi* prospérer. ●**pro'sperity** *n* prospérité *f*. ●**prosperous** *a* (*wealthy*) riche, prospère; (*thriving*) prospère.
prostate ['prɒsteɪt] *n* **p.** (**gland**) prostate *f*.
prostitute ['prɒstɪtjuːt] *n* (*woman*) prostituée *f*; **male p.** prostitué *m* ▮ *vt* **to p. oneself** se prostituer. ●**prostitution** [-'tjuːʃ(ə)n] *n* prostitution *f*.
prostrate ['prɒstreɪt] *a* (*prone*) sur le ventre; (*worshipper, servant*) prosterné; (*submissive*) soumis; (*exhausted*) prostré ▮ [prɒ'streɪt] *vt* **to p. oneself** se prosterner (**before** devant).
protagonist [prəʊ'tægənɪst] *n* protagoniste *mf*.
protect [prə'tekt] *vt* protéger (**from** de, **against** contre); (*interests*) sauvegarder. ●**protection** [-ʃ(ə)n] *n* protection *f*. ●**protective** *a* (*clothes, screen etc*) de protection; (*person, attitude etc*) protecteur (*f* -trice) (**to, towards** envers); (*barrier etc*) *Econ* protecteur (*f* -trice); **to be too** *or* **over p. towards** (*child*) surprotéger. ●**protector** *n* protecteur, -trice *mf*.
protein ['prəʊtiːn] *n* protéine *f*.
protest ['prəʊtest] *n* protestation *f* (**against** contre); **in p.** en signe de protestation (**at** contre); **under p.** contre son gré; **p. meeting/***etc* réunion *f*/*etc* de protestation ▮ [prə'test] *vt* protester (**that** que); (*one's innocence*) protester de ▮ *vi* protester (**against** contre); (*of students, demonstrators etc*) contester. ●**protester** *n* (*student etc*) contestataire *mf*.
Protestant ['prɒtɪstənt] *a* & *n* protestant, -ante (*mf*). ●**Protestantism** *n* protestantisme *m*.
protocol ['prəʊtəkɒl] *n* protocole *m*.
prototype ['prəʊtəʊtaɪp] *n* prototype *m*.
protracted [prə'træktɪd] *a* (*stay, lunch etc*) prolongé.
protractor [prə'træktər] *n* (*for measuring*) rapporteur *m*.
protrude [prə'truːd] *vi* dépasser; (*of tooth*) avancer; (*of balcony, cliff etc*) faire saillie. ●**protruding** *a* (*chin, veins, eyes*) saillant; (*tooth*) qui avance.
proud [praʊd] *a* (**-er, -est**) (*honoured,*

pleased) fier (**of** de, **to do** de faire); (*superior to others*, *arrogant*) orgueilleux. ● **proudly** *adv* fièrement; (*arrogantly*) orgueilleusement.

prove [pruːv] *vt* prouver (**that** que); **to p. oneself** faire ses preuves ▮ *vi* **to p. (to be) difficult**/*etc* s'avérer difficile/*etc*. ● **proven** *a* (*method etc*) éprouvé.

proverb ['prɒvɜːb] *n* proverbe *m*. ● **pro'verbial** *a* proverbial.

provide [prə'vaɪd] **1** *vt* (*supply*) fournir (**s.o. with sth** qch à qn); (*give*) donner, offrir (**to** à); **to p. s.o. with sth** (*equip*) pourvoir qn de qch.
▮ *vi* **to p. for s.o.** (*s.o.'s needs*) pourvoir aux besoins de qn; (*s.o.'s future*) assurer l'avenir de qn; **to p. for sth** (*make allowance for*) prévoir qch.
2 *vt* **to p. that** (*stipulate*) (*of contract etc*) stipuler que. ● **provided** *conj* **p. (that)** pourvu que (+ *sub*). ● **providing** *conj* **p. (that)** pourvu que (+ *sub*).

providence ['prɒvɪdəns] *n* providence *f*.

provident ['prɒvɪdənt] *a* (*person*) prévoyant; **p. society** *Br* société *f* de prévoyance.

province ['prɒvɪns] *n* province *f*; (*field of knowledge*) Fig domaine *m*, compétence *f*; **the provinces** la province; **in the provinces** en province. ● **pro'vincial** *a & n* provincial, -ale (*mf*).

provision [prə'vɪʒ(ə)n] *n* (*supply*) provision *f*; (*clause*) disposition *f*; **the p. of** (*supplying*) la fourniture de; **to make p. for** = **to provide for.**

provisional [prə'vɪʒən(ə)l] *a* provisoire. ● **provisionally** *adv* provisoirement.

proviso [prə'vaɪzəʊ] *n* (*pl* **-os**) stipulation *f*.

provocation [prɒvə'keɪʃ(ə)n] *n* provocation *f*.

provocative [prə'vɒkətɪv] *a* (*person*, *remark etc*) provocant; (*thought-provoking*) qui donne à penser.

provoke [prə'vəʊk] *vt* (*annoy*) agacer; (*rouse*, *challenge*) provoquer (*qn*) (**to do**, **into doing** à faire); (*cause*) provoquer (*réaction*, *accident etc*). ● **provoking** *a* (*annoying*) agaçant.

prow [praʊ] *n* (*of ship*) proue *f*.

prowess ['praʊes] *n* (*bravery*) courage *m*; (*skill*) talent *m*.

prowl [praʊl] *vi* **to p. (around)** rôder ▮ *n* **to be on the p.** rôder. ● **prowler** *n* rôdeur, -euse *mf*.

proximity [prɒk'sɪmɪtɪ] *n* proximité *f*.

proxy ['prɒksɪ] *n* **by p.** par procuration.

prude [pruːd] *n* prude *f*. ● **prudery** *n* pruderie *f*. ● **prudish** *a* prude.

prudent ['pruːdənt] *a* prudent. ● **prudence** *n* prudence *f*. ● **prudently** *adv* prudemment.

prune [pruːn] **1** *n* (*dried plum*) pruneau *m*. **2** *vt* (*tree*, *bush etc*) tailler, élaguer; (*speech etc*) Fig élaguer. ● **pruning** *n* (*of tree etc*) taille *f*; **p. shears** sécateur *m*.

pry [praɪ] **1** *vi* être indiscret; **to p. into** (*meddle*) se mêler de; (*s.o.'s reasons etc*)

chercher à découvrir. **2** *vt* **to p. open** *Am* forcer (en faisant levier). ● **prying** *a* (*habits*, *person etc*) indiscret.

PS [piː'es] *abbr* (*postscript*) P.-S.

psalm [sɑːm] *n* psaume *m*.

pseud [sjuːd] *n Br Fam* bêcheur, -euse *mf*.

pseudo- ['sjuːdəʊ] *pref* pseudo-.

pseudonym ['sjuːdənɪm] *n* pseudonyme *m*.

psyche ['saɪkɪ] *n* (*mind*) psyché *f*, structure *f* mentale.

psychiatry [saɪ'kaɪətrɪ] *n* psychiatrie *f*. ● **psychi'atric** *a* psychiatrique. ● **psychiatrist** *n* psychiatre *mf*.

psychic ['saɪkɪk] *a* (*méta*)psychique; **I'm not p.** *Fam* je ne suis pas devin ▮ *n* (*person*) médium *m*.

psycho- ['saɪkəʊ] *pref* psycho-. ● **psychoa'nalysis** *n* psychanalyse *f*. ● **psycho'analyst** *n* psychanalyste *mf*.

psychology [saɪ'kɒlədʒɪ] *n* psychologie *f*. ● **psycho'logical** *a* psychologique. ● **psychologist** *n* psychologue *mf*.

psychopath ['saɪkəʊpæθ] *n* psychopathe *mf*.

psychosis, *pl* **-oses** [saɪ'kəʊsɪs, -əʊsiːz] *n* psychose *f*.

psychosomatic [saɪkəʊsə'mætɪk] *a* psychosomatique.

PTO *abbr* (*please turn over*) TSVP.

pub [pʌb] *n Br* pub *m*.

puberty ['pjuːbətɪ] *n* puberté *f*.

pubic ['pjuːbɪk] *a* **p. hair** les poils *mpl* du pubis.

public ['pʌblɪk] *a* public (*f* -ique); (*library*, *swimming pool etc*) municipal; **to make a p. protest** protester publiquement; **in the p. eye** très en vue; **p. building** édifice *m* public; **p. company** société *f* par actions; **p. corporation** société *f* nationalisée; **p. figure** personnalité *f* connue; **p. house** *Br* pub *m*; **p. life** la vie publique, les affaires *fpl* publiques; **p. opinion** opinion *f* publique; **p. relations** relations *fpl* publiques; **p. school** *Br* école *f* privée; *Am* école *f* publique; **p. television** *Am* la télévision éducative.
▮ *n* public *m*; **in p.** en public; **a member of the p.** un simple particulier; **the sporting**/*etc* **p.** les amateurs *mpl* de sport/*etc*.

publican ['pʌblɪk(ə)n] *n Br* patron, -onne *mf* d'un pub.

publication [pʌblɪ'keɪʃ(ə)n] *n* (*book etc*) publication *f*; **the p. of** (*publishing*) la publication de.

publicity [pʌb'lɪsɪtɪ] *n* publicité *f*.

publicize ['pʌblɪsaɪz] *vt* (*make known*) rendre public; (*advertise*) faire de la publicité pour.

publicly ['pʌblɪklɪ] *adv* publiquement; **p.-owned company** entreprise *f* nationalisée.

public-spirited [pʌblɪk'spɪrɪtɪd] *a* **to be p.-spirited** avoir le sens civique.

publish ['pʌblɪʃ] *vt* (*news*, *results etc*) publier; (*book*, *author*) éditer, publier; **'published weekly'** 'paraît toutes les semaines'. ● **publishing** *n* (*profession*) édition *f*; **the p. of** la publication de. ● **publisher** *n* éditeur,

puck [pʌk] n (in ice hockey) palet m.

pucker ['pʌkər] vt to p. (up) (brow, lips) plisser ∎ vi to p. (up) se plisser.

pudding ['pudɪŋ] n pudding m; (dessert) Br dessert m; **black p.** Br boudin m; **Christmas p.** pudding m; **rice p.** riz m au lait.

puddle ['pʌd(ə)l] n flaque f (d'eau).

pudgy ['pʌdʒɪ] a (-ier, -iest) = **podgy**.

puerile [Br 'pjʊəraɪl, Am 'pjʊərəl] a puéril.

Puerto Rico [pwɜːtəʊ'riːkəʊ] n Porto Rico f.

puff [pʌf] n (of smoke) bouffée f; (of wind, air) bouffée f, souffle m; **to have run out of p.** Fam être à bout de souffle ∎ vi (blow, pant) souffler; **to p. at** (cigar) tirer sur ∎ vt (smoke etc) souffler (into dans); **to p. out** (cheeks etc) gonfler. ● **puffy** a (-ier, -iest) (swollen) gonflé.

puke [pjuːk] vi (vomit) Sl dégueuler.

pukka ['pʌkə] a Br Fam authentique.

pull [pʊl] n (attraction) attraction f; (force) force f; (influence) influence f; **to give sth a p.** tirer qch.

∎ vt (draw, tug) tirer; (tooth) arracher; (stopper) enlever; (trigger) appuyer sur; (muscle) se claquer; **to p. sth apart** or **to bits** or **to pieces** mettre qch en pièces; **to p. a face** faire la moue; **(to get s.o. to) p. strings** Fig se faire pistonner.

∎ vi (tug) tirer; (go, move) aller; **to p. at** or **on sth** tirer (sur) qch.

pull along vt (drag) traîner (to jusqu'à) ∎ **to pull away** vt (move) éloigner; (snatch) arracher (from à) ∎ vi (in vehicle) démarrer; **to p. away from** s'éloigner de ∎ **to pull back** vi (withdraw) se retirer ∎ vt retirer; (curtains) ouvrir ∎ **to pull down** vt (lower) baisser; (knock down) faire tomber; (demolish) démolir, abattre ∎ **to pull in** vt (drag into room etc) faire entrer (de force); (rope) ramener; (stomach) rentrer; (crowd) attirer ∎ vi (arrive) arriver; (stop in vehicle) se garer; **to p. into the station** (of train) entrer en gare ∎ **to pull off** vt (remove) enlever; (plan, deal etc) Fig mener à bien; **to p. it off** (be successful) réussir son coup ∎ **to pull on** vt (boots etc) mettre ∎ **to pull out** vt (tooth, hair etc) arracher; (cork, pin etc) enlever (from de); (from pocket, bag etc) tirer, sortir (from de); (troops) retirer ∎ vi (move out in vehicle to overtake) déboîter; (leave) (of train, person etc) partir; (withdraw) se retirer (from or of the negotiations/etc) des négociations/etc) ∎ **to pull over** vt (drag) traîner (qch, qn); (knock down) faire tomber ∎ vi (in vehicle) se ranger (sur le côté) ∎ **to pull round** vi (recover from illness) se remettre ∎ **to pull through** vi (survive illness etc) s'en tirer ∎ **to pull oneself together** vt se ressaisir ∎ **to pull up** vt (socks, Br blind, Am shade etc) remonter; (plant, tree etc) arracher; (stop) arrêter ∎ vi (in vehicle) s'arrêter. ● **pull-up** n (exercise on bars or rings) traction f.

pulley ['pʊlɪ] n poulie f.

pullout ['pʊlaʊt] n (in newspaper etc) supplément m détachable.

pullover ['pʊləʊvər] n pull(-over) m.

pulp [pʌlp] n (of fruit etc) pulpe f; (for paper) pâte f à papier; **in a p.** (crushed) en bouillie.

pulpit ['pʊlpɪt] n (in church) chaire f.

pulsate [pʌl'seɪt] vi produire des pulsations, battre; (vibrate) vibrer. ● **pulsation** [-ʃ(ə)n] n (heartbeat etc) pulsation f.

pulse [pʌls] n Med pouls m; (beating) pulsation f; (vibration) vibration f. ● **pulses** npl (plant seeds) graines fpl de légumineuse.

pulverize ['pʌlvəraɪz] vt (grind, defeat) pulvériser.

pumice ['pʌmɪs] n p. (stone) pierre f ponce.

pump [pʌmp] 1 n pompe f; **petrol p.** Br, **gas p.** Am pompe f à essence; **(petrol) p. attendant** Br pompiste mf ∎ vt pomper; (blood round body) faire circuler; (money, resources) Fig injecter (into dans); **to p. s.o.** (for information) tirer les vers du nez à qn; **to p. in** (liquid etc) refouler (à l'aide d'une pompe); **to p. out** (liquid etc) pomper (of de); **to p. air into, to p. up** (mattress etc) gonfler ∎ vi pomper; (of heart) battre.

2 n (shoe) (for sports) tennis m; (for dancing) escarpin m.

pumpkin ['pʌmpkɪn] n potiron m; **p. pie** Am tarte f au potiron.

pun [pʌn] n calembour m.

punch¹ [pʌntʃ] n (blow) coup m de poing; (force, vigour) Fig punch m; **to pack a p.** Boxing & Fig avoir du punch; **p. line** (of joke) astuce f finale ∎ vt (person) donner un coup de poing à; (s.o.'s nose etc) donner un coup de poing sur; (ball etc) frapper d'un coup de poing. ● **punch-up** n Br Fam bagarre f.

punch² [pʌntʃ] n (for paper) perforeuse f; (for tickets) poinçonneuse f; **p. card** carte f perforée ∎ vt (ticket) poinçonner; (with date) composter; (paper, card) perforer; **to p. a hole in sth** faire un trou dans qch.

punch³ [pʌntʃ] n (drink) punch m.

Punch [pʌntʃ] n P. **and Judy show** = guignol m.

punctilious [pʌŋk'tɪlɪəs] a pointilleux.

punctual ['pʌŋktʃʊəl] a (arriving on time) à l'heure; (regularly on time) ponctuel, exact. ● **punctu'ality** n ponctualité f, exactitude f. ● **punctually** adv (on time) à l'heure; (regularly) ponctuellement.

punctuate ['pʌŋktʃʊeɪt] vt ponctuer (with de). ● **punctuation** [-'eɪʃ(ə)n] n ponctuation f; **p. mark** signe m de ponctuation.

puncture ['pʌŋktʃər] n (in tyre) crevaison f; **to have a p.** crever ∎ vt (burst) crever (pneu, ballon etc); (pierce) piquer (peau, papier etc) ∎ vi (of Br tyre, Am tire) crever.

pundit ['pʌndɪt] n expert m, ponte m.

pungent ['pʌndʒənt] a âcre, piquant. ● **pungency** n âcreté f.

punish ['pʌnɪʃ] vt punir (for sth de qch, for doing or having done pour avoir fait); (treat *roughly*) *Fig* malmener (*adversaire etc*). ● **punishing** *a* (*tiring*) éreintant.

punishable ['pʌnɪʃəb(ə)l] *a* punissable (by de).

punishment ['pʌnɪʃmənt] *n* punition *f*, châtiment *m*; **capital p.** peine *f* capitale; **as (a) p. for** en punition de; **to take a (lot of) p.** (*damage*) *Fig* en encaisser.

punitive ['pjuːnɪtɪv] *a* (*measure etc*) punitif.

punk [pʌŋk] **1** *n* **p.** (*rock*) (*music*) le punk (rock); **p. rocker** (*fan*) punk *mf* ■ *a* punk *inv*. **2** *n* (*hoodlum*) *Am Fam* voyou *m*.

punnet ['pʌnɪt] *n* (*of strawberries*) *Br* barquette *f*.

punt [pʌnt] **1** *n* barque *f* (à fond plat). **2** *vi* (*bet*) *Br Fam* parier. ● **punting** *n* canotage *m*. ● **punter** *n Br* **1** (*gambler*) parieur, -euse *mf*. **2** (*customer*) *Fam* client, -ente *mf*.

puny ['pjuːnɪ] *a* (**-ier, -iest**) (*sickly*) chétif; (*small*) petit; (*effort*) faible.

pup [pʌp] *n* (*dog*) chiot *m*.

pupil ['pjuːp(ə)l] *n* **1** (*in school*) élève *mf*. **2** (*of eye*) pupille *f*.

puppet ['pʌpɪt] *n* marionnette *f*; **p. show** spectacle *m* de marionnettes ■ *a* (*government, leader*) fantoche.

puppy ['pʌpɪ] *n* (*dog*) chiot *m*.

purchase ['pɜːtʃɪs] *n* (*bought article*) achat *m*; **the p. of** (*buying*) l'achat *m* de ■ *vt* acheter (**from s.o.** à qn, **for s.o.** à *or* pour qn); **purchasing power** pouvoir *m* d'achat. ● **purchaser** *n* acheteur, -euse *mf*.

pure [pjʊər] *a* (**-er, -est**) pur.

purée ['pjʊəreɪ] *n* purée *f*.

purely ['pjʊəlɪ] *adv* (*only*) strictement; **p. and simply** purement et simplement.

purgatory ['pɜːgətrɪ] *n* purgatoire *m*.

purge [pɜːdʒ] *n Pol* purge *f* ■ *vt* purger (**of**de); (*political group*) épurer.

purify ['pjʊərɪfaɪ] *vt* purifier. ● **purification** [-'keɪʃ(ə)n] *n* purification *f*. ● **purifier** *n* (*for water*) épurateur *m*; (*for air*) purificateur *m*.

purist ['pjʊərɪst] *n* puriste *m*.

puritan ['pjʊərɪt(ə)n] *n & a* puritain, -aine (*mf*). ● **puri'tanical** *a* puritain.

purity ['pjʊərɪtɪ] *n* pureté *f*.

purl [pɜːl] *n* (*knitting stitch*) maille *f* à l'envers.

purple ['pɜːp(ə)l] *a* violet (*f* -ette); **to go** *or* **turn p.** (*with anger*) devenir pourpre; (*with shame*) devenir cramoisi ■ *n* violet *m*.

purport [pɜː'pɔːt] *vt* **to p. to be** (*claim*) prétendre être.

purpose ['pɜːpəs] *n* **1** (*aim*) but *m*; **for this p.** dans ce but; **on p.** exprès; **to no p.** inutilement; **to serve no p.** ne servir à rien; **for (the) purposes of** pour les besoins de. **2** (*determination, willpower*) résolution *f*; **to have a sense of p.** être résolu. ● **purpose-'built** *a* construit spécialement.

purposeful ['pɜːpəsfəl] *a* (*determined*) résolu. ● **purposefully** *adv* dans un but précis; (*resolutely*) résolument.

purposely ['pɜːpəslɪ] *adv* exprès.

purr [pɜːr] *vi* ronronner ■ *n* ronron(nement)

m.

purse [pɜːs] **1** *n* (*for coins*) porte-monnaie *m inv*; (*handbag*) *Am* sac *m* à main. **2** *vt* **to p. one's lips** pincer les lèvres.

purser ['pɜːsər] *n* (*on ship*) commissaire *m* du bord.

pursue [pə'sjuː] *vt* (*chase, seek, continue*) poursuivre (*animal, voleur, enquête, but etc*); (*fame, pleasure*) rechercher; (*course of action*) suivre. ● **pursuer** *n* poursuivant, -ante *mf*. ● **pursuit** *n* (*of person, glory etc*) poursuite *f*; (*activity, pastime*) occupation *f*; **to go in p. of s.o./sth** se mettre à la poursuite de qn/qch.

purveyor [pə'veɪər] *n* (*of goods*) fournisseur *m.*

pus [pʌs] *n* pus *m*.

push [pʊʃ] *n* (*shove*) poussée *f*; (*energy*) *Fig* dynamisme *m*; (*campaign*) campagne *f*; (*effort*) gros effort *m*; **to give s.o./sth a p.** pousser qn/qch; **to give s.o. the p.** (*dismiss*) *Br Fam* flanquer qn à la porte.

■ *vt* pousser (**to, as far as** jusqu'à); (*button*) appuyer sur; (*lever*) abaisser; (*product*) pousser la vente de; (*viewpoint etc*) mettre en avant; (*drugs*) *Fam* revendre; **to p. sth into/between** (*thrust*) enfoncer *or* fourrer qch dans/entre; **to p. s.o. into doing** (*urge*) pousser qn à faire; **to p. sth off the table** faire tomber qch de la table (en le poussant); **to p. s.o. off a cliff** pousser qn du haut d'une falaise; **to be pushing forty/etc** *Fam* friser la quarantaine/*etc*.

■ *vi* pousser; (*on button etc*) appuyer (**on** sur).

push about *or* **around** *vt* (*bully*) *Fam* marcher sur les pieds à (qn) ■ **to push aside** *vt* (*person, objection etc*) écarter ■ **to push away** *or* **back** *vt* repousser; (*curtains*) ouvrir ■ **to push down** *vt* (*button*) appuyer sur; (*lever*) abaisser ■ **to push for** *vt* faire pression pour obtenir (*qch*) ■ **to push in** *vi* (*in Br queue, Am line*) *Fam* resquiller ■ **to push off** *vi* (*leave*) *Fam* filer; **p. off!** *Fam* fiche le camp! ■ **to push on** *vi* (*go on*) continuer (**with sth** qch); (*in journey*) poursuivre sa route ■ **to push over** *vt* (*knock over*) renverser ■ **to push through** *vt* (*law*) faire adopter ■ *vti* **to p. (one's way) through** se frayer un chemin (**a crowd/etc** à travers une foule/*etc*) ■ **to push up** *vt* (*lever, sleeve, collar etc*) relever; (*increase*) augmenter, relever (*prix etc*).

pushbike ['pʊʃbaɪk] *n Br Fam* vélo *m*. ● **push-button** *n* bouton *m*; (*of phone*) touche *f*; **p.-button phone** téléphone *m* à touches; **push-button controls/operation** commande *f*/fonctionnement *m* automatique. ● **pushchair** *n Br* poussette *f* (pliante). ● **pushover** *n* **to be a** (*easy*) *Fam* être facile, être du gâteau. ● **push-up** *n* (*exercise*) *Am* pompe *f*.

pushed [pʊʃt] *a* **to be p.** (**for time**) (*rushed, busy*) être très bousculé.

pusher ['pʊʃər] *n* (*of drugs*) revendeur,

-euse *mf* (de drogue).

pushy ['pʊʃɪ] *a* (-ier, -iest) *Pej* (*self-assertive*) arrogant; (*in job*) arriviste.

puss(y) ['pʊs(ɪ)] *n* (*cat*) minou *m*, minet *m*.

put [pʊt] *vt* (*pt* & *pp* **put**, *pres p* **putting**) mettre; (*money, savings*) placer (**into** dans); (*problem, argument*) présenter (**to** à); (*question*) poser (**to** à); (*say*) dire; (*estimate*) évaluer (**at** à); **to p. pressure on sth/s.o.** faire pression sur qch/qn; **to p. a mark on sth** faire une marque sur qch; **to p. it bluntly** pour parler franc.

put across *vt* (*message, idea etc*) communiquer (**to** à) ∎ **to put aside** *vt* (*money, object*) mettre de côté ∎ **to put away** *vt* (*in its place*) ranger (*livre, voiture etc*); **to p. s.o. away** (*criminal*) mettre qn en prison; (*insane person*) enfermer qn ∎ **to put back** *vt* (*replace, postpone*) remettre; (*telephone receiver*) raccrocher; (*progress, clock, date*) retarder ∎ **to put by** *vt* (*money*) mettre de côté ∎ **to put down** *vt* (*on floor, table etc*) poser; (*passenger*) déposer; (*a deposit*) verser; (*revolt*) réprimer; (*write down*) inscrire; (*attribute*) attribuer (**to** à); (*kill*) faire piquer (*chien etc*) ∎ **to put forward** *vt* (*clock, meeting, argument*) avancer; (*opinion*) exprimer; (*candidate*) proposer (**for** à) ∎ **to put in** *vt* (*sth into box etc*) mettre dedans; (*insert*) introduire; (*add*) ajouter; (*install*) installer; (*present*) présenter; (*application, request*) faire; (*enrol*) inscrire (*qn*) (**for** à); (*spend*) passer (*une heure etc*) (**doing** à faire) ∎ *vi* **to p. in for** (*job etc*) faire une demande de; **to p. in at** (*of ship etc*) faire escale à ∎ **to put off** *vt* (*postpone*) renvoyer (à plus tard); (*passenger*) déposer; (*gas, radio*) fermer; (*dismay*) déconcerter; **to p. s.o. off** (*dissuade*) dissuader qn (**doing** de faire); (*disgust*) dégoûter qn (**sth** de qch); **to p. s.o. off doing** (*disgust*) ôter à qn l'envie de faire ∎ **to put on** *vt* (*clothes, shoe etc*) mettre; (*weight, accent*) prendre; (*film, play*) jouer; (*gas, radio*) mettre, allumer; (*record, cassette*) passer; (*clock*) avancer; **to p. s.o. on** (*tease*) *Am* faire marcher qn; **she p. me on to you** elle m'a donné votre adresse; **p. me on to him!** (*on phone*) passez-le-moi! ∎ **to put out** *vt* (*take outside*) sortir; (*arm, leg*) étendre;

(*hand*) tendre; (*tongue*) tirer; (*gas, light*) éteindre, fermer; (*bother, inconvenience*) déranger; (*upset*) déconcerter; (*issue*) publier; (*dislocate*) démettre ∎ **to put through** *vt* (*on phone*) passer (*qn*) (**to** à) ∎ **to put together** *vt* (*separate objects*) mettre ensemble; (*assemble*) assembler; (*compose*) composer; (*prepare*) préparer; (*collection*) faire ∎ **to put up** *vi* (*stay*) descendre (**at a hotel** à un hôtel) ∎ *vt* (*lift*) lever; (*window*) remonter; (*tent, statue, barrier, ladder*) dresser; (*flag*) hisser; (*building*) construire; (*umbrella*) ouvrir; (*picture, poster*) mettre; (*price, sales, numbers*) augmenter; (*resistance, plea, suggestion*) offrir; (*candidate*) proposer (**for** à); (*guest*) loger; **p.-up job** *Fam* coup *m* monté ∎ **to put up with** *vt* (*tolerate*) supporter (*qch, qn*).

putrid ['pjuːtrɪd] *a* putride. ●**putrify** *vi* se putréfier.

putt [pʌt] *n Golf* putt *m*. ●**putting** *n Golf* putting *m*; **p. green** green *m*.

putter ['pʌtər] *vi* **to p. around** *Am* bricoler.

putty ['pʌtɪ] *n* mastic *m* (*pour vitres*).

put-you-up ['pʊtjuːʌp] *n Br* canapé-lit *m*, convertible *m*.

puzzle ['pʌz(ə)l] *n* mystère *m*, énigme *f*; (*jigsaw*) puzzle *m*; (*game fitting boxes etc together*) casse-tête *m inv* ∎ *vt* laisser perplexe; **to p. out why/when/etc** essayer de comprendre pourquoi/quand/*etc*. ∎ *vi* **to p. over** (*problem, event*) se creuser la tête sur. ●**puzzled** *a* perplexe. ●**puzzling** *a* (*curious*) curieux; (*suprising*) surprenant.

PVC [piːviːsiː] *n* (*plastic*) PVC *m*; **P. belt**/*etc* ceinture *f*/*etc* en PVC.

pygmy ['pɪgmɪ] *n* pygmée *m*.

pyjama [pɪ'dʒɑːmə] *a* (*jacket etc*) *Br* de pyjama. ●**pyjamas** *npl Br* pyjama *m*; **a pair of p.** un pyjama; **to be in (one's) p.** être en pyjama.

pylon ['paɪlən] *n* pylône *m*.

pyramid ['pɪrəmɪd] *n* pyramide *f*.

Pyrenees [pɪrə'niːz] *npl* **the P.** les Pyrénées *fpl*.

Pyrex® ['paɪreks] *n* Pyrex® *m*; **P. dish**/*etc* plat *m*/*etc* en Pyrex.

python ['paɪθən] *n* (*snake*) python *m*.

Q

Q, q [kjuː] *n* Q, q *m*.

quack [kwæk] **1** *n (of duck)* coin-coin *m inv*. **2** *a & n* **q. (doctor)** charlatan *m*.

quad(rangle) ['kwɒd(ræŋg(ə)l)] *n (of college, school) Br* cour f.

quadruped ['kwɒdruped] *n* quadrupède *m*.

quadruple [kwɒ'druːp(ə)l] *vti* quadrupler.

quadruplets [kwɒ'druːplɪts] *(Fam* **quads** [kwɒdz]) *npl* quadruplés, -ées *mfpl*.

quaff [kwɒf] *vt (drink)* avaler.

quagmire ['kwægmaɪər] *n* bourbier *m*.

quail [kweɪl] *n (bird)* caille f.

quaint [kweɪnt] *a* **(-er, -est)** *(picturesque)* pittoresque; *(old-fashioned)* vieillot (f -otte); *(odd)* bizarre. ● **quaintness** *n* pittoresque *m*; *(old-fashionedness)* caractère *m* vieillot; *(oddness)* bizarrerie f.

quake [kweɪk] *n Fam* tremblement *m* de terre ‖ *vi* trembler **(with** de).

Quaker ['kweɪkər] *n* quaker, -eresse *mf*.

qualification [kwɒlɪfɪ'keɪʃ(ə)n] *n* **1** *(diploma)* diplôme *m*. **2** *(competence)* compétence f; *(professional background)* formation f; **qualifications** *(skills for job etc)* qualités *fpl* nécessaires **(for** pour, **to do** pour faire). **3** *(reservation)* réserve f.

qualify ['kwɒlɪfaɪ] **1** *vi* obtenir son diplôme *(as a doctor/etc* de médecin/etc); *Sport* se qualifier **(for** pour); **to q. for** *(post)* remplir les conditions requises pour ‖ *vt (make competent) & Sport* qualifier *(qn)* **(for sth** pour qch, **to do** pour faire).
2 *vt (modify)* faire une réserves à; *(opinion, statement)* nuancer; *Grammar* qualifier. ● **qualified** *a (able)* qualifié **(to do** pour faire); *(doctor etc)* diplômé; *(success)* limité; *(opinion)* nuancé; *(support)* conditionnel. ● **qualifying** *a* **q. exam** examen *m* d'entrée; **q. round** *Sport* épreuve f éliminatoire.

quality ['kwɒlɪtɪ] *n* qualité f; *a.* **product/***etc* produit *m/etc* de qualité. ● **qualitative** *a* qualitatif.

qualms [kwɑːmz] *npl (scruples)* scrupules *mpl*; *(anxieties)* inquiétudes *fpl*.

quandary ['kwɒndrɪ] *n* **in a q.** bien embarrassé; **to be in a q. about what to do** ne pas savoir quoi faire.

quantify ['kwɒntɪfaɪ] *vt* quantifier.

quantity ['kwɒntɪtɪ] *n* quantité f; **in q.** *(to purchase etc)* en grande(s) quantité(s); **q. surveyor** métreur *m* (vérificateur). ● **quantitative** *a* quantitatif.

quarantine ['kwɒrəntiːn] *n (for animal etc)* quarantaine f ‖ *vt* mettre en quarantaine.

quarrel ['kwɒrəl] *n* dispute f, querelle f; **to pick a q.** chercher des histoires **(with s.o.** à

qn) ‖ *vi (Br* **-ll-**, *Am* **-l-)** se disputer, se quereller **(with** avec); **to q. with sth** trouver à redire à qch. ● **quarrelling** *or Am* **quarreling** *n (quarrels)* disputes *fpl*, querelles *fpl*. ● **quarrelsome** *a* querelleur.

quarry ['kwɒrɪ] *n* **1** *(excavation to extract stone etc)* carrière f. **2** *(prey)* proie f.

quart [kwɔːt] *n* litre *m (mesure approximative) (Br = 1,14 litres, Am = 0,95 litre).*

quarter¹ ['kwɔːtər] *n* quart *m*; *(money) Am Can* quart *m* de dollar; *(division of year)* trimestre *m*; *(of fruit, moon)* quartier *m*; **to divide sth into quarters** diviser qch en quatre; **q. (of a) pound** quart *m* de livre; **a q. past nine** *Br*, **a q. after nine** *Am* neuf heures et or un quart; **a q. to nine** neuf heures moins le quart; **from all quarters** de toutes parts.

quarter² ['kwɔːtər] *n (district)* quartier *m*; **quarters** *(circles)* milieux *mpl*; **(living) quarters** logement(s) *m(pl)*; *(of soldier)* quartier(s) *m(pl)* ‖ *vt (troops)* cantonner.

quarterfinal [kwɔːtə'faɪn(ə)l] *n Sport* quart *m* de finale.

quarterly ['kwɔːtəlɪ] *a (magazine, payment etc)* trimestriel ‖ *adv* trimestriellement ‖ *n* publication f trimestrielle.

quartet(te) [kwɔː'tet] *n (music, players)* quatuor *m*; **(jazz) q.** quartette *m*.

quartz [kwɔːts] *n* quartz *m* ‖ *a (watch, clock etc)* à quartz.

quash [kwɒʃ] *vt (rebellion etc)* réprimer; *(legal verdict)* casser.

quasi- ['kweɪzaɪ] *pref* quasi-.

quaver ['kweɪvər] **1** *n (musical note) Br* croche f. **2** *vi (of voice etc)* chevroter ‖ *n* chevrotement *m*.

quay [kiː] *n (for boats)* quai *m*. ● **quayside** *n* **on the q.** sur les quais.

queasy ['kwiːzɪ] *a* **(-ier, -iest)** **to feel** or **be q.** avoir mal au cœur. ● **queasiness** *n* mal *m* au cœur.

Quebec [kwɪ'bek] *n* le Québec.

queen [kwiːn] *n* reine f; *Chess Cards* dame f; **the q. mother** la reine mère.

queer [kwɪər] *a* **(-er, -est)** *(odd)* bizarre; *(dubious)* louche; *(ill) Br Fam* patraque ‖ *n (homosexual) Offensive Sl* pédé *m*.

quell [kwel] *vt (revolt etc)* réprimer.

quench [kwentʃ] *vt (fire)* éteindre; **to q. one's thirst** se désaltérer.

querulous ['kwerʊləs] *a (complaining)* grognon (f -onne).

query ['kwɪərɪ] *n* question f; *(doubt)* doute *m* ‖ *vt (ask about)* poser des questions sur.

quest [kwest] *n* quête f **(for** de); **in q. of** en quête de.

question ['kwestʃ(ə)n] n question f; **there is some q. of it** il en est question; **there's no q. of it, it's out of the q.** c'est hors de question, il n'en est pas question; **without q.** incontestable(ment); **in q.** en question, dont il s'agit; **q. mark** point m d'interrogation; **q. master** (on television, radio etc) animateur, -trice mf.
❚ vt interroger (**about** sur); (doubt) mettre en question; **to q. whether** douter que (+ sub). ● **questioning** a (look etc) interrogateur ❚ n interrogation f.

questionable ['kwestʃ(ə)nəb(ə)l] a douteux, discutable.

questionnaire [kwestʃ(ə)'neər] n questionnaire m.

queue [kju:] n Br (of people) queue f; (of cars) file f; **to form a q., stand in a q.** faire la queue ❚ vi **(up)** Br faire la queue (**for the bus**/etc pour le bus/etc).

quibble ['kwɪb(ə)l] vi ergoter, discuter (**over** sur). ● **quibbling** n ergotage m.

quiche [ki:ʃ] n (tart) quiche f.

quick [kwɪk] 1 a (-er, -est) rapide; **q. to react** prompt à réagir; **be q.!** fais vite!; **to have a q. shower/meal**/etc se doucher/manger/etc en vitesse; **to be a q. worker** travailler vite ❚ adv (-er, -est) vite; **as q. as a flash** en un clin d'œil. 2 n **to cut s.o. to the q.** blesser qn au vif. ● **quick-'tempered** a irascible. ● **quick-'witted** a à l'esprit vif.

quicken ['kwɪk(ə)n] vt accélérer ❚ vi s'accélérer.

quickie ['kwɪkɪ] n (drink) Fam pot m (pris en vitesse).

quickly ['kwɪklɪ] adv vite.

quicksands ['kwɪksændz] npl sables mpl mouvants.

quid [kwɪd] n inv Br Fam livre f (sterling).

quiet ['kwaɪət] a (-er, -est) (silent, still, peaceful) tranquille, calme; (machine, vehicle) silencieux; (gentle) (person, temperament etc) doux (f douce); (not loud) (voice, music) doux (f douce); (sound) léger, doux (f douce); (private) (ceremony etc) intime; (colour) discret, **to be** or **keep q.** (shut up) se taire; (make no noise) ne pas faire de bruit; **q.!** silence!; **to keep q. about sth, keep sth q.** ne pas parler de qch; **on the q.** (secretly) Fam en cachette.
❚ vt calmer (qn).

quieten ['kwaɪət(ə)n] vt **to q. (down)** Br calmer (qn) ❚ vi **to q. down** Br se calmer.

quietly ['kwaɪətlɪ] adv tranquillement; (gently, not loudly) doucement; (silently) si-

lencieusement; (secretly) en cachette; (discreetly) discrètement. ● **quietness** n tranquillité f.

quill [kwɪl] n (pen) plume f (d'oie).

quilt [kwɪlt] n édredon m; **(continental) q.** (duvet) Br couette f ❚ vt (pad) matelasser; (stitch) piquer.

quintessence [kwɪn'tesəns] n quintessence f.

quintet(te) [kwɪn'tet] n quintette m.

quintuplets [Br kwɪn'tju:plɪts, Am -'tʌplɪts] (Fam **quins** [kwɪnz], Am **quints** [kwɪnts]) npl quintuplés, -ées mfpl.

quip [kwɪp] n (remark) boutade f ❚ vi (-pp-) faire des boutades ❚ vt dire sur le ton de la boutade.

quirk [kwɜːk] n bizarrerie f; (of fate etc) caprice m. ● **quirky** a (-ier, -iest) (odd) bizarre; (temperamental) capricieux.

quit [kwɪt] vt (pt & pp **quit** or **quitted**, pres p **quitting**) (leave) quitter; **to q. doing** arrêter de faire ❚ vi (give up) abandonner; (resign) démissionner.

quite [kwaɪt] adv (entirely) tout à fait; (really) vraiment; (rather) assez; **q. another matter** une tout autre affaire or question; **q. a genius** un véritable génie; **q. good** (not bad) pas mal (du tout); **q. (so)!** exactement!; **I q. understand** je comprends très bien or tout à fait; **q. a lot** pas mal (**of** de); **q. a (long) time ago** il y a pas mal de temps.

quits [kwɪts] a quitte (**with** envers); **to call it q.** en rester là.

quiver ['kwɪvər] vi (of person) frémir (**with** de); (of voice) trembler; (of flame) vaciller, trembler.

quiz [kwɪz] n (pl **quizzes**) (test) test m; (riddle) devinette f; **q. (programme)** (on television or radio) jeu-concours) m ❚ vt (-zz-) questionner. ● **quizmaster** n TV Radio animateur, -trice mf.

quizzical ['kwɪzɪk(ə)l] a (mocking) narquois; (perplexed) perplexe.

quorum ['kwɔːrəm] n quorum m.

quota ['kwəʊtə] n quota m.

quotation [kwəʊ'teɪʃ(ə)n] n citation f; (estimate) devis m; (on Stock Exchange) cote f; **q. marks** guillemets mpl; **in q. marks** entre guillemets.

quote [kwəʊt] vt citer; (reference number) rappeler; (price) indiquer; (price on Stock Exchange) coter ❚ vi **to q. from** (author, book) citer ❚ n = **quotation; in quotes** entre guillemets.

quotient ['kwəʊʃ(ə)nt] n quotient m.

R

R, r [ɑːr] *n* R, r *m*.

rabbi ['ræbaɪ] *n* rabbin *m*; **chief r.** grand rabbin.

rabbit ['ræbɪt] *n* lapin *m*.

rabble ['ræb(ə)l] *n* (*crowd*) cohue *f*; **the r.** *Pej* la populace.

rabies ['reɪbiːz] *n* (*disease*) rage *f*. ●**rabid** ['ræbɪd] *a* (*dog*) enragé; (*communist etc*) *Fig* fanatique.

raccoon [rə'kuːn] *n* (*animal*) raton *m* laveur.

race¹ [reɪs] *n* (*contest*) course *f* ▌*vt* (*horse*) faire courir; (*engine*) emballer; **to r.** (*against or with*) **s.o.** faire une course avec qn ▌*vi* (*run*) courir; (*of engine*) s'emballer; (*of pulse*) battre à tout rompre. ●**racing** *n* courses *fpl*; **r. car/bicycle** voiture *f*/vélo *m* de course; **r. driver** coureur *m* automobile.

race² [reɪs] *n* (*group*) race *f* ▌*a* (*prejudice etc*) racial; **r. relations** rapports *mpl* entre les races.

racecar ['reɪskɑːr] *n* Am voiture *f* de course. ●**racecourse** *n* champ *m* de courses. ●**racegoer** *n* turfiste *mf*. ●**racehorse** *n* cheval *m* de course. ●**racetrack** *n* (*for horses*) Am champ *m* de courses; (*for cars, bicycles*) Br piste *f*.

racial ['reɪʃəl] *a* racial. ●**racialism** *n* racisme *m*.

racism ['reɪsɪz(ə)m] *n* racisme *m*. ●**racist** *a* & *n* raciste (*mf*).

rack [ræk] **1** *n* (*for bottles, letters, records etc*) casier *m*; (*for drying dishes*) égouttoir *m*; (*set of shelves*) étagère *f*; (**luggage**) **r.** (*on bus, train etc*) filet *m* à bagages; (*on bicycle*) porte-bagages *m inv*; (**roof**) **r.** (*of car*) galerie *f*; (**drying**) **r.** séchoir *m* à linge.

2 *vt* **to r. one's brains** se creuser la cervelle.

3 *n* **to go to r. and ruin** (*of building*) tomber en ruine; (*of person*) aller à la ruine; (*of health*) se délabrer.

racket ['rækɪt] *n* **1** (*for tennis etc*) raquette *f*. **2** (*din*) vacarme *m*. **3** (*crime*) racket *m*; (*scheme*) combine *f*; **the drug(s) r.** le trafic de (la) drogue.

racketeer [rækɪ'tɪər] *n* racketteur *m*. ●**racketeering** *n* racket *m*.

racoon [rə'kuːn] *n* (*animal*) raton *m* laveur.

racy ['reɪsɪ] *a* (**-ier, -iest**) (*description, style etc*) piquant; (*suggestive*) osé.

radar ['reɪdɑːr] *n* radar *m*; **r. control/trap/etc** contrôle *m*/piège *m*/etc radar *inv*; **r. operator** radariste *m*.

radiant ['reɪdɪənt] *a* (*person, face etc*) rayonnant (**with** de), radieux; (*sun*) radieux. ●**radiance** *n* (*of face etc*) éclat *m*, rayonnement *m*; (*of sun*) éclat *m*. ●**radiantly** *adv* (*to shine*) avec éclat; **r. happy** rayonnant de joie.

radiate ['reɪdɪeɪt] *vt* (*emit*) dégager (*chaleur, lumière etc*); (*joy*) *Fig* rayonner de ▌*vi* (*of heat, lines*) rayonner (**from** de). ●**radiation** [-'eɪʃ(ə)n] *n* (*of heat etc*) rayonnement *m* (**of** de); (*radioactivity*) radiation *f*; (*rays*) irradiation *f*; **r. sickness** mal *m* des rayons.

radiator ['reɪdɪeɪtər] *n* (*of central heating, vehicle*) radiateur *m*.

radical ['rædɪk(ə)l] *a* radical ▌*n* (*person*) *Pol* radical, -ale *mf*.

radio ['reɪdɪəʊ] *n* (*pl* **-os**) radio *f*; **on** *or* **over the r.** à la radio; **car r.** autoradio *m*; **r. set** poste *m* (de) radio; **r. operator** radio *m*; **r. wave** onde *f* hertzienne ▌*vt* (*message*) transmettre (par radio) (**to** à); **to r. s.o.** appeler qn par radio. ●**radio-con'trolled** *a* radioguidé.

radioactive [reɪdɪəʊ'æktɪv] *a* radioactif. ●**radioac'tivity** *n* radioactivité *f*.

radiographer [reɪdɪ'ɒɡrəfər] *n* (*technician*) radiologue *mf*. ●**radiography** *n* radiographie *f*. ●**radiologist** *n* (*doctor*) radiologue *mf*. ●**radiology** *n* radiologie *f*.

radish ['rædɪʃ] *n* radis *m*.

radius, *pl* **-dii** ['reɪdɪəs, -dɪaɪ] *n* (*of circle*) rayon *m*; **within a r. of 10 km** dans un rayon de 10 km.

RAF [ɑːr'eɪ'ef] *n abbr* (*Royal Air Force*) armée *f* de l'air (britannique).

raffia ['ræfɪə] *n* raphia *m*.

raffle ['ræf(ə)l] *n* tombola *f*.

raft [rɑːft] *n* (*boat*) radeau *m*.

rafter ['rɑːftər] *n* (*beam*) chevron *m*.

rag [ræɡ] *n* **1** (*piece of old clothing*) haillon *m*, loque *f*; (*for dusting etc*) chiffon *m*; **in rags** (*clothes*) en loques; (*person*) en haillons; **r.-and-bone man** Br *Old-fashioned* chiffonnier *m*. **2** (*newspaper*) torchon *m*. **3** (*university procession*) Br carnaval *m* d'étudiants (*au profit d'œuvres de charité*).

ragamuffin ['ræɡəmʌfɪn] *n* va-nu-pieds *m inv*.

rage [reɪdʒ] *n* (*of person*) rage *f*; (*of sea*) furie *f*; **to fly into a r.** se mettre en rage; **to be all the r.** (*of fashion etc*) faire fureur ▌*vi* (*be angry*) rager; (*of storm, battle*) faire rage. ●**raging** *a* (*storm, fever*) violent; **a r. fire** un grand incendie; **in a r. temper** furieux.

ragged ['ræɡɪd] *a* (*clothes*) en loques; (*person*) en haillons; (*edge*) irrégulier.

rah-rah ['rɑːrɑː] *a* **r. skirt** jupette *f* à volants.

raid [reɪd] *n* (*military*) raid *m*; (*by police*) descente *f*; (*by thieves*) hold-up *m inv*; **air r.** raid *m* aérien, attaque *f* aérienne ▌*vt* faire un raid *or* une descente *or* un hold-up dans; (*of aircraft*) attaquer; (*fridge*, *Br* larder etc) *Fam* dévaliser. ● **raider** n (*criminal*) malfaiteur m; **raiders** (*soldiers*) commando m.

rail [reɪl] **1** n (*for train*) rail m; **by r.** (*to travel*) par le train; (*to send*) par chemin de fer; **to go off the rails** (*of train*) dérailler ▮ a (*ticket*) de chemin de fer; (*network*) ferroviaire; (*strike*) des cheminots. **2** n (*rod on balcony*) balustrade f; (*on stairs*, *for spotlight*) rampe f; (*curtain rod*) tringle f; (*towel*) **r.** *Br* porte-serviettes m inv.

railcard ['reɪlkɑːd] n carte f de chemin de fer.

railing ['reɪlɪŋ] n (*of balcony*) balustrade f; **railings** (*fence*) grille f.

railroad ['reɪlrəʊd] n *Am* = **railway**; **r. track** voie f ferrée.

railway ['reɪlweɪ] *Br* n (*system*) chemin m de fer; (*track*) voie f ferrée ▮ a (*ticket*) de chemin de fer; (*timetable*, *employee* etc) des chemins de fer; (*network*, *company*) ferroviaire; **r. carriage** voiture f; **r. line** (*route*) ligne f de chemin de fer; (*track*) voie f ferrée; **r. station** gare f. ● **railwayman** n *Br* (*pl* -**men**) cheminot m.

rain [reɪn] n pluie f; **in the r.** sous la pluie ▮ vi pleuvoir; **to r. (down)** (*of blows*, *bullets*) pleuvoir; **it's raining** il pleut.

rainbow ['reɪnbəʊ] n arc-en-ciel m. ● **rain check** n **I'll give you a r. check** (*for invitation*) *Am Fam* j'accepterai volontiers à une date ultérieure. ● **raincoat** n imper(méable) m. ● **raindrop** n goutte f de pluie. ● **rainfall** n (*amount*) précipitations fpl; (*shower*) chute f de pluie. ● **rainforest** n forêt f tropicale (humide). ● **rainproof** a imperméable. ● **rainstorm** n trombe f d'eau. ● **rainwater** n eau f de pluie. ● **rainy** a (-**ier**, -**iest**) pluvieux; **the r. season** la saison des pluies.

raise [reɪz] vt (*lift*) lever; (*sth heavy*) (sou)lever; (*child*, *family*, *animal*, *voice*, *statue*) élever; (*crops*) cultiver; (*salary*, *price*) augmenter, relever; (*temperature*) faire monter; (*question*, *protest*) soulever; (*taxes*, *blockade*) lever; **to r. a smile/a laugh** (*in others*) faire sourire/rire; **to r. s.o.'s hopes** faire naître les espérances de qn; **to r. money** réunir des fonds; **to r. a loan** obtenir un prêt.
▮ n (*pay rise*) *Am* augmentation f (de salaire).

raisin ['reɪz(ə)n] n raisin m sec.

rake [reɪk] n râteau m ▮ vt (*garden*) ratisser; **to r. (up)** (*leaves*) ratisser, ramasser (avec un râteau); **to r. in** (*money*) *Fam* ramasser à la pelle; **to r. through** (*drawers*, *papers*) fouiller dans; **to r. up the past** remuer le passé. ● **rake-off** n *Fam* ristourne f.

rally [ˈrælɪ] vt (*unite*, *win over*) rallier (**to** à); **to r. support** rallier des partisans (**for** autour de); **to r. one's strength** *Fig* reprendre ses forces ▮ vi se rallier (**to** à); (*recover*) reprendre ses forces; (*of share prices*) se raffermir, se redresser; **to r. round (s.o.)**

(*help*) venir en aide (à qn); **rallying point** point m de ralliement ▮ n (*political*) rassemblement m; (*car race*) rallye m; (*of share prices*) raffermissement m, redressement m.

ram [ræm] **1** n (*animal*) bélier m. **2** vt (-**mm**-) (*vehicle*) emboutir; (*ship*) heurter; **to r. sth into sth** enfoncer qch dans qch.

RAM [ræm] n abbr *Comptr* = **random access memory**.

ramble [ˈræmb(ə)l] **1** n (*hike*) randonnée f ▮ vi faire une randonnée *or* des randonnées. **2** vi **to r. on** (*talk at length*) discourir. ● **rambler** n promeneur, -euse mf.

rambling [ˈræmblɪŋ] **1** a (*house*) construit sans plan; (*spread out*) vaste; (*rose* etc) grimpant. **2** a (*speech*) décousu ▮ npl **ramblings** divagations fpl.

ramification [ræmɪfɪˈkeɪʃ(ə)n] n ramification f.

ramp [ræmp] n (*slope for wheelchair* etc) rampe f d'accès; (*in garage*) pont m (de graissage); (*stairs for aircraft*) passerelle f; **'r.'** (*road sign*) *Br* 'dénivellation'.

rampage [ˈræmpeɪdʒ] n **to go on the r.** (*of crowd*) se déchaîner; (*loot*) se livrer au pillage.

rampant [ˈræmpənt] a **to be r.** (*of crime*, *disease* etc) sévir.

rampart [ˈræmpɑːt] n rempart m.

ramshackle [ˈræmˌʃæk(ə)l] a délabré.

ran [ræn] pt of **run**.

ranch [rɑːntʃ] n *Am* ranch m; **r. house** maison f genre bungalow (sur sous-sol).

rancid [ˈrænsɪd] a rance.

rancour [ˈræŋkər] (*Am* **rancor**) n rancœur f.

random [ˈrændəm] n **at r.** au hasard ▮ a (*choice*) (fait) au hasard; (*sample*) prélevé au hasard; (*pattern*) irrégulier; **r. access** *Comptr* accès m aléatoire; **r. access memory** *Comptr* mémoire f vive; **r. check** (*by police*) contrôle-surprise m.

randy [ˈrændɪ] a (-**ier**, -**iest**) *Br Fam* excité.

rang [ræŋ] pt of **ring²**.

range [reɪndʒ] **1** n (*of gun*, *voice* etc) portée f; (*of singer's voice*) étendue f; (*of aircraft*, *ship*) rayon m d'action; (*of colours*, *prices*, *products*) gamme f; (*of sizes*) choix m; (*of temperature*) variations fpl; (*sphere*) *Fig* champ m, étendue f ▮ vi (*vary*) varier (**from** de, **to** à); (*extend*) s'étendre; (*roam*) errer, rôder.
  2 n (*of mountains*) chaîne f; (*grassland*) *Am* prairie f.
  3 n (*stove*) *Am* cuisinière f.
  4 n (*shooting or rifle*) **r.** (*at funfair*) stand m de tir; (*outdoors*) champ m de tir.

ranger [ˈreɪndʒər] n (*forest*) **r.** garde m forestier.

rank [ræŋk] **1** n (*position*, *class*) rang m; (*military grade*) grade m, rang m; **the r. and file** (*workers* etc) la base; **the ranks** (*men in army*, *numbers*) les rangs mpl (**of** de); **taxi r.** *Br* station f de taxi ▮ vti **to r. among** compter parmi. **2** a (-**er**, -**est**) (*smell*) fétide; (*vegeta-*

tion) luxuriant. **3** *a* (*thorough*) (*stupidity etc*) absolu.

rankle ['ræŋk(ə)l] *vi* it rankles (with me) je l'ai sur le cœur.

ransack ['rænsæk] *vt* (*search*) fouiller; (*plunder*) saccager.

ransom ['ræns(ə)m] *n* (*money*) rançon *f*; to hold s.o. to r. rançonner qn ▮ *vt* (*redeem*) racheter.

rant [rænt] *vi* to r. (and rave) tempêter (at contre).

rap [ræp] **1** *n* petit coup *m* sec ▮ *vi* (-pp-) frapper (at à) ▮ *vt* to r. s.o. over the knuckles taper sur les doigts de qn. **2** *n* r. (*music*) (*musique f*) rap *m*.

rapacious [rə'peɪʃəs] *a* (*greedy*) rapace.

rape [reɪp] *vt* violer ▮ *n* viol *m*. ● **rapist** *n* violeur *m*.

rapid ['ræpɪd] *a* rapide. ● **ra'pidity** *n* rapidité *f*. ● **rapidly** *adv* rapidement.

rapids ['ræpɪdz] *npl* (*of river*) rapides *mpl*.

rapport [ræ'pɔːr] *n* (*understanding*) rapport *m*.

rapt [ræpt] *a* (*attention*) profond.

rapture ['ræptʃər] *n* extase *f*; to go into raptures s'extasier (about sur). ● **rapturous** *a* (*welcome, applause*) enthousiaste.

rare [reər] *a* **1** (-er, -est) rare; (*first-rate*) *Fam* fameux; it's r. for her to do it il est rare qu'elle le fasse. **2** (*meat*) bleu; (*medium*) r. saignant. ● **rarely** *adv* rarement. ● **rareness** *n* rareté *f*. ● **rarity** *n* (*quality, object*) rareté *f*.

rarebit ['reəbɪt] *n* Welsh r. *Br* toast *m* chaud au fromage.

rarefied ['reərɪfaɪd] *a* raréfié.

raring ['reərɪŋ] *a* r. to start/etc impatient de commencer/etc.

rascal ['rɑːsk(ə)l] *n* coquin, -ine *mf*. ● **rascally** *a* (*child etc*) coquin; (*habit, trick etc*) de coquin.

rash [ræʃ] **1** *n* (*on skin*) (*red patches*) rougeurs *fpl*; (*spots*) (éruption *f* de) boutons *mpl*; to come out in a r. faire une éruption de boutons. **2** *a* (-er, -est) irréfléchi. ● **rashly** *adv* sans réfléchir. ● **rashness** *n* irréflexion *f*.

rasher ['ræʃər] *n* *Br* tranche *f* de lard.

rasp [rɑːsp] *n* (*file*) râpe *f*.

raspberry ['rɑːzbərɪ] *n* (*fruit*) framboise *f*; r. (bush) framboisier *m*.

rasping ['rɑːspɪŋ] *a* (*voice*) âpre; (*sound*) grinçant.

Rastafarian [ræstə'feərɪən] *n* & *a* rasta(fari) (*mf*) *inv*.

rat [ræt] **1** *n* rat *m*; r. poison mort-aux-rats *f*; the r. race *Fig* la course au bifteck, la jungle. **2** *vi* (-tt-) to r. on *Fam* (*denounce*) cafarder sur; (*desert*) lâcher; (*promise etc*) manquer à.

rate [reɪt] **1** *n* (*level, percentage*) taux *m*; (*speed*) vitesse *f*; (*price*) tarif *m*; the rates (*former tax on housing*) *Br* les impôts *mpl* locaux; exchange/interest/etc r. taux *m* de change/d'intérêt/etc; insurance rates primes *fpl* d'assurance; postage or postal r. tarif *m* postal; r. of flow débit *m*; at the r. of à une

vitesse de; (*amount*) à raison de; at this r. (*slow speed*) à ce train-là; at any r. en tout cas; the success r. (*chances*) les chances *fpl* de succès; (*candidates*) le pourcentage de reçus.

2 *vt* (*evaluate*) évaluer; (*regard*) considérer (as comme); (*deserve*) mériter; to r. highly apprécier (beaucoup); to be highly rated être très apprécié. ● **ratepayer** *n* (*formerly*) *Br* contribuable *mf*.

rather ['rɑːðər] *adv* (*preferably, quite*) plutôt; I'd r. stay j'aimerais mieux or je préférerais rester (than que); I'd r. you came j'aimerais mieux or je préférerais que vous veniez; r. than leave/etc plutôt que de partir/etc; r. more tired/etc un peu plus fatigué/etc (than que); it's r. nice c'est bien.

ratify ['rætɪfaɪ] *vt* ratifier. ● **ratification** [-'keɪʃ(ə)n] *n* ratification *f*.

rating ['reɪtɪŋ] *n* (*classification*) classement *m*; (*wage etc level*) indice *m*; credit r. (*of company, person*) degré *m* or réputation *f* de solvabilité; the ratings (*of television programme*) l'indice *m* d'écoute.

ratio ['reɪʃɪəʊ] *n* (*pl* -os) proportion *f*.

ration [*Br* 'ræʃ(ə)n, *Am* 'reɪʃ(ə)n] *n* ration *f*; rations (*food*) vivres *mpl* ▮ *vt* rationner; I was rationed to... ma ration était (de)..., j'avais droit à.... ● **rationing** *n* rationnement *m*.

rational ['ræʃən(ə)l] *a* (*thought, method etc*) rationnel; (*person*) raisonnable. ● **rationalize** *vt* (*organize*) rationaliser; (*explain*) justifier. ● **rationally** *adv* (*to behave etc*) raisonnablement.

rattle ['ræt(ə)l] **1** *n* (*baby's toy*) hochet *m*; (*of sports fan*) crécelle *f*.

2 *n* petit bruit *m* (sec); (*of keys etc*) cliquetis *m*; (*of gunfire*) crépitement *m* ▮ *vi* faire du bruit; (*of window*) trembler; (*of bottles*) cliqueter; (*of gunfire*) crépiter ▮ *vt* (*shake*) secouer; (*window*) faire trembler; (*keys*) faire cliqueter.

3 *vt* to r. s.o. (*make nervous*) *Fam* ébranler qn; to r. off (*poem etc*) *Fam* débiter (à toute vitesse).

rattlesnake ['ræt(ə)lsneɪk] *n* serpent *m* à sonnette.

ratty ['rætɪ] *a* (-ier, -iest) **1** (*shabby*) *Am Fam* minable. **2** to get r. (*annoyed*) *Br Fam* prendre la mouche.

raucous ['rɔːkəs] *a* (*noisy, rowdy*) bruyant.

raunchy ['rɔːntʃɪ] *a* (-ier, -iest) (*joke etc*) *Am Fam* cochon (*f* -onne), salé.

ravage ['rævɪdʒ] *vt* ravager. ● **ravages** *npl* (*of old age, time etc*) ravages *mpl*.

rave [reɪv] *vi* (*talk nonsense*) divaguer; (*rage*) tempêter (at contre); to r. about s.o./sth (*enthuse*) ne pas tarir d'éloges sur qn/qch ▮ *a* r. review *Fam* critique *f* dithyrambique. ● **raving** *a* to be a r. lunatic, be r. mad être fou furieux. ● **ravings** *npl* (*wild talk*) divagations *fpl*.

raven ['reɪv(ə)n] *n* corbeau *m*.

ravenous ['rævənəs] *a* (*appetite*) vorace; I'm

r. j'ai une faim de loup.

ravine [rə'viːn] *n* ravin *m*.

ravioli [rævɪ'oʊlɪ] *n* ravioli(s) *mpl*.

ravish ['rævɪʃ] *vt* (*rape*) *Lit* violenter.

ravishing ['rævɪʃɪŋ] *a* (*beautiful*) ravissant.
● **ravishingly** *adv* r. beautiful d'une beauté ravissante.

raw [rɔː] *a* (**-er, -est**) (*vegetable etc*) cru; (*sugar, data*) brut; (*skin*) écorché; (*wound*) à vif; (*immature*) inexpérimenté; (*weather*) rigoureux; **r. edge** bord *m* coupé; **r. material** matière *f* première; **to get a r. deal** *Fam* être mal traité.

Rawlplug® ['rɔːlplʌg] *n Br* cheville *f*.

ray [reɪ] *n* 1 (*of light, sun etc*) rayon *m*; (*of hope*) *Fig* lueur *f*. 2 (*fish*) raie *f*.

rayon ['reɪɒn] *n* rayonne *f* **I** *a* en rayonne.

raze [reɪz] *vt* **to r. (to the ground)** (*destroy*) raser.

razor ['reɪzər] *n* rasoir *m*; **r. blade** lame *f* de rasoir.

Rd *abbr* = **road.**

re [riː] *prep Com* en référence à.

re- [riː] *pref* ré-, re-, r-.

reach [riːtʃ] *vt* (*place, aim, distant object etc*) atteindre, arriver à; (*gain access to*) accéder à; (*of letter*) parvenir à (qn); (*contact*) joindre (qn); **to r. a conclusion** arriver à *or* parvenir à une conclusion; **to r. s.o. (over)** sth (*hand over*) passer qch à qn; **to r. out** one's arm (é)tendre le bras.
I *vi* (*extend*) s'étendre (to à); (*of voice*) porter; **to r. out** (*with arm*) (é)tendre le bras (**for** pour prendre).
I *n* portée *f*; *Boxing* allonge *f*; **within r. of** à portée de; (*near*) à proximité de; **within (easy) r.** (*object*) à portée de main; (*shops*) facilement accessible.

react [rɪ'ækt] *vi* réagir (**against** contre, **to** à).
● **reaction** [-ʃ(ə)n] *n* réaction *f*.

reactionary [rɪ'ækʃ(ə)nərɪ] *a* & *n* réactionnaire (*mf*).

reactor [rɪ'æktər] *n* réacteur *m* (*nucléaire*).

read [riːd] *vt* (*pt* & *pp* **read** [red]) lire; (*meter*) relever; (*of instrument*) indiquer; **to r. French/history/etc** (*at British university*) faire des études de français/d'histoire/*etc* **I** *vi* lire; **to r. well** (*of text*) se lire bien; **to r. to s.o.** faire la lecture à qn **I** *n* **to have a r.** *Fam* faire un peu de lecture; **this book is a good r.** *Fam* ce livre est agréable à lire. ● **readable** *a* (*handwriting, book etc*) lisible.

read about *vt* lire quelque chose sur (qn, qch) **I to read back** *vt* relire **I to read for** *vt* (*university degree*) *Br* préparer **I to read out** *vt* lire (qch) (à haute voix) **I to read over** *vt* relire **I to read through** *vt* (*skim*) parcourir **I to read up (on)** *vt* (*study*) étudier.

readdress [riːə'dres] *vt* (*letter*) faire suivre.

reader ['riːdər] *n* lecteur, -trice *mf*; (*book*) livre *m* de lecture. ● **readership** *n* lecteurs *mpl*, public *m*.

readily ['redɪlɪ] *adv* (*willingly*) volontiers; (*easily*) facilement. ● **readiness** *n* empressement *m* (**to do** à faire); **in r. for sth** prêt

pour qch.

reading ['riːdɪŋ] *n* lecture *f*; (*of meter*) relevé *m*; (*by instrument*) indication *f*; (*variant*) variante *f*; **it's light/heavy r.** c'est facile/difficile à lire; **r. book/room** livre *m*/salle *f* de lecture; **r. glasses** lunettes *fpl* pour lire; **r. lamp** (*on desk*) lampe *f* de bureau; (*at bedside*) lampe *f* de chevet; **r. matter** choses *fpl* à lire.

readjust [riːə'dʒʌst] *vt* (*instrument*) régler; (*salary*) réajuster **I** *vi* (*of person*) se réadapter (**to** à). ● **readjustment** *n* réglage *m*; (*of salary*) réajustement *m*; (*of person*) réadaptation *f*.

read-only [riːd'oʊnlɪ] *a* **r.-only memory** *Comptr* mémoire *f* morte.

ready ['redɪ] *a* (**-ier, -iest**) prêt (**to do** à faire, **for sth** à *or* pour qch); (*quick*) *Fig* prompt (**to do** à faire); **to get sth/s.o. r.** préparer qch/qn; **to get r.** se préparer (**for sth** à *or* pour qch, **to do** à faire); **r. cash, r. money** argent *m* liquide **I** *n* **to be at the r.** être tout prêt. ● **ready-'cooked** *a* tout cuit. ● **ready-'made** *a* (*article, food etc*) tout fait; **r.-made clothes** le prêt-à-porter; **to wear r.-made clothes** s'habiller en prêt-à-porter. ● **ready-to-wear** *a* **r.-to-wear clothes** le prêt-à-porter *m inv*.

real [rɪəl] *a* vrai, véritable; (*world, fact etc*) réel; **in r. life** dans la réalité; **in r. terms** dans la pratique; **it's the r. thing** *Fam* c'est du vrai de vrai; **r. estate** *Am* immobilier *m* **I** *adv Fam* vraiment; **r. stupid** vraiment bête **I** *n* **for r.** *Fam* pour de vrai.

realism ['rɪəlɪz(ə)m] *n* réalisme *m*. ● **realist** *n* réaliste *mf*. ● **rea'listic** *a* réaliste. ● **rea'listically** *adv* avec réalisme.

reality [rɪ'ælɪtɪ] *n* réalité *f*; **in r.** en réalité.

realize ['rɪəlaɪz] *vt* 1 (*know*) se rendre compte de, réaliser; (*understand*) comprendre (**that** que); **to r. that** (*know*) se rendre compte que. 2 (*carry out*) réaliser (*projet etc*); (*convert into cash*) réaliser (*actif, bénéfices*); (*achieve*) atteindre (*prix*). ● **realization** [-'zeɪʃ(ə)n] *n* 1 (*awareness*) (prise *f* de) conscience *f*. 2 (*of plan, assets etc*) réalisation *f*.

really ['rɪəlɪ] *adv* vraiment; **is it r. true?** est-ce bien vrai?

realm [relm] *n* (*kingdom*) royaume *m*; (*of science etc*) *Fig* domaine *m*; (*of dreams etc*) monde *m*.

realtor ['rɪəltər] *n Am* agent *m* immobilier.

ream [riːm] *n* (*of paper*) rame *f*.

reap [riːp] *vt* (*field, crop*) moissonner; (*profits etc*) *Fig* récolter.

reappear [riːə'pɪər] *vi* réapparaître.

reappraisal [riːə'preɪz(ə)l] *n* réévaluation *f*.

rear [rɪər] *n* 1 (*back part*) arrière *m*; (*of military column*) queue *f*; **in** *or* **at the r.** à l'arrière (**of** de); **from the r.** par derrière **I** *a* arrière *inv*, de derrière. 2 *vt* (*family, animals etc*) élever; (*one's head*) relever. 3 *vi* **to r. (up)** (*of horse*) se cabrer. ● **rearguard** *n* arrière-garde *f*. ● **rear-view 'mirror** *n* (*in vehicle*) rétroviseur *m*.

rearrange [ri:ə'reɪndʒ] *vt* (*hair*, *room*) réarranger; (*plans*) changer.

reason ['ri:z(ə)n] *n* (*cause*, *sense*) raison *f*; **the r. for/why or that...** la raison de/pour laquelle...; **for no r.** sans raison; **that stands to r.** c'est logique, cela va sans dire; **within r.** avec modération; **to do everything within r. to...** faire tout ce qu'il est raisonnable de faire pour...; **to have every r. to believe/etc** avoir tout lieu de croire/etc.
▮ *vi* raisonner; **to r. with s.o.** raisonner qn.
▮ *vt* **to r. that** calculer que. ● **reasoning** *n* raisonnement *m*.

reasonable ['ri:zənəb(ə)l] *a* raisonnable. ● **reasonably** *adv* (*to behave etc*) raisonnablement; (*fairly*, *rather*) assez; **r. fit** en assez bonne forme.

reassure [ri:ə'ʃʊər] *vt* rassurer. ● **reassuring** *a* rassurant. ● **reassurance** *n* réconfort *m*.

reawaken [ri:ə'weɪk(ə)n] *vt* (*interest etc*) réveiller. ● **reawakening** *n* réveil *m*.

rebate ['ri:beɪt] *n* (*discount on purchase*) ristourne *f*; (*refund*) remboursement *m* (*partiel*); (*tax refund*) remboursement *m* d'un trop-perçu d'impôt; (*reduction of tax*) dégrèvement *m* fiscal.

rebel ['reb(ə)l] *n* rebelle *mf*; (*against parents etc*) révolté, -ée *mf* ▮ a (*camp*, *chief*, *attack etc*) des rebelles ▮ [rɪ'bel] *vi* (-**ll**-) se révolter, se rebeller (**against** contre). ● **rebellion** [rɪ'beljən] *n* révolte *f*, rébellion *f*. ● **re'bellious** *a* (*child etc*) rebelle.

rebirth ['ri:bɜ:θ] *n* renaissance *f*.

rebound [rɪ'baʊnd] *vi* (*of ball*) rebondir; (*of stone*) ricocher; (*of lies*, *action etc*) *Fig* retomber (**on s.o.** sur qn) ▮ ['ri:baʊnd] *n* rebond *m*; (*of stone*) ricochet *m*; **to marry s.o. on the r.** épouser qn à cause d'une déception amoureuse.

rebuff [rɪ'bʌf] *vt* repousser ▮ *n* rebuffade *f*.

rebuild [ri:'bɪld] *vt* (*pt & pp* **rebuilt**) reconstruire.

rebuke [rɪ'bju:k] *vt* réprimander ▮ *n* réprimande *f*.

rebuttal [rɪ'bʌt(ə)l] *n* réfutation *f*.

recalcitrant [rɪ'kælsɪtrənt] *a* récalcitrant.

recall [rɪ'kɔ:l] *vt* (*remember*) se rappeler (**that** que, **doing** avoir fait); (*call back*) rappeler; **to r. sth to s.o.** rappeler qch à qn ▮ *n* (*calling back*) rappel *m*; **beyond r.** irrévocable; **my powers of r.** (*memory*) ma mémoire.

recant [rɪ'kænt] *vi* se rétracter.

recap [ri:'kæp] *vti* (-**pp**-) récapituler ▮ ['ri:kæp] *n* récapitulation *f*. ● **reca'pitulate** *vti* récapituler. ● **recapitulation** [-'leɪʃ(ə)n] *n* récapitulation *f*.

recapture [ri:'kæptʃər] *vt* (*prisoner etc*) reprendre; (*rediscover*) retrouver; (*recreate*) recréer ▮ *n* (*of prisoner*) arrestation *f*.

recede [rɪ'si:d] *vi* (*into the distance*) s'éloigner; (*of floods*) baisser. ● **receding** *a* (*forehead*) fuyant; **his hair(line) is r.** son front se dégarnit.

receipt [rɪ'si:t] *n* (*for payment*, *object left etc*)

reçu *m* (**for** de); (*for letter*, *parcel*) récépissé *m*, accusé *m* de réception; **receipts** (*takings*, *money received*) recettes *fpl*; **to acknowledge r.** accuser réception (**of** de); **on r. of** dès réception de.

receive [rɪ'si:v] *vt* recevoir; (*stolen goods*) receler. ● **receiving** *n* (*of stolen goods*) recel *m*.

receiver [rɪ'si:vər] *n* **1** (*of phone*) combiné *m*; (*radio*) récepteur *m*; **to pick up or lift the r.** (*of phone*) décrocher. **2** (*of stolen goods*) receleur, -euse *mf*; (*in bankruptcy*) *Br* administrateur *m* judiciaire. ● **receivership** *n* **to go into r.** être placé en règlement judiciaire.

recent ['ri:sənt] *a* récent; **in r. months** ces mois-ci. ● **recently** *adv* récemment; **as r. as** pas plus tard que.

receptacle [rɪ'septək(ə)l] *n* récipient *m*.

reception [rɪ'sepʃ(ə)n] *n* (*party*, *welcome*, *of radio etc*) réception *f*; **r. (desk)** réception *f*; **r. room** salle *f* de séjour. ● **receptionist** *n* secrétaire *mf*, réceptionniste *mf*.

receptive [rɪ'septɪv] *a* réceptif (**to an idea/etc** à une idée/etc); **r. to s.o.** compréhensif envers qn.

recess [*Br* rɪ'ses, *Am* 'ri:ses] *n* **1** (*Br holiday*, *Am vacation*) vacances *fpl*; (*between classes in school*) *Am* récréation *f*. **2** (*alcove*) renfoncement *m*; (*nook*) & *Fig* recoin *m*.

recession [rɪ'seʃ(ə)n] *n* (*economic*) récession *f*.

recharge [ri:'tʃɑ:dʒ] *vt* (*battery*) recharger. ● **rechargeable** *a* (*battery*) rechargeable.

recipe ['resɪpɪ] *n* (*for food*) & *Fig* recette *f* (**for sth** de qch, **for doing** pour faire).

recipient [rɪ'sɪpɪənt] *n* (*of award*, *honour*) récipiendaire *m*.

reciprocal [rɪ'sɪprək(ə)l] *a* réciproque.

reciprocate [rɪ'sɪprəkeɪt] *vt* (*compliment*) retourner; (*gesture*) faire à son tour ▮ *vi* (*do the same*) en faire autant.

recital [rɪ'saɪt(ə)l] *n* (*of music*) récital *m*.

recite [rɪ'saɪt] *vt* (*poem etc*) réciter; (*list*) énumérer. ● **recitation** [resɪ'teɪʃ(ə)n] *n* récitation *f*.

reckless ['rekləs] *a* (*rash*) imprudent. ● **recklessly** *adv* imprudemment.

reckon ['rek(ə)n] *vt* (*calculate*) calculer; (*count*) compter; (*consider*) considérer; (*think*) penser (**that** que) ▮ *vi* calculer; compter; **to r. with** (*take into account*) compter avec (*qch*, *qn*); (*deal with*) avoir affaire à (*qn*); **to r. on/without sth/s.o.** compter sur/sans qch/qn; **to r. on doing** compter or penser faire. ● **reckoning** *n* calcul(s) *m(pl)*.

reclaim [rɪ'kleɪm] *vt* **1** (*ask for back*) réclamer; (*luggage at airport*) récupérer. **2** (*land*) mettre en valeur; (*from sea*) assécher ▮ *n* **'baggage r.'** (*in airport*) 'récupération des bagages'.

recline [rɪ'klaɪn] *vi* (*of person*) être allongé; (*of head*) être appuyé ▮ *vt* (*head*) appuyer (**on** sur). ● **reclining seat** *n* siège *m* à dossier inclinable *or* réglable.

recluse [rɪ'kluːs] *n* reclus, -use *mf*.

recognition [rekəg'nɪʃ(ə)n] *n* reconnaissance *f*; **to change beyond** *or* **out of all r.** devenir méconnaissable; **to gain r.** être reconnu.

recognize ['rekəgnaɪz] *vt* reconnaître (**by** à, **that** que). ● **recognizable** *a* reconnaissable.

recoil [rɪ'kɔɪl] *vi* reculer (**from doing** à l'idée de faire, **from sth** à la vue de qch).

recollect [rekə'lekt] *vt* se souvenir de; **to r. that** se souvenir que **I** *vi* se souvenir. ● **recollection** [-'lekʃ(ə)n] *n* souvenir *m*.

recommend [rekə'mend] *vt* (*praise, support, advise*) recommander (**to** à, **for** pour); **to r. s.o. to do** recommander à qn de faire. ● **recommendation** [-'deɪʃ(ə)n] *n* recommandation *f*.

recompense ['rekəmpens] *vt* (*reward*) récompenser **I** *n* récompense *f*.

reconcile ['rekənsaɪl] *vt* (*person*) réconcilier (**with, to** avec); (*opinions, facts etc*) concilier; **to r. oneself to sth** se résigner à qch. ● **reconciliation** [-sɪlɪ'eɪʃ(ə)n] *n* réconciliation *f*.

reconditioned [riːkən'dɪʃ(ə)nd] *a* (*engine*) refait (à neuf).

reconnaissance [rɪ'kɒnɪsəns] *n* Mil reconnaissance *f*. ● **reconnoitre** [rekə'nɔɪtər] (*Am* **reconnoiter**) *vt* (*land, enemy troops*) reconnaître.

reconsider [riːkən'sɪdər] *vt* reconsidérer **I** *vi* revenir sur sa décision.

reconstruct [riːkən'strʌkt] *vt* (*crime*) reconstituer.

record 1 ['rekɔːd] *n* (*disc*) disque *m*; **r. library** discothèque *f*; **r. player** électrophone *m*.

2 *n* (*best performance*) Sport etc record *m*; **r. holder** détenteur, -trice *mf* du record **I** *a* (*time, number, quantity etc*) record *inv*; **in r. time** en un temps record; **a r. high** (*of unemployment etc*) un nouveau record, son niveau le plus élevé; **a r. low** son niveau le plus bas.

3 *n* (*report*) rapport *m*; (*register*) registre *m*; (*recording on tape etc*) enregistrement *m*; (*mention*) mention *f*; (*note*) note *f*; (*background*) antécédents *mpl*; (*case history*) dossier *m*; (*police*) **r.** casier *m* judiciaire; (*public*) **records** archives *fpl*; **to make** *or* **keep a r. of sth** noter qch; **on r.** (*fact, event*) attesté; **the highest figures on r.** les chiffres les plus élevés jamais enregistrés; **off the r.** à titre confidentiel; **their safety r.** leurs résultats *mpl* en matière de sécurité.

4 [rɪ'kɔːd] *vt* (*on tape etc, in register etc*) enregistrer; (*in diary*) noter; (*relate*) rapporter (**that** que) **I** *vi* (*on tape etc, of tape recorder etc*) enregistrer.

recorded [rɪ'kɔːdɪd] *a* enregistré; (*prerecorded*) (*TV programme*) en différé; (*fact*) attesté; **letter sent** (**by**) **r. delivery** *Br* = lettre *f* avec avis de réception.

recorder [rɪ'kɔːdər] *n* (*musical instrument*) flûte *f* à bec; (*tape*) **r.** magnétophone *m*; **video r.** magnétoscope *m*.

recording [rɪ'kɔːdɪŋ] *n* enregistrement *m*.

recount 1 [rɪ'kaunt] *vt* (*relate*) raconter. **2** ['riːkaunt] *n* (*of votes*) nouveau dépouillement *m* du scrutin.

recoup [rɪ'kuːp] *vt* (*loss*) récupérer.

recourse ['riːkɔːs] *n* recours *m*; **to have r. to** avoir recours à.

recover [rɪ'kʌvər] **1** *vt* (*get back*) retrouver, récupérer. **2** *vi* (*from illness, shock, surprise etc*) se remettre (**from** de); (*of economy, country, the Stock Market*) (*of currency, sales*) remonter. ● **recovery** *n* **1** (*from illness*) guérison *f*, rétablissement *m*; (*of economy, Stock Market*) redressement *m*; **she's making a good r.** elle est en bonne voie de guérison. **2** **the r. of sth** (*getting back*) la récupération de qch; **r. vehicle** *Br* dépanneuse *f*.

recreate [riːkrɪ'eɪt] *vt* recréer.

recreation [rekrɪ'eɪʃ(ə)n] *n* récréation *f*; **r. ground** terrain *m* de jeux. ● **recreational** *a* (*activity etc*) de loisir.

recrimination [rɪkrɪmɪ'neɪʃ(ə)n] *n* (*accusation*) contre-accusation *f*.

recruit [rɪ'kruːt] *n* recrue *f* **I** *vt* recruter; **to r. s.o. to do** (*persuade*) embaucher qn pour faire. ● **recruitment** *n* recrutement *m*.

rectangle ['rektæŋg(ə)l] *n* rectangle *m*. ● **rec'tangular** *a* rectangulaire.

rectify ['rektɪfaɪ] *vt* rectifier. ● **rectification** [-ɪ'keɪʃ(ə)n] *n* rectification *f*.

rector ['rektər] *n* (*priest*) pasteur *m* (anglican); (*of Scottish university*) président *m*.

rectum ['rektəm] *n* rectum *m*.

recuperate [rɪ'kuːpəreɪt] *vi* récupérer (*ses forces*) **I** *vt* récupérer. ● **recuperation** [-'reɪʃ(ə)n] *n* (*after illness*) rétablissement *m*.

recur [rɪ'kɜːr] *vi* (**-rr-**) (*of event*) se reproduire; (*of illness*) réapparaître; (*of theme*) revenir. ● **recurrence** [rɪ'kʌrəns] *n* répétition *f*; (*of illness*) réapparition *f*. ● **recurrent** *a* fréquent.

recycle [riː'saɪk(ə)l] *vt* (*material*) recycler.

red [red] *a* (**redder, reddest**) rouge; (*hair*) roux (*f* rousse); **to turn** *or* **go r.** rougir; **R. Cross** Croix-Rouge *f*; **R. Indian** Peau-Rouge *mf*; **r. light** (*traffic light*) feu *m* rouge; **the r.-light district** le quartier des prostituées; **r. tape** Fig paperasserie *f* (administrative).

I *n* (*colour*) rouge *m*; **in the r.** (*company*) dans le rouge, en déficit; (*account, person*) dans le rouge, à découvert. ● **red-'faced** *a* Fig rouge de confusion. ● **red-'handed** *adv* **to be caught r.-handed** être pris en flagrant délit. ● **red-'hot** *a* brûlant.

redcurrant [red'kʌrənt] *n* groseille *f*.

redden ['red(ə)n] *vti* rougir. ● **reddish** *a* rougeâtre; (*hair*) carotte *inv*. ● **redness** *n* rougeur *f*; (*of hair*) rousseur *f*.

redecorate [riː'dekəreɪt] *vt* (*room etc*) refaire **I** *vi* refaire la peinture et les papiers.

redeem [rɪ'diːm] *vt* (*restore to favour, buy back, free*) racheter; (*debt, loan*) rembourser; (*convert into cash*) réaliser; **redeeming feature** bon point *m*. ● **redemption**

[rɪ'dempʃ(ə)n] n rachat m; (of debt etc) remboursement m; (of asset) réalisation f; Rel rédemption f.

redeploy [riːdɪ'plɔɪ] vt (staff) réorganiser; (troops) redéployer.

redhead ['redhed] n roux m, rousse f.

redirect [riːdaɪ'rekt] vt (mail) faire suivre.

redo [riː'duː] vt (pt **redid**, pp **redone**) (exercise, house etc) refaire.

redolent ['redələnt] a r. of (suggestive) Lit évocateur (f -trice) de.

redress [rɪ'dres] n to seek r. demander réparation (for de).

reduce [rɪ'djuːs] vt réduire (to à, by de); (temperature) faire baisser; **at a reduced price** (ticket) à prix réduit; (goods) à prix réduit, au rabais. ●**reduction** [rɪ'dʌkʃ(ə)n] n réduction f; (of temperature) baisse f; (discount) réduction f, rabais m.

redundant [rɪ'dʌndənt] a (not needed) de trop, superflu; **to make r.** (worker) Br mettre au chômage, licencier. ●**redundancy** n (of worker) Br licenciement m; **compulsory r.** licenciement m sec; **voluntary r.** départ m volontaire; **r. pay(ment)** or **money** indemnité f de licenciement.

re-echo [riː'ekəʊ] vi résonner ■ vt (sound) répercuter; Fig répéter.

reed [riːd] n 1 (plant) roseau m. 2 (of clarinet etc) anche f ■ a (instrument) à anche.

re-educate [riː'edjʊkeɪt] vt (criminal, limb) rééduquer.

reef [riːf] n récif m, écueil m.

reek [riːk] vi puer; **to r. of sth** (smell, Fig suggest) puer qch ■ n puanteur f.

reel [riːl] n 1 (of thread, film) bobine f; (film itself) bande f; (of hose) dévidoir m; (for fishing line) moulinet m. 2 vi (stagger) chanceler; (of mind) chavirer; (of head) tourner. 3 vt **to r. off** (rattle off from memory) débiter à toute vitesse.

re-elect [riːɪ'lekt] vt réélire.

re-entry [riː'entrɪ] n (of spacecraft) rentrée f.

re-establish [riːɪ'stæblɪʃ] vt rétablir.

ref [ref] n abbr (referee) Sport Fam arbitre m.

refectory [rɪ'fektərɪ] n réfectoire m.

refer [rɪ'fɜːr] vi (-rr-) **to r. to** (mention) faire allusion à; (speak of) parler de; (apply to) s'appliquer à; (consult) se reporter à ■ vt **to r. sth to s.o.** (submit) soumettre qch à qn; **to r. s.o. to** (article, office etc) renvoyer qn à.

referee [refə'riː] n Football Boxing etc arbitre m; (for job applicant etc) répondant, -ante mf ■ vt (game, contest etc) arbitrer.

reference ['refərəns] n (in book etc, recommendation for job applicant) référence f; (indirect) allusion f (to à); (mention) mention f (to de); (connection) rapport m (to avec); **with** or **in r. to** concernant; **with** or **in r. to your letter** Com suite à votre lettre; **terms of r.** (of person, investigating body) compétence f; (of law) étendue f; **r. book** ouvrage m de référence.

referendum [refə'rendəm] n référendum m.

refill [riː'fɪl] vt remplir (à nouveau); (lighter, pen etc) recharger ■ ['riːfɪl] n recharge f; **a r.** (drink) un autre verre.

refine [rɪ'faɪn] vt (oil, sugar, manners) raffiner; (metal, ore) affiner; (technique, machine) perfectionner ■ vi **to r. upon** raffiner sur. ●**refined** a (person, manners etc) raffiné. ●**refinement** n (of person) raffinement m; (of sugar, oil) raffinage m; (of technique) perfectionnement m; **refinements** (technical improvements) améliorations fpl. ●**refinery** n raffinerie f.

refit [riː'fɪt] vt (-tt-) (ship) remettre en état ■ n remise f en état.

reflate [riː'fleɪt] vt (economy) relancer.

reflect [rɪ'flekt] 1 vt (light, image etc) refléter, réfléchir; (kindness etc) Fig refléter; **to be reflected** (of light etc) se refléter; **to r. sth on s.o.** (credit, honour) faire rejaillir qch sur qn ■ vi **to r. on s.o., be reflected on s.o.** (of prestige, honour etc) rejaillir sur qn; **to r. badly on s.o.** nuire à l'image de qn; **to r. well on s.o.** profiter à l'image de qn. 2 vi (think) réfléchir (on à) ■ vt **to r. that** penser que.

reflection [rɪ'flekʃ(ə)n] n 1 (image) & Fig reflet m; (reflecting) réflexion f (of de). 2 (thought, criticism) réflexion (on sur); **on r.** tout bien réfléchi.

reflector [rɪ'flektər] n réflecteur m.

reflex ['riːfleks] n & a réflexe (m); **r. action** réflexe m.

reflexion [rɪ'flekʃ(ə)n] n Br = **reflection**.

reflexive [rɪ'fleksɪv] a (verb) réfléchi.

refloat [riː'fləʊt] vt (ship, company) renflouer.

reform [rɪ'fɔːm] n réforme f; **r. school** Am centre m d'éducation surveillée ■ vt réformer; (person, conduct) corriger ■ vi (of person) se réformer. ●**reformer** n réformateur, -trice mf.

reformatory [rɪ'fɔːmət(ə)rɪ] n Am = **reform school**.

refrain [rɪ'freɪn] 1 vi s'abstenir (from doing de faire). 2 n (of song) & Fig refrain m.

refresh [rɪ'freʃ] vt (of bath, drink) rafraîchir; (of sleep, rest) délasser; **to r. oneself** (drink) se rafraîchir; **to r. one's memory** se rafraîchir la mémoire. ●**refreshing** a (drink, bath etc) rafraîchissant; (sleep) réparateur; (pleasant) agréable; (original) nouveau (f nouvelle).

refresher course [rɪ'freʃəkɔːs] n cours m de recyclage.

refreshments [rɪ'freʃmənts] npl (drinks) rafraîchissements mpl; (snacks) petites choses fpl à grignoter.

refrigerate [rɪ'frɪdʒəreɪt] vt (food) conserver au frais, réfrigérer. ●**refrigerator** n réfrigérateur m.

refuel [riː'fjʊəl] vi (Br -ll-, Am -l-) (of aircraft) se ravitailler ■ vt (aircraft) ravitailler.

refuge ['refjuːdʒ] n refuge m; **to take r.** se réfugier (in dans).

refugee [refjʊ'dʒiː] n réfugié, -ée mf.

refund [rɪ'fʌnd] vt rembourser ■ ['riːfʌnd] n remboursement m.

refurbish [riːˈfɜːbiʃ] vt remettre à neuf.

refusal [rɪˈfjuːz(ə)l] n refus m.

refuse¹ [rɪˈfjuːz] vt refuser (s.o. sth qch à qn, to do de faire) ▮ vi refuser.

refuse² [ˈrefjuːs] n Br (rubbish) ordures fpl, détritus m; (industrial waste materials) déchets mpl; **r. collector** éboueur m; **r. dump** dépôt m d'ordures.

refute [rɪˈfjuːt] vt réfuter.

regain [rɪˈɡeɪn] vt (lost ground, favour) regagner; (health, sight) retrouver; **to r. one's strength** retrouver or reprendre ses forces; **to r. consciousness** reprendre connaissance; **to r. possession of** reprendre possession de.

regal [ˈriːɡ(ə)l] a royal, majestueux.

regalia [rɪˈɡeɪlɪə] npl insignes mpl (royaux).

regard [rɪˈɡɑːd] vt (consider) considérer, regarder; (concern) regarder, concerner; **as regards** en ce qui concerne ▮ n considération f (for pour); **to have (a) high r. for s.o.** estimer qn; **without r. to** sans égard pour; **with r. to** en ce qui concerne; **to give or send one's regards to s.o.** transmettre son meilleur souvenir à qn. ●**regarding** prep en ce qui concerne.

regardless [rɪˈɡɑːdləs] a **r. of** (the danger etc) sans tenir compte de ▮ adv (all the same) quand même.

regatta [rɪˈɡætə] n régate(s) f(pl).

regency [ˈriːdʒənsɪ] n régence f. ●**regent** n régent, -ente mf; **prince r.** prince m régent.

regenerate [rɪˈdʒenəreɪt] vt régénérer.

reggae [ˈreɡeɪ] n (music) reggae m ▮ a (group, musician etc) reggae inv.

régime [reɪˈʒiːm] n (political etc) régime m.

regiment [ˈredʒɪmənt] n régiment m. ●**regi'mental** a (march etc) du régiment. ●**regimentation** [-teɪʃ(ə)n] n discipline f excessive.

region [ˈriːdʒ(ə)n] n région f; **in the r. of** (about) Fig environ; **in the r. of £50** dans les 50 livres, environ 50 livres. ●**regional** a régional.

register [ˈredʒɪstər] n registre m; (in school) cahier m d'appel; **electoral r.** liste f électorale; **to take the r.** (of teacher) faire l'appel. ▮ vt (birth, death) déclarer; (record, note) enregistrer; (vehicle) immatriculer; (express) exprimer; (indicate) indiquer; (letter, package) recommander; (realize) Fam réaliser. ▮ vi (enrol) s'inscrire (**for a course** à un cours); (in hotel) signer le registre; **it hasn't registered (with me)** Fam je n'ai pas encore réalisé ça. ●**registered** a (member) inscrit; (letter, package) recommandé; **r. trademark** marque f déposée; **to send by r.** Br post or Am mail envoyer en recommandé; **r. unemployed** Br inscrit au chômage; **to be r. disabled** être invalide titulaire d'une carte.

registrar [redʒɪˈstrɑːr] n Br officier m de l'état civil; (in university) secrétaire m général.

registration [redʒɪˈstreɪʃ(ə)n] n (enrolment) inscription f; (of complaint etc) enregistrement m; **r. (number)** (of vehicle) Br numéro

m d'immatriculation; **r. document** (of vehicle) Br = carte f grise.

registry [ˈredʒɪstrɪ] a & n **r. (office)** Br bureau m de l'état civil; **to get married in a r. office** se marier civilement or à la mairie.

regress [rɪˈɡres] vi régresser.

regret [rɪˈɡret] vt (-tt-) regretter (doing, to do de faire; that que (+ sub)); **I r. to hear that...** je suis désolé d'apprendre que... ▮ n regret m. ●**regretfully** adv **r., I...** à mon grand regret, je....

regrettable [rɪˈɡretəb(ə)l] a regrettable (that que (+ sub)). ●**regrettably** adv malheureusement; (poor, ill etc) fâcheusement.

regroup [riːˈɡruːp] vi se regrouper ▮ vt regrouper.

regular [ˈreɡjʊlər] a (steady, even) régulier; (surface) uni; (usual) habituel; (price, size) normal; (listener, reader) fidèle; (staff) permanent; (fool, slave etc) Fam vrai; **a r. guy** Am Fam un chic type ▮ n (in bar etc) habitué, -ée mf; (soldier) régulier m. ●**regu'larity** n régularité f. ●**regularly** adv régulièrement.

regulate [ˈreɡjʊleɪt] vt régler. ●**regulation** [-ˈleɪʃ(ə)n] n **1** regulations (rules) règlement m; **r. uniform/etc** uniforme m/etc réglementaire. **2** (regulating) réglage m.

rehabilitate [riːhəˈbɪlɪteɪt] vt (in public esteem) réhabiliter; (drug addict, alcoholic) désintoxiquer; (wounded soldier, disabled person etc) réadapter. ●**rehabilitation** [-ˈteɪʃ(ə)n] n (of drug addict etc) désintoxication f; (of soldier etc) réadaptation f.

rehash [riːˈhæʃ] vt (text) Pej remanier ▮ [ˈriːhæʃ] n **it's a r.** c'est du réchauffé.

rehearse [rɪˈhɜːs] vt (a play, piece of music etc) répéter; (prepare) Fig préparer ▮ vi répéter. ●**rehearsal** n (of play etc) répétition f.

reign [reɪn] n règne m; **in or during the r. of** sous le règne de ▮ vi régner (over sur).

reimburse [riːɪmˈbɜːs] vt rembourser (for de). ●**reimbursement** n remboursement m.

rein [reɪn] **1** n **to give free r. to** donner libre cours à. **2** vt **to r. in expenses** limiter les dépenses.

reindeer [ˈreɪndɪər] n inv renne m.

reinforce [riːɪnˈfɔːs] vt renforcer (with de); **reinforced concrete** béton m armé. ●**reinforcement** n renforcement m (of de); reinforcements (troops) renforts mpl.

reins [reɪnz] npl (for horse) rênes fpl; (for baby) bretelles fpl de sécurité (avec laisse).

reinstate [riːɪnˈsteɪt] vt réintégrer. ●**reinstatement** n réintégration f.

reissue [riːˈɪʃuː] vt (book) rééditer.

reiterate [riːˈɪtəreɪt] vt (say again) réitérer.

reject [rɪˈdʒekt] vt (offer, assumption etc) rejeter; (candidate, goods etc) refuser; (transplant) Med rejeter ▮ [ˈriːdʒekt] n (article) article m de rebut; **r. article** article m de deuxième choix; **r. shop** solderie f. ●**rejection** [rɪˈdʒekʃ(ə)n] n rejet m; (of candidate etc) refus m; Med rejet m.

rejoice [rɪˈdʒɔɪs] vi (celebrate) faire la fête;

(be delighted) se réjouir **(over** *or* **at** sth de qch, **in doing** de faire). ● **rejoicing(s)** n(pl) réjouissance(s) f(pl).

rejoin [rɪ'dʒɔɪn] **1** vt *(join up with)* rejoindre. **2** vi *(retort)* répliquer.

rejuvenate [rɪ'dʒuːvəneɪt] vt. rajeunir.

rekindle [riː'kɪnd(ə)l] vt rallumer.

relapse [rɪ'læps] n *(of sick person)* rechute f ▮ vi rechuter; **to r. into** *Fig* retomber dans.

relate [rɪ'leɪt] **1** vt *(narrate)* raconter **(that** que); *(report)* rapporter **(that** que). **2** vt *(connect)* établir un rapport entre *(faits etc)*; **to r. sth to** *(link)* rattacher qch à ▮ vi **to r. to** *(apply to)* se rapporter à; *(get along with)* s'entendre *ou* communiquer avec. ● **related** a *(linked)* lié **(to** à); *(languages, styles)* apparentés; **to be r. to s.o.** *(by family)* être parent de qn.

relation [rɪ'leɪʃ(ə)n] n *(relative)* parent, -ente mf; *(relationship)* rapport m, relation f *(between* entre, **with** avec*)*; **what r. are you to him?** quel est ton lien de parenté avec lui?; **international/etc relations** relations fpl internationales/etc; **sexual relations** rapports mpl sexuels.

relationship [rɪ'leɪʃ(ə)nʃɪp] n *(in family)* lien(s) m(pl) de parenté; *(relations)* relations fpl, rapports mpl; *(connection)* rapport m; **in r. to** relativement à.

relative ['relətɪv] **1** n *(person)* parent, -ente mf. **2** a relatif (**to** à); *(qualities etc of two or more people)* respectif; **r. to** *(compared to)* relativement à; **to be r. to** *(depend on)* être fonction de. ● **relatively** adv relativement.

relax [rɪ'læks] **1** vt *(person, mind)* détendre; ▮ vi se détendre; **r.!** *(calm down)* du calme! **2** vt *(grip, pressure etc)* relâcher; *(restrictions, control, principles)* assouplir. ● **relaxed** a *(person, atmosphere)* décontracté, détendu. ● **relaxing** a *(bath etc)* délassant.

relaxation [riːlæk'seɪʃ(ə)n] n **1** *(rest, recreation)* détente f; *(of body)* décontraction f. **2** *(of grip etc)* relâchement m; *(of restrictions etc)* assouplissement m.

relay ['riːleɪ] n relais m; **in relays** par relais; **r.** *(race)* course f de relais ▮ vt *(message etc)* *(by radio)* retransmettre; *(by letter etc)* *Fig* transmettre **(to** à).

release [rɪ'liːs] vt *(free)* libérer **(from** de); *(bomb, s.o.'s hand)* lâcher; *(spring)* déclencher; *(brake)* desserrer; *(film, record)* sortir; *(news, facts)* publier; *(smoke, trapped person)* dégager; *(tension)* éliminer. ▮ n *(of prisoner)* libération f; *(of film, book)* sortie f **(of** de); *(film)* nouveau film m; *(record)* nouveau disque m; *(relief)* *Fig* délivrance f; *(psychological)* défoulement m; **a merciful** *or* **happy r.** *(s.o.'s death)* une délivrance; **press r.** communiqué m de presse; **to be on general r.** *(of film)* *Br* passer dans toutes les salles.

relegate ['relɪgeɪt] vt reléguer **(to** à); **to be relegated** *(of team)* *Br* descendre en division inférieure, subir une relégation.

relent [rɪ'lent] vi *(change one's mind)* revenir

sur sa décision; *(be swayed)* se laisser fléchir.

relentless [rɪ'lentləs] a implacable.

relevant ['reləvənt] a *(apt)* pertinent **(to** à); *(fitting)* approprié; *(useful)* utile; *(significant)* important; **that's not r.** ça n'a rien à voir. ● **relevance** n pertinence f '**(to** à); *(significance)* intérêt m; *(connection)* rapport m **(to** avec).

reliable [rɪ'laɪəb(ə)l] a *(person, information, company etc)* fiable, sérieux, sûr; *(machine)* fiable. ● **reliability** n *(of person)* sérieux m, fiabilité f; *(of machine, information, company etc)* fiabilité f. ● **reliably** adv **to be r. informed that** tenir de source sûre que.

reliance [rɪ'laɪəns] n *(dependence)* dépendance f *(on* de); *(trust)* confiance f *(on* en). ● **reliant** a **to be r. on** *(dependent)* dépendre de; *(trusting)* avoir confiance en.

relic ['relɪk] n relique f; **relics** *(of the past)* vestiges mpl.

relief [rɪ'liːf] n *(from pain etc)* soulagement m *(from* à); *(help, supplies)* secours m; *(in art)* & *Geog* relief m; **tax r.** dégrèvement m; **to be on r.** *Am* recevoir l'aide sociale ▮ a *(train, bus etc)* supplémentaire; *(work, troops etc)* de secours; **r. road** *Br* route f de délestage.

relieve [rɪ'liːv] vt *(pain, suffering etc)* soulager; *(boredom)* dissiper; *(situation)* remédier à; *(take over from)* relayer *(qn)*; *(help)* secourir, soulager; **to r. s.o. of sth** *(rid)* débarrasser qn de qch; **to r. s.o. of his post** relever qn de ses fonctions; **to r. congestion in** *(street etc)* décongestionner; **to r. oneself** *(go to the lavatory)* *Hum Fam* se soulager.

religion [rɪ'lɪdʒ(ə)n] n religion f. ● **religious** a religieux; *(war, book)* de religion. ● **religiously** adv religieusement.

relinquish [rɪ'lɪŋkwɪʃ] vt *(give up)* abandonner; *(let go)* lâcher.

relish ['relɪʃ] n *(seasoning)* assaisonnement m; *(liking, taste)* goût m **(for** pour); *(pleasure)* plaisir m; **to eat with r.** manger de bon appétit ▮ vt *(food etc)* savourer; *(like)* aimer *(doing* faire).

reload [rɪ'ləʊd] vt *(gun, camera)* recharger.

relocate [*Br* riː'ləʊ'keɪt, *Am* riː'ləʊkeɪt] vi *(move to new place)* déménager; **to r. in** *or* **to** s'installer à.

reluctant [rɪ'lʌktənt] a *(greeting, gift, promise)* accordé sans enthousiasme *or* à contrecœur; **to be r.** *(to do)* être peu enthousiaste *(pour* faire); **a r. teacher/etc** un professeur/etc malgré lui. ● **reluctance** n manque m d'enthousiasme, répugnance f **(to do** à faire). ● **reluctantly** adv sans enthousiasme, à contrecœur.

rely [rɪ'laɪ] vi **to r. (up)on** *(count on)* compter sur; *(be dependent on)* dépendre de.

remain [rɪ'meɪn] **1** vi rester. **2** npl **remains** restes mpl; *(mortal)* **r.** dépouille f mortelle. ● **remaining** a qui reste(nt).

remainder [rɪ'meɪndər] **1** n reste m; **the r.** *(remaining people)* les autres mfpl; **the r. of the girls** les autres filles. **2** n *(book)* invendu *m* soldé ▮ *vt* (*book*) solder; **remaindered bookshop** solderie *f* de livres.

remand [rɪ'mɑːnd] *vt* **to r.** (**in custody**) (*in prison*) placer en détention préventive ▮ *n* **on r.** en détention préventive; **r. centre** *Br* centre *m* de détention préventive.

remark [rɪ'mɑːk] *n* remarque *f* ▮ *vt* (faire) remarquer (**that** que) ▮ *vi* **to r. on** faire des remarques sur. ●**remarkable** *a* remarquable (**for** par). ●**remarkably** *adv* remarquablement.

remarry [riː'mærɪ] *vi* se remarier.

remedial [rɪ'miːdɪəl] *a* (*measure*) de redressement; (*treatment*) thérapeutique; **r. class** cours *m* de rattrapage; **r. exercises** (*for handicapped people*) gymnastique *f* corrective.

remedy ['remɪdɪ] *vt* remédier à ▮ *n* remède *m* (**for** contre, à, de).

remember [rɪ'membər] *vt* se souvenir de, se rappeler; (*commemorate*) commémorer; **to r. that/doing** se rappeler que/d'avoir fait; **to r. to do** (*not forget to do*) penser à faire; **r. me to him** *or* **her!** rappelle-moi à son bon souvenir! ▮ *vi* se souvenir, se rappeler. ●**remembrance** *n* (*memory*) souvenir *m*; **in r. of** en souvenir de; **R. Day** *Br Can* = l'Armistice *m*.

remind [rɪ'maɪnd] *vt* rappeler (**s.o. of sth** qch à qn, **s.o. that** à qn que); **to r. s.o. to do** faire penser à qn à faire; **that** *or* **which reminds me!** à propos! ●**reminder** *n* (*of event & letter*) rappel *m*; (*note to do sth*) pensebête *m*; (*souvenir*) souvenir *m*; **it's a r.** (**for him** *or* **her**) **that...** c'est pour lui rappeler *or* faire penser que...; **to give s.o. a r. to do sth** faire penser à qn à faire qch, rappeler à qn de faire qch.

reminisce [remɪ'nɪs] *vi* raconter *or* se rappeler ses souvenirs (**about** de). ●**reminiscences** *npl* réminiscences *fpl*.

reminiscent [remɪ'nɪsənt] *a* **r. of** qui rappelle.

remiss [rɪ'mɪs] *a* négligent.

remission [rɪ'mɪʃ(ə)n] *n* (*in prison sentence*) remise *f* (de peine); (*forgiveness*) *Rel* rémission *f*.

remit [rɪ'mɪt] *vt* (**-tt-**) (*money*) envoyer. ●**remittance** [rɪ'mɪtəns] *n* (*sum*) paiement *m*.

remnant ['remnənt] *n* (*remaining part*) reste *m*; (*trace*) vestige *m*; (*of fabric*) coupon *m*; (*oddment*) fin *f* de série.

remodel [riː'mɒd(ə)l] *vt* (*Br* **-ll-**, *Am* **-l-**) remodeler (**on** sur).

remonstrate ['remənstreɪt] *vi* **to r. with s.o** faire des remontrances à qn.

remorse [rɪ'mɔːs] *n* remords *m*(*pl*) (**for** pour); **to show r.** faire preuve de remords; **without r.** sans remords; (*cruelly*) sans pitié. ●**remorseless** *a* implacable. ●**remorselessly** *adv* (*to hit etc*) implacablement.

remote [rɪ'məʊt] *a* (**-er**, **-est**) **1** (*far-off*) lointain, éloigné; (*isolated*) isolé; (*aloof*) *Fig* distant; **r. from** loin de; **r. control** télécommande *f*. **2** (*slight*) petit, vague; **not the**

remotest idea pas la moindre idée. ●**remotely** *adv* (*slightly*) un peu, vaguement; (*situated*) au loin; **not r. aware/etc** nullement conscient/*etc*. ●**remoteness** *n* éloignement *m*; (*isolation*) isolement *m*; (*aloofness*) *Fig* attitude *f* distante.

remould ['riːməʊld] *n Br* pneu *m* rechapé.

removable [rɪ'muːvəb(ə)l] *a* (*lining etc*) amovible.

removal [rɪ'muːv(ə)l] *n* enlèvement *m*; (*of furniture*) *Br* déménagement *m*; (*of obstacle etc*) suppression *f*; **r. man** *Br* déménageur *m*; **r. van** *Br* camion *m* de déménagement.

remove [rɪ'muːv] *vt* (*clothes, stain etc*) enlever (**from s.o.** à qn, **from sth** de qch); (*withdraw*) retirer; (*lead away*) emmener (**to** à); (*furniture*) *Br* déménager; (*obstacle, threat, word*) supprimer; (*fear, doubt*) dissiper; (*employee*) renvoyer; (**far**) **removed from** loin de.

remover [rɪ'muːvər] *n* (*for make-up*) démaquillant *m*; (*for nail polish*) dissolvant *m*; (*for paint*) décapant *m*; (*for stains*) détachant *m*.

remunerate [rɪ'mjuːnəreɪt] *vt* rémunérer. ●**remuneration** [-'reɪʃ(ə)n] *n* rémunération *f*.

renaissance [rə'neɪsəns] *n* (*in art etc*) renaissance *f*.

rename [riː'neɪm] *vt* (*street etc*) rebaptiser; (*file*) *Comptr* renommer.

render ['rendər] *vt* (*give, make*) rendre; (*piece of music*) interpréter; **to r. assistance to s.o.** prêter main-forte à qn. ●**rendering** *n* (*musical*) interprétation *f*; (*translation*) traduction *f*.

rendez-vous ['rɒndɪvuː, *pl* -vuːz] *n inv* rendez-vous *m inv*.

renegade ['renɪgeɪd] *n* renégat, -ate *mf*.

reneg(u)e [rɪ'niːg, *Br* rɪ'neɪg] *vi* **to r. on** (*promise etc*) revenir sur.

renew [rɪ'njuː] *vt* renouveler; (*resume*) reprendre; (*library book*) renouveler le prêt de. ●**renewed** *a* (*efforts*) renouvelés; (*attempt*) nouveau (*f* nouvelle); **with r. vigour/etc** avec un regain de vigueur/*etc*.

renewable [rɪ'njuːəb(ə)l] *a* (*passport, energy etc*) renouvelable.

renewal [rɪ'njuːəl] *n* renouvellement *m*; (*resumption*) reprise *f*; (*of strength*) regain *m*.

renounce [rɪ'naʊns] *vt* (*give up*) renoncer à; (*disown*) renier.

renovate ['renəveɪt] *vt* (*house etc*) rénover, restaurer; (*painting*) restaurer. ●**renovation** [-'veɪʃ(ə)n] *n* rénovation *f*; (*of painting*) restauration *f*.

renown [rɪ'naʊn] *n* renommée *f*. ●**renowned** *a* renommé (**for** pour).

rent [rent] *n* (*for house etc*) loyer *m*; **r. collector** encaisseur *m* de loyers ▮ *vt* louer; **to r. out** louer; **rented car** voiture *f* de location ▮ *vi* **this house/***etc* **rents at £100 per week** cette maison/*etc* se loue à 100 livres par semaine. ●**rent-'free** *adv* sans payer de loyer ▮ *a* gratuit.

rental ['rent(ə)l] *n* (*of television, car etc*)

(prix *m* de) location *f*; (*of telephone*) abonnement *m*.

renunciation [rɪnʌnsɪ'eɪʃ(ə)n] *n* (*giving up*) renonciation *f* (**of** à); (*disowning*) reniement *m* (**of** de).

reopen [riː'əʊpən] *vti* rouvrir. ● **reopening** *n* réouverture *f*.

reorganize [riː'ɔːgənaɪz] *vt* (*company, schedule etc*) réorganiser.

rep [rep] *n Fam* représentant, -ante *mf* de commerce.

repaid [riː'peɪd] *pt & pp of* **repay**.

repair [rɪ'peər] *vt* réparer ▮ *n* réparation *f*; **beyond r.** irréparable: **in good/bad r.** en bon/mauvais état; **'road under r.'** *Br* 'travaux'; **r. man** réparateur *m*; **r. woman** réparatrice *f*.

reparation [repə'reɪʃ(ə)n] *n* réparation *f* (**for** de); **reparations** (*money from defeated country*) réparations *fpl*.

repartee [repɑː'tiː] *n* (*sharp reply*) repartie *f*.

repatriate [riː'pætrɪeɪt] *vt* rapatrier.

repay [riː'peɪ] *vt* (*pt & pp* **repaid**) (*pay back*) rembourser; (*kindness*) payer de retour; (*reward*) récompenser (**for** de). ● **repayment** *n* remboursement *m*, récompense *f*.

repeal [rɪ'piːl] *vt* (*law*) abroger ▮ *n* abrogation *f*.

repeat [rɪ'piːt] *vt* répéter (**that** que); (*promise, threat*) réitérer; (*class*) redoubler; **to r. oneself** *or* **itself** se répéter ▮ *vi* répéter; **r. after me** répétez après moi; **I r., you're wrong** je le répète, vous avez tort; **to r. on s.o.** (*of food*) *Fam* revenir à qn ▮ *n* (*on TV, radio*) rediffusion *f*; **r. performance** (*of play*) deuxième représentation *f*. ● **repeated** *a* (*attempts etc*) répétés; (*efforts*) renouvelés. ● **repeatedly** *adv* de nombreuses fois, à maintes reprises.

repel [rɪ'pel] *vt* (**-ll-**) repousser. ● **repellent** *a* repoussant ▮ *n* **insect r.** crème *f* anti-insecte.

repent [rɪ'pent] *vi* se repentir (**of** de). ● **repentance** *n* repentir *m*. ● **repentant** *a* repentant.

repercussions [riːpə'kʌʃ(ə)nz] *npl* répercussions *fpl* (**on** sur).

repertoire ['repətwɑːr] *n Theatre & Fig* répertoire *m*. ● **repertory** *n Theatre & Fig* répertoire *m*; **r. (theatre)** théâtre *m* de répertoire.

repetition [repɪ'tɪʃ(ə)n] *n* répétition *f*. ● **repetitious** *or* **re'petitive** *a* répétitif.

replace [rɪ'pleɪs] *vt* (*take the place of*) remplacer (**by, with** par); (*put back*) remettre; **to r. the receiver** (*of phone*) raccrocher. ● **replacement** *n* (*substitution*) remplacement *m* (**of** de); (*person*) remplaçant, -ante *mf*; (*machine part*) pièce *f* de rechange.

replay ['riːpleɪ] *n Sport* match *m* rejoué; (**instant** *or* **action**) **r.** (*on TV*) répétition *f* immédiate (au ralenti) ▮ [riː'pleɪ] *vt* (*on tape recorder etc*) repasser (*cassette*).

replenish [rɪ'plenɪʃ] *vt* (*refill*) remplir (de

nouveau) (**with** de); (*renew*) renouveler.

replete [rɪ'pliːt] *a Lit* **r. with** rempli de; **r. (with food)** rassasié.

replica ['replɪkə] *n* copie *f* exacte.

reply [rɪ'plaɪ] *vti* répondre (**to** à, **that** que) ▮ *n* réponse *f*; **in r.** en réponse (**to** à).

report [rɪ'pɔːt] *n* (*account*) rapport *m*; (*of meeting*) compte rendu *m*; (*in media*) reportage *m*; (*rumour*) rumeur *f*; (*of gun*) détonation *f*; (*school*) **r.** *Br*, **r. card** *Am* bulletin *m* (scolaire); **government r.** rapport *m* du gouvernement; **weather r.** prévisions *fpl* météorologiques.

▮ *vt* (*give account of*) rapporter, rendre compte de; (*announce*) annoncer (**that** que); (*notify*) signaler (**to** à); (*denounce*) dénoncer (**to** à); (*in newspaper*) faire un reportage sur (*événement etc*).

▮ *vi* faire un rapport (**on** sur); (*of journalist*) faire un reportage (**on** sur); (*go*) se présenter (**to** à, **to s.o.** chez qn, **for work** au travail). ● **reported** *a* **r. speech** *Grammar* discours *m* indirect; **it is r. that** on dit que; **to be r. missing** être porté disparu. ● **reportedly** *adv* à ce qu'on dit. ● **reporting** *n* (*of journalist*) reportage *m*. ● **reporter** *n* reporter *m*.

repose [rɪ'pəʊz] *n Lit* repos *m*.

repository [rɪ'pɒzɪtərɪ] *n* dépôt *m*.

repossess [riːpə'zes] *vt* (*house, car etc*) reprendre possession de.

reprehensible [reprɪ'hensəb(ə)l] *a* répréhensible.

represent [reprɪ'zent] *vt* représenter. ● **representation** [-'teɪʃ(ə)n] *n* représentation *f*; **representations** (*complaints*) remontrances *fpl*.

representative [reprɪ'zentətɪv] *a* représentatif (**of** de) ▮ *n* représentant, -ante *mf*; *Pol Am* député *m*.

repress [rɪ'pres] *vt* (*feeling, anger, tears*) réprimer, refouler; (*uprising*) réprimer, mater; (*rebels*) mater; **to be repressed** (*frustrated*) être refoulé. ● **repression** [-ʃ(ə)n] *n* répression *f*. ● **repressive** *a* (*régime etc*) répressif; (*measures*) de répression.

reprieve [rɪ'priːv] *n* (*for condemned prisoner*) commutation *f*; (*temporary*) sursis *m*; *Fig* répit *m*, sursis *m* ▮ *vt* accorder une commutation *or* un sursis *or Fig* un répit à.

reprimand ['reprɪmɑːnd] *n* réprimande *f* ▮ *vt* réprimander.

reprint ['riːprɪnt] *n* (*reissue*) réimpression *f* ▮ [riː'prɪnt] *vt* réimprimer.

reprisal [rɪ'praɪz(ə)l] *n* **reprisals** représailles *fpl*; **as a r. for, in r. for** en représailles de.

reproach [rɪ'prəʊtʃ] *n* (*blame*) reproche *m*; (*shame*) honte *f*; **beyond r.** sans reproche ▮ *vt* reprocher (**s.o. for sth** qch à qn). ● **reproachful** *a* réprobateur. ● **reproachfully** *adv* d'un ton *or* d'un air réprobateur.

reprocess [riː'prəʊses] *vt* retraiter; **reprocessing plant** usine *f* de retraitement.

reproduce [riːprə'djuːs] *vt* reproduire ▮ *vi* (*of animals, plants etc*) se reproduire. ● **reproduction** [-'dʌkʃ(ə)n] *n* (*of sound, docu-*

ment etc) & *Biol Bot* reproduction *f*. ● **reproductive** *a* reproducteur.

reproof [rɪ'pruːf] *n Lit* réprobation *f*.

reptile ['reptaɪl] *n* reptile *m*.

republic [rɪ'pʌblɪk] *n* république *f*. ● **republican** *a* & *n* républicain, -aine (*mf*).

repudiate [rɪ'pjuːdɪeɪt] *vt* (*behaviour, violence etc*) condamner; (*offer*) repousser; (*accusation*) rejeter; (*spouse, idea*) répudier.

repugnant [rɪ'pʌgnənt] *a* répugnant; **he's r. to me** il me répugne. ● **repugnance** *n* répugnance *f* (**for** pour).

repulse [rɪ'pʌls] *vt* repousser. ● **repulsion** *-ʃ(ə)n*] *n* répulsion *f*. ● **repulsive** *a* (*face, person etc*) repoussant.

reputable ['repjʊtəb(ə)l] *a* de bonne réputation. ● **repute** [rɪ'pjuːt] *n* réputation *f*; **of r.** de bonne réputation. ● **re'puted** *a* to be r. to be être réputé pour être, passer pour être. ● **re'putedly** *adv* à ce qu'on dit.

reputation [repjʊ'teɪʃ(ə)n] *n* réputation *f*; **to have a r. for being frank/etc** or for frankness/etc avoir la réputation d'être franc/etc.

request [rɪ'kwest] *n* demande *f* (**for** de); **on r.** sur demande; **at s.o.'s r.** à la demande de qn; **by popular r.** à la demande générale; **r. stop** (*for bus*) *Br* arrêt *m* facultatif ▌ *vt* demander (*sth from or of s.o.* qch à qn, **s.o. to do** à qn de faire).

requiem ['rekwɪəm] *n* requiem *m inv*.

require [rɪ'kwaɪər] *vt* (*of thing*) (*necessitate*) demander; (*demand*) exiger; (*of person*) avoir besoin de (*qch, qn*); (*staff, employee*) rechercher; **to r. sth of s.o.** (*order*) exiger qch de qn; **to r. s.o. to do sth** exiger de qn qu'il fasse qch; (*ask*) demander à qn de faire qch; **if required** s'il le faut; **the required qualities/etc** les qualités *fpl/etc* qu'il faut; **required condition** condition *f* requise. ● **requirement** *n* (*need*) exigence *f*; (*condition*) condition *f* (requise).

requisite ['rekwɪzɪt] **1** *a* nécessaire. **2** *n* (*for travel etc*) article *m*; **toilet requisites** articles *mpl* or nécessaire *m* de toilette.

requisition [rekwɪ'zɪʃ(ə)n] *vt* réquisitionner ▌ *n* réquisition *f*.

reroute [riː'ruːt] *vt* (*aircraft etc*) dérouter.

rerun ['riːrʌn] *n* (*of film*) reprise *f*; (*of TV programme*) rediffusion *f*.

resale ['riːseɪl] *n* revente *f*.

resat [riː'sæt] *pt* & *pp* of **resit**.

reschedule [*Br* riː'ʃedjuːl, *Am* riː'skedʒuːl] *vt* (*meeting etc*) déplacer.

rescind [rɪ'sɪnd] *vt Jur* annuler; (*law*) abroger.

rescue ['reskjuː] *vt* (*save*) sauver; (*set free*) délivrer (**from** de) ▌ *n* (*action*) sauvetage *m* (**of** de); (*help, troops etc*) secours *mpl*; **to go/come to s.o.'s r.** aller/venir au secours de qn; **to the r.** à la rescousse ▌ *a* (*team, operation, attempt*) de sauvetage. ● **rescuer** *n* sauveteur *m*.

research [rɪ'sɜːtʃ] *n* recherches *fpl* (**on, into** sur); **some r.** des recherches, de la re-

cherche; **a piece of r.** (*work*) un travail de recherche ▌ *vi* faire des recherches (**on, into** sur). ● **researcher** *n* chercheur, -euse *mf*.

resemble [rɪ'zemb(ə)l] *vt* ressembler à. ● **resemblance** *n* ressemblance *f* (**to** avec).

resent [rɪ'zent] *vt* (*be angry about*) s'indigner de, ne pas aimer; (*be bitter about*) éprouver de l'amertume à l'égard de; **I r. that** ça m'indigne. ● **resentful** *a* to be r. éprouver de l'amertume. ● **resentment** *n* amertume *f*, ressentiment *m*.

reservation [rezə'veɪʃ(ə)n] *n* **1** (*booking*) réservation *f*; (*doubt etc*) réserve *f*; **to make a r.** réserver; **do you have a r.?** avez-vous réservé? **2** (*land for Indians, animals*) *Am* réserve *f*; **central r.** (*on road*) *Br* terre-plein *m*.

reserve [rɪ'zɜːv] **1** *vt* (*room, decision etc*) réserver; (*right*) se réserver; (*one's strength*) ménager; **to r. one's strength** ménager ses forces ▌ *n* (*reticence*) réserve *f*. **2** *n* (*land, stock*) réserve *f*; (*player*) (*in team*) remplaçant, -ante *mf*; **the reserves** (*troops*) les réserves *fpl*; **foreign exchange reserves** réserves *fpl* en devises; **nature r.** réserve *f* naturelle; **in r.** en réserve; **r. tank** (*of vehicle, aircraft*) réservoir *m* de secours. ● **reserved** *a* (*person, room*) réservé.

reservoir ['rezəvwɑːr] *n* (*of water etc*) & *Fig* réservoir *m*.

resettle [riː'set(ə)l] *vt* (*refugees*) implanter.

reshape [riː'ʃeɪp] *vt* (*industry etc*) réorganiser.

reshuffle [riː'ʃʌf(ə)l] *n* (*cabinet*) **r.** remaniement *m* (ministériel) ▌ *vt Pol* remanier.

reside [rɪ'zaɪd] *vi* résider.

residence ['rezɪdəns] *n* (*home*) résidence *f*; (*of students*) foyer *m*; **to take up r.** s'installer; **in r.** (*doctor*) sur place; (*students on campus*) *Br* sur le campus; (*in halls of residence*) *Br* rentrés; **r. permit** *Br* permis *m* de séjour.

resident ['rezɪdənt] **1** *n* habitant, -ante *mf*; (*of hotel*) pensionnaire *mf*; (*foreigner*) résident, -ente *mf* ▌ *a* résidant, qui habite sur place; (*doctor, nurse*) à demeure; (*population*) fixe; (*correspondent*) permanent; **to be r. in London** résider à Londres. **2** *n* (*doctor*) *Am* interne *mf*.

residential [rezɪ'denʃ(ə)l] *a* (*neighbourhood etc*) résidentiel.

residue ['rezɪdjuː] *n* résidu *m*. ● **residual** [rɪ'zɪdjʊəl] *a* (*pain, doubt*) qui subsiste.

resign [rɪ'zaɪn] *vt* (*one's post*) démissionner de; (*right, claim*) abandonner; **to r. oneself to sth/to doing** se résigner à qch/à faire ▌ *vi* démissionner (**from** de); **to r. from one's job** démissionner. ● **resigned** *a* (*person, attitude etc*) résigné.

resignation [rezɪg'neɪʃ(ə)n] *n* (*from job*) démission *f*; (*attitude*) résignation *f*.

resilient [rɪ'zɪlɪənt] *a* élastique; (*person*) *Fig* résistant. ● **resilience** *n* élasticité *f*; *Fig* résistance *f*.

resin ['rezɪn] *n* résine *f*.

resist [rɪ'zɪst] vt (attack, attacker etc) résister à; **to r. doing sth** se retenir de faire qch; **she can't r. cakes** elle ne peut pas résister devant des gâteaux; **he can't r. her** (indulgence) il ne peut rien lui refuser; (charm) il ne peut pas résister à son charme ▮ vi résister. ● **resistance** n résistance f (to à). ● **resistant** a résistant (to à); **r. to** (virus etc) rebelle à.

resit [riː'sɪt] vt (pt & pp **resat**, pres p **resitting**) (exam) Br repasser.

resolute ['rezəluːt] a résolu. ● **resolutely** adv résolument. ● **resolution** [-'luːʃ(ə)n] n résolution f.

resolve [rɪ'zɒlv] vt (problem etc) résoudre; **to r. to do sth** résoudre de faire qch; **to r.** that résoudre que; **to be resolved to do sth** être résolu à faire qch ▮ n résolution f.

resonant ['rezənənt] a (voice) réson(n)ant; **to be r. with** résonner de. ● **resonance** n résonance f.

resort [rɪ'zɔːt] 1 vi **to r. to sth** (turn to) avoir recours à qch; **to r. to doing sth** en venir à faire qch; **to r. to drink** se rabattre sur la boisson ▮ n (recourse) recours m (to à); **as a last r., in the last r.** en dernier ressort; **without r. to** sans recourir à. 2 n (Br holiday or Am vacation) n. station f de vacances; **seaside r.** Br, **beach r.** Am station f balnéaire; **ski r.** station f de ski.

resound [rɪ'zaʊnd] vi résonner (with de); Fig Lit avoir du retentissement. ● **resounding** a (success, victory, noise) retentissant.

resource [rɪ'sɔːs, rɪ'zɔːs] n (expedient, recourse) ressource f; **resources** (wealth, means) ressources fpl. ● **resourceful** a (person, scheme) ingénieux. ● **resourcefulness** n ingéniosité f, ressource f.

respect [rɪ'spekt] n respect m (for pour, de); (aspect) égard m; **with r. to, in r. of** en ce qui concerne; **with all due r.** sans vouloir vous vexer ▮ vt respecter. ● **respecta'bility** n respectabilité f.

respectable [rɪ'spektəb(ə)l] a (honourable, sizeable, quite good) respectable; (satisfying) (results, score etc) honnête; (clothes, behaviour) convenable. ● **respectably** adv (to dress etc) convenablement; (rather well) passablement.

respectful [rɪ'spektfəl] a respectueux (to envers, of de). ● **respectfully** adv respectueusement.

respective [rɪ'spektɪv] a respectif. ● **respectively** adv respectivement.

respiration [respɪ'reɪʃ(ə)n] n respiration f; **artificial r.** respiration f artificielle.

respite ['respɪt, Br 'respaɪt] n répit m.

resplendent [rɪ'splendənt] a Lit resplendissant.

respond [rɪ'spɒnd] vi répondre (to à); **to r. to treatment** bien réagir or réagir positivement au traitement. ● **response** n réponse f; **in r. to** en réponse à.

responsible [rɪ'spɒnsəb(ə)l] a responsable (for de, to s.o. devant qn); (job) à responsa-

bilités; **who's r. for...?** qui est chargé de...?, qui s'occupe de...? ● **responsi'bility** n responsabilité f. ● **responsibly** adv de façon responsable.

responsive [rɪ'spɒnsɪv] a (reacting) qui réagit bien; (alert) éveillé; (attentive) qui fait attention; **r. to** (kindness) sensible à; (suggestion) réceptif à. ● **responsiveness** n (bonne) réaction f.

respray [riː'spreɪ] vt (vehicle) repeindre.

rest¹ [rest] n (relaxation) repos m; (support) support m; **to have or take a r.** se reposer; **to set or put s.o.'s mind at r.** tranquilliser qn; **to come to r.** (of ball etc) s'immobiliser; (of bird, eyes) se poser (on sur); **r. home** maison f de repos; **r. room** Am toilettes fpl. ▮ vi (relax) se reposer; (be buried) reposer; **to r. on** (of argument, roof) reposer sur; **I won't r. till** je n'aurai de cesse que (+ sub); **to be resting on sth** (of hand etc) être posé sur qch; **a resting place** un lieu de repos.
▮ vt (lean) appuyer, poser (on sur); (base) fonder (on sur); (eyes etc) reposer; (horse etc) laisser reposer.

rest² [rest] n (remainder) reste m (of de); **the r.** (others) les autres mfpl; **the r. of the men/etc** les autres hommes/etc ▮ vi (remain) **r. assured** soyez assuré (that que); **it rests with you** to do il vous incombe de faire.

restaurant ['restərɒnt] n restaurant m; **r. car** (in train) Br wagon-restaurant m.

restful ['restfəl] a reposant.

restitution [restɪ'tjuːʃ(ə)n] n (compensation for damage) réparation f; **to make r. of sth** restituer qch.

restive ['restɪv] a (person, horse) rétif.

restless ['restləs] a agité. ● **restlessly** adv avec agitation. ● **restlessness** n agitation f.

restore [rɪ'stɔːr] vt (give back) rendre (to à); (order, peace, rights) rétablir; (building, painting) restaurer; **to r. s.o. to** (former condition, power etc) ramener qn à. ● **restoration** [restə'reɪʃ(ə)n] n (of building etc) restauration f; (of order, peace etc) rétablissement m.

restrain [rɪ'streɪn] vt (person) retenir, maîtriser; (crowd, anger, tears) contenir, retenir; (curb) contenir (inflation etc); **to r. s.o. from doing** retenir qn de faire; **to r. oneself** se retenir, se maîtriser. ● **restrained** a (feelings) contenu; (tone) mesuré. ● **restraint** n (moderation) retenue f, mesure f; (restriction) contrainte f; **wage r.** limitation f des salaires.

restrict [rɪ'strɪkt] vt limiter, restreindre (to à). ● **restricted** a (space, use) restreint; (sale) contrôlé. ● **restriction** [-ʃ(ə)n] n restriction f, limitation f (on de). ● **restrictive** a restrictif.

result [rɪ'zʌlt] n (outcome, success) résultat m; **as a r.** en conséquence; **as a r. of** par suite de ▮ vi résulter (from de); **to r. in** (lead to) aboutir à (échec, désespoir etc).

resume [rɪ'zjuːm] vti (begin or take again) reprendre; (se) remettre à; **to r. doing** se remettre à faire. ● **resumption** [rɪ'zʌmpʃ(ə)n] n reprise f.

résumé ['rezjʊmeɪ] n (summary) résumé m;

Am curriculum vitae *m inv.*

resurface [riː'sɜːfɪs] *vt* (*road*) refaire le revêtement de.

resurgence [rɪ'sɜːdʒəns] *n* réapparition *f.*

resurrect [rezə'rekt] *vt* (*custom*, *memory etc*) ressusciter. ●**resurrection** [-ʃ(ə)n] *n* résurrection *f.*

resuscitate [rɪ'sʌsɪteɪt] *vt Med* r(é)animer (*qn*). ●**resuscitation** [-'teɪʃ(ə)n] *n* r(é)animation *f.*

retail ['riːteɪl] *n* (vente *f* au) détail *m* ▮ *a* (*price*, *shop etc*) de détail ▮ *vi* se vendre (au détail) (**at** à) ▮ *vt* vendre (au détail), détailler ▮ *adv* (*to sell*) au détail. ●**retailer** *n* détaillant *m.*

retain [rɪ'teɪn] *vt* (*freshness*, *heat*, *hope etc*) conserver; (*hold back*, *remember*) retenir. ●**retainer** *n* (*fee*) acompte *m*, avance *f.* ●**retention** [rɪ'tenʃ(ə)n] *n* (*memory*) mémoire *f*; **the r. of** (*heat etc*) la conservation de. ●**retentive** *a* (*memory*) fidèle.

retaliate [rɪ'tælɪeɪt] *vi* riposter (**against s.o.** contre qn, **against an attack** à une attaque). ●**retaliation** [-'eɪʃ(ə)n] *n* riposte *f*, représailles *fpl*; **in r. for** en représailles de.

retarded [rɪ'tɑːdɪd] *a* (*mentally*) **r.** arriéré.

retch [retʃ] *vi* avoir un *or* des haut-le-cœur.

rethink [riː'θɪŋk] *vt* (*pt & pp* **rethought**) repenser.

reticent ['retɪsənt] *a* réticent. ●**reticence** *n* réticence *f.*

retina ['retɪnə] *n* (*of eye*) rétine *f.*

retire [rɪ'taɪər] **1** *vi* (*from work*) prendre sa retraite ▮ *vt* mettre (*qn*) à la retraite. **2** *vi* (*withdraw*) se retirer (**from** de, **to** à); (*go to bed*) aller se coucher. ●**retired** *a* (*no longer working*) retraité. ●**retiring** *a* **1** (*official*, *president etc*) sortant; **r. age** l'âge *m* de la retraite. **2** (*reserved*) réservé.

retirement [rɪ'taɪəmənt] *n* retraite *f*; **on** (**my**) **r.** dès mon départ à la *or* en retraite; **r. age** l'âge *m* de la retraite.

retort [rɪ'tɔːt] *vt* rétorquer ▮ *n* réplique *f.*

retrace [rɪ'treɪs] *vt* (*past event*) se remémorer, reconstituer; **to r. one's steps** revenir sur ses pas, rebrousser chemin.

retract [rɪ'trækt] **1** *vt* (*statement etc*) rétracter ▮ *vi* (*of person*) se rétracter. **2** *vt* (*claws*, *undercarriage etc*) rentrer. ●**retraction** [-ʃ(ə)n] *n* (*of statement*) rétractation *f.*

retrain [riː'treɪn] *vi* se recycler ▮ *vt* recycler. ●**retraining** *n* recyclage *m.*

retread ['riːtred] *n* pneu *m* rechapé.

retreat [rɪ'triːt] *n* (*withdrawal*) retraite *f*; (*place*) refuge *m* ▮ *vi* se retirer (**from** de); (*of troops etc*) battre en retraite.

retrial [riː'traɪəl] *n Jur* nouveau procès *m.*

retribution [retrɪ'bjuːʃ(ə)n] *n* châtiment *m.*

retrieve [rɪ'triːv] *vt* (*recover*) récupérer; (*rescue*) sauver (**from** de); (*loss*, *error*) réparer; (*data*) *Comptr* récupérer; (*honour*) rétablir. ●**retrieval** *n* récupération *f* (**of** de); **information r.** recherche *f* documentaire; *Comptr* recherche *f* de données. ●**retriever** *n* (*dog*) chien *m* d'arrêt.

retro- ['retrəʊ] *pref* rétro-.

retroactive [retrəʊ'æktɪv] *a* (*pay increase etc*) rétroactif. ●**retroactively** *adv* rétroactivement.

retrograde ['retrəgreɪd] *a* rétrograde.

retrospect ['retrəspekt] *n* **in r.** rétrospectivement.

retrospective [retrə'spektɪv] **1** *a* (*law*, *effect*) rétroactif. **2** *n* (*of film director*, *artist*) rétrospective *f.*

retune [riː'tjuːn] *vi* **to r. to** (*a different radio station or wavelength*) régler la radio sur.

return [rɪ'tɜːn] *vi* (*come back*) revenir; (*go back*) retourner; (*go back home*) rentrer; **to r. to** (*subject*) revenir à.
▮ *vt* (*give back*) rendre; (*put back*) remettre; (*bring back*) rapporter; (*send back*) renvoyer; (*profit*) rapporter; (*greeting*) répondre à; (*candidate in election*) élire; **'r. to sender'** 'retour à l'envoyeur'; **to r. s.o.'s phone call** rappeler qn.
▮ *n* retour *m*; (*on investment*) rendement *m*, rapport *m*; **returns** (*profits*) bénéfices *mpl*; (*results*) *Pol etc* résultats *mpl*; **r. (ticket)** *Br* (billet *m* d')aller et retour *m*; **tax r.** déclaration *f* de revenus; **many happy returns (of the day)!** bon anniversaire!; **in r.** (*exchange*) en échange (**for** de).
▮ *a* (*a trip*, *flight etc*) (de) retour; **r. match**, **r. game** match *m* retour. ●**returnable** *a* (*bottle*) consigné.

reunion [riː'juːnɪən] *n* réunion *f.* ●**reu'nite** *vt* réunir; **to be reunited with s.o.** retrouver qn; **to r. s.o. with s.o.** faire se retrouver qn et qn; **the whole family were reunited** tous les membres de la famille se sont retrouvés.

re-use [riː'juːz] *vt* réutiliser.

rev [rev] *n* (*of car engine*) *Fam* tour *m*; **r. counter** compte-tours *m inv* ▮ *vt* (**-vv-**) **to r. (up)** (*engine*) *Fam* faire ronfler.

Rev [rev] *abbr* **Reverend.**

revamp [riː'væmp] *vt* (*method*, *play etc*) *Fam* remanier.

reveal [rɪ'viːl] *vt* (*make known*) révéler (**that** que); (*make visible*) laisser voir. ●**revealing** *a* (*sign etc*) révélateur.

revel ['rev(ə)l] *vi* (*Br* **-ll-**, *Am* **-l-**) faire la fête; **to r. in sth** se délecter de qch. ●**revelling** (*Am* **reveling**) *n* **or revelry** *n* festivités *fpl.* ●**reveller** (*Am* **reveler**) *n* noceur, -euse *mf.*

revelation [revə'leɪʃ(ə)n] *n* révélation *f.*

revenge [rɪ'vendʒ] *n* vengeance *f*; *Sport* revanche *f*; **to have** *or* **get one's r.** se venger (**on s.o.** de qn, **on s.o. for sth** de qch sur qn); **in r.** pour se venger ▮ *vt* venger.

revenue ['revənjuː] *n* (*income*) revenu *m*; **the R.** *Br* le fisc, le service des impôts.

reverberate [rɪ'vɜːbəreɪt] *vi* (*of sound*) se répercuter; (*have an effect*) (*of news etc*) avoir des répercussions.

revere [rɪ'vɪər] *vt* révérer.

reverence ['revərəns] *n* révérence *f.*

reverend ['rev(ə)rənd] *a* **r. father** *Rel* révérend père *m* ▮ *n* **R. Smith** (*Anglican*) le révérend Smith; (*Catholic*) l'abbé *m* Smith;

(*Jewish*) le rabbin Smith.
reverent ['revərənt] *a* respectueux.
reversal [rɪ'vɜːsəl] *n* (*of situation*) renversement *m*; (*of policy, opinion*) revirement *m*;
r. (of fortune) revers *m* (de fortune).
reverse [rɪ'vɜːs] *a* (*opposite*) contraire;
(*image*) inverse; **in r. order** dans l'ordre inverse; **r. side** (*of coin etc*) revers *m*; (*of paper*) verso *m*.
▮ *n* contraire *m*; (*of coin, fabric etc*) revers
m; (*of paper*) verso *m*; (*setback*) Fig revers
m; **in r. (gear)** (*when driving*) en marche
arrière.
▮ *vt* (*situation*) renverser; (*order, policy*) inverser; (*decision*) annuler; (*bucket etc*) retourner; **to r. the charges** (*when phoning*) Br
téléphoner en PCV.
▮ *vti* Br **to r. (the car)** faire marche arrière;
to r. in/out rentrer/sortir en marche arrière;
to r. into a tree/*etc* rentrer dans un arbre/*etc*
en faisant marche arrière; **reversing lights** Br
feux *mpl* de recul.
reversible [rɪ'vɜːsəb(ə)l] *a* (*fabric etc*) réversible.
revert [rɪ'vɜːt] *vi* **to r. to** revenir à; (*of situation*) retourner à.
review [rɪ'vjuː] **1** *vt* (*book, film etc*) faire la
critique de; (*troops, one's life*) passer en revue; (*situation*) réexaminer; (*salary, opinion*)
réviser ▮ *n* (*of book, film etc*) critique *f*; (*of
troops*) revue *f*; (*of salary, opinion*) révision
f. **2** *n* (*magazine*) revue *f*. ● **reviewer** *n* critique *m*.
revile [rɪ'vaɪl] *vt* invectiver.
revise [rɪ'vaɪz] *vt* (*opinion, notes, text*) réviser ▮ *vi* (*for exam*) réviser (**for** pour). ● **revision** [rɪ'vɪʒ(ə)n] *n* révision *f*.
revitalize [riː'vaɪt(ə)laɪz] *vt* revitaliser.
revival [rɪ'vaɪvəl] *n* (*of custom, business,
play*) reprise *f*; (*of country*) essor *m*; (*of
faith, fashion, the arts*) renouveau *m*.
revive [rɪ'vaɪv] *vt* (*unconscious person,
memory, conversation*) ranimer; (*dying
person*) réanimer; (*custom, fashion, plan*)
ressusciter; (*hope, interest*) faire renaître ▮ *vi*
(*of unconscious person*) reprendre connaissance; (*of country, dying person*) ressusciter; (*of hope, interest*) renaître.
revoke [rɪ'vəʊk] *vt* (*decision*) annuler; (*contract*) révoquer.
revolt [rɪ'vəʊlt] **1** *n* révolte *f* ▮ *vi* (*rebel*) se
révolter (**against** contre). **2** *vt* (*disgust*) révolter. ● **revolting** *a* dégoûtant; (*injustice*) révoltant.
revolution [revə'luːʃ(ə)n] *n* révolution *f*.
● **revolutionary** *a & n* révolutionnaire (*mf*).
● **revolutionize** *vt* révolutionner.
revolve [rɪ'vɒlv] *vi* tourner (**around** autour
de). ● **revolving** *a* **r. chair** fauteuil *m* pivotant; **r. door(s)** (porte *f* à) tambour *m*.
revolver [rɪ'vɒlvər] *n* revolver *m*.
revue [rɪ'vjuː] *n* (*theatrical*) revue *f*.
revulsion [rɪ'vʌlʃ(ə)n] *n* **1** (*disgust*) dégoût
m; **to have a sense of r.** être rempli de dégoût. **2** (*change*) revirement *m*.

reward [rɪ'wɔːd] *n* récompense *f* (**for** de) ▮ *vt*
récompenser (**s.o. for sth** qn de *or* pour
qch). ● **rewarding** *a* (*worthwhile*) qui (en)
vaut la peine; (*satisfying*) satisfaisant;
(*financially*) rémunérateur.
rewind [riː'waɪnd] *vt* (*pt & pp* **rewound**)
(*tape*) rembobiner ▮ *vi* (*of tape*) se rembobiner.
rewire [riː'waɪər] *vt* (*house etc*) refaire
l'installation électrique de.
rewrite [riː'raɪt] *vt* (*pt* **rewrote**, *pp* **rewritten**)
récrire; (*edit*) réécrire.
rhapsody ['ræpsədɪ] *n* rhapsodie *f*.
rhesus ['riːsəs] *n* rhésus *m*; **r. positive/
negative** rhésus positif/négatif.
rhetoric ['retərɪk] *n* rhétorique *f*.
● **rhe'torical** *a* **r. question** question *f* de pure
forme.
rheumatism ['ruːmətɪz(ə)m] *n* rhumatisme
m; **to have r.** avoir des rhumatismes.
● **rheu'matic** *a* (*pain*) rhumatismal; (*person*)
rhumatisant.
Rhine [raɪn] *n* **the R.** le Rhin.
rhinoceros [raɪ'nɒsərəs] *n* rhinocéros *m*.
rhododendron [rəʊdə'dendrən] *n* rhododendron *m*.
Rhône [rəʊn] *n* **the R.** le Rhône.
rhubarb ['ruːbɑːb] *n* rhubarbe *f*.
rhyme [raɪm] *n* rime *f*; (*poem*) vers *mpl* ▮ *vi*
rimer (**with** avec).
rhythm ['rɪð(ə)m] *n* rythme *m*. ● **rhythmic(al)**
a rythmique.
rib [rɪb] *n* (*bone*) côte *f*; **to have a broken r.**
avoir une côte cassée.
ribald ['rɪb(ə)ld] *a* Lit grivois.
ribbon ['rɪbən] *n* ruban *m*; **to tear to ribbons**
mettre en lambeaux.
rice [raɪs] *n* riz *m*; **brown r.** riz complet.
● **ricefield** *n* rizière *f*.
rich [rɪtʃ] *a* (-**er**, -**est**) (*person, food etc*)
riche; (*profits*) gros; **r. in vitamins**/*etc* riche
en vitamines/*etc* ▮ **the r.** les riches *mpl*.
● **riches** *npl* richesses *fpl*. ● **richly** *adv* (*illustrated, dressed etc*) richement; (*deserved*)
amplement. ● **richness** *n* richesse *f*.
rick [rɪk] *vt* **to r. one's back** se tordre le dos.
rickets ['rɪkɪts] *npl* (*disease*) rachitisme *m*.
rickety ['rɪkɪtɪ] *a* (*furniture*) branlant.
rickshaw ['rɪkʃɔː] *n* pousse(-pousse) *m inv*.
ricochet ['rɪkəʃeɪ] *vi* ricocher ▮ *n* ricochet *m*.
rid [rɪd] *vt* (*pt & pp* **rid**, *pres p* **ridding**) débarrasser (**of** de); **to get r. of, r. oneself of** se
débarrasser de. ● **riddance** *n* **good r.!** Fam
bon débarras!
ridden ['rɪd(ə)n] *pp of* **ride**.
-ridden ['rɪd(ə)n] *suff* **debt-r.** criblé de
dettes; **disease-r.** en proie à la maladie.
riddle ['rɪd(ə)l] **1** *n* (*puzzle*) énigme *f*. **2** *vt*
cribler (**with** de); **riddled with** (*bullets, holes,
mistakes*) criblé de; (*corruption*) en proie à;
(*cancer*) rongé par.
ride [raɪd] *n* (*on bicycle, by car etc*) promenade *f*; (*distance*) trajet *m*; (*in taxi*) course *f*;
(*on merry-go-round*) tour *m*; **to go for a
(car) r.** faire une promenade (en voiture); **to**

give s.o. a r. (*in a car*) emmener qn en voiture; **to have a r. on** (*bicycle*) monter sur; **to take s.o. for a r.** (*deceive*) *Fam* mener qn en bateau.

‖ *vi* (*pt* **rode**, *pp* **ridden**) aller (à bicyclette, à moto, à cheval *etc*) (**to** à); **to r., go riding** (*on horse*) monter (à cheval); **to be riding in a car** être en voiture; **to r. up** (*of skirt*) remonter.

‖ *vt* (*a particular horse*) monter; (*distance*) faire (à cheval *etc*); **to r. a horse** *or* **horses** (*go riding*) monter à cheval; **I was riding (on) a bicycle/donkey** j'étais à bicyclette/à dos d'âne; **to know how to r. a bicycle** savoir faire de la bicyclette; **to r. a bicycle to** aller à bicyclette à; **may I r. your bicycle?** puis-je monter sur ta bicyclette?; **to r.** s.o. (*annoy*) *Am Fam* harceler qn.

rider ['raidər] *n* **1** (*on horse*) cavalier, -ière *mf*; (*cyclist*) cycliste *mf*. **2** (*to document*) annexe *f*; **to add a r. to** (*statement*) apporter une nuance *or* une précision à.

ridge [ridʒ] *n* (*of roof, mountain*) arête *f*.

ridicule ['ridikjuːl] *n* ridicule *m*; **to hold up to r.** tourner en ridicule; **object of r.** objet *m* de risée **‖** *vt* tourner en ridicule, ridiculiser.

ridiculous [ri'dikjuləs] *a* ridicule.

riding ['raidiŋ] *n* (*horse*) r. équitation *f*; **r. boots** bottes *fpl* de cheval; **r. school** école *f* d'équitation, manège *m*.

rife [raif] *a* (*widespread*) répandu.

riffraff ['rifræf] *n* racaille *f*.

rifle ['raif(ə)l] **1** *n* fusil *m*, carabine *f*. **2** *vt* (*drawers, pockets etc*) vider; **to r. through** (*search through*) fouiller dans (*papiers etc*).

rift [rift] *n* (*in political party*) scission *f*; (*disagreement*) désaccord *m*; (*crack in rock etc*) fissure *f*.

rig [rig] **1** *n* (oil) r. derrick *m*; (*at sea*) plateforme *f* pétrolière. **2** *vt* (**-gg-**) (*result, election etc*) *Pej* truquer; **to r. up** (*equipment*) installer; (*meeting etc*) *Fam* arranger. **3** *vt* (**-gg-**) **to r. out** (*dress*) *Br Fam* habiller. ● **rig-out** *n Br Fam* tenue *f*.

rigging ['rigiŋ] *n* (*ropes on ship*) gréement *m*.

right¹ [rait] **1** *a* (*correct*) bon (*f* **bonne**), exact, juste; (*fair*) juste; **r. angle** *Math* angle *m* droit; **to be r.** (*of person*) avoir raison (**to do** de faire); **it's the r. road** c'est la bonne route, c'est bien la route; **the r. choice/time/** *etc* le bon choix/moment/*etc*; **it's the r. time** (*accurate*) c'est l'heure exacte; **the clock is r.** la pendule est à l'heure; **he's the r. man** c'est l'homme qu'il faut; **the r. thing to do** la meilleure chose à faire; **it's not r. to steal** ce n'est pas bien de voler; **it doesn't look r.** il y a quelque chose qui ne va pas; **things will come r.** *Fam* ça s'arrangera; **to put r.** (*error*) corriger, rectifier; (*fix*) arranger; **to put s.o. r.** (*inform*) éclairer qn, détromper qn; **r.!** bien!; **that's r.** c'est ça, c'est exact.

‖ *adv* (*straight*) (tout) droit; (*completely*) tout à fait; (*correctly*) juste; (*well*) bien; **she did it r.** elle a bien fait; **r. round** tout autour

(sth de qch); **r. behind** juste derrière; **r. here** ici même; **r. away, r. now** tout de suite; **the R. Honourable...** (*address to Member of Parliament etc*) *Br* le Très Honorable....

‖ *n* **to be in the r.** avoir raison; **r. and wrong** le bien et le mal.

‖ *vt* (*error, wrong, boat, car*) redresser.

2 all r. *see* **all right**.

right² [rait] *a* (*not left*) (*hand, side etc*) droit **‖** *adv* à droite **‖** *n* droite *f*; **on** *or* **to the r.** à droite (**of** de). ● **right-hand** *a* à *or* de droite; **on the r.-hand side** à droite (**of** de); **r.-hand man** bras *m* droit. ● **right-'handed** *a* (*person*) droitier. ● **right-wing** *a* (*views, government etc*) de droite.

right³ [rait] *n* (*claim, entitlement*) droit *m* (**to** do de faire); **to have a r. to sth** avoir droit à qch; **he's famous in his own r.** il est luimême célèbre; **to have the r. of way** (*on road*) avoir la priorité; **human rights** les droits *mpl* de l'homme.

righteous ['raitʃəs] *a* (*person*) vertueux; (*cause, indignation*) juste.

rightful ['raitfəl] *a* légitime. ● **rightfully** *adv* légitimement.

rightly ['raitli] *adv* (*to guess etc*) bien, correctement; (*justifiably*) à juste titre; **r. or wrongly** à tort ou à raison.

rigid ['ridʒid] *a* rigide. ● **ri'gidity** *n* rigidité *f*. ● **rigidly** *adv* **r. opposed to** rigoureusement opposé à.

rigmarole ['rigmərəul] *n* (*process*) procédure *f* compliquée.

rigour ['rigər] (*Am* **rigor**) *n* rigueur *f*. ● **rigorous** *a* rigoureux.

rile [rail] *vt* (*annoy*) *Fam* agacer.

rim [rim] *n* (*of cup etc*) bord *m*; (*of wheel*) jante *f*; (*of spectacles*) monture *f*.

rind [raind] *n* (*of cheese*) croûte *f*; (*of bacon*) couenne *f*; (*of melon, lemon*) écorce *f*.

ring¹ [riŋ] *n* (*for curtain, in gym etc*) anneau *m*; (*for finger*) anneau *m*; (*for finger with jewel*) bague *f*; (*of people, chairs*) cercle *m*; (*of smoke, from napkin*) rond *m*; (*gang*) bande *f*; (*at circus*) piste *f*; *Boxing* ring *m*; (*burner on stove*) brûleur *m*; **diamond r.** bague *f* de diamants; **to have rings under one's eyes** avoir les yeux cernés; **r. road** *Br* route *f* de ceinture; (*on motorway*) périphérique *m*.

‖ *vt* (*round*) (*surround*) entourer (**with** de); (*item on list etc*) encadrer.

ring² [riŋ] *n* (*sound*) sonnerie *f*; **there's a r. on** someone; **to give s.o. a r.** (*phone call*) passer un coup de fil à qn; **it has a r. of truth (about it)** cela a un accent de vérité.

‖ *vi* (*pt* **rang**, *pp* **rung**) (*of bell, phone, person etc*) sonner; (*of sound, words*) retentir; (*of ears*) bourdonner; (*make a phone call*) téléphoner; **to r. for s.o.** sonner qn.

‖ *vt* sonner; **to r. s.o.** (*on phone*) téléphoner à qn; **to r. the bell** sonner; **to r. the doorbell** sonner à la porte; **that rings a bell** *Fam* ça me rappelle quelque chose. ● **ringing** *a* **r. tone** (*on phone*) *Br* sonnerie *f* **‖** *n* (*of bell*) sonnerie *f*; **a r. in one's ears** un bourdonnement dans les oreilles.

ring back (phone) rappeler ▌ vt to r. s.o. back rappeler qn ▌ to ring in vt (the New Year) carillonner ▌ to ring off vi (after phoning) raccrocher ▌ to ring out vi (of bell) sonner; (of sound) retentir ▌ to ring up vi (phone) téléphoner ▌ vt to r. s.o. up téléphoner à qn.

ringleader ['rɪŋliːdər] n Pej (of gang) chef m de bande; (of rebellion etc) meneur, -euse mf.

ringlet ['rɪŋlɪt] n (curl) anglaise f.

rink [rɪŋk] n (for ice-skating) patinoire f; (for roller-skating) skating m.

rinse [rɪns] vt rincer; to r. one's hands (remove soap) se rincer les mains; (wash) se passer les mains à l'eau; to r. out rincer ▌ n rinçage m; (hair colouring) shampooing m colorant; to give sth a r. rincer qch.

riot ['raɪət] n (uprising) émeute f; (fighting) bagarres fpl; (demonstration) manifestation f violente; a r. of colour Fig une orgie de couleurs; to run r. (of crowd) se déchaîner; the r. police = les CRS mpl ▌ vi (rise up) faire une émeute; (fight) se bagarrer. ●rioting n émeutes fpl; (fighting) bagarres fpl. ●rioter n émeutier, -ière mf; (vandal) casseur m; (demonstrator) manifestant, -ante mf violent(e).

riotous ['raɪətəs] a (crowd etc) tapageur; (children's play etc) plein d'exubérance; r. living vie f dissolue.

rip [rɪp] vt (-pp-) déchirer; to r. off (button etc) arracher (from de); to r. s.o. off (deceive) Fam rouler qn; to r. sth off (steal) Am Fam faucher qch; to r. out (telephone etc) arracher (from de); to r. sth up déchirer qch ▌ vi (of fabric) se déchirer; the explosion ripped through the building l'explosion souffla tout dans le bâtiment ▌ n déchirure f. ●rip-off n Fam it's a r.-off c'est du vol organisé, c'est de l'arnaque.

ripe [raɪp] a (-er, -est) mûr; (cheese) fait. ●ripen vti mûrir. ●ripeness n maturité f.

ripple ['rɪp(ə)l] n (on water) ride f; (of laughter) Fig cascade f ▌ vi (of water) se rider.

rise [raɪz] vi (pt rose, pp risen) (of temperature, balloon, price etc) monter, s'élever; (in society) s'élever; (of hope) grandir; (of sun, theatre curtain, wind) se lever; (of dough) lever; (get up from chair or bed) se lever; to r. in price augmenter de prix; to r. to the surface remonter à la surface; the river rises in... le fleuve prend sa source dans...; to r. (up) (rebel) se soulever (against contre); to r. to power accéder au pouvoir; to r. from the dead ressusciter; to r. to the occasion se montrer à la hauteur de la situation.

▌ n (in price, pressure etc) hausse f (in de); (of curtain in theatre) lever m; (in river) crue f; (of leader) Fig ascension f; (of technology, industry) essor m; (to power) accession f; (slope in ground) montée f; (hill) éminence f; his r. to fame son ascension vers la gloire; (pay) r. Br augmentation f (de salaire); to

give r. to sth donner lieu à qch.

riser ['raɪzər] n early r. lève-tôt mf inv; late r. lève-tard mf inv.

rising ['raɪzɪŋ] n (of curtain in theatre) lever m; (revolt) soulèvement m; (of river) crue f ▌ a (sun) levant (number) croissant; (tide) montant; (artist, politician etc) d'avenir; the r. generation la nouvelle génération; r. prices la hausse des prix.

risk [rɪsk] n risque m (of doing de faire, in doing à faire); at r. (person) en danger; (job) menacé; at your own r. à tes risques et périls ▌ vt (one's life, an accident etc) risquer; she won't r. leaving (take the risk) elle ne risquera pas à partir; let's r. it risquons le coup. ●riskiness n risques mpl. ●risky a (-ier, -iest) (full of risks) risqué.

rissole ['rɪsəʊl] n Br Culin croquette f.

rite [raɪt] n rite m; the last rites (for dying person) Rel les derniers sacrements mpl. ●ritual a & n rituel (m).

ritzy ['rɪtsɪ] a (-ier, -iest) Fam luxueux, classe inv.

rival ['raɪv(ə)l] a (company etc) rival; (forces, claim etc) opposé ▌ n rival, -ale mf ▌ vt (Br -ll-, Am -l-) (compete with) rivaliser avec (in de); (equal) égaler (in en). ●rivalry n rivalité f (between entre).

river ['rɪvər] n (small) rivière f; (flowing into sea) fleuve m; (of lava, tears etc) Fig fleuve m; the R. Thames la Tamise ▌ a (port, navigation etc) fluvial; r. bank rive f; r. bed lit m de rivière or de fleuve. ●riverside a & n (by the) r. au bord de l'eau.

rivet ['rɪvɪt] n (pin for metal) rivet m ▌ vt riveter; (eyes) Fig fixer (on sur); to be riveted to the TV set être cloué devant la télé. ●riveting a (story etc) fascinant.

Riviera [rɪvɪ'eərə] n the (French) R. la Côte d'Azur.

roach [rəʊtʃ] n (cockroach) Am cafard m.

road [rəʊd] n route f (to qui va à); (small) chemin m; (in town) rue f; (roadway) chaussée f; (path) Fig voie f, chemin m, route f (to de); A-r. Br = route f nationale; B-r. Br = route f départementale; the Paris r. la route de Paris; across or over the r. (building etc) en face; by r. par la route; get out of the r.! ne reste pas sur la chaussée!

▌ a (map, safety) routier; (accident) de la route; r. hog Fam chauffard m; to have r. sense (of pedestrian, child) avoir conscience des dangers de la rue; (of driver) avoir un bon sens de la conduite; r. sign panneau m (routier or de signalisation); r. works Br, r. work Am travaux mpl.

roadblock ['rəʊdblɒk] n barrage m routier. ●roadside a & n (by the) r. au bord de la route. ●roadway n chaussée f. ●roadworthy a (vehicle) en état de marche.

roam [rəʊm] vt parcourir ▌ vi errer, rôder; to r. (about) the streets (of child, dog etc) traîner dans les rues.

roar [rɔːr] vi (of lion, wind, engine) rugir; (of person, crowd) hurler; (of thunder) gronder;

to r. with laughter éclater de rire; **to r. past** (*of truck etc*) passer dans un bruit de tonnerre ∎ *vt* **to r. (out)** (*threat, order etc*) hurler ∎ *n* (*of lion etc*) rugissement *m*; (*of person etc*) hurlement *m*; (*of thunder*) grondement *m*. ●**roaring** *n* = **roar** *n* ∎ *a* **a r. fire** une belle flambée; **a r. success** un succès fou; **to do a r. trade** vendre beaucoup (**in** de).

roast [rəʊst] *vt* rôtir; (*coffee*) griller ∎ *vi* (*of meat*) rôtir; **we're roasting here** *Fam* on rôtit ici ∎ *n* (*meat*) rôti *m* ∎ *a* (*chicken etc*) rôti; **r. beef** rosbif *m*.

rob [rɒb] *vt* (**-bb-**) (*person*) voler; (*shop, bank, house*) dévaliser; (*by breaking in*) cambrioler; (*hold up*) attaquer; **to r. s.o. of sth** voler qch à qn; (*deprive*) priver qn de qch. ●**robber** *n* voleur, -euse *mf*. ●**robbery** *n* vol *m*; **it's daylight r.!** c'est du vol organisé; **armed r.** vol *m* à main armée.

robe [rəʊb] *n* (*dressing gown*) robe *f* de chambre; (*of priest, judge etc*) robe *f*.

robin ['rɒbɪn] *n* (*bird*) rouge-gorge *m*.

robot ['rəʊbɒt] *n* robot *m*. ●**ro'botics** *n* robotique *f*.

robust [rəʊ'bʌst] *a* robuste.

rock[1] [rɒk] **1** *vt* (*baby, boat*) bercer, balancer; (*branch, cradle*) balancer; (*violently*) (*of explosion etc*) secouer (*bâtiment etc*) ∎ *vi* (*sway gently*) se balancer; (*of building, ground*) trembler. **2** *n* (*music*) rock *m*.

rock[2] [rɒk] *n* (*substance*) roche *f*; (*boulder, rock face*) rocher *m*; (*stone*) *Am* pierre *f*; **a stick of r.**, **some r.** (*sweet*) *Br* un bâton de sucre d'orge; **r. face** paroi *f* rocheuse; **on the rocks** (*whisky*) avec des glaçons; (*marriage*) en pleine débâcle. ●**rock-'bottom** *n* point *m* le plus bas; **he has reached r.-bottom** il a touché le fond ∎ *a* (*prices*) les plus bas, très bas. ●**rock-climbing** *n* varappe *f*.

rockery ['rɒkərɪ] *n* (*in garden*) rocaille *f*.

rocket ['rɒkɪt] *n* fusée *f* ∎ *vi* (*of prices*) monter en flèche.

rocking chair ['rɒkɪŋtʃeər] *n* fauteuil *m* à bascule. ●**rocking horse** *n* cheval *m* à bascule.

rocky ['rɒkɪ] *a* (**-ier, -iest**) **1** (*road*) rocailleux; (*hill*) rocheux. **2** (*furniture etc*) branlant.

rod [rɒd] *n* (*wooden*) baguette *f*; (*metal*) tige *f*; (*of curtain*) tringle *f*; (*for fishing*) canne *f* (à pêche).

rode [rəʊd] *pt of* **ride**.

rodent ['rəʊdənt] *n* (*animal*) rongeur *m*.

rodeo [*Br* 'rəʊdɪəʊ, *Am* rəʊ'deɪəʊ] *n* (*pl* **-os**) *Am* rodéo *m*.

roe [rəʊ] *n* **1** (*eggs*) œufs *mpl* de poisson. **2 r.** (*deer*) chevreuil *m*.

rogue [rəʊg] *n* (*dishonest*) crapule *f*; (*mischievous*) coquin, -ine *mf*. ●**roguish** *a* (*smile etc*) coquin.

role [rəʊl] *n* rôle *m*.

roll [rəʊl] *n* (*of paper etc*) rouleau *m*; (*small bread loaf*) petit pain *m*; (*of fat, flesh*)

bourrelet *m*; (*of drum, thunder*) roulement *m*; (*list of names etc*) liste *f*; (*of ship*) roulis *m*; **r. of film** (rouleau *m* de) pellicule *f*; **to have a r. call** faire l'appel; **r. neck** (*neckline, sweater*) col *m* roulé. ∎ *vi* (*of ball, ship etc*) rouler; (*of person, animal*) se rouler; **to r. into a ball** (*of animal*) se rouler en boule; **to be rolling in money, be rolling in it** *Fam* rouler sur l'or. ∎ *vt* rouler (*qch, qn*). ●**rolling** *a* (*ground, gait*) onduleux.

roll down *vt* (*car window etc*) baisser; (*slope*) descendre (en roulant) ∎ **to roll in** *vi Fam* (*flow in*) affluer; (*of person*) s'amener ∎ **to roll on** *vt* (*paint, stocking*) mettre ∎ *vi Fam* **r. on tonight!** vivement ce soir! ∎ **to roll out** *vt* (*dough*) étaler ∎ **to roll over** *vi* (*many times*) se rouler; (*once*) se retourner ∎ *vt* retourner ∎ **to roll up** *vt* (*map, cloth*) rouler; (*sleeve, Br trousers, Am pants*) retrousser ∎ *vi* (*arrive*) *Fam* s'amener; **to r. up into a ball** (*of animal*) se rouler en boule.

roller ['rəʊlər] *n* (*for hair, painting etc*) rouleau *m*; **r. coaster** (*at funfair*) montagnes *fpl* russes. ●**roller-skate** *n* patin *m* à roulettes ∎ *vi* faire du patin à roulettes.

rollicking ['rɒlɪkɪŋ] **1** *a* joyeux (et bruyant). **2** *n* **to give s.o. a r.** (*tell off*) *Br Fam* engueuler qn.

rolling pin ['rəʊlɪŋpɪn] *n* rouleau *m* à pâtisserie.

roly-poly [rəʊlɪ'pəʊlɪ] *a Fam* grassouillet (*f* -ette).

ROM [rɒm] *n abbr Comptr* = **read-only memory.**

Roman ['rəʊmən] **1** *a & n* romain, -aine (*mf*). **2** *a & n* **R. Catholic** catholique (*mf*).

romance [rəʊ'mæns] **1** *n* (*love*) amour *m*; (*affair*) aventure *f* amoureuse; (*story*) histoire *f* or roman *m* d'amour; (*charm*) poésie *f*. **2** *a* **R. language** langue *f* romane.

Romania [rəʊ'meɪnɪə] *n* Roumanie *f*. ●**Romanian** *a* roumain ∎ *n* (*language*) roumain *m*; (*person*) Roumain, -aine *mf*.

romantic [rəʊ'mæntɪk] *a* (*of love, tenderness etc*) romantique; (*fanciful, imaginary*) romanesque ∎ *n* (*person*) romantique *mf*. ●**romantically** *adv* (*to behave*) de façon romantique. ●**romanticism** *n* romantisme *m*.

romp [rɒmp] *vi* s'ébattre (bruyamment); **to r. through an exam** avoir un examen les doigts dans le nez ∎ *n* ébats *mpl*.

rompers ['rɒmpəz] *npl* (*for baby*) barboteuse *f*.

roof [ruːf] *n* (*of building, vehicle*) toit *m*; (*of tunnel, cave*) plafond *m*; **r. of the mouth** voûte *f* du palais; **r. rack** (*of car*) galerie *f*. ●**roofing** *n* toiture *f*. ●**rooftop** *n* toit *m*.

rook [rʊk] *n* **1** (*bird*) corneille *f*. **2** *Chess* tour *f*.

rookie ['rʊkɪ] *n* (*new recruit*) *Fam* bleu *m*.

room [ruːm, rʊm] *n* **1** (*in house etc*) pièce *f*; (*bedroom*) chambre *f*; (*large, public*) salle *f*; **men's r., ladies' r.** *Am* toilettes *fpl*; **one's rooms** son appartement *m*; **in rooms** en meublé. **2** (*space*) place *f* (**for** pour); (**some**)

r. de la place; **there's r.** for doubt le doute est permis; **no r. for doubt** aucun doute possible. ● **rooming house** *n Am* maison *f* de rapport. ● **roommate** *n* camarade *mf* de chambre. ● **roomy** *a* (**-ier, -iest**) spacieux; (*clothes*) ample.

roost [ru:st] *vi* (*of bird*) se percher **❙** *n* perchoir *m*.

rooster ['ru:stər] *n* coq *m*.

root [ru:t] **1** *n* (*of plant etc*) & *Math* racine *f*; (*origin*) Fig origine *f*; (*cause*) cause *f*; **to pull up by the root(s)** déraciner; **to take r.** (*of plant*, Fig *person*) prendre racine; **roots** *fpl*; **to find one's roots** retrouver ses racines; **to put down (new) roots** (*of person*) s'enraciner; **r. beer** = boisson *f* gazeuse aux extraits végétaux; **r. cause** cause *f* première **❙** *vt* **to r. out** (*destroy*) extirper **❙** *vi* (*of plant cutting*) s'enraciner.

2 *vi* **to r. about** *or* **around for sth** fouiller pour trouver qch.

3 *vi* **to r. for** (*cheer, support*) *Fam* encourager. ● **rooted** *a* **deeply r.** bien enraciné (**in** dans); **r. to the spot** (*immobile*) cloué sur place. ● **rootless** *a* sans racines.

rope [rəup] *n* corde *f*; (*on ship*) cordage *m*; **to know the ropes** *Fam* être au courant **❙** *vt* (*tie*) lier; **to r. s.o. in** (*force to help*) *Fam* embrigader qn (**to do** pour faire); **to r. off** (*of police etc*) interdire l'accès de.

rop(e)y ['rəupɪ] *a* (**-ier, -iest**) *Br Fam* (*thing*) minable; (*person*) patraque.

rosary ['rəuzərɪ] *n Rel* chapelet *m*.

rose[1] [rəuz] *n* **1** (*flower*) rose *f*; (*colour*) rose *m*; **r. bush** rosier *m*. **2** (*of watering can*) pomme *f*. ● **rosebud** *n* bouton *m* de rose.

rose[2] [rəuz] *pt of* **rise**.

rosé ['rəuzeɪ] *n* (*wine*) rosé *m*.

rosemary ['rəuzmərɪ] *n* (*plant, herb*) romarin *m*.

rosette [rəu'zet] *n* (*prize*) *Sport* cocarde *f*; (*rose-shaped badge*) rosette *f*.

roster ['rɒstər] *n* liste *f* (de service).

rostrum ['rɒstrəm] *n* tribune *f*; (*for winning sportsman or sportswoman*) podium *m*.

rosy ['rəuzɪ] *a* (**-ier, -iest**) (*pink*) rose; (*future*) Fig tout en rose.

rot [rɒt] *n* pourriture *f*; (*nonsense*) *Br Fam* inepties *fpl* **❙** *vti* (**-tt-**) **to r.** (**away**) pourrir.

rota ['rəutə] *n* liste *f* (de service).

rotary ['rəutərɪ] *a* rotatif; **r. clothes dryer** (*washing line*) *Br* séchoir *m* parapluie **❙** *n* (*for traffic*) *Am* sens *m* giratoire. ● **rotation** [-'teɪʃ(ə)n] *n* rotation *f*; **in r.** à tour de rôle.

rotate [rəu'teɪt] *vi* tourner **❙** *vt* faire tourner; (*crops*) alterner.

rote [rəut] *n* **by r.** machinalement.

rotten ['rɒt(ə)n] *a* (*decayed*) (*fruit etc*) pourri; (*bad*) *Fam* moche; (*filthy*) *Fam* sale; (*corrupt*) pourri; **to feel r.** (*ill*) être mal fichu. ● **rottenness** *n* pourriture *f*. ● **rotting** *a* (*meat, fruit etc*) qui pourrit.

rotund [rəu'tʌnd] *a* (*round*) rond; (*plump*) rondelet (*f* -**ette**).

rouble ['ru:b(ə)l] (*Am* **ruble**) *n* (*currency*) rouble *m*.

rouge [ru:ʒ] *n* rouge *m* (à joues).

rough[1] [rʌf] *a* (**-er, -est**) (*surface*) rugueux, rude; (*plank, bark*) rugueux; (*ground*) inégal, accidenté; (*rocky*) rocailleux; (*climate, task, life, manners*) rude; (*sound*) âpre, rude; (*coarse*) grossier; (*brutal*) brutal; (*neighbourhood, weather*) mauvais; (*sea*) agité; (*justice*) *Br* sommaire; (*diamond*) brut; **a r. child** (*unruly*) un enfant dur; **in a r. voice** d'une voix rude; **to feel r.** (*ill*) *Br Fam* être mal fichu; **r. and ready** (*conditions, solution*) grossier (mais adéquat).

❙ *adv* **to sleep/live r.** *Br* coucher/vivre à la dure; **to play r.** jouer brutalement.

❙ *n* (*violent man*) *Fam* voyou *m*.

❙ *vt* **to r. it** *Fam* vivre à la dure; **to r. s.o. up** *Fam* malmener qn; **to r. up s.o.'s hair** ébouriffer les cheveux de qn. ● **rough-and-'tumble** *n* (*fight*) mêlée *f*; (*of s.o.'s life*) remue-ménage *m inv.* ● **roughen** *vt* rendre rude. ● **roughly[1]** *adv* (*not gently*) rudement; (*coarsely*) grossièrement; (*brutally*) brutalement. ● **roughness** *n* (*of surface, manners etc*) rudesse *f*; (*of ground*) inégalité *f*; (*coarseness*) grossièreté *f*; (*brutality*) brutalité *f*.

rough[2] [rʌf] *a* (**-er, -est**) (*calculation, figure, terms etc*) approximatif; **r. guess, r. estimate** approximation *f*; **r. book** *Br* cahier *m* de brouillon; **r. copy, r. draft** brouillon *m*; **r. paper** du papier brouillon; **a r. plan** l'ébauche *f* d'un projet **❙** *vt* **to r. out** (*plan*) ébaucher. ● **roughly[2]** *adv* (*approximately*) à peu (de choses) près.

roughage ['rʌfɪdʒ] *n* (*in food*) fibres *fpl* (alimentaires).

roulette [ru:'let] *n* roulette *f*.

round [raund] **1** *adv* autour; **all r., right r.** tout autour; **to go r. to s.o.'s** passer chez qn; **to ask s.o. r.** inviter qn chez soi; **he'll be r.** il passera; **r. here** par ici; **the long way r.** le chemin le plus long.

❙ *prep* autour de; **r. about** (*approximately*) environ; **r. (about) midday** vers midi, à environ midi; **to go r. a corner** tourner un coin; **to go r. the world** faire le tour du monde.

2 *a* (**-er, -est**) rond; **r. trip** *Am* aller (et) retour *m*.

3 *n* (*slice*) *Br* tranche *f*; (*sandwich*) *Br* sandwich *m*; (*in competition, election*) manche *f*; (*of golf*) partie *f*; *Boxing* round *m*; (*of talks*) série *f*; (*of drinks, visits*) tournée *f*; **to be on one's round(s), do one's round(s)** (*of milkman*) faire sa tournée; (*of doctor*) faire ses visites; (*of policeman*) faire sa ronde; **delivery r.** livraisons *fpl*, tournée *f*; **r. of applause** salve *f* d'applaudissements; **r. of ammunition** cartouche *f*, balle *f*.

4 *vt* **to r. a corner** (*in car*) prendre un virage; **to r. off** (*meal, speech etc*) terminer (**with** par); **to r. up** (*gather*) rassembler; (*price*) arrondir au chiffre supérieur.

rule

● **round-'shouldered** a voûté, aux épaules rondes.

roundabout ['raʊndəbaʊt] **1** a (method, route etc) indirect, détourné. **2** n Br (at funfair) manège m; (road junction) rond-point m (à sens giratoire).

rounded ['raʊndɪd] a arrondi. ● **roundness** n rondeur f.

rounders ['raʊndəz] npl sorte de baseball.

roundup ['raʊndʌp] n (of criminals) rafle f.

rouse [raʊz] vt (awaken) éveiller; **roused (to anger)** en colère; **to r. s.o. to action** inciter qn à agir. ● **rousing** a (welcome) enthousiaste; (speech) vibrant; (music) allègre.

rout [raʊt] n (defeat) déroute f ‖ vt mettre en déroute.

route 1 [ruːt] n itinéraire m; (of aircraft) route f; **sea r.** route f maritime; **bus r.** ligne f d'autobus ‖ vt (train etc) fixer l'itinéraire de. **2** [raʊt] n (delivery round) Am tournée f.

routine [ruːˈtiːn] **1** n (habit) routine f; (computer program) sous-programme m, routine f; **one's daily r.** (in office etc) son travail journalier; **the daily r.** (monotony) le train-train quotidien; **as a matter of r.** de façon systématique ‖ a (inquiry, work etc) de routine; Pej routinier. **2** n (on stage) numéro m.

rove [raʊv] vi errer ‖ vt parcourir. ● **roving** a (life) nomade; (ambassador) itinérant.

row¹ [raʊ] **1** n (line) rang m, rangée f; (one behind another) file f; **two days in a r.** deux jours de suite or d'affilée. **2** vi (in boat) ramer ‖ vt (boat) faire aller à la rame; (person) transporter en canot ‖ n to go for a r. canoter; **r. boat** Am bateau m à rames. ● **rowing** n canotage m; (as sport) aviron m; **r. boat** Br bateau m à rames.

row² [raʊ] n Fam (noise) vacarme m; (quarrel) dispute f ‖ vi Fam se disputer (with avec).

rowdy ['raʊdɪ] a (-ier, -iest) chahuteur (et brutal) ‖ n (person) Fam voyou m.

royal ['rɔɪəl] a royal; **R. Air Force** armée f de l'air (britannique) ‖ npl **the royals** Fam la famille royale. ● **royalist** a & n royaliste (mf). ● **royally** adv (to treat) royalement. ● **royalty 1** n (persons) personnages mpl royaux. **2** npl **royalties** (from book) droits mpl d'auteur; (from invention, on oil) royalties fpl.

rpm [ɑːpiːˈem] abbr (revolutions per minute) Aut tours/minute mpl.

Rt Hon Br Pol abbr **Right Honourable** (see right¹).

rub [rʌb] vt (-bb-) frotter; (person) frictionner, frotter; (polish) astiquer; **to r. shoulders with** Fig côtoyer, coudoyer; **to r. s.o. up** Br or **r. s.o.** Am **the wrong way** prendre qn à rebrousse-poil ‖ vi frotter ‖ n (massage) friction f; **to give sth a r.** frotter qch; (polish) astiquer qch.

rub down vt (mark) effacer; (tears) essuyer ‖ **to rub down** vt (person) frictionner; (wood, with sandpaper) poncer ‖ **to rub in** vt

(cream) faire pénétrer (en massant); **to r. it in** Pej Fam retourner le couteau dans la plaie ‖ **to rub off** vt (mark) effacer ‖ vi (of mark) partir; (of manners etc) Fig déteindre (on s.o. sur qn) ‖ **to rub out** vt (mark) effacer.

rubber ['rʌbər] n (substance) caoutchouc m; (eraser) gomme f; (for blackboard) Br brosse f (pour tableau); (contraceptive) Am Sl capote f; **r. stamp** tampon m. ● **rubber-'stamp** vt Pej approuver (sans discuter). ● **rubbery** a caoutchouteux.

rubbing alcohol ['rʌbɪŋælkəhɒl] n Am alcool m à 90°.

rubbish ['rʌbɪʃ] **1** n Br (waste) ordures fpl, détritus mpl; (industrial) déchets mpl; (junk) saleté(s) f(pl); (nonsense) Fig idioties fpl, absurdités fpl; **that's r.** (absurd) c'est absurde; (worthless) ça ne vaut rien; **r. bin** poubelle f; **r. dump** décharge f (publique), dépôt m d'ordures; (in garden) tas m d'ordures; (untidy place) dépotoir m. **2** vt **to r. s.o./sth** (criticize) Fam dénigrer qn/qch. ● **rubbishy** ['rʌbɪʃɪ] a (book, film etc) nul; (goods) de mauvaise qualité.

rubble ['rʌb(ə)l] n décombres mpl.

rubella [ruːˈbelə] n rubéole f.

ruble ['ruːb(ə)l] n (currency) Am rouble m.

ruby ['ruːbɪ] n (gem) rubis m.

rucksack ['rʌksæk] n sac m à dos.

ruckus ['rʌkəs] n (uproar) Fam chahut m.

rudder ['rʌdər] n gouvernail m.

ruddy ['rʌdɪ] a (-ier, -iest) **1** (complexion) coloré. **2** (bloody) Br Sl fichu.

rude [ruːd] a (-er, -est) (impolite) impoli (to envers); (coarse, insolent) grossier (to envers); (indecent) obscène; (shock) violent. ● **rudely** adv impoliment; (coarsely) grossièrement. ● **rudeness** n impolitesse f; (coarseness) grossièreté f; (indecency) obscénité f.

rudiments ['ruːdɪmənts] npl rudiments mpl. ● **rudi'mentary** a rudimentaire.

rueful ['ruːfəl] a Lit triste.

ruffian ['rʌfɪən] n voyou m.

ruffle ['rʌf(ə)l] **1** vt (hair) ébouriffer; (water) troubler; **to r. s.o.** (offend) froisser qn. **2** n (frill) ruche f.

rug [rʌg] n carpette f, petit tapis m; (over knees) plaid m; (bedside) **r.** descente f de lit.

rugby ['rʌgbɪ] n **r. (football)** rugby m. ● **rugger** n Br Fam rugby m.

rugged ['rʌgɪd] u (surface) rugueux, rude; (terrain, coast) accidenté; (person, features, manners) rude; (determination) Fig farouche.

ruin ['ruːɪn] n (destruction, rubble, building etc) ruine f; **in ruins** (building) en ruine ‖ vt (health, country, person etc) ruiner; (clothes) abîmer; (effect, meal, party etc) gâter. ● **ruined** a (person, country etc) ruiné; (building) en ruine. ● **ruinous** a ruineux.

rule [ruːl] **1** n (principle) règle f; (regulation) règlement m; (custom) coutume f; (authority) autorité f; Pol gouvernement m; **against the** Br **rules** or Am **rule** contraire au règlement; **as a (general) r.** en règle générale; **it's the** *or* **a r. that** il est de règle que (+ *sub*).

█ *vt* (*country*) gouverner; (*decide*) (*of judge, referee etc*) décider (**that** que); **to r. s.o.** (*dominate*) mener qn; **to r. sth out** (*exclude*) exclure qch.

█ *vi* (*of king etc*) régner (**over** sur); (*of judge*) statuer (**against** contre, **on** sur).

2 *n* (*for measuring*) règle *f*. ●**ruled** *a* (*paper*) réglé, ligné. ●**ruling** *a* (*passion, fear etc*) dominant; **the r. class** la classe dirigeante; **the r. party** *Pol* le parti au pouvoir █ *n* (*of judge, referee etc*) décision *f*.

ruler ['ruːlər] *n* **1** (*for measuring*) règle *f*. **2** (*king, queen etc*) souverain, -aine *mf*; (*political leader*) dirigeant, -ante *mf*.

rum [rʌm] *n* rhum *m*.

Rumania [ruːˈmeɪnɪə] *see* **Romania**.

rumble ['rʌmb(ə)l] *vi* (*of train, thunder, gun*) gronder; (*of stomach*) gargouiller █ *n* grondement *m*; (*of stomach*) gargouillement *m*.

ruminate ['ruːmɪneɪt] *vi* **to r. over** (*scheme etc*) ruminer.

rummage ['rʌmɪdʒ] *vi* **to r. (about)** farfouiller. ●**rummage sale** *n* (*used clothes etc*) *Am* vente *f* de charité.

rumour ['ruːmər] (*Am* **rumor**) *n* bruit *m*, rumeur *f*. ●**rumoured** *a* **it is r. that** on dit que.

rump [rʌmp] *n* (*of horse*) croupe *f*; (*of fowl*) croupion *m*; **r. steak** rumsteck *m*.

rumple ['rʌmp(ə)l] *vt* (*clothes*) chiffonner.

rumpus ['rʌmpəs] *n* (*noise*) *Fam* chahut *m*, vacarme *m*.

run [rʌn] *n* (*series*) série *f*; (*period*) période *f*; (*running*) course *f*; (*outing*) tour *m*; (*journey*) parcours *m*, trajet *m*; (*rush*) ruée *f* (**on** sur); (*trend*) tendance *f*; (*for skiing*) piste *f*; (*in cricket, baseball*) point *m*; *Cards* suite *f*; (*in stocking etc*) maille *f* filée; **to go for a r.** (*aller*) faire une course à pied; (*in vehicle*) (*aller*) faire un tour; **on the r.** (*prisoner etc*) en fuite; **to have the r. of** (*house etc*) avoir à sa disposition; **in the long r.** à la longue, avec le temps; **to have the runs** *Fam* avoir la diarrhée.

█ *vi* (*pt* **ran**, *pp* **run**, *pres p* **running**) courir; (*flee*) fuir; (*of river, nose, pen, Br tap or Am faucet*) couler; (*of colour in washing*) déteindre; (*of ink*) baver; (*melt*) fondre; (*of play, film*) se jouer; (*of contract*) être valide; (*last*) durer; (*pass*) passer; (*function*) (*of machine*) marcher; (*idle*) (*of engine*) tourner; (*of stocking, tights*) filer; **to r. down/in/out/** *etc* descendre/entrer/sortir/*etc* en courant; **to r. for president** être candidat à la présidence; **to r. with blood** ruisseler de sang; **to r. between** (*of bus etc*) faire le service entre; **to go running** (*as sport*) faire du jogging; **the road runs to...** la route va à...; **the river runs into the sea** le fleuve se jette dans la mer; **it runs into a hundred pounds** ça va chercher dans les cent livres; **it runs in the family** ça tient de famille.

█ *vt* (*risk*) courir; (*marathon etc*) courir,

prendre part à; (*horse*) faire courir; (*temperature, errand*) faire; (*machine*) faire fonctionner; (*engine*) faire tourner; (*drive*) conduire; (*furniture, goods*) transporter (**to** à); (*business, country etc*) diriger; (*courses, events*) organiser; (*film, play*) présenter; (*house*) tenir; (*computer program*) exécuter; (*newspaper article*) publier (**on** sur); (*bath*) faire couler; (*blockade*) forcer; **to r. a race** prendre part à une course; **to r. one's hand over** passer la main sur; **to r. one's eye over** jeter un coup d'œil à *or* sur; **to r. its course** (*of illness etc*) suivre son cours; **to r. 5 km** (*as sport*) faire 5 km de course à pied; **to r. a car** avoir une voiture.

run about *or* **around** *vi* courir çà et là; (*wander about*) se balader █ **to run across** *vt* (*meet*) tomber sur (*qn*) █ **to run along: run along!** filez! █ **to run away** *vi* (*flee*) s'enfuir, se sauver (**from** de) █ **to run back** *vt* (*person in vehicle*) ramener (**to** à) █ **to run down** *vt* (*pedestrian*) renverser; (*knock over and kill*) écraser; (*belittle*) *Fig* dénigrer; (*restrict*) limiter peu à peu █ **to run in** *vt* (*vehicle*) *Br* roder; **to r. s.o. in** (*of police*) *Br Fam* arrêter qn █ **to run into** *vt* (*meet*) tomber sur; (*crash into*) (*of vehicle, train etc*) percuter; **to r. into debt** s'endetter █ **to run off** *vi* (*flee*) s'enfuir (**with** avec) █ *vt* (*print*) tirer █ **to run out** *vi* (*of stocks*) s'épuiser; (*of lease*) expirer; (*of time*) manquer; **to r. out of time/ money** manquer de temps/d'argent; **we've r. out of coffee** on n'a plus de café; **I've r. out of** *Br* **petrol** *or Am* **gas** je suis tombé en panne d'essence █ *vt* **to r. s.o. out of** (*chase*) chasser qn de █ **to run over** *vi* (*of liquid*) déborder █ *vt* (*kill pedestrian*) écraser; (*knock down pedestrian*) renverser; (*notes, text*) revoir █ **to run round** *vt* (*surround*) entourer █ **to run through** *vt* (*recap*) revoir █ **to run up** *vt* (*debts, bill*) laisser s'accumuler.

runaway ['rʌnəweɪ] *n* fugitif, -ive *mf* █ *a* (*car, horse*) emballé; (*Br lorry, Am truck*) fou (*f* folle); (*inflation*) galopant; (*wedding*) clandestin; (*victory*) qu'on remporte haut la main.

run-down [rʌnˈdaʊn] *a* (*weak, tired*) à plat; (*district etc*) miteux, délabré.

rung[1] [rʌŋ] *n* (*of ladder*) barreau *m*.

rung[2] [rʌŋ] *pp of* **ring**[2].

runner ['rʌnər] *n* (*athlete*) coureur *m*; **r. bean** *Br* haricot *m* (grimpant).

runner-up [rʌnəˈrʌp] *n* (*in race etc*) second, -onde *mf*.

running ['rʌnɪŋ] *n* course *f*; (*of machine*) fonctionnement *m*; (*of business, country*) direction *f*; **to be in/out of the r.** être/ne plus être dans la course █ *a* **six days/***etc* **r.** six jours/*etc* de suite; **r. water** eau *f* courante; **a r. battle with** (*cancer, landlord etc*) une lutte continuelle avec; **to give a r. commentary** (**of**) (*on TV etc*) faire un commentaire simultané *or* en direct (de); **r. costs** (*of factory etc*) frais *mpl* d'exploitation; (*of car*) dépenses *fpl* courantes.

runny ['rʌnɪ] a (-ier, -iest) (cream, sauce etc) liquide; (nose) qui coule; **r. omelet(te)** omelette f baveuse.

run-of-the-mill [rʌnəvðə'mɪl] a ordinaire.

run-up ['rʌnʌp] n **in the r.-up to** (elections etc) dans la période qui précède.

runway ['rʌnweɪ] n (for aircraft) piste f (d'envol); (for fashion parade) Am podium m.

rupture ['rʌptʃər] n (hernia) hernie f; **the r. of** (breaking) la rupture de ▮ vt rompre; **to r. oneself** se donner une hernie.

rural ['rʊərəl] a rural.

ruse [ruːz] n (trick) ruse f.

rush¹ [rʌʃ] vi (move fast, throw oneself) se précipiter, se ruer (at sur, towards vers); (of blood) affluer (to à); (hurry) se dépêcher (to do de faire); (of vehicle) foncer; **to r. out** partir en vitesse.

▮ vt (attack) Mil foncer sur (l'ennemi); **to r. s.o.** (hurry) bousculer qn; **to r. s.o. to** Br **hospital** or Am **the hospital** transporter qn d'urgence à l'hôpital; **to r. (through) sth** (job, meal, order etc) faire, manger, envoyer etc qch en vitesse; **to be rushed into** (decision, answer etc) être forcé à prendre, donner etc.

▮ n ruée f (for vers, on sur); (confusion) bousculade f; (hurry) hâte f; (of orders) avalanche f; **to be in a r.** être pressé (to do de faire); **to leave/etc in a r.** partir/etc en vi-

tesse; **the gold r.** la ruée vers l'or; **the r. hour** l'heure f d'affluence; **a r. job** un travail d'urgence.

rush² [rʌʃ] n (plant) jonc m; **the rushes** les joncs.

rusk [rʌsk] n Br biscotte f.

russet ['rʌsɪt] a brun roux inv.

Russia ['rʌʃə] n Russie f. ● **Russian** a russe ▮ n (language) russe m; (person) Russe mf.

rust [rʌst] n rouille f ▮ vi (se) rouiller. ● **rustproof** a inoxydable. ● **rusty** a (-ier, -iest) (metal, Fig athlete, memory etc) rouillé.

rustic ['rʌstɪk] a rustique.

rustle ['rʌs(ə)l] **1** vi (of leaves) bruire; (of skirt) froufrouter ▮ n bruissement m; (of skirt) frou-frou m. **2** vt **to r. up** Fam (prepare) préparer (repas etc); **to r. up support** (find) se trouver des partisans. **3** vt (steal) Am voler (du bétail etc). ● **rustler** n (thief) Am voleur m de bétail.

rut [rʌt] n ornière f; **to be in a r.** Fig être encroûté.

rutabaga [ruːtə'beɪgə] n (swede) Am rutabaga m.

ruthless ['ruːθləs] a (attack, person etc) impitoyable, cruel; (in taking decisions) très ferme. ● **ruthlessly** adv (mercilessly) impitoyablement. ● **ruthlessness** n cruauté f.

rye [raɪ] n seigle m; **r. bread** pain m de seigle.

S

S, s [es] *n* S, s *m*.

Sabbath ['sæbəθ] *n* (*Jewish*) sabbat *m*; (*Christian*) dimanche *m*.

sabbatical [sə'bætɪk(ə)l] *a* (*university year, term etc*) sabbatique. ▮ *n* to be on s. être en congé sabbatique.

sabotage ['sæbətɑːʒ] *n* sabotage *m* ▮ *vt* saboter. ● **saboteur** [-'tɜːr] *n* saboteur, -euse *mf*.

sabre ['seɪbər] (*Am* **saber**) *n* (*sword*) sabre *m*.

saccharin ['sækərɪn] *n* saccharine *f*.

sachet ['sæʃeɪ] *n* (*of lavender etc*) sachet *m*; (*of shampoo*) dosette *f*.

sack [sæk] **1** *n* (*bag*) sac *m*. **2** *vt* (*dismiss from one's job*) *Fam* virer, renvoyer ▮ *n Fam* to get the s. se faire virer; to give s.o. the s. virer qn. **3** *vt* (*town etc*) mettre à sac, saccager. ● **sacking** *n* **1** (*cloth*) toile *f* à sac. **2** (*dismissal*) *Fam* renvoi *m*.

sacrament ['sækrəmənt] *n Rel* sacrement *m*.

sacred ['seɪkrɪd] *a* (*holy*) sacré.

sacrifice ['sækrɪfaɪs] *n* sacrifice *m* ▮ *vt* sacrifier (**to** à, **for** pour).

sacrilege ['sækrɪlɪdʒ] *n* sacrilège *m*. ● **sacri'legious** *a* sacrilège.

sacrosanct ['sækrəʊsæŋkt] *a Iron* sacrosaint.

sad [sæd] *a* (**sadder, saddest**) triste. ● **sadden** *vt* attrister. ● **sadly** *adv* tristement; (*unfortunately*) malheureusement; (*very*) (*inadequate etc*) très. ● **sadness** *n* tristesse *f*.

saddle ['sæd(ə)l] *n* selle *f*; to be in the s. (*in control*) *Fig* tenir les rênes ▮ *vt* (*horse*) seller; to s. s.o. with sth/s.o. (*debt, relative etc*) *Fam* coller qch/qn à qn. ● **saddlebag** *n* sacoche *f*.

sadism ['seɪdɪz(ə)m] *n* sadisme *m*. ● **sadist** *n* sadique *mf*. ● **sa'distic** *a* sadique.

sae [eseɪ'iː] *abbr Br* = stamped addressed envelope, *Am* = self-addressed envelope.

safari [sə'fɑːrɪ] *n* safari *m*; to be or go on s. faire un safari.

safe¹ [seɪf] *a* (**-er, -est**) (*person*) en sécurité; (*equipment, toy, animal*) sans danger; (*place, investment, method*) sûr; (*bridge, ladder*) solide; (*prudent*) prudent; (*winner*) assuré, garanti; s. (**and sound**) sain et sauf; it's s. to go out on peut sortir sans danger; **the safest thing to do) is...** le plus sûr est de...; s. from à l'abri de; to be on the s. side pour plus de sûreté; in s. hands en mains sûres; s. journey! bon voyage!; s. sex rapports *mpl* (sexuels) protégés. ● **safe-'conduct** *n* sauf-conduit *m*. ● **safe-deposit** *n* (*bank vault*) salle *f* des coffres. ● **safekeeping** *n* to give s.o. sth for s. donner qch à qn pour qu'il le garde en sécurité.

safe² [seɪf] *n* (*for money etc*) coffre-fort *m*.

safeguard ['seɪfgɑːd] *n* sauvegarde *f* (**against** contre) ▮ *vt* sauvegarder.

safely ['seɪflɪ] *adv* (*without accident*) sans accident; (*in a safe place*) en lieu sûr; (*securely*) (*locked etc*) solidement; (*without risk*) sans risque, sans danger.

safety ['seɪftɪ] *n* sécurité *f*; (*solidity*) solidité *f*; (*salvation*) salut *m* ▮ *a* (*belt, device, screen, margin*) de sécurité; (*pin, razor, chain, valve*) de sûreté; s. **curtain** (*in theatre*) rideau *m* de fer; s. **net** (*in circus*) filet *m* de sécurité; (*safeguard*) *Fig* filet *m*; s. **precaution** mesure *f* de sécurité.

saffron ['sæfrən] *n* safran *m*.

sag [sæg] *vi* (**-gg-**) (*of roof, ground, bed*) s'affaisser; (*of breasts*) tomber; (*of cheeks*) pendre; (*of knees, Fig interest rates, prices*) fléchir. ● **sagging** *a* (*roof, ground, bed*) affaissé; (*breasts*) tombant.

saga ['sɑːgə] *n* (*story*) saga *f*; (*bad sequence of events*) *Fig* feuilleton *m*.

sage [seɪdʒ] *n* **1** (*plant, herb*) sauge *f*. **2** (*wise man*) sage *m*.

Sagittarius [sædʒɪ'teərɪəs] *n* (*sign*) le Sagittaire.

sago ['seɪgəʊ] *n* (*cereal*) sagou *m*.

Sahara [sə'hɑːrə] *n* the S. (*desert*) le Sahara.

said [sed] *pt & pp of* say.

sail [seɪl] *vi* (*navigate*) naviguer; (*leave*) partir; (*as sport*) faire de la voile; (*glide*) *Fig* glisser; to s. **into port** entrer au port; to s. **round the world/an island** faire le tour du monde/d'une île en bateau; to s. **through an exam** *Fig* réussir un examen haut la main; to s. **through one's** *Br* **driving licence** *or Am* **driver's license** obtenir son permis de conduire haut la main.
▮ *vt* (*boat*) piloter; (*seas*) parcourir.
▮ *n* voile *f*; (*trip*) tour *m* en bateau; to set s. (*of boat*) partir (**for** à destination de). ● **sailing** *n* navigation *f*; (*sport*) voile *f*; (*departure*) départ *m*; (*crossing*) traversée *f*; s. **boat** *Br* voilier *m*.

sailboard ['seɪlbɔːd] *n* planche *f* (à voile). ● **sailboat** *n Am* voilier *m*.

sailor ['seɪlər] *n* marin *m*, matelot *m*.

saint [seɪnt] *n* saint *m*, sainte *f*; S. John saint Jean; s.'s day fête *f* (de saint). ● **saintly** *a* (**-ier, -iest**) saint.

sake [seɪk] *n* for my/your/his/etc s. pour moi/toi/lui/etc; for your father's s. pour (l'amour de) ton père; for your own s. pour ton bien; (**just) for the s. of eating/etc** simplement pour manger/etc; for heaven's or God's s. pour l'amour de Dieu.

salacious [sə'leɪʃəs] *a* obscène.

salad ['sæləd] n (dish of vegetables, fruit etc) salade f; **s. bowl** saladier m; **s. cream** Br mayonnaise f; **s. dressing** sauce f de salade.

salamander ['sæləmændər] n (lizard) salamandre f.

salami [sə'lɑ:mɪ] n salami m.

salary ['sælərɪ] n (professional) traitement m; (wage) salaire m. ● **salaried** a (person, staff) qui perçoit un traitement.

sale [seɪl] n vente f; **sale(s)** (at reduced prices) soldes mpl; **in a** or **the s., Am on s.** (cheaply) en solde; **on s.** (available) en vente; **(up) for s.** à vendre; **to put up for s.** mettre en vente; **s. price** prix m de solde; **sales check** or **slip** Am reçu m. ● **saleable** (Am **salable**) a vendable. ● **salesclerk** n Am vendeur, -euse mf. ● **salesman** n (pl **-men**) (in shop) vendeur m; (Br **travelling** or Am **traveling**) **s.** représentant m (de commerce). ● **saleswoman** n (pl **-women**) vendeuse f; (who travels) représentante f (de commerce).

salient ['seɪlɪənt] a (point, fact) marquant.

saliva [sə'laɪvə] n salive f. ● **'salivate** vi saliver.

sallow ['sæləʊ] a (-er, -est) jaunâtre.

sally ['sælɪ] vi **to s. forth** Hum sortir allégrement.

salmon ['sæmən] n saumon m.

salmonella [sælmə'nelə] n (poisoning) salmonellose f.

salon ['sælɒn] n beauty/hairdressing **s.** salon m de beauté/de coiffure.

saloon [sə'lu:n] n (car) Br berline f; (on ship) salon m; (bar) Am bar m; **s. bar** (of pub) Br salle f chic.

salt [sɔ:lt] n sel m; **bath salts** sels mpl de bain; **s. mine** mine f de sel; **s. water** eau f salée; **s.-water fish** poisson m de mer ∎ vt saler. ● **saltbeef** n bœuf m salé. ● **saltcellar** n Br salière f. ● **salt-'free** a sans sel. ● **saltshaker** n Am salière f. ● **salty** a (-ier, -iest) a salé.

salubrious [sə'lu:brɪəs] a salubre.

salutary [Br 'sæljʊtərɪ, Am -erɪ] a salutaire.

salute [sə'lu:t] n (of soldier) salut m; (of guns) salve f ∎ vt (greet) & Mil saluer ∎ vi (of soldier) faire un salut.

salvage ['sælvɪdʒ] vt (save) sauver (from de); (old iron etc to be used again) récupérer ∎ n (objects saved) objets mpl sauvés (d'un naufrage etc); (salvaging) sauvetage m (of de); (of old iron etc) récupération f (of de); **s. operation/etc** opération f/etc de sauvetage.

salvation [sæl'veɪʃ(ə)n] n salut m; **the S. Army** l'armée f du Salut.

same [seɪm] a même; **the (very) s. house as** (exactement) la même maison que ∎ pron **the s. le** même, la même, pl les mêmes; **the s. (thing)** la même chose; **it's all the s. to me** ça m'est égal; **all** or **just the s.** tout de même; **to do the s.** en faire autant. ● **sameness** n (monotony) monotonie f.

sample ['sɑ:mp(ə)l] n échantillon m; (of

blood) prélèvement m ∎ vt (wine, cheese etc) goûter, déguster; (product, recipe etc) essayer; (army life, prison life etc) goûter de. ● **sampling** n (of wine) dégustation f.

sanatorium [sænə'tɔ:rɪəm] n Br sanatorium m.

sanctify ['sæŋktɪfaɪ] vt sanctifier.

sanctimonious [sæŋktɪ'məʊnɪəs] a (person, manner) tartuffe.

sanction ['sæŋkʃ(ə)n] n (approval, punishment) sanction f ∎ vt (approve) sanctionner.

sanctity ['sæŋktɪtɪ] n sainteté f.

sanctuary [Br 'sæŋktʃʊərɪ, Am -erɪ] n (refuge) & Pol asile m; (for animals) réserve f; (holy place or area) sanctuaire m.

sand [sænd] n sable m; **the sands** (beach) la plage f ∎ vt (road) sabler; **to s. (down)** (wood etc) poncer. ● **sander** n (machine) ponceuse f.

sandbag ['sændbæg] n sac m de sable. ● **sandbank** n banc m de sable. ● **sandbar** n Am bac m à sable. ● **sandcastle** n château m de sable. ● **sandpaper** n papier m de verre ∎ vt (wood etc) poncer. ● **sandpit** n Br bac m à sable. ● **sandstone** n (rock) grès m. ● **sandstorm** n tempête f de sable.

sandal ['sænd(ə)l] n sandale f.

sandwich ['sænwɪdʒ] **1** n sandwich m; **cheese/etc s.** sandwich au fromage/etc; **hero** or **submarine s.** Am gros sandwich m coupé dans une baguette; **s. bar** Br snack-bar m (qui ne vend que des sandwichs); **s. course** Br formation f professionnelle en alternance. **2** vt **to s. (in)** (fit in) intercaler; **sandwiched in between** (caught) coincé entre.

sandy a **1** (-ier, -iest) (beach) de sable; (road, ground) sablonneux; (water) sableux. **2** (hair) blond roux inv.

sane [seɪn] a (-er, -est) (person) sain (d'esprit); (idea, attitude) raisonnable.

sang [sæŋ] pt of sing.

sanguine ['sæŋgwɪn] a (hopeful) optimiste.

sanitarium [sænɪ'teərɪəm] n Am sanatorium m.

sanitary [Br 'sænɪtərɪ, Am -erɪ] a (fittings, conditions) sanitaire; (clean) hygiénique; **s. towel** Br, **s. napkin** Am serviette f hygiénique.

sanitation [sænɪ'teɪʃ(ə)n] n hygiène f (publique); (plumbing etc) installations fpl sanitaires; **s. department** Am service m de collecte des ordures ménagères.

sanity ['sænɪtɪ] n (of person) santé f mentale; (reason) raison f.

sank [sæŋk] pt of sink[2].

Santa Claus ['sæntəklɔ:z] n le père Noël.

sap [sæp] **1** n (of tree, plant) sève f. **2** vt (-pp-) (weaken) miner (énergie etc).

sapphire ['sæfaɪər] n (jewel, needle) saphir m.

sarcasm ['sɑ:kæz(ə)m] n sarcasme m. ● **sar'castic** a sarcastique.

sardine [sɑ:'di:n] n sardine f.

Sardinia [sɑ:'dɪnɪə] n Sardaigne f.

sardonic [sɑ:'dɒnɪk] a sardonique.

sash [sæʃ] n 1 (on dress) ceinture f; (of mayor etc) écharpe f. 2 s. window fenêtre f à guillotine.

sat [sæt] pt & pp of sit.

Satan ['seɪt(ə)n] n Satan m. ● **sa'tanic** a satanique.

satchel ['sætʃ(ə)l] n cartable m.

satellite ['sætəlaɪt] n satellite m; s. (country) pays m satellite; s. dish (for TV programmes) antenne f satellite or parabolique; s. TV télévision f par satellite; s. picture (showing weather patterns) animation f satellite.

satiate ['seɪʃɪeɪt] vt rassasier.

satin ['sætɪn] n satin m; s. dress/etc robe f/etc de or en satin.

satire ['sætaɪər] n satire f (on contre). ● **sa'tirical** a satirique. ● **satirist** n écrivain m satirique. ● **satirize** vt faire la satire de.

satisfaction [sætɪsˈfækʃ(ə)n] n satisfaction f. ● **satisfactory** a satisfaisant.

satisfy ['sætɪsfaɪ] vt satisfaire (qn); (convince, persuade) persuader (qn) (that que); (demand, condition) satisfaire à; to s. oneself that s'assurer que; to s. oneself of sth or as to sth s'assurer de qch; to be satisfied (with) être satisfait (de) ▮ vi donner satisfaction. ● **satisfying** a satisfaisant; (meal, food) substantiel.

satsuma [sætˈsuːmə] n (fruit) satsuma f.

saturate ['sætʃəreɪt] vt (soak) tremper; (fill) saturer (with de). ● **saturation** [-ˈreɪʃ(ə)n] n saturation f; to reach s. point commencer à saturer or à être saturé.

Saturday [Br 'sætədɪ, Am -deɪ] n samedi m.

sauce [sɔːs] n 1 sauce f; tomato s. sauce tomate; s. boat saucière f. 2 (impudence) Fam toupet m. ● **saucy** a (-ier, -iest) (impudent) impertinent; (smart) (hat etc) Fam coquet.

saucepan ['sɔːspən] n casserole f.

saucer ['sɔːsər] n soucoupe f.

Saudi Arabia [Br saʊdɪəˈreɪbɪə, Am sɔːdɪəˈreɪbɪə] n Arabie f Séoudite.

sauerkraut ['saʊəkraʊt] n choucroute f.

sauna ['sɔːnə] n sauna m.

saunter ['sɔːntər] vi flâner.

sausage ['sɒsɪdʒ] n (cooked, for cooking) saucisse f; (dried, for slicing) saucisson m; s. roll Br (sorte de) friand m.

sauté ['səʊteɪ] a (potatoes etc) sauté ▮ vt Culin faire sauter.

savage ['sævɪdʒ] a (fierce) féroce; (brutal, cruel) brutal, sauvage; (primitive) sauvage ▮ n (brute) sauvage mf ▮ vt (of animal, critic etc) attaquer (férocement). ● **savagery** n (cruelty) sauvagerie f.

save¹ [seɪv] vt (rescue) sauver (from de); (keep) garder, réserver; (money, time) économiser, épargner; Comptr sauvegarder; (stamps) collectionner; (problems, trouble) éviter; to s. s.o. from doing sth (prevent) empêcher qn de faire qch; that will s. him or her (the bother of) going ça lui évitera d'y aller; to s. up (money) économiser.
▮ vi to s. (up) faire des économies (for sth, to

buy sth pour (s')acheter qch).
▮ n Football arrêt m. ● **saving** n (of time, money) économie f, épargne f (of de); (rescue) sauvetage m; (thrifty habit) l'épargne f; savings (money) économies fpl; savings account compte m d'épargne; savings bank caisse f d'épargne.

save² [seɪv] prep (except) sauf.

saveloy ['sævəlɔɪ] n Br cervelas m.

saviour ['seɪvjər] (Am savior) n sauveur m.

savour ['seɪvər] (Am savor) vt savourer ▮ n (taste, interest) saveur f. ● **savoury** (Am savory) a (food) (tasty) savoureux; (not sweet) salé; (tasty) savoureux; not very s. (neighbourhood etc) Fig peu recommandable.

saw¹ [sɔː] n scie f ▮ vt (pt sawed, pp sawn or sawed) scier; to s. off scier; a Br sawn-off or Am sawed-off shotgun un fusil à canon scié. ● **sawdust** n sciure f. ● **sawmill** n scierie f.

saw² [sɔː] pt of see¹.

saxophone ['sæksəfəʊn] n saxophone m.

say [seɪ] vt (pt & pp said [sed]) dire (to à, that que); (prayer) faire, dire; (of dial, watch etc) marquer; to s. again répéter; it is said that... on dit que...; what do you s. to a walk? que dirais-tu d'une promenade?; (let's) s. tomorrow disons demain; to s. the least c'est le moins que l'on puisse dire; to s. nothing of... sans parler de...; that's to s. c'est-à-dire que.
▮ vi dire; you don't s.! Fam sans blague!; I s.! Old-fashioned Br dites donc!; s.! Am Fam dis donc!; that goes without saying ça va sans dire.
▮ n to have one's s. dire ce que l'on a à dire, s'exprimer; to have no s. ne pas avoir voix au chapitre (in pour); to have a lot of s. avoir beaucoup d'influence.

saying ['seɪɪŋ] n dicton m, proverbe m.

scab [skæb] n 1 (of wound) croûte f. 2 (blackleg) Fam jaune m.

scaffold ['skæfəld] n (gallows) échafaud m; (for construction work) échafaudage m. ● **scaffolding** n échafaudage m.

scald [skɔːld] vt (burn, cleanse) ébouillanter; (sterilize) stériliser ▮ n brûlure f.

scale [skeɪl] 1 n (of map, wages etc) échelle f; (of numbers) série f; (in music) gamme f; s. of charges tarif m; on a small/large s. sur une petite/grande échelle; s. drawing dessin m à l'échelle; s. model modèle m réduit ▮ vt to s. down réduire (proportionnellement).
2 n (on fish) écaille f; (dead skin) squame f; (on teeth) tartre m ▮ vt (teeth) détartrer.
3 vt (climb) escalader (mur etc).

scales [skeɪlz] npl (for weighing) balance f; (bathroom) s. pèse-personne m; (baby) s. pèse-bébé m.

scallion ['skæljən] n (onion) Am oignon m vert.

scallop ['skɒləp] n coquille f Saint-Jacques.

scalp [skælp] n cuir m chevelu ▮ vt (cut off too much hair from) Fig Hum tondre (qn).

scalpel ['skælp(ə)l] n bistouri m, scalpel m.

scam [skæm] n (swindle) Fam escroquerie f, arnaque f.

scamp [skæmp] n coquin, -ine mf.

scamper ['skæmpər] vi to s. off or away détaler.

scampi ['skæmpɪ] npl scampi mpl.

scan [skæn] 1 vt (-nn-) (look at briefly) parcourir (des yeux); (scrutinize) scruter; (poetry) scander; (of radar) balayer. 2 n to have a s. (of pregnant woman) passer une échographie.

scandal ['skænd(ə)l] n (disgrace) scandale m; (gossip) médisances fpl; **to cause a s.** (of book, film etc) causer un scandale; (of conduct, attitude etc) faire (du) scandale. ●**scandalize** vt scandaliser. ●**scandalous** a scandaleux.

Scandinavia [skændɪ'neɪvɪə] n Scandinavie f. ●**Scandinavian** a scandinave ▮ n Scandinave mf.

scanner ['skænər] n (using X-rays) & Comptr scanner m; (using ultrasound) appareil m d'échographie.

scant [skænt] a (meal, amount) insuffisant; **s. attention/regard** peu d'attention/de cas. ●**scantily** adv insuffisamment; **s. dressed** à peine or légèrement vêtu. ●**scanty** a (-ier, -iest) insuffisant; (bikini etc) minuscule.

scapegoat ['skeɪpgəʊt] n bouc m émissaire.

scar [skɑːr] n cicatrice f ▮ vt (-rr-) marquer d'une cicatrice; (of experience etc) Fig marquer; **to be scarred for life** Fig être marqué à vie.

scarce [skeəs] a (-er, -est) (food, book, people etc) rare; **to make oneself s.** disparaître, débarrasser le plancher. ●**scarceness** or **scarcity** n (shortage) pénurie f; (rarity) rareté f.

scarcely ['skeəslɪ] adv à peine; **he s. talks** il parle à peine, il ne parle guère; **s. anything** presque rien; **s. ever** presque jamais.

scare [skeər] n peur f; **to give s.o. a s.** faire peur à qn; **bomb s.** alerte f à la bombe ▮ vt faire peur à; **to s. off** (person) faire fuir; (animal) effaroucher. ●**scared** a effrayé; **to be s.** (stiff) avoir (très) peur.

scarecrow ['skeəkrəʊ] n épouvantail m.

scaremonger ['skeəmʌŋgər] n alarmiste mf.

scarf [skɑːf] n (pl scarves) (long) écharpe f; (square, for women) foulard m.

scarlet ['skɑːlət] a écarlate; **s. fever** scarlatine f.

scary ['skeərɪ] a (-ier, -iest) Fam **it's s.** Fam ça fait peur.

scathing ['skeɪðɪŋ] a (remark etc) acerbe; **to be s. about** critiquer de façon acerbe.

scatter ['skætər] vt (disperse) disperser (foule, nuages etc); (throw or dot about) éparpiller (papiers etc); (spread) répandre ▮ vi (of crowd) se disperser. ●**scattering** n **a s. of houses/etc** quelques maisons/etc dispersées.

scatterbrain ['skætəbreɪn] n écervelé, -ée mf.

scatty ['skætɪ] a (-ier, -iest) Br Fam écervelé.

scavenge ['skævɪndʒ] vi fouiller dans les ordures (**for** pour trouver). ●**scavenger** n clochard, -arde mf (qui fait les poubelles).

scenario [sɪ'nɑːrɪəʊ] n (pl -os) (of film) & Fig scénario m.

scene [siːn] n (setting, fuss, part of play or film) scène f; (of crime, accident) lieu m; (incident) incident m; (situation) situation f; (view) vue f; **behind the scenes** (in theatre) & Fig dans les coulisses; **on the s.** sur les lieux; **to make** or **create a s.** faire une scène (à qn).

scenery ['siːnərɪ] n paysage m, décor m; (for play or film) décor(s) m(pl).

scenic ['siːnɪk] a (beauty) pittoresque; **the s. route** la route touristique.

scent [sent] n (fragrance, perfume) parfum m; (animal's track) & Fig piste f; **to throw the police/etc off the s.** dérouter la police/etc ▮ vt (room, handkerchief etc) parfumer (**with** de); (smell, sense) flairer.

sceptic ['skeptɪk] (Am **skeptic**) a & n sceptique (mf). ●**sceptical** a sceptique. ●**scepticism** n scepticisme m.

sceptre ['septər] (Am **scepter**) n sceptre m.

schedule [Br 'ʃedjuːl, Am 'skedjʊl] n (of work etc) programme m; (timetable) horaire m; (list) liste f; **to be on s.** (on time) être à l'heure; (up to date) être à jour; **to be ahead of s.** être en avance; **to be behind s.** (of person, train) avoir du retard; **according to s.** comme prévu.
▮ vt (to plan) prévoir; (event) fixer le programme or l'horaire de. ●**scheduled** a (planned) prévu; (service, flight, train etc) régulier; **s. stop** arrêt m normal or régulier; **she's s. to leave at 8** elle doit partir à 8 h.

scheme [skiːm] n (plan) plan m (to do pour faire); (idea) idée f; (dishonest trick) combine f, manœuvre f; (arrangement) arrangement m; (for profit-sharing, earning bonuses etc) système m ▮ vi manœuvrer. ●**scheming** a intrigant ▮ n Pej machinations fpl. ●**schemer** n intrigant, -ante mf.

schizophrenic [skɪtsə'frenɪk] a & n schizophrène (mf).

scholar ['skɒlər] n érudit, -ite mf; (specialist) spécialiste mf; (grant holder) boursier, -ière mf. ●**scholarly** a érudit, savant. ●**scholarship** n érudition f; (grant) bourse f (d'études). ●**scho'lastic** a scolaire.

school [skuːl] n école f; (teaching, lessons) classe f; (college) Am Fam université f; (within university) institut m, département m; **in** or **at s.** à l'école; **secondary s.** Br, **high s.** Am établissement m d'enseignement secondaire; **public s.** Br école f privée; Am école publique; **s. of motoring** Br auto-école f; **summer s.** cours mpl d'été or de vacances.
▮ a (year, book, equipment etc) scolaire; **s. bag** cartable m; **s. bus** car m scolaire; **s. fees** frais mpl de scolarité; **s. hours** les heures fpl de classe; **s. yard** Am cour f (de récréation). ●**schooling** n (learning) instruction f; (attendance) scolarité f.

294

schoolboy ['sku:lbɔɪ] n écolier m. ●school-children npl écoliers mpl. ●schooldays npl années fpl d'école. ●schoolfriend n camarade mf de classe. ●schoolgirl n écolière f. ●schoolhouse n école f. ●school-'leaver n Br jeune mf qui a terminé ses études secondaires. ●schoolmaster n Br (primary) instituteur m; (secondary) professeur m. ●schoolmate n camarade mf de classe. ●schoolmistress n Br (primary) institutrice f; (secondary) professeur m. ●schoolroom n salle f de classe. ●schoolteacher n (primary) instituteur, -trice mf; (secondary) professeur m.

schooner ['sku:nər] n (ship) goélette f.

sciatica [saɪ'ætɪkə] n (pain) sciatique f.

science ['saɪəns] n science f; to study s. étudier les sciences; s. subject matière f scientifique; s. teacher professeur m de sciences; s. fiction science-fiction f. ●scien'tific a scientifique. ●scientist n scientifique mf, savant m.

sci-fi ['saɪfaɪ] n Fam science-fiction f.

Scilly Isles ['sɪlɪaɪlz] npl the S. Isles les Sorlingues fpl.

scintillating ['sɪntɪleɪtɪŋ] a (conversation, wit) brillant.

scissors ['sɪzəz] npl ciseaux mpl; a pair of s. une paire de ciseaux.

sclerosis [sklɪ'rəʊsɪs] n (disease) sclérose f; multiple s. sclérose en plaques.

scoff [skɒf] 1 vt to s. at s.o./sth se moquer de qn/qch. 2 vti (eat) Br Fam bouffer.

scold [skəʊld] vt gronder, réprimander (for doing pour avoir fait). ●scolding n réprimande f; to get a s. se faire gronder.

scone [skəʊn, skɒn] n Br petit pain m au lait.

scoop [sku:p] n (shovel) pelle f (à main); (spoon-shaped for food) cuillère f; (in news-paper) exclusivité f; at one s. d'un seul coup ▌ vt (prizes) rafler; to s. out (hollow out) évi-der; (melon etc) préparer; to s. up ramasser (avec une pelle or une cuillère).

scoot [sku:t] vi (rush, leave) Fam filer.

scooter ['sku:tər] n (child's) trottinette f; (motorcycle) scooter m.

scope [skəʊp] n (range) étendue f; (of mind) envergure f; (competence) compétence(s) f(pl); (limits) limites fpl; s. for sth/for doing (opportunity) des possibilités fpl de qch/de faire; the s. of one's activity le champ de ses activités.

scorch [skɔːtʃ] vt (linen, grass etc) roussir ▌ n s. (mark) brûlure f légère. ●scorching a (day) torride; (sun, sand) brûlant. ●scorcher n Fam journée f torride.

score¹ [skɔːr] n (in sport) score m; (at cards) marque f; (music) partition f; (of film) musi-que f; to have a s. to settle (with s.o.) Fig avoir un compte à régler (avec qn); on that s. (in that respect) à cet égard.
▌ vt (point, goal) marquer; (exam mark) avoir; (success) remporter; (piece of music) adapter, arranger (for pour).

▌ vi marquer un point or un but; (count points) marquer les points. ●scoreboard n (in competition) tableau m d'affichage. ●scorer n (player who scores) marqueur m.

score² [skɔːr] n a s. (twenty) vingt a; (about twenty) une vingtaine (de); scores of Fig un grand nombre de.

score³ [skɔːr] vt 1 (cut) rayer; (paper, wood) marquer. 2 to s. off or out (delete) rayer.

scorn [skɔːn] vt mépriser ▌ n mépris m. ●scornful a méprisant; to be s. of mépriser. ●scornfully adv avec mépris.

Scorpio ['skɔːpɪəʊ] n (sign) le Scorpion.

scorpion ['skɔːpɪən] n scorpion m.

Scot [skɒt] n Écossais, -aise mf. ●Scotland n Écosse f. ●Scotsman n (pl -men) Écossais m. ●Scotswoman n (pl -women) Écossaise f. ●Scottish a écossais.

scotch [skɒtʃ] 1 a s. tape® Am scotch® m. 2 vt (rumour) étouffer; (attempt) faire échouer.

Scotch [skɒtʃ] n (whisky) scotch m.

scot-free [skɒt'fri:] adv sans être puni.

scoundrel ['skaʊndr(ə)l] n vaurien m.

scour ['skaʊər] vt (pan) récurer; (streets etc) Fig parcourir (for à la recherche de). ●scourer n tampon m à récurer.

scourge [skɜːdʒ] n fléau m.

scout [skaʊt] 1 n (soldier) éclaireur m; (boy) s. scout m, éclaireur m; girl s. Am éclaireuse f; s. camp camp m scout. 2 vi to s. round for (look for) chercher. ●scouting n scoutisme m.

scowl [skaʊl] vi se renfrogner; to s. at s.o. regarder qn d'un air mauvais. ●scowling a renfrogné.

Scrabble® ['skræb(ə)l] n Scrabble® m.

scraggy ['skrægɪ] a (-ier, -iest) (bony) mai-grichon, osseux; (unkempt) débraillé.

scram [skræm] vi (-mm-) Fam filer.

scramble ['skræmb(ə)l] 1 vi to s. for se ruer vers; to s. up (climb) grimper; to s. through traverser avec difficulté ▌ n ruée f (for vers). 2 vt (egg) brouiller; scrambled eggs œufs mpl brouillés. 3 vt (radio message) brouiller.

scrap [skræp] 1 n (piece) petit morceau m (of de); (of information, news) fragment m; scraps (food) restes mpl; not a s. of (truth, good sense etc) pas un brin de; s. paper (papier m) brouillon m.
2 n (metal) ferraille f; to sell for s. vendre à la casse; s. heap tas m de ferraille; s. yard casse f; s. dealer, s. merchant marchand m de ferraille; s. metal, s. iron ferraille f; to be on the s. heap Fig n'être plus bon à rien ▌ vt (-pp-) (get rid of) se débarrasser de; (ve-hicle) mettre à la ferraille; (plan, idea) Fig abandonner.
3 n Fam (fight) bagarre f; to get into a s. with s.o. en venir aux mains avec qn; (argu-ment) avoir des mots avec qn.

scrapbook ['skræpbʊk] n album m (pour collages etc).

scrape [skreɪp] vt racler, gratter; (skin, knee etc) érafler ▌ vi to s. against sth (rub) frotter contre qch ▌ *n* (*on skin*) éraflure *f*; (*sound*) raclement *m*; **to get into a s.** *Fam* s'attirer des ennuis. ●**scraping** *n* (*of butter etc*) mince couche *f*; **scrapings** (*of wood, dirt etc*) raclures *fpl*. ●**scraper** *n* racloir *m*.

scrape along *vi* (*manage financially*) se débrouiller ▌ **to scrape away** *or* **off** *vt* (*mud etc*) racler ▌ **to scrape through** *vti* **to s. through** (**an exam**) réussir (un examen) de justesse ▌ **to scrape together** *vt* (*money, people*) réunir (difficilement).

scratch [skrætʃ] *n* (*mark, injury*) éraflure *f*; (*on skin*) rayure *f*; **to have a s.** (*scratch oneself*) *Fam* se gratter; **to start from s.** (re)partir de zéro; **it isn't up to s.** ce n'est pas au niveau; **he isn't up to s.** il n'est pas à la hauteur.

▌ *vt* (*arm etc that itches*) gratter; (*skin, furniture, wall etc*) érafler; (*glass*) rayer; (*with claw*) griffer; (*one's name*) graver (**on** sur).

▌ *vi* (*relieve an itch*) se gratter; (*of cat etc*) griffer; (*of pen*) gratter, accrocher.

scrawl [skrɔːl] *vt* gribouiller ▌ *n* gribouillis *m*.

scrawny ['skrɔːnɪ] *a* (**-ier, -iest**) (*bony*) maigrichon (*f* -onne), osseux.

scream [skriːm] *vti* crier, hurler; **to s. at s.o.** crier après qn; **to s. with pain**/*etc* hurler de douleur/*etc* ▌ *n* cri *m* (perçant).

screech [skriːtʃ] *vi* (*cry*) crier, hurler; (*of Br tyres, Am tires*) grincer; (*of brakes*) hurler ▌ *n* cri *m*; grincement *m*; hurlement *m*.

screen [skriːn] 1 *n* (*of TV set, computer etc*) & *Fig* écran *m*; (*of data*) *Comptr* page-écran *f*; (**folding**) **s.** paravent *m*; **on s.** *Comptr* à l'écran.

2 *vt* (*hide*) cacher (**from s.o.** à qn); (*protect*) protéger (**from** de); (*a film*) projeter; (*visitors, documents*) filtrer; (*for cancer etc*) faire subir un test de dépistage à (*qn*) (**for** pour); **to s. off** (*hide*) cacher. ●**screening** *n* (*of film*) projection *f*; (*selection*) tri *m*; (*medical examination*) (test *m* de) dépistage *m*.

screenplay ['skriːnpleɪ] *n* (*of film*) *n* scénario *m*.

screw [skruː] *n* vis *f* ▌ *vt* visser (**to** à); **to s. down** *or* **on** visser; **to s. off** dévisser; **to s. up** (*paper*) chiffonner; (*mess up*) *Sl* gâcher; **to s. up one's eyes** plisser les yeux; **to s. one's face up** grimacer. ●**screwball** *n* & *a* *Am Fam* cinglé, -ée (*mf*). ●**screwdriver** *n* tournevis *m*. ●**screwy** *a* (**-ier, -iest**) (*idea, person etc*) farfelu.

scribble ['skrɪb(ə)l] *vti* griffonner ▌ *n* griffonnage *m*.

scribe [skraɪb] *n* scribe *m*.

scrimmage ['skrɪmɪdʒ] *n* *Am Football* mêlée *f*.

script [skrɪpt] *n* (*of film*) scénario *m*; (*of play*) texte *m*; (*in exam*) copie *f*; (*system of writing*) écriture *f*; (*handwriting*) script *m*. ●**scriptwriter** *n* (*for films*) scénariste *mf*, dialoguiste *mf*; (*for TV or radio*) dialoguiste *mf*.

Scripture(s) ['skrɪptʃə(z)] *n(pl)* *Rel* Écriture *f* (sainte), (Saintes) Écritures *fpl*.

scroll [skrəʊl] 1 *n* rouleau *m* (de parchemin); (*book*) manuscrit *m*. 2 *vi* (*of text*) *Comptr* défiler ▌ *vt* (*text*) *Comptr* faire défiler.

scrooge [skruːdʒ] *n* (*miser*) avare *m*, harpagon *m*.

scrounge [skraʊndʒ] *vt* (*meal*) se faire payer (**off** *or* **from s.o.** par qn); (*steal*) piquer (**off** *or* **from s.o.** à qn); **to s. money off** *or* **from s.o.** taper qn ▌ *vi* vivre en parasite; (*beg*) quémander; **to s. around for sth** *Pej* essayer de mettre la main sur qch. ●**scrounger** *n* parasite *m*.

scrub [skrʌb] 1 *vt* (**-bb-**) (*surface*) nettoyer (à la brosse), frotter; (*potato etc*) frotter; (*pan*) récurer, frotter; (*cancel*) *Fig* annuler; **to s. off** (*remove*) enlever (à la brosse *or* en frottant); **to s. out** (*erase*) *Fig* effacer ▌ *vi* (*scrub floors*) frotter les planchers; **scrubbing brush** brosse *f* dure ▌ **to give sth a s.** nettoyer qch (à la brosse), frotter qch; **s. brush** *Am* brosse *f* dure. 2 *n* (*land*) broussailles *fpl*.

scruff [skrʌf] *n* 1 **by the s. of the neck** par la peau du cou. 2 (*person*) *Fam* individu *m* débraillé. ●**scruffy** *a* (**-ier, -iest**) (*untidy*) débraillé; (*dirty*) malpropre.

scrum [skrʌm] *n* *Rugby* mêlée *f*.

scrumptious ['skrʌmpʃəs] *a* *Fam* (*cake, apple etc*) super bon, fameux.

scruple ['skruːp(ə)l] *n* scrupule *m*. ●**scrupulous** *a* scrupuleux. ●**scrupulously** *adv* (*conscientiously*) scrupuleusement; (*completely*) (*clean, honest etc*) absolument.

scrutinize ['skruːtɪnaɪz] *vt* scruter. ●**scrutiny** *n* examen *m* minutieux.

scuba ['skuːbə] *n* scaphandre *m* autonome; **s. diver** plongeur, -euse *mf*; **s. diving** la plongée sous-marine.

scuff [skʌf] *vt* **to s. (up)** (*scrape*) érafler (*chaussure*).

scuffle ['skʌf(ə)l] *n* bagarre *f*.

scullery ['skʌlərɪ] *n* *Br* arrière-cuisine *f*.

sculpt [skʌlpt] *vti* sculpter. ●**sculptress** *n* femme *f* sculpteur. ●**sculpture** *n* (*art, object*) sculpture *f* ▌ *vti* sculpter.

scum [skʌm] *n* 1 (*on liquid*) écume *f*. 2 *Pej* (*people*) racaille *f*; (*person*) salaud *m*; **the s. of society** la lie de la société.

scupper ['skʌpər] *vt* (*plan*) *Br Fam* saboter.

scurf [skɜːf] *n* (*dandruff*) pellicules *fpl*.

scurrilous ['skʌrɪləs] *a* (*criticism, attack*) haineux, violent et grossier.

scurry ['skʌrɪ] *vi* (*rush*) se précipiter, courir; **to s. off** décamper.

scurvy ['skɜːvɪ] *n* (*disease*) scorbut *m*.

scuttle ['skʌt(ə)l] 1 *vt* (*ship*) saborder. 2 *vi* **to s. off** filer.

scuzzy ['skʌzɪ] *a* (**-ier, -iest**) (*dirty*) *Am Sl* cradingue, cracra *inv*.

scythe [saɪð] *n* faux *f*.

sea [siː] *n* mer *f*; (**out**) **at s.** en mer; **by s.** par mer; **by** *or* **beside the s.** au bord de la mer; **to be all at s.** *Fig* nager complètement ▌ *a* (*level*, *breeze*) de la mer; (*water*, *fish*) de mer; (*air*, *salt*) marin; (*battle*, *power*) naval (*mpl* -als); (*route*) maritime; **s. bed**, **s. floor** fond *m* de la mer; **s. lion** otarie *f*; **s. voyage** voyage *m* par mer.

seaboard ['si:bɔːd] *n* littoral *m*. ● **seafarer** *n* marin *m*. ● **seafood** *n* fruits *mpl* de mer. ● **seafront** *n Br* front *m* de mer. ● **seagull** *n* mouette *f*. ● **seaman** *n* (*pl* -**men**) marin *m*. ● **seaplane** *n* hydravion *m*. ● **seaport** *n* port *m* de mer. ● **seashell** *n* coquillage *m*. ● **seashore** *n* bord *m* de la mer. ● **seasick** *a* **to be s.** avoir le mal de mer. ● **seasickness** *n* mal *m* de mer. ● **seaside** *n Br* bord *m* de la mer; **s. town/hotel/etc** ville *f*/hôtel *m/etc* au bord de la mer. ● **seaway** *n* route *f* maritime. ● **seaweed** *n* algue(s) *f(pl)*. ● **seaworthy** *a* (*ship*) en état de naviguer.

seal [si:l] **1** *n* (*animal*) phoque *m*.

2 *n* (*mark*, *design*) sceau *m*; (*of wax on document etc*) cachet *m* (de cire); (*rubber*, *putty etc for sealing*) joint *m*; (*on medicine bottle etc to make tamper-proof*) bague *f* or bande *f* de garantie ▮ *vt* (*document*, *container*) sceller; (*stick down*) cacheter (*enveloppe etc*); (*block*) boucher (*tuyau etc*); (*make airtight*) fermer hermétiquement; **to s. s.o.'s fate** décider du sort de qn; **to s. off a house/district/etc** (*of police*, *troops*) interdire l'accès d'une maison/d'un quartier/*etc*.

seam [si:m] *n* (*in cloth etc*) couture *f*; (*of coal*, *quartz etc*) veine *f*.

seamy ['si:mɪ] *a* (**-ier**, **-iest**) **the s. side** le côté peu reluisant (**of** de).

séance ['seɪɑ̃s] *n* séance *f* de spiritisme.

search [sɜːtʃ] *n* (*quest*) recherche *f* (**for** de); (*of person*, *place*) fouille *f*; **in s. of** à la recherche de; **to do a s. for sth** *Comptr* rechercher qch; **s. and replace** *Comptr* recherche *f* et remplacement *m*; **s. party** équipe *f* de secours.

▮ *vt* (*person*, *place*) fouiller (**for** pour trouver); (*study*) examiner (*document etc*); **to s. (through) one's papers/etc for sth** chercher qch dans ses papiers/*etc*; **to s. a file** *Comptr* examiner or consulter un fichier; **to s. a file for sth** rechercher qch dans un fichier.

▮ *vi* chercher; **to s. for sth** chercher qch. ● **searching** *a* (*look*) pénétrant; (*examination*) minutieux.

searchlight ['sɜːtʃlaɪt] *n* projecteur *m*.

season ['si:z(ə)n] **1** *n* saison *f*; **in the peak s.**, **in (the) high s.** en pleine *or* haute saison; **in the low** *or* **off s.** en basse saison; **a Truffaut s.** (*series of films*) un cycle Truffaut; **the festive s.** la période des fêtes; **'s.'s greetings'** 'meilleurs vœux'; **s. ticket** carte *f* d'abonnement.

2 *vt* (*food*) assaisonner; **highly seasoned dish** plat *m* relevé; **highly seasoned food** la cuisine relevée. ● **seasoning** *n Culin* assaisonnement *m*.

seasonable ['si:zənəb(ə)l] *a* (*weather*) de saison.

seasonal ['si:zən(ə)l] *a* (*work*, *change etc*)

saisonnier.

seasoned ['si:zənd] *a* (*worker etc*) expérimenté; (*soldier*) aguerri.

seat [si:t] *n* (*for sitting*, *centre*, *in parliament*) siège *m*; (*on train*, *bus*) banquette *f*; (*in theatre*, *Br cinema or Am movie theater*) fauteuil *m*; (*place*) place *f*; (*of Br trousers*, *Am pants*) fond *m*; **to take** *or* **have a s.** s'asseoir; **to be in the hot s.** (*in difficult position*) *Fig* être sur la sellette; **s. belt** ceinture *f* de sécurité.

▮ *vt* (*at table*) placer (*qn*); (*on one's lap*) asseoir (*qn*); **the room seats 50** la salle a 50 places (assises); **be seated!** asseyez-vous! ● **seated** *a* (*sitting*) assis. ● **seating** *n* (*seats*) places *fpl* assises; **the s. arrangements** la disposition des places; **s. capacity** nombre *m* de places assises; **s. plan** plan *m* de salle.

-seater ['si:tər] *suff* **two-s.** (*car*) voiture *f* à deux places.

secateurs [sekə'tɜːz] *npl Br* sécateur *m*.

secede [sɪ'si:d] *vi* faire sécession. ● **secession** [sɪ'seʃ(ə)n] *n* sécession *f*.

secluded [sɪ'klu:dɪd] *a* (*remote*) isolé. ● **seclusion** [-ʒ(ə)n] *n* solitude *f*.

second¹ ['sekənd] *a* deuxième, second; **every s. week** une semaine sur deux; **in s. (gear)** (*vehicle*) en seconde; **s. to none** sans pareil; **to be s. in command** commander en second.

▮ *adv* (*to say*) deuxièmement; **to come s.** (*in sport etc*) se classer deuxième; **the s. biggest** le deuxième en ordre de grandeur; **the s. richest country** le deuxième pays le plus riche; **my s. best** (*choice*) mon deuxième choix.

▮ *n* (*person*, *object*) deuxième *mf*, second, -onde *mf*; **Louis the S.** Louis Deux; **seconds** (*goods*) articles *mpl* de second choix.

▮ *vt* (*motion*, *proposal*) appuyer. ● **second-'class** *a* (*ticket on train etc*) de seconde (classe); (*mail*) non urgent; (*product*) de qualité inférieure. ● **second-'rate** *a* médiocre. ● **secondly** *adv* deuxièmement.

second² [sɪ'kənd] *n* (*part of minute*) seconde *f*; **s. hand** (*of clock*, *watch*) trotteuse *f*.

second³ [sɪ'kɒnd] *vt* (*employee*) *Br* détacher (**to** à). ● **secondment** *n Br* détachement *m*; **on s.** en (position de) détachement (**to** à).

secondary ['sekəndərɪ] *a* secondaire; **s. school** *Br* établissement *m* d'enseignement secondaire.

secondhand [sekənd'hænd] **1** *a & adv* (*not new*) d'occasion. **2** *a* (*report*, *news etc*) de seconde main.

secondly ['sekəndlɪ] *adv see* **second¹**.

secondment [sɪ'kɒndmənt] *n Br see* **second³**.

secrecy ['si:krəsɪ] *n* (*discretion*, *silence*) secret *m*; **in s.** en secret.

secret ['si:krɪt] *a* secret ▮ *n* secret *m*; **in s.** en secret; **it's an open s.** c'est le secret de Polichinelle. ● **secretly** *adv* secrètement, en secret.

secretary [*Br* 'sekrət(ə)rɪ, *Am* -erɪ] *n* secrétaire *mf*; **Foreign S.** *Br*, **S. of State** *Am* =

ministre *m* des Affaires étrangères. ●**se-cre'tarial** *a* (*work, post*) de secrétaire, de secrétariat; (*school*) de secrétariat. ●**se-cre'tariat** *n* (*in international organization*) secrétariat *m*.

secrete [sɪ'kri:t] *vt* (*of gland, animal etc*) sécréter. ●**secretion** [-ʃ(ə)n] *n* sécrétion *f*.

secretive [ˈsiːkrətɪv] *a* (*person*) cachottier; (*organization*) qui a le goût du secret; **to be s. about sth** être très discret sur qch. ●**secretively** *adv* (très) discrètement.

sect [sekt] *n* secte *f*. ●**sec'tarian** *a* & *n Pej* sectaire (*mf*).

section [ˈsekʃ(ə)n] *n* (*of town, country, book etc*) partie *f*; (*of road, forest etc*) section *f*, partie *f*; (*of machine, furniture*) élément *m*; (*department*) section *f*; (*in store*) rayon *m*; **the sports/etc s.** (*of newspaper*) la page des sports/etc. ●**section** *vt* (*separate*) séparer.

sector [ˈsektər] *n* secteur *m*.

secular [ˈsekjʊlər] *a* (*teaching etc*) laïque; (*music, art*) profane.

secure [sɪ'kjʊər] **1** *a* (*person, valuables*) en sûreté, en sécurité; (*place*) sûr; (*solid, firm*) solide; (*door, window*) bien fermé; (*certain*) assuré; **s. from** à l'abri de; (**emotionally**) **s.** sécurisé; **I feel s. knowing that...** je suis tranquille car je sais que... ‖ *vt* (*fasten*) attacher; (*window etc*) bien fermer; (*success, s.o.'s future etc*) *Fig* assurer; **to s. sth against** (*protect*) protéger qch de.
2 *vt* (*obtain*) procurer (**sth for s.o.** qch à qn); **to s. sth** (**for oneself**) se procurer qch. ●**securely** *adv* (*firmly*) solidement; (*safely*) en sûreté.

security [sɪ'kjʊərətɪ] *n* **1** sécurité *f*; (*for loan, bail*) caution *f*; **job s.** sécurité *f* de l'emploi; **to tighten s.** renforcer les mesures de sécurité; **s. firm** société *f* de surveillance; **s. guard** agent *m* de sécurité; (*transferring money*) convoyeur *m* de fonds; **she's a s. risk** elle constitue un risque *or* un danger pour la sécurité. **2 securities** (*stocks, bonds etc*) titres *mpl*, valeurs *fpl*.

sedan [sɪ'dæn] *n* (*saloon*) *Am* berline *f*.

sedate [sɪ'deɪt] **1** *a* calme. **2** *vt* mettre sous calmants. ●**sedation** [-ʃ(ə)n] *n* **under s.** sous calmants.

sedative [ˈsedətɪv] *n* calmant *m*.

sedentary [ˈsedəntərɪ] *a* sédentaire.

sediment [ˈsedɪmənt] *n* sédiment *m*.

sedition [sə'dɪʃ(ə)n] *n* sédition *f* ●**seditious** *a* séditieux.

seduce [sɪ'djuːs] *vt* séduire. ●**seducer** *n* séducteur, -trice *mf*. ●**seduction** [sɪ'dʌkʃ(ə)n] *n* séduction *f*. ●**seductive** *a* (*person, offer etc*) séduisant.

see¹ [siː] *vti* (*pt* **saw**, *pp* **seen**) voir; **we'll s. on verra** (bien); **I s.!** je vois!; **I can s. (clearly)** j'y vois clair; **I saw him run(ning)** je l'ai vu courir; **to s. reason** entendre raison; **to s. the joke** comprendre la plaisanterie; **s. who it is va voir qui c'est; s. you (later)!** à tout à l'heure!; **s. you (soon)!** à bientôt!; **to s. that** voir que; (*take care that*) veiller à ce que (+ *sub*); (*check*) s'assurer que (+ *indic*).

see² [siː] *n* (*of bishop*) siège *m* (épiscopal).

see about *vt* (*deal with*) s'occuper de; (*consider*) songer à ‖ **to see in** *vt* **to s. in the New Year** fêter la Nouvelle Année ‖ **to see off** *vt* accompagner (*qn*) (*à la gare etc*) ‖ **to see out** *vt* raccompagner (*qn*) ‖ **to see through** *vt* (*task*) mener à bonne fin; **to s. s.o. through** (*be enough for s.o.*) suffire à qn; **to s. through s.o.** deviner le jeu de qn ‖ **to see to** *vt* (*deal with*) s'occuper de (*qch, qn*); (*mend*) réparer (*qch*); **to s. to it that** (*take care that*) veiller à ce que (+ *sub*); (*check*) s'assurer que (+ *indic*); **to s. s.o. to** (*accompany*) raccompagner qn à.

seed [siːd] *n* graine *f*; (*in grape*) pépin *m*; (*source*) *Fig* germe *m*; *Tennis* tête *f* de série; **seed's** (*for sowing*) graines *fpl*; **to go to s.** (*of lettuce etc*) monter en graine. ●**seedbed** *n* (*for plants*) semis *m*; (*of rebellion etc*) *Fig* foyer *m*. ●**seedling** *n* (*plant*) semis *m*.

seedy [ˈsiːdɪ] *a* (**-ier, -iest**) miteux. ●**seediness** *n* aspect *m* miteux.

seeing [ˈsiːɪŋ] *conj* **s.** (**that**) vu que.

seek [siːk] *vt* (*pt* & *pp* **sought**) chercher (**to do** à faire); (*ask for*) demander (**from** à); **to s. (after)** rechercher; **to s. out** aller trouver.

seem [siːm] *vi* sembler (**to do** faire); **it seems that...** (*impression*) il semble que... (+ *sub or indic*); (*rumour*) il paraît que... (+ *indic*); **it seems to me that...** il me semble que... (+ *indic*); **we s. to know each other** il me semble qu'on se connaît; **I can't s. to do it** je n'arrive pas à le faire.

seeming [ˈsiːmɪŋ] *a* apparent. ●**seemingly** *adv* apparemment.

seemly [ˈsiːmlɪ] *a* convenable.

seen [siːn] *pp* of **see¹**.

seep [siːp] *vi* (*ooze*) suinter; **to s. into** s'infiltrer dans; **to s. through** filtrer à travers. ●**seepage** *n* (*oozing*) suintement *m*; (*infiltration*) infiltration(s) *f(pl)* (**into** dans); (*leak*) fuite *f*.

seersucker [ˈsɪəsʌkər] *n* seersucker *m*.

seesaw [ˈsiːsɔː] *n* (jeu *m* de) bascule *f*.

seethe [siːð] *vi* **to s. with anger** bouillir de colère; **to s. with people** (*swarm*) grouiller de monde.

see-through [ˈsiːθruː] *a* (*dress etc*) transparent.

segment [ˈsegmənt] *n* segment *m*; (*of orange*) quartier *m*.

segregate [ˈsegrɪgeɪt] *vt* séparer; (**racially**) **segregated** (*school*) où se pratique la ségrégation raciale. ●**segregation** [-'geɪʃ(ə)n] *n* ségrégation *f*.

Seine [seɪn] *n* **the S.** la Seine.

seize [siːz] **1** *vt* saisir; (*power, land*) s'emparer de ‖ *vi* **to s. (up)on** (*offer etc*) saisir. **2** *vi* **to s. up** (*of engine*) (se) gripper.

seizure [ˈsiːʒər] *n* (*of goods, property*) saisie *f*; (*attack of illness*) crise *f*, attaque *f*; **s. of power** prise *f* de pouvoir.

seldom [ˈseldəm] *adv* rarement.

select [sɪ'lekt] *vt* choisir (**from** parmi); (*candidates, players, pupils etc*) sélectionner ▮ *a* (*chosen*) choisi; (*exclusive*) sélect, chic *inv*. ● **selection** [-ʃ(ə)n] *n* sélection *f*.

selective [sɪ'lektɪv] *a* (*memory, recruitment etc*) sélectif; **to be s.** (*of person*) opérer un choix; (*choosy*) être difficile (**about sth** sur qch).

self [self] *n* (*pl* **selves**) **the s.** *Phil Psy* le moi; **he's back to his old s.** *Fam* il est redevenu lui-même. ● **self-addressed 'envelope** *n* enveloppe *f* timbrée à votre adresse. ● **self-a'ssurance** *n* assurance *f*. ● **self-a'ssured** *a* sûr de soi. ● **self-'catering** *a* *Br* où l'on fait la cuisine soi-même. ● **self-'centred** (*Am* -'centered) *a* égocentrique. ● **self-'cleaning** *a* (*oven*) autonettoyant. ● **self-con'fessed** *a* (*liar*) de son propre aveu. ● **self-'confidence** *n* assurance *f*. ● **self-'confident** *a* sûr de soi. ● **self-'conscious** *a* gêné. ● **self-'consciousness** *n* gêne *f*. ● **self-con'tained** *a* (*Br flat, Am apartment*) indépendant. ● **self-con'trol** *n* maîtrise *f* de soi. ● **self-de'feating** *a* qui a un effet contraire à celui qui est recherché. ● **self-de'fence** (*Am* -defense) *n* *Jur* légitime défense *f*; **in s.-defence** en légitime défense. ● **self-de'nial** *n* abnégation *f*. ● **self-determi'nation** *n* autodétermination *f*. ● **self-'discipline** *n* autodiscipline *f*. ● **self-em'ployed** *a* qui travaille à son compte. ● **self-es'teem** *n* amour-propre *m*. ● **self-'evident** *a* évident, qui va de soi. ● **self-ex'planatory** *a* qui tombe sous le sens, qui se passe d'explication. ● **self-'governing** *a* autonome. ● **self-im'portant** *a* suffisant. ● **self-in'dulgent** *a* qui ne se refuse rien. ● **self-'interest** *n* intérêt *m* (personnel). ● **self-made** *a* **to be s.-made** avoir réussi tout seul *or* par soi-même. ● **self-o'pinionated** *a* entêté. ● **self-'pity** *n* **to feel self-pity** s'apitoyer sur son propre sort. ● **self-'portrait** *n* autoportrait *m*. ● **self-po'ssessed** *a* assuré. ● **self-raising** *or Am* **self-rising 'flour** *n* farine *f* avec levure. ● **self-re'liant** *a* indépendant. ● **self-re'spect** *n* amour-propre *m*. ● **self-re'specting** *a* qui se respecte. ● **self-'righteous** *a* trop content de soi. ● **self-'sacrifice** *n* abnégation *f*. ● **self-'satisfied** *a* content de soi. ● **self-'service** *n* & *a* libre-service (*m inv*). ● **self-starter** *n* (*person*) personne *f* prête à prendre des initiatives. ● **self-'styled** *a* (*leader etc*) soi-disant. ● **self-su'fficient** *a* indépendant, qui a son indépendance. ● **self-su'pporting** *a* (*business, person*) financièrement indépendant. ● **self-'taught** *a* autodidacte.

selfish ['selfɪʃ] *a* égoïste; (*motive*) intéressé. ● **selfless** *a* désintéressé. ● **selfishness** *n* égoïsme *m*.

selfsame ['selfseɪm] *a* même.

sell [sel] *vt* (*pt & pp* **sold**) vendre; (*idea etc*) *Fig* faire accepter; **she sold it to me for twenty pounds** elle me l'a vendu vingt livres ▮ *vi* (*of product*) se vendre; (*of idea etc*) *Fig* être accepté. ● **sell-by date** *n* (*on product*) date *f* limite de vente. ● **selling price** *n* prix *m* de vente.

sell back *vt* revendre ▮ **to sell off** *vt* liquider ▮ **to sell out** *vt* **to have** *or* **be sold out of sth** n'avoir plus de qch; **this book is sold out** ce livre est épuisé ▮ **to sell up** *vi* (*sell one's house*) vendre sa maison; (*sell one's business*) vendre son affaire.

seller ['selər] *n* vendeur, -euse *mf*. ● **sellout** *n* **1 it was a s.** (*of play, film etc*) tous les billets ont été vendus. **2** (*betrayal*) trahison *f*.

sellotape® ['seləteɪp] *Br n* scotch® *m* ▮ *vt* scotcher.

semantic [sɪ'mæntɪk] *a* sémantique. ● **semantics** *n* sémantique *f*.

semaphore ['seməfɔːr] *n* (*system*) signaux *mpl* à bras; (*signalling device*) sémaphore *m*.

semblance ['sembləns] *n* semblant *m*.

semen ['siːmən] *n* sperme *m*.

semester [sɪ'mestər] *n* (*university term*) semestre *m*.

semi- ['semɪ] *pref* semi, demi-. ● **semiauto'matic** *a* semi-automatique. ● **semibreve** [-briːv] *n* (*musical note*) *Br* ronde *f*. ● **semi-circle** *n* demi-cercle *m*. ● **semi'circular** *a* semi-circulaire. ● **semi'colon** *n* point-virgule *m*. ● **semi-'conscious** *a* à demi conscient. ● **semide'tached** *a* **s. house** *Br* maison *f* jumelle. ● **semi'final** *n* (*in competition etc*) demi-finale *f*. ● **semiskilled** *a* **s. worker** ouvrier *m* spécialisé. ● **semi(trailer)** *n* (*truck*) *Am* semi-remorque *f*.

seminar ['semɪnɑːr] *n* (*university class*) séminaire *m*.

seminary ['semɪnərɪ] *n* *Rel* séminaire *m*.

Semite [*Br* 'siːmaɪt, *Am* 'semaɪt] *n* Sémite *mf*. ● **Se'mitic** *a* sémite; (*language*) sémitique.

semolina [semə'liːnə] *n* semoule *f*.

senate ['senɪt] *n* *Pol* sénat *m*; **the S.** *Am etc* le Sénat. ● **senator** *n* *Pol* sénateur *m*.

send [send] *vt* (*pt & pp* **sent**) envoyer (**to** à); **to s. s.o. for sth/s.o.** envoyer qn chercher qch/qn; **to s. s.o. crazy** *or* **mad** rendre qn fou/**to s. s.o. packing** *Fam* envoyer promener qn. ● **sender** *n* expéditeur, -trice *mf*; **'return to s.'** 'retour à l'expéditeur'.

send away *vt* envoyer (**to** à); (*dismiss*) renvoyer (*qn*) ▮ *vi* **to s. away for** commander (par courrier) ▮ **to send back** *vt* renvoyer ▮ **to send for** *vt* (*doctor etc*) faire venir, envoyer chercher; (*meal etc*) envoyer chercher; (*by mail*) commander (par courrier) ▮ **to send in** *vt* (*form, invoice etc*) envoyer; (*person into room etc*) faire entrer; (*troops*) envoyer ▮ **to send off** *vt* (*letter etc*) envoyer (**to** à); (*expel*) renvoyer (*joueur etc*) du terrain ▮ *vi* **to s. off for sth** commander qch (par courrier) ▮ **to send on** *vt* (*letter, luggage etc*) faire suivre ▮ **to send out** *vt* (*invitation etc*) envoyer; (*heat, sound, light*) émettre; (*from room etc*) faire sortir (*qn*) ▮ *vi* **to send out for** (*meal etc*) envoyer chercher ▮ **to send up** *vt* (*luggage, price etc*) faire monter; (*rocket, balloon*) lancer;

(*mock*) *Br Fam* parodier (*qn, qch*).

send-off ['sendɒf] *n* to give s.o. a s.-off *Fam* faire des adieux chaleureux à qn.

send-up ['sendʌp] *n Br Fam* parodie *f*.

senile ['si:naɪl] *a* gâteux, sénile. ● **se'nility** *n* gâtisme *m*, sénilité *f*.

senior ['si:nɪər] *a* (*older*) plus âgé; (*position, rank, executive*) supérieur; **s. teacher/partner** professeur *m*/associé *m* principal; **to be s.o.'s s., be s. to s.o.** être plus âgé que qn; (*in rank, status*) être au-dessus de qn; **Brown s.** Brown père; **s. citizen** personne *f* âgée; **s. year** (*in school, college*) *Am* dernière année *f*. ▮ *n* aîné, -ée *mf*; (*in school*) grand, grande *mf*; (*in last year of school or college*) *Am* étudiant, -ante *mf* de dernière année; *Sport* senior *mf*. ● **seni'ority** *n* (*in service*) ancienneté *f*; (*in rank*) supériorité *f*; (*in age*) priorité *f* d'âge.

sensation [sen'seɪʃ(ə)n] *n* sensation *f*. ● **sensational** *a* (*event*) qui fait sensation; (*newspaper, film etc*) à sensation; (*terrific*) *Fam* sensationnel.

sense [sens] *n* (*faculty, awareness, meaning*) sens *m*; **s. of smell** l'odorat *m*; **s. of hearing** (le sens de) l'ouïe *f*; **a s. of shame**/etc un sentiment de honte/etc; **a s. of warmth**/**pleasure** une sensation de chaleur/plaisir; **a s. of direction** le sens de l'orientation; **a s. of time** la notion de l'heure; **to have a s. of humour** avoir le sens de l'humour, avoir le sens de l'humour; **to have (good) s.** avoir du bon sens; **to have the s. to do sth** avoir l'intelligence de faire qch; **to bring s.o. to his senses** ramener qn à la raison; **to make s.** (*of story, action etc*) avoir un sens, tenir debout; **to make s. of** comprendre.
▮ *vt* sentir (intuitivement) (**that** que); (*have a foreboding of*) pressentir.

senseless ['senslɪs] *a* (*stupid, meaningless*) insensé; (*unconscious*) sans connaissance. ● **senselessness** *n* stupidité *f*.

sensibility [sensɪ'bɪlɪtɪ] *n* sensibilité *f*; **sensibilities** (*touchiness*) susceptibilité *f*.

sensible ['sensəb(ə)l] *a* (*wise*) raisonnable, sensé; (*clothes, shoes*) pratique.

sensitive ['sensɪtɪv] *a* (*responsive, painful*) sensible; (*delicate*) (*skin, question etc*) délicat; (*touchy*) susceptible (**about** à propos de); **to be s. to** (*the cold, light etc*) être sensible à. ● **sensi'tivity** *n* sensibilité *f* (*touchiness*) susceptibilité *f*.

sensor ['sensər] *n* détecteur *m*.

sensory ['sensərɪ] *a* (*organ*) sensoriel.

sensual ['senʃʊəl] *a* (*bodily, sexual*) sensuel. ● **sensu'ality** *n* sensualité *f*. ● **sensuous** *a* (*pleasing, refined*) sensuel. ● **sensuously** *adv* avec sensualité. ● **sensuousness** *n* sensualité *f*.

sent [sent] *pt* & *pp of* **send**.

sentence ['sentəns] **1** *n* (*words*) phrase *f*. **2** *n* (*punishment, in prison*) peine *f*; (*conviction*) condamnation *f*; **to pass s.** prononcer une condamnation (**on s.o.** contre qn); **to serve a**

s. purger une peine ▮ *vt* (*convicted criminal*) prononcer une condamnation contre; **to s. s.o. to 3 years (in prison)/to death** condamner qn à 3 ans de prison/à mort.

sentiment ['sentɪmənt] *n* sentiment *m*. ● **senti'mental** *a* sentimental. ● **sentimen'tality** *n* sentimentalité *f*.

sentry ['sentrɪ] *n* sentinelle *f*; **s. box** guérite *f*; **to be on s. duty** être de faction.

separate ['sepərət] *a* (*distinct*) séparé; (*independent*) indépendant; (*different*) différent; (*individual*) particulier ▮ ['sepəreɪt] *vt* séparer (**from** de) ▮ *vi* (*become detached*) se séparer (**from** de); (*of husband and wife*) se séparer. ● **'separately** *adv* séparément. ● **separation** [sepə'reɪʃ(ə)n] *n* séparation *f*.

separates ['sepərəts] *npl* (*garments*) coordonnés *mpl*.

separatist ['sepərətɪst] *n* séparatiste *mf*.

September [sep'tembər] *n* septembre *m*.

septic ['septɪk] *a* (*wound*) infecté; **to turn** or **go s.** s'infecter; **s. tank** fosse *f* septique.

sequel ['si:kw(ə)l] *n* suite *f*.

sequence ['si:kwəns] *n* (*order*) ordre *m*; (*series*) succession *f*; *Comptr Mus Cards* séquence *f*; **film s.** séquence de film; **in s.** dans l'ordre, successivement.

sequin ['si:kwɪn] *n* paillette *f*.

Serb [sɜ:b] *a* serbe ▮ *n* Serbe *mf*. ● **Serbia** *n* Serbie *f*.

serenade [serə'neɪd] *n* sérénade *f* ▮ *vt* donner une or la sérénade à.

serene [sə'ri:n] *a* serein. ● **serenity** *n* sérénité *f*.

sergeant ['sɑ:dʒənt] *n* (*in the army, air force*) sergent *m*; (*in the police force*) brigadier *m*.

serial ['sɪərɪəl] *n* (*story, film*) feuilleton *m*; **s. number** (*on appliance etc*) numéro de série; (*on Br banknote, Am bill*) numéro *m*. ● **serialize** *vt* (*in newspaper etc*) publier en feuilleton; (*on television or radio*) adapter en feuilleton.

series ['sɪəri:z] *n inv* série *f*; (*book collection*) collection *f*.

serious ['sɪərɪəs] *a* sérieux; (*illness, mistake, tone*) grave, sérieux; (*damage*) important; **s. money** *Fam* de grosses sommes *fpl* d'argent. ● **seriously** *adv* sérieusement; (*ill, damaged*) gravement; **to take s.o./sth s.** prendre qn/qch au sérieux. ● **seriousness** *n* sérieux *m*; (*of illness, situation etc*) gravité *f*; (*of damage*) importance *f*; **in all s.** sérieusement.

sermon ['sɜ:mən] *n* sermon *m*.

serpent ['sɜ:pənt] *n* serpent *m*.

serrated [sə'reɪtɪd] *a* (*knife*) à dents (de scie).

serum ['sɪərəm] *n* sérum *m*.

servant ['sɜ:vənt] *n* (*in house etc*) domestique *mf*; (*person who serves*) *Fig* serviteur *m*; **public s.** fonctionnaire *mf*.

serve [sɜ:v] *vt* (*master, cause etc*) servir; (*at table, in shop etc*) servir (**to s.o.** à qn, **s.o. with sth** qch à qn); (*of train, bus etc*) desservir (*un village, quartier etc*); (*supply* *with electricity etc*) alimenter; **to s. an apprenticeship** faire un apprentissage; **to s. a sentence** (*in prison*) purger une peine; **to s. a summons on s.o.** *Jur* remettre une assignation à qn; **it serves its purpose** ça fait l'affaire; **(it) serves you right!** *Fam* ça t'apprendra!; **to s. up** *or* **out a meal/etc** servir un repas/etc.

❚ *vi* servir (**as de**); **to s. on** (*committee, jury etc*) être membre de; **that serves to show/etc** ça sert à montrer/etc.

❚ *n Tennis* service *m*. **● server** *n* **cake s.** pelle *f* à tarte; **salad servers** couvert *m* à salade.

service ['sɜːvɪs] *n* (*serving, help, dishes etc*) & *Mil Rel Tennis* service *m*; (*machine or vehicle repair*) révision *f*; **to be of s.** to être utile à, rendre service à; **the (armed) services** les forces *fpl* armées; **s. (charge)** (*in restaurant*) service *m*; **s. department** (*workshop*) atelier *m*; **s. area** (*on motorway*) *Br* aire *f* de service; **s. station** station-service *f*. **❚** *vt* (*machine, vehicle*) réviser. **● servicing** *n* (*of machine, vehicle*) révision *f*.

serviceable ['sɜːvɪsəb(ə)l] *a* (*usable*) utilisable; (*useful*) commode; (*durable*) solide.

serviceman ['sɜːvɪsmən] *n* (*pl* **-men**) *n* militaire *m*.

serviette [sɜːvɪ'et] *n Br* serviette *f* (de table).

servile ['sɜːvaɪl] *a* servile.

serving ['sɜːvɪŋ] *n* (*of food*) portion *f*; **s. dish** plat *m* (de service).

session ['seʃ(ə)n] *n* (*meeting, period*) séance *f*; (*in university*) année *f* or trimestre *m* universitaire; *Am* semestre *m* universitaire; **the parliamentary s.** la session parlementaire.

set [set] **1** *n* (*of keys, needles, tools etc*) jeu *m*; (*of stamps, numbers*) série *f*; (*of people*) groupe *m*; (*of facts, laws*) & *Math* ensemble *m*; (*of books*) collection *f*; (*of dishes*) service *m*; (*of Br tyres, Am tires*) train *m*; (*kit*) trousse *f*; (*scenery of play or film*) décor *m*, scène *f*; (*stage for play or film*) plateau *m*; (*hairstyle*) mise *f* en plis; *Tennis* set *m*; **film s.** plateau *m* de tournage; **television** *or* **TV s.** téléviseur *m*; **radio s.** poste *m* de radio; **tea s.** service *m* à thé; **chess s.** (*pieces*) jeu *m* d'échecs; **construction s.** jeu *m* de construction; **painting s.** boîte *f* de couleurs *or* de peinture; **a s. of teeth** une rangée de dents, une denture; **the skiing/racing s.** le monde du ski/des courses; **s. theory** *Math* la théorie des ensembles.

2 *a* (*time, price etc*) fixe; (*lunch*) à prix fixe; (*school book etc*) au programme; (*speech*) préparé à l'avance; (*in one's habits*) régulier; (*situated*) situé; **s. phrase** expression *f* consacrée; **a s. purpose** un but déterminé; **the s. menu** le plat du jour; **to be dead s. against** être absolument opposé à; **to be s. on doing** être résolu à faire; **to be s. on sth** vouloir qch à tout prix; **all s.** (*ready*) prêt (*to do*) pour faire); **to be s. back from the road/etc** (*of house etc*) être en retrait de la route/etc.

3 *vt* (*pt* & *pp* **set**, *pres p* **setting**) (*put*)

mettre, poser; (*date, limit etc*) fixer; (*mechanism, clock*) régler; (*alarm clock*) mettre (**for** pour); (*arm etc in plaster*) plâtrer; (*task*) donner (**for s.o.** à qn); (*trap*) tendre (**for** à); (*problem*) poser; (*diamond*) monter; **to s. a (new) record** établir un (nouveau) record; **to s. a precedent** créer un précédent; **to have one's hair s.** se faire faire une mise en plis; **to s. loose** (*dog*) lâcher (**on contre**); **to s. s.o. crying/etc** faire pleurer/etc qn.

❚ *vi* (*of sun*) se coucher; (*of Br jelly, Am jello®*) prendre; (*of bone*) se ressouder.

set about *vt* (*begin*) commencer; **to s. about doing sth** se mettre à faire qch **❚ to set back** *vt* (*in time*) retarder (*qn*); (*cost*) *Fam* coûter (**à** *qn*) **❚ to set down** *vt* (*object*) déposer **❚ to set in** *vi* (*start*) commencer; (*arise*) surgir **❚ to set off** *vt* (*bomb*) faire exploser; (*mechanism*) déclencher; (*beauty, complexion*) *Fig* rehausser; **to s. s.o. off crying/etc** faire pleurer/etc qn **❚** *vi* (*leave*) partir **❚ to set out** *vt* (*display, explain*) exposer (**to** à); (*arrange*) disposer **❚** *vi* (*leave*) partir; **to s. out to do** entreprendre de faire **❚ to set up** *vt* (*tent, statue*) dresser; (*table etc*) installer; (*business*) créer, monter; (*meeting*) organiser; (*government*) établir; (*school*) fonder; (*inquiry*) ouvrir; **to s. s.o. up in business** lancer qn dans les affaires **❚** *vi* **to s. up in business** monter une affaire **❚ to set upon** *vt* (*attack*) attaquer (*qn*).

setback ['setbæk] *n* (*hitch*) revers *m*; (*in recovery of sick person*) rechute *f*.

setsquare ['setskweər] *n* (*for drawing*) *Br* équerre *f*.

settee [se'tiː] *n* canapé *m*.

setter ['setər] *n* chien *m* couchant.

setting ['setɪŋ] *n* (*surroundings*) cadre *m*; (*of sun*) coucher *m*; (*of diamond*) monture *f*.

settle ['set(ə)l] *vt* (*decide, arrange, pay*) régler; (*date*) fixer; (*place in position*) placer; (*person*) installer (*dans son lit etc*); (*nerves*) calmer; (*land*) coloniser; **let's s. things** arrangeons les choses; **that's (all) settled** (*decided*) c'est décidé *or* réglé.

❚ *vi* (*live*) s'installer, s'établir; (*of dust*) se déposer; (*of bird*) se poser; (*of snow*) tenir; **to s. into an armchair/etc** s'installer dans un fauteuil/etc; **to s. into one's job** s'habituer à son travail; **to s. with s.o.** régler qn; **may I s.?** (*pay*) puis-je régler? **● settled** *a* (*weather, period*) stable; (*habits*) régulier.

settle down *vi* (*in chair or house*) s'installer; (*calm down*) (*of nerves etc*) se calmer; (*in one's lifestyle*) se ranger; **to s. down into an armchair/etc** s'installer dans un fauteuil/etc; **to s. down in one's job** s'habituer à son travail; **to s. down to** (*get used to*) s'habituer à; **to s. down to work/to a task** se mettre au travail/à un travail **❚ to settle for** *vt* accepter, se contenter de **❚ to settle in** *vi* (*become established*) s'installer **❚ to settle up** *vi* (*pay*) régler; **to s. up with s.o.** régler qn.

settlement ['set(ə)lmənt] *n* (*agreement*)

accord *m*; (*payment*) règlement *m*; (*colony*) colonie *f*.

settler ['setlər] *n* colon *m*.

set-to [set'tu:] *n* (*pl* -os) (*quarrel*) Br Fam prise *f* de bec.

setup ['setʌp] *n* Fam situation *f*.

seven ['sev(ə)n] *a* & *n* sept (*m*). ● **seventh** *a* & *n* septième (*mf*).

seventeen ['sev(ə)nti:n] *a* & *n* dix-sept (*m*). ● **seven'teenth** *a* & *n* dix-septième (*mf*).

seventy ['sev(ə)ntɪ] *a* & *n* soixante-dix (*m*); **s.**-**one** soixante et onze. ● **seventieth** *a* & *n* soixante-dixième (*mf*).

sever ['sevər] *vt* sectionner, couper; (*relations*) Fig rompre. ● **severance** *n* (*of relations*) rupture *f*; **s. pay** indemnité *f* de licenciement.

several ['sev(ə)rəl] *a* & *pron* plusieurs (*of* d'entre).

severe [sə'vɪər] *a* (*tone, judge etc*) sévère; (*winter, training*) rigoureux; (*test*) dur; (*injury*) grave; (*blow, pain*) violent; (*cold, frost*) intense; (*overwork*) excessif; **to have a s. cold** avoir un gros rhume; **to be s. with s.o.** être sévère envers qn. ● **severely** *adv* (*to criticize, punish etc*) sévèrement; (*damaged, wounded*) gravement; **to be s. handicapped** *or* **disabled** souffrir d'un handicap sévère. ● **se'verity** *n* sévérité *f*; (*of winter etc*) rigueur *f*; (*of injury*) gravité *f*; (*of blow etc*) violence *f*.

sew [səʊ] *vti* (*pt* sewed, *pp* sewn [səʊn] *or* sewed) coudre; **to s. on** (*button*) (re)coudre; **to s. up** (*tear*) (re)coudre. ● **sewing** *n* couture *f*; **s. machine** machine *f* à coudre.

sewage ['su:ɪdʒ] *n* eaux *fpl* d'égout, eaux *fpl* usées. ● **sewer** ['su:ər] *n* égout *m*.

sewn [səʊn] *pp* of **sew**.

sex [seks] *n* (*gender, sexuality*) sexe *m*; (*activity*) relations *fpl* sexuelles; **the opposite s.** l'autre sexe; **to have s. with s.o.** coucher avec qn **i** *a* (*education, life, act etc*) sexuel; **s. appeal** sex-appeal *m*; **s. maniac** obsédé, -ée *mf* sexuel(le); **s. symbol** sex-symbol *m*. ● **sexist** *a* & *n* sexiste (*mf*).

sextet [sek'stet] *n* sextuor *m*.

sexual ['sekʃʊəl] *a* sexuel. ● **sexu'ality** *n* sexualité *f*. ● **sexy** *a* (-ier, -iest) (*book, clothes, person*) sexy *inv*; (*aroused*) qui a envie (de faire l'amour).

Seychelles [seɪ'ʃelz] *npl* **the S.** les Seychelles *fpl*.

sh! [ʃ] *int* chut! [ʃyt].

shabby ['ʃæbɪ] *a* (-ier, -iest) (*room etc*) minable; (*town*) miteux; (*person*) pauvrement vêtu; (*mean*) Fig mesquin. ● **shabbily** *adv* (*dressed*) pauvrement. ● **shabbiness** *n* aspect *m* minable; (*meanness*) Fig mesquinerie *f*.

shack [ʃæk] **1** *n* cabane *f*. **2** *vi* **to s. up with s.o.** *Pej* Fam se loger avec qn.

shackles ['ʃæk(ə)lz] *npl* chaînes *fpl*.

shade [ʃeɪd] *n* ombre *f*; (*of colour*) ton *m*, nuance *f*; (*of opinion, meaning*) nuance *f*; (*of lamp*) abat-jour *m inv*; **window s.** Am store *m*; **in the s.** à l'ombre; **a s. faster/**

taller/etc (*slightly*) un rien plus vite/plus grand/etc **i** *vt* (*of tree*) ombrager; (*protect*) abriter (**from** de); **to s. in** (*drawing*) ombrer. ● **shady** *a* (-ier, -iest) (*place*) ombragé; (*person, business, scheme etc*) Fig louche.

shadow ['ʃædəʊ] **1** *n* ombre *f*. **2** *a* Br Pol **s. cabinet** cabinet *m* fantôme; **the S. Education Secretary** le *or* la porte-parole de l'opposition sur les questions de l'éducation. **3** *vt* **to s. s.o.** (*follow*) filer qn. ● **shadowy** *a* (-ier, -iest) (*form etc*) obscur, vague.

shaft [ʃɑ:ft] *n* **1** (*of tool*) manche *m*; (*in machine*) arbre *m*; **s. of light** trait *m* de lumière. **2** (*of mine*) puits *m*; (*of Br lift, Am elevator*) cage *f*.

shaggy ['ʃægɪ] *a* (-ier, -iest) (*hair, beard*) broussailleux; (*dog, sheep etc*) à longs poils.

shake¹ [ʃeɪk] *vt* (*pt* shook, *pp* shaken) (*move up and down*) secouer; (*bottle, fist*) agiter; (*belief, resolution etc*) Fig ébranler; (*upset*) bouleverser, secouer; **to s. the windows** (*of shock*) ébranler les vitres; **to s. one's head** (*say no*) secouer la tête; **to s. hands with s.o.** serrer la main à qn; **we shook hands** nous nous sommes serré la main; **to s. off** (*dust etc*) secouer; (*cough, infection, pursuer*) Fig se débarrasser de; **to s. up** (*organization*) réorganiser, restructurer; **to s. s.o. up** (*disturb, rouse to action*) secouer qn; **to s. sth out of sth** (*remove*) secouer qch de qch; **s. yourself out of it!** Fam secoue-toi!

i *vi* (*of person, windows, voice etc*) trembler (**with** de).

i *n* secousse *f*; **to give sth a s.** secouer qch; **with a s. of his head** en secouant la tête; **in two shakes** (*soon*) Fam dans une minute. ● **shake-up** *n* Fig réorganisation *f*, restructuration *f*.

shake² [ʃeɪk] *n* (*milkshake*) milk-shake *m*.

shaky ['ʃeɪkɪ] *a* (-ier, -iest) (*trembling*) tremblant; (*ladder, table, chair etc*) branlant; (*memory, health*) chancelant; (*on one's legs, in a language*) mal assuré.

shall [ʃæl, unstressed ʃəl] *v aux* **1** (*future*) **I s. come, I'll come** je viendrai; **we s. not come, we shan't come** nous ne viendrons pas. **2** (*question*) **s. I leave?** veux-tu que je parte?; **s. we leave?** on part? **3** (*order*) **he s. do it if I order it** il devra le faire si je l'ordonne.

shallot [ʃə'lɒt] *n* (*onion*) Br échalote *f*.

shallow ['ʃæləʊ] *a* (-er, -est) (*water, river etc*) peu profond; (*argument, person etc*) Fig Pej superficiel **i** *npl* **the shallows** (*of river*) le bas-fond. ● **shallowness** *n* manque *m* de profondeur; Fig Pej caractère *m* superficiel.

sham [ʃæm] *n* (*pretence*) comédie *f*, feinte *f*; (*person*) imposteur *m*; **to be a s.** (*of jewel*) être faux; **it's a s.!** (*election promises etc*) c'est du bidon! **i** *a* (*false*) faux (*f* fausse); (*illness, emotion*) feint **i** *vt* (-mm-) feindre **i** *vi* **he's** (*only*) **shamming** il fait semblant.

shambles ['ʃæmb(ə)lz] *n* désordre *m*, pagaille *f*; **to be a s.** être en pagaille; **to make a s. of** (*room etc*) mettre en pagaille; (*one's* *life, an exercise etc*) rater.

shame [ʃeɪm] *n* (*feeling, disgrace*) honte *f*;
it's a s. c'est dommage (**to do** de faire); **it's a
s. (that)** c'est dommage que (+ *sub*); **what a
s.!** (quel) dommage!; **to put s.o. to s.** faire
honte à qn ▮ *vt* (*disgrace, make ashamed*)
faire honte à. ●**shamefaced** *a* (*embarrassed*)
honteux; (*bashful*) *Lit* timide.

shameful [ʃeɪmfəl] *a* honteux. ●**shamefully**
adv honteusement.

shameless [ʃeɪmləs] *a* (*brazen*) effronté;
(*indecent*) impudique. ●**shamelessly** *adv*
sans la moindre gêne.

shammy [ʃæmɪ] *n* **s. (leather)** *Fam* peau *f*
de chamois.

shampoo [ʃæmˈpuː] *n* shampooing *m* ▮ *vt*
(*carpet*) shampooiner; **to s. s.o.'s hair** faire
un shampooing à qn.

shandy [ʃændɪ] *n* (*beer*) *Br* panaché *m*.

shan't [ʃɑːnt] = **shall not**.

shanty¹ [ʃæntɪ] *n* (*hut*) baraque *f*. ●**shantytown** *n* bidonville *f*.

shanty² [ʃæntɪ] *n* **sea s.** chanson *f* de ma-
rins.

shape [ʃeɪp] *n* forme *f*; **in (good) s.** (*fit*) en
(pleine) forme; **to be in good/bad s.** (*of vehicle, house etc*) être en bon/mauvais état;
(*of business*) marcher bien/mal; **to take s.** (*of
plan, book etc*) prendre forme; (*progress
wall*) avancer; **in the s. of a pear/bell/**etc en
forme de poire/cloche/*etc*.
▮ *vt* (*fashion*) façonner (**into** en); (*one's life*)
Fig déterminer.
▮ *vi* **to s. up** (*of plans*) prendre (bonne)
tournure, s'annoncer bien; (*of pupil,
wrongdoer*) s'y mettre, s'appliquer; (*of patient*) faire des progrès. ●**-shaped** *suff* pear-
s.*/etc* en forme de poire/*etc*. ●**shapeless** *a*
(*object*) informe. ●**shapely** *a* (-**ier**, -**iest**)
(*woman, legs*) bien tourné.

share [ʃeər] *n* part *f* (**of**, **in** de); (*in company*) *Fin* action *f*; **one's (fair) s. of sth** sa part
de qch; **to do one's (fair) s.** fournir sa part
d'efforts; **stocks and shares** *Fin* valeurs *fpl*
(*boursières*).
▮ *vt* (*meal, joy, opinion etc*) partager (**with**
avec); (*characteristic*) avoir en commun; **to s.
sth out** (*distribute*) partager ou répartir qch
(**among** entre).
▮ *vi* partager; **to s. in sth** avoir sa part de
qch. ●**shareholder** *n* (*investor*) actionnaire
mf.

shark [ʃɑːk] *n* (*fish*) requin *m*; (*crook*) *Fig*
requin *m*.

sharp [ʃɑːp] **1** *a* (-**er**, -**est**) (*knife, blade etc*)
tranchant; (*pointed*) pointu; (*point, voice*)
aigu (*f* -**uë**); (*pace, mind*) vif; (*pain*) aigu (*f*
-**uë**), vif; (*bend, change*) brusque; (*taste*) piquant; (*words, wind, tone*) âpre; (*eyesight,
cry*) perçant; (*clear, distinct*) (*picture, difference etc*) net (*f* nette); (*lawyer, businessman
etc*) *Pej* peu scrupuleux; **she's very s.** (*has a
sharp mind*) elle a l'esprit vif; **to have s.
eyes, be s.-eyed** avoir la vue perçante; **s.
practice** *Pej* procédé(s) *m(pl)* malhonnête(s).

▮ *adv* **to stop s.** s'arrêter net; **five o'clock/**etc
s. cinq heures/*etc* pile; **s. right/left** tout de
suite à droite/à gauche.
2 *n Mus* dièse *m*.

sharpen [ʃɑːp(ə)n] *vt* (*knife*) aiguiser;
(*pencil*) tailler. ●**sharpener** *n* (*for pencils*)
taille-crayon(s) *m inv*; (*for blades*) aiguisoir
m.

sharply [ʃɑːplɪ] *adv* (*suddenly*) brusquement; (*harshly*) vivement; (*clearly*) nettement. ●**sharpness** *n* (*of blade*) tranchant *m*;
(*of picture*) netteté *f*.

sharpshooter [ʃɑːpʃuːtər] *n* tireur *m*
d'élite.

shatter [ʃætər] *vt* (*door, arm etc*) fracasser;
(*glass*) faire voler en éclats; (*career, health*)
briser; (*person, hopes*) anéantir ▮ *vi* (*smash*)
se fracasser; (*of glass*) voler en éclats.
●**shattered** *a* (*exhausted*) anéanti. ●**shatter-
ing** *a* (*defeat*) accablant; (*news, experience*)
bouleversant.

shave [ʃeɪv] *vt* (*person, head*) raser; **to s. off
one's beard/**etc se raser la barbe/*etc* ▮ *vi* se
raser ▮ *n* **to have a s.** se raser; **to have a close
s.** *Fig* l'échapper belle. ●**shaving** *n* (*strip of
wood etc*) copeau *m*; **he dislikes s.** il n'aime
pas se raser; **s. brush** blaireau *m*; **s. cream,
s. foam** crème *f* à raser. ●**shaven** a rasé (de
près). ●**shaver** *n* rasoir *m* électrique.

shawl [ʃɔːl] *n* châle *m*.

she [ʃiː] *pron* elle; **s. wants** elle veut; **she's a
happy woman** c'est une femme heureuse; **if I
were s.** si j'étais elle; **s. and I** elle et moi ▮ *n
Fam* femelle *f*; **it's a s.** (*baby*) c'est une fille;
she-bear ourse *f*.

sheaf [ʃiːf] *n* (*pl* **sheaves**) (*of corn*) gerbe *f*;
(*of paper*) liasse *f*.

shear [ʃɪər] *vt* tondre ▮ *npl* **shears** cisaille(s)
f(pl); **pruning shears** sécateur *m*. ●**shearing**
n tonte *f*.

sheath [ʃiːθ] *n* (*pl* -**s** [ʃiːðz]) (*container*)
fourreau *m*, gaine *f*; (*contraceptive*) préservatif *m*.

shed [ʃed] **1** *n* (*in garden*) abri *m* (de jardin);
(*for goods or machines*) hangar *m*; **bicycle s.**
abri *m* or remise *f* à vélos; **tool s.** cabane *f* à
outils. **2** *vt* (*pt* & *pp* **shed**, *pres p* **shedding**)
(*lose*) perdre; (*tears, blood*) verser, ré-
pandre; (*warmth etc*) répandre; (*get rid of*)
se défaire de; (*clothes*) enlever; **to s. light on
sth** *Fig* éclairer qch.

she'd [ʃiːd] = **she had** & **she would**.

sheen [ʃiːn] *n* lustre *m*.

sheep [ʃiːp] *n inv* mouton *m*. ●**sheepdog** *n*
chien *m* de berger. ●**sheepskin** *n* peau *f* de
mouton; **s. jacket** veste *f* en (peau de) mouton.

sheepish [ʃiːpɪʃ] *a* penaud. ●**sheepishly**
adv d'un air penaud.

sheer [ʃɪər] **1** *a* (*luck, madness etc*) pur;
(*impossibility etc*) absolu; **it's s. hard work**
ça demande du travail; **by s. determination/
hard work** à force de détermination/de tra-
vail. **2** *a* (*cliff*) à pic ▮ *adv* (*to rise*) à pic. **3** *a*
(*fabric*) très fin.

sheet [ʃiːt] n (on bed) drap m; (of paper etc) feuille f; (of glass, ice) plaque f; (dust cover) housse f; (canvas) bâche f; s. **metal** tôle f.

sheikh [ʃeɪk] n scheik m, cheik m.

shelf [ʃelf] n (pl **shelves**) étagère f, rayon m; (in shop) rayon m; (on cliff) saillie f; **set of shelves** étagères fpl, rayonnages mpl; **to be sold off the s.** être en vente dans tous les magasins.

shell [ʃel] 1 n (of egg, snail, nut etc) coquille f; (of tortoise, turtle, crab, lobster) carapace f; (seashell) coquillage m; (of peas) cosse f; (of building) carcasse f ■ vt (peas) écosser; (nut, shrimp) décortiquer. 2 n (explosive) obus m ■ vt (town etc) bombarder. 3 vt **to s. out a lot of money** Fam sortir or allonger pas mal d'argent. ● **shelling** n (with explosives) bombardement m. ● **shell suit** n survêtement m.

shellfish [ʃelfɪʃ] n inv (lobster, crab, shrimp) crustacé m; (mollusc) coquillage m ■ npl Culin (oysters etc) fruits mpl de mer.

shelter [ʃeltər] n (place, protection) abri m; **to take s.** se mettre à l'abri (from de); **to seek s.** chercher un abri ■ vt abriter (from de); (criminal) protéger ■ vi s'abriter. ● **sheltered** a (place) abrité; **to have led** or **had a s. life** avoir eu une vie très protégée.

shelve [ʃelv] vt (postpone) laisser en suspens.

shelving [ʃelvɪŋ] n (shelves) rayonnage(s) m(pl); **s. unit** (set of shelves) étagère f.

shepherd [ʃepəd] 1 n berger m; **s.'s pie** Br hachis m Parmentier. 2 vt **to s. s.o. in** faire entrer qn; **to s. s.o. around** piloter qn. ● **shepherdess** n bergère f.

sherbet [ʃɜːbət] n (powder) Br poudre f acidulée; (water ice) Am sorbet m.

sheriff [ʃerɪf] n Am shérif m.

sherry [ʃerɪ] n sherry m, xérès m.

Shetlands (The) [ðəˈʃetləndz] npl les îles fpl Shetland.

shh! [ʃ] int chut! [ʃʏt].

shield [ʃiːld] n (for protection) bouclier m; (on coat of arms) écu m; (protective screen, protection against sun, heat etc) écran m ■ vt protéger (from de).

shift [ʃɪft] n (change) changement m (of, in de); (period of work) poste m; (workers) équipe f; (standard) gear s. (on vehicle) Am levier m de vitesse; **s. work** travail m en équipe; **s. key** (on computer, typewriter) touche-majuscules f.
■ vt (move) bouger, déplacer; (arm, leg, head etc) bouger; (stain) enlever; (employee) muter (to à); **to s. places** changer de place; **to s. the responsibility/blame on to s.o.** rejeter la responsabilité/faute sur qn; **to s. gear(s)** (in vehicle) Am changer de vitesse; **to s. the scenery** (of stage play) changer le décor.
■ vi bouger; (of heavy object) se déplacer; (of views) changer; (pass) passer (to à); (go) aller (to à); **to s. to** (new town etc) déménager à; **to s. along** avancer; **to s. over** or **up** se

pousser. ● **shifting** a (views) changeant.

shiftless [ʃɪftləs] a (apathetic) mou (f molle); (lazy) paresseux.

shifty [ʃɪftɪ] a (-ier, -iest) (sly) sournois; (dubious) louche.

shilly-shally [ʃɪlɪʃælɪ] vi hésiter.

shimmer [ʃɪmər] vi chatoyer, miroiter ■ n chatoiement m, miroitement m.

shin [ʃɪn] n tibia m; **s. pad** (of hockey player etc) jambière f.

shindig [ʃɪndɪɡ] n Fam nouba f.

shine [ʃaɪn] vi (pt & pp **shone** [Br ʃɒn, Am ʃəʊn]) (of sun, light, shoes etc) & Fig briller; **the light/sun is shining in my eyes** la lumière/le soleil me tape dans les yeux; **the light is shining on the table** la lumière éclaire la table; **to s. with joy** (of face) rayonner de joie; (of eyes) briller de joie ■ vt (polish) faire briller; **to s. a light** or **Br torch** or **Am flashlight (on sth)** éclairer (qch); **s. your light!** éclairez! ■ n (on shoes, cloth) brillant m; (on metal etc) éclat m. ● **shining** a (bright, polished) brillant; **a shining example** of un bel exemple de.

shingle [ʃɪŋɡ(ə)l] n (on beach) galets mpl; (on roof) bardeau m.

shingles [ʃɪŋɡ(ə)lz] n (disease) zona m.

shiny [ʃaɪnɪ] a (-ier, -iest) (bright, polished) brillant; (clothes, through wear) lustré.

ship [ʃɪp] n navire m, bateau m; **by s. en bateau** ■ vt (-pp-) (send) expédier (par mer); (transport) transporter (par mer); (load on board) embarquer (on to sur). ● **shipping** n (traffic) navigation f; (ships) navires mpl; **s. agent** agent m maritime; **s. line** compagnie f de navigation.

shipbuilding [ʃɪpbɪldɪŋ] n construction f navale. ● **shipmate** n camarade m de bord. ● **shipment** n (goods) cargaison f, chargement m. ● **shipowner** n armateur m. ● **shipshape** a & adv en ordre. ● **shipwreck** n naufrage m. ● **shipwrecked** a naufragé; **to be s.** faire naufrage. ● **shipyard** n chantier m naval.

shire [ʃaɪər] n Br comté m.

shirk [ʃɜːk] vt (duty) se dérober à; (work) éviter de faire ■ vi tirer au flanc. ● **shirker** n tire-au-flanc m inv.

shirt [ʃɜːt] n chemise f; (of woman) chemisier m; (of sportsman) maillot m. ● **shirtfront** n plastron m. ● **shirtsleeves** npl in (one's) s. en bras de chemise.

shiver [ʃɪvər] vi frissonner (with de) ■ n frisson m; **to give s.o. the shivers** (creeps) donner le frisson à qn. ● **shivery** a **to be s.** (from the cold) être frissonnant; (from a fever) être fiévreux.

shoal [ʃəʊl] n (of fish) banc m.

shock [ʃɒk] n (emotional, physical) choc m; (impact, medical condition) choc m; (of explosion) secousse f; (electric) s. décharge f (électrique) (from sth en touchant qch); **a feeling of s.** un sentiment d'horreur; **to be suffering from s.** or **in a state of s.** être en état de choc; **to come as a s. to s.o.** stupéfier qn.

■ *a* (*tactics, troops*) de choc; **s. wave** onde *f* de choc; **s. effect/image/result/**etc effet *m*/image *f*/résultat *m*/-choc *inv*; **s. absorber** (*in vehicle etc*) amortisseur *m*.

■ *vt* (*offend*) choquer; (*surprise*) stupéfier; (*disgust*) dégoûter. ●**shocking** *a* affreux; (*outrageous*) scandaleux; (*indecent*) choquant. ●**shockingly** *adv* (*extremely, badly*) affreusement. ●**shocker** *n* **to be a s.** *Fam* être affreux *or* horrible. ●**shockproof** *a* résistant au choc.

shoddy ['ʃɒdɪ] *a* (**-ier, -iest**) (*goods etc*) de mauvaise qualité. ●**shoddily** *adv* (*made, done*) mal.

shoe [ʃuː] *n* chaussure *f*, soulier *m*; (*for horse*) fer *m*; (**brake**) **s.** (*in vehicle*) sabot *m* (de frein); **in your shoes** *Fig* à ta place; **s. polish** cirage *m*; **s. repair shop** cordonnerie *f*
■ *vt* (*pt & pp* **shod**) (*horse*) ferrer. ●**shoehorn** *n* chausse-pied *m*. ●**shoelace** *n* lacet *m*. ●**shoemaker** *n* fabricant *m* de chaussures; (*cobbler*) cordonnier *m*. ●**shoeshop** *n* magasin *m* de chaussures. ●**shoestring** *n* **on a s.** *Fig* avec peu d'argent (en poche).

shone [*Br* ʃɒn, *Am* ʃəʊn] *pt & pp of* **shine.**
shoo [ʃuː] *vt* **to s.** (**away**) chasser ■ *int* ouste!
shook [ʃʊk] *pt of* **shake**[1].
shoot[1] [ʃuːt] *vt* (*pt & pp* **shot**) (*kill*) tuer (d'un coup de feu), abattre; (*wound*) blesser (d'un coup de feu); (*execute*) fusiller; (*hunt*) chasser; (*gun*) tirer un coup de; (*bullet*) tirer; (*missile, Fig glance, questions*) lancer (**at** à); (*film, scene*) tourner; **to s. s.o. dead** tuer qn d'un coup de feu, abattre qn.
■ *vi* (*with gun, bow etc*) tirer (**at** sur); *Football etc* shooter. ●**shooting** *n* (*shots*) coups *mpl* de feu; (*murder*) meurtre *m*; (*execution*) fusillade *f*; (*of film, scene*) tournage *m*; (*hunting*) chasse *f*. ●**shoot-out** *n Fam* fusillade *f*.
shoot[2] [ʃuːt] *n* (*on plant*) pousse *f*.
shoot ahead *vi* (*move fast*) avancer à toute vitesse ■ **to shoot away** *vi* (*of vehicle, person etc*) partir à toute vitesse ■ **to shoot back** *vi* (*return fire*) riposter (à des coups de feu) ■ **to shoot down** *vt* (*aircraft*) abattre ■ **to shoot off** *vi* (*of vehicle, person etc*) partir à toute vitesse ■ **to shoot out** *vi* (*spurt out*) jaillir ■ **to shoot up** *vi* (*of price*) monter en flèche; (*grow*) pousser vite; (*spurt*) jaillir; (*of rocket*) s'élever.

shop [ʃɒp] **1** *n* magasin *m*; (*small*) boutique *f*; (*workshop*) atelier *m*; **at the baker's s.** à la boulangerie, chez le boulanger; **s. assistant** *Br* vendeur, -euse *mf*; **s. floor** (*workers*) *Br* ouvriers *mpl*; **s. front** *Br* devanture *f*; **s. steward** *Br* délégué, -ée *mf* syndical(e); **s. window** vitrine *f*.
■ *vi* (**-pp-**) faire ses courses (**at** chez); **to s. around** comparer les prix.
2 *vt* (**-pp-**) **to s. s.o.** *Br Fam* dénoncer qn (*à la police etc*). ●**shopping** *n* (*goods*) achats *mpl*; **to go s.** faire des courses *or* commis-

sions; **to do one's s.** faire ses courses *or* commissions.

■ *a* (*street, district*) commerçant; **s. bag/basket** sac *m*/panier *m* à provisions; **s. centre** centre *m* commercial; **s. list** liste *f* de commissions *or* de courses. ●**shopper** *n* (*customer*) client, -ente *mf*; (*bag*) *Br* sac *m* à provisions; **lots of shoppers** beaucoup de gens qui font leurs courses.
shopkeeper ['ʃɒpkiːpər] *n* commerçant, -ante *mf*. ●**shoplifter** *n* voleur, -euse *mf* à l'étalage. ●**shoplifting** *n* vol *m* à l'étalage. ●**shopsoiled** *or Am* **shopworn** *a* défraîchi.
shore [ʃɔːr] **1** *n* (*of sea, lake*) rivage *m*; (*coast*) côte *f*, bord *m* de (la) mer; (*beach*) plage *f*; **on s.** (*passenger*) à terre. **2** *vt* **to s. up** (*wall etc*) étayer; (*company, economy*) *Fig* consolider.
shorn [ʃɔːn] *a* (*head*) tondu; **s. of** (*stripped of*) *Lit* dénué de.
short [ʃɔːt] *a* (**-er, -est**) court; (*person, distance*) petit; (*syllable*) bref (*f* brève); (*impatient, curt*) brusque; **a s. time** *or* **while ago** il y a peu de temps; **to be s. of money/time** être à court d'argent/de temps; **we're s. of ten men** il nous manque dix hommes; **money/time is s.** l'argent/le temps manque; **in a s. time** *or* **while** dans un petit moment; **a s. time** *or* **while ago** il y a peu de temps; **I'll stay for a s. time** *or* **while** je resterai un petit moment; **s. of** (*except*) sauf; (*before*) avant; **not far s. of** pas loin de; **s. of a miracle** à moins d'un miracle; **to be s. for** (*of name*) être l'abréviation *or* le diminutif de; **in s. bref; **s. list** (*of applicants*) *Br* liste *f* de candidats retenus.
■ *adv* **to cut s.** (*hair*) couper court; (*visit etc*) raccourcir; (*person*) couper la parole à; **to go** *or* **get** *or* **run s. of** manquer de; **to get** *or* **run s.** manquer; **to stop s.** s'arrêter net.
■ *n El* (court-circuit *m*; (**a pair of**) **shorts** un short; (*boxer*) **shorts** caleçon *m*. ●**short cut** *n* raccourci *m*.
shortage ['ʃɔːtɪdʒ] *n* manque *m*, pénurie *f*; (*crisis*) crise *f*.
shortbread ['ʃɔːtbred] *n* sablé *m*. ●**short-'change** *vt* (*buyer*) ne pas rendre juste à. ●**short-'circuit** *n El* court-circuit *m* ■ *vt El & Fig* court-circuiter ■ *vi* (*of current*) *El* se mettre en court-circuit. ●**shortcoming** *n* défaut *m*. ●**shortfall** *n* manque *m*. ●**shorthand** *n* sténo *f*; **in s.** en sténo; **s. typist** sténodactylo *f*. ●**short-'handed** *a* à court de personnel. ●**short-'lived** *a* de courte durée, éphémère. ●**short'sighted** *a* myope; (*in one's judgments*) *Fig* myope, imprévoyant. ●**short'sightedness** *n* myopie *f*; *Fig* myopie *f*, imprévoyance *f*. ●**short-'sleeved** *a* à manches courtes. ●**short-'staffed** *a* à court de personnel. ●**short-'tempered** *a* irascible. ●**short-'term** *a* à court terme. ●**short-time 'working** *n Br* chômage *m* partiel.
shorten ['ʃɔːt(ə)n] *vt* (*dress, text, visit etc*) raccourcir.
shortening ['ʃɔːt(ə)nɪŋ] *n* (*cooking fat*) *Br*

matière f grasse.

shortly ['ʃɔːtlɪ] *adv* (*soon*) bientôt; **s. before/after** peu avant/après.

shortness ['ʃɔːtnəs] *n* (*of person*) petitesse *f*; (*of hair, stick, legs*) manque *m* de longueur.

shorts [ʃɔːts] *npl* (**a pair of**) **s.** un short; (**boxer**) **s.** caleçon *m*.

shot [ʃɒt] *pt & pp* shoot[1] ∎ *n* (*from gun*) coup *m*; (*bullet*) balle *f*; (*with camera*) prise *f* de vues; (*injection*) *Med* piqûre *f*; **to be a good s.** (*of person*) être bon tireur; **to have a s. at** (*doing*) **sth** essayer de faire qch; **it's a long s.** (*attempt*) c'est un coup à tenter; **big s.** (*important person*) *Fam* gros bonnet *m*; **like a s.** (*at once*) illico; **to be s. of s.o./sth** (*rid of*) *Fam* être débarrassé de qn/qch. ● **shot-gun** *n* fusil *m* (de chasse).

should [ʃʊd, *unstressed* ʃəd] *v aux* 1 (= *ought to*) **you s. do it** vous devriez le faire; **I s. have stayed** j'aurais dû rester; **that s. be Paul** ça doit être Paul. 2 (= *would*) **I s. like to stay** j'aimerais bien rester; **I s. like to** j'aimerais bien; **I s. hope so** j'espère bien; **it's strange (that) she s. say no** il est étrange qu'elle dise non. 3 (*possibility*) **if he s. come, s. he come** s'il vient.

shoulder ['ʃəʊldər] 1 *n* épaule *f*; **to have round shoulders** avoir le dos voûté, être voûté; (**hard**) **s.** (*of motorway*) *Br* bas-côté *m*, accotement *m* stabilisé; **s. bag** sac *m* à bandoulière; **s. blade** omoplate *f*; **s.-length hair** cheveux *mpl* mi-longs; **s. pad** (*on jacket*) épaulette *f*; **s. strap** (*on dress etc*) bretelle *f*. 2 *vt* (*responsibility*) endosser, assumer.

shout [ʃaʊt] *n* cri *m*; **to give s.o. a s.** appeler qn ∎ *vi* **to s. (out)** crier; **to s. to s.o. to do sth** crier à qn de faire qch; **to s. at s.o.** (*scold*) crier après qn ∎ *vt* **to s. (out)** (*insult etc*) crier; **to s. down** (*speaker*) huer. ● **shouting** *n* (*shouts*) cris *mpl*.

shove [ʃʌv] *n* poussée *f*; **to give a s. (to)** pousser ∎ *vt* pousser; (*put*) *Fam* fourrer; **to s. sth into sth** enfoncer *or* fourrer qch dans qch; **to s. s.o. around** *Fam* commander qn, régenter qn ∎ *vi* pousser; **to s. off** (*leave*) *Fam* ficher le camp, filer; **to s. over** (*move over*) *Fam* se pousser.

shovel ['ʃʌv(ə)l] *n* pelle *f* ∎ *vt* (**-ll-**, *Am* **-l-**) (*snow*) enlever à la pelle; (*grain etc*) pelleter; **to s. up** *or* **away** (*snow*) enlever à la pelle; **to s. up** (*leaves*) ramasser à la pelle; **to s. sth into sth** *Fam* fourrer qch dans qch.

show [ʃəʊ] *n Theatre TV* spectacle *m*; *Cinema* séance *f*; (*exhibition*) exposition *f*; (*of force, friendship etc*) démonstration *f*; (*pretence*) semblant *m* (**of** de); (*ostentation*) parade *f* (**of** de); **the Boat/Motor S.** *Br* le Salon de la Navigation/de l'Automobile; **film s.** séance *f* de cinéma; **horse s.** concours *m* hippique; **on s.** (*painting etc*) exposé; **to give a good s.** (*of sportsman, musician, actor etc*) *Br* jouer bien; **good s.!** bravo!; **it's (just) for s.** c'est pour l'effet; **to make a s. of** (*one's wealth etc*) faire parade de; **to make a s. of**

being angry faire semblant d'être en colère; **s. business** le monde du spectacle; **s. flat** *Br* appartement *m* témoin.

∎ *vt* (*pt* **showed**, *pp* **shown**) montrer (**to** à, **that** que); (*in exhibition*) exposer; (*film*) passer, donner; (*indicate*) indiquer, montrer; **to s. s.o. to the door** reconduire qn; **it (just) goes to s. that...** ça (dé)montre (bien) que...; **I'll s. him!** *Fam* je vais lui apprendre! ∎ *vi* (*be visible*) se voir; (*of film*) passer; **'now showing'** (*film*) 'à l'affiche' (**at** à).

show around *vt* **to s. s.o. around** faire visiter qn; **she was shown around the house** on lui a fait visiter la maison ∎ **to show in** *vt* (*visitor*) faire entrer ∎ **to show off** *vt* (*display*) *Pej* étaler (*richesses etc*); (*highlight*) faire valoir ∎ *vi Pej* crâner. ● **show-off** *n Pej* crâneur, -euse *mf*. ∎ **to show out** *vt* (*visitor*) reconduire ∎ **to show round** *vt* = **show around** ∎ **to show up** *vt* (*embarrass, humiliate*) mettre (*qn*) dans l'embarras; (*fault etc*) faire ressortir ∎ *vi* (*stand out*) ressortir (**against** contre); (*of error etc*) être visible; (*of person*) *Fam* arriver, s'amener.

showcase ['ʃəʊkeɪs] *n* vitrine *f*. ● **showdown** *n* confrontation *f*, conflit *m*. ● **showgirl** *n* (*in chorus etc*) girl *f*. ● **showjumping** *n Sport* jumping *m*. ● **showmanship** *n* art *m* de la mise en scène. ● **showpiece** *n* modèle *m* du genre. ● **showroom** *n* (*for cars etc*) salle *f* d'exposition.

shower ['ʃaʊər] *n* (*bathing, device*) douche *f*; (*of rain*) averse *f*; (*of blows*) déluge *m*; (*party*) *Am* réception *f* (*pour la remise de cadeaux*); **to have** *or* **take a s.** prendre une douche ∎ *vt* **to s. s.o. with** (*gifts, abuse etc*) couvrir qn de. ● **showery** *a* pluvieux.

showing ['ʃəʊɪŋ] *n* (*film show*) séance *f*, projection *f*; (*of team, player*) performance *f*.

shown [ʃəʊn] *pp* of show.

showy ['ʃəʊɪ] *a* (**-ier, -iest**) (*colour, hat*) voyant; (*person*) prétentieux.

shrank [ʃræŋk] *pt* of shrink 1.

shrapnel ['ʃræpn(ə)l] *n* éclats *mpl* d'obus.

shred [ʃred] *n* lambeau *m*; **not a s. of truth** *Fig* pas un grain de vérité; **not a s. of evidence** pas la moindre preuve ∎ *vt* (**-dd-**) mettre en lambeaux; (*cabbage, carrots*) râper. ● **shredder** *n Culin* râpe *f*; (*in office*) destructeur *m* de documents.

shrew [ʃruː] *n* (*woman*) *Pej* mégère *f*.

shrewd [ʃruːd] *a* (**-er, -est**) (*person, plan*) astucieux. ● **shrewdly** *adv* astucieusement. ● **shrewdness** *n* astuce *f*.

shriek [ʃriːk] *n* cri *m* (aigu) ∎ *vi* crier; **to s. with pain/laughter** hurler de douleur/de rire.

shrift [ʃrɪft] *n* **to get short s.** être traité sans ménagement.

shrill [ʃrɪl] *a* (**-er, -est**) aigu (*f* **-uë**), strident.

shrimp [ʃrɪmp] *n* crevette *f* (grise); (*small person*) *Pej* nabot, -ote *mf*; (*child*) *Pej* puce *f*.

shrine [ʃraɪn] *n* (*place of worship*) lieu *m* saint; (*tomb*) châsse *f*.

shrink [ʃrɪŋk] 1 vi (pt **shrank** or Am **shrunk**, pp **shrunk** or **shrunken**) (of clothes) rétrécir; (of aging person) se tasser; (of audience, amount etc) diminuer; **to s. from an obligation/etc** reculer devant une obligation/etc; **to s. from doing sth** reculer devant l'idée de faire qch ∎ vt rétrécir. 2 n (person) Am Hum psy(chiatre) m. ● **shrinkage** n rétrécissement m; (of audience etc) diminution f. ● **shrink-wrapped** a emballé sous pellicule plastique.

shrivel ['ʃrɪv(ə)l] vi (Br **-ll-**, Am **-l-**) **to s. (up)** se ratatiner ∎ vt **to s. (up)** ratatiner.

shroud [ʃraʊd] n linceul m; **a s. of mystery** Fig un voile de mystère ∎ vt **shrouded in mist** enseveli or enveloppé sous la brume; **shrouded in mystery** Fig enveloppé de mystère.

Shrove Tuesday [Br ʃrəʊv'tjuːzdɪ, Am - deɪ] n Mardi m gras.

shrub [ʃrʌb] n arbuste m. ● **shrubbery** n massif m d'arbustes.

shrug [ʃrʌg] vt (-gg-) **to s. one's shoulders** hausser les épaules; **to s. off** (dismiss) écarter (dédaigneusement) ∎ n haussement m d'épaules; **with a s. of his shoulders** en haussant les épaules.

shrunk(en) ['ʃrʌŋk(ən)] pp of **shrink** 1.

shudder ['ʃʌdər] vi (of person) frémir (**with** de); (of machine etc) vibrer; **I s. to think of it** je n'ose pas y penser ∎ n frémissement m; (of machine etc) vibration f.

shuffle ['ʃʌf(ə)l] 1 vt (cards) battre. 2 vti **to s. (one's feet)** traîner les pieds.

shun [ʃʌn] vt (-nn-) fuir, éviter.

shunt [ʃʌnt] vt (train, Fig conversation) aiguiller (**on to** sur); **we were shunted (to and fro)** Fam on nous a baladés (**from office to office/etc** de bureau en bureau/etc).

shush! [ʃʊʃ] int chut! [ʃyt].

shut [ʃʌt] vt (pt & pp **shut**, pp **shutting**) fermer; **to s. one's finger in a door/etc** se prendre le doigt dans une porte/etc ∎ vi (of door etc) se fermer; (of shop, museum etc) fermer; **the door doesn't s.** la porte ne ferme pas. ● **shutdown** n (of factory etc) fermeture f.

shut away vt (lock away) enfermer ∎ **to shut down** vt fermer ∎ vi (of shop) fermer (définitivement) ∎ **to shut in** vt (lock in) enfermer ∎ **to shut off** vt (gas etc) fermer; (engine) arrêter; (isolate) isoler ∎ **to shut out** vt (light) empêcher d'entrer; (view) boucher; (exclude) exclure (**of, from** de); **to s. s.o. out** (lock out accidentally) enfermer qn dehors ∎ **to shut up** vt (house etc) fermer; (lock up) enfermer (personne, objet précieux etc); (silence) Fam faire taire (qn) ∎ vi (be quiet) Fam se taire.

shutter ['ʃʌtər] n (on window) volet m; (of shop) rideau m (métallique); (of camera) obturateur m.

shuttle ['ʃʌt(ə)l] n (bus, train, plane etc) navette f; **space s.** navette spatiale; **s. service** navette f ∎ vi faire la navette ∎ vt (by bus,

train, plane etc) transporter.

shuttlecock ['ʃʌt(ə)lkɒk] n (in badminton) volant m.

shy [ʃaɪ] a (-er, -est) timide; **to be s. of doing sth** avoir peur de faire qch ∎ vi **to s. away from s.o./from doing sth** reculer devant qn/à l'idée de faire qch; **you're always shying away!** tu te défiles tout le temps! ● **shyness** n timidité f.

Siamese [saɪə'miːz] a **S. cat** chat m siamois; **S. twins** frères mpl siamois, sœurs fpl siamoises.

sibling ['sɪblɪŋ] n frère m, sœur f.

Sicily ['sɪsɪlɪ] n Sicile f. ● **Si'cilian** a sicilien ∎ n Sicilien, -ienne mf.

sick [sɪk] a (-er, -est) (ill) malade; (mind) malsain; (humour) noir; (cruel) sadique; (perverted) détraqué; **to be s.** (vomit) vomir; **to be off or away s., to be on s. leave** être en congé de maladie; **to feel s.** avoir mal au cœur; **to be s. (and tired) of sth/s.o.** Fam en avoir marre de qch/qn; **he makes me s.** Fam il m'écœure ∎ n (vomit) Br Fam vomi m; **the s.** (sick people) les malades mpl ∎ vi **to s.(up)** (vomit) Br Fam vomir ∎ vt **to s. sth up** Br Fam vomir qch. ● **sickbay** n infirmerie f. ● **sickbed** n lit m de malade.

sicken ['sɪkən] 1 vt écœurer. 2 vi **to be sickening for** (illness) Br couver; **you must be sickening for something** tu dois couver quelque chose. ● **sickening** a écœurant.

sickly ['sɪklɪ] a (-ier, -iest) maladif; (pale, faint) pâle; (taste) écœurant.

sickness ['sɪknɪs] n (illness) maladie f; (vomiting) vomissement(s) m(pl); **motion s.** (in car etc) mal m de la route; **s. benefit** Br prestations fpl d'assurance-maladie.

side [saɪd] n côté m; (of hill, animal) flanc m; (of road, river) bord m; (of beef) quartier m; (of question) aspect m; (of character) aspect m, facette f; (team) équipe f; (political party) parti m; **the right s.** (of fabric) l'endroit m; **the wrong s.** (of fabric) l'envers m; **at or by the s. of** (nearby) à côté de; **at or by my s.** à côté de moi, à mes côtés; **s. by s.** l'un à côté de l'autre; **to move to one s.** s'écarter; **on this s.** de ce côté; **on the other s.** de l'autre côté; **another s.** (TV channel) une autre chaîne; **it's on the big/etc s.** Fam c'est plutôt grand/etc; **to take sides with s.o.** se ranger du côté de qn; **she's on our s.** elle est de notre côté or avec nous; **to change sides** changer de camp; **to do sth on the s.** (as an extra) faire qch en plus; (illegally) faire qch au noir; **to earn money on the s.** (illegally) travailler au noir.

∎ a (lateral) latéral; (view, glance) de côté; (street) transversal; (effect, issue) secondaire. ∎ vi **to s. with s.o.** se ranger du côté de qn. ● **-sided** suff **ten-s.** à dix côtés.

sideboard ['saɪdbɔːd] n buffet m. ● **sideboards** npl (hair) Br pattes fpl. ● **sideburns** npl (hair) Am pattes fpl. ● **sidecar** n side-car m. ● **sidekick** n Fam associé, -ée mf. ● **side-**

light n (on vehicle) Br veilleuse f. ●**sideline** n (activity) activité f secondaire; (around playing field) ligne f de touche. ●**sidesaddle** adv **to ride** s. monter en amazone. ●**sidestep** vt (-pp-) éviter. ●**sidetrack** vt **to get sidetracked** s'écarter du sujet. ●**sidewalk** n Am trottoir m. ●**sideways** adv (to look, walk etc) de côté **I** a a s. **look/move/etc** un regard/mouvement/etc de côté.

siding ['saɪdɪŋ] n Rail voie f de garage.

sidle ['saɪd(ə)l] vi **to s. up to s.o.** s'approcher furtivement de qn.

siege [siːdʒ] n (by soldiers, police etc) siège m; **to lay s. to** faire le siège de, assiéger.

siesta [sɪ'estə] n sieste f; **to take** or **have a s.** faire la sieste.

sieve [sɪv] n tamis m; (for liquids) passoire f; (with coarse mesh for stones etc) crible m **I** vt tamiser. ●**sift** vt (flour etc) tamiser; (stones etc) cribler; **to s. out the truth** Fig dégager la vérité **I** vi **to s. through** (papers etc) examiner (à la loupe).

sigh [saɪ] n soupir m **I** vi soupirer; **to s. with relief** pousser un soupir de soulagement **-** vt **'yes', she sighed** 'oui', soupira-t-elle.

sight [saɪt] n vue f; (thing seen) spectacle m; (on gun) mire f; **to lose s. of** perdre de vue; **to catch s. of** apercevoir; **to come into s.** apparaître; **at first s.** à première vue; **by s.** de vue; **on s.** à vue; **in s.** (target, end, date etc) en vue; **out of s.** (hidden) caché; (no longer visible) disparu; **to disappear out of s. or from s.** disparaître; **keep out of s.!** ne te montre pas!; **he hates the s. of me** il ne peut pas me voir; **it's a lovely s.** c'est beau à voir; **the (tourist) sights** les attractions fpl touristiques; **to set one's sights on** (job etc) viser; **a s. longer/etc** Fam bien plus long/etc. **I** vt (land) apercevoir. ●**sighted** a qui voit, clairvoyant. ●**sighting** n **to make a s. of** voir.

sightseer ['saɪtsɪər] n touriste mf. ●**sightseeing** n **to go s., do some s.** faire du tourisme m.

sightly ['saɪtlɪ] a **not very s.** pas très beau à voir.

sign [saɪn] **1** n signe m; (notice) panneau m; (over shop, inn) enseigne f; **no s. of** aucune trace de; **to use s. language** parler par signes; **call s.** Radio indicatif m d'appel.
2 vt (put one's signature to) signer; **to s. sth away** or **over** céder qch (to à); **to s. on** or **up** (worker, soldier) engager.
I vi signer; **to s. for** (letter) signer le reçu de; **to s. in** (in hotel etc) signer le registre; **to s. off** (say goodbye) dire au revoir; **to s. on** (on the dole) Br s'inscrire au chômage; **to s. on** or **up** (of soldier, worker) s'engager; (for course) s'inscrire.

signal ['sɪgnəl] n signal m; **busy s.** (on telephone) Am sonnerie f 'occupé'; **traffic signals** feux mpl de circulation; **call s.** indicatif m d'appel; **s. box** Br, **s. tower** Am Rail poste m d'aiguillage **I** vt (Br -ll-, Am -l-) (be a sign of) indiquer; (arrival etc) signaler (to à); (message) communiquer (to à) **I** vi faire

des signaux; (of driver, with indicators) mettre son clignotant; **to s. (to) s.o. to do sth** faire signe à qn de faire qch. ●**signalman** n (pl -men) Rail aiguilleur m.

signature ['sɪgnətʃər] n signature f; **s. tune** indicatif m (musical). ●**signatory** n signataire mf.

signet ring ['sɪgnɪtrɪŋ] n chevalière f.

significant [sɪg'nɪfɪkənt] a (important, large) important; (meaningful) significatif. ●**significance** n (meaning) signification f; (importance) importance f. ●**significantly** adv (appreciably) sensiblement; **s., he...** fait significatif, il....

signify ['sɪgnɪfaɪ] vt (mean) signifier (that que); (make known) indiquer, signifier (to à).

signpost ['saɪnpəʊst] n poteau m indicateur **I** vt flécher.

Sikh [siːk] a sikh **I** n sikh, -e mf.

silence ['saɪləns] n silence m; **in s.** en silence **I** vt faire taire. ●**silencer** n (on car, gun) silencieux m.

silent ['saɪlənt] a (film, anger) muet (f muette); **to keep** or **be s.** garder le silence (about sur). ●**silently** adv silencieusement.

silhouette [sɪluː'et] n silhouette f. ●**silhouetted** a **to be s. against** se profiler contre.

silicon ['sɪlɪkən] n silicium m; **s. chip** puce f de silicium.

silicone ['sɪlɪkəʊn] n silicone f.

silk [sɪlk] n soie f. **s. dress/etc** robe f/etc de or en soie. ●**silky** a (-ier, -iest) soyeux.

sill [sɪl] n (of window) rebord m.

silly ['sɪlɪ] a (-ier, -iest) bête, idiot; **to do something s.** faire une bêtise; **to laugh oneself s.** mourir de rire; **s. fool,** Br Fam **s. billy** idiot, -ote mf **I** adv (to act, behave) bêtement. ●**silliness** n bêtise f.

silo ['saɪləʊ] n (pl -os) silo m.

silt [sɪlt] n vase f.

silver ['sɪlvər] n argent m; (plates etc) argenterie f; **£5 in s.** Br 5 livres en pièces d'argent **I** a (spoon etc) en argent, d'argent; (hair, colour) argenté; **s. jubilee** vingt-cinquième anniversaire m (d'un événement); **s. paper** Br papier m d'argent; **s. plate** argenterie f. ●**silver-'plated** a plaqué argent. ●**silversmith** n orfèvre m. ●**silverware** n argenterie f. ●**silvery** a (colour) argenté.

similar ['sɪmɪlər] a semblable (to à). ●**similarity** n ressemblance f (between entre, to avec). ●**similarly** adv de la même façon; (likewise) de même.

simile ['sɪmɪlɪ] n (comparison) comparaison f.

simmer ['sɪmər] vi (of vegetables etc) mijoter, cuire à feu doux; (of water) frémir; (of revolt, hatred etc) couver; **to s. with rage** bouillir de rage; **to s. down** (calm down) Fam se calmer **I** vt (vegetables etc) faire cuire à feu doux; (water) laisser frémir.

simper ['sɪmpər] vi sourire niaisement; (in

affected manner) minauder. ●**simpering** *a (person)* au sourire niais; minaudier.

simple ['sɪmp(ə)l] *a* (**-er, -est**) *(plain, basic, easy etc)* simple. ●**simple-'minded** *a* simple d'esprit. ●**simple-'mindedness** *n* simplicité *f* d'esprit. ●**simpleton** *n* nigaud, -aude *mf*. ●**sim'plicity** *n* simplicité *f*.

simplify ['sɪmplɪfaɪ] *vt* simplifier. ●**simplification** [-'keɪʃ(ə)n] *n* simplification *f*.

simplistic [sɪm'plɪstɪk] *a* simpliste.

simply ['sɪmplɪ] *adv (plainly, merely)* simplement; *(absolutely)* absolument.

simulate ['sɪmjʊleɪt] *vt* simuler.

simultaneous [*Br* sɪməl'teɪnɪəs, *Am* saɪməl-'teɪnɪəs] *a* simultané. ●**simultaneously** *adv* simultanément.

sin [sɪn] *n* péché *m* ▮ *vi* (**-nn-**) pécher.

since [sɪns] **1** *prep (in time)* depuis; **s. my departure** depuis mon départ ▮ *conj* depuis que; **s. she's been here** depuis qu'elle est ici; **it's a year s. I saw him** ça fait un an que je ne l'ai pas vu ▮ *adv (ever)* **s.** depuis. **2** *conj (because)* puisque.

sincere [sɪn'sɪər] *a* sincère. ●**sincerely** *adv* sincèrement; **yours s.** *Br*, **sincerely** *Am (in letter)* *Com* veuillez croire à mes sentiments dévoués. ●**sin'cerity** *n* sincérité *f*.

sinew ['sɪnjuː] *n Anat* tendon *m*.

sinful ['sɪnfəl] *a (guilt-provoking) (act etc)* coupable; *(shocking) (waste etc)* scandaleux; **he's s.** c'est un pécheur; **that's s.** c'est un péché.

sing [sɪŋ] *vti (pt* **sang**, *pp* **sung**) chanter; **to s. up** chanter plus fort. ●**singing** *n (of bird & musical technique)* chant *m*; *(way of singing)* façon *f* de chanter ▮ **s. lesson/teacher** leçon *f*/professeur *m* de chant. ●**singer** *n* chanteur, -euse *mf*.

Singapore [sɪŋgə'pɔːr] *n* Singapour *m*.

singe [sɪndʒ] *vt (cloth)* roussir; *(hair)* brûler; **to s. s.o.'s hair** *(at hairdresser's)* faire un brûlage à qn.

single ['sɪŋg(ə)l] *a (only one)* seul; *(room, bed)* pour une personne; *(unmarried)* célibataire; **not a s. book**/*etc* pas un seul livre/*etc*; **every s. day** tous les jours sans exception; **s. ticket** *Br* billet *m* simple; **s. parent** père *m* or mère *f* célibataire; **s.-parent family** famille *f* monoparentale; **s. party** *Pol* parti *m* unique; **s. European market** marché *m* unique européen.

▮ *n (ticket) Br* aller *m* (simple); *(record)* 45 tours *m inv*; **singles** *Tennis* simples *mpl*; **singles bar** bar *m* pour célibataires.

▮ *vt* **to s. out** *(choose)* choisir.

single-breasted [sɪŋg(ə)l'brestɪd] *a (jacket)* droit. ●**single-decker** *n (bus)* autobus *m* sans impériale. ●**single-handed** *a* sans aide. ●**single-minded** *a (person)* résolu, qui n'a qu'une idée en tête. ●**single-mindedly** *adv* résolument. ●**single-sex 'school** *n Br* école *f* non mixte.

singlet ['sɪŋglɪt] *n (garment) Br* maillot *m* de corps.

singly ['sɪŋglɪ] *adv (one by one)* un à un.

singsong ['sɪŋsɒŋ] *n* **to get together for a s.** se réunir pour chanter.

singular ['sɪŋgjʊlər] **1** *a (unusual)* singulier. **2** *a (form)* singulier; *(noun)* au singulier ▮ *n* singulier *m*; **in the s.** au singulier.

sinister ['sɪnɪstər] *a* sinistre.

sink¹ [sɪŋk] *n (in kitchen)* évier *m*; *(washbasin)* lavabo *m*.

sink² [sɪŋk] *vi (pt* **sank**, *pp* **sunk**) *(of ship, person etc)* couler; *(of water level, sun, price)* baisser; *(collapse, subside)* s'affaisser; **my heart sank** j'ai eu un pincement de cœur; **to s. (down) into** *(mud)* s'enfoncer dans; *(armchair)* s'affaler dans; **to s. in** *(of ink, water etc)* pénétrer; *(of fact, idea etc) Fam* rentrer (dans le crâne); **has that sunk in?** *Fam* as-tu compris ça?

▮ *vt (ship)* couler; *(well)* creuser; **to s. a knife**/*etc* **into sth** enfoncer un couteau/*etc* dans qch; **to s. money into a company**/*etc* investir de l'argent dans une société/*etc*; **a sinking feeling** un serrement de cœur.

sinner ['sɪnər] *n* pécheur *m*, pécheresse *f*.

sinuous ['sɪnjʊəs] *a* sinueux.

sinus [saɪnəs] *n Anat* sinus *m inv*. ●**sinusitis** [saɪnə'saɪtəs] *n* sinusite *f*; **to have s.** avoir or faire de la sinusite.

sip [sɪp] *vt* (**-pp-**) boire à petites gorgées ▮ *n (mouthful)* petite gorgée *f*; *(drop)* goutte *f*.

siphon ['saɪfən] *n* siphon *m* ▮ *vt* **to s. off** *(money) (draw off)* éponger; *(illegally)* détourner; *(liquid, Br petrol, Am gas)* siphonner.

sir [sɜːr] *n* monsieur *m*; **S. Walter Raleigh** *(title)* sir Walter Raleigh.

siren ['saɪərən] *n (of factory etc)* sirène *f*.

sirloin ['sɜːlɔɪn] *n (beef)* aloyau *m*.

sissy ['sɪsɪ] *n (boy, man) Fam* femmelette *f*.

sister ['sɪstər] *n* sœur *f*; *(nurse)* infirmière *f* en chef. ●**sister-in-law** *n (pl* **sisters-in-law**) belle-sœur *f*. ●**sisterly** *a* fraternel.

sit [sɪt] *vi (pp & pp* **sat**, *pres p* **sitting**) s'asseoir; *(for artist)* poser *(for* pour*)*; *(of assembly etc)* siéger, être en séance; **to s. at home** rester chez soi; **to be sitting** *(of person, cat etc)* être assis; **to be sitting on its perch** *(of bird)* être sur son perchoir; **she was sitting reading, she sat reading** elle était assise à lire ▮ *vt (child on chair etc)* asseoir; *(exam) Br* se présenter à.

sit around *vi (hang around)* traîner; *(do nothing)* ne rien faire ▮ **to sit back** *vi (in chair)* se caler; *(rest)* se reposer; *(do nothing)* ne rien faire ▮ **to sit down** *vi* s'asseoir; **to be sitting down** être assis ▮ *vt* **to s. (down) asseoir** qn ▮ **to sit for** *vt (exam) Br* se présenter à ▮ **to sit in on** *vt (lecture etc)* assister à ▮ **to sit on** *vt (jury etc)* être membre de; *(fact etc) Fam* garder pour soi ▮ **to sit out** *vt (event, dance)* ne pas prendre part à; *(film)* rester jusqu'au bout de ▮ **to sit through** *vt (film etc)* rester jusqu'au bout de ▮ **to sit up** *vi* **to s. up (straight)** s'asseoir (bien droit); **to s. up waiting for s.o.** *(at night)* ne pas se coucher en attendant qn.

sit-down ['sɪtdaʊn] *a* s.-down meal repas *m* servi à table; s.-down strike grève *f* sur le tas.

site [saɪt] *n* (*position*) emplacement *m*; (*archeological*) site *m*; (*building*) s. chantier *m*; launch(ing) s. aire *f* de lancement ▌ *vt* (*building*) placer.

sit-in ['sɪtɪn] *n* (*protest*) sit-in *m inv*.

sitter ['sɪtər] *n* (*for child*) baby-sitter *mf*.

sitting ['sɪtɪŋ] *n* séance *f*; (*for one's portrait*) séance *f* de pose; (*in restaurant*) service *m* ▌ *a* (*committee etc*) en séance; s. duck *Fam* victime *f* facile; s. tenant locataire *mf* en possession des lieux. ●**sitting room** *n* salon *m*.

situate ['sɪtʃəʊeɪt] *vt* situer; to be situated être situé. ●**situation** [-'eɪʃ(ə)n] *n* situation *f*.

six [sɪks] *a* & *n* six (*m*). ●**sixth** *a* & *n* sixième (*mf*); (*lower*) s. form *Br Sch* = classe *f* de première; (*upper*) s. form *Br Sch* = classe *f* terminale; a s. (*fraction*) un sixième.

sixteen [sɪk'stiːn] *a* & *n* seize (*m*). ●**sixteenth** *a* & *n* seizième (*mf*).

sixty ['sɪkstɪ] *a* & *n* soixante (*m*). ●**sixtieth** *a* & *n* soixantième (*mf*).

size [saɪz] 1 *n* (*of person, animal, clothes etc*) taille *f*; (*measurements*) dimensions *fpl*; (*of egg, fruit*) grosseur *f*; (*of packet*) taille *f*, grosseur *f*; (*of book*) grandeur *f*, format *m*; (*of town, damage, problem*) importance *f*, étendue *f*; (*of sum*) montant *m*, importance *f*; (*of shoes, gloves*) pointure *f*; (*of shirt*) encolure *f*; hip/chest s. tour *m* de hanches/de poitrine; it's the s. of... c'est grand comme... 2 *n* (*glue*) colle *f*. 3 *vt* to s. up (*person*) jauger; (*situation*) évaluer.

sizeable ['saɪzəb(ə)l] *a* assez grand *or* gros.

sizzle ['sɪz(ə)l] *vi* grésiller. ●**sizzling** *a* s. (hot) brûlant.

skate[1] [skeɪt] *n* patin *m* ▌ *vi* patiner. ●**skating** *n* patinage *m*; to go s. faire du patinage; s. rink (*ice-skating*) patinoire *f*; (*roller-skating*) skating *m*. ●**skateboard** *n* planche *f* à roulettes. ●**skater** *n* patineur, -euse *mf*.

skate[2] [skeɪt] *n* (*fish*) raie *f*.

skedaddle [skɪ'dæd(ə)l] *vi Fam* déguerpir.

skein [skeɪn] *n* (*of yarn*) écheveau *m*.

skeleton ['skelɪt(ə)n] *n* squelette *m* ▌ *a* (*crew, staff*) (réduit au) minimum, squelettique; s. key passe-partout *m inv*.

skeptic ['skeptɪk] *a* & *n Am* = sceptic.

sketch [sketʃ] *n* (*drawing*) croquis *m*, esquisse *f*; (*comic play*) sketch *m*; a rough s. of the situation/*etc* un résumé rapide de la situation/*etc* ▌ *vt* to s. (out) (*idea, view etc*) exposer brièvement; to s. in (*details*) ajouter ▌ *vi* faire un *or* des croquis. ●**sketchbook** *n* cahier *m* de croquis. ●**sketchy** *a* (-ier, -iest) incomplet, superficiel.

skew [skjuː] *n* on the s. de travers.

skewer ['skjʊər] *n* (*for meat etc*) broche *f*; (*for kebab*) brochette *f*.

ski [skiː] *n* (*pl* skis) ski *m*; s. boot chaussure *f* de ski; s. jump (*slope*) tremplin *m*; (*jump*) saut *m* à skis; s. lift remonte-pente *m*; s. mask *Am* cagoule *f*, passe-montagne *m*; s. pants fuseau *m*; s. run piste *f* de ski; s. tow téléski *m*; s. wax fart *m* ▌ *vi* (*pt* skied [skiːd], *pres p* skiing) faire du ski. ●**skiing** *n* (*sport*) ski *m* ▌ *a* (*school, clothes etc*) de ski; s. holiday *Br*, s. vacation *Am* vacances *fpl* de neige *or* aux sports d'hiver. ●**skier** *n* skieur, -euse *mf*.

skid [skɪd] 1 *vi* (-dd-) (*of vehicle*) déraper; to s. into sth déraper et heurter qch ▌ *n* dérapage *m*. 2 *a* s. row *Am* quartier *m* de clochards *or* de squats.

skill [skɪl] *n* habileté *f*, adresse *f* (at à); (*technique*) technique *f*; one's skills (*aptitudes*) ses compétences *fpl*. ●**skilful** *or Am* **skillful** *a* habile (at doing à faire, at sth en qch). ●**skilled** *a* habile (at doing à faire, at sth en qch); (*worker*) qualifié; (*work*) de spécialiste, de professionnel.

skillet ['skɪlɪt] *n Am* poêle *f* (à frire).

skim [skɪm] 1 *vt* (-mm-) (*milk*) écrémer; (*soup*) écumer; skimmed milk lait *m* écrémé. 2 *vti* (-mm-) to s. (over) (*surface*) effleurer; to s. through (*book*) parcourir.

skimp [skɪmp] *vi* (*on food, fabric etc*) lésiner (on sur). ●**skimpy** *a* (-ier, -iest) (*clothes*) étriqué; (*meal*) insuffisant.

skin [skɪn] *n* peau *f*; he has thick s. *Fig* c'est un dur; s. cancer cancer *m* de la peau; s. diving plongée *f* sous-marine; s. test cuti-(réaction) *f* ▌ *vt* (-nn-) (*fruit*) peler; (*animal*) écorcher. ●**skin-'deep** *a* superficiel. ●**skin-'tight** *a* moulant, collant.

skinflint ['skɪnflɪnt] *n* avare *mf*.

skinhead ['skɪnhed] *n Br* skin(head) *m*.

skinny ['skɪnɪ] *a* (-ier, -iest) maigre.

skint [skɪnt] *a* (*penniless*) *Br Fam* fauché.

skip[1] [skɪp] 1 *vi* (-pp-) (*hop about*) sautiller; (*with rope*) *Br* sauter à la corde; to s. off (*leave*) *Fam* filer; skipping rope *Br* corde *f* à sauter ▌ *n* petit saut *m*. 2 *vt* (-pp-) (*miss, omit*) sauter (*repas, classe, paragraphe etc*); to s. classes (*miss school*) sécher les cours; s. it! (*forget it*) *Fam* laisse tomber!

skip[2] [skɪp] *n* (*container for rubbish*) *Br* benne *f*.

skipper ['skɪpər] *n* (*of ship, team*) capitaine *m*.

skirmish ['skɜːmɪʃ] *n* accrochage *m*.

skirt [skɜːt] 1 *n* jupe *f*. 2 *vt* to s. round (*bypass, go round*) contourner ●**skirting board** *n* (*on wall*) *Br* plinthe *f*.

skit [skɪt] *n* (*play*) pièce *f* satirique; a s. on une parodie de.

skittish ['skɪtɪʃ] *a* (*person*) frivole; (*temperamental*) capricieux.

skittle ['skɪt(ə)l] *n Br* quille *f*; skittles (*game*) jeu *m* de quilles; to play skittles jouer aux quilles.

skive [skaɪv] *vi Br Fam* (*shirk*) tirer au flanc; to s. off (*slip away*) se défiler. ●**skiver** *n Br Fam* tire-au-flanc *m inv*.

skivvy ['skɪvɪ] *n Br Pej Fam* bonne *f* à tout faire, bon(n)iche *f*.

skulk 310

skulk [skʌlk] *vi* rôder (furtivement).
skull [skʌl] *n* crâne *m*. ● **skullcap** *n* calotte *f*.
skunk [skʌŋk] *n* (*animal*) mouffette *f*; (*person*) *Pej* salaud *m*.
sky [skaɪ] *n* ciel *m*. ● **sky-blue** *a* bleu ciel *inv*. ● **skydiving** *n* parachutisme *m* (en chute libre). ● **sky-high** *a* (*prices*) exorbitant. ● **skylark** *n* alouette *f*. ● **skylight** *n* lucarne *f*. ● **skyline** *n* (*outline of buildings*) ligne *f* d'horizon. ● **skyrocket** *vi* (*of prices*) *Fam* monter en flèche. ● **skyscraper** *n* gratte-ciel *m inv*.
slab [slæb] *n* (*of concrete etc*) bloc *m*; (*thin, flat*) plaque *f*; (*of chocolate*) tablette *f*, plaque *f*; (*of meat*) tranche *f* épaisse; (*paving stone*) dalle *f*.
slack [slæk] *a* (-er, -est) (*knot, spring*) lâche; (*discipline, security*) relâché, lâche; (*grip*) faible, mou (*f* molle); (*business*) calme; (*careless, negligent*) négligent; (*worker, student*) peu sérieux; **s. periods** (*weeks etc*) périodes *fpl* creuses; (*hours*) heures *fpl* creuses; **to be s.** (*of rope*) avoir du mou; (*in office etc*) être calme ▌ *vi* **to s. off** (*in effort*) se relâcher.
slacken [ˈslæk(ə)n] *vi* **to s. (off)** (*in effort*) se relâcher; (*of production, demand, speed, enthusiasm*) diminuer ▌ *vt* **to s. (off)** (*rope*) relâcher; (*pace, effort*) ralentir.
slacker [ˈslækər] *n* (*person*) *Fam* flemmard, -arde *mf*.
slackly [ˈslæklɪ] *adv* (*loosely*) lâchement. ● **slackness** *n* (*of person*) négligence *f*; (*of discipline*) relâchement *m*; (*of rope*) mou *m*; (*of trade*) stagnation *f*.
slacks [slæks] *npl* pantalon *m*.
slag [slæg] **1** *n* (*immoral woman*) *Offensive Br Sl* salope *f*, traînée *f*. **2** *vt* **to s. s.o. off** (*criticize*) *Br Sl* débiner qn, casser du sucre sur le dos de qn.
slagheap [ˈslæghiːp] *n* (*near mine*) terril *m*; (*near steelworks*) crassier *m*.
slain [sleɪn] *pp* of **slay**.
slake [sleɪk] *vt* (*thirst*) *Lit* étancher.
slalom [ˈslɑːləm] *n* (*ski race*) slalom *m*.
slam [slæm] **1** *vt* (-mm-) (*door, lid*) claquer; (*hit*) frapper violemment; **to s. (down)** (*put down*) poser violemment; **to s. on the brakes** écraser le frein, freiner à bloc ▌ *vi* (*of door*) claquer ▌ *n* claquement *m*. **2** *vt* (-mm-) (*criticize*) *Fam* critiquer (avec virulence).
slander [ˈslɑːndər] *n* diffamation *f*, calomnie *f* ▌ *vt* diffamer, calomnier.
slang [slæŋ] *n* argot *m* ▌ *a* (*word etc*) d'argot, argotique; **s. expression** expression *f* argotique. ● **slanging match** *n* *Br Fam* engueulade *f*.
slant [slɑːnt] *n* inclinaison *f*; (*point of view*) *Fig* angle *m* (**on** sur); (*bias*) *Fig* parti-pris *m*; **on a s.** penché; (*roof*) en pente ▌ *vi* (*of roof*) être en pente; (*of writing*) pencher ▌ *vt* (*writing*) faire pencher; (*news*) *Fig* présenter de façon partiale. ● **slanted** *or* **slanting** *a* penché; (*roof*) en pente.
slap [slæp] **1** *n* tape *f*, claque *f*; (*on face*) gifle

f ▌ *vt* (-pp-) (*person*) donner une tape à; **to s. s.o.'s face** gifler qn; **to s. s.o.'s bottom** donner une fessée à qn. **2** *vt* (-pp-) (*put*) mettre, flanquer; **to s. on** (*apply*) appliquer à la va-vite; (*add*) ajouter. **3** *adv* **s. in the middle** *Fam* en plein milieu.
slapdash [ˈslæpdæʃ] *a* (*person*) négligent; (*task*) fait à la va-vite ▌ *adv* (*carelessly*) à la va-vite.
slaphappy [slæpˈhæpɪ] *a* *Fam* (*negligent*) je-m'en-fichiste; (*carefree*) insouciant.
slapstick [ˈslæpstɪk] *a* & *n* **s.** (**comedy**) grosse farce *f*.
slap-up [ˈslæpʌp] *a* **s.-up meal** *Br Fam* gueuleton *m*.
slash [slæʃ] **1** *vt* (*cut with blade etc*) taillader, entailler; (*sever*) trancher ▌ *n* entaille *f*, taillade *f*. **2** *vt* (*reduce*) réduire radicalement; (*prices*) écraser.
slat [slæt] *n* (*in Br blind, Am shade*) lamelle *f*.
slate [sleɪt] **1** *n* ardoise *f*. **2** *vt* (*book etc*) *Br Fam* critiquer, démolir.
slaughter [ˈslɔːtər] *vt* (*people*) massacrer; (*animal*) abattre ▌ *n* massacre *m*; (*of animal*) abattage *m*. ● **slaughterhouse** *n* abattoir *m*.
Slav [slɑːv] *a* slave ▌ *n* Slave *mf*. ● **Sla'vonic** *a* (*language*) slave.
slave [sleɪv] *n* esclave *mf*; **the s. trade** *Hist* la traite des noirs; **s. driver** *Fig Pej* négrier *m* ▌ *vi* **to s. (away)** se crever (au travail), bosser comme une bête; **to s. away doing sth** s'escrimer à faire qch. ● **slavery** *n* esclavage *m*. ● **slavish** *a* servile.
slaver [ˈslævər] *vi* (*dribble*) baver (**over** sur) ▌ *n* bave *f*.
slay [sleɪ] *vt* (*pt* **slew**, *pp* **slain**) *Lit* tuer.
sleazy [ˈsliːzɪ] *a* (-ier, -iest) *Fam* (*bar room, affair etc*) sordide.
sledge [sledʒ] (*Am* **sled** [sled]) *n* *Br* luge *f*; (*horse-drawn*) traîneau *m*.
sledgehammer [ˈsledʒhæmər] *n* masse *f*.
sleek [sliːk] *a* (-er, -est) (*smooth*) lisse; (*shiny*) brillant; (*manner*) *Pej* onctueux.
sleep [sliːp] *n* sommeil *m*; **to have a s., get some s.** dormir; **to send s.o. to s.** endormir qn; **to go or get to s.** s'endormir; **to go to s.** (*of arm, foot, hand*) *Fam* s'engourdir.
▌ *vi* (*pt & pp* **slept**) dormir; (*spend the night*) coucher; **s. tight or well!** dors bien!; **I'll s. on it** *Fig* je déciderai demain, la nuit portera conseil.
▌ *vt* **this room sleeps six** on peut coucher *or* loger six personnes dans cette chambre; **to s. it off** *Fam*, **s. off a hangover** cuver son vin. ● **sleeping** *a* (*asleep*) endormi; **s. bag** sac *m* de couchage; **s. car** wagon-lit *m*; **s. pill** somnifère *m*; **s. quarters** chambre(s) *f(pl)*, dortoir *m*.
sleeper [ˈsliːpər] *n* **1** **to be a light/sound s.** avoir le sommeil léger/lourd. **2** *Br Rail* (*on track*) traverse *f*; (*bed in train*) couchette *f*; (*train*) train *m* couchettes. ● **sleepiness** *n* see **sleepy**. ● **sleepless** *a* (*night*) d'insomnie; (*hours*) sans sommeil.

sleepwalker ['sli:pwɔ:kər] *n* somnambule *mf*. ●**sleepwalking** *n* somnambulisme *m*.

sleepy ['sli:pɪ] *a* (-**ier**, -**iest**) (*town, voice etc*) endormi; **to be s.** (*of person*) avoir sommeil. ●**sleepiness** *n* torpeur *f*.

sleet [sli:t] *n* neige *f* fondue; (*sheet of ice*) *Am* verglas *m* ❚ *vi* **it's sleeting** il tombe de la neige fondue.

sleeve [sli:v] *n* (*of shirt etc*) manche *f*; (*of record*) pochette *f*; **to have something up one's s.** (*surprise, idea etc*) avoir quelque chose en réserve; **long-/short-sleeved** à manches longues/courtes.

sleigh [sleɪ] *n* traîneau *m*.

sleight [slaɪt] *n* **s. of hand** prestidigitation *f*.

slender ['slendər] *a* (*person*) mince, svelte; (*neck, hand*) fin; (*small, feeble*) *Fig* faible.

slept [slept] *pt & pp of* **sleep.**

sleuth [slu:θ] *n* (*detective*) *Hum* (fin) limier *m*.

slew [slu:] **1** *n* **a s. of** *Am Fam* un tas de, une tapée de. **2** *pt of* **slay.**

slice [slaɪs] *n* tranche *f*; (*portion*) *Fig* partie *f*, part *f* ❚ *vt* **to s.** (**up**) couper (en tranches); **to s. off** (*cut off*) couper.

slick [slɪk] **1** *a* (-**er**, -**est**) (*glib*) qui a la parole facile; (*manner*) mielleux; (*film, book*) bien fait mais superficiel; (*cunning*) astucieux; (*smooth, slippery*) lisse. **2** *n* **oil s.** nappe *f* de pétrole; (*large*) marée *f* noire.

slide [slaɪd] *n* (*in playground*) toboggan *m*; (*on ice*) glissoire *f*; (*for hair*) barrette *f*; *Phot* diapositive *f*; (*of microscope*) lamelle *f*, lame *f*; (*act of sliding*) glissade *f*; (*in value etc*) (légère) baisse *f*.

❚ *vi* (*pt & pp* **slid**) glisser; **to s. into a room/** *etc* se glisser dans une pièce/*etc.*

❚ *vt* (*letter etc*) glisser ●(**into** dans); (*table, chair etc*) faire glisser. ●**sliding** *a* (*door, panel*) coulissant; **s. roof** toit *m* ouvrant; **s. scale** (*in making calculations*) échelle *f* mobile.

slight [slaɪt] **1** *a* (-**er**, -**est**) (*noise, mistake, breeze etc*) léger, petit; (*chance*) faible; (*person, figure*) (*slim*) mince; (*frail*) frêle; **the slightest thing** la moindre chose; **not in the slightest** pas le moins du monde. **2** *vt* (*offend*) offenser; (*ignore*) bouder ❚ *n* affront *m* (**on** à). ●**slighting** *a* (*remark*) désobligeant.

slightly ['slaɪtlɪ] *adv* légèrement, un peu; **to know s.o. s.** connaître qn un peu; **s. built** fluet (*f* fluette).

slim [slɪm] *a* (**slimmer, slimmest**) mince ❚ *vi* (-**mm**-) maigrir. ●**slimmer** *n* *Br* personne *f* qui suit un régime amaigrissant. ●**slimming** *a* *Br* **s. diet** régime *m* amaigrissant; **s. food** aliment *m* qui ne fait pas grossir. ●**slimness** *n* minceur *f*.

slime [slaɪm] *n* boue *f* (visqueuse); (*of snail*) bave *f*. ●**slimy** *a* (-**ier**, -**iest**) (*muddy*) boueux; (*sticky, Fig smarmy*) visqueux.

sling [slɪŋ] **1** *n* (*weapon*) fronde *f*; (*toy*) lance-pierres *m inv*; (*for injured arm*) écharpe *f*; **in a s.** en écharpe. **2** *vt* (*pt & pp*

slung) (*throw*) jeter, lancer; (*hang*) suspendre; **to s. away** *or* **out** (*throw out*) *Fam* balancer. ●**slingshot** *n* *Am* lance-pierres *m inv*.

slip [slɪp] **1** *n* (*mistake*) erreur *f*; (*woman's undergarment*) combinaison *f*; **a s. of paper** (*bit*) un bout de papier; (*for filing*) une fiche de papier; **a s. (of the tongue)** un lapsus; **to give s.o. the s.** fausser compagnie à qn; **s. road** (*to or from motorway*) *Br* bretelle *f* (d'accès or de sortie).

2 *vi* (-**pp**-) glisser; (*of popularity, ratings*) *Fam* baisser; **to let s.** (*chance, oath, secret*) laisser échapper.

❚ *vt* (*slide*) glisser (**to** à, **into** dans); **it slipped her notice** ça lui a échappé; **it slipped his mind** ça lui est sorti de l'esprit; **to have a slipped** *Br* **disc** *or* *Am* **disk** avoir une hernie discale.

slip along *vi* **to s. along to s.o.'s** faire un saut chez qn ❚ **to slip away** *vi* (*escape*) s'esquiver ❚ **to slip back** *vi* retourner furtivement ❚ **to slip in** *vi* (*enter*) entrer furtivement ❚ **to slip into** *vt* (*room etc*) se glisser dans; (*bathrobe etc*) mettre, passer; (*habit*) prendre ❚ **to slip off** *vt* (*coat etc*) enlever ❚ **to slip on** *vt* (*coat etc*) mettre ❚ **to slip out** *vi* (*leave*) sortir furtivement; (*for a moment*) sortir (un instant); (*of secret*) s'éventer ❚ **to slip over** *vi* **to s. over to s.o.'s** faire un saut chez qn ❚ **to slip past** *vt* (*guard*) passer sans être vu de ❚ **to slip through** *vi* (*of error*) ne pas être remarqué ❚ *vt* **to s. through the crowd** se faufiler parmi la foule ❚ **to slip up** *vi* (*make a mistake*) *Fam* gaffer.

slipcover ['slɪpkʌvər] *n* *Am* housse *f*.

slipover ['slɪpəʊvər] *n* *Br* pull *m* sans manches.

slipper ['slɪpər] *n* pantoufle *f*.

slippery ['slɪpərɪ] *a* glissant.

slipshod ['slɪpʃɒd] *a* (*negligent*) négligent; (*slovenly*) négligé.

slip-up ['slɪpʌp] *Fam* gaffe *f*, erreur *f*.

slipway ['slɪpweɪ] *n* cale *f* de lancement.

slit [slɪt] *n* (*opening*) fente *f*; (*cut*) coupure *f* ❚ *vt* (*pt & pp* **slit**, *pres p* **slitting**) (*cut*) couper; (*tear*) déchirer; **to s. open** (*sack*) éventrer.

slither ['slɪðər] *vi* glisser; (*of snake*) se couler.

sliver ['slɪvər] *n* (*of wood*) éclat *m*; (*of cheese etc*) fine tranche *f*.

slob [slɒb] *n* *Fam* (*lazy person*) gros fainéant *m*; (*dirty person*) porc *m*.

slobber ['slɒbər] *vi* (*of dog, baby etc*) baver (**over** sur); **to s. over s.o.** (*kiss*) *Fam* faire des mamours à qn ❚ *n* bave *f*.

sloe [sləʊ] *n* (*fruit*) prunelle *f*.

slog [slɒg] *Br* **1** *n* **a (hard) s.** (*effort*) un gros effort; (*work*) un travail dur ❚ *vi* (-**gg**-) **to s.** (**away**) bosser, trimer. **2** *vt* (-**gg**-) (*ball, person*) donner un grand coup à.

slogan ['sləʊgən] *n* slogan *m*.

slop [slɒp] *n* **slops** eaux *fpl* sales ❚ *vi* (-**pp**-) **to s.** (**over**) (*spill*) se répandre ❚ *vt* répandre.

slope [sləʊp] *n* pente *f*; (*of mountain*)

versant *m*; (*for skiing*) piste *f*; (*slant of handwriting, pipe etc*) inclinaison *f* ▮ *vi* (*of ground, roof etc*) être en pente; (*of handwriting*) pencher; **to s. down** (*of path etc*) descendre en pente. ●**sloping** *a* (*roof etc*) en pente; (*handwriting*) penché.

sloppy ['slɒpɪ] *a* (**-ier, -iest**) (*work, appearance*) négligé; (*person*) négligent; (*sentimental*) sentimental; (*wet*) détrempé; (*watery*) liquide.

slosh [slɒʃ] *vt* (*pour, spill*) *Fam* renverser, répandre ▮ *vi* **to s. about** (*walk in water, mud etc*) patauger; (*splash in bath etc*) barboter. ●**sloshed** *a* (*drunk*) *Br Fam* bourré.

slot [slɒt] *n* (*slit*) fente *f*; (*groove*) rainure *f*; (*in radio or TV programme*) créneau *m*; **s. machine** (*for vending*) distributeur *m* automatique; (*for gambling*) machine *f* à sous ▮ *vt* (**-tt-**) (*insert*) insérer (**into** dans) ▮ *vi* s'insérer (**into** dans).

sloth [sləʊθ] *n Lit* paresse *f*.

slouch [slaʊtʃ] **1** *vi* ne pas se tenir droit; (*have a stoop*) avoir le dos voûté; (*in chair*) se vautrer (**in** dans); **to be slouching over one's desk/etc** être penché sur son bureau/*etc* ▮ *n* (*posture*) mauvaise tenue *f*; **with a s.** (*to walk*) en traînant les pieds; (*stooped*) le dos voûté. **2** *n Fam* (*person*) lourdaud, -aude *mf*; (*lazy*) paresseux, -euse *mf*; **he's no s.** il n'est pas empoté.

Slovakia [sləʊˈvækɪə] *n* Slovaquie *f*.
Slovenia [sləʊˈviːnɪə] *n* Slovénie *f*.

slovenly ['slʌvənlɪ] *a* négligé. ●**slovenliness** *n* (*of dress*) négligé *m*; (*carelessness*) négligence *f*.

slow [sləʊ] *a* (**-er, -est**) lent; (*business*) calme; (*party, event*) ennuyeux; **at (a) s. speed** à vitesse réduite; **to be a s. walker** marcher lentement; **to be s.** (*of clock, watch*) retarder; **to be five minutes s.** retarder de cinq minutes; **to be s. to act** *or* **in acting** être lent à agir; **in s. motion** au ralenti ▮ *adv* lentement ▮ *vt* **to s. down** *or* **up** ralentir; (*delay*) retarder ▮ *vi* **to s. down** *or* **up** ralentir. ●**slowly** *adv* lentement; (*bit by bit*) peu à peu. ●**slowness** *n* lenteur *f*.

slowcoach ['sləʊkəʊtʃ] *n Br Fam* tortue *f*, lambin, -ine *mf*. ●**slow-down** *n* ralentissement *m*; **s.-down** (*strike*) *Am* grève *f* perlée. ●**slow-'moving** *a* (*vehicle etc*) lent. ●**slowpoke** *n Am Fam* tortue *f*, lambin, -ine *mf*.

sludge [slʌdʒ] *n* gadoue *f*.

slue [sluː] *n Am Fam* = **slew 1**.

slug [slʌg] **1** *n* (*mollusc*) limace *f*. **2** *n* (*bullet*) *Am Sl* pruneau *m*. **3** *Am Fam vt* (**-gg-**) (*hit*) frapper ▮ *n* coup *m*, marron *m*.

sluggish ['slʌgɪʃ] *a* (*person*) (*lethargic*) amorphe, sans énergie; (*slow*) (*machine etc*) peu nerveux; (*business*) peu actif.

sluice [sluːs] *n* **s. (gate)** vanne *f*.

slum [slʌm] *n* (*house*) taudis *m*; **the slums** les quartiers *mpl* pauvres; **s. district** quartier *m* pauvre; **s. dwelling** taudis *m* ▮ *vt* (**-mm-**) **to s. it** *Fam* (*have lean times*) manger de la vache

enragée; (*mix with bad company*) s'encanailler. ●**slummy** *a* (**-ier, -iest**) sordide, pauvre.

slumber ['slʌmbər] *n Lit* sommeil *m*.

slump [slʌmp] **1** *n* baisse *f* soudaine (**in** de); (*in prices*) effondrement *m*; *Econ* crise *f* ▮ *vi* (*decrease*) baisser; (*of prices*) s'effondrer. **2** *vi* **to s. into** (*armchair etc*) s'affaisser dans.

slung [slʌŋ] *pt & pp of* **sling 2**.

slur [slɜːr] **1** *vt* (**-rr-**) (*word*) prononcer indistinctement; **to s. one's words** manger ses mots ▮ *n* **to speak with a s.** manger ses mots. **2** *n* (*insult*) insulte *f*; **to cast a s. on s.o.'s reputation** porter atteinte à la réputation de qn. ●**slurred** *a* (*speech*) indistinct.

slush [slʌʃ] *n* (*snow*) neige *f* fondue; (*mud*) gadoue *f*; **s. fund** *Pol Fam* caisse *f* noire. ●**slushy** *a* (**-ier, -iest**) (*road*) couvert de neige fondue.

slut [slʌt] *n Pej* (*immoral woman*) salope *f*, traînée *f*; (*untidy woman*) souillon *f*.

sly [slaɪ] *a* (**-er, -est**) (*deceitful*) sournois; (*cunning, crafty*) rusé ▮ *n* **on the s.** en cachette. ●**slyly** *adv* sournoisement; (*in secret*) en cachette.

smack [smæk] **1** *n* claque *f*; gifle *f*; fessée *f* ▮ *vt* (*person*) donner une claque à; **to s. s.o.'s face** gifler qn; **to s. s.o.('s bottom)** donner une fessée à qn. **2** *adv* **s. in the middle** *Fam* en plein milieu. **3** *vi* **to s. of** (*be suggestive of*) avoir des relents de. ●**smacking** *n* fessée *f*.

small [smɔːl] *a* (**-er, -est**) petit; **in the s. hours** au petit matin; **s. change** petite monnaie *f*; **s. talk** menus propos *mpl* ▮ *adv* (*to cut, chop*) menu ▮ *n* **the s. of the back** le creux *m* des reins. ●**smallness** *n* petitesse *f*. ●**small-minded** *a* à l'esprit étroit. ●**small-mindedness** *n* étroitesse *f* d'esprit. ●**small-scale** *a Fig* peu important. ●**small-time** *a* (*crook, dealer etc*) petit, sans grande envergure.

smallholding ['smɔːlhəʊldɪŋ] *n Br* petite ferme *f*.

smallpox ['smɔːlpɒks] *n* petite vérole *f*.

smarmy ['smɑːmɪ] *a* (**-ier, -iest**) *Pej Fam* visqueux, obséquieux.

smart[1] [smɑːt] *a* (**-er, -est**) (*in appearance*) élégant; (*clever*) intelligent; (*astute*) astucieux; (*quick*) rapide; **s. aleck** *Fam* je-sais-tout *mf inv*; **s. card** carte *f* à puce *or* à mémoire.

smart[2] [smɑːt] *vi* (*sting*) brûler, faire mal.

smarten ['smɑːt(ə)n] *vt* **to s. up** (*room etc*) embellir ▮ *vi* **to s. (oneself) up** (*make oneself spruce*) se faire beau, s'arranger.

smartly ['smɑːtlɪ] *adv* (*dressed*) avec élégance; (*quickly*) en vitesse; (*cleverly*) avec intelligence; (*astutely*) astucieusement. ●**smartness** *n* élégance *f*; (*cleverness*) intelligence *f*.

smash [smæʃ] *vt* (*break*) briser; (*shatter*) fracasser; (*record*) pulvériser; (*enemy*) écraser; **to s. s.o.'s face (in)** *Fam* casser la gueule à qn █ *vi* se briser █ *n* (*accident*) collision *f*; (*noise*) fracas *m*; (*blow*) coup *m*; **s. hit** *Fam* succès *m* fou. ● **smash-and-grab raid** *n Br* = vol *m* commis en défonçant une vitrine. ● **smash-down** *n* collision *f*.

smash down *or* **in** *vt* (*door*) enfoncer █ **to smash into** *vt* (*of vehicle*) (r)entrer dans (*lampadaire etc*) █ **to smash up** *vt* (*vehicle*) esquinter; (*room*) démolir tout dans.

smashing ['smæʃɪŋ] *a* (*wonderful*) *Br Fam* formidable. ● **smasher** *n* **to be a (real) s.** *Br Fam* être formidable.

smattering ['smætərɪŋ] *n* **a s. of French/etc** quelques notions *fpl* de français/etc.

smear [smɪər] *vt* (*coat*) enduire (**with** de); (*stain*) tacher (**with** de); (*smudge*) faire une trace sur █ *n* (*mark*) trace *f*; (*stain*) tache *f*; **s.** (**test**) *Med* frottis *m* (vaginal); **a s. on s.o.'s reputation/etc** (*attack*) une atteinte à la réputation/etc de qn; **s. campaign** campagne *f* de diffamation; **s. tactics** utilisation *f* systématique de la diffamation.

smell [smel] *n* odeur *f*; (**sense of**) **s.** odorat *m* █ *vt* (*pt & pp* **smelled** *or* **smelt**) sentir; (*of animal*) flairer █ *vi* (*stink*) sentir (mauvais); (*have a smell*) avoir une odeur; **to s. of smoke/etc** sentir la fumée/etc; **smelling salts** sels *mpl*. ● **smelly** *a* (**-ier, -iest**) **to be s.** sentir (mauvais).

smelt¹ [smelt] *pt & pp of* **smell**.

smelt² [smelt] *vt* (*ore*) fondre; **smelting works** fonderie *f*.

smidgen ['smɪdʒən] *n* **a s.** (*a little*) *Am Fam* un brin (of *m*).

smile [smaɪl] *n* sourire *m* █ *vi* sourire (**at s.o.** à qn, **at sth** de qch). ● **smiling** *a* souriant.

smirk [smɜːk] *n* (*smug*) sourire *m* suffisant; (*scornful*) sourire *m* goguenard.

smith [smɪθ] *n* (*blacksmith*) forgeron *m*.

smithereens [smɪðə'riːnz] *npl* **to smash sth to s.** briser qch en mille morceaux.

smitten ['smɪt(ə)n] *a Hum* **to be s. with s.o.** (*in love with*) être épris de qn; **to be s. with sth/s.o.** (*enthusiastic about*) être emballé par qch/qn.

smock [smɒk] *n* blouse *f*.

smog [smɒg] *n* brouillard *m* épais, smog *m*.

smoke [sməʊk] *n* fumée *f*; **to have a s.** fumer une cigarette *etc*; **s. detector** *or* **alarm** détecteur *m* de fumée; **s. screen** *Fig* écran *m* or rideau *m* de fumée.

█ *vt* (*cigarette etc*) fumer; **to s. out** (*room etc*) enfumer; **smoked salmon/etc** saumon *m/etc* fumé.

█ *vi* fumer; **'no smoking'** 'défense de fumer'; **smoking compartment** (*on train*) compartiment *m* fumeurs. ● **smokeless** *a* **s. fuel** combustible *m* non polluant. ● **smoker** *n* fumeur, -euse *mf*; (*train compartment*) compartiment *m* fumeurs. ● **smokestack** *n* cheminée *f* (d'usine). ● **smoky** *a* (**-ier, -iest**) (*room, air*) enfumé; (*ceiling, wall*) noirci de fumée; **it's s. here** il y a de la fumée ici.

smooth [smuːð] *a* (**-er, -est**) (*surface, skin etc*) lisse; (*road*) à la surface égale; (*move-*

ment) régulier, sans à-coups; (*flight*) agréable; (*cream*) onctueux; (*sea*) calme; (*person, manners*) *Pej* doucereux; **the s. running of** (*machine, service, business etc*) la bonne marche de █ *vt* **to s. down** (*hair, sheet, paper*) lisser; **to s. out** (*paper, sheet, dress etc*) lisser; (*crease*) faire disparaître; **to s. out** *or* **over** (*problems etc*) *Fig* aplanir. ● **smoothly** *adv* (*to land, pass off*) en douceur. ● **smoothness** *n* aspect *m* lisse; (*of road*) surface *f* égale.

smother ['smʌðər] *vt* **1** (*stifle*) étouffer. **2 to s. sth with sth** (*cover*) couvrir qch de qch; **to s. s.o. with kisses** *Fig* couvrir qn de baisers.

smoulder ['sməʊldər] (*Am* **smolder**) *vi* (*of fire*, *Fig passion etc*) couver.

smudge [smʌdʒ] *n* tache *f*, bavure *f* █ *vt* (*paper etc*) faire des taches sur, salir.

smug [smʌg] *a* (**smugger, smuggest**) (*smile etc*) béat; (*person*) content de soi, suffisant. ● **smugly** *adv* avec suffisance.

smuggle ['smʌg(ə)l] *vt* passer (en fraude); **smuggled goods** contrebande *f*. ● **smuggling** *n* contrebande *f*. ● **smuggler** *n* contrebandier, -ière *mf*.

smut [smʌt] *n inv* (*obscenity*) cochonneries *fpl*. ● **smutty** *a* (**-ier, -iest**) (*joke etc*) cochon.

snack [snæk] *n* (*meal*) casse-croûte *m inv*; **snacks** (*things to eat*) petites choses *fpl* à grignoter; (*Br sweets, Am candies*) friandises *fpl*; **to eat a s.** *or* **snacks** grignoter; **s. bar** snack(-bar) *m*.

snafu [snæ'fuː] *n* (*confusion*) *Sl* embrouillamini *m*.

snag [snæg] *n* **1** (*hitch*) inconvénient *m*, problème *m*, os *m*. **2** (*in cloth*) accroc *m*.

snail [sneɪl] *n* escargot *m*; **at a s.'s pace** comme une tortue.

snake [sneɪk] *n* (*reptile*) serpent *m*; **snakes and ladders** (*game*) le jeu de l'oie █ *vi* (*of river*) serpenter. ● **snakebite** *n* morsure *f* de serpent.

snap [snæp] **1** *vt* (**-pp-**) (*break*) casser (avec un bruit sec); (*fingers, whip*) faire claquer; **to s. up a bargain** sauter sur une occasion █ *vi* se casser net; (*of whip*) claquer; (*of person*) *Fig* parler sèchement (**at** à); **to s. off** (*break off*) se casser; **s. out of it!** *Fam* secoue-toi! █ *n* bruit *m* sec, claquement *m*; (*photo*) photo *f*; **s. (fastener)** pression *f*; **cold s.** (*weather*) coup *m* de froid.

2 *a* (*sudden*) soudain, brusque; **to make a s. decision** décider sans réfléchir.

snapdragon ['snæpdrægən] *n* (*flower*) gueule-de-loup *f*.

snappy ['snæpɪ] *a* (**-ier, -iest**) (*pace*) vif; **make it s.!** *Fam* dépêche-toi!

snapshot ['snæpʃɒt] *n* photo *f*, instantané *m*.

snare [sneər] *n* piège *m*.

snarl [snɑːl] *vi* gronder (en montrant les dents) █ *n* grondement *m*. ● **snarl-up** *n* (*traffic jam*) *Fam* embouteillage *m*; (*confusion*) *Fam* pagaille *f*.

snatch [snætʃ] *vt* saisir (*d'un geste vif*);

(some rest, a meal etc) Fig (réussir à) prendre; **to s. sth from s.o.** arracher qch à qn ▌ *n* **wages s.** *(theft)* vol *m* de l'argent de la paie.

snatches ['snætʃɪz] *npl (bits)* fragments *mpl* (of de).

snazzy ['snæzɪ] *a* (-ier, -iest) *Fam (flashy)* tapageur; *(smart)* élégant.

sneak [sniːk] **1** *vi (pt & pp Am* sneaked *or* snuck) **to s. in/out** entrer/sortir furtivement; **to s. off** s'esquiver ▌ *a* **a s. attack** une attaque-surprise; **to have a s. preview of a film/***etc* voir un film/*etc* en avant-première. **2** *n (telltale) Br Fam* rapporteur, -euse *mf* ▌ *vi* **to s. on s.o.** *(of child) Br Fam* rapporter sur qn. ●**sneaking** *a (suspicion)* vague; *(desire)* secret. ●**sneaky** *a* (-ier, -iest) *(sly) Fam* sournois.

sneaker ['sniːkər] *n (shoe)* (chaussure *f* de) tennis *m*.

sneer [snɪər] *vi* ricaner; **to s. at** se moquer de ▌ *n* ricanement *m*.

sneeze [sniːz] *n* éternuement *m* ▌ *vi* éternuer. ●**sneezy** *a* (-ier, -iest) **to be s.** ne pas arrêter d'éternuer.

snicker ['snɪkər] *n & vi Am* = **snigger**.

snide [snaɪd] *a (remark etc)* sarcastique.

sniff [snɪf] *vt* renifler; *(of dog)* flairer, renifler; **to s. glue** sniffer de la colle; **to s. out a bargain** Fig flairer une bonne affaire ▌ *vi* **to s. (at)** renifler ▌ *n* reniflement *m*; **to give a s.** renifler; **to take a s. at sth** renifler qch.

sniffle ['snɪf(ə)l] *vi* renifler ▌ *n* **to have a s. or the sniffles** Fam avoir un rhume.

snigger ['snɪgər] *vi* ricaner ▌ *n (petit)* ricanement *m*. ●**sniggering** *n* ricanement(s) *m(pl)*.

snip [snɪp] *n (bargain) Br Fam* bonne affaire *f*; *(piece)* petit bout *m (coupé)*; **to make a s.** couper ▌ *vt* (-pp-) **to s. (off)** couper.

sniper ['snaɪpər] *n Mil* tireur *m* embusqué *or* isolé.

snippet ['snɪpɪt] *n (of conversation)* bribe *f*.

snivel ['snɪv(ə)l] *vi (Br* -ll-*, Am* -l-*)* pleurnicher. ●**snivelling** *(Am* sniveling*) a* pleurnicheur.

snob [snɒb] *n* snob *mf*. ●**snobbery** *n* snobisme *m*. ●**snobbish** *a* snob *inv*.

snook [snuːk] *n* **to cock a s.** faire un pied de nez (at s.o. à qn).

snooker ['snuːkər] *n* snooker *m (sorte de jeu de billard)*.

snoop [snuːp] *vi* fourrer son nez partout; **to s. on s.o.** *(spy on)* espionner qn.

snooty ['snuːtɪ] *a* (-ier, -iest) *Fam* snob *inv*.

snooze [snuːz] *n* petit somme *m*; **to have a s.** faire un petit somme ▌ *vi* faire un petit somme.

snore [snɔːr] *vi* ronfler ▌ *n* ronflement *m*. ●**snoring** *n* ronflements *mpl*.

snorkel ['snɔːk(ə)l] *n (for underwater swimming)* tuba *m* ▌ *vi (Br* -ll-*, Am* -l-*)* faire de la plongée (avec un tuba).

snort [snɔːt] *vi (grunt)* grogner; *(sniff)* renifler; *(of horse)* renâcler ▌ *n (grunt)* grognement *m*.

snot [snɒt] *n Fam* morve *f*. ●**snotty** *a* (-ier,

-iest) *Fam (nose)* qui coule; *(handkerchief)* plein de morve; *(child)* morveux. ●**snottynosed** *a Fam* morveux.

snout [snaʊt] *n* museau *m*.

snow [snəʊ] *n* neige *f*; **s. tyres** *Br*, **s. tires** *Am* pneus *mpl* neige ▌ *vi* neiger; **it's snowing** il neige ▌ *vt* **to be snowed in** être bloqué par la neige; **to be snowed under with work** Fig être submergé de travail.

snowball ['snəʊbɔːl] Fig *n* boule *f* de neige ▌ *vi (increase)* faire boule de neige. ●**snowbound** *a* bloqué par la neige. ●**snow-capped** *a (mountain)* enneigé. ●**snowdrift** *n* congère *f*. ●**snowdrop** *n (flower)* perce-neige *m or f inv*. ●**snowfall** *n* chute *f* de neige. ●**snowflake** *n* flocon *m* de neige. ●**snowman** *n (pl* -men*)* bonhomme *m* de neige. ●**snowmobile** *n* motoneige *f*. ●**snowplough** *or Am* **snowplow** *n* chasse-neige *m inv*. ●**snowshoe** *n* raquette *f*. ●**snowstorm** *n* tempête *f* de neige. ●**snowy** *a* (-ier, -iest) *(weather, hills, day etc)* neigeux.

snub [snʌb] **1** *n* rebuffade *f* ▌ *vt* (-bb-) *(offer etc)* rejeter; **to s. s.o.** snober qn. **2** *a* **s. nose** nez *m* retroussé.

snuff [snʌf] **1** *vt* **to s. (out)** *(candle)* moucher. **2** *n* tabac *m* à priser. ●**snuffbox** *n* tabatière *f*.

snuffle ['snʌf(ə)l] *vi & n* = **sniffle**.

snug [snʌg] *a* (snugger, snuggest) *(house etc)* douillet *(f* -ette*)*, confortable; *(garment)* bien ajusté; **we're s. in this armchair** on est bien dans ce fauteuil; **s. in bed** bien au chaud dans son lit.

snuggle ['snʌg(ə)l] *vi* **to s. up to s.o.** se pelotonner contre qn.

so [səʊ] **1** *adv (to such a degree)* si, tellement *(that* que); *(thus)* ainsi, comme ça; **so that** *(purpose)* pour que (+ *sub*); *(result)* si bien que (+ *indic*); **so as to do** pour faire; **I think so** je le pense, je pense que oui; **do so!** faites-le!; **if so** oui; **is that so?** c'est vrai?; **so am I, so do I** *etc* moi aussi; **so much** *(to work, sing etc)* tant, tellement *(that* que); **so much courage/***etc* tant *or* tellement de courage/*etc (that* que); **so many** tant, tellement; **so many books/***etc* tant *or* tellement de livres/*etc (that* que); **so very fast/***etc* vraiment si vite/*etc*; **so on and so on** et ainsi de suite; **so long!** *Fam* au revoir! **2** *conj (therefore)* donc; *(in that case)* alors; **so what?** et alors? ●**So-and-so** *n* **Mr So-and-so** Monsieur Un tel. ●**so-'called** *a* prétendu, soi-disant *inv*. ●**so-so** *a Fam* comme ci comme ça.

soak [səʊk] *vt (drench)* tremper *(qn)*; *(washing, food)* faire tremper; **to be soaked through** *or* **to the skin** être trempé jusqu'aux os; **to s. up** absorber ▌ *vi (of washing etc)* tremper; **to s. in** *(of liquid)* s'infiltrer ▌ *n* **to give sth a s.** faire tremper qch. ●**soaked** *a (person)* trempé (jusqu'aux os). ●**soaking** *a & adv* **s. (wet)** trempé ▌ *n* **to get a s.** se faire tremper; **to give sth a s.** faire tremper qch.

soap [səʊp] *n* savon *m*; **s. opera** feuilleton *m*

(télé) à l'eau de rose; **s. powder** lessive *f* ▮ *vt*
to s. (down) savonner. ●**soapflakes** *npl* savon *m* en paillettes. ●**soapsuds** *npl* mousse
f de savon. ●**soapy** *a* (**-ier, -iest**) *a* savonneux.

soar [sɔːr] *vi* (*of bird etc*) s'élever; (*of price*)
monter (en flèche); (*of hope*) *Fig* grandir.

sob [sɒb] **n** sanglot *m* ▮ *vi* (**-bb-**) sangloter.
●**sobbing** *n* (*sobs*) sanglots *mpl*.

sober ['səʊbər] **1** *a* he's s. (*not drunk*) il n'est
pas ivre ▮ *vti* **to s. up** dessoûler. **2** *a* (*serious*)
sérieux, sensé; (*style, meal*) sobre. ●**soberly**
adv sobrement.

soccer ['sɒkər] *n* football *m*.

sociable ['səʊʃəb(ə)l] *a* (*person*) sociable,
aimable (to avec); (*evening*) amical. ●**sociably** *adv* (*to act, reply*) aimablement.

social ['səʊʃəl] *a* social; **s. club** club *m*; **s.
evening** soirée *f*; **s. gathering** réunion *f* mondaine; **to have a good s. life** sortir beaucoup;
s. science(s) sciences *fpl* humaines; **s. security** (*aid*) aide *f* sociale; (*retirement pension*)
Am pension *f* de retraite; **s. services, S. Security** = Sécurité *f* sociale; **Department of S.
Security** *Br* = ministère *m* de la Santé et de
la Sécurité sociale; **s. worker** assistant, -ante
mf social(e) ▮ **n** (*gathering*) réunion *f* (amicale).

socialism ['səʊʃəlɪz(ə)n] *n* socialisme *m*.
●**socialist** *a* & *n* socialiste (*mf*).

socialite ['səʊʃəlaɪt] *n* mondain, -aine *mf*.

socialize ['səʊʃəlaɪz] *vi* (*mix*) se mêler aux
autres; (*talk*) bavarder (**with** avec).

socially ['səʊʃəlɪ] *adv* socialement; (*to meet
s.o., behave*) en société.

society [sə'saɪətɪ] *n* (*community, club,
companionship etc*) société *f*; (*school or university club*) club *m* ▮ *a* (*wedding, news etc*)
mondain.

sociology [səʊsɪ'ɒlədʒɪ] *n* sociologie *f*. ●**socio'logical** *a* sociologique. ●**sociologist** *n* sociologue *mf*.

sock [sɒk] **1** *n* chaussette *f* **2** *vt* *Sl* (*hit*)
flanquer *or* coller un marron à (*qn*); **he
socked me on the jaw** il m'a flanqué *or* collé
un marron dans la figure.

socket ['sɒkɪt] *n* (*of electric plug*) *Br* prise *f*
de courant; (*of lamp*) *Br* douille *f*; (*of eye*)
orbite *f*; (*of bone*) cavité *f*.

sod [sɒd] *n* (*turf*) *Am* gazon *m*.

soda ['səʊdə] *n* **1** *Ch* soude *f*; **bicarbonate of
s., baking s.** bicarbonate *m* de soude; **washing s.** cristaux *mpl* de soude. **2** **s. (water)** eau
f gazeuse; **s. (pop)** *Am* soda *m*.

sodden ['sɒd(ə)n] *a* (*ground*) détrempé.

sodium ['səʊdɪəm] *n* *Ch* sodium *m*.

sofa ['səʊfə] *n* canapé *m*, divan *m*; **s. bed**
canapé-lit *m*.

soft [sɒft] *a* (**-er, -est**) (*gentle, not stiff*) doux
(*f* douce); (*butter, ground, paste, snow*) mou
(*f* molle); (*wood, heart, colour*) tendre;
(*flabby*) flasque, mou (*f* molle); (*easy*) facile;
(*indulgent*) indulgent; (*cowardly*) *Fam* poltron; (*stupid*) *Fam* ramolli; **it's too s.** (*radio
etc*) ce n'est pas assez fort; **s. drink** boisson *f*

non alcoolisée; **s. drugs** drogues *fpl* douces;
s. water eau *f* douce *or* non calcaire. ●**soft-'boiled** *a* (*egg*) à la coque.

soften ['sɒf(ə)n] *vt* (*object*) ramollir; (*colour,
light, voice*) adoucir ▮ *vi* se ramollir; (*of
colour etc*) s'adoucir.

softie ['sɒftɪ] *n* *Fam* sentimental, -ale *mf*;
(*weakling*) mauviette *f*.

softly ['sɒftlɪ] *adv* doucement. ●**softness** *n*
douceur *f*; (*of butter, ground, paste etc*)
mollesse *f*.

software ['sɒftweər] *n inv* (*of computer*) logiciel *m*; **s. package** progiciel *m*.

soggy ['sɒgɪ] *a* (**-ier, -iest**) (*ground*) détrempé; (*bread, Br biscuit, Am cookie*) ramolli.

soil [sɔɪl] **1** *n* (*earth*) sol *m*, terre *f*. **2** *vt*
(*dirty*) salir ▮ *vi* (*of fabric etc*) se salir.

solar ['səʊlər] *a* solaire; **s. power** énergie *f*
solaire.

sold [səʊld] *pt* & *pp* of **sell**.

solder [*Br* 'sɒldər, *Am* 'sɒdər] *vt* souder ▮ *n*
soudure *f*.

soldier ['səʊldʒər] **1** *n* soldat *m*, militaire *m*.
2 *vi* **to s. on** persévérer.

sole [səʊl] **1** *n* (*of shoe*) semelle *f*; (*of foot*)
plante *f* ▮ *vt* (*shoe*) ressemeler. **2** *a* (*only*)
seul, unique; (*exclusive*) (*rights, representative, responsibility*) exclusif; **s. trader** = entreprise *f* individuelle. **3** *n* (*fish*) sole *f*;
lemon s. limande *f*. ●**solely** *adv* uniquement;
you're s. to blame tu es seul coupable.

solemn ['sɒləm] *a* (*formal*) solennel; (*serious*) grave. ●**so'lemnity** *n* solennité *f*; gravité *f*. ●**solemnly** *adv* (*to promise*) solennellement; (*to say*) gravement.

solicit [sə'lɪsɪt] *vt* (*seek*) solliciter ▮ *vi* (*of
prostitute*) racoler.

solicitor [sə'lɪsɪtər] *n* (*for wills etc*) *Br* notaire *m*.

solid ['sɒlɪd] *a* (*car, character, meal, state
etc*) solide; (*wall, ball*) plein; (*gold, rock*)
massif; (*crowd, mass*) compact; **s. line** ligne *f*
continue; **frozen s.** entièrement gelé; **ten
days s.** dix jours d'affilée ▮ *n* *Ch* solide *m*;
solids (*foods*) aliments *mpl* solides; **the baby
is on solids** le bébé a commencé à manger
des aliments solides. ●**so'lidify** *vi* se solidifier. ●**so'lidity** *n* solidité *f*. ●**solidly** *adv*
(*built etc*) solidement; (*to support, vote*) en
masse.

solidarity [sɒlɪ'dærətɪ] *n* solidarité *f* (**with**
avec).

soliloquy [sə'lɪləkwɪ] *n* monologue *m*.

solitary ['sɒlɪtərɪ] *a* (*lonely, alone*) solitaire;
(*only*) seul; **s. confinement** (*in prison*) isolement *m* (cellulaire); **to be in s. confinement**
être mis en isolement, être isolé. ●**solitude**
n solitude *f*.

solo ['səʊləʊ] *n* (*pl* **-os**) *Mus* solo *m* ▮ *a* (*guitar, violin etc*) solo *inv* ▮ *adv* (*to play, sing*)
en solo; (*to fly*) en solitaire. ●**soloist** *n* *Mus*
soliste *mf*.

solstice ['sɒlstɪs] *n* solstice *m*.

soluble ['sɒljʊb(ə)l] *a* (*substance, problem*)

soluble.

solution [sə'luːʃ(ə)n] n 1 (to problem etc) solution f (to de). 2 (liquid) solution f.

solve [sɒlv] vt (problem etc) résoudre. ● **solveable** a soluble.

solvent ['sɒlvənt] 1 a (financially) solvable. 2 n Ch (dis)solvant m; **s. abuse** usage m de solvants hallucinogènes. ● **solvency** n (of company etc) solvabilité f.

Somalia [sə'mɑːliə] n Somalie f.

sombre ['sɒmbər] a sombre, triste.

some [sʌm] a 1 (amount, number) du, de la, des; **s. wine** du vin; **s. glue** de la colle; **s. water** de l'eau; **s. dogs** des chiens; **s. pretty flowers** de jolies fleurs.

2 (unspecified) un, une; **s. man (or other)** un homme (quelconque); **s. charm/time/etc** (a certain amount of) un certain charme/temps/etc; **I have s. anxiety** j'ai une certaine inquiétude or quelque inquiétude; **s. other way** un autre moyen, quelque autre moyen; **that's s. book!** Fam ça, c'est un livre!

3 (a few) quelques; (in contrast to others) certains; **s. days ago** il y a quelques jours; **s. people think that...** certaines personnes or certains pensent que..., il y a des gens qui pensent que....

▐ pron 1 (number) quelques-un(e)s, certain(e)s (of de, d'entre).

2 (a certain quantity) en; **I want s.** j'en veux; **do you have s.?** en as-tu?; **s. of it is over** il en reste un peu or une partie.

▐ adv (about) quelque; **s. ten years** quelque dix ans.

somebody ['sʌmbɒdɪ] pron = someone. ● **someday** adv un jour. ● **somehow** adv (in some way) d'une manière ou d'une autre; (for some reason) on ne sait pourquoi. ● **someone** pron quelqu'un; **at s.'s house** chez qn; **s. small/etc** quelqu'un de petit/etc. ● **someplace** adv Am quelque part. ● **something** pron quelque chose; **s. awful/etc** quelque chose d'affreux/etc; **s. of a liar/etc** un peu menteur/etc ▐ adv **she plays s. like...**, elle joue un peu comme...; **it was s. awful** c'était vraiment affreux. ● **sometime** 1 adv un jour; **s. in May/etc** au cours du mois de mai/etc; **s. before his departure** avant son départ. 2 a (former) ancien. ● **sometimes** adv quelquefois, parfois. ● **somewhat** adv quelque peu, assez. ● **somewhere** adv quelque part; **s. about fifteen** (approximately) environ quinze.

somersault ['sʌməsɔːlt] n (on ground) culbute f; (in air) saut m périlleux ▐ vi faire la or une culbute; (in air) faire un saut périlleux.

son [sʌn] n fils m. ● **son-in-law** n (pl sons-in-law) beau-fils m, gendre m.

sonar ['səʊnɑːr] n sonar m.

sonata [sə'nɑːtə] n (music) sonate f.

song [sɒŋ] n chanson f; (of bird) chant m. ● **songbook** n recueil m de chansons.

sonic ['sɒnɪk] a **s. boom** bang m (supersonique).

sonnet ['sɒnɪt] n (poem) sonnet m.

soon [suːn] adv (-er, -est) (in a short time) bientôt; (quickly) vite; (early) tôt; **he s. forgot about it** il l'oublia vite, il ne tarda pas à l'oublier; **s. after** peu après; **as s. as she leaves** aussitôt qu'elle partira; **no sooner had he spoken than...** à peine avait-il parlé que...; **I'd sooner leave** je préférerais partir; **I'd just as s. leave** j'aimerais autant partir; **sooner or later** tôt ou tard.

soot [sʊt] n suie f. ● **sooty** a (-ier, -iest) couvert de suie.

soothe [suːð] vt (pain, nerves, person) calmer. ● **soothing** a (ointment, words etc) calmant.

sophisticated [sə'fɪstɪkeɪtɪd] a (person, taste) raffiné; (machine, method, technology etc) sophistiqué.

sophomore ['sɒfəmɔːr] n Am étudiant, -ante mf de seconde année.

soporific [sɒpə'rɪfɪk] a (substance, speech etc) soporifique.

sopping ['sɒpɪŋ] a & adv **s. (wet)** trempé.

soppy ['sɒpɪ] a (-ier, -iest) Br Fam (silly) idiot, bête; (sentimental) sentimental.

soprano [sə'prɑːnəʊ] n (pl -os) (singer) soprano mf; (voice) soprano m.

sorbet ['sɔːbeɪ] n (water ice) sorbet m.

sorcerer ['sɔːsərər] n sorcier m.

sordid ['sɔːdɪd] a (act, street etc) sordide.

sore [sɔːr] a (-er, -est) (painful) douloureux; (angry) Am fâché (at contre); **she has a s. throat** elle a mal à la gorge; **he's still s.** (in pain) il a encore mal; **it's a s. point** Fig c'est un sujet délicat ▐ n (wound) plaie f. ● **sorely** adv (tempted, regretted) très; **it's s. needed** on en a grand besoin. ● **soreness** n (pain) douleur f.

sorrow ['sɒrəʊ] n chagrin m, peine f. ● **sorrowful** a triste.

sorry ['sɒrɪ] a (-ier, -iest) (sight, state etc) triste; **to be s.** (regret) être désolé, regretter (to do de faire); **I'm s. she can't come** je regrette qu'elle ne puisse pas venir; **I'm s. about the delay** excusez-moi de ce retard, je suis désolé de ce retard; **s.!** pardon!; **to say s.** demander pardon (to à); **to feel** or **be s. for s.o.** plaindre qn.

sort¹ [sɔːt] n espèce f, sorte f, genre m; **a s. of** une sorte or espèce de; **all sorts of** toutes sortes de; **what s. of drink/etc is it?** qu'est-ce que c'est comme boisson/etc?, c'est quel genre de boisson/etc?; **he's a good s.** Br Fam c'est un brave type; **s. of sad/etc** (somewhat) plutôt triste/etc.

sort² [sɔːt] vt (papers etc) trier; **to s. out** (classify, select) trier; (separate) séparer (from de); (arrange) arranger; (tidy) ranger; (problem) régler; **to s. s.o. out** Br Fam (punish) faire voir à qn; (beat) donner une raclée à qn ▐ vi **to s. through** (letters etc) trier; **sorting office** (for mail) Br centre m de tri. ● **sorter** n (person) trieur, -euse m f.

SOS [esəʊ'es] n abbr (save our souls) SOS m.

soufflé ['su:fleɪ] *n Culin* soufflé *m*.

sought [sɔːt] *pt & pp of* seek.

soul [səʊl] *n* âme *f*; **not a living s.** (*nobody*) personne, pas âme qui vive; **a good s.** *Fig* un brave type; **s. mate** âme *f* sœur. ●**soul-destroying** *a* abrutissant. ●**soul-searching** *n* examen *m* de conscience.

sound¹ [saʊnd] *n* son *m*; (*noise*) bruit *m*; **I don't like the s. of it** ça ne me plaît pas du tout; **s. archives** phonothèque *f*; **s. barrier** mur *m* du son; **s. bite** petite phrase *f* (*de politicien etc*); **s. effects** bruitage *m*; **s. engineer** ingénieur *m* du son; **s. recording** enregistrement *m* sonore; **s. wave** onde *f* sonore.

▌ *vt* (*bell, alarm etc*) sonner; (*bugle, horn*) sonner de; (*letter, syllable etc*) prononcer; **to s. one's horn** (*in vehicle*) klaxonner.

▌ *vi* (*of trumpet, bugle etc*) retentir, sonner; (*seem*) sembler; **to s. like** sembler être; (*resemble*) ressembler à; **it sounds like** *or* **as if it** semble que (+ *sub or indic*); **to s. off** (*about sth*) *Pej* (*boast*) se vanter (de qch); (*complain*) rouspéter (à propos de qch).

sound² [saʊnd] *a* (**-er, -est**) (*healthy*) sain; (*good, reliable*) (*construction, argument, quality, lungs etc*) solide; (*instinct, investment*) sûr; (*advice*) sensé; **a s. beating** une bonne correction; **it's s. sense** c'est du bon sens **▌** *adv* **s. asleep** profondément endormi. ●**soundly** *adv* (*asleep, to sleep*) profondément; (*reasoned*) solidement; (*beaten*) complètement. ●**soundness** *n* (*of mind*) santé *f*; (*of argument etc*) solidité *f*.

sound³ [saʊnd] *vt* (*test, measure*) sonder; **to s. s.o. out** sonder qn (**about** sur).

soundproof ['saʊndpru:f] *a* insonorisé **▌** *vt* insonoriser.

soundtrack ['saʊndtræk] *n* (*of film etc*) bande *f* sonore.

soup [su:p] *n* soupe *f*, potage *m*; **s. dish** *or* **plate** assiette *f* creuse; **to be in the s.** (*in trouble*) *Fam* être dans le pétrin.

sour ['saʊər] *a* (**-er, -est**) aigre; (*milk*) tourné; **to turn s.** (*of wine*) s'aigrir; (*of milk*) tourner; (*of friendship*) se détériorer; (*of conversation*) tourner au vinaigre **▌** *vi* (*of temper*) s'aigrir.

source [sɔːs] *n* (*origin*) source *f*; **s. of energy** source d'énergie.

south [saʊθ] *n* sud *m*; **(to the) s. of** au sud de.

▌ *a* (*coast*) sud *inv*; (*wind*) du sud; **S. America/Africa** Amérique *f*/Afrique *f* du Sud; **S. American** (*a*) sud-américain; (*n*) Sud-Américain, -aine *mf*; **S. African** (*a*) sud-africain; (*n*) Sud-Africain, -aine *mf*.

▌ *adv* au sud, vers le sud. ●**southbound** *a* (*traffic*) en direction du sud; (*carriageway*) *Br* sud *inv*. ●**south-'east** *n & a* sud-est *m & a inv*. ●**southerly** ['sʌðəlɪ] *a* (*point*) sud *inv*; (*direction, wind*) du sud. ●**southern** ['sʌðən] *a* (*town*) du sud; (*coast*) sud *inv*; **S. Italy** le Sud de l'Italie; **S. Africa** Afrique *f* australe. ●**southerner** ['sʌðənər] *n* habitant, -ante *mf* du Sud. ●**southward(s)** *a & adv* vers le sud.

●**south-'west** *n & a* sud-ouest *m & a inv*.

souvenir [su:və'nɪər] *n* (*object*) souvenir *m*.

sovereign ['sɒvrɪn] *n* souverain, -aine *mf* **▌** *a* (*State, authority*) souverain; (*rights*) de souveraineté. ●**sovereignty** *n* souveraineté *f*.

Soviet ['səʊvɪət] *a* soviétique; **the S. Union** (*former State*) l'Union *f* soviétique.

sow¹ [saʊ] *n* (*pig*) truie *f*.

sow² [səʊ] *vt* (*pt* sowed, *pp* sowed *or* sown) (*seeds, doubt etc*) semer; (*land*) ensemencer (**with** de).

soya ['sɔɪə] *n* **s. (bean)** *Br* graine *f* de soja. ●**soybean** *n* *Am* graine *f* de soja.

sozzled ['sɒz(ə)ld] *a* (*drunk*) *Sl* bourré.

spa [spɑː] *n* (*town*) station *f* thermale; (*spring*) source *f* minérale.

space [speɪs] *n* (*gap, emptiness, atmosphere*) espace *m*; (*period*) période *f*; (*for parking*) place *f*; **blank s.** espace *m*, blanc *m*; **outer s.** l'espace cosmique; **to take up s.** (*room*) prendre de la place; **in the s. of two hours/etc** en l'espace de deux heures/*etc*; **s. bar** (*on keyboard, typewriter*) barre *f* d'espacement; **s. heater** (*electric*) radiateur *m* **▌** *a* (*voyage, capsule etc*) spatial **▌** *vt* **to s. out** espacer. ●**spacing** *n* **in double/single spacing** (*to type*) à double/simple interligne. ●**spaceman** *n* (*pl* -**men**) astronaute *m*. ●**spaceship** *n or* **spacecraft** *n inv* engin *m* spatial. ●**spacesuit** *n* combinaison *f* spatiale. ●**spacewoman** *n* (*pl* -**women**) astronaute *f*.

spacious ['speɪʃəs] *a* spacieux, grand. ●**spaciousness** *n* grandeur *f*.

spade [speɪd] *n* **1** (*for garden*) bêche *f*; (*of child*) pelle *f*. **2** **spade(s)** *Cards* pique *m*. ●**spadework** *n* *Fig* travail *m* préparatoire; (*around problem or case*) débroussaillage *m*.

spaghetti [spə'getɪ] *n* spaghetti(s) *mpl*.

Spain [speɪn] *n* Espagne *f*.

span [spæn] *n* (*of arch*) portée *f*; (*of wings*) envergure *f*; (*of life*) *Fig* durée *f* **▌** *vt* (**-nn-**) (*of bridge etc*) enjamber (*rivière etc*); (*in time*) *Fig* couvrir, embrasser.

Spaniard ['spænjəd] *n* Espagnol, -ole *mf*. ●**Spanish** *a* espagnol **▌** *n* (*language*) espagnol *m*. ●**Spanish-A'merican** *a* hispano-américain **▌** *n* Hispano-Américain, -aine *mf*.

spaniel ['spænjəl] *n* épagneul *m*.

spank [spæŋk] *vt* donner une fessée à **▌** *n* **to give s.o. a s.** donner une fessée à qn. ●**spanking** *n* fessée *f*.

spanner ['spænər] *n* *Br* (*tool*) clef *f* (*à écrous*); **adjustable s.** clef *f* à molette.

spar [spɑːr] *vi* (*of boxer*) s'entraîner (**with** s.o. avec qn).

spare¹ [speər] **1** *a* (*extra, surplus*) de *or* en trop; (*clothes, Br tyre, Am tire*) de rechange; (*wheel*) de secours; (*available*) disponible; (*bed, room*) d'ami; **s. time** loisirs *mpl* **▌** *n* **s.** (*part*) (*for vehicle, machine etc*) pièce *f* détachée.

2 *vt* (*do without*) se passer de (*qn, qch*); (*efforts, s.o.'s feelings*) ménager; **to s. s.o.** (*not kill*) épargner qn; **to s. s.o.'s life** épargner la vie à qn; **to s. s.o. sth** (*grief, de-*

tails etc) épargner qch à qn; (*time*) accorder qch à qn; (*money*) donner qch à qn; **I can't s. the time** je n'ai pas le temps; **five to s.** (*extra*) cinq de trop.

spare² [speər] *a* (*lean*) maigre.

sparing ['speəriŋ] *a* **her s. use of** l'usage modéré qu'elle fait de; **to be s. with the** butter/etc ménager le beurre/etc. ● **sparingly** *adv* (*to use sth etc*) avec modération.

spark [spɑːk] **1** *n* étincelle *f.* **2** *vt* **to s. off** (*cause*) provoquer (*dispute etc*). ● **spark(ing) plug** *n* (*for vehicle*) bougie *f.*

sparkle ['spɑːk(ə)l] *vi* (*of diamond, star etc*) étinceler, scintiller ▮ *n* éclat *m.* ● **sparkling** *a* (*wine, water*) pétillant.

sparrow ['spærəu] *n* moineau *m.*

sparse [spɑːs] *a* clairsemé. ● **sparsely** *adv* (*populated, wooded etc*) peu; **s. furnished** à peine meublé.

spartan ['spɑːtən] *a* spartiate, austère.

spasm ['spæzəm] *n* (*of muscle*) spasme *m*; (*of coughing, jealousy etc*) Fig accès *m.* ● **spas'modic** *a* (*pain etc*) spasmodique; Fig intermittent.

spastic ['spæstɪk] *n* handicapé, -ée *mf* moteur.

spat [spæt] *pp & pp of* **spit 1.**

spate [speɪt] *n* **a s. of orders**/etc une avalanche de commandes/etc.

spatter ['spætər] *vt* (*clothes, person etc*) éclabousser (**with** de) ▮ *vi* **to s. over s.o.** (*of mud etc*) éclabousser qn.

spatula ['spætjulə] *n* spatule *f.*

spawn [spɔːn] *n* (*of fish etc*) frai *m* ▮ *vi* frayer ▮ *vt* (*bring about*) Fig engendrer.

speak [spiːk] *vi* (*pt* **spoke**, *pp* **spoken**) parler (**about, of** de); (*formally, in assembly*) prendre la parole; **so to s.** pour ainsi dire; **that speaks for itself** c'est évident; **to s. well of s.o./sth** dire du bien de qn/qch; **nothing to s.** of pas grand-chose; **Bob speaking!** (*on the telephone*) Bob à l'appareil!; **that's spoken for** c'est pris *or* réservé; **to s. out** *or* **up** (*boldly*) parler (franchement); **to s. up** (*more loudly*) parler plus fort.

▮ *vt* (*language*) parler; (*say*) dire; **to s. one's mind** dire ce que l'on pense. ● **speaking** *n* **public s.** l'art *m* oratoire ▮ *a* **to be on s. terms with s.o.** parler à qn; **English-/French-speaking** qui parle anglais/français, anglophone/francophone.

speaker ['spiːkər] *n* (*public*) orateur *m*; (*in dialogue*) interlocuteur, -trice *mf*; (*loudspeaker*) haut-parleur *m*; (*of stereo system*) enceinte *f*; **to be a Spanish/a bad**/etc **s.** parler espagnol/mal/etc.

spear [spɪər] *n* lance *f.* ● **spearhead** *vt* (*attack*) être le fer de lance de; (*campaign*) mener.

spearmint ['spɪəmint] *n* (*plant*) menthe *f* (verte) ▮ *a* (*Br sweet, Am candy*) à la menthe; (*flavour*) de menthe; (*chewing-gum*) mentholé.

spec [spek] *n* **on s.** (*as a gamble*) Br Fam à tout hasard.

special ['speʃəl] *a* spécial; (*care, attention*) (tout) particulier; (*favourite*) préféré; (*measures*) Pol extraordinaire; **by s. delivery** (*letter etc*) Br par exprès ▮ *n* **today's s.** (*in restaurant*) le plat du jour.

specialist ['speʃəlɪst] *n* spécialiste *mf* (**in** de) ▮ *a* (*dictionary, knowledge*) technique, spécialisé. ● **speci'ality** *n* Br spécialité *f.*

specialize ['speʃəlaɪz] *vi* se spécialiser (**in** dans). ● **specialized** *a* spécialisé.

specially ['speʃəlɪ] *adv* (*specifically*) spécialement; (*particularly*) particulièrement; (*on purpose*) (tout) spécialement.

specialty ['speʃəltɪ] *n* Am spécialité *f.*

species ['spiːʃiːz] *n inv* espèce *f.*

specific [spə'sɪfɪk] *a* précis, explicite; Phys Ch spécifique. ● **specifically** *adv* (*purposely*) expressément; (*exactly*) précisément; (*particularly*) spécifiquement.

specify ['spesɪfaɪ] *vt* spécifier (**that** que). ● **specification** [-'keɪʃ(ə)n] *n* spécification *f*; **specifications** (*of car, machine etc*) caractéristiques *fpl.*

specimen ['spesɪmɪn] *n* (*example, person*) spécimen *m*; (*of blood*) prélèvement *m*; (*of urine*) échantillon *m*; **s. signature** spécimen *m* de signature; **s. copy** (*of book etc*) spécimen *m.*

specious ['spiːʃəs] *a* spécieux.

speck [spek] *n* (*stain*) petite tache *f*; (*of dust*) grain *m*; (*dot*) point *m.*

speckled ['spek(ə)ld] *a* tacheté.

specs [speks] *npl* Fam lunettes *fpl.*

spectacle ['spektək(ə)l] *n* (*sight*) spectacle *m.* ● **spectacles** *npl* (*glasses*) lunettes *fpl.*

spectacular [spek'tækjulər] *a* spectaculaire. ● **spectacularly** *adv* de façon spectaculaire.

spectator [spek'teɪtər] *n* Sport etc spectateur, -trice *mf.*

spectre ['spektər] *n* (*menacing image*) spectre *m* (**of** de).

spectrum, *pl* **-tra** ['spektrəm, -trə] *n* Phys spectre *m*; (*range*) Fig gamme *f.*

speculate ['spekjuleɪt] *vi* (*financially, philosophically*) spéculer; **to s. about** (*make guesses*) s'interroger sur (*les motivations de qn etc*) ▮ *vt* **to s. that** (*guess*) conjecturer que. ● **speculation** [-'leɪʃ(ə)n] *n* Fin Phil spéculation *f*; (*guessing*) conjectures *fpl* (**about** sur). ● **speculator** *n* Fin spéculateur, -trice *mf.* ● **speculative** *a* Fin Phil spéculatif; **that's s.** (*guesswork*) c'est hypothétique.

sped [sped] *pt & pp of* **speed 1.**

speech [spiːtʃ] *n* (*talk, lecture*) discours *m* (**on, about** sur); (*power of language*) parole *f*; (*diction*) élocution *f*; (*spoken language of group*) langage *m*; **a short s.** une allocution *f*; **freedom of s.** liberté *f* d'expression; **part of s.** catégorie *f* grammaticale; **direct/indirect s.** Grammar discours *m* direct/indirect. ● **speechless** *a* muet (*f* muette) (**with** de).

speed [spiːd] **1** *n* (*rate of movement*) vitesse *f*; (*swiftness*) rapidité *f*; **s. limit** (*on road*) limitation *f* de vitesse; **at top** *or* **full s.** à toute vitesse ▮ *vt* (*pt & pp* **sped**) **to s. sth up** accé-

lérer qch ▌ *vi* to s. up (*of person*) aller plus
vite; (*of pace*) s'accélérer; **to s.** past passer à
toute vitesse (*sth devant qch*). **2** *vi* (*pt & pp*
speeded) (*drive too fast*) aller trop vite.
● **speeding** *n* (*in vehicle*) excès *m* de vitesse.

speedboat ['spiːdbəʊt] *n* vedette *f.*
● **spee'dometer** *n* (*in vehicle*) *Br* compteur
m (de vitesse). ● **speedway** *n Sport* piste *f* de
vitesse pour motos; (*for cars*) *Am* autodrome *m.*

speedy ['spiːdɪ] *a* (**-ier, -iest**) rapide. ● **spee-
dily** *adv* rapidement.

spell[1] [spel] *n* (*magic*) charme *m*, sortilège
m; (*curse*) sort *m*; *Fig* charme *m*; **to be
under a s.** être envoûté. ● **spellbound** *a*
(*audience etc*) captivé.

spell[2] [spel] *n* (*period*) (courte) période *f*;
(*while, moment*) moment *m*; **s. of duty** tour
m de service; **cold s.** vague *f* de froid.

spell[3] [spel] *vt* (*pt & pp* **spelled** *or* **spelt**)
(*write*) écrire; (*say aloud one letter at a time*)
épeler; (*of letters*) former (*mot*); (*mean*) *Fig*
signifier; **to be able to s.** savoir
l'orthographe; **how is it spelled** *or* **spelt?**
comment cela s'écrit-il?; **to s. out** expliquer
clairement; (*word one letter at a time*) épeler. ● **spelling** *n* orthographe *f*; **s. mistake** *or*
error faute *f* d'orthographe. ● **spellchecker** *n*
Comptr vérificateur *m* orthographique.

spend [spend] **1** *vt* (*pt & pp* **spent**) (*money*)
dépenser (**on** pour) ▌ *vi* dépenser. **2** *vt* (*pt &
pp* **spent**) (*time etc*) passer (**on sth** sur qch,
doing à faire); (*energy, care etc*) consacrer
(**on sth** à qch, **doing** à faire). ● **spending** *n*
dépenses *fpl*; **s. money** argent *m* de poche.
● **spender** *n* **to be a big s.** dépenser beaucoup. ● **spendthrift** *n* **to be a s.** être dépensier.

spent [spent] *pt & pp of* **spend** ▌ *a* (*used*) utilisé; (*energy*) épuisé; **s. bullet** douille *f* vide.

sperm [spɜːm] *n* (*pl* **sperm** *or* **sperms**)
sperme *m.*

spew [spjuː] *vt* vomir.

sphere [sfɪər] *n* (*of influence, action etc*) &
Geom Pol sphère *f*; (*of music, poetry etc*)
domaine *m*; **the social s.** le domaine social.
● **spherical** ['sferɪk(ə)l] *a* sphérique.

sphinx [sfɪŋks] *n* sphinx *m.*

spice [spaɪs] *n* épice *f*; (*interest etc*) *Fig* piment *m* ▌ *vt* (*food*) épicer; **to s. (up)** (*add
interest to*) pimenter (*récit etc*). ● **spicy** *a*
(**-ier, -iest**) (*food*) (*story etc*) *Fig* pimenté.

spick-and-span [spɪkən'spæn] *a* (*clean*)
impeccable.

spider ['spaɪdər] *n* araignée *f*; **s.'s web** toile *f*
d'araignée.

spiel [ʃpiːl] *n Fam* baratin *m.*

spike [spaɪk] *n* (*of metal*) pointe *f* ▌ *vt*
(*pierce*) transpercer. ● **spiky** *a* (**-ier, -iest**) (*a
stem, stick etc*) garni de pointes; (*hair*) tout
hérissé.

spill [spɪl] *vt* (*pt & pp* **spilled** *or* **spilt**) (*liquid*)
renverser, répandre (**on, over** sur) ▌ **to s. the
beans** *Fam* vendre la mèche ▌ *vi* se renverser, se répandre.

spill out *vt* (*empty*) vider (*café, verre etc*) ▌ *vi*
(*of coffee etc*) se renverser (**on, over** sur) ▌
to spill over *vi* (*of liquid*) déborder.

spin [spɪn] *n* (*motion*) tour *m*; (*car ride*) petit
tour *m*; (*on washing machine*) essorage *m*; **s.
dryer** essoreuse *f* ▌ *vt* (*pt & pp* **spun**, *pres p*
spinning) (*wheel, top*) faire tourner; (*web,
yarn, wool etc*) filer (**into** en); (*washing*)
essorer; (*story*) *Fig* débiter; **to s. out** (*speech
etc*) faire durer ▌ *vi* (*of spinner, spider*) filer;
to s. (round) (*of dancer, wheel, top, planet
etc*) tourner; (*of head, room*) *Fig* tourner;
(*of vehicle*) faire un tête-à-queue. ● **spinning**
n (*by hand*) filage *m*; (*process*) *Tech* filature
f; **s. top** toupie *f*; **s. wheel** rouet *m.*

spinach [*Br* 'spɪnɪdʒ, *Am* -ɪtʃ] *n* (*plant*) épinard *m*; (*food*) épinards *mpl.*

spindle ['spɪnd(ə)l] *n Tex* fuseau *m.*

spindly ['spɪndlɪ] *a* (**-ier, -iest**) (*legs, arms*)
grêle.

spin-dry ['spɪndraɪ] *vt* essorer. ● **spin dryer** *n*
essoreuse *f.*

spine [spaɪn] *n* (*backbone*) colonne *f* vertébrale; (*spike of animal or plant*) épine *f.*
● **spinal** *a* **s. column** colonne *f* vertébrale; **s.
cord** moelle *f* épinière; **s. injury** blessure *f* à
la colonne vertébrale. ● **spineless** *a Fig* mou
(*f* molle), faible.

spin-off ['spɪnɒf] *n* avantage *m* inattendu;
(*of process, book etc*) retombée *f.*

spinster ['spɪnstər] *n* célibataire *f*; *Pej* vieille
fille *f.*

spiral ['spaɪərəl] **1** *n* spirale *f* ▌ *a* en spirale;
(*staircase*) en colimaçon. **2** *vi* (*Br* **-ll-**, *Am*
-l-) (*of prices*) monter en flèche.

spire ['spaɪər] *n* (*of church*) flèche *f.*

spirit ['spɪrɪt] **1** *n* (*soul, ghost etc*) esprit *m*;
(*courage*) *Fig* courage *m*, vigueur *f*; **spirits**
(*drink*) alcool *m*, spiritueux *mpl*; **spirit(s)**
(*morale*) moral *m*; (*liquid for fuel, cleansing
etc*) alcool *m*; **in good spirits** de bonne humeur; **that's the right s.** c'est l'attitude qu'il
faut ▌ *a* (*lamp*) à alcool; **s. level** niveau *m* à
bulle (d'air).
2 *vt* **to s. away** (*person*) faire disparaître
mystérieusement; (*steal*) *Hum* subtiliser.
● **spirited** *a* (*campaign, attack*) vigoureux;
(*person, remark*) fougueux.

spiritual ['spɪrɪtʃʊəl] *a* (*life etc*) & *Rel* spirituel ▌ *n* (*Negro*) **s.** (negro-)spiritual *m.* ● **spiritualism** *n* spiritisme *m.* ● **spiritualist** *n* spirite *mf.*

spit [spɪt] **1** *n* (*on ground etc*) crachat *m*; (*in
mouth*) salive *f* ▌ *vi* (*pt & pp* **spat** *or* **spit**,
pres p **spitting**) cracher; (*splutter*) (*of fat,
fire*) crépiter ▌ *vt* cracher; **to s. out**
(re)cracher; **to be the spitting image** of s.o.
être le portrait (tout craché) de qn. **2** *n* (*for
meat*) broche *f.*

spite [spaɪt] **1** *n* **in s. of** malgré; **in s. of the
fact that** (*although*) bien que (+ *sub*). **2** *n*
(*dislike*) rancune *f* ▌ *vt* (*annoy*) contrarier.
● **spiteful** *a* méchant. ● **spitefully** *adv* méchamment.

spittle ['spɪt(ə)l] *n* crachat *m*; (*in mouth*) sa-

live f.
splash [splæʃ] vt (spatter) éclabousser (**with** de, **over** sur); (spill) répandre.
❚ vi (of mud, ink etc) faire des éclaboussures; (of waves) clapoter; **to s. over** sth/s.o. éclabousser qch/qn; **to s. (about)** (in river, mud) patauger; (in bath) barboter; **to s. out** (spend money) Fam claquer de l'argent.
❚ n (splashing) éclaboussement m; (of colour) Fig tache f; **s. (mark)** éclaboussure f; **s.!** plouf!
spleen [spli:n] n Anat rate f.
splendid ['splendɪd] a (wonderful, rich, beautiful etc) splendide. ●**splendour** (Am **splendor**) n splendeur f.
splint [splɪnt] n (for broken arm etc) attelle f.
splinter ['splɪntər] n (of wood etc) éclat m; (in finger) écharde f; **s. group** Pol groupe m dissident.
split [splɪt] n fente f; (tear) déchirure f; (of couple) rupture f; (in political party etc) scission f; **to do the splits** (in gymnastics) faire le grand écart; **one's s.** (share) Fam sa part.
❚ vt (pt & pp **split**, pres p **splitting**) (break apart) fendre; (tear) déchirer; **to s. (up)** (group) diviser; (money, work) partager (**between** entre); **to s. one's head open** s'ouvrir la tête; **to s. one's sides (laughing)** se tordre (de rire); **to s. hairs** (make trivial distinctions) couper les cheveux en quatre.
❚ vi se fendre; (tear) se déchirer; **to s. (up)** (of group) se diviser (**into** en); **to s. off** (become loose) se détacher (**from** de); **to s. up** (because of disagreement) (of couple, friends etc) se séparer; (of lovers) rompre; (disperse) (of crowd) se disperser.
❚ a a. second une fraction de seconde; **s.-level house** maison f à deux niveaux; **s.-level apartment** duplex m.
splitting ['splɪtɪŋ] a **to have a s. headache** avoir un mal de tête épouvantable.
split-up ['splɪtʌp] n (of couple) séparation f, rupture f.
splodge [splɒdʒ] or **splotch** [splɒtʃ] n (mark) tache f.
splurge [splɜ:dʒ] vi (spend money) Fam claquer de l'argent.
splutter ['splʌtər] vi (spit) (of person) crachoter; (of sparks, fat) crépiter; (stammer) bredouiller.
spoil [spɔɪl] vt (pt & pp **spoilt** or **spoiled**) (make unpleasant or less good) gâter; (damage, ruin) abîmer; (pleasure, life) gâcher, gâter; (pamper) gâter (qn). ●**spoilsport** n rabat-joie m inv.
spoils [spɔɪlz] npl (rewards) butin m.
spoke¹ [spəʊk] n (of wheel) rayon m.
spoke² [spəʊk] pt of speak. ●**spoken** pp of speak ❚ a (language etc) parlé; **to be softly s.** avoir la voix douce. ●**spokesman** (pl -men) or **spokesperson** or **spokeswoman** (pl -women) n porte-parole m inv (**for, of** de).

sponge [spʌndʒ] 1 n éponge f; **s. bag** Br trousse f de toilette; **s. cake** gâteau m de Savoie ❚ vt **to s. down/off** laver/enlever à l'éponge; **to s. oneself down** se laver à l'éponge. 2 vi **to s. off** or **on s.o.** Fam vivre aux crochets de qn ❚ vt **to s. sth off** s.o. Fam taper qn de qch. ●**sponger** n Fam parasite m. ●**spongy** a (-ier, -iest) spongieux.
sponsor ['spɒnsər] n (of appeal, advertiser etc) personne f assurant le patronage (**of** de); (for membership) parrain m, marraine f; (for loan) garant, -ante mf; Sport sponsor m ❚ vt (appeal etc) patronner; (member, company) parrainer; (match, sportsman etc) sponsoriser. ●**sponsorship** n patronage m; (member etc) parrainage m; Sport sponsoring m.
spontaneous [spɒn'teɪnɪəs] a spontané. ●**spontaneity** [spɒntə'neɪətɪ] n spontanéité f. ●**spontaneously** adv spontanément.
spoof [spu:f] n (parody) Fam parodie f (**on** de); **s. thriller** parodie f de film à suspense.
spooky ['spu:kɪ] a (-ier, -iest) Fam qui donne le frisson.
spool [spu:l] n bobine f.
spoon [spu:n] n cuillère f. ●**spoonfeed** vt (pt & pp **spoonfed**) (help) Fig mâcher le travail à. ●**spoonful** n cuillerée f.
sporadic [spə'rædɪk] a sporadique; **s. fighting** échauffourées fpl; **s. shooting** des tirs mpl sporadiques. ●**sporadically** adv sporadiquement.
sport¹ [spɔ:t] n sport m; **a (good) s.** (person) Fam un chic type; **to play s.** Br, **play sports** Am faire du sport; **sports club** club m sportif; **sports car/jacket/ground** voiture f/veste f/terrain m de sport; **sports results** résultats mpl sportifs. ●**sporting** a (attitude, conduct, person etc) sportif; **that's s. of you** Fig c'est chic de ta part.
sport² [spɔ:t] vt (wear) arborer.
sportsman ['spɔ:tsmən] n (pl -men) sportif m. ●**sportsmanlike** a sportif. ●**sportsmanship** n sportivité f. ●**sportswear** n vêtements mpl de sport. ●**sportswoman** n (pl -women) sportive f. ●**sporty** a (-ier, -iest) sportif.
spot¹ [spɒt] n (stain, mark) tache f; (dot) point m; (polka dot) pois m; (pimple) bouton m; (place) endroit m, coin m; (in TV show etc) numéro m; (advertising) spot m or message m publicitaire; (drop) goutte f; **a s. of** (bit) Fam un peu de; **to have a soft s. for** s.o. avoir un faible pour qn; **on the s.** sur place, sur les lieux; (at once) sur le coup; **to be in a (tight) s.** (difficulty) être dans le pétrin; (accident) **black s.** (on road) Br point m noir; **blind s.** (in vehicle) angle m mort; **bright s.** Fig point m positif; **s. cash** argent m comptant; **s. check** contrôle m au hasard or à l'improviste.
spot² [spɒt] vt (-tt-) (notice) apercevoir, remarquer.
spotless ['spɒtləs] a (clean) impeccable. ●**spotlessly** adv **s. clean** impeccable.
spotlight ['spɒtlaɪt] n (lamp) (in theatre) projecteur m; (for photography etc) spot m;

to be in the s. (*film star etc*) être sous le feu des projecteurs.

spot-on [spɒt'ɒn] *a Br Fam* tout à fait exact.

spotted ['spɒtɪd] *a* (*fur*) tacheté; (*dress etc*) à pois; (*stained*) taché.

spotty ['spɒtɪ] *a* (**-ier, -iest**) **1** (*face, person etc*) boutonneux. **2** (*patchy*) *Am* inégal.

spouse [spaʊs, spaʊz] *n* époux *m*, épouse *f*.

spout [spaʊt] **1** *n* (*of teapot, jug etc*) bec *m*; **to be up the** s. (*of hopes, plan etc*) *Br Sl* être fichu. **2** *vi* **to** s. (**out**) (*of liquid*) jaillir. **3** *vt* (*say*) *Pej* débiter.

sprain [spreɪn] *n* foulure *f*, entorse *f*; **to** s. **one's ankle/wrist** se fouler la cheville/le poignet.

sprang [spræŋ] *pt of* **spring¹**.

sprawl [sprɔːl] *vi* (*of town, person etc*) s'étaler; **to be sprawling** être étalé ∎ *n* **the urban** s. les banlieues *fpl* tentaculaires. ●**sprawling** *a* (*city*) tentaculaire.

spray [spreɪ] **1** *n* (*can, device*) bombe *f*, vaporisateur *m*; (*water drops*) (nuage *m* de) gouttelettes *fpl*; (*from sea*) embruns *mpl*; **hair** s. laque *f* à cheveux ∎ *vt* (*liquid, surface*) vaporiser; (*plant, crops*) arroser, traiter; (*car etc*) peindre à la bombe. **2** *n* (*of flowers*) petit bouquet *m*.

spread [spred] *vt* (*pt & pp* **spread**) (*stretch, open out*) étendre; (*legs, fingers*) écarter; (*distribute, strew*) répandre, étaler (*over* sur); (*paint, payment, visits, cards*) étaler; (*fear, knowledge*) répandre; (*news*) propager, répandre; (*germs, illness*) propager; **to** s. **out** étendre; (*fingers etc*) écarter; (*objects*) répandre, étaler; (*payments, visits etc*) étaler; (*people*) disperser.

∎ *vi* (*of fire, town, fog*) s'étendre; (*of epidemic*) se propager; (*of news*) se propager, se répandre; (*of fear*) se répandre; **to** s. **out** (*of people*) se disperser.

∎ *n* (*of fire, germs, ideas etc*) propagation *f*; (*of wealth*) répartition *f*; (*paste for sandwiches etc*) pâte *f* (à tartiner); (*meal*) festin *m*; **cheese** s. fromage *m* à tartiner. ●**spread-'eagled** *a* bras et jambes écartés. ●**spread-sheet** *n Comptr* tableur *m*.

spree [spriː] *n* **to go on a spending** s. faire des achats extravagants.

sprig [sprɪg] *n* (*branch of heather etc*) brin *m*; (*of parsley*) bouquet *m*.

sprightly ['spraɪtlɪ] *a* (**-ier, -iest**) alerte. ●**sprightliness** *n* vivacité *f*.

spring¹ [sprɪŋ] *n* (*metal device*) ressort *m*; (*leap*) bond *m* ∎ *vi* (*pt* **sprang**, *pp* **sprung**) (*leap*) bondir; **to** s. **into action** passer à l'action; **to** s. **from** (*stem from*) provenir de; **to** s. **up** (*appear*) surgir ∎ *vt* (*news*) annoncer brusquement (*on* à); (*surprise*) faire (**on** à); **to** s. **a leak** (*of boat*) commencer à faire eau. ●**springboard** *n* tremplin *m*. ●**springy** *a* (**-ier, -iest**) élastique.

spring² [sprɪŋ] *n* (*season*) printemps *m*; **in** (**the**) s. au printemps; s. **onion** *Br* oignon *m* vert. ●**spring-'cleaning** *n* nettoyage *m* de

printemps. ●**springlike** *a* printanier. ●**springtime** *n* printemps *m*.

spring³ [sprɪŋ] *n* (*of water*) source *f*; s. **water** eau *f* de source.

sprinkle ['sprɪŋk(ə)l] *vt* (*sand etc*) répandre (**on, over** sur); **to** s. **with water**, s. **water on** asperger d'eau, arroser; **to** s. **with** (*sugar, salt, flour*) saupoudrer de. ●**sprinkling** *n* a s. **of customers**/*etc* (*a few*) quelques (rares) clients/*etc*. ●**sprinkler** *n* (*in garden*) arroseur *m*.

sprint [sprɪnt] *n* (*race*) sprint *m* ∎ *vi* (*run*) sprinter. ●**sprinter** *n* sprinter *m*, sprinteuse *f*.

sprite [spraɪt] *n* (*fairy*) lutin *m*.

sprout [spraʊt] **1** *vi* (*of seed, bulb etc*) germer, pousser; **to** s. **up** (*grow*) pousser vite; (*appear*) surgir ∎ *vt* (*leaves*) pousser; (*beard, whiskers*) *Fig* laisser pousser. **2** *n* (**Brussels**) s. chou *m* de Bruxelles.

spruce¹ [spruːs] *a* (**-er, -est**) (*neat*) pimpant, net (*f* nette) ∎ *vt* **to** s. **oneself up** se faire beau (*or f* belle).

spruce² [spruːs] *n* (*tree*) épicéa *m*.

sprung [sprʌŋ] *pp of* **spring¹** ∎ *a* (*mattress, seat*) à ressorts.

spry [spraɪ] *a* (**spryer, spryest**) (*old person etc*) alerte.

spud [spʌd] *n* (*potato*) *Fam* patate *f*.

spun [spʌn] *pt & pp of* **spin**.

spur [spɜːr] *n* (*of horse rider*) éperon *m*; (*stimulus*) *Fig* aiguillon *m*; **to do sth on the** s. **of the moment** faire qch sur un coup de tête ∎ *vt* (**-rr-**) **to** s. **s.o. on** (*urge on*) aiguillonner qn.

spurious ['spjʊərɪəs] *a* faux (*f* fausse).

spurn [spɜːn] *vt* rejeter (avec mépris).

spurt [spɜːt] *vi* (*gush out*) (*of liquid*) jaillir; (*rush*) (*of person, animal*) foncer (**to** vers); **to** s. **out** (*of liquid*) jaillir ∎ *n* (*of liquid*) jaillissement *m*; (*of energy*) sursaut *m*; **a** s. **of activity/effort** un regain d'activité/d'effort; **to put on a** s. (*rush to place, in one's work etc*) foncer.

spy [spaɪ] *n* espion, -onne *mf* ∎ *a* (*story, film etc*) d'espionnage; s. **hole** (*peephole*) judas *m*; s. **ring** réseau *m* d'espionnage ∎ *vi* espionner; **to** s. **on s.o.** espionner qn ∎ *vt* (*notice*) *Lit* apercevoir. ●**spying** *n* espionnage *m*.

squabble ['skwɒb(ə)l] *vi* se chamailler (**over** à propos de) ∎ *n* chamaillerie *f*. ●**squabbling** *n* chamailleries *fpl*.

sq *a abbr* (*square*) carré.

squad [skwɒd] *n* (*group of policemen, soldiers etc*) escouade *f*; (*sports team*) équipe *f*; **the riot** s. la brigade anti-émeute; s. **car** *Br* voiture *f* de police.

squadron ['skwɒdrən] *n Mil* escadron *m*; *Nau Av* escadrille *f*.

squalid ['skwɒlɪd] *a* sordide. ●**squalor** *n* conditions *fpl* sordides.

squall [skwɔːl] *n* (*of wind*) rafale *f*.

squander ['skwɒndər] *vt* (*money, time etc*) gaspiller; **to** s. **one's savings on clothes/on a**

motorcycle gaspiller ses économies en vêtements/dans une moto.

square ['skweər] *n* carré *m*; (*on chessboard, graph paper etc*) case *f*; (*in town*) place *f*; (*drawing implement*) *Br* équerre *f*; **to start from s. one** repartir à zéro; **to be back to s. one** se retrouver à la case départ.

▮ *a* carré; (*in order, settled*) *Fig* en ordre; (*honest*) honnête; (*meal*) solide; **a s. meal** un repas solide; **we're (all) s.** (*quits*) *Fam* nous sommes quittes.

▮ *vt* (*settle*) mettre en ordre, régler; (*arrange*) arranger; (*number*) *Math* mettre au carré; (*reconcile*) faire cadrer.

▮ *vi* (*tally*) cadrer (**with** avec); **to s. up to** faire face à. ●**squarely** *adv* (*honestly*) honnêtement; (*exactly*) tout à fait; **to look at s.o. s. in the eye(s)** *or* **in the face** regarder qn bien en face.

squash [skwɒʃ] **1** *vt* (*crush*) écraser; (*squeeze*) serrer ▮ *n* **lemon/orange s.** *Br* (*concentrated*) sirop *m* de citron/d'orange; (*diluted*) citronnade *f*/orangeade *f*. **2** *n* (*game*) squash *m*. **3** *n* (*vegetable*) *Am* courge *f*. ●**squashy** *a* (-ier, -iest) (*soft*) mou (*f* molle).

squat [skwɒt] **1** *vi* (-tt-) **to s. (down)** s'accroupir; **to be squatting (down)** être accroupi. **2** *a* (*short and thick*) trapu. **3** *n* (*house*) squat *m*. ●**squatter** *n* squatter *m*.

squawk [skwɔːk] *vi* pousser des cris rauques ▮ *n* cri *m* rauque.

squeak [skwiːk] *vi* (*of door*) grincer; (*of shoe*) craquer; (*of mouse*) faire couic ▮ *n* grincement *m*; (*of shoe*) craquement *m*; (*of mouse*) couic *m*. ●**squeaky** *a* (-ier, -iest) (*door*) grinçant; (*shoe*) qui craque.

squeal [skwiːl] *vi* pousser des cris aigus; (*of Br tyres, Am tires*) crisser ▮ *n* cri *m* aigu; crissement *m*. **2** *vi* **to s. on s.o.** (*inform on*) *Fam* balancer qn.

squeamish ['skwiːmɪʃ] *a* facilement dégoûté, bien délicat.

squeegee ['skwiːdʒiː] *n* raclette *f* (à vitres).

squeeze [skwiːz] *vt* (*press*) presser; (*hand, arm, person*) serrer; **to s. the toothpaste** presser le tube de dentifrice; **to s. sth out of s.o.** (*information, secret etc*) arracher qch à qn; **to s. sth into sth** faire rentrer qch dans qch; **to s. (out)** (*juice etc*) faire sortir (**from** de).

▮ *vi* **to s. through/into**/*etc* (*force oneself*) se glisser par/dans/*etc*; **to s. in** trouver un peu de place; **to s. up** se serrer (**against** contre).

▮ *n* **to give sth a s.** presser qch; **to give s.o.'s hand/arm a s.** serrer la main/le bras à qn; **to give s.o. a s.** serrer qn dans ses bras; **it's a tight s.** il y a peu de place; **credit s.** *Fin* restrictions *fpl* de crédit. ●**squeezer** *n* **lemon s.** presse-citron *m inv*.

squelch [skweltʃ] **1** *vi* patauger (*en faisant floc-floc*). **2** *vt* (*silence*) *Fam* réduire (*qn*) au silence.

squid [skwɪd] *n* (*mollusc*) calmar *m*.

squiggle ['skwɪg(ə)l] *n* gribouillis *m*; (*line*) ligne *f* onduleuse.

squint [skwɪnt] *n* (*eye disorder*) strabisme *m*; **to have a s.** loucher ▮ *vi* loucher; (*in the sunlight etc*) plisser les yeux.

squire ['skwaɪər] *n* *Br* propriétaire *m* terrien.

squirm [skwɜːm] *vi* (*wriggle*) se tortiller; **to s. in pain** se tordre de douleur.

squirrel [*Br* 'skwɪrəl, *Am* 'skwɜːrəl] *n* écureuil *m*.

squirt [skwɜːt] **1** *vt* (*liquid*) faire gicler ▮ *vi* gicler ▮ *n* giclée *f*, jet *m*. **2** *n* **little s.** (*person*) *Fam* petit morveux *m*.

Sri Lanka [sriː'læŋkə] *n* Sri Lanka *m* or *f*.

St *abbr* **1** = Street. **2** = Saint.

stab [stæb] *vt* (-bb-) (*with knife etc*) poignarder; **to s. s.o. to death** tuer qn d'un coup *or* de coups de couteau *or* de poignard ▮ *n* **s. (wound)** coup *m* (de couteau *or* de poignard). ●**stabbing** *n* **there has been a s.** quelqu'un a été poignardé; **a s. pain** une douleur lancinante.

stability [stə'bɪlɪtɪ] *n* stabilité *f*; **mental s.** équilibre *m*.

stabilize ['steɪbɪlaɪz] *vt* stabiliser ▮ *vi* se stabiliser. ●**stabilizer** *n* (*in racing car etc*) stabilisateur *m*.

stable[1] ['steɪb(ə)l] *a* (-er, -est) stable; **mentally s.** (*person*) bien équilibré.

stable[2] ['steɪb(ə)l] *n* écurie *f*; **s. boy** lad *m*.

stack [stæk] **1** *n* (*heap*) tas *m*; **stacks of** (*lots of*) *Fam* un or des tas de ▮ *vt* **to s. (up)** entasser. **2** *n* **chimney s.** (*of factory etc*) tuyau *m* de cheminée. **3** *npl* **the stacks** (*in library*) la réserve *f*.

stadium ['steɪdɪəm] *n* *Sport* stade *m*.

staff [stɑːf] **1** *n* personnel *m*; (*of school, university*) professeurs *mpl*; (*of army*) état-major *m*; **to be on the s.** faire partie du personnel; **a member of (the) s.**, **a s. member** (*in office*) un(e) employé, -ée; (*in school*) un professeur; **chief of s.** *Mil* chef *m* d'état-major; **s. meeting** (*in school, university*) *Br* conseil *m* des professeurs; **s. room** (*in school etc*) *Br* salle *f* des professeurs ▮ *vt* pourvoir en personnel. **2** *n* (*stick*) *Lit* bâton *m*.

stag [stæg] *n* cerf *m*; **s. party** réunion *f* entre hommes.

stage[1] [steɪdʒ] *n* (*platform in theatre*) scène *f*; **the s.** (*profession*) le théâtre; **on s.** sur (la) scène; **s. door** entrée *f* des artistes; **to have s. fright** avoir le trac ▮ *vt* (*play*) monter; *Fig* organiser, effectuer; **it was staged** (*not real*) c'était un coup monté. ●**stage-hand** *n* machiniste *m*. ●**stage-manager** *n* régisseur *m*.

stage[2] [steɪdʒ] *n* (*phase*) stade *m*, étape *f*; (*of journey*) étape *f*; (*of track, road*) section *f*; **in (easy) stages** (*to travel*) par étapes; (*to pay*) en plusieurs fois; **at an early s.** au début (**of** de); **at this s. in the work** à ce stade des travaux; **at this s.** (*at this moment*) à l'heure qu'il est.

stagecoach ['steɪdʒkəʊtʃ] *n* *Hist* diligence *f*.

stagger ['stægər] **1** *vi* (*reel*) chanceler. **2** *vt* (*Br holidays, Am vacation etc*) étaler, échelonner. **3** *vt* **to s. s.o.** (*shock, amaze*) stupé-

fier qn. ●**staggering** *a* stupéfiant.
stagnant ['stægnənt] *a* stagnant. ●**stag'nate** *vi* stagner. ●**stagnation** [-'neɪʃ(ə)n] *n* stagnation *f*.
staid [steɪd] *a* posé, sérieux.
stain [steɪn] **1** *vt* (*mark, make dirty*) tacher (with de) ▎ *n* tache *f*; **s. remover** détachant *m*. **2** *vt* (*colour*) teinter (*du bois*); **stained glass window** vitrail *m* (*pl* vitraux) ▎ *n* (*colouring for wood*) teinture *f* (à bois); **a** *Br* **tin** *or* *Am* **can of** s. un bidon de teinture. ●**stainless steel** *n* acier *m* inoxydable, inox *m*; **s.-steel knife/etc** couteau *m/etc* en inox.
stair [steər] *n* **a** s. (*step*) une marche; **the stairs** (*staircase*) l'escalier *m*; **s. carpet** tapis *m* d'escalier. ●**staircase** *or* **stairway** *n* escalier *m*.
stake [steɪk] **1** *n* (*post*) pieu *m*; (*for plant*) tuteur *m*; **to be burned at the s.** mourir sur le bûcher ▎ *vt* **to s.** (**out**) (*land*) jalonner, délimiter; **to s. one's claim to sth** revendiquer qch. **2** *n* (*betting*) enjeu *m*; (*investment*) investissement *m*; **to have a s. in a company** (*interest*) posséder un intérêt *or* des intérêts dans une société; **at s.** en jeu; **there's a lot at s.** l'enjeu est considérable ▎ *vt* (*bet*) jouer (**on** sur).
stale [steɪl] *a* (-er, -est) (*bread*) rassis (*f* rassie); (*food*) pas frais (*f* fraîche); (*beer*) éventé; (*air*) vicié; (*smell*) de renfermé; (*news*) *Fig* vieux (*f* vieille); (*joke*) usé, vieux; (*artist*) manquant d'invention. ●**staleness** *n* (*of food*) manque *m* de fraîcheur.
stalemate ['steɪlmeɪt] *n* *Chess* pat *m*; *Fig* impasse *f*.
stalk [stɔːk] **1** *n* (*of plant*) tige *f*, queue *f*; (*of fruit*) queue *f*. **2** *vt* (*animal, criminal*) traquer. **3** *vi* **to s. out** (*walk proudly*) sortir d'un air digne; (*angrily*) sortir en colère.
stall [stɔːl] **1** *n* (*in market*) étal *m*, éventaire *m*; (*for newspapers, flowers*) *Br* kiosque *m*; (*in stable*) stalle *f*; **the stalls** (*in cinema, theatre*) *Br* l'orchestre *m*. **2** *vi* (*of car engine*) caler ▎ *vt* (*engine, car*) caler. **3** *vt* **to s. (for time)** chercher à gagner du temps.
stallion ['stæljən] *n* (*horse*) étalon *m*.
stalwart ['stɔːlwət] *a* (*supporter*) brave, fidèle ▎ *n* (*follower*) fidèle *mf*.
stamina ['stæmɪnə] *n* vigueur *f*, résistance *f*.
stammer ['stæmər] *vi* bégayer ▎ *vt* **to s. out** (*excuse etc*) bégayer ▎ *n* bégaiement *m*, **to have a s.** être bègue.
stamp [stæmp] **1** *n* (*for postage, instrument*) timbre *m*; (*mark*) cachet *m*, timbre *m*; **the s. of success/etc** *Fig* la marque de la réussite/ *etc*; **to be given the s. of approval** être approuvé; **men of your s.** les hommes de votre trempe; **s. collecting** philatélie *f*.
▎ *vt* (*document*) tamponner, timbrer; (*letter*) timbrer; (*metal*) estamper; **to s. sth on sth** (*affix*) apposer qch sur qch; **to s. out** (*rebellion, evil*) écraser; (*disease*) éradiquer; **stamped addressed envelope** *Br*, **stamped self-addressed envelope** *Am* enveloppe *f* tim-

brée à votre adresse.
2 *vti* **to s. (one's feet)** taper *or* frapper des pieds; **stamping ground** *Fam* lieu *m* favori.
stampede [stæm'piːd] *n* fuite *f* précipitée; (*rush*) ruée *f* ▎ *vi* fuir en désordre; (*rush*) se ruer.
stance [stɑːns] *n* position *f*.
stand [stænd] *n* (*position*) position *f*; (*support*) support *m*; (*at exhibition*) stand *m*; (*for spectators at sporting event*) tribune *f*; (*witness*) s. (*in court*) *Am* barre *f*; **to make a s.**, **take one's s.** prendre position (**against** contre); **news/flower s.** (*in street*) kiosque *m* à journaux/à fleurs; **hat s.** portemanteau *m*; **music s.** pupitre *m* à musique.
▎ *vt* (*pt & pp* **stood**) (*pain, journey etc*) supporter; (*put straight*) mettre (debout); **to s. a chance** avoir une chance; **I can't s. him** je ne ne peux pas le supporter; **I can't s. it** je ne supporte pas ça; **to s. s.o. sth** (*pay for*) *Br* payer qch à qn.
▎ *vi* être *or* se tenir (debout); (*get up*) se lever; (*remain*) rester (debout); (*be situated*) se trouver; (*be*) être; (*of object, argument*) reposer (**on** sur); (*be true*) tenir; (*of liquid*) reposer; **to s. to lose** risquer de perdre qch/s.o. risquer de perdre qch/qn.
stand about *or* **around** *vi* (*in street etc*) traîner ▎ **to stand aside** *vi* s'écarter ▎ **to stand back** *vi* reculer ▎ **to stand by** (*do nothing*) rester là (sans rien faire); (*be ready*) être prêt (à partir *or* à intervenir *etc*) ▎ *vt* (*one's opinion etc*) s'en tenir à; (*friend etc*) rester fidèle à ▎ **to stand down** *vi* (*withdraw*) se désister ▎ **to stand for** *vt* (*mean*) signifier; (*represent*) représenter; (*be candidate for*) *Br* être candidat à (*présidence etc*); (*put up with*) supporter ▎ **to stand in for** *vt* (*replace*) remplacer ▎ **to stand out** *vi* (*be visible or conspicuous*) ressortir (**against** sur) ▎ **to stand over** *vt* (*watch closely*) surveiller (*qn*) ▎ **to stand up** *vt* mettre debout; **to s. s.o. up** *Fam* poser un lapin à qn ▎ *vi* (*get up*) se lever ▎ **to stand up for** *vt* (*defend*) défendre ▎ **to stand up to** *vt* (*resist*) résister à; (*defend oneself against*) tenir tête à (*qn*).
standard¹ ['stændəd] **1** *n* (*norm*) norme *f*, critère *m*; (*level*) niveau *m*; (*of weight, gold*) étalon *m*; **standards (of behaviour)** principes *mpl*; **s. of living, living standards** niveau *m* de vie; **to be** *or* **come up to s.** (*of person*) être à la hauteur; (*of work etc*) être au niveau.
▎ *a* (*average*) ordinaire, courant; (*model, size*) standard *inv*; (*weight*) étalon *inv*; (*dictionary, book*) classique; **s. lamp** *Br* lampadaire *m*. ●**standardize** *vt* standardiser.
standard² ['stændəd] *n* (*flag*) étendard *m*.
standby ['stændbaɪ] *n* (*pl* -bys) **on s.** prêt à partir *or* à intervenir *etc* ▎ *a* (*battery etc*) de réserve; (*plane ticket*) sans garantie.
stand-in ['stændɪn] *n* remplaçant, -ante *mf* (**for** de); (*actor, actress*) doublure *f* (**for** de).
standing ['stændɪŋ] *a* debout *inv*; (*committee, offer, army*) permanent; **s. room**

places *fpl* debout; **s. order** (*in bank*) *Br* virement *m* automatique; **it's a s.** c'est un sujet de plaisanterie ∎ *n* (*reputation*) réputation *f*; (*social, professional*) rang *m*; (*financial*) situation *f*; **a friendship/***etc* **of six years' s.** (*duration*) une amitié/*etc* qui dure depuis six ans; **of long s.** de longue date.

stand-offish [stænd'ɒfɪʃ] *a* (*person*) distant, froid.

standpoint ['stændpɔɪnt] *n* point *m* de vue.

standstill ['stændstɪl] *n* **to bring sth to a s.** immobiliser qch; **to come to a s.** s'immobiliser; **at a s.** immobile; (*negotiations, industry*) paralysé.

stand-up ['stændʌp] *a* **s.-up comic** *or* **comedian** comique *m* (de scène).

stank [stæŋk] *pt of* **stink**.

stanza ['stænzə] *n* strophe *f*.

staple ['steɪp(ə)l] **1** *a* (*basic*) de base; **s. food** *or* **diet** nourriture *f* de base. **2** *n* (*for paper etc*) agrafe *f* ∎ *vt* agrafer. ● **stapler** *n* (*for paper etc*) agrafeuse *f*.

star [stɑːr] *n* étoile *f*; (*famous person*) vedette *f*, star *f*; **shooting s.** étoile *f* filante; **s. part** rôle *m* principal; **the Stars and Stripes, the S.-Spangled Banner** (*flag of the United States*) la bannière étoilée; **four-s.** (*petrol*) *Br* du super ∎ *vi* (**-rr-**) (*of actor, actress*) être la vedette (**in** de) ∎ *vt* (*of film*) avoir (*qn*) pour vedette.

starboard ['stɑːbəd] *n* (*right side in ship or aircraft*) tribord *m* ∎ *a* de tribord.

starch [stɑːtʃ] *n* (*for stiffening*) amidon *m*; (*in food*) fécule *f*; **starches** (*foods*) féculents *mpl* ∎ *vt* amidonner. ● **starchy** *a* (**-ier, -iest**); (*formal*) (*manner, person etc*) guindé; **s. food(s)** féculents *mpl*.

stardom ['stɑːdəm] *n* célébrité *f*.

stare [steər] *n* regard *m* (fixe) ∎ *vi* **to s. at s.o./sth** fixer qn/qch (du regard) ∎ *vt* **to s. s.o. in the face** dévisager qn.

starfish ['stɑːfɪʃ] *n* étoile *f* de mer.

stark [stɑːk] *a* (**-er, -est**) (*place*) désolé; (*austere*) austère; (*fact, reality*) brutal; **to be in s.·contrast to** contraster nettement avec; **the s. truth** la vérité toute nue ∎ *adv* **s. naked** complètement nu. ● **starkers** *a Br Sl* complètement nu, à poil.

starling ['stɑːlɪŋ] *n* étourneau *m*.

starlit ['stɑːlɪt] *a* (*night*) étoilé.

starry ['stɑːrɪ] *a* (**-ier, -iest**) (*sky, night*) étoilé. ● **starry-'eyed** *a* (*naïve*) ingénu, naïf.

start¹ [stɑːt] *n* commencement *m*, début *m*; (*of race*) départ *m*; (*lead in race, competition etc*) avance *f* (**on** sur); **to make a s.** commencer; **for a s.** pour commencer; **from the s.** dès le début.

∎ *vt* commencer; (*bottle, cake, packet*) entamer, commencer; (*fashion, campaign, offensive*) lancer; (*engine, vehicle*) mettre en marche; (*business*) fonder; **to s. a war** provoquer une guerre; **to s. a fire** (*deliberately*) (*in grate etc*) allumer un feu; (*accidentally*) provoquer un incendie; **to s. doing** *or* **to do** commencer *or* se mettre à faire.

∎ *vi* commencer (**with sth** par qch, **by doing** par faire); (*of vehicle*) démarrer; (*leave*) partir (**for** pour); (*in job*) débuter; **to s. with** (*firstly*) pour commencer; **starting from now/ten francs/***etc* à partir de maintenant/dix francs/*etc*. ● **starting** *a* (*point, line*) de départ; **s. post** (*in race*) ligne *f* de départ.

start² [stɑːt] *vi* (*be startled, jump*) sursauter ∎ *n* sursaut *m*; **to give s.o. a s.** faire sursauter qn.

start back *vi* (*return*) repartir ∎ **to start off** *vi* (*leave*) partir (**for** pour); (*in job*) débuter ∎ *vt* **to s. s.o. off on a career** lancer qn dans une carrière ∎ **to s. on** *vt* commencer (*qch*); **to s. s.o. on a career** lancer qn dans une carrière ∎ *vt* **to s. off** *vi* = **to start off** ∎ **to start up** *vt* (*engine, vehicle*) mettre en marche; (*business*) fonder ∎ *vi* (*of engine, vehicle*) démarrer.

starter ['stɑːtər] *n* (*device in vehicle*) démarreur *m*; (*course of meal*) hors-d'œuvre *m inv*, entrée *f*; (*soup*) potage *m*; (*runner*) partant; (*official in race*) starter *m*; **for starters** (*firstly*) *Fam* pour commencer.

startle ['stɑːt(ə)l] *vt* (*make jump*) faire sursauter; (*alarm*) *Fig* alarmer; (*surprise*) surprendre.

starvation [stɑː'veɪʃ(ə)n] *n* faim *f* ∎ *a* (*wage, ration etc*) de famine; **to be on a s. diet** (*to lose weight*) être à la diète.

starve [stɑːv] *vi* (*suffer*) souffrir de la faim; **to s. (to death)** mourir de faim; **I'm starving!** (*hungry*) je meurs de faim! ∎ *vt* (*make suffer*) faire souffrir de la faim; (*deprive*) *Fig* priver (**of** de); **to s. s.o. (to death)** laisser qn mourir de faim.

stash [stæʃ] *vt* **to s. away** *Fam* (*hide*) cacher; (*save up*) mettre de côté.

state¹ [steɪt] **1** *n* (*condition*) état *m*; (*pomp*) apparat *m*; **not in a (fit) s. to..., in no (fit) s. to...** hors d'état de...; **in (quite) a s.** (*bad shape*) dans un drôle d'état; **to lie in s.** (*of body*) être exposé.

2 *n* **s.** (*nation pect*) État *m*; **the States** *Fam* les États-Unis *mpl* ∎ *a* (*secret, document*) d'État; (*control, security*) de l'État; (*school, education*) *Br* public; **s. visit** voyage *m* officiel; **S. Department** *Am* Département *m* d'État. ● **stateless** *a* apatride; **s. person** apatride *mf*. ● **state-'owned** *a* étatisé.

state² [steɪt] *vt* déclarer (**that** que); (*opinion*) formuler; (*problem*) exposer; (*time, date*) fixer.

stately ['steɪtlɪ] *a* (**-ier, -iest**) majestueux; **s. home** *Br* château *m*.

statement ['steɪtmənt] *n* déclaration *f*; (*in court*) déposition *f*; (*bank*) **s., s. of account** relevé *m* de compte.

state-of-the-art [steɪtəvðɪ'ɑːt] *a* (*technology etc*) de pointe; (*up-to-date*) (*computer, television etc*) dernier cri *inv*.

statesman ['steɪtsmən] *n* (*pl* **-men**) homme *m* d'État. ● **statesmanship** *n* diplomatie *f*.

static ['stætɪk] *a* statique ∎ *n* (*noise on the radio etc*) parasites *mpl*.

station ['steɪʃ(ə)n] n (for trains) gare f; (underground) station f; (position) & Mil poste m; (social) rang m; (police) s. commissariat m or poste m (de police); space/observation/radio/etc s. station f spatiale/d'observation/de radio/etc; bus or Br coach s. gare f routière; service or Br petrol or Am gas s. station-service f; s. wagon (car) Am break m ● vt (position) placer, poster; to be stationed at/in (of troops) être en garnison à/en. ● stationmaster n Rail chef m de gare.

stationary ['steɪʃ(ə)rɪ] a (motionless) (vehicle) à l'arrêt; (person) immobile.

stationer ['steɪʃ(ə)nər] n papetier, -ière mf; s.'s (shop) papeterie f. ● stationery n (articles) articles mpl de bureau; (paper) papier m.

statistic [stə'tɪstɪk] n (fact) statistique f; statistics (science) la statistique. ● statistical a statistique.

statue ['stætʃuː] n statue f. ● statu'esque a (beauty, woman etc) sculptural.

stature ['stætʃər] n (height) stature f, taille f; (importance) Fig envergure f.

status ['steɪtəs] n (position) situation f; (legal, official) statut m; (prestige) standing m, prestige m; s. symbol marque f de standing; s. quo statu quo m inv.

statute ['stætʃuːt] n (law) loi f; statutes (of institution, club) statuts mpl. ● statutory a (right, duty etc) statutaire; s. holiday Br fête f légale.

staunch [stɔːntʃ] a (-er, -est) loyal, fidèle. ● staunchly adv loyalement.

stave [steɪv] 1 vt to s. off (disaster, danger) conjurer; to s. off hunger tromper la faim; to s. off s.o.'s attempt to do sth retarder qn dans sa tentative de faire qch. 2 n Mus portée f.

stay [steɪ] 1 n (visit) séjour m ● vi (remain) rester; (reside) loger; (visit) séjourner; to s. put ne pas bouger. 2 vt (hunger) tromper. ● stay-at-home n & a Pej casanier, -ière (mf). ● staying power n endurance f.

stay away vi (keep one's distance) ne pas s'approcher (from de); to s. away from (school, a meeting etc) ne pas aller à ● to stay behind vi rester en arrière ● to stay in vi (at home) rester à la maison; (of nail, screw, tooth etc) tenir ● to stay out vi (outside) rester dehors; (not come home) ne pas rentrer, to s. out of sth (not interfere in) ne pas se mêler de qch; (avoid) éviter qch ● to stay up vi (at night) ne pas se coucher; (of fence etc) tenir; to s. up late se coucher tard ● to stay with vt (plan, idea etc) ne pas lâcher.

St Bernard [Br sənt'bɜːnəd, Am seɪntbə'nɑːd] n (dog) saint-bernard m.

stead [sted] n to stand s.o. in good s. être bien utile à qn; in s.o.'s s. à la place de qn.

steadfast ['stedfɑːst] a (intention etc) ferme.

steady ['stedɪ] a (-ier, -iest) (firm, stable) stable; (hand) sûr, assuré; (progress, speed, demand) régulier, constant; (nerves) solide;

(staid) sérieux; a s. boyfriend un petit ami; a s. flood or stream of insults/etc un flot ininterrompu d'insultes/etc; to be s. (on one's feet) être solide sur ses jambes.
■ adv to go s. with s.o. Fam sortir avec qn.
■ vt (chair etc) maintenir (en place); (hand) assurer; (nerves) calmer; (wedge, prop up) caler; to s. oneself (stop oneself falling) reprendre son aplomb. ● steadily adv (to walk) d'un pas assuré; (gradually) progressivement; (regularly) régulièrement; (continuously) sans arrêt. ● steadiness n stabilité f, (of progress etc) régularité f.

steak [steɪk] n (beef) steak m, bifteck m; stewing s. bœuf m à pot-au-feu; s. and chips Br steak m frites; s. and kidney pie Br tourte f aux rognons et à la viande de bœuf. ● steakhouse n grill-(room) m.

steal¹ [stiːl] vti (pt stole, pp stolen) voler (from s.o. à qn).

steal² [stiːl] vi (pt stole, pp stolen) to s. in/out entrer/sortir furtivement. ● stealth [stelθ] n by s. furtivement. ● stealthy a (-ier, -iest) furtif.

steam [stiːm] n vapeur f; (on glass) buée f; to let off s. (unwind) Fam décompresser, se défouler; s. engine/iron locomotive f/fer m à vapeur ■ vt (food) cuire à la vapeur; to get steamed up (of glass) se couvrir de buée; (of person) Fam s'énerver ■ vi (of kettle etc) fumer; s. up (of glass) se couvrir de buée. ● steamer n (bateau m à) vapeur m; (ocean liner) paquebot m; (for food) = haut m de couscoussier.

steamroller ['stiːmrəʊlər] n rouleau m compresseur.

steamship ['stiːmʃɪp] n (bateau m à) vapeur m; (ocean liner) paquebot m.

steamy ['stiːmɪ] a (-ier, -iest) humide; (window) embué; (love affair, relationship etc) brûlant.

steel [stiːl] 1 n acier m; s. industry sidérurgie f. 2 vt to s. oneself s'armer de courage; to s. oneself against failure/etc s'endurcir contre l'échec/etc. ● steelworks n aciérie f.

steep [stiːp] 1 a (-er, -est) (stairs, slope etc) raide; (hill, path) escarpé; (price) Fig excessif. 2 vt (soak) tremper (in dans); steeped in (history, prejudice etc) Fig imprégné de. ● steeply adv (to rise) en pente raide; (of prices) Fig excessivement.

steeple ['stiːp(ə)l] n clocher m.

steeplechase ['stiːp(ə)ltʃeɪs] n (race) steeple-(chase) m.

steeplejack ['stiːp(ə)ldʒæk] n réparateur m de cheminées et de clochers.

steer [stɪər] vt (vehicle, person) diriger, piloter (towards vers); (ship, boat) diriger, gouverner ■ vi (of person) (in ship, boat) tenir le gouvernail, gouverner; (in vehicle) tenir le volant; to s. towards faire route vers; to s. clear of s.o./sth éviter qn/qch. ● steering n (in vehicle) direction f; s. wheel volant m.

stem [stem] 1 n (of plant etc) tige f; (of glass) pied m. 2 vt (-mm-) (stop) arrêter, contenir; **to s. the flow** *or* **tide of** (*refugees etc*) endiguer le flot de. **3** *vi* (**-mm-**) **to s. from** provenir de.

stench [stentʃ] *n* puanteur *f*.

stencil ['stens(ə)l] *n* (*metal, plastic*) pochoir *m*; (*paper, for typing*) stencil *m* ▌ *vt* (*Br* **-ll-**, *Am* **-l-**) (*notes etc*) polycopier.

stenographer [stə'nɒɡrəfər] *n* *Am* sténodactylo *f*. ● **stenography** *n* *Am* sténographie *f*.

step [step] *n* (*movement, sound*) pas *m*; (*of stairs*) marche *f*; (*on train, bus*) marchepied *m*; (*doorstep*) pas *m* de la porte; (*action*) *Fig* mesure *f*; (**flight of**) **steps** (*indoors*) escalier *m*; (*outdoors*) perron *m*; (**pair of**) **steps** (*ladder*) *Br* escabeau *m*; **s. by s.** pas à pas; **to keep in s.** marcher au pas; **to be in s. with** (*of opinions etc*) *Fig* être en accord avec. ▌ *vi* (**-pp-**) (*walk*) marcher (**on** sur); **s. this way!** (*venez*) par ici!.

step aside *vi* s'écarter ▌ **to step back** *vi* reculer ▌ **to step down** *vi* descendre (**from** de); (*withdraw*) *Fig* se retirer ▌ **to step forward** *vi* faire un pas en avant ▌ **to step in** *vi* (*enter*) entrer; (*into car*) monter; (*intervene*) *Fig* intervenir ▌ **to step into** *vt* (*car etc*) monter dans ▌ **to step off** *vt* (*chair etc*) descendre de ▌ **to step out** *vi* (*of car etc*) descendre (**of** de) ▌ **to step over** *vt* (*obstacle*) enjamber ▌ **to step up** *vt* (*increase*) augmenter, intensifier; (*speed up*) activer.

stepbrother ['stepbrʌðər] *n* demi-frère *m*. ● **stepdaughter** *n* belle-fille *f*. ● **stepfather** *n* beau-père *m*. ● **stepmother** *n* belle-mère *f*. ● **stepsister** *n* demi-sœur *f*. ● **stepson** *n* beau-fils *m*.

stepladder ['steplædər] *n* escabeau *m*.

stepping-stone ['stepɪŋstəʊn] *n* (*in career etc*) tremplin *m* (**to** pour arriver à).

stereo ['sterɪəʊ] *n* (*pl* **-os**) (*hi-fi, record player*) chaîne *f* (stéréo *inv*); (*sound*) stéréo(phonie) *f*; (*personal*) s. baladeur *m*; **in s.** en stéréo ▌ *a* (*record etc*) stéréo *inv*; (*broadcast*) en stéréo. ● **stereo'phonic** *a* stéréophonique.

stereotype ['sterɪətaɪp] *n* stéréotype *m*. ● **stereotyped** *a* stéréotypé.

sterile [*Br* 'steraɪl, *Am* 'sterəl] *a* stérile. ● **ste'rility** *n* stérilité *f*.

sterilize ['sterəlaɪz] *vt* stériliser. ● **sterilization** [-'zeɪʃ(ə)n] *n* stérilisation *f*.

sterling ['stɜːlɪŋ] *n* (*currency*) *Br* livre(s) *f*(*pl*) sterling *inv*; **the pound s.** la livre sterling *inv* ▌ *a* (*silver*) fin; (*quality, person*) *Fig* sûr.

stern [stɜːn] **1** *a* (**-er**, **-est**) sévère. **2** *n* (*of ship*) arrière *m*.

steroid ['stɪərɔɪd] *n* stéroïde *m*.

stethoscope ['steθəskəʊp] *n* stéthoscope *m*.

stetson ['stetsən] *n* *Am* chapeau *m* à larges bords.

stevedore ['stiːvədɔːr] *n* docker *m*.

stew [stjuː] *n* ragoût *m*; **to be in a s.** *Fig* être dans le pétrin; **s. pot, s. pan** cocotte *f* ▌ *vt* (*meat*) faire *or* cuire en ragoût; (*fruit*) faire cuire; **stewed fruit** compote *f* ▌ *vi* cuire.

● **stewing** *a* (*pears, apples etc*) à cuire.

steward ['stjuːəd] *n* (*on plane, ship*) steward *m*; (*in college, club etc*) intendant *m* (*préposé au ravitaillement*); **shop s.** *Br* délégué, -ée *mf* syndical(e). ● **stewar'dess** *n* (*on plane*) hôtesse *f*.

stick¹ [stɪk] *n* (*piece of wood, chalk, dynamite etc*) bâton *m*; (*for walking*) canne *f*; (*branch*) branche *f*; **in the sticks** (*countryside*) *Pej Fam* à la cambrousse; **to give s.o. some s.** (*scold*) *Br Fam* engueuler qn.

stick² [stɪk] *vt* (*pt & pp* **stuck**) (*glue*) coller; (*put*) *Fam* mettre, fourrer, coller; (*tolerate*) *Fam* supporter; **to s. sth into sth** fourrer *or* planter *or* enfoncer qch dans qch. ▌ *vi* attacher, adhérer (**to** à); (*of food in pan*) attacher (**to** dans); (*of drawer etc*) se coincer, se bloquer, être coincé *or* bloqué; (*remain*) *Fam* rester; **to s. to the facts** (*confine oneself to*) s'en tenir aux faits. ● **sticking plaster** *n Br* sparadrap *m*.

stick around *vi* (*hang around*) *Fam* rester dans les parages ▌ **to stick by** *vt* rester fidèle à (*qn*) ▌ **to stick down** *vt* (*envelope, stamp etc*) coller; (*put down*) *Fam* poser, coller ▌ **to stick on** *vt* (*stamp, label etc*) coller; (*hat, coat etc*) mettre ▌ **to stick out** *vt* (*tongue*) tirer; (*head or arm from window etc*) *Fam* sortir; **to s. it out** (*resist*) *Fam* tenir le coup ▌ *vi* (*of petticoat, balcony etc*) dépasser; (*of tooth*) avancer ▌ **to stick up** *vt* (*notice*) coller, afficher; (*hand*) *Fam* lever ▌ **to stick up for** *vt* défendre (*qn*, *qch*).

sticker ['stɪkər] *n* (*label*) autocollant *m*.

stickler ['stɪklər] *n* **to be a s. for** (*rules, discipline, details etc*) être intransigeant sur.

stick-on ['stɪkɒn] *a* (*label*) adhésif.

stick-up ['stɪkʌp] *n Fam* hold-up *m inv*.

sticky ['stɪkɪ] *a* (**-ier**, **-iest**) collant, poisseux; (*label*) adhésif; (*problem, matter*) *Fig* difficile.

stiff [stɪf] *a* (**-er**, **-est**) raide; (*leg, joint*) ankylosé; (*brush, paste*) dur; (*person*) *Fig* guindé, froid; (*difficult*) difficile; (*price*) élevé; (*whisky*) bien tassé; **to have a s. neck** avoir le torticolis; **to feel s.** être courbaturé *or* courbatu; **to be bored s.** *Fam* s'ennuyer à mourir; **frozen s.** *Fam* complètement gelé.

stiffen ['stɪf(ə)n] *vt* raidir ▌ *vi* se raidir.

stiffly ['stɪflɪ] *adv* (*coldly*) *Fig* froidement. ● **stiffness** *n* raideur *f*; (*hardness*) dureté *f*.

stifle ['staɪf(ə)l] *vt* (*feeling, person etc*) étouffer ▌ *vi* **it's stifling** on étouffe.

stigma ['stɪɡmə] *n* (*moral stain*) flétrissure *f*; **there's no s. attached to...** il n'y a aucune honte à.... ● **stigmatize** *vt* (*denounce*) dénoncer, stigmatiser; **to s. s.o. as** dénoncer qn (*publiquement*) comme.

stile [staɪl] *n* (*between fields etc*) échalier *m*.

stiletto [stɪ'letəʊ] *a* **s. heel** *Br* talon *m* aiguille.

still¹ [stɪl] *adv* encore, toujours; (*even*) encore; (*nevertheless*) tout de même; **better s., s. better** encore mieux.

still² [stɪl] *a* (**-er**, **-est**) (*not moving*) immobile; (*calm*) calme, tranquille; (*drink*) Br non gazeux; **to keep** *or* **stand** *or* **lie s.** rester tranquille; **s. life** (*painting, drawing*) nature *f* morte ▮ *n* (*photo of film*) photo *f* (*tirée d'un film*); **in the s. of the night** dans le silence de la nuit. ●**stillborn** (*baby*) *a* mort-né. ●**stillness** *n* immobilité *f*; (*calm*) calme *m*.

still³ [stɪl] *n* (*for making alcohol*) alambic *m*.

stilt [stɪlt] *n* (*pole*) échasse *f*.

stilted ['stɪltɪd] *a* (*speech, person etc*) guindé.

stimulate ['stɪmjuleɪt] *vt* stimuler. ●**stimulant** *n* (*drug etc*) stimulant *m*. ●**stimulation** [-'leɪʃ(ə)n] *n* stimulation *f*. ●**stimulus**, *pl* -**li** [-laɪ] *n* (*encouragement*) stimulant *m*; (*physiological*) stimulus *m*.

sting [stɪŋ] *vt* (*pt & pp* **stung**) (*of insect, ointment, wind etc*) piquer; (*of remark*) *Fig* blesser ▮ *vi* piquer ▮ *n* piqûre *f*; (*insect's organ*) dard *m*. ●**stinging** *a* (*pain, remark etc*) cuisant.

stingy ['stɪndʒɪ] *a* (-**ier**, -**iest**) avare, mesquin; **to be s. with** (*money, praise*) être avare de; (*food, wine*) être mesquin sur. ●**stinginess** *n* avarice *f*.

stink [stɪŋk] *n* puanteur *f*; **to cause** *or* **make a s.** (*trouble*) *Fam* faire du foin ▮ *vi* (*pt* **stank** *or* **stunk**, *pp* **stunk**) puer; (*of book, film etc*) *Fam* être infect; **to s. of smoke/etc** empester la fumée/etc ▮ *vt* **to s. out** (*room etc*) empester. ●**stinking** *a Fam* infect, sale. ●**stinker** *n Fam* (*person*) sale type *m*; (*question, task etc*) vacherie *f*.

stint [stɪnt] **1** *n* (*period*) période *f* de travail; (*share*) part *f* de travail. **2** *vi* **to s. on** (*food, money etc*) lésiner sur.

stipend ['staɪpend] *n* (*allowance for clergyman*) traitement *n*.

stipulate ['stɪpjuleɪt] *vt* stipuler (**that** que). ●**stipulation** [-'leɪʃ(ə)n] *n* stipulation *f*.

stir [stɜːr] *n* agitation *f*; **to give one's coffee/ etc a s.** remuer son café/etc; **to cause** *or* **create a s.** *Fig* faire du bruit.

▮ *vt* (-**rr**-) (*coffee, leaves etc*) remuer; (*excite*) *Fig* exciter; (*incite*) inciter (**s.o. to do** qn à faire); **to s. oneself** (*make an effort*) se secouer; **to s. up** (*memory*) réveiller; **to s. up trouble** (*of anarchist etc*) provoquer des troubles; (*in family etc*) semer la zizanie; **to s. up trouble for s.o.** attirer des ennuis à qn; **to s. up hatred** attiser les haines.

▮ *vi* (*move*) remuer, bouger. ●**stirring** *a* (*speech history*) émouvant.

stirrup ['stɪrəp] *n* étrier *m*.

stitch [stɪtʃ] *n* point *m*; (*in knitting*) maille *f*; (*in wound*) point *m* de suture; **a s. (in one's side)** (*pain*) un point de côté; **to be in stitches** *Fam* se tordre (de rire) ▮ *vt* **to s. (up)** (*sew up*) coudre; (*repair*) recoudre; (*wound*) suturer.

stoat [stəut] *n* (*animal*) hermine *f*.

stock [stɒk] *n* (*supply*) provision *f*, stock *m*, réserve *f*; (*of knowledge, jokes*) mine *f*; *Fin* valeurs *fpl*, titres *mpl*; (*family, descent*) souche *f*; (*soup*) bouillon *m*; (*cattle*) bétail *m*; **stocks and shares** *Fin* valeurs *fpl*, titres

mpl; **the stocks** *Hist* le pilori; **in s.** (*goods*) en magasin, en stock, disponible; **out of s.** (*goods*) épuisé, non disponible; **to take s.** *Fig* faire le point (**of** de); **s. reply/size** réponse *f*/taille *f* courante; **s. phrase** expression *f* toute faite; **the S. Exchange** *or* **Market** la Bourse.

▮ *vt* (*sell*) vendre; (*keep in store*) stocker; **to s. (up)** (*shop*) approvisionner; (*fridge, Br cupboard etc*) remplir; **well-stocked** (*shop*) bien approvisionné; (*fridge etc*) bien rempli.

▮ *vi* **to s. up** (*renew one's supplies of food etc*) s'approvisionner (**with** de, en).

stockade [stɒ'keɪd] *n* palissade *f*.

stockbroker ['stɒkbrəukər] *n* agent *m* de change. ●**stockcar** *n* stock-car *m*. ●**stockholder** *n Fin* actionnaire *mf*. ●**stockist** *n* dépositaire *mf*, stockiste *m*. ●**stockpile** *vt* stocker, amasser. ●**stockroom** *n* réserve *f*, magasin *m*. ●**stocktaking** *n Br Com* inventaire *m*.

stocking ['stɒkɪŋ] *n* (*garment*) bas *m*.

stocky ['stɒkɪ] *a* (-**ier**, -**iest**) trapu.

stodge [stɒdʒ] *n* (*food*) *Fam* étouffe-chrétien *m inv*. ●**stodgy** *a* (-**ier**, -**iest**) *Fam* (*food*) lourd, indigeste; (*person, style*) *Fig* compassé.

stoic ['stəuɪk] *a & n* stoïque (*mf*). ●**stoical** *a* stoïque. ●**stoicism** *n* stoïcisme *m*.

stoke [stəuk] *vt* (*fire*) entretenir; (*furnace*) alimenter; (*engine*) chauffer. ●**stoker** *n* (*of boiler, engine*) chauffeur *m*.

stole¹ [stəul] *n* (*shawl*) étole *f*.

stole², **stolen** [stəul, 'stəul(ə)n] *pt & pp* of **steal¹,²**.

stolid ['stɒlɪd] *a* (*manner, person*) impassible.

stomach ['stʌmək] **1** *n* (*for digestion*) estomac *m*; (*front of body*) ventre *m*. **2** *vt* (*put up with*) supporter. ●**stomach-ache** *n* mal *m* de ventre; **to have a s.-ache** avoir mal au ventre.

stone [stəun] *n* pierre *f*; (*pebble*) caillou *m*; (*in fruit*) noyau *m*; (*in kidney*) calcul *m*; (*weight*) *Br* = *6,348 kg*; **it's a stone's throw away** *Fig* c'est à deux pas d'ici ▮ *vt* lancer des pierres sur, lapider; (*fruit*) dénoyauter. ●**stonemason** *n* tailleur *m* de pierre, maçon *m*.

stone- [stəun] *pref* complètement. ●**stone-'broke** *a Am Sl* fauché. ●**stone-'cold** *a* complètement froid. ●**stone-'dead** *a* raide mort. ●**stone-'deaf** *a* sourd comme un pot.

stoned [stəund] *a* (*high on drugs*) *Fam* camé, défoncé (**on** à).

stony ['stəunɪ] *a* **1** (-**ier**, -**iest**) (*path etc*) caillouteux, pierreux. **2 s. broke** (*penniless*) *Br Sl* fauché.

stooge [stuːdʒ] *n* (*actor*) comparse *mf*; (*flunkey*) *Pej* larbin *m*; (*dupe*) *Pej* pigeon *m*.

stood [stud] *pt & pp* of **stand**.

stool [stuːl] *n* tabouret *m*.

stoop [stuːp] **1** *n* **to have a s.** être voûté ▮ *vi* se baisser; **to s. to doing/to sth** *Fig* s'abaisser à faire/à qch. **2** *n* (*in front of house*) *Am* perron *m*.

stop [stɒp] *n* (*place, halt*) arrêt *m*, halte *f*; (*for plane, ship*) escale *f*; (**full**) s. *Br Grammar* point *m*; **bus** s. arrêt *m* d'autobus; **to put a** s. **to sth** mettre fin à qch; **to make a** s. (*of vehicle etc*) s'arrêter; (*of plane*) faire escale; **to bring to a** s. (*vehicle etc*) arrêter; **to come to a** s. (*of vehicle etc*) s'arrêter; **without a** s. sans arrêt; s. **light** (*on vehicle*) *Br* (feu *m*) stop *m*; s. **sign** (*on road*) stop *m*. ▮ *vt* (**-pp-**) arrêter; (*end*) mettre fin à; (*Br cheque, Am check*) faire opposition à; **to** s. **s.o./sth** (**from**) **doing** (*prevent*) empêcher qn/ qch de faire.

▮ *vi* s'arrêter; (*of pain, conversation etc*) cesser; (*stay*) rester; **to** s. **eating/etc** s'arrêter de manger/etc; **to** s. **snowing/etc** cesser de neiger/etc.

stop by *vi* (*visit*) passer (s.o.'s chez qn) ▮ **to stop off** *or* **over** *vi* (*on journey*) s'arrêter ▮ **to stop up** (*sink, pipe, leak etc*) boucher.

stopcock ['stɒpkɒk] *n Br* robinet *m* d'arrêt. ● **stopgap** *n* bouche-trou *m* ▮ *a* (*solution etc*) intérimaire. ● **stopoff** *n* halte *f*; (*break in plane journey*) escale *f*. ● **stopover** *n* halte *f*, arrêt *m*; (*break in plane journey*) escale *f*; **to make a** s. faire halte; (*of plane*) faire escale. ● **stop-press** *n* (*informations fpl de*) dernière heure *f*. ● **stopwatch** *n* chronomètre *m*.

stoppage ['stɒpɪdʒ] *n* (*in work*) arrêt *m* de travail; (*strike*) débrayage *m*; (*in pay*) *Br* retenue *f*; (*blockage*) obstruction *f*.

stopper ['stɒpər] *n* bouchon *m*.

store [stɔːr] *n* (*supply*) provision *f*; (*of information, jokes etc*) Fig mine *f*; (*warehouse, depot*) entrepôt *m*; (*shop*) *Br* grand magasin *m*, *Am* magasin *m*; (*computer memory*) mémoire *f*; **department** s. grand magasin *m*; **to have sth in** s. **for s.o.** (*surprise*) réserver qch à qn; **to keep sth in** s. garder qch en réserve; **to set great** s. **by sth** attacher une grande importance à qch.

▮ *vt* (*in warehouse etc*) stocker; (*furniture*) entreposer; (*for future use*) mettre en réserve; (*file away*) ranger, classer; (*in memory*) *Comptr* mettre en mémoire. ● **storage** *n* emmagasinage *m*; (*for future use*) mise *f* en réserve; s. **space** *or* **room** espace *m* de rangement; s. **capacity** *Comptr* capacité *f* de mémoire.

store away *vt* (*put away, file away*) ranger; (*furniture*) entreposer ▮ **to store up** *vt* (*in warehouse etc*) stocker; (*for future use*) mettre en réserve.

storekeeper ['stɔːkiːpər] *n* (*shopkeeper*) *Am* commerçant, -ante *mf*; (*warehouseman*) *Br* magasinier *m*.

storeroom ['stɔːruːm] *n* (*in house*) débarras *m*; (*in office, shop*) réserve *f*.

storey ['stɔːrɪ] *n* (*of building*) *Br* étage *m*.

stork [stɔːk] *n* cigogne *f*.

storm [stɔːm] **1** *n* (*weather*) tempête *f*; (*thunderstorm*) orage *m*; s. **cloud** nuage *m* orageux; **a** s. **of protest** Fig une tempête de protestations; **to cause a** s. provoquer un

tollé général. **2** *vt* (*attack*) (*of soldiers, police etc*) prendre d'assaut. **3** *vi* **to** s. **out** (*angrily*) sortir comme une furie. ● **stormy** *a* (**-ier, -iest**) (*weather, meeting etc*) orageux; (*wind*) d'orage.

story¹ ['stɔːrɪ] *n* histoire *f*; (*newspaper article*) article *m*; s. (**line**) (*plot*) intrigue *f*; **short** s. *Liter* nouvelle *f*, conte *m*; **fairy** s. conte *m* de fées. ● **storybook** *n* livre *m* d'histoires. ● **storyteller** *n* conteur, -euse *mf*; (*liar*) *Fam* menteur, -euse *mf*.

story² ['stɔːrɪ] *n* (*of building*) *Am* étage *m*.

stout [staʊt] **1** *a* (**-er, -est**) (*person*) corpulent; (*stick, volume*) épais (*f* épaisse); (*shoes*) solide. **2** *n* (*beer*) *Br* bière *f* brune. ● **stoutness** *n* corpulence *f*.

stove [stəʊv] *n* (*for cooking*) cuisinière *f*; (*solid fuel*) fourneau *m*; (*portable*) réchaud *m*; (*for heating*) poêle *m*.

stow [stəʊ] **1** *vt* (*cargo*) arrimer; **to** s. **away** (*put away*) ranger. **2** *vi* **to** s. **away** (*on ship etc*) voyager clandestinement. ● **stowaway** *n* (*on ship etc*) passager, -ère *mf* clandestin(e).

straddle ['strædl] *vt* (*chair, fence*) se mettre *or* être à califourchon sur; (*step over, span*) enjamber; (*line in road*) (*of vehicle*) chevaucher.

straggle ['strægl] *vi* (*stretch*) s'étendre (en désordre); (*trail*) traîner (en désordre); **to** s. **in** entrer par petits groupes. ● **straggler** *n* traînard, -arde *mf*.

straight [streɪt] *a* (**-er, -est**) droit; (*hair*) raide; (*route*) direct; (*tidy*) en ordre; (*frank*) franc (*f* franche); (*refusal*) net (*f* nette); (*actor, role*) sérieux; **let's get** *or* **I want to get this** s. comprenons-nous bien; **to keep a** s. **face** garder son sérieux; **to put** *or* **set** s. (*tidy*) ranger.

▮ *n* **the** s. (*on race track etc*) la ligne droite. ▮ *adv* (*to walk etc*) droit; (*directly*) tout droit, directement; (*to drink gin, whisky etc*) sec; s. **away** (*at once*) tout de suite; s. **out, s. off** sans hésiter; s. **opposite** juste en face; s. **ahead** *or Br* **on** (*to walk etc*) tout droit; **to look** s. **ahead** regarder droit devant soi.

straightaway [streɪtə'weɪ] *adv* (*at once*) tout de suite.

straighten ['streɪt(ə)n] *vt* **to** s.(**out**) (*wire etc*) redresser; **to** s. (**up**) (*tie, hair, room*) arranger; **to** s. **things up** (*put the situation right*) arranger les choses.

straight-faced [streɪt'feɪst] *a* impassible.

straightforward [streɪt'fɔːwəd] *a* (*easy, clear*) simple; (*frank*) franc (*f* franche).

strain [streɪn] *n* tension *f*; (*tiredness*) fatigue *f*; (*mental stress*) tension *f* nerveuse; (*effort*) effort *m* ▮ *vt* (*rope, wire*) tendre excessivement; (*muscle*) se froisser; (*ankle, wrist*) se fouler; (*eyes*) fatiguer; (*voice*) forcer; (*rope, wire*) tendre excessivement; (*patience, friendship etc*) Fig mettre à l'épreuve; **to** s. **one's ears** (*to hear*) tendre l'oreille; **to** s. **one's back** se faire mal au dos; **to** s. **oneself** (*hurt oneself*) se faire mal; (*tire oneself*) se fatiguer ▮ *vi* fournir un effort (**to do** pour faire).

2 vt (soup etc) passer; (vegetables) égoutter.
3 n (breed) lignée f; (of virus) souche f; (streak) tendance f. ● **strains** npl (of music) accents mpl (of de).

strained [streɪnd] a (relations) tendu; (muscle) froissé; (ankle, wrist) foulé; (laugh) forcé.

strainer ['streɪnər] n passoire f.

strait [streɪt] n **1** strait(s) Geog détroit m. **2** in financial straits dans l'embarras.

straitjacket ['streɪtdʒækɪt] n camisole f de force.

straitlaced [streɪt'leɪst] a collet monté inv.

strand [strænd] n (of wool etc) brin m; (of hair) mèche f; (of story) Fig fil m.

stranded ['strændɪd] a (person, vehicle) en rade.

strange [streɪndʒ] a (-er, -est) (odd) étrange, bizarre; (unknown) inconnu; (new) nouveau (f nouvelle); **to feel s.** (in a new place) se sentir dépaysé. ● **strangely** adv étrangement; **s. (enough) she....** chose étrange elle.... ● **strangeness** n étrangeté f.

stranger ['streɪndʒər] n (unknown) inconnu, -ue mf; (outsider) étranger, -ère mf; **he's a s. here** il n'est pas d'ici; **she's a s. to me** elle m'est inconnue.

strangle ['stræŋg(ə)l] vt étrangler. ● **strangler** n étrangleur, -euse mf.

stranglehold ['stræŋg(ə)lhəʊld] n emprise f totale (on sur).

strap [stræp] n sangle f, courroie f; (on dress) bretelle f; (on watch) bracelet m; (on sandal) lanière f ‖ vt (-pp-) **s.** (**down** or **in**) attacher (avec une sangle or une courroie); **to s. s.o. in** (with seat belt) attacher qn avec une ceinture de sécurité.

strapping ['stræpɪŋ] a (well-built) robuste.

stratagem ['strætədʒəm] n stratagème m.

strategy ['strætədʒɪ] n stratégie f. ● **strategic** [strə'ti:dʒɪk] a stratégique.

stratum, pl **-ta** ['strɑ:təm, -tə] n couche f.

straw [strɔ:] n paille f; (drinking) s. paille f; **that's the last s.!** c'est le comble!

strawberry [Br 'strɔ:bərɪ, Am -berɪ] n fraise f ‖ a (flavour, ice cream) à la fraise; (jam) de fraises; (tart) aux fraises.

stray [streɪ] a (animal, bullet) perdu; **a few s. cars/etc** quelques rares voitures/etc; **a s. car/ etc** une voiture/etc isolée ‖ n animal m perdu ‖ vi s'égarer; **to s. from** (subject, path) s'écarter de; **don't s. too far** ne t'éloigne pas.

streak [stri:k] n (line) raie f; (of light) filet m; (of colour) strie f; (of paint) traînée f; (trace) Fig trace f; (tendency) tendance f; **grey/etc streaks** (in hair) mèches fpl grises/ etc; **to have a mad s.** avoir une tendance à la folie; **my literary s.** ma fibre littéraire. ● **streaked** a (marked) strié, zébré; (stained) taché (with de). ● **streaky** a (-ier, -iest) strié; (bacon) Br pas trop maigre.

stream [stri:m] n (brook) ruisseau m; (current) courant m; (flow) flot m; (in school) Br classe f (de niveau); **a steady s. of**

visitors/cars/insults/etc un flot ininterrompu de visiteurs/de voitures/d'insultes/etc ‖ vi ruisseler (**with** de); **to s. in** (of sunlight, people etc) entrer à flots.

streamer ['stri:mər] n (paper) serpentin m; (banner) banderole f.

streamline ['stri:mlaɪn] vt (work, method etc) rationaliser. ● **streamlined** a (shape) aérodynamique; (industry, production etc) rationalisé.

street [stri:t] n rue f; **s. door** porte f d'entrée; **s. lamp, s. light** lampadaire m; **s. map, s. plan** plan m des rues; **s. cred** Sl look m branché; **to have s. cred** Sl être branché; **that's (right) up my s.** Br Fam c'est dans mes cordes; **she's streets ahead** Br Fam elle est très en avance (**of** sur). ● **streetcar** n (tram) Am tramway m. ● **streetwise** a Fam averti, malin (f -igne).

strength [streŋθ] n force f; (health, energy) forces fpl; (of wood, fabric etc) solidité f; **on the s. of** Fig en vertu de; **in** or **at full s.** (of troops etc) au (grand) complet. ● **strengthen** vt (building, position etc) renforcer, consolider; (body, soul, limb) fortifier.

strenuous ['strenjʊəs] a (effort etc) vigoureux, énergique; (work) ardu; (active) actif; (tiring) fatigant. ● **strenuously** adv énergiquement.

strep [strep] a **s. throat** Am forte angine f.

stress [stres] n (pressure) pression f; (mental) stress m, tension f (nerveuse); (emphasis) & Grammar accent m; (on metal, structure etc) tension f; **under s.** (person) stressé, sous pression; (relationship) tendu ‖ vt insister sur; (word) accentuer; **to s. that** souligner que. ● **stressful** a stressant. ● **stress-related** a **to be s.-related** être dû au stress.

stretch [stretʃ] vt (rope, neck) tendre; (shoe, rubber) étirer; (meaning) Fig forcer; **to s. (out)** (arm, leg) étendre, allonger; **to s. (out) one's arm** (reach out) tendre le bras (**to take** pour prendre); **to s. one's legs** Fig se dégourdir les jambes; **to s. s.o.** Fig exiger un effort de qn; **to be (fully) stretched** (of budget etc) être tiré au maximum; **to s. out** (visit, stay, debate etc) prolonger.

‖ vi (of person, elastic) s'étirer; (of influence etc) s'étendre; **to s. (out)** (of rope, plain etc) s'étendre.

‖ n (area, duration) étendue f; (period of time) période f; (of road) tronçon m, partie f; (route, trip) trajet m; **ten/etc hours at a s.** dix/etc heures d'affilée; **for a long s. of time** (pendant) longtemps; **to do a three-year s.** (in prison) Fam faire trois ans de prison; **s. socks/etc** chaussettes fpl/etc extensibles; **s. nylon** nylon m stretch inv. ● **stretchmarks** npl (on body) vergetures fpl.

stretcher ['stretʃər] n brancard m.

strew [stru:] vt (pt strewed, pp strewed or strewn) (scatter) répandre; **strewn with** (covered) jonché de.

stricken ['strɪk(ə)n] a (town, region etc)

(with disaster) sinistré; **s. with panic** frappé de panique; **s. with illness** atteint de maladie.

strict [strɪkt] *a* (**-er, -est**) *(severe, absolute)* strict. ●**strictly** *adv* strictement; **s. forbidden** formellement interdit. ●**strictness** *n* sévérité *f*.

stride [straɪd] *n* (grand) pas *m*, enjambée *f*; **to make great strides** *Fig* faire de grands progrès ▮ *vi* (*pt* **strode**) **to s. across** *or* **over** enjamber; **to s. along/out/***etc* avancer/sortir/ *etc* à grands pas; **to s. up and down a room** arpenter une pièce.

strident ['straɪdənt] *a* strident.

strife [straɪf] *n inv* conflit(s) *m(pl)*.

strike [straɪk] **1** *n* *(military attack)* raid *m* (aérien); **an oil s.** *(discovery)* la découverte d'un gisement de pétrole ▮ *vt* (*pt & pp* **struck**) *(hit, impress)* frapper; *(collide with)* heurter; *(beat)* battre; *(a blow)* donner; *(a match)* frotter; *(gold, Fig problem etc)* trouver; *(coin)* frapper; **to s. the time** *(of clock)* sonner l'heure; **to s. a bargain** conclure un accord; **to s. a balance** trouver l'équilibre; **to s. oil** trouver du pétrole; **it strikes me that it** me semble que (+ *indic*); **it strikes me as possible** cela me semble être possible; **how did it s. you?** quelle impression ça t'a fait? ▮ *vi* *(attack)* attaquer.

2 *n* *(of workers)* grève *f*; **to go (out) on s.** se mettre en grève (**for** pour obtenir, **against** pour protester contre) ▮ *vi* (*pt & pp* **struck**) *(of workers)* faire grève. ●**strikebound** *a* paralysé par la grève *or* les grèves.

strike at *vt (attack)* attaquer ▮ **to strike back** *vi (retaliate)* riposter ▮ **to strike down** *vt (of illness etc)* terrasser *(qn)*; *(of disaster)* abattre *(qn)* ▮ **to strike off** *vt (from list)* rayer (**from** de); **to be struck off** *(of doctor)* être radié ▮ **to strike out** *vi (hit out)* donner des coups ▮ **to strike up** *vt* **to s. up a friend-ship** lier amitié (**with s.o.** avec qn).

striker ['straɪkər] *n (worker)* gréviste *mf*; *Football* buteur *m*.

striking ['straɪkɪŋ] *a (impressive)* frappant. ●**strikingly** *adv (beautiful, intelligent etc)* extraordinairement.

string [strɪŋ] *n* ficelle *f*; *(of anorak, apron etc)* cordon *m*; *(of violin, racket etc)* corde *f*; *(of onions, Fig insults)* chapelet *m*; *(of ve-hicles, people)* file *f*; *(of questions etc)* série *f*; **s. of pearls** collier *m* de perles; **s. of beads** collier *m*; *(for praying)* chapelet *m*; **to pull strings** *Fig* faire jouer ses relations; **to pull strings for s.o.** pistonner qn.

▮ *a (instrument, quartet)* à cordes; **s. bean** haricot *m* vert.

▮ *vt* (*pt & pp* **strung**) *(beads)* enfiler; **to s. up** *(hang up)* suspendre.

▮ *vi* **to s. along** *(follow) Fam* suivre; **to s. along with s.o.** *Fam* suivre qn. ●**stringed** *a (musical instrument)* à cordes.

stringent ['strɪndʒ(ə)nt] *a* rigoureux. ●**stringency** *n* rigueur *f*.

stringy ['strɪŋɪ] *a* (**-ier, -iest**) *(meat etc)*

filandreux.

strip [strɪp] **1** *n (piece)* bande *f*; *(of water)* bras *m*; **(thin) s.** *(of metal etc)* lamelle *f*; **landing s.** piste *f or* terrain *m* d'atterrissage; **s. cartoon, comic s.** bande *f* dessinée; **s. lighting** *Br* éclairage *m* au néon *or* fluorescent.

2 *vt* (**-pp-**) *(undress)* déshabiller; *(bed)* défaire; *(deprive)* dépouiller (**of** de); **to s. (down)** *(machine)* démonter; **to s. off** *(re-move)* enlever ▮ *vi* **to s. (off)** *(get undressed)* se déshabiller. ●**stripper** *n (woman)* strip-teaseuse *f*; **(paint) s.** décapant *m*. ●**strip'tease** *n* strip-tease *m*.

stripe [straɪp] *n* rayure *f*; *(on military uni-form)* galon *m*. ●**striped** *a* rayé (**with** de). ●**stripy** *a (fabric, pattern etc)* rayé.

strive [straɪv] *vi* (*pt* **strove**, *pp* **striven**) s'efforcer (**to do** de faire, **for** d'obtenir).

strobe [strəʊb] *a* **s. lighting** éclairage *m* stroboscopique.

strode [strəʊd] *pt of* **stride**.

stroke [strəʊk] *n (movement)* coup *m*; *(of pen, genius)* trait *m*; *(of brush)* touche *f*; *(of clock)* coup *m*; *(caress)* caresse *f*; *(illness)* coup *m* de sang, attaque *f*; **(swimming) s.** nage *f*; **at a s.** d'un coup; **a s. of luck** un coup de chance; **you haven't done a s.** *(of work)* tu n'as rien fait; **heat s.** *(sunstroke)* in-solation *f*; **four-s. engine** moteur *m* à quatre temps ▮ *vt (beard, cat etc)* caresser.

stroll [strəʊl] *n* promenade *f* ▮ *vi* se prome-ner, flâner; **to s. in/***etc* entrer/*etc* sans se presser. ●**strolling** *a (musician etc)* ambu-lant.

stroller ['strəʊlər] *n (for baby) Am* poussette *f*.

strong [strɒŋ] *a* (**-er, -est**) fort; *(shoes, chair, nerves etc)* solide; *(interest)* vif; *(measures)* énergique; *(supporter)* ardent; **they were sixty s.** ils étaient au nombre de soixante ▮ *adv* **to be going s.** aller toujours bien. ●**strongly** *adv (to protest, defend)* énergique-ment; *(to advise, remind, desire)* fortement; **s. built** solide; **to feel s. that** avoir la forte impression que.

strongarm ['strɒŋɑːm] *a* **s. tactics** la manière forte. ●**strongbox** *n* coffre-fort *m*. ●**strong-hold** *n* bastion *m*. ●**strongroom** *n* salle *f* des coffres. ●**strong-'willed** *a* résolu.

strove [strəʊv] *pt of* **strive**.

struck [strʌk] *pt & pp of* **strike 1, 2**.

structure ['strʌktʃər] *n* structure *f*; *(of build-ing)* gros œuvre *m*; *(building itself)* construc-tion *f*. ●**structural** *a* structural; *(building de-fect)* de construction; **s. damage** *(to building)* dommage *m* au gros œuvre.

struggle ['strʌg(ə)l] *n (fight)* lutte *f* **(to do** pour faire); *(effort)* effort *m*; **to put up a s.** résister; **to have a s. doing** *or* **to do sth** avoir du mal à faire qch.

▮ *vi (fight)* lutter, se battre (**with** avec); *(re-sist)* résister; *(move about wildly)* se dé-battre; **to be struggling** *(financially)* avoir du mal; **to s. to do** *(try hard)* s'efforcer de faire;

to s. out of sortir péniblement de; **to s. into** entrer péniblement dans; **to s. along** or on se débrouiller; **a struggling lawyer**/*etc* un avocat/*etc* qui a du mal à débuter.

strum [strʌm] *vt* (**-mm-**) (*guitar etc*) gratter de.

strung [strʌŋ] *pt & pp of* **string** ▌ *a* s. **out** (*things, people*) espacés; (*washing*) étendu; **people were s. out along the route** les gens étaient installés de loin en loin le long de la route.

strut [strʌt] **1** *vi* (**-tt-**) **to s.** (**about** or **around**) se pavaner. **2** *n* (*wood or metal support*) étai *m*.

stub [stʌb] **1** *n* (*of pencil, cigarette etc*) bout *m*; (*counterfoil of ticket, Br cheque, Am check*) talon *m* ▌ *vt* (**-bb-**) **to s. out** (*cigarette*) écraser. **2** *vt* (**-bb-**) **to s. one's toe** se cogner le doigt de pied (**on, against** contre).

stubble ['stʌb(ə)l] *n* (*on face*) barbe *f* de plusieurs jours.

stubborn ['stʌbən] *a* (*person*) entêté, opiniâtre; (*manner, efforts etc*) opiniâtre; (*cough*) rebelle, persistant. ● **stubbornly** *adv* opiniâtrement. ● **stubbornness** *n* entêtement *m*; opiniâtreté *f*; persistance *f*.

stubby ['stʌbɪ] *a* (**-ier, -iest**) (*finger etc*) gros (*f* grosse) et court, épais (*f* épaisse); (*person*) trapu.

stucco ['stʌkəʊ] *n* (*pl* **-os** or **-oes**) (*plaster*) stuc *m*.

stuck [stʌk] *pt & pp of* **stick**[2] ▌ *a* (*caught, jammed*) coincé; s. **in bed/indoors** cloué au lit/chez soi; **I'm s.** (*unable to carry on*) je ne sais pas quoi faire *or* dire *etc*; **I'm s. for an answer** je ne sais que répondre; **to be s. with sth/s.o.** se farcir qch/qn.

stuck-up [stʌˈkʌp] *a Fam* prétentieux, snob *inv*.

stud [stʌd] *n* **1** (*on football boot etc*) crampon *m*; (*earring*) clou *m* d'oreille; (**collar**) s. bouton *m* de col. **2** (*farm*) haras *m*; (*horses*) écurie *f*; (*stallion*) étalon *m*; (*virile man*) *Fam* mâle *m*. ● **studded** *a* (*boots, Br tyres, Am tires*) clouté; s. **with** (*covered*) *Fig* constellé de, parsemé de.

student ['stjuːdənt] *n* (*in university*) étudiant, -ante *mf*; (*in school*) élève *mf*; **music/ etc s.** étudiant, -ante en musique/*etc* ▌ *a* (*life, protest*) étudiant; (*restaurant, residence, grant*) universitaire.

studied ['stʌdɪd] *a* (*deliberate*) étudié.

studio ['stjuːdɪəʊ] *n* (*pl* **-os**) (*of painter etc*) & *Cinema TV etc* studio *m*; s. **audience** public *m* (présent dans le studio); s. **couch** canapé-lit *m*; s. **flat** *Br*, s. **apartment** *Am* studio *m*.

studious ['stjuːdɪəs] *a* (*person*) studieux. ● **studiously** *adv* (*carefully*) avec soin. ● **studiousness** *n* application *f*.

study ['stʌdɪ] *n* étude *f*; (*office*) bureau *m* ▌ *vt* (*learn, observe*) étudier ▌ *vi* étudier; **to s. to be a doctor**/*etc* faire des études pour devenir médecin/*etc*; **to s. for an exam** préparer un examen.

stuff [stʌf] **1** *n Fam* (*thing*) truc *m*, chose *f*; (*substance*) substance *f*; (*things*) trucs *mpl*, choses *fpl*; (*possessions*) affaires *fpl*; **s. (and nonsense)** idioties *fpl*, sottises *fpl*; **this s.'s good, it's good** s. c'est bon (ça).
2 *vt* (*cram, fill*) bourrer (**with** de); (*cushion, armchair etc*) rembourrer (**with** avec); (*animal*) empailler; (*put, thrust*) fourrer (**into** dans); (*chicken etc*) farcir; **to s. (up)** (*hole etc*) colmater; **my nose is stuffed (up)** j'ai le nez bouché. ● **stuffing** *n* (*padding*) bourre *f*; (*for chicken etc*) farce *f*.

stuffy ['stʌfɪ] *a* (**-ier, -iest**) (*room etc*) mal aéré; (*formal*) (*person, manner*) compassé; (*old-fashioned*) (*person, ideas etc*) vieux jeu *inv*; **it smells s.** ça sent le renfermé.

stumble ['stʌmb(ə)l] *vi* trébucher (**over** sur, **against** contre); **to s. across** or **on** (*find*) tomber sur; **stumbling block** (*obstacle*) pierre *f* d'achoppement (**to** sur la voie de).

stump [stʌmp] *n* (*of tree*) souche *f*; (*of limb*) moignon *m*; (*of pencil*) bout *m*; *Cricket* piquet *m*.

stumped ['stʌmpt] *a* **to be s. by sth** (*baffled*) ne pas savoir que penser de qch.

stun [stʌn] *vt* (**-nn-**) (*with a punch etc*) étourdir; (*animal*) assommer; (*amaze*) *Fig* stupéfier. ● **stunned** *a* (*amazed*) stupéfait (**by** par). ● **stunning** *a* (*news*) stupéfiant; (*terrific*) *Fam* sensationnel; **to deal a s. blow to** porter un coup terrible à.

stung [stʌŋ] *pt & pp of* **sting**.

stunk [stʌŋk] *pt & pp of* **stink**.

stunt [stʌnt] **1** *n* (*feat*) tour *m* (de force); (*in film*) cascade *f*; (*trick, ruse*) truc *m*; **publicity s.** coup *m* de pub; s. **man** (*in film*) cascadeur *m*; s. **woman** cascadeuse *f*. **2** *vt* (*growth*) retarder. ● **stunted** *a* (*person*) rabougri.

stupefy ['stjuːpɪfaɪ] *vt* (*of drink etc*) abrutir; (*amaze*) *Fig* stupéfier.

stupendous [stjuːˈpendəs] *a* prodigieux.

stupid ['stjuːpɪd] *a* stupide, bête; **to do/say a s. thing** faire/dire une stupidité *or* une sottise; s. **fool**, s. **idiot** idiot, -ote *mf*. ● **stupidity** *n* stupidité *f*. ● **stupidly** *adv* stupidement, bêtement.

stupor ['stjuːpər] *n* (*daze*) stupeur *f*.

sturdy ['stɜːdɪ] *a* (**-ier, -iest**) (*person, shoe etc*) robuste. ● **sturdiness** *n* robustesse *f*.

sturgeon ['stɜːdʒ(ə)n] *n* (*fish*) esturgeon *m*.

stutter ['stʌtər] *vi* bégayer ▌ *n* bégaiement *m*; **to have a s.** être bègue.

sty [staɪ] *n* (*for pigs*) porcherie *f*.

sty(e) [staɪ] *n* (*on eye*) orgelet *m*.

style [staɪl] *n* style *m*; (*fashion*) mode *f*; (*design of dress etc*) modèle *m*; (*of hair*) coiffure *f*; (*sort*) genre *m*; **to have s.** avoir de la classe; **in s.** (*in superior manner*) de la meilleure façon possible; (*to live, travel*) dans le luxe ▌ *vt* (*design*) créer; **to s. s.o.'s hair** coiffer qn; **he styles himself....** *Pej* il se fait appeler.... ● **styling** *n* (*cutting of hair*) coupe *f*.

stylish ['staɪlɪʃ] *a* chic *inv*, élégant. ● **stylishly** *adv* élégamment.

stylist ['staɪlɪst] *n* (**hair**) s. coiffeur, -euse *mf*.

stylistic [staɪ'lɪstɪk] *a* de style, stylistique.

stylized ['staɪlaɪzd] *a* stylisé.

stylus ['staɪləs] *n* (*of record player*) saphir *m*, pointe *f* de lecture.

suave [swɑːv] *a* (**-er, -est**) (*polite, urbane*) courtois; *Pej* doucereux.

sub- [sʌb] *pref* sous-, sub-.

subconscious [sʌb'kɒnʃəs] *a & n* subconscient (*m*). ● **subconsciously** *adv* inconsciemment.

subcontract [sʌbkən'trækt] *vt* sous-traiter. ● **subcontractor** *n* sous-traitant *m*.

subdivide [sʌbdɪ'vaɪd] *vt* subdiviser (**into** en). ● **subdivision** [-'vɪʒ(ə)n] *n* subdivision *f*.

subdue [səb'djuː] *vt* (*country, people*) soumettre, assujettir; (*feelings*) maîtriser. ● **subdued** *a* (*light*) atténué; (*voice, tone*) bas (*f* basse); (*reaction*) faible; (*person*) qui manque d'entrain.

subheading ['sʌbhedɪŋ] *n* sous-titre *m*.

subject¹ ['sʌbdʒɪkt] *n* **1** (*matter*) & *Grammar* sujet *m*; (*at school, university*) matière *f*; **s. matter** (*topic*) sujet *m*; (*content*) contenu *m*. **2** (*citizen*) ressortissant, -ante *mf*; (*of monarch*) sujet, -ette *mf*; (*person etc in experiment*) sujet *m*; **she's a British s.** c'est une sujette britannique.

subject² ['sʌbdʒekt] *a* (*tribe etc*) soumis; **to be s. to** (*prone to*) être sujet à (*maladie etc*); (*ruled by*) être soumis à (*loi, règle etc*); **it's s. to my agreement/your abiding by the rules** (*conditional upon*) c'est sous réserve de mon accord/de ton respect des règles; **prices are s. to change** les prix peuvent être modifiés ▌ [səb'dʒekt] *vt* soumettre (**to** à); (*expose*) exposer (**to** à). ● **subjection** [-ʃ(ə)n] *n* soumission *f* (**to** à).

subjective [səb'dʒektɪv] *a* subjectif. ● **subjectively** *adv* subjectivement. ● **subjec'tivity** *n* subjectivité *f*.

subjugate ['sʌbdʒʊgeɪt] *vt* subjuguer.

subjunctive [səb'dʒʌŋktɪv] *n Grammar* subjonctif *m*.

sublet [sʌb'let] *vt* (*pt & pp* **sublet**, *pres p* **subletting**) sous-louer.

sublimate ['sʌblɪmeɪt] *vt* (*one's feelings*) sublimer.

sublime [sə'blaɪm] *a* sublime; (*indifference, stupidity*) suprême ▌ *n* sublime *m*; **to go from the s. to the ridiculous** passer du sublime au grotesque.

submachine-gun [sʌbmə'ʃiːŋgʌn] *n* mitraillette *f*.

submarine ['sʌbməriːn] *n* sous-marin *m*.

submerge [səb'mɜːdʒ] *vt* (*flood, overwhelm*) submerger; (*immerse*) immerger (**in** dans) ▌ *vi* (*of submarine*) s'immerger.

submit [səb'mɪt] *vt* (**-tt-**) soumettre (**to** à); **I s. that** (*in court of law*) je suggère que ▌ *vi* se soumettre (**to** à). ● **submission** [-ʃ(ə)n] *n* soumission *f* (**to** à). ● **submissive** *a* (*person*) soumis; (*attitude*) de soumission. ● **submissively** *adv* avec soumission.

subnormal [sʌb'nɔːm(ə)l] *a* (*temperature*) au-dessous de la normale; **educationally s.** *Old-fashioned Pej* arriéré.

subordinate [sə'bɔːdɪnət] *a* subalterne; **s. to** subordonné à; **s. clause** *Grammar* proposition *f* subordonnée ▌ *n* subordonné, -ée *mf* ▌ [sə'bɔːdɪneɪt] *vt* subordonner (**to'** à). ● **subordination** [-'neɪʃ(ə)n] *n* subordination *f* (**to** à).

subpoena [səb'piːnə] *Jur vt* (*witness*) citer ▌ *n* (*summons*) citation *f*.

sub-post office [sʌb'pəʊstɒfɪs] *n Br* petit bureau *m* de poste.

subscribe [səb'skraɪb] *vi* (*pay money*) cotiser (**to** à); **to s. to** (*take out subscription*) s'abonner à (*journal etc*); (*be a subscriber*) être abonné à (*journal etc*); (*fund, idea*) souscrire à ▌ *vt* (*money*) donner (**to** à). ● **subscriber** *n* (*to newspaper etc, telephone user*) abonné, -ée *mf*. ● **subscription** [-'skrɪpʃ(ə)n] *n* (*to newspaper etc*) abonnement *m*; (*to fund, idea*) souscription *f*; (*to club etc*) cotisation *f*.

subsequent ['sʌbsɪkwənt] *a* postérieur (**to** à); **our s. problems** les problèmes que nous avons eus par la suite; **s. to** (*as a result of*) consécutif à. ● **subsequently** *adv* par la suite.

subservient [səb'sɜːvɪənt] *a* obséquieux; **to be s. to** (*a slave to*) être sous la dépendance de.

subside [səb'saɪd] *vi* (*of ground, building*) s'affaisser; (*of wind, flood, fever*) baisser; (*of threat, danger*) se dissiper. ● **'subsidence** *n* (*of ground*) affaissement *m*.

subsidiary [*Br* səb'sɪdɪərɪ, *Am* -erɪ] *a* accessoire; **s. subject** (*in university*) *Br* matière *f* secondaire ▌ *n* (*company*) filiale *f*.

subsidize ['sʌbsɪdaɪz] *vt* subventionner. ● **subsidy** *n* subvention *f*.

subsist [səb'sɪst] *vi* (*of person, doubts etc*) subsister. ● **subsistence** *n* subsistance *f*.

substance ['sʌbstəns] *n* substance *f*; (*firmness*) solidité *f*; **a man/woman of s.** un homme/une femme riche.

substantial [səb'stænʃ(ə)l] *a* important, considérable; (*meal*) copieux. ● **sub'stantially** *adv* considérablement, beaucoup; **s. true/etc** (*to a great extent*) en grande partie vrai/etc; **s. different** très différent.

substandard [sʌb'stændəd] *a* de qualité inférieure.

substantiate [səb'stænʃɪeɪt] *vt* prouver, justifier.

substitute ['sʌbstɪtjuːt] *n* (*thing*) produit *m* de remplacement; (*person*) remplaçant, -ante *mf* (**for** de); **s. teacher** suppléant, -ante *mf*; **there's no s. for...** rien ne peut remplacer... ▌ *vt* **to s. sth./s.o.** for substituer qch/qn à, remplacer qch/qn par ▌ *vi* **to s. for s.o.** remplacer qn. ● **substitution** [-'tjuːʃ(ə)n] *n* substitution *f*.

subterranean [sʌbtə'reɪnɪən] *a* souterrain.

subtitle ['sʌbtaɪt(ə)l] *n* (*of film*) sous-titre *m* ▌ *vt* (*film*) sous-titrer.

subtle ['sʌt(ə)l] *a* (**-er, -est**) subtil. ● **subtlety**

n subtilité *f*. ● **subtly** *adv* subtilement.

subtotal [sʌb'təʊt(ə)l] *n* sous-total *m*, total *m* partiel.

subtract [səb'trækt] *vt* soustraire (**from** de). ● **subtraction** [-ʃ(ə)n] *n* soustraction *f*.

subtropical [sʌb'trɒpɪk(ə)l] *a* subtropical.

suburb ['sʌbɜːb] *n* banlieue *f*; **the suburbs** la banlieue; **in the suburbs** en banlieue. ● **su'burban** *a* (*train, house etc*) de banlieue; (*accent*) de la banlieue, banlieusard; **that town is (quite) s.** cette ville fait (très) banlieue. ● **su'burbia** *n* la banlieue; **in s.** en banlieue.

subversive [səb'vɜːsɪv] *a* subversif. ● **subversion** [*Br* -ʃ(ə)n, *Am* -ʒ(ə)n] *n* subversion *f*. ● **subvert** *vt* (*system etc*) bouleverser; (*person*) corrompre.

subway ['sʌbweɪ] *n* (*under a road etc*) *Br* passage *m* souterrain; (*railroad*) *Am* métro *m*.

succeed [sək'siːd] **1** *vi* réussir (**in doing** à faire, **in sth** dans qch). **2** *vt* **to s. s.o.** (*follow*) succéder à qn **‖** *vi* **to s. to the throne** succéder à la couronne. ● **succeeding** *a* (*in past*) suivant; (*in future*) futur; (*consecutive*) consécutif.

success [sək'ses] *n* succès *m*, réussite *f*; **to make a s. of sth** réussir qch; **he was a s.** il a eu du succès; **it was a s.** c'était réussi; **her s. in the exam** sa réussite à l'examen; **s. story** réussite *f* complète *or* exemplaire.

successful [sək'sesfəl] *a* (*effort, venture etc*) couronné de succès, réussi; (*outcome*) heureux; (*company, businessman*) prospère; (*candidate in exam*) admis, reçu; (*candidate in election*) élu; (*writer, film etc*) à succès; **to be s.** réussir (**in** dans, **in an exam** à un examen, **in doing** à faire). ● **successfully** *adv* avec succès.

succession [sək'seʃ(ə)n] *n* succession *f*; **in s.** successivement; **ten days in s.** (*one after the other*) dix jours consécutifs; **in rapid s.** coup sur coup. ● **successive** *a* (*governments etc*) successif; **ten s. days** dix jours consécutifs. ● **successor** *n* successeur *m* (**of, to** de).

succinct [sək'sɪŋkt] *a* succinct.

succulent ['sʌkjʊlənt] *a* succulent.

succumb [sə'kʌm] *vi* (*yield*) succomber (**to** à).

such [sʌtʃ] *a* (*of this or that kind*) tel, telle; **s. a car/etc** une telle voiture/*etc*; **s. happiness/noise/etc** (*so much*) tant *or* tellement de bonheur/bruit/*etc*; **there's no s. thing** ça n'existe pas; **I said no s. thing** je n'ai rien dit de tel; **s. as** comme, tel que; **and s.** tel ou tel.

‖ *adv* (*so very*) si; (*in comparisons*) aussi; **s. long trips** de si longs voyages; **s. a large helping** une si grosse portion; **s. a kind woman as you** une femme aussi gentille que vous.

‖ *pron* **happiness/etc as s.** le bonheur/*etc* en tant que tel; **s. was my idea** telle était mon idée. ● **suchlike** *pron* & *a* **...and s.** ...et autres; **... and (other) s. tasty things...** et

autres choses succulentes.

suck [sʌk] *vt* sucer; (*of baby*) téter (*lait, biberon etc*); **to s. (up)** (*with straw, pump*) aspirer; **to s. up** *or* **in** (*absorb*) absorber **‖** *vi* (*of baby*) téter; **to s. at** (*pencil etc*) sucer; **to s. at its mother's breast** (*of baby*) téter sa mère.

sucker ['sʌkər] *n* **1** (*rubber pad*) ventouse *f*. **2** (*fool*) *Fam* pigeon *m*, dupe *f*.

suckle ['sʌk(ə)l] *vt* (*of woman*) allaiter **‖** *vi* (*of baby*) téter.

suction ['sʌkʃ(ə)n] *n* succion *f*; **s. pad** *or* **cup, s. disc** *Br*, **s. disk** *Am* ventouse *f*.

Sudan [suːˈdɑːn, -ˈdæn] *n* Soudan *m*.

sudden ['sʌd(ə)n] *a* soudain, subit; **all of a s.** tout à coup. ● **suddenly** *adv* tout à coup, subitement; **to die s.** mourir subitement. ● **suddenness** *n* soudaineté *f*.

suds [sʌdz] *npl* mousse *f* de savon.

sue [suː] *vt* poursuivre (en justice) **‖** *vi* engager des poursuites (judiciaires).

suede [sweɪd] *n* daim *m*; **s. coat/shoes/etc** manteau *m*/chaussures *fpl* de daim.

suet ['suːɪt] *n* graisse *f* de rognon.

suffer ['sʌfər] *vi* souffrir (**from** de); **to s. from pimples/the flu** avoir des boutons/la grippe; **your work/etc will s.** ton travail/*etc* s'en ressentira **‖** *vt* (*loss, damage, defeat etc*) subir; (*pain*) ressentir; (*tolerate*) souffrir (*affront etc*). ● **suffering** *n* souffrance(s) *f(pl)*. ● **sufferer** *n* (*from misfortune*) victime *f*; **AIDS s.** malade *mf* *or* victime *f* du SIDA; **asthma s.** asthmatique *mf*.

suffice [sə'faɪs] *vi* suffire.

sufficient [sə'fɪʃ(ə)nt] *a* (*quantity, number*) suffisant; **s. money/etc** (*enough*) suffisamment d'argent/*etc*; **to have s.** en avoir suffisamment. ● **sufficiently** *adv* suffisamment.

suffix ['sʌfɪks] *n Grammar* suffixe *m*.

suffocate ['sʌfəkeɪt] *vti* suffoquer, étouffer. ● **suffocation** [-'keɪʃ(ə)n] *n Med* étouffement *m*, asphyxie *f*; **to die of s.** mourir asphyxié *or* étouffé.

suffrage ['sʌfrɪdʒ] *n* (*right to vote*) suffrage *m*; **universal s.** le suffrage universel.

suffused [sə'fjuːzd] *a* **s. with light/tears** baigné de lumière/larmes.

sugar ['ʃʊɡər] *n* sucre *m*; **lump s.** sucre en morceaux; **brown s.** sucre brun; **s. beet/cane/tongs** betterave *f*/canne *f*/pince *f* à sucre; **s. bowl** sucrier *m*; **s. industry** industrie *f* sucrière **‖** *vt* (*tea etc*) sucrer. ● **sugar-free** *a* sans sucre. ● **sugary** *a* (*taste, tone*) sucré.

suggest [sə'dʒest] *vt* (*propose*) suggérer, proposer (**to** à, **doing** de faire, **that** que (+ *sub*)); (*evoke, imply*) suggérer; (*hint*) *Pej* insinuer. ● **suggestion** [-tʃ(ə)n] *n* suggestion *f*, proposition *f*; (*evocation*) suggestion *f*; *Pej* insinuation *f*. ● **suggestive** *a* (*word, gesture etc*) suggestif; **to be s.** of suggérer.

suicide ['suːɪsaɪd] *n* suicide *m*; **to commit s.** se suicider. ● **sui'cidal** *a* suicidaire.

suit[1] [suːt] **1** *n* (*man's*) costume *m*, complet *m*; (*woman's*) tailleur *m*; **flying/diving/ski s.** combinaison *f* de vol/plongée/ski. **2** *n* (*law-*

suit) procès *m*. **3** *n Cards* couleur *f*.

suit² [su:t] *vt* (*please, be acceptable to*) convenir à; (*of dress, colour etc*) aller (bien) à; (*adapt*) adapter (**to** à); **it suits me to stay** ça m'arrange de rester; **s. yourself!** comme tu voudras!; **suited to** (*job, activity*) fait pour; (*appropriate to*) qui convient à; **to be well suited** (*of couple etc*) être bien assorti.

suitability [su:tə'bɪlətɪ] *n* (*of remark etc*) à-propos *m*; (*of person*) aptitudes *fpl* (**for** pour); **I'm not sure of its s.** (*date etc*) je ne sais pas si ça convient.

suitable ['su:təb(ə)l] *a* qui convient (**for** à), convenable (**for** pour); (*dress, colour*) qui va (bien); (*example*) approprié; (*socially acceptable*) convenable. ● **suitably** *adv* convenablement.

suitcase ['su:tkeɪs] *n* valise *f*.

suite [swi:t] *n* (*rooms*) suite *f*; (*furniture*) mobilier *m*; **bedroom s.** (*furniture*) chambre *f* à coucher; **dining room s.** salle *f* à manger; **bathroom s.** meubles *mpl* de salle de bain.

suitor ['su:tər] *n* soupirant *m*.

sulfur ['sʌlfər] *Am* soufre *m*.

sulk [sʌlk] *vi* bouder. ● **sulky** *a* (**-ier, -iest**) boudeur.

sullen ['sʌlən] *a* maussade. ● **sullenly** *adv* d'un air maussade.

sully ['sʌlɪ] *vt Lit* souiller.

sulphur ['sʌlfər] (*Am* **sulfur**) *n* soufre *m*.

sultan ['sʌltən] *n* sultan *m*.

sultana [sʌl'tɑ:nə] *n* raisin *m* de Smyrne).

sultry ['sʌltrɪ] *a* (**-ier, -iest**) (*heat*) étouffant; *Fig* sensuel.

sum [sʌm] **1** *n* (*amount of money, total*) somme *f*; (*calculation*) calcul *m*; **sums** (*arithmetic*) le calcul; **s. total** résultat *m*. **2** *vt* (**-mm-**) **to s. up** (*facts etc*) récapituler, résumer; (*text*) résumer; (*situation*) évaluer; (*person*) jauger ▮ *vi* **to s. up** récapituler. ● **summing-'up** *n* (*pl* **summings-up**) résumé *m*.

summarize ['sʌməraɪz] *vt* résumer ▮ *vi* récapituler. ● **summary** *n* résumé *m* ▮ *a* (*brief*) sommaire.

summer ['sʌmər] *n* été *m*; **in⸱(the) s.** en été; **Indian s.** été indien *or* de la Saint-Martin ▮ *a* d'été; **s. camp** *Am* colonie *f* de vacances; **s. holidays** *Br*, **s. vacation** *Am* grandes vacances *fpl*. ● **summerhouse** *n* pavillon *m* (de gardien). ● **summertime** *n* été *m*; **in (the) s.** en été. ● **summery** *a* (*weather, temperature etc*) estival; (*dress, day etc*) d'été.

summit ['sʌmɪt] *n* (*of mountain, power etc*) sommet *m*; (*meeting*) *Pol* rencontre *f* au sommet; **s. conference/meeting** *Pol* conférence *f*/rencontre *f* au sommet.

summon ['sʌmən] *vt* (*call*) appeler; (*meeting, s.o. to meeting*) convoquer (**to** à); **to s. s.o. to do sth** sommer qn de faire qch; **to s. up courage/strength** rassembler son courage/ses forces.

summons ['sʌmənz] *n* (*to appear in court*) assignation *f* ▮ *vt* assigner.

sump [sʌmp] *n* (*in car engine*) *Br* carter *m* (à

huile).

sumptuous ['sʌmptʃʊəs] *a* somptueux. ● **sumptuousness** *n* somptuosité *f*.

sun [sʌn] *n* soleil *m*; **in the s.** au soleil; **the sun is shining** il fait (du) soleil ▮ *vt* (**-nn-**) **to s. oneself** se chauffer au soleil.

sunbaked ['sʌnbeɪkt] *a* brûlé par le soleil. ● **sunbathe** *vi* prendre un bain de soleil. ● **sunbeam** *n* rayon *m* de soleil. ● **sunbed** *n* lit *m* à ultraviolets. ● **sunblock** *n* (*cream*) écran *m* total. ● **sunburn** *n* (*tan*) bronzage *m*; (*soreness*) coup *m* de soleil. ● **sunburnt** *a* (*tanned*) bronzé; (*having sore skin*) brûlé par le soleil. ● **sundial** *n* cadran *m* solaire. ● **sundown** *n* coucher *m* du soleil. ● **sundrenched** *a* (*beach etc*) brûlé par le soleil. ● **sunflower** *n* tournesol *m*. ● **sunglasses** *npl* lunettes *fpl* de soleil. ● **sunhat** *n* chapeau *m* de soleil. ● **sunlamp** *n* lampe *f* à bronzer *or* à rayons ultraviolets. ● **sunlight** *n* (lumière *f* du) soleil *m*. ● **sunlit** *a* ensoleillé. ● **sun lotion** *n* crème *f* solaire. ● **sun lounge** *n* (*in house*) véranda *f*. ● **sunrise** *n* lever *m* du soleil. ● **sunroof** *n* (*in car*) toit *m* ouvrant. ● **sunset** *n* coucher *m* du soleil. ● **sunshade** *n* (*on table*) parasol *m*; (*portable*) ombrelle *f*. ● **sunshine** *n* soleil *m*. ● **sunspot** *n* (*resort*) *Br* lieu *m* de vacances au soleil. ● **sunstroke** *n* insolation *f*. ● **suntan** *n* bronzage *m*; **s. lotion/oil** crème *f*/huile *f* solaire. ● **suntanned** *a* bronzé. ● **sunup** *n Am* lever *m* du soleil.

sundae ['sʌndeɪ] *n* glace *f* aux fruits.

Sunday [*Br* 'sʌndɪ, *Am* -deɪ] *n* dimanche *m*; **S. school** = catéchisme *m*; **in one's S. best** dans ses habits du dimanche, endimanché.

sundry ['sʌndrɪ] *a* divers ▮ **in all and s.** tout le monde. ● **sundries** *npl Com* articles *mpl* divers.

sung [sʌŋ] *pp of* **sing**.

sunk [sʌŋk] *pp of* **sink²** ▮ *a* **I'm s.** *Fam* je suis fichu. ● **sunken** *a* (*rock, treasure etc*) submergé; (*eyes*) cave.

sunny ['sʌnɪ] *a* (**-ier, -iest**) (*day etc*) ensoleillé; **it's s.** il fait (du) soleil; **s. periods** *or* **intervals** éclaircies *fpl*.

super ['su:pər] *a Fam* super, sensationnel.

super- ['su:pər] *pref* super-.

superannuation [su:pərænjʊ'eɪʃ(ə)n] *n* (*money*) *Br* cotisations *fpl* (pour la) retraite.

superb [su:'pɜ:b] *a* superbe.

supercilious [su:pə'sɪlɪəs] *a* hautain.

superficial [su:pə'fɪʃ(ə)l] *a* superficiel. ● **superficially** *adv* superficiellement.

superfluous [su:'pɜ:flʊəs] *a* superflu.

superglue ['su:pəglu:] *n* colle *f* extra-forte.

superhuman [su:pə'hju:mən] *a* surhumain.

superimpose [su:pərɪm'pəʊz] *vt* superposer (**on** à).

superintendent [su:pərɪn'tendənt] *n* (*in police force*) commissaire *m*; (*manager*) responsable *mf*, directeur, -trice *mf*; **police s.** commissaire *m* de police.

superior [su:'pɪərɪər] *a* supérieur "(**to** à); (*goods*) de qualité supérieure ▮ *n* (*person*) supérieur, -eure *mf*. ● **superi'ority** *n* supé-

riorité f.
superlative [suːˈpɜːlətɪv] *a* sans pareil ▮ *a* &
n Grammar superlatif (*m*).
superman [ˈsuːpəmæn] *n* (*pl* -men)
surhomme *m*.
supermarket [ˈsuːpəmɑːkɪt] *n* supermarché
m.
supernatural [suːpəˈnætʃ(ə)rəl] *a* & *n* surnaturel (*m*).
superpower [ˈsuːpəpaʊər] *n Pol* superpuissance *f*.
supersede [suːpəˈsiːd] *vt* supplanter, remplacer.
supersonic [suːpəˈsɒnɪk] *a* supersonique.
superstar [ˈsuːpəstɑːr] *n* (*in films*) superstar
f.
superstition [suːpəˈstɪʃ(ə)n] *n* superstition *f*.
● **superstitious** *a* superstitieux.
supertanker [ˈsuːpətæŋkər] *n* pétrolier *m*
géant.
supervise [ˈsuːpəvaɪz] *vt* (*person, work*)
surveiller; (*office, research*) diriger. ● **supervision** [-ˈvɪʒ(ə)n] *n* (*of person etc*)
surveillance *f*; (*of office etc*) direction *f*.
● **supervisor** *n* surveillant, -ante *mf*; (*in
office*) chef *m* de service; (*in store*) chef *m*
de rayon; (*in university*) *Br* directeur, -trice
mf de thèse. ● **super'visory** *a* (*post*) de
surveillant(e).
supine [suːˈpaɪn] *a Lit* étendu sur le dos.
supper [ˈsʌpər] *n* dîner *m*, souper *m*; (*late-
night*) souper *m*; **to have s.** dîner, souper.
supple [ˈsʌp(ə)l] *a* souple. ● **suppleness** *n*
souplesse *f*.
supplement [ˈsʌplɪmənt] *n* (*addition, part of
newspaper*) supplément *m* (**to** à) ▮
[ˈsʌplɪment] *vt* compléter; **to s. one's income**
arrondir ses fins de mois. ● **supple'mentary** *a*
supplémentaire.
supplier [səˈplaɪər] *n Com* fournisseur *m*;
'**obtainable from your usual s.**' 'disponible
chez votre fournisseur habituel.'
supply [səˈplaɪ] *vt* (*provide*) fournir; (*with
gas, electricity, water*) alimenter (**with** en);
(*equip*) équiper, pourvoir (**with** de); **to s. a
need** subvenir à un besoin; **to s. s.o. with
sth, s. sth to s.o.** (*goods, facts etc*) fournir
qch à qn. ▮ *n* (*stock*) provision *f*, réserve *f*; **supplies**
(*equipment*) matériel *m*; **the s. of** (*act*) la
fourniture de; **the s. of gas/electricity/water
to** l'alimentation *f* en gaz/électricité/eau de;
(**food**) **supplies** vivres *mpl*; (**office**) **supplies**
fournitures *fpl* (de bureau); **s. and demand**
l'offre *f* et la demande; **to be in short s.**
manquer; **s. ship/train** navire *m*/train *m* ravi-
tailleur; **s. teacher** *Br* suppléant, -ante *mf*.
● **supplying** *n* (*provision*) fourniture *f*; (*feeding*) alimentation *f*.
support [səˈpɔːt] *vt* (*bear weight of*)
supporter, soutenir; (*help, encourage*) soutenir, appuyer; (*theory, idea*) appuyer; (*be in
favour of*) être en faveur de; (*family, wife,
husband etc*) subvenir aux besoins de; (*endure*) supporter.

▮ *n* (*help, encouragement*) soutien *m*, appui
m; (*object*) support *m*; **means of s.** moyens
mpl de subsistance; **income s.** *Br* allocation *f*
d'aide sociale; **in s. of** (*person*) en faveur de;
(*evidence, theory*) à l'appui de; **s. tights** (*for
varicose veins*) bas *mpl* à varices. ● **supporting** *a* (*role in play or film*) secondaire;
(*actor*) qui a un rôle secondaire.
supporter [səˈpɔːtər] *n* partisan *m*; *Football
etc* supporter *m*.
supportive [səˈpɔːtɪv] *a* **to be s. of s.o.** soutenir qn, être d'un grand soutien à qn; **she's
very s.** elle me soutient, elle (m')est d'un
grand soutien.
suppose [səˈpəʊz] *vti* supposer (**that** que);
I'm supposed to work or **be working** (*ought*)
je suis censé travailler; **he's s. to be rich** on
le dit riche; **I s.** (*so*) je pense; **I don't s. so, I
s. not** je ne pense pas; **you're tired, I s.** vous
êtes fatigué, je suppose; **s.** or **supposing we
go** (*suggestion*) si nous partions; **s.** or
supposing (**that**) **you're right** supposons que
tu aies raison. ● **supposed** *a* prétendu, soi-
disant *inv*; **the s. advantages/etc** les pré-
tendus or soi-disant avantages/etc. ● **supposedly** [-ɪdlɪ] *adv* soi-disant; **he went away, s.
to get help** il est parti soi-disant pour
chercher de l'aide. ● **supposition** *n*
[sʌpəˈzɪʃ(ə)n] supposition *f*.
suppository [*Br* səˈpɒzɪtərɪ, *Am* -ɔːrɪ] *n
Med* suppositoire *m*.
suppress [səˈpres] *vt* (*abuse etc*) supprimer;
(*feelings*) réprimer; (*scandal, yawn, revolt,
information*) étouffer. ● **suppression** [-ʃ(ə)n]
n suppression *f*; (*of feelings*) répression *f*; (*of
scandal etc*) étouffement *m*. ● **suppressor** *n*
(*electrical device*) dispositif *m* antiparasite.
supreme [suːˈpriːm] *a* suprême. ● **supremacy** *n* suprématie *f* (**over** sur).
supremo [suːˈpriːməʊ] *n* (*pl* -os) *Br Fam*
grand chef *m*.
surcharge [ˈsɜːtʃɑːdʒ] *n* (*extra charge*) supplément *m*; (*on stamp*) surcharge *f*; (*tax*)
surtaxe *f*.
sure [ʃʊər] *a* (-er, -est) sûr (**of** de, **that** que);
she's s. to accept c'est sûr qu'elle acceptera;
it's s. to snow il va sûrement neiger; **to make
s. of sth** s'assurer de qch; **for s.** à coup sûr,
pour sûr; **s.!, Fam s. thing!** bien sûr!; **s. enough** (*in effect*) en effet; **it s. is cold** *Am* il
fait vraiment froid; **be s. to do it!** ne manquez pas de le faire! ● **surefire** *a Fam* infaillible. ● **surely** *adv* (*certainly*) sûrement; **s. he
didn't refuse?** (*I think, I hope*) il n'a tout de
même pas refusé?
surety [ˈʃʊərətɪ] *n* caution *f*.
surf [sɜːf] *n* (*foam*) ressac *m*. ● **surfboard** *n*
planche *f* (de surf). ● **surfing** *n Sport* surf *m*;
to go s. faire du surf.
surface [ˈsɜːfɪs] *n* surface *f*; **s. area** superficie
f; **s. mail** courrier *m* par voie(s) de surface;
on the s. (*of water*) à la surface; (*of table,
wood etc*) en surface; (*to all appearances*)
Fig en apparence ▮ *vt* (*road*) revêtir ▮ *vi* (*of
swimmer etc*) remonter à la surface; (*of

person, thing etc) *Fam* réapparaître.
surfeit ['sɜːfɪt] *n* (*excess*) excès *m* (**of** de).
surge [sɜːdʒ] *n* (*of enthusiasm etc*) vague *f*; (*of anger, pride*) bouffe *f*; (*rise*) (*of prices etc*) montée *f*; (*in electrical current*) surtension *f* ∎ *vi* (*of crowd, hatred*) déferler; (*of prices etc*) monter (soudainement); **to s. forward** (*of person*) se lancer en avant.
surgeon ['sɜːdʒ(ə)n] *n* chirurgien *m*. ●**surgery** *n* (*doctor's office*) *Br* cabinet *m*; (*period, sitting*) consultation *f*; (*science*) chirurgie *f*; **to have** *or* **undergo s.** avoir une opération (**for** pour). ●**surgical** *a* chirurgical; **s. appliance** appareil *m* orthopédique; **s. spirit** *Br* alcool *m* à 90°.
surly ['sɜːlɪ] *a* (**-ier, -iest**) bourru. ●**surliness** *n* air *m* bourru.
surmise [sə'maɪz] *vt* conjecturer (**that** que).
surmount [sə'maʊnt] *vt* (*overcome, be on top of*) surmonter.
surname ['sɜːneɪm] *n* nom *m* de famille.
surpass [sə'pɑːs] *vt* surpasser (**in** en).
surplus ['sɜːpləs] *n* surplus *m* ∎ *a* (*goods*) en surplus; **some s. material**/*etc* (*left over*) un surplus de tissu/*etc*; **s. stock** surplus *mpl*.
surprise [sə'praɪz] *n* surprise *f*; **to give s.o. a s.** faire une surprise à qn; **to take s.o. by s.** prendre qn au dépourvu; **s. visit/result/***etc* visite *f*/résultat *m* inattendu(e) ∎ *vt* (*astonish*) étonner, surprendre; (*come upon*) surprendre. ●**surprised** *a* surpris (**that** que (+ *sub*), **at sth** de qch, **at seeing/***etc* de voir/*etc*); **I'm s. at his stupidity** sa bêtise m'étonne *or* me surprend; **I'm s. to see you** je suis surpris de te voir. ●**surprising** *a* surprenant. ●**surprisingly** *adv* étonnamment; **s. (enough) he...** chose étonnante il....
surrealistic [sərɪə'lɪstɪk] *a* (*strange*) *Fig* surréaliste.
surrender [sə'rendər] **1** *vi* (*give oneself up*) se rendre (**to** à); **to s. to the police** se livrer à la police ∎ *n* (*of soldiers etc*) capitulation *f*, reddition *f*. **2** *vt* (*hand over*) remettre, rendre (**to** à); (*right, claim*) renoncer à.
surreptitious [sʌrəp'tɪʃəs] *a* subreptice.
surrogate ['sʌrəgət] *n* substitut *m*; **s. mother** mère *f* porteuse.
surround [sə'raʊnd] *vt* entourer (**with** de); (*of army, police*) encercler; **surrounded by** entouré de. ●**surrounding** *a* environnant. ●**surroundings** *npl* (*of town etc*) environs *mpl*; (*setting*) cadre *m*.
surveillance [sɜː'veɪləns] *n* (*of prisoner etc*) surveillance *f*.
survey [sə'veɪ] *vt* (*look at*) regarder; (*review*) passer en revue; (*house etc*) inspecter; (*land*) arpenter ∎ ['sɜːveɪ] *n* (*investigation*) enquête *f*; (*of opinion*) sondage *m*; (*of house etc*) inspection *f*; **a (general) s. of** une vue générale de. ●**sur'veying** *n* arpentage *m*. ●**sur'veyor** *n* (*of land*) (arpenteur *m*) géomètre *m*; (*of house etc*) expert *m*.
survive [sə'vaɪv] *vi* (*of person, custom etc*) survivre ∎ *vt* survivre à (*qn, qch*). ●**survival** *n* (*act*) survie *f*; (*relic*) vestige *m*. ●**survivor**

n survivant, -ante *mf*.
susceptible [sə'septəb(ə)l] *a* (*sensitive*) sensible (**to** à); **s. to colds**/*etc* (*prone to*) prédisposé aux rhumes/*etc*. ●**suscepti'bility** *n* sensibilité *f*; (*to colds etc*) prédisposition *f*; **susceptibilities** susceptibilité(s) *f(pl)*.
suspect ['sʌspekt] *n* & *a* suspect, -ecte (*mf*) ∎ [sə'spekt] *vt* soupçonner (**s.o. of sth** de qch, **s.o. of doing** qn d'avoir fait); (*question, doubt*) suspecter, douter de (*l'honnête de qn etc*); **I s.** oui, **I s.** oui, j'imagine.
suspend [sə'spend] *vt* **1** (*hang*) suspendre (**from** à). **2** (*stop, postpone, dismiss*) suspendre; (*pupil*) renvoyer; (*passport etc*) retirer (provisoirement); **suspended sentence** *Jur* condamnation *f* avec sursis.
suspender [sə'spendər] *n* (*for stocking*) *Br* jarretelle *f*; **suspenders** (*for Br trousers, Am pants*) *Am* bretelles *fpl*; **s. belt** *Br* porte-jarretelles *m inv*.
suspension [sə'spenʃ(ə)n] *n* **1** (*of vehicle etc*) suspension *f*; **s. bridge** pont *m* suspendu. **2** (*stopping*) suspension *f*; (*of passport etc*) retrait *m* (provisoire).
suspense [sə'spens] *n* attente *f* (angoissée); (*in film, book etc*) suspense *m*; **in s.** (*person, Fig matter*) en suspens.
suspicion [sə'spɪʃ(ə)n] *n* soupçon *m*; **to arouse s.** éveiller les soupçons; **with s.** (*distrust*) avec méfiance; **to be under s.** être considéré comme suspect.
suspicious [sə'spɪʃəs] *a* (*person*) soupçonneux, méfiant; (*behaviour*) suspect; **s.(-looking)** (*suspect*) suspect; **to be s. of** *or* **about** (*distrust*) se méfier de. ●**suspiciously** *adv* (*to behave etc*) d'une manière suspecte; (*to consider etc*) avec méfiance.
suss [sʌs] *vt* *Br Fam* **to s. out** (*situation*) piger; **I can't s. out this machine** je ne pige pas comment cette machine marche.
sustain [sə'steɪn] *vt* (*effort, theory*) soutenir; (*weight*) supporter; (*with food*) nourrir; (*life*) maintenir; (*damage, loss, attack*) subir; (*injury*) recevoir. ●**sustainable** *a* (*growth rate etc*) qui peut être maintenu.
sustenance ['sʌstənəns] *n* (*food*) nourriture *f*; (*quality*) valeur *f* nutritive.
swab [swɒb] *n* (*pad for wound*) tampon *m*; (*specimen of fluid*) prélèvement *m*.
swagger ['swægər] *vi* (*walk*) parader ∎ *n* démarche *f* fanfaronne.
swallow ['swɒləʊ] **1** *vt* avaler; **to s. down** *or* **up** avaler; **to s. up** (*savings etc*) *Fig* engloutir ∎ *vi* avaler. **2** *n* (*bird*) hirondelle *f*.
swam [swæm] *pt of* **swim**.
swamp [swɒmp] *n* marécage *m*, marais *m* ∎ *vt* (*flood, overwhelm*) submerger (**with** de). ●**swampy** *a* (**-ier, -iest**) marécageux.
swan [swɒn] *n* cygne *m*.
swank [swæŋk] *vi* (*show off*) *Fam* crâner, fanfaronner.
swap [swɒp] *n* échange *m*; **swaps** (*stamps etc*) doubles *mpl* ∎ *vt* (**-pp-**) échanger (**for** contre); **to s. seats** *or* **places** changer de place ∎ *vi* échanger.

swarm [swɔːm] n (of bees, people etc) essaim m ▌ vi (of streets, insects, people etc) fourmiller (**with** de); **to s. in** (of people) entrer en foule.

swarthy ['swɔːðɪ] a (**-ier, -iest**) (dark) basané.

swastika ['swɒstɪkə] n (Nazi emblem) croix f gammée.

swat [swɒt] vt (**-tt-**) (fly etc) écraser.

sway [sweɪ] vi se balancer, osciller ▌ vt balancer; (person, public opinion etc) Fig influencer ▌ n balancement m; Fig influence f.

swear ['sweər] vt (pt **swore**, pp **sworn**) (promise) jurer (**to do** de faire, **that** que); **to s. an oath** prêter serment; **to s. s.o. to secrecy** faire jurer le silence à qn; **sworn enemies** ennemis mpl jurés ▌ vi (take an oath) jurer (**to sth** de qch); (curse) jurer, pester (**at** contre); **she swears by this lotion/her plumber**/etc elle ne jure que par cette lotion/son plombier/etc. ●**swearword** n gros mot m, juron m.

sweat [swet] n sueur f; **s. shirt** sweat-shirt m ▌ vi (of person) transpirer, suer; (of wall etc) suer (**with** de); **I'm sweating** je suis en sueur ▌ vt **to s. out** (a cold) se débarrasser de (en transpirant).

sweater ['swetər] n (garment) pull m.

sweatshop ['swetʃɒp] n = atelier m où les ouvriers sont exploités.

sweaty ['swetɪ] a (**-ier, -iest**) (shirt etc) plein de sueur; (hand) moite; (person) (tout) en sueur, (tout) en nage.

swede [swiːd] n (vegetable) Br rutabaga m.

Swede [swiːd] n Suédois, -oise mf. ●**Sweden** n Suède f. ●**Swedish** a suédois ▌ n (language) suédois m.

sweep [swiːp] n (with broom) coup m de balai; (movement) Fig (large) mouvement m; (curve) courbe f; **at one's.** (at one go) d'un seul coup; **to make a clean s.** (get rid of) faire table rase (**of** de); (victory) remporter une victoire totale ▌ vt (pt & pp **swept**) (with broom) balayer; (chimney) ramoner; (river) draguer ▌ vi balayer.

sweep along vt (carry off) emporter ▌ **to sweep aside** vt (dismiss) écarter (objection etc) ▌ **to sweep away** vt (leaves etc) balayer; (carry off) emporter ▌ **to sweep in** vi (of person) entrer rapidement or majestueusement ▌ **to sweep off** vt **to s. s.o. off** (take away) emmener qn (**to** à); **to s. s.o. off his or her feet** éblouir or conquérir qn ▌ **to sweep out** vt (room etc) balayer ▌ **to sweep through** vt (of fear etc) saisir (groupe etc); (of disease etc) ravager (pays etc) ▌ **to sweep up** vt (dust, floor etc) balayer ▌ vi balayer.

sweeping ['swiːpɪŋ] a (gesture) large; (change) radical; (statement) trop général.

sweepstake ['swiːpsteɪk] n (lottery) sweepstake m.

sweet [swiːt] a (**-er, -est**) (not sour) doux (f douce); (tea, coffee, cake etc) sucré; (child, house, cat) mignon (f mignonne), gentil (f -ille); (sound, smile) doux (f douce); (pleasant) agréable; (kind) aimable; **to have a s.**

tooth aimer les sucreries; **s. corn** Br maïs m; **s. pea** pois m de senteur; **s. potato** patate f douce; **s. shop** Br confiserie f; **s. talk** Fam cajoleries fpl, douceurs fpl.

▌ n (candy) Br bonbon m; (dessert) Br dessert m; **my s.!** (darling) mon ange! ●**sweet-smelling** a **to be s.-smelling** sentir bon.

sweetbread ['swiːtbred] n ris m de veau or d'agneau.

sweeten ['swiːt(ə)n] vt (tea, coffee etc) sucrer; Fig (offer, task) rendre plus alléchant; (person) amadouer. ●**sweetener** n (for tea etc) édulcorant m.

sweetheart ['swiːthɑːt] n petit ami m, petite amie f; **my s.!** (darling) mon ange!

sweetie ['swiːtɪ] n (darling) Fam chéri, -ie mf.

sweetly ['swiːtlɪ] adv (kindly) aimablement; (agreeably) agréablement; (softly) doucement. ●**sweetness** n douceur f; (taste) goût m sucré.

swell¹ [swel] vi (pt **swelled**, pp **swollen** or **swelled**) (of hand, leg etc) enfler; (of wood) gonfler; (of sails) se gonfler; (of river, numbers) grossir; **to s. up** (of hand etc) enfler ▌ vt (river, numbers) grossir. ●**swelling** n (on body) enflure f.

swell² [swel] 1 n (of sea) houle f. 2 a (very good) Am Fam formidable.

swelter ['sweltər] vi étouffer. ●**sweltering** a étouffant; **it's s.** on étouffe.

swept [swept] pt & pp of sweep.

swerve [swɜːv] vi (of vehicle) faire une embardée; (while running etc) faire un écart.

swift [swɪft] 1 a (**-er, -est**) rapide; **to be s. to act** être prompt à agir. 2 n (bird) martinet m. ●**swiftly** adv rapidement. ●**swiftness** n rapidité f.

swig [swɪg] n (of beer etc) lampée f; **to take a s.** avaler or boire une lampée.

swill [swɪl] vt (beer etc) Fam boire, siffler; **to s.** (**out** or **down**) laver (à grande eau).

swim [swɪm] n baignade f; **to go for a s.** se baigner, nager.

▌ vi (pt **swam**, pp **swum**, pres p **swimming**) nager; (as sport) faire de la natation; (of head, room) Fig tourner; **to go swimming** aller nager; **to s. away** se sauver (à la nage).

▌ vt (river) traverser à la nage; (length, crawl etc) nager. ●**swimming** n natation f; **s. cap** bonnet m de bain; **s. costume** Br maillot m de bain; **s. pool**, Br **s. baths** piscine f; **s. trunks** slip m de bain; (longer) caleçon m de bain. ●**swimmer** n nageur, -euse mf. ●**swimsuit** n maillot m de bain.

swindle ['swɪnd(ə)l] n escroquerie f ▌ vt escroquer; **to s. s.o. out of money** escroquer de l'argent à qn. ●**swindler** n escroc m.

swine [swaɪn] n inv (person) Pej salaud m.

swing [swɪŋ] n (in playground) balançoire f; (movement) balancement m; (of pendulum) oscillation f; (in opinion) revirement m; (rhythm) rythme m; **to be in full s.** (of party etc) battre son plein; **to get into the s.**

of things *Fam* se mettre dans le bain; **s. door** *Br* porte *f* de saloon.

▌**v i** (*pt & pp* **swung**) (*sway*) se balancer; (*of pendulum*) osciller; (*turn*) virer; **to s. round** (*turn suddenly*) virer, tourner; (*of person*) se retourner (vivement); (*of vehicle in collision*) faire un tête-à-queue; **to s. into action** passer à l'action. ●**swinging** *a Fam* (*trendy*) dans le vent; (*lively*) plein de vie; (*music*) entraînant; **s. door** *Am* porte *f* de saloon.

▌**vt** (*arms, legs etc*) balancer; (*axe*) brandir; (*influence*) *Fam* influencer; **to s. round** (*car etc*) faire tourner. ●**swinging** *a Fam* (*trendy*) dans le vent; (*lively*) plein de vie; (*music*) entraînant; **s. door** *Am* porte *f* de saloon.

swingeing ['swɪndʒɪŋ] *a* **s. cuts/increases** *Br* des réductions *fpl*/augmentations *fpl* considérables.

swipe [swaɪp] **1** *vti* **to s. (at)** (*hit*) (essayer de) frapper (*qn, qch*) ▌*n* grand coup *m*. **2** *vt* **to s. sth** (*steal*) *Fam* piquer qch (**from** s.o. à qn).

swirl [swɜːl] *vi* tourbillonner ▌*n* tourbillon *m*.

swish [swɪʃ] **1** *a* (*posh*) *Fam* rupin, chic. **2** *vi* (*of whip etc*) siffler; (*of fabric*) froufrouter ▌*n* (*of whip*) sifflement *m*; (*of fabric*) froufrou *m*.

Swiss [swɪs] *a* suisse; **S. roll** (*cake*) *Br* gâteau *m* roulé ▌*n inv* Suisse *m*, Suissesse *f*; **the S.** les Suisses *mpl*.

switch [swɪtʃ] *n* (*electrical*) bouton *m* (électrique), interrupteur *m*; (*change*) changement *m* (**in** de); (*reversal*) revirement *m* (**in** de); **light s.** bouton *m* (électrique).

▌*vt* (*money, employee etc*) transférer (**to** à); (*support, affection*) reporter (**to** sur, **from** de); (*exchange*) échanger (**for** contre); **to s. buses/etc** changer de bus/*etc*; **to s. places** *or* **seats** changer de place.

▌*vi* **to s. to** (*change to*) passer à. ●**switchback** *n* (*at funfair*) montagnes *fpl* russes. ●**switchblade** *n Am* couteau *m* à cran d'arrêt. ●**switchboard** *n Tel* standard *m*; **s. operator** standardiste *mf*.

switch off *vt* (*lamp, gas, radio etc*) éteindre; (*engine*) arrêter; (*electricity*) couper; **to s. itself off** (*of heating etc*) s'éteindre tout seul ▌*vi* (*switch off light, radio etc*) éteindre ▌**to switch on** *vt* (*lamp, gas, radio etc*) mettre, allumer; (*computer, iron etc*) allumer; (*engine*) mettre en marche ▌*vi* (*switch on light, radio etc*) allumer ▌**to switch over** *vi* (*change TV channels*) changer de chaîne; **to s. over to** (*change to*) passer à.

Switzerland ['swɪtsələnd] *n* Suisse *f*.

swivel ['swɪv(ə)l] *vi* (*Br* **-ll-**, *Am* **-l-**) **to s.** (*round*) (*of chair etc*) pivoter ▌*a* **s. chair** fauteuil *m* pivotant.

swollen ['swəʊl(ə)n] *pp of* **swell**[1] ▌*a* (*leg etc*) enflé; (*stomach*) gonflé.

swoon [swuːn] *vi Lit* se pâmer.

swoop [swuːp] **1** *vi* **to s. (down) on** (*of bird*) fondre sur. **2** *n* (*of police*) descente *f* ▌*vi* faire une descente (**on** dans).

swop [swɒp] *n, vt & vi* = **swap**.

sword [sɔːd] *n* épée *f*. ●**swordfish** *n* espadon *m*.

swore, sworn [swɔːr, swɔːn] *pt & pp of* **swear**.

swot [swɒt] *vti* (**-tt-**) **to s. (up)** (*study*) *Br Fam* potasser, bûcher; **to s. (up) for an exam** potasser *or* bûcher un examen; **to s. up on a subject** potasser *or* bûcher un sujet ▌*n Br Pej Fam* bûcheur, -euse *mf*.

swum [swʌm] *pp of* **swim**.

swung [swʌŋ] *pt & pp of* **swing**.

sycamore ['sɪkəmɔːr] *n* (*maple*) sycomore *m*; (*plane tree*) *Am* platane *m*.

sycophant ['sɪkəfænt] *n Lit* flagorneur, -euse *mf*.

syllable ['sɪləb(ə)l] *n* syllabe *f*.

syllabus ['sɪləbəs] *n* programme *m* (scolaire *or* universitaire).

symbol ['sɪmb(ə)l] *n* symbole *m*. ●**sym'bolic** *a* symbolique. ●**symbolism** *n* symbolisme *m*. ●**symbolize** *vt* symboliser.

symmetry ['sɪmɪtrɪ] *n* symétrie *f*. ●**sy'mmetrical** *a* symétrique.

sympathetic [sɪmpə'θetɪk] *a* (*showing pity*) compatissant; (*understanding*) compréhensif; **s. to s.o./sth** (*favourable*) bien disposé à l'égard de qn/qch. ●**sympathetically** *adv* avec compassion; avec compréhension.

sympathize ['sɪmpəθaɪz] *vi* **I s. (with you)** (*pity*) je suis désolé (pour vous); (*understanding*) je vous comprends. ●**sympathizer** *n Pol* sympathisant, -ante *mf*.

sympathy ['sɪmpəθɪ] *n* (*pity*) compassion *f*; (*understanding*) compréhension *f*; (*when someone dies*) condoléances *fpl*; (*solidarity*) solidarité *f* (**for** avec); (*political*) **sympathies** tendances *fpl* (politiques); **to be in s. with, have s. with** (*workers in dispute*) être du côté de; **to be in s. with s.o.'s opinion** être en accord avec les opinions de qn.

symphony ['sɪmfənɪ] *n* symphonie *f* ▌*a* (*orchestra, concert*) symphonique. ●**sym'phonic** *a* symphonique.

symposium [sɪm'pəʊzɪəm] *n* symposium *m*.

symptom ['sɪmptəm] *n Med & Fig* symptôme *m*; **to be s.-free** ne pas présenter de symptômes. ●**sympto'matic** *a* symptomatique (**of** de).

synagogue ['sɪnəgɒg] *n* synagogue *f*.

synchronize ['sɪŋkrənaɪz] *vt* synchroniser.

syndicate ['sɪndɪkət] *n* (*of businessmen*) syndicat *m*.

syndrome ['sɪndrəʊm] *n Med & Fig* syndrome *m*.

synod ['sɪnəd] *n* (*church council*) synode *m*.

synonym ['sɪnənɪm] *n* synonyme *m*. ●**sy'nonymous** *a* synonyme (**with** de).

synopsis, *pl* **-opses** [sɪ'nɒpsɪs, -psiːz] *n* résumé *m*, synopsis *m*; (*of film*) synopsis *m*.

syntax ['sɪntæks] *n* (*grammar*) syntaxe *f*.

synthesis, *pl* **-theses** ['sɪnθəsɪs, -θəsiːz] *n* synthèse *f*.

synthetic [sɪn'θetɪk] *a* synthétique.

syphilis ['sɪfɪlɪs] *n* syphilis *f*.

syphon ['saɪfən] *n & vt* = **siphon**.

Syria ['sɪrɪə] *n* Syrie *f*. ●**Syrian** *a* syrien ▌*n* Syrien, -ienne *mf*.

syringe [sə'rɪndʒ] n seringue f.

syrup ['sɪrəp] n sirop m; **(golden) s.** (treacle) Br mélasse f (raffinée). ● **syrupy** a sirupeux.

system ['sɪstəm] n (structure, network etc) & Anat Comptr etc système m; (human body) organisme m; (order) méthode f; **to get sth out of one's s.** Fam se libérer de qch; (anger etc) extérioriser qch; **the digestive s.** l'appareil m digestif; **the immune s.** le système immunitaire; **operating s.** Comptr système m d'exploitation; **s. disk** Comptr disque m système; **s. software** Comptr logiciel m système or d'exploitation; **systems analyst** analyste-programmeur, -euse mf.

systematic [sɪstə'mætɪk] a systématique. ● **systematically** adv systématiquement.

T

T, t [tiː] *n* T, t *m*. ●**T-junction** *n* (*of roads*) *Br* intersection *f* en T. ●**T-shirt** *n* tee-shirt *m*, T-shirt *m*.

ta! [tɑː] *int Br Sl* merci!

tab [tæb] *n* **1** (*cloth etc flap*) patte *f*; (*label*) étiquette *f*; (*loop*) attache *f*; **to keep tabs on s.o.** *Fam* surveiller qn (de près). **2** (*bill*) *Am* addition *f*; **to pick up the t.** (*for meal etc*) régler l'addition. **3** (*on computer, typewriter*) tabulateur *m*; **t. key** touche *f* de tabulation.

tabby ['tæbɪ] *a* **t. cat** chat *m* tigré, chatte *f* tigrée.

table¹ ['teɪb(ə)l] *n* **1** (*furniture*) table *f*; **bedside/card/operating t.** table de nuit/de jeu/d'opération; **to set** or *Br* **lay/clear the t.** mettre/débarrasser la table; (**sitting) at the t.** à table; **t. top** dessus *m* de table; **t. wine** vin *m* de table.
2 (*list*) table *f*; **t. of contents** table des matières. ●**tablecloth** *n* nappe *f*. ●**tablemat** *n* (*of cloth*) napperon *m*; (*hard*) dessous-de-plat *m inv*. ●**tablespoon** *n* = cuillère *f* à soupe. ●**tablespoonful** *n* = cuillerée *f* à soupe.

table² ['teɪb(ə)l] *vt* (*motion etc*) *Br* présenter; (*postpone*) *Am* ajourner.

tablet ['tæblɪt] *n* **1** (*pill*) comprimé *m*. **2** (*inscribed stone*) plaque *f*.

tabloid ['tæblɔɪd] *n* (*newspaper*) quotidien *m* populaire (*de petit format*).

taboo [tə'buː] *a & n* tabou (*m*).

tabulator ['tæbjʊleɪtər] *n* (*of computer, typewriter*) tabulateur *m*; **t. key** touche *f* de tabulation.

tacit ['tæsɪt] *a* tacite. ●**tacitly** *adv* tacitement.

taciturn ['tæsɪtɜːn] *a* taciturne.

tack [tæk] *n* **1** (*nail*) petit clou *m*, semence *f*; (*thumbtack*) *Am* punaise *f*; **to get down to brass tacks** *Fig* en venir aux faits ▮ *vt* **to t.** (**down**) clouer. **2** *n* (*stitch*) point *m* de bâti ▮ *vt* **to t.** (**down** *or* **on**) bâtir; **to t. on** (*add*) *Fig* (r)ajouter. **3** *vi* (*of ship*) louvoyer ▮ *n* (*course of action*) *Fig* voie *f*.

tackle ['tæk(ə)l] **1** *n* (*gear*) matériel *m*, équipement *m*. **2** *vt* (*task, problem etc*) s'attaquer à; (*thief etc*) saisir (à bras-le-corps); *Rugby* plaquer; *Football* tacler ▮ *n* *Rugby* plaquage *m*; *Football* tacle *m*.

tacky ['tækɪ] *a* (**-ier, -iest**) **1** (*wet, sticky*) pas sec (*f* sèche), collant. **2** *Fam* (*in appearance*) (*clothes, person etc*) moche; (*attitude*) moche; (*remark etc*) de mauvais goût.

taco ['tækəʊ] *n* (*pl* **-os**) *Am* crêpe *f* de maïs farcie.

tact [tækt] *n* tact *m*. ●**tactful** *a* (*remark etc*)

plein de tact, diplomatique; **to be t.** (*of person*) avoir du tact. ●**tactfully** *adv* avec tact. ●**tactless** *a* (*person, remark etc*) qui manque de tact. ●**tactlessly** *adv* sans tact.

tactic ['tæktɪk] *n* **a t.** une tactique; **tactics** la tactique. ●**tactical** *a* tactique.

tactile ['tæktaɪl] *a* tactile.

tadpole ['tædpəʊl] *n* têtard *m*.

taffy ['tæfɪ] *n* (*toffee*) *Am* caramel *m* (*dur*).

tag [tæg] **1** *n* (*label*) étiquette *f*; (*end piece*) bout *m* ▮ *vt* (**-gg-**) **to t. sth on** (*add*) *Fam* rajouter qch (to à). **2** *vi* (**-gg-**) **to t. along** (*follow*) suivre; **may I t. along (with you)?** est-ce que je peux venir (avec vous)?

Tahiti [tɑː'hiːtɪ] *n* Tahiti *m*.

tail [teɪl] *n* **1** (*of animal etc*) queue *f*; (*of shirt*) pan *m*; **tails** (*outfit*) queue-de-pie *f*, habit *m*; **the t. end** (*of film etc*) la fin (**of** de); (*of cloth, string etc*) le bout (**of** de); **heads or tails?** pile ou face? **2** *vt* (*follow*) suivre, filer. **3** *vi* **to t. off** (*lessen*) diminuer. **4** *vi* **the traffic is tailing back (for miles)** *Br* ça bouchonne (sur des kilomètres). ●**tailback** *n* (*of traffic*) *Br* bouchon *m*. ●**tailcoat** *n* queue-de-pie *f*. ●**tailgate** *n* (*of car*) *Br* hayon *m* ▮ *vt* **to t. s.o.** (*in vehicle*) *Am* coller au pare-chocs de qn. ●**taillight** *n* (*of vehicle*) *Am* feu *m* arrière *inv*.

tailor ['teɪlər] *n* (*person*) tailleur *m* ▮ *vt* (*garment*) façonner; (*adjust*) *Fig* adapter (**to, to** suit à). ●**tailor-'made** *a* fait sur mesure; **t.-made for** (*specially designed*) conçu pour; (*suited*) fait pour. ●**tailored** *a* **t. shirt** chemise *f* cintrée.

tainted ['teɪntɪd] *a* (*air*) pollué; (*food*) gâté; (*reputation, system etc*) *Fig* souillé.

Taiwan [taɪwɑːn] *n* Taiwan *m or f*.

take [teɪk] *vt* (*pt* **took**, *pp* **taken**) prendre; (*prize*) remporter; (*exam*) passer; (*choice*) faire; (*contain*) contenir; (*subtract*) *Math* soustraire (**from** de); (*tolerate*) supporter; (*bring*) amener (qn) (**to** à); (*by car*) conduire (qn) (**to** à); (*escort*) accompagner (qn) (**to** à); (*lead away*) emmener (qn) (**to** à); (*of road*) mener (qn) (**to** à); **to t. sth to s.o.** (ap)porter qch à qn; **to t. s.o. (out) to the theatre/etc** emmener qn au théâtre/etc; **to t. sth with one** emporter qch avec soi; **to t. s.o. home** (*on foot, by car etc*) ramener qn; **it takes an army/courage/etc** (*requires*) il faut une armée/du courage/etc (**to do** pour faire); **I took an hour to do it** *or* **over it** j'ai mis une heure à le faire, ça m'a pris une heure pour le faire; **I t. it that** je présume que.
▮ *n* (*recording of film*) prise *f* de vue(s).
▮ *vi* (*be successful*) (*of vaccination, fire etc*)

prendre.

take after *vt* to t. after s.o. *(be like)* ressembler à qn ∎ **to take along** *vt (object)* emporter; *(person)* emmener ∎ **to take apart** *vt (machine)* démonter ∎ **to take away** *vt (thing)* emporter; *(person)* emmener; *(remove)* enlever **(from** à); *(subtract) Math* soustraire **(from** de) ∎ **to take back** *vt* reprendre; *(return)* rapporter; *(statement)* retirer; *(accompany)* ramener *(qn)* **(to** à) ∎ **to take down** *vt (object)* descendre; *(notes)* prendre ∎ **to take in** *vt (chair, car etc)* rentrer; *(orphan)* recueillir; *(skirt)* reprendre; *(distance)* couvrir; *(include)* inclure, englober; *(understand)* comprendre; *(deceive) Fam* rouler ∎ **to take off** *vt (remove)* enlever; *(train, bus)* supprimer; *(lead away)* emmener; *(mimic)* imiter; *(deduct) Math* déduire **(from** de) ∎ *vi (of aircraft)* décoller ∎ **to take on** *vt (work, staff, passenger, shape)* prendre ∎ **to take out** *vt (from pocket etc)* sortir; *(stain)* enlever; *(tooth)* arracher; *(insurance policy, patent)* prendre; **to take s.o. out to the theatre/etc** emmener qn au théâtre/etc; **to t. it out on s.o.** *Fam* passer sa colère sur qn. ∎ **to take over** *vt (be responsible for the running of)* prendre la direction de *(compagnie, équipe, pays)*; *(buy out)* racheter *(compagnie)*; *(overrun)* envahir; **to t. over s.o.'s job** remplacer qn ∎ *vi (relieve)* prendre la relève **(from** de); *(succeed)* prendre la succession **(from** de); *(of dictator, general etc)* prendre le pouvoir ∎ **to take round** *vt (bring)* apporter *(qch)* **(to** à); amener *(qn)* **(to** à); *(distribute)* distribuer; *(visitor)* faire visiter ∎ **to take to** *vt* to t. to doing se mettre à faire; **I didn't t. to him/it** il/ça ne m'a pas plu ∎ **to take up** *vt (carry up)* monter; *(continue)* reprendre; *(space, time)* prendre; *(offer)* accepter; *(hobby)* se mettre à; *(hem)* raccourcir ∎ *vi* to t. up with s.o. se lier avec qn.

● **take-away** ['teɪkəweɪ] *Br a (meal)* à emporter ∎ *n (shop)* café *m* or restaurant *m* qui fait des plats à emporter; *(meal)* plat *m* à emporter. ● **takeoff** *n (of aircraft)* décollage *m* ● **take-out** *a & n Am* = take-away. ● **take-over** *n (of company)* rachat *m*; *Pol* prise *f* de pouvoir.

taken ['teɪk(ə)n] *a (seat)* pris; *(impressed)* impressionné **(with,** by par); to be t. ill tomber malade.

taking ['teɪkɪŋ] *n (capture of town etc)* prise *f*; **takings** *(money)* recette *f*.

talc [tælk] *n* = talcum powder. ● **talcum** ['tælkəm] *a* **t. powder** talc *m*.

tale [teɪl] *n (story)* conte *m*; *(account, report)* récit *m*; *(lie)* histoire *f*; **to tell tales** rapporter *(on s.o. sur qn)*.

talent ['tælənt] *n* talent *m*; *(talented people)* talents *mpl*; **to have a t. for** avoir du talent pour. ● **talented** *a* doué, talentueux.

talisman ['tælɪzmən] *n (pl -mans)* talisman *m*.

talk [tɔːk] *n (words)* propos *mpl*; *(gossip)* ba-

vardage(s) *m(pl)*; *(conversation)* conversation *f* **(about** à propos de); *(lecture)* exposé *m* **(on** sur); *(informal)* causerie *f* **(on** sur); *(interview)* entretien *m*; **talks** *(negotiations)* pourparlers *mpl*; **to have a t. with s.o.** parler avec qn; **there's t. of...** on parle de.... ∎ *vi* parler **(to** à; **with** avec; **about, of** de); *(chat)* bavarder; **to t. down to s.o.** parler à qn comme à un inférieur. ∎ *vt (nonsense)* dire; **to t. politics** parler politique; **to t. s.o. into doing/out of doing** persuader qn de faire/de ne pas faire; **to t. sth over** discuter (de) qch; **to t. s.o. round** persuader qn. ● **talking** *a* **t. film** film *m* parlant ∎ *n* **to do the t.** parler. ● **talking-to** *n* to give s.o. a t.-to passer un savon à qn.

talkative ['tɔːkətɪv] *a* bavard.

talker ['tɔːkər] *n* causeur, -euse *mf*; **she's a good t.** elle parle bien.

tall [tɔːl] *a (-er, -est) (person)* grand; *(tree, house etc)* haut; **how t. are you?** combien mesures-tu?; **a t. story** *Fig* une histoire invraisemblable *or* à dormir debout. ● **tallness** *n (of person)* grande taille *f*; *(of building etc)* hauteur *f*.

tallboy ['tɔːlbɔɪ] *n Br* grande commode *f*.

tally ['tælɪ] *vi* correspondre **(with** à).

talon ['tælən] *n (bird's claw)* serre *f*.

tambourine [tæmbə'riːn] *n* tambourin *m*.

tame [teɪm] *a (-er, -est) (animal, bird)* apprivoisé; *(person)* docile; *(book, play)* fade ∎ *vt (animal, bird)* apprivoiser; *(lion,* Fig *passion)* dompter.

tamper ['tæmpər] *vi* to t. with *(lock, car etc)* (essayer de) forcer; *(machine etc)* toucher à; *(text)* altérer. ● **tamper-proof** *a (lock)* inviolable; *(jar)* à fermeture de sécurité; **t.-proof seal** fermeture *f* de sécurité.

tampon ['tæmpon] *n* tampon *m (périodique)*.

tan [tæn] *n (suntan)* bronzage *m* ∎ *vi (-nn-)* bronzer. **2** *a (colour)* marron clair *inv*. **3** *vt (-nn-) (hide)* tanner.

tandem ['tændəm] *n* **1** *(bicycle)* tandem *m*. **2** **in t.** *(to work etc)* en tandem; **in t. with** *(at the same time as)* parallèlement à.

tang [tæŋ] *n (taste)* saveur *f* piquante; *(smell)* odeur *f* piquante. ● **tangy** *a (-ier, -iest)* piquant.

tangent ['tændʒənt] *n (line) Math* tangente *f*; **to go off at a t.** s'éloigner du sujet.

tangerine ['tændʒə'riːn] *n* mandarine *f*.

tangible ['tændʒəb(ə)l] *a* tangible.

tangle ['tæŋg(ə)l] *n* enchevêtrement *m*; **to get into a t.** *(of rope)* s'enchevêtrer; *(of hair)* s'emmêler; *(of person) Fig* se mettre dans une situation pas possible. ● **tangled** *a* enchevêtré; *(hair)* emmêlé; **to get t.** = to get into a tangle.

tango ['tæŋgəʊ] *n (pl -os)* tango *m*.

tank [tæŋk] *n* **1** *(for storing liquid or gas)* réservoir *m*; *(vat)* cuve *f*; *(fish)* t. aquarium *m*. **2** *(military vehicle)* char *m*, tank *m*. **3** *vi* to t. up on *(snacks, Br sweets, Am candy etc)* se remplir le ventre de.

tankard ['tæŋkəd] *n (beer mug) Br* chope *f*.

tanker ['tæŋkər] n (truck) camion-citerne m;
(oil) t. (ship) pétrolier m.

Tannoy® ['tænɔɪ] n over the T. Br au(x)
haut-parleur(s).

tantalizing ['tæntəlaɪzɪŋ] a (irrésistiblement)
tentant. ● **tantalizingly** adv d'une manière
tentante.

tantamount ['tæntəmaʊnt] a it's t. to cela
équivaut à.

tantrum ['tæntrəm] n colère f; to have a t.
(of child) faire une colère.

Tanzania [tænzə'nɪə] n Tanzanie f.

tap [tæp] 1 n (for water) Br robinet m; on t.
Fig disponible. 2 vti (-pp-) (hit) frapper légèrement, tapoter ▌ n petit coup m; t. dancing claquettes fpl. 3 vt (-pp-) (phone) placer
sur table d'écoute. 4 vt (-pp-) (resources)
exploiter.

tape [teɪp] 1 n ruban m; (sticky Br or adhesive) t. ruban adhésif; (bandage) sparadrap
m; t. measure mètre m (à) ruban ▌ vt (stick)
coller (avec du ruban adhésif). 2 n (for
sound or video recording) bande f (magnétique or vidéo); t. recorder magnétophone m;
t. deck platine f cassette ▌ vt (film, music,
voice etc) enregistrer; (event) faire une cassette de ▌ vi enregistrer.

taper ['teɪpər] 1 vi (of fingers etc) s'effiler; to
t. off Fig diminuer. 2 n (candle) bougie f
longue et fine; Rel cierge m. ● **tapered** a (Br
trousers, Am pants) à bas étroits. ● **tapering**
a (fingers) fuselé.

tapestry ['tæpɪstrɪ] n tapisserie f.

tapeworm ['teɪpwɜːm] n ver m solitaire.

tapioca [tæpɪ'əʊkə] n tapioca m.

tar [tɑːr] n goudron m ▌ vt (-rr-) goudronner.

tarantula [tə'ræntjʊlə] n (pl -as) tarentule f.

tardy ['tɑːdɪ] a (-ier, -iest) (belated) tardif;
(slow) lent.

target ['tɑːgɪt] n cible f; (objective) objectif
m; t. date date f fixée ▌ vt (campaign, product etc) destiner (at à); (age group etc) viser.

tariff ['tærɪf] n (tax) tarif m douanier; (price
list) Br tarif m.

tarmac ['tɑːmæk] n (on road) Br macadam
m (goudronné); (runway) piste f.

tarnish ['tɑːnɪʃ] vt ternir.

tarpaulin [tɑː'pɔːlɪn] n bâche f (gou-
dronnée); (plastic sheet) bâche f en plastique.

tarragon ['tærəgən] n (herb) estragon m.

tarry ['tærɪ] vi (remain) Lit rester.

tart [tɑːt] n (pie) (open) tarte f; (with pastry
on top) tourte f. 2 a (-er, -est) (sour, acid)
(taste, Fig remark) aigre. 3 n (prostitute) Br
Pej Fam poule f. 4 vt to t. up Br Pej Fam
(decorate) embellir; (dress) attifer. ● **tartness**
n (of taste, Fig remark) aigreur f.

tartan ['tɑːt(ə)n] n tartan m ▌ a (skirt etc)
écossais.

tartar ['tɑːtər] 1 a t. sauce sauce f tartare. 2 n
(on teeth) tartre m.

task [tɑːsk] n travail m, tâche f; to take s.o.
to t. prendre qn à partie; t. force Mil dé-

tachement m spécial; Pol commission f
spéciale.

tassel ['tas(ə)l] n (on clothes etc) gland m.

taste [teɪst] n goût m; (general idea) Fig idée
f, aperçu m; to get a t. for prendre goût à;
in good/bad t. de bon/mauvais goût; to have
a t. of sth goûter à qch; (try) goûter à qch;
(experience) goûter de qch ▌ vt (eat, drink,
enjoy) goûter; (try, sample) goûter à; (make
out the taste of) sentir (le goût de); (experience) goûter de ▌ vi to t. of or like sth avoir
un goût de qch; to t. delicious/etc avoir un
goût délicieux/etc; how does it t.? comment
le trouves-tu? ● **taste bud** n papille f gusta-
tive.

tasteful ['teɪstfəl] a de bon goût. ● **tastefully**
adv avec goût. ● **tasteless** a (food etc) sans
goût; (joke etc) Fig de mauvais goût. ● **tasty**
a (-ier, -iest) savoureux.

tat [tæt] see tit 1.

ta-ta! [tæ'tɑː] int Br Sl au revoir!

tattered ['tætəd] a (clothes) en lambeaux;
(person) déguenillé. ● **tatters** npl in t.
(clothes) en lambeaux.

tattoo [tæ'tuː] 1 n (pl -oos) (on arm, body
etc) tatouage m; to get a t. se faire tatouer ▌
vt tatouer. 2 n (pl -oos) Mil spectacle m militaire.

tatty ['tætɪ] a (-ier, -iest) (clothes etc) Br Fam
miteux.

taught [tɔːt] pt & pp of teach.

taunt [tɔːnt] vt railler ▌ n raillerie f. ● **taunt-
ing** a railleur.

Taurus ['tɔːrəs] n (sign) le Taureau.

taut [tɔːt] a (rope, wire etc, Fig person etc)
tendu.

tavern ['tævən] n taverne f.

tawdry ['tɔːdrɪ] a (-ier, -iest) Pej tape-à-l'œil
inv.

tawny ['tɔːnɪ] a (colour) fauve; t. owl (chouette f) hulotte f.

tax¹ [tæks] n (on goods) taxe f, impôt m; (income) t. impôts mpl (sur le revenu); road t.
Br taxe f sur les automobiles ▌ a fiscal; t.
collector percepteur m; t. relief dégrèvement
m (d'impôt); (road) t. disc Br = vignette f
(automobile) ▌ vt (person) imposer; (goods)
taxer. ● **taxable** a imposable. ● **taxation**
[tæk'seɪʃ(ə)n] n (taxes) impôts mpl; (act)
imposition f; the burden of t. le poids de
l'impôt. ● **tax-free** a exempt d'impôts. ● **tax-
man** n (pl -men) Br Fam percepteur m.
● **taxpayer** n contribuable mf.

tax² [tæks] vt (s.o.'s patience etc) mettre à
l'épreuve; (tire) fatiguer. ● **taxing** a (journey
etc) éprouvant.

taxi ['tæksɪ] 1 n taxi m; t. cab taxi m; t. rank
Br, t. stand Am station f de taxis. 2 vi (of
aircraft) rouler au sol.

TB [tiː'biː] n tuberculose f.

tea [tiː] n thé m; (snack) Br goûter m; (evening meal) Br repas m du soir; high t. Br
goûter m (dînatoire); to have t. prendre le
thé; (afternoon snack) goûter; t. break Br
pause-thé f; t. chest caisse f (à thé); t. cloth

(for drying dishes) torchon *m*; t. **party** thé *m*; t. **set** service *m* à thé; t. **strainer** passoire *f* à thé; **to sit at the t. table** s'asseoir à la table mise pour le thé *or* le repas du soir; t. **towel** *Br* torchon *m*.

teabag ['tiːbæg] *n* sachet *m* de thé. ●**teacup** *n* tasse *f* à thé. ●**tealeaf** *n* (*pl* -**leaves**) feuille *f* de thé. ●**teapot** *n* théière *f*. ●**tearoom** *n* salon *m* de thé. ●**teashop** *n Br* salon *m* de thé. ●**teaspoon** *n* petite cuillère *f*. ●**teaspoonful** *n* cuillerée *f* à café. ●**teatime** *n* l'heure *f* du thé.

teach [tiːtʃ] *vt* (*pt & pp* **taught**) apprendre (**s.o. sth** qch à qn, **that** que); (*in school, at university etc*) enseigner (**s.o. sth** qch à qn); **to t. s.o. (how) to do** apprendre à qn à faire; **to t. school** *Am* enseigner; **to t. oneself sth** apprendre qch tout seul ▌ *vi* enseigner. ●**teaching** *n* enseignement *m* ▌ *a* (*staff*) enseignant; (*method, material*) pédagogique; t. **hospital** *Br* centre *m* hospitalo-universitaire; **the t. profession** l'enseignement *m*; (*teachers*) le corps enseignant; t. **qualification** diplôme *m* permettant d'enseigner; **the t. staff** le personnel enseignant.

teacher ['tiːtʃər] *n* professeur *m*; (*in Br primary or Am elementary school*) instituteur, -trice *mf*.

teak [tiːk] *n* (*wood*) teck *m*; **a t. sideboard/***etc* un buffet/*etc* en teck.

team [tiːm] *n* équipe *f*; (*of horses, oxen*) attelage *m*; t. **mate** coéquipier, -ière *mf* ▌ *vi* **to t. up** faire équipe (**with s.o.** avec qn). ●**teamster** *n Am* routier *m*. ●**teamwork** *n* collaboration *f*.

tear[1] [teər] **1** *n* déchirure *f* ▌ *vt* (*pt* **tore**, *pp* **torn**) (*rip*) déchirer; (*snatch*) arracher (**from s.o.** à qn); **torn between** *Fig* tiraillé entre; **to t. s.o. away from sth** arracher qn à qch; **to t. down** (*house etc*) démolir; **to t. off** *or* **out** (*remove with force*) arracher; (*receipt, counterfoil, stamp etc*) détacher; **to t. up** déchirer ▌ *vi* (*of cloth etc*) se déchirer. **2** *vi* (*pt* **tore**, *pp* **torn**) **to t. along/away** *or* **off** (*rush*) aller/partir à toute vitesse.

tear[2] [tiər] *n* larme *f*; **in tears** en larmes; **close to** *or* **near (to) tears** au bord des larmes. ●**tearful** *a* (*eyes, voice*) larmoyant; (*person*) en larmes. ●**tearfully** *adv* en pleurant. ●**teargas** *n* gaz *m* lacrymogène.

tearaway ['teərəweɪ] *n Br Fam* casse-cou *m*.

tease [tiːz] *vt* taquiner; (*harshly*) tourmenter ▌ *n* (*person*) taquin, -ine *mf*. ●**teasing** *a* (*remark etc*) taquin. ●**teaser** *n* **1** (*person*) taquin, -ine *mf*. **2** (*question*) *Fam* colle *f*.

teat [tiːt] *n* (*of animal, Br of baby's bottle*) tétine *f*.

technical ['teknɪk(ə)l] *a* technique. ●**technicality** *n* (*detail*) détail *m* technique. ●**technically** *adv* techniquement; *Fig* théoriquement, en principe.

technician ['teknɪʃ(ə)n] *n* technicien, -ienne *mf*.

technique [tek'niːk] *n* technique *f*.

technocrat ['teknəkræt] *n* technocrate *m*.

technology [tek'nɒlədʒɪ] *n* technologie *f*; **the latest t.** la technologie la plus avancée; **alternative t.** les technologies douces. ●**technological** *a* technologique.

teddy ['tedɪ] *n* t. (**bear**) ours *m* (en peluche).

tedious ['tiːdɪəs] *a* fastidieux. ●**tediousness** *or* **tedium** *n* ennui *m*.

teem [tiːm] *vi* **1** (*swarm*) grouiller (**with** de). **2** **to t. (with rain)** pleuvoir à torrents. ●**teeming** *a* **1** (*crowd, street etc*) grouillant. **2 t. rain** pluie *f* torrentielle.

teenage ['tiːneɪdʒ] *a* (*boy, girl, behaviour*) adolescent; (*fashion, magazine etc*) pour adolescents. ●**teenager** *n* adolescent, -ente *mf*. ●**teens** *npl* **to be in one's t.** être adolescent.

teeny (weeny) ['tiːnɪ('wiːnɪ)] *a* (*tiny*) *Fam* minuscule.

tee-shirt ['tiːʃɜːt] *n* tee-shirt *m*.

teeter ['tiːtər] *vi* (*be unsteady*) chanceler; **to t. on the brink of ruin/disaster** *Fig* être à deux doigts de la ruine/du désastre.

teeth [tiːθ] *see* **tooth**.

teethe [tiːð] *vi* faire ses dents. ●**teething** *n* dentition *f*; t. **ring** anneau *m* de dentition; t. **troubles** *Fig* difficultés *fpl* de mise en route.

teetotal [tiː'təʊt(ə)l] *a* **to be t.** ne pas boire d'alcool. ●**teetotaller** (*Am* **teetotaler**) *n* personne *f* qui ne boit pas d'alcool.

tele- ['telɪ] *pref* télé-.

telecommunications [telɪkəmjuːnɪ'keɪʃ(ə)nz] *npl* télécommunications *fpl*.

telegram ['telɪgræm] *n* télégramme *m*.

telegraph ['telɪgrɑːf] *a* t. **pole/wire** poteau *m*/fil *m* télégraphique.

Telemessage® ['telɪmesɪdʒ] *n* (*in UK*) = télégramme *m* (téléphoné).

telepathy [tə'lepəθɪ] *n* télépathie *f*.

telephone ['telɪfəʊn] *n* téléphone *m*; **to be on the t.** (*speaking*) être au téléphone ▌ *a* (*call, line, message etc*) téléphonique; t. **booth**, *Br* t. **box** cabine *f* téléphonique; t. **directory** annuaire *m* du téléphone; t. **number** numéro *m* de téléphone ▌ *vi* téléphoner ▌ *vt* (*message*) téléphoner (**to** à); **to t. s.o.** téléphoner à qn. ●**te'lephonist** *n* standardiste *mf*.

telephoto ['telɪfəʊtəʊ] *a* t. **lens** téléobjectif *m*.

teleprinter ['telɪprɪntər] *n Br* téléscripteur *m*.

telescope ['telɪskəʊp] *n* télescope *m*. ●**telescopic** *a* (*umbrella, Br aerial, Am antenna*) télescopique.

teletext ['telɪtekst] *n* télétexte *m*.

teletypewriter [telɪ'taɪpraɪtər] *n Am* téléscripteur *m*.

televise ['telɪvaɪz] *vt* retransmettre à la télévision, téléviser.

television [telɪ'vɪʒ(ə)n] *n* télévision *f*; **on (the) t.** à la télévision; **to watch (the) t.** regarder la télévision ▌ *a* (*programme, screen etc*) de télévision; (*interview, report etc*) télévisé; t. **set** téléviseur *m*, poste *m* de télévision.

telex ['teleks] *n* (*service, message*) télex *m* ▮ *vt* envoyer par télex.

tell [tel] *vt* (*pt & pp* told) dire (*s.o. sth* qch à qn, *that* que); (*story*) raconter; (*distinguish*) distinguer (*from* de); (*know*) savoir; (*predict*) prédire (*l'avenir*); **to t. s.o. to do** dire à qn de faire qch; **to know how to t. the time** *or Am* **t. time** savoir lire l'heure; **to t. the difference** voir la différence (*between* entre); **to t. s.o. off** (*scold*) *Fam* disputer qn, gronder qn.
▮ *vi* dire; (*have an effect*) avoir un effet; (*know*) savoir; **to t. of** *or* **about sth/s.o.** parler de qch/qn; **to t. on s.o.** *Fam* rapporter sur qn.

teller ['telər] *n* (*bank*) **t.** guichetier, -ière *mf* (*de banque*).

telling ['telɪŋ] *a* (*smile etc*) révélateur; (*blow*) efficace.

telltale ['telteɪl] *a* **t. sign** signe *m* révélateur; **t. mark** trace *f* révélatrice ▮ *n Fam* rapporteur, -euse *mf*.

telly ['telɪ] *n Br Fam* télé *f*; **on the t.** à la télé.

temerity [tə'merɪtɪ] *n* témérité *f*.

temp [temp] *n* (*secretary etc*) *Br Fam* intérimaire *mf* ▮ *vi Br Fam* faire de l'intérim.

temper ['tempər] **1** *n* (*mood, nature*) humeur *f*; (*anger*) colère *f*; **to lose one's t.** se mettre en colère; **in a bad t.** de mauvaise humeur; **to have a (bad** *or* **an awful) t.** avoir un caractère de cochon. **2** *vt* (*moderate*) tempérer (*son enthousiasme etc*). **3** *vt* (*steel*) tremper.

temperament ['temp(ə)rəmənt] *n* tempérament *m*. ●**tempera'mental** *a* (*person, machine etc*) capricieux; (*inborn*) inné.

temperance ['temp(ə)rəns] *n* (*in drink*) tempérance *f*.

temperate ['tempərət] *a* (*climate etc*) tempéré.

temperature ['temp(ə)rətʃər] *n* température *f*; **to have a t.** avoir *or* faire de la température *or* de la fièvre.

tempest ['tempɪst] *n Lit* tempête *f*. ●**tem'pestuous** *a* (*meeting etc*) orageux.

template ['templət, -pleɪt] *n* (*of plastic, metal etc*) patron *m*.

temple ['temp(ə)l] *n* **1** (*religious building*) temple *m*. **2** *Anat* tempe *f*.

tempo ['tempəʊ] *n* (*pl* -os) (*of life, work etc*) rythme *m*; *Mus* tempo *m*.

temporal ['temp(ə)rəl] *a* temporel.

temporary [*Br* 'temp(ə)rərɪ, *Am* -erɪ] *a* provisoire; (*job, worker*) temporaire; (*secretary*) intérimaire. ●**temporarily** *adv* provisoirement.

tempt [tempt] *vt* tenter; **tempted to do** tenté de faire; **to t. s.o. to do** persuader qn de faire. ●**tempting** *a* tentant. ●**temptingly** *adv* d'une manière tentante; **the cake looked t. delicious** le gâteau avait l'air délicieux et il était bien tentant. ●**temptation** [-'teɪʃ(ə)n] *n* tentation *f*.

ten [ten] *a & n* dix (*m*).

tenable ['tenəb(ə)l] *a* (*argument*) défendable;

the post is t. for three years ce poste peut être occupé pendant trois ans.

tenacious [tə'neɪʃəs] *a* tenace. ●**tenacity** *n* ténacité *f*.

tenant ['tenənt] *n* locataire *nmf*. ●**tenancy** *n* (*lease*) location *f*; (*period*) occupation *f*.

tend [tend] **1** *vi* **to t. to do** avoir tendance à faire; **to t. towards** incliner vers. **2** *vt* (*look after*) s'occuper de. ●**tendency** *n* tendance *f* (**to do** à faire).

tendentious [ten'denʃəs] *a Pej* tendancieux.

tender¹ ['tendər] *a* (*soft, delicate, loving*) tendre; (*painful*) sensible. ●**tenderly** *adv* tendrement. ●**tenderness** *n* tendresse *f*; (*pain*) (*petite*) douleur *f*; (*of meat*) tendreté *f*.

tender² ['tendər] **1** *vt* (*offer*) offrir; **to t. one's resignation** donner sa démission. **2** *n* **to be legal t.** (*of money*) avoir cours. **3** *n* (*for services etc*) soumission *f* (**for** pour).

tendon ['tendən] *n Anat* tendon *m*.

tenement ['tenəmənt] *n* immeuble *m* (*de rapport*) (*Am dans un quartier pauvre*).

tenet ['tenɪt] *n* principe *m*.

tenfold ['tenfəʊld] *a* **t. increase** augmentation *f* par dix ▮ *adv* **to increase t.** (se) multiplier par dix.

tenner ['tenər] *n Br Fam* billet *m* de dix livres.

tennis ['tenɪs] *n* tennis *m*; **table t.** tennis de table; **t. court** court *m* (*de tennis*), tennis *m*.

tenor ['tenər] *n* **1** (*sense, course*) sens *m* général. **2** *Mus* ténor *m*.

tenpin ['tenpɪn] *a* **t. bowling** *Br* bowling *m*. ●**tenpins** *npl* quilles *fpl* ▮ *n sing* bowling *m*.

tense [tens] **1** *a* (-er, -est) (*person, muscle, situation*) tendu ▮ *vt* tendre, crisper ▮ *vi* **to t. (up)** (*of person, face*) se crisper. **2** *n* (*of verb*) temps *m*; **in the present/future t.** au présent/futur. ●**tenseness** *n* tension *f*. ●**tension** [-ʃ(ə)n] *n* tension *f*.

tent [tent] *n* tente *f*; **t. peg** *Br* piquet *m* de tente; **t. pole** *Br*, **t. stake** *Am* mât *m* de tente.

tentacle ['tentək(ə)l] *n* tentacule *m*.

tentative ['tentətɪv] *a* (*not definite*) provisoire; (*hesitant*) timide. ●**tentatively** *adv* provisoirement; (*hesitantly*) timidement.

tenterhooks ['tentəhʊks] *npl* **to be on t.** (*anxious*) être sur des charbons ardents.

tenth [tenθ] *a & n* dixième (*mf*); **a t.** un dixième.

tenuous ['tenjʊəs] *a* (*link, suspicion etc*) ténu.

tenure ['tenjər] *n* (*in job*) période *f* de jouissance; (*job security*) *Am* titularisation *f*.

tepid ['tepɪd] *a* (*liquid*) & *Fig* tiède.

term [tɜːm] *n* (*word*) terme *m*; (*period*) période *f*; (*duration*) durée *f*; (*of school or university year*) *Br* trimestre *m*; (*semester*) *Am* semestre *m*; **terms** (*conditions*) conditions *fpl*; (*prices*) prix *mpl*; **t. (of office)** *Pol* mandat *m*; **t. of abuse** insulte *f*; **to be on good/bad terms** être en bons/mauvais termes (**with s.o.** avec qn); **to be on close terms** être intime (**with** avec); **to buy sth on easy terms**

acheter qch avec facilités de paiement *or* à crédit; **in terms of** (*speaking of*) sur le plan de; **in real terms** dans la pratique; **to come to terms with** (*situation etc*) faire face à; (*person*) tomber d'accord avec; **in the long/short/medium t.** à long/court/moyen terme; **at (full) t.** (*baby*) à terme.

▮ *vt* (*name, call*) appeler; **this might be termed a catastrophe** on pourrait appeler ça une catastrophe.

terminal ['tɜːmɪn(ə)l] **1** *n* (*electronic*) terminal *m*; (*in electric circuit*) borne *f*; **computer t.** terminal *m* d'ordinateur; (**air**) **t.** aérogare *f*; (**bus**) **t.** gare *f* routière; (**oil**) **t.** terminal *m* (pétrolier). **2** *a* (*patient, illness*) incurable; **in its t. stage** (*illness*) en phase terminale. ●**terminally** *adv* **t. ill** (*patient*) incurable.

terminate ['tɜːmɪneɪt] *vt* mettre fin à; (*contract*) résilier; (*pregnancy*) interrompre ▮ *vi* se terminer. ●**termination** [-'neɪʃ(ə)n] *n* fin *f*; (*of contract*) résiliation *f*; (*of pregnancy*) interruption *f*.

terminology [tɜːmɪ'nɒlədʒɪ] *n* terminologie *f*.

terminus ['tɜːmɪnəs] *n* terminus *m*.

termite ['tɜːmaɪt] *n* (*insect*) termite *m*.

terrace ['terɪs] *n* (*next to house, on hill*) terrasse *f*; (*houses*) Br maisons *fpl* en bande; **the terraces** (*at football ground*) Br les gradins *mpl*. ●**terrace** *or* **terraced house** *n* Br maison *f* attenante aux maisons voisines.

terracota [terə'kɒtə] *n* terre *f* cuite.

terrain [tə'reɪn] *n* Mil Geol terrain *m*.

terrestrial [tə'restrɪəl] *a* terrestre.

terrible ['terəb(ə)l] *a* affreux, terrible. ●**terribly** *adv* (*badly, very*) affreusement.

terrier ['terɪər] *n* (*dog*) terrier *m*.

terrific [tə'rɪfɪk] *a* (*excellent, very great*) Fam formidable, terrible. ●**terrifically** *adv* Fam (*extremely*) terriblement; (*extremely well*) terriblement bien.

terrify ['terɪfaɪ] *vt* terrifier; **to be terrified of** avoir très peur de. ●**terrifying** *a* terrifiant. ●**terrifyingly** *adv* épouvantablement.

territory ['terɪtərɪ] *n* territoire *m*. ●**terr'itorial** *a* territorial; **the T. Army** Br l'armée *f* territoriale.

terror ['terər] *n* terreur *f*; (*child*) Fam polisson, -onne *mf*; **you little t.!** petit polisson!, petite polissonne! ●**terrorism** *n* terrorisme *m*. ●**terrorist** *n* & *a* terroriste (*mf*). ●**terrorize** *vt* terroriser.

terry(cloth) ['terɪ(klɒθ)] *n* tissu-éponge *m*.

terse [tɜːs] *a* laconique.

tertiary ['tɜːʃərɪ] *a* (*sector etc*) tertiaire; **t. education** enseignement *m* postscolaire.

Terylene® ['terɪliːn] *n* Br tergal® *m*.

test [test] *vt* (*try*) essayer; (*product, machine*) tester; (*pupil*) interroger; (*of doctor*) examiner (*les yeux etc*); (*analyse*) analyser (*le sang etc*); (*courage, nerves etc*) Fig éprouver.

▮ *n* (*trial*) essai *m*; (*of product*) test *m*; (*of s.o.'s knowledge*) Sch Univ interrogation *f*, test *m*; (*by doctor*) examen *m*; (*of blood etc*) analyse *f*; (*of courage etc*) Fig épreuve *f*; **eye t. examen** *m* de la vue; **driving t.** (examen *m* du) permis *m* de conduire.

▮ *a* **t.** pilot/flight pilote *m*/vol *m* d'essai; **t. drive** *or* **run** essai *m* sur route; **t. case** Jur affaire-test *f*; **t. match** Cricket etc match *m* international; **t. tube** éprouvette *f*; **t. tube baby** bébé *m* éprouvette.

testament ['testəmənt] *n* (*proof, tribute*) témoignage *m*; (*will*) testament *m*; **the Old/New T.** Rel l'Ancien/le Nouveau Testament.

testicle ['testɪk(ə)l] *n* Anat testicule *m*.

testify ['testɪfaɪ] *vi* (*in court etc*) témoigner (**against** contre); **to t. to sth** (*of person, event etc*) témoigner de qch ▮ *vt* **to t. that** (*in court etc*) témoigner que. ●**testi'monial** *n* références *fpl*, recommandation *f*. ●**testimony** *n* témoignage *m*.

testy ['testɪ] *a* (**-ier, -iest**) irritable.

tetanus ['tetənəs] *n* (*disease*) tétanos *m*.

tetchy ['tetʃɪ] *a* (**-ier, -iest**) irritable.

tête-à-tête [teɪtɑːteɪt] *n* tête-à-tête *m inv*.

tether ['teðər] **1** *vt* (*fasten*) attacher. **2** *n* **at the end of one's t.** à bout (de nerfs).

text [tekst] *n* texte *m*. ●**textbook** *n* manuel *m* (scolaire).

textile ['tekstaɪl] *a* & *n* textile (*m*).

texture ['tekstʃər] *n* (*of fabric, cake etc*) texture *f*; (*of paper, wood*) grain *m*.

Thai [taɪ] *a* thaïlandais ▮ *n* Thaïlandais, -aise *mf*. ●**Thailand** *n* Thaïlande *f*.

Thames [temz] *n* **the T.** la Tamise.

than [ðən, *stressed* ðæn] *conj* **1** que; **happier t.** plus heureux que; **less happy t.** moins heureux que; **he has more/less t. you** il en a plus/moins que toi; **she has fewer oranges t. plums** elle a moins d'oranges que de prunes. **2** (*with numbers*) de; **more t.** six plus de six.

thank [θæŋk] *vt* remercier (**for sth** de qch, **for doing** d'avoir fait); **t. you** merci (**for sth** pour *or* de qch, **for doing** d'avoir fait); **no, t. you** (non) merci; **t. God, t. heavens, t. goodness** Dieu merci.

▮ *npl* remerciements *mpl*; (**many**) **thanks!** merci (beaucoup)!; **thanks to** (*because of*) grâce à.

thankful ['θæŋkfəl] *a* reconnaissant (**for** de); **to be t. that** être bien heureux que (+ *sub*). ●**thankfully** *adv* (*gratefully*) avec reconnaissance; (*fortunately*) heureusement. ●**thankless** *a* ingrat.

Thanksgiving [θæŋks'gɪvɪŋ] *n* **T. (day)** (*holiday*) US Can jour *m* d'action de grâce(s).

that [ðət, *stressed* ðæt] **1** *conj* que; **to say t.** dire que.

2 *rel pron* (*subject*) qui; (*object*) que; (*with prep*) lequel, laquelle, *pl* lesquel(le)s; **the boy t. left** le garçon qui est parti; **the book t. I read** le livre que j'ai lu; **the carpet t. I put it on** le tapis sur lequel je l'ai mis; **the house t. she told me about** la maison dont elle m'a parlé; **the day/morning t. she arrived** le jour/matin où elle est arrivée.

3 *dem a* (*pl see* those) ce, cet (*before vowel or mute h*), cette; (*opposed to 'this'*) ... + -là; **t. day** ce jour; **ce jour-là; t. man** cet homme; cet homme-là; **t. girl** cette fille; cette fille-là.

4 *dem pron* (*pl see* those) ça, cela; ce; **t. (one)** celui-là *m*, celle-là *f*; **give me t.** donne-moi ça *or* cela; **I prefer t. (one)** je préfère celui-là; **before t.** avant ça *or* cela; **t.'s right** c'est juste; **who's t.?** qui est-ce?; **t.'s the house** c'est la maison; (*pointing*) voilà la maison; **what do you mean by t.?** qu'entends-tu par là?; **t. is (to say)…** c'est-à-dire…

5 *adv* (*so*) *Fam* si; **not t. good** pas si bon; **t. high** (*pointing*) haut comme ça; **t. much** (*to cost, earn etc*) (au)tant que ça.

thatch [θætʃ] *n* chaume *m*. ●**thatched** *a* (*roof*) de chaume; **t. cottage** chaumière *f*.

thaw [θɔː] *n* dégel *m* ▮ *vi* dégeler; (*of snow, ice*) fondre; (*of food*) décongeler; **it's thawing** ça dégèle; **to t. (out)** (*of person*) *Fig* se dégeler ▮ *vt* (*ice*) dégeler, faire fondre; (*snow*) faire fondre; **to t. (out)** (*food*) (faire) décongeler.

the [ðə, *before vowel* ði, *stressed* ðiː] *def art* le, l', la, *pl* les; **t. roof** le toit; **t. man** l'homme; **t. moon** la lune; **t. orange** l'orange; **t. boxes** les boîtes; **the smallest** le plus petit; **of t., from t.** du, de l', de la, *pl* des; **to t., at t.** au, à l', à la, *pl* aux; **Elizabeth t. Second** Élisabeth Deux; **Catherine t. Great** Catherine la Grande.

theatre [ˈθɪətər] (*Am* **theater**) *n* (*place, art*) & *Mil* théâtre *m*; (**operating**) **t.** (*in hospital*) *Br* salle *f* d'opération; **t. of operations** *Mil* théâtre *m* des opérations. ●**theatregoer** *n* amateur *m* de théâtre. ●**the'atrical** *a* théâtral; **t. company** troupe *f* de théâtre.

theft [θeft] *n* vol *m*.

their [ðeər] *poss a* leur, *pl* leurs; **t. house** leur maison *f*. ●**theirs** [ðeəz] *poss pron* le leur, la leur, *pl* les leurs; **this book is t.** ce livre est à eux *or* est le leur; **a friend of t.** un ami à eux.

them [ðəm, *stressed* ðem] *pron* les; (*after prep, 'than', 'it is'*) eux *mpl*, elles *fpl*; (*indirect*) leur; **I see t.** je les vois; **I give (to) t.** je leur donne; **with t.** avec eux, avec elles; **ten of t.** dix d'entre eux *or* elles; **all of t. came** tous sont venus, toutes sont venues; **I like all of t.** je les aime tous *or* toutes.

theme [θiːm] *n* thème *m*; **t. music** musique *f* (de film); **t. song** *or* **tune** chanson *f* (de film); **t. park** parc *m* (de loisirs) à thème.

themselves [ðemˈselvz] *pron* eux-mêmes *mpl*, elles-mêmes *fpl*; (*reflexive*) se, s'; (*after prep etc*) eux *mpl*, elles *fpl*; **they wash t.** ils *or* elles se lavent; **they think of t.** ils pensent à eux, elles pensent à elles.

then [ðen] **1** *adv* (*at that time*) à cette époque-là, alors; (*just a moment ago*) à ce moment-là; (*next*) ensuite, puis; **from t. on** dès lors; **before t.** avant cela; **until t.** jusque-là, jusqu'alors ▮ *a* **t. mayor/etc** le maire/etc d'alors. **2** *conj* (*therefore*) donc, alors.

theology [θɪˈɒlədʒɪ] *n* théologie *f*.

●**theo'logical** *a* théologique. ●**theo'logian** *n* théologien *m*.

theorem [ˈθɪərəm] *n* théorème *m*.

theory [ˈθɪərɪ] *n* théorie *f*; **in t.** en théorie. ●**theorize** *vi* développer *or* échafauder une théorie. ●**theo'retical** *a* théorique. ●**theo'retically** *adv* théoriquement. ●**theorist** *n* théoricien, -ienne *mf*.

therapy [ˈθerəpɪ] *n* thérapeutique *f*. ●**thera'peutic** *a* thérapeutique. ●**therapist** *n* thérapeute *mf*.

there [ðeər] *adv* là; (**down** *or* **over**) **t.** là-bas; **on t.** là-dessus; **she'll be t.** elle sera là, elle y sera; **t. is, t. are** il y a; (*pointing*) voilà; **t. he is** le voilà; **t. she is** la voilà; **t. they are** les voilà; **that man t.** cet homme-là; **t. (you are)!** (*take this*) tenez!; **t., (t.,) don't cry!** allons, allons, ne pleure pas! ●**therea'bout(s)** *adv* par là; (*in amount*) à peu près. ●**there'after** *adv* après cela. ●**thereby** *adv* de ce fait. ●**therefore** *adv* donc. ●**thereu'pon** *adv* sur ce.

thermal [ˈθɜːm(ə)l] *a* (*underwear*) en thermolactyl®; (*energy, unit*) thermique.

thermometer [θəˈmɒmɪtər] *n* thermomètre *m*.

thermonuclear [θɜːməʊˈnjuːklɪər] *a* thermonucléaire.

Thermos® [ˈθɜːməs] *n* (*pl* **-es**) **T.** (*Br* **flask** *or* *Am* **bottle**) thermos® *m or f inv*.

thermostat [ˈθɜːməstæt] *n* thermostat *m*.

thesaurus [θɪˈsɔːrəs] *n* dictionnaire *m* de synonymes.

these [ðiːz] **1** *dem a* (*sing see* this) ces; (*opposed to* 'those') … + -ci; **t. men** ces hommes-ci. **2** *dem pron* (*sing see* this) **t. (ones)** ceux-ci *mpl*, celles-ci *fpl*; **t. are my friends** ce sont mes amis.

thesis, *pl* **theses** [ˈθiːsɪs, ˈθiːsiːz] *n* thèse *f*.

they [ðeɪ] *pron* **1** ils *mpl*, elles *fpl*; (*stressed*) eux *mpl*, elles *fpl*; **t. go** ils vont, elles vont; **t. are doctors** ce sont des médecins. **2** (*people in general*) on; **t. say** on dit. ●**they'd** = **they had** & **they would**. ●**they'll** = **they will**.

thick [θɪk] *a* (**-er, -est**) épais (*f* épaisse); (*stupid*) *Fam* lourd; **to be t.** (*of friends*) *Fam* être très liés ▮ *adv* (*to spread*) en couche épaisse; (*to grow*) dru ▮ *n* **in the t. of battle** au cœur de la bataille. ●**thickly** *adv* (*to spread*) en couche épaisse; (*to grow*) dru; **t. populated/wooded** très peuplé/boisé.

thicken [ˈθɪk(ə)n] *vt* épaissir ▮ *vi* (*of fog etc*) s'épaissir; (*of cream, sauce etc*) épaissir. ●**thickness** *n* épaisseur *f*.

thicket [ˈθɪkɪt] *n* (*trees*) fourré *m*.

thickset [θɪkˈset] *a* (*person*) trapu. ●**thick-skinned** *a* (*person*) peu sensible, dur.

thief [θiːf] *n* (*pl* **thieves**) voleur, -euse *mf*; **stop t.!** au voleur! ●**thieve** *vti* voler. ●**thieving** *a* voleur ▮ *n* vol *m*.

thigh [θaɪ] *n* cuisse *f*. ●**thighbone** *n* fémur *m*.

thimble [ˈθɪmb(ə)l] *n* dé *m* (à coudre).

thin [θɪn] *a* (**thinner, thinnest**) (*slice, paper etc*) mince; (*person, leg*) maigre, mince;

(*soup*) peu épais (*f* épaisse); (*crowd, hair*) clairsemé; (*powder*) fin; (*excuse, profit*) *Fig* maigre, mince ▌ *adv* (*to spread*) en couche mince; (*to cut*) en tranches minces ▌ *vt* (-nn-) **to t. (down)** (*paint etc*) diluer ▌ *vi* **to t. out** (*of crowd, mist*) s'éclaircir. ●**thinly** *adv* (*to spread*) en couche mince; (*to cut*) en tranches minces; **t. disguised** à peine déguisé; **t. populated/wooded** peu peuplé/boisé. ●**thinness** *n* minceur *f*; (*of person, leg etc*) maigreur *f*.

thing [θɪŋ] *n* chose *f*; **one's things** (*belongings, clothes*) ses affaires *fpl*; **it's a funny t.** c'est drôle; **poor little t.!** pauvre petit!; **that's (just) the t.** voilà (exactement) ce qu'il faut; **how are things?**, *Fam* **how's things?** comment (ça) va?; **I'll think things over** j'y réfléchirai; **for one t....,** d'abord; **and for another t.** d'abord...et ensuite; **the tea things** *Br* (*set*) le service à thé; (*dishes*) la vaisselle. ●**thingamabob** *or Br* **thingummy** *n Fam* truc *m*, machin *m*.

think [θɪŋk] *vi* (*pt & pp* thought) penser (**about, of** à); **to t. (carefully)** réfléchir (**about, of** à); **to t. of doing** penser *or* songer à faire; **to t. highly of, to t. a lot of** penser beaucoup de bien de; **she doesn't t. much of it** ça ne lui dit pas grand-chose; **to t. better of it** se raviser; **I can't.t. of it** je n'arrive pas à m'en souvenir.

▌ *vt* penser (**that** que); **I t. so** je pense *or* crois que oui; **what do you t. of him?** que penses-tu de lui?; **I thought it difficult** je l'ai trouvé difficile; **to t. out** (*plan, method etc*) élaborer, concevoir; (*reply*) réfléchir sérieusement à; **to t. sth over** réfléchir à qch; **to t. sth through** réfléchir à qch sous tous les angles; **to t. sth up** (*invent*) inventer qch, avoir l'idée de qch.

▌ *n* **to have a t.** *Fam* réfléchir (**about** à); **t. tank** comité *m* d'experts. ●**thinking** *a* **t. person** personne *f* intelligente ▌ *n* (*opinion*) opinion *f*; **to my t.** à mon avis. ●**thinker** *n* penseur, -euse *mf*.

thinner [ˈθɪnər] *n* (*for paint etc*) diluant *m*.

thin-skinned [θɪnˈskɪnd] *a* (*person*) susceptible, chatouilleux.

third [θɜːd] *a* troisième; **t. person** *or* **party** tiers *m*; **t.-party insurance** assurance *f* au tiers; **the T. World** le Tiers-Monde *m* ▌ *n* troisième *mf*; **a t.** (*fraction*) un tiers ▌ *adv* **to come t.** (*in race etc*) se classer troisième. ●**thirdly** *adv* troisièmement.

third-class [θɜːdˈklɑːs] *a* de troisième classe; **t.-class degree** *Br* = licence *f* avec mention passable. ●**third-rate** *a* (très) inférieur.

thirst [θɜːst] *n* soif *f* (**for** de). ●**thirsty** *a* (-ier, -iest) *a* **to be** *or* **feel t.** avoir soif; **to make s.o. t.** donner soif à qn; **to be t. for** (*power etc*) *Fig* être assoiffé de.

thirteen [θɜːˈtiːn] *a & n* treize (*m*). ●**thirteenth** *a & n* treizième (*mf*).

thirty [ˈθɜːtɪ] *a & n* trente (*m*). ●**thirtieth** *a & n* trentième (*mf*).

this [ðɪs] **1** *dem a* (*pl see* these) ce, cet (*be-*fore vowel or mute h*); cette; (*opposed to* 'that'*) ... + -ci; **t. book** ce livre; ce livre-ci; **t. man** cet homme; cet homme-ci; **t. photo** cette photo; cette photo-ci. **2** *dem pron* (*pl see* these) ceci; ce; **t. (one)** celui-ci *m*, celle-ci *f*; **give me t.** donne-moi ceci; **I prefer t. (one)** je préfère celui-ci; **before t.** avant ceci; **who's t.?** qui est-ce?; **t. is Paul** c'est Paul; (*pointing*) voici Paul. **3** *adv* (*so*) **t. high** (*pointing*) haut comme ceci; **t. far** (*until now*) jusqu'ici.

thistle [ˈθɪs(ə)l] *n* chardon *m*.

thorax [ˈθɔːræks] *n Anat* thorax *m*.

thorn [θɔːn] *n* épine *f*. ●**thorny** *a* (-ier, -iest) (*bush*, *Fig* problem etc*) épineux.

thorough [ˈθʌrə] *a* (*careful, painstaking*) minutieux, consciencieux; (*knowledge, examination*) approfondi; (*liar, rogue*) parfait; (*disaster*) complet; **to give sth a t. washing/cleaning/etc** laver/nettoyer/etc à fond. ●**thoroughly** *adv* (*completely*) tout à fait; (*carefully*) avec minutie; (*to know, clean, wash etc*) à fond. ●**thoroughness** *n* minutie *f*; (*depth*) profondeur *f*.

thoroughbred [ˈθʌrəbred] *n* (*horse*) pursang *m inv*.

thoroughfare [ˈθʌrəfeər] *n* (*street*) artère *f*, rue *f*; **'no t.'** *Br* 'passage interdit'.

those [ðəʊz] **1** *dem a* (*sing see* that) ces; (*opposed to* 'these'*) ... + -là; **t. men** ces hommes; ces hommes-là. **2** *dem pron* (*sing see* that) **t. (ones)** ceux-là *mpl*, celles-là *fpl*; **t. are my friends** ce sont mes amis.

though [ðəʊ] **1** *conj* (*even*) **t.** bien que (+ *sub*); **as t.** comme si; **strange t. it may seem** si étrange que cela puisse paraître. **2** *adv* (*however*) pourtant, tout de même.

thought [θɔːt] *pt & pp of* think ▌ *n* pensée *f*; (*idea*) idée *f*, pensée *f*; (*careful*) **t.** réflexion *f*; **without (a) t. for** sans penser à; **to have second thoughts** changer d'avis; **on second thoughts** *Br*, **on second t.** *Am* à la réflexion.

thoughtful [ˈθɔːtfəl] *a* (*considerate, kind*) gentil, attentionné, prévenant; (*pensive*) pensif; (*serious*) sérieux. ●**thoughtfully** *adv* (*considerately*) gentiment. ●**thoughtfulness** *n* gentillesse *f*, prévenance *f*.

thoughtless [ˈθɔːtləs] *a* (*towards others*) pas très gentil; (*absent-minded*) étourdi. ●**thoughtlessly** *adv* (*inconsiderately*) pas très gentiment; (*absent-mindedly*) étourdiment.

thousand [ˈθaʊzənd] *a & n* mille *a & m inv*; **a t. pages** mille pages; **two t. pages** deux mille pages; **thousands of** des milliers de; **they came in their thousands** ils sont venus par milliers.

thrash [θræʃ] **1** *vt* **to t. s.o.** donner une correction à qn; (*defeat*) écraser qn; **to t. out** (*plan etc*) élaborer (à force de discussions). **2** *vi* **to t. around** *or* **about** (*struggle*) se débattre. ●**thrashing** *n* (*beating*) correction *f*.

thread [θred] *n* (*yarn*) & *Fig* fil *m*; (*of screw*) pas *m* ▌ *vt* (*needle, beads*) enfiler; **to t. one's way** se faufiler (**through the crowd/etc** parmi la foule/etc). ●**threadbare** *a* élimé, râpé.

threat [θret] *n* menace *f*; **to be a t.** to constituer une menace pour. ●**threaten** *vi* menacer ▌ *vt* menacer (**to do** de faire, **with sth** de qch). ●**threatening** *a* menaçant. ●**threateningly** *adv* (*to say etc*) d'un ton menaçant.

three [θriː] *a & n* trois (*m*); **t.-piece suite** *Br* canapé *m* et deux fauteuils. ●**three-'D** *a* (*film*) en 3-D. ●**three-di'mensional** *a* à trois dimensions. ●**threefold** *a* triple ▌ *adv* **to increase t.** tripler. ●**three-point 'turn** *n* *Aut* demi-tour *m* en trois manœuvres. ●**three-quarters** *n* *sing* **t.-quarters (of)** les trois quarts *mpl* (de); **it's t.-quarters full** c'est aux trois quarts plein. ●**threesome** *n* groupe *m* de trois personnes. ●**three-way** *a* (*division*) en trois; (*conversation*) à trois. ●**three-'wheeler** *n* (*tricycle*) tricycle *m*; (*car*) voiture *f* à trois roues.

thresh [θreʃ] *vt* (*wheat etc*) battre.

threshold ['θreʃhəʊld] *n* seuil *m*; **pain t.** seuil *m* de résistance à la douleur.

threw [θruː] *pt of* **throw**.

thrift [θrift] *n* (*virtue*) économie *f*. ●**thrifty** *a* (**-ier, -iest**) économe.

thrill [θril] *n* frisson *m*, émotion *f*; **to get a t. out of doing** prendre plaisir à faire qch ▌ *vt* (*delight*) réjouir; (*excite*) faire frissonner. ●**thrilled** *a* ravi (**with sth** de qch, **to do** de faire). ●**thrilling** *a* passionnant. ●**thriller** *n* film *m or* roman *m* à suspense.

thrive [θraɪv] *vi* (*of business, person, plant etc*) prospérer; **he *or* she thrives on hard work** le travail lui profite. ●**thriving** *a* prospère, florissant.

throat [θrəʊt] *n* gorge *f*; **to have a sore/scratchy t.** avoir mal/un peu mal à la gorge. ●**throaty** *a* (*voice*) rauque; (*person*) à la voix rauque.

throb [θrɒb] *vi* (**-bb-**) (*of heart*) palpiter; (*of engine*) vrombir; (*vibrate*) vibrer; **my finger is throbbing** mon doigt me fait des élancements ▌ *n* (*of heart*) palpitation *f*; (*of engine*) vrombissement *m*; (*in finger*) élancement *m*.

throes [θrəʊz] *npl* **in the t. of** au milieu de; (*illness, crisis*) en proie à; **in the t. of doing** en train de faire.

thrombosis [θrɒm'bəʊsɪs] *n* *Med* thrombose *f*; (*coronary*) infarctus *m*.

throne [θrəʊn] *n* trône *m*.

throng [θrɒŋ] *n* *Lit* foule *f* ▌ *vi* (*rush*) affluer ▌ *vt* (*station, street etc*) se presser dans; **it was thronged with people** c'était noir de monde.

throttle ['θrɒt(ə)l] **1** *n* (*of motorcycle etc*) poignée *f* des gaz; (*of aircraft etc*) commande *f* des gaz. **2** *vt* (*strangle*) étrangler.

through [θruː] *prep* (*place*) à travers; (*time*) pendant; (*means*) par; (*thanks to*) grâce à; **t. the window/door** par la fenêtre/porte; **to go *or* get in** (*forest etc*) traverser; (*hole etc*) passer par; (*wall etc*) passer à travers; **to speak t. one's nose** parler du nez; **Tuesday t. Saturday** *Am* de mardi à samedi.

▌ *adv* à travers; **to go t.** (*cross*) traverser; (*pass*) passer; **to let t.** laisser passer; **to be t.** (*finished*) *Am* avoir fini; **we're t.** (*it's over between us*) *Am* c'est fini entre nous; **I'm t. with the book** *Am* je n'ai plus besoin du livre; **all *or* right t.** (*to the end*) jusqu'au bout; **t. to *or* till** jusqu'à; **French t. and t.** français jusqu'au bout des ongles; **I'll put you t. (to him)** (*on telephone*) je vous le passe.

▌ *a* (*train, traffic, ticket*) direct; **'no t. road'** (*no exit*) *Br* 'voie sans issue'.

throughout ['θruːaʊt] *prep* **t. the neighbourhood/etc** dans tout le quartier/etc; **t. the day/etc** (*time*) pendant toute la journée/etc ▌ *adv* (*everywhere*) partout; (*all the time*) tout le temps.

throughway ['θruːweɪ] *n* *Am* = **thruway**.

throw [θrəʊ] *n* (*of stone etc*) jet *m*; *Sport* lancer *m*; (*of dice*) coup *m*; (*turn*) tour *m* ▌ *vt* (*pt* **threw,** *pp* **thrown**) jeter (**to, at** à); (*stone, ball*) lancer, jeter; (*hurl*) projeter; (*of horse*) désarçonner (*qn*); (*party, reception*) donner; (*baffle*) *Fam* dérouter.

throw away *vt* (*unwanted object*) jeter; (*waste, ruin*) *Fig* gâcher ▌ **to throw back** *vt* (*ball*) renvoyer (**to** à); (*one's head*) rejeter en arrière ▌ **to throw in** *vt* (*include as extra*) *Fam* donner en prime ▌ **to throw off** *vt* (*get rid of*) se débarrasser de ▌ **to throw out** *vt* (*unwanted object*) jeter; (*suggestion*) repousser; (*expel*) mettre (*qn*) à la porte; (*distort*) fausser (*calcul etc*) ▌ **to throw over** *vt* (*abandon*) abandonner ▌ **to throw up** *vt* *Fam* (*job*) laisser tomber; (*food*) rendre ▌ *vi* (*vomit*) *Fam* dégobiller.

throwaway ['θrəʊəweɪ] *a* (*disposable*) jetable, à jeter.

thrush [θrʌʃ] *n* **1** (*bird*) grive *f*. **2** (*infection*) muguet *m*.

thrust [θrʌst] *n* (*push, lunge, stab etc*) coup *m*; (*of argument*) poids *m*; (*dynamism*) allant *m* ▌ *vt* (*pt & pp* **thrust**) (*push*) pousser (avec force); (*put*) mettre; **to t. sth into sth** (*stick, knife, pin etc*) enfoncer qch dans qch; **to t. aside** (*reject*) écarter (brusquement) (*qch, qn*); **to t. sth/s.o. (up)on s.o.** *Fig* imposer qch/qn à qn.

thruway ['θruːweɪ] *n* *Am* autoroute *f*.

thud [θʌd] *n* bruit *m* sourd.

thug [θʌg] *n* voyou *m*.

thumb [θʌm] *n* pouce *m*; **with a t. index** (*book*) à onglets ▌ *vt* **to t. (through)** (*book etc*) feuilleter; **to t. a lift *or* a ride** *Fam* faire du stop. ●**thumbtack** *n* *Am* punaise *f*.

thump [θʌmp] *vt* (*person*) frapper, cogner sur; (*table, keyboard etc*) taper sur; **to t. one's head** (*on door etc*) se cogner la tête (**on** contre) ▌ *vi* frapper, cogner (**on** sur); (*of heart*) battre à grands coups ▌ *n* (*grand*) coup *m*; (*noise*) bruit *m* sourd. ●**thumping** *a* (*huge, great*) *Fam* énorme.

thunder ['θʌndər] *n* tonnerre *m* ▌ *vi* (*of guns, Fig person*) tonner; **it's thundering** (*weather*) il tonne; **to t. past** (*of train, truck etc*) passer (vite) dans un bruit de tonnerre. ●**thunderbolt** *n* coup *m* de foudre; (*event*)

Fig coup *m* de tonnerre. ●**thunderclap** *n* coup *m* de tonnerre. ●**thunderstorm** *n* orage *m*. ●**thunderstruck** *a* (*astonished*) *Lit* abasourdi.

Thursday [*Br* 'θɜːzdɪ, *Am* -deɪ] *n* jeudi *m*.

thus [ðʌs] *adv* ainsi.

thwart [θwɔːt] *vt* (*plan, person*) contrecarrer.

thyme [taɪm] *n* (*herb*) thym *m*.

thyroid ['θaɪrɔɪd] *a* & *n Anat* thyroïde (*f*); **t. complaint** maladie *f* de la thyroïde.

tiara [tɪ'ɑːrə] *n* (*woman's crown*) diadème *m*.

Tibet [tɪ'bet] *n* Tibet *m*.

tic [tɪk] *n* (*in face, limbs*) tic *m*.

tick [tɪk] **1** *n* (*of clock*) tic-tac *m* ▮ *vi* faire tic-tac; **to t. over** (*of engine, business, factory*) *Br* tourner au ralenti. **2** *Br n* (*mark on list etc*) coche *f*, = croix *f* ▮ *vt* **to t. (off)** (*on list etc*) cocher; **to t. s.o. off** (*reprimand*) *Fam* passer un savon à qn. **3** *n* (*moment*) *Br Fam* instant *m*. **4** *n* (*insect*) tique *f*. **5** *adv* **on t.** (*on credit*) *Br Fam* à crédit. ●**ticking** *n* (*of clock*) tic-tac *m*; **to give s.o. a t.-off** *Br Fam* passer un savon à qn.

ticket ['tɪkɪt] *n* billet *m*; (*for bus, Br underground, Am subway, cloakroom etc*) ticket *m*; (*for library*) carte *f*. (*fine for parking, speeding etc*) *Fam* contravention *f*, contredanse *f*; (*list of candidates*) *Am Pol* liste *f*; (**price**) **t.** étiquette *f*; **t. collector** contrôleur, -euse *mf*; **t. holder** personne *f* munie d'un billet; **t. office** guichet *m*; **t. scalper** *Am*, **t. tout** *Br* revendeur, -euse (en fraude).

tickle ['tɪk(ə)l] *vt* chatouiller; (*amuse*) *Fig* amuser ▮ *n* chatouillement *m*. ●**ticklish** *a* (*person*) chatouilleux; (*garment, fabric*) qui chatouille; (*problem*) *Fig* délicat.

tick-tack-toe [tɪktæk'təʊ] *n Am* morpion *m*.

tidal ['taɪd(ə)l] *a* (*river*) qui a une marée; **t. wave** raz-de-marée *m inv*; (*in public opinion etc*) *Fig* vague *f* de fond.

tidbit ['tɪdbɪt] *n* (*food*) *Am* bon morceau *m*.

tiddlywinks ['tɪdlɪwɪŋks] *n* jeu *m* de puce.

tide [taɪd] **1** *n* marée *f*; **against the t.** (*to swim etc*) & *Fig* à contre-courant; **the rising t. of discontent** le mécontentement grandissant. **2** *vt* **to t. s.o. over** (*help out*) dépanner qn. ●**tidemark** *n* (*on neck etc*) *Br Fig Hum* ligne *f* de crasse.

tidings ['taɪdɪŋz] *npl Lit* nouvelles *fpl*.

tidy ['taɪdɪ] *a* (-**ier**, -**iest**) (*place, toys etc*) bien rangé; (*clothes, hair*) soigné; (*person*) (*methodical*) ordonné; (*in appearance*) soigné; **a t. sum** *or* **amount** *Fam* une jolie *or* bonne somme; **to make t.** ranger ▮ *vt* **to t. sth** (**up** *or* **away**) ranger qch; **to t. out** (*drawer etc*) vider; **to t. oneself up** s'arranger ▮ *vi* **to t. up** ranger. ●**tidily** *adv* (*to put away etc*) soigneusement, avec soin. ●**tidiness** *n* (bon) ordre *m*; (*care*) soin *m*.

tie [taɪ] *n* (*around neck*) cravate *f*; (*string, strap etc*) & *Fig* lien *m*, attache *f*; (*on railroad track*) *Am* traverse *f*; *Sport* égalité *f* de points; (*drawn match*) match *m* nul ▮ *vt* (*fasten*) attacher, lier (**to** à); (*a knot*) faire (**in** à); (*shoe*) lacer; (*link*) lier (**to** à) ▮ *vi*

Sport finir à égalité de points; *Football* faire match, nul; (*in race*) être ex aequo.

tie down *vt* attacher; **to t. s.o. down to** (*date, place etc*) obliger qn à accepter ▮ **to tie in** *vi* (*be linked*) être lié; **to t. in with** (*tally with*) se rapporter à ▮ **to tie up** *vt* (*person, dog etc*) attacher; (*bind hand and foot*) ligoter; (*package*) ficeler; (*money*) *Fig* immobiliser; **to be tied up** (*linked*) être lié (**with** avec); (*busy*) *Fam* être occupé.

tier [tɪər] *n* (*of seats*) gradin *m*; (*of cake*) étage *m*.

tie-up ['taɪʌp] *n* (*link*) lien *m*; (*traffic jam*) *Am Fam* bouchon *m*.

tiff [tɪf] *n* petite querelle *f*.

tiger ['taɪgər] *n* tigre *m*. ●**tigress** *n* tigresse *f*.

tight [taɪt] *a* (**-er, -est**) (*clothes fitting too closely*) (trop) étroit, (trop) serré; (*skin-tight*) ajusté, collant; (*drawer, lid*) dur; (*knot, screw*) serré; (*rope, wire*) raide; (*control*) strict; (*schedule*) serré; (*with money*) *Fam* avare; (*drunk*) *Fam* gris; **a t. spot** *or* **corner** *Fam* une situation difficile; **it's a t. squeeze** il y a juste la place.

▮ *adv* (*hold, shut*) bien; (*to squeeze*) fort; **sleep t.!** dors bien!: **to sit t.** ne pas bouger. ●**tightly** *adv* (*to hold*) bien; (*to squeeze*) fort; **t. knit** (*close*) très uni. ●**tightness** *n* (*of garment*) étroitesse *f*; (*of control*) rigueur *f*; (*of rope*) tension *f*.

tighten ['taɪt(ə)n] *vt* **to t. (up)** (*bolt etc*) (res)serrer; (*rope*) tendre; (*security*) *Fig* renforcer ▮ *vi* **to t. up on** se montrer plus strict à l'égard de.

tightfisted [taɪt'fɪstɪd] *a* avare. ●**tight-fitting** *a* (*garment*) ajusté. ●**tightrope** *n* corde *f* raide. ●**tightwad** *n* (*miser*) *Am Fam* grippe-sou *m*.

tights [taɪts] *npl* (*garment*) *Br* collant(s) *mpl*; (**support**) **t.** (*for varicose veins*) bas *mpl* à varices.

tile [taɪl] *n* (*on roof*) tuile *f*; (*on wall or floor*) carreau *m* ▮ *vt* (*wall, floor*) carreler. ●**tiled** *a* (*roof*) de tuiles; (*wall, floor*) carrelé. ●**tiler** *n* carreleur *m*.

till [tɪl] **1** *prep* & *conj* = **until**. **2** *n* (*for money*) *Br* caisse *f* (enregistreuse); **t. receipt** ticket *m* de caisse. **3** *vt* (*land*) cultiver.

tiller ['tɪlər] *n* (*of boat*) barre *f*.

tilt [tɪlt] *vti* pencher ▮ *n* inclinaison *f*; (**at**) **full t.** à toute vitesse.

timber ['tɪmbər] *n* (*wood*) *Br* bois *m* (de construction); (*trees*) arbres *mpl* ▮ *a* (*house etc*) *Br* de *or* en bois. ●**timberyard** *n Br* entrepôt *m* de bois.

time [taɪm] *n* temps *m*; (*point in time*) moment *m*; (*period in history*) époque *f*; (*on clock*) heure *f*; (*occasion*) fois *f*; *Mus* mesure *f*; **in (the course of) t.**, **with (the passage of) t.** avec le temps; **it's t. (to do)** il est temps (de faire); **I have no t. to play**/*etc* je n'ai pas le temps de jouer/*etc*; **I have no t. to waste** je n'ai pas de temps à perdre; **some of the t.** (*not always*) une partie du temps; **most of the t.** la plupart du temps; **all of the t.** tout

le temps; **in a year's t.** dans un an; **a long t.** longtemps; **a short t.** peu de temps, un petit moment; **full-t.** à plein temps; **part-t.** à temps partiel; **to have a good** *or* **a nice t.** *(fun)* s'amuser (bien); **to have a hard t. doing** avoir du mal à faire; **to have t. off** avoir du temps libre; **in no t. (at all)** en un rien de temps; **(just) in t.** *(to arrive)* à temps **(for sth** pour qch, **to do** pour faire); **in my t.** *(formerly)* de mon temps; **from t. to t.** de temps en temps; **what t. is it?** quelle heure est-il?; **the right** *or* **exact t.** l'heure *f* exacte; **on t.** à l'heure; **at the same t.** en même temps **(as** que); *(simultaneously)* à la fois; **for the t. being** pour le moment; **at the** *or* **that t.** à ce moment-là; **at the present t.** à l'heure actuelle; **at times** parfois, par moments; **at one t.** à un moment donné; **this t. tomorrow** demain à cette heure-ci; **(the) next t. you come** la prochaine fois que tu viendras; **(the) last t.** la dernière fois; **one at a t.** un à un; **t. and (time) again** bien des fois, à plusieurs reprises; **ten times** ten dix fois dix; **t. bomb** bombe *f* à retardement; **t. lag** *(between events)* décalage *m*; **t. limit** délai *m*; **t. switch** = **timer**; **t. zone** fuseau *m* horaire.
▌ *vt (sportsman, worker etc)* chronométrer; *(activity, programme)* minuter; *(choose the time of)* choisir le moment de; *(to plan)* prévoir. ●**time-consuming** *a* qui prend du temps. ●**time-honoured** *a* consacré (par l'usage). ●**time-share** *n* multipropriété *f*.

timeless ['taɪmləs] *a* éternel.

timely ['taɪmlɪ] *a* à propos. ●**timeliness** *n* à-propos *m*.

timer ['taɪmər] *n (device)* minuteur *m*, compte-minutes *m inv*; *(sand-filled)* sablier *m*; *(built into appliance)* programmateur *m*; *(plugged into socket)* prise *f* programmable; *(to control lighting)* minuterie *f*.

timescale ['taɪmskeɪl] *n* période *f*.

timetable ['taɪmteɪb(ə)l] *n* horaire *m*; *(in school)* emploi *m* du temps.

timid ['tɪmɪd] *a (afraid)* craintif, timoré; *(shy)* timide. ●**timidly** *adv* timidement.

timing ['taɪmɪŋ] *n (of sportsman etc)* chronométrage *m*; *(of activity etc)* minutage *m*; *(judgment of artist etc)* rythme *m*; **the t. of** *(time)* le moment choisi pour; **what (good) t.!** quelle synchronisation!

tin [tɪn] *n (metal)* étain *m*; *(coated steel or iron)* fer-blanc *m*; *(can)* Br boîte *f*; **cake t.** moule *m* à gâteaux; **t. can** boîte *f* (en ferblanc); **t. opener** ouvre-boîtes *m inv*; **t. soldier** soldat *m* de plomb. ●**tinfoil** *n* papier *m* d'alu(minium).

tinge [tɪndʒ] *n* teinte *f*. ●**tinged** *a* **t. with** *(pink etc)* teinté de; *(jealousy etc)* Fig empreint de.

tingle ['tɪŋg(ə)l] *vi* picoter; **it's tingling** ça me picote. ●**tingly** *a* **t. feeling** sensation *f* de picotement.

tinker ['tɪŋkər] *vi* **to t. (about** *or* **around) with** bricoler.

tinkle ['tɪŋk(ə)l] *vi* tinter **▌** *n* tintement *m*; **to give s.o. a t.** *(phone s.o.)* Br Fam passer un coup de fil à qn.

tinned [tɪnd] *a* Br **t. pears/salmon/**etc poires *fpl*/saumon *m*/etc en boîte; **t. food** conserves *fpl*.

tinny ['tɪnɪ] *a (-ier, -iest) (sound)* métallique; *(vehicle, machine)* de mauvaise qualité.

tinplate ['tɪnpleɪt] *n* fer-blanc *m*.

tinsel ['tɪns(ə)l] *n* guirlandes *fpl* de Noël.

tint [tɪnt] *n* teinte *f*; *(for hair)* shampooing *m* colorant. ●**tinted** *a (paper, glass)* teinté; **t. glasses** verres *mpl* teintés.

tiny ['taɪnɪ] *a (-ier, -iest)* tout petit.

tip¹ [tɪp] **1** *n (end)* bout *m*; *(pointed)* pointe *f*. **2** *n (money)* pourboire *m* **▌** *vt (waiter etc)* donner un pourboire à. **3** *n (advice)* conseil *m*; *(information in betting on horses etc)* tuyau *m*; **to get a t.-off** se faire tuyauter **▌** *vt (-pp-)* **to t. a horse/**etc donner un cheval/etc gagnant; **to t. off** *(police)* prévenir. **4** *n Br (rubbish dump)* décharge *f*; **this room is a real t.** Fam cette pièce est un vrai dépotoir.

tip² [tɪp] *vt (-pp-)* **to t. (up** *or* **over)** *(tilt)* pencher, incliner; *(overturn)* faire basculer; **to t. (out)** *(liquid, load)* déverser **(into** dans) **▌** *vi* **to t. (up** *or* **over)** *(tilt)* pencher; *(overturn)* basculer.

tip-off ['tɪpɒf] *n see* tip¹ 3.

tipped [tɪpt] *a* **t. cigarette** cigarette *f* (à bout) filtre.

tipple ['tɪp(ə)l] *vi (drink)* Fam picoler.

tipsy ['tɪpsɪ] *a (-ier, -iest) (drunk)* éméché, gai.

tiptoe ['tɪptəʊ] *n* **on t.** sur la pointe des pieds **▌** *vi* marcher sur la pointe des pieds; **to t. into/out of a room** entrer dans une pièce/ sortir d'une pièce sur la pointe des pieds.

tiptop ['tɪptɒp] *a Fam* excellent.

tirade [taɪ'reɪd] *n* diatribe *f*.

tire¹ ['taɪər] *vt* fatiguer; **to t. s.o. out** *(exhaust)* épuiser qn **▌** *vi* se fatiguer. ●**tired** *a* fatigué; **to be t. of sth/s.o./doing** en avoir assez de qch/de qn/de faire; **to get t. of doing** se lasser de faire. ●**tiring** *a* fatigant. ●**tiredness** *n* fatigue *f*. ●**tireless** *a* infatigable. ●**tiresome** *a* ennuyeux.

tire² ['taɪər] *n Am* pneu *m* *(pl* pneus).

tissue ['tɪʃuː] *n (handkerchief)* mouchoir *m* en papier, kleenex® *m*; *Biol* tissu *m*; **t. (paper)** papier *m* de soie.

tit [tɪt] *n* **1** **to give t. for tat** rendre coup pour coup. **2** *(bird)* mésange *f*.

titbit ['tɪtbɪt] *n (food)* Br bon morceau *m*.

titillate ['tɪtɪleɪt] *vt* exciter.

title ['taɪt(ə)l] *n (name, claim)* & *Sport* titre *m*; **t. deed** titre *m* de propriété; **t. role** *(in film, play)* rôle *m* principal **▌** *vt (film)* intituler, titrer. ●**titled** *a (person)* titré. ●**titleholder** *n Sport* détenteur, -trice *mf* d'un *or* du titre.

titter ['tɪtər] *vi* rire bêtement.

tittle-tattle ['tɪt(ə)ltæt(ə)l] *n Fam* commérages *mpl*.

T-junction ['tiːdʒʌŋkʃ(ə)n] *n (of roads)* Br

intersection *f* en T.

to [tə, *stressed* tuː] *prep* **1** à; (*towards*) vers; (*of attitude, feelings*) envers; (*right up to*) jusqu'à; **give it to him** *or* **her** donne-le-lui; **to town on ville; to France** en France; **to Portugal** au Portugal; **to the butcher('s)/***etc* chez le boucher/*etc*; **the road to London** la route de Londres; **the train to Paris** le train pour Paris; **kind/cruel/***etc* **to s.o.** gentil/cruel/*etc* pour *or* envers qn; **from bad to worse** de mal en pis; **it's ten (minutes) to one** il est une heure moins dix; **ten to one** (*proportion*) dix contre un; **one person to a room** une personne par chambre.
2 (*with infinitive*) **to say/jump/***etc* dire/sauter/ *etc*; (**in order**) **to** do pour faire; **she tried to** elle a essayé; **wife/***etc***-to-be** future femme *fl etc.*
3 (*with adjective*) de; à; **happy/***etc* **to do** heureux/*etc* de faire; **it's easy/difficult/***etc* **to do** c'est facile/difficile/*etc* à faire.
❚ *adv* **to push the door to** fermer la porte; **to go** *or* **walk to and fro** aller et venir.

toad [təud] *n* crapaud *m*.

toadstool ['təudstuːl] *n* champignon *m* (vénéneux).

toast [təust] **1** *n* (*bread*) pain *m* grillé; **piece** *or* **slice of t.** tranche *f* de pain grillé, toast *m* ❚ *vt* (*bread*) (faire) griller. **2** *n* (*drink*) toast *m* ❚ *vt* (*person*) porter un toast à; (*success, event*) arroser. ● **toaster** *n* grille-pain *m inv*.

tobacco [tə'bækəu] *n* (*pl* **-os**) tabac *m*; **t. store** *Am* (bureau *m* de) tabac *m*. ● **tobacconist** *n* buraliste *mf*; **t.'s (shop)** *Br* (bureau *m* de) tabac *m*.

toboggan [tə'bɒgən] *n* luge *f*.

today [tə'deɪ] *adv* & *n* aujourd'hui (*m*).

toddle ['tɒd(ə)l] *vi* **to t. off** (*leave*) *Br Hum Fam* se sauver.

toddler ['tɒdlər] *n* enfant *mf* (en bas âge).

toddy ['tɒdɪ] *n* (**hot**) **t.** grog *m*.

to-do [tə'duː] *n* (*fuss*) *Fam* histoire *f*.

toe [təu] **1** *n* orteil *m*; **on one's toes** *Fig* vigilant. **2** *vt* **to t. the line** (*respect the rules*) se soumettre; **to t. the party line** respecter la ligne du parti. ● **toenail** *n* ongle *m* du pied.

toffee ['tɒfɪ] *n Br* caramel *m* (dur); **t. apple** pomme *f* d'amour. ● **toffee-nosed** *a Br Fam* crâneur (*f* -euse).

together [tə'geðər] *adv* ensemble; (*at the same time*) en même temps; **t. with** avec. ● **togetherness** *n* (*of group*) camaraderie *f*; (*of husband and wife*) intimité *f*.

togs [tɒgz] *npl* (*clothes*) *Sl* nippes *fpl*.

toil [tɔɪl] *n* labeur *m* ❚ *vi* travailler dur

toilet ['tɔɪlɪt] *n* (*room*) *Br* toilettes *fpl*; (*bowl, seat*) cuvette *f or* siège *m* des toilettes; **to go to the t.** *Br* aller aux toilettes; **t. flush** chasse *f* d'eau; **t. paper** papier *m* hygiénique; **t. requisites** articles *mpl* de toilette; **t. roll** rouleau *m* de papier hygiénique; **t. soap/water** savon *m*/eau *f* de toilette. ● **toiletries** *npl* articles *mpl* de toilette. ● **toilet-trained** *a* (*child*) propre.

token ['təukən] *n* (*metal Br disc or Am disk*)

jeton *m*; (*voucher*) bon *m*; (*sign, symbol*) témoignage *m*; **gift t.** *Br* chèque-cadeau *m*; **book t.** *Br* chèque-livre *m*; **record t.** *Br* chèque-disque *m* ❚ *a* symbolique.

told [təuld] *pt* & *pp of* **tell** ❚ *adv* **all t.** (*taken together*) en tout.

tolerable ['tɒlərəb(ə)l] *a* (*bearable*) tolérable; (*fairly good*) passable. ● **tolerably** *adv* (*fairly, fairly well*) passablement.

tolerant ['tɒlərənt] *a* tolérant (**of** à l'égard de). ● **tolerance** *n* tolérance *f*. ● **tolerantly** *adv* avec tolérance.

tolerate ['tɒləreɪt] *vt* tolérer.

toll [təul] **1** *n* (*fee*) péage *m*; **t. road/bridge/***etc* route *f*/pont *m*/*etc* à péage. **2** *n* **the death t.** le nombre de morts, le bilan en vies humaines; **to take a heavy t.** (*of accident etc*) faire beaucoup de victimes. **3** *vi* (*of bell*) sonner. ● **tollfree** *a* **t. number** (*on telephone*) *Am* = numéro *m* vert ❚ *adv* (*to call*) *Am* gratuitement.

tomato [*Br* tə'mɑːtəu, *Am* tə'meɪtəu] *n* (*pl* **-oes**) tomate *f*.

tomb [tuːm] *n* tombeau *m*. ● **tombstone** *n* pierre *f* tombale.

tomboy ['tɒmbɔɪ] *n* (*girl*) garçon *m* manqué.

tomcat ['tɒmkæt] *n* matou *m*.

tome [təum] *n* (*book*) tome *m*.

tomfoolery [tɒm'fuːlərɪ] *n* niaiserie(s) *f(pl)*.

tomorrow [tə'mɒrəu] *adv* & *n* demain (*m*); **t. morning/evening** demain matin/soir; **the day after t.** après-demain; **a week from t.**, *Br* **a week t.** demain en huit.

ton [tʌn] *n* tonne *f* (*Br* = 1016 kg, *Am* = 907 kg); **metric t.** tonne *f* (= 1000 kg); **tons of** (*lots of*) *Fam* des tonnes de.

tone [təun] *n* ton *m*; (*of telephone, radio*) tonalité *f*; **the engaged t.** (*on telephone*) *Br* la sonnerie 'occupé'; **in that t.** sur ce ton; **to set the t.** donner le ton; **she's t.-deaf** elle n'a pas d'oreille ❚ *vt* **to t. down** atténuer; **to t. up** (*muscles, skin*) tonifier ❚ *vi* **to t. in** (*blend in*) s'harmoniser (**with** avec).

tongs [tɒŋz] *npl* pinces *fpl*; **sugar t.** pince *f* à sucre; **curling t.** fer *m* à friser.

tongue [tʌŋ] *n* langue *f*; (*language*) *Lit* langue *f*; **t. in cheek** ironique(ment). ● **tongue-tied** *a* muet (*f* muette) (et gêné).

tonic ['tɒnɪk] *n* (*medicine*) fortifiant *m*; **t.** (**water**) eau *f* gazeuse (tonique); **gin and t.** gin-tonic *m*.

tonight [tə'naɪt] *adv* & *n* (*this evening*) ce soir (*m*); (*during the night*) cette nuit (*f*).

tonne [tʌn] *n* (*metric*) tonne *f*. ● **tonnage** *n* tonnage *m*.

tonsil ['tɒns(ə)l] *n* amygdale *f*. ● **tonsillectomy** *n* opération *f* des amygdales. ● **tonsillitis** [tɒnsə'laɪtəs] *n* **to have t.** avoir une angine *or* une amygdalite.

too [tuː] *adv* **1** (*excessively*) trop; **t. tired to play** trop fatigué pour jouer; **t. hard to solve** trop difficile à résoudre; **t. much, t. many** trop; **t. much salt/***etc* trop de sel/*etc*; **t. many people/***etc* trop de gens/*etc*; **one t. many** un de trop; **it's only t. true** ce n'est que trop vrai. **2** (*also*) aussi; (*moreover*) en plus.

took [tʊk] *pt of* take.

tool [tuːl] *n* outil *m*; **t. bag, t. kit** trousse *f* à outils.

toot [tuːt] *vti* **to t. (the horn)** *Aut* klaxonner.

tooth, *pl* **teeth** [tuːθ, tiːθ] *n* dent *f*; **front t.** dent de devant; **back t.** molaire *f*; **milk/ wisdom t.** dent de lait/de sagesse; **t. decay** carie *f* dentaire; **to have a sweet t.** aimer les sucreries; **long in the t.** (*old*) *Hum* chenu, vieux. **toothache** [ˈtuːθeɪk] *n* mal *m* de dents; **to have a t.** avoir mal aux dents. ●**toothbrush** *n* brosse *f* à dents. ●**tooth comb** *n* **to go through sth with a fine-t. comb** passer qch au peigne fin. ●**toothpaste** *n* dentifrice *m*. ●**toothpick** *n* cure-dent *m*.

top¹ [tɒp] *n* (*of mountain, tower, tree*) sommet *m*; (*of wall, ladder, page, dress*) haut *m*; (*of table, box, surface*) dessus *m*; (*of list*) tête *f*; (*of water*) surface *f*; (*of car*) toit *m*; (*of bottle, tube*) bouchon *m*; (*bottle cap*) capsule *f*; (*of saucepan*) couvercle *m*; (*of pen*) capuchon *m*; **pyjama t.** haut *m or* veste *f* de pyjama; (**at the) t. of the class** le premier de la classe; **on t. of** sur; (*in addition to*) *Fig* en plus de; **on t.** (*in bus etc*) en haut; **from t. to bottom** de fond en comble; **the big t.** (*circus*) le chapiteau; **over the t.** *Fam see* OTT.

▮ *a* (*drawer, shelf*) du haut, premier; (*step, layer*) dernier; (*upper*) supérieur; (*in rank, exam*) premier; (*chief*) principal; (*best*) meilleur; (*great, distinguished*) éminent; (*maximum*) maximum; ●**on the t. floor** au dernier étage; **in t. gear** (*vehicle*) en quatrième vitesse; **at t. speed** à toute vitesse; **t. copy** original *m*; **t. hat** (chapeau *m*) haut-de-forme *m*. ●**top-'flight** *a Fam* excellent. ●**top-'heavy** *a* trop lourd du haut. ●**top-level** *a* (*talks etc*) au sommet. ●**top-'notch** *a Fam* excellent. ●**top-'ranking** *a* (*official*) haut placé. ●**top-'secret** *a* ultra-secret.

top² [tɒp] *vt* (**-pp-**) (*exceed*) dépasser; **to t. up** *Br* (*glass etc*) remplir (de nouveau); (*coffee, tea, oil in car etc*) remettre; **and to t. it all...** et pour comble...; **topped with cream** nappé de crème; **topped with cherries** décoré de cerises. ●**topping** *n* (*of pizza*) garniture *f*; **with a t. of cream** nappé de crème.

top³ [tɒp] *n* (*spinning*) **t.** toupie *f*.

topaz [ˈtəʊpæz] *n* (*gem*) topaze *f*.

topic [ˈtɒpɪk] *n* sujet *m*. ●**topical** *a* d'actualité. ●**topi'cality** *n* actualité *f*.

topless [ˈtɒpləs] *a* (*woman*) aux seins nus.

topography [təˈpɒɡrəfɪ] *n* topographie *f*.

topping [ˈtɒpɪŋ] *n see* top².

topple [ˈtɒp(ə)l] *vi* **to t.** (**over**) tomber ▮ *vt* **to t. sth** (**over**) faire tomber qch.

topside [ˈtɒpsaɪd] *n* (*of beef*) *Br* gîte *m*.

topsy-turvy [tɒpsɪˈtɜːvɪ] *a & adv* sens dessus dessous [sɑ̃dsydsy].

torch [tɔːtʃ] *n* (*electric*) *Br* lampe *f* électrique; (*flame*) torche *f*, flambeau *m*. ●**torch-light** *n* **by t.** à la lumière des flambeaux *or* des torches ▮ *a* **t. procession** retraite *f* aux flambeaux.

tore [tɔːr] *pt of* tear¹.

torment [tɔːˈment] *vt* (*annoy*) agacer; (*make suffer*) tourmenter ▮ [ˈtɔːment] *n* tourment *m*.

tornado [tɔːˈneɪdəʊ] *n* (*pl* **-oes**) tornade *f*.

torpedo [tɔːˈpiːdəʊ] *n* (*pl* **-oes**) torpille *f*; **t. boat** torpilleur *m* ▮ *vt* torpiller.

torrent [ˈtɒrənt] *n* torrent *m*. ●**torrential** [təˈrenʃ(ə)l] *a* **t. rain** pluie *f* torrentielle.

torrid [ˈtɒrɪd] *a* (*love affair etc*) brûlant, passionné; (*climate, weather*) torride.

torso [ˈtɔːsəʊ] *n* (*pl* **-os**) torse *m*.

tortoise [ˈtɔːtəs] *n* tortue *f*. ●**tortoiseshell** *a* (*comb etc*) en écaille; (*spectacles*) à monture d'écaille.

tortuous [ˈtɔːtʃʊəs] *a* (*road etc*) sinueux; (*mind*) tortueux.

torture [ˈtɔːtʃər] *n* torture *f*, supplice *m*; **it's** (**sheer**) **t.!** *Fig* quel supplice! ▮ *vt* torturer. ●**torturer** *n* tortionnaire *m*.

Tory [ˈtɔːrɪ] *Pol n* tory *m* ▮ *a* tory *inv*.

toss [tɒs] *vt* (*throw*) jeter, lancer (**to** à); **to t. s.o.** (**about**) (*of boat, vehicle*) ballotter qn, faire tressauter qn; **to t. a coin** jouer à pile ou face; **to t. a pancake** retourner une crêpe; **to t. back one's head** rejeter sa tête en arrière.

▮ *vi* **to t.** (**about**), **t. and turn** (*in one's sleep*) se tourner et se retourner; **let's t. up, let's t.** (**up**) **for it** jouons-le à pile ou face.

▮ *n* **with a t. of the head** d'un mouvement brusque de la tête. ●**toss-up** *n* **it's a t.-up whether he leaves or stays** *Fam* il y a autant de chances pour qu'il parte que pour qu'il reste.

tot [tɒt] *n* **1** (*tiny*) **t.** petit(e) enfant *mf*. **2** *vt* (**-tt-**) **to t. up** (*total*) *Fam* additionner. **3** *n a* **t.** **of whisky/***etc Br* un doigt *or* un fond de whisky/*etc*.

total [ˈtəʊt(ə)l] **1** *a* total; **the t. sales** le total des ventes ▮ *n* total *m*; **in t.** au total ▮ *vt* (*Br* **-ll-**, *Am* **-l-**) (*of debt, invoice*) s'élever à; **to t.** (**up**) (*find the total of*) totaliser; **that totals $9** ça fait neuf dollars en tout. **2** *vt* (*Am* **-l-**) (*car etc*) *Am Fam* bousiller; **to be totaled** être une véritable épave. ●**totally** *adv* totalement.

totalitarian [təʊtælɪˈteərɪən] *a Pol* totalitaire.

tote [təʊt] **1** *n Br Sport Fam* pari *m* mutuel. **2** *vt* (*gun*) porter. ●**tote bag** *n Am* fourre-tout *m inv*.

toto [ˈtəʊtəʊ] **in t.** *adv* intégralement.

totter [ˈtɒtər] *vi* chanceler.

touch [tʌtʃ] *n* (*contact*) contact *m*; (*sense*) toucher *m*; (*of painter*) touche *f*; *Football Rugby* touche *f*; **a t. of** (*small amount*) un petit peu de, un soupçon de; **to put the finishing touches to** mettre la dernière touche à; **to be in t. with** (*person*) être en contact avec; (*situation*) être au courant de; **to be out of t. with** ne plus être en contact avec; (*situation*) ne plus être au courant de; **to get in t.** se mettre en contact (**with** avec); **we**

lost t. on s'est perdu de vue; **it's t. and go whether he'll live** (*uncertain*) ce n'est pas sûr du tout qu'il survivra.

▮ *vt* toucher; (*interfere with*, *eat*) toucher à; (*move emotionally*) toucher; (*equal*) *Fig* égaler; **I don't t. the stuff** (*beer etc*) je n'en bois jamais.

▮ *vi* (*of lines*, *hands*, *ends etc*) se toucher; **don't t.!** n'y *or* ne touche pas!; **he's always touching** c'est un touche-à-tout. ●**touched** *a* (*emotionally*) touché (**by** de); (*crazy*) *Fam* cinglé. ●**touching** *a* (*story etc*) touchant.

touch down *vi* (*of aircraft*) atterrir ▮ **to touch on** *vt* (*subject*) aborder ▮ **to touch up** *vt* (*photo etc*) retoucher.

touchdown ['tʌtʃdaʊn] *n* (*of aircraft*) atterrissage *m*; *Rugby Am Football* essai *m*.

touchline ['tʌtʃlaɪn] *n Football Rugby* (ligne *f* de) touche *f*.

touchy ['tʌtʃɪ] *a* (**-ier**, **-iest**) (*sensitive*) susceptible (**about** à propos de).

tough [tʌf] *a* (**-er**, **-est**) (*hard*) (*meat etc*) dur; (*sturdy*) solide; (*strong*) fort; (*difficult*, *harsh*) difficile, dur; (*relentless*) acharné; (*businessman*) dur en affaires; **t. guy** dur *m*; **t. luck!** *Fam* pas de chance!, quelle déveine! ▮ *n* (*tough guy*) *Old-fashioned Fam* dur *m*. ●**toughen** *vt* (*body*, *person*) endurcir; (*reinforce*) renforcer. ●**toughness** *n* dureté *f*; (*sturdiness*) solidité *f*; (*strength*) force *f*.

toupee ['tuːpeɪ] *n* postiche *m*.

tour [tʊər] *n* (*journey*) voyage *m*; (*visit*) visite *f*; (*by artist*, *team etc*) tournée *f*; (*on bicycle*, *on foot*) randonnée *f*; (*package*) t. voyage *m* organisé; **to be on t.** être en voyage; (*of artist etc*) être en tournée; **a t. of** (*France*) un voyage en; (*by artist etc*) une tournée en; (*on bicycle etc*) une randonnée en ▮ *vt* visiter; (*of artist etc*) être en tournée en *or* dans *etc*.' ●**touring** *n* tourisme *m*; **to go to t.** faire du tourisme.

tourism ['tʊərɪz(ə)m] *n* tourisme *m*. ●**tourist** *n* touriste *mf* ▮ *a* (*region etc*) touristique; **t. class** *Av etc* classe *f* touriste *inv*; **t. office** syndicat *m* d'initiative. ●**touristy** *a Pej Fam* (trop) touristique.

tournament ['tʊənəmənt] *n Sport & Hist* tournoi *m*.

tousled ['taʊz(ə)ld] *a* (*hair*) ébouriffé.

tout [taʊt] *vi* racoler; **to t. for** (*customers*) racoler ▮ *n* racoleur, -euse *mf*; **ticket t.** *Br* revendeur, -euse *mf* (en fraude) de billets.

tow [təʊ] *vt* (*car*, *boat*) remorquer; (*caravan*, *trailer*) tracter; **to t. away** (*vehicle*) (*by police etc*) emmener à la fourrière ▮ *n* **'on t.'** *Br*, **'in t.'** *Am* 'en remorque'; **t. truck** (*breakdown lorry*) *Am* dépanneuse *f*. ●**towpath** *n* chemin *m* de halage. ●**towrope** *n* (câble *m* de) remorque *f*.

toward(s) [*Br* təˈwɔːd(z), *Am* tɔːd(z)] *prep* vers; (*of feelings*) envers; **cruel/etc t.** s.o. cruel/etc envers qn; **money t. sth** de l'argent pour (acheter) qch.

towel ['taʊəl] *n* serviette *f* (de toilette); (*for dishes*) torchon *m*; **t. rail** *Br*, **t. rack** *Am*

porte-serviettes *m inv*. ●**towelling** *or Am* **toweling** *n* tissu-éponge *m*; **(kitchen) t.** *Am* essuie-tout *m inv*.

tower ['taʊər] *n* tour *f*; **t. block** *Br* tour *f*, immeuble *m*; **ivory t.** *Fig* tour *f* d'ivoire ▮ *vi* **to t. above** *or* **over** dominer. ●**towering** *a* très haut.

town [taʊn] *n* ville *f*; **in t.**, **(in)to t.** en ville; **out of t.** en province; **country t.** bourg *m*; **t. centre** centre-ville *m*; **t. clerk** *Br Hist* secrétaire *mf* de mairie; **t. council** *Br* conseil *m* municipal; **t. hall** *Br* mairie *f*; **t. planner** *Br* urbaniste *mf*; **t. planning** *Br* urbanisme *m*. ●**township** *n* (*in South Africa*) commune *f* (noire).

toxic ['tɒksɪk] *a* toxique; **t. waste** déchets *mpl* toxiques. ●**toxin** *n* toxine *f*.

toy [tɔɪ] *n* jouet *m*; **soft t.** (jouet *m* en) peluche *f* ▮ *a* (*gun*) d'enfant; (*house*, *car*, *train*) miniature *inv* ▮ *vi* **to t. with** (*idea etc*) caresser. ●**toyshop** *n* magasin *m* de jouets.

trace [treɪs] *n* trace *f* (**of** de); **to vanish** *or* **disappear without (a) t.** disparaître sans laisser de traces ▮ *vt* (*draw*) tracer; (*with tracing paper*) (dé)calquer; (*find*) retrouver (la trace de), dépister; (*follow*) suivre (la piste de) (**to** à); (*relate*) retracer; **to t. (back) to** (*one's family*, *ancestry*) faire remonter jusqu'à. ●**tracing** *n* (*drawing*) calque *m*; **t. paper** papier-calque *m inv*.

track [træk] *n* (*of animal*, *suspect*) piste *f*, trace *f*; (*of audio tape*, *sports stadium*) piste *f*; (*for trains*) voie *f*; (*path*) chemin *m*, piste *f*; (*of rocket*) trajectoire *f*; (*of record*) plage *f*; *Am Sch* classe *f* (de niveau); (*racetrack*) *Am* champ *m* de courses; **the tracks** (*of wheels*) les traces *fpl*; **to keep t. of** suivre; **to lose t. of** (*friend*) perdre de vue; (*argument*) perdre le fil de; **to make tracks** *Fam* se sauver; **to be on the right t.** être sur la bonne voie *or* piste; **off the beaten t.** (*remote*) loin des sentiers battus; **t. event** *Sport* épreuve *f* sur piste; **t. record** (*of person*, *company etc*) *Fig* antécédents *mpl*.

▮ *vt* **to t. (down)** (*find*) retrouver, dépister; (*pursue*) traquer. ●**tracker** *a* **t. dog** chien *m* policier. ●**tracking shot** *n* **to do a t. shot** *Cinema* faire un travelling. ●**track shoes** *npl Am* baskets *mpl*, tennis *mpl*. ●**tracksuit** *n* survêtement *m*.

tract [trækt] *n* (*stretch of land*) étendue *f*

traction ['trækʃ(ə)n] *n Tech* traction *f*.

tractor ['træktər] *n* tracteur *m*.

trade [treɪd] *n* commerce *m*; (*job*) métier *m*; (*exchange*) échange *m* ▮ *a* (*fair*, *balance*, *route*) commercial; (*price*) de (demi-)gros; (*secret*) de fabrication, commercial; (*barrier*) douanier; **t. union** *Br* syndicat *m*; **t. unionist** *Br* syndicaliste *mf* ▮ *vi* faire du commerce (**with** avec); **to t. in** (*sugar etc*) faire le commerce de ▮ *vt* (*exchange*) échanger (**for** contre); **to t. sth in** (*old article*) faire reprendre qch. ●**trade-in** *n Com* reprise *f*. ●**trade-off** *n* (*compromise*) compromis *m*.

trademark ['treɪdmɑːk] *n* marque *f* de fabrique; **(registered) t.** marque déposée.

trader ['treɪdər] *n* (*shopkeeper*) *Br*
commerçant, -ante *mf*; marchand, -ande *mf*;
(*street*) **t.** *Br* vendeur, -euse *mf* de rue.
● **tradesman** *n* (*pl* **-men**) *Br* commerçant *m*.

trading ['treɪdɪŋ] *n* commerce *m* ▮ *a* (*port,
debts, activity etc*) commercial; (*nation*)
commerçant; **t. estate** *Br* zone *f* industrielle.

tradition [trə'dɪʃ(ə)n] *n* tradition *f*.
● **tra'ditional** *a* traditionnel. ● **traditionalist** *n*
traditionaliste *mf*. ● **traditionally** *adv* traditionnellement.

traffic ['træfɪk] **1** *n* (*on road*) circulation *f*;
(*air, sea, rail*) trafic *m*; **heavy** *or* **busy t.**
beaucoup de circulation; **heavy t.** (*vehicles*)
poids *mpl* lourds; **t. circle** *Am* rond-point *m*;
t. cone *Br* cône *m* de chantier; **t. island** refuge *m* (*pour piétons*); **t. jam** embouteillage
m; **t. lights** feux *mpl* (de signalisation);
(*when red*) feu *m* rouge; **t. sign** panneau *m*
de signalisation.
2 *n* (*trade*) *Pej* trafic *m* (**in** de); **the drug t.** le
trafic de la drogue *or* des stupéfiants ▮ *vi*
(**-ck-**) trafiquer (**in** de). ● **trafficker** *n Pej*
trafiquant, -ante *mf*.

tragedy ['trædʒɪdɪ] *n* (*situation, drama etc*)
tragédie *f*. ● **tragic** *a* tragique. ● **tragically**
adv tragiquement.

trail [treɪl] *n* (*of smoke, blood, powder etc*)
traînée *f*; (*track*) piste *f*, trace *f*; (*path*)
sentier *m*; **in its t.** (*wake*) dans son sillage ▮
vt (*drag*) traîner; (*caravan*) tracter; (*follow*)
suivre (la piste de) ▮ *vi* (*on the ground etc*)
traîner; (*of plant*) ramper; **to t.** (**behind**) (*lag
behind*) traîner. ● **trailer** *n* **1** (*for car*) remorque *f*; (*caravan*) *Am* caravane *f*;
(*camper*) *Am* camping-car *m*. **2** (*advertisement for film etc*) bande *f* annonce.

train [treɪn] **1** *n* (*engine, transport*) train *m*;
(*underground*) rame *f*; **to go** *or* **come by t.**
prendre le train; **t. set** (*toy*) petit train *m*.
2 *n* (*procession*) file *f*; (*of events*) suite *f*; (*of
dress*) traîne *f*; **my t. of thought** le fil de ma
pensée.
3 *vt* (*teach, develop*) former (**to do** à faire);
Sport entraîner; (*animal, child*) dresser (**to
do** à faire); (*ear*) exercer; **to t. oneself to do**
s'entraîner à faire ▮ *vi* recevoir une formation (**as a doctor**/*etc* de médecin/etc); *Sport*
s'entraîner.
4 *vt* **to t. sth on s.o./sth** (*aim*) braquer qch
sur qn/qch. ● **trained** *a* (*skilled*) qualifié;
(*nurse, engineer etc*) diplômé; (*animal*)
dressé; (*ear*) exercé. ● **training** *n* formation *f*;
Sport entraînement *m*; (*of animal*) dressage
m; **to be in t.** *Sport* s'entraîner; **(teachers') t.
college** *Br* école *f* normale.

trainee [treɪ'niː] *n* & *a* stagiaire (*mf*).

trainer ['treɪnər] *n* (*of athlete, racehorse*) entraîneur *m*; (*of dog, lion etc*) dresseur *m*;
trainers (*shoes*) *Br* baskets *mpl*, tennis *mpl*.

traipse [treɪps] *vi Fam* **to t. around** (*tiredly*)
traîner les pieds; (*wander*) se balader; **to t.
in** se pointer, se ramener.

trait [treɪt] *n* (*of character*) trait *m*.

traitor ['treɪtər] *n* traître *m*.

trajectory [trə'dʒektərɪ] *n* trajectoire *f*.

tram [træm] *n* tram(way) *m*.

tramp [træmp] **1** *n* (*vagrant*) *Br* clochard,
-arde *mf*; (*woman*) *Pej* traînée *f*. **2** *vi* (*walk*)
marcher d'un pas lourd; (*hike*) marcher à
pied ▮ *vt* (*streets etc*) parcourir ▮ *n* (*sound*)
pas lourds *mpl*; **to go for a t.** (*hike*) faire une
randonnée *f*.

trample ['træmp(ə)l] *vti* **to t. sth** (**underfoot**),
t. on sth piétiner qch.

trampoline [træmpə'liːn] *n* trampoline *m*.

trance [trɑːns] *n* **to be in a t.** être en transe;
to go into a t. entrer en transe.

tranquil ['træŋkwɪl] *a* tranquille.
● **tran'quillity** *n* tranquillité *f*. ● **tranquillizer**
(*Am* **tranquilizer**) *n* (*drug*) tranquillisant *m*.

trans- [træns, trænz] *pref* trans-.

transact [træn'zækt] *vt* (*business*) traiter.
● **transaction** [-ʃ(ə)n] *n* (*in bank etc*) opération *f*; (*on Stock Market*) transaction *f*; **the t.
of business** la conduite des affaires.

transatlantic [trænzət'læntɪk] *a* transatlantique.

transcend [træn'send] *vt* transcender.
● **transcendent** *a* transcendant.

transcribe [træn'skraɪb] *vt* transcrire.
● **'transcript** *n* (*document*) transcription *f*.
● **transcription** [-skrɪpʃ(ə)n] *n* transcription
f.

transept ['trænsept] *n* (*in church*) transept
m.

transfer [træns'fɜːr] *vt* (**-rr-**) (*employee, prisoner, goods etc*) transférer (**to** à); (*political
power*) faire passer (**to** à); **to t. the charges**
Br téléphoner en PCV ▮ *vi* (*of employee,
prisoner etc*) être transféré (**to** à) ▮
['trænsfɜːr] *n* transfert *m* (**to** à); (*of political
power*) passation *f*; (*picture, design*) *Br* décalcomanie *f*; **bank** *or* **credit t.** virement *m*
(bancaire). ● **trans'ferable** *a* **not t.** (*on ticket*)
strictement personnel.

transform [træns'fɔːm] *vt* transformer (**into**
en). ● **transformation** [-fə'meɪʃ(ə)n] *n*
transformation *f*. ● **transformer** *n El*
transformateur *m*.

transfusion [træns'fjuːʒ(ə)n] *n* (**blood**) **t.**
transfusion *f* (sanguine).

transgress [trænz'gres] *vi* (*sin*) pécher.
● **transgression** [-ʃ(ə)n] *n* péché *m*, faute *f*.

transient ['trænzɪənt] *a* (*ephemeral*)
transitoire.

transistor [træn'zɪstər] *n* (*device*) transistor
m; **t. (radio)** transistor *m*.

transit ['trænzɪt] *n* transit *m*; **in t.** en transit;
t. lounge (*in airport*) *Br* salle *f* de transit.

transition [træn'zɪʃ(ə)n] *n* transition *f*.
● **transitional** *a* (*government etc*) de transition.

transitive ['trænsɪtɪv] *a Grammar* transitif.

transitory ['trænzɪtərɪ] *a* transitoire.

translate [træns'leɪt] *vt* traduire (**from** de,
into en). ● **translation** [-ʃ(ə)n] *n* traduction *f*;
(*into mother tongue*) *Sch* version *f*; (*from*

mother tongue) Sch thème *m.* ●**translator** *n* traducteur, -trice *mf.*

transmit [trænz'mɪt] *vt* (-tt-) (*send, pass*) transmettre **▌** *vti* (*broadcast*) émettre. ●**transmission** [-ʃ(ə)n] *n* transmission *f;* (*broadcast*) émission *f.* ●**transmitter** *n Radio TV* émetteur *m.*

transparent [træns'pærənt] *a* transparent. ●**transparency** *n* transparence *f;* (*photographic slide*) *Br* diapositive *f.*

transpire [træn'spaɪər] *vi* (*of secret etc*) s'ébruiter; (*happen*) *Fam* arriver; **it transpired that...** il s'est avéré que....

transplant [træns'plɑːnt] *vt* (*plant*) transplanter; (*organ*) (*surgically*) greffer, transplanter **▌** ['trænsplɑːnt] *n* (*surgical*) greffe *f,* transplantation *f.*

transport [træn'spɔːt] *vt* transporter **▌** ['trænspɔːt] *n* transport *m* (of de); (**means of**) **t.** moyen *m* de transport; **public t.** les transports en commun; **do you have t.?** es-tu motorisé?; **t. café** *Br* routier *m.* ●**transportation** [-'teɪʃ(ə)n] *n* transport *m;* (*means*) moyen *m* de transport; **do you have t.?** es-tu motorisé?

transpose [træns'pəʊz] *vt* transposer. ●**transposition** [-pə'zɪʃ(ə)n] *n* transposition *f.*

transvestite [trænz'vestaɪt] *n* travesti *m.*

trap [træp] *n* piège *m;* **t. door** trappe *f;* **to have a big t.** (*mouth*) *Sl* avoir une grande gueule; **shut your t.!** *Sl* ta gueule! **▌** *vt* (-pp-) (*animal*) prendre (au piège); (*jam, corner*) coincer; (*cut off by snow etc*) bloquer (**by** par); **to t. one's finger** se coincer le doigt (**in** dans). ●**trapper** *n* (*hunter*) trappeur *m.*

trapeze [trə'piːz] *n* (*in circus*) trapèze *m;* **t. artist** trapéziste *mf.*

trappings ['træpɪŋz] *npl* signes *mpl* extérieurs.

trash [træʃ] *n* (*nonsense*) bêtises *fpl;* (*junk*) bric-à-brac *m inv;* (*waste*) *Am* ordures *fpl;* (*riffraff*) *Am* racaille *f.* ●**trashcan** *n Am* poubelle *f.* ●**trashy** *a* (-ier, -iest) (*book, film etc*) qui ne vaut rien; (*goods*) de camelote.

trauma ['trɔːmə, 'traʊmə] *n* (*shock*) traumatisme *m.* ●**trau'matic** *a* traumatisant. ●**traumatize** *vt* traumatiser.

travel ['træv(ə)l] *vi* (*Br* -ll-, *Am* -l-) (*on journey*) voyager; (*move, go*) aller, se déplacer **▌** *vt* (*country, distance, road*) parcourir **▌** *n* **travel(s)** voyages *mpl;* **on one's travels** en voyage; **t. agency/agent** agence *f*/agent *m* de voyages; **t. book** (*account*) récit *m* de voyage(s); **t. brochure** dépliant *m* touristique; (*guide*) guide *m* touristique; **t. insurance** assurance *f* voyage. ●**travelled** (*Am* **traveled**) *a* **to be well** or **widely t.** avoir beaucoup voyagé. ●**travelling** (*Am* **traveling**) *n* voyages *mpl* **▌** *a* (*bag, clothes etc*) de voyage; (*expenses*) de déplacement; (*musician, circus*) ambulant.

traveller ['trævələr] (*Am* **traveler**) *n* voyageur, -euse *mf;* **traveller's cheque** *Br,* **traveler's check** *Am* chèque *m* de voyage.

travelogue ['trævəlɒg] (*Am* **travelog**) *n* (*book*) récit *m* de voyages.

travelsickness ['trævəlsɪknɪs] *n* (*in car*) mal *m* de la route; (*in aircraft*) mal *m* de l'air.

travesty ['trævəstɪ] *n* parodie *f;* **it was a t. of justice** ce fut une parodie de justice.

trawler ['trɔːlər] *n* (*ship*) chalutier *m.*

tray [treɪ] *n* plateau *m;* (*for office correspondence*) corbeille *f;* **baking t.** plaque *f* de four.

treacherous ['tretʃ(ə)rəs] *a* (*road, conditions*) très dangereux; (*journey*) parsemé d'embûches; (*person, action*) traître. ●**treacherously** *adv* (*to act etc*) traîtreusement; (*dangerously*) dangereusement. ●**treachery** *n* traîtrise *f.*

treacle ['triːk(ə)l] *n Br* mélasse *f.*

tread [tred] *vi* (*pt* **trod,** *pp* **trodden**) (*walk*) marcher (**on** sur); (*proceed*) *Fig* avancer **▌** *vt* (*path*) parcourir; **to t. sth into a carpet** étaler qch (avec les pieds) sur un tapis; **to t. the soil of one's native country** fouler le sol de sa patrie **▌** *n* (*step of stairs*) marche *f;* (*of Br tyre, Am tire*) bande *f* de roulement; (*footstep*) pas *m.*

treadmill ['tredmɪl] *n Pej Fig* routine *f.*

treason ['triːz(ə)n] *n* trahison *f.*

treasure ['treʒər] *n* trésor *m;* **she's a real t.** *Fig* c'est une vraie perle; **t. hunt** chasse *f* au trésor **▌** *vt* (*value*) tenir à, priser; (*keep*) conserver (précieusement). ●**treasurer** *n* trésorier, -ière *mf.* ●**Treasury** *n* the T. *Br Pol* = le ministère des Finances.

treat [triːt] **1** *vt* (*person, product etc*) traiter; (*patient, illness*) soigner, traiter; (*consider*) considérer (**as** comme); **to t. sth/s.o. with care** prendre soin de qch/qn; **to t. s.o. like a child/thief** traiter qn comme un enfant/un voleur; **to t. s.o. to sth** offrir qch à qn. **2** *n* (*special*) **t.** petit extra *m,* gâterie *f;* (*meal*) régal *m;* **to give s.o. a (special) t.** donner une surprise à qn; **it was a t. (for me) to do it** ça m'a fait plaisir de le faire.

treatment ['triːtmənt] *n* (*behaviour*) & *Med* traitement *m;* **his t. of her** la façon dont il la traite *or* la traitait *etc;* **rough t.** mauvais traitements *mpl.*

treatise ['triːtiːz] *n* (*book*) traité *m* (**on** de).

treaty ['triːtɪ] *n* (*between countries*) traité *m.*

treble ['treb(ə)l] *a* triple; **t. clef** *Mus* clef *f* de sol; **t. voice** *Mus* voix *f* de soprano **▌** *vti* tripler **▌** *n* le triple; **it's t. the price** c'est le triple du prix.

tree [triː] *n* arbre *m;* **Christmas t.** arbre *m* or sapin *m* de Noël; **family t.** arbre *m* généalogique. ●**tree-lined** *a* bordé d'arbres. ●**treetop** *n* cime *f* (d'un arbre). ●**tree-trunk** *n* tronc *m* d'arbre.

trek [trek] *vi* (-kk-) cheminer *or* voyager (péniblement); *Sport* marcher à pied; (*go*) *Fam* traîner **▌** *n* voyage *m* (pénible); *Sport* randonnée *f;* (*distance*) *Fam* tirée *f.*

trellis ['trelɪs] *n* treillage *m,* treillis *m.*

tremble ['tremb(ə)l] *vi* (*of person, voice etc*) trembler (**with** de). ●**tremor** *n* tremblement *m*; **(earth) t.** secousse *f* (sismique).

tremendous [trəˈmendəs] *a (huge)* énorme; *(dreadful)* terrible; *(wonderful)* formidable, terrible. ●**tremendously** *adv (enormously)* énormément; *(wonderfully)* formidablement.

trench [trentʃ] *n* tranchée *f*. ●**trenchcoat** *n* trench(-coat) *m*.

trend [trend] *n* tendance *f* **(towards** à**); the t.** *(fashion)* la mode; **to set** *or* **the t.** donner le ton, lancer *or* la mode. ●**trendy** *a* **(-ier, -iest)** *(person, clothes, topic etc)* Fam à la mode, dans le vent.

trepidation [trepɪˈdeɪʃ(ə)n] *n* inquiétude *f*.

trespass [ˈtrespəs] *vi* s'introduire sans autorisation **(on, upon** dans**); 'no trespassing'** 'entrée interdite'.

tresses [ˈtresɪz] *npl* Lit chevelure *f*.

trestle [ˈtres(ə)l] *n* tréteau *m*.

trial [ˈtraɪəl] *n (in court)* procès *m*; *(test)* essai *m*; *(ordeal)* épreuve *f*; **t. of strength** épreuve de force; **to go** *or* **be on t., stand t.** être jugé, passer en jugement; **to put s.o. on t.** juger qn; **by t. and error** par tâtonnements █ *a (period, flight etc)* d'essai; *(offer)* à l'essai; **t. run** *(of new product etc)* période *f* d'essai.

triangle [ˈtraɪæŋɡ(ə)l] *n* triangle *m*; *(setsquare)* Am équerre *f*. ●**triˈangular** *a* triangulaire.

tribe [traɪb] *n* tribu *f*. ●**tribal** *a* tribal. ●**tribesman** *n (pl* **-men)** membre d'une *or* de la tribu.

tribulations [trɪbjuˈleɪʃ(ə)nz] *npl* **(trials and) t.** tribulations *fpl*.

tribunal [traɪˈbjuːn(ə)l] *n* commission *f*; *(military)* tribunal *m*.

tributary [Br ˈtrɪbjʊtərɪ, Am -erɪ] *n* affluent *m*.

tribute [ˈtrɪbjuːt] *n* hommage *m*, tribut *m*; **to pay t.** to rendre hommage à.

trick [trɪk] *n (joke, deception, of conjurer etc)* tour *m*; *(clever method)* astuce *f*; *(habit)* manie *f*; **to play a t. on s.o.** jouer un tour à qn; **card t.** tour *m* de cartes; **that will do the t.** Fam ça fera l'affaire; **she never misses a t.** Fam rien ne lui échappe; **t. photo** photo *f* truquée; **t. question** question-piège *f* █ *vt (deceive)* tromper, attraper; **to t. s.o. into doing sth** amener qn à faire qch par la ruse. ●**trickery** *n* ruse *f*.

trickle [ˈtrɪk(ə)l] *n (of liquid)* filet *m*; **a t. of** *(letters, people etc)* Fig un petit nombre de █ *vi (flow)* couler (lentement), dégouliner, s'écouler lentement; **to t. in** *(of letters, people etc)* Fig arriver en petit nombre.

tricky [ˈtrɪkɪ] *a* **(-ier, -iest)** *(problem etc)* difficile, délicat; *(person)* rusé.

tricycle [ˈtraɪsɪk(ə)l] *n* tricycle *m*.

trier [ˈtraɪər] *n* **to be a t.** être persévérant.

trifle [ˈtraɪf(ə)l] **1** *n (insignificant thing, money)* bagatelle *f* █ *adv* **a t. small/too much/etc** un tantinet petit/trop/etc █ *vi* **to t. with** *(s.o.'s feelings)* jouer avec; *(person)* plaisanter avec. **2** *n (dessert)* Br diplomate *m*. ●**trifling** *a* insignifiant.

trigger [ˈtrɪɡər] *n (of gun)* gâchette *f* █ *vt* **to**

t. (off) *(start, cause)* déclencher. ●**trigger-happy** *a (gunman etc)* qui a la gâchette facile.

trilby [ˈtrɪlbɪ] *n* **t. (hat)** Br chapeau *m* mou.

trilingual [traɪˈlɪŋɡwəl] *a* trilingue.

trilogy [ˈtrɪlədʒɪ] *n* trilogie *f*.

trim [trɪm] **1** *a* **(trimmer, trimmest)** *(neat)* soigné, net *(f* nette); *(slim)* svelte █ *n* **in t.** *(fit)* en (bonne) forme. **2** *n (cut)* légère coupe *f*; *(haircut)* coupe *f* de rafraîchissement; **to have a t.** se faire rafraîchir les cheveux █ *vt* **(-mm-)** couper (un peu); *(fingernail, edge)* rogner; *(hair)* rafraîchir. **3** *n (on garment)* garniture *f*; *(on car)* garnitures *fpl* █ *vt* **(-mm-) to t. sth with** *(lace etc)* orner qch de. ●**trimmings** *npl* garniture(s) *f(pl)*; *(extras)* Fig accessoires *mpl*.

Trinity [ˈtrɪnɪtɪ] *n* **the T.** *(union)* Rel la Trinité.

trinket [ˈtrɪŋkɪt] *n* colifichet *m*.

trio [ˈtriːəʊ] *n (pl* **-os)** *(group)* & Mus trio *m*.

trip [trɪp] **1** *n (journey)* voyage *m*; *(outing)* excursion *f*; **to take a t. to** *(shops etc)* aller à. **2** *n (stumble)* faux pas *m* █ *vi* **(-pp-) to t.** *(over or up)* trébucher; **to t. over sth** trébucher contre qch █ *vt* **to t. s.o. up** faire trébucher qn. **3** *vi* **(-pp-)** *(walk gently)* marcher d'un pas léger.

tripe [traɪp] *n* **1** *(food)* tripes *fpl*. **2** *(nonsense)* Fam bêtises *fpl*.

triple [ˈtrɪp(ə)l] *a* triple █ *vti* tripler. ●**triplets** *npl (children)* triplés, -ées *mfpl*.

triplicate [ˈtrɪplɪkət] *n* **in t.** en trois exemplaires.

tripod [ˈtraɪpɒd] *n* trépied *m*.

tripper [ˈtrɪpər] *n* **day t.** Br excursionniste *mf*.

trite [traɪt] *a* banal *(mpl* -als). ●**triteness** *n* banalité *f*.

triumph [ˈtraɪʌmf] *n* triomphe *m* **(over** sur**)** █ *vi* triompher *(over* de). ●**triˈumphal** *a* triomphal. ●**triˈumphant** *a (team, army, gesture)* triomphant; *(success, welcome, return)* triomphal. ●**triˈumphantly** *adv* triomphalement.

trivia [ˈtrɪvɪə] *npl* vétilles *fpl*. ●**trivial** *a (unimportant)* insignifiant; *(trite)* banal *(mpl* -als). ●**triviˈality** *n* insignifiance *f*; *(triteness)* banalité *f*; **trivialities** banalités *fpl*. ●**trivialize** *vt (make unimportant)* minimiser.

trod, trodden [trɒd, ˈtrɒd(ə)n] *pt & pp of* **tread.**

trolley [ˈtrɒlɪ] *n (for luggage)* Br chariot *m*; *(in supermarket)* Br caddie® *m*; *(for shopping)* Br poussette *f* (de marché); *(trolleybus)* trolley *m*; **(tea) t.** Br table *f* roulante; *(for tea urn)* chariot *m*; **t. (car)** Am tramway *m*. ●**trolleybus** *n* trolleybus *m*.

trombone [trɒmˈbəʊn] *n (musical instrument)* trombone *m*.

troop [truːp] *n* bande *f*; *(group of soldiers)* troupe *f*; **the troops** *(army, soldiers)* les troupes *fpl*, la troupe █ *vi* **to t. in/out/etc** entrer/sortir/etc en masse. ●**trooping the colour** Br le salut du drapeau. ●**trooper** *n*

(state) t. *Am* membre *m* de la police montée.

trophy ['trəʊfɪ] *n* coupe *f*, trophée *m*.

tropic ['trɒpɪk] *n* tropique *m*; **in the tropics** sous les tropiques. ●**tropical** *a* tropical.

trot [trɒt] *n* (*of horse*) trot *m*; **on the t.** (*one after another*) *Fam* de suite ▮ *vi* (**-tt-**) trotter; **to t. off** *or* **along** (*leave*) *Br Hum Fam* se sauver ▮ *vt* **to t. out** (*say*) *Fam* débiter.

trouble ['trʌb(ə)l] *n* (*difficulty*) ennui(s) *m(pl)*; (*bother, effort*) peine *f*, mal *m*; (*inconvenience*) dérangement *m*; **trouble(s)** (*social unrest, illness*) & *Med* troubles *mpl*; **to be in t.** avoir des ennuis; **to get into t.** s'attirer des ennuis (**with** avec); **the t. (with you) is...** l'ennui (avec toi) c'est que...; **to go to the t. of doing, take the t. to do** se donner la peine *or* le mal de faire; **I didn't put her to any t.** je ne l'ai pas dérangée; **to find the t.** trouver le problème; *Br* un petit problème; **a t. spot** (*region in turmoil*) un point chaud; **it's one of the world's t. spots** c'est un point chaud du globe.
▮ *vt* (*inconvenience*) déranger, ennuyer; (*worry, annoy*) ennuyer; (*hurt*) faire mal à; (*grieve*) peiner; **to t. to do** se donner la peine de faire; **to t. oneself** se déranger. ●**troubled** *a* (*worried*) inquiet; (*period*) agité. ●**trouble-free** *a* (*machine, vehicle*) qui ne tombe jamais en panne, fiable.

troublemaker ['trʌb(ə)lmeɪkər] *n* (*in school*) élément *m* perturbateur; (*political*) fauteur *m* de troubles.

troubleshooter ['trʌb(ə)lʃuːtər] *n Tech* dépanneur *m*, expert *m*; *Pol* conciliateur, -trice *mf*; (*in firm*) expert *m* en gestion d'entreprise.

troublesome ['trʌb(ə)ls(ə)m] *a* ennuyeux, gênant; (*leg etc*) qui fait mal.

trough [trɒf] *n* **1** (*for drinking*) abreuvoir *m*; (*for feeding*) auge *f*. **2 t. of low pressure** *Met* dépression *f*.

trounce [traʊns] *vt* (*defeat*) écraser.

troupe [truːp] *n* (*of actors etc*) troupe *f*.

trousers ['traʊzəz] *npl Br* pantalon *m*; **a pair of t., some t.** un pantalon; **(short) t.** culottes *fpl* courtes. ●**trouser leg** *n* jambe *f* de pantalon.

trousseau ['truːsəʊ] *n* (*pl* **-eaux** *or* **-eaus** [-əʊz]) (*of bride*) trousseau *m*.

trout [traʊt] *n* truite *f*.

trowel ['traʊəl] *n* (*for cement or plaster*) truelle *f*; (*for plants*) déplantoir *m*

truant ['truːənt] *n* (*pupil, shirker*) absentéiste *mf*; **to play t.** sécher (la classe), faire l'école buissonnière. ●**truancy** *n Sch* absentéisme *m* scolaire.

truce [truːs] *n Mil* trêve *f*.

truck [trʌk] *n* **1** (*lorry*) camion *m*; *Br Rail* wagon *m* plat; **t. driver** camionneur *m*; (*long-distance*) routier *m*; **t. stop** (*restaurant*) *Am* routier *m*. **2 t. farmer** *Am* maraîcher, -ère *mf*. ●**trucker** *n Am* (*for goods*) transporteur *m* routier; (*driver*) camionneur *m*, routier *m*.

truculent ['trʌkjʊlənt] *a* agressif.

trudge [trʌdʒ] *vi* marcher d'un pas pesant.

true [truː] *a* (**-er, -est**) vrai; (*accurate*) exact; (*genuine*) vrai, véritable; **t. to** (*promise, person etc*) fidèle à; **t. to life** conforme à la réalité; **to come t.** se réaliser; **to hold t.** (*of argument etc*) valoir (**for** pour); **too t.!** *Fam* ah, ça oui! ●**truly** *adv* vraiment; (*faithfully*) fidèlement; **well and t.** bel et bien; **yours t.** (*in letter*) je vous prie d'agréer l'expression de mes sentiments distingués; **yours t.** (*myself*) *Fam Hum* votre (humble) serviteur.

truffle ['trʌf(ə)l] *n* (*mushroom*) truffe *f*.

truism ['truːɪz(ə)m] *n* lapalissade *f*.

trump [trʌmp] **1** *n Cards* atout *m*; **t. card** (*advantage*) *Fig* atout *m*. **2** *vt* **to t. up** (*charge, reason*) inventer (de toutes pièces).

trumpet ['trʌmpɪt] *n* trompette *f*; **t. player** trompettiste *mf*.

truncate [trʌŋ'keɪt] *vt* tronquer.

truncheon ['trʌntʃ(ə)n] *n* (*weapon*) matraque *f*.

trundle ['trʌnd(ə)l] *vti* **to t. along** rouler bruyamment.

trunk [trʌŋk] *n* (*of tree, body*) tronc *m*; (*of elephant*) trompe *f*; (*case*) malle *f*; (*of vehicle*) *Am* coffre *m*; **trunks** (*for swimming*) (*briefs*) slip *m* de bain; (*shorts*) caleçon *m* de bain; **t. call** *Old-fashioned Br Tel* communication *f* interurbaine; **t. road** *Br* route *f* nationale.

truss [trʌs] **1** *vt* **to t. (up)** (*prisoner etc*) ligoter. **2** *n* (*belt, bandage*) bandage *m* herniaire.

trust [trʌst] *n* (*faith*) confiance *f* (**in** en); (*financial group*) trust *m*; *Jur* fidéicommis *m*; **to take sth on t.** accepter qch de confiance ▮ *vt* (*person, judgment*) avoir confiance en, se fier à; (*instinct, promise*) se fier à; **to t. s.o. with sth, t. sth to s.o.** confier qch à qn; **to t. s.o. to do sth** (*rely on, expect*) compter sur qn pour faire qch; **I t. that** (*hope*) j'espère que ▮ *vi* **to t. in s.o.** avoir confiance en qn, se fier à qn; **to t. to luck** *or* **chance** se fier au hasard. ●**trusted** *a* (*friend, method etc*) éprouvé. ●**trusting** *a* confiant.

trustee [trʌs'tiː] *n* (*of school*) administrateur -trice *mf*; *Jur* fidéicommissaire *m*.

trustworthy ['trʌstwɜːðɪ] *a* digne de confiance, sûr.

truth [truːθ] *n* (*pl* **-s** [truːðz]) vérité *f*; **there's some t. in...** il y a du vrai dans.... ●**truthful** *a* (*statement etc*) véridique, vrai; (*person*) sincère. ●**truthfully** *adv* sincèrement.

try [traɪ] **1** *vt* (*attempt, sample, use*) essayer; (*s.o.'s patience etc*) mettre à l'épreuve; **to t. doing** *or* **to do** essayer de faire; **to t. one's hand at** s'essayer à; **to t. one's luck** tenter sa chance ▮ *vi* essayer (for sth d'obtenir qch); **to t. hard** faire un gros effort; **t. and come!** essaie de venir! ▮ *n* (*attempt*) & *Rugby* essai *m*; **to have a t.** essayer; **at (the) first t.** du premier coup.
2 *vt* (*person*) (*in court*) juger (**for** theft/*etc* pour vol/*etc*). ●**trying** *a* éprouvant, pénible.

try on *vt* (*clothes, shoes*) essayer ▮ **to try out**

vt (car, method, recipe etc) essayer; (person) mettre à l'essai.

tsar [zɑ:r] n tsar m.

T-shirt ['ti:ʃɜːt] n tee-shirt m, T-shirt m.

tub [tʌb] n (basin) baquet m; (bath) baignoire f; (for ice cream) Br pot m; (for flower, bush) Br bac m.

tuba ['tju:bə] n (musical instrument) tuba m.

tubby ['tʌbɪ] a (-ier, -iest) Fam grassouillet (f -ette).

tube [tju:b] n tube m; (underground railway) Br Fam métro m; (of Br tyre, Am tire) chambre f à air. ● tubing n (tubes) tubes mpl. ● tubular a tubulaire. ● tubeless a t. Br tyre or Am tire pneu m sans chambre.

tuberculosis [tju:bɜːkjʊ'ləʊsɪs] n tuberculose f.

TUC [ti:ju:'si:] n abbr (Trades Union Congress) Br = confédération f des syndicats britanniques.

tuck [tʌk] 1 vt (put) mettre; to t. away ranger; (hide) cacher; to t. in (shirt, blanket) rentrer; (person in bed) border; to t. up (sleeves) remonter. 2 n (fold in garment) rempli m. 3 vi Br Fam to t. in (eat) manger; to t. into (meal) attaquer ■ n t. shop (in school) Br boutique f à provisions.

Tuesday [Br 'tju:zdɪ, Am -deɪ] n mardi m.

tuft [tʌft] n (of hair, grass) touffe f.

tug [tʌg] vt (-gg-) (pull) tirer ■ vi tirer (at, on sur) ■ n to give sth a t. tirer (sur) qch. ● tug(boat) n remorqueur m.

tuition [tju:'ɪʃ(ə)n] n (teaching) enseignement m; (lessons) leçons fpl; (fee) frais mpl de scolarité.

tulip ['tju:lɪp] n tulipe f.

tumble ['tʌmb(ə)l] 1 vi to t. (down or over) (fall) dégringoler; (backwards) tomber à la renverse ■ n (fall) dégringolade f. 2 vi Br Sl (understand) to t. to sth réaliser qch; then I tumbled enfin j'ai réalisé or pigé. ● tumble dryer or drier n Br sèche-linge m inv.

tumbledown ['tʌmb(ə)ldaʊn] a délabré.

tumbler ['tʌmblər] n (drinking glass) gobelet m.

tummy ['tʌmɪ] n Fam ventre m; to have a t. ache avoir mal au ventre.

tumour ['tju:mər] (Am tumor) n tumeur f.

tumult ['tju:mʌlt] n tumulte m. ● tu'multuous a tumultueux.

tuna ['tju:nə] n t. (fish) thon m.

tune [tju:n] n (melody) air m; in t. (instrument) accordé; out of t. (instrument) désaccordé; to be or sing in t./out of t. chanter juste/faux; in t. with (harmony) Fig en accord avec; to the t. of £50 d'un montant de 50 livres, dans les 50 livres ■ vt to t. (up) (instrument) accorder; (engine) régler ■ vi to t. in (to) Radio TV se mettre à l'écoute (de), écouter. ● tuning n (of engine) réglage m; t. fork Mus diapason m.

tuneful ['tju:nfəl] a mélodieux.

tuner ['tju:nər] n (on radio) bouton m de réglage.

tunic ['tju:nɪk] n tunique f.

Tunisia [tju:'nɪzɪə] n Tunisie f. ● Tunisian a tunisien ■ n Tunisien, -ienne mf.

tunnel ['tʌn(ə)l] n tunnel m; (in mine) galerie f; the Channel T. le tunnel sous la Manche ■ vi (Br -ll-, Am -l-) percer un tunnel (into dans).

turban ['tɜːbən] n turban m.

turbine [Br 'tɜːbaɪn, Am 'tɜːbɪn] n turbine f.

turbulence ['tɜːbjʊləns] n (in air, social unrest) turbulences fpl.

turbulent ['tɜːbjʊlənt] a (person etc) turbulent.

tureen [Br tjʊ'ri:n, Am tə'ri:n] n (soup) t. soupière f.

turf [tɜːf] 1 n (grass) gazon m; piece of t. motte f de gazon; the t. (horseracing) le turf; t. accountant Br bookmaker m. 2 vt to t. out (get rid of) Br Fam jeter dehors.

turgid ['tɜːdʒɪd] a (style, language) ampoulé.

turkey ['tɜːkɪ] n dindon m, dinde f; (as food) dinde f.

Turkey ['tɜːkɪ] n Turquie f. ● Turk n Turc m, Turque f. ● Turkish a turc (f turque); T. bath/coffee bain m/café m turc; T. delight (Br sweet, Am candy) loukoum m ■ n (language) turc m.

turmoil ['tɜːmɔɪl] n confusion f, trouble m; in t. (country etc) en ébullition.

turn [tɜːn] n (movement, in game etc) tour m; (in road) tournant m; (of events, mind) tournure f; (feeling of illness) Br crise f; (shock) Br choc m; (theatrical act) numéro m; t. of phrase tour m or tournure f (de phrase); to take turns se relayer; in t. à tour de rôle; by turns tour à tour; in (one's) t. à son tour; it's your t. (to play) c'est à toi or (à) ton tour (de jouer); to do s.o. a good t. rendre service à qn; the t. of the century le début or la fin du siècle.

■ vt tourner; (mechanically) faire tourner; (mattress, pancake) retourner; to turn s.o./ sth into (change) changer or transformer qn/ qch en; to t. sth red/yellow rougir/jaunir qch; to t. sth on s.o. (aim) braquer qch sur qn; she has turned twenty elle a vingt ans passés; it has turned seven il est sept heures passées; it turns my stomach cela me soulève le cœur.

■ vi (of wheel, driver etc) tourner; (turn head or body) se (re)tourner (towards vers); (become) devenir; to t. red/yellow rougir/jaunir; to t. to (question, adviser etc) se tourner vers; to t. into (change) se changer or se transformer en.

turn against vt (person, one's country) se retourner contre ■ to turn around vi (of person) se retourner ■ to turn away vt (eyes) détourner (from de); (person) renvoyer ■ vi (stop facing) se détourner, détourner les yeux ■ to turn back vt (bed sheet, corner of page) replier; (person) renvoyer; (clock) reculer (to jusqu'à) ■ vi (return) retourner (sur ses pas) ■ to turn down vt (gas, radio etc) baisser; (fold down) rabattre; (refuse) refuser (qn, offre etc) ■ to turn in vt (hand in) rendre (**to** à); (*prisoner etc*) *Fam* livrer (à la police) **▮** *vi* (*go to bed*) *Fam* se coucher **▮ to turn off** *vt* (*light, radio etc*) éteindre; (*Br tap, Am faucet*) fermer; (*machine*) arrêter **▮** *vi* (*in vehicle*) tourner **▮ to turn on** *vt* (*light, radio etc*) mettre, allumer; (*Br tap, Am faucet*) ouvrir; (*machine*) mettre en marche; **to t. s.o. on** (*sexually*) *Fam* exciter qn **▮** *vi* **to t. on s.o.** (*attack*) attaquer qn **▮ to turn out** *vt* (*light*) éteindre; (*contents of box etc*) vider (**from** de); (*produce*) produire **▮** *vi* (*of crowds*) venir; (*happen*) se passer; **it turns out that** il s'avère que; **she turned out to be...** elle s'est révélée être... **▮ to turn over** *vt* (*page*) tourner **▮** *vi* (*of vehicle, person etc*) se retourner; (*of car engine*) tourner au ralenti **▮ to turn round** *vt* (*head, object*) tourner; (*vehicle*) faire faire demi-tour à **▮** *vi* (*of person*) se retourner; (*in vehicle*) faire demi-tour **▮ to turn up** *vt* (*radio, light etc*) mettre plus fort; (*collar*) remonter; (*unearth, find*) déterrer; **a turned-up nose** un nez retroussé **▮** *vi* (*arrive*) arriver; (*be found*) être retrouvé.

turncoat ['tɜːnkəʊt] *n* renégat, -at *mf*.

turner ['tɜːnər] *n* (*workman*) tourneur *m*.

turning ['tɜːnɪŋ] *n* (*street*) *Br* petite rue *f*; (*bend in road*) tournant *m*; **t. circle** *Br Aut* rayon *m* de braquage; **t. point** (*in time*) tournant *m*.

turnip ['tɜːnɪp] *n* navet *m*.

turn-off ['tɜːnɒf] *n* (*in road*) embranchement *m*. ●**turnout** *n* (*people*) assistance *f*; (*at polls*) participation *f*. ●**turnover** *n* (*sales*) *Com* chiffre *m* d'affaires; (*of stock*) *Com* rotation *f*; **staff t.** (*starting and leaving*) la rotation du personnel; **apple t.** *Br* chausson *m* (aux pommes).

turnpike ['tɜːnpaɪk] *n* *Am* autoroute *f* à péage.

turnstile ['tɜːnstaɪl] *n* (*gate*) tourniquet *m*.

turntable ['tɜːnteɪb(ə)l] *n* (*of record player*) platine *f*.

turnup ['tɜːnʌp] *n* (*on trousers*) *Br* revers *m*.

turpentine ['tɜːpəntaɪn] (*Br Fam* **turps** [tɜːps]) *n* térébenthine *f*.

turquoise ['tɜːkwɔɪz] *a* turquoise *inv*.

turret ['tʌrɪt] *n* tourelle *f*.

turtle ['tɜːt(ə)l] *n* tortue *f* de mer; (*living on land*) *Am* tortue *f*. ●**turtledove** *n* tourterelle *f*. ●**turtleneck** (*a sweater*) à col roulé **▮** *n* col *m* roulé.

tusk [tʌsk] *n* (*of elephant*) défense *f*.

tussle ['tʌs(ə)l] *n* bagarre *f*.

tutor ['tjuːtər] *n* professeur *m* particulier, répétiteur, -trice *mf*; (*in British university*) directeur, -trice *mf* d'études; (*in American university*) assistant, -ante *mf* **▮** *vt* donner des cours particuliers à. ●**tu'torial** *n* *Univ* = travaux *mpl* dirigés.

tut-tut! [tʌt'tʌt] *int* allons donc!

tuxedo [tʌk'siːdəʊ] *n* (*pl* -os) *Am* smoking *m*.

TV [tiː'viː] *n* télé *f*; **on TV** à la télé.

twaddle ['twɒd(ə)l] *n* fadaises *fpl*.

twang [twæŋ] *n* son *m* vibrant; (*nasal*) **t.** nasillement *m* **▮** *vi* (*of wire etc*) vibrer.

twee [twiː] *a* (*a fussy*) maniéré.

tweed [twiːd] *n* tweed *m*; **t. jacket/***etc* veste *f/etc* en tweed.

tweezers ['twiːzəz] *npl* pince *f* à épiler.

twelve [twelv] *a & n* douze (*m*). ●**twelfth** *a & n* douzième (*mf*).

twenty ['twentɪ] *a & n* vingt (*m*). ●**twentieth** *a & n* vingtième (*mf*).

twerp [twɜːp] *n* *Br Fam* crétin, -ine *mf*.

twice [twaɪs] *adv* deux fois; **t. as heavy/***etc* deux fois plus lourd/*etc*; **t. a month/***etc*, **t. monthly/***etc* deux fois par mois/*etc*.

twiddle ['twɪd(ə)l] *vti* **to t. (with)** sth (*pencil, knob etc*) tripoter qch; **to t. one's thumbs** se tourner les pouces.

twig [twɪg] **1** *n* (*of branch*) brindille *f*. **2** *vti* (**-gg-**) (*understand*) *Br Sl* piger.

twilight ['twaɪlaɪt] *n* crépuscule *m*.

twin [twɪn] *n* jumeau *m*, jumelle *f*; **identical t.** vrai jumeau, vraie jumelle; **t. brother** frère *m* jumeau; **t. sister** sœur *f* jumelle; **t. beds** lits *mpl* jumeaux; **t. town** ville *f* jumelée **▮** *vt* (**-nn-**) (*town*) jumeler. ●**twinning** *n* jumelage *m*.

twine [twaɪn] **1** *n* (*string*) ficelle *f*. **2** *vi* (*twist*) s'enlacer (**round** autour de).

twinge [twɪndʒ] *n* a **t.** (*of pain*) un élancement; **a t. of remorse** un pincement de remords.

twinkle ['twɪŋk(ə)l] *vi* (*of star*) scintiller; (*of eye*) pétiller **▮** *n* scintillement *m*; (*in eye*) pétillement *m*.

twirl [twɜːl] *vi* tournoyer **▮** *vt* faire tournoyer; (*moustache*) tortiller.

twist [twɪst] *vt* (*wire, arm etc*) tordre; (*roll*) enrouler (**round** autour de); (*weave together*) entortiller; (*knob*) tourner; (*truth etc*) *Fig* déformer; **to t. one's ankle** se tordre la cheville; **to t. s.o.'s arm** *Fig* forcer la main à qn; **to t. off** (*lid*) dévisser.

▮ *vi* (*wind*) s'entortiller (**round sth** autour de qch); (*of road, river*) serpenter.

▮ *n* torsion *f*; (*turn*) tour *m*; (*in rope*) entortillement *m*; (*bend in road*) tournant *m*; (*of lemon*) zeste *m*; (*in story*) *Fig* coup *m* de théâtre; (*in event*) *Fig* tournure *f*; **a road full of twists** une route qui fait des zigzags. ●**twisted** *a* (*ankle, wire, Fig mind*) tordu. ●**twister** *n* **tongue t.** mot *m* or expression *f* imprononçable.

twit [twɪt] *n* *Br Fam* idiot, -ote *mf*.

twitch [twɪtʃ] **1** *n* (*nervous*) tic *m* **▮** *vi* (*of person*) avoir un tic; (*of muscle*) se convulser. **2** *n* (*jerk*) secousse *f*.

twitter ['twɪtər] *vi* (*of bird*) pépier **▮** *n* pépiement *m*.

two [tuː] *a & n* deux (*m*). ●**two-cycle** *n* *Am* = **two-stroke**. ●**two-'faced** *a* *Fig* hypocrite. ●**two-'legged** *a* bipède. ●**two-piece** *n* (*woman's suit*) tailleur *m*; (*swimsuit*) deux-pièces *m inv*. ●**two-'seater** *n* (*car*) voiture *f* à deux places. ●**two-stroke** *n* **t.-stroke** (*engine*) *Br* deux-temps *m inv*. ●**two-way** *a* **t.-way traffic**

circulation *f* dans les deux sens; **t.-way radio** émetteur-récepteur *m*.

twofold ['tuːfəʊld] *a* double ∎ *adv* **to increase t.** doubler.

twosome ['tuːsəm] *n* couple *m*.

tycoon [taɪˈkuːn] *n* magnat *m*.

type¹ [taɪp] *n* **1** (*sort*) genre *m*, sorte *f*, type *m*; (*example*) type *m*; **blood t.** groupe *m* sanguin. **2** (*print*) caractères *mpl*; **in large t.** en gros caractères. ●**typeface** *n* (œil *m* de) caractère *m*. ●**typeset** *vt* (*pt & pp* **-set**, *pres p* **-setting**) composer. ●**typesetter** *n* compositeur, -trice *mf*.

type² [taɪp] *vti* (*write*) taper (à la machine) ∎ *vt* **to t.** in (*on computer*) entrer au clavier; **to t. out** (*letter*) taper. ●**typing** *n* dactylo(graphie) *f*; **a page of t.** une page dactylo-graphiée; **t. error** faute *f* de frappe. ●**typewriter** *n* machine *f* à écrire. ●**typewritten** *a* dactylographié. ●**typist** *n* dactylo *f*.

typhoid ['taɪfɔɪd] *n* **t.** (**fever**) typhoïde *f*.

typhoon [taɪˈfuːn] *n* (*storm*) typhon *m*.

typical ['tɪpɪk(ə)l] *a* typique (**of** de); (*customary*) habituel; **that's t.** (**of him**)! c'est bien lui! ●**typically** *adv* typiquement; (*as usual*) comme d'habitude. ●**typify** *vt* être typique de; (*symbolize*) représenter.

typo ['taɪpəʊ] *n* (*pl* **-os**) (*misprint*) *Fam* coquille *f*.

tyranny ['tɪrənɪ] *n* tyrannie *f*. ●**ty'rannical** *a* tyrannique. ●**tyrant** ['taɪərənt] *n* tyran *m*.

tyre ['taɪər] *n* *Br* pneu *m* (*pl* pneus); **t. pressure** pression *f* des pneus; **t. pressure gauge** manomètre *m*.

U

U, u [ju:] *n* U, u *m*. ●**U-turn** *n* (*in vehicle*) demi-tour *m*; (*change of policy etc*) Fig volte-face *f inv*.

ubiquitous [ju:'bɪkwɪtəs] *a* omniprésent.

udder ['ʌdər] *n* (*of cow etc*) pis *m*.

UFO [ju:ef'əʊ, 'ju:fəʊ] *n* (*pl* -Os) *abbr* (*unidentified flying object*) OVNI *m*.

ugh! [ɜ:(h)] *int* pouah!

Uganda [ju:'gændə] *n* Ouganda *m*.

ugly ['ʌglɪ]' *a* (-ier, -iest) laid, vilain. ●**ugliness** *n* laideur *f*.

UK [ju:'keɪ] *abbr* = United Kingdom.

Ukraine [ju:'kreɪn] *n* the U. l'Ukraine *f*.

ulcer ['ʌlsər] *n* ulcère *m*. ●**ulcerated** *a* ulcéré.

ulterior [ʌl'tɪərɪər] *a* u. motive arrière-pensée *f*.

ultimate ['ʌltɪmət] *a* (*final*, *last*) ultime; (*definitive*) définitif; (*basic*) fondamental; (*authority*) suprême. ●**ultimately** *adv* (*finally*) à la fin; (*fundamentally*) en fin de compte; (*subsequently*) à une date ultérieure.

ultimatum [ʌltɪ'meɪtəm] *n* ultimatum *m*; to give s.o. au u. lancer un ultimatum à qn.

ultra- ['ʌltrə] *pref* ultra-.

ultramodern [ʌltrə'mɒdən] *a* ultramoderne.

ultrasound ['ʌltrəsaʊnd] *n* (*scan*, *technique*) échographie *f*; (*vibration*) ultrason *m*; to have au u. *Fam* passer une échographie.

ultraviolet [ʌltrə'vaɪələt] *a* ultraviolet (*f* -ette).

umbilical [ʌm'bɪlɪk(ə)l] *a* u. cord cordon *m* ombilical.

umbrage ['ʌmbrɪdʒ] *n* to take u. *Lit* se froisser (at de).

umbrella [ʌm'brelə] *n* parapluie *m*; (*for sun*) parasol *m*; u. stand porte-parapluies *m inv*.

umpire ['ʌmpaɪər] *Sport n* arbitre *m* **‖** *vt* arbitrer.

umpteen [ʌmp'ti:n] *a* u. times/*etc* (*many*) *Fam* je ne sais combien de fois/*etc*. ●**umpteenth** *a Fam* énième.

un- [ʌn] *pref* in-, peu, non, sans.

UN [ju:'en] *abbr* = United Nations.

unabashed [ʌnə'bæʃt] *a* nullement déconcerté.

unabated [ʌnə'beɪtɪd] *a* to continue u. (*of rain*, *war etc*) continuer avec la même intensité.

unable [ʌn'eɪb(ə)l] *a* to be u. to do être incapable de faire; he's u. to swim il ne sait pas nager.

unabridged [ʌnə'brɪdʒd] *a* intégral.

unacceptable [ʌnək'septəb(ə)l] *a* inacceptable; it's u. that il est inacceptable que (+ sub).

unaccompanied [ʌnə'kʌmpənɪd] *a* (*person*) non accompagné; (*singing*) sans accompagnement.

unaccountable [ʌnə'kaʊntəb(ə)l] *a* inexplicable. ●**unaccountably** *adv* inexplicablement.

unaccounted [ʌnə'kaʊntɪd] *a* to be (still) u. for rester introuvable.

unaccustomed [ʌnə'kʌstəmd] *a* inaccoutumé; to be u. to sth/to doing ne pas être habitué à qch/à faire.

unadulterated [ʌnə'dʌltəreɪtɪd] *a* pur.

unaided [ʌn'eɪdɪd] *adv* (*to walk etc*) sans aide.

un-American [ʌnə'merɪk(ə)n] *a* (*disloyal*) antiaméricain.

unanimity [ju:nə'nɪmɪtɪ] *n* unanimité *f*. ●**unanimous** [ju:'nænɪməs] *a* unanime. ●**u'nanimously** *adv* à l'unanimité.

unappetizing [ʌn'æpɪtaɪzɪŋ] *a* peu appétissant.

unapproachable [ʌnə'prəʊtʃəb(ə)l] *a* (*person*) inabordable.

unarmed [ʌn'ɑ:md] *a* (*person*) non armé; u. combat combat *m* à mains nues.

unashamed [ʌnə'ʃeɪmd] *a* (*person*) sans honte; (*look*, *curiosity etc*) non dissimulé; she's u. about it elle n'en a pas honte. ●**unashamedly** [-ɪdlɪ] *adv* sans aucune honte.

unassailable [ʌnə'seɪləb(ə)l] *a* (*argument*, *reputation*) inattaquable.

unassuming [ʌnə'sju:mɪŋ] *a* modeste.

unattached [ʌnə'tætʃt] *a* (*independent*, *not married*) libre.

unattainable [ʌnə'teɪnəb(ə)l] *a* (*aim*, *goal*) inaccessible.

unattended [ʌnə'tendɪd] *adv* to leave sth/a child u. laisser qch/un enfant sans surveillance.

unattractive [ʌnə'træktɪv] *a* (*idea*, *appearance etc*) peu attrayant; (*ugly*) laid; (*character*) peu sympathique.

unauthorized [ʌn'ɔ:θəraɪzd] *a* non autorisé.

unavailable [ʌnə'veɪləb(ə)l] *a* (*person*, *funds*) qui n'est pas disponible; (*article in shop etc*) épuisé; to be u. for comment (*of politician etc*) rester injoignable.

unavoidable [ʌnə'vɔɪdəb(ə)l] *a* inévitable. ●**unavoidably** *adv* inévitablement; (*delayed*) pour une raison indépendante de sa volonté.

unaware [ʌnə'weər] *a* to be u. of sth ignorer qch; to be u. that ignorer que. ●**unawares** *adv* to catch s.o. u. prendre qn au dépourvu.

unbalanced [ʌn'bælənst] *a* (*mind*, *person*) déséquilibré.

unbearable [ʌn'beərəb(ə)l] *a* insupportable.

●**unbearably** *adv* insupportablement.
unbeatable [ʌn'biːtəb(ə)l] *a* imbattable.
●**unbeaten** *a* (*player*) invaincu; (*record*) non battu.
unbeknown(st) [ʌnbɪ'nəʊn(st)] *a* u. to s.o. à l'insu de qn.
unbelievable [ʌnbɪ'liːvəb(ə)l] *a* incroyable.
●**unbelieving** *a* incrédule.
unbend [ʌn'bend] *vi* (*pt & pp* unbent) (*relax*) se détendre. ●**unbending** *a* (*person, attitude etc*) inflexible.
unbias(s)ed [ʌn'baɪəst] *a* impartial.
unblock [ʌn'blɒk] *vt* (*sink etc*) déboucher.
unbolt [ʌn'bəʊlt] *vt* (*door*) déverrouiller.
unborn [ʌn'bɔːn] *a* u. child enfant *mf* à naître.
unbounded [ʌn'baʊndɪd] *a* (*enthusiasm, joy*) sans borne(s).
unbreakable [ʌn'breɪkəb(ə)l] *a* incassable. ●**unbroken** *a* (*intact*) intact; (*continuous*) continu; (*record*) non battu.
unbridled [ʌn'braɪd(ə)ld] *a* (*passion etc*) débridé.
unburden [ʌn'bɜːd(ə)n] *vt* to u. oneself (*reveal feelings etc*) s'épancher (**to** auprès de).
unbutton [ʌn'bʌt(ə)n] *vt* déboutonner.
uncalled-for [ʌn'kɔːldfɔːr] *a* déplacé, injustifié.
uncanny [ʌn'kænɪ] *a* (-ier, -iest) étrange, mystérieux.
unceasing [ʌn'siːsɪŋ] *a* incessant. ●**unceasingly** *adv* sans cesse.
unceremoniously [ʌnserɪ'məʊnɪəslɪ] *adv* (*to treat s.o.*) sans ménagement; (*to show s.o. out*) brusquement.
uncertain [ʌn'sɜːt(ə)n] *a* incertain (**about, of** de); it's u. whether *or* that il n'est pas certain que (+ *sub*); I'm u. whether to stay (or not) je ne sais pas très bien si je dois rester (ou pas). ●**uncertainty** *n* incertitude *f*.
unchanged [ʌn'tʃeɪndʒd] *a* inchangé. ●**unchanging** *a* immuable.
uncharitable [ʌn'tʃærɪtəb(ə)l] *a* peu charitable.
unchecked [ʌn'tʃekt] *adv* (*to spread etc*) sans que rien ne soit fait.
uncivil [ʌn'sɪv(ə)l] *a* impoli, incivil.
uncivilized [ʌn'sɪvɪlaɪzd] *a* barbare.
unclaimed [ʌn'kleɪmd] *a* (*Br luggage, Am baggage*) non réclamé.
uncle ['ʌŋk(ə)l] *n* oncle *m*.
unclear [ʌn'klɪər] *a* (*meaning*) qui n'est pas clair; (*result*) incertain; it's u. whether... on ne sait pas très bien si....
uncomfortable [ʌn'kʌmftəb(ə)l] *a* (*chair, house etc*) pas très confortable, peu confortable; (*heat, experience etc*) désagréable; (*feeling*) troublant; (*silence*) gêné; she feels or is u. (*uneasy*) elle est gênée (**about** de).
uncommitted [ʌnkə'mɪtɪd] *a* peu impliqué (**to** one's work/*etc* dans son travail/*etc*); (*politically*) non engagé.
uncommon [ʌn'kɒmən] *a* rare. ●**uncommonly** *adv* (*very*) extraordinairement; not u. (*fairly often*) assez souvent.

uncommunicative [ʌnkə'mjuːnɪkətɪv] *a* peu communicatif.
uncomplicated [ʌn'kɒmplɪkeɪtɪd] *a* simple.
uncompromising [ʌn'kɒmprəmaɪzɪŋ] *a* intransigeant.
unconcerned [ʌnkən'sɜːnd] *a* (*indifferent*) indifférent (**by,** with à); (*not anxious*) imperturbable.
unconditional [ʌnkən'dɪʃ(ə)nəl] *a* (*offer etc*) inconditionnel; (*surrender*) sans condition.
unconfirmed [ʌnkən'fɜːmd] *a* non confirmé.
uncongenial [ʌnkən'dʒiːnɪəl] *a* (*place, atmosphere etc*) peu agréable; (*person*) antipathique.
unconnected [ʌnkə'nektɪd] *a* (*facts, events etc*) sans rapport (**with** avec).
unconscious [ʌn'kɒnʃəs] *a* (*person*) sans connaissance; (*desire*) inconscient; u. of (*unaware of*) inconscient de ▮ *n* the u. *Psy* l'inconscient *m*. ●**unconsciously** *adv* inconsciemment.
uncontrollable [ʌnkən'trəʊləb(ə)l] *a* (*emotion, laughter*) irrépressible. ●**uncontrollably** *adv* (*to laugh, sob*) sans pouvoir s'arrêter.
unconventional [ʌnkən'venʃ(ə)nəl] *a* peu conventionnel; (*person*) anticonformiste.
unconvinced [ʌnkən'vɪnst] *a* to be *or* remain u. ne pas être convaincu (**of** de). ●**unconvincing** *a* peu convaincant.
uncooked [ʌn'kʊkt] *a* cru.
uncooperative [ʌnkəʊ'ɒp(ə)rətɪv] *a* peu coopératif.
uncork [ʌn'kɔːk] *vt* (*bottle*) déboucher.
uncouple [ʌn'kʌp(ə)l] *vt* (*Br railway carriage, Am railroad car etc*) dételer.
uncouth [ʌn'kuːθ] *a* grossier.
uncover [ʌn'kʌvər] *vt* (*conspiracy, saucepan etc*) découvrir.
unctuous ['ʌŋktʃʊəs] *a* (*insincere*) onctueux.
uncut [ʌn'kʌt] *a* (*film, play, version*) intégral; (*diamond*) brut.
undamaged [ʌn'dæmɪdʒd] *a* (*goods*) en bon état.
undated [ʌn'deɪtɪd] *a* (*Br cheque, Am check etc*) non daté.
undaunted [ʌn'dɔːntɪd] *a* nullement découragé.
undecided [ʌndɪ'saɪdɪd] *a* (*person*) indécis (**about** sur); I'm u. whether to do it or not je n'ai pas décidé si je le ferai ou non.
undefeated [ʌndɪ'fiːtɪd] *a* invaincu.
undeniable [ʌndɪ'naɪəb(ə)l] *a* incontestable.
under ['ʌndər] *prep* sous; (*less than*) moins de; (*according to*) selon; children u. nine les enfants de moins de *or* enfants au-dessous de neuf ans; u. the circumstances dans les circonstances; u. there là-dessous; u. it dessous; u. (the command of) s.o. sous les ordres de qn; u. (the terms of) an agreement selon un accord (**with** avec); u. age mineur; u. discussion/repair en discussion/réparation; to be u. way (*in progress*) être en cours; (*on the way*) être en route; to get u. way (*of campaign etc*) démarrer; to be u. the impression that avoir l'impression que ▮ *adv* au-

dessous.

under- [' ʌndər] *pref* sous-.

undercarriage [' ʌndəkærɪdʒ] *n (of aircraft)* train *m* d'atterrissage.

undercharge [ʌndə'tʃɑːdʒ] *vt* I **undercharged him (for it)** je ne (le) lui ai pas fait payer assez.

underclothes [' ʌndəkləuðz] *npl* sous-vêtements *mpl*.

undercoat [' ʌndəkəut] *n (of paint)* couche *f* de fond.

undercooked [ʌndə'kukt] *a* pas assez cuit.

undercover [ʌndə'kʌvər] *a (agent, operation etc)* secret.

undercurrent [' ʌndəkʌrənt] *n (in sea)* courant *m* (sous-marin); **an u. of discontent/etc** un mécontentement/etc sous-jacent.

undercut [ʌndə'kʌt] *vt (pt & pp* undercut, *pres p* undercutting*) (of competitor)* vendre moins cher que *(qn)*.

underdeveloped [ʌndədɪ'veləpt] *a (country, region)* sous-développé; *(limb etc)* pas assez développé.

underdog [' ʌndədɒg] *n (politically, socially)* opprimé, -ée *mf*; *(likely loser)* perdant, -ante *mf* probable.

underdone [ʌndə'dʌn] *a (food)* pas assez cuit; *(steak)* saignant.

underestimate [ʌndər'estɪmeɪt] *vt* sous-estimer.

underfed [ʌndə'fed] *a* sous-alimenté.

underfoot [ʌndə'fut] *adv* sous les pieds; **to trample sth u.** piétiner qch.

undergo [ʌndə'gəu] *vt (pt* underwent, *pp* undergone*)* subir.

undergraduate [ʌndə'grædʒuət] *n* étudiant, -ante *mf (de licence)*.

underground [' ʌndəgraund] *a* souterrain; *(secret)* Fig clandestin I *n (railway)* Br métro *m; (organization)* Pol résistance *f* I [ʌndə'graund] *adv* sous terre; **to go u.** *(of fugitive etc)* Fig passer dans la clandestinité.

undergrowth [' ʌndəgrəuθ] *n* sous-bois *m inv*.

underhand [ʌndə'hænd] *a (dishonest)* sournois.

underlie [ʌndə'laɪ] *vt (pt* underlay, *pp* underlain, *pres p* underlying*)* sous-tendre. ● **underlying** *a (basic)* fondamental; *(hidden)* profond.

underline [ʌndə'laɪn] *vt (word, text etc, Fig idea, fact etc)* souligner.

underling [' ʌndəlɪŋ] *n Pej* subalterne *mf*.

undermanned [ʌndə'mænd] *a (office etc)* à court de personnel.

undermine [ʌndə'maɪn] *vt (society, building, strength etc)* miner, saper.

underneath [ʌndə'niːθ] *prep* sous I *adv* (en) dessous; **the book u.** le livre d'en dessous I *n* **the u. (of)** le dessous (de).

undernourished [ʌndə'nʌrɪʃt] *a* sous-alimenté.

underpants [' ʌndəpænts] *npl (male underwear)* slip *m; (loose, long)* caleçon *m*.

underpass [' ʌndəpɑːs] *n (for pedestrians)*

passage *m* souterrain; *(for vehicles)* passage *m* inférieur.

underpay [ʌndə'peɪ] *vt* sous-payer. ● **underpaid** *a* sous-payé.

underpriced [ʌndə'praɪst] *a* **it's u.** le prix est trop bas, c'est bradé.

underprivileged [ʌndə'prɪvɪlɪdʒd] *a* défavorisé I **the u.** les défavorisés *mpl*.

underrate [ʌndə'reɪt] *vt* sous-estimer.

underscore [ʌndə'skɔːr] *vt (emphasize)* souligner *(fait etc)*.

underseal [' ʌndəsiːl] *vt (vehicle)* traiter contre la rouille.

undersecretary [ʌndə'sekrət(ə)rɪ] *n* Pol sous-secrétaire *mf*.

undershirt [' ʌndəʃɜːt] *n Am* maillot *m* de corps.

underside [' ʌndəsaɪd] *n* **the u. (of)** le dessous (de).

undersigned [' ʌndəsaɪnd] *a* soussigné; **I the u.** je soussigné(e).

undersized [ʌndə'saɪzd] *a* trop petit.

underskirt [' ʌndəskɜːt] *n* jupon *m*.

understaffed [ʌndə'stɑːft] *a* à court de personnel.

understand [ʌndə'stænd] *vti (pt & pp* understood*)* comprendre; **I u. that** *(hear)* je crois comprendre que, il paraît que; **I've been given to u. that** on m'a fait comprendre que. ● **understanding** *n (act, faculty)* compréhension *f; (agreement)* accord *m*, entente *f; (sympathy)* entente *f*; **on the u. that** à condition que (+ *sub)* I *a (person)* compréhensif. ● **understood** *a (agreed)* entendu; *(implied)* sous-entendu.

understandable [ʌndə'stændəb(ə)l] *a* compréhensible. ● **understandably** *adv* naturellement.

understatement [' ʌndəsteɪtmənt] *n* euphémisme *m*.

understudy [' ʌndəstʌdɪ] *n (actor, actress)* doublure *f*.

undertake [ʌndə'teɪk] *vt (pt* undertook, *pp* undertaken*) (task etc)* entreprendre; *(responsibility)* assumer; **to u. to do** entreprendre *or* se charger de faire. ● **undertaking** *n (task)* entreprise *f; (promise)* promesse *f;* **to give an u.** promettre (**that** que).

undertaker [' ʌndəteɪkər] *n* entrepreneur *m* de pompes funèbres.

undertone [' ʌndətəun] *n* **in an u.** à mi-voix; **an u. of** *(criticism, sadness etc)* Fig une nuance de.

undervalue [ʌndə'væljuː] *vt* sous-évaluer; **it's undervalued at ten pounds** ça vaut plus que dix livres.

underwater [ʌndə'wɔːtər] *a* sous-marin I *adv* sous l'eau.

underwear [' ʌndəweər] *n* sous-vêtements *mpl*.

underweight [ʌndə'weɪt] *a (person)* qui ne pèse pas assez; *(goods)* d'un poids insuffisant.

underworld [' ʌndəwɜːld] *n* **the u.** *(criminals)* le milieu, la pègre.

undesirable [ʌndɪ'zaɪərəb(ə)l] a peu souhaitable (**that** que (+ sub)); (person) indésirable ∎ n (person) indésirable mf.

undetected [ʌndɪ'tektɪd] a (crime etc) non découvert; **to go u.** (of crime etc) ne pas être découvert; (of person, gesture, joke etc) passer inaperçu.

undies ['ʌndɪz] npl (female underwear) Fam dessous mpl.

undignified [ʌn'dɪgnɪfaɪd] a qui manque de dignité.

undisciplined [ʌn'dɪsɪplɪnd] a indiscipliné.

undiscovered [ʌndɪ'skʌvəd] a **to remain u.** (of crime, body etc) ne pas être découvert.

undisputed [ʌndɪ'spjuːtɪd] a incontesté.

undistinguished [ʌndɪ'stɪŋgwɪʃt] a médiocre.

undisturbed [ʌndɪ'stɜːbd] a **to leave s.o. u.** ne pas déranger qn.

undivided [ʌndɪ'vaɪdɪd] a **my u. attention** toute mon attention.

undo [ʌn'duː] vt (pt **undid**, pp **undone**) défaire; (bound person) détacher; (hands) détacher, délier; (a wrong) réparer. ●**undoing** n (downfall) perte f, ruine f. ●**undone** a **to come u.** (of knot etc) se défaire; **to leave u.** (work etc) ne pas faire.

undoubted [ʌn'daʊtɪd] a indubitable. ●**undoubtedly** adv sans aucun doute, indubitablement.

undreamt-of [ʌn'dremtɒv] a insoupçonné.

undress [ʌn'dres] vi se déshabiller ∎ vt déshabiller; **to get undressed** se déshabiller.

undrinkable [ʌn'drɪŋkəb(ə)l] a imbuvable.

undue [ʌn'djuː] a excessif. ●**unduly** adv excessivement.

undulating ['ʌndjʊleɪtɪŋ] a (movement) onduleux; (countryside) vallonné.

undying [ʌn'daɪɪŋ] a (love etc) éternel.

unearned [ʌn'ɜːnd] a **u. income** rentes fpl.

unearth [ʌn'ɜːθ] vt (from ground) déterrer; (discover) Fig dénicher, déterrer.

unearthly [ʌn'ɜːθlɪ] a sinistre, mystérieux; **at an u. hour** Fam à une heure impossible.

uneasy [ʌn'iːzɪ] a (peace, situation) précaire; (silence) gêné; **to be** or **feel u.** (ill at ease) être mal à l'aise, être gêné; (worried) être inquiet.

uneatable [ʌn'iːtəb(ə)l] a (bad) immangeable; (poisonous) non comestible.

uneconomic(al) [ʌniːkə'nɒmɪk((ə)l)] a peu économique.

uneducated [ʌn'edʒʊkeɪtɪd] a (person) inculte; (accent) populaire.

unemotional [ʌnɪ'məʊʃən(ə)l] a (person, attitude) impassible; (speech) sans passion.

unemployed [ʌnɪm'plɔɪd] a au chômage, sans travail ∎ n **the u.** les chômeurs mpl. ●**unemployment** n chômage m; **u. benefit** Br allocation f de chômage.

unending [ʌn'endɪŋ] a interminable.

unenthusiastic [ʌnɪnθjuːzɪ'æstɪk] a peu enthousiaste.

unenviable [ʌn'envɪəb(ə)l] a peu enviable.

unequal [ʌn'iːkwəl] a inégal; **to be u. to** (task) ne pas être à la hauteur de. ●**unequalled** a (incomparable) inégalé.

unequivocal [ʌnɪ'kwɪvək(ə)l] a sans équivoque. ●**unequivocally** adv sans équivoque.

unerring [ʌn'ɜːrɪŋ] a infaillible.

unethical [ʌn'eθɪk(ə)l] a immoral.

uneven [ʌn'iːv(ə)n] a inégal.

uneventful [ʌnɪ'ventfəl] a (trip, life etc) sans histoires.

unexceptionable [ʌnɪk'sepʃ(ə)nəb(ə)l] a irréprochable.

unexpected [ʌnɪk'spektɪd] a inattendu. ●**unexpectedly** adv à l'improviste; (suddenly) subitement; (unusually) exceptionnellement.

unexplained [ʌnɪk'spleɪnd] a inexpliqué.

unfailing [ʌn'feɪlɪŋ] a (optimism, courage, support etc) inébranlable; (supply) inépuisable.

unfair [ʌn'feər] a injuste (**to s.o.** envers qn); (competition) déloyal. ●**unfairly** adv injustement. ●**unfairness** n injustice f.

unfaithful [ʌn'feɪθfəl] a infidèle (**to** à).

unfamiliar [ʌnfə'mɪlɪər] a inconnu, peu familier; **to be u. with sth** ne pas connaître qch.

unfashionable [ʌn'fæʃ(ə)nəb(ə)l] a (subject etc) démodé; (restaurant, district etc) peu chic inv, ringard; **it's u. to do it** il n'est pas de bon ton de faire.

unfasten [ʌn'fɑːs(ə)n] vt défaire.

unfavourable (Am **unfavorable**) [ʌn'feɪv(ə)rəb(ə)rl)] a défavorable.

unfeeling [ʌn'fiːlɪŋ] a insensible.

unfinished [ʌn'fɪnɪʃt] a inachevé; **to have some u. business** avoir une affaire à régler.

unfit [ʌn'fɪt] a (unwell) en mauvaise santé; (in bad shape) pas en forme; (unsuitable) impropre (**for sth** à qch, **to do** à faire); (unworthy) indigne (**for sth** de qch, **to do** de faire); (incapable) inapte (**for sth** à qch, **to do** à faire); **u. for human consumption** impropre à la consommation.

unflagging [ʌn'flægɪŋ] a (optimism, zeal) inlassable; (interest) soutenu.

unflappable [ʌn'flæpəb(ə)l] a Br Fam imperturbable.

unflattering [ʌn'flæt(ə)rɪŋ] a peu flatteur.

unflinching [ʌn'flɪntʃɪŋ] a (fearless) intrépide.

unfold [ʌn'fəʊld] vt déplier; (wings) déployer; (ideas, plan) Fig exposer ∎ vi (of story, view) se dérouler.

unforeseeable [ʌnfɔː'siːəb(ə)l] a imprévisible. ●**unforeseen** a imprévu.

unforgettable [ʌnfə'getəb(ə)l] a inoubliable.

unforgivable [ʌnfə'gɪvəb(ə)l] a impardonnable.

unfortunate [ʌn'fɔːtʃ(ə)nət] a malheureux; (event) fâcheux; **you were u.** tu n'as pas eu de chance. ●**unfortunately** adv malheureusement.

unfounded [ʌn'faʊndɪd] a (rumour, argument etc) sans fondement.

unfreeze [ʌn'friːz] vt (pt **unfroze**, pp **unfro-**

zen) (*funds etc*) dégeler.
unfriendly [ʌnˈfrendlɪ] *a* froid, peu aimable (to avec). ●**unfriendliness** *n* froideur *f*.
unfulfilled [ʌnfʊlˈfɪld] *a* (*desire*) insatisfait; (*plan, dream*) non réalisé; (*condition*) non rempli.
unfurl [ʌnˈfɜːl] *vt* (*flag etc*) déployer.
unfurnished [ʌnˈfɜːnɪʃt] *a* non meublé.
ungainly [ʌnˈgeɪnlɪ] *a* (*clumsy*) gauche.
unglued [ʌnˈgluːd] *a* to come u. (*confused etc*) *Am Fam* perdre les pédales, s'affoler.
ungodly [ʌnˈgɒdlɪ] *a* (*sinful*) impie; at an u. hour *Fam* à une heure impossible.
ungrammatical [ʌngrəˈmætɪk(ə)l] *a* non grammatical.
ungrateful [ʌnˈgreɪtfəl] *a* ingrat.
unguarded [ʌnˈgɑːdɪd] *a* in an u. moment dans un moment d'inattention.
unhappy [ʌnˈhæpɪ] *a* (-ier, -iest) (*sad*) malheureux, triste; (*worried*) inquiet; u. with or about sth (*not pleased*) mécontent de qch; he's u. about doing it ça le dérange de le faire. ●**unhappily** *adv* (*unfortunately*) malheureusement. ●**unhappiness** *n* tristesse *f*.
unharmed [ʌnˈhɑːmd] *a* (*person*) indemne, sain et sauf.
unhealthy [ʌnˈhelθɪ] *a* (-ier, -iest) (*person*) en mauvaise santé; (*climate, place, job*) malsain; (*lungs*) malade.
unheard-of [ʌnˈhɜːdɒv] *a* (*unprecedented*) inouï.
unheeded [ʌnˈhiːdɪd] *a* it went u. on n'en a pas tenu compte.
unhelpful [ʌnˈhelpfəl] *a* (*person*) peu serviable or obligeant; (*advice*) peu utile.
unhinge [ʌnˈhɪndʒ] *vt* (*person, mind*) déséquilibrer.
unholy [ʌnˈhəʊlɪ] *a* (-ier, -iest) impie; (*din*) *Fam* de tous les diables.
unhook [ʌnˈhʊk] *vt* (*picture, curtain*) décrocher; (*dress*) dégrafer.
unhoped-for [ʌnˈhəʊptfɔːr] *a* inespéré.
unhurried [ʌnˈhʌrɪd] *a* (*movement*) lent; (*stroll, journey*) fait sans hâte.
unhurt [ʌnˈhɜːt] *a* indemne, sain et sauf.
unhygienic [ʌnhaɪˈdʒiːnɪk] *a* pas très hygiénique.
unicorn [ˈjuːnɪkɔːn] *n* licorne *f*.
unidentified [ʌnaɪˈdentɪfaɪd] *a* u. flying object objet *m* volant non identifié.
uniform [ˈjuːnɪfɔːm] **1** *n* uniforme *m*. **2** *a* (*regular*) uniforme; (*temperature*) constant. ●**uniformed** *a* (*police officer etc*) en uniforme. ●**uni'formity** *n* uniformité *f*. ●**uniformly** *adv* uniformément.
unify [ˈjuːnɪfaɪ] *vt* unifier. ●**unification** [-ɪˈkeɪʃ(ə)n] *n* unification *f*.
unilateral [juːnɪˈlæt(ə)rəl] *a* unilatéral.
unimaginable [ʌnɪˈmædʒɪnəb(ə)l] *a* inimaginable. ●**unimaginative** *a* (*person, plan etc*) qui manque d'imagination.
unimpaired [ʌnɪmˈpeəd] *a* intact.
unimportant [ʌnɪmˈpɔːtənt] *a* peu important.
uninformative [ʌnɪnˈfɔːmətɪv] *a* peu in-

structif.
uninhabitable [ʌnɪnˈhæbɪtəb(ə)l] *a* inhabitable. ●**uninhabited** *a* inhabité.
uninhibited [ʌnɪnˈhɪbɪtɪd] *a* (*person*) sans complexes.
uninitiated [ʌnɪˈnɪʃɪeɪtɪd] *n* the u. les profanes *mpl*, les non-initiés.
uninjured [ʌnˈɪndʒəd] *a* indemne **I** *n* the u. les personnes *fpl* indemnes.
uninspiring [ʌnɪnˈspaɪərɪŋ] *a* (*subject etc*) pas très inspirant.
unintelligible [ʌnɪnˈtelɪdʒəb(ə)l] *a* inintelligible.
unintentional [ʌnɪnˈtenʃ(ə)nəl] *a* involontaire.
uninterested [ʌnˈɪntrɪstɪd] *a* indifférent (in à). ●**uninteresting** *a* (*book etc*) peu intéressant, inintéressant; (*person*) fastidieux.
uninterrupted [ʌnɪntəˈrʌptɪd] *a* ininterrompu.
uninvited [ʌnɪnˈvaɪtɪd] *adv* (*to arrive*) sans invitation. ●**uninviting** *a* peu attrayant.
union [ˈjuːnɪən] *n* union *f*; (*Br trade or Am labor union*) syndicat *m* **I** *a* syndical; (*Br trade or Am labor*) u. member syndiqué, -ée *mf*; the U. Jack le drapeau britannique. ●**unionist** *n* *Br* trade u., *Am* labor u. (*union member*) syndiqué, -ée *mf*; (*official*) syndicaliste *mf*. ●**unionize** *vt* syndiquer.
unique [juːˈniːk] *a* unique. ●**uniquely** *adv* exceptionnellement.
unisex [ˈjuːnɪseks] *a* (*clothes etc*) unisexe.
unison [ˈjuːnɪs(ə)n] *n* in u. à l'unisson (with de).
unit [ˈjuːnɪt] *n* unité *f*; (*of furniture etc*) élément *m*; (*system*) bloc *m*; (*group, team*) groupe *m*; psychiatric/heart u. service *m* de psychiatrie/cardiologie; research u. centre *m* de recherche; u. trust *Br Fin* fonds *m* commun de placement.
unite [juːˈnaɪt] *vt* unir; (*country, party*) unifier; United Kingdom Royaume-Uni *m*; United Nations (Organisation *f* des) Nations unies *fpl*; United States (of America) États-Unis *mpl* (d'Amérique) **I** *vi* (*of students etc*) s'unir.
unity [ˈjuːnɪtɪ] *n* (*cohesion*) unité *f*; (*harmony*) *Fig* harmonie *f*.
universal [juːnɪˈvɜːs(ə)l] *a* universel. ●**universally** *adv* universellement.
universe [ˈjuːnɪvɜːs] *n* univers *m*.
university [juːnɪˈvɜːsɪtɪ] *n* université *f*; to go to u. aller à l'université; at u. *Br* à l'université **I** *a* (*teaching, town, restaurant etc*) universitaire; (*student, teacher*) d'université.
unjust [ʌnˈdʒʌst] *a* injuste.
unjustified [ʌnˈdʒʌstɪfaɪd] *a* injustifié.
unkempt [ʌnˈkempt] *a* (*appearance*) négligé; (*hair*) mal peigné.
unkind [ʌnˈkaɪnd] *a* peu gentil (to s.o. avec qn); (*nasty*) méchant (to s.o. avec qn). ●**unkindly** *adv* méchamment.
unknowingly [ʌnˈnəʊɪŋlɪ] *adv* inconsciemment.

unknown [ʌnˈnəʊn] *a* inconnu; **u. to me, he had left** il était parti, ce que j'ignorais ∎ *n* (*person*) inconnu, -ue *mf*; **the u.** Phil l'inconnu *m*; **u. (quantity)** *Math & Fig* inconnue *f*.

unlawful [ʌnˈlɔːfəl] *a* illégal.

unleaded [ʌnˈledɪd] *a* (*Br petrol, Am gasoline*) sans plomb.

unleash [ʌnˈliːʃ] *vt* (*force etc*) déchaîner.

unless [ʌnˈles] *conj* à moins que (+ *sub*); **u. she comes** à moins qu'elle ne vienne; **u. you work harder, you'll fail** à moins de travailler plus dur, vous échouerez.

unlicensed [ʌnˈlaɪsənst] *a* **u. premises** *Br* établissement *m* sans licence de débit de boissons.

unlike [ʌnˈlaɪk] *a* différent ∎ *prep* **u. me, she...** à la différence de moi *or* contrairement à moi, elle...; **he's (very) u. his father** il n'est pas (du tout) comme son père; **that's u. him** ça ne lui ressemble pas.

unlikely [ʌnˈlaɪklɪ] *a* peu probable, improbable; (*unbelievable*) incroyable; (*implausible*) invraisemblable; **she's u. to win** il est peu probable qu'elle gagne. ● **unlikelihood** *n* improbabilité *f*.

unlimited [ʌnˈlɪmɪtɪd] *a* illimité.

unlisted [ʌnˈlɪstɪd] *a* (*phone number*) *Am* sur la liste rouge, qui ne figure pas à l'annuaire.

unload [ʌnˈləʊd] *vt* décharger.

unlock [ʌnˈlɒk] *vt* ouvrir (*avec une clef*).

unlucky [ʌnˈlʌkɪ] *a* (**-ier, -iest**) (*person*) malchanceux; (*number, colour etc*) qui porte malheur; **you're u.** tu n'as pas de chance. ● **unluckily** *adv* malheureusement.

unmade [ʌnˈmeɪd] *a* (*bed*) défait.

unmanageable [ʌnˈmænɪdʒəb(ə)l] *a* (*child*) difficile; (*hair*) difficile à coiffer; (*package, large book, size etc*) peu maniable.

unmanned [ʌnˈmænd] *a* (*spacecraft*) inhabité; (*ship*) sans équipage.

unmarked [ʌnˈmɑːkt] *a* (*not blemished*) sans marque; **u. police car** *Br* voiture *f* banalisée.

unmarried [ʌnˈmærɪd] *a* célibataire.

unmask [ʌnˈmɑːsk] *vt* démasquer.

unmentionable [ʌnˈmenʃ(ə)nəb(ə)l] *a* dont il ne faut pas parler; (*unpleasant*) innommable.

unmercifully [ʌnˈmɜːsɪf(ə)lɪ] *adv* sans pitié.

unmistakable [ʌnmɪˈsteɪkəb(ə)l] *a* (*obvious*) indubitable; (*face, voice etc*) facilement reconnaissable.

unmitigated [ʌnˈmɪtɪgeɪtɪd] *a* (*disaster*) absolu; (*folly*) pur.

unmoved [ʌnˈmuːvd] *a* **to be u.** (*feel no emotion*) être impassible (**by** devant), ne pas être ému (**by** par); (*be unconcerned*) être indifférent (**by** à).

unnamed [ʌnˈneɪmd] *a* (*person*) anonyme.

unnatural [ʌnˈnætʃ(ə)rəl] *a* (*not normal*) pas naturel; (*crime*) contre nature; (*affected*) qui manque de naturel. ● **unnaturally** *adv* **not u.** naturellement.

unnecessary [ʌnˈnesəs(ə)rɪ] *a* inutile;

(*superfluous*) superflu.

unnerve [ʌnˈnɜːv] *vt* déconcerter, désarçonner.

unnoticed [ʌnˈnəʊtɪst] *a* **to go u.** passer inaperçu.

unobstructed [ʌnəbˈstrʌktɪd] *a* (*road, view*) dégagé.

unobtainable [ʌnəbˈteɪnəb(ə)l] *a* impossible à obtenir.

unobtrusive [ʌnəbˈtruːsɪv] *a* discret.

unoccupied [ʌnˈɒkjʊpaɪd] *a* (*house, person*) inoccupé; (*seat*) libre.

unofficial [ʌnəˈfɪʃ(ə)l] *a* officieux; (*visit*) privé; (*strike*) sauvage. ● **unofficially** *adv* à titre officieux.

unorthodox [ʌnˈɔːθədɒks] *a* peu orthodoxe.

unpack [ʌnˈpæk] *vt* (*suitcase*) défaire; (*goods, belongings, contents*) déballer; **to u. a comb/etc from** sortir un peigne/etc de ∎ *vi* défaire sa valise; (*take out goods*) déballer.

unpaid [ʌnˈpeɪd] *a* (*bill, sum*) impayé; (*work, worker*) bénévole; (*leave*) non payé.

unpalatable [ʌnˈpælətəb(ə)l] *a* désagréable, déplaisant.

unparalleled [ʌnˈpærəleld] *a* sans égal.

unperturbed [ʌnpəˈtɜːbd] *a* nullement déconcerté.

unplanned [ʌnˈplænd] *a* (*visit, baby etc*) imprévu.

unpleasant [ʌnˈplezənt] *a* désagréable (**to s.o.** avec qn). ● **unpleasantness** *n* caractère *m* désagréable (**of** de); (*quarrel*) petite querelle *f*.

unplug [ʌnˈplʌg] *vt* (**-gg-**) (*appliance etc*) débrancher; (*unblock*) déboucher.

unpopular [ʌnˈpɒpjʊlər] *a* peu populaire, impopulaire; **to be u. with s.o.** ne pas plaire à qn.

unprecedented [ʌnˈpresɪdentɪd] *a* sans précédent.

unpredictable [ʌnprɪˈdɪktəb(ə)l] *a* imprévisible; (*weather*) indécis.

unprepared [ʌnprɪˈpeəd] *a* (*meal, room etc*) non préparé; (*speech*) improvisé; **to be u. for sth** (*not expect*) ne pas s'attendre à qch.

unprepossessing [ʌnpriːpəˈzesɪŋ] *a* peu avenant.

unpretentious [ʌnprɪˈtenʃəs] *a* sans prétention.

unprincipled [ʌnˈprɪnsɪp(ə)ld] *a* sans scrupules.

unprofessional [ʌnprəˈfeʃ(ə)nəl] *a* (*person, behaviour*) pas très professionnel.

unprovoked [ʌnprəˈvəʊkt] *a* **u. attack** agression *f* injustifiée.

unpublished [ʌnˈpʌblɪʃt] *a* (*text, writer*) inédit.

unpunished [ʌnˈpʌnɪʃt] *a* **to go u.** rester impuni.

unqualified [ʌnˈkwɒlɪfaɪd] *a* **1** (*teacher etc*) non diplômé; **he's u. to do it** il n'est pas qualifié pour faire. **2** (*support*) sans réserve; (*success, rogue, liar*) parfait.

unquestionable [ʌnˈkwestʃ(ə)nəb(ə)l] *a* incontestable. ● **unquestionably** *adv* incontestablement.

unravel [ʌnˈræv(ə)l] vt (Br -ll-, Am -l-) (threads etc) démêler; (mystery) Fig éclaircir.

unreal [ʌnˈrɪəl] a irréel. ●**unrea'listic** a peu réaliste.

unreasonable [ʌnˈriːz(ə)nəb(ə)l] a (person, attitude etc) qui n'est pas raisonnable; (price) excessif; **it's u. to do** ce n'est pas raisonnable de faire.

unrecognizable [ʌnrekəgˈnaɪzəb(ə)l] a méconnaissable.

unrelated [ʌnrɪˈleɪtɪd] a (facts etc) sans rapport (**to** avec); **we're u.** il n'y a aucun lien de parenté entre nous.

unrelenting [ʌnrɪˈlentɪŋ] a (person) implacable; (effort) acharné; **the u. pace of work** le rythme soutenu du travail.

unreliable [ʌnrɪˈlaɪəb(ə)l] a (person) peu sûr, peu sérieux; (machine) peu fiable.

unrelieved [ʌnrɪˈliːvd] a (constant) constant; (colour) uniforme; (monotony) absolu.

unremarkable [ʌnrɪˈmɑːkəb(ə)l] a médiocre.

unrepeatable [ʌnrɪˈpiːtəb(ə)l] a (offer) unique.

unrepentant [ʌnrɪˈpentənt] a impénitent; **the murderer was u.** le meurtrier n'a montré aucun remords.

unreservedly [ʌnrɪˈzɜːvɪdlɪ] adv sans réserve.

unrest [ʌnˈrest] n agitation f, troubles mpl.

unrestricted [ʌnrɪˈstrɪktɪd] a illimité; **u. access** libre accès m (**to** à).

unrewarding [ʌnrɪˈwɔːdɪŋ] a ingrat; (financially) peu rémunérateur.

unripe [ʌnˈraɪp] a (fruit) vert, pas mûr.

unrivalled [ʌnˈraɪvəld] a (Am **unrivaled**) a hors pair.

unroll [ʌnˈrəʊl] vt dérouler ▮ vi se dérouler.

unruffled [ʌnˈrʌf(ə)ld] a (person) calme.

unruly [ʌnˈruːlɪ] a (-ier, -iest) indiscipliné.

unsafe [ʌnˈseɪf] a (place, machine etc) dangereux; (person) en danger; (conviction) peu solide juridiquement; **u. sex** rapports mpl sexuels non protégés.

unsaid [ʌnˈsed] a **to leave sth u.** passer qch sous silence.

unsaleable [ʌnˈseɪləb(ə)l] a invendable.

unsatisfactory [ʌnsætɪsˈfækt(ə)rɪ] a peu satisfaisant. ●**un'satisfied** a insatisfait; **u. with** peu satisfait de.

unsavoury [ʌnˈseɪv(ə)rɪ] a (Am **unsavory**) a (person, place etc) répugnant.

unscathed [ʌnˈskeɪðd] a indemne.

unscheduled [Br ʌnˈʃedjuːld, Am ʌnˈskedʒʊld] a **u. stop** (on train, at place etc) arrêt m non prévu.

unscrew [ʌnˈskruː] vt dévisser.

unscrupulous [ʌnˈskruːpjʊləs] a (person, act) peu scrupuleux.

unseemly [ʌnˈsiːmlɪ] a inconvenant.

unseen [ʌnˈsiːn] **1** a (unnoticed) inaperçu. **2** n (translation) Br Sch Univ version f.

unselfish [ʌnˈselfɪʃ] a (person, motive etc) désintéressé.

unsettle [ʌnˈset(ə)l] vt (person) troubler. ●**unsettled** a (weather, situation) instable; (in one's mind) troublé; (in a job) mal à l'aise.

unshakeable [ʌnˈʃeɪkəb(ə)l] a (person, faith etc) inébranlable.

unshaven [ʌnˈʃeɪv(ə)n] a pas rasé.

unsightly [ʌnˈsaɪtlɪ] a laid, disgracieux.

unskilled [ʌnˈskɪld] a inexpert; (work) de manœuvre; **u. worker** ouvrier, -ière mf non qualifié(e), manœuvre m.

unsociable [ʌnˈsəʊʃəb(ə)l] a peu sociable.

unsocial [ʌnˈsəʊʃəl] a **to work u. hours** travailler en dehors des heures de bureau.

unsolved [ʌnˈsɒlvd] a (problem) non résolu; (mystery) inexpliqué; (crime) dont l'auteur n'est pas connu.

unsophisticated [ʌnsəˈfɪstɪkeɪtɪd] a simple.

unsound [ʌnˈsaʊnd] a (construction etc) peu solide; (method) peu sûr; (decision) peu judicieux; **he is of u. mind** il n'a pas toute sa raison.

unspeakable [ʌnˈspiːkəb(ə)l] a (horrible) innommable.

unspecified [ʌnˈspesɪfaɪd] a indéterminé.

unsporting [ʌnˈspɔːtɪŋ] a déloyal.

unstable [ʌnˈsteɪb(ə)l] a instable.

unsteady [ʌnˈstedɪ] a (hand, voice, step etc) mal assuré; (table, ladder etc) instable. ●**unsteadily** adv (to walk) d'un pas mal assuré.

unstinting [ʌnˈstɪntɪŋ] a (generosity) sans bornes; (praise) sans réserve.

unstoppable [ʌnˈstɒpəb(ə)l] a qu'on ne peut (pas) arrêter.

unstuck [ʌnˈstʌk] a **to come u.** (of stamp etc) se décoller; (fail) (of person) Br Fam se planter.

unsuccessful [ʌnsəkˈsesfəl] a (attempt etc) vain, infructueux; (outcome, candidate) malheureux; (application) non retenu; **to be u.** ne pas réussir (**in doing** à faire); (of book, film, artist etc) ne pas avoir de succès. ●**unsuccessfully** adv en vain, sans succès.

unsuitable [ʌnˈsuːtəb(ə)l] a qui ne convient pas (**for** à); (example) peu approprié; (manners, clothes) peu convenable. ●**unsuited** a **u. to** (job, activity) peu fait pour; **they're u.** (**to each other**) ils ne sont pas compatibles.

unsupervised [ʌnˈsuːpəvaɪzd] adv (to play etc) sans surveillance.

unsure [ʌnˈʃʊər] a incertain (**of, about** de).

unsuspecting [ʌnsəˈspektɪŋ] a qui ne se doute de rien.

unswerving [ʌnˈswɜːvɪŋ] a (loyalty etc) inébranlable.

unsympathetic [ʌnsɪmpəˈθetɪk] a incompréhensif; **u. to** indifférent à.

untangle [ʌnˈtæŋ(ə)l] vt (rope, hair etc) démêler.

untapped [ʌnˈtæpt] a (resources) inexploité.

untenable [ʌnˈtenəb(ə)l] a (position, argument) indéfendable.

unthinkable [ʌnˈθɪŋkəb(ə)l] a impensable, inconcevable; **it's u. that** c'est impensable or inconcevable que (+ sub).

untidy [ʌn'taɪdɪ] a (-ier, -iest) (clothes, hair) peu soigné; (room) en désordre; (person) (unmethodical) désordonné; (in appearance) peu soigné. ●**untidily** adv sans soin.

untie [ʌn'taɪ] vt (person, hands) détacher; (knot, parcel) défaire.

until [ʌn'tɪl] prep jusqu'à; **u. then** jusque-là; **I didn't come u. Monday** (in the past) je ne suis venu que lundi; **not u. tomorrow**/etc (in the future) pas avant demain/etc ‖ conj jusqu'à ce que (+ sub); **u. she comes** jusqu'à ce qu'elle vienne, en attendant qu'elle vienne; **do nothing u. I come** (before) ne fais rien avant que j'arrive.

untimely [ʌn'taɪmlɪ] a (moment, question etc) inopportun; (death) prématuré.

untiring [ʌn'taɪərɪŋ] a infatigable.

untold [ʌn'təʊld] a (wealth, quantity etc) incalculable.

untoward [ʌntə'wɔːd] a fâcheux, malencontreux.

untranslatable [ʌntræns'leɪtəb(ə)l] a intraduisible.

untroubled [ʌn'trʌb(ə)ld] a (calm) calme.

untrue [ʌn'truː] a faux (f fausse). ●**untruth** n contre-vérité f. ●**untruthful** a (person) menteur; (statement) mensonger.

unusable [ʌn'juːzəb(ə)l] a inutilisable.

unused 1 [ʌn'juːzd] a (new) neuf (f neuve); (not in use) inutilisé. **2** [ʌn'juːst] a **u. to sth/to doing** peu habitué à qch/à faire.

unusual [ʌn'juːʒʊəl] a exceptionnel, rare; (strange) étrange. ●**unusually** adv exceptionnellement.

unveil [ʌn'veɪl] vt dévoiler. ●**unveiling** n (ceremony) inauguration f.

unwanted [ʌn'wɒntɪd] a (useless) dont on n'a pas besoin, superflu; (child) non désiré.

unwarranted [ʌn'wɒrəntɪd] a injustifié.

unwavering [ʌn'weɪvərɪŋ] a (belief etc) inébranlable.

unwelcome [ʌn'welkəm] a (news, fact) fâcheux; (gift, visit) inopportun; (person) importun.

unwell [ʌn'wel] a indisposé.

unwieldy [ʌn'wiːldɪ] a (package etc) encombrant.

unwilling [ʌn'wɪlɪŋ] a **he's u. to do** il ne veut pas faire, il est peu disposé à faire. ●**unwillingly** adv à contrecœur.

unwind [ʌn'waɪnd] **1** vt (pt & pp unwound) (thread etc) dérouler ‖ vi se dérouler. **2** vi (relax) Fam décompresser.

unwise [ʌn'waɪz] a imprudent. ●**unwisely** adv imprudemment.

unwitting [ʌn'wɪtɪŋ] a involontaire. ●**unwittingly** adv involontairement.

unworkable [ʌn'wɜːkəb(ə)l] a (idea etc) impraticable.

unworthy [ʌn'wɜːðɪ] a indigne (of de).

unwrap [ʌn'ræp] vt (-pp-) ouvrir, défaire.

unwritten [ʌn'rɪt(ə)n] a (agreement) tacite, verbal.

unyielding [ʌn'jiːldɪŋ] a (person) inflexible.

unzip [ʌn'zɪp] vt (-pp-) ouvrir (la fermeture éclair® de).

up [ʌp] adv en haut; (in the air) en l'air; (of sun, hand) levé; (out of bed) levé, debout; (of building) construit; (finished) fini; **to come or go up** monter; **the road is u.** Br la route est en travaux; **prices are up** les prix ont augmenté (by de); **the level is up** (of river etc) le niveau a monté (by de); **up there** là-haut; **up above** au-dessus; **up on the roof** sur le toit; **further or higher up** plus haut; **up to** (as far as) jusqu'à; (task) Fig à la hauteur de; **to be up to doing** (able) être à même de faire; (in a position to) être en mesure de faire; **it's up to you to do it** c'est à toi de le faire; **that's or it's up to you** ça dépend de toi; **where are you up to?** (in book etc) où en es-tu?; **what are you up to?** Fam que fais-tu?; **what's up?** (what's the matter?) Fam qu'est-ce qu'il y a?; **time's up** c'est l'heure; **halfway up** (on hill etc) à mi-chemin; **to walk up and down** marcher de long en large; **to be well up in** (versed in) Fam s'y connaître en; **to be up against** (confront) être confronté à; **up** with the **workers**/etc! Fam vive(nt) les travailleurs/etc!

‖ prep (a hill) en haut de; (a tree) dans; (a ladder) sur; **to go up** (hill, stairs) monter; **to live up the street** habiter plus loin dans la rue; **halfway up the hill** à mi-côte.

‖ npl **to have ups and downs** avoir des hauts et des bas.

‖ vt (-pp-) (increase) Fam augmenter.

up-and-coming [ʌpənd'kʌmɪŋ] a plein d'avenir. ●**upbeat** a (optimistic, cheerful) Fam optimiste. ●**upbringing** n éducation f. ●**upcoming** a Am imminent. ●**up'date** vt mettre à jour. ●**up'grade** vt (job) revaloriser; (person) promouvoir. ●**up'hill 1** adv **to go u.** monter. **2** [ʌphɪl] a (struggle, task) pénible. ●**up'hold** vt (pt & pp upheld) maintenir. ●**upkeep** n entretien m. ●**uplift** [ʌp'lɪft] vt élever ‖ [ʌplɪft] n élévation f spirituelle. ●**upmarket** a Br (car, furniture etc) haut de gamme; (neighbourhood, accent) très chic inv; (person, crowd) BCBG inv. ●**upright 1** a & adv (straight) droit ‖ n (post) montant m. **2** a (honest) droit. ●**uprising** n insurrection f. ●**up'root** vt (plant, person) déraciner. ●**upside 'down** adv à l'envers; **to turn u. down** (room) tout chambouler dans; (plans etc) Fig chambouler. ●**upstairs** [ʌp'steəz] adv en haut; **to go u.** monter (l'escalier) ‖ [ʌpsteəz] a (people, room) du dessus. ●**up'stream** adv en amont. ●**upsurge** n (of interest) recrudescence f; (of anger) accès m. ●**uptake** n **to be quick on the u.** comprendre vite. ●**up'tight** a Fam (tense) crispé; (angry) en colère. ●**up-to-'date** a moderne; (information) à jour; (well-informed) au courant (on de). ●**upturn** n (improvement) amélioration f (in de); (rise) hausse f (in de). ●**up'turned** a (nose) retroussé. ●**upward** a (movement) ascendant; (path) qui monte; (trend) à la hausse. ●**upwards** adv vers le haut; **from**

five francs u. à partir de cinq francs; **u. of
fifty** cinquante et plus.

upheaval [ʌp'hiːv(ə)l] *n* bouleversement *m*.

upholster [ʌp'həʊlstər] *vt* (*pad*) rembourrer;
(*cover*) recouvrir. ●**upholsterer** *n* tapissier
m. ●**upholstery** *n* (*padding*) rembourrage
m; (*covering*) revêtement *m*; (*in car*) garniture *f*.

upon [ə'pɒn] *prep* sur.

upper ['ʌpər] **1** *a* supérieur; **u. class** aristocratie *f*; **to have/get the u. hand** avoir/
prendre le dessus; **u. circle** *Br Theatre* deuxième balcon *m*. **2** *n* (*of shoe*) dessus *m*,
empeigne *f*. ●**upper-'class** *a* aristocratique.
●**uppermost** *a* (*highest*) le plus haut; **to be u.**
(*on top*) être en dessus; (*in importance*) être
de la plus haute importance.

uppity ['ʌpɪtɪ] *a Fam* arrogant.

uproar ['ʌprɔːr] *n* vacarme *m*, tapage *m*.

upset [ʌp'set] *vt* (*pt & pp* upset, *pres p*
upsetting) (*knock over, spill*) renverser;
(*plans, stomach, routine etc*) déranger; **to u.
s.o.** (*make sad*) faire de la peine à qn, peiner qn; (*offend*) vexer qn; (*aggravate*)
exaspérer qn ▌*a* peiné; (*offended*) vexé; (*ag-
gravated*) exaspéré; **to have an u. stomach**
avoir l'estomac dérangé ▌ ['ʌpset] *n* (*in plans
etc*) dérangement *m* (in de); (*grief*) peine *f*;
to have a stomach u. avoir l'estomac dérangé.

upshot ['ʌpʃɒt] *n* résultat *m*.

upstart ['ʌpstɑːt] *n Pej* parvenu, -ue *mf*.

upstate [ʌp'steɪt] *a Am* du nord (*d'un État*);
u. New York le nord de l'État de New York
▌ *adv* **to go u.** aller vers le nord (*d'un État*).

uranium [jʊ'reɪnɪəm] *n* uranium *m*.

urban ['ɜːbən] *a* urbain.

urbane [ɜː'beɪn] *a* courtois, urbain.

urchin ['ɜːtʃɪn] *n* polisson, -onne *mf*.

urge [ɜːdʒ] *vt* **to u. s.o. to do** (*advise*) conseiller vivement à qn de faire; **to u. on**
(*person, team etc*) encourager ▌ *n* forte envie
f, besoin *m*.

urgency ['ɜːdʒənsɪ] *n* urgence *f*; (*of tone, request etc*) insistance *f*. ●**urgent** *a* urgent,
pressant; (*tone*) insistant; (*letter*) urgent.
●**urgently** *adv* d'urgence; (*insistently*) avec
insistance.

urinal [jʊ'raɪn(ə)l] *n* urinoir *m*.

urine ['jʊ(ə)rɪn] *n* urine *f*. ●**urinate** *vi* uriner.

urn [ɜːn] *n* urne *f*; (*for coffee or tea*) fontaine
f.

Uruguay ['jʊərəgwaɪ] *n* Uruguay *m*.

us [əs, *stressed* ʌs] *pron* nous; **(to) us** (*indirect*) nous; **she sees us** elle nous voit; **he gives
(to) us** il nous donne; **with us** avec nous; **all
of us** nous tous; **let's** *or* **let us eat!** mangeons!

US [juː'es] *abbr* = United States.

USA [juːes'eɪ] *abbr* = United States of America.

usage ['juːsɪdʒ] *n* (*custom*) & *Ling* usage *m*.

use [juːs] *n* emploi *m*, usage *m*; (*way of
using*) emploi *m*, utilisation *f* (*d'une machine
etc*); (*usefulness*) utilité *f*; **to have the u. of**

avoir l'usage de; **to make u. of** se servir de;
in u. en usage; **not in u., out of u.** hors
d'usage; **ready for u.** prêt à l'emploi; **to be
of u.** être utile, servir; **it's no u. crying/etc** ça
ne sert à rien de pleurer/etc; **what's the u. of
worrying/etc?** à quoi bon s'inquiéter/etc?, à
quoi ça sert de s'inquiéter/etc?; **I have no u.
for it** je n'en ai pas l'usage, qu'est-ce que je
ferais de ça?; **he's no u.** (*hopeless*) il est nul.
▌ [juːz] *vt* se servir de, utiliser, employer (as
comme; to do, for doing pour faire); **it's
used to do** *or* **for doing** ça sert à; **it's
used as** ça sert de; **I u. it to clean** je m'en
sers pour nettoyer, ça me sert à nettoyer; **to
u. (up)** (*fuel etc*) consommer; (*supplies*)
épuiser; (*money*) dépenser. ●**use-by date** *n*
(*on product*) date *f* limite d'utilisation.

used 1 [juːzd] *a* (*secondhand*) d'occasion;
(*stamp*) oblitéré. **2** [juːst] *v aux* **I u. to sing/
etc** avant, je chantais/etc; **she u. to jog every
Sunday** elle faisait du jogging ` tous les di-
manches ▌ *a* **to be u. to sth/to doing**
(*accustomed*) être habitué à qch/à faire; **to
get u. to sth/s.o.** s'habituer à qch/qn.

useful ['juːsfəl] *a* utile (to à); **to come in u.**
être utile; **to make oneself u.** se rendre utile.
●**usefulness** *n* utilité *f*. ●**useless** *a* inutile;
(*unusable*) inutilisable; (*person*) nul, incompétent.

user ['juːzər] *n* (*of road, train, telephone etc*)
usager *m*; (*of machine, dictionary*) utilisateur, -trice *mf*. ●**user-friendly** *a Comptr* convivial.

usher ['ʌʃər] *n* (*in church or theatre*) placeur
m; (*in law court*) huissier *m* ▌ *vt* **to u. in**
faire entrer (qn); (*period etc*) *Fig* inaugurer.
●**ushe'rette** *n* (*in Br cinema, Am movie
theater etc*) ouvreuse *f*.

USSR [juːeses'ɑːr] *n abbr* (Union of Soviet
Socialist Republics) (*former State*) URSS *f*.

usual ['juːʒʊəl] *a* habituel, normal; **as u.**
comme d'habitude; **it's her u. practice** c'est
son habitude ▌ *n* **the u.** (*food, excuse etc*)
Fam la même chose que d'habitude. ●**usually** *adv* d'habitude.

usurer ['juːʒərər] *n* usurier, -ière *mf*.

usurp [juː'zɜːp] *vt* usurper.

utensil [juː'tens(ə)l] *n* ustensile *m*; **kitchen u.**
ustensile de cuisine.

uterus ['juːt(ə)rəs] *n Anat* utérus *m*.

utilitarian [juːtɪlɪ'teərɪən] *a* utilitaire.

utility [juː'tɪlətɪ] *n* **(public) u.** service *m* public; **u. room** pièce *f* servant de buanderie et
de débarras; **u. software** *Comptr* utilitaire *m*;
u. vehicle véhicule *m* utilitaire.

utilize ['juːtɪlaɪz] *vt* utiliser. ●**utilization** [-
'zeɪʃ(ə)n] *n* utilisation *f*.

utmost ['ʌtməʊst] *a* **the u. ease/etc** (*greatest*)
la plus grande facilité/etc; **the u. danger/
limit/etc** (*extreme*) un danger/une limite/etc
extrême ▌ *n* **to do one's u.** faire tout son
possible (**to do** pour faire).

utopia [juː'təʊpɪə] *n* (*perfect place*) utopie *f*.
●**utopian** *a* utopique.

utter ['ʌtər] **1** *a* complet, total; (*folly, lie*)

pur; (*idiot, scoundrel, liar*) parfait; **it's u. nonsense** c'est complètement absurde. **2** *vt* (*cry, sigh*) pousser; (*word*) dire; (*threat*) proférer. ●**utterance** *n* (*remark etc*) déclaration

f; *Ling* énoncé *m*; **to give u. to** exprimer. ●**utterly** *adv* complètement.

U-turn ['juːtɜːn] *n* (*in vehicle*) demi-tour *m*; (*change of policy etc*) *Fig* volte-face *f inv*.

V

V, v [viː] *n* V, v *m*. ● **V.-neck** *a* (*sweater etc*) à col en V ‖ *n* col *m* en V.

vacant ['veɪkənt] *a* (*room, seat*) libre; (*post*) vacant; (*look*) vague, dans le vide; **'situations v.'** (*in newspaper*) *Br* 'offres *fpl* d'emploi'. ● **vacancy** *n* (*post*) poste *m* vacant; (*room*) chambre *f* libre; **'no vacancies'** (*in hotel*) 'complet'. ● **vacantly** *adv* **to gaze v.** regarder dans le vide.

vacate [*Br* və'keɪt, *Am* 'veɪkeɪt] *vt* quitter.

vacation [veɪ'keɪʃ(ə)n] *n Am* vacances *fpl*; **to be/go/go away on v.** être/aller/partir en vacances. ● **vacationer** *n Am* vacancier, -ière *mf*.

vaccinate ['væksɪneɪt] *vt* vacciner. ● **vaccination** [-'neɪʃ(ə)n] *n* vaccination *f*. ● **vaccine** [væk'siːn] *n* vaccin *m*.

vacillate ['væsɪleɪt] *vi* (*hesitate*) hésiter.

vacuum ['vækjʊəm] *n* vide *m*; **v. cleaner** aspirateur *m*; **v. flask** *Br* thermos® *m* or *f* *inv* ‖ *vt* (*room*) passer l'aspirateur dans; (*carpet etc*) passer l'aspirateur sur. ● **vacuum-packed** *a* emballé sous vide.

vagabond ['vægəbɒnd] *n* vagabond, -onde *mf*.

vagary ['veɪgərɪ] *n* caprice *m*.

vagina [və'dʒaɪnə] *n* vagin *m*.

vagrant ['veɪgrənt] *n Jur* vagabond, -onde *mf*. ● **vagrancy** *n Jur* vagabondage *m*.

vague [veɪg] *a* (**-er, -est**) vague; (*outline, memory, photo*) flou; **I haven't got the vaguest idea** je n'en ai pas la moindre idée; **he was v.** (**about it**) il est resté vague. ● **vaguely** *adv* vaguement.

vain [veɪn] *a* (**-er, -est**) **1** (*attempt, hope*) vain; **in v.** en vain; **her efforts were in v.** ses efforts ont été inutiles. **2** (*conceited*) vaniteux. ● **vainly** *adv* (*in vain*) vainement.

valentine ['væləntaɪn] *n* (*card*) carte *f* de la Saint-Valentin; (**Saint**) **V.'s Day** la Saint-Valentin.

valet ['vælɪt, 'væleɪ] *n* valet *m* de chambre.

valiant ['væljənt] *a* courageux. ● **valour** (*Am* **valor**) *n* bravoure *f*.

valid ['vælɪd] *a* (*ticket, motive etc*) valable. ● **validate** *vt* valider. ● **va'lidity** *n* validité *f*; (*of argument*) justesse *f*.

valley ['vælɪ] *n* vallée *f*.

valuable ['væljʊəb(ə)l] *a* (*object*) de (grande) valeur; (*help, time etc*) *Fig* précieux ‖ *npl* **valuables** objets *mpl* de valeur.

value ['væljuː] *n* valeur *f*; **to be of great/little v.** (*of object*) valoir cher/peu (cher); **it's good v.** (**for money**) ça a un bon rapport qualité/prix; **v. added tax** *Br* taxe *f* à la valeur ajoutée ‖ *vt* (*appreciate*) attacher de la valeur à; (*assess*) évaluer. ● **valuation** [-'eɪʃ(ə)n] *n* (*by expert*) expertise *f*; (*assessment*) évaluation *f*. ● **valuer** *n* expert *m*.

valve [vælv] *n* (*of machine, car*) soupape *f*; (*in radio*) lampe *f*; (*of Br tyre, Am tire*) valve *f*; (*of heart*) valvule *f*.

vampire ['væmpaɪər] *n* vampire *m*.

van [væn] *n* (*small*) camionnette *f*, fourgonnette *f*; (*large*) camion *m*; (**guard's**) **v.** (*on train*) *Br* fourgon *m*.

vandal ['vænd(ə)l] *n* vandale *mf*. ● **vandalism** *n* vandalisme *m*. ● **vandalize** *vt* saccager.

vanguard ['vængɑːd] *n* **in the v. of** (*progress etc*) à l'avant-garde de.

vanilla [və'nɪlə] *n* vanille *f* ‖ *a* (*ice cream*) à la vanille; **v. flavour** parfum *m* vanille.

vanish ['vænɪʃ] *vi* disparaître; **to v. into thin air** se volatiliser.

vanity ['vænɪtɪ] *n* vanité *f*; **v. case** vanity *m inv*.

vanquish ['væŋkwɪʃ] *vt* vaincre.

vantage point ['vɑːntɪdʒpɔɪnt] *n* (*place*) (bon) point *m* de vue; (*point of view*) point *m* de vue, angle *m*.

vapour ['veɪpər] (*Am* **vapor**) *n* vapeur *f*; (*on glass*) buée *f*.

variable ['veərɪəb(ə)l] *a* variable.

variance ['veərɪəns] *n* **at v.** en désaccord (**with** avec).

variant ['veərɪənt] *a* différent ‖ *n* variante *f*.

variation [veərɪ'eɪʃ(ə)n] *n* variation *f*.

varicose ['værɪkəʊs] *a* **v. veins** varices *fpl*.

variety [və'raɪətɪ] *n* **1** (*diversity*) variété *f*; **a v. of opinions/reasons/etc** (*many*) diverses opinions/raisons/etc; **a v. of articles/products** toute une gamme d'articles/de produits. **2** (*entertainment*) variétés *fpl*; **v. show** spectacle *m* de variétés.

various ['veərɪəs] *a* divers. ● **variously** *adv* diversement.

varnish ['vɑːnɪʃ] *vt* vernir ‖ *n* vernis *m*; **nail v.** *Br* vernis *m* à ongles.

vary ['veərɪ] *vti* varier (**from** de). ● **varied** *a* varié. ● **varying** *a* variable.

vase [*Br* vɑːz, *Am* veɪs] *n* vase *m*.

vasectomy [və'sektəmɪ] *n* vasectomie *f*.

Vaseline® ['væsəliːn] *n* vaseline *f*.

vast [vɑːst] *a* vaste, immense. ● **vastly** *adv* (*very*) infiniment, extrêmement. ● **vastness** *n* immensité *f*.

vat [væt] *n* cuve *f*.

VAT [viːeɪ'tiː, væt] *n abbr* (*value added tax*) *Br* TVA *f*.

Vatican ['vætɪkən] *n* **the V.** le Vatican.

vaudeville ['vɔːdəvɪl] *n* (*entertainment*) *Am* variétés *fpl*; **v. show** spectacle *m* de variétés.

vault [vɔːlt] **1** n (in bank) salle f des coffres; (tomb) caveau m; (roof) voûte f; (cellar) cave f. **2** vti (jump) sauter.

VCR [viːsiːˈɑːr] n abbr (video cassette recorder) magnétoscope m.

VD [viːˈdiː] n abbr (venereal disease) maladie f vénérienne, MST f; **VD clinic** (in hospital) Br service m de vénérologie.

VDU [viːdiːˈjuː] n abbr (visual display unit) moniteur m.

veal [viːl] n (meat) veau m.

veer [vɪər] vi (of car) virer; (of wind) tourner; (of road) décrire un virage; **to v. off the road** quitter la route.

vegan [ˈviːgən] n végétaliste mf.

vegeburger [ˈvedʒɪbɜːgər] n burger m végétarien.

vegetable [ˈvedʒtəb(ə)l] n légume m; **v. garden** (jardin m) potager m; **v. kingdom** règne m végétal; **v. oil** huile f végétale. ● **vege'tarian** a & n végétarien, -ienne (mf). ● **vegetation** [-ɪˈteɪʃ(ə)n] n végétation f.

vegetate [ˈvedʒɪteɪt] vi (of person) Pej végéter.

vehement [ˈvɪəmənt] a (feeling, speech) véhément; (attack) violent. ● **vehemently** adv avec véhémence; (to attack) violemment.

vehicle [ˈviːɪk(ə)l] n véhicule m; **heavy goods v.** Br poids m lourd.

veil [veɪl] n (covering) & Fig voile m ■ vt (face, truth etc) voiler. ● **veiled** a (criticism, woman etc) voilé.

vein [veɪn] n (in body or rock) veine f; (in leaf) nervure f; (mood) Fig esprit m.

Velcro® [ˈvelkrəʊ] n Velcro® m.

vellum [ˈveləm] n (paper, skin) vélin m.

velocity [vəˈlɒsɪtɪ] n vélocité f.

velvet [ˈvelvɪt] n velours m ■ a de velours. ● **velvety** a velouté.

vendetta [venˈdetə] n vendetta f.

vending machine [ˈvendɪŋməʃiːn] n distributeur m automatique.

vendor [ˈvendər] n vendeur, -euse mf.

veneer [vəˈnɪər] n (wood) placage m; (appearance) Fig vernis m.

venerable [ˈven(ə)rəb(ə)l] a vénérable. ● **venerate** vt vénérer.

venereal [vəˈnɪərɪəl] a (disease etc) vénérien.

venetian [vəˈniːʃ(ə)n] a **v. blind** store m vénitien.

Venezuela [veneˈzweɪlə] n Venezuela m.

vengeance [ˈvendʒəns] n vengeance f; **with a v.** (to work, study etc) furieusement; (to rain, catch up etc) pour de bon.

venison [ˈvenɪs(ə)n] n venaison f.

venom [ˈvenəm] n (poison) & Fig venin m. ● **venomous** a (speech, snake etc) venimeux.

vent [vent] **1** n (hole) orifice m; (for air) bouche f d'aération; (in jacket) fente f. **2** n **to give v. to** (feeling etc) donner libre cours à ■ vt (one's anger) décharger (on sur).

ventilate [ˈventɪleɪt] vt (tunnel, workshop etc) ventiler; (bedroom etc) aérer. ● **ventilation** [-ˈleɪʃ(ə)n] n (of tunnel etc) ventilation

f; (of bedroom etc) aération f. ● **ventilator** n (in wall etc) ventilateur m; (for sick person) respirateur m artificiel.

ventriloquist [venˈtrɪləkwɪst] n ventriloque mf.

venture [ˈventʃər] n entreprise f (risquée); **my v. into** mon incursion f dans ■ vt (opinion) hasarder; **to v. to do** (dare) oser faire ■ vi s'aventurer, se risquer (into dans).

venue [ˈvenjuː] n lieu m de rencontre or de rendez-vous.

veranda(h) [vəˈrændə] n véranda f.

verb [vɜːb] n verbe m. ● **verbal** a (promise, skill etc) verbal.

verbatim [vɜːˈbeɪtɪm] a & adv mot pour mot.

verbose [vɜːˈbəʊs] a (person, text) verbeux.

verdict [ˈvɜːdɪkt] n verdict m.

verdigris [ˈvɜːdɪgrɪs] n vert-de-gris m inv.

verge [vɜːdʒ] n (of road) Br accotement m, bord m; **on the v. of ruin/tears/etc** au bord de la ruine/des larmes/etc; **on the v. of a discovery** à la veille d'une découverte; **on the v. of doing sth** sur le point de faire qch ■ vi **to v. on** friser, frôler; (of colour) tirer sur.

verger [ˈvɜːdʒər] n (church official) bedeau m.

verify [ˈverɪfaɪ] vt vérifier; (passport) contrôler. ● **verification** [-ˈkeɪʃ(ə)n] n vérification f; (of passport) contrôle m.

veritable [ˈverɪtəb(ə)l] a véritable.

vermicelli [vɜːmɪˈselɪ] n (pasta) vermicelle(s) m(pl).

vermin [ˈvɜːmɪn] n (animals) animaux mpl nuisibles; (insects, people) vermine f.

vermouth [ˈvɜːməθ] n vermouth m.

vernacular [vəˈnækjʊlər] n (of region) dialecte m.

versatile [Br ˈvɜːsətaɪl, Am ˈvɜːsət(ə)l] a (mind) souple; (tool, computer, material) polyvalent; **he's v.** il a des talents variés, il est polyvalent. ● **versa'tility** n souplesse f; **his v.** la variété de ses talents.

verse [vɜːs] n (part of song) couplet m; (of poem) strophe f; (poetry) poésie f; (of Bible) verset m; **in v.** en vers.

versed [vɜːst] a (well) **v. in** versé dans.

version [Br ˈvɜːʃ(ə)n, Am ˈvɜːʒ(ə)n] n version f.

versus [ˈvɜːsəs] prep contre.

vertebra, pl **-ae** [ˈvɜːtɪbrə, -iː] n vertèbre f.

vertical [ˈvɜːtɪk(ə)l] a vertical ■ n verticale f. ● **vertically** adv verticalement.

vertigo [ˈvɜːtɪgəʊ] n (fear of falling) vertige m.

verve [vɜːv] n fougue f.

very [ˈverɪ] **1** adv très; **I'm v. hot** j'ai très chaud; **v. much** beaucoup; **the v. first** le tout premier; **at the v. least/most** tout au moins/plus; **at the v. latest** au plus tard. **2** a (actual) même; **his v. brother** son frère même; **at the v. end** (of play, book etc) tout à la fin; **to the v. end** jusqu'au bout.

vespers [ˈvespəz] npl (church service) vêpres fpl.

vessel ['ves(ə)l] n (ship) vaisseau m; (receptacle) récipient m; (for blood, sap etc) vaisseau m.

vest [vest] n tricot m or maillot m de corps; (woman's) chemise f (américaine); (waistcoat) Am gilet m.

vested ['vestɪd] a v. interests Pol etc intérêts(s) m(pl); she's got a v. interest in Fig elle est directement intéressée dans.

vestige ['vestɪdʒ] n vestige m; not a v. of truth/good sense pas un grain de vérité/de bon sens.

vestry ['vestrɪ] n (in church) sacristie f.

vet [vet] 1 n vétérinaire mf. 2 vt (-tt-) Br (document) examiner de près; (candidate) se renseigner à fond sur. • **veteri'narian** n Am vétérinaire mf. • **veterinary** a vétérinaire; v. **surgeon** Br vétérinaire mf.

veteran ['vet(ə)rən] n vétéran m; (war) n. ancien combattant m █ a v. golfer/etc golfeur/etc expérimenté.

veto ['viːtəʊ] n (pl -oes) (refusal) veto m inv; (power) droit m de veto █ vt mettre or opposer son veto à.

vex [veks] vt contrarier, fâcher; **vexed question** question f controversée.

VHF [viːeɪtʃ'ef] n abbr (very high frequency) **on VHF** en VHF, sur modulation de fréquence.

via [Br 'vaɪə, Am 'vɪə] prep via, par.

viable ['vaɪəb(ə)l] a (plan, company, baby etc) viable. • **via'bility** n viabilité f.

viaduct ['vaɪədʌkt] n viaduc m.

vibrant ['vaɪbrənt] a (person) plein de vie or d'énergie; (speech) vibrant; (colour) vif; a city v. with activity une ville palpitante d'activité.

vibrate [vaɪ'breɪt] vi vibrer. • **vibration** [-'breɪʃ(ə)n] n vibration f. • **vibrator** n vibromasseur m.

vicar ['vɪkər] n (in Church of England) pasteur m. • **vicarage** n presbytère m.

vicarious [vɪ'keərɪəs] a (emotion) ressenti indirectement. • **vicariously** adv (to experience sth) indirectement.

vice [vaɪs] n 1 (depravity) vice m; (fault) vice m, défaut m; v. **squad** brigade f des mœurs. 2 (tool) Br étau m.

vice- [vaɪs] pref vice-. • **vice-'chancellor** n (of British university) président m.

vice versa [vaɪs(ɪ)'vɜːsə] adv vice versa.

vicinity [və'sɪnɪtɪ] n environs mpl; in the v. of (place, Fig amount) aux environs de.

vicious ['vɪʃəs] a (spiteful) méchant; (violent) brutal; v. **circle** cercle m vicieux; v. **dog** chien m (très) méchant. • **viciously** adv (spitefully) méchamment; (violently) brutalement. • **viciousness** n (spite) méchanceté f; (violence) brutalité f.

vicissitudes [vɪ'sɪsɪtjuːdz] npl vicissitudes fpl.

victim ['vɪktɪm] n victime f; to be the v. of être victime de; to fall v. to (disease etc) contracter; (s.o.'s charms etc) succomber à; the accident victims les victimes de l'accident.

victimize ['vɪktɪmaɪz] vt persécuter. • **victimization** [-'zeɪʃ(ə)n] n persécution f.

victor ['vɪktər] n Old-fashioned vainqueur m.

Victorian [vɪk'tɔːrɪən] a victorien █ n Victorien, -ienne mf.

victory ['vɪktərɪ] n victoire f. • **vic'torious** a victorieux.

video ['vɪdɪəʊ] n (cassette) cassette f; v. **cassette** vidéocassette f; v. (**recorder**) magnétoscope m; **on v.** sur cassette; to **make a v. of** faire une cassette de █ a (game, camera etc) vidéo inv █ vt (event) faire une (vidéo)cassette de; (TV programme) enregistrer au magnétoscope. • **videodisk** n vidéodisque m. • **videotape** n bande f vidéo.

vie [vaɪ] vi (pres p **vying**) rivaliser (**with** avec).

Vienna [vɪ'enə] n Vienne m or f.

Vietnam [Br vjet'næm, Am -'nɑːm] n Viêt Nam m. • **Vietna'mese** a vietnamien █ n Vietnamien, -ienne mf.

view [vjuː] n vue f; (opinion) opinion f, avis m; to **come into v.** apparaître; in **full v. of everyone** à la vue de tous; in **my v.** (opinion) à mon avis; **on v.** (exhibit) exposé; in **v. of** (considering) compte tenu de, étant donné; **with a v. to doing** afin de faire █ vt (regard) considérer; (house) visiter. • **viewer** n 1 TV téléspectateur, -trice mf. 2 (for slides) visionneuse f. • **viewfinder** n (in camera) viseur m. • **viewpoint** n point m de vue.

vigil ['vɪdʒɪl] n veille f; (over sick person or corpse) veillée f.

vigilant ['vɪdʒɪlənt] a vigilant. • **vigilance** n vigilance f.

vigilante [vɪdʒɪ'læntɪ] n Pej membre m d'une milice privée.

vigour ['vɪgər] (Am **vigor**) n vigueur f. • **vigorous** a (person, speech etc) vigoureux.

vile [vaɪl] a (-er, -est) (base) infâme, vil; (unpleasant) abominable.

vilify ['vɪlɪfaɪ] vt diffamer.

villa ['vɪlə] n grande maison f; (Br holiday or Am vacation home) maison f de vacances.

village ['vɪlɪdʒ] n village m. • **villager** n villageois, -oise mf.

villain ['vɪlən] n (scoundrel) canaille f; (in story or play) méchant m, traître m. • **villainous** a infâme. • **villainy** n infamie f.

vindicate ['vɪndɪkeɪt] vt justifier. • **vindication** [-'keɪʃ(ə)n] n justification f.

vindictive [vɪn'dɪktɪv] a vindicatif.

vine [vaɪn] n (grapevine) vigne f; v. **grower** viticulteur m. • **vineyard** ['vɪnjəd] n vignoble m.

vinegar ['vɪnɪgər] n vinaigre m.

vintage ['vɪntɪdʒ] 1 n (year) année f. 2 a (wine) de grand cru; (car) d'époque; (film) classique; (good) Fig bon; **it's v.** Shaw/etc c'est du meilleur Shaw/etc.

vinyl ['vaɪn(ə)l] n vinyle m; v. **seats**/etc sièges mpl/etc en vinyle.

viola [vɪ'əʊlə] n (musical instrument) alto m.

violate ['vaɪəleɪt] vt (agreement etc) violer.

● **violation** [-'leɪʃ(ə)n] n violation f.

violence ['vaɪələns] n violence f. ● **violent** a violent; **a v. dislike** une aversion vive (of pour). ● **violently** adv violemment; **to be v. sick** (vomit) Br être pris de violents vomissements.

violet ['vaɪələt] **1** a (colour) violet (f -ette) **I** n violet m. **2** n (plant) violette f.

violin [vaɪə'lɪn] n violon m; **v. concerto/etc** concerto m/etc pour violon. ● **violinist** n violoniste mf.

VIP [vi:aɪ'pi:] n abbr (very important person) personnage m de marque.

viper ['vaɪpər] n vipère f.

viral ['vaɪrəl] a (infection, disease etc) viral.

virgin ['vɜ:dʒɪn] n vierge f; **to be a v.** (of woman, man) être vierge **I** a (territory, forest etc) vierge; **v. snow** neige f d'une blancheur virginale. ● **vir'ginity** n virginité f; **to lose one's v.** perdre sa virginité.

Virgo ['vɜ:gəu] n (sign) la Vierge.

virile [Br 'vɪraɪl, Am 'vɪrəl] a viril. ● **vi'rility** n virilité f.

virtual ['vɜ:tʃuəl] a **1** it was a v. failure/etc ce fut en fait un échec/etc. **2** Phys Comptr virtuel; **v. reality** réalité f virtuelle. ● **virtually** adv (in fact) en fait; (almost) pratiquement.

virtue ['vɜ:tʃu:] n **1** (goodness, chastity) vertu f; (advantage) mérite m, avantage m. **2** by or in v. of en raison de. ● **virtuous** a vertueux.

virtuoso, pl **-si** [vɜ:tʃu'əusəu, -si:] n virtuose mf. ● **virtuosity** [-'ɒsɪtɪ] n virtuosité f.

virulent ['vɪrulənt] a virulent. ● **virulence** n virulence f.

virus ['vaɪ(ə)rəs] n Med Comptr virus m; **to come down with a v.** attraper un virus; **v. infection** infection f virale.

visa ['vi:zə] n visa m.

Visa® ['vi:zə] n V. (card) carte f Visa®.

vis-à-vis [vi:zə'vi:] prep vis-à-vis de.

viscount ['vaɪkaunt] n vicomte m. ● **viscountess** n vicomtesse f.

viscous ['vɪskəs] a visqueux.

vise [vaɪs] n (tool) Am étau m.

visible ['vɪzəb(ə)l] a visible. ● **visi'bility** n visibilité f. ● **visibly** adv visiblement.

vision ['vɪʒ(ə)n] n (eyesight, foresight etc) vision f; **a man/a woman of v.** Fig un homme/ une femme qui voit loin. ● **visionary** a & n visionnaire (mf).

visit ['vɪzɪt] n (call, tour) visite f; (stay) séjour m **I** vt (place) visiter; **to visit s.o.** (call on) rendre visite à qn; (stay with) faire un séjour chez qn **I** vi être en visite (Am with chez). ● **visiting** n visites fpl; **to go v.** aller en visites; **v. hours/Br card** heures fpl/carte f de visite. ● **visitor** n visiteur, -euse mf; (guest) invité, -ée mf; (in hotel) client, -ente mf.

visor ['vaɪzər] n (of helmet) visière f.

vista ['vɪstə] n (view of place etc) vue f; (of future) Fig perspective f.

visual ['vɪʒuəl] a visuel; **v. aid** (in teaching) support m visuel. ● **visualize** vt (imagine) se

représenter; (foresee) envisager.

vital ['vaɪt(ə)l] a essentiel; **it's v. that** il est essentiel que (+ sub); **of v. importance** d'importance capitale; **v. statistics** (of woman) mensurations fpl. ● **vitally** adv (important etc) extrêmement.

vitality [vaɪ'tælɪtɪ] n vitalité f.

vitamin [Br 'vɪtəmɪn, Am 'vaɪtəmɪn] n vitamine f; **v. tablet** comprimé m de vitamines.

vitriol ['vɪtrɪəl] n (acid, Fig bitter speech) vitriol m. ● **vitri'olic** a (attack, speech etc) au vitriol.

viva ['vaɪvə] n (oral examination) Br Univ Fam (examen m) oral m.

vivacious [vɪ'veɪʃəs] a plein d'entrain.

vivid ['vɪvɪd] a (imagination, recollection etc) vif; (description) vivant. ● **vividly** adv (to describe) de façon vivante; **to remember sth v.** avoir un vif souvenir de qch.

vivisection [vɪvɪ'sekʃ(ə)n] n vivisection f.

vixen ['vɪksən] n (fox) renarde f.

V-neck [vi:'nek] a (sweater etc) à col en V **I** n col m en V.

vocabulary [Br və'kæbjulərɪ, Am -erɪ] n vocabulaire m.

vocal ['vəuk(ə)l] a (cords, music) vocal; (outspoken, noisy, critical) qui se fait entendre. ● **vocalist** n chanteur, -euse mf.

vocation [vəu'keɪʃ(ə)n] n vocation f. ● **vocational** a professionnel; **v. course** cours m de formation professionnelle; **v. school** établissement m d'enseignement professionnel; **v. training** formation f professionnelle.

vociferous [və'sɪf(ə)rəs] a bruyant.

vodka ['vɒdkə] n vodka f.

vogue [vəug] n vogue f; **in v.** en vogue.

voice [vɔɪs] n voix f; **at the top of one's v.** à tue-tête **I** vt (opinion, feeling etc) formuler, exprimer.

void [vɔɪd] **1** n vide m **I** a v. of (lacking in) Lit dépourvu de. **2** a (not valid) (contract etc) nul.

volatile [Br 'vɒlətaɪl, Am 'vɒlət(ə)l] a (person) versatile, changeant; (situation) explosif.

volcano [vɒl'keɪnəu] n (pl -oes) volcan m. ● **volcanic** [-'kænɪk] a volcanique.

volition [və'lɪʃ(ə)n] n of one's own v. de son propre gré.

volley ['vɒlɪ] n (of gunfire) salve f; (of blows) volée f; (of insults) Fig bordée f; Tennis volée f. ● **volleyball** n Sport volley(-ball) m.

volt [vəult] n El volt m. ● **voltage** n voltage m.

volume ['vɒlju:m] n (book, capacity, loudness) volume m; **v. control** (on TV, radio) bouton m de (réglage du) volume. ● **voluminous** [və'lu:mɪnəs] a volumineux.

voluntary [Br 'vɒlənt(ə)rɪ, Am -erɪ] a volontaire; (unpaid) bénévole. ● **voluntarily** adv volontairement; (on an unpaid basis) bénévolement.

volunteer [vɒlən'tɪər] n volontaire mf **I** vi se proposer (for sth pour qch, to do pour faire); (*for the army etc*) s'engager comme volontaire (**for** dans) ▮ *vt* (*information etc*) offrir (spontanément).

voluptuous [və'lʌptʃuəs] *a* voluptueux, sensuel.

vomit ['vɒmɪt] *vti* vomir ▮ *n* (*matter*) vomi *m*.

voracious [və'reɪʃəs] *a* (*appetite, reader etc*) vorace.

vote [vəut] *n* vote *m*; (*right to vote*) droit *m* de vote; **to win votes** gagner des voix; **v. of no confidence** *or* **of censure** motion *f* de censure; **v. of thanks** discours *m* de remerciement ▮ *vt* (*funds, bill etc*) voter; (*person*) élire; **to be voted president/etc** être élu président/etc ▮ *vi* voter; **to v.** *Br* **Labour/** *Am* **Democrat/etc** voter travailliste/ démocrate/etc. ●**voting** *n* (*of funds etc*) vote

m (**of** de); (*polling*) scrutin *m*. ●**voter** *n* (*elector*) électeur, -trice *mf*.

vouch [vautʃ] *vi* **to v. for s.o./sth** répondre de qn/qch.

voucher ['vautʃər] *n Br* (*for meals, gift etc*) chèque *m*; (*for price reduction*) bon *m* de réduction.

vow [vau] *n* vœu *m* ▮ *vt* (*obedience etc*) jurer (**to** à); **to v. to do** jurer de faire, faire le vœu de faire.

vowel ['vauəl] *n* voyelle *f*.

voyage ['vɔɪɪdʒ] *n* voyage *m* (par mer).

vulgar ['vʌlgər] *a* vulgaire. ●**vul'garity** *n* vulgarité *f*.

vulnerable ['vʌln(ə)rəb(ə)l] *a* vulnérable. ●**vulnera'bility** *n* vulnérabilité *f*.

vulture ['vʌltʃər] *n* vautour *m*.

W

W, w [ˈdʌb(ə)lju:] *n* W, w *m*.

wacky [ˈwæki] *a* (**-ier, -iest**) *Fam* farfelu.

wad [wɒd] *n* (*of papers, Br banknotes, Am bills etc*) liasse *f*; (*of cloth, Br cotton wool, Am absorbent cotton*) tampon *m*.

waddle [ˈwɒd(ə)l] *vi* (*of duck, Fig person*) se dandiner.

wade [weɪd] *vi* **to w. through** (*mud, water etc*) patauger dans; (*book etc to the very end*) *Fig* venir péniblement à bout de; **I'm wading through this book** j'avance péniblement dans ce livre. ●**wading pool** *n Am* (*inflatable*) piscine *f* gonflable; (*purpose-built*) pataugeoire *f*.

wafer [ˈweɪfər] *n* 1 (*biscuit*) gaufrette *f*; *Rel* hostie *f*. 2 *Comptr* tranche *f*.

waffle [ˈwɒf(ə)l] 1 *n* (*talk*) *Br Fam* blabla *m*, verbiage *m* ▌ *vi Br Fam* parler pour ne rien dire, blablater. 2 *n* (*cake*) gaufre *f*.

waft [wɒft] *vi* (*of smell etc*) flotter.

wag [wæg] 1 *vt* (**-gg-**) (*tail, finger*) remuer, agiter ▌ *vi* (*of tail*) remuer; **tongues are wagging** *Pej* on en jase, les langues vont bon train. 2 *n* (*joker*) farceur, -euse *mf*.

wage [weɪdʒ] 1 *n* **wage(s)** salaire *m*, paie *f*; **a living w.** un salaire qui permet de vivre; **w. claim** *or* **demand** revendication *f* salariale; **w. earner** salarié, -ée *mf*; (*breadwinner*) soutien *m* de famille; **w. freeze** blocage *m* des salaires; **w. increase** *or Br* **rise** augmentation *f* de salaire; **w. packet** *Br* (*envelope*) enveloppe *f* de paie; (*net pay*) paie *f*.
2 *vt* (*campaign*) mener; **to w. war** faire la guerre (**on** à).

wager [ˈweɪdʒər] *n* pari *m* ▌ *vt* parier (**that** que).

waggle [ˈwæg(ə)l] *vti* remuer.

wag(g)on [ˈwægən] *n* (*of train*) *Br* wagon *m* (de marchandises); (*horse-drawn*) chariot *m*; **to be on the w.** (*no longer drinking*) *Fam* être au régime sec.

waif [weɪf] *n* enfant *mf* abandonné(e).

wail [weɪl] *vi* (*cry out, complain*) gémir; (*of siren*) hurler ▌ *n* gémissement *m*; (*of siren*) hurlement *m*.

waist [weɪst] *n* taille *f*; **stripped to the w.** torse nu, nu jusqu'à la ceinture. ●**waistband** *n* (*part of garment*) ceinture *f*. ●**waistcoat** [ˈweɪskəʊt] *n Br* gilet *m*. ●**waistline** *n* taille *f*.

wait [weɪt] 1 *n* attente *f*; **to lie in w.** (**for**) guetter ▌ *vi* attendre; **to w. for s.o./sth** attendre qn/qch; **w. till** *or* **until I've gone, w. for me to go** attends que je sois parti; **to keep s.o. waiting** faire attendre qn; **w. and see!** attends voir!; **I can't w. to do it** j'ai hâte de le faire.
2 *vi* (*serve*) **to w. at table** servir à table; **to w. on s.o.** servir qn. ●**waiting** *n* attente *f*; **'no w.'** (*street sign*) *Br* 'arrêt interdit' ▌ *a* **w. list/room** liste *f*/salle *f* d'attente.

wait about *or* **around** *vi* attendre; **to w. about** *or* **around for s.o./sth** attendre qn/qch ▌ **to wait behind** *vi* rester ▌ **to wait up** *vi* veiller; **to w. up for s.o.** attendre le retour de qn avant de se coucher.

waiter [ˈweɪtər] *n* garçon *m* (de café), serveur *m*; **w.!** garçon! ●**waitress** *n* serveuse *f*; **w.!** mademoiselle!

waive [weɪv] *vt* (*renounce*) renoncer à, abandonner; **to w. a requirement** (**for s.o.**) dispenser qn d'une condition requise.

wake¹ [weɪk] *vi* (*pt* **woke**, *pp* **woken**) **to w. (up)** se réveiller; **to w. up to** (*fact etc*) prendre conscience de ▌ *vt* **to w. (up)** réveiller. ●**waking** *a* **to spend one's waking hours working/etc** passer ses journées à travailler/etc.

wake² [weɪk] *n* 1 (*of ship*) & *Fig* sillage *m*; **in the w. of** *Fig* dans le sillage de, à la suite de. 2 (*beside dead person*) veillée *f* mortuaire.

waken [ˈweɪkən] *vi Lit* éveiller ▌ *vi Lit* s'éveiller.

Wales [weɪlz] *n* pays *m* de Galles; **the Prince of W.** le prince de Galles.

walk [wɔːk] *n* promenade *f*; (*shorter*) (petit) tour *m*; (*way of walking*) démarche *f*; (*pace*) pas *m*; (*path*) allée *f*, chemin *m*; **to go for a w., take a w.** faire une promenade; (*shorter*) faire un (petit) tour; **to take for a w.** (*baby, dog*) promener; **five minutes' w. (away)** à cinq minutes à pied; **from all walks of life** *Fig* de toutes conditions sociales.
▌ *vi* marcher; (*stroll*) se promener; (*go on foot*) aller à pied; **w.!** (*don't run*) ne cours pas!
▌ *vt* (*distance*) faire à pied; (*streets*) (par)courir; (*take for a walk*) promener (*bébé, chien*); **to w. s.o. to** (*station etc*) accompagner qn à; **to w. s.o. home** raccompagner qn (chez lui). ●**walking** *n* marche *f* (à pied) ▌ *a* **w. corpse/dictionary** (*person*) *Fig* un cadavre/dictionnaire ambulant; **at a w. pace** au pas. ●**walking stick** *n* canne *f*.

walk away *vi* s'éloigner, partir (**from** de); **to w. away with sth** (*steal*) *Fam* faucher qch ▌ **to walk in** *vi* entrer; **to w. into a tree/etc** rentrer dans un arbre/etc; **to w. into a trap** tomber dans un piège ▌ **to walk off** *vi* = **walk away** ▌ **to walk out** *vi* (*leave*) partir; (*of* *workers*) *Br* se mettre en grève; **to w. out on s.o.** (*desert*) laisser tomber qn, abandonner qn ∎ **to walk over** *vi* **to w. over to** (*go up to*) s'approcher de.

walker ['wɔːkər] *n* marcheur, -euse *mf*; (*for pleasure*) promeneur, -euse *mf*. ●**walkout** *n* (*strike*) grève *f* surprise; (*from meeting*) départ *m* (en signe de protestation). ●**walkover** *n* (*in contest etc*) victoire *f* facile. ●**walkway** *n* moving w. trottoir *m* roulant.

walkie-talkie [wɔːkɪ'tɔːkɪ] *n* talkie-walkie *m*.

Walkman® ['wɔːkmən] *n* (*pl* **Walkmans**) baladeur *m*.

wall [wɔːl] *n* mur *m*; (*of cabin, tunnel, stomach etc*) paroi *f*; **a w. of ice** *Fig* une muraille de glace; **a. w. of smoke** *Fig* un rideau de fumée; **to go to the w.** (*of company*) *Fig* faire faillite ∎ **a** (*map etc*) mural ∎ *vt* **to w. up** (*door etc*) murer. ●**walled** *a* **w. city** ville *f* fortifiée. ●**wallflower** *n* (*plant*) giroflée *f*; **to be a w.** (*at dance*) faire tapisserie. ●**wallpaper** *n* papier *m* peint ∎ *vt* tapisser. ●**wall-to-wall 'carpet(ing)** *n* moquette *f*.

wallet ['wɒlɪt] *n* portefeuille *m*.

wallop ['wɒləp] *vt* (*hit*) *Fam* taper sur ∎ *n* (*blow*) *Fam* grand coup *m*.

wallow ['wɒləʊ] *vi* **to w. in the mud/**Fig **in vice/**etc se vautrer dans la boue/*Fig* le vice/*etc*.

wally ['wɒlɪ] *n Br Fam* (*idiot*) andouille *f*; **you w.!** espèce d'andouille!

walnut ['wɔːlnʌt] *n* (*nut*) noix *f*; (*tree, wood*) noyer *m*.

walrus ['wɔːlrəs] *n* (*animal*) morse *m*.

waltz [*Br* wɔːls, *Am* wɒlts] *n* valse *f* ∎ *vi* valser.

wan [wɒn] *a* (*pale*) *Lit* pâle.

wand [wɒnd] *n* (*magic*) **w.** baguette *f* (magique).

wander ['wɒndər] *vi* (*of thoughts*) vagabonder; (*of person*) (*roam*) errer, vagabonder; (*stroll*) flâner; **to w. from** (*path, Fig subject*) s'écarter de; **to w. in/out/**etc (*go or come leisurely*) entrer/sortir/*etc* (tranquillement); **my mind's wandering** je suis distrait ∎ *vt* **to w. the streets** errer dans les rues. ●**wandering** *a* (*life, tribe*) vagabond, nomade ∎ *npl* **my wanderings** mes vagabondages *mpl*. ●**wanderer** *n* vagabond, -onde *mf*.

wander about *or* **around** *vi* (*roam*) errer, vagabonder; (*stroll*) flâner ∎ **to wander off** *vi* (*go away*) s'éloigner; **to w. off the path/**Fig **the subject** s'écarter du chemin/*Fig* du sujet.

wane [weɪn] *vi* (*of moon, fame, strength etc*) décroître ∎ *n* **to be on the w.** (*of fame etc*) décroître, être en déclin.

wangle ['wæŋɡ(ə)l] *vt Br Fam* (*obtain*) se débrouiller pour obtenir; (*avoiding payment*) carotter (**from** à).

want [wɒnt] *vt* vouloir (**to do** faire); (*ask for*) demander (qn); (*need*) avoir besoin de; **I w. him to go** je veux qu'il parte; **you w. to try** (*should*) *Br* tu devrais essayer; **you're wanted on the phone** on vous demande au téléphone; **'situations wanted'** (*in newspa-*

per) *Br* 'demandes *fpl* d'emploi'.

∎ *vi* **not to w. for sth** (*not lack*) ne pas manquer de qch.

∎ *n* (*lack*) manque *m* (**of** de); (*poverty*) besoin *m*; **for w. of** par manque de; **for w. of money/time** faute d'argent/de temps; **for w. of anything better** faute de mieux; **your wants** (*needs*) tes besoins *mpl*. ●**wanted** *a* (*criminal, man*) recherché par la police; **to feel w.** sentir qu'on vous aime. ●**wanting** *a* (*inadequate*) insuffisant; **to be w.** (*lacking, missing*) manquer (**in** de).

wanton ['wɒntən] *a* (*gratuitous*) gratuit; (*immoral*) *Old-fashioned* impudique.

war [wɔːr] *n* guerre *f*; **at w.** en guerre (**with** avec); **to go to w.** entrer en guerre (**with** avec); **to declare w.** déclarer la guerre (**on** à) ∎ *a* (*wound, crime, criminal, zone etc*) de guerre; **w. memorial** monument *m* aux morts.

warble ['wɔːb(ə)l] *vi* (*of bird*) gazouiller.

ward¹ [wɔːd] *n* **1** (*in hospital*) salle *f*. **2** (*child*) *Jur* pupille *mf*. **3** (*electoral division*) *Br* circonscription *f* électorale.

ward² [wɔːd] *vt* **to w. off** (*blow, anger*) détourner; (*danger, illness*) éviter.

warden ['wɔːd(ə)n] *n* (*of Br institution, Am prison*) directeur, -trice *mf*; (*of park*) *Br* gardien, -ienne *mf*; (**traffic**) **w.** *Br* contractuel, -elle *mf*.

warder ['wɔːdər] *n Br* gardien *m* (de prison).

wardrobe ['wɔːdrəʊb] *n* (*Br cupboard, Am closet*) penderie *f*; (*clothes*) garde-robe *f*.

warehouse, *pl* **-ses** ['weəhaʊs, -zɪz] *n* entrepôt *m*.

wares [weəz] *npl* marchandises *fpl*.

warfare ['wɔːfeər] *n* guerre *f*. ●**warhead** *n* (*of missile*) ogive *f*.

warily ['weərɪlɪ] *adv* avec précaution.

warlike ['wɔːlaɪk] *a* guerrier.

warm [wɔːm] *a* (-er, -est) chaud; (*iron, oven*) moyen; (*welcome, thanks etc*) *Fig* chaleureux; **to be or feel w.** avoir chaud; **it's** (**nice and**) **w.** (*of weather*) il fait (agréablement) chaud; **to get w.** (*of person, room etc*) se réchauffer; (*of food, water*) chauffer.

∎ *vt* **to w. (up)** (*person, food etc*) réchauffer; (*car engine*) faire chauffer.

∎ *vi* **to w. up** (*of person, room, engine*) se réchauffer; (*of food, water*) chauffer; (*of discussion*) *Fig* s'échauffer; **to w. to s.o.** *Fig* se prendre de sympathie pour qn. ●**warm-hearted** *a* chaleureux. ●**warming** *n* **global w.** réchauffement *m* de la planète. ●**warmly** *adv* (*to wrap up etc*) chaudement; (*to welcome, thank etc*) *Fig* chaleureusement. ●**warmth** *n* chaleur *f*.

warmonger ['wɔːmʌŋɡər] *n* fauteur *m* de guerre.

warn [wɔːn] *vt* avertir, prévenir (**that** que); **to w. s.o. against** *or* **off sth** mettre qn en garde contre qch; **to w. s.o. against doing** conseiller à qn de ne pas faire. ●**warning** *n* avertissement *m*; (*advance notice*) (pré)avis *m*; (*device*) alarme *f*, alerte *f*; **without w.**

sans prévenir; **gale/storm** w. avis *m* de coup de vent/de tempête; **a word or note of** w. une mise en garde; **w. light** (*on appliance*) voyant *m* lumineux; **(hazard)** w. **lights** *Br Aut* feux *mpl* de détresse; **w. triangle** triangle *m* de présignalisation.

warp [wɔːp] 1 *vt* (*wood etc*) voiler; (*judgment, person etc*) Fig pervertir; **a warped mind** un esprit tordu; **a warped account** un récit déformé ▮ *vi* (*of door etc*) se voiler. 2 *n Tex* chaîne *f*.

warpath ['wɔːpɑːθ] *n* **to be on the** w. (*angry*) Fam être d'humeur massacrante.

warrant ['wɒrənt] 1 *n Jur* mandat *m*; **I have a** w. **for your arrest** j'ai un mandat d'arrêt contre vous; **search** w. mandat *m* de perquisition. 2 *vt* (*justify*) justifier; **I w. you that....** (*declare confidently*) je vous assure que.... ● **warranty** *n Com* garantie *f*; **under** w. sous garantie.

warren ['wɒrən] *n* (**rabbit**) w. garenne *f*.

warring ['wɔːrɪŋ] *a* (*countries etc*) en guerre; (*ideologies etc*) Fig en conflit.

warrior ['wɒrɪər] *n* guerrier, -ière *mf*.

Warsaw ['wɔːsɔː] *n* Varsovie *m or f*.

warship ['wɔːʃɪp] *n* navire *m* de guerre.

wart [wɔːt] *n* verrue *f*.

wartime ['wɔːtaɪm] *n* **in** w. en temps de guerre.

wary ['weərɪ] *a* (**-ier, -iest**) prudent; **to be** w. **of s.o./sth** se méfier de qn/qch; **to be** w. **of doing sth** hésiter beaucoup à faire qch.

was [wəz, *stressed* wɒz] *see* be.

wash [wɒʃ] *n* (*clothes*) lessive *f*; (*rough water from ship*) sillage *m*; **to have a** w. se laver; **to give sth a** w. laver qch; **to do the** w. *Am* faire la lessive; **in the** w. à la lessive ▮ *vt* laver; (*flow over*) (*of sea etc*) baigner (*côte etc*); **to** w. **one's hands** se laver les mains (Fig **of sth** de qch); **to be washed ashore** (*of driftwood etc*) être rejeté sur le rivage ▮ *vi* (*have a wash*) se laver.

washable ['wɒʃəb(ə)l] *a* lavable.

wash away *vt* (*stain*) faire partir (en lavant); **to** w. **s.o./sth away** (*of sea etc*) emporter qn/qch ▮ *vi* (*of stain*) partir (au lavage) ▮ **to wash down** *vt* (*vehicle, deck*) laver à grande eau; (*food*) arroser (**with** de) ▮ **to wash off** *vti* = **wash away** ▮ **to wash out** *vt* (*bowl, cup etc*) laver; (*stain*) faire partir (en lavant) ▮ *vi* (*of stain*) partir (au lavage) ▮ **to wash up** *vt* (*dishes, forks etc*) *Br* laver ▮ *vi* (*do the dishes*) *Br* faire la vaisselle; (*have a wash*) *Am* se laver.

washbasin ['wɒʃbeɪs(ə)n] *n Br* lavabo *m*. ● **washcloth** *n Am* gant *m* de toilette.

washed-out [wɒʃt'aut] *a* (*tired*) *Fam* lessivé. ● **washed-'up** *a* (**all**) w.-up (*person, plan*) *Fam* fichu.

washer ['wɒʃər] *n* (*ring*) rondelle *f*, joint *m*.

washing ['wɒʃɪŋ] *n* (*act*) lavage *m*; (*clothes*) lessive *f*, linge *m*; **to do the** w. faire la lessive; w. **line** corde *f* à linge; w. **machine** machine *f* à laver; w. **powder** *Br* lessive *f*. ● **washing-up** *n Br* vaisselle *f*; **to do the** w.-

up faire la vaisselle; **w.-up liquid** produit *m* pour la vaisselle.

washout ['wɒʃaut] *n Fam* (*event etc*) fiasco *m*; (*person*) nullité *f*. ● **washroom** *n Am* toilettes *fpl*.

wasp [wɒsp] *n* guêpe *f*.

wastage ['weɪstɪdʒ] *n* gaspillage *m*; (*losses*) pertes *fpl*; **some** w. (*of goods, staff etc*) du déchet.

waste [weɪst] *n* gaspillage *m*; (*of time*) perte *f*; (*Br rubbish, Am garbage*) déchets *mpl*; **wastes** (*land*) étendue *f* déserte; w. **disposal unit** *Br* broyeur *m* d'ordures; w. **material or products** déchets *mpl*; w. **ground** (*in town*) *Br* terrain *m* vague; w. **land** (*uncultivated*) terres *fpl* incultes; (*in town*) terrain *m* vague; w. **paper** vieux papiers *mpl*; w. **pipe** tuyau *m* d'évacuation.

▮ *vt* (*money, food etc*) gaspiller; (*time, opportunity*) perdre; **to** w. **one's time on frivolities/etc** gaspiller son temps en frivolités/etc, perdre son temps à des frivolités/etc; **to** w. **one's life** gâcher sa vie.

▮ *vi* **to** w. **away** dépérir. ● **wasted** *a* (*effort*) inutile; (*body etc*) émacié.

wastebin ['weɪstbɪn] *n* (*in kitchen*) poubelle *f*.

wasteful ['weɪstfəl] *a* (*person*) gaspilleur; (*process*) peu économique.

wastepaper ['weɪstpeɪpər] *n* vieux papiers *mpl*; w. **basket** corbeille *f* (à papier).

watch [wɒtʃ] 1 *n* (*small clock*) montre *f*. 2 *n* (*over suspect, baby etc*) surveillance *f*; (*on ship*) quart *m*; **to keep (a)** w. **over or on s.o./sth** surveiller qn/qch; **to keep a close** w. **on** surveiller de près; **to keep** w. faire le guet; **to be on the** w. **(for)** guetter ▮ *vt* regarder; (*observe*) observer; (*suspect, baby, luggage etc*) surveiller; (*be careful of*) faire attention à ▮ *vi* regarder; **to** w. **(out) for sth/ s.o.** (*wait for*) guetter qch/qn; **to** w. **out** (*take care*) faire attention (**for** à); w. **out!** attention!; **to** w. **over** surveiller.

watchdog ['wɒtʃdɒg] *n* chien *m* de garde.

watchful ['wɒtʃfəl] *a* vigilant.

watchmaker ['wɒtʃmeɪkər] *n* horloger, -ère *mf*. ● **watchman** *n* (*pl* **-men**) **night** w. veilleur *m* de nuit. ● **watchstrap** *n* bracelet *m* de montre. ● **watchtower** *n* tour *f* de guet.

water ['wɔːtər] *n* eau *f*; **by** w. en bateau; **under** w. (*road, field etc*) inondé; (*to swim*) sous l'eau; **at high** w. à marée haute; **hard/ soft** w. eau *f* calcaire/douce; **it doesn't hold** w. (*of theory etc*) Fig ça ne tient pas debout; **in hot** w. Fig dans le pétrin; w. **cannon** lance *f* à eau; w. **heater** chauffe-eau *m inv*; w. **ice** *Br* sorbet *m*; w. **lily** nénuphar *m*; w. **main** conduite *f* d'eau; w. **pistol** pistolet *m* à eau; w. **polo** *Sport* water-polo *m*; w. **power** énergie *f* hydraulique; w. **rates** *Br* taxes *fpl* sur l'eau; w. **skiing** ski *m* nautique; w. **tank** réservoir *m* d'eau; w. **tower** château *m* d'eau; w. **wings** manchons *mpl* (de natation).

▮ *vt* (*plant etc*) arroser; **to** w. **down** (*wine etc*) couper (d'eau); (*text etc*) édulcorer.

❚ *vi* (*of eyes*) larmoyer; **it makes his mouth w.** ça lui fait venir l'eau à la bouche.
● **watering** *n* (*of plant etc*) arrosage *m*.
● **watering can** *n* arrosoir *m*.

watercolour ['wɔːtəkʌlər] (*Am* **-color**) *n* (*picture*) aquarelle *f*; (*paint*) couleur *f* pour aquarelle. ● **watercress** *n* cresson *m* (de fontaine). ● **waterfall** *n* chute *f* d'eau.
● **waterfront** *n* (*at seaside*) front *m* de mer; (*at docks*) quais *mpl*. ● **waterhole** *n* (*in desert*) point *m* d'eau. ● **waterline** *n* (*on ship*) ligne *f* de flottaison. ● **waterlogged** *a* délavé.
● **watermark** *n* (*in paper*) filigrane *m*.
● **watermelon** *n* pastèque *f*. ● **waterproof** *a* (*material*) imperméable. ● **water-repellent** *a* déperlant. ● **watershed** *n* (*turning point*) tournant *m* (décisif). ● **watertight** *a* (*container etc*) étanche. ● **waterway** *n* voie *f* navigable. ● **waterworks** *n* (*place*) station *f* hydraulique.

watery ['wɔːtəri] *a* (*soup etc*) trop liquide; (*colour*) délavé; (*eyes*) larmoyant; **w. tea** *or* **coffee** de la lavasse.

watt [wɒt] *n* El watt *m*.

wave [weiv] *n* (*of sea*) vague *f*; (*in hair*) ondulation *f*; (*sign*) signe *m* (de la main); *Radio Phys* onde *f*; (*of enthusiasm, protests etc*) *Fig* vague *f*; **medium/short w.** *Radio* ondes *fpl* moyennes/courtes; **long w.** *Radio* grandes ondes, ondes longues; **shock w.** (*from bomb blast etc*) & *Fig* onde *f* de choc.
❚ *vi* (*with hand*) faire signe (de la main); (*of flag*) flotter; **to w. to s.o.** (*greet*) saluer qn de la main.
❚ *vt* (*arm, flag etc*) agiter; (*s.o.'s hair*) onduler; **to w. s.o. on** faire signe à qn d'avancer; **to w. aside** (*objection etc*) écarter. ● **waveband** *n Radio* bande *f* de fréquence. ● **wavelength** *n Radio* & *Fig* longueur *f* d'onde; **on the same w.** *Fig* sur la même longueur d'onde.

waver ['weivər] *vi* (*of person, flame etc*) vaciller.

wavy ['weivi] *a* (**-ier, -iest**) (*line*) onduleux; (*hair*) ondulé.

wax [wæks] **1** *n* cire *f*; (*for ski*) fart *m* ❚ *vt* cirer; (*ski*) farter; (*car*) lustrer ❚ *a* (*candle, doll etc*) de cire; **w. paper** (*for wrapping etc*) *Am* papier *m* paraffiné. **2** *vi* (*of moon*) croître. **3** *vi* **to w. lyrical/merry** (*become*) *Lit* se faire lyrique/gai. ● **waxworks** *npl* (*place*) musée *m* de cire; (*dummies*) moulages *mpl* de cire.

way¹ [wei] *n* (*path, road*) chemin *m* (**to** de); (*direction*) sens *m*, direction *f*; (*distance*) distance *f*; **all the w., the whole w.** (*to talk etc*) pendant tout le chemin; **this w.** par là; **which w.?** par où?; **to lose one's w.** se perdre; **I'm on my w.** (*coming*) j'arrive; (*going*) je pars; **to make one's w. towards** se diriger vers; **he made his w. out/ home** il est sorti/rentré; **the w. there** l'aller *m*; **the w. back** le retour; **the w. in** l'entrée *f*; **the w. out** la sortie; **a w. out of** (*problem etc*) *Fig* une solution à; **the w. is clear** *Fig* la voie

est libre; **across the w.** en face; **on the w.** en route (**to** pour); **by w. of** (*via*) par; (*as*) *Fig* comme; **out of the w.** (*isolated*) isolé; **to go out of one's w. to do sth** se donner du mal pour faire qch; **by the w. ....** *Fig* à propos...; **to be** *or* **stand in s.o.'s w.** être sur le chemin de qn; **she's in my w.** (*hindrance*) *Fig* elle me gêne; **to get out of the w., make w.** s'écarter; **to give w.** céder; (*in vehicle*) *Br* céder le passage *or* la priorité (**to** à); **a long w.** (*away or off*) très loin; **it's the wrong w. up** c'est dans le mauvais sens; **do it the other w. round** fais le contraire.
❚ *adv* (*behind etc*) très loin; **w. ahead** très en avance (**of** sur).

way² [wei] *n* (*manner*) façon *f*; (*means*) moyen *m*; (*condition*) état *m*; (*habit*) habitude *f*; (*particular*) égard *m*; **one's ways** (*behaviour*) ses manières *fpl*; **to get one's own w.** obtenir ce qu'on veut; (**in**) **this w.** de cette façon; **in a w.** (*to some extent*) dans un certain sens; **w. of life** mode *m* de vie, façon *f* de vivre; **no w.!** (*certainly not*) *Fam* pas question!; **w. to go!** *Am Sl* c'est géant!

wayfarer ['weifeərər] *n* voyageur, -euse *mf*.

waylay [wei'lei] *vt* (*pt & pp* **-laid**) (*attack*) attaquer par surprise; (*stop*) *Fig* arrêter au passage.

way-out [wei'aut] *a Fam* extraordinaire.

wayside ['weisaid] *n* **by the w.** au bord de la route.

wayward ['weiwəd] *a* rebelle, capricieux.

WC [dʌb(ə)lju:'si:] *n* w-c *mpl*.

we [wiː] *pron* **1** nous; **we go** nous allons; **we teachers** nous autres professeurs; **we are right — not you** (*stressed*) nous, nous avons raison — pas vous. **2** (*indefinite*) on; **we never know** on ne sait jamais; **we all make mistakes** tout le monde peut se tromper.

weak [wiːk] *a* (**-er, -est**) faible; (*tea, coffee*) léger; **to have a w. stomach/kidneys/etc** avoir l'estomac/les reins/etc fragiles(s). ● **weakly** *adv* faiblement. ● **weakness** *n* faiblesse *f*; (*of stomach etc*) fragilité *f*; (*fault*) point *m* faible; **a w. for** (*liking*) un faible pour.

weaken ['wiːkən] *vt* affaiblir ❚ *vi* faiblir.

weakling ['wiːkliŋ] *n* (*in body*) mauviette *f*; (*in character*) faible *mf*.

weak-willed ['wiːkwild] *a* faible, mou (*f* molle).

weal [wiːl] *n* (*wound on skin*) marque *f*, zébrure *f*.

wealth [welθ] *n* (*money, natural resources*) richesse(s) *f(pl)*; **a w. of** (*abundance*) *Fig* une profusion de. ● **wealthy** *a* (**-ier, -iest**) riche ❚ *n* **the w.** les riches *mpl*.

wean [wiːn] *vt* (*baby*) sevrer.

weapon ['wepən] *n* arme *f*. ● **weaponry** *n* armements *mpl*.

wear [weər] **1** *vt* (*pt* **wore**, *pp* **worn**) (*have on body*) porter; (*put on*) mettre; **to have nothing to w.** n'avoir rien à se mettre; **to w. a strange smile/look** *Fig* avoir un drôle d'air/de sourire ❚ *n* **men's/sports w.** vêtements *mpl* pour hommes/de sport; **evening w.** tenue *f* de soirée.

2 *vt* (*pt* **wore**, *pp* **worn**) (*material, Fig patience etc*) user ▮ *vi* (*last*) faire de l'usage, durer; (*become worn*) s'user ▮ *n* (*use*) usage *m*; **w. (and tear)** usure *f*. ●**wearing** *a* (*tiring*) épuisant.

wear away *vt* (*clothes, Fig patience etc*) user ▮ *vi* (*of material*) s'user; (*of colours, ink*) s'effacer ▮ **to wear down** *vt* = **wear out** ▮ **to wear off** *vi* (*of colour, Fig pain etc*) disparaître, passer ▮ **to wear on** *vi* (*of time*) passer ▮ **to wear out** *vt* (*clothes, Fig patience etc*) user; **to w. s.o. out** épuiser qn ▮ *vi* (*of clothes etc*) s'user; (*of patience*) Fig s'épuiser.

weary ['wɪərɪ] *a* (**-ier, -iest**) (*tired*) fatigué, Lit las (*f* lasse) (**of doing** de faire); (*tiring*) fatigant; (*look, smile*) las (*f* lasse) ▮ *vi* **to w. of** se lasser de. ●**wearily** *adv* avec lassitude. ●**weariness** *n* lassitude *f*.

weasel ['wiːz(ə)l] *n* belette *f*.

weather ['weðər] *n* temps *m*; **what's the w. like?** quel temps fait-il?; **in (the) hot w.** par temps chaud; **under the w.** (*ill*) patraque ▮ *a* **w. chart/conditions/station**/*etc* carte *f*/ conditions/*fpl* station *f*/*etc* météorologique(s); **w. forecast** prévisions *fpl* météorologiques, météo *f*; **w. report** (*bulletin m*) météo *f*; **w. vane** girouette *f* ▮ *vt* (*storm, hurricane etc*) essuyer; (*crisis*) Fig surmonter. ●**weather-beaten** *a* (*face, person*) tanné, hâlé. ●**weathercock** *n* girouette *f*. ●**weatherman** *n* (*pl* **-men**) (*on TV or radio*) Fam présentateur *m* météo.

weave [wiːv] *vt* (*pt* **wove**, *pp* **woven**) (*cloth, Fig plot*) tisser; (*basket, garland*) tresser ▮ *vi* Tex tisser; **to w. in and out of** (*crowd, cars etc*) Fig se faufiler entre ▮ *n* (*style*) tissage *m*. ●**weaving** *n* tissage *m*. ●**weaver** *n* tisserand, -ande *mf*.

web [web] *n* (*of spider*) toile *f*; (*of lies*) Fig tissu *m*. ●**webbed** *a* (*foot*) palmé. ●**webbing** *n* (*in chair*) sangles *fpl*.

wed [wed] *vt* (**-dd-**) (*marry*) épouser; (*qualities etc*) Fig allier (**to** à) ▮ *vi* se marier. ●**wedded** *a* (*bliss, life*) conjugal.

we'd [wiːd] = **we had & we would**.

wedding ['wedɪŋ] *n* mariage *m*; **golden/silver w.** noces *fpl* d'or/d'argent ▮ *a* (*cake*) de noces; (*anniversary, present*) de mariage; (*dress*) de mariée; **his** *or* **her w. day** le jour de son mariage; **w. ring** Br, **w. band** Am alliance *f*.

wedge [wedʒ] *n* (*under wheel, table etc*) cale *f*; (*for splitting*) coin *m*; **w. heel** (*of shoe*) semelle *f* compensée ▮ *vt* (*wheel, table etc*) caler; (*push*) enfoncer (**into** dans); **wedged (in) between** (*caught, trapped*) coincé entre.

wedlock ['wedlɒk] *n* **born out of w.** illégitime.

Wednesday [Br 'wenzdɪ, Am -deɪ] *n* mercredi *m*.

wee [wiː] *a* (*tiny*) Fam tout petit.

weed [wiːd] *n* (*plant*) mauvaise herbe *f*; (*weak person*) Fam mauviette *f*; **w. killer** désherbant *m* ▮ *vti* désherber ▮ *vt* **to w. out**

Fig éliminer (**from** de). ●**weedy** *a* (**-ier, -iest**) (*person*) Fam maigre et chétif.

week [wiːk] *n* semaine *f*; **the w. before last** pas la semaine dernière, celle d'avant; **the w. after next** pas la semaine prochaine, celle d'après; **tomorrow w.** Br, **a w. tomorrow** Br, **a w. from tomorrow** Am demain en huit. ●**weekday** *n* jour *m* de semaine, jour *m* ouvrable.

weekend [Br wiːk'end, Am 'wiːkend] *n* week-end *m*; **at** *or* **on** *or* **over the w.** ce week-end, pendant le week-end.

weekly ['wiːklɪ] *a* hebdomadaire ▮ *adv* toutes les semaines ▮ *n* (*magazine*) hebdomadaire *m*.

weep [wiːp] *vi* (*pt & pp* **wept**) pleurer; (*of wound*) suinter; **to w. for s.o.** pleurer qn ▮ *vt* (*tears*) pleurer. ●**weeping willow** *n* saule *m* pleureur.

weewee ['wiːwiː] *n* Fam pipi *m*; **to do** *or* **have a w.** faire pipi.

weft [weft] *n* Tex trame *f*.

weigh [weɪ] *vt* peser; **to w. sth/s.o. down** (*with load etc*) surcharger qch/qn (**with** de); **to w. down a branch**/*etc* (*of fruit*) faire plier une branche/*etc*; **to be weighed down by** (*of branch etc*) plier sous le poids de; **weighed down with worry**/*etc* Fig accablé de soucis/*etc*; **to w. up** (*goods, chances etc*) peser ▮ *vi* peser; **it's weighing on my mind** ça me tracasse; **to w. down on s.o.** (*of worries etc*) accabler qn. ●**weighing-machine** *n* balance *f*.

weight [weɪt] *n* poids *m*; **by w.** au poids; **to put on w.** grossir; **to lose w.** maigrir; **to carry w.** (*of argument etc*) Fig avoir du poids (**with** pour); **to pull one's w.** (*do one's share*) faire sa part du travail ▮ *vt* **to w. (down)** (*hold down*) faire tenir qch avec un poids; **to w. sth/s.o. down with sth** (*overload*) surcharger qch/qn de qch. ●**weight lifter** *n* haltérophile *mf*. ●**weight lifting** *n* haltérophilie *f*.

weighting ['weɪtɪŋ] *n* Br (*on salary*) indemnité *f* de résidence; **London w.** indemnité de résidence pour Londres.

weightless ['weɪtləs] *a* (*in space*) en état d'apesanteur. ●**weightlessness** *n* apesanteur *f*.

weighty ['weɪtɪ] *a* (**-ier, -iest**) (*heavy*) lourd; (*argument, subject*) Fig de poids.

weir [wɪər] *n* (*across river*) barrage *m*.

weird [wɪəd] *a* (**-ier, -iest**) (*odd*) bizarre; (*eerie*) mystérieux.

welcome ['welkəm] *a* (*pleasant*) agréable; (*timely*) opportun; **to be w.** (*warmly received, of person*) être bien reçu; **w.!** bienvenue!; **w. back!** bienvenue!; **you're always w.** vous êtes toujours le *or* la bienvenu(e); **to make s.o. (feel) w.** faire bon accueil à qn; **to feel w.** se sentir bien accueilli; **I don't feel w.** je me sens de trop; **you're w.!** (*after 'thank you'*) il n'y a pas de quoi!; **a coffee/a break would be w.** un café/une pause ne ferait pas de mal; **to be w. to do** (*free*) être libre de faire; **you're w. to (take** *or* **use) my bike** mon vélo est à ta disposition; **you're w. to it!** *Iron* grand bien vous fasse!

▌ *n* accueil *m*; **to extend a w. to s.o.** (*greet*) souhaiter la bienvenue à qn.

▌ *vt* accueillir; (*warmly*) faire bon accueil à; (*be glad of*) se réjouir de; **I w. you!** (*say welcome to you*) je vous souhaite la bienvenue! ● **welcoming** *a* (*smile etc*) accueillant; (*speech, words*) de bienvenue.

weld [weld] *vt* **to w. (together)** souder; (*groups etc*) Fig unir ▌ *n* (*joint*) soudure *f*. ● **welding** *n* soudure *f*. ● **welder** *n* soudeur *m*.

welfare ['welfeər] *n* (*physical, material*) bien-être *m*; (*spiritual*) santé *f*; (*public aid*) aide *f* sociale; **public w.** (*good*) le bien public; **to be on w.** *Am Fam* percevoir des allocations; **the w. state** (*in Great Britain*) l'État-providence *m*; **w. work** assistance *f* sociale.

well¹ [wel] **1** *n* (*for water*) puits *m*; (*of stairs, Br lift, Am elevator*) cage *f*; (**oil**) **w.** puits de pétrole. **2** *vi* **to w. up** (*rise*) monter.

well² [wel] *adv* (*better, best*) bien; **to do w.** (*succeed*) réussir; **you'd do w. to refuse** tu ferais bien de refuser; **w. done!** bravo!; **I, you, she** *etc* **might (just) as w. have left** il valait mieux partir, autant valait partir; **it's just as w. that** (*lucky*) heureusement que...; **as w.** (*also*) aussi; **as w. as** aussi bien que; **as w. as two cats, he has...** en plus de deux chats, il a....

▌ *a* **she's w.** (*healthy*) elle va bien; **he's not a w. man** c'est un homme malade; **to get w.** se remettre; **all's w.** tout va bien; **that's all very w., but...** tout ça c'est très joli, mais....

▌ *int* eh bien!; **w., w.!** (*surprise*) tiens, tiens!; **huge, w., quite big** énorme, enfin, assez grand.

we'll [wi:l] = **we will** *or* **we shall.**

well-behaved [welbɪ'heɪvd] *a* sage. ● **well-'being** *n* bien-être *m*. ● **well-'built** *a* (*person, car*) solide. ● **well-'founded** *a* bien fondé. ● **well-'heeled** *a* (*rich*) *Fam* nanti. ● **well-in'formed** *a* (*person, newspaper*) bien informé. ● **well-'known** *a* (*bien*) connu. ● **well-'mannered** *a* bien élevé. ● **well-'meaning** *a* bien intentionné. ● **well-nigh** *adv* presque. ● **well-'off** *a* riche, aisé. ● **well-'read** *a* instruit. ● **well-'spoken** *a* (*person*) qui a un accent cultivé, qui parle bien. ● **well-'thought-of** *a* hautement considéré. ● **well-thought-out** *a* bien conçu. ● **well-'timed** *a* opportun. ● **well-to-'do** *a* riche, aisé. ● **well-'tried** *a* (*method*) éprouvé. ● **well-'trodden** *a* (*path*) battu. ● **well-wishers** *npl* admirateurs, -trices *mfpl*. ● **well-woman clinic** *n Br* centre *m* de dépistage gynécologique. ● **well-'worn** *a* (*clothes, carpet*) usagé.

wellington ['welɪŋtən] *n* **w. (boot)** *Br* botte *f* de caoutchouc. ● **welly** *n Br Fam* botte *f* de caoutchouc.

welsh [welʃ] *vi* **to w. on** (*debt, promise*) ne pas honorer.

Welsh [welʃ] *a* gallois; **W. rabbit** *or* **rarebit**

(*grilled cheese*) *Br* toast *m* au fromage ▌ *n* (*language*) gallois *m*; **the W.** (*people*) les Gallois *mpl*. ● **Welshman** *n* (*pl* **-men**) Gallois *m*. ● **Welshwoman** *n* (*pl* **-women**) Galloise *f*.

wench [wentʃ] *n Old-fashioned Hum* jeune fille *f*.

wend [wend] *vt* **to w. one's way** s'acheminer (**to** vers).

went [went] *pt of* **go 1.**

wept [wept] *pt of* **weep.**

were [wər, *stressed* wɜːr] *see* **be.**

werewolf ['weəwʊlf] *n* (*pl* **-wolves**) loup-garou *m*.

west [west] *n* ouest *m*; **(to the) w. of** à l'ouest de; **the W.** *Pol* l'Occident *m*.

▌ *a* (*coast*) ouest *inv*; (*wind*) d'ouest; **W. Africa** Afrique *f* occidentale; **W. Indian** (*a*) antillais; (*n*) Antillais, -aise *mf*; **the W. Indies** les Antilles *fpl*; **the W. Country** *Br* le sud-ouest de l'Angleterre.

▌ *adv* à l'ouest, vers l'ouest. ● **westbound** *a* (*traffic*) en direction de l'ouest; (*carriageway*) *Br* ouest *inv*. ● **westerly** *a* (*point*) ouest *inv*; (*direction*) de l'ouest; (*wind*) d'ouest. ● **western** *a* (*coast*) ouest *inv*; (*culture etc*) *Pol* occidental; **W. Europe** Europe *f* de l'Ouest ▌ *n* (*film*) western *m*. ● **westerner** *n* habitant, -ante *mf* de l'Ouest; *Pol* occidental, -ale *mf*. ● **westernize** *vt* occidentaliser. ● **westward(s)** *a* & *adv* vers l'ouest.

wet [wet] *a* (**wetter, wettest**) mouillé; (*damp, rainy*) humide; (*day, month*) de pluie; **'w. paint'** 'peinture fraîche'; **the ink is w.** l'encre est fraîche; **to be w. through** être trempé; **to get w.** se mouiller; **it's w.** (*raining*) il pleut; **he's w.** (*weak-willed*) *Fam* c'est une lavette; **w. blanket** *Fig* rabat-joie *m inv*; **w. nurse** nourrice *f*; **w. suit** combinaison *f* de plongée ▌ *n* **the w.** (*rain*) la pluie; (*damp*) l'humidité *f* ▌ *vt* (**-tt-**) mouiller. ● **wetness** *n* humidité *f*.

we've [wi:v] = **we have.**

whack [wæk] *n* (*blow*) grand coup *m* ▌ *vt* donner un grand coup à. ● **whacked** *a* **w. (out)** (*tired*) *Br Fam* claqué. ● **whacking** *a* (*big*) *Br Fam* énorme.

whale [weɪl] *n* baleine *f*. ● **whaling** *n* pêche *f* à la baleine.

wham! [wæm] *int* vlan!

wharf [wɔːf] *n* (*pl* **wharfs** *or* **wharves**) (*for ships*) quai *m*.

what [wɒt] **1** *a* quel, quelle, *pl* quel(le)s; **w. book?** quel livre?; **w. a fool/etc!** quel idiot/etc!; **I know w. book it is** je sais quel livre c'est; **w. little she has** le peu qu'elle a.

2 *pron* (*in questions*) qu'est-ce qui; (*object*) (qu'est-ce) que; (*after prep*) quoi; **w.'s happening?** qu'est-ce qui se passe?; **w. does he do?** qu'est-ce qu'il fait?, que fait-il?; **w. is it?** qu'est-ce que c'est?; **w.'s that book?** c'est quoi ce livre?; **w.!** (*surprise*) quoi!, comment!; **w.'s it called?** comment ça s'appelle?; **w. for?** pourquoi?; **w. about me/etc?** et moi/etc?; **w. about leaving/etc?** si on partait/etc?

3 *pron* (*indirect, relative*) (*subject*) ce qui; (*object*) ce que; **I know w. will happen/w.**

she'll do je sais ce qui arrivera/ce qu'elle fera; **w. happens is...** ce qui arrive c'est que...; **w. I need** ce dont j'ai besoin.

whatever [wɒt'evər] *a* **w. (the) mistake/etc** (*no matter what*) quelle que soit l'erreur/etc; **of w. size** de n'importe quelle taille; **no chance w.** pas la moindre chance; **nothing w.** rien du tout ▮ *pron* (*no matter what*) quoi que (+ *sub*); **w. you do** quoi que tu fasses; **w. happens** quoi qu'il arrive; **do w. is important** fais tout ce qui est important; **do w. you want** fais tout ce que tu veux.

what's-it ['wɒtsɪt] *n* (*thing*) *Fam* machin *m*.

whatsoever [wɒtsəʊ'evər] *a & pron* = **whatever.**

wheat [wiːt] *n* blé *m*, froment *m*. ● **wheatgerm** *n* germes *mpl* de blé.

wheedle ['wiːd(ə)l] *vt* **to w. s.o.** enjôler qn (*into doing pour qu'il fasse*); **to w. sth out of s.o.** obtenir qch de qn par la flatterie.

wheel [wiːl] **1** *n* roue *f*; **at the w.** (*of vehicle*) au volant; (*of boat*) à la barre; **w. clamp** (*for vehicle*) sabot *m* (de Denver) ▮ *vt* (*bicycle etc*) pousser ▮ *vi* (*turn*) tourner. **2** *vi* **to w. and deal** *Fam* faire des combines. ● **wheelbarrow** *n* brouette *f*. ● **wheelchair** *n* fauteuil *m* roulant.

wheeze [wiːz] **1** *vi* respirer bruyamment. **2** *n* (*scheme*) *Br Fam* combine *f*. ● **wheezy** *a* (**-ier, -iest**) poussif.

whelk [welk] *n* (*mollusc*) buccin *m*.

when [wen] *adv* quand ▮ *conj* quand, lorsque; (*whereas*) alors que; **w. I finish, w. I've finished** quand j'aurai fini; **w. I saw him** *or* **w. I'd seen him, I left** après l'avoir vu, je suis parti; **the day/moment w.** le jour/moment où; **I talked about w....** j'ai parlé de l'époque où....

whenever [wen'evər] *conj* (*at whatever time*) quand; (*each time that*) chaque fois que.

where [weər] *adv* où; **w. are you from?** d'où êtes-vous? ▮ *conj* (*là*) où; (*whereas*) alors que; **I found it w. she'd left it** je l'ai trouvé là où elle l'avait laissé; **the place/house w.** l'endroit/la maison où; **I went to w. he was** je suis allé à l'endroit où il était; **that's w. you'll find it** c'est là que tu le trouveras. ● **whereabouts** *adv* où (donc) ▮ *n* **his w.** l'endroit *m* où il est. ● **where's as** *conj* alors que. ● **whereby** *adv* par quoi. ● **whereupon** *adv* sur quoi. ● **'wherewithal** *n* **to have the w. to do sth** avoir de quoi faire qch.

wherever [weər'evər] *conj* **w. you go** (*everywhere*) partout où tu iras, où que tu ailles; **I'll go w. you like** (*anywhere*) j'irai (là) où vous voudrez.

whet [wet] *vt* (**-tt-**) (*appetite, desire etc*) aiguiser.

whether ['weðər] *conj* si; **I don't know w. to leave** je ne sais pas si je dois partir; **w. she does it or not** qu'elle le fasse ou non; **w. now or tomorrow** que ce soit maintenant ou demain; **it's doubtful w.** il est douteux que (+ *sub*).

which [wɪtʃ] **1** *a* (*in questions etc*) quel,

quelle, *pl* quel(le)s; **w. hat?** quel chapeau?; **in w. case** auquel cas.

2 *rel pron* (*subject*) qui; (*object*) que; (*after prep*) lequel, laquelle, *pl* lesquel(le)s; (*after clause*) (*subject*) ce qui; (*object*) ce que; **the house w. is old** la maison qui est vieille; **the book w. I like** le livre que j'aime; **the table w. I put it on** la table sur laquelle je l'ai mis; **the film of w. she was speaking** le film dont *or* duquel elle parlait; **she's ill, w. is sad** elle est malade, ce qui est triste; **he lies, w. I don't like** il ment, ce que je n'aime pas; **after w.** (*whereupon*) après quoi.

3 *pron* **w. (one)** (*in questions*) lequel, laquelle, *pl* lesquel(le)s; **w. (one) of us?** lequel *or* laquelle d'entre nous *or* de nous?; **w. (ones) are the best of the books?** quels sont les meilleurs de ces livres?

4 *pron* **w. (one)** (*the one that*) (*subject*) celui qui, celle qui, *pl* ceux qui, celles qui; (*object*) celui *etc* que; **show me w. (one) is red** montrez-moi celui *or* celle qui est rouge; **I know w. (ones) you want** je sais ceux *or* celles que vous désirez.

whichever [wɪtʃ'evər] *a & pron* **w. book/etc** *or* **w. of the books/etc you buy** quel que soit le livre/etc que tu achètes; **take w. books** *or* **w. of the books interest you** prenez les livres qui vous intéressent; **take w. (one) you like** prends celui *or* celle que tu veux; **w. (ones) remain** ceux *or* celles qui restent.

whiff [wɪf] *n* (*puff*) bouffée *f*; (*smell*) odeur *f*.

while [waɪl] *conj* (*when*) pendant que; (*although*) bien que (+ *sub*); (*as long as*) tant que; (*whereas*) tandis que; **w. eating/etc** (*in the course of*) en mangeant/etc ▮ *n* **a w.** un moment, quelque temps; **all the w.** tout le temps ▮ *vt* **to w. away the time** passer le temps (**doing** à faire). ● **whilst** [waɪlst] *conj Br* = **while.**

whim [wɪm] *n* caprice *m*; **on a w.** sur un coup de tête.

whimper ['wɪmpər] *vi* (*of dog, person*) gémir faiblement; (*snivel*) pleurnicher ▮ *n* faible gémissement *m*; **without a w.** (*complaint*) sans se plaindre.

whimsical ['wɪmzɪk(ə)l] *a* (*look, idea*) bizarre; (*person*) fantasque, capricieux.

whine [waɪn] *vi* (*of dog, person etc*) gémir; (*complain*) *Fig* se plaindre ▮ *n* gémissement *m*; (*complaint*) plainte *f*.

whip [wɪp] *n* fouet *m*; (*person*) *Br Pol* chef *m* de file ▮ *vt* (**-pp-**) (*person, eggs etc*) fouetter; (*defeat*) *Fam* dérouiller; **whipped cream** crème *f* fouettée ▮ *vi* (*rush*) aller à toute vitesse. ● **whip-round** *n Br Fam* collecte *f*.

whip off *vt* (*take off*) *Fam* enlever brusquement ▮ **to whip out** *vt* (*from pocket etc*) *Fam* sortir brusquement (**from de**) ▮ **to whip round** *vi* (*rush*) *Fam* faire un saut (**to s.o.'s** chez qn) ▮ **to whip up** *vt* (*interest etc*) susciter; (*eggs etc*) fouetter; (*meal*) *Fam* préparer rapidement.

whirl [wɜːl] *vi* **to w. (round)** tourbillonner,

tournoyer; (*of spinning top*) tourner ▮ *vt* **to w. (round)** faire tourbillonner; (*spinning top*) faire tourner ▮ *n* tourbillon *m*. ●**whirlpool** *n* tourbillon *m*; w. **bath** *Am* bain *m* à remous. ●**whirlwind** *n* tourbillon *m* (de vent).

whirr [wɜːr] *vi* (*of engine, insect wing*) vrombir; (*of spinning top*) ronronner ▮ *n* vrombissement *m*; (*of spinning top*) ronronnement *m*.

whisk [wɪsk] **1** *n* (*for eggs etc*) fouet *m* ▮ *vt* fouetter. **2** *vt* **to away** *or* **off** (*tablecloth etc*) enlever rapidement; (*person*) emmener rapidement; (*chase away*) chasser.

whiskers ['wɪskəz] *npl* (*of cat*) moustaches *fpl*; (*beard*) barbe *f*; (*Br moustache, Am mustache*) moustache *f*; (**side**) **w.** favoris *mpl*.

whisky, *Am* **whiskey** ['wɪskɪ] *n* whisky *m*.

whisper ['wɪspər] *vti* chuchoter; **to w. sth to s.o.** chuchoter qch à l'oreille de qn; **w. to me!** chuchote à mon oreille! ▮ *n* chuchotement *m*; (*rumour*) *Fig* rumeur *f*, bruit *m*.

whist [wɪst] *n Br* (*card game*) whist *m*; **w. drive** tournoi *m* de whist.

whistle ['wɪs(ə)l] *n* sifflement *m*; (*object*) sifflet *m*; **to blow the** *or* **one's w.** siffler, donner un coup de sifflet; **to give a w.** siffler ▮ *vti* siffler; **to w. for** (*dog, taxi*) siffler.

Whit [wɪt] *a* **W. Sunday** *Br* dimanche *m* de Pentecôte.

white [waɪt] *a* (**-er, -est**) blanc (*f* blanche); **to go** *or* **turn w.** blanchir; **w. coffee** *Br* café *m* au lait; **w. elephant** *Fig* objet *m or* projet *m etc* inutile; **w. lie** pieux mensonge *m*; **w. man** blanc *m*; **w. woman** blanche *f*; **w. spirit** white-spirit *m* ▮ *n* (*colour, of egg, of eye*) blanc *m*; (*person*) blanc *m*, blanche *f*. ●**white-collar 'worker** *n* employé, -ée *mf* de bureau. ●**whiten** *vti* blanchir. ●**whiteness** *n* blancheur *f*. ●**whitewash** *n* (*for walls etc*) badigeon *m* ▮ *vt* (*wall etc*) badigeonner; (*person*) *Fig* blanchir; (*events, s.o.'s faults*) camoufler.

whiting ['waɪtɪŋ] *n inv* (*fish*) merlan *m*.

Whitsun ['wɪts(ə)n] *n Br* la Pentecôte.

whittle ['wɪt(ə)l] *vt* **to w. down** (*wood*) tailler; (*price etc*) *Fig* rogner.

whizz [wɪz] **1** *vi* (*rush*) aller à toute vitesse; **to w. past** *or* **by** passer à toute vitesse; **to w. through the air** (*of bullet, spear etc*) fendre l'air. **2** *a* **w. kid** *Fam* petit prodige *m*.

who [huː] *pron* qui; **w. did it?** qui (est-ce qui) a fait ça?; **the woman w.** la femme qui; **w. did you see?** tu as vu qui?; **w. were you talking to?** à qui est-ce que tu parlais?

whoever [huː'evər] *pron* (*no matter who*) (*subject*) qui que ce soit qui; (*object*) qui que ce soit que; **w. has seen this** (*anyone who*) quiconque a *or* celui qui a vu cela; **w. you are** qui que vous soyez; **this man, w. he is** cet homme, quel qu'il soit; **w. did that?** qui donc a fait ça?

whodunit [huː'dʌnɪt] *n* (*detective story*) *Fam* polar *m*.

whole [həʊl] *a* entier; (*intact*) intact; **the w.**

time tout le temps; **the w. apple** toute la pomme, la pomme (tout) entière; **the w. truth** toute la vérité; **the w. world** le monde entier; **the w. lot** le tout; **w. food** aliment *m* complet; **to swallow sth w.** avaler qch tout rond ▮ *n* (*unit*) tout *m*; (*total*) totalité *f*; **the w. of the village** le village (tout) entier, tout le village; **the w. of the night** toute la nuit; **on the w., as a w.** dans l'ensemble. ●**whole-'hearted** *a or* **whole-'heartedly** *adv* sans réserve. ●**wholemeal** *or Am* **wholewheat** *a* (*bread*) complet.

wholesale ['həʊlseɪl] *n* **to deal in w.** faire de la vente en gros ▮ *a* (*price etc*) de gros; (*destruction etc*) *Fig* en masse; **w. business** *or* **trade** commerce *m* de gros ▮ *adv* (*to buy or sell one article*) au prix de gros; (*in bulk*) en gros; (*to destroy etc*) *Fig* en masse. ●**wholesaler** *n* grossiste *m*.

wholesome ['həʊlsəm] *a* (*food, climate etc*) sain.

wholly ['həʊlɪ] *adv* entièrement.

whom [huːm] *pron* (*object*) que; (*in questions and after prep*) qui; **w. did she see?** qui a-t-elle vu?; **the man w. you know** l'homme que tu connais; **with w.** avec qui; **of w.** dont.

whooping cough ['huːpɪŋkɒf] *n* coqueluche *f*.

whoops! [wʊps] *int* (*apology etc*) oups!

whopping ['wɒpɪŋ] *a* (*big*) *Fam* énorme. ●**whopper** *n Fam* chose *f* énorme.

whore [hɔːr] *n* (*prostitute*) putain *f*.

whose [huːz] *poss pron & a* à qui, de qui; **w. book is this?, w. is this book?** à qui est ce livre?; **w. daughter are you?** de qui es-tu la fille?; **the woman w. book I have** la femme dont *or* de qui j'ai le livre; **the man w. mother I spoke to** l'homme à la mère de qui j'ai parlé.

why [waɪ] **1** *adv* pourquoi; **w. not?** pourquoi pas? ▮ *conj* **the reason w. they...** la raison pour laquelle ils... ▮ *npl* **the whys and wherefores** le pourquoi et le comment. **2** *int* (*surprise*) eh bien!, tiens!

wick [wɪk] *n* (*of candle, lighter, oil lamp*) mèche *f*.

wicked ['wɪkɪd] *a* (*evil*) méchant; (*mischievous*) malicieux. ●**wickedly** *adv* méchamment; (*mischievously*) malicieusement. ●**wickedness** *n* méchanceté *f*.

wicker ['wɪkər] *n* osier *m*; **w. basket** panier *m* d'osier; **w. chair** fauteuil *m* en osier. ●**wickerwork** *n* (*objects*) vannerie *f*.

wicket ['wɪkɪt] *n* (*cricket stumps*) guichet *m*.

wide [waɪd] *a* (**-er, -est**) large; (*ocean, desert*) vaste; (*choice, variety, knowledge*) grand; **to be three metres w.** avoir trois mètres de large.
▮ *adv* (*to open*) tout grand; (*to fall, shoot*) loin du but; **wide-'awake** *a* (*alert, not sleeping*) éveillé. ●**widely** *adv* (*to travel*) beaucoup; (*to broadcast, spread*) largement; **w. different** très différent; **it's w. thought** *or* **believed that...** on pense généralement que.... ●**widen** *vt* élargir ▮ *vi* s'élargir.

● **wideness** n largeur f.
widespread ['waidspred] a (très) répandu.
widow ['wɪdəu] n veuve f. ● **widowed** a to be w. (of man) devenir veuf; (of woman) devenir veuve; **her w. uncle** son oncle qui est veuf. ● **widower** n veuf m.
width [wɪdθ] n largeur f.
wield [wi:ld] vt (brandish) brandir (bâton etc); (handle) manier (outil etc); **to w. power** Fig exercer le pouvoir.
wife [waɪf] n (pl **wives**) femme f, épouse f. ● **wife-to-be** n future femme f or épouse f.
wig [wɪg] n perruque f.
wiggle ['wɪg(ə)l] vt agiter; **to w. one's hips** tortiller des hanches ▮ vi (of worm etc) se tortiller; (of tail) remuer.
wild [waɪld] a (-er, -est) (animal, flower, region etc) sauvage; (enthusiasm, sea) déchaîné; (idea, life) fou (f folle); (look) farouche; (angry) furieux (with contre); **w. with joy/anger/etc** fou de joie/colère/etc; **I'm not w. about it** (plan etc) Fam ça ne m'emballe pas; **to be w. about s.o.** (very fond of) être dingue de qn; **to grow w.** (of plant) pousser à l'état sauvage; **to run w.** (of animals) courir en liberté; (of crowd) se déchaîner; **the W. West** Am le Far West ▮ npl **the wilds** les régions fpl sauvages. ● **wild-card character** n Compt caractère m joker. ● **wildcat 'strike** n grève f sauvage. ● **wild-'goose chase** n fausse piste f. ● **wildlife** n faune f, animaux mpl sauvages.
wilderness ['wɪldənəs] n désert m; (overgrown garden etc) jungle f.
wildly ['waɪldlɪ] adv (madly) follement; (violently) violemment.
wile [waɪl] n ruse f, artifice m.
wilful ['wɪlfəl] (Am **willful**) a (intentional, obstinate) volontaire. ● **wilfully** adv volontairement.
will¹ [wɪl] v aux **he will come, he'll come** (future tense) il viendra (**won't he?** n'est-ce pas?); **you will not come, you won't come** tu ne viendras pas (**will you?** n'est-ce pas?); **will you have a tea?** veux-tu prendre un thé?; **w. you be quiet!** veux-tu te taire!; **I w.!** (yes) oui!; **it won't open** ça ne veut pas s'ouvrir, ça ne s'ouvre pas.
will² [wɪl] **1** vt (intend, wish) Old-fashioned vouloir (**that** que (+ sub)); **to w. oneself to do** faire un effort de volonté pour faire ▮ n volonté f; **ill w.** mauvaise volonté; **free w.** libre arbitre m; **of one's own free w.** de son plein gré; **against one's w.** à contrecœur; **at w.** (to leave etc) quand on veut; (to choose) à volonté. **2** n (legal document) testament m.
willing ['wɪlɪŋ] **1** vt (a helper, worker) de bonne volonté; (help, advice etc) spontané; **to be w. to do** être disposé or prêt à faire, vouloir bien faire ▮ n to show w. faire preuve de bonne volonté. ● **willingly** adv (with pleasure) volontiers; (voluntarily) volontairement. ● **willingness** n (goodwill) bonne volonté f; **her w. to do** (enthusiasm) son empressement m à faire.

willow ['wɪləu] n (tree, wood) saule m.
willowy ['wɪləuɪ] a (person) gracile, svelte.
willpower ['wɪlpauər] n volonté f.
willy-nilly [wɪlɪ'nɪlɪ] adv bon gré mal gré, de gré ou de force.
wilt [wɪlt] vi (of plant) dépérir; (of enthusiasm etc) Fig décliner.
wily [waɪlɪ] a (-ier, -iest) rusé.
wimp [wɪmp] n (weakling) Fam femmelette f, mauviette f.
win [wɪn] n (victory) victoire f ▮ vi (pt & pp **won**, pres p **winning**) gagner ▮ vt (money, race etc) gagner; (prize) gagner, remporter; (victory) remporter; (fame) acquérir; (friends) se faire; **to w. s.o. over** or Br **round** gagner qn (**to** à). ● **winning** a (number, horse etc) gagnant; (team) victorieux; (goal) décisif; (smile) engageant ▮ npl **winnings** gains mpl.
wince [wɪns] vi faire une grimace (de douleur, dégoût etc); **without wincing** sans sourciller.
winch [wɪntʃ] n treuil m ▮ vt **to w. (up)** hisser au treuil.
wind¹ [wɪnd] n vent m; (breath) souffle m; **to have w.** (in stomach) avoir des gaz; **to get w. of sth** entendre parler de qch; **there's something in the w.** Fig il y a quelque chose dans l'air; **w. instrument** Mus instrument m à vent ▮ vt (of blow etc) couper le souffle à qn. ● **windbreak** n (fence, trees) brise-vent m inv. ● **windcheater** or Am **windbreaker** n blouson m, coupe-vent m inv. ● **windfall** n (piece of fruit) fruit m abattu par le vent; (unexpected money) Fig aubaine f. ● **windmill** n moulin m à vent. ● **windpipe** n trachée f. ● **windscreen** or Am **windshield** n (of vehicle) pare-brise m inv; **w. wiper** essuie-glace m inv. ● **windsurfer** n (person) véliplanchiste mf; (board) planche f à voile. ● **windsurfing** n **to go w.** faire de la planche à voile. ● **windswept** a (street etc) balayé par les vents. ● **windy** a (-ier, -iest) **it's w.** (of weather) il y a du vent; **w. day** jour m de grand vent; **w. place** endroit m plein de vent.
wind² [waɪnd] vt (pt & pp **wound**) (roll) enrouler (**round** autour de); (clock) remonter ▮ vi (of river, road) serpenter. ● **winding** a (road etc) sinueux; (staircase) tournant. ● **winder** n (of watch) remontoir m.
wind down [waɪnd] vt (car window) baisser ▮ vi (relax) Fam se détendre ▮ **to wind up** vt (clock) remonter; (meeting, speech etc) terminer; **to w. s.o. up** (annoy) Br Fam faire marcher qn ▮ vi (end up) finir (**doing par** faire); **to w. up with sth/s.o.** se retrouver avec qch/qn.
window ['wɪndəu] n fenêtre f; (pane) vitre f, carreau m; (in vehicle or train) vitre f; (in shop) vitrine f; (counter) guichet m; **French w.** Br porte-fenêtre f; **w. box** jardinière f; **w. cleaner** Br, **w. washer** Am laveur, -euse mf de carreaux; **w. dresser** étalagiste mf; **w. ledge** Br = **windowsill**; **to go w. shopping** faire du lèche-vitrines. ● **windowpane** n vitre

f, carreau m. ● **windowsill** n (inside) appui m
de (la) fenêtre; (outside) rebord m de (la)
fenêtre.
windy ['wɪndɪ] a see wind¹.
wine [waɪn] n vin m; w. **bar/bottle** bar m/
bouteille f à vin; w. **cellar** cave f (à vin); w.
grower viticulteur m; w. **list** carte f des vins;
w. **taster** dégustateur, -trice mf de vins; w.
tasting dégustation f de vins; w. **waiter**
sommelier m ▌ vt to w. **and dine s.o.** offrir à
dîner et à boire à qn. ● **wineglass** n verre m
à vin. ● **wine-growing** a viticole.
wing [wɪŋ] n aile f; the **wings** (in theatre)
coulisses fpl; **to take s.o. under one's w.** Fig
prendre qn sous son aile. ● **winged** a ailé.
● **winger** n Football etc ailier m. ● **wingspan**
n envergure f.
wink [wɪŋk] vi faire un clin d'œil (at, to à);
(of light) clignoter ▌ n clin m d'œil.
winkle ['wɪŋk(ə)l] n (sea animal) bigorneau
m.
winner ['wɪnər] n (of contest etc) gagnant,
-ante mf; (of argument, fight) vainqueur m;
that **idea/etc is a w.** Fam c'est une idée/etc
en or. ● **winning** a & npl see **win**.
winter ['wɪntər] n hiver m; **in (the) w.** en hiver; a **w.'s day** un jour d'hiver ▌ a d'hiver.
● **wintertime** n hiver m. ● **wintry** a hivernal;
w. **day** jour m d'hiver.
wipe [waɪp] vt essuyer; to w. **one's feet/hands**
s'essuyer les pieds/les mains; **to w. away** or
off or **up** (liquid) essuyer; **to w. out** (clean)
essuyer; (destroy) anéantir; (erase) effacer ▌
vi to w. **up** (dry the dishes) essuyer la
vaisselle ▌ n to **give sth a w.** donner un coup
de torchon or d'éponge à qch. ● **wiper** n
(for Br windscreen, Am windshield) essuie-
glace m inv.
wire ['waɪər] n fil m; w. **mesh** or **netting**
grillage m ▌ vt to w. **(up)** (house) faire
l'installation électrique de; to w. **sth (up) to**
sth (connect electrically) relier qch à qch; to
w. **a hall (up) for sound** sonoriser une salle.
● **wiring** n (system) installation f électrique;
(wires) fils mpl électriques.
wirecutters ['waɪəkʌtəz] npl pince f cou-
pante.
wireless ['waɪələs] n (set) Old-fashioned Br
TSF f, radio f.
wiry ['waɪərɪ] a (-ier, -iest) maigre et
nerveux.
wisdom ['wɪzdəm] n (knowledge) sagesse f;
(advisability) prudence f; w. **tooth** dent f de
sagesse.
wise [waɪz] a (-er, -est) (in knowledge) sage;
(advisable) prudent; (learned) savant; **to put**
s.o. w./be w. to Fam mettre qn/être au courant de; w. **guy** Fam gros malin m. ● **wise-**
crack n Fam (joke) astuce f; (sarcastic remark) sarcasme m. ● **wisely** adv prudemment.
-wise [waɪz] suff (with regard to) **money/**
etc **-wise** question argent/etc.
wish [wɪʃ] vt souhaiter, vouloir (to do faire);
I w. **(that) you could help me/could have**

helped me je voudrais que/j'aurais voulu que
vous m'aidiez; I w. I **hadn't done that** je regrette d'avoir fait ça; **if you w.** si tu veux; I
w. **you (a) happy birthday/(good) luck** je
vous souhaite (un) bon anniversaire/bonne
chance; I w. I **could** si seulement je pouvais.
▌ vi to w. **for sth** souhaiter qch; I **wished for**
him to recover quickly j'ai souhaité qu'il se
rétablisse vite; **as you w.** comme vous voulez.
▌ n (specific) souhait m, vœu m; (general)
désir m; the w. **for sth/to do** le désir de qch/
de faire; **best wishes, all good wishes** (in
greeting card) meilleurs vœux mpl; (in letter)
amitiés fpl, bien amicalement; **send him my**
best wishes fais-lui mes amitiés. ● **wishbone**
n fourchette f, lunette f. ● **wishful** a it's w.
thinking (on your part) tu rêves, tu prends
tes désirs pour la réalité.
wishy-washy ['wɪʃɪwɒʃɪ] a (taste, colour)
fade, fadasse.
wisp [wɪsp] n (of smoke) volute f; (of hair)
fine mèche f; (of straw) brin m; a **(mere) w.**
of a girl Hum une fillette toute menue.
wisteria [wɪ'stɪərɪə] n (plant) glycine f.
wistful ['wɪstfəl] a mélancolique et rêveur.
● **wistfully** adv d'un ton rêveur, avec mélancolie.
wit [wɪt] n 1 (humour) esprit m; (person)
homme m or femme f d'esprit. 2 **wit(s)** (intelligence) intelligence f; he **didn't have the**
w. **to do it** il n'a pas eu l'intelligence de le
faire; **to be at one's wits'** or **wit's end** ne plus
savoir que faire.
witch [wɪtʃ] n sorcière f. ● **witchcraft** n
sorcellerie f. ● **witch-hunt** n Pol chasse f
aux sorcières.
with [wɪð] prep 1 avec; **come w. me** viens
avec moi; w. **no hat/gloves/etc** sans chapeau/
gants/etc; I'll **be right w. you** je suis à vous
dans une seconde; I'm w. **you** (I understand)
Fam je te suis; **to be w. it** (up-to-date) Fam
être dans le vent.
2 (at the house, flat etc of) chez; **she's staying**
w. **me** elle loge chez moi; **it's a habit w. me**
Fig c'est une habitude chez moi.
3 (cause) de; **to jump w. joy** sauter de joie;
to be ill with measles être malade de la rougeole.
4 (instrument, means) avec; de; **to write w. a**
pen écrire avec un or au stylo; **to walk w. a**
stick marcher avec une canne; **to fill w.** remplir de; **satisfied w.** satisfait de; w. **my own**
eyes de mes propres yeux; w. **two hands** à
deux mains.
5 (description) à; a **woman w. blue eyes** une
femme aux yeux bleus.
6 (despite) malgré; w. **all his faults** malgré
tous ses défauts.
withdraw [wɪð'drɔː] vt (pt withdrew, pp
withdrawn) (person, money, troops, claim
etc) retirer (**from** de) ▌ vi (of person, troops,
candidate etc) se retirer (**from** de). ● **with-**
drawn a (person) renfermé. ● **withdrawal** n
retrait m; **to suffer from w. symptoms** (of

drug addict etc) être en manque.

wither ['wɪðər] *vi* (*of plant etc*) se flétrir ▮ *vt* flétrir. ● **withered** *a* (*plant*) flétri; (*limb*) atrophié; (*old man etc*) desséché. ● **withering** *a* (*look*) foudroyant; (*remark*) cinglant.

withhold [wɪð'həʊld] *vt* (*pt & pp* **withheld**) (*permission, help etc*) refuser (**from** à); (*decision*) différer; (*money*) retenir (**from** de); (*information etc*) cacher (**from** à).

within [wɪð'ɪn] *adv* à l'intérieur ▮ *prep* (*place, box etc*) à l'intérieur de, dans; **w. 10km** (**of**) (*less than*) à moins de 10 km (de); (*inside an area of*) dans un rayon de 10 km (de); **w. a month** (*to return etc*) avant un mois; (*to finish sth*) en moins d'un mois; (*to pay*) sous un mois; **it's w. my means** c'est dans (les limites de) mes moyens; **to live w. one's means** vivre selon ses moyens; **w. sight** en vue.

without [wɪð'aʊt] *prep* sans; **w. a tie/etc** sans cravate/etc; **w. doing** sans faire; **to do w. sth/s.o.** se passer de qch/qn.

withstand [wɪð'stænd] *vt* (*pt & pp* **withstood**) résister à.

witness ['wɪtnɪs] *n* (*person*) témoin *m*; (*testimony*) témoignage *m*; **to bear w. to** témoigner de; **w. box** *Br*, **w. stand** *Am* barre *f* (des témoins) ▮ *vt* (*accident etc*) être (le) témoin de; (*document*) signer (pour attester l'authenticité de).

witty ['wɪtɪ] *a* (**-ier, -iest**) spirituel. ● **witticism** *n* bon mot *m*, mot *m* d'esprit. ● **wittiness** *n* esprit *m*.

wives [waɪvz] *see* **wife**.

wizard ['wɪzəd] *n* magicien *m*; (*genius*) *Fig* génie *m*, as *m*. ● **wizardry** *n* *Fig* génie *m*.

wizened ['wɪz(ə)nd] *a* ratatiné.

wobble ['wɒb(ə)l] *vi* (*of chair etc*) branler, être bancal; (*of cyclist, pile etc*) osciller; (*of Br jelly, Am jello®, leg*) trembler; (*of wheel*) tourner de façon irrégulière. ● **wobbly** *a* (*table, chair etc*) branlant, bancal (*mpl* -als); (*tooth*) branlant; **to be w. = to wobble**.

woe [wəʊ] *n* malheur *m*. ● **woeful** *a* triste.

wok [wɒk] *n* (*pan for cooking*) wok *m*.

woke, woken [wəʊk, 'wəʊkən] *pt & pp of* **wake¹**.

wolf [wʊlf] **1** *n* (*pl* **wolves**) loup *m*; **w. whistle** sifflement *m* admiratif (*au passage d'une femme*). **2** *vt* **to w.** (**down**) (*food*) engloutir.

woman, *pl* **women** ['wʊmən, 'wɪmɪn] *n* femme *f*; **young w.** jeune femme; **she's a London w.** c'est une Londonienne; **w. doctor** femme *f* médecin; **women drivers** les femmes *fpl* au volant; **w. friend** amie *f*; **w. teacher** professeur *m* femme; **women's** (*clothes, attitudes etc*) féminin; **women's rights** droits *mpl* des femmes *or* de la femme. ● **womanhood** *n* (*quality*) féminité *f*; **to reach w.** devenir (une) femme. ● **womanizer** *n* *Pej* coureur *m* (de femmes *or* de jupons). ● **womanly** *a* féminin.

womb [wuːm] *n* utérus *m*.

women ['wɪmɪn] *see* **woman**.

won [wʌn] *pt & pp of* **win**.

wonder ['wʌndər] **1** *n* (*marvel*) merveille *f*, miracle *m*; (*feeling*) émerveillement *m*; **in w.** (*to watch etc*) émerveillé; (**it's**) **no w.** ce n'est pas étonnant (**that que** (+ *sub*)); **it's a w. she wasn't killed** c'est un miracle qu'elle n'ait pas été tuée; **to work wonders** (*of medicine etc*) faire merveille ▮ *vi* (*marvel*) s'étonner (**at** de) ▮ *vt* **I w. that** *je or* ça m'étonne que (+ *sub*).

2 *vt* (*ask oneself*) se demander (**if** si, **why** pourquoi) ▮ *vi* (*ask oneself questions*) s'interroger (**about** au sujet de, sur); **I was just wondering** je réfléchissais.

wonderful ['wʌndəfəl] *a* (*excellent, astonishing*) merveilleux. ● **wonderfully** *adv* (*beautiful, hot etc*) merveilleusement; (*to do, work etc*) à merveille.

wonky ['wɒŋkɪ] *a* (**-ier, -iest**) *Br Fam* (*table etc*) bancal (*mpl* -als); (*hat, picture*) de travers.

won't [wəʊnt] = **will not**.

woo [wuː] *vt* (*woman*) faire la cour à, courtiser; (*voters etc*) chercher à plaire à.

wood [wʊd] *n* (*material, forest*) bois *m*. ● **woodcut** *n* gravure *f* sur bois. ● **wooded** *a* (*valley etc*) boisé. ● **wooden** *a* de *or* en bois; (*manner, dancer, actor etc*) *Fig* raide. ● **woodland** *n* région *f* boisée. ● **woodlouse** *n* (*pl* **-lice**) cloporte *m*. ● **woodpecker** *n* (*bird*) pic *m*. ● **woodwind** *n* **the w.** (*musical instruments*) les bois *mpl*. ● **wood pigeon** *n* (*pigeon m*) ramier *m*. ● **woodwork** *n* (*school subject*) menuiserie *f*. ● **woodworm** *n* (*larvae*) vers *mpl* (du bois); **it has w.** c'est vermoulu. ● **woody** *a* (**-ier, -iest**) (*hill etc*) boisé; (*stem etc*) ligneux.

wool [wʊl] *n* laine *f* **w. cloth/garment** tissu *m*/vêtement *m* de laine; **the w. industry** l'industrie *f* lainière; **w. shop** magasin *m* de laines. ● **woollen** (*Am* **woolen**) *a* (*dress etc*) en *or* de laine; **the w. industry** l'industrie lainière ▮ *npl* **woollens** *Br*, **woolens** *Am* (*garments*) lainages *mpl*. ● **woolly** *a* (**-ier, -iest**) laineux; (*unclear*) *Fig* nébuleux ▮ *n* (*garment*) *Br Fam* lainage *m*.

word [wɜːd] *n* mot *m*; (*spoken*) parole *f*, mot *m*; (*promise*) parole *f*; (*command*) ordre *m*; (*news*) nouvelles *fpl*; **words** (*of song etc*) paroles *fpl*; **to have a w. with s.o.** (*speak to*) parler à qn; (*advise, criticize*) avoir un mot avec qn; **to keep one's w.** tenir sa promesse; **in other words** autrement dit; **w. for w.** (*to report sth*) mot pour mot; (*to translate sth*) mot à mot; **by w. of mouth** de vive voix; **I have no w. from** je suis sans nouvelles de; **to send w. that...** faire savoir que...; **to leave w. that...** faire dire que...; **the last w. in** (*latest development*) le dernier cri en matière de; **w. processing** traitement *m* de texte; **w. processor** machine *f* à *or* de traitement de texte.

▮ *vt* (*express*) formuler, rédiger. ● **wording** *n* termes *mpl*. ● **wordy** *a* (**-ier, -iest**) verbeux.

wore [wɔːr] *pt of* **wear**.

work [wɜːk] *n* travail *m*; (*product, book etc*)

œuvre f, ouvrage m; (*building or repair work*) travaux *mpl*; **to be at w.** travailler; **hard w.** travail *m* dur; **it's h. work (doing that)** c'est très dur (de faire ça); **farm w.** travaux *mpl* agricoles; **out of w.** au chômage; **a day off w.** un jour de congé *or* de repos; **he's off w.** il n'est pas allé travailler; **the works** (*of clock etc*) le mécanisme; **gas works** (*factory*) *Br* usine f à gaz; **w. force** main-d'œuvre f; **a heavy w. load** beaucoup de travail; **w. permit** permis *m* de travail; **w. station** poste *m* de travail.

▮ *vi* travailler; (*of machine etc*) marcher, fonctionner; (*of drug*) agir; **to w. loose** (*of knot, screw*) se desserrer; (*of tooth*) se mettre à branler; (*of result, agreement, aim*) travailler à.

▮ *vt* (*person*) faire travailler; (*machine*) faire marcher; (*mine*) exploiter; (*miracle*) faire; (*metal, wood etc*) travailler.

workable ['wɜːkəb(ə)l] *a* (*plan, idea etc*) praticable.

workaholic [wɜːkə'hɒlɪk] *n Fam* bourreau *m* de travail. ● **'workbench** *n* établi *m*. ● **workday** *n Am* = **working day.** ● **'workman** *n* (*pl -men*) ouvrier *m*. ● **'workmanship** *n* maîtrise f, travail *m*. ● **'workmate** *n Br* camarade *mf* de travail. ● **'workout** *n Sport* séance f d'entraînement *m*. ● **'workroom** *n* salle f de travail. ● **'workshop** *n* (*place, study course*) atelier *m*. ● **'work-shy** *a Br* peu enclin au travail. ● **workto-'rule** *n Br* grève f du zèle.

work at *vt* (*improve*) travailler (*son français etc*) **▮ to work off** *vt* (*debt*) payer en travaillant; (*excess fat*) se débarrasser de (par l'exercice); (*one's anger*) passer **▮ to work on** *vt* (*book, problem*) travailler à; (*improve*) travailler (*son français etc*); (*principle etc*) se baser sur **▮ to work out** *vi* (*succeed*) marcher; (*do exercises*) s'entraîner; **it works out at 50 francs** ça fait 50 francs **▮** *vt* (*calculate*) calculer; (*problem*) résoudre; (*scheme, plan*) préparer; (*understand*) comprendre **▮ to work up** *vt* **to w. up an appetite** s'ouvrir l'appétit; **to w. up enthusiasm** s'enthousiasmer (*for pour*); **to w. one's way up** (*rise socially etc*) faire du chemin; **to get worked up** s'énerver **▮** *vi* **it works up to** (*climax*) ça tend vers; **to w. up to sth** en venir à qch.

worker ['wɜːkər] *n* travailleur, -euse *mf*; (*manual*) ouvrier, -ière *mf*; (*office*) employé, -ée *mf* (de bureau); **blue-collar w.** col *m* bleu.

working ['wɜːkɪŋ] *a* (*day, clothes etc*) de travail; **w. population** population f active; **a w. wife** une femme qui travaille; **Monday is a w. day** *Br* on travaille le lundi, lundi est un jour ouvré; **w. class** classe f ouvrière; **in w. order** en état_de marche **▮** *npl* **the workings of** (*clock etc*) le mécanisme de. ● **workingclass** *a* ouvrier.

world [wɜːld] *n* monde *m*; **all over the w.** dans le monde entier; **the richest/etc in the world** le *or* la plus riche/etc du monde; **to**

think the w. of penser énormément de bien de; **it did me the** *or* **a w. of good** ça m'a drôlement fait du bien; **why in the w....?** pourquoi diable...?; **out of this w.** (*wonderful*) *Fam* formidable.

▮ *a* (*war, production etc*) mondial; (*champion, record*) du monde; **the W. Cup** *Football* la Coupe du Monde. ● **world-'famous** *a* de renommée mondiale. ● **worldly** *a* (*pleasures*) de ce monde; (*person*) qui a l'expérience du monde. ● **world'wide** *a* universel, mondial **▮** *adv* dans le monde entier.

worm [wɜːm] **1** *n* ver *m*. **2** *vt* **to w. one's way into** s'insinuer dans; **to w. sth out of s.o.** soutirer qch à qn. ● **worm-eaten** *a* (*wood*) vermoulu; (*fruit*) véreux.

worn [wɔːn] *pp of* **wear ▮** *a* (*clothes, Br tyre, Am tire etc*) usé. ● **worn-'out** *a* (*object*) complètement usé; (*person*) épuisé.

worry ['wʌrɪ] *n* souci *m*; **to be a w.** faire du souci (**to s.o.** à qn) **▮** *vi* s'inquiéter (**about sth** de qch, **about s.o.** pour qn) **▮** *vt* inquiéter; **to w. oneself sick** se ronger les sangs. ● **worried** *a* inquiet (**about au sujet de**); **to be w. sick** se ronger les_sangs. ● **worrying** *a* (*news etc*) inquiétant. ● **worrier** *n* anxieux, -euse *mf*. ● **worryguts** *or Am* **worrywart** *n Fam* anxieux, -euse *mf*.

worse [wɜːs] *a* pire, plus mauvais (**than** que); **to get w.** se détériorer; **he's getting w.** (*in health*) il va de plus en plus mal; (*in behaviour*) il se conduit de plus en plus mal.

▮ *adv* plus mal (**than que**); **I could do w.** je pourrais faire pire; **from bad to w.** de mal en pis; **she's w. off (than before)** sa situation est pire qu'avant; (*financially*) elle est encore plus pauvre qu'avant.

▮ *n* **there's w. (to come)** il y a pire encore; **a change for the w.** une détérioration.

worsen ['wɜːs(ə)n] *vi* (*of illness, situation etc*) empirer; **your chances are worsening** tes chances se détériorent **▮** *vt* empirer.

worship ['wɜːʃɪp] *n* culte *m*; **his W. the Mayor** *Br* Monsieur le Maire **▮** *vt* (*-pp-*) (*person, god*) adorer; (*money*) *Pej* avoir le culte de **▮** *vi* (*pray*) faire ses dévotions (**at** à). ● **worshipper** *n* (*in church*) fidèle *mf*; (*of person, money etc*) adorateur, -trice *mf*.

worst [wɜːst] *a* pire, plus mauvais **▮** *adv* (**the**) **w.** le plus mal; **to come off w.** (*in struggle etc*) avoir le dessous **▮** *n* **the w.** (*one*) (*object, person*) le *or* la pire, le *or* la plus mauvais(e); **the w. (thing) is that...** le pire c'est que...; **at (the) w.** au pire; **to be at its w.** (*of crisis etc*) avoir atteint son paroxysme; **the situation is at its w.** la situation est on ne peut plus mauvaise; **to get the w. of it** (*in struggle etc*) avoir le dessous; **the w. is yet to come** on n'a pas encore vu le pire.

worsted ['wʊstɪd] *n* laine f peignée.

worth [wɜːθ] *n* valeur f; **to buy 50 pence w. of chocolates** acheter pour cinquante pence de chocolats **▮** *a* **to be w. sth** valoir qch; **how much** *or* **what is it w.?** ça vaut combien?; **it's w. a great deal** *or* **a lot** (*be valuable,* *important*) avoir beaucoup de valeur; **the film's (well) seeing** le film vaut la peine *or Fam* le coup d'être vu; **it's w. (one's) while** ça (en) vaut la peine *or Fam* le coup; **it's w. (while) waiting** ça vaut la peine *or Fam* le coup d'attendre. ● **worthless** *a* qui ne vaut rien.

worthwhile [wɜːθˈwaɪl] *a* (*book, film etc*) qui vaut la peine d'être lu, vu *etc*; (*activity*) qui (en) vaut la peine; (*plan, contribution*) valable; (*cause*) louable; (*satisfying*) qui donne des satisfactions.

worthy [ˈwɜːðɪ] *a* (**-ier, -iest**) (*person*) digne; (*cause, act*) louable; **to be w. of sth/s.o.** être digne de qch/qn ∎ *n* (*person*) notable *m*.

would [wʊd, *unstressed* wəd] *v aux* **1** (*past tense of 'will'*) (=*conditional tense in French*) **I w. stay, I'd stay** je resterais; **he w. have done it** il l'aurait fait; **I said she'd come** j'ai dit qu'elle viendrait. **2** (*willingness, ability etc*) **w. you help me, please?** voulez-vous m'aider, s'il vous plaît?; **she wouldn't help me** elle n'a pas voulu m'aider; **w. you like some tea?** voudriez-vous (prendre) du thé?; **the wound wouldn't heal** la blessure ne voulait pas cicatriser. **3** (*habit*) (= *used to*) **I w.** see her every day je la voyais chaque jour. ● **would-be** *a* (*musician etc*) soi-disant *inv*.

wound¹ [wuːnd] *vt* (*hurt*) blesser; **the wounded** les blessés *mpl* ∎ *n* blessure *f*.

wound² [waʊnd] *pt & pp of* **wind²**.

wove, woven [wəʊv, ˈwəʊv(ə)n] *see* weave.

wow! [waʊ] *int Fam* oh là là!

WP [dʌb(ə)ljuːˈpiː] *n abbr* **word processor**.

wrangle [ˈræŋg(ə)l] *n* dispute *f* ∎ *vi* se disputer.

wrap [ræp] *vt* (**-pp-**) **to w. (up)** envelopper; (*parcel*) emballer; **wrapped up in** (*engrossed*) *Fig* absorbé par ∎ *vti* **to w. (oneself) up** (*dress warmly*) se couvrir ∎ *n* (*shawl*) châle *m*; (*cape*) pèlerine *f*; **plastic w.** *Am* film *m* plastique. ● **wrapping** *n* (*action, material*) emballage *m*; **w. paper** papier *m* d'emballage. ● **wrapper** *n* (*of Br sweet, Am candy*) papier *m*; (*of book*) jaquette *f*.

wrath [rɒθ] *n Lit* courroux *m*.

wreak [riːk] *vt* **to w. vengeance** on se venger de; **to w. havoc on** ravager.

wreath [riːθ] *n* (*pl* **-s** [riːðz]) (*of flowers*) (*on head, for funeral etc*) couronne *f*.

wreck [rek] *n* (*ship*) épave *f*; (*sinking*) naufrage *m*; (*train etc*) train *m etc* accidenté; (*person*) épave *f* (humaine); **to be a nervous w.** être à bout de nerfs ∎ *vt* (*break, destroy*) détruire; (*ship*) provoquer le naufrage de; (*spoil*) *Fig* gâcher; (*career, hopes etc*) *Fig* briser, détruire. ● **wreckage** *n* (*of plane, train etc*) débris *mpl*. ● **wrecker** *n* **1** (*truck*) *Am* dépanneuse *f*. **2** (*destructive child*) brise-fer *m inv*.

wren [ren] *n* (*bird*) roitelet *m*.

wrench [rentʃ] *vt* **1** (*tool*) *Am* clef *f* (à écrous); (*adjustable*) **w.** clef à molette; **monkey w.** clef anglaise. **2** (*tug at*) tirer sur; (*twist*) tordre; **to w. sth from s.o.** arracher

qch à qn ∎ *n* mouvement *m* de torsion; (*emotional distress*) *Fig* déchirement *m*.

wrest [rest] *vt* **to w. sth from s.o.** arracher qch à qn.

wrestle [ˈres(ə)l] *vi* lutter (**with** avec qn); **to w. with a problem/etc** *Fig* se débattre avec un problème/*etc*. ● **wrestling** *n* (*sport*) lutte *f*; (**all-in**) **w.** (*with relaxed rules*) catch *m*. ● **wrestler** *n* lutteur, -euse *mf*; (*in all-in wrestling*) catcheur, -euse *mf*.

wretch [retʃ] *n* (*unfortunate person*) malheureux, -euse *mf*; (*rascal*) misérable *mf*. ● **wretched** [-ɪd] *a* (*poor, pitiful*) misérable; (*dreadful*) affreux; (*annoying*) maudit.

wriggle [ˈrɪg(ə)l] *vi* **to w. (about)** se tortiller; (*of fish*) frétiller; **to w. out of** (*difficulty, task etc*) esquiver ∎ *vt* (*toes, fingers*) tortiller.

wring [rɪŋ] *vt* (*pt & pp* **wrung**) **to w. (out)** (*clothes by hand*) tordre; (*water*) faire sortir; **I'll w. your neck** *Fig* je vais te tordre le cou; **to w. sth out of s.o.** *Fig* arracher qch à qn; **to be wringing wet** (*of person*) être trempé jusqu'aux os; (*of garment*) être (trempé) à tordre.

wrinkle [ˈrɪŋk(ə)l] *n* (*on skin*) ride *f*; (*in cloth or paper*) pli *m* ∎ *vt* (*skin*) rider; (*cloth, paper*) plisser ∎ *vi* (*of skin*) se rider; (*of cloth etc*) faire des plis.

wrist [rɪst] *n* poignet *m*. ● **wristwatch** *n* montre *f*.

writ [rɪt] *n* acte *m* judiciaire; **to issue a w. against s.o.** assigner qn (en justice).

write [raɪt] *vti* (*pt* **wrote**, *pp* **written**) écrire. ● **write-off** *n* **to be a (complete) w.-off** (*of vehicle*) *Br* être une véritable épave. ● **write-protected** *a* (*diskette*) *Comptr* protégé (en écriture). ● **write-up** *n* (*report in newspaper*) compte rendu *m*.

write away for *vt* (*details etc*) écrire pour demander ∎ **to write back** vi répondre ∎ **to write down** vt noter ∎ **to write in** vi *Radio TV* écrire (**for information/etc** pour demander des renseignements/*etc*) ∎ **to write off** vt (*debt*) passer aux profits et pertes; **to w. off for** = **write away for** ∎ **to write out** vt (*list, Br cheque, Am check etc*) écrire; (*copy*) recopier ∎ **to write up** vt (*notes, diary*) mettre à jour; **to w. up for** = **write away for**.

writer [ˈraɪtər] *n* auteur *m* (**of** de); (*literary*) écrivain *m*.

writhe [raɪð] *vi* (*in pain etc*) se tordre.

writing [ˈraɪtɪŋ] *n* (*handwriting*) écriture *f*; (*literature*) littérature *f*; **writings** (*of author*) écrits *mpl*; **to put sth (down) in w.** mettre qch par écrit; **there's some w.** (*on page*) il y a quelque chose d'écrit; **w. desk** secrétaire *m*; **w. pad** (*for letters etc*) bloc *m* de papier à lettres; (*for notes*) bloc-notes *m*; **w. paper** papier *m* à lettres.

written [ˈrɪt(ə)n] *pp of* **write**.

wrong [rɒŋ] *a* (*sum, idea etc*) faux, (*f* fausse), erroné; (*direction, time etc*) mauvais; (*unfair*) injuste; **to be w.** (*of person*) avoir tort (**to do** de faire); (*mistaken*) se tromper; **it's w. to swear/etc** (*morally*) c'est mal de jurer/*etc*; **it's the w. road** ce n'est pas la bonne route, c'est la mauvaise route; **you're the w. man** (*for job etc*) tu n'es pas l'homme qu'il faut; **the clock's w.** la pendule n'est pas à l'heure; **something's w.** quelque chose ne va pas; **something's w. with the phone/TV/***etc* le téléphone/la télévision/*etc* ne marche pas bien; **something's w. with her arm/leg/***etc* elle a quelque chose au bras/à la jambe/*etc*; **nothing's w.** tout va bien; **what's w. with you?** qu'est-ce que tu as?; **the w. way round** *or* **up** à l'envers; **to rub s.o. up the w. way** *Fig* prendre qn à rebrousse-poil. ▮ *adv* mal; **to go w.** (*of plan*) mal tourner; (*of vehicle, machine*) tomber en panne; (*of clock, watch, camera*) se détraquer; (*of person*) se tromper; **to get the date/day/***etc* se tromper de date/de jour/*etc*; **to get the w.**

number (*on phone*) se tromper de numéro. ▮ *n* (*injustice*) injustice *f*; (*evil*) mal *m*; **to be in the w.** être dans son tort, avoir tort; **right and w.** le bien et le mal. ▮ *vt* faire (du) tort à (*qn*). ●**wrongdoer** *n* (*criminal*) malfaiteur *m*. ●**wrongful** *a* (*accusation etc*) injustifié; **w. arrest** arrestation *f* arbitraire. ●**wrongfully** *adv* à tort. ●**wrongly** *adv* (*incorrectly*) (*to inform, translate etc*) mal; (*to suspect, accuse, condemn, claim etc*) à tort.

wrote [rəʊt] *pt of* write.

wrought [rɔːt] *a* **w. iron** fer *m* forgé. ●**wrought-'iron** *a* (*gate etc*) en fer forgé.

wrung [rʌŋ] *pt* & *pp of* wring.

wry [raɪ] *a* (wryer, wryest) (*comment, smile etc*) ironique; **to pull a w. face** grimacer. ●**wryly** *adv* d'un air ironique.

X

X, x [eks] *n* X, x *m*.

xenophobia [*Br* zenə'fəʊbɪə, *Am* ziːnəʊ-] *n* xénophobie *f*.

Xerox® [ˈzɪərɒks] *n* photocopie *f* ▮ *vt* photocopier.

Xmas [ˈkrɪsməs] *n Fam* Noël *m*.

X-ray [ˈeksreɪ] *n* (*photo*) radio(graphie) *f*; (*beam*) rayon *m* X; **to have an X-ray** passer une radio; **X-ray examination** examen *m* radioscopique ▮ *vt* (*person, organ etc*) radiographier.

xylophone [ˈzaɪləfəʊn] *n* xylophone *m*.

Y

Y, y [waɪ] *n* Y, y *m*.

yacht [jɒt] *n* yacht *m*. ●**yachting** *n* yachting *m*.

yank [jæŋk] *vt Fam* tirer d'un coup sec; **to y. sth off** *or* **out** arracher qch ▮ *n Fam* coup *m* sec.

Yank(ee) [ˈjæŋk(ɪ)] *n Fam* Ricain, -aine *mf*, *Pej* Amerloque *mf*.

yap [jæp] *vi* (-pp-) (*of dog*) japper; (*jabber*) *Fam* jacasser.

yard [jɑːd] *n* **1** (*of house, farm, school, prison etc*) cour *f*; (*for storage*) dépôt *m*, chantier *m*; (*garden*) *Am* jardin *m* (à l'arrière d'une maison); **builder's y.** *Br* chantier *m* de construction. **2** (*measure*) yard *m* (= 91,44 cm). ●**yardstick** *n* (*criterion*) critère *m*; **the y. against which...** le critère selon lequel....

yarn [jɑːn] *n* **1** (*thread*) fil *m*. **2** (*tale*) *Fam* longue histoire *f*.

yawn [jɔːn] *vi* bâiller ▮ *n* bâillement *m*. ●**yawning** *a* (*gulf etc*) béant.

yeah [jeə] *adv* (*yes*) *Fam* ouais.

year [jɪər] *n* an *m*, année *f*; (*of wine*) année *f*; **school/tax/***etc* **y.** année *f* scolaire/fiscale/*etc*; **this y.** cette année; **in the y. 1995** en (l'an) 1995; **he's ten years old** il a dix ans; **New Y.** Nouvel An, Nouvelle Année; **y. in y. out** une année après l'autre; **New Year's Day** le jour de l'An; **New Year's Eve** la Saint-Sylvestre. ●**yearbook** *n* annuaire *m*. ●**yearly**

a annuel ▮ *adv* annuellement; **twice y.** deux fois par an.

yearn [jɜːn] *vi* **to y. for s.o.** languir après qn; **to y. for sth** avoir très envie de qch; **to y. to do** avoir très envie de faire. ●**yearning** *n* (*desire*) grande envie *f* (**for** de, **to do** de faire); (*nostalgia*) nostalgie *f*.

yeast [jiːst] *n* levure *f*.

yell [jel] *vti* **to y.** (**out**) hurler; **to y. at s.o.** (*scold*) crier après qn ▮ *n* hurlement *m*.

yellow [ˈjeləʊ] **1** *a* & *n* (*colour*) jaune (*m*) ▮ *vi* jaunir. **2** *a* (*cowardly*) *Fam* froussard. ●**yellowish** *a* jaunâtre.

yelp [jelp] *vi* (*of dog*) japper ▮ *n* jappement *m*.

Yemen [ˈjemən] *n* Yémen *m*.

yen [jen] *n* **1** (*desire*) grande envie *f* (**for** de, **to do** de faire). **2** (*currency*) yen *m*.

yes [jes] *adv* oui; (*contradicting negative question*) si; **aren't you coming? — y. (I am)!** tu ne viens pas? — si! ▮ *n* oui *m inv*.

yesterday [*Br* ˈjestədɪ, *Am* -deɪ] *adv* & *n* hier (*m*); **y. morning/evening** hier matin/soir; **the day before y.** avant-hier.

yet [jet] **1** *adv* encore; (*already*) déjà; **she hasn't come** (**as**) **y.** elle n'est pas encore venue; **has he come y.?** est-il déjà arrivé?; **the best y.** le meilleur jusqu'ici; **y. more complicated** (*even more*) encore plus compliqué; **not** (**just**) **y.**, *Br* **not y. awhile** pas pour l'instant. **2** *conj* (*nevertheless*) pourtant.

yew [juː] *n* (*tree, wood*) if *m*.

Yiddish ['jɪdɪʃ] *n* & *a* yiddish (*m*).

yield [jiːld] *n* (*of farm etc*) rendement *m*; (*profit*) rapport *m* ▌ *vt* (*produce*) produire, rendre; (*profit*) rapporter; (*give up*) céder (**to à**) ▌ *vi* (*surrender, give way*) céder (**to à**); (*of tree, land etc*) rendre; **'y.'** (*road sign*) *Am* 'cédez la priorité *or* le passage'.

yippee! [jɪ'piː] *int Fam* hourra!

yob(bo) ['jɒb(əʊ)] *n* (*pl* **yob(bo)s** *Br Fam Pej*) loubar(d) *m*.

yoga ['jəʊgə] *n* yoga *m*.

yog(h)urt [*Br* 'jɒgət, *Am* 'jəʊgɜːt] *n* yaourt *m*.

yoke [jəʊk] *n* (*for oxen*) & *Fig* joug *m*.

yokel ['jəʊk(ə)l] *n Pej* plouc *m*.

yolk [jəʊk] *n* jaune *m* (d'œuf).

yonder ['jɒndər] *adv Lit* là-bas.

you [juː] *pron* **1** (*polite form singular*) vous; (*familiar form singular*) tu; (*polite and familiar form plural*) vous; (*object*) vous; te, t'; *pl* vous; (*after prep, 'than', 'it is'*) vous; toi; *pl* vous; (**to**) **y.** (*indirect*) vous; te, t'; *pl* vous; **y. are** vous êtes; tu es; **I see y.** je vous vois; je te vois; **I give it to y.** je vous le donne; je te le donne; **with y.** avec vous; avec toi; **y. teachers** vous autres professeurs; **y. idiot!** espèce d'imbécile!
2 (*indefinite*) on; (*object*) vous; te, t'; *pl* vous; **y. never know on ne sait jamais; it surprises y.** cela vous surprend; cela te surprend. ● **you'd = you had & you would.** ● **you'll = you will.**

young [jʌŋ] *a* (**-er, -est**) jeune; **my young(er) brother** mon (frère) cadet; **my young(er)**

sister ma (sœur) cadette; **her youngest brother** le cadet de ses frères; **my youngest sister** la cadette de mes sœurs; **the youngest son/daughter** le cadet/la cadette ▌ *n* (*of animals*) petits *mpl*; **the y.** (*people*) les jeunes *mpl*; **she's my youngest** (*daughter*) c'est ma petite dernière. ● **young-looking** *a* qui a l'air jeune. ● **youngster** *n* jeune *mf*.

your [jɔːr] *poss a* (*polite form singular, polite and familiar form plural*) votre, *pl* vos; (*familiar form singular*) ton, ta, *pl* tes; (*one's*) son, sa, *pl* ses.

yours [jɔːz] *poss pron* le vôtre, la vôtre, *pl* les vôtres; (*familiar form singular*) le tien, la tienne, *pl* les tien(ne)s; **this book is y.** ce livre est à vous *or* est le vôtre; ce livre est à toi *or* est le tien; **a friend of y.** un ami à vous; un ami à toi.

yourself [jɔː'self] *pron* (*polite form*) vous-même; (*familiar form*) toi-même; (*reflexive*) vous; te, t'; (*after prep*) vous; toi; **you wash y.** vous vous lavez; tu te laves. ● **yourselves** *pron pl* vous-mêmes; (*reflexive & after prep*) vous.

youth [juːθ] *n* (*pl* **-s** [juːðz]) (*age, young people*) jeunesse *f*; (*young man*) jeune *m*; **y. club** maison *f* des jeunes. ● **youthful** *a* (*person*) jeune; (*quality, smile etc*) juvénile, jeune. ● **youthfulness** *n* jeunesse *f*.

you've [juːv] **= you have.**

yoyo ['jəʊjəʊ] *n* (*pl* **-os**) yo-yo *m inv*.

yucky ['jʌkɪ] *a Fam* dégueulasse.

yummy ['jʌmɪ] *a* (**-ier, -iest**) *Fam* délicieux.

yuppie ['jʌpɪ] *n* jeune cadre *m* dynamique, jeune loup *m*.

Z

Z, z [*Br* zed, *Am* ziː] *n* Z, z *m*.

zany ['zeɪnɪ] *a* (**-ier, -iest**) (*idea, person etc*) farfelu.

zap [zæp] *vt Comptr* effacer. ● **zapper** *n* (*for TV channels*) télécommande *f*.

zeal [ziːl] *n* zèle *m*. ● **zealous** ['zeləs] *a* zélé. ● **zealously** *adv* avec zèle.

zebra ['ziːbrə, *Br* 'zebrə] *n* zèbre *m*; **z. crossing** *Br* passage *m* pour piétons.

zenith ['zenɪθ] *n* zénith *m*.

zero ['zɪərəʊ] *n* (*pl* **-os**) zéro *m*; **z. hour** (*for military operation*) *Fig* l'heure H.

zest [zest] *n* **1** (*enthusiasm*) entrain *m*; (*spice*) *Fig* piquant *m*; **z. for living** appétit *m* de vivre. **2** (*of lemon, orange*) zeste *m*.

zigzag ['zɪgzæg] *n* zigzag *m* ▌ *a* & *adv* en zigzag ▌ *vi* (**-gg-**) zigzaguer.

Zimbabwe [zɪm'bɑːbweɪ] *n* Zimbabwe *m*.

zinc [zɪŋk] *n* (*metal*) zinc *m*.

zip [zɪp] **1** *n* **z.** (*fastener*) *Br* fermeture *f* éclair®; **z. pocket** poche *f* à fermeture éclair® ▌ *vt* (**-pp-**) **to z.** (**up**) fermer (avec une fermeture éclair®). **2** *n* (*vitality*) *Fam* entrain *m* ▌ *vi* (**-pp-**) (*go quickly*) aller comme

l'éclair. **3** *a* **z. code** *Am* code *m* postal. ● **zipper** *n Am* fermeture *f* éclair®.

zit [zɪt] *n* (*pimple*) *Am Fam* bouton *m*.

zither ['zɪðər] *n* cithare *f*.

zodiac ['zəʊdɪæk] *n* zodiaque *m*; **sign of the z.** signe *m* du zodiaque.

zombie ['zɒmbɪ] *n* (*spiritless person*) *Fam* robot *m*, zombie *m*.

zone [zəʊn] *n* zone *f*; (*division of city*) secteur *m*; **time z.** fuseau *m* horaire. ● **zoning** *n* (*in city planning*) *Am* zonage *m*.

zonked [zɒŋkt] *a* **z.** (**out**) *Sl* (*exhausted*) vanné; (*on drugs*) défoncé.

zoo [zuː] *n* (*pl* **zoos**) zoo *m*; **z. keeper** gardien, **-ienne** *mf* de zoo. ● **zoological** [zuːə'lɒdʒɪk(ə)l] *a* zoologique. ● **zoology** [zuː'blədʒɪ] *n* zoologie *f*.

zoom [zuːm] **1** *vi* (*rush*) se précipiter; **to z. past** passer comme un éclair. **2** *n* **z. lens** zoom *m* ▌ *vi* **to z. in** (*with camera*) faire un zoom, zoomer (**on** sur).

zucchini [zuː'kiːnɪ] *n* (*pl* **-ni** *or* **-nis**) *Am* courgette *f*.

zwieback ['zwiːbæk] *n* (*rusk*) *Am* biscotte *f*.

FRENCH VERB CONJUGATIONS

Regular Verbs

	-ER Verbs	**-IR Verbs**	**-RE Verbs**
Infinitive	*donn/er*	*fin/ir*	*vend/re*
1 Present	je donne	je finis	je vends
	tu donnes	tu finis	tu vends
	il donne	il finit	il vend
	nous donnons	nous finissons	nous vendons
	vous donnez	vous finissez	vous vendez
	ils donnent	ils finissent	ils vendent
2 Imperfect	je donnais	je finissais	je vendais
	tu donnais	tu finissais	tu vendais
	il donnait	il finissait	il vendait
	nous donnions	nous finissions	nous vendions
	vous donniez	vous finissiez	vous vendiez
	ils donnaient	ils finissaient	ils vendaient
3 Past historic	je donnai	je finis	je vendis
	tu donnas	tu finis	tu vendis
	il donna	il finit	il vendit
	nous donnâmes	nous finîmes	nous vendîmes
	vous donnâtes	vous finîtes	vous vendîtes
	ils donnèrent	ils finirent	ils vendirent
4 Future	je donnerai	je finirai	je vendrai
	tu donneras	tu finiras	tu vendras
	il donnera	il finira	il vendra
	nous donnerons	nous finirons	nous vendrons
	vous donnerez	vous finirez	vous vendrez
	ils donneront	ils finiront	ils vendront
5 Subjunctive	je donne	je finisse	je vende
	tu donnes	tu finisses	tu vendes
	il donne	il finisse	il vende
	nous donnions	nous finissions	nous vendions
	vous donniez	vous finissiez	vous vendiez
	ils donnent	ils finissent	ils vendent
6 Imperative	donne	finis	vends
	donnons	finissons	vendons
	donnez	finissez	vendez
7 Present participle	donnant	finissant	vendant
8 Past participle	donné	fini	vendu

Note The conditional is formed by adding the following endings to the infinitive: -ais, -ais, -ait, -ions, -iez, -aient. Final 'e' is dropped in infinitives ending '-re'.

SPELLING ANOMALIES OF -ER VERBS

Verbs in **-ger** (eg **manger**) take an extra e before endings beginning with o or a: *Present* je mange, nous mangeons; *Imperfect* je mangeais, nous mangions; *Past historic* je mangeai, nous mangeâmes; *Present participle* mangeant. Verbs in **-cer** (eg **commencer**) change c to ç before endings beginning with o or a: *Present* je commence, nous commençons; *Imperfect* je commençais, nous commencions; *Past historic* je commençai, nous commençâmes; *Present participle* commençant. Verbs containing mute e in their penultimate syllable fall into two groups. In the first (eg **mener, peser, lever**), e becomes è before an unpronounced syllable in the present and subjunctive, and in the future and conditional tenses (eg je **mène**, ils **mèneront**). The second group contains most verbs ending in **-eler** and **-eter** (eg **appeler, jeter**). These verbs change l to ll and t to tt before an unpronounced syllable in the present and subjunctive, and in the future and conditional tenses (eg je **mène**, ils **mèneront**). The second group contains most verbs ending in **-eler** and **-eter** (eg **appeler, jeter**). These verbs change l to ll and t to tt before an unpronounced syllable (eg j'appelle, ils appelleront; je jette, ils jetteront). However, the following verbs in **-eler** and **-eter** fall into the first group in which e changes to è before mute e (eg je modèle, ils modèleront; j'achète, ils achèteront): **ciseler, déceler, démanteler, geler, marteler, modeler, peler, receler; acheter, crocheter, fureter, haleter**. Derived verbs (eg **dégeler, racheter**) are conjugated in the same way. Verbs containing é acute in their penultimate syllable change é to è before the unpronounced endings of the present and subjunctive only (eg je cède but je céderai). Verbs in **-yer** (eg **essuyer**) change y to i before an unpronounced syllable in the present and subjunctive, and in the future and conditional tenses (eg j'essuie, ils essuieront). In verbs in **-ayer** (eg **balayer**), y may be retained before mute e (eg je balaie or balaye, ils balaieront or balayeront).

IRREGULAR VERBS

Listed below are those verbs considered to be the most useful. Forms and tenses not given are fully derivable, such as the third person singular of the present tense which is normally formed by substituting 't' for the final 's' of the first person singular, eg 'crois' becomes 'croit', 'dis' becomes 'dit'. Note that the endings of the past historic fall into three categories, the 'a' and 'i' categories shown at *donner*, and at *finir* and *vendre*, and the 'u' category which has the following endings: -us, -ut, -ûmes, -ûtes, -urent. Most of the verbs listed below form their past historic with 'u'. The imperfect may usually be formed by adding -ais, -ait, -ions, -iez, -aient to the stem of the first person plural of the present tense, eg 'je buvais' etc may be derived from 'nous buvons' (stem 'buv-' and ending '-ons'); similarly, the present participle may generally be formed by substituting -ant for -ons (eg buvant). The future may usually be formed by adding -ai, -as, -a, -ons, -ez, -ont to the infinitive or to an infinitive without final 'e' where the ending is -re (eg conduire). The imperative usually has the same forms as the second persons singular and plural and first person plural of the present tense.

1 = Present   2 = Imperfect   3 = Past historic   4 = Future
5 = Subjunctive   6 = Imperative   7 = Present participle
8 = Past participle   n = nous   v = vous   † verbs conjugated with **être** only.

abattre	*like* **battre**
absoudre	1 j'absous, n absolvons 2 j'absolvais 3 j'absolus (*rarely used*) 5 j'absolve 7 absolvant 8 absous, absoute
†s'abstenir	*like* **tenir**
abstraire	1 j'abstrais, n abstrayons 2 j'abstrayais 3 *none* 5 j'abstraie 7 abstrayant 8 abstrait
accourir	*like* **courir**
accroître	*like* **croître** *except* 8 accru

accueillir	*like* **cueillir**
acquérir	1 j'acquiers, n acquérons 2 j'acquérais 3 j'acquis
	4 j'acquerrai 5 j'acquière 7 acquérant 8 acquis
adjoindre	*like* **joindre**
admettre	*like* **mettre**
advenir	*like* **venir** (*but third person only*)
†aller	1 je vais, tu vas, il va, n allons, v allez, ils vont 4 j'irai
	5 j'aille, n allions, ils aillent 6 va, allons, allez (*but note* vas-y)
apercevoir	*like* **recevoir**
apparaître	*like* **connaître**
appartenir	*like* **tenir**
apprendre	*like* **prendre**
asseoir	1 j'assieds, il assied, n asseyons, ils asseyent 2 j'asseyais
	3 j'assis 4 j'assiérai 5 j'asseye 7 asseyant 8 assis
astreindre	*like* **atteindre**
atteindre	1 j'atteins, n atteignons, ils atteignent 2 j'atteignais 3 j'atteignis
	4 j'atteindrai 5 j'atteigne 7 atteignant 8 atteint
avoir	1 j'ai, tu as, il a, n avons, v avez, ils ont 2 j'avais 3 j'eus
	4 j'aurai 5 j'aie, il ait, n ayons, ils aient 6 aie, ayons, ayez
	7 ayant 8 eu
battre	1 je bats, il bat, n battons 5 je batte
boire	1 je bois, n buvons, ils boivent 2 je buvais 3 je bus
	5 je boive, n buvions 7 buvant 8 bu
bouillir	1 je bous, n bouillons, ils bouillent 2 je bouillais
	3 *not used* 5 je bouille 7 bouillant
braire	(*defective*) 1 il brait, ils braient 4 il braira, ils brairont
circonscrire	*like* **écrire**
circonvenir	*like* **tenir**
clore	*like* **éclore**
combattre	*like* **battre**
commettre	*like* **mettre**
comparaître	*like* **connaître**
complaire	*like* **plaire**
comprendre	*like* **prendre**
compromettre	*like* **mettre**
concevoir	*like* **recevoir**
conclure	1 je conclus, n concluons, ils concluent 5 je conclue
concourir	*like* **courir**
conduire	1 je conduis, n conduisons 3 je conduisis 5 je conduise 8 conduit
confire	*like* **suffire**
connaître	1 je connais, il connaît, n connaissons 3 je connus
	5 je connaisse 7 connaissant 8 connu
conquérir	*like* **acquérir**
consentir	*like* **mentir**
construire	*like* **conduire**
contenir	*like* **tenir**
contraindre	*like* **craindre**
contredire	*like* **dire** *except* 1 v contredisez
convaincre	*like* **vaincre**
convenir	*like* **tenir**
corrompre	*like* **rompre**
coudre	1 je couds, il coud, n cousons, ils cousent 3 je cousis 5 je couse
	7 cousant 8 cousu
courir	1 je cours, n courons 3 je courus 4 je courrai 5 je coure 8 couru

couvrir	1 je couvre, n couvrons 2 je couvrais 5 je couvre 8 couvert
craindre	1 je crains, n craignons, ils craignent 2 je craignais 3 je craignis 4 je craindrai 5 je craigne 7 craignant 8 craint
croire	1 je crois, n croyons, ils croient 2 je croyais 3 je crus 5 je croie, n croyions 7 croyant 8 cru
croître	1 je crois, il croît, n croissons 2 je croissais 3 je crûs 5 je croisse 7 croissant 8 crû, crue
cueillir	1 je cueille, n cueillons 2 je cueillais 4 je cueillerai 5 je cueille 7 cueillant
cuire	1 je cuis, n cuisons 2 je cuisais 3 je cuisis 5 je cuise 7 cuisant 8 cuit
débattre	*like* **battre**
décevoir	*like* **recevoir**
déchoir	(*defective*) 1 je déchois 2 *none* 3 je déchus 4 je déchoirai 6 *none* 7 *none* 8 déchu
découdre	*like* **coudre**
découvrir	*like* **couvrir**
décrire	*like* **écrire**
décroître	*like* **croître** *except* 8 décru
†se dédire	*like* **dire**
déduire	*like* **conduire**
défaillir	1 je défaille, n défaillons 2 je défaillais 3 je défaillis 5 je défaille 7 défaillant 8 défailli
défaire	*like* **faire**
démentir	*like* **mentir**
démettre	*like* **mettre**
†se départir	*like* **mentir**
dépeindre	*like* **atteindre**
déplaire	*like* **plaire**
déteindre	*like* **atteindre**
détenir	*like* **tenir**
détruire	*like* **conduire**
†devenir	*like* **tenir**
†se dévêtir	*like* **vêtir**
devoir	1 je dois, n devons, ils doivent 2 je devais 3 je dus 4 je devrai 5 je doive, n devions 6 *not used* 7 devant 8 dû, due, *pl* dus, dues
dire	1 je dis, n disons, v dites 2 je disais 3 je dis 5 je dise 7 disant 8 dit
disconvenir	*like* **tenir**
disjoindre	*like* **joindre**
disparaître	*like* **connaître**
dissoudre	*like* **absoudre**
distraire	*like* **abstraire**
dormir	*like* **mentir**
†échoir	(*defective*) 1 il échoit 2 *none* 3 il échut, ils échurent 4 il échoira 6 *none* 7 échéant 8 échu
éclore	1 il éclôt, ils éclosent 8 éclos
éconduire	*like* **conduire**
écrire	1 j'écris, n écrivons 2 j'écrivais 3 j'écrivis 5 j'écrive 7 écrivant 8 écrit
élire	*like* **lire**
émettre	*like* **mettre**
émouvoir	*like* **mouvoir** *except* 8 ému
enclore	*like* **éclore**

Irregular French Verbs

encourir	*like* **courir**
endormir	*like* **mentir**
enduire	*like* **conduire**
enfreindre	*like* **atteindre**
†s'enfuir	*like* **fuir**
enjoindre	*like* **joindre**
†s'enquérir	*like* **acquérir**
†s'ensuivre	*like* **suivre** (*but third person only*)
entreprendre	*like* **prendre**
entretenir	*like* **tenir**
entrevoir	*like* **voir**
entrouvrir	*like* **couvrir**
envoyer	4 j'enverrai
†s'éprendre	*like* **prendre**
équivaloir	*like* **valoir**
éteindre	*like* **atteindre**
être	1 je suis, tu es, il est, n sommes, v êtes, ils sont 2 j'étais 3 je fus 4 je serai 5 je sois, n soyons, ils soient 6 sois, soyons, soyez 7 étant 8 été
étreindre	*like* **atteindre**
exclure	*like* **conclure**
extraire	*like* **abstraire**
faillir	(*defective*) 3 je faillis 4 je faillirai 8 failli
faire	1 je fais, n faisons, v faites, ils font 2 je faisais 3 je fis 4 je ferai 5 je fasse 7 faisant 8 fait
falloir	(*impersonal*) 1 il faut 2 il fallait 3 il fallut 4 il faudra 5 il faille 6 *none* 7 *none* 8 fallu
feindre	*like* **atteindre**
foutre	1 je fous, n foutons 2 je foutais 3 *none* 5 je foute 7 foutant 8 foutu
frire	(*defective*) 1 je fris, tu fris, il frit 4 je frirai (*rare*) 6 fris (*rare*) 8 frit (*for other persons and tenses use* faire frire)
fuir	1 je fuis, n fuyons, ils fuient 2 je fuyais 3 je fuis 5 je fuie 7 fuyant 8 fui
geindre	*like* **atteindre**
haïr	1 je hais, il hait, n haïssons
inclure	*like* **conclure**
induire	*like* **conduire**
inscrire	*like* **écrire**
instruire	*like* **conduire**
interdire	*like* **dire** *except* 1 v interdisez
interrompre	*like* **rompre**
intervenir	*like* **tenir**
introduire	*like* **conduire**
joindre	1 je joins, n joignons, ils joignent 2 je joignais 3 je joignis 4 je joindrai 5 je joigne 7 joignant 8 joint
lire	1 je lis, n lisons 2 je lisais 3 je lus 5 je lise 7 lisant 8 lu
luire	*like* **nuire**
maintenir	*like* **tenir**
maudire	1 je maudis, n maudissons 2 je maudissais 3 je maudis 4 je maudirai 5 je maudisse 7 maudissant 8 maudit
méconnaître	*like* **connaître**
médire	*like* **dire** *except* 1 v médisez
mentir	1 je mens, n mentons 2 je mentais 5 je mente 7 mentant

Irregular French Verbs

mettre	1 je mets, n mettons 2 je mettais 3 je mis 5 je mette 7 mettant 8 mis
moudre	1 je mouds, il moud, n moulons 2 je moulais 3 je moulus 5 je moule 7 moulant 8 moulu
†mourir	1 je meurs, n mourons, ils meurent 2 je mourais 3 je mourus 4 je mourrai 5 je meure, n mourions 7 mourant 8 mort
mouvoir	1 je meus, n mouvons, ils meuvent 2 je mouvais 3 je mus *(rare)* 4 je mouvrai 5 je meuve, n mouvions 8 mû, mue, *pl* mus, mues
†naître	1 je nais, il naît, n naissons 2 je naissais 3 je naquis 4 je naîtrai 5 je naisse 7 naissant 8 né
nuire	1 je nuis, n nuisons 2 je nuisais 3 je nuisis 5 je nuise 7 nuisant 8 nui
obtenir	*like* **tenir**
offrir	*like* **couvrir**
omettre	*like* **mettre**
ouvrir	*like* **couvrir**
paître	*(defective)* 1 il paît 2 il paissait 3 *none* 4 il paîtra 5 il paisse 7 paissant 8 *none*
paraître	*like* **connaître**
parcourir	*like* **courir**
parfaire	*like* **faire** *except present tense, infinitive and past participle only*
†partir	*like* **mentir**
†parvenir	*like* **tenir**
peindre	*like* **atteindre**
percevoir	*like* **recevoir**
permettre	*like* **mettre**
plaindre	*like* **craindre**
plaire	1 je plais, il plaît, n plaisons 2 je plaisais 3 je plus 5 je plaise 7 plaisant 8 plu
pleuvoir	*(impersonal)* 1 il pleut 2 il pleuvait 3 il plut 4 il pleuvra 5 il pleuve 6 *none* 7 pleuvant 8 plu
poindre	*(defective)* 1 il point 4 il poindra 8 point
poursuivre	*like* **suivre**
pourvoir	*like* **voir** *except* 3 je pourvus *and* 4 je pourvoirai
pouvoir	1 je peux *or* je puis, tu peux, il peut, n pouvons, ils peuvent 2 je pouvais 3 je pus 4 je pourrai 5 je puisse 6 *not used* 7 pouvant 8 pu
prédire	*like* **dire** *except* 1 v prédisez
prendre	1 je prends, il prend, n prenons, ils prennent 2 je prenais 3 je pris 5 je prenne 7 prenant 8 pris
prescrire	*like* **écrire**
pressentir	*like* **mentir**
prévaloir	*like* **valoir** *except* 5 je prévale
prévenir	*like* **tenir**
prévoir	*like* **voir** *except* 4 je prévoirai
produire	*like* **conduire**
promettre	*like* **mettre**
promouvoir	*like* **mouvoir** *except* 8 promu
proscrire	*like* **écrire**
†provenir	*like* **tenir**
rabattre	*like* **battre**
rasseoir	*like* **asseoir**
réapparaître	*like* **connaître**
recevoir	1 je reçois, n recevons, ils reçoivent 2 je recevais 3 je reçus

Irregular French Verbs

	4 je recevrai 5 je reçoive, n recevions, ils reçoivent 7 recevant
	8 reçu
reconduire	*like* conduire
reconnaître	*like* connaître
reconquérir	*like* acquérir
reconstruire	*like* conduire
recoudre	*like* coudre
recourir	*like* courir
recouvrir	*like* couvrir
récrire	*like* écrire
recueillir	*like* cueillir
†redevenir	*like* tenir
redire	*like* dire
réduire	*like* conduire
réécrire	*like* écrire
réélire	*like* lire
refaire	*like* faire
rejoindre	*like* joindre
relire	*like* lire
reluire	*like* nuire
remettre	*like* mettre
†renaître	*like* naître
rendormir	*like* mentir
renvoyer	*like* envoyer
†se repaître	*like* paître
reparaître	*like* connaître
†repartir	*like* mentir
repeindre	*like* atteindre
repentir	*like* mentir
reprendre	*like* prendre
reproduire	*like* conduire
résoudre	1 je résous, n résolvons 2 je résolvais 3 je résolus
	5 je résolve 7 résolvant 8 résolu
ressentir	*like* mentir
resservir	*like* mentir
ressortir	*like* mentir
restreindre	*like* atteindre
retenir	*like* tenir
retransmettre	*like* mettre
†revenir	*like* tenir
revêtir	*like* vêtir
revivre	*like* vivre
revoir	*like* voir
rire	1 je ris, n rions 2 je riais 3 je ris 5 je rie, n riions 7 riant 8 ri
rompre	*regular except* 1 il rompt
rouvrir	*like* couvrir
satisfaire	*like* faire
savoir	1 je sais, n savons, il savent 2 je savais 3 je sus 4 je saurai
	5 je sache 6 sache, sachons, sachez 7 sachant 8 su
séduire	*like* conduire
sentir	*like* mentir
servir	*like* mentir
sortir	*like* mentir
souffrir	*like* couvrir

soumettre	*like* **mettre**
sourire	*like* **rire**
souscrire	*like* **écrire**
soustraire	*like* **abstraire**
soutenir	*like* **tenir**
†se souvenir	*like* **tenir**
subvenir	*like* **tenir**
suffire	1 je suffis, n suffisons 2 je suffisais 3 je suffis 5 je suffise 7 suffisant 8 suffi
suivre	1 je suis, n suivons 2 je suivais 3 je suivis 5 je suive 7 suivant 8 suivi
surprendre	*like* **prendre**
†survenir	*like* **tenir**
survivre	*like* **vivre**
taire	1 je tais, n taisons 2 je taisais 3 je tus 5 je taise 7 taisant 8 tu
teindre	*like* **atteindre**
tenir	1 je tiens, n tenons, ils tiennent 2 je tenais 3 je tins, tu tins, il tint, n tînmes, v tîntes, ils tinrent 4 je tiendrai 5 je tienne 7 tenant 8 tenu
traduire	*like* **conduire**
traire	*like* **abstraire**
transcrire	*like* **écrire**
transmettre	*like* **mettre**
transparaître	*like* **connaître**
tressaillir	*like* **défaillir**
vaincre	1 je vaincs, il vainc, n vainquons 2 je vainquais 3 je vainquis 5 je vainque 7 vainquant 8 vaincu
valoir	1 je vaux, il vaut, n valons 2 je valais 3 je valus 4 je vaudrai 5 je vaille 6 *not used* 7 valant 8 valu
†venir	*like* **tenir**
vêtir	1 je vêts, n vêtons 2 je vêtais 5 je vête 7 vêtant 8 vêtu
vivre	1 je vis, n vivons 2 je vivais 3 je vécus 5 je vive 7 vivant 8 vécu
voir	1 je vois, n voyons 2 je voyais 3 je vis 4 je verrai 5 je voie, n voyions 7 voyant 8 vu
vouloir	1 je veux, il veut, n voulons, ils veulent 2 je voulais 3 je voulus 4 je voudrai 5 je veuille 6 veuille, veuillons, veuillez 7 voulant 8 voulu

VERBES ANGLAIS IRRÉGULIERS

Infinitif	Prétérit	Participe passé
arise	arose	arisen
awake	awoke	awoken
be	was, were	been
bear	bore	borne
beat	beat	beaten
become	became	become
begin	began	begun
bend	bent	bent
bet	bet, betted	bet, betted
bid	bade, bid	bidden, bid
bind	bound	bound
bite	bit	bitten
bleed	bled	bled
blow	blew	blown
break	broke	broken
breed	bred	bred
bring	brought [brɔːt]	brought
broadcast	broadcast	broadcast
build	built	built
burn	burnt, burned	burnt, burned
burst	burst	burst
buy	bought [bɔːt]	bought
cast	cast	cast
catch	caught [kɔːt]	caught
choose	chose	chosen
cling	clung	clung
come	came	come
cost	cost	cost
creep	crept	crept
cut	cut	cut
deal	dealt [delt]	dealt
dig	dug	dug
dive	dived, *Am* dove [dəʊv]	dived
do	did	done
draw	drew	drawn
dream	dreamed, dreamt [dremt]	dreamed, dreamt
drink	drank	drunk
drive	drove	driven
dwell	dwelt	dwelt
eat	ate [*Br* et, *Am* eɪt]	eaten
fall	fell	fallen
feed	fed	fed
feel	felt	felt
fight	fought [fɔːt]	fought
find	found	found
flee	fled	fled
fling	flung	flung
fly	flew	flown
forbid	forbade, forbad	forbidden
forecast	forecast	forecast

Verbes anglais irréguliers

Infinitif	Prétérit	Participe passé
foresee	foresaw	foreseen
forget	forgot	forgotten
forgive	forgave	forgiven
forsake	forsook (*rare*)	forsaken
freeze	froze	frozen
get	got	got, *Am* gotten
give	gave	given
go	went	gone
grind	ground	ground
grow	grew	grown
hang	hung, hanged	hung, hanged
have	had	had
hear	heard [hɜːd]	heard
hide	hid	hidden
hit	hit	hit
hold	held	held
hurt	hurt	hurt
keep	kept	kept
kneel	knelt, kneeled	knelt, kneeled
know	knew	known
lay	laid	laid
lead	led	led
lean	leant [lent], leaned	leant, leaned
leap	leapt [lept], leaped	leapt, leaped
learn	learnt, learned	learnt, learned
leave	left	left
lend	lent	lent
let	let	let
lie	lay	lain
light	lit, lighted	lit, lighted
lose	lost	lost
make	made	made
mean	meant [ment]	meant
meet	met	met
mislay	mislaid	mislaid
mislead	misled	misled
mistake	mistook	mistaken
misunderstand	misunderstood	misunderstood
mow	mowed	mown, mowed
outdo	outdid	outdone
overcome	overcame	overcome
overdo	overdid	overdone
overtake	overtook	overtaken
pay	paid	paid
put	put	put
quit	quit, quitted	quit, quitted
read	read [red]	read
redo	redid	redone
rewind	rewound	rewound
rid	rid	rid
ride	rode	ridden
ring	rang	rung
rise	rose	risen

Verbes anglais irréguliers

Infinitif	Prétérit	Participe passé
run	ran	run
saw	sawed	sawn, sawed
say	said [sed]	said
see	saw	seen
seek	sought [sɔːt]	sought
sell	sold	sold
send	sent	sent
set	set	set
sew	sewed	sewn, sewed
shake	shook [ʃʊk]	shaken
shed	shed	shed
shine	shone [*Br* ʃɒn, *Am* ʃəʊn]	shone
shoot	shot	shot
show	showed	shown, showed
shrink	shrank	shrunk, shrunken
shut	shut	shut
sing	sang	sung
sink	sank	sunk
sit	sat	sat
sleep	slept	slept
slide	slid	slid
sling	slung	slung
slit	slit	slit
smell	smelt, smelled	smelt, smelled
sow	sowed	sown, sowed
speak	spoke	spoken
speed	sped, speeded	sped, speeded
spell	spelt, spelled	spelt, spelled
spend	spent	spent
spill	spilt, spilled	spilt, spilled
spin	spun	spun
spit	spat, spit	spat, spit
split	split	split
spoil	spoilt, spoiled	spoilt, spoiled
spread	spread	spread
spring	sprang	sprung
stand	stood [stʊd]	stood
steal	stole	stolen
stick	stuck	stuck
sting	stung	stung
stink	stank, stunk	stunk
stride	strode	stridden (*rare*)
strike	struck	struck
string	strung	strung
strive	strove	striven
swear	swore	sworn
sweep	swept	swept
swell	swelled	swollen, swelled
swim	swam	swum
swing	swung	swung
take	took [tʊk]	taken
teach	taught [tɔːt]	taught
tear	tore	torn

Verbes anglais irréguliers

Infinitif	Prétérit	Participe passé
tell	told	told
think	thought [θɔːt]	thought
throw	threw	thrown
thrust	thrust	thrust
tread	trod	trodden
undergo	underwent	undergone
understand	understood	understood
undertake	undertook	undertaken
upset	upset	upset
wake	woke	woken
wear	wore	worn
weave	wove	woven
weep	wept	wept
win	won [wʌn]	won
wind	wound [waʊnd]	wound
withdraw	withdrew	withdrawn
withhold	withheld	withheld
withstand	withstood	withstood
wring	wrung	wrung
write	wrote	written

A

A, a [a] *nm* A, a.

a [a] *voir* **avoir**.

à [a] *prép* (**à** + **le** = **au** [o], **à** + **les** = **aux** [o]) **1** (*direction: lieu*) to; (*temps*) till, to; **aller à Paris** to go to Paris; **de 3 à 4 h** from 3 till *ou* to 4 (o'clock).

2 (*position: lieu*) at, in; (*surface*) on; (*temps*) at; **être au bureau/à la ferme/au jardin/à Paris** to be at *ou* in the office/on *ou* at the farm/in the garden/in Paris; **à la maison** at home; **à l'horizon** on the horizon; **à 8 h** at 8 (o'clock); **à mon arrivée** on (my) arrival; **à lundi!** see you (on) Monday!

3 (*description*) **l'homme à la barbe** the man with the beard; **verre à liqueur** liqueur glass.

4 (*attribution*) **donner/prêter qch à qn** to give/lend sth to s.o., give/lend s.o. sth.

5 (*devant inf*) **apprendre à lire** to learn to read; **travail à faire** work to do; **maison à vendre** house for sale; **'à louer'** *Br* 'to let', *Am* 'to rent'; **prêt à partir** ready to leave.

6 (*appartenance*) **c'est (son livre) à lui** it's his (book); **c'est à vous de** (*décider, protester etc*) it's up to you to; (*lire, jouer etc*) it's your turn to; **à toi!** your turn!

7 (*prix*) for; **pain à 2F** loaf for 2F.

8 (*poids*) by; **vendre au kilo** to sell by the kilo.

9 (*vitesse*) **100 km à l'heure** 100 km an *ou* per hour.

10 (*moyen, manière*) **à bicyclette** by bicycle; **à la main** by hand; **à pied** on foot; **au crayon** with a pencil, in pencil; **à l'encre** in ink; **au galop** at a gallop; **à la française** in the French style *ou* way; **deux à deux** two by two.

11 (*appel*) **au voleur!** (stop) thief!; **au feu!** (there's a) fire!

abaisser [abese] *vt* to lower; **a. qn** to humiliate s.o. **▮ s'abaisser** *vpr* (*barrière*) to lower; (*température*) to drop; **s'a. à faire** to stoop to doing. **●abaissement** [-esmã] *nm* (*chute*) drop.

abandon [abãdõ] *nm* abandonment; desertion; (*de droit*) surrender; (*de sportif*) withdrawal; (*naturel*) abandon; (*confiance*) lack of restraint; **à l'a.** in a neglected state.

abandonner [abãdɔne] *vt* (*travail, tentative*) to give up, abandon; (*endroit, animal*) to desert, abandon; (*droit*) to surrender **▮** *vi* to give up; (*sportif*) to withdraw **▮ s'abandonner** *vpr* (*se confier*) to open up; (*se détendre*) to let oneself go; **s'a. à** to give oneself up to, abandon oneself to.

abasourdir [abazurdir] *vt* to stun, astound.

abat-jour [abaʒur] *nm inv* lampshade.

abats [aba] *nmpl* offal; (*de volaille*) giblets.

abattant [abatã] *nm* leaf, flap.

abattis [abati] *nmpl* giblets.

abattoir [abatwar] *nm* slaughterhouse.

abattre* [abatr] *vt* (*mur*) to knock down; (*arbre*) to cut down, fell; (*personne, gros gibier*) to shoot; (*vache etc*) to slaughter; (*animal blessé*) to put down; (*avion*) to shoot down; (*déprimer*) *Fig* to demoralize; (*épuiser*) *Fig* to exhaust.

▮ s'abattre *vpr* (*tomber*) to collapse; (*oiseau*) to swoop down (**sur** on); **s'a. sur** (*pluie*) to come down on; (*tempête*) to hit. **●abattage** *nm* (*d'arbre*) felling; (*de vache etc*) slaughter(ing). **●abattement** *nm* (*faiblesse*) exhaustion; (*désespoir*) dejection.

abattu, -ue [abaty] *a* (*triste*) dejected, demoralized; (*faible*) in poor shape, at a low ebb.

abbaye [abei] *nf* abbey.

abbé [abe] *nm* (*chef d'abbaye*) abbot; (*prêtre*) priest. **●abbesse** *nf* abbess.

abcès [apsɛ] *nm* abscess.

abdiquer [abdike] *vti* to abdicate. **●abdication** *nf* abdication.

abdomen [abdɔmɛn] *nm* stomach, abdomen. **●abdominal, -e, -aux** *a* abdominal. **●abdominaux** *nmpl* (*muscles*) abdominal muscles.

abeille [abɛj] *nf* bee.

aberrant, -ante [aberã, -ãt] *a* (*idée etc*) ludicrous, absurd. **●aberration** *nf* (*égarement*) aberration; (*idée*) ludicrous idea; **dire des aberrations** to talk sheer nonsense.

abhorrer [abɔre] *vt* to abhor, loathe.

abîme [abim] *nm* abyss, chasm, gulf.

abîmer [abime] *vt* to spoil, damage **▮ s'abîmer** *vpr* to get spoilt; **s'a. dans ses pensées** *Litt* to lose oneself in one's thoughts.

abject, -e [abʒɛkt] *a* abject, despicable.

abjurer [abʒyre] *vti* to abjure.

ablation [ablɑsjõ] *nf* (*d'organe*) removal.

ablutions [ablysjõ] *nfpl* ablutions.

abnégation [abnegɑsjõ] *nf* self-sacrifice, abnegation.

aboiement [abwamã] *nm voir* **aboyer**.

abois (aux) [ozabwa] *adv* at bay.

abolir [abɔlir] *vt* to abolish. **●abolition** *nf* abolition.

abominable [abɔminabl] *a* terrible. **●abominablement** *adv* terribly.

abondant, -ante [abõdã, -ãt] *a* plentiful, abundant. **●abondamment** *adv* abundantly. **●abondance** *nf* abundance (**de** of); **une a. de** plenty of, an abundance of; **en a.** in abundance; **années d'a.** years of plenty.

●**abonder** *vi* to abound (**en** in).

abonné, -ée [abɔne] *nmf* (*à un journal, au téléphone*) subscriber; (*de train, d'un théâtre*) & *Sport* season ticket holder; (*du gaz etc*) consumer. ●**abonnement** *nm* subscription; (**carte d'**)a. (*de train, de théâtre*) season ticket. ●**s'abonner** *vpr* (*à un journal etc*) to subscribe, take out a subscription (**à** to); *Rail Théâtre etc* to buy a season ticket.

abord [abɔr] *nm* 1 (*accès*) **d'un a. facile** easy to approach. 2 (*vue*) **au premier a.** at first sight. ●**abordable** *a* (*prix, marchandises*) affordable; (*personne*) approachable.

abord (d') [dabɔr] *adv* (*avant tout*) first; (*au début*) (at) first.

aborder [abɔrde] *vi* to land ∎ *vt* (*personne*) to approach, accost; (*lieu*) to approach, reach; (*problème*) to tackle, approach; (*attaquer*) to board (*ship*); (*heurter*) to run foul of (*ship*). ●**abordage** *nm* (*d'un bateau*) (*assaut*) boarding; (*accident*) collision.

abords [abɔr] *nmpl* (*environs*) surroundings; **aux a. de** around, nearby.

aborigène [abɔriʒɛn] *a* & *nm* aboriginal.

aboutir [abutir] *vi* to succeed; **a. à** to end at, lead to, end up in; **n'a. à rien** to come to nothing. ●**aboutissants** *nmpl voir* **tenants**. ●**aboutissement** *nm* (*résultat*) outcome; (*succès*) success.

aboyer [abwaje] *vi* to bark. ●**aboiement** *nm* bark; **aboiements** barking.

abrasif, -ive [abrazif, -iv] *a* & *nm* abrasive.

abréger [abreʒe] *vt* (*récit*) to shorten, abridge; (*mot*) to abbreviate. ●**abrégé** *nm* summary; **en a.** (*phrase*) in shortened form; (*mot*) in abbreviated form.

abreuver [abrœve] *vt* (*cheval*) to water ∎ **s'abreuver** *vpr* to drink. ●**abreuvoir** *nm* (*lieu*) watering place; (*récipient*) drinking trough.

abréviation [abrevjasjɔ̃] *nf* abbreviation.

●**abri** [abri] *nm* shelter; **a. (de jardin)** (garden) shed; **à l'a. de** (*vent*) sheltered from; (*besoin*) safe from; **sans a.** homeless.

Abribus® [abribys] *nm* bus shelter.

abricot [abriko] *nm* apricot. ●**abricotier** *nm* apricot tree.

abriter [abrite] *vt* (*protéger*) to shelter; (*loger*) to house ∎ **s'abriter** *vpr* to (take) shelter.

abroger [abrɔʒe] *vt* to repeal.

abrupt, -e [abrypt] *a* (*pente, versant etc*) steep, sheer, abrupt; (*personne*) abrupt.

abrutir [abrytir] *vt* **a. qn** (*travail, télévision etc*) to turn s.o. into a vegetable; (*alcool*) to stupefy s.o.; (*propagande*) to brutalize s.o. ●**abruti, -ie** *nmf* idiot ∎ *a* idiotic.

absence [apsɑ̃s] *nf* absence. ●**absent, -ente** *a* (*personne*) absent, away; (*chose*) missing; **air a.** faraway look ∎ *nmf* absentee. ●**absentéisme** *nm* absenteeism. ●**s'absenter** *vpr* to go away.

abside [apsid] *nf* (*d'une église*) apse.

absolu, -ue [apsɔly] *a* absolute. ●**absolument** *adv* absolutely.

absolution [apsɔlysjɔ̃] *nf* absolution.

absorber [apsɔrbe] *vt* to absorb; (*manger*) to eat; (*médicament*) to take. ●**absorbant, -ante** *a* (*papier*) absorbent; (*travail, lecture*) absorbing. ●**absorption** *nf* absorption.

absoudre* [apsudr] *vt Rel Jur etc* to absolve.

abstenir* (s') [sapstənir] *vpr* (*ne pas voter*) to abstain; **s'a. de qch/de faire** to refrain from sth/from doing. ●**abstention** *nf Pol* abstention.

abstinence [apstinɑ̃s] *nf* abstinence.

abstraire* [apstrɛr] *vt* to abstract. ●**abstrait, -aite** *a* abstract. ●**abstraction** *nf* abstraction; **faire a. de** to disregard, leave aside.

absurde [apsyrd] *a* absurd ∎ *nm* absurd. ●**absurdité** *nf* absurdity; **dire des absurdités** to talk nonsense.

abus [aby] *nm* abuse, misuse (**de** of); (*de nourriture*) over-indulgence (**en** in); (*injustice*) abuse; **a. d'alcool** alcohol abuse; **a. de tabac** excessive smoking. ●**abuser 1** *vi* to go too far; **a. de** (*situation, personne*) to take unfair advantage of; (*autorité*) to abuse, misuse; (*friandises etc*) to over-indulge in. 2 **s'abuser** *vpr* to be mistaken.

abusif, -ive [abyzif, -iv] *a* excessive; **emploi a.** *Ling* improper use, misuse. ●**abusivement** *adv* (*employer un mot*) improperly.

acabit [akabi] *nm* **de cet a.** *Péj* of that ilk ou sort.

acacia [akasja] *nm* (*arbre*) acacia.

académie [akademi] *nf* academy; (*administration scolaire*) = (regional) education authority. ●**académicien, -ienne** *nmf* academician. ●**académique** *a* academic.

acajou [akaʒu] *nm* mahogany; **cheveux a.** auburn hair.

acariâtre [akarjɑtr] *a* cantankerous.

accablement [akabləmɑ̃] *nm* dejection.

accabler [akable] *vt* to overwhelm (**de** with); **a. d'injures** to heap insults upon; **accablé de dettes** (over)burdened with debt; **accablé de chaleur** overcome by heat; **chaleur accablante** oppressive heat.

accalmie [akalmi] *nf* lull.

accaparer [akapare] *vt* to monopolize; (*personne*) *Fam* to take up all the time of.

accéder [aksede] *vi* **a. à** (*lieu*) to reach, have access to; (*pouvoir, trône, demande*) to accede to.

accélérer [akselere] *vi* (*dans un véhicule*) to accelerate ∎ *vt* (*travaux etc*) to speed up; (*allure, pas*) to quicken, speed up. ●**s'accélérer** *vpr* to speed up. ●**accélérateur** *nm* (*pédale etc*) accelerator. ●**accélération** *nf* acceleration; (*des travaux etc*) speeding up.

accent [aksɑ̃] *nm* accent; (*sur une syllabe*) stress; **mettre l'a. sur** to stress ∎ **accentuation** *nf* accentuation. ●**accentuer** *vt* to emphasize, accentuate, stress ∎ **s'accentuer** *vpr* to become more pronounced.

accepter [aksɛpte] *vt* to accept; **a. de faire** to agree to do. ●**acceptable** *a* acceptable. ●**acceptation** *nf* acceptance.

acception [aksɛpsjɔ̃] *nf* sense, meaning.

accès [aksɛ] *nm* **1** access (à to); **'a. interdit'** 'no entry'; **les a. de** (*routes*) the approaches to. **2** (*de folie, colère, toux*) fit; (*de fièvre*) bout, attack. ● **accessible** *a* accessible; (*personne*) approachable. ● **accession** *nf* accession (à-to); (*à un traité*) adherence; **a. à la propriété** home ownership.

accessoire [akseswar] *a* secondary. ● **accessoires** *nmpl* (*de théâtre*) props; (*de voiture etc*) accessories; **a. de toilette** toilet requisites, toiletries.

accident [aksidɑ̃] *nm* accident; **a. d'avion/de train** plane/train crash; **par a.** by accident, by chance. ● **accidenté, -ée** *a* (*terrain*) uneven; (*région*) hilly; (*voiture*) damaged (in an accident) ‖ *nmf* accident victim, casualty. ● **accidentel, -elle** *a* accidental. ● **accidentellement** *adv* accidentally, unintentionally.

acclamer [aklame] *vt* to cheer, acclaim. ● **acclamations** *nfpl* cheers.

acclimater [aklimate] *vt*, **s'acclimater** *vpr Br* to acclimatize, *Am* acclimate. ● **acclimatation** *nf Br* acclimatization, *Am* acclimation.

accointances [akwɛ̃tɑ̃s] *nfpl* (*relations*) *Péj* contacts.

accolade [akɔlad] *nf* (*embrassade*) embrace; (*signe*) *Typ* brace, bracket.

accoler [akɔle] *vt* to place (side by side) (à against).

accommoder [akɔmɔde] *vt* to adapt; (*assaisonner*) to prepare; **s'a. à** to adapt (oneself) to; **s'a. de** to make the best of. ● **accommodant, -ante** *a* accommodating, easy to please. ● **accommodement** *nm* arrangement, compromise.

accompagner [akɔ̃paɲe] *vt* (*personne*) to go *ou* come with, accompany, escort; (*chose, musicien*) to accompany; **s'a. de** to be accompanied by, go with. ● **accompagnateur, -trice** *nmf* (*musical*) accompanist; (*de touristes etc*) guide. ● **accompagnement** *nm Mus* accompaniment.

accomplir [akɔ̃plir] *vt* to carry out, fulfil, accomplish. ● **accompli, -ie** *a* accomplished. ● **accomplissement** *nm* fulfilment.

accord [akɔr] *nm* agreement; (*harmonie*) harmony; (*musical*) chord; **être d'a.** to agree, be in agreement (**avec** with); **d'a.!** all right!

accordéon [akɔrdeɔ̃] *nm* accordion; **en a.** (*chaussette etc*) wrinkled.

accorder [akɔrde] *vt* (*donner*) to grant; (*instrument*) to tune; (*verbe, adjectif*) to make agree ‖ **s'accorder** *vpr* (*s'entendre*) to get along; (*mots*) to agree (**avec** with).

accoster [akɔste] *vt* to accost; (*navire, quai etc*) to come alongside ‖ *vi Nau* to berth.

accotement [akɔtmɑ̃] *nm* roadside, shoulder, *Br* verge.

accoucher [akuʃe] *vi* to give birth (**de** to) ‖ *vt* (*enfant*) to deliver. ● **accouchement** *nm* delivery. ● **accoucheur** *nm* (*médecin*) a. obstetrician.

accouder (s') [sakude] *vpr* **s'a. à** *ou* **sur** to lean on (*with one's elbows*). ● **accoudoir** *nm* armrest.

accoupler [akuple] *vt* (*roues, bœufs etc*) to couple (à to) ‖ **s'accoupler** *vpr* (*animaux*) to mate (à with). ● **accouplement** *nm* coupling; (*d'animaux*) mating.

accourir* [akurir] *vi* to come running, run over.

accoutrement [akutrəmɑ̃] *nm Péj* garb, dress.

accoutumer [akutyme] *vt* to accustom. ● **s'accoutumer** *vpr* to get accustomed (à to); **comme à l'accoutumée** as usual. ● **accoutumance** *nf* familiarization (à with); (*dépendance*) *Méd* addiction.

accréditer [akredite] *vt* (*ambassadeur*) to accredit; (*rumeur*) to lend credence to.

accroc [akro] *nm* (*déchirure*) tear; (*difficulté*) hitch, snag.

accrocher [akrɔʃe] *vt* (*déchirer*) to catch; (*fixer*) to hook; (*suspendre*) to hang up (on a hook); (*heurter*) to hit, knock ‖ *vi* (*affiche etc*) to grab one's attention ‖ **s'accrocher** *vpr* (*ne pas céder*) to persevere; (*se disputer*) *Fam* to clash; **s'a. à** (*se cramponner etc*) to cling to; (*s'écorcher*) to catch oneself on. ● **accrochage** *nm* (*de véhicules*) minor collision, knock; (*friction*) *Fam* clash. ● **accrocheur, -euse** *a* (*personne*) tenacious; (*affiche etc*) eyecatching, catchy.

accroître* [akrwatr] *vt* to increase ‖ **s'accroître** *vpr* to increase, grow. ● **accroissement** *nm* increase; growth.

accroupir (s') [sakrupir] *vpr* to squat *ou* crouch (down). ● **accroupi, -ie** *a* squatting, crouching.

accueil [akœj] *nm* welcome, reception. ● **accueillir*** *vt* to receive, welcome, greet. ● **accueillant, -ante** *a* welcoming.

acculer [akyle] *vt* **a. qn à qch** to drive s.o. to *ou* against sth.

accumuler [akymyle] *vt*, **s'accumuler** *vpr* to pile up, accumulate. ● **accumulateur** *nm* accumulator, battery. ● **accumulation** *nf* accumulation.

accuser [akyze] *vt* (*dénoncer*) to accuse; (*rendre responsable*) to blame (**de** for); (*révéler*) to show; (*faire ressortir*) to bring out; **a. réception** to acknowledge receipt (**de** of); **a. le coup** to stagger under the blow. ● **accusé, -ée 1** *nmf* **l'a.** the accused; (*cour d'assises*) the defendant. **2** *a* (*trait etc*) prominent. ● **accusateur, -trice** *a* (*regard*) accusing; (*document*) incriminating ‖ *nmf* accuser. ● **accusation** *nf* accusation; (*au tribunal*) charge.

acerbe [asɛrb] *a* bitter, caustic.

acéré, -ée [asere] *a* sharp.

acétate [asetat] *nm* acetate. ● **acétique** *a* acetic.

achalandé, -ée [aʃalɑ̃de] *a* **bien a.** (*magasin*) well-stocked.

acharner (s') [saʃarne] *vpr* **s'a. sur** (*attaquer*) to set upon, lay into; **s'a. contre**

(*poursuivre*) to pursue (relentlessly); **s'a. à faire** to struggle to do, try desperately to do. ●**acharné, -ée** *a* (*effort, travail*) relentless; (*combat*) fierce, furious ▮ *nmf* (*du jeu etc*) fanatic. ●**acharnement** *nm* (*au travail*) (stubborn) determination; (*dans un combat*) fury.

achat [aʃa] *nm* purchase; **achats** shopping.

acheminer [aʃmine] *vt* to dispatch ▮ **s'acheminer** *vpr* to proceed (**vers** towards).

acheter [aʃte] *vti* to buy, purchase; **a. à qn** (*vendeur*) to buy from s.o.; (*pour qn*) to buy for s.o. ●**acheteur, -euse** *nmf* buyer, purchaser; (*dans un magasin*) shopper.

achever [aʃve] *vt* to finish (off); **a. de faire qch** (*personne*) to finish doing sth; **a. qn** (*tuer*) to finish s.o. off ▮ **s'achever** *vpr* to end, finish. ●**achèvement** *nm* completion.

achoppement [aʃɔpmã] *nm* **pierre d'a.** stumbling block.

acide [asid] *a* acid, sour ▮ *nm* acid. ●**acidité** *nf* acidity.

acier [asje] *nm* steel. ●**aciérie** *nf* steelworks.

acné [akne] *nf* acne.

acolyte [akɔlit] *nm Péj* confederate, associate.

acompte [akɔ̃t] *nm* part payment, deposit.

à-côté [akote] *nm* (*d'une question*) side issue; **à-côtés** (*gains*) little extras.

à-coup [aku] *nm* jerk, jolt; **sans à-coups** smoothly; **par à-coups** in fits and starts.

acoustique [akustik] *a* acoustic ▮ *nf* acoustics.

acquérir* [akerir] *vt* (*acheter*) to purchase; (*obtenir*) to acquire, gain; **s'a. une réputation/etc** to win a reputation/etc; **être acquis à** (*idée, parti*) to be a supporter of. ●**acquéreur** *nm* purchaser. ●**acquis** *nm* experience. ●**acquisition** *nf* (*achat*) purchase; (*de connaissances etc*) acquisition.

acquiescer [akjese] *vi* to acquiesce (**à** to). ●**acquiescement** *nm* acquiescence.

acquit [aki] *nm* receipt; **'pour a.'** 'paid'; **par a. de conscience** to ease one's conscience.

acquitter [akite] *vt* (*dette*) to clear, pay; (*accusé*) to acquit; **s'a. de** (*devoir, promesse*) to discharge; **s'a. envers qn** to repay s.o. ●**acquittement** *nm* (*d'un accusé*) acquittal; (*de dette*) payment.

âcre [ɑkr] *a* bitter, acrid, pungent.

acrobate [akrɔbat] *nmf* acrobat. ●**acrobatie(s)** [-basi] *nf(pl)* acrobatics. ●**acrobatique** *a* acrobatic.

acrylique [akrilik] *a & nm* acrylic.

acte [akt] *nm* (*action*) act, deed; (*de pièce de théâtre*) act; **un a. de courage/bonté/etc** an act of courage/kindness/etc; **un a. terroriste** a terrorist action *ou* act; **a. de naissance** birth certificate; **prendre a. de** to take note of.

acteur, -trice [aktœr, -tris] *nmf* actor, actress.

actif, -ive [aktif, -iv] *a* active ▮ *nm* Grammaire active; (*d'une entreprise*) assets; **à son a.** to one's credit; (*vols, meurtres*) *Hum* to one's name.

action [aksjɔ̃] *nf* action; (*en Bourse*) share.

●**actionnaire** *nmf* shareholder.

actionner [aksjɔne] *vt* to set in motion, activate, actuate.

activer [aktive] *vt* (*accélérer*) to speed up; **a. le feu** (*avec un tisonnier*) to stoke up the fire; (*en soufflant*) to fan the fire ▮ **s'activer** *vpr* to bustle about; (*se dépêcher*) *Fam* to get a move on.

activiste [aktivist] *nmf* activist.

activité [aktivite] *nf* activity; **en a.** (*personne*) fully active; (*volcan*) active.

actuaire [aktɥɛr] *nmf* actuary.

actualité [aktɥalite] *nf* (*d'un problème*) topicality; (*événements*) current events; **actualités** (*télévisées*) news; **d'a.** topical.

actuel, -elle [aktɥɛl] *a* (*présent*) present; (*contemporain*) topical. ●**actuellement** *adv* at present, at the present time.

acuité [akɥite] *nf* (*de douleur*) acuteness; (*de vision*) keenness.

acupuncture [akypɔ̃ktyr] *nf* acupuncture. ●**acupuncteur, -trice** *nmf* acupuncturist.

adage [adaʒ] *nm* (*maxime*) adage.

adapter [adapte] *vt* to adapt; (*ajuster*) to fit (**à** to); **s'a. à** (*s'habituer*) to adapt to, adjust to; (*tuyau etc*) to fit. ●**adaptable** *a* adaptable. ●**adaptateur, -trice** *nmf* adapter. ●**adaptation** *nf* adjustment; (*de roman, pièce*) adaptation.

additif [aditif] *nm* additive.

addition [adisjɔ̃] *nf* addition; (*au restaurant*) Br bill, Am check. ●**additionner** *vt* to add (**à** to); (*nombres*) to add up.

adepte [adɛpt] *nmf* follower.

adéquat, -ate [adekwa, -at] *a* appropriate.

adhérer [adere] *vi* **a. à** (*coller*) to stick to; (*s'inscrire*) to join; (*pneu*) to grip (*road*). ●**adhérence** *nf* (*de pneu*) grip. ●**adhérent, -ente** *nmf* member.

adhésif, -ive [adezif, -iv] *a* adhesive, sticky ▮ *nm* adhesive. ●**adhésion** *nf* membership; (*accord*) support.

adieu, -x [adjø] *int & nm* farewell, goodbye.

adipeux, -euse [adipø, -øz] *a* (*tissu*) fatty; (*visage*) fat.

adjacent, -ente [adʒasã, -ãt] *a* (*maison, angles etc*) adjacent.

adjectif [adʒɛktif] *nm* adjective.

adjoindre* [adʒwɛ̃dr] *vt* (*associer*) to appoint (*s.o.*) as an assistant (**à** to); (*ajouter*) to add; **s'a. qn** to appoint s.o. ●**adjoint, -ointe** *nmf & a* assistant; **a. au maire** deputy mayor.

adjudant [adʒydã] *nm* warrant officer.

adjuger [adʒyʒe] *vt* (*accorder*) to award (*prize etc*); **s'a. qch** *Fam* to grab sth for oneself.

adjurer [adʒyre] *vt* to beseech, entreat.

admettre* [admɛtr] *vt* (*laisser entrer, accueillir*) to admit; (*reconnaître*) to admit, acknowledge (**que** that); (*autoriser, tolérer*) to allow; (*supposer*) to admit, suppose; (*candidat*) to pass; **être admis à** (*examen*) to have passed.

administrer [administre] *vt* (*gérer, donner*) to administer. ●**administrateur, -trice** *nmf* administrator. ● **administratif, -ive** a administrative. ● **administration** nf administration; l'A. (service public) government service, the Civil Service.

admirer [admire] vt to admire. ● **admirable** a admirable. ● **admirateur, -trice** nmf admirer. ● **admiratif, -ive** a admiring. ● **admiration** nf admiration.

admissible [admisibl] a (tolérable) .acceptable, admissible; (après un concours) eligible (à for). ● **admission** nf admission.

adolescent, -ente [adɔlesã, -ãt] nmf adolescent, teenager ▮ a teenage. ● **adolescence** nf adolescence, Fam teens.

adonner (s') [sadɔne] vpr s'a. à (boisson) to take to; (étude) to devote oneself to.

adopter [adɔpte] vt to adopt. ● **adoptif, -ive** a (fils, patrie) adopted. ● **adoption** nf adoption; suisse d'a. Swiss by adoption.

adorer [adɔre] vt (dieu etc) to worship; (chose, personne) to love, adore; a. faire to love ou adore doing. ● **adorable** a adorable. ● **adoration** nf worship, adoration; être en a. devant to worship, love, adore.

adosser [adose] vt a. qch à to lean sth back against; s'a. à to lean back against.

adoucir [adusir] vt (voix, traits etc) to soften; (boisson) to sweeten; (chagrin) to mitigate, ease ▮ s'adoucir vpr (temps) to turn milder; (caractère) to mellow. ● **adoucissement** nm a. de la température milder weather.

adrénaline [adrenalin] nf adrenalin(e).

adresse [adrɛs] nf 1 (domicile) address. 2 (habileté) skill. ● **adresser** vt (lettre) to send; (compliment, remarque etc) to address; (coup) to direct, aim; (personne) to direct (à to); a. la parole à to speak to; s'a. à to speak to (aller trouver) to go and see; (bureau) to inquire at; (être destiné à) to be aimed at.

Adriatique [adriatik] nf l'A. the Adriatic.

adroit, -oite [adrwa, -wat] a skilful, clever.

adulation [adylɑsjɔ̃] nf adulation.

adulte [adylt] nmf adult, grown-up ▮ a (personne, animal, attitude etc) adult; être a. to be an adult ou a grown-up.

adultère [adyltɛr] a adulterous ▮ nm adultery.

advenir* [advənir] v imp to occur; a. de (devenir) to become of; advienne que pourra come what may.

adverbe [advɛrb] nm adverb. ● **adverbial, -e, -aux** a adverbial.

adversaire [advɛrsɛr] nmf opponent, adversary. ● **adverse** a opposing.

adversité [advɛrsite] nf adversity.

aérer [aere] vt (chambre, classe etc) to air (out), ventilate; (lit) to air (out) ▮ s'aérer vpr Fam to get some air. ● **aéré, -ée** a (pièce etc) airy; (texte) nicely spaced, uncluttered. ● **aération** nf ventilation.

aérien, -ienne [aerjɛ̃, -jɛn] a (transport, attaque etc) air; (photo) aerial; (câble) overhead; (léger) airy; ligne aérienne airline.

aérobic [aerɔbik] nf aerobics.

aéro-club [aerɔklœb] nm flying club. ● **aérodrome** nm aerodrome. ● **aérodynamique** a streamlined, aerodynamic. ● **aérogare** nf air terminal. ● **aéroglisseur** nm hovercraft. ● **aérogramme** nm air letter. ● **aéromodélisme** nm model aircraft building and flying. ● **aéronautique** nf aeronautics. ● **aéronavale** nf = Br Fleet Air Arm, = Am Naval Air Force. ● **aéroport** nm airport. ● **aéroporté, -ée** a airborne. ● **aérosol** nm aerosol.

affable [afabl] a affable.

affaiblir [afeblir] vt, s'affaiblir vpr to weaken.

affaire [afɛr] nf (question) matter, affair; (marché) deal; (firme) concern, business; (scandale) affair; (procès) case; affaires (commerce) business; (d'intérêt public, personnel) affairs; (effets) belongings, things; avoir a. à to have to deal with; c'est mon a. that's my business ou affair ou concern; faire une bonne a. to get a good deal, get a bargain; ça fera l'a. that will do nicely; c'est toute une a. (histoire) it's quite a business.

affairer (s') [safere] vpr to run ou bustle about, busy oneself. ● **affairé, -ée** a busy.

affaisser (s') [afese] vpr (personne) to collapse; (plancher) to cave in, give way; (sol) to subside. ● **affaissement** [afɛsmã] nm (du sol) subsidence.

affaler (s') [afale] vpr to flop down, collapse.

affamé, -ée [afame] a starving; a. de (gloire etc) hungry for.

affecter [afɛkte] vt (nommer à un poste) to post; (destiner) to earmark, assign; (feindre, émouvoir) to affect. ● **affecté, -ée** a (manières, personne) affected. ● **affectation** nf (de fonctionnaire etc) posting; (de somme etc) assignment; (simulation) affectation.

affectif, -ive [afɛktif, -iv] a emotional.

affection [afɛksjɔ̃] nf (attachement) affection; (maladie) ailment. ● **affectionner** vt to be fond of. ● **affectionné, -ée** a loving.

affectueux, -euse [afɛktɥø, -øz] a affectionate, loving.

affermir [afɛrmir] vt (autorité) to strengthen; (muscles) to tone up; (voix) to steady.

affiche [afiʃ] nf notice; (publicitaire etc) poster; Th (play) bill. ● **afficher** vt (avis, affiche etc) to put up, stick ou post up; (concert, réunion etc) to put up a notice about; (sentiment) Péj to display; Ordinat to display (message). ● **affichage** nm (bill-)posting, Ordinat display, 'a. interdit' 'stick no bills'; panneau d'a. Br hoarding, Am billboard.

affilée (d') [dafile] adv (à la suite) in a row, at a stretch.

affiler [afile] vt to sharpen.

affilier (s') [safilje] vpr s'a. à to join, become affiliated to. ● **affiliation** nf affiliation.

affiner [afine] vt to refine.

affinité [afinite] nf affinity.

affirmatif, -ive [afirmatif, -iv] a (ton) assertive, positive; (proposition) affirmative; il a été a. he was quite positive ▮ nf répondre par l'affirmative to reply in the affirmative.

affirmer [afirme] *vt* to assert; (*proclamer solennellement*) to affirm. ●**affirmation** *nf* assertion.

affleurer [aflœre] *vi* to appear on the surface.

affliger [afliʒe] *vt* to distress; **affligé de** stricken *ou* afflicted with.

affluence [aflyãs] *nf* crowd; **heure(s) d'a.** rush hour(s).

affluent [aflyã] *nm* tributary.

affluer [aflye] *vi* (*sang*) to flow, rush; (*gens*) to flock. ●**afflux** *nm* flow; (*arrivée*) influx.

affoler [afɔle] *vt* to drive crazy; (*effrayer*) to terrify ▮ **s'affoler** *vpr* to panic. ●**affolant, -ante** *a* terrifying. ●**affolement** *nm* panic.

affranchir [afrɑ̃ʃir] *vt* (*timbrer*) to stamp (*letter*); (*émanciper*) to free. ●**affranchissement** *nm* **tarifs d'a.** postage.

affréter [afrete] *vt* (*avion*) to charter; (*navire*) to freight.

affreux, -euse [afrø, -øz] *a* horrible, dreadful, awful. ●**affreusement** *adv* dreadfully, awfully.

affriolant, -ante [afriɔlɑ̃, -ɑ̃t] *a* enticing.

affront [afrɔ̃] *nm* insult, affront; **faire un a. à** to insult.

affronter [afrɔ̃te] *vt* to confront, face; (*mauvais temps, difficultés etc*) to brave. ●**affrontement** *nm* confrontation.

affubler [afyble] *vt Péj* to dress, rig out (**de** in).

affût [afy] *nm* **à l'a. de** *Fig* on the lookout for.

affûter [afyte] *vt* (*outil*) to sharpen, grind.

Afghanistan [afganistɑ̃] *nm* Afghanistan.

afin [afɛ̃] *prép* **a. de** (+ *inf*) in order to ▮ *conj* **a. que** (+ *sub*) so that.

Afrique [afrik] *nf* Africa. ●**africain, -aine** *a* & African ▮ *nmf* A., **Africaine** African.

agacer [agase] *vt* (*personne*) to irritate, annoy. ●**agacement** *nm* irritation.

âge [ɑʒ] *nm* age; **quel â. as-tu?** how old are you?; **avant l'â.** before one's time; **d'un certain â.** middle-aged; **d'un â. avancé** elderly; **l'â. adulte** adulthood; **la force de l'â.** the prime of life; **le moyen â.** the Middle Ages. ●**âgé, -ée** *a* old, elderly; **â. de six ans** six years old; **un enfant â. de six ans** a six-year-old child.

agence [aʒɑ̃s] *nf* agency; (*succursale*) branch office; **a. immobilière** *Br* estate agent's office, *Am* real estate office.

agencer [aʒɑ̃se] *vt* to arrange; **bien agencé** (*maison etc*) well laid-out; (*phrase*) well put-together. ●**agencement** *nm* (*de maison etc*) layout.

agenda [aʒɛ̃da] *nm Br* diary, *Am* datebook.

agenouiller (s') [saʒnuje] *vpr* to kneel (down); **être agenouillé** to be kneeling (down).

agent [aʒɑ̃] *nm* agent; **a. (de police)** policeman; **a. de change** stockbroker; **a. immobilier** *Br* estate agent, *Am* real estate agent.

aggloméré [aglɔmere] *nm* (*bois*) chipboard, fibreboard.

agglomérer (s') [saglɔmere] *vpr* (*s'entasser*) to conglomerate. ●**agglomération** *nf* conglomeration; (*habitations*) built-up area; (*ville*) town.

aggraver [agrave] *vt* to worsen, make worse; (*peine*) *Jur* to increase ▮ **s'aggraver** *vpr* to worsen, get worse. ●**aggravation** *nf* worsening.

agile [aʒil] *a* agile, nimble. ●**agilité** *nf* agility, nimbleness.

agir [aʒir] **1** *vi* to act; **a. auprès de** to intercede with. **2 s'agir** *v imp* **il s'agit d'argent**/*etc* it's a question *ou* matter of money/*etc*, it concerns money/*etc*; **de quoi s'agit-il?** what is it?, what's it about?; **il s'agit de se dépêcher**/*etc* we have to hurry/*etc*. ●**agissant, -ante** *a* active, effective. ●**agissements** *nmpl Péj* dealings.

agitation [aʒitasjɔ̃] *nf* (*de la mer*) roughness; (*d'une personne*) restlessness; (*nervosité*) agitation; (*de la rue*) bustle; (*politique*) unrest.

agiter [aʒite] *vt* (*remuer*) to stir; (*secouer*) to shake; (*brandir*) to wave; (*troubler*) to agitate; (*discuter*) to debate ▮ **s'agiter** *vpr* (*enfant*) to fidget; (*peuple*) to stir. ●**agité, -ée** *a* (*mer*) rough; (*personne*) restless, agitated; (*enfant*) fidgety, restless. ●**agitateur, -trice** *nmf* (political) agitator.

agneau, -x [aɲo] *nm* lamb.

agonie [agɔni] *nf* death throes; **être à l'a.** to be suffering the pangs of death. ●**agoniser** *vi* to be dying.

agrafe [agraf] *nf* hook; (*pour papiers*) staple. ●**agrafer** *vt* to fasten, do up, hook; (*papiers*) to staple. ●**agrafeuse** *nf* stapler.

agrandir [agrɑ̃dir] *vt* to enlarge; (*grossir*) to magnify ▮ **s'agrandir** *vpr* to expand, grow. ●**agrandissement** *nm* (*de ville*) expansion; (*de maison*) extension; (*de photo*) enlargement.

agréable [agreabl] *a* pleasant, agreeable, nice. ●**agréablement** [-əmɑ̃] *adv* pleasantly.

agréer [agree] *vt* to accept; **veuillez a. l'expression de mes salutations distinguées** (*dans une lettre*) *Br* yours faithfully, *Am* sincerely. ●**agréé, -ée** *a* (*fournisseur, centre*) approved.

agrégation [agregasjɔ̃] *nf* competitive examination for recruitment of lycée teachers. ●**agrégé, -ée** *nmf* teacher who has passed the *agrégation*.

agrément [agremɑ̃] *nm* (*attrait*) charm; (*accord*) assent; **voyage d'a.** pleasure trip. ●**agrémenter** *vt* to embellish; **a. un récit d'anecdotes** to pepper a story with anecdotes.

agrès [agre] *nmpl* (*de voilier*) tackle, rigging; (*de gymnastique*) *Br* apparatus, *Am* equipment.

agresser [agrese] *vt* to attack; (*dans la rue etc, pour voler*) to mug. ●**agresseur** *nm* attacker; (*dans la rue etc*) mugger; (*dans un conflit*) aggressor. ●**agression** *nf* attack; (*dans la rue etc*) mugging; (*d'un État*) aggression.

agressif, -ive [agrɛsif, -iv] a aggressive.
● **agressivité** nf aggressiveness.

agricole [agrikɔl] a (ouvrier, machine) farm;
(peuple) agricultural, farming; **travaux agricoles** farm work.

agriculteur [agrikyltœr] nm farmer. ● **agriculture** nf farming, agriculture.

agripper [agripe] vt to clutch, grip; **s'a. à** to cling to, clutch, grip.

agronomie [agrɔnɔmi] nf agronomics.

agrumes [agrym] nmpl citrus fruit(s).

aguerri, -ie [ageri] a seasoned, hardened.

aguets (aux) [ozagɛ] adv on the lookout.

aguicher [agiʃe] vt to tease, excite.
● **aguichant, -ante** a enticing.

ah! [a] int ah!, oh!

ahurir [ayrir] vt (étonner) to astound, bewilder; **avoir l'air ahuri** to look astounded ou utterly bewildered. ● **ahuri, -ie** nmf idiot.

ai [e] voir **avoir**.

aide [ɛd] nf help, assistance, aid; **à l'a. de** with the help ou aid of **I** nmf (personne) assistant; **a. familiale** Br home help, Am mother's helper. ● **aide-électricien** nm electrician's Br mate ou Am helper. ● **aide-mémoire** nm inv (livre scolaire) handbook (of facts etc). ● **aide-soignante** nf Br nursing auxiliary, Am nurse's aid.

aider [ede] vt to help, assist, aid (**à faire** to do); **s'a. de** to make use of.

aïe [aj] int ouch!, ow!

aie(s), aient [ɛ] voir **avoir**.

aïeul, -e [ajœl] nmf Litt grandfather, grandmother.

aïeux [ajø] nmpl Litt forefathers, forebears.

aigle [ɛgl] nm eagle.

aiglefin [ɛgləfɛ̃] nm haddock.

aigre [ɛgr] a (acide) sour; (voix, vent, parole) sharp, cutting. ● **aigre-doux, -douce** a bittersweet. ● **aigreur** nf sourness; (de ton) sharpness; **aigreurs** heartburn.

aigrette [ɛgrɛt] nf (de plumes) tuft.

aigrir (s') [segrir] vpr (vin) to turn sour;
(caractère) to sour. ● **aigri, -ie** [egri] a (personne) embittered, bitter.

aigu, -uë [egy] a (douleur, crise etc) acute;
(dents) sharp, pointed; (voix) shrill.

aiguille [egɥij] nf (à coudre, de pin) needle;
(de montre) hand; (de balance) pointer; **a.** (rocheuse) peak.

aiguiller [egɥije] vt (train) Br to shunt, Am switch; (personne) Fig to steer, direct. ● **aiguillage** nm (de voie ferrée) Br points, Am switches. ● **aiguilleur** nm Rail signalman; **a. du ciel** air traffic controller.

aiguillon [egɥijɔ̃] nm (dard) sting; (stimulant) spur. ● **aiguillonner** vt to spur (on).

aiguiser [eg(ɥ)ize] vt (affiler) to sharpen;
(appétit) to whet.

ail [aj] nm garlic.

aile [ɛl] nf wing; (de moulin) sail;
(d'automobile) Br wing, Am fender; **battre de l'a.** to be in a bad way; **d'un coup d'a.** (avion) in continuous flight. ● **ailé, -ée** [ele] a winged. ● **aileron** nm (de requin) fin;

(d'avion) aileron; (d'oiseau) wing tip. ● **ailier** [elje] nm Football wing(er).

aile(s), aillent [aj] voir **aller**[1].

ailleurs [ajœr] adv somewhere else, elsewhere; **partout a.** everywhere else; **d'a.** (du reste) besides, anyway; **par a.** (en outre) moreover; (autrement) otherwise.

ailloli [ajoli] nm garlic mayonnaise.

aimable [ɛmabl] a (gentil) kind; (sympathique) likeable, amiable; (agréable) pleasant.
● **aimablement** [-əmɑ̃] adv kindly.

aimant[1] [ɛmɑ̃] nm magnet. ● **aimanter** vt to magnetize.

aimant[2], **-ante** [ɛmɑ̃, -ɑ̃t] a loving.

aimer [eme] vt to love; **a.** (**bien**) (apprécier) to like, be fond of; **a. faire** to like doing ou to do; **j'aimerais qu'il vienne** I would like him to come; **a. mieux** to prefer; **j'aime(rais) mieux qu'elle reste** I'd prefer ou I'd rather she stayed; **ils s'aiment** they're in love.

aine [ɛn] nf groin.

aîné, -ée [ene] a (de deux frères etc) elder, older; (de plus de deux) eldest, oldest **I** nmf (enfant) elder ou older (child); eldest ou oldest (child); **c'est mon a.** he's my senior.

ainsi [ɛ̃si] adv (comme ça) (in) this ou that way, thus; (alors) so; **a. que** as well as; **et a. de suite** and so on; **pour a. dire** so to speak.

air [ɛr] nm **1** air; **prendre l'a.** to get some (fresh) air; **en plein a.** in the open (air), outdoors; **en l'a.** (jeter) (up) in(to) the air; (paroles, menaces) empty; (projets) uncertain, (up) in the air; **ficher** ou **flanquer en l'a.** Fam (jeter) to chuck away; (gâcher) to mess up, upset; **dans l'a.** (grippe, idées) about, around.

2 (expression) look, appearance; **avoir l'a.** (fatigué etc) to look, seem; **avoir l'a.** d'un **professeur/etc** to look like a teacher/etc; **avoir l'a. de dire la vérité/etc** to look as if one is telling the truth/etc; **a. de famille** family likeness.

3 (mélodie) tune; **a. d'opéra** aria.

aire [ɛr] nf (de stationnement etc) & Géom area; (d'oiseau) eyrie; **a. de lancement** launching site; **a. d'atterrissage** landing place ou strip; **a de jeux** (children's) play area; **a. de repos** (sur autoroute) rest area.

airelle [ɛrɛl] nf Br bilberry, Am blueberry.

aisance [ɛzɑ̃s] nf (facilité) ease; (prospérité) easy circumstances, affluence.

aise [ɛz] nf **à l'a.** (dans un vêtement etc) comfortable; (dans une situation) at ease; (fortuné) comfortably off; **aimer ses aises** to like one's comforts; **mal à l'a.** uncomfortable, ill at ease. ● **aisé, -ée** [eze] a (fortuné) comfortably off; (naturel) free and easy; (facile) easy. ● **aisément** adv easily.

aisselle [ɛsɛl] nf armpit.

ait [ɛ] voir **avoir**.

ajonc(s) [aʒɔ̃] nm(pl) gorse, furze.

ajouré, -ée [aʒure] a (dentelle etc) openwork.

ajourner [aʒurne] vt to postpone, adjourn.
● **ajournement** nm postponement, adjourn-

ment.

ajout [aʒu] *nm* addition. ● **ajouter** *vti* to add (à to); **s'a. à** to add to.

ajuster [aʒyste] *vt* (*pièce, salaires*) to adjust; (*coiffure*) to arrange; (*coup*) to aim; **a. à** (*adapter*) to fit to. ● **ajusté, -ée** *a* (*serré*) close-fitting. ● **ajustement** *nm* adjustment. ● **ajusteur** *nm* (*ouvrier*) fitter.

alaise [alɛz] *nf* (waterproof) undersheet.

alambic [alɑ̃bik] *nm* still.

alambiqué, -ée [alɑ̃bike] *a* convoluted.

alanguir [alɑ̃gir] *vt* to make languid.

alarme [alarm] *nf* (*signal, inquiétude*) alarm; **jeter l'a.** to cause alarm; **a. antivol/ d'incendie** burglar/fire alarm. ● **alarmer** *vt* to alarm; **s'a.** to become alarmed at.

Albanie [albani] *nf* Albania. ● **albanais, -aise** *a* Albanian ▮ *nmf* **A., Albanaise** Albanian.

albâtre [albɑtr] *nm* alabaster.

albatros [albatros] *nm* albatross.

albinos [albinos] *nmf & a inv* albino.

album [albɔm] *nm* (*de timbres etc*) album; (*de dessins*) sketchbook.

alcali [alkali] *nm* alkali. ● **alcalin, -ine** *a* alkaline.

alchimie [alʃimi] *nf* alchemy.

alcool [alkɔl] *nm* alcohol; (*spiritueux*) spirits; **a. à 90%** *Br* surgical spirit, *Am* rubbing alcohol; **a. à brûler** *Br* methylated spirit(s), *Am* wood alcohol; **lampe à a.** spirit lamp. ● **alcoolique** *a & nmf* alcoholic. ● **alcoolisée** *af* **boisson a.** alcoholic drink. ● **alcoolisme** *nm* alcoholism. ● **alcootest**® *nm* breath test; (*appareil*) breathalyzer.

alcôve [alkov] *nf* alcove.

aléas [alea] *nmpl* hazards, risks. ● **aléatoire** *a* (*résultat*) uncertain; (*sélection, nombre*) random; (*accès*) *Ordinat* random.

alentour [alɑ̃tur] *adv* round about, around; **d'a.** surrounding. ● **alentours** *nmpl* surroundings, vicinity; **aux a. de** in the vicinity of.

alerte [alɛrt] 1 *a* (*leste*) agile, spry; (*éveillé*) alert. 2 *nf* alarm; **en état d'a.** on the alert; **a. aérienne** air-raid warning. ● **alerter** *vt* to warn, alert.

alezan, -ane [alzɑ̃, -an] *a & nmf* (*cheval*) chestnut.

algarade [algarad] *nf* (*dispute*) altercation.

algèbre [alʒɛbr] *nf* algebra. ● **algébrique** *a* algebraic.

Alger [alʒe] *nm ou f* Algiers.

Algérie [alʒeri] *nf* Algeria. ● **algérien, -ienne** *a* Algerian ▮ *nmf* **A., Algérienne** Algerian.

algue(s) [alg] *nf(pl)* seaweed.

alias [aljɑs] *adv* alias.

alibi [alibi] *nm* alibi.

aliéner [aljene] *vt* to alienate; **s'a. qn** to alienate s.o. ● **aliéné, -ée** *nmf* insane person; *Péj* lunatic. ● **aliénation** *nf* alienation; *Méd* derangement.

aligner [aline] *vt* to line up, align; **les a.** *Arg* to fork out, pay up ▮ **s'aligner** *vpr* (*personnes*) to fall into line, line up; (*dirigeant*) to align oneself; (*gouvernement, pays*) to align itself (**sur** with). ● **alignement** *nm*

alignment.

aliment [alimɑ̃] *nm* food. ● **alimentaire** *a* (*ration, industrie etc*) food; **produits alimentaires** foods. ● **alimentation** *nf* (*action*) feeding; (*en eau, électricité etc*) supply(ing); (*régime*) diet, nutrition; (*nourriture*) food; **magasin d'a.** grocer's, grocery store. ● **alimenter** *vt* (*nourrir*) to feed; (*fournir*) to supply (**en** with); (*débat, feu*) to fuel.

alinéa [alinea] *nm* paragraph.

alité, -ée [alite] *a* bedridden.

allaiter [alete] *vti* (*femme*) to (breast)feed (*baby*); (*animal*) to suckle.

allant [alɑ̃] *nm* drive, energy, zest.

allécher [aleʃe] *vt* to tempt, entice.

allée [ale] *nf* (*de parc etc*) path; (*bordée d'arbres*) walk, avenue; (*de cinéma, supermarché etc*) aisle; (*devant une maison*) drive(way); **allées et venues** comings and goings, running about.

allégation [alegasjɔ̃] *nf* assertion, allegation.

alléger [aleʒe] *vt* to make lighter, alleviate. ● **allégé, -ée** *a* (*fromage etc*) low-fat.

allégorie [alegɔri] *nf* allegory.

allègre [alegr] *a* gay, lively, cheerful. ● **allégresse** *nf* gladness, rejoicing.

alléguer [alege] *vt* (*excuse*) to put forward.

alléluia [aleluja] *nm* hallelujah.

Allemagne [almaɲ] *nf* Germany. ● **allemand, -ande** *a* German ▮ *nmf* **A., Allemande** German ▮ *nm* (*langue*) German.

aller¹* [ale] 1 *vi* (*aux être*) to go; (*montre etc*) to work, go; **a. à** (*convenir à*) to suit; **a. avec** (*vêtement*) to go with, match; **a. bien/mieux** (*personne*) to be well/better; **va voir!** go and see!; **comment vas-tu?, (comment) ça va?** how are you?; **ça va!** all right!; fine!; **ça va (comme ça)!** that's enough!; **allez-y** go on, go ahead; **j'y vais** I'm coming; **allons (donc)!** come on!, come off it!; **allez! au lit!** come on *ou* go on, (to) bed!; **ça va de soi** that's obvious.

2 *v aux* (*futur proche*) **il va savoir/venir**/*etc* he'll know/come/*etc*, he's going to know/come/*etc*; **il va partir** he's about to leave, he's going to leave.

3 **s'en aller** [sɑ̃ale] *vpr* to go away; (*tache*) to come out.

aller² [ale] *nm* outward journey; **a. (simple)** *Br* single (ticket), *Am* one-way (ticket); **a. (et) retour** *Br* return (ticket), *Am* round-trip (ticket).

allergie [alɛrʒi] *nf* allergy. ● **allergique** *a* allergic (**à** to).

alliage [aljaʒ] *nm* alloy.

alliance [aljɑ̃s] *nf* (*anneau*) wedding ring; (*de pays*) alliance; *Rel* covenant; (*mariage*) marriage.

allier [alje] *vt* (*associer*) to combine (**à** with); (*pays*) to ally (**à** with) ▮ **s'allier** *vpr* (*couleurs*) to combine; (*pays*) to become allied (**à** with, to); **s'a. à** (*famille*) to ally oneself with. ● **allié, -ée** *nmf* ally.

alligator [aligatɔr] *nm* alligator.

allô [alo] *int Tél* hello!, hullo!, hallo!

allocation [alɔkasjɔ̃] *nf* (*somme*) allowance, benefit; **a. (de) chômage** unemployment benefit; **a. (de) logement** housing benefit, = rent allowance; **allocations familiales** child benefit.

allocution [alɔkysjɔ̃] *nf* (short) speech, address.

allonger [alɔ̃ʒe] *vt* (*bras*) to stretch out; (*jupe*) to lengthen; (*sauce*) to thin ▌ *vi* (*jours*) to get longer ▌ **s'allonger** *vpr* to stretch out. ●**allongé, -ée** *a* (*étiré*) elongated.

allouer [alwe] *vt* to allocate.

allumer [alyme] *vt* (*feu, pipe etc*) to light; (*électricité, radio*) to turn *ou* switch on; (*désir, colère*) Fig to arouse, kindle ▌ **s'allumer** *vpr* (*lumière, lampe*) to come on; (*yeux*) Fig to light up; (*feu, guerre*) to flare up. ●**allumage** *nm* lighting; (*de véhicule*) ignition. ●**allume-gaz** *nm inv* gas lighter. ●**allumeuse** *nf* (*femme*) teaser.

allumette [alymɛt] *nf* match.

allure [alyr] *nf* (*vitesse*) pace; (*de véhicule*) speed; (*démarche*) gait, walk; (*maintien*) bearing; (*air*) look; **allures** (*conduite*) ways.

allusion [alyzjɔ̃] *nf* reference, allusion; (*voilée*) hint; **faire a. à** to refer *ou* allude to; (*en termes voilés*) to hint at.

almanach [almana] *nm* almanac.

aloi [alwa] *nm* **de bon a.** genuine, worthy.

alors [alɔr] *adv* (*en ce cas-là*) so, then; (*en ce temps-là*) then; **a. que** (*lorsque*) when; (*tandis que*) whereas; **et a.?** so what?; **a., tu viens?** are you coming then?, are you coming or what?

alouette [alwɛt] *nf* (sky)lark.

alourdir [alurdir] *vt* to weigh down ▌ **s'alourdir** *vpr* to become heavy *ou* heavier. ●**alourdi, -ie** *a* heavy.

aloyau [alwajo] *nm* sirloin.

alpaga [alpaga] *nm* (*tissu*) alpaca.

alpage [alpaʒ] *nm* mountain pasture. ●**Alpes** *nfpl* **les A.** the Alps. ●**alpestre** *ou* **alpin, -ine** *a* alpine.

alphabet [alfabɛ] *nm* alphabet. ●**alphabétique** *a* alphabetical. ●**alphabétiser** *vt* to teach to read and write.

alpinisme [alpinism] *nm* mountaineering. ●**alpiniste** *nmf* mountaineer.

altercation [altɛrkasjɔ̃] *nf* altercation.

altérer [altere] *vt* **1** (*denrée, santé*) to impair, spoil; (*voix, vérité*) to distort; (*monnaie, texte*) to falsify. **2** (*donner soif à*) to make thirsty ▌ **s'altérer** *vpr* (*santé, relations*) to deteriorate. ●**altération** *nf* deterioration, change (**de** in); (*de visage*) distortion.

alternatif, -ive [alternatif, -iv] *a* alternating. ●**alternative** *nf* alternative; **des alternatives de** (*joie et de tristesse etc*) alternate periods of. ●**alternativement** *adv* alternately.

alterner [alterne] *vti* to alternate. ●**alterné, -ée** *a* alternate. ●**alternance** *nf* alternation.

altesse [altɛs] *nf* (*titre*) Highness.

altier, -ière [altje, -jɛr] *a* haughty.

altitude [altityd] *nf* height, altitude.

alto [alto] *nm* (*instrument de musique*) viola.

aluminium [alyminjɔm] *nm* Br aluminium, Am aluminum; **papier (d')a., Fam papier (d')alu** tinfoil.

alunir [alynir] *vi* to land on the moon.

alvéole [alveɔl] *nf* (*de ruche*) cell; (*dentaire*) socket. ●**alvéolé, -ée** *a* honeycombed.

amabilité [amabilte] *nf* kindness; **faire des amabilités à** to show kindness to.

amadouer [amadwe] *vt* to coax, persuade.

amaigrir [amegrir] *vt* to make thin(ner); **régime amaigrissant** Br slimming diet, Am weight reduction diet. ●**amaigri, -ie** *a* thin(ner). ●**amaigrissement** *nm* (*de malade*) weight loss; (*volontaire*) dieting, Br slimming.

amalgame [amalgam] *nm* (*mélange*) mixture, combination. ●**amalgamer** *vt*, **s'amalgamer** *vpr* to blend, mix, combine.

amande [amɑ̃d] *nf* almond.

amant [amɑ̃] *nm* lover.

amarre [amar] *nf* (mooring) rope, hawser; **amarres** moorings. ●**amarrer** *vt* (*bateau*) to moor; (*corde, paquet etc*) to secure, make fast.

amas [ama] *nm* heap, pile. ●**amasser** *vt* to pile up; (*fortune, argent*) to amass; (*preuves*) to amass, gather ▌ **s'amasser** *vpr* to pile up; (*gens*) to gather.

amateur [amatœr] *nm* (*d'art etc*) lover; (*sportif*) amateur; (*acheteur*) Fam taker; **d'a.** (*talent*) amateur; (*travail*) Péj amateurish; **une équipe d'a.** an amateur team. ●**amateurisme** *nm* Sport amateurism; Péj amateurishness.

amazone [amazɔn] *nf* horsewoman; **monter en a.** to ride sidesaddle.

ambages (sans) [sɑ̃zabaʒ] *adv* to the point, in plain language.

ambassade [ɑ̃basad] *nf* embassy. ●**ambassadeur, -drice** *nmf* ambassador.

ambiance [ɑ̃bjɑ̃s] *nf* atmosphere. ●**ambiant, -ante** *a* surrounding.

ambigu, -uë [ɑ̃bigy] *a* ambiguous. ●**ambiguïté** [-ɥite] *nf* ambiguity.

ambitieux, -euse [ɑ̃bisjø, -øz] *a* ambitious. ●**ambition** *nf* ambition. ●**ambitionner** *vt* to aspire to; **il ambitionne de faire/d'être** his ambition is to do/be.

ambre [ɑ̃br] *nm* (*jaune*) amber; (*gris*) ambergris.

ambulance [ɑ̃bylɑ̃s] *nf* ambulance. ●**ambulancier, -ière** *nmf* ambulance driver.

ambulant, -ante [ɑ̃bylɑ̃, -ɑ̃t] *a* travelling, itinerant; **marchand a.** (street) hawker.

âme [ɑm] *nf* soul; **je n'ai pas rencontré â. qui vive** I didn't meet a (living) soul; **état d'â.** state of mind; **â. sœur** soul mate; **â. damnée** evil genius, henchman; **avoir charge d'âmes** to be responsible for human life.

améliorer [ameljɔre] *vt*, **s'améliorer** *vpr* to improve. ●**amélioration** *nf* improvement.

amen [amɛn] *adv* amen.

aménager [amenaʒe] *vt* (*arranger, installer*) to fit out, Br fit up (**en** as); (*bateau*) to fit out; (*transformer*) to convert (**en** into); (*construire*) to set up; (*ajuster*) to adjust; (*région,* *ville*) to develop. ● **aménagement** *nm* fitting out; conversion; setting up; adjustment; development.

amende [amɑ̃d] *nf* fine; **infliger une a. à** to impose a fine on; **faire a. honorable** to make an apology.

amender [amɑ̃de] *vt* (*texte de loi*) to amend; (*terre*) to improve ‖ **s'amender** *vpr* to mend *ou* improve one's ways.

amener [amne] *vt* to bring; (*causer*) to bring about ‖ **s'amener** *vpr Fam* to come along.

amenuiser (s') [samənɥize] *vpr* to grow smaller, dwindle.

amer, -ère [amɛr] *a* bitter. ● **amèrement** *adv* bitterly.

Amérique [amerik] *nf* America; **A. du Nord/du Sud** North/South America. ● **américain, -aine** *a* American ‖ *nmf* **A.**, **Américaine** American.

amerrir [amerir] *vi* to make a sea landing; (*cabine spatiale*) to splash down.

amertume [amɛrtym] *nf* bitterness.

améthyste [ametist] *nf* amethyst.

ameublement [amœbləmɑ̃] *nm* furniture.

ameuter [amøte] *vt* (*soulever*) to stir up; (*attrouper*) to gather, muster; (*voisins*) to bring out ‖ **s'ameuter** *vpr* to gather, muster.

ami, -ie [ami] *nmf* friend; (*de la nature, des livres etc*) lover (**de** of); **petit a.** boyfriend; **petite amie** girlfriend ‖ *a* friendly.

amiable (à l') [alamjabl] *a* amicable ‖ *adv* amicably.

amiante [amjɑ̃t] *nm* asbestos.

amical, -e, -aux [amikal, -o] *a* friendly. ● **amicalement** *adv* in a friendly manner.

amicale [amikal] *nf* association.

amidon [amidɔ̃] *nm* starch. ● **amidonner** *vt* to starch.

amincir [amɛ̃sir] *vt* to make thin(ner) ‖ *vi* (*personne*) to grow slim ‖ **s'amincir** *vpr* to become thinner.

amiral, -aux [amiral, -o] *nm* admiral. ● **amirauté** *nf* admiralty.

amitié [amitje] *nf* friendship; (*amabilité*) kindness; **amitiés** kind regards; **prendre qn en a.** to take a liking to s.o.

ammoniac [amɔnjak] *nm* (*gaz*) ammonia. ● **ammoniaque** *nf* (*liquide*) ammonia.

amnésie [amnezi] *nf* amnesia. ● **amnésique** *a* amnesic.

amniocentèse [amnjosɛ̃tɛz] *nf* amniocentesis.

amnistie [amnisti] *nf* amnesty.

amocher [amɔʃe] *vt Arg* to mess up, bash.

amoindrir [amwɛ̃drir] *vt*, **s'amoindrir** *vpr* to decrease, diminish.

amollir [amɔlir] *vt* to soften; (*affaiblir*) to weaken.

amonceler [amɔ̃sle] *vt*, **s'amonceler** *vpr* to pile up. ● **amoncellement** [-sɛlmɑ̃] *nm* heap, pile.

amont (en) [ɑ̃namɔ̃] *adv* upstream.

amoral, -e, -aux [amɔral, -o] *a* amoral.

amorce [amɔrs] *nf* (*début*) start; (*de pêcheur*) bait; (*détonateur*) fuse, detonator;

(*de pistolet d'enfant*) cap. ● **amorcer** *vt* to start; (*hameçon*) to bait; (*pompe*) to prime. ● **s'amorcer** *vpr* to start.

amorphe [amɔrf] *a* listless, apathetic.

amortir [amɔrtir] *vt* (*coup*) to cushion, absorb; (*bruit*) to deaden; (*dette*) to pay off; (*achat*) to recoup the costs on. ● **amortissement** *nm* (*d'un emprunt*) redemption. ● **amortisseur** *nm* (*de véhicule*) shock absorber.

amour [amur] *nm* love; (*liaison*) romance, love; (*Cupidon*) Cupid; **pour l'a. de** for the sake of; **mon a.** my darling, my love. ● **amour-propre** *nm* self-respect, self-esteem. ● **s'amouracher** *vpr Péj* to become infatuated (**de** with). ● **amoureux, -euse** *nmf* lover ‖ *a* (*de personne*) in love; **a. de qn** in love with s.o.; **a. de la gloire/etc** *Litt* enamoured of glory/*etc*.

amovible [amɔvibl] *a* removable, detachable.

ampère [ɑ̃pɛr] *nm Él* amp(ere).

amphi [ɑ̃fi] *nm* (*à l'université*) *Fam* lecture hall.

amphibie [ɑ̃fibi] *a* amphibious ‖ *nm* amphibian.

amphithéâtre [ɑ̃fiteatr] *nm* (*romain*) amphitheatre; (*à l'université*) lecture hall.

ample [ɑ̃pl] *a* (*vêtement*) full, ample, roomy; (*provision*) full; (*vues*) broad. ● **amplement** *adv* amply, fully; **a. suffisant** ample. ● **ampleur** *nf* (*de robe*) fullness; (*importance, étendue*) scale, extent; **prendre de l'a.** (*maladie etc*) to grow.

amplifier [ɑ̃plifje] *vt* (*son, courant*) to amplify; (*accroître*) to develop; (*exagérer*) to magnify ‖ **s'amplifier** *vpr* (*bruit etc*) to increase. ● **amplificateur** *nm* amplifier. ● **amplification** *nf* (*extension*) increase.

amplitude [ɑ̃plityd] *nf* (*d'un désastre etc*) magnitude.

ampoule [ɑ̃pul] *nf* (*électrique*) (light) bulb; (*aux pieds etc*) blister; (*de médicament*) phial.

ampoulé, -ée [ɑ̃pule] *a* (*style etc*) turgid.

amputer [ɑ̃pyte] *vt* **1** (*membre*) to amputate; **a. qn de la jambe/etc** to amputate s.o.'s leg/ *etc*. **2** (*texte*) to cut, curtail (**de** by). ● **amputation** *nf* **1** (*de membre*) amputation. **2** (*de texte*) (drastic) cut (**de** in).

amuse-gueule [amyzgœl] *nm inv* cocktail snack, appetizer.

amuser [amyze] *vt* (*divertir*) to amuse, entertain; (*occuper*) to divert the attention of ‖ **s'amuser** *vpr* to enjoy oneself, have fun; (*en chemin*) to dawdle, loiter; **s'a. avec** to play with; **s'a. à faire** to amuse oneself doing. ● **amusant, -ante** *a* amusing. ● **amusement** *nm* amusement; (*jeu*) game.

amygdales [amidal] *nfpl* tonsils.

an [ɑ̃] *nm* year; **il a dix ans** he's ten (years old); **par a.** (*dix fois an*) per year; **bon a., mal a.** taking the good and bad years together; **Nouvel A.** New Year.

anachronisme [anakrɔnism] *nm* anachronism.

anagramme [anagram] *nf* anagram.

analogie [analɔʒi] *nf* analogy. ● **analogue** *a* similar ▮ *nm* analogue.

analphabète [analfabɛt] *a* & *nmf* illiterate. ● **analphabétisme** *nm* illiteracy.

analyse [analiz] *nf* analysis; **a. grammaticale** parsing; **a. du sang/d'urine** blood/urine test. ● **analyser** *vt* to analyse; (*phrase*) to parse. ● **analytique** *a* analytic(al).

ananas [anana(s)] *nm* pineapple.

anarchie [anarʃi] *nf* anarchy. ● **anarchique** *a* anarchic. ● **anarchiste** *nmf* anarchist ▮ *a* anarchistic.

anathème [anatɛm] *nm Rel* anathema.

anatomie [anatɔmi] *nf* anatomy. ● **anatomique** *a* anatomical.

ancestral, -e, -aux [ɑ̃sɛstral, -o] *a* ancestral.

ancêtre [ɑ̃sɛtr] *nm* ancestor.

anche [ɑ̃ʃ] *nf* (*de clarinette etc*) reed.

anchois [ɑ̃ʃwa] *nm* anchovy.

ancien, -ienne [ɑ̃sjɛ̃, -jɛn] *a* (*vieux*) old; (*meuble*) antique; (*qui n'est plus*) former, ex-, old; (*antique*) ancient; (*dans une fonction*) senior; **a. élève** *Br* old boy, *Am* alumnus; **a. combattant** *Br* ex-serviceman, *Am* veteran.
▮ *nmf* (*par l'âge*) elder; (*dans une fonction*) senior; **les anciens** (*auteurs, peuples*) the ancients. ● **anciennement** *adv* formerly. ● **ancienneté** *nf* age; (*dans une fonction*) seniority.

ancre [ɑ̃kr] *nf* anchor; **jeter l'a.** to (cast) anchor; **lever l'a.** to weigh anchor. ● **ancrer** *vt* **1** (*navire*) to anchor; **être ancré** *ou* at anchor. **2** (*idée, sentiment*) to root, fix; **ancré dans** rooted in.

Andorre [ɑ̃dɔr] *nf* Andorra.

andouille [ɑ̃duj] *nf* **1** (*idiot*) nitwit; **espèce d'a.!** *Fam* (you) nitwit! **2** (*charcuterie*) sausage (*made from chitterlings*).

âne [ɑn] *nm* (*animal*) donkey, ass; (*personne*) *Péj* ass; **bonnet d'â.** *Br* dunce's cap, *Am* dunce cap.

anéantir [aneɑ̃tir] *vt* to annihilate, wipe out, destroy ▮ **s'anéantir** *vpr* to vanish. ● **anéanti, -ie** *a* (*épuisé*) exhausted; (*stupéfait*) dismayed; (*accablé*) overwhelmed. ● **anéantissement** *nm* annihilation; (*abattement*) dejection.

anecdote [anɛkdɔt] *nf* anecdote. ● **anecdotique** *a* anecdotal.

anémie [anemi] *nf* an(a)emia. ● **anémique** *a* an(a)emic. ● **s'anémier** *vpr* to become an(a)emic.

anémone [anemɔn] *nf* anemone.

ânerie [ɑnri] *nf* stupidity; (*action etc*) stupid thing. ● **ânesse** *nf* she-ass.

anesthésie [anɛstezi] *nf* an(a)esthesia; **a. générale/locale** general/local an(a)esthetic. ● **anesthésier** *vt* to an(a)esthetize. ● **anesthésique** *nm* an(a)esthetic.

anfractuosité [ɑ̃fraktyozite] *nf* crevice, cleft.

ange [ɑ̃ʒ] *nm* angel; **être aux anges** to be in seventh heaven. ● **angélique** *a* angelic.

angélus [ɑ̃ʒelys] *nm* (*prière*) angelus.

angine [ɑ̃ʒin] *nf* sore throat; **a. de poitrine** angina (pectoris).

anglais, -aise [ɑ̃glɛ, -ɛz] *a* English ▮ *nmf* **A.**, **Anglaise** Englishman, Englishwoman; **les A.** the English ▮ *nm* (*langue*) English ▮ *af* **filer à l'anglaise** *Br* to take French leave, slip away, abscond.

angle [ɑ̃gl] *nm* (*point de vue*) & *Géom* angle; (*coin de rue*) corner.

Angleterre [ɑ̃glətɛr] *nf* England.

anglican, -ane [ɑ̃glikã, -an] *a* & *nmf* Anglican.

anglicisme [ɑ̃glisism] *nm* Anglicism. ● **angliciste** *nmf* English specialist.

anglo- [ɑ̃glo] *préf* Anglo-. ● **anglo-normand, -ande** *a* Anglo-Norman; **îles a.-normandes** Channel Islands. ● **anglophile** *a* & *nmf* anglophile. ● **anglophone** *a* English-speaking ▮ *nmf* English speaker. ● **anglo-saxon, -onne** *a* & *nmf* Anglo-Saxon.

angoisse [ɑ̃gwas] *nf* (great) anxiety, anguish, distress. ● **angoissant, -ante** *a* distressing. ● **angoissé, -ée** *a* (*personne*) distressed, in anguish; (*geste, cri*) anguished.

angora [ɑ̃gɔra] *nm* (*laine*) angora; **pull/etc en a.** angora sweater/etc.

anguille [ɑ̃gij] *nf* eel.

angulaire [ɑ̃gylɛr] *a* **pierre a.** cornerstone. ● **anguleux, -euse** *a* (*visage*) angular.

anicroche [anikrɔʃ] *nf* hitch, snag.

animal, -aux [animal, -o] *nm* animal; (*personne mal élevée*) brute, animal ▮ *a* (*règne, graisse etc*) animal.

animateur, -trice [animatœr, -tris] *nmf* (*de télévision*) *Br* compere, *Am* master of ceremonies, emcee; (*de club*) leader, organizer; (*d'entreprise*) driving force, spirit.

animer [anime] *vt* (*débat, groupe*) to lead; (*soirée*) to liven up, enliven; (*mécanisme*) to drive; (*inspirer, faire agir*) (*espoir, ambition, sentiment*) to drive, spur on, animate (*s.o.*); **a. la course** *Sport* to set the pace; **la joie/l'enthousiasme qui animait son regard** *ou* **son visage** the joy/enthusiasm which made his face light up.
▮ **s'animer** *vpr* (*rue etc*) to come to life; (*yeux*) to light up, brighten up. ● **animé, -ée** *a* (*rue, réunion*) lively; (*conversation*) lively, animated; (*doué de vie*) animate. ● **animation** *nf* (*des rues*) activity; (*de réunion*) liveliness; (*de visage*) brightness; *Cinéma* animation.

animosité [animozite] *nf* animosity.

anis [ani(s)] *nm* (*boisson, parfum*) aniseed; **boisson/etc à l'a.** aniseed drink/etc. ● **anisette** *nf* (*liqueur*) anisette.

ankylose [ɑ̃kiloz] *nf* stiffening. ● **s'ankyloser** *vpr* to stiffen up. ● **ankylosé, -ée** *a* stiff.

annales [anal] *nfpl* annals.

anneau, -x [ano] *nm* ring; (*de chaîne*) link.

année [ane] *nf* year; **bonne a.!** Happy New Year!

annexe [anɛks] *nf* (*bâtiment*) annex(e) ▮ *a* (*pièces*) appended; **bâtiment a.** annex(e).

●**annexer** *vt* (*pays*) to annex; (*document*) to append. ●**annexion** *nf* annexation.

annihiler [aniile] *vt* to destroy, annihilate.

anniversaire [anivɛrsɛr] *nm* (*d'événement*) anniversary; (*de naissance*) birthday **I** *a* (*date*) anniversary.

annonce [anɔ̃s] *nf* (*avis*) announcement; (*publicitaire*) advertisement; (*indice*) sign; **petites annonces** classified advertisements, *Br* small ads. ●**annoncer** *vt* (*signaler*) to announce, report; (*vente*) to advertise; (*être l'indice de*) to indicate, be a sign of; **a. le printemps** to herald spring; **s'a. pluvieux/ difficile/etc** to look like being rainy/difficult/ *etc*. ●**annonceur** *nm* (*à la radio, télévision*) announcer; (*publicitaire*) advertiser.

Annonciation [anɔ̃sjasjɔ̃] *nf* Annunciation.

annoter [anɔte] *vt* to annotate. ●**annotation** *nf* annotation.

annuaire [anɥɛr] *nm* yearbook; (*téléphonique*) phone book, directory.

annuel, -elle [anɥɛl] *a* annual, yearly. ●**annuellement** *adv* annually. ●**annuité** *nf* annual *Br* instalment *ou Am* installment.

annulaire [anɥlɛr] *nm* ring *ou* third finger.

annuler [anɥle] *vt* (*visite etc*) to cancel; (*mariage*) to annul; (*jugement*) to quash **I s'annuler** *vpr* to cancel each other out. ●**annulation** *nf* cancellation; (*de mariage*) annulment; (*de jugement*) quashing.

anodin, -ine [anɔdɛ̃, -in] *a* harmless; (*remède*) ineffectual.

anomalie [anɔmali] *nf* (*bizarrerie*) anomaly; (*difformité*) abnormality.

ânon [anɔ̃] *nm* baby donkey.

ânonner [anɔne] *vt* (*en hésitant*) to stumble through; (*d'une voix monotone*) to drone out (*poem etc*).

anonymat [anɔnima] *nm* anonymity; **garder l'a.** to remain anonymous. ●**anonyme** *a & nmf* anonymous (person).

anorak [anɔrak] *nm* anorak.

anorexie [anɔrɛksi] *nf* anorexia. ●**anorexique** *a & nmf* anorexic.

anormal, -e, -aux [anɔrmal, -o] *a* abnormal; (*enfant*) educationally subnormal.

ANPE [aenpeø] *nf abrév* (*agence nationale pour l'emploi*) employment office, = *Br* Jobcentre.

anse [ɑ̃s] *nf* **1** (*de tasse, panier etc*) handle. **2** (*baie*) cove.

antagonisme [ɑ̃tagɔnism] *nm* antagonism. ●**antagoniste** *a* antagonistic **I** *nmf* antagonist.

antan (d') [dɑ̃tɑ̃] *a Litt* of long ago.

antarctique [ɑ̃tarktik] *a* antarctic **I** *nm* **l'A.** the Antarctic, Antarctica.

antécédent [ɑ̃tesedɑ̃] *nm Grammaire* antecedent; **antécédents** past history.

antenne [ɑ̃tɛn] *nf* (*de radio etc*) *Br* aerial, *Am* antenna; (*d'insecte*) antenna, feeler; **a. chirurgicale** (*pour les accidentés de la route*) emergency medical unit; **sur** *ou* **à l'a.** on the air; **passer à l'a.** to come on the air.

antérieur, -e [ɑ̃terjœr] *a* (*précédent*) former,

previous, earlier; (*placé devant*) front; **membre a.** forelimb; **a. à** prior to. ●**antérieurement** *adv* previously. ●**antériorité** *nf* precedence.

anthologie [ɑ̃tɔlɔʒi] *nf* anthology.

anthropologie [ɑ̃trɔpɔlɔʒi] *nf* anthropology.

anthropophage [ɑ̃trɔpɔfaʒ] *nm* cannibal. ●**anthropophagie** *nf* cannibalism.

antiaérien, -ienne [ɑ̃tiaerjɛ̃, -jɛn] *a* **canon a.** antiaircraft gun; **abri a.** air-raid shelter.

antiatomique [ɑ̃tiatɔmik] *a* **abri a.** fallout shelter.

antibiotique [ɑ̃tibjɔtik] *nm* antibiotic; **sous antibiotiques** on antibiotics.

antibrouillard [ɑ̃tibrujar] *a & nm* (**phare**) **a.** fog lamp.

anticancéreux, -euse [ɑ̃tikɑ̃serø, -øz] *a* **centre a.** cancer hospital.

antichambre [ɑ̃tiʃɑ̃br] *nf* antechamber.

antichoc [ɑ̃tiʃɔk] *a inv* shockproof.

anticiper [ɑ̃tisipe] *vti* **a.** (**sur**) to anticipate. ●**anticipé, -ée** *a* (*retraite etc*) early; (*paiement*) advance; **avec mes remerciements anticipés** thanking you in advance. ●**anticipation** *nf* anticipation; **par a.** in advance; **d'a.** (*roman, film etc*) science-fiction.

anticlérical, -e, -aux [ɑ̃tiklerikal, -o] *a* anticlerical.

anticonformiste [ɑ̃tikɔ̃fɔrmist] *a & nmf* nonconformist.

anticonstitutionnel, -elle [ɑ̃tikɔ̃stitysjɔnɛl] *a* unconstitutional.

anticorps [ɑ̃tikɔr] *nm* antibody.

anticyclone [ɑ̃tisiklon] *nm* anticyclone.

antidater [ɑ̃tidate] *vt* to backdate, antedate.

antidémocratique [ɑ̃tidemɔkratik] *a* undemocratic.

antidérapant, -ante [ɑ̃tiderapɑ̃, -ɑ̃t] *a* (*surface etc*) non-skid.

antidote [ɑ̃tidɔt] *nm* antidote.

antigel [ɑ̃tiʒɛl] *nm* antifreeze.

Antilles [ɑ̃tij] *nfpl* **les A.** the West Indies. ●**antillais, -aise** *a* West Indian **I** *nmf* A., Antillaise West Indian.

antilope [ɑ̃tilɔp] *nf* antelope.

antimite [ɑ̃timit] *nm* **de l'a.** mothballs.

antiparasite [ɑ̃tiparazit] *a* **dispositif a.** (*de moteur etc*) suppressor.

antipathie [ɑ̃tipati] *nf* antipathy. ●**antipathique** *a* unpleasant; **elle m'est a.** I find her unpleasant.

antipodes [ɑ̃tipɔd] *nmpl* **aux a.** (*partir*) to the antipodes; **aux a. de** at the opposite end of the world from; (*la vérité, la réalité*) *Fig* poles apart from.

antique [ɑ̃tik] *a* ancient. ●**antiquaire** *nmf* antique dealer. ●**antiquité** *nf* (*temps, ancienneté*) antiquity; (*objet ancien*) antique; **antiquités** (*monuments etc*) antiquities.

antirabique [ɑ̃tirabik] *a* (anti-)rabies.

antirouille [ɑ̃tiruj] *a inv* antirust.

antisémite [ɑ̃tisemit] *a* anti-Semitic. ●**antisémitisme** *nm* anti-Semitism.

antiseptique [ɑ̃tisɛptik] *a & nm* antiseptic.

antisudoral, -aux [ɑ̃tisydɔral, -o] *nm* antiperspirant.

antithèse [ãtitɛz] *nf* antithesis.

antituberculeux, -euse [ãtitybɛrkylø, -øz] *a* (*vaccin etc*) tuberculosis.

antivol [ãtivɔl] *nm* anti-theft lock *ou* device.

antonyme [ãtɔnim] *nm* antonym.

antre [ãtr] *nm* (*de lion etc*) den.

anus [anys] *nm* anus.

Anvers [ãvɛr(s)] *nm ou f* Antwerp.

anxiété [ãksjete] *nf* anxiety. ● **anxieux, -euse** *a* anxious **I** *nmf* worrier.

août [u(t)] *nm* August. ● **aoûtien, -ienne** [ausjɛ̃, -jɛn] *nmf* August *Br* holidaymaker *ou Am* vacationer.

apaiser [apɛze] *vt* (*personne*) to calm, pacify; (*scrupules, faim*) to appease; (*douleur*) to soothe; (*craintes*) to calm, allay **I** **s'apaiser** *vpr* (*personne, colère*) to calm down; (*tempête, douleur*) to die down. ● **apaisant, -ante** *a* (*propos etc*) soothing. ● **apaisements** *nmpl* reassurances.

apanage [apanaʒ] *nm* privilege, monopoly (de of).

aparté [aparte] *nm Théâtre* aside; (*dans une réunion*) private exchange; **en a.** in private.

apartheid [aparted] *nm* apartheid.

apathie [apati] *nf* apathy. ● **apathique** *a* apathetic, listless.

apatride [apatrid] *nmf* stateless person.

apercevoir* [apɛrsəvwar] *vt* to see; (*brièvement*) to catch a glimpse of; (*comprendre*) to perceive; **s'a. de** to realize, notice; **s'a. que** to realize *ou* notice that. ● **aperçu** *nm* overall view, general outline; (*intuition*) insight.

apéritif [aperitif] *nm* aperitif. ● **apéro** *nm Fam* aperitif.

apesanteur [apəzɑ̃tœr] *nf* weightlessness.

à-peu-près [apøprɛ] *nm inv* vague approximation.

apeuré, -ée [apœre] *a* frightened, scared.

aphone [afɔn] *a* voiceless; **je suis a. aujourd'hui** I've lost my voice today.

aphorisme [afɔrism] *nm* aphorism.

aphrodisiaque [afrɔdizjak] *nm & a* aphrodisiac.

aphte [aft] *nm* mouth ulcer. ● **aphteuse** *af* **fièvre a.** foot-and-mouth disease.

apiculture [apikyltyr] *nf* beekeeping. ● **apiculteur, -trice** *nmf* beekeeper.

apitoyer [apitwaje] *vt* to move (to pity); **s'a. sur** to pity. ● **apitoiement** *nm* pity, commiseration.

aplanir [aplanir] *vt* (*terrain*) to level; (*difficulté*) to iron out, smooth out.

aplatir [aplatir] *vt* to flatten (out) **I** **s'aplatir** *vpr* (*s'étendre*) to lie flat; (*s'humilier*) to grovel; (*tomber*) *Fam* to fall flat on one's face; **s'a. contre** to flatten oneself against. ● **aplati, -ie** *a* flat. ● **aplatissement** *nm* (*état*) flatness.

aplomb [aplɔ̃] *nm* self-possession, self-assurance; *Péj* impudence; **d'a.** (*meuble etc*) level, straight; (*personne*) (*sur ses jambes*) steady; (*bien portant*) in good shape; **tomber d'a.** (*soleil*) to beat down.

apocalypse [apɔkalips] *nf* apocalypse; **d'a.**

(*vision etc*) apocalyptic. ● **apocalyptique** *a* apocalyptic.

apogée [apɔʒe] *nm* (*de la lune etc*) apogee; (*de règne, carrière etc*) *Fig* peak, apogee.

apolitique [apɔlitik] *a* apolitical.

Apollon [apɔlɔ̃] *nm* Apollo.

apologie [apɔlɔʒi] *nf* defence, vindication. ● **apologiste** *nmf* apologist.

apoplexie [apɔplɛksi] *nf* apoplexy. ● **apoplectique** *a* apoplectic.

apostolat [apɔstɔla] *nm* (*prosélytisme*) proselytism; (*mission*) calling. ● **apostolique** *a* apostolic.

apostrophe [apɔstrɔf] *nf* **1** (*signe*) apostrophe. **2** (*interpellation*) sharp *ou* rude remark. ● **apostropher** *vt* to shout at.

apothéose [apɔteoz] *nf* final triumph, apotheosis.

apôtre [apotr] *nm* apostle.

apparaître* [aparɛtr] *vi* (*se montrer, sembler*) to appear.

apparat [apara] *nm* pomp; **tenue/etc d'a.** ceremonial *ou* formal dress/etc.

appareil [aparɛj] *nm* (*instrument, machine etc*) apparatus; (*électrique*) appliance; (*téléphonique*) telephone; (*avion*) aircraft; (*digestif etc*) *Anat* system; (*législatif etc*) *Pol* machinery; **a. (photo)** camera; **a. (auditif)** hearing aid; **a. (dentaire)** brace; **qui est à l'a.?** (*au téléphone*) who's speaking?

appareiller [apareje] **1** *vi* (*navire*) to get under way. **2** *vt* (*assortir*) to match (up).

apparence [aparɑ̃s] *nf* appearance; (*vestige*) semblance; **en a.** outwardly; **sous l'a. de** under the guise of; **sauver les apparences** to keep up appearances. ● **apparemment** [-amɑ̃] *adv* apparently. ● **apparent, -ente** *a* apparent; (*très visible*) conspicuous.

apparenter (s') [saparɑ̃te] *vpr* (*ressembler*) to be similar *ou* akin (à to). ● **apparenté, -ée** *a* (*semblable*) similar; (*allié*) related.

appariteur [aparitœr] *nm Univ Br* porter, *Am* = janitor.

apparition [aparisjɔ̃] *nf* appearance; (*fantôme*) apparition.

appartement [apartəmɑ̃] *nm Br* flat, *Am* apartment.

appartenir* [apartənir] **1** *vi* to belong (à to); **il ne vous appartient pas de le critiquer** it's not your responsibility *ou* job to criticize him. **2** **s'appartenir** *vpr* to be one's own master. ● **appartenance** *nf* membership (à of).

appât [apɑ] *nm* (*amorce*) bait; (*attrait*) lure. ● **appâter** *vt* (*attirer*) to lure.

appauvrir [apovrir] *vt* to make poorer, impoverish **I** **s'appauvrir** *vpr* to become poorer *ou* impoverished. ● **appauvrissement** *nm* impoverishment.

appel [apɛl] *nm* (*cri, attrait etc*) call; (*demande pressante & en justice*) appeal; (*recrutement*) *Mil* call-up; **a. téléphonique** telephone call; **faire l'a.** (*à l'école*) to take the register; *Mil* to have a roll call; **faire a.** to appeal to, call upon; (*nécessiter*) to call for.

appeler [aple] *vt* (*personne, nom etc*) to call;

(en criant) to call out to; *(recruter) Mil* to call up; *(nécessiter)* to call for; **a. à l'aide to** call for help; **en a. à** to appeal to; **il est appelé à de hautes fonctions/etc** he is marked out for high office/etc; **être appelé à témoigner/etc** to be called upon to give evidence/etc.

▮ **s'appeler** *vpr* to be called; **il s'appelle Paul** his name is Paul. ● **appelé** *nm Mil* conscript. ● **appellation** *nf (nom)* term; **a. contrôlée** guaranteed vintage *(trade name guaranteeing quality of wine)*.

appendice [apɛ̃dis] *nm (du corps, de livre)* appendix; *(d'animal)* appendage. ● **appendicite** *nf* appendicitis.

appentis [apɑ̃ti] *nm (bâtiment)* lean-to, shed.

appesantir (s') [apəzɑ̃tir] *vpr* to become heavier; **s'a. sur** *(sujet)* to dwell upon.

appétit [apeti] *nm* appetite *(de* for*)*; **mettre qn en a.** to whet s.o.'s appetite; **bon a.!** enjoy your meal! ● **appétissant, -ante** *a* appetizing.

applaudir [aplodir] *vti* to applaud, clap; **a. à** *(approuver)* to applaud. ● **applaudissements** *nmpl* applause.

applicable [aplikabl] *a* applicable. ● **application** *nf (action, soin)* application; **mettre en a.** *(loi, décision)* to put into effect.

applique [aplik] *nf* wall lamp.

appliquer [aplike] *vt* to apply *(à* to*)*; *(surnom, baiser, gifle)* to give *(à* to*)*; *(loi, décision)* to put into effect; **s'a. à** *(un travail)* to apply oneself to; **s'a. à faire** to take pains to do; **cette décision/etc s'applique à...** *(concerne)* this decision/etc applies to.... ● **appliqué, -ée** *a (travailleur)* painstaking; *(sciences)* applied.

appoint [apwɛ̃] *nm* contribution; **faire l'a.** to give the correct money *ou* change.

appointements [apwɛ̃tmɑ̃] *nmpl* salary.

appontement [apɔ̃tmɑ̃] *nm* landing stage.

apport [apɔr] *nm* contribution.

apporter [apɔrte] *vt* to bring.

apposer [apoze] *vt (sceau, signature)* to affix. ● **apposition** *nf Grammaire* apposition.

apprécier [apresje] *vt (aimer, percevoir)* to appreciate; *(évaluer)* to assess, estimate *(distance etc)*. ● **appréciable** *a* appreciable. ● **appréciation** *nf (opinion de professeur)* comment *(sur* on*)*; *(de distance etc)* assessment.

appréhender [apreɑ̃de] *vt (craindre)* to dread *(de faire* doing*)*; *(arrêter)* to arrest, apprehend. ● **appréhension** *nf (crainte)* anxiety, apprehension *(de* about*)*.

apprendre* [aprɑ̃dr] *vti (étudier)* to learn; *(événement, fait)* to hear of, learn of; *(nouvelle)* to hear; **a. à faire** to learn to do; **a. qch à qn** *(enseigner)* to teach s.o. sth; *(informer)* to tell s.o. sth; **a. à qn à faire** to teach s.o. to do; **a. que** to learn that; *(être informé)* to hear that.

apprenti, -ie [aprɑ̃ti] *nmf* apprentice; *(débutant)* novice. ● **apprentissage** *nm* apprenticeship; *(d'une langue)* learning *(de* of*)*; **faire**

l'a. de *Fig* to learn the experience of *(suffering, love etc)*.

apprêter (s') [aprete] *vpr* to get ready, prepare *(à faire* to do*)*.

apprivoiser [aprivwaze] *vt* to tame ▮ **s'apprivoiser** *vpr* to become tame. ● **apprivoisé, -ée** *a* tame.

approbation [aprɔbasjɔ̃] *nf* approval. ● **approbateur, -trice** *a* approving.

approchable [aprɔʃabl] *a (personne)* approachable.

approche [aprɔʃ] *nf* approach.

approcher [aprɔʃe] *vt (chaise etc)* to bring up, draw up *(de* to, close to*)*; *(personne)* to come *ou* get close to, approach. ▮ *vi* to draw near(er), get close(r) *(de* to*)*, approach. ▮ **s'approcher** *vpr* to come *ou* get near(er) *(de* to*)*; **il s'est approché de moi** he came up to me. ● **approchant, -ante** *a* similar. ● **approché, -ée** *a* approximate.

approfondir [aprɔfɔ̃dir] *vt (trou, puits etc)* to dig deeper; *(question, idée)* to go into thoroughly; *(mystère)* to plumb the depths of. ● **approfondi, -ie** *a (étude, examen etc)* thorough. ● **approfondissement** *nm* deepening; *(examen)* thorough examination.

approprié, -ée [aprɔprije] *a* appropriate.

approprier (s') [aprɔprije] *vpr* **s'a. qch** to take sth, help oneself to sth.

approuver [apruve] *vt (autoriser)* to approve; *(apprécier)* to approve of.

approvisionner [aprɔvizjɔne] *vt (ville etc)* to supply *(with* provisions*)*; *(magasin)* to stock ▮ **s'approvisionner** *vpr* to get one's supplies *(de, en* of*)*. ● **approvisionnements** *nmpl* stocks, supplies.

approximatif, -ive [aprɔksimatif, -iv] *a* approximate. ● **approximativement** *adv* approximately. ● **approximation** *nf* approximation.

appui [apɥi] *nm* support; *(pour coude etc)* rest; *(de fenêtre)* sill; **à hauteur d'a.** breast-high.

appuyer [apɥije] *vt (soutenir)* to support *(candidate etc)*; **a. qch sur/contre** *(poser)* to rest *ou* lean sth on/against; *(presser)* to press sth on/against; **s'a. sur** to lean on, rest on; *(compter)* to rely on; *(se baser)* to base oneself on.

▮ *vi* **a. sur** *(bouton, levier etc)* to press; *(mot, argument)* to stress; *(être posé sur)* to rest on.

âpre [ɑpr] *a* harsh, rough; **a. au gain** grasping.

après [aprɛ] **1** *prép (temps)* after; *(espace)* beyond; **a. un an** after a year; **a. le pont** beyond the bridge; **a. coup** afterwards, after the event; **a. tout** after all; **a. quoi** after which; **a. avoir mangé** after eating; **a. qu'il t'a vu** after he saw you; **jour a. jour** day after day ▮ *adv* after(wards); **l'année d'a.** the following year; **et a.?** and then what?; *(et alors)* so what? **2** *prép* **d'a.** *(selon)* according to.

après-demain [aprɛdmɛ̃] *adv* the day after tomorrow. ● **après-guerre** *nm* post-war period; **d'a.-guerre** post-war. ● **après-midi** *nm ou f inv* afternoon. ● **après-rasage** *nm* aftershave (lotion). ● **après-shampooing** *nm* (hair) conditioner. ● **après-ski** *nm* ankle boot, snow boot.

a priori [aprijɔri] *adv* at the very outset, without going into the matter ❚ *nm inv* Phil premiss; (*préjugé*) prejudice.

à-propos [aprɔpo] *nm* timeliness, aptness.

apte [apt] *a* suited (à to), capable (à of). ● **aptitude** *nf* aptitude, capacity (à, pour for); **avoir des aptitudes pour qch** to have an aptitude for sth.

aquarelle [akwarɛl] *nf* watercolour.

aquarium [akwarjɔm] *nm* aquarium.

aquatique [akwatik] *a* aquatic.

aqueduc [akdyk] *nm* aqueduct.

aquilin [akilɛ̃] *am* **nez a.** aquiline nose.

arabe [arab] *a* (*peuple etc*) Arab; (*langue etc*) Arabic; **chiffres arabes** Arabic numerals; **désert a.** Arabian desert ❚ *nmf* A. Arab ❚ *nm* (*langue*) Arabic. ● **Arabie** *nf* Arabia; **A. Séoudite** Saudi Arabia.

arabesque [arabɛsk] *nf* arabesque. –

arable [arabl] *a* arable.

arachide [araʃid] *nf* peanut, groundnut.

araignée [areɲe] *nf* spider.

arbalète [arbalɛt] *nf* crossbow.

arbitraire [arbitrɛr] *a* arbitrary.

arbitre [arbitr] *nm* Football Boxe referee; Tennis umpire; (*d'un litige*) arbitrator; (*maître absolu*) arbiter; **libre a.** free will. ● **arbitrer** *vt* to referee; to umpire; to arbitrate. ● **arbitrage** *nm* refereeing; umpiring; arbitration.

arborer [arbɔre] *vt* (*insigne, vêtement*) to sport, display.

arbre [arbr] *nm* tree; (*de transmission*) shaft, axle. ● **arbrisseau, -x** *nm* shrub. ● **arbuste** *nm* (small) shrub, bush.

arc [ark] *nm* (*arme*) bow; (*voûte*) arch; (*de cercle*) arc; **tir à l'a.** archery. ● **arcade** *nf* arch(way); **arcades** arcade, arches; **l'a. sourcilière** the arch of the eyebrows.

arc-boutant [arkbutɑ̃] *nm* (*pl* arcs-boutants) flying buttress. ● **s'arc-bouter** *vpr* **s'a.** à **ou** **contre** to support *ou* brace oneself against.

arceau, -x [arso] *nm* (*de voûte*) arch.

arc-en-ciel [arkɑ̃sjɛl] *nm* (*pl* arcs-en-ciel) rainbow.

archaïque [arkaik] *a* archaic.

archange [arkɑ̃ʒ] *nm* archangel.

arche [arʃ] *nf* (*voûte*) arch; **l'a. de Noé** Noah's ark.

archéologie [arkeɔlɔʒi] *nf* arch(a)eology. ● **archéologique** *a* arch(a)eological. ● **archéologue** *nmf* arch(a)eologist.

archer [arʃe] *nm* archer, bowman.

archet [arʃɛ] *nm* (*de violon etc*) bow.

archétype [arketip] *nm* archetype.

archevêque [arʃəvɛk] *nm* archbishop.

archicomble [arʃikɔbl] *a* jam-packed.

archipel [arʃipɛl] *nm* archipelago.

archiplein, -pleine [arʃiplɛ̃, -plɛn] *a* chock-full, Br chock-a-block.

architecte [arʃitɛkt] *nm* architect. ● **architecture** *nf* architecture.

archives [arʃiv] *nfpl* archives, records. ● **archiviste** *nmf* archivist.

arctique [arktik] *a* arctic ❚ *nm* **l'A.** the Arctic.

ardent, -ente [ardɑ̃, -ɑ̃t] *a* (*actif, passionné*) ardent, fervent; (*empressé*) eager; (*soleil*) scorching. ● **ardemment** [-amɑ̃] *adv* eagerly, fervently. ● **ardeur** *nf* (*énergie*) enthusiasm, fervour, ardour; (*chaleur*) Litt heat.

ardoise [ardwaz] *nf* slate.

ardu, -ue [ardy] *a* (*travail etc*) arduous.

are [ar] *nm* (*mesure*) = 100 square metres.

arène [arɛn] *nf* (*pour taureaux*) bullring; (*romaine, politique*) arena; **arènes** bullring; (*romaines*) amphitheatre.

arête [arɛt] *nf* (*de poisson*) bone; (*de cube, dé etc*) edge, ridge; (*de montagne*) ridge.

argent [arʒɑ̃] *nm* (*métal*) silver; (*monnaie*) money; **a. comptant** *ou* **liquide** cash. ● **argenté, -ée** *a* (*plaqué*) silver-plated; (*couleur*) silvery. ● **argenterie** *nf* silverware.

Argentine [arʒɑ̃tin] *nf* Argentina. ● **argentin, -ine** *a* Argentinian ❚ *nmf* A., **Argentine** Argentinian.

argile [arʒil] *nf* clay. ● **argileux, -euse** *a* clayey.

argot [argo] *nm* slang. ● **argotique** *a* (*terme*) slang; (*texte, discours*) full of slang, slangy.

arguer [argɥe] *vi* **a. de qch** to put forward sth as an argument. ● **argumentation** *nf* arguments, argumentation. ● **argumenter** *vi* to argue.

argument [argymɑ̃] *nm* argument.

argus [argys] *nm* guide to secondhand cars.

arguties [argysi] *nfpl* specious arguments, quibbling.

aride [arid] *a* arid, barren.

aristocrate [aristɔkrat] *nmf* aristocrat. ● **aristocratie** [-asi] *nf* aristocracy. ● **aristocratique** *a* aristocratic.

arithmétique [aritmetik] *nf* arithmetic ❚ *a* arithmetical.

arlequin [arləkɛ̃] *nm* harlequin.

armateur [armatœr] *nm* shipowner.

armature [armatyr] *nf* (*charpente*) framework; (*de lunettes, tente*) frame.

arme [arm] *nf* weapon; **armes** weapons, arms; **a. à feu** firearm; **prendre les armes** to take up arms; **à armes égales** on equal terms. ● **armes** *nfpl* (*d'une ville etc*) (coat of) arms.

armée [arme] *nf* army; **a. de l'air** air force; **a. active/de métier** regular/professional army.

armer [arme] *vt* (*personne etc*) to arm (**de** with); (*fusil*) to cock; (*appareil photo*) to wind on; (*navire*) to equip; (*béton*) to reinforce ❚ **s'armer** *vpr* to arm oneself (**de** with). ● **armement(s)** *nm(pl)* arms.

armistice [armistis] *nm* armistice.

armoire [armwar] *nf* (*penderie*) Br wardrobe, Am closet; **a. à pharmacie** medicine chest *ou* cabinet.

armoiries [armwari] *nfpl* (coat of) arms.

armure [armyr] *nf* armour.

armurier [armyrje] *nm* gunsmith.

arôme [arom] *nm* (*goût*) flavour; (*odeur*) (pleasant) smell, aroma. ● **aromate** *nm* spice. ● **aromatique** *a* aromatic.

arpenter [arpɑ̃te] *vt* (*terrain*) to survey; (*trottoir etc*) to pace up and down. ● **arpenteur** *nm* (land) surveyor.

arqué, -ée [arke] *a* (*nez, sourcil etc*) arched, curved; (*jambes*) bandy.

arrache-pied (d') [daraʃpje] *adv* relentlessly, steadfastly.

arracher [araʃe] *vt* (*clou, dent etc*) to pull out; (*cheveux, page*) to tear out, pull out; (*plante*) to pull up; (*masque*) to tear off, pull off; **a. qch à qn** to snatch sth from s.o.; (*aveu, argent, promesse*) to force sth out of s.o.; **a. un bras à qn** (*obus etc*) to blow s.o.'s arm off; **a. qn de son lit** to drag s.o. out of bed. ● **arrachage** *nm* (*de plante*) pulling up.

arraisonner [arɛzɔne] *vt* (*navire*) to board and examine.

arranger [arɑ̃ʒe] *vt* (*chambre, visite, cheveux etc*) to fix up, arrange; (*voiture, texte etc*) to put right; (*différend*) to settle, *Br* sort out; **a. qn** (*maltraiter*) *Fam* to give s.o. a going-over; **je vais à. ça** I'll fix that; **ça m'arrange** that suits me (fine).

▌ s'arranger *vpr* (*se mettre d'accord*) to come to an agreement *ou* arrangement; (*finir bien*) to turn out fine; (*se réparer*) to be put right; **s'a. pour faire** to arrange to do, manage to do. ● **arrangeant, -ante** *a* accommodating. ● **arrangement** *nm* arrangement.

arrestation [arɛstasjɔ̃] *nf* arrest.

arrêt [arɛ] *nm* (*halte, endroit*) stop; (*action*) stopping; (*de tribunal*) decree; **a. du cœur** cardiac arrest; **temps d'a.** pause; **à l'a.** stationary; **a. de travail** (*grève*) stoppage; (*congé*) sick leave; **sans a.** constantly, nonstop.

arrêté¹ [arete] *nm* order, decision.

arrêté², -ée [arete] *a* (*projet*) fixed; (*volonté*) firm.

arrêter [arete] *vt* to stop; (*appréhender*) to arrest; (*regard, date*) to fix; (*plan*) to draw up **▌** *vi* to stop; **il n'arrête pas de critiquer/** *etc* he's always criticizing/etc, he doesn't stop criticizing/etc **▌ s'arrêter** *vpr* to stop; **s'a. de faire** to stop doing.

arrhes [ar] *nfpl* (*acompte*) deposit.

arrière [arjɛr] **1** *adv* **en a.** (*marcher, tomber etc*) backwards; (*rester*) behind; (*regarder*) back, behind; **en a. de qn/qch** behind s.o./sth **▌** *nm* (*de maison etc*) back, rear; **à l'a. in** *ou* at the back **▌** *a inv* (*siège etc*) back, rear; **faire marche a.** to reverse, back. **2** *nm Football* (full) back.

arriéré, -ée [arjere] **1** *a* (*enfant*) (mentally) retarded; (*idée*) backward. **2** *nm* (*dette*) arrears.

arrière-boutique [arjerbutik] *nm* back room (*of a shop*). ● **arrière-garde** *nf* rearguard. ● **arrière-goût** *nm* aftertaste. ● **arrière-grand-mère** *nf* great-grand-mother. ● **arrière-**

grand-père *nm* (*pl* **arrière-grands-pères**) great-great-father. ● **arrière-pays** *nm* hinterland. ● **arrière-pensée** *nf* ulterior motive. ● **arrière-plan** *nm* background. ● **arrière-saison** *nf* end of season, (late) *Br* autumn *ou Am* fall. ● **arrière-train** *nm* hindquarters.

arrimer [arime] *vt* (*fixer*) to rope down.

arriver [arive] *vi* (*aux être*) (*venir*) to arrive, come; (*survenir*) to happen; (*réussir*) to succeed; **a. à** (*atteindre*) to reach; **a. à faire** to manage to do, succeed in doing; **a. à qn** to happen to s.o.; **il m'arrive d'oublier/**etc I (sometimes) forget/etc, I happen (sometimes) to forget/etc; **en a. à faire** to get to the point of doing. ● **arrivant, -ante** *nmf* new arrival. ● **arrivée** *nf* arrival; (*ligne, poteau*) (winning) post. ● **arrivage** *nm* consignment. ● **arriviste** *nmf Péj* social climber.

arrogant, -ante [arɔgɑ̃, -ɑ̃t] *a* arrogant. ● **arrogance** *nf* arrogance.

arroger (s') [sarɔʒe] *vpr* (*droit etc*) to assume (falsely).

arrondir [arɔ̃dir] *vt* (*somme, chiffre, angle, jupe*) to round off; (*rendre rond*) to make round (*pebble etc*). ● **arrondi, -ie** *a* rounded.

arrondissement [arɔ̃dismɑ̃] *nm* (*d'une ville*) district.

arroser [aroze] *vt* (*terre*) to water; (*repas*) to wash down; (*succès*) to drink to. ● **arrosage** *nm* watering; (*d'une réussite etc*) *Fam* celebration. ● **arrosoir** *nm* watering can.

arsenal, -aux [arsənal, -o] *nm* (*naval*) dockyard; (*quantité d'armes*) *Fig* arsenal.

arsenic [arsənik] *nm* arsenic.

art [ar] *nm* art; **film/critique d'a.** art film/critic; **arts ménagers** home economics, domestic science.

artère [artɛr] *nf* (*veine*) artery; (*rue*) main road. ● **artériel, -ielle** *a* arterial.

artichaut [artiʃo] *nm* artichoke; **fond d'a.** artichoke heart.

article [artikl] *nm* (*de presse, de commerce*) & *Grammaire* article; (*dans un contrat, catalogue*) item; **a. de fond** feature (article); **articles de toilette** toiletries; **articles de voyage** travel goods; **à l'a. de la mort** at death's door.

articuler [artikyle] *vt* (*mot etc*) to articulate **▌ s'articuler** *vpr* (*membre*) to articulate; (*idées etc*) to connect. ● **articulation** *nf* **1** (*de membre*) joint; **a. (du doigt)** knuckle. **2** (*prononciation*) articulation.

artifice [artifis] *nm* trick, contrivance; **feu d'a.** (*spectacle*) firework display, fireworks.

artificiel, -ielle [artifisjɛl] *a* artificial. ● **artificiellement** *adv* artificially.

artillerie [artijri] *nf* artillery. ● **artilleur** *nm* gunner.

artisan [artizɑ̃] *nm* craftsman, artisan. ● **artisanal, -e, -aux** *a* craftsman's trade; **objet a.** object made by craftsmen. ● **artisanat** *nm* (*métier*) craftsman's trade; (*classe*) artisan class.

artiste [artist] *nmf* artist; (*acteur, musicien*) performer, artist. ● **artistique** *a* artistic.

as [ɑs] *nm* (*carte, champion*) ace; **a. du volant/de la mécanique** brilliant *ou* crack driver/mechanic/*etc*.

ascendant [asɑ̃dɑ̃] *a* ascending, upward ▮ *nm* ascendancy, power; **ascendants** ancestors. ● **ascendance** *nf* ancestry.

ascenseur [asɑ̃sœr] *nm Br* lift, *Am* elevator.

ascension [asɑ̃sjɔ̃] *nf* ascent; **l'A.** Ascension Day.

ascète [asɛt] *nmf* ascetic. ● **ascétique** *a* ascetic. ● **ascétisme** *nm* asceticism.

Asie [azi] *nf* Asia. ● **Asiate** *nmf* Asian. ● **asiatique** *a* Asian ▮ *nmf* **A.** Asian.

asile [azil] *nm* (*abri*) refuge, shelter; (*pour vieillards*) home; **a. (d'aliénés)** *Péj* (lunatic) asylum; **a. politique** (political) asylum; **a. de paix** haven of peace.

aspect [aspɛ] *nm* (*air*) appearance; (*vue*) sight; (*perspective*) & *Grammaire* aspect.

asperger [aspɛrʒe] *vt* (*par jeu ou accident*) to splash (**de** with); (*pour humecter*) to spray, sprinkle (**de** with); **s'a. de parfum** to spray oneself with perfume.

asperges [aspɛrʒ] *nfpl* asparagus.

aspérité [asperite] *nf* bump, uneven bit.

asphalte [asfalt] *nm* asphalt.

asphyxie [asfiksi] *nf* suffocation. ● **asphyxier** *vt* to suffocate, asphyxiate ▮ **s'asphyxier** *vpr* to suffocate; (*volontairement*) to suffocate oneself.

aspic [aspik] *nm* (*vipère*) asp.

aspirant [aspirɑ̃] *nm* (*candidat*) candidate.

aspirateur [aspiratœr] *nm* vacuum cleaner, *Br* hoover®; **passer (à) l'a.** to vacuum, hoover.

aspirer [aspire] **1** *vt* (*liquide*) to suck up; (*respirer*) to breathe in, inhale. **2** *vi* **a.** (*bonheur, gloire etc*) to aspire to. ● **aspiré, -ée** *a* (*son, lettre*) aspirate(d). ● **aspiration** *nf* suction; inhaling; (*ambition*) aspiration.

aspirine [aspirin] *nf* aspirin.

assagir (s') [sasaʒir] *vpr* to settle down.

assaillir [asajir] *vt* to attack; **a. de** (*questions etc*) to assail with. ● **assaillant** *nm* attacker, assailant.

assainir [asenir] *vt* (*purifier*) to clean up; (*marché, économie etc*) to stabilize.

assaisonner [asɛzɔne] *vt* to season. ● **assaisonnement** *nm* seasoning.

assassin [asasɛ̃] *nm* murderer; (*d'homme politique etc*) assassin. ● **assassinat** *nm* murder; assassination. ● **assassiner** *vt* to murder; (*homme politique etc*) to assassinate.

assaut [aso] *nm* onslaught, attack, assault; **prendre d'a.** to (take by) storm.

assécher [asefe] *vt* to drain.

assemblée [asɑ̃ble] *nf* (*personnes réunies*) gathering; (*réunion*) meeting; (*parlement*) assembly; (*de fidèles*) congregation.

assembler [asɑ̃ble] *vt* to put together, assemble ▮ **s'assembler** *vpr* to gather, assemble. ● **assemblage** *nm* (*montage*) assembly; (*réunion d'objets*) collection.

asséner [asene] *vt* (*coup*) to deal, strike.

assentiment [asɑ̃timɑ̃] *nm* assent, consent.

asseoir* [aswar] *vt* (*personne*) to sit (down), seat (**sur** on); (*fondations*) to lay; (*autorité, réputation*) to establish; **a. une théorie/etc sur** to base a theory/etc on ▮ **s'asseoir** *vpr* to sit (down).

assermenté, -ée [asɛrmɑ̃te] *a* (*témoin etc*) sworn.

assertion [asɛrsjɔ̃] *nf* assertion.

asservir [asɛrvir] *vt* to enslave. ● **asservissement** *nm* enslavement.

assez [ase] *adv* enough; **a. de pain/de gens/ etc** enough bread/people/etc; **j'en ai a.** I've had enough (**de** of); **a. grand/intelligent/etc** (*suffisamment*) big/clever/etc enough (*pour faire* to do); **a. fatigué/etc** (*plutôt*) fairly *ou* rather *ou* quite tired/etc.

assidu, -ue [asidy] *a* (*toujours présent*) regular; (*appliqué*) diligent, assiduous; **a. auprès de qn** attentive to s.o. ● **assiduité** *nf* (*d'élève etc*) regularity; (*empressement*) attentiveness. ● **assidûment** *adv* diligently, assiduously.

assiéger [asjeʒe] *vt* (*ville*) to besiege; (*magasin, vedette, guichet*) to mob, crowd round; (*importuner*) to pester, harry; **assiégé de** (*demandes*) besieged with; (*maux*) beset by. ● **assiégeant, -ante** *nmf* besieger.

assiette [asjɛt] *nf* **1** (*récipient*) plate; **a. anglaise** *Culin Br* (assorted) cold meats, *Am* cold cuts. **2** (*à cheval*) seat; **il n'est pas dans son a.** he's feeling out of sorts. ● **assiettée** *nf* plateful.

assigner [asiɲe] *vt* (*attribuer*) to assign (*task etc*) (**à** to); (*en justice*) to summon, subpoena. ● **assignation** *nf* *Jur* subpoena, summons.

assimiler [asimile] *vt* (*comprendre, absorber*) to assimilate ▮ **s'assimiler** *vpr* (*immigrants*) to assimilate, become assimilated (**à** with). ● **assimilation** *nf* assimilation.

assis, -ise[1] [asi, -iz] (*pp de asseoir*) *a* sitting (down), seated; (*situation*) stable, secure; **rester a.** to remain seated; **place assise** seat (*on bus etc*).

assise[2] [asiz] *nf* (*base*) foundation; **assises** (*cour*) assizes; (*d'un parti etc*) congress; **cour d'assises** court of assizes.

assistance [asistɑ̃s] *nf* **1** (*assemblée*) audience; (*nombre de personnes présentes*) attendance, turnout. **2** (*aide*) assistance; **l'A. (publique)** the Welfare Service; **enfant de l'A.** child in care.

assister [asiste] **1** *vt* (*aider*) to help, assist. **2** *vi* **a.** (*réunion, cours etc*) to attend, be present at; (*accident*) to witness. ● **assistant, -ante** *nmf* assistant; **les assistants** (*spectateurs*) the members of the audience; (*témoins*) the onlookers; **assistant(e) social(e)** social worker; **assistante maternelle** *Br* child minder, *Am* baby-sitter.

association [asɔsjasjɔ̃] *nf* association; (*amitié, alliance*) partnership, association.

associer [asɔsje] *vt* to associate (**à** with); **a. qn à** (*ses travaux, une affaire*) to involve s.o.

in; (*profits*) to give s.o. a share in ▮ **s'associer** *vpr* to join forces, form an association; **s'a. à** (*collaborer*) to associate with, join forces with; (*aux vues ou au chagrin de qn*) to share; (*s'harmoniser*) to combine with. ●**associé, -ée** *nmf* partner, associate ▮ *a* associate.

assoiffé, -ée [aswafe] *a* thirsty (de for).

assombrir [asɔ̃brir] *vt* (*obscurcir*) to darken; (*attrister*) to cast a cloud over, fill with gloom ▮ **s'assombrir** *vpr* (*ciel, visage, avenir*) to cloud over.

assommer [asɔme] *vt* (*personne*) to knock unconscious; (*animal*) to stun, brain; (*ennuyer*) to▪bore stiff. ●**assommant, -ante** *a* tiresome, boring.

assomption [asɔ̃psjɔ̃] *nf* Rel Assumption.

assortir [asɔrtir] *vt*, **s'assortir** *vpr* to match. ●**assorti, -ie** *a* 1 **bien a.** (*magasin*) well-stocked. 2 (*objet semblable*) matching; **fromages/etc assortis** assorted cheeses/etc; **époux bien assortis** well-matched couple. ●**assortiment** *nm* assortment.

assoupir [asupir] *vt* (*personne*) to make drowsy; (*douleur, sentiment etc*) Fig to dull ▮ **s'assoupir** *vpr* to doze off; (*douleur*) Fig to subside. ●**assoupi, -ie** *a* (*personne*) drowsy. ●**assoupissement** *nm* drowsiness.

assouplir [asuplir] *vt* (*étoffe, muscles*) to make supple; (*corps*) to limber up; (*caractère*) to soften; (*règles*) to ease, relax. ●**assouplissement** *nm* **exercices d'a.** limbering-up exercises.

assourdir [asurdir] *vt* (*personne*) to deafen; (*son*) to muffle. ●**assourdissant, -ante** *a* deafening.

assouvir [asuvir] *vt* to appease, satisfy.

assujettir [asyʒetir] *vt* (*soumettre*) to subject (à to); (*peuple*) to subjugate; (*fixer*) to secure; **s'a.** à to subject oneself to, submit to. ●**assujettissant, -ante** *a* (*travail*) exacting. ●**assujettissement** *nm* subjection; (*contrainte*) constraint.

assumer [asyme] *vt* (*tâche, rôle*) to assume, take on; (*emploi*) to take up, assume.

assurance [asyrɑ̃s] *nf* (*aplomb*) (self-) assurance; (*promesse*) assurance; (*contrat*) insurance; **a. au tiers/tous risques** third-party/comprehensive insurance; **assurances sociales** Br = national insurance, Am = social security.

assurer [asyre] *vt* (*par un contrat*) to insure; (*travail etc*) to carry out; (*rendre sûr*) Br to ensure, Am insure (*success etc*); (*fixer*) to secure; **a. à qn que** to assure s.o. that; **a. qn de qch, a. qch à qn** to assure s.o. of sth. ▮ **s'assurer** *vpr* (*par un contrat*) to insure oneself, get insured (**contre** against); **s'a. l'aide/etc de qn** (*se procurer*) to secure s.o.'s help/etc; **s'a. que/de** to make sure that/of. ●**assuré, -ée** *a* (*succès*) assured, certain; (*pas*) firm, secure; (*air*) (self-)assured, (self-) confident ▮ *nmf* policyholder, insured person. ●**assurément** *adv* certainly, assuredly. ●**assureur** *nm* insurer.

astérisque [asterisk] *nm* asterisk.

asthme [asm] *nm* asthma. ●**asthmatique** *a* & *nmf* asthmatic.

asticot [astiko] *nm* Br maggot, Am worm.

asticoter [astikɔte] *vt* (*agacer*) Fam to bug.

astiquer [astike] *vt* to polish.

astre [astr] *nm* star.

astreindre* [astrɛ̃dr] *vt* **a. qn à** (*discipline*) to compel s.o. to accept; **a. qn à faire** to compel s.o. to do. ●**astreignant, -ante** *a* exacting. ●**astreinte** *nf* constraint.

astrologie [astrɔlɔʒi] *nf* astrology. ●**astrologique** *a* astrological. ●**astrologue** *nm* astrologer.

astronaute [astronot] *nmf* astronaut. ●**astronautique** *nf* space travel.

astronomie [astrɔnɔmi] *nf* astronomy. ●**astronome** *nm* astronomer. ●**astronomique** *a* astronomical.

astuce [astys] *nf* (*pour faire qch*) knack, trick; (*invention*) gadget; (*plaisanterie*) clever joke, wisecrack; (*jeu de mots*) pun; (*finesse*) astuteness; **les astuces du métier** the tricks of the trade. ●**astucieux, -euse** *a* clever, astute.

atelier [atəlje] *nm* (*d'ouvrier etc*) workshop; (*de peintre*) studio.

atermoyer [atermwaje] *vi* to procrastinate.

athée [ate] *a* atheistic ▮ *nmf* atheist. ●**athéisme** *nm* atheism.

athénée [atene] *nm* (*lycée belge*) Br secondary school, Am high school.

Athènes [atɛn] *nm ou f* Athens.

athlète [atlet] *nmf* athlete. ●**athlétique** *a* athletic. ●**athlétisme** *nm* athletics.

atlantique [atlɑ̃tik] *a* Atlantic ▮ *nm* **l'A.** the Atlantic.

atlas [atlɑs] *nm* atlas.

atmosphère [atmɔsfer] *nf* atmosphere. ●**atmosphérique** *a* atmospheric.

atome [atom] *nm* atom. ●**atomique** [atɔmik] *a* (*énergie etc*) atomic; **bombe a.** atom *ou* atomic bomb.

atomiser [atɔmize] *vt* (*liquide*) to spray; (*région*) to destroy (*by atomic weapons*). ●**atomiseur** *nm* spray.

atone [atɔn] *a* (*personne*) (*sans énergie*) lifeless; (*regard*) vacant.

atours [atur] *nmpl* Hum finery.

atout [atu] *nm* trump (card); (*avantage*) Fig asset, trump card; **l'a. est cœur** hearts are trumps.

âtre [ɑtr] *nm* (*foyer*) hearth.

atroce [atrɔs] *a* atrocious; (*crime*) heinous, atrocious. ●**atrocité** *nf* (*cruauté*) atrociousness; **atrocités** (*horreurs*) atrocities.

atrophie [atrɔfi] *nf* atrophy. ●**atrophié, -ée** *a* (*jambe etc*) atrophied.

attabler (s') [satable] *vpr* to sit down at the table. ●**attablé, -ée** *a* (*seated*) at the table.

attache [ataʃ] *nf* (*objet*) attachment, fastening; **attaches** (*liens*) links.

attaché-case [ataʃekez] *nm* attaché case.

attachement [ataʃmɑ̃] *nm* (*affection*) attachment (à to).

attacher [ataʃe] vt (lier) to tie (up), attach (à to); (boucler, fixer) to fasten; **a. de l'importance/de la valeur à qch** to attach great importance/value to sth; **cette obligation m'attache à lui** this obligation binds me to him; **s'a. à** (se lier) to become attached to (s.o.); (se consacrer) to apply oneself to (task, project etc); (adhérer) to stick to.

▮ vi (en cuisant) to stick. ● **attachant, -ante** a (enfant etc) likeable; (roman) appealing. ● **attaché, -ée 1** nmf (de presse, diplomatique etc) attaché. **2** a **être a. à** (ami etc) to be attached to; **nous sommes attachés** we're very attached (to each other).

attaque [atak] nf attack; **a. aérienne** air raid; **d'a.** in tip-top shape, on top form.

attaquer [atake] vt, **s'a. à** to attack; (difficulté, sujet) to tackle ▮ vi to attack. ● **attaquant, -ante** nmf attacker.

attarder (s') [satarde] vpr (en chemin) to dawdle, loiter; (chez qn) to linger (on), stay on; **s'a. sur** ou **à** (détails etc) to linger over; **s'a. derrière qn** to lag behind s.o. ● **attardé, -ée** a (enfant etc) backward; (passant) late.

atteindre* [atɛ̃dr] vt (parvenir à) to reach; (cible) to hit; (idéal) to achieve, attain; (blesser) to hit, wound; (toucher) to affect; (offenser) to hurt, wound; **être atteint de** (maladie) to be suffering from.

atteinte [atɛ̃t] nf attack; **porter a. à** to attack, undermine; **a. à** (honneur) slur on; **hors d'a.** (objet, personne) out of reach; (réputation) unassailable.

atteler [atle] vt (bêtes) to harness, hitch up; (remorque) to hook up; **s'a. à** (travail etc) to apply oneself to. ● **attelage** nm (crochet) hook (for towing); (bêtes) team.

attenant, -ante [atnɑ̃, -ɑ̃t] a a. (à) adjoining.

attendre [atɑ̃dr] vt (personne, train etc) to wait for, Litt await; (escompter) to expect (de of, from); **elle attend un bébé** she's expecting a baby; **le bonheur/etc qui vous attend** the happiness/etc that awaits you; **a. que qn vienne** to wait for s.o. to come, wait until s.o. comes; **a. d'être informé** to wait to be informed.

▮ vi to wait; **faire a. qn** to keep s.o. waiting; **se faire a.** (réponse, personne etc) to be a long time coming; **attends voir!** Fam let me see!; **en attendant** meanwhile; **en attendant que** (+ sub) until.

▮ **s'attendre** vpr **s'a. à qch/à faire qch** to expect sth/to do sth, **s'a. à ce que qn fasse qch** to expect s.o. to do sth. ● **attendu, -ue 1** a (avec joie) eagerly-awaited; (prévu) expected. **2** prép considering; **a. que** considering that.

attendrir [atɑ̃drir] vt **1** (émouvoir) to move (to compassion). **2** (viande) to tenderize ▮ **s'attendrir** vpr to be moved (sur by). ● **attendri, -ie** a compassionate. ● **attendrissant, -ante** a moving. ● **attendrissement** nm compassion.

attentat [atɑ̃ta] nm attempt on s.o.'s life, murder attempt; (contre un principe etc) crime, outrage (à against); **a.** (à la bombe) (bomb) attack. ● **attenter** vi **a. à** (la vie de qn) to make an attempt on; Fig to attack, undermine.

attente [atɑ̃t] nf (temps) wait(ing); (espérance) expectation(s); **une a. prolongée** a long wait; **contre toute a.** against all expectations; **être dans l'a. de** to be waiting for; **salle d'a.** waiting room.

attentif, -ive [atɑ̃tif, -iv] a (personne) attentive; (travail, examen) careful; **a. à** (ses devoirs etc) mindful of; (l'orthographe, la ponctuation) careful about; **a. à plaire/etc** anxious to please/etc. ● **attentivement** adv attentively.

attention [atɑ̃sjɔ̃] nf attention; **attentions** (égards) consideration; **faire** ou **prêter a. à** (écouter, remarquer) to pay attention to; **faire a. à** (prendre garde) to be careful of; **faire a. (à ce) que** (+ sub) to be careful that; **a.!** watch out!, look out!, be careful!; **a. à la voiture!** watch out for the car!, Br mind the car! ● **attentionné, -ée** a considerate.

atténuer [atenɥe] vt to mitigate, attenuate; **circonstances atténuantes** extenuating circumstances ▮ **s'atténuer** vpr (douleur, tempête etc) to subside.

atterrer [atere] vt to dismay.

atterrir [aterir] vi (avion) to land. ● **atterrissage** nm landing; **a. forcé** crash ou emergency landing.

attester [ateste] vt to testify to; **a. que** to testify that. ● **attestation** nf (document) declaration, certificate.

attifer [atife] vt Fam Péj to dress up, rig out.

attirail [atiraj] nm (équipement) Fam gear.

attirance [atirɑ̃s] nf attraction (pour for).

attirer [atire] vt (faire venir) to attract, draw; (plaire à) to attract; (attention) to attract, catch; **a. l'attention de qn sur** to draw s.o.'s attention to; **a. qch à qn** (ennuis etc) to bring s.o. sth; (gloire etc) to win ou earn s.o. sth; **a. sur soi** (colère de qn) to bring down upon oneself; **a. qn dans** (coin, piège) to lure s.o. into.

▮ **s'attirer** vpr (ennuis etc) to bring upon oneself; (sympathie de qn) to win. ● **attirant, -ante** a attractive.

attiser [atize] vt (feu) to poke; (sentiment) Fig to rouse.

attitré, -ée [atitre] a (représentant) appointed; (marchand) regular.

attitude [atityd] nf attitude; (maintien) bearing.

attraction [atraksjɔ̃] nf (force, centre d'intérêt) attraction; **attractions** (manèges etc) attractions, rides.

attrait [atrɛ] nm attraction.

attrape [atrap] nf (objet) trick. ● **attrape-nigaud** nm (ruse) trick.

attraper [atrape] vt (ballon, maladie, voleur, train etc) to catch; (accent, contravention etc) to pick up; **se laisser a.** (duper) to get taken in ou tricked; **se faire a.** (gronder) Fam to get a telling-off. ● **attrapade** nf (gronderie)

Fam telling-off.

attrayant, -ante [atrɛjɑ̃, -ɑ̃t] *a* attractive.

attribuer [atribɥe] *vt* (*donner*) to assign (*role, funds etc*) (**à** to); (*décerner*) to award (*prize etc*) (**à** to); (*imputer, reconnaître*) to attribute, ascribe (*responsibility etc*) (**à** to). ● **attribuable** *a* attributable. ● **attribution** *nf* assignment; (*de prix*) awarding; **attributions** (*compétence*) powers.

attribut [atriby] *nm* (*adjectif*) predicate adjective; (*caractéristique*) attribute.

attrister [atriste] *vt* to sadden.

attrouper [atrupe] *vt*, **s'attrouper** *vpr* to gather. ● **attroupement** *nm* (disorderly) crowd.

au [o] *voir* **à**.

aubaine [obɛn] *nf* (**bonne**) **a.** stroke of good luck, godsend.

aube [ob] *nf* dawn; **dès l'a.** at the crack of dawn.

aubépine [obepin] *nf* hawthorn.

auberge [obɛrʒ] *nf* inn; **a. de jeunesse** youth hostel. ● **aubergiste** *nmf* innkeeper.

aubergine [obɛrʒin] *nf* *Br* aubergine, *Am* eggplant.

aucun, -une [okœ̃, -yn] *a* no, not any; **il n'a a. talent** he has no talent, he doesn't have any talent; **a. professeur n'est venu** no teacher has come ∎ *pron* none, not any; **il n'en a a.** he has none (at all), he doesn't have any (at all); **a. d'entre nous** none of us; **a. des deux** neither of the two; **plus qu'a.** more than any(one); **d'aucuns** some (people). ● **aucunement** *adv* not at all.

audace [odas] *nf* (*courage*) daring, boldness; (*impudence*) audacity; **audaces** (*de style etc*) daring innovations. ● **audacieux, -euse** *a* daring, bold.

au-dedans, au-dehors, au-delà [odədɑ̃, odəɔr, odəla] *voir* **dedans** *etc*.

au-dessous [odəsu] *adv* (*à l'étage inférieur*) downstairs; (*moins*) below, under ∎ *prép* **au-d. de** (*arbre etc*) below, under, beneath; (*âge, prix*) under; (*température*) below; **au-d. de sa tâche** not up to *ou* unequal to one's task.

au-dessus [odəsy] *adv* (*à l'étage supérieur*) upstairs; (*d'une pile*) on top; (*prix, température*) above, over ∎ *prép* **au-d. de** above; (*âge, température, prix*) over; (*posé sur*) on top of.

au-devant de [odəvɑ̃də] *prép* **aller au-d. de** (*personne*) to go to meet; (*danger*) to court; (*désirs de qn*) to anticipate.

audible [odibl] *a* audible.

audience [odjɑ̃s] *nf* (*entretien*) audience; (*de tribunal*) hearing.

audio [odjo] *a inv* (*cassette etc*) audio. ● **audiophone** *nm* hearing aid. ● **audio-visuel, -elle** *a* audio-visual.

auditeur, -trice [oditœr, -tris] *nmf* (*de la radio*) listener; **les auditeurs** the audience; **a. libre** (*à l'université*) auditor (*student allowed to attend classes but not to sit examinations*).

audition [odisjɔ̃] *nf* (*ouïe*) hearing; (*séance musicale*) recital; (*d'acteurs*) audition; (*de témoins*) examination. ● **auditionner** *vti* to audition. ● **auditoire** *nm* audience. ● **auditorium** *nm* concert hall; (*studio*) recording studio (*for recitals*).

auge [oʒ] *nf* (feeding) trough.

augmenter [ɔgmɑ̃te] *vt* to increase (**de** by); (*salaire, prix, impôt*) to raise, increase, put up; **a. qn** to give s.o. a *Br* rise *ou Am* raise ∎ *vi* to increase (**de** by); (*prix, population*) to rise, go up, increase. ● **augmentation** *nf* increase (**de** in, of); **a. de salaire** *Br* (pay) rise, *Am* raise; **a. de prix** price rise *ou* increase.

augure [ɔgyr] *nm* (*présage*) omen; (*devin*) oracle; **être de bon/mauvais a.** to be a good/ bad omen. ● **augurer** *vt* to augur, predict.

aujourd'hui [oʒurdɥi] *adv* today; (*actuellement*) nowadays, today; **a. en quinze** two weeks from today; **jusqu'à a.** to this very day; **les problèmes/etc d'a.** today's problems/etc, the problems/etc of today.

aumône [omon] *nf* alms; **faire l'a. à** to give alms to.

aumônier [omonje] *nm* chaplain.

auparavant [oparavɑ̃] *adv* (*avant*) before(hand); (*d'abord*) first.

auprès de [opredə] *prép* (*assis, situé etc*) by, close to, next to; (*en comparaison de*) compared to; **agir a. du ministre/etc** to use one's influence with the minister/etc; **accès a. de qn** access to s.o.

auquel [okɛl] *voir* **lequel**.

aura, aurait *etc* [ora, orɛ] *voir* **avoir**.

auréole [oreɔl] *nf* (*de saint etc*) halo; (*laissée par une tache*) ring.

auriculaire [orikylɛr] *nm* **l'a.** the little finger.

aurore [oror] *nf* dawn, daybreak.

ausculter [ɔskylte] *vt* (*malade*) to examine (*with a stethoscope*); (*cœur*) to listen to.

auspices [ɔspis] *nmpl* **sous les a. de** under the auspices of.

aussi [osi] *adv* **1** (*comparaison*) as; **a. lourd/ etc que** as heavy/etc as. **2** (*également*) too, also, as well; **moi a.** so do, can, am *etc* I; **a. bien que** as well as. **3** (*tellement*) so; **un repas a. délicieux** such a delicious meal, so delicious a meal. **4** *conj* (*donc*) therefore.

aussitôt [osito] *adv* immediately, at once; **a. que** as soon as; **a. levé, il partit** as soon as he was up, he left; **a. dit, a. fait** no sooner said than done.

austère [ɔstɛr] *a* austere. ● **austérité** *nf* austerity.

austral, -e, *mpl* **-als** [ɔstral] *a* southern.

Australie [ɔstrali] *nf* Australia. ● **australien, -ienne** *a* Australian ∎ *nmf* **A., Australienne** Australian.

autant [otɑ̃] *adv* **1 a. de...que** (*quantité*) as much...as; (*nombre*) as many...as; **il a a. d'argent/de pommes que vous** he has as much money/as many apples as you.

2 a. de (*tant de*) so much; (*nombre*) so many; **je n'ai jamais vu a. d'argent/de pommes** I've never seen so much money/so many apples; **pourquoi manges-tu a.?** why

are you eating so much?
3 a. que (*lire, souffrir etc*) as much as; **il lit a. que vous/que possible** he reads as much as you/as possible; **il n'a jamais souffert a.** he's never suffered as *ou* so much; **a. que je sache** as far as I know; **d'a. (plus) que** all the more (so) since; **d'a. moins que** even less since; **a. avouer/etc** we, you *etc* might as well confess/etc; **en faire/dire a.** to do/say the same; **j'aimerais a. aller au musée** I'd just as soon go to the museum.

autel [otɛl] *nm* altar.

auteur [otœr] *nm* (*de livre*) author, writer; (*de chanson*) composer; (*de procédé*) originator; (*de crime*) perpetrator; (*d'accident*) cause; **droit d'a.** copyright; **droits d'a.** royalties.

authenticité [otãtisite] *nf* authenticity. ● **authentifier** *vt* to authenticate. ● **authentique** *a* genuine, authentic.

autiste [otist] *ou* **autistique** *a* autistic.

auto [oto] *nf* car; **autos tamponneuses** bumper cars, dodgems.

auto- [oto] *préf* self-.

autobiographie [otobjɔgrafi] *nf* autobiography. ● **autobiographique** *a* autobiographical.

autobus [otobys] *nm* bus.

autocar [otokar] *nm* bus, *Br* coach.

autochtone [otɔktɔn] *a* & *nmf* native.

autocollant, -ante [otokɔlɑ̃, -ɑ̃t] *a* (*enveloppe, timbre etc*) self-seal ▮ *nm* sticker.

autocrate [otokrat] *nm* autocrat. ● **autocratique** *a* autocratic.

autocuiseur [otokɥizœr] *nm* pressure cooker.

autodéfense [otodefɑ̃s] *nf* self-defence.

autodestruction [otodɛstryksjɔ̃] *nf* self-destruction.

autodidacte [otodidakt] *a* & *nmf* self-taught (person).

autodrome [otodrom] *nm* racetrack, *Br* motor-racing track.

auto-école [otoekɔl] *nf* driving school, *Br* school of motoring.

autographe [otograf] *nm* autograph.

automate [otomat] *nm* automaton. ● **automation** *nf* automation. ● **automatisation** *nf* automation. ● **automatiser** *vt* to automate.

automatique [otomatik] *a* automatic. ● **automatiquement** *adv* automatically.

automitrailleuse [otomitrajøz] *nf Br* armoured *ou Am* armored car.

automne [otɔn] *nm* autumn, *Am* fall. ● **automnal, -e, -aux** *a* autumnal.

automobile [otomɔbil] *nf* car, *Br* motorcar, *Am* automobile; **l'a., le sport a.** motoring; **Salon de l'A.** *Br* Motor Show, *Am* Auto Show; **canot a.** motor boat. ● **automobiliste** *nmf* motorist.

autonome [otonɔm] *a* (*région etc*) autonomous, self-governing; (*personne*) *Fig* independent; (*ordinateur*) standalone. ● **autonomie** *nf* autonomy.

autopsie [otɔpsi] *nf* autopsy, post-mortem.

autoradio [otoradjo] *nm* car radio.

autorail [otoraj] *nm* railcar.

autoriser [otɔrize] *vt* (*permettre*) to permit (**à faire** to do); (*donner une autorité à*) to authorize (**à faire** to do). ● **autorisé, -ée** *a* (*qualifié*) authoritative. ● **autorisation** *nf* permission, authorization.

autorité [otɔrite] *nf* authority; **faire a.** (*livre etc*) to be authoritative. ● **autoritaire** *a* authoritarian.

autoroute [otorut] *nf Br* motorway, *Am* highway, *Am* freeway.

auto-stop [otostɔp] *nm* hitchhiking; **faire de l'a.** to hitchhike. ● **auto-stoppeur, -euse** *nmf* hitchhiker.

autour [otur] *adv* around, round; **tout a.** all around *ou* round ▮ *prép* **a. de** around, round; (*environ*) around, round about.

autre [otr] *a* & *pron* other; **un a. livre** another book; **un a.** another (one); **d'autres** others; **d'autres médecins/livres/etc** other doctors/books/etc; **as-tu d'autres questions?** have you any other *ou* further questions?; **qn/personne/rien d'a.** s.o./no one/nothing else; **a. chose/part** something/somewhere else; **qui/quoi d'a.?** who/what else?; **l'un l'a., les uns les autres** each other; **l'un et l'a.** both (of them); **l'un ou l'a.** either (of them); **ni l'un ni l'a.** neither (of them); **les autres** the others; **les uns...les autres** some...others; **nous/vous autres Anglais** we/you English; **d'un moment à l'a.** any moment (now); **...et d'autres** ...and so on.

autrefois [otrəfwa] *adv* in the past, long ago, in times gone by.

autrement [otrəmɑ̃] *adv* (*différemment*) differently; (*sinon*) otherwise; (*plus*) far more (**que** than); **pas a. satisfait/etc** not particularly satisfied/etc.

Autriche [otriʃ] *nf* Austria. ● **autrichien, -ienne** *a* Austrian ▮ *nmf* **A., Autrichienne** Austrian.

autruche [otryʃ] *nf* ostrich.

autrui [otrɥi] *pron* others, other people.

auvent [ovɑ̃] *nm* (*de tente, magasin*) awning, canopy.

aux [o] *voir* **à**.

auxiliaire [ɔksiljɛr] *a* (*verbe, machine, troupes etc*) auxiliary ▮ *nm* (*verbe*) auxiliary ▮ *nmf* (*aide*) helper, auxiliary.

auxquels, -elles [okɛl] *voir* **lequel**.

av. *abrév* **avenue**.

avachir (s') [savaʃir] *vpr* (*soulier, personne*) to become flabby *ou* limp.

avait [avɛ] *voir* **avoir**.

aval (en) [ɑ̃naval] *adv* downstream (**de** from).

avalanche [avalɑ̃ʃ] *nf* avalanche; (*de lettres etc*) flood, avalanche.

avaler [avale] *vt* to swallow; (*livre*) *Fig* to devour; **a. ses mots** to mumble ▮ *vi* to swallow; **j'ai avalé de travers** it went down the wrong way.

avance [avɑ̃s] *nf* (*marche, acompte*) advance; (*de coureur, chercheur etc*) lead;

avances (*diplomatiques*) overtures; (*à une femme*) advances; **à l'a., d'a., par a.** in advance; **en a.** (*arriver, partir*) early; (*avant l'horaire prévu*) ahead (of time); (*dans son développement*) ahead, in advance; (*montre etc*) fast; **en a. sur** (*qn, son époque etc*) ahead of, in advance of; **avoir une heure d'a.** (*train etc*) to be an hour early.

avancé, -ée *a* (*âge, enfant, état etc*) advanced; (*saison*) well advanced.

avancée [avɑ̃se] *nf* projection, overhang.

avancement [avɑ̃smɑ̃] *nm* (*de personne*) promotion; (*de travail*) progress.

avancer [avɑ̃se] *vt* (*date, réunion*) to bring forward; (*main, chaise, pion*) to move forward; (*travail*) to speed up; (*argent, thèse*) to advance; (*montre*) to put forward.

▮ *vi* (*personne, véhicule etc*) to move forward, advance; (*travail*) to progress, advance; (*faire saillie*) to jut out (*sur* over); **a. de cinq minutes** (*montre*) to be five minutes fast; **alors, ça avance?** is everything progressing well?; **ça n'avance à rien de pleurer/etc** it's no help crying/etc.

▮ **s'avancer** *vpr* to move forward, advance; (*faire saillie*) to jut out; **elle s'avança vers moi** she came *ou* moved towards me.

avanie [avani] *nf* affront, insult.

avant [avɑ̃] *prép* before; **a. de voir** before seeing; **a. qu'il (ne) parte** before he leaves; **a. huit jours** within a week; **a. tout** above all; **a. toute chose** first and foremost; **a. peu** before long.

▮ *adv* before; **en a.** (*mouvement*) forward; (*en tête*) ahead; **en a. de** in front of; **bien a. dans** (*creuser etc*) very deep(ly) into; **la nuit d'a.** the night before.

▮ *nm* (*de navire, voiture etc*) front; (*joueur*) *Football* forward; **à l'a.** in (the) front; **monter à l'a.** to get *ou* go in (the) front.

▮ *a inv* (*pneu etc*) front.

avantage [avɑ̃taʒ] *nm* advantage; (*bénéfice*) *Fin* benefit; **tu as a. à le faire** it's worth your while to do it; **tirer a. de** to benefit from; **avantages en nature** fringe benefits. ●**avantager** *vt* (*favoriser*) to favour; (*faire valoir*) to show off to advantage.

avantageux, -euse [avɑ̃taʒø, -øz] *a* (*prix etc*) worthwhile, attractive; (*flatteur*) flattering; *Péj* conceited; **a. pour qn** advantageous to s.o.

avant-bras [avɑ̃bra] *nm inv* forearm. ●**avant-centre** *nm* (*joueur*) centre-forward. ●**avant-coureur** *am* **un signe a.-coureur de** qch a sign heralding sth. ●**avant-dernier, -ière** *a* & *nmf* last but one. ●**avant-garde** *nf* (*d'armée*) advance guard; **d'a.-garde** (*idée, film etc*) avant-garde. ●**avant-goût** *nm* foretaste. ●**avant-guerre** *nm ou f* pre-war period; **d'a.-guerre** pre-war. ●**avant-hier** [avɑ̃tjɛr] *adv* the day before yesterday. ●**avant-première** *nf* preview. ●**avant-propos** *nm inv* foreword. ●**avant-veille** *nf* **l'a.-veille (de)** two days before.

avare [avar] *a* miserly; **a. de** (*compliments*

etc) sparing of ▮ *nmf* miser. ●**avarice** *nf* miserliness, avarice.

avarie(s) [avari] *nf(pl)* damage. ●**avarié, -ée** *a* (*aliment*) rotting, rotten.

avatar [avatar] *nm Péj Fam* misadventure.

avec [avɛk] *prép* with; (*envers*) to(wards); **méchant/aimable/etc a. qn** nasty/kind/etc to s.o.; **a. ça qu'est-ce que je vous sers?** what else can I bring you?; **et a. ça?** (*dans un magasin*) *Fam* anything else? ▮ *adv* **il est venu a.** (*son chapeau etc*) *Fam* he came with it.

avenant, -ante [avnɑ̃, -ɑ̃t] *a* (*visage etc*) pleasing, attractive ▮ *nm* **à l'a.** in keeping (de with).

avènement [avɛnmɑ̃] *nm* **l'a. de** the coming *ou* advent of; (*roi*) the accession of.

avenir [avnir] *nm* future; **à l'a.** (*désormais*) in future; **d'a.** (*personne, métier*) with future prospects.

aventure [avɑ̃tyr] *nf* adventure; (*en amour*) affair; **à l'a.** (*marcher etc*) aimlessly; **dire la bonne a. à qn** to tell s.o.'s fortune; **tenter l'a.** to try one's luck. ●**aventurer** *vt* to risk; (*remarque*) to venture; (*réputation*) to risk ▮ **s'aventurer** *vpr* to venture (**sur** on to, **à faire** to do). ●**aventureux, -euse** *a* (*personne, vie*) adventurous; (*risqué*) risky. ●**aventurier, -ière** *nmf* adventurer.

avenue [avny] *nf* avenue.

avérer (s') [savere] *vpr* (*juste etc*) to prove (to be); **il s'avère que** it turns out that. ●**avéré, -ée** *a* (*fait etc*) established.

averse [avɛrs] *nf* shower, downpour.

aversion [avɛrsjɔ̃] *nf* aversion (**pour** to).

avertir [avɛrtir] *vt* (*mettre en garde, menacer*) to warn; (*informer*) to notify, inform. ●**averti, -ie** *a* (*public etc*) informed. ●**avertissement** *nm* warning; (*dans un livre*) foreword. ●**avertisseur** *nm* (*klaxon®*) horn; **a. d'incendie** fire alarm.

aveu, -x [avø] *nm* confession; **passer aux aveux** to make a confession; **de l'a. de** by the admission of.

aveugle [avœgl] *a* blind; **devenir aveugle** to go blind ▮ *nmf* blind man, blind woman; **les aveugles** the blind. ●**aveuglément** [-emɑ̃] *adv* blindly.

aveugler [avœgle] *vt* (*éblouir*) & *Fig* to blind. ●**aveuglement** [-əmɑ̃] *nm* (*égarement*) complete lack of judgment.

aveuglette (à l') [alavœglɛt] *adv* blindly; **chercher qch à l'a.** to grope for sth.

aviateur, -trice [avjatœr, -tris] *nmf* airman, airwoman. ●**aviation** *nf* (*industrie, science*) aviation; (*armée de l'air*) air force; (*avions*) aircraft *inv*; **l'a.** (*activité*) flying; **base d'a.** air base.

avide [avid] *a* (*d'argent*) greedy (de for); **a. d'apprendre/etc** (*désireux*) eager to learn/etc. ●**avidement** *adv* greedily. ●**avidité** *nf* greed.

avilir [avilir] *vt* to degrade, debase.

avion [avjɔ̃] *nm* plane, aircraft *inv*, *Br* aeroplane, *Am* airplane; **a. à réaction** jet; **a. de chasse** fighter (plane); **a. de ligne** airliner;

par a. (*lettre*) airmail; **en a., par a.** (*voyager*) by plane, by air; **aller en a.** to fly, go by plane *ou* by air (**à** to).

aviron [avirɔ̃] *nm* oar; **l'a.** (*sport*) rowing; **faire de l'a.** to row; **champion d'a.** rowing champion.

avis [avi] *nm* opinion; (*d'un tribunal, d'une assemblée*) judgment; (*communiqué*) notice; (*conseil*) & *Fin* advice; **à mon a.** in my opinion, to my mind; **changer d'a.** to change one's mind.

aviser [avize] *vt* to advise, inform; (*voir*) to notice; **s'a. de qch** to realize sth suddenly; **s'a. de faire** to venture to do. ●**avisé, -ée** *a* prudent, wise (**de faire** to do); **bien/mal a.** well-/ill-advised.

aviver [avive] *vt* (*couleur*) to bring out; (*douleur*) to sharpen.

avocat, -ate [avɔka, -at] **1** *nmf* lawyer, *Br* barrister, *Am* attorney, *Am* counselor; (*d'une cause*) *Fig* advocate. **2** *nm* (*fruit*) avocado (pear).

avoine [avwan] *nf* oats; **farine d'a.** oatmeal.

avoir* [avwar] **1** *v aux* to have; **je l'ai vu** I have *ou* I've seen him; **je l'avais vu** I had *ou* I'd seen him.
2 *vt* (*posséder*) to have; (*obtenir*) to get; (*porter*) to have on, wear; (*tromper*) *Fam* to take for a ride; **il a he has**, he's got; **qu'est-ce que tu as?** what's the matter with you?, what's wrong with you?; **j'ai à lui parler** I have to speak to her; **j'ai à faire** I have things to do; **il n'a qu'à essayer** he only has to try; **a. faim/chaud/***etc* to be *ou* feel hungry/hot/*etc*; **a. cinq ans/***etc* to be five (years old)/*etc*; **en a. pour longtemps** to be busy for quite a while; **j'en ai pour dix minutes** this will take me ten minutes; (*ne bougez pas*) I'll be with you in ten minutes; **en a. pour son argent** to get *ou* have one's

money's worth; **j'en ai eu pour dix francs** it cost me ten francs; **en a. après** *ou* **contre** to have a grudge against.
3 *v imp* **il y a** there is, *pl* there are; **il y a six ans** six years ago; **il n'y a pas de quoi!** (*en réponse à 'merci'*) don't mention it!; **qu'est-ce qu'il y a?** what's the matter?, what's wrong?
4 *nm* assets, property; (*d'un compte*) credit.

avoisiner [avwazine] *vt* to border on. ●**avoisinant, -ante** *a* neighbouring, nearby.

avorter [avɔrte] *vi* (*femme*) to miscarry, abort; (*projet etc*) *Fig* to miscarry, fail; (**se faire**) **a.** (*femme*) to have *ou* get an abortion. ●**avortement** *nm* abortion; (*de projet etc*) *Fig* failure.

avouer [avwe] *vt* to confess, admit (**que** that, **à** to); (*crime*) to confess to, admit to; **s'a. vaincu** to admit defeat **‖** *vi* (*coupable*) to confess. ●**avoué, -ée** *a* (*ennemi, but*) declared, avowed **‖** *nm Br* solicitor, *Am* attorney.

avril [avril] *nm* April; **un poisson d'a.** (*farce*) an April fool joke.

axe [aks] *nm* (*ligne*) *Math Astronomie etc* axis; (*essieu*) axle; (*d'une politique*) broad direction; **grands axes** (*routes*) main roads. ●**axer** *vt* to centre (**sur** on); **il est axé sur** his mind is drawn towards.

axiome [aksjom] *nm* axiom.

ayant [ɛjɑ̃], **ayez** [ɛje], **ayons** [ɛjɔ̃] *voir* avoir.

azalée [azale] *nf* (*plante*) azalea.

azimuts [azimyt] *nmpl* **dans tous les a.** *Fam* here there and everywhere, all over the place; **tous a.** (*guerre, publicité etc*) all-out.

azote [azɔt] *nm* nitrogen.

azur [azyr] *nm* azure, (sky) blue; **la Côte d'A.** the (French) Riviera.

azyme [azim] *a* (*pain*) unleavened.

B

B, b [be] *nm* B, b.
baba [baba] *n* **b. au rhum** rum baba.
babeurre [babœr] *nm* buttermilk.
babillard [babijar] *nm Can* notice board.
babiller [babije] *vi* to babble. ● **babillage** *nm* babble.
babines [babin] *nfpl* (*lèvres*) chops.
babiole [babjɔl] *nf* (*objet*) knick-knack; (*futilité*) trifle.
bâbord [bɑbɔr] *nm* (*de bateau, d'avion*) port (side).
babouin [babwɛ̃] *nm* baboon.
baby-foot [babifut] *nm inv* table *ou* miniature football.
bac [bak] *nm* **1** (*bateau*) ferry(boat). **2** (*cuve*) tank; **b. à glace** ice tray (*in refrigerator*); **b. à légumes** vegetable compartment, crisper; **b. à laver** washtub. **3** *abrév* = **baccalauréat**.
baccalauréat [bakalɔrea] *nm* school leaving certificate, = *Br* GCE A-levels, = *Am* high school diploma.
bâche [bɑʃ] *nf* (*de toile*) tarpaulin; (*de plastique*) plastic sheet. ● **bâcher** *vt* to cover over (*with a tarpaulin ou plastic sheet*).
bachelier, -ière [baʃəlje, -jɛr] *nmf* holder of the *baccalauréat*.
bachot [baʃo] *nm abrév* = **baccalauréat**. ● **bachoter** *vi* to cram (*for an exam*).
bacille [basil] *nm* germ.
bâcler [bɑkle] *vt* (*travail*) to dash off carelessly, botch (up).
bactérie [bakteri] *nfpl* bacteria. ● **bactériologique** *a* bacteriological; **la guerre b.** germ warfare.
badaud, -aude [bado, -od] *nmf* (inquisitive) onlooker, bystander.
baderne [badɛrn] *nf* **vieille b.** *Péj* old fogey, old fuddy-duddy.
badge [badʒ] *nm Br* badge, *Am* button.
badigeon [badiʒɔ̃] *nm* whitewash, *Br* distemper. ● **badigeonner** *vt* (*mur*) to whitewash, *Br* distemper; (*de peinture*) to daub (with paint); (*écorchure*) to paint *ou* coat (with antiseptic).
badin, -ine [badɛ̃, -in] *a* (*peu sérieux*) lighthearted, playful. ● **badiner** *vi* to jest, joke; **b. avec** (*prendre à la légère*) to trifle with. ● **badinage** *nm* banter, jesting.
baffe [baf] *nf Fam* slap (in the face).
bafouer [bafwe] *vt* to mock *ou* scoff at.
bafouiller [bafuje] *vti* to stammer, splutter.
bâfrer [bɑfre] *vi Fam* to stuff oneself (with food).
bagage [bagaʒ] *nm* (*valise etc*) piece of luggage *ou* baggage; (*connaissances*) *Fig* (fund of) knowledge; **bagages** (*ensemble des valises*) luggage, baggage; **faire ses bagages** to pack (one's bags); **plier bagages** to pack one's bags (and leave). ● **bagagiste** *nm* baggage handler.
bagarre [bagar] *nf* fight, brawl; **des bagarres éclatèrent** fights *ou* fighting broke out *ou* erupted; **aimer la b.** to like a fight *ou* a brawl; **chercher la b.** to look for a fight; **b. générale** free-for-all. ● **bagarrer** *vi Fam* to fight, struggle **‖ se bagarrer** *vpr* to fight, brawl; (*se disputer*) to fight, quarrel.
bagatelle [bagatɛl] *nf* trifle; **la b. de 1 000 francs** *Iron* the trifling sum of 1,000 francs.
bagne [baɲ] *nm* convict prison; (*outre-mer*) penal colony; **c'est le b. ici** *Fig* this place is a real sweatshop *ou Br* workhouse. ● **bagnard** *nm* convict.
bagnole [baɲɔl] *nf Fam* car.
bagou(t) [bagu] *nm Fam* glibness; **avoir du b.** to have the gift of the gab.
bague [bag] *nf* (*anneau*) ring; (*de cigare*) band. ● **bagué** *am* **doigt b.** ringed finger.
baguenauder [bagnode] *vi*, **se baguenauder** *vpr* to loaf around, saunter.
baguette [bagɛt] *nf* (*canne*) stick; (*de chef d'orchestre*) baton; (*pain*) (long thin) loaf, baguette; **baguettes** (*de tambour*) drumsticks; (*pour manger*) chopsticks; **b. (magique)** (magic) wand; **mener qn à la b.** to rule s.o. with an iron hand.
bahut [bay] *nm* (*meuble*) chest, cabinet; (*lycée*) *Fam* school.
baie [bɛ] *nf* **1** (*de côte*) bay. **2** (*petit fruit*) berry. **3** (*fenêtre*) picture window.
baignade [bɛɲad] *nf* (*bain*) swim, *Br* bathe; (*activité*) swimming, *Br* bathing; (*endroit*) bathing place.
baigner [beɲe] *vt* (*immerger*) to bathe; (*enfant*) *Br* to bath, *Am* bathe; **les rivages** (*mer*) to wash the shores; **baigné de sueur/lumière** bathed in sweat/light; **baigné de sang** blood-soaked, soaked in blood.
‖ *vi* **b. dans** (*tremper*) (*aliment*) to be steeped in (*sauce etc*).
‖ se baigner *vpr* to go swimming *ou Br* bathing; (*dans une baignoire*) to have *ou* take a bath; **des gens qui se baignent** people swimming *ou Br* bathing. ● **baigneur, -euse 1** *nmf* swimmer, *Br* bather. **2** (*poupée*) baby doll.
baignoire [beɲwar] *nf* bath (tub).
bail, *pl* **baux** [baj, bo] *nm* lease. ● **bailleur** *nm* **b. de fonds** financial backer.
bâiller [bɑje] *vi* to yawn; (*chemise etc*) to be half-open; (*porte*) to be *ou* stand ajar. ● **bâillement** *nm* (*de personne*) yawn.

bâillon [bɑjɔ̃] *nm* gag. ●**bâillonner** *vt* (*victime, presse etc*) to gag.
bain [bɛ̃] *nm* bath; (*de mer*) swim, *Br* bathe; **prendre un b. de soleil** to sunbathe; **salle de bain(s)** bathroom; **être dans le b.** (*au courant*) *Fam* to have *Br* got *ou Am* gotten into the swing of things; **petit/grand b.** (*piscine*) shallow/deep end; **b. de bouche** mouthwash. ●**bain-marie** *nm* (*pl* **bains-marie**) (*casserole*) double boiler.
baïonnette [bajɔnɛt] *nf* bayonet.
baiser [beze] **1** *vt* **b. qn au front/sur la joue** to kiss s.o. on the forehead/cheek ▮ *nm* kiss; **bons baisers** (*dans une lettre*) (with) love. **2** *vt* (*duper*) *Fam* to con.
baisse [bɛs] *nf* fall, drop (*de* in); **en b.** (*température*) falling; (*popularité*) declining.
baisser [bese] *vt* (*voix, prix etc*) to lower, drop; (*tête*) to bend; (*radio, chauffage etc*) to turn down ▮ *vi* (*prix, niveau, température etc*) to go down, drop; (*soleil*) to go down, sink; (*marée*) to go out, ebb; (*santé, popularité, qualité*) *Fig* to decline ▮ **se baisser** *vpr* to bend down, stoop.
bajoues [baʒu] *nfpl* (*joues d'animal ou de personne*) chops.
bal, *pl* **bals** [bal] *nm* (*réunion de grand apparat*) ball; (*populaire*) dance; (*lieu*) dance hall.
balade [balad] *nf* *Fam* walk; (*en voiture*) drive; (*excursion*) tour. ●**balader** *vt* *Fam* (*enfant etc*) to take for a walk *ou* drive; (*objet*) to trail around ▮ **se balader** *vpr Fam* (*à pied*) to (go for a) walk; (*excursionner*) to tour (around); **se b.** (*en voiture*) to go for a drive. ●**baladeur** *nm* Walkman®, (personal) stereo. ●**baladeuse** *nf* inspection lamp.
balafre [balafr] *nf* (*cicatrice*) scar; (*blessure*) gash, slash. ●**balafré, -ée** *a* scarred; (*blessé*) gashed, slashed.
balai [bale] *nm* broom; **b. mécanique** carpet sweeper; **manche à b.** broomstick; (*d'avion, de jeu vidéo*) joystick; **donner un coup de b.** to sweep up. ●**balai-brosse** *nm* (*pl* **balais-brosses**) garden brush *ou* broom (*for scrubbing paving stones*).
balance [balɑ̃s] *nf* (*instrument*) (pair of) scales; (*de comptes*) balance; **la b. des pouvoirs** the balance of power; **la B.** (*signe*) Libra; **mettre en b.** to balance, weigh up.
balancer [balɑ̃se] *vt* (*hanches, tête, branches*) to sway; (*bras*) to swing; (*lancer*) *Fam* to toss, *Br* chuck; (*se débarrasser de*) *Fam* to toss out, *Br* chuck out; **b. un compte** to balance an account.
▮ **se balancer** *vpr* (*personne*) to swing (from side to side); (*arbre, bateau etc*) to sway; **je m'en balance!** I couldn't care less! ●**balancé, -ée** *a* **bien b.** (*phrase*) well-balanced; (*personne*) *Fam* well-built. ●**balancement** *nm* swaying; (*de bras*) swinging.
balancier [balɑ̃sje] *nm* (*d'horloge*) pendulum; (*de montre*) balance wheel.
balançoire [balɑ̃swar] *nf* (*suspendue*) swing; (*bascule*) seesaw.

balayer [baleje] *vt* (*chambre etc*) to sweep (out); (*rue, feuilles etc*) to sweep (up); (*enlever, chasser*) to sweep away; (*parcourir*) (*lumière de phare etc*) to sweep across (*beach etc*); **le vent balayait la plaine** the wind swept the plain. ●**balayage** *nm* sweeping (*out ou up ou* away).
balayette [balejet] *nf* (hand) brush; (*balai*) short-handled broom.
balayeur, -euse [balejœr, -øz] *nmf* (*personne*) roadsweeper. ●**balayeuse** *nf* (*véhicule*) roadsweeper.
balbutier [balbysje] *vti* to stammer. ●**balbutiement** *nm* balbutiement(s) stammering; **en être à ses premiers balbutiements** (*science etc*) to be in its infancy.
balcon [balkɔ̃] *nm* balcony; (*de théâtre, opéra*) *Br* dress circle, *Am* mezzanine.
baldaquin [baldakɛ̃] *nm* (*de lit etc*) canopy.
Baléares [balear] *nfpl* **les B.** the Balearic Islands.
baleine [balɛn] *nf* (*animal*) whale; (*fanon*) whalebone; (*de parapluie*) rib. ●**baleinier** *nm* (*navire*) whaler. ●**baleinière** *nf* whaleboat.
balise [baliz] *nf* (*de navigation*) *Nau* beacon; *Av* (ground) light; (*routière*) road sign. ●**baliser** *vt* to mark with beacons *ou* lights; (*route*) to signpost. ●**balisage** *nm Nau* beacons; *Av* lighting; (*routier*) signposting.
balistique [balistik] *a* ballistic.
balivernes [balivern] *nfpl Vieilli* balderdash, nonsense.
Balkans [balkɑ̃] *nmpl* **les B.** the Balkans.
ballade [balad] *nf* (*légende, poème long*) ballad; (*musicale, poème court*) ballade.
ballant, -ante [balɑ̃, -ɑ̃t] *a* (*bras, jambes*) dangling.
ballast [balast] *nm* ballast.
balle [bal] *nf* (*de tennis, golf etc*) ball; (*projectile*) bullet; (*paquet*) bale; **balles** (*francs*) *Fam* francs; **faire des balles** (*au tennis*) to knock the ball about; **se renvoyer la b.** *Fig* to pass the buck (to each other).
ballet [bale] *nm* ballet. ●**ballerine** *nf* ballerina.
ballon [balɔ̃] *nm* (*jouet d'enfant, dirigeable*) balloon; (*de sport*) ball; **b. de football** *Br* football, *Am* soccer ball; **b. d'eau chaude** hot-water tank; **lancer un b. d'essai** *Fig* to put out a feeler; **être un b. d'oxygène pour qn** *Fig* to be a (real) shot in the arm *ou* boost for s.o.
ballonné [balɔne] *am* (*ventre, estomac*) bloated, swollen.
ballot [balo] *nm* (*paquet*) bundle; (*imbécile*) *Fam* idiot.
ballottage [balɔtaʒ] *nm* (*scrutin*) second ballot (*no candidate having achieved the required number of votes*).
ballotter [balɔte] *vti* to shake (about); **ballotté entre** (*sentiments contraires*) torn between.
balnéaire [balneer] *a* **station b.** *Br* seaside resort, *Am* beach resort.
balourd, -ourde [balur, -urd] *nmf* (clumsy

oaf. ●**balourdise** *nf* clumsiness, oafishness; (*gaffe*) blunder.
Baltique [baltik] *nf* **la B.** the Baltic.
balustrade [balystrad] *nf* (hand)rail, railing(s).
bambin [bɑ̃bɛ̃] *nm* tiny tot, toddler.
bambou [bɑ̃bu] *nm* bamboo; **canne/etc de b.** bamboo stick/etc.
ban [bɑ̃] *nm* (*applaudissements*) round of applause; (*de tambour*) roll; **bans** (*de mariage*) banns; **mettre qn au b. de** to cast s.o. out from, outlaw s.o. from; **un (triple) b. pour...** three cheers for..., a big hand for....
banal, -e, *mpl* **-als** [banal] *a* (*fait, accident etc*) commonplace, banal; (*idée, propos*) banal, trite. ●**banalité** *nf* banality; **banalités** (*propos*) banalities.
banalisée [banalize] *af* **voiture (de police) b.** unmarked (police) car.
banane [banan] *nf* banana; (*sac de skieur etc*) waist pouch, *Br* bum bag, *Am* fanny pack. ●**bananier** *nm* (*arbre*) banana tree.
banc [bɑ̃] *nm* (*siège*) bench; (*établi de menuisier etc*) work(bench); (*de poissons*) shoal; **b. des accusés** (*dans un tribunal*) dock; **b. d'église** pew; **b. de neige** *Can* snowbank; **b. de sable** sandbank; **b. d'essai** *Fig* testing ground.
bancaire [bɑ̃kɛr] *a* **compte/chèque/etc b.** bank account/*Br* cheque *ou Am* check/etc; **opération b.** banking operation.
bancal, -e, *mpl* **-als** [bɑ̃kal] *a* (*personne*) bandy, bow-legged; (*boiteux*) who limps; (*meuble*) wobbly; (*idée*) *Fig* shaky.
bandage [bɑ̃daʒ] *nm* (*pansement*) bandage.
bandana [bɑ̃dana] *nm* bandan(n)a.
bande [bɑ̃d] *nf* **1** (*de terrain, papier etc*) strip; (*de film*) reel; (*de journal*) wrapper; (*rayure*) stripe; (*pansement*) bandage; (*sur la chaussée*) line; (*de fréquences*) *Radio* band; **b. (magnétique)** tape; **b. vidéo** videotape; **b. sonore** sound track; **une b. dessinée** a comic strip, a strip cartoon; **aimer la b. dessinée** to like comic strips *ou Br* comics; **par la b.** (*de façon détournée*) indirectly.
2 (*groupe*) gang, troop, band; (*de chiens*) pack; (*d'oiseaux*) flock; **on a fait b. à part** we split into our own group; **b. d'idiots!** you bunch *ou Br* load of idiots!
bandeau, -x [bɑ̃do] *nm* (*sur les yeux*) blindfold; (*pour la tête*) headband; (*pansement*) head bandage.
bander [bɑ̃de] *vt* (*blessure etc*) to bandage; (*yeux*) to blindfold; (*muscle*) to tense; (*arc*) to bend.
banderole [bɑ̃drɔl] *nf* (*de manifestants*) banner; (*publicitaire*) streamer.
bandit [bɑ̃di] *nm* robber, gangster; (*enfant*) *Fam* rascal. ●**banditisme** *nm* **le b.** crime.
bandoulière [bɑ̃duljɛr] *nf* shoulder strap; **en b.** slung across the shoulder.
banjo [bɑ̃dʒo] *nm* banjo.
banlieue [bɑ̃ljø] *nf* **la b.** the suburbs, the outskirts; **une b.** a suburb; **en b.** in the suburbs; **la proche/grande b.** the inner/outer

suburbs; **de b.** (*maison, magasin etc*) suburban; **train de b.** commuter train. ●**banlieusard, -arde** *nmf* (*habitant*) suburbanite; (*voyageur*) commuter; **c'est un b.** he lives in the suburbs, he's a suburbanite.
banne [ban] *nf* (*de magasin*) awning.
bannière [banjɛr] *nf* (*drapeau*) banner.
bannir [banir] *vt* (*exiler*) to banish (**de** from); (*supprimer*) to banish, ban (**de** from). ●**bannissement** *nm* (*de personne*) banishment.
banque [bɑ̃k] *nf* bank; (*activité*) banking; **b. de données** *Ordinat* data bank; **b. du sang** blood bank.
banqueroute [bɑ̃krut] *nf* (*frauduleux*) bankruptcy.
banquet [bɑ̃kɛ] *nm* banquet.
banquette [bɑ̃kɛt] *nf* (*de véhicule, train*) (bench) seat.
banquier [bɑ̃kje] *nm* banker.
banquise [bɑ̃kiz] *nf* ice floe *ou* field.
baptême [batɛm] *nm* christening, baptism; (*de navire etc*) *Fig* christening; **b. du feu** baptism of fire; **b. de l'air** first flight. ●**baptiser** *vt* (*enfant*) to christen, baptize; (*appeler*) *Fig* to christen (*ship etc*).
baquet [bakɛ] *nm* tub, basin.
bar [bar] *nm* **1** (*lieu, comptoir, meuble*) bar. **2** (*poisson marin*) bass.
baragouin [baragwɛ̃] *nm* gibberish, gabble. ●**baragouiner** *vt* (*langue*) to gabble a few words of ∎ *vi* to gabble away, talk gibberish.
baraque [barak] *nf* hut, shack; (*maison*) *Fam* house, place; (*taudis*) hovel; (*de foire*) stall. ●**baraquement** *nm* (makeshift) huts.
baratin [baratɛ̃] *nm* *Fam* sweet talk; (*de vendeur*) sales talk, (sales) patter. ●**baratiner** *vt* (*fille*) *Br* to chat up, *Am* sweet-talk.
barbare [barbar] *a* (*manières, action, crime*) barbaric; (*peuple, invasions*) barbarian ∎ *nmf* barbarian. ●**barbarie** *nf* (*cruauté*) barbarity. ●**barbarisme** *nm* (*faute de langage*) barbarism.
barbe [barb] *nf* beard; **une b. de trois jours** three days' growth of beard; **se faire la b.** to shave; **à la b. de** under the (very) nose(s) of; **rire dans sa b.** to laugh up one's sleeve; **la b.!** *Fam* enough!, cut it out!; **quelle b.!** *Fam* what a drag *ou* bore!; **b. à papa** *Br* candyfloss, *Am* cotton candy.
barbecue [barbəkju] *nm* barbecue.
barbelé [barbəle] *am* **fil de fer b.** barbed wire. ●**barbelés** *nmpl* barbed wire.
barber [barbe] *vt* *Fam* to bore (stiff) ∎ **se barber** *vpr Fam* to be *ou* get bored (stiff). ●**barbant, -ante** *a Fam* boring.
barbiche [barbiʃ] *nf* goatee (beard).
barbiturique [barbityrik] *nm* barbiturate.
barboter [barbɔte] **1** *vi* (*s'agiter*) to splash about, paddle. **2** *vt* (*voler*) *Fam* to snatch, *Br* pinch, filch. ●**barboteuse** *nf* (*de bébé*) rompers, play suit.
barbouiller [barbuje] *vt* (*salir*) to smear; (*gribouiller*) to scribble; (*peindre*) to daub; **avoir l'estomac** *ou* **le cœur barbouillé** *Fam* to

feel queasy. ●**barbouillage** *nm* (*de confiture etc*) smear; (*au stylo etc*) scribble; (*de peinture*) daub; (*action de peindre*) daubing.

barbu, -ue [barby] *a* bearded.

barda [barda] *nm* (*bagages*) *Fam* gear; (*de soldat*) kit.

bardé, -ée [barde] *a* b. de décorations/etc covered with decorations/*etc*.

barder [barde] *v imp* ça va b.! *Fam* there'll be fireworks!, there'll be (real) trouble!

barème [barɛm] *nm* (*des tarifs*) table; (*des salaires*) scale; (*livre de comptes*) ready reckoner.

baril [bari(l)] *nm* barrel; b. de poudre powder keg; b. de lessive box of laundry detergent.

bariolé, -ée [barjɔle] *a* brightly-coloured.

barjo [barʒo] *a inv* (*fou*) *Fam* nutty, *Br* bonkers.

barman, *pl* **-men** *ou* **-mans** [barman, -mɛn, -man] *nm Br* barman, *Am* bartender.

baromètre [barɔmɛtr] *nm* barometer.

baron [barɔ̃] *nm* baron. ●**baronne** *nf* baroness.

baroque [barɔk] **1** *a* (*idée etc*) bizarre, weird. **2** *a & nm Archit Mus etc* baroque.

baroud [barud] *nm* b. d'honneur gallant last stand *ou* fight.

barque [bark] *nf* (small) boat.

barrage [baraʒ] *nm* (*sur une route*) roadblock; (*sur un fleuve*) dam; (*de petite rivière*) weir; b. d'une rue the closure of a street; b. de police police roadblock; tir de b. barrage fire.

barre [bar] *nf* (*de fer, bois, chocolat etc*) bar; (*de bateau*) helm; (*trait*) line, stroke; b. de soustraction minus sign; b. d'espacement (*d'ordinateur, de machine à écrire*) space bar; b. fixe *Sport* horizontal bar.

barreau, -x [baro] *nm* (*de fenêtre etc*) bar; (*d'échelle*) rung; le b. (*profession des avocats*) the bar.

barrer [bare] **1** *vt* (*route etc*) (*police*) to close (off); (*obstruer*) (*éboulis etc*) to block (off); (*porte*) to bar; (*chèque*) to cross; (*phrase*) to cross out; (*bateau*) to steer; b. la route à qn, b. qn to bar s.o.'s way; **'rue barrée'** 'road closed'. **2** se barrer *vpr Arg* to beat it, *Br* hop it, make off.

barrette [barɛt] *nf* (*pince*) *Br* (hair)slide, *Am* barrette.

barreur [barœr] *nm* (*de bateau*) cox.

barricade [barikad] *nf* barricade. ●**barricader** *vt* to barricade ▌ se barricader *vpr* (*forcené etc*) to barricade oneself (dans in); (*pour être seul*) to shut oneself away.

barrière [barjɛr] *nf* (*porte*) gate; (*clôture*) fence; (*obstacle, mur*) barrier.

barrique [barik] *nf* (large) barrel.

baryton [baritɔ̃] *nm* baritone.

bas¹, basse [bɑ, bɑs] *a* (*table, prix etc*) low; (*âme, action*) vile, base, mean; (*partie de ville etc*) lower; (*origine*) lowly; au b. mot at the very least; enfant en b. âge young child; avoir la vue basse to be short-sighted; le b.

peuple *Péj* the lower classes; coup b. *Boxe* blow below the belt.

▌ *adv* low; (*parler*) in a whisper, softly; mettre b. (*animal*) to give birth; mettre b. les armes to lay down one's arms; jeter b. to overthrow; plus b. further *ou* lower down; sauter à b. du lit to jump out of bed; à b. les dictateurs/etc! down with dictators/*etc*!

▌ *nm* (*de côte, page, mur etc*) bottom, foot; tiroir/étagère/etc du b. bottom drawer/shelf/ *etc*; en b. down (below); (*par l'escalier*) downstairs; en *ou* au b. de at the foot *ou* bottom of; de haut en b. from top to bottom.

bas² [bɑ] *nm* (*chaussette*) stocking; b. à varices support stockings; b. de laine (*économies*) nest egg.

basané, -ée [bazane] *a* (*visage etc*) tanned.

bas-bleu [bɑblø] *nm* (*pl* **-bleus**) (*femme*) *Péj* bluestocking.

bas-côté [bakote] *nm* (*de route*) roadside, shoulder, *Br* verge.

bascule [baskyl] *nf* (*balançoire*) seesaw; (*balance à*) b. weighing machine; cheval/ fauteuil à b. rocking horse/chair. ●**basculer** *vti* (*personne*) to topple over; (*benne*) to tip up.

base [bɑz] *nf* **1** (*de colonne, triangle etc*) & *Ch Math etc* base; (*principe fondamental*) basis; bases (*d'un argument, accord etc*) basis; salaire/etc de b. basic pay/*etc*; produit à b. de lait/citron milk-/lemon-based product; militant de b. rank-and-file militant. **2** (*militaire etc*) base. ●**baser** *vt* to base (sur on); se b. sur to base oneself on.

bas-fond [bɑfɔ̃] *nm* (*eau*) shallows; (*terrain*) low ground; les bas-fonds (*population*) *Péj* the dregs.

basilic [bazilik] *nm* (*plante, aromate*) basil.

basilique [bazilik] *nf* basilica.

basket(-ball) [baskɛt(bol)] *nm* basketball.

baskets [baskɛt] *nfpl* (*chaussures*) *Br* trainers, *Am* track shoes.

basque [bask] *a* Basque ▌ *nmf* B. Basque. ●**basques** *nfpl* (*pans de veste*) skirts.

basse [bas] **1** *voir* bas¹. **2** *nf Mus* bass.

basse-cour [baskur] *nf* (*pl* **basses-cours**) farmyard, *Am* barnyard.

bassement [bɑsmɑ̃] *adv* basely, meanly. ●**bassesse** *nf* baseness, meanness; (*action*) vile *ou* base *ou* mean act.

bassin [basɛ̃] *nm* **1** (*pièce d'eau*) pond; (*port*) dock; (*de piscine*) pool; (*cuvette*) bowl, basin; (*rade*) dock. **2** (*du corps*) pelvis. **3** (*région*) basin; b. houiller coalfield. ●**bassine** *nf* bowl.

bassiner [basine] *vt* (*ennuyer*) *Fam* to bore.

basson [basɔ̃] *nm* (*instrument*) bassoon; (*musicien*) bassoonist.

bastingage [bastɛ̃gaʒ] *nm* (ship's) rail, bulwarks.

bastion [bastjɔ̃] *nm* (*d'un parti etc*) bastion, stronghold.

bastringue [bastrɛ̃g] *nm* (*tapage*) *Arg* shindig, din; (*attirail*) *Arg* paraphernalia.

bas-ventre [bavɑ̃tr] *nm* lower abdomen; (*sexe*) *Fam* genitals.

bat [ba] *voir* battre.

bât [ba] *nm* packsaddle.

bataclan [bataklɑ̃] *nm Fam* paraphernalia; **et tout le b.** *Fam* and all the rest of it.

bataille [batɑj] *nf* battle; (*jeu de cartes*) beggar-my-neighbour. ● **batailler** *vi* to fight, battle. ● **batailleur, -euse** *nmf* fighter ▍ *a* fond of fighting.

bataillon [batɑjɔ̃] *nm* batallion.

bâtard, -arde [bɑtar, -ard] *a & nmf* bastard; **chien b.** mongrel; **œuvre bâtarde** hybrid work.

bateau, -x [bato] **1** *nm* boat; (*grand*) ship. **2** *a inv* (*question, sujet etc*) trite, hackneyed. ● **bateau-citerne** *nm* (*pl* **bateaux-citernes**) tanker. ● **bateau-mouche** *nm* (*pl* **bateaux-mouches**) (*sur la Seine*) pleasure boat.

batifoler [batifɔle] *vi Hum* to play *ou* fool *ou Br* lark about.

bâtiment [bɑtimɑ̃] *nm* (*édifice*) building; (*navire*) vessel; **le b., l'industrie du b.** the building trade; **ouvrier du b.** building worker.

bâtir [bɑtir] *vt* (*construire*) to build; (*coudre*) to baste, tack; **terrain à b.** building site. ● **bâti, -ie** *a* **bien b.** well-built ▍ *nm* (*charpente*) frame, support. ● **bâtisse** *nf Péj* building. ● **bâtisseur, -euse** *nmf* builder (**de** of).

bâton [bɑtɔ̃] *nm* (*canne*) stick; (*de maréchal, d'agent*) baton; **b. de rouge** lipstick; **donner des coups de b. à qn** to beat s.o. (with a stick); **parler à bâtons rompus** to ramble from one subject to another; **mettre des bâtons dans les roues à qn** to put obstacles in s.o.'s way.

battage [bataʒ] *nm* **1** (*du blé*) threshing; (*publicité*) *Fam* publicity, hype, ballyhoo.

battant [batɑ̃] *nm* **1** (*de cloche*) tongue; (*vantail de porte etc*) flap; **porte à deux battants** double door. **2** (*personne*) fighter.

battante [batɑ̃t] *af* **pluie b.** driving rain; **porte b.** *Br* swing door, *Am* swinging door.

battement [batmɑ̃] *nm* **1** (*de tambour etc*) beat(ing); (*de paupières*) blink(ing); **b. de cœur** heartbeat; **avoir des battements de cœur** to have palpitations. **2** (*délai*) interval.

batterie [batri] *nf* (*pour voiture, de canons etc*) battery; **la b.** (*d'un orchestre*) the drums; **b. de cuisine** set of pots and pans and dishes.

batteur [batœr] *nm* **1** (*musicien*) drummer, percussionist. **2 b. à œufs** egg beater.

battre* [batr] **1** *vt* (*frapper, vaincre*) to beat; (*à coups redoublés*) to batter, pound; (*blé*) to thresh; (*cartes*) to shuffle; (*œufs*) to beat; (*pays, chemins*) to scour; **b. la mesure** to beat time; **b. qn à mort** to batter *ou* beat s.o. to death; **b. pavillon** to fly a flag.

▍ *vi* to beat; (*porte*) to bang; **b. des mains** to clap (one's hands); **b. des paupières** to blink; **b. des ailes** (*oiseau*) to flap its wings; **le vent fait b. la porte** the wind bangs the door.

2 se battre *vpr* to fight (**avec** with, **pour** for).

battu [baty] *am* **le chemin** *ou* **sentier b.** the beaten track.

baudet [bodɛ] *nm* donkey.

baume [bom] *nm* (*résine, Fig consolation*) balm.

baux [bo] *voir* **bail**.

bavard, -arde [bavar, -ard] *a* (*élève etc*) talkative; (*commère*) gossipy ▍ *nmf* chatterbox; (*commère*) gossip. ● **bavarder** *vi* to chat, chatter; (*commère*) to gossip; (*divulguer des secrets*) to blab. ● **bavardage** *nm* chatting, chatter(ing); (*de commère*) gossip(ing).

bave [bav] *nf* dribble, slobber; (*de chien enragé*) foam; (*de limace*) slime. ● **baver** *vi* to dribble, slobber; (*chien enragé*) to foam; (*stylo*) to smudge; **en b.** *Fam* to have a rough time of it.

bavette [bavɛt] *nf* bib.

baveux, -euse [bavø, -øz] *a* (*bouche*) slobbery; (*omelette*) runny.

bavoir [bavwar] *nm* bib.

bavure [bavyr] *nf* (*tache*) smudge; (*erreur*) blunder; **sans b.** (*impeccable(ment)*) flawless(ly), perfect(ly).

bazar [bazar] *nm* (*magasin, marché*) bazaar; (*désordre*) mess, clutter; (*attirail*) *Fam* stuff, gear. ● **bazarder** [bazarde] *vt Fam* to sell off, get rid of.

bazooka [bazuka] *nm* bazooka.

BCBG [besebeʒe] *a inv abrév* (*bon chic bon genre*) stylish, classy.

bd *abrév* **boulevard**.

BD [bede] *nf abrév* **bande dessinée**.

béant, -ante [beɑ̃, -ɑ̃t] *a* (*plaie*) gaping; (*gouffre*) yawning.

béat, -ate [bea, -at] *a* (*air, sourire*) *Péj* smug; (*heureux*) *Hum* blissful. ● **béatitude** *nf Hum* bliss.

beau (*or* **bel** *before vowel or mute h*), **belle**, *pl* **beaux, belles** [bo, bɛl] *a* (*fleur, histoire etc*) beautiful; (*femme*) beautiful, attractive; (*homme*) handsome, good-looking; (*voyage, temps, discours etc*) fine, lovely, beautiful; (*occasion, talent*) fine; **au b. milieu** right in the middle (**de** of); **j'ai b. crier/essayer/***etc* it's no use (my) shouting/trying/*etc*; **un b. morceau** a good *ou* sizeable bit; **ce n'est pas b. de mentir** it isn't nice *ou* right to lie; **de plus belle** (*recommencer, hurler etc*) worse than ever; **bel et bien** really.

▍ *nm* **le b.** the beautiful; **faire le b.** (*chien*) to sit up and beg; **le plus b. de l'histoire** the best part of the story.

▍ *nf* **belle** (*aux cartes etc*) deciding game; (*femme*) beauty.

beaucoup [boku] *adv* (*lire etc*) a lot, a great deal; **aimer b.** to like very much; **s'intéresser b. à** to be very interested in; **b. de** (*livres etc*) many, a lot *ou* a great deal of; (*courage etc*) a lot *ou* a great deal of, much; **pas b. d'argent/***etc* not much money/*etc*; **j'en ai b.** (*quantité*) I have a lot; (*nombre*) I have lots *ou* many; **b. plus/moins** much more/less, a lot more/less (**que** than); (*nombre*) many *ou* a lot more/a lot fewer (**que** than); **b. trop** (*quantité*) much too much; (*nombre*) much too many; **beaucoup trop petit/etc** much too small/etc; **de b.** by far; **b. sont...** many are....

beau-fils [bofis] *nm* (*pl* **beaux-fils**) (*d'un précédent mariage*) stepson; (*gendre*) son-in-law. ● **beau-frère** *nm* (*pl* **beaux-frères**) brother-in-law. ● **beau-père** *nm* (*pl* **beaux-pères**) father-in-law; (*second mari de la mère*) stepfather.

beauté [bote] *nf* (*qualité, femme*) beauty; **institut** *ou* **salon de b.** beauty salon *ou* parlour; **en b.** (*gagner, finir etc*) magnificently; **être en b.** to look one's very best; **de toute b.** very beautiful.

beaux-arts [bozar] *nmpl* fine arts. ● **beaux-parents** *nmpl* parents-in-law.

bébé [bebe] *nm* baby; **b.-lion/etc** (*pl* **bébés-lions/etc**) baby lion/etc.

bébête [bebɛt] *a Fam* silly.

bec [bɛk] *nm* (*d'oiseau*) beak, bill; (*de cruche*) spout, lip; (*de plume*) nib; (*bouche*) *Fam* mouth; (*de flûte etc*) mouthpiece; **coup de b.** peck; **b. de gaz** gas lamp; **clouer le b. à qn** *Fam* to shut s.o. up; **tomber sur un b.** *Fam* to come up against a serious snag. ● **bec-de-cane** *nm* (*pl* **becs-de-cane**) door handle.

bécane [bekan] *nf Fam* bike.

bécarre [bekar] *nm* (*signe musical*) natural.

bécasse [bekas] *nf* (*oiseau*) woodcock; (*personne*) *Fam* simpleton.

bêche [bɛʃ] *nf* spade. ● **bêcher** [beʃe] *vt* **1** (*cultiver*) to dig. **2** (*critiquer*) to criticize; (*snober*) to snub. ● **bêcheur, -euse** *nmf* snob.

bécot [beko] *nm Fam* kiss. ● **bécoter** *vt, se bécoter vpr Fam* to kiss.

becquée [beke] *nf* beakful; **donner la b. à** (*oiseau, enfant*) to feed. ● **becqueter** *vt* (*picorer*) to peck (at); (*manger*) *Fam* to eat.

bedaine [bədɛn] *nf Fam* potbelly, paunch.

bedeau, -x [bədo] *nm* beadle, verger.

bedon [bədɔ̃] *nm Fam* potbelly, paunch. ● **bedonnant, -ante** *a* potbellied, paunchy.

bée [be] *af* **bouche b.** open-mouthed.

beffroi [befrwa] *nm* belfry.

bégayer [begeje] *vi* to stutter, stammer. ● **bégaiement(s)** *nm* stuttering, stammering.

bégonia [begɔnja] *nm* begonia.

bègue [bɛg] *nmf* stutterer, stammerer **ǁ** *a* **être b.** to stutter, stammer.

bégueule [begœl] *a* prudish **ǁ** *nf* prude.

béguin [begɛ̃] *nm* **avoir le b. pour qn** *Fam Vieilli* to have taken a fancy to s.o.

beige [bɛʒ] *a & nm* beige.

beignet [bɛɲɛ] *nm* (*pâtisserie*) fritter.

Beijing [beidʒiŋ] *nm ou f* Beijing.

bel [bɛl] *voir* **beau.**

bêler [bele] *vi* to bleat. ● **bêlement(s)** [bɛlmã] *nm(pl)* bleating.

belette [bəlɛt] *nf* weasel.

Belgique [bɛlʒik] *nf* Belgium. ● **belge** *a* Belgian **ǁ** *nmf* **B.** Belgian.

bélier [belje] *nm* (*animal, machine*) ram; **le B.** (*signe*) Aries.

belle [bɛl] *voir* **beau.**

belle-fille [bɛlfij] *nf* (*pl* **belles-filles**) (*d'un précédent mariage*) stepdaughter; (*épouse d'un fils*) daughter-in-law. ● **belle-mère** *nf* (*pl* **belles-mères**) mother-in-law; (*seconde épouse du père*) stepmother. ● **belle-sœur** *nf* (*pl* **belles-sœurs**) sister-in-law.

belligérant, -ante [beliʒerã, -ãt] *a & nm* belligerent.

belliqueux, -euse [bɛlikø, -øz] *a* (*enfant, ton etc*) aggressive; (*peuple etc*) warlike.

belvédère [bɛlveder] *nm* (*plate-forme ou terrasse sur une route*) viewing place, view-point.

bémol [bemɔl] *nm* (*signe musical*) flat.

bénédiction [benediksjɔ̃] *nf* blessing.

bénéfice [benefis] *nm* (*financier*) profit; (*avantage*) benefit; **b.** (*ecclésiastique*) living, benefice.

bénéficiaire [benefisjɛr] *nmf* beneficiary **ǁ** *a* (*opération, société etc*) profit-making; **marge/solde b.** profit margin/balance.

bénéficier [benefisje] *vi* **b. de** to benefit from, have the benefit of.

bénéfique [benefik] *a* beneficial.

Bénélux [benelyks] *nm* Benelux.

benêt [bənɛ] *nm* simpleton **ǁ** *am* simple-minded.

bénévole [benevɔl] *a & nmf* voluntary *ou* unpaid (worker).

bénin, -igne [benɛ̃, -iɲ] *a* (*tumeur, critique*) benign; (*accident, maladie*) minor.

bénir [benir] *vt* to bless; (*remercier, exalter*) to give thanks to. ● **bénit, -ite** *a* (*pain*) consecrated; **eau bénite** holy water.

bénitier [benitje] *nm* (holy-water) stoup.

benjamin, -ine [bɛ̃ʒamɛ̃, -in] *nmf* youngest child; (*sportif*) young junior.

benne [bɛn] *nf* (*de camion*) (movable) container; (*de grue*) scoop; (*à charbon*) tub, skip; (*de téléphérique*) cable car; **camion à b. basculante** dump truck; **b. à ordures** *Br* skip, *Am* Dumpster®.

béotien, -ienne [beɔsjɛ̃, -jɛn] *nmf* (*inculte*) philistine.

béquille [bekij] *nf* (*canne*) crutch; (*de moto*) stand.

bercail [bɛrkaj] *nm* (*famille etc*) *Hum* fold; **rentrer au b.** to return to the fold.

berceau, -x [bɛrso] *nm* cradle.

bercer [bɛrse] *vt* (*balancer*) to rock; (*apaiser*) to soothe, lull; (*leurrer*) to delude (de with); **se b. d'illusions** to delude oneself. ● **berceuse** *nf* lullaby.

béret [berɛ] *nm* beret.

berge [bɛrʒ] *nm* (*rive*) (raised) bank.

berger [bɛrʒe] *nm* **1** shepherd; **chien (de) b.** sheepdog. **2** *nm* **b. allemand** *Br* Alsatian (dog), *Am* German shepherd. ● **bergère** *nf* shepherdess. ● **bergerie** *nf* sheepfold.

berline [bɛrlin] *nf* (*voiture*) *Br* (four-door) saloon, *Am* sedan.

berlingot [bɛrlɛ̃go] *nm* (*bonbon aux fruits*)

Br boiled sweet, *Am* hard candy; (*à la menthe*) mint; (*emballage*) (milk) carton.
berlue [bɛrly] *nf* **avoir la b.** to be seeing *ou* imagining things.
bermuda [bɛrmyda] *nm* Bermuda shorts, Bermudas.
Bermudes [bɛrmyd] *nfpl* Bermuda.
berne (en) [ɑ̃bɛrn] *adv* (*drapeau*) at half-mast.
berner [bɛrne] *vt* to fool, hoodwink.
besogne [bəzɔɲ] *nf* job, task, work *inv*.
● **besogneux, -euse** *a* needy.
besoin [bəzwɛ̃] *nm* need; **avoir b. de** to need; **au b.** if necessary, if need be; **dans le b.** in need, needy; **faire ses besoins** to relieve oneself, go to the *Br* toilet *ou Am* lavatory.
bestial, -e, -aux [bɛstjal, -o] *a* bestial, brutish.
bestiaux [bɛstjo] *nmpl* livestock; (*bovins*) cattle.
bestiole [bɛstjɔl] *nf* (*insecte*) bug, *Br* creepy-crawly, *Am* creepy-crawler.
bétail [betaj] *nm* livestock; (*bovins*) cattle.
bête[1] [bɛt] *nf* animal; (*insecte*) bug, creature; **b. de somme** beast of burden; **b. à bon dieu** *Br* ladybird, *Am* ladybug; **b. noire** *Br* pet hate, *Am* pet peeve; **chercher la petite b.** (*critiquer*) to pick holes.
bête[2] [bɛt] *a* stupid, silly; **être b. comme ses pieds** *ou* **comme une oie** to be as stupid *ou* as silly as they come. ● **bêtement** *adv* stupidly; **tout b.** quite simply. ● **bêtise** [betiz] *nf* stupidity, silliness; (*action, parole*) stupid *ou* silly thing; (*bagatelle*) mere trifle.
béton [betɔ̃] *nm* concrete; **mur/etc en b.** concrete wall/etc; **b. armé** reinforced concrete. ● **bétonnière** *nf ou* **bétonneuse** *nf* cement *ou* concrete mixer.
betterave [bɛtrav] *nf* (*plante*) *Br* beetroot, *Am* beet; **b. sucrière** *ou* **à sucre** sugar beet.
beugler [bøgle] *vi* (*taureau*) to bellow; (*vache*) to moo; (*radio*) *Fig* to blare (out).
beur [bœr] *nm* = North African born in France of immigrant parents.
beurre [bœr] *nm* butter; **b. d'anchois** anchovy paste. ● **beurrer** *vt* to butter. ● **beurrier** *nm* butter dish.
beuverie [bøvri] *nf* drinking session, *Br* booze-up.
bévue [bevy] *nf* blunder, mistake.
biais [bjɛ] *nm* (*moyen détourné*) device, expedient; (*aspect*) angle; **regarder de b.** to look at sidelong; **traverser en b.** to cross at an angle.
biaiser [bjeze] *vi* to prevaricate, hedge.
bibelot [biblo] *nm* (small) ornament, trinket.
biberon [bibrɔ̃] *nm* (feeding) bottle; **nourrir au b.** to bottlefeed.
bible [bibl] *nf* bible; **la B.** the Bible. ● **biblique** *a* biblical.
bibliobus [biblijɔbys] *nm* mobile library.
bibliographie [biblijɔgrafi] *nf* bibliography.
bibliothèque [biblijɔtɛk] *nf* library; (*meuble*) bookcase; (*à la gare*) bookstall. ● **bibliothécaire** *nmf* librarian.

bic® [bik] *nm* ballpoint, *Br* biro®.
bicarbonate [bikarbɔnat] *nm* bicarbonate.
bicentenaire [bisɑ̃tnɛr] *nm* bicentenary, bicentennial.
biceps [bisɛps] *nm* (*muscle*) biceps.
biche [biʃ] *nf* doe, hind; **ma b.** (*ma chérie*) my pet.
bichonner [biʃɔne] *vt* (*personne*) to doll up; (*voiture etc*) to take loving care of.
bicolore [bikɔlɔr] *a* two-coloured.
bicoque [bikɔk] *nf Péj* shack, hovel.
bicyclette [bisiklɛt] *nf* bicycle; **la b.** (*sport*) cycling; **aller à b.** to cycle.
bide [bid] *nm* (*ventre*) *Fam* belly; **faire un b.** (*film, roman etc*) *Arg* to flop.
bidet [bidɛ] *nm* (*cuvette*) bidet.
bidon [bidɔ̃] **1** *nm* (*d'essence*) can; (*pour boissons*) canteen; (*ventre*) *Fam* belly. **2** *nm* **du b.** (*mensonge*) *Fam* bull, baloney ▌ *a inv* (*simulé*) *Fam* phoney, fake.
bidonner (se) [səbidɔne] *vpr Fam* to have a good laugh.
bidonville [bidɔ̃vil] *nf* shantytown.
bidule [bidyl] *nm* (*chose*) *Fam* whatsit, *Br* thingummy.
bielle [bjɛl] *nf* (*de moteur*) connecting rod.
bien [bjɛ̃] *adv* well; **il joue b.** he plays well; **je vais b.** I'm fine *ou* well; **b. fatigué/souvent/etc** (*très*) very tired/often/etc; **merci b.!** thanks very much!; **b.!** fine!, right!; **elle ferait b. de partir** she'd do well to leave; **tu as b. fait** you did right; **c'est b. fait (pour lui)** it serves him right; **b. du courage/etc** a lot of courage/etc; **b. des fois/des gens/etc** lots of *ou* many times/people/etc; **je l'ai b. dit** (*intensif*) I *did* say so; **c'est b. compris?** is that quite understood?; **c'est b. toi?** is it really you?
▌ *a inv* (*convenable*) all right, fine; (*agréable*) nice, fine; (*compétent, bon*) good, fine; (*à l'aise*) comfortable, fine; (*beau*) attractive; (*en forme*) well; (*moralement*) nice; **une fille b.** (*moralement*) a nice *ou* respectable girl; **ce n'est pas b. de mentir/etc** it's not nice *ou* right to lie/etc.
▌ *nm* (*avantage*) good; (*chose, capital*) possession; **ça te fera du b.** it will do you good; **pour ton b.** for your own good; **le b. et le mal** good and evil; **biens de consommation** consumer goods. ● **bien-aimé, -ée** *a* & *nmf* beloved. ● **bien-être** *nm* well-being. ● **bien-fondé** *nm* validity, soundness.
bienfaisance [bjɛ̃fəzɑ̃s] *nf* benevolence, charity; **œuvre de b.** charity, charitable *ou* benevolent organization; **fête de b.** charity fair *ou Br* fête.
bienfaisant, -ante [bjɛ̃fəzɑ̃, -ɑ̃t] *a* beneficial.
bienfait [bjɛ̃fɛ] *nm* (*générosité*) favour; (*remède, climat etc*) beneficial effect; **bienfaits** benefits, blessings.
bienfaiteur, -trice [bjɛ̃fɛtœr, -tris] *nmf* benefactor, benefactress.
bienheureux, -euse [bjɛ̃nœrø, -øz] *a* blessed, blissful.

biennal, -e, -aux [bjenal, -o] *a* biennial.

bien que [bjɛ̃k(ə)] *conj* (+ *sub*) although.

bienséant, -ante [bjɛ̃seɑ̃, -ɑ̃t] *a* proper. ● **bienséance** *nf* propriety.

bientôt [bjɛ̃to] *adv* soon; **à b.!** see you soon!; **il est b. dix heures/***etc* it's nearly ten o'clock/*etc*.

bienveillant, -ante [bjɛ̃vɛjɑ̃, -ɑ̃t] *a* kindly. ● **bienveillance** *nf* kindliness.

bienvenu, -ue [bjɛ̃vny] *a* welcome ▮ *nmf* **soyez le b.!** welcome!; **être le** *ou* **la bienvenu(e)** (*somme d'argent etc*) to be welcome. ● **bienvenue** *nf* welcome; **souhaiter la b. à** to welcome s.o.

bière [bjɛr] *nf* **1** (*boisson*) beer; **b. pression** *Br* draught beer, *Am* draft beer. **2** (*cercueil*) coffin.

biffer [bife] *vt* to cross *ou* strike out.

bifteck [biftɛk] *nm* steak; **gagner son b.** *Fam* to earn one's (daily) bread.

bifurquer [bifyrke] *vi* (*route etc*) to fork, branch off; (*véhicule*) to turn off, fork, branch off. ● **bifurcation** *nf* fork, junction.

bigame [bigam] *a* bigamous ▮ *nmf* bigamist. ● **bigamie** *nf* bigamy.

bigarré, -ée [bigare] *a* (*bariolé*) (*étoffe etc*) mottled; (*hétéroclite*) (*foule, société etc*) motley, mixed.

bigler [bigle] *vi* (*loucher*) *Fam* to squint ▮ *vti* **b. (sur)** *qn/qch* (*lorgner*) *Fam* to leer at s.o./ sth. ● **bigleux, -euse** *a* *Fam* cock-eyed.

bigorneau, -x [bigɔrno] *nm* (*coquillage*) winkle.

bigot, -ote [bigo, -ɔt] *nmf* *Péj* churchy person ▮ *a* *Péj* churchy, over-devout.

bigoudi [bigudi] *nm* (hair) curler *ou* roller.

bigrement [bigrəmɑ̃] *adv* *Fam* awfully.

bijou, -x [biʒu] *nm* jewel; (*ouvrage élégant*) *Fig* gem. ● **bijouterie** *nf* (*commerce*) *Br* jeweller's shop, *Am* jewelry shop; (*bijoux*) *Br* jewellery, *Am* jewelry. ● **bijoutier, -ière** *nmf* *Br* jeweller, *Am* jeweler.

bikini [bikini] *nm* bikini.

bilan [bilɑ̃] *nm* (*financier*) balance sheet; (*résultat*) outcome; (*d'un accident*) (casualty) toll; **b. de santé** checkup; **faire le b.** to make an assessment (**de**).

bilboquet [bilbɔkɛ] *nm* cup-and-ball (game).

bile [bil] *nf* bile; **se faire de la b.** *Fam* to worry, fret. ● **bilieux, -euse** *a* bilious.

bilingue [bilɛ̃g] *a* bilingual.

billard [bijar] *nm* (*jeu*) billiards; (*table*) billiard table; (*table d'opération*) *Fam* operating table; **b. électrique** pinball machine; **b. anglais** snooker; **b. américain** pool; **c'est du b.** *Fam* it's a cinch, it's as easy as can be.

bille [bij] *nf* (*d'enfant*) marble; (*de billard*) billiard ball; **stylo à b.** ballpoint (pen), *Br* biro®; **jouer aux billes** to play marbles.

billet [bijɛ] *nm* ticket; **b.** (**de banque**) *Br* (bank)note, *Am* bill; **b. aller, b. simple** *Br* single ticket, *Am* one-way ticket; **b. (d')aller et retour** *Br* return ticket, *Am* round trip ticket; **b. doux** love letter.

billion [biljɔ̃] *nm* trillion.

billot [bijo] *nm* (*de bois*) block.

bimensuel, -elle [bimɑ̃syɛl] *a* bimonthly, *Br* fortnightly.

bimoteur [bimɔtœr] *a* a twin-engined.

binaire [binɛr] *a* binary.

biner [bine] *vt* to hoe. ● **binette** *nf* hoe; (*visage*) *Arg* mug, face.

biochimie [bjɔʃimi] *nf* biochemistry. ● **biochimique** *a* biochemical.

biodégradable [bjɔdegradabl] *a* biodegradable.

biographie [bjɔgrafi] *nf* biography. ● **biographe** *nmf* biographer. ● **biographique** *a* biographical.

biologie [bjɔlɔʒi] *nf* biology. ● **biologique** *a* biological; (*légumes etc*) organic. ● **biologiste** *nm* biologist.

bip [bip] *nm* bleeper.

bipède [bipɛd] *nm* biped.

bique [bik] *nf* *Fam* nanny-goat.

Birmanie [birmani] *nf* Burma. ● **birman, -ane** *a* Burmese ▮ *nmf* **B., Birmane** Burmese.

bis¹ [bis] *adv* (*cri*) (*au théâtre etc*) encore; (*dans une chanson etc*) repeat; **4 bis** (*numéro*) 4A ▮ *nm* (*au théâtre etc*) encore.

bis², bise [bi, biz] *a* *Br* greyish-brown, *Am* grayish-brown.

bisbille [bisbij] *nf* squabble; **en b. avec qn** *Fam* at loggerheads with s.o.

biscornu, -ue [biskɔrny] *a* (*objet*) distorted, misshapen; (*idée*) cranky.

biscotte [biskɔt] *nf* (*pain*) Melba toast; (*pour bébé, de régime*) rusk, *Am* zwieback.

biscuit [biskɥi] *nm* (*sucré*) *Br* biscuit, *Am* cookie; (*salé*) *Br* biscuit, *Am* cracker; **b. de Savoie** sponge (cake). ● **biscuiterie** *nf* *Br* biscuit *ou* *Am* cookie factory.

bise [biz] *nf* **1** (*vent*) north wind. **2** (*baiser*) *Fam* kiss.

biseau, -x [bizo] *nm* bevel *ou* *Br* bevelled *ou* *Am* beveled edge; **en b.** *Br* bevelled, *Am* beveled.

bison [bizɔ̃] *nm* (American) buffalo, bison.

bisou [bizu] *nm* *Fam* kiss.

bisser [bise] *vt* (*musicien, acteur*) to encore.

bissextile [bisɛkstil] *a* **année b.** leap year.

bistouri [bisturi] *nm* scalpel, lancet.

bistre [bistr] *a* *inv* bistre, dark-brown.

bistro(t) [bistro] *nm* bar, café.

bitume [bitym] *nm* (*revêtement*) asphalt.

bivouac [bivwak] *nm* (*campement*) bivouac. ● **bivouaquer** *vi* (*camper*) to bivouac.

bizarre [bizar] *a* peculiar, odd, bizarre. ● **bizarrement** *adv* oddly, peculiarly. ● **bizarrerie** *nf* peculiarity.

blabla(bla) [blabla(bla)] *nm* claptrap, bunkum.

blafard, -arde [blafar, -ard] *a* pale, pallid.

blague [blag] *nf* **1** (*plaisanterie, farce*) *Fam* joke; (*absurdités*) *Fam* nonsense; **sans b.!** you're joking! **2 b. (à tabac)** (tobacco) pouch. ● **blaguer** *vi* to be joking ▮ *vt* **b. qn** *Fam* to tease s.o. ● **blagueur, -euse** *nmf* joker.

blair [blɛr] *nm* (*nez*) *Arg* snout, *Br* conk.

blairer

32

blairer [blere] vt je ne peux pas le b. Arg I can't stomach him.

blaireau, -x [blɛro] nm 1 (animal) badger. 2 (brosse) (shaving) brush.

blâme [blɑm] nm (critique) criticism; (réprimande) rebuke. ● **blâmable** a blameworthy. ● **blâmer** vt (critiquer) to criticize, blame; (réprimander) to rebuke.

blanc, blanche [blɑ̃, blɑ̃ʃ] 1 a white; (page etc) blank; **nuit blanche** sleepless night; **voix blanche** expressionless voice.

█ nmf (personne) white man ou woman.

█ nm (couleur) white; (de poulet) breast, white meat; (espace, interligne) blank; **b. (d'œuf)** (egg) white; **le b.** (linge) whites; **magasin de b.** Br linen shop, Am = store selling bedding etc; **laisser qch en b.** to leave sth blank; **chèque en b.** blank Br cheque ou Am check; **cartouche à b.** blank (cartridge); **tirer à b.** to fire a blank ou blanks; **chauffé à b.** white-hot; **saigner qn à b.** to bleed s.o. white.

2 nf (note de musique) Br minim, Am half-note. ● **blanchâtre** a whitish. ● **blancheur** nf whiteness.

blanchir [blɑ̃ʃir] vt to make white, whiten; (mur) to whitewash; (draps) to launder; (du chou etc) to blanch; (argent) Fig to launder; **b. qn** (disculper) to clear s.o. █ vi to turn white, whiten. ● **blanchissage** nm laundering. ● **blanchisserie** nf (lieu) laundry. ● **blanchisseur, -euse** nmf laundryman, laundrywoman.

blanquette [blɑ̃kɛt] nf b. de veau veal stew in white sauce.

blasé, -ée [blaze] a blasé.

blason [blazɔ̃] nm (écu) coat of arms; (science) heraldry.

blasphème [blasfɛm] nf blasphemy. ● **blasphématoire** a (propos) blasphemous. ● **blasphémer** vi to blaspheme.

blatte [blat] nf cockroach.

blazer [blazœr] nm blazer.

blé [ble] nm wheat, Br corn; (argent) Arg bread.

bled [blɛd] nm (village, ville etc) Péj Fam dump of a place.

blême [blɛm] a sickly pale, wan; **b. de colère** livid with anger.

blesser [blese] vt to injure, hurt; (avec un couteau, une balle etc) to wound; (offenser) to hurt, offend, wound; **se b. le** ou **au bras/** etc to hurt one's arm/etc. ● **blessant, -ante** a (parole, personne) hurtful. ● **blessé, -ée** nmf casualty, injured ou wounded person. ● **blessure** nf injury; (avec un couteau etc) wound.

blet, blette [blɛ, blɛt] a (poire etc) Litt overripe.

bleu, -e [blø] a (mpl bleus) blue; **b. de colère** blue in the face; **steak b.** (très saignant) very rare steak █ nm (pl -s) (couleur) blue; (contusion) bruise; (vêtement) Br overalls, Am overall; (nouvelle recrue) raw recruit; **bleus de travail** Br overalls, Am overall; **se faire un b. au**

genou/etc to bruise one's knee/etc. ● **bleuâtre** a bluish. ● **bleu ciel** a inv sky-blue. ● **bleuir** vti to turn blue. ● **bleuté, -ée** a bluish.

bleuet [bløɛ] nm cornflower.

blinder [blɛ̃de] vt (véhicule, abri etc) to armour(-plate). ● **blindé, -ée** a (voiture, train etc) armoured, armour-plated; **porte blindée** reinforced steel door; **une vitre blindée** bulletproof glass █ nm (char) armoured vehicle.

bloc [blɔk] nm (de pierre etc) block; (de papier) pad; (masse compacte) unit; (de pays, parti) bloc; en b. (démissionner etc) all together; **accepter/refuser qch en b.** to accept/refuse sth wholly ou outright; **à b.** (visser, serrer etc) tight, hard; **travailler à b.** Fam to work flat out. ● **bloc-notes** nm (pl blocs-notes) writing pad.

blocage [blɔkaʒ] nm (des roues) locking; (psychologique) mental block; **b. des prix** price freeze; **faire un b.** to have a mental block (par rapport à in).

blocus [blɔkys] nm blockade.

blond, -onde [blɔ̃, -ɔ̃d] a fair(-haired), blond █ nm fair-haired man; (couleur) blond █ nf fair-haired woman, blonde; (bière) blonde Br lager, light ou Br pale ale. ● **blondeur** nf fairness, blondness.

bloquer [blɔke] vt (obstruer) to block; (coincer) to jam; (roue) to lock; (freins) to slam ou jam on; (salaires, prix, crédits) to freeze; (grouper) to group together; (ville) to blockade; **bloqué par la neige/la glace** snowbound/icebound █ se **bloquer** vpr (mécanisme) to jam, stick; (roue) to lock.

blottir (se) [səblɔtir] vpr (dans un coin etc) to crouch; (dans son lit) to snuggle down; **se b. contre** to huddle up to, snuggle up to.

blouse [bluz] nf (tablier) smock, overall; (corsage) blouse. ● **blouson** nm Br windcheater, Am windbreaker.

blue-jean(s) [bludʒin(z)] nm jeans, denims.

bluff [blœf] nm bluff. ● **bluffer** vti to bluff.

boa [bɔa] nm (serpent, tour de cou) boa.

bobard [bɔbar] nm Fam fib, yarn, tall story.

bobine [bɔbin] nf (de fil, film etc) spool, Br reel; (pour machine à coudre) spool, bobbin; (électrique) coil.

bobo [bɔbo] nm (langage enfantin) hurt, pain; **j'ai b., ça fait b.** it hurts.

bocage [bɔkaʒ] nm Géog landscape of fields surrounded by hedges.

bocal, -aux [bɔkal, -o] nm glass jar; (à poissons) bowl.

bock [bɔk] nm (récipient) beer glass; (contenu) glass of beer.

body [bɔdi] nm (sous-vêtement) body stocking.

bœuf, pl -fs [bœf, bø] nm (animal) ox (pl oxen), bullock; (viande) beef.

bof! [bɔf] int (indifférence, doute etc) Fam don't know and don't care!, big deal!

bohème [bɔɛm] a & nmf bohemian. ● **bohémien, -ienne** a & nmf gipsy.

boire* [bwar] vt to drink; (absorber) to soak

up; (*paroles*) *Fig* to take *ou* drink in; **b. un coup** to have a drink; **offrir à b. à qn** to offer s.o. a drink; **b. à petits coups** to sip **I** *vi* to drink.

bois¹ [bwa] *voir* boire.

bois² [bwa] *nm* (*matière, forêt*) wood; (*de construction*) timber; (*gravure*) woodcut; **les b.** (*de cerf*) the antlers; (*flûte etc*) woodwind instruments; **en** *ou* **de b.** wooden; **b. de chauffage** firewood; **b. de lit** bedstead. ●**boisé, -ée** *a* wooded, woody. ●**boiserie(s)** *nf(pl)* Br panelling, *Am* paneling.

boisson [bwasɔ̃] *nf* drink.

boit [bwa] *voir* boire.

boîte [bwat] *nf* **1** box; (*de conserve*) Br tin, *Am* can; (*de bière*) can; **b. aux** *ou* **à lettres** letterbox; **mettre qn en b.** *Fam* to pull s.o.'s leg. **2** (*lieu de travail*) *Fam* place of work; (*entreprise*) *Fam* company, firm; (*bureau*) *Fam* office; **b. de nuit** nightclub. ●**boîtier** *nm* (*de montre etc*) case.

boiter [bwate] *vi* (*personne, cheval etc*) to limp. ●**boiteux, -euse** *a* (*personne etc*) lame; (*meuble*) wobbly; (*projet etc*) *Fig* shaky.

bol [bɔl] *nm* (*récipient*) bowl; **prendre un b. d'air** to get a breath of fresh air; *Fam* **avoir du b.** to be lucky; **coup de b.** *Fam* stroke of luck.

bolide [bɔlid] *nm* (*véhicule*) racing car, racer.

Bolivie [bɔlivi] *nf* Bolivia. ●**bolivien, -ienne** *a* Bolivian **I** *nmf* **B., Bolivienne** Bolivian.

bombarder [bɔ̃barde] *vt* (*ville etc*) to bomb; (*avec des obus*) to shell; **b. qn** *Fam* (*nommer*) to pitchfork s.o. (**à un poste** into a job); **b. de** (*questions*) to bombard with; (*objets*) to pelt with. ●**bombardement** *nm* bombing; (*avec des obus*) shelling. ●**bombardier** *nm* (*avion*) bomber.

bombe [bɔ̃b] *nf* **1** (*projectile*) bomb; (*de laque, peinture etc*) spray (can); **b. artisanale** homemade bomb; **faire l'effet d'une b.** *Fig* to be a bombshell, be totally unexpected; **faire la b.** *Fam* to have a binge. **2** (*chapeau*) riding hat *ou* cap.

bomber [bɔ̃be] **1** *vi* (*gonfler*) to bulge **I** *vt* **b. la poitrine** to throw out one's chest. **2** *vi* (*véhicule etc*) *Fam* to bomb *ou* Br belt along. **3** *vt* (*peindre*) to spray (*graffiti etc*). ●**bombé, -ée** *a* (*vitre etc*) rounded; (*route*) cambered.

bon¹, bonne [bɔ̃, bɔn] *a* **1** (*satisfaisant etc*) good; **avoir de bons résultats** to get good results.

2 (*agréable*) nice, good; **il fait b. se reposer** it's nice *ou* good to rest; **b. anniversaire!** happy birthday!; **bonne année!** Happy New Year!

3 (*charitable*) kind, good (**avec qn** to s.o.).

4 (*qui convient*) right; **le b. choix/moment/livre/etc** the right choice/moment/book/etc.

5 (*approprié, apte*) fit; **b. à manger** fit to eat; **b. pour le service** (*soldat*) fit for service; **ce n'est b. à rien** it's useless; **comme b. te semble** as you think fit *ou* best; **c'est b. à savoir** it's worth knowing.

6 (*prudent*) wise, good; **croire** *ou* **juger b. de**

partir/*etc* to think it wise *ou* good to leave/*etc*.

7 (*compétent*) good; **b. en français/etc** good at French/*etc*.

8 (*valable*) good; **ce billet est encore b.** this ticket is still good.

9 (*intensif*) **un b. moment** a good while; **dix bonnes minutes** a good ten minutes.

10 (*locutions*) **à quoi b.?** what's the use *ou* point *ou* good?; **pour de b.** really (and truly), in earnest; **tenir b.** to stand firm; **ah b.?** is that so?

11 *nm* **avoir du b.** to have some good points *ou* some merit; **les bons** the good.

I *adv* **sentir b.** to smell good; **il fait b.** it's nice (and warm).

bon² [bɔ̃] *nm* (*billet*) coupon, Br voucher; (*titre*) Fin bond; (*formulaire*) slip.

bonasse [bɔnas] *a* feeble, soft.

bonbon [bɔ̃bɔ̃] *nm* Br sweet, *Am* candy. ●**bonbonnière** *nf* Br sweet box, *Am* candy box.

bonbonne [bɔ̃bɔn] *nf* (*bouteille*) demijohn.

bond [bɔ̃] *nm* leap, bound; (*de balle*) bounce; **faire un b.** to leap (into the air); (*prix*) to shoot up; **se lever d'un b.** (*du lit*) to jump out of bed; (*d'une chaise*) to leap up; **faire faux b. à qn** to stand s.o. up, let s.o. down (*by not turning up*).

bonde [bɔ̃d] *nf* (*bouchon*) plug; (*trou*) plug-hole.

bondé, -ée *a* packed, crammed.

bondir [bɔ̃dir] *vi* to leap, bound.

bonheur [bɔnœr] *nm* happiness; (*chance*) good luck, good fortune; **par b.** luckily; **au petit b.** haphazardly.

bonhomie [bɔnɔmi] *nf* good-heartedness.

bonhomme, *pl* **bonshommes** [bɔnɔm, bɔ̃zɔm] **1** *nm* fellow, guy; **b. de neige** snowman; **aller son petit b. de chemin** to go along *ou* jog along in one's own sweet way. **2** *a inv* good-hearted.

boniment(s) [bɔnimɑ̃] *nm(pl)* (*bobard*) clap-trap; (*baratin*) patter.

bonjour [bɔ̃ʒur] *nm & int* good morning; (*après-midi*) good afternoon; **donner le b. à qn, dire b. à qn** to say hello to s.o.

bonne¹ [bɔn] *voir* bon¹.

bonne² [bɔn] *nf* (*domestique*) maid; **b. d'enfants** nanny.

bonnement [bɔnmɑ̃] *adv* **tout b.** simply.

bonnet [bɔnɛ] *nm* (*de ski, douche etc*) cap; (*de femme, d'enfant*) hat, bonnet; (*de soutien-gorge*) cup; **gros b.** *Fam* bigshot, bigwig; **b. d'âne** Br dunce's cap, *Am* dunce cap. ●**bonneterie** *nf* hosiery.

bonsoir [bɔ̃swar] *nm & int* (*en rencontrant qn*) good evening; (*en quittant qn*) goodbye; (*au coucher*) good night.

bonté [bɔ̃te] *nf* kindness, goodness.

bonus [bɔnys] *nm* no claims bonus (*for car driver*).

boom [bum] *nm* (*économique*) boom.

bord [bɔr] *nm* (*rebord*) edge; (*rive*) bank; (*de vêtement*) border; (*de chapeau*) brim; (*de *verre*) rim, brim, edge; **au b. de la mer/route** at *ou* by the seaside/roadside; **b. du trottoir** *Br* kerb, *Am* curb; **au b. de** (*précipice, désespoir, ruine etc*) on the brink *ou* verge of; **au b. des larmes** on the verge of tears; **à bord d'un bateau/d'un avion** on board a boat/a plane; **monter à b.** to go on board; **être le seul maître à b.** (*bateau, entreprise etc*) to be the one in charge; **jeter par-dessus b.** to throw overboard.

bordeaux [bɔrdo] **1** *nm* (*vin*) Bordeaux (wine); (*rouge*) claret. **2** *a inv* maroon.

bordée [bɔrde] *nf* (*salve*) *Nau* broadside; (*d'injures*) *Fig* torrent, volley.

bordel [bɔrdɛl] *nm* **1** *Fam* brothel. **2** (*désordre*) *Fam* mess.

border [bɔrde] *vt* (*lit, personne*) to tuck in; (*vêtement*) to edge; **b. la rue/etc** (*maisons, arbres etc*) to line the street/etc.

bordereau, -x [bɔrdəro] *nm* (*relevé*) docket, statement; (*formulaire*) note.

bordure [bɔrdyr] *nf* border; **en b. de** bordering on.

borgne [bɔrɲ] *a* (*personne*) one-eyed, blind in one eye; (*hôtel etc*) *Fig* shady.

borne [bɔrn] *nf* (*pierre*) boundary mark; *Él* terminal; **bornes** (*limites*) *Fig* bounds; **b. kilométrique** = milestone; **dépasser** *ou* **franchir les bornes** to go too far.

borner [bɔrne] *vt* (*limiter*) to confine; **se b. à** to confine oneself to. ●**borné, -ée** *a* (*personne*) narrow-minded; (*intelligence*) narrow, limited.

Bosnie [bɔzni] *nf* Bosnia.

bosquet [bɔskɛ] *nm* grove, thicket, copse.

bosse [bɔs] *nf* (*dans le dos*) hump; (*enflure*) bump, lump; (*de terrain*) bump; **avoir la b. des langues/des maths/etc** *Fam* to have a flair for languages/*Br* maths *ou* *Am* math/etc; **il a roulé sa b.** *Fam* he's been around, *Br* he's knocked about the world.

bossu, -ue [bɔsy] *a* hunchbacked; **dos b.** hunchback ▮ *nmf* (*personne*) hunchback.

bosseler [bɔsle] *vt* (*déformer*) to dent; (*orfèvrerie*) to emboss.

bosser [bɔse] *vi Fam* to work (hard).

bot [bo] *am* **pied b.** clubfoot.

botanique [bɔtanik] *a* botanical ▮ *nf* botany.

botte [bɔt] *nf* **1** (*chaussure*) boot. **2** (*de fleurs, radis etc*) bunch. ●**botter** *vt* (*ballon etc*) *Fam* to boot. ●**bottier** *nm* bootmaker. ●**bottillon** *nm ou* **bottine** *nf* (*ankle*) boot.

Bottin® [bɔtɛ̃] *nm* phone book.

bouc [buk] *nm* billy goat; (*barbe*) goatee; **b. émissaire** scapegoat.

boucan [bukɑ̃] *nm Fam* din, racket, row.

bouche [buʃ] *nf* mouth; **faire la petite** *ou* **fine b.** *Péj* to turn up one's nose; **une fine b.** a gourmet; **b. de métro** métro entrance; **b. d'égout** drain opening, manhole; **b. d'incendie** fire hydrant; **le b.-à-bouche** the kiss of life. ●**bouchée** *nf* mouthful.

boucher¹ [buʃe] **1** *vt* (*évier, nez, gouttière etc*) to stop up, block (up); (*bouteille*) to cork; (*vue, rue, artère*) to block; **se b. le nez**

to hold one's nose. ●**bouché, -ée** *a* (*vin*) bottled; (*temps*) overcast; (*personne*) *Fig* stupid, dense. ●**bouche-trou** *nm* stopgap.

boucher² [buʃe] *nm* butcher. ●**boucherie** *nf* butcher's (shop); (*carnage*) butchery.

bouchon [buʃɔ̃] *nm* **1** stopper, top; (*de liège*) cork; (*de tube, bidon*) cap, top; (*de canne à pêche*) float. **2** (*embouteillage*) traffic jam.

boucle [bukl] *nf* **1** (*de ceinture*) buckle; (*de fleuve, route*) & *Av* loop; (*de ruban*) bow; **b. d'oreille** earring. **2** **b.** (*de cheveux*) curl.

boucler [bukle] **1** *vt* (*attacher*) to fasten, buckle; (*travail etc*) to finish off; (*enfermer, fermer*) *Fam* to lock up, shut; (*budget*) to balance; (*circuit*) to lap; (*encercler*) to surround, cordon off; **b. la boucle** *Av* to loop the loop; **b. ses valises** (*se préparer à partir*) to get ready to leave; **boucle-la!** *Fam* shut up! **2** *vt* (*cheveux*) to curl ▮ *vi* to be curly. ●**bouclé, -ée** *a* (*cheveux*) curly.

bouclier [buklije] *nm* shield.

bouddhiste [budist] *a & nmf* Buddhist.

bouder [bude] *vi* to sulk ▮ *vt* (*personne, plaisirs etc*) to steer clear of. ●**bouderie** *nf* sulkiness. ●**boudeur, -euse** *a* sulky, moody.

boudin [budɛ̃] *nm Br* black pudding, *Am* blood sausage.

boue [bu] *nf* mud. ●**boueux, -euse** **1** *a* muddy. **2** *nm Br* dustman, *Am* garbage collector.

bouée [bwe] *nf* buoy; **b. de sauvetage** lifebuoy; **b.** (*gonflable*) (*d'enfant*) (inflatable) rubber ring.

bouffe [buf] *nf Fam* food, grub, *Br* nosh. ●**bouffer¹** *vti* (*manger*) *Fam* to eat.

bouffée [bufe] *nf* (*de fumée*) puff; (*de parfum*) whiff; (*d'orgueil, etc*) burst, fit; **b. de chaleur** (*malaise*) hot flush.

bouffer² [bufe] *vi* (*cheveux, jupe etc*) to puff out. ●**bouffant, -ante** *a* **manche bouffante** puff(ed) sleeve. ●**bouffi, -ie** *a* (*yeux, visage etc*) puffy.

bouffon, -onne [bufɔ̃, -ɔn] *a* farcical ▮ *nm* buffoon. ●**bouffonneries** *nfpl* antics, buffoonery.

bouge [buʒ] *nm* (*bar*) dive; (*taudis*) hovel.

bougeoir [buʒwar] *nm* candlestick.

bougeotte [buʒɔt] *nf* **avoir la b.** *Fam* to have the fidgets.

bouger [buʒe] *vi* to move; (*agir*) to stir; (*rétrécir*) to shrink ▮ *vt* to move ▮ **se bouger** *vpr Fam* to move.

bougie [buʒi] *nf* candle; (*pour moteur*) *Aut* sparking *ou* spark plug, *Am* spark plug.

bougon, -onne [bugɔ̃, -ɔn] *a Fam* grumpy ▮ *nmf* grumbler, grouch. ●**bougonner** *vi Fam* to grumble, grouch.

bougre [bugr] *nm* fellow, *Br* bloke; (*enfant méchant*) (little) devil. ●**bougrement** *adv* (*déçu etc*) *Arg* damned; **il l'a b. mérité** he damned deserved it.

bouillabaisse [bujabɛs] *nf* fish soup.

bouillie [buji] *nf* porridge; (*pour bébé*) cereal; **réduire qch/***Fam* **qn en b.** to crush sth/*Fam* s.o. to a pulp.

bouillir* [bujir] *vi* to boil; **b. à gros bouillons** to bubble, boil hard; **faire b. qch** to boil sth; **b. de colère/d'impatience/**etc to be seething with anger/impatience/etc. ● **bouillant, -ante** *a* (*aliment*) *Fam* filling, stodgy.

bouilloire [bujwar] *nf* kettle.

bouillon [bujɔ̃] *nm* (*aliment*) broth, stock; (*bulles*) bubbles. ● **bouillonner** *vi* to bubble.

bouillotte [bujɔt] *nf* hot water bottle.

boulanger, -ère [bulɑ̃ʒe, -ɛr] *nmf* baker. ● **boulangerie** *nf* baker's (shop).

boule [bul] *nf* (*sphère*) ball; **boules** (*jeu*) bowls; **b. de neige** snowball; **se mettre en b.** (*chat etc*) to curl up into a ball; (*en colère*) *Fam* to fly off the handle; **faire b. de neige** (*grossir*) to snowball; **perdre la b.** *Fam* to go round the bend, go out of one's mind; **boules Quiès®** earplugs.

bouleau, -x [bulo] *nm* (silver) birch.

bouledogue [buldɔg] *nm* bulldog.

boulet [bulɛ] *nm* (*de forçat*) ball and chain; **b. de canon** cannonball.

boulette [bulɛt] *nf* (*de papier*) ball, pellet; (*de viande*) meatball; (*gaffe*) *Fam* blunder.

boulevard [bulvar] *nm* boulevard.

bouleverser [bulvɛrse] *vt* (*déranger*) to turn upside down; (*émouvoir*) to upset (greatly), distress; (*vie de qn, pays*) to disrupt. ● **bouleversant, -ante** *a* upsetting, distressing. ● **bouleversement** *nm* upheaval.

boulimique [bulimik] *a* **être b.** to be a compulsive eater.

boulon [bulɔ̃] *nm* bolt.

boulot¹ [bulo] *nm* (*emploi*) *Fam* job.

boulot², -otte [bulo, -ɔt] *a* dumpy, plump.

boum [bum] **1** *int* & *nm* bang. **2** *nf* (*surprise-partie*) *Fam* party.

bouquet [bukɛ] *nm* (*de fleurs*) bunch, bouquet; (*d'arbres*) clump; (*de vin*) bouquet; (*crevette*) prawn; (*de feu d'artifice*) grand finale; **c'est le b.!** that's the last straw!

bouquin [bukɛ̃] *nm Fam* book. ● **bouquiner** *vti Fam* to read. ● **bouquiniste** *nmf* second-hand bookseller.

bourbeux, -euse [burbø, -øz] *a* muddy. ● **bourbier** *nm* (*lieu, Fig situation*) quagmire, morass.

bourde [burd] *nf* blunder, *Br* bloomer.

bourdon [burdɔ̃] *nm* (*insecte*) bumblebee. ● **bourdonner** *vi* to buzz, hum. ● **bourdonnement** *nm* buzzing, humming.

bourg [bur] *nm* (*small*) market town. ● **bourgade** *nf* (large) village.

bourgeois, -oise [burʒwa, -waz] *a* & *nmf* middle-class (person); *Péj* bourgeois. ● **bourgeoisie** *nf* middle class; *Pol* bourgeoisie.

bourgeon [burʒɔ̃] *nm* bud. ● **bourgeonner** *vi* to bud; (*nez etc*) *Fam* to be pimply.

bourgmestre [burgmɛstr] *nm* (*en Belgique, Suisse*) burgomaster.

bourgogne [burgɔɲ] *nm* (*vin*) Burgundy.

bourlinguer [burlɛ̃ge] *vi* (*voyager*) *Fam* to get around, *Br* knock about.

bourrade [burad] *nf* (*du coude etc*) shove.

bourrage [buraʒ] *nm* **b. de crâne** brainwashing.

bourrasque [burask] *nf* squall, gust of wind.

bourratif, -ive [buratif, -iv] *a* (*aliment*) *Fam* filling, stodgy.

bourreau, -x [buro] *nm* executioner; **b. d'enfants** child batterer; **b. de travail** workaholic.

bourrelet [burlɛ] *nm* weather strip; **b. de graisse** roll of fat, *Hum* spare *Br* tyre *ou Am* tire.

bourrer [bure] **1** *vt* to stuff, cram (**de** with); (*pipe*) to fill; (*coussin*) to stuff, fill; **b. qn de coups** to thrash s.o.; **b. le crâne à qn** to brainwash s.o. **2 se bourrer** *vpr* (*s'enivrer*) *Fam* to get plastered. ● **bourré, -ée** *a* (*ivre*) *Fam* plastered.

bourrique [burik] *nf* (she-)ass.

bourru, -ue [bury] *a* surly, rough.

bourse [burs] *nf* (*sac*) purse; (*d'études*) *Br* grant, scholarship; **la B.** the Stock Exchange *ou* Market; **sans b. délier** without spending a penny. ● **boursier, -ière 1** *a* **opération/**etc **boursière** Stock Exchange *ou* Market transaction/etc. **2** *nmf* (*élève, étudiant*) *Br* grant holder, scholar.

boursouflé, -ée [bursufle] *a* (*visage etc*) puffy; (*style*) *Fig* inflated.

bousculer [buskyle] *vt* (*heurter, pousser*) to jostle; (*presser*) to rush, push; **b. qch** (*renverser*) to knock sth over; **b. les habitudes/**etc to turn one's habits/etc upside down. ● **bousculade** *nf* jostling, rush.

bouse [buz] *nf* **une b. (de vache)** a cowpat; **de la b. (de vache)** cow dung.

bousiller [buzije] *vt Fam* to mess up, wreck.

boussole [busɔl] *nf* compass.

bout [bu] *nm* end; (*de langue, canne, doigt*) tip; (*de papier, pain, ficelle*) bit; **un b. de temps/chemin** a little while/way; **au b. d'un moment** after a while; **jusqu'au b.** (*lire, rester etc*) (right) to the end; **à b. (de forces)** exhausted; **à b. de souffle** out of breath; **à b. de bras** at arm's length; **pousser qn à b.** to try s.o.'s patience, exasperate s.o.; **venir à b. de** (*travail*) to get through; (*adversaire*) to get the better of; **à tout b. de champ** at every turn, every minute; **à b. portant** point-blank.

boutade [butad] *nf* (*plaisanterie*) quip, witticism.

boute-en-train [butɑ̃trɛ̃] *nm inv* (*personne*) live wire.

bouteille [butɛj] *nf* bottle; (*de gaz*) cylinder.

bouteur [butœr] *nm* bulldozer.

boutique [butik] *nf* shop; (*d'un grand couturier*) boutique. ● **boutiquier, -ière** *nmf Péj* shopkeeper.

boutoir [butwar] *nm* **coup de b.** staggering blow.

bouton [butɔ̃] *nm* (*bourgeon*) bud; (*au visage etc*) pimple, spot; (*de vêtement*) button; (*poussoir*) (push-)button; (*de porte, de télévision*) knob; **b. de manchette** cuff link.

●**bouton-d'or** *nm* (*pl* **boutons-d'or**) buttercup. ●**bouton-pression** *nm* (*pl* **boutons-pression**) *Br* press-stud, *Am* snap (fastener). ●**boutonner** *vt*, **se boutonner** *vpr* to button (up).

boutonneux, -euse [butɔnø, -øz] *a* pimply, spotty.

boutonnière [butɔnjɛr] *nf* buttonhole.

bouture [butyr] *nf* (*plante*) cutting.

bouvreuil [buvrœj] *nm* (*oiseau*) bullfinch.

bovin, -ine [bɔvɛ̃, -in] *a* bovine. ●**bovins** *nmpl* cattle.

bowling [boliŋ] *nm* bowling, *Br* tenpin bowling, *Am* tenpins; (*lieu*) bowling alley.

box, *pl* **boxes** [bɔks] *nm* (*garage*) individual *ou Br* lockup garage; (*d'écurie*) (loose) box; (*de dortoir*) cubicle; (*des accusés*) dock.

boxe [bɔks] *nf* boxing. ●**boxer** *vi Sport* to box **I** *vt Fam* to whack, punch. ●**boxeur** *nm* boxer.

boyau, -x [bwajo] *nm* (*intestin*) gut; (*corde*) catgut; (*de bicyclette*) (racing) tyre *ou Am* tire.

boycotter [bɔjkɔte] *vt* to boycott. ●**boycottage** *nm* boycott.

BP [bepe] *nf abrév* (*boîte postale*) PO Box.

bracelet [braslɛ] *nm* bracelet, bangle; (*de montre*) *Br* strap, *Am* band.

braconner [brakɔne] *vi* to poach. ●**braconnier** *nm* poacher.

brader [brade] *vt* to sell off cheaply. ●**braderie** *nf* open-air (clearance) sale.

braguette [bragɛt] *nf* (*de pantalon*) fly, *Br* flies.

braille [braj] *nm* Braille; **en b.** in Braille.

brailler [braje] *vti* to bawl. ●**braillard, -arde** *a* bawling.

braire* [brɛr] *vi* (*âne*) to bray.

braise(s) [brɛz] *nf(pl)* embers, live coals. ●**braiser** [breze] *vt* (*viande etc*) to braise.

brancard [brãkar] *nm* (*civière*) stretcher; (*de charrette*) shaft. ●**brancardier** *nm* stretcher-bearer.

branche [brãʃ] *nf* (*d'arbre, d'une science etc*) branch; (*de compas*) leg, arm; (*de lunettes*) side (piece). ●**branchages** *nmpl* (*cut ou fallen*) branches.

branché, -ée [brãʃe] *a* (*informé, à la mode*) *Fam* with it, trendy.

brancher [brãʃe] *vt* (*lampe etc*) to plug in; (*installer*) to connect. ●**branchement** *nm* (*électrique*) connection.

brandir [brãdir] *vt* to brandish, flourish.

brandon [brãdɔ̃] *nm* (*paille, bois*) firebrand.

branle [brãl] *nm* impetus; **mettre qch en b.** to set sth in motion. ●**branle-bas** *nm inv* turmoil. ●**branler** *vi* to be shaky, shake. ●**branlant, -ante** *a* (*table etc*) wobbly, shaky.

braquer [brake] **1** *vt* (*arme etc*) to point, aim (**sur** at); (*yeux*) to fix; **b. qn** (*irriter*) to antagonize s.o.; **b. qn contre qn** to set *ou* turn s.o. against s.o. **2** *vi* (*en voiture*) to turn the steering wheel, steer. ●**braquage** *nm* (*de roues*) steering; **rayon de b.** turning circle.

bras [bra] *nm* arm; **en b. de chemise** in one's shirtsleeves; **b. dessus b. dessous** arm in arm; **à b. ouverts** with open arms; **se retrouver avec qch/qn sur les b.** *Fig* to be left with sth/s.o. on one's hands; **son b. droit** *Fig* his right-hand man; **à tour de b.** with all one's might; **faire un** *ou* **le b. d'honneur** *Fam* to make an obscene gesture (**à qn** to s.o.); **prendre** *ou* **attraper qn à b.-le-corps** to seize *ou* grasp s.o. round the waist.

brasier [brazje] *nm* blaze, inferno.

brassard [brasar] *nm* armband.

brasse [bras] *nf* (*nage*) breaststroke; (*mesure*) fathom; **b. papillon** butterfly stroke.

brassée [brase] *nf* armful.

brasser [brase] *vt* to mix; (*bière*) to brew. ●**brassage** *nm* mixture; (*de bière*) brewing. ●**brasserie** *nf* (*usine*) brewery; (*café*) brasserie.

brasseur [brasœr] *nm* **b. d'affaires** big businessman.

brassière [brasjɛr] *nf* (*de bébé*) *Br* vest, *Am* undershirt.

bravache [bravaʃ] *nm* braggart.

bravade [bravad] *nf* **par b.** out of bravado.

brave [brav] *a & nm* (*hardi*) brave (man); (*honnête*) good (man). ●**bravement** *adv* bravely.

braver [brave] *vt* (*règles, ordres etc*) to defy; (*danger*) to brave, defy.

bravo [bravo] *int* well done, *Br* good show **I** *nm* cheer.

bravoure [bravur] *nf* bravery.

break [brɛk] *nm Br* estate car, *Am* station wagon.

brebis [brəbi] *nf* ewe; **b. galeuse** (*indésirable*) black sheep.

brèche [brɛʃ] *nf* gap, breach; **battre en b.** (*attaquer*) to attack (mercilessly).

bredouille [brəduj] *a* **rentrer b.** to come back empty-handed.

bredouiller [brəduje] *vti* to mumble.

bref, brève [brɛf, brɛv] *a* brief, short **I** *adv* (**enfin**) **b.** in a word.

breloque [brəlɔk] *nf* charm, trinket.

Brésil [brezil] *nm* Brazil. ●**brésilien, -ienne** *a* Brazilian **I** *nmf* **B., Brésilienne** Brazilian.

Bretagne [brətaɲ] *nf* Brittany. ●**breton, -onne** *a* Breton **I** *nmf* **B., Bretonne** Breton.

bretelle [brətɛl] *nf* strap; (*route d'accès*) access road; (*sortie d'autoroute*) *Br* exit road, *Am* exit ramp; **bretelles** (*pour pantalon*) *Br* braces, *Am* suspenders.

breuvage [brœvaʒ] *nm* drink, brew.

brève [brɛv] *voir* **bref.**

brevet [brəvɛ] *nm* diploma; **b. des collèges** = *Br* GCSE (*examination for 16-year-olds*); **b.** (**d'invention**) patent. ●**breveter** *vt* to patent. ●**breveté, -ée** *a* (*technicien*) qualified.

bréviaire [brevjɛr] *nm Rel* breviary.

bribes [brib] *nfpl* scraps, bits.

bric-à-brac [brikabrak] *nm inv* bric-à-brac, jumble, junk.

bricole [brikɔl] *nf* (*objet, futilité*) trifle.

bricoler [brikɔle] *vi* to do odd jobs **I** *vt* (*réparer*) to patch up; (*fabriquer*) to put together. ●**bricolage** nm (passe-temps) do-it-yourself; (petits travaux) odd jobs; **salon/rayon du b.** do-it-yourself exhibition/department. ●**bricoleur, -euse** nmf handyman, handywoman.

bride [brid] nf (de cheval) bridle; **à b. abattue** at full gallop. ●**brider** vt (cheval) to bridle; (personne, désir) to curb; (poulet) to truss; **avoir les yeux bridés** to have slanting eyes.

bridge [bridʒ] nm (jeu) bridge.

brièvement [brievmɑ̃] adv briefly. ●**brièveté** nf shortness, brevity.

brigade [brigad] nf (de gendarmerie) squad; (de soldats) brigade; **b. des mœurs** vice squad. ●**brigadier** nm (de police) police sergeant; (dans l'armée) corporal.

brigand [brigɑ̃] nm robber; (enfant) rascal.

briguer [brige] vt (honneur, poste etc) to covet; (faveurs, suffrages) to court.

brillant, -ante [brijɑ̃, -ɑ̃t] a (luisant) shining; (astiqué) shiny; (couleur) bright; (doué, remarquable) Fig brilliant ▮ nm shine; (de couleur) brightness; (de conversation etc) Fig brilliance; (diamant) diamond. ●**brillamment** adv brilliantly.

briller [brije] vi to shine; **ses yeux brillaient de colère/etc** his eyes shone with anger/etc; **faire b.** (meuble etc) to polish (up).

brimer [brime] vt to bully. ●**brimade** nf (entre élèves) bullying, Br ragging, Am hazing; (humiliation) Fig vexation.

brin [brɛ̃] nm (d'herbe) blade; (de corde, fil) strand; (de muguet) spray; **un b. de** Fig a bit of.

brindille [brɛ̃dij] nf twig.

bringue [brɛ̃g] nf **faire la b.** Fam to go on a binge, have a wild time.

bringuebaler [brɛ̃gbale] vi (objets dans un véhicule) to shake about (all over the place); (véhicule) to rattle along.

brio [brijo] nm (virtuosité) brilliance.

brioche [brijɔʃ] nf **1** (pâtisserie) brioche (light sweet bun). **2** (ventre) Fam paunch.

brique [brik] nf brick; (de lait, jus de fruit) carton.

briquer [brike] vt to polish (up).

briquet [brike] nm (cigarette) lighter.

brise [briz] nf breeze.

briser [brize] vt to break; (en morceaux) to smash, break; (espoir, carrière) to wreck, shatter; (fatiguer) to exhaust ▮ **se briser** vpr to break. ●**brisants** nmpl reefs. ●**brise-lames** nm inv breakwater.

britannique [britanik] a British ▮ nmf B. Briton, British subject; **les Britanniques** the British.

broc [bro] nm pitcher, jug.

brocanteur, -euse [brɔkɑ̃tœr, -øz] nmf secondhand dealer (in furniture etc).

broche [brɔʃ] nf (pour rôtir) spit; (bijou) brooch; (pour fracture) pin; **faire cuire à la b.** to cook on a spit. ●**brochette** nf (tige) skewer; (plat) kebab.

broché, -ée [brɔʃe] a **livre b.** paperback;

édition brochée paperback edition.

brochet [brɔʃɛ] nm (poisson) pike.

brochure [brɔʃyr] nf brochure, booklet, pamphlet.

brocolis [brɔkɔli] nmpl broccoli.

broder [brɔde] vt to embroider (de with). ●**broderie** nf embroidery; **faire de la b.** to embroider.

broncher [brɔ̃ʃe] vi (bouger) to budge; (reculer) to flinch; (protester, regimber) to balk.

bronches [brɔ̃ʃ] nfpl bronchial tubes. ●**bronchite** nf bronchitis; **avoir une b.** to have bronchitis.

bronze [brɔ̃z] nm bronze.

bronzer [brɔ̃ze] vt to tan; **se (faire) b.** to sunbathe, get a (sun)tan ▮ vi to get (sun)tanned. ●**bronzage** nm (sun)tan, Br sunburn.

brosse [brɔs] nf brush; **donner un coup de b. à qch** to give sth a brush; **b. à dents** toothbrush; **cheveux en b.** crew cut. ●**brosser** vt to brush; **b. un tableau de** to give an outline of; **se b. les dents/les cheveux** to brush one's teeth/one's hair.

brouette [brwɛt] nf wheelbarrow.

brouhaha [bruaa] nm hubbub.

brouillard [brujar] nm fog; **il y a du b.** it's foggy.

brouille [bruj] nf disagreement, quarrel. ●**brouiller**[1] vt (amis) to cause a split between ▮ **se brouiller** vpr to fall out (avec with).

brouiller[2] [bruje] vt (papiers, idées etc) to mix up; (œufs) to scramble; (émission radio) to jam; **b. la vue à qn** to blur s.o.'s vision ▮ **se brouiller** vpr (idées) to be ou get confused; (temps) to cloud over; (vue) to get blurred.

brouillon[1] [brujɔ̃] nm rough draft.

brouillon[2], **-onne** [brujɔ̃, -ɔn] a (confus) disorganized, unmethodical.

broussailles [brusaj] nfpl bushes, undergrowth.

brousse [brus] nf **la b.** the bush.

brouter [brute] vti to graze.

broyer [brwaje] vt to grind; (doigt, bras) to crush; **b. du noir** to be (down) in the dumps.

bru [bry] nf daughter-in-law.

brugnon [brynɔ̃] nm (fruit) nectarine.

bruine [bruin] nf drizzle. ●**bruiner** v imp to drizzle; **il bruine** it's drizzling.

bruissement [bruismɑ̃] nm (de feuilles) rustle, rustling.

bruit [brui] nm noise, sound; (nouvelle) rumour; **faire du b.** to make a noise. ●**bruitage** nm (de cinéma) sound effects.

brûlant, -ante [brylɑ̃, -ɑ̃t] a (objet, soleil, soupe etc) burning (hot); (sujet) Fig red-hot.

brûlé, -ée [bryle] **1** nm **odeur de b.** smell of burning. **2** a **cerveau b.**, **tête brûlée** hothead.

brûle-pourpoint (à) [abrylpurpwɛ̃] adv (dire etc) point-blank.

brûler [bryle] vt to burn; (consommer) to use up, burn (gas, electricity etc); (signal, station) to go through (without stopping); **b. un feu (rouge)** to go through ou jump the lights; **ce désir le brûlait** this desire consumed him ▮ vi to burn; **b. (d'envie) de faire qch** to be dying to do sth; **ça brûle** (*temps*) it's baking *ou* scorching ‖ **se brûler** *vpr* to burn oneself.

brûlure [brylyr] *nf* burn; **brûlures d'estomac** heartburn.

brume [brym] *nf* mist, haze. ● **brumeux, -euse** *a* misty, hazy; (*obscur*) Fig hazy.

brun, brune [brœ̃, bryn] *a* brown; (*cheveux*) dark, brown; (*personne*) dark-haired ‖ *nm* (*couleur*) brown ‖ *nmf* dark-haired person. ● **brunette** *nf* brunette. ● **brunir** *vt* (*peau*) to tan ‖ *vi* to turn brown; (*cheveux*) to get *ou* go darker.

brushing [brœʃiŋ] *nm* blow-dry; **faire un b. à qn** to blow-dry s.o.'s hair.

brusque [brysk] *a* (*manière, personne etc*) abrupt, blunt; (*subit*) sudden, abrupt. ● **brusquement** *adv* suddenly, abruptly. ● **brusquer** *vt* to rush. ● **brusquerie** *nf* abruptness, bluntness.

brut, brute [bryt] *a* (*pétrole*) crude; (*diamant*) rough; (*sucre*) unrefined; (*soie*) raw; (*poids, revenu*) gross.

brutal, -e, -aux [brytal, -o] *a* (*violent*) savage, brutal; (*enfant*) rough; (*franchise, réponse*) crude, blunt; (*fait*) stark. ● **brutaliser** *vt* to ill-treat. ● **brutalité** *nf* (*violence, acte*) brutality. ● **brute** *nf* brute.

Bruxelles [brysɛl] *nm ou f* Brussels.

bruyant, -ante [brɥijɑ̃, -ɑ̃t] *a* noisy. ● **bruyamment** *adv* noisily.

bruyère [brɥijɛr] *nf* (*plante*) heather; (*terrain*) heath.

bu, bue [by] *pp de* **boire**.

buanderie [bɥɑ̃dri] *nf* (*lieu*) laundry.

bûche [byʃ] *nf* log; **ramasser une b.** Fam Br to come a cropper, Am take a spill. ● **bûcher[1]** *nm* (*local*) woodshed; (*supplice*) stake.

bûcher[2] [byʃe] *vt* (*étudier*) Fam to slave *ou* Br slog away at, bone up on ‖ *vi* to slave *ou* Br slog away, bone up. ● **bûcheur, -euse** *nmf Br* swot, *Am* grind.

bûcheron [byʃrɔ̃] *nm* lumberjack, woodcutter.

budget [bydʒɛ] *nm* budget. ● **budgétaire** *a* budgetary; **année b.** financial year.

buée [bɥe] *nf* mist, condensation.

buffet [byfɛ] *nm* (*armoire*) sideboard; (*table, repas*) buffet.

buffle [byfl] *nm* buffalo.

buis [bɥi] *nm* (*arbre*) box; (*bois*) boxwood.

buisson [bɥisɔ̃] *nm* bush.

buissonnière [bɥisɔnjɛr] *af* **faire l'école b.** to play Br truant *ou* Am hookey.

bulbe [bylb] *nm* bulb. ● **bulbeux, -euse** *a* bulbous.

Bulgarie [bylgari] *nf* Bulgaria. ● **bulgare** *a*

Bulgarian ‖ *nmf* **B.** Bulgarian.

bulldozer [byldozœr] *nm* bulldozer.

bulle [byl] *nf* **1** bubble; (*de bande dessinée*) balloon. **2** (*décret du pape*) bull.

bulletin [byltɛ̃] *nm* (*météo*) report; (*scolaire*) Br report, Am report card; (*communiqué, revue*) bulletin; (*de bagages*) Br ticket, Am check; **b. d'informations** news bulletin; **b. de paie** Br pay slip, Am pay stub; **b. de vote** ballot paper.

buraliste [byralist] *nmf* (*à la poste*) clerk; (*au tabac*) tobacconist.

bureau, -x [byro] *nm* **1** (*table*) desk. **2** (*lieu*) office; (*comité*) board; **b. de change** foreign exchange office, bureau de change; **b. de location** (*pour spectacles*) box office; **b. de tabac** Br tobacconist's (shop), Am tobacco store.

bureaucrate [byrokrat] *nmf* bureaucrat. ● **bureaucratie** [-asi] *nf* bureaucracy.

bureautique [byrotik] *nf* office automation.

burette [byrɛt] *nf* (*de garage*) oilcan; (*de table*) cruet.

burin [byrɛ̃] *nm* (*outil*) (cold) chisel.

burlesque [byrlɛsk] *a* (*idée etc*) ludicrous; (*genre*) burlesque.

bus[1] [bys] *nm* bus.

bus[2] [by] *pt de* **boire**.

busqué [byske] *am* **nez b.** hooked nose.

buste [byst] *nm* (*torse, sculpture*) bust. ● **bustier** *nm* long-line bra(ssiere).

but[1] [by(t)] *nm* (*objectif*) aim, goal; (*cible*) target; Football goal; **de b. en blanc** (*soudain, sans prévenir*) point-blank; **aller droit au b.** to go straight to the point; **j'ai pour b. de...** my aim is to....

but[2] [by] *pt de* **boire**.

butane [bytan] *nm* (*gaz*) butane, Br Calor gas.

buter [byte] **1** *vi* **b. contre** to stumble over; (*difficulté*) Fig to come up against. **2 se buter** *vpr* (*s'entêter*) to become *ou* be obstinate. ● **buté, -ée** *a* obstinate.

butin [bytɛ̃] *nm* loot, haul, booty.

butiner [bytine] *vi* (*abeille*) to gather pollen and nectar.

butoir [bytwar] *nm* (*pour train*) buffer; (*de porte*) stopper, Br stop.

butor [bytɔr] *nm Péj* lout, oaf, boor.

butte [byt] *nf* mound, hillock; **être en b. à** (*calomnie, ridicule etc*) to be exposed to *ou* a butt for.

buvable [byvabl] *a* drinkable. ● **buveur, -euse** *nmf* drinker; **c'est un grand** *ou* **gros b.** he's a heavy drinker.

buvard [byvar] *a & nm* (**papier**) **b.** blotting paper.

buvette [byvɛt] *nf* refreshment bar.

C

C, c [se] *nm* C, c.
c *abrév* centime.
c' [s] *voir* ce[1].
ça [sa] *pron dém* (*abrév de cela*) (*pour dé-signer*) that; (*plus près*) this; (*sujet indéfini*) it, that; **qu'est-ce que c'est que ça?** what (on earth) is that *ou* this?; **ça dépend** it *ou* that depends; **c'est qui/quoi ça?** who's/what's that?; **ça m'amuse que...** it amuses me that...; **où/quand/comment/etc ça?** where?/when?/how?/etc; **ça va (bien)?** how's it going?, how are things?; **ça va!** fine!, OK!; **ça alors!** (*surprise, indignation*) how about that!, well I never!; **c'est ça** that's right, that's it; **et avec ça?** (*dans un magasin*) *Fam* anything else?
çà [sa] *adv* **çà et là** here and there.
caban [kabã] *nm* (*veste de sport*) *Br* pea jacket, *Am* peacoat.
cabane [kaban] *nf* hut, cabin; (*de jardin*) shed; **c. à outils** tool shed; **c. (à lapins)** (*rabbit*) hutch.
cabaret [kabarɛ] *nm* night club, cabaret.
cabas [kaba] *nm* shopping bag.
cabillaud [kabijo] *nm* (fresh) cod.
cabine [kabin] *nf* (*de bateau*) cabin; (*télépho-nique*) phone booth, *Br* phone box; (*de ca-mion*) cab; (*d'ascenseur*) cage, *Am* car; **c. (de bain)** *Br* beach hut, *Am* cabana; (*à la piscine*) cubicle; **c. (de pilotage)** cockpit; (*d'un grand avion*) flight deck; **c. spatiale** space capsule; **c. d'essayage** fitting room; **c. d'aiguillage** signal box.
cabinet [kabinɛ] *nm* (*de médecin*) *Br* surg-ery, *Am* office; (*d'avocat*) office, *Br* chambers; (*clientèle de médecin ou d'avocat*) practice; (*de ministre*) department; **cabinets** (*toilettes*) *Br* toilet, *Am* lavatory; **c. de toi-lette** (*small*) bathroom; **c. de travail** study.
câble [kabl] *nm* cable; (*cordage*) rope; **la télévision par c.** cable television; **le c.** *TV* cable. ● **câbler** *vt* (*message*) to cable; **être câblé** *TV* to have cable (television).
caboche [kabɔʃ] *nf* (*tête*) *Fam* nut, noggin.
cabosser [kabɔse] *vt* to dent.
caboteur [kabɔtœr] *nm* (*bateau*) coaster.
cabotin, -ine [kabɔtɛ̃, -in] *nmf* (*acteur*) ham actor; (*actrice*) ham actress; (*enfant etc*) *Fig* play-actor. ● **cabotinage** *nm* histrionics, play-acting.
cabrer (se) [səkabre] *vpr* (*cheval*) to rear (up); (*personne*) to rebel.
cabri [kabri] *nm* (*chevreau*) kid.
cabrioles [kabriɔl] *nfpl* **faire des c.** (*sauts*) to cavort, caper (about).
cabriolet [kabriɔlɛ] *nm* (*voiture*) convertible.

caca [kaka] *nm* (*dans le langage enfantin*) *Fam* number two, *Br* pooh; **faire c.** to do a number two *ou Br* a pooh.
cacah(o)uète [kakawɛt] *nf* peanut.
cacao [kakao] *nm* (*boisson*) cocoa.
cacatoès [kakatɔɛs] *nm* cockatoo.
cachalot [kaʃalo] *nm* sperm whale.
cache-cache [kaʃkaʃ] *nm inv* hide-and-seek; **jouer à cache-c.** to play hide and seek. ● **cache-col** *nm inv* scarf, muffler.
cachemire [kaʃmir] *nm* (*tissu*) cashmere.
cache-nez [kaʃne] *nm inv* scarf, muffler.
cacher [kaʃe] *vt* to hide, conceal (à from); **je ne cache pas que...** I don't hide the fact that...; **c. la lumière à qn** to stand in s.o.'s light ‖ **se cacher** *vpr* to hide.
cache-sexe [kaʃsɛks] *nm inv* G-string.
cachet [kaʃɛ] *nm* (*sceau*) seal; (*de la poste*) postmark; (*comprimé*) tablet; (*d'acteur etc*) fee; (*originalité*) distinctive character. ● **cacheter** *vt* (*lettre*) to seal.
cachette [kaʃɛt] *nf* hiding place; **en c.** in se-cret; **en c. de qn** without s.o. knowing.
cachot [kaʃo] *nm* dungeon.
cachotteries [kaʃɔtri] *nfpl* secretiveness; (*petits secrets*) little mysteries. ● **cachottier, -ière** *a & nmf* secretive (person).
cacophonie [kakɔfɔni] *nf* cacophony.
cactus [kaktys] *nm* cactus.
cadastre [kadastr] *nm* (*registre*) land re-gister.
cadavre [kadavr] *nm* corpse. ● **cadavérique** *a* (*teint*) deathly pale; **rigidité c.** rigor mortis.
caddie® [kadi] *nm* (supermarket) *Br* trolley *ou Am* cart.
cadeau, -x [kado] *nm* present, gift; **faire c. de qch à qn** to let s.o. have sth (to keep).
cadenas [kadna] *nm* padlock. ● **cadenasser** *vt* to padlock.
cadence [kadɑ̃s] *nf* (*taux, vitesse*) rate; (*de chanson etc*) rhythm; (*accords*) *Mus* ca-dence; **en c.** in time. ● **cadencé, -ée** *a* rhythmical.
cadet, -ette [kadɛ, -ɛt] *a* (*de deux frères etc*) younger; (*de plus de deux*) youngest ‖ *nmf* (*enfant*) younger (child); (*de plus de deux*) youngest (child); (*sportif*) junior; **c'est mon c.** he's my junior.
cadran [kadrɑ̃] *nm* (*de téléphone etc*) dial; (*de montre*) face; **c. solaire** sundial; **faire le tour du c.** to sleep round the clock.
cadre [kadr] *nm* **1** (*de photo, vélo etc*) frame; (*décor*) setting; (*sur un imprimé*) box; **dans le c. de** (*limites, contexte*) within the frame-work *ou* scope of, as part of. **2** (*d'entreprise*) executive, manager; **cadres** (*personnel*) (*mili-

taires) officers; (*d'entreprise*) management, managers.

cadrer [kadre] *vi* to tally (**avec** with) ∎ *vt* (*image*) to centre. ●**cadreur** *nm* cameraman.

caduc, -uque [kadyk] *a* (*usage*) obsolete; (*feuilles*) deciduous; (*loi etc*) null and void.

cafard, -arde [kafar, -ard] **1** *nmf* (*espion*) sneak. **2** *nm* (*insecte*) cockroach. **3** *nm* **avoir le c.** to be (down) in the dumps; **ça me donne le c.** it makes me depressed, it depresses me. ●**cafardeux, -euse** *a* (*personne*) (down) in the dumps; (*qui donne le cafard*) depressing.

café [kafe] *nm* coffee; (*bar*) café; **c. au lait, c. crème** *Br* white coffee, coffee with milk; **c. noir, c. nature** black coffee; **c. glacé** iced coffee; **c. soluble** *ou* **instantané** instant coffee; **tasse de c.** cup of black coffee. ●**caféine** *nf* caffeine. ●**cafétéria** *nf* cafeteria. ●**cafetier** *nm* café owner. ●**cafetière** *nf* coffeepot; (*électrique*) percolator.

cafouiller [kafuje] *vi* *Fam* to make a mess of things, get into a mess. ●**cafouillage** *nm* *Fam* mess, muddle, snafu.

cage [kaʒ] *nf* cage; (*d'ascenseur*) shaft; *Football* goal (area); **c. (d'escalier)** (stair)well; **c. thoracique** rib cage.

cageot [kaʒo] *nm* crate, box.

cagibi [kaʒibi] *nm* (storage) room, cubbyhole.

cagneux, -euse [kaɲø, -øz] *a* knock-kneed.

cagnotte [kaɲɔt] *nf* (*caisse commune*) kitty.

cagoule [kagul] *nf* (*de bandit, moine*) hood; (*d'enfant*) *Br* balaclava, *Am* ski mask.

cahier [kaje] *nm* notebook; (*d'écolier*) exercise book; **c. de brouillon** *Br* rough book, *Am* = scratch pad; **c. d'appel** register (*in school*).

cahin-caha [kaɛ̃kaa] *adv* **aller c.-caha** (*personne, vie*) to jog along (with ups and downs).

cahot [kao] *nm* jolt, bump. ●**cahoter** *vt* to jolt, bump ∎ *vi* (*véhicule*) to jolt along. ●**cahoteux, -euse** *a* (*route, chemin*) bumpy.

caïd [kaid] *nm* *Fam* bigshot, leader.

caille [kaj] *nf* (*oiseau*) quail.

cailler [kaje] *vti*, **se cailler** *vpr* (*sang*) to clot, congeal; (*lait*) to curdle; **faire c.** (*lait*) to curdle; **ça caille** *Fam* it's freezing cold. ●**caillot** *nm* (blood) clot.

caillou, -x [kaju] *nm* stone; (*sur la plage*) pebble. ●**caillouté, -ée** *a* (*allée etc*) gravelled. ●**caillouteux, -euse** *a* stony.

Caire [kɛr] *nm* **le C.** Cairo.

caisse [kɛs] *nf* **1** (*boîte*) case, box; (*cageot*) crate; (*de véhicule*) body. **2** (*guichet*) *Br* cash desk, *Br* pay desk, *Am* cashier's window; (*de supermarché*) checkout; (*fonds*) fund; (*bureau*) cashier's office, *Br* paying-in office; **c. (enregistreuse)** *Br* till, cash register; **c. d'épargne** savings bank; **recettes/etc de c.** cash takings/*etc*. **3** (*tambour*) drum; **la grosse c.** the big *ou* bass drum.

caissier, -ière [kesje, -jɛr] *nmf* cashier; (*de supermarché*) checkout *Br* assistant *ou* *Am*

clerk.

cajoler [kaʒɔle] *vt* (*câliner*) to pamper, make a fuss of, cosset. ●**cajolerie(s)** *nf(pl)* pampering.

cajou [kaʒu] *nm* (*pl* **-s**) cashew; **noix de c.** cashew nut.

cake [kɛk] *nm* fruit cake.

calamité [kalamite] *nf* calamity.

calandre [kalɑ̃dr] *nf* (*de véhicule*) radiator grille.

calcaire [kalkɛr] *a* (*eau*) hard; (*terrain*) chalky ∎ *nm* *Géol* limestone.

calciné, -ée [kalsine] *a* charred, burnt to a cinder.

calcium [kalsjɔm] *nm* calcium.

calcul [kalkyl] *nm* **1** (*opérations*) calculation; (*estimation*) calculation, reckoning; (*discipline*) arithmetic; (*différentiel*) calculus. **2** (*du rein etc*) stone; **c. rénal** kidney stone.

calculateur [kalkylatœr] *nm* calculator, computer. ●**calculatrice** *nf* (*ordinateur*) calculator.

calculer [kalkyle] *vt* (*compter*) to calculate, reckon; (*évaluer, combiner*) to calculate. ●**calculé, -ée** *a* (*risque etc*) calculated.

calculette [kalkylɛt] *nf* (pocket) calculator.

cale [kal] *nf* **1** (*pour maintenir*) wedge. **2** (*de bateau*) hold; **c. sèche** dry dock.

calé, -ée [kale] *a* *Fam* (*instruit*) clever (**en qch** at sth); (*difficile*) (*problème etc*) tough.

caleçon [kalsɔ̃] *nm* underpants, boxer shorts; **c. de bain** swimming *ou* *Br* bathing trunks.

calembour [kalɑ̃bur] *nm* pun, play on words.

calendrier [kalɑ̃drije] *nm* (*mois et jours*) calendar; (*programme*) timetable.

cale-pied [kalpje] *nm* (*de bicyclette*) toe-clip.

calepin [kalpɛ̃] *nm* (pocket) notebook.

caler [kale] **1** *vt* (*meuble etc*) to wedge (up); (*appuyer*) to prop (up); **ça cale l'estomac** *Fam* it fills you up. **2** *vt* (*moteur*) to stall ∎ *vi* to stall; (*abandonner*) *Fam* to give up.

calfeutrer [kalføtre] *vt* (*avec du bourrelet*) *Br* to draughtproof, *Am* to draftproof; **se c. (chez soi)** to shut oneself away *ou* up, hole up.

calibre [kalibr] *nm* (*diamètre*) calibre; (*d'œuf*) grade; **de ce c.** (*bêtise etc*) of such a degree, of this degree. ●**calibrer** *vt* (*œufs*) to grade.

calice [kalis] *nm* (*vase*) *Rel* chalice.

calicot [kaliko] *nm* (*tissu*) calico.

Californie [kalifɔrni] *nf* California.

californien, -ienne [kalifurʃɔ̃] *adv* astride; **se mettre à c. sur** to straddle.

câlin, -ine [kalɛ̃, -in] *a* (*enfant, ton etc*) affectionate ∎ *nm* cuddle. ●**câliner** *vt* (*cajoler*) to make a fuss of; (*caresser*) to cuddle. ●**câlineries** *nfpl* affectionate ways.

calleux, -euse [kalø, -øz] *a* (*main etc*) covered in calluses, horny.

calligraphie [kaligrafi] *nf* calligraphy.

calmant [kalmɑ̃] *nm* (*pour la nervosité*) sedative; (*la douleur*) painkiller; **sous calmants** under sedation; (*pour la douleur*) on painkillers.

calmar [kalmar] *nm* (*mollusque*) squid.

calme [kalm] *a* (*flegmatique*) calm, cool; (*journée, sommeil etc*) quiet, calm ∎ *nm* calm(ness); **du c.!** keep quiet!; (*pas de panique*) keep calm!; **dans le c.** (*travailler, étudier*) in peace and quiet.

calmer [kalme] *vt* (*douleur*) to soothe; (*inquiétude*) to calm; (*ardeur*) to damp down; **c. qn** to calm s.o. (down) ∎ **se calmer** *vpr* to calm down.

calomnie [kalɔmni] *nf* slander; (*par écrit*) libel. ●**calomnier** *vt* to slander; (*par écrit*) to libel. ●**calomnieux, -euse** *a* (*paroles` etc*) slanderous; (*texte*) libellous.

calorie [kalɔri] *nf* calorie.

calorifuge [kalɔrifyʒ] *a* (heat-)insulating. ●**calorifuger** *vt* (*tuyaux*) to lag.

calot [kalo] *nm* (*de soldat*) forage cap.

calotte [kalɔt] *nf* (*de prêtre*) skull cap; (*gifle*) *Fam* slap; **c. glaciaire** icecap.

calque [kalk] *nm* (*dessin*) tracing; (*imitation*) (exact *ou* carbon) copy; (**papier-**)**c.** tracing paper. ●**calquer** *vt* to trace; (*imiter*) to copy; **c. sur** to model on.

calumet [kalymɛ] *nm* **c. de la paix** peace pipe.

calvaire [kalver] *nm Rel* calvary; *Fig* ordeal.

calvitie [kalvisi] *nf* baldness.

camarade [kamarad] *nmf* friend, pal, chum; *Pol* comrade; **c. d'atelier** *Br* workmate *ou Am* work colleague (*in factory*); **c. de classe** classmate; **c. d'école** school friend; **c. de jeu** playmate; **c. de travail** *Br* workmate, *Am* work colleague. ●**camaraderie** *nf* friendship, companionship.

Cambodge [kãbɔdʒ] *nm* Cambodia.

cambouis [kãbwi] *nm* (dirty) oil, grease.

cambrer [kãbre] *vt* to arch; **c. les reins** *ou* le **buste** to throw out one's chest ∎ **se cambrer** *vpr* to throw back one's shoulders. ●**cambrure** *nf* curve; (*de pied*) arch, instep.

cambrioler [kãbrijɔle] *vt Br* to burgle, *Am* burglarize. ●**cambriolage** *nm* burglary. ●**cambrioleur, -euse** *nmf* burglar.

came [kam] *nf Tech* cam; **arbre à cames** camshaft.

camée [kame] *nm* (*pierre*) cameo.

caméléon [kameleɔ̃] *nm* (*reptile*) chameleon.

camélia [kamelja] *nm* camellia.

camelot [kamlo] *nm* street peddler *ou Br* hawker, *Am* huckster. ●**camelote** *nf* cheap goods, junk.

camembert [kamãber] *nm* Camembert (cheese).

camer (se) [səkame] *vpr Fam* to get high (on drugs).

caméra [kamera] *nf* (TV *ou* film) camera. ●**cameraman** *nm* (*pl* **-mans** *ou* **-men**) cameraman.

caméscope [kameskɔp] *nm* camcorder.

camion [kamjɔ̃] *nm Br* lorry, *Am* truck; **c. de déménagement** *Br* removal van, *Am* moving van. ●**camion-benne** *nm* (*pl* **camions-bennes**) *Br* dustcart, *Am* garbage truck.

●**camion-citerne** *nm* (*pl* **camions-citernes**) *Br* tanker, *Am* tank truck. ●**camionnage** *nm Br* (road) haulage, *Am* trucking. ●**camionnette** *nf* van. ●**camionneur** *nm* (*conducteur*) *Br* lorry *ou Am* truck driver; (*entrepreneur*) *Br* haulage contractor, *Am* trucker.

camisole [kamizɔl] *nf* **c. de force** straitjacket.

camomille [kamɔmij] *nf* (*plante*) camomile; (*tisane*) camomile tea.

camoufler [kamufle] *vt* to camouflage; (*la vérité etc*) *Fig* to cover up, conceal. ●**camouflage** *nm* camouflage; *Fig* covering up, concealing.

camp [kã] *nm* camp; **feu de c.** campfire; **lit de c.** camp bed; **c. de concentration** concentration camp; **elle est dans mon c.** (*jeu*) she's on my side; **ficher** *ou* **foutre le c.** *Arg* to clear off.

campagne [kãpaɲ] *nf* **1** country(side); **à la c.** in the country. **2** (*électorale, militaire etc*) campaign (**pour** for, **contre** against); **c. de presse/publicité** press/publicity campaign. ●**campagnard, -arde** *a* **accent/style/etc c.** country accent/style/etc ∎ *nm* countryman ∎ *nf* countrywoman.

campanile [kãpanil] *nm* belltower.

camper [kãpe] *vi* to camp ∎ *vt* (*personnage*) to portray (boldly); (*chapeau etc*) to place *ou* plant boldly ∎ **se camper** *vpr* to plant oneself (boldly) (**devant** in front of). ●**campement** *nm* encampment, camp. ●**campeur, -euse** *nmf* camper.

camphre [kãfr] *nm* camphor.

camping [kãpiŋ] *nm* (*activité*) camping; (*terrain*) camp(ing) site; **faire du c.** to go camping, camp; **ils font du c.** (*généralement*) they go camping, they camp; (*ici*) they are camping. ●**camping-car** *nm* camper.

campus [kãpys] *nm* (*universitaire*) campus.

camus, -use [kamy] *a* (*personne*) snub-nosed; **nez c.** snub nose.

Canada [kanada] *nm* Canada. ●**canadien, -ienne** *a* Canadian ∎ *nmf* **C., Canadienne** Canadian. ●**canadienne** *nf* fur-lined jacket.

canaille [kanaj] *nf* rogue, scoundrel ∎ *a* (*manière, accent etc*) vulgar, cheap.

canal, -aux [kanal, -o] *nm* (*pour péniches etc*) canal; (*de télévision, bras de mer*) channel; (*du corps, conduite*) duct; **par le c. de via**, through.

canalisation [kanalizasjɔ̃] *nf* (*de gaz etc*) mains, main pipe.

canaliser [kanalize] *vt* (*rivière, fleuve*) to canalize; (*foule, énergies*) *Fig* to channel.

canapé [kanape] *nm* **1** (*siège*) sofa, couch, *Br* settee. **2** (*tranche de pain*) canapé.

canard [kanar] *nm* **1** duck; (*mâle*) drake. **2** (*fausse note*) false note. **3** (*journal*) *Péj* rag.

canarder [kanarde] *vt* (*faire feu sur*) to fire at *ou* on.

canari [kanari] *nm* canary.

cancans [kãkã] *nmpl* (malicious) gossip. ●**cancaner** *vi* to gossip. ●**cancanier, -ière** *a* gossipy.

cancer [kɑ̃sɛr] *nm* cancer; **le C.** (*signe*) Cancer; **c. de l'estomac**/*etc* stomach/*etc* cancer. ● **cancéreux, -euse** *a* cancerous ▌ *nmf* cancer patient. ● **cancérigène** *a* carcinogenic. ● **cancérologue** *nmf* cancer specialist.

cancre [kɑ̃kr] *nm* (*mauvais élève*) dunce.

cancrelat [kɑ̃krəla] *nm* cockroach.

candélabre [kɑ̃delabr] *nm* candelabra.

candeur [kɑ̃dœr] *nf* innocence, artlessness. ● **candide** *a* artless, innocent.

candidat, -ate [kɑ̃dida, -at] *nmf* candidate; (*à un poste*) applicant, candidate; **être** *ou* **se porter c. à** to apply for. ● **candidature** *nf* application; (*aux élections*) candidacy; **poser sa c.** to apply (à for).

cane [kan] *nf* (*female*) duck. ● **caneton** *nm* duckling.

canette [kanɛt] *nf* **1** (*de bière*) (small) bottle. **2** (*bobine*) spool.

canevas [kanva] *nm* (*toile*) canvas; (*ébauche*) framework, outline.

caniche [kaniʃ] *nm* poodle.

canicule [kanikyl] *nf* scorching heat; **la c.** (*période*) the summer heat, the dog days.

canif [kanif] *nm* penknife.

canine [kanin] **1** *af* (*espèce, race*) canine; **exposition c.** dog show. **2** *nf* (*dent*) canine (tooth).

caniveau, -x [kanivo] *nm* gutter (*in street*).

canne [kan] *nf* (*walking*) stick; (*de bambou*) cane; (*de roseau*) reed; **c. à pêche** fishing rod; **c. à sucre** sugar cane.

cannelle [kanɛl] *nf* (*écorce, épice*) cinnamon.

cannelure [kanlyr] *nf* groove; (*de colonne*) flute.

cannette [kanɛt] *nf* = **canette.**

cannibale [kanibal] *nmf* cannibal ▌ *a* (*tribu etc*) cannibalistic. ● **cannibalisme** *nm* cannibalism.

canoë [kanɔe] *nm* canoe; (*sport*) canoeing. ● **canoëiste** *nmf* canoeist.

canon¹ [kanɔ̃] *nm* (*big*) gun; (*ancien, à boulets*) cannon; (*de fusil etc*) barrel; **c. lisse** smooth bore; **de la chair à c.** cannon fodder. ● **canonnade** *nf* gunfire. ● **canonnier** *nm* gunner.

canon² [kanɔ̃] *nm* (*règle*) canon.

cañon [kanɔ̃] *nm* canyon.

canoniser [kanɔnize] *vt Rel* to canonize.

canot [kano] *nm* boat; **c. de sauvetage** lifeboat; **c. pneumatique** rubber dinghy. ● **canoter** *vi* to go boating, boat. ● **canotage** *nm* boating.

cantaloup [kɑ̃talu] *nm* (*melon*) cantaloup(e).

cantate [kɑ̃tat] *nf* (*chant*) cantata.

cantatrice [kɑ̃tatris] *nf* opera singer.

cantine [kɑ̃tin] *nf* **1** (*réfectoire*) canteen; **manger à la c.** (*écolier*) *Br* to have school dinners, *Am* to have school lunch. **2** (*coffre*) tin trunk.

cantique [kɑ̃tik] *nm* hymn.

canton [kɑ̃tɔ̃] *nm* (*en France*) district (*division of arrondissement*); (*en Suisse*) canton. ● **cantonal, -e, -aux** *a* divisional; (*en Suisse*) cantonal.

cantonade (à la) [alakɑ̃tɔnad] *adv* (*parler etc*) to all and sundry, to everyone in general.

cantonner [kɑ̃tɔne] *vt* (*soldat*) to billet; (*confiner*) to confine ▌ *vi* (*soldat*) to be billeted ▌ **se cantonner** *vpr* to confine oneself (**dans sa chambre**/*etc* to one's room/*etc*). ● **cantonnement** *nm* (*lieu*) billet, quarters.

cantonnier [kɑ̃tɔnje] *nm* road mender.

canular [kanylar] *nm* practical joke, hoax.

canyon [kanjɔ̃] *nm* canyon.

caoutchouc [kautʃu] *nm* rubber; (*élastique*) rubber band; **caoutchoucs** (*chaussures*) galoshes, (rubber) overshoes; **c. mousse**® foam (*for cushion etc*). ● **caoutchouter** *vt* to rubberize. ● **caoutchouteux, -euse** *a* rubbery.

CAP [seape] *nm abrév* (*certificat d'aptitude professionnelle*) technical and vocational diploma.

cap [kap] *nm Géog* cape, headland; (*direction*) *Nau* course; **mettre le c. sur** to steer a course for; **changer de c.** to change course; **franchir** *ou* **doubler le c. de** (*difficulté*) to get over the worst of; **franchir** *ou* **doubler le c. de la trentaine**/*etc* to turn thirty/*etc*; **franchir le c. des mille employés** (*limite*) to pass the one-thousand employee mark.

capable [kapabl] *a* capable, able; **c. de faire** able to do, capable of doing; **elle est bien c. de faire ça** (*susceptible*) she's quite likely to do that, she's quite capable of doing that. ● **capacité** *nf* ability, capacity; (*contenance*) capacity.

cape [kap] *nf* cape; (*grande*) cloak.

CAPES [kapɛs] *nm abrév* (*certificat d'aptitude professionnelle à l'enseignement secondaire*) teaching diploma.

capillaire [kapilɛr] *a* **huile/lotion c.** hair oil/lotion.

capitaine [kapitɛn] *nm* captain.

capital, -e, -aux [kapital, -o] **1** *a* (*importance, élément etc*) major, fundamental, capital; (*peine*) capital; (*péché*) deadly. **2** *af* **lettre capitale** capital letter. **3** *nm* (*argent*) capital. ● **capitale** *nf* (*lettre, ville*) capital. ● **capitaux** *nmpl* (*argent*) capital.

capitaliser [kapitalize] *vt* (*accumuler*) to build up ▌ *vi* to save (up).

capitalisme [kapitalism] *nm* capitalism. ● **capitaliste** *a* & *nmf* capitalist.

capiteux, -euse [kapitø, -øz] *a* (*vin, parfum*) heady.

capitonner [kapitɔne] *vt* to pad, upholster. ● **capitonnage** *nm* (*garniture*) padding, upholstery.

capituler [kapityle] *vi* to surrender, capitulate. ● **capitulation** *nf* surrender, capitulation.

caporal, -aux [kapɔral, -o] *nm* corporal.

capot [kapo] *nm* (*de véhicule*) *Br* bonnet, *Am* hood.

capote [kapɔt] *nf* (*de véhicule*) *Br* hood, *Am* (convertible) top; (*manteau de soldat*) great-

coat; **c. (anglaise)** (*préservatif*) *Fam* condom.
capoter [kapɔte] *vi* (*véhicule*) to overturn.
câpre [kɑpr] *nf* (*condiment*) caper.
caprice [kapris] *nm* (*passing*) whim, caprice.
● **capricieux, -euse** *a* temperamental, capricious.
Capricorne [kaprikɔrn] *nm* **le C.** (*signe*) Capricorn.
capsule [kapsyl] *nf* (*spatiale, de médicament*) capsule; (*de bouteille, pistolet d'enfant*) cap.
capter [kapte] *vt* (*signal, radio*) to pick up; (*attention*) to capture, win; (*faveur*) to win; (*eau*) to draw off.
captif, -ive [kaptif, -iv] *a & nmf* captive.
● **captivité** *nf* captivity; **en c.** in captivity.
captiver [kaptive] *vt* to fascinate, captivate.
● **captivant, -ante** *a* fascinating.
capture [kaptyr] *nf* catch, capture. ● **capturer** *vt* (*animal, criminel etc*) to capture.
capuche [kapyʃ] *nf* hood. ● **capuchon** *nm* hood; (*de moine*) cowl; (*pèlerine*) hooded (rain)coat; (*de stylo*) cap, top.
capucine [kapysin] *nf* (*plante*) nasturtium.
caquet [kakɛ] *nm* (*bavardage*) cackle. ● **caqueter** *vi* (*poule, personne*) to cackle. ● **caquetage** *nm* cackle.
car [kar] **1** *conj* because, for. **2** *nm* bus, *Br* coach; **c. de police** police van.
carabine [karabin] *nf* rifle; **c. à air comprimé** airgun.
carabiné, -ée [karabine] *a Fam* (*rhume, grippe etc*) violent; (*punition, amende*) very stiff.
caracoler [karakɔle] *vi* to prance, caper.
caractère[1] [karaktɛr] *nm* (*lettre*) character; **petits caractères** small letters; **caractères d'imprimerie** (block) capitals *ou* letters; **en caractères gras** in bold type *ou* characters.
caractère[2] [karaktɛr] *nm* (*tempérament, nature*) character, nature; (*attribut*) characteristic; **aucun c. de gravité** no serious element; **son c. inégal** his *ou* her uneven temper; **avoir bon c.** to be good-natured.
caractériel, -ielle [karakterjɛl] *a* **troubles caractériels** emotional disorder ▮ *a & nmf* disturbed (child).
caractériser [karakterize] *vt* to characterize; **se c. par** to be characterized by.
caractéristique [karakteristik] *a & nf* characteristic.
carafe [karaf] *nf* decanter, carafe.
caramboler [karɑ̃bɔle] *vt* (*véhicule*) to smash into. ● **carambolage** *nm* pile-up, multiple collision.
caramel [karamɛl] *nm* caramel; (*bonbon dur*) *Br* toffee, *Am* taffy.
carapace [karapas] *nf* (*de tortue etc*) & *Fig* shell.
carat [kara] *nm* carat; **or à dix-huit carats** eighteen-carat gold.
caravane [karavan] *nf* (*pour camper*) *Br* caravan, *Am* trailer; (*dans le désert*) caravan; **c. publicitaire** publicity convoy. ● **caravaning** *ou* **caravanage** *nm* caravanning.
carbone [karbɔn] *nm* carbon; (**papier**) **c.**

carbon (paper).
carboniser [karbɔnize] *vt* to burn (to ashes), char; (*substance*) to carbonize; **mourir carbonisé** to be burned to death.
carburant [karbyrɑ̃] *nm* (*essence etc*) fuel. ● **carburateur** *nm Br* carburettor, *Am* carburetor.
carcan [karkɑ̃] *nm* (*de torture*) iron collar; (*contrainte, règles etc*) yoke.
carcasse [karkas] *nf* (*os*) carcass; (*d'immeuble etc*) frame, shell.
cardiaque [kardjak] *a* **être c.** to have a weak heart; **crise/problème c.** heart attack/trouble; **arrêt c.** cardiac arrest ▮ *nmf* heart patient.
cardinal, -e, -aux [kardinal, -o] **1** *a* (*nombre, point*) cardinal. **2** *nm Rel* cardinal.
cardiologue [kardjɔlɔg] *nmf* heart specialist.
Carême [karɛm] *nm* Lent.
carence [karɑ̃s] *nf* (*en vitamines etc*) deficiency; (*impuissance*) inadequacy, incompetence.
carène [karɛn] *nf* (*de navire*) hull. ● **caréné, -ée** *a* (*voiture, avion etc*) streamlined.
caresse [karɛs] *nf* caress; **faire des caresses à** = caresser.
caresser [karese] *vt* (*animal, enfant etc*) to stroke, pat; (*femme, homme*) to caress; (*espoir*) to cherish. ● **caressant, -ante** *a* loving, very affectionate.
cargaison [kargɛzɔ̃] *nf* cargo, freight. ● **cargo** *nm* cargo boat, freighter.
caricature [karikatyr] *nf* caricature. ● **caricatural, -e, -aux** *a* ludicrous; **portrait c.** portrait in caricature. ● **caricaturer** *vt* to caricature.
carie [kari] *nf* **la c.** (*dentaire*) tooth decay; **une c.** a cavity. ● **cariée** *af* **dent c.** decayed *ou* bad tooth.
carillon [karijɔ̃] *nm* (*cloches*) chimes, peal; (*horloge*) chiming clock; (*de porte*) door chime. ● **carillonner** *vi* to chime, peal.
carlingue [karlɛ̃g] *nf* (*fuselage d'avion*) cabin.
carnage [karnaʒ] *nm* carnage.
carnassier, -ière [karnasje, -jɛr] *a* carnivorous ▮ *nm* carnivore.
carnaval, pl -als [karnaval] *nm* carnival.
carné [karne] *am* **régime c.** meat diet.
carnet [karnɛ] *nm* notebook; (*de timbres, chèques, adresses etc*) book; **c. de notes** *Br* school report, *Am* report card; **c. de route** logbook; **c. de vol** (*d'avion*) logbook.
carnivore [karnivɔr] *a* carnivorous ▮ *nm* carnivore.
carotte [karɔt] *nf* carrot.
carotter [karɔte] *vt Arg* to wangle, cadge (**à qn** from s.o.).
carpe [karp] *nf* carp.
carpette [karpɛt] *nf* rug.
carré, -ée [kare] *a* square; (*honnête en affaires*) plain-dealing; **mètre/etc c.** square metre/*etc* ▮ *nm* square; (*de jardin*) patch; (*sur un navire*) messroom; **c. de soie** (square) silk scarf.
carreau, -x [karo] *nm* (*vitre*) (window) pane; (*pavé*) tile; (*sol*) tiled floor; (*couleur*) *Cartes*

carreler 44

diamonds; **à carreaux** (*nappe etc*) check(ed);
se tenir à c. to watch one's step; **rester sur le
c.** to be left for dead; (*candidat*) *Fig* to be
left out in the cold.

carreler [karle] *vt* to tile. ●**carrelage** *nm*
(*sol*) tiled floor; (*action*) tiling.

carrefour [karfur] *nm* crossroads.

carrelet [karlɛ] *nm* (*poisson*) *Br* plaice, *Am*
flounder.

carrément [karemã] *adv* (*dire, répondre etc*)
bluntly; (*complètement*) downright, well and
truly.

carrer (se) [səkare] *vpr* to settle down
firmly.

carrière [karjɛr] *nf* **1** (*terrain*) quarry. **2**
(*métier*) career.

carrosse [karɔs] *nm Hist* (horse-drawn)
carriage. ●**carrossable** *a* (*chemin*) suitable
for vehicles. ●**carrosserie** *nf* (*de véhicule*)
body(work).

carrousel [karuzɛl] *nm* (*tourbillon*) *Fig*
whirl, merry-go-round.

carrure [karyr] *nf* build, breadth of
shoulders; (*valeur*) *Fig* calibre.

cartable [kartabl] *nm* (*d'écolier*) school bag;
(*à bretelles*) satchel.

carte [kart] *nf* **1** card; (*de lecteur*) ticket;
(*routière*) map; (*marine, météo*) chart; **c.
(postale)** (post)card; **c. (à jouer)** (playing)
card; **jouer aux cartes** to play cards; **c. de
crédit** credit card; **c. d'identité bancaire**
bank card; **c. de visite** *Br* visiting card, *Am*
calling card; (*professionnelle*) business card;
c. grise vehicle registration document; **avoir
c. blanche** *Fig* to have a free hand. **2** (*au
restaurant*) menu; **c. des vins** wine list; **manger à la c.** to have an à la carte meal.

cartel [kartɛl] *nm* (*entreprises*) cartel.

carter [kartɛr] *nm* (*de moteur*) crankcase; (*de
bicyclette*) chain guard.

cartilage [kartilaʒ] *nm* cartilage.

carton [kartɔ̃] *nm* cardboard; (*boîte*) cardboard box, carton; **c. à dessin** portfolio; **en
c.-pâte** (*faux*) *Péj* pasteboard; **faire un c. sur
qn/qch** *Fam* to take a potshot at s.o./sth.
●**cartonner** *vt* (*livre*) to case; **livre cartonné**
hardback. ●**cartonnage** *nm* (*emballage*)
cardboard package.

cartouche [kartuʃ] *nf* cartridge; (*de cigarettes*) carton; (*vidéo*) cassette. ●**cartouchière** *nf* (*ceinture*) cartridge belt.

cas [kɑ] *nm* case; **en tout c.** in any case *ou*
event; **en aucun c.** on no account; **en c. de
besoin** if need be; **en c. d'accident** in the
event of an accident; **en c. d'urgence** in an
emergency; **au c. où elle tomberait** if she
should fall; **pour le c. où il pleuvrait** in case
it rains; **faire c. de/peu de c. de qn/qch** to set
great/little store by s.o./sth.

casanier, -ière [kazanje, -jɛr] *a & nmf*
home-loving (person); (*pantouflard*) *Péj*
stay-at-home (person).

casaque [kazak] *nf* (*de jockey*) shirt, blouse.

cascade [kaskad] *nf* **1** waterfall; (*série*)
(*d'ennuis, de problèmes etc*) *Fig* spate; **en c.**

in succession. **2** (*de cinéma*) stunt. ●**cascadeur, -euse** *nmf* stunt man, stunt woman.

case [kɑz] *nf* **1** pigeonhole; (*de tiroir*)
compartment; (*d'échiquier etc*) square; (*de
formulaire*) box. **2** (*hutte*) hut, cabin.

caser [kaze] *vt Fam* (*ranger*) to put *ou* stash
(away), place (**dans** in); **c. qn** (*dans un logement*) to find a place for s.o.; (*dans un travail*) to find a job for s.o.; (*marier*) to marry
s.o. off ▌ **se caser** *vpr* to settle down.

caserne [kazɛrn] *nf* (*pour soldats*) barracks;
c. de pompiers fire station.

casier [kazje] *nm* pigeonhole, compartment;
(*meuble à tiroirs*) filing cabinet; (*fermant à
clef, à consigne automatique*) locker; **c. à
bouteilles/à disques** bottle/record rack; **c. judiciaire** criminal *ou* police record.

casino [kazino] *nm* casino.

casque [kask] *nm* helmet; (*de coiffeur*)
(hair) dryer; **c. (à écouteurs)** headphones; **les
Casques bleus** the UN peace-keeping force.
●**casqué, -ée** *a* helmeted, wearing a helmet.

casquer [kaske] *vi Fam* to pay up, cough
up, fork out.

casquette [kaskɛt] *nf* (*coiffure*) cap.

cassant, -ante [kasɑ̃, -ɑ̃t] *a voir* **casser.**

cassation [kasasjɔ̃] *nf* **Cour de c.** supreme
court of appeal.

casse¹ [kɑs] *nf* **1** (*action*) breakage; (*objets*)
breakages; (*grabuge*) *Fam* trouble; **mettre à
la c.** to scrap; **vendre à la c.** to sell for scrap.
2 (*d'imprimerie*) case; **haut de c.** upper case;
bas de c. lower case; (*lettre*) lower-case
letter.

casse² [kɑs] *nm* (*cambriolage*) *Arg* break-in.

casse-cou [kasku] *nmf inv* (*personne*) *Fam*
daredevil. ●**casse-croûte** *nm inv* snack.
●**casse-gueule** *nm inv* (*endroit*) *Fam* death
trap, danger spot ▌ *a inv* (*entreprise etc*) *Fam*
(highly) dangerous. ●**casse-noisettes** *nm inv*
ou **casse-noix** *nm inv* nut-cracker(s).
●**casse-pieds** *nmf inv* (*personne*) *Fam* pain
in the neck. ●**casse-tête** *nm inv* **1**
(*problème*) headache; (*jeu*) puzzle, brain
teaser. **2** (*massue*) club.

casser [kase] **1** *vt* to break; (*noix*) to crack;
elle me casse les pieds *Fam* she's getting on
my nerves; **il me casse la tête** *Fam* he's giving me a headache; **c. la tête** *Fam* to rack
one's brains; **c. la figure à qn** *Fam* to smash
s.o.'s face in; **se c. la figure** (*tomber*) *Fam Br*
to come a cropper, *Am* take a spill; **ça ne
casse rien** *Fam* it's nothing special; **ça vaut
50F à tout c.** *Fam* it's worth 50F at the very
most ▌ *vi*, **se casser** *vpr* to break; **il ne s'est
pas cassé** *Iron Fam* he didn't bother himself
ou exhaust himself.
2 *vt* (*annuler*) *Jur* to nullify, annul; **c. un jugement** to quash a sentence.
3 *vt* (*dégrader*) to dismiss from the army,
cashier (*officier*). ●**cassant, -ante** *a* (*fragile*)
brittle; (*brusque*) curt, abrupt; (*fatigant*)
Fam exhausting. ●**casseur** *nm* (*d'épaves de
voitures*) *Br* breaker, scrap dealer *ou* *Br*
merchant; (*manifestant*) demonstrator who

damages property.

casserole [kasrɔl] *nf* (sauce)pan.

cassette [kasɛt] *nf* (*pour magnétophone*) cassette; (*pour magnétoscope*) video, cassette; **sur c.** (*film*) on video; **faire une c. de** (*film*) to make a video of.

cassis 1 [kasis] *nm* (*fruit*) blackcurrant; (*boisson*) blackcurrant liqueur. 2 [kasi] *nm* (*obstacle*) dip (*across road*).

cassoulet [kasulɛ] *nm* stew (*of meat and beans*).

cassure [kasyr] *nf* (*fissure, rupture*) break; (*de l'écorce terrestre*) fault.

castagnettes [kastaɲɛt] *nfpl* castanets.

caste [kast] *nf* caste; **esprit de c.** class consciousness.

castor [kastɔr] *nm* beaver.

castrer [kastre] *vt* to castrate; (*chat*) to neuter. ● **castration** *nf* castration; (*de chat*) neutering.

cataclysme [kataklism] *nm* cataclysm. ● **cataclysmique** *a* cataclysmic.

catacombes [katakɔ̃b] *nfpl* catacombs.

catalogue [katalɔg] *nm Br* catalogue, *Am* catalog. ● **cataloguer** *vt* (*livres etc*) *Br* to catalogue, *Am* catalog; **c. qn** *Péj* to categorize s.o.

catalyseur [katalizœr] *nm Ch & Fig* catalyst.

catalytique [katalitik] *a* **pot c.** (*de véhicule*) catalytic converter.

cataphote® [katafɔt] *nm* (*de vélo etc*) reflector; (*sur la route*) cat's eye.

cataplasme [kataplasm] *nm* (*pour malade*) poultice.

catapulte [katapylt] *nf* (*de porte-avions*) catapult. ● **catapulter** *vt* to catapult.

cataracte [katarakt] *nf* 1 (*maladie des yeux*) cataract. 2 (*cascade*) falls, cataract.

catastrophe [katastrɔf] *nf* disaster, catastrophe; **atterrir en c.** to make an emergency landing. ● **catastrophique** *a* disastrous, catastrophic.

catastrophé, -ée [katastrɔfe] *a* (*attristé*) shattered.

catch [katʃ] *nm* (all-in) wrestling. ● **catcheur, -euse** *nmf* wrestler.

catéchisme [kateʃism] *nm Rel* catechism.

catégorie [kategɔri] *nf* category.

catégorique [kategɔrik] *a* categorical. ● **catégoriquement** *adv* (*refuser etc*) categorically.

cathédrale [katedral] *nf* cathedral.

catholicisme [katɔlisism] *nm* Catholicism. ● **catholique** *a* & *nmf* (Roman) Catholic; **pas (très) c.** (*affaire, personne*) *Fig* shady, (rather) dubious.

catimini (en) [ɑ̃katimini] *adv* on the sly.

cauchemar [koʃmar] *nm* nightmare; **faire un c.** to have a nightmare.

cause [koz] *nf* cause; (*procès*) case; **une bonne** *ou* **noble c.** a good *ou* worthy cause; **à c. de** because of, on account of; **pour c. de** on account of; **et pour c.!** for a very good reason!; **en (toute) connaissance de c.** in full knowledge of the facts; **mettre en c.** (*la bonne foi de qn etc*) to (call into) question; (*personne*) to implicate (**dans** in); **votre probité n'est pas en c.** your integrity is not in question.

causer [koze] 1 *vt* (*provoquer*) to cause. 2 *vi* (*bavarder*) to chat (**de** about); (*discourir*) to talk; (*dire des secrets*) to blab. ● **causant, -ante** *a Fam* chatty, talkative. ● **causerie** *nf* talk. ● **causette** *nf* **faire la c.** *Fam* to have a little chat.

caustique [kostik] *a* (*substance, esprit*) caustic.

cauteleux, -euse [kotlø, -øz] *a* wily, sly.

cautériser [koterize] *vt Méd* to cauterize.

caution [kosjɔ̃] *nf* surety; **sous c.** on bail; **pour libérer qn de prison**) bail; **sous c.** on bail; **c'est sujet à c.** (*nouvelle etc*) it's very doubtful. ● **cautionner** *vt* (*approuver*) to sanction. ● **cautionnement** *nm* (*garantie*) surety.

cavalcade [kavalkad] *nf Fam* stampede; (*défilé*) cavalcade.

cavale [kaval] *nf* **en c.** *Arg* on the run. ● **cavaler** *vi Fam* to run, rush.

cavalerie [kavalri] *nf* (*soldats*) cavalry; (*de cirque*) horses.

cavalier, -ière [kavalje, -jɛr] 1 *nmf* rider ▮ *nm* (*soldat*) trooper, cavalryman; *Échecs* knight ▮ *af* **allée cavalière** bridle path. 2 *nmf* (*pour danser etc*) partner, escort. 3 *a* (*insolent*) offhand. ● **cavalièrement** *adv* offhandedly.

cave [kav] 1 *nf* cellar. 2 *a* (*yeux*) sunken, hollow. ● **caveau, -x** *nm* (*sépulture*) (burial) vault.

caverne [kavɛrn] *nf* cave, cavern; **homme des cavernes** caveman.

caverneux, -euse [kavɛrnø, -øz] *a* (*voix, rire*) hollow, deep-sounding.

caviar [kavjar] *nm* caviar(e).

cavité [kavite] *nf* hollow, cavity.

CCP [sesepe] *nm abrév* (*compte chèque postal*) *Br* PO Giro account, *Am* Post Office checking account.

CD [sede] *nm abrév* (*disque compact*) CD.

ce¹ [s(ə)] (**c'** *before e and é*) *pron dém* **1** it, that; **c'est toi/bon/demain/etc** it's *ou* that's you/good/tomorrow/etc; **c'est un médecin** he's a doctor; **ce sont eux qui...** they are the people *ou* the ones who...; **qui est-ce?** (*en général*) who is it?; (*en montrant qn*) who is that?; **c'est à elle de jouer** it's her turn to play; **est-ce que tu viens?** are you coming?; **sur ce** at this point, thereupon.

2 (*pour reprendre une proposition*) **ce que, ce qui** what; **je sais ce qui est bon/ce que tu veux** I know what is good/what you want; **elle est malade, ce qui est triste/ce que je ne savais pas** she's ill, which is sad/which I didn't know; **ce que c'est beau!** it's so beautiful!, how beautiful it is!

ce², **cette**, *pl* **ces** [s(ə), sɛt, se] (**ce** *becomes* **cet** *before a vowel or mute h*) *a dém* this, that, *pl* these, those; (**+ -ci**) *this*, *pl* these; (**+ -là**) *that*, *pl* those; **cet homme** this *ou* that man; **cet homme-ci** this man; **cet**

homme-là that man.

ceci [səsi] *pron dém* this; **écoutez bien c.** listen to this.

cécité [sesite] *nf* blindness.

céder [sede] *vt* to give up (à to); (*propriété, bien*) to transfer; **c. sa place à qn** to give up one's seat to s.o.; let s.o. have one's seat; **je lui ai cédé mon tour** I let him have my turn; **c. le pas à qn** to give way *ou* precedence to s.o. ▮ *vi* (*personne*) to give in, give way (à to); (*branche, chaise etc*) to give way.

cédille [sedij] *nf* Grammaire cedilla.

cèdre [sedr] *nm* (*arbre, bois*) cedar.

CEE [seøø] *abrév* (*Communauté économique européenne*) EEC.

CEI [seøi] *nf abrév* (*Communauté des États Indépendants*) CIS.

ceinture [sɛ̃tyr] *nf* belt; (*de robe de chambre*) cord; (*taille*) waist; (*de remparts*) girdle; **petite/grande c.** (*ligne de bus etc*) inner/outer circle; **c. de sécurité** (*de véhicule etc*) seatbelt; **c. de sauvetage** *Br* lifebelt, *Am* life preserver.

ceinturer [sɛ̃tyre] *vt* to seize round the waist; *Rugby* to tackle; (*ville*) to surround.

cela [s(ə)la] *pron dém* (*pour désigner*) that; (*sujet indéfini*) it, that; **c. m'attriste que...** it saddens me that...; **quand/comment/***etc* **c.?** when?/how?/*etc*; **c'est c.** that is so.

célèbre [selɛbr] *a* famous. ● **célébrité** *nf* fame; (*personne*) celebrity.

célébrer [selebre] *vt* to celebrate. ● **célébra-tion** *nf* celebration (de of).

céleri [sɛlri] *nm* (*en branches*) celery.

céleste [selɛst] *a* celestial, heavenly.

célibat [seliba] *nm* (*de prêtre*) celibacy. ● **cé-libataire** *a* (*non marié*) single, unmarried; (*chaste*) (*prêtre etc*) celibate ▮ *nm* bachelor ▮ *nf* unmarried woman.

celle *voir* celui.

cellier [selje] *nm* storeroom (*for wine etc*).

cellophane® [selɔfan] *nf* cellophane®; **sous c.** in cellophane.

cellule [selyl] *nf* cell. ● **cellulaire** *a* (*tissu, membrane*) cellular; **téléphone c.** cellular phone; **voiture c.** *Br* prison van, *Am* patrol wagon.

celluloïd [selylɔid] *nm* celluloid.

cellulite [selylit] *nf* (*inflammation*) cellulitis.

cellulose [selyloz] *nf* cellulose.

celtique *ou* **celte** [sɛltik, sɛlt] *a* Celtic.

celui, celle, *pl* **ceux, celles** [səlɥi, sɛl, sø, sɛl] *pron dém* **1** the one, *pl* those, the ones; **c. de Jean** John's (one); **ceux de Jean** John's (ones), those of John; **c. qui appartient à Jean** the one that belongs to John. **2** (+ -ci) this one, *pl* these (ones); (*dont on vient de parler*) the latter; (+ -là) that one, *pl* those (ones); (*dont on vient de parler*) the former; **ceux-ci sont gros** these (ones) are big; **elle alla voir son amie, mais celle-ci était absente** she went to see her friend but she was out.

cendre [sɑ̃dr] *nf* ash. ● **cendré, -ée** *a* (*che-veux*) ash(-coloured). ● **cendrée** *nf* (*de stade*) cinder track.

cendrier [sɑ̃drije] *nm* ashtray.

Cendrillon [sɑ̃drijɔ̃] *nm* Cinderella.

censé, -ée [sɑ̃se] *a* **être c. faire** to be supposed to do; **il n'est pas c. le savoir** he's not supposed to know.

censeur [sɑ̃sœr] *nm* (*de films, journaux etc*) censor; (*de lycée*) *Br* assistant headmaster, *Am* assistant principal. ● **censure** *nf* **la c.** (*examen*) censorship; (*comité, service*) the (board of) censors, the censor; **motion de c.** (*à l'Assemblée*) censure motion. ● **censurer** *vt* (*film etc*) to censor; (*critiquer*) to censure (*s.o., the government etc*).

cent [sɑ̃] ([sɑ̃t] *pl* [sɑ̃z] *before vowel and mute h except* **un** *and* **onze**) *a & nm* hundred; **c. pages** a *ou* one hundred pages; **deux cents pages** two hundred pages; **deux c. trois pages** two hundred and three pages; **cinq pour c.** five per cent. ● **centaine** *nf* **une c. (de)** about a hundred; **des centaines de** hundreds of; **plusieurs centaines** several hundred. ● **centenaire** *a & nmf* centenarian ▮ *nm* (*anniversaire*) centenary. ● **centième** *a & nmf* hundredth; **un c.** a hundredth.

centigrade [sɑ̃tigrad] *a* centigrade.

centime [sɑ̃tim] *nm* centime.

centimètre [sɑ̃timetr] *nm* centimetre; (*ru-ban*) tape measure.

central, -e, -aux [sɑ̃tral, -o] **1** *a* central; **pou-voir c.** (power of) central government. **2** *nm* **c. (téléphonique)** (telephone) exchange. ● **centrale** *nf* (*usine*) *Br* power station, *Am* power plant. ● **centraliser** *vt* to centralize.

centre [sɑ̃tr] *nm* centre; **c. commercial** shop-ping centre *ou* mall; **c. hospitalo-universitaire** = teaching hospital. ● **centre-ville** *nm* (*pl* **centres-villes**) *Br* city *ou* town centre, *Am* downtown area. ● **centrer** *vt* to centre.

centrifuge [sɑ̃trifyʒ] *a* centrifugal. ● **centrifu-geuse** *nf* (*pour fruits etc*) *Br* liquidizer, juice extractor.

centuple [sɑ̃typl] *nm* **x est le c. de y** x is a hundred times y; **au c.** a hundredfold. ● **centupler** *vti* to increase a hundredfold.

cep [sɛp] *nm* vine stock. ● **cépage** *nm* vine.

cependant [səpɑ̃dɑ̃] *conj* however, yet.

céramique [seramik] *nf* (*matière*) ceramic; (*art*) pottery, ceramics; **de** *ou* **en c.** ceramic.

cerceau, -x [sɛrso] *nm* hoop.

cercle [sɛrkl] *nm* (*forme, groupe, étendue*) circle; **c. vicieux** vicious circle.

cercueil [sɛrkœj] *nm* coffin.

céréale [sereal] *nf* cereal.

cérébral, -e, -aux [serebral, -o] *a* (*du cerveau*) cerebral; (*activité, travail etc*) *Fig* mental, cerebral.

cérémonie [seremɔni] *nf* ceremony; **tenue de c.** ceremonial dress; **sans c.** (*inviter, manger*) informally; **faire des cérémonies** *Fam* to make a lot of fuss. ● **cérémonial,** *pl* **-als** *nm* ceremonial. ● **cérémonieux, -euse** *a* ceremo-nious.

cerf [sɛr] *nm* deer *inv*; (*mâle*) stag. ● **cerf-volant** *nm* (*pl* **cerfs-volants**) (*jouet*) kite.

47 **chamois**

cerise [s(ə)riz] *nf* cherry. ●**cerisier** *nm* cherry tree.

cerne [sɛrn] *nm* (*cercle, marque*) ring. ●**cerner** *vt* to surround; (*problème*) to define; **avoir les yeux cernés** to have rings under one's eyes.

certain, -aine [sɛrtɛ̃, -ɛn] **1** *a* (*sûr*) certain, sure; **il est** *ou* **c'est c. que tu réussiras** you're certain *ou* sure to succeed; **je suis c. de réussir** I'm certain *ou* sure I'll be successful *ou* of being successful; **être c. de qch** to be certain *ou* sure of sth.
2 *a* (*imprécis, difficile à fixer*) certain; *pl* certain, some; **un c. temps** a certain (amount of) time. ●**certainement** *adv* certainly. ●**certains** *pron pl* some (people), certain people; (*choses*) some.

certes [sɛrt] *adv Litt* indeed, most certainly.

certificat [sɛrtifika] *nm* certificate.

certifier [sɛrtifje] *vt* to certify; **je vous certifie que** I assure you that. ●**certifié, -ée** *a* (*professeur*) qualified.

certitude [sɛrtityd] *nf* certainty; **avoir la c.** **que** to be certain that.

cerveau, -x [sɛrvo] *nm* (*organe*) brain; (*intelligence*) mind, brain(s); **rhume de c.** head cold; **fuite des cerveaux** brain drain.

cervelas [sɛrvəla] *nm Br* saveloy, = salami.

cervelle [sɛrvɛl] *nf* (*substance*) brain; (*plat*) brains; **tête sans c.** scatterbrain.

ces *voir* **ce**[2].

CES [seœs] *nm abrév* (*collège d'enseignement secondaire*) *Br* = comprehensive school (*lower forms only, covering the 11-14 age group*), *Am* = junior high school.

césarienne [sezarjɛn] *nf* (*opération*) Caesarean (section).

cessation [sɛsasjɔ̃] *nf* (*arrêt, fin*) suspension.

cesse [sɛs] *nf* **sans c.** constantly; **elle n'a (pas) eu de c. que je n'accepte** she had no rest until I accepted....

cesser [sese] *vti* to stop; **faire c.** to put a stop *ou* halt to; **c. de faire qch** to stop doing sth; **il ne cesse (pas) de parler** he doesn't stop talking; **cela a cessé d'exister** that has ceased to exist. ●**cessez-le-feu** *nm inv* cease-fire.

cession [sɛsjɔ̃] *nf* (*de bien etc*) transfer.

c'est-à-dire [sɛtadir] *conj* that is (to say), in other words.

cet, cette *voir* **ce**[2].

ceux *voir* **celui**.

chacal, *pl* -als [ʃakal] *nm* jackal.

chacun, -une [ʃakœ̃, -yn] *pron* each (one), every one; (*tous le monde*) everyone; (**à) c. son tour!** wait your turn!

chagrin [ʃagrɛ̃] **1** *nm* grief, sorrow; **avoir du c.** to be very upset; **faire du c. à qn** to make s.o. very upset. **2** *a* (*air, voix etc*) *Litt* doleful. ●**chagriner** *vt* to upset, distress.

chahut [ʃay] *nm* (*bruit*) racket, uproar. ●**chahuter** *vi* to create a racket *ou* an uproar ‖ *vt* (*professeur*) to rowdy with, *Br* play up. ●**chahuteur, -euse** *nmf* rowdy.

chai [ʃɛ] *nm* wine and spirits storehouse.

chaîne [ʃɛn] *nf* chain; (*de télévision*) channel, network; (*de montagnes*) chain, range; (*de bateau*) cable; (*d'étoffe*) warp; **chaînes** (*liens*) *Fig* shackles, chains; **c. de montage** assembly line; **travail à la c.** production-line work; **c. haute fidélité, c. hi-fi** hi-fi (system); **c. compacte** music centre; **c. de magasins** chain of shops *ou* Am stores; **collision en c.** (*accident de la route*) multiple collision; **réaction en c.** chain reaction. ●**chaînette** *nf* (small) chain. ●**chaînon** *nm* (*anneau, lien*) link.

chair [ʃɛr] *nf* flesh; (**couleur) c.** flesh-coloured; **en c. et en os** in the flesh; **la c. de poule** goose pimples *ou* bumps, gooseflesh; **bien en c.** plump; **c. à saucisses** sausage meat.

chaire [ʃɛr] *nf* (*d'université*) chair; *Rel* pulpit.

chaise [ʃɛz] *nf* chair; **c. longue** (*siège pliant*) deckchair; **c. d'enfant, c. haute** high-chair.

chaland [ʃalɑ̃] *nm* barge, lighter.

châle [ʃal] *nm* shawl.

chalet [ʃalɛ] *nm* chalet.

chaleur [ʃalœr] *nf* heat; (*douce*) warmth; (*d'un accueil, d'une voix etc*) warmth; (*des convictions*) ardour; (*d'une discussion*) heat. ●**chaleureux, -euse** *a* (*accueil etc*) warm. ●**chaleureusement** *adv* warmly.

challenge [ʃalɑ̃ʒ] *nm* (*sportif*) challenge match.

chaloupe [ʃalup] *nf* (*bateau*) launch.

chalumeau, -x [ʃalymo] *nm* blowtorch, *Br* blowlamp; (*flûte*) pipe.

chalut [ʃaly] *nm* trawl net, drag net. ●**chalutier** *nm* (*bateau*) trawler.

chamailler (se) [səʃamaje] *vpr* to squabble, bicker. ●**chamailleries** *nfpl* squabbling, bickering.

chamarré, -ée [ʃamare] *a* (*robe etc*) richly coloured; **c. de** (*décorations etc*) *Péj* bedecked with.

chambard [ʃɑ̃bar] *nm Fam* (*tapage*) rumpus, *Br* row. ●**chambarder** *vt* to turn upside down; **il a tout chambardé dans sa chambre/** *etc* he's turned everything upside down in his room/etc.

chambouler [ʃɑ̃bule] *vt* (*pièce, affaires etc*) *Fam* to make a complete mess of, turn upside down.

chambre [ʃɑ̃br] *nf* (*bed*)room; (*au parlement, au tribunal*) & *Tech Anat* chamber; **c. à coucher** bedroom; (*mobilier*) bedroom suite; **c. à air** (*de pneu*) inner tube; **c. d'ami** guest *ou* spare room; **c. de commerce** chamber of commerce; **C. des Communes** (*parlement*) *Br* House of Commons; **c. forte** strongroom; **c. noire** (*de photographe*) darkroom; **garder la c.** to stay indoors. ●**chambrée** *nf* (*de soldats*) barrack room. ●**chambrer** *vt* (*vin*) to bring to room temperature.

chameau, -x [ʃamo] *nm* camel.

chamois [ʃamwa] **1** *nm* (*animal*) chamois; **peau de c.** shammy, chamois, *Br* wash leather. **2** *a inv* buff(-coloured).

champ [ʃɑ̃] nm field; (domaine) Fig scope, field, range; **le c. des investigations** the scope ou field of the investigations; **le c. de ses activités** the scope ou range of his activities; **c. de bataille** battlefield; **c. de courses** Br racecourse, Am racetrack; **c. de foire** fairground; **c. de tir** (terrain) rifle range; **laisser le c. libre à qn** to leave the field open for s.o.

champagne [ʃɑ̃paɲ] nm champagne; **c. brut** extra-dry champagne.

champêtre [ʃɑ̃pɛtr] a (bal, vie etc) country, rural.

champignon [ʃɑ̃piɲɔ̃] nm 1 (végétal) mushroom; **c. vénéneux** toadstool, poisonous mushroom; **c. atomique** mushroom cloud. 2 (accélérateur) Fam accelerator pedal.

champion, -onne [ʃɑ̃pjɔ̃, -jɔn] nmf champion. ●**championnat** nm championship.

chance [ʃɑ̃s] nf luck; (probabilité de réussir, occasion) chance; **avoir de la c.** to be lucky; **tenter** ou **courir sa c.** to try one's luck; **c'est une c. que je sois arrivé** it's lucky that I came; **mes chances de succès** my chances of success. ●**chanceux, -euse** a lucky.

chanceler [ʃɑ̃sle] vi to stagger, totter; (courage, détermination) Fig to falter. ●**chancelant, -ante** a (pas, santé) faltering, shaky.

chancelier [ʃɑ̃səlje] nm (allemand etc) chancellor. ●**chancellerie** nf (d'ambassade) chancellery.

chancre [ʃɑ̃kr] nm (maladie) & Fig canker.

chandail [ʃɑ̃daj] nm (thick) sweater ou Br jersey.

chandelier [ʃɑ̃dəlje] nm candlestick.

chandelle [ʃɑ̃dɛl] nf candle; **voir trente-six chandelles** Fig to see stars; **en c.** (tir) straight into the air.

change [ʃɑ̃ʒ] nm (de devises) exchange; **le contrôle des changes** exchange control; **donner le c. à qn** to deceive s.o.

changer [ʃɑ̃ʒe] vt (modifier, remplacer, échanger) to change; **c. qn/qch en** to change s.o./sth into; **c. un bébé** to change a baby; **ça la changera de ne pas travailler** it'll be a change for her not to be working.
█ vi to change; **c. de voiture/d'adresse/etc** to change one's car/address/etc; **c. de train/de bus/de côté** to change trains/buses/sides; **c. de place** to change ou swap places (avec qn with s.o.); **c. de vitesse/de cap/de couleur** to change gear/course/colour; **c. de sujet** to change the subject; **du café, pour c. du thé?** some coffee, to make a change from tea?
█ **se changer** vpr to change (one's clothes). ●**changeant, -ante** a (temps) changeable; (humeur) fickle; (couleurs) changing. ●**changement** nm change; **aimer le c.** to like change. ●**changeur** nm moneychanger; **c. de monnaie** change machine.

chanoine [ʃanwan] nm (personne) Rel canon.

chanson [ʃɑ̃sɔ̃] nf song. ●**chant** nm singing; (chanson) song; (hymne) hymn; **c. de Noël** Christmas carol.

chanter [ʃɑ̃te] vi to sing; (psalmodier) to chant; (coq) to crow; **si ça te chante** Fam if you feel like it; **faire c. qn** to blackmail s.o.
█ vt to sing; (glorifier) to sing of (exploits etc); (dire) Fam to say. ●**chantant, -ante** a (air, voix) melodious. ●**chantage** nm blackmail. ●**chanteur, -euse** nmf singer.

chantier [ʃɑ̃tje] nm (building) site; (sur route) roadworks; (entrepôt) builder's yard; **c. naval** shipyard, dockyard; **mettre un travail en c.** to get a task under way.

chantonner [ʃɑ̃tɔne] vti to hum.

chantre [ʃɑ̃tr] nm Rel cantor.

chanvre [ʃɑ̃vr] nm hemp; **c. indien** (plante) cannabis.

chaos [kao] nm chaos. ●**chaotique** a chaotic.

chaparder [ʃaparde] vt Fam to steal, filch, Br pinch (à from).

chapeau, -x [ʃapo] nm hat; (de champignon, roue) cap; **c.!** well done!; **donner un coup de c.** (pour saluer etc) to raise one's hat (à qn to s.o.); **c. mou** Br trilby, Am fedora. ●**chapelier** nm hatter, hatmaker.

chapelet [ʃaplɛ] nm rosary; **dire son c.** to tell one's beads; **un c. de saucisses/d'injures/etc** a string of sausages/abuse/etc.

chapelle [ʃapɛl] nf chapel; **c. ardente** chapel of rest.

chapelure [ʃaplyr] nf breadcrumbs.

chaperon [ʃaprɔ̃] nm chaperon(e). ●**chaperonner** vt to chaperon(e).

chapiteau, -x [ʃapito] nm (de cirque) big top; (pour expositions etc) tent, Br marquee; (de colonne) Archit capital.

chapitre [ʃapitr] nm (de livre etc) & Rel chapter; **sur le c.** de on the subject of.

chapitrer [ʃapitre] vt to scold, lecture.

chaque [ʃak] a each, every.

char [ʃar] nm (romain) chariot; (de carnaval) float; (voiture) Can Fam car; **c. (d'assaut)** (tank) tank; **c. à bœufs** oxcart.

charabia [ʃarabja] nm Fam gibberish.

charade [ʃarad] nf (énigme) riddle; (mimée) charade.

charbon [ʃarbɔ̃] nm coal; (pour dessiner) charcoal; **c. de bois** (combustible) charcoal; **sur des charbons ardents** on tenterhooks, like a cat on hot bricks. ●**charbonnages** nmpl coalmines, Br collieries. ●**charbonnier, -ière** a basin **c.** coal basin; **industrie charbonnière** coal industry █ nm coal merchant.

charcuter [ʃarkyte] vt (opérer) Fam Péj to cut up (badly).

charcuterie [ʃarkytri] nf pork butcher's shop; (aliments) cooked (pork) meats. ●**charcutier, -ière** nmf pork butcher.

chardon [ʃardɔ̃] nm (plante) thistle.

chardonneret [ʃardɔnrɛ] nm (oiseau) goldfinch.

charge [ʃarʒ] nf (poids) load; (fardeau) burden; (électrique, accusation, attaque militaire) charge; (fonction) office; **charges** (financières) financial obligations; (dépenses) expenses; (*de locataire*) (maintenance) charges; **charges sociales** Br national insurance contributions, Am Social Security contributions; **un enfant/parent à c.** a dependent child/relative; **à la c. de qn** (*personne*) dependent on s.o.; (*frais*) payable by s.o.; **prendre en c.** to take charge of, take responsibility for.

charger [ʃarʒe] vt to load; (*soldats, batterie*) to charge; (*passager*) Fam to pick up; **se c. de** (*enfant, tâche etc*) to take charge of; **c. qn de** (*tâche etc*) to entrust s.o. with; (*impôts etc*) to burden s.o. with; (*paquets etc*) to load s.o. with; **se c. de faire qch** to undertake to do sth; **c. qn de faire qch** to instruct s.o. to do sth. ● **chargé, -ée** a (*véhicule, arme etc*) loaded; (*journée, programme etc*) busy, heavy; (*langue*) coated; **c. de** (*personne, véhicule etc*) loaded with (*packages etc*); (*arbre, navire etc*) laden with (*fruit, goods etc*); **il est c. de balayer/etc** his job is to sweep/etc ▮ nmf **c. de cours** Univ (temporary) lecturer. ● **chargement** nm (*action*) loading; (*objet*) load. ● **chargeur** nm (*d'arme à feu*) magazine; **c. (de piles)** (battery) charger.

chariot [ʃarjo] nm (*à bagages etc*) Br trolley, Am cart; (*de ferme*) waggon; (*de machine à écrire*) carriage.

charitable [ʃaritabl] a charitable (**pour, envers** towards).

charité [ʃarite] nf (*secours, vertu*) charity; (*acte*) act of charity; **faire la c.** to give to charity; **faire la c. à** (*mendiant*) to give (money) to.

charivari [ʃarivari] nm Fam hubbub, hullabaloo.

charlatan [ʃarlatã] nm charlatan, quack.

charme [ʃarm] nm **1** charm; (*magie*) spell; **se porter comme un c.** to be the very picture of health. **2** (*arbre*) hornbeam.

charmer [ʃarme] vt to charm; **je suis charmé de vous voir** I'm delighted to see you. ● **charmant, -ante** a charming. ● **charmeur, -euse** nmf charmer ▮ a (*sourire, air etc*) winning, engaging, bewitching.

charnel, -elle [ʃarnɛl] a carnal.

charnier [ʃarnje] nm mass grave.

charnière [ʃarnjɛr] nf hinge; Fig meeting point (de between).

charnu, -ue [ʃarny] a fleshy.

charogne [ʃarɔɲ] nf carrion.

charpente [ʃarpɑ̃t] nf frame(work); (*de personne*) build. ● **charpenté, -ée** a **bien c.** solidly built. ● **charpenterie** nf carpentry. ● **charpentier** nm carpenter.

charpie [ʃarpi] nf **mettre en c.** (*déchirer*) & Fig to tear to shreds.

charrette [ʃarɛt] nf cart. ● **charrier 1** vt (*transporter*) to cart; (*rivière*) to carry along, wash down (*sand etc*). **2** vti (*taquiner*) Fam to tease.

charrue [ʃary] nf Br plough, Am plow.

charte [ʃart] nf (*loi*) charter.

charter [ʃartɛr] nm (*vol*) charter (flight); (*avion*) charter plane.

chas [ʃa] nm eye (*of a needle*).

chasse¹ [ʃas] nf hunting, hunt; (*poursuite*) chase; (*avions*) fighter forces; **c. sous-marine** underwater fishing; **c. à courre** hunting; **avion/pilote de c.** fighter plane/pilot; **chien de c.** retriever; **tableau de c.** (*animaux abattus*) bag; **faire la c. à** to hunt for; **donner la c. à** to give chase to; **c. à l'homme** manhunt.

chasse² [ʃas] nf **c. d'eau** Br toilet ou Am lavatory flush; **tirer la c.** to flush the Br toilet ou Am lavatory.

châsse [ʃas] nf shrine.

chassé-croisé [ʃasekrwaze] nm (pl **chassés-croisés**) Fig confused coming(s) and going(s).

chasser [ʃase] vt (*animal*) to hunt; (*faisan, perdrix etc*) to shoot; (*papillon*) to chase; (*faire partir*) to chase (*s.o.*) away, drive (*s.o.*) away ou off; (*employé*) to dismiss; (*mouche*) to brush away ▮ vi to hunt; (*déraper*) to skid. ● **chasseur, -euse** nmf hunter; **c. de têtes** (*pour le compte d'une entreprise*) headhunter ▮ nm (*d'hôtel*) Br pageboy, Am bellboy; (*avion*) fighter; **c. à pied** infantryman. ● **chasse-neige** nm inv Br snowplough, Am snowplow.

châssis [ʃasi] nm frame; (*d'automobile*) chassis.

chaste [ʃast] a chaste, pure. ● **chasteté** nf chastity.

chat [ʃa] nm cat; **avoir un c. dans la gorge** to have a frog in one's throat; **avoir d'autres chats à fouetter** to have other fish to fry; **il n'y avait pas un c.** there wasn't a soul (around); **c. perché** (*jeu*) tag.

châtaigne [ʃatɛɲ] nf chestnut. ● **châtaignier** nm chestnut tree. ● **châtain** a inv (chestnut) brown.

château, -x [ʃato] nm (*forteresse*) castle; (*palais*) palace, stately home; **c. fort** fortified castle; **châteaux en Espagne** Fig castles in the air; **c. d'eau** water tower; **c. de cartes** Fig house of cards.

châtelain, -aine [ʃatlɛ̃, -ɛn] nmf lord of the manor, lady of the manor.

châtier [ʃatje] vt Litt to chastise, castigate; (*style*) to refine.

châtiment [ʃatimã] nm punishment.

chaton [ʃatɔ̃] nm **1** (*chat*) kitten. **2** (*de bague*) setting, mounting. **3** (*d'arbre*) catkin.

chatouiller [ʃatuje] vt (*pour faire rire*) to tickle; (*exciter, plaire à*) Fig to titillate. ● **chatouillement** nm ou **chatouillis** nm tickle; (*action*) tickling. ● **chatouilleux, -euse** a ticklish; (*irritable*) touchy.

chatoyer [ʃatwaje] vi to glitter, sparkle.

châtrer [ʃatre] vt to castrate.

chatte [ʃat] nf (she-)cat; **ma (petite) c.** Fam my darling.

chatteries [ʃatri] nfpl cuddles; (*friandises*) delicacies.

chatterton [ʃatɛrtɔn] nm (adhesive) insulating tape.

chaud, chaude [ʃo, ʃod] a hot; (*doux*)

warm; (*fervent*) (*partisan, plaidoyer etc*) ardent; **pleurer à chaudes larmes** to cry bitterly ∎ *nm* heat; (*modéré*) warmth; **avoir c.** to be hot; to be warm; **il fait c.** it's hot; it's warm; **être au c.** to be in the warm(th); **ça ne me fait ni c. ni froid** it makes no difference to me, it leaves me completely indifferent. ●**chaudement** *adv* warmly; (*avec passion*) (*plaider, défendre, discuter*) ardently.

chaudière [ʃodjɛr] *nf* boiler.

chauffage [ʃofaʒ] *nm* heating.

chauffard [ʃofar] *nm* road hog, reckless driver.

chauffer [ʃofe] *vt* (*chaussures*) to put on; (*fournir*) to supply with footwear; **c. qn** to put shoes on to s.o.; **c. du 40** to take a size 40 shoe; **ce soulier te chausse bien** this shoe fits (you) well ∎ **se chausser** *vpr* to put on one's shoes. ●**chausse-pied** *nm* shoehorn.

chaussette [ʃosɛt] *nf* sock.

chausson [ʃosɔ̃] *nm* slipper; (*de danse*) shoe; (*de bébé*) bootee; **c. (aux pommes)** apple turnover.

chaussure [ʃosyr] *nf* shoe; **chaussures à semelles compensées** platform shoes; **chaussures de ski** ski boots; **il travaille dans la c.** he works in footwear *ou* in the shoe business.

chauve [ʃov] *a* & *nmf* bald (person).

chauve-souris [ʃovsuri] *nf* (*pl* **chauves-souris**) (*animal*) bat.

chauvin, -ine [ʃovɛ̃, -in] *a* chauvinistic ∎ *nmf* chauvinist. ●**chauvinisme** *nm* chauvinism.

chaux [ʃo] *nf* lime; **blanc de c.** whitewash.

chavirer [ʃavire] *vti* (*bateau etc*) to capsize.

chef [ʃɛf] *nm* 1 leader, head; (*de tribu*) chief; (*cuisinier*) chef; **commandant/rédacteur en c.** commander/editor in chief; **c'est un c.!** (*personne remarquable*) he's an ace!; **c. d'atelier** (shop) foreman; **c. de bande** ringleader; gang leader; **c. d'entreprise** company head; **c. d'équipe** foreman; **c. d'État** head of state; **c. d'état-major** chief of staff; **c. de famille** head of the family; **c. de** file leader; **c. de gare** stationmaster; **c. d'orchestre** conductor; **c. de service** head of department. **2 de son propre c.** on one's own authority.

chef-lieu [ʃɛfljø] *nm* (*pl* **chefs-lieux**) chief town (*of a département*).

chef-d'œuvre [ʃɛdœvr] *nm* (*pl* **chefs-d'œuvre**) masterpiece.

cheik [ʃɛk] *nm* sheik.

chemin [ʃ(ə)mɛ̃] *nm* 1 road, path; (*trajet, direction*) way; **beaucoup de c. à faire** a long way to go; **dix minutes de c.** ten minutes' walk; **se mettre en c.** to set out, start out; **faire du c.** to come a long way; (*idée*) to make considerable headway; **c. faisant** on the way; **à mi-c.** half-way. **2 c. de fer** *Br* railway, *Am* railroad.

cheminée [ʃ(ə)mine] *nf* (*âtre*) fireplace; (*encadrement*) mantelpiece; (*sur le toit*) chimney; (*de navire*) funnel.

cheminer [ʃ(ə)mine] *vi* to proceed (on foot), continue on one's way; (*péniblement*) to trudge (along) on foot; (*évoluer*) *Fig* to progress. ●**cheminement** *nm* *Fig* progress.

cheminot [ʃ(ə)mino] *nm* *Br* railway *ou* *Am* railroad employee.

chemise [ʃ(ə)miz] *nf* shirt; (*couverture cartonnée*) folder; **c. de nuit** (*de femme*) nightdress. ●**chemiserie** *nf* men's shirt and underwear) shop. ●**chemisette** *nf* short-sleeved shirt. ●**chemisier** *nm* (*vêtement*) blouse.

chenal, -aux [ʃənal, -o] *nm* channel.

chenapan [ʃ(ə)napɑ̃] *nm* *Hum* rogue, scoundrel.

chêne [ʃɛn] *nm* (*arbre, bois*) oak.

chenet [ʃ(ə)nɛ] *nm* andiron, firedog.

chenil [ʃ(ə)ni(l)] *nm* *Br* kennels, *Am* kennel; **mettre un chien dans un c.** to put a dog in *Br* kennels *ou* *Am* a kennel.

chenille [ʃ(ə)nij] *nf* caterpillar; (*de char etc*) caterpillar track.

cheptel [ʃɛptɛl] *nm* livestock.

chèque [ʃɛk] *nm* *Br* cheque, *Am* check; **c. de voyage** *Br* traveller's cheque, *Am* traveler's check. ●**chèque-repas** *nm* (*pl* **chèques-repas**) *Br* luncheon voucher, *Am* meal ticket. ●**chéquier** *nm* *Br* cheque book, *Am* checkbook.

cher, chère [ʃɛr] **1** *a* (*aimé*) dear (à to) ∎ *nmf* **mon c.** my dear fellow; **ma chère** my dear (woman). **2** *a* (*coûteux*) (*objet, magasin etc*) expensive, dear (*après le nom*); (*quartier, hôtel etc*) expensive; **ça coûte c.** that's expensive; **la vie chère** the high cost of living; **payer c.** (*objet*) to pay a lot for; (*erreur etc*) *Fig* to pay dearly for. ●**chèrement** *adv* (*aimer, payer*) dearly.

chercher [ʃɛrʃe] *vt* to look for; (*du secours, la paix etc*) to seek; (*dans un dictionnaire*) to look up (*word*); **c. ses mots** to fumble for one's words; **aller c. qn/qch** to (go and) get *ou* fetch s.o./sth; **venir c. qn/qch** to call for s.o./sth, come and get *ou* fetch s.o./sth; **c. à faire** to attempt to do; **tu l'as bien cherché!**

it's your own fault!, you asked for it! ●**chercheur, -euse** *nmf* research worker; **c. d'or** gold-digger.

chérir [ʃerir] *vt* to cherish. ●**chéri, -ie** *a* dearly loved, beloved ▮ *nmf* darling.

chérot [ʃero] *am* **c'est c.** *Fam* it's pricey.

cherté [ʃerte] *nf* high cost, expensiveness.

chétif, -ive [ʃetif, -iv] *a* puny; (*dérisoire*) (*vie, repas etc*) wretched.

cheval, -aux [ʃ(ə)val, -o] *nm* horse; **c. (vapeur)** *Aut* horsepower; **à c.** on horseback; **faire du c.** to go *Br* horse riding *ou Am* horseback riding; **être à à c. sur** to be straddling; **être à c. sur les principes** to be a stickler for principle; **monter sur ses grands chevaux** to get excited; **c. à bascule** rocking horse; **c. d'arçons** *Sport* vaulting horse; **c. de bataille** (*dada*) hobbyhorse; **chevaux de bois** (*manège*) merry-go-round.

chevaleresque [ʃ(ə)valrɛsk] *a* chivalrous.

chevalet [ʃ(ə)vale] *nm* (*de peintre*) easel; (*de menuisier etc*) trestle.

chevalier [ʃ(ə)valje] *nm* knight.

chevalière [ʃ(ə)valjɛr] *nf* signet ring.

chevaline [ʃ(ə)valin] *af* **boucherie c.** horse butcher's (shop).

chevauchée [ʃ(ə)voʃe] *nf* (horse) ride.

chevaucher [ʃ(ə)voʃe] *vt* to straddle ▮ *vi* **se chevaucher** *vpr* to overlap.

chevelu, -ue [ʃ(ə)vly] *a* long-haired, hairy. ●**chevelure** *nf* (head of) hair.

chevet [ʃ(ə)ve] *nm* bedhead; **table/livre de c.** bedside table/book; **au c. de** at the bedside of.

cheveu, -x [ʃ(ə)vø] *nm* **un c.** a hair; **cheveux** hair; **avoir les cheveux noirs** to have black hair; **couper les cheveux en quatre** *Fig* to split hairs; **tiré par les cheveux** (*argument*) far-fetched.

cheville [ʃ(ə)vij] *nf* (*du pied*) ankle; (*pour vis*) (wall) plug; (*pour meuble*) peg, pin; **c. ouvrière** *Fig* linchpin; **en c. avec qn** *Fam* in cahoots with (s.o.); **elle ne vous arrive pas à la c.** *Fig* she can't hold a candle to you. ●**cheviller** *vt* (*meuble*) to pin, peg.

chèvre [ʃɛvr] *nf* goat; (*femelle*) nanny-goat. ●**chevreau, -x** *nm* (*petit de la chèvre*) kid.

chèvrefeuille [ʃɛvrəfœj] *nm* honeysuckle.

chevreuil [ʃəvrœj] *nm* roe deer; (*viande*) venison.

chevron [ʃəvrɔ̃] *nm* (*poutre*) rafter; (*signe de grade militaire*) stripe, chevron; **à chevrons** (*tissu, veste etc*) herringbone.

chevronné, -ée [ʃəvrɔne] *a* (*professeur etc*) seasoned, experienced.

chevroter [ʃəvrɔte] *vi* (*voix*) to quaver, tremble.

chez [ʃe] *prép* **c. qn** at s.o.'s house, flat *etc*; **il est c. Jean/c.** **l'épicier** he's at John's (place)/at the grocer's; **il va c. Jean/c.** **l'épicier** he's going to John's (place)/to the grocer's; **c. moi, c. nous** at home; **je vais c. moi** I'm going home; **faites comme c. vous** make yourself at home; **c. les Suisses/les jeunes** among the Swiss/the young; **c. Camus**

in (the work of) Camus; **c. l'homme** in man; **chez les mammifères** in mammals; **une habitude c. elle** a habit with her; **c. Mme Dupont** (*adresse*) care of *ou* c/o Mme Dupont. ●**chez-soi** *nm inv* **un c.-soi** a home (of one's own).

chialer [ʃjale] *vi* (*pleurer*) *Fam* to cry.

chic [ʃik] **1** *a inv* smart, stylish; (*gentil*) *Fam* nice, decent ▮ *int* **c. (alors)!** great! ▮ *nm* style, elegance. **2** *nm* **avoir le c. pour faire** to have the knack of doing.

chicane [ʃikan] *nf* (*querelle*) quibble. ●**chicaner** *vt* to quibble with (s.o.) ▮ *vi* to quibble.

chicanes [ʃikan] *nfpl* (*obstacles*) zigzag barriers.

chiche [ʃiʃ] **1** *a* mean, niggardly; **c. de** sparing of. **2** *int* (*défi*) *Fam* I bet (you) I do, can *etc*; **c. que je parte sans lui!** I bet (you) I leave without him!

chichis [ʃiʃi] *nmpl* **faire des c.** to make a lot of fuss.

chicorée [ʃikɔre] *nf* (*à café*) chicory *inv*; (*pour salade*) endive.

chien [ʃjɛ̃] *nm* dog; **c. d'aveugle** guide dog; **c. d'arrêt** pointer, retriever; **un mal de c.** *Fam* an awful lot of trouble; **temps de c.** *Fam* rotten *or* filthy weather; **une vie de c.** *Fig* a dog's life; **entre c. et loup** at dusk, in the twilight. ●**chien-loup** *nm* (*pl* **chiens-loups**) wolfhound. ●**chienne** *nf* dog, bitch.

chiendent [ʃjɛ̃dɑ̃] *nm* (*plante*) couch grass; **brosse de c.** scrubbing brush.

chiffon [ʃifɔ̃] *nm* rag; **c. (à poussière)** *Br* duster, *Am* dustcloth. ●**chiffonner** *vt* to crumple; (*ennuyer*) *Fig* to bother, distress. ●**chiffonnier** *nm* ragman.

chiffre [ʃifr] *nm* figure, number; (*romain, arabe*) numeral; (*code*) cipher; **c. d'affaires** (sales) turnover. ●**chiffrer** *vt* (*montant*) to assess, work out; (*message*) to cipher, code ▮ *vi* to mount up ▮ **se chiffrer** *vpr* **se c. à** to amount to, work out at.

chignon [ʃiɲɔ̃] *nm* bun, chignon.

Chili [ʃili] *nm* Chile. ●**chilien, -ienne** *a* Chilean ▮ *nmf* **C., Chilienne** Chilean.

chimère [ʃimɛr] *nf* fantasy, (wild) dream. ●**chimérique** *a* fanciful.

chimie [ʃimi] *nf* chemistry. ●**chimique** *a* chemical. ●**chimiste** *nmf* (research) chemist.

chimiothérapie [ʃimjɔterapi] *nf* chemotherapy.

chimpanzé [ʃɛ̃pɑze] *nm* chimpanzee.

Chine [ʃin] *nf* China. ●**chinois, -oise** *a* Chinese ▮ *nmf* **C., Chinoise** Chinese man *ou* woman, Chinese *inv*; **les C.** the Chinese ▮ *nm* (*langue*) Chinese. ●**chinoiser** *vi* to quibble. ●**chinoiserie** *nf* (*objet*) Chinese curio; **chinoiseries** (*bizarreries*) *Fig* weird complications.

chiner [ʃine] *vi* (*brocanteur etc*) to hunt for bargains.

chiot [ʃjo] *nm* pup(py).

chiper [ʃipe] *vt* *Fam* to swipe, *Br* pinch (**à** from).

chipie [ʃipi] *nf* **vieille c.** (*femme*) *Péj* old crab or shrew.

chipoter [ʃipɔte] *vi* **1** (*discuter*) to quibble. **2** (*manger*) to nibble.

chips [ʃips] *nfpl Br* (potato) crisps, *Am* chips.

chiquenaude [ʃiknod] *nf* flick (of the finger).

chiromancie [kirɔmɑ̃si] *nf* palmistry.

chirurgie [ʃiryrʒi] *nf* surgery. ● **chirurgical, -e, -aux** *a* surgical. ● **chirurgien** *nm* surgeon.

chlore [klɔr] *nm* chlorine. ● **chlorer** *vt* to chlorinate; **eau chlorée** chlorinated water.

chloroforme [klɔrɔfɔrm] *nm* chloroform.

choc [ʃɔk] *nm* (*d'objets*) impact, shock; (*émotion, traumatisme*) shock; (*collision, bruit*) crash; (*des opinions, entre manifestants etc*) clash.

chocolat [ʃɔkɔla] *nm* chocolate; **c. à croquer** *Br* plain *ou Am* bittersweet chocolate; **c. au lait** milk chocolate; **c. glacé** *Br* choc-ice, *Am* (chocolate) ice-cream bar **▮** *a inv* chocolate(-coloured). ● **chocolaté, -ée** *a* a chocolate-flavoured.

chœur [kœr] *nm* (*chanteurs, nef*) *Rel* choir; (*composition musicale*) & *Fig* chorus; **en c.** (all) together, in chorus.

choir [ʃwar] *vi* **laisser c. qn** *Fam* to turn one's back on s.o.

choisir [ʃwazir] *vt* to choose, pick, select. ● **choisi, -ie** *a* (*œuvres*) selected; (*terme, langage*) well-chosen; (*public*) select.

choix [ʃwa] *nm* choice; (*assortiment*) selection; **morceau de c.** choice piece; **au c. du client** according to choice.

choléra [kɔlera] *nm* cholera.

cholestérol [kɔlesterɔl] *nm* cholesterol.

chômer [ʃome] *vi* (*ouvrier etc*) to be unemployed; **jour chômé** (public) holiday. ● **chômage** *nm* unemployment; **au c.** unemployed; **mettre en c. technique** to lay off, *Br* make redundant. ● **chômeur, -euse** *nmf* unemployed person; **les chômeurs** the unemployed.

chope [ʃɔp] *nf* beer mug, *Br* tankard; (*contenu*) pint.

choquer [ʃɔke] *vt* (*scandaliser*) to shock (*s.o.*); (*commotionner*) to shake (*s.o.*) up; (*verres*) to clink. ● **choquant, -ante** *a* (*propos, images etc*) shocking, offensive.

choral, -e, mpl -als [kɔral] *a* choral. ● **chorale** *nf* choral society. ● **choriste** *nmf* chorister.

chorégraphe [kɔregraf] *nmf* choreographer. ● **chorégraphie** *nf* choreography.

chose [ʃoz] *nf* thing; **état de choses** state of affairs; **dis-lui bien des choses de ma part** remember me to him *ou* her; **par la force des choses** through force of circumstance; **monsieur C.** Mr What's-his-name; **se sentir tout c.** *Fam* (*décontenancé, malade*) to feel all funny.

chou, -x [ʃu] *nm* cabbage; **choux de Bruxelles** Brussels sprouts; **mon c.!** my pet!; **c. à la crème** cream puff. ● **chou-fleur** *nm* (*pl* choux-fleurs) cauliflower.

choucas [ʃuka] *nm* jackdaw.

chouchou, -oute [ʃuʃu, -ut] *nmf* (*favori*) *Fam* pet, darling. ● **chouchouter** *vt* to pamper.

choucroute [ʃukrut] *nf* sauerkraut.

chouette [ʃwɛt] *nf* (*oiseau*) owl. **2** *a* (*chic*) *Fam* super, great **▮** *int* **c.!** super!, great!

choyer [ʃwaje] *vt* to pamper.

chrétien, -ienne [kretjɛ̃, -jɛn] *a* & *nmf* Christian. ● **Christ** [krist] *nm* Christ. ● **christianisme** *nm* Christianity.

chrome [krom] *nm* chromium, chrome. ● **chromé, -ée** *a* chromium- *ou* chrome-plated.

chromosome [krɔmozom] *nm* chromosome.

chronique¹ [krɔnik] *a* (*malade, chômage etc*) chronic.

chronique² [krɔnik] *nf* (*à la radio*) report; (*dans le journal*) column; (*annales*) chronicle. ● **chroniqueur** *nm* (*historien*) chronicler; (*journaliste*) reporter, columnist.

chronologie [krɔnɔlɔʒi] *nf* chronology. ● **chronologique** *a* chronological.

chronomètre [krɔnɔmɛtr] *nm* stopwatch. ● **chronométrer** *vt* (*course etc*) to time. ● **chronométreur** *nm* (*de course*) timekeeper.

chrysanthème [krizɑ̃tɛm] *nm* chrysanthemum.

CHU [seaʃy] *nm abrév* **centre hospitalo-universitaire.**

chuchoter [ʃyʃɔte] *vti* to whisper. ● **chuchotement** *nm* whisper(ing). ● **chuchoteries** *nfpl Fam* whispering.

chuinter [ʃwɛ̃te] *vi* (*vapeur*) to hiss.

chut! [ʃyt] *int* sh!, shush! [ʃuʃ].

chute [ʃyt] *nf* fall; (*défaite*) (down)fall; **c. d'eau** waterfall; **c. de neige** snowfall; **c. de pluie** rainfall; **c. des cheveux** hair loss; **être en c. libre** (*monnaie etc*) to be in free fall, be plummeting. ● **chuter** *vi Fam* to fall.

Chypre [ʃipr] *nf* Cyprus. ● **chypriote** *a* Cypriot **▮** *nmf* **C.** Cypriot.

ci [si] *pron dém* **comme ci comme ça** so so.

-ci [si] *adv* **1** **par-ci, par-là** here and there. **2** *voir* ce², celui.

ci-après [siapre] *adv* below, hereafter. ● **ci-contre** *adv* opposite. ● **ci-dessous** *adv* below. ● **ci-dessus** *adv* above. ● **ci-gît** *adv* here lies (*on gravestones*). ● **ci-inclus, -use** *a ou* **ci-joint, -jointe** *a* (*inv before n*) (*dans une lettre*) enclosed (herewith).

cible [sibl] *nf* target.

ciboulette [sibulɛt] *nf* (*condiment*) chives.

cicatrice [sikatris] *nf* scar.

cicatriser [sikatrize] *vt*, **se cicatriser** *vpr* to heal (up) (*leaving a scar*). ● **cicatrisation** *nf* healing (up).

cidre [sidr] *nm* cider.

Cie *abrév* (*compagnie*) Co.

ciel [sjɛl] *nm* **1** (*pl* ciels) sky; **à c. ouvert** (*piscine etc*) open-air; **c. de lit** canopy. **2** (*pl* cieux [sjø]) (*paradis*) heaven; **juste c.!** good heavens!; **sous d'autres cieux** *Hum* in other climes.

cierge [sjɛrʒ] nm Rel candle.

cigale [sigal] nf (insecte) cicada.

cigare [sigar] nm cigar. ● **cigarette** nf cigarette.

cigogne [sigɔɲ] nf stork.

cil [sil] nm (eye)lash.

cime [sim] nf (d'un arbre) top; (d'une montagne) & Fig peak.

ciment [simã] nm cement. ● **cimenter** vt to cement.

cimetière [simtjɛr] nm cemetery; (autour d'une église) graveyard; **c. de voitures** scrapyard, Br breaker's yard, Am auto graveyard.

ciné [sine] nm Fam = **cinéma**. ● **ciné-club** nm film club ou society. ● **cinéaste** nmf film maker. ● **cinéphile** nmf film buff.

cinéma [sinema] nm (art) cinema; (salle) Br cinema, Am movie theater; **faire du c.** to make movies ou films; **aller au c.** to go to the movies ou Br the cinema; **acteur/etc de c.** movie ou film actor. ● **cinémascope** nm cinemascope. ● **cinémathèque** nf film library; (salle) film theatre. ● **cinématographique** a **industrie/technique/etc c.** film industry/technique/etc.

cinglé, -ée [sɛ̃gle] a Fam crazy.

cingler [sɛ̃gle] vt to lash. ● **cinglant, -ante** a (vent, remarque) cutting, biting.

cinoche [sinɔʃ] nm Fam Br cinema, Am movie theater.

cinq [sɛ̃k] nm five ▌ a ([sɛ̃] before consonant) five. ● **cinquième** a & nmf fifth; **un c.** a fifth.

cinquante [sɛ̃kãt] a & nm fifty. ● **cinquantaine** nf **une c. (de)** about fifty; **avoir la c.** (âge) to be about fifty. ● **cinquantenaire** a & nmf fifty-year-old (person) ▌ nm fiftieth anniversary. ● **cinquantième** a & nmf fiftieth.

cintre [sɛ̃tr] nm coathanger; Archit arch. ● **cintré, -ée** a (porte etc) arched; (veste etc) tailored, slim-fitting, Br fitted.

cirage [siraʒ] nm (shoe) polish.

circoncis [sirkɔ̃si] am circumcised. ● **circoncision** nf circumcision.

circonférence [sirkɔ̃ferãs] nf circumference.

circonflexe [sirkɔ̃flɛks] a Grammaire circumflex.

circonlocution [sirkɔ̃lɔkysjɔ̃] nf circumlocution.

circonscription [sirkɔ̃skripsjɔ̃] nf division, district; **c. (électorale)** Br constituency, Am district.

çirconscrire* [sirkɔ̃skrir] vt (incendie etc) to contain, bring under control; (question, problème etc) to define.

circonspect, -ecte [sirkɔ̃spɛ(kt), -ɛkt] a cautious, circumspect. ● **circonspection** nf caution.

circonstance [sirkɔ̃stãs] nf circumstance; **pour/en la c.** for/on this occasion; **de c.** (habit, parole etc) appropriate, befitting the occasion. ● **circonstancié, -ée** a detailed. ● **circonstanciel, -ielle** a Grammaire adverbial.

circonvenir* [sirkɔ̃vnir] vt to circumvent.

circuit [sirkɥi] nm (électrique, sportif etc) circuit; (voyage) tour, trip; (détour) round-about way.

circulaire [sirkyler] a circular ▌ nf (lettre) circular.

circulation [sirkylasjɔ̃] nf circulation; (automobile) traffic. ● **circuler** vi (sang, lettre etc) to circulate; (véhicule, train) to travel, go, move; (passant) to walk about; (rumeur, nouvelles) to go round, circulate; **faire c.** (lettre, rumeur, plat etc) to circulate; (piétons etc) to move on; **circulez!** keep moving!

cire [sir] nf wax; (pour meubles) polish, wax. ● **cirer** vt to polish. ● **ciré** nm (vêtement) oilskin(s). ● **cireur** nm bootblack. ● **cireuse** nf (appareil) floor polisher. ● **cireux, -euse** a waxy.

cirque [sirk] nm circus.

cirrhose [siroz] nf **c. (du foie)** cirrhosis (of the liver).

cisaille(s) [sizaj] nf(pl) (garden) shears. ● **ciseau, -x** nm (de menuisier) chisel; **(une paire de) ciseaux** (a pair of) scissors. ● **ciseler** vt to chisel.

citadelle [sitadɛl] nf citadel.

cité [site] nf city; **c. (ouvrière)** Br housing estate (for workers), Am housing project ou development; **c. universitaire** Br (students') halls of residence, Am university dormitory complex. ● **citadin, -ine** nmf city dweller ▌ a **vie/etc citadine** city ou urban life/etc.

citer [site] vt to quote; (témoin etc) to summon; (soldat) to mention, cite. ● **citation** nf quotation; (au tribunal) summons; (d'un soldat) mention, citation.

citerne [sitɛrn] nf (réservoir) tank.

cithare [sitar] nf zither.

citoyen, -enne [sitwajɛ̃, -ɛn] nmf citizen. ● **citoyenneté** nf citizenship.

citron [sitrɔ̃] nm lemon; **c. pressé** (fresh) lemon juice. ● **citronnade** nf lemon drink, Br lemon squash, Am lemonade.

citrouille [sitruj] nf pumpkin.

civet [sivɛ] nm stew; **c. de lièvre** jugged hare.

civière [sivjɛr] nf stretcher.

civil, -e [sivil] 1 a (guerre, mariage, droits etc) civil; (non militaire) civilian; (courtois) civil; **année civile** calendar year. **2** nm civilian; **dans le c.** in civilian life; **en c.** (policier) in plain clothes; (soldat) in civilian clothes. ● **civilité** nf civility.

civilisation [sivilizasjɔ̃] nf civilization.

civiliser [sivilize] vt to civilize ▌ **se civiliser** vpr to become civilized.

civique [sivik] a (droit, sens etc) civic; **instruction c.** (des enfants) civics. ● **civisme** nm good citizenship.

clair, -e [klɛr] a (net, limpide, évident) clear; (éclairé) light; (pâle) (tissu, fond etc) light- (-coloured); (sauce, chevelure) thin; **bleu/vert c.** light blue/green; **robe bleu/vert c.** light-blue/-green dress; **il fait c.** it's light ou bright ▌ adv (voir) clearly ▌ nm **c. de lune** moonlight; **au c. de lune** in the moonlight; **passer le plus c. de son temps à faire** to spend the major *ou* greater part of one's time doing; **tirer au c.** (*question etc*) to clarify. ●**clairement** *adv* clearly.

claire-voie [klɛrvwa] *nf* **à c.-voie** (*barrière, caisse*) openwork; (*porte*) louvre(d).

clairière [klɛrjɛr] *nf* clearing.

clairon [klɛrɔ̃] *nm* bugle; (*soldat*) bugler. ●**claironner** *vt* (*annoncer*) to trumpet forth (*news etc*).

clairsemé, -ée [klɛrsəme] *a* (*cheveux, auditoire etc*) sparse.

clairvoyant, -ante [klɛrvwajɑ̃, -ɑ̃t] *a* (*perspicace*) clear-sighted. ●**clairvoyance** *nf* clear-sightedness.

clamer [klame] *vt* (*innocence, mécontentement etc*) to proclaim; **c. que** to proclaim that. ●**clameur** *nf* clamour, outcry.

clan [klɑ̃] *nm* (*en Écosse*) clan; (*petit groupe*) *Péj* clique, set.

clandestin, -ine [klɑ̃dɛstɛ̃, -in] *a* (*rencontre etc*) secret, clandestine; (*journal, mouvement*) underground; **passager c.** stowaway. ●**clandestinité** *nf* **entrer dans la c.** to go underground.

clapet [klapɛ] *nm* (*de pompe etc*) valve; (*bouche*) *Arg* trap.

clapier [klapje] *nm* (*rabbit*) hutch.

clapoter [klapote] *vi* (*vagues*) to lap. ●**clapotement** *nm ou* **clapotis** *nm* lap(ping).

claque [klak] *nf* smack, slap.

claquer [klake] *vt* (*porte*) to slam, bang; (*gifler*) to smack, slap; (*fouet*) to crack; (*fatiguer*) *Fam* to tire out; (*dépenser*) *Arg* to blow (*one's money*); **se c. un muscle** to pull a muscle; **faire c.** (*doigts*) to snap; (*langue*) to click; (*fouet*) to crack.

I *vi* (*porte*) to slam, bang; (*drapeau*) to flap; (*coup de feu*) to ring out; (*mourir*) *Fam* to die; (*tomber en panne*) *Fam* to break down; **c. des mains** to clap one's hands; **elle claque des dents** her teeth are chattering; **se faire un c.** to pull a muscle. ●**claquement** *nm* (*de porte*) slam(ming).

claquemurer (se) [səklakmyre] *vpr* to shut oneself up, hole up (**dans** in).

claquettes [klakɛt] *nfpl* tap dancing.

clarifier [klarifje] *vt* to clarify. ●**clarification** *nf* clarification.

clarinette [klarinɛt] *nf* clarinet.

clarté [klarte] *nf* (*lumière*) light; (*éclat*) brightness; (*précision*) clarity, clearness (*of explanation etc*); **avec c.** clearly.

classe [klɑs] *nf* (*division, qualité, leçon, élèves etc*) class; **aller en c.** to go to school; (*salle de*) **c.** class(room); **en c. de sixième** *Br* in the first year, *Am* in fifth grade; **c. ouvrière/moyenne** working/middle class; **avoir de la c.** to have class; **de première c.** (*billet, compartiment etc*) first-class.

classer [klɑse] *vt* (*photos, spécimens etc*) to classify; (*papiers*) to file; (*candidats*) to grade; **c. une affaire** to consider a matter closed; **se c. parmi** to rank *ou* be classed among; **se c. premier** to come first; **bâtiment**

classé *Br* listed building. ●**classement** *nm* classification; (*de papiers*) filing; (*de candidats*) grading; (*rang*) class; (*en sport*) placing. ●**classeur** *nm* (*meuble*) filing cabinet; (*portefeuille*) (loose leaf) file *ou* binder.

classifier [klasifje] *vt* to classify. ●**classification** *nf* classification.

classique [klasik] *a* classical; (*typique*) classic **I** *nm* (*œuvre, auteur*) classic. ●**classicisme** *nm* classicism.

clause [kloz] *nf* clause.

claustrophobie [klostrɔfɔbi] *nf* claustrophobia. ●**claustrophobe** *a* claustrophobic.

clavecin [klavsɛ̃] *nm Mus* harpsichord.

clavicule [klavikyl] *nf* collarbone.

clavier [klavje] *nm* keyboard.

clé, clef [kle] *nf* key; (*outil*) *Br* spanner, *Am* wrench; (*de sol etc*) *Mus* clef; **fermer à c.** to lock; **sous c.** under lock and key; **c. de contact** ignition key; **c. de voûte** (*d'une politique etc*) keystone; **poste/industrie c.** key post/industry; **clés en main** (*acheter une maison etc*) ready to move in; **prix clés en main** (*voiture*) on-the-road price.

clément, -ente [klemɑ̃, -ɑ̃t] *a* (*juge*) lenient, clement; (*temps*) mild, clement. ●**clémence** *nf* (*de juge*) leniency, clemency; (*de temps*) mildness.

clémentine [klemɑ̃tin] *nf* clementine.

clerc [klɛr] *nm Rel* cleric; (*de notaire*) clerk. ●**clergé** *nm* clergy. ●**clérical, -e, -aux** *a Rel* clerical.

cliché [kliʃe] *nm* (*de photo*) negative; (*idée*) cliché.

client, -ente [klijɑ̃, -ɑ̃t] *nmf* (*de magasin etc*) customer; (*d'un avocat etc*) client; (*d'un médecin*) patient; (*d'hôtel*) guest. ●**clientèle** *nf* customers, clientele; (*d'un avocat*) practice, clientele; (*d'un médecin*) practice, patients; **accorder sa c. à** to give one's custom to.

cligner [kliɲe] *vi* **c. des yeux** (*ouvrir et fermer*) to blink; (*fermer à demi*) to screw up one's eyes; **c. de l'œil** to wink.

clignoter [kliɲote] *vi* to blink; (*lumière*) to flicker; (*feu de circulation*) to flash; (*étoile*) to twinkle. ●**clignotant** *nm* (*de véhicule*) *Br* indicator, *Am* directional signal.

climat [klima] *nm* (*d'une région etc*) & *Fig* climate. ●**climatique** *a* climatic.

climatisation [klimatizasjɔ̃] *nf* air-conditioning. ●**climatiser** *vt* to air-condition. ●**climatisé, -ée** *a* air-conditioned.

clin d'œil [klɛ̃dœj] *nm* wink; **en un c. d'œil** in no time (at all).

clinique [klinik] *a* clinical **I** *nf* (*hôpital*) (private) clinic.

clinquant, -ante [klɛ̃kɑ̃, -ɑ̃t] *a* (*bijoux etc*) tawdry.

clip [klip] *nm* (*vidéo*) (promotional) video (*of rock group etc*).

clique [klik] *nf* (*petit groupe*) *Péj* clique; (*musiciens*) (drum and bugle) band.

cliqueter [klikte] *vi* (*clefs, pièces de monnaie etc*) to jangle, clink; (*chaînes, épées*) to rattle, clank. ●**cliquetis** *nm* jangling, clink-

ing; (de chaînes etc) rattling, clanking.
clivage [kliva3] nm split, division (de in).
cloaque [klɔak] nm cesspool.
clochard, -arde [klɔʃar, -ard] nmf down-and-out, Br tramp.
cloche [klɔʃ] nf 1 bell; **c. à fromage** cheese cover. 2 (personne) Fam idiot, oaf. ●**clocher 1** nm bell tower; (en pointe) steeple; **querelles de c.** petty local quarrels; **esprit de c.** parochialism. **2** vi **il y a quelque chose qui cloche** there's something wrong ou amiss. ●**clochette** nf (small) bell.
cloche-pied (à) [aklɔʃpje] adv **sauter à c.-pied** to hop on one foot.
cloison [klwazɔ̃] nf partition; (entre générations etc) barrier. ●**cloisonner** vt (pièce) to partition; (activités etc) Fig to compartmentalize.
cloître [klwatr] nm cloister. ●**se cloîtrer** vpr to shut oneself away, cloister oneself.
clope [klɔp] nm ou f (cigarette) Fam Br fag, smoke, Am butt.
clopin-clopant [klɔpɛ̃klɔpɑ̃] adv **aller c.-clopant** to hobble.
cloque [klɔk] nf (au pied etc) blister.
clore* [klɔr] vt (débat, lettre) to close. ●**clos, close** a (incident etc) closed; **espace c.** enclosed space ▌nm (enclosed) field.
clôture [klotyr] nf (barrière) fence, enclosure; (fermeture) closing. ●**clôturer** vt to enclose; (compte, séance etc) to close.
clou [klu] nm nail; (furoncle) boil; **le c. (du spectacle)** Fam the star attraction; **les clous** (passage) Br the pedestrian crossing, Am the crosswalk; **des clous!** Fam nothing doing!, no way! ●**clouer** vt (planche, tapis etc) to nail (down); **cloué au lit** confined to (one's) bed; **cloué sur place** nailed to the spot; **le bec à qn** Fam to shut s.o. up. ●**cloué, -ée** a (chaussures) hobnailed; (ceinture, pneus) studded; **passage c.** Br pedestrian crossing, Am crosswalk.
clown [klun] nm clown; **faire le c.** to clown around.
club [klœb] nm (association) club.
cm abrév (centimètre) cm.
co- [kɔ] préf co-.
coaguler [kɔagyle] vti, **se coaguler** vpr (sang) to clot.
coaliser (se) [sɔkɔalize] vpr to form a coalition, join forces. ●**coalition** nf coalition.
coasser [kɔase] vi (grenouille) to croak.
cobaye [kɔbaj] nm (animal, Fig dans une expérience) guinea pig.
cobra [kɔbra] nm (serpent) cobra.
coca [kɔka] nm (Coca-Cola®) coke.
cocagne [kɔkaɲ] nf **pays de c.** dreamland, land of plenty.
cocaïne [kɔkain] nf cocain.
cocarde [kɔkard] nf rosette; (sur un chapeau) cockade; (d'avion) roundel. ●**cocardier, -ière** a (chauvin) flag-waving.
cocasse [kɔkas] a droll, comical. ●**cocasserie** nf drollery.
coccinelle [kɔksinɛl] nf 1 (insecte) Br lady-

bird, Am ladybug. **2** (voiture) Fam beetle.
cocher¹ [kɔʃe] vt Br to tick (off), Am to check (off).
cocher² [kɔʃe] nm coachman. ●**cochère** af **porte c.** main gateway.
cochon, -onne [kɔʃɔ̃, -ɔn] **1** nm pig; (mâle) hog; **c. d'Inde** guinea pig. **2** nmf (personne sale) (dirty) pig; (salaud) swine ▌a (histoire, film) dirty. ●**cochonnerie(s)** nf(pl) Fam (obscénité(s)) filth; (nourriture) junk food; (pacotille) trash, Br rubbish.
cocktail [kɔktɛl] nm (boisson) cocktail; (réunion) cocktail party.
coco [kɔko] nm **noix de c.** coconut. ●**cocotier** nm coconut palm.
cocon [kɔkɔ̃] nm cocoon.
cocorico [kɔkɔriko] int & nm cock-a-doodle-doo; **faire c.** (crier victoire) Fam to give three cheers for France, wave the flag.
cocotte [kɔkɔt] nf (marmite) casserole; **c. minute®** pressure cooker.
cocu [kɔky] nm Fam cuckold.
code [kɔd] nm code; **codes, phares c.** (de véhicule) Br dipped headlights, Am low beams, dimmers; **se mettre en c.** Br to dip one's headlights, Am switch on one's low beams ou dimmers; **C. de la route** Br Highway Code, Am traffic regulations; **c. à barres** (sur produit) bar code. ●**code-barres** nm bar code. ●**coder** vt (message etc) to code. ●**codifier** vt (législation) to codify.
coefficient [kɔefisjɑ̃] nm (nombre) coefficient; **c. d'erreur** margin of error; **c. de sécurité** safety margin.
coéquipier, -ière [kɔekipje, -jɛr] nmf team mate.
cœur [kœr] nm heart; (couleur) Cartes hearts; **au c. de** (ville, hiver etc) in the middle ou heart of; **par c.** (off) by heart; **ça me soulève le c.** that turns my stomach; **opération à c. ouvert** open-heart operation; **parler à c. ouvert** to speak freely; **avoir mal au c.** to feel sick; **avoir le c. gros** ou **serré** to have a heavy heart; **ça me tient à c.** that's important to me, that's close to my heart; **avoir bon c.** to be kind-hearted; **de bon c.** (offrir) willingly, with a good heart; (rire) heartily; **si le c. vous en dit** if you so desire.
coexister [kɔegziste] vi to coexist. ●**coexistence** nf coexistence.
coffre [kɔr] nm chest; (de banque) safe; (de voiture) Br boot, Am trunk; (d'autocar) luggage ou baggage compartment. ●**coffre-fort** (pl **coffres-forts**) safe. ●**coffret** nm (à bijoux, cigares etc) box.
cogiter [kɔʒite] vi Iron to cogitate.
cognac [kɔɲak] nm cognac.
cogner [kɔɲe] vti to knock, bang (à la porte/etc on the door/etc); **c. qn** Arg (frapper) to thump s.o.; (tabasser) to beat s.o. up; **se c. la tête/etc** to knock ou bang one's head/etc; **se c. à qch** to knock ou bang into sth.
cohabiter [kɔabite] vi to live together; **c. avec** to live with. ●**cohabitation** nf living to-

gether; *Pol Fam* power sharing.
cohérent, -ente [kɔerɑ̃, -ɑ̃t] *a* (*discours*) coherent; (*conduite*) consistent; (*argument*) consistent, coherent. ●**cohérence** *nf* coherence; consistency. ●**cohésion** *nf* cohesion, cohesiveness.
cohorte [kɔɔrt] *nf* (*groupe*) troop, band.
cohue [kɔy] *nf* crowd, mob; (*bousculade*) crush.
coiffe [kwaf] *nf* headdress.
coiffer [kwafe] *vt* (*chapeau*) to put on; (*surmonter*) *Fig* to cap; (*être à la tête de*) to head (*a company etc*); **c. qn** to do s.o.'s hair; **c. qn d'un chapeau** to put a hat on s.o.; **elle est bien coiffée** her hair looks very nice ∎ **se coiffer** *vpr* to do one's hair; **se c. d'un chapeau** to put on a hat. ●**coiffeur, coiffeuse**[1] *nmf* (*pour hommes*) barber, hairdresser; (*pour dames*) hairdresser. ●**coiffeuse**[2] *nf* (*meuble*) dressing table. ●**coiffure** *nf* hat, headgear; (*arrangement*) hairstyle; (*métier*) hairdressing.
coin [kwɛ̃] *nm* (*angle*) corner; (*endroit*) spot; (*de terre, de ciel*) patch; (*cale*) wedge; **du c.** (*magasin, gens etc*) local; **dans le c. in the** (local) area; **au c. du feu** by the fireside; **petit c.** (*toilettes*) *Fam Br* loo, *Am* bathroom, *Am* john.
coincer [kwɛ̃se] *vt* (*mécanisme, tiroir etc*) to jam; (*caler*) to wedge; **c. qn** *Fam* to catch s.o., corner s.o. ∎ **se coincer** *vpr* (*mécanisme etc*) to get stuck *ou* jammed; **se c. le doigt** to get one's finger stuck. ●**coincé, -ée** *a* (*tiroir etc*) stuck, jammed; (*personne*) *Fam* stuck.
coïncider [kɔɛ̃side] *vi* to coincide (**avec** with). ●**coïncidence** *nf* coincidence.
coin-coin [kwɛ̃kwɛ̃] *nm inv* (*de canard*) quack.
coing [kwɛ̃] *nm* (*fruit*) quince.
coke [kɔk] *nm* (*combustible*) coke.
col [kɔl] *nm* (*de chemise etc*) collar; (*de bouteille*) neck; (*de montagne*) pass; **c. roulé** *Br* polo neck, *Am* turtleneck; **c. de l'utérus** cervix.
colère [kɔlɛr] *nf* anger; **une c.** (*accès*) a fit of anger; **faire une c.** (*enfant*) to throw ou have a tantrum; **en c.** angry (**contre** with); **mettre qn en c.** to make s.o. angry; **se mettre en c.** to lose one's temper, get angry (**contre** with); **elle est partie en c.** she left angrily. ●**coléreux, -euse** *ou* **colérique** *a* quick-tempered.
colibri [kɔlibri] *nm* hummingbird.
colifichet [kɔlifiʃɛ] *nm* trinket.
colimaçon (en) [ɑ̃kɔlimasɔ̃] *adv* **escalier en c.** spiral staircase.
colin [kɔlɛ̃] *nm* (*poisson*) hake.
colique [kɔlik] *nf Br* diarrhoea, *Am* diarrhea; (*douleur*) stomach pain, colic.
colis [kɔli] *nm* parcel, package.
collaborer [kɔlabɔre] *vi* collaborate (**avec** with, **à** on); **c. à** (*journal, recherche etc*) to contribute to. ●**collaborateur, -trice** *nmf* collaborator; (*d'un journal etc*) contributor. ●**collaboration** *nf* collaboration; (*à un*

journal) contribution.
collage [kɔlaʒ] *nm* (*œuvre, jeu etc*) collage.
collant, -ante [kɔlɑ̃, -ɑ̃t] **1** *a* (*papier*) sticky; (*vêtement*) skin-tight; **être c.** (*importun*) *Fam* to be a pest. **2** *nm Br* tights, *Am* pantyhose; (*maillot pour la danse*) leotard.
collation [kɔlasjɔ̃] *nf* (*repas*) light meal.
colle [kɔl] *nf* (*transparente*) glue; (*blanche*) paste; (*question*) *Fam* poser, teaser; (*interrogation*) *Arg* oral; (*retenue*) *Arg* detention.
collecte [kɔlɛkt] *nf* (*quête*) collection. ●**collecter** *vt* to collect.
collectif, -ive [kɔlɛktif, -iv] *a* collective; **billet c.** group ticket; **hystérie/démission/etc collective** mass hysteria/resignation/etc. ●**collectivement** *adv* collectively. ●**collectivité** *nf* (*groupe*) community.
collection [kɔlɛksjɔ̃] *nf* collection. ●**collectionner** *vt* (*timbres, tableaux etc*) to collect. ●**collectionneur, -euse** *nmf* collector.
collège [kɔlɛʒ] *nm Br* (secondary) school, *Am* (high) school; (*électoral, sacré*) college; **c. d'enseignement secondaire** voir **CES.** ●**collégien** *nm* schoolboy. ●**collégienne** *nf* schoolgirl.
collègue [kɔlɛg] *nmf* colleague.
coller [kɔle] *vt* (*timbre etc*) to stick; (*à la colle transparente*) to glue; (*à la colle blanche*) to paste; (*enveloppe*) to stick (down); (*deux objets*) to stick together; (*affiche*) to stick up; (*papier peint*) to hang; (*mettre*) *Fam* to put, shove; **c. son nez/son oreille/etc contre** to press one's nose/ear/etc against; **c. qn** (*embarrasser*) *Fam* to stump s.o., catch s.o. out; **c. un élève** (*consigner*) to keep a pupil in (detention); **être collé à** (*examen*) *Fam* to fail, flunk; **se c. contre** to cling (close) to; **se c. qn/qch** *Fam* to get stuck with s.o./sth.
∎ *vi* (*être collant*) to be sticky; (*vêtement*) to cling; (*tenir*) to stick; **c. à** (*papier etc*) to stick to; (*s'adapter*) to fit; **ça colle!** *Fam* everything's just fine! ●**colleur, -euse** *nmf* **c. d'affiches** billsticker.
collet [kɔlɛ] *nm* (*piège*) snare; **prendre qn au c.** to grab s.o. by the scruff of the neck; **elle est/ils sont c. monté** she is/they are prim and proper *ou* straitlaced.
collier [kɔlje] *nm* (*bijou*) necklace; (*de chien, cheval, pour tuyau etc*) collar; **c. (de barbe)** narrow beard, fringe of beard.
colline [kɔlin] *nf* hill.
collision [kɔlizjɔ̃] *nf* (*de véhicules*) collision; (*bagarre, conflit*) clash; **entrer en c. avec** to collide with.
colloque [kɔlɔk] *nm* symposium.
collusion [kɔlyzjɔ̃] *nf* collusion.
colmater [kɔlmate] *vt* (*fuite, fente*) to seal; (*trou*) to fill in; **c. une brèche** *Mil* to close *ou* seal a gap.
colombe [kɔlɔ̃b] *nf* dove.
Colombie [kɔlɔ̃bi] *nf* Columbia. ●**colombien, -ienne** *a* Columbian ∎ *nmf* **C., Colombienne** Columbian.

colon [kɔlɔ̃] *nm* settler, colonist; (*enfant*) child taking part in a *Br* holiday camp *ou Am* vacation camp.

côlon [kolɔ̃] *nm* (*intestin*) colon.

colonial, -e, -aux [kɔlɔnjal, -o] *a* colonial. ● **colonialisme** *nm* colonialism.

colonie [kɔlɔni] *nf* colony; **c. de vacances** *Br* (children's) holiday camp, *Am* (children's) vacation *ou* summer camp.

coloniser [kɔlɔnize] *vt* (*pays*) to colonize. ● **colonisateur, -trice** *a* colonizing ‖ *nmf* colonizer. ● **colonisation** *nf* colonization.

colonel [kɔlɔnɛl] *nm* (*d'infanterie*) colonel.

colonne [kɔlɔn] *nf* column; **c. vertébrale** spine; **se ranger en c. par deux** to line up in two columns. ● **colonnade** *nf* colonnade.

colorer [kɔlɔre] *vt* to colour; **c. en vert/etc** to colour green/*etc*. ● **colorant, -ante** *a* & *nm* colouring. ● **coloré, -ée** *a* (*verre, liquide etc*) coloured; (*teint*) ruddy, reddish; (*style, foule*) colourful. ● **coloration** *nf* colouring, colour. ● **coloriage** *nm* colouring; (*dessin*) coloured drawing; **album de coloriages** colouring book. ● **colorier** *vt* (*dessin etc*) to colour (in). ● **coloris** *nm* (*nuance*) shade; (*effet des couleurs*) colouring.

colosse [kɔlɔs] *nm* giant, colossus. ● **colossal, -e, -aux** *a* colossal, gigantic.

colporter [kɔlpɔrte] *vt* to peddle, hawk.

coltiner [kɔltine] *vt* (*objet lourd*) *Fam* to lug, haul ‖ **se coltiner** *vpr* (*tâche pénible*) *Fam* to take on, tackle.

coma [kɔma] *nm* coma; **dans le c.** in a coma.

combat [kɔ̃ba] *nm* fight; (*de soldats*) combat; **c. de boxe/catch** boxing/wrestling match. ● **combatif, -ive** *a* (*personne*) eager to fight; (*instinct, esprit*) fighting.

combattre* [kɔ̃batr] *vt* (*personne, incendie etc*) to fight; (*maladie, inflation etc*) to fight, combat ‖ *vi* to fight. ● **combattant, -ante** *nmf* (*soldat*) combattant; (*bagarreur*) *Fam* fighter, brawler ‖ *a* (*unité, troupe*) fighting.

combien [kɔ̃bjɛ̃] **1** *adv* (*quantité*) how much; (*nombre*) how many; **c. de** (*temps, argent etc*) how much; (*gens, livres etc*) how many.
2 *adv* (*à quel point*) how; **tu verras c. il est bête** you'll see how silly he is; **tu sais c. je t'aime** you know how (much) I love you.
3 *adv* (*distance*) **c. y a-t-il d'ici à...?** how far is it to...?
4 *nm inv* **le c. sommes-nous?** *Fam* what date is it?, what's the date?; **tous les c.?** (*fréquence*) *Fam* how often?

combinaison [kɔ̃binɛzɔ̃] *nf* **1** combination; (*manœuvre*) scheme. **2** (*vêtement de femme*) slip; (*de mécanicien*) *Br* boiler suit, *Am* overalls; **c. de vol/plongée/ski** flying/diving/ski suit; **c. spatiale** spacesuit.

combine [kɔ̃bin] *nf* (*truc, astuce*) *Fam* trick.

combiner [kɔ̃bine] *vt* (*assembler, disposer*) to combine; (*calculer*) to devise (*means, plot etc*). ● **combiné** *nm* (*de téléphone*) receiver.

comble¹ [kɔ̃bl] *nm* **le c. du bonheur/etc** the height of happiness/*etc*; **au c. de la joie** overjoyed; **pour c.** (*de malheur*) to crown it *ou*

cap it all; **c'est un** *ou* **le c.!** that's the limit! ● **combles** *nmpl* (*mansarde*) attic, loft; **sous les c.** beneath the roof, in the loft *ou* attic.

comble² [kɔ̃bl] *a* (*bondé*) (*salle, bus, train etc*) packed, full.

combler [kɔ̃ble] *vt* (*trou, lacune etc*) to fill; (*perte*) to make good; (*vœu*) to fulfil; **c. son retard** to make up lost time; **c. qn de cadeaux** to shower s.o. with gifts; **c. qn de joie** to fill s.o. with joy; **je suis comblé** I'm completely fulfilled, I have all I wish; **vous me comblez!** you're too good to me!

combustible [kɔ̃bystibl] *nm* fuel ‖ *a* combustible. ● **combustion** *nf* combustion.

comédie [kɔmedi] *nf* comedy; (*complication*) *Fam* fuss, *Br* palaver; **c. musicale** musical; **jouer la c.** *Fig* to put on an act, pretend, play-act; **c'est de la c.** (*c'est faux*) it's a sham. ● **comédien** *nm* (*acteur, Fig hypocrite*) actor. ● **comédienne** *nf* (*actrice, Fig hypocrite*) actress.

comestible [kɔmɛstibl] *a* edible. ● **comestibles** *nmpl* foods.

comète [kɔmɛt] *nf* comet.

comique [kɔmik] *a* (*amusant*) funny, comical; (*acteur, style etc*) comic; (*auteur*) **c.** comedy writer ‖ *nm* comedy; (*acteur*) comic (*actor*); **le c.** (*genre*) comedy; (*d'une histoire etc*) the comical side (**de** of).

comité [kɔmite] *nm* committee; **c. de gestion** board of (management); **en petit c.** in a small group.

commandant [kɔmɑ̃dɑ̃] *nm* (*d'un navire*) captain; (*grade*) (*dans l'infanterie*) major; (*dans l'aviation*) squadron leader; **c. de bord** (*d'un avion*) captain.

commande [kɔmɑ̃d] *nf* **1** (*achat*) order; **sur c.** to order. **2** *Tech* control; *Ordinat* command; **c. à distance** remote control. ● **commandes** *nfpl* **les c.** (*d'un avion etc*) the controls; **tenir les c.** (*diriger*) to be at the helm (*of a company etc*).

commandement [kɔmɑ̃dmɑ̃] *nm* (*autorité*) command; *Rel* commandment.

commander¹ [kɔmɑ̃de] *vt* (*diriger, exiger, dominer*) to command; (*faire fonctionner*) (*bouton, manette etc*) to control (*sth*) ‖ *vi* **c. à** (*ses passions etc*) to have control over; **c. à qn de faire** to command s.o. to do.

commander² [kɔmɑ̃de] *vt* (*acheter*) to order.

commanditaire [kɔmɑ̃diter] *nm* (*d'une société*) *Br* sleeping *ou* limited partner, *Am* silent partner.

commando [kɔmɑ̃do] *nm* commando.

comme [kɔm] *adv* & *conj* **1** **un peu c.** a bit like; **c. moi/elle/etc** like me/her/etc; **c. cela** like that.
2 as; **il écrit c. il parle** he writes as he speaks; **blanc c. neige** (as) white as snow; **c. si** as if; **c. pour faire** as if to do; **c. par hasard** as if by chance; **je le connais c. médecin** (*en tant que*) I know him as a doctor; **je vous le donne c. cadeau** I give it to you as a gift; **qu'as-tu c. diplômes?** what do you have in the way of certificates?; **joli c. tout** *Fam* very

pretty, *Br* ever so pretty; **c. quoi** (*disant que*) to the effect that; (*ce qui prouve que*) so, which goes to show that.
▮ *adv* (*exclamatif*) **regarde c. il pleut!** look how it's raining!; **c. c'est petit!** isn't it small!
▮ *conj* (*temps*) as; (*cause*) as, since; **c. elle entrait** (just) as she was coming in; **c. tu es mon ami** as *ou* since you're my friend.
commémorer [kɔmemɔre] *vt* to commemorate. ●**commémoratif, -ive** *a* commemorative. ●**commémoration** *nf* commemoration.
commencer [kɔmãse] *vti* to begin, start (**à faire** to do, doing; **par qch** with sth; **par faire** by doing); **pour c.** to begin with. ●**commencement** *nm* beginning, start; **au c.** at the beginning *ou* start.
comment [kɔmã] *adv* how; **c. le sais-tu?** how do you know?; **et c.!** and how!, you bet!; *Br* not half!; **c.?** (*répétition*) pardon?, what?; (*surprise*) what?; **c.!** (*indignation*) what!; **c. est-il?** what is he like?; **c. faire?** what's to be done?; **c. t'appelles-tu?** what's your name?; **c. allez-vous?** how are you?
commentaire [kɔmãtɛr] *nm* (*explications*) commentary; (*remarque*) comment. ●**commentateur, -trice** *nmf* commentator. ●**commenter** *vt* to comment (up)on.
commérage(s) [kɔmeraʒ] *nm(pl)* gossip.
commerçant, -ante [kɔmɛrsã, -ãt] *nmf* shopkeeper; **c. en gros** wholesale dealer ▮ *a* (*personne*) business-minded; **rue/quartier commerçant(e)** shopping street/area; **nation commerçante** trading nation.
commerce [kɔmɛrs] *nm* trade, commerce; (*magasin*) shop, business; **c. de gros** wholesale trade; **maison/voyageur/etc de c.** commercial establishment/traveller/etc; **chambre de c.** chamber of commerce; **faire du c.** to trade (**avec** with); **dans le c.** (*objet*) on sale) in the *Br* shops *ou Am* stores. ●**commercer** *vi* to trade. ●**commercial, -e, -aux** *a* commercial; **relations commerciales** business *ou* trade relations. ●**commercialiser** *vt* to market.
commère [kɔmɛr] *nf* (*femme*) gossip.
commettre* [kɔmɛtr] *vt* (*délit etc*) to commit; (*erreur*) to make.
commis [kɔmi] *nm* (*de magasin*) *Br* assistant, *Am* clerk; (*de bureau*) *Br* clerk, *Am* clerical worker.
commissaire [kɔmisɛr] *nm* (*d'une course*) steward; **c. (de police)** police *Br* superintendent *ou Am* chief; **c. aux comptes** auditor; **c. du bord** (*d'un navire*) purser. ●**commissaire-priseur** *nm* (*pl commissaires-priseurs*) auctioneer. ●**commissariat** *nm* **c. (de police)** (central) police station.
commission [kɔmisjɔ̃] *nf* (*course*) errand; (*message*) message; (*réunion*) commission, committee; (*pourcentage sur une vente etc*) commission (**sur** on); **faire les commissions** to do the shopping. ●**commissionnaire** *nm* messenger; (*agent commercial*) agent.
commode [kɔmɔd] **1** *a* (*pratique*) handy; (*simple*) easy; **il n'est pas c.** (*pas aimable*)

he's unpleasant; (*difficile*) he's a tough one. **2** *nf Br* chest of drawers, *Am* dresser. ●**commodément** *adv* comfortably. ●**commodité** *nf* convenience.
commotion [kɔmosjɔ̃] *nf* shock; **c. (cérébrale)** concussion. ●**commotionner** *vt* to shake up.
commuer [kɔmɥe] *vt* (*peine*) *Jur* to commute (**en** to).
commun, -une [kɔmœ̃, -yn] **1** *a* (*collectif, habituel, comparable*) common; (*frais, cuisine etc*) shared; (*action, démarche*) joint; **ami c.** mutual friend; **peu c.** uncommon; **en c.** in common; **transports en c.** public transport; **avoir** *ou* **mettre en c.** to share; **vivre en c.** to live together; **elle n'a rien de c. avec** she has nothing in common with; **ils n'ont rien de c.** they have nothing in common. **2** *nm* **le c. des mortels** ordinary mortals. ●**communément** [kɔmynemã] *adv* commonly.
communauté [kɔmynote] *nf* community; **la C. européenne** the European Community. ●**communautaire** *a* **vie/etc c.** community life/etc.
commune [kɔmyn] *nf* (*municipalité française*) commune; **les Communes** (*parlement*) *Br* the Commons. ●**communal, -e, -aux** *a* communal, local, municipal.
communicatif, -ive [kɔmynikatif, -iv] *a* (*personne*) communicative; (*contagieux*) infectious.
communication [kɔmynikasjɔ̃] *nf* communication; **c. (téléphonique)** (telephone) call; **mauvaise c.** (*au téléphone*) bad line.
communier [kɔmynje] *vi* to receive Holy Communion. ●**communiant, -ante** *nmf Rel* communicant. ●**communion** *nf* communion; *Rel* (Holy) Communion.
communiquer [kɔmynike] *vt* (*information, enthousiasme etc*) to communicate, pass on; (*document, maladie*) to pass on; (*mouvement*) to impart, communicate; **se c. à** (*feu, rire*) to spread to ▮ *vi* (*personne, pièces etc*) to communicate (**avec** with). ●**communiqué** *nm* (*avis*) (official) statement, communiqué; (*publicitaire*) message; **c. de presse** press release.
communisme [kɔmynism] *nm* communism. ●**communiste** *a* & *nmf* communist.
communs [kɔmœ̃] *nmpl* (*bâtiments*) outbuildings.
commutateur [kɔmytatœr] *nm* (*bouton électrique*) switch.
compact, -e [kɔ̃pakt] *a* (*foule, amas*) dense; (*appareil, véhicule*) compact; **disque c.** compact *Br* disc *ou Am* disk.
compagne [kɔ̃paɲ] *nf* (*camarade*) friend; (*épouse, maîtresse*) companion.
compagnie [kɔ̃paɲi] *nf* (*présence, société, firme, soldats*) company; **tenir c. à qn** to keep s.o. company; **en c. de qn** in the company of s.o.
compagnon [kɔ̃paɲɔ̃] *nm* companion; (*ouvrier*) workman; **c. de route** travelling

companion, fellow traveller; **c. de jeu** playmate; **c. de travail** fellow worker, Br workmate.

comparaître* [kɔ̃parɛtr] vi (devant un tribunal) to appear (in court) (**devant** before).

comparer [kɔ̃pare] vt to compare (**à** to, with) ∎ **se comparer** vpr to be compared (**à**, with). ●**comparé, -ée** a (science, grammaire etc) comparative. ●**comparable** a comparable (**à** to, with). ●**comparaison** nf comparison (**avec** with); (image, métaphore) simile; **en c. de** in comparison with. ●**comparatif, -ive** a (méthode etc) comparative ∎ nm Grammaire comparative.

comparse [kɔ̃pars] nmf (complice) minor accomplice, stooge.

compartiment [kɔ̃partimã] nm compartment. ●**compartimenter** vt to compartmentalize, divide up.

comparution [kɔ̃parysjɔ̃] nf (devant un tribunal) appearance (in court).

compas [kɔ̃pa] nm 1 (pour mesurer etc) Br (pair of) compasses, Am compass. 2 (boussole de marin) compass.

compassé, -ée [kɔ̃pase] a (affecté) starchy, stiff.

compassion [kɔ̃pasjɔ̃] nf compassion.

compatible [kɔ̃patibl] a compatible (**avec** with). ●**compatibilité** nf compatibility.

compatir [kɔ̃patir] vi to sympathize; **c. à la douleur/etc de qn** to share in s.o.'s grief/etc. ●**compatissant, -ante** a sympathetic.

compatriote [kɔ̃patrijɔt] nmf compatriot.

compenser [kɔ̃pɑ̃se] vt to make up for, compensate for ∎ vi to compensate; **pour c.** to make up for it, to compensate. ●**compensation** nf compensation; **en c.** in compensation (**de** for), to compensate.

compère [kɔ̃pɛr] nm accomplice.

compétent, -ente [kɔ̃petɑ̃, -ɑ̃t] a competent. ●**compétence** nf competence; **compétences** skills, abilities.

compétition [kɔ̃petisjɔ̃] nf competition; (épreuve sportive) event; **esprit/sport de c.** competitive spirit/sport. ●**compétitif, -ive** a competitive. ●**compétitivité** nf competitiveness.

compiler [kɔ̃pile] vt (documents) to compile.

complainte [kɔ̃plɛ̃t] nf (chanson) lament.

complaire* (**se**) [sakɔ̃plɛr] vpr **se c. dans qch/à faire** to delight in sth/in doing.

complaisant, -ante [kɔ̃plɛzɑ̃, -ɑ̃t] a kind, obliging; (indulgent, satisfait de soi) self-indulgent, complacent. ●**complaisance** nf kindness, (vanité) self-indulgence, complacency.

complément [kɔ̃plemã] nm Grammaire complement; **le c.** (le reste) the rest; **un c. d'information** additional information; **c. circonstanciel** adverbial phrase; **c. d'agent** agent; **c. d'objet direct/indirect** direct/indirect object. ●**complémentaire** a complementary; (détails) additional.

complet, -ète [kɔ̃plɛ, -ɛt] 1 a complete; (train, hôtel, étude, examen etc) full; (ali-

ment) whole; **au (grand) c.** (groupe etc) in full strength. 2 nm (costume) suit. ●**complètement** adv completely.

compléter [kɔ̃plete] vt to complete; (ajouter à) to complement; (somme) to make up ∎ **se compléter** vpr (personnes, caractères) to complement each other.

complexe [kɔ̃plɛks] 1 a complex. 2 nm (sentiment, construction) complex; **avoir des complexes** to be hung up, have hang-ups. ●**complexé, -ée** a Fam hung up, inhibited. ●**complexité** nf complexity.

complication [kɔ̃plikasjɔ̃] nf complication; (complexité) complexity.

complice [kɔ̃plis] nm accomplice ∎ a (regard) knowing; (silence, attitude) conniving; **être c. de** (crime etc) to be a party to. ●**complicité** nf complicity.

compliment [kɔ̃plimã] nm (éloge) compliment; **compliments** (félicitations) congratulations; **mes compliments!** congratulations; **faire des compliments à qn** to compliment ou congratulate s.o. ●**complimenter** vt to compliment (**sur, pour** on).

compliquer [kɔ̃plike] vt to complicate ∎ **se compliquer** vpr (situation) to get complicated. ●**compliqué, -ée** a complicated; (mécanisme, structure etc) intricate, complicated; (histoire, problème etc) involved, complicated.

complot [kɔ̃plo] nm plot, conspiracy (**contre** against). ●**comploter** [kɔ̃plɔte] vti to plot (**de faire** to do).

comporter [kɔ̃pɔrte] 1 vt (impliquer) to involve, contain; (comprendre en soi, présenter) to contain, comprise, have. 2 **se comporter** vpr to behave; (joueur, voiture) to perform. ●**comportement** nm behaviour; (de joueur etc) performance.

composer [kɔ̃poze] vt (former, constituer) to make up, compose; (musique, visage) to compose; (texte à imprimer) to set (up); **c. un numéro** (au téléphone) to dial a number; **se c. de, être composé de** to be made up ou composed of ∎ vi (étudiant etc) to take an examination; **c. avec** (l'ennemi etc) to come to terms with. ●**composant** nm (chimique, électronique) component. ●**composante** nf (d'une idée, d'un ensemble etc) component. ●**composé, -ée** a (mot etc) & Ch compound; **temps c.** compound tense; **passé c.** perfect (tense) ∎ nm compound.

compositeur, -trice [kɔ̃pozitœr, -tris] nmf (musicien) composer; (typographe) typesetter.

composition [kɔ̃pozisjɔ̃] nf (action) composing, making up; Typ typesetting; (symphonie, dissertation) & Ch composition; (examen) test, class exam; **c. française** (examen) French essay ou composition.

composter [kɔ̃pɔste] vt (billet) to cancel, punch.

compote [kɔ̃pɔt] nf Br stewed fruit, Am sauce; **c. de pommes** Br stewed apples, Am applesauce. ●**compotier** nm fruit dish.

compréhensible [kɔ̃preɑ̃sibl] *a* understandable, comprehensible. ● **compréhensif, -ive** *a* (*personne*) understanding. ● **compréhension** *nf* understanding.

comprendre* [kɔ̃prɑ̃dr] *vt* to understand; (*comporter*) to include, comprise; **je n'y comprends rien** I can't make head or tail of it, I don't understand a thing about it; **se faire c.** to make oneself understood; **ça se comprend** that's understandable.

compris, -ise [kɔ̃pri, -iz] *a* (*inclus*) included (**dans** in); **frais c.** including expenses; **tout c.** (all) inclusive; **y c.** including; **c. entre** (situated) between; **(c'est) c.!** it's agreed!

compresse [kɔ̃pres] *nf* (*pansement*) compress.

compresseur [kɔ̃preseœr] *a* **rouleau c.** steamroller.

comprimé [kɔ̃prime] *nm* (*médicament*) tablet.

comprimer [kɔ̃prime] *vt* (*air, gaz, artère*) to compress; (*colère, sentiment etc*) to repress; (*dépenses*) to reduce. ● **compression** *nf* compression; (*du personnel etc*) reduction.

compromettre* [kɔ̃prɔmetr] *vt* to compromise. ● **compromis** *nm* compromise. ● **compromission** *nf* compromising action, compromise.

comptabiliser [kɔ̃tabilize] *vt* (*compter*) to count, make a count of.

comptable [kɔ̃tabl] *nmf* bookkeeper; (*expert*) accountant. ● **comptabilité** *nf* (*comptes*) accounts; (*science*) bookkeeping, accountancy; (*service*) accounts department.

comptant [kɔ̃tɑ̃] *am* **argent c.** (hard) cash ▌*adv* **payer c.** to pay (in) cash; (**au**) **c.** (*acheter, vendre*) for cash.

compte [kɔ̃t] *nm* (*comptabilité*) account; (*calcul*) count; (*nombre*) (right) number; **avoir un c. en banque** to have a bank account; **c. chèque** *Br* cheque account, *Am* checking account; **tenir c. de** to take into account; **c. tenu de** considering; **entrer en ligne de c.** to be taken into account; **se rendre c. de** to realize; **rendre c. de** (*exposer*) to report on; (*justifier*) to account for; **demander des comptes à qn** to call s.o. to account; **faire le c. de** to count; **travailler à son c.** to work for oneself; **s'installer à son c.** to set up (in business) on one's own; **pour le c. de** on behalf of; **pour mon c.** for my part; **sur le c. de qn** about s.o.; **en fin de c.** all things considered; **à bon c.** (*acheter*) cheap(ly); **s'en tirer à bon c.** to get off lightly; **avoir un c. à régler avec qn** to have a score to settle with s.o.; **c. à rebours** countdown. ● **compte-gouttes** *nm inv* (*pour médicament*) dropper; **au c.-gouttes** (*utiliser, donner etc*) very sparingly. ● **compte-tours** *nm inv* (*de véhicule*) tachometer, *Br* rev counter.

compter [kɔ̃te] *vt* (*calculer*) to count; (*prévoir*) to allow, reckon; (*considérer*) to consider; (*payer*) to pay; **c. faire** (*espérer*) to expect to do; (*avoir l'intention de*) to intend

to do; **c. qch à qn** (*facturer*) to charge s.o. for sth; **il compte deux ans de service** he has two years' service; **ses jours sont comptés** his *ou* her days are numbered; **sans c.** (*sans parler de*) not to mention.

▌*vi* (*calculer, avoir de l'importance*) to count; **c. sur qn** (*se fier à*) to rely on s.o., count on s.o.; **c. avec qch/qn** to reckon with sth/s.o.; **c. parmi** to be (numbered) among; **à c. de demain** as from tomorrow, starting (from) tomorrow. ● **compteur** *nm* (*électrique*) meter; **c.** (**de vitesse**) (*de véhicule*) speedometer; **c.** (**kilométrique**) *Br* milometer, *Br* clock, *Am* odometer; **c. Geiger** Geiger counter.

compte rendu [kɔ̃trɑ̃dy] *nm* report; (*de livre, film etc*) review.

comptoir [kɔ̃twar] *nm* **1** (*de magasin*) counter; (*de café*) bar; (*de bureau*) (reception) desk. **2** (*commercial*) branch, agency.

compulser [kɔ̃pylse] *vt* (*notes, archives etc*) to examine.

comte [kɔ̃t] *nm* (*noble*) count; *Br* earl. ● **comté** *nm* county. ● **comtesse** *nf* countess.

con, conne [kɔ̃, kɔn] *a* (*idiot*) *Fam* (damn) stupid ▌*nmf Fam* (damn) stupid fool.

concave [kɔ̃kav] *a* concave.

concéder [kɔ̃sede] *vt* to concede, grant (**à** to, **que** that).

concentrer [kɔ̃sɑ̃tre] *vt* to concentrate; (*attention, esprit, énergie*) to focus, concentrate ▌**se concentrer** *vpr* (*réfléchir*) to concentrate. ● **concentré, -ée** *a* (*lait*) condensed; (*solution, Javel, boisson*) concentrated; (*attentif*) concentrating (hard) ▌*nm* **c. de tomates** tomato purée. ● **concentration** *nf* concentration.

concentrique [kɔ̃sɑ̃trik] *a* concentric.

concept [kɔ̃sept] *nm* concept. ● **conception** *nf* (*idée*) & *Méd* conception.

concerner [kɔ̃serne] *vt* to concern; **en ce qui me concerne** as far as I'm concerned. ● **concernant** *prép* concerning.

concert [kɔ̃ser] *nm* (*de musique*) concert; (*de louanges, protestations etc*) *Fig* chorus; **de c.** (*agir*) together, in concert.

concerter [kɔ̃serte] *vt* (*attaque, projet etc*) to devise (*in agreement*) ▌**se concerter** *vpr* to consult together. ● **concerté, -ée** *a* (*plan etc*) concerted. ● **concertation** *nf* (*dialogue*) *Br* dialogue, *Am* dialog.

concerto [kɔ̃sɛrto] *nm* concerto.

concession [kɔ̃sesjɔ̃] *nf* concession (**à** to); (*terrain*) plot (of land). ● **concessionnaire** *nmf* (*automobile etc*) (authorized) dealer, agent.

concevoir* [kɔ̃səvwar] **1** *vt* (*imaginer, éprouver, engendrer*) to conceive; (*comprendre*) to understand; **ainsi conçu** (*dépêche, lettre etc*) worded as follows. **2** *vi* (*femme*) to conceive. ● **concevable** *a* conceivable.

concierge [kɔ̃sjɛrʒ] *nmf* caretaker, *Am* janitor.

concile [kɔ̃sil] *nm Rel* council.

concilier [kɔ̃silje] *vt* (*choses*) to reconcile; **se**

c. l'amitié/*etc* de qn to win (over) s.o.'s friendship/*etc*. ●**conciliant, -ante** *a* (*ton, geste etc*) *a* conciliatory. ●**conciliateur, -trice** *nmf* conciliator. ●**conciliation** *nf* conciliation.

concis, -ise [kɔ̃si, -is] *a* concise, terse. ●**concision** *nf* concision.

concitoyen, -enne [kɔ̃sitwajɛ̃, -ɛn] *nmf* fellow citizen.

conclure* [kɔ̃klyr] *vt* (*terminer, régler*) to conclude; **c. que** (*déduire*) to conclude that; **c. un marché** to make a deal *ou* bargain ▮ *vi* (*orateur etc*) to conclude; **c. à la culpabilité**/*etc* **de qn** to conclude that s.o. is guilty/*etc*. ●**concluant, -ante** *a* (*argument etc*) *a* conclusive. ●**conclusion** *nf* conclusion; **en c.** in conclusion.

concombre [kɔ̃kɔ̃br] *nm* cucumber.

concordance [kɔ̃kɔrdɑ̃s] *nf* agreement; (*de situations, résultats*) similarity; **c. des temps** *Grammaire* sequence of tenses.

concorde [kɔ̃kɔrd] *nf* concord, harmony.

concorder [kɔ̃kɔrde] *vi* (*faits etc*) to agree; (*caractères*) to match; **c. avec** to match. ●**concordant, -ante** *a* in agreement.

concourir* [kɔ̃kurir] *vi* (*candidat*) to compete (**pour** for); (*converger*) to converge; **c. à** (*un but, un succès etc*) to contribute to.

concours [kɔ̃kur] *nm* (*examen*) competitive examination; (*jeu*) competition; (*aide*) assistance; (*de circonstances*) combination; **c. hippique** horse show, show-jumping event.

concret, -ète [kɔ̃krɛ, -ɛt] *a* concrete. ●**concrétiser** *vt* to give concrete form to ▮ **se concrétiser** *vpr* to materialize.

conçu, -ue [kɔ̃sy] *pp de* **concevoir** ▮ *a* **c. pour faire/pour qn** designed to do/for s.o.; **bien c.** (*maison, véhicule etc*) well designed.

concubine [kɔ̃kybin] *nf* (*maîtresse*) concubine. ●**concubinage** *nm* cohabitation; **vivre en c.** to live together as husband and wife.

concurrent, -ente [kɔ̃kyrɑ̃, -ɑ̃t] *nmf* competitor. ●**concurrence** *nf* competition; **faire c.** **à** to compete with; **jusqu'à c. de 100 F**/*etc* up to the amount of 100 francs/*etc*. ●**concurrencer** *vt* to compete with. ●**concurrentiel, -ielle** *a* (*prix, offre etc*) competitive.

condamnation [kɔ̃danasjɔ̃] *nf* (*peine de prison etc*) sentence; (*censure*) condemnation.

condamner [kɔ̃dane] *vt* to condemn; (*accusé*) to sentence (**à** to); (*porte*) to block up, bar; (*pièce*) to keep locked; **c. qn à une amende** to fine s.o. ●**condamné, -ée** *nmf* (*à mort*) condemned man, condemned woman; **être c.** (*malade*) to be a hopeless case, be terminally ill.

condenser [kɔ̃dɑ̃se] *vt*, **se condenser** *vpr* to condense. ●**condensation** *nf* (*buée*) *Fam* condensation.

condescendre [kɔ̃dɛsɑ̃dr] *vi* to condescend (**à faire** to do). ●**condescendant, -ante** *a* condescending. ●**condescendance** *nf* condescension.

condiment [kɔ̃dimɑ̃] *nm* condiment.

condisciple [kɔ̃disipl] *nm* (*écolier*) classmate, schoolfellow; (*étudiant*) fellow student.

condition [kɔ̃disjɔ̃] *nf* (*état, stipulation, rang*) condition; **conditions** (*clauses, tarifs*) terms; **à c. de faire, à c. que l'on fasse** providing *ou* provided (that) one does; **mettre qn en c.** (*endoctriner*) to condition s.o.; **sans c.** (*capitulation*) unconditional; (*se rendre etc*) unconditionally. ●**conditionnel, -elle** *a* (*promesse etc*) conditional ▮ *nm* *Grammaire* conditional.

conditionner [kɔ̃disjɔne] *vt* **1** (*influencer*) to condition. **2** (*emballer*) to package. ●**conditionné, -ée** *a* (*réflexe*) conditioned; **à air c.** (*pièce etc*) air-conditioned. ●**conditionnement** *nm* conditioning; (*emballage*) packaging.

condoléances [kɔ̃dɔleɑ̃s] *nfpl* sympathy, condolences; **carte de c.** sympathy card.

conducteur, -trice [kɔ̃dyktœr, -tris] **1** *nmf* (*de véhicule, train*) driver. **2** *a* & *nm* (*corps*) **c.** (*non isolant*) conductor; (**fil**) **c.** (*électrique*) lead (wire).

conduire* [kɔ̃dɥir] **1** *vt* to lead; (*véhicule*) to drive; (*eau*) to carry; (*affaire, électricité etc*) to conduct; **c. qn à** (*accompagner*) to take s.o. to. **2 se conduire** *vpr* to behave.

conduit [kɔ̃dɥi] *nm* duct.

conduite [kɔ̃dɥit] *nf* conduct, behaviour; (*de véhicule*) driving (**de** of); (*d'eau, de gaz*) main; (*d'entreprise etc*) conduct; **c. à gauche/droite** (*volant*) left-hand/right-hand drive; **faire un bout de c. à qn** to go with s.o. part of the way; **sous la c. de qn** under the guidance of s.o.

cône [kon] *nm* cone.

confection [kɔ̃fɛksjɔ̃] *nf* making (**de** of); **vêtements de c.** ready-to-wear clothes; **magasin de c.** *Br* clothes shop, *Am* clothing store. ●**confectionner** *vt* (*gâteau, robe*) to make.

confédération [kɔ̃federasjɔ̃] *nf* confederation. ●**confédéré, -ée** *a* confederate.

conférence [kɔ̃ferɑ̃s] *nf* (*réunion*) conference; (*exposé*) lecture; **en c.** in a meeting, in conference; **c. de presse** press conference. ●**conférencier, -ière** *nmf* lecturer.

conférer [kɔ̃fere] *vt* (*attribuer, donner*) to confer (**à** on).

confesser [kɔ̃fese] *vt* to confess ▮ **se confesser** *vpr Rel* to confess (**à** to). ●**confesseur** *nm* (*prêtre*) confessor. ●**confession** *nf* confession. ●**confessionnal, -aux** *nm Rel* confessional. ●**confessionnel, -elle** *a* (*école*) *Rel* denominational.

confettis [kɔ̃feti] *nmpl* confetti.

confiance [kɔ̃fjɑ̃s] *nf* trust, confidence; **faire c. à qn, avoir c. en qn** to trust s.o.; **c. en soi** (self-)confidence; **poste/abus de c.** position/breach of trust; **homme de c.** reliable man; **en toute c.** (*acheter, dire etc*) quite confidently; **poser la question de c.** to ask for a vote of confidence. ●**confiant, -ante** *a* trusting; (*sûr de soi*) confident; **être c. en qn/dans qch** to have confidence in s.o./sth.

confidence [kɔ̃fidɑ̃s] *nf* (*secret*) confidence; **en c.** in confidence; **faire une c. à qn** to confide in s.o. ●**confident** *nm* (*personne*) confidant. ●**confidente** *nf* confidante. ●**confidentiel, -ielle** *a* confidential.

confier [kɔ̃fje] *vt* **c. à qn** (*enfant, objet*) to give s.o. to look after, entrust s.o. with; **c. un secret/etc à qn** to confide a secret/etc to s.o.; **se c. à qn** to confide in s.o.

configuration [kɔ̃figyrasjɔ̃] *nf* (*d'un lieu*) layout; (*de matériel informatique*) configuration.

confiner [kɔ̃fine] *vt* to confine ▌ *vi* **c. à** to border on ▌ **se confiner** *vpr* to confine oneself (**dans** to). ●**confiné, -ée** *a* (*atmosphère*) stuffy.

confins [kɔ̃fɛ̃] *nmpl* confines.

confire* [kɔ̃fir] *vt* (*cornichon*) to pickle; (*fruit*) to preserve.

confirmer [kɔ̃firme] *vt* to confirm (**que** that); **c. qn dans sa résolution** to confirm s.o.'s resolve. ●**confirmation** *nf* confirmation.

confiserie [kɔ̃fizri] *nf* (*magasin*) Br sweet shop, *Am* candy store; **confiseries** (*produits*) confectionery, *Br* sweets, *Am* candy. ●**confiseur, -euse** *nmf* confectioner.

confisquer [kɔ̃fiske] *vt* to confiscate (**à qn** from s.o.). ●**confiscation** *nf* confiscation.

confit [kɔ̃fi] *a* **fruits confits** crystallized *ou* candied fruit. ●**confiture** *nf* jam, preserves.

conflit [kɔ̃fli] *nm* conflict. ●**conflictuel, -elle** *a* (*relation*) conflict-provoking; **situation conflictuelle** situation of conflict.

confluent [kɔ̃flyɑ̃] *nm* (*jonction*) confluence.

confondre [kɔ̃fɔ̃dr] *vt* (*choses, personnes*) to mix up, confuse; (*consterner, étonner*) to confound; (*amalgamer*) to merge, fuse; **c. qch/qn avec** to mistake sth/s.o. for ▌ **se confondre** *vpr* (*s'unir*) (*couleurs etc*) to merge; **se c. en excuses** to be very apologetic.

conforme [kɔ̃fɔrm] *a* **c. à** in accordance with, in keeping with; (*modèle*) true to; **copie c. à l'original** true copy, copy true to the original. ●**conformément** *adv* **c. à** in accordance with.

conformer [kɔ̃fɔrme] *vt* (*attitude, politique etc*) *vt* to model, adapt ▌ **se conformer** *vpr* to conform (**à** to).

conformisme [kɔ̃fɔrmism] *nm* conformity, conformism. ●**conformiste** *a* & *nmf* conformist.

conformité [kɔ̃fɔrmite] *nf* conformity.

confort [kɔ̃fɔr] *nm* comfort. ●**confortable** *a* comfortable.

confrère [kɔ̃frɛr] *nm* colleague. ●**confrérie** *nf* Rel brotherhood.

confronter [kɔ̃frɔ̃te] *vt* (*témoins etc*) to confront (**avec** with); (*expériences, résultats etc*) to compare; (*textes*) to collate, compare; **confronté à** (*difficulté etc*) confronted with. ●**confrontation** *nf* confrontation; (*d'expériences, de textes etc*) comparison.

confus, -use [kɔ̃fy, -yz] *a* (*esprit, situation, bruit*) confused; (*idée, style*) confused, jumbled; (*gêné*) embarrassed; **je suis c.!** (*dé-*

solé*) I'm terribly sorry!; (*comblé de bienfaits*) I'm overwhelmed! ●**confusément** *adv* indistinctly, vaguely. ●**confusion** *nf* confusion; (*gêne, honte*) embarrassment.

congé [kɔ̃ʒe] *nm* (*vacances*) *Br* holiday, *Am* vacation; (*absence du travail*) leave (of absence); (*avis pour locataire*) notice (to quit); (*pour salarié*) notice (of dismissal); **c. de maladie** sick leave; **c. de maternité** maternity leave; **congés payés** *Br* paid holidays, *Am* paid vacation; **donner son c. à** (*employé, locataire*) to give notice to; **prendre c. de qn** to take leave of s.o.

congédier [kɔ̃ʒedje] *vt* (*domestique etc*) to dismiss.

congeler [kɔ̃ʒle] *vt* to freeze. ●**congélateur** *nm* freezer, deep-freeze; **compartiment c.** (*de réfrigérateur*) freezer. ●**congélation** *nf* freezing.

congénère [kɔ̃ʒener] *nmf* fellow creature. ●**congénital, -e, -aux** *a* congenital.

congère [kɔ̃ʒer] *nf* snowdrift.

congestion [kɔ̃ʒɛstjɔ̃] *nf* congestion; **c. cérébrale** stroke. ●**congestionner** *vt* to congest. ●**congestionné, -ée** *a* (*visage*) flushed.

Congo [kɔ̃go] *nm* Congo. ●**congolais, -aise** *a* Congolese ▌ *nmf* **C.**, **Congolaise** Congolese.

congratuler [kɔ̃gratyle] *vt* Iron to congratulate (**sur** on).

congrégation [kɔ̃gregasjɔ̃] *nf* (*de prêtres etc*) congregation.

congrès [kɔ̃grɛ] *nm* congress. ●**congressiste** *nmf* delegate (**to** a congress).

conifère [kɔnifer] *nm* (*arbre*) conifer.

conique [kɔnik] *a* conical, cone-shaped.

conjecture [kɔ̃ʒektyr] *nf* conjecture. ●**conjectural, -e, -aux** *a* conjectural. ●**conjecturer** *vt* to conjecture, surmise.

conjoint, -jointe [kɔ̃ʒwɛ̃, -ʒwɛ̃t] **1** *a* (*problèmes, action etc*) joint. **2** *nm* spouse; **conjoints** husband and wife. ●**conjointement** *adv* jointly.

conjonction [kɔ̃ʒɔ̃ksjɔ̃] *nf* Grammaire conjunction.

conjonctivite [kɔ̃ʒɔ̃ktivit] *nf* conjunctivitis.

conjoncture [kɔ̃ʒɔ̃ktyr] *nf* circumstances; **la c. (économique)** the economic situation. ●**conjoncturel, -elle** *a* (*prévisions, données etc*) economic.

conjugal, -e, -aux [kɔ̃ʒygal, -o] *a* (*vie*) married, conjugal; **bonheur c.** married *ou* marital bliss; **foyer c.** marital home.

conjuguer [kɔ̃ʒyge] *vt* (*verbe*) to conjugate; (*efforts*) to combine ▌ **se conjuguer** *vpr* (*verbe*) to be conjugated. ●**conjugaison** *nf* Grammaire conjugation.

conjurer [kɔ̃ʒyre] *vt* (*danger*) to avert; (*mauvais sort*) to ward off; **c. qn** to beg s.o., implore (**de faire** to do). ●**conjuré, -ée** *nmf* conspirator. ●**conjuration** *nf* (*complot*) conspiracy.

connaissance [kɔnesɑ̃s] *nf* knowledge; (*personne*) acquaintance; **connaissances** (*science*) knowledge (**en** of); **faire la c. de**

qn, **faire c. avec qn** (*inconnu*) to meet s.o., make s.o.'s acquaintance; (*ami, époux etc*) to get to know s.o.; **à ma c.** as far as I know; **avoir c. de** to be aware of; **perdre/reprendre c.** to lose/regain consciousness; **sans c.** unconscious; **prendre c. d'une lettre/etc** to read a letter/*etc*. ● **connaisseur** *nm* connoisseur.

connaître* [kɔnɛtr] *vt* to know; (*rencontrer*) to meet; (*un succès*) to have; (*un malheur*) to experience; **faire c. qch** (*publier, faire découvrir*) to make sth known; **faire c. qn** (*présenter*) to introduce s.o.; (*rendre célèbre*) to make s.o. known **‖ se connaître** *vpr* (*amis etc*) to get to know each other; **nous nous connaissons déjà** we've met before; **s'y c. à** *ou* **en qch** to know (all) about sth; **il ne se connaît plus** he's losing his cool.

connecter [kɔnɛkte] *vt* (*appareil électrique*) to connect. ● **connexe** *a* (*matières*) allied. ● **connexion** *nf* (*électrique*) connection.

connerie [kɔnri] *nf Fam* (*bêtise*) (damn) stupidity; (*action*) (damn) stupid thing; **conneries** (*paroles*) (damn) stupid nonsense.

connivence [kɔnivãs] *nf* connivance.

connotation [kɔnɔtasjɔ̃] *nf* connotation.

connu, -ue [kɔny] *pp de* **connaître ‖** *a* (*célèbre*) well-known.

conquérir* [kɔkerir] *vt* (*pays, marché etc*) to conquer (*charmer*) to win (*s.o.*) over. ● **conquérant, -ante** *nmf* conqueror. ● **conquête** *nf* conquest; **faire la c. de** (*pays, marché etc*) to conquer.

consacrer [kɔsakre] *vt* (*temps, vie etc*) to devote (à to); (*église etc*) to consecrate; (*coutume*) to establish, sanction, consecrate; **expression consacrée** accepted *ou* set phrase; **se c. à** to devote oneself to.

consciemment [kɔsjamã] *adv* consciously.

conscience [kɔsjãs] *nf* **1** (*psychologique*) consciousness; **la c. de qch** the awareness *ou* consciousness of sth; **c. de soi** self-awareness; **avoir/prendre c. de** to be/become aware *ou* conscious of; **perdre c.** (*s'évanouir*) to lose consciousness. **2** (*morale*) conscience; **avoir bonne/mauvaise c.** to have a clear/guilty conscience; **c. professionnelle** conscientiousness. ● **consciencieux, -euse** *a* conscientious.

conscient, -ente [kɔsjã, -ãt] *a* (*non évanoui*) conscious; **c. de** aware *ou* conscious of.

conscrit [kɔskri] *nm* (*soldat*) conscript. ● **conscription** *nf* conscription, *Am* draft.

consécration [kɔsekrasjɔ̃] *nf* (*d'une église etc*) consecration; (*confirmation*) sanction, consecration.

consécutif, -ive [kɔsekytif, -iv] *a* consecutive; **c. à** following upon. ● **consécutivement** *adv* consecutively.

conseil¹ [kɔsɛj] *nm* **un c.** a piece of advice, some advice; **des conseils** advice; (**expert-**)**c.** consultant.

conseil² [kɔsɛj] *nm* (*assemblée*) council, committee; **c. d'administration** board of dir-

ectors; **c. de classe** = teacher-student-parent progress meeting; **c. des ministres** (*réunion*) cabinet meeting.

conseiller¹ [kɔseje] *vt* (*guider, recommander*) to advise; **c. qch à qn** to recommend sth to s.o.; **c. à qn de faire** to advise s.o. to do.

conseiller², -ère [kɔseje, -jɛr] *nmf* (*expert*) consultant, adviser; (*d'un conseil*) *Br* councillor, *Am* councilor; **c. municipal** *Br* town councillor, *Am* councilman *ou* -woman.

consentir* [kɔsãtir] *vi* **c. à** to consent to **‖** *vt* (*prêt, remise etc*) to grant (à to). ● **consentement** *nm* consent.

conséquence [kɔsekãs] *nf* consequence; (*conclusion*) conclusion; **en c.** accordingly; **agir en c.** to take appropriate action, act accordingly; **sans c.** (*importance*) of no importance.

conséquent, -ente [kɔsekã, -ãt] *a* logical; (*important*) *Fam* important.

conséquent (par) [parkɔsekã] *adv* consequently.

conservateur, -trice [kɔsɛrvatœr, -tris] **1** *a* & *nmf Pol* Conservative. **2** *nm* (*de musée*) curator; (*de bibliothèque*) (chief) librarian. **3** *nm* (*pour aliment*) preservative. ● **conservatisme** *nm* conservatism.

conservation [kɔsɛrvasjɔ̃] *nf* preservation; **instinct de c.** instinct for self-preservation.

conservatoire [kɔsɛrvatwar] *nm* school, academy (*of music, drama*).

conserve [kɔsɛrv] *nf* **conserves** canned *ou Br* tinned food; **de** *ou* **en c.** canned, *Br* tinned; **mettre en c.** to can, *Br* tin.

conserver [kɔsɛrve] *vt* (*ne pas perdre*) to keep, retain (*one's job etc*); (*fruits, vie, tradition etc*) to preserve; **c. son calme** *ou* **son sang-froid** to keep one's calm **‖ se conserver** *vpr* (*aliment*) to keep. ● **conservé, -ée** *a* **bien c.** (*vieillard*) well-preserved.

considérable [kɔsiderabl] *a* considerable.

considérer [kɔsidere] *vt* to consider (**que** that); **c. qn** (*faire cas de*) to respect s.o.; **c. comme** to consider to be, regard as; **tout bien considéré** all things considered. ● **considération** *nf* (*motif, examen*) consideration; (*respect*) regard, esteem; **considérations** (*remarques*) observations; **prendre qch en c.** to take sth into consideration.

consigne [kɔsiɲ] *nf* (*instruction*) orders; (*de gare*) *Br* left-luggage office, *Am* baggage checkroom; (*punition*) *Scol* detention; (*de soldat*) confinement to barracks; (*somme*) deposit; **c. automatique** (*de gare*) *Br* luggage lockers, *Am* baggage lockers. ● **consignation** *nf* (*somme*) deposit. ● **consigner** *vt* (*bouteille*) to charge a deposit on; (*bagages*) *Br* to deposit in the left-luggage office, *Am* to check; (*écrire*) to record (*note etc*); (*élève*) to keep in (*as punishment*); (*soldat*) to confine (to barracks); (*salle*) to seal off, close. ● **consigné, -ée** *a* (*bouteille*) returnable.

consistant, -ante [kɔsistã, -ãt] *a* (*sauce, bouillie*) thick; (*repas, Fig argument*) solid.

●**consistance** *nf* (*de liquide*) consistency; **sans c.** (*rumeur*) unfounded; (*esprit*) irresolute.

consister [kɔ̃siste] *vi* **c. en/dans** to consist of/in; **c. à faire** to consist in doing.

consistoire [kɔ̃sistwar] *nm* *Rel* council.

console [kɔ̃sɔl] *nf* (*d'ordinateur, de jeux*) console.

consoler [kɔ̃sɔle] *vt* to comfort, console; **se c. de** (*la mort de qn etc*) to get over. ●**consolation** *nf* comfort, consolation.

consolider [kɔ̃sɔlide] *vt* (*mur etc*) to strengthen; (*position, argument etc*) *Fig* to strenghten, consolidate. ●**consolidation** *nf* strengthening; (*de position etc*) *Fig* strengthening, consolidation.

consommateur, -trice [kɔ̃sɔmatœr, -tris] *nmf* consumer; (*au café*) customer. ●**consommation** *nf* consumption; (*boisson*) drink; **biens/société de c.** consumer goods/society.

consommé, -ée [kɔ̃sɔme] **1** *a* (*achevé*) (*art, habileté*) consummate. **2** *nm* clear meat soup, consommé.

consommer [kɔ̃sɔme] *vt* (*aliment, carburant etc*) to consume; (*crime, œuvre*) *Litt* to accomplish ▮ *vi* (*au café*) to drink; **c. beaucoup/peu** (*véhicule*) to be heavy/light on *Br* petrol *ou Am* gas.

consonance [kɔ̃sɔnɑ̃s] *nf* (*accord*) consonance; **consonances** (*sons*) sounds.

consonne [kɔ̃sɔn] *nf* consonant.

consortium [kɔ̃sɔrsjɔm] *nm* (*entreprises*) consortium.

consorts [kɔ̃sɔr] *nmpl* **et c.** *Péj* and people of that ilk.

conspirer [kɔ̃spire] *vi* **1** (*comploter*) to plot, conspire (**contre** against). **2 c. à faire** (*concourir*) to conspire to do. ●**conspirateur, -trice** *nmf* plotter, conspirator. ●**conspiration** *nf* plot, conspiracy.

conspuer [kɔ̃spɥe] *vt* (*orateur etc*) to boo.

constant, -ante [kɔ̃stɑ̃, -ɑ̃t] *a* constant ▮ *nf* (*nombre*) constante. ●**constamment** *adv* constantly. ●**constance** *nf* constancy.

constat [kɔ̃sta] *nm* (*official*) report; **dresser un c. d'échec** to acknowledge one's failure.

constater [kɔ̃state] *vt* to note, observe (**que** that); (*vérifier*) to establish; (*faire un procès-verbal de*) to record (*facts etc*) ▮ *vi* **je ne fais que c.** I'm merely stating a fact. ●**constatation** *nf* (*remarque*) observation.

constellation [kɔ̃stelasjɔ̃] *nf* constellation. ●**constellé, -ée** *a* **c. d'étoiles/de joyaux/***etc* studded with stars/jewels/*etc*.

consterner [kɔ̃stɛrne] *vt* to distress, upset greatly, dismay. ●**consternation** *nf* distress, (profound) dismay.

constiper [kɔ̃stipe] *vt* to constipate. ●**constipé, -ée** *a* constipated; (*gêné*) *Fam* embarrassed, stiff. ●**constipation** *nf* constipation.

constituer [kɔ̃stitɥe] *vt* (*composer*) to make up; (*représenter*) to represent; (*organiser*) to form (*government team etc*); (*instituer*) to appoint (*committee etc*); **cela constitue un**

crime that constitutes a crime; **constitué de** made up of; **se c. prisonnier** to give oneself up. ●**constituant, -ante** *a* (*éléments*) component, constituent; **assemblée constituante** constituent assembly.

constitutif, -ive [kɔ̃stitysif, -iv] *a* constituent.

constitution [kɔ̃stitysjɔ̃] *nf* (*santé, lois d'un pays*) constitution; (*fondation*) formation (**de** of); (*composition*) composition. ●**constitutionnel, -elle** *a* constitutional.

constructeur [kɔ̃stryktœr] *nm* builder; (*fabricant*) maker (**de** of). ●**constructif, -ive** *a* constructive. ●**construction** *nf* (*de pont etc*) building, construction (**de** of); (*édifice*) building, structure; (*de théorie etc, phrase*) construction; **matériaux/jeu de c.** building materials/set; **en c.** under construction.

construire* [kɔ̃strɥir] *vt* (*maison, route etc*) to build, construct; (*phrase, théorie etc*) to construct.

consul [kɔ̃syl] *nm* consul. ●**consulaire** *a* consular. ●**consulat** *nm* consulate.

consulter [kɔ̃sylte] **1** *vt* to consult ▮ **se consulter** *vpr* to consult (each other), confer. **2** *vi* (*médecin*) *Br* to hold surgery, *Am* hold office hours. ●**consultatif, -ive** *a* (*comité, rôle etc*) consultative, advisory. ●**consultation** *nf* consultation; **cabinet de c.** (*de médecin*) *Br* surgery, *Am* (doctor's) office; **heures de c.** (*de médecin*) *Br* surgery hours, *Am* office hours.

consumer [kɔ̃syme] *vt* (*détruire, miner*) to consume.

contact [kɔ̃takt] *nm* contact; (*toucher*) touch; (*de véhicule*) ignition; **être en c. avec** to be in touch *ou* contact with; **prendre c.** to get in touch (**avec** with); **entrer en c. avec** to come into contact with; **prise de c.** first meeting; **mettre/couper le c.** (*dans un véhicule*) to switch on/off the ignition; **lentilles** *ou* **verres de c.** contact lenses. ●**contacter** *vt* to contact.

contagieux, -euse [kɔ̃taʒjø, -øz] *a* (*maladie, rire*) contagious, infectious; **c'est c.** it's catching *ou* contagious. ●**contagion** *nf* (*de maladie*) infection, contagion; (*de rire, bâillement etc*) contagiousness.

contaminer [kɔ̃tamine] *vt* to contaminate. ●**contamination** *nf* contamination.

conte [kɔ̃t] *nm* tale; **c. de fées** fairy tale *ou* story.

contempler [kɔ̃tɑ̃ple] *vt* to gaze at, contemplate. ●**contemplation** *nf* contemplation; **être** *ou* **rester en c. devant qch/qn** to gaze at sth/s.o.

contemporain, -aine [kɔ̃tɑ̃pɔrɛ̃, -ɛn] *a* & *nmf* contemporary.

contenance [kɔ̃tnɑ̃s] *nf* **1** (*contenu d'un récipient*) capacity. **2** (*allure*) bearing; **perdre c.** to lose one's composure.

contenir* [kɔ̃tnir] *vt* (*renfermer*) to hold; (*avoir comme capacité*) to hold; (*contrôler*) to hold back, contain ▮ **se contenir** *vpr* to contain oneself. ●**contenant** *nm* **le c.** the container. ●**conteneur** *nm* (*pour marchandises, verre*) container.

content, -ente [kɔ̃tã, -ãt] **1** *a* pleased, happy, glad (**de faire** to do); **c. de qn/qch** pleased *ou* happy with s.o./sth; **c. de soi** self-satisfied; **non c. de mentir/d'avoir menti** not content with lying/with having lied. **2** *nm* **avoir son c.** to have had one's fill (**de** of).

contenter [kɔ̃tãte] *vt* to satisfy, please; **se c. de** to be content *ou* happy with, content oneself with. ●**contentement** *nm* contentment, satisfaction.

contentieux [kɔ̃tãsjø] *nm* (*affaires*) matters in dispute; (*service*) legal *ou* claims department.

contenu [kɔ̃tny] *nm* (*de récipient*) contents; (*de texte, film etc*) content.

conter [kɔ̃te] *vt* (*histoire etc*) to tell, relate (à to). ●**conteur, -euse** *nmf* storyteller.

contestable [kɔ̃tɛstabl] *a* (*argument etc*) debatable.

contestataire [kɔ̃tɛstatɛr] *a* **étudiant/ouvrier c.** student/worker protester ▎ *nmf* protester. ●**contestation** *nf* (*opposition politique*) protest; (*discussion*) dispute; **faire de la c.** to protest.

conteste (sans) [sɑ̃kɔ̃tɛst] *adv* unquestionably, indisputably.

contester [kɔ̃tɛste] **1** *vi* (*étudiants etc*) to protest ▎ *vt* to protest against. **2** *vt* (*fait etc*) to dispute, contest. ●**contesté, -ée** *a* (*théorie, dirigeant etc*) controversial.

contexte [kɔ̃tɛkst] *nm* context.

contigu, -uë [kɔ̃tigy] *a* (*maisons etc*) adjoining; **c. à** adjoining, adjacent to. ●**contiguïté** *nf* close proximity.

continent [kɔ̃tinã] *nm* continent; (*opposé à une île*) mainland. ●**continental, -e, -aux** *a* continental.

contingent [kɔ̃tɛ̃ʒã, -ãt] **1** *a* (*accidentel*) contingent. **2** *nm* (*armée*) contingent; (*part, quota*) quota. ●**contingences** *nfpl* contingencies.

continu, -ue [kɔ̃tiny] *a* continuous. ●**continuel, -elle** *a* continual. ●**continuellement** *adv* continually.

continuer [kɔ̃tinɥe] *vt* to continue, carry on (**à** *ou* **de faire** doing); (*prolonger*) to continue (*straight line etc*) ▎ *vi* to continue, go on. ●**continuation** *nf* continuation; **bonne c.!** *Fam* I hope the rest of it goes well. ●**continuité** *nf* continuity.

contondant [kɔ̃tɔ̃dã] *am* **instrument c.** (*arme*) blunt instrument.

contorsion [kɔ̃tɔrsjɔ̃] *nf* contortion. ●**se contorsionner** *vpr* to contort oneself. ●**contorsionniste** *nmf* contortionist.

contour [kɔ̃tur] *nm* outline, contour; **contours** (*de route, rivière*) twists, bends.

contourner [kɔ̃turne] *vt* (*colline etc*) to go round, skirt; (*difficulté, loi*) to get round. ●**contourné, -ée** *a* (*style*) convoluted, tortuous.

contraception [kɔ̃trasɛpsjɔ̃] *nf* contraception. ●**contraceptif, -ive** *a* & *nm* contracep-

tive.

contracter [kɔ̃trakte] *vt* (*muscle, habitude, dette etc*) to contract ▎ **se contracter** *vpr* (*cœur etc*) to contract. ●**contraction** *nf* contraction.

contractuel, -elle [kɔ̃traktɥɛl] **1** *nmf* *Br* traffic warden, *Am* meter man *ou* maid. **2** *a* (*politique etc*) contractual.

contradicteur [kɔ̃tradiktœr] *nm* contradictor. ●**contradiction** *nf* contradiction; **être en c. avec** to be at variance with, contradict. ●**contradictoire** *a* (*propos etc*) contradictory; (*rapports, théories*) conflicting; **débat c.** debate.

contraindre* [kɔ̃trɛ̃dr] *vt* to compel, force (**à faire** to do) ▎ **se contraindre** *vpr* to compel *ou* force oneself (**à faire** to do); (*se gêner*) to restrain oneself. ●**contraignant, -ante** *a* (*horaire etc*) constraining, restricting. ●**contraint, -ainte** *a* (*air, ton etc*) forced, constrained. ●**contrainte** *nf* (*pression*) constraint; (*gêne*) constraint, restraint; **sous la c.** under duress.

contraire [kɔ̃trɛr] *a* opposite; (*défavorable*) (*destin*) adverse; (*vent*) adverse, contrary; **c. à** contrary to ▎ *nm* opposite; (**bien**) **au c.** on the contrary. ●**contrairement** *adv* **c. à** (*information etc*) contrary to; **c. à qn** unlike s.o.

contrarier [kɔ̃trarje] *vt* (*projet, action etc*) to spoil, thwart; (*personne*) to annoy. ●**contrariant, -ante** *a* (*action etc*) annoying; (*personne*) difficult, perverse. ●**contrariété** *nf* annoyance.

contraste [kɔ̃trast] *nm* contrast. ●**contraster** *vi* to contrast (**avec** with); **faire c. qch avec** to contrast sth with.

contrat [kɔ̃tra] *nm* contract.

contravention [kɔ̃travãsjɔ̃] *nf* (*pour stationnement interdit*) (*parking*) ticket; (*amende*) fine; **en c. à** (*loi etc*) in contravention of.

contre [kɔ̃tr] **1** *prép* & *adv* against; (*en échange de*) (in exchange) for; **échanger c.** to exchange for; **fâché c.** angry with; **s'abriter c.** to shelter from; **il va s'appuyer c.** he's going to lean against it; **six voix c. deux** six votes to two; **Nîmes c. Arras** (*match*) Nîmes versus *ou* against Arras; **un médicament c.** (*toux, grippe etc*) a medicine for; **par c.** on the other hand; **tout c. qch/qn** close to sth/s.o.

2 *nm* (*riposte d'escrimeur etc*) counter.

contre- [kɔ̃tr] *préf* counter-.

contre-attaque [kɔ̃tratak] *nf* counterattack. ●**contre-attaquer** *vt* to counterattack.

contrebalancer [kɔ̃trəbalãse] *vt* to counterbalance; (*compenser*) *Fig* to offset.

contrebande [kɔ̃trəbãd] *nf* (*fraude*) smuggling, contraband; (*marchandises*) smuggled goods, contraband; **tabac/etc de c.** smuggled *ou* contraband tobacco/etc; **faire de la c.** to smuggle; **passer qch en c.** to smuggle sth. ●**contrebandier, -ière** *nmf* smuggler.

contrebas (en) [ãkɔ̃trəba] *adv* & *prép* **en c.**

(de) down below.
contrebasse [kɔ̃trəbas] nf (*instrument de musique*) double-bass.
contrecarrer [kɔ̃trəkare] vt (*projet, personne etc*) to thwart, frustrate.
contrecœur (à) [akɔ̃trəkœr] adv reluctantly.
contrecoup [kɔ̃trəku] nm (indirect) effect *ou* consequence; **par c.** as an indirect consequence.
contre-courant (à) [akɔ̃trəkurɑ̃] adv against the current.
contredanse [kɔ̃trədɑ̃s] nf (*amende pour stationnement interdit etc*) Fam ticket.
contredire* [kɔ̃trədir] vt to contradict **I se contredire** vpr to contradict oneself.
contrée [kɔ̃tre] nf region, land.
contre-espionnage [kɔ̃trɛspjɔnaʒ] nm counter-espionage.
contrefaçon [kɔ̃trəfasɔ̃] nf counterfeiting, forgery; (*objet imité*) counterfeit, forgery. ● **contrefaire*** vt (*parodier*) to mimic; (*déguiser*) to disguise (*voice, truth etc*); (*monnaie etc*) to counterfeit, forge.
contreforts [kɔ̃trəfɔr] nmpl (*montagnes*) foothills.
contre-indiqué, -ée [kɔ̃trɛ̃dike] a (*médicament, mesure etc*) dangerous, not recommended.
contre-jour (à) [akɔ̃trəʒur] adv against the (sun)light.
contremaître [kɔ̃trəmɛtr] nm foreman.
contre-offensive [kɔ̃trɔfɑ̃siv] nf counter-offensive.
contrepartie [kɔ̃trəparti] nf compensation; **en c.** in exchange.
contre-performance [kɔ̃trəperfɔrmɑ̃s] nf (*de sportif*) bad performance.
contre-pied [kɔ̃trəpje] nm **prendre le c.-pied d'une opinion/attitude** to take (exactly) the opposite view/attitude; **à c.-pied** Sport on the wrong foot.
contre-plaqué [kɔ̃trəplake] nm plywood.
contrepoids [kɔ̃trəpwa] nm (*poids, Fig personne*) counterbalance; **faire c. à qch** to counterbalance sth.
contrepoint [kɔ̃trəpwɛ̃] nm (*motif musical*) counterpoint.
contrer [kɔ̃tre] vt (*personne, attaque*) to counter.
contre-révolution [kɔ̃trərevɔlysjɔ̃] nf counter-revolution.
contresens [kɔ̃trəsɑ̃s] nm misinterpretation; (*en traduisant*) mistranslation; (*non-sens*) absurdity; **à c.** (*interpréter qch etc*) the wrong way; **prendre une rue à c.** to go down *ou* up a street the wrong way.
contresigner [kɔ̃trəsiɲe] vt to countersign.
contretemps [kɔ̃trətɑ̃] nm hitch, mishap; **à c.** (*arriver, intervenir etc*) at the wrong moment.
contre-torpilleur [kɔ̃trətɔrpijœr] nm (*navire*) destroyer, torpedo boat.
contrevenir* [kɔ̃trəvnir] vi **c. à** (*loi etc*) to contravene.
contre-vérité [kɔ̃trəverite] nf untruth.

contribuer [kɔ̃tribɥe] vi to contribute (**à** to). ● **contribuable** nmf taxpayer. ● **contribution** nf contribution; (*impôt*) tax; **contributions** (*administration*) tax office; **mettre qn à c.** to use s.o.'s services.
contrit, -ite [kɔ̃tri, -it] a (*air etc*) contrite. ● **contrition** nf contrition.
contrôle [kɔ̃trol] nm (*vérification*) inspection, check(ing) (**de** of); (*des prix, de la qualité*) control; (*maîtrise*) control; (*sur bijou*) hallmark; **un c.** (*examen*) a check (**sur** on); **le c. de soi(-même)** self-control; **le c. des naissances** birth control; **un c. d'identité** an identity check.
contrôler [kɔ̃trole] vt (*examiner*) to inspect, check; (*maîtriser, surveiller*) to control **I se contrôler** vpr (*se maîtriser*) to control oneself. ● **contrôleur, -euse** nmf (*de train, bus etc*) Br (ticket) inspector, Am conductor; (*au quai*) ticket collector; **c. de la navigation aérienne, c. aérien** air-traffic controller.
contrordre [kɔ̃trɔrdr] nm **il y a c.** there's a change of orders.
controverse [kɔ̃trɔvɛrs] nf controversy. ● **controversé, -ée** a (*film, personnage etc*) controversial.
contumace (par) [parkɔ̃tymas] adv (*condamné*) in one's absence, in absentia.
contusion [kɔ̃tyzjɔ̃] nf bruise. ● **contusionner** vt to bruise.
convaincre* [kɔ̃vɛ̃kr] vt to convince (**de** of); (*accusé*) to prove guilty (**de** of); **c. qn de faire** to persuade s.o. to do. ● **convaincant, -ante** a convincing. ● **convaincu, -ue** a (*certain*) convinced (**de** of, **que** that).
convalescent, -ente [kɔ̃valesɑ̃, -ɑ̃t] nmf convalescent **I** a **être c.** to convalesce. ● **convalescence** nf convalescence; **être en c.** to convalesce; **maison de c.** convalescent home.
convenable [kɔ̃vnabl] a (*acceptable*) suitable; (*correct*) (*tenue, manières etc*) decent, proper, respectable. ● **convenablement** adv suitably; (*s'habiller, être payé etc*) decently, properly.
convenance [kɔ̃vnɑ̃s] nf **convenances** (*usages*) convention(s), proprieties; **à sa c.** to one's satisfaction *ou* taste.
convenir* [kɔ̃vnir] vi **1 c. à** (*être fait pour*) to be suitable for; (*plaire à, aller à*) to suit; **ça convient** (*date etc*) that's suitable. **2 c. de** (*lieu, prix etc*) to agree upon; (*erreur*) to admit; **c. que** to admit that **I** v imp **il convient de faire** it's advisable to do; (*selon les usages*) it is proper *ou* fitting to do. ● **convenu, -ue** a (*prix etc*) agreed; **comme c.** as agreed.
convention [kɔ̃vɑ̃sjɔ̃] nf (*accord*) agreement, convention; (*règle, Am réunion de parti politique*) convention; **c. collective** collective bargaining; **de c.** (*sentiment, paroles etc*) conventional. ● **conventionné, -ée** a (*prix, tarif*) regulated (by voluntary agreement); **médecin c.** = Br National Health Service doctor (*bound by agreement with the State*).

conventionnel, -elle [kɔ̃vɑ̃sjɔnɛl] *a* conventional.

convergent, -ente [kɔ̃vɛrʒɑ̃, -ɑ̃t] *a* converging, convergent. ● **convergence** *nf* convergence. ● **converger** *vi* to converge.

conversation [kɔ̃vɛrsasjɔ̃] *nf* conversation. ● **converser** *vi* to converse (**avec** with).

conversion [kɔ̃vɛrsjɔ̃] *nf* conversion. ● **convertir** *vt* to convert (**à** to, **en** into) **I se convertir** *vpr* to be converted, convert. ● **converti, -ie** *nmf* convert. ● **convertible I** *nm* (**canapé**) **c.** sofa bed, *Br* bed settee.

convexe [kɔ̃vɛks] *a* convex.

conviction [kɔ̃viksjɔ̃] *nf* (*certitude, croyance*) conviction; **pièce à c.** (*dans un procès*) exhibit.

convier [kɔ̃vje] *vt* to invite (**à une soirée**/*etc* to a party/*etc*, **à faire** to do).

convive [kɔ̃viv] *nmf* guest (*at table*).

convivial, -e, -aux [kɔ̃vivjal, -o] *a* (*ordinateur*) user-friendly.

convoi [kɔ̃vwa] *nm* (*véhicules, personnes etc*) convoy; (*train*) train; **c.** (**funèbre**) funeral procession.

convoiter [kɔ̃vwate] *vt* to desire, envy, covet. ● **convoitise** *nf* desire, envy.

convoquer [kɔ̃vɔke] *vt* (*candidats, membres etc*) to summon *ou* invite (to attend); (*assemblée, comité etc*) to convene, summon; **c. qn à** to summon *ou* invite s.o. to. ● **convocation** *nf* (*lettre*) (written) notice to attend; (*action*) summoning; (*d'assemblée etc*) convening, summoning; (*ordre*) summons to attend.

convoyer [kɔ̃vwaje] *vt* to escort. ● **convoyeur** *nm* (*navire*) escort ship; **c. de fonds** security guard (*transporting money etc*).

convulser [kɔ̃vylse] *vt* to convulse. ● **convulsif, -ive** *a* convulsive. ● **convulsion** *nf* convulsion.

coopérer [kɔɔpere] *vi* to co-operate (**à** in, **avec** with). ● **coopératif, -ive** *a* co-operative **I** *nf* co-operative (society). ● **coopération** *nf* co-operation (**entre** between).

coopter [kɔɔpte] *vt* (*candidat etc*) to co-opt.

coordonner [kɔɔrdɔne] *vt* to co-ordinate. ● **coordonnées** *nfpl* (*adresse, téléphone*) *Fam* contact address and phone number, particulars, details; *Math* co-ordinates. ● **coordination** *nf* co-ordination.

copain [kɔpɛ̃] *nm Fam* (*camarade*) pal; (*petit ami*) boyfriend; **être c. avec** to be pals with.

copeau, -x [kɔpo] *nm* (*de bois*) shaving.

copie [kɔpi] *nf* copy; (*devoir, examen*) paper. ● **copier** *vti* to copy; (*tricher*) (*élève*) to copy, crib (**sur qn** from s.o.). ● **copieur, -euse** *nmf* (*élève etc*) copycat, copier **I** *nm* (*machine*) photocopier.

copieux, -euse [kɔpjø, -øz] *a* (*repas*) plentiful, copious; (*notes, texte*) copious.

copilote [kɔpilɔt] *nm* co-pilot.

copine [kɔpin] *nf Fam* (*camarade*) pal; (*petite amie*) girlfriend; **être c. avec** to be pals with.

copropriété [kɔprɔprijete] *nf* joint ownership; (**immeuble en**) **c.** *Br* block of flats in joint ownership, *Am* condominium.

copulation [kɔpylasjɔ̃] *nf* copulation.

coq [kɔk] *nm* rooster, cock; **c. au vin** (*chicken cooked in wine*) coq au vin; **passer du c. à l'âne** to jump from one subject to another.

coque [kɔk] *nf* **1** (*de noix*) shell; (*fruit de mer*) cockle; **œuf à la c.** boiled egg. **2** (*de navire*) hull.

coquelicot [kɔkliko] *nm* poppy.

coqueluche [kɔklyʃ] *nf* **1** (*maladie*) whooping cough. **2 être la c. de** (*admiré*) to be the darling of.

coquet, -ette [kɔkɛ, -ɛt] *a* (*chic*) smart; (*joli*) pretty; (*provocant*) coquettish, flirtatious; (*somme, bénéfice*) *Fam* tidy **I** *nf* coquette, flirt. ● **coquetterie** *nf* (*élégance*) smartness; (*goût de la toilette*) dress sense; (*galanterie*) coquetry.

coquetier [kɔktje] *nm* egg cup.

coquille [kɔkij] *nf* shell; (*faute d'imprimerie*) misprint; **c. Saint-Jacques** (*mollusque*) scallop. ● **coquillage** *nm* (*mollusque*) shellfish *inv*; (*coquille*) shell.

coquin, -ine [kɔkɛ̃, -in] *nmf* rascal **I** *a* mischievous, rascally; (*histoire, sous-vêtements etc*) naughty.

cor [kɔr] *nm* (*instrument de musique*) horn; **c.** (**au pied**) corn; **réclamer** *ou* **demander qch/qn à c. et à cri** to clamour for sth/s.o.

corail, -aux [kɔraj, -o] *nm* coral.

Coran [kɔrɑ̃] *nm* **le C.** the Koran.

corbeau, -x [kɔrbo] *nm* crow; (**grand**) **c.** raven.

corbeille [kɔrbɛj] *nf* basket; **c. à papier** waste paper basket.

corbillard [kɔrbijar] *nm* hearse.

cordage [kɔrdaʒ] *nm* (*de voilier etc*) rope.

corde [kɔrd] *nf* rope; (*plus mince*) (*fine*) cord; (*de raquette, violon etc*) string; **c.** (**raide**) (*d'acrobate*) tightrope; **monter à la c.** to climb up a rope; **instrument à cordes** (*violon etc*) string(ed) instrument; **c. à linge** (*washing ou clothes*) line; **c. à sauter** *Br* skipping rope, *Am* jump rope; **usé jusqu'à la c.** threadbare; **cordes vocales** vocal cords; **prendre un virage à la c.** (*conducteur*) to hug a bend; **ce n'est pas dans mes cordes** *Fam* it's not my line *ou* business *ou* province. ● **cordée** *nf* roped (climbing) party. ● **cordelette** *nf* (*fine*) cord. ● **cordon** *vt* (*raquette*) to string.

cordial, -e, -aux [kɔrdjal, -o] *a* (*accueil, personne etc*) warm, cordial **I** *nm* (*remontant*) tonic, cordial. ● **cordialité** *nf* warmth, cordiality.

cordon [kɔrdɔ̃] *nm* (*de tablier, sac etc*) string; (*de rideau*) cord, rope; (*d'agents de police*) cordon; (*décoration*) ribbon, sash; (*ombilical*) cord. ● **cordon-bleu** *nm* (*pl* **cordons-bleus**) first-class cook, cordon bleu (cook).

cordonnier [kɔrdɔnje] *nm* shoe repairer, cobbler. ● **cordonnerie** *nf* shoe repair *ou* repairer's shop.

Corée [kɔre] *nf* Korea. ●**coréen, -enne** *a* Korean ▌ *nmf* C., **Coréenne** Korean.

coriace [kɔrjas] *a* (*aliment, personne*) tough.

corne [kɔrn] *nf* (*de chèvre etc*) horn; (*de cerf*) antler; (*matière, instrument*) horn; (*au pied etc*) hard skin; (*angle, pli*) corner.

cornée [kɔrne] *nf* (*de l'œil*) cornea.

corneille [kɔrnɛj] *nf* crow.

cornemuse [kɔrnəmyz] *nf* bagpipes.

corner [kɔrne] **1** *vt* (*page*) to turn down the corner of, dog-ear. **2** *vi* (*véhicule*) to sound its horn. **3** [kɔrnɛr] *nm* Football corner.

cornet [kɔrne] *nm* **1** (*de glace*) cone, *Br* cornet; **c. (de papier)** (paper) cone. **2 c. (à pistons)** (*instrument de musique*) cornet.

corniaud [kɔrnjo] *nm* (*chien*) mongrel; (*imbécile*) *Fam* drip, twit.

corniche [kɔrniʃ] *nf* (*route*) cliff road; (*en haut d'un mur etc*) cornice.

cornichon [kɔrniʃɔ̃] *nm* (*concombre*) gherkin; (*niais*) *Fam* twit, clod, *Br* clot.

cornu, -ue [kɔrny] *a* (*diable, animal*) horned.

corollaire [kɔrɔlɛr] *nm* corollary.

corporation [kɔrpɔrasjɔ̃] *nf* (*gens du même métier*) trade association, professional body.

corps [kɔr] *nm* Anat Ch Fig etc body; **c. électoral** electorate; **c. enseignant** teaching profession; **c. d'armée/diplomatique** army/diplomatic corps; **garde du c.** bodyguard; **un c. de bâtiment** a main building; **c. et âme** body and soul; **lutter c. à c.** to fight hand-to-hand; **à son c. défendant** under protest; **prendre c.** (*projet*) to take shape; **donner c. à** (*rumeur, idée*) to give substance to; **faire c. avec** to form a part of, belong with; **perdu c. et biens** (*navire etc*) lost with all hands; **esprit de c.** corporate spirit.

corporel, -elle [kɔrpɔrɛl] *a* (*besoin etc*) bodily; **châtiment c.** coporal punishment.

corpulent, -ente [kɔrpylɑ̃, -ɑ̃t] *a* stout, corpulent. ●**corpulence** *nf* stoutness, corpulence.

corpus [kɔrpys] *nm* (*ensemble d'exemples*) corpus.

correct, -e [kɔrɛkt] *a* (*exact*) correct; (*bienséant, honnête, décent*) proper, correct; (*passable*) adequate. ●**correctement** *adv* correctly; (*se conduire, agir*) properly; (*fonctionner*) adequately.

correcteur, -trice [kɔrɛktœr, -tris] **1** *a* **verres correcteurs** corrective lenses. **2** *nmf* (*d'examen*) examiner; (*d'épreuves d'imprimerie*) proofreader. **3** *nm* **c. d'orthographe** Ordinat spell-checker.

correction [kɔrɛksjɔ̃] *nf* (*rectification etc*) correction; (*punition*) thrashing; (*exactitude, bienséance*) correctness; **la c. de** (*devoirs, examen*) the marking of; **c. d'épreuves** Typ proofreading.

correctionnel, -elle [kɔrɛksjɔnɛl] *a* **tribunal c.** *Br* magistrates' court, *Am* police court ▌ *nf* = **tribunal correctionnel.**

corrélation [kɔrelɑsjɔ̃] *nf* correlation.

correspondance [kɔrɛspɔ̃dɑ̃s] *nf* (*relation, lettres*) correspondence; (*de train, d'autocar*) *Br* connection, *Am* transfer.

correspondre [kɔrɛspɔ̃dr] **1** *vi* (*s'accorder*) to correspond (à to, with); (*pièces*) to communicate; **c. avec** (*train*) to connect with ▌ **se correspondre** *vpr* (*idées, ensembles etc*) to correspond; (*pièces*) to communicate. **2** *vi* (*écrire*) to correspond (**avec** with). ●**correspondant, -ante** *a* corresponding ▌ *nmf* (*reporter*) correspondent; (*d'un élève, d'un adolescent*) *Br* pen friend, *Am* pen pal; (*au téléphone*) caller.

corrida [kɔrida] *nf* bullfight.

corridor [kɔridɔr] *nm* corridor.

corriger [kɔriʒe] *vt* (*texte, injustice etc*) to correct; (*épreuve*) to read; (*devoir*) to mark, correct; (*châtier*) to beat, punish; **c. qn de** (*défaut*) to cure s.o. of; **se c. de** to cure oneself of. ●**corrigé** *nm* (*d'un exercice etc*) model (answer), correct version, key.

corroborer [kɔrɔbɔre] *vt* to corroborate.

corroder [kɔrɔde] *vt* to corrode. ●**corrosif, -ive** *a* corrosive. ●**corrosion** *nf* corrosion.

corrompre* [kɔrɔ̃pr] *vt* to corrupt; (*soudoyer*) to bribe; (*aliment, eau*) to taint. ●**corrompu, -ue** *a* corrupt; (*altéré*) tainted. ●**corruption** *nf* (*par l'argent*) bribery; (*vice*) corruption.

corsage [kɔrsaʒ] *nm* (*chemisier*) blouse; (*de robe*) bodice.

corsaire [kɔrsɛr] *nm* (*marin*) Hist privateer.

Corse [kɔrs] *nf* Corsica. ●**corse** *a* Corsican ▌ *nmf* C. Corsican.

corser [kɔrse] *vt* (*récit, action*) to heighten; **l'affaire se corse** things are hotting up. ●**corsé, -ée** *a* (*café*) strong; (*vin*) full-bodied; (*sauce, Fig histoire*) spicy; (*problème*) tough; (*addition de restaurant*) steep.

corset [kɔrse] *nm* corset.

cortège [kɔrtɛʒ] *nm* (*défilé*) procession; (*suite*) (*de prince etc*) retinue; **c. officiel** (*automobiles*) motorcade.

corvée [kɔrve] *nf* chore, drudgery; (*de soldat*) fatigue (duty).

cosaque [kɔzak] *nm* Cossack.

cosmétique [kɔsmetik] *a* & *nm* (**produit**) **c.** cosmetic, beauty care product.

cosmopolite [kɔsmɔpɔlit] *a* cosmopolitan.

cosmos [kɔsmɔs] *nm* (*univers*) cosmos; (*espace*) outer space. ●**cosmique** *a* cosmic. ●**cosmonaute** *nmf* cosmonaut.

cosse [kɔs] *nf* (*de pois etc*) pod.

cossu, -ue [kɔsy] *a* (*personne*) well-to-do; (*maison, voiture etc*) opulent.

costaud [kɔsto] *a Fam* brawny, beefy, strong ▌ *nm Fam* strong man.

costume [kɔstym] *nm* (*déguisement*) costume, dress; (*complet*) suit. ●**costumer** *vt* **c. qn** to dress s.o. up (**en** as); **se c. en** to dress up as; **bal costumé** costume ball, *Br* fancy-dress ball.

cote [kɔt] *nf* (*marque de classement*) mark, letter, number; (*tableau des valeurs*) (official) listing; (*des valeurs boursières*) quotation; (*évaluation, popularité*) rating; (*de cheval*) odds (**de** on); **c. d'alerte** danger level.

côte [kot] *nf* **1** (*os*) rib; (*de mouton*) chop; (*de veau*) cutlet; **à côtes** (*étoffe*) ribbed; **c. à c.** side by side; **se tenir les côtes** to split one's sides (laughing). **2** (*montée*) hill; (*versant*) hillside. **3** (*littoral*) coast.

côté [kote] *nm* side; (*direction*) way; **de l'autre c.** on the other side (**de** of); (*direction*) the other way; **de ce c.** (*passer*) this way; **du c. de** (*vers, près de*) towards; **de c.** (*se jeter, mettre de l'argent etc*) to one side; (*regarder, faire un pas*) sideways, to one side; **à c.** close by, nearby; (*pièce*) in the other room; (*maison*) next door; **la maison (d')à c.** the house next door; **à c. de** next to, beside; (*comparaison*) compared to; **passer à c.** (*balle*) to fall wide (**de** of); **venir de tous côtés** to come from all directions; **d'un c.** on the one hand; **de mon c.** for my part; **à mes côtés** by my side; **laisser de c.** (*travail*) to neglect; (**du**) **c. argent**/*etc Fam* as regards money/*etc*, moneywise/*etc*; **le bon c.** (*d'une affaire*) the bright side (**de** of).

coteau, -x [kɔto] *nm* (small) hill; (*versant*) hillside.

côtelé, -ée [kotle] *a* (*étoffe*) ribbed; **velours c.** cord(uroy).

côtelette [kotlɛt] *nf* (*d'agneau, de porc*) chop; (*de veau*) cutlet.

coter [kote] *vt* (*valeur boursière*) to quote. ● **coté, -ée** *a* **bien c.** highly rated.

coterie [kɔtri] *nf* (*clan*) *Péj* set, clique.

côtier, -ière [kotje, -jɛr] *a* coastal; (*pêche*) inshore.

cotiser [kɔtize] *vi* (*à un cadeau, pour la retraite etc*) to contribute (**à** to, **pour** towards); **c. à un club**/*etc* to subscribe to a club/*etc* ■ **se cotiser** *vpr Br* to club together, *Am* club in (**pour acheter** to buy). ● **cotisation** *nf* (*de club etc*) dues, subscription; (*de retraite, chômage etc*) contribution(s).

coton [kɔtɔ̃] *nm* cotton; **c. (hydrophile)** *Br* cotton wool, *Am* (absorbent) cotton. ● **cotonnade** *nf* cotton (fabric). ● **cotonnier, -ière** *a* **industrie**/*etc* cotonnière cotton industry/*etc*.

côtoyer [kotwaje] *vt* (*route, rivière*) to run along, skirt; (*la misère, la folie etc*) *Fig* to be ou come close to; **c. qn** (*fréquenter*) to rub shoulders with s.o.

cotte [kɔt] *nf* (*de travail*) overalls.

cou [ku] *nm* neck; **sauter au c. de qn** to throw one's arms around s.o.; **jusqu'au c.** (*endetté etc*) up to one's eyes ou ears.

couchage [kuʃaʒ] *nm* **sac de c.** sleeping bag; **matériel de c.** bedding.

couche [kuʃ] *nf* **1** (*épaisseur*) layer; (*de peinture*) coat; (*de roche*) stratum; **couches sociales** levels of society, social strata. **2** (*linge de bébé*) *Br* nappy, *Am* diaper. **3 faire une fausse c.** (*femme*) to have a miscarriage; **les couches** (*accouchement*) confinement. ● **couche-culotte** *nf* (*pl* **couches-culottes**) baby's trainer pants lined with a disposable *Br* nappy ou *Am* diaper.

coucher [kuʃe] *vt* to put to bed; (*héberger*) to put up; (*allonger*) to lay (down ou out); (*blé*) to flatten; **c. (par écrit)** to put down (in writing); **c. qn en joue** to aim at s.o. ■ *vi* to sleep (**avec** with) ■ **se coucher** *vpr* to go to bed; (*s'allonger*) to lie flat ou down; (*soleil*) to set, go down ■ *nm* (*moment*) bedtime; **l'heure du c.** bedtime; **au c.** at bedtime; **le c. du soleil** sunset. ● **couchant** *am* **soleil c.** setting sun ■ *nm* (*aspect*) **le c.** (*ouest*) the west. ● **couché, -ée** *a* **être c.** to be in bed; (*étendu*) to be lying (down).

couchette [kuʃɛt] *nf* (*de train*) sleeper, sleeping berth, *Br* couchette; (*de bateau*) bunk.

couci-couça [kusikusa] *adv Fam* so-so.

coucou [kuku] **1** *nm* (*oiseau*) cuckoo; (*pendule*) cuckoo clock; (*fleur*) cowslip. **2** *int* **c.!** (*à cache-cache*) peek-a-boo!

coude [kud] *nm* elbow; (*de chemin, rivière*) bend; **se serrer** ou **se tenir les coudes** to help one another, stick together; **c. à c.** side by side; **coup de c.** poke ou dig with one's elbow; (*léger*) nudge; **pousser qn du c.** to nudge s.o.

coudoyer [kudwaje] *vt* to rub shoulders with.

cou-de-pied [kudpje] *nm* (*pl* **cous-de-pied**) instep.

coudre* [kudr] *vti* to sew.

couenne [kwan] *nf* (*de porc*) crackling, rind.

couette [kwɛt] *nf* (*édredon*) duvet, *Br* continental quilt.

couffin [kufɛ̃] *nm* (*de bébé*) *Br* Moses basket, *Am* bassinet.

couic! [kwik] *int* eek!, squeak! ● **couiner** *vi Fam* (*animal, enfant*) to squeal, squeak; (*pleurer*) to whine.

couillon [kuj3] *nm* (*idiot*) *Arg* drip, cretin.

coulage [kulaʒ] *nm* (*de métal, statue*) casting; (*gaspillage*) *Fam* wastage.

coulée [kule] *nf* (*de métal*) casting; **c. de lave** lava flow; **c. de boue** mud slide.

couler¹ [kule] *vi* (*eau, rivière etc*) to flow; (*robinet, nez, sueur*) to run; (*fuir*) (*robinet*) to leak; *Fig* **faire c. un bain** to run a bath; **faire c. le sang** to cause bloodshed; **ça coule de source** (*c'est évident*) that's completely obvious.

■ *vt* (*métal, statue*) to cast; (*vie*) *Fig* to spend, lead; (*jours*) to spend; (*glisser*) to slip (*rope etc*); **se c. dans** (*passer*) to slip into; **se la c. douce** to have things easy. ● **coulant, -ante** *a* (*style*) flowing; (*caractère*) easygoing.

couler² [kule] *vi* (*bateau, nageur*) to sink; **c. à pic** to sink to the bottom ■ *vt* to sink; (*discréditer*) *Fig* to discredit.

couleur [kulœr] *nf* colour; (*colorant*) paint; *Cartes* suit; **couleurs** (*teint*) colour; **reprendre des couleurs** to get one's colour back; **c. chair** flesh-coloured; **de c.** (*homme, habit etc*) coloured; **boîte de couleurs** box of paints, paint box; **photo/film**/*etc* **en couleurs** colour photo/film/*etc*; **téléviseur** ou **télévision c.** ou **en couleurs** colour television ou TV set; **haut en c.** colourful!; **sous c. de faire** while pretending to do.

couleuvre [kulœvr] *nf* (grass) snake.

coulisse [kulis] *nf* **1** (*de porte*) runner; **porte à c.** sliding door. **2 dans les coulisses** (*au théâtre*) in the wings, backstage; **dans la c.** (*caché*) *Fig* behind the scenes. ●**coulissant, -ante** *a* (*porte, fenêtre*) sliding.

couloir [kulwar] *nm* corridor; (*de circulation, d'une piste*) lane; (*dans un bus*) gangway; **c. aérien** air corridor *ou* lane.

coup [ku] *nm* blow, knock; (*léger*) tap, touch; (*choc moral*) blow; (*de fusil, canon, revolver etc*) shot; (*de crayon, d'horloge, de raquette etc*) stroke; (*aux échecs etc*) move; (*fois*) *Fam* time; **donner des coups à** to hit; **c. de brosse** brush(-up); **c. de chiffon** wipe (with a rag); **c. de sonnette** ring (on a bell); **c. de dents** bite; **c. de chance** stroke of luck; **c. d'état** coup; **c. dur** *Fam* nasty blow; **sale c.** dirty trick; **mauvais c.** piece of mischief; **c. franc** *Football* free kick; **tenter le c.** *Fam* to have a go *ou* try; **réussir son c.** to bring it off; **faire les quatre cents coups** to get into all kinds of mischief; **tenir le c.** to hold out; **avoir/attraper le c.** to have/get the knack; **sous le c. de** (*émotion etc*) under the influence of; **il est dans le c.** *Fam* he's in the know; **après c.** afterwards, after the event; **sur le c. de midi** on the stroke of twelve; **sur le c.** (*alors*) at the time; **tué sur le c.** killed outright; **à c. sûr** for sure; **c. sur c.** (*à la suite*) one after the other, in quick succession; **tout à c., tout d'un c.** suddenly; **à tout c.** at every go; **d'un seul c.** (*avaler etc*) in one go; (*soudain*) all of a sudden; **du premier c.** *Fam* (at the) first go; **du c.** (*de ce fait*) as a result; **pour le c.** this time. ●**coup-de-poing** *nm* (*pl* **coups-de-poing**) **c.-de-poing** (**américain**) knuckle-duster.

coupable [kupabl] *a* guilty (**de** of); (*plaisir, désir*) guilty, sinful; **déclarer qn c.** to convict s.o., find s.o. guilty ▌ *nmf* guilty person, culprit.

coupe [kup] *nf* **1** (*trophée*) cup; (*à fruits*) dish; (*à boire*) goblet, glass. **2** (*de vêtement etc*) cut; (*plan*) section; **c. de cheveux** haircut.

coupe-circuit [kupsirkɥi] *nm inv* (*fusible*) cutout, circuit breaker. ●**coupe-file** *nm inv* (*carte*) official pass. ●**coupe-gorge** *nm inv* cut-throat alley. ●**coupe-ongles** *nm inv* (finger nail) clippers. ●**coupe-papier** *nm inv* paper knife. ●**coupe-vent** *nm Br* windcheater, *Am* windbreaker.

couper [kupe] *vt* to cut; (*arbre*) to cut down; (*téléphone, vivres etc*) to cut off; (*courant, radio, télévision etc*) to switch off; (*voyage*) to break (off); (*faim, appétit, souffle etc*) to take away; (*vin*) to water down; (*morceler*) to cut up; (*croiser*) to cut across; **c. la parole à qn** to cut s.o. short; **se faire c. les cheveux** to get one's hair cut.

▌ *vi* to cut; (*aux cartes*) to cut; (*prendre un raccourci*) to take a short cut; **c. à** (*corvée*)

Fam to get out of; **ne coupez pas!** (*au téléphone*) hold the line!

▌ **se couper** *vpr* (*routes*) to intersect; (*se trahir*) to give oneself away; **se c. au** *ou* **le doigt** to cut one's finger. ●**coupant, -ante** *a* sharp ▌ *nm* (cutting) edge. ●**coupé** *nm* (*voiture*) coupé.

couperet [kuprɛ] *nm* (*de boucher*) (meat) chopper; (*de guillotine*) blade.

couperosé, -ée [kuprozε] *a* (*visage*) blotchy.

couple [kupl] *nm* couple. ●**coupler** *vt* to couple, connect.

couplet [kuplɛ] *nm* verse.

coupole [kupɔl] *nf* dome.

coupon [kupɔ̃] *nm* (*tissu*) remnant, oddment; (*pour la confection d'un vêtement*) length; (*ticket, titre*) coupon; **c. réponse** reply coupon.

coupure [kupyr] *nf* cut; (*de journal*) *Br* cutting, *Am* clipping; (*billet*) *Br* banknote, *Am* bill; **c. d'électricité** *ou* **de courant** blackout, *Br* power cut.

cour [kur] *nf* **1** court(yard); (*de gare*) forecourt; **c.** (**de récréation**) (*d'école*) *Br* playground, *Am* school yard. **2** (*de roi, tribunal*) court; **c. d'appel** Court of Appeal, Appeal Court. **3** (*de femme, d'homme*) courtship; **faire la c. à qn** to court s.o., woo s.o.

courage [kuraʒ] *nm* courage; (*zèle*) spirit; **perdre c.** to lose heart *ou* courage; **s'armer de c.** to pluck up courage; **bon c.!** good luck! ●**courageux, -euse** *a* courageous; (*énergique*) spirited. ●**courageusement** *adv* courageously.

couramment [kuramɑ̃] *adv* (*parler*) fluently; (*souvent*) frequently.

courant, -ante [kurɑ̃, -ɑ̃t] **1** *a* (*fréquent*) common; (*modèle, taille*) standard; (*compte, année, langage*) current; (*affaires*) routine; **eau courante** running water; **le dix/etc c.** *Com* the tenth/etc of this month, *Br* the tenth/etc inst(ant). **2** *nm* (*de l'eau, électrique*) current; **c. d'air** *Br* draught, *Am* draft; **dans le c. du mois/etc** during the course of the month/etc; **être au c.** to know (de about); (**à jour**) to be up-to-date; **mettre qn au c. de** to tell s.o. about.

courbature [kurbatyr] *nf* (muscular) ache. ●**courbaturé, -ée** *a* aching (all over).

courbe [kurb] *a* curved ▌ *nf* curve. ●**courber** *vti* to bend ▌ **se courber** *vpr* (*personne*) to bend (down); **se c. devant qn** *Fig* to bow down to s.o.

courge [kurʒ] *nf Br* marrow, *Am* squash. ●**courgette** *nf Br* courgette, *Am* zucchini.

courir* [kurir] *vi* to run; (*se hâter*) to rush; (*à bicyclette, en auto*) to race; **en courant** (*vite*) in a rush; **le bruit court que...** there's a rumour going around that...; **c. après qn** to run after s.o.; **faire c.** (*nouvelle*) to spread; **il court encore** (*voleur, assassin etc*) he's still at large.

▌ *vt* (*risque*) to run; (*épreuve sportive*) to run (in); (*danger*) to face; (*rues, monde*) to roam; (*magasins, cafés*) to go round; (*filles*) to run after. ●**coureur** *nm* (*sportif*) runner; (*cycliste*) cyclist; (*automobile*) racing driver; (*galant*) *Péj* womanizer.

couronne [kurɔn] *nf* (*de roi, reine etc*) crown; (*pour enterrement*) wreath; (*de dent*) crown. ●**couronner** *vt* (*roi etc*) to crown; (*auteur, ouvrage*) to award a prize to; **leurs efforts ont été couronnés de succès** their efforts were successful. ●**couronné, -ée** *a* (*tête*) crowned; **roman c.** prize novel. ●**couronnement** *nm* (*de roi etc*) coronation; (*d'une carrière, d'une œuvre etc*) crowning achievement.

courrier [kurje] *nm* mail, *Br* post; (*transport*) postal *ou* mail service; (*rubrique de journal*) column; **j'ai du c. à faire** I have (some) letters to write; **par retour du c.** *Br* by return of post, *Am* by return mail.

courroie [kurwa] *nf* (*attache*) strap; (*de transmission, ventilateur*) belt.

courroux [kuru] *nm Litt* wrath.

cours [kur] *nm* **1** (*de maladie, rivière, astre, pensées etc*) course; (*cote d'une monnaie etc*) rate, price; **c. d'eau** river, stream; **suivre son c.** (*déroulement*) to follow its course; **avoir c.** (*monnaie*) to be legal tender; (*théorie*) to be current; **en c.** (*travail*) in progress; (*année*) current; (*affaires*) outstanding; **en c. de route** on the way; **au c. de** during; **donner libre c. à** (*sa joie, sa colère etc*) to give free rein to. **2** (*leçon*) class; (*série de leçons*) course; (*conférence*) lecture; (*établissement*) school; (*manuel*) textbook; **faire c.** (*professeur*) to teach; **c. magistral** lecture; **des c. du soir** evening classes.
3 (*allée*) avenue.

course¹ [kurs] *nf* (*action*) run(ning); (*épreuve de vitesse*) & *Fig* race; (*trajet*) journey, trip, run; (*excursion*) hike; (*de projectile etc*) path, flight; **courses** (*de chevaux*) races; **faire la c. avec qn** to race (with) s.o.; **il n'est plus dans la c.** (*dépassé*) he's out of touch; **cheval de c.** racehorse; **voiture de c.** racing car.

course² [kurs] *nf* (*commission*) errand; **courses** (*achats*) shopping; **faire une c.** to run an errand; **faire les courses** to do the shopping.

coursier, -ière [kursje, -jer] *nmf* messenger.

court, courte [kur, kurt] **I** *a* short; **c'est un peu c.** *Fam* that's not very much **I** *adv* (*couper, s'arrêter*) short; **couper c. à** (*entretien etc*) to cut short; **tout c.** quite simply; **à c. d'argent/etc** short of money/etc; **pris de c.** caught unawares. **2** *nm* Tennis court.
●**court-bouillon** *nm* (*pl* **courts-bouillons**) court-bouillon (spiced water for cooking fish). ●**court-circuit** *nm* (*pl* **courts-circuits**) (*coupure d'électricité*) short-circuit. ●**court-circuiter** *vt* to short-circuit.

courtier, -ière [kurtje, -jer] *nmf* broker.
●**courtage** *nm* brokerage.

courtisan [kurtizɑ̃] *nm* (*d'un roi etc*) courtier. ●**courtisane** *nf* (*d'un roi etc*)

courtesan. ●**courtiser** *vt* to court.

courtois, -oise [kurtwa, -waz] *a* courteous. ●**courtoisie** *nf* courtesy.

couru, -ue [kury] *a* (*spectacle, lieu*) popular; **c'est c. (d'avance)** *Fam* it's a sure thing.

couscous [kuskus] *nm* (*plat*) couscous.

cousin, -ine [kuzɛ̃, -in] **1** *nmf* cousin. **2** *nm* (*insecte*) (*long-legged*) mosquito.

coussin [kusɛ̃] *nm* cushion.

cousu, -ue [kuzy] *a* .sewn; **c. main** hand-sewn.

coût [ku] *nm* cost. ●**coûter** *vti* to cost; **ça coûte combien?** how much is it?, how much does it cost?; **ça lui en coûte de faire** it pains him *ou* her to do that; **coûte que coûte** at all costs; **ça coûte les yeux de la tête** that costs the earth; **cette erreur va vous c. cher** that error will cost you dearly. ●**coûtant** *am* **prix c.** *Br* cost *ou Am* wholesale price.

couteau, -x [kuto] *nm* knife; **coup de c.** stab; **donner un coup de c. à qn** to stab s.o.; **être à couteaux tirés** to be at daggers drawn (**avec qn** with s.o.); **visage en lame de c.** hatchet face; **retourner le c. dans la plaie** *Fig* to rub it in.

coûteux, -euse [kutø, -øz] *a* costly, expensive.

coutume [kutym] *nf* custom; **avoir c. de faire** to be accustomed to doing; **comme de c.** as usual; **plus que de c.** more than is customary. ●**coutumier, -ière** *a* customary.

couture [kutyr] *nf* sewing, needlework; (*métier*) dressmaking; (*raccord*) seam; **faire de la c.** to sew; **maison de c.** fashion house. ●**couturier** *nm* fashion designer. ●**couturière** *nf* dressmaker.

couvent [kuvɑ̃] *nm* (*pour religieuses*) convent; (*pour moines*) monastery; (*pensionnat*) convent school.

couver [kuve] *vt* (*œufs*) to sit on, hatch; (*projet*) *Fig* to hatch; (*maladie*) to be getting; **c. qn** to pamper s.o.; **c. qn/qch des yeux** (*convoiter*) to look at s.o./sth enviously **I** *vi* (*poule*) to brood; (*feu*) *Br* to smoulder, *Am* smolder; (*mal, complot*) to be brewing. ●**couvée** *nf* (*petits oiseaux*) brood; (*œufs*) clutch. ●**couveuse** *nf* (*pour nouveaux-nés, œufs*) incubator.

couvercle [kuverkl] *nm* lid, cover.

couvert¹ [kuver] **1** *nm* (*cuillère, fourchette, couteau*) (set of) cutlery; (*au restaurant*) cover charge; **mettre le c.** to set *ou Br* lay the table; **table de cinq couverts** table set *ou Br* laid for five. **2** *nm* **sous (le) c. de** (*apparence*) under cover of; **se mettre à c.** to take cover.

couvert², -erte [kuver, -ert] *pp de* **couvrir I** *a* covered (**de** with, in); (*ciel*) overcast.

couverture [kuvertyr] *nf* (*de lit*) blanket; (*de livre etc, garantie, troupes*) cover; (*de toit*) roofing; **les couvertures** (*de lit*) the blankets, the covers; **c. chauffante** electric blanket; **c. de voyage** travelling rug.

couvre-chef [kuvrəʃef] *nm Hum* headgear. ●**couvre-feu** *nm* (*pl* **-x**) curfew; **décréter le**

c.-feu to impose a curfew. ● **couvre-lit** *nm* bedspread. ● **couvre-pied(s)** *nm* quilt.

couvrir* [kuvrir] *vt* to cover (**de** with); (*voix*) to drown; **c. qn de cadeaux** to shower s.o. with gifts; **c. qn de bijoux** to lavish *Br* jewellery *ou Am* jewelry upon s.o. ∎ **se couvrir** *vpr* (*s'habiller*) to wrap up, cover up; (*se coiffer*) to cover one's head; (*ciel*) to cloud over. ● **couvreur** *nm* roofer.

cow-boy [kɔbɔj] *nm* cowboy.

CPE [sepeø] *nmf abrév* (*Conseiller, -ère Principal(e) d'Éducation*) official in charge of disciplinary matters etc in a *lycée* or *collège*, *Am* = dean.

CQFD [sekyefde] *abrév* (*ce qu'il fallait démontrer*) QED.

crabe [krab] *nm* crab.

crac! [krak] *int* (*objet qui casse*) snap!; (*choc*) bang!, smash!

crachat [kraʃa] *nm* spit, spittle.

cracher [kraʃe] *vi* to spit; (*stylo*) to splutter; (*radio*) to crackle; **c. sur qch** (*dédaigner*) *Fam* to turn one's nose up at sth ∎ *vt* to spit (out). ● **craché** *am* **c'est son portrait tout c.** *Fam* that's the spitting image of him *ou* her.

crachin [kraʃɛ̃] *nm* (*fine*) drizzle.

crack [krak] *nm* (*champion*) *Fam* ace, wizard, real champ.

craie [krɛ] *nf* chalk; **écrire qch à la c.** to write sth in chalk.

craindre* [krɛ̃dr] *vt* (*personne, mort, douleur* etc) to be afraid of, fear; (*chaleur, froid* etc) to be sensitive to; **c. de faire** to be afraid of doing; **je crains qu'elle ne vienne** I'm afraid *ou* I fear (that) she might come; **c. pour qch/qn** to fear for sth/s.o.; **ne craignez rien** don't be afraid, have no fear; **'craint l'humidité'** (*médicament* etc) 'store in a dry place'.

crainte [krɛ̃t] *nf* fear; **de c. de faire** for fear of doing; **de c. que** (+ *sub*) for fear that. ● **craintif, -ive** *a* timid.

cramoisi, -ie [kramwazi] *a* crimson.

crampe [krɑ̃p] *nf* (*musculaire*) cramp.

crampon [krɑ̃pɔ̃] *nm* (*personne*) *Fam* leech, hanger-on.

cramponner (se) [səkrɑ̃pɔne] *vpr* to hold on; **se c. à** to hold on to, cling to.

crampons [krɑ̃pɔ̃] *nmpl* (*de chaussures*) studs.

cran [krɑ̃] *nm* **1** (*entaille*) notch; (*de ceinture*) hole; **c. d'arrêt** *ou* **de sûreté** (safety) catch; **couteau à c. d'arrêt** *Br* flick-knife, *Am* switchblade. **2** (*de cheveux*) wave. **3** (*audace*) *Fam* pluck, guts. **4 être à c.** (*excédé*) *Fam* to be on edge.

crâne [krɑn] *nm* skull; (*tête*) *Fam* head. ● **crânienne** *af* **boîte c.** skull, cranium.

crâner [krɑne] *vi Péj* to show off, swagger.

crapaud [krapo] *nm* toad.

crapule [krapyl] *nf* villain, (filthy) scoundrel. ● **crapuleux, -euse** *a* (*crime, affaire*) vile, sordid.

craqueler [krakle] *vt*, **se craqueler** *vpr* (*terre, émail* etc) to crack.

craquer [krake] *vi* (*branche*) to snap; (*bois sec*) to crack; (*sous la dent*) to crunch; (*chaussure*) to creak; (*se déchirer*) to split, rip; (*projet, entreprise* etc) to come apart at the seams, crumble; (*personne*) to break down, reach breaking point ∎ *vt* (*faire*) **c.** (*allumette*) to strike. ● **craquement** *nm* snapping *ou* cracking *ou* creaking (sound).

crasse [kras] **1** *nf* filth. **2** *a* (*ignorance*) crass. ● **crasseux, -euse** *a* filthy.

cratère [krater] *nm* crater.

cravache [kravaʃ] *nf* horsewhip, riding crop.

cravate [kravat] *nf* (*autour du cou*) tie. ● **cravaté, -ée** *a* wearing a tie.

crawl [krol] *nm* (*nage*) crawl. ● **crawlé** *am* **dos c.** backstroke.

crayeux, -euse [krɛjø, -øz] *a* chalky.

crayon [krɛjɔ̃] *nm* (*en bois*) pencil; **c. de couleur** coloured pencil; (*en cire*) crayon; **c. à bille** ballpoint (pen). ● **crayonner** *vt* to pencil.

créance [kreɑ̃s] *nf* **1** (*dette*) claim (*for money*). **2 lettres de c.** (*d'ambassadeur*) credentials. ● **créancier, -ière** *nmf* creditor.

créateur, -trice [kreatœr, -tris] *nmf* creator ∎ *a* creative; **esprit c.** creativeness. ● **créatif, -ive** *a* creative. ● **création** *nf* creation. ● **créativité** *nf* creativity.

créature [kreatyr] *nf* (*être*) creature.

crécelle [kresɛl] *nf* (*de supporter*) rattle.

crèche [krɛʃ] *nf* (*de Noël*) manger, *Br* crib; (*pour enfants*) (day) nursery, *Br* crèche. ● **crécher** *vi Arg* to bed down, hang out.

crédible [kredibl] *a* credible. ● **crédibilité** *nf* credibility.

crédit [kredi] *nm* (*influence, prêt d'argent*) credit; **crédits** (*sommes*) funds; **acheter/payer qch à c.** to buy sth/pay for sth on credit *ou* on easy terms; **faire c.** (*prêter*) to give credit (à to). ● **créditer** *vt* (*compte, personne*) to credit (**de** with). ● **créditeur** *am* **solde c.** credit balance; **son compte est c.** his account is in credit, he is in credit.

credo [kredo] *nm* creed.

crédule [kredyl] *a* gullible, credulous. ● **crédulité** *nf* credulity.

créer [kree] *vt* to create.

crémaillère [kremajɛr] *nf* **pendre la c.** to have a house-warming (party).

crématoire [krematwar] *a* **four c.** crematorium. ● **crémation** *nf* cremation.

crématorium [krematɔrjɔm] *nm Br* crematorium, *Am* crematory.

crème [krɛm] *nf* cream; (*dessert*) cream dessert; **café c.** coffee with cream *ou* milk, *Br* white coffee; **c. Chantilly** whipped cream, Chantilly cream; **c. glacée** ice cream; **c. à raser** shaving cream; **c. anglaise** custard ∎ *a inv* cream(-coloured) ∎ *nm* (*café*) coffee with cream *ou* milk, *Br* white coffee. ● **crémerie** *nf* (*magasin*) dairy (shop). ● **crémeux, -euse** *a* creamy. ● **crémier, -ière** *nmf* dairyman, dairywoman.

créneau, -x [kreno] *nm* (*d'un marché*) market opportunity, niche, gap; *TV Radio* slot; **créneaux** (de château) Br crenellations, Am crenelations; **faire un c.** (se garer) to park between two vehicles.

créole [kreɔl] a creole ∎ nmf Creole ∎ nm (langue) Creole.

crêpe [krɛp] **1** nf (dessert) pancake. **2** nm (tissu) crepe; (caoutchouc) crepe (rubber). ● **crêperie** nf pancake bar.

crépi, -ie [krepi] a & nm roughcast.

crépiter [krepite] vi to crackle. ● **crépitement** nm crackling (sound).

crépu, -ue [krepy] a (cheveux, personne) frizzy.

crépuscule [krepyskyl] nm twilight, dusk. ● **crépusculaire** a **lueur c.** twilight glow.

crescendo [kreʃɛndo] adv & nm inv crescendo.

cresson [kresɔ̃] nm (water)cress.

crête [krɛt] nf (de montagne, d'oiseau, de vague) crest; **c. de coq** cockscomb.

Crète [krɛt] nf Crete.

crétin, -ine [kretɛ̃, -in] nmf cretin, idiot ∎ a idiotic, cretinous.

creuser [krøze] **1** vt (terre, sol) to dig (a hole ou holes in); (trou, puits) to dig; (évider) to hollow (out) (tree etc); (idée) Fig to go into thoroughly; **ça creuse l'estomac** it whets the appetite; **un visage creusé de rides** a face furrowed with wrinkles. **2 se creuser** vpr (joues etc) to become hollow; (abîme) Fig to form; **se c. la tête** ou **la cervelle** to rack one's brains.

creuset [krøzɛ] nm (récipient) crucible; (lieu) Fig melting pot.

creux, -euse [krø, -øz] a (tube, joues, paroles etc) hollow; (estomac) empty; (sans activité) slack; **assiette creuse** soup plate ∎ nm hollow; (moment) slack period; **le c. des reins** the small of the back; **le c. de l'estomac** the pit of the stomach; **avoir un c. à l'estomac** to be hungry.

crevaison [krəvɛzɔ̃] nf (de pneu) flat, Br puncture.

crevasse [krəvas] nf (trou) crevice, crack; (de glacier) crevasse; **avoir des crevasses aux mains** to have chapped hands. ● **crevasser** vt, **se crevasser** vpr (mur, sol etc) to crack; (peau) to chap.

crève [krɛv] nf (rhume) Fam bad cold.

crever [krəve] vi (bulle etc) to burst; (pneu) to burst, Br puncture; (mourir) Fam to die; **c. d'orgueil** to be bursting with pride; **c. de rire** Fam to split one's sides (laughing); **c. d'ennui/de froid** Fam to be bored/to freeze to death; **c. de faim** Fam to be starving; **je crève de chaud** Fam I'm boiling (hot) ou baking.

∎ vt (ballon, bulle etc) to burst; (œil) to put ou knock out; **c. qn** Fam to wear s.o. out; **ça (vous) crève les yeux** Fam it's staring you in the face; **ça crève le cœur** it's heartbreaking. ● **crevant, -ante** a Fam (fatigant) exhausting; (drôle) hilarious, Br killing. ● **crevé, -ée** a Fam (fatigué) worn out, Br dead beat; (mort) dead. ● **crève-cœur** nm inv heartbreak.

crevette [krəvɛt] nf (grise) shrimp; (rose) prawn.

cri [kri] nm (de joie, surprise) cry, shout; (de peur) scream; (de douleur, d'alarme) cry; (appel) call, cry; **c. de guerre** war cry; **un chapeau/etc dernier c.** the latest hat/etc. ● **criard, -arde** a **1** (enfant) bawling; (son) screeching. **2** (couleur) gaudy, showy.

criant, -ante [krijɑ̃, -ɑ̃t] a (injustice, preuve etc) glaring.

crible [kribl] nm sieve. ● **cribler** vt to sift; **criblé de balles/dettes/etc** riddled with bullets/debts/etc.

cric [krik] nm (instrument pour véhicule) jack.

cricket [krikɛt] nm Sport cricket.

crier [krije] vi to shout (out), cry (out); (de peur) to scream; (oiseau) to chirp; (grincer) (charnière etc) to creak, squeak; **c. au scandale** to call it scandalous, say it's a scandal; **c. après qn** Fam to shout at s.o.; **parlez sans c.** talk without shouting ∎ vt (injure, ordre) to shout (out); (son innocence, la vérité etc) to proclaim; **c. vengeance** to cry out for vengeance. ● **crieur, -euse** nmf **c. de journaux** newspaper seller.

crime [krim] nm crime; (assassinat) murder. ● **criminalité** nf crime (in general), criminal practice. ● **criminel, -elle** a criminal ∎ nmf criminal; (assassin) murderer.

crin [krɛ̃] nm horsehair; **c. végétal** vegetable fibre; **à tous crins** (pacifiste, socialiste etc) out-and-out. ● **crinière** nf mane.

crique [krik] nf creek, cove.

criquet [krikɛ] nm locust.

crise [kriz] nf crisis; (accès) (de nerfs etc) attack; (de colère, rire, toux etc) fit; (pénurie) shortage; **c. de conscience** (moral) dilemma.

crisper [krispe] vt (visage) to make tense; (poing) to clench; (muscle) to tense; **c. qn** Fam to aggravate s.o., irritate s.o.; **se c. sur** (main) to grip tightly. ● **crispant, -ante** a Fam aggravating, irritating. ● **crispé, -ée** a (personne) tense. ● **crispation** nf (agacement) irritation, aggravation.

crisser [krise] vi (pneu, roue) to screech; (neige) to crunch.

cristal, -aux [kristal, -o] nm crystal; **cristaux** (objets) crystal(ware); **cristaux (de soude)** (pour nettoyer) washing soda. ● **cristallin, -ine** a (eau, son) crystal-clear. ● **cristalliser** vti, **se cristalliser** vpr to crystallize.

critère [kritɛr] nm criterion.

critérium [kriterjɔm] nm (épreuve sportive) eliminating heat.

critiquable [kritikabl] a open to criticism.

critique [kritik] a (situation, phase etc) critical ∎ nf (reproche) criticism; (analyse de film, livre etc) review; (de texte philosophique) critique; **faire la c. de** (film etc) to review; **affronter la c.** to confront the critics ∎ nm critic. ● **critiquer** vt to criticize; (roman etc) to assess critically.

croasser [krɔase] vi (corbeau) to caw.
Croatie [krɔasi] nf Croatia.
croc [kro] nm (crochet) hook; (dent) fang.
croc-en-jambe [krɔkɑ̃ʒɑ̃b] nm (pl crocs-en-jambe) = croche-pied.
croche [krɔʃ] nf (note de musique) Br quaver, Am eighth (note).
croche-pied [krɔʃpje] nm faire un c.-pied à qn to trip s.o. up.
crochet [krɔʃɛ] nm (pour accrocher) & Boxe hook; (aiguille) crochet hook; (travail) crochet; (de cambrioleur) picklock; (parenthèse) (square) bracket; faire qch au c. to crochet sth; faire un c. (personne) to make a detour ou side trip; (pour éviter) to swerve; (route) to make a sudden turn; vivre aux crochets de qn Fam to sponge off ou on s.o. ● crocheter vt (serrure) to pick.
crochu, -ue [krɔʃy] a (nez) hooked; (doigts) claw-like.
crocodile [krɔkɔdil] nm crocodile.
crocus [krɔkys] nm (fleur) crocus.
croire* [krwar] vt to believe; (estimer) to think, believe (que that); j'ai cru la voir I thought I saw her; je crois que oui I think ou believe so; je n'en crois pas mes yeux I can't believe my eyes; à l'en c. according to him ou her; il se croit malin/quelque chose he thinks he's smart/quite something ▮ vi to believe (à, en in).
croisé¹ [krwaze] nm Hist crusader. ● croisade nf Hist & Fig crusade.
croiser [krwaze] vt (jambes, ligne etc) to cross; (bras) to fold, cross; c. qn to pass ou meet s.o. ▮ vi (navire) to cruise; (veston) to fold over ▮ se croiser vpr (voitures etc) to pass ou meet (each other); (routes) to cross, intersect; (lettres) to cross in the mail ou Br post; (regards) to meet. ● croisé², -ée a (bras) folded, crossed; (veston) double-breasted; mots croisés crossword; tirs croisés crossfire; race croisée crossbreed ▮ nf croisée (fenêtre) casement; croisée des chemins crossroads. ● croisement nm (de routes) crossroads, intersection; (action) crossing; (de véhicules) passing.
croiseur [krwazœr] nm (navire de guerre) cruiser.
croisière [krwazjer] nf cruise; faire une c. to go on a cruise; vitesse de c. (de véhicule, navire, Fig entreprise etc) cruising speed.
croître* [krwatr] vi (plante) to grow; (augmenter) to grow, increase; (lune) to wax. ● croissant, -ante 1 nm crescent; (pâtisserie) croissant. 2 a (nombre etc) growing. ● croissance nf growth.
croix [krwa] nf cross; la C.-Rouge the Red Cross.
croque-mitaine [krɔkmiten] nm bogeyman. ● croque-monsieur nm inv toasted cheese and ham sandwich. ● croque-mort nm Fam undertaker's assistant.
croquer [krɔke] 1 vt (manger) to crunch ▮ vi (fruit etc) to be crunchy, crunch. 2 vt (peindre) to sketch; joli à c. pretty as a picture. ● croquant, -ante a (biscuit etc) crunchy. ● croquette nf (de pommes de terre etc) croquette.
croquet [krɔke] nm (jeu) croquet.
croquis [krɔki] nm sketch.
crosse [krɔs] nf (de fusil) butt; (de hockey) stick; (d'évêque) crook.
crotte [krɔt] nf (de lapin etc) droppings, Br mess; c. de chien dog dirt, Br dog's mess. ● crottin nm (horse) dung.
crotté, -ée a (bottes etc) muddy.
crouler [krule] vi (édifice, projet etc) to crumble, collapse; c. sous une charge (porteur etc) to totter beneath a burden; c. sous le travail to be snowed under with work; faire c. (immeuble etc) to bring down. ● croulant, -ante a (mur etc) tottering ▮ nm (vieux) Fam old-timer.
croupe [krup] nf (de cheval) rump; monter en c. (à cheval) to ride pillion. ● croupion nm (de poulet) Br parson's nose, Am pope's nose.
croupier [krupje] nm (au casino) croupier.
croupir [krupir] vi (eau) to stagnate, become foul; c. dans l'ignorance/le vice/etc to wallow in ignorance/vice/etc; eau croupie stagnant water.
croustiller [krustije] vi to be crusty; (biscuit) to be crunchy. ● croustillant, -ante a (pain) crusty; (biscuit) crunchy; (histoire) Fig spicy, juicy.
croûte [krut] nf (de pain etc) crust; (de fromage) rind; (de plaie) scab; casser la c. Fam to have a snack; gagner sa c. Fam to earn one's bread and butter. ● croûton nm crust (at end of loaf); croûtons (avec soupe) croûtons.
croyable [krwajabl] a credible, believable; pas c. unbelievable, incredible. ● croyance nf belief (à, en in). ● croyant, -ante a être c. to be a believer ▮ nmf believer.
CRS [seeres] nmpl abrév (Compagnies républicaines de sécurité) riot police, State security police.
cru, crue¹ [kry] pp de croire.
cru, crue² [kry] 1 a (aliment) raw; (lumière) glaring; (propos) crude; monter à c. to ride bareback. 2 nm (vignoble) vineyard; un grand c. (vin) a vintage wine; vin du c. local wine.
cruauté [kryote] nf cruelty (envers to).
cruche [kryʃ] nf pitcher, jug.
crucial, -e, -aux [krysjal, -o] a crucial.
crucifier [krysifje] vt to crucify. ● crucifix [krysifi] nm crucifix. ● crucifixion nf crucifixion.
crudité [krydite] nf (grossièreté) crudeness. ● crudités nfpl (légumes) assorted raw vegetables.
crue [kry] nf (de cours d'eau) swelling, flood; en c. (rivière, fleuve) in spate.
cruel, -elle [kryɛl] a cruel (envers, avec to).
crûment [krymɑ̃] adv crudely.
crustacés [krystase] nmpl Culin shellfish inv.

crypte [kript] *nf* crypt.
Cuba [kyba] *nm* Cuba. ●**cubain, -aine** *a* Cuban ▌*nmf* C., Cubaine Cuban.
cube [kyb] *nm* cube; **cubes** (*jeu*) building blocks ▌**a mètre/etc c.** cubic metre/*etc*. ●**cubique** *a* (*forme*) cubic.
cueillir* [kœjir] *vt* to pick, gather; (*un baiser*) to snatch; (*voleur*) *Fam* to pick up, *Br* run in. ●**cueillette** *nf* picking, gathering; (*fruits cueillis*) harvest.
cuiller, cuillère [kɥijer] *nf* spoon; **petite c., c. à café** teaspoon; **c. à soupe** soup spoon, tablespoon. ●**cuillerée** *nf* spoonful; **c. à café** teaspoonful; **c. à soupe** tablespoonful.
cuir [kɥir] *nm* leather; (*peau épaisse d'un animal vivant*) hide; **c. chevelu** scalp.
cuirasse [kɥiras] *nf Hist* breastplate. ●**se cuirasser** *vpr* to steel oneself (**contre** against). ●**cuirassé** *nm* battleship.
cuire* [kɥir] *vt* (*aliment, plat etc*) to cook; (*à l'eau*) to boil; **c.** (**au four**) to bake; (*viande*) to roast ▌*vi* (*aliment*) to cook; (*à l'eau*) to boil; (*au four*) to bake; (*viande*) to roast; **faire c. qch** to cook sth; **faire trop c. qch** to overcook sth; **on cuit!** (*il fait trop chaud*) it's scorching *ou* baking hot.
cuisant, -ante [kɥizɑ̃, -ɑ̃t] *a* (*affront, blessure etc*) stinging.
cuisine [kɥizin] *nf* (*pièce*) kitchen; (*art*) cookery, cooking, cuisine; (*préparation*) cooking; (*aliments*) cooking food; (*intrigues politiques*) scheming; **faire la c.** to cook, do the cooking; **faire de la bonne c.** to be a good cook; **livre de c.** cookery *ou* cook book; **haute c.** high-class cooking *ou* cookery. ●**cuisiner** *vti* to cook; **c. qn** (*interroger*) *Fam* to grill s.o. ●**cuisinier, -ière** *nmf* cook. ●**cuisinière** *nf* (*appareil*) *Br* cooker, stove, *Am* range.
cuisse [kɥis] *nf* thigh; (*de poulet, mouton*) leg.
cuisson [kɥisɔ̃] *nm* (*d'aliments*) cooking.
cuit, cuite [kɥi, kɥit] *pp de* **cuire**. **1** *a* cooked; **bien c.** well done *ou* cooked; **trop c.** overdone, overcooked; **pas assez c.** underdone, undercooked. **2** *a* **nous sommes cuits** (*pris*) *Fam* we're finished *ou Br* done for.
cuite [kɥit] *nf* **prendre une c.** *Fam* to get plastered *ou* drunk.
cuivre [kɥivr] *nm* (*rouge*) copper; (*jaune*) brass; **cuivres** (*ustensiles, clairon etc*) brass. ●**cuivré, -ée** *a* copper-coloured, coppery.
cul [ky] *nm* (*derrière*) *Fam* backside; (*de bouteille, verre, pot*) bottom. ●**cul-de-jatte** *nm* (*pl* **culs-de-jatte**) legless cripple. ●**cul-de-sac** *nm* (*pl* **culs-de-sac**) dead end, *Br* cul-de-sac.
culasse [kylas] *nf* (*de moteur*) cylinder head; (*d'une arme à feu*) breech.
culbute [kylbyt] *nf* (*saut*) somersault; (*chute*) (backward) tumble; **faire une c.** to tumble (backwards); (*acrobate*) to somersault. ●**culbuter** *vi* to tumble over (backwards) ▌*vt* (*personne, chaise*) to knock over.

culinaire [kyliner] *a* (*art*) culinary; **recette c.** cooking recipe.
culminer [kylmine] *vi* (*montagne*) to reach its highest point, peak (**à** at); (*colère*) *Fig* to reach a peak; **point culminant** (*de réussite, montagne etc*) peak.
culot [kylo] *nm* **1** (*aplomb*) *Fam* nerve, *Br* cheek. **2** (*d'ampoule, de lampe etc*) base. ●**culotté, -ée** *a* **être c.** *Fam* to have plenty of nerve *ou Br* cheek.
culotte [kylɔt] *nf* (*de sportif*) (pair of) shorts; (*de femme*) *Br* (pair of) knickers, *Am* (pair of) panties; **culottes** (**courtes**) (*de jeune garçon*) *Br* short trousers, *Am* short pants; **c. de cheval** riding breeches.
culpabilité [kylpabilite] *nf* guilt.
culte [kylt] *nm* (*de dieu*) worship; (*religion*) form of worship, religion; (*service protestant*) service; (*admiration*) *Fig* cult; **film/etc c.** cult film/*etc*.
cultiver [kyltive] *vt* (*terre*) to farm, cultivate; (*plantes, légumes*) to grow; (*goût, relations etc*) to cultivate ▌**se cultiver** *vpr* to improve *ou* cultivate one's mind. ●**cultivé, -ée** *a* (*esprit, personne*) cultured, cultivated. ●**cultivateur, -trice** *nmf* farmer.
culture [kyltyr] *nf* **1** (*action*) farming, cultivation; (*agriculture*) farming; (*de légumes*) growing; **cultures** (*terres*) fields (under cultivation); (*plantes*) crops. **2** (*éducation, civilisation*) culture; **c. générale** general knowledge. ●**culturel, -elle** *a* cultural.
culturisme [kyltyrism] *nm* body building.
cumin [kymɛ̃] *nm* (*plante*) cumin; (*graines*) caraway; **graines de c.** caraway seeds.
cumul [kymyl] *nm* **c. de fonctions** plurality of offices. ●**cumulatif, -ive** *a* cumulative. ●**cumuler** *vt* **c. deux fonctions** to hold two offices (at the same time).
cupide [kypid] *a* avaricious. ●**cupidité** *nf* avarice, cupidity.
Cupidon [kypidɔ̃] *nm* Cupid.
curable [kyrabl] *a* curable.
cure [kyr] *nf* **1** (*pour malade*) (course of) treatment, cure; **faire une c. de repos** to go on a rest cure. **2** (*fonction*) office (of a parish priest); (*résidence*) presbytery. ●**curatif, -ive** *a* (*traitement etc*) curative.
curé [kyre] *nm* (parish) priest.
curer [kyre] *vt* (*fossé, canal etc*) to clean out; **se c. le nez/les dents** to pick one's nose/teeth. ●**cure-dent** *nm* toothpick. ●**cure-ongles** *nm inv* nail cleaner. ●**cure-pipe** *nm* pipe cleaner.
curieux, -euse [kyrjø, -øz] *a* (*bizarre*) curious; (*indiscret*) inquisitive, curious (**de** about); **c. de savoir** curious to know ▌*nmf* inquisitive *ou* curious person; (*badaud*) onlooker. ●**curieusement** *adv* curiously. ●**curiosité** *nf* (*de personne, forme etc*) curiosity; (*chose*) curiosity; (*spectacle*) unusual sight.
curriculum (**vitæ**) [kyrikylɔm(vite)] *nm inv Br* curriculum (vitae), *Am* résumé.
curseur [kyrsœr] *nm* (*d'ordinateur*) cursor.
cutané, -ée [kytane] *a* **maladie cutanée** skin

condition. ●**cuti(-réaction)** *nf* skin test.
cuve [kyv] *nf* vat; (*réservoir*) & *Phot* tank.
●**cuvée** *nf* (*récolte de vin*) vintage. ●**cuver** *vt*
c. son vin *Fam* to sleep it off. ●**cuvette** *nf*
(*récipient*) & *Geog* basin, bowl; (*des cabinets*) bowl, pan.
CV [seve] *nm abrév* (*curriculum vitæ*) *Br* CV,
Am résumé.
cyanure [sjanyr] *nm* cyanide.
cybernétique [sibɛrnetik] *nf* cybernetics.
cycle [sikl] *nm* **1** (*série, révolution*) cycle. **2**
(*bicyclette*) cycle. ●**cyclable** *a* **piste c.** cycle
ou bicycle path. ●**cyclique** *a* cyclic(al).
cyclisme [siklism] *nm* (*sport*) cycling.
●**cycliste** *nmf* cyclist ▍ *a* **course c.** cycle *ou*
bicycle race; **champion c.** cycling champion;

coureur c. racing cyclist.
cyclomoteur [siklɔmɔtœr] *nm* moped.
cyclone [siklon] *nm* cyclone.
cygne [siɲ] *nm* swan; **chant du c.** (*dernière
œuvre*) swan song.
cylindre [silɛ̃dr] *nm* cylinder; (*de rouleau
compresseur*) roller. ●**cylindrée** *nf* (*de véhicule, moteur*) (engine) capacity. ●**cylindrique** *a* cylindrical.
cymbale [sɛ̃bal] *nf* cymbal.
cynique [sinik] *a* cynical ▍ *nmf* cynic. ●**cynisme** *nm* cynicism.
cyprès [siprɛ] *nm* (*arbre*) cypress.
Cypriote [siprijɔt] *a* Cypriot ▍ *nmf* C. Cypriot.
cytise [sitiz] *nf* (*plante*) laburnum.

D

D, d [de] *nm* D, d.

d' [d] *voir* de[1,2].

d'abord [dabɔr] *adv* (*en premier lieu*) first; (*au début*) (at) first.

dactylo [daktilo] *nf* (*personne*) typist; (*action*) typing. ●**dactylographie** *nf* typing. ●**dactylographier** *vt* to type.

dada [dada] *nm* (*manie*) hobby horse, pet subject.

dadais [dadɛ] *nm* (**grand**) d. big oaf.

dahlia [dalja] *nm* dahlia.

daigner [dɛɲe] *vt* d. faire to condescend *ou* deign to do.

daim [dɛ̃] *nm* fallow deer; (*mâle*) buck; (*cuir*) suede.

dais [de] *nm* (*de lit, feuillage etc*) canopy.

dalle [dal] *nf* paving stone; (*funèbre*) (flat) gravestone. ●**dallage** *nm* (*action, surface*) paving. ●**dallé, -ée** *a* (*pièce, cour etc*) paved.

daltonien, -ienne [daltɔnjɛ̃, -jen] *a & n* colour-blind (person). ●**daltonisme** *nm* colour blindness.

dame [dam] *nf* **1** lady; (*mariée*) married woman. **2** *Échecs Cartes* queen; (*au jeu de dames*) king; (**jeu de**) **dames** *Br* draughts, *Am* checkers. ●**damer** *vt* (*au jeu de dames*) to crown; **le pion à qn** to outsmart s.o. ●**damier** *nm* *Br* draughtboard, *Am* checkerboard.

damner [dane] *vt* to damn; **faire d.** *Fam* to torment, drive mad **▌ se damner** *vpr* to be damned. ●**damnation** *nf* damnation.

dancing [dãsiŋ] *nm* dance hall.

dandiner (se) [sədãdine] *vpr* (*canard, personne*) to waddle.

dandy [dãdi] *nm* dandy.

Danemark [danmark] *nm* Denmark. ●**danois, -oise** *a* Danish **▌** *nmf* D., Danoise Dane **▌** *nm* (*langue*) Danish.

danger [dãʒe] *nm* danger; **en d.** in danger *ou* jeopardy; **mettre en d.** to endanger, jeopardize; **en cas de d.** in an emergency; **en d. de mort** in mortal danger, in peril of death; **'d. de mort'** (*panneau*) 'danger'; **courir un d.** to run a serious risk; **à l'abri du d.** out of danger; **sans d.** (*se promener etc*) safely; **être sans d.** to be safe; **pas de d.!** *Fam* no way!, *Br* no fear! ●**dangereux, -euse** *a* (*endroit, maladie, personne etc*) dangerous (**pour** to). ●**dangereusement** *adv* dangerously.

dans [dã] **1** *prép* in; (*changement de lieu*) into; (*à l'intérieur de*) inside; **d. le jardin/ journal** in the garden/newspaper; **d. la boîte** in *ou* inside the box; **d. Paris** in Paris (itself); **mettre d.** to put in(to); **entrer d.** to go in(to); **d. un rayon de** within (a radius of); **marcher d. les rues** (*à travers*) to walk through *ou* around the streets; **d. ces circonstances** under *ou* in these circumstances.

2 (*provenance*) from, out of; **boire/prendre/ etc d.** to drink/take/*etc* from *ou* out of.

3 (*temps futur*) in; **d. deux jours/***etc* in two days/*etc*, in two days'/*etc* time.

4 (*quantité approximative*) about; **d. les dix francs/***etc* about ten francs/*etc*.

danse [dãs] *nf* dance; (*art*) dancing; **musique de d.** dance music; **professeur de d.** dancing teacher. ●**danser** *vti* to dance; **je ne sais pas sur quel pied d.** I am all at sea. ●**danseur, -euse** *nmf* dancer; **danseuse étoile** prima ballerina; **en danseuse** (*cycliste*) standing on the pedals.

Danube [danyb] *nm* le D. the Danube.

dard [dar] *nm* (*d'insecte*) sting; (*de serpent*) tongue. ●**darder** *vt* *Litt* (*flèche*) to shoot; (*regard*) to flash, dart; **le soleil dardait ses rayons** the sun cast down its burning rays.

dare-dare [dardar] *adv* *Fam* at *ou* on the double.

date [dat] *nf* date; **amitié/***etc* **de longue d.** long-standing friendship/*etc*, friendship/*etc* of long standing; **faire d.** (*événement*) to mark an important date, be epoch-making; **en d. du...** dated the...; **d. d'expiration** *Br* expiry or *Am* expiration date; **d. limite** deadline; **d. limite de vente** sell-by date; **d. de naissance** date of birth. ●**datation** *nf* dating. ●**dater** *vt* (*lettre etc*) to date **▌** *vi* (*être dépassé*) to date, be dated; **d. de** to date from, date back to; **à d. du 20/de demain** as from the 20th/ tomorrow. ●**dateur** *nm* (*de montre*) date indicator **▌** *a & nm* (**tampon**) d. date stamp.

datif [datif] *nm* *Grammaire* dative.

datte [dat] *nf* (*fruit*) date. ●**dattier** *nm* date palm.

daube [dob] *nf* **bœuf en d.** braised beef stew.

dauphin [dofɛ̃] *nm* (*mammifère marin*) dolphin.

daurade [dorad] *nf* sea bream.

davantage [davãtaʒ] *adv* (*quantité*) more; (*temps*) longer; **d. de temps/d'argent/***etc* more time/money *etc*; **d. que** more than; (*plus longtemps que*) longer than.

de[1] [d(ə)] (**d'** before a vowel or mute h; **de** + **le** = **du**, **de** + **les** = **des**) *prép* **1** (*complément d'un nom*) of; **les rayons du soleil** the rays of the sun, the sun's rays; **le livre de Paul** Paul's book; **la ville de Paris** the town of Paris; **un livre de Flaubert** a book by Flaubert; **un pont de fer** an iron bridge; **le train de Londres** the London train; **une**

augmentation/diminution de salaire/*etc* an increase/decrease in salary/*etc*.

2 (*complément d'un adjectif*) **digne de** worthy of; **heureux de partir** happy to leave; **content de qch/qn** pleased with sth/s.o.

3 (*complément d'un verbe*) **parler de** to speak of *ou* about; **se souvenir de** to remember; **décider de faire** to decide to do; **empêcher qn de faire** to stop *ou* prevent s.o. from doing; **traiter qn de lâche** to call s.o. a coward.

4 (*provenance: lieu & temps*) from; **venir/ dater de** to come/date from; **mes amis du village** my friends from the village, my village friends; **le train de Londres** the train from London; **sortir de** (*chambre, boîte etc*) to come out of.

5 (*agent*) **accompagné de** accompanied by; **entouré de** surrounded by *ou* with.

6 (*moyen*) **armé de** armed with; **se nourrir de** to live on.

7 (*manière*) **d'une voix douce** in *ou* with a gentle voice.

8 (*cause*) **puni de son impatience**/*etc* punished for his impatience/*etc*; **mourir de faim** to die of hunger; **sauter de joie** to jump for joy.

9 (*temps*) **travailler de nuit/de jour** to work by night/by day; **six heures du matin** six o'clock in the morning.

10 (*mesure*) **avoir six mètres de haut, être haut de six mètres** to be six metres high; **retarder qn/qch de deux heures** to delay s.o./ sth by two hours; **homme de trente ans** thirty-year-old man; **gagner cent francs de l'heure** to earn a hundred francs an hour.

de² [d(ə)] *art partitif* some; **elle boit du vin** she drinks (some) wine; **il ne boit pas de vin** (*négation*) he doesn't drink (any) wine; **est-ce que vous buvez du vin?** (*interrogatif*) do you drink (any) wine?; **elle achète des épinards** she buys (some) spinach; **il y en a six de tués** (*avec un nombre*) there are six killed; **une(e) de trop** one too many.

de³ [d(ə)] *art indéf pl* **de, des** some; **des fleurs/garçons**/*etc* (some) flowers/boys/*etc*; **de jolies fleurs** (*devant un adjectif*) (some) pretty flowers; **d'agréables soirées** (some) pleasant evenings.

dé¹ [de] *nm* (*à jouer*) dice; (*à coudre*) thimble; **les dés** the dice; **jouer aux dés** to play dice; **les dés sont jetés** *Fig* the die is cast; **couper en dés** (*pommes de terre etc*) to dice.

déambuler [deãbyle] *vi* to stroll, saunter.

débâcle [debakl] *nf* (*d'une armée*) rout; (*ruine*) *Fig* downfall; (*des glaces*) breaking up.

déballer [debale] *vt* to unpack; (*étaler*) to display. ●**déballage** *nm* unpacking; (*étalage*) display.

débandade [debãdad] *nf* (*mad*) rush, stampede; **à la d.** in confusion; **tout va à la d.** everything's going to rack and ruin.

débaptiser [debatize] *vt* (*rue, chien etc*) to rename.

débarbouiller [debarbuje] *vt* **d. qn** to wash s.o.'s face; **se d.** to wash one's face.

débarcadère [debarkadɛr] *nm* quay, wharf, landing stage.

débardeur [debardœr] *nm* **1** (*docker*) docker, stevedore. **2** (*vêtement*) *Br* slipover, *Am* (*sweater*) vest.

débarquer [debarke] *vt* (*passagers*) to land; (*marchandises*) to unload; **d. qn** (*congédier*) *Fam* to sack s.o., throw s.o. out ▮ *vi* (*passagers*) to land, disembark; (*être naïf*) *Fam* to be not quite with it; **d. chez qn** *Fam* to turn up suddenly at s.o.'s place. ●**débarquement** *nm* landing; (*de marchandises*) unloading; (*d'une armée*) landing.

débarras [debara] *nm Br* lumber room, *Am* storeroom; **bon d.!** *Fam* good riddance! ●**débarrasser** *vt* (*chambre, table etc*) to clear (**de** of); **d. qn de** (*ennemi, soucis etc*) to rid s.o. of; (*manteau etc*) to relieve s.o. of; **se d. de qn/qch** to get rid of s.o./sth, rid oneself of s.o./sth.

débat [deba] *nm* discussion, debate; **débats** (*d'un procès ou au Parlement*) proceedings. ●**débattre*** *vt* to discuss, debate; **d.** (**d'**)**une question** to discuss a question; **prix à d.** price to be negotiated ▮ **se débattre** *vpr* to struggle *ou* fight (to get free), put up a fight.

débauche [deboʃ] *nf* debauchery; **une d. de** (*excès*) a wealth *ou* profusion of. ●**débauché, -ée** *a* (*libertin*) debauched, profligate ▮ *nmf* debauchee, profligate.

débaucher [deboʃe] *vt* **d. qn** (*licencier*) to lay s.o. off; (*détourner*) *Fam* to entice s.o. away from his work.

débile [debil] *a* (*esprit, enfant etc*) weak, feeble; *Péj Fam* stupid, idiotic ▮ *nmf* (*imbécile*) *Fam* idiot, moron. ●**débilité** *nf* debility, weakness; **débilités** (*niaiseries*) *Fam* sheer nonsense. ●**débiliter** *vt* to debilitate, weaken.

débiner [debine] **1** *vt* (*décrier*) *Fam* to run down. **2 se débiner** *vpr* (*s'enfuir*) *Arg* to beat it, *Br* hop it, bolt.

débit [debi] *nm* **1** (*vente*) turnover, sales; (*de fleuve*) (rate of) flow; (*d'un orateur*) delivery; **d. de boissons** bar, café; **d. de tabac** *Br* tobacconist's shop, *Am* tobacco store. **2** (*compte*) debit.

débiter [debite] *vt* **1** (*découper*) to cut up, slice up (**en** into); (*vendre*) to sell; (*fournir*) to produce, yield; (*dire*) *Péj* to utter, spout. **2** (*compte*) to debit. ●**débiteur, -trice** *nmf* debtor ▮ *a* **solde d.** debit balance; **son compte est d.** his account is in debit, he is in debit.

déblais [deblɛ] *nmpl* (*terre*) earth; (*décombres*) rubble. ●**déblayer** [debleje] *vt* (*terrain, décombres*) to clear.

débloquer [deblɔke] **1** *vt* (*mécanisme*) to unjam; (*freins*) to release; (*compte, prix*) to unfreeze; **d. des crédits** to unfreeze funds. **2** *vi* (*divaguer*) *Fam* to talk nonsense, talk through one's hat.

déboires [debwar] *nmpl* disappointments, setbacks.

déboiser [debwaze] vt (terrain) to clear (of trees).

déboîter [debwate] 1 vt (tuyau) to disconnect; se d. l'épaule/etc to dislocate one's shoulder/etc. 2 vi (véhicule) to pull out, change lanes. ●**déboîtement** nm (d'un os) dislocation.

débonnaire [debɔnɛr] a good-natured, easy-going.

déborder [debɔrde] vi (fleuve, liquide) to overflow; (en bouillant) to boil over; (en coloriant) to go over the edge; **l'eau déborde du vase** the water is running over the top of the vase ou is overflowing the vase; **c'est la goutte d'eau qui fait d. le vase** Fig that's the last straw; **d. de joie/vie/etc** Fig to be overflowing ou bubbling over with joy/life/etc.
▮ vt (dépasser) to go ou extend beyond; (faire saillie) to stick out from; (dans une bataille) & Football etc to outflank; **débordé de travail/de visites** snowed under with work/visits. ●**débordement** nm overflowing; (de joie, activité) outburst.

débouché [debuʃe] nm (carrière) (career) opening ou prospect; (marché pour produit) outlet; (de rue) exit; (de vallée etc) opening.

déboucher [debuʃe] 1 vt (bouteille) to open, uncork; (bouchon vissé) to uncap; (lavabo, tuyau) to clear, unblock. 2 vi (surgir) to emerge, come out (de from); **d. sur** (rue) to lead out onto, lead into; (aboutir à) Fig to lead to.

débouler [debule] vi (arriver) Fam to burst in, turn up.

déboulonner [debulɔne] vt to unbolt; **d. qn** Fam (renvoyer) to sack ou fire s.o.; (discréditer) to bring s.o. down.

débourser [deburse] vt to pay out.

debout [d(ə)bu] adv standing (up); **mettre d.** (planche etc) to stand up, put upright; **se mettre d.** to stand ou get up; **se tenir ou rester d.** (personne) to stand (up), remain standing (up); **elle est très faible, elle tient à peine d.** she's very weak, she can hardly stand; **cet édifice tient encore d.** this building is still standing; **ça ne tient pas d.** (théorie etc) that doesn't hold water ou make sense; **être d.** (levé) to be up (and about); **d.!** get up!

déboutonner [debutɔne] vt to unbutton, undo ▮ **se déboutonner** vpr (personne) to undo one's buttons.

débraillé, -ée [debraje] a (tenue etc) slovenly, sloppy ▮ nm slovenliness, sloppiness.

débrancher [debrɑ̃ʃe] 1 vt (appareil électrique) to unplug, disconnect. 2 vi (se détendre) Fam to take it easy.

débrayer [debreje] vi 1 (conducteur) to press the clutch, let out the clutch; Br declutch. 2 (se mettre en grève) to stop work. ●**débrayage** (grève) strike, walk-out.

débridé, -ée [debride] a (effréné) unbridled.

débris [debri] nmpl fragments, scraps; (restes) remains; (détritus) Br rubbish, Am garbage.

débrouiller [debruje] 1 vt (écheveau etc) to unravel, disentangle; (affaire) to sort out. 2 **se débrouiller** vpr Fam to manage, get by, make out; **se d. pour faire** to manage (somehow) to do. ●**débrouillard, -arde** a Fam smart, resourceful. ●**débrouillardise** nf Fam smartness, resourcefulness.

débroussailler [debrusaje] vt (chemin) to clear (of brushwood); (problème, sujet etc) Fig to clarify.

débusquer [debyske] vt (gibier, personne) to drive out, dislodge.

début [deby] nm beginning, start; **au d.** at the beginning; **dès le d.** (right) from the start ou beginning; **les débuts de l'automobile/etc** the beginnings ou infancy of the car industry/etc; **faire ses débuts** (sur la scène etc) to make one's debut.

débuter [debyte] vi to start, begin; (dans une carrière) to start out in life; (sur la scène etc) to make one's debut. ●**débutant, -ante** nmf beginner ▮ a **c'est un pianiste d.** he's learning to play the piano, he's a novice pianist.

déca [deka] nm Fam decaffeinated coffee.

deçà (en) [ɑ̃d(ə)sa] adv (on) this side ▮ prép **en d. de** (on) this side of; **être en d. de la vérité/etc** Fig to be some way from the truth/etc.

décacheter [dekaʃte] vt (lettre etc) to open, unseal.

décade [dekad] nf (dix jours) period of ten days; (décennie) decade.

décadent, -ente [dekadɑ̃, -ɑ̃t] a decadent. ●**décadence** nf decadence, decay.

décaféiné, -ée [dekafeine] a decaffeinated.

décalcomanie [dekalkɔmani] nf (image) Br transfer, Am decal.

décaler [dekale] vt 1 (dans le temps) to change ou shift the time of (departure etc); (dans l'espace) to shift ou move (slightly), change ou shift the position of (chair etc). 2 (ôter les cales de) to unwedge. ●**décalage** nm (écart) gap (entre between); (entre des faits, idées etc) discrepancy; **d. horaire** time difference; **souffrir du d. horaire** to suffer from jet lag.

décalque [dekalk] nm tracing. ●**décalquer** vt (dessin) to trace.

décamper [dekɑ̃pe] vi to run off, clear out.

décanter [dekɑ̃te] vt (liquide) to (allow to) settle, clarify; **d. ses idées** to clarify one's ideas ▮ **se décanter** vpr (idées, situation) to become clearer, settle.

décaper [dekape] vt (métal) to clean, scrape down; (surface peinte) to strip; (avec du papier de verre) to sand (down). ●**décapant** nm cleaning agent; (pour enlever la peinture) paint remover ou stripper. ●**décapeur** nm **d. thermique** hot-air paint stripper.

décapiter [dekapite] vt to behead, decapitate.

décapotable [dekapɔtabl] a & nf (voiture) convertible.

décapsuler [dekapsyle] vt **d. une bouteille** to take the top ou cap off a bottle, uncap a

décarcasser 80

bottle. ●**décapsuleur** *nm* bottle-opener.
décarcasser (se) [sədekarkase] *vpr Fam* to
flog oneself to death (**pour faire** doing).
décathlon [dekatlɔ̃] *nm Sport* decathlon.
décéder [desede] *vi* to die. ●**décédé, -ée** *a*
deceased.
déceler [desle] *vt* (*trouver*) to detect, uncover; (*révéler*) to reveal.
décembre [desɑ̃br] *nm* December.
décennie [deseni] *nf* decade.
décent, -ente [desɑ̃, -ɑ̃t] *a* (*bienséant,
acceptable*) decent. ●**décemment** [-amɑ̃] *adv*
decently. ●**décence** *nf* decency.
décentraliser [desɑ̃tralize] *vt* to decentralize. ●**décentralisation** *nf* decentralization.
déception [desɛpsjɔ̃] *nf* disappointment.
décerner [deserne] *vt* (*prix etc*) to award;
(*mandat d'arrêt etc*) to issue.
décès [desɛ] *nm* death.
décevoir* [des(ə)vwar] *vt* to disappoint.
●**décevant, -ante** *a* disappointing.
déchaîner [deʃene] *vt* (*colère, violence*) to
unleash, let loose; **d. l'enthousiasme/les rires**
to set off wild enthusiasm/a storm of laughter ‖ **se déchaîner** *vpr* (*tempête, rires*) to
break out; (*foule*) to run riot *ou* amok;
(*personne*) to fly into a rage. ●**déchaîné, -ée**
a (*foule, flots*) wild, raging. ●**déchaînement**
[-ɛnmɑ̃] *nm* (*de rires, de haine etc*) outburst;
(*de violence*) outbreak, eruption; **le d. de la
tempête** the raging of the storm.
déchanter [deʃɑ̃te] *vi Fam* to become disillusioned.
décharge [deʃarʒ] *nf Jur* discharge; **d. (publique)** *Br* (rubbish) dump *ou* tip, *Am* (garbage) dump; **d. (électrique)** (electric) shock,
(electrical) discharge; **recevoir une d. (électrique)** to get a shock *ou* an electric shock; **à
la d. de qn** in s.o.'s *Br* defence *ou Am* defense.
décharger [deʃarʒe] *vt* to unload; (*batterie*)
to discharge; (*accusé*) to discharge, exonerate; **d. qn de** (*travail etc*) to relieve s.o. of;
d. son arme sur qn to fire one's weapon at
s.o.; **d. sa colère sur qn** to vent one's anger
on s.o. ‖ **se décharger** *vpr* (*batterie*) to go
flat; **se d. sur qn du soin de faire qch** to unload onto s.o. *ou Br* offload onto s.o. the
job of doing sth. ●**déchargement** *nm* unloading.
décharné, -ée [deʃarne] *a* skinny, bony.
déchausser [deʃose] **1** *vt* **d. qn** to take s.o.'s
shoes off; **se d.** to take one's shoes off. **2 se
déchausser** *vpr* (*dent*) to get loose.
dèche [dɛʃ] *nf* **être dans la d.** *Fam* to be flat
broke.
déchéance [deʃeɑ̃s] *nf* (*déclin*) decay, decline, degradation.
déchet [deʃɛ] *nm* **déchets** (*restes*) scraps,
waste; **il y a du d.** there's some waste *ou*
wastage.
déchiffrer [deʃifre] *vt* (*message*) to decipher;
(*mauvaise écriture*) to make out, decipher.
déchiqueter [deʃikte] *vt* to tear to shreds,
cut to bits. ●**déchiqueté, -ée** *a* (*drapeau etc*)

(all) in shreds; (*côte*) jagged.
déchirer [deʃire] *vt* (*page etc*) to tear (up),
rip (up); (*vêtement*) to tear, rip; (*ouvrir*) to
tear *ou* rip open; (*retirer*) to tear out
(*voucher etc*); (*pays, groupe*) to tear apart;
un cri/etc déchira l'air a loud cry/etc pierced
the air *ou* rang out; **ce bruit me déchire les
oreilles** this noise is ear-splitting.
‖ **se déchirer** *vpr* (*robe etc*) to tear, rip; **se d.
un muscle** to tear a muscle. ●**déchirant,
-ante** *a* (*douloureux*) heart-breaking; (*aigu*)
ear-splitting. ●**déchirement** *nm* (*souffrance*)
heartbreak; **déchirements** (*divisions au sein
d'une famille etc*) deep rifts. ●**déchirure** *nf*
tear, rip; **d. musculaire** torn muscle.
déchoir* [deʃwar] *vi* (*personne*) to lose
prestige and status. ●**déchu, -ue** *a* **ange d.**
fallen angel; **être d. de ses droits/etc** to have
forfeited one's rights/etc.
décibel [desibel] *nm* decibel.
décidé, -ée [deside] *a* (*air, ton*) determined,
decided; (*net, pas douteux*) (*goût etc*) decided; **c'est d.** it's settled; **être d. à faire** to
be determined to do *ou* decided about
doing.
décidément [desidemɑ̃] *adv* certainly, really, undoubtedly.
décider [deside] *vt* (*opération, envoi etc*) to
decide on; **d. que** to decide that; **d. de faire**
to decide to do; **d. qn (à faire)** to persuade
s.o. (to do) ‖ *vi* **d. d'un voyage/etc** to decide
on a journey/etc; **cela va d. de votre destin**
that will decide your fate.
‖ **se décider** *vpr* (*question*) to be decided; **se
d. (à faire)** to make up one's mind (to do);
se d. pour qch to decide on sth *ou* in favour
of sth. ●**décideur, -euse** *nmf* decision-
maker.
décilitre [desilitr] *nm* decilitre.
décimal, -e, -aux [desimal, -o] *a* decimal.
●**décimale** *nf* decimal.
décimer [desime] *vt* to decimate.
décimètre [desimɛtr] *nm* decimetre; **double
d.** ruler.
décisif, -ive [desizif, -iv] *a* (*bataille etc*) decisive; (*moment*) crucial. ●**décision** *nf* decision (**de faire** to do); (*fermeté*) determination; **prendre une d.** to make a decision;
avec d. decisively.
déclamer [deklame] *vt* to recite, declaim;
Péj to spout. ●**déclamatoire** *a Péj* bombastic.
déclaration [deklarasjɔ̃] *nf* declaration; (*de
vol, décès etc*) notification; (*commentaire*)
statement, comment; **d. d'impôts** *ou* **de revenus** (*formulaire*) tax return.
déclarer [deklare] *vt* to declare; (*annoncer*)
to state, declare (**que** that); (*vol, décès etc*)
to notify; **d. qn coupable** to convict s.o., find
s.o. guilty (**de** of); **d. la guerre** to declare
war (**à** on).
‖ **se déclarer** *vpr* (*incendie, maladie*) to
break out; (*s'expliquer*) to declare one's
views; **se d. contre** to come out against.
déclasser [deklase] *vt* (*livres etc*) to put out

of order; (*hôtel etc*) to downgrade; **d. qn** *Sport* to relegate s.o. (in the placings).

déclencher [deklɑ̃ʃe] *vt* (*mécanisme*) to set *ou* trigger off, start (off); (*attaque*) to launch; (*provoquer*) to trigger off, start, spark off (*crisis, reaction etc*); **d. le travail** (*accouchement*) to induce labour **I se déclencher** *vpr* (*alarme, sonnerie*) to go off; (*attaque, grève*) to start. ● **déclenchement** *nm* (*d'un appareil*) release.

déclic [deklik] *nm* (*bruit*) click; (*mécanisme*) catch, trigger.

déclin [deklɛ̃] *nm* decline; (*du jour*) close; (*de la lune*) wane.

déclinaison [deklinɛzɔ̃] *nf* Grammaire declension.

décliner [dekline] **1** *vi* (*forces etc*) to decline, wane; (*jour*) to draw to a close. **2** *vt* (*refuser*) to decline. **3** *vt* (*réciter*) to state.

déclivité [deklivite] *nf* slope.

déclouer [deklue] *vt* (*caisse etc*) to take the nails out of.

décocher [dekɔʃe] *vt* (*flèche*) to shoot, fire; (*coup*) to let fly, aim; (*regard*) to flash.

décoder [dekɔde] *vt* (*message*) to decode. ● **décodeur** *nm* Ordinat TV decoder.

décoiffer [dekwafe] *vt* **d. qn** to mess up s.o.'s hair; **se d.** to mess up one's hair; (*enlever son chapeau*) to take off one's hat.

décoincer [dekwɛ̃se] *vt* (*engrenage*) to unjam.

décoller [dekɔle] **1** *vi* (*avion etc*) to take off; **elle ne décolle pas d'ici** *Fam* she won't leave *ou* budge, she's staying put. **2** *vt* (*timbre etc*) to unstick **I se décoller** *vpr* to come unstuck. ● **décollage** *nm* (*d'avion*) takeoff.

décolleté, -ée [dekɔlte] *a* (*robe*) low-cut **I** *nm* (*de robe*) low neckline; (*de femme*) bare neck and shoulders.

décoloniser [dekɔlɔnize] *vt* to decolonize. ● **décolonisation** *nf* decolonization.

décolorer [dekɔlɔre] *vt* (*tissu*) to fade, discolour; (*cheveux*) to bleach **I se décolorer** *vpr* (*tissu*) to fade. ● **décolorant** *nm* bleach. ● **décoloration** *nf* discolo(u)ration; bleaching.

décombres [dekɔ̃br] *nmpl* rubble, ruins, debris.

décommander [dekɔmɑ̃de] *vt* (*marchandises, invitation*) to cancel; (*invités*) to put off **I se décommander** *vpr* to cancel (one's appointment).

décomposer [dekɔ̃poze] *vt* Ch to decompose; (*lumière*) to split; (*phrase*) to break down; (*visage*) to distort **I se décomposer** *vpr* (*pourrir*) to decompose; (*visage*) (*marqué par la fatigue etc*) to become drawn *ou* haggard. ● **décomposition** *nf* decomposition.

décompresser [dekɔ̃prese] *vi* (*se détendre*) *Fam* to unwind.

décompression [dekɔ̃prɛsjɔ̃] *nf* decompression.

décompte [dekɔ̃t] *nm* (*soustraction*) deduction; (*détail*) breakdown. ● **décompter** *vt* to deduct.

déconcentrer (se) [sədekɔ̃sɑ̃tre] *vpr* to lose one's concentration.

déconcerter [dekɔ̃sɛrte] *vt* to disconcert.

déconfit, -ite [dekɔ̃fi, -it] *a* downcast. ● **déconfiture** *nf* Fam (*state of*) collapse *ou* defeat; (*faillite*) financial ruin.

décongeler [dekɔ̃ʒle] *vt* (*faire*) **d.** (*aliment*) to thaw, defrost **I** *vi* **mettre qch à d.** to thaw *ou* defrost sth.

décongestionner [dekɔ̃ʒɛstjɔne] *vt* (*rue, poumons etc*) to relieve congestion in.

déconnecter [dekɔnɛkte] *vt* (*appareil électrique*) to disconnect; (*sujets*) to keep separate.

déconner [dekɔne] *vi* (*divaguer*) Fam to talk a lot of nonsense.

déconseiller [dekɔ̃seje] *vt* **d. qch à qn** to advise s.o. against sth; **d. à qn de faire** to advise s.o. against doing; **c'est déconseillé** it is not advisable.

déconsidérer [dekɔ̃sidere] *vt* to discredit.

décontaminer [dekɔ̃tamine] *vt* to decontaminate.

décontenancer [dekɔ̃tnɑ̃se] *vt* to disconcert **I se décontenancer** *vpr* to lose one's composure, become flustered.

décontracter [dekɔ̃trakte] *vt* (*muscle etc*) to relax **I se décontracter** *vpr* to relax. ● **décontraction** *nf* relaxation.

déconvenue [dekɔ̃vny] *nf* disappointment.

décor [dekɔr] *nm* (*de théâtre, cinéma etc*) scenery, decor; (*paysage*) scenery; (*d'intérieur*) decoration; (*cadre, ambiance*) setting; **les décors** (*de théâtre etc*) the scenery; **un d. de théâtre/cinéma** a stage/film set; **entrer dans le d.** (*véhicule*) Fam to run off the road (*into a tree etc*).

décorer [dekɔre] *vt* (*maison, soldat etc*) to decorate (**de** with). ● **décorateur, -trice** *nmf* (*interior*) decorator; *Théâtre* stage designer; *Cinéma* set designer. ● **décoratif, -ive** *a* decorative. ● **décoration** *nf* (*ornement, action, médaille*) decoration.

décortiquer [dekɔrtike] *vt* (*graine*) to husk; (*homard etc*) to shell; (*texte*) Fam to take to pieces, dissect.

découcher [dekuʃe] *vi* to stay out all night.

découdre* [dekudr] *vt* (*ourlet, bouton*) to unstitch **I** *vi* **en d. (avec qn)** Fam to fight it out (with s.o.) **I se découdre** *vpr* to come unstitched.

découler [dekule] *vi* **d. de** to follow from.

découper [dekupe] *vt* (*viande, poulet etc*) to carve; (*article de journal etc*) to cut out; (*papier*) to cut up; **se d. sur** (*silhouette etc*) to stand out against. ● **découpé, -ée** *a* (*côte*) jagged. ● **découpage** *nm* (*image*) cutout; (*de poulet etc*) carving; (*d'article etc*) cutting out. ● **découpure** *nf* (*contour*) jagged outline; (*morceau*) cutout, piece cut out.

découplé, -ée [dekuple] *a* **bien d.** (*personne*) well-built, strapping.

décourager [dekuraʒe] *vt* (*dissuader*) to discourage (**de faire** from doing); (*démoraliser*) to dishearten, discourage **I se décourager** *vpr* to get discouraged *ou* disheartened.

● **découragement** *nm* discouragement.

décousu, -ue [dekuzy] *a* unstitched; (*propos, idées*) *Fig* disconnected.

découvert, -erte [dekuvɛr, -ɛrt] **1** *a* (*terrain*) open; (*tête etc*) bare; **à d.** exposed, unprotected; **agir à d.** to act openly. **2** *nm* (*d'un compte*) overdraft.

découverte [dekuvɛrt] *nf* discovery; **partir** *ou* **aller à la d. de** qch to go in search of sth.

découvrir* [dekuvrir] *vt* (*trésor, terre etc*) to discover; (*secret, vérité etc*) to find out, discover; (*casserole etc*) to take the lid off; (*dénuder*) to uncover, expose; (*voir*) to perceive; **d. que** to discover *ou* find out that; **faire d. qch à qn** to disclose sth to s.o.
█ **se découvrir** *vpr* (*dans son lit*) to push the bedcovers off; (*enlever son chapeau*) to take one's hat off; (*ciel*) to clear (up).

décrasser [dekrase] *vt* (*nettoyer*) to clean; (*éduquer*) to take the rough edges off (*s.o.*).

décrépit, -ite [dekrepi, -it] *a* (*vieillard*) decrepit. ● **décrépitude** *nf* (*des institutions etc*) decay.

décret [dekrɛ] *nm* decree. ● **décréter** *vt* to order, decree.

décrier [dekrije] *vt* to run down, disparage.

décrisper [dekrispe] *vt* (*atmosphère*) to lighten; (*situation*) to ease █ **se décrisper** *vpr* to relax.

décrire* [dekrir] *vt* to describe.

décrocher¹ [dekrɔʃe] *vt* (*détacher*) to unhook; (*tableau etc*) to take down; (*obtenir*) *Fam* to get, land (*contract etc*); **d.** (le téléphone) to pick up the phone; **le téléphone est décroché** the phone is off the hook █ **se décrocher** *vpr* (*tableau etc*) to fall down; (*poisson*) to come unhooked.

décrocher² [dekrɔʃe] *vi Fam* (*abandonner*) to give up; (*perdre le fil*) to be unable to follow, lose track.

décroître* [dekrwatr] *vi* (*mortalité etc*) to decrease, decline; (*eaux*) to subside; (*jours*) to get shorter, *Br* draw in. ● **décroissance** *nf* decrease, decline (de in, of).

décrotter [dekrɔte] *vt* (*chaussures*) to clean *ou* scrape (the mud off). ● **décrottoir** *nm* shoe scraper.

décrue [dekry] *nf* (*des eaux*) fall *ou* drop in the water level.

décrypter [dekripte] *vt* (*message*) to decipher, decode.

déçu, -ue [desy] *pp de* **décevoir** █ *a* disappointed.

déculotter (se) [sədekylɔte] *vpr* to take off one's *Br* trousers *ou Am* pants. ● **déculottée** *nf Fam* thrashing; **prendre une d.** to get a thrashing.

décupler [dekyple] *vti* (*forces etc*) to increase tenfold.

dédaigner [dedeɲe] *vt* (*personne, richesse etc*) to scorn, despise; (*repas*) to turn up one's nose at; (*offre*) to spurn; (*ne pas tenir compte de*) to disregard. ● **dédaigneux, -euse** *a* scornful, disdainful (de of).

dédain [dedɛ̃] *nm* scorn, disdain (**pour, de** for).

dédale [dedal] *nm* maze, labyrinth.

dedans [d(ə)dɑ̃] *adv* inside; **de d.** from (the) inside, from within; **en d.** on the inside; **au-d. (de), au d. (de)** inside; **au-d. ou au d. de lui-même** inwardly; **tomber d.** (*trou*) to fall in (it); **donner (en plein) d., tomber en plein d.** (*être dupé*) *Fam* to fall in, fall for it; **mettre qn d.** *Fam* (*en prison*) to put s.o. inside; (*tromper*) to take s.o. in; **je me suis mis d.** (*je me suis trompé*) *Fam* I made a real blunder; **je me suis fait rentrer d.** (*accident de voiture*) *Fam* someone went *ou* crashed into me █ *nm* **le d.** the inside.

dédicace [dedikas] *nf* dedication, inscription. ● **dédicacer** *vt* (*livre etc*) to inscribe, dedicate (à to).

dédier [dedje] *vt* (*livre, église etc*) to dedicate (à to).

dédire* (se) [sədedir] *vpr* to go back on one's word; **se d. d'une promesse**/*etc* to go back on one's promise/*etc*. ● **dédit** *nm* (*somme*) forfeit, penalty (*for breaking contract etc*).

dédommager [dedɔmaʒe] *vt* to compensate (de for). ● **dédommagement** *nm* compensation.

dédouaner [dedwane] *vt* **1** (*marchandises*) to clear through customs. **2 d. qn** to restore s.o.'s good name.

dédoubler [deduble] *vt* (*classe etc*) to split into two; **d. un train** to run an extra train █ **se dédoubler** *vpr* to be in two places at once. ● **dédoublement** *nm* **d. de la personnalité** *Psy* split personality.

déduire* [deduir] *vt* (*retirer*) to deduct (de from); (*conclure*) to deduce (de from). ● **déductible** *a* (*frais*) deductible, allowable. ● **déduction** *nf* (*raisonnement, décompte etc*) deduction.

déesse [deɛs] *nf* goddess.

défaillir* [defajir] *vi* (*s'évanouir*) to faint; (*forces, mémoire*) to fail, flag; **sans d.** without flinching. ● **défaillant, -ante** *a* (*personne*) faint; (*témoin*) defaulting. ● **défaillance** *nf* (*évanouissement*) fainting fit; (*faiblesse*) weakness; (*panne*) fault; **une d. cardiaque** heart failure; **une d. de mémoire** a lapse of memory.

défaire* [defɛr] *vt* (*nœud etc*) to undo, untie; (*valises*) to unpack; (*installation*) to take down; (*coiffure*) to mess up; **d. qn de** to rid s.o. of █ **se défaire** *vpr* (*nœud etc*) to come undone *ou* untied; **se d. de** to get rid of. ● **défait, -aite** *a* (*lit*) unmade; (*cheveux*) dishevelled, untidy; (*visage*) drawn; (*armée*) defeated.

défaite [defɛt] *nf* defeat. ● **défaitisme** *nm* defeatism.

défalquer [defalke] *vt* (*frais etc*) to deduct (de from).

défaut [defo] *nm* (*faiblesse de caractère*) fault, shortcoming, failing, defect; (*de fabrication*) defect; (*de diamant etc*) flaw; (*désavantage*) drawback; **le d. de la cuirasse** the chink in the armour; **avoir un d.** (*appareil*) to be defective, have a defect; **faire d.** to be lacking; **le temps me fait d.** I lack time; **à d. de** for want of; **prendre qn en d.** to catch s.o. out; **ou, à d....** or, failing that...; **calculer qch par d.** to calculate sth to the nearest decimal point; **condamner qn par d.** to sentence s.o. in his *ou* her absence; **police/ lecteur par d.** Ordinat default font/drive.

défaveur [defavœr] *nf* disfavour. ●**défavorable** *a* unfavourable (à to). ●**défavoriser** *vt* to put at a disadvantage, be unfair to.

défection [defɛksjɔ̃] *nf* defection, desertion; **faire d.** to desert; (*ne pas venir*) to fail to turn up.

défectueux, -euse [defɛktɥø, -øz] *a* faulty, defective. ●**défectuosité** *nf* defectiveness; (*défaut*) defect (**de** in).

défendre [defɑ̃dr] **1** *vt* (*protéger*) to defend (**contre** against); **se défendre** *vpr* to defend oneself; **se d. de** (*pluie etc*) to protect oneself from; **se d. de faire** (*s'empêcher de*) to refrain from doing; **je me défends (bien) en anglais/etc** *Fam* I can hold my own in English/etc.
2 *vt* **d. à qn de faire qch** (*interdire*) to forbid s.o. to do sth, not allow s.o. to do sth; **d. qch à qn** to forbid s.o. sth. ●**défendable** *a* defensible.

défense [defɑ̃s] *nf* **1** (*protection*) Br defence, Am defense; **assurer la d. de qn** Jur to conduct the case for the defence; **prendre la d. de qn** to defend s.o.; **en état de légitime d.** acting in self-defence; **sans d.** Br defenceless, Am defenseless.
2 (*interdiction*) **'d. de fumer'** 'no smoking'; **'d. (absolue) d'entrer'** '(strictly) no entry', '(strictly) no admittance'.
3 (*d'éléphant*) tusk.

défenseur [defɑ̃sœr] *nm* defender; (*des faibles*) protector, defender.

défensif, -ive [defɑ̃sif, -iv] *a* defensive ∎ *nf* **sur la défensive** on the defensive.

déférent, -ente [deferɑ̃, -ɑ̃t] *a* deferential. ●**déférence** *nf* deference.

déférer [defere] **1** *vt* (*suspect*) to refer (à to).
2 *vi* **d. à l'avis de qn** to defer to s.o.'s opinion.

déferler [defɛrle] *vi* (*vagues*) to break; (*haine etc*) to erupt; **d. dans** *ou* **sur** (*foule*) to surge *ou* sweep into.

défi [defi] *nm* challenge; **lancer un d. à qn** to challenge s.o.; **mettre qn au d. de faire qch** to defy *ou* dare *ou* challenge s.o. to do sth; **relever un d.** to take up *ou* accept a challenge.

déficient, -ente [defisjɑ̃, -ɑ̃t] *a* (*faible*) deficient. ●**déficience** *nf* (*faiblesse, manque*) deficiency.

déficit [defisit] *nm* deficit. ●**déficitaire** *a* (*budget etc*) in deficit; (*récolte etc*) Fig short, insufficient.

défier¹ [defje] *vt* (*provoquer*) to challenge (à to); (*braver*) to defy; **d. qn à la course/etc** to challenge s.o. to a race/etc; **d. qn de faire**

qch to defy *ou* challenge s.o. to do sth.

défier² (se) [sədefje] *vpr* **se d. de** *Litt* to distrust. ●**défiance** *nf* distrust (**de** of). ●**défiant, -ante** *a* distrustful (**à l'égard de** of).

défigurer [defigyre] *vt* (*visage*) to disfigure; (*vérité etc*) to distort. ●**défiguré, -ée** *a* (*personne*) disfigured.

défilé [defile] *nm* **1** (*cortège*) procession; (*de manifestants*) march; (*de soldats*) parade, Br march-past; (*de visiteurs*) stream, succession. **2** (*couloir de montagne*) gorge, pass.

défiler [defile] *vi* (*manifestants*) to march (**devant** past); (*soldats*) to march (past), file past; (*paysage, jours*) to pass by; (*visiteurs*) to keep coming and going, stream in and out; (*images*) to flash by (on the screen); (*données*) Ordinat to scroll.
∎ **se défiler** *vpr* Fam (*s'éloigner*) to sneak off; (*éviter d'agir*) to cop out.

définir [definir] *vt* to define. ●**défini, -ie** *a* definite; **article d.** Grammaire definite article. ●**définition** *nf* definition; (*de mots croisés*) clue.

définitif, -ive [definitif, -iv] *a* final, definitive ∎ *nf* **en définitive** in the final analysis, finally. ●**définitivement** *adv* (*partir, exclure*) permanently, for good.

déflagration [deflagrasjɔ̃] *nf* explosion.

déflation [deflasjɔ̃] *nf* Econ deflation.

déflorer [deflɔre] *vt* (*idée, sujet*) to spoil the freshness of.

défoncer [defɔ̃se] **1** *vt* (*porte, mur etc*) to smash in *ou* down; (*trottoir, route etc*) to dig up, break up. **2 se défoncer** *vpr* (*drogué*) Fam to get high (**à** on). ●**défoncé, -ée** *a* **1** (*route*) full of potholes, bumpy. **2** (*drogué*) Fam high.

déformation [defɔrmasjɔ̃] *nf* (*de fait etc*) distortion; (*de goût*) corruption; (*de membre*) deformity; **c'est de la d. professionnelle** it's a case of being conditioned by one's job, it's an occupational hazard.

déformer [defɔrme] *vt* (*objet*) to put *ou* knock out of shape; (*doigt, main*) to deform; (*faits, image etc*) to distort; (*goût*) to corrupt ∎ **se déformer** *vpr* to lose its shape. ●**déformé, -ée** *a* (*objet*) misshapen; (*corps etc*) deformed, misshapen; **chaussée déformée** uneven road surface, bumpy road.

défouler (se) [sədefule] *vpr* Fam to let off steam.

défraîchir (se) [sədefrɛʃir] *vpr* (*étoffe etc*) to lose its freshness, become faded.

défrayer [defreje] *vt* **d. la chronique** to be the talk of the town; **d. qn** to pay *ou* defray s.o.'s expenses.

défricher [defriʃe] *vt* (*terrain*) to clear (for cultivation); (*sujet etc*) Fig to open up.

défriser [defrize] *vt* (*cheveux*) to straighten; **d. qn** (*contrarier*) Fam to ruffle *ou* annoy s.o.

défroisser [defrwase] *vt* (*papier*) to smooth out.

défroqué, -ée [defrɔke] *a* (*prêtre*) defrocked.

défunt, -unte [defœ̃, -œ̃t] *a* (*mort*) departed; **son d. mari** her late husband ∎ *nmf* **le d., la défunte** the deceased, the departed.

dégager [degaʒe] *vt* (*passage, voie*) to clear (**de** of); (*odeur*) to give off; (*chaleur*) to give out; (*responsabilité*) to disclaim; (*idée, conclusion*) to bring out; (*objet en gage*) Vieilli to redeem; **d. qn de** (*décombres*) to free s.o. from, pull s.o. out of; (*promesse*) to release s.o. from; **cette robe dégage la taille** this dress leaves the waist free and easy.
∎ *vi Football* to clear the ball (down the pitch); **dégagez!** *Fam* clear the way!, clear off!
∎ **se dégager** *vpr* (*rue, ciel*) to clear; **se d. de** (*personne*) to release oneself from (*promise*); to get free from, free oneself from (*rubble*); (*odeur, gaz etc*) to come out of, issue *ou* emanate from (*kitchen etc*); (*vérité, impression*) to emerge from. ● **dégagé, -ée** *a* (*ciel*) clear; (*allure, ton*) easy-going, casual; (*vue*) open. ● **dégagement** *nm* **1** (*action*) clearing; (*d'odeur*) emanation; (*de chaleur*) emission; (*de promesse*) release; (*de décombres*) freeing; *Football* clearance, kick; **itinéraire de d.** (*de route*) relief road. **2** (*espace libre*) clearing; (*de maison*) passage.

dégainer [degene] *vti* (*arme*) to draw.

dégarnir [degarnir] *vt* to clear, empty; (*compte*) to strip; (*arbre de Noël*) to take down the decorations from ∎ **se dégarnir** *vpr* (*crâne*) to go bald; (*salle*) to clear, empty. ● **dégarni, -ie** *a* (*salle*) empty, bare; (*tête*) balding; **front d.** receding hairline.

dégâts [dega] *nmpl* damage; **limiter les d.** *Fig* to prevent matters getting worse, limit the damage.

dégel [deʒɛl] *nm* thaw; ● **dégeler** *vt* to thaw (out); (*crédits*) to unfreeze ∎ *vi* to thaw (out); **faire d. qch, mettre qch à d.** to thaw sth (out) ∎ *v imp* to thaw; **il dégèle** it's thawing ∎ **se dégeler** *vpr* (*personne, situation*) *Fig* to thaw (out).

dégénérer [deʒenere] *vi* (*se déverser*) to degenerate (**en** into). ● **dégénéré, -ée** *a* & *nmf* degenerate. ● **dégénérescence** *nf* degeneration.

dégingandé, -ée [deʒɛ̃gɑ̃de] *a* gangling, lanky.

dégivrer [deʒivre] *vt* (*réfrigérateur*) to defrost; (*voiture, avion*) to de-ice.

déglinguer (se) [sədeglɛ̃ge] *vpr Fam* to fall to bits. ● **déglingué, -ée** *a* falling to bits, in bits.

dégobiller [degɔbije] *vt Fam* to spew up.

dégonfler [degɔ̃fle] *vt* (*pneu etc*) to let the air out of, let down ∎ **se dégonfler** *vpr* (*pneu etc*) to go down; (*se montrer lâche*) *Fam* to chicken out, get cold feet. ● **dégonflé, -ée** *a* (*pneu*) flat; (*lâche*) *Fam* chicken, yellow ∎ *nmf Fam* yellow belly.

dégorger [degɔrʒe] *vi* (*se déverser*) to discharge (**dans** into); **faire d.** (*escargots etc*) to salt, cover with salt.

dégot(t)er [degɔte] *vt Fam* to find, turn up.

dégouliner [deguline] *vi* to trickle, drip.

dégourdir [degurdir] *vt* (*doigts etc*) to take the numbness out of; **d. qn** *Fig* to smarten *ou* wise s.o. up, sharpen s.o.'s wits ∎ **se dégourdir** *vpr* to smarten up, wise up; **se d. les jambes** to stretch one's legs. ● **dégourdi, -ie** *a* (*malin*) smart, sharp.

dégoût [degu] *nm* disgust; **le d. de** (*la vie, les gens etc*) disgust for; **avoir du d. pour qch** to have a (strong) dislike *ou* distaste for sth.

dégoûter [degute] *vt* to disgust; **d. qn de qch** to put s.o. off sth, *Am* (be enough to) make s.o. sick of sth; **se d. de** to take a (strong) dislike to, become disgusted with. ● **dégoûtant, -ante** *a* disgusting. ● **dégoûté, -ée** *a* disgusted; **être d. de** to be sick of *ou* disgusted with *ou* by *ou* at; **elle est partie dégoûtée** she left in disgust; **il n'est pas d.** (*difficile*) he's not too fussy; **faire le d.** to be fussy.

dégradation [degradɑsjɔ̃] *nf Ch Mil etc* degradation; (*de situation, état etc*) deterioration; **dégradations** (*dégâts*) damage.

dégrader [degrade] *vt* **1** (*avilir*) to degrade; (*mur etc*) to deface, damage ∎ **se dégrader** *vpr* (*édifice, situation*) to deteriorate; (*s'avilir*) to degrade onself. **2** *vt* (*couleur*) to shade off. ● **dégradant, -ante** *a* degrading. ● **dégradé** *nm* (*de couleur*) shading off, gradation.

dégrafer [degrafe] *vt* (*vêtement*) to unfasten, undo, unhook.

dégraisser [degrese] *vt* **1** (*bœuf*) to take the fat off; (*bouillon*) to skim. **2** (*entreprise*) *Fam* to slim down, trim down the size of (*by laying off workers*).

degré [dəgre] *nm* **1** (*d'angle, de température etc*) & *Mus Méd etc* degree; **enseignement du premier/second d.** *Br* primary *ou Am* elementary education/secondary education; **avare/etc au plus haut d.** extremely miserly/ *etc*. **2** (*gradin*) *Litt* step.

dégrever [degrave] *vt* (*contribuable*) to reduce the tax burden on.

dégriffé, -ée [degrife] *a* **vêtement d.** unlabelled designer garment (*sold in seconds store*).

dégringoler [degrɛ̃gɔle] *vi* to tumble (down); **faire d. qch** to topple sth over ∎ *vt* (*escalier*) to rush down. ● **dégringolade** *nf* tumble.

dégriser [degrize] *vt* **d. qn** *Fig* to sober s.o. (up).

dégrossir [degrosir] *vt* (*travail*) to rough out; **d. qn** *Fig* to refine s.o.

déguerpir [degɛrpir] *vi Fam* to clear off *ou* out, make tracks.

dégueulasse [degœlas] *a Fam* (*sale*) filthy; (*révoltant*) disgusting; (*mauvais*) lousy.

dégueuler [degœle] *vt* (*vomir*) *Fam* to puke.

déguiser [degize] *vt* (*pour tromper*) to disguise; **d. qn en** (*costumer*) to dress s.o. up as, disguise s.o. as ∎ **se déguiser** *vpr* to dress oneself up (**en** as); (*pour tromper*) to disguise oneself (**en** as). ● **déguisement** *nm* disguise; (*de bal costumé etc*) *Br* fancy dress, costume.

déguster [degyste] **1** vt (goûter) to taste, sample; (apprécier) to relish. **2** vi (subir des coups) Fam to cop it, get a good hiding. ● **dégustation** nf tasting, sampling.

déhancher (se) [sədeɑ̃ʃe] vpr (femme etc) to sway ou wiggle one's hips; (boiteux) to walk lop-sided.

dehors [dəɔr] adv outside, out; (hors de chez soi) out; (à l'air) outdoors, outside; **en d.** on the outside; **en d. de la maison**/etc outside the house/etc; **en d. de la ville/fenêtre** out of town/the window; **en d. de** (excepté) Fig apart from; **déjeuner/jeter**/etc **d.** to lunch/throw/etc out; **mettre qn d.** Fam to throw s.o. out; (employé) to fire s.o., sack s.o. ▌nm (extérieur) outside; **des dehors** (aspect) outward appearance; **sous des d. timides**/etc beneath an outward appearance of shyness/etc.

déjà [deʒa] adv already; **est-il d. parti?** has he left yet ou already?; **elle l'a d. vu** she's seen it before, she's already seen it; **c'est d. pas mal** Fam that's not bad at all; **quand partez-vous, d.?** Fam when did you say you're leaving ou you were leaving?

déjeuner [deʒœne] vi (à midi) to (have) lunch; (le matin) to (have) breakfast ▌nm lunch; **petit d.** breakfast.

déjouer [deʒwe] vt (intrigue, plans) to thwart, foil.

déjuger (se) [sədeʒyʒe] vpr to go back on one's opinion ou decision.

delà [d(ə)la] adv **au-d. (de), au d. (de),** par-d., par d. beyond; **au-d. du pont**/etc beyond ou past the bridge/etc ▌nm **l'au-d.** the (world) beyond.

délabrer (se) [sədelabre] vpr (édifice) to become dilapidated, fall into disrepair; (santé) to give out, fail, become impaired. ● **délabré, -ée** a (bâtiment) dilapidated. ● **délabrement** [-əmɑ̃] nm (de bâtiment) dilapidation, disrepair; (de santé) impaired state.

délacer [delase] vt (chaussures) to undo.

délai [dele] nm time limit; (répit, sursis) extra time, extension; **dans un d. de dix jours** within ten days; **sans d.** without delay; **dans les plus brefs délais** as soon as possible; **dernier d.** final date.

délaisser [delese] vt (négliger) to neglect; (abandonner) to forsake, desert, abandon.

délasser [delase] vt, **se délasser** vpr to relax. ● **délassement** nm relaxation, diversion.

délateur, -trice [delatœr, -tris] nmf informer.

délavé, -ée [delave] a (tissu, jean) faded; (ciel) watery; (terre) waterlogged.

délayer [deleje] vt (mélanger) to mix (with liquid); (discours, texte) Fig to pad out.

delco [delko] nm (de véhicule) distributor.

délecter (se) [sədelekte] vpr **se d. de qch/à faire** to (take) delight in sth/in doing. ● **délectable** a delectable. ● **délectation** nf delight.

déléguer [delege] vt to delegate (à to). ● **délégué, -ée** nmf delegate. ● **délégation** nf delegation.

délestage [delɛstaʒ] nm **itinéraire de d.** alternative route (to relieve congestion).

délester [delɛste] vt (couper le courant dans) to cut the power in (as a relief measure); **d. qn de** (voler à qn) Fam to relieve s.o. of.

délibérer [delibere] vi (se consulter) to deliberate, confer (de about); (réfléchir) to deliberate (sur upon). ● **délibéré, -ée** a (résolu) determined; (intentionnel) deliberate; **de propos d.** deliberately. ● **délibérément** adv (à dessein) deliberately. ● **délibération** nf deliberation.

délicat, -ate [delika, -at] a (santé, travail etc) delicate; (question) tricky, delicate; (geste) tactful; (exigeant) particular; **des procédés peu délicats** unscrupulous methods. ● **délicatement** adv delicately; (avec tact) tactfully. ● **délicatesse** nf delicacy; (tact) tact(fulness).

délice [delis] nm delight. ● **délices** nfpl delights. ● **délicieux, -euse** a (mets, fruit etc) delicious; (endroit, parfum etc) delightful.

délié, -ée [delje] **1** a (esprit) sharp, subtle; (doigts) nimble; (écriture) fine; **avoir la langue déliée** to be talkative. **2** nm (d'une lettre) (thin) upstroke.

délier [delje] vt to untie, undo; (langue) Fig to loosen; **d. qn de** to release s.o. from ▌ **se délier** vpr **les langues se délient** people start talking, tongues are loosened.

délimiter [delimite] vt (terrain) to mark off; (sujet) to define. ● **délimitation** nf (de terrain) demarcation; (de sujet) definition.

délinquant, -ante [delɛ̃kɑ̃, -ɑ̃t] a & nmf delinquent. ● **délinquance** nf delinquency.

délire [delir] nm (maladie) delirium; (exaltation) frenzy; **c'est du d.** Fam it's utter madness. ● **délirer** vi (patient) to be delirious; (dire n'importe quoi) to rave; **d. de** (joie etc) to be wild with. ● **délirant, -ante** a (malade) delirious; (joie) frenzied, wild; (déraisonnable) utterly absurd.

délit [deli] nm Br offence, Am offense; **d. d'initié** (à la Bourse) insider trading ou dealing.

délivrer [delivre] vt **1** (prisonnier, otage) to release, (set) free; (pays) to free, deliver; **d. qn de** (souci, obligation etc) to rid s.o. of. **2** (passeport, billet etc) to issue (à to). **3** (marchandises) to deliver. ● **délivrance** nf release; deliverance; issue; (soulagement) relief.

déloger [deloʒe] vt to force ou drive out; (soldats) to dislodge.

déloyal, -e, -aux [delwajal, -o] a disloyal; (concurrence) unfair. ● **déloyauté** nf disloyalty; (de concurrence) unfairness; (action) disloyal act.

delta [dɛlta] nm (de fleuve) delta.

deltaplane® [dɛltaplan] nm (engin) hangglider; **faire du d.** to practise ou do hanggliding, go hang-gliding.

déluge [delyʒ] nm flood; (de pluie) downpour; (de compliments, coups) shower, deluge.

déluré

86

déluré, -ée [delyre] *a* (*malin*) smart, sharp; (*fille trop hardie*) brazen.
démagogie [demagɔʒi] *nf* demagogy. ●**démagogue** *nmf* demagogue.
demain [d(ə)mɛ̃] *adv* tomorrow; **à d.!** see you tomorrow!; **ce n'est pas d. la veille** *Fam* that won't happen for a (quite a) while.
demande [d(ə)mãd] *nf* request (**de qch for** sth); (*d'emploi*) application; (*de renseignements*) inquiry; *Econ* demand; (*question*) question; **d. (en mariage)** proposal (of marriage); **demandes d'emploi** (*dans le journal*) jobs wanted, *Br* situations wanted.
demander [d(ə)mãde] *vt* to ask for; (*emploi*) to apply for; (*autorisation*) to request, ask for; (*charité*) to beg for; (*prix*) to charge; (*nécessiter, exiger*) to require; **d. le chemin/l'heure** to ask the way/the time; **d. qch à qn** to ask s.o. for sth; **d. à qn de faire qch** to ask s.o. to do sth; **d. si/où** to ask *ou* inquire whether/where; **on te demande!** you're wanted!; **ça demande du temps/une heure** it takes time/an hour; **je peux vous d. votre nom?** may I ask your name?; **d. qn en mariage** to propose (marriage) to s.o.; **elle est très demandée** she's in great demand.
 se demander *vpr* to wonder, ask oneself (**pourquoi** why, **si** if).
démanger [demãʒe] *vti* to itch; **son bras le démange** his arm itches; **ça me démange de...** (*j'ai très envie de*) I'm itching to.... ●**démangeaison** *nf* itch; **avoir des démangeaisons** to be itching; **j'ai une d. au bras** my arm's itching.
démanteler [demãtle] *vt* (*organisation etc*) to break up; (*bâtiment*) to demolish.
démantibuler [demãtibyle] *vt* (*meuble etc*) *Fam* to smash up, knock to pieces.
démaquiller (se) [sədemakije] *vpr* to take off one's make-up. ●**démaquillant** *nm* make-up remover.
démarcation [demarkasjɔ̃] *nf* demarcation.
démarche [demarʃ] *nf* walk, gait, step; **d. intellectuelle** thought process; **faire des démarches** to go through the process (**pour faire** of doing), take the necessary steps (**pour faire** to do); **faire une d.** *ou* **des démarches auprès de qn** to approach s.o. (**pour faire** to do).
démarcheur, -euse [demarʃœr, -øz] *nmf* (*vendeur*) door-to-door salesman *ou* saleswoman.
démarquer [demarke] *vt* (*prix*) to mark down; **se d. de** (*marquer une différence*) to dissociate oneself from.
démarrer [demare] *vi* (*moteur de voiture etc*) to start (up); (*partir en voiture*) to move *ou* drive off; (*entreprise etc*) *Fig* to get off the ground **|** *vt* (*commencer*) *Fam* to start. ●**démarrage** *nm* (*de voiture*) start; **d. en côte** hill start. ●**démarreur** *nm* (*de voiture*) starter.
démasquer [demaske] *vt* to expose, unmask.
démêler [demele] *vt* to disentangle, untangle; **d. une affaire** *Fig* to disentangle a

matter. ●**démêlé** *nm* (*dispute*) squabble; **avoir des démêlés avec la justice/son patron** (*ennuis*) to have a brush with *or* unpleasant dealings with the law/one's boss.
démembrer [demãbre] *vt* (*pays etc*) to dismember, carve up.
déménager [demenaʒe] *vi* to move (out), move house **|** *vt* (*meubles*) *Br* to (re)move, *Am* move. ●**déménagement** *nm* move, moving (house); (*de meubles*) *Br* removal, moving (of); **camion de d.** *Br* removal van, *Am* moving van. ●**déménageur** *nm* *Br* removal man, *Am* (furniture) mover.
démener (se) [sədemne] *vpr* to fling oneself about; **se d. pour faire qch** to spare no effort to do sth.
dément, -ente [demã, -ãt] *a* insane; (*génial*) *Fam* fantastic **|** *nmf* lunatic. ●**démence** *nf* insanity. ●**démentiel, -ielle** *a* insane.
démentir [demãtir] *vt* (*nouvelle, fait etc*) to deny; (*témoin*) to contradict. ●**démenti** *nm* denial; **opposer un d. à qch** to make a formal denial of sth.
démerder (se) [sədemerde] *vpr* (*se débrouiller*) *Fam* to manage (by oneself).
démesure [deməzyr] *nf* excess. ●**démesuré, -ée** *a* excessive, inordinate.
démettre* [demetr] *vt* **1 se d. l'épaule/***etc* to dislocate one's shoulder/etc. **2 d. qn de ses fonctions** to dismiss s.o. from his post; **se d. de ses fonctions** to resign.
demeurant (au) [odəmœrã] *adv* for all that, nonetheless, after all.
demeure [dəmœr] *nf* **1** (*belle maison*) mansion. **2 à d.** permanently. **3 mettre qn en d. de faire qch** to summon *ou* instruct s.o. to do sth.
demeuré, -ée *a* *Fam* (mentally) retarded.
demeurer [dəmœre] *vi* **1** (*aux être*) (*rester*) to remain; **en d. là** (*affaire etc*) to rest there. **2** (*aux avoir*) (*habiter*) to live, reside.
demi, -ie [d(ə)mi] *a* half; **d.-journée** half-day; **une heure et demie** an hour and a half; (*horloge*) half past one **|** *adv* (**à**) **d. plein** half-full; **à d. nu** half-naked; **dormir à d.** to be half asleep; **ouvrir à d.** to open halfway; **faire les choses à d.** to do things by halves **|** *nmf* (*moitié*) half **|** *nm* (*verre*) (half-pint) glass of beer; *Football* half-back **|** *nf* **demie** (*à l'horloge*) half-hour.
demi-cercle [d(ə)misɛrkl] *nm* semicircle. ●**demi-douzaine** *nf* **une d.-douzaine (de)** a half-dozen, half a dozen. ●**demi-finale** *nf* *Sport* semifinal. ●**demi-frère** *nm* stepbrother, half brother. ●**demi-heure** *nf* **une d.-heure** a half-hour, half an hour. ●**demi-livre** *nf* half a pound. ●**demi-mesure** *nf* half-measure. ●**demi-mot** *nm* **tu comprendras à d.-mot** you'll understand without my having to spell it out. ●**demi-pension** *nf* *Br* half-board, *Am* breakfast and one meal. ●**demi-pensionnaire** *nmf* *Br* day boarder, *Am* day student. ●**demi-saison** *nf* **de d.-saison** (*vêtement*) between seasons. ●**demi-sel** *a inv* (*beurre*) slightly salted; (*fromage*) **d.-sel** cream

cheese. ● **demi-sœur** nf stepsister, half sister.
● **demi-tarif** nm & a inv (billet) (à) d.-tarif half-price. ● **demi-tour** nm Br about turn, Am about face; (en voiture) U-turn; **faire d.-tour** (à pied) to turn back; (en voiture) to make a U-turn.

déminéralisée [demineralize] af eau d. (pour voiture, fer à repasser) distilled water.

démis, -mise [demi, -miz] a avoir l'épaule démise to have a dislocated shoulder.

démission [demisjɔ̃] nf resignation; **donner sa d.** to hand in or give in one's resignation. ● **démissionner** vi to resign.

démobiliser [demɔbilize] vt to demobilize. ● **démobilisation** nf demobilization.

démocrate [demɔkrat] nmf democrat ▌ a democratic. ● **démocratie** [-asi] nf democracy. ● **démocratique** a democratic.

démoder (se) [sədemɔde] vpr to go out of fashion. ● **démodé, -ée** a old-fashioned.

démographie [demɔgrafi] nf demography.

demoiselle [d(ə)mwazɛl] nf (jeune fille) young lady; (célibataire) single woman, Vieilli spinster; **d. d'honneur** (à un mariage) bridesmaid; (de reine) maid of honour.

démolir [demɔlir] vt (maison etc) to knock ou pull down, demolish; (jouet etc) to wreck, demolish; (projet, autorité) Fig to wreck, shatter; **d. qn** (battre, discréditer) Fam to tear s.o. to pieces, demolish s.o. ● **démolition** nf demolition; **en d.** being demolished.

démon [demɔ̃] nm demon; **petit d.** (enfant) little devil; **le d.** the Devil. ● **démoniaque** a devilish, fiendish.

démonstratif, -ive [demɔ̃stratif, -iv] a demonstrative; **adjectif d.** demonstrative adjective ▌ nm Grammaire demonstrative.

démonstration [demɔ̃strasjɔ̃] nf demonstration; **faire une d.** Math to give a demonstration; **faire la d. d'un appareil**/etc to demonstrate an appliance/etc; **d. de force** show of force. ● **démonstrateur, -trice** nmf (dans un magasin etc) demonstrator.

démonter [demɔ̃te] vt (mécanisme) to dismantle, take apart; (installation, tente) to take down; **d. qn** (troubler) to disconcert s.o.; **une mer démontée** a stormy sea ▌ **se démonter** vpr to come apart; (installation etc) to come down; (personne) Fig to be put out ou disconcerted.

démontrer [demɔ̃tre] vt to demonstrate, show.

démoraliser [demɔralize] vt to demoralize ▌ **se démoraliser** vpr to become demoralized. ● **démoralisation** nf demoralization.

démordre [demɔrdr] vi **il ne démordra pas de son opinion**/etc he won't budge from his opinion/etc, he's sticking to his opinion/etc.

démouler [demule] vt (gâteau) to turn out (from its mould).

démuni, -e [demyni] a (sans argent) penniless, destitute.

démunir [demynir] vt **d. qn de** to deprive s.o. of; **se d. de** to part with.

démystifier [demistifje] vt (public etc) to disabuse; (idée etc) to debunk.

dénationaliser [denasjɔnalize] vt to denationalize.

dénaturer [denatyre] vt (propos, faits etc) to misrepresent, distort; (goût) to alter. ● **dénaturé, -ée** a (parents, goût) unnatural.

dénégation [denegasjɔ̃] nf denial.

déneiger [deneʒe] vt to clear of snow.

dénicher [deniʃe] vt (trouver) to dig up, turn up; (ennemi, fugitif) to hunt out, flush out.

dénier [denje] vt to deny; (responsabilité) to disclaim, deny; (droit) to deny; **d. qch à qn** to deny s.o. sth.

dénigrer [denigre] vt to denigrate, disparage. ● **dénigrement** nm denigration, disparagement.

dénivellation [denivɛlasjɔ̃] nf unevenness; (pente) gradient; **dénivellations** (relief) bumps.

dénombrer [denɔ̃bre] vt to count, number.

dénominateur [denɔminatœr] nm Math & Fig denominator.

dénommer [denɔme] vt to name. ● **dénommé, -ée** nmf un d. Dupont a man named Dupont. ● **dénomination** nf designation.

dénoncer [denɔ̃se] vt (injustice etc) to denounce (à to); **d. qn** (au professeur) to tell on s.o., inform on s.o. (à to) ▌ **se dénoncer** vpr (à la police etc) to give oneself up (à to); (au professeur) to own up (à to). ● **dénonciateur, -trice** nmf informer; (élève) telltale. ● **dénonciation** nf denunciation.

dénoter [denɔte] vt to denote.

dénouement [denumɑ̃] nm outcome, ending; (au théâtre) dénouement.

dénouer [denwe] vt (nœud, corde) to undo, untie; (cheveux) to let down, undo; (situation, intrigue) to unravel; (problème, crise) to clear up ▌ **se dénouer** vpr (nœud) to come undone ou untied; (cheveux) to come undone.

dénoyauter [denwajote] vt (prune etc) Br to stone, Am to pit.

denrée [dɑ̃re] nf food(stuff); **denrées alimentaires** foods, foodstuffs; **denrées périssables** perishable foods or foodstuffs, perishables.

dense [dɑ̃s] a dense. ● **densité** nf density.

dent [dɑ̃] nf tooth (pl teeth); (de roue) cog; (de fourchette) prong; (de timbre-poste) perforation; **d. de lait/sagesse** milk/wisdom tooth; **faire ses dents** (enfant) to be teething; **coup de d.** bite; **rien à se mettre sous la d.** nothing to eat; **manger à belles dents/du bout des dents** to eat whole-heartedly/half-heartedly; **être sur les dents** (énervé) to be on edge; (surmené) to be exhausted; **avoir une d. contre qn** to have it in for s.o.; **couteau en dents de scie** serrated knife; **résultats en dents de scie** Fig irregular results showing ups and downs, good and bad results. ● **dentaire** a dental. ● **dentée** af roue d. cogwheel.

dentelé, -ée [dɑ̃tle] a (côte) jagged; (feuille) serrated. ● **dentelure** nf jagged outline.

dentelle [dɑ̃tɛl] *nf* lace.

dentier [dɑ̃tje] *nm* (set of) false teeth, denture(s).

dentifrice [dɑ̃tifris] *nm* toothpaste.

dentiste [dɑ̃tist] *nmf* dentist; **chirurgien d.** dental surgeon. ● **dentition** *nf* (*dents*) (set of) teeth.

dénuder [denyde] *vt* to (lay) bare. ● **dénudé, -ée** *a* bare.

dénué, -ée [denɥe] *a* **d. de sens/d'intérêt/***etc* devoid of sense/interest/*etc*.

dénuement [denymɑ̃] *nm* destitution; **dans le d.** poverty-stricken.

déodorant [deɔdɔrɑ̃] *nm* deodorant.

dépanner [depane] *vt* (*voiture, télévision etc*) to get going (again), repair; **d. qn** *Fam* to help s.o. out. ● **dépannage** *nm* (emergency) repair; **voiture/service de d.** *Br* breakdown *ou* recovery vehicle/service. ● **dépanneur** *nm* (*de télévision*) repairman; (*de voiture*) *Br* breakdown mechanic, emergency car mechanic. ● **dépanneuse** *nf* (*voiture*) *Br* breakdown lorry, *Am* wrecker, tow truck.

dépareillé, -ée [depareje] *a* (*chaussure etc*) odd, not matching; (*collection*) incomplete.

départ [depar] *nm* departure; (*de course etc*) start; **c'est le jour des départs en vacances** it's the start of the *Br* holidays *or Am* vacation; **point/ligne de d.** starting point/post; **salaire de d.** starting salary; **au d.** at the outset, at the start; **dès le d.** (right) from the start; **au d. de Paris/***etc* (*excursion etc*) leaving *ou* departing from Paris/*etc*; **à mon d. de Paris** when I left Paris.

départager [departaʒe] *vt* (*concurrents*) to decide between; **d. les votes** to give the casting vote.

département [departəmɑ̃] *nm* department. ● **départemental, -e, -aux** *a* departmental; **route départementale** secondary road, *Br* = B road.

départir* (se) [sədepartir] *vpr* **se d. de** (*attitude*) to depart from, abandon.

dépasser [depɑse] *vt* (*véhicule, bicyclette etc*) *Br* to overtake, pass; (*endroit*) to go past, go beyond; (*prévisions, date limite etc*) to exceed, go beyond; **d. qn** (*en hauteur*) to be taller than s.o.; (*surclasser*) to be ahead of s.o.; **ça me dépasse** *Fig* that's (quite) beyond me ∥ *vi* (*jupon, clou etc*) to stick out, show. ● **dépassé, -ée** *a* (*démodé*) outdated; (*incapable*) unable to cope. ● **dépassement** *nm* (*en voiture*) *Br* overtaking, passing.

dépayser [depeize] *vt* *Br* to disorientate, *Am* disorient. ● **dépaysement** *nm* disorientation; (*changement*) change of scenery.

dépecer [depəse] *vt* (*animal*) to cut up, carve up.

dépêche [depɛʃ] *nf* telegram; (*diplomatique*) dispatch. ● **dépêcher** *vt* to dispatch ∥ **se dépêcher** *vpr* to hurry (up).

dépeigner [depeɲe] *vt* **d. qn** to make s.o.'s hair untidy. ● **dépeigné, -ée** *a* **être d.** to have untidy hair; **sortir d.** to go out with untidy hair.

dépeindre* [depɛ̃dr] *vt* to depict, describe.

dépenaillé, -ée [depənaje] *a* in tatters *ou* rags.

dépendant, -ante [depɑ̃dɑ̃, -ɑ̃t] dependent (de on). ● **dépendance** *nf* dependence; **sous la d. de qn** under s.o.'s domination. ● **dépendances** *nfpl* (*bâtiments*) outbuildings.

dépendre [depɑ̃dr] **1** *vi* to depend (de on, upon); **d. de** (*appartenir à*) to belong to; (*être soumis à*) to be dependent on; **ça dépend de toi** that depends on you, that's up to you. **2** *vt* (*décrocher*) to take down.

dépens [depɑ̃] *nmpl* **aux d. de** at the expense of; **apprendre à ses d.** to learn to one's cost.

dépense [depɑ̃s] *nf* (*frais*) expense, expenditure (*no pl*); (*d'électricité etc*) consumption; (*physique*) exertion; (*action*) spending; **faire** *ou* **engager des dépenses** to incur expenses, spend money. ● **dépenser** *vt* (*argent*) to spend; (*électricité etc*) to use; (*forces*) to exert; (*énergie*) to expend ∥ **se dépenser** *vpr* to exert oneself.

dépensier, -ière [depɑ̃sje, -jɛr] *a* wasteful, extravagant.

déperdition [deperdisjɔ̃] *nf* (*de chaleur etc*) loss.

dépérir [deperir] *vi* (*personne*) to waste away; (*plante*) to wither; (*santé etc*) to decline. ● **dépérissement** *nm* (*baisse*) decline.

dépêtrer (se) [sadepetre] *vpr* *Fam* to extricate oneself (de from).

dépeupler [depœple] *vt* to depopulate. ● **dépeuplement** [-əmɑ̃] *nm* depopulation.

dépilatoire [depilatwar] *nm* hair-remover.

dépister [depiste] *vt* (*criminel etc*) to track down; (*maladie*) to detect. ● **dépistage** *nm* (*de maladie*) detection.

dépit [depi] *nm* resentment, pique, chagrin; **en d. de** in spite of; **en d. du bon sens** (*mal*) atrociously; **par d.** out of pique.

dépiter [depite] *vt* to vex, pique, chagrin ∥ **se dépiter** *vpr* to feel resentment *ou* pique *ou* chagrin. ● **dépité, -ée** *a* vexed, miffed.

déplacement [deplasmɑ̃] *nm* (*voyage*) (business *ou* professional) trip; (*d'ouragan, de troupes*) movement; **être en d.** (*homme d'affaires etc*) to be travelling (around); **frais de d.** *Br* travelling *ou Am* traveling expenses.

déplacer [deplase] *vt* (*vase, meuble etc*) to shift, move; (*fonctionnaire*) to transfer ∥ **se déplacer** *vpr* (*aiguille d'une montre etc*) to move; (*personne, animal etc*) to move (about); (*marcher*) to walk (around); (*voyager*) to travel (around *ou* about), get about. ● **déplacé, -ée** *a* (*mal à propos*) out of place; **personne déplacée** (*réfugié*) displaced person.

déplaire* [depler] *vi* **d. à qn** to displease s.o.; **ça me déplaît** I don't like it; **cet aliment lui déplaît** he *ou* she dislikes this food; **il se déplaît à Paris** he doesn't like it in Paris; **n'en déplaise à** *Iron* with all due respect to ∥ *v imp* **il me déplaît de faire** I dislike doing, it displeases me to do. ● **déplaisant, -ante** *a* unpleasant, displeasing. ● **déplaisir** nm displeasure.

déplantoir [deplɑ̃twar] nm (garden) trowel.

déplier [deplije] vt to open out, unfold. ● **dépliant** nm (prospectus) leaflet.

déplorer [deplɔre] vt (regretter) to deplore; (la mort de qn) to mourn (over), lament (over); **d. que** (+ sub) to deplore the fact that, regret that. ● **déplorable** a regrettable, deplorable, lamentable.

déployer [deplwaje] vt (ailes) to spread; (journal, carte etc) to unfold, spread (out); (courage, énergie etc) to display; (troupes) to deploy ▮ **se déployer** vpr (drapeau) to unfurl. ● **déploiement** nm (démonstration) display; (d'une armée) deployment.

dépoli, -ie [depɔli] a verre d. frosted glass.

déporter [depɔrte] vt 1 (dévier) to carry ou veer (off course). 2 (exiler) Hist to deport (to a penal colony); (dans un camp de concentration) Hist to send to a concentration camp, deport. ● **déporté, -ée** nmf Hist deportee; (concentration camp) inmate. ● **déportation** nf Hist deportation; internment (in a concentration camp).

déposer [depoze] vt (poser) to put down; (laisser) to leave; (argent, lie) to deposit; (plainte) to lodge; (ordures) to dump; (marque de fabrique) to register; (armes) to lay down; (gerbe) to lay; (projet de loi) to introduce; (souverain) to depose; **d. qn** (en voiture) to drop s.o. (off), put s.o. off; **d. une lettre à la poste/boîte** to drop a letter in the post/in the box, mail a letter; **d. de l'argent sur un compte** to deposit money in an account; **d. son bilan** (entreprise) to go into liquidation, file for bankruptcy.

▮ vi Jur to testify; (liquide) to leave a deposit.

▮ **se déposer** vpr (poussière, lie) to settle.

dépositaire [depoziter] nmf (vendeur) agent; (de secret) custodian.

déposition [depozisjɔ̃] nf (au tribunal etc) statement; (de souverain) deposing.

déposséder [deposede] vt to deprive, dispossess (de of).

dépôt [depo] nm (de vin) deposit, sediment; (à la banque) deposit; (d'autobus, de trains) depot; (entrepôt) warehouse; (prison) jail; **d.** (calcaire) (de chaudière etc) deposit; **d. d'une gerbe** the laying of a wreath; **d. d'ordures** Br rubbish ou Am garbage dump; **d.-vente** (pour vêtements) = secondhand clothes shop; **laisser qch à qn en d.** to give s.o. sth for safekeeping ou in trust.

dépotoir [depotwar] nm Br rubbish dump, Am garbage dump; **classe d.** = class for children without scholastic ability.

dépouille [depuj] nf (d'un animal) hide, skin; (de serpent) slough; **les dépouilles** (butin) the spoils; **d. (mortelle)** (d'un défunt) mortal remains.

dépouiller [depuje] vt (animal) to skin, flay; (analyser) to go through, analyse (results etc); **d. de** (déposséder) to deprive of; (dé-

garnir) to strip of; **se d. de** to rid ou divest oneself of, cast off; **d. un scrutin** to count votes. ● **dépouillé, -ée** a (arbre) bare; (style) austere, spare; **d. de** bereft of. ● **dépouillement** nm (de document etc) analysis; (privation) deprivation; (sobriété) austerity; **d. du scrutin** counting of the votes.

dépourvu, -ue [depurvy] a **d. de** devoid of; **prendre qn au d.** to catch s.o. unawares ou off his ou her guard.

dépraver [deprave] vt to deprave. ● **dépravé, -ée** a depraved. ● **dépravation** nf depravity.

déprécier [depresje] vt (monnaie, immeuble etc) to depreciate; (dénigrer) to disparage ▮ **se déprécier** vpr (baisser) to depreciate, lose (its) value. ● **dépréciation** nf depreciation.

déprédations [depredɑsjɔ̃] nfpl damage, ravages.

dépression [depresjɔ̃] nf (sur le sol) & Psy depression; **zone de d.** trough of low pressure; **d. (nerveuse)** nervous breakdown; **faire de la d.** to be suffering from depression, be in a state of depression; **d. économique** slump. ● **dépressif, -ive** a depressive.

déprime [deprim] nf **la d.** (dépression) Fam the blues, depression. ● **déprimer** vt to depress. ● **déprimé, -ée** a depressed.

depuis [dəpɥi] prép since; **d. lundi/1990** since Monday/1990; **d. qu'elle est partie** since she left; **j'habite ici d. un mois** I've been living here for a month; **d. quand êtes-vous là?, d. combien de temps êtes-vous là?** how long have you been here?; **d. Paris jusqu'à Londres** from Paris to London; **d. peu/longtemps** for a short/long time; **je le connais d. toujours** I've known him all my life; **d. des siècles** Fam for ages; **d. le temps que je le connais!** I've known him for ages! ▮ adv since (then), ever since.

députation [depytasjɔ̃] nf (groupe) deputation, delegation; **candidat à la d.** parliamentary candidate. ● **député** nm delegate, deputy; (à l'Assemblée nationale) deputy, = Br MP, = Am congressman, congresswoman.

déraciner [derasine] vt (arbre, Fig personne etc) to uproot; (préjugés etc) to eradicate, root out. ● **déracinement** nm uprooting; (de préjugés etc) eradication.

dérailler [deraje] vi 1 (train) to jump the rails, be derailed; **faire d.** to derail. 2 (divaguer) Fam to talk drivel, talk through one's hat. ● **déraillement** nm (de train) derailment. ● **dérailleur** nm (de bicyclette) derailleur (gear change).

déraisonnable [derezɔnabl] a unreasonable. ● **déraisonner** vi to talk nonsense.

déranger [derɑ̃ʒe] vt (affaires) to disturb, upset; (projets) to mess up, upset; (vêtements) to mess up; **d. qn** to disturb ou bother ou trouble s.o.; **je viendrai si ça ne te dérange pas** I'll come if that won't put you out ou if that isn't imposing; **ça vous dérange si je fume?** do you mind if I smoke?; **avoir l'estomac dérangé** to have an upset sto-

mach; **il a l'esprit dérangé** he's deranged.
∎ **se déranger** *vpr* to put oneself to a lot of
trouble (**pour faire** to do); (*se déplacer*) to
move; **ne te dérange pas!** don't bother!,
don't trouble yourself! ●**dérangement** *nm*
(*gêne*) bother, inconvenience; **excusez-moi
pour le d.** I'm sorry to disturb *ou* bother *ou*
trouble you; **ça vaut le d.** (*musée etc*) it's
well worth the trouble (going), it's well
worth it; **en d.** (*téléphone etc*) out of order.

déraper [derape] *vi* (*véhicule*) to skid;
(*personne*) *Fam* to slip. ●**dérapage** *nm* skid;
(*des prix, de l'inflation*) *Fig* loss of control
(**de** over).

dératé [derate] *nm* **courir comme un d.** to
run like mad.

dérèglement [dereglǝmɑ̃] *nm* (*de mécanisme
etc*) breakdown; (*d'esprit*) disorder; (*d'estomac*) upset.

dérégler [deregle] *vt* (*télévision, mécanisme*)
to put out of order; (*estomac, habitudes*) to
upset; (*esprit*) to unsettle ∎ **se dérégler** *vpr*
(*montre, appareil*) to go wrong. ●**déréglé,
-ée** *a* (*appareil*) out of order; (*vie, mœurs*)
dissolute, wild.

dérider [deride] *vt*, **se dérider** *vpr* to cheer
up.

dérision [derizjɔ̃] *nf* derision, mockery;
tourner en d. to mock, deride; **par d.** deris-
ively; **rires de d.** derisive laughter. ●**dérisoire** *a* ridiculous, derisory.

dérivatif [derivatif] *nm* distraction (**à** from).

dérive [deriv] *nf* (*en bateau*) drift; **partir à la
d.** (*navire*) to drift out to sea; **aller à la d.**
(*navire*) to go adrift; (*entreprise etc*) *Fig* to
drift (**towards** ruin).

dériver [derive] *vi* (*bateau*) to drift; **d. de**
(*venir*) to derive from, be derived from ∎ *vt*
(*cours d'eau*) to divert; **d. un mot du latin/**
etc to derive a word from Latin/*etc*. ●**dérivé** *nm* (*mot, substance chimique*) derivative; (*produit*) by-product. ●**dérivation** *nf*
(*de cours d'eau*) diversion; (*de mot*) derivation; (*déviation*) bypass.

dermatologie [dermatɔlɔʒi] *nf* dermatology.

dernier, -ière [dernje, -jɛr] *a* last; (*nouvelles,
mode*) latest; (*étage*) top; (*degré*) highest; **le
d. rang** the back *ou* last row; **hôtel de d.
ordre** third-rate hotel; **ces derniers mois**
these past few months, these last *ou* final
months; **les dix dernières minutes** the last *ou*
final ten minutes; **de la dernière importance**
of (the) utmost importance; **en d.** last.
∎ *nmf* last (person *ou* one); **ce d.** (*de deux*)
the latter; (*de plusieurs*) the last-mentioned;
être le d. de la classe to be (at the) bottom
of the class; **le d. des derniers** the lowest of
the low; **le d. de mes soucis** the least of my
worries; **avoir le d. mot** to have the last *ou*
final word. ●**dernier-né, dernière-née** *nmf*
youngest (child). ●**dernièrement** *adv* recently.

dérobade [derɔbad] *nf* dodge, evasion.

dérober [derɔbe] *vt* (*voler*) to steal (**à** from);
(*cacher*) to hide (**à** from) ∎ **se dérober** *vpr* to

get out of one's obligations; (*s'esquiver*) to
slip away; (*éviter de répondre*) to dodge the
issue; **se d. à** (*obligations*) to shirk, get out
of; **se d. aux regards** to hide from view,
escape notice; **ses jambes se sont dérobées
sous lui** his legs gave way beneath him.
●**dérobé, -ée** *a* (*porte etc*) hidden, secret; **à
la dérobée** (*adv*) on the sly, stealthily.

dérogation [derɔgasjɔ̃] *nf* exemption,
(special) dispensation.

déroger [derɔʒe] *vi* **d. à une règle/**etc to depart from a rule/*etc*.

dérouiller [deruje] *vt* **d. qn** (*battre*) *Fam* to
thrash *ou* thump s.o.; **se d. les jambes** *Fam*
to stretch one's legs.

dérouler [derule] *vt* (*tapis etc*) to unroll; (*fil*)
to unwind ∎ **se dérouler** *vpr* (*événement*) to
take place; (*paysage, souvenirs*) to unfold;
(*récit*) to develop. ●**déroulement** *nm* (*d'une
action*) unfolding, development; (*cours*)
course.

déroute [derut] *nf* (*d'une armée*) rout.

dérouter [derute] *vt* (*avion, navire*) to divert, reroute; (*candidat etc*)˙ to baffle;
(*poursuivant*) to throw off the scent.

derrick [derik] *nm* oil rig, derrick.

derrière [derjɛr] *prép & adv* behind; **d. moi**
behind me, *Am* in back of me; **assis d.** (*dans
une voiture*) sitting in the back; **par d.** (*attaquer*) from behind, from the rear ∎ *nm* (*de
maison etc*) back, rear; (*fesses*) behind,
bottom; **patte de d.** hind leg; **roue de d.** back
ou rear wheel.

des [de] = **de** + **les** (*voir* de[1,2,3] & **le**).

dès [de] *prép* from; **d. le début** (right) from
the start; **d. cette époque** (as) from that
time, from that time on *ou* forward; **d.
maintenant** from now on; **d. son enfance**
since *ou* from (his *ou* her) childhood; **d. le
sixième siècle** as early as *ou* as far back as
the sixth century; **d. l'aube** at (the crack of)
dawn; **d. qu'elle viendra** as soon as she
comes.

désabusé, -ée [dezabyze] *a* disillusioned,
disenchanted.

désaccord [dezakɔr] *nm* disagreement; **être
en d. avec qn** to be at odds with s.o., be in
disagreement with s.o. ●**désaccordé, -ée** *a*
(*violon etc*) out of tune.

désaccoutumer (se) [sǝdezakutyme] *vpr* **se
d. de qch/de faire qch** to lose the habit of
sth/of doing sth.

désaffecté, -ée [dezafɛkte] *a* (*gare etc*) disused.

désaffection [dezafɛksjɔ̃] *nf* loss of affection, disaffection (**pour** for).

désagréable [dezagreabl] *a* unpleasant, disagreeable. ●**désagréablement** [-ǝmɑ̃] *adv*
unpleasantly.

désagréger [dezagreʒe] *vt*, **se désagréger**
vpr to disintegrate, break up. ●**désagréga-
tion** *nf* disintegration.

désagrément [dezagremɑ̃] *nm* annoyance,
trouble.

désaltérer [dezaltere] *vt* **d. qn** to quench

s.o.'s thirst █ se **désaltérer** *vpr* to quench one's thirst. ●**désaltérant, -ante** *a* thirst-quenching.

désamorcer [dezamɔrse] *vt* (*obus,* *Fig conflit etc*) to defuse.

désappointer [dezapwɛte] *vt* to disappoint.

désapprouver [dezapruve] *vt* to disapprove of █ *vi* to disapprove. ●**désapprobateur, -trice** *a* disapproving. ●**désapprobation** *nf* disapproval.

désarçonner [dezarsɔne] *vt* (*jockey*) to throw, unseat; (*déconcerter*) *Fig* to confound, nonplus, throw.

désarmer [dezarme] *vt* (*soldat, nation etc*) to disarm; **d. qn** (*franchise, attitude etc*) to disarm s.o. █ *vi* (*pays*) to disarm; (*céder*) to let up. ●**désarmant, -ante** *a* (*charme etc*) disarming. ●**désarmé, -ée** *a* (*sans défense*) unarmed; *Fig* helpless. ●**désarmement** *nm* (*de nation*) disarmament.

désarroi [dezarwa] *nm* (*angoisse*) distress; **être en plein d.** to be in a state of utter distress.

désarticulé, -ée [dezartikyle] *a* (*pantin, clown*) double-jointed.

désastre [dezastr] *nm* disaster. ●**désastreux, -euse** *a* disastrous.

désavantage [dezavɑ̃taʒ] *nm* (*inconvénient*) drawback, disadvantage; (*gêne*) disadvantage, handicap. ●**désavantager** *vt* to put at a disadvantage, handicap. ●**désavantageux, -euse** *a* disadvantageous.

désaveu, -x [dezavø] *nm* repudiation.

désavouer [dezavwe] *vt* (*livre, personne etc*) to disown, repudiate █ se **désavouer** *vpr* to retract.

désaxé, -ée [dezakse] *a & nmf* unbalanced (person).

desceller [desele] *vt* (*pierre etc*) to loosen █ se **desceller** *vpr* to come loose.

descendant, -ante [desɑ̃dɑ̃, -ɑ̃t] **1** *a* descending; **marée descendante** outgoing tide. **2** *nmf* (*personne*) descendant. ●**descendance** *nf* (*enfants*) descendants; (*origine*) descent.

descendre [desɑ̃dr] *vi* (*aux être*) to come *ou* go down, descend (**de from**); (*d'un train etc*) to get off *ou* out, alight (**de from**); (*d'un arbre*) to climb down (**de from**); (*nuit, thermomètre*) to fall; (*marée*) to go out; **d. à l'hôtel** to put up at a hotel; **d. chez un ami** to stay with a friend; **d. de** (*être issu de*) to be descended from; **d. de cheval** to dismount; **d. en courant/flânant/**etc to run/stroll/*etc* down; **elle est descendue bien bas** she has stooped very low.

█ *vt* (*aux avoir*) (*escalier*) to come *ou* go down, descend; (*objet*) to bring *ou* take down; (*avion*) to bring *ou* shoot down; **d. qn** (*tuer*) *Fam* to bump s.o. off.

descente [desɑ̃t] *nf* (*d'avion*) descent; (*en parachute*) drop; (*pente*) slope; (*de police*) raid (**dans** upon); **il fut accueilli à sa d. d'avion** he was met as he got off the plane; **d. à skis** downhill run; **d. de lit** (*tapis*) bed-

side rug.

descriptif, -ive [dɛskriptif, -iv] *a* descriptive. ●**description** *nf* description.

déségrégation [desegregasjɔ̃] *nf* desegregation.

désemparé, -ée [dezɑ̃pare] *a* (*personne*) at a total loss, all adrift, distraught; (*navire*) crippled.

désemplir [dezɑ̃plir] *vi* **ce magasin/**etc **ne désemplit pas** this shop/*etc* is always crowded *ou* is never empty.

désenchanter [dezɑ̃ʃɑ̃te] *vt* to disenchant. ●**désenchantement** *nm* disenchantment.

désencombrer [dezɑ̃kɔ̃bre] *vt* (*passage etc*) to clear.

désenfler [dezɑ̃fle] *vi* (*genou, cheville etc*) to go down, become less swollen.

déséquilibre [dezekilibr] *nm* (*inégalité, disproportion*) imbalance; (*mental*) unbalance; **en d.** (*meuble etc*) unsteady. ●**déséquilibrer** *vt* to throw off balance; (*esprit, personne*) *Fig* to unbalance.

désert, -erte [dezɛr, -ɛrt] *a* deserted; **île déserte** desert island █ *nm* desert, wilderness. ●**désertique** *a* **région/**etc **d.** desert region/*etc*.

déserter [dezɛrte] *vti* to desert. ●**déserteur** *nm* (*soldat*) deserter. ●**désertion** *nf* desertion.

désespérer [dezɛspere] *vi* to despair (**de of**) █ *vt* to drive to despair █ se **désespérer** *vpr* to (be in) despair. ●**désespérant, -ante** *a* (*enfant etc*) that drives one to despair, hopeless. ●**désespéré, -ée** *a* (*personne*) in despair, despairing; (*cas, situation*) desperate, hopeless; (*efforts, cris*) desperate █ *nmf* (*suicidé*) person driven to despair *ou* desperation. ●**désespérément** *adv* desperately.

désespoir [dezɛspwar] *nm* despair; **au d.** in despair; **en d. de cause** in desperation, as a (desperate) last resort.

déshabiller [dezabije] *vt* to undress, strip █ se **déshabiller** *vpr* to get undressed, undress.

déshabituer [dezabitɥe] *vt* **d. qn de** to break s.o. of the habit of.

désherber [dezɛrbe] *vti* to weed. ●**désherbant** *nm* weed killer.

déshériter [dezerite] *vt* to disinherit. ●**déshérité, -ée** *a* (*pauvre*) underprivileged; (*dépourvu de dons naturels, laid*) ill-favoured.

déshonneur [dezɔnœr] *nm* dishonour, disgrace.

déshonorer [dezɔnɔre] *vt* to disgrace, dishonour. ●**déshonorant, -ante** *a* dishonourable.

déshydrater [dezidrate] *vt* to dehydrate █ se **déshydrater** *vpr* to become dehydrated.

désigner [dezine] *vt* (*montrer*) to point to, point out; (*choisir*) to appoint, designate; (*signifier*) to indicate, designate; **il est tout désigné pour ce travail** he's just the person for the job. ●**désignation** *nf* designation.

désillusion [dezilyzjɔ̃] *nf* disillusion(ment). ●**désillusionner** *vt* to disillusion.

désinence [dezinɑ̃s] *nf* *Grammaire* ending.

désinfecter [dezɛ̃fɛkte] vt to disinfect. ● **désinfectant, -ante** nm & a disinfectant. ● **désinfection** nf disinfection.

désinformation [dezɛ̃fɔrmɑsjɔ̃] nf (dans la presse) disinformation, misinformation.

désintégrer (se) [sədezɛ̃tegre] vpr to disintegrate. ● **désintégration** nf disintegration.

désintéresser (se) [sədezɛ̃terese] vpr se d. de to lose interest in, take no further interest in. ● **désintéressé, -ée** a (altruiste) disinterested. ● **désintéressement** [-ɛsmɑ̃] nm (altruisme) disinterestedness. ● **désintérêt** nm lack of interest.

désintoxiquer [dezɛ̃tɔksike] vt (alcoolique, drogué) to treat for alcoholism ou drug abuse; **se faire d.** to follow treatment for alcoholism ou drug abuse.

désinvolte [dezɛ̃vɔlt] a (dégagé) easy-going, casual; (insolent) offhand, casual. ● **désinvolture** nf casualness; (insolence) offhandedness.

désir [dezir] nm desire, wish; **prendre ses désirs pour des réalités** to indulge in wishful thinking. ● **désirable** a desirable. ● **désirer** vt to want, desire; (convoiter) to desire; **je désire venir** I would like to come, I wish ou want to come; **je désire que tu viennes** I want you to come; **ça laisse à d.** it leaves something ou a lot to be desired.

désireux, -euse [deziɾø, -øz] a d. de faire qch anxious ou eager to do sth.

désister (se) [sədeziste] vpr (candidat etc) to withdraw. ● **désistement** nm withdrawal.

désobéir [dezɔbeir] vi to disobey; **d. à qn** to disobey s.o. ● **désobéissant, -ante** a disobedient. ● **désobéissance** nf disobedience (à to).

désobligeant, -ante [dezɔbliʒɑ̃, -ɑ̃t] a disagreeable, unkind.

désodorisant [dezɔdɔrizɑ̃] nm air freshener.

désœuvré, -ée [dezœvre] a idle, unoccupied. ● **désœuvrement** [-əmɑ̃] nm idleness.

désoler [dezɔle] vt to distress, upset (very much). ● **se désoler** vpr to be distressed ou upset (de at). ● **désolant, -ante** a distressing, upsetting. ● **désolé, -ée** a (région) desolate; (affligé) distressed; **être d.** (navré) to be sorry (que (+ sub) that, de faire to do). ● **désolation** nf (peine) distress, grief.

désolidariser (se) [sədesɔlidarize] vpr to dissociate oneself (de from).

désopilant, -ante [dezɔpilɑ̃, -ɑ̃t] a hilarious, screamingly funny.

désordonné, -ée [dezɔrdɔne] a (personne, chambre) untidy, messy.

désordre [dezɔrdr] nm (de papiers, affaires, idées) mess, muddle, disorder; (dans une classe) disturbance; (de cheveux, pièce) untidiness; **en d.** untidy, messy; **de graves désordres** (émeutes) serious disturbances ou unrest.

désorganiser [dezɔrganize] vt to disorganize. ● **désorganisé, -ée** a (dans son travail etc) disorganized. ● **désorganisation** nf disorganisation.

désorienter [dezɔrjɑ̃te] vt **d. qn** Br to disorientate ou Am disorient s.o., make s.o. lose his ou her bearings; (déconcerter) to bewilder s.o. ● **désorientation** nf disorientation.

désormais [dezɔrmɛ] adv from now on, in future, henceforth.

désosser [dezose] vt (viande) to bone.

despote [dɛspɔt] nm tyrant, despot. ● **despotique** a tyrannical, despotic. ● **despotisme** nm tyranny, despotism.

desquels, desquelles [dekɛl] voir **lequel**.

dessaisir (se) [sədesezir] vpr se **d. de qch** to part with sth, relinquish sth.

dessaler [desale] vt (poisson etc) to remove the salt from (by smoking).

dessécher [desefe] vt (végétation) to dry up, wither; (bouche, gorge) to parch, dry; (fruits) to desiccate, dry; (cœur) Fig to harden; **une vieille femme toute desséchée** a wizened ou withered old woman **I se dessécher** vpr (plante) to wither, dry up; (peau) to dry (up), get dry.

dessein [desɛ̃] nm aim, design; **dans le d. de faire qch** with the aim of doing sth; **à d.** intentionally.

desserrer [desere] vt (ceinture etc) to loosen, slacken; (poing) to open, unclench; (frein) to release; **il n'a pas desserré les dents** he didn't open his mouth **I se desserrer** vpr to come loose.

dessert [desɛr] nm dessert, Br sweet.

desserte [desɛrt] nf **assurer la d. de** (village etc) to provide a (bus ou train) service to.

desservir [desɛrvir] vt **1** (table) to clear (away). **2 d. qn** to harm s.o., do s.o. a disservice. **3 le car/etc dessert ce village** the bus/etc provides a service to ou stops at this village; **ce quartier est bien desservi** this district is well served by public transport.

dessin [desɛ̃] nm drawing; (rapide) sketch; (motif) design, pattern; (contour) outline; **d. animé** (film) cartoon; **d. humoristique** (dans un journal) cartoon; **école de d.** art school; **planche à d.** drawing board.

dessinateur, -trice [desinatœr, -tris] nmf drawer, sketcher; **d. humoristique** cartoonist; **d. de modes** dress designer; **d. industriel** Br draughtsman, Am draftsman.

dessiner [desine] vt to draw; (rapidement) to sketch; (meuble, robe etc) to design; (indiquer) to outline, trace; **d. (bien) la taille** (vêtement) to show off the figure **I se dessiner** vpr (colline etc) to stand out, be outlined; (projet) to take shape.

dessoûler [desule] vti Fam to sober up.

dessous [dəsu] adv under(neath), beneath, below; **en d.** (sous) under(neath); **par-d.** (passer) under(neath); **agir en d.** to act in an underhand way; **rire en d.** to laugh furtively; **être au-d. de tout** to be utterly dreadful (in one's work, behaviour etc).

I nm underside, underneath; **des d.** (vêtements) underclothes; **drap de d.** bottom sheet; **vêtement de d.** undergarment; **d. de table** bribe, Br backhander; **les gens du d.**

the people downstairs *ou* below; **avoir le d.** to get the worst of it. ● **dessous-de-plat** *nm inv* table mat.

dessus [dəsy] *adv* (*marcher, écrire*) on it; (*monter*) on top (of it), on it; (*lancer, passer*) over it; **de d. la table** off *ou* from the table; **par-d.** (*sauter etc*) over (it); **par-d. tout** above all.

I *nm* top; (*de chaussure*) upper; **drap de d.** top sheet; **vêtement de d.** outer garment; **avoir le d.** to have the upper hand, get the best of it; **reprendre le d.** (*se remettre*) to get back into one's stride; **les gens du d.** the people upstairs *ou* above. ● **dessus-de-lit** *nm inv* bedspread.

déstabiliser [destabilize] *vt* to destabilize.

destin [dɛstɛ̃] *nm* fate, destiny; **c'est le d.!** it's fate!, it was meant to be! ● **destinée** *nf* fate, destiny (*of an individual*).

destinataire [dɛstinatɛr] *nmf* addressee.

destination [dɛstinasjɔ̃] *nf* **1** (*lieu*) destination; **à d. de** (*train etc*) (going) to, (bound) for; **arriver à d.** to reach one's destination. **2** (*usage*) purpose.

destiner [dɛstine] *vt* **d. qch à qn** to intend *ou* mean sth for s.o.; **d. qn à** (*carrière, fonction*) to intend *ou* destine s.o. for; **se d. à** (*carrière etc*) to intend *ou* mean to take up; **destiné à mourir/etc** (*condamné*) destined *ou* fated to die/etc.

destituer [dɛstitɥe] *vt* (*fonctionnaire etc*) to dismiss (from office). ● **destitution** *nf* dismissal.

destructeur, -trice [dɛstryktœr, -tris] *a* destructive **I** *nmf* (*personne*) destroyer. ● **destructif, -ive** *a* destructive.

destruction [dɛstryksjɔ̃] *nf* destruction.

désuet, -ète [desɥɛ, -ɛt] *a* obsolete, antiquated. ● **désuétude** *nf* **tomber en d.** (*expression etc*) to become obsolete.

désunir [dezynir] *vt* (*famille etc*) to divide, disunite. ● **désunion** *nf* disunity, dissension.

détachant [detaʃɑ̃] *nm* stain remover.

détachement [detaʃmɑ̃] *nm* **1** (*indifférence*) detachment. **2** (*de fonctionnaire*) (temporary) transfer; (*de troupes*) detachment.

détacher¹ [detaʃe] *vt* (*ceinture, vêtement*) to undo; (*mains, personne*) to untie; (*ôter*) to take off, detach; (*mots*) to pronounce clearly; **d. qn** (*libérer*) to untie s.o., let s.o. loose; (*affecter*) to transfer s.o. (on assignment) (**à** to); **d. les yeux de qn/qch** to take one's eyes off s.o./sth; **'détachez en suivant les pointillés'** 'tear off along the dotted line'.

I se détacher *vpr* (*chien, prisonnier*) to break loose; (*se dénouer*) to come undone; **se d. (de qch)** (*fragment*) to come off (sth); **se d. de ses amis/etc** to break away from one's friends/etc; **se d. (sur)** (*ressortir*) to stand out (against). ● **détaché, -ée** *a* **1** (*nœud*) loose, undone. **2** (*air, ton etc*) detached.

détacher² [detaʃe] *vt* (*linge etc*) to remove the spots *ou* stains from.

détail [detaj] *nm* **1** detail; **en d.** in detail; en-

trer dans les détails to go into detail; **le d. de** (*dépenses etc*) a breakdown *ou* detailing of. **2 magasin/prix de d.** retail store/price; **vendre au d.** to sell retail; (*par petites quantités*) to sell separately; **faire le d.** (*magasin*) to retail to the public.

détaillant [detajɑ̃] *nm* retailer.

détailler [detaje] *vt* **1** (*énumérer*) to detail. **2** (*vendre*) to sell in small quantities *ou* separately; (*au détail*) to (sell) retail. ● **détaillé, -ée** *a* (*récit, facture etc*) detailed.

détaler [detale] *vi Fam* to run off.

détartrer [detartre] *vt* (*chaudière, dents etc*) to scale.

détaxer [detakse] *vt* (*denrée etc*) to reduce the tax on; (*supprimer*) to take the tax off; **produit détaxé** duty-free article.

détecter [detɛkte] *vt* to detect. ● **détecteur** *nm* (*appareil*) detector; **d. de fumée** smoke detector. ● **détection** *nf* detection.

détective [detɛktiv] *nm* **d. (privé)** (private) detective.

déteindre* [detɛ̃dr] *vi* (*couleur ou étoffe au lavage*) to run; (*au soleil*) to fade; **ton tablier bleu a déteint sur ma chemise** the blue of your apron has come off on(to) my shirt; **d. sur qn** (*influencer*) to leave one's mark on s.o.

dételer [dɛtle] *vt* (*chevaux*) to unhitch, unharness.

détendre [detɑ̃dr] *vt* (*arc etc*) to slacken, relax; (*atmosphère*) to ease; **d. qn** to relax s.o. **I se détendre** *vpr* (*arc etc*) to slacken, get slack; (*atmosphère*) to ease; (*se reposer*) to relax; (*rapports*) to become less strained. ● **détendu, -ue** *a* (*visage, atmosphère*) relaxed; (*ressort, câble*) slack.

détenir* [det(ə)nir] *vt* (*record, pouvoir, titre etc*) to hold; (*secret, objet volé*) to be in possession of; (*prisonnier*) to hold, detain. ● **détenu, -ue** *nmf* prisoner. ● **détenteur, -trice** *nmf* (*de record etc*) holder. ● **détention** *nf* (*d'armes*) possession; (*captivité*) detention; **placer qn en d. préventive** *Br* to remand s.o. in custody, imprison s.o. (*while awaiting trial*).

détente [detɑ̃t] *nf* **1** (*repos*) relaxation; (*d'arc*) slackening; (*de relations*) easing of tension, (*entre deux pays*) détente; (*saut*) leap, spring. **2** (*gâchette*) trigger.

détergent [detɛrʒɑ̃] *nm* detergent.

détériorer [deterjɔre] *vt* (*abîmer*) to damage **I se détériorer** *vpr* (*empirer*) to deteriorate. ● **détérioration** *nf* damage (**de** to); (*d'une situation etc*) deterioration (**de** in).

détermination [detɛrminasjɔ̃] *nf* (*fermeté*) determination; (*résolution*) resolve.

déterminer [detɛrmine] *vt* (*préciser*) to determine; (*causer*) to bring about; **d. qn à faire qch** to induce s.o. to do sth, make s.o. (decide) to do sth; **se d. à faire qch** to resolve *ou* determine to do sth. ● **déterminant, -ante** *a* (*motif*) deciding, determining; (*rôle*) decisive **I** *nm Grammaire* determiner. ● **déterminé, -ée** *a* (*précis*) specific; (*résolu*) détermined.

déterrer [detere] *vt* to dig up, unearth.

détester [detɛste] *vt* to hate, detest; **d. faire** to hate doing *ou* to do, detest doing. ● **détestable** *a* awful, dreadful, foul.

détonateur [detɔnatœr] *nm* detonator. ● **détonation** *nf* explosion, blast.

détonner [detɔne] *vi* (*contraster*) to jar, be out of place.

détour [detur] *nm* (*crochet*) detour; (*de route etc*) bend, curve; **sans d.** (*parler*) without beating around *ou* about the bush; **faire des détours** (*route*) to wind.

détourner [deturne] *vt* (*dévier*) to divert (*river, procession etc*); (*tête*) to turn (away); (*avion*) to hijack; (*conversation, sens*) to change; (*fonds*) to embezzle, misappropriate; (*coups*) to ward off; **d. qn de** (*son devoir, ses amis*) to take *ou* turn s.o. away from; (*sa route*) to lead s.o. away from; (*projet*) to talk s.o. out of; **d. les yeux** to look away, Litt avert one's eyes.

▮ se détourner *vpr* to turn aside *ou* away; **se d. de** (*chemin*) to wander *ou* stray from. ● **détourné, -ée** *a* (*chemin, moyen*) roundabout, indirect. ● **détournement** *nm* (*de cours d'eau*) diversion; (*d'avion*) hijack(ing); **d. (de fonds)** embezzlement; **d. de mineur** seduction of a minor; (*enlèvement*) abduction of a minor.

détracteur, -trice [detraktœr, -tris] *nmf* detractor.

détraquer [detrake] *vt* (*mécanisme etc*) to break, put out of order **▮ se détraquer** *vpr* (*machine*) to go wrong; **se d. l'estomac** to upset one's stomach; **se d. la santé** to ruin one's health. ● **détraqué, -ée** *a* (*appareil etc*) out of order; (*cerveau*) deranged **▮** *nmf* (*obsédé*) sex maniac.

détremper [detrɑ̃pe] *vt* to soak, saturate; **des terres détrempées** waterlogged *ou* saturated ground.

détresse [detrɛs] *nf* distress; **en d.** (*navire, âme*) in distress; **dans la d.** (*misère*) in (great) distress.

détriment de (au) [odetrimɑ̃də] *prép* to the detriment of.

détritus [detritys] *nmpl* Br rubbish, Am garbage.

détroit [detrwa] *nm* (*bras de mer*) strait(s), sound.

détromper [detrɔ̃pe] *vt* **d. qn** to undeceive s.o., put s.o. right **▮ se détromper** *vpr* **détrompez-vous!** don't you believe it!

détrôner [detrone] *vt* (*souverain*) to dethrone; (*supplanter*) to supersede, oust.

détrousser [detruse] *vt* (*voyageur etc*) Litt to rob.

détruire* [detrɥir] *vt* (*ravager, tuer*) to destroy; (*santé etc*) to ruin, wreck, destroy.

dette [dɛt] *nf* debt; **avoir des dettes** to be in debt; **faire des dettes** to run into *ou* get into debt.

DEUG [dœg] *nm abrév* (*diplôme d'études universitaires générales*) degree taken after two

years' study at university.

deuil [dœj] *nm* (*affliction, vêtements*) mourning; (*mort de qn*) bereavement; **être en d., porter le d.** to be in mourning.

deux [dø] *a & nm* two; **d. fois** twice, two times; **mes d. sœurs** both my sisters, my two sisters; **tous (les) d.** both; **en moins de d.** Fam in no time (at all). ● **deux-pièces** *nm inv* (*maillot de bain*) bikini; (*appartement*) two-roomed Br flat *ou* Am apartment. ● **deux-points** *nm inv* (*ponctuation*) colon. ● **deux-roues** *nm inv* two-wheeled vehicle. ● **deux-temps** *nm inv* (*moteur*) two-stroke *ou* Am two-cycle (engine).

deuxième [døzjɛm] *a & nmf* second. ● **deuxièmement** *adv* secondly.

dévaler [devale] *vt* (*escalier etc*) to race *ou* hurtle *ou* rush down **▮** *vi* (*tomber*) to tumble down, come tumbling down.

dévaliser [devalize] *vt* (*personne, banque etc*) to rob; (*maison*) to clean out, strip of everything.

dévaloriser [devalɔrize] **1** *vt* (*diplôme etc*) to reduce in value, devalue; (*contribution etc*) to play down the value of, devalue **▮ se dévaloriser** *vpr* (*diplômes*) to become devalued. **2** *vt* (*humilier etc*) to devalue, disparage. ● **dévalorisation** *nf* (*de diplôme etc*) loss of value.

dévaluer [devalɥe] *vt* (*monnaie, théorie*) to devalue. ● **dévaluation** *nf* devaluation.

devancer [dəvɑ̃se] *vt* to get *ou* be ahead of; (*question etc*) to anticipate, forestall; (*surpasser*) to outstrip; **tu m'as devancé** (*action*) you did it before me; (*lieu*) you got there before me.

devancier, -ière [dəvɑ̃sje, -jɛr] *nmf* predecessor.

devant [dəvɑ̃] *prép & adv* in front (of); **d.** (*l'hôtel/etc*) in front (of the hotel/*etc*); **passer d.** (*l'église/etc*) to go past (the church/*etc*); **marcher d.** (*qn*) to walk in front (of s.o.) *ou* ahead (of s.o.); **assis d.** (*dans une voiture*) sitting in the front; **par d.** from *ou* at the front; **loin d.** a long way ahead *ou* in front; **d. le danger** (*confronté à*) in the face of danger; **d. mes yeux/la loi** before my eyes/ the law; **l'avenir est d. toi** the future is ahead of you.

▮ *nm* front; **roue/porte de d.** front wheel/ door; **patte de d.** foreleg; **aller au-d. des désirs de qn** to anticipate s.o.'s desires; **prendre les devants** (*action*) to take the initiative.

devanture [dəvɑ̃tyr] *nf* (*vitrine*) shop window; (*façade*) shop front.

dévaster [devaste] *vt* to ruin, devastate. ● **dévastation** *nf* devastation.

déveine [devɛn] *nf* Fam tough *ou* bad luck.

développer [devlɔpe] *vt* (*muscles, idées, commerce etc*) to develop; (*photo*) to develop, process **▮ se développer** *vpr* to develop. ● **développement** *nm* development; (*d'une photo*) developing, processing; **les pays en voie de d.** the developing countries.

devenir* [dəvnir] vi (aux être) to become; (vieux, difficile etc) to get, become, grow; (rouge, bleu etc) to turn, go, become; **d. un papillon/un homme/**etc to grow into a butterfly/a man/etc; **d. médecin** to become a doctor; **qu'est-il devenu?** what has become of him ou it?; (en cherchant) where has he ou it got to?; **qu'est-ce que tu deviens?** Fam how are you doing?

dévergonder (se) [sədevɛrgɔ̃de] vpr to fall into dissolute ways. ● **dévergondé, -ée** a dissolute, licentious, shameless.

déverser [devɛrse] vt (liquide, rancune) to pour out; (bombes, ordures) to dump ▮ **se déverser** vpr (liquide) to empty, pour out (dans into).

dévêtir [devetir] vt, **se dévêtir** vpr Litt to undress.

dévier [devje] vt (circulation, conversation) to divert; (coup, rayons) to deflect ▮ vi (de ses principes etc) to deviate (de from); (de sa route) to veer (off course). ● **déviation** nf (chemin) bypass; (itinéraire provisoire) Br diversion, Am detour; (de circulation) deviation; (de coup etc) deflection.

devin [dəvɛ̃] nm soothsayer; **je ne suis pas d.** Fam I can't predict what will happen.

deviner [dəvine] vt to guess (que that); (avenir) to predict; (apercevoir) to make out; **d. (le jeu de) qn** to see through s.o. ● **devinette** nf riddle.

devis [dəvi] nm estimate (of cost of work to be done).

dévisager [deviza̧ʒe] vt **d. qn** to stare at s.o.

devise [dəviz] nf (légende) motto; (monnaie) currency; **devises (étrangères)** foreign currency; **d. forte/faible** strong/weak currency.

dévisser [devise] vt to unscrew, undo ▮ **se dévisser** vpr (se desserrer) to come loose; (bouchon) to unscrew.

dévoiler [devwale] vt (secret etc) to disclose; (statue) to unveil ▮ **se dévoiler** vpr (mystère) to come to light.

devoir*1 [dəvwar] v aux 1 (nécessité) **je dois refuser** I must refuse, I have (got) to refuse; **j'ai dû refuser** I had to refuse.

2 (forte probabilité) **il doit être tard** it must be late; **elle a dû oublier** she must have forgotten; **il ne doit pas être bête** he can't be stupid; **cela devait arriver** it had to happen.

3 (obligation) **tu dois apprendre tes leçons** you must learn your lessons; **vous devriez rester** you should stay, you ought to stay; **il aurait dû venir** he should have come, he ought to have come.

4 (événement prévu) **elle doit venir** she's supposed to be coming, she's due to come, she should be coming; **le train devait arriver à midi** the train was due (to arrive) at noon; **je devais le voir** I was (due) to see him.

devoir*2 [dəvwar] 1 vt to owe; **d. de l'argent/100 francs à qn** to owe s.o. money/100 francs, owe money/100 francs to s.o.; **l'argent qui m'est dû** the money due to ou owing to me, the money owed (to) me; **se d.**

à sa famille/etc to have to devote oneself to one's family/etc; **comme il se doit** as is proper.

2 nm (obligation) duty; **présenter ses devoirs à qn** to pay one's respects to s.o.; **devoir(s)** (exercice(s) à faire à la maison) homework; **d. sur table** class exam(ination); **faire ses devoirs** to do one's homework.

dévolu, -ue [devɔly] 1 nm **jeter son d. sur qch/qn** to set one's heart on sth/s.o. 2 a **d. à qn** (pouvoirs, tâche) vested in s.o., allotted to s.o.

dévorer [devɔre] vt (manger) to eat up, gobble up, devour; (incendie) to engulf, devour; (tourmenter, lire) to devour; **d. qn/qch du regard** to eye s.o./sth. ● **dévorant, -ante** a (faim) ravenous; (passion) devouring.

dévot, -ote [devo, -ɔt] a & nmf devout ou pious (person). ● **dévotion** nf devotion.

dévouer (se) [sədevwe] vpr (à une tâche) to dedicate oneself, devote oneself (à to); **se d. (pour qn)** (se sacrifier) to sacrifice oneself (for s.o.). ● **dévoué, -ée** a (ami, femme etc) devoted (à qn to s.o.); (soldat, domestique etc) dedicated. ● **dévouement** [-umã] nm devotion, dedication; (de héros) devotion to duty.

dévoyé, -ée [devwaje] a & nmf delinquent.

dextérité [dɛksterite] nf dexterity, skill.

diabète [djabɛt] nm (maladie) diabetes. ● **diabétique** a & nmf diabetic.

diable [djɑbl] nm (diable); **le d.** the Devil; **habiter au d.** to live miles from anywhere; **faire qch à la d.** to do something anyhow; **se débattre comme un beau d.** to struggle with all one's might; **tirer le d. par la queue** to live from hand to mouth; **il fait un vent de tous les diables** there's the devil of a wind; **c'est bien le d. si...** I'll be damned if...; **quel d., cet enfant!** what a little devil that child is!; **d.!** heavens!; **où/pourquoi d.?** where/why the devil? ● **diabolique** a diabolical, devilish.

diabolo [djabɔlo] nm **d. menthe** (boisson) lemonade ou Am lemon soda flavoured with mint syrup.

diacre [djakr] nm (ecclésiastique) deacon.

diadème [djadɛm] nm (bijou féminin) tiara.

diagnostic [djagnɔstik] nm diagnosis. ● **diagnostiquer** vt to diagnose.

diagonal, -e, -aux [djagɔnal, -o] a diagonal. ● **diagonale** nf diagonal (line); **en d.** diagonally; **lire qch en d.** to skim through sth.

diagramme [djagram] nm (schéma) diagram; (courbe) graph.

dialecte [djalɛkt] nm dialect.

dialogue [djalɔg] nm conversation; (de film, pièce de théâtre etc) & Pol etc Br dialogue, Am dialog. ● **dialoguer** vi to have a conversation; (négocier) Pol etc to hold a Br dialogue ou Am dialog.

dialyse [djaliz] nf Méd dialysis.

diamant [djamã] nm diamond.

diamètre [djametr] nm diameter. ● **diamétralement** adv **d. opposés** (avis etc) diametrically opposed, poles apart.

diapason [djapazɔ̃] nm (pour la musique) tuning fork; **être/se mettre au d. de** (en harmonie) Fig to be/get in tune with.

diaphragme [djafragm] nm diaphragm.

diapositive, Fam **diapo** [djapozitiv, djapo] nf (colour) slide, transparency.

diarrhée [djare] nf diarrh(o)ea.

diatribe [djatrib] nf diatribe.

dictateur [diktatœr] nm dictator. ● **dictatorial, -e, -aux** a dictatorial. ● **dictature** nf dictatorship; **alors, c'est la d.!** Fam this is absolute tyranny!

dicter [dikte] vt to dictate (à to). ● **dictée** nf dictation; **prendre une lettre/etc sous la d.** to take down a letter/etc (that has been dictated). ● **dictaphone**® nm dictaphone®.

diction [diksjɔ̃] nf diction, elocution.

dictionnaire [diksjɔnɛr] nm dictionary.

dicton [diktɔ̃] nm saying, adage, dictum.

didactique [didaktik] a didactic.

dièse [djɛz] a & nm Mus sharp.

diesel [djezɛl] a & nm (moteur) d. diesel (engine).

diète [djɛt] nf (jeûne) starvation diet; (régime) (strict) diet; **mettre qn à la d.** to put s.o. on a starvation diet ou on a (strict) diet. ● **diététicien, -ienne** [djetetisjɛ̃, -jɛn] nmf dietician. ● **diététique** nf dietetics **∎** a **aliment** ou **produit d.** health food; **magasin/restaurant/etc d.** health-food shop/restaurant/etc.

dieu, -x [djø] nm god; **D.** God; **le bon D.** God, the Lord God; **on lui donnerait le bon D. sans confession** butter wouldn't melt in his mouth; **D. seul le sait!** God only knows!; **D. merci!** thank God!, thank goodness!; **laisse-moi tranquille, bon D.!** Fam leave me alone, for God's sake!

diffamation [difamasjɔ̃] nf defamation; (en paroles) slander; (par écrit) libel; **campagne de d.** smear campaign; **procès en d.** action for slander; (pour un écrit) action for libel. ● **diffamatoire** a (paroles) slanderous; (écrit) libellous.

diffamer [difame] vt (en paroles) to slander; (par écrit) to libel.

différé [difere] nm **en d.** (émission) (pre)recorded.

différence [diferɑ̃s] nf difference (de in); **à la d. de** unlike; **faire la d. entre** to make a distinction between.

différencier [diferɑ̃sje] vt to differentiate (de from) **∎** se **différencier** vpr to differ (de from).

différend [diferɑ̃] nm difference (of opinion).

différent, -ente [diferɑ̃, -ɑ̃t] a different; **différents** (divers) different, various; **d. de** different from ou to, unlike; **au cours de mes différents voyages** during my different ou various trips. ● **différemment** [-amɑ̃] adv differently (de from, to).

différentiel, -ielle [diferɑ̃sjɛl] a differential.

différer [difere] **1** vi to differ (de from). **2** vt (remettre) to postpone, defer.

difficile [difisil] a difficult; (exigeant) fussy,

hard ou difficult to please; **c'est d. à faire** it's hard ou difficult to do; **il (nous) est d. de faire ça** it's hard ou difficult (for us) to do that. ● **difficilement** adv with difficulty; **d. lisible** not easy to read.

difficulté [difikylte] nf difficulty (à faire in doing); **en d.** in a difficult situation.

difforme [difɔrm] a deformed, misshapen. ● **difformité** nf deformity.

diffus, -use [dify, -yz] a (lumière, style) diffuse.

diffuser [difyze] vt (émission, nouvelle etc) to broadcast; (lumière, chaleur) to diffuse; (livre) to distribute. ● **diffusion** nf broadcasting; (de connaissances, de lumière etc) diffusion; (de livre) distribution.

digérer [diʒere] vt to digest; (endurer) Fam to stomach **∎** vi to digest; **avoir du mal à d.** to have trouble digesting. ● **digeste** ou **digestible** a digestible.

digestif, -ive [diʒɛstif, -iv] a (tube, sucs etc) digestive **∎** nmf after-dinner liqueur.

digestion [diʒɛstjɔ̃] nf digestion.

digitale [diʒital] af **empreinte d.** fingerprint.

digne [diɲ] a (méritant) worthy; (air, attitude etc) dignified; **d. de qn** worthy of s.o.; **d. d'admiration/etc** worthy of ou deserving of admiration/etc; **il n'est pas d. d'exister** he's not fit to live; **d. de foi** reliable. ● **dignement** [-əmɑ̃] adv with dignity.

dignitaire [diɲitɛr] nm dignitary.

dignité [diɲite] nf dignity; **manquer de d.** to have no self-respect.

digression [digresjɔ̃] nf digression.

digue [dig] nf dike, dyke; (en bord de mer) sea wall.

dilapider [dilapide] vt to squander, waste.

dilater [dilate] vt, se **dilater** vpr to expand, dilate. ● **dilatation** nf expansion, dilation.

dilatoire [dilatwar] a **manœuvre** ou **moyen d.** delaying tactic.

dilemme [dilɛm] nm dilemma.

dilettante [diletɑ̃t] nmf Péj dabbler, amateur; **faire qch en d.** to dabble in sth.

diligence [diliʒɑ̃s] nf **1** (rapidité) speedy efficiency. **2** (véhicule) Hist stagecoach.

diligent, -ente [diliʒɑ̃, -ɑ̃t] a (prompt) speedy and efficient; (soin) diligent.

diluer [dilɥe] vt (liquide, substance) to dilute (dans in). ● **dilution** nf dilution.

diluvienne [dilyvjɛn] af **pluie d.** torrential rain.

dimanche [dimɑ̃ʃ] nm Sunday.

dimension [dimɑ̃sjɔ̃] nf (mesure) dimension; (taille) size; **à deux dimensions** two-dimensional; **pièces de même d.** rooms of the same size.

diminuer [diminɥe] vt to reduce, decrease; (frais) to cut down (on), reduce; (forces physiques, mérite) to diminish, lessen, reduce; **d. qn** (rabaisser) to diminish s.o., lessen s.o.; **il est très diminué depuis l'accident** he has been far less able-bodied since the accident.

∎ vi (réserves, nombre) to decrease, diminish; (*jours*) to get shorter, draw in; (*prix, profits*) to decrease, drop. ● **diminution** *nf* reduction, decrease (**de** in).

diminutif, -ive [diminytif, -iv] *a & nm* Grammaire diminutive ▮ *nm* (*prénom*) nickname.

dinde [dɛ̃d] *nf* turkey (hen); (*viande*) turkey. ● **dindon** *nm* turkey (cock); **être le d. de la farce** (*victime*) to be the fall guy.

dîner [dine] *vi* to have dinner, dine; (*au Canada, en Belgique etc*) to (have) lunch ▮ *nm* dinner; lunch; (*soirée*) dinner party. ● **dîneur, -euse** *nmf* diner.

dînette [dinɛt] *nf* (*jouet*) doll's dinner service *ou* set; (*jeu*) doll's dinner party.

dingue [dɛ̃g] *a Fam* crazy, nuts, screwy ▮ *nmf Fam* nutcase.

dinosaure [dinozɔr] *nm* dinosaur.

diocèse [djɔsɛz] *nm* (*évêché*) diocese.

diphtérie [difteri] *nf* diphtheria.

diphtongue [diftɔ̃g] *nf* (*en phonétique*) diphthong.

diplomate [diplɔmat] *nmf* (*ambassadeur etc*) diplomat; (*négociateur habile*) diplomatist ▮ *a* (*habile, plein de tact*) diplomatic. ● **diplomatie** [-asi] *nf* (*tact*) & Pol diplomacy; (*carrière*) diplomatic service. ● **diplomatique** *a* Pol diplomatic.

diplôme [diplom] *nm* certificate, diploma; (*d'université*) degree. ● **diplômé, -ée** *a & nmf* qualified (person); **être d. (de)** Univ to be a graduate (of).

dire* [dir] *vt* (*mot, avis etc*) to say; (*vérité, secret, heure etc*) to tell; (*penser*) to think (**de** of, about); **d. des bêtises** to talk nonsense; **d. qch à qn** to tell s.o. sth, say sth to s.o.; **d. à qn que** to tell s.o. that, say to s.o. that; **d. à qn de faire qch** to tell s.o. to do sth; **d. que oui/non** to say yes/no; **d. du mal/du bien de** to speak ill/well of; **elle dit que tu mens** she says (that) you're lying; **on dirait un château** it looks like a castle; **on dirait du Mozart** it sounds like Mozart; **on dirait du cabillaud** it tastes like cod; **que diriez-vous d'un verre de vin?** what would you say to a glass of wine?; **on dirait que** it would seem that; **dit-il** he said; **dit-on** they say; **ça ne me dit rien** (*envie*) I don't feel like *ou* Br fancy that; (*souvenir*) it doesn't ring a bell; **ça ne me dit rien qui vaille** it doesn't sound good to me; **dites donc!** look here!, Br Vieilli I say!; **autrement dit** in other words; **ceci dit** having said this; **à vrai d.** to tell the truth; **à l'heure dite** at the agreed time; **ça ne se dit pas** that's not said; **ça vous dit de rester?** do you feel like staying?; **ça va sans d.** that goes without saying; **c'est beaucoup d.** that's going too far; **il se dit malade/etc** he says he's ill/etc; **comment ça se dit en anglais?** how do you say that in English?

▮ *nm* **au d. de** according to; **les dires de** (*déclarations*) the statements of.

direct, -e [dirɛkt] *a* direct; (*chemin*) straight, direct; (*manière*) straightforward, direct; **train d.** fast train, Br through train; **être en**

rapport d. avec qn/qch to be in direct contact with s.o./sth ▮ *nm* **en d.** (*émission*) live; **un d. du gauche** Boxe a straight left. ● **directement** [-əmɑ̃] *adv* directly; (*immédiatement*) straight (away), directly.

directeur, -trice [dirɛktœr, -tris] *nmf* director; (*d'entreprise*) manager(ess), director; (*de journal*) editor; (*d'école*) Br headmaster, Am principal ▮ *a* (*principe*) guiding; **idées** *ou* **lignes directrices** guidelines.

direction [dirɛksjɔ̃] *nf* **1** (*sens*) direction; **en d. de** (*train*) (going) to, for. **2** (*de société, club*) running, management; (*d'études*) supervision; (*sur une voiture*) steering; **avoir la d. de** to be in charge of; **prendre la d. de** (*parti etc*) to take charge of; **sous la d. de** (*orchestre*) conducted by; **la d.** (*équipe dirigeante*) the management; **un poste de d.** a management post; **la d. du personnel** the personnel department.

directive [dirɛktiv] *nf* directive, instruction.

dirigeable [diriʒabl] *a & nm* (*ballon*) d. airship, dirigible.

dirigeant, -ante [diriʒɑ̃, -ɑ̃t] *a* (*classe*) ruling ▮ *nm* (*de pays*) leader; (*d'entreprise, club*) manager.

diriger [diriʒe] *vt* (*société, club*) to run, manage, direct; (*parti, groupe, débat, cheval*) to lead; (*véhicule*) to steer; (*orchestre*) to conduct; (*études*) to supervise, direct; (*conscience*) to guide; (*orienter*) to turn (**vers** towards); (*arme, lumière*) to point, direct (**vers** towards); **se d. vers** (*lieu, objet*) to make one's way towards, head *ou* make for; (*dans une carrière*) to turn towards. ● **dirigé, -ée** *a* (*économie*) planned.

dirigisme [diriʒism] *nm* **d. (économique)** state control.

dis, disant [di, dizɑ̃] *voir* dire.

discerner [disɛrne] *vt* (*voir*) to make out, discern; (*différencier*) to distinguish. ● **discernement** [-əmɑ̃] *nm* discernment, discrimination.

disciple [disipl] *nm* disciple, follower.

discipline [disiplin] *nf* (*règle, matière*) discipline. ● **disciplinaire** *a* disciplinary.

discipliner [discipline] *vt* (*contrôler, éduquer*) to discipline ▮ **se discipliner** *vpr* to discipline oneself. ● **discipliné, -ée** *a* well-disciplined.

discontinu, -ue [diskɔ̃tiny] *a* (*ligne*) discontinuous; (*bruit etc*) intermittent. ● **discontinuer** *vi* **sans d.** without stopping.

disconvenir* [diskɔ̃vnir] *vi* **je n'en disconviens pas** I don't deny it.

discorde [diskɔrd] *nf* discord. ● **discordance** *nf* (*de caractères*) clash, conflict; (*de son*) discord. ● **discordant, -ante** *a* (*son*) discordant; (*témoignages*) conflicting; (*couleurs*) clashing.

discothèque [diskɔtɛk] *nf* record library; (*club*) discotheque, disco; **aller en d.** to go to a disco *ou* discotheque.

discours [diskur] *nm* speech; (*écrit littéraire*) discourse; **tenir de longs d. à qn sur qch** to go on and on to s.o. about sth. ● **discourir** *vi* (*longuement*) to hold forth, ramble on.

discourtois, -oise [diskurtwa, -waz] *a* discourteous.

discrédit [diskredi] *nm* disrepute, discredit; **jeter le d. sur qn** to bring s.o. into disrepute.

discréditer [diskredite] *vt* to discredit, bring into disrepute ▮ **se discréditer** *vpr* (*personne*) to become discredited.

discret, -ète [diskre, -εt] *a* (*personne, manière etc*) discreet; (*vêtement*) simple. ● **discrètement** *adv* discreetly; (*s'habiller*) simply.

discrétion [diskresjɔ̃] *nf* discretion; **vin/etc à d.** as much wine/etc as one wants; **laisser qch à la d. de qn** to leave sth to s.o.'s discretion. ● **discrétionnaire** *a* discretionary.

discrimination [diskriminɑsjɔ̃] *nf* (*ségrégation*) discrimination. ● **discriminatoire** *a* discriminatory.

disculper [diskylpe] *vt* to exonerate (*de* from).

discussion [diskysjɔ̃] *nf* discussion; (*conversation*) talk; (*querelle*) argument; **pas de d.!** no argument!

discutable [diskytabl] *a* arguable, debatable.

discuter [diskyte] *vt* to discuss, (*familièrement*) to talk over; (*contester*) to question; **ça peut se d., ça se discute** that's arguable ▮ *vi* (*parler*) to talk (**de** about, **avec** with); (*répliquer*) to argue; **d. de** *ou* **sur qch** to discuss sth. ● **discuté, -ée** *a* (*auteur*) much discussed *ou* debated; (*théorie, question*) disputed, controversial.

dise, disent [diz] *voir* **dire.**

disette [dizεt] *nf* food shortage.

diseuse [dizøz] *nf* **d. de bonne aventure** fortune-teller.

disgrâce [disgrɑs] *nf* disgrace, disfavour. ● **disgracier** *vt* to disgrace.

disgracieux, -euse [disgrasjø, -øz] *a* ungainly.

disjoindre* [disʒwεdr] *vt* (*questions*) to treat separately. ● **disjoint, -ointe** *a* (*questions*) unconnected, separate.

disjoncter [disʒɔ̃kte] *vi* (*compteur etc*) to cut out; (*s'effondrer*) *Fam* to crack up, have a breakdown.

disjoncteur [disʒɔ̃ktœr] *nm* (*interrupteur*) circuit breaker.

dislocation [dislɔkɑsjɔ̃] *nf* (*de membre*) dislocation.

disloquer [dislɔke] *vt* (*membre*) to dislocate; (*meuble, machine*) to break ▮ **se disloquer** *vpr* (*meuble etc*) to fall apart; (*cortège*) to break up; **se d. le bras** to dislocate one's arm.

disons [dizɔ̃] *voir* **dire.**

disparaître* [disparεtr] *vi* to disappear; (*être porté manquant*) to go missing; (*mourir*) to die; (*coutume etc*) to die out, disappear; **d. en mer** to be lost at sea; **faire d.** to remove, get rid of. ● **disparu, -ue** *a* (*soldat etc*) missing, lost; **être porté d.** to be reported missing. ▮ *nmf* (*absent*) missing person; (*mort*) departed. ● **disparition** *nf* dis-

appearance; (*mort*) death; **espèce en voie de d.** endangered species.

disparate [disparat] *a* ill-assorted.

disparité [disparite] *nf* disparity (**entre, de** between).

dispendieux, -euse [dispɑ̃djø, -øz] *a* expensive, costly.

dispensaire [dispɑ̃sεr] *nm* community health centre.

dispense [dispɑ̃s] *nf* exemption; **d. d'âge** waiving of the age limit. ● **dispenser** *vt* (*soins, bienfaits etc*) to dispense; **d. qn de qch** (*obligation*) to exempt *ou* excuse s.o. from sth; **je vous dispense de vos réflexions/** *etc* I can dispense with your comments/*etc*; **se d. de faire qch** to spare oneself the bother of doing sth.

disperser [dispεrse] *vt* (*papiers, foule etc*) to disperse, scatter; (*brouillard*) to break up; (*collection*) to break up; (*efforts*) to dissipate ▮ **se disperser** *vpr* (*foule etc*) to disperse; **elle se disperse trop** she tries to do too many things at once. ● **dispersion** *nf* (*d'une armée, du brouillard etc*) dispersal; (*d'une collection*) break(ing) up.

disponible [dispɔnibl] *a* (*article, personne etc*) available; (*place*) available, spare; (*esprit*) alert. ● **disponibilité** *nf* availability; **disponibilités** (*fonds*) available funds; **être en d.** to be temporarily transferred to other duties *ou* released from one's duties.

dispos [dispo] *am* (*personne*) fit, in fine fettle; **frais et d.** refreshed.

disposé, -ée [dispoze] *a* **bien/mal d.** in a good/bad mood; **bien d. envers** *ou* **à l'égard de** well-disposed towards; **d. à faire qch** prepared *ou* disposed to do sth.

disposer [dispoze] *vt* (*objets*) to arrange; (*troupes*) to dispose; **d. qn à** (*la bonne humeur etc*) to dispose *ou* incline s.o. towards; **se d. à faire qch** to prepare to do sth ▮ *vi* **d. de qch** to have sth at one's disposal; (*utiliser*) to make use of sth; **d. de qn** *Péj* to take advantage of s.o.

dispositif [dispozitif] *nm* (*mécanisme*) device; **d. policier** police presence; **d. de défense** (*de l'armée*) *Br* defence *ou* *Am* defense system; **d. antiparasite** (*de radio*) suppressor.

disposition [dispozisjɔ̃] *nf* arrangement; (*de troupes*) disposition; (*humeur*) frame of mind; (*tendance*) tendency, (pre)disposition (**à** to); (*de maison, page*) layout; (*clause d'un contrat etc*) provision; **dispositions** (*aptitudes*) ability, aptitude (**pour** for); **être** *ou* **rester** *ou* **se tenir à la d. de qn** to be *ou* remain at s.o.'s disposal *ou* service; **prendre ses** *ou* **des dispositions** (*préparatifs*) to make arrangements, prepare; (*pour l'avenir*) to make provision; **dans de bonnes dispositions à l'égard de qn** well-disposed towards s.o.

disproportion [disprɔpɔrsjɔ̃] *nf* disproportion. ● **disproportionné, -ée** *a* disproportionate.

dispute [dispyt] *nf* quarrel. ● **disputer** *vt* (*match*) to play; (*rallye*) to compete in;

(*combat de boxe etc*) to compete in, fight; (*droit etc*) to contest, dispute; **d. qch à qn** (*prix, première place etc*) to fight with s.o. for *ou* over sth, contend with s.o. for sth; **d. le terrain** to fight every inch of the way; **d. qn** (*gronder*) *Fam* to tell s.o. off ▮ **se disputer** *vpr* to quarrel (**avec** with); (*match*) to take place; **se d. qch** to fight over sth.

disqualifier [diskalifje] *vt* (*équipe, athlète etc*) to disqualify ▮ **se disqualifier** *vpr* (*perdre son crédit*) to become discredited. ● **disqualification** *nf* (*d'équipe etc*) disqualification.

disque [disk] *nm* (*de musique*) record; (*cercle*) *Br* disc, *Am* disk; (*d'ordinateur*) disk; *Sport* discus; **d. compact** compact *Br* disc *ou Am* disk. ● **disquaire** *nmf* record dealer. ● **disquette** *nf* (*d'ordinateur*) floppy (disk), diskette.

dissection [disɛksjɔ̃] *nf* dissection.

dissemblable [disɑ̃blabl] *a* dissimilar (à to).

disséminer [disemine] *vt* (*graines, mines etc*) to scatter; (*idées*) *Fig* to disseminate. ● **dissémination** *nf* scattering; (*d'idées*) *Fig* dissemination.

dissension [disɑ̃sjɔ̃] *nf* dissension.

disséquer [diseke] *vt* to dissect.

disserter [diserte] *vi* **d. sur** to comment upon, discuss. ● **dissertation** *nf* (*au lycée etc*) essay.

dissident, -ente [disidɑ̃, -ɑ̃t] *a* & *nmf* dissident. ● **dissidence** *nf* dissidence.

dissimulation [disimylasjɔ̃] *nf* concealment; (*duplicité*) deceit.

dissimuler [disimyle] *vt* (*cacher*) to hide, conceal (**à** from) ▮ *vi* (*feindre*) to pretend ▮ **se dissimuler** *vpr* to hide (oneself), conceal oneself. ● **dissimulé, -ée** *a* (*renfermé, hypocrite*) secretive.

dissipation [disipasjɔ̃] *nf* (*de brouillard*) clearing; (*indiscipline*) misbehaviour; (*débauche*) *Litt* dissipation.

dissiper [disipe] *vt* (*brouillard, malentendu*) to clear up, dispel; (*craintes*) to dispel; (*fortune*) to squander, dissipate; **d. qn** to distract s.o., lead s.o. astray ▮ **se dissiper** *vpr* (*brume*) to clear, lift; (*craintes*) to disappear; (*élève*) to misbehave. ● **dissipé, -ée** *a* (*élève*) unruly; (*vie*) dissipated.

dissocier [disɔsje] *vt* to dissociate (**de** from).

dissolu, -ue [disɔly] *a* (*vie etc*) dissolute.

dissolution [disɔlysjɔ̃] *nf* dissolution.

dissolvant, -ante [disɔlvɑ̃, -ɑ̃t] *a* & *Ch* solvent ▮ *nm* solvent; (*pour vernis à ongles*) nail polish remover.

dissoudre* [disudr] *vt*, **se dissoudre** *vpr* to dissolve.

dissuader [disɥade] *vt* to dissuade, deter (**de qch** from sth, **de faire** from doing). ● **dissuasif, -ive** *a* (*effet*) deterrent; **être d.** to be a deterrent. ● **dissuasion** *nf* dissuasion; **force de d.** (*de l'armée*) deterrent.

distance [distɑ̃s] *nf* distance; **à deux mètres de d.** two metres apart; **à d.** at *ou* from a distance; **garder ses distances** to keep one's

distance (**vis-à-vis de** from); **tenir qn à d.** to keep s.o. at a distance; **commandé à d.** remote-controlled; **à quelle d. se trouve la poste?** how far is it to the post office?

distancer [distɑ̃se] *vt* to leave behind, outstrip.

distant, -ante [distɑ̃, -ɑ̃t] *a* distant; (*personne*) aloof, distant; **d. de dix kilomètres** (*éloigné*) ten kilometres away; (*à intervalles*) ten kilometres apart.

distendre [distɑ̃dr] *vt*, **se distendre** *vpr* to distend.

distiller [distile] *vt* to distil. ● **distillation** *nf* distillation. ● **distillerie** *nf* (*lieu*) distillery.

distinct, -incte [distɛ̃, -ɛ̃kt] *a* (*différent*) distinct, separate (**de** from); (*net*) clear, distinct. ● **distinctement** [-ɔmɑ̃] *adv* distinctly, clearly. ● **distinctif, -ive** *a* distinctive. ● **distinction** *nf* (*différence, raffinement*) distinction.

distinguer [distɛ̃ge] *vt* (*différencier*) to distinguish; (*voir*) to make out; (*choisir*) to single out; **d. le bien du mal** to tell good from evil ▮ **se distinguer** *vpr* (*s'illustrer*) to distinguish oneself; **se d. de** (*différer*) to be distinguishable from; **se d. par sa beauté/etc** to stand out on account of one's beauty/etc, be conspicuous *ou* remarkable for one's beauty/etc. ● **distingué, -ée** *a* (*bien élevé, éminent*) distinguished; **sentiments distingués** (*formule épistolaire de politesse*) *Br* yours faithfully, *Am* sincerely.

distorsion [distɔrsjɔ̃] *nf* (*du corps, d'une image etc*) distortion.

distraction [distraksjɔ̃] *nf* amusement, distraction; (*étourderie*) (fit of) absent-mindedness. ● **distraire*** *vt* (*divertir*) to entertain, amuse; **d. qn (de)** (*détourner*) to distract s.o. (from) ▮ **se distraire** *vpr* to amuse oneself, enjoy oneself. ● **distrait, -aite** *a* absent-minded. ● **distraitement** *adv* absent-mindedly. ● **distrayant, -ante** *a* entertaining.

distribuer [distribɥe] *vt* (*donner*) to hand *ou* give out, distribute; (*courrier*) to deliver; (*cartes*) to deal; (*répartir*) to distribute; (*eau*) to supply; **bien distribué** (*appartement*) well-arranged.

distributeur [distribytœr] *nm* (*sur une voiture, de films etc*) & *Com* distributor; **d.** (*automatique*) vending machine; **d. de billets** (*de train*) ticket machine; (*de billets de banque*) cash machine *ou Br* dispenser.

distribution [distribysjɔ̃] *nf* distribution; (*du courrier*) delivery; (*de l'eau*) supply; (*acteurs de cinéma*) cast; **d. des prix** prize-giving.

district [distrikt] *nm* district.

dit¹, dite [di, dit] *pp de* **dire** ▮ *a* (*convenu*) agreed; (*surnommé*) called.

dit², dites [di, dit] *voir* **dire**.

divaguer [divage] *vi* (*dérailler*) to rave, talk drivel. ● **divagations** *nfpl* ravings.

divan [divɑ̃] *nm* divan, couch.

divergent, -ente [divɛrʒɑ̃, -ɑ̃t] *a* diverging, divergent. ● **divergence** *nf* divergence. ● **diverger** *vi* to diverge (**de** from).

divers, -erse [divɛr, -ɛrs] a (varié) varied, diverse; **divers(es)** (distincts) various; **d. groupes** (plusieurs) various ou sundry groups. ●**diversement** adv in various ways.

diversifier [divɛrsifje] vt to diversify ▮ **se diversifier** vpr (économie, entreprise etc) to diversify.

diversion [divɛrsjɔ̃] nf diversion.

diversité [divɛrsite] nf diversity.

divertir [divɛrtir] vt to entertain, amuse ▮ **se divertir** vpr to enjoy oneself, amuse oneself. ●**divertissement** nm entertainment, amusement.

dividende [dividɑ̃d] nm (bénéfice) & Math dividend.

divin, -ine [divɛ̃, -in] a divine. ●**divinité** nf divinity.

diviser [divize] vt, **se diviser** vpr to divide (en into). ●**divisible** a divisible. ●**division** nf division.

divorce [divɔrs] nm divorce. ●**divorcer** vi to get ou to be divorced, divorce; **d. d'avec qn** to divorce s.o. ●**divorcé, -ée** a divorced (**d'avec** from) ▮ nmf divorcee.

divulguer [divylge] vt to divulge. ●**divulgation** nf divulgence.

dix [dis] ([di] before consonant, [diz] before vowel) a & nm ten. ●**dixième** [dizjɛm] a & nmf tenth; **un d.** a tenth.

dix-huit [dizɥit] a & nm eighteen. ●**dix-huitième** a & nmf eighteenth. ●**dix-neuf** [diznœf] a & nm nineteen. ●**dix-neuvième** a & nmf nineteenth. ●**dix-sept** [disset] a & nm seventeen. ●**dix-septième** a & nmf seventeenth.

dizaine [dizɛn] nf **une d.** (de) about ten.

do [do] nm (note de musique) C.

docile [dɔsil] a submissive, docile. ●**docilité** nf submissiveness, docility.

dock [dɔk] nm (bassin) dock; (magasin) warehouse. ●**docker** [dɔkɛr] nm docker.

docteur [dɔktœr] nm (en médecine, d'université) doctor (**ès, en of**). ●**doctorat** nm doctorate, = PhD (**ès, en in**).

doctrine [dɔktrin] nf doctrine. ●**doctrinaire** a & nmf Péj doctrinaire.

document [dɔkymɑ̃] nm document. ●**documentaire** a documentary ▮ nm (film) documentary. ●**documentaliste** nmf information officer; (à l'école) (school) librarian.

documentation [dɔkymɑ̃tasjɔ̃] nf (documents) documentation, (brochure(s)) literature; (renseignements) information.

documenter [dɔkymɑ̃te] vt (informer) to document ▮ **se documenter** vpr to collect information ou material. ●**documenté, -ée** a (bien ou très) d. (personne) well-informed; **un article/etc solidement d.** a well-documented article/etc.

dodeliner [dɔdline] vi **d. de la tête** to nod (one's head).

dodo [dodo] nm (langage enfantin) **faire d.** to sleep; **aller au d.** Br to go to bye-byes, Am go beddy-bye.

dodu, -ue [dɔdy] a chubby, plump.

dogme [dɔgm] nm dogma. ●**dogmatique** a dogmatic. ●**dogmatisme** nm dogmatism.

dogue [dɔg] nm (chien) mastiff.

doigt [dwa] nm finger; **d. de pied** toe; **petit d.** little finger, Am pinkie; **un d. de vin/etc** a drop of wine/etc; **à deux doigts de** within an ace of; **montrer qn du d.** to point one's finger at s.o.; **savoir qch sur le bout du d.** to have sth at one's finger tips; **elle ne lèvera pas le petit d. pour vous aider** she won't lift a finger to help you; **c'est mon petit d. qui me l'a dit** a little birdie told me.

doigté [dwate] nm Mus fingering, touch; (savoir-faire) tact, expertise.

dois, doit [dwa] voir **devoir**[1,2].

doléances [dɔleɑ̃s] nfpl (plaintes) grievances.

dollar [dɔlar] nm dollar.

domaine [dɔmɛn] nm (terres) estate, domain; (sphère) province, domain.

dôme [dom] nm dome.

domestique [dɔmɛstik] a (vie, marché, produit etc) domestic; **querelle/etc d.** family ou domestic quarrel/etc; **travaux domestiques** housework; **à usage d.** for household ou domestic use; **animal d.** domestic animal, pet ▮ nmf servant. ●**domestiquer** vt to domesticate.

domicile [dɔmisil] nm home; (demeure légale) abode; **travailler à d.** to work at home; **livrer à d.** (pain etc) to deliver (to the house); **dernier d. connu** last known address; **quitter le d. conjugal** to leave the (marital) home. ●**domicilié, -ée** a resident (**à, chez** at).

dominateur, -trice [dɔminatœr, -tris] a domineering. ●**domination** nf domination.

dominer [dɔmine] vt to dominate; (situation, sentiment) to master, dominate; (être supérieur à) to surpass, outclass; (tour, rocher) to tower above, dominate (valley, building etc); **d. le monde** to rule the world. ▮ vi (être le plus fort) to be dominant, dominate; (être le plus important) to predominate. ▮ **se dominer** vpr to control oneself. ●**dominant, -ante** a dominant. ●**dominante** nf dominant feature; Mus dominant.

dominicain, -aine [dɔminikɛ̃, -ɛn] 1 a & nmf Rel Dominican. 2 a Géog Dominican; **la République dominicaine** the Dominican Republic ▮ nmf **D., Dominicaine** Dominican.

dominical, -e, -aux [dɔminikal, -o] a **repos/promenade/etc dominical(e)** Sunday rest/walk/etc.

domino [dɔmino] nm domino; **dominos** (jeu) dominoes.

dommage [dɔmaʒ] nm 1 (c'est) **d.!** it's a pity ou a shame! (que that); **quel d.!** what a pity ou a shame!; **c'est (bien) d. qu'elle ne soit pas venue** it's a (great) pity ou shame she didn't come. 2 (tort) prejudice, harm; **dommages** (dégâts) damage; **dommages-intérêts** (somme due) damages.

dompter [dɔ̃te] vt (animal) to tame; (passions, rebelles) to subdue. ●**dompteur, -euse**

nmf (*de lions*) lion tamer.

DOM-TOM [dɔmtɔm] *nmpl abrév* (*départements et territoires d'outre-mer*) (French) overseas departments and territories.

don [dɔ̃] *nm* (*cadeau, aptitude*) gift; (*charité*) donation; **le d. du sang**/*etc* (the) giving of blood/*etc*; **faire d. de qch** to give sth; **avoir le d. de** (*le chic pour*) to have the knack of.

donateur, -trice [dɔnatœr, -tris] *nmf* (*d'un tableau etc*) donor. ● **donation** *nf* (*d'un tableau etc*) donation.

donc [dɔ̃(k)] *conj* so, then; (*par conséquent*) so, therefore; **asseyez-vous d.!** (*intensif*) will you sit down!, sit down then!; **qui/quoi d.?** who?/what?; **allons d.!** come on!; **dis d.!** *Fam* excuse me!

donjon [dɔ̃ʒɔ̃] *nm* (*de château*) keep.

donne [dɔn] *nf Cartes* deal.

données [dɔne] *nfpl* (*information*) data; (*de problème*) (known) facts; (*d'un roman*) basic elements.

donner [dɔne] *vt* to give; (*récolte, résultat*) to produce; (*sa place*) to give up; (*cartes*) to deal; (*pièce, film*) to put on; **pourriez-vous me d. l'heure?** could you tell me *ou* give me the time?; **d. un coup à** to hit, give a blow to; **d. le bonjour à qn** to say hello to s.o.; **d. qch à réparer** to take sth (in) to be repaired; **d. à manger à qn** to give s.o. something to eat, feed s.o.; **d. à manger à un chat**/*etc* to feed a cat/*etc*; **d. raison à qn** to say s.o. is right; **elle m'a donné de ses nouvelles** she told me how she was *ou* how she was doing; **ça donne soif/faim** it makes you thirsty/ hungry; **je lui donne trente ans** I'd say *ou* guess she *ou* she was thirty; **ça n'a rien donné** (*efforts*) it hasn't got us anywhere; **c'est donné** *Fam* it's dirt cheap; **étant donné** (*la situation etc*) considering, in view of; **étant donné que** seeing (that), considering (that); **à un moment donné** at some stage.

■ *vi* **d. sur** (*fenêtre*) to overlook, look out onto; (*porte*) to open onto; **d. dans** (*piège*) to fall into; **ne plus savoir où d. de la tête** *Fam* not to know which way to turn.

■ **se donner** *vpr* (*se consacrer*) to devote oneself (à to); **se d. du mal** to go to a lot of trouble (**pour faire** to do); **s'en d. à cœur joie** to have a whale of a time, enjoy oneself to the full.

donneur, -euse [dɔnœr, -øz] *nmf* giver; (*de sang, d'organe*) donor; *Cartes* dealer.

dont [dɔ̃] *pron rel* (= *de qui, duquel, de quoi etc*) (*personne*) of whom; (*chose*) of which; (*appartenance: personne*) whose, of whom; (*appartenance: chose*) of which, whose; **une mère d. le fils est malade** a mother whose son is ill; **la fille d. il est fier** the daughter he is proud of *ou* of whom he is proud; **les outils d. j'ai besoin** the tools I need; **la façon d. elle joue** the way (in which) she plays; **cinq enfants d. deux filles** five children two of whom are daughters, five children including two daughters; **voici ce d. il s'agit** here's what it's about.

doper [dɔpe] *vt* (*cheval, sportif*) to dope ■ **se doper** *vpr* to take *ou* use dope. ● **doping** *nm* (*action*) doping; (*substance*) dope.

dorénavant [dɔrenavɑ̃] *adv* henceforth.

dorer [dɔre] *vt* (*objet*) to gild; **d. la pilule à qn** to sugar the pill for s.o.; **se (faire) d. au soleil** to bask in the sun ■ *vi* (*à la cuisson*) to brown. ● **doré, -ée** *a* (*objet*) gilt, gold; (*couleur*) golden ■ *nm* (*couche*) gilt. ● **dorure** *nf* gilding.

dorloter [dɔrlɔte] *vt* to pamper, coddle.

dormir* [dɔrmir] *vi* to sleep; (*être endormi*) to be asleep; (*argent*) *Fig* to lie idle; **avoir envie de d.** to feel sleepy; **dormez tranquille!** (*sans soucis*) set your mind at rest!, rest easy!; **histoire à d. debout** tall story, cock-and-bull story; **eau dormante** stagnant water.

dortoir [dɔrtwar] *nm* dormitory.

dos [do] *nm* (*de personne, d'animal etc*) back; (*de livre*) spine; (*de nez*) bridge; '**voir au d.**' (*verso*) 'see over'; **voir qn de d.** to have a back view of s.o.; **mettre qch sur le d. de qn** (*accusation*) to pin sth on s.o.; **avoir qn sur le d.** to have s.o. on one's back *ou* breathing down one's neck; **j'en ai plein le d.** *Fam* I'm sick of it.

dose [doz] *nf* dose; (*quantité administrée*) dosage; **forcer la d.** (*exagérer*) to overdo it. ● **doser** *vt* (*remède*) to measure out the dose of; (*équilibrer*) to strike the correct balance between. ● **dosage** *nm* measuring out (*of dose*); (*équilibre*) balance; **faire le d. de =** doser. ● **doseur** *nm* **bouchon d.** measuring cap.

dossard [dɔsar] *nm* (*de sportif*) number (*fixed on back*).

dossier [dɔsje] *nm* **1** (*de siège*) back. **2** (*papiers, documents*) file, dossier; (*classeur*) folder, file.

dot [dɔt] *nf* dowry.

doter [dɔte] *vt* (*hôpital etc*) to endow; **d. de** (*matériel*) to equip with; (*qualité*) to endow with. ● **dotation** *nf* (*à un hôpital etc*) endowment; (*en matériel*) equipping.

douane [dwan] *nf* customs; **passer la d.** to go through customs. ● **douanier, -ière** *nm* customs officer ■ *a* **union**/*etc* **douanière** customs union/*etc*.

doublage [dublaʒ] *nm* (*de film*) dubbing.

double [dubl] *a* double; (*rôle, avantage etc*) twofold, double; **en d. exemplaire** in duplicate; **enfermer qn à d. tour** to lock s.o in; **fermer une porte à d. tour** to double-lock a door; **doubles rideaux** lined curtains, *Am* (thick) drapes ■ *adv* double ■ *nm* (*de personne*) double; (*copie*) copy, duplicate; (*de timbre*) swap, duplicate; **le d. (de)** (*quantité*) twice as much (as); **je l'ai en d.** I have two of them. ● **doublement** *adv* doubly ■ *nm* doubling.

doubler [duble] **1** *vt* (*augmenter*) to double; (*vêtement*) to line; (*film*) to dub; (*acteur*) to stand in for; (*classe à l'école*) to repeat; (*cap*) (*en bateau*) to round; **se d. de** to be coupled with ■ *vi* (*augmenter*) to double; **d.**

doublure 102

de volume/*etc* to double in volume/*etc*. **2** *vti* (*en voiture*) *Br* to overtake, pass.

doublure [dublyr] *nf* (*étoffe*) lining; (*au théâtre*) understudy; (*au cinéma*) stand-in, double.

douce [dus] *voir* **doux**. ●**doucement** *adv* (*délicatement*) gently; (*à voix basse*) softly; (*lentement*) slowly; (*sans bruit*) quietly; (*sans à-coups*) smoothly; (*assez bien*) *Fam* so-so. ●**douceur** *nf* (*de miel etc*) sweetness; (*de peau etc*) softness; (*de temps*) mildness; (*de personne*) gentleness; **douceurs** (*sucreries*) *Br* sweets, *Am* candies; **la voiture a démarré en d.** the car started smoothly.

douche [duʃ] *nf* shower; **prendre une d.** to have *ou* take a shower; **être sous la d.** to be in the shower. ●**doucher** *vt* **d. qn** to give s.o. a shower ‖ **se doucher** *vpr* to have *ou* take a shower.

doué, -ée [dwe] *a* gifted, talented (**en** at); (*intelligent*) clever; **d. de raison**/*etc* gifted with reason/*etc*; **il est d. pour** he has a gift *ou* talent for.

douille [duj] *nf* (*d'ampoule électrique*) socket; (*de cartouche*) case.

douillet, -ette [dujɛ, -ɛt] *a* (*lit etc*) soft, snug, *Br* cosy, *Am* cozy; **tu es d.** (*délicat*) you're such a baby.

douleur [dulœr] *nf* (*mal*) pain; (*chagrin*) sorrow, grief. ●**douloureux, -euse** *a* (*maladie, membre, décision, perte etc*) painful.

doute [dut] *nm* doubt; **doutes** (*méfiance*) doubts, misgivings; **sans d.** no doubt, probably; **sans aucun d.** without (any *ou* a) doubt; **mettre qch en d.** to cast doubt on sth; **dans le d.** uncertain, doubtful; **ça ne fait pas de d.** there is no doubt about it.

douter [dute] *vi* to doubt; **d. de qch/qn** to doubt sth/s.o.; **d. que** (+ *sub*) to doubt whether *ou* that; **ne d. de rien** *Fam* to have lots of *ou Br* bags of self-confidence ‖ **se douter** *vpr* **se d. de qch** to suspect sth; **je m'en doute** I would think so, I suspect so.

douteux, -euse [dutø, -øz] *a* doubtful; (*louche, médiocre*) dubious; **il est d. que** (+ *sub*) it's doubtful whether *ou* that.

douve(s) [duv] *nf(pl)* (*de château*) moat.

Douvres [duvr] *nm ou f* Dover.

doux, douce [du, dus] *a* (*miel, son etc*) sweet; (*peau, lumière, drogue etc*) soft; (*temps, climat*) mild; (*personne, pente etc*) gentle; (*émotion, souvenir etc*) pleasant; **d. comme un agneau** as gentle as a lamb; **faire qch en douce** to do sth on the quiet.

douze [duz] *a & nm* twelve. ●**douzaine** *nf* (*douze*) dozen; (*environ*) about twelve; **une d. d'œufs**/*etc* a dozen eggs/*etc*. ●**douzième** *a & nmf* twelfth; **un d.** a twelfth.

doyen, -enne [dwajɛ̃, -ɛn] *nmf* (*d'université, ecclésiastique*) dean; **d. (d'âge)** oldest person.

draconien, -ienne [drakɔnjɛ̃, -jɛn] *a* (*mesures*) drastic.

dragée [draʒe] *nf* sugared almond; **tenir la d. haute à qn** (*tenir tête à qn*) *Fig* to stand up to s.o.

dragon [dragɔ̃] *nm* (*animal*) dragon; (*soldat*) *Hist* dragoon; **c'est un vrai d.** (*personne autoritaire*) *Fam* he's *ou* she's a real dragon.

drague [drag] *nf* (*appareil*) dredge; (*filet*) drag net.

draguer [drage] *vt* **1** (*rivière etc*) to dredge. **2** (*faire du baratin à*) *Fam Br* to chat (*s.o.*) up, *Am* smooth-talk (*s.o.*).

drainer [drene] *vt* to drain.

dramaturge [dramatyrʒ] *nmf* dramatist.

drame [dram] *nm* drama; (*catastrophe*) tragedy. ●**dramatique** *a* dramatic; **critique d.** drama critic; **auteur d.** playwright, dramatist; **film d.** drama. ●**dramatiser** *vt* (*exagérer*) to dramatize.

drap [dra] *nm* (*de lit*) sheet; (*tissu*) cloth; **d. housse** fitted sheet; **d. de bain** bath towel; **être dans de beaux draps** (*dans une situation difficile*) to be in a fine mess.

drapeau, -x [drapo] *nm* flag; **être sous les drapeaux** (*soldat*) to be doing one's military service.

draper [drape] *vt* to drape (**de** with) ‖ **se draper** *vpr* **se d. dans sa dignité** *Fig* to stand on one's dignity. ●**draperie** *nf* (*étoffe*) drapery.

dresser [drese] **1** *vt* (*échelle, statue*) to put up, erect; (*oreille*) to prick up; (*liste*) to draw up, make out; (*piège*) to set, lay ‖ **se dresser** *vpr* (*personne*) to stand up; (*statue, montagne*) to rise up, stand; **se d. contre** (*abus*) to stand up against. **2** *vt* (*animal*) to train; (*personne*) *Péj* to drill, teach. ●**dressage** *nm* training. ●**dresseur, -euse** *nmf* trainer.

dribbler [drible] *vti Football* to dribble.

drogue [drɔg] *nf* (*médicament*) *Péj* drug; **une d.** (*stupéfiant*) a drug; **la d.** drugs, dope. ●**droguer** *vt* (*victime*) to drug; (*malade*) to dose up ‖ **se droguer** *vpr* to take drugs, be on drugs; (*malade*) to dose oneself up. ●**drogué, -ée** *nmf* drug addict.

droguerie [drɔgri] *nf* hardware *Br* shop *ou Am* store. ●**droguiste** *nmf* owner of a *droguerie*.

droit¹ [drwa] *nm* (*privilège*) right; (*d'inscription etc*) fee(s), dues; **le d.** (*science juridique*) law; **d. d'entrée** entrance fee; **droits de douane** (customs) duty, customs duties; **droits de l'homme** human rights; **droits d'auteur** royalties; **à bon d.** rightly; **avoir d. à** to be entitled to; **avoir le d. de faire qch** to be entitled to do sth, have the right to do sth.

droit², droite¹ [drwa, drwat] *a* (*route, ligne etc*) straight; (*vertical*) (*mur etc*) upright, straight; (*angle*) right; (*veston*) single-breasted; (*honnête*) *Fig* upright ‖ *adv* straight; **tout d.** straight *ou* right ahead; **aller d. au but** to get *ou* go straight to the point. ●**droite²** *nf* (*ligne*) straight line.

droit³, droite³ [drwa, drwat] *a* (*côté, bras etc*) right ‖ *nm* (*coup*) *Boxe* right. ●**droite⁴** *nf* **la d.** (*côté*) the right (side); *Pol* the right (wing); **à d.** (*tourner*) (to the) right; (*rouler, se tenir etc*) on the right, on the right(-hand)

103 **dyslexique**

side; **de d.** (*fenêtre etc*) right-hand; (*candidat etc*) right-wing; **mener une politique de d.** to follow right-wing policies; **voter à d.** to vote right-wing; **à d. de** on *ou* to the right of; **à d. et à gauche** (*voyager etc*) here, there and everywhere.

droitier, -ière [drwatje, -jɛr] *a & nmf* right-handed (person).

droiture [drwatyr] *nf* uprightness.

drôle [drol] *a* funny; **d. d'air/de type** funny look/fellow; **faire une d. de tête** to pull a face. ●**drôlement** *adv* funnily; (*extrêmement*) *Fam* terribly, dreadfully.

dromadaire [drɔmadɛr] *nm* dromedary.

dru, drue [dry] *a* (*herbe etc*) thick, dense ▮ *adv* **tomber d.** (*pluie*) to pour down *ou* come down heavily; **pousser d.** to grow thick(ly).

du [dy] = **de + le** (*voir de*[1,2,3] **& le**).

dû, due [dy] *a* **d. à** (*accident etc*) due to; **en bonne et due forme** (*compléter etc*) in due form ▮ *nm* due; (*argent*) dues.

dualité [dɥalite] *nf* duality.

dubitatif, -ive [dybitatif, -iv] *a* (*regard etc*) dubious.

duc [dyk] *nm* duke. ●**duché** *nm* duchy. ●**duchesse** *nf* duchess.

duel [dɥɛl] *nm* duel.

dûment [dymã] *adv* duly.

dune [dyn] *nf* (sand) dune.

duo [dɥo] *nm Mus* duet; **d. comique** comic duo.

dupe [dyp] *nf* dupe, fool ▮ *a* **d. de** duped by, fooled by; **il n'est pas d.** he's no fool, he's well aware of it. ●**duper** *vt* to fool, dupe.

duplex [dyplɛks] *nm Br* split-level flat, *Am* duplex; (*émission en*) **d.** (*de télévision*) link-up.

duplicata [dyplikata] *nm inv* duplicate.

duplicateur [dyplikatœr] *nm* (*machine*) duplicator.

duplicité [dyplisite] *nf* duplicity, deceit.

duquel [dykɛl] *voir* **lequel.**

dur, dure [dyr] *a* (*substance*) hard; (*difficile*) hard, tough; (*viande*) tough; (*hiver, ton*) harsh; (*personne*) hard, harsh; (*œuf*) hard-boiled; (*brosse, carton*) stiff; **d. d'oreille** hard of hearing; **d. à cuire** *Fam* hard-bitten, tough (*travailler*) hard; **croire à qch d. comme fer** to have a cast-iron belief in sth ▮ *nm* (*personne*) *Fam* tough guy. ●**durement** *adv* harshly. ●**dureté** *nf* (*de substance*) hardness; (*d'hiver, de ton*) harshness; (*de viande*) toughness.

durable [dyrabl] *a* durable, lasting.

durant [dyrã] *prép* during; **d. l'hiver/etc** during the winter/etc; **des heures d.** for hours and hours.

durcir [dyrsir] *vti, se durcir vpr* to harden. ●**durcissement** *nm* hardening.

durée [dyre] *nf* (*de film, d'événement etc*) length; (*période*) duration; (*de pile électrique*) life; **de longue d.** (*bonheur etc*) lasting; **chômage de longue d.** long-term unemployment; **disque de longue d.** long-playing record; **pile longue d.** long-life battery; **de courte d.** (*attente etc*) short; (*bonheur etc*) short-lived.

durer [dyre] *vi* to last; **ça dure depuis...** it's been going on for....

durillon [dyrijɔ̃] *nm* callus.

DUT [deyte] *nm abrév* (*diplôme universitaire de technologie*) university technical qualification taken two or three years after the *baccalauréat*.

duvet [dyvɛ] *nm* **1** (*d'oiseau, de visage*) down. **2** (*sac*) sleeping bag. ●**duveté, -ée** *ou* **duveteux, -euse** *a* downy.

dynamique [dinamik] *a* dynamic ▮ *nf* (*force*) dynamic force, thrust. ●**dynamisme** *nm* dynamism.

dynamite [dinamit] *nf* dynamite. ●**dynamiter** *vt* to dynamite.

dynamo [dinamo] *nf* dynamo.

dynastie [dinasti] *nf* dynasty.

dysenterie [disãtri] *nf* (*maladie*) dysentery.

dyslexique [dislɛksik] *a & nmf* dyslexic.

E

E, e [ə, ø] *nm* E, e.

eau, -x [o] *nf* water; **il est tombé beaucoup d'e.** a lot of rain fell; **e. douce** (*non salée*) fresh water; **e. du robinet** tap water; **e. salée** salt water; **e. plate** still water; **e. gazeuse** sparkling *ou* carbonated *ou Br* fizzy water; **e. de Cologne** eau de Cologne; **e. de toilette** toilet water; **grandes eaux** (*d'un parc*) ornamental fountains; **tomber à l'e.** (*projet*) *Fam* to fall through; **ça lui fait venir l'e. à la bouche** it makes his *ou* her mouth water; **tout en e.** sweating; **prendre l'e.** (*bateau, chaussure etc*) to take water, leak; **tu apportes de l'e. à mon moulin** you're strengthening *ou* confirming my argument. ● **eau-de-vie** *nf* (*pl* **eaux-de-vie**) brandy. ● **eau-forte** *nf* (*pl* **eaux-fortes**) (*gravure*) etching.

ébahir [ebair] *vt* to astound, dumbfound, amaze. ● **ébahissement** *nm* amazement.

ébattre (s') [sebatr] *vpr* to run about, play about, frolic. ● **ébats** *nmpl* frolics.

ébauche [eboʃ] *nf* (*esquisse*) (rough) outline, (rough) sketch; (*début*) beginnings; **première e.** rough *ou* first draft. ● **ébaucher** *vt* (*projet, tableau, œuvre*) to sketch out, outline; **e. un sourire** to give a faint smile ‖ **s'ébaucher** *vpr* to take shape.

ébène [eben] *nf* (*bois*) ebony.

ébéniste [ebenist] *nm* cabinet-maker. ● **ébénisterie** *nf* cabinet-making.

éberlué, -ée [eberlɥe] *a Fam* dumbfounded.

éblouir [ebluir] *vt* to dazzle. ● **éblouissement** *nm* (*aveuglement*) dazzling, dazzle; (*émerveillement*) feeling of wonder; (*malaise*) fit of dizziness.

éboueur [ebwœr] *nm Br* dustman, *Am* garbage collector.

ébouillanter [ebujɑ̃te] *vt* to scald ‖ **s'ébouillanter** *vpr* to scald oneself.

ébouler (s') [sebule] *vpr* (*falaise etc*) to crumble; (*terre, roches*) to fall. ● **éboulement** *nm* landslide. ● **éboulis** *nm* (mass of) fallen debris.

ébouriffé, -ée [eburife] *a* dishevelled; **il est tout é.** he looks *ou* his is all dishevelled, his hair is all dishevelled.

ébranler [ebrɑ̃le] *vt* (*mur, confiance etc*) to shake; (*santé*) to weaken, affect; (*personne*) to shake, shatter ‖ **s'ébranler** *vpr* (*train, cortège etc*) to move off. ● **ébranlement** *nm* (*secousse*) shaking, shock; (*nerveux*) shock.

ébrécher [ebreʃe] *vt* (*assiette*) to chip; (*lame*) to nick. ● **ébréchure** *nf* chip; (*de lame*) nick.

ébriété [ebrijete] *nf* **en état d'é.** under the influence of drink.

ébrouer (s') [sebrue] *vpr* (*se secouer*) to shake oneself (about); (*souffler*) to snort.

ébruiter [ebrɥite] *vt* (*nouvelle etc*) to make known, divulge.

ébullition [ebylisjɔ̃] *nf* boiling; **être en é.** (*eau*) to be boiling; (*ville etc*) *Fig* to be in turmoil; **porter à é.** to bring to the boil.

écaille [ekaj] *nf* (*de poisson*) scale; (*de tortue, d'huître*) shell; (*pour lunettes*) tortoise-shell. ● **écailler 1** *vt* (*poisson*) to scale; (*huître*) to shell. **2 s'écailler** *vpr* (*peinture*) to flake (off), peel.

écarlate [ekarlat] *a & nf* scarlet.

écarquiller [ekarkije] *vt* **é. les yeux** to open one's eyes wide.

écart [ekar] *nm* (*intervalle*) gap, distance; (*embardée, mouvement*) swerve; (*différence*) difference (**de** in, **entre** between); **écarts de** (*conduite, langage etc*) lapses in; **faire le grand é.** (*de gymnaste*) to do the splits; **à l'é.** out of the way; **tenir qn à l'é.** (*ne pas gener au courant*) to keep s.o. out of things; **à l'é. de** away from, clear of.

écartelé, -ée [ekartəle] *a* **é. entre** (*tiraillé*) torn between.

écartement [ekartəmɑ̃] *nm* (*espace*) gap, distance (**de** between).

écarter [ekarte] *vt* (*objets*) to move apart, move away from each other; (*jambes*) to open, spread; (*rideaux*) to open, draw (aside); (*crainte, idée*) to brush aside, dismiss; (*carte*) to discard; **é. qch de qch** to move sth away from sth; **é. qn de** (*exclure*) to keep s.o. out of; (*éloigner*) to keep *ou* take s.o. away from.
‖ **s'écarter** *vpr* (*s'éloigner*) to move away (**de** from); (*se séparer*) to move aside (**de** from); **s'é. de** (*sujet, bonne route*) to stray *ou* deviate from. ● **écarté, -ée** *a* (*endroit*) remote; **les jambes écartées** with legs (wide) apart.

ecchymose [ekimoz] *nf* bruise.

ecclésiastique [eklezjastik] *a* ecclesiastical ‖ *nm* ecclesiastic, clergyman.

écervelé, -ée [eservəle] *a* scatterbrained ‖ *nmf* scatterbrain.

échafaud [eʃafo] *nm* (*pour exécution*) scaffold.

échafaudage [eʃafodaʒ] *nm* (*de peintre etc*) scaffolding *inv*, scaffold; (*tas*) heap; (*système*) fabric. ● **échafauder** *vi* to put up (some) scaffolding *ou* a scaffold ‖ *vt* (*projet etc*) to put together, think up.

échalas [eʃala] *nm* **grand é.** tall skinny person.

échalote [eʃalɔt] *nf* shallot, scallion.

échancré, -ée [eʃɑ̃kre] *a* (*encolure*) Vshaped, scooped. ●**échancrure** nf (de robe) opening.

échange [eʃɑ̃ʒ] nm exchange; **en é.** in exchange (**de for**). ●**échanger** vt to exchange (**contre for**).

échangeur [eʃɑ̃ʒœr] nm (intersection) Aut interchange.

échantillon [eʃɑ̃tijɔ̃] nm sample. ●**échantillonnage** nm (collection) range (of samples).

échappatoire [eʃapatwar] nf way out, means of escape, evasion.

échappement [eʃapmɑ̃] nm (de véhicule) **tuyau d'é.** exhaust pipe; **pot d'é.** (tuyau) exhaust; (silencieux) Br silencer, Am muffler.

échapper [eʃape] vi **é. à qn** to escape from s.o.; **é. à la mort/un danger/etc** to escape death/a danger/etc; **son nom m'échappe** his ou her name escapes me; **ça m'a échappé** (je n'ai pas compris) I didn't catch it; **ça lui a échappé (des mains)** it slipped out of his ou her hands; **laisser é.** (cri) to let out; (objet, occasion) to let slip.
█ **s'échapper** vpr (s'enfuir) to escape (**de from**); (s'éclipser) to slip away; (gaz, eau) to escape, come out; (cycliste) to pull ou break away. ●**échappée** nf **1** (de cycliste) breakaway. **2** (vue) vista.

écharde [eʃard] nf (de bois) splinter.

écharpe [eʃarp] nf scarf; (de maire) sash; **avoir le bras en é.** to have one's arm in a sling; **prendre en é.** (de biais) (véhicule) to hit sideways.

écharper [eʃarpe] vt **é. qn** to cut s.o. to bits.

échasse [eʃas] nf (bâton) stilt. ●**échassier** nm wading bird.

échauder [eʃode] vt **être échaudé, se faire é.** (décu) Fig to be taught a lesson.

échauffer [eʃofe] vt (moteur) to overheat; (esprits) to excite █ **s'échauffer** vpr (discussion, sportif) to warm up. ●**échauffement** nm (de moteur) overheating; (de sportif) warm(ing)-up.

échauffourée [eʃofure] nf (bagarre) clash, brawl, skirmish.

échéance [eʃeɑ̃s] nf (date limite) date (due), Br expiry ou Am expiration date; (paiement) payment (due); **à brève/longue é.** (projet, emprunt) short-/long-term; **faire face à ses échéances** to meet one's (regular) payments.

échéant (le cas) [ləkazeʃeɑ̃] adv if the occasion should arise, possibly.

échec [eʃɛk] nm **1** (insuccès) failure; **faire é. à** (inflation etc) to hold in check. **2 les échecs** (jeu) chess; **en é.** in check; **é.!** check!; **é. et mat!** checkmate!

échelle [eʃɛl] nf **1** (marches) ladder; **faire la courte é. à qn** to give s.o. Br a leg up ou Am a boost. **2** (dimension, mesure) scale; **à l'é. nationale/etc** on a national/etc scale.

échelon [eʃlɔ̃] nm (d'échelle) rung; (de fonctionnaire) grade; (dans une organisation) echelon; **à l'é. régional/national** on a regional/national level.

échelonner [eʃlɔne] vt (paiements) to spread out, space out █ **s'échelonner** vpr to be spread out.

écheveau, -x [eʃ(ə)vo] nm (de laine) skein; (d'une intrigue etc) muddle, tangle.

échevelé, -ée [eʃəv(ə)le] a (ébouriffé) dishevelled; (course, danse etc) Fig wild.

échine [eʃin] nf Anat backbone, spine; **courber l'é.** (céder) to kowtow (**devant qn to s.o.**).

échiner (s') [seʃine] vpr (s'évertuer) Fam to knock oneself out (**à faire doing**).

échiquier [eʃikje] nm (plateau) chessboard.

écho [eko] nm (d'un son) echo; (réponse) response; **échos** (dans la presse) gossip (items), local news; **avoir des échos de** to hear some news about; **se faire l'é. de** (opinions etc) to echo.

échographie [ekografi] nf (ultrasound) scan; **passer une é.** (femme enceinte) to have a scan.

échoir* [eʃwar] vi (terme) to expire; **é. à qn** (part) to fall to s.o.

échouer [eʃwe] **1** vi to fail; **é. à** (examen) to fail; **faire é. un projet** to wreck a plan; **faire é. un complot/etc** to foil a plot/etc. **2** vi, **s'échouer** vpr (navire) to run aground.

éclabousser [eklabuse] vt to splash, spatter (**de with**); (salir) Fig to tarnish the image of █ **s'éclabousser** vpr (en faisant la vaisselle etc) to splash oneself, get oneself splashed. ●**éclaboussure** nf splash, spatter.

éclair [ekler] **1** nm (lumière) flash; (d'orage) flash of lightning. **un é. de génie** a flash of genius. **2** nm (gâteau) éclair. **3** a inv **visite/raid é.** lightning visit/raid.

éclairage [eklɛraʒ] nm (de pièce etc) lighting; (point de vue) light.

éclaircie [eklɛrsi] nf (durée) sunny spell; (dans le ciel) clear patch.

éclaircir [eklɛrsir] vt (couleur etc) make lighter, lighten; (mystère, question) to clear up, clarify; (sauce) to thin out █ **s'éclaircir** vpr (ciel) to clear (up); (situation etc) to become clear(er); (devenir moins dense) to thin out; **s'é. la voix** to clear one's throat. ●**éclaircissement** nm (explication) explanation, clarification; **demander des éclaircissements** to ask for an ou some explanation.

éclairer [eklere] vt (pièce etc) to light (up); **é. qn** (avec une lampe etc) to give s.o. some light; (informer) to enlighten s.o. (**sur about**); **é. une situation/etc d'un jour nouveau** to shed ou throw new light on a situation/etc █ vi (lampe) to give light; **é. bien/mal** to give good/poor light █ **s'éclairer** vpr (visage) to light up, brighten up; (question, situation) to become clear(er); **s'é. à la bougie** to use candlelight; **s'é. à l'électricité** to have electric lighting. ●**éclairé, -ée** a (averti) enlightened; **bien/mal é.** (illuminé) well/badly lit.

éclaireur, -euse [eklɛrœr, -øz] nmf (boy) scout, (girl) guide █ nm (soldat) scout.

éclat [ekla] nm **1** (de la lumière) brightness; (de phare) Aut glare; (du feu) blaze; (de dia-

mant) glitter, sparkle; (*splendeur*) brilliance, radiance; (*de la jeunesse*) bloom. **2** (*fragment de verre ou de bois*) splinter; (*de rire, colère*) (out)burst; **é. d'obus** shrapnel; **éclats de voix** noisy outbursts, shouts.

éclatant, -ante [eklatɑ̃, -ɑ̃t] *a* (*lumière, couleur, succès*) brilliant; (*beauté, santé*) radiant; (*vérité*) blinding; (*bruyant*) (*rire etc*) loud, piercing; **être é. de santé**/*etc* to be radiant *ou* glowing with health/*etc*.

éclater [eklate] *vi* (*pneu, obus etc*) to burst; (*bombe, pétard*) to go off, explode; (*verre*) to shatter, break into pieces; (*guerre, incendie*) to break out; (*orage, scandale*) to break; (*parti*) to break up; **é. de rire** to burst out laughing; **é. en sanglots** to burst into tears. ● **éclatement** *nm* (*de pneu etc*) bursting; (*de bombe etc*) explosion; (*de parti*) break-up.

éclectique [eklɛktik] *a* eclectic.

éclipse [eklips] *nf* (*du soleil, d'une célébrité etc*) eclipse. ● **éclipser** *vt* to eclipse ∎ **s'éclipser** *vpr* (*soleil*) to be eclipsed; (*partir*) *Fam* to slip away.

éclopé, -ée [eklope] *a & nmf* lame *ou* limping (person).

éclore* [eklɔr] *vi* (*œuf*) to hatch; (*fleur*) to open (out), blossom. ● **éclosion** *nf* hatching; (*de fleur*) opening, blossoming.

écluse [eklyz] *nf* (*de canal*) lock.

écœurer [ekœre] *vt* (*aliment etc*) to make (s.o.) feel sick; (*au moral*) to sicken, nauseate. ● **écœurant, -ante** *a* disgusting, sickening. ● **écœurement** *nm* (*répugnance*) nausea, disgust.

école [ekɔl] *nf* school; (*militaire*) academy; **à l'é.** in *ou* at school; **aller à l'é.** to go to school; **é. de danse/dessin** dancing/art school; **é. normale** *Br* teachers' training college, *Am* teachers' college; **é. publique** *Br* state school, *Am* public school; **é. privée** private school; **les grandes écoles** university establishments giving high-level professional training; **faire é.** to gain a following; **faire l'é. buissonnière** to play *Br* truant *ou Am* hookey. ● **écolier, -ière** *nmf* schoolboy, schoolgirl.

écologie [ekɔlɔʒi] *nf* ecology. ● **écologique** *a* ecological. ● **écologiste** *a* (*programme etc*) environmentalist ∎ *nmf* (*partisan*) environmentalist.

éconduire* [ekɔ̃dɥir] *vt* (*repousser*) to reject.

économe [ekɔnɔm] **1** *a* thrifty, economical. **2** *nmf* (*de collège etc*) bursar, steward.

économie [ekɔnɔmi] *nf* (*activité économique, vertu*) economy; **économies** (*argent*) savings; **une é.** *de* (*gain*) a saving of; **faire une é. de temps** to save time; **faire des économies** to save (up); **faire des économies d'énergie** to conserve *ou* save energy; **é. politique** economics; **é. dirigée** planned economy. ● **économique** *a* (*doctrine etc*) economic; **science é.** economics. **2** (*bon marché, avantageux*) economical. ● **économiquement** *adv* economic-

ally.

économiser [ekɔnɔmize] *vt* (*forces, argent, énergie etc*) to save ∎ *vi* to economize (**sur** on).

économiste [ekɔnɔmist] *nmf* economist.

écoper [ekɔpe] **1** *vt* (*bateau*) to bail out, *Br* bale out. **2** *vi Fam* to get the blame, *Br* cop it; **é. (de)** (*punition*) to get, *Br* cop.

écorce [ekɔrs] *nf* (*d'arbre*) bark; (*de fruit*) peel, skin; **l'é. terrestre** the earth's crust.

écorcher [ekɔrʃe] *vt* (*érafler*) to graze; (*animal*) to skin, flay; (*langue étrangère*) *Fig* to murder; (*nom*) *Fig* to mispronounce; **é. les oreilles à qn** to grate on s.o.'s ears ∎ **s'écorcher** *vpr* to graze oneself. ● **écorchure** *nf* graze.

Écosse [ekɔs] *nf* Scotland. ● **écossais, -aise** *a* Scottish; (*tissu*) tartan; (*whisky*) Scotch ∎ *nmf* **É., Écossaise** Scot.

écosser [ekɔse] *vt* (*pois*) to shell.

écot [eko] *nm* (*quote-part*) share.

écouler [ekule] **1** *vt* (*se débarrasser de*) to dispose of; (*marchandises*) to sell (off), clear. **2** **s'écouler** *vpr* (*eau*) to flow out, run out; (*temps*) to pass, elapse; (*foule*) to disperse. ● **écoulé, -ée** *a* (*années etc*) past. ● **écoulement** *nm* **1** (*de liquide, véhicules*) flow; (*de temps*) passage. **2** (*de marchandises*) sale, selling.

écourter [ekurte] *vt* (*séjour, discours etc*) to cut short; (*texte, tige etc*) to shorten.

écoute [ekut] *nf* listening; **être à l'é.** (*à la radio etc*) to be tuned in, be listening in (**de** to); **rester à l'é.** to stay tuned, keep listening; **être à l'é. de qn** to listen (sympathetically) to s.o.; **heure de grande é.** *Radio* peak listening time; *TV* peak viewing time; **écoutes téléphoniques** phone tapping.

écouter [ekute] *vt* to listen to; (*radio*) to listen (in) to ∎ *vi* to listen; (*aux portes etc*) to eavesdrop, listen; **faire é. qch à qn** (*disque etc*) to play s.o. sth; **si je m'écoutais** if I did what I wanted; **il s'écoute parler** he likes the sound of his own voice. ● **écouteur** *nm* (*de téléphone*) earpiece; **écouteurs** (*casque*) earphones, headphones.

écrabouiller [ekrabuje] *vt Fam* to crush to a pulp.

écran [ekrɑ̃] *nm* screen; **le petit é.** television.

écraser [ekraze] *vt* (*broyer*) to crush; (*fruit, insecte*) to squash, crush; (*cigarette*) to put out; (*piéton*) *Aut* to run over; (*vaincre*) to crush (*revolt, enemy etc*); (*dominer*) *Fig* to outstrip; **écrasé de travail/douleur** overwhelmed with work/grief; **se faire é. (par une voiture)** to get run over (by a car); **se faire é. (au tennis/***etc*) to be thrashed *ou Fam* clobbered (at tennis/*etc*). ∎ **s'écraser** *vpr* (*avion, voiture*) to crash (**contre** into); **s'é. dans** (*foule*) to crush *ou* squash into. ● **écrasant, -ante** *a* (*victoire, chaleur etc*) overwhelming. ● **écrasé** *am* **nez é.** snub nose. ● **écrasement** *nm* (*d'insecte, de révolte etc*) crushing.

écrémer [ekreme] *vt* (*lait*) to skim, cream;

(*collection etc*) *Fig* to cream off the best from; **lait écrémé** skimmed *ou* skim milk.

écrevisse [ekrəvis] *nf* (*crustacé*) crayfish *inv*.

écrier (s') [sekrije] *vpr* to exclaim, cry out (**que that**).

écrin [ekrɛ̃] *nm* (jewel) case.

écrire* [ekrir] *vt* to write; (*noter*) to write (down); (*en toutes lettres*) to spell; **é. à la machine** to type ▮ *vi* to write ▮ **s'écrire** *vpr* (*mot*) to be spelled *ou* spelt; **comment ça s'écrit?** how do you spell it? ● **écrit** *nm* written document, paper; (*examen*) written paper; **écrits** (*œuvres*) writings; **par é.** in writing.

écriteau, -x [ekrito] *nm* notice, sign.

écriture [ekrityr] *nf* (*système*) writing; (*personnelle*) (hand)writing; **écritures** *Com* accounts; **les Écritures** (*la Bible*) the Scripture(s).

écrivain [ekrivɛ̃] *nm* author, writer.

écrou [ekru] *nm* (*de boulon*) nut.

écrouer [ekrue] *vt* to imprison.

écrouler (s') [sekrule] *vpr* (*édifice, blessé etc*) to collapse; **être écroulé de fatigue** to be dropping with exhaustion; **être écroulé (de rire)** *Fam* to be doubled up (with laughter). ● **écroulement** *nm* collapse.

écru, -ue [ekry] *a* (*tissu*) unbleached; (*pull etc*) made out of unbleached material; **toile écrue** unbleached linen; **soie écrue** raw silk.

ECU [eky] *nm abrév* (*European Currency Unit*) ECU.

écueil [ekœj] *nm* (*rocher*) reef; (*obstacle*) *Fig* pitfall.

écuelle [ekɥɛl] *nf* (*bol*) bowl.

éculé, -ée [ekyle] *a* (*chaussure*) worn out at the heel; (*plaisanterie etc*) *Fig* hackneyed.

écume [ekym] *nf* (*de mer, bave d'animal etc*) foam; (*de pot-au-feu etc*) scum. ● **écumer** *vt* (*pot-au-feu etc*) to skim; (*piller*) to plunder ▮ *vi* to foam (**de rage** with anger). ● **écumoire** *nf* (*ustensile*) skimmer.

écureuil [ekyrœj] *nm* squirrel.

écurie [ekyri] *nf* stable.

écusson [ekysɔ̃] *nm* (*en étoffe*) badge.

écuyer, -ère [ekɥije, -ɛr] *nmf* (*cavalier*) (horse) rider, equestrian.

eczéma [ɛgzema] *nm* (*maladie*) eczema.

édenté, -ée [edɑ̃te] *a* toothless.

EDF [ədɛf] *nm abrév* (*Électricité de France*) *Br* (French) Electricity Board, *Am* (French) Electric Company.

édicter [edikte] *vt* to enact, decree.

édifice [edifis] *nm* building, edifice; (*ensemble organisé*) *Fig* edifice. ● **édification** *nf* construction; (*instruction morale*) edification; *Iron* enlightenment. ● **édifier** *vt* (*bâtiment*) to erect, construct; (*théorie*) to construct; **é. qn** (*moralement*) to edify s.o.; (*détromper*) *Iron* to enlighten s.o.

Édimbourg [edɛ̃bur] *nm ou f* Edinburgh.

édit [edi] *nm Hist* edict.

éditer [edite] *vt* (*publier*) to publish; (*annoter*) & *Ordinat* to edit. ● **éditeur, -trice** *nmf* publisher; (*commentateur*) editor. ● **édition**

nf (*livre, journal*) edition; (*métier, diffusion*) publishing.

éditorial, -aux [editɔrjal, -o] *nm* (*article*) editorial, *Br* leader. ● **éditorialiste** *nmf* editorial *ou Br* leader writer.

édredon [edrədɔ̃] *nm* eiderdown.

éducateur, -trice [edykatœr, -tris] *nmf* educator.

éducatif, -ive [edykatif, -iv] *a* educational.

éducation [edykasjɔ̃] *nf* (*enseignement*) education; (*façon d'élever*) upbringing, education; **é. physique** physical education *ou* training; **é. sexuelle** sex education; **l'É. nationale** = Department of Education; **avoir de l'é.** to have good manners, be well-bred. ● **éduquer** *vt* (*à l'école*) to educate (*s.o.*); (*à la maison*) to bring (*s.o.*) up, educate (*s.o.*); (*esprit*) to educate, train.

effacé, -ée [efase] *a* (*modeste*) self-effacing. ● **effacement** *nm* (*modestie*) self-effacement.

effacer [efase] *vt* (*gommer*) to rub out, erase; (*en lavant*) to wash out; (*avec un chiffon*) to wipe away; (*souvenir*) *Fig* to blot out, erase ▮ **s'effacer** *vpr* (*souvenir, couleur etc*) to fade; (*se placer en retrait*) to step *ou* draw aside.

effarer [efare] *vt* to scare, alarm. ● **effarant, -ante** *a Fam* incredible. ● **effarement** *nm* alarm.

effaroucher [efaruʃe] *vt* to scare away, frighten away ▮ **s'effaroucher** *vpr* to take fright, be scared.

effectif, -ive [efɛktif, -iv] **1** *a* (*réel*) effective, real. **2** *nm* (*de classe etc*) total number, size; (*d'une armée etc*) (total) strength; **effectifs** (*employés, soldats*) manpower. ● **effectivement** *adv* (*en effet*) actually, effectively.

effectuer [efɛktɥe] *vt* (*expérience, geste difficile etc*) to carry out, perform; (*paiement, trajet etc*) to make.

efféminé, -ée [efemine] *a* effeminate.

effervescent, -ente [efɛrvesɑ̃, -ɑ̃t] *a* (*mélange, jeunesse*) effervescent. ● **effervescence** *nf* (*exaltation*) excitement, effervescence; (*de liquide*) effervescence.

effet [efɛ] *nm* **1** (*résultat*) effect; (*impression*) impression, effect (**sur on**); **en è.** indeed, in fact; **à cet e.** to this end, for this purpose; **sous l'e. de la colère** (*agir*) in anger, out of anger; **e. de serre** greenhouse effect; **faire de l'e.** (*remède etc*) to be effective; **rester sans e.** to have no effect; **donner de l'e. à une balle** (*au tennis*) to spin a ball; **il mé fáit l'e. d'être fatigué** he seems to me to be tired; **ce n'est pas l'e. du hasard si...** it is not simply a matter of chance if.... **2 e. de commerce** bill, draft.

effets [efɛ] *nmpl* (*vêtements*) clothes, things.

efficace [efikas] *a* (*mesure etc*) effective; (*personne*) efficient. ● **efficacité** *nf* effectiveness; (*de personne*) efficiency.

effigie [efiʒi] *nf* effigy; **pièce de monnaie à l'e. de la reine** coin bearing the queen's head *ou* a portrait of the queen.

effilé, -ée [efile] *a* (*doigt, lame etc*) tapering,

long and slender.

effilocher (s') [sefilɔʃe] *vpr* to fray.

efflanqué, -ée [eflɑ̃ke] *a* emaciated.

effleurer [eflœre] *vt* (*frôler*) to skim, touch (lightly); (*question*) *Fig* to touch on; **e. qn** (*pensée etc*) to cross s.o.'s mind.

effondrer (s') [sefɔ̃dre] *vpr* (*projet, édifice, Bourse, personne*) to collapse; (*toit*) to cave in, collapse; **avoir l'air effondré** to look completely dejected. ●**effondrement** *nm* collapse; (*des cours de la Bourse*) collapse, slump; (*abattement*) (complete) dejection.

efforcer (s') [sefɔrse] *vpr* **s'e. de faire** to try (hard) *ou* endeavour *ou* strive to do.

effort [efɔr] *nm* effort; **sans e.** (*réussir etc*) effortlessly; **faire des efforts** to try (hard), make an effort; **allons! encore un petit e.!** come on, one more try!, come on, a bit more effort!

effraction [efraksjɔ̃] *nf* **pénétrer par e.** (*cambrioleur*) to break in; **vol avec e.** housebreaking.

effranger (s') [sefrɑ̃ʒe] *vpr* to fray.

effrayer [efreje] *vt* to frighten, scare ∎ **s'effrayer** *vpr* to be frightened *ou* scared. ●**effrayant, ante** *a* frightening, scary; (*extraordinaire*) *Fam* incredible.

effréné, -ée [efrene] *a* unrestrained, wild.

effriter (s') [sefrite] *vpr* to crumble (away); **la roche effritée** the crumbling rock.

effroi [efrwɑ] *nm* (*frayeur*) dread. ●**effroyable** *a* dreadful, appalling. ●**effroyablement** *adv* dreadfully.

effronté, -ée [efrɔ̃te] *a* (*enfant etc*) insolent, *Br* cheeky, brazen. ●**effronterie** *nf* insolence, *Br* cheek, effrontery.

effusion [efyzjɔ̃] *nf* **1 e. de sang** bloodshed. **2** (*manifestation de tendresse*) emotional outburst, effusion; **avec e.** effusively.

égal, -e, -aux [egal, -o] *a* equal (**à** to); (*uniforme, régulier*) even; **ça m'est é.** I don't care, it's all the same to me; **combattre à armes égales** to fight on equal terms; *Sport* **faire jeu é.** to be evenly matched; **se trouver à égale distance de** to be equidistant from ∎ *nmf* (*personne*) equal; **traiter qn d'é. à é.** *ou* **en é.** to treat s.o. as an equal; **sans é.** without match. ●**également** *adv* (*au même degré*) equally; (*aussi*) also, as well. ●**égaler** *vt* to equal, match (**en** in); **3 plus 4 égale(nt) 7** 3 plus 4 equals 7.

égaliser [egalize] *vt* to equalize; (*terrain*) to level ∎ *vi Sport* to equalize. ●**égalisation** *nf Sport* equalization; (*de terrain*) levelling.

égalité [egalite] *nf* equality; (*régularité*) evenness; **à é.** (**de score**) *Sport* even, equal (in points); **signe d'é.** *Math* equals sign. ●**égalitaire** *a* egalitarian.

égard [egar] *nm* **à l'é. de** (*envers*) towards; (*concernant*) with respect *ou* regard to; **à cet é.** in this respect; **à certains égards** in some respects; **eu é. à** considering, in consideration of; **avoir des égards pour qn** to have respect *ou* consideration for s.o.

égarement [egarmɑ̃] *nm* mental confusion ∎

égarements (*actes immoraux*) wild aberrations.

égarer [egare] *vt* (*objet*) to mislay; **é. qn** (*dérouter*) to mislead s.o.; (*aveugler, troubler*) to lead s.o. astray, misguide s.o. ∎ **s'égarer** *vpr* to lose one's way, get lost; (*objet*) to get mislaid, go astray; (*esprit*) to wander, become confused.

égayer [egeje] *vt* (*pièce*) to brighten up; **é. qn** (*réconforter, amuser*) to cheer s.o. up, amuse s.o. ∎ **s'égayer** *vpr* to amuse oneself, have fun (**aux dépens de qn** at s.o.'s expense).

égide [eʒid] *nf* **sous l'é. de** under the aegis of.

églantier [eglɑ̃tje] *nm* (*arbre*) wild rose. ●**églantine** *nf* (*fleur*) wild rose.

église [egliz] *nf* church.

égocentrique [egɔsɑ̃trik] *a* egocentric.

égoïsme [egɔism] *nm* selfishness, egoism. ●**égoïste** *a* selfish, egoistic(al) ∎ *nmf* selfish person, egoist.

égorger [egɔrʒe] *vt* to cut *ou* slit the throat of.

égosiller (s') [segozije] *vpr* to scream one's head off, bawl out.

égotisme [egɔtism] *nm* egotism.

égout [egu] *nm* sewer; **eaux d'é.** sewage.

égoutter [egute] *vt* (*vaisselle*) to drain; (*légumes*) to strain, drain ∎ *vi*, **s'égoutter** *vpr* (*vaisselle, légumes*) to drain; (*linge*) to drip; **laisser la vaisselle é.** to leave the dishes to drain (off). ●**égouttoir** *nm* (*panier*) (dish) drainer.

égratigner [egratiɲe] *vt* to scratch ∎ **s'égratigner** (*en tombant*) to scratch oneself. ●**égratignure** *nf* scratch.

égrener [egrəne] *vt* (*raisins*) to pick off; (*épis*) to shell; **é. son chapelet** *Rel* to count one's beads; **l'horloge égrène les heures** the clock slowly marks the hours.

Égypte [eʒipt] *nf* Egypt. ●**égyptien, -ienne** [-sjɛ̃, -sjɛn] *a* Egyptian ∎ *nmf* **E., Égyptienne** Egyptian.

eh! [e] *int* hey!; **eh bien!** well!

éhonté, -ée [eɔ̃te] *a* shameless; **mensonge é.** barefaced lie.

éjecter [eʒɛkte] *vt* to eject; **se faire é.** *Fam* to get thrown out. ●**éjectable** *a* **siège é.** (*dans un avion*) ejector seat. ●**éjection** *nf* ejection.

élaborer [elabɔre] *vt* (*système etc*) to elaborate. ●**élaboration** *nf* elaboration.

élaguer [elage] *vt* (*arbre, texte etc*) to prune.

élan [elɑ̃] *nm* **1** (*vitesse*) momentum, impetus; (*impulsion*) impulse; (*fougue*) fervour, spirit; **un é. de tendresse/etc** an outburst *ou* a surge of affection/etc; **prendre son é.** (*sportif*) to take a run (up); **d'un seul é.** in one bound. **2** (*animal*) elk.

élancé, -ée [elɑ̃se] *a* (*personne, taille etc*) slender.

élancer [elɑ̃se] **1** *vi* (*abcès etc*) to give shooting pains. **2** **s'élancer** *vpr* (*bondir*) to leap *ou* rush (forward); **s'é. vers le ciel** (*tour*) to soar up (high) into the sky. ●**élancement** *nm* shooting pain.

élargir [elarʒir] 1 vt (chemin) to widen; (vêtement) to let out; (esprit, débat) to broaden ▮ **s'élargir** vpr (sentier etc) to widen out; (vêtement) to stretch. 2 vt (prisonnier) to free.

élastique [elastik] a (objet, gaz, métal) elastic; (règlement, notion) flexible, supple ▮ nm (lien) rubber band, Br elastic band; (tissu) elastic. ●**élasticité** nf elasticity.

élection [elɛksjɔ̃] nf election; **é. partielle** by-election. ●**électeur, -trice** nmf voter, elector. ●**électoral, -e, -aux** a **campagne électorale** election campaign; **liste électorale** register of electors; **collège é.** electoral college. ●**électorat** nm (électeurs) electorate, voters.

électricien [elɛktrisjɛ̃] nm electrician. ●**électricité** nf electricity; **coupure d'é.** blackout, Br power cut. ●**électrifier** vt (voie ferrée) to electrify. ●**électrique** a (pendule, décharge) electric; (courant, fil) electric(al); (effet) Fig electric; **bleu é.** electric blue. ●**électriser** vt (animer) Fig to electrify.

électrocardiogramme [elɛktrɔkardjɔgram] nm electrocardiogram.

électrochoc [elɛktrɔʃɔk] nm (traitement) electric shock treatment.

électrocuter [elɛktrɔkyte] vt to electrocute.

électrode [elɛktrɔd] nf Él electrode.

électrogène [elɛktrɔʒɛn] a **groupe é.** Él generator.

électroménager [elɛktrɔmenaʒe] am **appareil é.** household electrical appliance.

électron [elɛktrɔ̃] nm electron. ●**électronicien, -ienne** nmf electronics engineer. ●**électronique** a electronic; **microscope é.** electron microscope ▮ nf electronics.

électrophone [elɛktrɔfɔn] nm record player.

élégant, -ante [elegɑ̃, -ɑ̃t] a (style, solution etc) elegant; (bien habillé) smart, elegant. ●**élégamment** [-amɑ̃] adv elegantly; smartly. ●**élégance** nf elegance; **avec é.** elegantly; (s'habiller) smartly, elegantly.

élégie [eleʒi] nf elegy.

élément [elemɑ̃] nm (composante, personne, substance chimique) element; (de meuble) unit; (d'ensemble) Math member; (éléments (notions) rudiments, elements; **être dans son é.** (milieu) to be in one's element. ●**élémentaire** a basic; (cours, école etc) elementary.

éléphant [elefɑ̃] nm elephant. ●**éléphantesque** a (énorme) Fam elephantine.

élevage [elvaʒ] nm breeding, rearing (de of); **é. de bovins** cattle rearing; **faire l'é. de** to breed, rear.

élévateur [elevatœr] am **chariot é.** forklift truck.

élévation [elevasjɔ̃] nf raising; Géom elevation; **é. de** (hausse) rise in (level etc).

élevé, -ée [elve] a (haut) high; (noble) noble; **bien/mal é.** well-/bad-mannered.

élève [elɛv] nmf (à l'école) pupil.

élever [elve] vt (prix, voix, objection etc) to raise; (enfant) to bring up, raise; (animal) to breed, rear; (âme) to uplift, raise ▮ **s'élever**

vpr (prix, ton, montagne etc) to rise; (cerf-volant) to rise into the sky; (monument) to be put up; **un cri s'éleva dans la foule** a shout went up from the crowd; **s'é. à** (prix etc) to amount to; **s'é. contre** to rise up against.

éleveur, -euse [elvœr, -øz] nmf breeder.

élider [elide] vt **é. une voyelle** to elide a vowel.

éligible [eliʒibl] a Pol eligible (à for).

élimé, -ée [elime] a (tissu) threadbare, worn thin.

éliminer [elimine] vt to eliminate. ●**élimination** nf elimination. ●**éliminatoire** a **épreuve é.** Sport qualifying round, heat; Scol qualifying exam; **note é.** Scol disqualifying mark. ●**éliminatoires** nfpl Sport qualifying rounds.

élire* [elir] vt Pol to elect (à to).

élision [elizjɔ̃] nf (d'une voyelle) elision.

élite [elit] nf elite (de of); **les élites** the elite; **troupes/etc d'é.** crack ou elite troops/etc.

elle [ɛl] pron f 1 (sujet) she; (chose, animal) it; **elles** they; **e. est** she is; it is; **elles sont** they are. 2 (complément) her; (chose, animal) it; **elles** them; **pour e.** for her; **pour elles** for them; **plus grande qu'e./qu'elles** taller than her/them. ●**elle-même** pron herself; (chose, animal) itself; **elles-mêmes** themselves.

ellipse [elips] nf Géom ellipse. ●**elliptique** a elliptical.

élocution [elɔkysjɔ̃] nf diction; **défaut d'é.** speech defect.

éloge [elɔʒ] nm (compliment) praise; (panégyrique) eulogy; **faire l'é. de** to praise; **prononcer l'é. funèbre de qn** to deliver a eulogy in praise of s.o. (deceased person). ●**élogieux, -euse** a laudatory.

éloigné, -ée [elwaɲe] a (lieu) far away, remote; (date, parent) distant; **é. de** (village, maison etc) far (away) from; (très différent) far removed from.

éloignement [elwaɲ(ə)mɑ̃] nm remoteness, distance; (absence) separation (de from); **avec l'é.** (avec le recul) with time.

éloigner [elwaɲe] vt (chose, personne) to move ou take away (de from); (malade, moustiques) to keep away; (crainte, idée) to get rid of, banish; (échéance) to put off; **é. qn de** (sujet, but) to take ou get s.o. away from ▮ **s'éloigner** vpr (partir) to move ou go away (de from); (dans le passé) to become (more) remote; **s'é. de** (sujet, but) to get away from.

élongation [elɔ̃gasjɔ̃] nf Méd pulled muscle; **se faire une é.** to pull a muscle.

éloquent, -ente [elɔkɑ̃, -ɑ̃t] a eloquent. ●**éloquence** nf eloquence.

élu, -ue [ely] pp de **élire** ▮ a **le peuple é.** Rel the chosen people ▮ nmf Pol elected member ou representative; **les élus** Rel the chosen, the elect; **l'heureux é., l'heureuse élue** (futur mari, future femme) the lucky man/woman.

élucider [elyside] vt to elucidate.

élucubrations [elykybrasjɔ̃] nfpl Péj fanciful

learned theories.

éluder [elyde] *vt* to elude, evade.

Elysée [elize] *nm* (**le palais de**) **l'É.** the Élysée palace (*French President's residence*).

émacié, -ée [emasje] *a* emaciated.

émail, -aux [emaj, -o] *nm* enamel; **casserole/etc en é.** enamel saucepan/*etc*. ● **émailler** *vt* to enamel.

émaillé, -ée [emaje] *a* **é. de fautes/etc** (*texte*) peppered with errors/*etc*.

émanciper [emãsipe] *vt* (*femmes*) to emancipate ▮ **s'émanciper** *vpr* to become emancipated. ● **émancipation** *nf* emancipation; **l'é. de la femme** the emancipation of women.

émaner [emane] *vt* **é. de** to come from, emanate from. ● **émanation** *nf* **des émanations** (*odeurs*) smells; (*vapeurs*) fumes; **émanations toxiques** toxic fumes; **une é. du pouvoir** *Fig* an expression of power.

émarger [emarʒe] *vt* (*signer*) to sign ▮ *vi* (*recevoir un salaire*) to draw one's salary.

emballer [ãbale] **1** *vt* (*dans une caisse etc*) to pack; (*dans du papier*) to wrap (up). **2** *vt* (*moteur*) to race; **e. qn** (*passionner*) *Fam* to thrill s.o., enthuse s.o. ▮ **s'emballer** *vpr* (*personne*) *Fam* to get carried away; (*cheval*) to bolt; (*moteur*) to race. ● **emballé, -ée** *a Fam* enthusiastic. ● **emballage** *nm* (*action*) packing; wrapping; (*caisse*) packaging; (*papier d'*)**e.** wrapping (paper). ● **emballement** *nm Fam* (sudden) enthusiasm.

embarcadère [ãbarkadεr] *nm* quay, wharf, landing stage.

embarcation [ãbarkasjɔ̃] *nf* (small) boat.

embardée [ãbarde] *nf* (*dans un véhicule*) (sudden) swerve; **faire une e.** to swerve.

embargo [ãbargo] *nm* embargo; **imposer/ lever un e.** to impose/lift an embargo.

embarquer [ãbarke] *vt* (*passagers*) to take on board, embark; (*marchandises*) to load (up); (*voler*) *Fam* to walk off with; **e. qn** (*au commissariat etc*) *Fam* to cart s.o. off; **e. qn dans** (*affaire*) *Fam* to involve s.o. in, launch s.o. into ▮ *vi*, **s'embarquer** *vpr* to (go on) board, embark; **s'e. dans** (*aventure etc*) *Fam* to embark on. ● **embarquement** *nm* (*de passagers*) boarding.

embarras [ãbara] *nm* (*gêne*, *malaise*) embarrassment; (*difficulté*) difficulty, trouble; (*obstacle*) obstacle; **dans l'e.** in difficulty, in an awkward situation; (*financièrement*) in difficulties; **n'avoir que l'e. du choix** to be able to pick and choose, have an enormous choice.

embarrasser [ãbarase] *vt* (*obstruer*) to clutter, encumber; **e. qn** to be in s.o.'s way; (*déconcerter*) to embarrass s.o., bother s.o.; **s'e. de** to burden oneself with; (*se soucier*) to bother oneself about. ● **embarrassant, -ante** *a* (*paquet*) cumbersome; (*question*) embarrassing.

embauche [ãboʃ] *nf* (*action*) hiring; (*travail*) work; **possibilité d'e.** (job) vacancy; **bureau d'e.** employment office. ● **embaucher** *vt* (*ouvrier*) to hire, take on.

embaumer [ãbome] **1** *vt* (*parfumer*) to give a sweet smell to ▮ *vi* to smell sweet. **2** *vt* (*cadavre*) to embalm.

embellie [ãbeli] *nf* bright *ou* calm spell (of weather).

embellir [ãbelir] *vt* (*pièce*, *personne*) to make (more) attractive; (*texte*, *vérité*) to embellish ▮ *vi* (*jeune fille etc*) to blossom out. ● **embellissement** *nm* improvement, embellishment.

emberlificoter [ãbεrlifikɔte] *vt* (*empêtrer*) *Fam* to tangle (*s.o.*) up; **se laisser e. dans** (*affaire etc*) *Fig* to get tangled up in.

embêter [ãbete] *vt Fam* (*agacer*) to annoy, bother; (*ennuyer*) to bore ▮ **s'embêter** *vpr Fam* to get bored. ● **embêtant, -ante** *a Fam* annoying. ● **embêtement** [-tmã] *nm Fam* **un e.** (some) trouble *ou* bother; **des embêtements** bother, trouble.

emblée (d') [dãble] *adv* right away.

emblème [ãblεm] *nm* emblem.

embobiner [ãbɔbine] *vt* (*tromper*) *Fam* to take (*s.o.*) in, hoodwink (*s.o.*).

emboîter [ãbwate] *vt*, **s'emboîter** *vpr* (*tuyau(x)*) to fit together, fit into each other; **e. le pas à qn** to follow close on s.o.'s heels; (*imiter*) *Fig* to follow in s.o.'s footsteps.

embonpoint [ãbɔ̃pwε̃] *nm* plumpness.

embouché, -ée [ãbuʃe] *a* **mal e.** coarse, foul-mouthed.

embouchure [ãbuʃyr] *nf* (*de fleuve*) mouth; (*d'un instrument à vent*) mouthpiece.

embourber (s') [sãburbe] *vpr* (*véhicule*) & *Fig* to get bogged down.

embourgeoiser (s') [sãburʒwaze] *vpr* to become middle-class.

embout [ãbu] *nm* (*de canne*) tip, end piece; (*de seringue*) nozzle.

embouteillage [ãbutejaʒ] *nm* traffic jam.

embouteillé, -ée [ãbuteje] *a* (*rue*) congested; **route embouteillée sur 5 km** road with a 5-km-long traffic jam; **lignes téléphoniques embouteillées** jammed telephone lines.

emboutir [ãbutir] *vt* (*voiture*) to knock *ou* crash into; (*métal*) to stamp, emboss; **il a eu l'arrière embouti** someone knocked *ou* crashed into the back of his car; **elle s'est fait e. par un camion** *a Br* lorry *ou Am* truck knocked into her *ou* crashed into her.

embrancher (s') [sãbrãʃe] *vpr* (*voie*, *route*) to branch off. ● **embranchement** *nm* (*de voie*) junction, fork; (*division du règne animal*) branch.

embraser [ãbraze] *vt* to set ablaze ▮ **s'embraser** *vpr* (*prendre feu*) to flare up. ● **embrasement** *nm* (*troubles*) flare-up.

embrasser [ãbrase] *vt* **e. qn** (*donner un baiser à*) to kiss s.o.; (*serrer contre soi*) to embrace *ou* hug s.o.; **e. une croyance/un sujet/** *etc* to embrace a belief/subject/*etc*; **e. qch du regard** to take in the whole of sth (at one glance) ▮ **s'embrasser** *vpr* to kiss (each other). ● **embrassade** *nf* embrace, hug.

embrasure [ãbrazyr] *nf* (*de fenêtre*, *porte*)

opening; **dans l'e. de la porte** in the doorway.

embrayer [ɑ̃breje] *vi* to let in *ou* engage the clutch. ●**embrayage** *nm* (*mécanisme, pédale d'une voiture*) clutch.

embrigader [ɑ̃brigade] *vt Péj* to recruit.

embrocher [ɑ̃brɔʃe] *vt* (*volaille etc*) to put on a spit, skewer; **e. qn** (*avec une épée*) *Fam* to skewer s.o.

embrouiller [ɑ̃bruje] *vt* (*fils*) to tangle (up); (*papiers etc*) to mix up, muddle (up); **e. qn** to confuse s.o., get s.o. muddled; **tu vas m'e. les idées** you're going to get me confused ▮ **s'embrouiller** *vpr* to get confused *ou* muddled (**dans** in, with). ●**embrouille** *nf Fam* muddle; **un sac d'embrouilles** a confused mess, a muddle of the first order. ●**embrouillamini** *nm Fam* muddle, mix-up.

embroussaillé, -ée [ɑ̃brusaje] *a* (*barbe, chemin*) bushy.

embruns [ɑ̃brœ̃] *nmpl* (sea) spray.

embryon [ɑ̃brijɔ̃] *nm* embryo. ●**embryonnaire** *a Méd & Fig* embryonic.

embûches [ɑ̃byʃ] *nfpl* (*difficultés*) traps, pitfalls; **tendre des e. à qn** to set traps for s.o.; **semé d'e.** full of pitfalls.

embuer [ɑ̃bɥe] *vt* (*vitre, yeux*) to mist up; **des yeux embués de larmes** eyes misted over with tears.

embusquer (s') [sɑ̃byske] *vpr* to lie in ambush. ●**embuscade** *nf* ambush.

éméché, -ée [emeʃe] *a* (*ivre*) *Fam* tipsy.

émeraude [emrod] *nf & a* emerald.

émerger [emerʒe] *vi* to emerge (**de** from).

émeri [emri] *nm* **toile/papier (d')é.** emery cloth/paper.

émérite [emerit] *a* **professeur é.** emeritus professor.

émerveiller [emɛrveje] *vt* to amaze, fill with wonder ▮ **s'émerveiller** *vpr* to marvel, be filled with wonder (**de** at). ●**émerveillement** *nm* wonder, amazement.

émettre* [emɛtr] *vt* (*lumière, son etc*) to give out, emit; (*message radio*) to broadcast, transmit; (*timbre, monnaie*) to issue; (*opinion, vœu*) to express; (*cri*) to utter; (*chèque*) to draw; (*emprunt*) to float. ●**émetteur** *nm* (**poste**) é. *Radio* transmitter.

émeute [emøt] *nf* riot. ●**émeutier, -ière** *nmf* rioter.

émiettor [emjete] *vt,* **s'émietter** *vpr* (*pain etc*) to crumble.

émigrer [emigre] *vi* (*personne*) to emigrate. ●**emigrant, -ante** *nmf* emigrant. ●**émigré, -ée** *nmf* exile, émigré ▮ *a* **travailleur é.** migrant worker. ●**émigration** *nf* emigration.

éminent, -ente [eminɑ̃, -ɑ̃t] *a* eminent. ●**éminemment** [-amɑ̃] *adv* eminently. ●**éminence** *nf* **1** (*colline*) hillock. **2 son É.** (**le cardinal**) (*titre honorifique*) his Eminence (the Cardinal); **une é. grise** (*conseiller*) *Fig* an éminence grise.

émir [emir] *nm* emir. ●**émirat** *nm* emirate.

émissaire [emiser] *nm* emissary.

émission [emisjɔ̃] *nf* (*programme de radio*

etc) programme, broadcast; (*diffusion*) transmission; (*de timbre, monnaie*) issue; (*de lumière, son etc*) emission (**de** of).

emmagasiner [ɑ̃magazine] *vt* to store (up); **e. de l'énergie/**Fig **des souvenirs** to store energy/Fig memories.

emmanchure [ɑ̃mɑ̃ʃyr] *nf* (*de vêtement*) arm hole.

emmêler [ɑ̃mele] *vt* (*fil, cheveux etc*) to tangle (up) ▮ **s'emmêler** *vpr* to get tangled.

emménager [ɑ̃menaʒe] *vi* (*dans un logement*) to move in; **e. dans** to move into. ●**emménagement** *nm* moving in.

emmener [ɑ̃mne] *vt* to take (**à** to); (*prisonnier*) to take away; **e. qn faire une promenade** to take s.o. for a walk; **e. qn en voiture (à l'aéroport/**etc**)** to give s.o. a *Br* lift *ou Am* ride *ou* drive s.o. (to the airport/etc).

emmerder [ɑ̃mɛrde] *vt Arg* to annoy, bug; (*ennuyer*) to bore stiff ▮ **s'emmerder** *vpr Arg* to get bored stiff. ●**emmerdement** *nm Arg* bother, trouble. ●**emmerdeur, -euse** *nmf* (*personne*) *Arg* pain in the neck.

emmitoufler (s') [sɑ̃mitufle] *vpr* to wrap (oneself) up (**dans** in).

emmurer [ɑ̃myre] *vt* (*personne*) to wall in.

émoi [emwa] *nm* excitement; **en é.** agog, excited.

émoluments [emɔlymɑ̃] *nmpl* (*de fonctionnaire*) remuneration.

émotion [emosjɔ̃] *nf* (*sentiment*) emotion; (*trouble*) excitement; **donner des émotions à qn** (*faire peur à qn*) to give s.o. a scare; **aimer les émotions fortes** to love thrills. ●**émotif, -ive** *a* emotional. ●**émotionné, -ée** *a Fam* upset.

émousser [emuse] *vt* (*pointe*) to blunt; (*sentiment*) *Fig* to dull. ●**émoussé, -ée** *a* (*pointe*) blunt; (*sentiment*) *Fig* dulled.

émouvoir* [emuvwar] *vt* (*affecter*) to move, touch ▮ **s'émouvoir** *vpr* to be moved *ou* touched. ●**émouvant, -ante** *a* moving, touching.

empailler [ɑ̃paje] *vt* (*animal*) to stuff.

empaler [ɑ̃pale] *vt* to impale.

empaqueter [ɑ̃pakte] *vt* to pack(age).

emparer (s') [sɑ̃pare] *vpr* **s'e. de** to take, grab, seize; (*otage*) to seize.

empâter (s') [sɑ̃pate] *vpr* to fill out, get fat(ter). ●**empâté, -ée** *a* fleshy, fat.

empêcher [ɑ̃peʃe] *vt* to prevent, stop; **e. qn de faire** to prevent *ou* stop s.o. (from) doing; **e. l'accès d'un lieu** to prevent access to a place; **n'empêche qu'elle a raison** *Fam* all the same she's right; **n'empêche!** *Fam* all the same!; **elle ne peut pas s'e. de rire** she can't help laughing; **ça ne m'empêche pas de dormir** *Fig* I don't lose any sleep over it. ●**empêchement** [-ɛʃmɑ̃] *nm* difficulty, hitch; **avoir un e.** to have something come up at the last minute (*to prevent or delay an action*).

empereur [ɑ̃prœr] *nm* emperor.

empeser [ɑ̃pəze] *vt* to starch.

empester [ɑ̃peste] *vt* (*tabac etc*) to stink of;

(*pièce*) to make stink, stink out; **e. qn** to stink s.o. out ▮ *vi* to stink.

empêtrer (s') [sɑ̃petre] *vpr* to get entangled (**dans** in).

emphase [ɑ̃faz] *nf* pomposity. ●**emphatique** *a* pompous.

empiéter [ɑ̃pjete] *vi* **e. sur** to encroach (up)on. ●**empiétement** *nm* encroachment.

empiffrer (s') [sɑ̃pifre] *vpr* Fam to gorge *ou* stuff oneself (**de** with).

empiler [ɑ̃pile] *vt*, **s'empiler** *vpr* to pile up (**sur** on); **s'e. dans** (*personnes*) to pile into (*building, car etc*). ●**empilement** *nm* (*tas*) pile.

empire [ɑ̃pir] *nm* (*territoires*) empire; (*autorité*) hold, influence; **sous l'e. de la peur**/*etc* in the grip of fear/*etc*.

empirer [ɑ̃pire] *vi* to worsen, get worse.

empirique [ɑ̃pirik] *a* empirical. ●**empirisme** *nm* empiricism.

emplacement [ɑ̃plasmɑ̃] *nm* (*d'une construction*) site, location; (*de stationnement*) place.

emplâtre [ɑ̃plɑtr] *nm* (*cataplasme*) plaster.

emplette [ɑ̃plɛt] *nf* purchase; **faire des emplettes** to do some shopping.

emplir [ɑ̃plir] *vt*, **s'emplir** *vpr* to fill (**de** with).

emploi [ɑ̃plwa] *nm* **1** (*usage*) use; **e. du temps** timetable; **mode d'e.** directions (for use). **2** (*travail*) job, position, employment; **l'e.** (*travail*) *Écon Pol* employment; **sans e.** unemployed.

employer [ɑ̃plwaje] *vt* (*utiliser*) to use; **e. qn** (*occuper*) to employ s.o. ▮ **s'employer** *vpr* (*expression etc*) to be used; **s'e. à faire** to devote oneself to doing. ●**employé, -ée** *nmf* employee; **e. de banque** bank clerk *ou* employee; **e. de bureau** office worker, clerk; **e. de maison** domestic employee; **e. des postes/**etc postal/*etc* worker. ●**employeur, -euse** *nmf* employer.

empocher [ɑ̃pɔʃe] *vt* (*argent*) to pocket.

empoigner [ɑ̃pwaɲe] *vt* (*saisir*) to grab, grasp ▮ **s'empoigner** *vpr* to come to blows, fight. ●**empoignade** *nf* (*querelle*) fight.

empoisonner [ɑ̃pwazɔne] *vt* (*personne, aliment, atmosphère etc*) to poison; (*empester*) to stink out; (*gâter, altérer*) to trouble, bedevil; **e. qn** (*embêter*) Fam to get on s.o.'s nerves; **e. la vie à qn** Fam to make s.o.'s life a misery ▮ **s'empoisonner** *vpr* (*par accident*) to be poisoned; (*volontairement*) to poison oneself; (*s'ennuyer*) Fam to get bored stiff. ●**empoisonnant, -ante** *a* (*embêtant*) Fam irritating. ●**empoisonnement** *nm* poisoning; (*ennui*) Fam trouble, problem.

emporter [ɑ̃pɔrte] *vt* (*prendre*) to take (away) (**avec soi** with one); (*enlever*) to take away; (*prix, trophée*) to carry off; (*décision*) to carry; (*entraîner*) to carry along *ou* away; (*par le vent*) to blow off *ou* away; (*par les vagues*) to sweep away; (*par la maladie*) to carry off; **pizza**/etc à *Br* take-away *ou* Am take-out pizza/*etc*; **l'e. sur qn** to get the

upper hand over s.o.; **il l'a emporté** he won; **se laisser e.** Fig to get carried away (**par** by); **elle ne l'emportera pas au paradis** she'll soon be smiling on the other side of her face. ▮ **s'emporter** *vpr* to lose one's temper (**contre** with). ●**emporté, -ée** *a* (*caractère*) hot-tempered. ●**emportement** *nm* anger; **emportements** fits of anger.

empoté, -ée [ɑ̃pɔte] *a* Fam clumsy.

empourprer (s') [sɑ̃purpre] *vpr* to turn crimson.

empreint, -einte [ɑ̃prɛ̃, -ɛ̃t] *a* **e. de** *Litt* stamped with, heavy with.

empreinte [ɑ̃prɛ̃t] *nf* (*marque*) & *Fig* mark, stamp; **e. (digitale)** fingerprint; **e. (de pas)** footprint.

empresser (s') [sɑ̃prese] *vpr* **s'e. de faire** to hasten to do; **s'e. auprès de qn** to busy oneself with s.o., be attentive to s.o.; **s'e. autour de qn** to rush around s.o. ●**empressé, -ée** *a* eager, attentive; **e. à faire** eager to do. ●**empressement** [-ɛsmɑ̃] *nm* (*hâte*) eagerness; (*auprès de qn*) attentiveness.

emprise [ɑ̃priz] *nf* hold, ascendancy (**sur** over).

emprisonner [ɑ̃prizɔne] *vt* to jail, imprison; (*enfermer*) *Fig* to confine. ●**emprisonnement** *nm* imprisonment.

emprunt [ɑ̃prœ̃] *nm* (*argent etc*) loan; (*mot*) *Ling* borrowed word; **un e. à** *Ling* a borrowing from; **l'e. de qch** the borrowing of sth; **d'e.** borrowed; **nom d'e.** assumed name. ●**emprunter** *vt* (*argent, objet*) to borrow (**à qn** from s.o.); (*route etc*) to use; (*nom*) to assume; **e. à** (*tirer de*) to derive *ou* borrow from.

emprunté, -ée [ɑ̃prœ̃te] *a* (*gêné*) ill-at-ease.

empuantir [ɑ̃pɥɑ̃tir] *vt* to make stink, stink out.

ému, -ue [emy] *pp de* **émouvoir** ▮ *a* (*attendri*) moved; (*attristé*) upset; (*apeuré*) nervous; **une voix émue** a voice charged with emotion, an emotional voice.

émulation [emylasjɔ̃] *nf* (*sentiment*) & *Ordinat* emulation.

émule [emyl] *nmf* imitator, follower.

en¹ [ɑ̃] *prép* **1** (*lieu*) in; (*direction*) to; **être en ville/en France** to be in town/in France; **aller en ville/en France** to go (in)to town/to France.

2 (*temps*) in; **en février** in February; **en été** in summer; **d'heure en heure** from hour to hour.

3 (*moyen, état etc*) by; in; on; at; **en avion** by plane; **en groupe** in a group; **en fleur** in flower; **en vain** in vain; **en congé** on leave; **en mer** at sea; **en guerre** at war.

4 (*matière*) in; **en bois** in wood, wooden; **chemise en nylon** nylon shirt; **c'est en or** it's (made of) gold.

5 (*domaine*) **étudiant en lettres** humanities *ou Br* arts student; **docteur en médecine** doctor of medicine.

6 (*comme*) **en cadeau** as a present; **en ami** as a friend.

7 (+ *participe présent*) en mangeant/chantant/*etc* while eating/singing/*etc*; en apprenant que... on hearing that...; en souriant smiling, with a smile; en ne disant rien by saying nothing; sortir en courant to run out.
8 (*transformation*) into; traduire en français/*etc* to translate into French/*etc*.

en² [ɑ̃] *pron & adv* **1** (= *de là*) from there; j'en viens I've just come from there.
2 (= *de ça, lui, eux etc*) il en est content he's pleased with it *ou* him *ou* them; en parler to talk about it; en mourir to die *ou* from it; elle m'en frappa she struck me with it; il s'en souviendra he'll remember it.
3 (*partitif*) some; j'en ai I have some; en veux-tu? do you want some *ou* any?; donne-lui-en give some to him *ou* her; je t'en supplie I beg you (to).

ENA [ena] *nf abrév* (*École nationale d'administration*) school training top civil servants.
● **énarque** *nmf* student *ou* former student of ENA.

encablure [ɑ̃kablyr] *nf* à quelques encablures du rivage a short distance (away) from the shore.

encadrer [ɑ̃kadre] *vt* (*tableau*) to frame; (*entourer d'un trait*) to circle (*word*); (*étudiants, troupes*) to supervise, train; (*prisonnier, accusé*) to flank; je ne peux pas l'e. *Fam* I can't stand him *ou* her. ● **encadrement** *nm* (*action*) framing; (*d'étudiants etc*) supervision; (*de porte, photo*) frame; personnel d'e. training and supervisory staff.

encaissé, -ée [ɑ̃kese] *a* (*vallée*) deep.

encaisser [ɑ̃kese] *vt* (*argent, loyer etc*) to collect; (*chèque*) to cash; (*coup*) *Fam* to take; je ne peux pas l'e. *Fam* I can't stand him *ou* her. ● **encaissement** [-ɛsmɑ̃] *nm* (*de loyer etc*) collection; (*de chèque*) cashing.

encapuchonné, -ée [ɑ̃kapyʃɔne] *a* hooded.

encart [ɑ̃kar] *nm* (*feuille*) insert; e. publicitaire publicity insert.

en-cas [ɑ̃kɑ] *nm inv* (*repas*) snack.

encastrer [ɑ̃kastre] *vt* to build in (dans to), embed (dans into).

encaustique [ɑ̃kostik] *nf* (wax) polish. ● **encaustiquer** *vt* to wax, polish.

enceinte [ɑ̃sɛ̃t] **1** *af* (*femme*) pregnant; e. de six mois/*etc* six months/*etc* pregnant. **2** *nf* (*muraille*) (surrounding) wall; (*espace*) enclosure; e. (acoustique) (loud)speakers; dans l'e. de within, inside.

encens [ɑ̃sɑ̃] *nm* incense. ● **encensoir** *nm Rel* censer.

encercler [ɑ̃sɛrkle] *vt* to surround, encircle.

enchaîner [ɑ̃ʃene] *vt* (*animal*) to chain (up); (*prisonnier*) to put in chains, chain (up); (*idées etc*) to link (up), connect ▮ *vi* (*continuer à parler*) to continue ▮ **s'enchaîner** *vpr* (*idées etc*) to be linked (up). ● **enchaînement** [-ɛnmɑ̃] *nm* (*succession*) chain, series; (*liaison*) link(ing) (de between, of); (*en gymnastique ou danse*) enchaînement.

enchanter [ɑ̃ʃɑ̃te] *vt* (*ravir*) to delight, enchant; (*ensorceler*) to bewitch, enchant. ● **en-**

chanté, -ée *a* (*ravi*) delighted (de with, que (+ *sub*) that); (*magique*) enchanted; e. de faire votre connaissance! pleased to meet you! ● **enchantement** *nm* (*ravissement*) delight; (*magie, effet*) enchantment; comme par e. as if by magic. ● **enchanteur** *a* delightful, enchanting ▮ *nm* (*sorcier*) magician.

enchâsser [ɑ̃ʃɑse] *vt* (*diamant*) to set, embed.

enchère [ɑ̃ʃɛr] *nf* (*offre*) bid; vente aux enchères auction; mettre qch aux enchères to put sth up for auction, auction sth. ● **enchérir** *vi* e. sur qn to outbid s.o. ● **enchérisseur** *nm* bidder.

enchevêtrer [ɑ̃ʃvetre] *vt* to (en)tangle ▮ **s'enchevêtrer** *vpr* to get entangled (dans in). ● **enchevêtrement** [-vɛtrəmɑ̃] *nm* tangle, entanglement.

enclave [ɑ̃klav] *nf* enclave. ● **enclaver** *vt* to enclose (completely).

enclencher [ɑ̃klɑ̃ʃe] *vt Tech* to engage.

enclin, -ine [ɑ̃klɛ̃, -in] *a* e. à inclined *ou* prone to.

enclos [ɑ̃klo] *nm* (*terrain, clôture*) enclosure. ● **enclore*** *vt* (*terrain*) to enclose.

enclume [ɑ̃klym] *nf* anvil.

encoche [ɑ̃kɔʃ] *nf* nick, notch (à in).

encoignure [ɑ̃kwaɲyr] *nf* corner.

encoller [ɑ̃kɔle] *vt* (*papier peint etc*) to paste.

encolure [ɑ̃kɔlyr] *nf* (*de cheval, vêtement*) neck; (*tour du cou*) collar (size); robe à e. carrée/*etc* square-neck(ed)/*etc* dress.

encombre (sans) [sɑ̃zɑ̃kɔbr] *adv* without a hitch.

encombrer [ɑ̃kɔ̃bre] *vt* (*pièce, couloir etc*) to clutter up (de with); (*rue*) to congest, clog (de with); e. qn to hamper s.o.; s'e. de to burden *ou* saddle oneself with. ● **encombrant, -ante** (*paquet*) bulky, cumbersome; (*présence*) awkward. ● **encombré, -ée** *a* (*lignes téléphoniques, route etc*) jammed. ● **encombrement** *nm* (*d'objets*) clutter; (*de rue*) traffic jam; (*volume*) bulk(iness).

encontre de (à l') [alɑ̃kɔ̃trədə] *adv* against.

encore [ɑ̃kɔr] *adv* **1** (*toujours*) still; tu es e. là? are you still here?
2 (*avec négation*) yet; pas e. not yet; ne pars pas e. don't go yet; je ne suis pas e. prêt I'm not ready yet, I'm still not ready.
3 (*de nouveau*) again; essaie e. try again.
4 (*de plus, en plus*) e. un café another coffee, one more coffee; e. une fois (once) again, once more; e. un autre (one), one more; e. du pain (some) more bread; que veut-il e.? what else *ou* more does he want?; e. quelque chose something else; qui/quoi e.? who/what else?; chante e. sing some more.
5 (*avec comparatif*) even, still; e. mieux even better, better still.
6 (*aussi*) mais e. but also.
7 si e. (*si seulement*) if only; et e.! (*à peine*) if that!, only just!
8 e. que (+ *sub*) although.

encourager [ɑ̃kuraʒe] *vt* to encourage (à faire to do). ● **encourageant, -ante** *a* encouraging. ● **encouragement** *nm* encouragement.

encourir* [ãkurir] *vt* (*amende etc*) *Litt* to incur.

encrasser [ãkrase] *vt* to clog up (with dirt) ∎ **s'encrasser** *vpr* to get clogged up.

encre [ãkr] *nf* ink; **e. de Chine** *Br* Indian *ou* *Am* India ink; **e. sympathique** invisible ink; **faire couler beaucoup d'e.** to be much written about. ● **encrier** *nm* inkpot, inkwell.

encroûter (s') [sãkrute] *vpr Péj* to get into a rut, get set in one's ways; **s'e. dans** (*habitude*) to get stuck *ou* set in.

encyclique [ãsiklik] *nf Rel* encyclical.

encyclopédie [ãsiklɔpedi] *nf* encyclop(a)edia. ● **encyclopédique** *a* encyclop(a)edic.

endémique [ãdemik] *a* endemic.

endetter [ãdete] *vt* **e. qn** to get s.o. into debt ∎ **s'endetter** *vpr* to get into debt. ● **endettement** *nm* (*dettes*) debts.

endeuiller [ãdœje] *vt* to plunge into mourning.

endiablé, -ée [ãdjable] *a* (*rythme etc*) frantic, wild.

endiguer [ãdige] *vt* (*fleuve*) to dam (up); (*réprimer*) *Fig* to stem.

endimanché, -ée [ãdimãʃe] *a* in one's Sunday best.

endive [ãdiv] *nf* chicory *inv*, endive.

endoctriner [ãdɔktrine] *vt* to indoctrinate. ● **endoctrinement** *nm* indoctrination.

endolori, -ie [ãdɔlɔri] *a* painful, aching.

endommager [ãdɔmaʒe] *vt* to damage.

endormir* [ãdɔrmir] *vt* (*enfant etc*) to put to sleep; (*ennuyer*) to send to sleep; (*soupçons etc*) to lull; (*douleur*) to deaden ∎ **s'endormir** *vpr* to fall asleep, go to sleep. ● **endormi, -ie** *a* asleep, sleeping; (*indolent*) *Fam* sluggish.

endosser [ãdose] *vt* **1** (*vêtement*) to put on, *Litt* don. **2** (*responsabilité*) to assume. **3** (*chèque*) to endorse.

endroit [ãdrwa] *nm* **1** place, spot; **à cet e. du récit** at this point in the story; **par endroits** in places. **2** (*de tissu*) right side; **à l'e.** (*vêtement*) right side out, the right way round.

enduire* [ãdɥir] *vt* to smear, coat (**de** with). ● **enduit** *nm* coating; (*de mur*) plaster.

endurant, -ante [ãdyrã, -ãt] *a* hardy, tough. ● **endurance** *nf* endurance.

endurcir [ãdyrsir] *vt* **e. qn à** (*douleur etc*) to harden s.o. to; **s'e.** (*personne*) to become hardened (**à** to). ● **endurci, -ie** (*insensible*) hardened; **célibataire e.** confirmed bachelor. ● **endurcissement** *nm* hardening.

endurer [ãdyre] *vt* to endure, bear.

énergie [enɛrʒi] *nf* energy; **avec é.** (*protester etc*) forcefully. ● **énergétique** *a* **aliment é.** energy food; **dépense é.** expenditure of energy; **ressources énergétiques** energy resources. ● **énergique** *a* (*dynamique*) energetic; (*remède*) powerful; (*mesure*, *ton*) forceful. ● **énergiquement** *adv* (*protester etc*) energetically.

énergumène [enɛrgymɛn] *nmf Péj* rowdy hothead, fanatical ranter.

énerver [enɛrve] *vt* **é. qn** (*irriter*) to get on s.o.'s nerves; (*rendre nerveux*) to make s.o. nervous ∎ **s'énerver** *vpr* to get worked up. ● **énervé, -ée** *a* on edge, irritated. ● **énervement** *nm* irritation, nervousness.

enfance [ãfãs] *nf* childhood; **petite e.** infancy, early childhood; **dans son e.** (*science etc*) in its infancy; **c'est l'e. de l'art** it's child's play. ● **enfanter** *vt Litt* to give birth to ∎ *vi Litt* to give birth. ● **enfantillage(s)** *nm* childishness. ● **enfantin, -ine** *a* (*voix*, *joie*) childlike; (*simple*) easy; (*puéril*) childish; (*langage*, *jeu*) children's.

enfant [ãfã] *nmf* child (*pl* children); **e. en bas âge** infant; **e. trouvé** foundling; **e. de chœur** *Rel* altar boy; **e. prodige** child prodigy; **e. prodigue** prodigal son; **e. gâté** spoiled *ou* spoilt child; **c'est un e. de** (*originaire*) he's a native of; **attendre un e.** to expect a baby *ou* a child; **c'est un jeu d'e.** it's child's play ∎ *a inv* **bon e.** (*caractère*) good-natured.

enfer [ãfɛr] *nm* hell; **d'e.** (*bruit*, *vision*) infernal; **feu d'e.** roaring fire; **à un train d'e.** at breakneck speed; **un plan/etc d'e.** *Fam* a hell of a (good) plan/*etc*.

enfermer [ãfɛrme] *vt* (*personne etc*) to lock up, shut up; (*objet précieux*) to lock up, shut away; **s'e. dans** (*chambre etc*) to lock *ou* shut oneself (up) in; (*attitude etc*) *Fig* to maintain stubbornly.

enferrer (s') [sãfɛre] *vpr* **s'e. dans** to get caught up in.

enfiévré, -ée [ãfjevre] *a* (*surexcité*) feverish.

enfilade [ãfilad] *nf* (*série*) row, string; **des pièces en e.** a suite of rooms.

enfiler [ãfile] *vt* (*aiguille*) to thread; (*perles etc*) to string; (*vêtement*) *Fam* to pull on, slip on; (*rue*, *couloir*) to take; **s'e. dans** (*rue etc*) to take; **s'e. tout le travail** *Fam* to take on *ou* get landed with all the work.

enfin [ãfɛ̃] *adv* (*à la fin*) finally, at last; (*en dernier lieu*) lastly; (*en somme*) in a word; (*conclusion résignée*) well; **e. bref** (*en somme*) *Fam* in a word; **mais e.** but; (*mais*) **e.!** for heaven's sake!; **il est grand, e. pas trop petit** he's tall — well, not too short anyhow.

enflammer [ãflame] *vt* to set fire to, ignite; (*allumette*) to light; (*irriter*) to inflame (*throat etc*); (*imagination*, *colère*) to excite, inflame ∎ **s'enflammer** *vpr* to catch fire, ignite; **s'e. de colère** to flare up. ● **enflammé, -ée** *a* (*discours*) fiery.

enfler [ãfle] *vt* (*rivière*, *membre etc*) to swell ∎ *vi* (*membre etc*) to swell (up). ● **enflure** *nf* swelling.

enfoncer [ãfɔ̃se] *vt* (*clou etc*) to knock in, bang in, drive in; (*porte*, *voiture*) to smash in; (*chapeau*) to push *ou* force down; **e. dans** qch (*couteau*, *mains etc*) to plunge into sth; **e. des portes ouvertes** *Fig* to persist in stating the obvious ∎ *vi*, **s'enfoncer** *vpr* (*s'enliser*) to sink (**dans** into); **s'e. dans** (*pénétrer*) to plunge into, disappear (deep) into. ● **enfoncé, -ée** *a* (*yeux*) sunken.

enfouir [ãfwir] *vt* to bury.

enfourcher [ãfurʃe] *vt* (*cheval etc*) to mount, bestride.

enfourner [ãfurne] *vt* to put in the oven.

enfreindre* [ãfrɛ̃dr] *vt Litt* to infringe.

enfuir* (s') [sãfμir] *vpr* to run away *ou* off, flee (de from).

enfumer [ãfyme] *vt* (*pièce*) to fill with smoke; (*personne*) to smoke out.

engager [ãgaʒe] *vt* (*discussion, combat*) to start; (*bijou etc*) to pawn; (*parole*) to pledge; (*capitaux*) to tie up, invest; (*clef etc*) to insert (dans into); **e. qn** (*embaucher*) to hire s.o., engage s.o.; (*lier*) to bind s.o., commit s.o.; **e. qn dans** (*affaire etc*) to involve s.o. in; **e. qn à faire** (*exhorter*) to urge s.o. to do; **e. la bataille avec** to join battle with.
■ **s'engager** *vpr* (dans l'armée) to enlist; (*sportif*) to enter (one's name); (*action, jeu*) to start; (*au service d'une cause*) to commit oneself; **s'e. à faire** to undertake to do, commit oneself to doing; **s'e. dans** (*voie*) to enter; (*affaire etc*) to get involved in. ● **engageant, -ante** *a* engaging, inviting. ● **engagé, -ée** *a* (*écrivain etc*) committed. ● **engagement** *nm* (*promesse*) commitment; (*commencement*) start; (*de recrues*) enlistment; (*dans une compétition sportive*) entry; (*combat militaire*) engagement; **sans e. de votre part** without obligation (on your part); **prendre l'e. de faire** to undertake to do.

engelure [ãʒlyr] *nf* chilblain.

engendrer [ãʒãdre] *vt* (*causer*) to generate, engender; (*procréer*) to beget.

engin [ãʒɛ̃] *nm* machine, device; **e. spatial** spaceship; **e. explosif** explosive device.

englober [ãglɔbe] *vt* to include, embrace.

engloutir [ãglutir] *vt* (*nourriture*) to wolf (down), gobble (up); (*faire disparaître*) to swallow up, engulf.

engorger [ãgɔrʒe] *vt* to block up, clog.

engouement [ãgumã] *nm* (*sudden*) craze (pour for).

engouffrer [ãgufre] *vt* **1** (*avaler*) to wolf (down); (*fortune*) to consume. **2 s'engouffrer** *vpr* **s'e. dans** to sweep *ou* rush into.

engourdir [ãgurdir] *vt* (*membre*) to numb; (*esprit*) to dull ■ **s'engourdir** *vpr* to go numb; (*esprit*) to become dull(ed). ● **engourdissement** *nm* numbness; (*d'esprit*) dullness.

engrais [ãgrɛ] *nm* (*naturel*) manure; (*chimique*) fertilizer.

engraisser [ãgrese] *vt* (*animal*) to fatten (up); (*personne*) *Fam* to fatten up ■ *vi*, **s'engraisser** *vpr* to get fat, put on weight.

engrenage [ãgrənaʒ] *nm Tech* gears; *Fig* mesh, chain, web.

engueuler [ãgœle] *vt* **e. qn** *Fam* to give s.o. hell, bawl s.o. out, swear at s.o. ■ **s'engueuler** *vpr Fam* to bawl each other out, (have a) row. ● **engueulade** *nf Fam* (*réprimande*) bawling out, dressing-down; (*dispute*) row, *Br* slanging match.

enhardir [ãardir] *vt* to make bold *ou* bolder; **s'e. à faire** to pluck up courage to do, make s.o. bold (as) to do.

énième [enjɛm] *a Fam* umpteenth, nth.

énigme [enigm] *nf* riddle, enigma. ● **énigmatique** *a* enigmatic.

enivrer [ãnivre] *vt* (*soûler, troubler*) to intoxicate ■ **s'enivrer** *vpr* to get drunk (de on).

enjamber [ãʒãbe] *vt* to step over; (*pont etc*) to span (*river etc*). ● **enjambée** *nf* stride.

enjeu, -x [ãʒø] *nm* (*mise*) stake(s).

enjoindre* [ãʒwɛ̃dr] *vt* **e. à qn de faire** *Litt* to order s.o. to do.

enjôler [ãʒole] *vt* to wheedle, coax.

enjoliver [ãʒolive] *vt* to embellish.

enjoliveur [ãʒolivœr] *nm* (*de roue*) hubcap.

enjoué, -ée [ãʒwe] *a* playful, cheerful. ● **enjouement** *nm* playfulness.

enlacer [ãlase] *vt* to entwine; (*serrer dans ses bras*) to clasp.

enlaidir [ãledir] *vt* to make ugly ■ *vi* to grow ugly.

enlevé, -ée [ãl(ə)ve] *a* (*scène, danse etc*) well-rendered.

enlever [ãl(ə)ve] *vt* to take away *ou* off, remove (à qn from s.o.); (*vêtement*) to take off, remove; (*tache*) to take out, lift, remove; (*enfant etc*) to kidnap, abduct; (*ordures*) to collect ■ **s'enlever** *vpr* (*tache*) to come out; (*vernis*) to come off. ● **enlèvement** *nm* (*d'enfant*) kidnapping, abduction; (*d'un objet*) removal; (*des ordures*) collection.

enliser (s') [sãlize] *vpr* (*véhicule*) & *Fig* to get bogged down (dans in).

enneigé, -ée [ãneʒe] *a* snow-covered. ● **enneigement** [-ɛʒmã] *nm* snow coverage; **bulletin d'e.** snow report.

ennemi, -ie [ɛnmi] *nmf* enemy ■ *a* (*personne*) hostile (de to); **pays/soldat e.** enemy country/soldier.

ennui [ãnμi] *nm* boredom; (*mélancolie*) weariness; **un e.** (*tracas*) (some) trouble *ou* bother; **des ennuis** trouble, bother; **l'e., c'est que...** the annoying thing is that....

ennuyer [ãnμije] *vt* (*agacer*) to annoy, bother; (*préoccuper*) to bother; (*fatiguer*) to bore; **si ça ne t'ennuie pas** if you don't mind ■ **s'ennuyer** *vpr* to get bored. ● **ennuyé, -ée** *a* (*air*) bored; **je suis très e.** (*confus*) I feel bad *ou* badly (about it). ● **ennuyeux, -euse** *a* (*fastidieux*) boring; (*contrariant*) annoying.

énoncé [enõse] *nm* (*de texte*) wording, terms; (*phrase*) *Ling* utterance.

énoncer [enõse] *vt* to state, express.

enorgueillir (s') [sãnɔrgœjir] *vpr* **s'e. de** to pride oneself on.

énorme [enɔrm] *a* enormous, huge, tremendous. ● **énormément** *adv* enormously, tremendously; **e. de** an enormous *ou* tremendous amount of. ● **énormité** *nf* (*dimension*) enormity; (*faute*) blunder.

enquérir* (s') [sãkerir] *vpr* **s'e. de** to inquire about.

enquête [ãkɛt] *nf* (*de police etc*) investigation; (*judiciaire, administrative*) inquiry; (*sondage*) survey. ● **enquêter** [ãkete] *vi* (*po-*

lice etc) to investigate; **e. sur** (*crime*) to investigate. ● **enquêteur, -euse** *nmf* (*policier etc*) investigator; (*sondeur*) researcher.

enquiquiner [ãkikine] *vt Fam* to annoy, bug.

enraciner (s') [sãrasine] *vpr* to take root; **enraciné dans** (*personne, souvenir*) rooted in; **bien enraciné** (*préjugé etc*) deep-rooted.

enrager [ãraʒe] *vi* to be furious (**de faire** about doing); **faire e. qn** to get on s.o.'s nerves. ● **enrageant, -ante** *a* infuriating. ● **enragé, -ée** *a* (*chien*) rabid, mad; (*joueur etc*) *Fam* fanatical (**de** about); **devenir e.** (*furieux*) to become furious; **rendre qn e.** to make s.o. furious.

enrayer [ãreje] *vt* (*maladie etc*) to check ▮ **s'enrayer** *vpr* (*fusil*) to jam.

enregistrer [ãr(ə)ʒistre] *vt* **1** (*par écrit, sur bande*) to record; (*sur registre*) to register; (*constater*) to note, register; (**faire**) **e. ses bagages** (*à l'aéroport*) to check in, check one's luggage in. **2** (*musique, émission etc*) to record; **ça enregistre** it's recording. ● **enregistrement** *nm* (*d'un acte*) registration; (*sur bande etc*) recording; **l'e. des bagages** (*à l'aéroport*) (luggage) check-in; **se présenter à l'e.** to check in. ● **enregistreur, -euse** *a* **appareil e.** recording apparatus; **caisse enregistreuse** cash register.

enrhumer (s') [sãryme] *vpr* to catch a cold; **être enrhumé** to have a cold.

enrichir [ãriʃir] *vt* to enrich (**de** with) ▮ **s'enrichir** *vpr* (*personne*) to get rich. ● **enrichissement** *nm* enrichment.

enrober [ãrɔbe] *vt* to coat (**de** in); **enrobé de chocolat** chocolate-coated.

enrôler [ãrole] *vt*, **s'enrôler** *vpr* to enlist. ● **enrôlement** *nm* enlistment.

enrouer (s') [sãrwe] *vpr* to get hoarse. ● **enroué, -ée** *a* hoarse.

enrouler [ãrule] *vt* (*fil etc*) to wind; (*tapis, cordage etc*) to roll up; **s'e. dans** (*couvertures*) to wrap *ou* roll oneself up in; **s'e. sur** *ou* **autour de qch** to wind round sth.

ensabler [ãsable] *vt*, **s'ensabler** *vpr* (*port*) to silt up.

ensanglanté, -ée [ãsãglãte] *a* bloodstained.

enseigne [ãsɛɲ] **1** *nf* (*de magasin etc*) sign; **e. lumineuse** neon sign; **logés à la même e.** *Fig* in the same boat. **2** *nm* **e. de vaisseau** *Br* lieutenant, *Am* ensign.

enseigner [ãsɛɲe] *vt* to teach; **e. qch à qn** to teach s.o. sth ▮ *vi* to teach. ● **enseignant, -ante** [-ɛɲã, -ãt] *nmf* teacher ▮ *a* **corps e.** teaching profession. ● **enseignement** [-ɛɲ(ə)mã] *nm* education; (*action, métier*) teaching; **e. privé** private education; **e. libre** private (and religious) education; **e. public** *Br* state *ou* *Am* public education; **e. par correspondance** tuition *ou* education by correspondence; **être dans l'e.** to be a teacher.

ensemble [ãsãbl] **1** *adv* together; **aller (bien) e.** (*couleurs etc*) to go together; (*personnes*) to be well-matched.

2 *nm* (*d'objets*) group, set; *Math* set; (*vêtement féminin*) outfit; *Mus* ensemble; (*mobilier*) suite; (*harmonie*) unity; **l'e. du personnel** (*totalité*) the whole (of the) staff; **l'e. des enseignants** all (of) the teachers; **dans l'e.** on the whole; **vue/etc d'e.** general view/*etc*; **grand e.** (*quartier*) housing *Br* complex *ou* *Am* development; (*ville*) = *Br* new town, = *Am* planned community. ● **ensembler** *nm* (interior) decorator.

ensemencer [ãs(ə)mãse] *vt* (*terre*) to sow.

ensevelir [ãsəvlir] *vt* to bury.

ensoleillé, -ée [ãsɔleje] *a* (*endroit, journée*) sunny.

ensommeillé, -ée [ãsɔmeje] *a* sleepy.

ensorceler [ãsɔrsəle] *vt* (*envoûter, séduire*) to bewitch. ● **ensorcellement** [-ɛlmã] *nm* (*séduction*) spell.

ensuite [ãsɥit] *adv* (*puis*) next, then; (*plus tard*) afterwards.

ensuivre* (s') [sãsɥivr] *v imp Litt* **il s'ensuit que** it follows that; **et tout ce qui s'ensuit** and all the rest of it, and everything that follows on from that.

entacher [ãtaʃe] *vt* (*honneur etc*) to sully.

entaille [ãtaj] *nf* (*fente*) notch; (*blessure*) gash, slash. ● **entailler** *vt* to notch; (*blesser*) to gash, slash.

entame [ãtam] *nf* first slice.

entamer [ãtame] *vt* (*pain, peau etc*) to cut (into); (*bouteille, boîte etc*) to start (on); (*négociations etc*) to enter into, start; (*capital*) to eat *ou* break into; (*métal, plastique*) to damage; (*résolution, réputation*) to shake; (*sujet*) to broach.

entartrer [ãtartre] *vt*, **s'entartrer** *vpr* (*chaudière etc*) *Br* to fur up, *Am* scale.

entasser [ãtase] *vt*, **s'entasser** *vpr* (*objets*) to pile up, heap up; (**s')e. dans** (*passagers etc*) to crowd *ou* pack *ou* pile into; **ils s'entassaient sur la plage** they were crowded *ou* packed (together) on the beach. ● **entassement** *nm* (*tas*) pile, heap; (*de gens*) crowding.

entendement [ãtãdmã] *nm* (*faculté*) understanding.

entendre [ãtãdr] *vt* to hear; (*comprendre*) to understand; (*vouloir*) to intend, mean; **e. parler de** to hear of; **e. dire que** to hear (it said) that; **e. raison** to listen to reason; **laisser e. à qn que** to give s.o. to understand that.

▮ **s'entendre** *vpr* (*être entendu*) to be heard; (*être compris*) to be understood; **s'e. (sur)** (*être d'accord*) to agree (on); (**bien) s'e. (avec qn)** (*s'accorder*) to get along *ou* *Br* on (with s.o.); **on ne s'entend plus!** (*à cause du bruit etc*) we can't hear ourselves speak!; **s'y entend** (*est expert*) he knows all about that.

entendu, -ue *a* (*convenu*) agreed; (*compris*) understood; (*sourire, air*) knowing; **e.!** all right!; **bien e.** of course.

entente [ãtãt] *nf* (*accord*) agreement, understanding; (**bonne) e.** (*amitié*) good relation-

ship, harmony.
entériner [ɑ̃terine] vt to ratify.
enterrer [ɑ̃tere] vt (défunt etc) to bury; (projet) Fig to scrap. ●**enterrement** [-ɛrmɑ̃] nm
burial; (funérailles) funeral.
en-tête [ɑ̃tɛt] nm (de papier) heading; **papier
à en-tête** Br headed paper, Am letterhead.
entêter (s') [sɑ̃tete] vpr to persist (à faire in
doing). ●**entêté, -ée** a (têtu) stubborn; (persévérant) persistent. ●**entêtement** [ɑ̃tɛtmɑ̃]
nm stubbornness; (à faire qch) persistence.
enthousiasme [ɑ̃tuzjasm] nm enthusiasm.
●**enthousiasmer** vt to fill with enthusiasm,
enthuse; **s'e. pour** to get ou get enthusiastic
about ou over, enthuse over. ●**enthou-
siasmant, -ante** a (nouvelle etc) exciting,
thrilling. ●**enthousiaste** a enthusiastic.
enticher (s') [sɑ̃tiʃe] vpr **s'e. de** to become
infatuated with.
entier, -ière [ɑ̃tje, -jɛr] 1 a (total) whole, entire; (intact) intact; (absolu) absolute, complete, entire; **payer place entière** to pay full
price; **le pays tout e.** the whole ou entire
country; **nombre e.** Math whole number; **lait
e.** whole milk, Br full-cream milk ▌ nm
(unité) whole; **en e., dans son e.** in its
entirety, completely. 2 a (caractère,
personne) uncompromising, unyielding. ●**entièrement** adv entirely.
entité [ɑ̃tite] nf entity.
entonner [ɑ̃tɔne] vt (air) to start singing.
entonnoir [ɑ̃tɔnwar] nm (ustensile) funnel.
entorse [ɑ̃tɔrs] nf 1 Méd sprain; **se faire une
e. à la cheville/etc** to sprain one's ankle/etc. 2
une e. à (règlement) an infringement of.
entortiller [ɑ̃tɔrtije] vt **e. qch autour de qch**
(dans du papier etc) to wrap sth around sth;
e. qn Fam to dupe s.o., get round s.o.
●**s'entortiller** vpr (lierre etc) to wind, twist.
●**entortillé, -ée** a (phrase etc) convoluted.
entourage [ɑ̃turaʒ] nm (proches) circle of
family and friends.
entourer [ɑ̃ture] vt to surround (de with);
(envelopper) to wrap (de in); **entouré de**
surrounded by; **e. qn de ses bras** to put one's
arms round s.o.; **s'e. de** to surround oneself
with; **il est très entouré** (soutenu) he has lots
of supportive people around him.
entourloupette [ɑ̃turlupɛt] nf Fam nasty
trick.
entracte [ɑ̃trakt] nm (de théâtre) Br interval,
Am intermission.
entraide [ɑ̃trɛd] nf mutual aid. ●**s'entraider**
[sɑ̃trede] vpr to help each other.
entrailles [ɑ̃traj] nfpl entrails.
entrain [ɑ̃trɛ̃] nm spirit, liveliness; **plein d'e.**
lively; **sans e.** lifeless, spiritless.
entraînant, -ante [ɑ̃trɛnɑ̃, -ɑ̃t] a (musique)
lively, captivating.
entraîner [ɑ̃trene] 1 vt (charrier) to carry ou
sweep away; (causer) to bring about; (impliquer) to entail, involve; (roue) Tech to
drive; **e. qn** (emmener) to lead ou draw s.o.
(away); (de force) to drag s.o. (away); (attirer) Péj to lure s.o.; (charmer) to carry s.o.

away; **e. qn à faire** (amener) to lead s.o. to
do.
2 vt (athlète, cheval etc) to train (à for) ▌
s'entraîner vpr to train oneself (à faire qch
to do sth); Sport to train. ●**entraînement**
[-ɛnmɑ̃] nm **1** Sport training. **2** (élan)
impulse; Tech drive. ●**entraîneur** [-ɛnœr] nm
(d'athlète) coach, trainer; (de cheval) trainer.
entrave [ɑ̃trav] nf (obstacle) Fig hindrance (à
to). ●**entraver** vt to hinder, hamper.
entre [ɑ̃tr(ə)] prép between; (parmi)
among(st); **l'un d'e. vous** one of you; (soit
dit) **e. nous** between you and me; **se dévorer
e. eux** (réciprocité) to devour each other; **e.
deux âges** middle-aged; **e. autres (choses)**
among other things; **e. les mains de** in the
hands of; **être pris e. deux feux** (soldat) &
Fig to be caught in the crossfire; **elle est e. la
vie et la mort** it's touch and go whether
she'll live.
entrebâiller [ɑ̃trəbaje] vt (porte) to open
slightly. ●**entrebâillé, -ée** a slightly open,
ajar. ●**entrebâillement** nm **se tenir/etc dans
l'e. de la porte** to stand/etc by the half-open
door. ●**entrebâilleur** nm **e.** (de porte) door
chain.
entrechoquer (s') [sɑ̃trəʃɔke] vpr (bouteilles
etc) to chink, knock against each other.
entrecôte [ɑ̃trəkot] nf (Br boned ou Am
filleted) rib steak.
entrecouper [ɑ̃trəkupe] vt (entremêler) to
punctuate (de with), intersperse (de with).
entrecroiser [ɑ̃trəkrwaze] vt, **s'entrecroiser**
vpr (fils) to interlace; (routes) to intersect.
entre-deux-guerres [ɑ̃trədøgɛr] nm inv
inter-war period.
entrée [ɑ̃tre] nf (action) entry, entrance;
(porte) entrance; (accès) admission, entry
(de to); (vestibule) entrance hall, entry; (billet) ticket (for admission); (plat) first course,
entrée; Ordinat input; (mot dans un dictionnaire) entry; **à son e.** as he ou she came in;
faire son e. (dans une salle etc) to make
one's entrance; **à l'e. de l'hiver** at the outset
ou beginning of winter; **'e. interdite'** 'no entry', 'no admittance'; **'e. libre'** 'admission
free'; **e. en matière** (d'un discours) opening,
introduction; **e. en vigueur** (d'une loi etc)
date of application; **e. en sixième/etc** Scol =
Br entering ou going into the first form, =
Am entering the sixth grade; **e. de service**
service ou Br tradesmen's entrance; **e. des
artistes** (au théâtre) stage door.
entrefaites (sur ces) [syrsezɑ̃trəfɛt] adv at
that moment.
entrefilet [ɑ̃trəfilɛ] nm (dans un journal)
(news) item.
entrejambe [ɑ̃trəʒɑ̃b] nm (de pantalon,
partie du corps) crutch, crotch.
entrelacer [ɑ̃trəlase] vt, **s'entrelacer** vpr to
intertwine.
entremêler [ɑ̃trəmele] vt, **s'entremêler** vpr
to intermingle.
entremets [ɑ̃trəmɛ] nm (plat) dessert, Br
sweet.

entremetteur, -euse [ɑ̃trəmɛtœr, -øz] *nmf* Péj go-between.
entremise [ɑ̃trəmiz] *nf* intervention; **par l'e. de qn** through s.o.
entreposer [ɑ̃trəpoze] *vt* to store; *Jur* to bond. ●**entrepôt** *nm* warehouse; *(de la douane) Jur* bonded warehouse.
entreprendre* [ɑ̃trəprɑ̃dr] *vt (travail, voyage etc)* to undertake, start on; **e. de faire** to undertake to do. ●**entreprenant, -ante** *a* enterprising; *(galant)* brash, forward.
entrepreneur [ɑ̃trəprənœr] *nm (en bâtiment)* (building) contractor.
entreprise [ɑ̃trəpriz] *nf* **1** *(firme)* company, firm. **2** *(opération)* undertaking.
entrer [ɑ̃tre] *vi (aux* **être**) *(aller)* to go in, enter; *(venir)* to come in, enter; **e. dans** to go into; *(pièce)* to come *ou* go into, enter; *(club)* to join, enter; *(carrière)* to enter, go into; **e. dans un arbre**/*etc (en voiture etc)* to crash into a tree/*etc*; **e. à l'université**/*etc* to go to *ou* start university/*etc*; **e. en action** to go into action; **e. en ébullition** to start boiling; **e. dans les détails** to go into detail; **faire/laisser e. qn** to show/let s.o. in; **entrez!** come in! ▮ *vt* **e. des données dans un ordinateur** to enter *ou* input *ou* key data into a computer.
entresol [ɑ̃trəsɔl] *nm* mezzanine (floor), entresol.
entre-temps [ɑ̃trətɑ̃] *adv* meanwhile.
entretenir* [ɑ̃trət(ə)nir] *vt* **1** *(voiture, maison etc)* to maintain; *(relations, souvenir)* to keep up; *(famille)* to keep, maintain; *(sentiment)* to entertain; **e. sa forme/sa santé** to keep fit/healthy.
2 e. qn to talk to s.o. about; **s'e. de** to talk about (**avec** with). ●**entretenu, -ue** *a* **bien/mal e.** *(maison etc)* well-/badly-kept; **femme entretenue** kept woman.
entretien [ɑ̃trətjɛ̃] *nm* **1** *(de route, maison etc)* maintenance, upkeep; *(subsistance)* keep. **2** *(dialogue)* conversation; *(entrevue)* interview.
entre-tuer (s') [sɑ̃trətɥe] *vpr* to kill each other.
entrevoir* [ɑ̃trəvwar] *vt (rapidement)* to catch a glimpse of; *(pressentir)* to (fore)see.
entrevue [ɑ̃trəvy] *nf* interview.
entrouvrir* [ɑ̃truvrir] *vt*, **s'entrouvrir** *vpr* to half-open. ●**entrouvert, -erte** *a (porte, fenêtre)* half-open, ajar.
énumérer [enymere] *vt* to list, enumerate. ●**énumération** *nf* listing, enumeration.
envahir [ɑ̃vair] *vt* to invade; *(herbe etc)* to overrun *(garden etc)*; **e. qn** *(doute, peur etc)* to overcome s.o. ●**envahissant, -ante** *a (voisin etc)* intrusive. ●**envahissement** *nm* invasion. ●**envahisseur** *nm* invader.
enveloppant, -ante [ɑ̃vlɔpɑ̃, -ɑ̃t] *a (séduisant)* captivating.
enveloppe [ɑ̃vlɔp] *nf (pour lettre)* envelope; *(de colis)* wrapping; *(de pneu)* casing; *(d'oreiller)* cover; *(apparence)* Fig exterior; **mettre sous e.** to put into an envelope; **e.**

timbrée à votre adresse *Br* stamped addressed envelope, *Am* stamped self-addressed envelope.
envelopper [ɑ̃vlɔpe] *vt* to wrap (up) *(dans* in); **e. la ville** *(brouillard etc)* to blanket *ou* envelop the town; **enveloppé de mystère** shrouded *ou* enveloped in mystery ▮ **s'envelopper** *vpr* to wrap oneself (up) *(dans* in).
envenimer [ɑ̃v(ə)nime] *vt (plaie)* to make septic; *(querelle)* Fig to embitter, envenom ▮ **s'envenimer** *vpr (plaie)* to turn septic; *Fig* to become embittered *ou* acrimonious.
envergure [ɑ̃vɛrgyr] *nf* **1** *(d'avion, d'oiseau)* wingspan. **2** *(de personne)* calibre; *(ampleur)* scope, importance; **de grande e.** *(réforme etc)* wide-ranging, far-reaching.
envers [ɑ̃vɛr] **1** *prép Br* towards, *Am* toward(s), to; **e. et contre tous** in the face of all opposition. **2** *nm (de tissu)* wrong side; *(de médaille)* reverse side; **à l'e.** *(chaussette)* inside out; *(pantalon)* back to front; *(la tête en bas)* upside down; *(à contresens)* the wrong way.
envie [ɑ̃vi] *nf* **1** *(jalousie)* envy; *(désir)* longing, desire; **avoir e. de qch** to want sth; **j'ai e. de faire** I feel like doing, I would like to do; **elle meurt d'e. de faire** she's dying *ou* longing to do; **ça me fait e.** I really like that. **2** *(peau autour des ongles)* Fam hangnail. ●**envier** *vt* to envy *(qch à qn* s.o. sth). ●**envieux, -euse** *a* & *nmf* envious (person); **faire des envieux** to cause envy.
environ [ɑ̃virɔ̃] *adv (à peu près)* about. ●**environs** *nmpl* outskirts, surroundings; **aux environs de** *(Paris, Noël, dix francs etc)* around, in the vicinity of.
environner [ɑ̃virɔne] *vt* to surround. ●**environnant, -ante** *a* surrounding. ●**environnement** *nm* environment.
envisager [ɑ̃vizaʒe] *vt* to consider; *(imaginer comme possible) Br* to envisage, *Am* envision, consider; **e. de faire** to consider *ou* contemplate doing. ●**envisageable** *a* conceivable; **pas e.** not thinkable.
envoi [ɑ̃vwa] *nm (action)* dispatch, sending; *(paquet)* package, consignment; **e. contre remboursement** cash on delivery; **coup d'e.** *Football* kick-off.
envol [ɑ̃vɔl] *nm (d'oiseau)* taking flight; *(d'avion)* takeoff; **piste d'e.** *Av* runway. ●**s'envoler** *vpr (oiseau)* to fly away; *(avion)* to take off; *(chapeau etc)* to blow away; *(espoir) Fig* to vanish. ●**envolée** *nf (élan) Fig* flight.
envoûter [ɑ̃vute] *vt* to bewitch. ●**envoûtement** *nm* bewitchment.
envoyer* [ɑ̃vwaje] *vt* to send; *(lancer)* to throw; *(gifle)* to give; **e. chercher qn** to send for s.o.; **e. promener qn** Fam to send s.o. packing ▮ **s'envoyer** *vpr (repas etc)* to put *ou* stash away; *(travail etc)* to take on, do. ●**envoyé, -ée** *nmf* envoy; **e. spécial** *(reporter)* special correspondent. ●**envoyeur** *nm* sender; **'retour à l'e.'** 'return to sender'.

épagneul, -eule [epaɲœl] *nmf* spaniel.

épais, -aisse [epɛ, -ɛs] *a* thick; (*esprit*) dull. ● **épaisseur** *nf* thickness; (*dimension*) depth; **avoir 1 mètre d'é.** to be 1 metre thick. ● **épaissir** [epesir] *vt* to thicken ▌ *vi*, **s'épaisser** *vpr* to thicken; (*grossir*) to fill out; **le mystère s'épaissit** the mystery is deepening.

épancher [epɑ̃ʃe] *vt* (*cœur*) *Fig* to pour out ▌ **s'épancher** *vpr* (*parler*) to pour out one's heart, open up, unburden oneself. ● **épanchement** *nm* (*aveu*) outpouring; *Méd* effusion.

épanouir (s') [sepanwir] *vpr* (*fleur*) to blossom, open out; (*personne*) *Fig* to blossom (out), fulfil oneself; (*visage*) to beam. ● **épanoui, -ie** *a* (*fleur, personne*) in full bloom; (*visage*) beaming. ● **épanouissement** *nm* (*éclat*) full bloom; (*de la personnalité*) fulfilment.

épargne [eparɲ] *nf* saving (de of); (*qualité, vertu*) thrift; (*sommes d'argent*) savings. ● **épargner** *vt* (*argent*) to save; (*denrée rare etc*) to be sparing with; (*ennemi etc*) to spare; **e. qch à qn** (*ennuis, chagrin etc*) to spare s.o. sth. ● **épargnant, -ante** *nmf* saver.

éparpiller [eparpije] *vt*, **s'éparpiller** *vpr* to scatter; (*efforts*) to dissipate. ● **épars, éparse** *a* scattered.

épaté, -ée [epate] *a* (*nez*) flat. ● **épatement** *nm* flatness.

épater [epate] *vt* *Fam* to stun, astound. ● **épatant, -ante** *a* *Fam* marvellous, stunning.

épaule [epol] *nf* shoulder. ● **épauler** *vt* (*fusil*) to raise (to one's shoulder); **é. qn** (*aider*) to back s.o. up. ● **épaulette** *nf* (*d'une veste*) shoulder pad.

épave [epav] *nf* (*bateau, Fig personne*) wreck.

épée [epe] *nf* sword; **un coup d'é.** a sword thrust.

épeler [ep(ə)le] *vt* (*mot*) to spell.

éperdu, -ue [eperdy] *a* wild, frantic (**de** with); (*besoin*) desperate; (*regard*) distraught. ● **éperdument** *adv* (*aimer qn*) madly; (*travailler*) frantically; **elle s'en moque e.** she couldn't care less.

éperon [ep(ə)rɔ̃] *nm* (*de cavalier, coq*) spur. ● **éperonner** *vt* (*cheval, personne*) to spur (on).

épervier [epervje] *nm* sparrowhawk.

éphémère [efemɛr] *a* short lived, ephemeral.

épi [epi] *nm* (*de blé etc*) ear; (*mèche de cheveux*) tuft of hair.

épice [epis] *nf* (*aromate*) spice. ● **épicer** *vt* to spice. ● **épicé, -ée** *a* (*plat, récit etc*) spicy.

épicier, -ière [episje, -jɛr] *nmf* grocer. ● **épicerie** *nf* (*magasin*) *Br* grocer's (shop), *Am* grocery (store); **rayon é.** grocery department; **é. fine** delicatessen.

épidémie [epidemi] *nf* epidemic. ● **épidémique** *a* epidemic.

épiderme [epiderm] *nm* (*peau*) skin.

épier [epje] *vt* (*observer*) to watch closely; (*occasion*) to watch out for; **é. qn** to spy on s.o.

épilepsie [epilɛpsi] *nf* epilepsy. ● **épileptique** *a* & *nmf* epileptic.

épiler [epile] *vt* (*jambe*) to remove unwanted hair(s) from; (*sourcil*) to pluck.

épilogue [epilɔg] *nm* epilogue.

épinard [epinar] *nm* (*plante*) spinach; **épinards** (*feuilles*) spinach.

épine [epin] *nf* **1** (*de plante*) thorn; (*d'animal*) spine, prickle. **2 é. dorsale** *Anat* spine. ● **épineux, -euse** *a* (*tige, question*) thorny.

épingle [epɛ̃gl] *nf* pin; **é. de ou à nourrice, é. de sûreté** safety pin; **é. à linge** *Br* clothes peg, *Am* clothes pin; **é. à cheveux** hairpin; **virage en é. à cheveux** hairpin bend; **tiré à quatre épingles** immaculately turned out. ● **épingler** *vt* to pin; **é. qn** (*arrêter*) *Fam* to nab s.o.

Epiphanie [epifani] *nf* Epiphany.

épique [epik] *a* epic.

épiscopal, -e, -aux [episkɔpal, -o] *a* episcopal.

épisode [epizod] *nm* episode; **feuilleton en six épisodes** serial in six episodes *ou* parts, six-part serial. ● **épisodique** *a* occasional, episodic; (*accessoire*) minor.

épitaphe [epitaf] *nf* epitaph.

épithète [epitɛt] *nf* epithet; *Grammaire* attribute.

épître [epitr] *nf* epistle.

éploré, -ée [eplɔre] *a* (*veuve, air*) tearful.

éplucher [eplyʃe] *vt* (*carotte, pomme etc*) to peel; (*salade*) to clean; (*texte*) *Fig* to dissect. ● **épluchure** *nf* peeling.

éponge [epɔ̃ʒ] *nf* sponge; **jeter l'é.** *Fig* to throw in the towel. ● **éponger** *vt* (*liquide*) to sponge up, mop up; (*carrelage*) to sponge (down), mop; (*dette etc*) to absorb; **s'é. le front** to mop one's brow.

épopée [epɔpe] *nf* epic.

époque [epɔk] *nf* (*date*) time, period; (*historique*) age; **meubles d'é.** period furniture; **à l'é.** at the *ou* that time.

épouse [epuz] *nf* wife.

épouser [epuze] *vt* **1 é. qn** to marry s.o. **2** (*opinion etc*) to espouse; (*forme*) to assume, adopt.

épousseter [epuste] *vt* to dust.

époustoufler [epustufle] *vt* *Fam* to astound.

épouvantable [epuvɑ̃tabl] *a* terrifying; (*très mauvais*) appalling.

épouvantail [epuvɑ̃taj] *nm* (*à oiseaux*) scarecrow.

épouvante [epuvɑ̃t] *nf* (*peur*) terror; (*appréhension*) dread; **film d'é.** horror film. ● **épouvanter** *vt* to terrify.

époux [epu] *nm* husband; **les é.** the husband and wife.

éprendre* (s') [seprɑ̃dr] *vpr* **s'é. de qn** to fall in love with s.o. ● **épris, -ise** *a* in love (**de** with).

épreuve [eprœv] *nf* (*examen*) test; (*sportive*) event, heat; (*malheur*) hardship, ordeal, trial; (*photo*) print; (*texte imprimé*) proof;

éprouver 120

mettre à l'é. to put to the test; à toute é. (*patience*) unfailing; (*nerfs*) rock-solid; à l'é. du feu/des balles bulletproof/fireproof.

éprouver [epruve] *vt* to test, try; (*sentiment etc*) to feel, experience; é. qn (*mettre à l'épreuve*) to put s.o. to the test; (*faire souffrir*) to distress s.o. ● **éprouvant, -ante** *a* (*pénible*) trying. ● **éprouvé, -ée** *a* (*sûr*) well-tried.

éprouvette [epruvɛt] *nf* test tube; **bébé é.** test tube baby.

EPS [əpeɛs] *nf abrév* (*Éducation physique et sportive*) *Br* PE, *Am* Phys Ed.

épuiser [epɥize] *vt* (*personne, provisions, sujet*) to exhaust ‖ **s'épuiser** *vpr* (*réserves, patience*) to run out; **s'é. à faire** to exhaust oneself doing. ● **épuisant, -ante** *a* exhausting. ● **épuisé, -ée** *a* exhausted; (*marchandise*) out of stock; (*édition*) out of print; **é. de fatigue** exhausted. ● **épuisement** *nm* exhaustion.

épuisette [epɥizɛt] *nf* fishing net (*on pole*).

épurer [epyre] *vt* to purify; (*personnel etc*) to purge; (*goût*) to refine. ● **épuration** *nf* purification; (*de personnel etc*) purging; **station d'é.** purification *Br* works *ou Am* plant.

équateur [ekwatœr] *nm* equator; **sous l'é.** at *ou* on the equator. ● **équatorial, -e, -aux** *a* equatorial.

équation [ekwasjɔ̃] *nf Math* equation.

équerre [ekɛr] *nf* **é.** (**à dessiner**) *Br* setsquare, *Am* triangle; **d'é.** straight, square; **monter à la corde en é.** to pull oneself up a rope using one's hands only.

équestre [ekɛstr] *a* (*statue, sports etc*) equestrian.

équilibre [ekilibr] *nm* balance; **tenir *ou* mettre en é.** to balance (**sur** on); **se tenir en é.** to (keep one's) balance; **garder/perdre l'é.** to keep/lose one's balance. ● **équilibriste** *nmf* tightrope walker.

équilibrer [ekilibre] *vt* (*budget etc*) to balance ‖ **s'équilibrer** *vpr* (*équipes etc*) to (counter)balance each other; (*comptes etc*) to balance.

équinoxe [ekinɔks] *nm* equinox.

équipage [ekipaʒ] *nm* (*sur un navire, un avion etc*) crew.

équipe [ekip] *nf* team; (*d'ouvriers*) gang; **é. de nuit** night shift; **l'é. des secours** the search party; **faire é. avec qn** to team up with s.o. ● **équipier, -ière** *nmf* team member.

équipée [ekipe] *nf* escapade.

équiper [ekipe] *vt* to equip (**de** with) ‖ **s'équiper** *vpr* to equip oneself. ● **équipement** *nm* equipment; (*de camping, ski etc*) gear, equipment.

équitation [ekitasjɔ̃] *nf Br* (horse) riding, *Am* (horseback) riding; **faire de l'é** to go riding.

équité [ekite] *nf* fairness. ● **équitable** *a* fair, equitable. ● **équitablement** [-əmɑ̃] *adv* fairly.

équivalent, -ente [ekivalɑ̃, -ɑ̃t] *a & nm* equivalent. ● **équivalence** *nf* equivalence. ● **équivaloir** *vi* **é. à** to be equivalent to.

équivoque [ekivɔk] *a* (*ambigu*) equivocal;

(*douteux*) dubious; **sans é.** (*déclaration etc*) unequivocal ‖ *nf* ambiguity.

érable [erabl] *nm* (*arbre, bois*) maple.

érafler [erafle] *vt* to graze, scratch. ● **éraflure** *nf* graze, scratch.

éraillée [eraje] *af* **voix e.** rasping voice.

ère [ɛr] *nf* era; **avant notre è.** BC; **l'an 800 de notre è.** the year 800 AD.

érection [erɛksjɔ̃] *nf* (*de monument etc*) erection.

éreinter [erɛ̃te] *vt* (*fatiguer*) to exhaust; (*critiquer*) to tear to pieces, slam, *Br* slate.

ergot [ɛrgo] *nm* (*de coq*) spur.

ergoter [ɛrgɔte] *vi* to quibble, cavil.

ériger [eriʒe] *vt* to erect; **s'é. en** to set oneself up as.

ermite [ɛrmit] *nm* hermit.

érosion [erozjɔ̃] *nf* erosion. ● **éroder** *vt* to erode.

érotique [erɔtik] *a* erotic. ● **érotisme** *nm* eroticism.

errer [ɛre] *vi* to wander, roam. ● **errant, -ante** *a* wandering, roving; **chien/chat e.** stray dog/cat.

erreur [ɛrœr] *nf* (*faute*) mistake, error; (*action blâmable, opinion fausse*) error; **par e.** by mistake, in error; **dans l'e.** mistaken; **sauf e. de ma part** unless I'm mistaken; **e. judiciaire** miscarriage of justice; **faire e.** (*au téléphone*) to dial the wrong number. ● **erroné, -ée** *a* erroneous.

ersatz [ɛrzats] *nm* substitute.

éructer [erykte] *vi Litt* to belch.

érudit, -ite [erydi, -it] *a* scholarly, erudite ‖ *nmf* scholar. ● **érudition** *nf* scholarship, erudition.

éruption [erypsjɔ̃] *nf* (*de volcan*) eruption; (*de colère*) outburst (**de** of); (*de boutons*) rash.

es *voir* **être**.

ès [ɛs] *prép* of; **licencié/docteur ès lettres** = BA/PhD.

escabeau, -x [ɛskabo] *nm* stepladder, *Br* (pair of) steps; (*tabouret*) stool.

escadre [ɛskadr] *nf Nau Av* fleet, squadron. ● **escadrille** *nf* (*groupe d'avions*) flight. ● **escadron** *nm* squadron.

escalade [ɛskalad] *nf* climbing; (*des prix, de la violence etc*) & *Mil* escalation. ● **escalader** *vt* to climb, scale.

escale [ɛskal] *nf Av* stop(over); (*lieu*) *Nau* port of call; **faire e. à** (*avion*) to stop (over) at; (*navire*) to put in at; **vol sans e.** non-stop flight; **faire une e. technique** to make a refuelling stop.

escalier [ɛskalje] *nm* stairs, staircase; **l'é., les escaliers** the stairs; **e. mécanique *ou* roulant** escalator; **e. de secours** fire escape; **e. de service** service stairs.

escalope [ɛskalɔp] *nf* (*viande*) escalope.

escamoter [ɛskamɔte] *vt* (*faire disparaître*) to make vanish; (*esquiver*) to dodge. ● **escamotable** *a Tech* retractable.

escampette [ɛskɑ̃pɛt] *nf* **prendre la poudre d'e.** *Fam* to run away, leg it, *Br* scarper.

escapade [ɛskapad] *nf* (*excursion*) jaunt; **faire une e.** to run off.

escargot [ɛskargo] *nm* snail.

escarmouche [ɛskarmuʃ] *nf* skirmish.

escarpé, -ée [ɛskarpe] *a* steep. ● **escarpement** *nm* (*côte*) steep slope.

escarpin [ɛskarpɛ̃] *nm* (*soulier*) pump, *Br* court shoe.

escient [ɛsjɑ̃] *nm* **à bon e.** judiciously, discerningly, wisely.

esclaffer (s') [ɛsklafe] *vpr* to roar with laughter.

esclandre [ɛsklɑ̃dr] *nm* (*noisy*) scene.

esclave [ɛsklav] *nmf* slave; **être l'e. de** to be a slave to. ● **esclavage** *nm* slavery.

escompte [ɛskɔ̃t] *nm* discount; **taux d'e.** bank rate. ● **escompter** *vt* **1** (*espérer*) to anticipate (**faire** doing), expect (**faire** to do). **2** *Com* to discount.

escorte [ɛskɔrt] *nf* (*troupe, navires, cortège etc*) escort. ● **escorter** *vt* to escort.

escouade [ɛskwad] *nf* (*petite troupe*) squad.

escrime [ɛskrim] *nf* *Sport* fencing; **faire de l'e.** to fence. ● **escrimeur, -euse** *nmf* fencer.

escrimer (s') [sɛskrime] *vpr* to slave away (**à faire** at doing).

escroc [ɛskro] *nm* crook, swindler. ● **escroquer** *vt* **e. qn** to swindle s.o.; **e. qch à qn** to swindle s.o. out of sth. ● **escroquerie** *nf* swindling; **une e.** a swindle; **c'est de l'e.** it's a rip-off.

espace [ɛspas] *nm* space; **e. vert** garden, park; **e. aérien** air space. ● **espacer** *vt* to space out; **espacés d'un mètre** (spaced out) one metre apart ▌ **s'espacer** *vpr* (*maisons, visites etc*) to become less frequent.

espadon [ɛspadɔ̃] *nm* swordfish.

espadrille [ɛspadrij] *nf* rope-soled sandal.

Espagne [ɛspaɲ] *nf* Spain. ● **espagnol, -ole** *a* Spanish ▌ *nmf* E., Espagnole Spaniard ▌ *nm* (*langue*) Spanish.

espèce [ɛspɛs] *nf* (*race*) species; (*genre*) kind, sort; **un e. d'idiot, une e. d'idiote** *Fam* a silly fool; **e. d'idiot!/de maladroit!/etc** *Fam* (you) silly fool!/oaf!/etc. ● **espèces** *nfpl* (*argent*) **en espèces** in cash.

espérance [ɛsperɑ̃s] *nf* hope; **avoir des espérances** to have expectations; **e. de vie** life expectancy.

espérer [ɛspere] *vt* to hope for; **e. que** to hope that; **e. faire** to hope to do ▌ *vi* to hope; **e. en qn/qch** to trust in s.o./sth; **j'espère (bien)!** I hope so!

espiègle [ɛspjɛgl] *a* mischievous. ● **espièglerie** *nf* mischievousness; (*farce*) mischievous trick.

espion, -onne [ɛspjɔ̃, -ɔn] *nmf* spy. ● **espionnage** *nm* spying, espionage. ● **espionner** *vt* to spy on ▌ *vi* to spy.

esplanade [ɛsplanad] *nf* esplanade.

espoir [ɛspwar] *nm* hope; **avoir de l'e.** to have hope(s); **il n'y a plus d'e.** (*il va mourir*) there's no hope for him; **sans e.** (*cas etc*) hopeless; **les espoirs de la danse/du cinéma/etc** the young hopefuls of the dancing/film/etc world.

esprit [ɛspri] *nm* (*attitude, fantôme*) spirit; (*intellect*) mind; (*humour*) wit; (*être humain*) person; **venir à l'e. de qn** to cross s.o.'s mind; **avoir de l'e.** to be witty; **avoir l'e. large/étroit** to be broad-/narrow-minded; **avoir l'e. de contradiction** to be argumentative; **perdre l'e.** to go out of one's mind.

esquimau, -aude, -aux [ɛskimo, -od, -o] **1** *a* Eskimo ▌ *nmf* E., Esquimaude Eskimo. **2** *nm* (*glace*) *Br* choc-ice (*on a stick*), *Am* ice-cream bar.

esquinter [ɛskɛ̃te] *vt* *Fam* (*voiture etc*) to damage, bash; (*critiquer*) to slam, pan (*author, film etc*); **s'e. la santé** to damage one's health; **s'e. à faire** (*se fatiguer*) to wear oneself out doing.

esquisse [ɛskis] *nf* (*croquis, plan*) sketch. ● **esquisser** *vt* to sketch; **e. un geste** to make a (slight) gesture.

esquive [ɛskiv] *nf* *Boxe* dodge; **e. de** (*question*) dodging of, evasion of. ● **esquiver** *vt* (*coup, problème*) to dodge ▌ **s'esquiver** *vpr* to slip away.

essai [ɛsɛ] *nm* (*preuve*) test, trial; (*tentative*) try, attempt; *Rugby* try; *Littér* essay; **à l'e.** (*objet*) *Com* on approval, on trial; **pilote d'e.** test pilot; **période d'e.** trial period; **coup d'e.** first attempt.

essaim [ɛsɛ̃] *nm* swarm (*of bees etc*).

essayer [ɛseje] *vt* to try (**de faire** to do); (*vêtement*) to try on; (*méthode*) to try (out); **s'e. à qch/à faire** to try one's hand at sth/at doing. ● **essayage** *nm* (*de costume*) fitting; **salon d'e.** fitting room.

essence [ɛsɑ̃s] *nf* **1** (*carburant*) *Br* petrol, *Am* gas; (*extrait*) essence; **poste d'e.** filling station. **2** *Phil* essence. **3** (*d'arbres*) species.

essentiel, -ielle [ɛsɑ̃sjɛl] *a* essential (**à, pour** for) ▌ *nm* **l'e.** the main thing *ou* point; (*quantité*) the main part (**de** of). ● **essentiellement** *adv* essentially.

essieu, -x [ɛsjø] *nm* axle.

essor [ɛsɔr] *nm* (*de pays, d'entreprise etc*) development, rise, expansion; **en plein e.** (*industrie etc*) booming.

essorer [ɛsɔre] *vt* (*linge*) to wring; (*dans une essoreuse*) to spin-dry; (*dans une machine à laver*) to spin. ● **essoreuse** *nf* (*à main*) wringer; (*électrique*) spin dryer; (*à salade*) salad spinner.

essouffler [ɛsufle] *vt* to make (s.o.) out of breath ▌ **s'essouffler** *vpr* to get out of breath.

essuyer [ɛsɥije] **1** *vt* to wipe ▌ **s'essuyer** *vpr* to wipe oneself. **2** *vt* (*subir*) to suffer. ● **essuie-glace** *nm inv* *Br* windscreen wiper, *Am* windshield wiper. ● **essuie-mains** *nm inv* (hand) towel.

est¹ [ɛ] *voir* être.

est² [ɛst] *nm* east; **à l'e.** in the east; (*direction*) (to the) east (**de** of); **d'e.** (*vent*) east(erly); **de l'e.** eastern ▌ *a inv* (*côte*) east(ern).

estafilade [ɛstafilad] *nf* gash, slash.

estampe [ɛstãp] nf (gravure) print.

estampille [ɛstãpij] nf mark, stamp.

esthète [ɛstɛt] nmf Br aesthete, Am esthete.

esthéticienne [ɛstetisjɛn] nf beautician.

esthétique [ɛstetik] a Br aesthetic, Am esthetic.

estime [ɛstim] nf esteem, regard.

estimer [ɛstime] vt (tableau etc) to value (à at); (calculer) to estimate; (apprécier) to appreciate; (juger) to consider (que that); **e. dangereux/etc de faire qch** to consider it dangerous/etc to do sth; **e. qn** to have (a) high regard for s.o., esteem s.o.; **s'e. heureux/etc** to consider oneself happy/etc. ●**estimable** a respectable. ●**estimation** nf (de mobilier etc) valuation; (calcul) estimation.

estival, -e, -aux [ɛstival, -o] a travail/température/etc **estival(e)** summer work/temperature/etc. ●**estivant, -ante** nmf Br holidaymaker, Am vacationer.

estomac [ɛstɔma] nm stomach.

estomaquer [ɛstɔmake] vt Fam to flabbergast.

estomper [ɛstõpe] vt (rendre flou) to blur **s'estomper** vpr to become blurred.

estrade [ɛstrad] nf (tribune) platform.

estragon [ɛstragõ] nm (plante, condiment) tarragon.

estropier [ɛstrɔpje] vt to cripple, maim. ●**estropié, -ée** nmf cripple.

estuaire [ɛstɥɛr] nm estuary.

esturgeon [ɛstyrʒõ] nm (poisson) sturgeon.

et [e] conj and; **vingt et un**/etc twenty-one/etc; **et moi?** what about me?

étable [etabl] nf cowshed.

établi [etabli] nm (de menuisier) (work)bench.

établir [etablir] vt to establish; (installer) to set up; (plan, chèque, liste) to draw up **s'établir** vpr (habiter) to settle; (épicier etc) to set up shop as, set (oneself) up as. ●**établissement** nm (action, bâtiment, institution) establishment; (commercial) company, establishment, firm; **é. scolaire** school.

étage [etaʒ] nm (d'immeuble) floor, Br storey, Am story; (de fusée etc) stage; **à l'é.** upstairs; **au premier é.** on the Br first ou Am second floor; **maison à deux étages** Br two-storeyed ou Am two-storied house. ●**étager (s'), s'étager** vpr (rochers, maisons etc) to range above one another.

étagère [etaʒɛr] nf shelf; (meuble) shelving unit.

étai [etɛ] nm Tech prop, stay.

étain [etɛ̃] nm (métal) tin; (de gobelet etc) pewter.

étais, était [etɛ] voir être.

étal, pl étals [etal] nm (au marché) stall.

étalage [etalaʒ] nm display; (vitrine) display window; **faire é. de** to show off, make a show ou display of. ●**étalagiste** nmf window dresser.

étaler [etale] vt (disposer) to lay out; (en vitrine) to display; (beurre etc) to spread; (vacances, paiements) to stagger; (érudition etc)

to show off **s'étaler** vpr (s'affaler) Fam to sprawl; **s'é. (de tout son long)** (tomber) Fam to fall flat; **s'é. sur** (congés, paiements etc) to be spread over. ●**étalement** nm (des vacances, paiements etc) staggering.

étalon [etalõ] nm **1** (cheval) stallion. **2** (modèle) standard; **é.-or** gold standard.

étanche [etãʃ] a watertight; (montre) waterproof.

étancher [etãʃe] vt (sang) to stop the flow of; (soif) to quench, slake.

étang [etã] nm pond.

étant [etã] p prés de être.

étape [etap] nf (de voyage etc) stage; (lieu) stop(over); **faire é. à** to stop off ou over at; **par (petites) étapes** in (easy) stages; **brûler les étapes** (dans sa carrière etc) to race ahead.

état [eta] nm **1** (condition, manière d'être) state; (registre, liste) statement, list; **en bon é.** in good condition; **en é. de marche** in working order; **en é. de faire** in a position to do; **hors d'é. de faire** not in a position to do; **é. d'esprit** state ou frame of mind; **é. d'âme** mood; **é. civil** civil status (birth, marriage, death etc); **é. de choses** situation, state of affairs; **é. des lieux** inventory of fixtures; **à l'é. brut** in a raw state; **à l'é. neuf** as new; **de son é.** (métier) by trade; **faire é. de** (mention) to mention, put forward; **(ne pas) être dans son é. normal** (not) to be one's usual self; **être dans un é. second** to be in a daze, be spaced out; **être dans tous ses états** (affolé) Fam to be all worked up; **mettre qn en é. d'arrestation** to put s.o. under arrest; **remettre qch en é.** (réparer) to repair sth.
2 É. (nation) State; **homme d'É.** statesman. ●**étatisé, -ée** a state-controlled, state-owned.

état-major [etamaʒɔr] nm (pl états-majors) (d'un parti etc) senior staff.

Etats-Unis [etazyni] nmpl É.-Unis (d'Amérique) United States (of America).

étau, -x [eto] nm (instrument) Br vice, Am vise.

étayer [eteje] vt to prop up, support.

été¹ [ete] nm summer.

été² [ete] pp de être.

éteindre* [etɛ̃dr] vt (feu, cigarette etc) to put out, extinguish; (lampe etc) to turn ou switch off; (dette, espoir) to extinguish **vi** to switch off **s'éteindre** vpr (feu) to go out; (personne) to pass away; (race) to die out; (amour) to die. ●**éteint, -einte** a (feu, bougie) out; (lampe, lumière) off; (volcan, race, amour) extinct; (voix) faint.

étendard [etãdar] nm (drapeau) standard.

étendre [etãdr] vt (linge) to hang out; (nappe) to spread (out); (beurre) to spread; (agrandir) to extend; **é. le bras**/etc to stretch out one's arm/etc; **é. qn** to stretch s.o. out **s'étendre** vpr (personne) to stretch (oneself) out; (plaine etc) to stretch; (feu) to spread; (pouvoir) to extend; **s'é. sur** (sujet) to dwell on. ●**étendu, -ue** a (forêt, vocabulaire etc) extensive; (personne) stretched out. ●**eten-**

due *nf* (*importance*) extent; (*surface*) area; (*d'eau*), expanse, stretch.
éternel, -elle [etɛrnɛl] *a* eternal. ●**éternellement** *adv* eternally, for ever. ●**éterniser** *vt* Litt to perpetuate ▮ **s'éterniser** *vpr* (*débat etc*) to drag on endlessly; (*visiteur etc*) Fam to stay for ever. ●**éternité** *nf* eternity.
éternuer [etɛrnчe] *vi* to sneeze. ●**éternuement** [-ymã] *nm* sneeze.
êtes [ɛt] *voir* **être**.
éther [etɛr] *nm* ether.
Ethiopie [etjɔpi] *nf* Ethiopia. ●**éthiopien, -ienne** *a* Ethiopian ▮ *nmf* É., Éthiopienne Ethiopian.
éthique [etik] *a* ethical ▮ *nf* Phil ethics; **l'é. puritaine**/*etc* the Puritan/*etc* ethic.
ethnie [ɛtni] *nf* ethnic group. ●**ethnique** *a* ethnic.
étinceler [etɛ̃s(ə)le] *vi* to sparkle. ●**étincelle** *nf* spark; **faire des étincelles** Fam (*personne*) to scintillate, be brilliant; (*scandale etc*) to cause sparks to fly.
étioler (s') [setjɔle] *vpr* to wilt, wither.
étiqueter [etik(ə)te] *vt* to label. ●**étiquette** *nf* **1** (*marque*) label. **2** (*protocole*) (diplomatic *ou* court) etiquette.
étirer [etire] *vt* to stretch ▮ **s'étirer** *vpr* to stretch (oneself).
étoffe [etɔf] *nf* material, cloth, fabric; **avoir l'é. d'un héros**/*etc* to be the stuff heroes/*etc* are made of.
étoffer [etɔfe] *vt* to fill out; (*texte*) to make more meaty ▮ **s'étoffer** *vpr* (*personne*) to fill out.
étoile [etwal] *nf* **1** star; **é. filante** shooting star; **à la belle é.** in the open; **être né sous une bonne é.** to be born under a lucky star. **2 é. de mer** starfish. ●**étoilé, -ée** *a* (*ciel, nuit*) starry; (*vitre*) cracked (*star-shaped*); **é. de** (*rubis etc*) studded with; **la bannière étoilée** Am the Star-Spangled Banner.
étonner [etɔne] *vt* to surprise, astonish ▮ **s'étonner** *vpr* to be surprised *ou* astonished (**de qch** at sth, **que** (+ *sub*) that). ●**étonnant, -ante** *a* (*ahurissant*) surprising; (*remarquable*) amazing. ●**étonnement** *nm* surprise, astonishment.
étouffer [etufe] *vt* (*tuer*) to suffocate, smother; (*bruit*) to muffle; (*feu*) to smother; (*révolte, sentiment*) to stifle; (*scandale*) to hush up; **é. qn** (*chaleur*) to stifle s.o.; (*aliment, colère*) to choke s.o. ▮ *vi* to suffocate; **on étouffe!** it's stifling!; **é. de colère** to choke with anger ▮ **s'étouffer** *vpr* (*en mangeant*) to choke, gag (**sur, avec** on); (*mourir*) to suffocate. ●**étouffant, -ante** *a* (*air*) stifling. ●**étouffement** *nm* Méd suffocation.
étourdi, -ie [eturdi] *a* thoughtless ▮ *nmf* scatterbrain. ●**étourderie** *nf* thoughtlessness; **une (faute d')é.** a thoughtless blunder.
étourdir [eturdir] *vt* to stun, daze; (*vin, vitesse*) to make dizzy; (*abrutir*) to deafen. ●**étourdissant, -ante** *a* (*bruit*) deafening; (*remarquable*) stunning. ●**étourdissement** *nm* dizziness; (*malaise*) dizzy spell.

étourneau, -x [eturno] *nm* starling.
étrange [etrãʒ] *a* strange, odd. ●**étrangement** *adv* strangely, oddly. ●**étrangeté** *nf* strangeness, oddness.
étranger, -ère [etrãʒe, -ɛr] *a* (*d'un autre pays*) foreign; (*non familier*) strange (**à** to); **il m'est é.** he's unknown to me ▮ *nmf* foreigner; (*inconnu*) stranger; **à l'é.** abroad; **de l'é.** from abroad.
étrangler [etrãgle] *vt* **é. qn** (*tuer*) to strangle s.o.; (*col*) to choke s.o. ▮ **s'étrangler** *vpr* (*de colère, en mangeant*) to choke. ●**étranglé, -ée** *a* (*voix*) choking; (*passage*) constricted. ●**étranglement** *nm* (*d'une victime*) strangulation. ●**étrangleur, -euse** *nmf* strangler.
être* [ɛtr] **1** *vi* to be; **il est tailleur** he's a tailor; **est-ce qu'elle vient?** is she coming?; **il vient, n'est-ce pas?** he's coming, isn't he?; **est-ce qu'il aime le thé?** does he like tea?; **nous sommes dix** there are ten of us; **nous sommes le dix** today is the tenth (of the month); **où en es-tu?** how far have you Br got *ou* Am gotten?; **il a été à Paris** (*est allé*) he has been to Paris; **elle est de Paris** she's from Paris; **elle est de la famille** she's one of the family; **il est cinq heures** it's five (o'clock); **il était une fois** once upon a time, there was; **c'est à lire pour demain** (*obligation*) this has to be read for tomorrow; **c'est à voir absolument** (*exposition etc*) it's well worth seeing; **c'est à lui** it's his; **il n'est plus** (*il est mort*) he is dead; **si j'étais vous** if I were *ou* was you; **cela étant** that being so.
2 *v aux* (*avec venir, partir etc*) to have; **elle est (déjà) arrivée** she has (already) arrived; **nous y sommes toujours bien reçus** (*passif*) we are always well received.
3 *nm* (*personne*) being; **ê. humain** human being; **ê. vivant** living being; **les êtres chers** the loved ones.
étreindre* [etrɛ̃dr] *vt* to grip; (*avec amour*) to embrace. ●**étreinte** *nf* grip; (*amoureuse etc*) embrace.
étrenner [etrene] *vt* to use *ou* wear for the first time.
étrennes [etrɛn] *nfpl* New Year gift; (*gratification*) = Christmas tip *ou* Br box.
étrier [etrije] *nm* stirrup; **mettre le pied à l'é. à qn** to help s.o. get off to a good start.
étriper (s') [setripe] *vpr* Fam to fight (each other) to the kill.
étriqué, -ée [etrike] *a* (*vêtement*) tight, skimpy; (*esprit, vie*) narrow.
étroit, -oite [etrwa, -at] *a* narrow; (*vêtement*) tight; (*lien, collaboration etc*) close; (*discipline*) strict; **être à l'é.** to be cramped. ●**étroitement** *adv* (*surveiller etc*) closely. ●**étroitesse** *nf* narrowness; (*de lien etc*) closeness; **é. d'esprit** narrow-mindedness.
étude [etyd] *nf* **1** (*action, ouvrage*) study; Scol study room; **à l'é.** (*projet*) under consideration; **é. de marché** Com market survey *ou* study; **faire des études de** (*médecine etc*) to study. **2** (*de notaire etc*) office.

étudiant, -ante [etydjã, -ãt] *nmf* student; **être é. en médecine/droit/***etc* to be a medical/law/*etc* student **‖** *a* (*vie etc*) student.

étudier [etydje] *vti* to study.

étui [etɥi] *nm* (*à lunettes, à cigarettes etc*) case; (*de revolver*) holster.

étymologie [etimɔlɔʒi] *nf* etymology.

eu, eue [y] *pp de* **avoir.**

eucalyptus [økaliptys] *nm* (*arbre*) eucalyptus.

Eucharistie [økaristi] *nf Rel* Eucharist.

eugénisme [øʒenism] *nm* eugenics.

euh! [ø] *int* hem!, er!, well!

euphémisme [øfemism] *nm* euphemism.

euphorie [øfɔri] *nf* euphoria.

eurent [yr] *voir* **avoir.**

euro- [øro] *préf* Euro-.

eurocrate [ørɔkrat] *nmf* Eurocrat.

eurodollar [ørɔdɔlar] *nm* Eurodollar.

Europe [ørɔp] *nf* Europe; **l'E. (des douze)** the Twelve (countries of the Common Market). ● **européen, -enne** *a* European **‖** *nmf* **E., Européenne** European.

eurosceptique [øroseptik] *a* Eurosceptic.

eut [y] *voir* **avoir.**

euthanasie [øtanazi] *nf* euthanasia.

eux [ø] *pron* (*sujet*) they; (*complément*) them; (*réfléchi, emphase*) themselves. ● **eux-mêmes** *pron* themselves.

évacuer [evakɥe] *vt* to evacuate; (*liquide*) to drain off. ● **évacuation** *nf* evacuation.

évader (s') [sevade] *vpr* to escape (**de** from). ● **évadé, -ée** *nmf* escaped prisoner.

évaluer [evalɥe] *vt* (*fortune etc*) to estimate; (*meuble etc*) to value. ● **évaluation** *nf* estimation; (*de meuble etc*) valuation.

évangile [evãʒil] *nm* gospel; **É.** Gospel; **parole d'é.** *Fig* gospel (truth). ● **évangélique** *a* evangelical.

évanouir (s') [sevanwir] *vpr* (*personne*) to faint, pass *ou* black out; (*espoir, crainte etc*) to vanish. ● **évanoui, -ie** *a Méd* unconscious. ● **évanouissement** *nm* (*syncope*) blackout, fainting fit; (*disparition*) vanishing.

évaporer (s') [sevapɔre] *vpr* to evaporate; (*disparaître*) *Fam* to vanish into thin air. ● **évaporation** *nf* evaporation.

évasé, -ée [evaze] *a* (*jupe etc*) flared.

évasif, -ive [evazif, -iv] *a* evasive.

évasion [evazjɔ̃] *nf* escape (**d'un lieu** from a place, **devant un danger/***etc* from a danger/*etc*); (*hors de la réalité*) escapism; **é. fiscale** tax evasion; **é. de capitaux** flight of capital.

évêché [eveʃe] *nm* (*territoire*) bishopric, see.

éveil [evɛj] *nm* awakening; **en é.** on the alert; **donner l'é. à** to alert; **activité d'é.** (*à l'école*) early-learning *ou* awareness activity.

éveiller [eveje] *vt* (*susciter*) to arouse; **é. qn** to awake(n) s.o. **‖ s'éveiller** *vpr* to awake(n) (**à** to); (*sentiment, idée*) to be aroused. ● **éveillé, -ée** *a* awake; (*vif*) lively, alert.

événement [evɛnmã] *nm* event.

éventail [evãtaj] *nm* **1** (*instrument portatif*) fan; **en é.** (*orteils*) spread out. **2** (*choix*) range.

éventer [evãte] *vt* **1** (*secret*) to discover. **2 é. qn** to fan s.o. **3 s'éventer** *vpr* (*bière, vin, parfum etc*) to turn stale. ● **eventé, -ée** *a* (*bière, parfum, vin etc*) stale.

éventrer [evãtre] *vt* (*oreiller etc*) to rip open; (*animal*) to open up.

éventuel, -elle [evãtɥel] *a* possible. ● **éventuellement** *adv* possibly. ● **éventualité** *nf* possibility; **dans l'é. de** in the event of.

évêque [evɛk] *nm* bishop.

évertuer (s') [severtɥe] *vpr* **s'é. à faire** to do one's utmost to do, struggle to do.

éviction [eviksjɔ̃] *nf* (*de concurrent, président etc*) ousting.

évident, -ente [evidã, -ãt] *a* obvious, evident (**que** that); (*facile*) *Fam* easy. ● **évidemment** [-amã] *adv* obviously, certainly. ● **évidence** *nf* obviousness; **une é.** an obvious fact; **nier l'é.** to deny the obvious; **être en é.** to be conspicuous *ou* in evidence; **mettre en é.** (*fait*) to underline; **se rendre à l'é.** to face the facts.

évider [evide] *vt* to hollow out.

évier [evje] *nm* (kitchen) sink.

évincer [evɛ̃se] *vt* (*concurrent, président etc*) to oust (**de** from).

éviter [evite] *vt* to avoid (**de faire** doing); **é. qch à qn** to spare *ou* save s.o. sth; **je voulais é. que vous ne vous déplaciez pour rien** I wanted to save you coming for nothing.

évoluer [evɔlɥe] *vi* **1** (*changer*) to develop, change; (*société, idée, situation*) to evolve. **2** (*se déplacer*) to move; (*maladie*) to develop; (*danseurs, soldats etc*) *Br* to manœuvre, *Am* maneuver. ● **évolué, -ée** *a* (*pays*) advanced; (*personne*) enlightened. ● **évolution** *nf* **1** (*changement*) development; evolution. **2** (*d'un danseur etc*) movement.

évoquer [evɔke] *vt* to evoke, call to mind. ● **évocateur, -trice** *a* evocative. ● **évocation** *nf* evocation, recalling.

ex [ɛks] *nmf* (*mari, femme*) *Fam* ex.

ex- [ɛks] *préf* ex-; **ex-mari** ex-husband.

exacerber [ɛgzaserbe] *vt* (*douleur etc*) to exacerbate.

exact, -e [ɛgzakt] *a* (*précis*) exact, accurate; (*juste, vrai*) correct, right, exact; (*ponctuel*) punctual. ● **exactement** [-amã] *adv* exactly. ● **exactitude** *nf* accuracy; correctness; exactness; (*ponctualité*) punctuality.

exactions [ɛgzaksjɔ̃] *nfpl* (*actes de violence*) acts of violence.

ex aequo [ɛgzeko] *adv* **être classés ex ae.** *Sport* to tie, be equally placed.

exagérer [ɛgzaʒere] *vt* to exaggerate **‖** *vi* (*parler*) to exaggerate; (*agir*) to overdo it, go too far. ● **exagéré, -ée** *a* excessive. ● **exagérément** *adv* excessively. ● **exagération** *nf* exaggeration; (*excès*) excessiveness.

exalter [ɛgzalte] *vt* (*glorifier*) to exalt; (*passionner*) to fire, stir. ● **exaltant, -ante** *a* stirring. ● **exalté, -ée** *a* (*sentiment*) impassioned, wild **‖** *nmf Péj* fanatic. ● **exaltation** *nf* (*délire*) elation, excitement.

examen [ɛgzamɛ̃] *nm* examination; (*bac etc*)

exam(ination); **e. blanc** mock exam(ination). ● **examinateur, -trice** *nmf* examiner. ● **examiner** *vt* (*considérer, regarder*) to examine.

exaspérer [ɛgzaspere] *vt* (*énerver*) to aggravate, exasperate. ● **exaspération** *nf* exasperation, aggravation.

exaucer [ɛgzose] *vt* (*désir*) to grant; **e. qn** to grant s.o.'s wish(es).

excavation [ɛkskavɑsjɔ̃] *nf* (*trou*) hollow.

excéder [ɛksede] *vt* 1 (*dépasser*) to exceed. 2 **é. qn** (*énerver*) to exasperate s.o. ● **excédent** *nm* surplus, excess; **e. de bagages** excess luggage *ou* Am baggage. ● **excédentaire** *a* **poids/etc e.** excess weight/etc.

excellent, -ente [ɛkselã, -ãt] *a* excellent. ● **excellence** *nf* 1 excellence; **par e.** above all else *ou* all others. 2 **E.** (*titre*) Excellency. ● **exceller** *vi* to excel (**en qch, dans qch** in sth; **à faire** in doing).

excentrique [ɛksãtrik] 1 *a & nmf* (*original*) eccentric. 2 *a* (*quartier*) remote. ● **excentricité** *nf* (*bizarrerie*) eccentricity.

excepté[1] [ɛksɛpte] *prép* except. ● **excepté**[2], **-ée** *a* except (for); **les femmes exceptées** except (for) the women. ● **excepter** *vt* to except.

exception [ɛksɛpsjɔ̃] *nf* exception; **à l'e. de** except (for), with the exception of; **faire e.** to be an exception. ● **exceptionnel, -elle** *a* exceptional. ● **exceptionnellement** *adv* exceptionally.

excès [ɛksɛ] *nm* excess; **des e. (de table)** over-eating; **e. de vitesse** (*dans un véhicule*) speeding; **faire un e. de vitesse** to speed. ● **excessif, -ive** *a* excessive. ● **excessivement** *adv* excessively.

excitation [ɛksitɑsjɔ̃] *nf* (*agitation*) excitement; **e. à** (*haine etc*) incitement to.

exciter [ɛksite] *vt* (*faire naître*) to excite, rouse, stir (*desire, anger etc*); **e. qn** (*énerver*) to provoke s.o.; **e. qn à faire** to incite s.o. to do ▮ **s'exciter** *vpr* (*devenir nerveux*) to get excited. ● **excitant, -ante** *a* Fam exciting ▮ *nm* stimulant. ● **excité, -ée** *a* excited. ● **excitable** *a* excitable.

exclamer (s') [sɛksklame] *vpr* to exclaim. ● **exclamatif, -ive** *a* exclamatory. ● **exclamation** *nf* exclamation.

exclure* [ɛksklyr] *vt* (*écarter*) to exclude (de from); (*chasser*) to expel (de from); **e. qch** (*rendre impossible*) to preclude sth. ● **exclu, -ue** *a* (*solution etc*) out of the question; (*avec une date*) exclusive.

exclusif, -ive [ɛksklyzif, -iv] *a* (*droit, modèle, préoccupation*) exclusive. ● **exclusivement** *adv* exclusively. ● **exclusivité** *nf* Com exclusive rights; (*dans la presse*) scoop; **en e.** (*film*) having an exclusive showing (à at).

exclusion [ɛksklyzjɔ̃] *nf* exclusion; **à l'e. de** with the exception of.

excommunier [ɛkskɔmynje] *vt* to excommunicate. ● **excommunication** *nf* excommunication.

excréments [ɛkskremã] *nmpl* excrement.

excroissance [ɛkskrwasãs] *nf* (out)growth.

excursion [ɛkskyrsjɔ̃] *nf* trip, outing, excursion, tour; (*à pied*) hike.

excuse [ɛkskyz] *nf* (*prétexte*) excuse; **excuses** (*regrets*) apology; **faire des excuses** to apologize (à to); **toutes mes excuses** (my) sincere apologies. ● **excuser** *vt* (*justifier, pardonner*) to excuse (**qn d'avoir fait, qn de faire** s.o. for doing) ▮ **s'excuser** *vpr* to apologize (**de** for, **auprès de** to); **excusez-moi!, je m'excuse!** excuse me!

exécrer [ɛgzekre] *vt* to loathe. ● **exécrable** *a* atrocious.

exécuter [ɛgzekyte] *vt* 1 (*travail, projet, tâche etc*) to carry out, execute; (*jouer*) Mus to perform; (*broderie, statue etc*) to produce; (*programme informatique*) to run.
2 **e. qn** (*tuer*) to execute s.o.
3 **s'exécuter** *vpr* to comply. ● **exécutant, -ante** *nmf* (*musicien*) performer; (*ouvrier, employé etc*) subordinate (*who carries out orders*). ● **exécutable** *a* practicable. ● **exécution** *nf* 1 carrying out, execution; performance; production; **mettre à e.** to put into effect, carry out. 2 (*mise à mort*) execution.

exécutif [ɛgzekytif] *am* **pouvoir e.** executive power ▮ *nm* l'e. Pol the executive.

exemplaire [ɛgzãplɛr] 1 *a* exemplary. 2 *nm* (*livre etc*) copy; **photocopier un document en double e.** to make two photocopies of a document.

exemple [ɛgzãpl] *nm* example; **par e.** for example, for instance; **donner l'e.** to set an example (à to); **prendre e. sur qn** to follow s.o.'s example; **faire un e.** (*pour dissuader*) to make an example (of someone); **c'est un e. de vertu/etc** he's a model of virtue/etc; (*ça*) **par e.!** Fam good heavens!

exempt, -empte [ɛgzã, -ãt] *a* **e. de** (*dispensé de*) exempt from; (*sans*) free from. ● **exempter** [ɛgzãte] *vt* to exempt (de from). ● **exemption** [ɛgzãpsjɔ̃] *nf* exemption.

exercer [ɛgzɛrse] *vt* (*voix, droits*) to exercise; (*autorité, influence*) to exert (**sur** over); (*profession*) Br to practise *ou* Am practice; **e. qn à** (*couture etc*) to train s.o. in; **e. qn à faire** to train s.o. to do ▮ *vi* (*médecin etc*) Br to practise, Am practice ▮ **s'exercer** *vpr* (*influence etc*) to be exerted; **s'e. (à qch)** (*sportif etc*) Br to practise (sth), Am practice (sth); **s'e. à faire** Br to practise *ou* Am practice doing.

exercice [ɛgzɛrsis] *nm* (*physique etc*) & Scol exercise; Mil drill, exercise; (*de métier*) practice; **l'e. de** (*pouvoir etc*) the exercise of; **en e.** (*fonctionnaire*) in office; (*médecin etc*) in practice; **faire de l'e., prendre de l'e.** to (take) exercise.

exhaler [ɛgzale] *vt* (*odeur etc*) to give off.

exhaustif, -ive [ɛgzostif, -iv] *a* exhaustive.

exhiber [ɛgzibe] *vt* to exhibit, show. ● **exhibition** *nf* exhibition. ● **exhibitionniste** *nmf* exhibitionist.

exhorter [ɛgzɔrte] *vt* to urge, exhort (**à faire** to do).

exhumer [ɛgzyme] vt (cadavre) to exhume; (vestiges) to dig up.

exiger [ɛgziʒe] vt to demand, require (de from, que (+ sub) that). ● **exigeant, -ante** a demanding, exacting. ● **exigence** nf demand, requirement; **exigences** (revendications) demands; **d'une grande e.** very demanding.

exigu, -uë [ɛgzigy] a (appartement etc) cramped, tiny. ● **exiguïté** nf crampedness.

exil [ɛgzil] nm exile. ● **exiler** vt to exile **‖** **s'exiler** vpr to go into exile. ● **exilé, -ée** nmf (personne) exile.

existence [ɛgzistɑ̃s] nf (fait d'exister) existence; (vie) existence, life; **e. heureuse** happy life; **moyen d'e.** means of existence. ● **existentialisme** nm existentialism. ● **exister** vi to exist **‖** v imp **il existe...** (sing) there is ...; (pl) there are.... ● **existant, -ante** a existing.

exode [ɛgzɔd] nm exodus; **e. rural** rural depopulation ou exodus.

exonérer [ɛgzɔnere] vt Fin to exempt (de from). ● **exonération** nf exemption.

exorbitant, -ante [ɛgzɔrbitɑ̃, -ɑ̃t] a exorbitant.

exorbité, -ée [ɛgzɔrbite] a **yeux exorbités** bulging eyes.

exorciser [ɛgzɔrsize] vt to exorcize. ● **exorcisme** nm exorcism.

exotique [ɛgzɔtik] a exotic. ● **exotisme** nm exoticism.

expansif, -ive [ɛkspɑ̃sif, -iv] a expansive, effusive.

expansion [ɛkspɑ̃sjɔ̃] nf (d'un commerce, pays, gaz) expansion; **en (pleine) e.** (fast ou rapidly) expanding.

expatrier (s') [sɛkspatrije] vpr to leave one's country. ● **expatrié, -ée** a & nmf expatriate.

expectative [ɛkspɛktativ] nf **être dans l'e.** to be waiting to see what happens.

expédient [ɛkspedjɑ̃] nm (moyen) expedient.

expédier [ɛkspedje] vt 1 (envoyer) to send off. 2 (affaires, client) to dispose of quickly, dispatch. ● **expéditeur, -trice** nmf sender. ● **expéditif, -ive** a expeditious, quick. ● **expédition** nf 1 (envoi) dispatch. 2 (voyage) expedition.

expérience [ɛksperjɑ̃s] nf (connaissance) experience; (scientifique) experiment; **faire l'e. de qch** to experience sth; **avoir de l'e.** to have experience; **être sans e.** to have no experience; **un homme d'e.** a man of experience. ● **expérimental, -e, -aux** a experimental. ● **expérimentation** nf experimentation.

expérimenter [ɛksperimɑ̃te] vt Phys Ch to try out, experiment with **‖** vi to experiment. ● **expérimenté, -ée** a experienced.

expert, -erte [ɛkspɛr, -ɛrt] a expert, skilled (en in) **‖** nm expert (en on, in); (d'assurances) valuer. ● **expert-comptable** nm (pl **experts-comptables**) = Br chartered accountant, = Am certified public accountant. ● **expertise** nf (évaluation) (expert) appraisal; (compétence) expertise;

(rapport) expert's report; **e. judiciaire** expert opinion.

expier [ɛkspje] vt (péchés, crime) to expiate, atone for. ● **expiation** nf expiation (de of).

expirer [ɛkspire] 1 vti to breathe out. 2 vi (mourir) to pass away; (finir, cesser) to expire. ● **expiration** nf 1 (respiration) breathing out. 2 (échéance) Br expiry, Am expiration; **arriver à e.** to expire.

explication [ɛksplikɑsjɔ̃] nf explanation; (mise au point) discussion; **e. de texte** Scol literary appreciation.

explicite [ɛksplisit] a explicit. ● **explicitement** adv explicitly.

expliquer [ɛksplike] vt to explain (à to, que that) **‖** **s'expliquer** vpr to explain oneself; (discuter) to talk things over, have it out (avec with); **s'e. qch** (comprendre) to understand sth; **ça s'explique** that is understandable. ● **explicable** a understandable. ● **explicatif, -ive** a explanatory.

exploit [ɛksplwa] nm feat, exploit.

exploiter [ɛksplwate] vt 1 (champs) to farm; (ferme, entreprise) to run; (mine) to work; (profiter de) Fig to exploit (situation). 2 (abuser de) Péj to exploit (s.o.). ● **exploitant, -ante** nmf **e. (agricole)** farmer. ● **exploitation** nf 1 (de champs) farming; (de ferme etc) running; (de mine) working; **e. (agricole)** farm; **e. industrielle** concern. 2 Péj exploitation.

explorer [ɛksplɔre] vt to explore. ● **explorateur, -trice** nmf explorer. ● **exploration** nf exploration.

exploser [ɛksploze] vi (gaz etc) to explode; (bombe) to blow up, explode; **e. (de colère)** Fam to explode, blow up; **faire e.** (bombe) to explode. ● **explosif, -ive** a & nm explosive. ● **explosion** nf explosion; (de colère, joie) outburst.

exporter [ɛkspɔrte] vt to export (**vers** to, **de** from). ● **exportateur, -trice** nmf exporter **‖** a exporting. ● **exportation** nf (produit) export; (action) export(ation), exporting.

exposer [ɛkspoze] vt (présenter, soumettre) & Phot to expose (à to); (tableau etc) to exhibit; (marchandises) to display; (idée, théorie) to set out; (vie, réputation) to risk, endanger; **s'e. à** to expose oneself to. ● **exposant, -ante** nmf exhibitor. ● **exposé, -ée 1** a **bien e.** (édifice) having a good exposure; **e. au sud/etc** facing south/etc. 2 nm (compte rendu) account (de of); (présentation) talk; Scol paper.

exposition [ɛkspozisjɔ̃] nf (d'objets d'art) exhibition; (de marchandises etc) display; (au danger etc) & Phot exposure (à to); (de maison etc) aspect; **É. universelle** Br the World Fair, Am the World's Fair.

exprès¹ [ɛksprɛ] adv on purpose, intentionally; (spécialement) specially; **comme (par) un fait e.** almost as if it was meant to be.

exprès², -esse [ɛksprɛs] 1 a (ordre, condition) express. 2 a inv **lettre/colis e.** express letter/parcel. ● **expressément** [-emɑ̃] adv ex-

pressly.
express [ɛkspres] a & nm inv (train) express; (café) espresso.
expressif, -ive [ɛkspresif, -iv] a expressive. ● **expression** nf (phrase, mine etc) expression; **réduire qch à sa plus simple e.** Fig to reduce sth to its simplest form ou bare bones. ● **exprimer** vt to express ▌ **s'exprimer** vpr to express oneself.
exproprier [ɛksproprije] vt to seize the property of by compulsory purchase.
expulser [ɛkspylse] vt to expel (de from); (joueur) to send off; (locataire) to evict. ● **expulsion** nf expulsion; (de joueur) sending off; (de locataire) eviction.
expurger [ɛkspyrʒe] vt to expurgate.
exquis, -ise [ɛkski, -iz] a (nourriture) delicious, exquisite.
exsangue [ɛksɑ̃g] a (visage etc) bloodless.
extase [ɛkstaz] nf ecstasy, rapture; **tomber en e. devant qch** to be in raptures over sth. ● **s'extasier** vpr to be in raptures (sur over, about). ● **extasié, -ée** a ecstatic.
extensible [ɛkstɑ̃sibl] a expandable. ● **extension** nf extension; (essor) expansion.
exténuer [ɛkstenɥe] vt (fatiguer) to exhaust. ● **exténué, -ée** a exhausted.
extérieur, -e [ɛksterjœr] a (monde etc) outside; (surface) outer, external; (signe) outward, external; (politique) foreign; **e. à** external to; **signe e. de richesse** outward sign of wealth ▌ nm outside, exterior; **à l'e. (de)** outside; **à l'e.** (match) away; **tourner un film en e.** to shoot a film on location. ● **extérieurement** adv externally; (en apparence) outwardly. ● **extérioriser** vt to express.
exterminer [ɛkstermine] vt to exterminate, wipe out. ● **extermination** nf extermination.
externat [ɛksterna] nm (école) day school.
externe [ɛkstern] 1 a external. 2 nmf (élève) day pupil; Méd non-resident hospital medical student, Am extern.

extincteur [ɛkstɛ̃ktœr] nm fire extinguisher. ● **extinction** nf (de feu) extinguishing; (de race) extinction; **e. de voix** loss of voice.
extirper [ɛkstirpe] vt to eradicate ▌ **s'extirper** vpr **s'e. de** (endroit) Fam to get out of, drag oneself out of.
extorquer [ɛkstorke] vt to extort (à from). ● **extorsion** nf extortion; **e. de fonds** (crime) extorsion.
extra [ɛkstra] 1 a inv (très bon) Fam topquality. 2 nm inv Culin (extra-special) treat; (serviteur) extra hand ou help.
extra- [ɛkstra] préf extra-. ● **extra-fin, -fine** a extra-fine. ● **extra-fort, -forte** a extra-strong.
extradition [ɛkstradisjɔ̃] nf extradition. ● **extrader** vt to extradite.
extraire* [ɛkstrɛr] vt to extract (de from); (charbon) to mine. ● **extraction** nf extraction. ● **extrait** nm extract; **un e. de naissance** a (copy of one's) birth certificate.
extralucide [ɛkstralysid] a & nf clairvoyant.
extraordinaire [ɛkstraordinɛr] a extraordinary; **si par e.** if by some remote chance. ● **extraordinairement** adv exceptionally; (très, bizarrement) extraordinarily.
extraterrestre [ɛkstraterɛstr] a & nmf extraterrestrial.
extravagant, -ante [ɛkstravagɑ̃, -ɑ̃t] a extravagant. ● **extravagance** nf extravagance.
extraverti, -ie [ɛkstraverti] nmf extrovert.
extrême [ɛkstrɛm] a extreme; **l'e. droite/ gauche** Pol the far ou extreme right/left ▌ nm extreme; **pousser à l'e.** to take ou carry to extremes. ● **Extrême-Orient** nm Far East. ● **extrêmement** adv extremely. ● **extrémiste** a & nmf extremist. ● **extrémité** nf (bout) extremity, end; **extrémités** (excès) extremes; (pieds et mains) extremities.
exubérant, -ante [ɛgzyberɑ̃, -ɑ̃t] a exuberant. ● **exubérance** nf exuberance.
exulter [ɛgzylte] vi to exult, rejoice. ● **exultation** nf exultation.
exutoire [ɛgzytwar] nm outlet (à for).

F

F, f [ɛf] *nm* F, f.
F *abrév* franc(s).
fa [fa] *nm* (*note de musique*) F.
fable [fabl] *nf* fable.
fabricant, -ante [fabrikɑ̃, -ɑ̃t] *nmf* manufacturer. ● **fabrication** *nf* manufacture; **f. artisanale** small-scale manufacture; **(de) f. artisanale** (*pull etc*) hand-made; **bombe de f. artisanale** home-made bomb; **de f. française** of French make.
fabrique [fabrik] *nf* factory; **marque de f.** trade mark.
fabriquer [fabrike] *vt* (*objet*) to make; (*en usine*) to manufacture; (*récit*) *Péj* to fabricate, make up; **qu'est-ce qu'il fabrique?** *Fam* what's he up to?
fabuler [fabyle] *vi* to make up stories, tell lies.
fabuleux, -euse [fabylø, -øz] *a* (*légendaire, incroyable*) fabulous.
fac [fak] *nf abrév* (*faculté*) *Fam* university; **à la f.** *Br* at university, *Am* at school.
façade [fasad] *nf* (*de bâtiment*) front, façade; (*apparence*) *Fig* pretence, façade; **de f.** (*luxe etc*) sham.
face [fas] *nf* face; (*de cube, montagne etc*) side; (*de monnaie*) head; **en f.** opposite; **en f. de** opposite, facing; (*en présence de*) in front of, face to face with; **f. à** (*vis-à-vis*) facing; **f. à face** face to face; **f. à un problème** faced with a problem, in the face of a problem; **faire f. à** (*situation*) to face, face up to; **regarder qn en f.** to look s.o. in the face; **sauver/perdre la f.** to save/lose face; **se voiler la f.** *Fig* to hide from reality; **(photo) de f.** full-face (photo). ● **face à face** *nm inv* **f. à f. télévisé** face-to-face TV encounter.
facétie [fasesi] *nf* joke, jest. ● **facétieux, -euse** [-esjø, -øz] *a* (*personne*) facetious.
facette [fasɛt] *nf* (*de diamant, problème etc*) facet.
fâcher [faʃe] *vt* to anger **I** **se fâcher** *vpr* to get angry *ou* annoyed (**contre** with); **se f. avec qn** (*se brouiller*) to fall out with s.o. ● **fâché, -ée** *a* (*air*) angry; (*amis*) on bad terms; **f. avec** *ou* **contre qn** angry *ou* annoyed with s.o.; **être f. avec l'orthographe** *Fam* to be a hopeless speller, be unable to get on with spelling; **f. de qch** sorry about sth. ● **fâcheux, -euse** *a* (*nouvelle etc*) unfortunate.
facho [faʃo] *a & nmf* *Fam* fascist.
facile [fasil] *a* easy; (*caractère, humeur*) easy-going; (*banal*) *Péj* facile; **c'est f. à faire** it's easy to do; **il nous est f. de faire ça** it's easy for us to do that; **f. à vivre** easy to get along

with, easygoing. ● **facilement** *adv* easily. ● **facilité** *nf* (*simplicité*) easiness; (*à faire qch*) ease; **facilités de paiement** *Com* easy terms; **avoir des facilités pour qch** to have an aptitude for sth; **avoir toutes facilités pour faire qch** to have every facility *ou* opportunity to do sth. ● **faciliter** *vt* to make easier, facilitate.
façon [fasɔ̃] *nf* **1** way; **la f. dont elle parle** the way (in which) she talks; **de quelle f.?** how?; **f. (d'agir)** behaviour; **façons** (*manières*) manners; **une f. de parler** a manner of speaking; **à la f. de** in the fashion of; **de toute f.** anyway, anyhow; **d'une certaine f.** in some way; **de f. à so as to; de f. à ce qu'on vous comprenne** so as to be understood, so that you may be understood; **de f. générale** generally speaking; **d'une f. ou d'une autre** one way or another; **à ma f.** my way, (in) my own way; **faire des façons** to make a fuss; **accepter qch sans f.** to accept sth without fuss; **table f. chêne** imitation oak table.
2 (*coupe de vêtement*) cut, style.
façonner [fasone] *vt* (*travailler, former*) to fashion, shape; (*fabriquer*) to manufacture.
facteur [faktœr] *nm* **1** *Br* postman, *Am* mailman. **2** (*élément*) factor. ● **factrice** *nf* *Fam* *Br* postwoman, *Am* mail woman.
factice [faktis] *a* false, artificial; **diamant/etc f.** imitation diamond/etc.
faction [faksjɔ̃] *nf* **1** (*groupe politique*) faction. **2** **de f.** (*soldat*) on guard (duty), on sentry duty.
facture [faktyr] *nf* *Com* bill, invoice. ● **facturer** *vt* to bill, invoice.
facultatif, -ive [fakyltatif, -iv] *a* (*travail etc*) optional; **arrêt f.** *Br* request stop; **matière/ épreuve facultative** (*à l'école*) optional subject/test paper.
faculté [fakylte] *nf* **1** (*aptitude*) faculty; (*possibilité*) freedom (**de faire** to do); **une grande/etc f. de travail** a great/etc capacity for work. **2** (*d'université*) faculty; **à la f.** *Br* at university, *Am* at school.
fadaises [fadɛz] *nfpl* twaddle, nonsense.
fade [fad] *a* insipid; (*nourriture*) bland. ● **fadasse** *a* *Fam* wishy-washy.
fagot [fago] *nm* bundle (of firewood).
fagoter [fagote] *vt* *Péj* to dress, rig out.
faible [fɛbl] *a* weak, feeble; (*bruit, voix*) faint; (*vent, quantité, chances*) slight; (*revenus*) small; **f. en anglais/etc** poor at English/ etc.
I *nm* (*personne*) weakling; **les faibles** the weak; **f. d'esprit** feeble-minded person; **avoir un f. pour** to have a weakness *ou* a

soft spot for. ●**faiblement** [-əmã] adv weakly; (légèrement) slightly; (éclairer, parler) faintly. ●**faiblesse** nf weakness, feebleness; (de bruit etc) faintness; (de vent etc) slightness; (de revenus) smallness; (défaut, syncope) weakness.

faiblir [feblir] vi (forces) to weaken; (courage, vue) to fail; (vent) to slacken.

faïence [fajãs] nf (matière) earthenware; **faïences** (objets) crockery, earthenware.

faille[1] [faj] nf Géol fault; Fig flaw.

faille[2] [faj] voir **falloir**.

faillible [fajibl] a fallible.

faillir* [fajir] vi **1** il a failli tomber he almost ou nearly fell. **2** f. à un devoir to fail in a duty.

faillite [fajit] nf Com bankruptcy; Fig failure; **faire f.** to go bankrupt.

faim [fɛ̃] nf hunger; **avoir f.** to be hungry; **donner f. à qn** to make s.o. hungry; **manger à sa f.** to eat one's fill; **rester sur sa f.** to remain hungry; **mourir de f.** to die of starvation; (avoir très faim) Fig to be starving.

fainéant, -ante [feneɑ̃, -ɑ̃t] a idle ▮ nmf idler. ●**fainéanter** vi to idle. ●**fainéantise** nf idleness.

faire* [fɛr] **1** vt (bruit, faute, gâteau, voyage, repas etc) to make; (devoir, ménage, dégâts etc) to do; (rêve, chute) to have; (sourire) to give; (promenade, sieste) to have, take; (guerre) to wage, make; **ça fait dix mètres de large** (mesure) it's ou that's ten metres wide; **ça fait dix francs** (prix) it's ou that's ten francs; **2 et 2 font 4** 2 and 2 are 4; **qu'a-t-il fait (de)?** what's he done (with)?; **que f.?** what's to be done? **f. du tennis/du piano/etc** to play tennis/the piano/etc; **f. du droit/de la médecine/etc** to study law/medicine/etc; **f. du bien à qn** to do s.o. good; **f. du mal à qn** to hurt ou harm s.o.; **f. l'idiot** to act ou play the fool; **il fera un bon médecin** he'll be ou make a good doctor; **ça ne fait rien** that doesn't matter; **comment as-tu fait pour...?** how did you manage to...?; **il ne fait que travailler** he does nothing but work, he keeps on working; **je ne fais que d'arriver** I've just arrived; **oui, fit-elle** yes, she said.

2 vi (agir) to do; (paraître) to look; **f. comme chez soi** to make yourself at home; **faites donc!** please do!; **elle ferait bien de partir** she'd do well to leave; **il fait vieux/etc** he looks old/etc; **il fait (bien) son âge** he looks his age.

3 v imp **il fait beau/froid/etc** it's fine/cold/etc; **il fait du vent/soleil/etc** it's windy/sunny/etc; **quel temps fait-il?** what's the weather like?; **ça fait deux ans que je ne l'ai pas vu** I haven't seen him for two years, it's (been) two years since I saw him; **ça fait un an que je suis là** I've been here for a year.

4 v aux (+ inf): **f. construire une maison** to have ou get a house built (à qn for s.o., par qn by s.o.); **f. crier/souffrir/etc** qn to make s.o. shout/suffer/etc; **se f. couper les cheveux** to have one's hair cut; **se f. craindre/obéir/**

etc to make oneself feared/obeyed/etc; **se f. tuer/renverser/etc** to get ou be killed/knocked down/etc.

5 se faire vpr (fabrication) to be made; (activité) to be done; **se f. des illusions** to have illusions; **se f. des amis** to make friends; **se f. vieux/etc** (devenir) to get old/etc; **il se fait tard** it's getting late; **comment se fait-il que?** how is it that?; **ça se fait beaucoup** people do that a lot; **se f. à** to get used to, adjust to; **ne t'en fais pas!** don't worry!

faire-part [fɛrpar] nm inv (de mariage etc) announcement.

fais, fait [fɛ] voir **faire**.

faisable [fəzabl] a feasible.

faisan [fəzɑ̃] nm (oiseau) pheasant.

faisandé, -ée [fəzɑ̃de] a (gibier) high.

faisceau, -x [fɛso] nm (lumineux) beam; (de tiges etc) bundle; **un f. de preuves** Fig a (solid) body of proof.

fait, faite [fɛ, fɛt] **1** pp de voir **faire** ▮ a (fromage) ripe; (yeux) made up; (ongles) polished; (homme) grown; **tout f.** ready made; **bien f.** (jambes, corps etc) shapely; **c'est bien f. (pour toi)!** it serves you right!

2 nm event, occurrence; (donnée, réalité) fact; **du f.** de on account of; **au f.** (à propos) by the way; **en f.** in fact; **en f. de** in the matter of; **f. divers** (rubrique de journal) (miscellaneous) news item; **prendre qn sur le f.** to catch s.o. red-handed ou in the act; **aller au f., en venir au f.** to get to the point; **faits et gestes** actions; **prendre f. et cause pour qn** to stand up for s.o., fight s.o.'s cause; **mettre qn devant un f. accompli** to present s.o. with a fait accompli.

faîte [fɛt] nm (haut) top; (apogée) Fig height.

faites [fɛt] voir **faire**.

faitout [fɛtu] nm stewing pot, casserole.

falaise [falɛz] nf cliff.

falloir* [falwar] **1** v imp **il faut qch/qn** I, you, we etc need sth/s.o.; **il lui faut un stylo** he ou she needs a pen; **il faut partir/etc** I, you, we etc have to go/etc; **il faut que je parte** I have to go; **il faudrait qu'elle reste** she ought to stay; **il faut un jour** it takes a day (**pour faire** to do); **comme il faut** proper(ly); **s'il le faut** if need be.

2 s'en falloir v imp **il s'en est fallu de peu qu'il ne pleure,** peu s'en est fallu qu'il ne pleure he almost cried; **tant s'en faut** far from it.

falsifier [falsifje] vt (texte etc) to falsify. ●**falsification** nf falsification.

famé, -ée (mal) [malfame] a of ill repute.

famélique [famelik] a ill-fed, starving.

fameux, -euse [famø, -øz] a (célèbre) famous; (excellent) Fam first-class; **pas f.** Fam not much good.

familial, -aux [familjal, -o] a **ennuis/etc familiaux** family problems/etc.

familier, -ière [familje, -jɛr] a (bien connu) familiar (à to); (amical) friendly, informal; (locution) colloquial, familiar; **f. avec qn** (over)familiar with s.o.; **animal f.** pet ▮ nm (*de club etc*) regular visitor. ●**familiariser** *vt* to familiarize (**avec** with) **‖ se familiariser** *vpr* to familiarize oneself (**avec** with). ●**familiarité** *nf* familiarity (**avec** with); **familiarités** *Péj* liberties. ●**familièrement** *adv* familiarly; (*parler*) informally.

famille [famij] *nf* family; **en f.** (*dîner etc*) with one's family; **un père de f.** a family man.

famine [famin] *nf* famine.

fan [fan] *nm* (*admirateur*) *Fam* fan.

fana [fana] *nmf Fam* fan; **être f. de** to be crazy about.

fanal, -aux [fanal, -o] *nm* lantern, light.

fanatique [fanatik] *a* fanatical **‖** *nmf* fanatic. ●**fanatisme** *nm* fanaticism.

faner (se) [səfane] *vpr* (*fleur, beauté*) to fade. ●**fané, -ée** *a* faded.

fanfare [fɑ̃far] *nf* (*orchestre*) brass band; (*air, musique*) fanfare; **réveil en f.** *Fam* rude awakening.

fanfaron, -onne [fɑ̃farɔ̃, -ɔn] *a* boastful **‖** *nmf* braggart.

fanfreluches [fɑ̃frəlyʃ] *nfpl Péj* trimmings, frills.

fange [fɑ̃ʒ] *nf Litt* mud, mire.

fanion [fanjɔ̃] *nm* (*drapeau*) pennant.

fantaisie [fɑ̃tezi] *nf* (*caprice*) whim, fancy; (*imagination*) imagination, fantasy; **bouton/bijoux/etc f.** novelty *ou* fancy button/*Br* jewellery *ou* *Am* jewelry/etc. ●**fantaisiste** *a* (*pas sérieux*) fanciful; (*excentrique*) unorthodox.

fantasme [fɑ̃tasm] *nm* (*rêve*) fantasy. ●**fantasmer** *vi* to fantasize (**sur** about).

fantasque [fɑ̃task] *a* whimsical.

fantassin [fɑ̃tasɛ̃] *nm* (*militaire*) infantryman.

fantastique [fɑ̃tastik] *a* (*imaginaire, excellent*) fantastic.

fantoche [fɑ̃tɔʃ] *nm* & *a* puppet.

fantôme [fɑ̃tom] *nm* ghost, phantom **‖** *a* **ville/train/etc f.** ghost town/train/etc; **firme f.** bogus company *ou* firm.

faon [fɑ̃] *nm* (*animal*) fawn.

faramineux, -euse [faraminø, -øz] *a Fam* fantastic.

farce¹ [fars] *nf* practical joke, prank; (*pièce de théâtre*) farce; **magasin de farces et attrapes** joke shop; **faire une f. à qn** to play a practical joke *ou* a prank on s.o. ●**farceur, -euse** *nmf* (*blagueur*) practical joker, wag.

farce² [fars] *nf* (*viande*) stuffing. ●**farcir** *vt* 1 (*poulet etc*) to stuff. 2 **se f. qn/qch** *Fam* to put up with s.o./sth.

fard [far] *nm* make-up. ●**farder** *vt* (*acteur etc*) to make up; (*vérité*) to camouflage **‖ se farder** *vpr* (*se maquiller*) to make up; **se f. les yeux/le visage** to put on eye/face make-up.

fardeau, -x [fardo] *nm* burden, load.

farfelu, -ue [farfəly] *a Fam* crazy, bizarre **‖** *nmf Fam* weirdo.

farfouiller [farfuje] *vi Fam* to rummage (**dans** in).

fariboles [faribɔl] *nfpl Fam* nonsense.

farine [farin] *nf* (*de blé*) flour; **f. d'avoine** oatmeal. ●**farineux, -euse** *a* floury, powdery.

farouche [faruʃ] *a* 1 (*timide*) shy, unsociable; (*animal*) easily scared. 2 (*acharné*) fierce. ●**farouchement** *adv* fiercely.

fart [far(t)] *nm* (*ski*) wax. ●**farter** *vt* (*skis*) to wax.

fascicule [fasikyl] *nm* volume.

fasciner [fasine] *vt* to fascinate. ●**fascination** *nf* fascination.

fascisme [faʃism] *nm* fascism. ●**fasciste** *a* & *nmf* fascist.

fasse(s), fassent [fas] *voir* **faire.**

faste [fast] *nm* ostentation, display **‖** *a* **jour/période f.** lucky *ou* auspicious day/period.

fastidieux, -euse [fastidjø, -øz] *a* tedious, dull.

fatal, -e, *mpl* **-als** [fatal] *a* (*mortel*) fatal; (*inévitable*) inevitable; (*moment, ton*) fateful; **c'était f.!** it was bound to happen! ●**fatalement** *adv* inevitably. ●**fataliste** *a* fatalistic **‖** *nmf* fatalist. ●**fatalité** *nf* (*destin*) fate. ●**fatidique** *a* (*jour, date*) fateful.

fatigant, -ante [fatigɑ̃, -ɑ̃t] *a* (*épuisant*) tiring; (*ennuyeux*) tiresome.

fatigue [fatig] *nf* tiredness, fatigue, weariness.

fatiguer [fatige] *vt* to tire, fatigue; (*yeux*) to strain; (*ennuyer*) to bore **‖** *vi* (*moteur*) to strain **‖ se fatiguer** *vpr* (*se lasser*) to get tired, tire (**de** of); (*travailler*) to tire oneself out (**à faire** doing). ●**fatigué, -ée** *a* tired, weary (**de** of).

fatras [fatra] *nm* jumble, muddle.

faubourg [fobur] *nm* suburb. ●**faubourien, -ienne** *a* (*accent etc*) suburban, common.

fauché, -ée [foʃe] *a* (*sans argent*) *Fam* broke.

faucher [foʃe] *vt* 1 (*herbe*) to mow; (*blé*) to reap; **f. qn** (*faire tomber brutalement*) *Fig* to knock s.o. down, mow s.o. down. 2 (*voler*) *Fam* to snatch, *Br* pinch. ●**faucheuse** *nf* (*machine*) reaper.

faucille [fosij] *nf* (*instrument*) sickle.

faucon [fokɔ̃] *nm* (*oiseau*) hawk, falcon; (*personne*) *Fig* hawk.

faudra, faudrait [fodra, fodrɛ] *voir* **falloir.**

faufiler (se) [səfofile] *vpr* to edge *ou* inch one's way (**dans** through; **into**; **entre** between).

faune [fon] *nf* wildlife, fauna; (*gens*) *Péj* set.

faussaire [fosɛr] *nm* forger.

fausse [fos] *voir* **faux¹.** ●**faussement** *adv* falsely.

fausser [fose] *vt* (*réalité etc*) to distort; (*clé etc*) to buckle; **f. compagnie à qn** to give s.o. the slip.

fausseté [foste] *nf* (*d'un raisonnement etc*) falseness; (*hypocrisie*) duplicity.

faut [fo] *voir* **falloir.**

faute [fot] *nf* (*erreur*) mistake; (*responsabilité*) fault; (*péché*) sin; (*délit*) offence; *Football* foul; **c'est de ta f.,** *Fam* **c'est ta f.** it's your fault, you're to blame; **f. de temps/etc** for lack of time/etc; **f. de mieux** for want of anything better; **en f.** at fault; **sans f.** without fail; **faire une f.** to make a mistake; **f. d'impression** printing error; **f. de français** grammatical error (*in French*); **f. de jeunesse** youthful error.

fauteuil [fotœj] *nm* armchair; (*de président*) chair; (*roulant*) wheelchair; **f. pivotant** swivel chair; **f. d'orchestre** *Théâtre etc* seat in the *Br* stalls *ou Am* orchestra; **arriver dans un f.** *Fam* to win hands down.

fauteur [fotœr] *nm* **f. de troubles** troublemaker.

fautif, -ive [fotif, -iv] *a* (*personne*) at fault; (*erroné*) faulty.

fauve [fov] **1** *nm* wild animal *ou* beast, big cat; **chasse aux grands fauves** big game hunting. **2** *a & nm* (*couleur*) fawn.

faux¹, fausse [fo, fos] *a* (*pas vrai*) false, untrue; (*pas exact*) wrong; (*inauthentique*) false; (*monnaie*) forged, counterfeit; (*voix*) out of tune; **f. diamant/etc** imitation *ou* false diamond/*etc*; **f. nez/etc** false nose/*etc*; **f. col** detachable collar; **f. départ** false start; **f. ami** *Ling* false friend; **faire fausse route** to take the wrong road; *Fig* to be on the wrong track; **faire un f. mouvement** to make a sudden (awkward) movement; **faire une fausse note** (*musicien*) to play a wrong note; **avoir tout f.** *Fam* to get it all wrong. **▌** *adv* (*chanter*) out of tune. **▌** *nm* (*contrefaçon*) forgery. ● **faux-filet** *nm* (*viande*) sirloin. ● **faux-fuyant** *nm* subterfuge. ● **faux-monnayeur** *nm* counterfeiter.

faux² [fo] *nf* (*instrument*) scythe.

faveur [favœr] *nf* favour; **en f. de** (*au profit de*) in aid *ou* favour of; **de f.** (*billet*) complimentary; (*traitement, régime*) preferential. ● **favorable** *a* favourable (à to). ● **favori, -ite** *a & nmf* favourite. ● **favoriser** *vt* to favour. ● **favoritisme** *nm* favouritism.

favoris [favori] *nmpl* sideburns, *Br* sideboards, side whiskers.

fax [faks] *nm* (*appareil, message*) fax. ● **faxer** [fakse] *vt* (*message*) to fax.

fébrile [febril] *a* feverish. ● **fébrilité** *nf* feverishness.

fécond, -onde [fekɔ̃, -ɔ̃d] *a* (*femme, idée etc*) fertile. ● **féconder** *vt* to fertilize. ● **fécondité** *nf* fertility.

fécule [fekyl] *nf* starch. ● **féculents** *nmpl* (*aliments*) carbohydrates.

fédéral, -e, -aux [federal, -o] *a* federal. ● **fédération** *nf* federation. ● **fédérer** *vt* to federate.

fée [fe] *nf* fairy. ● **féerie** *nf* *Théâtre* fantasy extravaganza; *Fig* fairy-like spectacle. ● **féerique** *a* fairy(-like), magical.

feindre* [fɛ̃dr] *vt* to feign, affect, sham; **f. de faire** to pretend to do. ● **feint, feinte** *a* feigned, sham. ● **feinte** *nf* sham, *Br* pretence, *Am* pretense; *Boxe Mil* feint.

fêler [fele] *vt*, **se fêler** *vpr* (*tasse etc*) to crack. ● **fêlure** *nf* crack.

félicité [felisite] *nf* bliss, felicity.

féliciter [felisite] *vt* to congratulate (**qn de** *ou* **sur** s.o. on); **se f. de** to congratulate oneself on. ● **félicitations** *nfpl* congratulations (**pour** on).

félin, -ine [felɛ̃, -in] *a & nm* feline.

femelle [fəmɛl] *a & nf* (*animal*) female.

féminin, -ine [feminɛ̃, -in] *a* (*prénom, hormone etc*) female; (*trait, intuition, pronom etc*) feminine; (*mode, revue, équipe etc*) women's. ● **féministe** *a & nmf* feminist. ● **féminité** *nf* femininity.

femme [fam] *nf* woman (*pl* women); (*épouse*) wife; **f. médecin** woman doctor; **f. de ménage** cleaning woman *ou* lady, maid; **f. de chambre** (chamber)maid; **f. d'affaires** businesswoman; **f. au foyer** housewife; **f.-objet** woman as a sex object; **bonne f.** *Fam* woman.

fémur [femyr] *nm* thighbone, femur.

fendiller (se) [səfɑ̃dije] *vpr* to crack.

fendre [fɑ̃dr] *vt* (*bois etc*) to split; (*foule*) to force one's way through; (*air*) to cleave; (*cœur*) *Fig* to break, rend; **jupe fendue** slit skirt **▌ se fendre** *vpr* (*se fissurer*) to crack; **se f. de 50 francs/etc** *Fam* to fork out 50 francs/*etc*; **se f. la gueule** *Fam* to laugh one's head off.

fenêtre [f(ə)nɛtr] *nf* window.

fenouil [fənuj] *nm* fennel.

fente [fɑ̃t] *nf* (*de tirelire, palissade, jupe etc*) slit; (*de rocher*) split, crack.

féodal, -e, -aux [feɔdal, -o] *a* feudal.

fer [fɛr] *nm* iron; (*partie métallique de qch*) metal (part); **f. forgé** wrought iron; **barre de** *ou* **en f.** iron bar; **boîte en f.** can, *Br* tin; **fil de f.** wire; **f. à cheval** horseshoe; **f.** (*à repasser*) iron (*for clothes*); **f. à friser** curling tongs; **f. de lance** *Fig* spearhead; **santé de f.** *Fig* cast-iron health; **main/volonté de f.** *Fig* iron hand/will. ● **fer-blanc** *nm* (*pl* **fers-blancs**) tin(-plate).

fera, ferait *etc* [fəra, fərɛ] *voir* **faire.**

férié [ferje] *am* **jour f.** (public) holiday.

ferme¹ [fɛrm] *nf* farm; (*maison*) farm(house).

ferme² [fɛrm] *a* (*beurre, décision etc*) firm; (*pas, voix*) steady; (*pâte*) stiff; (*autoritaire*) firm (avec with) **▌** *adv* (*discuter*) keenly; (*travailler, boire*) hard; **s'ennuyer f.** to be bored stiff; **tenir f.** to stand firm *ou* fast. ● **fermement** [-əmɑ̃] *adv* firmly.

ferment [fɛrmɑ̃] *nm* ferment. ● **fermentation** *nf* fermentation. ● **fermenter** *vi* to ferment.

fermer [fɛrme] *vt* to close, shut; (*gaz, radio etc*) to turn *ou* switch off; (*vêtement*) to do up; (*passage*) to block; (à clef) to lock; **f. un magasin/etc** (*définitivement*) to close *ou* shut (down) a shop/*etc*; **f. la marche** to bring up the rear; **ferme-la!, la ferme!** *Fam* shut up! **▌** *vi*, **se fermer** *vpr* to close, shut. ● **fermé, -ée** *a* (*porte, magasin etc*) closed, shut; (*route, circuit etc*) closed; (*gaz etc*) off.

fermeté [fɛrməte] *nf* firmness; (*de geste, voix*) steadiness.

fermeture [fɛrmətyr] *nf* closing, closure; (*heure*) closing time; (*mécanisme*) catch; **f. éclair®** *Br* zip (fastener), *Am* zipper; **f.**

annuelle annual closure.

fermier, -ière [fɛrmje, -jɛr] *nmf* farmer ▮ *a* **poulet**/*etc* **f.** farm chicken/*etc.*

fermoir [fɛrmwar] *nm* clasp, (snap) fastener.

féroce [feros] *a* fierce, savage, ferocious. ● **férocité** *nf* ferocity, fierceness.

feront [fərɔ̃] *voir* **faire.**

ferraille [fɛraj] *nf* scrap metal, *Br* old iron; **mettre à la f.** to scrap. ● **ferrailleur** *nm* scrap metal dealer *ou Br* merchant.

ferré, -ée [fɛre] *a* (*canne*) metal-tipped; **voie ferrée** *Br* railway, *Am* railroad; (*rails*) track.

ferrer [fɛre] *vt* (*cheval*) to shoe.

ferronnerie [fɛrɔnri] *nf* ironwork.

ferroviaire [fɛrɔvjɛr] *a* **compagnie f.** *Br* railway company, *Am* railroad company; **catastrophe f.** rail disaster.

ferry [fɛri] *nm* ferry.

fertile [fɛrtil] *a* (*terre, imagination*) fertile; **f. en incidents** eventful. ● **fertiliser** *vt* to fertilize. ● **fertilité** *nf* fertility.

fervent, -ente [fɛrvã, -ãt] *a* fervent ▮ *nmf* devotee (**de** of). ● **ferveur** *nf* fervour.

fesse [fɛs] *nf* buttock; **les fesses** one's behind. ● **fessée** *nf* spanking.

festin [fɛstɛ̃] *nm* (*banquet*) feast.

festival, *pl* **-als** [fɛstival] *nm Mus Cinéma etc* festival; **nous avons assisté à un (vrai) f.** *Fig* we witnessed a dazzling performance *ou* display.

festivités [fɛstivite] *nfpl* festivities.

festoyer [fɛstwaje] *vi* to feast, carouse.

fête [fɛt] *nf* (*civile*) holiday; (*religieuse*) festival, feast; (*entre amis*) party; **f. de famille** family celebration; **f. du village** village fair *ou* fête; **f. des Mères** Mother's Day; **f. du travail** Labour Day; **jour de f.** (*public*) holiday; **f. nationale** national holiday; **les fêtes (de Noël et du nouvel an)** the Christmas holidays; **air de f.** festive air; **faire la f.** to have a good time, make merry, revel; **c'est sa f.** it's his *ou* her saint's day; **on va te faire ta f.!** *Fam* you're in for it! ● **fêter** *vt* (*événement*) to celebrate.

fétiche [fetiʃ] *nm* (*objet de culte*) fetish; (*mascotte*) *Fig* mascot.

fétide [fetid] *a* fetid, stinking.

feu¹, -x [fø] *nm* fire; (*de réchaud etc*) burner; (*lumière*) *Aut Nau Av* light; **les feux (tricolores)** traffic lights; **feux de détresse** (hazard) warning lights; **feux de croisement** *Br* dipped headlights, *Am* low beams; **feux de position** (*de véhicule*) parking lights; **tous feux éteints** (*rouler etc*) without lights; **f. rouge** *Aut* (*lumière*) red light; (*objet*) traffic lights; **coup de f.** (*bruit*) gunshot; **feux croisés** *Mil* crossfire; **en f.** on fire, ablaze; **dans le f. de la dispute**/*etc Fig* in the heat of the argument/*etc*; **mettre le f. à** to set fire to; **mettre le f. aux poudres** *Fig* to spark things off; **faire du f.** to light *ou* make a fire; **prendre f.** to catch fire; **donner du f. à qn** to give s.o. a light; **avez-vous du f.?** have you got a light?; **donner le f. vert** *Fig* to give the go-ahead (**à** to); **faire cuire à f. doux** to cook on a low light *ou*

heat; **ne pas faire long f.** *Fig* not to last very long; **au f.!** (there's a) fire!; **f.! Mil** fire!

feu² [fø] *a inv* late; **f. ma tante** my late aunt.

feuille [fœj] *nf* leaf; (*de papier etc*) sheet; (*de température*) chart; (*de journal*) newssheet; **f. d'impôt** tax form *ou* return; **f. de paie** *Br* pay slip, *Am* pay stub; **f. de maladie** form given by doctor to patient for claiming reimbursement from the Social Security; **f. de présence** attendance sheet. ● **feuillage** *nm* leaves, foliage. ● **feuillu, -ue** *a* leafy.

feuillet [fœje] *nm* (*de livre*) leaf. ● **feuilleter** *vt* (*livre*) to flip *ou* leaf through; **pâte feuilletée** *Br* puff pastry, *Am* puff paste, flaky pastry. ● **feuilleté** *nm* **f. au fromage**/*etc* cheese/*etc* pastry.

feuilleton [fœjtɔ̃] *nm* (*roman, film etc*) serial; **f. (télévisé)** television serial.

feutre [føtr] *nm* felt; (*chapeau*) felt hat; (*crayon*) **f.** felt-tip(ped) pen. ● **feutré, -ée** *a* (*lainage*) matted; (*bruit*) muffled; **à pas feutrés** silently. ● **feutrine** *nf* lightweight felt.

fève [fɛv] *nf* (broad) bean; (*de la Galette des Rois*) charm (*hidden in Twelfth Night Cake*).

février [fevrije] *nm* February.

fiable [fjabl] *a* reliable. ● **fiabilité** *nf* reliability.

fiacre [fjakr] *nm Hist* hackney carriage.

fiancer (se) [səfjãse] *vpr* to become engaged (**avec** to). ● **fiancé** *nm* fiancé; **fiancés** engaged couple. ● **fiancée** *nf* fiancée. ● **fiançailles** *nfpl* engagement.

fiasco [fjasko] *nm* fiasco; **faire f.** to be a fiasco.

fibre [fibr] *nf* fibre; **f. (alimentaire)** roughage, (dietary) fibre; **f. de verre** fibreglass; **fibres optiques** optical fibres; **câble en fibres optiques** fibre-optic cable.

ficelle [fisɛl] *nf* **1** string; **connaître les ficelles (d'un métier)** to know the ropes. **2** (*pain*) long thin loaf. ● **ficeler** *vt* to tie up.

fiche [fiʃ] *nf* **1** (*carte*) index *ou* record card; (*papier*) form, slip; **f. technique** data record; **f. de paie** *Br* pay slip, *Am* pay stub; **f. d'état civil** record of civil status (*birth details and marital status*). **2** *Él* (*broche*) pin; (*prise*) plug. ● **fichier** *nm* card index, file; *Ordinat* file.

fiche(r) [fiʃ(e)] *vt* (*pp fichu*) *Fam* (faire) to do; (*donner*) to give; (*jeter*) to throw; (*mettre*) to put; **f. le camp** to shove off; **fiche-moi la paix!** leave me alone!; **se f. de qn** to make fun of s.o.; **je m'en fiche!** I don't give a damn!; **je me suis fichu dedans** I goofed, I made a *Br* boob *ou Am* booboo.

ficher [fiʃe] *vt* **1** (*enfoncer*) to drive in. **2** (*renseignement sur une personne*) to put on file.

fichu, -ue [fiʃy] **1** *a Fam* (*mauvais*) lousy, rotten; (*capable*) able (**de faire** to do); **mal f.** (*malade*) not well; **c'est f.** (*abîmé*) *Fam* it's had it; **il est f.** (*condamné*) he's had it, *Br* he's done for. **2** *nm* (head) scarf.

fictif, -ive [fiktif, -iv] *a* fictitious. ● **fiction** *nf* fiction.

fidèle [fidɛl] *a* faithful (à to) **‖** *nmf* faithful supporter; *(client)* regular (customer); **les fidèles** *(croyants)* the faithful; *(à l'église)* the congregation. ● **fidèlement** *adv* faithfully. ● **fidélité** *nf* fidelity, faithfulness.

fief [fjɛf] *nm (spécialité, chasse gardée)* domain.

fieffé, -ée [fjefe] *a* **un f. menteur** an out-and-out liar.

fiel [fjɛl] *nm* gall.

fier (se) [səfje] *vpr* **se f. à** to trust.

fier, fière [fjɛr] *a* proud (de of); **un f. culot** *Fam* a rare impudence *ou Br* cheek; **avoir fière allure** to cut a fine figure. ● **fièrement** *adv* proudly. ● **fierté** *nf* pride.

fièvre [fjɛvr] *nf (maladie)* fever; *(agitation)* frenzy; **avoir de la f.** to have a temperature *ou* a fever. ● **fiévreux, -euse** *a* feverish.

figer [fiʒe] *vt (liquide)* to congeal; **f. qn** *(paralyser) Fig* to freeze s.o. **‖** *vi (liquide)* to congeal **‖ se figer** *vpr (liquide)* to congeal; *(sourire, personne) Fig* to freeze. ● **figé, -ée** *a (locution)* set, fixed; *(regard)* frozen; *(société)* fossilized.

fignoler [fiɲɔle] *vt Fam* to round off meticulously, refine. ● **fignolé, -ée** *a Fam* meticulous.

figue [fig] *nf* fig; **mi-f., mi-raisin** *(accueil etc)* neither good nor bad, mixed. ● **figuier** *nm* fig tree.

figurant, -ante [figyrã, -ãt] *nmf Cinéma Théâtre* extra.

figure [figyr] *nf* 1 *(visage)* face. 2 *(personnage)* & *Géom* figure; *(de livre)* figure, illustration; **faire f. de favori** to be considered the favourite; **f. de style** stylistic device. ● **figurine** *nf* statuette.

figurer [figyre] *vt* to represent **‖** *vi* to appear, figure **‖ se figurer** *vpr* to imagine; **figurez-vous que...?** would you believe that...? ● **figuré, -ée** *a (sens)* figurative **‖** *nm* **au f.** figuratively.

fil [fil] *nm* 1 *(de coton, pensée etc)* thread; *(lin)* linen; **f. dentaire** dental floss; **de f. en aiguille** bit by bit; **donner du f. à retordre à qn** to give s.o. a lot of heartache; **cousu de f. blanc** plain for all to see, as plain as day. 2 *(métallique)* wire; **f. de fer** wire; **f. à plomb** plumbline; **passer un coup de f. à qn** to give s.o. a ring, call s.o. up; **au bout du f.** *(au téléphone)* on the line. 3 *(de couteau)* edge. 4 **au f. de l'eau/des jours** with the current/the passing of time.

filament [filamã] *nm Biol Él* filament.

filandreux, -euse [filãdrø, -øz] *a (viande)* stringy; *(phrase) Fig* long-winded.

filature [filatyr] *nf* 1 *(usine)* textile mill. 2 *(de policiers etc)* shadowing; **prendre qn en f.** to shadow s.o.

file [fil] *nf* line; *(couloir) Aut* lane; **f. d'attente** *Br* queue, *Am* line; **en f. (indienne)** in single file; **chef de f.** leader; **(se) mettre en f.** to line up; **être en double f.** *(voiture)* to be double-parked.

filer [file] 1 *vt (coton etc)* to spin. 2 *vt* **f. qn**

(suivre) to shadow s.o., tail s.o. 3 *vt Fam* **f. qch à qn** *(objet)* to slip s.o. sth; **f. un coup de pied/etc à qn** to give s.o. a kick/etc. 4 *vi (partir)* to rush off, shoot off, bolt; *(aller vite)* to speed along; *(temps)* to fly; *(bas, collant)* to run, *Br* ladder; *(liquide)* to trickle, run; **filez!** beat it!, *Br* hop it!; **f. entre les doigts de qn** to slip through s.o.'s fingers;   **f.   doux**   to   be obedient.

filet [filɛ] *nm* 1 *(à bagages) (dans un train etc)* (luggage) rack; *(de pêche)* & *Sport* net; **f. (à provisions)** string *ou* net bag *(for shopping)*; **coup de f.** *(opération de police)* police haul. 2 *(d'eau)* trickle. 3 *(de poisson, viande)* fillet.

filial, -e, -aux [filjal, -o] *a* filial.

filiale [filjal] *nf* subsidiary (company).

filiation [filjasjɔ̃] *nf* relationship.

filière [filjɛr] *nf (de drogue)* network; **suivre la f. (normale)** *(pour obtenir qch)* to go through the official channels; *(employé)* to work one's way up; **remonter la f.** *(police)* to go back through the network (to reach the person at the top).

filigrane [filigran] *nm (sur papier)* watermark.

filin [filɛ̃] *nm Nau* rope.

fille [fij] *nf* 1 girl; **petite f.** (little *ou* young) girl; **jeune f.** girl, young lady; **vieille f.** *Péj* old maid; **f. (publique)** *Péj* prostitute. 2 *(parenté)* daughter. ● **fille-mère** *nf (pl* **filles-mères)** *Péj* unmarried mother. ● **fillette** *nf* little girl.

filleul [fijœl] *nm* godson. ● **filleule** *nf* goddaughter.

film [film] *nm* 1 film, movie; *(pour photo)* film; **f. muet/parlant** silent/talking film *ou* movie; **f. policier** thriller; **f. d'aventures** adventure film *ou* movie; **le f. des événements** *Fig* the sequence of events. 2 **f. plastique** *Br* clingfilm, *Am* plastic wrap. ● **filmer** *vt (personne, scène)* to film.

filon [filɔ̃] *nm Géol* seam; **trouver le (bon) f.** *Fam* to strike it lucky.

filou [filu] *nm* rogue, crook.

fils [fis] *nm* son; **Dupont f.** Dupont junior.

filtre [filtr] *nm* filter; **(à bout) f.** *(cigarette)* (filter-)tipped; **(bout) f.** filter tip. ● **filtrer** *vt* to filter; *(personne, nouvelles)* to scrutinize **‖** *vi* to filter (through).

fin [fɛ̃] *nf* 1 end; **mettre f. à** to put an end *ou* a stop; **prendre f.** to come to an end; **tirer à sa f.** to draw to an end *ou* a close; **sans f.** endless; **à la f.** in the end; **arrêtez, à la f.!** stop, for heaven's sake!; **f. de semaine** weekend; **f. mai** at the end of May; **c'est la f. de tout!** *Fam* we've had it!, that's the last straw! 2 *(but)* end, aim; **arriver à ses fins** to achieve one's ends *ou* aims; **à cette f.** to this end.

fin, fine [fɛ̃, fin] *a (pointe, tissu etc)* fine; *(peu épais)* thin; *(plat)* delicate, choice; *(esprit, oreille)* sharp; *(observation)* sharp, fine; *(intelligent)* clever; **au f. fond de** in the depths of; **f. gourmet** gourmet; **jouer au plus f. avec qn** to try and be smarter than s.o. ∎ *adv* (*couper, moudre*) finely; (*écrire*) small.

final, -e, -aux *ou* **-als** [final, -o] *a* final ∎ *nm Mus* finale. ●**finale** *nf Sport* final; *Grammaire* final syllable ∎ *nm Mus* finale. ●**finalement** *adv* finally; (*en somme*) after all. ●**finaliste** *nmf Sport* finalist.

finance [finɑ̃s] *nf* finance. ●**financer** *vt* to finance. ●**financement** *nm* financing.

financier, -ière [finɑ̃sje, -jɛr] *a* financial ∎ *nm* financier. ●**financièrement** *adv* financially.

fine [fin] *nf* liqueur brandy.

finement [finmɑ̃] *adv* (*couper, broder etc*) finely; (*agir*) cleverly; **f. joué** nicely played.

finesse [finɛs] *nf* (*de pointe etc*) fineness; (*de taille etc*) thinness; (*de plat*) delicacy; (*d'esprit, de goût*) finesse; **finesses** (*de langue*) niceties.

finir [finir] *vt* to finish; (*discours, vie*) to end, finish ∎ *vi* to finish, end; **f.** *bien/mal* (*histoire, film etc*) to have a happy/unhappy ending; **f. de faire** (*achever*) to finish doing; (*cesser*) to stop doing; **f. par faire** to end up *ou* finish up doing; **f. par qch** to finish (up) *ou* end (up) with sth; **en f. avec** to put an end to, finish with; **elle n'en finit pas de pleurer** there's nothing that can make her stop crying; **il finira tout seul** (*il mourra tout seul*) he'll come to a lonely end. ●**fini, -ie** *a* (*produit*) finished; (*univers etc*) & *Math* finite; **c'est f.** it's over *ou* finished; **il est f.** (*trop vieux*) he's finished ∎ *nm* (*poli*) finish. ●**finissant, -ante** *a* (*siècle etc*) declining. ●**finish** *nm Sport* final burst, finish; **avoir qn au f.** (*à l'usure*) *Fam* to get s.o. in the end. ●**finition** *nf* (*action*) *Tech* finishing; (*résultat*) finish.

Finlande [fɛ̃lɑ̃d] *nf* Finland. ●**finlandais, -aise** *a* Finnish ∎ *nmf* **F.**, **Finlandaise** Finn. ●**finnois, -oise** *a* Finnish ∎ *nmf* **F.**, **Finnoise** Finn ∎ *nm* (*langue*) Finnish.

fiole [fjɔl] *nf* phial, flask.

firme [firm] *nf* (*entreprise*) firm, company.

fisc [fisk] *nm* tax authorities, = *Br* Inland Revenue, = *Am* Internal Revenue. ●**fiscal, -e, -aux** *a* **droit/etc f.** tax *ou* fiscal law/etc; **charges fiscales** taxes; **fraude fiscale** tax fraud *ou* evasion. ●**fiscalité** *nf* tax system; (*charges*) taxation.

fission [fisjɔ̃] *nf Phys* fission.

fissure [fisyr] *nf* split, crack, fissure. ●**se fissurer** *vpr* to split, crack.

fiston [fistɔ̃] *nm Fam* son, sonny.

fixateur [fiksatœr] *nm Phot* fixer; (*pour cheveux*) setting lotion.

fixation [fiksasjɔ̃] *nf* (*action*) fixing; (*dispositif*) fastening, binding; *Psy* fixation.

fixe [fiks] *a* fixed; (*prix, heure*) set, fixed; **idée f.** obsession; **regard f.** stare; **être au beau f.** (*temps*) to be set fair ∎ *nm* (*paie*) fixed salary. ●**fixement** [-əmɑ̃] *adv* **regarder f.** to stare at.

fixer [fikse] *vt* (*attacher*) to fix (à to); (*choix*)

to settle; (*date, règle etc*) to decide, fix; **f.** (**du regard**) to stare at; **être fixé** (*décidé*) to be decided; **comme ça on est fixé!** (*renseigné*) we've got the picture! ∎ **se fixer** *vpr* (*regard*) to become fixed; (*s'établir*) to settle.

flacon [flakɔ̃] *nm* small bottle, flask.

flageoler [flaʒɔle] *vi* to shake, tremble.

flageolet [flaʒɔlɛ] *nm* (*haricot*) (dwarf) kidney bean.

flagrant, -ante [flagrɑ̃, -ɑ̃t] *a* (*injustice etc*) flagrant, glaring; **pris en f. délit** caught in the act *ou* red-handed.

flair [flɛr] *nm* **1** (*d'un chien etc*) (sense of) smell, scent. **2** (*clairvoyance*) intuition, flair. ●**flairer** *vt* to smell, sniff at; (*discerner*) *Fig* to smell, sense.

flamand, -ande [flamɑ̃, -ɑ̃d] *a* Flemish ∎ *nmf* **F.**, **Flamande** Fleming ∎ *nm* (*langue*) Flemish.

flamant [flamɑ̃] *nm* **f.** (**rose**) (*oiseau*) flamingo.

flambant [flɑ̃bɑ̃] *adv* **f. neuf** brand new.

flambeau, -x [flɑ̃bo] *nm* torch.

flambée [flɑ̃be] *nf* blaze; (*de colère, des prix etc*) *Fig* surge; (*de violence*) flare-up, eruption.

flamber [flɑ̃be] **1** *vi* to burn, blaze ∎ *vt* (*aiguille*) *Méd* to sterilize; (*poulet*) to singe; **bananes flambées** flambéed bananas. **2** *vi* (*jouer*) *Fam* to gamble for big money. ●**flambeur** *nm Fam* big gambler.

flamboyer [flɑ̃bwaje] *vi* to blaze, flame.

flamme [flam] *nf* flame; (*ardeur*) *Fig* fire; **en flammes** on fire. ●**flammèche** *nf* spark.

flan [flɑ̃] *nm* (*dessert*) custard tart *ou* pie, baked custard; **rester comme deux ronds de f.** *Fam* to be flabbergasted.

flanc [flɑ̃] *nm* side; (*d'une armée, d'un animal*) flank; **tirer au f.** *Arg* to shirk, idle.

flancher [flɑ̃ʃe] *vi Fam* to give in, weaken.

Flandre(s) [flɑ̃dr] *nf(pl)* Flanders.

flanelle [flanɛl] *nf* (*tissu*) flannel.

flâner [flɑne] *vi* to stroll, dawdle. ●**flânerie** *nf* (*action*) strolling; (*promenade*) stroll.

flanquer [flɑ̃ke] *vt* **1** to flank (de with). **2** *Fam* (*jeter*) to chuck; (*donner*) to give; **f. qn à la porte** to throw s.o. out.

flaque [flak] *nf* puddle, pool.

flash, *pl* **flashes** [flaʃ] *nm* **1** *Phot* (*éclair*) flashlight; (*dispositif*) flash(gun). **2** **f.** (**d'informations**) (*à la radio ou télévision*) (news) flash. ●**flasher** *vi* **f. sur qch/qn** *Fam* to fall for sth/s.o., fall in love with sth/s.o.

flasque [flask] *a* flabby, floppy.

flatter [flate] *vt* to flatter; **se f. d'être malin/de réussir** to flatter oneself on being smart/on being able to succeed. ●**flatté, -ée** *a* flattered (de qch by sth, de faire to do, que that). ●**flatterie** *nf* flattery. ●**flatteur, -euse** *nmf* flatterer ∎ *a* flattering.

fléau, -x [fleo] *nm* **1** (*catastrophe*) scourge; (*personne*) plague, bane. **2** *Agr* flail.

flèche [flɛʃ] *nf* arrow; (*d'église*) spire; **monter en f.** (*prix*) to shoot up, (sky)rocket; **celui-là, ce n'est pas une f.** *Fam* he's a bit slow to understand things. ●**flécher** [fleʃe] *vt* to signpost (with arrows). ●**fléchette** *nf* dart; **fléchettes** (*jeu*) darts.

fléchir [fleʃir] *vt* (*membre*) to flex, bend; **f. qn** *Fig* to move s.o., persuade s.o. **‖** *vi* (*membre*) to bend; (*poutre*) to sag; (*faiblir*) to give way; (*baisser*) to fall off.

flegme [flɛgm] *nm* composure. ●**flegmatique** *a* phlegmatic, stolid.

flemme [flɛm] *nf Fam* laziness; **il a la f.** he can't be bothered, he's just too lazy. ●**flemmard, -arde** *a Fam* lazy **‖** *nmf Fam* lazybones.

flétrir [fletrir] **1** *vt*, **se flétrir** *vpr* to wither. **2** *vt* **f. la réputation de qn** to cast a slur on s.o.'s reputation.

fleur [flœr] *nf* flower; (*d'arbre*, *d'arbuste*) blossom; **en fleur(s)** in flower, in bloom; (*arbre etc*) in blossom; **à fleurs** (*tissu*) flowered, flowery, floral; **à ou dans la f. de l'âge** in the prime of life; **à f. d'eau** just above the water; **la fine f. de la marine française/***etc* the cream of the French navy/*etc*; **arriver comme une f.** (*innocemment*) *Fam* to arrive innocent and unsuspecting; **faire une f. à qn** *Fam* to do s.o. a favour; **il a un côté f. bleue** he has a romantic side.

fleurir [flœrir] *vi* to flower, bloom; (*arbre etc*) to blossom; (*art, commerce etc*) *Fig* to flourish **‖** *vt* (*table etc*) to decorate with flowers. ●**fleuri, -ie** *a* (*fleur, jardin*) in bloom; (*tissu*) flowered, flowery, floral; (*teint*) florid; (*style*) flowery, florid.

fleuriste [flœrist] *nmf* florist.

fleuve [flœv] *nm* river.

flexible [flɛksibl] *a* pliable, flexible. ●**flexibilité** *nf* flexibility.

flexion [flɛksjɔ̃] *nf* **1** *Anat* flexion, flexing. **2** *Grammaire* inflexion.

flic [flik] *nm* (*agent de police*) *Fam* cop, policeman.

flinguer [flɛ̃ge] *vt* **f. qn** *Arg* to shoot s.o.

flipper [flipœr] *nm* (*jeu*) pinball; (*appareil*) pinball machine.

flirt [flœrt] *nm* (*rapports*) flirtation; (*personne*) flirt. ●**flirter** *vi* to flirt (**avec** with).

flocon [flɔkɔ̃] *nm* (*de neige*) flake; (*de laine*) flock; **flocons de maïs** cornflakes; **flocons d'avoine** porridge oats; **il neige à gros flocons** big flakes of snow are falling. ●**floconneux, -euse** *a* fluffy.

floraison [flɔrezɔ̃] *nf* flowering; **en pleine f.** in full bloom. ●**floral, -e, -aux** *a* floral. ●**floralies** *nfpl* flower show.

flore [flɔr] *nf* flora.

florissant, -ante [flɔrisɑ̃, -ɑ̃t] *a* flourishing.

flot [flo] *nm* (*de souvenirs, larmes etc*) flood, stream; (*marée*) floodtide; **les flots** (*la mer*) the waves; **à f.** (*bateau, personne*) afloat; **remettre qn à f.** to restore s.o.'s fortunes; **couler à flots** (*argent, vin etc*) to flow freely; **le soleil entrait à flots** the sun was streaming in.

flotte [flɔt] *nf* **1** (*de bateaux, d'avions*) fleet. **2** *Fam* (*pluie*) rain; (*eau*) water. ●**flottille** *nf Nau* flotilla.

flottement [flɔtmɑ̃] *nm* (*hésitation*) indecision.

flotter [flɔte] *vi* to float; (*drapeau*) to fly; (*cheveux*) to flow; (*pensées*) to drift; (*pleuvoir*) *Fam* to rain. ●**flottant, -ante** *a* **1** (*bois, dette etc*) floating; (*vêtement*) flowing, loose. **2** (*esprit*) indecisive. ●**flotteur** *nm* (*de ligne de pêche, d'hydravion etc*) float.

flou, -e [flu] *a* (*photo*) fuzzy, blurred; (*idée*) hazy, fuzzy **‖** *nm* fuzziness; **f. artistique** *Photo Cinéma* soft focus (effect); *Fig* vagueness.

fluctuant, -ante [flyktɥɑ̃, -ɑ̃t] *a* (*prix, opinions*) fluctuating. ●**fluctuations** *nfpl* fluctuation(s) (**de** in).

fluet, -ette [flɥɛ, -ɛt] *a* thin, slender.

fluide [flɥid] *a* (*liquide*) & *Fig* fluid **‖** *nm* (*liquide*) fluid. ●**fluidité** *nf* fluidity.

fluo [flyo] *a inv* (*couleur etc*) luminous, fluorescent, dayglo.

fluorescent, -ente [flyɔresɑ̃, -ɑ̃t] *a* fluorescent.

flûte [flyt] **1** *nf* (*instrument de musique*) flute. **2** *nf* (*verre*) champagne glass. **3** *int* heck!, darn!, dash it! ●**flûté, -ée** *a* (*voix*) piping. ●**flûtiste** *nmf Br* flautist, *Am* flutist.

fluvial, -e, -aux [flyvjal, -o] *a* **navigation/***etc* **fluviale** river navigation/*etc*.

flux [fly] *nm* (*abondance*) flow; **f. et reflux** ebb and flow.

focal, -e, -aux [fɔkal, -o] *a* focal. ●**focaliser** *vt* (*intérêt etc*) to focus.

fœtus [fetys] *nm Br* foetus, *Am* fetus.

foi [fwa] *nf* faith; **sur la f. de** on the strength of; **être de bonne/mauvaise f.** to be/not to be (completely) sincere, to be in good/bad faith; **avoir la f.** (*être croyant*) to have faith; **ma f., oui!** yes, indeed!

foie [fwa] *nm* liver; **f. gras** foie gras (*goose liver paste*); **crise de f.** bout of indigestion.

foin [fwɛ̃] *nm* hay; **faire du f.** (*scandale*) *Fam* to make a stink.

foire [fwar] *nf* fair; **faire la f.** *Fam* to have a ball, go on a binge.

fois [fwa] *nf* time; **une f.** once; **deux f.** twice, two times; **trois f.** three times; **deux f. trois** two times three; **chaque f. que** whenever, each time (that); **une f. qu'il sera arrivé** (*dès que*) once he has arrived; **à la f.** at the same time, at once; **à la f. riche et heureux** both rich and happy; **une autre f.** (*elle fera attention etc*) next time; **des f.** *Fam* sometimes; **non mais des f.!** *Fam* you must be joking!; **une f. pour toutes, une bonne f.** once and for all; **payer qch en plusieurs f.** to pay for sth in several instalments.

foison [fwazɔ̃] *nf* **à f.** in plenty. ●**foisonner** *vi* to abound (**de, en** in). ●**foisonnement** *nm* abundance.

fol [fɔl] *voir* **fou.**

folâtre [fɔlɑtr] *a* playful. ●**folâtrer** *vi* to romp, frolic.

folichon, -onne [fɔliʃɔ̃, -ɔn] *a* **pas f.** not much fun, not very funny.

folie [fɔli] *nf* madness, insanity; **faire une f.**

to do a foolish thing; (*dépense*) to be very *ou* wildly extravagant; **faire des folies pour qn** to do anything for s.o.; **aimer qn à la f.** to be madly in love with s.o.

folklore [fɔlklɔr] *nm* folklore. ●**folklorique** *a* **1 musique/etc** f. folk music/etc. **2** (*pas sérieux*) *Fam* lightweight, trivial, silly.

folle [fɔl] *voir* **fou. ●follement** *adv* madly.

fomenter [fɔmɑ̃te] *vt* (*révolte etc*) *Litt* to foment.

foncé, -ée [fɔ̃se] *a* (*couleur*) dark.

foncer [fɔ̃se] **1** *vi* (*aller vite*) to tear *ou* charge along; **f. sur qn** to charge into *ou* at s.o. **2** *vti* (*couleur*) to darken. ●**fonceur, -euse** *nmf Fam* dynamic *ou* go-ahead person.

foncier, -ière [fɔ̃sje, -jɛr] *a* **1** fundamental, basic. **2** (*propriété*) landed; **crédit/etc f.** land loan/etc. ●**foncièrement** *adv* fundamentally.

fonction [fɔ̃ksjɔ̃] *nf* (*rôle*) & *Math* function; (*emploi*) office, post, duty; **f. publique** the public *ou* civil service; **faire f. de** (*personne*) to act as; (*objet*) to serve *ou* act as; **en f. de** according to; **prendre ses fonctions** to take up one's post *ou* duties; **touche de f.** *Ordinat* function key. ●**fonctionnaire** *nmf* civil servant. ●**fonctionnel, -elle** *a* functional.

fonctionner [fɔ̃ksjɔne] *vi* (*machine etc*) to work, operate, function; (*organisation*) to function; **faire f.** to operate, work. ●**fonctionnement** *nm* working.

fond [fɔ̃] *nm* (*de boîte, jardin, vallée etc*) bottom; (*de salle, armoire etc*) back; (*arrière-plan*) background; (*de problème, débat etc*) essence; (*contenu*) content; **au f. de** at the bottom of; (*salle etc*) at the back of; **f. de teint** foundation cream; **f. sonore** background music; **un f. de bon sens** a stock of good sense; **un f. de vin/etc** a drop of wine/ etc; **au f., dans le f.** basically, in essence; **à f.** (*connaître etc*) thoroughly; **de f. en comble** from top to bottom; **course/coureur de f.** long-distance race/runner; **ski de f.** cross-country skiing; **bruit de f.** background noise; **toucher le f. (du désespoir)** to have hit rock-bottom; **user ses fonds de culotte sur les bancs d'une école** to spend a great deal of time at a school.

fondamental, -e, -aux [fɔ̃damɑ̃tal, -o] *a* fundamental, basic.

fonder [fɔ̃de] *vt* (*ville etc*) to found; (*commerce*) to set up; (*famille*) to start; (*se*) **f. sur** to base (oneself) on; **être fondé à croire/etc** to be justified in thinking/etc; **bien fondé** well-founded. ●**fondement** *nm* foundation. ●**fondateur, -trice** *nmf* founder **▮** **membre f.** founding member. ●**fondation** *nf* (*création, œuvre*) foundation (de of).

fonderie [fɔ̃dri] *nf* (*usine*) smelting works, foundry.

fondre [fɔ̃dr] *vt* to melt; (*métal*) to melt down, smelt; (*cloche*) to cast; (*amalgamer*) *Fig* to fuse (avec with); **faire f.** (*sucre etc*) to dissolve **▮** *vi* to melt; (*se dissoudre*) to dissolve; **f. en larmes** to burst into tears; **f. sur**

to swoop on **▮** **se fondre** *vpr* to merge; fuse; **se f. en eau** (*glaçon etc*) to melt away; **se f. dans** (*la brume etc*) to disappear *ou* merge into. ●**fondant, -ante** *a* (*fruit*) which melts in the mouth. ●**fondu** *nm* **f. enchaîné** *Cinéma* dissolve.

fonds [fɔ̃] **1** *nmpl* (*argent*) funds. **2** *nm* un **f.** (**de commerce**) a business. **3** *nm* (*culturel etc*) *Fig* fund.

font [fɔ̃] *voir* **faire.**

fontaine [fɔ̃tɛn] *nf* (*construction*) fountain; (*source*) spring.

fonte [fɔ̃t] *nf* **1** (*de la neige*) melting; (*d'acier*) smelting. **2** (*fer*) cast iron; **en f.** (*poêle etc*) cast-iron.

fonts [fɔ̃] *nmpl* **f. baptismaux** *Rel* font.

football [futbol] *nm Br* football, soccer. ●**footballeur, -euse** *nmf Br* footballer, soccer player.

footing [futiŋ] *nm Sport* jogging; **faire du f.** to jog, go jogging.

forage [fɔraʒ] *nm* drilling, boring.

forain, -aine [fɔrɛ̃, -ɛn] *a* (*marchand*) itinerant; **fête foraine** (fun)fair.

forçat [fɔrsa] *nm* (*prisonnier*) convict.

force [fɔrs] *nf* force; (*physique, morale*) strength; (*nucléaire*) power; **de toutes ses forces** with all one's strength; **les forces armées** the armed forces; **de f.** by force, forcibly; **en f.** (*attaquer, venir*) in force; **à f. de lire/etc** through reading/etc, after much reading/etc; **cas de f. majeure** circumstances beyond one's control; **dans la f. de l'âge** in the prime of life; **à f. de** through sheer force of, by dint of; **par la f. des choses** through force of circumstances; **à f., il va se mettre en colère** *Fam* he'll end up losing his temper.

forcé, -ée [fɔrse] *a* forced (**de faire** to do); **un sourire f.** a forced smile; **c'est f.** *Fam* it's inevitable *ou* obvious. ●**forcément** *adv* inevitably, obviously; **pas f.** not necessarily.

forcené, -ée [fɔrsəne] *a* frantic, frenzied **▮** *nmf* madman, madwoman.

forcer [fɔrse] *vt* (*porte, attention etc*) to force; (*voix*) to strain; (*sens*) to stretch; **f. qn à faire qch** to force *ou* compel s.o. to do sth; **f. la main à qn** to force s.o.'s hand; **f. la dose** *Fam* to exaggerate things **▮** *vi* (*y aller trop fort*) to overdo it **▮** **se forcer** *vpr* to force oneself (**à faire** to do).

forceps [fɔrsɛps] *nm* forceps.

forcir [fɔrsir] *vi* (*grossir*) to fill out.

forer [fɔre] *vt* to drill, bore. ●**foret** *nm* drill.

forêt [fɔrɛ] *nf* forest; **f. vierge** virgin forest. ●**forestier, -ière** *a* **chemin/etc f.** forest road/ etc **▮** *nm* (**garde**) **f.** *Br* forester, *Am* (forest) ranger.

forfait [fɔrfɛ] *nm* **1** (*prix*) all-inclusive price; **travailler à f.** to work for a lump sum. **2** **déclarer f.** (*joueur*) to withdraw from the game. **3** (*crime*) *Litt* heinous crime. ●**forfaitaire** **à prix f.** all-inclusive price.

forge [fɔrʒ] *nf* forge. ●**forger** *vt* (*métal, liens etc*) to forge; (*inventer*) to make up. ●**forgé, -ée a fer f.** wrought iron. ●**forgeron** *nm* (black)smith.

formaliser (se) [sǝfɔrmalize] *vpr* to take *Br* offence *ou Am* offense (**de** at).

formalité [fɔrmalite] *nf* formality.

format [fɔrma] *nm* size, format.

formater [fɔrmate] *vt* (*disquette*) to format. ●**formatage** *nm* formatting.

formation [fɔrmasjɔ̃] *nf* formation; (*éducation*) education, training; **f. permanente** continuing education. ●**formateur, -trice** *a* formative ▮ *nmf* instructor, teacher.

forme [fɔrm] *nf* (*contour*) shape, form; (*manière, genre*) form; **formes** (*de femme*) figure; **en f. de** in the form of; **en f. d'aiguille/de poire/etc** needle-/pear-/etc shaped; **dans les formes** in the accepted way, in due form; **en (pleine) f.** in good shape *ou* form, on form; **en bonne et due f.** in due form; **sans autre f. de procès** unceremoniously; **prendre f.** to take shape; **y mettre les formes** to do things tactfully.

formel, -elle [fɔrmɛl] *a* (*structure, logique etc*) formal; (*démenti*) categorical, formal; (*preuve*) positive, formal. ●**formellement** *adv* (*interdire*) strictly.

former [fɔrme] *vt* (*groupe, caractère etc*) to form; (*apprenti etc*) to train ▮ **se former** *vpr* (*apparaître*) to form; (*institution*) to be formed. ●**formé, -ée** *a* (*personne*) fully-formed.

formidable [fɔrmidabl] *a* terrific, tremendous.

formulaire [fɔrmylɛr] *nm* (*feuille*) form.

formule [fɔrmyl] *nf* **1** formula; (*phrase*) (set) expression; (*méthode*) method; **f. de politesse** polite form of address; **f. de vacances** *Br* holiday programme, *Am* vacation program. **2** (*feuille*) form. ●**formulation** *nf* formulation. ●**formuler** *vt* to formulate.

fort¹, forte [fɔr, fɔrt] *a* strong; (*pluie, mer, chute de neige*) heavy; (*voix, radio*) loud; (*fièvre*) high; (*élève*) bright; (*pente*) steep; (*chances*) good; (*femme, homme*) heavy, large; (*ville*) fortified; **f. en** (*maths etc*) good at; **c'est plus f. qu'elle** she can't help it; **c'est un peu f.** *Fam* that's a bit much; **à plus forte raison** all the more reason.

▮ *adv* **1** (*frapper*) hard; (*pleuvoir*) hard, heavily; (*parler*) loud(ly); (*serrer*) tight; **sentir f.** to have a strong smell; **respirer f.** to breathe deeply *ou* heavily. **2** (*très*) *Litt* very; (*beaucoup*) *Litt* very much.

▮ *nm* **c'est/ce n'est pas son f.** that's/that's not his *ou* her strong point; **les forts** the strong; **au plus f. de** in the thick of. ●**fortement** [fɔrtǝmã] *adv* greatly; (*frapper*) hard.

fort² [fɔr] *nm Hist Mil* fort. ●**forteresse** *nf* fortress.

fortifié, -ée [fɔrtifje] *a* (*ville, camp*) fortified. ●**fortification** *nf* fortification.

fortifier [fɔrtifje] *vt* to strengthen, fortify ▮ **se fortifier** *vpr* (*malade*) to fortify oneself. ●**for-**

tifiant *nm Méd* tonic.

fortuit, -uite [fɔrtɥi, -it] *a* **rencontre/etc fortuite** chance meeting/etc. ●**fortuitement** *adv* by chance.

fortune [fɔrtyn] *nf* (*argent, hasard*) fortune; **faire f.** to make one's fortune; **avoir de la f.** to have (private) means; **moyens/etc de f.** makeshift means/etc; **dîner à la f. du pot** to take pot luck; **faire contre mauvaise f. bon cœur** to smile in the face of adversity. ●**fortuné, -ée** *a* (*riche*) well-to-do.

forum [fɔrɔm] *nm* forum.

fosse [fos] *nf* (*trou*) pit; (*tombe*) grave; **f. d'aisances** cesspool.

fossé [fose] *nm* ditch; (*douve*) moat; (*désaccord*) *Fig* gulf, gap.

fossette [fosɛt] *nf* dimple.

fossile [fɔsil] *nm & a* fossil.

fossoyeur [foswajœr] *nm* gravedigger.

fou (*or* **fol** *before vowel or mute h*), **folle** [fu, fɔl] *a* (*personne, projet etc*) mad, insane, crazy; (*succès, temps*) tremendous; (*envie*) wild, mad; (*espoir*) foolish; (*cheval, camion*) runaway; **f. à lier** raving mad; **f. de** (*musique, personne etc*) mad *ou* wild *ou* crazy about; **f. de joie** wildly happy, wild with joy; **ils ont le f. rire** they can't stop laughing ▮ *nmf* madman, madwoman ▮ *nm* (*bouffon*) jester; *Échecs* bishop; **faire le f.** to play the fool.

foudre [fudr] *nf* **la f.** lightning; **coup de f.** *Fig* love at first sight. ●**foudroyer** *vt* to strike by lightning; *Él* to electrocute; (*malheur etc*) *Fig* to strike (*s.o.*) down; **f. qn du regard** to give s.o. an angry glare. ●**foudroyant, -ante** *a* (*succès, vitesse etc*) staggering. ●**foudroyé, -ée** *a* (*stupéfait*) thunderstruck.

fouet [fwɛ] *nm* whip; *Culin* (egg-)whisk; **coup de f.** lash (with a whip); **de plein f.** smack in the face; **heurter une voiture de plein f.** to hit a car head-on. ●**fouetter** *vt* to whip; (*œufs*) to whisk; (*pluie etc*) to lash (*face, windows etc*); **crème fouettée** whipped cream.

fougère [fuʒɛr] *nf* fern.

fougue [fug] *nf* fire, ardour. ●**fougueux, -euse** *a* fiery, ardent.

fouille [fuj] *nf* **1** (*de personne, bagages etc*) search. **2** *nfpl* **fouilles (archéologiques)** excavation, dig. ●**fouiller 1** *vt* (*personne, maison etc*) to search ▮ *vi* **f. dans** (*tiroir etc*) to search *ou* rummage through. **2** *vti* (*creuser*) to dig. ●**fouillé, -ée** *a* **une étude/etc très fouillée** a very thorough *ou* detailed study/etc.

fouillis [fuji] *nm* jumble, mess.

fouine [fwin] *nf* (*animal*) stone marten.

fouiner [fwine] *vi Fam* to nose about (**dans** in). ●**fouineur, -euse** *a Fam* nosy ▮ *nmf Fam* nosy parker.

foulard [fular] *nm* (head)scarf.

foule [ful] *nf* crowd; **en f.** in mass; **une f. de** (*objets etc*) a mass of; **un bain de f.** a walkabout.

foulée [fule] *nf* (*de coureur, cheval etc*) stride; **courir à grandes/petites foulées** to run taking long strides/short steps; **dans la f.** *Fam* at one and the same time.

fouler [fule] *vt* to press; (*sol*) to tread; **f. aux pieds** to trample on; **se f. la cheville**/*etc* to sprain one's ankle/*etc*; **il ne se foule pas** *Fam* he doesn't exactly exert himself. ●**foulure** *nf* sprain.

four [fur] *nm* **1** oven; (*de potier etc*) kiln. **2 petit f.** (*gâteau*) (small) fancy cake. **3** (*pièce de théâtre, film etc*) flop; **faire un f.** to flop.

fourbe [furb] *a* deceitful **l** *nmf* cheat. ●**fourberie** *nf* deceit.

fourbi [furbi] *nm* (*choses*) *Fam* stuff, gear, rubbish.

fourbu, -ue [furby] *a* (*fatigué*) exhausted, *Br* dead beat.

fourche [furʃ] *nf* fork; **f. à foin** pitchfork. ●**fourcher** *vi* (*arbre etc*) to fork; **ma langue a fourché** I made a slip of the tongue. ●**fourchette** *nf* **1** (*pour manger*) fork. **2** (*de salaires etc*) bracket. ●**fourchu, -ue** *a* forked.

fourgon [furgɔ̃] *nm* (*camion*) van; (*mortuaire*) hearse; (*de train*) *Br* luggage van, *Am* baggage car; **f. cellulaire** *Br* prison van, *Am* patrol wagon; **f. postal** *Br* postal van (*on train*), *Am* mail car. ●**fourgonnette** *nf* (small) van.

fourmi [furmi] *nf* **1** (*insecte*) ant. **2 avoir des fourmis dans les jambes**/*etc* to have pins and needles in one's legs/*etc*. ●**fourmilière** *nf* anthill. ●**fourmiller** *vi* **1** (*grouiller*) to teem, swarm (**de** with). **2** (*démanger*) to tingle.

fournaise [furnεz] *nf* (*chambre etc*) *Fig* furnace.

fourneau, -x [furno] *nm* (*poêle*) stove; (*four*) furnace; **haut f.** blast furnace.

fournée [furne] *nf* (*de pain, gens*) batch.

fournil [furni] *nm* bakery.

fournir [furnir] *vt* to supply, provide; (*effort*) to make; **f. qch à qn** to supply s.o. with sth **l** **se fournir** *vpr* to get one's supplies (**chez** from), shop (**chez** at). ●**fourni, -ie** *a* (*barbe*) bushy; **bien f.** (*boutique*) well-stocked. ●**fournisseur** *nm* (*commerçant*) supplier. ●**fourniture** *nf* (*action*) supply(ing) (**de** of); **fournitures** (*objets*) supplies; **fournitures scolaires** educational supplies, school equipment.

fourrage [furaʒ] *nm* fodder.

fourrager [furaʒe] *vi Fam* to rummage (**dans** in, through).

fourreau, -x [furo] *nm* (*gaine*) sheath.

fourré, -ée [fure] **1** *a* (*gant etc*) fur-lined; (*gâteau*) jam- *ou* cream-filled; **coup f.** (*traîtrise*) *Fam* stab in the back. **2** *nm Bot* thicket.

fourrer [fure] **1** *vt* (*gâteau, chou etc*) to fill; (*vêtement*) to fur-line. **2** *vt Fam* (*mettre*) to stick; **f. qch dans la tête de qn** to knock sth into s.o.'s head; **f. son nez dans qch** to poke one's nose into sth **l** **se fourrer** *vpr* to *ou* stick oneself (**dans** in); **se f. le doigt dans l'œil** *Fam* to kid *ou* delude oneself.

fourre-tout [furtu] *nm inv* (*pièce*) junk room; (*sac*) *Br* holdall, *Am* carryall.

fourrière [furjεr] *nf* (*lieu*) pound.

fourrure [furyr] *nf* (*vêtement, de chat etc*) fur. ●**fourreur** *nm* furrier.

fourvoyer (se) [səfurvwaje] *vpr Litt* to go astray.

foutre* [futr] *vt Fam* = **fiche(r)**. ●**foutu, -ue** *a Fam* = **fichu 1**. ●**foutaise** *nf Fam* bull, *Br* rubbish, *Br* rot.

foyer [fwaje] *nm* (*maison, famille*) home; (*d'étudiants etc*) hostel; (*lieu de réunion*) club; (*âtre*) hearth; (*de théâtre*) foyer; *Géom Phys* focus; **f. de** (*maladie etc*) seat of; (*énergie, lumière*) source of; **fonder un f.** to start a family.

fracas [fraka] *nm* din; (*d'un objet qui tombe*) crash. ●**fracasser** *vt*, **se fracasser** *vpr* to smash. ●**fracassant, -ante** *a* (*nouvelle, film etc*) sensational.

fraction [fraksjɔ̃] *nf* fraction. ●**fractionner** *vt*, **se fractionner** *vpr* to split (up).

fracture [fraktyr] *nf* fracture; **se faire une f. au bras**/*etc* to fracture one's arm/*etc*. ●**fracturer** *vt* (*porte etc*) to break (open); **se f. la jambe**/*etc* to fracture one's leg/*etc*.

fragile [fraʒil] *a* (*verre, santé etc*) fragile; (*enfant etc*) frail; (*équilibre*) shaky. ●**fragilité** *nf* fragility; (*d'un enfant etc*) frailty.

fragment [fragmɑ̃] *nm* fragment. ●**fragmentaire** *a* fragmentary, fragmented. ●**fragmentation** *nf* fragmentation. ●**fragmenter** *vt* to fragment, divide.

frais¹, fraîche [frε, frεʃ] *a* (*poisson, souvenir etc*) fresh; (*température*) cool, fresh, (*plutôt désagréable*) chilly; (*boisson*) cold, cool; (*œufs*) *Br* new-laid, fresh; (*peinture*) wet; (*nouvelles*) recent; **connaître qn de fraîche date** to have known s.o. for a short time; **être f. et dispos** to be refreshed; **servir f.** (*vin etc*) to serve chilled; **boire f.** to drink something cold *ou* cool; **il fait f.** it's cool; (*froid*) it's chilly.

l *nm* **prendre le f.** to get some fresh air; **mettre qch au f.** to put sth in a cool place; (*au réfrigérateur*) to refrigerate sth. ●**fraîchement** *adv* **1** (*récemment*) freshly. **2** (*accueillir etc*) coolly. ●**fraîcheur** *nf* freshness; (*de température, boisson*) coolness; (*désagréable*) chilliness. ●**fraîchir** *vi* (*temps*) to get cooler *ou* chillier, freshen.

frais² [frε] *nmpl* expenses; **à mes f.** at my (own) expense; **à grands f.** at great expense; **faire des f.**, **se mettre en f.** to go to some expense; **faire les f.** to bear the cost (**de** of); **j'en ai été pour mes f.** I wasted my time and effort; **faux f.** incidental expenses; **f. généraux** running expenses, *Br* overheads, *Am* overhead; **f. de scolarité** school *ou* tuition fees; **f. d'inscription** (*à l'université*) registration fees; (*dans un club*) enrolment fee(s).

fraise [frεz] *nf* **1** (*fruit*) strawberry. **2** (*de dentiste*) drill. ●**fraisier** *nm* (*plante*) strawberry plant.

framboise [frɑ̃bwaz] *nf* raspberry. ●**framboisier** *nm* raspberry cane.

franc¹, franche [frɑ̃, frɑ̃ʃ] *a* **1** (*personne, ré-*

ponse etc) frank; (*visage, gaieté*) open; (*net*) clear; (*cassure, coupe*) clean. **2** (*zone*) free; **coup f.** Football free kick; **f. de port** postpaid, *Br* carriage paid. ●**franchement** *adv* (*honnêtement*) frankly; (*vraiment*) really; (*sans ambiguïté*) clearly.

franc² [frɑ̃] *nm* (*monnaie*) franc.

France [frɑ̃s] *nf* France. ●**français, -aise** *a* French **‖** *nmf* F. Frenchman; **Française** Frenchwoman; **les F.** the French **‖** *nm* (*langue*) French.

franchir [frɑ̃ʃir] *vt* (*fossé*) to jump (over), clear; (*frontière, seuil etc*) to cross; (*porte*) to go through; (*distance*) to cover; (*limites*) to exceed; (*mur du son*) to break (through), go through. ●**franchissable** *a* (*rivière, col*) passable.

franchise [frɑ̃ʃiz] *nf* **1** frankness; (*de visage etc*) openness; **en toute f.** quite frankly. **2** (*exemption*) *Com* exemption; **en f.** (*produit*) duty-free; **'f. postale'** 'official paid'. **3** (*permis de vendre*) *Com* franchise.

franc-maçon [frɑ̃masɔ̃] *nm* (*pl* **francs-maçons**) Freemason. ●**franc-maçonnerie** *nf* Freemasonry.

franco [frɑ̃ko] *adv* **f. (de port)** postpaid, *Br* carriage paid.

franco- [frɑ̃ko] *préf* Franco-.

francophile [frɑ̃kɔfil] *a* & *nmf* francophile.

francophone [frɑ̃kɔfɔn] *a* French-speaking **‖** *nmf* French speaker. ●**francophonie** *nf* **la f.** the French-speaking community.

franc-tireur [frɑ̃tirœr] *nm* irregular (*soldier*).

frange [frɑ̃ʒ] *nf* (*de cheveux*) *Br* fringe, *Am* bangs; (*de vêtement etc*) fringe.

frangin [frɑ̃ʒɛ̃] *nm* *Fam* brother. ●**frangine** *nf* *Fam* sister.

franquette (à la bonne) [alabɔnfrɑ̃kɛt] *adv* without ceremony.

frappe [frap] *nf* **1** (*dactylographie*) typing; (*de dactylo etc*) touch; **faute de f.** typing error. **2 force de f.** *Mil* strike force.

frapper [frape] *vt* (*battre*) to strike, hit; (*monnaie*) to mint; **f. qn** (*surprendre, affecter*) to strike s.o.; (*impôt, mesure etc*) to hit s.o.; **frappé de stupeur** astounded, flabbergasted; **j'ai été frappé d'apprendre sa mort** I was astounded *ou* very upset to hear of his death **‖** *vi* (*à la porte etc*) to knock, bang (à at); **du pied** to stamp (one's foot); **f dans ses mains** to clap one's hands; **f. à toutes les portes** *Fig* to try everywhere; **'entrez sans f.'** 'come in — no need to knock' **‖ se frapper** *vpr* (*s'inquiéter*) *Fam* to worry. ●**frappant, -ante** *a* striking. ●**frappé, -ée** *a* (*vin*) chilled; (*fou*) *Fam* crazy, nutty.

frasques [frask] *nfpl* pranks, escapades.

fraternel, -elle [fratɛrnɛl] *a* fraternal, brotherly. ●**fraterniser** *vi* to fraternize (**avec** with). ●**fraternité** *nf* fraternity, brotherhood.

fraude [frod] *nf* (*crime*) fraud; (*à un examen*) cheating; (*faire*) **passer qch en f.** to smuggle sth; **prendre qn en f.** to catch s.o. cheating; **f. fiscale** tax fraud *ou* evasion. ●**frauder** *vt* to defraud **‖** *vi* (*à un examen*)

to cheat (à in); **f. sur** (*poids etc*) to cheat on *ou* over. ●**fraudeur, -euse** *nmf* defrauder. ●**frauduleux, -euse** *a* fraudulent.

frayer [freje] *vt* (*voie etc*) to clear; **se f. un chemin** *ou* **un passage** to clear a way, force one's way (**à travers, dans** through).

frayeur [frejœr] *nf* fear, fright.

fredaines [frədɛn] *nfpl* pranks, escapades.

fredonner [frədɔne] *vt* to hum.

freezer [frizœr] *nm* (*de réfrigérateur*) freezer.

frégate [fregat] *nf* (*navire*) frigate.

frein [frɛ̃] *nm* brake; **donner un coup de f.** to brake hard; **mettre un f. à** *Fig* to put a curb on; **f. à main** handbrake. ●**freiner** *vi* (*dans un véhicule*) to brake **‖** *vt* (*gêner*) *Fig* to check, curb. ●**freinage** *nm* *Aut* braking.

frelaté, -ée [frəlate] *a* (*vin etc*) & *Fig* adulterated.

frêle [frɛl] *a* frail, fragile.

frelon [frəlɔ̃] *nm* (*guêpe*) hornet.

frémir [fremir] *vi* (*trembler*) to shake, shudder (**de** with); (*feuille*) to quiver; (*eau chaude*) to simmer. ●**frémissement** *nm* shaking; (*de feuille*) quivering; (*d'eau chaude*) simmering; (*frisson*) shudder; (*de plaisir*) thrill.

frêne [frɛn] *nm* (*arbre, bois*) ash.

frénésie [frenezi] *nf* frenzy. ●**frénétique** *a* frenzied, frantic.

fréquent, -ente [frekɑ̃, -ɑ̃t] *a* frequent. ●**fréquemment** [frekamɑ̃] *adv* frequently. ●**fréquence** *nf* frequency.

fréquenter [frekɑ̃te] *vt* (*lieu*) to visit, frequent; (*école, église*) to attend; **f. qn** to see *ou* visit s.o. **‖ se fréquenter** *vpr* (*fille et garçon*) to see each other, go out together; (*voisins*) to see each other socially. ●**fréquenté, -ée** *a* **très f.** (*lieu*) very busy; **mal f.** of ill repute; **bien f.** reputable, of good repute. ●**fréquentable** *a* **peu f.** (*personne, endroit*) not very commendable. ●**fréquentation** *nf* visiting; **fréquentations** (*personnes*) company; **avoir de mauvaises fréquentations** to keep bad company.

frère [frɛr] *nm* brother.

fresque [frɛsk] *nf* (*œuvre peinte*) fresco; **une f. historique** *Littér* the portrait of a period.

fret [frɛ] *nm* freight.

frétiller [fretije] *vi* (*poisson*) to wriggle; **f. d'impatience** to quiver with impatience; **f. de joie** to tingle with excitement.

fretin [frətɛ̃] *nm* **menu f.** (*poissons*) fry; (*personnes*) *Fig* small fry.

friable [frijabl] *a* crumbly.

friand, -ande [frijɑ̃, -ɑ̃d] *a* **f. de** fond of, partial to. ●**friandises** *nfpl* (*confiseries*) *Br* sweets, *Am* candies; (*pâtisseries*) *Br* titbits, *Am* tidbits.

fric [frik] *nm* (*argent*) *Fam* cash, dough.

fric-frac [frikfrak] *nm* (*cambriolage*) *Fam Vieilli* break-in.

friche (en) [ɑ̃friʃ] *adv* fallow; **laisser une terre en f.** to let a piece of land lie fallow.

friction [friksjɔ̃] *nf* **1** massage, rub(-down); (*de cheveux*) lotion. **2** (*désaccord*) friction.

● **frictionner** vt to rub (down).
frigidaire® [friʒidɛr] nm fridge. ● **frigo** nm
Fam fridge. ● **frigorifié, -ée** a (personne) Fam
very cold. ● **frigorifique** a (vitrine) refri-
gerated; **wagon f.** refrigerator Br van ou Am
car; **camion f.** refrigerator truck.
frigide [friʒid] a frigid. ● **frigidité** nf frigidity.
frileux, -euse [frilø, -øz] a être f. to feel the
cold, be a chilly person.
frime [frim] nf Fam sham, show. ● **frimer** vi
Fam (faire l'important) to show off; (bluffer)
to sham.
frimousse [frimus] nf Fam little face.
fringale [frɛ̃gal] nf Fam raging appetite.
fringant, -ante [frɛ̃gɑ̃, -ɑ̃t] a (allure etc)
dashing.
fringues [frɛ̃g] nfpl (vêtements) Fam togs,
clothes. ● **se fringuer** vpr Fam to get dressed
up.
friper [fripe] vt to crumple ∎ **se friper** vpr to
get crumpled. ● **fripé, -ée** a (visage)
crumpled, wrinkled.
fripier, -ière [fripje, -jɛr] nmf secondhand
clothes dealer.
fripon, -onne [fripɔ̃, -ɔn] nmf (escroc) Vieilli
rascal; (enfant) Fam rascal ∎ a mischievous,
rascally.
fripouille [fripuj] nf rogue, scoundrel.
friqué, -ée [frike] a (riche) Fam loaded.
frire* [frir] vti to fry; faire f. to fry.
frise [friz] nf Archit frieze.
friser [frize] 1 vti (cheveux) to curl, wave; f.
les cheveux à qn to curl ou wave s.o.'s hair.
2 vt (effleurer) to skim; (accident etc) to be
within an ace of; f. la trentaine to be close
to thirty; f. le ridicule to be almost ridiculous. ● **frisé, -ée** a curly. ● **frisette** nf ringlet,
little curl.
frisquet [friskɛ] am chilly, coldish.
frisson [frisɔ̃] nm shiver; (de peur) shudder;
avoir des frissons to be shivering; donner le
f. à qn to give s.o. the creeps ou shivers.
● **frissonner** vi (de froid) to shiver; (de peur
etc) to shudder (de with).
frit, frite [fri, -it] pp de frire ∎ a (poisson etc)
fried. ● **frites** nfpl Br chips, Am French fries.
● **friteuse** nf (deep) fryer, Br chip pan.
● **friture** nf (matière) (frying) oil ou fat; (aliment) fried fish; (bruit) Radio Tél crackling.
frivole [frivɔl] a frivolous. ● **frivolité** nf frivolity.
froc [frɔk] nm Fam (pair of) Br trousers ou
Am pants.
froid, froide [frwa, frwad] a cold; garder la
tête froide to keep a cool head ∎ nm cold;
avoir/prendre f. to be/catch cold; avoir f.
aux mains/etc to have cold hands/etc; il fait
f. it's cold; coup de f. (rhume) chill; jeter un
f. to cast a chill (dans over); démarrer à f.
(véhicule) to start (from) cold; être en f. to
be on bad terms (avec qn with s.o.); n'avoir
pas f. aux yeux to have plenty of nerve.
● **froidement** adv coldly. ● **froideur** nf (insensibilité) coldness.
froisser [frwase] 1 vt, **se froisser** vpr (tissu

etc) to crumple, rumple; **se f. un muscle** to
strain a muscle. 2 vt f. qn to offend s.o.; **se
f.** to take Br offence ou Am offense (de at).
frôler [frole] vt (toucher) to brush against,
touch lightly; (raser) to skim; (la mort etc) to
come within an ace of.
fromage [frɔmaʒ] nm cheese; **f. blanc** soft
white cheese; **f. frais** fromage frais; **f. de
chèvre** goat cheese, goat's milk cheese. ● **fro-
mager, -ère** a industrie/etc fromagère cheese
industry/etc ∎ nm (fabricant) cheesemaker.
● **fromagerie** (magasin) nf cheese shop.
froment [frɔmɑ̃] nm wheat.
fronce [frɔ̃s] nf (pli dans un tissu) gather,
fold. ● **froncer** vt 1 (étoffe) to gather. 2 f. les
sourcils to frown. ● **froncement** nm f. de
sourcils frown.
fronde [frɔ̃d] nf 1 (arme) sling. 2 (sédition)
revolt.
front [frɔ̃] nm forehead, brow; Mil Pol front;
f. de mer sea front; de f. (heurter) head-on;
(côte à côte) abreast; (à la fois) (all) at once;
faire f. à to face.
frontière [frɔ̃tjɛr] nf border, frontier ∎ a inv
ville/etc f. border town/etc. ● **frontalier, -ière**
a ville/etc **frontalière** border ou frontier
town/etc.
fronton [frɔ̃tɔ̃] nm Archit pediment.
frotter [frɔte] vt to rub; (pour nettoyer) to
scrub, rub; (plancher) to scrub; (allumette)
to strike; **se f. le dos** to scrub one's back; **se
f. à qn** (défier) to meddle with s.o., provoke
s.o. ∎ vi to rub; (nettoyer, laver) to scrub.
● **frottement** nm rubbing; Tech friction.
froufrous [frufru] nmpl (bruit) rustling; **froufrous** (dentelles, volants etc) frills.
frousse [frus] nf Fam funk, fear; avoir la f.
to be scared. ● **froussard, -arde** nmf Fam
coward.
fructifier [fryktifje] vi (arbre, capital) to bear
fruit; faire f. son capital to make one's capital grow. ● **fructueux, -euse** a (profitable)
fruitful.
frugal, -e, -aux [frygal, -o] a frugal. ● **fruga-
lité** nf frugality.
fruit [frɥi] nm fruit; des fruits, les fruits fruit;
fruits de mer seafood; fruits secs dried fruit;
porter ses fruits (placement etc) to bear fruit.
● **fruité, -ée** a fruity. ● **fruitier, -ière** a arbre f.
fruit tree ∎ nmf Br fruiterer, fruit seller.
frusques [frysk] nfpl (vêtements) Fam togs,
clothes.
fruste [fryst] a (personne) rough.
frustrer [frystre] vt f. qn to frustrate s.o.; f.
qn de qch to deprive s.o. of sth. ● **frustré,
-ée** a frustrated. ● **frustration** nf frustration.
fuel [fjul] nm (fuel) oil, heating oil.
fugace [fygas] a fleeting.
fugitif, -ive [fyʒitif, -iv] 1 nmf runaway, fugitive. 2 a (passager) fleeting.
fugue [fyg] nf 1 (œuvre musicale) fugue. 2
(escapade) flight; faire une f. to run away.
● **fuguer** Fam to run away.
fuir* [fɥir] vi to run away, flee; (gaz, robinet,
stylo etc) to leak; (temps) Litt to fly ∎ vt (évi-

ter) to shun, avoid. ● **fuite** *nf* (*évasion*) flight (de from); (*de gaz etc*) leak(age); (*de documents*) *Fig* leak; **en f.** on the run; **prendre la f.** to take flight, run away *ou* off; **f. des cerveaux** brain drain; **délit de f.** *Aut* hit-and-run *Br* offence *ou* *Am* offense.

fulgurant, -ante [fylgyrã, -ãt] *a* **progrès fulgurants** spectacular progress; **vitesse fulgurante** lightning speed; **douleur fulgurante** searing pain.

fulminer [fylmine] *vi* (*personne*) to thunder forth (**contre** against).

fumée [fyme] *nf* smoke; (*vapeur*) steam, fumes; **fumées** (*de vin*) fumes.

fumer [fyme] *vi* to smoke; (*liquide brûlant*) to steam ▮ *vt* to smoke. ● **fumé, -ée** *a* (*poisson, verre etc*) smoked. ● **fumeur, -euse** *nmf* smoker; **compartiment fumeurs** (*de train*) smoking compartment. ● **fume-cigarette** *nm* cigarette holder.

fumet [fyme] *nm* aroma, smell.

fumeux, -euse [fymø, -øz] *a* (*idée etc*) *Fig* hazy, woolly.

fumier [fymje] *nm* manure, dung; (*tas*) dung-hill.

fumigation [fymigɑsjɔ̃] *nf* fumigation.

fumigène [fymiʒɛn] *a* **bombe**/*etc* **f.** smoke bomb/*etc*.

fumiste [fymist] *nmf* (*étudiant etc*) *Fam* time-waster, good-for-nothing. ● **fumisterie** *nf Fam* farce, con.

funambule [fynãbyl] *nmf* tightrope walker.

funèbre [fynɛbr] *a* (*lugubre*) gloomy; **service/marche f.** funeral service/march. ● **funérailles** *nfpl* funeral. ● **funéraire** *a* **salon f.** funeral parlour *ou* *Am* home; **frais**/*etc* **funéraires** funeral expenses/*etc*.

funeste [fynɛst] *a* (*désastreux*) catastrophic.

funiculaire [fynikylɛr] *nm* funicular.

fur et à mesure (au) [ofyreamzyr] *adv* as one goes along, progressively; **au f. et à m. de vos besoins/votre progression** as your needs dictate/your progress dictates; **au f. et à m. que** as.

furent [fyr] *voir* être.

furet [fyrɛ] *nm* (*animal*) ferret.

fureter [fyr(ə)te] *vi Péj* to pry *ou* ferret about. ● **fureteur, -euse** *a* inquisitive, prying ▮ *nmf* inquisitive person.

fureur [fyrœr] *nf* (*violence*) fury; (*colère*) rage, fury; (*passion*) passion (**de** for); **en f.**

furious; **faire f.** (*mode etc*) *Fam* to be all the rage. ● **furibond, -onde** *a* furious. ● **furie** *nf* (*colère, mégère*) fury. ● **furieux, -euse** *a* (*violent, en colère*) furious (**contre** with, at); (*vent*) raging; (*coup*) *Fig* tremendous; **avoir une furieuse envie de faire qch** to have a tremendous urge to do sth.

furoncle [fyrɔ̃kl] *nm* (*sur la peau*) boil.

furtif, -ive [fyrtif, -iv] *a* furtive, stealthy.

fusain [fyzɛ̃] *nm* **1** (*crayon, dessin*) charcoal; **dessin au f.** charcoal drawing. **2** (*arbrisseau*) spindle tree.

fuseau, -x [fyzo] *nm* **1** (*pantalon*) ski pants. **2 f. horaire** time zone. **3** *Tex* spindle; **en f.** (*jambes*) spindly. ● **fuselé, -ée** *a* slender.

fusée [fyze] *nf* rocket; (*d'obus*) fuse; **f. éclairante** flare; **f. de détresse** flare, distress signal.

fuselage [fyzlaʒ] *nm* (*d'avion*) fuselage.

fuser [fyze] *vi* (*rires etc*) to burst forth.

fusible [fyzibl] *nm* *Él* fuse.

fusil [fyzi] *nm* rifle, gun; (*de chasse*) shotgun; **coup de f.** gunshot, report; **un bon f.** (*personne*) a good shot. ● **fusillade** *nf* (*tirs*) gunfire; (*exécution*) shooting. ● **fusiller** *vt* (*exécuter*) to shoot; **f. qn du regard** *Fam* to glare at s.o., give s.o. a glaring look.

fusion [fyzjɔ̃] *nf* **1** melting; *Phys Biol* fusion; **point de f.** melting point; **métal en f.** molten metal. **2** (*de sociétés*) *Com* merger; (*union*) fusion. ● **fusionner** *vti* (*sociétés*) *Com* to merge.

fustiger [fystiʒe] *vt* (*critiquer*) *Litt* to castigate.

fut [fy] *voir* être.

fût [fy] *nm* **1** (*tonneau*) barrel, cask. **2** (*d'arbre*) trunk. ● **futaie** *nf* timber forest.

futal, *pl* **-als** [fytal] *nm Fam* (pair of) *Br* trousers *ou* *Am* pants.

futé, -ée [fyte] *a* cunning, smart.

futile [fytil] *a* (*propos, prétexte etc*) frivolous, futile; (*personne*) frivolous; (*tentative, action*) futile. ● **futilité** *nf* futility; **futilités** (*bagatelles*) trifles.

futur, -ure [fytyr] *a* future; **future mère** mother-to-be ▮ *nmf* **f.** (*mari*) husband-to-be; **future** (*épouse*) wife-to-be ▮ *nm* future; *Grammaire* future (tense).

fuyant [fɥijã] *p prés de* fuir. ● **fuyant, -ante** *a* (*front, ligne*) receding; (*personne*) evasive. ● **fuyard** *nm* (*soldat*) runaway, deserter.

G

G, g [ʒe] *nm* G, g.
gabardine [gabardin] *nf* (*tissu, imperméable*) gabardine.
gabarit [gabari] *nm* size, dimension.
gâcher [gɑʃe] *vt* **1** (*gâter*) to spoil; (*occasion, argent*) to waste; (*vie, travail*) to mess up. **2** (*plâtre*) to mix. ●**gâchis** *nm* (*gaspillage*) waste; (*désordre*) mess.
gâchette [gɑʃɛt] *nf* (*d'arme à feu*) trigger; **appuyer sur la g.** to pull the trigger.
gadget [gadʒɛt] *nm* gadget.
gadoue [gadu] *nf* (*boue*) dirt, sludge; (*neige*) slush.
gaffe [gaf] *nf* **1** (*bévue*) *Fam* blunder, *Am* booboo, *Br* gaffe. **2 faire g.** to take care, be careful. ●**gaffer** *vi Fam* to blunder, *Am* make a booboo. ●**gaffeur, -euse** *nmf Fam* blunderer.
gag [gag] *nm* (*effet comique*) *Cinéma Théâtre etc* (sight) gag.
gaga [gaga] *a Fam* senile, gaga.
gage [gaʒ] *nm* **1** (*garantie*) security; (*promesse*) pledge; (*témoignage*) proof; **mettre qch en g.** to pawn sth; **donner qch en g. de fidélité/etc** to give sth as a token of one's fidelity/etc. **2** (*au jeu*) forfeit. ●**gages** *nmpl* (*salaire*) pay; **tueur à gages** hired killer, hitman.
gager [gaʒe] *vt* **g. que** *Litt* to wager that. ●**gageure** [gaʒyr] *nf Litt* (impossible) wager.
gagnant, -ante [gaɲɑ̃, -ɑ̃t] *a* (*billet, cheval*) winning ▮ *nmf* winner.
gagner [gaɲe] **1** *vt* (*par le travail*) to earn; (*mériter*) *Fig* to earn; **g. sa vie** to earn one's living; **g. des mille et des cents** to earn a bundle *ou Br* a packet.
2 *vt* (*par le jeu*) to win; (*réputation, estime etc*) *Fig* to win, gain; **g. qn** to win s.o. over (à to); **g. une heure/etc** (*économiser*) to save an hour/etc; **g. du temps** (*temporiser*) to gain time; **g. du terrain/du poids** to gain ground/ weight; **g. de la place** to save space ▮ *vi* (*être vainqueur*) to win; **g. à être connu** to be well worth getting to know; **g. sur tous les tableaux** to win on all counts, win all along the line.
3 *vt* (*atteindre*) to reach; **g. qn** (*sommeil, faim etc*) to overcome s.o. ▮ *vi* (*incendie etc*) to spread, gain. ●**gagne-pain** *nm inv* (*emploi*) job, livelihood.
gai, gaie [ge] *a* (*personne, air etc*) cheerful, happy, jolly; (*ivre*) merry, tipsy; (*couleur, pièce*) bright, cheerful. ●**gaiement** *adv* cheerfully. ●**gaieté** *nf* (*de personne etc*) cheerfulness, gaiety, jollity.
gaillard, -arde [gajar, -ard] *a* vigorous; (*gri-*

vois) coarse ▮ *nm* (*robuste*) strapping fellow; (*type*) *Fam* fellow.
gain [gɛ̃] *nm* (*profit*) gain, profit; (*avantage*) *Fig* advantage; **gains** (*salaire*) earnings; (*au jeu*) winnings; **un g. de temps** a saving of time; **obtenir g. de cause** to win one's case.
gaine [gɛn] *nf* **1** (*sous-vêtement*) girdle. **2** (*étui*) sheath.
gala [gala] *nm* gala, official reception.
galant, -ante [galɑ̃, -ɑ̃t] *a* (*homme*) gallant; (*ton, propos*) *Hum* amorous ▮ *nm* suitor. ●**galanterie** *nf* (*courtoisie*) gallantry.
galaxie [galaksi] *nf* galaxy.
galbe [galb] *nm* curve, contour. ●**galbé, -ée** *a* (*jambes*) shapely.
gale [gal] *nf* **la g.** (*maladie*) the itch, scabies; (*d'un chien*) mange; **une (mauvaise) g.** (*personne*) *Fam* a pest.
galère [galɛr] *nf* (*navire*) *Hist* galley. ●**galérien** *nm Hist & Fig* galley slave. ●**galérer** *vi Fam* to struggle hard, have a hard time.
galerie [galri] *nf* **1** (*passage, salle, magasin etc*) gallery; *Théâtre* balcony; **g. (d'art)** (art) gallery; **g. marchande** (shopping) mall; **amuser la g.** *Fig* to amuse people *ou* the audience. **2** (*porte-bagages*) *Aut* roof rack.
galet [galɛ] *nm* pebble, stone; **galets** shingle, pebbles.
galette [galɛt] *nf* **1** (*gâteau*) round, flat, flaky cake; (*crêpe*) pancake. **2** (*argent*) *Fam* dough, money.
galeux, -euse [galø, -øz] *a* (*chien*) mangy.
galimatias [galimatja] *nm* gibberish.
galipette [galipet] *nf Fam* (*roulade*) somersault.
Galles [gal] *nfpl* **pays de G.** Wales. ●**gallois, -oise** *a* Welsh ▮ *nm* (*langue*) Welsh ▮ *nmf* **G.** Welshman; **Galloise** Welshwoman.
gallicisme [galisism] *nm* (*mot etc*) gallicism.
galon [galɔ̃] *nm* (*ruban*) braid; (*de soldat*) stripe; **prendre du g.** *Mil & Fig* to get promoted.
galop [galo] *nm* gallop; **aller au g.** to gallop; **g. d'essai** *Fig* trial run. ●**galopade** *nf* (*ruée*) stampede. ●**galoper** *vi* (*cheval*) to gallop; (*personne*) to rush; **inflation galopante** galloping inflation.
galopin [galɔpɛ̃] *nm* urchin, rascal.
galvaniser [galvanize] *vt* (*métal*) & *Fig* to galvanize.
galvauder [galvode] *vt* (*talent, avantage etc*) to debase, misuse.
gambade [gɑ̃bad] *nf* leap, caper. ●**gambader** *vi* to leap *ou* frisk about.
gambas [gɑ̃bas] *nfpl* scampi.
Gambie [gɑ̃bi] *nf* **la G.** The Gambia.

gamelle [gamɛl] *nf Fam* pan; *(de chien)* bowl; *(d'ouvrier)* lunch tin *ou* box; **se prendre une g.** *(tomber, subir un échec) Br* to come a cropper, *Am* take a spill.

gamin, -ine [gamɛ̃, -in] *nmf (enfant) Fam* kid **‖** a playful, naughty. ● **gaminerie** *nf* playfulness; *(acte)* naughty prank.

gamme [gam] *nf Mus* scale; *(éventail)* range; **téléviseur/etc haut/bas de g.** top-of-the-range/bottom-of-the-range television/*etc.*

gammée [game] *af* **croix g.** swastika.

gang [gɑ̃g] *nm (de malfaiteurs)* gang. ● **gangster** *nm* gangster.

Gange [gɑ̃ʒ] *nm* **le G.** the Ganges.

gangrène [gɑ̃grɛn] *nf* gangrene. ● **se gangrener** [səgɑ̃grəne] *vpr (jambe etc)* to become gangrenous.

gant [gɑ̃] *nm* glove; **g. de boxe** boxing glove; **g. de toilette** face cloth, cloth glove *(for washing);* **boîte à gants** glove compartment; **aller comme un g. à qn** *(vêtement etc)* to fit s.o. like a glove; **jeter/relever le g.** *Fig* to throw down/take up the gauntlet. ● **ganté, -ée** *a (main)* gloved; *(personne)* wearing gloves.

garage [garaʒ] *nm (pour véhicules)* garage; **voie de g.** *(pour trains)* siding; *Fig* dead end. ● **garagiste** *nmf* garage mechanic; *(propriétaire)* garage owner.

garant, -ante [garɑ̃, -ɑ̃t] *nmf (personne) Jur* guarantor; **se porter g. de** to guarantee, vouch for **‖** *nm (garantie)* guarantee.

garantie [garɑ̃ti] *nf* guarantee; *(caution)* security; *(protection) Fig* safeguard; **garantie(s)** *(de police d'assurance)* cover. ● **garantir** *vt* to guarantee *(contre* against); **g. à qn que** to assure *ou* guarantee s.o. that; **g. qch de** *(protéger)* to protect sth from.

garce [gars] *nf Péj Fam* bitch.

garçon [garsɔ̃] *nm* boy, lad; *(jeune homme)* young man; *(célibataire)* bachelor; **g. (de café)** waiter; **g. d'honneur** *(d'un mariage)* best man; **g. manqué** tomboy; **vieux g.** (old) bachelor; *(comportement)* boyish. ● **garçonnet** *nm* little boy. ● **garçonnière** *nf* bachelor *Br* flat *ou Am* apartment.

garde [gard] **1** *nm (gardien)* guard; *(soldat)* guardsman; **g. champêtre** rural policeman; **g. du corps** bodyguard; **G. des Sceaux** Justice Minister.

2 *nf (d'enfants, de bagages etc)* care, custody *(de* of); **avoir la g. de** to be in charge of; **faire bonne g.** to keep a close watch; **prendre g.** to pay attention *(à qch* to sth), be careful *(à qch* of sth); **prendre g. de ne pas faire** to be careful not to do; **mettre qn en g.** to warn s.o. *(contre* against); **mise en g.** warning; **être de g.** to be on duty; *(soldat)* to be on guard duty; **monter la g.** to stand *ou* mount guard; **être sur ses gardes** to be on one's guard; **chien de g.** watchdog; **g. à vue** *(police)* custody.

3 *nf (escorte, soldats)* guard.

garde-à-vous [gardavu] *nm inv Mil* (position of) attention; **se mettre au g.-à-vous** to stand at *ou* to attention. ● **garde-boue** *nm inv Br* mudguard, *Am* fender. ● **garde-chasse** *nm (pl* gardes-chasses*)* gamekeeper. ● **garde-chiourme** *nm (surveillant sévère)* martinet. ● **garde-côte** *nm (personne)* coastguard. ● **garde-fou** *nm* railing(s), parapet. ● **garde-malade** *nmf (pl* gardes-malades*)* nurse. ● **garde-manger** *nm inv (armoire)* food safe; *(pièce)* pantry, *Br* larder. ● **garde-robe** *nf (habits, armoire)* wardrobe.

garder [garde] *vt (maintenir, conserver, mettre de côté)* to keep; *(vêtement)* to keep on; *(surveiller)* to watch (over); *(défendre)* to guard; *(enfant)* to look after, watch; *(habitude)* to keep up; **g. qn** *(retenir)* to keep s.o.; **g. la chambre** to stay in one's (bed)room, keep to one's room; **g. le lit** to stay in bed.

‖ se garder *vpr (aliment)* to keep; **se g. de qch** *(éviter)* to beware of sth; **se g. de faire qch** to take care not to do sth.

garderie [gardəri] *nf Br* crèche, *Br* (day) nursery, *Am* daycare center.

gardien, -ienne [gardjɛ̃, -jɛn] *nmf (d'immeuble, d'hôtel etc)* caretaker, *Am* janitor; *(de prison)* (prison) guard, *Br* warder; *(de zoo, parc)* keeper; *(de musée) Br* attendant, *Am* guard; **g. de but** *Football* goalkeeper; **gardienne d'enfants** *Br* child minder, *Am* baby-sitter; **g. de nuit** night watchman; **g. de la paix** policeman; **g. de** *(libertés etc) Fig* guardian of **‖** *am* **ange g.** guardian angel.

gardon [gardɔ̃] *nm (poisson)* roach; **frais comme un g.** in the pink, fresh as a daisy, full of beans.

gare [gar] **1** *nf (pour trains)* station; **g. routière** bus *ou Br* coach station. **2** *int* **g. à** watch *ou* look out for; **g. à toi!** watch *ou* look out!; **sans crier g.** without warning.

garer [gare] *vt (voiture etc)* to park; *(au garage)* to garage **‖ se garer** *vpr (automobiliste)* to park; **se g. de qch** *(se protéger)* to get out of the way of sth, steer clear of sth.

gargariser (se) [səgargarize] *vpr* to gargle. ● **gargarisme** *nm* gargle.

gargote [gargɔt] *nf Péj* cheap eating house.

gargouille [garguj] *nf Archit* gargoyle.

gargouiller [garguje] *vi (fontaine, eau)* to gurgle; *(ventre)* to rumble. ● **gargouillis** *ou* **gargouillement** *nm* gurgling; *(de ventre)* rumbling.

garnement [garnəmɑ̃] *nm* rascal, urchin.

garnir [garnir] *vt (équiper)* to fit out, furnish *(de* with); *(remplir)* to fill; *(magasin)* to stock *(de* with); *(tissu)* to line; *(orner)* to decorate, adorn *(de* with); *(enjoliver)* to trim *(robe etc)* *(de* with); *(couvrir)* to cover; *Culin* to garnish **‖ se garnir** *vpr (lieu)* to fill (up) *(de* with). ● **garni, -ie** *a (plat)* served with vegetables; **bien g.** *(portefeuille etc) Fig* well-lined. ● **garniture** *nf Culin* garnish, trimmings; *(de véhicule)* fittings, upholstery; **g. de frein** brake lining; **g. de lit** bed linen.

garnison [garnizɔ̃] *nf (troupes)* garrison.

garrot [garo] *nm* **1** *(de cheval)* withers. **2**

(*lien*) *Méd* tourniquet.

gars [gɑ] *nm Fam* fellow, guy.

gas-oil [gozwal] *nm* diesel (oil).

gaspiller [gaspije] *vt* to waste. ● **gaspillage** *nm* waste.

gastrique [gastrik] *a* gastric.

gastronome [gastrɔnɔm] *nmf* gourmet. ● **gastronomie** *nf* gastronomy.

gâteau, -x [gɑto] *nm* cake; **g. de riz** rice pudding; **g. sec** *Br* (sweet) biscuit, *Am* cookie; **c'était du g.** (*facile*) *Fam* it was a piece of cake.

gâter [gɑte] *vt* to spoil; (*plaisir, vue*) to mar, spoil ▮ **se gâter** *vpr* (*aliment, dent*) to go bad; (*temps, situation*) to get worse; (*relations*) to turn sour. ● **gâté, -ée** *a* (*dent, fruit etc*) bad. ● **gâteries** *nfpl* (*sucreries*) treats.

gâteux, -euse [gɑtø, -øz] *a* senile, soft in the head.

gauche¹ [goʃ] *a* (*côté, main etc*) left ▮ *nf* **la g.** (*côté*) the left (side); *Pol* the left (wing); **à g.** (*tourner etc*) (to the) left; (*marcher, se tenir*) on the left, on the left(-hand) side; **de g.** (*fenêtre etc*) left-hand; (*parti, politique etc*) left-wing; **à g. de** on *ou* to the left of. ● **gaucher, -ère** *a* & *nmf* left-handed (person). ● **gauchisant, -ante** *a Pol* leftish. ● **gauchiste** *a* & *nmf Pol* (extreme) leftist.

gauche² [goʃ] *a* (*maladroit*) awkward. ● **gauchement** *adv* awkwardly. ● **gaucherie** *nf* awkwardness; (*acte*) blunder.

gauchir [goʃir] *vti* to warp.

gaufre [gofr] *nf* (*pâtisserie*) waffle. ● **gaufrette** *nf* wafer (biscuit).

gaule [gol] *nf* long pole; *Pêche* fishing rod.

Gaule [gol] *nf* (*pays*) *Hist* Gaul. ● **gaulois, -oise** *a* Gallic; (*propos etc*) *Fig* earthy, bawdy, broad ▮ *nmpl* **les G.** *Hist* the Gauls. ● **gauloiserie** *nf* bawdy *ou* broad joke.

gausser (se) [sɔgose] *vpr Litt* to poke fun (de at).

gaver [gave] *vt* (*animal*) to force-feed; (*personne*) *Fig* to cram (de with) ▮ **se gaver** *vpr* to gorge *ou* stuff oneself (de with).

gaz [gɑz] *nm inv* gas; **usine à g.** gasworks; **réchaud/masque/etc à g.** gas stove/mask *etc*; **chambre à g.** gas chamber; **g. carbonique** carbon dioxide; **g. d'échappement** (*de véhicule*) exhaust fumes; **avoir des g.** to have wind *ou* flatulence; **il y a de l'eau dans le g.** we're running into difficulties, things aren't going smoothly.

Gaza [gaza] *nf* Gaza; **la bande de G.** the Gaza Strip.

gaze [gɑz] *nf* (*tissu*) gauze.

gazelle [gazɛl] *nf* (*animal*) gazelle.

gazer [gaze] **1** *vi* (*aller vite*) *Fam* to whizz along; **ça gaze!** everything's just fine! **2** *vt Mil* to gas.

gazette [gazɛt] *nf* (*journal*) *Vieilli* newspaper.

gazeux, -euse [gazø, -øz] *a* (*état*) gaseous; (*boisson, eau*) *Br* fizzy, carbonated. ● **gazomètre** *nm Br* gasometer, gas storage tank.

gazinière [gazinjɛr] *nf Br* gas cooker, *Am*

gas stove.

gazole [gɑzɔl] *nm voir* **gas-oil**.

gazon [gɑzɔ̃] *nm* grass, lawn.

gazouiller [gazuje] *vi* (*oiseau*) to chirp; (*bébé, ruisseau*) to babble. ● **gazouillis** *ou* **gazouillement** *nm* chirping; (*de bébé etc*) babbling.

GDF [ʒedeɛf] *nm abrév* (*Gaz de France*) (French) Gas Company.

geai [ʒɛ] *nm* (*oiseau*) jay.

géant, -ante [ʒeɑ̃, -ɑ̃t] *nmf* giant ▮ *a* giant; **c'est g.!** *Fam* it's terrific *ou* brilliant!

Geiger [ʒeʒɛr] *nm* **compteur G.** Geiger counter.

geindre* [ʒɛ̃dr] *vi* to whine, whimper.

gel [ʒɛl] *nm* **1** (*temps, glace*) frost; (*de crédits*) *Écon* freezing. **2** (*pour cheveux etc*) gel. ● **geler** *vti* to freeze; **on gèle ici** it's freezing here ▮ *v imp* **il gèle** it's freezing. ● **gelé, -ée** *a* frozen; (*doigts, mains, pieds*) *Méd* frostbitten. ● **gelée** *nf* **1** frost; **g. blanche** ground frost. **2** (*de fruits, de viande*) jelly; **œufs en g.** jellied eggs.

gélatine [ʒelatin] *nf* gelatin(e).

gélule [ʒelyl] *nf* (*médicament*) capsule.

Gémeaux [ʒemo] *nmpl* **les G.** (*signe*) Gemini.

gémir [ʒemir] *vi* to groan, moan. ● **gémissement** *nm* groan, moan.

gencive [ʒɑ̃siv] *nf* (*de la bouche*) gum.

gendarme [ʒɑ̃darm] *nm* gendarme, policeman (*soldier performing police duties*). ● **gendarmerie** *nf* police force; (*local*) police headquarters.

gendre [ʒɑ̃dr] *nm* son-in-law.

gène [ʒɛn] *nm* (*élément du chromosome*) gene.

gêne [ʒɛn] *nf* (*trouble physique*) discomfort; (*confusion*) embarrassment; (*dérangement*) bother, trouble; **dans la g.** (*à court d'argent*) in financial difficulties.

généalogie [ʒenealɔʒi] *nf* genealogy. ● **généalogique** *a* genealogical; **arbre g.** family tree.

gêner [ʒene] *vt* (*déranger, irriter*) to bother, annoy; (*troubler*) to embarrass; (*mouvement, action*) to hamper, hinder; (*circulation*) *Aut* to hold up, block; **g. qn** (*vêtement*) to be uncomfortable on s.o.; (*par sa présence*) to be in s.o.'s way; **ça ne me gêne pas** I don't mind (**si** if).

▮ **se gêner** *vpr* (*se déranger*) to put oneself out; **ne te gêne pas pour moi!** don't mind me! ● **gênant, -ante** *a* (*objet*) cumbersome; (*présence, situation*) awkward; (*bruit, personne*) annoying. ● **gêné, -ée** *a* (*intimidé*) embarrassed; (*mal à l'aise*) awkward, uneasy; (*silence, sourire*) awkward; (*sans argent*) short of money.

général, -e, -aux [ʒeneral, -o] **1** *a* (*global, commun*) general; **en g.** in general. **2** *nm* (*officier dans l'armée*) general; **oui, mon g.!** yes, general! ● **générale** *nf Théâtre* dress rehearsal. ● **généralement** *adv* generally; **g. parlant** broadly *ou* generally speaking.

●**généralité** nf generality.
généralisation [ʒeneralizasjɔ̃] nf generalization. ●**généraliser** vti to generalize ▮ **se généraliser** vpr to become general ou widespread.
généraliste [ʒeneralist] nm (médecin) general practitioner, GP.
générateur [ʒeneratœr] nm ou **génératrice** nf Él generator.
génération [ʒenerasjɔ̃] nf generation.
générer [ʒenere] vt to generate.
généreux, -euse [ʒenerø, -øz] a generous (de with). ●**généreusement** adv generously. ●**générosité** nf generosity.
générique [ʒenerik] nm (de film) credits ▮ a produit g. generic ou unbranded product.
genèse [ʒənɛz] nf genesis.
genêt [ʒənɛ] nm (plante) broom.
génétique [ʒenetik] nf genetics ▮ a (code, empreinte etc) genetic; **manipulation g.** genetic engineering ou manipulation.
Genève [ʒənɛv] nm ou f Geneva.
génial, -e, -aux [ʒenjal, -o] a (personne, invention) brilliant; (formidable) Fam fantastic.
génie [ʒeni] nm 1 (aptitude, personne) genius; inventeur/etc **de g.** inventor/etc of genius; **avoir le g. pour faire/de qch** to have a genius for doing/for sth. 2 g. civil civil engineering; g. génétique/informatique genetic/computer engineering; g. militaire engineering corps. 3 (esprit) genie, spirit; **bon/mauvais g.** good/evil genie.
génisse [ʒenis] nf (vache) heifer.
génital, -e, -aux [ʒenital, -o] a genital; organes génitaux genitals.
génocide [ʒenɔsid] nm genocide.
genou, -x [ʒ(ə)nu] nm knee; **être à genoux** to be kneeling (down); **se mettre à genoux** to kneel (down); **prendre qn sur ses genoux** to take s.o. on one's lap ou knee; **écrire sur ses genoux** to write on one's lap. ●**genouillère** nf Football etc knee pad.
genre [ʒɑ̃r] nm 1 (espèce) kind, sort; (attitude) manner, way; g. **humain** mankind; g. **de vie** way of life; **ce n'est pas son g.** that's not like him. 2 Littér Cinéma genre; Grammaire gender; Biol genus.
gens [ʒɑ̃] nmpl ou nfpl people; **jeunes g.** young people; (hommes) young men; **de petites g.** people of humble means; g. **de maison** (domestiques) domestic servants.
gentil, -ille [ʒɑ̃ti, -ij] a (agréable) nice, pleasant; (aimable) kind, nice; (mignon) pretty; g. **avec qn** nice ou kind to s.o.; **sois g.** (sage) be good. ●**gentillesse** nf kindness; **avoir la g. de faire qch** to be kind enough to do sth. ●**gentiment** adv (aimablement) kindly; (sagement) nicely.
gentilhomme, pl **gentilshommes** [ʒɑ̃tijɔm, ʒɑ̃tizɔm] nm (noble) Hist gentleman.
géographie [ʒeɔgrafi] nf geography. ●**géographique** a geographical.
geôlier, -ière [ʒolje, -jɛr] nmf jailer, Br gaoler.

géologie [ʒeɔlɔʒi] nf geology. ●**géologique** a geological. ●**géologue** nmf geologist.
géomètre [ʒeɔmɛtr] nm surveyor.
géométrie [ʒeɔmetri] nf geometry; à g. **variable** Fig ever-changing, volatile. ●**géométrique** a geometric(al).
géostationnaire [ʒeostasjɔnɛr] a (satellite) geostationary.
géranium [ʒeranjɔm] nm (plante) geranium.
gérant, -ante [ʒerɑ̃, -ɑ̃t] nmf manager, manageress; g. **d'immeubles** landlord's agent. ●**gérance** nf (gestion) management.
gerbe [ʒɛrb] nf (de blé) sheaf; (de fleurs) bunch; (d'eau) spray; (d'étincelles) shower.
gercer [ʒɛrse] vi, **se gercer** vpr (peau, lèvres) to become chapped; **avoir les lèvres gercées** to have chapped lips. ●**gerçure** nf chap, crack; **avoir des gerçures aux mains** to have chapped hands.
gérer [ʒere] vt (commerce, budget etc) to manage.
germain, -aine [ʒɛrmɛ̃, -ɛn] a cousin g. first cousin.
germanique [ʒɛrmanik] a Germanic.
germe [ʒɛrm] nm (microbe) germ; (de plante) shoot; (d'une idée) Fig seed, germ. ●**germer** vi (graine) to start to grow; (pomme de terre) to sprout; (idée) Fig to germinate.
gérondif [ʒerɔ̃dif] nm Grammaire gerund.
gésir [ʒezir] vi (être étendu) Litt to be lying; **il gît/gisait** he is/was lying; **ci-gît** here lies.
gestation [ʒɛstasjɔ̃] nf gestation.
geste [ʒɛst] nm gesture; **ne pas faire un g.** (ne pas bouger) not to make a move; **faire un g. de la main** to wave one's hand; **faire un g.** (intervenir) to do something positive, make a (positive) gesture; **faire un beau g.** to make a noble gesture. ●**gesticuler** vi to gesticulate.
gestion [ʒɛstjɔ̃] nf (action) management; g. **du personnel/de patrimoine** personnel/property management. ●**gestionnaire** nmf administrator.
geyser [ʒɛzɛr] nm Géol geyser.
Ghana [gana] nm Ghana.
ghetto [gɛto] nm ghetto.
gibecière [ʒib(ə)sjɛr] nf shoulder bag.
gibier [ʒibje] nm (animaux etc) game; **le gros g.** big game.
giboulée [ʒibule] nf shower, downpour; **giboulées de mars** = April showers.
gicler [ʒikle] vi (liquide) to spurt, squirt, (boue) to splash; **faire g.** to spurt, squirt. ●**giclée** nf jet, spurt. ●**gicleur** nm (de carburateur) Aut jet.
gifle [ʒifl] nf slap (in the face). ●**gifler** vt g. **qn** to slap s.o., slap s.o.'s face.
gigantesque [ʒigɑ̃tɛsk] a gigantic.
gigogne [ʒigɔɲ] a **table g.** nest of tables.
gigot [ʒigo] nm leg of mutton ou lamb.
gigoter [ʒigɔte] vi Fam to wriggle, fidget.
gilet [ʒile] nm (cardigan); (de costume) Br waistcoat, Am vest; g. **de sauvetage** life jacket; g. **pare-balles** bulletproof Br

jacket *ou Am* vest.

gin [dʒin] *nm* (*eau-de-vie*) gin.

gingembre [ʒɛ̃ʒɑ̃br] *nm* (*plante, condiment*) ginger.

girafe [ʒiraf] *nf* giraffe.

giratoire [ʒiratwar] *a* sens g. *Aut Br* roundabout, *Am* traffic circle.

girl [gœrl] *nf* (*danseuse*) chorus girl.

girofle [ʒirɔfl] *nm* clou de g. *Bot* clove.

giroflée [ʒirɔfle] *nf* wallflower.

girouette [ʒirwɛt] *nf Br* weathercock, *Am* weathervane; (*personne*) *Fig* weathercock.

gisement [ʒizmɑ̃] *nm* (*de minerai, pétrole*) deposit.

gitan, -ane [ʒitɑ̃, -an] *nmf* (Spanish) gipsy.

gîte [ʒit] *nm* (*abri*) resting place; **g. rural** furnished *Br* holiday *ou Am* vacation accommodation (*farmhouse, cottage etc*); **donner le g. et le couvert à qn** to give s.o. room and board.

gîter [ʒite] *vi* (*navire*) to list.

givre [ʒivr] *nm* frost, hoarfrost. ● **se givrer** *vpr* (*pare-brise etc*) to ice up, frost up. ● **givré, -ée** *a* frost-covered; (*fou*) *Fam* nuts, crazy.

glabre [glabr] *a* (*visage*) smooth.

glace [glas] *nf* **1** (*eau gelée*) ice; (*crème glacée*) ice cream. **2** (*vitre*) window; (*miroir*) mirror; (*verre*) plate glass; **briser la g.** *Fig* to break the ice; **il est resté de g.** he showed no emotion.

glacer* [glase] **1** *vt* (*durcir*) to freeze; (*sang*) *Fig* to chill; **g. qn** (*paralyser, transir*) to chill s.o. ∎ **se glacer** *vpr* **mon sang s'est glacé dans mes veines** my blood ran cold. **2** *vt* (*gâteau*) to ice, (*au jus*) to glaze; (*papier*) to glaze. ● **glaçant, -ante** *a* (*attitude etc*) chilling, icy. ● **glacé, -ée** *a* **1** (*eau, pièce*) icecold, icy; (*vent*) freezing, icy; (*accueil*) *Fig* icy, chilly; **avoir les pieds/etc glacés** to have icy *ou* frozen *ou* ice-cold feet/*etc*. **2** (*thé, café*) iced; (*fruit, marron*) candied; (*papier*) glazed. ● **glaçage** *nm* (*de gâteau etc*) icing.

glacial, -e, -aux [glasjal, -o] *a* icy.

glacier [glasje] *nm* **1** *Géol* glacier. **2** (*vendeur*) ice-cream man.

glacière [glasjɛr] *nf* (*boîte, endroit*) icebox.

glaçon [glasɔ̃] *nm Culin* ice cube; *Géol* block of ice; (*sur le toit*) icicle.

glaïeul [glajœl] *nm* (*plante*) gladiolus.

glaire [glɛr] *nf Méd* phlegm.

glaise [glɛz] *nf* clay.

gland [glɑ̃] *nm* **1** *Bot* acorn. **2** (*pompon*) tassel.

glande [glɑ̃d] *nf* gland.

glander [glɑ̃de] *vi Fam* to fritter away one's time ∎ *vt* (*faire*) *Fam* to do.

glaner [glane] *vt* (*blé, renseignement etc*) to glean.

glapir [glapir] *vi* to yelp, yap.

glas [glɑ] *nm* (*de cloche*) knell; **on sonne le g.** the bell is tolling.

glauque [glok] *a* sea-green; (*sinistre*) *Fam* shady.

glisse [glis] *nf* (**sports de**) **g.** = sliding and gliding sports (*skiing, surfing etc*).

glisser [glise] *vi* (*involontairement*) to slip; (*volontairement*) (*sur glace etc*) to slide; (*sur l'eau*) to glide; **g. sur** (*sujet*) *Fig* to slide *ou* gloss over; **faire g. un tiroir**/*etc* to slide a drawer/*etc*; **ça glisse** it's slippery; **ça m'a glissé des mains** it slid out of my hands ∎ *vt* (*introduire*) to slip (**dans** into); (*murmurer*) to whisper; **se g. dans/sous** to slip into/under; **se laisser g. le long de la gouttière**/*etc* to slide down the drainpipe/*etc*. ● **glissant, -ante** *a* slippery. ● **glissade** *nf* (*involontaire*) slip; (*volontaire*) slide. ● **glissement** *nm* **g. à gauche** *Pol* swing *ou* shift to the left; **g. de terrain** *Géol* landslide; **g. de sens** shift in meaning.

glissière [glisjɛr] *nf* groove; **porte à g.** sliding door; **fermeture à g.** *Br* zip (fastener), *Am* zipper; **g. de sécurité** *Aut* crash barrier.

global, -e, -aux [glɔbal, -o] *a* total, global; **somme globale** lump sum; **méthode globale** (*à l'école*) word recognition. ● **globalement** *adv* collectively, as a whole.

globe [glɔb] *nm* globe; **g. de l'œil** eyeball; **g.** (**terrestre**) (terrestrial) globe.

globule [glɔbyl] *nm* **globules blancs/rouges** (*du sang*) white/red corpuscles.

globuleux, -euse [glɔbylø, -øz] *a* **yeux g.** protruding eyes.

gloire [glwar] *nf* (*renommée, louange, mérite*) glory; (*personne célèbre*) celebrity; **se faire g. de** to glory in; **à la g. de** in praise of. ● **glorieux, -euse** *a* (*plein de gloire*) glorious. ● **glorifier** *vt* to glorify; **se g. de qch** to glory in sth.

glossaire [glɔsɛr] *nm* glossary.

glouglou [gluglu] *nm* (*de liquide*) *Fam* gurgle. ● **glouglouter** *vi Fam* to gurgle.

glousser [gluse] *vi* (*poule*) to cluck; (*personne*) to chuckle. ● **gloussement** *nm* cluck(ing); (*de personne*) chuckle, chuckling.

glouton, -onne [glutɔ̃, -ɔn] *a* greedy, gluttonous ∎ *nmf* glutton. ● **gloutonnerie** *nf* gluttony.

gluant, -ante [glyɑ̃, -ɑ̃t] *a* sticky.

glucose [glykoz] *nm* glucose.

glycérine [gliserin] *nf* glycerin(e).

glycine [glisin] *nf* (*plante*) wisteria.

gnome [gnom] *nm* (*nain*) gnome.

gnon [ɲɔ̃] *nm Fam* blow, punch; **se prendre un g. dans la figure** *Fam* to get punched in the face.

go (tout de) [tudəgo] *adv* out of the blue, all of a sudden.

goal [gol] *nm Football* goalkeeper.

gobelet [gɔblɛ] *nm* tumbler; (*de plastique, papier*) cup.

gober [gɔbe] *vt* (*œuf, mouche etc*) to swallow (whole); (*propos*) *Fam* to swallow.

godasse [gɔdas] *nf Fam* shoe.

godet [gɔdɛ] *nm* (*récipient*) pot; (*verre*) *Fam* drink.

godillot [gɔdijo] *nm Fam* clodhopper, (heavy) shoe.

goéland [gɔelɑ̃] *nm* (sea)gull.

goélette [gɔelɛt] *nf* schooner.

gogo [gogo] *nm* (*homme naïf*) *Fam* sucker.

gogo (à) [agogo] *adv Fam* **whisky**/*etc* à g. whisky/*etc* galore.

goguenard, -arde [gɔgnar, -ard] *a* mocking.

goguette (en) [ãgɔgɛt] *adv* (*un peu ivre*) *Fam* merry, tight tipsy.

goinfre [gwɛ̃fr] *nm* (*glouton*) *Fam* pig, guzzler. ● **se goinfrer** *vpr Fam* to stuff oneself (de with), to gut (de on).

golf [gɔlf] *nm* golf; (*terrain*) golf course. ● **golfeur, -euse** *nmf* golfer.

golfe [gɔlf] *nm* gulf, bay.

gomme [gɔm] *nf* 1 (*substance*) gum. 2 (à *effacer*) eraser, *Br* rubber. 3 **mettre toute la g.** *Fam* (*accélérer*) to pull out all the stops; (*en voiture*) to put one's foot down. ● **gommé, -ée** *a* (*papier*) gummed. ● **gommer** *vt* (*effacer*) to rub out, erase.

gomme (à la) [alagɔm] *adv Fam* useless.

gond [gɔ̃] *nm* (*de porte etc*) hinge; **sortir de ses gonds** *Fig* to lose one's temper.

gondole [gɔ̃dɔl] *nf* (*bateau*) gondola. ● **gondolier** *nm* gondolier.

gondoler [gɔ̃dɔle] 1 *vi*, **se gondoler** *vpr* (*planche*) to warp. 2 **se gondoler** *vpr* (*rire*) *Fam* to split one's sides.

gonflable [gɔ̃flabl] *a* inflatable.

gonfler [gɔ̃fle] *vt* to swell; (*pneu*) to pump up, inflate; (*en soufflant*) to blow up; (*poitrine*) to swell out; (*grossir*) *Fig* to inflate ▮ *vi*, **se gonfler** *vpr* to swell; **se g. d'orgueil** to swell up with pride. ● **gonflé, -ée** *a* swollen; **être g.** *Fam* (*courageux*) to have plenty of pluck; (*insolent*) to have plenty of nerve. ● **gonflement** *nm* swelling. ● **gonfleur** *nm* (air) pump.

gong [gɔ̃g] *nm* gong.

gorge [gɔrʒ] *nf* 1 throat; (*seins*) *Litt* bust; **rire à g. déployée** to roar with laughter; **faire des gorges chaudes de qch** *Fig* to have a field day pouring scorn on sth. 2 *Géog* gorge.

gorgé, -ée [gɔrʒe] *a* **g. de** (*saturé*) gorged with.

gorgée [gɔrʒe] *nf* mouthful (*of wine etc*); **petite g.** sip; **d'une seule g.** in *ou* at one gulp.

gorger [gɔrʒe] *vt* (*remplir*) to stuff (de with); **se g. de** to stuff *ou* gorge oneself with.

gorille [gɔrij] *nm* 1 (*animal*) gorilla. 2 (*garde du corps*) *Fam* bodyguard.

gosier [gozje] *nm* throat, windpipe.

gosse [gɔs] *nmf* (*enfant*) *Fam* kid, youngster.

gothique [gɔtik] *a & nm* Gothic.

gouache [gwaʃ] *nf* (*peinture*) gouache.

goudron [gudrɔ̃] *nm* tar. ● **goudronner** *vt* to tar.

gouffre [gufr] *nm* gulf, chasm.

goujat [guʒa] *nm* churl, lout.

goulasch [gulaʃ] *nf* (*plat*) goulash.

goulot [gulo] *nm* (*de bouteille*) neck; **boire au g.** to drink from the bottle.

goulu, -ue [guly] *a* greedy. ● **goulûment** *adv* greedily.

goupille [gupij] *nf* (*cheville*) pin.

goupiller [gupije] *vt* (*arranger*) *Fam* to work out, arrange ▮ **se goupiller** *vpr* **ça s'est bien goupillé** *Fam* it worked out (well); **ça s'est mal goupillé** *Fam* it didn't work out.

gourde [gurd] *nf* 1 (à *eau*) water bottle, flask. 2 (*personne*) *Péj Fam* chump, oaf.

gourdin [gurdɛ̃] *nm* club, cudgel.

gourer (se) [sɔgure] *vpr Fam* to make a mistake.

gourmand, -ande [gurmã, -ãd] *a* (over)fond of food *ou* eating, *Péj* greedy; **g. de** fond of; **être g.** (**de sucreries**) to have a sweet tooth ▮ *nmf* hearty eater, *Péj* glutton. ● **gourmandise** *nf* (over)fondness for food, *Péj* gluttony; **gourmandises** (*mets*) delicacies.

gourmet [gurmɛ] *nm* gourmet, epicure.

gourmette [gurmɛt] *nf* identity bracelet *ou* chain.

gousse [gus] *nf* **g. d'ail** clove of garlic.

goût [gu] *nm* taste; **de bon g.** in good taste; **sans g.** tasteless; **par g.** from *ou* by choice; **avoir du g.** (*personne*) to have good taste; **avoir un g. de noisette**/*etc* to taste of hazelnut/*etc*; **prendre g. à** something to take a liking to sth; **quelque chose dans ce g.-là!** *Fam* something of that sort *ou* order!

goûter [gute] *vt* (*aliment*) to taste; (*apprécier*) to relish, enjoy; **g. à qch** to taste (a little of) sth; **g. de** (*pour la première fois*) to try out, taste ▮ *vi* to have an afternoon snack, *Br* have tea ▮ *nm* afternoon snack, *Br* tea.

goutte [gut] *nf* 1 drop; **couler g. à g.** to drip. 2 (*maladie*) gout. ● **goutte-à-goutte** *nm inv Méd* drip. ● **gouttelette** *nf* droplet. ● **goutter** *vi* (*eau, robinet, nez*) to drip (de from).

gouttière [gutjɛr] *nf* (*d'un toit*) gutter; (*verticale*) drainpipe.

gouvernail [guvɛrnaj] *nm* (*pale*) rudder; (*barre*) helm.

gouvernante [guvɛrnãt] *nf* governess.

gouvernement [guvɛrnəmã] *nm* government. ● **gouvernemental, -e, -aux** *a* politique/*etc* **gouvernementale** government policy/*etc*; **l'équipe gouvernementale** the government.

gouverner [guvɛrne] *vti Pol & Fig* to govern, rule. ● **gouvernants** *nmpl* rulers. ● **gouverneur** *nm* governor.

grabuge [grabyʒ] *nm* **il y a du g.** (*querelle*) *Fam* there's a rumpus.

grâce [grɑs] *nf* 1 (*charme*) & *Rel* grace; (*avantage*) favour; (*miséricorde*) mercy; **crier g.** to cry for mercy; **de bonne/mauvaise g.** with good/bad grace; **g. présidentielle** presidential pardon; **délai de g.** (*pour payer les impôts etc*) days of grace; **donner le coup de g. à** to finish off; **faire g. de qch à qn** to spare s.o. sth; **être dans les bonnes grâces de qn** to be in favour with s.o.; **rendre g. à qn** to give thanks to s.o. 2 *prép* **g. à** thanks to.

gracier [grasje] *vt* (*condamné*) to pardon.

gracieux, -euse [grasjø, -øz] *a* 1 (*élégant*) graceful; (*aimable*) gracious. 2 (*gratuit*) gratuitous; **à titre g.** free (of charge). ● **gracieu-**

sement *adv* gracefully; (*aimablement*) graciously; (*gratuitement*) free (of charge).

gracile [grasil] *a Litt* slender.

gradation [gradɑsjɔ̃] *nf* gradation.

grade [grad] *nm* (*militaire etc*) rank; **monter en g.** to be promoted. ●**gradé** *nm* (*dans l'armée*) non-commissioned officer.

gradins [gradɛ̃] *nmpl* (*d'amphithéâtre etc*) seats in tiers, rows of seats; (*de stade*) *Br* terraces, *Am* bleachers.

graduel, -elle [gradɥɛl] *a* gradual.

graduer [gradɥe] *vt* (*règle*) to graduate; (*exercices*) to grade (*for difficulty*), make gradually more difficult.

graffiti [grafiti] *nmpl* graffiti.

grain [grɛ̃] *nm* 1 (*de blé etc*) & *Fig* grain; (*de café*) bean; (*de poussière*) speck; (*de chapelet*) bead; **grains** (*céréales*) grain; **le g.** (*de cuir, papier*) the grain; **g. de beauté** mole; (*sur le visage*) beauty spot; **g. de raisin** grape; **avoir un g.** *Fam* to be not quite right in the head; **mettre son g. de sel** *Fam* to put one's oar in. 2 (*averse*) shower.

graine [grɛn] *nf* seed; **une mauvaise g.** (*enfant*) a rotten egg, *Br* a bad lot; **en prendre de la g.** to profit *ou* learn from someone's example.

graisse [grɛs] *nf* fat; (*lubrifiant*) grease. ●**graissage** *nm* (*de véhicule*) lubrication. ●**graisser** *vt* to grease. ●**graisseux, -euse** *a* (*vêtement etc*) greasy, oily; (*bourrelets, tissu*) fatty.

grammaire [gramer] *nf* grammar; **livre de g.** grammar (book). ●**grammatical, -e, -aux** *a* grammatical.

gramme [gram] *nm* gram(me).

grand, grande [grɑ̃, grɑ̃d] *a* big, large; (*en hauteur*) tall; (*chaleur, découverte, âge, mérite, ami etc*) great; (*bruit*) loud, great; (*différence*) wide, big, great; (*adulte, mûr, plus âgé*) grown up, big; (*maître, officier*) grand; (*âme*) noble; **g. frère/etc** (*plus âgé*) big brother/etc; **le g. air** the open air; **il est g.** **temps que je parte** it's high time that I left; **il n'y avait pas g. monde** there were not many people.

❚ *adv* **g. ouvert** (*yeux, fenêtre*) wide-open; **ouvrir g.** to open wide; **en g.** on a grand *ou* large scale.

❚ *nmf* (*à l'école*) senior; (*adulte*) grown-up. ●**grandement** *adv* (*beaucoup*) greatly; (*généreusement*) grandly; **avoir g. de quoi vivre** to have plenty to live on.

grand-chose [grɑ̃ʃoz] *pron* **pas g.-chose** not much.

Grande-Bretagne [grɑ̃dbrətaɲ] *nf* Great Britain.

grandeur [grɑ̃dœr] *nf* (*importance, gloire*) greatness; (*dimension*) size, magnitude; (*majesté, splendeur*) grandeur; **g. nature** life-size; **g. d'âme** generosity; **avoir la folie des grandeurs** to have delusions of grandeur.

grandiose [grɑ̃djoz] *a* grandiose, grand.

grandir [grɑ̃dir] *vi* to grow; (*bruit*) to grow louder; **g. de 2 cm** to grow 2 cm ❚ *vt*

(*grossir*) to magnify; **g. qn** (*faire paraître plus grand*) to make s.o. seem taller.

grand-mère [grɑ̃mɛr] *nf* (*pl* **grands-mères**) grandmother. ●**grand-père** *nm* (*pl* **grands-pères**) grandfather. ●**grands-parents** *nmpl* grandparents.

grand-route [grɑ̃rut] *nf* main road.

grange [grɑ̃ʒ] *nf* barn.

granit(e) [granit] *nm* granite.

granule [granyl] *nm* granule.

graphique [grafik] *a* (*signe, art*) graphic ❚ *nm* graph; *Ordinat* graphic.

grappe [grap] *nf* (*de fruits etc*) cluster; **g. de raisin** bunch of grapes.

grappin [grapɛ̃] *nm* **mettre le g. sur** *Fam* to grab hold of.

gras, grasse [grɑ, grɑs] *a* (*personne, ventre etc*) fat; (*aliment*) fatty; (*graisseux*) greasy, oily; (*plante, contour*) thick; (*rire*) throaty, deep; (*toux*) loose, phlegmy; **matières grasses** *Culin* fat; **foie g.** foie gras (*goose liver paste*); **caractères g.** bold type ❚ *nm* (*de viande*) fat. ●**grassement** *adv* **g. payé** handsomely paid. ●**grassouillet, -ette** *a* plump.

gratifier [gratifje] *vt* **g. qn de** to present *ou* favour s.o. with. ●**gratification** *nf* (*prime*) bonus.

gratin [gratɛ̃] *nm* 1 **macaronis/chou-fleur au g.** (*plat*) *Br* macaroni/cauliflower cheese, *Am* macaroni/cauliflower and cheese. 2 (*élite*) *Fam* upper crust. ●**gratiner** *vt* to cook (*sth*) au gratin.

gratis [gratis] *adv* free (of charge), gratis.

gratitude [gratityd] *nf* gratitude.

gratte-ciel [gratsjel] *nm inv* skyscraper.

gratte-papier [gratpapje] *nm inv* (*employé*) *Péj* pen-pusher.

gratter [grate] *vt* (*avec un outil etc*) to scrape; (*avec les ongles, les griffes etc*) to scratch; (*boue*) to scrape off; (*effacer*) to scratch out; **ça me gratte** *Fam* it itches, I have an itch ❚ *vi* (*à la porte etc*) to scratch; (*tissu*) to be scratchy ❚ **se gratter** *vpr* to scratch oneself. ●**grattoir** *nm* scraper.

gratuit, -uite [gratɥi, -ɥit] *a* (*billet etc*) free; (*hypothèse, acte*) gratuitous. ●**gratuité** *nf* **la g. de l'enseignement/etc** free education/etc. ●**gratuitement** *adv* free (of charge); (*sans motif*) gratuitously.

gravats [grava] *nmpl* rubble, debris.

grave [grav] *a* (*maladie, faute etc*) serious; (*juge, visage*) grave; (*voix*) deep, low, solemn; **ce n'est pas g.!** it's not important!; **accent g.** grave [grɑːv] accent. ●**gravement** *adv* (*malade, menacé*) seriously; (*dignement*) gravely.

graver [grave] *vt* (*sur métal etc*) to engrave; (*sur bois*) to carve; (*disque*) to cut; (*dans sa mémoire*) to imprint, engrave. ●**graveur** *nm* engraver.

gravier [gravje] *nm* gravel. ●**gravillon** *nm* gravel; **gravillons** gravel, *Br* (loose) chippings.

gravir [gravir] *vt* to climb (*with effort*); **g. les échelons** *Fig* to climb the ladder.

gravité [gravite] nf 1 (de situation etc) seriousness; (solennité) gravity; **accident sans g.** minor accident. 2 Phys gravity; **centre de g.** centre of gravity.

graviter [gravite] vi to revolve (autour around). ●**gravitation** nf gravitation.

gravure [gravyr] nf (image) print; (action, art) engraving; (à l'eau forte) etching; (de disque) recording; **g. sur bois** (objet) woodcut.

gré [gre] nm **à son g.** (goût) to his ou her taste; (désir) as he ou she pleases; **de son plein g.** of one's own free will; **de bon g.** willingly; **contre le g. de qn** against s.o.'s will; **bon g. mal g.** willy-nilly, reluctantly; **de g. ou de force** one way or another, willynilly; **au g. de** (vent etc) at the mercy of; **savoir g. de qch à qn** to be thankful to s.o. for sth.

Grèce [grɛs] nf Greece. ●**grec, grecque** a Greek ▮ nm **G., Grecque** Greek ▮ nm (langue) Greek.

greffe [grɛf] nf 1 (de peau, d'arbre etc) graft; (d'organe) transplant. 2 nm Jur record office. ●**greffer** vt (peau etc) & Bot to graft (à on to); (organe) to transplant. ●**greffier** nm clerk (of the court). ●**greffon** nm (de peau) & Bot graft.

grégaire [greger] a (instinct) gregarious.

grêle [grɛl] 1 nf hail; **g. de balles/etc** Fig hail of bullets/etc. 2 a (fin) spindly, (very) slender ou thin. ●**grêler** v imp to hail; **il grêle** it's hailing. ●**grêlon** nm hailstone.

grêlé, -ée [grele] a (visage) pockmarked.

grelot [grəlo] nm (small round) bell (that jingles).

grelotter [grəlɔte] vi to shiver (de with).

grenade [grənad] nf 1 (fruit) pomegranate. 2 (projectile) grenade. ●**grenadine** nf pomegranate syrup, grenadine.

grenat [grəna] a inv (couleur) dark red.

grenier [grənje] nm (de maison) attic; Agr granary.

grenouille [grənuj] nf frog.

grès [grɛ] nm (roche) sandstone; (poterie) stoneware.

grésiller [grezije] vi Culin to sizzle; Radio to crackle.

grève [grɛv] nf 1 strike; **se mettre en g.** to go (out) on strike; **g. de la faim** hunger strike; **g. du zèle** Br work-to-rule, Am rule-book slow down; **g. perlée** Br go-slow, Am slowdown (strike); **g. sauvage/sur le tas** wildcat/sit-down strike; **g. tournante** strike by rota. 2 (de mer) shore; (de rivière) bank. ●**gréviste** nmf striker.

gribouiller [gribuje] vti to scribble. ●**gribouillis** nm scribble.

grief [grijɛf] nm (plainte) grievance; **faire g. de qch à qn** to hold sth against s.o.

grièvement [grijɛvmɑ̃] adv **g. blessé** seriously ou badly injured.

griffe [grif] nf 1 (ongle) claw; **sous la g. de qn** (pouvoir) in s.o.'s clutches. 2 (de couturier) (designer) label; (tampon) printed signature; (d'auteur) Fig mark, stamp. ●**griffé, -ée** a vêtements griffés designer clothes. ●**griffer** vt to scratch, claw.

griffonner [grifɔne] vt to scribble, scrawl. ●**griffonnage** nm scribble, scrawl.

grignoter [griɲɔte] vti to nibble.

gril [gril] nm (ustensile de cuisine) Br grill, Am broiler. ●**grillade** [grijad] nf (viande) Br grill, Br grilled meat, Am broiled meat. ●**grille-pain** nm inv toaster. ●**griller** vt (viande) Br to grill, Am broil; (pain) to toast; (café) to roast; (ampoule électrique) to blow; (brûler) to scorch; (cigarette) Fam to smoke; **g. un feu rouge** (en voiture etc) Fam to drive through ou jump a red light ▮ vi to mettre à g. Br to put on the grill, Am to broil; **on grille ici** Fam it's scorching; **g. de faire qch** Fam to be itching to do sth; **se faire g.** Fam to get one's fingers burnt; **il est grillé** (dévoilé) Fam his game's up, he's had it.

grille [grij] nf (clôture) railings; (porte) (iron) gate; (de fourneau, foyer) grate; (de radiateur de voiture) grid, grille; (des salaires) Fig scale; (grilles (de fenêtre) bars, grating; g. (des horaires) schedule; **g. de mots croisés** crossword puzzle grid. ●**grillage** nm wire mesh ou netting.

griller [grije] vt & vi voir **gril.**

grillon [grijɔ̃] nm (insecte) cricket.

grimace [grimas] nf (pour faire rire) (funny) face; (de dégoût, douleur) grimace; **faire des grimaces/la g.** to make faces/a face. ●**grimacer** vi to make faces ou a face; (de dégoût etc) to grimace (de with).

grimer [grime] vt, **se grimer** vpr (acteur) to make up.

grimper [grɛ̃pe] vi to climb (à qch up sth); (prix) Fam to rocket ▮ vt to climb. ●**grimpant, -ante** a plante/etc grimpante climbing plant/etc.

grincer [grɛ̃se] vi to creak, grate; **g. des dents** to grind ou gnash one's teeth. ●**grincement** nm creaking, grating; (des dents) grinding.

grincheux, -euse [grɛ̃ʃø, -øz] a grumpy, bad-tempered.

gringalet [grɛ̃galɛ] nm (homme) Péj puny runt, weakling.

grippe [grip] nf 1 (maladie) flu, influenza; **g. intestinale** gastric flu. 2 **prendre qch/qn en g.** to take a strong dislike to sth/s.o. ●**grippé, -ée** a être g. to have (the) flu.

gripper [gripe] vi, **se gripper** vpr (moteur) to seize up.

grippe-sou [gripsu] nm skinflint, miser.

gris, grise [gri, griz] a Br grey, Am gray; (temps) dull, grey; (ivre) tipsy ▮ nm Br grey, Am gray. ●**grisaille** nf (de vie) dullness, Br greyness, Am grayness. ●**grisâtre** a Br greyish, Am grayish.

griser [grize] vt (vin etc) to make (s.o.) tipsy, intoxicate (s.o.); (air vif, succès etc) to exhilarate (s.o.). ●**griserie** nf intoxication; (du succès etc) exhilaration.

grisonner [grizɔne] vi (cheveux, personne) to

go *Br* grey *ou Am* gray. ●**grisonnant, -ante**
a Br greying, *Am* graying; **avoir les tempes
grisonnantes** to be going grey at the temples.
grisou [grizu] *nm* (*gaz*) firedamp; **coup de g.**
firedamp explosion.

grive [griv] *nf* (*oiseau*) thrush.

grivois, -oise [grivwa, -waz] *a* bawdy. ●**gri-
voiserie** *nf* (*propos*) bawdy talk.

grizzli [grizli] *nm* grizzly bear.

Groenland [grɔɛnlɑ̃d] *nm* Greenland.

grog [grɔg] *nm* (*boisson*) grog, toddy.

grogner [grɔɲe] *vi* (*personne*) to grumble,
growl (**contre** at); (*cochon*) to grunt. ●**grognement** *nm* grumble, growl; (*de cochon*)
grunt. ●**grognon** *am* grumpy, peevish.

grommeler [grɔm(ə)le] *vti* to grumble, mutter.

gronder [grɔ̃de] *vi* (*chien*) to growl; (*tonnerre*, *camion*) to rumble **▌** *vt* (*réprimander*) to
scold, tell off. ●**grondement** *nm* growl; (*de
tonnerre etc*) rumble. ●**gronderie** *nf* scolding.

groom [grum] *nm Br* page (boy), *Am*
bellboy.

gros, grosse [gro, gros] *a* big; (*gras*) fat;
(*épais*) thick; (*effort*, *progrès*) great;
(*somme*, *fortune*) large; (*averse*, *rhume*, *mer*)
heavy; (*faute*) serious, gross; (*bruit*) loud;
(*traits*, *laine*, *fil*) coarse; **g. mot** swear word.
▌ *adv* **gagner g.** to earn big money; **risquer
g.** to take a big risk; **écrire g.** to write big;
en g. (*globalement*) roughly; (*écrire*) in big
letters; (*vendre*) in bulk, wholesale; **en avoir
g. sur le cœur** to be bitter.
▌ *nmf* (*personne*) fat man, fat woman.
▌ *nm* **le g.** the bulk of; **commerce/maison/
prix/etc de g.** wholesale trade/company/
prices/*etc*.

groseille [grozɛj] *nf* (white *ou* red) currant;
g. à maquereau gooseberry.

grossesse [grosɛs] *nf* pregnancy.

grosseur [grosœr] *nf* **1** (*volume*) size; (*obésité*) weight. **2** (*tumeur*) lump.

grossier, -ière [grosje, -jɛr] *a* (*tissu*, *traits*)
rough, coarse; (*personne*, *manières*) rude,
coarse; (*erreur*) gross; (*idée*, *solution*) rough,
crude; (*instrument*) crude; **ruse grossière**
crude trick; **être g. envers qn** (*incorrect*) to
be rude to s.o. ●**grossièrement** *adv* (*calculer*) roughly; (*répondre*) coarsely, rudely; (*se
tromper*) grossly. ●**grossièreté** *nf* roughness,
coarseness; (*vulgarité*) rudeness; (*mot*) rude
word.

grossir [grosir] *vi* (*personne*) to put on
weight; (*fleuve*) to swell; (*bosse*, *foule*,
nombre etc) to swell, get bigger; (*bruit*) to
get louder **▌** *vt* to swell; (*exagérer*) *Fig* to
magnify **▌** *vti* (*verre*, *loupe etc*) to magnify;
verre grossissant magnifying glass. ●**grossissement** *nm* increase in weight; (*de bosse etc*)
swelling, increase in size; (*de microscope etc*)
magnification.

grossiste [grosist] *nmf Com* wholesaler.

grosso modo [grosomɔdo] *adv* (*en gros*)
roughly.

grotesque [grɔtɛsk] *a* (*risible*) ludicrous,
grotesque.

grotte [grɔt] *nf* cave, grotto.

grouiller [gruje] **1** *vi* (*rue*, *fourmis*, *foule etc*)
to be swarming (**de** with). **2 se grouiller** *vpr*
(*se hâter*) *Fam* to step on it. ●**grouillant,
-ante** *a* swarming (**de** with).

groupe [grup] *nm* group; **g. sanguin** blood
group; **g. scolaire** (*bâtiments*) school block.
●**groupement** *nm* (*action*) grouping;
(*groupe*) group. ●**grouper** *vt* to group (together) **▌ se grouper** *vpr* to group (together),
band together.

groupie [grupi] *nf* groupie.

grue [gry] *nf* (*machine*, *oiseau*) crane.

gruger [gryʒe] *vt Litt* to swindle, dupe; **se
faire g.** to get swindled *ou* duped.

grumeau, -x [grymo] *nm* (*dans une sauce
etc*) lump. ●**grumeleux, -euse** *a* lumpy.

gruyère [gryjɛr] *nm* gruyère (cheese).

Guadeloupe [gwadlup] *nf* Guadeloupe.

Guatemala [gwatemala] *nm* Guatemala.

gué [ge] *nm* ford; **passer à g.** to ford.

guenilles [gənij] *nfpl* rags (and tatters).

guenon [gənɔ̃] *nf* female monkey.

guépard [gepar] *nm* cheetah.

guêpe [gɛp] *nf* wasp. ●**guêpier** *nm* (*nid*)
wasp's nest; (*piège*) *Fig* trap.

guère [gɛr] *adv* (**ne**)... **g.** hardly, scarcely; **il
ne sort g.** he hardly *ou* scarcely goes out;
elle ne le fait g. plus she hardly *ou* scarcely
does it any more.

guéridon [geridɔ̃] *nm* pedestal table.

guérilla [gerija] *nf* guerrilla warfare. ●**guérillero** *nm* guerrilla.

guérir [gerir] *vt* (*personne*, *maladie*) to cure
(**de** of); (*blessure*) to heal **▌** *vi* (*personne*) to
get better, recover; (*blessure*) to heal;
(*rhume*) to get better; (*de* (*maladie*) to get
over, recover from **▌ se guérir** *vpr* to get
better. ●**guéri, -ie** *a* cured, better, well; **être
g. de qch/qn** (*débarrassé*) *Fig* to have got
over sth/s.o., be finished with sth/s.o. ●**guérison** *nf* (*de personne*) recovery; (*de maladie*) cure; (*de blessure*) healing. ●**guérisseur, -euse** *nmf* faith healer.

guérite [gerit] *nf Mil* sentry box.

Guernesey [gɛrnəze] *nm ou f* Guernsey.

guerre [gɛr] *nf* war; (*chimique etc*) warfare;
en g. at war (**avec** with); **faire la g.** to wage
ou make war (**à** on, against); **crime/cri/etc de
g.** war crime/cry/*etc*; **g. d'usure** war of attrition; **conseil de g.** court-martial; **c'est de
bonne g.** that's fair enough; **j'ai accepté de g.
lasse** I accepted, unable to resist any longer.
●**guerrier, -ière** *a* **danse guerrière** war dance;
chant g. battle song; **nation guerrière** warlike nation **▌** *nmf* warrior. ●**guerroyer** *vi Litt*
to war.

guet [gɛ] *nm* **faire le g.** to be on the lookout.
●**guetter** *vt* to be on the lookout for, watch
(out) for; (*gibier*) to lie in wait for.
●**guetteur** *nm* (*soldat*) lookout.

guet-apens [gɛtapɑ̃] *nm* (*pl* **guets-apens**)
ambush.

guêtre [gɛtr] *nf* gaiter.

gueule [gœl] *nf* (*d'animal, de canon*) mouth; (*de personne*) *Fam* mouth; (*figure*) *Fam* face; **avoir la g. de bois** *Fam* to have a hangover; **faire la g.** *Fam* to sulk; **faire une g. d'enterrement** *Fam* to look thoroughly depressed. ● **gueuler** *vti Fam* to bawl (out). ● **gueuleton** *nm* (*repas*) *Fam Br* blow-out, feast.

gui [gi] *nm* (*plante*) mistletoe.

guichet [giʃɛ] *nm* (*de gare, cinéma etc*) ticket office; (*de banque etc*) window; (*de théâtre*) box office, ticket office; **à guichets fermés** *Théâtre etc* with all tickets sold in advance. ● **guichetier, -ière** *nmf* (*de banque etc*) *Br* counter clerk, *Am* teller; (*à la gare*) ticket office clerk.

guide [gid] 1 *nm* (*personne, livre etc*) guide. 2 *nf* (*éclaireuse*) (girl) guide. ● **guides** *nfpl* (*rênes*) reins. ● **guider** *vt* to guide; **se g. sur un manuel/etc** to use a handbook/etc as a guide.

guidon [gidɔ̃] *nm* (*bicyclette*) handlebar(s).

guigne [giɲ] *nf* (*malchance*) *Fam* bad luck.

guignol [giɲɔl] *nm* (*spectacle*) = Punch and Judy show; **faire le g.** *Fam* to clown about *ou* around.

guillemets [gijmɛ] *nmpl Typ* inverted commas, quotation marks; **entre g.** in inverted commas, in quotation marks.

guilleret, -ette [gijrɛ, -ɛt] *a* lively, perky.

guillotine [gijɔtin] *nf* guillotine. ● **guillotiner** *vt* to guillotine.

guimauve [gimov] *nf* (*plante, confiserie*) marshmallow.

guimbarde [gɛ̃bard] *nf* (*voiture*) *Fam Br* old banger, *Am* (old) wreck.

guindé, -ée [gɛ̃de] *a* (*peu naturel*) stiff; (*style*) stilted.

Guinée [gine] *nf* Guinea.

guingois (de) [dəgɛ̃gwa] *adv Fam* askew, *Br* skew-whiff.

guirlande [girlɑ̃d] *nf* garland, wreath.

guise [giz] *nf* **agir à sa g.** to have one's own way; **n'en faire qu'à sa g.** to do as one pleases; **en g. de** by way of.

guitare [gitar] *nf* guitar. ● **guitariste** *nmf* guitarist.

guttural, -e, -aux [gytyral, -o] *a* guttural.

Guyane [gɥijan] *nf* Guyana.

gymnase [ʒimnɑz] *nm* gymnasium. ● **gymnaste** *nmf* gymnast. ● **gymnastique** *nf* gymnastics.

gynécologie [ʒinekɔlɔʒi] *nf Br* gynaecology, *Am* gynecology. ● **gynécologue** *nmf Br* gynaecologist, *Am* gynecologist.

gyrophare [ʒirofar] *nm* (*de voiture de police etc*) revolving light, flashing light.

H

H, h [aʃ] *nm* H, h; **l'heure H** zero hour; **bombe H** H-bomb.

ha! [ʼɑ] *int* ah!, oh!; **ha, ha!** (*rire*) ha-ha!

habile [abil] *a* skilful, clever (**à qch** at sth, **à faire** at doing); **h. de ses doigts** dexterous, clever *ou* good with one's fingers. ● **habilement** *adv* skilfully, cleverly. ● **habileté** *nf* skill, ability.

habilité, -ée [abilite] *a* (legally) authorized (**à faire** to do).

habiller [abije] *vt* to dress (**de** in); (*fournir en vêtements*) to clothe; (*couvrir*) to cover (**de** with); **h. qn en soldat**/*etc* (*déguiser*) to dress s.o. up as a soldier/*etc*; **un rien l'habille** she looks good in anything ‖ **s'habiller** *vpr* to dress (oneself), get dressed; (*avec élégance*) to dress up. ● **habillé, -ée** *a* dressed (**de** in, **en** as); (*costume, robe*) smart, dressy. ● **habillement** *nm* (*vêtements*) clothing, clothes.

habit [abi] *nm* costume, outfit; (*tenue de soirée*) evening dress, tails; **habits** (*vêtements*) clothes.

habitable [abitabl] *a* (in)habitable; (*maison*) fit to live in.

habitat [abita] *nm* (*d'animal, de plante*) habitat; (*conditions*) housing, living conditions.

habitation [abitɑsjɔ̃] *nf* house, dwelling; (*action de résider*) living.

habiter [abite] *vi* to live (**à, en, dans in**) ‖ *vt* (*maison, région*) to live in; (*planète*) to inhabit. ● **habitant, -ante** *nmf* (*de pays etc*) inhabitant; (*de maison*) occupant, resident. ● **habité, -ée** *a* (*région*) inhabited; (*maison*) occupied.

habitude [abityd] *nf* habit; **avoir l'h. de qch** to be used to sth; **avoir l'h. de faire** to be used to doing, be in the habit of doing; **prendre l'h. de faire** to get into the habit of doing; **prendre de bonnes habitudes** to take on some good habits; **prendre de mauvaises habitudes** to get into *ou* pick up (some) bad habits; **d'h.** usually; **comme d'h.** as usual.

habituel, -elle [abityɛl] *a* usual, customary. ● **habituellement** *adv* usually.

habituer [abitye] *vt* **h. qn à** to accustom s.o. to; **être habitué à qch/à faire** to be used *ou* accustomed to sth/to doing ‖ **s'habituer** *vpr* to get accustomed; **s'h. à** to get used *ou* accustomed to. ● **habitué, -ée** *nmf* regular (customer *ou* visitor).

hache [ʼaʃ] *nf* axe, *Am* ax. ● **hachette** *nf* hatchet.

hacher [ʼaʃe] *vt* (*au couteau*) to chop (up); (*avec un appareil*) *Br* to mince, *Am* grind; (*déchiqueter*) to cut to pieces. ● **haché, -ée** *a* **1** (*viande*) *Br* minced, *Am* ground; (*légumes*)

chopped. **2** (*style*) jerky, broken, staccato. ● **hachis** *nm* (*viande*) *Br* mince, *Br* minced *ou Am* ground meat; **h. Parmentier** shepherd's pie. ● **hachoir** *nm* (*couteau*) chopper; (*appareil*) *Br* mincer, *Am* grinder.

hachures [ʼaʃyr] *nfpl* shading, hatching. ● **hachurer** *vt* to shade in, hatch.

hagard, -arde [ʼagar, -ard] *a* wild-looking, frantic.

haie [ʼɛ] *nf* (*clôture*) hedge; (*rangée*) row; (*de coureur*) *Sport* hurdle; (*de chevaux*) *Sport* fence, hurdle; **course de haies** (*coureurs*) hurdle race; (*chevaux*) steeplechase; **h. d'honneur** guard of honour; **faire la h.** to line up, form a line.

haillons [ʼajɔ̃] *nmpl* rags (and tatters).

haine [ʼɛn] *nf* hatred, hate. ● **haineux, -euse** *a* full of hatred.

haïr* [ʼair] *vt* to hate. ● **haïssable** *a* hateful, detestable.

halage [ʼalaʒ] *nm voir* **haler**.

hâle [ʼɑl] *nm* suntan. ● **hâlé, -ée** *a* (*par le soleil*) suntanned.

haleine [alɛn] *nf* breath; **hors d'h.** out of breath; **perdre h.** to get out of breath; **reprendre h.** to get one's breath back, catch one's breath; **travail de longue h.** long-term and exacting task; **tenir qn en h.** to hold s.o. in suspense.

haler [ʼale] *vt* (*bateau*) to tow. ● **halage** *nm* towing; **chemin de h.** towpath.

haleter [ʼal(ə)te] *vi* to pant, gasp (for breath). ● **haletant, -ante** *a* panting, gasping.

hall [ʼol] *nm* (*de gare*) main hall, concourse; (*de maison*) hall(way); (*d'hôtel*) lobby, hall.

halle [ʼal] *nf* (covered) market; **les halles** the central food market.

hallucination [alysinɑsjɔ̃] *nf* hallucination. ● **hallucinant, -ante** *a* extraordinary.

halo [ʼalo] *nm* (*auréole*) halo.

halogène [ʼalɔʒɛn] *a* (*lampe etc*) halogen.

halte [ʼalt] *nf* (*arrêt*) stop, *Mil* halt; (*lieu*) stopping place, *Mil* halting place; **faire h.** to stop ‖ *int* stop!, *Mil* halt!

haltères [altɛr] *nmpl* weights, dumbbells. ● **haltérophile** [ʼɑburgœr] *nm* weight lifter ● **haltérophilie** *nf* weight lifting.

hamac [ʼamak] *nm* hammock.

hamburger [ʼɑburgœr] *nm* hamburger.

hameau, -x [ʼamo] *nm* hamlet.

hameçon [amsɔ̃] *nm* (fish) hook; **mordre à l'h.** *Pêche & Fig* to swallow the bait, rise to the bait.

hamster [ʼamster] *nm* hamster.

hanche [ʼɑ̃ʃ] *nf* hip.

hand(-)ball [ʼɑ̃dbal] *nm Sport* handball.

153 **havre**

handicap ['ãdikap] *nm* (*désavantage*) & *Sport* handicap. ● **handicaper** *vt* to handicap.

handicapé, -ée ['ãdikape] *a* handicapped ∎ *nmf* handicapped person; **h. moteur** spastic; **h. physique/mental** physically/mentally handicapped person.

hangar ['ãgar] *nm* (*entrepôt*) shed; (*pour avions*) hangar.

hanneton ['an(ə)tɔ̃] *nm* (*insecte*) cockchafer.

hanter ['ãte] *vt* (*fantôme etc*) to haunt (*house etc*); (*souvenir etc*) to haunt, obsess (*s.o.*). ● **hanté, -ée** *a* (*maison etc*) haunted.

hantise ['ãtiz] *nf* **la h. de** an obsession with.

happer ['ape] *vt* (*saisir*) to catch, snatch; (*par la gueule*) to snap up.

haras ['ara] *nm* stud farm.

harasser ['arase] *vt* (*fatiguer*) to exhaust. ● **harassé, -ée** *a* exhausted.

harceler ['arsəle] *vt* to harass, torment (**de** with). ● **harcèlement** *nm* harassment; **h. sexuel** sexual harassment.

hardi, -ie ['ardi] *a* bold, daring. ● **hardiment** *adv* boldly. ● **hardiesse** *nf* boldness, daring; **une h.** (*action*) an audacity.

harem ['arɛm] *nm* harem.

hareng ['arã] *nm* herring; **h. saur** smoked herring.

hargne ['arɲ] *nf* aggressive bad temper. ● **hargneux, -euse** *a* bad-tempered, aggressive.

haricot ['ariko] *nm* bean; **h. blanc** haricot bean; **h. vert** green bean, *Br* French bean; **h. rouge** kidney bean; **h. de mouton** mutton stew; **c'est la fin des haricots** *Fam* the game's up, it's all over.

harmonica [armɔnika] *nm* harmonica, mouthorgan.

harmonie [armɔni] *nf* harmony. ● **harmonieux, -euse** *a* harmonious. ● **harmonique** *a* & *nm Mus* harmonic. ● **harmoniser** *vt* **s'harmoniser** *vpr* to harmonize. ● **harmonium** *nm* (*instrument de musique*) harmonium.

harnacher ['arnaʃe] *vt* (*cheval etc*) to harness. ● **harnais** *nm* (*de cheval, bébé*) harness.

harpe ['arp] *nf* harp. ● **harpiste** *nmf* harpist.

harpon ['arpɔ̃] *nm* harpoon. ● **harponner** *vt* (*baleine*) to harpoon; **h. qn** (*arrêter au passage*) *Fam* to waylay s.o., collar s.o.

hasard ['azar] *nm* **le h.** chance; **un h.** (*coïncidence*) a coincidence; **un heureux h.** a stroke of luck; **un malheureux h.** a rotten piece of luck; **par h.** by chance; **par le plus grand des hasards** by a (sheer) fluke; **si par h.** if by any chance; **au h.** at random, haphazardly; **à tout h.** just in case; **les hasards de la vie/etc** the fortunes of life/etc.

hasarder ['azarde] *vt* (*remarque, démarche*) to venture, hazard; (*vie, réputation*) *Litt* to risk; **se h. dans** to venture into; **se h. à faire** to risk doing, venture to do.

hasardeux, -euse ['azardø, -øz] *a* risky, hazardous.

haschisch ['aʃiʃ] *nm* hashish.

hâte ['at] *nf* haste, speed; (*impatience*) eager-ness; **à la h., en (toute) h.** in a hurry, hurriedly, in haste; **avoir h. de faire** (*désireux*) to be eager to do, be in a hurry to do. ● **hâter** *vt* (*pas, départ etc*) to hasten ∎ **se hâter** *vpr* to hurry, make haste (**de faire** to do). ● **hâtif, -ive** *a* (*conclusion, jugement etc*) hasty, hurried; (*développement*) precocious; (*fruit*) early.

hausse ['os] *nf* rise (**de** in); **en h.** rising. ● **hausser** *vt* (*prix, voix etc*) to raise; (*épaules*) to shrug; **se h. sur la pointe des pieds** to stand on tip-toe.

haut, haute ['o, 'ot] *a* (*montagne etc*) high; (*de taille*) tall; (*note de musique, rang, température etc*) high; **la mer est haute** it's high tide; **le h. Rhin** the upper Rhine; **à haute voix, à voix haute** aloud, in a loud voice; **en haute mer** out at sea; **h. de 5 mètres** 5 metres high *ou* tall; **h. fonctionnaire** high-ranking civil servant; **haute trahison** high treason; **la haute couture** high fashion, haute couture; **la haute coiffure** haute coiffure; **la haute société** high society; **la haute bourgeoisie** the upper middle class; **un instrument de haute précision** a precision instrument; **un renseignement/etc de la plus haute importance** news/etc of the utmost importance; **avoir une haute opinion de qn** to have a high opinion of s.o.; **obtenir qch de haute lutte** to get sth after a hard struggle.

∎ *adv* (*voler, viser etc*) high (up); (*parler*) loud, loudly; **tout h.** (*lire, penser*) aloud, out loud; **h. placé** (*personne*) in a high position; **plus h.** (*dans un texte*) above, further back; **emporter** *ou* **gagner h. la main** to win hands down.

∎ *nm* (*partie haute*) top; **en h. de** at the top of; **en h.** (*loger*) upstairs; (*regarder*) up; (*mettre*) on (the) top; **d'en h.** (*de la partie haute, du ciel etc*) from high up, from up above; **avoir 5 mètres de h.** to be 5 metres high *ou* tall; **des hauts et des bas** *Fig* ups and downs.

hautain, -aine ['otɛ̃, -ɛn] *a* haughty.

hautbois ['obwa] *nm* (*instrument de musique*) oboe.

haut-de-forme ['od(ə)fɔrm] *nm* (*pl* **hauts-de-forme**) top hat.

hautement ['otmã] *adv* (*tout à fait, très*) highly. ● **hauteur** *nf* height; (*colline*) hill; (*orgueil*) *Péj* haughtiness; *Mus* pitch; **à h. de 100 000 francs/etc** for a sum of 100,000 francs/etc; **à la h. de** (*objet*) level with; (*rue*) opposite; **arriver à la h. de qch** (*mesurer*) to reach (the level of) sth; **à la h. de la situation** up to *ou* equal to the situation; **il n'est pas à la h.** he isn't up to it; **saut en h.** *Sport* high jump.

haut-le-cœur ['ol(ə)kœr] *nm inv* **avoir des h.-le-cœur** (*nausée*) to retch, gag.

haut lo-corps ['ol(ə)kɔr] *nm inv* (*sursaut*) sudden start, jump.

haut-parleur ['oparlœr] *nm* loudspeaker.

hâve ['av] *a* gaunt, emaciated.

havre ['avr] *nm Litt* (*refuge*) haven; **h. de**

paix haven of peace.
Haye (La) [la'ɛ] *nf* The Hague.
hayon ['ajɔ̃, 'ɛjɔ̃] *nm* (*porte de voiture*) hatchback, tailgate.
hé! [e] *int* **hé (là)** (*appel*) hey!; **hé! hé!** (*appréciation, moquerie*) well, well!
hebdomadaire [ɛbdɔmadɛr] *a* weekly ▌ *nm* (*publication*) weekly.
héberger [ebɛrʒe] *vt* to put up, accommodate. ●**hébergement** *nm* accommodation; **centre d'h.** shelter.
hébété, -ée [ebete] *a* dazed, stupefied.
hébreu, -x [ebrø] *am* Hebrew ▌ *nm* (*langue*) Hebrew. ●**hébraïque** *a* Hebrew.
Hébrides [ebrid] *nfpl* **les H.** the Hebrides.
hécatombe [ekatɔ̃b] *nf* (great) slaughter.
hectare [ɛktar] *nm* hectare (= 2.47 acres).
hégémonie [eʒemɔni] *nf* supremacy, hegemony.
hein! [ɛ̃] *int* (*surprise, interrogation*) *Fam* eh!
hélas! ['elɑs] *int* unfortunately, alas!
héler ['ele] *vt* (*taxi etc*) to hail.
hélice [elis] *nf* (*d'avion, de navire*) propeller.
hélicoptère [elikɔptɛr] *nm* helicopter. ●**héliport** *nm* heliport.
hellénique [elenik] *a* Hellenic, Greek.
hem! ['ɛm] *int* (a)hem!, hm!
hémicycle [emisikl] *nm* semicircle; *Pol Fr* (French) National Assembly.
hémisphère [emisfɛr] *nm* hemisphere.
hémophile [emɔfil] *a* h(a)emophilic ▌ *nmf* h(a)emophiliac. ●**hémophilie** *nf* h(a)emophilia.
hémorragie [emɔraʒi] *nf* *Méd* h(a)emorrhage; (*de capitaux*) outflow, drain; **h. cérébrale** stroke; **faire une h.** to h(a)emorrhage, have a h(a)emorrhage.
hémorroïdes [emɔrɔid] *nfpl* piles, h(a)emorrhoids.
hennir ['enir] *vi* (*cheval*) to neigh. ●**hennissement** *nm* neigh(ing).
hep! ['ɛp] *int* hey!, hey there!
hépatite [epatit] *nf* hepatitis.
herbe [ɛrb] *nf* grass; (*pour soigner*) herb; **mauvaise h.** weed; **fines herbes** (*assaisonnement*) herbs; **blé(s) en h.** green wheat; **poète/etc en h.** *Fig* budding poet/etc; **couper l'h. sous le pied de qn** to cut the ground from under s.o.'s feet; **fumer de l'herbe** (*haschisch*) *Fam* to smoke grass. ●**herbage** *nm* grassland. ●**herbeux, -euse** *a* grassy. ●**herbicide** *nm* weed killer. ●**herbivore** *a* grass-eating, herbivorous. ●**herbu, -ue** *a* grassy.
hercule [ɛrkyl] *nm* Hercules, strong man. ●**herculéen, -enne** *a* herculean.
hérédité [eredite] *nf* heredity. ●**héréditaire** *a* hereditary.
hérésie [erezi] *nf* heresy. ●**hérétique** *a* heretical ▌ *nmf* heretic.
hérisser ['erise] *vt* (*poils*) to bristle (up); **h. qn** (*irriter*) to ruffle s.o.'s feathers, ruffle s.o. ▌ **se hérisser** *vpr* (*poils*) to bristle (up); (*personne*) *Fig* to get ruffled. ●**hérissé, -ée** *a*

(*cheveux*) bristly; (*cactus*) prickly; **h. de** bristling with.
hérisson ['erisɔ̃] *nm* (*animal*) hedgehog.
hériter [erite] *vti* to inherit (**qch de qn** sth from s.o.); **h. de qch** to inherit sth. ●**héritage** *nm* (*biens*) inheritance; (*culturel, politique etc*) *Fig* heritage. ●**héritier** *nm* heir; **h. de la couronne** *ou* **du trône** heir to the throne. ●**héritière** *nf* heiress.
hermétique [ɛrmetik] *a* airtight, hermetically sealed; (*obscur*) *Fig* impenetrable. ●**hermétiquement** *adv* hermetically.
hermine [ɛrmin] *nf* (*animal, fourrure*) ermine.
hernie ['ɛrni] *nf* (*d'organe*) hernia, rupture; (*de pneu*) swelling.
héron ['erɔ̃] *nm* (*oiseau*) heron.
héros ['ero] *nm* hero. ●**héroïne** [erɔin] *nf* **1** (*femme*) heroine. **2** (*drogue*) heroin. ●**héroïque** [erɔik] *a* heroic. ●**héroïsme** [erɔism] *nm* heroism.
hésiter [ezite] *vi* to hesitate (**sur** over, about; **entre** between; **à faire** to do); (*en parlant*) to falter, hesitate. ●**hésitant, -ante** *a* (*personne*) hesitant; (*pas, voix*) unsteady, faltering, wavering. ●**hésitation** *nf* hesitation; **avec h.** hesitantly.
hétéroclite [eterɔklit] *a* (*disparate*) motley.
hétérogène [eterɔʒɛn] *a* diverse, heterogeneous.
hêtre ['ɛtr] *nm* (*arbre, bois*) beech.
heu! ['ø] *int* (*hésitation*) er!
heure [œr] *nf* (*mesure*) hour; (*moment*) time; **quelle h. est-il?** what time is it?; **il est six heures** it's six (o'clock); **six heures moins cinq** five to six; **six heures cinq** *Br* five past six, *Am* five after six; **à l'h.** (*arriver*) on time; (*être payé*) by the hour; **dix kilomètres à l'h.** ten kilometres an hour; **à l'h. qu'il est** (by) now; **de bonne h.** early; **nouvelle de dernière h.** latest *ou* last-minute news; **à une h. avancée (de la nuit)** at a late hour, late at night; **tout à l'h.** (*futur*) in a few moments, later; (*passé*) a moment ago; **à tout à l'h.!** (*au revoir*) see you soon!; **à toute h.** (*continuellement*) at all hours; **24 heures sur 24** 24 hours a day; **d'h. en h.** hourly, hour by hour; **faire des heures supplémentaires** to work *ou* do overtime; **heures creuses** off-peak *ou* slack periods; **l'h. d'affluence, l'h. de pointe** (*circulation etc*) (the) rush hour; (*dans les magasins*) (the) peak period; **l'h. de pointe** (*électricité etc*) (the) peak period; **h. d'été** summer time.
heureux, -euse [œrø, -øz] *a* happy; (*chanceux*) lucky, fortunate; (*issue, changement*) successful; (*expression, choix*) apt; **h. de qch/de voir qn** (*satisfait*) happy *ou* pleased *ou* glad about sth/to see s.o.; **je suis h. que vous puissiez venir** I'm happy *ou* pleased *ou* glad you can come ▌ *adv* (*vivre, mourir*) happily. ●**heureusement** *adv* (*par chance*) fortunately, luckily, happily (**pour** for); (*avec succès*) successfully; (*exprimer*) aptly.

heurt [‘œr] nm bump, knock; (d'opinions etc) Fig clash; **sans heurts** smoothly.

heurter vt (cogner) to hit, knock, bump (**contre** against); (mur, piéton) to bump into, hit; **h. qn** (choquer) to offend s.o., upset s.o.; **se h. à** to bump into, hit; (difficultés) Fig to come up against. ●**heurté, -ée** a (couleurs, tons) clashing; (style, rythme) jerky. ●**heurtoir** nm (door) knocker.

hexagone [ɛgzagɔn] nm hexagon; **l'H.** Fig France. ●**hexagonal, -e, -aux** a hexagonal; (français) Fam French.

hiatus [jatys] nm Fig hiatus, gap.

hiberner [ibɛrne] vi to hibernate. ●**hibernation** nf hibernation.

hibou, -x [ibu] nm owl.

hic [‘ik] nm **voilà le h.** Fam that's the snag.

hideux, -euse [idø, -øz] a hideous.

hier [(i)jɛr] adv & nm yesterday; **h. soir** last ou yesterday night, yesterday evening; **ça ne date pas d'h.** that's been going on for quite a while; **elle n'est pas née d'h.** Fig she wasn't born yesterday.

hiérarchie [‘jerarʃi] nf hierarchy. ●**hiérarchique** a (ordre) hierarchical; **par la voie h.** through (the) official channels. ●**hiérarchiser** vt (emploi, valeurs) to grade.

hi-fi [‘ifi] a inv & nf inv hi-fi.

hilare [ilar] a merry. ●**hilarant, -ante** a (drôle) hilarious. ●**hilarité** nf (sudden) laughter.

hindou, -oue [ɛ̃du] a Hindu ∎ nmf Hindu.

hippie [‘ipi] nmf hippie.

hippique [ipik] a **concours h.** horse show, show-jumping event. ●**hippodrome** nm racecourse, racetrack (for horses).

hippopotame [ipɔpɔtam] nm hippopotamus.

hirondelle [irɔ̃dɛl] nf (oiseau) swallow.

hirsute [irsyt] a (personne, barbe) unkempt, shaggy.

hispanique [ispanik] a Spanish, Hispanic ∎ nmf H. (aux États-Unis) Hispanic.

hisser [‘ise] vt (voile, drapeau, fardeau etc) to hoist, raise ∎ **se hisser** vpr to raise oneself (up).

histoire [istwar] nf (science, événements) history; (récit) story; (affaire) Fam business, matter; **des histoires** Fam (mensonges) lies, stories; (façons, chichis) fuss; **faire des histoires à qn** Fam to cause s.o. trouble; **toute une h.** Fam (problème) quite a lot of trouble; (chichis) quite a lot of fuss; **h. de voir/etc** Fam (so as) to see/etc; **h. de rire** Fam for (the sake of) a laugh; **sans histoires** (voyage etc) uneventful.

historien, -ienne [istɔrjɛ̃, -jɛn] nmf historian.

historique [istɔrik] a historical; (lieu, événement) historic ∎ nm **faire l'h. de** to give an historical account of.

hiver [ivɛr] nm winter. ●**hivernal, -e, -aux** a froid/etc **h.** winter ou wint(e)ry cold/etc.

HLM [‘aʃɛlɛm] nm ou f abrév (habitation à loyer modéré) Br = council flats, Am = low-rent apartment building (sponsored by government).

hocher [‘ɔʃe] vt **h. la tête** (pour dire oui) to nod one's head; (pour dire non) to shake one's head. ●**hochement** nm **h. de tête** nod; (pour dire non) shake of the head.

hochet [‘ɔʃɛ] nm (jouet) rattle.

hockey [‘ɔkɛ] nm hockey; **h. sur glace** ice hockey; **h. sur gazon** field hockey.

holà! [‘ɔla] int (arrêtez) hold on!, stop!; (pour appeler) hello! ∎ nm inv **mettre le h. à qch** to put a stop to sth.

hold-up [‘ɔldœp] nm inv (attaque) holdup, Fam stick-up.

Hollande [‘ɔlɑ̃d] nf Holland. ●**hollandais, -aise** a Dutch ∎ nmf H. Dutchman; Hollandaise Dutchwoman; **les H.** the Dutch ∎ nm (langue) Dutch.

holocauste [ɔlɔkost] nm (massacre) holocaust.

homard [‘ɔmar] nm lobster.

homélie [ɔmeli] nf homily.

homéopathie [ɔmeɔpati] nf hom(o)eopathy.

homicide [ɔmisid] nm murder, homicide; **h. involontaire** ou **par imprudence** manslaughter; **h. volontaire** murder.

hommage [ɔmaʒ] nm tribute, homage (**à** to); **rendre h. à** to pay (a) tribute to, pay homage to; **faire qch en h. à qn/qch** to do sth as a tribute to s.o. ou in homage to s.o.; **présenter ses hommages à une femme** to pay one's respects to a lady.

homme [ɔm] nm man (pl men); **l'h.** (espèce) man(kind); **des vêtements d'h.** men's clothes; **d'h. à h.** man to man; **l'h. de la rue** Fig the man in the street; **h. d'affaires** businessman; **les grands hommes** great men; **il n'est pas h. à vous laisser tomber** he's not the sort of man to let you down. ●**homme-grenouille** nm (pl **hommes-grenouilles**) frogman.

homogène [ɔmɔʒɛn] a homogeneous. ●**homogénéité** nf homogeneity.

homologue [ɔmɔlɔg] a equivalent (**de** to) ∎ nmf counterpart, opposite number.

homologuer [ɔmɔlɔge] vt to approve ou re-cognize officially, validate.

homonyme [ɔmɔnim] nm (mot) homonym; (personne, lieu) namesake.

homosexuel, -elle [ɔmɔsɛksɥɛl] a & nmf homosexual. ●**homosexualité** nf homosexuality.

Hongrie [‘ɔ̃gri] nf Hungary. ●**hongrois, -oise** a Hungarian ∎ nmf H., Hongroise Hungarian ∎ nm (langue) Hungarian.

honnête [ɔnɛt] a (intègre) honest, (satisfaisant, raisonnable) decent, fair. ●**honnêtement** adv honestly; (raisonnablement) decently. ●**honnêteté** nf honesty.

honneur [ɔnœr] nm (dignité, faveur) honour; (mérite) credit; **en l'h. de** in honour of; **faire h. à** (sa famille etc) to be a credit to; (par sa présence) to do honour to; (promesse etc) to honour; (repas) Fam to do justice to; **être à l'h.** to have the place of honour; **invité d'h.** guest of honour; **membre d'h.** honorary member; **donner sa parole d'h.** to give one's word of honour; **avoir la place d'h.** to have pride of place *ou* the place of honour.

honorable [ɔnɔrabl] *a* honourable; (*résultat, salaire etc*) *Fig* respectable. ● **honorabilité** *nf* respectability.

honoraire [ɔnɔrɛr] *a* (*membre*) honorary. ● **honoraires** *nmpl* (*d'avocat etc*) fees.

honorer [ɔnɔre] *vt* to honour (**de** with); **h. qn** (*conduite etc*) to do credit to s.o.; **s'h. d'être** *a* to pride oneself *ou* itself on being. ● **honorifique** *a* (*titre*) honorary.

honte [ˈɔt] *nf* shame; **avoir h.** to be *ou* feel ashamed (**de qch/de faire** of sth/to do *ou* of doing); **faire h. à qn** to put s.o. to shame; **sans fausse h.** unselfconsciously, quite openly. ● **honteux, -euse** *a* (*confus*) ashamed, shamefaced; (*scandaleux*) shameful; **être h. de** to be ashamed of. ● **honteusement** *adv* shamefully.

hop! [ˈɔp] *int* **allez, h.!** jump!, move!; (*pars*) off you go!

hôpital, -aux [ɔpital, -o] *nm* hospital; **à l'h.** *Br* in hospital, *Am* in the hospital.

hoquet [ɔkɛ] *nm* hiccup; **avoir le h.** to have (the) hiccups. ● **hoqueter** *vi* to hiccup.

horaire [ɔrɛr] *a* (*salaire etc*) hourly; (*vitesse*) per hour ▮ *nm* timetable, schedule.

horde [ˈɔrd] *nf* (*troupe*) *Péj* horde.

horizon [ɔrizɔ̃] *nm* horizon; (*vue, paysage*) view; **à l'h.** on the horizon.

horizontal, -e, -aux [ɔrizɔ̃tal, -o] *a* horizontal. ● **horizontalement** *adv* horizontally.

horloge [ɔrlɔʒ] *nf* clock. ● **horloger, -ère** *nmf* watchmaker. ● **horlogerie** *nf* (*magasin*) watchmaker's (shop); (*industrie*) watchmaking.

hormis [ˈɔrmi] *prép* *Litt* save, except (for).

hormone [ɔrmɔn] *nf* hormone. ● **hormonal, -e, -aux** *a* **traitement/etc h.** hormone treatment/etc.

horoscope [ɔrɔskɔp] *nm* horoscope.

horreur [ɔrœr] *nf* horror; **des horreurs** (*propos*) horrible things; **faire h. à** to disgust; **avoir h. de** to hate, loathe; **quelle h.!** how revolting!, how awful!

horrible [ɔribl] *a* horrible, awful. ● **horriblement** *adv* horribly.

horrifiant, -ante [ɔrifjɑ̃, -ɑ̃t] *a* horrifying, horrific. ● **horrifié, -ée** *a* horrified.

horripiler [ɔripile] *vt* to exasperate.

hors [ˈɔr] *prép* **h. de** (*maison, boîte etc*) out of, outside; (*danger, haleine etc*) *Fig* out of; **h. de doute** beyond doubt; **h. de soi** (*furieux*) beside oneself; **être h. concours** to be non-competing, not to be in the competition; **être h. jeu** *Football* to be offside. ● **hors-bord** *nm inv* speedboat; **moteur h.-bord** outboard motor. ● **hors-d'œuvre** *nm inv* (*plat*) hors-d'œuvre, starter. ● **hors-jeu** *nm inv* *Football* offside. ● **hors-la-loi** *nm inv* outlaw. ● **hors service** *a inv* (*appareil etc*) out of order. ● **hors-taxe** *a inv* (*magasin, objet*) duty-free.

hortensia [ɔrtɑ̃sja] *nm* (*arbrisseau*) hydrangea.

horticulteur, -trice [ɔrtikyltœr, -tris] *nmf* horticulturalist. ● **horticole** *a* horticultural. ● **horticulture** *nf* horticulture.

hospice [ɔspis] *nm* (*pour vieillards*) geriatric hospital.

hospitalier, -ière [ɔspitalje, -jɛr] *a* **1** (*accueillant*) hospitable. **2 personnel/etc h.** hospital staff/etc; **centre h.** hospital (complex). ● **hospitaliser** *vt* to hospitalize. ● **hospitalité** *nf* hospitality.

hostie [ɔsti] *nf* (*pain*) *Rel* host.

hostile [ɔstil] *a* hostile (**à** to, towards). ● **hostilité** *nf* hostility (**envers** to, towards); **hostilités** *Mil* hostilities.

hôte [ot] **1** *nm* (*qui reçoit*) host. **2** *nmf* (*invité*) guest. ● **hôtesse** *nf* hostess; **h. (de l'air)** (air) hostess.

hôtel [otɛl] *nm* hotel; **h. particulier** mansion, town house; **h. de ville** *Br* town hall, *Am* city hall; **h. des ventes** auction rooms; **h. des impôts** (main) tax office. ● **hôtelier, -ière** *nmf* hotel-keeper, hotelier ▮ *a* **industrie/etc hôtelière** hotel industry/etc. ● **hôtellerie** *nf* **1** (*auberge*) inn, hostelry. **2** (*métier*) hotel trade.

hotte [ˈɔt] *nf* **1** (*panier*) basket (*carried on back*); **la h. du Père Noël** *Br* Father Christmas's sack, *Am* Santa's sack. **2** (*de cheminée etc*) hood; **h. (aspirante)** hood (*over Br cooker or Am stove*).

houblon [ˈublɔ̃] *nm* **le h.** (*plante*) hops.

houille [ˈuj] *nf* coal; **h. blanche** hydro-electric power. ● **houiller, -ère** *a* **bassin h.** coalfield; **industrie/etc houillère** coal industry/etc ▮ *nf* **houillère** coalmine, *Br* colliery.

houle [ˈul] *nf* (*de mer*) swell, surge. ● **houleux, -euse** *a* (*mer*) rough; (*réunion etc*) *Fig* stormy.

houlette [ulɛt] *nf* **sous la h. de qn** *Fig* under the leadership *ou* stewardship of s.o.

houppette [ˈupɛt] *nf* powder puff.

hourra [ˈura] *nm & int* hurray, hurrah.

houspiller [ˈuspije] *vt* to scold, upbraid.

housse [ˈus] *nf* (protective) cover.

houx [ˈu] *nm* holly.

HS [aʃɛs] *a inv* *abrév* (*hors service*) (*personne*) *Fam* out of commission.

hublot [ˈyblo] *nm* (*de navire, d'avion*) porthole.

huche [ˈyʃ] *nf* **h. à pain** bread box *ou* chest.

hue! [ˈy] *int* gee up! (*to horse*).

huer [ˈɥe] *vt* to boo. ● **huées** *nfpl* boos.

huile [ɥil] *nf* **1** oil; **huiles essentielles** essential *ou* plant oils; **peinture à l'h.** oil painting; **mer d'h.** *Fig* dead calm sea; **jeter de l'h. sur le feu** *Fig* to add fuel to the flames; **h. de coude** *Fam* elbow grease. **2** (*personnage*) *Fam* bigshot. ● **huiler** *vt* to oil. ● **huileux, -euse** *a* oily.

huis [ɥi] *nm* **à h. clos** *Jur* in camera.

huissier [ɥisje] *nm* **1** (*introducteur*) usher. **2** (*officier*) *Jur* bailiff.

huit [ˈɥit] *a* ([ˈɥi] *before consonant*) eight; **h. jours a week** ▮ *nm* eight; **dimanche/etc en h.** *Br* a week on Sunday/etc, *Am* a week from Sunday/etc. ● **huitaine** *nf* (about) eight; (*se-*

maine) week; **une h. (de)** about eight. ● **hui-tième** *a* & *nmf* eighth; **un h.** an eighth; **être en h. de finale** *Sport* to be in the last sixteen.

huître [ɥitr] *nf* oyster.

hululer ['ylyle] *vi* (*hibou*) to hoot.

humain, -aine [ymɛ̃, -ɛn] *a* human; (*compa-tissant*) humane **I** *nmpl* **les humains** humans. ● **humainement** *adv* (*possible etc*) humanly; (*avec humanité*) humanely. ● **humaniser** *vt* (*prison, ville etc*) to humanize, make more humane. ● **humanitaire** *a* humanitarian. ● **hu-manité** *nf* (*genre humain, sentiment*) human-ity.

humble [œbl] *a* humble. ● **humblement** [-əmɑ̃] *adv* humbly.

humecter [ymɛkte] *vt* to moisten, damp(en).

humer ['yme] *vt* (*respirer*) to breathe in; (*sentir*) to smell.

humeur [ymœr] *nf* (*caprice*) mood, humour; (*caractère*) temperament; (*irritation*) bad temper; **bonne h.** (*gaieté*) good humour; **être/mettre qn de bonne/mauvaise h.** to be/ put s.o. in a good/bad mood; **d'h. égale** even-tempered.

humide [ymid] *a* damp, wet; (*saison, route*) wet; (*main, yeux*) moist; **climat/temps h.** (*chaud*) humid climate/weather; (*froid, plu-vieux*) damp *ou* wet climate/weather. ● **humi-difier** *vt* to humidify. ● **humidité** *nf* humidity; (*plutôt froide*) damp(ness); (*vapeur*) moisture.

humilier [ymilje] *vt* to humiliate, humble. ● **humiliant, -ante** *a* humiliating. ● **humilia-tion** *nf* humiliation. ● **humilité** *nf* humility.

humour [ymur] *nm* humour; **avoir de l'h.** *ou* **beaucoup d'h.** *ou* **le sens de l'h.** to have a sense of humour; **h. noir** black *ou* sick hu-mour. ● **humoriste** *nmf* humorist. ● **humo-ristique** *a* (*ton etc*) humorous.

huppé, -ée ['ype] *a* (*riche*) *Fam* high-class, posh.

hurler ['yrle] *vi* (*loup, vent*) to howl; (*personne*) to scream, yell (out); **h. avec les loups** *Fig* to follow the herd *ou* the crowd **I** *vt* (*slogans, injures etc*) to scream, yell out. ● **hurlement** *nm* howl; (*de personne*) scream, yell.

hurluberlu [yrlyberly] *nm* eccentric scatter-brain.

hutte ['yt] *nf* hut.

hybride [ibrid] *a* & *nm* hybrid.

hydrater [idrate] *vt* (*peau*) to moisturize; **crème hydratante** moisturizing cream.

hydraulique [idrolik] *a* hydraulic.

hydravion [idravjɔ̃] *nm* seaplane.

hydrocarbure [idrokarbyr] *nm* hydrocarbon.

hydro-électrique [idroelɛktrik] *a* hydro-electric.

hydrogène [idrɔʒɛn] *nm* hydrogen.

hydrophile [idrofil] *a* **coton h.** *Br* cotton wool, *Am* (absorbent) cotton.

hyène [jɛn] *nf* (*animal*) hyena.

hygiaphone [iʒjafon] *nm* (hygienic) grill (*for speaking through in booking office etc*).

hygiène [iʒjɛn] *nf* hygiene. ● **hygiénique** *a* hygienic; (*serviette, conditions*) sanitary; (*promenade*) healthy; **papier h.** toilet paper.

hymne [imn] *nm* Rel Littér hymn; **h. national** national anthem.

hyper- [iper] *préf* hyper-.

hypermarché [ipermarʃe] *nm* hypermarket.

hypermétrope [ipermetrop] *a* & *nmf* long-sighted (person).

hypertension [ipertɑ̃sjɔ̃] *nf* **h. artérielle** high blood pressure; **faire de l'h.** to have high blood pressure.

hypnose [ipnoz] *nf* hypnosis. ● **hypnotique** *a* hypnotic. ● **hypnotiser** *vt* to hypnotize. ● **hypnotiseur** *nm* hypnotist. ● **hypnotisme** *nm* hypnotism.

hypoallergénique [ipoalerʒenik] *a* hypo-allergenic.

hypocalorique [ipokalɔrik] *a* (*régime, ali-ment etc*) low-calorie, calorie-reduced.

hypocondriaque [ipokɔ̃drijak] *a* & *nmf* hypochondriac.

hypocrisie [ipokrizi] *nf* hypocrisy. ● **hypo-crite** *a* hypocritical **I** *nmf* hypocrite. ● **hypo-critement** *adv* hypocritically.

hypodermique [ipodermik] *a* hypodermic.

hypokhâgne [ipokaɲ] *nf* Scol Fam = first-year arts class preparing to compete for en-trance to the *École normale supérieure*.

hypothèque [ipotek] *nf* mortgage. ● **hypothéquer** *vt* (*maison, Fig avenir*) to mortgage.

hypothèse [ipotez] *nf* (*supposition*) assump-tion; (*en sciences*) hypothesis; **dans l'h. où...** supposing (that).... ● **hypothétique** *a* hypothetical.

hystérie [isteri] *nf* hysteria. ● **hystérique** *a* hysterical.

I

I, i [i] *nm* I, i.

iceberg [isbɛrg, ajsbɛrg] *nm* iceberg.

ici [isi] *adv* here; **par i.** (*passer*) this way; (*habiter*) around here, hereabouts; **jusqu'i.** (*temps*) up to now; (*lieu*) as far as this *ou* here; **d'i. à mardi** by Tuesday, between now and Tuesday; **d'i. à une semaine** within a week; **d'i. peu** before long; **i. Dupont!** (*au téléphone*) this is Dupont!, Dupont speaking!; **je ne suis pas d'i.** I'm a stranger around here; **les gens d'i.** the people (from) around here, the locals. ● **ici-bas** *adv* on earth.

icône [ikon] *nf* Rel & Ordinat icon.

idéal, -e, -aux *ou* **-als** [ideal, -o] *a & nm* ideal; **l'i.** (*valeurs spirituelles*) ideals; **c'est l'i.** *Fam* that's the ideal thing. ● **idéalement** *adv* ideally. ● **idéaliser** *vt* to idealize. ● **idéalisme** *nm* idealism. ● **idéaliste** *a* idealistic ▮ *nmf* idealist.

idée [ide] *nf* idea (de of, que that); **i. fixe** obsession; **changer d'i.** to change one's mind; **il m'est venu à l'i. que** it occurred to me that; **se faire une i.** de to imagine, get *ou* have an idea of; **se faire des idées** *Fam* to imagine things; **avoir dans l'i. de faire qch** to have it in mind to do sth; **avoir son i. sur qch** to have one's own idea(s) *ou* opinion(s) about sth; **avoir des idées** *Fam* to be full of good ideas; **avoir des idées noires** (*de suicide*) to be suicidal, have black thoughts; (*le cafard*) to be depressed; **avoir une i. derrière la tête** to have an idea at the back of one's mind.

idem [idɛm] *adv* ditto.

identifier [idãtifje] *vt* to identify (à, avec with); **s'i. à** *ou* **avec** to identify (oneself) with. ● **identification** *nf* identification.

identique [idãtik] *a* identical (à to, with).

identité [idãtite] *nf* identity; **carte d'i** identity card.

idéologie [ideɔlɔʒi] *nf* ideology. ● **idéologique** *a* ideological.

idiome [idjom] *nm* (*langue*) idiom. ● **idiomatique** *a* idiomatic.

idiot, -ote [idjo, -ɔt] *a* silly, idiotic ▮ *nmf* idiot. ● **idiotie** [-ɔsi] *nf* (*état*) idiocy; **une i.** a silly *ou* an idiotic thing.

idole [idɔl] *nf* idol; **être l'i. des jeunes** *Fig* to be a teenage idol. ● **idolâtrer** *vt* *Litt* to idolize.

idylle [idil] *nf* (*amourette*) romance.

idyllique [idilik] *a* (*merveilleux*) idyllic.

if [if] *nm* yew (tree).

IFOP [ifɔp] *nm* abrév (*Institut français d'opinion publique*) (French) market and opinion research institute.

igloo [iglu] *nm* igloo.

ignare [iɲar] *a* Péj ignorant ▮ *nmf* ignoramus.

ignifugé, -ée [iɲifyʒe] *a* fireproof(ed).

ignoble [iɲɔbl] *a* vile, revolting.

ignorant, -ante [iɲɔrɑ̃] *a* ignorant (de of). ● **ignorance** *nf* ignorance.

ignorer [iɲɔre] *vt* not to know, be ignorant of; **j'ignore si** I don't know if; **je n'ignore pas les difficultés** I am not unaware of the difficulties; **i. qn** (*être indifférent à*) to ignore s.o., cold-shoulder s.o. ● **ignoré, -ée** *a* (*inconnu*) unknown.

il [il] *pron m* (*personne*) he; (*chose, animal, impersonnel*) it; **il est** he is; it is; **il pleut** it's raining; **il est vrai que** it's true that; **il y a** there is; *pl* there are; **il y a six ans** (*temps écoulé*) six years ago; **il y a une heure qu'il travaille** (*durée*) he has been working for an hour; **qu'est-ce qu'il y a?** what's the matter?, what's wrong?; **il n'y a pas de quoi!** don't mention it!; **il doit/peut y avoir** there must/may be.

île [il] *nf* island; **les îles Britanniques** the British Isles.

illégal, -e, -aux [il(l)egal, -o] *a* illegal. ● **illégalité** *nf* illegality.

illégitime [il(l)eʒitim] *a* (*enfant, revendication*) illegitimate; (*non fondé*) unfounded.

illettré, -ée [il(l)etre] *a & nmf* illiterate.

illicite [il(l)isit] *a* unlawful, illicit.

illico [il(l)iko] *adv* **i.** (*presto*) *Fam* straightaway.

illimité, -ée [il(l)imite] *a* unlimited.

illisible [il(l)izibl] *a* (*écriture*) illegible; (*livre*) unreadable.

illogique [il(l)ɔʒik] *a* illogical.

illuminer [il(l)ymine] *vt* to light up, illuminate ▮ **s'illuminer** *vpr* (*visage, personne, ciel*) to light up. ● **illuminé, -ée** *a* (*monument*) floodlit, lit up. ● **illumination** *nf* (*action, lumière*) illumination.

illusion [il(l)yzjɔ̃] *nf* illusion (sur about); **i. d'optique** optical illusion; **se faire des illusions** to delude oneself (sur about). ● **s'illusionner** *vpr* to delude oneself (sur about). ● **illusionniste** *nmf* conjurer. ● **illusoire** *a* illusory, illusive.

illustre [il(l)ystr] *a* famous, illustrious.

illustrer [il(l)ystre] *vt* (*d'images, par des exemples*) to illustrate (de with) ▮ **s'illustrer** *vpr* to become famous. ● **illustré, -ée** *a* (*livre, magazine*) illustrated ▮ *nm* (*périodique*) Br comic, Am comic book. ● **illustration** *nf* illustration.

îlot [ilo] *nm* **1** (*île*) small island. **2** (*maisons*) block.

ils [il] *pron mpl* they; **ils sont** they are.

image [imaʒ] *nf* picture; (*ressemblance, symbole*) image; (*dans une glace*) reflection; **i. de marque** (*de firme etc*) (public) image; **i. de synthèse** *Ordinat* computer generated image. ● **imagé, -ée** *a* (*style*) colourful, full of imagery.

imaginable [imaʒinabl] *a* imaginable. ● **imaginaire** *a* imaginary. ● **imaginatif, -ive** *a* imaginative.

imagination [imaʒinɑsjɔ̃] *nf* imagination; **des imaginations** *Litt* imaginings.

imaginer [imaʒine] *vt* (*envisager, supposer*) to imagine; (*inventer*) to devise ∎ **s'imaginer** *vpr* (*se figurer*) to imagine (**que** that); (*se voir*) to picture ou imagine oneself.

imbattable [ɛ̃batabl] *a* unbeatable.

imbécile [ɛ̃besil] *a* idiotic ∎ *nmf* idiot, imbecile. ● **imbécillité** *nf* (*état*) imbecility; **une i.** (*action, parole*) an idiotic thing.

imberbe [ɛ̃bɛrb] *a* beardless.

imbiber [ɛ̃bibe] *vt* to soak (**de** with, in) ∎ **s'imbiber** *vpr* to become soaked.

imbriquer (s') [sɛ̃brike] *vpr* (*questions etc*) to overlap, be interconnected ou bound up with each other.

imbroglio [ɛ̃brɔɡlijo] *nm* muddle, foul-up.

imbu, -ue [ɛ̃by] *a* **i.** de imbued with.

imbuvable [ɛ̃byvabl] *a* undrinkable; (*personne*) *Fam* insufferable.

imiter [imite] *vt* to imitate; (*contrefaire*) to forge; **i. qn** (*pour rire*) to mimic s.o., take s.o. off; (*faire comme*) to do the same as s.o., follow suit. ● **imitateur, -trice** *nmf* imitator; (*artiste de théâtre*) impersonator, mimic. ● **imitatif, -ive** *a* imitative. ● **imitation** *nf* imitation.

immaculé, -ée [imakyle] *a* (*sans tache, sans péché*) immaculate.

immangeable [ɛ̃mɑ̃ʒabl] *a* inedible.

immanquable [ɛ̃mɑ̃kabl] *a* inevitable.

immatriculer [imatrikyle] *vt* to register; **se faire i.** to register. ● **immatriculation** *nf* registration.

immédiat, -ate [imedja, -at] *a* immediate ∎ *nm* **dans l'i.** for the time being. ● **immédiatement** *adv* immediately.

immense [imɑ̃s] *a* immense, vast. ● **immensément** *adv* immensely. ● **immensité** *nf* immensity, vastness.

immerger [imɛrʒe] *vt* to immerse, put under water ∎ **s'immerger** *vpr* (*sous-marin*) to submerge. ● **immersion** *nf* immersion; (*de sous-marin*) submersion; **séjour linguistique en i. totale** period abroad consisting of total immersion in a foreign language.

immettable [ɛ̃metabl] *a* (*vêtement*) unfit to be worn.

immeuble [imœbl] *nm* building; (*d'habitation*) *Br* block of flats, *Am* apartment building; (*de bureaux*) office building, *Br* office block.

immigrer [imigre] *vi* to immigrate. ● **immigrant, -ante** *nmf* immigrant. ● **immigré, -ée** *a & nmf* immigrant; **travailleur i.** immigrant

worker. ● **immigration** *nf* immigration.

imminent, -ente [iminɑ̃, -ɑ̃t] *a* imminent. ● **imminence** *nf* imminence.

immiscer (s') [simise] *vpr* to interfere (**dans** in).

immobile [imɔbil] *a* still, motionless. ● **immobiliser** *vt* to bring to a stop, immobilize; (*arrêter*) to stop ∎ **s'immobiliser** *vpr* to come to a stop ou a standstill. ● **immobilité** *nf* stillness; (*inactivité*) immobility.

immobilier, -ière [imɔbilje, -jɛr] *a* **marché/ etc i.** property market/*etc*; **vente immobilière** sale of property; **agence immobilière** *Br* estate agency, *Am* real estate office; **agent i.** *Br* estate agent, *Am* real estate agent.

immodéré, -ée [imɔdere] *a* immoderate.

immoler [i(m)mɔle] *vt* (*sacrifier*) *Litt* to sacrifice. ∎ **s'immoler** *vpr* **s'i. par le feu** (*se suicider*) to set fire to oneself.

immonde [i(m)mɔ̃d] *a* filthy. ● **immondices** *nfpl* refuse, *Br* rubbish, *Am* garbage.

immoral, -e, -aux [i(m)mɔral, -o] *a* immoral. ● **immoralité** *nf* immorality.

immortel, -elle [i(m)mɔrtɛl] *a* immortal; **les Immortels** (*académiciens*) the members of the *Académie Française*. ● **immortaliser** *vt* to immortalize. ● **immortalité** *nf* immortality.

immuable [i(m)mɥabl] *a* immutable, unchanging.

immuniser [i(m)mynize] *vt* to immunize (**contre** against); **immunisé contre** (*à l'abri de*) *Méd & Fig* immune to ou from. ● **immunitaire** *a* (*déficience, système etc*) *Méd* immune. ● **immunité** *nf* immunity; **i. parlementaire** parliamentary immunity.

impact [ɛ̃pakt] *nm* impact (**sur** on).

impair, -e [ɛ̃pɛr] *1 a* (*nombre*) odd, uneven. *2 nm* (*maladresse*) blunder.

imparable [ɛ̃parabl] *a* (*coup etc*) unavoidable.

impardonnable [ɛ̃pardɔnabl] *a* unforgivable.

imparfait, -aite [ɛ̃parfɛ, -ɛt] *1 a* (*connaissance etc*) imperfect. *2 nm* (*temps*) *Grammaire* imperfect.

impartial, -e, -aux [ɛ̃parsjal, -o] *a* fair, impartial, unbiased. ● **impartialité** *nf* impartiality.

impartir [ɛ̃partir] *vt* to grant (**à** to); **dans le temps qui nous est imparti** within the stipulated time ou the time allowed.

impasse [ɛ̃pɑs] *nf* (*rue*) dead end, blind alley; (*situation*) *Fig* stalemate, impasse; **dans l'i.** (*négociations*) in deadlock.

impassible [ɛ̃pasibl] *a* impassive, unmoved. ● **impassibilité** *nf* impassiveness.

impatient, -ente [ɛ̃pasjɑ̃, -ɑ̃t] *a* impatient; **i. de faire** eager ou impatient to do. ● **impatiemment** [-amɑ̃] *adv* impatiently. ● **impatience** *nf* impatience. ● **impatienter** *vt* to annoy, make impatient ∎ **s'impatienter** *vpr* to get impatient.

impavide [ɛ̃pavid] *a* *Litt* impassive.

impayable [ɛ̃pɛjabl] *a* (*comique*) *Fam* hilarious, priceless.

impayé, -ée [ɛ̃peje] *a* unpaid.

impeccable [ɛ̃pekabl] *a* (*propre*) immaculate, impeccable. ●**impeccablement** [-əmɑ̃] *adv* impeccably, immaculately.

impénétrable [ɛ̃penetrabl] *a* (*forêt, mystère etc*) impenetrable.

impénitent, -ente [ɛ̃penitɑ̃, -ɑ̃t] *a* unrepentant.

impensable [ɛ̃pɑ̃sabl] *a* unthinkable.

imper [ɛ̃pɛr] *nm Fam* raincoat, *Br* mac.

impératif, -ive [ɛ̃peratif, -iv] *a* (*consigne, ton*) imperative ‖ *nm* (*mode*) *Grammaire* imperative.

impératrice [ɛ̃peratris] *nf* empress.

imperceptible [ɛ̃persɛptibl] *a* imperceptible (à to).

imperfection [ɛ̃pɛrfɛksjɔ̃] *nf* imperfection.

impérial, -e, -aux [ɛ̃perjal, -o] *a* imperial. ●**impérialisme** *nm* imperialism.

impériale [ɛ̃perjal] *nf* (*d'autobus*) top deck; **autobus à i.** double-decker (bus).

impérieux, -euse [ɛ̃perjø, -øz] *a* (*autoritaire*) imperious; (*besoin*) pressing, imperative.

imperméable [ɛ̃pɛrmeabl] 1 *a* impervious (à to); (*tissu, manteau*) waterproof. 2 *nm* raincoat, *Br* mackintosh. ●**imperméabilisé, -ée** *a* waterproof.

impersonnel, -elle [ɛ̃pɛrsɔnɛl] *a* impersonal.

impertinent, -ente [ɛ̃pɛrtinɑ̃, -ɑ̃t] *a* impertinent (envers to). ●**impertinence** *nf* impertinence.

imperturbable [ɛ̃pɛrtyrbabl] *a* (*personne*) unruffled, imperturbable.

impétueux, -euse [ɛ̃petɥø, -øz] *a* impetuous. ●**impétuosité** *nf* impetuosity.

impie [ɛ̃pi] *a Litt* ungodly, impious.

impitoyable [ɛ̃pitwajabl] *a* ruthless, pitiless, merciless.

implacable [ɛ̃plakabl] *a* implacable, relentless.

implant [ɛ̃plɑ̃] *nm* (*dentaire*) implant; **faire des implants** (*cheveux*) to have hair grafts.

implanter [ɛ̃plɑ̃te] *vt* (*industrie, mode etc*) to establish ‖ **s'implanter** *vpr* to become established. ●**implantation** *nf* establishment.

implicite [ɛ̃plisit] *a* implicit. ●**implicitement** *adv* implicitly.

impliquer [ɛ̃plike] *vt* (*entraîner*) to imply; **i. que** (*supposer*) to imply that; **i. qn** (*engager*) to implicate s.o. (dans in). ●**implication** *nf* (*conséquence, participation*) implication.

implorer [ɛ̃plɔre] *vt* to implore (qn de faire s.o. to do).

impoli, -ie [ɛ̃pɔli] *a* rude, impolite. ●**impolitesse** *nf* impoliteness, rudeness; **une i.** an act of rudeness.

impondérables [ɛ̃pɔ̃derabl] *nmpl* imponderables.

impopulaire [ɛ̃pɔpylɛr] *a* unpopular.

important, -ante [ɛ̃pɔrtɑ̃, -ɑ̃t] *a* (*personnage, événement etc*) important; (*quantité, somme etc*) large, considerable; (*dégâts, retard*) considerable, great ‖ *nm* **l'i.,**

c'est de... the important thing is to....
●**importance** *nf* importance, significance; (*taille*) size; (*de dégâts*) extent; **attacher de l'i. à qch** to attach importance to sth; **ça n'a pas d'i.** it doesn't matter.

importer [ɛ̃pɔrte] 1 *v imp* to matter, be important (à to); **il importe de faire** it's important to do; **peu importe, n'importe** it doesn't matter; **n'importe qui/quoi/où/quand/comment** anyone/anything/anywhere/any time/anyhow.
2 *vt* (*marchandises etc*) to import (de from). ●**importateur, -trice** *nmf* importer ‖ *a* importing. ●**importation** *nf* (*objet*) import; (*action*) import(ing), importation; **d'i.** (*article*) imported.

importun, -une [ɛ̃pɔrtœ̃, -yn] *a* troublesome, intrusive ‖ *nmf* nuisance, intruder. ●**importuner** *vt* to inconvenience, trouble.

imposer [ɛ̃poze] 1 *vt* **i. qch à qn** to impose sth on s.o.; **i. le respect** to command *ou* compel respect ‖ *vi* **en i. à qn** to impress s.o., command *ou* compel respect from s.o. ‖ **s'imposer** *vpr* (*chez qn*) *Péj* to impose; (*s'affirmer*) to assert oneself, compel recognition; (*être nécessaire*) to be essential; (*aller de soi*) to stand out clearly.
2 *vt* (*taxer*) to tax. ●**imposant, -ante** *a* imposing. ●**imposable** *a Fin* taxable. ●**imposition** *nf Fin* taxation.

impossible [ɛ̃pɔsibl] *a* impossible (à faire to do); **il (nous) est i. de faire** it is impossible (for us) to do; **il est i. que** (+ *sub*) it is impossible that; **ça m'est i.** I cannot possibly; **i. n'est pas français** there's no such thing as 'impossible' ‖ *nm* **faire l'i.** to do the impossible. ●**impossibilité** *nf* impossibility.

imposteur [ɛ̃pɔstœr] *nm* impostor. ●**imposture** *nf* deception.

impôt [ɛ̃po] *nm* tax; **impôts** (*contributions*) (income) tax, taxes; **i. sur le revenu** income tax; **impôts locaux** local taxes, *Br* = council tax; **(service des) impôts** tax authorities.

impotent, -ente [ɛ̃pɔtɑ̃, -ɑ̃t] *a* crippled, disabled ‖ *nmf* cripple, invalid.

impraticable [ɛ̃pratikabl] *a* (*chemin etc*) impassable; (*projet etc*) impracticable.

imprécis, -ise [ɛ̃presi, -iz] *a* imprecise. ●**imprécision** *nf* lack of precision.

imprégner [ɛ̃preɲe] *vt* to permeate, saturate, impregnate (de with) ‖ **s'imprégner** *vpr* to become permeated *ou* saturated *ou* impregnated (de with); **imprégné de** (*idées*) imbued *ou* infused with. ●**imprégnation** *nf* saturation.

imprenable [ɛ̃prənabl] *a* (*forteresse etc*) impregnable; **vue i.** unimpeded view; (*belle*) magnificent view.

impresario [ɛ̃presarjo] *nm* (business) manager, impresario.

impression [ɛ̃presjɔ̃] *nf* 1 impression; **avoir l'i. que** to have the feeling *ou* impression that, be under the impression that; **il donne l'i. d'être fatigué** he gives the impression of being tired; **faire (une) bonne i. à qn** to make a good impression on s.o. 2 (*de livre etc*) printing.

impressionner [ɛ̃presjɔne] *vt* (*émouvoir, troubler*) to make a strong impression on; (*influencer*) to impress. ● **impressionnant, -ante** *a* impressive. ● **impressionnable** *a* impressionable.

imprévisible [ɛ̃previzibl] *a* unforeseeable. ● **imprévoyance** *nf* lack of foresight. ● **imprévoyant, -ante** *a* shortsighted. ● **imprévu, -ue** *a* unexpected, unforeseen ▮ *nm* **en cas d'i.** in case of anything unexpected.

imprimer [ɛ̃prime] *vt* **1** (*livre etc*) to print; (*trace*) to impress (**dans** in); (*cachet*) to stamp. **2 i. un mouvement à** *Tech* to impart motion *ou* movement to. ● **imprimante** *nf* (*d'ordinateur*) printer. ● **imprimé** *nm* (*formulaire*) printed form; **imprimé(s)** (*par la poste*) printed matter. ● **imprimerie** *nf* (*technique*) printing; (*lieu*) *Br* printing works, *Am* print shop. ● **imprimeur** *nm* printer.

improbable [ɛ̃prɔbabl] *a* improbable, unlikely. ● **improbabilité** *nf* improbability, unlikelihood.

impromptu, -ue [ɛ̃prɔ̃pty] *a* & *adv* impromptu.

impropre [ɛ̃prɔpr] *a* inappropriate; **i. à qch** unfit for sth; **i. à la consommation** unfit for human consumption. ● **impropriété** *nf* (*incorrection*) *Ling* impropriety.

improviser [ɛ̃prɔvize] *vti* to improvise. ● **improvisation** *nf* improvisation.

improviste (à l') [alɛ̃prɔvist] *adv* unexpectedly; **une visite à l'i.** an unexpected visit; **prendre qn à l'i.** to catch s.o. unawares.

imprudent, -ente [ɛ̃prydɑ̃, -ɑ̃t] *a* (*personne, action*) careless, rash; **il est i. de** it is unwise *ou* foolish to. ● **imprudemment** [-amɑ̃] *adv* carelessly. ● **imprudence** *nf* carelessness, foolishness; **commettre une i.** to do something foolish.

impudent, -ente [ɛ̃pydɑ̃, -ɑ̃t] *a* impudent. ● **impudence** *nf* impudence.

impudique [ɛ̃pydik] *a* lewd.

impuissant, -ante [ɛ̃pɥisɑ̃, -ɑ̃t] *a* helpless; *Méd* impotent; **i. à faire qch** powerless to do sth. ● **impuissance** *nf* helplessness; *Méd* impotence.

impulsif, -ive [ɛ̃pylsif, -iv] *a* impulsive. ● **impulsion** *nf* impulse; **donner une i. à** (*élan*) *Fig* to give an impetus *ou* impulse to.

impunément [ɛ̃pynemɑ̃] *adv* with impunity. ● **impuni, -ie** *a* unpunished.

impur, -e [ɛ̃pyr] *a* impure. ● **impureté** *nf* impurity.

imputer [ɛ̃pyte] *vt* to attribute, impute (**à** to); (*affecter*) to charge (*expenses etc*) (**à** to). ● **imputable** *a* attributable (**à** to). ● **imputation** *nf* (*accusation*) charge, accusation.

inabordable [inabɔrdabl] *a* (*prix*) prohibitive; (*lieu*) inaccessible; (*personne*) unapproachable.

inacceptable [inaksɛptabl] *a* unacceptable.

inaccessible [inaksesibl] *a* inaccessible.

inaccoutumé, -ée [inakutyme] *a* unusual,

unaccustomed.

inachevé, -ée [inaʃve] *a* unfinished.

inactif, -ive [inaktif, -iv] *a* inactive. ● **inaction** *nf* inactivity, inaction. ● **inactivité** *nf* inactivity.

inadapté, -ée [inadapte] *a* (*personne*) maladjusted; (*moyens etc*) unsuited (**à** to); **enfance inadaptée** maladjusted children ▮ *nmf* maladjusted person. ● **inadaptation** *nf* maladjustment.

inadmissible [inadmisibl] *a* unacceptable, inadmissible.

inadvertance (par) [parinadvɛrtɑ̃s] *adv* inadvertently.

inaltérable [inalterabl] *a* (*matière*) that does not deteriorate; (*couleur*) fast; (*sentiment*) unchanging.

inamical, -e, -aux [inamikal, -o] *a* unfriendly.

inanimé, -ée [inanime] *a* (*mort*) lifeless; (*évanoui*) unconscious; (*matière*) inanimate.

inanité [inanite] *nf* (*vanité*) futility.

inanition [inanisjɔ̃] *nf* **mourir d'i.** to die of starvation.

inaperçu, -ue [inapersy] *a* **passer i.** to go unnoticed.

inapplicable [inaplikabl] *a* inapplicable (**à** to).

inappliqué, -ée [inaplike] *a* (*élève etc*) inattentive.

inappréciable [inapresjabl] *a* invaluable.

inapte [inapt] *a* unsuited (**à qch** to sth), inept (**à qch** at sth); (*soldat*) unfit. ● **inaptitude** *nf* ineptitude, incapacity.

inarticulé, -ée [inartikyle] *a* (*son*) inarticulate.

inattaquable [inatakabl] *a* unassailable.

inattendu, -ue [inatɑ̃dy] *a* unexpected.

inattentif, -ive [inatɑ̃tif, -iv] *a* inattentive, careless; **i. à** (*soucis, danger etc*) heedless of. ● **inattention** *nf* lack of attention; **dans un moment d'i.** in a moment of distraction; **faute d'i.** careless mistake, slip.

inaudible [inodibl] *a* inaudible.

inaugurer [inogyre] *vt* (*politique, édifice*) to inaugurate; (*école, congrès*) to open, inaugurate; (*statue*) to unveil. ● **inaugural, -e, -aux** *a* inaugural. ● **inauguration** *nf* inauguration; (*d'école etc*) opening; (*de statue*) unveiling.

inauthentique [inotɑ̃tik] *a* not authentic.

inavouable [inavwabl] *a* shameful.

incalculable [ɛ̃kalkylabl] *a* incalculable.

incandescent, -ente [ɛ̃kɑ̃desɑ̃, -ɑ̃t] *a* white-hot, incandescent.

incapable [ɛ̃kapabl] *a* incapable; **i. de faire** unable to do, incapable of doing ▮ *nmf* (*personne*) incompetent. ● **incapacité** *nf* incapacity, inability (**de faire** to do); (*invalidité*) disability, incapacity.

incarcérer [ɛ̃karsere] *vt* to incarcerate. ● **incarcération** *nf* incarceration.

incarné, -ée [ɛ̃karne] *a* **1** **être la gentillesse/** *etc* **incarnée** (*personnifié*) to be the very embodiment of kindness/*etc*. **2** (*ongle*) ingrown.

incarner [ɛ̃karne] vt to embody, incarnate. ● **incarnation** nf embodiment, incarnation.

incartade [ɛ̃kartad] nf indiscretion, prank.

incassable [ɛ̃kasabl] a unbreakable.

incendie [ɛ̃sɑ̃di] nm fire; **i. criminel** arson; **i. de forêt** forest fire. ● **incendiaire** nmf arsonist ▮ a (bombe) incendiary; (paroles) inflammatory. ● **incendier** vt to set fire to, set on fire.

incertain, -aine [ɛ̃sɛrtɛ̃, -ɛn] a uncertain; (temps) unsettled; (entreprise) chancy; (contour) indistinct. ● **incertitude** nf uncertainty.

incessamment [ɛ̃sesamɑ̃] adv without delay, shortly.

incessant, -ante [ɛ̃sesɑ̃, -ɑ̃t] a continual, incessant.

inceste [ɛ̃sɛst] nm incest. ● **incestueux, -euse** a incestuous.

inchangé, -ée [ɛ̃ʃɑ̃ʒe] a unchanged.

incidence [ɛ̃sidɑ̃s] nf (influence) effect.

incident [ɛ̃sidɑ̃] nm incident; (accroc) hitch.

incinérer [ɛ̃sinere] vt (ordures) to incinerate; (cadavre) to cremate. ● **incinération** nf incineration; (de cadavre) cremation.

inciser [ɛ̃size] vt to make an incision in. ● **incision** nf (entaille) incision.

incisif, -ive¹ [ɛ̃sizif, -iv] a incisive, sharp.

incisive² [ɛ̃siziv] nf (dent) incisor (tooth).

inciter [ɛ̃site] vt to urge, incite (à faire to do). ● **incitation** nf incitement (à to).

incliner [ɛ̃kline] vt (courber) to bend; (pencher) to tilt, incline; **i. la tête** (approuver) to nod one's head; (saluer) to bow (one's head); **i. qn à faire qch** Fig to make s.o. inclined to do sth, incline s.o. to do sth. ▮ vi **i. à** Fig Litt to be inclined towards. ▮ **s'incliner** vpr (se courber) to bow (down); (chemin) to slope down; (bateau) to heel over; (s'avouer vaincu) Fig to admit defeat. ● **inclinaison** nf incline, slope. ● **inclination** nf (de tête) nod; (salut) bow; (goût) inclination.

inclure* [ɛ̃klyr] vt to include; (enfermer) to enclose. ● **inclus, -use** a inclusive; **du quatre jusqu'au dix mai i.** from the fourth to the tenth of May inclusive; **jusqu'à lundi i.** up to and including (next) Monday. ● **inclusion** nf inclusion.

incognito [ɛ̃kɔnito] adv incognito; **garder l'i.** to remain incognito.

incohérent, -ente [ɛ̃kɔerɑ̃, -ɑ̃t] a incoherent. ● **incohérence** nf incoherence.

incollable [ɛ̃kɔlabl] a (personne) Fam unbeatable, infallible; **riz i.** non-stick rice.

incolore [ɛ̃kɔlɔr] a colourless; (vernis, verre) clear.

incomber [ɛ̃kɔbe] vi **i. à qn** (devoir) to fall to s.o.; **il lui incombe de faire** it's his ou her duty ou responsiblity to do.

incommensurable [ɛ̃kɔmɑ̃syrabl] a immeasurable, immense.

incommode [ɛ̃kɔmɔd] a awkward. ● **incommodité** nf awkwardness.

incommoder [ɛ̃kɔmɔde] vt to bother, annoy. ● **incommodant, -ante** a annoying.

incomparable [ɛ̃kɔparabl] a incomparable.

incompatible [ɛ̃kɔpatibl] a incompatible, inconsistent (avec with). ● **incompatibilité** nf incompatibility, inconsistency; **divorcer pour i. d'humeur** to get divorced on account of mutual incompatibility.

incompétent, -ente [ɛ̃kɔpetɑ̃, -ɑ̃t] a incompetent. ● **incompétence** nf incompetence.

incomplet, -ète [ɛ̃kɔplɛ, -ɛt] a incomplete; (fragmentaire) scrappy, sketchy.

incompréhensible [ɛ̃kɔpreɑ̃sibl] a incomprehensible.

incompréhensif, -ive [ɛ̃kɔpreɑ̃sif, -iv] a lacking understanding. ● **incompréhension** nf lack of understanding.

incompris, -ise [ɛ̃kɔpri, -iz] a misunderstood ▮ nmf greatly misunderstood person.

inconcevable [ɛ̃kɔs(ə)vabl] a inconceivable.

inconciliable [ɛ̃kɔsiljabl] a irreconcilable.

inconditionnel, -elle [ɛ̃kɔdisjɔnel] a unconditional.

inconfort [ɛ̃kɔfɔr] nm lack of comfort. ● **inconfortable** a uncomfortable.

incongru, -ue [ɛ̃kɔgry] a unseemly, incongruous.

inconnu, -ue [ɛ̃kɔny] a unknown (à to) ▮ nmf (étranger) stranger; (auteur) unknown ▮ nm **l'i.** the unknown ▮ nf **inconnue** Math unknown (quantity).

inconscient, -ente [ɛ̃kɔsjɑ̃, -ɑ̃t] a unconscious; (imprudent) thoughtless, senseless; **i. de qch** unaware of sth ▮ nm **l'i.** Psy the unconscious. ● **inconsciemment** [-amɑ̃] adv unconsciously. ● **inconscience** nf (physique) unconsciousness; (irréflexion) utter thoughtlessness.

inconséquence [ɛ̃kɔsekɑ̃s] nf inconsistency.

inconsidéré, -ée [ɛ̃kɔsidere] a thoughtless.

inconsistant, -ante [ɛ̃kɔsistɑ̃, -ɑ̃t] a (caractère) weak, soft; (film, roman) flimsy; (sauce, crème) runny, watery.

inconsolable [ɛ̃kɔsɔlabl] a heartbroken, cut up, inconsolable.

inconstant, -ante [ɛ̃kɔstɑ̃, -ɑ̃t] a fickle. ● **inconstance** nf fickleness.

incontestable [ɛ̃kɔtɛstabl] a undeniable, indisputable. ● **incontesté, -ée** a undisputed.

incontinent, -ente [ɛ̃kɔtinɑ̃, -ɑ̃t] a incontinent.

incontournable [ɛ̃kɔturnabl] a Fig inevitable, inescapable; (film) unmissable; (auteur etc) who cannot be ignored.

incontrôlé, -ée [ɛ̃kɔtrole] a unchecked. ● **incontrôlable** a (invérifiable) unverifiable; (indomptable) (enfant etc) uncontrollable.

inconvenant, -ante [ɛ̃kɔvnɑ̃, -ɑ̃t] a improper. ● **inconvenance** nf impropriety.

inconvénient [ɛ̃kɔvenjɑ̃] nm (désavantage) drawback; (risque) risk; **si vous n'y voyez pas d'i.** if you have no objection(s); **l'i. c'est que....** the annoying thing is that....

incorporer [ɛ̃kɔrpore] vt (introduire, admettre) to incorporate (dans into); (ingré-

dient) to blend (**à** with); (*recrue*) *Mil* to enlist, *Br* enrol, *Am* enroll. ●**incorporation** *nf* incorporation (**de** of); *Mil* enlistment, *Br* enrolment, *Am* enrollment.

incorrect, -e [ɛ̃kɔrɛkt] *a* (*inexact*) incorrect; (*grossier*) impolite; (*inconvenant*) improper. ●**incorrection** *nf* (*faute*) impropriety, error; (*inconvenance*) impropriety; **une i.** (*grossièreté*) an impolite word *ou* act.

incorrigible [ɛ̃kɔriʒibl] *a* incorrigible.

incorruptible [ɛ̃kɔryptibl] *a* incorruptible.

incrédule [ɛ̃kredyl] *a* incredulous. ●**incrédulité** *nf* disbelief, incredulity.

increvable [ɛ̃krəvabl] *a* (*pneu etc*) puncture-proof; (*robuste*) *Fam* tireless.

incriminer [ɛ̃krimine] *vt* to incriminate.

incroyable [ɛ̃krwajabl] *a* incredible, unbelievable. ●**incroyablement** [-əmɑ̃] *adv* incredibly. ●**incroyant, -ante** *a* unbelieving ▮ *nmf* unbeliever.

incrusté, -ée [ɛ̃kryste] *a* **i. de** (*orné*) inlaid with; **i. de tartre** encrusted with scale, scaled up. ●**incrustation** *nf* (*ornement*) inlay; (*action*) inlaying.

incruster (s') [sɛ̃kryste] *vpr* (*chez qn*) *Fam* to be difficult to get rid of, outstay one's welcome, dig oneself in.

incubation [ɛ̃kybasjɔ̃] *nf* incubation.

inculper [ɛ̃kylpe] *vt* (*accuser*) to charge (**de** with), indict (**de** for). ●**inculpé, -ée** *nmf* **l'i.** the accused. ●**inculpation** *nf* charge, indictment.

inculquer [ɛ̃kylke] *vt* to instil (**à** into).

inculte [ɛ̃kylt] *a* (*terre*) uncultivated; (*personne*) uneducated.

incurable [ɛ̃kyrabl] *a* incurable.

incursion [ɛ̃kyrsjɔ̃] *nf* incursion, inroad (**dans** into).

incurver [ɛ̃kyrve] *vt* to curve.

Inde [ɛ̃d] *nf* India.

indécent, -ente [ɛ̃desɑ̃, -ɑ̃t] *a* indecent. ●**indécemment** [-amɑ̃] *adv* indecently. ●**indécence** *nf* indecency.

indéchiffrable [ɛ̃deʃifrabl] *a* undecipherable.

indécis, -ise [ɛ̃desi, -iz] *a* (*victoire, résultat*) undecided; (*indistinct*) vague; **être i.** (*hésiter*) to be undecided; (*de tempérament*) to be indecisive *ou* irresolute. ●**indécision** *nf* indecisiveness, indecision.

indéfectible [ɛ̃defektibl] *a* unfailing.

indéfendable [ɛ̃defɑ̃dabl] *a* indefensible.

indéfini, -ie [ɛ̃defini] *a* (*indéterminé*) indefinite; (*imprécis*) undefined; **article/pronom/adjectif i.** *Grammaire* indefinite article/pronoun/adjective. ●**indéfiniment** *adv* indefinitely. ●**indéfinissable** *a* indefinable.

indéformable [ɛ̃defɔrmabl] *a* (*vêtement*) which keeps its shape.

indélébile [ɛ̃delebil] *a* (*encre, souvenir*) indelible.

indélicat, -ate [ɛ̃delika, -at] *a* (*grossier*) indelicate; (*malhonnête*) unscrupulous.

indemne [ɛ̃dɛmn] *a* unhurt, unscathed.

indemniser [ɛ̃dɛmnize] *vt* to indemnify,

compensate (**de** for). ●**indemnisation** *nf* compensation. ●**indemnité** *nf* (*dédommagement*) compensation, indemnity; (*allocation*) allowance.

indémontable [ɛ̃demɔ̃tabl] *a* that cannot be taken apart.

indéniable [ɛ̃denjabl] *a* undeniable.

indépendant, -ante [ɛ̃depɑ̃dɑ̃, -ɑ̃t] *a* independent (**de** of); (*chambre*) self-contained; (*journaliste etc*) freelance. ●**indépendamment** [-amɑ̃] *adv* independently (**de** of); **i. de** (*sans aucun égard à*) apart from. ●**indépendance** *nf* independence. ●**indépendantiste** *nmf* freedom fighter.

indescriptible [ɛ̃deskriptibl] *a* indescribable.

indésirable [ɛ̃dezirabl] *a & nmf* undesirable.

indestructible [ɛ̃destryktibl] *a* indestructible.

indéterminé, -ée [ɛ̃determine] *a* indeterminate. ●**indétermination** *nf* (*doute*) indecision.

index [ɛ̃dɛks] *nm* (*doigt*) forefinger, index finger; (*liste*) index.

indexer [ɛ̃dɛkse] *vt* *Écon* to index-link, tie (**sur** to).

indicateur, -trice [ɛ̃dikatœr, -tris] **1** *nm Rail* guide, timetable; *Tech* indicator, gauge. **2** *a* **poteau i.** signpost; **panneau i.** road sign. **3** *nmf* (*espion*) (*police*) informer.

indicatif, -ive [ɛ̃dikatif, -iv] **1** *a* indicative (**de** of); **à titre i.** for information ▮ *nm* (à la *radio*) signature tune; **i. (téléphonique)** *Br* dialling code, *Am* area code. **2** *nm* (*mode*) *Grammaire* indicative.

indication [ɛ̃dikasjɔ̃] *nf* indication (**de** of); (*renseignement*) (piece of) information; (*directive*) instruction; **indications** (*pour aller quelque part*) directions.

indice [ɛ̃dis] *nm* (*dans une enquête*) clue; (*indication*) sign; **i. des prix/du coût de la vie/** *etc* price/cost of living/*etc* index; **l'i. d'écoute** (*de télévision ou de radio*) the ratings, the audience rating.

indien, -ienne [ɛ̃djɛ̃, -jɛn] *a* Indian ▮ *nmf* **I., Indienne** Indian.

indifférent, -ente [ɛ̃diferɑ̃, -ɑ̃t] *a* indifferent (**à** to); **ça m'est i.** that's all the same to me. ●**indifféremment** [-amɑ̃] *adv* indifferently. ●**indifférence** *nf* indifference (**à** to).

indigène [ɛ̃diʒɛn] *a & nmf* native.

indigent, -ente [ɛ̃diʒɑ̃, -ɑ̃t] *a* (very) poor. ●**indigence** *nf* poverty.

indigeste [ɛ̃diʒɛst] *a* indigestible. ●**indigestion** *nf* (attack of) indigestion.

indigne [ɛ̃diɲ] *a* (*personne*) unworthy; (*chose*) shameful; **i. de qn/qch** unworthy of s.o./sth. ●**indignité** *nf* unworthiness; **une i.** (*honte*) an indignity.

indigner [ɛ̃diɲe] *vt* **i. qn** to make s.o. indignant ▮ **s'indigner** *vpr* to be *ou* become indignant (**de** at). ●**indigné, -ée** *a* indignant. ●**indignation** *nf* indignation.

indigo [ɛ̃digo] *nm & a inv* (*couleur*) indigo.

indiquer [ɛ̃dike] *vt* (*montrer*) to show, indicate; (*dire*) to tell, point out; (*recommander*) to recommend; **i. du doigt** to point to *ou* at.

●**indiqué, -ée** a (conseillé) recommended; (adéquat) appropriate; **à l'heure indiquée** at the appointed time.

indirect, -e [ɛ̃dirɛkt] a indirect. ●**indirectement** [-əmɑ̃] adv indirectly.

indiscipline [ɛ̃disiplin] nf lack of discipline. ●**indiscipliné, -ée** a unruly.

indiscret, -ète [ɛ̃diskrɛ, -ɛt] a (curieux) Péj inquisitive, prying; (indélicat) indiscreet, tactless. ●**indiscrétion** nf indiscretion.

indiscutable [ɛ̃diskytabl] a indisputable.

indispensable [ɛ̃dispɑ̃sabl] a essential, indispensable.

indisposer [ɛ̃dispoze] vt (incommoder) to make unwell, upset; **i. qn (contre soi)** (mécontenter) to antagonize s.o. ●**indisposé, -ée** a (malade) indisposed, unwell. ●**indisposition** nf indisposition.

indissoluble [ɛ̃disɔlybl] a (liens etc) solid, indissoluble.

indistinct, -incte [ɛ̃distɛ̃(kt), -ɛ̃kt] a unclear, indistinct. ●**indistinctement** [-ɛ̃ktəmɑ̃] adv indistinctly; (également) without distinction.

individu [ɛ̃dividy] nm individual; Péj individual, character.

individualiser [ɛ̃dividɥalize] vt to individualize.

individualiste [ɛ̃dividɥalist] a individualistic ❙ nmf individualist.

individualité [ɛ̃dividɥalite] nf (originalité) individuality.

individuel, -elle [ɛ̃dividɥɛl] a individual. ●**individuellement** adv individually.

indivisible [ɛ̃divizibl] a indivisible.

Indochine [ɛ̃dɔʃin] nf Indo-China.

indolent, -ente [ɛ̃dɔlɑ̃, -ɑ̃t] a indolent. ●**indolence** nf indolence.

indolore [ɛ̃dɔlɔr] a painless.

indomptable [ɛ̃dɔ̃(p)tabl] a (volonté etc) indomitable. ●**indompté, -ée** a (animal) untamed.

Indonésie [ɛ̃dɔnezi] nf Indonesia.

indubitable [ɛ̃dybitabl] a beyond doubt.

indue [ɛ̃dy] af **à une heure i.** at an ungodly hour; **à des heures indues** at all hours, at ungodly hours.

induire* [ɛ̃dɥir] vt **i. qn en erreur** to lead s.o. astray.

indulgent, -ente [ɛ̃dylʒɑ̃, -ɑ̃t] a indulgent (envers to, avec with). ●**indulgence** nf indulgence.

industrie [ɛ̃dystri] nf industry. ●**industrialisé, -ée** a industrialized. ●**industriel, -elle** a industrial ❙ nm industrialist.

inébranlable [inebrɑ̃labl] a (certitude, personne) unshakeable, unwavering.

inédit, -ite [inedi, -it] a (texte) unpublished; (nouveau) Fig original.

ineffable [inefabl] a Litt inexpressible, ineffable.

inefficace [inefikas] a (mesure, effort etc) ineffective, ineffectual; (personne) inefficient. ●**inefficacité** nf ineffectiveness; inefficiency.

inégal, -e, -aux [inegal, -o] a unequal; (sol,

humeur) uneven. ●**inégalable** a incomparable. ●**inégalé, -ée** a unequalled. ●**inégalité** nf (injustice) inequality; (physique) difference; (irrégularité) unevenness; **inégalités de la route/etc** (bosses) bumps in the road/etc.

inélégant, -ante [inelegɑ̃, -ɑ̃t] a coarse, inelegant.

inéligible [ineliʒibl] a (candidat) ineligible.

inéluctable [inelyktabl] a inescapable.

inénarrable [inenarabl] a (comique) indescribably funny.

inepte [inɛpt] a absurd, inept. ●**ineptie** [inɛpsi] nf absurdity, ineptitude.

inépuisable [inepɥizabl] a inexhaustible.

inerte [inɛrt] a inert; (corps) lifeless. ●**inertie** [inɛrsi] nf inertia.

inespéré, -ée [inɛspere] a unhoped-for.

inestimable [inɛstimabl] a priceless.

inévitable [inevitabl] a inevitable, unavoidable.

inexact, -e [inɛgzakt] a (erroné) inaccurate, inexact; **c'est i.!** it's incorrect! ●**inexactitude** nf inaccuracy, inexactitude; (manque de ponctualité) lack of punctuality.

inexcusable [inɛkskyzabl] a inexcusable.

inexistant, -ante [inɛgzistɑ̃, -ɑ̃t] a nonexistent.

inexorable [inɛgzɔrabl] a inexorable.

inexpérience [inɛksperjɑ̃s] nf inexperience. ●**inexpérimenté, -ée** a (personne) inexperienced; (machine, arme) untested.

inexplicable [inɛksplikabl] a inexplicable. ●**inexpliqué, -ée** a unexplained.

inexploré, -ée [inɛksplɔre] a unexplored.

inexpressif, -ive [inɛkspresif, -iv] a expressionless.

inexprimable [inɛksprimabl] a beyond words, inexpressible.

in extremis [inɛkstremis] adv at the very last minute.

inextricable [inɛkstrikabl] a inextricable.

infaillible [ɛ̃fajibl] a infallible. ●**infaillibilité** nf infallibility.

infaisable [ɛ̃fəzabl] a (travail etc) that cannot be done.

infamant, -ante [ɛ̃famɑ̃, -ɑ̃t] a ignominious.

infâme [ɛ̃fam] a (odieux) (action etc) vile, infamous; (taudis) squalid; (aliment) vile, revolting. ●**infamie** nf infamy.

infanterie [ɛ̃fɑ̃tri] nf infantry.

infantile [ɛ̃fɑ̃til] a (maladie, réaction) infantile.

infarctus [ɛ̃farktys] nm **un i.** Méd a coronary.

infatigable [ɛ̃fatigabl] a tireless, indefatigable.

infect, -e [ɛ̃fɛkt] a (odeur) foul; (goût, café etc) lousy, vile.

infecter [ɛ̃fɛkte] **1** vt (air) to contaminate, foul. **2** vt Méd to infect ❙ **s'infecter** vpr to get infected. ●**infectieux, -euse** a infectious. ●**infection** nf **1** Méd infection. **2** (odeur) stench.

inférer [ɛ̃fere] vt (conclure) Litt to infer (de from, que that).

inférieur, -e [ɛ̃ferjœr] a (*partie*) lower; (*qualité, personne etc*) inferior; **à l'étage i.** on the floor below; **i. à** inferior to; (*plus petit que*) smaller than; **i. à la moyenne** (*note, intelligence etc*) below average ❚ *nmf* (*personne*) *Péj* inferior. ● **infériorité** *nf* inferiority.

infernal, -e, -aux [ɛ̃fɛrnal, -o] a infernal; (*insupportable*) (*enfant*) diabolical.

infester [ɛ̃fɛste] *vt* to infest, overrun (**de** with). ● **infesté, -ée** a **i. de requins/de fourmis/etc** shark/ant/*etc*-infested.

infidèle [ɛ̃fidɛl] a unfaithful (**à** to). ● **infidélité** *nf* unfaithfulness; **une i.** (*acte*) an infidelity.

infiltrer (s') [sɛ̃filtre] *vpr* (*liquide*) to seep *ou* percolate (through) (**dans** into); (*lumière*) to filter (through) (**dans** into); **s'i. dans** (*groupe, esprit*) *Fig* to infiltrate. ● **infiltration** *nf* (*de personne, idée, liquide*) infiltration.

infime [ɛ̃fim] a (*très petit*) tiny.

infini, -ie [ɛ̃fini] a infinite ❚ *nm Math Phot* infinity; *Phil* infinite; **à l'i.** (*beaucoup*) endlessly, ad infinitum; *Math* to infinity. ● **infiniment** *adv* infinitely; (*regretter, remercier*) very much. ● **infinité** *nf* **une i.** de an infinite amount of.

infinitif [ɛ̃finitif] *nm Grammaire* infinitive.

infirme [ɛ̃firm] a disabled, crippled ❚ *nmf* disabled person. ● **infirmité** *nf* disability.

infirmer [ɛ̃firme] *vt* to invalidate.

infirmerie [ɛ̃firməri] *nf* sick room, sickbay, infirmary. ● **infirmier** *nm* male nurse. ● **infirmière** *nf* nurse; **i. diplômée d'État** = *Br* State Registered Nurse; = *Am* Registered Nurse.

inflammable [ɛ̃flamabl] a (in)flammable.

inflammation [ɛ̃flamɑsjɔ̃] *nf Méd* inflammation.

inflation [ɛ̃flɑsjɔ̃] *nf Écon* inflation. ● **inflationniste** a *Écon* inflationary.

infléchir [ɛ̃fleʃir] *vt* (*courber*) to inflect, bend; (*modifier*) to shift. ● **inflexion** *nf* bend; (*de voix*) tone, inflexion; **une i. de la tête** a nod.

inflexible [ɛ̃flɛksibl] a inflexible.

infliger [ɛ̃fliʒe] *vt* to inflict (**à** on); (*amende*) to impose (**à** on).

influence [ɛ̃flyɑ̃s] *nf* influence; **sous l'i. de la drogue** under the influence of drugs; **sous l'i. de la colère** in the grip of anger. ● **influencer** *vt* to influence. ● **influençable** a easily influenced. ● **influent, -ente** a influential. ● **influer** *vi* **i. sur** to influence.

informateur, -trice [ɛ̃fɔrmatœr, -tris] *nmf* informant.

informaticien, -ienne [ɛ̃fɔrmatisjɛ̃, -jɛn] *nmf* computer scientist.

information [ɛ̃fɔrmɑsjɔ̃] *nf* information; (*nouvelle*) piece of news; (*enquête*) *Jur* inquiry, investigation; **les informations** (*à la radio ou télévision*) the news.

informatique [ɛ̃fɔrmatik] *nf* (*science*) computer science, computing; (*technique*) data processing ❚ a **programme/matériel/etc i.** computer program/hardware/*etc*. ● **informatisation** *nf* computerization. ● **informatiser** *vt* to computerize.

informe [ɛ̃fɔrm] a shapeless.

informer [ɛ̃fɔrme] *vt* to inform (**de** of, about; **que** that) ❚ **s'informer** *vpr* to inquire (**de** about; **si** if, whether).

infortune [ɛ̃fɔrtyn] *nf* misfortune. ● **infortuné, -ée** a ill-fated, hapless.

infraction [ɛ̃fraksjɔ̃] *nf* (*délit*) *Br* offence, *Am* offense; **i. à** breach of, infringement of.

infranchissable [ɛ̃frɑ̃ʃisabl] a (*mur, fleuve*) impassable; (*difficulté*) *Fig* insuperable.

infrarouge [ɛ̃fraruʒ] a (*rayons etc*) infrared.

infroissable [ɛ̃frwasabl] a crease-resistant.

infructueux, -euse [ɛ̃fryktɥø, -øz] a fruitless.

infuser [ɛ̃fyze] *vt* (*faire*) **i.** (*thé*) to brew, infuse; **laisser i. le thé** to leave the tea to brew *ou* infuse. ● **infusion** *nf* (*tisane*) (herb *ou* herbal) tea, infusion.

ingénier (s') [sɛ̃ʒenje] *vpr* to exercise one's wits (**à faire** in order to do).

ingénieur [ɛ̃ʒenjœr] *nm* engineer; **femme i.** woman engineer. ● **ingénierie** [-iri] *nf* engineering; **i. mécanique** mechanical engineering.

ingénieux, -euse [ɛ̃ʒenjø, -øz] a ingenious. ● **ingéniosité** *nf* ingenuity.

ingénu, -ue [ɛ̃ʒeny] a artless, naïve.

ingérer (s') [sɛ̃ʒere] *vpr* to interfere (**dans** in). ● **ingérence** *nf* interference (**dans** in).

ingrat, -ate [ɛ̃gra, -at] a (*personne*) ungrateful (**envers** to); (*tâche*) thankless; (*sol*) barren; (*visage, physique*) unattractive; **l'âge i.** the awkward age. ● **ingratitude** *nf* ingratitude.

ingrédient [ɛ̃gredjɑ̃] *nm* ingredient.

inguérissable [ɛ̃gerisabl] a incurable.

ingurgiter [ɛ̃gyrʒite] *vt* to gulp down.

inhabitable [inabitabl] a uninhabitable. ● **inhabité, -ée** a uninhabited.

inhabituel, -elle [inabitɥɛl] a unusual.

inhalateur [inalatœr] *nm Méd* inhaler. ● **inhalation** *nf* inhalation; **faire des inhalations** to inhale.

inhérent, -ente [inerɑ̃, -ɑ̃t] a inherent (**à** in).

inhibé, -ée [inibe] a inhibited. ● **inhibition** *nf* inhibition.

inhospitalier, -ière [inɔspitalje, -jɛr] a inhospitable.

inhumain, -aine [inymɛ̃, -ɛn] a (*cruel, terrible*) inhuman.

inhumer [inyme] *vt* to bury, inter. ● **inhumation** *nf* burial.

inimaginable [inimaʒinabl] a unimaginable.

inimitable [inimitabl] a inimitable.

inimitié [inimitje] *nf* enmity.

ininflammable [inɛ̃flamabl] a (*tissu etc*) non-flammable.

inintelligent, -ente [inɛ̃teliʒɑ̃, -ɑ̃t] a unintelligent.

inintelligible [inɛ̃teliʒibl] a unintelligible.

inintéressant, -ante [inɛ̃teresɑ̃, -ɑ̃t] a uninteresting.

ininterrompu, -ue [inɛ̃terɔ̃py] a continuous, uninterrupted.

inique [inik] *a* iniquitous. ● **iniquité** *nf* iniquity.

initial, -e, -aux [inisjal, -o] *a* initial. ● **initiale** *nf* (*lettre*) initial. ● **initialement** *adv* initially.

initiative [inisjativ] *nf* **1** initiative; **avoir l'esprit d'i.** to have plenty of initiative, show initiative; **de ma propre i.** on my own initiative. **2** **syndicat d'i.** tourist office.

initier [inisje] *vt* to initiate (à into); **s'i. à** (*art, science*) to become acquainted with *ou* initiated into. ● **initié, -ée** *nmf* initiate; **les initiés** the initiated. ● **initiateur, -trice** *nmf* initiator. ● **initiation** *nf* initiation.

injecter [ɛ̃ʒɛkte] *vt* to inject; **injecté de sang** bloodshot. ● **injection** *nf* injection.

injoignable [ɛ̃ʒwaɲabl] *a* **il est i.** he cannot be reached *ou* contacted, he's unavailable.

injonction [ɛ̃ʒɔ̃ksjɔ̃] *nf* order, injunction.

injure [ɛ̃ʒyr] *nf* insult; **injures** abuse, insults. ● **injurier** *vt* to insult, abuse, swear at. ● **injurieux, -euse** *a* abusive, insulting (**pour** to).

injuste [ɛ̃ʒyst] *a* (*contraire à la justice*) unjust; (*non équitable*) unfair. ● **injustice** *nf* injustice.

injustifiable [ɛ̃ʒystifjabl] *a* unjustifiable. ● **injustifié, -ée** *a* unjustified.

inlassable [ɛ̃lɑsabl] *a* untiring.

inné, -ée [ine] *a* innate, inborn.

innocent, -ente [inɔsɑ̃, -ɑ̃t] *a* innocent (**de** of) **I** *nmf Jur* innocent person; (*idiot*) simpleton. ● **innocemment** [-amɑ̃] *adv* innocently. ● **innocence** *nf* innocence; **agir en toute i.** to act in all innocence. ● **innocenter** *vt* **i. qn** to clear s.o. (**de** of).

innombrable [inɔ̃brabl] *a* countless, innumerable.

innommable [inɔmabl] *a* (*dégoûtant*) unspeakable, foul.

innover [inɔve] *vi* to innovate. ● **innovateur, -trice** *nmf* innovator. ● **innovation** *nf* innovation.

inoccupé, -ée [inɔkype] *a* unoccupied.

inoculer [inɔkyle] *vt* **i. qch à qn** to infect *ou* inoculate s.o. with sth. ● **inoculation** *nf* (*vaccination*) inoculation.

inodore [inɔdɔr] *a* odourless.

inoffensif, -ive [inɔfɑ̃sif, -iv] *a* harmless, inoffensive.

inonder [inɔ̃de] *vt* to flood, inundate; (*mouiller*) to soak; **inondé de** (*envahi*) inundated with; **inondé de soleil** bathed in sunlight. ● **inondable** *a* (*chaussée etc*) liable to flooding. ● **inondation** *nf* flood; (*action*) flooding (**de** of).

inopérant, -ante [inɔperɑ̃, -ɑ̃t] *a* inoperative.

inopiné, -ée [inɔpine] *a* unexpected.

inopportun, -une [inɔpɔrtœ̃, -yn] *a* inopportune.

inoubliable [inublijabl] *a* unforgettable.

inouï, -e [inwi] *a* incredible, extraordinary.

inox [inɔks] *nm* stainless steel; **couteau/etc en i.** stainless-steel knife/*etc*. ● **inoxydable** *a* (*couteau etc*) stainless-steel; **acier i.** stainless steel.

inqualifiable [ɛ̃kalifjabl] *a* (*indigne*) unspeakable.

inquiet, -iète [ɛ̃kjɛ, -jɛt] *a* worried, anxious (**de** about).

inquiéter [ɛ̃kjete] *vt* (*préoccuper*) to worry; (*police*) to bother, harass (*suspect etc*) **I** **s'inquiéter** *vpr* to worry (**de** about). ● **inquiétant, -ante** *a* worrying.

inquiétude [ɛ̃kjetyd] *nf* anxiety, concern, worry.

inquisiteur, -trice [ɛ̃kizitœr, -tris] *a* (*regard*) *Péj* inquisitive. ● **inquisition** *nf* inquisition; **c'est de l'i.!** is this the Inquisition?.

insaisissable [ɛ̃sezisabl] *a* elusive.

insalubre [ɛ̃salybr] *a* unhealthy, insalubrious.

insanités [ɛ̃sanite] *nfpl* (*idioties*) absurdities.

insatiable [ɛ̃sasjabl] *a* insatiable.

insatisfait, -aite [ɛ̃satisfɛ, -ɛt] *a* unsatisfied, dissatisfied.

inscription [ɛ̃skripsjɔ̃] *nf* writing down; (*sur écriteau, de médaille etc*) inscription; (*immatriculation*) *Br* enrolment, *Am* enrollment, registration; **frais d'i.** (*à l'université*) registration fees; (*dans un club*) enrolment fee(s); **date des inscriptions** (*à l'université*) registration date.

inscrire* [ɛ̃skrir] *vt* to write *ou* put down; (*sur un registre*) to register; (*graver*) to inscribe; **i. qn** *Br* to enrol s.o., *Am* enroll s.o. **I** **s'inscrire** *vpr* to put one's name down, *Br* enrol, *Am* enroll (**à** at); (*à l'université*) to register (**à** at); **s'i. à** (*club, parti*) to join, enrol in; (*examen*) to enter *ou* enrol *ou* register for; **s'i. dans** (**le cadre de**) to be part of; **s'i. en faux contre** to deny absolutely.

insecte [ɛ̃sɛkt] *nm* insect. ● **insecticide** *nm & a* insecticide.

insécurité [ɛ̃sekyrite] *nf* insecurity.

INSEE [inse] *nm abrév* (*Institut national de la statistique et des études économiques*) (French) national institute of statistics and economic studies.

insémination [ɛ̃seminɑsjɔ̃] *nf* **i. artificielle** *Méd* artificial insemination.

insensé, -ée [ɛ̃sɑ̃se] *a* senseless, absurd.

insensible [ɛ̃sɑ̃sibl] *a* (*indifférent*) insensitive (**à** to); (*graduel*) imperceptible, very slight. ● **insensiblement** [-amɑ̃] *adv* imperceptibly. ● **insensibilité** *nf* insensitivity.

inséparable [ɛ̃separabl] *a* inseparable (**de** from).

insérer [ɛ̃sere] *vt* to insert (**dans** into, in); **s'i. dans** (*société, groupe*) to become accepted by, become part of. ● **insertion** *nf* insertion; **l'i. des chômeurs/etc** the (social) integration of the unemployed/*etc*.

INSERM [insɛrm] *nm abrév* (*Institut national de la santé et de la recherche médicale*) (French) national institute of health and medical research.

insidieux, -euse [ɛ̃sidjø, -øz] *a* insidious.

insigne [ɛ̃siɲ] *nm* badge, emblem; **les insignes de** (*de maire etc*) the insignia of.

insignifiant, -ante [ɛ̃siɲifjɑ̃, -ɑ̃t] *a* insignificant, unimportant. ● **insignifiance** *nf* insignificance.

insinuer [ɛ̃sinɥe] *vt Péj* to insinuate (**que** that) **I s'insinuer** *vpr* to insinuate oneself (**dans** into). ● **insinuation** *nf* insinuation.

insipide [ɛ̃sipid] *a* insipid.

insister [ɛ̃siste] *vi* to insist (**pour faire on** doing); (*persévérer*) *Fam* to persevere; **i. sur** (*détail, syllabe etc*) to stress; **i. pour que** (+ *sub*) to insist that. ● **insistant, -ante** *a* insistent, persistent. ● **insistance** *nf* insistence, persistence.

insolation [ɛ̃sɔlasjɔ̃] *nf Méd* sunstroke.

insolent, -ente [ɛ̃sɔlɑ̃, -ɑ̃t] *a* (*impoli*) insolent; (*luxe*) indecent. ● **insolence** *nf* insolence.

insolite [ɛ̃sɔlit] *a* unusual, strange.

insoluble [ɛ̃sɔlybl] *a* insoluble.

insolvable [ɛ̃sɔlvabl] *a Fin* insolvent.

insomnie [ɛ̃sɔmni] *nf* insomnia; **avoir des insomnies** to have insomnia; **nuit d'i.** sleepless night. ● **insomniaque** *nmf* insomniac.

insondable [ɛ̃sɔ̃dabl] *a* unfathomable.

insonoriser [ɛ̃sɔnɔrize] *vt* to soundproof, insulate. ● **insonorisation** *nf* soundproofing, insulation.

insouciant, -ante [ɛ̃susjɑ̃, -ɑ̃t] *a* carefree; **i. de** unconcerned about. ● **insouciance** *nf* carefree attitude, lack of concern.

insoumis, -ise [ɛ̃sumi, -iz] *a* rebellious. ● **insoumission** *nf* rebelliousness.

insoupçonnable [ɛ̃supsɔnabl] *a* beyond suspicion. ● **insoupçonné, -ée** *a* unsuspected.

insoutenable [ɛ̃sutnabl] *a* (*insupportable*) unbearable; (*théorie*) untenable.

inspecter [ɛ̃spɛkte] *vt* to inspect. ● **inspecteur, -trice** *nmf* inspector. ● **inspection** *nf* inspection.

inspirer [ɛ̃spire] **1** *vt* to inspire; **i. qch à qn** to inspire s.o. with sth; **s'i. de** to take one's inspiration from. **2** *vi Méd* to breathe in. ● **inspiré, -ée** *a* inspired; **être bien i. de faire** to have the good idea to do. ● **inspiration** *nf* **1** inspiration. **2** *Méd* breathing in.

instable [ɛ̃stabl] *a* (*meuble*) shaky, unsteady; (*temps*) unsettled; (*situation, caractère*) unstable. ● **instabilité** *nf* unsteadiness; (*de situation etc*) instability.

installer [ɛ̃stale] *vt* (*appareil, meuble etc*) to install, put in; (*étagère*) to put up; (*équiper*) to fit out, fix up; **i. qn** (*dans une fonction, un logement*) to install s.o. (**dans** in).
I s'installer *vpr* (*s'asseoir, s'établir*) to settle (down); (*médecin etc*) to set oneself up; **s'i. dans** (*maison, hôtel*) to move into. ● **installateur** *nm* fitter. ● **installation** *nf* putting in; fitting out; installation; moving in; **installations** (*appareils*) fittings, installations; (*bâtiments*) facilities.

instamment [ɛ̃stamɑ̃] *adv* insistently.

instance [ɛ̃stɑ̃s] *nf* (*juridiction, autorité*) authority; **tribunal de première i.** = magistrates' court; **en i. de divorce** waiting for a divorce; **en i. de départ** about to depart. ● **instances** *nfpl* céder aux **i. de qn** to give in

to s.o.'s requests.

instant [ɛ̃stɑ̃] *nm* moment, instant; **à l'i.** a moment ago; **à l'i.** (**même**) **où** just as; **pour l'i.** for the moment; **dès l'i.** **que** from the moment that; (*puisque*) seeing that. ● **instantané, -ée** *a* instantaneous; **café i.** instant coffee **I** *nm* (*photo*) snapshot.

instar [ɛ̃star] *nm* **à l'i. de qn** *Litt* after the fashion of s.o.

instaurer [ɛ̃stɔre] *vt* to found, set up.

instigateur, -trice [ɛ̃stigatœr, -tris] *nmf* instigator. ● **instigation** *nf* instigation.

instinct [ɛ̃stɛ̃] *nm* instinct; **d'i.** instinctively, by instinct. ● **instinctif, -ive** *a* instinctive.

instituer [ɛ̃stitɥe] *vt* (*règle, régime*) to establish, institute.

institut [ɛ̃stity] *nm* institute; **i. de beauté** beauty salon *ou* parlour; **i. universitaire de technologie** technical college (*conferring two-year degrees*), *Br* = polytechnic.

instituteur, -trice [ɛ̃stitytœr, -tris] *nmf Br* primary *ou Am* elementary school teacher.

institution [ɛ̃stitysjɔ̃] *nf* (*organisation, règle, structure etc*) institution; (*école*) private school; **les institutions** (**républicaines**) (republican) institutions. ● **institutionnel, -elle** *a* institutional.

instructif, -ive [ɛ̃stryktif, -iv] *a* instructive.

instruction [ɛ̃stryksjɔ̃] *nf* education, schooling; (*militaire*) training; *Jur* investigation; **instructions** (*ordres*) instructions; (*mode d'emploi*) instructions, directions. ● **instructeur** *nm* (*moniteur*) & *Mil* instructor.

instruire* [ɛ̃strɥir] *vt* to teach, educate; *Mil* to train; **i. une affaire/un procès** to conduct the investigation for a case/trial; **i. qn de** to inform *ou* instruct s.o. of **I s'instruire** *vpr* to educate oneself; **s'i. de** to inquire about. ● **instruit, -uite** *a* educated.

instrument [ɛ̃strymɑ̃] *nm* instrument; (*outil*) implement, tool; **i. à vent** wind instrument; **les instruments de bord** (*d'un avion*) the instruments. ● **instrumental, -e, -aux** *a Mus* instrumental. ● **instrumentiste** *nmf Mus* instrumentalist.

insu de (à l') [alɛ̃syd(ə)] *prép* without the knowledge of; **elle tremblait/souriait**/*etc* **à son i.** she was shaking/smiling/*etc* without realizing it.

insuccès [ɛ̃syksɛ] *nm* failure.

insuffisant, -ante [ɛ̃syfizɑ̃, -ɑ̃t] *a* (*en qualité*) inadequate; (*en quantité*) insufficient, inadequate. ● **insuffisance** *nf* inadequacy.

insulaire [ɛ̃syler] *a* insular **I** *nmf* Islander.

insuline [ɛ̃sylin] *nf Méd* insulin.

insulte [ɛ̃sylt] *nf* insult (**à** to). ● **insulter** *vt* to insult.

insupportable [ɛ̃sypɔrtabl] *a* unbearable.

insurger (s') [sɛ̃syrʒe] *vpr* to rise (up), rebel (**contre** against). ● **insurgé, -ée** *nmf* & *a* insurgent, rebel. ● **insurrection** *nf* insurrection, uprising.

insurmontable [ɛ̃syrmɔ̃tabl] *a* insurmountable, insuperable.

intact, -e [ɛ̃takt] *a* intact.

intangible [ētāʒibl] *a* intangible.

intarissable [ētarisabl] *a* inexhaustible.

intégral, -e, -aux [ētegral, -o] *a* full, complete; (*édition*) unabridged; **version intégrale** (*de film*) uncut version; **bronzage i.** all-over tan, whole-body tan; **casque i.** (*de motard*) full-face crash helmet. ● **intégralement** *adv* in full, fully. ● **intégralité** *nf* whole (**de** of); **dans son i.** in full.

intègre [ētɛgr] *a* upright, honest. ● **intégrité** *nf* integrity.

intégrer [ētegre] *vt* to integrate (**dans** in) ▮ **s'intégrer** *vpr* to become integrated, adapt. ● **intégrante** *af* **faire partie i. de** to be part and parcel of. ● **intégration** *nf* integration; **politique d'i. des immigrés** integration policy (*for immigrants*).

intégrisme [ētegrism] *nm* fundamentalism.

intellectuel, -elle [ētelektɥɛl] *a* & *nmf* intellectual.

intelligent, -ente [ēteliʒā, -āt] *a* intelligent, clever. ● **intelligemment** [-amā] *adv* intelligently. ● **intelligence** *nf* (*faculté*) intelligence; **intelligences** *Mil Pol* secret relations; **i. artificielle** *Ordinat* artificial intelligence; **avoir l'i. de qch** (*compréhension*) to have an understanding of sth; **avoir l'i. de faire qch** to have the sense *ou* intelligence to do sth; **d'i. avec qn** in complicity with s.o.; **vivre en bonne i. avec qn** to be on good terms with s.o.

intelligentsia [inteligɛnsja] *nf* intelligentsia.

intelligible [ēteliʒibl] *a* intelligible. ● **intelligibilité** *nf* intelligibility.

intempérance [ētāperās] *nf* intemperance.

intempéries [ētāperi] *nfpl* **les i.** the elements, bad weather.

intempestif, -ive [ētāpestif, -iv] *a* untimely.

intenable [ētnabl] *a* (*position*) untenable; (*enfant*) *Fam* unruly, uncontrollable.

intendant, -ante [ētādā, -āt] *nmf* *Scol* bursar. ● **intendance** *nf* *Scol* bursar's office.

intense [ētās] *a* intense; (*trafic, circulation*) heavy. ● **intensément** *adv* intensely. ● **intensif, -ive** *a* intensive.

intensifier [ētāsifje] *vt*, **s'intensifier** *vpr* to intensify.

intensité [ētāsite] *nf* intensity.

intenter [ētāte] *vt* **i. un procès à qn** *Jur* to institute proceedings against s.o.

intention [ētāsjɔ̄] *nf* intention; *Jur* intent; **avoir l'i. de faire** to intend to do; **à l'i. de qn** for s.o.; **à votre i.** for you; **sans i. de nuire** without ill intent, without meaning any harm. ● **intentionné, -ée** **a bien i.** well-intentioned; **mal i.** ill-intentioned. ● **intentionnel, -elle** *a* intentional, wilful. ● **intentionnellement** *adv* intentionally.

inter- [ēter] *préf* inter-.

interactif, -ive [ēteraktif, -iv] *a* *Ordinat* interactive.

interaction [ēteraksjɔ̄] *nf* interaction.

intercalaire [ēterkaler] *a* & *nm* (**feuille**) **i.** (*dans un classeur*) divider.

intercaler [ēterkale] *vt* to insert.

intercéder [ētersede] *vt* to intercede (**auprès de** with, **en faveur de** on behalf of).

intercepter [ētersepte] *vt* to intercept. ● **interception** *nf* interception.

interchangeable [ēterʃāʒabl] *a* interchangeable.

interclasse [ēterklas] *nm* *Scol* break (between classes).

intercontinental, -e, -aux [ēterkɔ̄tinātal, -o] *a* intercontinental.

interdépendant, -ante [ēterdepādā, -āt] *a* interdependent.

interdire* [ēterdir] *vt* to forbid, not to allow (**qch à qn** s.o. sth); (*film, meeting etc*) to ban; **i. à qn de faire qch** (*médecin, père etc*) not to allow s.o. to do sth, forbid s.o. to do sth; (*santé etc*) to prevent s.o. from doing sth, not allow s.o. to do sth. ● **interdit, -ite** *a* **1** forbidden, not allowed; **il est i. de** it is forbidden to; **'stationnement i.'** 'no parking'. **2** (*étonné*) nonplussed. ● **interdiction** *nf* ban (**de** on); **'i. de fumer'** 'no smoking'.

intéresser [ēterese] *vt* to interest; (*concerner*) to concern; **s'i. à** to take an interest in, be interested in. ● **intéressant, -ante** *a* (*captivant*) interesting; (*prix etc*) attractive, worthwhile; **faire l'i.** *Péj* to draw attention to oneself. ● **intéressé, -ée** *a* (*avide*) self-interested; (*motif*) selfish; (*concerné*) concerned ▮ *nmf* **l'i.** the interested party.

intérêt [ētere] *nm* interest; *Péj* self-interest; **intérêts** (*d'un placement*) interest; **tu as i. à faire** it would pay you to do, you'd do well to do; **avoir des intérêts dans** *Com* to have a financial interest in *ou* a stake in.

interface [ēterfas] *nf* *Ordinat* interface.

intérieur, -e [ēterjœr] *a* (*cour, paroi*) inner, interior; (*poche*) inside; (*politique, vol*) internal, domestic; (*vie, sentiment*) inner, inward; (*mer*) inland; **dans son for i.** *Litt* in one's heart of hearts.
▮ *nm* (*de boîte etc*) inside (**de** of); (*de maison*) interior, inside; (*de pays*) interior; **à l'i.** (**de**) inside; **à l'i. de nos frontières** within the country; **d'i.** (*vêtement, jeux*) indoor; **femme d'i.** home-loving woman; **ministère de l'I.** *Br* Home Office, *Am* Department of the Interior. ● **intérieurement** *adv* (*dans le cœur*) inwardly.

intérim [ēterim] *nm* **pendant l'i.** in the interim; **assurer l'i.** to deputize (**de** for); **président**/*etc* **par i.** acting president/*etc*. ● **intérimaire** *a* temporary, interim ▮ *nmf* (*fonctionnaire*) deputy; (*secrétaire*) temporary.

interligne [ēterliɲ] *nm* (*dans un texte*) space (between the lines), spacing.

interlocuteur, -trice [ēterlɔkytœr, -tris] *nmf* *Pol etc* negotiator; **mon i.** the person I am, was *etc* speaking to.

interloqué, -ée [ēterlɔke] *a* dumbfounded.

interlude [ēterlyd] *nm* (*à la télévision*) interlude.

intermède [ētermɛd] *nm* (*interruption*) & *Théâtre* interlude.

intermédiaire [ɛ̃tɛrmedjɛr] *a* intermediate ▮ *nmf* intermediary; **par l'i.** de through (the medium of); **vendre sans i.** to sell direct (*to the consumer*).

interminable [ɛ̃tɛrminabl] *a* endless, interminable.

intermittent, -ente [ɛ̃tɛrmitã, -ãt] *a* intermittent. ● **intermittence** *nf* **par i.** intermittently.

international, -e, -aux [ɛ̃tɛrnasjɔnal, -o] *a* international ▮ *nm* (*joueur de football etc*) international.

interne [ɛ̃tɛrn] **1** *a* (*douleur etc*) internal; (*oreille*) inner. **2** *nmf* (*élève*) boarder; **i.** (**des hôpitaux**) *Br* houseman, *Am* intern. ● **internat** *nm* (*école*) boarding school.

interner [ɛ̃tɛrne] *vt* (*prisonnier*) to intern; (*aliéné*) to confine. ● **internement** *nm* internment; (*d'aliéné*) confinement.

interpeller [ɛ̃tɛrpele] *vt* (*appeler*) to shout at *ou* to, address sharply; (*dans une réunion*) to question; (*police*) to take in (s.o.) for questioning; (*problème, misère, chômage etc*) to be of concern to (s.o.). ● **interpellation** *nf* sharp address; (*dans une réunion*) questioning; (*de police*) arrest.

interphone [ɛ̃tɛrfɔn] *nm* intercom.

interplanétaire [ɛ̃tɛrplanetɛr] *a* interplanetary.

interpoler [ɛ̃tɛrpɔle] *vt* to interpolate.

interposer (s') [sɛ̃tɛrpoze] *vpr* (*dans une dispute etc*) to intervene (**dans** in); **s'i. entre** to come between; **par personne interposée** through a third party.

interprète [ɛ̃tɛrprɛt] *nmf* *Ling* interpreter; (*chanteur*) singer; (*au théâtre, de musique*) performer; (*porte-parole*) spokesman, spokeswoman; **faire l'i.** *Ling* to interpret. ● **interprétariat** *nm* (*métier*) *Ling* interpreting. ● **interprétation** *nf* interpretation; (*au théâtre, en musique*) performance. ● **interpréter** *vt* (*expliquer*) to interpret; (*chanter*) to sing; (*jouer sur scène*) to play, perform; (*morceau de musique*) to perform.

interroger [ɛ̃tɛrɔʒe] *vt* to question; (*de façon prolongée*) to interrogate; (*faits*) to examine. ● **interrogateur, -trice** *a* (*air*) questioning. ● **interrogatif, -ive** *a & nm* *Grammaire* interrogative. ● **interrogation** *nf* (*question*) question; (*action*) questioning; interrogation; examination; (*épreuve orale ou écrite*) test. ● **interrogatoire** *nm* (*par la police*) interrogation.

interrompre* [ɛ̃tɛrɔ̃pr] *vt* to interrupt, break off; **i. qn** to interrupt s.o. ▮ **s'interrompre** *vpr* (*personne*) to break off, stop. ● **interrupteur** *nm* (*électrique*) switch. ● **interruption** *nf* interruption; (*des hostilités, du courant*) break (**de** in); **sans i.** without a break.

intersection [ɛ̃tɛrseksjɔ̃] *nf* intersection.

interstice [ɛ̃tɛrstis] *nm* crack, chink.

interurbain, -aine [ɛ̃tɛryrbɛ̃, -ɛn] *a & nm* (**téléphone**) **i.** long-distance telephone service.

intervalle [ɛ̃tɛrval] *nm* (*écart*) gap, space; (*temps*) interval; **dans l'i.** (*entretemps*) in the meantime; **par intervalles** (every) now and then, at intervals.

intervenir* [ɛ̃tɛrvənir] *vi* (*s'interposer, agir*) to intervene; (*survenir*) to occur; (*opérer*) *Méd* to operate; **être intervenu** (*accord*) to be reached. ● **intervention** *nf* intervention; **i.** (**chirurgicale**) operation.

intervertir [ɛ̃tɛrvɛrtir] *vt* to invert. ● **interversion** *nf* inversion.

interview [ɛ̃tɛrvju] *nf* (*d'un journaliste etc*) interview. ● **interviewer** [-vjuve] *vt* to interview.

intestin [ɛ̃tɛstɛ̃] *nm* bowel, intestine. ● **intestinal, -e, -aux** *a* intestinal; **grippe intestinale** gastric flu.

intime [ɛ̃tim] *a* intimate; (*ami*) close, intimate; (*vie, journal, mariage*) private; (*pièce, coin*) cosy; (*cérémonie*) quiet ▮ *nmf* close *ou* intimate friend. ● **intimement** *adv* intimately. ● **intimité** *nf* (*familiarité*) intimacy; (*vie privée*) privacy; (*de pièce etc*) cosiness; **dans l'i.** (*mariage etc*) in private.

intimider [ɛ̃timide] *vt* to intimidate, frighten. ● **intimidation** *nf* intimidation.

intituler [ɛ̃tityle] *vt* to entitle ▮ **s'intituler** *vpr* to be entitled.

intolérable [ɛ̃tɔlerabl] *a* intolerable (**que** (+*sub*) that). ● **intolérance** *nf* intolerance. ● **intolérant, -ante** *a* intolerant (**de** of).

intonation [ɛ̃tɔnasjɔ̃] *nf* *Ling* intonation; (*ton*) tone.

intoxiquer [ɛ̃tɔksike] *vt* (*empoisonner*) to poison; (*influencer*) *Pol etc* to brainwash ▮ **s'intoxiquer** *vpr* to be *ou* become poisoned. ● **intoxiqué, -ée** *nmf* addict. ● **intoxication** *nf* poisoning; *Pol etc* brainwashing; **i. alimentaire** food poisoning.

intra- [ɛ̃tra] *préf* intra-.

intraduisible [ɛ̃tradɥizibl] *a* difficult to translate, untranslatable.

intraitable [ɛ̃trɛtabl] *a* uncompromising.

intransigeant, -ante [ɛ̃trãziʒã, -ãt] *a* intransigent. ● **intransigeance** *nf* intransigence.

intransitif, -ive [ɛ̃trãzitif, -iv] *a & nm* *Grammaire* intransitive.

intraveineux, -euse [ɛ̃travɛnø, -øz] *a* *Méd* intravenous.

intrépide [ɛ̃trepid] *a* (*courageux*) fearless, intrepid; (*obstiné*) headstrong. ● **intrépidité** *nf* fearlessness.

intrigue [ɛ̃trig] *nf* intrigue; (*de film, roman etc*) plot. ● **intrigant, -ante** *nmf* schemer. ● **intriguer 1** *vi* to scheme, intrigue. **2** *vt* **i. qn** (*intéresser*) to intrigue s.o., puzzle s.o.

intrinsèque [ɛ̃trɛ̃sɛk] *a* intrinsic. ● **intrinsèquement** *adv* intrinsically.

introduire* [ɛ̃trɔdɥir] *vt* (*présenter*) to introduce, bring in; (*insérer*) put in (**dans** to); to insert (**dans** into); (*faire entrer*) to show (s.o.) in; **s'i. dans** to get into. ● **introduction** *nf* (*texte, action*) introduction.

introspectif, -ive [ɛ̃trɔspektif, -iv] *a* introspective. ● **introspection** *nf* introspection.

introuvable [ɛ̃truvabl] *a* nowhere to be

found.
introverti, -ie [ɛ̃trɔvɛrti] *nmf* introvert.
intrus, -use [ɛ̃try, -yz] *nmf* intruder. ● **intrusion** *nf* intrusion (**dans** into).
intuition [ɛ̃tɥisjɔ̃] *nf* intuition. ● **intuitif, -ive** *a* intuitive.
inusable [inyzabl] *a Fam* hard-wearing, durable.
inusité, -ée [inyzite] *a* (*mot, forme etc*) unused.
inutile [inytil] *a* useless, unnecessary; **c'est i. de crier** it's pointless *ou* useless to shout. ● **inutilement** *adv* (*vainement*) needlessly. ● **inutilité** *nf* uselessness.
inutilisable [inytilizabl] *a* unusable. ● **inutilisé, -ée** *a* unused.
invaincu, -ue [ɛ̃vɛ̃ky] *a Sport* unbeaten.
invalide [ɛ̃valid] *a* & *nmf* disabled (person); **i. de guerre** disabled ex-soldier.
● **invalider** [ɛ̃valide] *vt* to invalidate.
invariable [ɛ̃varjabl] *a* invariable. ● **invariablement** [-əmɑ̃] *adv* invariably.
invasion [ɛ̃vɑzjɔ̃] *nf* invasion.
invective [ɛ̃vɛktiv] *nf* invective. ● **invectiver** *vt* to abuse ▮ *vi* **i. contre** to inveigh against.
invendable [ɛ̃vɑ̃dabl] *a* unsaleable. ● **invendu, -ue** *a* unsold ▮ *nmpl* **invendus** unsold articles; (*journaux*) unsold copies.
inventaire [ɛ̃vɑ̃tɛr] *nm* (*liste*) *Com* inventory; (*étude*) *Fig* survey; **faire l'i.** *Com* to do the stocktaking (**de** of).
inventer [ɛ̃vɑ̃te] *vt* (*créer*) to invent; (*imaginer*) to make up. ● **inventeur, -trice** *nmf* inventor. ● **inventif, -ive** *a* inventive. ● **invention** *nf* invention.
inverse [ɛ̃vɛrs] *a* (*sens*) opposite; (*ordre*) reverse; *Math* inverse ▮ *nm* **l'i.** the reverse, the opposite. ● **inversement** [-əmɑ̃] *adv* conversely. ● **inverser** *vt* (*ordre*) to reverse. ● **inversion** *nf* Grammaire Anat etc inversion.
investigation [ɛ̃vɛstigɑsjɔ̃] *nf* investigation.
investir [ɛ̃vɛstir] **1** *vt* (*capitaux*) to invest (**dans** in) ▮ *vi* to invest (**dans** in). **2** *vt* **i. qn de** (*fonction etc*) to invest s.o. with. ● **investissement** *nm* (*placement*) investment. ● **investiture** *nf Pol* nomination.
invétéré, -ée [ɛ̃vetere] *a* inveterate.
invincible [ɛ̃vɛ̃sibl] *a* invincible.
invisible [ɛ̃vizibl] *a* invisible.
inviter [ɛ̃vite] *vt* to invite; **i. qn à faire qch** to invite *ou* ask s.o. to do sth; (*inciter*) to tempt s.o. to do sth; **s'i.** (**chez qn**) to gatecrash. ● **invité, -ée** *nmf* guest. ● **invitation** *nf* invitation.
invivable [ɛ̃vivabl] *a* unbearable; (*personne*) *Fam* insufferable.
involontaire [ɛ̃vɔlɔ̃tɛr] *a* (*geste etc*) unintentional, involuntary. ● **involontairement** *adv* accidentally, involuntarily.
invoquer [ɛ̃vɔke] *vt* (*argument etc*) to put forward; (*appeler*) to call upon, invoke. ● **invocation** *nf* invocation (**à** to).
invraisemblable [ɛ̃vrɛsɑ̃blabl] *a* incredible; (*improbable*) improbable. ● **invraisemblance** *nf* improbability.

invulnérable [ɛ̃vylnerabl] *a* invulnerable.
iode [jɔd] *nm* **teinture d'i.** (*antiseptique*) iodine.
ira, irait *etc* [ira, irɛ] *voir* **aller**[1].
Irak [irak] *nm* Iraq. ● **irakien, -ienne** *a* Iraqi ▮ *nmf* **I., Irakienne** Iraqi.
Iran [irɑ̃] *nm* Iran. ● **iranien, -ienne** *a* Iranian ▮ *nmf* **I., Iranienne** Iranian.
irascible [irasibl] *a* irascible.
iris [iris] *nm* (*de l'œil, plante*) iris.
Irlande [irlɑ̃d] *nf* Ireland; **I. du Nord** Northern Ireland. ● **irlandais, -aise** *a* Irish ▮ *nmf* **I.** Irishman; **Irlandaise** Irishwoman; **les I.** the Irish ▮ *nm* (*langue*) Irish.
ironie [irɔni] *nf* irony. ● **ironique** *a* ironic(al).
iront [irɔ̃] *voir* **aller**[1].
irradier [iradje] *vt* to irradiate; **aliments irradiés** irradiated food.
irraisonné, -ée [irezɔne] *a* irrational.
irréconciliable [irekɔ̃siljabl] *a* irreconcilable.
irrécupérable [irekyperabl] *a* (*objet*) beyond repair *ou* redemption; (*personne*) beyond redemption.
irrécusable [irekyzabl] *a* irrefutable.
irréel, -elle [ireɛl] *a* unreal.
irréfléchi, -ie [irefleʃi] *a* thoughtless, unthinking.
irréfutable [irefytabl] *a* irrefutable.
irrégulier, -ière [iregylje, -jɛr] *a* irregular. ● **irrégularité** *nf* irregularity.
irrémédiable [iremedjabl] *a* irreparable.
irremplaçable [irɑ̃plasabl] *a* irreplaceable.
irréparable [ireparabl] *a* (*véhicule etc*) beyond repair; (*tort, perte*) irreparable.
irrépressible [irepresibl] *a* (*rires etc*) irrepressible.
irréprochable [ireprɔʃabl] *a* beyond reproach, irreproachable.
irrésistible [irezistibl] *a* (*personne, charme etc*) irresistible.
irrésolu, -ue [irezɔly] *a* irresolute.
irrespirable [irɛspirabl] *a* (*air*) unbreathable; *Fig* stifling.
irresponsable [irɛspɔ̃sabl] *a* (*personne*) irresponsable.
irrévérencieux, -euse [ireverɑ̃sjø, -øz] *a* irreverent.
irréversible [ireversibl] *a* irreversible.
irrévocable [irevɔkabl] *a* irrevocable.
irriguer [irige] *vt* to irrigate. ● **irrigation** *nf* irrigation.
irriter [irite] *vt* to irritate ▮ **s'irriter** *vpr* to get angry (**de, contre** at). ● **irritant, -ante** *a* irritating ▮ *nm* irritant. ● **irritable** *a* irritable. ● **irritation** *nf* (*colère*) & *Méd* irritation.
irruption [irypsjɔ̃] *nf* **faire i. dans** to burst into.
islam [islam] *nm* Islam. ● **islamique** *a* Islamic.
Islande [islɑ̃d] *nf* Iceland. ● **islandais, -aise** *a* Icelandic ▮ *nmf* **I., Islandaise** Icelander.
isocèle [izɔsɛl] *a* **triangle i.** isoceles triangle.
isoler [izɔle] *vt* to isolate (**de** from); (*du froid etc*) & *Él* to insulate ▮ **s'isoler** *vpr* to cut oneself off, isolate oneself. ● **isolant, -ante** *a*

insulating ▌ *nm* insulating material. ●**isolé, -ée** *a* isolated; (*écarté*) remote, isolated; **i. de cut off** *ou* isolated from. ●**isolation** *nf* insulation. ●**isolement** *nm* isolation. ●**isolément** *adv* in isolation, singly.

isoloir [izɔlwar] *nm Br* polling *ou Am* voting booth.

isorel® [izɔrɛl] *nm* hardboard.

Israël [israɛl] *nm* Israel. ●**israélien, -ienne** *a* Israeli ▌ *nmf* **I., Israélienne** Israeli. ●**israélite** *a* Jewish ▌ *nm* Jew ▌ *nf* Jew, Jewess.

issu [isy] *a* **être i. de** to come from.

issue [isy] *nf* (*sortie*) way out, exit; (*solution*) *Fig* way out; (*résultat*) outcome; **rue** *etc* **sans i.** dead end; **situation** *etc* **sans i.** *Fig* dead end; **à l'i. de** at the close of.

isthme [ism] *nm* (*bande de terre*) isthmus.

Italie [itali] *nf* Italy. ●**italien, -ienne** *a* Italian ▌ *nmf* **I., Italienne** Italian ▌ *nm* (*langue*) Italian.

italique [italik] *a* (*lettre etc*) italic ▌ *nm* italics; **en i.** in italics.

itinéraire [itinɛrɛr] *nm* route, itinerary.

itinérant, -ante [itinerɑ̃, -ɑ̃t] *a* itinerant, *Br* travelling, *Am* traveling.

IUT [iyte] *nm abrév* **institut universitaire de technologie.**

IVG [iveʒe] *nf abrév* (*interruption volontaire de grossesse*) (voluntary) abortion.

ivoire [ivwar] *nm* ivory; **statuette/etc en i.** *ou* **d'i.** ivory statuette/etc.

ivre [ivr] *a* drunk (**de** with); **i. de joie/etc** wild with joy/etc; **i. de bonheur** wildly happy. ●**ivresse** *nf* drunkenness; **en état d'i.** under the influence of drink. ●**ivrogne** *nmf* drunk(ard).

J

J, j [ʒi] *nm* J, j; **le jour J.** D-day.

j' [ʒ] *voir* **je.**

jacasser [ʒakase] *vi* (*personne, pie*) to chatter.

jachère (en) [ãʒaʃɛr] *adv* (*champ etc*) fallow; **être en j.** to lie fallow.

jacinthe [ʒasɛ̃t] *nf* hyacinth.

jacuzzi [ʒakuzi] *nm* (*baignoire*) jacuzzi.

jade [ʒad] *nm* (*pierre*) jade.

jadis [ʒadis] *adv* long ago, once.

jaguar [ʒagwar] *nm* (*animal*) jaguar.

jaillir [ʒajir] *vi* (*liquide*) to spurt (out), gush (out); (*lumière*) to beam out, shine forth. (*cri*) to burst out; (*étincelle*) to fly out; (*vérité*) to burst forth. ●**jaillissement** *nm* (*de liquide*) gush.

jais [ʒɛ] *nm* (*noir*) de j. jet-black.

jalon [ʒalɔ̃] *nm* (*piquet*) marker; **poser les jalons** *Fig* to prepare the way (**de for**). ●**jalonner** *vt* to mark (out); (*border*) to line.

jaloux, -ouse [ʒalu, -uz] *a* jealous (**de of**). ●**jalouser** *vt* to envy. ●**jalousie** *nf* 1 jealousy. 2 (*persienne*) venetian blind.

Jamaïque [ʒamaik] *nf* Jamaica.

jamais [ʒamɛ] *adv* 1 (*négatif*) never; **sans j. sortir** without ever going out; **elle ne sort j.** she never goes out; **à tout j.** (absolutely) never! 2 (*positif*) ever; **à (tout) j.** for ever; **si j.** if ever.

jambe [ʒãb] *nf leg*; **j. de pantalon** *Br* trouser leg, *Am* pants leg; **à toutes jambes** as fast as one can; **prendre ses jambes à son cou** *Fig* to take to one's heels; **être dans les jambes de qn** (*gêner*) to be under s.o.'s feet; **faire qch par dessus la j.** *Fam* to do sth any old how; **ça me fait une belle j.!** *Fam* that does me a fat lot of good.

jambon [ʒãbɔ̃] *nm* (*charcuterie*) ham. ●**jambonneau, -x** *nm* knuckle of ham.

jante [ʒãt] *nf* (*de roue*) rim.

janvier [ʒãvje] *nm* January.

Japon [ʒapɔ̃] *nm* Japan. ●**japonais, -aise** *a* Japanese ▮ *nmf* **J., Japonaise** Japanese man *ou* woman, Japanese *inv*; **les J.** the Japanese ▮ *nm* (*langue*) Japanese.

japper [ʒape] *vi* (*chien etc*) to yap, yelp. ●**jappement** *nm* yap, yelp.

jaquette [ʒakɛt] *nf* (*d'homme*) tailcoat, morning coat; *Br* (*de livre*) jacket; **se faire la j.** *Fam* to buzz off, *Br* skip off.

jardin [ʒardɛ̃] *nm* garden; **j. d'enfants** kindergarten, *Br* playschool; **j. public** park; (*plus petit*) gardens. ●**jardinage** *nm* gardening. ●**jardiner** *vi* to do the garden *ou* the gardening, be gardening. ●**jardinerie** *nf* garden centre.

jardinier [ʒardinje] *nm* gardener. ●**jardinière** *nf* (*personne*) gardener; (*caisse à fleurs*) window box; **j. (de légumes)** mixed vegetable dish; **j. d'enfants** kindergarten teacher.

jargon [ʒargɔ̃] *nm* jargon.

jarret [ʒarɛ] *nm* back of the knee.

jarretelle [ʒartɛl] *nf* (*de gaine*) *Br* suspender, *Am* garter. ●**jarretière** *nf* (*autour de la jambe*) garter.

jaser [ʒaze] *vi* (*bavarder*) to jabber.

jasmin [ʒasmɛ̃] *nm* (*arbuste*) jasmine; **thé au j.** jasmine tea.

jatte [ʒat] *nf* (*bol*) bowl.

jauge [ʒoʒ] *nf* 1 (*instrument*) gauge. 2 (*capacité*) capacity; *Nau* tonnage. ●**jauger** *vt* (*personne*) *Fig* Litt to size up.

jaune [ʒon] 1 *a* yellow ▮ *nm* (*couleur*) yellow; **j. d'œuf** (egg) yolk. 2 *nm* (*ouvrier*) *Péj* blackleg, scab ▮ *adv* **rire j.** to give a forced laugh. ●**jaunâtre** *a* yellowish. ●**jaunir** *vti* (to turn) yellow. ●**jaunisse** *nf* (*maladie*) jaundice.

Javel (eau de) [odʒavɛl] *nf* bleach. ●**javelliser** *vt* to chlorinate.

javelot [ʒavlo] *nm* javelin.

jazz [dʒaz] *nm* jazz.

je [ʒ(ə)] *pron* (**j'** before vowel or mute **h**) I; **je suis** I am.

jean® [dʒin] *nm* (pair of) jeans.

jeep® [dʒip] *nf* jeep®.

je-m'en-fichisme [ʒmãfiʃism] *ou* **je-m'en-foutisme** [ʒmãfutism] *nm inv* *Fam* couldn't-care-less attitude.

jérémiades [ʒeremjad] *nfpl* *Fam* lamentations, whining.

jerrycan [(d)ʒerikan] *nm* *Br* petrol *ou* *Am* gasoline can; (*pour l'eau*) water can.

jersey [ʒɛrze] *nm* (*tissu*) jersey.

Jersey [ʒɛrze] *nf* Jersey.

jésuite [ʒezɥit] *nm* Jesuit.

Jésus [ʒezy] *nm* Jesus; **J.-Christ** Jesus Christ; **avant/après J.-Christ** BC/AD.

jet [ʒɛ] *nm* throw; (*de vapeur*) burst, gush, jet; (*de lumière*) flash; (*de tuyau d'arrosage*) nozzle; **j. d'eau** fountain; **premier j.** (*ébauche*) first draft; **d'un seul j.** in one go.

jetable [ʒ(ə)tabl] *a* (*rasoir etc*) disposable.

jetée [ʒ(ə)te] *nf* pier, jetty.

jeter [ʒ(ə)te] *vt* to throw (**à** to, **dans** into); (*à la poubelle*) to throw away; (*ancre, sort, regard*) to cast; (*bases*) to lay; (*cri, son*) to let out, utter; (*éclat, lueur*) to throw out, give out; (*noter*) to jot down; **j. un coup d'œil sur** *ou* **à** to have *ou* take a look at; (*rapidement*) to glance at; **j. l'argent par les fenêtres** *Fig* to throw money down the drain.

se jeter *vpr* to throw oneself; **se j. sur** to pounce on, fall on; **se j. contre** *(véhicule)* to crash into; **se j. dans** *(fleuve)* to flow into; **se j. à l'eau** *(plonger)* to jump into the water; *(se décider) Fig* to take the plunge.

jeton [3(ə)tɔ̃] *nm (pièce)* token; *(au jeu)* chip.

jeu, -x [3ø] *nm* **1** game; *(amusement)* play; *(d'argent)* gambling; *Théâtre* acting; *Mus* playing; **j. de mots** play on words, pun; **jeux de société** parlour *ou* indoor *ou* party games; **j. télévisé** television quiz; **maison de jeux** gambling club; **en j.** *(en cause)* at stake; *(forces etc)* at work; **entrer en j.** to come into play; **d'entrée de j.** from the outset, from the word go; **tirer son épingle du j.** *(obtenir un bénéfice)* to play one's game profitably; **elle a beau j. de critiquer/etc** it's easy for her to criticize/etc; **c'est un j. d'enfant!** it's child's play! **2** *(série complète)* set; *(de cartes)* deck, *Br* pack; *(cartes en main)* hand; **j. d'échecs** *(boîte, pièces)* chess set. **3** *(de ressort, verrou) Tech* play.

jeudi [3ødi] *nm* Thursday.

jeun (à) [a3œ̃] *adv* on an empty stomach; **être à j.** to have eaten no food.

jeune [3œn] *a* young; *(inexpérimenté)* inexperienced; **Dupont j.** Dupont junior; **d'allure j.** young-looking; **jeunes gens** young people ∎ *nmf* young person; **les jeunes** young people. ●**jeunesse** *nf* youth; *(apparence)* youthfulness; **la j.** *(jeunes)* the young, youth.

jeûne [3øn] *nm* fast; *(action)* fasting. ●**jeûner** *vi* to fast.

joaillier, -ière [3ɔaje, -jɛr] *nmf Br* jeweller, *Am* jeweler. ●**joaillerie** *nf Br* jewellery, *Am* jewelry; *(magasin) Br* jewellery *ou Am* jewelry shop.

jockey [3ɔkɛ] *nm* jockey.

jogging [dʒɔgiŋ] *nm Sport* jogging; *(survêtement)* jogging suit; **faire du j.** to jog, go jogging.

joie [3wa] *nf* joy, delight; **feu de j.** bonfire.

joindre* [3wɛ̃dr] *vt (mettre ensemble, relier)* to join; *(efforts)* to combine; *(insérer dans une enveloppe)* to enclose (**à** with); *(ajouter)* to add (**à** to); **j. qn** *(contacter)* to get in touch with s.o.; **j. les deux bouts** *Fig* to make ends meet; **se j. à** *(un groupe etc)* to join ∎ **joint, jointe** *a (efforts)* joint, combined; **à pieds joints** with feet together ∎ *nm (articulation) Tech* joint; *(d'étanchéité)* seal; *(de robinet)* washer; **j. de culasse** gasket. ●**jointure** *nf Anat* joint.

joker [3ɔkɛr] *nm Cartes* joker.

joli, -ie [3ɔli] *a* nice, lovely; *(femme, enfant)* pretty. ●**joliment** *adv* nicely; *(très, beaucoup) Fam* awfully.

jonc [3ɔ̃] *nm (plante)* (bul)rush.

joncher [3ɔ̃ʃe] *vt* to litter (**de** with); **jonché de** strewn *ou* littered with.

jonction [3ɔ̃ksjɔ̃] *nf (de routes etc)* junction.

jongler [3ɔ̃gle] *vi* to juggle (**avec** with). ●**jongleur, -euse** *nmf* juggler.

jonquille [3ɔ̃kij] *nf* daffodil.

Jordanie [3ɔrdani] *nf* Jordan.

joue [3u] *nf (du visage)* cheek; **mettre en j. un fusil** to aim a rifle; **en j.!** (take) aim!; **danser j. contre j.** to dance cheek to cheek.

jouer [3we] *vi* to play; *(acteur)* to act; *(au tiercé etc)* to gamble, bet; *(à la Bourse)* to gamble; *(entrer en jeu)* to come into play; *(être important)* to count; **j. au tennis/aux cartes/etc** to play tennis/cards/etc; **j. du piano/du violon/etc** to play the piano/violin/etc; **j. aux courses** to bet on the horses; **j. des coudes** to use one's elbows; **faire j. un ressort** to release *ou* trigger a spring; **la clef jouait dans la serrure** the key was loose in the lock *ou* didn't fit the lock; **à toi de j.!** it's your turn (to play)!

∎ *vt (musique, tour, jeu, rôle)* to play; *(pièce de théâtre)* to perform, put on; *(film)* to show, put on; *(risquer)* to gamble, bet (**sur** on); *(cheval)* to bet on; **j. gros jeu** to play for high stakes; **se j. de** *(se moquer)* to scoff at; *(difficultés)* to make light of.

jouet [3wɛ] *nm* toy; **le j. de qn** *Fig* s.o.'s plaything.

joueur, -euse [3wœr, -øz] *nmf* player; *(au tiercé etc)* gambler; **beau j., bon j.,** good loser.

joufflu, -ue [3ufly] *a (visage)* chubby; *(enfant)* chubby-cheeked.

joug [3u] *nm Agr & Fig* yoke.

jouir [3wir] *vi* **1 j. de** *(savourer, avoir)* to enjoy. **2** *(éprouver le plaisir sexuel)* to have an orgasm, come. ●**jouissance** *nf* enjoyment; *(usage) Jur* use.

joujou, -x [3u3u] *nm Fam* toy.

jour [3ur] *nm* day; *(lumière)* (day)light; *(ouverture)* gap, opening; **il fait j.** it's (day)light; **de j. en j.** day by day, daily; **du j. au lendemain** overnight; **au j. le j.** from day to day; **en plein j., au grand j.** in broad daylight; **de nos jours** nowadays, these days; **sous un j. nouveau** *Fig* in a different light; **le j. de l'An** New Year's day; **les beaux jours** *(l'été)* summer; **mettre qch à j.** to bring sth up to date; **mettre qch au j.** to bring sth into the open; **se faire j.** to come to light; **donner le j. à qn** to give birth to s.o.; **mettre fin à ses jours** to commit suicide; **quel j. sommes-nous?** what day is it?; **il y a dix ans j. pour j.** ten years ago to the day; **elle et lui, c'est le j. et la nuit!** *Fam* she and he are as different as night and day *ou Br* as chalk and cheese.

journal, -aux [3urnal, -o] *nm* (news)paper; *(spécialisé)* journal; *(intime)* diary; *(parlé) (à la radio)* (radio) news; **j. (télévisé)** (TV) news; **j. de bord** *(de navire)* logbook. ●**journalisme** *nm* journalism. ●**journaliste** *nmf* journalist. ●**journalistique** *a (style etc)* journalistic.

journalier, -ière [3urnalje, -jɛr] *a* daily.

journée [3urne] *nf* day; **pendant la j.** during the day(time); **toute la j.** all day (long). ●**journellement** *adv* daily.

jovial, -e, -aux [3ɔvjal, -o] *a* jovial, jolly.

● **jovialité** *nf* jollity.

joyau, -aux [ʒwajo] *nm* jewel.

joyeux, -euse [ʒwajø, -øz] *a* merry, happy, joyful; **j. anniversaire!** happy birthday!; **j. Noël!** merry *ou Br* happy Christmas!

jubilé [ʒybile] *nm* (golden) jubilee.

jubiler [ʒybile] *vi* to be jubilant. ● **jubilation** *nf* jubilation.

jucher [ʒyʃe] *vt*, **se jucher** *vpr* to perch (**sur** on).

judaïque [ʒydaik] *a* Jewish. ● **judaïsme** *nm* Judaism.

judas [ʒyda] *nm* (*de porte*) peephole, spy hole.

judiciaire [ʒydisjɛr] *a* judicial, legal.

judicieux, -euse [ʒydisjø, -øz] *a* sensible, judicious.

judo [ʒydo] *nm* judo. ● **judoka** *nmf* judo expert.

juge [ʒyʒ] *nm* judge; **j. d'instruction** examining magistrate; **j. de paix, j. d'instance** Justice of the Peace; **j. de touche** *Football* linesman; **j. de filet** *Tennis* linesman. ● **juge-arbitre** *nm* (*pl* **juges-arbitres**) *Sport* referee, umpire.

jugé (au) [oʒyʒe] *adv* by guesswork.

jugement [ʒyʒmɑ̃] *nm* judg(e)ment; (*verdict*) *Jur* sentence; **passer en j.** (*au tribunal*) to stand trial; **le J. dernier** *Rel* the Last Judg(e)ment.

jugeote [ʒyʒɔt] *nf Fam* commonsense.

juger [ʒyʒe] *vt* (*personne, question etc*) to judge; (*au tribunal*) to try (*s.o.*); (*estimer*) to consider (**que** that); **j. utile/***etc* **de faire** to consider it useful/*etc* to do. ▮ *vi* **j. de** to judge; **jugez de ma surprise/***etc* imagine my surprise/*etc*.

juguler [ʒygyle] *vt* to check, suppress.

juif, juive [ʒɥif, ʒɥiv] *a* Jewish ▮ *nm* **J.** Jew ▮ *nf* **Juive** Jew(ess), Jewish woman *ou* girl.

juillet [ʒɥijɛ] *nm* July.

juin [ʒɥɛ̃] *nm* June.

jumeau, -elle, *pl* **-eaux, -elles** [ʒymo, -ɛl] *a* **frère** *ou* **sœur jumelle** twin brother/sister; **lits jumeaux** twin beds ▮ *nmf* twin. ● **jumeler** *vt* (*villes*) to twin. ● **jumelage** *nm* twinning.

jumelles [ʒymɛl] *nfpl* (*pour regarder*) binoculars; **j. de théâtre** opera glasses.

jument [ʒymɑ̃] *nf* mare.

jungle [ʒœ̃gl] *nf* jungle.

junior [ʒynjɔr] *nm & a inv Sport* junior.

junte [ʒœ̃t] *nf Pol* junta.

jupe [ʒyp] *nf* skirt. ● **jupon** *nm* petticoat.

jurer [ʒyre] **1** *vi* (*dire un gros mot*) to swear (**contre** at). **2** *vt* (*promettre*) to swear (**que** that, **de faire** to do) ▮ *vi* **j. de qch** to swear to sth. **3** *vi* (*contraster*) to clash (**avec** with). ● **juré, -ée** *a* **ennemi j.** sworn enemy ▮ *nm* Jur

juror.

juridiction [ʒyridiksjɔ̃] *nf* jurisdiction.

juridique [ʒyridik] *a* legal. ● **juriste** *nmf* legal expert, jurist.

juron [ʒyrɔ̃] *nm* swearword, oath.

jury [ʒyri] *nm* Jur jury; (*examinateurs*) board (of examiners), jury.

jus [ʒy] *nm* (*fruits*) juice; (*viande*) gravy; (*café*) *Fam* coffee; **j. d'orange** orange juice; **prendre du j.** (*électricité*) *Fam* to get a shock.

jusque [ʒysk] *prép* **jusqu'à** (*espace*) as far as, (right) up to; (*temps*) until, (up) till, to; (*même*) even; **jusqu'à dix francs/***etc* (*limite*) up to ten francs/*etc*; **jusqu'en mai/***etc* until May/*etc*; **jusqu'où?** how far?; **jusqu'ici** as far as this; (*temps*) until now; **jusqu'à présent** up till now; **jusqu'à un certain point** up to a point; **jusqu'à la limite de ses forces** to the point of exhaustion; **j. dans/sous/***etc* right into/under/*etc*; **j. chez moi** as far as my place; **en avoir j.-là** *Fam* to be fed up.
▮ *conj* **jusqu'à ce qu'il vienne** until he comes.

juste [ʒyst] *a* (*équitable*) fair, just; (*légitime*) just; (*exact*) right, correct, accurate; (*étroit*) tight; (*remarque*) sound; (*voix*) *Mus* true; **un peu j.** (*quantité, qualité*) barely enough; **très j.!** quite so *ou* right!; **à 3 heures juste(s)** on the stroke of 3.
▮ *adv* (*deviner, compter*) correctly, right, accurately; (*chanter*) in tune; (*seulement, exactement*) just; **au j.** exactly; **tout j.** (*à peine, seulement*) only just; **calculer au plus j.** to work things out at the minimum price; **c'était j.!** (*il était temps*) it was a near thing!; **un peu j.** (*mesurer, compter*) a bit on the short side; **comme de j.** *Fam* as one would expect.
▮ *nm* (*homme*) just man. ● **justement** [-əmɑ̃] *adv* exactly, precisely, just; (*avec justesse ou justice*) justly.

justesse [ʒystɛs] *nf* (*exactitude*) accuracy; **de j.** (*éviter, gagner etc*) just.

justice [ʒystis] *nf* justice; (*autorités*) law; **en toute j.** in all fairness; **rendre j. à qn** to do justice to s.o.; **rendre la j.** to dispense justice; **passer en j.** to stand trial. ● **justicier, -ière** *nmf* dispenser of justice.

justifier [ʒystifje] *vt* to justify ▮ *vi* **j. de qch** to prove sth ▮ **se justifier** *vpr* Jur to clear oneself (**de**); (*attitude etc*) to be justified. ● **justifiable** *a* justifiable. ● **justificatif, -ive** *a* **document j.** supporting document, written proof. ● **justification** *nf* justification; (*preuve*) proof.

jute [ʒyt] *nm* (*fibre*) jute.

juteux, -euse [ʒytø, -øz] *a* juicy.

juvénile [ʒyvenil] *a* youthful.

juxtaposer [ʒykstapoze] *vt* to juxtapose. ● **juxtaposition** *nf* juxtaposition.

K

K, k [kɑ] *nm* K, k.
kaki [kaki] *a inv* & *nm* khaki.
kaléidoscope [kaleidɔskɔp] *nm* kaleidoscope.
kangourou [kãguru] *nm* **1** (*animal*) kangaroo. **2**® (*porte-bébé*) baby sling.
karaté [karate] *nm Sport* karate.
kart [kart] *nm Sport* (go-)kart, go-cart.
● **karting** [-iŋ] *nm Sport* (go-)karting.
kascher [kaʃɛr] *a inv Rel* kosher.
kayak [kajak] *nm* (*bateau*) canoe.
Kenya [kenja] *nm* Kenya.
képi [kepi] *nm* (*coiffure militaire*) cap, kepi.
kermesse [kɛrmɛs] *nf* charity fair *ou Br* fête; (*en Belgique etc*) village fair.
kérosène [kerozɛn] *nm* kerosene, aviation fuel.
kibboutz [kibuts] *nm* kibbutz.
kidnapper [kidnape] *vt* to kidnap. ● **kidnappeur, -euse** *nmf* kidnapper.
kilo [kilo] *nm* kilo. ● **kilogramme** *nm* kilogram(me).
kilomètre [kilɔmɛtr] *nm* kilometre. ● **kilométrage** *nm Aut* = mileage. ● **kilométrique** *a* **borne k.** = milestone.

kilo-octet [kilɔɔktɛ] *nm Ordinat* kilobyte.
kilowatt [kilɔwat] *nm* kilowatt.
kimono [kimɔno] *nm* (*tunique*) kimono.
kinésithérapie [kineziterapi] *nf* physiotherapy. ● **kinésithérapeute** *nmf* physiotherapist.
kiosque [kjɔsk] *nm* (*à fleurs etc*) kiosk, *Br* stall; **k. à journaux** news stand, newspaper kiosk *ou Br* stall; **k. à musique** bandstand.
kit [kit] *nm* (self-assembly) kit; **meuble en k.** self-assembly (furniture) unit.
kiwi [kiwi] *nm* (*oiseau, fruit*) kiwi.
klaxon® [klaksɔn] *nm* (*de véhicule*) horn. ● **klaxonner** *vi* to sound one's horn, *Br* hoot, *Am* honk.
km *abrév* (*kilomètre*) km. ● **km/h** *abrév* (*kilomètre-heure*) kph,= mph.
k.-o. [kɑo] *a inv* **mettre qn k.-o.** *Boxe* to knock s.o. out.
Koweït [kɔwɛjt] *nm* Kuwait. ● **koweïtien, -ienne** *a* Kuwaiti ❚ *nmf* **K., Koweïtienne** Kuwaiti.
kyrielle [kirjɛl] *nf* **une k. de** (*reproches etc*) a long string of; (*vedettes etc*) a whole series *ou* crowd of.
kyste [kist] *nm Méd* cyst.

L

L, l [ɛl] *nm* L, l.

l', la [l, la] *voir* **le**.

la [la] *nm* (*note de musique*) A; **donner le la** *Mus* to give an A.

là [la] **1** *adv* (*lieu*) there; (*chez soi*) in, home; **je reste là** I'll stay here; **c'est là que** *ou* **où** that's where; **c'est là ton erreur** that's *ou* there's your mistake; **là où il est** where he is; **à cinq mètres de là** five metres away; **de là son échec** (*cause*) hence his *ou* her failure; **jusque-là** (*lieu*) as far as that; **passe par là** go that way.

2 *adv* (*temps*) then; **jusque-là** up till then.

3 *int* **oh là là!** oh dear!; **alors là!** well!; **là, là!** (*pour rassurer*) there, there!

4 *voir* **ce², celui**.

là-bas [labɑ] *adv* over there.

label [label] *nm* (*sur un produit*) label, mark (*of quality, origin etc*).

labeur [labœr] *nm Litt* toil.

labo [labo] *nm Fam* lab. ●**laboratoire** *nm* laboratory; **l. de langues** language laboratory.

laborieux, -euse [labɔrjø, -øz] *a* (*pénible*) laborious; (*personne*) industrious; **les classes laborieuses** the working classes.

labour [labur] *nm Br* ploughing, *Am* plowing; (*avec une bêche*) digging over. ●**labourer** *vt* (*avec une charrue*) *Br* to plough, *Am* plow; (*avec une bêche*) to dig over; (*visage etc*) *Fig* to furrow. ●**laboureur** *nm Br* ploughman, *Am* plowman.

labyrinthe [labirɛt] *nm* maze, labyrinth.

lac [lak] *nm* lake.

lacer [lase] *vt* to lace (up). ●**lacet** *nm* **1** (*shoe- ou boot-*)**lace**. **2** (*de route*) twist, zigzag; **route en l.** winding *ou* zigzag road.

lacérer [lasere] *vt* (*papier etc*) to tear; (*visage etc*) to lacerate.

lâche [lɑʃ] **1** *a* cowardly ▮ *nmf* coward. **2** *a* (*détendu*) loose, slack. ●**lâchement** *adv* in a cowardly manner. ●**lâcheté** *nf* cowardice; **une l.** (*action*) a cowardly act.

lâcher [lɑʃe] *vt* (*main, objet etc*) to let go of; (*bombe*) to drop, release; (*pigeon, colombe*) to release; (*place, études*) to give up; (*juron*) to utter, let slip; (*secret*) to let out; **l. qn** *Fam* (*laisser tranquille*) to leave s.o. (alone); (*abandonner*) to drop s.o.; **l. prise** to let go; **lâche-moi les baskets** *ou* **basquettes!** *Fam* get off my back! ▮ *vi* (*corde*) to give way ▮ *nm* release. ●**lâcheur, -euse** *nmf Fam* deserter.

laconique [lakɔnik] *a* laconic.

lacrymogène [lakrimɔʒɛn] *a* **gaz l.** tear gas.

lacté, -ée [lakte] *a* **régime l.** milk diet; **la Voie lactée** the Milky Way.

lacune [lakyn] *nf* gap, deficiency.

lad [lad] *nm* stable boy, groom.

là-dedans [lad(ə)dɑ] *adv* (*lieu*) in there, inside. ●**là-dessous** *adv* underneath. ●**là-dessus** *adv* on there; (*monter*) on top; (*alors*) thereupon. ●**là-haut** *adv* up there; (*à l'étage*) upstairs.

lagon [lagɔ] *nm* (*small*) lagoon. ●**lagune** *nf* lagoon.

laid, laide [lɛ, lɛd] *a* ugly; (*ignoble*) wretched. ●**laideur** *nf* ugliness.

laine [lɛn] *nf* wool; **de l., en l.** *Br* woollen, *Am* woolen. ●**lainage** *nm* (*vêtement*) *Br* woolly, woollen garment; (*étoffe*) woollen material; **lainages** (*vêtements*) woollens. ●**laineux, -euse** *a* woolly.

laïque [laik] *a* (*école*) non-denominational; (*vie*) secular; (*tribunal*) lay ▮ *nmf* (*non-prêtre*) layman, laywoman.

laisse [lɛs] *nf Br* lead, leash; **tenir en l.** to keep on a *Br* lead *ou* leash.

laisser [lese] *vt* to leave; **l. qn partir/entrer/** *etc* (*permettre*) to let s.o. go/come in/*etc*; **l. qch à qn** (*confier, donner*) to let s.o. have sth, leave sth with s.o.; **laissez-moi le temps de le faire** give me *ou* leave me time to do it; **l. qn seul** to leave s.o. alone *ou* by one-self; **je vous laisse** I'm leaving now; **je vous le laisse pour 100 francs** I'll let you have it for 100 francs; **se l. aller/faire** to let oneself go/be pushed around; **se l. surprendre par l'orage** to get caught out by the storm. ●**laissé(e)-pour-compte** *nmf* (*personne*) misfit, reject. ●**laisser-aller** *nm inv* careless-ness, slovenliness; ●**laissez-passer** *nm inv* (*sauf-conduit*) pass.

lait [lɛ] *nm* milk; **l. entier/demi-écrémé/** **écrémé** whole/semi-skimmed/skimmed milk; **dent de l.** milk tooth; **frère/sœur de l.** foster-brother/-sister. ●**laitage** *nm* milk prod-uct *ou* food. ●**laiterie** *nf* dairy. ●**laiteux, -euse** *a* milky. ●**laitier, -ière** *a* **produit l.** dairy product. ▮ *nm* (*livreur*) milkman; (*vendeur*) dairyman ▮ *nf* **laitière** dairywoman.

laiton [lɛtɔ] *nm* brass.

laitue [lety] *nf* lettuce.

laïus [lajys] *nm Fam* speech.

lama [lama] *nm* (*animal*) llama.

lambeau, -x [lɑbo] *nm* shred, bit; **mettre en lambeaux** to tear to shreds; **tomber en lambeaux** to fall to bits.

lambin, -ine [lɑbɛ̃, -in] *Fam nmf* dawdler ▮ *a* **être l.** to dawdle, be a dawdler. ●**lambiner** *vi Fam* to dawdle.

lambris [lɑbri] *nm* panelling. ●**lambrisser** *vt* to panel.

lame [lam] *nf* **1** (*de couteau, rasoir etc*)

blade; (*de métal*) strip, plate; **l. de parquet** floorboard. **2** (*vague*) wave; **l. de fond** groundswell.

lamelle [lamɛl] *nf* thin strip; **l. de verre** (*pour microscope*) slide.

lamenter (se) [səlamɑ̃te] *vpr* to moan, lament; **se l. sur** to lament (over). ● **lamentable** *a* (*mauvais*) terrible, deplorable; (*voix, cri*) mournful. ● **lamentation** *nf* lament(ation).

laminé, -ée [lamine] *a* (*métal*) laminated.

lampadaire [lɑ̃padɛr] *nm Br* standard lamp, *Am* floor lamp; (*de rue*) street lamp.

lampe [lɑ̃p] *nf* lamp; (*au néon*) light; (*de vieille radio*) valve, *Am* (*vacuum*) tube; **l. de poche** *Br* torch, *Am* flashlight; **l. à pétrole** oil lamp; **l. de bureau** desk lamp *ou* light.

lampée [lɑ̃pe] *nf Fam* gulp.

lampion [lɑ̃pjɔ̃] *nm* Chinese lantern.

lance [lɑ̃s] *nf* spear; (*de tournoi*) *Hist* lance; (*extrémité de tuyau*) nozzle; **l. d'incendie** fire hose.

lance-flammes [lɑ̃sflam] *nm inv* flame thrower. ● **lance-pierres** *nm inv* catapult. ● **lance-roquettes** *nm inv* rocket launcher.

lancer [lɑ̃se] *vt* (*jeter*) to throw (à to); (*avec force*) to hurl; (*fusée, produit, navire etc*) to launch; (*appel, ultimatum etc*) to issue; (*cri*) to utter; (*bombe*) to drop; (*regard*) to cast (à at); (*moteur*) to start; **'au revoir!' nous lança-t-il gaiement** 'goodbye' he called out *ou* said cheerfully to us.

❚ **se lancer** *vpr* (*se précipiter*) to rush; **se l. dans** (*aventure, discussion*) to launch into.

❚ *nm* **un l.** a throw; **le l.** de the throwing of. ● **lancée** *nf* momentum; **continuer sur sa l.** to keep going (*under one's initial momentum*). ● **lancement** *nm Sport* throwing; (*de fusée, navire etc*) launch(ing); **prix de l.** introductory price.

lancinant, -ante [lɑ̃sinɑ̃, -ɑ̃t] *a* (*douleur*) shooting; (*obsédant*) haunting.

landau [lɑ̃do] *nm* (*pl* **landaus**) *Br* pram, *Am* baby carriage.

lande [lɑ̃d] *nf* moor, heath.

langage [lɑ̃gaʒ] *nm* (*système, faculté d'expression*) language; **l. machine/naturel** *Ordinat* computer/natural language.

lange [lɑ̃ʒ] *nm* (baby) blanket; (*couche*) *Br* nappy, *Am* diaper. ● **langer** *vt* (*bébé*) to change.

langouste [lɑ̃gust] *nf* (spiny) lobster. ● **langoustine** *nf* (Dublin Bay) prawn, Norway lobster.

langue [lɑ̃g] *nf* tongue; *Ling* language; **l. maternelle** mother tongue; **langues vivantes** modern languages; **langues mortes** dead *ou* ancient languages; **de l. anglaise/française** English-/French-speaking; **mauvaise l.** (*personne*) gossip; **tenir sa l.** *Fig* to keep a secret; **donner sa l. au chat** *Fig* to give up; **avoir un cheveu sur la l.** *Fig* to lisp; **avoir la l. bien pendue** *Fig* to have the gift of the gab; **avoir un mot sur le bout de la l.** *Fig* to have a word on the tip of one's tongue.

● **languette** *nf* (*patte*) tongue.

langueur [lɑ̃gœr] *nf* languor. ● **languir** *vi* to languish (**après** for, after); (*conversation*) to flag. ● **languissant, -ante** *a* languid; (*conversation*) flagging.

lanière [lanjɛr] *nf* strap; (*d'étoffe*) strip.

lanterne [lɑ̃tɛrn] *nf* lantern; (*électrique*) lamp; **lanternes** (*de véhicule*) parking lights, *Br* sidelights.

lanterner [lɑ̃tɛrne] *vi* to loiter.

lapalissade [lapalisad] *nf* statement of the obvious, truism.

laper [lape] *vt* (*boire*) to lap up ❚ *vi* to lap.

lapider [lapide] *vt* to stone.

lapin [lapɛ̃] *nm* rabbit; **mon (petit) l.!** my dear!; **poser un l. à qn** *Fam* to stand s.o. up.

laps [laps] *nm* **un l. de temps** a lapse of time.

lapsus [lapsys] *nm* slip (of the tongue).

laquais [lakɛ] *nm Hist & Fig* lackey.

laque [lak] *nf* lacquer; **l. à cheveux** (hair) lacquer. ● **laquer** *vt* to lacquer; **canard laqué** *Culin* Peking duck.

laquelle [lakɛl] *voir* **lequel**.

larbin [larbɛ̃] *nm Péj* flunkey.

larcin [larsɛ̃] *nm Litt* petty theft.

lard [lar] *nm* (*gras*) (pig's) fat; **l. fumé** smoked bacon. ● **lardon** *nm Culin* strip of bacon *ou* fat.

large [larʒ] *a* wide, broad; (*vêtement*) loose; (*grand*) large; (*généreux*) liberal; **l. de six mètres** six metres wide; **l. d'esprit** broad-minded; **avoir les idées larges** to be broad-minded.

❚ *adv* (*calculer*) liberally, broadly; **ne pas en mener l.** *Fam* to be very sheepish.

❚ *nm* breadth, width; **avoir six mètres de l.** to be six metres wide; **le l.** (*mer*) the open sea; **au l. de Cherbourg** *Nau* off Cherbourg; **être au l. dans** (*vêtement*) to have lots of room in. ● **largement** [-əmɑ̃] *adv* widely; (*ouvrir*) easily; (*au moins*) easily; (*servir, payer*) liberally; **avoir l. le temps** to have plenty of time, have ample time. ● **largesse** *nf Litt* generosity, largesse; **largesses** (*dons*) generous gifts. ● **largeur** *nf* width, breadth; (*d'esprit*) breadth.

larguer [large] *vt* (*bombe, parachutiste*) to drop; **l. qn** (*se débarrasser de*) *Fam* to drop s.o.; **l. les amarres** *Nau* to cast off; **je suis largué** (*perdu*) *Fam* I'm all at sea.

larme [larm] *nf* tear; (*goutte*) *Fam* drop; **avoir les larmes aux yeux** to have tears in one's eyes; **en larmes** in tears; **rire aux larmes** to laugh till one cries. ● **larmoyer** *vi* (*yeux*) to water.

larve [larv] *nf* (*d'insecte*) larva, grub.

larvé, -ée [larve] *a* latent, underlying.

larynx [larɛ̃ks] *nm* larynx ● **laryngite** *nf* (*inflammation*) laryngitis.

las, lasse [lɑ, lɑs] *a* tired, weary (**de** of). ● **lasser** *vt* to tire, weary; **se l. de** to tire of. ● **lassitude** *nf* tiredness, weariness.

lasagne [lazaɲ] *nf* lasagna.

lascar [laskar] *nm Fam* (clever) fellow.

lascif, -ive [lasif, -iv] *a* lascivious.

laser [lazɛr] *nm* laser; **rayon l.** laser beam.
lasso [laso] *nm* lasso; **prendre au l.** to lasso.
latent, -ente [latã, -ãt] *a* latent.
latéral, -e, -aux [lateral, -o] *a* latéral; **rue latérale** side street.
latin, -ine [latɛ̃, -in] *a* Latin ▮ *nmf* L., Latine Latin ▮ *nm* (*langue*) Latin; **j'y perds mon l.** *Fam* I can't make head or tail of it.
latitude [latityd] *nf Géog & Fig* latitude.
latrines [latrin] *nfpl* latrines.
latte [lat] *nf* slat, lath; (*de plancher*) board.
lauréat, -ate [lɔrea, -at] *nmf* (prize)winner ▮ *a* prize-winning.
laurier [lɔrje] *nm* (*arbre*) laurel, bay; **du l.** (*assaisonnement*) bay leaves; **s'endormir sur ses lauriers** to rest on one's laurels.
lavabo [lavabo] *nm* washbasin, sink; **lavabos** (*toilettes*) *Br* toilet(s), *Am* washroom.
lavande [lavãd] *nf* lavender.
lave [lav] *nf Géol* lava.
lave-auto [lavoto] *nm Can* car wash. ●**lave-glace** *nm Br* windscreen *ou Am* windshield washer. ●**lave-linge** *nm inv* washing machine. ●**lave-vaisselle** *nm inv* dishwasher.
laver [lave] *vt* to wash; **l. qn de** (*soupçon etc*) *Fig* to clear s.o. of ▮ **se laver** *vpr* to wash (oneself), *Am* wash up; **se l. les mains** to wash one's hands (*Fig* de of). ●**lavable** *a* washable. ●**lavage** *nm* washing; **l. de cerveau** *Psy* brainwashing. ●**laverie** *nf* (*automatique*) *Br* launderette, *Am* Laundromat®. ●**lavette** *nf* dish cloth; (*homme*) *Péj* drip. ●**laveur** *nm* **l. de carreaux** window *Br* cleaner *ou Am* washer. ●**lavoir** *nm* (*bâtiment*) washhouse.
laxatif, -ive [laksatif, -iv] *nm & a* laxative.
laxisme [laksism] *nm* permissiveness, laxity. ●**laxiste** *a* permissive, lax.
layette [lɛjɛt] *nf* baby clothes, layette.
le, la, *pl* **les** [l(ə), la, le] (**le & la** *become* **l'** *before a vowel or mute h*) **1** *art déf* (**à** + **le** = **au, à** + **les** = **aux;** **de** + **le** = **du, de** + **les** = **des**) the; **le garçon** the boy; **la fille** the girl; **les petits/rouges/**etc the little ones/red ones/etc; **mon ami le plus intime** my closest friend; **venez, les enfants!** come, children!
2 (*généralisation, abstraction*) **la beauté/vie/**etc beauty/life/etc; **la France** France; **les Français** the French; **les hommes** men; **aimer le café** to like coffee.
3 (*possession*) **il ouvrit la bouche** he opened his mouth; **se blesser au pied** to hurt one's foot; **avoir les cheveux blonds** to have blond hair.
4 (*mesure*) **dix francs le kilo** ten francs a kilo.
5 (*temps*) **elle vient le lundi/le matin** she comes on Mondays/in the morning(s); **elle passe le soir** she comes over in the evening(s); **l'an prochain** next year; **une fois l'an** once a year.
▮ *pron* (*homme*) him; (*femme*) her; (*chose, animal*) it; **les them; je la vois** I see her; I see it; **je le vois** I see him; I see it; **je les vois** I see them; **es-tu fatigué? — je le suis** are

you tired? — I am; **je le crois** I think so.
leader [lidœr] *nm Pol* leader.
lécher [leʃe] *vt* to lick; **se l. les doigts** to lick one's fingers. ●**lèche-vitrines** *nm* **faire du l.-vitrines** *Fam* to go window-shopping.
leçon [ləsɔ̃] *nf* lesson; **faire la l. à qn** to lecture s.o.; **servir de l. à qn** to teach s.o. a lesson.
lecteur, -trice [lɛktœr, -tris] *nmf* reader; (*à l'université*) (foreign language) assistant; **l. de cassettes/de CD** cassette/CD player; **l. de disques** *ou* **de disquettes** *Ordinat* disk drive. ●**lecture** *nf* reading; **lectures** (*livres*) books; **l. optique** *Ordinat* optical character reading; **tête de l.** (tape) head; **faire la l. à qn** to read to s.o.; **de la l.** some reading matter; **donner l. des résultats/**etc to read out the results/etc.
légal, -e, -aux [legal, -o] *a* legal; **médecine légale** forensic medicine. ●**légalement** *adv* legally. ●**légaliser** *vt* to legalize. ●**légalité** *nf* legality (de of); **respecter la l.** to respect the law; **rester dans la l.** to keep within the law.
légation [legasjɔ̃] *nf Pol* legation.
légende [leʒãd] *nf* **1** (*histoire*) legend. **2** (*de plan, carte*) key, legend; (*de photo*) caption. ●**légendaire** *a* legendary.
léger, -ère [leʒe, -ɛr] *a* light; (*bruit, fièvre, faute etc*) slight; (*café, thé, argument*) weak; (*bière, tabac*) mild; (*frivole*) frivolous; (*irréfléchi*) careless; **agir/**etc **à la légère** to act/etc rashly. ●**légèrement** *adv* lightly; (*un peu*) slightly; (*à la légère*) rashly. ●**légèreté** *nf* lightness; (*frivolité*) frivolity.
légiférer [leʒifere] *vi* to legislate.
légion [leʒjɔ̃] *nf Mil & Fig* legion; **L. d'honneur** Legion of Honour. ●**légionnaire** *nm* (*de la Légion étrangère*) legionnaire.
législatif, -ive [leʒislatif, -iv] *a* legislative; (*élections*) parliamentary. ●**législation** *nf* legislation. ●**législature** *nf* (*période*) term of office (*of legislative body*).
légitime [leʒitim] *a* (*action, enfant etc*) legitimate; **être en état de l. défense** to be acting in *Br* self-defence *ou Am* self-defense. ●**légitimité** *nf* legitimacy.
legs [lɛg] *nm* (*don*) *Jur* legacy, bequest; (*héritage*) *Fig* legacy. ●**léguer** *vt* to bequeath (à to).
légume [legym] **1** *nm* vegetable. **2** *nf* **grosse l.** (*personne*) *Fam* bigwig, bigshot.
lendemain [lãdmɛ̃] *nm* **le l.** the next day; (*avenir*) *Fig* the future; **le l. de** the day after; **le l. matin** the next morning.
lent, lente [lã, lãt] *a* slow. ●**lentement** *adv* slowly. ●**lenteur** *nf* slowness.
lentille [lãtij] *nf* **1** (*plante, graine*) lentil. **2** (*verre*) lens.
léopard [leɔpar] *nm* leopard.
lèpre [lɛpr] *nf* leprosy. ●**lépreux, -euse** *a* leprous ▮ *nmf* leper.
lequel, laquelle, *pl* **lesquels, lesquelles** [ləkɛl, lakɛl, lekɛl] (+ **à** = **auquel, à laquelle, auxquel(le)s;** + **de** = **duquel, de laquelle, desquel(le)s**) *pron rel* (*chose, animal*) which; (*personne*) who, (*indirect*) whom;

dans l. in which; **parmi lesquels** (*choses, animaux*) among which; (*personnes*) among whom ▌ *pron interrogatif* which (one); **l. préférez-vous?** which (one) do you prefer?

les [le] *voir* **le.**

lesbienne [lɛsbjɛn] *nf & af* lesbian.

léser [leze] *vt* (*personne*) to wrong.

lésiner [lezine] *vi* to be stingy (**sur** with).

lésion [lezjɔ̃] *nf* (*blessure*) lesion.

lessive [lesiv] *nf* (*produit*) (laundry) detergent, *Br* washing powder; (*linge*) washing; **faire la l.** to do the wash(ing). ● **lessiver** *vt* to scrub, wash. ● **lessiveuse** *nf* (laundry) boiler.

lessivé, -ée [lesive] *a* (*fatigué*) *Fam* shattered.

lest [lɛst] *nm* ballast. ● **lester** *vt* to ballast, weight down; (*remplir*) *Fam* to overload.

leste [lɛst] *a* (*agile*) nimble; (*grivois*) coarse.

léthargie [letarʒi] *nf* lethargy. ● **léthargique** *a* lethargic.

lettre [lɛtr] *nf* (*missive, caractère*) letter; **en toutes lettres** (*mot*) in full; (*nombre*) in words; **obéir à des instructions à la l.** to obey instructions to the letter; **l. ouverte** open letter; **les lettres** (*discipline*) arts, humanities; **homme de lettres** man of letters; **c'est passé comme une l. à la poste** *Fam* it was a cinch, it went off without a problem *ou* a hitch. ● **lettré, -ée** *a* well-read ▌ *nmf* scholar.

leucémie [løsemi] *nf* leuk(a)emia.

leur [lœr] **1** *a poss* their; **l. chat** their cat; **leurs voitures** their cars ▌ *pron poss* **le l., la l., les leurs** theirs. **2** *pron inv* (*indirect*) (to) them; **il l. est facile de...** it's easy for them to....

leurre [lœr] *nm* illusion; (*tromperie*) trickery. ● **leurrer** *vt* to delude.

lever [l(ə)ve] *vt* to lift (up), raise; (*blocus, interdiction, immunité parlementaire*) to lift; (*séance*) to close; (*camp*) to strike; (*impôts, armée*) to levy; **l. les yeux** to look up. ▌ *vi* (*pâte*) to rise; (*blé*) to come up. ▌ *se lever vpr* to get up; (*soleil, rideau*) to rise; (*jour*) to break; (*brume*) to clear, lift. ▌ *nm* **le l. du soleil** sunrise; **le l. du rideau** (*au théâtre*) the curtain (up). ● **levant, -ante** *a* (*soleil*) rising ▌ *nm* **le l.** the east. ● **levé, -ée** *a* **être l.** (*debout*) to be up. ● **levée** *nf* (*d'interdiction*) lifting; (*du courrier*) collection; (*d'impôts*) levying; **l. de boucliers** *Fig* public outcry.

levier [ləvje] *nm* lever; (*pour soulever*) crowbar; **l. de vitesse** (*dans une voiture*) *Br* gear lever, *Am* gear shift.

lèvre [lɛvr] *nf* lip; **du bout des lèvres** half-heartedly, grudgingly.

lévrier [levrije] *nm* greyhound.

levure [ləvyr] *nf* yeast.

lexique [lɛksik] *nm* vocabulary, glossary.

lézard [lezar] *nm* lizard.

lézarde [lezard] *nf* crack, split. ● **lézarder 1** *vi Fam* to bask in the sun. **2 se lézarder** *vpr* to crack, split.

liaison [ljɛzɔ̃] *nf* (*rapport*) connection; (*rou-*

tière etc) link; (*entre mots*) & *Mil* liaison; **l.** (*amoureuse*) love affair; **en l. avec qn** in contact with s.o.

liane [ljan] *nf* jungle vine, liana.

liant, -ante [ljɑ̃, -ɑ̃t] *a* sociable.

liasse [ljas] *nf* bundle.

Liban [libɑ̃] *nm* Lebanon. ● **libanais, -aise** *a* Lebanese ▌ *nmf* **L., Libanaise** Lebanese.

libeller [libele] *vt* (*contrat etc*) to word, draw up; (*chèque*) to make out. ● **libellé** *nm* wording.

libellule [libelyl] *nf* dragonfly.

libéral, -e, -aux [liberal, -o] *a & nmf* liberal. ● **libéraliser** *vt* to liberalize. ● **libéralisme** *nm* liberalism. ● **libéralité** *nf Litt* liberality; (*don*) liberal gift.

libérer [libere] *vt* (*prisonnier etc*) to (set) free, release; (*pays, esprit*) to liberate (**de** from); **l. qn de** to free s.o. of *ou* from ▌ **se libérer** *vpr* to free oneself, get free (**de** of, from). ● **libérateur, -trice** *a* (*sentiment etc*) liberating ▌ *nmf* liberator. ● **libération** *nf* freeing, release; (*de pays etc*) liberation; **l. conditionnelle** *Jur* parole; **la L.** *Hist Fr* the Liberation.

liberté [liberte] *nf* freedom, liberty; **en l. provisoire** *Jur* on bail; **mettre qn en l.** to free s.o., release s.o.; **mise en l.** release.

libraire [librɛr] *nmf* bookseller. ● **librairie** *nf* (*magasin*) bookshop.

libre [libr] *a* free (**de qch** from sth, **de faire** to do); (*voie*) clear; (*place*) vacant, free; (*école*) private (and religious); **l. arbitre** free will; **l. penseur** freethinker; **temps l.** spare *ou* free time; **être l. comme l'air** to be as free as a bird. ● **libre-échange** *nm Écon* free trade. ● **libre-service** *nm* (*pl* **libres-services**) (*système, magasin etc*) self-service. ● **librement** [-əmɑ̃] *adv* freely.

Libye [libi] *nf* Libya. ● **libyen, -enne** *a* Libyan ▌ *nmf* **L., Libyenne** Libyan.

licence [lisɑ̃s] *nf Sport* permit; *Com Littér Br* licence, *Am* license; *Univ* (Bachelor's) degree; **l. ès lettres/sciences** arts/science degree, = *Br* BA/BSc = *Am* BA/BS. ● **licencié, -ée** *a & nmf* graduate; **l. ès lettres/sciences** Bachelor of Arts/Science, = *Br* BA/BSc, = *Am* BA/BS.

licencier [lisɑ̃sje] *vt* (*employé*) to lay off, make redundant. ● **licenciement** *nm* lay-off, *Br* redundancy; **l. économique** lay-off *ou Br* redundancy (*for economic reasons*).

licite [lisit] *a* licit, lawful.

licorne [likɔrn] *nf* unicorn.

lie [li] *nf* (*de vin*) dregs.

liège [ljɛʒ] *nm* (*matériau*) cork.

lien [ljɛ̃] *nm* (*rapport*) link, connection; (*ficelle etc*) tie; **l. de parenté** family tie; **les liens (sacrés) du mariage** the (sacred) bonds of marriage.

lier [lje] *vt* (*attacher*) to tie (up), bind; (*relier*) to link (up), connect; (*conversation, amitié*) to strike up; **l. qn** (*unir, engager*) to bind s.o.; **amis très liés** very close friends ▌ **se lier** *vpr* (*idées etc*) to tie in, link together; **se l.**

avec qn to make friends with s.o.

lierre [ljɛr] *nm* ivy.

lieu, -x [ljø] *nm* place; **les lieux** (*locaux*) the premises; **être sur les lieux** to be on the spot; **sur les lieux du crime/de l'accident** at the scene of the crime/accident; **avoir l.** to take place, be held; **donner l. à qch** to give rise to sth; **au l. de** instead of; **en premier l.** in the first place, firstly; **en dernier l.** lastly; **s'il y a l.** if necessary; **l. commun** commonplace; **l. public** public place; **l. de vacances** *Br* holiday *ou Am* vacation destination *ou* spot; **avoir l. de faire** (*des raisons*) to have good reason to do; **tenir l. de qch** to serve as sth; **se plaindre en haut l.** to complain to people in high places. ● **lieu-dit** *nm* (*pl* **lieux-dits**) *Géog* locality.

lieue [ljø] *nf* (*mesure*) *Hist* league.

lieutenant [ljøtnɑ̃] *nm* lieutenant.

lièvre [ljɛvr] *nm* hare.

lifting [liftiŋ] *nm* face lift.

ligament [ligamɑ̃] *nm* ligament.

ligne [liɲ] *nf* (*trait, contour, transport*) line; (*belle silhouette etc*) figure; (*rangée*) row, line; (**se**) **mettre en l.** to line up; **en l.** (*au téléphone*) connected, through; **les grandes lignes** (*de train*) the main line (services); *Fig* the broad outline; **à la l.** *Grammaire* new paragraph; **sur toute la l.** *Fig* all the way down the line, from start to finish; **entrer en l. de compte** to be taken into account, count; **faire entrer en l. de compte** to take into account; **garder la l.** *Fam* to stay slim, keep one's figure; **pilote de l.** airline pilot.

lignée [liɲe] *nf* line, ancestry; **dans la l. de** *Fig* in the line *ou* tradition of.

ligoter [ligɔte] *vt* to tie up.

ligue [lig] *nf* (*alliance*) league. ● **se liguer** *vpr* to join together, conspire, gang up (**contre** against).

lilas [lila] *nm* lilac ▌ *a inv* (*couleur*) lilac.

limace [limas] *nf* (*mollusque*) slug.

limaille [limaj] *nf* filings.

limande [limɑ̃d] *nf* (*poisson*) lemon sole, dab.

lime [lim] *nf* (*outil*) file. ● **limer** *vt* to file.

limier [limje] *nm* (*chien*) bloodhound; **fin l.** (*policier*) good detective *ou* sleuth.

limitatif, -ive [limitatif, -iv] *a* restrictive. ● **limitation** *nf* limitation; (*de vitesse, poids*) limit.

limite [limit] *nf* limit (**a** to); (*de propriété, jardin etc*) boundary; **les limites** (*d'un terrain de football*) the boundary lines; **dépasser la l.** *ou* **les limites** to go beyond the bounds; **sans l.** unlimited, limitless; **jusqu'à la l. de ses forces** to the point of exhaustion; **à la l.** if absolutely necessary.

▌ *a* (*cas*) extreme; (*vitesse, âge etc*) maximum; **date l.** latest date, deadline; **date l. de vente** (*sur produit*) sell-by date.

limiter [limite] *vt* to limit, restrict; (**à** to); (*délimiter*) to border; **se l. à faire** to limit *ou* restrict oneself to doing.

limoger [limɔʒe] *vt* (*destituer*) to dismiss.

limonade [limɔnad] *nf* (carbonated *ou Br* fizzy) lemonade.

limpide [lɛ̃pid] *a* (*eau, explication*) clear, crystal-clear. ● **limpidité** *nf* clearness.

lin [lɛ̃] *nm Bot* flax; (*tissu*) linen; **huile de l.** linseed oil.

linceul [lɛ̃sœl] *nm* shroud.

linéaire [lineɛr] *a* linear.

linge [lɛ̃ʒ] *nm* (*vêtements*) linen; (*à laver*) washing, linen; (*torchon*) cloth; **l. (de corps)** underwear; **petit l.** small items to be washed; **l. de maison** household linen. ● **lingerie** *nf* (*de femmes*) underwear; (*pièce*) linen room.

lingot [lɛ̃go] *nm* ingot; **l. d'or** gold bar.

linguiste [lɛ̃gɥist] *nmf* linguist. ● **linguistique** *a* linguistic ▌ *nf* linguistics.

lino [lino] *nm* lino. ● **linoléum** *nm* linoleum.

linotte [linɔt] *nf* (*oiseau*) linnet; **tête de l.** *Fig* scatterbrain.

lion [ljɔ̃] *nm* lion; **le L.** (*signe*) Leo. ● **lionceau, -x** *nm* lion cub. ● **lionne** *nf* lioness.

liquéfier [likefje] *vt*, **se liquéfier** *vpr* to liquefy.

liqueur [likœr] *nf* liqueur.

liquide [likid] *a* liquid; **argent l.** ready cash ▌ *nm* liquid; **du l.** (*argent*) ready cash.

liquider [likide] *vt* (*dette, stock etc*) to clear, liquidate; (*société*) to wind up, liquidate; (*affaire, travail*) *Fam* to wind up, finish off; **l. qn** (*tuer*) *Fam* to liquidate s.o. ● **liquidation** *nf* (*de dette etc*) clearing, liquidation; (*de société*) winding up, liquidation; **vente de l.** clearance sale; **l. totale du stock** stock clearance sale.

lire¹* [lir] *vti* to read.

lire² [lir] *nf* (*monnaie*) lira.

lis¹ [lis] *nm* (*plante, fleur*) lily.

lis², lisant, lise(nt) *etc* [li, lizɑ̃, liz] *voir* **lire¹**.

liseron [lizrɔ̃] *nm* (*plante*) convolvulus.

lisible [lizibl] *a* (*écriture*) legible; (*livre*) readable. ● **lisiblement** [-əmɑ̃] *adv* legibly.

lisière [lizjɛr] *nf* edge, border.

lisse [lis] *a* smooth. ● **lisser** *vt* to smooth; (*plumes*) to preen.

liste [list] *nf* list; **l. électorale** *Br* register of electors, *Am* voting register, electoral roll; **sur la l. rouge** (*numéro de téléphone*) *Br* ex-directory, *Am* unlisted; **faire une l. de qch** to make (out) a list of sth.

lit¹ [li] *nm* bed; **l. d'enfant** *Br* cot, *Am* crib; **lits superposés** bunk beds; **se mettre au l.** to go (in)to bed; **garder le l.** to stay in bed; **faire le l.** to make the bed. ● **literie** *nf* bedding, bedclothes.

lit² [li] *voir* **lire¹**.

litanie [litani] *nf* **1** (*énumération*) long list (**de** of). **2 litanies** (*prière*) *Rel* litany.

litière [litjɛr] *nf* (*couche de paille*) litter.

litige [litiʒ] *nm* dispute; *Jur* litigation. ● **litigieux, -euse** *a* contentious.

litre [litr] *nm Br* litre, *Am* liter.

littéraire [literɛr] *a* literary. ● **littérature** *nf* literature.

littéral, -e, -aux [literal, -o] *a* literal. ● **litté-**

ralement *adv* literally.

littoral, -e, -aux [litɔral, -o] *a* coastal ▮ *nm* coast(line).

liturgie [lityrʒi] *nf* liturgy. ●**liturgique** *a* liturgical.

livide [livid] *a* (*pâle*) (ghastly) pale, pallid.

livraison [livrɛzɔ̃] *nf voir* **livrer.**

livre [livr] **1** *nm* book; **l. de poche** paperback (book); **l. de bord** *Nau* logbook; **le l., l'industrie du l.** the book industry. **2** *nf* (*monnaie, poids*) pound. ●**livresque** *a* (*savoir*) bookish.

livrée [livre] *nf* (*uniforme*) livery.

livrer [livre] *vt* (*marchandises*) to deliver (**à** to); (*secret*) to give away; **l. qn à** (*la police etc*) to give s.o. over *ou* up to; **l. bataille** to do *ou* join battle.

  ▮ **se livrer** *vpr* (*se rendre*) to give oneself up (**à** to); (*se confier*) to confide (**à** in); **se l. à** (*habitude, excès etc*) to indulge in; (*activité*) to devote oneself to; (*désespoir, destin*) to abandon oneself to. ●**livraison** *nf* delivery. ●**livreur, -euse** *nmf* delivery man, delivery woman.

livret [livrɛ] *nm* (*registre*) book; *Mus* libretto; **l. scolaire** school report book; **l. de famille** family registration book; **l. de caisse d'épargne** bankbook, *Br* passbook.

lobe [lɔb] *nm* (*de l'oreille*) lobe.

local, -e, -aux [lɔkal, -o] **1** *a* local. **2** *nm* (*pièce*) room; **locaux** (*bâtiment*) premises. ●**localement** *adv* locally. ●**localiser** *vt* (*déterminer*) to locate; (*limiter*) to localize.

localité [lɔkalite] *nf* locality.

locataire [lɔkatɛr] *nmf* tenant; (*chez le propriétaire*) lodger, *Am* roomer.

location [lɔkasjɔ̃] *nf* (*de maison etc*) renting; (*de voiture*) renting, *Br* hiring; (*par propriétaire*) renting (out), *Br* letting; (*de voiture*) renting (out), *Br* hiring (out); (*à bail*) leasing; (*réservation*) booking; (*loyer*) rental, rent; (*bail*) lease; **bureau de l.** booking office; **en l.** on hire; **voiture de l.** rented *ou Br* hired car; **l.-vente** (*crédit-bail*) leasing with option to buy.

lock-out [lɔkawt] *nm inv* (*industriel*) lockout.

locomotion [lɔkɔmosjɔ̃] *nf* **moyen de l.** means of transport *ou* locomotion.

locomotive [lɔkɔmotiv] *nf* (*de train*) engine, locomotive.

locuteur [lɔkytœr] *nm Ling* speaker. ●**locution** *nf* phrase, idiom; *Grammaire* phrase.

loge [lɔʒ] *nf* (*de concierge*) lodge; (*d'acteur*) dressing-room; (*de spectateur*) *Théâtre* box; **être aux premières loges** *Fig* to have a ringside seat.

loger [lɔʒe] *vt* (*recevoir, mettre*) to accommodate, house; (*héberger*) to put up; **être logé et nourri** to have board and lodging.

  ▮ *vi* (*à l'hôtel etc*) to put up, *Br* lodge; (*habiter*) to live; (*trouver à*) **se l.** to find somewhere to live; (*temporairement*) to find somewhere to stay; **la balle se logea dans le mur** the bullet lodged (itself) in the wall. ●**logeable** *a* habitable. ●**logement** *nm*

accommodation, lodging; (*habitat*) housing; (*appartement*) *Br* flat, *Am* apartment; (*maison*) house; **le l.** housing. ●**logeur, -euse** *nmf* landlord, landlady.

loggia [lɔdʒja] *nf* (*balcon*) loggia.

logiciel [lɔʒisjɛl] *nm* (*d'ordinateur*) software *inv.*

logique [lɔʒik] *a* logical ▮ *nf* logic. ●**logiquement** *adv* logically.

logistique [lɔʒistik] *nf* logistics.

logo [lɔgo] *nm* logo.

loi [lwa] *nf* law; (*du Parlement*) act; **projet de l.** *Pol* bill; **faire la l.** to lay down the law (**à** to).

loin [lwɛ̃] *adv* far (away *ou* off); **Boston est l. (de Paris)** Boston is a long way away (from Paris); **plus l.** further, farther; (*ci-après*) further on; **aller l.** (*dans la vie*) *Fig* to go far; **aller trop l.** *Fig* to go too far; **au l.** in the distance, far away; **de l.** from a distance; (*de beaucoup*) by far; **de l. en l.** every so often; **c'est l. tout ça** (*passé*) that was a long time ago; **l. de là** *Fig* far from it. ●**lointain, -aine** *a* distant, far-off; (*ressemblance, rapport etc*) remote ▮ *nm* **dans le l.** in the distance.

loir [lwar] *nm* (*animal*) dormouse.

loisir [lwazir] *nm* **avoir le l. de faire qch** to have the time to do sth; **moment de l.** moment of leisure; (*tout*) **à l.** (*en prenant tout son temps*) at leisure; (*autant qu'on le désire*) as much as one would like; **loisirs** (*temps libre*) spare time, (time); (*distractions*) leisure *ou* spare-time activities.

Londres [lɔ̃dr] *nm ou f* London. ●**londonien, -ienne** *a* London, of London ▮ *nmf* **L., Londonienne** Londoner.

long, longue [lɔ̃, lɔ̃g] *a* long; **être l.** (**à faire**) to be a long time *ou* slow (in doing); **l. de deux mètres** two metres long.

  ▮ *nm* **avoir deux mètres de l.** to be two metres long; (**tout**) **le l. de** (*espace*) (all) along; **tout le l. de** (*temps*) throughout; **de l. en large** (*marcher etc*) up and down; **en l. et en large** thoroughly; **en l.** lengthwise; **à la longue** in the long run; **tomber de tout son l.** to fall flat (on one's face).

  ▮ *adv* **en savoir/en dire l. sur** to know/say a lot about; **leur attitude en disait l.** their attitude said a lot *ou* spoke volumes. ●**long-courrier** *nm* (*avion*) long-distance airliner.

longer [lɔ̃ʒe] *vt* to go *ou* pass along; (*forêt, mer*) to skirt; (*mur*) to hug.

longévité [lɔ̃ʒevite] *nf* longevity.

longitude [lɔ̃ʒityd] *nf* longitude.

longtemps [lɔ̃tɑ̃] *adv* (for) a long time; **trop/avant l.** too/before long; **aussi l. que** as long as.

longue [lɔ̃g] *voir* **long.** ●**longuement** *adv* at length. ●**longuet, -ette** *a Fam* (fairly) lengthy. ●**longueur** *nf* length; **longueurs** (*de texte, film*) over-long passages; **saut en l.** *Sport* long jump, *Am* broad jump; **à l. de journée** all day long; **l. d'onde** (*à la radio*) & *Fig* wavelength.

longue-vue [lɔ̃gvy] *nf* (*pl* **longues-vues**) telescope.

lopin [lɔpɛ̃] *nm* **l. de terre** plot *ou* patch of land.

loquace [lɔkas] *a* loquacious, talkative.

loque [lɔk] *nf* **l.** (**humaine**) (*personne*) human wreck.

loques [lɔk] *nfpl* rags.

loquet [lɔkɛ] *nm* latch.

lorgner [lɔrɲe] *vt* (*regarder, convoiter*) to eye.

lors [lɔr] *adv* **l. de** at the time of; **depuis l., dès l.** from then on; **dès l. que** (*puisque*) since.

lorsque [lɔrsk(ə)] *conj* when.

losange [lɔzɑ̃ʒ] *nm* (*forme*) diamond, lozenge.

lot [lo] *nm* **1** (*de loterie*) prize; **gros l.** top prize, jackpot. **2** (*de marchandises etc*) batch. ●**loterie** *nf* lottery, raffle.

lotion [losjɔ̃] *nf* lotion.

lotir [lɔtir] *vt* (*terrain*) to divide into lots; **bien loti** *Fig* favoured by fortune. ●**lotissement** *nm* (*terrain*) building plot; (*habitations*) housing *Br* estate *ou Am* development.

loto [lɔto] *nm* (*jeu*) lotto.

louable [lwabl] *a* praiseworthy, laudable.

louange [lwɑ̃ʒ] *nf* praise; **à la l. de** in praise of.

louche [luʃ] **1** *nf* (*cuillère*) ladle. **2** *a* (*suspect*) shady, fishy.

loucher [luʃe] *vi* to squint; **l. sur** *Fam* to eye.

louer [lwe] *vt* **1** (*prendre en location*) to rent (*house, flat etc*); (*voiture*) to rent, *Br* hire; (*donner en location*) to rent (out), *Br* let; (*voiture*) to rent (out), *Br* hire (out); (*réserver*) to book; **l. à bail** to lease; **maison/chambre à l.** house/room to rent *ou Br* to let.
2 (*exalter*) to praise (**de** for); **se l. de** to be highly satisfied with.

loufoque [lufɔk] *a* (*fou*) *Fam* nutty, crazy.

loukoum [lukum] *nm* Turkish delight.

loup [lu] *nm* wolf; **avoir une faim de l.** to be ravenous. ●**loup-garou** *nm* (*pl* **loups-garous**) werewolf.

loupe [lup] *nf* magnifying glass.

louper [lupe] *vt Fam* (*train etc*) to miss; (*examen*) to fail; (*travail*) to mess up.

lourd, lourde [lur, lurd] *a* heavy (*Fig de* with); (*temps, chaleur*) close, sultry; (*faute*) gross; (*tâche*) arduous; (*esprit*) dull ▮ *adv* **peser l.** (*malle etc*) to be heavy. ●**lourdaud, -aude** *a* loutish, oafish ▮ *nmf* lout, oaf. ●**lourdement** [-əmɑ̃] *adv* heavily. ●**lourdeur** *nf* heaviness; (*d'esprit*) dullness.

loutre [lutr] *nf* otter.

louve [luv] *nf* she-wolf. ●**louveteau, -x** *nm* (*animal*) wolf cub; (*scout*) cub (scout).

louvoyer [luvwaje] *vi* (*tergiverser*) to hedge, be evasive.

loyal, -e, -aux [lwajal, -o] *a* (*honnête*) fair, honest (**envers** to); (*dévoué*) loyal (**envers,** to). ●**loyalement** *adv* fairly; (*avec dévoue-*

ment) loyally. ●**loyauté** *nf* (*honnêteté*) fairness, honesty; (*dévouement*) loyalty.

loyer [lwaje] *nm* rent.

lu [ly] *pp de* **lire¹.**

lubie [lybi] *nf* whim.

lubrifier [lybrifje] *vt* to lubricate. ●**lubrifiant** *nm* lubricant.

lubrique [lybrik] *a Litt* lewd, lustful.

lucarne [lykarn] *nf* (*fenêtre*) dormer window, skylight.

lucide [lysid] *a* lucid. ●**lucidité** *nf* lucidity.

lucratif, -ive [lykratif, -iv] *a* lucrative.

lueur [lɥœr] *nf* (*lumière*) & *Fig* glimmer.

luge [lyʒ] *nf Br* sledge, *Am* sled, toboggan.

lugubre [lygybr] *a* gloomy, lugubrious.

lui [lɥi] *pron mf* (*complément indirect*) (to) him; (*femme*) (to) her; (*chose, animal*) (to) it; **je le lui ai montré** I showed it to him *ou* to her; **il lui est facile de...** it's easy for him *ou* her to....
▮ *pron m* **1** (*après une préposition*) him; **pour/avec/etc lui** for/with/*etc* him; **elle pense à lui** she thinks of him; **il ne pense qu'à lui** he only thinks of himself.
2 (*complément direct*) him; **elle n'aime que lui** she only loves him; **elle n'écoute ni lui ni personne** she doesn't listen to him or to anybody.
3 (*sujet*) **elle est plus grande que lui** she's taller than he is *ou* than him; **lui, il ne viendra pas** (*emphatique*) he won't come; **c'est lui qui me l'a dit** he is the one who told me. ●**lui-même** *pron* himself; (*chose, animal*) itself.

luire* [lɥir] *vi* to shine, gleam. ●**luisant, -ante** *a* (*métal etc*) shiny.

lumbago [lɔ̃bago] *nm* lumbago.

lumière [lymjɛr] *nf* light; **à la l. de** by the light of; (*grâce à*) *Fig* in the light of; **faire toute la l. sur** *Fig* to clear up; **mettre en l.** *Fig* to bring to light; **le siècle des lumières** the Age of Enlightenment. ●**luminaire** *nm* (*appareil*) lighting appliance.

lumineux, -euse [lyminø, -øz] *a* (*idée, ciel etc*) bright, brilliant; (*cadran, corps etc*) luminous; **faisceau l.** beam of light; **source lumineuse** light source. ●**luminosité** *nf* luminosity.

lunaire [lynɛr] *a* lunar; **clarté l.** light *ou* brightness of the moon.

lunatique [lynatik] *a* temperamental.

lunch [lœ̃ʃ, lœ̃tʃ] *nm* buffet lunch, snack.

lundi [lœ̃di] *nm* Monday.

lune [lyn] *nf* moon; **l. de miel** honeymoon; **être dans la l.** to have one's head in the clouds, be up in the clouds. ●**luné, -ée** *a* **être bien/mal l.** *Fam* to be in a good/bad mood.

lunette [lynɛt] *nf* **1 lunettes** glasses, spectacles; (*de protection, plongée*) goggles; **lunettes de soleil** sunglasses. **2** (*astronomique*) telescope; **l. arrière** (*de voiture*) rear window.

lurette [lyrɛt] *nf* **il y a belle l.** *Fam* a long time ago.

luron [lyrɔ̃] *nm* **gai l.** gay fellow.

lustre [lystr] *nm* (*éclairage*) chandelier; (*éclat*) lustre. ●**lustré, -ée** *a* (*par l'usure*) shiny.

lustres [lystr] *nmpl* **depuis des l.** *Fam* for ages and ages.

luth [lyt] *nm* (*instrument de musique*) lute.

lutin [lytɛ̃] *nm* elf, imp, goblin.

lutte [lyt] *nf* fight, struggle; *Sport* wrestling; **l. des classes** class warfare *ou* struggle. ●**lutter** *vi* to fight, struggle; *Sport* to wrestle. ●**lutteur, -euse** *nmf* fighter; *Sport* wrestler.

luxation [lyksasjɔ̃] *nf* (*de l'épaule etc*) dislocation; **se faire une l. à l'épaule/etc** to dislocate one's shoulder/*etc*.

luxe [lyks] *nm* luxury; **un l. de** a wealth of; **article de l.** luxury article; **modèle de l.** de luxe model. ●**luxueux, -euse** *a* luxurious.

Luxembourg [lyksãbur] *nm* Luxembourg.

luxure [lyksyr] *nf* lewdness, lust.

luxuriant, -ante [lyksyrjã, -ãt] *a* luxuriant.

luzerne [lyzɛrn] *nf* (*plante*) *Br* lucerne, *Am* alfalfa.

lycée [lise] *nm Br* (secondary) school, *Am* high school; **l. technique** *ou* **professionnel** vocational *ou* technical school ●**lycéen, -enne** *nmf* pupil *ou* student (*at a lycée*).

lymphathique [lɛ̃fatik] *a* (*apathique*) sluggish.

lyncher [lɛ̃ʃe] *vt* to lynch. ●**lynchage** *nm* lynching.

lynx [lɛ̃ks] *nm* lynx; **avoir des yeux de l.** to have eyes like a hawk.

lyophiliser [ljɔfilize] *vt* (*café etc*) to freeze-dry.

lyre [lir] *nf* (*instrument de musique antique*) lyre.

lyrique [lirik] *a* (*poème etc*) lyric; (*passionné*) *Fig* lyrical; **artiste l.** opera singer. ●**lyrisme** *nm* lyricism.

lys [lis] *nm* (*plante, fleur*) lily.

M

M, m [ɛm] *nm* M, m.
m *abrév* (*mètre*) metre.
M [məsjø] *abrév* = Monsieur.
m' [m] *voir* me.
ma [ma] *voir* mon.
macabre [makɑbr] *a* macabre, gruesome.
macadam [makadam] *nm* (*goudron*) tarmac.
macaron [makarɔ̃] *nm* 1 (*gâteau*) macaroon.
 2 (*insigne*) (round) badge.
macaroni(s) [makarɔni] *nm(pl)* macaroni.
macédoine [masedwan] *nf* m. (de légumes)
 mixed vegetables; **m.** (de fruits) fruit salad.
macérer [masere] *vti* (*fruits etc*) to soak.
 ● **macération** *nf* soaking.
mâcher [mɑʃe] *vt* to chew; **m. le travail à qn**
 to go over all s.o.'s work for him, make
 s.o.'s task easy; **il ne mâche pas ses mots** he
 doesn't mince matters *ou* his words.
machiavélique [makjavelik] *a* Machiavellian.
machin, -ine [maʃɛ̃, -ʃin] *nmf Fam* (*chose*)
 what's-it; **M.** (*personne*) what's-his-name;
 Machine what's-her-name.
machinal, -e, -aux [maʃinal, -o] *a* instinctive, unconscious, mechanical. ● **machinale-**
 ment *adv* instinctively, unconsciously, mechanically.
machination [maʃinɑsjɔ̃] *nf* machination.
machine [maʃin] *nf* (*appareil, avion, système*
 etc) machine; (*locomotive, moteur*) engine;
 machines *Tech* machines, (heavy) machinery; **m. à calculer** calculator; **m. à coudre**
 sewing machine; **m. à écrire** typewriter; **m. à**
 laver washing machine; **m. à laver la**
 vaisselle dishwasher; **m. à ou de traitement**
 de texte word processor; **salle des machines**
 (*de bateau*) engine room. ● **machinerie** *nf*
 (*de bateau*) engine room. ● **machiniste** *nm*
 (*conducteur*) driver; (*au théâtre*) stage-hand.
macho [matʃo] *Fam nm* macho *m* ▮ *a* (*f inv*)
 (*attitude etc*) macho.
mâchoire [mɑʃwar] *nf* jaw.
mâchonner [mɑʃɔne] *vt* to chew, munch.
maçon [masɔ̃] *nm* builder; (*briques*)
 bricklayer; (*pierres*) mason. ● **maçonnerie** *nf*
 (*travaux*) building work; (*ouvrage de bri-*
 ques) brickwork; (*de pierres*) masonry,
 stonework.
macro-instruction [makroɛ̃stryksjɔ̃] *nf*
 Ordinat macro.
maculer [makyle] *vt Litt* to stain (**de** with).
Madagascar [madagaskar] *nf* Madagascar.
madame, *pl* **mesdames** [madam, medam] *nf*
 madam; **oui m.** yes (madam); **bonjour**
 mesdames good morning (ladies); **Madame**
 ou **Mme Legras** Mrs Legras; **Madame** (*dans*

une lettre) Dear Madam.
madeleine [madlɛn] *nf* (small) sponge cake.
mademoiselle, *pl* **mesdemoiselles**
 [madmwazɛl, medmwazɛl] *nf* miss; **oui m.**
 yes (miss); **bonjour mesdemoiselles** good
 morning (ladies); **Mademoiselle** *ou* **Mlle Le-**
 gras Miss Legras; **Mademoiselle** (*dans une*
 lettre) Dear Madam.
madère [madɛr] *nm* (*vin*) Madeira.
Madère [madɛr] *nf* (*île*) Madeira.
madone [madɔn] *nf Rel* madonna.
madrier [madrije] *nm* (*poutre*) beam.
maestro [maestro] *nm Mus* maestro.
maf(f)ia [mafja] *nf* Mafia.
magasin [magazɛ̃] *nm Br* shop, *Am* store;
 (*entrepôt*) warehouse; (*d'arme*) & *Phot* magazine; **grand m.** department store; **en m.** in
 stock. ● **magasinier** *nm* warehouseman.
magazine [magazin] *nm* (*revue*) magazine.
magie [maʒi] *nf* magic. ● **magicien, -ienne**
 nmf magician. ● **magique** *a* (*baguette etc*)
 magic; (*mystérieux, enchanteur*) magical.
magistral, -e, -aux [maʒistral, -o] *a*
 masterly, magnificent; **cours m.** lecture.
 ● **magistralement** *adv* magnificently.
magistrat [maʒistra] *nm* magistrate. ● **magi-**
 strature *nf* judiciary, magistracy.
magma [magma] *nm* (*roche*) magma; (*mé-*
 lange) *Fig* jumble.
magnanime [maɲanim] *a* magnanimous.
magnat [magna] *nm* tycoon, magnate.
magner (se) [səmaɲe] *vpr Fam* to hurry up.
magnésium [maɲezjɔm] *nm* magnesium.
magnétique [maɲetik] *a* magnetic. ● **magné-**
 tiser *vt* to magnetize. ● **magnétisme** *nm*
 magnetism.
magnétophone [maɲetɔfɔn] (*Fam* **magnéto**)
 nm tape recorder; **m. à cassettes** cassette recorder. ● **magnétoscope** *nm* video recorder,
 VCR, *Br* video.
magnifique [maɲifik] *a* magnificent. ● **magni-**
 ficence *nf* magnificence. ● **magnifiquement** *adv*
 magnificently.
magnolia [maɲɔlja] *nm* (*arbre*) magnolia.
magot [mago] *nm* (*économies*) *Fam* nest egg,
 hoard.
magouille(s) [maguj] *nf(pl) Fam* wheeling
 and dealing, (shady) scheming.
magret [magrɛ] *nm* **m. de canard** *Br* fillet *ou*
 Am filet of duck.
mai [mɛ] *nm* May.
maigre [mɛgr] *a* thin, lean; (*viande*) lean;
 (*fromage, yaourt*) low-fat; (*repas, salaire,*
 espoir) meagre; **faire m.** to abstain from
 meat. ● **maigrement** [-əmɑ̃] *adv* (*chichement*)
 meagrely. ● **maigreur** *nf* thinness; (*de*

viande) leanness; *(médiocrité) Fig* meagreness. ●**maigrichon, -onne** [mɛg-] *a & nmf Fam* skinny (person). ●**maigrir** [megrir] *vi* to get thin(ner) **‖** *vt Litt* to make thin(ner).

maille [mɑj] *nf (de tricot)* stitch; *(de filet)* mesh; **m. filée** *(de bas)* run, *Br* ladder; **avoir m. à partir avec qn** *Fig* to have an argument *ou* a brush with s.o. ●**maillon** *nm (de chaîne)* link.

maillet [mɑjɛ] *nm (outil)* mallet.

maillot [mɑjo] *nm (de sportif)* jersey, shirt; *(de danseur)* leotard, tights; **m. (de corps)** *Br* vest, *Am* undershirt; **m. (de bain)** *(de femme)* swimsuit; *(d'homme)* (swimming) trunks; **être m. jaune** to be the overall leader of the Tour de France *(who wears a yellow jersey)*.

main [mɛ̃] *nf* hand; **tenir à la m.** to hold in one's hand; **à la m.** *(faire, écrire etc)* by hand; **haut les mains!** hands up!; **donner un coup de m. à qn** *Fig* to lend s.o. a (helping) hand; **avoir le coup de m.** *(habileté)* to have the knack; **sous la m.** at hand, handy; **la m. dans la m.** hand in hand; **en venir aux mains** to come to blows; **avoir la m. heureuse** *Fig* to be lucky *(in what one does)*; **mettre la dernière m. à qch** to put the finishing touches to sth; **demander la m. d'une femme** to ask for a woman's hand (in marriage); **faire la m. basse sur qch** *(police etc)* to seize sth, take sth away; **mettre la m. à la pâte** to do one's bit, lend a hand; **ne pas y aller de m.** morte not to pull punches; **j'y mettrais ma m. au feu** *Fig* I'd stake my all *ou* my life on it; **remettre qch en m. propre** to hand sth over in person; **attaque/vol à m.** armée armed attack/robbery; **homme de m.** henchman, hired man; **m. courante** handrail; **prêter m.-forte à qn** to lend assistance to s.o.

main-d'œuvre [mɛ̃dœvr] *nf (pl mains-d'œuvre) (travail)* manpower, labour; *(salariés)* work *ou* labour force.

-

mainmise [mɛ̃miz] *nf (prise)* seizure **(de** by, **sur** of); *(influence) Péj* stranglehold **(sur** over).

maint, mainte [mɛ̃, mɛ̃t] *a Litt* many a; **maintes fois, à maintes reprises** many a time.

maintenant [mɛ̃t(ə)nã] *adv* now; *(de nos jours)* nowadays; **m. que** now that; **dès m.** from now on.

maintenir* [mɛ̃t(ə)nir] *vt (conserver)* to keep, maintain; *(retenir)* to hold, keep; *(affirmer)* to maintain *(que* that) **‖ se maintenir** *vpr (durer)* to be maintained; *(rester)* to keep; *(malade, vieillard)* to hold one's own; **se m. en forme** to keep in shape *ou* in trim. ●**maintien** *nm (action)* maintenance **(de** of); *(allure)* bearing.

maire [mɛr] *nm* mayor. ●**mairie** *nf Br* town hall, *Am* city hall; *(administration) Br* town council, *Am* city hall.

mais [mɛ] *conj* but; **m. oui, m. si** yes of course; **m. non** definitely not.

maïs [mais] *nm (céréale) Br* maize, *Am* corn;

farine de m. *Br* cornflour, *Am* cornstarch.

maison [mɛzɔ̃] *nf (bâtiment)* house; *(chez-soi, asile)* home; *(entreprise)* company, firm; *(famille)* household; **à la m.** at home; **aller à la m.** to go home; **rentrer à la m.** to go *ou* come (back) home; **m. individuelle** detached house; **la M. Blanche** *Am* the White House; **m. de la culture** arts *ou* cultural centre; **m. d'étudiants** student hostel; **m. des jeunes** youth club; **m. de repos** rest home; **m. de retraite** old people's home; **m. de santé** *(pour malades)* nursing home **‖** *a inv (tartes etc)* homemade. ●**maisonnée** *nf* household. ●**maisonnette** *nf* small house.

maître [mɛtr] *nm* master; **se rendre m. de** *(incendie)* to bring under control; *(pays)* to conquer; **être m. de la situation** to be in control of *ou* master of the situation; **m. de soi** in control of oneself; **m. d'école** teacher; **m. d'hôtel** *(restaurant)* head waiter; **m. de maison** host; **m. nageur** *(sauveteur)* swimming instructor (and lifeguard); **m. chanteur** blackmailer; **coup de m.** master stroke.

maîtresse [mɛtrɛs] *nf* mistress; **m. d'école** teacher; **m. de maison** hostess; *(ménagère)* housewife; **être m. de la situation** to be in control of the situation **‖** *af (idée, poutre)* main; *(carte)* master.

maîtrise [mɛtriz] *nf (habileté, contrôle)* mastery **(de** of); *(diplôme)* Master's degree **(de** in); **m. (de soi)** self-control. ●**maîtriser** *vt (incendie)* to (bring under) control; *(émotion)* to master, control; *(sujet)* to master; **m. qn** to overpower s.o., subdue s.o. **‖ se maîtriser** *vpr* to control oneself.

majesté [maʒɛste] *nf* majesty; **Votre M.** *(titre)* Your Majesty. ●**majestueux, -euse** *a* majestic, stately.

majeur [maʒœr] **1** *a (important)* & *Mus* major; **être m.** *Jur* to be of age; **la majeure partie de** most of; **en majeure partie** for the most part. **2** *nm (doigt)* middle finger.

majorer [maʒɔre] *vt* to raise, increase. ●**majoration** *nf (hausse)* increase **(de** in).

majorette [maʒɔrɛt] *nf (drum)* majorette.

majorité [maʒɔrite] *nf* majority **(de** of); *(âge) Jur* coming of age, majority; *(gouvernement)* government, party in office; **en m.** in the *ou* a majority; *(pour la plupart)* in the main. ●**majoritaire** *a* **scrutin m.** first-past-the-post voting system; **être m.** to be in the *ou* a majority; **être m. aux élections** to win the elections.

Majorque [maʒɔrk] *nf* Majorca.

majuscule [maʒyskyl] *a* capital **‖** *nf* capital letter.

mal, maux [mal, mo] **1** *nm (douleur)* pain; *(dommage)* harm; *(maladie)* illness; *(malheur)* misfortune; *Phil Rel* evil; **dire du m. de qn** to say bad things about s.o., speak ill of s.o.; **m. de dents** toothache; **m. de gorge** sore throat; **m. de tête** headache; **m. de ventre** stomach-ache; **avoir le m. de mer** to be seasick; **m. du pays** homesickness; **avoir le m. du pays** to be homesick; **avoir m. à la**

malade

186

tête/à la gorge/etc to have a headache/sore throat/etc; ça (me) fait m., j'ai m. it hurts (me); faire du m. à qn to harm s.o., hurt s.o.; avoir du m. à faire to have trouble (in) doing; se donner du m. pour faire to go to a lot of trouble to do; le bien et le m. good and evil.
2 adv (travailler etc) badly; (entendre, comprendre) not too well; aller m. (projet etc) to be going badly; (personne) Méd to be bad or ill; prendre m. to catch a chill, catch cold; m. (à l'aise) uncomfortable; se trouver m. to (feel) faint; (ce n'est) pas m.! (mauvais) (that's) not bad!; pas m. (beaucoup) Fam quite a lot (de of); c'est m. de mentir/etc (moralement) it's wrong to lie/etc; de m. en pis from bad to worse; m. renseigner/interpréter/etc to misinform/misinterpret/etc.

malade [malad] a ill, sick; (arbre, dent) diseased; (estomac, jambe) bad; être m. du foie/cœur to have a bad liver/heart ∎ nmf sick person; (d'un médecin) patient; les malades the sick. ●**maladie** nf illness, disease, sickness. ●**maladif, -ive** a (personne) sickly; (morbide) morbid.

maladroit, -oite [maladrwa, -wat] a (malhabile) clumsy, awkward; (indélicat) tactless. ●**maladresse** nf clumsiness, awkwardness; (indélicatesse) tactlessness; (bévue) blunder.

malaise [malɛz] nm (angoisse) uneasiness, malaise; (indisposition) feeling of faintness ou discomfort ou dizziness; avoir un m. to feel faint ou dizzy.

malaisé, -ée [maleze] a difficult.

Malaisie [malɛzi] nf Malaysia.

malaria [malarja] nf malaria.

malavisé, -ée [malavize] a ill-advised (de faire to do).

malaxer [malakse] vt (pétrir) to knead; (mélanger) to mix. ●**malaxeur** nm Tech mixer.

malchance [malʃɑ̃s] nf bad luck; une m. (mésaventure) a mishap; jouer de m. to have no luck at all, have a run of bad luck. ●**malchanceux, -euse** a unlucky.

malcommode [malkɔmɔd] a awkward.

mâle [mal] a male; (viril) manly ∎ nm male.

malédiction [malediksjɔ̃] nf curse.

maléfice [malefis] nm evil spell. ●**maléfique** a evil, baleful.

malencontreux, -euse [malɑ̃kɔ̃trø, -øz] a unfortunate.

malentendant, -ante [malɑ̃tɑ̃dɑ̃, -ɑ̃t] nmf person who is hard of hearing.

malentendu [malɑ̃tɑ̃dy] nm misunderstanding.

malfaçon [malfasɔ̃] nf defect.

malfaisant, -ante [malfəzɑ̃, -ɑ̃t] a evil, harmful.

malfaiteur [malfɛtœr] nm criminal.

malformation [malfɔrmasjɔ̃] nf malformation.

malgré [malgre] prép in spite of; m. tout for all that, after all; m. soi (à contrecœur) reluctantly.

malhabile [malabil] a clumsy.

malheur [malœr] nm (événement) misfortune; (accident) mishap; (malchance) bad luck, misfortune; par m. unfortunately. ●**malheureusement** adv unfortunately. ●**malheureux, -euse** a (triste) unhappy, miserable; (fâcheux) unfortunate; (malchanceux) unlucky, unfortunate ∎ nmf (infortuné) poor man ou woman, (poor) wretch; (indigent) needy person.

malhonnête [malɔnɛt] a dishonest. ●**malhonnêteté** nf dishonesty; une m. (action) a dishonest act.

malice [malis] nf mischievousness. ●**malicieux, -euse** a mischievous.

malin, -igne [malɛ̃, -iɲ] a (astucieux) clever, smart; prendre un m. plaisir à faire qch to take a malicious delight in ou take malicious pleasure in doing sth; c'est (vraiment) m.! Iron Fam that's (really) clever!; tumeur maligne Méd malignant tumour. ●**malignité** nf (méchanceté) malice, maliciousness; Méd malignancy.

malingre [malɛ̃gr] a puny, sickly.

malintentionné, -ée [malɛ̃tɑ̃sjɔne] a ill-intentioned (à l'égard de towards).

malle [mal] nf (coffre) trunk; (de véhicule) Br boot, Am trunk. ●**mallette** nf small suitcase; (pour documents) attaché case.

malléable [maleabl] a malleable.

malmener [malmɔne] vt to manhandle, treat badly.

malnutrition [malnytrisjɔ̃] nf malnutrition.

malodorant, -ante [malɔdɔrɑ̃, -ɑ̃t] a smelly.

malotru, -ue [malɔtry] nmf boor, lout.

malpoli, -ie [malpɔli] a Fam rude, bad-mannered.

malpropre [malprɔpr] a (sale) dirty. ●**malpropreté** nf dirtiness.

malsain, -aine [malsɛ̃, -ɛn] a unhealthy, unwholesome.

malséant, -ante [malseɑ̃, -ɑ̃t] a unseemly.

malt [malt] nm malt.

Malte [malt] nf Malta. ●**maltais, -aise** a Maltese ∎ nmf M., Maltaise Maltese.

maltraiter [maltrete] vt to ill-treat.

malveillant, -ante [malvejɑ̃, -ɑ̃t] a malevolent. ●**malveillance** nf malevolence, ill will.

malvenu, -ue [malvəny] a (déplacé) uncalled-for.

maman [mamɑ̃] nf Br mum(my), Am mom(my).

mamelle [mamɛl] nf (d'animal) teat; (de vache) udder. ●**mamelon** nm 1 (de femme) nipple. 2 (colline) hillock.

mamie [mami] nf grandma, granny.

mammifère [mamifɛr] nm mammal.

manche [mɑ̃ʃ] 1 nf (de vêtement) sleeve; Sport Cartes round; la M. Géog the Channel. 2 nm (d'outil etc) handle; m. à balai broomstick; (d'avion, d'ordinateur) joystick; c'est une autre paire de manches! Fam that's quite another matter ou story, it's a different ball game. ●**manchette** nf 1 (de chemise etc) cuff. 2 (de journal) headline. ●**manchon** nm (en fourrure) muff.

manchot, -ote [mɑ̃ʃo, -ɔt] **1** *a* & *nmf* one-armed *ou* one-handed (person). **2** *nm* (*oiseau*) penguin.

mandarin [mɑ̃darɛ̃] *nm* (*lettré influent*) *Péj* mandarin.

mandarine [mɑ̃darin] *nf* (*fruit*) tangerine, mandarin (orange).

mandat [mɑ̃da] *nm* **1** **m. postal** money order. **2** (*pouvoir*) & *Pol* mandate; *Jur* power of attorney; **m. d'arrêt** warrant (**contre qn** for s.o.'s arrest); **m. de perquisition** search warrant. ●**mandataire** *nmf* (*délégué*) representative, proxy. ●**mandater** *vt* to delegate; (*député*) *Pol* to give a mandate to.

manège [manɛʒ] *nm* **1** (*à la foire*) merry-go-round, *Br* roundabout; (*lieu*) riding-school; (*piste*) ring, manège; (*exercice*) horsemanship. **2** (*intrigue*) ploy, trickery (*no pl*), wiles.

manette [manɛt] *nf* lever, handle.

mangeoire [mɑ̃ʒwar] *nf* (feeding) trough.

manger [mɑ̃ʒe] *vt* to eat; (*corroder*) to eat into; (*essence, électricité*) *Fig* to guzzle; (*fortune*) *Fig* to eat up; **donner à m.** to feed ▮ *vi* to eat; **on mange bien ici** the food is good here; **m. à sa faim** to have enough to eat ▮ *nm* (*nourriture*) food. ●**mangeable** *a* eatable. ●**mangeaille** *nf Péj* (bad) food. ●**mangeur, -euse** *nmf* eater; **être un gros m.** to be a big eater.

mangue [mɑ̃g] *nf* (*fruit*) mango.

manie [mani] *nf* mania, craze (**de** for). ●**maniaque** *a* fussy, finicky ▮ *nmf Br* fusspot, *Am* fussbudget; **un m. de la propreté**/*etc* a maniac for cleanliness/*etc*.

manier [manje] *vt* to handle; **se m. bien** (*véhicule etc*) to handle well. ●**maniabilité** *nf* (*de véhicule etc*) *Br* manoeuvrability, *Am* maneuverability. ●**maniable** *a* easy to handle. ●**maniement** *nm* handling; **m. d'armes** *Mil* drill.

manière [manjɛr] *nf* way, manner; **manières** (*politesse*) manners; **de toute m.** anyway, anyhow; **de cette m.** (in) this way; **de m. à faire** so as to do; **à ma m.** my way, (in) my own way; **la m. dont elle parle** the way (in which) she talks; **d'une m. générale** generally speaking; **faire des manières** (*simagrées*) to make a fuss; (*être affecté*) to put on airs. ●**maniéré, -ée** *a* affected; (*style*) mannered.

manif [manif] *nf abrév* (*manifestation*) *Fam* demo.

manifeste [manifɛst] **1** *a* (*évident*) manifest, patent, obvious. **2** *nm Pol* manifesto. ●**manifestement** [-əmɑ̃] *adv* patently, manifestly.

manifester [manifɛste] **1** *vi* (*dans la rue*) to demonstrate. **2** *vt* (*sa colère etc*) to show, manifest ▮ **se manifester** *vpr* (*maladie, sentiment etc*) to show *ou* manifest itself; (*apparaître*) to appear. ●**manifestant, -ante** *nmf* demonstrator. ●**manifestation** *nf* **1** (*défilé*) demonstration; (*réunion, fête*) event. **2** (*expression*) expression, manifestation; (*de symptômes*) appearance.

manigance [manigɑ̃s] *nf* little scheme.

●**manigancer** *vt* to plot.

manipuler [manipyle] *vt* (*manier*) to handle; (*faits, électeurs*) *Péj* to manipulate. ●**manipulation** *nf* handling; *Péj* manipulation (**de** of); **manipulations** *Pol Péj* manipulation; **manipulations génétiques** genetic engineering *ou* manipulation.

manivelle [manivɛl] *nf* (*pour voiture*) crank.

mannequin [mankẽ̝] *nm* (*personne*) (fashion) model; (*statue*) dummy.

manœuvre [manœvr] **1** *nm* (*ouvrier*) labourer, unskilled worker. **2** *nf* (*opération*) & *Mil Br* manoeuvre, *Am* maneuver; (*action*) manœuvring; (*intrigue*) scheme. ●**manœuvrer** *vt* (*véhicule, personne etc*) *Br* to manoeuvre, *Am* maneuver; (*machine*) to operate ▮ *vi Br* to manoeuvre, *Am* maneuver.

manoir [manwar] *nm* manor house.

manomètre [manɔmɛtr] *nm* (*pour pneus*) pressure gauge.

manque [mɑ̃k] *nm* lack (**de** of); (*lacune*) gap; **manques** (*défauts*) shortcomings; **m. à gagner** loss of profit.

manquer [mɑ̃ke] *vt* (*cible, train, chance etc*) to miss; (*ne pas réussir*) to make a mess of, ruin.
▮ *vi* (*faire défaut*) to be short *ou* lacking; (*être absent*) to be absent; (*être en moins*) to be missing *ou* short; (*échouer*) to fail; **m. de** (*pain, argent etc*) to be short of; (*attention, cohérence etc*) to lack; **m. à son devoir** to fail in one's duty; **m. à sa parole** to break one's word; **m. à l'appel** (*à l'école*) to miss the register; *Mil* to miss (*by*) roll call; **ça manque de sel**/*etc* there isn't enough salt/*etc*, it lacks salt/*etc*; **elle/cela lui manque** he misses her/that; **le temps lui manque** he's short of time, he has no time; **ça n'a pas manqué** that was bound to happen; **je ne manquerai pas de venir** I won't fail to come; **ne manquez pas de venir** don't forget to come; **je n'y manquerai pas** I won't forget; **elle a manqué (de) tomber** she nearly fell; **le cœur m'a manqué** my courage failed me.
▮ *v imp* **il manque/il nous manque dix tasses** there are/we are ten cups short. ●**manquant, -ante** *a* missing. ●**manqué, -ée** *a* (*médecin, pilote etc*) failed; (*livre*) unsuccessful. ●**manquement** *nm* breach (**à** of).

mansarde [mɑ̃sard] *nf* attic.

mansuétude [mɑ̃sɥetyd] *nf Litt* indulgence, kindness.

manteau, -x [mɑ̃to] *nm* coat.

manucure [manykyr] *nmf* manicurist. ●**manucurer** *vt Fam* to manicure.

manuel, -elle [manɥɛl] **1** *a* (*travail etc*) manual. **2** *nm* (*livre*) handbook, manual; **m. scolaire** textbook.

manufacture [manyfaktyr] *nf* factory. ●**manufacturé, -ée** *a* (*produit*) manufactured.

manuscrit [manyskri] *nm* manuscript; (*tapé à la machine*) typescript.

manutention [manytɑ̃sjɔ̃] *nf* handling (*of goods*). ●**manutentionnaire** *nmf* packer.

mappemonde [mapmɔ̃d] *nf* map of the

world; (*sphère*) globe.

maquereau, -x [makro] *nm* (*poisson*) mackerel.

maquette [makɛt] *nf* (scale) model.

maquiller [makije] *vt* (*visage*) to make up; (*voiture etc*) *Péj* to tamper with; (*vérité etc*) *Péj* to fake, falsify ▮ **se maquiller** *vpr* to make (oneself) up. ● **maquillage** *nm* (*fard*) make-up.

maquis [maki] *nm* (*arbustes*) scrub, bush; *Mil Hist* maquis.

maraîcher, -ère [mareʃe, -ɛʃer] *nmf Br* market gardener, *Am* truck farmer ▮ *a* **culture maraîchère** *Br* market gardening, *Am* truck farming.

marais [marɛ] *nm* marsh, bog; **m. salant** saltern, saltworks.

marasme [marasm] *nm* **m. économique/ politique/***etc* economic/political/*etc* stagnation.

marathon [maratɔ̃] *nm* marathon.

maraudeur, -euse [marodœr, -øz] *nmf* petty thief.

marbre [marbr] *nm* marble. ● **marbré, -ée** *a* (*verre etc*) mottled, marbled; **gâteau m.** marble cake. ● **marbrier** *nm* (*funéraire*) monumental mason.

marc [mar] *nm* (*eau-de-vie*) marc, brandy; **m.** (**de café**) coffee grounds.

marchand, -ande [marʃɑ̃, -ɑ̃d] *nmf Br* shopkeeper, *Am* storekeeper, trader; (*de vins, charbon*) merchant; (*de voitures, meubles*) dealer; **m. de bonbons** confectioner; **m. de journaux** (*dans la rue*) newsvendor; (*dans un magasin*) *Br* newsagent, *Am* news dealer; **m. de légumes** *Br* greengrocer, *Am* produce dealer; **m. de poissons** fishmonger; **m. de couleurs** hardware merchant *ou* dealer ▮ *a* **valeur marchande** market value; **prix m.** trade price.

marchander [marʃɑ̃de] *vi* to haggle, bargain ▮ *vt* (*objet, prix*) to haggle over. ● **marchandage** *nm* haggling, bargaining.

marchandise(s) [marʃɑ̃diz] *nf(pl)* goods, merchandise.

marche [marʃ] *nf* 1 (*d'escalier*) step, stair. 2 (*trajet*) walk; *Mil Mus* march; (*rythme*) pace; (*de train, véhicule*) movement; (*de maladie, d'événement*) progress, course; **la m.** (*action*) *Sport* walking; **faire m. arrière** (*en voiture*) *Br* to reverse, *Am* back up; **un train/véhicule en m.** a moving train/vehicle; **mettre qch en m.** to start sth (up); **la bonne m. de** (*opération, machine*) the smooth running of; **la m. à suivre** (*procédure*) the correct procedure; **dans le sens de la m.** (*dans un train etc*) facing the front *ou* the engine.

marché [marʃe] *nm* (*lieu*) & *Écon* market; (*contrat*) deal; **faire son** *ou* **le m.** to do one's shopping (*in the market*); **vendre (à) bon m.** to sell cheap(ly); **par-dessus le m.** *Fig* into the bargain; **vendre au m. noir** to sell on the black market; **le m. du travail** the labour market; **le M. commun** the Common Market; **le m. unique européen** the single

European market. ▮ *a inv* **être bon m.** to be cheap; **voiture(s)/***etc* **bon m.** cheap car(s)/*etc*; **c'est meilleur m.** it's cheaper.

marchepied [marʃəpje] *nm* (*de train, bus*) step(s); (*de voiture*) running board.

marcher [marʃe] *vi* (*à pied*) to walk; (*poser le pied*) to tread, step (**dans** in); (*train, véhicule etc*) to run, go, move; (*soldats*) to march; (*fonctionner*) to work, go, run; (*prospérer*) to go well; **faire m.** (*machine*) to work; (*entreprise*) to run; (*tromper*) *Fam* to kid (*s.o.*); **ça marche?** *Fam* how's it going?; **elle va m.** (*accepter*) *Fam* she'll go along (with it). ● **marcheur, -euse** *nmf* walker.

mardi [mardi] *nm* Tuesday; **M. gras** Shrove Tuesday.

mare [mar] *nf* (*étang*) pond; (*flaque*) pool.

marécage [mareka ʒ] *nm* swamp, marsh. ● **marécageux, -euse** *a* swampy, marshy.

maréchal, -aux [mareʃal, -o] *nm* (*dans l'armée française*) marshal. ● **maréchal-ferrant** *nm* (*pl* **maréchaux-ferrants**) blacksmith.

marée [mare] *nf* tide; (*poissons*) fresh (sea) fish; **m. haute/basse** high/low tide; **m. noire** oil slick.

marelle [marɛl] *nf* (*jeu*) hopscotch; **jouer à la m.** to play hopscotch.

marémotrice [maremɔtris] *af* **usine m.** tidal power station.

margarine [margarin] *nf* margarine, *Br* marge.

marge [marʒ] *nf* (*de cahier etc*) margin; **en m. de** (*en dehors de*) on the fringe(s) of, on the periphery of; **m. de sécurité** safety margin. ● **marginal, -e, -aux** *a* (*secondaire, asocial*) marginal ▮ *nmf* misfit, drop-out; (*bizarre*) weirdo.

marguerite [margərit] *nf* (*fleur*) daisy, marguerite.

mari [mari] *nm* husband.

mariage [marja ʒ] *nm* marriage; (*cérémonie*) wedding; (*mélange*) *Fig* blend, marriage; **demande en m.** proposal (of marriage).

marier [marje] *vt* (*couleurs*) to blend; **m. qn** (*prêtre, maire etc*) to marry s.o.; **m. qn avec** qn to marry s.o. (off) to s.o. ▮ **se marier** *vpr* to get married, marry; **se m. avec qn** to get married to s.o., marry s.o. ● **marié, -ée** *a* married ▮ *nm* (bride)groom; **les mariés** the bride and (bride)groom; **les jeunes mariés** the newly-weds. ● **mariée** *nf* bride.

marijuana [mariʒɥana] *nf* marijuana.

marin, -ine [marɛ̃, -in] *a* (*flore*) marine; (*mille*) nautical; **air/sel/***etc* **m.** sea air/salt/*etc*; **costume m.** sailor suit ▮ *nm* sailor, seaman. ● **marine** *nf* **m.** (**de guerre**) navy; **m. marchande** merchant navy ▮ *a* & *nm inv* (bleu) **m.** (*couleur*) navy (blue).

marina [marina] *nf* marina.

mariner [marine] *vti Culin* to marinate.

marionnette [marjɔnɛt] *nf* puppet; (*à fils*) marionette.

maritalement [maritalmɑ̃] *adv* **vivre m.** to

live together (as husband and wife).

maritime [maritim] *a* (*droit, climat etc*) maritime; **port m.** seaport; **gare m.** harbour station; **les Provinces maritimes** *Can* the Maritime Provinces.

marjolaine [marʒɔlɛn] *nf* (*aromate*) marjoram.

mark [mark] *nm* (*monnaie*) mark.

marmaille [marmɑj] *nf* (*enfants*) *Fam Péj* kids.

marmelade [marmǝlad] *nf* **m.** (**de fruits**) *Br* stewed fruit, *Am* fruit compote; **en m.** (*trop cuit*) cooked to a pulp *ou* mush; **avoir le nez en m.** *Fig* to get one's nose reduced to a pulp *ou* mush.

marmite [marmit] *nf* (cooking) pot.

marmonner [marmɔne] *vti* to mutter.

marmot [marmo] *nm* (*enfant*) *Fam* kid.

marmotte [marmɔt] *nf* (*animal*) marmot; **dormir comme une m.** to sleep like a log.

marmotter [marmɔte] *vti* to mumble.

Maroc [marɔk] *nm* Morocco. ● **marocain, -aine** *a* Moroccan ▮ *nmf* M., Marocaine Moroccan.

maroquinerie [marɔkinri] *nf* (*magasin*) leather goods shop. ● **maroquinier** *nm* leather goods dealer.

marotte [marɔt] *nf* (*passion*) *Fam* fad, craze.

marque [mark] *nf* (*trace, signe*) mark; (*de produit*) make, brand; (*points*) *Sport* score; **m. de fabrique** trademark; **m. déposée** (registered) trademark; **la m. de** (*preuve*) the stamp of; **de m.** (*hôte, visiteur*) distinguished; (*produit*) of quality.

marquer [marke] *vt* (*par une marque*) to mark; (*écrire*) to note down; (*indiquer*) to show, mark; (*point, but*) *Sport* to score; **m. qn** *Sport* to mark s.o.; **m. les points** *Sport* to keep (the) score; **m. le coup** *Fam* to mark the event.
▮ *vi* (*laisser une trace*) to leave a mark; (*date, événement*) to stand out; *Sport* to score. ● **marquant, -ante** *a* (*remarquable*) outstanding; **un fait m.** a highlight, an outstanding episode *ou* event. ● **marqué, -ée** *a* (*différence, accent etc*) marked, pronounced. ● **marqueur** *nm* (*crayon feutre*) marker.

marquis [marki] *nm* marquis. ● **marquise** *nf* 1 marchioness. 2 (*auvent*) glass canopy.

marraine [marɛn] *nf* godmother.

marre [mar] *nf* **en avoir m.** *Fam* to be fed up (**de** with).

marrer (se) [sǝmare] *vpr Fam* to have a good laugh. ● **marrant, -ante** *a Fam* funny, hilarious ▮ *nmf* **c'est un m.** *Fam* he's a good laugh, he's a real comedian.

marron[1] [marɔ̃] 1 *nm* chestnut; (*couleur*) (chestnut) brown; **m. (d'Inde)** horse chestnut ▮ *a inv* (*couleur*) (chestnut) brown. 2 *nm* (*coup*) *Fam* punch, clout. ● **marronnier** *nm* (horse) chestnut tree.

marron[2], -onne [marɔ̃, -ɔn] *a* (*médecin etc*) bogus.

mars [mars] *nm* March.

marsouin [marswɛ̃] *nm* porpoise.

marteau, -x [marto] *nm* hammer; (*de porte*) (door)knocker; **m. pneumatique** pneumatic drill. ● **marteau-piqueur** *nm* (*pl* marteaux-piqueurs) pneumatic drill. ● **marteler** *vt* to hammer. ● **martèlement** *nm* hammering.

martial, -e, -aux [marsjal, -o] *a* martial; **cour martiale** court-martial; **loi martiale** martial law; **arts martiaux** martial arts.

martien, -ienne [marsjɛ̃, -jɛn] *nmf* & *a* Martian.

martinet [martinɛ] *nm* (*fouet*) (small) whip.

Martinique [martinik] *nf* Martinique. ● **martiniquais, -aise** *a* Martinican ▮ *nmf* M., Martiniquaise Martinican.

martin-pêcheur [martɛ̃peʃœr] *nm* (*pl* martins-pêcheurs) (*oiseau*) kingfisher.

martyr, -yre[1] [martir] *nmf* (*personne*) martyr; **enfant m.** battered child. ● **martyre[2]** *nm* (*souffrance*) martyrdom; **souffrir le m.** to suffer unbearably *ou* atrociously, go through agony. ● **martyriser** *vt* to torture; (*enfant*) to batter.

marxisme [marksism] *nm* Marxism. ● **marxiste** *a* & *nmf* Marxist.

mascara [maskara] *nm* mascara.

mascarade [maskarad] *nf* masquerade.

mascotte [maskɔt] *nf* mascot.

masculin, -ine [maskylɛ̃, -in] *a* male; (*viril*) masculine, manly; (*nom etc*) *Grammaire* masculine; (*vêtement, équipe*) men's ▮ *nm Grammaire* masculine. ● **masculinité** *nf* masculinity.

masochisme [mazɔʃism] *nm* masochism. ● **masochiste** *nmf* (*Fam* maso) masochist ▮ *a* masochistic.

masque [mask] *nm* mask; **m. à gaz/oxygène** gas/oxygen mask. ● **masquer** *vt* (*dissimuler*) to mask (**à** from); (*cacher à la vue*) to block off.

massacre [masakr] *nm* slaughter, massacre; **jeu de m.** = *Br* Aunty Sally; **ce fut un m.** *Fig* it was a wholesale *ou* real massacre. ● **massacrer** *vt* to slaughter, massacre; (*abîmer*)` *Fam* to ruin. ● **massacrant, -ante** *a* (*humeur*) excruciating.

massage [masaʒ] *nm* massage.

masse [mas] *nf* 1 (*volume*) mass; (*gros morceau, majorité*) bulk (**de** of); **en m.** (*arriver etc*) in large numbers; **départ en m.** mass *ou* wholesale departure; **manifestation de m.** mass demonstration; **la m.** (*foule*) the masses; **les masses** (*peuple*) the masses; **une m. de** (*tas*) a mass of; **des masses de** *Fam* masses of; **pas des masses** *Fam* not that much, not massively. 2 (*outil*) sledgehammer. 3 *Él Br* earth, *Am* ground.

masser [mase] 1 *vt* (*pétrir*) to massage. 2 **se masser** *vpr* (*foule*) to form, mass. ● **masseur** *nm* masseur. ● **masseuse** *nf* masseuse.

massif, -ive [masif, -iv] 1 *a* massive; (*or, chêne etc*) solid; **départs massifs** mass departure(s). 2 *nm* (*d'arbres, de fleurs*) clump; *Géog* massif. ● **massivement** *adv* (*en masse*) in large numbers.

massue [masy] *nf* (*bâton*) club.

mastic [mastik] *nm* (*pour vitres*) putty; (*pour bois*) filler; **m.** (*silicone*) mastic **∎** *a inv* (*imperméable etc*) putty-coloured.

mastiquer [mastike] *vt* **1** (*vitre*) to putty; (*bois*) to fill; (*porte*) to mastic. **2** (*mâcher*) to chew, masticate.

mastoc [mastɔk] *a inv Péj Fam* massive.

mastodonte [mastɔdɔ̃t] *nm* (*personne*) *Péj* monster; (*véhicule*) enormous vehicle, *Br* juggernaut.

masturber (se) [səmastyrbe] *vpr* to masturbate. ● **masturbation** *nf* masturbation.

masure [mazyr] *nf* tumbledown house.

mat, mate [mat] **1** *a* (*papier, couleur*) mat(t); (*bruit*) dull. **2** *am inv* & *nm* Échecs (check)mate; **faire m.** to (check)mate; **mettre qn m.** to (check)mate s.o.

mât [mɑ] *nm* (*de navire*) mast; (*poteau*) pole.

match [matʃ] *nm Sport Br* match, *Am* game; **m. nul** tie, draw; **m. aller** first leg; **m. retour** second *ou* return leg.

matelas [matla] *nm* mattress; **m. pneumatique** air bed. ● **matelassé, -ée** *a* (*tissu*) quilted, padded; (*meuble*) padded.

matelot [matlo] *nm* sailor, seaman.

mater [mate] *vt* (*enfant etc*) to subdue.

matérialiser [materjalize] *vt*, **se matérialiser** *vpr* to materialize. ● **matérialisation** *nf* materialization.

matérialisme [materjalism] *nm* materialism. ● **matérialiste** *a* materialistic **∎** *nmf* materialist.

matériau [materjo] *nm* material; **matériaux** (*de construction*) building material(s); (*de roman, enquête etc*) *Fig* material.

matériel, -ielle [materjɛl] **1** *a* (*dégâts etc*) material; (*personne*) *Péj* materialistic; (*financier*) financial; (*pratique*) practical. **2** *nm* (*de camping*) equipment, material(s); (*d'ordinateur*) hardware *inv*. ● **matériellement** *adv* materially; **m. impossible** physically impossible.

maternel, -elle [matɛrnɛl] *a* (*amour, femme etc*) maternal, motherly; (*parenté, réprimande*) maternal **∎** *nf* (*école*) **maternelle** *Br* (state) nursery school, *Am* kindergarten. ● **materner** *vt* to mother. ● **maternité** *nf* (*état*) motherhood, maternity; (*hôpital*) maternity hospital *ou* unit; (*grossesse*) pregnancy; **congé/allocation/etc de m.** maternity leave/allowance/etc.

mathématique [matematik] *a* mathematical. ● **mathématiques** *nfpl* mathematics. ● **mathématicien, -ienne** *nmf* mathematician. ● **maths** [mat] *nfpl Fam Br* maths, *Am* math; **être en m. sup/spé** *Fam* to be in the first-/second-year mathematics class preparing for the *grandes écoles.*

matière [matjɛr] *nf* (*à l'école*) subject; (*de livre*) subject matter; (*substance*) material, matter (*no pl*); **la m.** *Phys* matter; **m. première** raw material; **en m. d'art/etc** as regards art/etc, in art/etc; **s'y connaître en m. de** to be experienced in; **en la m.** (*sur ce sujet*) on the subject.

Matignon [matiɲɔ̃] *nm* (**l'hôtel**) **M.** the Hotel Matignon (*French Prime Minister's office*).

matin [matɛ̃] *nm* morning; **le m.** (*chaque matin*) in the morning(s); **à sept heures du m.** at seven in the morning; **tous les mardis matin(s)** every Tuesday morning; **de bon m., au petit m., de grand m.** very early (in the morning); **du m. au soir** from morning till night; **le 8 au m.** on the morning of the 8th; **médicament à prendre m., midi et soir** medicine to be taken three times a day. ● **matinal, -e, -aux** *a* (*personne*) early; **soleil m.** morning sun; **être m.** to be an early riser.

matinée [matine] *nf* morning; *Théâtre Cinéma* matinée; **faire la grasse m.** to sleep late, *Br* lie in.

matou [matu] *nm* tomcat.

matraque [matrak] *nf* (*de policier*) *Br* truncheon, *Am* night stick, *Am* billy (club); (*de malfaiteur*) *Br* cosh, club. ● **matraquer** *vt* (*frapper*) to club; (*publicité etc*) to plug. ● **matraquage** *nm* **m.** (**publicitaire**) plugging, publicity build-up.

matrice [matris] *nf Math* matrix.

matricielle [matrisjɛl] *af* **imprimante m.** *Ordinat* dot matrix printer.

matricule [matrikyl] *nm* (registration) number **∎** *a* **numéro m.** registration number; **livret m.** army registration document.

matrimonial, -e, -aux [matrimɔnjal, -o] *a* matrimonial.

mâture [mɑtyr] *nf* (*de navire*) masts.

maturité [matyrite] *nf* maturity. ● **maturation** *nf* maturing.

maudire* [modir] *vt* to curse. ● **maudit, -ite** *a* (*sacré*) (ac)cursed, damned.

maugréer [mogree] *vi* to growl, grumble (**contre** at).

Maurice (île) [ilmɔris] *nf* Mauritius.

mausolée [mozɔle] *nm* mausoleum.

maussade [mosad] *a* (*personne etc*) bad-tempered, moody, glum; (*temps*) gloomy.

mauvais, -aise [movɛ, -ɛz] *a* bad; (*méchant, malveillant*) wicked, evil; (*mal choisi*) wrong; (*mer*) rough; **plus m.** worse; **le plus m.** the worst; **il fait m.** the weather's bad; **être m. en anglais/etc** to be bad at English/etc; **être en mauvaise santé** to be in bad *ou* ill *ou* poor health **∎** *adv* **ça sent m.** it smells bad **∎** *nm* **le bon et le m.** the good and the bad.

mauve [mov] *a* & *nm* (*couleur*) mauve.

mauviette [movjɛt] *nf* (*personne*) *Péj* weakling.

maux [mo] *voir* **mal**.

maxime [maksim] *nf* maxim.

maximum [maksimɔm] *nm* maximum; **le m. de** (*force etc*) the maximum (amount of); **au m.** as much as possible; (*tout au plus*) at most **∎** *a* maximum; **la température/etc m.** maximum temperature/etc; **bénéfices/etc maximums** maximum profits/etc. ● **maximal, -e, -aux** *a* maximum.

mayonnaise [majɔnɛz] *nf* mayonnaise.

mazout [mazut] *nm* (fuel) oil.

me [m(ə)] (**m'** *before vowel or mute h*) *pron*

1 (*complément direct*) me; **il me voit** he sees me. **2** (*indirect*) (to) me; **elle me parle** she speaks to me; **tu me l'as dit** you told me. **3** (*réfléchi*) myself; **je me lave** I wash myself.

méandres [meɑ̃dr] *nmpl* meander(ing)s.

mec [mɛk] *nm* (*individu*) *Arg* guy, bloke.

mécanicien [mekanisjɛ̃] *nm* mechanic; (*de train*) *Br* train driver, *Am* engineer.

mécanique [mekanik] *a* mechanical; **jouet m.** wind-up toy ▮ *nf* (*science*) mechanics; (*mécanisme*) mechanism. ●**mécanisme** *nm* mechanism.

mécaniser [mekanize] *vt* to mechanize. ●**mécanisation** *nf* mechanization.

mécène [mesɛn] *nm* patron (of the arts).

méchant, -ante [meʃɑ̃, -ɑ̃t] *a* (*cruel*) wicked, malicious, evil; (*désagréable*) nasty; (*enfant*) naughty; (*chien*) vicious; **chien m.!** beware of the dog!; **ce n'est pas m.** (*grave*) *Fam* it's nothing much; **être de méchante humeur** to be in a terrible *ou* foul mood. ●**méchamment** [-amɑ̃] *adv* (*cruellement*) maliciously; (*très*) *Fam* terribly. ●**méchanceté** *nf* malice, wickedness; **une m.** (*parole*) a malicious word; (*acte*) a malicious act.

mèche [mɛʃ] *nf* **1** (*de cheveux*) lock; **se faire faire des mèches** (*reflets*) to have highlights put in one's hair. **2** (*de bougie*) wick; (*de pétard*) fuse; (*de perceuse*) drill, bit; **vendre la m.** *Fig* to spill the beans, give the game away. **3** **être de m. avec qn** (*complicité*) *Fam* to be in collusion *ou* cahoots with s.o.

méconnaître* [mekɔnɛtr] *vt* to ignore; (*méjuger*) to fail to appreciate. ●**méconnu, -ue** *a* unrecognized. ●**méconnaissable** *a* unrecognizable.

mécontent, -ente [mekɔ̃tɑ̃, -ɑ̃t] *a* dissatisfied, discontented (**de** with). ●**mécontenter** *vt* to displease, dissatisfy. ●**mécontentement** *nm* dissatisfaction, discontent.

Mecque (la) [lamɛk] *nf* Mecca.

médaille [medaj] *nf* (*décoration*) & *Sport* medal; (*bijou*) medallion; (*pour chien*) name tag; **être m. d'or/d'argent** *Sport* to be a gold/silver medallist. ●**médaillé, -ée** *nmf* medal holder. ●**médaillon** *nm* (*bijou*) locket, medallion; (*ornement*) *Archit* medallion.

médecin [medsɛ̃] *nm* doctor, physician; **m. généraliste** general practitioner; **m. de famille** family doctor; **m. traitant** regular doctor. ●**médecine** *nf* medicine; **médecines douces** alternative medicines; **étudiant en m.** medical student. ●**médical, -e, -aux** *a* medical. ●**médicament** *nm* medicine. ●**médicinal, -e, -aux** *a* medicinal. ●**médico-légal, -e, -aux** *a* (*laboratoire*) forensic.

média [medja] *nm* medium; **médias** (mass) media. ●**médiatique** *a* campagne/événement/*etc* **m.** media campaign/event/*etc*.

médiateur, -trice [medjatœr, -tris] *nmf* mediator ▮ *a* mediating. ●**médiation** *nf* mediation.

médical, -e, -aux [medikal, -o] *a voir* médecin.

médiéval, -e, -aux [medjeval, -o] *a* medi(a)eval.

médiocre [medjɔkr] *a* second-rate, mediocre. ●**médiocrement** [-əmɑ̃] *adv* (*pas très*) not very; (*pas très bien*) not very well. ●**médiocrité** *nf* mediocrity.

médire* [medir] *vi* **m. de qn** to speak ill of s.o., slander s.o. ●**médisance(s)** *nf(pl)* malicious gossip, slander; **une m.** a piece of malicious gossip.

méditer [medite] *vt* (*conseil etc*) to meditate on; **m. de faire** to consider doing ▮ *vi* to meditate (**sur** on). ●**méditatif, -ive** *a* meditative. ●**méditation** *nf* meditation.

Méditerranée [mediterane] *nf* **la M.** the Mediterranean. ●**méditerranéen, -enne** *a* Mediterranean.

médium [medjɔm] *nm* (*spirite*) medium.

méduse [medyz] *nf* jellyfish.

méduser [medyze] *vt* to stun, dumbfound.

meeting [mitiŋ] *nm* *Pol Sport* meeting, rally.

méfait [mefɛ] *nm* *Jur* misdeed; **méfaits** (*dégâts*) ravages.

méfier (se) [səmefje] *vpr* **se m. de** to distrust, mistrust; (*faire attention à*) to watch out for, beware of; **méfie-toi!** watch out!, beware!; **je me méfie** I'm suspicious *ou* distrustful. ●**méfiant, -ante** *a* suspicious, distrustful. ●**méfiance** *nf* distrust, mistrust.

mégalomane [megalɔman] *nmf* megalomaniac. ●**mégalomanie** *nf* megalomania.

méga-octet [megaɔktɛ] *nm* *Ordinat* megabyte.

mégaphone [megafɔn] *nm* *Br* loudhailer, megaphone.

mégarde (par) [parmegard] *adv* inadvertently, by mistake.

mégère [meʒɛr] *nf* (*femme*) *Péj* shrew.

mégot [mego] *nm* cigarette butt *ou* end.

meilleur, -e [mejœr] *a* better (**que** than); **le m. résultat/moment/***etc* the best result/moment/*etc* ▮ *nmf* **le m., la meilleure** the best (one).

mélancolie [melɑ̃kɔli] *nf* melancholy, gloom. ●**mélancolique** *a* melancholy, gloomy.

mélange [melɑ̃ʒ] *nm* mixture, blend; (*opération*) mixing. ●**mélanger** *vt* (*mêler*) to mix; (*brouiller*) to mix up, muddle ▮ **se mélanger** *vpr* to mix; (*idées etc*) to get mixed up *ou* muddled.

mélasse [melas] *nf* *Br* treacle, *Am* molasses.

mêler [mele] *vt* to mix, mingle (**à** with); (*odeurs, thèmes*) to combine; (*brouiller*) to mix up, muddle; **m. qn à** (*impliquer*) to involve s.o. in.

▮ **se mêler** *vpr* to mix, mingle (**à** with); **se m. à la foule** to join the crowd, mingle with the crowd; **se m. de** (*s'ingérer dans*) to meddle in; **mêle-toi de ce qui te regarde!** mind your own business! ●**mêlé, -ée** *a* mixed (**de** with). ●**mêlée** *nf* (*bataille*) rough-and-tumble; *Rugby* scrum(mage).

méli-mélo [melimelo] *nm* (*pl* **mélis-mélos**) *Fam* muddle.

mélodie [melɔdi] *nf* melody. ●**mélodieux,**

-euse *a* melodious. ●**mélodique** *a* melodic.
●**mélomane** *nmf* music lover.

mélodrame [melɔdram] *nm* melodrama.
●**mélodramatique** *a* melodramatic.

melon [m(ə)lɔ̃] *nm* 1 (*fruit*) melon. 2 (*chapeau*) m. *Br* bowler (hat), *Am* derby.

membrane [mãbran] *nf* membrane.

membre [mãbr] *nm* 1 (*bras, jambe*) limb. 2 (*d'un groupe*) member.

même [mɛm] 1 *a* (*identique*) same; en m. temps at the same time (que as); le m. jour/*etc* the same day/*etc*; le jour/*etc* m. (*exact*) the very day/*etc*; il est la bonté m. he is kindness itself; lui-m./vous-m./*etc* himself/yourself/*etc* ▮ *pron* le m., la m. the same (one); j'ai les mêmes I have the same (ones); cela revient au m. it amounts to the same thing.
2 *adv* (*y compris, aussi*) even; m. si even if; ici m. in this very place; tout de m., quand m. all the same; de m. likewise; de m. que just as; être à m. de to be in a position to; dormir/*etc* à m. le sol to sleep/*etc* on the ground; boire à m. la bouteille to drink (straight) from the bottle.

mémento [memɛ̃to] *nm* (*aide-mémoire*) handbook; (*agenda*) notebook.

mémoire [memwar] 1 *nf* memory; de m. d'homme in living memory; à la m. de in memory of; m. morte/vive *Ordinat* read only/random access memory. 2 *nm* (*requête*) petition; *Univ* dissertation; mémoires *Littér* memoirs. ●**mémorable** *a* memorable.

mémorandum [memɔrãdɔm] *nm* *Pol Com* memorandum.

mémorial, -aux [memɔrjal, -o] *nm* (*monument*) memorial.

menace [mənas] *nf* threat, menace. ●**menacer** *vt* to threaten (de faire to do). ●**menaçant, -ante** *a* threatening.

ménage [menaʒ] *nm* (*entretien*) housekeeping; (*couple*) couple, household; faire le m. to do the housework; faire bon m. avec to get on happily with. ●**ménager¹, -ère** *a* appareil m. domestic *ou* household appliance; travaux ménagers housework ▮ *nf* ménagère (*femme*) housewife.

ménager² [menaʒe] *vt* (*arranger*) to prepare *ou* arrange (carefully); (*épargner*) to use sparingly, be careful with; (*fenêtre, escalier etc*) to build; m. qn to treat *ou* handle s.o. carefully *ou* gently. ●**ménagement** *nm* (*soin*) care; sans m. (*brutalement*) brutally.

ménagerie [menaʒri] *nf* menagerie.

mendier [mãdje] *vi* to beg ▮ *vt* to beg for. ●**mendiant, -ante** *nmf* beggar. ●**mendicité** *nf* begging.

menées [məne] *nfpl* schemings, intrigues.

mener [məne] *vt* (*personne, vie etc*) to lead; (*enquête, tâche etc*) to carry out; (*affaires*) to run; (*bateau*) to command; m. une campagne to wage a campaign; m. qn à (*accompagner*) to take s.o. to; m. qch à bien *Fig* to carry sth through; ça ne mène à rien it won't *ou* doesn't get you *ou* us *etc* anywhere ▮ *vi*

Sport to lead; m. à (*rue etc*) to lead to. ●**meneur, -euse** *nmf* (*de révolte*) (ring)leader.

méningite [menɛ̃ʒit] *nf* (*maladie*) meningitis.

ménopause [menɔpoz] *nf* menopause.

menottes [mənɔt] *nfpl* handcuffs.

mensonge [mãsɔ̃ʒ] *nm* lie; (*action*) lying. ●**mensonger, -ère** *a* untrue, false.

menstruation [mãstryasjɔ̃] *nf* menstruation.

mensuel, -elle [mãsɥɛl] *a* monthly ▮ *nm* (*revue*) monthly. ●**mensualité** *nf* monthly payment. ●**mensuellement** *adv* monthly.

mensurations [mãsyrasjɔ̃] *nfpl* measurements.

mental, -e, -aux [mãtal, -o] *a* mental. ●**mentalité** *nf* mentality.

menthe [mãt] *nf* mint.

mention [mãsjɔ̃] *nf* mention, reference; (*annotation*) comment; (*à un examen*) = distinction; m. passable/assez bien/bien/très bien *Scol* = grade D/C/B/A pass; faire m. de qch to mention sth; 'rayez les mentions inutiles' 'delete as appropriate'. ●**mentionner** *vt* to mention.

mentir* [mãtir] *vi* to lie, tell lies *ou* a lie (à to). ●**menteur, -euse** *nmf* liar ▮ *a* lying.

menton [mãtɔ̃] *nm* chin.

menu, -ue [məny] 1 *nm* (*liste des plats*) & *Ordinat* menu. 2 *a* (*petit*) tiny; (*mince*) slender, fine; (*peu important*) minor, petty ▮ *adv* (*hacher*) small, finely ▮ *nm* par le m. in detail.

menuisier [mənɥizje] *nm* carpenter, joiner. ●**menuiserie** *nf* carpentry, joinery; (*ouvrage*) woodwork.

méprendre (se) [səmeprãdr] *vpr* se m. sur *Litt* to be mistaken about. ●**méprise** *nf* mistake.

mépris [mepri] *nm* contempt (pour for), scorn (de for); au m. de without regard to; avoir le m. des convenances/*etc* to scorn convention/*etc*. ●**mépriser** *vt* to despise, scorn. ●**méprisant, -ante** *a* contemptuous, scornful.

méprisable [meprizabl] *a* despicable.

mer [mɛr] *nf* sea; (*marée*) tide; en m. at sea; par m. by sea; aller à la m. to go to the seaside *ou* the coast; prendre la m. to go out to sea, set sail; un homme à la m.! man overboard!

mercantile [mɛrkãtil] *a* *Péj* money-grabbing.

mercenaire [mɛrsənɛr] *a* & *nm* mercenary.

mercerie [mɛrsəri] *nf* (*magasin*) *Br* haberdasher's, *Am* notions store. ●**mercier, -ière** *nmf* *Br* haberdasher, *Am* notions dealer *ou* merchant.

merci [mɛrsi] 1 *int* & *nm* thank you, thanks (de, pour for); (non) m.! no, thank you! 2 *nf* à la m. de at the mercy of; tenir qn à sa m. to have s.o. at one's mercy.

mercredi [mɛrkrədi] *nm* Wednesday.

mercure [mɛrkyr] *nm* mercury.

merde! [mɛrd] *int* *Fam* (bloody) hell!

mère [mɛr] *nf* mother; m. de famille mother (of a family); m. porteuse surrogate mother;

la m. Dubois *Fam* old Mrs Dubois; **maison m.** *Com* parent company *ou* firm.
méridien [meridjɛ̃] *nm* meridian.
méridional, -e, -aux [meridjɔnal, -o] *a* southern (*Europe*) Mediterranean.
meringue [mərɛ̃g] *nf* (*gâteau*) meringue.
merisier [mərizje] *nm* (*bois*) cherry.
mérite [merit] *nm* merit; **homme de m.** (*valeur*) man of worth. ● **mériter** *vt* (*être digne de*) to deserve; (*valoir*) to be worth; **m. de réussir/etc** to deserve to succeed/etc. ● **méritant, -ante** *a* deserving. ● **méritoire** *a* commendable.
merlan [mɛrlɑ̃] *nm* 1 (*poisson*) whiting. 2 (*coiffeur*) *Fam* hairdresser.
merle [mɛrl] *nm* blackbird.
merveille [mɛrvɛj] *nf* wonder, marvel; **les sept Merveilles du monde** the seven wonders of the world; **à m.** wonderfully (well); **faire des merveilles** (*médicament etc*) to work wonders.
merveilleux, -euse [mɛrvɛjø, -øz] *a* wonderful, *Br* marvellous, *Am* marvelous ‖ *nm* **le m.** (*surnaturel*) the supernatural. ● **merveilleusement** *adv* wonderfully.
mes [me] *voir* **mon.**
mésange [mezɑ̃ʒ] *nf* (*oiseau*) tit.
mésaventure [mezavɑ̃tyr] *nf* slight mishap, misfortune, misadventure.
mesdames [medam] *voir* **madame.**
mesdemoiselles [medmwazɛl] *voir* **mademoiselle.**
mésentente [mezɑ̃tɑ̃t] *nf* disagreement, misunderstanding.
mesquin, -ine [mɛskɛ̃, -in] *a* mean, petty. ● **mesquinerie** *nf* meanness, pettiness; **une m.** an act of meanness.
mess [mɛs] *nm inv* (*salle*) *Mil* mess.
message [mesaʒ] *nm* message. ● **messager, -ère** *nmf* messenger.
messagerie [mesaʒri] *nf* **m. électronique** electronic mail; **messageries** *Com* courier service.
messe [mɛs] *nf* mass (*church service*); **faire des messes basses** *Fam* to whisper, mutter under one's breath.
Messie [mesi] *nm* Messiah.
messieurs [mesjø] *voir* **monsieur.**
mesure [məzyr] *nf* (*dimension*) measurement; (*action*) measure; (*retenue*) moderation; (*cadence*) *Mus* time, beat; **fait sur m.** made to measure; **à m. que** *ou* **as** as soon *ou* as fast as; **dans la m. où** in so far as; **dans une certaine m.** to a certain extent; **être en m. de** to be able to, be in a position to; **dépasser la m.** to exceed the bounds; **prendre la m. de** (*problème etc*) to size up.
mesurer [məzyre] *vt* to measure; (*juger, estimer*) to calculate, assess, measure; (*argent, temps*) to ration (out); **m. 1 mètre 83** (*personne*) to be six feet tall; (*objet*) to measure six feet; **se m. à** *ou* **avec qn** *Fig* to pit oneself against s.o. ● **mesuré, -ée** *a* (*pas, ton*) measured; (*personne*) moderate.
met [mɛ] *voir* **mettre.**

métal, -aux [metal, -o] *nm* metal. ● **métallique** *a* (*éclat, reflet*) metallic; **pont/etc m.** metal bridge/etc. ● **métallisé, -ée** *a* **bleu/etc m.** metallic blue/etc.
métallo [metalo] *nm abrév* (*métallurgiste*) *Fam* steelworker.
métallurgie [metalyrʒi] *nf* (*industrie*) steel industry; (*science*) metallurgy. ● **métallurgique** *a* **usine m.** steelworks. ● **métallurgiste** *a* & *nm* (*ouvrier*) **m.** steelworker.
métamorphose [metamɔrfoz] *nf* metamorphosis. ● **métamorphoser** *vt*, **se métamorphoser** *vpr* to transform (**en** into).
métaphore [metafɔr] *nf* metaphor. ● **métaphorique** *a* metaphorical.
métaphysique [metafizik] *a* metaphysical.
météo [meteo] *nf* (*bulletin*) weather forecast.
météore [meteɔr] *nm* meteor. ● **météorite** *nm* meteorite.
météorologie [meteɔrɔlɔʒi] *nf* (*science*) meteorology; (*service*) weather bureau. ● **météorologique** *a* meteorological; **bulletin/station/etc m.** weather report/station/etc.
méthode [metɔd] *nf* (*manière, soin*) method; (*livre*) course. ● **méthodique** *a* methodical.
méticuleux, -euse [metikylø, -øz] *a* meticulous.
métier [metje] *nm* 1 (*travail*) job; (*manuel*) trade; (*intellectuel*) profession; (*habileté*) professional skill; **homme de m.** specialist; **tailleur/etc de son m.** tailor/etc by trade; **il est du m.** he's in the trade *ou* profession, he's an expert. **2 m.** (**à tisser**) loom.
métis, -isse [metis] *a* & *nmf* half-caste.
métrage [metraʒ] *nm* 1 surveying. 2 (*tissu*) length; (*de film*) footage; **long m.** (*film*) full length film; **court m.** (*film*) short (film).
mètre [mɛtr] *nm* (*mesure*) *Br* metre, *Am* meter; (*règle*) (metre) rule; **m. carré** square metre; **m. (à ruban**) tape measure. ● **métrer** *vt* (*terrain*) to survey. ● **métreur** *nm* quantity surveyor. ● **métrique** *a* metric.
métro [metro] *nm* *Br* underground, *Am* subway.
métropole [metrɔpɔl] *nf* (*ville*) metropolis; (*pays*) mother country. ● **métropolitain, -aine** *a* metropolitan.
mets [mɛ] *nm* (*aliment*) dish.
mettable [metabl] *a* wearable.
metteur en scène [metœrɑ̃sɛn] *nm* *Théâtre* producer; *Cinéma* director.
mettre* [mɛtr] *vt* to put; (*table*) to set, *Br* lay; (*vêtement, lunettes*) to put on, wear; (*chauffage, radio etc*) to put on, switch on; (*réveil*) to set (à for); **m. dix heures/etc à venir** (*consacrer*) to take ten hours/etc coming *ou* to come; **j'ai mis une heure** it took me an hour; **m. 100 francs/etc** to spend 100 francs/etc (*pour une robe/etc* on a dress/etc); **m. en colère** to make angry; **m. à l'aise** (*rassurer*) to put *ou* set at ease; (*dans un fauteuil etc*) to make comfortable; **m. en liberté** to free; **m. en bouteille(s)** to bottle; **m. du soin à faire** to take care to do; **mettons que** (+ *sub*) let's suppose that.

se mettre *vpr* (*se placer*) to put oneself; (*debout*) to stand; (*assis*) to sit; (*objet*) to go, be put; **se m. en short/pyjama/***etc* to get into one's shorts/pyjamas/*etc*; **se m. à table** to sit (down) at the table; **se m. à l'aise** to make oneself comfortable; **se m. à la cuisine/au salon/***etc* to go into the kitchen/dining room/*etc*; **se m. au travail** to start work; **se m. à faire qch** to start doing sth; **le temps s'est mis au beau/au froid/à la pluie** the weather has turned fine/cold/rainy; **se m. en rapport avec qn** to get in touch with s.o.; **se m. le doigt dans l'œil** *Fam* to be badly mistaken.

meuble [mœbl] *nm* piece of furniture; **meubles** furniture. ● **meubler** *vt* to furnish; (*remplir*) *Fig* to fill. ● **meublé** *nm* furnished *Br* flat *ou Am* apartment.

meugler [møgle] *vi* (*vache*) to moo, *Litt* low. ● **meuglement(s)** *nm(pl)* mooing, *Litt* lowing.

meule [møl] *nf* **1** (*de foin*) haystack. **2** (*pour moudre*) millstone.

meunier, -ière [mønje, -jɛr] *nmf* miller.

meurt [mœr] *voir* **mourir.**

meurtre [mœrtr] *nm* murder. ● **meurtrier, -ière** *nmf* murderer █ *a* deadly, murderous.

meurtrir [mœrtrir] *vt* to bruise. ● **meurtrissure** *nf* bruise.

meute [møt] *nf* (*de chiens, de créanciers etc*) pack.

Mexique [mɛksik] *nm* Mexico. ● **mexicain, -aine** *a* Mexican █ *nmf* M., Mexicaine Mexican.

mezzanine [mɛdzanin] *nf* (*dans une pièce*) mezzanine floor.

mi [mi] *nm* (*note de musique*) E.

mi- [mi] *préf* **la mi-mars/***etc* mid March/*etc*; **à mi-distance** midway, mid-distance; **cheveux mi-longs** shoulder-length hair.

miaou [mjau] *int* miaow. ● **miauler** [mjole] *vi* (*chat*) to miaow, mew. ● **miaulement(s)** *nm(pl)* miaowing, mewing.

mi-bas [miba] *nm inv* knee sock.

miche [miʃ] *nf* round loaf.

mi-chemin (à) [amiʃmɛ̃] *adv* halfway.

mi-clos, -ose [miklo, -oz] *a* half-closed.

micmac [mikmak] *nm* (*manigance*) *Fam* intrigue.

mi-corps (à) [amikɔr] *adv* (up) to the waist.

mi-côte (à) [amikot] *adv* halfway up *ou* down (the hill).

micro [mikro] *nm* **1** microphone, mike. **2** (*ordinateur*) micro(-computer). ● **microphone** *nm* microphone.

micro- [mikro] *préf* micro-.

microbe [mikrɔb] *nm* germ, microbe.

microcosme [mikrɔkɔsm] *nm* microcosm.

microfiche [mikrɔfiʃ] *nf* microfiche.

microfilm [mikrɔfilm] *nm* microfilm.

micro-informatique [mikroɛ̃fɔrmatik] *nf* microcomputing.

micro-onde [mikrɔɔ̃d] *nf* microwave; **four à micro-ondes** microwave oven.

micro-ordinateur [mikroɔrdinatœr] *nm* microcomputer.

microprocesseur [mikroprɔsesœr] *nm* microprocessor.

microscope [mikrɔskɔp] *nm* microscope. ● **microscopique** *a* miscroscopic.

midi [midi] *nm* **1** (*heure*) twelve o'clock, noon, midday; (*heure du déjeuner*) lunchtime; **chercher m. à quatorze heures** to make unnecessary complications for oneself. **2** (*sud*) south; **le M.** the south of France.

mie [mi] *nf* **la m.** the soft part of the bread; **pain de m.** sandwich loaf.

miel [mjɛl] *nm* honey. ● **mielleux, -euse** *a* (*parole, personne*) *Fig* smooth, unctuous.

mien, mienne [mjɛ̃, mjɛn] *pron poss* **le m., la mienne** mine, *Br* my one; **les miens, les miennes** mine, *Br* my ones; **les deux miens** my two █ *nmpl* **les miens** (*ma famille*) my (own) people.

miette [mjɛt] *nf* (*de pain etc*) crumb; **réduire qch en miettes** to smash sth to pieces; **elle ne perd pas une m. du spectacle** *Fam* not one scrap of the show is passing her by, she's taking the whole show in.

mieux [mjø] *adv & a* better (**que** than); (*plus à l'aise*) more comfortable; (*plus beau*) better-looking; **le m., la m., les m.** (*convenir, être etc*) the best; (*de deux*) the better; **le m. serait de...** the best thing would be to...; **tu ferais m. de partir** you had better leave; **de m. en m.** better and better; **je ne demande pas m.** there's nothing I'd like better (**que de faire** than to do).

█ *nm* (*amélioration*) improvement; **faire de son m.** to do one's best; **faites au m.** do the best you can.

mièvre [mjɛvr] *a* (*doucereux*) *Péj* mannered, wishy-washy.

mignon, -onne [miɲɔ̃, -ɔn] *a* (*charmant*) cute; (*gentil*) nice.

migraine [migrɛn] *nf* headache; *Méd* migraine.

migration [migrɑsjɔ̃] *nf* migration. ● **migrant, -ante** *a & nmf* (**travailleur**) **m.** migrant worker, migrant.

mijoter [miʒɔte] *vt* (*faire cuire*) to cook (lovingly); (*lentement*) to simmer; (*complot*) *Fam* to brew █ *vi* to simmer.

mil [mil] *nm inv* (*dans les dates*) a *ou* one thousand; **l'an deux m.** the year two thousand.

milice [milis] *nf* militia. ● **milicien** *nm* militiaman.

milieu, -x [miljø] *nm* (*centre*) middle; (*cadre, groupe social*) environment; (*entre extrêmes*) middle course; (*espace*) *Phys* medium; **milieux littéraires/militaires/***etc* literary/military/*etc* circles; **au m. de** in the middle of; **au m. du danger** in the midst of danger; **le juste m.** the happy medium; **le m.** (*de malfaiteurs*) the underworld.

militaire [militɛr] *a* military; **service m.** military service █ *nm* serviceman; (*dans l'armée de terre*) soldier.

militer [milite] *vi* (*personne*) to be a militant; (*arguments etc*) to militate (**pour** in favour of, **contre** against). ● **militant, -ante** a & nmf militant.

mille [mil] **1** a & nm inv thousand; **m. hommes/etc** a ou one thousand men/etc; **deux m.** two thousand; **mettre dans le m.** Fig to hit the bull's-eye; **je vous le donne en m.** you'll never guess. **2** nm m. (**marin**) (*mesure*) nautical mile. ● **mille-pattes** nm inv (*insecte*) centipede. ● **millième** a & nmf thousandth; **un m.** a thousandth. ● **millier** nm thousand; **un m. (de)** a thousand or so; **par milliers** in their thousands.

millefeuille [milfœj] nm (*gâteau*) cream puff, Am napoleon.

millénaire [milenɛr] nm millennium.

millésime [milezim] nm date (on wine etc).

millet [mijɛ] nm Bot millet.

milli- [mili] préf milli-.

milliard [miljar] nm billion, thousand million. ● **milliardaire** a & nmf multimillionaire, billionaire.

millimètre [milimɛtr] nm millimetre.

million [miljɔ̃] nm million; **un m. de livres/etc** a million pounds/etc; **deux millions** two million. ● **millionième** a & nmf millionth. ● **millionnaire** nmf millionaire.

mime [mim] nmf (*acteur*) mime; **le m.** (*art*) mime. ● **mimer** vti to mime. ● **mimique** nf (*mine*) (funny) face.

mimétisme [mimetism] nm (de caméléon etc) & Fig mimicry; **agir par m.** to mimic ou copy s.o.'s attitudes etc.

mimosa [mimoza] nm (arbre, fleur) mimosa.

minable [minabl] a (lieu, personne) shabby; (*médiocre*) pathetic.

minaret [minarɛ] nm (de mosquée) minaret.

minauder [minode] vi to simper, make a show of affectation.

mince [mɛ̃s] **1** a thin; (*élancé, svelte*) slim; (*insignifiant*) slim, paltry. **2** int **m. (alors)!** Fam oh heck!, Br blast (it)! ● **minceur** nf thinness; (*sveltesse*) slimness. ● **mincir** vi to get slim(mer), grow slim.

mine [min] nf **1** appearance; (*physionomie*) look; (*santé*) **avoir bonne/mauvaise m.** (*santé*) to look well/ill; **faire m. de faire qch** to appear to do sth, make as if to do sth; **faire grise m.** to look anything but pleased; **m. de rien** (*discrètement*) Fam quite casually. **2** (*gisement*) & Fig mine; **m. de charbon** coalmine. **3** (de crayon) lead. **4** (engin explosif) mine.

miner [mine] vt **1** (saper) Fig to undermine; **m. qn** (chagrin, maladie etc) to wear s.o. down. **2** (terrain) to mine.

minerai [minrɛ] nm ore.

minéral, -e, -aux [mineral, -o] a & nm mineral.

minéralogique [mineralɔʒik] a **plaque m.** (de véhicule) Br number ou Am license plate.

minet, -ette [minɛ, -ɛt] nmf **1** (chat) Fam puss. **2** (personne) Fam fashion-conscious ou trendy young man ou woman.

mineur, -e [minœr] nm **1** (ouvrier) miner. **2** a (jeune, secondaire) & Mus minor ▌ nmf Jur minor. ● **minier, -ière** a industrie/etc **minière** mining industry/etc.

mini- [mini] préf mini-.

miniature [minjatyr] nf miniature ▌ a inv **train/etc m.** miniature train/etc.

minibus [minibys] nm minibus.

minichaîne [miniʃɛn] nf mini (hi-fi) system.

minijupe [miniʒyp] nf miniskirt.

minime [minim] a a trifling, minimal, minor. ● **minimiser** vt to minimize.

minimum [minimɔm] nm minimum; **le m. de** (force etc) the minimum (amount of); **au (grand) m.** at the very least ▌ a minimum; **la température/etc m.** the minimum temperature/etc; **bénéfices/etc minimums** minimum profits/etc. ● **minimal, -e, -aux** a minimum, minimal.

ministère [ministɛr] nm ministry; (*gouvernement*) government, cabinet; **m. de Intérieur** = Br Home Office, = Am Department of the Interior. ● **ministériel, -ielle** a ministerial; **remaniement/etc m.** cabinet ou government reshuffle/etc.

ministre [ministr] nm Pol Rel minister; **m. de l'Intérieur** = Br Home Secretary, = Am Secretary of the Interior; **m. de la Justice** Justice Minister, = Br Lord Chancellor, = Am Attorney General; **m. de l'Économie et des Finances** Finances Minister, = Br Chancellor of the Exchequer, = Am Secretary of the Treasury; **m. de la Culture** Arts Minister; **m. d'État** minister without portfolio.

Minitel® [minitɛl] nm telephone-connected terminal for data bank consultation (run by French phone company).

minois [minwa] nm joli/petit/etc **m.** pretty/little/etc face.

minorer [minɔre] vt to reduce.

minorité [minɔrite] nf minority; **en m.** in the ou a minority. ● **minoritaire** a parti/etc **m.** minority party/etc; **être m.** to be in the ou a minority.

Minorque [minɔrk] nf Minorca.

minou [minu] nm (chat) Fam puss.

minuit [minɥi] nm midnight, twelve o'clock.

minus [minys] nm (individu) Péj Fam moron.

minuscule [minyskyl] **1** a (petit) tiny, minute. **2** a & nf (lettre) **m.** small letter.

minute [minyt] nf minute; **à la m.** (tout de suite) this (very) minute; **d'une m. à l'autre** any minute (now) ▌ a inv aliments ou plats **m.** convenience food(s). ● **minuter** vt to time. ● **minuterie** nf time switch (for lighting in a stairway etc). ● **minuteur** nm timer.

minutie [minysi] nf meticulousness. ● **minutieux, -euse** a meticulous.

mioche [mjɔʃ] nmf (enfant) Fam kid, youngster.

mirabelle [mirabɛl] nf mirabelle plum.

miracle [mirakl] nm miracle; **par m.** miraculously. ● **miraculeux, -euse** a miraculous.

mirador [miradɔr] nm Mil watchtower.

mirage [miraʒ] nm mirage.

mire [mir] *nf* **point de m.** (*cible*) & *Fig* target.

mirifique [mirifik] *a Hum* fabulous.

mirobolant, -ante [mirɔbɔlɑ̃, -ɑ̃t] *a Fam* fantastic.

miroir [mirwar] *nm* mirror. ●**miroiter** *vi* to gleam, shimmer.

mis, mise¹ [mi, miz] *pp de* **mettre ‖** *a* **bien m.** (*vêtu*) well dressed.

misanthrope [mizɑ̃trɔp] *nmf* misanthropist ‖ *a* misanthropic.

mise² [miz] *nf* **1** (*action de mettre*) putting; **m. en marche** starting up; **m. en service** putting into service; **m. en scène** *Théâtre* production; *Cinéma* direction; **m. à feu** (*de fusée*) blast-off; **m. à la retraite** pensioning off; **m. au point** *voir* **point¹**. **2** (*argent*) stake. **3** (*tenue*) attire.

miser [mize] *vt* (*argent*) to stake (**sur** on) ‖ *vi* **m. sur** (*cheval*) to back; (*compter sur*) *Fam* to bank on.

misère [mizɛr] *nf* (*grinding*) poverty; (*malheur*) misery; (*bagatelle*) trifle. ●**misérable** *a* miserable, wretched; (*très pauvre*) destitute, poor; (*logement, quartier*) seedy, slummy ‖ *nmf* (*malheureux*) (poor) wretch; (*indigent*) pauper; (*scélérat*) scoundrel, miserable wretch. ●**miséreux, -euse** *a* destitute ‖ *nmf* pauper.

miséricorde [mizerikɔrd] *nf* mercy. ●**miséricordieux, -euse** *a* merciful.

misogyne [mizɔʒin] *nmf* misogynist.

missile [misil] *nm* (*fusée*) missile.

mission [misjɔ̃] *nf* mission; (*tâche*) task; **m. accomplie** mission accomplished. ●**missionnaire** *nm* & *a* missionary.

missive [misiv] *nf* (*lettre*) *Litt* missive.

mistral [mistral] *nm* **le m.** (*vent*) the mistral.

mite [mit] *nf* (*clothes*) moth; (*du fromage etc*) mite. ●**mité, -ée** *a* moth-eaten.

mi-temps [mitɑ̃] *nf* (*pause*) *Sport* half-time; (*période*) *Sport* half; **travailler/etc à mi-t.** to work/*etc* part-time ‖ *nm* part-time job *ou* work; **prendre un mi-t.** to take on a part-time job *ou* part-time work.

miteux, -euse [mitø, -øz] *a* shabby.

mitigé, -ée [mitiʒe] *a* (*zèle etc*) moderate, lukewarm; (*mêlé*) *Fam* mixed.

mitonner [mitɔne] *vt* (*cuire à petit feu*) to simmer gently.

mitoyen, -enne [mitwajɛ̃, -ɛn] *a* **mur m.** common wall (*shared by two properties*).

mitraille [mitraj] *nf* gunfire. ●**mitrailler** *vt* to machinegun; (*photographier*) *Fam* to click *ou* snap away at. ●**mitraillette** *nf* machinegun (*portable*). ●**mitrailleur** *a* **fusil m.** machinegun (*portable*). ●**mitrailleuse** *nf* machinegun (*heavy*).

mi-voix (à) [amivwa] *adv* in an undertone.

mixe(u)r [miksœr] *nm* (*pour mélanger*) (food) mixer; (*pour rendre liquide*) liquidizer.

mixte [mikst] *a* mixed; (*école*) coeducational, *Br* mixed; (*commission, tribunal*) joint.

mixture [mikstyr] *nf Péj* mixture.

MLF [ɛmɛlɛf] *nm abrév* (*Mouvement de libération de la femme*) Women's Liberation Movement.

Mlle [madmwazɛl] *abrév* = **Mademoiselle.**

MM [mesjø] *abrév* = **Messieurs.**

mm *abrév* (*millimètre*) mm.

Mme [madam] *abrév* = **Madame.**

mobile [mɔbil] **1** *a* (*pièce*) moving; (*panneau*) mov(e)able; (*personne*) mobile; (*feuillets*) detachable, loose; (*reflets*) changing; **échelle m.** sliding scale; **fête m.** mov(e)able feast ‖ *nm* (*décoration*) mobile. **2** *nm* (*motif*) motive (**de** for). ●**mobilité** *nf* mobility.

mobilier [mɔbilje] *nm* furniture.

mobiliser [mɔbilize] *vti* to mobilize. ●**mobilisation** *nf* mobilization.

mobylette® [mɔbilɛt] *nf* moped.

mocassin [mɔkasɛ̃] *nm* (*chaussure*) moccasin.

moche [mɔʃ] *a Fam* (*laid*) ugly; **c'est m.** (*mal*) it's lousy *ou* rotten.

modalités [mɔdalite] *nfpl* methods (**de** of).

mode [mɔd] **1** *nf* fashion; (*industrie*) fashion trade; **à la m.** fashionable, in fashion; **à la m. de** in the manner of; **passé de m.** out of fashion. **2** *nm* mode, method; **m. d'emploi** directions (for use); **m. de vie** way of life. **3** *nm Grammaire* mood.

modèle [mɔdɛl] *nm* (*schéma, exemple, personne*) model; **m.** (**réduit**) (scale) model; **grand/petit m.** large/small size *ou* version ‖ *a* **élève/petite fille/etc m.** model pupil/girl/*etc*. ●**modeler** *vt* to model (**sur** on); **se m. sur** to model oneself on. ●**modelage** *nm* (*de statue etc*) *Br* modelling, *Am* modeling.

modéliste [mɔdelist] *nmf Tex* stylist, designer.

modem [mɔdɛm] *nm Ordinat* modem.

modéré, -ée [mɔdere] *a* moderate. ●**modérément** *adv* moderately.

modérer [mɔdere] *vt* to moderate, restrain; (*vitesse, température etc*) to reduce ‖ **se modérer** *vpr* to restrain oneself. ●**modérateur, -trice** *a* moderating ‖ *nmf* moderator. ●**modération** *nf* moderation, restraint; (*de vitesse etc*) reduction; **avec m.** in moderation.

moderne [mɔdɛrn] *a* modern ‖ *nm* **le m.** (*mobilier*) modern furniture. ●**modernisation** *nf* modernization. ●**moderniser** *vt, se* **moderniser** *vpr* to modernize. ●**modernisme** *nm* modernism.

modeste [mɔdɛst] *a* modest. ●**modestement** [-əmɑ̃] *adv* modestly. ●**modestie** *nf* modesty.

modifier [mɔdifje] *vt* to alter, modify ‖ **se modifier** *vpr* to alter. ●**modification** *nf* alteration, modification.

modique [mɔdik] *a* (*prix, somme etc*) modest. ●**modicité** *nf* modesty.

module [mɔdyl] *nm* module.

moduler [mɔdyle] *vt* to modulate. ●**modulation** *nf* modulation; **m. de fréquence** *Radio* FM (*frequency modulation*).

moelle [mwal] *nf* (*d'os*) marrow; **m. épinière**

spinal cord.

moelleux, -euse [mwalø, -øz] *a* (*lit, tissu*) soft; (*voix, vin*) mellow.

mœurs [mœr(s)] *nfpl* (*morale*) morals; (*habitudes*) habits, customs.

mohair [mɔɛr] *nm* mohair.

moi [mwa] *pron* **1** (*après une préposition*) me; **pour/avec/etc moi** for/with/*etc* me.
2 (*complément direct*) me; **laissez-moi** leave me.
3 (*complément indirect*) (to) me; **montrez-le-moi** show it to me, show it me.
4 (*sujet*) I; **c'est moi qui vous le dis!** I'm telling you!; **il est plus grand que moi** he's taller than I am *ou* than me; **moi, je veux bien** (*emphatique*) that's OK by me.
5 *nm inv Psy* self, ego. ●**moi-même** *pron* myself.

moignon [mwaɲɔ̃] *nm* stump.

moindre [mwɛ̃dr] *a* **être m.** (*moins grand*) to be less; **la m. erreur/etc** the slightest mistake/*etc*; **le m. doute/etc** the slightest *ou* least doubt/*etc*; **le m.** (*de mes problèmes etc*) the least (de of); (*de deux problèmes etc*) the lesser (de of); **c'est un m. mal** it's a lesser evil, it's the lesser of two evils.

moine [mwan] *nm* monk, friar.

moineau, -x [mwano] *nm* sparrow.

moins [mwɛ̃] **1** *adv* ([mwɛz] before vowel) less (**que** than); **m. de** (*temps, travail etc*) less (**que** than), not so much (**que** as); (*gens, livres etc*) fewer (**que** than), not so many (**que** as); (*cent francs etc*) less than; **m. grand/froid/etc** not as big/cold/*etc* (**que** as); **le m., la m., les m.** (*travailler etc*) the least; **le m. grand, la m. grande, les m. grand(e)s** the smallest; **de m. en m.** [dəmɛ̃zɑ̃mwɛ̃] less and less; **au m., du m.** at least; **qch de m., qch en m.** (*qui manque*) sth missing; **dix ans/etc de m.** ten years/*etc* less; **en m.** (*personne, objet*) less; (*personnes, objets*) fewer; **les m. de vingt ans** those under twenty, the under-twenties; **à m. que** (+ *sub*) unless.
2 *prép Math* minus; **deux heures m. cinq** five to two; **il fait m. dix (degrés)** it's minus ten (degrees).

mois [mwa] *nm* month; **au m. de juin/etc** in (the month of) June/*etc*.

moisir [mwazir] *vi* to go *Br* mouldy *ou Am* moldy; (*attendre*) *Fam* to hang *ou* wait around *ou* about. ●**moisi, -ie** *a Br* mouldy, *Am* moldy **‖** *nm Br* mould, *Am* mold, mildew; **sentir le m.** to smell musty. ●**moisissure** *nf* mould, mildew.

moisson [mwasɔ̃] *nf* harvest. ●**moissonner** *vt* to harvest. ●**moissonneuse-batteuse** *nf* (*pl* **moissonneuses-batteuses**) combine-harvester.

moite [mwat] *a* sticky, moist. ●**moiteur** *nf* stickiness, moistness.

moitié [mwatje] *nf* half; **la m. de la pomme/etc** half (of) the apple/*etc*; **à m.** (*remplir etc*) halfway; **à m. fermé/cru/etc** half closed/raw/*etc*; **à m. prix** (at *ou* for) half-price; **réduire qch de m.** to reduce sth by half; **m.-moitié**

Fam so-so; **partager m.-moitié** *Fam* to split fifty-fifty.

moka [mɔka] *nm* (*café*) mocha; (*gâteau*) mocha *ou* coffee cake.

mol [mɔl] *voir* **mou**.

molaire [mɔlɛr] *nf* (*dent*) back tooth, molar.

molécule [mɔlekyl] *nf* molecule.

moleskine [mɔlɛskin] *nf* imitation leather.

molester [mɔlɛste] *vt* to manhandle.

molette [mɔlɛt] *nf* **clé à m.** adjustable wrench *ou Br* spanner.

mollasse [mɔlas] *a* (*flasque*) *Péj* flabby. ●**mollasson, -onne** *Fam* a lazy **‖** *nmf* lazybones.

molle [mɔl] *voir* **mou**. ●**mollement** *adv* feebly; (*paresseusement*) lazily. ●**mollesse** *nf* softness; (*faiblesse*) feebleness. ●**mollir** *vi* to go soft; (*courage*) to flag.

mollet [mɔlɛ] **1** *nm* (*de jambe*) calf. **2** *a* **œuf m.** soft-boiled egg.

molleton [mɔltɔ̃] *nm* soft thick flannel. ●**molletonné, -ée** *a* (*survêtement etc*) fleece-lined, fleecy.

mollusque [mɔlysk] *nm* mollusc.

môme [mom] *nmf* (*enfant*) *Fam* kid.

moment [mɔmɑ̃] *nm* (*instant*) moment; (*période*) time; **en ce m.** at the moment; **par moments** at times; **au m. de partir** when just about to leave; **au m. où** just as, when; **du m. que** (*puisque*) seeing that; **à ce m.-là** (*à ce moment précis*) at that (very) moment, at that time; (*dans ce cas*) then. ●**momentané, -ée** *a* momentary. ●**momentanément** *adv* temporarily, for the moment.

momie [mɔmi] *nf* (*cadavre*) mummy.

mon, ma, *pl* **mes** [mɔ̃, ma, me] (**ma** *becomes* **mon** [mɔ̃n] *before a vowel or mute h*) *a poss* my; **mon père** my father; **ma mère** my mother; **mon ami(e)** my friend; **mes parents** my parents.

Monaco [mɔnako] *nf* Monaco.

monarque [mɔnark] *nm* monarch. ●**monarchie** *nf* monarchy. ●**monarchique** *a* monarchic.

monastère [mɔnastɛr] *nm* monastery.

monceau, -x [mɔ̃so] *nm* heap, pile.

mondain, -aine [mɔ̃dɛ̃, -ɛn] *a* **réunion/etc mondaine** society gathering/*etc*. ●**mondanités** *nfpl* (*événements*) social events.

monde [mɔ̃d] *nm* world; (*milieu social*) set; **du m.** (*gens*) people; (*beaucoup de gens*) a lot of people; **un m. fou** a tremendous crowd; **le m. entier** the whole world; **tout le m.** everybody; **le (grand) m.** (high) society; **mettre qn au m.** to give birth to s.o.; **venir au m.** to come into the world; **tu te moques du m.!** you can't be serious!, you're crazy!; **pas le moins du m.!** not in the least *ou* slightest!; **c'est le m. à l'envers** it's a mad world! ●**mondial, -e, -aux** *a* (*crise, renommée etc*) worldwide; **guerre mondiale** world war. ●**mondialement** *adv* the (whole) world over. **monégasque** [mɔnegask] *a* Monegasque **‖** *nmf* M. Monegasque.

monétaire [mɔnetɛr] *a* monetary.

mongolien, -ienne [mɔ̃gɔljɛ̃, -jɛn] *Méd a* mongol ▮ *nmf* mongol, person with Down's syndrome. ●**mongolisme** *nm* Down's syndrome.

moniteur, -trice [mɔnitœr, -tris] **1** *nmf* instructor; (*de colonie de vacances*) assistant, *Am* camp counselor. **2** *nm* (*écran*) Ordinat *etc* monitor.

monnaie [mɔnɛ] *nf* (*devise*) currency, money; (*pièces*) change; **pièce de m.** coin; (**petite**) **m.** (small) change; **faire de la m.** to get change; **faire de la m. à qn** to give s.o. change (**sur un billet** for a *Br* note *ou Am* bill); **c'est m. courante** *Fig* it's very frequent; **Hôtel de la M.** mint. ●**monnayer** *vt* (*talent etc*) to cash in on; (*bien, titre*) to convert into cash.

mono [mɔnɔ] *a inv* (*disque etc*) mono.

mono- [mɔnɔ] *préf* mono-.

monocle [mɔnɔkl] *nm* monocle.

monocorde [mɔnɔkɔrd] *a* (*voix etc*) monotonous.

monologue [mɔnɔlɔg] *nm Br* monologue, *Am* monolog.

monoparentale [mɔnɔparɑ̃tal] *af* **famille m.** one-parent family.

monophonie [mɔnɔfɔni] *nf* **en m.** in mono.

monoplace [mɔnɔplas] *a & nmf* (*avion, voiture*) single-seater.

monopole [mɔnɔpɔl] *nm* monopoly. ●**monopoliser** *vt* to monopolize.

monoski [mɔnɔski] *nm* monoski; **faire du m.** to monoski.

monosyllabe [mɔnɔsilab] *nm* monosyllable. ●**monosyllabique** *a* monosyllabic.

monotone [mɔnɔtɔn] *a* monotonous. ●**monotonie** *nf* monotony.

monseigneur [mɔ̃sɛɲœr] *nm* (*évêque*) His *ou* Your Grace; (*prince*) His *ou* Your Highness.

monsieur, *pl* **messieurs** [məsjø, mesjø] *nm* man, gentleman; **oui m.** yes; (*avec déférence*) yes sir; **oui messieurs** yes (gentlemen); **M. Legras** Mr Legras; **Messieurs** *ou* **MM Legras** Messrs Legras; **tu vois ce m.?** do you see that man *ou* gentleman?; **Monsieur** (*dans une lettre*) Dear Sir.

monstre [mɔ̃str] *nm* monster ▮ *a* (*énorme*) *Fam* colossal. ●**monstrueux, -euse** *a* (*abominable, énorme*) monstrous. ●**monstruosité** *nf* (*horreur*) monstrosity.

mont [mɔ̃] *nm* (*montagne*) mount; **être toujours par monts et par vaux** to be forever on the move.

montage [mɔ̃taʒ] *nm Tech* assembling, assembly; *Cinéma* editing.

montagne [mɔ̃taɲ] *nf* mountain; **la m.** (*zone*) the mountains; **montagnes russes** (*attraction foraine*) roller coaster. ●**montagnard, -arde** *nmf* mountain dweller ▮ *a* **peuple/etc m.** mountain people/*etc.* ●**montagneux, -euse** *a* mountainous.

montant, -ante 1 *nm* (*somme*) amount. **2** *nm* (*de barrière*) post; (*d'échelle*) upright. **3** *a* (*marée*) rising; (*col*) stand-up; (*robe*) high-necked; (*chemin*) uphill; (*mouvement*) upward; **chaussure montante** boot.

mont-de-piété [mɔ̃dpjete] *nm* (*pl* **monts-de-piété**) pawnshop.

monte-charge [mɔ̃tʃarʒ] *nm inv* service *Br* lift *ou Am* elevator.

montée [mɔ̃te] *nf* (*ascension*) climb, ascent; (*chemin*) slope; (*des prix, des eaux*) rise.

monter [mɔ̃te] *vi* (*aux être*) (*personne*) to go *ou* come up; (*s'élever*) (*ballon etc*) to go up; (*grimper*) to climb (up) (**sur** onto); (*prix*) to go up, rise; (*marée*) to come in; (*avion*) to climb; **m. dans un véhicule** to get in(to) a vehicle; **m. dans un train** to get on(to) a train; **m. sur** *ou* **à une échelle**/*etc* to climb up a ladder/*etc*; **m. sur le trône** to become king *ou* queen; **m. en courant**/*etc* to run/*etc* up; **m. (à cheval)** *Sport* to ride (a horse); **le vin me monte à la tête** wine goes to my head.

▮ *vt* (*aux avoir*) (*côte etc*) to climb (up); (*objet*) to bring *ou* take up; (*cheval*) to ride; (*tente, affaire*) to set up; (*machine*) to assemble; (*bijou*) to set, mount; (*complot*) to mount; (*pièce de théâtre*) to stage, mount; **m. l'escalier** to go *ou* come upstairs *ou* up the stairs; **faire m. qn** to show s.o. up; **m. qn contre qn** to set s.o. against s.o.; **coup monté** frame-up.

▮ **se monter** *vpr* (*s'irriter*) *Fam* to get angry (**contre** with); **se m. à** (*frais*) to amount to. ●**monté, -ée** *a* (*police*) mounted.

monteur, -euse [mɔ̃tœr, -øz] *nmf Tech* fitter; *Cinéma* editor.

montre [mɔ̃tr] *nf* **1** (wrist)watch; **course contre la m.** *Sport & Fig* race against time, race against the clock. **2 faire m. de qch** to show sth. ●**montre-bracelet** *nf* (*pl* **montres-bracelets**) wristwatch.

Montréal [mɔ̃real] *nm ou f* Montreal.

montrer [mɔ̃tre] *vt* to show (**à** to); **m. qn/qch du doigt** to point at s.o./sth; **m. à qn à faire qch** to show s.o. how to do sth ▮ **se montrer** *vpr* to show oneself, appear; **se m. courageux/etc** (*être*) to be courageous/*etc*.

monture [mɔ̃tyr] *nf* **1** (*de lunettes*) frame; (*de bijou*) setting. **2** (*cheval*) mount.

monument [mɔnymɑ̃] *nm* monument; **m. historique** ancient monument; **m. aux morts** war memorial. ●**monumental, -e, -aux** *a* (*imposant, énorme etc*) monumental.

moquer (se) [səmɔke] *vpr* **se m. de** to make fun of; (*personne*) to make fun of, make a fool of; **je m'en moque!** *Fam* I couldn't care less! ●**moquerie** *nf* mockery. ●**moqueur, -euse** *a* mocking.

moquette [mɔkɛt] *nf Br* fitted carpet(s), *Am* wall-to-wall carpeting.

moral, -e, -aux [mɔral, -o] *a* moral ▮ *nm* **le m.** spirits, morale. ●**morale** *nf* (*d'histoire etc*) moral; (*principes*) morals; (*code*) moral code; **faire la m. à qn** to lecture s.o. ●**moralement** *adv* morally. ●**moraliser** *vi* to moralize. ●**moraliste** *nmf* moralist. ●**moralité** *nf* (*mœurs*) morality; (*de fable, récit etc*) moral.

moratoire [mɔratwar] *nm* moratorium.

morbide [mɔrbid] *a* morbid.

morceau, -x [mɔrso] *nm* piece, bit; (*de sucre*) lump; (*de viande*) cut; (*d'une œuvre littéraire*) extract. ● **morceler** *vt* (*terrain*) to divide up.

mordicus [mɔrdikys] *adv* **soutenir**/*etc* m. **Fam** to maintain/*etc* stubbornly.

mordiller [mɔrdije] *vt* to nibble.

mordre [mɔrdr] *vti* to bite; **ça mord Pêche** I have a bite. ● **mordant, -ante** 1 *a* (*voix, manière*) scathing; (*froid*) biting; (*personne, ironie*) caustic. 2 *nm* (*énergie*) punch.

mordu, -ue [mɔrdy] *pp de* **mordre** ▌ *nmf* **un m. du** *ou* **de jazz**/*etc* **Fam** a jazz/*etc* fan.

morfondre (se) [səmɔrfɔ̃dr] *vpr* to get bored (waiting), mope (about).

morgue [mɔrg] *nf* (*lieu*) mortuary, morgue.

moribond, -onde [mɔribɔ̃, -ɔ̃d] *a & nmf* dying *ou* moribund (person).

morne [mɔrn] *a* dismal, gloomy, dull.

morose [mɔroz] *a* morose, sullen.

morphine [mɔrfin] *nf* morphine.

mors [mɔr] *nm* (*de harnais*) bit; **prendre le m. aux dents** (*cheval*) to take the bit between its teeth.

morse [mɔrs] *nm* 1 Morse (code). 2 (*animal*) walrus.

morsure [mɔrsyr] *nf* bite.

mort¹ [mɔr] *nf* death; **mettre à m.** to put to death; **se donner la m.** to kill oneself, take one's own life; **en vouloir à m. à qn** to bear s.o. an almighty grudge, be dead set against s.o.; **un silence de m.** a deathly silence; **la m. dans l'âme** (*accepter qch etc*) with a heavy heart. ● **mortalité** *nf* death rate, mortality. ● **mortel, -elle** *a* (*hommes, ennemi, danger etc*) mortal; (*accident*) fatal; (*ennuyeux*) **Fam** deadly (dull); (*pâleur*) deathly ▌ *nmf* mortal. ● **mortellement** *adv* (*blessé*) fatally.

mort², morte [mɔr, mɔrt] *a* (*personne, plante, ville etc*) dead; **m. de fatigue** dead tired; **m. de froid** numb with cold; **m. de peur** frightened to death; **m. ou vif** dead or alive; **être ivre m.** to be dead drunk.

▌ *nmf* dead man, dead woman; **les morts** the dead; **de nombreux morts** (*victimes*) many casualties *ou* deaths; **le jour** *ou* **la fête des Morts** All Souls' Day. ● **morte-saison** *nf* (*pl* **mortes-saisons**) off season (period). ● **mort-né, mort-née** *a* (*enfant*) & Fig stillborn.

mortier [mɔrtje] *nm* mortar.

mortifier [mɔrtifje] *vt* to mortify.

mortuaire [mɔrtɥɛr] *a* **couronne**/*etc* m. funeral wreath/*etc*.

morue [mɔry] *nf* cod.

morve [mɔrv] *nf* (*nasal*) mucus. ● **morveux, -euse** *a* (*enfant*) **Fam** Péj snotty(-nosed).

mosaïque [mɔzaik] *nf* mosaic.

Moscou [mɔsku] *nm ou f* Moscow.

mosquée [mɔske] *nf* mosque.

mot [mo] *nm* word; **envoyer un m. à qn** to drop a line to s.o.; **m. à** *ou* **pour m.** word for word; **un bon m.** a witticism; **mots croisés** crossword (puzzle); **m. de passe** password; **m. d'ordre Pol** resolution, order; (*slo-*

gan) watchword; **avoir le dernier m.** to have the last word; **avoir son m. à dire** to have something to say, have one's say.

motard [mɔtar] *nm* **Fam** motorcyclist.

motel [mɔtɛl] *nm* motel.

moteur¹ [mɔtœr] *nm* (*de véhicule etc*) engine, motor; (*électrique*) motor.

moteur², -trice [mɔtœr, -tris] *a* (*nerf, muscle*) motor; **force motrice** driving force; **voiture à quatre roues motrices** four-wheel drive (car).

motif [mɔtif] *nm* 1 (*raison*) reason, motive (de for). 2 (*dessin*) pattern.

motion [mosjɔ̃] *nf* Pol motion; **on a voté une m. de censure** a vote of no confidence was given.

motiver [mɔtive] *vt* (*inciter, causer*) to motivate; (*justifier*) to justify. ● **motivé, -ée** *a* motivated. ● **motivation** *nf* motivation.

moto [mɔto] *nf* motorcycle, motorbike. ● **motocycliste** *nmf* motorcyclist.

motorisé, -ée [mɔtorize] *a* motorized.

motrice [mɔtris] *nf* (*train*) Br motor coach, Am motor car.

motte [mɔt] *nf* (*de terre*) lump, clod; (*de beurre*) block.

mou (*or* **mol** *before vowel or mute h*), **molle** [mu, mɔl] *a* soft; (*sans énergie*) feeble ▌ *nm* **avoir du m.** (*cordage*) to be slack.

mouchard, -arde [muʃar, -ard] *nmf* Péj informer. ● **moucharder** *vt* **m. qn Fam** to inform on s.o.

mouche [muʃ] *nf* (*insecte*) fly; **prendre la m.** (*se fâcher*) to fly off the handle, fly into a temper; **quelle m. l'a piqué?** Fam what has Br got *ou* Am gotten into him?, what's eating him?; **faire m.** to hit the bull's-eye. ● **moucheron** *nm* (*insecte*) gnat, midge.

moucher [muʃe] *vt* **m. qn** to wipe s.o.'s nose ▌ **se moucher** *vpr* to blow one's nose.

moucheté, -ée [muʃte] *a* speckled, spotted.

mouchoir [muʃwar] *nm* handkerchief; (*en papier*) tissue.

moudre* [mudr] *vt* (*café, blé*) to grind.

moue [mu] *nf* long face, pout; **faire la m.** to pull a (long) face, pout.

mouette [mwɛt] *nf* (sea)gull.

moufle [mufl] *nf* (*gant*) mitten, mitt.

mouiller [muje] 1 *vt* to wet, make wet; **se faire m. par la pluie** to get wet ▌ **se mouiller** *vpr* to get (oneself) wet; (*se compromettre*) Fam to get involved (*by taking risks*). 2 **m. l'ancre Nau** to (drop) anchor ▌ *vi* Nau to anchor. ● **mouillé, -ée** *a* wet (**de** with). ● **mouillage** *nm* Nau (*action*) anchoring; (*lieu*) anchorage.

moule¹ [mul] *nm* Br mould, Am mold; **m. à gâteaux** cake tin. ● **mouler** *vt* Br to mould, Am mold; (*statue*) to cast; **m. qn** (*vêtement*) to fit s.o. tightly. ● **moulant, -ante** *a* (*vêtement*) tight-fitting. ● **moulage** *nm* moulding; (*de statue*) casting; (*objet*) cast. ● **moulure** *nf* Archit moulding.

moule² [mul] *nf* (*mollusque*) mussel.

moulin [mulɛ̃] *nm* mill; (*moteur*) Fam

moulinet 200

engine; **m. à vent** windmill; **m. à café** coffee grinder; **m. à paroles** *Fam* chatterbox, windbag.

moulinet [mulinɛ] *nm* **1** (*de canne à pêche*) reel. **2 faire des moulinets** (*avec un bâton*) to twirl one's stick.

moulu, -ue [muly] *pp de* **moudre ‖** *a* (*café*) ground; (*éreinté*) dead tired.

mourir* [murir] *vi* (*aux* **être**) to die (de of, from); **m. de froid** to die of exposure; **m. de fatigue/d'ennui** *Fig* to be dead tired/bored; **m. de peur** *Fig* to be frightened to death; **m. de rire** *Fig* to laugh oneself silly; **s'ennuyer à m.** to be bored to death; **je meurs de faim!** *Fig* I'm starving! **‖ se mourir** *vpr Litt* to be dying. ●**mourant, -ante** *a* dying; (*voix*) faint **‖** *nmf* dying person.

mousquetaire [muskətɛr] *nm Mil Hist* musketeer.

mousse [mus] **1** *nf* (*plante*) moss. **2** *nf* (*écume*) foam, froth; (*de bière*) froth; (*de savon*) lather; **m. à raser** shaving foam. **3** *nf* **m. au chocolat/etc** *Culin* chocolate/etc mousse. **4** *nm* (*marin*) ship's boy. ●**mousser** *vi* (*bière etc*) to froth; (*savon*) to lather; (*eau savonneuse*) to foam. ●**mousseux, -euse** *a* frothy; (*vin*) sparkling **‖** *nm* sparkling wine. ●**moussu, -ue** *a* mossy.

mousseline [muslin] *nf* (*coton*) muslin.

mousson [musɔ̃] *nf* (*vent*) monsoon.

moustache [mustaʃ] *nf* **moustache(s)** (*d'homme*) *Br* moustache, *Am* mustache; **moustaches** (*de chat etc*) whiskers. ●**moustachu, -ue** *a* wearing a moustache.

moustique [mustik] *nm* mosquito. ●**moustiquaire** *nf* mosquito net; (*en métal*) screen.

moutard [mutar] *nm* (*enfant*) *Fam* kid.

moutarde [mutard] *nf* mustard.

mouton [mutɔ̃] *nm* sheep *inv*; (*viande*) mutton; **moutons** (*sur la mer*) *Br* white horses, *Am* whitecaps; (*poussière*) bits of dust; **peau de m.** sheepskin.

mouvement [muvmɑ̃] *nm* (*geste, groupe, déplacement etc*) & *Mus* movement; (*de colère*) outburst; (*impulsion*) impulse; **en m.** in motion. ●**mouvementé, -ée** *a* (*vie, voyage etc*) eventful.

mouvoir* [muvwar] *vi, se mouvoir* *vpr* to move; **mû par** (*mécanisme*) driven by. ●**mouvant, -ante** *a* (*changeant*) changing; **sables mouvants** quicksands.

moyen¹, -enne [mwajɛ̃, -ɛn] *a* average; (*format, entreprise etc*) medium(-sized); **classe moyenne** middle class **‖** *nf* average; **en moyenne** on average; **la moyenne d'âge** the average age; **avoir la moyenne** (*à un examen*) *Br* to get a pass mark, *Am* get a pass; (*à un devoir*) to get fifty per cent, *Br* get half marks. ●**moyennement** *adv* averagely, moderately.

moyen² [mwajɛ̃] *nm* (*procédé, façon*) means, way (**de faire** of doing, to do); **moyens** (*capacités*) ability, powers; (*argent, ressources*) means; **au m. de** by means of; **il n'y a pas m. de faire** it's not possible to do; **je n'ai pas**

les moyens (*argent*) I can't afford it; **par mes propres moyens** under my own steam; **utiliser les grands moyens** to take extreme measures; (**avec**) **les moyens du bord** (with) the means at one's disposal, (with) the available means.

moyennant [mwajɛnɑ̃] *prép* (*pour*) (in return) for; (*avec*) with; **m. finance** for money, for a fee.

moyeu, -x [mwajø] *nm* (*de roue*) hub.

Mozambique [mɔzɑ̃bik] *nm* Mozambique.

MST [ɛmɛste] *nf abrév* (*maladie sexuellement transmissible*) sexually transmitted disease.

mucosités [mykozite] *nfpl* mucus.

mue [my] *nf* (*d'animal*) *Br* moulting, *Am* molting; (*de voix*) breaking of the voice. ●**muer** [mɥe] *vi* (*animal*) *Br* to moult, *Am* molt; (*voix*) to break; **se m. en** *Litt* to become transformed into.

muet, -ette [mɥɛ, -ɛt] *a* (*infirme*) dumb; (*de surprise etc*) speechless; (*film, reproche etc*) silent; (*voyelle etc*) *Grammaire* silent, mute **‖** *nmf* dumb person.

mufle [myfl] *nm* **1** (*d'animal*) muzzle, nose. **2** (*individu*) *Péj* lout.

mugir [myʒir] *vi* (*bœuf*) to bellow; (*vache*) to moo; (*vent*) *Fig* to roar. ●**mugissement(s)** *nm(pl)* bellow(ing); (*de vache*) moo(ing); (*de vent*) roar(ing).

muguet [mygɛ] *nm* lily of the valley.

mule [myl] *nf* **1** (*pantoufle*) mule. **2** (*animal*) (she-)mule. ●**mulet¹** *nm* (he-)mule.

mulet² [mylɛ] *nm* (*poisson*) mullet.

multi- [mylti] *préf* multi-.

multicolore [myltikɔlɔr] *a* multicoloured.

multinationale [myltinasjɔnal] *nf* multinational.

multiple [myltipl] *a* (*nombreux*) numerous; (*varié*) multiple **‖** *nm Math* multiple. ●**multiplication** *nf* multiplication; (*augmentation*) increase. ●**multiplicité** *nf* multiplicity. ●**multiplier** *vt* to multiply **‖** *se multiplier* *vpr* to increase; (*se reproduire*) to multiply.

multitude [myltityd] *nf* multitude.

municipal, -e, -aux [mynisipal, -o] *a* municipal; **conseil m.** *Br* town *ou* *Am* city council. ●**municipalité** *nf* (*corps*) *Br* town *ou* *Am* city council; (*commune*) municipality.

munir [mynir] *vt* **m. de** to provide *ou* equip with; **se m. de** to provide oneself with; **muni de** (*papiers, arme etc*) in possession of.

munitions [mynisjɔ̃] *nfpl* ammunition.

muqueuse [mykøz] *nf* mucous membrane.

mur [myr] *nm* wall; **m. du son** sound barrier; **au pied du m.** *Fig* with one's back to the wall. ●**muraille** *nf* (high) wall. ●**mural, -e, -aux** *a* **carte/etc murale** wall map/etc; **peinture murale** mural (painting). ●**murer** *vt* (*porte*) to wall up; **m. qn** to wall s.o. in; **se m. dans le silence** *Fig* to retreat into silence.

mûr, mûre¹ [myr] *a* (*fruit etc*) ripe; (*personne*) mature; **d'âge m.** of mature years, middle-aged. ●**mûrement** *adv* (*réfléchir*) carefully; **m. réfléchi** (*décision etc*) carefully thought out. ●**mûrir** *vti* (*fruit*) to ripen; (*personne*) to mature.

mûre² [myr] *nf* (*baie*) blackberry.

muret [myrɛ] *nm* low wall.

murmure [myrmyr] *nm* murmur. ● **murmurer** *vti* to murmur.

musc [mysk] *nm* (*parfum*) musk.

muscade [myskad] *nf* nutmeg.

muscadet [myskadɛ] *nm* (*vin*) Muscadet.

muscat [myska] *nm* (**raisin**) **m.** muscat (grape); (**vin**) **m.** muscatel (wine).

muscle [myskl] *nm* muscle. ● **musclé, -ée** *a* (*bras etc*) muscular, brawny. ● **musculaire** *a* (*force, douleur etc*) muscular. ● **musculature** *nf* muscles.

museau, -x [myzo] *nm* (*de chien, chat etc*) nose, muzzle; (*de porc*) snout. ● **museler** *vt* (*animal, Fig presse etc*) to muzzle. ● **muselière** *nf* (*appareil*) muzzle.

musée [myze] *nm* museum; **m. de peinture** (*public*) art gallery. ● **muséum** *nm* (natural history) museum.

musette [myzɛt] *nf* 1 (*d'ouvrier*) duffel bag, kit bag. **2 bal m.** popular dance (*with accordion band*).

music-hall [myzikol] *nm* (*salle*) variety theatre, *Am* vaudeville theater; (*genre*) variety, *Am* vaudeville.

musique [myzik] *nf* music; (*fanfare militaire*) band. ● **musical, -e, -aux** *a* musical. ● **musicien, -ienne** *nmf* musician ▌ *a* être très/assez **m.** to be very/quite musical.

musulman, -ane [myzylmã, -an] *a & nmf* Muslim, Moslem.

muter [myte] *vt* (*employé*) to transfer. ● **mutant, -ante** *a & nm* mutant. ● **mutation** *nf* 1 (*d'employé*) transfer; **en pleine m.** *Fig* undergoing profound change. **2** *Biol* mutation.

mutiler [mytile] *vt* to mutilate, maim; **être mutilé** to be disabled. ● **mutilé, -ée** *nmf* **m. de guerre** disabled *Br* ex-serviceman *ou Am*

veteran; **m. du travail** disabled worker. ● **mutilation** *nf* mutilation.

mutin¹, -ine [mytẽ, -in] *a* (*espiègle*) full of fun, saucy.

mutin² [mytẽ] *nm* (*rebelle*) mutineer. ● **se mutiner** *vpr* to mutiny. ● **mutiné, -ée** *a* mutinous. ● **mutinerie** *nf* mutiny.

mutisme [mytism] *nm* (stubborn) silence.

mutualité [mytɥalite] *nf* mutual insurance. ● **mutualiste** *nmf* member of a *Br* friendly *ou Am* benefit society.

mutuel, -elle¹ [mytɥɛl] *a* (*réciproque*) mutual. ● **mutuellement** *adv* (*l'un l'autre*) each other (mutually); **s'aider m.** to help each other (mutually), give mutual help to each other.

mutuelle² [mytɥɛl] *nf Br* friendly society, *Am* benefit society.

myope [mjɔp] *a & nmf Méd & Fig* shortsighted (person). ● **myopie** *nf Méd & Fig* shortsightedness.

myosotis [mjozɔtis] *nm* (*plante*) forget-me-not.

myrtille [mirtij] *nf* (*baie*) bilberry, whortleberry.

mystère [mistɛr] *nm* mystery; **faire des mystères** to be secretive, make a mystery of things; **faire qch en grand m.** to do sth in greaty secrecy, make a great mystery of doing sth. ● **mystérieux, -euse** *a* mysterious.

mystifier [mistifje] *vt* to fool, deceive, hoax. ● **mystification** *nf* hoax.

mystique [mistik] *a* mystical ▌ *nmf* (*personne*) mystic ▌ *nf* mystique (**de** of). ● **mysticisme** *nm* mysticism.

mythe [mit] *nm* myth. ● **mythique** *a* mythical. ● **mythologie** *nf* mythology. ● **mythologique** *a* mythological.

mythomane [mitɔman] *nmf* compulsive liar.

myxomatose [miksɔmatoz] *nf* myxomatosis.

N

N, n [ɛn] *nm* N, n.

n' [n] *voir* ne.

nabot [nabo] *nm Péj* midget.

nacelle [nasɛl] *nf* (*de ballon*) basket, car, gondola; (*de landau*) carriage, *Br* carrycot.

nacre [nakr] *nf* mother-of-pearl. ● **nacré, -ée** *a* pearly.

nage [naʒ] *nf* (*swimming*) stroke; **n. libre** freestyle; **traverser une rivière/etc à la n.** to swim across a river/etc; **en n.** *Fig* sweating.

nageoire [naʒwar] *nf* (*de poisson*) fin; (*de phoque*) flipper.

nager [naʒe] *vi* to swim; (*flotter*) to float; **je nage dans le bonheur** I'm blissfully happy, my happiness knows no bounds; **je nage complètement** (*je suis perdu*) *Fam* I'm all at sea ‖ *vt* (*crawl etc*) to swim. ● **nageur, -euse** *nmf* swimmer.

naguère [nagɛr] *adv Litt* not long ago.

naïf, -ïve [naif, -iv] *a* naïve, simple ‖ *nmf* simpleton.

nain, naine [nɛ̃, nɛn] *nmf* dwarf ‖ *a* arbre/haricot/etc **n.** dwarf tree/bean/etc.

naissance [nɛsɑ̃s] *nf* (*de personne, d'animal*) birth; (*de cou*) base; **donner n. à** (*enfant*) to give birth to; (*rumeur etc*) *Fig* to give rise to; **de n.** from birth.

naître* [nɛtr] *vi* to be born; (*sentiment, difficulté*) to arise (*de* from); (*jour*) to dawn; **faire n.** (*soupçon, industrie etc*) to give rise to, create; **à** (*l'amour etc*) *Litt* to awaken to; **il n'est pas né de la dernière pluie** *Fam* he wasn't born yesterday. ● **naissant, -ante** *a* (*amitié etc*) incipient, just beginning to develop.

naïveté [naivte] *nf* naïveté, naïvety.

nana [nana] *nf Fam* girl, broad.

nantir [nɑ̃tir] *vt* **n. de** to provide with. ● **nanti, -ie** *a* (*riche*) well-off, affluent ‖ *nmpl* **les nantis** *Péj* the well-off, the affluent.

NAP [nap] *a inv abrév* (*Neuilly, Auteuil, Passy*) (*élégant*) trendy, smart.

naphtaline [naftalin] *nf* mothballs.

nappe [nap] *nf* **1** table cloth. **2** (*d'eau*) sheet; (*de gaz, pétrole*) layer; (*de brouillard*) blanket. ● **napperon** *nm* (*soft*) table mat; (*pour vase etc*) (*cloth ou* soft) mat.

napper [nape] *vt* (*gâteau etc*) to top, coat (**de chocolat**/etc with chocolate/etc).

narcotique [narkɔtik] *a & nm* narcotic.

narguer [narge] *vt* to flout, mock.

narine [narin] *nf* nostril.

narquois, -oise [narkwa] *a* sneering.

narration [narasjɔ̃] *nf* (*récit, acte, art*) narration. ● **narrateur, -trice** *nmf* narrator.

nasal, -e, -aux [nazal, -o] *a* nasal.

nase [naz] *a Fam* (*personne*) exhausted, *Br* dead beat; (*objet*) kaput, *Br* done for.

naseau, -x [nazo] *nm* (*de cheval*) nostril.

nasiller [nazije] *vi* (*personne*) to speak with a twang; (*micro, radio*) to crackle. ● **nasillard, -arde** *a* (*voix*) nasal; (*micro etc*) crackling.

natal, -e, mpl -als [natal] *a* (*pays etc*) native; **sa maison natale** the house where he *ou* she was born. ● **natalité** *nf* birthrate.

natation [natasjɔ̃] *nf* swimming.

natif, -ive [natif, -iv] *a & nmf* native; **être n. de** to be a native of.

nation [nasjɔ̃] *nf* nation; **les Nations Unies** the United Nations. ● **national, -e, -aux** *a* national; **fête nationale** national holiday. ● **nationale** *nf* (*route*) *Br* main *ou* trunk *ou* A road, *Am* (*state*) highway. ● **nationaliser** *vt* to nationalize. ● **nationaliste** *a Péj* nationalistic ‖ *nmf* nationalist. ● **nationalité** *nf* nationality.

Nativité [nativite] *nf Rel* Nativity.

natte [nat] *nf* **1** (*de cheveux*) *Br* plait, *Am* braid. **2** (*tapis*) mat, (*piece of*) matting. ● **natter** *vt Br* to plait, *Am* braid. ● **nattage** *n* (*matière*) matting.

naturaliser [natyralize] *vt* (*personne*) *Pol* to naturalize. ● **naturalisation** *nf* naturalization.

nature [natyr] *nf* (*monde naturel, caractère*) nature; **de toute n.** of every kind; **être de n. à faire qch** to be likely to do sth; **payer en n.** to pay in kind; **n. morte** (*tableau*) still life; **plus grand que n.** larger than life; **seconde n.** second nature ‖ *a inv* (*omelette, yaourt etc*) plain; (*thé*) without milk. ● **naturaliste** *nmf* naturalist. ● **naturiste** *nmf* nudist, naturist.

naturel, -elle [natyrɛl] *a* natural; **mort naturelle** death from natural causes ‖ *nm* (*caractère*) nature; (*simplicité*) naturalness. ● **naturellement** *adv* naturally.

naufrage [nofraʒ] *nm* (ship)wreck; (*ruine*) *Litt Fig* ruin; **faire n.** to be (ship)wrecked. ● **naufragé, -ée** *a & nmf* shipwrecked (person).

nausée [noze] *nf* nausea, sickness. ● **nauséabond, -onde** *a* nauseating, sickening.

nautique [notik] *a* nautical; **ski n.** water skiing; **sports nautiques** water sports.

naval, -e, mpl -als [naval] *a* naval; **constructions navales** shipbuilding.

navet [navɛ] *nm* **1** (*légume*) turnip. **2** (*film etc*) *Fam* flop, dud.

navette [navɛt] *nf* (*transport*) shuttle (service); **faire la n.** (*véhicule, personne etc*) to shuttle back and forth (**entre** between); **n. spatiale** space shuttle.

navigable [navigabl] *a* (*fleuve*) navigable.

●**navigabilité** *nf* (*de bateau*) seaworthiness; (*d'avion*) airworthiness.

navigant, -ante [navigɑ̃, -ɑ̃t] *a* personnel n. *Av* flight crew; **hôtesse navigante** flight attendant.

navigateur [navigatœr] *nm* (*de navire, d'avion*) navigator; **n. solitaire** solo navigator, lone sailor. ●**navigation** *nf* (*pilotage*) navigation; (*trafic de bateaux*) shipping.

naviguer [navige] *vi* (*bateau*) to sail; (*piloter, voler*) to navigate.

navire [navir] *nm* ship.

navrer [navre] *vt* to upset (greatly), distress, grieve. ●**navrant, -ante** *a* upsetting. ●**navré, -ée** *a* (*air*) grieved; **je suis n.** I'm (terribly) sorry (**de faire** to do).

nazi, -ie [nazi] *a* & *nmf* *Pol Hist* Nazi.

ne [n(ə)] (**n'** before vowel or mute *h*; used to form negative verb with **pas, jamais, personne, rien** etc) *adv* 1 (+ *pas*) not; **il ne boit pas** he does not *ou* doesn't drink; **elle n'ose (pas)** she doesn't dare; **n'importe** it doesn't matter. 2 (+*que*) (*restriction*) only; **il n'a qu'une sœur** he only has one sister. 3 (*with* **craindre, avoir peur** *etc*) **je crains qu'il ne parte** I'm afraid he'll leave.

né, née [ne] *pp de* **naître** born; **il est né en 1945** he was born in 1945; **née Dupont** née Dupont ▌*a* born; **c'est un poète/etc-né** he's a born poet/etc.

néanmoins [neɑ̃mwɛ̃] *adv* nevertheless, nonetheless.

néant [neɑ̃] *nm* nothingness, void; (*sur un formulaire*) = none.

nébuleux, -euse [nebylø, -øz] *a* hazy, nebulous.

nécessaire [neseser] *a* necessary; (*inéluctable*) inevitable ▌*nm* **le n.** (*biens*) the necessities; **le strict n.** the bare necessities; **n. de couture** sewing *Br* box *ou* *Am* basket, *Br* workbox; **n. de toilette** *Br* sponge bag, dressing case; **faire le n.** to do what's necessary *ou* the necessary. ●**nécessairement** *adv* necessarily; (*échouer* etc) inevitably.

nécessité [nesesite] *nf* necessity. ●**nécessiter** *vt* to require, necessitate.

nécessiteux, -euse [nesesitø, -øz] *a* needy.

nécrologie [nekrɔlɔʒi] *nf* obituary.

nectarine [nɛktarin] *nf* (*fruit*) nectarine.

néerlandais, -aise [neerlɑ̃de, -ez] *a* Dutch ▌*nmf* N. Dutchman; **Néerlandaise** Dutchwoman ▌*nm* (*langue*) Dutch.

nef [nɛf] *nf* (*d'église*) nave.

néfaste [nefast] *a* (*influence* etc) harmful (à to).

négatif, -ive [negatif, -iv] *a* negative ▌*nm* (*de photo*) negative ▌*nf* **répondre par la négative** to answer in the negative. ●**négation** *nf* denial, negation (**de** of); *Grammaire* negation; (*mot*) negative.

négligeable [negliʒabl] *a* negligible.

négligent, -ente [negliʒɑ̃, -ɑ̃t] *a* careless, negligent. ●**négligemment** [-amɑ̃] *adv* negligently, carelessly. ●**négligence** *nf* (*dé-*

faut) carelessness, negligence; (*faute*) (careless) error.

négliger [negliʒe] *vt* (*personne, travail, conseil* etc) to neglect; **n. de faire qch** to neglect to do sth ▌**se négliger** *vpr* (*négliger sa tenue ou sa santé*) to neglect oneself. ●**négligé, -ée** *a* (*tenue*) untidy, neglected; (*travail*) careless ▌*nm* (*de tenue*) untidiness; (*vêtement*) negligee.

négocier [negɔsje] *vi* (*discuter, traiter*) to negotiate ▌*vt* (*régler*) & *Fin* to negotiate. ●**négociant, -ante** *nmf* merchant, trader. ●**négociable** *a* *Fin* negotiable. ●**négociateur, -trice** *nmf* negotiator. ●**négociation** *nf* negotiation.

nègre [nɛgr] 1 *a* (*art, sculpture* etc) Negro. 2 *nm* (*écrivain*) ghost writer.

neige [nɛʒ] *nf* snow; **n. fondue** sleet; **n. carbonique** dry ice; **aller à la n.** to go skiing; **classe de n.** *Scol* winter sports class. ●**neiger** *v imp* to snow; **il neige** it's snowing. ●**neigeux, -euse** *a* snowy.

nénuphar [nenyfar] *nm* water lily.

néo [neɔ] *préf* neo-.

néon [neɔ̃] *nm* (*gaz*) neon; **éclairage au n.** neon lighting.

néophyte [neɔfit] *nmf* novice.

néo-zélandais, -aise [neɔzelɑ̃de, -ez] *a* of *ou* from New Zealand ▌*nmf* N.-Zélandais, N.-Zélandaise New Zealander.

nerf [nɛr] *nm* nerve; **crise de nerfs** (fit of) hysterics; **du n.!, un peu de n.!** *Fam* buck up!; **ça me tape sur les nerfs** *Fam* it gets on my nerves; **être sur les nerfs** *Fig* to be keyed up *ou* het up; **avoir du n.** (*vigueur*) *Fam* to have guts. ●**nerveux, -euse** *a* (*agité*) nervous; **cellule/etc nerveuse** nerve cell/etc; **système n.** nervous system; **une voiture nerveuse** a car that has good acceleration. ●**nervosité** *nf* nervousness.

nervure [nɛrvyr] *nf* (*de feuille*) vein.

nescafé® [nɛskafe] *nm* instant coffee.

n'est-ce pas? [nɛspɑ] *adv* isn't he?, don't you, won't they? *etc*; **il fait beau, n'est-ce pas?** the weather's fine, isn't it?

net, nette [nɛt] 1 *a* (*image, refus*) clear; (*coupure, linge*) clean; (*soigné*) neat; (*copie*) fair; **je veux en avoir le cœur n.** *Fig* I want to get to the bottom of it once and for all ▌*adv* (*casser, couper*) clean; (*tuer*) outright; (*refuser*) flat(ly); (*parler*) plainly; **s'arrêter n.** to stop dead. 2 *a* (*poids, prix* etc) net. ●**nettement** *adv* clearly, plainly; (*bien plus*) definitely. ●**netteté** *nf* clearness; (*de travail*) neatness.

nettoyer [nɛtwaje] *vt* to clean (up); (*plaie*) to cleanse, clean (up); (*vider, ruiner*) *Fam* to clean out. ●**nettoiement** *nm* cleaning; **service du n.** refuse *ou* *Am* garbage collection. ●**nettoyage** *nm* cleaning; **n. à sec** dry cleaning.

neuf¹, neuve [nœf, nœv] *a* new; **quoi de n.?** what's new(s)? ▌*nm* **remettre qch à n.** to make sth as good as new, do sth up; **il y a du n.** there's been something new.

neuf² [nœf] *a* & *nm* ([nœv] before **heures** &

ans) nine. ● **neuvième** a & nmf ninth.
neurasthénique [nørastenik] a depressed.
neutre [nøtr] 1 a (pays, personne etc) neutral
▮ nm Él neutral. 2 a & nm Grammaire neu-
ter. ● **neutraliser** vt to neutralize. ● **neutralité**
nf neutrality.
neveu, -x [nəvø] nm nephew.
névralgie [nevralʒi] nf headache; Méd neur-
algia. ● **névralgique** a centre n. Fig nerve
centre.
névrose [nevroz] nf neurosis. ● **névrosé, -ée**
a & nmf neurotic.
nez [ne] nm nose; **n. à n.** face to face (avec
with); **rire/etc au n. de qn** to laugh/etc in
s.o.'s face; **parler du n.** to speak through
one's nose; **avoir qch sous le n.** Fam to have
sth under one's very nose; **mener qn par le
bout du n.** Fig to lead s.o. by the nose; **avoir
un verre dans le n.** (être ivre) Fam to have
had one too many; **mettre le n. dehors** Fam
to stick one's nose outside; **ça se voit comme
le n. au milieu de la figure** Fam it's as plain
as the nose on your face.
ni [ni] conj ni...ni (+ ne) neither...nor; **ni
Pierre ni Paul ne sont venus** neither Peter
nor Paul came; **il n'a ni faim ni soif** he's
neither hungry nor thirsty; **sans manger ni
boire** without eating or drinking; **ni l'un(e) ni
l'autre** neither (of them).
niais, -aise [njɛ, -ɛz] a silly, simple ▮ nmf
simpleton. ● **niaiserie** nf silliness; **niaiseries**
(paroles) nonsense.
Nicaragua [nikaragwa] nm Nicaragua.
niche [niʃ] nf (de chien) Br kennel, Am doghouse; (cavité) niche, recess.
nicher [niʃe] vi (oiseau) to nest ▮ **se nicher**
vpr (oiseau) to nest; (se cacher) to hide oneself. ● **nichée** nf (chiens) litter; (oiseaux, enfants) brood.
nickel [nikɛl] nm (métal) nickel.
nicotine [nikɔtin] nf nicotine.
nid [ni] nm nest; **n. de poules** pothole (in
road).
nièce [njɛs] nf niece.
nième [ɛnjɛm] a nth.
nier [nje] vt to deny (que that) ▮ vi (accusé)
to deny the charge.
nigaud, -aude [nigo, -od] nmf silly fool.
Nigéria [niʒerja] nm Nigeria.
Nil [nil] nm le N. the Nile.
n'importe [nɛ̃pɔrt] voir importer 1.
nippon, -one ou **-onne** [nipɔ̃, -ɔn] a Japanese.
niveau, -x [nivo] nm (hauteur) level; (degré,
compétence) standard, level; **n. de vie**
standard of living; **n. à bulle (d'air)** spirit level; **au n. de qn** (élève etc) up to s.o.'s
standard; **se mettre au n.** to get up to (the
required) standard. ● **niveler** vt (surface) to
level; (fortunes etc) to even (up).
noble [nɔbl] a noble ▮ nmf nobleman, noblewoman. ● **noblement** [-əmɑ̃] adv nobly.
● **noblesse** nf (caractère, classe) nobility.
noce(s) [nɔs] nf(pl) wedding; **noces
d'argent/d'or** silver/golden wedding; **faire la**
noce Fam to have a good time, make merry.
● **noceur, -euse** nmf Fam reveller, hell-
raiser.
nocif, -ive [nɔsif, -iv] a harmful. ● **nocivité**
nf harmfulness.
noctambule [nɔktɑ̃byl] nmf (personne) night
bird ou prowler.
nocturne [nɔktyrn] a nocturnal; **tapage n.**
Jur disturbance (at night) ▮ nf (de magasins
etc) late night opening; (match en) n. Sport
Br floodlit match, Am night game.
Noël [nɔɛl] nm Christmas; **le père N.** Br
Father Christmas, Santa Claus.
nœud [nø] nm 1 knot; (ruban) bow; **n. coulant** slipknot, noose; **n. papillon** bow tie; **le
n. du problème** the crux of the problem; **j'ai
un n. à l'estomac** Fig I feel bloated. 2 (mesure) Nau knot.
noir, noire [nwar] a black; (nuit, lunettes etc)
dark; (idées) gloomy; (âme, crime) vile;
(misère) dire; **roman n.** thriller; **film n.** film
noir; **une rue noire de monde** Fig a street
swarming with ou thick with people; **il fait
n.** it's dark; **il fait nuit noire** it's pitch-dark.
▮ nm (couleur) black; (obscurité) dark; N.
(homme) black; **vendre au (marché) n.** to
sell on the black market.
▮ nf noire (note de musique) Br crotchet, Am
quarter note; **Noire** (femme) black.
● **noirceur** nf blackness; (d'une action etc) vi-
leness. ● **noircir** vt to make black, blacken ▮
vi, **se noircir** vpr to turn black.
noisette [nwazɛt] nf hazelnut. ● **noisetier** nm
hazel (tree).
noix [nwa] nf (du noyer) walnut; **n. de coco**
coconut; **n. du Brésil** Brazil nut; **n. de
beurre** knob of butter; **à la n.** Fam trashy,
awful.
nom [nɔ̃] nm name; Grammaire noun; **n. de
famille** surname; **n. de jeune fille** maiden
name; **n. propre** Grammaire proper noun;
au n. de qn on s.o.'s behalf; **sans n.** (anonyme) nameless; (vil) vile; **n. d'un chien!**
Fam oh hell!, for heaven's sake!
nomade [nɔmad] a nomadic ▮ nmf nomad.
nombre [nɔ̃br] nm number; **ils sont au ou du
dix** there are ten of them; **ils sont au ou du
n. de** (parmi) they're among; **le plus grand
n. de** the majority of.
nombreux, -euse [nɔ̃brø, -øz] a (amis,
livres etc) numerous, many; (famille, collection etc) large; **peu n.** few; **venir n.** to come
in large numbers.
nombril [nɔ̃bri] nm navel.
nominal, -e, -aux [nɔminal, -o] a nominal.
nomination [nɔminasjɔ̃] nf appointment, nomination.
nommer [nɔme] vt (appeler) to name; **n. qn**
(désigner) to appoint s.o. (à un poste/etc to a
post/etc); **n. qn président** to nominate ou
appoint s.o. chairman ▮ **se nommer** vpr
(s'appeler) to be called. ● **nommément** adv
by name.
non [nɔ̃] adv & nm inv no; **n.!** no!; **tu viens
ou n.?** are you coming or not?; **n. seulement**

not only; **n. (pas) que** (+ *sub*)... not that...; **n. sans regret**/*etc* not without regret/*etc*; **je crois que n.** I don't think so; **(ni) moi n. plus** neither do, am, can *etc* I; **c'est bien, n.?** *Fam* it's all right, isn't it?; **(ah) ça n.!** *Fam* definitely not (that)!; **une place n. réservée** an unreserved seat.

non- [nɔ̃] *préf* non-.

nonante [nɔnɑ̃t] *a & nm (en Belgique, en Suisse)* ninety.

nonchalant, -ante [nɔ̃ʃalɑ̃, -ɑ̃t] *a* nonchalant, apathetic. ●**nonchalance** *nf* nonchalance, apathy.

non-conformiste [nɔ̃kɔ̃fɔrmist] *a & nmf* nonconformist.

non-fumeur, -euse [nɔ̃fymœr, -øz] *nmf* non-smoker.

non-lieu [nɔ̃ljø] *nm* **bénéficier d'un n.-lieu** *Jur* to have one's case dismissed (*through lack of evidence*).

non-retour [nɔ̃rətur] *nm* **point de n.-retour** point of no return.

non-sens [nɔ̃sɑ̃s] *nm inv* absurdity.

non-violence [nɔ̃vjɔlɑ̃s] *nf* non-violence.

nord [nɔr] *nm* north; **au n.** in the north; (*direction*) (to the) north (**de** of); **du n.** (*vent, direction*) northerly; (*ville*) northern; (*gens*) from *ou* in the north; **Amérique/Afrique du N.** North America/Africa; **l'Europe du N.** Northern Europe; **le grand N.** the Far North, the Arctic regions.

▮ *a inv* (*côte*) north(ern). ●**nord-africain, -aine** *a* North African ▮ *nmf* **N.-Africain, N.-Africaine** North African. ●**nord-américain, -aine** *a* North American ▮ *nmf* **N.-Américain, N.-Américaine** North American. ●**nord-est** *nm & a inv* north-east. ●**nord-ouest** *nm & a inv* north-west.

nordique [nɔrdik] *a* Scandinavian ▮ *nmf* **N.** Scandinavian; *Can* Northern Canadian.

noria [nɔrja] *nf* **une n. d'ambulances**/*etc* a fleet of ambulances/*etc*.

normal, -e, -aux [nɔrmal, -o] *a* normal. ●**normale** *nf* norm, normality; **au-dessus/au-dessous de la n.** above/below normal. ●**normalement** *adv* normally. ●**normaliser** *vt* (*uniformiser*) to standardize; (*relations etc*) to normalize.

normand, -ande [nɔrmɑ̃, -ɑ̃d] *a* Norman ▮ *nmf* **N., Normande** Norman. ●**Normandie** *nf* Normandy.

norme [nɔrm] *nf* norm; **normes de sécurité** safety standards.

Norvège [nɔrvɛʒ] *nf* Norway. ●**norvégien, -ienne** *a* Norwegian ▮ *nmf* **N., Norvégienne** Norwegian ▮ *nm* (*langue*) Norwegian.

nos [no] *voir* **notre**.

nostalgie [nɔstalʒi] *nf* nostalgia. ●**nostalgique** *a* nostalgic.

notable [nɔtabl] *a* (*fait etc*) notable ▮ *nm* (*personne*) notable. ●**notablement** [-əmɑ̃] *adv* (*sensiblement*) notably.

notaire [nɔtɛr] *nm* lawyer, *Br* solicitor, notary (public).

notamment [nɔtamɑ̃] *adv* particularly, not-

ably.

note [nɔt] *nf* (*de musique, remarque etc*) note; (*chiffrée*) (*à l'école*) *Br* mark, *Am* grade; (*facture*) *Br* bill, *Am* check; **prendre n. de qch, prendre qch en n.** to make a note of sth; **prendre des notes** to take notes.

noter [nɔte] *vt* (*remarquer*) to note, notice; (*écrire*) to note down; (*devoir etc*) *Br* to mark, *Am* grade; **être bien noté** (*personne*) to be highly rated.

notice [nɔtis] *nf* (*mode d'emploi*) instructions; (*résumé, préface*) note.

notifier [nɔtifje] *vt* **n. qch à qn** to notify s.o. of sth.

notion [nɔsjɔ̃] *nf* notion, idea; **notions** (*éléments*) rudiments; **avoir des notions de chimie**/*etc* to know the rudiments of *ou* have a smattering of chemistry/*etc*.

notoire [nɔtwar] *a* (*criminel, bêtise*) notorious; (*fait*) well-known. ●**notoriété** *nf* (*renom*) fame; (*de fait*) general recognition; **il est de n. publique que...** it's public *ou* common knowledge that....

notre, pl nos [nɔtr, no] *a poss* our. ●**nôtre** *pron poss* **le** *ou* **la n., les nôtres** ours ▮ *nmpl* **les nôtres** (*parents etc*) our own (people); **serez-vous des nôtres?** (*à notre dîner etc*) will you join us?

nouba [nuba] *nf* **faire la n.** *Fam* to have a good time, make merry.

nouer [nwe] *vt* (*lacets etc*) to tie, knot; (*amitié, conversation*) *Fig* to strike up; **avoir la gorge nouée** to have a lump in one's throat. ●**noueux, -euse** *a* (*bois*) knotty; (*doigts*) gnarled.

nougat [nuga] *nm* nougat.

nouille [nuj] *nf* (*idiot*) *Fam* drip.

nouilles [nuj] *nfpl* noodles.

nounours [nunurs] *nm* teddy bear.

nourrice [nuris] *nf* (*assistante maternelle*) (children's) nurse, *Br* child minder; (*qui allaite*) wet nurse; **mettre un enfant en n.** to put a child out to nurse.

nourrir [nurir] *vt* (*alimenter*) to feed; (*espoir etc*) *Fig* to nourish; (*esprit*) to enrich; **enfant nourri au sein** breastfed child ▮ *vi* (*aliment*) to be nourishing. ▮ **se nourrir** *vpr* to eat; **se n. de** to feed on. ●**nourrissant, -ante** *a* nourishing.

nourrisson [nurisɔ̃] *nm* infant.

nourriture [nurityr] *nf* food.

nous [nu] *pron* **1** (*sujet*) we; **n. sommes** we are **2** (*complément direct*) us; **il n. connaît** he knows us. **3** (*complément indirect*) (to) us; **il n. l'a donné** he gave it to us, he gave us it. **4** (*réfléchi*) ourselves; **n. n. lavons** we wash ourselves. **5** (*réciproque*) each other; **n. n. détestons** we hate each other. ●**nous-mêmes** *pron* ourselves.

nouveau (*or* **nouvel** *before vowel or mute h*), **nouvelle**[1], *pl* **nouveaux, nouvelles** [nuvo, nuvɛl] *a* new; **on craint de nouvelles inondations** (*d'autres*) further *ou* fresh flooding is feared ▮ *nmf* (*à l'école*) new boy, new girl ▮ *nm* **du n.** something new ▮ *adv* **de n., à n.**

again. ●**nouveau-né, -ée** *a* & *nmf* new-born (baby). ●**nouveau-venu** *nm ou* **nouvelle-venue** *nf* newcomer.

nouveauté [nuvote] *nf* novelty, newness; **nouveautés** (*livres*) new books; (*disques*) new releases; (*vêtements*) new fashions; **une n.** (*objet*) a novelty.

nouvelle² [nuvɛl] *nf* **1 nouvelle(s)** (*informations*) news; **une n.** a piece of news, some news; **la n. de sa mort** the news of her death; **les nouvelles sont bonnes/mauvaises** the news is good/bad; **j'ai des nouvelles** I have some news; **avoir des nouvelles de qn** to have *ou* get news about *ou* of s.o.; **demander des nouvelles de qn** to ask *ou* inquire after *ou* about s.o. **2** (*récit*) short story.

Nouvelle-Calédonie [nuvɛlkaledɔni] *nf* New Caledonia.

Nouvelle-Zélande [nuvɛlzelɑ̃d] *nf* New Zealand.

novateur, -trice [nɔvatœr, -tris] *nmf* innovator ‖ *a* innovative.

novembre [nɔvɑ̃br] *nm* November.

novice [nɔvis] *nmf* novice ‖ *a* inexperienced.

noyade [nwajad] *nf* drowning.

noyau, -x [nwajo] *nm* (*de fruit*) stone, *Am* pit; (*d'atome, de cellule*) nucleus; (*groupe*) group; **un n. d'opposants** a hard core of opponents; **un n. dur** (*de groupe*) a hard core.

noyauter [nwajote] *vt Pol* to infiltrate. ●**noyautage** *nm* infiltration.

noyer¹ [nwaje] *vt* (*personne etc*) to drown; (*terres*) to flood; **n. son chagrin dans le vin** to drown one's sorrows (in wine); **n. le poisson** *Fig* to sidestep the issue (*by giving a complex reply*) ‖ **se noyer** *vpr* to drown; (*se suicider*) to drown oneself; **se n. dans le détail** to get bogged down in details. ●**noyé, -ée** *nmf* (*mort*) drowned man *ou* woman ‖ *a* **être n.** (*perdu*) *Fig* to be out of one's depth; **être n. dans la masse** *Fig* to be lumped in with the rest.

noyer² [nwaje] *nm* (*arbre*) walnut tree.

nu, nue [ny] *a* (*personne, vérité*) naked; (*mains, chambre*) bare; **tout nu** (stark) naked, (in the) nude; **tête nue, nu-tête** bareheaded; **voir qch à l'œil nu** to see sth with the naked eye; **mettre qch à nu** (*exposer*) to lay sth bare; **se mettre nu** to strip off ‖ *nm* (*femme, homme, œuvre*) nude.

nuage [nɥaʒ] *nm* cloud; **un n. de lait** *Fig* a dash of milk; **être sur son petit n.** to have one's head in the clouds. ●**nuageux, -euse** *a* (*ciel*) cloudy.

nuance [nɥɑ̃s] *nf* (*de couleurs*) shade, nuance; (*de sens*) nuance; (*de regret*) tinge, nuance. ●**nuancer** *vt* (*teintes*) to blend, shade; (*pensée*) to qualify. ●**nuancé, -ée** *a*

(*jugement*) qualified.

nucléaire [nykleɛr] *a* nuclear; **centrale n.** nuclear power station ‖ *nm* (*énergie*) nuclear energy.

nudisme [nydism] *nm* nudism. ●**nudiste** *nmf* nudist; **camp de nudistes** nudist camp. ●**nudité** *nf* nudity, nakedness; (*de mur etc*) bareness.

nuée [nɥe] *nf* **une n. de** *Litt* (*foule*) a host of; (*groupe compact*) a cloud of.

nues [ny] *nfpl* **tomber des n.** to be astounded; **porter qn aux n.** to praise s.o. to the skies.

nuire* [nɥir] *vi* **n. à** (*personne, intérêts etc*) to harm. ●**nuisible** *a* harmful.

nuit [nɥi] *nf* night; (*obscurité*) dark(ness); **il fait n.** it's dark; **la n.** (*se promener etc*) at night; **cette n.** (*aujourd'hui*) tonight; (*hier*) last night; **avant la n.** before nightfall; **n. d'hôtel** overnight stay in a hotel; **oiseau de n.** night bird; **bonne n.** good night. ●**nuitée** *nf* overnight stay (*in hotel etc*).

nul, nulle [nyl] **1** *a* (*médiocre*) hopeless, useless; (*risque etc*) non-existent, nil; (*non valable*) *Jur* null (and void); **faire match n.** *Sport* to tie, draw. **2** *a* (*aucun*) no; **nulle part** nowhere; **sans n. doute** without any doubt ‖ *pron m* (*aucun*) *Litt* no one. ●**nullard, -arde** *nmf Fam* useless person. ●**nullement** *adv* not at all. ●**nullité** *nf* (*d'un élève etc*) uselessness; (*personne*) useless person.

numéraire [nymerɛr] *nm* cash, currency.

numéral, -e, -aux [nymeral, -o] *a* & *nm* numeral.

numérique [nymerik] *a* a numerical; (*montre, clavier, données etc*) digital. ‖

numéro [nymero] *nm* number; (*de journal*) issue, number; (*au cirque*) act; **un n. de danse/de chant** a dance/song number; **n. vert** *Tél* = 0-800 number, = *Am* tollfree number; **n. gagnant** (*au jeu*) winning number; **quel n.!** (*personne*) *Fam* what a character! ●**numéroter** *vt* (*pages, sièges*) to number. ●**numérotage** *nm* numbering.

nu-pieds [nypje] *a inv* barefoot ‖ *nmpl* open sandals.

nuptial, -e, -aux [nypsjal, -o] *a* (*chambre*) bridal; **cérémonie/etc nuptiale** wedding ceremony/etc.

nuque [nyk] *nf* back *ou* nape of the neck.

nurse [nœrs] *nf* nanny, (children's) nurse.

nutritif, -ive [nytritif, -iv] *a* nutritious, nutritive. ●**nutrition** *nf* nutrition. ●**nutritionnel, -elle** *a* nutritional.

nylon [nilɔ̃] *nm* (*fibre*) nylon; **chemise/etc en n.** nylon shirt/etc.

nymphe [nɛ̃f] *nf* nymph. ●**nymphomane** *nf Péj* nymphomaniac.

O

O, o [o] *nm* O, o.

oasis [ɔazis] *nf* oasis.

obédience [ɔbedjɑ̃s] *nf* (*politique*) allegiance.

obéir [ɔbeir] *vi* to obey; **o. à qn/qch** to obey s.o./sth.; **être obéi** to be obeyed; **o. à qn au doigt et à l'œil** to obey s.o. dutifully *ou* strictly, do s.o.'s bidding. ● **obéissant, -ante** *a* obedient. ● **obéissance** *nf* obedience (à to).'

obélisque [ɔbelisk] *nm* (*monument*) obelisk.

obèse [ɔbɛz] *a* & *nmf* obese (person). ● **obésité** *nf* obesity.

objecter [ɔbʒɛkte] *vt* (*prétexte*) to put forward, plead; **o. que** to object that; **on lui objecta son jeune âge** they objected that he *ou* she was too young. ● **objecteur** *nm* **o. de conscience** conscientious objector. ● **objection** *nf* objection; **si vous n'y voyez pas d'o.** if you have no objection(s).

objectif, -ive [ɔbʒɛktif, -iv] **1** *nm.* (*but*) objective; (*d'appareil photo*) lens; **o. de vente** *Com* sales target. **2** *a* (*opinion etc*) objective. ● **objectivement** *adv* objectively. ● **objectivité** *nf* objectivity.

objet [ɔbʒɛ] *nm* (*chose, sujet, but*) object; (*de toilette*) article; **faire l'o. de** (*étude, critiques etc*) to be the subject of; (*soins, surveillance*) to be given, receive; **objets trouvés** (*bureau*) *Br* lost property, *Am* lost and found; **o. d'art** objet d'art; **sans o.** (*inquiétude etc*) groundless.

obligation [ɔbligasjɔ̃] *nf* (*devoir, nécessité*) obligation; *Fin* bond; **se trouver dans l'o. de faire qch** to feel compelled *ou* obliged to do sth; **sans o. de votre part** without obligation (on your part). ● **obligatoire** *a* compulsory, obligatory; (*inévitable*) *Fam* inevitable. ● **obligatoirement** *adv* (*fatalement*) inevitably; **tu dois o. le faire** you have to do it.

obligeant, -ante [ɔbliʒɑ̃, -ɑ̃t] *a* obliging, kind. ● **obligeamment** [-amɑ̃] *adv* obligingly. ● **obligeance** *nf* kindness.

obliger [ɔbliʒe] *vt* **1** (*contraindre*) to force, compel, oblige (à faire to do); (*engager*) to bind; **être obligé de faire** to have to do, be compelled *ou* obliged to do. **2** (*rendre service à*) to oblige; **être obligé à qn de qch** to be obliged to s.o. for sth. ● **obligé, -ée** *a* (*obligatoire*) necessary; (*fatal*) *Fam* inevitable.

oblique [ɔblik] *a* oblique; **regard o.** sidelong glance; **en o.** at an (oblique) angle. ● **obliquer** *vi* (*véhicule etc*) to turn off.

oblitérer [ɔblitere] *vt* (*timbre*) to cancel; (*billet, carte*) to stamp; **timbre oblitéré** (*non*

neuf) used stamp. ● **oblitération** *nf* cancellation; (*de billet etc*) stamping.

oblong, -ongue [ɔblɔ̃, -ɔ̃g] *a* oblong.

obnubilé, -ée [ɔbnybile] *a* (*obsédé*) obsessed (par with).

obscène [ɔpsɛn] *a* obscene. ● **obscénité** *nf* obscenity.

obscur, -e [ɔpskyr] *a* (*noir*) dark; (*peu clair, inconnu, humble*) obscure. ● **obscurcir** *vt* (*pièce*) to make dark(er), darken; (*rendre peu intelligible*) to obscure (*text, ideas etc*) ▮ **s'obscurcir** *vpr* (*ciel*) to get dark(er), cloud over, darken; (*vue*) to become dim. ● **obscurément** *adv* obscurely. ● **obscurité** *nf* dark(ness); (*de texte, d'acteur etc*) obscurity; **rester dans l'o.** to be *ou* remain in the dark.

obséder [ɔpsede] *vt* to obsess, haunt. ● **obsédant, -ante** *a* haunting, obsessive. ● **obsédé, -ée** *nmf* maniac (de for); **o. sexuel** sex maniac.

obsèques [ɔpsɛk] *nfpl* funeral; **faire des o. nationales à qn** to give s.o. a state funeral.

obséquieux, -euse [ɔpsekjø, -øz] *a* obsequious.

observateur, -trice [ɔpsɛrvatœr, -tris] *a* observant ▮ *nmf* observer.

observation [ɔpsɛrvasjɔ̃] *nf* (*étude, remarque*) observation; (*reproche*) rebuke, (critical) remark; (*de règle etc*) observance; **en o.** (*malade*) under observation.

observatoire [ɔpsɛrvatwar] *nm* observatory; (*endroit élevé*) lookout post; (*d'une armée*) observation post.

observer [ɔpsɛrve] *vt* (*regarder*) to watch, observe; (*remarquer, respecter*) to observe; **faire o. qch à qn** to point sth out to s.o.

obsession [ɔpsesjɔ̃] *nf* obsession. ● **obsessif, -ive** *a* (*peur etc*) obsessive. ● **obsessionnel, -elle** *a* *Psy* obsessive.

obstacle [ɔpstakl] *nm* obstacle; **faire o. à** to stand in the way of.

obstétrique [ɔpstetrik] *nf* *Méd* obstetrics.

obstiner (s') [sɔpstine] *vpr* to be persistent *ou* obstinate; **s'o. à faire** to persist in doing. ● **obstiné, -ée** *a* stubborn, persistent, obstinate. ● **obstination** *nf* stubbornness, obstinacy, persistence.

obstruction [ɔpstryksjɔ̃] *nf* (*gêne, tactique politique, au football etc*) obstruction; **faire de l'o.** (*homme politique, footballeur etc*) to be obstructive. ● **obstruer** *vt* to obstruct.

obtempérer [ɔptɑ̃pere] *vi* to obey (an order); **o. à** to obey.

obtenir [ɔptənir] *vt* to get, obtain, secure. ● **obtention** *nf* obtaining, getting.

obturer [ɔptyre] *vt* (*trou etc*) to stop *ou* close

up. ●**obturateur** *nm* (*d'appareil photo*) shutter; (*dans une conduite d'eau etc*) valve.

obtus, -use [ɔpty, -tyz] *a* (*angle, esprit*) obtuse.

obus [ɔby] *nm* (*projectile*) shell.

occasion [ɔkazjɔ̃] *nf* **1** (*chance*) chance, opportunity (**de faire** to do); (*circonstance*) occasion; **à l'o.** on occasion, when the occasion arises; **à l'o. de** on the occasion of; **pour les grandes occasions** for special *ou* important occasions. **2** (*prix avantageux*) bargain; (*objet non neuf*) secondhand buy; **d'o.** secondhand, used.

occasionner [ɔkazjɔne] *vt* to cause; **o. qch à qn** to cause s.o. sth.

occident [ɔksidɑ̃] *nm* **l'O.** *Pol* the West. ●**occidental, -e, -aux** *a Géog Pol* western **l** *nmpl* **les occidentaux** *Pol* Westerners. ●**occidentalisé, -ée** *a Pol* Westernized.

occulte [ɔkylt] *a* occult.

occupant, -ante [ɔkypɑ̃, -ɑ̃t] *a* (*armée*) occupying **l** *nmf* (*habitant*) occupant **l** *nm* (*soldats ennemis*) forces of occupation, occupier.

occupation [ɔkypasjɔ̃] *nf* (*activité, travail etc*) occupation; **l'o. de** (*action*) the occupation of; **l'O.** *Hist* the Occupation; **armée d'o.** occupying forces, army of occupation.

occupé, -ée [ɔkype] *a* busy (**à faire** doing); (*place, maison etc*) occupied; (*ligne téléphonique*) *Br* engaged, *Am* busy; (*taxi*) hired.

occuper [ɔkype] *vt* (*maison, pays, usine etc*) to occupy; (*place, temps*) to take up, occupy; (*poste*) to hold, occupy; **o. qn** (*jeu, travail*) to keep s.o. busy *ou* occupied, occupy s.o.; (*ouvrier etc*) to employ s.o.; **o. qn à qch** to keep s.o. occupied *ou* busy doing sth; **o. ses loisirs** to occupy one's spare *ou* leisure time.

l s'occuper *vpr* to keep (oneself) busy (**à faire** doing); **s'o. de** (*affaire, problème etc*) to deal with; (*politique*) to be engaged in; **s'o. de qn** (*malade etc*) to take care of s.o.; (*client*) to see to s.o., deal with s.o.; **occupe-toi de tes affaires!** mind your own business!; **est-ce qu'on s'occupe de vous?** (*dans un magasin*) are you being served *ou* seen to?

occurrence [ɔkyrɑ̃s] *nf Ling* occurrence; **en l'o.** in this case, in the circumstances, as it happens *ou* happened.

océan [ɔseɑ̃] *nm* ocean; **un o. de verdure** *Litt* a sea of greenery; **un o. de larmes** *Litt* a deluge of tears. ●**océanique** *a* oceanic.

ocre [ɔkr] *nm & a inv* (*couleur*) ochre.

octave [ɔktav] *nf Mus* octave.

octet [ɔktɛ] *nm Ordinat* byte.

octobre [ɔktɔbr] *nm* October.

octogénaire [ɔktɔʒenɛr] *nmf* octogenarian.

octogone [ɔktɔgɔn] *nm* octagon. ●**octogonal, -e, -aux** *a* octagonal.

octroi [ɔktrwa] *nm Litt* granting. ●**octroyer** *vt Litt* to grant (**à** to).

oculaire [ɔkylɛr] *a* **témoin o.** eyewitness; **globe o.** eyeball. ●**oculiste** *nmf* eye specialist.

ode [ɔd] *nf* (*poème*) ode.

odeur [ɔdœr] *nf* smell, odour; (*de fleur*) scent; **une o. de brûlé** a smell of burning. ●**odorant, -ante** *a* sweet-smelling. ●**odorat** *nm* sense of smell.

odieux, -euse [ɔdjø, -øz] *a* horrible, odious, obnoxious.

œcuménique [ekymenik] *a Rel* (o)ecumenical.

œil, *pl* **yeux** [œj, jø] *nm* eye; **avoir les yeux noirs/etc** to have black/etc eyes; **avoir de grands yeux** to have big *ou* wide eyes; **lever/ baisser les yeux** to look up/down; **fermer les yeux sur qch** *Fig* to turn a blind eye to sth; **je n'ai pas fermé l'o. (de la nuit)** I didn't close my eyes *ou* sleep a wink (all night); **coup d'o.** (*regard*) look, glance; **jeter un coup d'o. sur** to (have a) look *ou* glance at; **à vue d'o.** visibly; **à mes yeux** in my eyes; **à l'o.** (*gratuitement*) *Fam* free; **avoir qch sous les yeux** to have sth before one's very eyes *ou* right in front of one; **regarder qn dans les yeux** to look at s.o. in the eyes *ou* face; **être les yeux dans les yeux** to be staring into each other's eyes; **faire les gros yeux à qn** to scowl at s.o.; **faire de l'o. à qn** *Fam* to make eyes at s.o.; **avoir qn à l'o.** (*surveiller*) to keep an eye on s.o.; **ne pas avoir les yeux dans sa poche** to be very observant, have sharp eyes; **o. poché, o. au beurre noir** *Fig* black eye; **l'o. du cyclone** the eye of the storm *ou* cyclone; **ouvre l'o.!** keep your eyes open!; **mon o.!** *Fam* (*incrédulité*) my foot!; (*refus*) no way!, no chance!; **entre quat'z'yeux** [katzjø] (*en privé*) *Fam* in private. ●**œil-de-bœuf** *nm* (*pl* **œils-de-bœuf**) bull's-eye window.

œillade [œjad] *nf* (*clin d'œil*) wink.

œillères [œjɛr] *nfpl* (*de cheval*) & *Fig Br* blinkers, *Am* blinders.

œillet [œjɛ] *nm* **1** (*plante*) carnation. **2** (*trou de ceinture etc*) eyelet.

œuf, *pl* **œufs** [œf, ø] *nm* egg; **œufs** (*de poisson*) (hard) roe; **o. sur le plat** fried egg; **o. dur** hard-boiled egg; **œufs brouillés** scrambled eggs; **o. de Pâques** Easter egg; **étouffer qch dans l'o.** *Fig* to nip *ou* stifle sth in the bud.

œuvre [œvr] *nf* (*travail, livre etc*) work; **o. de charité** (*organisation*) charity; **o. d'art** work of art; **l'o. de** (*production artistique etc*) the works of; **mettre en o.** (*employer*) to make use of; **mettre tout en o.** to do everything possible (**pour faire** to do); **se mettre à l'o.** to set to work. ●**œuvrer** *vi Litt* to work.

offense [ɔfɑ̃s] *nf* insult; *Rel* transgression. ●**offenser** *vt* to offend; **s'o. de qch** to take *Br* offence *ou* *Am* offense at sth. ●**offensant, -ante** *a* offensive.

offensif, -ive [ɔfɑ̃sif, -iv] *a* offensive **l** *nf* (*attaque*) offensive; **offensive du froid** sudden cold spell, onslaught of the cold weather.

offert, -erte [ɔfɛr, -ɛrt] *pp de* **offrir**.

office [ɔfis] *nm* **1** *Rel* service. **2** (*pièce près de* la cuisine) pantry. **3** (établissement) office, bureau; **d'o.** (être promu etc) automatically; **faire o.** de to serve as; **ses bons offices** (service) one's good offices.

officiel, -ielle [ɔfisjɛl] a (acte etc) official; **le Journal O.** official government publication giving details of laws and important announcements ∎ nm (personnage) official. ● **officiellement** adv officially.

officier [ɔfisje] **1** nm (dans l'armée etc) officer. **2** vi Rel to officiate.

officieux, -euse [ɔfisjø, -øz] a unofficial.

offre [ɔfr] nf offer; (aux enchères) bid; **l'o. et la demande** Écon supply and demand; **offres d'emploi** (dans un journal) job vacancies, Br situations vacant; **appel d'offres** invitation to tender, invitation for tenders. ● **offrande** nf offering.

offrir* [ɔfrir] vt (donner en cadeau) to give; (proposer) to offer; **o. qch à qn** (donner) to give s.o. sth, give sth to s.o.; (proposer) to offer s.o. sth, offer sth to s.o.; **o. à qn de l'héberger**/etc to offer to put s.o. up/etc; **o. sa démission (à qn)** to offer (s.o.) one's resignation ∎ **s'offrir** vpr (cadeau etc) to treat oneself to; (se proposer) to offer oneself (**comme** as); **s'o. aux regards** (spectacle etc) to greet one's eyes. ● **offrant** nm **au plus o.** to the highest bidder.

offusquer [ɔfyske] vt to offend, shock; **s'o.** de to take Br offence ou Am offense at.

ogive [ɔʒiv] nf (de fusée) nose cone; **o. nucléaire** nuclear warhead.

ogre [ɔgr] nm ogre.

oh! [o] int oh!, o!

ohé! [ɔe] int hey (there)!

oie [wa] nf goose (pl geese).

oignon [ɔɲɔ̃] nm (légume) onion; (de fleur) bulb; **en rang d'oignons** Fam in a straight ou neat row; **occupe-toi de tes oignons!** Fam mind your own business!

oiseau, -x [wazo] nm bird; **à vol d'o.** as the crow flies; **o. rare** (être irremplaçable) Hum rare bird, perfect gem; **drôle d'o.** (individu) Péj Br queer ou odd fish, Am oddball; **'attention! le petit o. va sortir!'** 'watch the birdie!'

oiseux, -euse [wazø, -øz] a (inutile) idle, vain.

oisif, -ive [wazif, -iv] a (inactif) idle ∎ nmf idler. ● **oisiveté** nf idleness.

oléoduc [ɔleɔdyk] nm oil pipeline.

olfactif, -ive [ɔlfaktif, -iv] a olfactory.

olive [ɔliv] nf (fruit) olive; **huile d'o.** olive oil ∎ a inv (couleur) (vert) **o.** olive (green). ● **olivier** nm (arbre) olive tree.

olympique [ɔlɛ̃pik] a (jeux, record, piscine etc) Olympic; **jeux olympiques d'hiver** Winter Olympics.

ombilical, -e, -aux [ɔ̃bilikal, -o] a umbilical; **cordon o.** umbilical cord.

ombrage [ɔ̃braʒ] nm **1** (ombre) shade. **2** **prendre o. de qch** Litt to take umbrage at sth. ● **ombrager** vt to give shade to. ● **ombragé, -ée** a shady. ● **ombrageux, -euse** a (caractère, personne) touchy.

ombre [ɔ̃br] nf (d'arbre etc) shade; (de personne, objet) shadow; **30° à l'o.** 30° in the shade; **dans l'o.** (comploter etc) Fig in secret; **rester dans l'o.** (effacé) to remain in the background; **sans l'o. d'un doute** without the shadow of a doubt; **sans l'o. d'un reproche/remords**/etc without the slightest trace of blame/remorse/etc; **il y a une o. au tableau** Fig there's a fly in the ointment.

ombrelle [ɔ̃brɛl] nf sunshade, parasol.

omelette [ɔmlɛt] nf omelet(te); **o. au fromage**/etc cheese/etc omelet(te); **o. norvégienne** baked Alaska.

omettre* [ɔmɛtr] vt to omit (**de faire** to do). ● **omission** nf omission.

omni- [ɔmni] préf omni-. ● **omnipotent, -ente** a omnipotent.

omnibus [ɔmnibys] a & nm (**train**) **o.** slow train (stopping at all stations).

omoplate [ɔmɔplat] nf shoulder blade.

on [ɔ̃] (sometimes **l'on** [lɔ̃]) pron (les gens) they, people; (nous) we, one; (vous) you, one; **on frappe** (quelqu'un) someone's knocking; **on dit** they say, people say, it is said; **on m'a dit que...** I was told that...; **on me l'a donné** it was given to me, I was given it.

once [ɔ̃s] nf (mesure) & Fig ounce.

oncle [ɔ̃kl] nm uncle.

onctueux, -euse [ɔ̃ktɥø, -øz] a (liquide, crème) creamy; (manières, paroles) Fig smooth.

onde [ɔ̃d] nf (à la radio) & Phys wave; **grandes ondes** long wave; **ondes courtes/moyennes** short/medium wave; **sur les ondes** (sur l'antenne) on the radio.

ondée [ɔ̃de] nf (pluie) Litt (sudden) shower.

on-dit [ɔ̃di] nm inv rumour, hearsay.

ondoyer [ɔ̃dwaje] vi to undulate.

ondulation [ɔ̃dylɑsjɔ̃] nf undulation; (de cheveux) wave. ● **onduler** vi to undulate; (cheveux) to be wavy. ● **ondulé, -ée** a wavy.

onéreux, -euse [ɔnerø, -øz] a costly.

ongle [ɔ̃gl] nm (finger)nail.

onglet [ɔ̃glɛ] nm (entaille de canif etc) (nail) groove; **à onglets** (dictionnaire etc) with a thumb index.

ont [ɔ̃] voir avoir.

ONU [ɔny] nf abrév (Organisation des nations unies) UN.

onyx [ɔniks] nm (pierre semi-précieuse) onyx.

onze [ɔ̃z] a & nm eleven. ● **onzième** a & nmf eleventh.

opale [ɔpal] nf (pierre semi-précieuse) opal.

opaque [ɔpak] a opaque. ● **opacité** nf opacity.

OPA [ɔpea] nf abrév (offre publique d'achat) Com takeover bid.

opéra [ɔpera] nm (musique) opera; (édifice) opera house; **o. rock** rock opera. ● **opéra-comique** nm (pl opéras-comiques) comic opera. ● **opérette** nf operetta.

opérateur, -trice [ɔperatœr, -tris] nmf (de prise de vues) cameraman; (sur machine)

opération [ɔperɑsjɔ̃] *nf* (*action*) & *Méd Mil Math etc* operation; *Fin* deal; **o. à cœur ouvert** open-heart surgery; **faire une o. portes ouvertes** (*école etc*) to open one's doors to the public; **théâtre des opérations** *Mil* theatre of operations. ● **opérationnel, -elle** *a* operational. ● **opératoire** *a* (*de chirurgie*) (*méthode etc*) operative; **choc o.** post-operative shock; **bloc o.** operating *ou* surgical wing.

opérer [ɔpere] **1** *vt* (*en chirurgie*) (*personne, organe etc*) to operate on (**de** for); (*tumeur*) to operate on, remove; **se faire o.** to have an operation **‖** *vi* (*chirurgien*) to operate.
2 *vt* (*exécuter*) to carry out; (*choix*) to make **‖** *vi* (*agir*) to work, act; (*procéder*) to proceed **‖ s'opérer** *vpr* (*se produire*) to take place. ● **opérant, -ante** *a* (*efficace*) operative. ● **opéré, -ée** *nmf* patient (*operated on*).

ophtalmologue [ɔftalmɔlɔg] *nmf* opthalmologist.

opiner [ɔpine] *vi* **o.** (**de la tête**) to nod assent.

opiniâtre [ɔpinjɑtr] *a* stubborn, obstinate. ● **opiniâtreté** *nf* stubbornness, obstinacy.

opinion [ɔpinjɔ̃] *nf* opinion (**sur** about, on); **o. publique** public opinion; **mon opinion est faite** my mind is made up.

opium [ɔpjɔm] *nm* opium.

opportun, -une [ɔpɔrtœ̃, -yn] *a* opportune, timely. ● **opportunément** *adv* opportunely. ● **opportunisme** *nm* opportunism. ● **opportunité** *nf* timeliness.

opposé, -ée [ɔpoze] *a* (*direction etc*) opposite; (*opinions*) opposite, opposing; (*intérêts, équipe*) opposing; (*couleurs*) contrasting; **être o. à** to be opposed to **‖** *nm* **l'o.** the opposite (**de** of); **à l'o.** (*côté*) on the opposite side (**de** from, to); **à l'o. de** (*contrairement à*) contrary to.

opposer [ɔpoze] *vt* (*résistance, argument*) to put up (**à** against); (*équipes, rivaux*) to bring together, set against each other; (*couleurs etc*) to contrast; **o. qn à qn** to set s.o. against s.o.; **o. qch à qch** (*objet*) to place sth opposite sth; **match qui oppose...** match between...
‖ s'opposer *vpr* (*équipes*) to play against each other, confront each other; (*couleurs*) to contrast; **s'o. à** (*mesure, personne etc*) to be opposed to, oppose; **je m'y oppose** I'm opposed to it, I oppose. ● **opposant, -ante** *a* opposing **‖** *nmf* opponent.

opposition [ɔpozisjɔ̃] *nf* opposition (**à** to); **faire o. à** to oppose; (*chèque*) to stop; **par o. à** as opposed to.

oppresser [ɔprese] *vt* (*gêner*) to oppress. ● **oppressant, -ante** *a* oppressive. ● **oppresseur** *nm Pol* oppressor. ● **oppressif, -ive** *a* (*loi etc*) oppressive. ● **oppression** *nf* oppression. ● **opprimer** *vt* (*tyranniser*) to oppress. ● **opprimés** *nmpl* **les o.** the oppressed.

opter [ɔpte] *vi* **o. pour** to opt for.

opticien, -ienne [ɔptisjɛ̃, -jɛn] *nmf* optician.

optimisme [ɔptimism] *nm* optimism. ● **optimiste** *a* optimistic **‖** *nmf* optimist.

optimum [ɔptimɔm] *nm* & *a* optimum; **la température o.** the optimum temperature. ● **optimal, -e, -aux** *a* optimal.

option [ɔpsjɔ̃] *nf* (*choix*) option; (*chose*) optional extra; (*à l'école*) *Br* option, *Br* optional subject, *Am* elective (subject).

optique [ɔptik] *a* (*verre, fibres*) optical **‖** *nf* optics; (*aspect*) *Fig* perspective; **d'o.** (*instrument, appareil etc*) optical; **illusion d'o.** optical illusion.

opulent, -ente [ɔpylɑ̃, -ɑ̃t] *a* opulent. ● **opulence** *nf* opulence.

or [ɔr] **1** *nm* gold; **montre/chaîne/etc en or** gold watch/chain/etc; **règle/âge/cheveux d'or** golden rule/age/hair; **cœur d'or** heart of gold; **mine d'or** goldmine; (*trésor*) *Fig* goldmine; **affaire en or** (*achat*) bargain; (*commerce*) *Fig* goldmine; **or noir** (*pétrole*) *Fig* black gold. **2** *conj* (*cependant*) now, well.

oracle [ɔrakl] *nm* oracle.

orage [ɔraʒ] *nm* (thunder)storm. ● **orageux, -euse** *a* stormy.

oraison [ɔrɛzɔ̃] *nf* prayer; **o. funèbre** funeral oration.

oral, -e, -aux [ɔral, -o] *a* oral **‖** *nm* (*examen scolaire ou universitaire*) oral.

orange [ɔrɑ̃ʒ] *nf* (*fruit*) orange; **o. pressée** (fresh) orange juice **‖** *a* & *nm inv* (*couleur*) orange; **carte o.** monthly *ou* weekly season ticket (*for Paris métro and buses*). ● **orangeade** *nf* orangeade. ● **orangé, -ée** *a* & *nm* (*couleur*) orange. ● **oranger** *nm* orange tree.

orang-outan(g) [ɔrɑ̃utɑ̃] *nm* (*pl* **orangs-outan(g)s**) orang-outang.

orateur [ɔratœr] *nm* speaker, orator.

orbite [ɔrbit] *nf* (*d'astre etc*) & *Fig* orbit; (*d'œil*) socket; **mettre sur o.** (*fusée etc*) to put into orbit. ● **orbital, -e, -aux** *a* **station/etc orbitale** space station/etc.

orchestre [ɔrkɛstr] *nm* (*classique*) orchestra; (*de jazz*) band; (*places*) *Théâtre Br* stalls, *Am* orchestra. ● **orchestrer** *vt* (*organiser*) & *Mus* to orchestrate.

orchidée [ɔrkide] *nf* orchid.

ordinaire [ɔrdinɛr] *a* (*habituel, normal*) ordinary, *Am* regular; (*médiocre*) ordinary, average; **d'o., à l'o.** usually; **comme d'o.**, **comme à l'o.** as usual; **de l'essence o.** *Br* two-star (petrol), *Am* regular. ● **ordinairement** *adv* usually.

ordinal, -e, -aux [ɔrdinal, -o] *a* (*nombre*) ordinal.

ordinateur [ɔrdinatœr] *nm* computer; **o. personnel** personal computer; **o. portable** lap-top *ou* portable computer.

ordination [ɔrdinasjɔ̃] *nf Rel* ordination.

ordonnance [ɔrdɔnɑ̃s] *nf* **1** (*de médecin*) prescription. **2** (*de juge*) order, ruling. **3** (*disposition*) arrangement. **4** (*soldat*) orderly.

ordonner [ɔrdɔne] *vt* **1** (*enjoindre*) to order (**que** (+ *sub*) that); **o. à qn de faire** to order s.o. to do. **2** (*agencer*) to arrange, order. **3** (*médicament etc*) to prescribe. **4** (*prêtre*) to ordain; **il a été ordonné prêtre** he has been ordained (as) a priest. ●**ordonné, -ée** a (*personne, maison etc*) tidy, orderly.

ordre [ɔrdr] *nm* (*commandement, classement, structure etc*) order; (*absence de désordre*) tidiness (*of room, person etc*); **en o.** (*chambre etc*) tidy; **mettre en o., mettre de l'o. dans** to tidy (up); **jusqu'à nouvel o.** until further notice; **de l'o. de** (*environ*) of the order of; **du même o.** of the same order, similar; **de premier o.** first-rate; **à l'o. du jour** (*au programme*) on the agenda; (*d'actualité*) of topical interest; **par o. d'âge** in order of age; **les forces de l'o.** the police; **l'o. public** law and order; **assurer le maintien de l'o.** to maintain order; **entrer dans les orders** *Rel* to take holy orders; **donnez-moi un o. de grandeur** give me a rough estimate (*of price etc*); **à vos ordres!** *Mil* yes sir!

ordures [ɔrdyr] *nfpl* (*déchets*) *Br* rubbish, *Am* garbage; **mettre qch aux o.** to throw sth out (in the *Br* rubbish *ou Am* garbage). ●**ordurier, -ière** a (*plaisanterie etc*) lewd.

oreille [ɔrɛj] *nf* ear; **faire la sourde o.** to take no notice, refuse to listen, turn a deaf ear; **être tout oreilles** to be all ears; **casser les oreilles à qn** to deafen s.o.; **mettre la puce à l'o. de qn** to make s.o. suspicious.

oreiller [ɔreje] *nm* pillow.

oreillons [ɔrɛjɔ̃] *nmpl* (*maladie*) mumps.

ores et déjà (d') [dɔrzedeʒa] *adv* henceforth.

orfèvre [ɔrfɛvr] *nm* goldsmith, silversmith. ●**orfèvrerie** *nf* (*magasin*) goldsmith's *ou* silversmith's shop; (*objets*) gold *ou* silver plate.

organe [ɔrgan] *nm* *Anat & Fig* organ; (*porte-parole*) mouthpiece. ●**organique** a organic. ●**organisme** *nm* **1** (*corps*) body; *Anat Biol* organism. **2** (*bureaux etc*) organization.

organisateur, -trice [ɔrganizatœr, -tris] *nmf* organizer.

organisation [ɔrganizasjɔ̃] *nf* (*arrangement, association*) organization.

organiser [ɔrganize] *vt* to organize ▮ **s'organiser** *vpr* to organize oneself, get organized. ●**organisé, -ée** a (*esprit, groupe etc*) organized. ●**organiseur** *nm* (*agenda*) o. Filofax®.

organiste [ɔrganist] *nmf Mus* organist.

orgasme [ɔrgasm] *nm* orgasm.

orge [ɔrʒ] *nf* barley.

orgie [ɔrʒi] *nf* orgy.

orgue [ɔrg] *nm* (*instrument de musique*) organ; **o. de Barbarie** barrel organ ▮ *nfpl* **orgues** organ; **grandes orgues** great organ.

orgueil [ɔrgœj] *nm* pride. ●**orgueilleux, -euse** a proud.

orient [ɔrjɑ̃] *nm* **l'O.** the Orient, the East; **Moyen-O., Proche-O.** Middle East; **Extrême-O.** Far East. ●**oriental, -e, -aux** a (*côte, pays etc*) eastern; (*du Japon, de la Chine*) far-eastern, oriental ▮ *nmf* **O., Orientale** Oriental.

orientable [ɔrjɑ̃tabl] a (*lampe etc*)

adjustable, flexible; (*bras de machine*) movable.

orientation [ɔrjɑ̃tasjɔ̃] *nf* direction; (*action*) positioning, directing; (*de maison*) aspect, orientation; (*tendance politique, littéraire etc*) trend; **o. professionnelle** careers' advice, vocational guidance; **sens de l'o.** sense of direction.

orienter [ɔrjɑ̃te] *vt* (*lampe, antenne etc*) to position, direct; (*voyageur, élève etc*) to direct (**vers** towards); (*maison*) *Br* to orientate, *Am* orient ▮ **s'orienter** *vpr* to find one's bearings *ou* direction; **s'o. vers** (*carrière etc*) to move towards, take a direction towards. ●**orienté, -ée** a (*film etc*) slanted; **o. à l'ouest** (*appartement etc*) facing west.

orifice [ɔrifis] *nm* opening, orifice.

originaire [ɔriʒinɛr] a **être o. de** (*natif*) to be a native of.

original, -e, -aux [ɔriʒinal, -o] **1** a (*idée, artiste, version etc*) original ▮ *nm* (*texte, tableau etc*) original. **2** a & *nmf* (*bizarre*) eccentric. ●**originalité** *nf* originality; (*étrangeté*) eccentricity.

origine [ɔriʒin] *nf* origin; **à l'o.** originally; **d'o.** (*pneu etc*) original; **pays d'o.** country of origin. ●**originel, -elle** a (*sens, péché, habitant etc*) original.

orme [ɔrm] *nm* (*arbre, bois*) elm.

ornement [ɔrnəmɑ̃] *nm* ornament. ●**ornemental, -e, -aux** a ornamental. ●**ornementation** *nf* ornamentation. ●**ornementé, -ée** a adorned, ornamented (**de** with). ●**orner** [ɔrne] *vt* to decorate, adorn (**de** with). ●**orné, -ée** a (*syle etc*) ornate.

ornière [ɔrnjɛr] *nf* (*sillon*) rut; **sortir de l'o.** (*de la routine*) *Litt* to get out of the rut.

orphelin, -ine [ɔrfəlɛ̃, -in] *nmf* orphan ▮ a orphaned. ●**orphelinat** *nm* orphanage.

ORSEC [ɔrsɛk] *abrév* (*Organisation des secours*) **plan O.** programme of response to major disasters via the emergency services.

orteil [ɔrtɛj] *nm* toe; **gros o.** big toe.

orthodoxe [ɔrtɔdɔks] a orthodox ▮ *nmpl* **les orthodoxes** the orthodox. ●**orthodoxie** *nf* orthodoxy.

orthographe [ɔrtɔgraf] *nf* spelling. ●**orthographique** a (*règles etc*) spelling. ●**orthographier** *vt* to spell.

orthopédie [ɔrtɔpedi] *nf* orthop(a)edics.

ortie [ɔrti] *nf* nettle.

os [ɔs, *pl* o *ou* ɔs] *nm* bone; **être trempé jusqu'aux os** to be soaked to the skin; **on lui voit les os** he's all skin and bone; **nous n'y ferons pas de vieux os** (*dans un endroit*) we won't stay there long; **tomber sur un os** (*difficulté*) *Fam* to hit a snag.

OS [ɔɛs] *nm abrév* = **ouvrier spécialisé**.

oscar [ɔskar] *nm* (*récompense cinématographique*) Oscar.

osciller [ɔsile] *vi Tech* to oscillate; (*se balancer*) to swing, sway; (*pendule*) to swing; (*hésiter*) to waver; (*varier*) to fluctuate (**entre** between); (*flamme*) to flicker. ●**oscillation** *nf Tech* oscillation; (*de l'opinion*) fluctuation.

oseille [ozɛj] *nf* **1** (*plante potagère*) sorrel. **2** (*argent*) *Fam* dough.

oser [oze] *vti* to dare; **o. faire qch** to dare (to) do sth. ●**osé, -ée** *a* bold, daring.

osier [ozje] *nm* wicker; **panier d'o.** wicker basket.

ossature [ɔsatyr] *nf* (*du corps*) frame; (*de bâtiment*) & *Fig* framework. ●**osselets** *nmpl* (*jeu*) jacks, *Br* knucklebones. ●**ossements** *nmpl* (*de cadavres*) bones.

osseux, -euse [ɔsø, -øz] *a* (*maigre*) bony; **tissu**/*etc* **o.** bone tissue/*etc*.

ostensible [ɔstɑ̃sibl] *a* conspicuous. ●**ostensiblement** [-əmɑ̃] *adv* conspicuously.

ostentation [ɔstɑ̃tɑsjɔ̃] *nf* ostentation. ●**ostentatoire** *a* ostentatious.

ostréiculteur, -trice [ɔstreikyltœr, -tris] *nmf* oyster farmer.

otage [ɔtaʒ] *nm* hostage; **prendre qn en o.** to take s.o. hostage.

OTAN [ɔtɑ̃] *nf abrév* (*Organisation du traité de l'Atlantique Nord*) NATO.

otarie [ɔtari] *nf* (*animal*) sea lion.

ôter [ote] *vt* to take away, remove (**à qn** from s.o.); (*vêtement*) to take off, remove; (*déduire*) to take (away); **ôte-toi de là!** *Fam* get out of the way!

otite [ɔtit] *nf* ear infection.

oto-rhino [ɔtorino] *nmf* (*médecin*) *Fam* ear, nose and throat specialist.

ou [u] *conj* or; **ou bien** or else; **ou elle ou moi** either her or me; **pour ou contre nous** for or against us.

où [u] *adv & pron* where; **le jour où** the day when, the day on which; **la table où** the table on which; **l'état où** the condition in which; **par où?** which way?; **d'où?** where from?; **d'où ma surprise**/*etc* hence my surprise/*etc*; **le pays d'où** the country from which; **où qu'il soit** wherever he may be.

ouate [wat] *nf* (*pour pansement*) *Br* cotton wool, *Am* absorbent cotton.

oubli [ubli] *nm* (*défaut*) forgetfulness; **l'o. de qch** forgetting sth; **un o.** a lapse of memory; (*dans une liste etc*) an oversight; **tomber dans l'o.** to fall into oblivion.

oublier [ublije] *vt* to forget (**de faire** to do); (*faute*) to overlook ▮ **s'oublier** *vpr* (*traditions etc*) to be forgotten; (*personne*) *Fig* to forget oneself.

oubliettes [ublijɛt] *nfpl* (*de château*) dungeon; **être tombé aux o.** (*personne, projet etc*) to be long forgotten, have sunk into oblivion.

oublieux, -euse [ublijø, -øz] *a* forgetful (**de** of).

ouest [wɛst] *nm* west; **à l'o.** in the west; (*direction*) (to the) west (**de** of); **d'o.** (*vent*) west(erly); **de l'o.** western; **l'Europe de l'O.** Western Europe ▮ *a inv* (*côte*) west(ern).

ouf! [uf] *int* (*soulagement*) what a relief!, phew!

Ouganda [ugɑ̃da] *nm* Uganda.

oui [wi] *adv & nm inv* yes; **o.!** yes!; (**ah,**) **ça**

o.! oh yes (indeed!); **les o.** (*votes*) the ayes; **tu viens, o. ou non?** are you coming or aren't you?; **je crois que o.** I think so; **si o.** if so; **pour un o. pour un non** (*battre qn etc*) for the slightest thing *ou* reason.

ouï-dire [widir] *nm inv* hearsay; **par o.-dire** by hearsay.

ouïe¹ [wi] *nf* hearing; **être tout o.** *Hum* to be all ears.

ouïe²! [uj] *int* ouch!

ouïes [wi] *nfpl* (*de poisson*) gills.

ouille! [uj] *int* ouch!

ouragan [uragɑ̃] *nm* hurricane.

ourler [urle] *vt* to hem. ●**ourlet** *nm* hem.

ours [urs] *nm* bear; **o. blanc/gris** polar/grizzly bear; **o. (mal léché)** *Péj* uncouth lout, brute. ●**ourse** *nf* she-bear; **la Grande O.** (*étoiles*) *Br* the Plough, *Am* the Big Dipper.

oursin [ursɛ̃] *nm* (*animal*) sea urchin.

ouste! [ust] *int* *Fam* scram!

out [ˈaut] *a inv* (*dépassé*) *Fam* past it, out of it.

outil [uti] *nm* tool. ●**outiller** *vt* to equip. ●**outillage** *nm* tools; (*d'une usine*) equipment.

outrage [utraʒ] *nm* insult (**à** to). **o. à magistrat** *Jur* contempt (of court). ●**outrager** *vt* to insult, offend. ●**outrageant, -ante** *a* insulting, offensive.

outrance [utrɑ̃s] *nf* (*excès*) excess; **à o.** (*travailler etc*) to excess; **guerre à o.** all-out war. ●**outrancier, -ière** *a* excessive.

outre [utr] *prép* besides ▮ *adv* **en o.** besides, moreover; **o. mesure** inordinately; **passer o.** to take no notice (**à** of). ●**outre-Manche** *adv* across the Channel. ●**outre-mer** *adv* overseas; **d'o.-mer** (*marché etc*) overseas; **territoires d'o.-mer** overseas territories.

outrepasser [utrəpase] *vt* (*limite etc*) to go beyond, exceed.

outrer [utre] *vt* to exaggerate, overdo; **o. qn** (*indigner*) to outrage s.o. ●**outré, -ée** *a* (*révolté*) outraged; (*excessif*) exaggerated.

outsider [awtsajdœr] *nm* (*cheval etc*) outsider.

ouvert, -erte [uvɛr, -ɛrt] *pp de* **ouvrir** ▮ *a* open; (*robinet, gaz etc*) on; **à bras ouverts** with open arms. ●**ouvertement** [-əmɑ̃] *adv* openly. ●**ouverture** *nf* opening; (*trou*) hole; (*avance*) & *Mus* overture; (*d'objectif d'appareil photo*) aperture; **o. d'esprit** open-mindedness.

ouvrable [uvrabl] *a* **jour o.** working *ou* *Am* work day.

ouvrage [uvraʒ] *nm* (*travail, livre, objet*) work; (*couture*) (needle)work; **un o.** (*travail*) a piece of work. ●**ouvragé, -ée** *a* (*bijou etc*) finely worked.

ouvreuse [uvrøz] *nf* (*de cinéma*) usherette.

ouvrier, -ière [uvrije, -jɛr] *nmf* worker; **o. qualifié/spécialisé** skilled/semiskilled worker; **o. agricole** farm labourer *ou* worker ▮ *a* (*législation etc*) industrial; (*quartier, origine etc*) working-class; **classe ouvrière** working class.

ouvrir* [uvrir] *vt* to open (up); (*gaz, radio*

etc) to turn on, switch on; (*inaugurer*) to open; (*hostilités*) to begin; (*appétit*) to whet; (*liste, procession*) to head ▮ *vi* to open; (*ouvrir la porte*) to open (up) ▮ **s'ouvrir** *vpr* (*porte, boîte, fleur etc*) to open (up); **s'o. la jambe** to cut one's leg open; **s'o. à qn, o. son cœur à qn** *Fig* to open one's heart to s.o., open up to s.o. (**de qch** about sth). ●**ouvre-boîte** *nm Br* tin opener, *Am* can-opener. ●**ouvre-bouteille** *nm* bottle opener.

ovaire [ɔvɛr] *nm Anat* ovary.

ovale [ɔval] *a & nm* oval.

ovation [ɔvasjɔ̃] *nf* (standing) ovation.

overdose [ɔvœrdoz] *nf* overdose (of drugs).

OVNI [ɔvni] *nm abrév* (*objet volant non identifié*) UFO.

oxyde [ɔksid] *nm Ch* oxide; **o. de carbone** carbon monoxide. ●**oxyder** *vt*, **s'oxyder** *vpr* to oxidize.

oxygène [ɔksiʒɛn] *nm* oxygen; **masque/tente/etc à o.** oxygen mask/tent/etc. ●**oxygéner** *vt* (*cheveux*) to bleach ▮ **s'oxygéner** *vpr Fam* to breathe *ou* get some fresh air. ●**oxygéné, -ée** *a* **eau oxygénée** (hydrogen) peroxide; **cheveux blonds oxygénés** peroxide blonde hair, bleached hair.

ozone [ozon] *nm Ch* ozone; **couche d'o.** ozone layer.

P

P, p [pe] *nm* P, p.

PAC [pak] *nf abrév (politique agricole commune)* CAP.

pachyderme [paʃidɛrm] *nm* elephant.

pacifier [pasifje] *vt* to pacify. ● **pacification** *nf* pacification.

pacifique [pasifik] **1** *a (manifestation etc)* peaceful; *(personne, peuple)* peace-loving. **2** *a (côte etc)* Pacific; **Océan P.** Pacific Ocean ▮ *nm* **le P.** the Pacific.

pacifiste [pasifist] *a & nmf* pacifist.

pack [pak] *nm (de lait etc)* carton.

pacotille [pakɔtij] *nf (camelote)* trash; **bijou de p.** trashy *ou* cheap piece of *Br* jewellery *ou Am* jewelry.

pacte [pakt] *nm* pact. ● **pactiser** *vi* **p. avec qn** to be in league with s.o.

pactole [paktɔl] *nm Fig* gold mine.

paf! [paf] **1** *int* bang!, crash! **2** *a inv (ivre) Fam* plastered, *Br* sozzled.

pagaie [pagɛ] *nf* paddle. ● **pagayer** *vi (ramer)* to paddle.

pagaïe, pagaille [pagaj] *nf (désordre) Fam* mess, shambles; **en p.** *Fam* in a mess; **avoir des livres/etc en p.** *Fam* to have loads *ou* heaps of books/etc.

paganisme [paganism] *nm* paganism.

page [paʒ] **1** *nf (de livre etc)* page; **mise en p.** page make-up *ou* layout; **p. de garde** flyleaf; **les pages jaunes (de l'annuaire)** the yellow pages *(in phone book)*; **p. de publicité** *Radio* commercial break; **p. précédente/suivante** *Ordinat* page up/down; **à la p.** *(personne) Fig* up-to-date. **2** *nm (à la cour) Hist* page (boy).

page-écran [paʒekrã] *nf (pl pages-écrans) Ordinat* screen, screenful.

paginer [paʒine] *vt* to paginate. ● **pagination** *nf* pagination.

pagne [paɲ] *nm* loincloth.

pagode [pagɔd] *nf* pagoda.

paie [pɛ] *nf* pay, wages. ● **paiement** *nm* payment.

païen, -enne [pajɛ̃, -ɛn] *a & nmf* pagan, heathen.

paillasse [pajas] *nf* **1** *(matelas)* straw mattress. **2** *(d'un évier)* draining board.

paillasson [pajasɔ̃] *nm* (door)mat.

paille [paj] *nf* straw; *(pour boire)* (drinking) straw; **homme de p.** *Fig* stooge, man of straw; **tirer à la courte p.** to draw lots; **sur la p.** *Fig* penniless; **feu de p.** *Fig* flash in the pan.

paillette [pajɛt] *nf (d'habit)* sequin; **paillettes** *(de savon, lessive)* flakes; *(d'or)* gold dust. ● **pailleté, -ée** *a (robe etc)* sequined.

pain [pɛ̃] *nm* bread; **un p.** a loaf (of bread); **petit p.** roll; **p. grillé** toast; **p. complet** wholemeal bread; **p. de mie** sandwich loaf; **p. de savon/de cire** bar of soap/wax; **p. de seigle** rye bread; **p. de sucre** sugar loaf; **avoir du p. sur la planche** *(travail) Fig* to have a lot on one's plate.

pair, -e [pɛr] **1** *a (numéro)* even. **2** *nm (personne)* peer; **hors p.** unrivalled, without equal; **aller de p.** to go hand in hand *(avec* with); **au p.** *(étudiante etc)* au pair; **travailler au p.** to work as an au pair.

paire [pɛr] *nf* pair (de of).

paisible [pezibl] *a (vie, endroit etc)* peaceful; *(caractère, personne)* quiet, placid. ● **paisiblement** [-əmã] *adv* peacefully.

paître* [pɛtr] *vi* to graze; **envoyer qn p.** *Fam* to send s.o. packing.

paix [pɛ] *nf* peace; *(traité)* peace treaty; **en p.** *(vivre, laisser etc)* in peace *(avec* with); **être en p. avec** *(pays, sa conscience etc)* to be at peace with; **signer la p. avec qn** to sign a peace treaty with s.o.; **avoir la p.** to have (some) peace and quiet.

Pakistan [pakistã] *nm* Pakistan. ● **pakistanais, -aise** *a* Pakistani ▮ *nmf* **P., Pakistanaise** Pakistani.

palabres [palabr] *nmpl* palaver, long-winded discussions.

palace [palas] *nm* luxury hotel.

palais [palɛ] *nm* **1** *(château)* palace; **P. de justice** law courts; **p. des sports** sports stadium *ou* centre. **2** *Anat* palate.

palan [palã] *nm (de navire etc)* hoist.

pâle [pɑl] *a* pale; **être p. comme un linge** to be as white as a sheet; **se faire porter p.** *Fam* to report sick.

Palestine [palɛstin] *nf* Palestine. ● **palestinien, -ienne** *a* Palestinian ▮ *nmf* **P., Palestinienne** Palestinian.

palet [palɛ] *nm (hockey sur glace)* puck.

paletot [palto] *nm (manteau)* (short) overcoat; *(gilet) Fam* (knitted) cardigan; **ils nous sont tombés sur le p.** *Fam* they attacked us, they jumped *ou* fell on us.

palette [palɛt] *nf* **1** *(de peintre)* palette. **2** *(support pour marchandises)* pallet.

pâleur [pɑlœr] *nf* paleness, pallor. ● **pâlir** *vi* to turn *ou* go pale (de with).

palier [palje] *nm* **1** *(d'escalier)* landing; **être voisins de p.** to live on the same floor. **2** *(niveau)* level; *(phase de stabilité)* plateau; **par paliers** *(étapes)* in stages.

palissade [palisad] *nf* fence (of stakes).

pallier [palje] *vt (difficultés etc)* to alleviate. ● **palliatif** *nm* palliative.

palmarès [palmarɛs] *nm* prize list; (*des chansons*) hit-parade.

palme [palm] *nf* **1** palm (leaf); (*symbole*) *Fig* palm. **2** (*de nageur*) flipper. ● **palmier** *nm* palm (tree).

palmé, -ée [palme] *a* (*patte, pied*) webbed.

palombe [palɔ̃b] *nf* wood pigeon.

pâlot, -otte [pɑlo, -ɔt] *a Fam* pale.

palourde [palurd] *nf* (*mollusque*) clam.

palper [palpe] *vt* to feel, finger. ● **palpable** *a* tangible.

palpiter [palpite] *vi* (*cœur*) to throb, palpitate; (*frémir*) (*animal etc*) to quiver. ● **palpitant, -ante** *a* (*film etc*) thrilling. ● **palpitations** *nfpl* (*du cœur*) palpitations; (*d'animal etc*) quivering.

pâmer (se) [səpɑme] *vpr* **se p.** de (*joie etc*) to be ecstatic with; (*effroi etc*) to be *Br* paralysed *ou Am* paralyzed with.

pamphlet [pɑ̃flɛ] *nm* lampoon.

pamplemousse [pɑ̃pləmus] *nm* grapefruit.

pan [pɑ̃] **1** *nm* (*de chemise*) tail; (*de ciel*) patch; **p. de mur** section of wall. **2** *int* bang!

pan- [pɑ̃, pan] *préf* Pan-.

panacée [panase] *nf* panacea.

panachage [panaʃaʒ] *nm* **p. électoral** = splitting one's vote between candidates from different parties.

panache [panaʃ] *nm* (*plume*) plume; **avoir du p.** (*fière allure*) to have panache; **un p. de fumée** a plume of smoke.

panaché, -ée [panaʃe] **1** *a* (*bigarré, hétéroclite*) motley. **2** *a & nm* (*demi*) **p.** *Br* shandy (*beer and lemonade*).

Panama [panama] *nm* Panama.

pan-bagnat [pɑ̃baɲa] *nm* (*pl* **pans-bagnats**) large round sandwich filled with lettuce, tomatoes, egg etc.

pancarte [pɑ̃kart] *nf* sign, notice; (*de manifestant*) placard.

pancréas [pɑ̃kreas] *nm Anat* pancreas.

panda [pɑ̃da] *nm* (*animal*) panda.

pané, -ée [pane] *a* (*poisson etc*) breaded.

panier [panje] *nm* (*ustensile, contenu*) basket; **p. à linge** *Br* linen basket, *Am* (clothes) hamper; **p. à salade** (*ustensile*) salad basket; (*voiture*) *Fam Br* police van, *Br* prison van, *Am* patrol wagon; **marquer un p.** *Sport* to score a basket; **jeter qch au p.** to throw sth into the (wastepaper) basket. ● **panier-repas** *nm* (*pl* **paniers-repas**) *Br* packed lunch, *Am* (brown-bag) lunch.

panique [panik] *nf* panic; **pris de p.** panic-stricken ‖ *a* **peur p.** panic fear. ● **paniquer** *vi* to panic. ● **paniqué, -ée** *a* panic-stricken.

panne [pan] *nf* breakdown; **tomber en p.** to break down; **être en p.** to have broken down; **p. d'électricité** blackout, *Br* power cut; **tomber en p. sèche** to run out of *Br* petrol *ou Am* gas; **trouver la p.** to locate the cause of the trouble, find the problem; **il m'a fait le coup de la p.** he pretended we'd run out of *Br* petrol *ou Am* gas.

panneau, -x [pano] *nm* **1** (*écriteau*) sign, notice, board; **p. (de signalisation)** road *ou* traffic sign; **p. (d'affichage)** (*publicité*) *Br* hoarding, *Am* billboard. **2** (*de porte etc*) panel; **tomber dans le p.** *Fam* to let oneself be tricked *ou Br* fall in, fall for it. ● **panonceau, -x** *nm* (*enseigne*) sign.

panoplie [panɔpli] *nf* **1** (*jouet*) outfit. **2** (*gamme*) (wide) range, assortment.

panorama [panɔrama] *nm* view, panorama. ● **panoramique** *a* panoramic; **écran p.** *Cinéma* wide screen.

panse [pɑ̃s] *nf Fam* paunch, belly. ● **pansu, -ue** *a* potbellied.

panser [pɑ̃se] *vt* (*main, plaie etc*) to dress, bandage; (*personne*) to dress the wound(s) of, bandage (up); (*cheval*) to groom. ● **pansement** *nm* (*bande*) dressing, bandage; **p. adhésif** *Br* sticking plaster, *Am* Band-Aid®; **refaire le p.** to change the dressing.

pantalon [pɑ̃talɔ̃] *nm* (pair of) *Br* trousers *ou Am* pants; **deux pantalons** two pairs of *Br* trousers *ou Am* pants; **en p.** *Br* in trousers, *Am* in pants.

pantelant, -ante [pɑ̃tlɑ̃, -ɑ̃t] *a* gasping (for breath).

panthère [pɑ̃tɛr] *nf* (*animal*) panther.

pantin [pɑ̃tɛ̃] *nm* (*jouet*) puppet, jumping jack; (*personne*) *Péj* puppet.

pantois, -oise [pɑ̃twa, -waz] *a* flabbergasted; **elle en est restée pantoise** she was flabbergasted.

pantoufle [pɑ̃tufl] *nf* slipper. ● **pantouflard, -arde** *nmf Fam* stay-at-home, *Am* homebody.

PAO [peao] *nf abrév* (*publication assistée par ordinateur*) DTP.

paon [pɑ̃] *nm* peacock.

papa [papa] *nm* dad(dy); **fils à p.** *Péj* rich man's son, daddy's boy; **de p.** (*désuet*) *Fam Péj* outdated.

papaye [papaj] *nf* (*fruit*) pawpaw, papaya.

pape [pap] *nm* pope. ● **papauté** *nf* papacy.

paperasse(s) [papras] *nf(pl) Péj* papers. ● **paperasserie** *nf Péj* (official) papers; (*procédure*) red tape.

papeterie [papetri] *nf* (*magasin*) stationer's shop; (*articles*) stationery; (*fabrique*) paper mill. ● **papetier, -ière** *nmf* stationer.

papi [papi] *nm* grand(d)ad.

papier [papje] *nm* (*matière*) paper; **un p.** (*feuille*) a sheet *ou* piece of paper; (*formulaire*) a form; (*dans un journal*) an article; **sac/etc en p.** paper bag/etc; **papiers (d'identité)** (identity) papers; **p. hygiénique** toilet paper; **p. à lettres** writing paper; **du p. journal** (some) newspaper; **p. peint** wallpaper; **p. de verre** sandpaper; **être dans les petits papiers de qn** to be in s.o.'s good books.

papillon [papijɔ̃] *nm* **1** (*insecte*) butterfly; (*écrou*) *Br* butterfly nut, *Am* wing nut; **p. (de nuit)** moth. **2** (*contravention*) *Fam* (parking) ticket.

papoter [papɔte] *vi* to prattle. ● **papotage(s)** *nm(pl)* prattle.

paprika [paprika] *nm* (*condiment*) paprika.

papy [papi] *nm* grand(d)ad.
Pâque [pɑk] *nf* la **P.** *Rel* Passover.
paquebot [pakbo] *nm* (*ocean*) liner.
pâquerette [pakrɛt] *nf* daisy.
Pâques [pɑk] *nm sing* & *nfpl* Easter.
paquet [pakɛ] *nm* (*de bonbons, sucre etc*)
packet; (*colis*) package; (*de cigarettes*) pack,
Br packet; (*de cartes*) *Br* pack, deck; y
mettre le p. (*toute son énergie*) *Fam* to pull
out all the stops.
par [par] *prép* **1** (*agent, manière, moyen*) by;
choisi/frappé/etc p. chosen/hit/*etc* by; **p. mer**
by sea; **p. le train** by train; **p. le travail/la**
force/etc by *ou* through work/force/*etc*; ap-
prendre p. un ami to learn from *ou* through
a friend; **commencer p. qch** (*récit etc*) to begin with sth; **p. erreur** by mistake; **p. chance**
fortunately, by a stroke of luck; **p. mal-**
chance unfortunately, as ill luck would have
it.
2 (*lieu*) through; **p. la porte/le tunnel/etc**
through *ou* by the door/tunnel/*etc*; jeter/
regarder **p. la fenêtre** to throw/look out (of)
the window; **p. ici/là** (*aller*) this/that way;
(*habiter*) around here/there; **p. les rues**
through the streets.
3 (*motif*) out of, from; **p. pitié/respect/etc** out
of *ou* from pity/respect/*etc*.
4 (*temps*) on; in; **p. un jour d'hiver/etc** on a
winter's day/*etc*; **p. ce froid** in this cold; **p. le**
passé in the past.
5 (*distributif*) **dix fois p. an/mois/etc** ten times
a *ou* per year/month/*etc*; **cent francs p.**
personne a hundred francs a *ou* per person;
deux p. deux two by two; **p. deux fois** twice.
6 (*trop*) **p. trop aimable/etc** far too kind/*etc*.
para [para] *nm* (*soldat*) *Fam* para(trooper).
para- [para] *préf* para-.
parabole [parabɔl] *nf* **1** (*récit*) parable. **2**
Math parabola.
parabolique [parabɔlik] *a* **antenne p.** satellite dish.
parachever [paraʃve] *vt* to perfect.
parachute [paraʃyt] *nm* parachute. ● para-
chuter *vt* to parachute; (*nommer*) *Fam* to
pitchfork (*s.o.*) (**à un poste** into a job).
● **parachutisme** *nm* parachute jumping.
● **parachutiste** *nmf* parachutist; (*soldat*)
paratrooper.
parade [parad] *nf* **1** (*spectacle, défilé mili-*
taire) parade; (*étalage*) show, parade. **2** *Boxe*
Escrime parry; (*riposte*) *Fig* reply. ● **parader**
vi to parade, show off.
paradis [paradi] *nm* heaven, paradise.
● **paradisiaque** *a* (*endroit etc*) *Fig* heavenly.
paradoxe [paradɔks] *nm* paradox. ● para-
doxal, -e, -aux *a* paradoxical. ● **paradoxale-**
ment *adv* paradoxically.
parafe [paraf] *nm* = **paraphe.** ● **parafer** *vt* =
parapher.
paraffine [parafin] *nf* paraffin (wax).
parages [paraʒ] *nmpl* region, area (**de** of);
dans ces p. in these parts.
paragraphe [paragraf] *nm* paragraph.
Paraguay [paragwɛ] *nm* Paraguay.

paraître* [parɛtr] **1** *vi* (*sembler*) to seem,
look, appear; (*apparaître, se montrer*) to
appear ▮ *v imp* **il paraît qu'il va partir** it
appears *ou* seems (that) he's leaving; **à ce**
qu'il paraît apparently, it would seem. **2** *vi*
(*livre*) to come out, be published; **faire p.**
qch to bring out sth, publish sth.
parallèle [paralɛl] **1** *a* (*comparable*) & *Math*
parallel (**à** with, to); **il a deux vies parallèles**
(*séparées*) he has two separate lives; **le**
marché p. *Com* the unofficial *ou* black
market. **2** *nm* (*comparaison*) & *Géog*
parallel. ● **parallèlement** *adv* **p. à** parallel to.
paralyser [paralize] *vt Br* to paralyse, *Am*
paralyze. ● **paralysie** *nf* paralysis. ● **paralyti-**
que *a* & *nmf* paralytic.
paramédical, -e, -aux [paramedikal, -o] *a*
(*carrière etc*) paramedical.
paramètre [parametr] *nm* parameter.
paramilitaire [paramiliter] *a* (*organisation*
etc) paramilitary.
paranoïa [paranɔja] *nf* paranoia. ● **paranoïa-**
que *a* & *nmf* paranoid.
parapet [parapɛ] *nm* parapet.
paraphe [paraf] *nm* initials, signature;
(*traits*) flourish. ● **parapher** *vt* to initial, sign.
paraphrase [parafraz] *nf* paraphrase. ● **para-**
phraser *vt* to paraphrase.
parapluie [paraplɥi] *nm* umbrella.
parasite [parazit] *nm* (*personne, organisme*)
parasite; **parasites** (*à la radio*) interference ▮
a parasitic(al).
parasol [parasɔl] *nm* sunshade, parasol.
paratonnerre [paratɔner] *nm* lightning *Br*
conductor *ou* *Am* rod.
paravent [paravɑ̃] *nm* (folding) screen.
parc [park] *nm* **1** park; (*de château*) grounds;
p. d'attractions amusement park; **p. naturel**
nature reserve. **2** (*de bébé*) (play) pen; (*à*
moutons, à bétail) pen; **p.** (**de stationnement**)
Br car park, *Am* parking lot; **p. à huîtres**
oyster bed. **3 p. automobile** (*d'un pays*)
number of vehicles on the road.
parcelle [parsɛl] *nf* fragment, particle;
(*terrain*) plot; (*de vérité*) *Fig* grain.
parce que [pars(ə)] *conj* because.
parchemin [parʃəmɛ̃] *nm* parchment.
parcimonie [parsimɔni] *nf* **avec p.** parsimoniously. ● **parcimonieux, -euse** *a* parsimonious.
par-ci, par-là [parsiparla] *adv* here, there
and everywhere.
parcmètre [parkmetr] *nm* parking meter.
parcourir* [parkurir] *vt* (*région*) to travel all
over, tour, scour; (*distance*) to cover; (*texte*)
to glance through. ● **parcours** *nm* (*itinéraire*)
route; (*distance*) distance; (*voyage*) trip,
journey; **p. de golf** (*terrain*) golf course.
par-delà [pardəla] *voir* **delà.**
par-derrière [parderjɛr] *voir* **derrière.**
par-dessous [pardəsu] *prép* & *adv*
under(neath).
pardessus [pardəsy] *nm* overcoat.
par-dessus [pardəsy] *prép* & *adv* over (the
top of); **p.-dessus tout** above all; **en avoir**

p.-dessus la tête *Fam* to be completely fed up.
par-devant [pardəvã] *voir* devant.
pardon [pardɔ̃] *nm* forgiveness, pardon; **p.!** (*excusez-moi*) sorry!; **p.?** (*pour demander*) excuse me?, *Am* pardon me?; **demander p.** to apologize (à to). ● **pardonner** *vt* to forgive; **p. qch à qn/à qn d'avoir fait qch** to forgive s.o. for sth/for doing sth *ou* for having done sth. ● **pardonable** *a* forgivable.
pare-balles [parbal] *a inv* **gilet p.-balles** bulletproof *Br* jacket *ou Am* vest.
pare-brise [parbriz] *nm inv* (*de véhicule*) *Br* windscreen, *Am* windshield.
pare-chocs [parʃɔk] *nm inv* (*de véhicule*) bumper.
pare-feu [parfø] *nm inv* (*de cheminée*) fireguard.
pareil, -eille [parɛj] *a* similar; **p. à** the same as, similar to; **être pareils** to be the same, be similar *ou* alike; **un p. désordre/etc, un désordre/etc p.** such a mess/etc; **en p. cas** in such a case ▌ *adv Fam* the same ▌ *nmf* (*personne*) equal; **sans p.** unparalleled, unique; **il n'a pas son p. pour laver les carreaux** there's no one quite like him when it comes to cleaning windows; **rendre la pareille à qn** to treat s.o. the same way. ● **pareillement** *adv* in the same way; (*aussi*) likewise.
parement [parmã] *nm* (*de pierre, de vêtement*) facing.
parent, -ente [parã, -ãt] *nmf* relative, relation ▌ *nmpl* (*père et mère*) parents ▌ *a* related (de to). ● **parental, -e, -aux** *a* (*autorité etc*) parental; **congé p.** parental leave. ● **parenté** *nf* (*lien*) relationship; (*en sociologie*) kinship.
parenthèse [parãtɛz] *nf* (*signe*) *Br* bracket, *Am* parenthesis; (*digression*) digression; **entre parenthèses** *Br* in brackets, *Am* in parentheses.
paréo [pareo] *nm* (*vêtement de plage*) pareu, pareo.
parer [pare] **1** *vt* (*coup*) to parry, ward off ▌ *vi* **p. à** (*éventualité etc*) to be prepared for. **2** *vt* (*orner*) to adorn (de with).
paresse [parɛs] *nf* laziness, idleness. ● **paresser** *vi* to laze (about). ● **paresseux, -euse** *a* lazy, idle ▌ *nmf* lazy person, lazybones.
parfaire* [parfɛr] *vt* to perfect. ● **parfait, -aite** *a* perfect; **p.!** excellent! ▌ *nm Grammaire* perfect (tense). ● **parfaitement** *adv* perfectly; (*certainement*) certainly.
parfois [parfwa] *adv* sometimes.
parfum [parfœ̃] *nm* (*odeur*) fragrance, scent; (*goût*) flavour; (*liquide*) perfume, scent; **être au p.** *Fam* to be in the know.
parfumer [parfyme] *vt* to perfume, scent; (*glace, crème etc*) to flavour (à with) ▌ **se parfumer** *vpr* to put on perfume; (*habituellement*) to wear perfume. ● **parfumé, -ée** *a* (*savon, fleur, mouchoir*) scented; **p. au café/etc** coffee-/etc flavoured. ● **parfumerie** *nf* (*magasin*) perfume shop.
pari [pari] *nm* bet, *Litt* wager; **paris** (*sur les* chevaux*) betting, bets; **p. mutuel urbain** = *Br* the tote, *Am* pari-mutuel; **faire un p.** to make a bet; **tenir un p.** to take up a bet; **les paris sont ouverts** *Fig* it's anyone's guess. ● **parier** *vti* to bet (**sur** on, **que** that); **il y a fort à p. que...** the odds are that.... ● **parieur, -euse** *nmf* (*aux courses*) better, punter.
Paris [pari] *nm ou f* Paris. ● **parisien, -ienne** *a* (*accent etc*) Parisian; **la banlieue parisienne** the Paris suburbs ▌ *nmf* **P., Parisienne** Parisian.
parité [parite] *nf* parity.
parjure [parʒyr] *nm* perjury ▌ *nmf* perjurer. ● **se parjurer** *vpr* to perjure oneself.
parka [parka] *nm* parka.
parking [parkiŋ] *nm* (*lieu*) car park, *Am* parking lot; **'p. autorisé'** 'parking is permitted'.
par-là [parla] *adv voir* par-ci.
parlement [parləmã] *nm* parliament. ● **parlementaire** *a* parliamentary ▌ *nmf* member of parliament.
parlementer [parləmãte] *vi* (*négocier*) to negotiate, parley (**avec** with); **p. avec qn** (*discuter longuement*) *Fam* to have a long discussion with s.o.
parler [parle] *vi* to talk, speak (**de** about, of; **à** to); **tu parles!** (*je n'en crois pas un mot*) *Fam* you must be joking!; **sans p. de...** not to mention...; **p. par gestes** *Fig* to use sign language; **n'en parlons plus!** enough said!, let's forget it!; **faire p. un prisonnier/etc** to make a prisoner/etc talk ▌ *vt* (*langue*) to speak; **p. affaires/etc** to talk business/etc ▌ **se parler** *vpr* (*langue*) to be spoken; **ils ne se parlent plus** they're not speaking to each other, they're not on speaking terms ▌ *nm* speech; (*régional*) dialect. ● **parlant, -ante** *a* (*film*) talking; (*regard etc*) eloquent ▌ *adv* **professionnellement/etc p.** professionally/etc speaking. ● **parlé, -ée** *a* (*langue*) spoken.
parloir [parlwar] *nm* (*de couvent, prison*) visiting room.
parmi [parmi] *prép* among(st).
parodie [parɔdi] *nf* parody. ● **parodier** *vt* to parody.
paroi [parwa] *nf* wall; (*de maison*) inside wall; (*de rocher*) (rock) face.
paroisse [parwas] *nf* parish. ● **paroissial, -e, -aux** *a* **registre/salle/etc paroissial(e)** parish register/hall/etc. ● **paroissien, -ienne** *nmf* parishioner.
parole [parɔl] *nf* (*mot, promesse*) word; (*faculté, langage*) speech; **paroles** (*d'une chanson*) words, lyrics; **adresser la p. à qn** to speak to s.o.; **prendre la p.** to speak, make a speech; **demander la p.** to ask to speak; **perdre la p.** to lose one's tongue; **tenir sa p.** to keep one's word; **je te crois sur p.** I take your word for it; **libéré sur p.** *Jur* free(d) on parole; **ma p.!** my word!
paroxysme [parɔksism] *nm* (*de douleur etc*) height.
parpaing [parpɛ̃] *nm* concrete block, breeze-

block.

parquer [parke] vt (*bœufs*) to pen; (*gens*) Péj to herd together, confine; (*véhicule*) to park.

parquet [parkɛ] nm 1 (parquet) floor(ing). 2 Jur Public Prosecutor's office.

parrain [parɛ̃] nm Rel godfather; (*qui finance, dans un club etc*) sponsor. ●**parrainer** vt (*course etc*) to sponsor. ●**parrainage** nm sponsorship.

pars, part¹ [par] *voir* partir.

parsemer [parsəme] vt to strew, dot (de with). ●**parsemé, -ée** a p. de (*sol*) scattered ou strewn with.

part² [par] nf (*portion*) share, part; (*de gâteau*) portion; **prendre p.** à (*activité*) to take part in; (*la joie etc de qn*) to share; **d'e toutes parts** from ou on all sides; **de p. et d'autre** on both sides; **d'une p...., d'autre p.** on the one hand..., on the other hand; **d'autre p.** (*d'ailleurs*) moreover; **de p. en p.** right through; **de la p. de** (*provenance*) from; **c'est de la p. de qui?** (*au téléphone*) who's speaking?; **pour ma p.** as far as I'm concerned; **quelque p.** somewhere; **nulle p.** nowhere; **autre p.** somewhere else; **à p.** (*mettre, prendre*) aside; (*excepté*) apart from; (*séparément*) apart; (*personne*) different, not like the others; **un cas/une place/etc à p.** a separate ou special case/place/etc; **membre à p. entière** full member; **faire p. de qch à qn** to inform s.o. of sth.

partage [partaʒ] nm dividing (up), division; (*de gâteau, trésor etc*) sharing; (*distribution*) sharing out; (*sort*) Fig lot; **procéder au p. de** = partager; **donner qch à qn en p.** to bestow on s.o. ou give to s.o. as one's share ou lot.

partager [partaʒe] vt (*repas, frais, joie etc*) to share (avec with); (*diviser*) to divide (up); (*distribuer*) to share out ▌ **se partager** vpr (*bénéfices etc*) to share (between themselves etc); **se p. entre** to divide one's time between. ●**partagé, -ée** a (*avis etc*) divided; **p. entre** (*sentiments*) torn between.

partance (en) [ɑ̃partɑ̃s] adv (*train etc*) about to depart (**pour** for).

partant, -ante [partɑ̃, -ɑ̃t] 1 nm (*coureur, cheval etc*) starter ▌ 2 a **être p. pour qch/pour faire qch** Fam to be ready for sth/to do sth.

partenaire [partənɛr] nmf (*coéquipier etc*) & partner; **partenaires sociaux** labour and management.

parterre [partɛr] nm 1 (*de jardin etc*) flower bed. 2 Théâtre Br stalls, Am orchestra. 3 (*public*) audience.

parti [parti] nm party; **un beau p.** (*pour un mariage*) a desirable ou fitting match (*socially*); **prendre un p.** to make a decision ou choice, follow a course; **prendre p. pour qn** to side with s.o.; **tirer p. de qch** to turn sth to (good) account; **p. pris** (*préjugé*) prejudice; **être de p. pris** to be prejudiced (**contre** against).

partial, -e, -aux [parsjal, -o] a biased. ●**partialité** nf bias.

participe [partisip] nm Grammaire participle.

participer [partisipe] vi **p. à** (*jeu etc*) to take part in, participate in; (*frais, joie etc*) to share (in). ●**participant, -ante** nmf participant. ●**participation** nf participation; (*d'un acteur*) (personal) appearance, collaboration; (*part du capital*) Com stake, interest; **p. (aux frais)** contribution (*toward expenses*); **p. aux bénéfices** Com profit-sharing; **taux de p. électorale** turnout (*of voters in election*).

particularité [partikylarite] nf peculiarity.

particule [partikyl] nf 1 particle. 2 **avoir un nom à p.** to have a handle to one's name.

particulier, -ière [partikylje, -jɛr] a (*spécial, spécifique*) particular; (*privé*) private; (*bizarre*) peculiar; **p.** à peculiar to; **en p.** (*surtout*) in particular; (*à part*) in private; **cas p.** special case; **leçon particulière** private lesson ou tuition ▌ nm private individual ou citizen; **vente de p. à p.** private sale. ●**particulièrement** adv particularly; **tout p.** especially.

partie [parti] nf part; (*de cartes, tennis etc*) game; Jur party; (*métier*) line, field; **une p. de chasse** a shooting party; **en p.** partly, in part; **en grande p.** mainly; **faire p. de** to be a part of; (*club etc*) to belong to; (*comité*) to be on; **ça n'a pas été une p. de plaisir** it was no picnic; **ce n'est que p. remise** it has been put off for the time being, there's been a temporary postponement. ●**partiel, -ielle** a partial ▌ nm (**examen**) **p.** Univ term exam. ●**partiellement** adv partially.

partir* [partir] vi (aux être) (*aller, disparaître*) to go; (*s'en aller*) to go (off), leave; (*se mettre en route*) to set off; (*s'éloigner*) to go (away); (*coup de feu*) to go off; (*flèche*) to shoot off; (*tache*) to come out; (*bouton*) to come off; (*moteur*) to start; **p. en vacances** to go on Br holiday ou Am vacation; **p. en voiture** to go by car, drive; **p. de** (*lieu*) to leave from; (*commencer par*) to start (off) with; **à p. de** (*date, prix*) from; **p. bien/mal** to get off to a good/bad start; **je pars du principe que...** I'm working on the assumption that...; **il est parti de rien** he started with nothing; **ça part du cœur** it comes from the heart; **ça partait d'un bon sentiment** it was with the best of intentions; **je pars!** I'm going; **c'est parti!** off we go! ●**parti, -ie** a **bien p.** off to a good start.

partisan [partizɑ̃] nm supporter, follower; (*combattant*) partisan ▌ a (*esprit*) Péj partisan; **être p. de qch/de faire** to be in favour of sth/of doing.

partition [partisjɔ̃] nf Mus score.

partout [partu] adv everywhere; **p. où tu vas** ou **iras** everywhere ou wherever you go; **p. sur la table/etc** all over the table/etc; Tennis **15 p.** 15 all.

paru, -ue [pary] pp de paraître. ●**parution** nf (*de livre etc*) publication.

parure [paryr] nf (*toilette*) finery; (*bijoux*) Br jewellery, Am jewelry.

parvenir* [parvənir] vi (aux être) **p. à** (*lieu*) to reach; (*objectif*) to achieve; **p. à faire qch**

to manage to do sth. ●**parvenu, -ue** *nmf Péj* upstart.

parvis [parvi] *nm* square (*in front of church etc*).

pas¹ [pɑ] *adv* (*négatif*) not; (ne)... p. not; je ne sais p. I do not *ou* don't know; je n'ai p. compris I didn't understand; je voudrais ne p. sortir I would like not to go out; p. de pain/de café/*etc* no bread/coffee/*etc*; p. encore not yet; p. du tout not at all; p. beaucoup not much; (*quantité*) not many; elle chantera — p. moi! she'll sing — not me!

pas² [pɑ] *nm* 1 step, pace; (*allure*) pace; (*bruit*) footstep; (*trace*) footprint; à deux p. (de) close by; aller au p. to go at a walking pace; rouler au p. (*véhicule*) to go dead slow(ly); marcher au p. (cadencé) to march in step; faire les cent p. to walk up and down; revenir sur ses p. to go back on one's tracks; marcher à p. de loup to creep (silently); marcher à grands p. to take big strides, walk with big strides; faire le premier p. *Fig* to make the first move; faire ses premiers p. to take one's first steps; faire un faux p. (*en marchant*) to stumble; (*faute*) *Fig* to make a blunder; avancer p. à p. to move forward one step at a time, advance step by step; le p. de la porte the doorstep. 2 (*de vis*) thread. 3 *Géog* straits; le p. de Calais the Straits of Dover.

pascal, -e, -aux, [paskal, -o] *a* semaine/messe/*etc* pascale Easter week/mass/*etc*.

passable [pɑsabl] *a* (*travail, résultat etc*); (just) average; mention p. (à un examen) pass. ●**passablement** [-əmɑ̃] *adv* acceptably; (*beaucoup*) quite a lot.

passage [pɑsaʒ] *nm* (*action*) passing, passage; (*traversée*) crossing, passage; (*extrait*) passage; (*couloir*) passage(way); (*chemin*) path; (*court séjour*) visit, stay; p. clouté *ou* pour piétons *Br* (pedestrian) crossing, *Am* crosswalk; p. souterrain *Br* subway, *Am* underpass; p. à niveau *Br* level crossing, *Am* grade crossing; 'p. interdit' 'no through traffic'; avoir le p. to have the right of way; 'cédez le p.' (au carrefour) *Br* 'give way', *Am* 'yield'; être de p. to be passing through (à Paris/*etc* Paris/*etc*); hôte de p. passing guest; obstruer le p. to block the way.

passager, -ère [pɑsaʒe, -ɛr] 1 *nmf* passenger; p. clandestin stowaway. 2 *a* (*de courte durée*) passing, temporary. ●**passagèrement** *adv* temporarily.

passant, -ante [pɑsɑ̃, -ɑ̃t] 1 *a* (*rue*) busy **‖** *nmf* passer-by. 2 *nm* (*de ceinture etc*) loop.

passe [pɑs] *nf Football etc* pass; mot de p. password; une mauvaise p. *Fig* a bad patch; être en p. de faire qch to be on the road to doing sth.

passé, -ée [pɑse] 1 *a* (*temps etc*) past; (*couleur*) faded; il est dix heures passées it's after *ou Br* gone ten (o'clock); être passé (*personne*) to have

been (and gone); (*orage*) to be over; avoir vingt ans passés to be over twenty **‖** *nm* (*temps, vie passée*) past; *Grammaire* past (tense). 2 *prép* after; p. huit heures after eight (o'clock).

passe-montagne [pɑsmɔ̃taɲ] *nm Br* balaclava, *Am* ski mask.

passe-partout [pɑspartu] *nm inv* (*clef*) master key **‖** *a inv* (*compliment, phrase*) allpurpose.

passe-passe [pɑspɑs] *nm inv* tour de p.-passe conjuring trick.

passe-plat [pɑsplɑ] *nm* service *ou* serving hatch.

passeport [pɑspɔr] *nm* passport.

passer [pɑse] *vi* (*aux être ou avoir*) (*aller*) to go, pass (de from, à to); (*traverser*) to go through *ou* over; (*facteur, laitier*) to come; (*temps*) to pass (by), go by; (*film, programme*) to be shown, be on; (*douleur, mode*) to pass; (*couleur*) to fade; (*courant*) to flow; (*loi*) to be passed; p. devant (*maison etc*) to go past *ou* by, pass (by); p. à *ou* par Paris to pass through Paris; p. à la boulangerie *ou* chez le boulanger to go round to the baker's; p. à la radio to come *ou* go on the radio; p. à l'ennemi/à la caisse to go over to the enemy/*Br* the cash desk *ou Am* the cashier's window; laisser p. (*personne, lumière*) to let through *ou* in; (*occasion*) to let slip; p. prendre to fetch, pick up; p. voir qn to drop in on s.o.; p. pour (*riche etc*) to be taken for; faire p. qn pour to pass s.o. off as; faire p. qch sous/dans/*etc* to slide *ou* push sth under/into/*etc*; faire p. un réfugié/*etc* to smuggle a refugee/*etc* (en Suisse/*etc* into Switzerland/*etc*); p. sur (*détail etc*) to overlook, pass over; p. en (*seconde etc*) (à l'école) to go *ou* move up into; (*en voiture*) to change up to; p. capitaine/*etc* to be promoted captain/*etc*; ça passe (*c'est passable*) that'll do; en passant (*dire qch*) in passing.

‖ *vt* (*aux avoir*) (*frontière etc*) to cross, pass; (*maison etc*) to pass, go past; (*mettre*) to put; (*omettre*) to overlook; (*temps*) to spend, pass (à faire doing); (*disque*) to play, put on; (*film, programme*) to show, put on; (*loi, motion*) to pass; (*chemise*) to slip on, put on; (*examen*) to take, *Br* sit (for); (*thé*) to strain; (*café*) to filter; (*commande*) to place; (*accord*) to conclude; (*limites*) to go beyond; (*visite médicale*) to have; p. (son tour) to pass; p. qch à qn (*prêter*) to pass *ou* hand sth to s.o.; (*caprice etc*) to grant s.o. sth; (*pardonner*) to excuse s.o. sth; p. un coup d'éponge/*etc* à qch to go over sth with a sponge/*etc*; p. sa colère sur qn to vent one's anger on s.o.; j'ai passé l'âge de faire ça I'm too old to do that, I've passed the age for doing that; je vous passe... (au téléphone) I'm putting you through to....

‖ se passer *vpr* (se produire) to take place, happen; (*douleur*) to go (away), pass; se p. de to do *ou* go without; cela se passe de commentaires it needs no comment; ça s'est

bien passé it went off well.
passerelle [pɑsrɛl] nf (pont) footbridge; (voie d'accès de bateau, d'avion) gangway.
passe-temps [pɑstɑ̃] nm inv pastime.
passeur, -euse [pɑsœr, -øz] nmf 1 (batelier) ferryman, ferrywoman. 2 (contrebandier) smuggler.
passible [pɑsibl] a p. de (peine) Jur liable to.
passif, -ive [pasif, -iv] 1 a (rôle, personne etc) passive ▮ nm Grammaire passive. 2 nm (dettes d'une entreprise etc) liabilities. ●**passivité** nf passiveness, passivity.
passion [pɑsjɔ̃] nf passion; **avoir la p. des voitures/d'écrire/etc** to have a passion ou a great love for cars/writing/etc. ●**passionnel, -elle** a crime p. crime of passion.
passionner [pɑsjɔne] vt to thrill, fascinate; **se p. pour** to have a passion for. ●**passionnant, -ante** a thrilling. ●**passionné, -ée** a passionate; **p. de qch** passionately fond of sth ▮ nmf fan (de of). ●**passionnément** adv passionately.
passoire [pɑswar] nf (pour liquides) sieve; (à thé) strainer; (à légumes) colander; **ce goal est une vraie p.** Fig this goalkeeper is hopeless at saving goals.
pastel [pastɛl] nm pastel; **dessin au p.** pastel drawing ▮ a inv **ton p.** pastel shade ou tone.
pastèque [pastɛk] nf watermelon.
pasteur [pastœr] nm Rel pastor.
pasteurisé, -ée [pastœrize] a (lait, beurre etc) pasteurized.
pastiche [pastiʃ] nm pastiche.
pastille [pastij] nf pastille, lozenge.
pastis [pastis] nm aniseed liqueur, pastis.
pastoral, -e, -aux [pastɔral, -o] a pastoral.
patate [patat] nf Fam spud, potato.
patatras! [patatra] int crash!
pataud, -aude [pato, -od] a clumsy, oafish.
patauger [patoʒe] vi (marcher) to wade (in the mud etc); (barboter) to splash about; (s'empêtrer) Fam to flounder. ●**pataugeoire** nf Br paddling pool, Am wading pool (large, purpose-built).
patchwork [patʃwœrk] nm patchwork.
pâte [pɑt] nf (substance) paste; **p. (à pain), p. (à gâteau)** dough; **p. (à tarte)** pastry; **p. (à frire)** batter; **pâtes (alimentaires)** pasta; **p. d'amandes** almond paste; **p. de fruits** fruit jelly; **fromage à p. molle** soft cheese; **p. à modeler** Br plasticine®, modelling clay; **p. dentifrice** toothpaste; **mettre la main à la p.** Fig to get down to it, do one's bit.
pâté [pɑte] nm 1 (charcuterie) pâté; **p. (en croûte)** meat pie. 2 **p. (de sable)** sand castle; **p. de maisons** block of houses. 3 (tache d'encre) (ink) blot.
pâtée [pɑte] nf (pour chien) dog food; (pour chat) cat food.
patelin [patlɛ̃] nm Fam village.
patent, -ente [patɑ̃, -ɑ̃t] a patent, obvious.
patère [patɛr] nf (coat) peg.
paternel, -elle [patɛrnɛl] a (amour etc) paternal, fatherly; (parenté, réprimande) pa-

ternal. ●**paternalisme** nm paternalism. ●**paternité** nf (état) paternity, fatherhood; (de livre) authorship.
pâteux, -euse [pɑtø, -øz] a (substance) doughy, pasty; (style) Fig woolly; **une langue pâteuse** (après une maladie etc) a coated tongue; **avoir la bouche ou la langue pâteuse** (après s'être enivré) to have a mouth full of Br cotton wool ou Am cotton.
pathétique [patetik] a a moving ▮ nm pathos.
pathologie [patɔlɔʒi] nf pathology. ●**pathologique** a pathological.
patibulaire [patibylɛr] a **avoir une mine p.** to look sinister.
patient, -ente [pasjɑ̃, -ɑ̃t] 1 a patient. 2 nmf (malade) patient. ●**patiemment** [-amɑ̃] adv patiently. ●**patienter** vi to wait (patiently).
patience [pasjɑ̃s] nf patience; **prendre p.** to have patience; **perdre p.** to lose patience; **faire une p.** (jeu de cartes) to play a game of patience.
patin [patɛ̃] nm skate; (pour le parquet) cloth pad (used for walking); **p. à glace** ice skate; **p. à roulettes** roller-skate; **p. de frein** (de véhicule) brake shoe.
patine [patin] nf patina.
patiner [patine] vi Sport to skate; (roue) to spin around; (véhicule) to slip (and slide); (embrayage) to slip. ●**patinage** nm Sport skating; **p. artistique** figure skating. ●**patineur, -euse** nmf (sportif) skater. ●**patinoire** nf (piste) skating rink, ice rink.
patio [patjo] nm patio (of Spanish-style house).
pâtir [pɑtir] vi **p. de** to suffer from.
pâtisserie [pɑtisri] nf pastry, cake; (magasin) cake shop; (art) cake ou pastry making. ●**pâtissier, -ière** nmf pastrycook and cake shop owner ▮ a **crème pâtissière** confectioner's cream.
patois [patwa] nm Ling patois.
patraque [patrak] a (malade) Fam under the weather.
patriarche [patrijarʃ] nm patriarch.
patrie [patri] nf (native) country; (ville) birth place.
patrimoine [patrimwan] nm (biens) & Fig heritage; **p. génétique** genetic inheritance.
patriote [patrijɔt] nmf patriot ▮ a (personne) patriotic. ●**patriotique** a (chant etc) patriotic. ●**patriotisme** nm patriotism.
patron, -onne [patrɔ̃, -ɔn] 1 nmf (chef) boss, employer; (propriétaire) owner (de of); (gérant) manager, manageress; (de bar) landlord, landlady. 2 nmf Rel patron saint. 3 nm (modèle de papier) (en couture) pattern.
patronage [patrɔnaʒ] nm 1 (protection) patronage. 2 (centre) youth club. ●**patronner** vt to sponsor.
patronat [patrɔna] nm employers. ●**patronal, -e, -aux** a (syndicat etc) employers'.
patronyme [patrɔnim] nm family name.
patrouille [patruj] nf patrol. ●**patrouiller** vi to patrol. ●**patrouilleur** nm (navire) patrol boat.

patte [pat] nf **1** (membre) leg; (de chat, chien) paw; (main) Fam hand; **marcher à quatre pattes** to crawl, walk on all fours. **2** (languette) tongue; (de poche) flap.

pattes [pat] nfpl (favoris) sideburns, Br sideboards.

pâturage [patyraʒ] nm pasture.

pâture [patyr] nf (nourriture) food; (intellectuelle) Fig fodder; **donner qch en p. à la presse/etc** Fig to serve sth up ou feed sth to the press/etc.

paume [pom] nf (de main) palm.

paumer [pome] vt Fam to lose. ●**paumé, -ée** nmf (malheureux) Fam down-and-out, loser ▮ a **un coin** ou **trou p.** (sans attrait) Fam a dump.

paupière [popjɛr] nf eyelid.

paupiette [popjɛt] nf **p. de veau** slice of veal rolled around stuffing.

pause [poz] nf (arrêt) break; (dans le discours etc) pause.

pauvre [povr] a (indigent, malheureux, insuffisant) poor; (terre, vocabulaire) impoverished, poor; **p. en** (calories etc) low in; (ressources etc) low on ▮ nmf (indigent, malheureux) poor man, poor woman; **les pauvres** the poor. ●**pauvrement** [-əmɑ̃] adv poorly. ●**pauvreté** nf (besoin) poverty; (insuffisance) poorness.

pavaner (se) [səpavane] vpr to strut (about).

paver [pave] vt to pave. ●**pavé** nm **un p.** a paving stone; (de vieille chaussée) a cobblestone; **sur le p.** Fig on the streets. ●**pavage** nm (travail, revêtement) paving.

pavillon [pavijɔ̃] nm **1** (maison) (detached) house; (d'hôpital) ward; (d'exposition) pavilion; (de chasse) lodge. **2** (drapeau) flag; **p. de complaisance** flag of convenience.

pavoiser [pavwaze] vi (exulter) to rejoice; **il n'y a pas de quoi p.** there's nothing to crow ou rejoice about ▮ vt to deck out with flags.

pavot [pavo] nm (cultivé) poppy.

payable [pɛjabl] a payable.

paye [pɛj] nf pay, wages. ●**payement** nm payment.

payer [peje] vt (personne, somme) to pay; (service, objet) to pay for; (récompenser) to repay; **p. qn pour faire qch** to pay s.o. to do ou for doing sth; **p. qch à qn** (offrir en cadeau) Fam to treat s.o. to sth; **tu me le paieras!** Fam you'll pay for this! ▮ vi (personne, métier, crime) to pay. ▮ **se payer** vpr **se p. qch** (s'acheter) Fam to treat oneself to sth; **se p. la tête de qn** Fam to make fun of s.o. ●**payant, -ante** [pɛjɑ̃, -ɑ̃t] a (hôte, spectateur) paying, who pays; (place, entrée) that one has to pay for; (rentable) worthwhile.

pays [pei] nm country; (région) region; (village) village; **p. des rêves/du soleil** land of dreams/sun; **du p.** (vin, gens etc) local.

paysage [peizaʒ] nm landscape, scenery; **p. urbain** urban landscape. ●**paysagiste** nmf landscape gardener.

paysan, -anne [peizɑ̃, -an] nmf (small) farmer; (rustre) Péj peasant ▮ a **coutume/etc paysanne** rural ou country custom/etc; **le monde p.** the farming world ou community.

Pays-Bas [peiba] nmpl **les P.-Bas** the Netherlands.

PCV [peseve] abrév (paiement contre vérification) **téléphoner en PCV** Br to reverse the charges, Am call collect.

PDG [pedeʒe] abrév = **président directeur général.**

péage [peaʒ] nm (droit) toll; (lieu) tollbooth, tollgate; **autoroute à p.** Br toll motorway, Am turnpike.

peau, -x [po] nf skin; (de fruit) peel, skin; (cuir) hide, skin; (fourrure) fur, pelt; **se mettre dans la p. de qn** Fig to put oneself in s.o.'s shoes; **avoir qn dans la p.** to be crazy about s.o.; **faire p. neuve** Fig to turn over a new leaf; **laisser sa p. dans** (aventure etc) Fam to lose one's life in; **j'aurai sa p.!** Fam I'll get him ou kill him!; **être bien/mal dans sa p.** Fam to feel happy and contented/unhappy and discontented. ●**Peau-Rouge** nmf (pl **Peaux-Rouges**) (Red) Indian.

pêche¹ [pɛʃ] nf (activité) fishing; (poissons) catch; **p.** (à la ligne) angling; **aller à la p.** to go fishing. ●**pêcher¹** vi to fish ▮ vt (attraper) to catch; (chercher à prendre) to fish for; (dénicher) Fam to dig up. ●**pêcheur** nm fisherman; (à la ligne) angler.

pêche² [pɛʃ] nf (fruit) peach; **avoir une peau de p.** to have soft and velvety skin; **avoir la p.** Fam to feel on top of the world. ●**pêcher²** nm (arbre) peach tree.

péché [peʃe] nm sin; **avoir un p. mignon** to have a weakness ou penchant. ●**pécher** vi to sin; **p. par orgueil/etc** to be too proud/etc. ●**pécheur, -eresse** nmf sinner.

pectoraux [pɛktɔro] nmpl (muscles) chest muscles.

pécule [pekyl] nm **un p.** (économies) (some) savings, a nest egg.

pécuniaire [pekynjɛr] a monetary.

pédagogie [pedagɔʒi] nf (science) education, teaching methods. ●**pédagogique** a educational. ●**pédagogue** nmf teacher.

pédale [pedal] nf **1** pedal; **p. de frein** footbrake (pedal); **mettre la p. douce** (aller moins vite) Fam to slow down, ease up; **perdre les pédales** Fam to lose one's marbles. **2** (homosexuel) Péj Fam pansy, queer ●**pédaler** vi to pedal.

pédalo [pedalo] nm pedal boat, pedalo.

pédant, -ante [pedɑ̃, -ɑ̃t] nmf pedant ▮ a pedantic. ●**pédantisme** nm pedantry.

pédé [pede] nm (homosexuel) Péj Fam queer.

pédiatre [pedjatr] nmf children's doctor, p(a)ediatrician.

pédibus [pedibys] adv Fam on foot.

pédicure [pedikyr] nmf Br chiropodist, Am podiatrist.

pedigree [pedigre] nm (de chien, cheval etc) pedigree.

pègre [pɛgr] *nf* **la p.** the (criminal) underworld.

peigne [pɛɲ] *nm* comb; **se donner un coup de p.** to give one's hair a comb; **passer au p. fin** *Fig* to go through with a fine-tooth comb. ●**peigner** *vt* (*cheveux*) to comb; **p. qn** to comb s.o.'s hair **‖ se peigner** *vpr* to comb one's hair.

peignoir [pɛɲwar] *nm Br* dressing gown, *Am* bathrobe; **p. (de bain)** bathrobe.

peinard, -arde [pɛnar, -ard] *a Fam* quiet (and easy).

peindre* [pɛ̃dr] *vt* to paint; (*décrire*) *Fig* to depict, paint; **p. en bleu/etc** to paint blue/etc **‖** *vi* to paint.

peine [pɛn] *nf* **1** (*châtiment*) punishment; **la p. de mort** the death penalty *ou* sentence; **p. de prison** prison sentence; **'défense d'entrer sous p. d'amende'** 'trespassers will be prosecuted *ou* fined'.
2 (*chagrin*) sorrow, grief; **avoir de la p.** to be upset *ou* sad; **faire de la p. à qn** to upset s.o., cause pain *ou* sorrow to s.o.
3 (*effort, difficulté*) trouble; **se donner de la p.** *ou* **beaucoup de p.** to go to a lot of trouble (**pour faire** to do); **avec p.** with difficulty; **ça vaut la p. d'attendre/etc** it's worth (while) waiting/etc; **ce n'est pas** *ou* **ça ne vaut pas la p.** it's not worth it *ou* worth bothering *ou* worth while.

peine (à) [apɛn] *adv* hardly, scarcely.

peiner [pɛne] **1** *vt* to upset, sadden, grieve. **2** *vi* to labour, struggle.

peintre [pɛ̃tr] *nm* (*artiste*) painter; **p. (en bâtiment)** (house) painter, *Br* (painter and) decorator. ●**peinture** *nf* (*tableau, activité*) painting; (*matière*) paint; **'p. fraîche'** 'wet paint'. ●**peinturlurer** *vt Fam* to daub with colour; **se p. (le visage)** to paint one's face.

péjoratif, -ive [peʒɔratif, -iv] *a* pejorative, derogatory.

Pékin [pekɛ̃] *nm ou f* Peking.

pékinois [pekinwa] *nm* (*chien*) pekin(g)ese.

pelage [pəlaʒ] *nm* (*d'animal*) coat, fur.

pelé, -ée [pəle] *a* bare.

pêle-mêle [pɛlmɛl] *adv* in disorder.

peler [pəle] *vt* (*fruit*) to peel; **se p. facilement** (*fruit*) to peel easily **‖** *vi* (*personne, peau*) to peel; **je pèle de froid** *Fam* I'm freezing cold, I'm perishing (with cold).

pèlerin [pɛlrɛ̃] *nm* pilgrim. ●**pèlerinage** *nm* pilgrimage.

pélican [pelikã] *nm* (*oiseau*) pelican.

pelisse [pəlis] *nf* fur-lined coat.

pelle [pɛl] *nf* shovel; (*d'enfant*) spade; **p. à tarte** cake server; **p. à poussière** dustpan; **à la p.** (*argent etc*) *Fam* galore; **ramasser** *ou* **prendre une p.** (*tomber*) *Fam Br* to come a cropper, *Am* take a spill. ●**pelletée** *nf* shovelful. ●**pelleteuse** *nf Tech* mechanical digger *ou* shovel, excavator.

pellicule [pelikyl] *nf* (*pour photos*) film; (*couche*) layer, film; **pellicules** (*dans les cheveux*) dandruff.

pelote [plɔt] *nf* (*de laine*) ball; (*à épingles*) pincushion; **p. (basque)** *Sport* pelota.

peloter [plɔte] *vt* (*palper*) *Péj Fam* to paw.

peloton [p(ə)lɔtɔ̃] *nm* **1** (*cyclistes*) pack, bunch, main body; **p. de tête** leading pack *ou* bunch. **2** (*de soldats*) squad; **p. d'exécution** firing squad. **3** (*de ficelle*) ball.

pelotonner (se) [səp(ə)lɔtɔne] *vpr* to curl up (into a ball).

pelouse [p(ə)luz] *nf* lawn; *Sport* enclosure.

peluche [p(ə)lyʃ] *nf* **1** (*tissu*) plush; (**jouet en**) **p.** soft toy; **chien/etc en p.** (*jouet*) furry dog/etc; **ours en p.** teddy bear. **2 peluches** (*flocons*) fluff, lint. ●**pelucher** *vi* to get fluffy *ou* linty. ●**pelucheux, -euse** *a* fluffy, linty.

pelure [p(ə)lyr] *nf* (*épluchure*) peeling; **une p.** a (piece of) peeling.

pénal, -e, -aux [penal, -o] *a* (*code etc*) penal. ●**pénalisation** *nf Rugby etc* penalty. ●**pénaliser** *vt Rugby etc & Jur* to penalize (**pour** for). ●**pénalité** *nf Rugby etc & Jur* penalty.

penalty, pl -ties [penalti, -iz] *nm Football* penalty.

penaud, -aude [pəno, -od] *a* sheepish.

penchant [pɑ̃ʃɑ̃] *nm* (*goût*) liking (**pour** for); (*tendance*) inclination (**à qch** towards sth).

pencher [pɑ̃ʃe] *vt* (*objet*) to tilt; (*tête*) to lean **‖** *vi* (*arbre etc*) to lean (over); **p. pour** *Fig* to be inclined towards **‖ se pencher** *vpr* to lean (over *ou* forward); **se p. par la fenêtre** to lean out of the window; **se p. sur** (*problème etc*) to examine. ●**penché, -ée** *a* leaning.

pendable [pɑ̃dabl] *a* **faire un tour p.** to play a wicked *ou* diabolical trick (**à qn** on s.o.).

pendaison [pɑ̃dɛzɔ̃] *nf* hanging.

pendant¹ [pɑ̃dɑ̃] *prép* (*au cours de*) during; **p. la nuit** during the night; **p. deux mois** (*pour une période de*) for two months; **p. que** while, whilst.

pendentif [pɑ̃dɑ̃tif] *nm* (*collier*) pendant.

penderie [pɑ̃dri] *nf Br* wardrobe, *Am* closet.

pendre [pɑ̃dr] *vti* to hang (**à** from); **p. qn** to hang s.o. **‖ se pendre** *vpr* (*se suicider*) to hang oneself; (*se suspendre*) to hang (**à** from). ●**pendant², -ante** **1** *a* hanging; (*langue*) hanging out; (*joues*) sagging; (*question*) *Fig* pending. **2** *nm* **p. (d'oreille)** drop earring. **3** *nm* **le p. de** the companion piece to. ●**pendu, -ue** *a* (*objet*) hanging (**à** from); **être p. au téléphone** *Fam* to be never off the phone **‖** *nmf* hanged man, hanged woman.

pendule [pɑ̃dyl] **1** *nf* clock. **2** *nm* (*balancier*) pendulum. ●**pendulette** *nf* small clock.

pénétrer [penetre] *vi* **p. dans** to enter; (*profondément*) to penetrate (into) **‖** *vt* (*pluie etc*) to penetrate (*sth*); **se p. d'une idée** to become convinced of an idea. ●**pénétrant, -ante** *a* (*esprit, froid etc*) penetrating, keen. ●**pénétration** *nf* penetration.

pénible [penibl] *a* (*difficile*) difficult; (*douloureux*) painful, distressing; (*ennuyeux*) tiresome; (*agaçant*) annoying. ●**péniblement** [-əmã] *adv* with difficulty; (*avec douleur*) painfully.

péniche [peniʃ] *nf* barge; **p. de débarquement** (*de l'armée*) landing craft.

pénicilline [penisilin] *nf* penicillin.

péninsule [penɛ̃syl] *nf* peninsula. ●**péninsulaire** *a* peninsular.

pénis [penis] *nm* penis.

pénitence [penitɑ̃s] *nf* (*punition*) punishment; (*peine*) *Rel* penance; (*regret*) penitence; **faire p.** to repent. ●**pénitent, -ente** *nmf Rel* penitent.

pénitencier [penitɑ̃sje] *nm* prison. ●**pénitentiaire** *a* **régime/etc p.** prison system/etc.

pénombre [penɔ̃br] *nf* half-light, (semi-) darkness.

pense-bête [pɑ̃sbɛt] *nm* reminder.

pensée [pɑ̃se] *nf* **1** thought; **à la p. de faire qch** at the thought of doing sth. **2** (*fleur*) pansy.

penser [pɑ̃se] *vi* to think (à of, about); **p. à qch/à faire qch** (*ne pas oublier*) to remember sth/to do sth; **p. à tout** (*prévoir*) to think of everything; **j'y pense** I'm thinking about it; **penses-tu!** you must be joking!, not at all! **▮** *vt* to think (que that); (*concevoir*) to think out; (*imaginer*) to imagine (que that); **je pensais rester** (*intention*) I was thinking of staying, I thought I'd stay; **je pense réussir** (*espoir*) I hope to succeed; **que pensez-vous de...?** what do you think of *ou* about...?; **p. du bien de qn/qch** to think highly of s.o./sth. ●**pensant, -ante** *a* **bien p.** *Péj* orthodox. ●**penseur** *nm* thinker.

pensif, -ive [pɑ̃sif, -iv] *a* thoughtful, pensive.

pension [pɑ̃sjɔ̃] *nf* **1** boarding school; (*somme à payer*) board; **être en p.** to board, be a boarder (**chez** with); **p.** (**de famille**) guesthouse, boarding house; **p. complète** *Br* full board, *Am* American plan. **2** (*de retraite etc*) pension; **p. alimentaire** maintenance allowance. ●**pensionnaire** *nmf* (*élève*) boarder; (*d'hôtel*) resident; (*de famille*) lodger. ●**pensionnat** *nm* boarding school; (*élèves*) boarders. ●**pensionné, -ée** *nmf* pensioner.

pentagone [pɛ̃tagɔn] *nm* **le P.** *Am Mil* the Pentagon.

pentathlon [pɛ̃tatlɔ̃] *nm Sport* pentathlon.

pente [pɑ̃t] *nf* slope; **être en p.** to slope, be sloping; **être sur la mauvaise p.** *Fig* to be on the slippery slope.

Pentecôte [pɑ̃tkot] *nf Br* Whitsun, *Am* Pentecost.

pénurie [penyri] *nf* scarcity, shortage (**de** of).

pépère [pepɛr] **1** *nm Fam* grand(d)ad. **2** *a* (*tranquille*) *Fam* quiet (and easy).

pépier [pepje] *vi* (*oiseau*) to cheep, chirp.

pépin [pepɛ̃] *nm* **1** (*de fruit*) *Br* pip, *Am* seed, pit. **2** (*ennui*) *Fam* hitch, bother. **3** (*parapluie*) *Fam* umbrella, *Br* brolly.

pépinière [pepinjɛr] *nf* (*pour plantes*) nursery; (*école etc*) *Fig* seedbed, training ground (**de** for).

pépite [pepit] *nf* (*gold*) nugget.

péquenaud, -aude [pekno, -od] *nmf Péj Fam* peasant, (country) bumpkin.

perçant, -ante [pɛrsɑ̃, -ɑ̃t] *a* (*cri*, *froid*) piercing; (*yeux*) sharp, keen.

percée [pɛrse] *nf* (*dans une forêt etc*) opening; (*avance technologique*, *attaque militaire*) breakthrough.

perce-neige [pɛrsənɛʒ] *nm ou f inv* (*plante*) snowdrop.

perce-oreille [pɛrsɔrɛj] *nm* (*insecte*) earwig.

percepteur [pɛrsɛptœr] *nm* tax collector. ●**perceptible** *a* perceptible (à to), noticeable. ●**perception** *nf* **1** (*bureau*) tax office; (*d'impôt*) collection. **2** (*sensation*) perception.

percer [pɛrse] *vt* (*trouer*) to pierce; (*avec une perceuse*) to drill (a hole in); (*trou*, *ouverture*) to make, drill; (*mystère etc*) to uncover; **p. une dent** (*bébé*) to cut a tooth **▮** *vi* (*soleil*, *ennemi*, *sentiment*) to break *ou* come through; (*abcès*) to burst; (*acteur etc*) to make a name for oneself. ●**perceuse** *nf* (*outil*) drill.

percevoir* [pɛrsəvwar] *vt* **1** (*sensation*) to perceive; (*son*) to hear. **2** (*impôt*) to collect.

perche [pɛrʃ] *nf* **1** (*bâton*) pole; **saut à la p.** pole vaulting; **tendre la p. à qn** *Fig* to give s.o. a helping hand. **2** (*poisson*) perch. **3** **une grande p.** (*personne*) *Fam* a beanpole. ●**perchiste** *nm* pole vaulter.

percher [pɛrʃe] *vi* (*oiseau*) to perch; (*volailles*) to roost; (*loger*) *Fam* to hang out **▮** *vt* (*placer*) *Fam* to perch **▮ se percher** *vpr* (*oiseau*, *personne*) to perch. ●**perché, -ée** *a* perched. ●**perchoir** *nm* perch; (*de volailles*) roost; *Pol Fam* seat of the president of the National Assembly; **descends de ton p.!** *Fam* come off your high horse!

percolateur [pɛrkɔlatœr] *nm* (*de restaurant*) percolator.

percussion [pɛrkysjɔ̃] *nf Mus* percussion.

percutant, -ante [pɛrkytɑ̃, -ɑ̃t] *a Fig* powerful.

percuter [pɛrkyte] *vt* (*véhicule*) to crash into **▮** *vi* **p. contre** to crash into.

perdant, -ante [pɛrdɑ̃, -ɑ̃t] *a* (*billet*) losing **▮** *nmf* loser.

perdition (en) [ɑ̃pɛrdisjɔ̃] *adv* (*navire*) in distress.

perdre [pɛrdr] *vt* to lose; (*gaspiller*) to waste; (*habitude*) to get out of; **p. de vue** to lose sight of; **il a perdu son père** he lost his father; **sa passion du jeu/etc l'a perdu** his passion for gambling/etc was his undoing. **▮** *vi* to lose; (*récipient*, *tuyau*) to leak; **j'y perds** I lose out, I lose on the deal. **▮ se perdre** *vpr* (*s'égarer*) to get lost; (*disparaître*) to disappear; **se p. dans les détails** to be *ou* get bogged down in details; **je m'y perds** I'm lost *ou* confused; **nous nous sommes perdus de vue** we lost touch, we lost sight of each other. ●**perdu, -ue** *a* lost; (*gaspillé*) wasted; (*malade*) finished; (*lieu*) isolated, in the middle of nowhere; **à ses moments perdus** in one's spare time; **une balle perdue** a stray bullet; **c'est du temps p.** it's a waste of time.

perdrix [perdri] *nf* partridge. ● **perdreau, -x**
nm young partridge.

père [per] *nm* father; **Dupont p.** Dupont senior; **le p. Jean** *Fam* old John; **le p. Martin**
Rel Father Martin; **mon p.!** *Rel* father!

péremptoire [perãptwar] *a* peremptory.

perfection [perfɛksjɔ̃] *nf* perfection; **à la p.**
perfectly.

perfectionner [perfɛksjɔne] *vt* to improve,
perfect ∎ **se perfectionner** *vpr* **se p. en
anglais/***etc* to improve one's English/*etc*.
● **perfectionné, -ée** *a* (*machine etc*) advanced.
● **perfectionnement** *nm* improvement (de in,
par rapport à on); **cours de p.** refresher
course, advanced *ou Br* improvers' course.

perfectionniste [perfɛksjɔnist] *nmf*
perfectionist.

perfide [perfid] *a Litt* treacherous,
perfidious. ● **perfidie** *nf Litt* treachery.

perforer [perfɔre] *vt* (*pneu, intestin etc*) to
perforate; (*billet, carte*) to punch; **carte
perforée** punch card. ● **perforateur** *nm*
(*appareil*) drill. ● **perforation** *nf* perforation;
(*trou*) punched hole. ● **perforatrice** *nf*
(*machine*) (card) punch. ● **perforeuse** *nf*
(*machine*) (paper) punch.

performance [performãs] *nf* (*d'athlète, de
machine etc*) performance. ● **performant,
-ante** *a* (highly) efficient.

perfusion [perfyzjɔ̃] *nf* (*injection*) (intravenous) drip; **être sous p.** to be on a drip.

péricliter [periklite] *vi* to go to rack and
ruin.

péridurale [peridyral] *af & nf* (**anesthésie**) **p.**
epidural; **accoucher sous p.** to give birth
under an epidural.

péril [peril] *nm* danger, peril; **à tes risques et
périls** at your own risk; **mettre qch en p.** to
jeopardize *ou* endanger sth; **mettre qn en p.**
to put s.o. in danger. ● **périlleux, -euse** *a*
dangerous, perilous; **saut p.** somersault (*in
mid air*).

périmer [perime] *vi*, **se périmer** *vpr* **laisser
qch (se) p.** to allow sth to expire. ● **périmé,
-ée** *a* (*billet*) expired; (*désuet*) outdated.

périmètre [perimɛtr] *nm* perimeter.

période [perjɔd] *nf* period. ● **périodique** *a*
periodic ∎ *nm* (*revue*) periodical.

péripétie [peripesi] *nf* (unexpected) event.

périphérie [periferi] *nf* (*limite*) periphery;
(*banlieue*) outskirts.

périphérique [periferik] *a* (*quartier etc*) outlying, peripheral; **radio p.** radio station
broadcasting from outside France ∎ *nm & a*
(*boulevard*) **p.** *Br* (mótorway) ring road, *Am*
beltway. ● **périphériques** *nmpl Ordinat* peripherals.

périphrase [perifraz] *nf* circumlocution.

périple [peripl] *nm* trip, tour.

périr [perir] *vi Litt* to perish, die. ● **périssable** *a* (*denrée*) perishable.

périscope [periskɔp] *nm* periscope.

perle [perl] *nf* (*bijou*) pearl; (*de bois, verre
etc*) bead; (*personne*) *Fig* gem, pearl;
(*erreur*) *Iron* howler, gem. ● **perler** *vi* (*sueur*)

to form beads; **grève perlée** *Br* go-slow, *Am*
slow-down strike.

permanent, -ente [permanã, -ãt] **1** *a* a permanent; (*spectacle*) *Cinéma* continuous; (*comité*) standing. **2** *nf* **permanente** (*coiffure*)
perm. ● **permanence** *nf* permanence; (*salle
d'étude*) study room; (*service, bureau*) duty
office; **être de p.** to be on duty; **en p.**
permanently.

perméable [permeabl] *a* permeable.

permettre* [permɛtr] *vt* to allow, permit; **p.
à qn de faire qch** (*permission, possibilité*) to
allow *ou* permit s.o. to do sth; **permettez!
excuse me!; vous permettez?** may I? ∎ **se
permettre** *vpr* **se p. de faire** to allow oneself
to do, take the liberty to do; **je ne peux pas
me p. de l'acheter** I can't afford to buy it.

permis, -ise [permi, -iz] *a* allowed,
permitted ∎ *nm* (*autorisation*) *Br* licence, *Am*
license, permit; **p. de conduire** (*carte*) *Br*
driving licence, *Am* driver's license; **passer
son p. de conduire** to take one's driving *ou*
road test; **p. à point** (*système*) points system
for *Br* driving licence *ou Am* driver's license; **p. de travail** work permit; **p. de séjour** residence permit.

permission [permisjɔ̃] *nf* permission; (*congé
militaire*) leave; **demander la p.** to ask
permission (**de faire** to do).

permuter [permyte] *vt* to change round *ou*
over, permutate. ● **permutation** *nf* permutation.

pernicieux, -euse [pernisjø, -øz] *a* (*maladie*) pernicious; (*nuisible*) *Litt* pernicious.

pérorer [perɔre] *vi Péj* to speechify.

Pérou [peru] *nm* Peru.

perpendiculaire [perpãdikylɛr] *a & nf*
perpendicular (**à** to).

perpétrer [perpetre] *vt* (*crime*) to perpetrate.

perpétuel, -elle [perpetɥɛl] *a* perpetual; (*incessant*) continual; (*fonction, rente*) for life.
● **perpétuellement** *adv* perpetually. ● **perpétuer** *vt* to perpetuate. ● **perpétuité (à)** *adv* in
perpetuity; **condamnation à p.** life sentence,
sentence for life.

perplexe [perplɛks] *a* perplexed, puzzled.
● **perplexité** *nf* perplexity.

perquisition [perkizisjɔ̃] *nf* (house) search
(*by police*). ● **perquisitionner** *vi* to search.

perron [perɔ̃] *nm* (front) steps.

perroquet [perɔke] *nm* parrot.

perruche [peryʃ] *nf Br* budgerigar, *Am*
parakeet.

perruque [peryk] *nf* wig.

persan, -ane [persã, -an] *a* (*langue, tapis,
chat etc*) Persian ∎ *nm* (*langue*) Persian.

persécuter [persekyte] *vt* (*opprimer*) to
persecute; (*importuner*) to harass. ● **persécu-
teur, -trice** *nmf* persecutor. ● **persécution** *nf*
persecution.

persévérer [persevere] *vi* to persevere (**dans**
in). ● **persévérant, -ante** *a* persevering.
● **persévérance** *nf* perseverance.

persienne [persjɛn] *nf* (outside) shutter.

persil [persi] *nm* parsley. ● **persillé, -ée** *a*

225 **petit**

(plat) sprinkled with parsley.

Persique [persik] *a* **le golfe P.** the Persian Gulf.

persister [persiste] *vi* to persist (**à faire** in doing, **dans qch** in sth). ● **persistant, -ante** *a* persistent; **à feuilles persistantes** *(arbre etc)* evergreen. ● **persistance** *nf* persistence.

personnage [personaʒ] *nm (célébrité)* (important) person; *Théâtre Littér* character.

personnaliser [personalize] *vt* to personalize; *(voiture)* to customize.

personnalité [personalite] *nf (individualité, personnage)* personality.

personne [person] **1** *nf* person; **deux/etc personnes** two/etc people; **grande p.** grown-up, adult; **p. âgée** elderly person; **jolie p.** pretty girl *ou* woman; **en p.** in person; **être bien de sa p.** to be very good-looking; **être content de sa (petite) p.** to be pleased with oneself.
2 *pron (négatif)* nobody, no one; **(ne)...p.** nobody, no one; **je ne vois p.** I don't see anybody *ou* anyone; **p. ne saura** nobody *ou* no one will know; **mieux que p.** better than anybody *ou* anyone.

personnel, -elle [personɛl] **1** *a* personal; *(joueur, jeu)* individualistic. **2** *nm* staff, personnel. ● **personnellement** *adv* personally.

personnifier [personifje] *vt* to personify. ● **personnification** *nf* personification.

perspective [perspektiv] *nf (art)* perspective; *(idée, possibilité etc)* prospect (**de** of); *(de paysage etc)* view; *(point de vue)* Fig viewpoint, perspective; **en p.** *Fig* in view, in prospect.

perspicace [perspikas] *a* shrewd. ● **perspicacité** *nf* shrewdness.

persuader [persɥade] *vt* to persuade (**qn de faire** s.o. to do); **être persuadé que** to be convinced that ▮ **se persuader** *vpr* **se p. que** to convince oneself that, be convinced that. ● **persuasif, -ive** *a* persuasive. ● **persuasion** *nf* persuasion; *(croyance)* conviction.

perte [pert] *nf* loss; *(gaspillage)* waste *(de temps/d'argent* of time/money); *(ruine)* ruin; **à p. de vue** as far as the eye can see; **en pure p.** *(inutilement)* completely for nothing; **p. sèche** absolute *ou* complete loss; **vendre qch à p.** to sell sth at a loss; **courir à sa p.** to be heading for disaster *ou* ruin; **vouloir la p. de qn** *(mort, ruine)* to seek s.o.'s destruction.

pertinent, -ente [pertinã, -ãt] *a* relevant, pertinent. ● **pertinemment** [-amã] *adv* **savoir p. que** to know for a fact that. ● **pertinence** *nf* relevance.

perturber [pertyrbe] *vt (trafic, cérémonie etc)* to disrupt; *(ordre public, personne)* to disturb. ● **perturbé, -ée** *a (troublé)* Fam perturbed. ● **perturbateur, -trice** *a (élément)* disruptive ▮ *nmf* troublemaker. ● **perturbation** *nf* disruption; *(crise)* upheaval; **p. atmosphérique** atmospheric disturbance; **semer la p.** to spread disruption.

péruvien, -ienne [peryvjɛ̃, -jɛn] *a* Peruvian

▮ *nmf* **P., Péruvienne** Peruvian.

pervenche [pervã ʃ] *nf (plante)* periwinkle; *(contractuelle)* Fam Br (woman) traffic warden, *Am* meter maid.

pervers, -erse [pɛrvɛr, -ɛrs] *a* wicked, perverse; *(dépravé)* perverted ▮ *nmf* pervert. ● **perversion** *nf* perversion. ● **perversité** *nf* perversity. ● **pervertir** *vt* to pervert. ● **perverti, -ie** *nmf* pervert.

pesage [pəzaʒ] *nm* weighing.

pesant, -ante [pəzã, -ãt] *a* heavy, weighty ▮ *nm* **valoir son p. d'or** to be worth one's *ou* its weight in gold. ● **pesamment** [-amã] *adv* heavily. ● **pesanteur** *nf* heaviness; *(force)* Phys gravity.

pesée [pəze] *nf* weighing; *Boxe* weigh-in; *(effort)* pressure.

peser [pəze] *vt* to weigh; **p. le pour et le contre** to weigh up the pros and the cons; **p. ses mots** to choose one's words carefully, weigh one's words; **elle pèse 20 millions** *Fam* she's worth 20 million ▮ *vi* to weigh; **p. lourd** to be heavy; *(argument etc)* Fig to carry (a lot of) weight; **p. sur** *(appuyer)* to bear down upon; *(influer)* to bear upon; **p. sur qn** *(menace)* to hang over s.o.; **p. sur l'estomac** to lie (heavily) on the stomach. ● **pèse-bébé** *nm* (baby) scales. ● **pèse-lettre** *nm* (letter) scales. ● **pèse-personne** *nm* (bathroom) scales.

pessimisme [pesimism] *nm* pessimism. ● **pessimiste** *a* pessimistic ▮ *nmf* pessimist.

peste [pest] *nf (maladie)* plague; *(personne, enfant)* Fig pest.

pester [peste] *vi* to curse; **p. contre qch/qn** to curse sth/s.o.

pestilentiel, -ielle [pestilãsjɛl] *a* fetid, stinking.

pétale [petal] *nm* petal.

pétanque [petãk] *nf (jeu)* bowls.

pétarades [petarad] *nfpl (de moto etc)* backfiring. ● **pétarader** *vi* to backfire.

pétard [petar] *nm (explosif)* firecracker, *Br* banger.

péter [pete] *vi* Fam *(éclater)* to go bang *ou* pop; *(se rompre)* to snap.

pétiller [petije] *vi (champagne, eau etc)* to sparkle, fizz; *(yeux)* to sparkle; *(bois, feu)* to crackle. ● **pétillant, -ante** *a (eau, vin, yeux)* sparkling.

petit, -ite [p(ə)ti, -it] *a* small, little; *(de taille)* short; *(bruit, coup, espoir)* slight; *(jeune)* little; *(mesquin, insignifiant)* petty; **tout p.** tiny; **un p. Français** a (little) French boy; **une bonne petite employée** a good little worker; **se faire tout p.** *Fam (être gêné)* to want to find a corner to hide in; **se faire tout p. devant une femme** to satisfy a woman's every whim; **c'est une petite nature** he's *ou* she's a weak sort of person.

▮ *nmf* (little) boy, (little) girl; *(personne)* small person; *Scol* junior; **petits** *(d'animal)* young; *(de chien)* pups, young; *(de chat)* kittens, young.

▮ *adv* **écrire p.** to write small; **p. à p.** little

by little. ●**petit-beurre** *nm* (*pl* petits-beurre) *Br* butter biscuit, *Am* butter cookie. ●**petit-bourgeois, petite-bourgeoise** *a* (*mpl* petits-bourgeois) *a Péj* middle-class. ●**petit-suisse** *nm* (*pl* petits-suisses) soft cheese (*for dessert*).

petitement [p(ə)titmã] *adv* (*chichement*) shabbily, poorly. ●**petitesse** *nf* (*de taille*) smallness; (*mesquinerie*) pettiness.

petit-fils [p(ə)tifis] *nm* (*pl* petits-fils) grandson, grandchild. ●**petite-fille** *nf* (*pl* petites-filles) granddaughter, grandchild. ●**petits-enfants** *nmpl* grandchildren.

pétition [petisjõ] *nf* petition.

pétrifier [petrifje] *vt* (*de peur, d'émoi etc*) to petrify.

pétrin [petrɛ̃] *nm Fam* (*situation*) fix; être dans le p. to be in a fix.

pétrir [petrir] *vt* to knead.

pétrole [petrɔl] *nm* oil, petroleum; p. (lampant) *Br* paraffin, *Am* kerosene; nappe de p. (*sur la mer*) oil slick. ●**pétrolier, -ière** *a* industrie/etc pétrolière oil industry/etc ▮ *nm* (*navire*) oil tanker. ●**pétrolifère** *a* gisement p. oil field.

pétulant, -ante [petylã, -ãt] *a* exuberant.

pétunia [petynja] *nm* (*plante*) petunia.

peu [pø] *adv* (*manger, lire etc*) not much, little; **elle mange p.** she doesn't eat much, she eats little; **un p.** (*lire, surpris etc*) a little, a bit; **p. de sel/de temps**/etc not much salt/time/etc, little salt/time/etc; **un p. de fromage**/etc a little cheese/etc, a bit of cheese/etc; **le p. de fromage que j'ai** the little cheese I have; **p. de gens/de livres**/etc few people/ books/etc, not many people/books/etc; **p. sont...** few are...; **un (tout) petit p.** a (tiny) little bit; **p. intéressant/souvent**/etc not very interesting/often/etc; **p. de chose** not much; **p. à p.** little by little, gradually; **à p.** près more or less; **p. après/avant** shortly after/before; **pour un p. je l'aurais jeté dehors** I very nearly threw him out.

peuplade [pœplad] *nf* tribe.

peuple [pœpl] *nm* (*nation, masse*) people; **les gens du p.** the common people.

peupler [pœple] *vt* to populate, people. ●**peuplé, -ée** *a* (*région etc*) populated (**de** by); **très/peu**/etc p. highly/sparsely/etc populated. ●**peuplement** *nm* (*action*) populating; **zone de p.** population zone, area of population.

peuplier [pøplije] *nm* (*arbre, bois*) poplar.

peur [pœr] *nf* fear; **avoir p.** to be afraid *ou* frightened *ou* scared (**de** qch/qn of sth/s.o.; **de faire** qch to do sth, of doing sth); **faire p. à** qn to frighten *ou* scare s.o.; **de p. qu'il ne parte** for fear that he would leave, for fear of his leaving; **de p. de faire** qch for fear of doing sth. ●**peureux, -euse** *a* easily frightened, fearful.

peut, peux [pø] *voir* pouvoir 1.

peut-être [pøtɛtr] *adv* perhaps, maybe; **p.-être qu'il viendra, p.-être viendra-t-il** perhaps *ou* maybe he'll come.

peuvent, peux [pœv, pø] *voir* **pouvoir 1.**

phallique [falik] *a* a phallic. ●**phallocrate** *nm Péj* male chauvinist (pig).

pharaon [faraõ] *nm Hist* Pharaoh.

phare [far] *nm* (*pour bateaux*) lighthouse; (*de véhicule*) headlight, *Br* headlamp; **faire un appel de phares** (*en voiture*) to flash one's lights; **rouler pleins phares** (*en voiture*) to drive on full headlights.

pharmacie [farmasi] *nf Br* chemist's shop, *Am* drugstore; (*science*) pharmacy; (*armoire*) medicine cabinet. ●**pharmaceutique** *a* pharmaceutical. ●**pharmacien, -ienne** *nmf Br* chemist, pharmacist, *Am* druggist.

pharynx [farɛ̃ks] *nm Anat* pharynx.

phase [faz] *nf* phase; **être en p.** *Fig* to be in perfect harmony (**avec** qn with s.o.).

phénomène [fenɔmɛn] *nm* phenomenon; (*personne*) *Fam* eccentric. ●**phénoménal, -e, -aux** *a* phenomenal.

philanthrope [filãtrɔp] *nmf* philanthropist. ●**philanthropique** *a* philanthropic.

philatélie [filateli] *nf* stamp collecting, philately. ●**philatélique** *a* philatelic. ●**philatéliste** *nmf* stamp collector, philatelist.

philharmonique [filarmɔnik] *a* (*orchestre*) philharmonic.

Philippines [filipin] *nfpl* **les P.** the Philippines.

philosophe [filɔzɔf] *nmf* philosopher ▮ *a* (*résigné, sage*) philosophical. ●**philosopher** *vi* to philosophize (**sur** about). ●**philosophie** *nf* philosophy. ●**philosophique** *a* philosophical.

philtre [filtr] *nm* love potion.

phobie [fɔbi] *nf* phobia.

phonétique [fɔnetik] *a* phonetic ▮ *nf* phonetics.

phonographe [fɔnɔgraf] *nm Br* gramophone, *Am* phonograph.

phoque [fɔk] *nm* (*animal*) seal.

phosphate [fɔsfat] *nm Ch* phosphate.

phosphore [fɔsfɔr] *nm Ch* phosphorus. ●**phosphorescent, -ente** *a* luminous, phosphorescent.

photo [fɔto] *nf* photo; (*art*) photography; **p. d'identité** ID photo; **prendre une p. de, prendre en p.** to take a photo of; **se faire prendre en p.** to have one's photo taken; **il veut ma p.?** *Fam* who does he think he's staring at? ▮ *a inv* **appareil p.** camera. ●**photogénique** *a* photogenic. ●**photographe** *nmf* photographer. ●**photographie** *nf* (*art*) photography; (*image*) photograph. ●**photographier** *vt* to photograph. ●**photographique** *a* photographic.

photocopie [fɔtɔkɔpi] *nf* photocopy. ●**photocopier** *vt* to photocopy. ●**photocopieur** *nm ou* **photocopieuse** *nf* (*machine*) photocopier.

photomaton® [fɔtɔmatõ] *nm* (*appareil*) photo booth.

phrase [fraz] *nf* (*mots*) sentence.

physicien, -ienne [fizisjɛ̃, -jɛn] *nmf* physicist.

physiologie [fizjɔlɔʒi] *nf* physiology.

●**physiologique** a physiological.
physionomie [fizjɔnɔmi] nf face.
physique [fizik] **1** a physical **l** nm (corps, aspect) physique; **au p. comme au moral** physically and morally. **2** nf (science) physics. ●**physiquement** adv physically.
phytothérapie [fitɔterapi] nf herbal medicine.
piaffer [pjafe] vi (cheval) to stamp; **p. d'impatience** Fig to fidget impatiently.
piailler [pjaje] vi (oiseau) to cheep; (enfant) Fam to squeal.
piano [pjano] nm piano; **p. droit/à queue** upright/grand piano. ●**pianiste** nmf pianist. ●**pianoter** vi to thump away at the piano; Fig to drum one's fingers.
piaule [pjol] nf (chambre) Fam room, pad.
PIB [peibe] nm abrév (produit intérieur brut) GDP.
pic [pik] nm **1** (cime) peak. **2** (outil) pick(axe); **p. à glace** ice pick. **3** (oiseau) woodpecker.
pic (à) [apik] adv (verticalement) sheer; **couler à p.** to sink to the bottom; **la falaise tombe à p.** the cliff is sheer, there's a sheer drop; **tomber ou arriver à p.** Fig to come at the right moment ou in the nick of time.
pichenette [piʃnɛt] nf **faire une p.** to flick one's finger.
pichet [piʃɛ] nm jug, pitcher.
pickpocket [pikpɔkɛt] nm pickpocket.
picoler [pikɔle] vi Fam to tipple, booze.
picorer [pikɔre] vti to peck.
picoter [pikɔte] vt (yeux) to make smart; (jambes) to make tingle; **les yeux me picotent** my eyes are smarting.
pie [pi] **1** nf (oiseau) magpie. **2** a inv (couleur) piebald.
pièce [pjes] nf **1** (de maison etc) room. **2** (morceau, objet etc) piece; (de pantalon) patch; (écrit de dossier) document; **p. (de monnaie)** coin; **p. (de théâtre)** play; **p. (d'artillerie)** gun; **p. d'identité** identity card, proof of identity; **p. d'eau** pool, pond; **pièces détachées** ou **de rechange** (de véhicule etc) spare parts; **pièces justificatives** supporting documents; **avec pièces à l'appui** with supporting documents; **p. montée** = tiered wedding cake; **cinq dollars/etc (la) p.** five dollars/etc each; **travailler à la p.** to do piecework; **mettre qch en pièces** to tear sth to pieces ou to shreds.
pied [pje] nm foot (pl feet); (de lit, d'arbre, de colline) foot; (de meuble) leg; (de verre, lampe) base; (d'appareil photo) stand; **un p. de salade** a head of lettuce; **à p.** on foot; **aller à p.** to walk, go on foot; **au p. de** at the foot ou bottom of; **au p. de la lettre** Fig literally; **coup de p.** kick; **donner un coup de p.** to kick (**à qn** s.o.); **avoir p.** (nageur) to have a footing, touch the bottom; **sur p.** (debout, levé) up and about; **sur ses pieds** (malade guéri) up and about; **sur un p. d'égalité** on an equal footing; **sur le p. de guerre** on a war footing; **comme un p.** (mal)

Fam dreadfully; **faire un p. de nez à qn** to thumb one's nose at s.o.; **mettre qch sur p.** (organiser) to set sth up; **attendre qn de p. ferme** to be ready and waiting for s.o.; **remplacer qn au p. levé** to replace s.o. at a moment's notice; **ça lui fera les pieds!** Fam that will serve him right!; **c'est le p.!** Fam it's fantastic ou terrific! ●**pied-noir** nmf (pl **pieds-noirs**) Algerian-born Frenchman ou Frenchwoman.
piédestal, -aux [pjedestal, -o] nm pedestal.
piège [pjeʒ] nm (pour animal) & Fig trap. ●**piéger** vt (animal) to trap; (voiture etc) to booby-trap; **colis/voiture/lettre piégé(e)** parcel/car/letter bomb; **engin piégé** booby trap.
pierre [pjɛr] nf stone; (précieuse) gem, stone; **p. (à briquet)** flint; **geler à p. fendre** to freeze hard; **faire d'une p. deux coups** Fig to kill two birds with one stone. ●**pierreries** nfpl gems, precious stones. ●**pierreux, -euse** a stony.
piété [pjete] nf piety.
piétiner [pjetine] vt (sol etc) to trample (on) **l** vi to stamp (one's feet); (marcher sur place) to mark time; (ne pas avancer) Fig to make no headway.
piéton [pjetɔ̃] nm pedestrian. ●**piétonne** ou **piétonnière** a **rue p.** pedestrian(ized) street; **zone p.** Br pedestrian precinct, pedestrianized area.
piètre [pjɛtr] a Litt wretched, poor.
pieu, -x [pjø] nm **1** (piquet) post, stake. **2** (lit) Fam bed.
pieuvre [pjœvr] nf octopus.
pieux, -euse [pjø, -øz] a pious.
pif [pif] nm (nez) Fam nose. ●**pif(omètre) (au)** adv (sans calcul) Fam at a rough guess.
pigeon [piʒɔ̃] nm pigeon; (personne) Fam dupe; **p. voyageur** carrier pigeon. ●**pigeonner** vt (voler) Fam to rip off.
piger [piʒe] vti Fam to understand.
pigment [pigmã] nm pigment. ●**pigmentation** nf pigmentation.
pignon [piɲɔ̃] nm (de maison etc) gable; **avoir p. sur rue** Fig to be in a position of some standing, be established and respected.
pile [pil] **1** nf (électrique) battery; (atomique) pile; **radio à piles** battery radio. **2** nf (tas) pile; **en p.** in a pile. **3** nf **p. (ou face)?** heads (or tails)?; **jouer à p. ou face** to toss up. **4** nf (de pont) pier. **5** adv **s'arrêter p.** Fam to stop short ou dead; **à deux heures p.** Fam on the dot of two.
piler [pile] **1** vt (amandes etc) to grind; (ail) to crush. **2** vi (en voiture) Fam to stop dead. ●**pilonner** vt (sous les obus) to bombard, shell.
pilier [pilje] nm pillar.
pilon [pilɔ̃] nm (de poulet) drumstick.
piller [pije] vti to loot, pillage. ●**pillage** nm looting, pillage. ●**pillard, -arde** nmf looter.
pilori [pilɔri] nm **mettre au p.** Fig to pillory.
pilote [pilɔt] nm (d'avion, de bateau) pilot; (de voiture, char) driver; (guide) Fig guide;

p. de ligne airline pilot ▮ **a usine**/*etc*(-)**p.** pilot factory/*etc*. ● **piloter** *vt* (*avion*) to fly, pilot; (*bateau*) to pilot; (*voiture*) to drive; **p. qn** *Fig* to show s.o. around. ● **pilotage** *nm* piloting; **poste de p.** cockpit; **école de p.** flying school; **être sur p. automatique** to be on automatic pilot.

pilotis [pilɔti] *nm* (*pieux*) *Archit* piles; **construit sur p.** built on piles.

pilule [pilyl] *nf* pill; **prendre la p.** (*femme*) to be on the pill; **arrêter la p.** to go off the pill; **avaler la p.** *Fig* to swallow the bitter pill.

piment [pimã] *nm* pepper, pimento. ● **pimenté, -ée** *a* (*plat*) *& Fig* spicy.

pimpant, -ante [pɛ̃pɑ̃, -ɑ̃t] *a* pretty, spruce.

pin [pɛ̃] *nm* (*arbre, bois*) pine; **pomme de p.** pine cone.

pinailler [pinaje] *vi Fam* to quibble, split hairs.

pinard [pinar] *nm* (*vin*) *Fam* wine.

pince [pɛ̃s] *nf* (*outil*) pliers; (*de cycliste*) clip; (*levier*) crowbar; **pinces** (*de crabe*) pincers; **p. à linge** (*clothes*) *Br* peg *ou Am* pin; **p. à épiler** tweezers; **p. à ongles** nail clippers; **p. à sucre** sugar tongs; **p. (à cheveux)** *Br* hairgrip, *Am* bobby pin; **serrer la p. à qn** *Fam* to shake s.o.'s hand.

pincer [pɛ̃se] *vt* to pinch; (*corde*) *Mus* to pluck; **p. qn** (*arrêter*) *Fam* to nab s.o., *Br* pinch s.o.; **se p. le doigt** to get one's finger caught (**dans** in). ● **pincé, -ée** *a* (*air*) stiff, constrained. ● **pincée** *nf* (*de sel etc*) pinch (**de** of). ● **pincettes** *nfpl* (*fire*) tongs; (*d'horloger*) tweezers; **il n'est pas à prendre avec des p.** (*il est de mauvaise humeur*) he's like a bear with a sore head. ● **pinçon** *nm* pinch (mark).

pinceau, -x [pɛ̃so] *nm* (paint)brush.

pince-sans-rire [pɛ̃sɑ̃rir] *nm inv* person of dry humour.

pinède [pinɛd] *nf* pine forest.

pingouin [pɛ̃gwɛ̃] *nm* penguin, auk.

ping-pong [piŋpɔ̃g] *nm* table tennis, ping-pong.

pingre [pɛ̃gr] *a* stingy ▮ *nmf* skinflint.

pin's [pinz] *nm inv* badge, lapel pin.

pinson [pɛ̃sɔ̃] *nm* (*oiseau*) chaffinch.

pintade [pɛ̃tad] *nf* guinea fowl.

pin-up [pinœp] *nf inv* (*fille*) pinup.

pioche [pjɔʃ] *nf* pick(axe). ● **piocher** *vti* (*creuser*) to dig (with a pick); (*aux cartes*) to take (a card) from the pile.

pion [pjɔ̃] *nm* **1** (*au jeu de dames*) piece; *Échecs & Fig* pawn. **2** (*surveillant de lycée*) *Fam* master (in charge of discipline).

pionnier [pjɔnje] *nm* pioneer.

pipe [pip] *nf* (*de fumeur*) pipe; **fumer la p.** to smoke a pipe.

pipeau, -x [pipo] *nm* (*flûte*) pipe.

pipeline [piplin] *nm* pipeline.

pipi [pipi] *nm* **faire p.** *Fam* to go for a pee.

pique [pik] **1** *nm* (*couleur*) *Cartes* spades. **2** *nf* (*allusion*) cutting remark. **3** *nf* (*arme*) pike.

pique-assiette [pikasjɛt] *nmf inv* scrounger.

pique-nique [piknik] *nm* picnic. ● **pique-niquer** *vi* to picnic.

piquer [pike] *vt* (*percer*) to prick; (*langue, yeux*) to sting; (*coudre*) to (machine-)stitch; (*édredon, couvre-lit*) to quilt; (*curiosité*) to rouse; **p. qn** (*abeille*) to sting s.o.; (*serpent*) to bite s.o.; *Méd* to give s.o. an injection; (*arrêter*) *Fam* to nab *ou Br* pinch s.o.; **p. qn au vif** to cut s.o. to the quick; **p. qch dans** (*enfoncer*) to stick into; **p. qch** (*voler*) *Fam* to steal sth, *Br* pinch sth; **p. une colère** *Fam* to fly into a rage; **p. une crise (de nerfs)** *Fam* to throw a fit; **p. une tête** *Fam* to plunge headlong; **p. un cent mètres** *Fam* to put on a sprint; **faire p. un chien**/*etc* to have a dog/*etc* put to sleep.

▮ *vi* (*avion*) to dive; (*moutarde etc*) to be hot.

▮ **se piquer** *vpr* to prick oneself; **se p. au doigt** to prick one's finger; **se p. de faire qch** *Litt* to pride oneself on being able to do sth. ● **piquant, -ante** *a* (*plante, barbe*) prickly; (*sauce, goût*) pungent, piquant; (*froid*) biting; (*mot*) cutting; (*détail*) spicy ▮ *nm* (*de plante*) prickle, thorn; (*d'animal*) spine, prickle. ● **piqué, -ée** *a* (*meuble*) worm-eaten; (*fou*) *Fam* crazy ▮ *nm* (*en avion*) (nose)dive; **descente en p.** (*en avion*) nosedive.

piquet [pikɛ] *nm* **1** (*pieu*) stake, picket; (*de tente*) peg. **2 p. (de grève)** picket (line), strike picket. **3 au p.** (*à l'école*) in the corner.

piqueté, -ée [pikte] *a* **p. de** dotted with.

piqûre [pikyr] *nf* (*d'abeille*) sting; (*de serpent*) bite; (*d'épingle*) prick; *Méd* injection; (*point*) stitch; (*trou*) hole; **faire une p. à qn** to give s.o. an injection.

pirate [pirat] *nm* pirate; **p. de l'air** hijacker; **p. (informatique)** hacker ▮ **a radio**/*etc* **p.** pirate radio/*etc*; **édition/CD**/*etc* **p.** pirated edition/CD/*etc*. ● **piratage** *nm* (*recopiage illégal*) pirating. ● **piraterie** *nf* piracy; (*acte*) act of piracy; **p. (aérienne)** hijacking.

pire [pir] *a* worse (**que** than); **le p. moment/résultat**/*etc* the worst moment/result/*etc* ▮ *nmf* **le ou la p.** the worst (one); **le p. de tout** the worst (thing) of all; **au p.** at (the very) worst; **s'attendre au p.** to expect the (very) worst.

pirogue [pirɔg] *nf* canoe, dugout.

pis [pi] **1** *nm* (*de vache*) udder. **2** *a inv & adv* *Litt* worse; **de mal en p.** from bad to worse ▮ *nm* **le p.** *Litt* the worst.

pis-aller [pizale] *nm inv* (*personne, solution*) stopgap.

piscine [pisin] *nf* swimming pool.

pissenlit [pisɑ̃li] *nm* dandelion.

pisser [pise] *vi Fam* to have a pee; **il pissait le sang** there was blood gushing out of him.

pistache [pistaʃ] *nf* (*graine, parfum*) pistachio.

piste [pist] *nf* (*traces*) track, trail; *Sport* (race)track; (*de cirque*) ring; (*de patinage*) rink; (*pour chevaux*) racecourse, racetrack; (*de magnétophone*) track; **p. (d'envol ou**

d'atterrissage) runway; **p. cyclable** *Br* cycle track, *Am* bicycle path; **p. de danse** dance floor; **p. de ski** ski run *ou* slope; **tour de p.** *Sport* lap; **jeu de p.** treasure hunt.

pistolet [pistɔlɛ] *nm* gun, pistol; (*de peintre*) spray gun; **p. à eau** water pistol.

piston [pistɔ̃] *nm* **1** (*de véhicule*) piston. **2 avoir du p.** (*appui*) *Fam* to have connections. ●**pistonner** *vt* (*appuyer*) *Fam* to pull strings for.

pita [pita] *nm* pitta bread.

pitié [pitje] *nf* pity; **j'ai p. de lui, il me fait p.** I feel sorry for him, I pity him. ●**piteux, -euse** *a Iron* pitiful; **en p. état** in a pitiful *ou* sorry state. ●**pitoyable** *a* pitiful.

piton [pitɔ̃] *nm* **1** (*à crochet*) hook. **2** *Géog* peak.

pitre [pitr] *nm* clown. ●**pitrerie(s)** *nf(pl)* clowning.

pittoresque [pitɔrɛsk] *a* picturesque.

pivert [pivɛr] *nm* (green) woodpecker.

pivoine [pivwan] *nf* (*plante*) peony.

pivot [pivo] *nm* pivot; (*personne*) *Fig* linchpin, mainspring. ●**pivoter** *vi* (*personne*) to swing round; (*fauteuil*) to swivel; (*porte*) to revolve.

pizza [pidza] *nf* pizza. ●**pizzeria** *nf* pizzeria, pizza parlour.

PJ [peʒi] **1** *nf abrév* (*police judiciaire*) = *Br* CID, = *Am* FBI. **2** *abrév* (*pièce(s) jointe(s)*) enc, encl.

placage [plakaʒ] *nm* (*revêtement*) facing; (*en bois*) veneer.

placard [plakar] *nm* **1** (*armoire*) *Br* cupboard, *Am* closet. **2 p. publicitaire** advertising poster. ●**placarder** *vt* (*affiche*) to stick up.

place [plas] *nf* (*endroit, rang*) & *Sport* place; (*espace*) room; (*lieu public*) square; (*siège*) seat, place; (*emploi*) job, position; **p. (de parking)** parking place *ou* space; **p. de train/bus/etc** train/bus/*etc* fare; **p. (forte)** (*forteresse*) fortress; **p. (financière)** (*money*) market; **à la p.** (*échange*) instead (de of); **à votre p.** in your place; **sur p.** on the spot; **sur la p. de Paris** in (the city of) Paris; **en p.** (*objet*) in place; **mettre qch en p.** (*installer*) to set sth up; (*ranger*) to put sth in its place; **changer de p.** to change places; **changer qch de p.** to move sth; **faire de la p.** (à qn) to make room (for s.o.); **se mettre à la p. de qn** to put oneself in s.o.'s place *ou* shoes; **ne pas tenir en p.** to be unable to keep still, **faire p. à** to give way to; **faire p. nette** to make a clean sweep of things.

placer [plase] *vt* (*mettre*) to put, place; (*situer*) to place, position; (*invité, spectateur*) to seat; (*argent*) to invest, place (**dans** in); (*vendre*) to place, sell; **je n'ai pas pu p. un mot** I couldn't get a word in *Br* edgeways *ou Am* edgewise.

  se placer *vpr* (*debout*) to (go and) stand; (*s'asseoir*) to (go and) sit; (*objet*) to be put *ou* placed; (*cheval, coureur*) to be placed; **se p. troisième/etc** *Sport* to come *ou* be third/

etc. ●**placé, -ée** *a* (*objet*) & *Sport* placed; **bien/mal p. pour faire qch** in a good/bad position to do sth; **les gens haut placés** people in high places. ●**placement** *nm* (*d'argent*) investment; **bureau de p.** (*dans une école*) placement *ou* employment office.

placide [plasid] *a* placid.

plafond [plafɔ̃] *nm* ceiling. ●**plafonnier** *nm* (*de voiture*) roof light.

plage [plaʒ] *nf* **1** beach; (*ville*) (seaside) resort. **2** (*sur disque*) track. **3 p. arrière** (*de voiture*) (back) window shelf, parcel shelf.

plagiat [plaʒja] *nm* plagiarism. ●**plagier** *vt* to plagiarize.

plaid [plɛd] *nm* travelling rug.

plaider [plede] *vti* (*défendre*) *Jur* to plead. ●**plaideur, -euse** *nmf* litigant. ●**plaidoirie** *nf* (*d'un avocat*) speech (for the *Br* defence *ou Am* defense). ●**plaidoyer** *nm* plea.

plaie [plɛ] *nf* (*blessure*) wound; (*coupure*) cut; (*corvée, personne*) *Fig* nuisance.

plaignant, -ante [plɛɲɑ̃, -ɑ̃t] *nmf* (*à un procès*) plaintiff.

plain-pied (de) [dəplɛ̃pje] *adv* on the same level, on one level.

plaindre* [plɛ̃dr] **1** *vt* to feel sorry for, pity. **2 se plaindre** *vpr* (*protester*) to complain (about, **que** that); **se p. de** (*maux de tête etc*) to complain of *ou* about. ●**plainte** *nf* complaint; (*cri*) moan, groan; **porter p. contre qn** to lodge *ou* make a complaint against s.o.; **porter p. contre X** to make a complaint against person *ou* persons unknown.

plaine [plɛn] *nf Géog* plain.

plaintif, -ive [plɛ̃tif, -iv] *a* sorrowful, plaintive.

plaire* [plɛr] *vi* & *v imp* **p. à qn** to please s.o.; **elle lui plaît** he likes her, she pleases him; **ça me plaît** I like it ▌ *v imp* **il me plaît de faire** I like doing; **s'il vous** *ou* **te plaît** please ▌ **se plaire** *vpr* (*l'un l'autre*) to like each other; **se p. à Paris/etc** to like it *ou* enjoy in Paris/*etc*.

plaisance [plɛzɑ̃s] *nf* **bateau de p.** pleasure boat; **navigation de p.** yachting.

plaisant, -ante [plɛzɑ̃, -ɑ̃t] *a* (*drôle*) amusing; (*agréable*) pleasing ▌ *nm* **mauvais p.** joker. ●**plaisanter** *vi* to joke, jest (**sur** about); **p. avec qch** to trifle with sth; **on ne plaisante pas avec la drogue/etc** drugs/*etc* are no joking matter; **tu plaisantes!** you're joking! ▌ *vt* to tease. ●**plaisanterie** *nf* joke, jest; (*bagatelle*) trifle; **par p.** for a joke. ●**plaisantin** *nm* joker.

plaisir [plɛzir] *nm* pleasure; **faire p. à qn** to please s.o.; **pour le p.** for fun, for the fun of it; **au p. (de vous revoir)** see you again sometime; **faites-moi le p. de...** would you be good enough to....

plan¹ [plɑ̃] *nm* **1** (*projet, dessin*) plan; (*de ville*) map, plan; *Géom* plane; **au premier p.** in the foreground; **au second p.** *Phot* in the background; **passer au second p.** *Fig* to be forced into the background; **gros p.** *Phot Cinéma* close-up; **sur le p. politique/etc, au p.**

politique/*etc* from the political/*etc* viewpoint, politically/*etc*; **sur le même p.** on the same level *ou* plane; **de premier p.** of importance, major; **p. d'eau** stretch of water; **laisser en p.** (*abandonner*) *Fam* to ditch.

plan¹, plane [plɑ̃, plan] *a* (*plat*) even, flat.

planche [plɑ̃ʃ] *nf* **1** board, plank; **p. à repasser/à dessin** ironing/drawing board; **p.** (**à roulettes**) skateboard; **p.** (**à voile**) sailboard; **p.** (**de surf**) surfboard; **faire de la p.** (**à voile**) to go windsurfing; **faire la p.** to float on one's back; **monter sur les planches** (*au théâtre*) to go on the stage. **2** (*illustration*) plate. **3** (*de légumes*) bed, plot.

plancher¹ [plɑ̃ʃe] *nm* floor.

plancher² [plɑ̃ʃe] *vi Arg* to be questioned (*in an exam*) (**sur** on).

planer [plane] *vi* (*oiseau*) to glide, hover; (*avion etc*) to glide; **p. sur qn/qch** (*mystère*) to hang over s.o./sth; **vol plané** glide/gliding. ● **planeur** *nm* (*avion*) glider.

planète [planɛt] *nf* planet. ● **planétaire** *a* planetary. ● **planétarium** *nm* planetarium.

planifier [planifje] *vt* *Écon* to plan. ● **planification** *nf Écon* planning. ● **planning** *nm* (*emploi du temps*) schedule; **p. familial** family planning.

planisphère [planisfɛr] *nm* planisphere.

planque [plɑ̃k] *nf* **1** (*travail*) *Fam* cushy job. **2** (*lieu*) *Fam* hideout. ● **planquer** *vt,* **se planquer** *vpr Fam* to hide.

plant [plɑ̃] *nm* (*plante*) seedling; (*de légumes etc*) bed.

plantation [plɑ̃tasjɔ̃] *nf* (*action*) planting; (*terrain*) bed; (*de café, d'arbres etc*) plantation.

plante [plɑ̃t] *nf* **1** *Bot* plant; **p. verte, p. d'appartement** house plant; **jardin des plantes** botanical gardens. **2 p. des pieds** sole (of the foot).

planter [plɑ̃te] *vt* (*fleur, arbre etc*) to plant; (*clou, couteau*) to drive in; (*tente, drapeau*) to put up; (*mettre*) to put (**sur** on, **contre** against); (*regard*) to fix (**sur** on); **p. là qn** to leave s.o. standing ∎ **se planter** *vpr* (*tomber*) *Fam* to fall over; (*échouer*) *Fam* to fail; **se p. devant** to come *ou* go and stand in front of, to plant oneself in front of. ● **planté, -ée** *a* (*immobile*) standing; **bien p.** (*personne*) sturdy.

planteur [plɑ̃tœr] *nm* plantation owner.

planton [plɑ̃tɔ̃] *nm* (*soldat*) orderly.

plantureux, -euse [plɑ̃tyrø, -øz] *a* (*repas etc*) abundant; (*femme*) buxom.

plaque [plak] *nf* plate; (*de verre, métal*) sheet, plate; (*de verglas*) sheet; (*de marbre*) slab; (*de chocolat*) bar; (*commémorative*) plaque; (*tache*) *Méd* blotch; **p. chauffante** (*de cuisine*) hotplate; **p. tournante** (*carrefour*) *Fig* centre; **p. minéralogique, p. d'immatriculation** (*de véhicule*) *Br* number *ou* *Am* license plate; **p. dentaire** (dental) plaque.

plaquer [plake] *vt* (*métal, bijou*) to plate; (*bois*) to veneer; (*cheveux*) to plaster

(down); *Rugby* to tackle; (*aplatir*) to flatten (**contre** against); (*abandonner*) *Fam* to give (*sth*) up; **p. qn** *Fam* to ditch s.o.; **se p. contre** to flatten oneself against. ● **plaqué, -ée** *a* (*bijou*) plated; **p. or** gold-plated ∎ *nm* **p. or** gold plate. ● **plaquage** *nm Rugby* tackle.

plasma [plasma] *nm* (*du sang*) plasma.

plastic [plastik] *nm* plastic explosive. ● **plastiquer** *vt* to blow up.

plastique [plastik] *a* (*art, substance*) plastic; **matière** ∎ plastic ∎ *nm* (*matière*) plastic; **en p.** (*bouteille etc*) plastic.

plastron [plastrɔ̃] *nm* shirtfront.

plat, plate [pla, plat] **1** *a* flat; (*mer*) calm, smooth; (*fade*) flat, dull; **à fond p.** flat-bottomed; **à p. ventre** flat on one's face; **à p.** (*pneu, batterie*) flat; (*épuisé*) *Fam* exhausted; **poser à p.** to put *ou* lay (down) flat; **tomber à p.** (*être un échec*) to fall flat; **assiette plate** dinner plate; **eau plate** still water; **calme p.** dead calm; **faire à qn des plates excuses** to make a humble apology to s.o. ∎ *nm* (*de la main*) flat.

2 *nm* (*récipient, nourriture*) dish; (*partie du repas*) course; **'p. du jour'** (*au restaurant*) 'today's special'; **mettre les petits plats dans les grands** *Fig* to put on a marvellous spread; **elle en a fait tout un p.** *Fam* she made a great big fuss about it.

platane [platan] *nm* plane tree.

plateau, -x [plato] *nm* (*pour servir*) tray; (*de balance*) pan; (*de tourne-disque*) turntable; (*de cinéma, télévision*) set; (*de théâtre*) stage; *Géog* plateau; **p. à fromages** cheeseboard.

plate-bande [platbɑ̃d] *nf* (*pl* **plates-bandes**) flower bed; **marcher sur les plates-bandes de qn** *Fam* to poke one's nose into s.o.'s business.

plate-forme [platform] *nf* (*pl* **plates-formes**) platform; **p.-forme pétrolière** oil rig.

platine [platin] **1** *nm* (*métal*) platinum ∎ *a inv* (*couleur*) platinum; **blond p.** platinum blond. **2** *nf* (*d'électrophone, de magnétophone*) deck. ● **platiné, -ée** *a* (*cheveux*) platinum, platinum-blond(e).

platitude [platityd] *nf* platitude.

plâtre [plɑtr] *nm* (*matière*) plaster; **un p.** (*pour jambe cassée*) a plaster cast; **dans le p.** (*jambe, bras etc*) in plaster; **les plâtres** (*d'une maison etc*) the plasterwork; **p. à mouler** plaster of Paris; **essuyer les plâtres** *Fam* to be the first to suffer (*as the result of a new situation*). ● **plâtrer** *vt* (*mur*) to plaster; (*membre*) to put in plaster. ● **plâtrage** *nm* plastering. ● **plâtrier** *nm* plasterer.

plausible [plozibl] *a* plausible.

play-back [plebak] *nm inv* **chanter en p.-back** to mime to a tape *ou* record.

plébiscite [plebisit] *nm* plebiscite.

plein, pleine [plɛ̃, plɛn] *a* (*rempli, complet*) full; (*paroi*) solid; (*ivre*) *Fam* tight; **p. de** full of; **en pleine mer** out at sea, on the open sea; **en pleine figure** right in the face; **en pleine nuit** in the middle of the night; **en p. jour** in broad daylight; **en pleine campagne**

in the heart of the country; **à la pleine lune** at full moon; **p. à craquer** crammed full, full to bursting; **être p. aux as** (riche) Fam to be rolling in it.

▌prép & adv **des billes p. les poches** pockets full of marbles; **du chocolat p. la figure** chocolate all over one's face; **p. de lettres/ d'argent**/etc (beaucoup de) Fam lots of letters/money/etc; **à p.** (travailler) to full capacity.

▌nm **faire le p.** (d'essence) Aut to fill up (the tank); **battre son p.** (fête) to be in full swing. ●**pleinement** adv fully.

pléonasme [pleɔnasm] nm (expression) redundancy.

pléthore [pletɔr] nf plethora.

pleurer [plœre] vi to cry, weep (**sur** over); **p. de rire** to laugh till one cries ▌ vt (regretter) to mourn (for); **p. toutes les larmes de son corps** to cry one's eyes out. ●**pleureur** am **saule p.** weeping willow. ●**pleurnicher** vi to snivel, grizzle. ●**pleurs (en)** adv in tears.

pleurésie [plørezi] nf (maladie) pleurisy.

pleuvoir* [pløvwar] v imp to rain; **il pleut** it's raining; **il pleut des cordes** Fig it's raining cats and dogs ▌ vi (coups etc) to rain down (**sur** on).

Plexiglas® [pleksiglɑs] nm Br Perspex®, Am lucite.

pli [pli] nm **1** (de papier etc) fold; (de jupe, robe) pleat; (de pantalon, de bouche) crease; (de bras) bend; (faux) p. crease; **mise en plis** (coiffure) set; **ça n'a pas fait un p.** (ça n'a pas manqué) Fam it was bound to happen. **2** (enveloppe) envelope, letter; **sous p. séparé** under separate cover. **3** Cartes trick. **4** (habitude) habit; **prendre le p. de faire qch** to get into the habit of doing sth.

pliable [plijabl] a (facile à plier) pliable.

plier [plije] vt to fold; (courber) to bend; **p. qn** to submit s.o. to; **p. bagages** to pack one's bags (and leave) ▌ vi (branche) to bend ▌ **se plier** vpr (lit, chaise etc) to fold (up); **se p. à** to submit to, give in to. ●**pliant, -ante** a (chaise etc) folding; (parapluie) telescopic ▌ nm folding stool. ●**pliage** nm (manière) fold; (action) folding.

plinthe [plɛ̃t] nf Br skirting board, Am baseboard.

plisser [plise] vt (jupe, robe) to pleat; (lèvres) to pucker; (front) to wrinkle, crease; (yeux) to screw up; (froisser) to crease. ●**plissé, -ée** a (tissu, jupe) pleated.

plomb [plɔ̃] nm (métal) lead; (fusible) fuse; (poids pour rideau etc) lead weight; **plombs** (de chasse) lead shot, buckshot; **essence sans p.** unleaded Br petrol ou Am gasoline; **tuyau**/etc **de p.** ou **en p.** lead pipe/etc; **de p.** (sommeil) Fig heavy; (soleil) blazing; (ciel) leaden; **ça lui mettra du p. dans la cervelle** Fig that will knock some sense into him.

plomber [plɔ̃be] vt (dent) to fill; (colis) to seal (with lead). ●**plombé, -ée** a (teint) leaden. ●**plombage** nm (de dent) filling.

plombier [plɔ̃bje] nm plumber. ●**plomberie**

nf (métier, installations) plumbing.

plonger [plɔ̃ʒe] vi (personne, avion etc) to dive, plunge; (route, regard) Fig to plunge ▌ vt (mettre, enfoncer) to plunge, thrust (**dans** into); **se p. dans** (lecture etc) to immerse oneself in. ●**plongeant, -ante** a (décolleté) plunging; **vue plongeante** bird's-eye view. ●**plongé, -ée** a **dans** (lecture, pensées etc) immersed ou engrossed in; **p. dans l'obscurité** plunged into darkness. ●**plongée** nf diving; (de sous-marin) submersion; **p. (sous-marine)** (skin ou scuba) diving; **en p. (sous-marin)** submerged. ●**plongeoir** nm diving board. ●**plongeon** nm dive. ●**plongeur, -euse** nmf **1** diver. **2** (employé de restaurant) dishwasher.

plouf [pluf] nm & int splash.

ployer [plwaje] vti Litt to bend.

plu [ply] pp de **plaire, pleuvoir.**

pluie [plɥi] nf rain; **une p.** (averse) a shower; **sous la p.** in the rain; **pluies acides** acid rain; **une p. de pierres/coups**/etc a shower ou deluge of stones/blows/etc; **sous une p. d'applaudissements** beneath a deluge of applause.

plume [plym] nf **1** (d'oiseau) feather. **2** (pour écrire) His quill (pen); **(pointe de stylo en acier)** (pen) nib; **stylo à p.** (fountain) pen; **vivre de sa p.** Fam to live by one's pen. ●**plumage** nm plumage. ●**plumeau, -x** nm feather duster. ●**plumer** vt (volaille) to pluck; **p. qn** (voler) Fig to fleece s.o. ●**plumet** nm plume. ●**plumier** nm pencil box, pen box.

plupart (la) [laplypar] nf most; **la p. des cas/** etc most cases/etc; **la p. du temps** most of the time; **la p. d'entre eux** most of them; **pour la p.** mostly.

pluriel, -ielle [plyrjɛl] a & nm Grammaire plural; **au p.** in the plural; **nom au p.** plural noun.

plus¹ [ply] ([plyz] before vowel, [plys] in end position) **1** adv comparatif (travailler etc) more (**que** than); **p. d'un kilo/de dix**/etc (quantité, nombre) more than a kilo/ten/etc; **p. de thé**/etc (davantage) more tea/etc; **p. beau/rapidement**/etc more beautiful/rapidly/ etc (**que** than); **p. tard** later; **p. petit** smaller; **de p. en p.** more and more; **de p. en p. vite** quicker and quicker; **p. ou moins** more or less; **en p.** in addition (**de** to); **au p.** at most; **de p.** more (**que** than); (en outre) moreover; **les enfants (âgés) de p. de dix ans** children over ten; **j'ai dix ans de p. qu'elle** I'm ten years older than she is; **il est p. de cinq heures** it's after five (o'clock); **p. il crie p. il s'enroue** the more he shouts the more hoarse he gets.

2 adv superlatif **le p.** (travailler etc) (the) most; **le p. beau/**etc the most beautiful/etc (**de** in); (de deux) the more beautiful/etc; **le p. grand/**etc the biggest/etc (**de** in); (de deux) the bigger/etc; **j'ai le p. de livres** I have (the) most books; **j'en ai le p.** I have the most.

plus² [ply] adv de négation (**ne**)... **p.** no

more; **il n'a p. de pain** he has no more bread, he doesn't have any more bread; **il ne reste p. rien** there's no more left, there's nothing else left; **tu n'es p. jeune** you're not young any more *ou* any longer, you're no longer young; **elle ne le fait p.** she no longer does it, she doesn't do it any more *ou* any longer; **je ne la reverrai p.** I won't see her again; **je ne voyagerai p. jamais** I'll never travel again *ou* any more.

plus³ [plys] *prép* plus; **deux p. deux font quatre** two plus two are four; **il fait p. deux (degrés)** it's two degrees above freezing **I** *nm* **le signe p.** the plus sign.

plusieurs [plyzjœr] *a & pron pl* several.

plus-que-parfait [plyskəparfɛ] *nm Grammaire* pluperfect.

plus-value [plyvaly] *nf (bénéfice)* profit.

plutonium [plytɔnjɔm] *nm* plutonium.

plutôt [plyto] *adv* rather *(que than)*.

pluvieux, -euse [plyvjø, -øz] *a* rainy, wet.

PME [peɛmø] *nf abrév (petite et moyenne entreprise)* small company.

PMU [peɛmy] *abrév* = **pari mutuel urbain.**

PNB [peɛnbe] *nm abrév (produit national brut)* GNP.

pneu [pnø] *nm (pl pneus) (de roue) Br* tyre, *Am* tire. ● **pneumatique** *a* **matelas p.** air-bed; **canot p.** rubber dinghy; **marteau p.** pneumatic drill.

pneumonie [pnømɔni] *nf* pneumonia.

poche [pɔʃ] *nf* pocket; *(de kangourou etc)* pouch; *(sac en papier etc)* bag; **poches** *(sous les yeux)* bags; **livre de p.** paperback; **argent de p.** pocket money; **faire des poches** *(pantalon)* to be baggy; **faire les poches à qn** *Fam* to go through s.o.'s pockets; **j'ai un franc en p.** I have one franc on me; **elle connaît Paris comme sa poche** she knows Paris like the back of her hand. ● **pochette** *nf (sac)* bag, envelope; *(d'allumettes)* book; *(de disque)* sleeve, jacket; *(sac à main)* (clutch) bag; *(mouchoir)* pocket handkerchief.

pocher [pɔʃe] *vt* 1 *(œufs)* to poach. 2 **p. l'œil à qn** to give s.o. a black eye. ● **poché, -ée** *a* **œil p.** black eye.

podium [pɔdjɔm] *nm (plate-forme)* podium, rostrum.

poêle [pwal] 1 *nm* stove. 2 *nf* **p. (à frire)** frying pan.

poème [pɔɛm] *nm* poem. ● **poésie** *nf (art)* poetry; **une p.** *(poème)* a poem, a piece of poetry. ● **poète** *nm* poet **I** *a* **femme p.** woman poet, poetess. ● **poétique** *a* poetic.

pognon [pɔɲɔ̃] *nm (argent) Fam* dough.

poids [pwa] *nm* weight; **au p.** by weight; **de p.** *(argument etc)* influential; **p. lourd** *(camion) Br* lorry, *Am* truck; *(personne) Boxe* heavyweight; **p. plume** *Boxe* featherweight; *Fig* small slender person; **lancer le p.** *Sport* to put *ou* hurl the shot.

poignant, -ante [pwaɲɑ̃, -ɑ̃t] *a (souvenir etc)* poignant.

poignard [pwaɲar] *nm* dagger; **coup de p.** stab. ● **poignarder** *vt* to stab.

poigne [pwaɲ] *nf (étreinte)* grip.

poignée [pwaɲe] *nf (quantité)* handful *(de* of*)*; *(de porte, casserole etc)* handle; *(d'épée)* hilt; **p. de main** handshake; **donner une p. de main à** to shake hands with.

poignet [pwaɲɛ] *nm* wrist; *(de chemise)* cuff.

poil [pwal] *nm* hair; *(pelage)* coat, fur; **poils** *(de brosse)* bristles; *(de tapis)* pile; *(d'étoffe)* nap; **à p.** *(nu) Fam* (stark) naked; **au p.** *(parfait) Fam* top-rate; **de bon/mauvais p.** *Fam* in a good/bad mood; **de tout p.** *Fam* of all kinds. ● **poilu, -ue** *a* hairy.

poinçon [pwɛ̃sɔ̃] *nm (outil)* awl, bradawl; *(marque de bijou)* hallmark. ● **poinçonner** *vt (billet)* to punch; *(bijou)* to hallmark. ● **poinçonneuse** *nf (machine)* punch.

poindre* [pwɛ̃dr] *vi (jour) Litt* to dawn.

poing [pwɛ̃] *nm* fist; **coup de p.** punch.

point¹ [pwɛ̃] *nm (lieu, score, question etc)* point; *(sur i, à l'horizon etc)* dot; *(tache)* spot; *(unité d'une note) Scol* mark, point; *(de couture)* stitch; **être sur le p. de faire** to be about to do, be on the point of doing; **p. (final)** *Br* full stop, *Am* period; **p. d'exclamation** exclamation *Br* mark *ou Am* point; **p. d'interrogation** question mark; **points de suspension** suspension points; **p. de vue** *(opinion)* point of view, viewpoint; *(endroit) (arriver etc)* at the right moment; **à p.** *(steak)* medium rare; **jusqu'à un certain p.** up to a point; **déprimé/etc au p. que...** depressed/etc to such an extent that...; **mal en p.** in bad shape; **mettre au p.** *(appareil photo)* to focus; *(moteur)* to tune; *(technique etc)* to elaborate, perfect; *(éclaircir) Fig* to clarify, clear up; **mise au p.** focusing; *(de moteur)* tuning, tune-up; *(de technique etc)* elaboration; *Fig* clarification; **faire le p.** *Fig* to take stock, sum up; **au p. mort** *(en voiture)* in neutral; *Fig* at a standstill; **p. noir** *(de la circulation)* (accident) black spot; **p. du jour** daybreak; **p. de côté** *(douleur)* stitch (in one's side); **mettre les points sur les i** *Fig* to dot one's i's (and cross one's t's); **un p., c'est tout!** that's final!, *Am* period! ● **point-virgule** *nm (pl points-virgules)* semicolon.

point² [pwɛ̃] *adv Litt* = **pas¹.**

pointe [pwɛ̃t] *nf (extrémité)* tip, point; *(clou)* nail; *(de grille)* spike; *Géog* headland; *(maximum) Fig* peak; **sur la p. des pieds** on tiptoe; **en p.** pointed; **de p.** *(technologie, industrie etc)* state-of-the-art; **à la p. de** *(progrès etc) Fig* in *ou* at the forefront of; **une p. d'humour/etc** a touch of humour/etc; **faire des pointes** *(danseuse)* to danse on points.

pointer [pwɛ̃te] 1 *vt (cocher) Br* to tick (off), *Am* check (off). 2 *vt (braquer)* to point **(sur,** vers** at). 3 *vi (employé)* to clock in; *(à la sortie)* to clock out. 4 *vi (apparaître)* to appear; **p. vers** to point upwards towards. 5 **se pointer** *vpr (arriver) Fam* to show up. ● **pointage** *nm (de personnel)* clocking in; *(à la sortie)* clocking out.

pointillé [pwɛtije] nm dotted line; **ligne en p.** dotted line.

pointilleux, -euse [pwɛtijø, -øz] a fussy, particular.

pointu, -ue [pwɛty] a (en pointe) pointed; (voix) shrill.

pointure [pwɛtyr] nf (de chaussure, gant) size.

poire [pwar] nf 1 (fruit) pear; **couper la p. en deux** Fig to compromise. 2 (figure) Fam mug. 3 (personne) Fam sucker. ● **poirier** nm pear tree.

poireau, -x [pwaro] nm leek.

poireauter [pwarote] vi (attendre) Fam to kick one's heels.

pois [pwa] nm (légume) pea; (dessin) (polka) dot; **petits p.** Br (garden) peas, Am peas; **p. chiche** chickpea; **à p.** (vêtement) spotted, dotted.

poison [pwazɔ̃] nm poison.

poisse [pwas] nf Fam bad luck.

poisseux, -euse [pwasø, -øz] a sticky.

poisson [pwasɔ̃] nm fish; **p. rouge** goldfish; **les Poissons** (signe) Pisces; **un p. d'avril** (farce) an April fool joke; **faire un p. d'avril à qn** to make an April fool of s.o. ● **poissonnerie** nf fish shop. ● **poissonnier, -ière** nmf fishmonger.

poitrine [pwatrin] nf Anat chest; (de femme) bust, bosom; (de veau, mouton) Culin breast.

poivre [pwavr] nm pepper. ● **poivrer** vt to pepper. ● **poivré, -ée** a (piquant) peppery; (plaisanterie) Fig spicy. ● **poivrier** nm (plante) pepper plant; (ustensile) pepperpot. ● **poivrière** nf pepperpot.

poivron [pwavrɔ̃] nm (légume) pepper, capsicum.

poivrot, -ote [pwavro, -ɔt] nm Fam drunk(ard).

poker [pɔker] nm Cartes poker.

polar [pɔlar] nm (roman) Fam whodunit.

polariser [pɔlarize] vt to polarize.

pôle [pol] nm Géog pole; **p. Nord/Sud** North/South Pole. ● **polaire** a polar.

polémique [pɔlemik] a controversial, polemical ‖ nf controversy, polemic.

poli, -ie [pɔli] 1 a (courtois) polite (avec to, with). 2 a (lisse, brillant) polished ‖ nm (aspect) polish. ● **poliment** adv politely.

police [pɔlis] nf 1 police; **faire ou assurer la p.** to maintain order (dans in); **p. secours** emergency services; **p. mondaine ou des mœurs** = vice squad. 2 **p.** (d'assurance) (insurance) policy. 3 **p. de caractères** Typ Ordinat font. ● **policier** a enquête/etc policière police inquiry/etc; **chien p.** police dog; **roman p.** dsetective novel ‖ nm policeman, detective.

polichinelle [pɔliʃinɛl] nm (marionnette) Punch; (personne) Péj buffoon; **secret de p.** open secret.

polio [pɔljo] nf abrév (poliomyélite) (maladie) polio. ● **poliomyélite** nf poliomyelitis.

polir [pɔlir] vt (métal etc) to polish.

polisson, -onne [pɔlisɔ̃, -ɔn] a naughty ‖ nmf rascal.

politesse [pɔlitɛs] nf politeness; **une p.** (parole) a polite word; (action) an act of politeness.

politique [pɔlitik] a political; **homme p.** politician ‖ nf (activité, science) politics; (mesures, manières de gouverner) policies; **une p.** (tactique) a policy; **faire de la p.** to be in politics, be a politician. ● **politicien, -ienne** nmf Péj politician. ● **politiser** vt to politicize.

pollen [pɔlɛn] nm pollen.

polluer [pɔlɥe] vt to pollute. ● **polluant** nm pollutant. ● **pollueur, -euse** a polluting ‖ nmf polluter. ● **pollution** nf pollution.

polo [pɔlo] nm 1 (chemise) sweat shirt. 2 Sport polo.

polochon [pɔlɔʃɔ̃] nm (traversin) Fam bolster.

Pologne [pɔlɔɲ] nf Poland. ● **polonais, -aise** a Polish ‖ nmf P., **Polonaise** Pole ‖ nm (langue) Polish.

poltron, -onne [pɔltrɔ̃, -ɔn] a cowardly ‖ nmf coward.

polycopier [pɔlikɔpje] vt to duplicate, mimeograph. ● **polycopié** nm Univ duplicated course notes, mimeographed copy (of lecture etc).

polyester [pɔliɛster] nm polyester; **chemise/etc en p.** polyester shirt/etc.

polygame [pɔligam] a polygamous ‖ nm polygamist.

Polynésie [pɔlinezi] nf Polynesia.

polype [pɔlip] nm (tumeur) polyp.

polytechnique [pɔliteknik] a & nf **École p., P.** University institution specializing in engineering. ● **polytechnicien, -ienne** nmf student ou graduate of the École polytechnique.

polyvalent, -ente [pɔlivalɑ̃, -ɑ̃t] 1 a (rôle) multi-purpose, varied; (personne) all-round. 2 a & nf (école) **polyvalente** Can = Br secondary school, = Am high school.

pommade [pɔmad] nf ointment.

pomme [pɔm] nf 1 apple; **p. d'Adam** Anat Adam's apple. 2 **p. de terre** potato; **pommes frites** Br chips, Am French fries; **pommes chips** potato Br crisps ou Am chips; **pommes vapeur** steamed potatoes. 3 (locutions) **tomber dans les pommes** Fam to faint; **être haut comme trois pommes** Fam to be knee-high to a grasshopper; **ma p.** (moi) Fam yours truly. 4 (d'arrosoir) rose. ● **pommier** nm apple tree.

pommette [pɔmɛt] nf cheekbone; **pommettes saillantes** high cheekbones.

pompe [pɔ̃p] nf 1 pump; **p. à essence** Br petrol ou Am gas station; **p. à incendie** fire engine; **coup de p.** Fam (sudden) feeling of exhaustion. 2 nf (chaussure) Fam shoe. 3 nf (en gymnastique) Br press-up, Am push-up. 4 nfpl **pompes funèbres** undertaker's; **entrepreneur des pompes funèbres** undertaker. 5 nf Scol crib. 6 nf (splendeur) pomp. 7 (locution) **être à côté de ses pompes** not to be feeling one's usual self.

pomper [pɔ̃pe] *vt* to pump; *(eau)* to pump out (**de** of); *(absorber)* to soak up; **p. qn** *(épuiser) Fam* to tire s.o. out; **tu me pompes (l'air)** *Fam* you're getting on my nerves **‖** *vi* to pump.

pompeux, -euse [pɔ̃pø, -øz] *a* pompous.

pompier [pɔ̃pje] *nm* fireman; **voiture des pompiers** fire engine.

pompiste [pɔ̃pist] *nmf Br* petrol *ou Am* gas station attendant.

pompon [pɔ̃pɔ̃] *nm (ornement)* pompon.

pomponner [pɔ̃pɔne] *vt* to doll up **‖ se pomponner** *vpr* to doll oneself up.

ponce [pɔ̃s] *nf* **(pierre) p.** pumice (stone). ● **poncer** *vt* to rub down, sand. ● **ponceuse** *nf (machine)* sander.

poncho [pɔ̃ʃo] *nm* poncho.

ponctuation [pɔ̃ktɥasjɔ̃] *nf* punctuation. ● **ponctuer** *vt* to punctuate (**de** with).

ponctuel, -elle [pɔ̃ktɥɛl] *a* **1** *(à l'heure)* punctual. **2** *(unique) Br* one-off, *Am* one-of-a-kind. ● **ponctualité** *nf* punctuality.

pondéré, -ée [pɔ̃dere] *a* level-headed. ● **pondération** *nf* level-headedness.

pondre [pɔ̃dr] *vt (œuf)* to lay; *(livre, discours) Fam* to produce **‖** *vi (poule)* to lay (eggs *ou* an egg).

poney [pɔnɛ] *nm* pony.

pont [pɔ̃] *nm* bridge; *(de bateau)* deck; **p. (de graissage)** *(pour véhicule)* ramp; **p. aérien** airlift; **faire le p.** *Fig* to take the intervening day(s) off *(between two holidays)*; **faire un p. d'or à qn** to give s.o. a golden hello. ● **pont-levis** *nm (pl ponts-levis)* drawbridge.

ponte [pɔ̃t] **1** *nf (d'œufs)* laying. **2** *nm (personne) Fam* bigwig, bigshot.

pontife [pɔ̃tif] *nm* **(souverain) p.** pope. ● **pontifical, -e, -aux** *a* papal, pontifical.

ponton [pɔ̃tɔ̃] *nm* pontoon, floating landing stage.

pop [pɔp] *nm & a inv (musique)* pop.

popote [pɔpɔt] *nf (cuisine) Fam* cooking.

populace [pɔpylas] *nf Péj* rabble.

populaire [pɔpylɛr] *a (qui plaît) (personne, gouvernement etc)* popular; *(quartier, milieu)* working-class; *(expression)* colloquial; **art p.** folk art. ● **populariser** *vt* to popularize. ● **popularité** *nf* popularity (**auprès de** with).

population [pɔpylasjɔ̃] *nf* population. ● **populeux, -euse** *a* populous, crowded.

porc [pɔr] *nm* pig; *(viande)* pork; *(personne) Péj* swine.

porcelaine [pɔrsəlɛn] *nf* china, porcelain.

porc-épic [pɔrkepik] *nm (pl porcs-épics) (animal)* porcupine.

porche [pɔrʃ] *nm* porch.

porcherie [pɔrʃəri] *nf (pig)sty.

pore [pɔr] *nm* pore. ● **poreux, -euse** *a* porous.

pornographie [pɔrnɔgrafi] *nf* pornography. ● **pornographique** *a (Fam* **porno)** pornographic.

port [pɔr] *nm* **1** port, harbour; **arriver à bon p.** *Fig* to arrive safely. **2** *(d'armes)* carrying;

(de barbe) wearing; *(prix)* carriage, postage; *(attitude)* bearing.

portable [pɔrtabl] *a (portatif)* portable; *(robe etc)* wearable **‖** *nm (ordinateur)* laptop (computer).

portail [pɔrtaj] *nm (de jardin)* gate; *(de cathédrale etc)* portal.

portant, -ante [pɔrtã, -ãt] *a* **à bien p.** in good health.

portatif, -ive [pɔrtatif, -iv] *a* portable.

porte [pɔrt] *nf* door, *(passage)* doorway; *(de jardin)* gate, *(passage)* gateway; *(de ville)* entrance, *Hist* gate; *(de slalom)* gate, pair of flags; **p. (d'embarquement)** *(d'aéroport)* (departure) gate; **Alger, p. de...** Algiers, gateway to...; **p. d'entrée** front door; **p. coulissante** sliding door; **faire du p.-à-porte** to go from door to do selling *ou* canvassing; **mettre à la p.** *(jeter dehors)* to throw out; *(renvoyer)* to fire, *Br* sack. ● **porte-fenêtre** *nf (pl portes-fenêtres) Br* French window, *Am* French door.

porte-avions [pɔrtavjɔ̃] *nm inv* aircraft carrier. ● **porte-bagages** *nm inv* luggage rack. ● **porte-bébé** *nm (nacelle) Br* carrycot, *Am* baby basket; *(kangourou®)* baby sling. ● **porte-bonheur** *nm inv (fétiche)* (lucky) charm. ● **porte-cartes** *nm inv* card holder *ou* case. ● **porte-clefs** *nm inv* key ring. ● **porte-documents** *nm inv* briefcase. ● **porte-drapeau, -x** *nm (soldat)* standard bearer. ● **porte-jarretelles** *nm inv Br* suspender *ou Am* garter belt. ● **porte-monnaie** *nm inv* purse. ● **porte-parapluie** *nm inv* umbrella stand. ● **porte-plume** *nm inv* pen *(for dipping in ink)*. ● **porte-revues** *nm inv* newspaper rack. ● **porte-savon** *nm* soapdish. ● **porte-serviettes** *nm inv Br* towel rail, *Am* towel rack. ● **porte-voix** *nm inv* loudspeaker, megaphone.

portée [pɔrte] *nf* **1** *(de fusil etc)* range; **à la p. de qn** within reach of s.o.; *(richesse, plaisir etc) Fig* within s.o.'s grasp; **à p. de la main** within (easy) reach; **à p. de voix** within earshot; **hors de p.** out of reach. **2** *(animaux)* litter. **3** *(importance, effet)* significance, import. **4** *Mus* stave.

portefeuille [pɔrtəfœj] *nm* wallet; *(de ministre, d'actions etc)* portfolio.

portemanteau, -x [pɔrtmãto] *nm (sur pied)* hatstand, *Br* hallstand; *(crochet)* coat *ou* hat peg.

porte-parole [pɔrtparɔl] *nm inv* spokesperson; *(homme)* spokesman; *(femme)* spokeswoman (**de** for, of).

porter [pɔrte] *vt* to carry; *(vêtement, lunettes, barbe etc)* to wear; *(trace, responsabilité, fruits etc)* to bear; *(regard)* to cast; *(attaque)* to make (**contre** against); *(inscrire)* to enter, write down; *(coup)* to strike; *(sentiment)* to have (**à** for); **p. qch à** *(apporter)* to take *ou* bring sth to; **p. qn à faire** *(pousser)* to lead *ou* prompt s.o. to do; **p. bonheur/malheur** to

bring good/bad luck; **se faire p. malade** to
report sick.

▌ *vi* (*voix*) to carry; (*canon*) to fire; (*vue*) to
extend; **p. (juste)** (*coup*) to hit the mark;
(*reproche*) to hit home; **p. sur** (*concerner*) to
bear on; (*accent*) to fall on; (*reposer sur*) to
rest on; (*heurter*) to strike.

▌ **se porter** *vpr* (*vêtement*) to be worn; **se p.
bien/mal** to be well/ill; **comment te portes-
tu?** how are you?; **se p. candidat** to stand as
a candidate. ● **portant, -ante a bien p.** in
good health. ● **porté, -ée** *a* **p. à croire/**etc inclined to believe/etc; **p. sur qch** fond of sth.

porteur, -euse [pɔrtœr, -øz] *nm* (*de bagages*) porter ▌ *nmf* (*malade*) carrier; (*de
nouvelles, chèque*) bearer; **p. sain** *Méd*
carrier (*who displays no symptoms*) ▌ *a* (*situation économique etc*) buoyant; **marché p.**
growth *ou* buoyant market; **mère porteuse**
surrogate mother.

portier [pɔrtje] *nm* doorkeeper, porter.
● **portière** *nf* (*de véhicule, train*) door.
● **portillon** *nm* gate.

portion [pɔrsjɔ̃] *nf* (*partie*) portion; (*de
nourriture*) helping, portion.

portique [pɔrtik] *nm* **1** *Archit* portico. **2** (*de
balançoire etc*) crossbar, frame.

porto [pɔrto] *nm* (*vin*) port.
Porto Rico [pɔrtoriko] *nm* Puerto Rico.

portrait [pɔrtrɛ] *nm* portrait; **être le p. de**
(*son père etc*) to be the image of; **faire un p.**
to paint *ou* draw a portrait (**de** of); **p. en
pied** full-length portrait. ● **portrait-robot** *nm*
(*pl* **portraits-robots**) identikit (picture),
photofit.

portuaire [pɔrtɥɛr] *a* **installations portuaires**
port *ou* harbour facilities.

Portugal [pɔrtygal] *nm* Portugal. ● **portugais,
-aise** *a* Portuguese ▌ *nmf* **P.** Portuguese man,
Portuguese *inv*; **Portugaise** Portuguese woman, Portuguese *inv*; **les P.** the Portuguese ▌
nm (*langue*) Portuguese.

pose [poz] *nf* **1** (*installation*) putting up; (*de
sonnette etc*) putting in; (*de mine etc*) laying.
2 (*attitude de modèle*), affectation) pose; *Phot*
exposure (time).

posé, -ée *a* (*calme*) calm, staid.
● **posément** *adv* calmly.

poser [poze] *vt* to put (down); (*papier peint,
rideaux*) to put up; (*sonnette, chauffage*) to
put in; (*mine, moquette, fondations*) to lay;
(*question*) to ask (**à** qn s,o); (*conditions,
principe*) to lay down; **p. sa candidature** to
apply, put in one's application (**à** for); **ça
pose la question de...** it poses the question
of....

▌ *vi* (*modèle etc*) to pose (**pour** for).

▌ **se poser** *vpr* (*oiseau, avion*) to land;
(*problème, question*) to arise; **se p. sur**
(*yeux*) to fix on; **se p. en chef/**etc to set oneself up as *ou* pose as a leader/etc; **la question
se pose!** this question should be asked!

positif, -ive [pozitif, -iv] *a* positive. ● **positivement** *adv* positively.

position [pozisjɔ̃] *nf* (*attitude, emplacement,*

opinion etc) position; **prendre p.** *Fig* to take
a stand (**contre** against); **prise de p.** stand;
rester sur ses positions to stand one's
ground.

posologie [pozɔlɔʒi] *nf* (*de médicament*)
dosage, directions.

posséder [pɔsede] *vt* to possess; (*maison,
bien etc*) to own, possess; (*bien connaître*) to
master; (*duper*) *Fam* to fool. ● **possesseur**
nm possessor; owner. ● **possessif, -ive** *a*
(*personne, adjectif etc*) possessive ▌ *nm*
Grammaire possessive. ● **possession** *nf*
possession; **en p. de qch** in possession of
sth; **prendre p. de qch** to take possession of
sth.

possibilité [pɔsibilite] *nf* possibility; **la p. de
faire qch** the chance *ou* possibility to do sth.

possible [pɔsibl] *a* possible (**à faire** to do); **il
(nous) est p. de faire** it is possible (for us)
to do it; **il est p. que** (+ *sub*) it is possible
that; **si p.** if possible; **le plus tôt/**etc **p.** as
soon/etc as possible; **autant que p.** as far as
possible; **le plus p.** as much *ou* as many as
possible ▌ *nm* **faire (tout) son p.** to do one's
utmost (**pour faire** to do); **dans la mesure du
p.** as far as possible.

post- [pɔst] *préf* post-.

postal, -e, -aux [pɔstal, -o] *a* postal; **boîte
postale** PO Box; **code p.** *Br* postcode, *Am*
zip code.

postdater [pɔstdate] *vt* to postdate.

poste [pɔst] **1** *nf* (*service*) post, mail; (*bureau
de*) post office; **Postes (et Télécommunications)** (*administration*) Post Office; **par la p.**
by post, by mail; **p. aérienne** airmail; **mettre
qch à la p.** to post sth, mail sth.

2 *nm* (*lieu, emploi*) post; **p. de secours** first
aid post; **p. de police** police station; **p.
d'essence** *Br* petrol *ou* *Am* gas station; **p.
d'incendie** fire point (*containing fire-fighting
equipment*); **p. d'aiguillage** *Br* signal box,
Am signal tower.

3 *nm* (*appareil de radio ou de télévision*) set;
Tél extension. ● **poster 1** *vt* (*lettre*) to post,
mail. **2** *vt* **p. un soldat/**etc (*placer*) to post *ou*
station a soldier/etc. **3** [pɔster] *nm* poster.

postérieur, -e [pɔsterjœr] *a* **1** (*document etc*)
later; **p. à** after. **2** *nm* (*derrière*) *Fam* posterior.

postérité [pɔsterite] *nf* posterity.

posthume [pɔstym] *a* posthumous; **à titre p.**
posthumously.

postiche [pɔstiʃ] *a* (*barbe etc*) false.

postier, -ière [pɔstje, -jɛr] *nmf* postal worker.

postillonner [pɔstijɔne] *vi* to sputter.

post-scriptum [pɔstskriptɔm] *nm inv* postscript.

postuler [pɔstyle] **1** *vi* **p.** (**à un emploi**) to apply for a job. **2** *vt* (*poser comme postulat*) to
postulate. ● **postulant, -ante** *nmf* applicant.

posture [pɔstyr] *nf* posture.

pot [po] *nm* **1** pot; (*à confiture*) jar, pot; (*à
lait*) jug; (*à bière*) mug; (*de crème, yaourt*)
carton; (*de bébé*) potty; **p. de chambre**

chamber pot; **p. de fleurs** flower pot; **prendre un p.** *Fam* to have a drink. **2** *Fam* (*chance*) luck; **avoir du p.** to be lucky.

potable [pɔtabl] *a* drinkable; (*passable*) *Fam* tolerable; **'eau p.'** 'drinking water'.

potage [pɔtaʒ] *nm* soup.

potager, -ère [pɔtaʒe, -ɛr] *a* **jardin p.** vegetable garden; **plante potagère** vegetable ▮ *nm* vegetable garden.

potasser [pɔtase] *vt* (*examen*) *Fam* to cram for ▮ *vi Fam* to cram.

pot-au-feu [pɔtofø] *nm inv* (*plat*) beef stew.

pot-de-vin [podvɛ̃] *nm* (*pl* **pots-de-vin**) bribe.

pote [pɔt] *nm* (*ami*) *Fam* pal, buddy.

poteau, -x [pɔto] *nm* post; **p. indicateur** signpost; **p. d'arrivée** *Sport* winning *ou* finishing post; **p. télégraphique** telegraph pole.

potelé, -ée [pɔtle] *a* plump, chubby.

potence [pɔtɑ̃s] *nf* (*gibet*) gallows.

potentiel, -ielle [pɔtɑ̃sjɛl] *a & nm* potential.

poterie [pɔtri] *nf* (*art*) pottery; **une p.** a piece of pottery; **des poteries** (*objets*) pottery. ● **potier** *nm* potter.

potin [pɔtɛ̃] *nm* (*bruit*) *Fam* row. ● **potins** *nmpl* (*cancans*) gossip.

potion [posjɔ̃] *nf* potion.

potiron [pɔtirɔ̃] *nm* pumpkin.

pot-pourri [popuri] *nm* (*pl* **pots-pourris**) *Mus* medley.

pou, -x [pu] *nm* louse; **poux** lice.

poubelle [pubɛl] *nf Br* dustbin, *Am* garbage can.

pouce [pus] *nm* **1** thumb; **un coup de p.** *Fam* a helping hand; **se tourner les pouces** *Fam* to twiddle one's thumbs. **2** (*mesure*) *Hist & Fig* inch.

poudre [pudr] *nf* powder; **p. (à canon)** (*explosif*) gunpowder; **en p.** (*lait*) powdered; (*chocolat*) drinking; **sucre en p.** *Br* castor *ou* caster sugar, *Am* finely ground sugar; **mettre le feu aux poudres** *Fig* to spark off a crisis, create an explosive situation. ● **poudrer** *vt* to powder ▮ **se poudrer** *vpr* (*femme*) to powder one's face *ou* nose. ● **poudreux, -euse** *a* powdery ▮ *nf* **poudreuse** (*neige*) powder snow. ● **poudrier** *nm* (powder) compact. ● **poudrière** *nf* powder magazine; (*région*) *Fig* powder keg.

pouf [puf] **1** *int* thump! **2** *nm* (*siège*) pouf(fe).

pouffer [pufe] *vi* **p. (de rire)** to burst out laughing, guffaw.

pouilleux, -euse [pujø, -øz] *a* (*sordide*) miserable; (*mendiant*) lousy.

poulailler [pulaje] *nm* **1** henhouse, (hen) coop. **2** **le p.** (*de théâtre*) *Fam* the gods, the gallery.

poulain [pulɛ̃] *nm* (*cheval*) foal; **le p. de qn** *Fig* s.o.'s protégé.

poule [pul] *nf* **1** hen; *Culin* fowl; **mère p.** overprotective mother; **être une p. mouillée** (*lâche*) to be chicken; **oui, ma p.!** *Fam* yes, my pet! **2** (*femme*) *Péj* tart, *Am* broad. ● **poulet** *nm* **1** (*poule, coq*) chicken. **2** (*policier*) *Fam* cop.

pouliche [puliʃ] *nf* (*jument*) filly.

poulie [puli] *nf* pulley.

poulpe [pulp] *nm* octopus.

pouls [pu] *nm Méd* pulse; **prendre le p. de qn** to take s.o.'s pulse.

poumon [pumɔ̃] *nm* lung; **à pleins poumons** (*respirer*) deeply; (*crier*) loudly; **p. d'acier** iron lung.

poupe [pup] *nf* (*de bateau*) stern, poop; **avoir le vent en p.** *Fig* to be favoured by fortune.

poupée [pupe] *nf* doll.

poupin [pupɛ̃] *a* **visage p.** baby face.

poupon [pupɔ̃] *nm* (*bébé*) baby; (*poupée*) doll.

pour [pur] **1** *prép* for; **p. toi/moi/**etc for you/me/etc; **faites-le p. lui** do it for him, do it for his sake; **partir p. Paris/l'Italie/**etc to leave for Paris/Italy/etc; **elle va partir p. cinq ans** she's leaving for five years; **elle est p.** she's in favour; **p. faire qch** (in order) to do sth, so as to do sth; **p. que tu saches** so (that) you may know; **p. quoi faire?** what for?; **trop petit/poli/**etc **p. faire qch** too small/polite/etc to do sth; **assez grand/**etc **p. faire qch** big/etc enough to do sth; **p. femme/base/**etc as a wife/basis/etc; **p. cela** for that reason; **p. ma part, p. moi** (*quant à moi*) as for me; **jour p. jour/heure p. heure** to the day/hour; **dix p. cent** ten per cent; **acheter p. cinq francs de bonbons** to buy five francs' worth of *Br* sweets *ou* *Am* candies; **p. intelligent/**etc **qu'il soit** however clever/etc he may be; **ce n'est pas p. me plaire** it doesn't exactly please me.

2 *nm* **le p. et le contre** the pros and cons.

pourboire [purbwar] *nm* tip (*money*).

pourcentage [pursɑ̃taʒ] *nm* percentage.

pourchasser [purʃase] *vt* to pursue.

pourparlers [purparle] *nmpl* negotiations, talks; **p. de paix** peace talks.

pourpre [purpr] *a & nm* purple.

pourquoi [purkwa] *adv & conj* why; **p. pas?** why not? ▮ *nm inv* reason (*de* for); **le p. et le comment** the whys and wherefores.

pourra, pourrait *etc* [pura, purɛ] *voir* **pouvoir 1**.

pourrir [purir] *vi* to rot ▮ *vt* to rot; **p. qn** *Fig* to corrupt s.o. ● **pourri, -ie** *a* (*fruit, temps, personne etc*) rotten. ● **pourriture** *nf* rot, rottenness; (*personne*) *Péj* swine.

poursuite [pursɥit] *nf* **1** chase, pursuit; (*du bonheur, de créancier*) pursuit (*de* of); (*continuation*) continuation; **se mettre à la p. de** to go after, chase (after), go in pursuit of. **2** *nfpl* **poursuites (judiciaires)** legal proceedings (*contre* against).

poursuivre* [pursɥivr] **1** *vt* (*courir après*) to chase, go after, pursue; (*harceler, relancer*) to hound, pursue; (*obséder*) to haunt; (*but, idéal etc*) to pursue. **2** *vt* **p. qn (en justice)** (*au criminel*) to prosecute s.o.; (*au civil*) to sue s.o. **3** *vt* (*lecture, voyage etc*) to carry on (with), continue (with), pursue ▮ *vi*, **se poursuivre** *vpr* to continue, go on.

● **poursuivant, -ante** *nmf* pursuer.

pourtant [purtɑ̃] *adv* yet, nevertheless; **et p.** and yet.

pourtour [purtur] *nm* perimeter.

pourvoir * [purvwar] *vt* to provide (de with); **être pourvu de** to have, be provided with ▮ *vi* **p. à** (*besoins etc*) to provide for. ● **pourvoyeur, -euse** *nmf* supplier.

pourvu que [purvyk(ə)] *conj* (*condition*) provided *ou* providing (that); (*souhait*) **p. qu'elle soit là!** I only hope (that) she's there!

pousse [pus] *nf* **1** (*bourgeon*) shoot, sprout; **pousses de bambou** bamboo shoots. **2** (*croissance*) growth.

pousse-café [puskafe] *nm inv* after-dinner liqueur.

poussée [puse] *nf* (*pression*) pressure; (*coup*) push; (*d'ennemi*) thrust, push; (*de fièvre etc*) outbreak; (*de l'inflation*) upsurge.

pousser [puse] **1** *vt* to push; (*du coude*) to nudge, poke; (*cri*) to utter; (*soupir*) to heave; (*moteur, machine*) to drive hard; (*re-cherches*) to pursue; **p. qn à faire qch** to urge s.o. to do sth; **p. qn à bout** to push s.o. to his *ou* her limits; **p. trop loin** (*gentillesse etc*) to carry too far ▮ *vi* to push; **p. jusqu'à Paris**/*etc* to push on as far as Paris/*etc* ▮ **se pousser** *vpr* (*se déplacer*) to move up *ou* over.

2 *vi* (*croître*) to grow; **faire p.** (*plante, barbe etc*) to grow; **se laisser p. les cheveux** to let one's hair grow. ● **poussé, -ée** *a* (*travail, études*) advanced.

poussette [puset] *nf Br* pushchair, *Am* stroller; **p. canne** *Br* (baby) buggy, *Am* (collapsible) stroller; **p.** (**de marché**) shopping *Br* trolley *ou Am* cart.

poussière [pusjɛr] *nf* dust; **dix francs et des poussières** *Fam* a bit over ten francs. ● **poussiéreux, -euse** *a* dusty.

poussif, -ive [pusif, -iv] *a* short-winded, puffing.

poussin [pusɛ̃] *nm* (*poulet*) chick.

poutre [putr] *nf* (*en bois*) beam; (*en acier*) girder. ● **poutrelle** *nf* girder.

pouvoir * [puvwar] **1** *v aux* (*capacité*) can, be able to; (*permission, éventualité*) may, can; **je peux deviner** I can guess, I'm able to guess; **tu peux entrer** you may *ou* can come in; **il peut être sorti** he may *ou* might be out; **elle pourrait/pouvait venir** she might/could come, **j'ai pu l'obtenir** I managed to get it; **j'aurais pu l'obtenir** I could have *Br* got it *ou Am* gotten it; **je n'en peux plus** I'm utterly exhausted ▮ *v imp* **il peut neiger** it may snow ▮ **se pouvoir** *vpr* **il se peut qu'elle parte** (it's possible that) she might leave.

2 *nm* (*capacité, autorité*) power; (*procuration*) power of attorney; **les pouvoirs publics** the authorities; **au p.** (*parti etc*) in power; **il n'est pas en mon p. de vous aider** it's not in my power to help you; **p. d'achat** purchasing power.

poux [pu] *voir* pou.

pragmatique [pragmatik] *a* pragmatic.

praire [prɛr] *nf* (*mollusque*) clam.

prairie [preri] *nf* meadow.

praline [pralin] *nf* praline; (*amande*) sugared almond. ● **praliné, -ée** *a* (*glace etc*) praline-flavoured.

praticable [pratikabl] *a* (*chemin, projet*) practicable.

praticien, -ienne [pratisjɛ̃, -jɛn] *nmf* practitioner.

pratique [pratik] **1** *a* (*connaissance, personne, outil etc*) practical. **2** *nf* (*exercice, procédé*) practice; (*expérience*) practical experience; **la p. de la natation/du golf**/*etc* swimming/golfing/*etc*; **mettre qch en p.** to put sth into practice; **en p.** (*en réalité*) in practice.

pratiquement [pratikmɑ̃] *adv* (*presque*) practically; (*en réalité*) in practice.

pratiquer [pratike] *vt* (*sport, art etc*) *Br* to practise, *Am* practice; (*football*) to play, practise; (*trou, route*) to make; (*opération*) to carry out; **p. la natation** to go swimming ▮ *vi Br* to practise, *Am* practice. ● **pratiquant, -ante** *a* (*catholique etc*) practising ▮ *nmf* churchgoer.

pré [pre] *nm* meadow.

pré- [pre] *préf* pre-.

préalable [prealabl] *a* prior, preliminary, previous; **p. à** prior to ▮ *nm* precondition, prerequisite; **au p.** beforehand. ● **préalable-ment** [-amɑ̃] *adv* beforehand.

préambule [preɑ̃byl] *nm* (*de loi*) preamble; *Fig* prelude (à to).

préau, -x [preo] *nm* (*d'une école*) covered *Br* playground *ou Am* school yard.

préavis [preavi] *nm* (*de grève, licenciement etc*) (advance) notice (**de** of); **sans p.** without warning, without any notice.

précaire [prekɛr] *a* precarious.

précaution [prekosjɔ̃] *nf* (*mesure*) precaution; (*prudence*) caution; **par p.** as a precaution; **prendre la p. de faire qch** to take the precaution of doing sth. ● **précautionneux, -euse** *a* cautious.

précédent, -ente [presedɑ̃, -ɑ̃t] **1** *a* previous, preceding, earlier ▮ *nmf* previous one. **2** *nm* (*exemple, fait*) a precedent; **sans p.** unprecedented. ● **précédemment** [-amɑ̃] *adv* previously. ● **précéder** *vti* to precede; **faire p. qch de qch** to precede sth by sth.

précepte [presɛpt] *nm* precept.

précepteur, -trice [preseptœr, -tris] *nmf* (*private*) tutor.

prêcher [preʃe] *vti* to preach; **p. qn** *Rel* & *Fig* to preach to s.o.

précieux, -euse [presjø, -øz] *a* precious.

précipice [presipis] *nm* chasm, precipice, abyss.

précipiter [presipite] *vt* (*hâter*) to hasten, rush; (*jeter*) to throw, hurl; (*plonger*) to plunge (**dans** into) ▮ **se précipiter** *vpr* (*se je-ter*) to throw *ou* hurl oneself; (*foncer*) to rush (**à, sur** on to); (*s'accélérer*) to speed up. ● **précipité, -ée** *a* hasty. ● **précipitamment** [-amɑ̃] *adv* hastily. ● **précipitation** *nf* **1** haste.

2 **précipitations** (*pluie*) precipitation.

précis, -ise [presi, -iz] 1 *a* precise; (*idée, mécanisme*) accurate, precise; **à deux heures précises** at two o'clock sharp *ou* precisely. 2 *nm* (*résumé*) summary; (*manuel*) handbook. ● **précisément** *adv* precisely. ● **précision** *nf* precision; (*de mécanisme etc*) accuracy, precision; (*détail*) detail; (*explication*) explanation.

préciser [presize] *vt* to specify (**que that**) **se préciser** *vpr* to become clear(er).

précoce [prekɔs] *a* (*fruit, mariage, mort etc*) early; (*enfant*) precocious. ● **précocité** *nf* (*d'enfant*) precociousness; (*de fruit etc*) earliness.

préconçu, -ue [prekɔ̃sy] *a* preconceived.

préconiser [prekɔnize] *vt* to advocate (**que that**).

précurseur [prekyrsœr] *nm* forerunner, precursor **a un signe p. de qch** a sign heralding sth.

prédécesseur [predesesœr] *nm* predecessor.

prédestiné, -ée [predɛstine] *a* fated, predestined (**à faire to do**).

prédicateur [predikatœr] *nm* preacher.

prédilection [predilɛksjɔ̃] *nf* (special) liking; **de p.** favourite.

prédire* [predir] *vt* to predict (**que that**). ● **prédiction** *nf* prediction.

prédisposer [predispoze] *vt* to predispose (**à qch to sth, à faire to do**). ● **prédisposition** *nf* predisposition.

prédominer [predɔmine] *vi* to predominate. ● **prédominant, -ante** *a* predominant. ● **prédominance** *nf* predominance.

préfabriqué, -ée [prefabrike] *a* prefabricated.

préface [prefas] *nf* preface. ● **préfacer** *vt* to preface.

préfecture [prefɛktyr] *nf* prefecture; **p. de police** Paris police headquarters. ● **préfectoral, -e, -aux** *a* (*décision etc*) prefectoral.

préférable [preferabl] *a* preferable (**à to**).

préférence [preferɑ̃s] *nf* preference (**pour for**); **de p.** preferably; **de p. à** in preference to. ● **préférentiel, -ielle** *a* preferential.

préférer [prefere] *vt* to prefer (**à to**); **p. faire qch** to prefer to do sth; **je préférerais rester** I would rather stay, I would prefer to stay. ● **préféré, -ée** *a & nmf* favourite.

préfet [prefɛ] *nm* prefect (*chief administrator in a department*); **p. de police** prefect of police (*Paris chief of police*).

préfigurer [prefigyre] *vt* to herald, foreshadow.

préfixe [prefiks] *nm Grammaire* prefix.

préhistoire [preistwar] *nf* prehistory. ● **préhistorique** *a* prehistoric.

préjudice [prezydis] *nm Jur* prejudice, harm; **porter p. à** to prejudice, harm. ● **préjudiciable** *a* prejudicial (**à to**).

préjugé [prezyze] *nm* (*parti pris*) prejudice; **avoir des préjugés** to be prejudiced (**contre against**); **être plein de préjugés** to be full of prejudice.

préjuger [prezyze] *vi* **p. de** (*réponse de qn etc*) to anticipate; **j'ai préjugé de mes forces** I misjudged my strength.

prélasser (se) [səprelase] *vpr* to lounge (about *ou* around).

prélat [prela] *nm Rel* prelate.

prélever [prel(ə)ve] *vt* (*échantillon*) to take (**sur from**); (*somme*) to deduct (**sur from**). ● **prélèvement** *nm* (*d'échantillon*) taking; (*de somme*) deduction; **p. automatique** (*à la banque*) *Br* standing order, *Br* direct debit, *Am* automatic deduction.

préliminaire [preliminɛr] *a* preliminary **nmpl préliminaires** preliminaries.

prélude [prelyd] *nm* prelude (**à to**).

prématuré, -ée [prematyre] *a* premature **nm** (*bébé*) premature baby. ● **prématurément** *adv* prematurely, too soon.

préméditer [premedite] *vt* to premeditate. ● **préméditation** *nf Jur* premeditation; **meurtre/etc avec p.** premeditated murder/etc.

prémices [premis] *nfpl* **les p. de** *Litt* the (very) beginnings of.

premier, -ière [prəmje, -jɛr] *a* first; (*enfance*) early; (*page de journal*) front, first; (*qualité, nécessité, importance*) prime; (*état*) original; (*notion, cause*) basic; (*danseuse, rôle*) leading; (*inférieur*) bottom; (*supérieur*) top; **nombre p.** *Math* prime number; **le p. rang** the front *ou* first row; **à la première occasion** at the earliest opportunity; **P. ministre** Prime Minister, Premier.

nmf first (one); **arriver le p.** *ou* **en p.** to arrive first; **être le p. de la classe** to be (at the) top of the class.

nm (*date*) first; (*étage*) *Br* first *ou Am* second floor; **le p. de l'an** New Year's Day.

première (*wagon, billet*) first class; *Scol* = *Br* sixth form, = *Am* twelfth grade; (*vitesse*) first (gear); (*événement historique*) first; **passer en première** (*élève*) *Br* to go up into the sixth form, *Am* to enter the twelfth grade; (*en voiture*) to go into first gear. ● **premier-né** *nm*, **première-née** *nf* first-born (child). ● **premièrement** *adv* firstly.

prémisse [premis] *nf* premiss.

prémonition [premɔnisjɔ̃] *nf* premonition. ● **prémonitoire** *a* **un rêve p.** a dream which is a premonition.

prémunir [premynir] *vt Litt* to safeguard (**contre against**).

prenant, -ante [prənɑ̃, -ɑ̃t] *a* (*travail, film etc*) engrossing; (*voix*) engaging.

prénatal, -e, mpl -als [prenatal] *a Br* antenatal, *Am* prenatal.

prendre* [prɑ̃dr] *vt* to take (**à qn from s.o.**); (*attraper*) to catch, get; (*voyager par*) to take, travel by (*train etc*); (*douche, bain*) to take, have; (*repas, boisson*) to have; (*nouvelles*) to get; (*acheter*) to get; (*photo*) to take; (*ton, air*) to put on; (*pensionnaire*) to take (in); (*engager*) to take (*s.o.*) (on); (*chercher*) to pick up, get; **p. qn pour** (*un autre*) to mistake s.o. for, take s.o. for; (*considérer*) to take s.o. for; **p. qn** (*doute* *etc*) to seize s.o.; **p. feu** to catch fire; **p. du temps/une heure/***etc* to take time/an hour/*etc*; **p. de la place** to take up room; **p. du poids/ de la vitesse** to put on weight/speed; **p. l'eau** (*bateau, chaussure etc*) to take water, leak; **p. l'air** (*se promener*) to get some fresh air; **passer p. qn** to come and get s.o.; **p. un coup de poing dans la figure** *Fam* to get a punch in the face; **à tout p.** on the whole; **qu'est-ce qui te prend?** what's *Br* got *ou Am* gotten into you?

▮ *vi* (*feu*) to catch; (*ciment, gelée*) to set; (*greffe, vaccin*) to take; (*mode*) to catch on.

▮ **se prendre** *vpr* (*médicament*) to be taken; (*s'accrocher*) to get caught; (*eau*) to freeze; **se p. les pieds/***etc* **dans qch** to get one's feet/ *etc* caught in sth; **se p. pour un génie/***etc* to think one is a genius/*etc*; **s'y p. pour faire qch** to go *ou* set about doing sth; **s'en p. à** (*critiquer, attaquer*) to attack; (*accuser*) to blame; **se p. à faire** to begin to do sth; **je me suis pris au jeu** *Fig* I got really involved in it, I really got to like it.

preneur, -euse [prənœr, -øz] *nmf* taker, buyer.

prénom [prenɔ̃] *nm* first name. ● **prénommer** *vt* to name; **il se prénomme Daniel** his first name is Daniel.

préoccuper [preɔkype] *vt* (*inquiéter*) to worry; (*absorber*) to preoccupy ▮ **se préoccuper** *vpr* **se p. de** to be worried about; (*s'intéresser à*) to be concerned *ou* preoccupied about. ● **préoccupant, -ante** *a* worrying. ● **préoccupé, -ée** *a* worried. ● **préoccupation** *nf* worry; (*idée, problème*) preoccupation, concern.

préparatifs [preparatif] *nmpl* preparations (de for). ● **préparation** *nf* preparation. ● **préparatoire** *a* preparatory.

préparer [prepare] *vt* to prepare (qch pour sth for); (*repas etc*) to get ready, prepare; (*examen*) to prepare (for), study for; **p. qch à qn** to prepare sth for s.o.; **p. qn à** (*examen*) to prepare *ou* coach s.o. for.

▮ **se préparer** *vpr* to get (oneself) ready, prepare oneself (à *ou* pour qch for sth); (*orage*) to brew; threaten; **se p. à faire qch** to prepare to do sth.

prépondérant, -ante [prepɔ̃derɑ̃, -ɑ̃t] *a* dominant. ● **prépondérance** *nf* dominance.

préposé, -ée [prepoze] *nmf* employee; (*facteur*) postman, postwoman.

préposer [prepoze] *vt* **p. qn à qch** to put s.o. in charge of sth.

préposition [prepozisjɔ̃] *nf Grammaire* preposition.

préretraite [prerətrɛt] *nf* early retirement.

prérogative [prerɔgativ] *nf* prerogative.

près [prɛ] *adv* **p. de** (*qn, qch*) near (to), close to; **p. de deux ans/***etc* (*presque*) nearly two years/*etc*; **p. de partir/***etc* about to leave/*etc*; **tout p.** nearby (de qn/qch s.o./sth), close by (de qn/qch s.o./sth); **de p.** (*lire, suivre, examiner*) closely; **à peu de chose p.** almost; **à cela p.** except for that; **voici le**

chiffre à un franc p. here is the figure given or take a franc; **calculer au franc p.** to calculate to the nearest franc.

présage [prezaʒ] *nm* omen, foreboding. ● **présager** *vt* to forebode.

presbyte [prɛsbit] *a* & *nmf* long-sighted (person). ● **presbytie** [-bisi] *nf* long-sightedness.

presbytère [prɛsbitɛr] *nm Rel* presbytery.

préscolaire [preskɔlɛr] *a* (*âge, enseignement etc*) preschool.

prescrire* [preskrir] *vt* (*médicament*) to prescribe. ● **prescription** *nf* (*instruction*) & *Jur* prescription.

préséance [preseɑ̃s] *nf* precedence (sur over).

présence [prezɑ̃s] *nf* presence; (à *l'école etc*) attendance (à at); **feuille de p.** attendance sheet; **en p.** (*personnes*) face to face; **en p. de** in the presence of; **p. d'esprit** presence of mind; **faire acte de p.** to put in an appearance.

présent¹, -ente [prezɑ̃, -ɑ̃t] **1** *a* (*non absent*) present (à at, dans in); **les personnes présentes** those present. **2** *a* (*actuel*) present ▮ *nm* (*temps*) present; *Grammaire* present (tense); **à p.** at present, now; **dès à p.** as from now.

présent² [prezɑ̃] *nm* (*cadeau*) *Litt* present; **faire p. de qch à qn** *Litt* to present s.o. with sth.

présentable [prezɑ̃tabl] *a* presentable.

présentateur, -trice [prezɑ̃tatœr, -tris] *nmf* (*de télévision*) announcer, presenter. ● **présentation** *nf* presentation; (*de personnes*) introduction; **p. de mode** fashion show; **faire les présentations** to make the introductions.

présenter [prezɑ̃te] *vt* (*offrir, animer, exposer etc*) to present; (*montrer*) to present, show; **p. qn à qn** to introduce *ou* present s.o. to s.o. ▮ *vi* **elle présente bien** *Fam* she has (a) good presentation, she presents herself well ▮ **se présenter** *vpr* to introduce *ou* present oneself (à to); (*chez qn*) to show up; (*occasion etc*) to arise; **se p. à** (*examen*) to take, *Br* sit for; (*élections*) to run in, stand in; (*emploi*) to apply for; (*autorités*) to report to; **ça se présente bien** it looks promising.

présentoir [prezɑ̃twar] *nm* (*étagère*) (display) stand.

préservatif [prezɛrvatif] *nm* condom, sheath.

préserver [prezɛrve] *vt* to protect, preserve (de from). ● **préservation** *nf* protection, preservation.

présidence [prezidɑ̃s] *nf* (*de nation*) presidency; (*de firme etc*) chairmanship. ● **président, -ente** *nmf* (*de nation*) president; (*de réunion, firme*) chairman, chairwoman; **p. directeur général** *Br* (chairman and) managing director, *Am* chief executive officer; **p. du jury** (*d'examen*) chief examiner; (*de tribunal*) foreman of the jury. ● **présidentiable** *a* **être p.** to be a possible presidential candi-

présider [prezide] vt (réunion etc) to chair, preside over ▮ vi to preside.

présomption [prezɔ̃psjɔ̃] nf (supposition, suffisance) presumption.

présomptueux, -euse [prezɔ̃ptɥø, -øz] a presumptuous.

presque [prɛsk(ə)] adv almost, nearly; **p. jamais/rien** hardly ever/anything.

presqu'île [prɛskil] nf peninsula.

pressant, -ante [prɛsɑ̃, -ɑ̃t] a voir presser.

presse [prɛs] nf (journaux, appareil) press; Typ (printing) press; **conférence/agence de p.** press ou news conference/agency.

pressé, -ée [prese] a voir presser.

presse-citron [presitrɔ̃] nm inv lemon squeezer. ● **presse-papiers** nm inv paperweight. ● **presse-purée** nm inv (potato) masher.

pressentir* [presɑ̃tir] vt (deviner) to sense (que that). ● **pressentiment** nm foreboding, presentiment.

presser [prese] vt (serrer) to squeeze, press; (bouton) to press; (fruit) to squeeze; (départ etc) to hasten; **p. qn** to hurry s.o. (de faire to do); (assaillir) to harass s.o.; **p. qn de questions** to bombard s.o. with questions; **p. le pas** to speed up.
▮ vi (temps) to press; (affaire) to be urgent ou pressing; **rien ne presse** there's no hurry.
▮ **se presser** vpr (se serrer) to squeeze (together); (se hâter) to hurry (de faire to do); (se grouper) to crowd, swarm; **presse-toi (de partir)** hurry up (and go). ● **pressant, -ante** a urgent, pressing. ● **pressé, -ée** a (personne) in a hurry; (travail) pressing, urgent; (air) hurried.

pressing [presiŋ] nm (magasin) dry cleaner's.

pression [presjɔ̃] nf 1 pressure; **faire p. sur qn** to put pressure on s.o., pressurize s.o.; **bière (à la) p.** Br draught beer, Am draft beer. 2 (bouton) snap (fastener).

pressoir [preswar] nm (wine) press.

pressuriser [presyrize] vt (avion) to pressurize. ● **pressurisation** nf pressurization.

prestance [prestɑ̃s] nf (imposing) presence.

prestation [prestasjɔ̃] nf 1 (allocation) allowance, benefit; **prestations sociales** Br social security benefits, Am welfare payments. 2 (performance) performance.

prestidigitateur, -trice [prestidiʒitatœr, -tris] nmf conjurer. ● **prestidigitation** nf tour de p. conjuring trick.

prestige [prestiʒ] nm prestige. ● **prestigieux, -euse** a prestigious.

presto [presto] adv Fam voir illico.

présumer [prezyme] vt to presume (que that); **p. de qch** to overestimate sth.

présupposer [presypoze] vt to presuppose (que that).

prêt¹, prête [prɛ, prɛt] a (préparé, disposé) ready (à faire to do, à qch for sth); **être fin p.** to be all ready ou all set; **il est p. à tout**

pour l'épouser he's prepared to do anything ou he would do anything to marry her. ● **prêt-à-porter** [prɛtaportɛ] nm (pl prêts-à-porter) ready-to-wear clothes.

prêt² [prɛ] nm (emprunt) loan. ● **prêt-logement** nm (pl prêts-logement) mortgage.

prétendre [pretɑ̃dr] vt to claim (que that); (vouloir) to intend (faire to do); **p. être/savoir** to claim to be/to know; **elle se prétend riche** she claims to be rich ▮ vi **p. à** (titre etc) to lay claim to. ● **prédendant** nm (amoureux) suitor. ● **prétendu, -ue** a so-called. ● **prétendument** adv supposedly.

prétentieux, -euse [pretɑ̃sjø, -øz] a conceited ou pretentious (person). ● **prétention** nf (vanité) pretension; (revendication, ambition) claim; **sans p.** (film, robe etc) unpretentious.

prêter [prete] vt (argent, objet) to lend (à to); (aide, concours) to give (à to); (attribuer) to attribute (à to); **p. attention** to pay attention (à to); **p. serment** to take an oath ▮ vi **p. à** (phrase etc) to lend itself to ▮ **se prêter** vpr **p. à** (consentir à) to agree to; (sujet etc) to lend itself to. ● **prêteur, -euse** [pretœr, -øz] nmf (d'argent) lender; **p. sur gages** pawnbroker.

prétérit [preterit] nm Grammaire preterite (tense).

prétexte [pretɛkst] nm excuse, pretext; **sous p. de/que** on the pretext of/that; **sous aucun p.** under any circumstances. ● **prétexter** vt to plead (que that).

prêtre [prɛtr] nm priest; **grand p.** high priest.

preuve [prœv] nf preuve(s) proof, evidence; **faire p. de qch** to show sth; **faire ses preuves** (personne) to prove oneself; (méthode) to prove itself.

prévaloir* [prevalwar] vi to prevail (contre against, sur over).

prévenant, -ante [prevnɑ̃, -ɑ̃t] a considerate. ● **prévenance(s)** nf(pl) (gentillesse) consideration.

prévenir* [prevnir] vt 1 (avertir) to warn (que that); (aviser) to inform, tell (que that). 2 (désir, question) to anticipate; (malheur) to avert. ● **prévenu, -ue** nmf (inculpé) defendant, accused. 2 a prejudiced (contre against). ● **préventif, -ive** a preventive. ● **prévention** nf 1 prevention; **p. routière** road safety. 2 (opinion) prejudice.

prévisible [previzibl] a foreseeable.

prévision [previzjɔ̃] nf (opinion etc) forecast; **en p. de** in expectation of; **prévisions météorologiques** weather forecast.

prévoir* [prevwar] vt (anticiper) to foresee (que that); (prédire) to forecast (que that); (temps) to forecast; (organiser) to plan (for); (préparer) to provide, make provision for; **un repas est prévu** a meal is provided; **au moment prévu** at the appointed time; **comme prévu** as expected, as planned; **prévu pour** (véhicule, appareil etc) designed for.

prévoyant, -ante [prevwajɑ̃, -ɑ̃t] a **être p.** to have foresight. ● **prévoyance** nf foresight;

société de p. *Br* provident society, *Am* benefit society.

prier [prije] 1 *vi Rel* to pray ▮ *vt* p. Dieu pour qu'il nous accorde qch to pray (to God) for sth. 2 *vt* p. qn de faire to ask *ou* request s.o. to do; (*implorer*) to beg s.o. to do; **je vous en prie** (*faites donc, allez-y*) please; (*en réponse à 'merci'*) don't mention it; **je vous prie** please; **se faire** p. to wait to be asked; **il ne s'est pas fait** p. he didn't need much persuading.

prière [prijer] *nf Rel* prayer; (*demande*) request; p. **de répondre**/*etc* please answer/*etc*.

primaire [primer] *a* primary; **école** p. *Br* primary school, *Am* elementary school; **secteur** p. *Écon* primary sector ▮ *nm Br* primary *ou Am* elementary education; **entrer en** p. to enter *Br* primary *ou Am* elementary school.

primauté [primote] *nf* (*importance*) primacy; **donner la** p. à qch to give priority to sth.

prime [prim] 1 *nf* (*d'employé*) bonus; (*d'État*) subsidy; **en** p. (*cadeau*) as a free gift; p. (**d'assurance**) (insurance) premium; p. **de fin d'année** = Christmas bonus; p. **de transport** transport allowance; p. **de licenciement** severance pay, *Br* redundancy payment. 2 *a* **de** p. **abord** at the very first glance.

primé, -ée [prime] *a* (*animal, film etc*) prize-winning.

primer [prime] *vi* to excel, prevail ▮ *vt* to prevail over.

primeurs [primœr] *nfpl* early fruit and vegetables.

primevère [primver] *nf* primula; (*à fleurs jaunes*) primrose.

primitif, -ive [primitif, -iv] *a* (*société, art etc*) primitive; (*état, sens*) original ▮ *nm* (*artiste*) primitive. ● **primitivement** *adv* originally.

primo [primo] *adv* first(ly).

primordial, -e, -aux [primordjal, -o] *a* vital (**de faire** to do).

prince [prɛ̃s] *nm* prince. ● **princesse** *nf* princess. ● **princier, -ière** *a* princely. ● **principauté** *nf* principality.

principal, -e, -aux [prɛ̃sipal, -o] *a* main, chief, principal ▮ *nm* (*de collège*) principal, *Br* headmaster; **le** p. (*essentiel*) the main *ou* chief thing. ● **principalement** *adv* mainly.

principe [prɛ̃sip] *nm* principle; **en** p. theoretically, in principle; (*normalement*) as a rule; **par** p. on principle.

printemps [prɛ̃tɑ̃] *nm* (*saison*) spring. ● **printanier, -ière** *a* **température**/*etc* **printanière** spring-like temperature/*etc*.

priorité [prijorite] *nf* priority; (*sur route*) **la** p. (*en voiture*) the right of way; **avoir la** p. to have (the) right of way; **la** p. à **droite** (*du Code de la route*) right of way to traffic coming from the right; **'cédez la** p.' *Br* 'give way', *Am* 'yield'; **en** p. as a matter of priority. ● **prioritaire** *a* **secteur**/*etc* **être** p. to have priority; (*en voiture*) to have (the) right of way.

pris, prise¹ [pri, priz] *pp de* **prendre** ▮ *a* (*place*) taken; (*crème, mayonnaise, ciment*)

set; (*nez*) congested; (*gorge*) infected; (*eau*) frozen; **être (très)** p. (*occupé*) to be (very) busy; p. **de** (*peur, panique*) stricken with.

prise² [priz] *nf* taking; (*objet saisi*) catch; (*manière d'empoigner*) grip, hold; (*de ville etc*) hold; (*de ville*) capture, taking; (*de tabac*) pinch; p. (**de courant**) *Él* (*mâle*) plug; (*femelle*) socket; p. **multiple** *Él* adaptor; p. **de sang** blood test; **faire une** p. **de sang à qn** to give s.o. a blood test; p. **de contact** first meeting; p. **de position** *Fig* stand; p. **de conscience** awareness; p. **d'air** air vent; p. **d'otages** hostage-taking; p. **de son** (sound) recording; p. **de vue(s)** *Cinéma Phot* (*action*) shooting; (*résultat*) shot; **être aux prises avec qn/qch** *Fig* to be struggling *ou* battling with s.o./sth.

priser [prize] 1 *vt* (*tabac, cocaïne etc*) to sniff (up one's nostrils); **tabac à** p. snuff ▮ *vi* to take snuff. 2 *vt* (*estimer*) to prize.

prisme [prism] *nm* prism.

prison [prizɔ̃] *nf* prison, jail, *Br* gaol; (*réclusion*) imprisonment; **être en** p. to be in prison *ou* in jail; **mettre qn en** p. to send s.o. to prison, jail s.o. ● **prisonnier, -ière** *nmf* prisoner; **faire qn** p. to take s.o. prisoner.

privation [privasjɔ̃] *nf* deprivation (**de** of); **privations** (*sacrifices*) hardships.

privatiser [privatize] *vt* to privatize.

privé, -ée [prive] *a* private; **en** p. (*seul à seul*) in private ▮ *nm* **dans le** p. in private life; *Com etc Fam* in the private sector.

priver [prive] *vt* to deprive (**de** of); **se** p. **de** to do without, deprive oneself of.

privilège [privilɛʒ] *nm* privilege. ● **privilégié, -ée** *a & nmf* privileged (person).

prix [pri] *nm* 1 (*d'un objet, du succès etc*) price; **à tout** p. at all costs; **à aucun** p. on no account; **hors (de)** p. exorbitant; **attacher du** p. **à** to attach importance to; **menu à** p. **fixe** set price menu; **faire un** p. **à qn** to give s.o. a special price. 2 (*récompense*) prize.

pro- [pro] *préf* pro-.

probable [prɔbabl] *a* likely, probable; **peu** p. unlikely. ● **probabilité** *nf* probability, likelihood; **selon toute** p. in all probability. ● **probablement** [-əmɑ̃] *adv* probably.

probant, -ante [prɔbɑ̃, -ɑ̃t] *a* conclusive.

probité [prɔbite] *nf* (*honnêteté*) integrity.

problème [prɔblɛm] *nm* problem. ● **problématique** *a* doubtful, problematic.

procédé [prɔsede] *nm* process; (*conduite*) behaviour.

procéder [prɔsede] *vi* (*agir*) to proceed, (*se conduire*) to behave; p. **à** (*enquête etc*) to carry out. ● **procédure** *nf* (*méthode*) procedure; (*règles juridiques*) procedure; (*procès*) proceedings.

procès [prɔsɛ] *nm* (*criminel*) trial; (*civil*) lawsuit; **faire un** p. **à qn** to take s.o. to court.

processeur [prɔsesœr] *nm* (*d'ordinateur*) processor.

procession [prɔsesjɔ̃] *nf* procession.

processus [prɔsesys] *nm* process.

procès-verbal, -aux [prɔsɛvɛrbal, -o] *nm* (*contravention*) (traffic) fine, ticket; (*de réunion*) minutes; (*constat de juge etc*) report.

prochain, -aine [prɔʃɛ̃, -ɛn] **1** *a* next; (*mort, arrivée*) impending; (*mariage*) forthcoming; (*avenir*) near; **un jour p.** one day soon ∎ **f à la prochaine!** *Fam* see you soon!; **à la prochaine (station)** at the next station. **2** *nm* (*semblable*) fellow (man). ● **prochainement** *adv* shortly, soon.

proche [prɔʃ] *a* (*espace*) near, close; (*temps*) close (at hand); (*parent, ami*) close; (*avenir*) near; **p. de** near (to), close to; **une maison/** *etc* **p.** a house/*etc* nearby *ou* close by; **le P.-Orient** the Middle East. ● **proches** *nmpl* close relations.

proclamer [prɔklame] *vt* to proclaim, declare (**que** that); **p. qn roi** to proclaim s.o. king. ● **proclamation** *nf* proclamation, declaration.

procréer [prɔkree] *vt* to procreate. ● **procréation** *nf* procreation. **p. médicalement assistée** artifical fertilization.

procuration [prɔkyrasjɔ̃] *nf* power of attorney; **par p.** (*voter etc*) by proxy.

procurer [prɔkyre] *vt* **p. qch à qn** (*personne*) to obtain sth for s.o.; **ce travail me procure bien des satisfactions** this work brings me *ou* affords me great satisfaction; **se p. qch** to obtain sth.

procureur [prɔkyrœr] *nm* **p. (de la République)** = *Br* public prosecutor, = *Am* district attorney.

prodige [prɔdiʒ] *nm* (*miracle*) wonder; (*personne*) prodigy. ● **prodigieux, -euse** *a* prodigious, extraordinary.

prodigue [prɔdig] *a* (*dépensier*) wasteful, prodigal.

prodiguer [prɔdige] *vt* **p. qch à qn** to lavish sth on s.o.

production [prɔdyksjɔ̃] *nf* production; (*de la terre*) yield. ● **producteur, -trice** *nmf Com Cinéma* producer ∎ *a* producing; **pays p. de pétrole** oil-producing country. ● **productif, -ive** *a* (*terre, réunion etc*) productive. ● **productivité** *nf* productivity.

produire* [prɔdɥir] **1** *vt* (*fabriquer, présenter etc*) to produce; (*causer*) to produce, bring about. **2 se produire** *vpr* (*événement etc*) to happen, occur; (*sur scène*) to perform. ● **produit** *nm* (*article*) product; (*pour la vaisselle*) liquid; (*d'une vente, d'une collecte*) proceeds; **produits** (*de la terre*) produce; **p. (chimique)** chemical; **p. de beauté** cosmetic; **p. de consommation courante** basic consumer product; **p. national brut** gross national product; **p. intérieur brut** gross domestic product.

proéminent, -ente [prɔeminɑ̃, -ɑ̃t] *a* prominent.

prof [prɔf] *nm Fam* = **professeur.**

profane [prɔfan] **1** *nmf* lay person. **2** *a* (*art etc*) secular.

profaner [prɔfane] *vt* to profane, desecrate. ● **profanation** *nf* profanation, desecration.

proférer [prɔfere] *vt* to utter.

professer [prɔfese] **1** *vt Litt* to profess (**que** that). **2** *vi* (*enseigner*) to teach.

professeur [prɔfesœr] *nm* teacher; (*à l'université*) *Br* lecturer, *Am* professor; (*titulaire d'une chaire*) professor.

profession [prɔfesjɔ̃] *nf* **1** occupation, vocation; (*manuelle*) trade; **p. libérale** profession; **sans p.** not gainfully employed; **de p.** (*chanteur etc*) professional, by profession. **2 p. de foi** *Rel* profession of faith; *Fig* declaration of principles. ● **professionnel, -elle** *a* professional; (*école*) vocational ∎ *nmf* (*non amateur*) professional.

profil [prɔfil] *nm* (*de personne, objet*) profile; **de p.** (viewed) from the side, in profile. ● **profiler** *vt* to outline, profile ∎ **se profiler** *vpr* to be outlined *ou* profiled (**sur** against).

profit [prɔfi] *nm* profit; (*avantage*) advantage, profit; **tirer p. de** to benefit from *ou* by, profit by; **mettre à p.** to turn to good account, make good use of; **au p. de** for the benefit of. ● **profitable** *a* (*utile*) beneficial, profitable (**à** to). ● **profiter** *vi* **p. de** to take advantage of; **p. à qn** to benefit s.o., be of benefit to s.o. ● **profiteur, -euse** *nmf Péj* profiteer.

profond, -onde [prɔfɔ̃, -ɔ̃d] *a* deep; (*esprit, joie, erreur etc*) profound, great; (*cause*) underlying; **p. de deux mètres** two metres deep ∎ *adv* (*pénétrer etc*) deep ∎ *nm* **au plus p. de** in the depths of. ● **profondément** *adv* deeply; (*dormir*) soundly; (*triste, souhaiter*) profoundly; (*extrêmement*) thoroughly. ● **profondeur** *nf* depth; (*de joie etc*) profoundness; **profondeurs** depths (**de** of); **à six mètres de p.** at a depth of six metres; **en p.** (*étudier etc*) in depth.

profusion [prɔfyzjɔ̃] *nf* profusion; **à p.** in profusion.

progéniture [prɔʒenityr] *nf* (*enfants*) *Litt ou Hum* offspring.

progiciel [prɔʒisjɛl] *nm* (*pour ordinateur*) (software) package.

programmable [prɔgramabl] *a* programmable. ● **programmation** *nf* programming.

programmateur [prɔgramatœr] *nm* (*de four etc*) timer.

programme [prɔgram] *nm Br* programme, *Am* program; (*d'une matière*) *Scol* syllabus; (*d'ordinateur*) program; **p. (d'études)** (*d'une école*) curriculum. ● **programmer** *vt* (*ordinateur etc*) to program; (*au cinéma, à la radio, à la télévision*) to schedule, *Br* programme, *Am* program. ● **programmeur, -euse** *nmf* (computer) programmer.

progrès [prɔgrɛ] *nm & nmpl* progress; **faire des p.** to make (good) progress. ● **progresser** *vi* to progress. ● **progressif, -ive** *a* gradual, progressive. ● **progression** *nf* progression. ● **progressiste** *a & nmf Pol* progressive. ● **progressivement** *adv* gradually, progressively.

prohiber [prɔibe] *vt* to prohibit, forbid.

● **prohibitif, -ive** *a* prohibitive. ● **prohibition** *nf* prohibition.

proie [prwa] *nf* prey; **oiseau de p.** bird of prey; **être en p. à** *Fig* to be (a) prey to, be tortured by; **être la p. des flammes** to be consumed by fire.

projecteur [prɔʒɛktœr] *nm* (*de monument*) floodlight; (*de prison, de l'armée*) search-light; *Théâtre* spot(light); *Cinéma* projector.

projectile [prɔʒɛktil] *nm* missile.

projection [prɔʒɛksjɔ̃] *nf* (*lancement*) hurling, projection; (*de film, d'ombre*) projection; (*séance*) showing; **salle de p.** film theatre.

projet [prɔʒɛ] *nm* plan; (*ébauche*) draft; (*entreprise, étude*) project; **faire des projets d'avenir** to make plans for the future.

projeter [prɔʒte] *vt* **1** (*lancer*) to hurl, project. **2** (*film, ombre*) to project; (*lumière*) to flash. **3** (*voyage, fête etc*) to plan; **p. de faire qch** to plan to do sth.

prolétaire [prɔleter] *nmf* proletarian. ● **prolétariat** *nm* proletariat. ● **prolétarien, -ienne** *a* proletarian.

proliférer [prɔlifere] *vi* to proliferate. ● **prolifération** *nf* proliferation.

prolifique [prɔlifik] *a* prolific.

prolixe [prɔliks] *a* verbose, wordy.

prologue [prɔlɔg] *nm* prologue (**de, à** to).

prolonger [prɔlɔ̃ʒe] *vt* to extend, prolong ▌ **se prolonger** *vpr* (*séance, rue, effet*) to continue. ● **prolongateur** *nm* (*rallonge*) *El* extension cord. ● **prolongation** *nf* (*dans le temps*) extension; **prolongations** *Football* extra time. ● **prolongement** *nm* (*dans l'espace*) extension.

promenade [prɔm(ə)nad] *nf* (*à pied*) walk; (*en voiture*) drive, ride; (*en vélo, à cheval*) ride; (*action*) *Sport* walking; (*lieu*) walk, promenade; **faire une p. = se promener.**

promener [prɔm(ə)ne] *vt* to take for a walk *ou* ride; (*visiteur*) to take *ou* show around; (*chien*) to walk; **p. qch sur qch** (*main, regard*) to run sth over sth; **envoyer p.** *Fam* to send packing ▌ **se promener** *vpr* (*à pied*) to (go for a) walk; (*en voiture*) to (go for a) drive *ou* ride. ● **promeneur, -euse** *nmf* stroller, walker.

promesse [prɔmɛs] *nf* promise; **tenir sa p.** to keep one's promise.

promettre* [prɔmɛtr] *vt* to promise (**qch à qn** s.o. sth, **que** that); **p. de faire qch** to promise to do sth; **c'est promis** it's a promise ▌ *vi* **p.** (*beaucoup*) *Fig* to be promising ▌ **se promettre** *vpr* **se p. qch** to promise oneself sth; **se p. de faire qch** to resolve to do sth. ● **prometteur, -euse** *a* promising.

promontoire [prɔmɔ̃twar] *nm* *Géog* headland.

promoteur [prɔmɔtœr] *nm* **p. (immobilier)** property developer.

promotion [prɔmɔsjɔ̃] *nf* **1** promotion; **en p.** (*produit*) on (special) offer. **2** (*élèves*) *Univ* year. ● **promouvoir*** *vt* (*personne, produit etc*) to promote; **être promu** (*employé*) to be promoted (**à** to).

prompt, prompte [prɔ̃, prɔ̃t] *a* swift, prompt, quick. ● **promptitude** *nf* swiftness, promptness.

promulguer [prɔmylge] *vt* to promulgate.

prôner [prone] *vt* (*vanter*) to extol; (*préconiser*) to advocate.

pronom [prɔnɔ̃] *nm* *Grammaire* pronoun. ● **pronominal, -e, -aux** *a* *Grammaire* pronominal.

prononcer [prɔnɔ̃se] *vt* (*articuler*) to pronounce; (*dire*) to utter; (*discours*) to deliver; (*jugement*) to pronounce, pass ▌ *vi* (*juge etc*) to pronounce; (*articuler*) to pronounce ▌ **se prononcer** *vpr* (*mot*) to be pronounced; (*personne*) to reach a decision (**sur** about, on); **se p. pour/contre qch** to come out in favour of/against sth. ● **prononcé, -ée** *a* (*visible*) pronounced, marked. ● **prononciation** *nf* pronunciation.

pronostic [prɔnɔstik] *nm* (*prévision*) & *Sport* forecast. ● **pronostiquer** *vt* to forecast.

propagande [prɔpagɑ̃d] *nf* propaganda. ● **propagandiste** *nmf* propagandist.

propager [prɔpaʒe] *vt*, **se propager** *vpr* to spread. ● **propagation** *nf* spread(ing).

propension [prɔpɑ̃sjɔ̃] *nf* propensity (**à qch** for sth, **à faire** to do).

prophète [prɔfɛt] *nm* prophet. ● **prophétie** [-fesi] *nf* prophecy. ● **prophétique** *a* prophetic. ● **prophétiser** *vti* to prophesy.

propice [prɔpis] *a* favourable (**à** to).

proportion [prɔpɔrsjɔ̃] *nf* proportion; *Math* ratio; **proportions** (*dimensions*) proportions; **en p. de** in proportion to; **hors de p.** out of proportion (**avec** to); **l'affaire a pris des proportions considérables** the affair has blown up into a scandal. ● **proportionnel, -elle** *a* proportional (**à** to) ▌ *nf* **proportionnelle** (*scrutin*) proportional representation. ● **proportionner** *vt* to proportion (**à** to). ● **proportionné, -ée** *a* proportionate (**à** to); **bien p.** well *ou* nicely proportioned.

propos [prɔpo] **1** *nmpl* (*paroles*) remarks, utterances. **2** *nm* (*sujet*) subject; **à p. de** about; **à tout p.** for no reason, at every turn; **à p. de rien** for no reason. **3** *nm* (*intention*) purpose. **4** *adv* **à p.** (*arriver etc*) at the right time; **à p.!** by the way!; **juger à p. de faire qch** to consider it fit to do sth.

proposer [prɔpoze] *vt* (*suggérer*) to suggest, propose (**qch à qn sth** to s.o., **que** (+ *sub*) that); (*offrir*) to offer (**qch à qn** s.o. sth, **de faire** to do); (*candidat*) to put forward, propose; **je te propose de rester** I suggest (that) you stay ▌ **se proposer** *vpr* **se p. pour faire qch** to offer to do sth; **se p. de faire qch** to propose *ou* mean to do sth. ● **proposition** *nf* suggestion, proposal; (*de paix*) proposal, (*affirmation*) proposition; *Grammaire* clause.

propre¹ [prɔpr] *a* clean; (*soigné*) neat; (*honnête*) decent; **p. comme un sou neuf** squeaky clean ▌ *nm* **mettre qch au p.** to make a fair copy of sth; **c'est du p.!** *Fam* what a shocking way to behave! ● **proprement¹** [-əmɑ̃] *adv* (*avec propreté*) cleanly; (*avec netteté*) neatly; (*comme il faut*) decently. ● **propreté** *nf* cleanliness; (*netteté*) neatness.

propre² [prɔpr] **1** *a* (*à soi*) own; **par mes propres moyens** under my own steam; **mon p. argent** my own money; **ses propres mots** his very *ou* his own words.
2 *a* (*qui convient*) right, proper; **p. à** (*attribut, coutume etc*) peculiar to; (*approprié*) well-suited to; **p. à faire qch** likely to do sth; **sens p.** literal meaning; **nom p.** proper noun ▮ *nm* **le p. de** (*qualité*) the distinctive quality of; **au p.** (*au sens propre*) literally. ● **proprement²** [-əmã] *adv* (*strictement*) strictly; **à p. parler** strictly speaking; **le village/etc p. dit** the village/etc proper *ou* itself.

propriétaire [prɔprijetɛr] *nmf* owner; (*d'hôtel*) proprietor, owner; (*qui loue*) landlord, landlady; **p. foncier** landowner.

propriété [prɔprijete] *nf* **1** (*bien, maison*) property; (*droit*) ownership, property. **2** (*qualité*) property. **3** (*de mot*) suitability.

propulser [prɔpylse] *vt* (*faire avancer, projeter*) to propel. ● **propulsion** *nf* propulsion.

prosaïque [prɔzaik] *a* prosaic, pedestrian.

proscrire* [prɔskrir] *vt* (*exiler*) to proscribe, banish; (*interdire*) to ban. ● **proscrit, -ite** *nmf* (*personne*) exile.

prose [proz] *nf* prose.

prospecter [prɔspɛkte] *vt* (*sol*) to prospect; (*pétrole*) to prospect for; (*région*) Com to canvass. ● **prospecteur, -trice** *nmf* prospector. ● **prospection** *nf* prospecting; Com canvassing.

prospectus [prɔspɛktys] *nm* leaflet, prospectus.

prospère [prɔspɛr] *a* (*florissant*) thriving, prosperous; (*riche*) prosperous. ● **prospérer** *vi* to thrive, flourish, prosper. ● **prospérité** *nf* prosperity.

prostate [prɔstat] *nf* Anat prostate (gland).

prosterner (se) [səprɔstɛrne] *vpr* to prostrate oneself (**devant** before). ● **prosterné, -ée** *a* prostrate.

prostituer [prɔstitɥe] *vt* to prostitute ▮ **se prostituer** *vpr* to prostitute oneself. ● **prostituée** *nf* prostitute. ● **prostitution** *nf* prostitution.

prostré, -ée [prɔstre] *a* (*accablé*) prostrate. ● **prostration** *nf* prostration.

protagoniste [prɔtagɔnist] *nmf* protagonist.

protecteur, -trice [prɔtɛktœr, -tris] *nmf/a* protector; (*mécène*) patron ▮ *a* (*geste, crème etc*) & Écon protective; (*ton, air*) patronizing. ● **protection** *nf* protection; (*mécénat*) patronage; **de p.** (*écran etc*) protective; **assurer la p. de qn** to ensure s.o.'s safety; **p. sociale** social security. ● **protectionnisme** *nm* Écon protectionism.

protéger [prɔteʒe] *vt* to protect (**de** from, **contre** against); (*appuyer*) Fig to patronize ▮ **se protéger** *vpr* to protect oneself. ● **protégé** *nm* protégé. ● **protégée** *nf* protégée. ● **protège-cahier** *nm* exercise book cover.

protéine [prɔtein] *nf* protein.

protestant, -ante [prɔtɛstã, -ãt] *a* & *nmf* Protestant. ● **protestantisme** *nm* Protestantism.

protester [prɔtɛste] *vi* to protest (**contre** against); **p. de son innocence/etc** to protest one's innocence/etc ▮ *vt* to protest (**que** that). ● **protestataire** *a* (*tendances etc*) anti-Establishment ▮ *nmf* protester. ● **protestation** *nf* protest (**contre** against); **protestations** (*d'amitié*) declarations (**de** of).

prothèse [prɔtɛz] *nf* (**appareil de) p.** (*membre*) artificial limb; **p. dentaire** dental prosthesis, false tooth *ou* teeth.

protocole [prɔtɔkɔl] *nm* protocol.

prototype [prɔtɔtip] *nm* prototype.

protubérance [prɔtyberãs] *nf* protuberance. ● **protubérant, -ante** *a* (*yeux*) bulging; (*menton*) protruding.

proue [pru] *nf* (*de navire*) bow(s), prow.

prouesse [prues] *nf* feat, exploit.

prouver [pruve] *vt* to prove (**que** that).

Provence [prɔvãs] *nf* Provence. ● **provençal, -e, -aux** *a* Provençal ▮ *nmf* **P., Provençale** Provençal.

provenir* [prɔv(ə)nir] *vi* **p. de** to come from. ● **provenance** *nf* origin; **en p. de** from.

proverbe [prɔvɛrb] *nm* proverb. ● **proverbial, -e, -aux** *a* proverbial.

providence [prɔvidãs] *nf* providence. ● **providentiel, -ielle** *a* providential.

province [prɔvɛ̃s] *nf* province; **la p.** the provinces; **en p.** in the provinces; **de p.** (*ville etc*) provincial. ● **provincial, -e, -aux** *a* & *nmf* provincial.

proviseur [prɔvizœr] *nm* (*de lycée*) Br headmaster, Br headmistress, Am principal.

provision [prɔvizjɔ̃] *nf* **1** (*réserve*) supply, stock; **provisions** (*achats*) shopping; (*nourriture*) food; **panier/sac à provisions** shopping basket/bag. **2** (*somme*) funds; (*acompte*) advance payment; **chèque sans p.** Br dud cheque, Am bad check.

provisoire [prɔvizwar] *a* temporary, provisional; **à titre p.** temporarily, provisionally. ● **provisoirement** *adv* temporarily, provisionally.

provoquer [prɔvɔke] *vt* **1** (*causer*) to bring about, provoke; (*désir*) to arouse. **2** (*défier*) to provoke (*s.o.*). ● **provocant, -ante** *a* provocative. ● **provocateur** *nm* troublemaker. ● **provocation** *nf* provocation.

proxénète [prɔksenɛt] *nm* pimp.

proximité [prɔksimite] *nf* closeness, proximity; **à p.** close by; **à p. de** close to.

prude [pryd] *a* prudish ▮ *nf* prude.

prudent, -ente [prydã, -ãt] *a* (*circonspect*) cautious, careful; (*sage*) sensible. ● **prudemment** [-amã] *adv* cautiously, carefully; (*sagement*) sensibly. ● **prudence** *nf* caution, care, prudence; (*sagesse*) wisdom; **par p.** as a precaution.

prune [pryn] *nf* (*fruit*) plum. ● **pruneau, -x** *nm* prune. ● **prunier** *nm* plum tree.

prunelle [prynɛl] *nf* **1** (*de l'œil*) pupil; **il tient à ses enfants comme à la p. de ses yeux** his children are the apple of his eye *ou* his pride and joy. **2** (*fruit*) sloe.

P.-S. [pees] *abrév* (*post-scriptum*) PS.

psaume [psom] *nm* psalm.

pseudo- [psødo] *préf* pseudo-.

pseudonyme [psødɔnim] *nm* pseudonym.

psychanalyse [psikanaliz] *nf* psychoanalysis. ● **psychanalyste** *nmf* psychoanalyst.

psychédélique [psikedelik] *a* (*vision, musique etc*) psychedelic.

psychiatre [psikjatr] *nmf* psychiatrist. ● **psychiatrie** *nf* psychiatry. ● **psychiatrique** *a* psychiatric.

psychique [psiʃik] *a* mental, psychic.

psycho [psiko] *préf* psycho-.

psychologie [psikɔlɔʒi] *nf* psychology. ● **psychologique** *a* psychological. ● **psychologue** *nmf* psychologist; **p. scolaire** educational psychologist.

psychose [psikoz] *nf* psychosis.

PTT [petete] *nfpl* (*Postes, Télégraphes, Téléphones*) Post Office, = *Br* GPO.

pu [py] *pp de* **pouvoir** 1.

puant, -ante [pɥɑ̃, -ɑ̃t] *a* stinking. ● **puanteur** *nf* stink, stench.

pub [pyb] *nf Fam* (*réclame*) advertising; (*annonce*) ad.

puberté [pyberte] *nf* puberty.

public, -ique [pyblik] *a* public; **dette publique** national debt; **ennemi p. numéro un** public enemy number one **I** *nm* public; (*de spectacle*) audience; **le grand p.** the general public; **film grand p.** film suitable for the general public, film of mass appeal; **en p.** in public. ● **publiquement** *adv* publicly.

publication [pyblikasjɔ̃] *nf* (*action, livre etc*) publication. ● **publier** *vt* to publish.

publicité [pyblisite] *nf* publicity (**pour** for); (*réclame*) advertising, publicity; (*annonce*) advertisement; (*à la radio ou télévision*) commercial; *Fig* publicity (**autour de** surrounding); **agence de p.** advertising agency; **faire de la p. pour qch** to advertise sth. ● **publicitaire** *a* **agence/etc p.** advertising agency/etc; **film/etc p.** promotional film/etc **I** *nmf* advertising executive.

puce [pys] *nf* **1** flea; **le marché aux puces, les puces** the flea market. **2** (*d'un ordinateur*) (micro)chip, silicon chip.

puceron [pysrɔ̃] *nm* greenfly.

pudeur [pydœr] *nf* (sense of) modesty; **attentat à la p.** *Jur* indecency. ● **pudibond, -onde** *a* prudish. ● **pudique** *a* modest.

puer [pɥe] *vi* to stink **I** *vt* to stink of.

puériculture [pɥerikyltyr] *nf* infant care, child care. ● **puéricultrice** *nf* children's nurse.

puéril, -e [pɥeril] *a* puerile. ● **puérilité** *nf* puerility.

puis [pɥi] *adv* then; **et p.** (*en plus*) and besides; **et p. quoi?** and so what?

puiser [pɥize] *vt* to draw, take (**dans** from) **I** *vi* **p. dans** to dip into.

puisque [pɥisk(ə)] *conj* since, as.

puissant, -ante [pɥisɑ̃, -ɑ̃t] *a* powerful.

● **puissamment** [-amɑ̃] *adv* powerfully.

● **puissance** *nf* (*force, nation*) & *Math Tech* power; **en p.** (*talent, danger etc*) potential.

puisse(s), puissent *etc* [pɥis] *voir* **pouvoir** 1.

puits [pɥi] *nm* well; (*de mine*) shaft; **un p. de science** *Fig* a fund of knowledge.

pull(-over) [pyl(ɔvɛr)] *nm* sweater, *Br* jumper, pullover.

pulluler [pylyle] *vi Péj* to swarm.

pulmonaire [pylmɔnɛr] *a* **congestion/etc p.** congestion/etc of the lungs.

pulpe [pylp] *nf* (*de fruits*) pulp.

pulsation [pylsasjɔ̃] *nf* (heart)beat.

pulvériser [pylverize] *vt* (*liquide*) to spray; (*broyer*) & *Fig* to pulverize; **p. un record** *Sport Fam* to smash a record. ● **pulvérisateur** *nm* spray, atomizer. ● **pulvérisation** *nf* (*de liquide*) spraying.

puma [pyma] *nm* (*animal*) puma.

punaise [pynɛz] *nf* **1** (*insecte*) bug (*bedbug etc*). **2** (*clou*) *Br* drawing pin, *Am* thumbtack. ● **punaiser** *vt* (*fixer*) to pin (up).

punch [pɔ̃ʃ] *nm* **1** (*boisson*) punch. **2** [pœnʃ] (*énergie*) *Fam* punch.

punir [pynir] *vt* to punish; **p. qn de qch/pour avoir fait qch** to punish s.o. for sth/for doing *ou* having done sth. ● **punissable** *a* punishable (**de** by). ● **punition** *nf* punishment.

punk [pœnk] *nmf* punk **I** *a inv* (*musique etc*) punk.

pupille [pypij] *nf* **1** (*de l'œil*) pupil. **2** *nmf* (*enfant sous tutelle*) ward; **p. de la Nation** war orphan.

pupitre [pypitr] *nm* (*d'écolier*) desk; (*d'orateur*) lectern; *Ordinat* console; **p. à musique** music stand.

pur, pure [pyr] *a* pure; (*alcool*) neat, straight. ● **purement** *adv* purely; **p. et simplement** (*refuser etc*) purely and simply. ● **pureté** *nf* purity.

purée [pyre] *nf* purée; **p. (de pommes de terre)** mashed potatoes, *Br* mash.

purgatoire [pyrgatwar] *nm* purgatory.

purge [pyrʒ] *nf Pol Méd* purge.

purger [pyrʒe] *vt* **1** (*conduite*) *Tech* to drain, clear; (*débarrasser*) *Litt* to purge, rid (**de** of). **2** (*peine de prison*) to serve.

purifier [pyrifje] *vt* to purify. ● **purification** *nf* purification; **p. ethnique** ethnic cleansing.

purin [pyrɛ̃] *nm* liquid manure.

puriste [pyrist] *nmf Grammaire* purist.

puritain, -aine [pyritɛ̃, -ɛn] *a* & *nmf* puritan.

pur-sang [pyrsɑ̃] *nm inv* (*cheval*) thoroughbred.

pus¹ [py] *nm* (*liquide*) pus, matter.

pus², put [py] *voir* **pouvoir** 1.

putain [pytɛ̃] *nf Péj Vulg* whore.

putois [pytwa] *nm* (*animal*) polecat.

putréfier [pytrefje] *vt*, **se putréfier** *vpr* to putrefy. ● **putréfaction** *nf* putrefaction.

puzzle [pœzl] *nm* (jigsaw) puzzle, jigsaw.

p.-v. [peve] *nm inv abrév* (*procès-verbal*) (traffic) fine.

PVC [pevese] *nm* (*matière plastique*) PVC.
pygmée [pigme] *nm* pygmy.
pyjama [piʒama] *nm* Br pyjamas, *Am* pajamas; **un p.** a pair of *Br* pyjamas *ou Am* pajamas; **pantalon de p.** *Br* pyjama trousers, *Am* pajama bottoms; **être en p.** to be in *Br* pyjamas *ou Am* pajamas.

pylône [pilon] *nm* pylon.
pyramide [piramid] *nf* pyramid.
Pyrénées [pirene] *nfpl* **les P.** the Pyrenees.
Pyrex® [pirɛks] *nm* Pyrex®; **plat**/*etc* **en P.** Pyrex dish/*etc*.
pyromane [pirɔman] *nmf* arsonist, firebug.
python [pitɔ̃] *nm* (*serpent*) python.

Q

Q, q [ky] *nm* Q, q.
QCM [kyseɛm] *nm abrév* (*questionnaire à choix multiple*) multiple choice question paper.
QI [kyi] *nm inv abrév* (*quotient intellectuel*) IQ.
qu' [k] *voir* que.
quadragénaire [kwadraʒenɛr] (*Fam* **quadra**) *a* forty-year-old; **être q.** to be in one's forties **∎** *nmf* person in his *ou* her forties.
quadriller [kadrije] *vt* (*police etc*) to be positioned throughout, comb, cover (*town etc*).
quadrillage [kadrijaʒ] *nm* (*lignes*) squares. ●**quadrillé, -ée** *a* (*papier*) squared.
quadrupède [k(w)adrypɛd] *nm* quadruped.
quadruple [k(w)adrypl] *a* **q. de** fourfold **∎** *nm* **le q. de** four times as much as. ●**quadrupler** *vti* to quadruple. ●**quadruplés, -ées** *nmfpl* (*enfants*) quadruplets, quads.
quai [ke] *nm* Nau (*pour passagers*) quay; (*pour marchandises*) wharf; (*de fleuve*) embankment, bank; (*de gare*) platform.
qualification [kalifikasjɔ̃] *nf* **1** (*action, à un match etc*) qualifying, qualification. **2** (*nom*) description, designation. ●**qualificatif** *nm* (*mot*) term.
qualifier [kalifje] **1** *vt* (*décrire*) to describe (**de** as); **q. qn de menteur/etc** to call s.o. a liar/etc. **2** *vt* (*équipe etc*) to qualify (**pour qch** for sth, **pour faire** to do) **∎ se qualifier** *vpr* (*équipe etc*) to qualify (**pour** for). **3** *vt* Grammaire to qualify. ●**qualifié, -ée** *a* (*équipe etc*) that has qualified; (*ouvrier, main-d'œuvre*) skilled; **q. pour faire qch** qualified to do sth.
qualité [kalite] *nf* quality; (*condition sociale etc*) occupation, status; **produit/etc de q.** high-quality product/etc; **en sa q. de** in one's capacity as. ●**qualitatif, -ive** *a* qualitative.
quand [kɑ̃] *conj & adv* when; **q. je viendrai** when I come; **c'est pour q.?** (*réunion, mariage*) when is it?; **q. bien même vous le feriez** even if you did it; **q. même** *Fam* all the same.
quant (à) [kɑ̃ta] *prép* as for.
quantifier [kɑ̃tifje] *vt* to quantify. ●**quantitatif, -ive** *a* quantitative.
quantité [kɑ̃tite] *nf* quantity; **une q., des quantités** (*beaucoup*) a lot (**de** of); **en q.** (*abondamment*) in abundance, in plenty.
quarante [karɑ̃t] *a & nm* forty; **un q.-cinq tours** (*disque*) a single. ●**quarantaine** *nf* **1 une q. (de)** (*nombre*) (about) forty; **avoir la q.** (*âge*) to be about forty. **2** *Méd* quarantine; **mettre qn en q.** to quarantine s.o.; (*exclure*) *Fig Br* to send s.o. to Coventry,

Am give s.o. the silent treatment. ●**quarantième** *a & nmf* fortieth.
quart [kar] *nm* **1** quarter; **q. (de litre)** quarter litre, quarter of a litre; **q. d'heure** quarter of an hour; **une heure et q.** an hour and a quarter; **il est une heure et q.** it's a quarter *Br* past *ou Am* after one; **une heure moins le q.** quarter to one; **jouer les quarts de finale** *Sport* to play in the quarter finals; **passer un mauvais q. d'heure** *Fig* to have a bad *ou* rough time (of it). **2** (*sur un bateau*) watch; **être de q.** to be on watch.
quarté [karte] *nm* system of betting on four horses in the same race.
quartette [kwartɛt] *nm* (*jazz*) quartet(te).
quartier [kartje] **1** *nm* neighbourhood, district, quarter; **de q.** (*cinéma etc*) local; **les gens du q.** the local people; **les beaux quartiers** the rich neighbourhoods; **le Q. latin** the Latin Quarter. **2** *nm* (*de pomme, lune*) quarter; (*d'orange*) segment. **3** *nm(pl)* **quartier(s)** (*cantonnement*) *Mil* quarters; **q. général** headquarters.
quart-monde [karmɔ̃d] *nm* **le q.-monde** the Fourth World (*the poorest countries in the world*).
quartz [kwarts] *nm* quartz; **montre/etc à q.** quartz watch/etc.
quasi [kazi] *adv* almost. ●**quasi-** *préf* near; **q.-obscurité** near darkness. ●**quasiment** *adv* almost.
quatorze [katɔrz] *a & nm* fourteen. ●**quatorzième** *a & nmf* fourteenth.
quatre [katr] *a & nm* four; **son q. heures** (*goûter*) *Fam* one's afternoon snack; **se mettre en q.** *Fig* to go out of one's way (**pour faire** to do); **manger comme q.** *Fam* to eat like a horse; **un de ces q.** *Fam* some day soon. ●**quatrième** *a & nmf* fourth. ●**quatrièmement** *adv* fourthly.
quatre-vingt(s) [katrəvɛ̃] *a & nm* eighty; **q.-vingts ans** eighty years; **q.-vingt-un** eighty-one, **page q.-vingt** page eighty. ●**quatre-vingt-dix** *a & nm* ninety.
quatuor [kwatɥɔr] *nm* (*musique, musiciens*) quartet(te). **q. à cordes** string quartet(te).
que [k(ə)] (**qu'** *before a vowel or mute h*) **1** *conj* that; **je pense qu'elle restera** I think (that) she'll stay; **qu'elle vienne ou non** whether she comes or not; **qu'il s'en aille!** let him leave!; **ça fait un an q. je suis là** I've been here for a year; **ça fait un an q. je suis parti** I left a year ago.
2 (ne)...q.** only; **tu n'as qu'un franc** you only have one franc.

3 (*comparaison*) than; (*avec aussi, même, tel, autant*) as; **plus/moins** âgé q. **lui** older/younger than him; **aussi sage/fatigué**/*etc* q. as wise/tired/*etc* as; **le même q.** the same as.
4 *adv* (**ce**) **qu'il est bête!** (*comme*) he's really stupid!, how stupid he is!; **q. de gens!** (*combien*) what a lot of people!
5 *pron rel objet* (*chose*) that, which; (*personne*) that, whom; (*temps*) when; **le livre q. j'ai** the book (that *ou* which) I have; **l'ami q. j'ai** the friend (that *ou* whom) I have; **un jour qu'il faisait beau** one day when the weather was fine, one fine day.
6 *pron interrogatif* what; **q. fait-il?, qu'est-ce qu'il fait?** what is he doing?; **qu'est-ce qui est dans ta poche?** what's in your pocket?; **q. préférez-vous?** which do you prefer?

Québec [kebɛk] *nm* le Q. Quebec.

quel, quelle [kɛl] **1** *a interrogatif* what, which; (*qui*) who; **q. livre/acteur préférez-vous?** which *ou* what book/actor do you prefer?; **q. est cet homme?** who is that man?; **je sais q. est ton but** I know what your aim is; **je ne sais à q. employé m'adresser** I don't know which clerk to ask ∎ *pron interrogatif* which (one); **q. est le meilleur?** which (one) is the best?
2 *a exclamatif* **q. idiot!** what a fool!; **q. joli bébé!** what a pretty baby!
3 *a rel* **q. qu'il soit** (*chose*) whatever it may be; (*personne*) whoever it *ou* he may be.

quelconque [kɛlkɔ̃k] *a* **1** any (whatever), some (or other); **une raison q.** any reason (whatever *ou* at all), some reason (or other).
2 (*banal*) ordinary.

quelque [kɛlk(ə)] **1** *a* some; **q. jour** some day; **quelques femmes/livres**/*etc* some *ou* a few women/books/*etc*; **les quelques amies qu'elle a** the few friends she has.
2 *adv* (*environ*) about, some; **q. peu** somewhat; **cent francs et q.** *Fam* a hundred francs and a bit; **q. grand qu'il soit** however tall he may be; **q. numéro qu'elle choisisse** whichever number she chooses.
3 *pron* **q. chose** something; (*interrogation*) anything, something; **il a q. chose** (*un problème*) *Fig* there's something the matter with him; **q. chose d'autre** something else; **q. chose de grand**/*etc* something big/*etc*; **q. chose de plus pratique/de moins lourd**/*etc* something more practical/less heavy *ou* not so heavy/*etc*.
4 *adv* **q. part** somewhere; (*interrogation*) anywhere, somewhere.

quelquefois [kɛlkəfwa] *adv* sometimes.

quelques-uns, -unes [kɛlkəzœ̃, -yn] *pron pl* some.

quelqu'un [kɛlkœ̃] *pron* someone, somebody; (*interrogation*) anyone, anybody, someone, somebody; **q. d'intelligent**/*etc* someone clever/*etc*.

quémander [kemãde] *vt* to beg for.

qu'en-dira-t-on [kɑ̃diratɔ̃] *nm inv* (*propos*) gossip.

quenelle [kənɛl] *nf Culin* quenelle, fish *ou*

meat roll.

querelle [kərɛl] *nf* quarrel, dispute; **chercher q. à qn** to try to pick a fight with s.o. ●**se quereller** *vpr* to quarrel. ●**querelleur, -euse** *a* quarrelsome.

question [kɛstjɔ̃] *nf* question; (*affaire, problème*) matter, question, issue; **il est q. de** (*on parle de*) there's some talk about, there's some question of (*faire doing*); **il a été q. de vous** we *ou* they talked about you; **il n'en est pas q.** it's out of the question, there's no question of it; **en q.** in question; **hors de q.** out of the question; **(re)mettre qch en q.** to call sth in question, question sth. ●**questionnaire** *nm* questionnaire. ●**questionner** *vt* to question (**sur** about).

quête [kɛt] *nf* **1** (*collecte*) collection; **faire la q.** to collect money. **2** (*recherche*) quest (**de** for); **en q. de** in quest *ou* search of. ●**quêter** [kete] *vt* to seek, beg for ∎ *vi* to collect money.

queue [kø] *nf* **1** (*d'animal*) tail; (*de fleur*) stem, stalk; (*de fruit*) stalk; (*de poêle*) handle; (*de train, cortège*) rear; (*de comète*) trail; (*de robe*) train; **q. de cheval** (*coiffure*) ponytail; **à la q. de** (*classe*) at the bottom of; **la q. leu leu** (*marcher*) in single file; **faire une q. de poisson** (*en voiture*) to cut in (**à qn** in front of s.o.); **ça n'a ni q. ni tête** (*histoire etc*) it just doesn't make sense.
2 (*file*) *Br* queue, *Am* line; **faire la q.** *Br* to queue up, *Am* line up.
3 (*de billard*) cue. ●**queue-de-pie** *nf* (*pl* **queues-de-pie**) (*habit*) tails.

qui [ki] *pron interrogatif* (*personne*) who; (*en complément*) whom; **q. (est-ce qui) est là?** who's there?; **q. désirez-vous voir?, q. est-ce que vous désirez voir?** who(m) do you want to see?; **à q. est ce livre?** whose book is this?; **q. encore?, q. d'autre?** who else?; **je demande q. a téléphoné** I'm asking who phoned.
∎ *pron rel* **1** (*sujet*) (*personne*) who, that; (*chose*) which, that; **l'homme q. est là** the man who's here *ou* that's here; **la maison q. se trouve en face** the house which is *ou* that's opposite.
2 (*sans antécédent*) **q. que vous soyez** whoever you are, whoever you may be; **amène q. tu veux** bring along anyone you like *ou* whoever you like; **q. que ce soit** anyone.
3 (*après prép*) **la femme de q. je parle** the woman I'm talking about *ou* about whom I'm talking; **l'ami sur l'aide de q. je compte** the friend on whose help I rely.

quiche [kiʃ] *nf* quiche; **q. lorraine** quiche lorraine.

quiconque [kikɔ̃k] *pron* (*celui qui*) whoever; (*n'importe qui*) anyone.

quiétude [kjetyd] *nf Litt* quiet; **en toute q.** (*partir ou*) with an easy mind.

quignon [kiɲɔ̃] *nm* chunk (of bread).

quille [kij] *nf* **1** (*de navire*) keel. **2** (*de jeu*) (bowling) pin, *Br* skittle; **jouer aux quilles** to bowl, *Br* play skittles. **3** (*jambe*) *Fam* leg.

quincaillier, -ière [kɛ̃kaje, -jɛr] *nmf* Br ironmonger, hardware dealer. ●**quincaillerie** *nf* (*magasin*) hardware shop; (*objets*) hardware.

quinine [kinin] *nf* (*médicament*) quinine.

quinquennal, -e, -aux [kɛ̃kenal, -o] *a* **plan/** *etc* **q.** five-year plan/*etc.*

quinte [kɛ̃t] *nf* **q. (de toux)** coughing fit.

quintessence [kɛ̃tesɑ̃s] *nf* quintessence.

quintette [kɛ̃tɛt] *nm* (*musique, musiciens*) quintet(te).

quintuple [kɛ̃typl] *a* **q. de** fivefold ▮ *nm* **le q. de** five times as much as. ●**quintupler** *vti* to increase fivefold. ●**quintuplés, -ées** *nmfpl* (*enfants*) quintuplets, quins.

quinze [kɛ̃z] *a & nm* fifteen; **q. jours** two weeks, Br fortnight; **le q. de France** *Rugby* the French fifteen. ●**quinzaine** *nf* **une q. (de)** (*nombre*) (about) fifteen; **q. (de jours)** two weeks, Br fortnight. ●**quinzième** *a & nmf* fifteenth.

quiproquo [kiprɔko] *nm* misunderstanding.

quittance [kitɑ̃s] *nf* (*reçu*) receipt; **q. de loyer** rent receipt.

quitte [kit] *a* even, quits (**envers** with); **q. à faire** even if it means doing; **en être q. pour une amende/***etc* to (be lucky enough to) get off with a fine/*etc.*

quitter [kite] *vt* to leave; (*ôter*) to take off;

q. qn des yeux to take one's eyes off s.o. ▮ *vi* **ne quittez pas!** (*au téléphone*) hold on!, hold the line! ▮ **se quitter** *vpr* (*se séparer*) to part, say goodbye.

qui-vive (sur le) [syrləkiviv] *adv* on the alert.

quoi [kwa] *pron* what; (*après prép*) which; **à q. penses-tu?** what are you thinking about?; **après q.** after which; **ce à q. je m'attendais** what I was expecting; **de q. manger/***etc* something to eat/*etc*; (*assez*) enough to eat/ *etc*; **de q. écrire** something to write with; **q. que je dise** whatever I say; **q. que ce soit** anything (at all); **q. qu'il en soit** be that as it may; **il n'y a pas de q.!** (*en réponse à 'merci'*) don't mention it!; **q.?** what?; **c'est un idiot, q.!** (*non traduit*) *Fam* he's a fool!; **et puis q. encore!** really, what next!

quoique [kwak(ə)] *conj* (+ *sub*) (al)though; **quoiqu'il soit pauvre** (al)though he's pour.

quolibet [kɔlibɛ] *nm Litt* gibe.

quorum [k(w)ɔrɔm] *nm* quorum.

quota [k(w)ɔta] *nm* quota.

quote-part [kɔtpar] *nf* (*pl* **quotes-parts**) share.

quotidien, -ienne [kɔtidjɛ̃, -jɛn] *a* (*journalier*) daily; (*banal*) everyday ▮ *nm* daily (paper). ●**quotidiennement** *adv* daily.

quotient [kɔsjɑ̃] *nm* quotient.

R

R, r [ɛr] nm R, r.

rab [rab] nm Fam abrév **rabiot**.

rabâcher [rabaʃe] vt to repeat endlessly ▮ vi to repeat oneself (over and over again). ●**rabâchage** nm endless repetition.

rabais [rabɛ] nm (price) reduction, discount; **acheter/etc au r.** to buy/etc cheap(ly) ou at a reduction.

rabaisser [rabese] vt (dénigrer) to belittle, humble; **r. à** (ravaler) to reduce to.

rabat-joie [rabaʒwa] nm inv killjoy.

rabattre* [rabatr] vt (baisser) to pull ou put down; (refermer) to close (down); (replier) to fold down ou over; (déduire) to take off; **en r.** (prétentieux) Fig to climb down (from one's high horse) ▮ **se rabattre** vpr (se refermer) to close; (barrière) to come down; (après avoir doublé un véhicule) to cut in (**devant** in front of); **se r. sur** Fig to fall back on.

rabbin [rabɛ̃] nm rabbi; **grand r.** chief rabbi.

rabibocher [rabibɔʃe] vt (réconcilier) Fam to patch it up between ▮ **se rabibocher** vpr Fam to patch it up (**avec** with).

rabiot [rabjo] nm (surplus) Fam extra (helping); **faire du r.** Fam to work extra time.

râblé, -ée [rɑble] a stocky, thickset.

rabot [rabo] nm (outil) plane. ●**raboter** vt to plane.

raboteux, -euse [rabɔtø, -øz] a uneven, rough.

rabougri, -ie [rabugri] a (personne, plante) stunted.

rabrouer [rabrue] vt to snub, rebuff.

racaille [rakaj] nf rabble, riffraff.

raccommoder [rakɔmɔde] **1** vt (linge) to mend; (chaussette) to darn. **2** vt (réconcilier) Fam to reconcile ▮ **se raccommoder** vpr Fam to become reconciled, Br make it up (**avec** with). ●**raccommodage** nm (de linge) mending; (de chaussette) darning.

raccompagner [rakɔ̃paɲe] vt to see ou take back (home); **r. qn à la porte** to see s.o. to the door, see s.o. out.

raccord [rakɔr] nm (dispositif) connection, connector; (de papier peint) join; **r. (de peinture)** touch-up. ●**raccorder** vt, **se raccorder** vpr to connect (up), join (up) (**à** with, to). ●**raccordement** nm (action, résultat) connection.

raccourcir [rakursir] vt to shorten ▮ vi to get shorter; (au lavage) to shrink. ●**raccourci** nm **1** (chemin) short cut. **2** (tournure) concise turn of phrase; **en r.** (histoire etc) in a nutshell, in brief.

raccroc (par) [parrakro] adv by a fluke, by

(a lucky) chance.

raccrocher [rakrɔʃe] vt (objet tombé) to hang back up; (téléphone) to put down; (relier) to connect (**à** with, to); (client) to accost ▮ vi (au téléphone) to hang up, Br ring off; (sportif) Fam to hang up one's hat, retire ▮ **se raccrocher** vpr **se r. à** to hold on to, cling to; (se rapporter à) to link (up) with.

race [ras] nf (groupe ethnique) race; (animale) breed; **chien de r.** pedigree dog. ●**racé, -ée** a (cheval) thoroughbred; (personne) distinguished. ●**racial, -e, -aux** a racial. ●**racisme** nm racism, racialism. ●**raciste** a & nmf racist, racialist.

rachat [raʃa] nm (de marchandises) repurchase; (de firme) take-over; Rel redemption. ●**racheter** vt to buy back; (objet d'occasion) to buy; (firme) to take over, buy out; (pécheur, dette) to redeem; (compenser) to make up for; **r. un manteau/une voiture/etc** to buy another coat/car/etc; **r. des chaussettes/du pain/etc** to buy (some) more socks/bread/etc ▮ **se racheter** vpr to make amends, redeem oneself.

racine [rasin] nf (de plante, personne etc) & Math root; **prendre r.** (plante, Fig personne) to take root.

racket [rakɛt] nm (activité) racketeering.

raclée [rakle] nf Fam thrashing, hiding.

racler [rakle] vt to scrape; (enlever) to scrape off; **se r. la gorge** to clear one's throat. ●**raclette** nf **1** scraper; (à vitres) squeegee. **2** (plat) raclette (potatoes and melted cheese). ●**racloir** nm scraper. ●**raclures** nfpl (déchets) scrapings.

racoler [rakɔle] vt (prostituée, vendeur etc) to accost (s.o.). ●**racolage** nm (de prostituée) soliciting; (de vendeur etc) touting. ●**racoleur, -euse** nmf (vendeur etc) tout; (prostituée) prostitute (who solicits).

raconter [rakɔ̃te] vt (histoire) to tell, relate; (décrire) to describe; **r. qch à qn** (vacances etc) to tell s.o. about sth; **r. à qn que** to tell s.o. that, say to s.o. that; **qu'est-ce que tu racontes?** Fam what are you talking about? ●**racontars** nmpl gossip, stories.

racornir [rakɔrnir] vt (dessécher) to harden ▮ **se racornir** vpr to get hard.

radar [radar] nm radar; **contrôle r.** (pour véhicules etc) radar control; **elle marche au r.** Fam she's like a zombie going through the motions (through over-tiredness etc). ●**radariste** nmf radar operator.

rade [rad] nf **1** (bassin) (natural) harbour. **2** **laisser qn en r.** Fam to leave s.o. stranded, abandon s.o.; **rester en r.** *Fam* to be left behind.

radeau, -x [rado] *nm* raft.

radiateur [radjatœr] *nm* (*à eau*) radiator; (*électrique, à gaz*) heater; (*de chauffage central, voiture*) radiator.

radiation [radjɑsjɔ̃] *nf* **1** *Phys* radiation. **2** (*suppression*) removal (de from).

radical, -e, -aux [radikal, -o] *a* radical ▮ *nm* (*d'un mot*) stem ▮ *nmf Pol* radical.

radier [radje] *vt* to strike *ou* cross off (de from).

radieux, -euse [radjø, -øz] *a* (*personne, visage*) beaming, radiant; (*soleil*) brilliant; (*temps*) glorious.

radin, -ine [radɛ̃, -in] *a Fam* stingy ▮ *nmf Fam* skinflint.

radio [radjo] **1** *nf* radio; (*poste*) radio (set); **à la r.** on the radio. **2** *nf* (*des poumons etc*) X-ray; **passer** *ou* **faire une r.** to have an X-ray, be X-rayed; **faire passer une r. à qn** to give s.o. an X-ray. **3** *nm* (*opérateur*) radio operator. ● **radio-réveil** *m* (*pl* radios-réveils) radio alarm clock.

radioactif, -ive [radjoaktif, -iv] *a* radioactive. ● **radioactivité** *nf* radioactivity.

radiodiffuser [radjodifyse] *vt* to broadcast (on the radio). ● **radiodiffusion** *nf* broadcasting.

radiographie [radjografi] *nf* (*photo*) X-ray; (*technique*) radiography. ● **radiographier** *vt* to X-ray. ● **radiologie** *nf Méd* radiology. ● **radiologue** *nmf* (*technicien*) radiographer; (*médecin*) radiologist.

radiophonique [radjofɔnik] *a* **émission/etc r.** radio broadcast/etc. ● **radiotélévisé, -ée** *a* broadcast on radio and television.

radis [radi] *nm* radish; **r. noir** horseradish; **je n'ai plus un r.** *Fam* I don't have a bean.

radoter [radɔte] *vi* to ramble (on), drivel (on). ● **radotage** *nm* (*propos*) drivel.

radoucir (se) [sǝradusir] *vpr* to calm down; (*temps*) to become milder. ● **radoucissement** *nm* **r.** (*du temps*) milder weather.

rafale [rafal] *nf* (*vent*) gust, squall; (*de mitrailleuse*) burst; (*de balles*) hail.

raffermir [rafɛrmir] *vt* to strengthen; (*muscles etc*) to tone up ▮ **se raffermir** *vpr* to become stronger.

raffiné, -ée [rafine] *a* (*pétrole, sucre, Fig personne etc*) refined.

raffinement [rafinmɑ̃] *nm* (*de personne*) refinement.

raffiner [rafine] *vt* (*pétrole, sucre, Fig manières*) to refine. ● **raffinage** *nm* (*du pétrole, sucre*) refining. ● **raffinerie** *nf* refinery.

raffoler [rafɔle] *vi* **r. de** (*aimer*) to be mad *ou* wild about, be very fond of.

raffut [rafy] *nm Fam* din, row.

rafiot [rafjo] *nm* (*bateau*) *Péj* (old) tub.

rafistoler [rafistɔle] *vt Fam* to patch up.

rafle [rɑfl] *nf* (*police*) raid.

rafler [rɑfle] *vt* (*enlever*) *Fam* to swipe, make off with.

rafraîchir [rafreʃir] *vt* to cool (down); (*re-*

---

mettre à neuf) to brighten up; (*personne*) to refresh; **r. la mémoire à qn** to refresh s.o.'s memory ▮ *vi* **mettre à r.** *Culin* to chill ▮ **se rafraîchir** *vpr* (*boire*) to refresh oneself; (*se laver*) to freshen (oneself) up; (*temps*) to get cooler. ● **rafraîchissant, -ante** *a* refreshing. ● **rafraîchissement** *nm* **1** (*de température*) cooling. **2** (*boisson*) cold drink.

ragaillardir [ragajardir] *vt* to buck up.

rage [raʒ] *nf* **1** (*colère*) rage; **r. de dents** violent toothache; **faire r.** (*incendie, tempête*) to rage. **2** (*maladie*) rabies. ● **rager** *vi* (*personne*) *Fam* to rage, fume. ● **rageant, -ante** *a Fam* infuriating. ● **rageur, -euse** *a* bad-tempered, furious.

ragots [rago] *nmpl Fam* gossip.

ragoût [ragu] *nm Culin* stew.

ragoûtant, -ante [ragutɑ̃, -ɑ̃t] *a* **peu r.** (*mets, personne*) unsavoury.

raid [rɛd] *nm* (*aérien, militaire*) raid.

raide [rɛd] *a* (*rigide, guindé*) stiff; (*côte*) steep; (*cheveux*) straight; (*corde etc*) tight; **c'est r.!** (*exagéré*) *Fam* that's a bit hard to swallow, that's a bit much!; **il est complètement r.** *Fam* he's blind drunk ▮ *adv* (*grimper*) steeply; **tomber r. mort** to drop dead. ● **raideur** *nf* stiffness; steepness. ● **raidillon** *nm* (*pente*) short steep rise. ● **raidir** *vt*, **se raidir** *vpr* to stiffen; (*corde*) to tighten; (*position*) *Fig* to harden; **se r. contre** *Fig* to steel oneself against.

raie [rɛ] *nf* **1** (*trait*) line; (*de tissu, zèbre*) stripe; (*de cheveux*) *Br* parting, *Am* part. **2** (*poisson*) skate, ray.

rail [rɑj] *nm* (*barre*) rail (for train); **le r.** (*transport*) rail.

railler [raje] *vt* to mock, make fun of. ● **raillerie** *nf* gibe, mocking remark. ● **railleur, -euse** *a* mocking.

rainure [renyr] *nf* groove.

raisin [rezɛ̃] *nm* **1** (*faculté, motif*) grapes; **grain de r.** grape; **manger du r.** *ou* **des raisins** to eat grapes; **r. sec** raisin.

raison [rezɔ̃] *nf* **1** (*faculté, motif*) reason; **la r. de mon absence/etc** the reason for my absence/etc; **la r. pour laquelle je...** the reason (why *ou* that) I...; **pour raisons de famille/de santé/etc** for family/health/etc reasons; **en r. de** (*cause*) on account of; **à r. de** (*proportion*) at the rate of; **à plus forte r.** all the more so; **plus que de r.** (*boire etc*) much too much, much more than one should; **r. de plus** all the more reason (**pour faire** to do, for doing); **mariage de r.** marriage of convenience; **avoir r. de qn/qch** to get the better of s.o./sth; **entendre r.** to listen to reason; **se faire une r.** to put up with *ou* accept the situation, resign oneself.
2 avoir r. to be right (**de faire** to do, in doing); **donner r. à qn** to agree with s.o.; (*événement etc*) to prove s.o. right; **avec r.** rightly.

raisonnable [rezɔnabl] *a* reasonable. ● **raisonnablement** [-ǝmɑ̃] *adv* reasonably. ● **raisonner** [rezɔne] *vi* (*penser*) to reason;

(*discuter*) to argue ▮ *vt* **r. qn** to reason with s.o. ●**raisonné, -ée** *a* (*projet*) well-thought-out. ●**raisonnement** *nm* (*faculté, activité*) reasoning; (*propositions*) argument. ●**raisonneur, -euse** *a* *Péj* argumentative ▮ *nmf* *Péj* arguer.

rajeunir [raʒœnir] *vt* to make (*s.o.*) (feel *ou* look) younger; (*personnel*) to infuse new blood into; (*moderniser*) to modernize, update; (*personne âgée*) to rejuvenate ▮ *vi* to get *ou* feel *ou* look younger. ●**rajeunissant, -ante** *a* (*crème etc*) rejuvenating. ●**rajeunissement** *nm* (*de personne âgée*) rejuvenation; **le r. de la population** the population getting younger.

rajout [raʒu] *nm* addition. ●**rajouter** *vt* to add (à to); **en r.** *Fig* to overdo it, exaggerate.

rajuster [raʒyste] *vt* (*mécanisme*) to readjust; (*vêtements, lunettes*) to straighten, adjust; (*cheveux*) to rearrange ▮ **se rajuster** *vpr* to straighten *ou* tidy oneself up.

râle [rɑl] *nm* (*de blessé*) groan; (*de mourant*) death rattle. ●**râler** *vi* (*blessé*) to groan; (*mourant*) to give the death rattle; (*protester*) *Fam* to grouse, moan. ●**râleur, -euse** *nmf* *Fam* grouser, moaner.

ralentir [ralɑ̃tir] *vti*, **se ralentir** *vpr* to slow down. ●**ralenti** *nm* (*de cinéma, télévision*) slow motion; **au r.** (*filmer etc*) in slow motion; (*vivre, travailler*) at a slower pace; **tourner au r.** (*moteur, usine*) *Br* to tick over, idle, *Am* turn over. ●**ralentissement** *nm* slowing down, slowdown; **un r. sur 10 km** a 10 km (traffic) holdup *ou* *Br* tailback, slow-moving traffic for 10 km.

rallier [ralje] *vt* (*rassembler*) to rally; (*rejoindre*) to rejoin; **r. qn à** (*convertir*) to win s.o. over to ▮ **se rallier** *vpr* (*se regrouper*) to rally; **se r. à un point de vue/etc** to come over *ou* round to a point of view/etc.

rallonge [ralɔ̃ʒ] *nf* (*de table*) extension; (*fil électrique*) extension (lead); **une r.** (**de**) (*supplément*) *Fam* (some) extra; **nom à r.** *Fam* *Br* double-barrelled name, name with a handle. ●**rallonger** *vti* to lengthen.

rallumer [ralyme] *vt* (*feu, pipe etc*) to light again, relight; (*lampe*) to switch on again; (*conflit, haine*) to rekindle ▮ **se rallumer** *vpr* (*guerre, incendie*) to flare up again.

rallye [rali] *nm* (*course automobile*) rally.

ramage [ramaʒ] *nm* (*d'oiseaux*) song, warbling. ●**ramages** *nmpl* (*dessin*) foliage.

ramassé, -ée [ramase] *a* (*trapu*) squat, stocky; (*recroquevillé*) huddled; (*concis*) compact.

ramasser [ramase] **1** *vt* (*prendre par terre, réunir*) to pick up; (*ordures, copies*) to collect, pick up; (*fruits, coquillages*) to gather; (*rhume, amende*) *Fam* to pick up, get; **r. une bûche** *ou* **une pelle** (*tomber*) *Fam* to fall flat on one's face, *Br* come a cropper, *Am* take a spill. **2 se ramasser** *vpr* (*se pelotonner*) to curl up; (*tomber*) *Fam* to fall flat on one's face, *Br* come a cropper; (*échouer*)

Fam to come to grief, fail. ●**ramassage** *nm* picking up; (*d'ordures etc*) collection; (*de fruits etc*) gathering; **r. scolaire** school bus service.

ramassis [ramasi] *nm* **r. de** (*voyous, vieux livres etc*) *Péj* bunch of.

rambarde [rɑ̃bard] *nf* guardrail.

rame [ram] *nf* **1** (*aviron*) oar. **2** (*de métro*) train. **3** (*de papier*) ream. ●**ramer** *vi* to row; (*s'évertuer*) *Fam* to struggle hard, work hard. ●**rameur, -euse** *nmf* rower.

rameau, -x [ramo] *nm* branch; **le dimanche des Rameaux, les Rameaux** *Rel* Palm Sunday.

ramener [ramne] *vt* to bring *ou* take (*s.o.*) back; (*paix, ordre, calme etc*) to restore, bring back; (*remettre en place*) to put back; **r. à** (*réduire à*) to reduce to; **r. à la vie** to bring back to life; **cela m'a ramené quinze ans en arrière** that took me back fifteen years ▮ **se ramener** *vpr* (*arriver*) *Fam* to turn up; **se r. à** (*problème etc*) to boil down to.

ramier [ramje] *nm* (*pigeon*) **r.** wood pigeon.

ramification [ramifikɑsjɔ̃] *nf* ramification.

ramollir [ramɔlir] *vt*, **se ramollir** *vpr* to soften. ●**ramolli, -ie** *a* soft; (*personne*) soft-headed.

ramoner [ramɔne] *vt* (*cheminée*) to sweep. ●**ramonage** *nm* (chimney) sweeping. ●**ramoneur** *nm* (chimney)sweep.

rampe [rɑ̃p] *nf* **1** (*d'escalier*) banister(s). **2** (*pente*) ramp, slope; **r. (d'accès)** ramp; **r. de lancement** (*de fusées etc*) launch(ing) pad. **3** (*projecteurs de théâtre*) footlights; **être sous les feux de la r.** (*célèbre*) to be in the limelight.

ramper [rɑ̃pe] *vi* to crawl; (*plante*) to creep; **r. devant qn** *Fig* to cringe *ou* crawl to s.o.

rancard [rɑ̃kar] *nm* (*rendez-vous*) *Fam* date, appointment; (*renseignement*) *Arg* tip.

rancart [rɑ̃kar] *nm* **mettre au r.** *Fam* to throw out, scrap.

rance [rɑ̃s] *a* rancid. ●**rancir** *vi* to turn rancid.

ranch [rɑ̃tʃ] *nm* ranch.

rancœur [rɑ̃kœr] *nf* rancour, resentment.

rançon [rɑ̃sɔ̃] *nf* ransom; **la r. de** (*inconvénient*) the price of (*success, fame etc*). ●**rançonner** *vt* to hold to ransom.

rancune [rɑ̃kyn] *nf* grudge; **garder r. à qn** to bear s.o. a grudge; **sans r.!** no hard feelings! ●**rancunier, -ière** *a* spiteful, vindictive, resentful.

randonnée [rɑ̃dɔne] *nf* (*à pied*) hike, walk; (*en vélo*) ride; **r. équestre** horse ride, pony trek.

rang [rɑ̃] *nm* (*rangée*) row, line; (*classement, grade*) rank; **les rangs** (*soldats*) the ranks (**de** of); **les rangs de ses ennemis** (*nombre*) *Fig* the ranks of his enemies; **se mettre en rang(s)** to line up (**par trois/etc** in threes/etc); **en r. d'oignons** in a straight *ou* neat row; **par r. de** in order of. ●**rangée** *nf* row, line.

ranger [rɑ̃ʒe] *vt* (*papiers, vaisselle etc*) to put away; (*chambre etc*) to tidy (up); (*chiffres,* *mots*) to arrange; (*voiture*) to park; **r. un auteur/etc parmi** to rank an author/etc among.

■ **se ranger** *vpr* (*élèves etc*) to line up; (*s'écarter*) to stand aside; (*voiture*) to pull over; (*s'assagir*) to settle down; **se r. à l'avis de qn** to fall in with s.o.'s opinion. ● **rangé, -ée** *a* (*chambre etc*) tidy; (*personne*) steady; (*bataille*) pitched. ● **rangement** *nm* putting away; (*de chambre etc*) tidying (up); (*espace*) storage space; **rangements** (*placards*) storage space; **faire du r.** to do some tidying up.

ranimer [ranime] *vt* (*réanimer, revigorer*) to revive; (*feu*) to poke, stir; (*querelle*) to revive, rekindle; (*encourager*) to spur on.

rapace [rapas] **1** *nm* (*oiseau*) bird of prey. **2** *a* (*avide*) grasping.

rapatrier [rapatrije] *vt* to repatriate. ● **rapatriement** *nm* repatriation.

râpe [rɑp] *nf Culin* grater; shredder; (*lime*) rasp. ● **râper** *vt* (*fromage etc*) to grate; (*carottes*) to shred, (*finement*) to grate; (*bois*) to rasp. ● **râpé, -ée 1** *a* (*fromage etc*) grated; (*carottes*) shredded; grated ■ *nm* grated cheese. **2** *a* (*vêtement*) threadbare.

rapetisser [raptise] *vt* to make (look) smaller; (*vêtement*) to shorten ■ *vi* to get smaller; (*au lavage*) to shrink; (*jours*) to get shorter.

râpeux, -euse [rɑpø, -øz] *a* rough.

raphia [rafja] *nm* raffia.

rapide [rapid] *a* fast, quick, rapid; (*pente*) steep ■ *nm* (*train*) express (train); (*de fleuve*) rapid. ● **rapidement** *adv* fast, quickly, rapidly. ● **rapidité** *nf* speed, rapidity.

rapiécer [rapjese] *vt* to patch (up).

rappel [rapɛl] *nm* (*de diplomate etc*) recall; (*évocation, souvenir*) reminder; (*paiement*) back pay; (*au théâtre*) curtain call; (*vaccination*) **r.** booster (injection); **r. à l'ordre** call to order; **descendre en r.** (*en alpinisme*) to abseil.

rappeler [rap(ə)le] *vt* (*pour faire revenir, au téléphone*) to call back; (*souvenir, diplomate*) to recall; **r. qch à qn** (*redire*) to remind s.o. of sth ■ *vi* (*au téléphone*) to call back ■ **se rappeler** *vpr* (*histoire, personne etc*) to remember, recall, recollect; **r. que** to remember *ou* recall *ou* recollect that.

rappliquer [raplike] *vi* (*arriver*) *Fam* to show up.

rapport [rapɔr] *nm* **1** (*lien*) connection, link; **rapports** (*entre personnes*) relations; **rapports (sexuels)** (sexual) intercourse, sexual relations; **par r. à** compared to *ou* with; (*envers*) towards; **se mettre en r. avec qn** to get in touch with s.o.; **en r. avec** in keeping with; **sous le r. de** from the point of view of; **homme bien sous tous rapports** nice man in every respect; **ça n'a aucun r.!** it has nothing to do with it! **2** (*revenu, rendement*) return, yield. **3** (*récit*) report.

rapporter [rapɔrte] **1** *vt* (*apporter*) to bring *ou* take back; (*ajouter*) to add ■ *vi* (*chien*) to retrieve. **2** *vt* (*récit*) to report; (*mot célèbre*)

to repeat ■ *vi* (*moucharder*) *Fam* to tell tales. **3** *vt* (*profit*) to bring in, yield ■ *vi* (*investissement*) to bring in a good return. **4** *vt* **r. qch à** (*rattacher*) to relate sth to ■ **se rapporter** *vpr* **se r. à** to relate to, be connected with; **s'en r. à** to rely on. ● **rapporteur, -euse 1** *nmf* (*mouchard*) telltale. **2** *nm* (*d'un procès etc*) reporter. **3** *nm* (*instrument*) *Géom* protractor.

rapprocher [raprɔʃe] *vt* to bring closer (*de* to); (*chaise*) to pull up (*de* to); (*réconcilier*) to bring together; (*réunir*) to join; (*comparer*) to compare (*de* to, with) ■ **se rapprocher** *vpr* to come *ou* get closer (*de* to); (*se réconcilier*) to come together, be reconciled; (*ressembler*) to be close (*de* to). ● **rapproché, -ée** *a* close, near; (*yeux*) close-set; (*fréquent*) frequent. ● **rapprochement** *nm* reconciliation; (*rapport*) connection; (*comparaison*) comparison.

rapt [rapt] *nm* (*d'enfant*) abduction.

raquette [rakɛt] *nf* (*de tennis*) racket; (*de ping-pong*) bat.

rare [rar] *a* rare; (*argent, main-d'œuvre etc*) scarce; (*barbe, herbe*) sparse; **il est r. que** (+ *sub*) it's seldom *ou* rare that. ● **se raréfier** *vpr* (*denrées etc*) to get scarce. ● **rarement** *adv* rarely, seldom. ● **rareté** *nf* rarity; (*de main-d'œuvre etc*) scarcity; **une r.** (*objet*) a rarity.

ras, rase [rɑ, rɑz] *a* (*cheveux*) close-cropped; (*herbe, poil*) short; (*mesure*) full; **en rase campagne** in the open country; **à r. bord** (*remplir*) to the brim; **au r. de, à r. de** very close to; **voler au r. du sol** (*avion etc*) to fly very close to the ground, hedge-hop; **en avoir r. le bol** *Fam* to be fed up (*de* with); **pull (au) r. du cou** *ou* **à col r.** crew-neck(ed) pullover ■ *adv* (*coupé*) short.

RAS [ɛrɑɛs] *abrév* (*rien à signaler*) nothing to report, all OK.

rase-mottes [rɑzmɔt] *nm inv* **voler en r.-mottes, faire du r.-mottes** (*avion etc*) to hedge-hop, fly close to the ground.

raser [rɑze] **1** *vt* (*menton, personne*) to shave; (*barbe, moustache*) to shave off ■ **se raser** *vpr* to (have a) shave. **2** *vt* (*démolir*) to knock down, raze to the ground. **3** *vt* (*frôler*) to skim, brush. **4** *vt* (*ennuyer*) *Fam* to bore. ● **rasant, -ante** *a Fam* boring. ● **rasé, -ée** *a* **être bien r.** to have shaved, be clean-shaven; **mal r.** unshaven. ● **rasage** *nm* shaving. ● **raseur, -euse** *nmf Fam* bore.

rasoir [rɑzwar] **1** *nm* razor; (*électrique*) shaver. **2** *a inv Fam* boring.

rassasier [rasazje] *vti* to satisfy; **être rassasié** to have had enough (*de* of).

rassembler [rasɑ̃ble] *vt* (*gens, objets*) to gather (together), assemble; (*courage*) to summon up, muster; **r. des données** to gather *ou* collect data ■ **se rassembler** *vpr* to gather, assemble. ● **rassemblement** *nm* (*action, groupe*) gathering.

rasseoir* (se) [səraswar] *vpr* to sit down again.

rassis, *f* **rassie** [rasi] *a* (*pain*, *brioche etc*) stale. ●**rassir** *vti* to turn stale.

rassurer [rasyre] *vt* to reassure; **rassure-toi** don't worry, set your mind at rest. ●**rassurant**, **-ante** *a* (*nouvelle*) reassuring, comforting.

rat [ra] *nm* rat; **r. de bibliothèque** *Fig* bookworm; **petit r. de l'Opéra** young ballet pupil (*at the Paris Opera House*).

ratatiner (se) [səratatine] *vpr* to shrivel (up); (*vieillard*) to become wizened.

ratatouille [ratatuj] *nf* **r. (niçoise)** *Culin* ratatouille.

rate [rat] *nf Anat* spleen.

râteau, **-x** [rɑto] *nm* (*outil*) rake.

râtelier [rɑtəlje] *nm* **1** (*support pour outils*, *armes etc*) rack. **2** (*dentier*) *Fam* set of false teeth.

rater [rate] *vt* (*bus*, *cible*, *occasion etc*) to miss; (*travail*, *gâteau etc*) to ruin, spoil; (*examen*) to fail; (*vie*) to waste; **il n'en rate pas une** *Fam* he's always putting his foot in it ▌ *vi* (*projet etc*) to fail; **ça n'a pas raté** *Fam* inevitably that happened (again), it had to happen (again). ●**raté**, **-ée 1** *nmf* (*personne*) failure. **2** *nmpl* **avoir des ratés** (*moteur*) to backfire. ●**ratage** *nm* (*échec*) *Fam* failure.

ratifier [ratifje] *vt* to ratify. ●**ratification** *nf* ratification.

ration [rasjɔ̃] *nf* ration; **r. de** *Fig* share of. ●**rationner** *vt* (*vivres*, *personne*) to ration. ●**rationnement** *nm* rationing.

rationaliser [rasjɔnalize] *vt* to rationalize. ●**rationalisation** *nf* rationalization.

rationnel, **-elle** [rasjɔnɛl] *a* (*pensée*, *méthode*) rational.

ratisser [ratise] *vt* **1** (*allée etc*) to rake; (*feuilles etc*) to rake up. **2** (*fouiller*) to comb. **3 r. qn** (*au jeu*) *Fam* to clean s.o. out.

raton [ratɔ̃] *nm* **r. laveur** rac(c)oon.

RATP [cratep] *nf abrév* (*Régie autonome de transports parisiens*) = Paris municipal transport authority.

rattacher [rataʃe] *vt* (*lacets etc*) to tie up again; (*incorporer*, *joindre*) to join (à to); (*idée*, *question*) to link (à to); **r. qn à son pays/sa famille**/*etc* to bind s.o. to his *ou* her country/family/*etc*; **se r. à** to be linked to. ●**rattachement** *nm* (*annexion*) joining (à to).

rattraper [ratrape] *vt* to catch; (*prisonnier etc*) to recapture; (*temps perdu*, *erreur*) to make up for; **r. qn** (*rejoindre*) to catch up with s.o., catch s.o. up; **elle a été rattrapée** (*à un examen*) she was allowed to get through *ou* to pass ▌ **se rattraper** *vpr* to catch up; (*après une erreur*) to make up for it; **se r. à** (*branche etc*) to catch hold of. ●**rattrapage** *nm* **cours de r.** *Scol* remedial classes; **r. des prix/salaires** adjustment of prices/wages (*to the cost of living*).

rature [ratyr] *nf* crossing out, deletion. ●**raturer** *vt* to cross out, delete.

rauque [rok] *a* (*voix*) hoarse, raucous, rough.

ravages [ravaʒ] *nmpl* havoc, devastation; (*du temps*, *de la maladie*) ravages; **faire des r.** to cause *ou* wreak havoc, cause widespread damage; (*femme*) to break many hearts. ●**ravager** *vt* to devastate, ravage.

ravaler [ravale] *vt* **1** (*façade etc*) to clean (and restore). **2** (*sanglots*, *salive*) to swallow; (*colère*) *Fig* to stifle, suppress; (*orgueil*) to swallow. **3** (*avilir*) *Litt* to lower. ●**ravalement** *nm* (*de façade etc*) cleaning (and restoration).

ravi, **-ie** [ravi] *a* delighted (**de** with, **de faire** to do, **que** that).

ravier [ravje] *nm* hors-d'œuvre dish.

ravigoter [ravigɔte] *vt Fam* to buck up.

ravin [ravɛ̃] *nm* ravine, gully.

ravioli [ravjɔli] *nmpl* ravioli.

ravir [ravir] *vt* **1** (*plaire à*) to delight; **chanter**/*etc* **à r.** to sing/*etc* delightfully. **2** (*emporter*) to snatch (à from). ●**ravissant**, **-ante** *a* beautiful, lovely, delightful. ●**ravissement** *nm* (*extase*) ecstasy, sheer delight. ●**ravisseur**, **-euse** *nmf* kidnapper.

raviser (se) [səravize] *vpr* to change one's mind.

ravitailler [ravitaje] *vt* to provide with supplies (**en** of), supply (**en** with); (*avion*) to refuel ▌ **se ravitailler** *vpr* to stock up (with supplies). ●**ravitaillement** *nm* supplying; (*d'avion*) refuelling; (*denrées*) supplies; **aller au r.** (*faire des courses*) *Fam* to stock up, get stocks in.

raviver [ravive] *vt* (*feu*, *sentiment*) to revive; (*couleurs*) to brighten up.

rayer [reje] *vt* (*érafler*) to scratch; (*mot etc*) to cross out; **r. qn d'une liste** to cross *ou* strike s.o. off a list. ●**rayé**, **-ée** *a* (*verre*, *disque etc*) scratched; (*tissu*, *pantalon etc*) striped; (*papier*) lined, ruled. ●**rayure** *nf* scratch; (*bande*) stripe; **à rayures** striped.

rayon [rejɔ̃] *nm* **1** (*de lumière*, *soleil etc*) ray; (*de cercle*) radius; (*de roue*) spoke; (*d'espoir*) *Fig* ray; **r. X** X-ray; **r. d'action** range; **dans un r. de** within a radius of. **2** (*planche*) shelf; (*de magasin*) department. **3** (*de ruche*) honeycomb. **4 elle en connaît un r.** *Fam* she knows an awful lot (about it), *Br* she's well up (on it). ●**rayonnage** *nm* shelving, shelves.

rayonner [rejɔne] *vi* to radiate; (*dans une région*) to travel around (*from a central base*); **r. de joie** to beam with joy. ●**rayonnant**, **-ante** *a* (*visage etc*) beaming, radiant (**de** with). ●**rayonnement** *nm* (*éclat*) radiance; (*influence*) influence; (*radiation*) radiation.

rayure [rejyr] *nf voir* **rayer**.

raz-de-marée [radmare] *nm inv* tidal wave; (*bouleversement*) *Fig* upheaval; **r.-de-marée électoral** landslide, massive swing (of votes).

razzia [ra(d)zja] *nf* **faire une r. sur qch** (*tout enlever*) *Fam* to raid sth.

re- [r(ə)] *préf* re-.

ré [re] *nm* (*note de musique*) D.

ré- [re] *préf* re-.

réabonner (se) [səreabɔne] *vpr* to renew one's subscription (à to). ●**réabonnement**

nm renewal of subscription.

réacteur [reaktœr] *nm* (*d'avion*) jet engine; (*nucléaire*) reactor.

réaction [reaksjɔ̃] *nf* reaction; **r. en chaîne** chain reaction; **avion à r.** jet (aircraft); **moteur à r.** jet engine. ● **réactionnaire** *a* & *nmf* (*Fam* **réac**) reactionary.

réadapter [readapte] *vt*, **se réadpter** *vpr* to readjust (**à** to). ● **réadaptation** *nf* readjustment.

réaffirmer [reafirme] *vt* to reaffirm.

réagir [reaʒir] *vi* to react (**contre** against, **à** to); (*se secouer*) *Fig* to shake oneself out of it.

réaliser [realize] *vt* (*projet etc*) to carry out, realize; (*rêve, ambition*) to fulfil; (*bénéfices, économies*) to make; (*film*) to direct; (*capital*) to realize; (*se rendre compte*) to realize (**que** that).

‖ se réaliser *vpr* (*vœu*) to come true; (*projet*) to materialize, be carried out; (*personne*) to fulfil oneself. ● **réalisable** *a* (*plan*) workable; (*rêve*) attainable. ● **réalisateur, -trice** *nmf* (*de film*) director. ● **réalisation** *nf* realization; (*de rêve*) fulfilment; (*de film*) direction; (*œuvre*) achievement.

réalisme [realism] *nm* realism. ● **réaliste** *a* realistic ‖ *nmf* realist.

réalité [realite] *nf* reality; **en r.** in fact, in reality; **prendre ses désirs pour des réalités** to indulge in wishful thinking.

réanimation [reanimɑsjɔ̃] *nf* resuscitation; (*service de*) **r.** intensive care unit. ● **réanimer** *vt* (*malade*) to revive, resuscitate.

réapparaître* [reaparɛtr] *vi* to reappear. ● **réapparition** *nf* reappearance.

réarmer [rearme] *vt* (*fusil etc*) to reload ‖ *vi*, **se réarmer** *vpr* (*pays*) to rearm. ● **réarmement** *nm* rearmament.

rébarbatif, -ive [rebarbatif, -iv] *a* forbidding, *Br* off-putting.

rebâtir [r(ə)bɑtir] *vt* to rebuild.

rebattu, -ue [r(ə)baty] *a* (*sujet*) hackneyed.

rebelle [rəbɛl] *a* (*enfant, esprit etc*) rebellious; (*mèche*) unruly; (*fièvre*) stubborn; **troupes rebelles** rebel troops; **être r. à** (*enfant etc*) to resist (*discipline etc*); (*organisme etc*) to be resistant to ‖ *nmf* rebel. ● **se rebeller** *vpr* to rebel (**contre** against). ● **rébellion** *nf* rebellion.

rebiffer (se) [sər(ə)bife] *vpr* *Fam* to rebel.

rebiquer [r(ə)bike] *vi* (*mèche, col etc*) to stick up.

reboiser [r(ə)bwaze] *vti* to reafforest.

rebond [r(ə)bɔ̃] *nm* bounce; (*par ricochet*) rebound; **faux r.** bad bounce. ● **rebondir** *vi* to bounce; (*par ricochet*) to rebound; (**faire**) **r.** (*affaire, discussion etc*) to get going again. ● **rebondissement** *nm* new development (**de** in).

rebondi, -ie [r(ə)bɔ̃di] *a* chubby, rounded.

rebord [r(ə)bɔr] *nm* edge; (*de plat etc*) rim; (*de vêtement*) hem; **r. de (la) fenêtre** windowsill, window ledge.

reboucher [r(ə)buʃe] *vt* (*flacon*) to put the

top back on; (*trou*) to fill in again.

rebours (à) [ar(ə)bur] *adv* the wrong way.

rebrousse-poil (à) [ar(ə)bruspwal] *adv* **prendre qn à r.-poil** *Fig* to rub s.o. up the wrong way.

rebrousser [r(ə)bruse] *vt* **r. chemin** to turn back.

rebuffade [rəbyfad] *nf* rebuff.

rébus [rebys] *nm* rebus (*word guessing game*).

rebut [rəby] *nm* **mettre qch au r.** to throw sth out, scrap sth; **le r. de la société** *Péj* the dregs of society.

rebuter [r(ə)byte] *vt* (*décourager*) *Br* to put off, dishearten; (*choquer*) to repel. ● **rebutant, -ante** *a Br* off-putting, disheartening; (*choquant*) revolting, repellent.

récalcitrant, -ante [rekalsitrɑ̃, -ɑ̃t] *a* recalcitrant.

recaler [r(ə)kale] *vt* **r. qn** *Scol Fam* to fail s.o., flunk s.o.; **être recalé, se faire r.** *Scol Fam* to fail, flunk.

récapituler [rekapityle] *vti* to recapitulate. ● **récapitulation** *nf* recapitulation.

recel [rəsɛl] *nm* receiving stolen goods, fencing; harbouring. ● **receler** *ou* **recéler** *vt* (*mystère, secret etc*) to contain; (*objet volé*) to receive; (*malfaiteur*) to harbour. ● **receleur** *ou* **recéleur, -euse** *nmf* receiver (*of stolen goods*), fence.

recenser [r(ə)sɑ̃se] *vt* (*population*) to take a census of; (*inventorier*) to make an inventory of. ● **recensement** *nm* census; (*d'objets*) inventory.

récent, -ente [resɑ̃, -ɑ̃t] *a* recent. ● **récemment** [-amɑ̃] *adv* recently.

récépissé [resepise] *nm* (*reçu*) receipt.

récepteur [reseptœr] *nm* (*téléphone etc*) receiver. ● **réceptif, -ive** *a* receptive (**à** to). ● **réception** *nf* (*accueil, soirée*) & *Radio* reception; (*de lettre etc*) receipt; (*d'hôtel etc*) reception (desk); **dès r. de** on receipt of; **avec accusé de r.** with acknowledgement of receipt. ● **réceptionniste** *nmf* receptionist.

récession [resesjɔ̃] *nf Écon* recession.

recette [r(ə)sɛt] *nf* **1** *Culin* & *Fig* recipe (**de** for). **2** (*argent, bénéfice*) takings; (*bureau*) tax office; **recettes** (*rentrées*) *Com* receipts; **faire r.** *Fig* to be a success.

recevoir* [rəs(ə)vwar] *vt* to receive; (*accueillir*) to welcome; (*obtenir*) to get, receive; (*accepter*) to accept; (*candidat*) to pass; **être reçu à un examen** to pass an exam(ination); **être reçu premier** to come first ‖ *vi* to have guests, receive visitors; (*médecin*) to see patients. ● **recevable** *a* (*excuse etc*) admissible. ● **receveur, -euse** *nmf* (*d'autobus*) *Br* (bus) conductor, *Br* (bus) conductress; (*des postes*) postmaster, postmistress; (*des impôts*) tax collector.

rechange (de) [dər(ə)ʃɑ̃ʒ] *a* (*outil, pièce etc*) spare; (*solution etc*) alternative; **vêtements/chaussures de r.** a change of clothes/shoes.

rechapé, -ée [r(ə)ʃape] *a* **pneu r.** retread, *Br* remould.

réchapper [reʃape] *vi* **r. de** *ou* **à** (*accident etc*) to come through; **en r.** to escape with one's life.

recharge [r(ə)ʃarʒ] *nf* (*de stylo etc*) refill. ●**recharger** *vt* (*fusil, appareil photo, camion*) to reload; (*briquet, stylo etc*) to refill; (*batterie*) to recharge.

réchaud [reʃo] *nm* (portable) stove.

réchauffer [reʃofe] *vt* (*personne, aliment etc*) to warm up ‖ **se réchauffer** *vpr* to warm oneself up; (*temps*) to get warmer. ●**réchauffé** *nm* **c'est du r.** *Fig Péj* it's old hat. ●**réchauffement** *nm* (*de température*) rise (de in); **le r. de la planète** global warming.

rêche [rɛʃ] *a* rough, harsh.

recherche [r(ə)ʃɛrʃ] *nf* **1** search, quest (de for); **à la r. de** in search of; **se mettre à la r. de** to go in search of, search for. **2 la r., des recherches** (*scientifique*) *etc*) research (**sur** on, into); **faire des recherches** to (do) research; (*enquêter*) to make investigations. **3** (*raffinement*) studied elegance; *Péj* affectation.

rechercher [r(ə)ʃɛrʃe] *vt* (*personne, objet*) to search *ou* hunt for; (*cause, faveur, perfection*) to seek. ●**recherché, -ée** *a* **1** (*très demandé*) in great demand; (*rare*) much sought-after; **r. pour meurtre** wanted for murder. **2** (*élégant*) elegant; *Péj* affected.

rechigner [r(ə)ʃiɲe] *vi* (*renâcler*) to jib (**à** qch at sth, **à faire** at doing).

rechute [r(ə)ʃyt] *nf* (*après une guérison*) relapse; **faire une r.** to have a relapse. ●**rechuter** *vi* (*malade*) to (have a) relapse.

récidive [residiv] *nf* (*de malfaiteur*) further *Br* offence *ou Am* offense; (*de maladie*) recurrence (de of). ●**récidiver** *vi* (*malfaiteur*) to commit a further *Br* offence *ou Am* offense; (*maladie*) to recur. ●**récidiviste** *nmf* (*malfaiteur*) repeat offender, reoffender.

récif [resif] *nm* reef.

récipient [resipjɑ̃] *nm* container, receptacle.

réciproque [resiprɔk] *a* mutual, reciprocal ‖ *nf* (*inverse*) opposite; **rendre la r. à qn** to get even with s.o. ●**réciprocité** *nf* reciprocity. ●**réciproquement** *adv* (*l'un l'autre*) each other; **et r.** and vice versa.

récit [resi] *nm* (*histoire*) story; (*compte rendu*) account; **faire le r. de qch** to give an account of sth, tell about sth.

récital, *pl* **-als** [resital] *nm* (*concert*) recital.

réciter [resite] *vt* to recite. ●**récitation** *nf* (*poème*) poem (*learnt by heart and recited aloud*); (*action, matière*) recitation.

réclame [reklam] *nf* advertising; (*annonce*) advertisement; **en r.** (*en promotion*) on (special) offer ‖ *a inv* **vente r.** (bargain) sale.

réclamer [reklame] *vt* (*demander, nécessiter*) to call for, demand; (*redemander*) to ask for (*sth*) back; (*revendiquer*) to claim (*one's due, compensation etc*) ‖ *vi* to complain ‖ **se réclamer** *vpr* **se r. de qn** to invoke s.o.'s authority, claim s.o.'s support. ●**réclamation** *nf* complaint; (**bureau des**) **réclamations** complaints department.

reclasser [r(ə)klase] *vt* (*fiches etc*) to reclassify.

reclus, -use [rəkly, -yz] *a* (*vie, existence*) cloistered; **vivre** *ou* **être r.** to lead a cloistered life ‖ *nmf* recluse.

réclusion [reklyzjɔ̃] *nf* **r. (criminelle)** imprisonment; **r. (criminelle) à perpétuité** life imprisonment.

recoiffer (se) [sər(ə)kwafe] *vpr* (*se peigner*) to do *ou* comb one's hair.

recoin [rəkwɛ̃] *nm* nook, recess.

recoller [r(ə)kɔle] *vt* (*objet cassé*) to stick back together; (*enveloppe*) to stick back down.

récolte [rekɔlt] *nf* (*action*) harvest; (*produits*) crop, harvest; (*de documents etc*) *Fig* crop. ●**récolter** *vt* to harvest, gather (in); (*recueillir*) *Fig* to collect, gather; (*coups*) *Fam* to get.

recommandable [r(ə)kɔmɑ̃dabl] *a* **peu r.** not very commendable.

recommandation [r(ə)kɔmɑ̃dasjɔ̃] *nf* **1** (*appui, conseil*) recommendation. **2** (*de lettre etc*) registration.

recommander [r(ə)kɔmɑ̃de] *vt* (*appuyer, conseiller*) to recommend (**à** to, **pour** for); **r. à qn de faire qch** to recommend s.o. to do sth; **r. son âme à Dieu** to commend one's soul to God; **lettre recommandée** registered letter ‖ **se recommander** *vpr* **se r. de qn** to invoke s.o.'s authority *ou* support, use s.o. as a reference. ●**recommandé** *nm* **envoyer qch en r.** to send sth by registered *Br* post *ou* mail.

recommencer [r(ə)kɔmɑ̃se] *vti* to start *ou* begin again. ●**recommencement** *nm* (*reprise*) renewal (**de** of).

récompense [rekɔ̃pɑ̃s] *nf* reward (**pour, de** for); (*prix*) award; **en r. de qch** in return for sth. ●**récompenser** *vt* to reward (**de, pour** for).

réconcilier [rekɔ̃silje] *vt* to reconcile ‖ **se réconcilier** *vpr* to settle one's differences, become reconciled, *Br* make it up (**avec** with). ●**réconciliation** *nf* reconciliation.

reconduire* [r(ə)kɔ̃dɥir] *vt* **1 r. qn** to see *ou* take s.o. back; (*à la porte*) to show s.o. out. **2** (*mesures, bail etc*) to renew. ●**reconduction** *nf* renewal.

réconfort [rekɔ̃fɔr] *nm* comfort. ●**réconforter** *vt* to comfort; (*revigorer*) to fortify. ●**réconfortant, -ante** *a* comforting; (*boisson etc*) fortifying.

reconnaissant, -ante [r(ə)kɔnɛsɑ̃, -ɑ̃t] *a* grateful, thankful (**à qn de qch** to s.o. for sth). ●**reconnaissance¹** *nf* (*gratitude*) gratitude.

reconnaître* [r(ə)kɔnɛtr] *vt* to recognize (**à qch** by sth); (*admettre*) to admit, acknowledge, recognize (**que** that); (*terrain*) *Mil* to reconnoitre; (*enfant*) to recognize (legally); **être reconnu coupable** to be found guilty ‖ **se reconnaître** *vpr* (*s'orienter*) to find one's bearings; **se r. coupable** to admit one's guilt. ●**reconnu, -ue** *a* (*chef, fait*) acknowledged, recognized. ● **reconnaissable** *a* recognizable (à qch by sth). ● **reconnaissance²** *nf* recognition; *(aveu)* acknowledgement; *Mil* reconnaissance; **r. de dette** IOU; **envoyer qn en r.** *Mil* to send s.o. on a reconnaissance mission.

reconquérir* [r(ə)kɔ̃kerir] *vt* (territoire) to regain, reconquer; (liberté) to regain, win back; **r. qn** to win back s.o.'s love.

reconsidérer [r(ə)kɔ̃sidere] *vt* to reconsider.

reconstituant, -ante [r(ə)kɔ̃stitɥɑ̃, -ɑ̃t] *a* **aliment/régime r.** food/diet which restores one's strength.

reconstituer [r(ə)kɔ̃stitɥe] *vt* (armée, parti) to reconstitute; (crime, quartier) to reconstruct; (faits) to piece together; (fortune) to build up again. ● **reconstitution** *nf* reconstitution; (de crime etc) reconstruction.

reconstruire* [r(ə)kɔ̃strɥir] *vt* (ville, fortune) to rebuild. ● **reconstruction** *nf* rebuilding.

reconvertir [r(ə)kɔ̃vertir] **1** *vt* (bâtiment etc) to reconvert. **2 se reconvertir** *vpr* to take up a new form of employment. ● **reconversion** *nf* reconversion; (recyclage) retraining.

recopier [r(ə)kɔpje] *vt* to copy out; **r. qch d'un livre/au tableau** to copy sth from a book/the blackboard; **r. un fichier sur une disquette** *Ordinat* to copy a file to a floppy disk.

record [r(ə)kɔr] *nm & a inv Sport* record.

recoucher (se) [sər(ə)kuʃe] *vpr* to go back to bed.

recoudre* [r(ə)kudr] *vt* (bouton) to sew (back) on; (vêtement) to stitch (up).

recouper [r(ə)kupe] *vt* (témoignage etc) to tally with, confirm ▌ **se recouper** *vpr* to tally, match *ou* tie up. ● **recoupement** *nm* cross-check(ing).

recourbé, -ée [r(ə)kurbe] *a* (clou etc) bent; (nez) hooked.

recours [r(ə)kur] *nm* recourse (à to); *Jur* appeal; **avoir r. à** to resort to; (personne) to turn to; **notre dernier r.** our last resort. ● **recourir*** *vi* **r. à** to resort to; (personne) to turn to.

recouvrer [r(ə)kuvre] *vt* (santé etc) to recover.

recouvrir* [r(ə)kuvrir] *vt* (livre, meuble, sol etc) to cover; (de nouveau) to recover; (cacher) *Fig* to conceal, mask.

récréation [rekreasjɔ̃] *nf* recreation; (temps) *Scol Br* break, *Br* playtime, *Am* recess.

récrier (se) [sərekrije] *vpr* (protester) *Litt* to protest vehemently.

récriminer [rekrimine] *vi* to complain bitterly (contre about). ● **récriminations** *nfpl* (bitter) complaints, recriminations.

récrire* [rekrir] *vt* (lettre etc) to rewrite.

recroqueviller (se) [sər(ə)krɔkvije] *vpr* (papier, personne) to curl up.

recrudescence [rəkrydesɑ̃s] *nf* new *ou* renewed outbreak (de of).

recrue [rəkry] *nf* recruit. ● **recruter** *vt* to recruit. ● **recrutement** *nm* recruitment.

rectangle [rektɑ̃gl] *nm* rectangle. ● **rectangulaire** *a* rectangular.

rectifier [rektifje] *vt* (erreur etc) to correct, rectify; (ajuster) to adjust. ● **rectificatif** *nm* (document) amendment, correction. ● **rectification** *nf* correction, rectification.

recto [rekto] *nm* front (of the page); **r. verso** on both sides (of the page).

rectorat [rektɔra] *nm* (bureau) Education Office.

reçu, -ue [r(ə)sy] *pp de* recevoir ▌ *a* (idée) conventional, received; (usages etc) accepted; (candidat) successful ▌ *nm* (récépissé) receipt.

recueil [r(ə)kœj] *nm* (ouvrage) anthology, collection (de of).

recueillir* [r(ə)kœjir] **1** *vt* to collect, gather; (suffrages) to win, get; (prendre chez soi) to take (s.o.) in. **2 se recueillir** *vpr* to meditate; (devant un monument) to stand in silence. ● **recueilli, -ie** *a* (air) meditative. ● **recueillement** *nm* meditation.

recul [r(ə)kyl] *nm* (d'armée, de négociateur, de maladie) retreat; (éloignement) distance; (déclin) decline; (mouvement de) **r.** (de véhicule) backward movement; **avoir un mouvement de r.** (personne) to recoil, start back; **phare de r.** (de véhicule) *Br* reversing light, *Am* backup light. ● **reculade** *nf Péj* retreat.

reculer [r(ə)kyle] *vi* to move *ou* step back; (en voiture) to reverse, *Am* back up; (armée) to retreat; (épidémie, glacier) to recede, retreat; (renoncer) to back down, retreat; (diminuer) to decline; **r. devant** *Fig* to shrink *ou* recoil from ▌ *vt* to push *ou* move back; (différer) to postpone. ● **reculé, -ée** *a* (endroit, temps) remote.

reculons (à) [arkylɔ̃] *adv* backwards.

récupérer [rekypere] *vt* (objet prêté) to get back, recover; (ferraille etc) to salvage; (heures) to make up; (mouvement, personne etc) *Pol Péj* to take over, convert ▌ *vi* to get one's strength back, recover, recuperate. ● **récupération** *nf* recovery; (de ferraille etc) salvage.

récurer [rekyre] *vt* (casserole etc) to scrub, scour; **poudre à r.** scouring powder.

récuser [rekyze] *vt* to challenge ▌ **se récuser** *vpr* to decline to give an opinion.

recycler [r(ə)sikle] *vt* **1** (matériaux) to recycle. **2** (reconvertir) to retrain (s.o.) ▌ **se recycler** *vpr* to retrain. ● **recyclage** *nm* (de matériaux) recycling; (de personne) retraining.

rédacteur, -trice [redaktœr, -tris] *nmf* writer; (de journal) editor; (de dictionnaire etc) compiler; **r. en chef** (de journal) editor (in chief). ● **rédaction** *nf* (action) writing; (de contrat) drawing up; (devoir de français) essay, composition; (journalistes) editorial staff; (bureaux) editorial offices.

reddition [redisjɔ̃] *nf* surrender.

redemander [rəd(ə)mɑ̃de] *vt* (pain etc) to ask for more; **r. qch à qn** to ask s.o. for sth back.

rédemption [redɑ̃psjɔ̃] *nf Rel* redemption.

redescendre [r(ə)desɑ̃dr] *vi* (*aux* être) to come ou go back down ∎ *vt* (*aux* avoir) (*objet*) to bring ou take back down.

redevable [rəd(ə)vabl] *a* être r. de qch à qn (*argent*) to owe s.o. sth; *Fig* to be indebted to s.o. for sth.

redevance [r(ə)d(ə)vɑ̃s] *nf* (*taxe de télévision*) *Br* licence fee; **r. (téléphonique)** (telephone) rental charge ou fee.

redevenir* [r(ə)dəv(ə)nir] *vi* (*aux* être) to become again.

rediffusion [rədifyzjɔ̃] *nf* (*de film etc*) repeat.

rédiger [rediʒe] *vt* to write; (*contrat*) to draw up; (*dictionnaire etc*) to compile.

redire* [r(ə)dir] **1** *vt* to repeat. **2** *vi* avoir ou trouver à r. à qch to find fault with sth. ●**redite** *nf* (pointless) repetition.

redondant, -ante [r(ə)dɔ̃dɑ̃, -ɑ̃t] *a* (*style*) redundant.

redonner [r(ə)dɔne] *vt* to give back; (*donner plus*) to give more (*bread etc*); **r. un franc/** *etc* to give another franc/*etc*.

redoubler [r(ə)duble] *vti* **1** to increase; **r. de patience/***etc* to be much more patient/*etc*; **à coups redoublés** (*frapper etc*) harder and harder, very hard. **2 r. (une classe)** to repeat a year ou *Am* a grade. ●**redoublant, -ante** *nmf* pupil repeating a year ou *Am* a grade. ●**redoublement** *nm* increase (de in); *Scol* repeating a year ou *Am* a grade.

redouter [r(ə)dute] *vt* to dread (de faire doing). ●**redoutable** *a* formidable, fearsome.

redresser [r(ə)drese] *vt* (*objet tordu etc*) to straighten (out); (*économie, situation, tort*) to put right ∎ **se redresser** *vpr* (*se mettre assis*) to sit up; (*debout*) to stand up; (*pays, situation etc*) to put itself right, right itself. ●**redressement** [-ɛsmɑ̃] *nm* (*essor*) recovery; **plan de r.** recovery plan.

réduction [redyksjɔ̃] *nf* reduction (de in); (*prix réduit*) discount; **en r.** (*copie, modèle etc*) small-scale.

réduire* [redyir] *vt* to reduce (à to, de by); **r. en cendres** to reduce to ashes; **r. qn à** (*contraindre à*) to reduce s.o. to (*silence, inaction etc*) ∎ *vi* (**faire**) **r.** (*sauce*) to reduce, boil down ∎ **se réduire** *vpr* **se r. à** (*se ramener à*) to come down to, amount to; **se r. en cendres/***etc* to be reduced to ashes/*etc*. ●**réduit, -uite 1** *a* (*prix, vitesse*) reduced; (*moyens*) limited; (*modèle*) small-scale. **2** *nm* (*pièce*) *Péj* tiny room, cubbyhole; (*recoin*) recess.

réécrire* [reekrir] *vt* (*texte*) to rewrite.

rééduquer [reedyke] *vt* (*membre*) *Méd* to re-educate; **r. qn** to rehabilitate s.o., reeducate s.o. ●**rééducation** *nf* (*de membre*) re-education; (*de personne*) rehabilitation; **faire de la r.** to have physiotherapy.

réel, -elle [reel] *a* real ∎ *nm* **le r.** reality. ●**réellement** *adv* really.

réélire* [reelir] *vt* to re-elect.

réévaluer [reevalye] *vt* (*monnaie*) to revalue; (*salaires*) to reassess, upgrade. ●**réévaluation**

nf revaluation; (*de salaires*) reassessment, upgrading.

réexpédier [reekspedje] *vt* (*faire suivre*) to forward (*letter etc*); (*à l'envoyeur*) to return.

refaire* [r(ə)fɛr] *vt* (*exercice, travail etc*) to do again, redo; (*chambre*) to do up, redo; (*erreur, voyage etc*) to make again; (*réparer*) to do up, redo; (*duper*) *Fam* to take in; **se faire r. le nez/***etc* to have one's nose/*etc* reshaped. ●**réfection** *nf* repair(ing).

réfectoire [refɛktwar] *nm* dining hall, refectory.

référendum [referɑ̃dɔm] *nm* referendum.

référer [refere] *vi* **en r. à** to refer the matter to ∎ **se référer** *vpr* **se r. à** to refer to. ●**référence** *nf* reference; **avoir des références** (*domestique*) to have references.

refermer [r(ə)fɛrme] *vt*, **se refermer** *vpr* to close ou shut (again).

refiler [r(ə)file] *vt* (*donner*) *Fam* to palm off (à on).

réfléchir [refleʃir] **1** *vt* (*image*) to reflect ∎ **se réfléchir** *vpr* to be reflected. **2** *vi* (*penser*) to think (à, sur about) ∎ *vt* **r. que** to realize that. ●**réfléchi, -ie** *a* (*personne*) thoughtful, reflective; (*action, décision*) carefully thought-out; **c'est tout r.** my mind is made up; **verbe r.** reflexive verb. ●**réflecteur** *nm* reflector.

reflet [r(ə)flɛ] *nm* (*image*) & *Fig* reflection; (*lumière*) glint; (*couleur*) tint. ●**refléter** *vt* (*image, sentiment etc*) to reflect ∎ **se refléter** *vpr* to be reflected.

refleurir [rəflœrir] *vi* to bloom ou flower again.

réflexe [reflɛks] *nm* & *a* reflex.

réflexion [reflɛksjɔ̃] *nf* **1** (*de lumière etc*) reflection. **2** (*méditation*) thought, reflection; (*remarque*) remark; **r. faite, à la r.** on second *Br* thoughts ou *Am* thought, on reflection.

refluer [r(ə)flye] *vi* (*eaux*) to ebb, flow back; (*foule*) to surge back. ●**reflux** *nm* (*de la mer*) ebb; (*de la foule*) backward surge.

réforme *nf* **1** (*changement*) reform. **2** (*de soldat*) discharge. ●**réformateur, -trice** *nmf* reformer. ●**réformer 1** *vt* to reform ∎ **se réformer** *vpr* to mend one's ways. **2** *vt* (*soldat*) to discharge as unfit, *Br* invalid out (of the army).

refouler [r(ə)fule] *vt* to force ou drive back; (*sentiment*) to repress; (*larmes*) to hold back. ●**refoulé, -ée** *a* (*personne*) repressed. ●**refoulement** *nm* *Psy* repression.

réfractaire [refraktɛr] *a* **r. à** resistant to.

refrain [r(ə)frɛ̃] *nm* (*de chanson*) chorus, refrain; (*rengaine*) *Fig* tune; **c'est toujours le même r.** it's always the same old story ou tune.

refréner [refrene] *vt* to curb, check.

réfrigérer [refriʒere] *vt* to refrigerate. ●**réfrigérant, -ante** *a* (*accueil, air*) icy. ●**réfrigérateur** *nm* refrigerator. ●**réfrigération** *nf* refrigeration.

refroidir [r(ə)frwadir] *vt* to cool (down);

(*ardeur etc*) *Fig* to cool, damp, *Br* dampen; **r. qn** (*décourager*) to cool *ou* damp s.o.'s enthusiasm ▪ *vi* to get cold, cool down ▪ **se refroidir** *vpr* (*prendre froid*) *Fam* to catch cold; (*temps*) to get cold; (*ardeur etc*) *Fig* to cool (off). ●**refroidissement** *nm* cooling; (*rhume*) chill; **r. de la température** fall in the temperature.

refuge [r(ə)fyʒ] *nm* refuge; (*pour piétons*) (traffic) island; (*de montagne*) (mountain) hut.

réfugier (se) [səfeyʒje] *vpr* to take refuge. ●**réfugié, -ée** *nmf* refugee.

refus [r(ə)fy] *nm* refusal; **ce n'est pas de r.** *Fam* I won't say no. ●**refuser** *vt* to refuse (**qch à qn** s.o. sth, **de faire** to do); (*offre, invitation*) to turn down, refuse; (*candidat*) to fail; (*client*) to turn away, refuse ▪ **se refuser** *vpr* (*plaisir etc*) to deny oneself; **se r. à** (*l'évidence etc*) to refuse to accept, reject; **se r. à croire/etc** to refuse to believe/etc.

réfuter [refyte] *vt* to refute.

regagner [r(ə)ɡaɲe] *vt* (*récupérer*) to regain, get back; (*revenir à*) to get back to. ●**regain** *nm* (*renouveau*) renewal; **un r. d'énergie/etc** renewed energy/etc.

régal, *pl* -**als** [reɡal] *nm* treat. ●**régaler** *vt* to treat to a feast *ou* delicious meal; **r. de** to treat to ▪ **se régaler** *vpr* to have a feast *ou* delicious meal.

regard [rəɡar] *nm* 1 (*coup d'œil, expression*) look; (*fixe*) stare, gaze; **jeter un r. sur** to glance at; **chercher qn/qch du r.** to look (a)round for s.o./sth; **parcourir qch du r.** to cast a glance at sth; **attirer les regards** to attract attention; **dévorer qn/qch du r.** to eye s.o./sth. 2 **au r. de** in regard to; **en r. de** compared with.

regarder [rəɡarde] 1 *vt* to look at; (*fixement*) to stare at, gaze at; (*observer*) to watch; (*considérer*) to consider, regard (**comme as**); **r. qn faire qch** to watch s.o. do sth ▪ *vi* to look; (*fixement*) to stare, gaze; (*observer*) to watch; **r. à** (*dépense, qualité etc*) to pay attention to; **y r. à deux fois avant de faire qch** to think twice before doing sth; **r. vers** (*maison etc*) to face; **r. par la fenêtre** to look through the window ▪ **se regarder** *vpr* (*personnes*) to look at each other; **se r. en chiens de faïence** to glare at each other.
2 *vt* (*concerner*) to concern; **ça ne te regarde pas!** it's none of your business! ●**regardant, -ante** *a* (*économe*) careful (with money).

régate [reɡat] *nf* regatta.

régence [reʒɑ̃s] *nf* regency.

régénérer [reʒenere] *vt* to regenerate.

régenter [reʒɑ̃te] *vt* to rule over.

régie [reʒi] *nf* (*entreprise*) state-owned company; (*de théâtre*) stage management; (*de cinéma, télévision*) production department.

regimber [r(ə)ʒɛ̃be] *vi* to balk (**contre** at).

régime [reʒim] *nm* 1 (*politique*) (form of) government; *Péj* regime. 2 (*alimentaire*) diet; **se mettre au r.** to go on a diet; **suivre un r.**

to be on a diet; **chocolat/etc de r.** diet chocolate/etc. 3 (*de moteur*) speed; **à ce r.** *Fig* at this rate. 4 (*de bananes, dattes*) bunch.

régiment [reʒimɑ̃] *nm* (*de soldats*) regiment; **un r. de** (*quantité*) *Fam* a host of.

région [reʒjɔ̃] *nf* region, area; **la r. parisienne** the Paris region. ●**régional, -e, -aux** *a* regional.

régir [reʒir] *vt* (*déterminer*) to govern.

régisseur [reʒisœr] *nm* (*de propriété*) steward; (*de théâtre*) stage manager; (*de cinéma*) assistant director.

registre [rəʒistr] *nm* register.

réglable [reɡlabl] *a* (*siège etc*) adjustable. ●**réglage** *nm* adjustment; (*de moteur*) tuning.

règle [reɡl] *nf* 1 (*principe*) rule; **en r.** (*papiers d'identité etc*) in order; **être/se mettre en r. avec qn** to be/put oneself straight with s.o.; **en r. générale** as a (general) rule; **dans les règles de l'art** according to the rule book, in the proper way. 2 (*instrument*) ruler; **r. à calcul** slide rule. ●**règles** *nfpl* (*de femme*) (monthly) period.

règlement [rɛɡləmɑ̃] *nm* 1 (*arrêté*) regulation; (*règles*) regulations; **contraire au r.** *Br* against the rules, *Am* against the rule. 2 (*de conflit, problème etc*) settling; (*paiement*) payment; **r. de comptes** *Fig* (violent) settling of scores. ●**réglementaire** *a* in accordance with the regulations; **tenue r.** *Mil* regulation uniform. ●**réglementation** *nf* 1 (*action*) regulation. 2 (*règles*) regulations. ●**réglementer** *vt* to regulate.

régler [reɡle] 1 *vt* (*problème, conflit etc*) to settle; (*mécanisme*) to adjust, regulate; (*moteur*) to tune; (*papier*) to rule; **se r. sur** to model oneself on. 2 *vti* (*payer*) to pay; **r. qn** to settle up with s.o.; **r. son compte à qn** *Fig* to settle old scores with s.o. ●**réglé, -ée** *a* (*vie*) ordered; (*papier*) ruled.

réglisse [reɡlis] *nf Br* liquorice, *Am* licorice.

règne [rɛɲ] *nm* reign; (*animal, minéral, végétal*) kingdom. ●**régner** *vi* (*roi, silence etc*) to reign (**sur** over); (*prédominer*) to prevail; **faire r. l'ordre** to maintain (law and) order.

regorger [r(ə)ɡɔrʒe] *vi* **r. de** to be overflowing with.

régresser [reɡrese] *vi* to regress. ●**régression** *nf* regression; **en r.** on the decline.

regret [r(ə)ɡrɛ] *nm* regret; **à r.** with regret; **avoir le r. ou être au r. de faire qch** to be sorry to do sth. ●**regretter** [r(ə)ɡrɛte] *vt* to regret; **r. qn** to miss s.o.; **je regrette, je le regrette** I'm sorry; **r. que** (+ *sub*) to be sorry that, regret that. ●**regrettable** *a* unfortunate, regrettable.

regrouper [r(ə)ɡrupe] *vt*, **se regrouper** *vpr* to gather together.

régulariser [reɡylarize] *vt* (*situation etc*) to regularize.

régulation [reɡylasjɔ̃] *nf* (*action*) regulation.

régulier, -ière [reɡylje, -jɛr] *a* regular; (*progrès, vitesse*) steady; (*légal*) legal, lawful;

(*honnête*) honest; (*clergé*) regular; .**verbe r.** regular verb. ●**régularité** *nf* regularity; (*du progrès etc*) steadiness; (*de jugement etc*) legality. ●**régulièrement** *adv* regularly; (*normalement*) normally.

réhabiliter [reabilite] *vt* (*dans l'estime publique*) to rehabilitate.

réhabituer (se) [sǝreabitɥe] *vpr* se **r. à qch/à faire qch** to get used to sth/to doing sth again.

rehausser [rǝose] *vt* to raise; (*faire valoir*) to enhance.

réimpression [reɛ̃presjɔ̃] *nf* (*livre*) reprint.

rein [rɛ̃] *nm* kidney; **les reins** (*dos*) the back, the small of the back; **avoir mal aux reins** to have a backache, have low back pain; **r. artificiel** *Méd* kidney machine.

reine [rɛn] *nf* queen; **la r. mère** the queen mother; **la r. Élisabeth** Queen Elizabeth.

reine-claude [rɛnklod] *nf* greengage.

réinsertion [reɛ̃sɛrsjɔ̃] *nf* **r. sociale** rehabilitation (*of young criminals etc*).

réintégrer [reɛ̃tegre] *vt* **1** (*fonctionnaire etc*) to reinstate. **2** (*lieu*) to return to. ●**réintégration** *nf* reinstatement.

réitérer [reitere] *vt* to repeat.

rejaillir [r(ǝ)ʒajir] *vi* to spurt (up *ou* out); **r. sur** *Fig* to rebound on.

rejet [r(ǝ)ʒɛ] *nm* **1** (*refus*) & *Méd* rejection. **2** (*pousse, branche*) shoot. ●**rejeter** *vt* to throw back; (*offre, greffe etc*) to reject; (*épave*) to cast up; (*vomir*) to bring up; **r. une erreur/** *etc* **sur qn** to put the blame for a mistake/*etc* on s.o.

rejeton [rǝʒ(ǝ)tɔ̃] *nm* (*enfant*) *Fam* kid.

rejoindre* [r(ǝ)ʒwɛdr] *vt* (*famille, lieu etc*) to get *ou* go back to; (*régiment*) to rejoin, go *ou* get back to; (*route, rue*) to join; **r. qn** (*se joindre à*) to join *ou* meet s.o.; (*rattraper*) to catch up with s.o. **I se rejoindre** *vpr* (*personnes, routes, rues*) to meet.

réjouir [reʒwir] *vt* to delight **I se réjouir** *vpr* to be delighted (**de** at, about; **de faire** to do). ●**réjoui, -ie** *a* (*air*) joyful. ●**réjouissant, -ante** *a* (*nouvelles etc*) cheering; **ce n'est pas r.!** (*amusant*) no joking matter! ●**réjouissance** *nf* rejoicing; **réjouissances** festivities, rejoicings.

relâche [r(ǝ)lɑʃ] *nf* (*au cinéma, au théâtre*) (temporary) closure; **faire r.** (*théâtre, cinéma*) to close; (*bateau*) to put in (**dans un port** at a port); **sans r.** without a break.

relâcher [r(ǝ)lɑʃe] **1** *vt* (*corde etc*) to slacken; (*discipline, étreinte*) to relax; **r. qn** to release s.o. **I se relâcher** *vpr* to slacken; (*discipline*) to get lax. **2** *vi* (*bateau*) to put in. ●**relâché, -ée** *a* lax. ●**relâchement** *nm* (*de corde etc*) slackness; (*de discipline*) slackening.

relais [r(ǝ)lɛ] *nm* (*dispositif*) (*de radio, télévision*) & *Él* relay; **r. de télévision** (*station*) television relay station; (*course de*) **r.** *Sport* relay (race); **r. routier** *Br* transport café, *Am* truck stop (*café*); **prendre le r.** to take over (**de** from); **par r.** in relays.

relance [r(ǝ)lɑ̃s] *nf* (*reprise*) revival. ●**relancer** *vt* to throw back; (*moteur*) to restart; (*industrie etc*) to put back on its feet; **r. qn** (*solliciter*) to pester s.o.

relater [r(ǝ)late] *vt Litt* to relate (**que** that).

relatif, -ive [r(ǝ)latif, -iv] *a* relative (**à** to). ●**relativement** *adv* (*assez*) relatively; **r. à** compared to, relative to.

relation [r(ǝ)lasjɔ̃] *nf* (*rapport*) relation(ship); (*ami*) acquaintance; **entrer/être en relations avec** to come into/be in contact with; **avoir des relations** (*amis influents*) to have connections; **relations internationales/** *etc* international/*etc* relations.

relax(e) [rǝlaks] *a Fam* relaxed, informal.

relaxer (se) [sǝr(ǝ)lakse] *vpr* to relax. ●**relaxation** *nf* relaxation.

relayer [r(ǝ)leje] *vt* to take over from (*s.o.*), relieve (*s.o.*); (*émission*) to relay **I se relayer** *vpr* to take (it in) turns (**pour faire** to do); *Sport* to take over from one another.

reléguer [r(ǝ)lege] *vt* (*objet etc*) to relegate (**à** to); (*équipe*) *Br* to relegate, *Am* demote (**en** to).

relent [rǝlɑ̃] *nm* stench, smell.

relève [r(ǝ)lɛv] *nf* (*remplacement*) relief; **prendre la r.** to take over (**de** from).

relevé [rǝl(ǝ)ve] *nm* list; (*de dépenses*) statement; (*de compteur*) reading; **r. (de compte)** (bank) statement; **r. (de notes)** *Scol* list of *Br* marks *ou Am* grades.

relèvement [rǝlɛvmɑ̃] *nm* (*d'économie, de pays*) recovery; (*augmentation*) (*des impôts etc*) raising, increase.

relever [rǝl(ǝ)ve] *vt* to raise; (*ramasser*) to pick up; (*personne tombée*) to help up; (*chaise etc*) to put up straight; (*col*) to turn up; (*manches*) to roll up; (*cahiers, copies etc*) to collect; (*copier*) to note down; (*faute*) to pick out, point out; (*compteur*) to read; (*traces*) to find; (*défi*) to accept; (*sauce*) to season; (*relayer*) to relieve; (*rehausser*) to enhance; (*économie, pays*) to put back on its feet; (*mur*) to rebuild; **r. qn de ses fonctions** to relieve s.o. of his *ou* her duties. **I vi r. de** (*dépendre de*) to come under; (*maladie*) to get over. **I se relever** *vpr* (*personne tombée*) to get up; **se r. de** (*malheur*) to recover from; (*ruines*) to rise from.

relief [rǝljef] *nm* (*forme, ouvrage*) relief; **en r.** (*cinéma*) three-D; (*livre*) pop-up; **mettre qch en r.** *Fig* to highlight sth. ●**reliefs** *nmpl* (*de repas*) remains.

relier [rǝlje] *vt* to connect, link (**à** to); (*ensemble*) to link (together); (*livre*) to bind.

religion [r(ǝ)liʒjɔ̃] *nf* religion; (*foi*) faith. ●**religieux, -euse** *a* religious; **mariage r.** church wedding **I** *nm* monk. ●**religieuse** *nf* **1** *nf* nun. **2** (*gâteau*) cream bun.

reliquat [r(ǝ)lika] *nm* (*de dette etc*) remainder.

relique [r(ǝ)lik] *nf* relic.

relire* [r(ǝ)lir] *vt* to read again, reread.

reliure [rǝljyr] *nf* (*couverture de livre*) binding; (art) bookbinding.

reluire* [r(ə)lɥir] vi to shine, gleam; **faire r.** (polir) to shine, polish up. ●**reluisant, -ante** a shiny; **peu r.** Fig far from brilliant.

reluquer [r(ə)lyke] vt Fam to eye (up).

remâcher [r(ə)maʃe] vt (souvenirs etc) Fig to brood over.

remanier [r(ə)manje] vt (texte) to revise; (ministère) to reshuffle. ●**remaniement** nm (de texte) revision; (ministériel) reshuffle.

remarier (se) [sər(ə)marje] vpr to remarry.

remarquable [rəmarkabl] a remarkable (par for). ●**remarquablement** [-əmã] adv remarkably.

remarque [r(ə)mark] nf remark; (écrite) note; **je lui en ai fait la r.** I remarked on it to him ou her.

remarquer [rəmarke] vt 1 (apercevoir) to notice (que that); **faire r.** to point out (à to, que that); **se faire r.** to attract attention; **remarque!** Br mind you!, you know! 2 (dire) to remark (que that).

remballer [rãbale] vt to repack, pack up; **il s'est fait r.** Fam he was sent packing.

rembarrer [rãbare] vt Fam to rebuff, snub.

remblai [rãblɛ] nm (terres) embankment. ●**remblayer** vt (route) to bank up; (trou) to fill in.

rembobiner [rãbɔbine] vt, **se rembobiner** vpr (bande) to rewind.

rembourrer [rãbure] vt (fauteuil, matelas etc) to stuff, pad; (épaules de veston) to pad. ●**rembourré, -ée** a (fauteuil etc) padded, stuffed. ●**rembourrage** nm (action, matière) stuffing, padding.

rembourser [rãburse] vt to pay back, repay; (billet) to refund. ●**remboursement** nm repayment; (de billet) refund; **envoi contre r.** cash on delivery.

remède [r(ə)mɛd] nm cure, remedy; (médicament) medicine. ●**remédier** vi r. à to remedy.

remémorer (se) [sər(ə)memɔre] vpr (histoire etc) Litt to recollect, recall.

remercier [r(ə)mɛrsje] vt 1 to thank (de qch, pour qch for sth); **je vous remercie d'être venu** thank you for coming; **je vous remercie** (non merci) no thank you. 2 (congédier) to dismiss. ●**remerciements** nmpl thanks.

remettre* [r(ə)mɛtr] vt to put back, replace; (vêtement) to put back on; (donner) to hand over (à to); (restituer) to give back (à to); (démission, devoir) to hand in; (différer) to postpone (à until); (ajouter) to add more ou another; **r. qn** (reconnaître) to place s.o., remember s.o.; **r. en question** ou **cause** to call into question; **r. en état** to repair; **r. à jour** to bring up to date; **r. les pendules à l'heure** to put the clocks back ou forward, put the clocks on the correct time; **r. les idées en place** to sort things out, clear things up; **r. une montre à l'heure** to set a watch to the correct time, reset a watch; **ça te remettra les idées en place** that will clear your mind ou help you to see straight; **r. ça** Fam to start again.

█ **se remettre** vpr se r. à (activité) to go back to; **se r. à qch** to start to do sth again; **se r. de** (chagrin, maladie) to get over, recover from; **s'en r. à** to rely on.

réminiscences [reminisãs] nfpl (vague) recollections, reminiscences.

remise [r(ə)miz] nf 1 (de lettre etc) delivery; **la r. de diplômes** graduation; **r. en cause** ou **question** calling into question; **r. en état** repair(ing); **r. à niveau** bringing up to standard; **r. en jeu** Football throw-in. 2 (rabais) discount. 3 **r. de peine** Jur remission. 4 (local) shed; (garage) garage.

remiser [r(ə)mize] vt to put away.

rémission [remisjɔ̃] nf (de péché, maladie) & Jur remission; **sans r.** (travailler etc) relentlessly.

remmener [rãm(ə)ne] vt to take back.

remontée [r(ə)mɔ̃te] nf 1 (de pente etc) ascent; (d'eau, de prix) rise. 2 **r. mécanique** ski lift.

remonte-pente [r(ə)mɔ̃tpãt] nm ski lift.

remonter [r(ə)mɔ̃te] vi (aux être) to come ou go back up; (niveau, prix) to rise again, go back up; (dans le temps) to go back (à to); **r. dans** (voiture) to get ou go back in(to); (bus, train) to get ou go back on(to); **r. sur** (cheval, vélo) to get back on(to), remount; **r. à dix ans**/etc to go back ten years/etc.

█ vt (aux avoir) (escalier, pente) to come ou go back up; (porter) to bring ou take back up; (montre) to wind up; (relever) to raise; (col) to turn up; (objet démonté) to put back together, reassemble; (garde-robe etc) to restock; **r. qn** (ragaillardir) to buck s.o. up; **r. le moral à qn** to cheer s.o. up; **r. la pente** Fig to get back on to one's feet (after a hard struggle); **être (très) remonté contre qn** Fam to be (really) furious with ou mad at s.o.; **se faire r. les bretelles** Fam to get rapped over the knuckles, get a serious talking-to. ●**remontant, -ante** a (boisson) fortifying █ nm (médicament) tonic.

remontoir [r(ə)mɔ̃twar] nm (de mécanisme, montre) winder.

remontrance [r(ə)mɔ̃trãs] nf reprimand; **faire des remontrances à qn** to reprimand s.o., remonstrate with s.o.

remontrer [r(ə)mɔ̃tre] vt to show again; **en r. à qn** to prove one's superiority over s.o.

remords [r(ə)mɔr] nm & nmpl remorse; **avoir des r.** to feel remorse.

remorque [r(ə)mɔrk] nf (de voiture etc) trailer; (câble de) r. towrope; **prendre en r.** to tow; **en r.** Br on tow, Am in tow. ●**remorquer** vt (voiture, bateau) to tow. ●**remorqueur** nm tug(boat).

remous [r(ə)mu] nm eddy; (de foule) bustle; (agitation) Fig turmoil.

rempailler [rãpaje] vt (chaise) to redo the straw bottom of.

rempart [rãpar] nm rampart.

remplacer [rãplase] vt to replace (par with, by); (succéder à) to take over from; (tempo-

rairement) to stand in for. ● **remplaçant, -ante** *nmf* (*personne*) replacement; (*enseignant*) substitute teacher, *Br* supply teacher; (*d'une équipe*) reserve. ● **remplacement** *nm* replacement; **assurer le r. de** qn to stand in for s.o.; **en r. de** in place of.

remplir [rɑ̃plir] *vt* to fill (up) (de with); (*fiche, formulaire etc*) to fill out, *Br* fill in; (*condition, devoir*) *Br* to fulfil, *Am* fulfill; (*fonctions*) to perform ▌ **se remplir** *vpr* to fill (up). ● **rempli, -ie** *a* full (de of). ● **remplissage** *nm* filling; (*verbiage*) *Péj* padding, *Br* waffle; **faire du r.** to pad, *Br* waffle.

remporter [rɑ̃pɔrte] *vt* **1** (*objet*) to take back. **2** (*prix, victoire*) to win; (*succès*) to achieve.

remuer [r(ə)mɥe] *vt* (*bouger*) to move; (*café etc*) to stir; (*salade*) to toss; (*terre*) to turn over; **r. qn** (*émouvoir*) to move s.o. ▌ *vi* to move; (*gigoter*) to fidget; (*se rebeller*) to stir ▌ **se remuer** *vpr* to move; (*se démener*) *Fam* to go to a lot of trouble, exert oneself. ● **remuant, -ante** *a* (*enfant*) restless, fidgety. ● **remue-ménage** *nm inv* commotion.

rémunérer [remynere] *vt* (*personne*) to pay; (*travail*) to pay for. ● **rémunérateur, -trice** *a* lucrative, remunerative. ● **rémunération** *nf* payment (de for).

renâcler [r(ə)nɑkle] *vi* **1** (*cheval*) to snort. **2 r. à** *Fam* to jib at, balk at.

renaître* [r(ə)nɛtr] *vi* (*fleur*) to grow again; (*espoir, industrie*) to revive; **r. de ses cendres** *Fig* to rise from its ashes. ● **renaissance** *nf* rebirth, renaissance.

renard [r(ə)nar] *nm* fox.

renchérir [rɑ̃ʃerir] *vi* **r. sur ce que** qn **dit**/*etc*, **r. sur** qn to go one further than s.o. in what one says/*etc*.

rencontre [rɑ̃kɔ̃tr] *nf* meeting; (*inattendue*) & *Mil* encounter; (*sportive*) *Br* match, *Am* game; (*sportive*) meeting point *ou* place; **amours**/*etc* **de r.** casual love affairs/*etc*; **aller à la r. de** qn to go to meet s.o. ● **rencontrer** *vt* to meet; (*difficulté, obstacle*) to come up against, encounter; (*trouver*) to come across, find; (*heurter*) to hit; (*équipe*) *Sport* to play ▌ **se rencontrer** *vpr* to meet.

rendement [rɑ̃dmɑ̃] *nm* (*d'un champ*) yield; (*d'un investissement*) return, yield; (*de personne, machine*) output.

rendez-vous [rɑ̃devu] *nm inv* appointment; (*d'amoureux*) date; (*lieu*) meeting place; **donner r.-vous à** qn, **prendre r.-vous avec** qn to make an appointment with s.o.; **recevoir sur r.-vous** (*médecin etc*) to see patients by appointment.

rendormir* (**se**) [sərɑ̃dɔrmir] *vpr* to go back to sleep.

rendre [rɑ̃dr] *vt* (*restituer*) to give back, return; (*son*) to give; (*hommage*) to pay; (*justice*) to dispense; (*jugement*) to pronounce, give; (*armes*) to surrender; (*invitation*) to return; (*santé*) to restore; (*exprimer, traduire*) to render; (*vomir*) to throw up, bring up; **r. célèbre/plus grand/possible**/*etc* to

make famous/bigger/possible/*etc*; **r. la monnaie à** qn to give s.o. his *ou* her change; **r. l'âme** to pass away, die.

▌ *vi* (*vomir*) to throw up, *Br* be sick; (*arbre, terre*) to yield.

▌ **se rendre** *vpr* (*capituler*) to surrender (à to); (*aller*) to go (à to); **se r. à** (*évidence, ordres*) to submit to; **se r. malade/utile**/*etc* to make oneself ill/useful/*etc*.

rendu, -ue [rɑ̃dy] *a* **être r.** (*arrivé*) to have arrived.

renégat, -ate [renega, -at] *nmf* renegade.

rênes [rɛn] *nfpl* reins.

renfermer [rɑ̃fɛrme] *vt* to contain ▌ **se renfermer** *vpr* **se r.** (**en soi-même**) to withdraw into oneself. ● **renfermé, -ée** **1** *a* (*personne*) withdrawn. **2** *nm* **sentir le r.** (*chambre etc*) to smell stuffy.

renflé, -ée [rɑ̃fle] *a* bulging. ● **renflement** [-əmɑ̃] *nm* bulge.

renflouer [rɑ̃flue] *vt* (*navire, entreprise*) to refloat; **r. les caisses de l'État** to replenish the State coffers.

renfoncement [rɑ̃fɔ̃smɑ̃] *nm* recess; **dans le r. d'une porte** in a doorway.

renforcer [rɑ̃fɔrse] *vt* to strengthen, reinforce. ● **renforcement** *nm* reinforcement, strengthening.

renfort [rɑ̃fɔr] *nm* **des renforts** (*troupes etc*) reinforcements; (*aide*) *Fig* backup, additional help; **personnel**/*etc* **de r.** backup staff/*etc*; **à grand r. de** *Fig* with (the help of) a great deal of.

renfrogner (**se**) [sərɑ̃frɔɲe] *vpr* to scowl. ● **renfrogné, -ée** *a* scowling, sullen.

rengaine [rɑ̃gɛn] *nf* **la même r.** *Péj Fam* the same old story *ou* song *ou* tune.

rengorger (**se**) [sərɑ̃gɔrʒe] *vpr* *Fig* to give oneself airs.

renier [rənje] *vt* (*ami, pays etc*) to disown; (*foi, opinion*) to renounce. ● **reniement** *nm* disowning; (*de foi etc*) renunciation.

renifler [r(ə)nifle] *vti* to sniff. ● **reniflement** *nm* sniff.

renne [rɛn] *nm* reindeer.

renom [rənɔ̃] *nm* (*popularité*) renown; (*réputation*) reputation (de for); **de r., de grand r.** (*ouvrage, artiste etc*) (very) famous, renowned. ● **renommé, -ée** *a* famous, renowned (**pour** for). ● **renommée** *nf* fame, renown; (*réputation*) reputation.

renoncer [r(ə)nɔ̃se] *vi* **r. à** qch to give sth up, abandon sth; **r. à faire** qch to give up (the idea of) doing sth. ● **renoncement** *nm ou* **renonciation** *nf* renunciation (à of).

renouer [rənwe] **1** *vt* (*lacet etc*) to retie. **2** *vt* (*reprendre*) to renew ▌ *vi* **r. avec** qch (*tradition, mode etc*) to revive sth; **r. avec** qn to take up with s.o. again.

renouveau, -x [r(ə)nuvo] *nm* revival.

renouveler [r(ə)nuv(ə)le] *vt* to renew; (*erreur, question*) to repeat ▌ **se renouveler** *vpr* (*incident*) to happen again, recur; (*cellules, sang*) to be renewed. ● **renouvelable** *a* renewable. ● **renouvellement** *nm* renewal.

rénover [renɔve] vt (édifice, meuble etc) to renovate; (institution, méthode) to reform. ● **rénovation** nf renovation; (d'institution etc) reform.

renseigner [rãsεɲe] vt to inform, give some information to (sur about) ▌ **se renseigner** vpr to find out, inquire, make inquiries (sur about). ● **renseignement** nm (piece of) information; **renseignements** information; (pour la défense d'un pays) Mil intelligence; **les renseignements (téléphoniques)** Br directory inquiries, Am information; **prendre ou demander des renseignements** to make inquiries; **service de renseignements** Mil intelligence service.

rentable [rãtabl] a profitable. ● **rentabilité** nf profitability.

rente [rãt] nf (private) income; (pension) pension; **avoir des rentes** to have private means. ● **rentier, -ière** nmf person of private means.

rentrée [rãtre] nf 1 (retour) return; (de parlement) reopening, reassembly; (d'acteur etc) comeback; **r. (des classes)** beginning of term ou of the school year; **faire sa r.** (acteur etc) to make one's comeback. 2 (des foins etc) bringing in; **rentrées d'argent** (cash) receipts; **les rentrées d'impôts** tax receipts.

rentrer [rãtre] vi (aux être) to go ou come back, return; (chez soi) to go ou come (back) home; (entrer) to go ou come in; (entrer de nouveau) to go ou come back in; (écoles, tribunaux) to reopen, start again; (argent) to come in; **r. dans** (entrer dans) to go ou come into; (entrer de nouveau dans) to go ou come back into; (pays, famille) to return to; (heurter) to crash into; (s'emboîter dans) to fit into; (catégorie) to come under; **r. (en classe)** to go back to school; **r. dans ses frais** to recover one's expenses; **tout est rentré dans l'ordre** everything returned to normal; **je lui suis rentré dedans** (frapper) Fam I laid into ou pitched into him ou her.
▌ vt (aux avoir) to bring ou take in; (voiture) to put away; (chemise) to tuck in; (griffes) to draw in. ● **rentré, -ée** a (colère) suppressed; (yeux) sunken.

renverse (à la) [alarãvεrs] adv (tomber) backwards, on one's back.

renverser [rãvεrse] vt (mettre à l'envers) to turn upside down; (faire tomber) to knock over ou down; (piéton) to knock down, run over; (liquide) to spill, knock over; (courant, ordre) to reverse; (gouvernement) to overthrow, overturn; (tête) to tip back, tilt back.
▌ **se renverser** vpr (en arrière) to lean back; (bouteille, vase etc) to fall over; (liquide) to spill. ● **renversant, -ante** a (nouvelle etc) Fam astounding. ● **renversement** nm (de situation) reversal; (de gouvernement) overthrow.

renvoi [rãvwa] nm 1 return; (d'employé) dismissal; (d'élève) expulsion; (ajournement) postponement; (dans un livre) (cross) refer-

ence. 2 (rot) belch, burp. ● **renvoyer** vt to send back, return; (employé) to dismiss; (élève) to expel; (importun) to send away; (balle etc) to throw back; (lumière, image etc) to reflect; (ajourner) to postpone (à until); **r. qn à** (adresser à) to refer s.o. to; **r. un lecteur à** to refer a reader to; **cette note (nous) renvoie au chapitre dix** this note refers us to chapter ten.

réorganiser [reɔrganize] vt to reorganize. ● **réorganisation** nf reorganization.

réouverture [reuvεrtyr] nf reopening.

repaire [r(ə)pεr] nm den.

repaître (se) [sərəpεtr] vpr se r. de (sang) Fig Litt to wallow in.

répandre [repãdr] vt (liquide) to spill; (nouvelle, joie) to spread; (odeur) to give off; (lumière, larmes, sang, chargement) to shed; (gravillons etc) to scatter; (dons, bienfaits) to lavish ▌ **se répandre** vpr (nouvelle, peur etc) to spread; (liquide) to spill; **se r. dans** (fumée, odeur) to spread through; **se r. en louanges/etc** to pour forth praise/etc. ● **répandu, -ue** a (opinion, usage) widespread; (épars) scattered.

reparaître [r(ə)parεtr] vi to reappear.

réparer [repare] vt to repair, mend; (erreur) to put right; (forces) to restore; (faute) to make amends for; (perte) to make good; **faire r. qch** to get sth repaired. ● **réparable** a (montre etc) repairable. ● **réparateur, -trice** nmf repairer ▌ a (sommeil) refreshing. ● **réparation** nf repair(ing); (compensation) amends, compensation (de for); **réparations** Mil Hist reparations; **en r.** under repair; **faire des réparations sur qch** to do some repairs to ou on sth.

reparler [r(ə)parle] vi r. de to talk about again.

repartie [reparti] nf (réponse vive) repartee.

repartir [r(ə)partir] vi (aux être) to set off again; (s'en retourner) to go back; (reprendre) to start again; **r. à ou de zéro** to start from scratch again, go back to square one.

répartir [repartir] vt to distribute; (partager) to share (out); (classer) to divide (up); (étaler dans le temps) to spread (out) (sur over). ● **répartition** nf distribution; (partage) sharing; (classement) division.

repas [r(ə)pɑ] nm meal; **prendre un r.** to have ou eat a meal.

repasser [r(ə)pɑse] 1 vi to come ou go back ▌ vt (traverser) to go back over; (examen) to take again, Br resit; (leçon, rôle) to go over; (film) to show again; (bande magnétique) to play back; (maladie, travail) Fam to pass on (à to). 2 vt (linge) to iron. 3 vt (couteau) to sharpen. ● **repassage** nm ironing.

repêcher [r(ə)pεʃe] vt (objet) to fish out; (candidat) Fam to allow to pass.

repeindre [rəpεdr] vt to repaint.

repenser [r(ə)pãse] vt to rethink.

repentir [r(ə)pɑtir] nm repentance. ● **se repentir** vpr Rel to repent (de of); **se r. de**

qch/d'avoir fait qch (*regretter*) to be sorry for sth/for doing sth, regret sth/doing sth. ● **repentant, -ante** *ou* **repenti, -ie** *a* repentant.

répercuter [repɛrkyte] *vt* (*son*) to echo ∎ **se répercuter** *vpr* to echo, reverberate; **se r. sur** *Fig* to have repercussions on. ● **répercussion** *nf* repercussion.

reperdre [rəpɛrdr] *vt* to lose again.

repère [r(ə)pɛr] *nm* (*guide*) mark; (*jalon*) marker; **point de r.** (*espace, temps*) landmark, point of reference. ● **repérer** *vt* to locate; (*remarquer*) *Fam* to spot ∎ **se repérer** *vpr* to get one's bearings.

répertoire [repɛrtwar] *nm* 1 index; (*carnet*) (indexed) notebook; (*de fichiers*) *Ordinat* directory; **r. d'adresses** address book. 2 (*de théâtre*) repertoire. ● **répertorier** *vt* to index.

répéter [repete] *vt* to repeat; (*pièce de théâtre, rôle, symphonie etc*) to rehearse; **r. à qn que** to tell s.o. again that; **je te l'ai répété cent fois** I've told you a hundred times; **des tentatives répétées** repeated attempts ∎ *vi* to repeat; **répétez après moi** repeat *ou* say after me ∎ **se répéter** *vpr* (*radoter*) to repeat oneself; (*événement*) to happen again, repeat itself. ● **répétitif, -ive** *a* repetitive. ● **répétition** *nf* repetition; (*au théâtre etc*) rehearsal; **r. générale** (*final*) dress rehearsal.

répétiteur, -trice [repetitœr, -tris] *nmf* tutor.

repiquer [r(ə)pike] *vt* 1 (*plante*) to plant out. 2 (*disque*) to tape, record (on tape).

répit [repi] *nm* rest, respite; **sans r.** ceaselessly.

replacer [r(ə)plase] *vt* to replace, put back.

replanter [rəplɑ̃te] *vt* to (re)plant.

repli [r(ə)pli] *nm* fold; *Mil* withdrawal; **les replis de l'âme** the innermost recesses of the soul.

replier [r(ə)plije] 1 *vt* to fold (up); (*siège*) to fold up; (*couverture, couteau*) to fold back; (*ailes, jambes*) to tuck in ∎ **se replier** (*siège*) to fold up; (*couverture, couteau*) to fold back. 2 *vt*, **se replier** *vpr* (*armée*) to withdraw; **se r. sur soi-même** *Fig* to withdraw into oneself.

réplique [replik] *nf* 1 (*réponse*) (sharp) reply; (*riposte*) retort; (*d'acteur*) lines; **pas de r.!** no answering back!; **sans r.** (*argument*) irrefutable. 2 (*copie*) replica. ● **répliquer** *vt* to reply (sharply) (**que** that); (*riposter*) to retort (**que** that) ∎ *vi* (*être impertinent*) to answer back.

répondre [repɔ̃dr] *vi* to answer, reply; (*être impertinent*) to answer back; (*réagir*) to respond (**à** to); **r. à qn** to answer s.o., reply to s.o.; (*avec impertinence*) to answer s.o. back; **r. à** (*lettre, question, objection*) to answer, reply to; (*besoin*) to meet, answer; (*salut*) to return; (*correspondre à*) to correspond to; **r. de** (*garantir*) to answer for (*s.o., sth*).

∎ *vt* (*remarque etc*) to answer *ou* reply with; **r. que** to answer *ou* reply that. ● **répondant, -ante** 1 *nmf* guarantor. 2 *nm* **avoir du r.** *Fam* to have money behind one. ● **répondeur** *nm*

r. (*téléphonique*) answering machine. (*réaction*)

réponse [repɔ̃s] *nf* answer, reply; (*réaction*) response (**à** to); **en r. à** in answer *ou* reply *ou* response to.

report [r(ə)pɔr] *nm* (*de rendez-vous etc*) postponement; (*transcription*) transfer; (*de somme*) carrying forward.

reportage [r(ə)pɔrtaʒ] *nm* (news) report, article; (*en direct*) commentary; (*métier*) reporting.

reporter[1] [r(ə)pɔrte] *vt* to take back; (*différer*) to put off, postpone (**à** until); (*transcrire*) to transfer (**sur** to); (*somme*) to carry forward (**sur** to); **se r. à** (*texte etc*) to refer to; (*en esprit*) to go *ou* think back to.

reporter[2] [r(ə)pɔrtɛr] *nm* reporter.

repos [r(ə)po] *nm* rest; (*tranquillité*) peace (and quiet); (*de l'esprit*) peace of mind; **r.!** (*commandement*) *Mil* at ease!; **jour de r.** day off; **de tout r.** (*situation etc*) safe.

reposer [r(ə)poze] 1 *vt* (*objet*) to put back down; (*problème, question*) to raise again. 2 *vt* (*délasser*) to rest, relax; **r. sa tête sur** (*appuyer*) to rest one's head on. ∎ *vi* (*être enterré*) to rest, lie; **r. sur** (*bâtiment*) to be built on; (*théorie etc*) to be based on, rest on; **laisser r.** (*liquide*) to allow to settle.

∎ **se reposer** *vpr* to rest; **se r. sur qn** to rely on s.o.; **se r. sur ses lauriers** to rest on one's laurels. ● **reposant, -ante** *a* restful, relaxing. ● **reposé, -ée** *a* rested, fresh.

repousser [r(ə)puse] 1 *vt* to push back; (*écarter*) to push away; (*attaque, ennemi*) to beat off, *Litt* repulse; (*importun etc*) to turn away; (*différer*) to put off, postpone; (*décliner*) to reject; (*dégoûter*) to repel. 2 *vi* (*cheveux, feuilles etc*) to grow again. ● **repoussant, -ante** *a* repulsive, repellent.

répréhensible [repreɑ̃sibl] *a* reprehensible, blameworthy.

reprendre* [r(ə)prɑ̃dr] *vt* (*objet*) to take back; (*évadé, ville*) to recapture; (*passer prendre*) to pick up again; (*souffle*) to get back; (*activité*) to resume, take up again; (*refrain*) to take up; (*vêtement*) to alter; (*corriger*) to correct; (*blâmer*) to admonish; (*pièce de théâtre*) to put on again; (*texte*) to go back over; **r. de la viande/un œuf/**etc to take (some) more meat/another egg/etc; **r. ses esprits** to come round; **r. des forces** to get one's strength back, recover one's strength; **je jure qu'on ne m'y reprendra plus** *Fam* I swear it's the last time I'll do that, I swear I won't be caught out doing that again.

∎ *vi* (*plante*) to take root again; (*recommencer*) to start (up) again, resume; (*affaires*) to pick up; (*parler*) to go on, continue.

∎ **se reprendre** *vpr* (*se ressaisir*) to get a grip on oneself; (*se corriger*) to correct oneself; **s'y r. à deux/plusieurs fois** to have another go/several goes (at it).

représailles [r(ə)prezɑj] *nfpl* reprisals, retaliation.

résistance

265

représenter [r(ə)prezɑ̃te] *vt* to represent; (*pièce de théâtre*) to perform ▌ **se représenter** *vpr* (*s'imaginer*) to imagine. ● **représentant, -ante** *nmf* representative; **r. de commerce** (travelling) salesman *ou* saleswoman, sales representative. ● **représentatif, -ive** *a* representative (**de** of). ● **représentation** *nf* representation; (*de théâtre*) performance.

répression [represjɔ̃] *nf* suppression, repression; (*mesures de contrôle*) *Pol* repression. ● **répressif, -ive** *a* repressive. ● **réprimer** *vt* (*sentiment, révolte etc*) to suppress, repress.

réprimande [reprimɑ̃d] *nf* reprimand. ● **réprimander** *vt* to reprimand.

repris [r(ə)pri] *nm* **r. de justice** hardened criminal.

reprise [r(ə)priz] *nf* (*recommencement*) resumption; (*de pièce de théâtre*) revival; (*à la radio ou télévision*) repeat; (*raccommodage d'un tissu*) mend; *Boxe* round; (*économique*) recovery, revival; (*d'un locataire*) money for fittings; (*de marchandise*) taking back; (*pour nouvel achat*) *Br* part exchange, trade-in; **reprises** (*de moteur*) acceleration; **à plusieurs reprises** on several occasions. ● **repriser** *vt* (*chaussette etc*) to mend, darn.

réprobation [reprɔbasjɔ̃] *nf* disapproval. ● **réprobateur, -trice** *a* disapproving.

reproche [r(ə)prɔʃ] *nm* criticism, reproach; **faire des reproches à qn** to criticize s.o., reproach s.o.; **sans r.** beyond reproach. ● **reprocher** *vt* **r. qch à qn** to criticize *ou* blame *ou* reproach s.o. for sth; **n'avoir rien à se r.** to have nothing to reproach *ou* blame oneself for; **qu'as-tu à r. à ce livre?** what do you have against this book?

reproduire* [r(ə)prɔdɥir] **1** *vt* (*modèle, son etc*) to copy, reproduce ▌ **se reproduire** *vpr* (*animaux*) to breed, reproduce. **2 se reproduire** *vpr* (*incident etc*) to happen again, recur. ● **reproducteur, -trice** *a* reproductive. ● **reproduction** *nf* (*d'animaux*) breeding, reproduction; (*de son etc*) reproduction; (*copie*) copy.

réprouver [repruve] *vt* to disapprove of, condemn.

reptile [reptil] *nm* reptile.

repu, -ue [rəpy] *a* (*rassasié*) satiated.

république [repyblik] *nf* republic. ● **républicain, -aine** *a* & *nmf* republican.

répudier [repydje] *vt* to repudiate.

répugnant, -ante [repynɑ̃, -ɑ̃t] *a* repulsive, disgusting, repugnant. ● **répugnance** *nf* disgust, repugnance, loathing (**pour** for); (*manque d'enthousiasme*) reluctance. ● **répugner** *vi* **r. à qn** to be repulsive *ou* repugnant to s.o.; **r. à faire qch** to be loath to do sth.

répulsion [repylsjɔ̃] *nf* repulsion.

réputation [repytasjɔ̃] *nf* reputation; **avoir la r. d'être franc** to have a reputation for being frank *ou* for frankness; **connaître qn de r.** to know s.o. by reputation. ● **réputé, -ée** *a* (*célèbre*) renowned (**pour** for); **r. pour être très intelligent/etc** reputed to be very intelligent/

etc.

requérir [rəkerir] *vt* (*nécessiter*) to demand, require; (*peine de prison*) to call for. ● **requis, -ise** *a* required, requisite.

requête [rəkɛt] *nf* request; (*auprès d'un juge etc*) petition.

requiem [rekɥijɛm] *nm inv* requiem.

requin [r(ə)kɛ̃] *nm* (*poisson*) & *Fig* shark.

requinquer [rəkɛ̃ke] *vt Fam* to buck up, perk up.

réquisition [rekizisjɔ̃] *nf* requisition. ● **réquisitionner** *vt* to requisition, commandeer.

réquisitoire [rekizitwar] *nm* (*critique*) indictment (**contre** of).

RER [ɛrøɛr] *nm abrév* (*Réseau express régional*) express rail network serving Paris and its suburbs.

rescapé, -ée [rɛskape] *a* surviving ▌ *nmf* survivor.

rescousse (à la) [alarɛskus] *adv* to the rescue.

réseau, -x [rezo] *nm* network; **r. d'espionnage** spy ring *ou* network.

réservation [rezɛrvasjɔ̃] *nf* reservation, booking.

réserve [rezɛrv] *nf* **1** (*provision*) stock, reserve; (*entrepôt*) storeroom; (*de bibliothèque*) stacks; **la r.** *Mil* the reserve; **les réserves** (*soldats*) the reserves; **en r.** in reserve. **2** (*de chasse, pêche*) preserve; (*indienne*) reservation; **r. naturelle** nature reserve. **3** (*discrétion, réticence*) reserve; (*restriction, doute*) reservation; **sans r.** (*admiration etc*) unqualified; **sous r. de** subject to; **sous toutes réserves** without guarantee.

réserver [rezɛrve] *vt* to reserve; (*garder*) to save, keep (**à** for); (*marchandises*) to put aside (**à** for); (*place, table*) to book, reserve; (*sort, surprise etc*) to hold in store (**à** for); **se r. pour qch** to save oneself for sth; **se r. de faire qch** to reserve the right to do sth. ● **réservé, -ée** *a* (*personne, place*) reserved; **être r. dans ses propos/etc** (*prudent*) to be guarded *ou* cautious in one's speech/etc.

réservoir [rezɛrvwar] *nm* (*lac*) reservoir; (*citerne*) tank; **r. d'essence** *Br* petrol *ou* *Am* gas tank.

résidence [rezidɑ̃s] *nf* residence; **r. secondaire** second home; **r. universitaire** *Br* hall of residence, *Am* dormitory. ● **résident, -ente** *nmf* (foreign) resident. ● **résidentiel, -ielle** *a* (*quartier*) residential. ● **résider** *vi* to be resident, reside (**à, en, dans** in); **r. dans** (*consister dans*) to lie in.

résidu [rezidy] *nm* residue, waste.

résigner (se) [sərezine] *vpr* to resign oneself (**à qch** to sth, **à faire** to doing). ● **résignation** *nf* resignation.

résilier [rezilje] *vt* (*contrat*) to terminate. ● **résiliation** *nf* termination.

résille [rezij] *nf* (*pour cheveux*) hairnet.

résine [rezin] *nf* resin.

résistance [rezistɑ̃s] *nf* resistance (**à** to); (*conducteur*) *Él* (heating) element; **plat de r.** main dish; **la R.** *Hist* the Resistance.

résister [reziste] *vi* r. à to resist; (*chaleur, fatigue, souffrance*) to withstand; (*se défendre contre*) to stand up to; r. à l'analyse to stand up to analysis. ●**résistant, -ante** *a* tough, strong; r. à la chaleur heat-resistant; r. au choc shockproof ∎ *nmf Hist* Resistance fighter.

résolu, -ue [rezɔly] *pp de* **résoudre** ∎ *a* determined, resolute; r. à faire determined *ou* resolved to do. ●**résolument** *adv* resolutely. ●**résolution** *nf* (*décision*) decision, resolution; (*fermeté*) determination.

résonance [rezɔnãs] *nf* resonance.

résonner [rezɔne] *vi* (*cri etc*) to ring out, resound; (*salle, voix*) to echo (**de** with).

résorber [rezɔrbe] *vt* (*chômage*) to reduce; (*excédent*) to absorb ∎ **se résorber** *vpr* to be reduced; (*excédent*) to be absorbed. ●**résorption** *nf* reduction; (*d'excédent*) absorption.

résoudre* [rezudr] *vt* (*problème*) to solve; (*difficulté*) to clear up, resolve; r. de faire qch to decide *ou* resolve to do sth; se r. à faire qch (*se résigner*) to bring oneself to do sth, resign oneself to do sth.

respect [respɛ] *nm* respect (**pour, de** for); mes respects à my regards *ou* respects to; tenir qn en r. to hold s.o. in check. ●**respectabilité** *nf* respectability. ●**respectable** *a* (*honorable, important*) respectable. ●**respecter** *vt* to respect; qui se respecte self-respecting; r. la loi to abide by *ou* obey *ou* respect the law; faire r. la loi to enforce the law. ●**respectueux, -euse** *a* respectful (**envers** to, **de** of).

respectif, -ive [respɛktif, -iv] *a* respective. ●**respectivement** *adv* respectively.

respirer [respire] *vi* to breathe; (*reprendre haleine*) to get one's breath back; (*être soulagé*) to breathe again ∎ *vt* to breathe (in); (*exprimer*) *Fig* to exude, radiate. ●**respiration** *nf* breathing; (*haleine*) breath; r. artificielle *Méd* artificial respiration. ●**respiratoire** *a* troubles/*etc* **respiratoires** breathing *ou* respiratory trouble/*etc*.

resplendir [resplãdir] *vi* to shine; (*visage*) to glow (**de** with). ●**resplendissant, -ante** *a* (*visage*) glowing, radiant (**de** with).

responsable [respɔ̃sabl] *a* responsible (**de qch** for sth, **devant qn** to s.o.) ∎ *nmf* (*chef*) person in charge; (*dans une organisation*) official; (*coupable*) person responsible (**de** for). ●**responsabilité** *nf* responsibility; (*légale*) liability.

resquiller [reskije] *vi* (*au cinéma, dans le métro etc*) to avoid paying; (*sans attendre*) *Br* to jump the queue, *Am* cut in (line). ●**resquilleur, -euse** *nmf Br* queue-jumper, *Am* person who cuts in (line).

ressaisir (se) [sər(ə)sezir] *vpr* to pull oneself together.

ressasser [r(ə)sase] *vt* (*ruminer*) to keep going over; (*répéter*) to keep trotting out.

ressemblance [r(ə)sãblãs] *nf* likeness, resemblance (**avec** to). ●**ressembler** *vi* r. à to

look *ou* be like, resemble; **cela ne lui ressemble pas** (*ce n'est pas son genre*) that's not like him *ou* her ∎ **se ressembler** *vpr* to look *ou* be alike. ●**ressemblant, -ante** *a* portrait *etc* r. good likeness.

ressentiment [r(ə)sãtimã] *nm* resentment.

ressentir* [r(ə)sãtir] *vt* to feel; **se r. de qch** (*personne*) to feel the effects of sth; (*chose*) to show the effects of sth.

resserre [r(ə)ser] *nf* storeroom; (*remise*) shed.

resserrer [r(ə)sere] *vt* (*nœud, boulon etc*) to tighten; (*contracter*) to close (up), contract; (*liens*) *Fig* to strengthen ∎ **se resserrer** *vpr* to tighten; (*amitié*) to become closer; (*se contracter*) to close (up), contract; (*route etc*) to narrow.

resservir* [r(ə)servir] **1** *vi* (*outil etc*) to come in useful (again). **2 se resservir** *vpr* se r. de (*plat etc*) to have another helping of.

ressort [r(ə)sɔr] *nm* **1** (*objet*) spring. **2** (*énergie*) spirit. **3 du r.** de within the competence of; **en dernier r.** (*décider etc*) as a last resort, in the last resort.

ressortir¹* [r(ə)sɔrtir] *vi* (*aux être*) **1** to go *ou* come back out; (*film*) to be shown again. **2** (*se voir*) to stand out; **faire r.** to bring out; **il ressort de** (*résulte*) it emerges from.

ressortir² [r(ə)sɔrtir] *vi* (*conjugated like* **finir**) **r. à** *Litt* to fall within the scope of.

ressortissant, -ante [r(ə)sɔrtisã, -ãt] *nmf* (*citoyen*) national.

ressource [r(ə)surs] **1** *nfpl* (*moyens*) resources; (*argent*) resources, means. **2** *nf* (*recours*) recourse; (*possibilité*) possibility (**de** faire of doing); **dernière r.** last resort.

ressusciter [resysite] *vi* to rise from the dead; (*malade, pays*) to recover, revive ∎ *vt* (*mort*) to raise; (*malade, mode*) to revive.

restant, -ante [restã, -ãt] *a* remaining; **poste restante** *Br* poste restante, *Am* general delivery ∎ *nm* **le r.** the rest, the remainder; **un r. de viande**/*etc* some left-over meat/*etc*.

restaurant [restɔrã] *nm* restaurant.

restaurer [restɔre] **1** *vt* (*réparer, rétablir*) to restore. **2 se restaurer** *vpr* to have something to eat. ●**restaurateur, -trice** *nmf* **1** (*hôtelier, hôtelière*) restaurant owner. **2** (*de tableaux*) restorer. ●**restauration** *nf* **1** (*hôtellerie*) catering. **2** (*de tableau etc*) restoration.

reste [rest] *nm* rest, remainder (**de** of); *Math* remainder; **restes** remains (**de** of); (*de repas*) leftovers; **au r., du r.** moreover, besides; **il est parti sans demander son r.** he left without further ado, he left discreetly.

rester [reste] *vi* (*aux être*) to stay, remain; (*calme, jeune etc*) to keep, stay, remain; (*subsister*) to be left, remain; **il reste du pain**/*etc* there's some bread/*etc* left (over); **il me reste une minute**/*etc* I have one minute/*etc* left; **l'argent qui lui reste** the money he *ou* she has left; **reste à savoir** it remains to be seen; **il me reste deux choses à faire** I still have two things to do; **il me reste à vous remercier** it remains for me to thank you; **il n'en reste pas moins que...** the fact remains that..., it's nevertheless the case that...; **en r. à** to stop at; **restons-en là** let's leave it at that; **r. sur sa faim** to remain hungry; **les oignons me sont restés sur l'estomac** the onions are lying on my stomach; **elle a failli y r.** *Fam* that was very nearly the end of her.

restituer [restitɥe] *vt* **1** (*rendre*) to return, restore (**à** to). **2** (*son*) to reproduce; (*énergie*) to release. ● **restitution** *nf* return.

restreindre* [restrɛ̃dr] *vt* to limit, restrict (**à** to). **█ se restreindre** *vpr* to decrease; (*faire des économies*) to cut back *ou* down. ● **restreint, -einte** *a* limited, restricted (**à** to). ● **restrictif, -ive** *a* restrictive. ● **restriction** *nf* restriction; **sans r.** unreservedly.

résultat [rezylta] *nm* (*score, d'examen etc*) result; (*conséquence*) outcome, result; **avoir qch pour r.** to result in sth. ● **résulter** *vi* **r. de** to result from.

résumer [rezyme] *vt* (*abréger*) to summarize (*text, thought etc*); (*récapituler*) to sum up (*situation etc*) **█ se résumer** *vpr* (*orateur etc*) to sum up; **se r. à** (*se réduire à*) to boil down to. ● **résumé** *nm* summary; **en r.** in short; (*en récapitulant*) to sum up.

résurgence [rezyrʒɑ̃s] *nf* (*de la criminalité etc*) resurgence (**de** in).

résurrection [rezyrɛksjɔ̃] *nf* resurrection.

rétablir [retablir] *vt* (*communications, ordre, peine de mort etc*) to restore; (*vérité*) to re-establish; (*malade*) to restore to health; (*employé*) to reinstate **█ se rétablir** *vpr* to be restored; (*malade*) to recover. ● **rétablissement** *nm* restoring, restoration; (*de vérité*) re-establishment; (*après une maladie*) recovery; **faire un r.** *Gymnastique* to do a pull-up, heave *ou* pull oneself up.

retaper [r(ə)tape] *vt* (*maison, voiture etc*) to do up; (*lit*) to straighten; (*malade*) *Fam* to buck up.

retard [r(ə)tar] *nm* lateness; (*sur un programme etc*) delay; (*de région*) backwardness; **en r.** late; **en r. dans qch** behind in sth; **en r. sur qn/qch** behind s.o./sth.; **rattraper** *ou* **combler son r.** to catch up; **avoir du r.** to be late; (*sur un programme*) to be behind (schedule); (*montre*) to be slow; **avoir une heure de r.** to be an hour late; **prendre du r.** (*montre*) to lose (time); (*personne*) to fall behind; **sans r.** without delay; **elle est en r. pour son âge** she's behind for her age; **il a un métro de r.** *Fam* he's slow on the uptake, he lags miles behind. ● **retardataire** *a* (*qui arrive en retard*) late; *enfant r. Méd* slow learner **█** *nmf* latecomer. ● **retardement** *nm* **bombe à r.** time bomb, delayed-action bomb.

retarder [r(ə)tarde] *vt* to delay; (*date, montre, départ*) to put back; **r. qn** (*dans une activité*) to put s.o. behind **█** *vi* (*montre*) to be slow; **r. de cinq minutes** to be five minutes slow; **r. (sur son temps)** (*personne*) to be be-

hind the times. ● **retardé, -ée** *a* (*enfant*) backward **█** *nmf* backward child.

retenir* [rət(ə)nir] *vt* (*empêcher d'agir, contenir*) to hold back; (*souffle, attention*) to hold; (*réserver*) to book; (*se souvenir de*) to remember; (*fixer*) to hold (in place), secure; (*chiffre*) *Math* to carry; (*chaleur, odeur*) to retain; (*candidature, proposition*) to accept; (*invité, suspect etc*) to detain, keep; (*déduire*) to take off; **r. qn prisonnier** to keep *ou* hold s.o. prisoner; **r. qn de faire qch** to stop s.o. (from) doing sth.
█ se retenir *vpr* (*se contenir*) to restrain oneself; **se r. de faire qch** to stop oneself (from) doing sth; **se r. à** to cling to.

retentir [r(ə)tɑ̃tir] *vi* to ring (out) (**de** with). ● **retentissant, -ante** *a* resounding; (*scandale*) major. ● **retentissement** *nm* (*effet*) effect; **avoir un grand r.** (*film etc*) to create a stir.

retenue [rət(ə)ny] *nf* **1** (*modération*) restraint. **2** (*de salaire*) deduction, *Br* stoppage; (*chiffre*) *Math* figure carried over. **3** (*punition*) *Scol* detention; **en r.** in detention.

réticent, -ente [retisɑ̃, -ɑ̃t] *a* (*réservé*) reticent; (*hésitant*) reluctant. ● **réticence** *nf* reticence; (*hésitation*) reluctance.

rétine [retin] *nf* (*de l'œil*) retina.

retirer [r(ə)tire] *vt* to withdraw; (*sortir*) to take out; (*ôter*) to take off; (*éloigner*) to take away; (*aller chercher*) to pick up; (*offre, plainte, candidature, argent*) to withdraw, take back; **r. qch à qn** (*permis etc*) to take sth away from s.o.; **r. qch de** (*gagner*) to derive sth from **█ se retirer** *vpr* to withdraw, retire (**de** from); (*mer*) to ebb. ● **retiré, -ée** *a* (*lieu, vie*) secluded.

retomber [r(ə)tɔ̃be] *vi* to fall (again); (*pendre*) to hang (down); (*après un saut*) to land; (*intérêt*) to slacken; **r. dans** (*l'oubli, le chaos*) to sink back into; (*le péché*) to lapse into; **r. dans l'erreur** to be wrong again; **r. sur qn** (*responsabilité, frais*) to fall on s.o.; (*dans la rue*) *Fam* to bump into s.o. again. ● **retombées** *nfpl* (*radioactives*) fallout; (*conséquences*) *Fig* repercussions, effects.

rétorquer [retɔrke] *vt* **r. que** to retort that.

retors, -orse [rətɔr, -ɔrs] *a* wily, crafty.

rétorsion [retɔrsjɔ̃] *nf* (*d'un État*) retaliation; **mesure de r.** reprisal.

retouche [r(ə)tuʃ] *nf* (*de vêtement etc*) alteration; (*de photo etc*) touching up. ● **retoucher** *vt* (*vêtement, texte*) to alter; (*photo, tableau*) to touch up, retouch.

retour [r(ə)tur] *nm* return; (*de fortune*) reversal; **être de r.** to be back (**de** from); **en r.** (*en échange*) in return; **par r. (du courrier)** *Br* by return (of post), *Am* by return mail; **à mon retour** when I get *ou* got back (**de** from); **r. en arrière** flashback; **r. de flamme** *Fig* backlash; **match r.** return *Br* match *ou* *Am* game.

retourner [r(ə)turne] *vt* (*aux avoir*) (*matelas, steak etc*) to turn over; (*terre etc*) to turn; (*vêtement, sac etc*) to turn inside out; (*ta-*

bleau etc) to turn round; (*compliment, lettre*) to return; (*maison*) *Fam* to turn upside down; **r. contre qn** (*argument*) to turn against s.o.; (*arme*) to turn on s.o.; **r. qn** (*bouleverser*) *Fam* to upset s.o., shake s.o.; **savoir de quoi il retourne** to know what it's all about.
■ *vi* (*aux être*) to go back, return.
■ **se retourner** *vpr* (*pour regarder*) to turn round, look round *ou* back; (*sur le dos*) to turn over *ou* round; (*dans son lit*) to toss and turn; (*voiture*) to overturn; **s'en r.** to go back; **se r. contre** *Fig* to turn against. ● **retournement** *nm* **le r. de la situation** the sudden change in the situation, the dramatic turn of events.

retracer [r(ə)trase] *vt* (*histoire etc*) to retrace.

rétracter [retrakte] *vt*, **se rétracter** *vpr* to retract. ● **rétractation** *nf* (*désaveu*) retraction.

retrait [r(ə)trɛ] *nm* withdrawal; (*de bagages, billets*) collection; (*de mer*) ebb(ing); **en r.** (*maison etc*) set back; **ligne en r.** indented line; **commencer un paragraphe en r.** to indent a paragraph; **rester en r.** to stay in the background.

retraite [r(ə)trɛt] *nf* **1** (*d'employé*) retirement; (*pension*) (retirement) pension; (*refuge*) retreat, refuge; **r. anticipée** early retirement; **prendre sa r.** to retire; **à la r.** retired; **mettre qn à la r.** to pension s.o. off. **2** (*d'une armée*) retreat; **r. aux flambeaux** torchlight procession *ou* Br tattoo; **battre en r.** *Mil & Fig* to beat a retreat. ● **retraité, -ée** *a* retired ■ *nmf* senior citizen, *Br* (old age) pensioner.

retraitement [r(ə)trɛtmɑ̃] *nm* reprocessing; **usine de r.** (*des déchets nucléaires*) (*nuclear*) reprocessing plant.

retrancher [r(ə)trɑ̃ʃe] **1** *vt* (*passage etc*) to cut (**de** from); (*argent, quantité*) to deduct (**de** from). **2 se retrancher** *vpr* (*soldat, gangster etc*) to entrench oneself; **se r. dans/derrière** *Fig* to take refuge in/behind. ● **retranchement** *nm* **pousser qn dans ses derniers retranchements** to drive s.o. to the wall *ou* into a corner.

retransmettre* [r(ə)trɑ̃smɛtr] *vt* to broadcast. ● **retransmission** *nf* broadcast.

rétrécir [retresir] *vt* to narrow; (*vêtement*) to take in ■ *vi* (*au lavage*) to shrink ■ **se rétrécir** *vpr* (*rue etc*) to narrow. ● **rétréci, -ie** *a* (*esprit, rue*) narrow.

rétribuer [retribɥe] *vt* to pay, remunerate; (*travail*) to pay for. ● **rétribution** *nf* payment, remuneration.

rétro [retro] *a inv* (*personne, idée etc*) old-fashioned.

rétro- [retro] *préf* retro-.

rétroactif, -ive [retrɔaktif, -iv] *a* (*mesure etc*) retroactive; **augmentation avec effet r.** retroactive (pay) increase.

rétrograde [retrɔgrad] *a* retrograde. ● **rétrograder** *vi* (*reculer*) to move back; (*civilisation etc*) to go backwards; (*en

voiture) to change down ■ *vt* (*fonctionnaire, officier*) to demote.

rétroprojecteur [retrɔprɔʒɛktœr] *nm* overhead projector.

rétrospectif, -ive [retrɔspɛktif, -iv] *a* (*sentiment etc*) retrospective ■ *nf* **rétrospective** (*de films, tableaux*) retrospective. ● **rétrospectivement** *adv* in retrospect.

retrousser [r(ə)truse] *vt* (*manches*) to roll up; (*jupe etc*) to hitch up, tuck up ● **retroussé, -ée** *a* (*nez*) turned-up, snub.

retrouver [r(ə)truve] *vt* to find (again); (*rejoindre*) to meet (again); (*forces, santé*) to get back, regain; (*se rappeler*) to recall; (*découvrir*) to rediscover ■ **se retrouver** *vpr* (*chose*) to be found (again); (*se trouver*) to find oneself (back); (*se rencontrer*) to meet (again); **s'y r.** (*s'orienter*) to find one's way *ou* bearings. ● **retrouvailles** *nfpl* reunion.

rétroviseur [retrɔvizœr] *nm* (*de véhicule*) (rear-view) mirror.

réunion [reynjɔ̃] *nf* (*séance*) meeting; (*d'objets*) collection, gathering; (*d'éléments divers*) combination; (*jonction*) joining.

Réunion [reynjɔ̃] *nf* **la R.** Réunion.

réunir [reynir] *vt* (*objets*) to collect, gather; (*convoquer*) to call together, assemble; (*relier*) to join; (*rapprocher*) to bring together; (*qualités, etc*) to combine. ● **réuni, -ie** *a* **amis/etc réunis** friends/etc (all) together; **éléments réunis** combined elements.

réussir [reysir] *vi* to succeed, be successful (**à faire** in doing); (*à un examen*) to pass; (*plante*) to thrive; **r. à qn** to work out well for s.o.; (*aliment, climat*) to agree with s.o.; **r. à un examen** to pass an exam(ination) ■ *vt* to make a success of. ● **réussi, -ie** *a* successful. ● **réussite** *nf* **1** success. **2 faire des réussites** *Cartes* to play patience.

revaloir [r(ə)valwar] *vt* **je vous le revaudrai** (*en bien ou en mal*) I'll pay you back.

revaloriser [r(ə)valɔrize] *vt* (*monnaie*) to revalue; (*salaires*) to raise. ● **revalorisation** *nf* revaluation; (*de salaires*) raising.

revanche [r(ə)vɑ̃ʃ] *nf* revenge; (*d'un match*) return game; **en r.** on the other hand.

rêve [rɛv] *nm* dream; **faire un r.** to have a dream; **maison/voiture/etc de r.** dream house/car/etc. ● **rêvasser** *vi* to daydream.

revêche [rəvɛʃ] *a* bad-tempered, surly.

réveil [revɛj] *nm* waking (up); *Fig* awakening; (*pendule*) alarm (clock); **à son r.** when he wakes (up) *ou* woke (up).

réveiller [reveje] *vt* (*personne*) to wake (up); (*sentiment, souvenir*) *Fig* to revive, awaken ■ **se réveiller** *vpr* to wake (up); *Fig* to revive, awaken. ● **réveillé, -ée** *a* awake. ● **réveille-matin** *nm inv* alarm (clock).

réveillon [revɛjɔ̃] *nm* (*repas*) midnight supper (*on Christmas Eve or New Year's Eve*). ● **réveillonner** *vi* to take part in a réveillon.

révéler [revele] *vt* to reveal (**que** that) ■ **se révéler** *vpr* to be revealed; **se r. facile/etc** to turn out to be easy/etc. ● **révélateur, -trice** *a* revealing; **r. de** indicative of. ● **révélation** nf revelation.

revenant [rəv(ə)nɑ̃] nm ghost; **voilà un r.!** Fam look who's here!, hello, stranger!

revendiquer [r(ə)vɑ̃dike] vt to claim; (exiger) to demand. ● **revendicatif, -ive** a mouvement/etc **r.** protest movement/etc. ● **revendication** nf claim; (exigence) demand; (action) claiming; demanding.

revendre [r(ə)vɑ̃dr] vt to resell; **avoir (de) qch à r.** Fig to have sth to spare. ● **revendeur, -euse** nmf retailer; (d'occasion) secondhand dealer; **r. (de drogue)** drug pusher; **r. de billets** Br ticket tout, Am ticket scalper. ● **revente** nf resale.

revenir* [rəv(ə)nir] vi (aux être) to come back, return; (mot) to come ou crop up; (date) to come round again; **r. à cents francs/etc** to come to ou cost a hundred francs/etc; **le dîner nous est revenu à cent francs** the dinner cost us a hundred francs; **r. cher** to work out expensive, cost a lot; **r. à** (activité, sujet) to go back to, return to; (se résumer à) to boil down to; **r. à qn** (forces, mémoire) to come back to s.o., return to s.o.; (honneur) to fall to s.o.; **r. à soi** to come round ou to; **r. de** (surprise) to get over; **r. sur** (décision, promesse) to go back on; (passé, question) to go back over; **r. sur ses pas** to retrace one's steps; **faire r.** (aliment) to brown; **sa tête ne me revient pas** Fam I don't like the look of him; **je n'en reviens pas!** Fam I can't get over it!; **elle revient de loin** Fig she's back in the running (after almost having been at death's door etc).

revenu [rəv(ə)ny] nm income (de from); (d'un État) revenue (de from); **déclaration de revenus** tax return.

rêver [reve] vi to dream (de of, de faire of doing) **‖** vt to dream (que that); (désirer) to dream of. ● **rêvé, -ée** a ideal.

réverbération [reverberasjɔ̃] nf (de lumière) reflection; (de son) reverberation.

réverbère [reverber] nm street lamp.

reverdir [rəverdir] vi to turn green (again).

révérence [reverɑ̃s] nf reverence; (salut d'homme) bow; (salut de femme) curts(e)y; **faire une r.** (homme) to bow; (femme) to curts(e)y. ● **révérer** vt to revere.

révérend, -ende [reverɑ̃, -ɑ̃d] a & nm Rel reverend.

rêverie [revri] nf daydream; (activité) daydreaming.

revers [r(ə)ver] nm (de veste) lapel; (de pantalon) Br turnup, Am cuff; (d'étoffe) wrong side; (de pièce d'argent) reverse; Tennis backhand; (coup du sort) setback; **d'un r. de la main** with the back of one's hand; **le r. de la médaille** Fig the other side of the coin.

reverser [rəverse] vt (café, vin etc) to pour more; (argent) Fig to pay back (**sur un compte** into an account).

réversible [reversibl] a reversible.

revêtir* [r(ə)vetir] vt to cover (de with); (habit) to put on; (route) to surface; (caractère, forme) to assume; **r. qn** (habiller) to dress s.o. (de in); **r. un document de** (signature) to provide a document with. ● **revêtement** [-vɛtmɑ̃] nm (surface) covering; (de route) surface.

rêveur, -euse [revœr, -øz] a dreamy **‖** nmf dreamer.

revient [rəvjɛ̃] nm **prix de r.** Br cost price, Am wholesale price.

revigorer [r(ə)vigɔre] vt (personne) to revive.

revirement [r(ə)virmɑ̃] nm (changement) Br about-turn, Am about-face; (de situation, d'opinion, de politique) reversal.

réviser [revize] vt (leçon) to revise; (machine, voiture) to service, overhaul; (jugement, règlement etc) to review. ● **révision** nf (de leçon) revision; (de machine etc) service, overhaul; (de jugement etc) review.

revisser [rəvise] vt (bouchon etc) to screw on.

revivre* [r(ə)vivr] vi to live again; **faire r.** to revive **‖** vt (incident etc) to relive.

révocation [revɔkasjɔ̃] nf **1** (de fonctionnaire) dismissal. **2** (de contrat etc) revocation.

revoici [r(ə)vwasi] prép **me r.** here I am again.

revoilà [r(ə)vwala] prép **la r.** there she is again.

revoir* [r(ə)vwar] vt to see (again); (texte, leçon) to revise; **au r.** goodbye.

révolte [revɔlt] nf rebellion, revolt. ● **révolter** **1** vt to sicken, revolt. **2 se révolter** vpr to rebel, revolt (**contre** against). ● **révoltant, -ante** a (honteux) revolting. ● **révolté, -ée** nmf rebel.

révolu, -ue [revɔly] a (époque) past; **avoir trente ans révolus** to be over thirty (years of age).

révolution [revɔlysjɔ̃] nf (changement, rotation) revolution. ● **révolutionnaire** a & nmf revolutionary. ● **révolutionner** vt (transformer) to revolutionize.

revolver [revɔlver] nm gun, revolver.

révoquer [revɔke] vt **1** (fonctionnaire) to dismiss. **2** (contrat etc) to revoke.

revue [r(ə)vy] nf **1** (magazine) magazine; (spécialisée) journal. **2** (de music-hall) variety show. **3** Mil review; **passer en r.** to review.

révulser [revylse] vt to repulse, disgust. ● **révulsé, -ée** a (visage) contorted; (yeux) with the whites showing.

rez-de-chaussée [red(ə)ʃose] nm inv Br ground floor, Am first floor.

rhabiller (se) [sərabije] vpr to get dressed again.

rhapsodie [rapsɔdi] nf rhapsody.

rhésus [rezys] nm **r. positif/négatif** rhesus positive/negative.

rhétorique [retɔrik] nf rhetoric.

Rhin [rɛ̃] nm **le R.** the Rhine.

rhinocéros 270

rhinocéros [rinɔserɔs] *nm* rhinoceros.
rhododendron [rɔdɔdɛ̃drɔ̃] *nm* rhododendron.
Rhône [ron] *nm* le R. the Rhone.
rhubarbe [rybarb] *nf* rhubarb.
rhum [rɔm] *nm* rum.
rhumatisme [rymatism] *nm* (*maladie*) rheumatism; **avoir des rhumatismes** to have rheumatism. ● **rhumatisant, -ante** *a* & *nmf* rheumatic. ● **rhumatismal, -e, -aux** *a* (*douleur*) rheumatic.
rhume [rym] *nm* cold; **r. de cerveau** head cold; **r. des foins** hay fever.
ri [ri] *pp de* rire.
riant, -ante [rjɑ̃, -ɑ̃t] *p prés de* rire ▮ *a* cheerful, smiling.
ribambelle [ribɑ̃bɛl] *nf* **une r. d'enfants/etc** a mass *ou* swarm of children/etc.
ricaner [rikane] *vi* (*sarcastiquement*) Br to snigger, Am snicker; (*bêtement*) to giggle.
riche [riʃ] *a* rich; (*personne, pays*) rich, wealthy; **r. en** (*vitamines, minérai etc*) rich in ▮ *nmf* rich *ou* wealthy person; **les riches** the rich. ● **richement** *a* (*vêtu, illustré etc*) richly. ● **richesse** *nf* wealth; (*d'étoffe, de sol, de vocabulaire*) richness; **richesses** (*trésor*) riches; (*ressources*) wealth.
ricin [risɛ̃] *nm* **huile de r.** castor oil.
ricocher [rikɔʃe] *vi* to rebound, ricochet. ● **ricochet** *nm* rebound, ricochet; **par r.** Fig as an indirect result.
rictus [riktys] *nm* grin, grimace.
ride [rid] *nf* (*de visage*) wrinkle; (*sur l'eau*) ripple. ● **rider** *vt* (*visage*) to wrinkle; (*eau*) to ripple ▮ **se rider** *vpr* to wrinkle. ● **ridé, -ée** *a* wrinkled.
rideau, -x [rido] *nm* curtain; (*métallique, de magasin*) shutter; (*écran*) Fig screen (de of).
ridicule [ridikyl] *a* ridiculous, ludicrous ▮ *nm* (*moquerie*) ridicule; (*défaut*) absurdity; (*de situation etc*) ridiculousness; **tourner en r.** to ridicule. ● **ridiculiser** *vt* to ridicule ▮ **se ridiculiser** *vpr* to make a fool of oneself.
rien [rjɛ̃] *pron* nothing; **il ne sait r.** he knows nothing, he doesn't know anything; **r. du tout** nothing at all; **r. d'autre/de bon/etc** nothing else/good/etc; **r. de tel** nothing like it; **il n'y avait r. que des filles** there were only girls there; **de r.!** (*je vous en prie*) don't mention it!; **ça ne fait r.** it doesn't matter; **ce n'est r.** it's nothing; (*en réponse à 'merci'*) don't mention it!; **trois fois r.** (*chose insignifiante*) next to nothing; **avoir qch pour r.** (*à bas prix*) to get sth for next to nothing; **pour r. au monde** never in your life, never in a thousand years; **il n'en est r.** (*ce n'est pas vrai*) nothing of the kind; **je n'en ai r. à faire** Fam I couldn't care less; **comme si de r. n'était** as if nothing had happened.
▮ *nm* (mere) nothing, trifle; **un r.** a hint *ou* touch of; **en un r. de temps** (*vite*) in no time; **un r. trop petit/etc** just a bit too small/etc; **pleurer/etc pour un r.** to cry/etc for the slightest thing.
rieur, -euse [rijœr, -øz] *a* cheerful.

rigide [riʒid] *a* rigid; (*carton, muscle*) stiff; (*personne*) Fig inflexible; (*éducation*) strict. ● **rigidité** *nf* rigidity; (*de carton etc*) stiffness; (*de personne*) inflexibility; (*d'éducation*) strictness.
rigole [rigɔl] *nf* (*conduit*) channel; (*filet d'eau*) rivulet.
rigoler [rigɔle] *vi* Fam to laugh; (*s'amuser*) to have fun *ou* a laugh; (*plaisanter*) to joke (avec about). ● **rigolade** *nf* Fam fun; (*chose ridicule*) joke, farce; **prendre qch à la r.** to make a joke out of sth. ● **rigolo, -ote** *a* Fam funny ▮ *nmf* Fam joker.
rigueur [rigœr] *nf* rigour; (*de climat etc*) harshness; (*de personne etc*) strictness; (*précision*) precision; **être de r.** to be the rule; **à la r.** if absolutely necessary, Br at a pinch, Am in a pinch; **politique de r.** (*de gouvernement*) austerity policies *ou* programme; **tenir r. à qn de qch** Fig to hold sth against s.o. ● **rigoureux, -euse** *a* rigorous; (*climat, punition*) harsh; (*personne, morale, sens*) strict.
rillettes [rijɛt] *nfpl* potted minced pork.
rime [rim] *nf* rhyme. ● **rimer** *vi* to rhyme (avec with); **ça ne rime à rien** it makes no sense.
rimmel® [rimɛl] *nm* mascara.
rincer [rɛ̃se] *vt* to rinse; (*verre*) to rinse (out). ● **rinçage** *nm* rinsing; (*opération*) rinse.
ring [riŋ] *nm* (boxing) ring.
ringard, -arde [rɛ̃gar, -ard] *a* (*démodé*) Fam old-fashioned, unfashionable, fuddy-duddy.
ripaille [ripaj] *nf* Fam feast.
riposte [ripɔst] *nf* (*réponse*) retort; (*attaque*) counter(attack). ● **riposter** *vi* to retort; **r. à** (*attaque*) to counter; (*insulte*) to reply to ▮ *vt* **r. que** to retort that.
riquiqui [rikiki] *a inv* (*trop petit*) Fam tiny.
rire* [rir] *vi* to laugh (de at); (*s'amuser*) to have a good time; (*plaisanter*) to joke; **r. aux éclats** to laugh out loud, roar with laughter; **faire qch pour r.** to do sth for a joke *ou* laugh; **se r. de qch** (*difficulté etc*) to laugh sth off ▮ *nm* laugh; **rires** laughter; **le r.** (*activité*) laughter; **le fou r.** the giggles.
ris [ri] *nm* **r. de veau** Culin (calf) sweetbread.
risée [rize] *nf* mockery; **être la r. de** to be the laughing stock of.
risible [rizibl] *a* laughable.
risque [risk] *nm* risk; **au r. de faire qch** at the risk of doing sth; **les risques du métier** occupational hazards; **à vos risques et périls** at your own risk; **assurance tous risques** comprehensive *ou* all risks insurance.
risquer [riske] *vt* to risk; (*question, regard*) to venture, hazard; **r. de faire qch** to stand a good chance of doing sth; **se r. à faire qch** to dare to do sth; **se r. dans** to venture into. ● **risqué, -ée** *a* risky; (*plaisanterie*) daring, risqué.
ristourne [risturn] *nf* discount.
rite [rit] *nm* rite; (*habitude*) Fig ritual. ● **rituel, -elle** *a* & *nm* ritual.
rivage [rivaʒ] *nm* shore.

rival, -e, -aux [rival, -o] *a & nmf* rival. ●**rivaliser** *vi* to compete (**avec** with, **de** in). ●**rivalité** *nf* rivalry.

rive [riv] *nf* (*de fleuve*) bank; (*de lac*) shore.

rivé, -ée [rive] *a* **clou r.** clinched nail; **r. à** (*chaise etc*) *Fig* riveted to; **r. sur** qn/qch (*yeux, regard*) *Fig* riveted on s.o./sth. ●**rivet** *nm* (*tige*) rivet. ●**riveter** *vt* to rivet (together).

riverain, -aine [rivrɛ̃, -ɛn] *a* riverside; lakeside ▮ *nmf* riverside resident; (*de lac*) lakeside resident; (*de rue*) resident.

rivière [rivjɛr] *nf* river.

rixe [riks] *nf* brawl, scuffle.

riz [ri] *nm* rice; **r. blanc/complet** white/brown rice; **r. au lait** rice pudding. ●**rizière** *nf* paddy (field), ricefield.

RMI [ɛrɛmi] *nm abrév* (*Revenu minimum d'insertion*) = *Br* income support, = *Am* welfare.

RN *abrév* = **route nationale.**

robe [rɔb] *nf* (*de femme*) dress; (*d'ecclésiastique, de juge*) robe; (*de professeur*) gown; (*pelage*) coat; **r. de soirée** *ou* **du soir** evening dress *ou* gown; **r. de grossesse/de mariée** maternity/wedding dress; **r. de chambre** *Br* dressing gown, *Am* bathrobe; **r. chasuble** pinafore (dress); **pomme de terre en r. des champs** *Br* jacket potato, baked potato.

robinet [rɔbinɛ] *nm Br* tap, *Am* faucet; **eau du r.** tap water.

robot [rɔbo] *nm* robot; **r. ménager** food processor, *Br* liquidizer. ●**robotique** *nf* robotics.

robuste [rɔbyst] *a* sturdy, robust. ●**robustesse** *nf* robustness.

roc [rɔk] *nm* rock.

rocade [rɔkad] *nf* (*route*) bypass.

rocaille [rɔkɑj] *nf* (*terrain*) rocky ground; (*de jardin*) rockery. ●**rocailleux, -euse** *a* rocky, stony; (*voix*) harsh.

rocambolesque [rɔkɑ̃bɔlɛsk] *a* (*aventure etc*) fantastic.

roche [rɔʃ] *nf ou* **rocher** [rɔʃe] *nm* (*bloc, substance*) rock. ●**rocheux, -euse** *a* rocky.

rock [rɔk] *nm* (*musique*) rock ▮ *a inv* **chanteur/opéra/etc r.** rock singer/opera/etc. ●**rockeur, -euse** *nmf* rocker, rock fan.

rodéo [rɔdeo] *nm* (*aux États-Unis*) rodeo.

roder [rɔde] *vt* (*moteur, voiture*) *Br* to run in, *Am* break in; **être rodé** (*personne*) *Fig* to have *Br* got *ou Am* gotten the hang of things. ●**rodage** *nm Br* running in, *Am* breaking in.

rôder [rode] *vi* to roam (around *ou* about); (*suspect*) to prowl (around *ou* about). ●**rôdeur, -euse** *nmf* prowler.

rogne [rɔɲ] *nf Fam* anger, bad temper; **être en r.** to be in a temper; **se mettre en r.** to blow one's top, lose one's temper.

rogner [rɔɲe] *vt* to trim, clip; (*réduire*) to cut ▮ *vi* **r. sur** (*réduire*) to cut down on. ●**rognures** *nfpl* clippings, trimmings.

rognon [rɔɲɔ̃] *nm Culin* kidney.

roi [rwa] *nm* king; **fête** *ou* **jour des Rois**

Twelfth Night; **galette des Rois** Twelfth Night cake.

roitelet [rwatlɛ] *nm* (*oiseau*) wren.

rôle [rol] *nm* role, part; (*d'un père etc*) job; **à tour de r.** in turn.

roller [rɔlœr] *nm* roller skate.

romain, -aine [rɔmɛ̃, -ɛn] **1** *a* Roman ▮ *nmf* **R., Romaine** Roman. **2** *nf* (*laitue*) *Br* cos (lettuce), *Am* romaine.

roman¹ [rɔmɑ̃] *nm* novel; (*histoire*) *Fig* story; **r. d'aventures/d'amour** adventure/love story; **r.-fleuve** saga; **r.-photo** photo romance. ●**romancé, -ée** *a* (*histoire*) fictional. ●**romancier, -ière** *nmf* novelist.

roman², -ane [rɔmɑ̃, -an] *a* (*langue*) Romance; *Archit* Romanesque.

romanesque [rɔmanɛsk] *a* romantic; (*incroyable*) fantastic.

romanichel, -elle [rɔmaniʃɛl] *nmf* gipsy.

romantique [rɔmɑ̃tik] *a* romantic. ●**romantisme** *nm* romanticism.

romarin [rɔmarɛ̃] *nm* (*arbuste, condiment*) rosemary.

rompre* [rɔ̃pr] *vt* to break; (*pourparlers, relations*) to break off; (*digue*) to burst ▮ *vi* to break (*Fig* **avec** with); (*digue*) to burst; (*fiancés*) to break it off ▮ **se rompre** *vpr* (*corde etc*) to break; (*digue*) to burst. ●**rompu, -ue** *a* **1** (*fatigué*) exhausted. **2 r. à** (*expérimenté*) *Litt* experienced in.

romsteck [rɔmstɛk] *nm* rump steak.

ronces [rɔ̃s] *nfpl* (*branches*) brambles.

ronchonner [rɔ̃ʃɔne] *vi Fam* to grouse, grumble.

rond, ronde¹ [rɔ̃, rɔ̃d] *a* round; (*gras*) plump; (*honnête*) straight; (*ivre*) *Fam* tight; **chiffre r.** whole number; **r. comme une queue de pelle** *Fam* blind drunk; **ouvrir des yeux ronds** to be wide-eyed with astonishment, look astonished.

▮ *adv* **tourner r.** (*machine etc*) to run smoothly; **dix francs tout r.** ten francs exactly.

▮ *nm* (*cercle*) circle, ring; (*objet*) ring; (*tranche*) slice; **ronds** (*argent*) *Fam* money; **r. de serviette** napkin ring; **en r.** (*s'asseoir etc*) in a ring *ou* circle; **tourner en r.** (*toupie etc*) & *Fig* to go round and round. ●**rondelet, -ette** *a* chubby; (*somme*) *Fig* tidy. ●**rondement** *adv* (*efficacement*) briskly; (*franchement*) straight. ●**rond-de-cuir** *nm* (*pl* **ronds-de-cuir**) *Péj* pen pusher. ●**rond-point** *nm* (*pl* **ronds-points**) *Aut Br* roundabout, *Am* traffic circle.

ronde² [rɔ̃d] *nf* (*de soldat*) round; (*de policier*) beat, round; (*danse*) round (dance); (*note de musique*) *Br* semibreve, *Am* whole note; **à la r.** around; (*boire*) in turn; **faire sa r.** (*gardien etc*) to do one's rounds.

rondelle [rɔ̃dɛl] *nf* (*tranche*) slice; *Tech* washer.

rondeur [rɔ̃dœr] *nf* roundness; (*du corps*) plumpness, **rondeurs** (*de femme*) curves; (*embonpoint*) plumpness.

rondin [rɔ̃dɛ̃] *nm* log.

ronéotyper [rɔneɔtipe] *vt* to duplicate, roneo.

ronflant, -ante [rɔ̃flɑ̃, -ɑ̃t] *a* (*langage etc*) *Péj* high-flown; (*feu*) roaring.

ronfler [rɔ̃fle] *vi* (*personne*) to snore; (*moteur*) to hum. ● **ronflement** *nm* snore; (*de moteur*) hum; **ronflements** snoring; (*de moteur*) humming.

ronger [rɔ̃ʒe] *vt* to gnaw (at); (*ver, mer, rouille*) to eat into (*sth*); **r. qn** (*maladie, chagrin*) to consume s.o.; **r. son frein** (*personne*) *Fig* to champ at the bit; **se r. les ongles** to bite one's nails; **se r. les sangs** (*s'inquiéter*) *Fam* to worry oneself sick. ● **rongeur** *nm* (*animal*) rodent.

ronronnement [rɔ̃rɔnmɑ̃] *nm* (*Fam* **ronron**) purr(ing). ● **ronronner** *vi* to purr.

roquefort [rɔkfɔr] *nm* Roquefort (cheese).

roquette [rɔkɛt] *nf Mil* rocket.

rosace [rozas] *nf* (*figure*) rosette; (*d'église*) rose window.

rosbif [rɔsbif] *nm* **du r.** (*rôti*) roast beef; (*à rôtir*) roasting beef; **un r.** a joint of roast *ou* roasting beef.

rose [roz] **1** *nf* (*fleur*) rose; **envoyer qn sur les roses** *Fam* to send s.o. packing; **découvrir le pot aux roses** *Fam* to find out what's been going on. **2** *a* (*couleur*) pink; (*situation, teint*) rosy **∎** *nm* pink; **vieux r.** soft pink; **r. bonbon** bright pink. ● **rosé, -ée** *a* pinkish **∎** *a* & *nm* (*vin*) rosé. ● **rosier** *nm* rose bush. ● **roseraie** *nf* rose garden.

roseau, -x [rozo] *nm* (*plante*) reed.

rosée [roze] *nf* dew.

rosette [rozɛt] *nf* (*d'un officier*) rosette; (*nœud*) bow.

rosse [rɔs] *a* & *nf Fam* nasty (person).

rosser [rɔse] *vt* to thrash. ● **rossée** *nf Fam* thrashing.

rossignol [rɔsiɲɔl] *nm* **1** (*oiseau*) nightingale. **2** (*crochet*) picklock.

rot [ro] *nm Fam* burp, belch. ● **roter** *vi Fam* to burp, belch.

rotation [rɔtasjɔ̃] *nf* rotation; (*de stock*) turnover. ● **rotatif, -ive** *a* rotary **∎** *nf* rotary press.

rotin [rɔtɛ̃] *nm* cane, rattan.

rôtir [rotir] *vti*, **se rôtir** *vpr* to roast; **faire r.** to roast; **se r. au soleil** *Fam* to roast in the sun. ● **rôti** *nm* **du r.** roasting meat; (*cuit*) roast meat; **un r.** a joint; **r. de porc/de bœuf** (joint of) roast pork/beef. ● **rôtissoire** *nf* (roasting) spit.

rotule [rɔtyl] *nf* kneecap; **être sur les rotules** *Fam* to be exhausted *ou Br* dead beat.

roturier, -ière [rɔtyrje, -jɛr] *nmf* commoner.

rouage [rwaʒ] *nm* (*de montre etc*) (working) part; (*d'organisation etc*) *Fig* cog.

roublard, -arde [rublar, -ard] *a Fam* wily, foxy.

rouble [rubl] *nm* (*monnaie*) r(o)uble.

roucouler [rukule] *vi* (*oiseau, Fig amoureux*) to coo.

roue [ru] *nf* wheel; **r.** (**dentée**) cog(wheel); **faire la r.** (*paon*) to spread its tail; (*se pavaner*) *Fig* to strut; **être en r. libre** *Aut* to free-

wheel; **partir sur les chapeaux de r.** *Fam* to drive off at high speed; **les deux roues** two-wheeled vehicles.

roué, -ée [rwe] *a* & *nmf* sly *ou* calculating (person).

rouer [rwe] *vt* **r. qn de coups** to beat s.o. black and blue.

rouet [rwɛ] *nm* spinning wheel.

rouge [ruʒ] *a* red; (*fer*) red-hot **∎** *nm* (*couleur*) red; (*vin*) *Fam* red wine; **r.** (**à lèvres**) lipstick; **r.** (**à joues**) rouge; **le feu est au r.** the (traffic) lights are red **∎** *nmf* (*personne*) *Pol* Red. ● **rougeâtre** *a* reddish. ● **rougeaud, -aude** *a* red-faced. ● **rouge-gorge** *nm* (*pl* **rouges-gorges**) robin.

rougeoyer [ruʒwaje] *vi* to glow (red).

rougeur [ruʒœr] *nf* redness; (*due à la honte*) blush(ing); **rougeurs** *Méd* rash, red spots *ou* blotches.

rougir [ruʒir] *vti* to redden, turn red **∎** *vi* (*de honte*) to blush (**de** with); (*de colère, de joie*) to flush (**de** with), go red.

rougeole [ruʒɔl] *nf* measles.

rouget [ruʒɛ] *nm* (*poisson*) mullet.

rouille [ruj] *nf* rust **∎** *a inv* (*couleur*) rust-(-coloured). ● **rouiller** *vi* to rust **∎** **se rouiller** *vpr* to rust; (*esprit, sportif etc*) *Fig* to get rusty. ● **rouillé, -ée** *a* rusty.

roulade [rulad] *nf* **1** *Sport* **r. avant/arrière** forward/backward roll; **faire r.** to do a roll. **2** *Culin* **r. de poisson/**etc rolled fish/etc.

rouleau, -x [rulo] *nm* (*outil, vague*) roller; (*de papier, pellicule etc*) roll; **r. à pâtisserie** rolling pin; **r. compresseur** steamroller.

roulement [rulmɑ̃] *nm* (*bruit*) rumbling, rumble; (*de tambour, de tonnerre, d'yeux*) roll; (*ordre*) rotation; **par r.** in rotation; **r. à billes** *Tech* ball bearing.

rouler [rule] *vt* to roll; (*brouette*) to push, wheel; (*crêpe, ficelle, manches etc*) to roll up; **r. qn** (*duper*) *Fam* to cheat s.o. **∎** *vi* to roll; (*train, voiture*) to go, travel; (*conducteur*) to drive; **r. sur** (*conversation*) to turn on; **r. sur l'or** (*être riche*) to be rolling in it; **ça roule!** *Fam* everything's fine! **∎** **se rouler** *vpr* to roll; **se r. dans** (*couverture etc*) to roll oneself (up) in. ● **roulant, -ante** *a* (*escalier, trottoir*) moving; (*meuble*) on wheels; **chaise roulante** wheelchair; **un feu r. de questions** *Fig* a barrage of questions. ● **roulé** *nm* (*gâteau*) Swiss roll.

roulette [rulɛt] *nf* (*de meuble*) castor; (*de dentiste*) drill; (*jeu*) roulette.

roulis [ruli] *nm* (*de navire*) roll(ing).

roulotte [rulɔt] *nf* (*de gitan*) caravan.

Roumanie [rumani] *nf* Romania. ● **roumain, -aine** *a* Romanian **∎** *nmf* **R., Roumaine** Romanian **∎** *nm* (*langue*) Romanian.

round [rawnd, rund] *nm Boxe* round.

roupiller [rupije] *vi Fam* to sleep, *Br* kip.

rouquin, -ine [rukɛ̃, -in] *a Fam* red-haired **∎** *nmf Fam* redhead.

rouspéter [ruspete] *vi Fam* to complain, grumble. ● **rouspéteur, -euse** *nmf Fam* grumbler.

rousse [rus] *voir* **roux.**

rousseur [rusœr] *nf (de chevelure)* redness; **tache de r.** freckle. ●**roussir** *vt (brûler)* to scorch, singe ▮ *vi (feuilles)* to turn brown; **faire r.** *Culin* to brown. ●**roussi** *nm* **ça sent le r.** there's a a slight smell of something burning.

rouste [rust] *nf Fam* severe thrashing, good hiding.

routard, -arde [rutar, -ard] *nmf* traveller on foot, backpacker.

route [rut] *nf* road **(de** to); *(itinéraire)* way, route; *(aérienne, maritime)* route; *(chemin) Fig* path, way; **r. nationale** *Br* main *ou* trunk *ou* A road, *Am* (state) highway; **r. départementale** secondary road, *Br* B road; **grand-r., grande r.** main road; **Code de la r.** *Br* Highway Code, *Am* traffic regulations; **en r.** on the way, en route; **en r.!** let's go!; **par la r.** by road; **sur la bonne r.** *Fig* on the right track; **faire fausse r.** *Fig* to be on the wrong track; **mettre en r.** *(voiture etc)* to start (up); **se mettre en r.** to set out **(pour** for); **une heure de r.** *Aut* an hour's drive; **faire r. vers Paris/etc** to head for Paris/etc; **faire de la r.** to do a lot of driving; **bonne r.!** have a good trip!; **leurs routes se sont croisées** *Fig* their paths crossed.

routier, -ière [rutje, -jɛr] *a* **carte/sécurité/etc routière** road map/safety/etc; **réseau r.** road network ▮ *nm (camionneur)* (long distance) *Br* lorry *ou Am* truck driver; *(restaurant) Br* transport café, *Am* truck stop.

routine [rutin] *nf* routine; **contrôle de r.** routine check. ●**routinier, -ière** *a (personne)* addicted to routine; **travail/etc r.** routine work/etc.

rouvrir* [ruvrir] *vti,* **se rouvrir** *vpr* to reopen.

roux, rousse [ru, rus] *a (cheveux)* red, ginger; *(personne)* red-haired ▮ *nmf* redhead.

royal, -e, -aux [rwajal, -o] *a (famille, palais etc)* royal; *(cadeau, festin etc)* fit for a king; *(salaire)* princely. ●**royalement** *adv (traiter)* royally; **je m'en fiche r.** *Fam* I couldn't care less (about it). ●**royaliste** *a* & *nmf* royalist.

royaume [rwajom] *nm* kingdom. ●**Royaume-Uni** *nm* United Kingdom.

royauté [rwajote] *nf (monarchie)* monarchy.

ruade [rɥad] *nf (d'âne etc)* kick.

ruban [rybã] *nm* ribbon; *(de chapeau)* band; **r. adhésif** sticky *ou* adhesive tape.

rubéole [rybeɔl] *nf* German measles, rubella.

rubis [rybi] *nm (pierre)* ruby; *(de montre)* jewel.

rubrique [rybrik] *nf (article de journal)* column; *(catégorie, titre)* heading.

ruche [ryʃ] *nf* (bee)hive.

rude [ryd] *a (pénible)* tough; *(hiver, voix)* harsh; *(grossier)* crude; *(rêche)* rough; *(remarquable) Fam* tremendous. ●**rudement** *adv (parler, traiter)* harshly; *(frapper, tomber)* hard; *(très) Fam* awfully. ●**rudesse**

nf harshness.

rudiments [rydimã] *nmpl* rudiments. ●**rudimentaire** *a* rudimentary.

rudoyer [rydwaje] *vt* to treat harshly.

rue [ry] *nf* street; **être à la r.** *(sans domicile)* to be on the streets. ●**ruelle** *nf* alley(way).

ruer [rɥe] **1** *vi (cheval)* to kick (out). **2 se ruer** *vpr (foncer)* to rush, fling oneself **(sur** at). ●**ruée** *nf* rush; **la r. vers l'or** the gold rush.

rugby [rygbi] *nm* rugby. ●**rugbyman,** *pl* **-men** [rygbiman, -mɛn] *nm* rugby player.

rugir [ryʒir] *vi* to roar. ●**rugissement** *nm* roar.

rugueux, -euse [rygø, -øz] *a* rough. ●**rugosité** *nf* roughness; **rugosités** *(aspérités)* rough spots, roughness.

ruine [rɥin] *nf (décombres, destruction, faillite etc)* ruin; **en r.** *(bâtiment)* in ruins; **tomber en r.** *(bâtiment)* to become a ruin, crumble; *(mur)* to crumble. ●**ruiner** *vt (personne, santé, pays etc)* to ruin ▮ **se ruiner** *vpr (en dépensant)* to be(come) ruined, ruin oneself. ●**ruineux, -euse** *a (goûts, projet)* ruinously expensive; *(dépense)* ruinous.

ruisseau, -x [rɥiso] *nm* stream; *(caniveau)* gutter. ●**ruisseler** *vi* to stream (de with).

rumeur [rymœr] *nf (protestation)* clamour; *(murmure)* murmur; *(nouvelle)* rumour.

ruminer [rymine] *vi (vache)* to chew the cud ▮ *vt (méditer) Fig* to ponder on, ruminate over.

rumsteak [rɔmstɛk] *nm* rump steak.

rupture [ryptyr] *nf* break(ing); *(de fiançailles, relations)* breaking off; *(de pourparlers)* breakdown (de in); *(brouille)* breakup, split; *(d'organe) Méd* rupture; **être en r. de stock** to be out of stock; **r. de contrat** breach of contract.

rural, -e, -aux [ryral, -o] *a (population etc)* rural; **vie/école/etc rurale** country life/school/etc; **exode r.** rural depopulation *ou* exodus. ●**ruraux** *nmpl* country people.

ruse [ryz] *nf (subterfuge)* trick; **la r.** *(habileté)* cunning; *(fourberie)* trickery. ●**rusé, -ée** *a* cunning, crafty ▮ *nmf* **c'est un r.** he's a cunning *ou* crafty one. ●**ruser** *vi* to resort to trickery.

Russie [rysi] *nf* Russia. ●**russe** *a* Russian ▮ *nmf* R. Russian ▮ *nm (langue)* Russian.

rustique [rystik] *a (meuble)* rustic.

rustre [rystr] *nm* lout, churl.

rut (en) [ãryt] *nm (animal) Br* on heat, *Am* in heat.

rutabaga [rytabaga] *nm (racine) Br* swede, *Am* rutabaga.

rutilant, -ante [rytilã, -ãt] *a* gleaming, glittering.

RV *abrév* = **rendez-vous.**

rythme [ritm] *nm* rhythm; *(de travail)* rate, tempo; *(de la vie)* pace; **au r. de trois par jour** at a *ou* the rate of three a day. ●**rythmé, -ée** *ou* **rythmique** *a* rhythmic(al).

S

S, s [ɛs] *nm* S, s.
s' [s] *voir* se, si.
sa [sa] *voir* son².
SA *abrév (société anonyme) Com Br* plc, *Am* Inc.
sabbat [saba] *nm* (Jewish) Sabbath.
sabbatique [sabatik] *a (année universitaire etc)* sabbatical; **prendre une année s.** to take a year's sabbatical.
sable [sabl] *nm* sand; **sables mouvants** quicksand(s). ●**sabler** *vt (route)* to sand; **s. le champagne** to celebrate with champagne. ●**sableux, -euse** *a (eau)* sandy.
sablier [sablije] *nm* hourglass; *Culin* egg timer. ●**sablière** *nf (carrière)* sandpit.
sablonneux, -euse [sablɔnø, -øz] *a (terrain)* sandy.
sablé¹ [sable] *nm* shortbread *Br* biscuit *ou Am* cookie. ●**sablé², -ée** *a* **pâte sablée** short-crust pastry.
saborder [sabɔrde] *vt (navire)* to scuttle; *(entreprise) Fig* to shut down, wind up.
sabot [sabo] *nm* **1** *(de cheval etc)* hoof. **2** *(chaussure)* clog. **3** *Aut* **s. (de frein)** (brake) shoe; **s. (de Denver)** (wheel) clamp.
saboter [sabɔte] *vt (machine, Fig projet etc)* to sabotage; *(bâcler)* to botch. ●**sabotage** *nm* sabotage; **un s., un acte de s.** an act of sabotage. ●**saboteur, -euse** *nmf* saboteur.
sabre [sabr] *nm* sabre, sword.
sabrer [sabre] *vt Fam (élève, candidat)* to give a thoroughly bad *Br* mark *ou Am* grade to; **se faire s. à un examen** to get a thoroughly bad *Br* mark *ou Am* grade in an exam.
sac [sak] *nm* **1** bag; *(grand et en toile)* sack; **s. (à main)** handbag; **s. à dos** rucksack; **s. de voyage** travelling bag; **prendre qn la main dans le s.** *Fig* to catch s.o. red-handed; **je les mets dans le même s.** *Fam* in my opinion they're as bad as each other *ou* they're all the same; **l'affaire est dans le s.!** *Fam* it's in the bag! **2 mettre à s.** *(ville) Mil* to sack.
saccade [sakad] *nf* jerk, jolt; **par saccades** in fits and starts, jerkily. ●**saccadé, -ée** *a (geste, style)* jerky.
saccager [sakaʒe] *vt (détruire)* to wreck; *(ville, région) Mil* to sack; *(bouleverser) Fig* to turn upside down.
saccharine [sakarin] *nf* saccharin.
sacerdoce [saserdɔs] *nm (fonction) Rel* priesthood; *Fig* vocation.
sachant, sache(s), sachent *etc* [saʃɑ̃, saʃ] *voir* savoir.
sachet [saʃɛ] *nm* (small) bag; *(de lavande etc)* sachet; **s. de thé** teabag.

sacoche [sakɔʃ] *nf* bag; *(de vélo, moto)* saddlebag; *(d'écolier)* satchel; **s. du facteur** *Br* postman's *ou Am* mailman's bag.
sacquer [sake] *vt Fam (renvoyer)* to sack; *(élève)* to give a thoroughly bad *Br* mark *ou Am* grade to; **je ne peux pas le s.** *Fam* I can't stand him.
sacre [sakr] *nm (de roi)* coronation; *(d'évêque)* consecration. ●**sacrer** *vt (roi)* to crown; *(évêque)* to consecrate.
sacré, -ée [sakre] *a (saint)* sacred; **un s. menteur/etc** *Fam* a damned liar/etc. ●**sacrement** *adv Fam (très)* damn(ed); *(beaucoup)* a hell of a lot.
sacrement [sakrəmɑ̃] *nm Rel* sacrament.
sacrifice [sakrifis] *nm* sacrifice. ●**sacrifier** *vt* to sacrifice (à to, pour for) **‖** *vi* **s. à** *(mode etc)* to pander to **‖ se sacrifier** *vpr* to sacrifice oneself (à to, pour for).
sacrilège [sakrilɛʒ] *nm* sacrilege **‖** *a* sacrilegious.
sacristie [sakristi] *nf* vestry. ●**sacristain** *nm* sexton.
sacro-saint, -sainte [sakrosɛ̃, -sɛ̃t] *a Iron* sacrosanct.
sadisme [sadism] *nm* sadism. ●**sadique** *a* sadistic **‖** *nmf* sadist.
safari [safari] *nm* safari; **faire un s.** to be *ou* go on safari; **un s.-photo** a photographic safari.
safran [safrɑ̃] *nm (condiment)* saffron.
sagace [sagas] *a* shrewd, sagacious. ●**sagacité** *nf* shrewdness.
sage [saʒ] *a* wise; *(enfant)* good, well-behaved; *(modéré)* moderate **‖** *nm* wise man, sage. ●**sagement** *adv* wisely; *(avec calme)* quietly. ●**sagesse** *nf (philosophie)* wisdom; *(calme)* good behaviour; *(modération)* moderation.
sage-femme [saʒfam] *nf (pl* sages-femmes*)* midwife.
Sagittaire [saʒitɛr] *nm* **le S.** *(signe)* Sagittarius.
Sahara [saara] *nm* **le S.** the Sahara (desert).
saigner [seɲe] *vti* to bleed; **s. du nez** to have a nosebleed; **saigné à blanc** *Fig* bled white; **se s. aux quatre veines pour qn** *Fig* to make major sacrifices for s.o. ●**saignant, -ante** [seɲɑ̃, -ɑ̃t] *a (viande)* rare, underdone. ●**saignée** *nf* **1** *Méd* bleeding, blood-letting; *(perte) Fig* heavy loss. **2 la s. du bras** *Anat* the bend of the arm. ●**saignement** *nm* bleeding; **s. de nez** nosebleed.
saillant, -ante [sajɑ̃, -ɑ̃t] *a* projecting, jutting out; *(trait etc) Fig* salient. ●**saillie** *nf* projection; **en s., faisant s.** projecting.

275   **sanatorium**

sain, saine [sɛ̃, sɛn] a healthy; (moralement)
sane; (jugement) sound; (nourriture) wholesome, healthy; **s. et sauf** safe and sound, unhurt. ●**sainement** adv (vivre) healthily; (raisonner) sanely.

saindoux [sɛ̃du] nm lard.

saint, sainte [sɛ̃, sɛ̃t] a holy; (personne)
saintly; **s. Jean** Saint John; **la Sainte Vierge**
the Blessed Virgin; **sainte nitouche** Fam Iron
little innocent ▮ nmf saint. ●**saint-bernard**
nm (chien) St Bernard. ●**Saint-Esprit** nm
Holy Spirit. ●**saint-frusquin** nm **tout le s.-
frusquin** Fam the whole kit and caboodle.
●**saint-honoré** nm Saint-Honoré (choux pastry ring filled with confectioner's sugar).
●**Saint-Siège** nm Holy See. ●**Saint-Sylvestre**
nf New Year's Eve.

sainteté [sɛ̃tte] nf holiness; (de personne)
saintliness; **Sa S.** (le pape) His Holiness.

saint-glinglin (à la) [alasɛ̃glɛ̃glɛ̃] adv **à la
s.-glinglin** Fam never in you life, never in a
month of Sundays.

sais [sɛ] voir **savoir**.

saisie [sezi] nf Jur seizure; **s. de données**
Ordinat data capture, keyboarding; **opérateur de s.** Ordinat keyboard operator.

saisir [sezir] **1** vt to grab (hold of), seize;
(occasion) to jump at, seize; (comprendre)
to understand, grasp; Jur to seize; (frapper)
Fig to strike; **se s. de** to grab (hold of),
seize. **2** vt (viande) to fry briskly. ●**saisi, -ie**
a **s. de** (joie, peur etc) overcome by; **s. par la
ressemblance/etc** struck by the likeness/etc.
●**saisissant, -ante** a (film etc) gripping; (contraste, ressemblance) striking. ●**saisissement**
nm (émotion) shock.

saison [sɛzɔ̃] nf season; **en/hors s.** in/out of
season; **en pleine** ou **haute s.** in (the) high
season; **en basse s.** in the low season; **la s.
des pluies** the rainy season. ●**saisonnier,
-ière** a seasonal.

sait [sɛ] voir **savoir**.

salade [salad] nf **1** (laitue) lettuce; **s. (verte)**
(green) salad; **s. de fruits/de tomates/etc**
fruit/tomato/etc salad; **s. niçoise** salade niçoise (lettuce, tomatoes, olives, anchovies,
eggs etc). **2** (désordre) Fam mess. ●**salades**
nfpl (mensonges) Fam stories, nonsense.
●**saladier** nm salad bowl.

salaire [salɛr] nm wage(s), salary.

salaison [salɛzɔ̃] nf Culin salting; **salaisons**
(denrées) salt(ed) meat ou fish.

salamandre [salamɑ̃dr] nf (animal) salamander.

salami [salami] nm (saucisson) salami.

salarial, -e, -aux [salarjal, -o] a accord/etc s.
wage agreement/etc. ●**salarié, -ée** a a wage-
earning ▮ nmf wage earner.

salaud [salo] nm Fam Péj bastard, swine.

sale [sal] a dirty; (dégoûtant) filthy; (mauvais) nasty; (couleur) dingy; **s. coup** Fam
dirty trick; **s. temps** Fam rotten ou awful
weather; **avoir une s. gueule** Fam to look
rotten ou awful. ●**salement** adv (se conduire, manger) disgustingly. ●**saleté** nf dirti-

ness; filthiness; (crasse) dirt, filth; (action)
Fig dirty trick; (camelote) Fam junk, Br
rubbish, Am garbage; **saletés** (détritus) Br
rubbish, Am garbage; (obscénités) filth.

saler [sale] vt Culin to salt. ●**salé, -ée** a **1**
(goût, plat) salty; (aliment) salted; (grivois)
Fig spicy; **eau salée** salt water. **2** (excessif)
Fam steep. ●**salière** nf Br saltcellar, Am
saltshaker.

salir [salir] vt to (make) dirty; (réputation)
Fig to tarnish, sully ▮ **se salir** vpr to get
dirty. ●**salissant, -ante** a (métier) dirty,
messy; (étoffe) that shows the dirt. ●**salissure** nf (tache) dirty mark.

salive [saliv] nf saliva. ●**saliver** vi to salivate.

salle [sal] nf room; (très grande, publique)
hall; (de théâtre) theatre, auditorium; (de cinéma) Br cinema, Am movie theater;
(d'hôpital) ward; (public de théâtre)
audience, house; **s. à manger** dining room;
s. de bain(s) bathroom; **s. d'eau** shower
room; **s. de classe** classroom; **s. de concert**
concert hall; **s. d'embarquement** (d'aéroport)
departure lounge; **s. d'exposition** Com showroom; **s. de jeux** (pour enfants) games room;
(avec machines à sous) amusement arcade;
(de casino) gaming room; **s. d'opération**
(d'hôpital) operating Br theatre ou Am
room.

salon [salɔ̃] nm living room, sitting room, Br
lounge; (exposition) show; **s. de beauté/de
coiffure** beauty/hairdressing salon; **s. de thé**
tearoom(s).

salope [salɔp] nf (femme) Fam Vulg bitch,
cow. ●**saloper** vt (salir) Fam to mess up.
●**saloperie** nf Fam (action) dirty trick; (camelote) junk, Br rubbish, Am garbage; **des
saloperies** (propos) filthy talk ou remarks,
filth.

salopette [salɔpɛt] nf (d'enfant, d'ouvrier)
Br dungarees, Am overalls.

salsifis [salsifi] nf Bot Culin salsify.

saltimbanque [saltɛ̃bɑ̃k] nmf (travelling)
acrobat.

salubre [salybr] a healthy, salubrious. ●**sa-
lubrité** nf healthiness; **s. publique** public
health.

saluer [salɥe] vt to greet; (en partant) to take
one's leave of, say goobye to; (de la main)
to wave to; (de la tête) to nod to; Mil to salute; **s. qn comme** Fig to hail s.o. as.

salut [saly] **1** nm greeting; (de la main) wave;
(de la tête) nod; Mil salute ▮ int Fam hello!,
hi!; (au revoir) bye! **2** nm (du peuple etc) salvation; (sauvegarde) safety. ●**salutation** nf
greeting; **je vous prie d'accepter mes salutations distinguées** (dans une lettre) Br yours
faithfully, Am sincerely.

salutaire [salytɛr] a salutary.

salve [salv] nf salvo.

samedi [samdi] nm Saturday.

SAMU [samy] nm abrév (service d'assistance
médicale d'urgence) emergency medical
service.

sanatorium [sanatɔrjɔm] nm sanatorium.

sanctifier [sɑ̃ktifje] *vt* to sanctify.

sanction [sɑ̃ksjɔ̃] *nf* (*approbation, peine*) sanction. ● **sanctionner** *vt* (*confirmer, approuver*) to sanction; (*punir*) to punish.

sanctuaire [sɑ̃ktɥɛr] *nm Rel* sanctuary.

sandale [sɑ̃dal] *nf* sandal.

sandwich [sɑ̃dwitʃ] *nm* sandwich; **s. au fromage/etc** cheese/etc sandwich.

sang [sɑ̃] *nm* blood; **coup de s.** *Méd* stroke; **être en s.** to be covered in blood; **avoir du s. bleu** (*être noble*) to be blue-blooded, have blue blood; **avoir le s. chaud** to be hot-tempered; **se faire du mauvais s.** *Fam* to worry, fret; **mon s. n'a fait qu'un tour** *Fig* my heart missed a beat. ● **sanglant, -ante** *a* bloody; (*critique, reproche*) scathing.

sang-froid [sɑ̃frwa] *nm* self-control, calm; **garder son s.-froid** to keep calm, keep one's head; **avec s.-froid** calmly; **tuer/etc de s.-froid** to kill/etc in cold blood.

sangle [sɑ̃gl] *nf* (*de selle, parachute*) strap.

sanglier [sɑ̃glije] *nm* wild boar.

sanglot [sɑ̃glo] *nm* sob. ● **sangloter** *vi* to sob.

sangsue [sɑ̃sy] *nf* leech.

sanguin, -ine [sɑ̃gɛ̃, -in] 1 *a* (*tempérament*) full-blooded; **vaisseau/groupe/etc s.** blood vessel/group/etc. 2 *nf* **sanguine** (*fruit*) blood orange, ruby-red orange.

sanguinaire [sɑ̃ginɛr] *a* blood-thirsty.

sanitaire [sanitɛr] *a* (*conditions*) sanitary; (*personnel*) medical; **installation s.** bathroom fittings; **règlement s.** health regulations.

sans [sɑ̃] ([sɑ̃z] *before vowel and mute h*) *prép* without; **s. faire** without doing; **s. qu'il le sache** without him *ou* his knowing; **s. cela, s. quoi** otherwise; **s. plus** (but) no more than that; **s. faute/exception** without fail/exception; **s. importance/travail** unimportant/unemployed; **s. argent/manches** penniless/sleeveless; **ça va s. dire** that goes without saying. ● **sans-abri** *nmf inv* homeless person; **les s.-abri** the homeless. ● **sans-cœur** *nmf inv Fam* heartless person. ● **sans-faute** *inv* **faire un s.-faute** *Équitation etc* to do a clear round; *Fig* not to put a foot wrong, turn in a faultless performance. ● **sans-gêne** *a inv* inconsiderate ▌ *nm inv* lack of consideration. ● **sans-travail** *nmf inv* unemployed person.

santé [sɑ̃te] *nf* health; **en bonne/mauvaise s.** in good/bad health, well/not well, fit/unfit; (**à votre**) **s.!** (*en trinquant*) your (good) health!, cheers!; **boire à la s. de qn** to drink to s.o.'s (good) health; **maison de s.** nursing home.

santiag [sɑ̃tjag] *nf Fam* cowboy boot.

saoul [su] *a & nm* = soûl.

saper [sape] *vt* to undermine; **s. le moral à qn** to undermine *ou* sap s.o.'s morale.

sapeur-pompier [sapœrpɔ̃pje] *nm* (*pl* sapeurs-pompiers) fireman.

saphir [safir] *nm* (*pierre*) sapphire; (*d'électrophone*) sapphire, stylus.

sapin [sapɛ̃] *nm* (*arbre, bois*) fir; **s. de Noël** Christmas tree.

sarbacane [sarbakan] *nf* (*jouet*) peashooter.

sarcasme [sarkasm] *nm* sarcasm; **un s.** a piece of sarcasm. ● **sarcastique** *a* sarcastic.

sarcler [sarkle] *vt* (*jardin etc*) to weed.

Sardaigne [sardɛɲ] *nf* Sardinia. ● **sarde** *a* Sardinian ▌ *nmf* S. Sardinian.

sardine [sardin] *nf* sardine; **sardines à l'huile** sardines in oil; **serrés comme des sardines** *Fam* squashed like sardines.

sardonique [sardɔnik] *a* sardonic.

SARL [ɛsɑɛrɛl] *abrév* (*société à responsabilité limitée*) *Br* Ltd, *Am* Inc.

sarment [sarmɑ̃] *nm* vine shoot.

sarrasin [sarazɛ̃] *nm* buckwheat.

sas [sas] *nm* (*de bateau, d'avion*) airlock; **s. de sécurité** security screen.

Satan [satɑ̃] *nm* Satan. ● **satané, -ée** *a* (*maudit*) *Fam* damned. ● **satanique** *a* satanic.

satellite [satelit] *nm* satellite; **télévision par s.** satellite TV; **antenne s.** satellite dish; **pays s.** *Pol* satellite (country).

satiété [sasjete] *nf* **à s.** (*boire, manger*) one's fill; (*répéter*) ad nauseam.

satin [satɛ̃] *nm* satin. ● **satiné, -ée** *a* satiny, silky.

satire [satir] *nf* satire (**contre** on). ● **satirique** *a* satiric(al).

satisfaction [satisfaksjɔ̃] *nf* satisfaction; **donner s. à qn** to give s.o. (complete) satisfaction. ● **satisfaire*** *vt* to satisfy (*s.o.*) ▌ *vi* **s. à** (*conditions, engagement etc*) *Br* to fulfil, *Am* fulfill. ● **satisfaisant, -ante** *a* (*acceptable*) satisfactory. ● **satisfait, -aite** *a* satisfied, content (**de** with).

saturateur [satyratœr] *nm* (*de radiateur*) humidifier.

saturer [satyre] *vt* to saturate (**de** with). ● **saturation** *nf* saturation; **arriver à s.** to reach saturation point.

satyre [satir] *nm Fam* sex fiend.

sauce [sos] *nf* sauce; (*jus de viande*) gravy; **s. tomate** tomato sauce. ● **saucière** *nf* sauce boat; (*pour jus de viande*) gravy boat.

saucisse [sosis] *nf* sausage; **s. de Strasbourg** beef sausage; **s. de Francfort** frankfurter. ● **saucisson** *nm* (cold) sausage.

sauf¹ [sof] *prép* except (**que** that); **s. avis contraire** unless you hear otherwise; **s. erreur** errors excepted, barring error(s).

sauf², sauve [sof, sov] *a* (*honneur*) intact, saved; **avoir la vie sauve** to be unharmed. ● **sauf-conduit** *nm* (*document*) safe-conduct.

sauge [soʒ] *nf Bot Culin* sage.

saugrenu, -ue [sograny] *a* preposterous.

saule [sol] *nm* willow; **s. pleureur** weeping willow.

saumâtre [somɑtr] *a* (*eau*) briny, brackish.

saumon [somɔ̃] *nm* salmon ▌ *a inv* (*couleur*) salmon (pink).

saumure [somyr] *nf* (pickling) brine.

sauna [sona] *nm* sauna.

saupoudrer [sopudre] *vt* to sprinkle (**de** with).

saur [sɔr] *am* **hareng s.** smoked herring.

saura, saurait *etc* [sora, sorɛ] *voir* savoir.

saut [so] *nm* jump, leap; **faire un s.** to jump, leap; **faire un s.** (**chez qn**) to drop in (on s.o.), *Br* pop round (to s.o.); **au s. du lit** on getting out of bed; **s. à la corde** *Br* skipping, *Am* jumping rope; **s. à l'élastique** bungee jumping; **s. en parachute** parachute jump; (*activité*) parachute jumping; **triple s.** *Sport* triple jump.

sauté, -ée [sote] *a & nm Culin* sauté. ● **sauteuse** *nf* (shallow) pan.

sauter [sote] *vi* to jump, leap; (*bombe*) to go off, explode; (*poudrière etc*) to go up, blow up; (*fusible*) to blow; (*se détacher*) to come off; **faire s.** (*détruire*) to blow up; (*arracher*) to tear off; (*casser*) to break; (*renvoyer*) *Fam* to get rid of, fire; (*fusible*) to blow; *Culin* to sauté; **s. à la corde** *Br* to skip, *Am* jump rope; **ça saute aux yeux** it's obvious; **elle m'a sauté dessus** *Fam* she pounced on me.
❚ *vt* (*franchir*) to jump (over); (*mot, repas, classe, cours, ligne*) to skip. ● **saute-mouton** *nm* (*jeu*) leapfrog.

sauterelle [sotrɛl] *nf* grasshopper.

sautes [sot] *nfpl* (*d'humeur, de température*) sudden changes (**de** in).

sautiller [sotije] *vi* to hop.

sautoir [sotwar] *nm Sport* jumping area.

sauvage [sovaʒ] *a* (*animal, plante etc*) wild; (*tribu, homme*) primitive; (*cruel*) savage; (*farouche*) unsociable, shy; (*illégal*) unauthorized ❚ *nmf* unsociable person; (*brute*) savage. ● **sauvagerie** *nf* unsociability; (*cruauté*) savagery.

sauve [sov] *a voir* **sauf².**

sauvegarde [sovgard] *nf* safeguard (**contre** against); (*copie*) *Ordinat* backup. ● **sauvegarder** *vt* to safeguard; *Ordinat* to save; (*copier*) to back up.

sauver [sove] **1** *vt* to save; (*d'un danger*) to rescue (**de** from); (*matériel*) to salvage; **s. la vie à qn** to save s.o.'s life. **2 se sauver** *vpr* (*s'enfuir*) to run away *ou* off; (*partir*) *Fam* to get off, go. ● **sauve-qui-peut** *nm inv* stampede. ● **sauvetage** *nm* rescue; **canot de s.** lifeboat; **ceinture de s.** *Br* lifebelt, *Am* life preserver; **radeau de s.** life raft. ● **sauveteur** *nm* rescuer. ● **sauveur** *nm* saviour.

sauvette (à la) [alasovɛt] *adv* **vendre à la s.** to peddle *ou* hawk on the streets (*illegally*).

savane [savan] *nf* savanna(h).

savant, -ante [savã, -ãt] *a* learned, scholarly; (*manœuvre etc*) masterly, clever ❚ *nm* scientist. ● **savamment** [-amã] *adv* learnedly; (*avec habileté*) cleverly, skilfully.

savate [savat] *nf* old shoe *ou* slipper.

saveur [savœr] *nf* (*goût*) flavour; (*piment*) *Fig* savour.

Savoie [savwa] *nf* Savoy.

savoir* [savwar] *vt* to know; (*nouvelle*) to know, have heard; **j'ai su la nouvelle** I heard *ou* got to know the news; **s. lire/nager/**etc to know how to read/swim/etc; **faire s. à qn que** to inform *ou* tell s.o. that; **à s.** (*c'est-à-dire*) that is, namely; **je ne saurais pas** I could

not, I cannot; (**pas**) **que je sache** (not) as far as I know; **je n'en sais rien** I have no idea, I don't know; **en s. long sur** to know a lot about; **un je ne sais quoi** a something or other.
❚ *nm* (*culture*) learning, knowledge. ● **savoir-faire** *nm inv* know-how, ability. ● **savoir-vivre** *nm inv* good manners.

savon [savõ] *nm* **1** soap; (*morceau*) (bar of) soap. **2 passer un s. à qn** (*gronder*) *Fam* to give s.o. a dressing-down *ou* a talking-to. ● **savonner** *vt* to wash with soap. ● **savonnette** *nf* bar of soap. ● **savonneux, -euse** *a* soapy.

savourer [savure] *vt* to enjoy, savour, relish. ● **savoureux, -euse** *a* tasty; (*histoire etc*) *Fig* juicy.

savoyard, -arde [savwajar, -ard] *a* Savoyard ❚ *nmf* **S.**, Savoyarde Savoyard.

saxophone [saksɔfɔn] *nm* saxophone. ● **saxo** *nm* (*instrument*) *Fam* sax.

saynette [sɛnɛt] *nf* playlet.

sbire [sbir] *nm* (*homme de main*) *Péj* henchman.

scabreux, -euse [skabrø, -øz] *a* obscene.

scalp [skalp] *nm* (*chevelure*) scalp. ● **scalper** *vt* to scalp.

scalpel [skalpɛl] *nm* scalpel.

scandale [skãdal] *nm* scandal; (*tapage*) uproar; **faire s.** (*livre etc*) to scandalize people; **faire un s.** to make a scene. ● **scandaleux, -euse** *a* shocking, outrageous, scandalous. ● **scandaleusement** *adv* outrageously. ● **scandaliser** *vt* to scandalize, shock ❚ **se scandaliser** *vpr* to be shocked *ou* scandalized (**de** by, **que** (+ *sub*) that).

scander [skãde] *vt* (*vers*) to scan; (*slogan*) to chant.

Scandinavie [skãdinavi] *nf* Scandinavia. ● **scandinave** *a* Scandinavian ❚ *nmf* **S.** Scandinavian.

scanner [skanɛr] *nm Méd Ordinat* scanner.

scaphandre [skafãdr] *nm* (*de plongeur*) diving suit; (*de cosmonaute*) spacesuit; **s. autonome** aqualung. ● **scaphandrier** *nm* diver.

scarabée [skarabe] *nm* beetle.

scarlatine [skarlatin] *nf* scarlet fever.

scarole [skarɔl] *nf* endive.

sceau, -x [so] *nm* (*cachet, cire*) seal. ● **sceller** *vt* **1** (*document etc*) to seal. **2** (*fixer*) *Tech* to cement in, embed. ● **scellés** *nmpl* (*cachets de cire*) seals; **mettre les s.** (*sur une porte etc*) to put on the seals.

scélérat, -ate [selera, -at] *nmf Litt* scoundrel.

scel-o-frais® [selɔfrɛ] *nm Br* clingfilm, *Am* plastic wrap.

scénario [senarjo] *nm* (*plan de film*) scenario; (*dialogues de film*) film script, screenplay; (*déroulement*) *Fig* scenario. ● **scénariste** *nmf* (*de cinéma*) scriptwriter.

scène [sɛn] *nf* **1** (*de théâtre*) scene; (*plateau*) stage; (*décors, partie de pièce*) scene; (*action*) action; **mettre en s.** (*pièce, film*) to direct; **entrer en s.** (*acteur*) to come on, go on; **sur la s. internationale** *Fig* on the international scene. **2** (*dispute*) scene; **faire une s.** (**à qn**) to make *ou* create a scene; **elle m'a fait une s.** she made *ou* created a scene; **s. de ménage** domestic quarrel.

scepticisme [sɛptisism] *nm Br* scepticism, *Am* skepticism. ● **sceptique** *a Br* sceptical, *Am* skeptical ▌ *nmf Br* sceptic, *Am* skeptic.

scheik [ʃɛk] *nm* sheikh.

schéma [ʃema] *nm* diagram; *Fig* outline. ● **schématique** *a* diagrammatic; (*succinct*) sketchy. ● **schématiser** *vt* to represent diagrammatically; (*simplifier*) to oversimplify.

schizophrène [skizɔfrɛn] *a* & *nmf* schizophrenic.

sciatique [sjatik] *nf* (*douleur*) sciatica.

scie [si] *nf* (*outil*) saw; **s. électrique** power saw; **s. musicale** musical saw. ● **scier** *vt* to saw. ● **scierie** *nf* sawmill.

sciemment [sjamã] *adv* knowingly.

science [sjãs] *nf* science; (*savoir*) knowledge; (*habileté*) skill; **sciences humaines** social science(s); **sciences naturelles** biology; **étudier les sciences** to study science. ● **science-fiction** *nf* science fiction. ● **scientifique** *a* scientific ▌ *nmf* scientist.

scinder [sɛ̃de] *vt*, **se scinder** *vpr* to divide, split.

scintiller [sɛ̃tije] *vi* to sparkle, glitter; (*étoile*) to twinkle. ● **scintillement** *nm* sparkling; (*d'étoile*) twinkling.

scission [sisjɔ̃] *nf* (*de parti etc*) split (**de** in); **s. de l'atome** splitting of the atom.

sciure [sjyr] *nf* sawdust.

sclérose [skleroz] *nf Méd* sclerosis; *Fig* ossification; **s. en plaques** multiple sclerosis. ● **sclérosé, -ée** *a* (*société etc*) *Fig* ossified.

scolaire [skɔlɛr] *a* **année/etc s.** school year/ *etc*; **enfant d'âge s.** child of school age; **progrès scolaires** progress at school, academic progress. ● **scolariser** *vt* (*enfant*) to send to school, put in school; (*pays*) to provide with schools. ● **scolarité** *nf* schooling; **s. obligatoire/gratuite** compulsory/free schooling; **certificat de s.** certificate of attendance (*at school or university*); **pendant ma s.** during my school years.

scoliose [skɔljoz] *nf Méd* curvature of the spine.

scooter [skutɛr] *nm* (motor) scooter; **s. des mers** jet ski.

scorbut [skɔrbyt] *nm* (*maladie*) scurvy.

score [skɔr] *nm Sport* score.

scories [skɔri] *nfpl* (*résidu*) slag.

scorpion [skɔrpjɔ̃] *nm* scorpion; **le S.** (*signe*) Scorpio.

scotch [skɔtʃ] *nm* **1** (*boisson*) Scotch, whisky. **2®** (*ruban adhésif*) *Br* sellotape®, *Am* scotch tape®. ● **scotcher** *vt Br* to sellotape, *Am* to tape.

scout, -e [skut] *a* & *nm* scout. ● **scoutisme** *nm* scout movement, scouting.

script [skript] *nm* (*écriture*) printing.

scripte [skript] *nf* (*de cinéma*) continuity girl.

scrupule [skrypyl] *nm* scruple; **sans scrupules** unscrupulous; (*agir*) unscrupulously. ● **scrupuleux, -euse** *a* scrupulous. ● **scrupuleusement** *adv* scrupulously.

scruter [skryte] *vt* to examine, scrutinize.

scrutin [skrytɛ̃] *nm* voting, ballot; (*opérations électorales*) poll(ing); **premier/etc tour de s.** first/*etc* ballot *ou* round.

sculpter [skylte] *vt* (*statue, pierre etc*) to sculpture, sculpt; (*bois*) to carve; **s. qch dans** to sculpture sth out of; to carve sth out of. ● **sculpteur** *nm* sculptor. ● **sculptural, -e, -aux** *a* (*beauté, femme etc*) statuesque. ● **sculpture** *nf* (*art, œuvre*) sculpture; **s. sur bois** woodcarving.

SDF [ɛsdeɛf] *nm abrév* (*sans domicile fixe*) person of no fixed abode.

se [s(ə)] (**s'** *before vowel or mute h*) *pron* **1** (*complément direct*) himself; (*féminin*) herself; (*non humain*) itself; (*indéfini*) oneself; *pl* themselves; **il se lave** he washes himself; **ils** *ou* **elles se lavent** they wash themselves.

2 (*indirect*) to himself; to herself; to itself; to oneself; **se dire** to say to oneself; **elle se dit** she says to herself.

3 (*réciproque*) each other, one another; (*indirect*) to each other, to one another; **ils s'aiment** they love each other *ou* one another; **ils** *ou* **elles se parlent** they speak to each other *ou* one another.

4 (*possessif*) **il se lave les mains** he washes his hands; **elle se lave les mains** she washes her hands.

5 (*passif*) **ça se fait** that is done; **ça se vend bien** it sells well.

séance [seãs] *nf* **1** (*de cinéma*) showing, performance. **2** (*d'assemblée etc*) session, sitting; (*de travail etc*) session; **s.** (**de pose**) (*chez un peintre*) sitting. **3 s. tenante** at once.

séant, -ante [seã, -ãt] **1** *a* (*convenable*) *Litt* seemly, proper. **2** *nm* **se mettre sur son s.** to sit up.

seau, -x [so] *nm* bucket, pail.

sec, sèche [sɛk, sɛʃ] *a* dry; (*fruits, légumes*) dried; (*ton*) curt, harsh; (*maigre*) spare; (*cœur*) *Fig* hard; **frapper un coup s.** to knock (sharply), bang; **bruit s.** (*rupture*) snap ▌ *adv* (*boire*) *Br* neat, *Am* straight; (*frapper, pleuvoir*) hard ▌ *nm* **à s.** dried up, dry; (*sans argent*) *Fam* broke; **au s.** in a dry place.

sécateur [sekatœr] *nm* pruning shears, *Br* secateurs.

sécession [sesesjɔ̃] *nf* secession; **faire s.** to secede.

sèche [sɛʃ] *voir* **sec.** ● **sèche-cheveux** *nm inv* hair dryer. ● **sèche-linge** *nm inv Br* tumble dryer, *Am* (clothes) dryer.

sécher [seʃe] **1** *vti* to dry ▌ **se sécher** *vpr* to dry oneself. **2** *vt* (*cours*) *Scol Fam* to skip ▌ *vi* (*ignorer*) *Scol Fam* to be stumped; (*être absent*) *Scol* to skip lessons *ou* classes. ● **séchage** *nm* drying.

sécheresse [seʃrɛs] *nf* dryness; (*de ton*) curtness; *Mét* drought.

séchoir [seʃwar] nm (appareil) dryer; s. à linge drying rack, clothes horse.

second, -onde¹ [sgɔ̃, -ɔ̃d] a & nmf second; de seconde main secondhand ▌ nm (adjoint) second in command; (étage) Br second floor, Am third floor ▌ nf seconde Rail etc second class; Scol = Br fifth form, = Am eleventh grade; (vitesse) Aut second (gear). ●**secondaire** a secondary; école s. Br secondary school, Am high school.

seconde² [sgɔ̃d] nf (instant) second.

seconder [sgɔ̃de] vt to assist.

secouer [s(ə)kwe] vt to shake; (paresse, poussière) to shake off; s. qn (maladie, nouvelle etc) to shake s.o. up; s. qch de qch (enlever) to shake sth out of sth; s. la tête (réponse affirmative) to nod (one's head); (réponse négative) to shake one's head ▌ se secouer vpr (faire un effort) Fam to shake oneself out of it.

secourir [s(ə)kurir] vt to assist, help. ●secourable a (personne) helpful. ●secourisme nm first aid. ●secouriste nmf first-aid worker.

secours [s(ə)kur] nm assistance, help; des secours (aux victimes) aid, relief; le s., les s. Mil relief; (premiers) s. Méd first aid; au s.! help!; porter s. à qn to give s.o. assistance ou help; sortie de s. emergency exit; équipe de s. rescue team; roue de s. spare wheel.

secousse [s(ə)kus] nf jolt, jerk; (psychologique) shock; (dans un tremblement de terre) tremor.

secret, -ète [sɔkrɛ, -ɛt] a secret; (cachottier) secretive ▌ nm secret; (discrétion) secrecy; s. d'État state secret; en s. in secret, secretly; dans le s. (au courant) in on the secret; au s. (en prison) in solitary confinement.

secrétaire [sɔkretɛr] 1 nmf secretary; s. médicale (doctor's) receptionist; s. d'État Secretary of State; s. de mairie town clerk; s. de rédaction (de journal) Br subeditor, Am copyeditor. 2 nm (meuble) writing desk. ●secrétariat nm (bureau) secretary's office; (d'organisation internationale) secretariat; (métier) secretarial work; école/travail de s. secretarial school/work.

sécréter [sekrete] vt Méd Biol to secrete. ●sécrétion nf secretion.

secte [sɛkt] nf sect. ●sectaire a & nmf Péj sectarian.

secteur [sɛktœr] nm Mil Écon sector; (de ville) district; (domaine) Fig area; (de réseau) Él supply area; (ligne) Él mains; branché sur le s. plugged into the mains; s. primaire/secondaire Écon primary/secondary sector.

section [sɛksjɔ̃] nf section; (de ligne d'autobus) fare stage; Mil platoon. ●sectionner vt to divide (into sections); (artère, doigt) to sever.

séculaire [sekylɛr] a (tradition etc) age-old.

séculier, -ière [sekylje, -jɛr] a (clergé etc) secular.

secundo [s(ə)gɔ̃do] adv secondly.

sécurité [sekyrite] nf (matérielle) safety; (tranquillité) security; s. routière road safety; S. sociale = social services, Social Security; ceinture/marge/normes/etc de s. safety belt/margin/standards/etc; s. de l'emploi job security; en s. safe; (tranquille) secure. ●sécuriser vt to reassure (s.o.), make (s.o.) feel (emotionally) secure.

sédatif [sedatif] nm sedative.

sédentaire [sedɑ̃tɛr] a sedentary.

sédiment [sedimɑ̃] nm sediment.

séditieux, -euse [sedisjø, -øz] a seditious. ●sédition nf sedition.

séduire* [seduir] vt to charm, attract; (plaire à) to appeal to; (abuser de) to seduce. ●séduisant, -ante a attractive. ●séducteur, -trice a seductive ▌ nmf seducer. ●séduction nf attraction.

segment [sɛgmɑ̃] nm segment. ●segmenter vt to segment, divide into segments.

ségrégation [segregasjɔ̃] nf segregation.

seiche [sɛʃ] nf cuttlefish.

seigle [sɛgl] nm rye; pain de s. rye bread.

seigneur [sɛɲœr] nm (noble, maître) Hist lord; le S. Rel the Lord.

sein [sɛ̃] nm breast; Fig bosom; bout de s. nipple; donner le s. à (enfant) to breastfeed; au s. de (parti, fédération, famille etc) within; (bonheur etc) in the midst of.

Seine [sɛn] nf la S. the Seine.

séisme [seism] nm earthquake.

seize [sɛz] a & nm sixteen. ●seizième a & nmf sixteenth.

séjour [seʒur] nm stay; (salle de) s. living room. ●séjourner vi to stay.

sel [sɛl] nm salt; (piquant) Fig spice; (humour) wit; sels Méd (smelling) salts; s. de mer sea salt; sels de bain bath salts.

sélect, -e [selɛkt] a Fam select.

sélectif, -ive [selɛktif, -iv] a selective. ●sélection nf selection. ●sélectionner vt to select. ●sélectionneur nm (sportif etc) selector.

self(-service) [sɛlf(sɛrvis)] nm self-service restaurant ou shop.

selle [sɛl] nf (de cheval) saddle. ●seller [sele] vt (cheval) to saddle.

selles [sɛl] nfpl les s. Méd bowel movements, stools, Br motions.

sellette [sɛlɛt] nf sur la s. (personne) Fig under examination, in the hot seat.

selon [s(ə)lɔ̃] prép according to (que whether); c'est s. Fam it (all) depends.

Seltz (eau de) [odsɛls] nf soda (water).

semailles [s(ə)maj] nfpl (travail) sowing; (période) seedtime.

semaine [s(ə)mɛn] nf week; en s. (opposé à week-end) in the week; à la s. by the week, weekly; à la petite s. (politique etc) Fam shortsighted.

sémantique [semɑ̃tik] a semantic ▌ nf semantics.

sémaphore [semafɔr] nm (pour bateaux ou trains) semaphore.

semblable [sɑ̃blabl] a similar (à to); être

semblables to be alike *ou* similar; **de semblables propos**/*etc* (*tels*) such remarks/*etc* ▌ *nm* fellow (creature); **toi et tes semblables** you and your kind.

semblant [sãblã] *nm* **faire s.** to pretend (**de faire** to do); **un s.** de a semblance of.

sembler [sãble] *vi* to seem (**à** to); **il (me) semble vieux** he seems *ou* looks old (to me); **s. être/faire** to seem to be/to do ▌ *v imp* **il semble que** (+ *sub ou indic*) it seems that, it looks as if; **il me semble que** I think that, it seems to me that; **quand bon lui semble** when he *ou* she sees fit.

semelle [s(ə)mɛl] *nf* (*de chaussure*) sole; (*intérieure*) insole; **ne pas quitter qn d'une s.** Fig to be always at s.o.'s heels.

semer [s(ə)me] *vt* **1** (*graines*) to sow; (*jeter*) Fig to strew; (*répandre*) to spread; **semé de** Fig strewn with, dotted with. **2** (*concurrent, poursuivant*) to shake off. ● **semence** *nf* seed; (*clou*) tack. ● **semeur, -euse** *nmf* sower (de of).

semestre [s(ə)mɛstr] *nm* half-year; *Univ* semester. ● **semestriel, -ielle** *a* half-yearly.

semi- [səmi] *préf* semi-.

séminaire [seminɛr] *nm* **1** *Univ* seminar. **2** *Rel* seminary. ● **séminariste** *nm* *Rel* seminarist.

semi-remorque [səmirəmɔrk] *nm* (*camion*) Br articulated lorry, Am semi(trailer), Am trailer truck.

semis [s(ə)mi] *nm* sowing; (*terrain*) seedbed; (*plant*) seedling.

sémite [semit] *a* Semitic ▌ *nmf* S. Semite. ● **sémitique** *a* (*langue*) Semitic.

semonce [səmɔ̃s] *nf* reprimand; **coup de s.** (*de navire*) warning shot.

semoule [s(ə)mul] *nf* semolina.

sempiternel, -elle [sãpiternɛl] *a* endless, ceaseless.

sénat [sena] *nm* *Pol* senate. ● **sénateur** *nm* *Pol* senator.

sénile [senil] *a* senile. ● **sénilité** *nf* senility.

senior [senjɔr] *nm* & *a inv* *Sport* senior.

sens [sãs] *nm* **1** (*faculté, raison, instinct*) sense; **avoir le s. de l'humour** to have a sense of humour; **avoir du bon s.** to have (good) sense, be sensible; **cela tombe sous le s.** that's perfectly obvious; **à mon s.** to my mind; **s. commun** commonsense.
2 (*signification*) meaning, sense; **ça n'a pas de s.** that doesn't make sense; **dans un certain s.** in a way.
3 (*direction*) direction; **s. giratoire** *Aut* Br roundabout, Am traffic circle, Am rotary; **s. interdit** *ou* **unique** (*rue*) one-way street; **'s. interdit'** 'no entry'; **à s. unique** (*rue*) one-way; **s. dessus dessous** [sãd(ə)syd(ə)su] upside down; **dans le s. des aiguilles d'une montre** clockwise; **dans le s. inverse des aiguilles d'une montre** Br anticlockwise, Am counterclockwise.

sensation [sãsasjɔ̃] *nf* feeling, sensation; **faire s.** to cause *ou* create a sensation; **à s.** (*film, roman etc*) Péj sensational. ● **sensa-**

tionnel, -elle *a* sensational; (*excellent*) Fam fantastic, sensational.

sensé, -ée [sãse] *a* sensible.

sensible [sãsibl] *a* sensitive (**à** to); (*douloureux*) tender, sore; (*perceptible*) perceptible; (*progrès, différence etc*) noticeable, appreciable. ● **sensiblement** [-əmã] *adv* (*notablement*) appreciably; (*à peu près*) more or less. ● **sensibiliser** *vt* **s. qn à** (*problème etc*) to make s.o. alive to *ou* aware of. ● **sensibilité** *nf* sensitivity.

sensoriel, -ielle [sãsɔrjɛl] *a* sensory.

sensuel, -elle [sãsɥɛl] *a* (*sexuel*) sensual; (*musique, couleur etc*) sensuous. ● **sensualité** *nf* sensuality; (*de musique etc*) sensuousness.

sentence [sãtãs] *nf* **1** (*jugement*) Jur sentence. **2** (*maxime*) maxim.

senteur [sãtœr] *nf* (*odeur*) scent.

sentier [sãtje] *nm* path.

sentiment [sãtimã] *nm* feeling; **avoir le s. que** to have a feeling that; **meilleurs sentiments** (*sur une carte de visite etc*) best wishes. ● **sentimental, -e, -aux** *a* sentimental; **vie**/*etc* **sentimentale** love life/*etc*. ● **sentimentalité** *nf* sentimentality.

sentinelle [sãtinɛl] *nf* sentry.

sentir* [sãtir] *vt* to feel; (*odeur*) to smell; (*goût*) to taste; (*racisme etc*) to smack of; (*se rendre compte de*) to sense, be conscious of; **s. le moisi/le parfum**/*etc* to smell musty/of perfume/*etc*; **s. le poisson**/*etc* (*avoir le goût de*) to taste of fish/*etc*; **je ne peux pas le s.** (*supporter*) Fam I can't stand *ou* bear him; **se s. fatigué/humilié**/*etc* to feel tired/humiliated/*etc*; **se faire s.** (*effet etc*) to make itself felt ▌ *vi* to smell; **s. bon/mauvais** to smell good/bad. ● **senti, -ie** *a* **bien s.** (*cruel, direct*) (*remarque etc*) hard-hitting.

séparation [separasjɔ̃] *nf* separation; (*en deux*) division, split; (*départ*) parting.

séparer [separe] *vt* to separate (**de** from); (*diviser en deux*) to divide, split (up); (*cheveux*) to part; **plus rien ne nous sépare de la victoire** nothing (else) stands between us and victory, there is nothing keeping us from victory ▌ **se séparer** *vpr* (*se quitter*) to part; (*couple*) to separate; (*assemblée, cortège*) to disperse, break up; (*se détacher*) to split off; **se s. de** (*objet aimé, chien etc*) to part with. ● **séparé, -ée** *a* (*distinct*) separate; (*époux*) separated (**de** from). ● **séparément** *adv* separately.

sept [sɛt] *a* & *nm* seven. ● **septième** *a* & *nmf* seventh; **un s.** a seventh.

septante [sɛptãt] *a* & *nm* (*en Belgique, en Suisse*) seventy.

septembre [sɛptãbr] *nm* September.

septennat [sɛptena] *nm* *Pol* seven-year term (of office).

septentrional, -e, -aux [sɛptãtrijɔnal, -o] *a* northern.

sépulcre [sepylkr] *nm* (*tombeau*) sepulchre.

sépulture [sepyltyr] *nf* burial; (*lieu*) burial place.

séquelles [sekɛl] *nfpl* (*de maladie etc*) after-effects; (*de guerre*) aftermath.

séquence [sekãs] *nf* Ordinat Mus Cartes sequence; **s. de film** film sequence.

séquestrer [sekɛstre] *vt* to confine (illegally), lock up. ●**séquestration** *nf* (illegal) confinement.

sera, serait *etc* [s(ə)ra, s(ə)rɛ] *voir* être.

Serbie [sɛrbi] *nf* Serbia. ●**serbe** *a* Serbian ▮ *nmf* S. Serbian.

serein, -eine [sərɛ̃, -ɛn] *a* serene. ●**sérénité** *nf* serenity.

sérénade [serenad] *nf* serenade.

sergent [sɛrʒã] *nm* Mil sergeant.

série [seri] *nf* series; (*ensemble*) set; **s. noire** Fig series *ou* string of disasters; **de s.** (*article*, voiture etc) standard; **fabrication en s.** mass production; **fins de s.** Com oddments, ends of lines; **hors s.** Fig outstanding.

sérier [serje] *vt* (*problèmes etc*) to grade (in order of difficulty).

sérieux, -euse [serjø, -øz] *a* (*personne*, doute etc) serious; (*de bonne foi*) genuine, serious; (*fiable*) reliable; (*bénéfices*) substantial; **de sérieuses chances de...** a good chance of... ▮ *nm* seriousness; (*fiabilité*) reliability; **prendre qn/qch au s.** to take s.o./sth seriously; **garder son s.** to keep a straight face; **manquer de s.** (*travailleur*) to lack application; **se prendre (trop) au s.** to take oneself (too) seriously. ●**sérieusement** adv seriously; (*travailler*) conscientiously.

serin [s(ə)rɛ̃] *nm* canary.

seriner [s(ə)rine] *vt* **s. qch à qn** Fig to repeat sth to s.o. over and over again.

seringue [s(ə)rɛ̃g] *nf* syringe.

serment [sɛrmã] *nm* (*affirmation solennelle*) oath; (*promesse*) pledge; **prêter s.** to take an oath; **faire le s. de faire qch** to swear to do sth; **sous s.** Jur on *ou* under oath.

sermon [sɛrmɔ̃] *nm* (*de prêtre etc*) sermon; (*discours*) Péj lecture. ●**sermonner** *vt* (*faire la morale à*) to lecture.

séropositif, -ive [seropozitif, -iv] *a* Méd HIV positive. ●**séronégatif, -ive** *a* Méd HIV negative.

serpe [sɛrp] *nf* bill(hook).

serpent [sɛrpã] *nm* snake; **s. à sonnette** rattlesnake.

serpenter [sɛrpãte] *vi* (*sentier etc*) to meander.

serpentin [sɛrpãtɛ̃] *nm* (*ruban*) streamer.

serpillière [sɛrpijɛr] *nf* floor cloth.

serpolet [sɛrpɔlɛ] *nm* (*plante*, aromate) wild thyme.

serrage [seraʒ] *nm* (*de vis etc*) tightening; **le s. des freins** applying the brakes.

serre [sɛr] *nf* greenhouse. ●**serres** *nfpl* (*d'oiseau*) claws, talons.

serre-livres [sɛrlivr] *nm inv* bookend.

serrement [sɛrmã] *nm* **s. de cœur** heavy-hearted feeling; **s. de gorge** tightening in one's throat.

serrer [sere] *vt* (*tenir*) to grip, clasp; (*presser*) to squeeze, press; (*nœud*, vis, corde) to

tighten; (*poing*) to clench; (*taille*) to hug; (*pieds*) to pinch; (*frein*) to apply, put on; (*rapprocher*) to close up; (*rangs*) Mil to close; **s. la main à qn** to shake hands with s.o.; **s. les dents** Fig to grit one's teeth; **s. qn** (*embrasser*) to hug s.o.; (*vêtement*) to be too tight for s.o.; **s. qn de près** (*talonner*) to be close behind s.o.

▮ *vi* **s. à droite** (*en voiture*) to keep (to the) right.

▮ **se serrer** *vpr* (*se rapprocher*) to squeeze up *ou* together; **se s. contre** to squeeze up against. ●**serré, -ée** *a* (*nœud*, budget, vêtement*) tight; (*gens*) packed (together); (*lutte*) close; (*rangs*) serried; (*dense*) dense, thick; **avoir le cœur s.** Fig to have a heavy heart; **avoir la gorge serrée** Fig to have a lump in one's throat.

serre-tête [sɛrtɛt] *nm inv* headband.

serrure [seryr] *nf* lock. ●**serrurier** *nm* locksmith.

sertir [sɛrtir] *vt* (*diamant etc*) to set.

sérum [serɔm] *nm* serum.

servante [sɛrvãt] *nf* (maid)servant.

serveur, -euse [sɛrvœr, -øz] *nmf* waiter, waitress; (*au bar*) barman, barmaid.

serviable [sɛrvjabl] *a* helpful, obliging. ●**serviabilité** *nf* helpfulness.

service [sɛrvis] *nm* service; (*travail*) duty; (*pourboire*) service (charge); (*dans une entreprise*) department; Tennis serve, service; **un s.** (*aide*) a favour; **rendre s.** to be of service (à qn to s.o.), help (à qn s.o.); **rendre un mauvais s. à qn** to do s.o. a disservice; **ça pourrait rendre s.** Fam that might come in useful; **s. (non) compris** service (not) included; **s. après-vente** (*d'un magasin etc*) aftersales service; **s. d'ordre** (*policiers*) police; **être de s.** to be on duty; **être au s.** Tennis to be serving, be the one to serve; **faire son s.** (*militaire*) to do one's military service; **s. à café/à thé** coffee/tea service *ou* set; **à votre s.!** at your service!

serviette [sɛrvjɛt] *nf* 1 towel; **s. de bain/de toilette** bath/hand towel; **s. hygiénique** sanitary Br towel *ou* Am napkin; **s. (de table)** napkin, Br serviette. 2 (*sac*) briefcase. ●**serviette-éponge** *nf* (pl serviettes-éponges) terry towel.

servile [sɛrvil] *a* servile; (*imitation*) slavish. ●**servilité** *nf* servility; slavishness.

servir* [sɛrvir] 1 *vt* to serve (**qch à qn** s.o. with sth, sth to s.o.); (*convive*) to wait on ▮ *vi* to serve ▮ **se servir** *vpr* (*à table*) to help oneself (de to).

2 *vi* (*être utile*) to be useful, serve; **s. à qch/à faire qch** (*objet*) to be used for sth/to do *ou* for doing sth; **ça ne s.** à rien it's useless, it's no good *ou* use (de faire doing); **à quoi ça sert de protester/etc** what's the use *ou* good of protesting/etc; **s. de qch** (*objet*) to be used for sth, serve as sth; **ça me sert à faire/de qch** I use it to do *ou* for doing/as sth; **s. à qn de guide/etc** to act as a guide/etc to s.o.

3 **se servir** *vpr* **se s. de** (*utiliser*) to use.

serviteur [sɛrvitœr] *nm* servant. ● **servitude** *nf* (*esclavage*) servitude; (*contrainte*) *Fig* constraint.

ses [se] *voir* son².

session [sesjɔ̃] *nf* session.

set [sɛt] *nm* **1** *Tennis* set. **2** s. (de table) (*napperon*) place mat.

seuil [sœj] *nm* doorstep; (*entrée*) doorway; (*limite*) *Fig* threshold; **au s. de** *Fig* on the threshold of.

seul, seule [sœl] **1** *a* (*sans compagnie*) alone; **tout s.** by oneself, on one's own, all alone; **se sentir s.** to feel lonely *ou* alone ∎ *adv* (**tout**) **s.** (*rentrer, vivre etc*) by oneself, alone, on one's own; (*parler*) to oneself; **s. à s.** (*parler*) in private.
2 *a* (*unique*) only; **la seule femme/***etc* the only *ou* sole woman/*etc*; **un s. chat/***etc* only one cat/*etc*; **une seule fois** only once; **pas un s. livre/***etc* not a single book/*etc*; **seuls les garçons..., les garçons seuls...** only the boys... ∎ *nmf* **le s., la seule** the only one; **un s., une seule** only one, one only; **pas un s.** not (a single) one.

seulement [sœlmɑ̃] *adv* only; **non s.... mais encore...** not only... but (also)...; **pas s.** (*même*) not even; **sans s. faire** without even doing.

sève [sɛv] *nf* (*de plante*) & *Fig* sap.

sévère [sever] *a* severe; (*parents, professeur, juge etc*) strict. ● **sévèrement** *adv* severely; (*élever qn*) strictly. ● **sévérité** *nf* severity; (*de parents etc*) strictness.

sévices [sevis] *nmpl* brutality; **s. à enfant** child abuse.

sévir [sevir] *vi* (*fléau*) *Fig* to rage; **s. contre** to deal severely with.

sevrer [səvre] *vt* (*enfant*) to wean; **s. de** (*priver*) *Fig* to deprive of.

sexe [sɛks] *nm* (*catégorie, sexualité*) sex; (*organes*) genitals; **l'autre s.** the opposite sex. ● **sexiste** *a* & *nmf* sexist. ● **sexualité** *nf* sexuality. ● **sexuel, -elle** *a* sexual; **éducation/vie/***etc* **sexuelle** sex education/life/*etc*; **avoir des relations sexuelles** to have sex, have sexual relations (**avec qn** with s.o.).

sextuor [sɛkstyɔr] *nm* sextet.

seyant, -ante [sejɑ̃, -ɑ̃t] *a* (*vêtement*) becoming.

shampooing [ʃɑ̃pwɛ̃] *nm* shampoo; **s. colorant rinse; faire un s. à qn** to shampoo s.o.'s hair.

shérif [ʃerif] *nm* (*anx États-Unis*) sheriff.

shooter [ʃute] **1** *vti* *Football* to shoot. **2 se shooter** *vpr* (*avec une drogue*) *Fam* to inject oneself (à with).

short [ʃɔrt] *nm* (pair of) shorts.

si¹ [si] **1** (= s' [s] *before* **il, ils**) *conj* if; **si je pouvais** if I could; **s'il vient** if he comes; **si j'étais roi** if I were *ou* was king; **je me demande si** I wonder whether *ou* if; **si on restait?** (*suggestion*) what if we stayed?; **si je dis ça, c'est que...** I say this because...; **si ce n'est** (*sinon*) if not; **si oui** if so; **si non** if not; **si seulement** if only; **même si** even if.
2 *adv* (*tellement*) so; **pas si riche que toi/que tu crois** not as rich as you/as you think; **un si bon dîner** such a good dinner; **si grand qu'il soit** however big he may be; **si bien que** with the result that, so much so that.
3 *adv* (*après négative*) yes; **tu ne viens pas? – si!** you're not coming? – yes (I am)!

si² [si] *nm* (*note de musique*) B.

siamois, -oise [sjamwa, -waz] *a* Siamese; **frères s., sœurs siamoises** Siamese twins.

Sicile [sisil] *nf* Sicily.

SIDA [sida] *nm abrév* (*syndrome immuno-déficitaire acquis*) AIDS; **malade/virus du S.** AIDS victim/virus. ● **sidéen, -enne** *ou* **sidatique** *nmf* AIDS sufferer *ou* victim.

sidérer [sidere] *vt Fam* to stagger.

sidérurgie [sideryrʒi] *nf* iron and steel industry. ● **sidérurgique** *a* **industrie/***etc* **s.** iron and steel industry/*etc*.

siècle [sjɛkl] *nm* century; (*époque*) age; **depuis des siècles** *Fam* for ages (and ages).

siège [sjɛʒ] *nm* **1** (*meuble, centre, au parlement etc*) seat; (*d'autorité, de parti etc*) headquarters; **s. (social)** (*d'entreprise*) head office. **2** *Mil* siege; **mettre le s. devant** to lay siege to. ● **siéger** *vi* (*assemblée etc*) to sit.

sien, sienne [sjɛ̃, sjɛn] *pron poss* **le s., la sienne, les sien(ne)s** his; (*de femme*) hers; (*de chose*) its; **les deux siens** his *ou* her two ∎ *nmpl* **les siens** (*sa famille*) one's (own) people ∎ *nfpl* **faire des siennes** to be up to one's tricks again.

sieste [sjɛst] *nf* siesta; **faire la s.** to take *ou* have a nap.

siffler [sifle] *vi* (*avec un sifflet*) to blow one's whistle; (*gaz, serpent*) to hiss; (*en respirant*) to wheeze ∎ *vt* (*chanson*) to whistle; (*chien*) to whistle to; (*faute, fin de match*) *Sport* to blow one's whistle for; (*acteur, pièce*) to boo; (*boisson*) *Fam Br* to knock back; **se faire s.** (*acteur etc*) to be booed. ● **sifflement** *nm* whistling; whistle; (*de gaz etc*) hiss(ing).

sifflet [sifle] *nm* (*instrument*) whistle; **sifflets** (*des spectateurs*) booing, boos; (**coup de) s.** (*son*) whistle. ● **siffloter** *vti* to whistle.

sigle [sigl] *nm* (*initiales*) abbreviation; (*prononcé comme un mot*) acronym.

signal, -aux [siɲal, -o] *nm* signal; **s. d'alarme** (*dans un train*) alarm, *Br* communication cord; **signaux routiers** road signs.

signalement [siɲalmɑ̃] *nm* (*de personne*) description, particulars.

signaler [siɲale] **1** *vt* (*faire remarquer*) to point out (à qn to s.o., que that); (*indiquer*) to indicate, signal; (*dénoncer à la police etc*) to report (à to). **2 se signaler** *vpr* **se s. par** (*sa présence d'esprit, son courage etc*) to distinguish oneself by.

signalétique [siɲaletik] *a* **fiche s.** descriptive notice, description.

signalisation [siɲalizasjɔ̃] *nf* signalling; (*sur les routes*) signposting; **s. (routière)** (*signaux*) road signs.

signature [siɲatyr] *nf* signature; (*action*)

signing. ● **signataire** *nmf* signatory. ● **signer 1** *vt* to sign. **2 se signer** *vpr* (*chrétien*) to cross oneself.

signe [siɲ] *nm* (*indice*) sign, indication; **s. particulier/de ponctuation** distinguishing/ punctuation mark; **s. (astrologique)** (astrological) sign; **en s. de protestation/etc** as a sign of protest/etc; **faire s. à qn** (*geste*) to motion (to) s.o. (*de faire* to do); (*contacter*) to get in touch with s.o.; **faire s. que oui** to nod (one's head); **faire s. que non** to shake one's head; **faire le s. de croix** to make a *ou* the sign of the cross; **ne pas donner s. de vie** to give no sign of life.

signet [siɲɛ] *nm* bookmark.

signification [siɲifikasjɔ̃] *nf* meaning. ● **significatif, -ive** *a* significant, meaningful; **s. de** indicative of.

signifier [siɲifje] *vt* to mean, signify (**que** that); **s. qch à qn** (*faire connaître*) to make sth known to s.o., signify sth to s.o.

silence [silɑ̃s] *nm* silence; *Mus* rest; **en s.** in silence; **garder le s.** to keep quiet *ou* silent (**sur** about). ● **silencieux, -euse 1** *a* silent. **2** *nm* (*de voiture*) *Br* silencer, *Am* muffler; (*d'arme*) silencer. ● **silencieusement** *adv* silently.

silex [silɛks] *nm* (*roche*) flint.

silhouette [silwɛt] *nf* outline; (*en noir*) silhouette; (*ligne du corps*) figure.

silicium [silisjɔm] *nm* silicon; **pastille de s.** silicon chip. ● **silicone** *nf* silicone.

sillage [sijaʒ] *nm* (*de bateau*) wake; **dans le s. de** *Fig* in the wake of.

sillon [sijɔ̃] *nm* furrow; (*de disque*) groove.

sillonner [sijɔne] *vt* (*traverser*) to cross; (*en tous sens*) to criss-cross.

silo [silo] *nm* silo.

simagrées [simagre] *nfpl* airs (and graces); (*minauderies*) fuss.

similaire [similɛr] *a* similar. ● **similitude** *nf* similarity.

similicuir [similikɥir] *nm* imitation leather.

simple [sɛ̃pl] *a* simple; (*non multiple*) single; (*employé, particulier*) ordinary; **c'est s. comme bonjour** *Fam* it's dead easy, it's as easy as pie; **c'est tout s.** *Fam* it's quite simple, this is how it is **‖** *nmf* **s. d'esprit** simpleton **‖** *nm* *Tennis* singles; **passer du s. au double** to double, increase by a factor of two. ● **simplement** [-əmɑ̃] *adv* simply. ● **simplet, -ette** *a* (*personne*) a bit simple. ● **simplicité** *nf* simplicity.

simplifier [sɛ̃plifje] *vt* to simplify. ● **simplification** *nf* simplification.

simpliste [sɛ̃plist] *a* simplistic.

simulacre [simylakr] *nm* **un s. de** (*procès etc*) *Litt* a *Br* pretence *ou* *Am* pretense of.

simuler [simyle] *vt* to simulate; (*feindre*) to feign. ● **simulateur, -trice 1** *nmf* (*hypocrite*) shammer; (*tire-au-flanc*) malingerer. **2** *nm* (*appareil*) simulator. ● **simulation** *nf* simulation; (*feinte*) feigning.

simultané, -ée [simyltane] *a* simultaneous. ● **simultanément** *adv* simultaneously.

sincère [sɛ̃sɛr] *a* sincere. ● **sincèrement** *adv* sincerely. ● **sincérité** *nf* sincerity; **en toute s.** quite sincerely.

sinécure [sinekyr] *nf* sinecure; **ce n'est pas une s.** *Fam* it's no rest cure.

Singapour [sɛ̃gapur] *nm* Singapore.

singe [sɛ̃ʒ] *nm* monkey, ape. ● **singer** *vt* (*imiter*) to ape, mimic. ● **singeries** *nfpl* antics, clowning; **faire des s.** to clown around *ou* about.

singulariser (se) [səsɛ̃gylarize] *vpr* to draw attention to oneself.

singulier, -ière [sɛ̃gylje, -jɛr] **1** *a* (*peu ordinaire*) peculiar, odd; **combat s.** single combat. **2** *a* & *nm* *Grammaire* singular; **au s.** in the singular; **nom au s.** singular noun. ● **singularité** *nf* peculiarity. ● **singulièrement** *adv* (*notamment*) particularly; (*beaucoup*) extremely.

sinistre [sinistr] **1** *a* (*effrayant*) sinister; (*triste*) grim, (deadly) dull. **2** *nm* disaster; (*incendie*) fire; (*dommage*) *Jur* damage. ● **sinistré, -ée** *a* (*population, région etc*) disaster-stricken **‖** *nmf* disaster victim.

sinon [sinɔ̃] *conj* (*autrement*) otherwise, or else; (*sauf*) except (**que** that); (*si ce n'est*) if not.

sinueux, -euse [sinɥø, -øz] *a* winding. ● **sinuosités** *nfpl* twists (and turns).

sinus [sinys] *nm inv* *Anat* sinus. ● **sinusite** *nf* sinusitis; **avoir** *ou* **faire de la s.** to have sinusitis.

siphon [sifɔ̃] *nm* siphon; (*d'évier*) trap, *Br* U-bend.

siphonné, -ée [sifɔne] *a* *Fam* round the bend, crazy.

sirène [sirɛn] *nf* **1** (*d'usine etc*) siren. **2** (*femme*) mermaid.

sirop [siro] *nm* syrup; (*à diluer*) *Br* (fruit) cordial, fruit drink; **s. contre la toux** cough medicine *ou* mixture *ou* syrup. ● **syrupeux, -euse** *a* syrupy.

siroter [sirɔte] *vt* *Fam* to sip (at).

sis, sise [si, siz] *a* *Jur* situated.

sismique [sismik] *a* seismic; **secousse s.** earth tremor.

site [sit] *nm* (*endroit*) site; (*environnement*) setting; (*pittoresque*) beauty spot; **s. (touristique)** (*monument etc*) place of interest; **s. protégé** protected site (*on which building is not allowed*); **s. classé** place of historical importance, historical site.

sitôt [sito] *adv* **s. que** as soon as; **s. levée, elle partit** as soon as she was up, she left, **s. après** immediately after; **pas de s.** not for some time.

situation [sitɥasjɔ̃] *nf* situation, position; (*emploi*) position; **s. de famille** marital status. ● **situer** *vt* to situate, locate **‖** **se situer** *vpr* (*se trouver*) to be situated. ● **situé, -ée** *a* (*maison etc*) situated (**à** in).

six [sis] ([si] *before consonant*, [siz] *before vowel*) *a* & *nm* six. ● **sixième** [sizjɛm] *a* & *nmf* sixth; **un s.** a sixth **‖** *nf* *Scol* = *Br* first form; = *Am* sixth grade.

Skaï 284

Skaï® [skaj] *nm* imitation leather, leather-ette.

sketch [skɛtʃ] *nm* (*pl* sketches) (*de théâtre*) sketch.

ski [ski] *nm* (*objet*) ski; (*sport*) skiing; **faire du s.** to ski; **s. acrobatique** hotdogging; **s. alpin** downhill *ou* alpine skiing; **s. de fond** cross-country skiing; **s. nautique** water skiing. ●**skier** *vi* to ski. ●**skiable** *a* (*piste*) skiable, fit for skiing. ●**skieur, -euse** *nmf* skier.

slalom [slalɔm] *nm* Sport slalom; **faire du s.** to slalom.

slave [slav] *a* Slav; (*langue*) Slavonic ▮ *nmf* S. Slav.

slip [slip] *nm* (*d'homme*) briefs, underpants, *Br* pants; (*de femme*) panties, *Br* knickers, *Br* pants; **s. de bain** (swimming) trunks; (*d'un bikini*) briefs.

slogan [slɔgɑ̃] *nm* slogan.

Slovaquie [slɔvaki] *nf* Slovakia.

Slovénie [slɔveni] *nf* Slovenia.

slow [slo] *nm* slow dance.

SME [ɛsɛmə] *nm abrév* (*Système monétaire européen*) EMS.

SMIC [smik] *nm abrév* (*salaire minimum interprofessionnel de croissance*) guaranteed minimum wage. ●**smicard, -arde** *nmf* minimum wage earner.

smoking [smɔkiŋ] *nm* (*veston, costume*) dinner jacket, *Am* tuxedo.

snack(-bar) [snak(bar)] *nm* snack bar.

SNCF [ɛsɛnseef] *nf abrév* (*Société nationale des chemins de fer français*) *Br* French railways, *Am* French railroad system.

sniffer [snife] *vt* **s. de la colle** *Arg* to sniff glue.

snob [snɔb] *nmf* snob ▮ *a* snobbish; **elles sont snobs** they're snobbish, they're snobs. ●**snober** *vt* **s. qn** to snub s.o. ●**snobisme** *nm* snobbery.

sobre [sɔbr] *a* sober. ●**sobriété** *nf* sobriety.

sobriquet [sɔbrikɛ] *nm* nickname.

sociable [sɔsjabl] *a* sociable. ●**sociabilité** *nf* sociability.

social, -e, -aux [sɔsjal, -o] *a* social. ●**socialisme** *nm* socialism. ●**socialiste** *a* & *nmf* socialist.

société [sɔsjete] *nf* society; (*compagnie*) company; **s. anonyme** (*entreprise*) *Br* (public) limited company, *Am* incorporated company. ●**sociétaire** *nmf* (*d'une association*) member.

sociologie [sɔsjɔlɔʒi] *nf* sociology. ●**sociologique** *a* sociological. ●**sociologue** *nmf* sociologist.

socle [sɔkl] *nm* (*de statue, colonne*) plinth, pedestal; (*de lampe*) base.

socquette [sɔkɛt] *nf* ankle sock.

soda [sɔda] *nm* (*à l'orange etc*) *Br* fizzy drink, *Am* soda (pop).

sœur [sœr] *nf* sister; (*religieuse*) sister, nun; **bonne s.** *Fam* nun; **et ta s.!** *Fam* tell me another!, tell that to the marines!

sofa [sɔfa] *nm* sofa, settee.

soi [swa] *pron* oneself; **chacun pour s.** every

man for himself; **en s.** in itself; **chez s.** at home; **prendre sur s.** to get a grip on oneself; **cela va de soi** it's self-evident (**que** that); **amour/conscience de s.** self-love/awareness. ●**soi-même** *pron* oneself.

soi-disant [swadizɑ̃] *a inv* so-called ▮ *adv* supposedly.

soie [swa] *nf* **1** silk. **2** (*de porc etc*) bristle. ●**soierie** *nf* (*tissu*) silk.

soient [swa] *voir* **être.**

SOFRES [sɔfrɛs] *nf abrév* (*Société française d'études par sondages*) public opinion polling institute.

soif [swaf] *nf* thirst (*Fig* de for); **avoir s.** to be thirsty; **avoir s. de liberté/etc** *Fig* to thirst for freedom/etc; **donner s. à qn** to make s.o. thirsty.

soigner [swaɲe] *vt* to look after, take care of; (*malade*) to tend, nurse; (*maladie*) to treat; (*présentation, travail*) to take care over; **se faire s.** to have (medical) treatment. ▮ **se soigner** *vpr* to take care of oneself, look after oneself. ●**soigné, -ée** *a* (*vêtement*) neat, tidy; (*travail*) careful; (*personne*) well-groomed.

soigneux, -euse [swaɲø, -øz] *a* careful (**de** with); (*propre*) neat, tidy. ●**soigneusement** *adv* carefully.

soin [swɛ̃] *nm* care; (*ordre*) tidiness, neatness; **soins** *Méd* treatment, care; **avoir** *ou* **prendre s. de qch/de faire qch** to take care of sth/to do sth; **être aux petits soins avec qn** to wait hand and foot on s.o., fuss over s.o.; **les premiers soins** first aid; **soins de beauté** beauty care *ou* treatment; **aux bons soins de** (*sur lettre*) care of, c/o; **avec s.** carefully, with care.

soir [swar] *nm* evening; **le s.** (*chaque soir*) in the evening(s); **à neuf heures du s.** at nine in the evening; **repas du s.** evening meal. ●**soirée** *nf* evening; (*réunion*) party; **s. dansante** dance.

sois, soit¹ [swa] *voir* **être.**

soit² **1** [swa] *conj* (*à savoir*) that is (to say); **s.... s....** either... or...; **s. une droite...** *Math* given a straight line.... **2** [swat] *adv* (*oui*) very well.

soixante [swasɑ̃t] *a* & *nm* sixty. ●**soixantaine** *nf* **une s.** (**de**) (*nombre*) (about) sixty; **avoir la s.** (*âge*) to be about sixty. ●**soixantième** *a* & *nmf* sixtieth.

soixante-dix [swasɑ̃tdis] *a* & *nm* seventy. ●**soixante-dixième** *a* & *nmf* seventieth.

soja [sɔʒa] *nm* (*plante*) soya; **graines de s.** soya bean; **germes** *ou* **pousses de s.** beansprouts.

sol¹ [sɔl] *nm* ground; (*plancher*) floor; (*territoire, terrain*) soil.

sol² [sɔl] *nm* (*note de musique*) G.

solaire [sɔlɛr] *a* solar; (*rayons, chaleur*) sun's; **crème/huile s.** sun(tan) lotion/oil.

solarium [sɔlarjɔm] *nm* solarium.

soldat [sɔlda] *nm* soldier; **simple s.** private.

solde [sɔld] **1** *nm* (*de compte, à payer*) balance. **2** *nm* **en s.** (*acheter*) at a bargain price, in the sales, *Am* on sale; **soldes** (*marchandises*) sale goods; (*vente*) (clearance) sale(s); **faire les soldes** to go round the sales. **3** *nf* (*de soldat*) pay; **à la s. de qn** *Fig* *Péj* in s.o.'s pay.

solder [sɔlde] **1** *vt* (*articles*) to clear, sell off. **2** *vt* (*compte*) to pay the balance of. **3 se solder** *vpr* **se s. par un échec/etc** to end in failure/*etc*. ● **soldé, -ée** *a* (*article etc*) reduced. ● **solderie** *nf* *Br* discount *ou* reject shop, *Am* discount outlet.

sole [sɔl] *nf* (*poisson*) sole.

soleil [sɔlɛj] *nm* sun; (*chaleur, lumière*) sunshine; (*fleur*) sunflower; **au s.** in the sun; **il fait (du) s.** it's sunny, the sun's shining; **coup de s.** *Méd* sunburn; **prendre un bain de s.** to sunbathe.

solennel, -elle [sɔlanɛl] *a* solemn. ● **solennellement** *adv* solemnly. ● **solennité** [-anite] *nf* solemnity.

solex® [sɔlɛks] *nm* moped.

solfège [sɔlfɛʒ] *nm* rudiments of music.

solidaire [sɔlidɛr] *a* **être s.** (*ouvriers etc*) to show solidarity, be as one (**de** with); (*pièce de machine*) to be interdependent (**de** with). ● **solidairement** *adv* jointly. ● **se solidariser** *vpr* to show solidarity (**avec** with). ● **solidarité** *nf* solidarity; (*d'éléments*) interdependence.

solide [sɔlid] *a* (*voiture, nourriture, caractère, état etc*) solid; (*argument, nerfs etc*) sound; (*vigoureux*) robust ▮ *nm Ch* solid. ● **solidement** *adv* solidly. ● **se solidifier** *vpr* to solidify. ● **solidité** *nf* solidity; (*d'argument etc*) soundness.

soliste [sɔlist] *nmf Mus* soloist.

solitaire [sɔlitɛr] *a* (*vie, passant etc*) solitary; (*tout seul*) all alone ▮ *nmf* loner; (*ermite*) recluse, hermit; **en s.** on one's own; **traversée en s.** solo *ou* single-handed crossing. ● **solitude** *nf* solitude; **aimer la s.** to like being alone.

solive [sɔliv] *nf* joist, beam.

solliciter [sɔlisite] *vt* (*audience, emploi etc*) to seek; (*tenter*) *Litt* to tempt, entice; **s. qn** (*faire appel à*) to appeal to s.o. (**de faire** to do); **être (très) sollicité** (*personne*) to be in (great) demand. ● **sollicitation** *nf* (*demande*) appeal; (*tentation*) temptation. ● **sollicitude** [sɔlisityd] *nf* solicitude, concern.

solo [sɔlo] *a inv & nm Mus* solo.

solstice [sɔlstis] *nm* solstice.

soluble [sɔlybl] *a* (*substance, problème*) soluble; **café s.** instant coffee.

solution [sɔlysjɔ̃] *nf* (*d'un problème etc*) solution (**de** to); (*action, mélange chimique*) solution.

solvable [sɔlvabl] *a Fin* solvent. ● **solvabilité** *nf Fin* solvency.

solvant [sɔlvɑ̃] *nm Ch* solvent.

Somalie [sɔmali] *nf* Somalia.

sombre [sɔ̃br] *a* dark; (*triste*) sombre, gloomy; **il fait s.** it's dark.

sombrer [sɔ̃bre] *vi* (*bateau*) to sink, founder; **s. dans** (*folie, sommeil etc*) *Fig* to sink into.

sommaire [sɔmɛr] *a* summary; (*repas, tenue*) scant ▮ *nm* summary, synopsis.

sommation [sɔmasjɔ̃] *nf Jur* summons; (*de policier etc*) warning.

somme [sɔm] **1** *nf* sum; **faire la s. de** to add up; **en s., s. toute** in short. **2** *nm* (*sommeil*) nap; **faire un s.** to to take *ou* have a nap.

sommeil [sɔmɛj] *nm* sleep; (*envie de dormir*) sleepiness, drowsiness; **avoir s.** to be *ou* feel sleepy *ou* drowsy; **être en plein s.** to be fast asleep; **laisser une affaire/etc en s.** *Fig* to put a matter/*etc* aside. ● **sommeiller** *vi* to doze; (*faculté, qualité*) *Fig* to lie dormant *ou* idle.

sommelier [sɔməlje] *nm* wine waiter.

sommer [sɔme] *vt* **s. qn de faire qch** (*enjoindre*) *Litt & Jur* to summon s.o. to do sth.

sommes [sɔm] *voir* **être**.

sommet [sɔmɛ] *nm* top; (*de montagne*) summit, top; (*de la gloire etc*) *Fig* height, summit; **conférence au s.** summit (conference).

sommier [sɔmje] *nm* (*de lit*) base; **s. à ressorts** spring base.

sommité [sɔmite] *nf* leading light, top person (**de** in).

somnambule [sɔmnɑ̃byl] *nmf* sleepwalker; **être s.** to sleepwalk. ● **somnambulisme** *nm* sleepwalking.

somnifère [sɔmnifɛr] *nm* sleeping pill.

somnolence [sɔmnɔlɑ̃s] *nf* drowsiness, sleepiness. ● **somnolent, -ente** *a* drowsy, sleepy. ● **somnoler** *vi* to doze, drowse.

somptuaire [sɔ̃ptɥɛr] *a* (*dépenses etc*) *Litt* extravagant.

somptueux, -euse [sɔ̃ptɥø, -øz] *a* sumptuous, magnificent. ● **somptuosité** *nf* sumptuousness, magnificence.

son¹ [sɔ̃] *nm* **1** (*bruit*) sound. **2** (*de grains*) bran.

son², sa, *pl* **ses** [sɔ̃, sa, se] (*sa becomes* **son** [sɔ̃n] *before a vowel or mute h*) *a poss* his; (*de femme*) her; (*de chose*) its; (*indéfini*) one's; **son père/sa mère** his *ou* her *ou* one's father/mother; **son ami(e)** his *ou* her *ou* one's friend; **sa durée** its duration.

sonate [sɔnat] *nf Mus* sonata.

sondage [sɔ̃daʒ] *nm* (*de mer*) sounding; (*de terrain*) drilling; *Méd* probing; **s. (d'opinion)** opinion poll.

sonde [sɔ̃d] *nf Géol* drill; *Nau* sounding line; *Méd* probe; (*pour l'alimentation*) (feeding) tube; **s. spatiale** space probe.

sonder [sɔ̃de] *vt* (*rivière etc*) to sound; (*terrain*) to drill; (*atmosphère*) & *Méd* to probe; (*personne, l'opinion*) *Fig* to sound out.

songe [sɔ̃ʒ] *nm* dream.

songer [sɔ̃ʒe] *vi* **s. à qch/à faire qch** to think of sth/of doing sth ▮ *vt* **s. que** to consider *ou* think that. ● **songeur, -euse** *a* thoughtful, pensive.

sonner [sɔne] *vi* to ring; (*cor, cloches etc*) to sound; **on a sonné (à la porte)** someone has rung the (door)bell; **midi a sonné** it has struck twelve ∎ vt (cloche) to ring; (domestique) to ring for; (cor etc) to sound; (l'heure) to strike; (assommer) to knock out.

● **sonnant, -ante** a en espèces sonnantes et trébuchantes in coin of the realm; **à cinq**/etc **heures sonnantes** on the stroke of five/etc. ● **sonné, -ée** a **1 trois**/etc **heures sonnées** Br gone ou past three/etc o'clock. **2** Fam (fou) crazy; (assommé) dazed, groggy.

sonnerie [sɔnri] nf (son) ring(ing); (de cor etc) sound; (appareil) bell; (au bout du fil) Br ringing tone, Am ring; **s. 'occupé'** Br engaged tone, Am busy signal.

sonnette [sɔnɛt] nf bell; **coup de s.** ring; **s. d'alarme** alarm (bell).

sonnet [sɔnɛ] nm (poème) sonnet.

sonore [sɔnɔr] a (rire) loud; (salle, voix) resonant; **effets/ondes/etc sonores** sound effects/waves/etc. ● **sonorité** nf (de salle) acoustics, resonance; (de violon etc) tone.

sonorisation [sɔnɔrizasjɔ̃] nf (Fam sono) (matériel) sound equipment ou system. ● **sonoriser** vt (salle) to wire for sound; (film) to add sound to.

sont [sɔ̃] voir être.

sophistiqué, -ée [sɔfistike] a sophisticated.

soporifique [sɔpɔrifik] a (médicament, discours etc) soporific.

soprano [sɔprano] Mus nmf (personne) soprano ∎ nm (voix) soprano.

sorbet [sɔrbɛ] nm Culin Br water ice, sorbet.

sorcellerie [sɔrsɛlri] nf witchcraft, sorcery. ● **sorcier** nm sorcerer ∎ am ce n'est pas s.! Fam there's nothing complicated about it!, it's dead easy! ● **sorcière** nf witch; **chasse aux sorcières** Pol witch-hunt.

sordide [sɔrdid] a (acte, affaire etc) sordid; (maison etc) squalid.

sornettes [sɔrnɛt] nfpl (propos) Péj twaddle, nonsense.

sort [sɔr] nm **1** (destin, hasard) fate; (condition) lot. **2** (maléfice) spell.

sortable [sɔrtabl] a (personne, vêtement) presentable; **elle n'est pas s.!** Fam we etc can't really take you anywhere!

sortant, -ante [sɔrtɑ̃, -ɑ̃t] a (numéro) winning; (député etc) outgoing.

sorte [sɔrt] nf sort, kind (de of); **toutes sortes de** all sorts ou kinds of; **en quelque s.** in a way, as it were; **de (telle) s. que tu apprennes** so that ou in such a way that you may learn; **de la s.** (de cette façon) in that way; **faire en s. que** (+ sub) to see to it that.

sortie [sɔrti] nf **1** (porte) exit, way out; (action de sortir) leaving, exit, departure; (de scène) exit; (promenade à pied) walk; (en voiture) drive; (excursion) outing, trip; (au cinéma etc) evening out; (de film, disque) release; (de livre, modèle etc) appearance; Ordinat output; (de devises, marchandises) export; **sorties** (argent) outgoings; **à la s. de l'école** when the children come out of school; **l'heure de la s. de qn** the time at which s.o. leaves; **première s.** (de

convalescent etc) first time out; **être de s.** (pour s'amuser etc) to be out, be having time out. **2 s. de bain** (peignoir) bathrobe.

sortilège [sɔrtilɛʒ] nm (magic) spell.

sortir* [sɔrtir] vi (aux être) to go out, leave; (venir) to come out; (pour s'amuser, danser etc) to go out; (film, modèle etc) to come out; (numéro gagnant) to come up; **s. de** (endroit) to leave; (université) to be a graduate of; (famille, milieu) to come from; (légalité, limites) to go beyond; (compétence) to be outside; (sujet) to stray from; (gonds, rails) to come off; **s. de table** to leave the table; **s. de terre** (plante, fondations) to come up; **s. de l'ordinaire** ou **du commun** to be out of the ordinary; **s. indemne** to escape unhurt (de from).

∎ vt (aux avoir) to take out (de of); (film, modèle, livre etc) to bring out; (dire) Fam to come out with; (expulser) Fam to throw out.

∎ **se sortir** vpr **s'en s.**, **se s. d'affaire** to get ou pull ou come through.

∎ nm **au s. de l'hiver**/etc at the end of winter/etc; **au s. du lit** on getting out of bed.

SOS [ɛsoɛs] nm SOS; **lancer un SOS** to send (out) an SOS; **SOS médecins** emergency medical services.

sosie [sozi] nm (de personne) double.

sot, sotte [so, sɔt] a foolish ∎ nmf fool. ● **sottement** adv foolishly. ● **sottise** nf foolishness; (action, parole) foolish thing; **faire des sottises** (enfant) to be naughty, misbehave.

sou [su] nm (monnaie) Hist sou; **sous** (argent) Fam money; **elle n'a pas un ou le s.** she doesn't have a penny, she's penniless; **n'avoir pas un s. de bon sens**/etc not to have an ounce of good sense/etc; **dépenser jusqu'à son dernier s.** to spend every last penny ou one's last penny; **machine à sous** fruit machine, Am slot machine, one-armed bandit.

soubresaut [subrəso] nm (sudden) start, jolt.

souche [suʃ] nf (d'arbre) stump; (de carnet) stub, counterfoil; (de vigne, famille) stock.

souci [susi] nm (inquiétude) worry, concern; (préoccupation) concern (de for); **se faire du s.** to worry, be worried; **ça lui donne du s.** it worries him ou her. ● **se soucier** vpr **se s. de** to be worried ou concerned about; **se s. de qch comme de l'an quarante** Fam not to give a hoot about sth. ● **soucieux, -euse** a worried, concerned (de qch about sth); **s. de plaire**/etc anxious to please/etc.

soucoupe [sukup] nf saucer; **s. volante** flying saucer.

soudain, -aine [sudɛ̃, -ɛn] a sudden ∎ adv suddenly. ● **soudainement** adv suddenly. ● **soudaineté** nf suddenness.

Soudan [sudɑ̃] nm Sudan.

soude [sud] nf Ch soda; **cristaux de s.** washing soda.

souder [sude] vt (avec de la soudure) to solder; (par soudure autogène ou soudure à *l'arc*) to weld; (*groupes etc*) *Fig* to unite (closely); **lampe à s.** blowlamp ∎ **se souder** *vpr* (*os*) to knit (together). ● **soudure** *nf* soldering; (*substance*) solder; **s. (autogène)** welding.

soudoyer [sudwaje] *vt* to bribe.

souffle [sufl] *nm* puff, blow; (*haleine*) breath; (*respiration*) breathing; (*de bombe etc*) blast; (*inspiration*) *Fig* inspiration; **s. (d'air)** breath of air; **reprendre son s.** to get one's breath back. ● **souffler** *vi* to blow; (*haleter*) to puff; **laisser s. qn** (*reprendre haleine*) to let s.o. get his breath back ∎ *vt* (*bougie*) to blow out; (*fumée, poussière, verre*) to blow; (*par une explosion*) to blow down, blast; (*chuchoter*) to whisper; (*voler*) *Fam* to swipe, *Br* pinch (à from); (*étonner*) *Fam* to astound, flabbergast; **s. une réplique à qn** (*acteur*) to give s.o. a prompt; **ne pas s. mot** not to breathe a word. ● **soufflet** *nm* **1** (*instrument*) bellows. **2** (*de train, d'autobus*) concertina vestibule. **3** (*gifle*) *Litt* slap. ● **souffleur, -euse** *nmf* (*de théâtre*) prompter.

soufflé [sufle] *nm Culin* soufflé.

souffrance [sufrãs] *nf* **1 souffrance(s)** suffering. **2 en s.** (*colis etc*) unclaimed; (*affaire*) in abeyance.

souffreteux, -euse [sufrətø, -øz] *a* sickly.

souffrir* [sufrir] **1** *vi* to suffer; **s. de** to suffer from; (*gorge, pieds etc*) to have trouble with; **faire s. qn** (*physiquement*) to hurt s.o.; (*moralement*) to make s.o. suffer, hurt s.o.; **ta réputation en souffrira** your reputation will suffer. **2** *vt* (*endurer*) to suffer; **je ne peux pas le s.** *Fam* I can't bear him. **3** *vt* (*exception*) to admit of. ● **souffrant, -ante** *a* unwell.

soufre [sufr] *nm Br* sulphur, *Am* sulfur.

souhait [swɛ] *nm* wish; **à vos souhaits!** (*après un éternuement*) bless you!; **à s.** perfectly. ● **souhaiter** [swete] *vt* (*bonheur etc*) to wish for; **s. qch à qn** to wish s.o. sth; **s. faire** to hope to do; **s. que** (+ *sub*) to hope that. ● **souhaitable** *a* desirable.

souiller [suje] *vt* to soil, dirty; (*déshonorer*) *Fig* to sully, tarnish. ● **souillon** *nf* slut, slovenly woman.

soûl, soûle [su, sul] **1** *a* drunk. **2** *nm* **tout son s.** (*boire etc*) to one's heart's content. ● **soûler** *vt* to make (s.o.) drunk ∎ **se soûler** *vpr* to get drunk.

soulager [sulaʒe] *vt* to relieve (de of). ● **soulagement** *nm* relief.

soulever [sul(ə)ve] *vt* to lift (up), raise; (*poussière, question*) to raise; (*le peuple, l'opinion*) to stir up; (*sentiment*) to arouse; **cela me soulève le cœur** it makes me feel sick, it turns my stomach ∎ **se soulever** *vpr* (*malade etc*) to lift oneself (up); (*se révolter*) to rise (up). ● **soulèvement** [-ɛvmã] *nm* (*révolte*) (up)rising.

soulier [sulje] *nm* shoe; **être dans ses petits souliers** *Fam* to feel awkward.

souligner [suliɲe] *vt* (*d'un trait*) to underline; (*faire remarquer*) to emphasize, under-

line; **s. que** to emphasize that.

soumettre* [sumɛtr] **1** *vt* (*pays, rebelles*) to subdue, subjugate; **s. à** (*assujettir*) to subject to ∎ **se soumettre** *vpr* to submit (à to). **2** *vt* (*présenter*) to submit (à to). ● **soumis, -ise** *a* (*docile*) submissive; **s. à** subject to. ● **soumission** *nf* **1** submission; (*docilité*) submissiveness. **2** (*offre*) *Com* tender, bid.

soupape [supap] *nf* valve; **s. de sécurité** (*appareil, Fig exutoire*) safety valve.

soupçon [supsɔ̃] *nm* suspicion; **un s. de** (*quantité*) *Fig* a hint *ou* touch of; **au-dessus de tout s.** above suspicion. ● **soupçonner** *vt* to suspect (de of, **d'avoir fait** of doing, **que** that). ● **soupçonneux, -euse** *a* suspicious.

soupe [sup] *nf* soup; **s. populaire** (*endroit*) soup kitchen; **être s. au lait** *Fam* to be hot-tempered *ou* quick-tempered; **un gros plein de s.** (*obèse*) *Fam* fatso, *Péj* fat lump. ● **soupière** *nf* (soup) tureen.

soupente [supãt] *nf* (*sous le toit*) loft.

souper [supe] *nm* supper ∎ *vi* to have supper.

soupeser [supəze] *vt* (*objet dans la main*) to feel the weight of; (*arguments etc*) *Fig* to weigh up.

soupir [supir] *nm* sigh. ● **soupirer** *vi* to sigh; **s. après** to yearn for. ● **soupirant** *nm* (*amoureux*) suitor.

soupirail, -aux [supiraj, -o] *nm* basement window.

souple [supl] *a* (*cuir, membre, personne etc*) supple; (*tolérant*) (*personne etc*) flexible. ● **souplesse** *nf* suppleness; (*adaptabilité*) flexibility.

source [surs] *nf* **1** (*point d'eau*) spring; **eau de s.** spring water; **prendre sa s.** (*rivière*) to rise (à at, dans in). **2** (*origine*) source; **s. d'énergie** source of energy; **s. lumineuse** light source; **tenir qch de s. sûre** to have sth on good authority.

sourcil [sursi] *nm* eyebrow. ● **sourciller** *vi* **ne pas s.** *Fig* not to bat an eyelid.

sourd, sourde [sur, surd] **1** *a* deaf (*Fig* à to); **être s. comme un pot** *Fam* to be stone-deaf, be as deaf as a post ∎ *nmf* deaf person. **2** *a* (*douleur*) dull; **bruit s.** thump; **lutte sourde** silent *ou* secret struggle. ● **sourd-muet** (*pl* **sourds-muets**), **sourde-muette** (*pl* **sourdes-muettes**) *a* a deaf and dumb ∎ *nmf* deaf and dumb person, *Péj* deaf mute.

sourdine [surdin] *nf* (*dispositif*) *Mus* mute; **en s.** *Fig* quietly, secretly.

souricière [surisjɛr] *nf* mousetrap; *Fig* trap.

sourire* [surir] *vi* to smile (à at); **s. à qn** (*fortune*) to smile on s.o. ∎ *nm* smile; **faire un s. à qn** to give s.o. a smile.

souris [suri] *nf* (*animal*) & *Ordinat* mouse (*pl* mice).

sournois, -oise [surnwa, -waz] *a* sly, underhand. ● **sournoisement** *adv* slyly. ● **sournoiserie** *nf* slyness.

sous [su] *prép* (*position*) under, underneath, beneath; (*rang*) under; **s. la pluie** in the rain; **nager s. l'eau** to swim underwater; **s.**

calmants under sedation; **s. cet angle** from that angle *ou* point of view; **s. le nom de** under the name of; **s. Charles X** under Charles X; **travailler s.** DOS *Ordinat* to work in DOS; **s. peu** (*bientôt*) shortly.

sous- [su] *préf* (*subordination, subdivision*) sub-; (*insuffisance*) under-.

sous-alimenté, -ée [suzalimãte] *a* underfed, undernourished. ● **sous-alimentation** *nf* malnutrition, undernourishment.

sous-bois [subwa] *nm* undergrowth.

sous-chef [suʃɛf] *nmf* second-in-command.

souscrire* [suskrir] *vi* **s. à** (*payer, approuver*) to subscribe to. ● **souscription** *nf* subscription.

sous-développé, -ée [sudevlɔpe] *a* (*pays etc*) underdeveloped.

sous-directeur, -trice [sudirektœr, -tris] *nmf* assistant manager, assistant manageress.

sous-emploi [suzãplwa] *nm* underemployment.

sous-entendre [suzãtãdr] *vt* to imply. ● **sous-entendu** *nm* insinuation.

sous-estimer [suzɛstime] *vt* to underestimate.

sous-jacent, -ente [suʒasã, -ãt] *a* underlying.

sous-louer [sulwe] *vt* (*appartement*) to sublet.

sous-main [sumɛ̃] *nm inv* desk pad.

sous-marin, -ine [sumarɛ̃, -in] *a* underwater; **plongée sous-marine** skin *ou* scuba diving ▮ *nm* submarine.

sous-officier [suzɔfisje] *nm* noncommissioned officer, NCO.

sous-payer [supeje] *vt* (*ouvrier etc*) to underpay.

sous-préfet [suprefɛ] *nm* subprefect (*chief administrative officer in an arrondissement*). ● **sous-préfecture** *nf* subprefecture.

sous-produit [suprɔdɥi] *nm* by-product.

soussigné, -ée [susine] *a & nmf* undersigned; **je s.** I the undersigned.

sous-sol [susɔl] *nm* (*d'immeuble*) basement; *Géol* subsoil.

sous-titre [sutitr] *nm* subtitle. ● **sous-titrer** *vt* (*film*) to subtitle.

soustraire* [sustrer] *vt* to remove; *Math* to take away, subtract (**de** from); **s. qn à** (*danger etc*) to shield *ou* protect s.o. from ▮ **se soustraire** *vpr* **se s. à** to escape from; (*devoir, obligation*) to avoid. ● **soustraction** *nf Math* subtraction.

sous-traiter [sutrete] *vi* (*usine etc*) to subcontract ▮ *vt* (*affaire etc*) to subcontract. ● **sous-traitant** *nm* subcontractor. ● **sous-traitance** *nf* **travailler en s.-traitance avec qn** to work as a subcontractor with s.o.

sous-verre [suver] *nm inv* (*encadrement*) (frameless) glass mount.

sous-vêtement [suvɛtmã] *nm* undergarment; **sous-vêtements** underwear.

soutane [sutan] *nf* (*de prêtre*) cassock.

soute [sut] *nf* (*de bateau*) hold.

soutenir* [sut(ə)nir] *vt* to support, hold up;

(*opinion*) to uphold, maintain; (*candidat etc*) to back, support; (*malade*) to sustain; (*effort, intérêt*) to sustain, keep up; (*thèse*) to defend; (*résister à*) to withstand; **s. que** to maintain that ▮ **se soutenir** *vpr* (*blessé etc*) to hold oneself up (straight); (*se maintenir, durer*) to be sustained. ● **soutenu, -ue** *a* (*attention, effort*) sustained; (*style*) lofty.

souterrain, -aine [suterɛ̃, -ɛn] *a* underground ▮ *nm* underground passage.

soutien [sutjɛ̃] *nm* support; (*personne*) supporter; **s. de famille** breadwinner. ● **soutien-gorge** *nm* (*pl* soutiens-gorge) bra.

soutirer [sutire] *vt* **s. qch à qn** to extract *ou* get sth from s.o.

souvenir [suvnir] *nm* memory, recollection; (*objet*) memento; (*cadeau*) keepsake; (*pour touristes*) souvenir; **en s. de** in memory of; **mon bon s. à...** (give) my regards to..., my best regards to.... ● **se souvenir*** *vpr* **se s. de** to remember, recall; **se s. que** to remember *ou* recall that.

souvent [suvã] *adv* often; **peu s.** seldom; **le plus s.** usually, more often than not.

souverain, -aine [suv(ə)rɛ̃, -ɛn] *a* sovereign; (*extrême*) (*mépris etc*) supreme; **un remède s. contre** a guaranteed *ou Litt* sovereign remedy against ▮ *nmf* sovereign. ● **souveraineté** *nf* sovereignty.

soviétique [sɔvjetik] *Hist a* Soviet; **l'Union s.** the Soviet Union ▮ *nmf* Soviet citizen.

soyeux, -euse [swajø, -øz] *a* silky.

soyons, soyez [swajɔ̃, swaje] *voir* être.

SPA [espea] *nf abrév* (*Société protectrice des animaux*) = *Br* RSPCA, = *Am* ASPCA.

spacieux, -euse [spasjø, -øz] *a* spacious, roomy.

spaghetti(s) [spageti] *nmpl* spaghetti.

sparadrap [sparadra] *nm* (*pour pansement*) *Br* sticking plaster, *Am* adhesive tape.

spasme [spasm] *nm* spasm. ● **spasmodique** *a* spasmodic.

spatial, -e, -aux [spasjal, -o] *a* **station**/*etc* **spatiale** space station/*etc*; **engin s.** spaceship, spacecraft.

spatule [spatyl] *nf* spatula.

speaker [spikœr] *nm ou* **speakerine** [spikrin] *nf* (*de télévision ou radio*) announcer.

spécial, -e, -aux [spesjal, -o] *a* special; (*bizarre*) peculiar. ● **spécialement** *adv* (*exprès*) specially; (*en particulier*) especially, particularly; **pas s.** *Fam* not particularly, not especially.

spécialiser (se) [səspesjalize] *vpr* to specialize (**dans** in). ● **spécialisation** *nf* specialization. ● **spécialiste** *nmf* specialist. ● **spécialité** *nf Br* speciality, *Am* specialty.

spécifier [spesifje] *vt* to specify (**que** that).

spécifique [spesifik] *a* (*particulier*) & *Phys Ch* specific.

spécimen [spesimen] *nm* specimen; (*livre etc*) specimen copy.

spectacle [spɛktakl] *nm* **1** (*vue*) sight, spectacle; **se donner en s.** *Péj* to make an exhibition of oneself. **2** (*représentation*) show; **le s.**

(industrie) show business; **salle de s.** *(théâtre)* theatre; *(cinéma) Br* cinema, *Am* movie theater. ●**spectateur, -trice** *nmf Sport* spectator; *(au théâtre, cinéma etc)* member of the audience; *(témoin)* onlooker, witness; **spectateurs** *(au théâtre, cinéma etc)* audience.

spectaculaire [spɛktakyler] *a* spectacular.

spectre [spɛktr] *nm* 1 *(fantôme)* spectre, ghost. 2 *(solaire)* spectrum.

spéculer [spekyle] *vi Fin Phil* to speculate; **s. sur** *(tabler sur)* to bank *ou* rely on. ●**spéculateur, -trice** *nmf Fin* speculator. ●**spéculatif, -ive** *a Fin Phil* speculative. ●**spéculation** *nf Fin Phil* speculation.

spéléologie [speleɔlɔʒi] *nf (activité) Br* potholing, caving, *Am* spelunking. ●**spéléologue** *nmf Br* potholer, *Am* spelunker.

sperme [spɛrm] *nm* sperm, semen.

sphère [sfɛr] *nf (boule, domaine)* sphere. ●**sphérique** *a* spherical.

sphinx [sfɛ̃ks] *nm* sphinx.

spirale [spiral] *nf* spiral.

spirite [spirit] *nmf* spiritualist. ●**spiritisme** *nm* spiritualism.

spirituel, -elle [spirityɛl] *a* 1 *(amusant)* witty. 2 *(pouvoir, vie etc)* spiritual.

spiritueux [spirityø] *nmpl (boissons)* spirits.

splendide [splɑ̃did] *a (merveilleux, riche, beau etc)* splendid. ●**splendeur** *nf (richesse, beauté)* splendour.

spongieux, -euse [spɔ̃ʒjø, -øz] *a* spongy.

spontané, -ée [spɔ̃tane] *a* spontaneous. ●**spontanéité** *nf* spontaneity. ●**spontanément** *adv* spontaneously.

sporadique [spɔradik] *a* sporadic.

sport [spɔr] *nm* sport; **faire du s.** to play *Br* sport *ou Am* sports; **(de) s.** *(chaussures, vêtements)* casual, sports; **voiture/veste/terrain de s.** sports car/jacket/ground. ●**sportif, -ive** *a (personne)* fond of *Br* sport *ou Am* sports; *(attitude, esprit)* sportsmanlike, sporting; *(association, journal, résultats)* sports, sporting; *(allure)* athletic ▮ *nmf* sportsman, sportswoman. ●**sportivité** *nf* sportsmanship.

spot [spɔt] *nm* 1 *(lampe)* spotlight, *Fam* spot. 2 **s.** *(publicitaire)* *(à la radio, télévision etc)* commercial.

sprint [sprint] *nm Sport* sprint. ●**sprinter** *vt* to sprint ▮ *nm* [-œr] sprinter. ●**sprinteuse** *nf* sprinter.

square [skwar] *nm* public garden.

squash [skwaʃ] *nm (jeu)* squash.

squat [skwat] *nm* squat. ●**squatteur, -euse** *nmf* squatter. ●**squatter** *vi* to squat ▮ *nm* [-œr] squatter.

squelette [skəlɛt] *nm* skeleton. ●**squelettique** *a (personne, maigreur)* skeleton-like; *(exposé)* sketchy.

stable [stabl] *a* stable. ●**stabilisateur** *nm* stabilizer. ●**stabiliser** *vt* to stabilize ▮ **se stabiliser** *vpr* to stabilize. ●**stabilité** *nf* stability.

stade [stad] *nm* 1 *Sport* stadium. 2 *(phase)* stage.

stage [staʒ] *nm (période)* training period; *(cours)* (training) course; **faire un s.** to undergo training, do a (training) course; **être en s.** to be undergoing training, be on a (training) course. ●**stagiaire** *a & nmf* trainee.

stagner [stagne] *vi* to stagnate. ●**stagnant, -ante** *a* stagnant. ●**stagnation** *nf* stagnation.

stalle [stal] *nf (dans une écurie) & Rel* stall.

stand [stɑ̃d] *nm (d'exposition etc)* stand, stall; **s. de ravitaillement** *Sport* pit; **s. de tir** *(de foire)* shooting range; *(militaire)* firing range.

standard [stɑ̃dar] 1 *nm (téléphonique)* switchboard. 2 *a inv (modèle etc)* standard. ●**standardiser** *vt* to standardize. ●**standardiste** *nmf* (switchboard) operator.

standing [stɑ̃diŋ] *nm* standing, status; **immeuble de (grand) s.** *Br* luxury block of flats, *Am* luxury apartment building.

starter [starter] *nm* 1 *(de véhicule)* choke. 2 *Sport* starter.

station [stasjɔ̃] *nf (de métro, d'observation, de radio etc)* station; *(de ski etc)* resort; *(d'autobus)* stop; **s. de taxis** *Br* taxi rank, *Am* taxi stand; **s. debout** standing (position); **s. (thermale)** spa. ●**station-service** *nf (pl stations-service)* service station, *Br* petrol *ou Am* gas station.

stationnaire [stasjɔner] *a* stationary.

stationner [stasjɔne] *vi (être garé)* to be parked; *(se garer)* to park. ●**stationnement** *nm* parking.

statique [statik] *a* static.

statistique [statistik] *nf (donnée)* statistic; **la s.** *(téchniques)* statistics ▮ *a* statistical.

statue [staty] *nf* statue. ●**statuette** *nf* statuette.

statuer [statɥe] *vi* **s. sur** *(juge etc)* to rule on.

statu quo [statykwo] *nm inv* status quo.

stature [statyr] *nf* stature.

statut [staty] *nm* 1 *(position)* status. 2 **statuts** *(règles)* statutes. ●**statutaire** *a* statutory.

steak [stɛk] *nm* steak.

stencil [stɛnsil] *nm* stencil.

sténo [steno] *nf (personne)* stenographer; *(sténographie)* shorthand, stenography; **prendre qch en s.** to take sth down in shorthand. ●**sténodactylo** *nf Br* shorthand typist, *Am* stenographer. ●**sténographie** *nf* shorthand, stenography.

stéréo [stereo] *nf* stereo; **en s.** in stereo ▮ *a inv (disque etc)* stereo. ●**stéréophonique** *a* stereophonic.

stéréotype [stereɔtip] *nm* stereotype. ●**stéréotypé, -ée** *a* stereotyped.

stérile [steril] *a* sterile; *(terre)* barren. ●**stérilisation** *nf* sterilization. ●**stériliser** *vt* to sterilize. ●**stérilité** *nf* sterility; *(de terre)* barrenness.

stérilet [sterilɛ] *nm* IUD, coil.

stéroïde [sterɔid] *nm* steroid.

stéthoscope [stetɔskɔp] *nm* stethoscope.

steward [stiwart] *nm (d'avion, de bateau)* steward.

stigmate [stigmat] *nm Fig* mark, stigma (**de** of). ●**stigmatiser** *vt (dénoncer)* to stigma-

tize.
stimuler [stimyle] *vt* to stimulate. ●**stimulant**
nm *Fig* stimulus; (*médicament*) stimulant.
●**stimulateur** *nm* s. **cardiaque** pacemaker.
●**stimulation** *nf* stimulation.
stimulus [stimylys] *nm* (*pl* stimuli [-li])
(*physiologique*) stimulus.
stipuler [stipyle] *vt* to stipulate (**que** that).
●**stipulation** *nf* stipulation.
stock [stɔk] *nm* (*de marchandises*) & *Fig*
stock (**de** of); **en s.** in stock. ●**stocker** *vt*
(*provisions etc*) to store, (keep in) stock.
●**stockage** *nm* stocking.
stoïque [stɔik] *a* stoic(al). ●**stoïcisme** *nm*
stoicism.
stop [stɔp] 1 *int* stop ▮ *nm* (*panneau*) *Aut*
stop sign; (*feu arrière de véhicule*) brake
light, *Br* stoplight. 2 *nm* **faire du s.** *Fam* to
hitchhike. ●**stopper** 1 *vti* to stop. 2 *vt* (*vêtement*) to mend (invisibly). ●**stoppage** *nm*
(invisible) mending.
store [stɔr] *nm* *Br* blind, *Am* (window)
shade; (*de magasin*) awning.
strabisme [strabism] *nm* squint.
strapontin [strapɔ̃tɛ̃] *nm* tip-up *ou* folding
seat.
stratagème [strataʒɛm] *nm* stratagem, ploy.
stratège [strateʒ] *nm* strategist. ●**stratégie** *nf*
strategy. ●**stratégique** *a* strategic.
stress [strɛs] *nm inv* stress. ●**stressant, -ante**
a stressful. ●**stressé, -ée** *a* under stress.
strict, -e [strikt] *a* (*principes, professeur etc*)
strict; (*tenue, vérité*) plain; **le s. minimum**
the bare minimum; **mon droit le plus s.** my
basic right; **dans la plus stricte intimité** in the
strictest privacy. ●**strictement** [-əmɑ̃] *adv*
strictly; (*vêtu*) plainly.
strident, -ente [stridɑ̃, -ɑ̃t] *a* shrill, strident.
strie [stri] *nf* (*sillon*) groove; (*de couleur etc*)
streak. ●**strier** *vt* to streak.
strip-tease [striptiz] *nm* striptease. ●**strip-
teaseuse** *nf* stripper.
strophe [strɔf] *nf* verse, stanza.
structure [stryktyr] *nf* structure. ●**structural,
-e, -aux** *a* structural. ●**structurer** *vt* to
structure.
stuc [styk] *nm* stucco.
studieux, -euse [stydjø, -øz] *a* studious;
(*vacances etc*) devoted to study.
studio [stydjo] *nm* (*de cinéma, télévision,
peintre*) studio; (*logement*) *Br* studio flat,
Am studio apartment.
stupéfait, -aite [stypefɛ, -ɛt] *a* amazed,
astounded (**de** at, by). ●**stupéfaction** *nf*
amazement.
stupéfier [stypefje] *vt* to amaze, astound.
●**stupéfiant, -ante** 1 *a* amazing, astounding.
2 *nm* drug, narcotic.
stupeur [stypœr] *nf* 1 (*étonnement*) amazement. 2 (*inertie*) stupor.
stupide [stypid] *a* stupid. ●**stupidement** *adv*
stupidly. ●**stupidité** *nf* stupidity; (*action,
parole*) stupid thing.
style [stil] *nm* style; **meubles de s.** period
furniture. ●**stylisé, -ée** *a* stylized. ●**styliste**

nmf (*de mode etc*) designer. ●**stylistique** *a*
stylistic.
stylé, -ée [stile] *a* well-trained.
stylo [stilo] *nm* pen; **s. à bille** ballpoint
(pen), *Br* biro®; **s. à encre, s.-plume**
fountain pen.
su, sue [sy] *pp* de **savoir**.
suave [sɥav] *a* (*odeur, voix*) sweet.
subalterne [sybaltɛrn] *a* & *nmf* subordinate.
subconscient, -ente [sypkɔ̃sjɑ̃, -ɑ̃t] *a* & *nm*
subconscious.
subdiviser [sybdivize] *vt* to subdivide (**en**
into). ●**subdivision** *nf* subdivision.
subir [sybir] *vt* to undergo; (*conséquences,
défaite, perte, tortures*) to suffer; (*influence*)
to be under; **faire s. qch à qn** to subject s.o.
to sth, inflict sth on s.o.; **s. qn** (*supporter*)
Fam to put up with s.o.
subit, -ite [sybi, -it] *a* sudden. ●**subitement**
adv suddenly.
subjectif, -ive [sybʒɛktif, -iv] *a* subjective.
●**subjectivement** *adv* subjectively. ●**subjectivité** *nf* subjectivity.
subjonctif [sybʒɔ̃ktif] *nm* *Grammaire* subjunctive.
subjuguer [sybʒyge] *vt* to subjugate, subdue;
(*envoûter*) to captivate.
sublime [syblim] *a* & *nm* sublime.
sublimer [syblime] *vt* (*passion etc*) to sublimate.
submerger [sybmɛrʒe] *vt* to submerge; (*envahir*) *Fig* to overwhelm; **plaine/etc sub-
mergée** flooded plain/etc; **submergé de travail** *Fig* overwhelmed with work, snowed
under with work; **submergé par** (*ennemi,
foule etc*) swamped by. ●**submersible** *nm*
submarine.
subodorer [sybɔdɔre] *vt* *Fam* to sense,
scent.
subordonner [sybɔrdɔne] *vt* to subordinate
(**à** to). ●**subordonné, -ée** *a* subordinate (**à**
to); **être s. à** (*dépendre de*) to depend on ▮
nmf subordinate. ●**subordination** *nf* subordination.
subreptice [sybrɛptis] *a* surreptitious. ●**sub-
repticement** *adv* surreptitiously.
subside [sypsid] *nm* grant, subsidy.
subsidiaire [sybsidjɛr] *a* a subsidiary; **question
s.** (*de concours*) deciding question.
subsister [sybziste] 1 *vi* (*rester*) to remain;
(*doutes, souvenirs, traditions etc*) to linger
(on), subsist ▮ *v imp* to remain; **il subsiste un
doute/une erreur** there remains some doubt/
an error. 2 *vi* (*vivre*) (*personne*) to get by,
subsist. ●**subsistance** *nf* subsistence.
substance [sypstɑ̃s] *nf* substance; **en s.** *Fig*
in essence. ●**substantiel, -ielle** *a* substantial.
substantif [sypstɑ̃tif] *nm* *Grammaire* noun.
substituer [sypstitɥe] *vt* to substitute (*qch,
qn*) (**à** for); **se s. à qn** to take the place of
s.o., substitute for s.o.; (*représenter*) to substitute for s.o. ●**substitution** *nf* substitution;
produit de s. substitute (product).
substitut [sypstity] *nm* (*produit de remplacement*) substitute (**de** for); (*magistrat*) deputy

public prosecutor; **s. du sucre**/etc sugar/etc substitute.

subterfuge [sypterfyʒ] nm subterfuge.

subtil, -e [syptil] a subtle. ● **subtilité** nf subtlety.

subtiliser [syptilize] vt (dérober) Fam to make off with, swipe.

subvenir* [sybvənir] vi **s. à** (besoins, frais) to meet.

subvention [sybvɑ̃sjɔ̃] nf subsidy. ● **subventionner** vt to subsidize.

subversif, -ive [sybversif, -iv] a subversive. ● **subversion** nf subversion.

suc [syk] nm (gastrique, de fruit) juice; (de plante) sap.

succédané [syksedane] nm substitute (de for).

succéder [syksede] vi **s. à qn** to succeed s.o.; **s. à qch** to follow sth, come after sth ∎ **se succéder** vpr (choses) to follow one another; (personnes) to succeed ou follow one another.

succès [syksɛ] nm success; **s. de librairie** (livre) best-seller; **avoir du s.** to be successful, be a success; **à s.** (auteur, film etc) successful; **avec s.** successfully.

successeur [syksesœr] nm successor. ● **successif, -ive** a successive. ● **successivement** adv successively. ● **succession** nf succession (de of, à to); (série) sequence (de of); (patrimoine) inheritance, estate; **prendre la s. de qn** to succeed s.o.

succinct, -incte [syksɛ̃, -ɛ̃t] a succinct, brief.

succion [sy(k)sjɔ̃] nf suction.

succomber [sykɔ̃be] vi **1** (mourir) to die; **s. à ses blessures** to die of one's wounds. **2 s. à** (céder à) to succumb to, give in to.

succulent, -ente [sykylɑ̃, -ɑ̃t] a succulent.

succursale [sykyrsal] nf (de magasin etc) branch; **magasin à succursales multiples** chain store, Br multiple store.

sucer [syse] vt to suck. ● **sucette** nf lollipop; (tétine) Br dummy, comforter, Am pacifier.

sucre [sykr] nm sugar; (morceau) sugar lump; **s. cristallisé** granulated sugar; **s. en morceaux** lump sugar; **s. en poudre, s. semoule** Br castor ou caster sugar, Am finely ground sugar; **s. d'orge** barley sugar.

sucrer [sykre] vt to sugar, sweeten. ● **sucré, -ée** a sweet, sugary; (artificiellement) sweetened; (doucereux) Fig sugary, syrupy.

sucrerie [sykrəri] nf **1** (usine) sugar refinery. **2 sucreries** (bonbons) Br sweets, Am candy.

sucrier, -ière [sykrije, -jer] a industrie/etc sucrière sugar industry/etc ∎ nm (récipient) sugar bowl.

sud [syd] nm south; **au s.** in the south; (direction) (to the) south (de of); **du s.** (vent, direction) southerly; (ville) southern; (gens) from ou in the south; **Amérique/Afrique du S.** South America/Africa; **l'Europe du S.** Southern Europe.
∎ a inv (côte) south(ern). ● **sud-africain, -aine** a South African ∎ nmf S.-Africain, S.-

Africaine South African. ● **sud-américain, -aine** a South American ∎ nmf S.-Américain, S.-Américaine South American. ● **sud-est** nm & a inv south-east. ● **sud-ouest** nm & a inv south-west.

Suède [sɥɛd] nf Sweden. ● **suédois, -oise** a Swedish ∎ nmf S., Suédoise Swede ∎ nm (langue) Swedish.

suer [sɥe] vi (personne, mur etc) to sweat; **faire s. qn** Fam to get on s.o.'s nerves; **se faire s.** Fam to be bored stiff ∎ vt **s. sang et eau** Fig to sweat blood. ● **sueur** nf sweat; **(tout) en s.** sweating; **avoir des sueurs froides** Fam to break out in a cold sweat.

suffire* [syfir] vi to be enough ou sufficient, suffice (à for); **votre promesse me suffit** your promise is enough ou sufficient for me; **ça suffit!** that's enough! ∎ v imp **il suffit de faire** one only has to do; **il suffit d'une goutte/d'une heure**/etc **pour faire** a drop/an hour/etc is enough to do; **il ne me suffit pas de faire** I'm not satisfied with doing ∎ **se suffire** vpr **se s.** (**à soi-même**) to be self-sufficient.

suffisance [syfizɑ̃s] nf (vanité) conceit.

suffisant, -ante [syfizɑ̃, -ɑ̃t] a **1** sufficient, adequate. **2** (vaniteux) conceited. ● **suffisamment** [-amɑ̃] adv sufficiently; **s. de** enough, sufficient.

suffixe [syfiks] nm Grammaire suffix.

suffoquer [syfɔke] vti to choke, suffocate; **s. qn** (étonner) Fig to astound s.o., stagger s.o. ● **suffocant, -ante** a stifling, suffocating. ● **suffocation** nf suffocation; (sensation) feeling of suffocation.

suffrage [syfraʒ] nm Pol (voix) vote; **droit de s.** suffrage; **s. universel** universal suffrage; **suffrages exprimés** (valid) votes cast; **remporter tous les suffrages** to win universal approval.

suggérer [sygʒere] vt (proposer) to suggest (à to, **de faire** doing, **que** (+ sub) that); (évoquer) to suggest. ● **suggestif, -ive** a suggestive. ● **suggestion** nf suggestion.

suicide [sɥisid] nm suicide.. ● **suicidaire** a suicidal. ● **se suicider** vpr to commit suicide. ● **suicidé, -ée** nmf suicide (victim).

suie [sɥi] nf soot.

suif [sɥif] nm tallow.

suinter [sɥɛ̃te] vi to ooze, seep. ● **suintement** nm oozing, seeping.

suis [sɥi] voir **être, suivre**.

Suisse [sɥis] nf Switzerland; **S. allemande/romande** German-speaking/French-speaking Switzerland. ● **suisse** a Swiss ∎ nmf S. Swiss; **les Suisses** the Swiss. ● **Suissesse** nf Swiss woman ou girl, Swiss inv.

suite [sɥit] nf (reste) rest; (continuation) continuation; (de film, roman) sequel; (série) series, sequence; (appartement, escorte) & Mus suite; (cohérence) order; **suites** (séquelles) effects; (résultats) consequences; **faire s. (à)** to follow; **donner s. à** (demande etc) to follow up; **prendre la s. de qn** to take over from s.o.; **attendre la s.** to wait and see what happens next; **avoir de la s. dans les**

idées to be single-minded (of purpose); **par la s.** afterwards; **par s. de** as a result of; **à la s.** one after another; **à la s. de** (*derrière*) behind; (*événement, maladie etc*) as a result of; **de s.** (*deux jours etc*) in a row.

suivant¹, -ante [sɥivɑ̃, -ɑ̃t] *a* next, following; (*ci-après*) following **‖** *nmf* next (one); **au s.!** next!, next person! ● **suivant²** *prép* (*selon*) according to.

suivi, -ie [sɥivi] *a* (*régulier*) regular, steady; (*cohérent*) coherent; (*article*) regularly on sale, generally available; **peu/très s.** (*cours*) poorly/well attended.

suivre* [sɥivr] *vt* to follow; (*accompagner*) to go with, accompany; (*cours*) to attend, go to; (*malade*) to treat; **s.** (**des yeux** *ou* **du regard**) to watch; **s. son chemin** to go on one's way; **s. l'exemple de qn** to follow s.o.'s example; **s. le mouvement** to follow the crowd *ou* trend, *Fam* go with the flow; **s. l'actualité** to follow events *ou* the news; **se s.** to follow each other.
‖ *vi* to follow; (*courrier, lettre etc*) to forward; **'à s.'** 'to be continued'; **comme suit** as follows.

sujet¹, -ette [syʒɛ, -ɛt] *a* **s. à** (*maladie etc*) subject *ou* liable to; **s. à caution** (*information, nouvelle etc*) unconfirmed **‖** *nmf* (*personne*) *Pol* subject.

sujet² [syʒɛ] *nm* **1** (*question*) & *Grammaire* subject; (*d'examen*) question; **au s. de** about; **à quel s.?** about what? **2** (*raison*) cause; **sujet(s) de dispute** grounds for dispute. **3** *nm* (*individu*) subject; **un mauvais s.** (*garçon*) a rotten egg; **un brillant s.** a brilliant student.

sulfurique [sylfyrik] *a* (*acide*) *Br* sulphuric, *Am* sulfuric.

sultan [syltɑ̃] *nm* sultan.

summum [sɔmɔm] *nm* (*comble*) *Fig* height.

super [sypɛr] **1** *a inv* (*bon*) *Fam* great, super. **2** *nm* (*supercarburant*) *Br* four-star (petrol), *Am* premium *ou* hi(gh)-test gas.

superbe [sypɛrb] *a* superb.

supercarburant [sypɛrkarbyrɑ̃] *nm* high-octane *Br* petrol *ou* *Am* gasoline.

supercherie [sypɛrʃəri] *nf* deception.

supérette [sypɛrɛt] *nf* mini supermarket, convenience store.

superficie [sypɛrfisi] *nf* surface; (*dimensions*) area. ● **superficiel, -ielle** *a* superficial. ● **superficiellement** *adv* superficially.

superflu, -ue [sypɛrfly] *a* superfluous.

super-grand [sypɛrgrɑ̃] *nm* *Pol Fam* superpower.

supérieur, -e [sypɛrjœr] *a* (*étages, partie etc*) upper; (*qualité, air, ton*) superior; **à l'étage s.** on the floor above; **s. à** (*meilleur que*) superior to, better than; (*plus grand que*) above, greater than; **s. à la moyenne** above average; **études supérieures** higher *ou* university studies **‖** *nmf* superior. ● **supériorité** *nf* superiority.

superlatif, -ive [sypɛrlatif, -iv] *a* & *nm* *Grammaire* superlative.

supermarché [sypɛrmarʃe] *nm* supermarket.

superposer [sypɛrpoze] *vt* (*objets*) to put on top of each other; (*images etc*) to superimpose.

superproduction [sypɛrprɔdyksjɔ̃] *nf* (*film*) blockbuster.

superpuissance [sypɛrpɥisɑ̃s] *nf* *Pol* superpower.

supersonique [sypɛrsɔnik] *a* supersonic.

superstar [sypɛrstar] *nf* superstar.

superstitieux, -euse [sypɛrstisjø, -øz] *a* superstitious. ● **superstition** *nf* superstition.

superviser [sypɛrvize] *vt* to supervise.

supplanter [syplɑ̃te] *vt* to take the place of.

suppléer [syplee] *vi* **s. à** (*compenser*) to make up for **‖** *vt* *Litt* (*remplacer*) to replace; (*compenser*) to make up for. ● **suppléant, -ante** *a & nmf* (*personne*) substitute, replacement; (*professeur*) **s.** substitute *ou* *Br* supply teacher.

supplément [syplemɑ̃] *nm* (*argent*) extra charge, supplement; (*de revue, livre*) supplement; **en s.** extra; **s. de** (*information, travail etc*) extra, additional; **payer un s.** to pay extra, pay a supplement. ● **supplémentaire** *a* extra, additional.

supplication [syplikasjɔ̃] *nf* plea, entreaty.

supplice [syplis] *nm* torture; **au s.** *Fig* in agony. ● **supplicier** *vt* to torture.

supplier [syplije] *vt* **s. qn de faire qch** to beg *ou* implore s.o. to do sth; **je vous en supplie!** I beg *ou* implore you! ● **suppliant, -ante** *a* (*regard etc*) imploring.

support [sypɔr] *nm* **1** support; (*d'instrument etc*) stand. **2** (*moyen*) *Fig* medium; **s. audiovisuel** audio-visual aid.

supporter¹ [sypɔrte] *vt* (*malheur, conséquences etc*) to bear, endure; (*résister à*) to withstand (*heat etc*); (*soutenir*) to support (*arch etc*); (*frais*) to bear; (*affront etc*) to suffer; **je ne peux pas la s.** I can't bear her. ● **supportable** *a* bearable; (*excusable, passable*) tolerable.

supporter² [sypɔrtɛr] *nm* (*de football etc*) supporter.

supposer [sypoze] *vt* to suppose, assume (**que** that); (*impliquer*) to imply (**que** that); **à s.** *ou* **en supposant que** (+ *sub*) supposing (that). ● **supposition** *nf* assumption, supposition.

suppositoire [sypozitwar] *nm* suppository.

supprimer [syprime] *vt* to get rid of, remove; (*mot, passage*) to cut out, delete; (*train etc*) to cancel; (*tuer*) to do away with; (*institution, loi*) to abolish; (*journal etc*) to suppress; **s. des emplois** to axe jobs; **s. qch à qn** to take sth away from s.o. **‖ se supprimer** *vpr* (*se suicider*) to do away with oneself. ● **suppression** *nf* removal; (*de mot etc*) deletion; (*de train etc*) cancellation; (*d'emplois*) axing; (*de loi etc*) abolition; (*de journal etc*) suppression.

supputer [sypyte] *vt* to calculate, compute.

suprématie [sypremasi] *nf* supremacy.

suprême [syprɛm] *a* supreme.

sur [syr] *prép* on, upon; (*par-dessus*) over; (*au sujet de*) on, about; **six s.** dix six out of ten; **un jour s. deux** every other day; **six mètres s.** dix six metres by ten; **s. les trois heures** at about three o'clock; **coup s. coup** blow after *ou* upon blow; **s. ce** after which, and then; (*maintenant*) and now; **s. votre gauche** to *ou* on your left; **mettre/monter/etc s.** to put/climb/etc on (to); **aller/tourner/etc s.** to go/turn/etc towards; **aller s. ses vingt/etc ans** to be approaching twenty/etc; **être s. le départ** to be about to leave.

sur- [syr] *préf* over-.

sûr, sûre [syr] *a* sure, certain (de of, que that); (*digne de confiance*) reliable; (*lieu*) safe; (*avenir*) secure; (*goût*) discerning; (*jugement*) sound; (*main*) steady; **c'est s. que** (+ *indic*) it's certain that; **s. de soi** self-assured; **être s. de son coup** *Fam* to be quite sure of oneself; **bien s.!** of course!

surabondant, -ante [syrabɔ̃dɑ̃, -ɑ̃t] *a* overabundant.

suranné, -ée [syrane] *a* outmoded.

surarmement [syrarməmɑ̃] *nm* excessive arms build-up.

surboum [syrbum] *nf Fam* party.

surcharge [syrʃarʒ] *nf* 1 overloading; (*poids*) extra load; **s. de travail** extra work; **en s.** (*passagers etc*) extra. 2 (*correction de texte etc*) alteration; (*de timbre-poste*) surcharge. ● **surcharger** *vt* (*voiture, personne etc*) to overload (de with).

surchauffer [syrʃofe] *vt* to overheat.

surchoix [syrʃwa] *a inv* (*produit etc*) top-quality.

surclasser [syrklase] *vt* to outclass.

surcroît [syrkrwa] *nm* increase (de in); **de s., par s.** in addition.

surdité [syrdite] *nf* deafness.

surdose [syrdoz] *nf* (*de drogue*) overdose.

surdoué, -ée [syrdwe] *nmf* (exceptionally) gifted child, child who has a genius-level IQ.

surélever [syrelve] *vt* to raise (the height of).

sûrement [syrmɑ̃] *adv* certainly; (*sans danger*) safely.

surenchère [syrɑ̃ʃɛr] *nf* (*offre d'achat*) higher bid; **s. électorale** *Fig* bidding for votes. ● **surenchérir** *vi* to bid higher (**sur** than).

surestimer [syrɛstime] *vt* to overestimate; (*tableau etc*) to overvalue.

sûreté [syrte] *nf* safety; (*de l'État*) security; (*garantie*) surety; (*de geste*) sureness; (*de jugement*) soundness; **être en s.** to be safe; **mettre qch/qn en s.** to put sth/s.o. in a safe place; **épingle/etc de s.** safety pin/etc; **pour plus de s.** to be on the safe side.

surexcité, -ée [syrɛksite] *a* overexcited.

surf [sœrf] *nm Sport* surfing; **faire du s.** to surf, go surfing.

surface [syrfas] *nf* surface; (*dimensions*) (surface) area; **faire s.** (*sous-marin etc*) to surface; (*magasin à*) **grande s.** hypermarket; **de s.** (*politesse etc*) superficial.

surfait, -aite [syrfɛ, -ɛt] *a* overrated.

surgelé, -ée [syrʒəle] *a* (*viande etc*) (deep-)frozen. ● **surgelés** *nmpl* (deep-)frozen foods.

surgir [syrʒir] *vi* to appear suddenly (de from); (*problème etc*) to arise.

surhomme [syrɔm] *nm* superman. ● **surhumain, -aine** *a* superhuman.

sur-le-champ [syrləʃɑ̃] *adv* immediately.

surlendemain [syrlɑ̃dəmɛ̃] *nm* **le s.** two days later; **le s. de** two days after.

surligner [syrliɲe] *vt* to highlight (*with a highlighter*). ● **surligneur** *nm* highlighter (pen).

surmener [syrməne] *vt*, **se surmener** *vpr* to overwork. ● **surmenage** *nm* overwork.

surmonter [syrmɔ̃te] *vt* 1 (*obstacle, peur etc*) to get over, overcome. 2 (*être placé sur*) to be on top of, top.

surnager [syrnaʒe] *vi* to float.

surnaturel, -elle [syrnatyrɛl] *a & nm* supernatural.

surnom [syrnɔ̃] *nm* nickname. ● **surnommer** *vt* to nickname.

surnombre [syrnɔ̃br] *nm* **en s.** too many; **je suis en s.** I am one too many.

surpasser [syrpase] *vt* to surpass (**en** in) ■ **se surpasser** *vpr* to excel *ou* surpass oneself.

surpeuplé, -ée [syrpœple] *a* overpopulated.

surplace [syrplas] *nm* **faire du s.** (*dans un embouteillage*) & *Fig* to be hardly moving, be unable to make any headway.

surplomb [syrplɔ̃] *nm* **en s.** overhanging. ● **surplomber** *vti* to overhang.

surplus [syrply] *nm* surplus; **les surplus agricoles/etc** agricultural/etc surpluses.

surprendre* [syrprɑ̃dr] *vt* (*étonner*) to surprise; (*prendre sur le fait*) to catch; (*secret*) to discover; (*conversation*) to overhear; **se s. à faire qch** to find oneself doing sth. ● **surprenant, -ante** *a* surprising. ● **surpris, -ise** *a* surprised (de at, que (+ *sub*) that); **je suis s. de te voir** I'm surprised to see you. ● **surprise** *nf* surprise; **prendre qn par s.** to catch s.o. unawares. ● **surprise-partie** *nf* (*pl* surprises-parties*) party.

surproduction [syrprɔdyksjɔ̃] *nf* excess supply, overproduction.

surréaliste [syrealist] *a* (*poète, peintre etc*) surrealist; (*bizarre*) *Fam* surrealistic.

surréservation [syrrezɛrvasjɔ̃] *nf* overbooking.

sursaut [syrso] *nm* (sudden) start *ou* jump; **s. d'énergie/etc** burst of energy/etc; **se réveiller en s.** to wake up with a start. ● **sursauter** *vi* to jump, start.

sursis [syrsi] *nm* (*à l'armée*) deferment; (*répit*) *Fig* reprieve; **un an (de prison) avec s.** a one-year suspended sentence.

surtaxe [syrtaks] *nf* surcharge.

surtout [syrtu] *adv* especially; (*avant tout*) above all; **s. pas** certainly not; **s. que** *Fam* especially since *ou* as.

surveiller [syrveje] *vt* (*garder*) to watch, keep an eye on; (*contrôler*) to supervise; (*épier*) to watch; **s. son langage/sa santé** *Fig*

to watch one's language/health.
‖ se surveiller *vpr* Litt to watch oneself.
● **surveillant, -ante** *nmf* (*de lycée*) supervisor
(in charge of discipline); (*de prison*) prison
guard, *Br* warder; (*de chantier*) supervisor;
s. de plage lifeguard. ● **surveillance** *nf* watch
(**sur** over); (*de travaux, d'ouvriers*) supervision; (*de la police*) surveillance, observation;
tromper la s. de ses gardiens to escape from
one's guards (*by eluding their vigilance*); **à
prendre sous s. médicale** (*médicament*) to be
taken under medical supervision.

survenir* [syrvənir] *vi* to occur; (*personne*)
to turn up.

survêtement [syrvɛtmɑ̃] *nm* (*vêtement de
sport*) tracksuit.

survie [syrvi] *nf* survival. ● **survivre*** *vi* to
survive (**à qch** sth); **s. à qn** to outlive s.o.,
survive s.o. ● **survivant, -ante** *nmf* survivor.
● **survivance** *nf* (*chose*) survival, relic.

survol [syrvɔl] *nm* **le s. de** (*en avion etc*)
flying over; (*question*) *Fig* the overview of.
● **survoler** *vt* to fly over; (*question etc*) *Fig* to
go over (quickly), skim (superficially).

survolté, -ée [syrvɔlte] *a* (*surexcité*) worked
up.

sus (en) [ɑ̃sys] *adv* Litt in addition.

susceptible [syseptibl] *a* **1** (*ombrageux*)
touchy, sensitive. **2 s. de** (*interprétations etc*)
open to; **s. de faire qch** likely *ou* liable to do
sth; (*capable*) able to do sth. ● **susceptibilité**
nf touchiness, sensitiveness.

susciter [sysite] *vt* (*sentiment*) to arouse;
(*ennuis, obstacles etc*) to create.

suspect, -ecte [syspe(kt), -ɛkt] *a* suspicious,
suspect; **s. de qch** suspected of sth **‖** *nmf*
suspect. ● **suspecter** *vt* to suspect (**de qch** of
sth, **de faire** of doing); (*bonne foi etc*) to
question, suspect, doubt.

suspendre [syspɑ̃dr] *vt* **1** (*accrocher*) to
hang (up) (**à** on); **se s. à** to hang from. **2**
(*destituer, interrompre, différer*) to suspend.
● **suspendu, -ue** *a* **s. à** hanging from; **pont s.**
suspension bridge; **être s. aux paroles de qn**
Fig to hang upon s.o.'s every word.
● **suspension** *nf* **1** (*d'hostilités, d'employé, de
véhicule*) suspension; **points de s.** (*ponctuation*) dots, suspension points. **2** (*lustre*) hanging lamp.

suspens (en) [ɑ̃syspɑ̃] *adv* **1** (*affaire, travail*) in abeyance. **2** (*dans l'incertitude*) in
suspense.

suspense [syspɛns] *nm* suspense; **film à s.**
thriller, suspense film.

suspicion [syspisjɔ̃] *nf* suspicion.

susurrer [sysyre] *vti* to murmur.

suture [sytyr] *nf* (*opération*) stitching, suture;
point de s. stitch (*in wound*). ● **suturer** *vt* to
stitch up.

svelte [svɛlt] *a* slender. ● **sveltesse** *nf*
slenderness.

SVP [ɛsvepe] *abrév* (*s'il vous plaît*) please.

syllabe [silab] *nf* syllable.

symbole [sɛ̃bɔl] *nm* symbol. ● **symbolique** *a*
symbolic; (*salaire, cotisation, loyer*) nominal;
geste s. symbolic *ou* token gesture; **grève/
paiement s.** token strike/payment. ● **symboliser** *vt* to symbolize. ● **symbolisme** *nm*
symbolism.

symétrie [simetri] *nf* symmetry. ● **symétrique** *a* symmetrical.

sympa [sɛ̃pa] *a inv Fam* = **sympathique.**

sympathie [sɛ̃pati] *nf* liking, affection;
(*affinité*) affinity; (*condoléances*) sympathy;
avoir de la s. pour qn to be fond of s.o.
● **sympathique** *a* nice, pleasant; (*accueil,
geste*) friendly. ● **sympathiser** *vi* fo get along
well, *Br* get on well (**avec** with). ● **sympathisant, -ante** *nmf* (*d'un parti politique*)
sympathizer.

symphonie [sɛ̃fɔni] *nf* symphony. ● **symphonique** *a* symphonic; **orchestre s.** symphony
orchestra.

symposium [sɛ̃pozjɔm] *nm* symposium.

symptôme [sɛ̃ptom] *nm* *Méd* & *Fig*
symptom. ● **symptomatique** *a* symptomatic
(**de** of).

synagogue [sinagɔg] *nf* synagogue.

synchroniser [sɛ̃krɔnize] *vt* to synchronize.

syncope [sɛ̃kɔp] *nf* (*évanouissement*) blackout; **tomber en s.** to black out.

syndicat [sɛ̃dika] *nm* **1** (*d'ouvriers etc*) (*Br
trade ou Am labor*) union; (*de patrons etc*)
association. **2 s. d'initiative** tourist (information) office. ● **syndical, -e, -aux** *a* **réunion**/*etc*
syndicale (*Br* trade *ou Am* labor) union
meeting/*etc*. ● **syndicalisme** *nm Br* trade *ou
Am* labor unionism. ● **syndicaliste** *nmf Br*
trade *ou Am* labor unionist **‖** *a* **esprit/idéal/**
etc **s.** union spirit/ideal/*etc*.

syndiquer [sɛ̃dike] *vt* to unionize **‖ se syndiquer** *vpr* (*adhérer*) to join a (*Br* trade *ou
Am* labor) union. ● **syndiqué, -ée** *nmf* (*Br*
trade *ou Am* labor) union member.

syndrome [sɛ̃drom] *nm Méd* & *Fig* syndrome; **s. immunodéficitaire acquis** acquired
immune deficiency syndrome.

synode [sinɔd] *nm Rel* synod.

synonyme [sinɔnim] *a* synonymous (**de**
with) **‖** *nm* synonym.

syntaxe [sɛ̃taks] *nf* (*grammaire*) syntax.

synthèse [sɛ̃tez] *nf* synthesis. ● **synthétique**
a synthetic.

synthétiseur [sɛ̃tetizœr] *nm* synthesizer.

syphilis [sifilis] *nf* (*maladie*) syphilis.

Syrie [siri] *nf* Syria. ● **syrien, -ienne** *a* Syrian
‖ *nmf* **S., Syrienne** Syrian.

système [sistɛm] *nm* (*structure, réseau etc*)
& *Anat* system; **le s. immunitaire** the
immune system; **le s. nerveux** the nervous
system; **le s. D** *Fam* resourcefulness; **s.
d'exploitation** *Ordinat* operating system;
courir sur le s. à qn *Fam* to get on s.o.'s
nerves. ● **systématique** *a* systematic; (*soutien*) unconditional. ● **systématiquement** *adv*
systematically.

T

T, t [te] *nm* T, t.

t' [t] *voir* **te.**

ta [ta] *voir* **ton¹.**

tabac [taba] **1** *nm* tobacco; (*magasin*) *Br* tobacconist's (shop), *Am* tobacco store; **t. (à priser)** snuff. **2** *nm* **passer qn à t.** *Fam* to beat s.o. up; **passage à t.** beating up. **3** *a inv* (*couleur*) buff.

tabasser [tabase] *vt Fam* to beat up; **se faire t.** to be *ou* get beaten up.

tabatière [tabatjɛr] *nf* (*boîte*) snuffbox.

table [tabl] *nf* **1** (*meuble*) table; (*d'école*) desk; (*nourriture*) fare; **t. de nuit/ d'opération/de jeu** bedside/operating/card table; **t. basse** coffee table; **t. à repasser** ironing board; **t. roulante** *Br* (tea) trolley, *Am* (serving) cart; **t. à rallonges** pull-out *ou* extending table; **t. ronde** (*réunion*) (round-table) conference; **mettre/débarrasser la t.** to set *ou* Br lay/clear the table; **être à t.** to be sitting at the table; **à t.!** (food's) ready!; **faire t. rase** *Fig* to make a clean sweep (**de** of); **mettre qn sur t. d'écoute** to tap s.o.'s phone.
2 (*liste*) table; **t. des matières** table of contents.

tableau, -x [tablo] *nm* **1** (*peinture*) picture, painting; (*image, description*) picture; (*scène de théâtre*) scene; **t. de maître** (*peinture*) old master. **2** (*panneau*) board; (*liste*) list; (*graphique*) chart; **t. (noir)** (black)board; **t. d'affichage** *Br* notice board, *Am* bulletin board; **t. de bord** (*de véhicule*) dashboard; **t. de contrôle** *Tech* control panel; **t. des départs/arrivées** (*de gare, d'aéroport*) departures/arrivals board; **avoir le t. d'honneur** *Scol Br* to get one's name on the merit list, *Am* make the honor roll.

tabler [table] *vi* **t. sur** to count *ou* rely on.

tablette [tablɛt] *nf* (*de chocolat*) bar, slab; (*de lavabo etc*) shelf; (*de cheminée*) mantelpiece.

tableur [tablœr] *nm Ordinat* spreadsheet.

tablier [tablije] *nm* **1** (*vêtement*) apron; (*d'écolier*) smock; **rendre son t.** (*démissionner*) *Fam* to give notice. **2** (*de pont*) roadway.

tabou [tabu] *a & nm* taboo.

taboulé [tabule] *nm* (*plat*) tabbouleh.

tabouret [taburɛ] *nm* stool.

tabulateur [tabylatœr] *nm* (*d'ordinateur, de machine à écrire*) tabulator.

tac [tak] *nm* **répondre du t. au t.** to give tit for tat.

tache [taʃ] *nf* spot, mark; (*salissure*) stain; **faire t.** (*détonner*) *Péj* to jar, stand out; **faire**
t. d'huile *Fig* to spread. ● **tacher** *vt*, **se tacher** *vpr* (*tissu etc*) to stain ‖ *vi* (*vin etc*) to stain.

tâche [taʃ] *nf* task, job; **travailler à la t.** to do piecework; **se tuer à la t.** *Fig* to work oneself to death.

tâcher [taʃe] *vi* **t. de faire qch** to try *ou* endeavour to do sth.

tâcheron [taʃrɔ̃] *nm* drudge.

tacheté, -ée [taʃte] *a* speckled, spotted.

tacite [tasit] *a* tacit. ● **tacitement** *adv* tacitly.

taciturne [tasityrn] *a* taciturn.

tacot [tako] *nm* (*voiture*) *Fam* (old) wreck, *Br* banger.

tact [takt] *nm* tact; **avoir du t.** to be tactful.

tactile [taktil] *a* tactile.

tactique [taktik] *a* tactical ‖ *nf* **la t.** tactics; **une t.** a tactic.

tag [tag] *nm* tag (*spray-painted graffiti*). ● **tagueur, -euse** *nmf* graffiti artist, tagger.

Tahiti [taiti] *nm* Tahiti. ● **tahitien, -ienne** [taisjɛ̃, -jɛn] *a* Tahitian ‖ *nmf* **T., Tahitienne** Tahitian.

taie [tɛ] *nf* **t. d'oreiller** pillowcase, pillowslip.

taillade [tajad] *nf* gash, slash. ● **taillader** *vt* to gash, slash.

taille¹ [taj] *nf* **1** (*hauteur*) height; (*dimension, mesure*) size; **de haute t.** (*personne*) tall; **de petite t.** short; **de t. moyenne** (*objet, personne*) medium-sized; **être de t. à faire qch** *Fig* to be capable of doing sth; **de t.** (*erreur, objet*) *Fam* enormous. **2** (*ceinture*) waist; **tour de t.** waist measurement.

taille² [taj] *nf* cutting; (*de haie etc*) trimming; (*d'arbre*) pruning; (*de vêtement etc*) cutting out; (*forme*) cut. ● **tailler 1** *vt* to cut; (*haie, barbe*) to trim; (*arbre*) to prune; (*crayon*) to sharpen; (*vêtement*) to cut out; **se t. la part du lion** to take the lion's share. **2 se tailler** *vpr* (*partir*) *Fam* to beat it, make tracks. ● **taillé, -ée** *a* **t. en athlète/etc** built like an athlete/etc; **t. pour faire qch** *Fig* cut out for doing sth.

taille-crayon(s) [tajkrɛjɔ̃] *nm inv* pencil-sharpener. ● **taille-haie(s)** [tajɛ] *nm inv* (*garden*) shears; (*électrique*) hedge trimmer.

tailleur [tajœr] *nm* **1** (*personne*) tailor. **2** (*costume féminin*) suit.

taillis [taji] *nm* copse, coppice.

tain [tɛ̃] *nm* (*de glace*) silvering; **glace sans t.** two-way mirror.

taire* [tɛr] *vt* to say nothing about ‖ *vi* **faire t. qn** to silence s.o. ‖ **se taire** *vpr* (*ne rien dire*) to keep quiet (**sur qch** about sth); (*cesser de parler*) to stop talking, fall silent; **tais-toi!** be *ou* keep quiet!, shut up!

Taiwan [tajwan] *nm ou f* Taiwan.

talc [talk] *nm* talcum powder.

talé, -ée [tale] *a (fruit)* bruised.

talent [talɑ̃] *nm* talent; **avoir du t. pour qch** to have a talent for sth. ● **talentueux, -euse** *a* talented.

talion [taljɔ̃] *nm* **la loi du t.** *(vengeance)* the law of retaliation, an eye for an eye.

talisman [talismɑ̃] *nm* talisman.

talkie-walkie [talkiwalki] *nm (poste)* walkie-talkie.

taloche [talɔʃ] *nf (gifle) Fam* clout, smack.

talon [talɔ̃] *nm* **1** heel; **(chaussures à) talons hauts** high heels, high-heeled shoes; **talons aiguilles** stiletto heels; **tourner les talons** to walk away; **c'est son t. d'Achille** it's his Achilles' heel. **2** *(de chèque, carnet)* stub, counterfoil; *(bout de pain)* crust; *(de jambon)* heel. ● **talonnette** *nf (pour chaussure)* lift, heel cushion.

talonner [talɔne] *vt (fugitif etc)* to follow on the heels of; *(ballon) Rugby* to heel; *(harceler) Fig* to hound, dog.

talus [taly] *nm* slope, embankment.

tambour [tɑ̃bur] *nm* **1** *(de machine etc, instrument de musique)* drum; *(personne)* drummer. **2** *(porte)* revolving door; **sans t. ni trompette** quietly, without fuss. ● **tambourin** *nm* tambourine. ● **tambouriner** *vi (avec les doigts etc)* to drum **(sur** on).

tamis [tami] *nm* sieve. ● **tamiser** *vt (farine etc)* to sift; *(lumière)* to filter, subdue.

Tamise [tamiz] *nf* la T. the Thames.

tampon [tɑ̃pɔ̃] *nm* **1** *(marque, instrument)* stamp; **t. buvard** blotter; **t. encreur** ink(ing) pad; **lettre à renvoyer avant minuit le t. de la poste faisant foi** letter to be postmarked no later than midnight. **2** *(bouchon)* plug, stopper; *(de coton etc)* wad, pad; *(pour pansement)* swab; **t. hygiénique** *ou* **périodique** tampon; **t. à récurer** scrubbing *ou* scouring pad. **3** *(de train etc)* & *Fig* buffer; **état t.** buffer state.

tamponner [tɑ̃pɔne] **1** *vt (lettre, document etc)* to stamp. **2** *vt (visage etc)* to dab; *(plaie)* to swab. **3** *vt (train, voiture)* to crash into **▮ se tamponner** *vpr* to crash into each other. ● **tamponneuses** *afpl* **autos t.** dodgems, bumper cars.

tam-tam [tamtam] *nm (tambour)* tom-tom.

tandem [tɑ̃dɛm] *nm* **1** *(bicyclette)* tandem. **2** *(duo) Fig* duo, pair; **travailler/etc en t.** to work/etc in tandem.

tandis que [tɑ̃dik(ə)] *conj (pendant que)* while; *(contraste)* whereas, while.

tangent, -ente [tɑ̃ʒɑ̃, -ɑ̃t] *a* **1** *Géom* tangential (à to). **2** *(juste) Fam* touch and go, close. ● **tangente** *nf Géom* tangent.

tangible [tɑ̃ʒibl] *a* tangible.

tango [tɑ̃go] *nm* tango.

tanguer [tɑ̃ge] *vi (bateau, avion)* to pitch. ● **tangage** *nm (de bateau, d'avion)* pitching.

tanière [tanjɛr] *nf* den, lair.

tank [tɑ̃k] *nm (char d'assaut)* tank.

tanker [tɑ̃kɛr] *nm (navire)* tanker.

tanner [tane] *vt (cuir)* to tan. ● **tanné, -ée** *a (visage)* weather-beaten, tanned.

tant [tɑ̃] *adv (travailler etc)* so much **(que** that); **t. de** *(pain, temps etc)* so much **(que** that); *(gens, choses etc)* so many **(que** that); **t. de fois** so often, so many times; **t. que** *(autant que)* as much as; *(aussi fort que)* as hard as; *(aussi longtemps que)* as long as; **en t. que** *(considéré comme)* as; **t. bien que mal** more or less, somehow or other; **t. mieux!** good!, I'm glad!; **t. pis!** too bad!, pity!; **t. mieux pour toi!** good for you!; **t. pis pour toi!** that's too bad!, that's a pity for you!; **t. soit peu** (even) remotely *ou* slightly; **un t. soit peu** somewhat; **t. s'en faut** far from it.

tante [tɑ̃t] *nf* aunt.

tantinet [tɑ̃tine] *nm* & *adv* **un t.** a tiny bit (de of).

tantôt [tɑ̃to] *adv* **1** **t....t.** sometimes... sometimes, now... now. **2** *(cet après-midi)* this afternoon.

taon [tɑ̃] *nm* horsefly, gadfly.

tapage [tapaʒ] *nm* din, uproar. ● **tapageur, -euse** *a* **1** *(bruyant)* rowdy. **2** *(criard)* flashy.

tape [tap] *nf* slap.

tape-à-l'œil [tapalœj] *a inv* flashy, gaudy.

tapée [tape] *nf* **une t. de** *Fam* heaps of, *Br* a load of.

taper [tape] **1** *vt (enfant, cuisse)* to slap; *(table)* to bang; **t. qn** *(emprunter de l'argent à qn) Fam* to touch s.o., tap s.o. (de for).

▮ *vi (soleil)* to beat down; **t. sur qch** to bang on sth; **t. du pied** to stamp one's foot; **t. à la porte** to bang on the door; **t. sur qn** *(critiquer) Fam* to run s.o. down, knock s.o.; **t. sur les nerfs de qn** *Fam* to get on s.o.'s nerves; **t. dans** *(provisions etc) Fam* to dig into; **t. dans l'œil à qn** *Fam* to take s.o.'s fancy.

▮ se taper *vpr (travail) Fam* to do, take on; *(repas, vin) Fam* to put away.

2 *vti* **t.** **(à la machine)** to type. ● **tapant, -ante** *a* **à midi t.** at twelve sharp; **à huit heures tapant(es)** at eight sharp.

tapeur, -euse [tapœr, -øz] *nmf Fam* person who borrows money.

tapioca [tapjɔka] *nm* tapioca.

tapir (se) [sətapir] *vpr* to crouch (down). ● **tapi, -ie** *a* crouching, crouched.

tapis [tapi] *nm* carpet; **t. de bain** bathmat; **t. roulant** *(pour marchandises)* conveyor belt; *(pour personnes)* moving walkway; **t. de sol** groundsheet; **t. de table** table cover; **envoyer qn au t.** *(abattre)* to floor s.o.; **mettre sur le t.** *(sujet)* to bring up for discussion; **dérouler le t. rouge** to put out the red carpet. ● **tapis-brosse** *nm* doormat.

tapisser [tapise] *vt (mur)* to (wall)paper; *(de tentures etc)* to hang with tapestry; *(recouvrir) Fig* to cover. ● **tapisserie** *nf (papier peint)* wallpaper; *(broderie)* tapestry; **faire t.** *(jeune fille etc)* to be a wallflower. ● **tapissier, -ière** *nmf (qui pose des tissus etc)* upholsterer; **t.(-décorateur)** interior decorator.

tapoter [tapɔte] *vt* to tap; *(joue)* to pat ‖ *vi* t. sur to tap (on).

taquin, -ine [takɛ̃, -in] *a* (fond of) teasing ‖ *nmf* tease(r). ●**taquiner** *vt* to tease; *(inquiéter, agacer)* to bother. ●**taquinerie(s)** *nf(pl)* teasing.

tarabiscoté, -ée [tarabiskɔte] *a* over-elaborate.

tarabuster [tarabyste] *vt (idée etc)* to trouble *(s.o.)*, worry *(s.o.)*.

tarauder [tarode] *vt Litt* to torment.

tard [tar] *adv* late; **plus** t. later (on); **au plus** t. at the latest; **sur le** t. late in life.

tarder [tarde] *vi (lettre, saison)* to be a long time coming; **t. à faire qch** to take one's time doing sth; *(différer)* to delay (in) doing sth; **ne tardez pas** *(agissez tout de suite)* don't delay; **elle ne va pas t.** she won't be long; **sans t.** without delay; **il me tarde de faire** I long to do.

tardif, -ive [tardif, -iv] *a* late; *(regrets)* belated. ●**tardivement** *adv* late.

tare [tar] *nf* 1 *(poids)* tare. 2 *(défaut)* Fig defect. ●**taré, -ée** *a (corrompu)* corrupt; *(dégénéré)* defective; *(fou)* Fam mad, idiotic.

tarentule [tarɑ̃tyl] *nf* tarantula.

targette [tarʒet] *nf* (flat) door bolt.

targuer (se) [sətarge] *vpr* **se t. de qch/de faire** to boast about sth/about doing.

tarif [tarif] *nm (prix)* rate; *(de train etc)* fare; *(tableau)* price list, Br tariff; **plein t.** full price; *(de train, bus etc)* full fare. ●**tarification** *nf (prix)* fixing.

tarir [tarir] *vti*, **se tarir** *vpr (fleuve etc) & Fig* to dry up; **ne pas t. d'éloges sur qn** Fig to rave about s.o.

tarot [taro] *nm* tarot; **jeu de t.** *(cartes)* deck *ou Br* pack of tarot cards.

tartare [tartar] *a* **sauce t.** tartar sauce.

tarte [tart] 1 *nf* (open) pie, tart; **ce n'est pas de la t.!** *Fam* it isn't easy!, it's no piece of cake! 2 *a inv Fam (sot)* silly; *(laid)* ugly. ●**tartelette** *nf* (small) tart.

tartine [tartin] *nf* slice of bread; **t. (de beurre/de confiture)** slice of bread and butter/jam. ●**tartiner** *vt (beurre etc)* to spread; **fromage à t.** cheese spread.

tartre [tartr] *nm (de bouilloire)* scale, Br fur; *(de dents)* plaque, tartar.

tas [tɑ] *nm* pile, heap; **un** *ou* **des t. de** *(beaucoup)* Fam lots of; **mettre en t.** to pile *ou* heap up; **former qn sur le t.** *(au travail)* Fam to train s.o. on the job.

tasse [tɑs] *nf* cup; **t. à café** coffee cup; **t. à thé** teacup; **boire la t.** Fam to·swallow a mouthful *(when swimming)*.

tasser [tɑse] *vt* to pack, squeeze *(sth, s.o.)* *(dans into)*; *(terre)* to pack down; **un café/etc bien tassé** *(fort)* Fam a (good) strong coffee/etc ‖ **se tasser** *vpr (se serrer)* to squeeze up; *(sol)* to sink, collapse; *(se voûter)* to become bowed; **ça va se t.** *(s'arranger)* Fam things will pan out (all right).

tâter [tɑte] *vt* to feel; *(sonder)* Fig to sound out ‖ *vi* **t. de** *(prison, métier)* to have a taste

of, experience ‖ **se tâter** *vpr (hésiter)* to be in *ou* of two minds.

tatillon, -onne [tatijɔ̃, -ɔn] *a Fam* finicky.

tâtonner [tɑtɔne] *vi* to grope about, feel one's way. ●**tâtonnement** *nm* **par t.** *(procéder)* by trial and error. ●**tâtons (à)** *adv* **avancer à** t. to feel one's way (along); **chercher à** t. to grope for.

tatouer [tatwe] *vt (corps, dessin)* to tattoo; **se faire t.** to get a tattoo; **se faire t. un bateau sur le bras** to get a boat tatooed on one's arm. ●**tatouage** *nm (dessin)* tattoo; *(action)* tattooing.

taudis [todi] *nm* slum, hovel.

taule [tol] *nf (chambre)* Fam room; *(prison)* Arg Br nick, Br jug, Am can.

taupe [top] *nf (animal, espion)* mole. ●**taupinière** *nf* molehill.

taureau, -x [tɔro] *nm* bull; **le T.** *(signe)* Taurus. ●**tauromachie** *nf* bull-fighting.

taux [to] *nm* rate; **t. d'alcool/de cholestérol/etc** alcohol/cholesterol/etc level; **t. d'intérêt/de change** interest/exchange rate; **t. de natalité** birth rate.

taverne [tavern] *nf* tavern.

taxe [taks] *nf (impôt)* tax; *(de douane)* duty; *(prix)* official price; **t. à la valeur ajoutée** value-added tax; **t. de séjour** tourist tax. ●**taxation** *nf (imposition)* taxation (de of); *(fixation du prix)* (price) assessment (de of).

taxer [takse] *vt* 1 *(produit, personne, firme etc)* to tax; *(fixer le prix de)* to fix *ou* assess the price of *(product, service etc)*. 2 **t. qn de** to accuse s.o. of. 3 **t. qch à qn** *(prendre, voler)* Fam to swipe sth from s.o. ●**taxé, -ée** *a (produit etc)* taxed.

taxi [taksi] *nm* taxi.

taxiphone® [taksifɔn] *nm* pay phone.

tchador [tʃadɔr] *nm (voile)* chador.

tchatche [tʃatʃ] *nf* **avoir la t.** Fam to be a real windbag *ou* gasbag.

Tchécoslovaquie [tʃekɔslɔvaki] *nf* Czechoslovakia. ●**tchèque** *a* Czech; **la République** t. the Czech Republic ‖ *nmf* T. Czech ‖ *nm (langue)* Czech.

TD [tede] *nm abrév* = **travaux dirigés** *(voir travail)*.

te [t(ə)] *(t' before vowel or mute h) pron* 1 *(complément direct)* you; **je te vois** I see you. 2 *(indirect)* (to) you; **il te parle** he speaks to you; **elle te l'a dit** she told you. 3 *(réfléchi)* yourself; **tu te laves** you wash yourself.

technicien, -ienne [tɛknisjɛ̃, -jɛn] *nmf* technician. ●**technique** *a* technical ‖ *nf* technique. ●**techniquement** *adv* technically. ●**technocrate** *nm* technocrat. ●**technologie** *nf* technology. ●**technologique** *a* technological.

teck [tɛk] *nm (bois)* teak.

teckel [tekɛl] *nm (chien)* dachshund.

tee-shirt [tiʃœrt] *nm* tee-shirt.

teindre* [tɛ̃dr] *vt* to dye; **t. en rouge/etc** to dye red/etc ‖ **se teindre** *vpr* **se t. (les cheveux)** to dye one's hair.

teint [tɛ̃] *nm* 1 *(de visage)* complexion. 2 **bon**

ou **grand t.** *(tissu)* colourfast; **bon t.** *(catholique etc) Fig Hum* staunch.

teinte [tɛ̃t] *nf* shade, tint; **une t. de** *(dose) Fig* a tinge of. ● **teinter** *vt* to tint; *(bois)* to stain; **se t. de** *(remarque, ciel) Fig* to be tinged with.

teinture [tɛ̃tyr] *nf* dyeing; *(produit)* dye. ● **teinturerie** *nf (boutique)* (dry) cleaner's. ● **teinturier, -ière** *nmf* dry cleaner.

tel, telle [tɛl] *a* such; **t. livre/homme/etc** such a book/man/etc; **un t. intérêt/etc** such interest/etc; **de tels mots/etc** such words/etc; **t. que** such as, like; **t. que je l'ai laissé** just as I left it; **laissez-le t. quel** leave it just as it is; **en tant que t.,** **comme t.** as such; **t. ou t.** such and such; **rien de t. que...** (there's) nothing like...; **rien de t.** nothing like it; **Monsieur Un t.** Mr So-and-so; **t. père t. fils** like father like son.

télé [tele] *nf (téléviseur) Fam* TV; *Br* telly; **à la t.** on TV, *Br* on the telly; **regarder la t.** to watch TV *ou Br* on the telly.

télé- [tele] *préf* tele-.

télébenne [teleben] *nf ou* **télécabine** [telekabin] *nf (cabine, système)* cable car.

télécarte® [telekart] *nf* phonecard.

télécommande [telekɔmɑ̃d] *nf* remote control. ● **télécommander** *vt* to operate by remote control.

télécommunications [telekɔmynikasjɔ̃] *nfpl* telecommunications.

télécopie [telekɔpi] *nf* fax. ● **télécopieur** *nm* fax (machine).

téléfilm [telefilm] *nm* TV film.

télégramme [telegram] *nm* telegram.

télégraphe [telegraf] *nm* telegraph. ● **télégraphie** *nf* telegraphy. ● **télégraphier** *vt (message)* to wire, cable *(que* that). ● **télégraphique** *a* **poteau/fil/etc t.** telegraph pole/wire/etc; **style t.** *Fig* telegraphic style. ● **télégraphiste** *nm (messager)* telegraph boy.

téléguider [telegide] *vt* to operate by remote control, radio-control. ● **téléguidage** *nm* radio control.

télématique [telematik] *nf* telematics, computer communications.

téléobjectif [teleɔbʒɛktif] *nm* telephoto lens.

télépathie [telepati] *nf* telepathy.

téléphérique [teleferik] *nm (système)* cable car, cableway.

téléphone [telefɔn] *nm (tele)phone;* **coup de t.** (phone) call; **passer un coup de t. à qn** to give s.o. a ring *ou* a call; **au t.** on the (tele)phone; **avoir le t.** to be on the (tele)phone; **t. portatif** mobile phone; **t. sans fil** cordless phone; **apprendre qch par le t. arabe** *Fig* to hear about sth through *ou* on the grapevine. ● **téléphoner** *vt (nouvelle etc)* to (tele)phone (à to) ▮ *vi* to (tele)phone; **t. à qn** to (tele)phone s.o., call s.o. (up). ● **téléphonique** *a* **appel/etc t.** telephone call/etc. ● **téléphoniste** *nmf* operator, *Br* telephonist.

téléprompteur [teleprɔ̃ptœr] *nm* teleprompter, *Br* autocue.

télescope [teleskɔp] *nm* telescope. ● **télesco-**

-pique *a* telescopic.

télescoper [teleskɔpe] *vt (voiture, train etc)* to smash into; **se t.** to smash into each other. ● **télescopage** *nm* smash.

téléscripteur [teleskriptœr] *nm (appareil)* teleprinter, *Am* teletypewriter.

télésiège [telesjɛʒ] *nm* chair lift.

téléski [teleski] *nm* ski tow.

téléspectateur, -trice [telespɛktatœr, -tris] *nmf (television)* viewer.

télétravail [teletravaj] *nm* home work *ou* working, teleworking.

téléviser [televize] *vt* to televise; **journal télévisé** television news. ● **téléviseur** *nm* television (set). ● **télévision** *nf* television; **à la t.** on (the) television; **regarder la t.** to watch (the) television; **programme/etc de t.** television programme/etc.

télex [telɛks] *nm (service, message)* telex.

telle [tɛl] *voir* **tel.**

tellement [tɛlmɑ̃] *adv (si)* so; *(tant)* so much; **t. grand/etc que** so big/etc that; **crier/etc t. que** to shout/etc so much that; **t. de travail/etc** so much work/etc; **t. de soucis/etc** so many worries/etc; **tu aimes ça? - pas t.!** *(pas beaucoup)* do you like it? - not much *ou* a lot!; **personne ne peut le supporter, t. il est bavard** nobody can stand him, he's so talkative.

tellurique [telyrik] *a* **secousse t.** earth tremor.

téméraire [temerɛr] *a* rash, reckless. ● **témérité** *nf* rashness, recklessness.

témoigner [temwaɲe] **1** *vi (devant un tribunal)* to give evidence, testify *(contre* against); **t. de qch** *(personne, attitude etc)* to testify to sth ▮ *vt* **t. que** *(attester)* to testify that. **2** *vt (gratitude etc)* to show *(à qn* (to) s.o.). ● **témoignage** *nm* **1** evidence, testimony; *(récit)* account; **faux t.** *(délit)* perjury. **2** *(d'affection etc) Fig* token, sign (of) of; **en t. de** as a token *ou* sign of.

témoin [temwɛ̃] **1** *nm* witness; **t. oculaire** eyewitness; **t. à charge/à décharge** witness for the prosecution/*Br* defence *ou Am* defense; **être t. de** *(accident etc)* to witness ▮ *a* **appartement t.** *Br* show flat, *Am* model apartment. **2** *nm (de relais)* baton.

tempe [tɑ̃p] *nf Anat* temple.

tempérament [tɑ̃peramɑ̃] *nm* **1** *(caractère)* temperament; *(physique)* constitution. **2** **acheter à t.** to buy on *Br* hire purchase *ou Am* on the installment plan.

tempérance [tɑ̃perɑ̃s] *nf* temperance; **société de t.** temperance society.

température [tɑ̃peratyr] *nf* temperature; **avoir** *ou* **faire de la t.** *(fièvre)* to have a temperature.

tempéré, -ée [tɑ̃pere] *a (climat, zone)* temperate.

tempérer [tɑ̃pere] *vt Litt* to temper.

tempête [tɑ̃pɛt] *nf* storm; **t. de neige** snowstorm, blizzard.

tempêter [tɑ̃pete] *vi (crier)* to storm, rage *(contre* against).

temple [tɑ̃pl] *nm* (*romain, grec etc*) temple; (*protestant*) church.

tempo [tɛmpo] *nm* tempo.

temporaire [tɑ̃pɔrɛr] *a* temporary. ●**temporairement** *adv* temporarily.

temporel, -elle [tɑ̃pɔrɛl] *a* temporal; (*terrestre*) wordly.

temporiser [tɑ̃pɔrize] *vi* to procrastinate, play for time.

temps¹ [tɑ̃] *nm* (*durée, période, moment*) time; *Grammaire* tense; (*étape*) stage; **t. d'arrêt** pause, break; **t. mort** (*dans un film etc*) *Fig* slow period, slack moment; **en t. utile** in due course, in time; **en t. de guerre** in wartime, in time of war; **avoir/trouver le t.** to have/find (the) time (**de faire** to do); **il est t.** it is time (**de faire** to do); **il était t.!** it was about time (too)!; **il est (grand) t. que vous partiez** it's (high) time you left; **ces derniers t.** lately; **de t. en t.** [dətɑ̃zɑ̃tɑ̃], **de t. à autre** [dətɑ̃zaotr] from time to time, now and again; **en t. utile** [ɑ̃tɑ̃zytil] in good *ou* due time; **en même t.** at the same time (**que** as); **à t.** (*arriver*) in time; **à plein t.** (*travailler etc*) full-time; **à t. partiel** (*travailler etc*) part-time; **dans le t.** (*autrefois*) once, at one time; **avec le t.** (*à la longue*) in time; **tout le t.** all the time; **de mon t.** in my time; **t. de mes parents**/*etc* in my parents'/*etc* time; **pendant un t.** for a while *ou* time; **par les t. qui courent** *Fam* at the present time, in the present climate; **moteur à quatre t.** four-stroke engine, *Am* four-cycle engine.

temps² [tɑ̃] *nm* (*climat*) weather; **il fait beau/mauvais t.** the weather's fine/bad; **quel t. fait-il?** what's the weather like?

tenable [tənabl] *a* bearable.

tenace [tənas] *a* stubborn, tenacious. ●**ténacité** *nf* stubbornness, tenacity.

tenailler [tənaje] *vt* (*faim, remords*) to rack, torture (*s.o.*).

tenailles [tənaj] *nfpl* (*outil*) pincers.

tenancier, -ière [tənɑ̃sje, -jɛr] *nmf* (*d'hôtel etc*) manager, manageress.

tenant, -ante [tənɑ̃, -ɑ̃t] **1** *nmf* **le t. du titre** (*champion*) the title holder. **2** *nm* (*partisan*) supporter (**de** of).

tenants [tənɑ̃] *nmpl* **les t. et les aboutissants d'une question**/*etc* the ins and outs of a question/*etc*.

tendance [tɑ̃dɑ̃s] *nf* (*penchant*) tendency; (*évolution*) trend (**à towards**); **avoir t. à faire qch** to tend to do sth, have a tendency to do sth.

tendancieux, -euse [tɑ̃dɑ̃sjø, -øz] *a Péj* tendentious.

tendeur [tɑ̃dœr] *nm* (*à bagages*) elastic strap, *Am* bungee.

tendon [tɑ̃dɔ̃] *nm Anat* tendon, sinew.

tendre¹ [tɑ̃dr] **1** *vt* to stretch; (*main*) to hold out (**à qn** to *s.o.*); (*bras, jambe*) to stretch out; (*cou*) to strain, crane; (*muscle*) to tense, flex; (*arc*) to bend; (*piège*) to set, lay; (*filet*) to spread; (*tapisserie*) to hang; **t. qch à qn** to hold out sth to *s.o.*; **t. l'oreille** *Fig* to

prick up one's ears ∎ **se tendre** *vpr* (*rapports*) to become strained.

2 *vi* **t. à qch/à faire qch** to tend towards sth/ to do sth. ●**tendu, -ue** *a* (*corde*) tight, taut; (*personne, situation, muscle*) tense; (*main*) held out; (*rapports*) strained.

tendre² [tɑ̃dr] *a* **1** (*viande*) tender; (*bois, couleur, peau*) soft; (*peau*) delicate, tender; **depuis ma plus t. enfance** since I've been a young child. **2** (*personne*) affectionate (**avec** to), loving; (*parole, regard etc*) tender, loving. ●**tendrement** [-əmɑ̃] *adv* tenderly, lovingly. ●**tendresse** *nf* (*affection*) affection, tenderness. ●**tendreté** *nf* (*de viande*) tenderness.

ténèbres [tenɛbr] *nfpl* darkness, gloom. ●**ténébreux, -euse** *a* dark, gloomy; (*mystérieux*) mysterious.

teneur [tənœr] *nf* (*de lettre etc*) content; **t. en alcool**/*etc* alcohol/*etc* content (**de** of).

tenir* [tənir] *vt* (*à la main etc*) to hold; (*promesse, comptes, hôtel*) to keep; (*rôle*) to play; (*propos*) to utter; **t. sa droite** (*conducteur*) to keep to the right; **t. la route** (*véhicule*) to hold the road; **t. sa langue** *Fig* to hold one's tongue; **t. pour** to regard as; **t. propre/chaud**/*etc* to keep clean/hot/*etc*; **je le tiens!** (*je l'ai attrapé*) I've got him!; **je le tiens de** (*fait etc*) I got it from; (*caractère héréditaire*) I get it from.

∎ *vi* (*nœud etc*) to hold; (*neige, coiffure*) to last, hold; (*résister*) to hold out; (*offre*) to stand; **t. à qn/qch** to be attached to *ou* fond of *s.o.*/sth; **t. à la vie** to value life; **t. à faire qch** to be anxious to do sth; **t. dans qch** (*être contenu*) to fit into sth; **t. de qn** to take after *s.o.*; **tenez!** (*prenez*) here (you are)!; **tiens!** (*surprise*) well!, hey!; **ça tient à sa maladie**/*etc* it's due to his illness/*etc*.

∎ *v imp* **il ne tient qu'à vous** it's up to you (**de faire** to do).

∎ **se tenir** *vpr* (*avoir lieu*) to be held; (*rester*) to keep, remain; **se t. debout** to stand (up); **se t. droit** to stand up *ou* sit up straight; **se t. par la main** to hold hands; **se t. bien** to behave oneself; **se t. à qch** to hold on to sth; **s'en t. à qch** (*se limiter à*) to stick to sth; **savoir à quoi s'en t.** to know what's what; **tout se tient** *Fig* it all hangs together.

tennis [tenis] *nm* tennis; (*terrain*) (tennis) court; **t. de table** table tennis ∎ *nmpl* (*chaussures*) *Br* plimsolls, *Br* pumps, *Am* sneakers.

ténor [tenɔr] *nm Mus* tenor.

tension [tɑ̃sjɔ̃] *nf* (*tension*; **t. (artérielle)** blood pressure; **t. d'esprit** mental effort, concentration; **avoir de la t. (artérielle)** to have high blood pressure.

tentacule [tɑ̃takyl] *nm* tentacle.

tente [tɑ̃t] *nf* tent.

tenter¹ [tɑ̃te] *vt* (*essayer*) to try; **t. de faire qch** to try *ou* attempt to do sth. ●**tentative** *nf* attempt; **t. de suicide** suicide attempt.

tenter² [tɑ̃te] *vt* (*faire envie à etc*) to tempt; **tenté de faire qch** tempted to do sth. ●**tentant, -ante** *a* tempting. ●**tentation** *nf* temptation.

tenture [tɑ̃tyr] nf (wall) hanging; (de porte) drape, curtain.

tenu, -ue [təny] pp de tenir ▌ a t. de faire qch obliged to do sth; **bien/mal t.** (maison etc) well/badly kept.

ténu, -ue [teny] a (fil etc) fine; (soupçon, différence) tenuous; (voix) thin.

tenue [təny] nf 1 (vêtements) clothes, outfit; (aspect) appearance; **t. de combat** (uniforme) battle ou Br combat dress; **t. de soirée** evening dress; **être en petite t.** to be scantily dressed. **2** (conduite) (good) behaviour; (maintien) posture; **manquer de t.** to lack (good) manners. **3** (de maison, hôtel) running; (de comptes) keeping. **4 t. de route** (de véhicule) road-holding.

ter [tɛr] a (à 4 t. (numéro) 4B.

térébenthine [terebɑ̃tin] nf turpentine.

tergal® [tɛrgal] nm Br Terylene®, Am Dacron®.

tergiverser [tɛrʒivɛrse] vi Litt to procrastinate.

terme [tɛrm] nm 1 (mot) term. **2** (date limite) time (limit), date; (fin) Litt end; **mettre un t. à qch** to put an end to sth; **à court/long t.** (conséquences, projet etc) short-/long-term; **être né avant/à t.** to be born prematurely/at (full) term. **3 moyen t.** (solution) middle course. **4 en bons/mauvais termes** on good/ bad terms (avec qn with s.o.). **5** (loyer) rent; (jour) rent day; (période) rental period.

terminal, -e, -aux [tɛrminal, -o] 1 a final; (phase de maladie) terminal ▌ a & nf (classe) **terminale** Scol = Br sixth form, = Am twelfth grade. **2** nm (d'ordinateur, pétrolier) terminal.

terminer [tɛrmine] vt to end; (achever) to finish, complete ▌ **se terminer** vpr to end (par with, en in). ● **terminaison** nf (de mot) ending.

terminologie [tɛrminɔlɔʒi] nf terminology.

terminus [tɛrminys] nm terminus.

termite [tɛrmit] nm (insecte) termite.

terne [tɛrn] a (couleur, journée etc) dull, drab; (personne) dull. ● **ternir** vt (métal, réputation) to tarnish; (meuble, miroir) to dull ▌ **se ternir** vpr (métal) to tarnish.

terrain [tɛrɛ̃] nm (sol) & Fig ground; (étendue) land; (à bâtir) plot, site; (pour opérations militaires) & Géol terrain; **un t.** a piece of land; **t. de camping** campsite; **t. de football/rugby** football/rugby pitch; **t. de golf** golf course; **t. de jeu(x)** (pour enfants) playground; (stade) Br playing field, Am athletic field; **t. de sport** Br sports ground, Br playing field, Am athletic field; **t. d'aviation** airfield; **t. vague** waste ground, Am vacant lot; **céder/gagner/perdre du t.** (armée etc) & Fig to give/gain/lose ground; **tâter le t.** Fig to see how the land lies, sound things out; **trouver un t. d'entente** to find a common ground; **être sur son t.** to be on familiar ground; **véhicule tout t.** ou **tous terrains** off-road ou all-terrain vehicle.

terrasse [tɛras] nf 1 (balcon, plate-forme) terrace; (toit) terrace (roof). **2** (de café) Br pavement ou Am sidewalk area; **à la t.** outside.

terrassement [tɛrasmɑ̃] nm (travail) excavation.

terrasser [tɛrase] vt (adversaire) to floor, knock down; (accabler) Fig to overcome.

terrassier [tɛrasje] nm labourer, Br navvy.

terre [tɛr] nf (matière, monde) earth; (sol) ground; (opposé à mer, étendue) land; **terres** (domaine) land, estate; **El** Br earth, Am ground; **la t.** (le monde) the earth; **la T.** (planète) Earth; **à** ou **par t.** (tomber) to the ground; (poser) on the ground; **par t.** (assis, couché etc) on the ground; **aller à t.** (marin etc) to go ashore; **sous t.** underground; **t. cuite** (baked) clay, earthenware; **poterie/etc en t. cuite** earthenware pottery/etc; **t. battue** (de court de tennis) hard surface. ● **terre-à-terre** a inv down-to-earth. ● **terre-plein** nm (earth) platform; (au milieu de la route) Br central reservation, Am median strip.

terreau [tɛro] nm compost.

terrer (se) [sətere] vpr (fugitif, animal) to hide, go to ground ou earth.

terrestre [tɛrɛstr] a (vie, joies etc) earthly; **animal/transport/etc t.** land animal/transportation/etc; **la surface t.** the earth's surface; **globe t.** globe, terrestrial globe.

terreur [tɛrœr] nf terror; **vivre dans la t. de l'armée/etc** to live in terror of the army/etc. ● **terrible** a awful, terrible; (formidable) Fam terrific; **pas t.** Fam nothing special, not terribly good. ● **terriblement** [-əmɑ̃] adv (extrêmement) terribly.

terreux, -euse [tɛrø, -øz] a (goût) earthy; (sale) grubby; (couleur) dull; (teint) ashen.

terrien, -ienne [tɛrjɛ̃, -jɛn] a land-owning; **propriétaire t.** landowner ▌ nmf (habitant de la terre) earth dweller, earthling.

terrier [tɛrje] nm 1 (de lapin etc) burrow. **2** (chien) terrier.

terrifier [tɛrifje] vt to terrify. ● **terrifiant, -ante** a terrifying; (extraordinaire) incredible.

terrine [tɛrin] nf (récipient) terrine; (pâté) pâté.

territoire [tɛritwar] nm territory. ● **territorial, -e, -aux** a territorial; **eaux territoriales** territorial waters.

terroir [tɛrwar] nm (sol) soil; (région) region; **accent/etc du t.** rural accent/etc.

terroriser [tɛrɔrize] vt to terrorize. ● **terrorisme** nm terrorism. ● **terroriste** a & nmf terrorist.

tertiaire [tɛrsjɛr] a tertiary; **secteur t.** service ou tertiary sector.

tertre [tɛrtr] nm hillock, mound.

tes [te] voir ton¹.

tesson [tɛsɔ̃] nm **t. de bouteille** piece ou fragment of broken bottle.

test [tɛst] nm test. ● **tester** vt (élève, produit) to test.

testament [tɛstamɑ̃] nm 1 (document) will; (œuvre) Fig testament. **2 Ancien/Nouveau T.**

Rel Old/New Testament.

testicule [testikyl] *nm Anat* testicle.

tétanos [tetanos] *nm (maladie)* tetanus.

têtard [tetar] *nm* tadpole.

tête [tɛt] *nf* head; *(visage)* face; *(cheveux)* (head of) hair; *(cerveau)* brain; *(d'arbre)* top; *(de lit, clou, cortège)* head; *(de page, liste)* top, head; **(coup de) t.** *Football* header; **t. nucléaire** nuclear warhead; **tenir t. à qn** *(s'opposer à)* to stand up to s.o.; **faire la t.** *(bouder)* to sulk; **faire une t.** *Football* to head the ball; **avoir/faire une drôle de t.** to have/give a funny look; **tomber la t. la première** to fall headlong *ou* head first; **calculer qch de t.** to work sth out in one's head; **se mettre dans la t. de faire qch** to get it into one's head to do sth; **perdre la t.** *Fig* to lose one's head; **à t. reposée** at one's leisure; **à la t. de** *(entreprise, parti)* at the head of; *(classe)* at the top of; **de la t. aux pieds** from head *ou* top to toe; **t. nue** bare-headed; **en t.** *(d'une course etc)* in the lead; **se payer la t. de qn** *Fam* to make fun of s.o.; **j'en ai par-dessus la t.** *Fam* I've had enough of it; **ça me prend la t.** *Fam* it gets on my nerves *ou* under my skin; **tu n'as pas de t.!** *Fam* you're a scatterbrain!

tête-à-queue [tɛtakø] *nm inv* **faire un t.-à-queue** *(en voiture)* to spin right round. ● **tête-à-tête** *adv* **(en) t.-à-tête** *(seul)* in private, alone together **I** *nm inv* tête-à-tête. ● **tête-bêche** *adv* head to tail.

téter [tete] *vt (lait, biberon etc)* to suck; **t. sa mère** *(bébé)* to feed *ou* suck at one's mother's breast; **le bébé tète** the baby is being fed (at the breast); **donner à t. à** to feed, suckle. ● **tétée** *nf (de bébé)* feed. ● **tétine** *nf* **1** *(de biberon)* *Br* teat, *Am* nipple; *(sucette)* *Br* dummy, *Am* pacifier. **2** *(de vache)* udder. ● **téton** *nm Fam* breast.

têtu, -ue [tety] *a* stubborn, obstinate.

texte [tɛkst] *nm* text; *(de théâtre)* lines, text; *(de devoir scolaire)* subject; *(morceau choisi)* *Littér* passage. ● **textuel, -elle** *a (traduction)* literal. ● **textuellement** *adv* word for word.

textile [tɛkstil] *a & nm* textile.

texture [tɛkstyr] *nf* texture.

TGV [teʒeve] *abrév* = **train à grande vitesse.**

Thaïlande [tailãd] *nf* Thailand. ● **thaïlandais, -aise** *a* Thai **I** *nmf* **T., Thaïlandaise** Thai.

thé [te] *nm (boisson, réunion)* tea. ● **théière** *nf* teapot.

théâtre [teatr] *nm (art, lieu)* theatre; *(œuvres)* drama; *(d'un crime etc)* *Fig* scene; **t. des opérations** *Mil* theatre of operations; **faire du t.** to act. ● **théâtral, -e, -aux** *a* theatrical.

thème [tɛm] *nm* theme; *(traduction)* *Scol* translation, *Br* prose (composition).

théologie [teɔlɔʒi] *nf* theology. ● **théologien** *nm* theologian. ● **théologique** *a* theological.

théorème [teɔrɛm] *nm* theorem.

théorie [teɔri] *nf* theory; **en t.** in theory. ● **théoricien, -ienne** *nmf* theorist, theoreti-cian. ● **théorique** *a* theoretical. ● **théorique-**

ment *adv* theoretically.

thérapeutique [terapøtik] *a* therapeutic **I** *nf (traitement)* therapy. ● **thérapie** *nf Psy* ther-apy.

thermal, -e, -aux [tɛrmal, -o] *a* **station thermale** spa; **eaux thermales** hot *ou* thermal springs.

thermique [tɛrmik] *a (énergie, unité)* thermal.

thermomètre [tɛrmɔmɛtr] *nm* thermometer.

thermonucléaire [tɛrmɔnykleɛr] *a* thermo-nuclear.

thermos® [tɛrmɔs] *nm ou f inv* Thermos® *(Br* flask *ou Am* bottle), *Br* vacuum flask.

thermostat [tɛrmɔsta] *nm* thermostat.

thèse [tɛz] *nf (proposition, ouvrage)* thesis.

thon [tɔ̃] *nm* tuna (fish).

thorax [tɔraks] *nm Anat* thorax.

thym [tɛ̃] *nm (plante, aromate)* thyme.

thyroïde [tiroid] *a & nf Anat* thyroid.

Tibet [tibɛ] *nm* Tibet.

tibia [tibja] *nm* shin bone, tibia.

tic [tik] *nm (contraction)* twitch, tic; *(manie)* *Fig* mannerism.

ticket [tikɛ] *nm* ticket; **t. de quai** *(de gare)* platform ticket; **t. modérateur** portion of the cost of medical treatment paid by the in-sured person.

tic(-)tac [tiktak] *int & nm inv* tick-tock.

tiède [tjɛd] *a (luke)*warm, tepid; *(vent, cli-mat)* mild; *(accueil, partisan)* half-hearted. ● **tiédeur** *nf (luke)*warmness, tepidness; *(de vent etc)* mildness; *(d'accueil etc)* half-heartedness. ● **tiédir** *vi* to cool (down); *(de-venir plus chaud)* to warm up **I** *vt* to cool (down); *(chauffer)* to warm (up).

tien, tienne [tjɛ̃, tjɛn] *pron poss* **le t., la tienne, les tien(ne)s** yours; **les deux tiens** your two **I** *nmpl* **les tiens** *(ta famille)* your (own) people.

tiens, tient [tjɛ̃] *voir* tenir.

tiercé [tjɛrse] *nm (pari)* place betting *(on the horses)*; **jouer/gagner au t.** = to bet/win on the horses.

tiers, tierce [tjɛr, tjɛrs] *a* third **I** *nm (frac-tion)* third; *(personne)* third party; **assurance au t.** third-party insurance; **t. provisionnel** interim tax payment *(one third of previous year's tax)*. ● **Tiers-Monde** *nm* Third World.

tifs [tif] *nmpl Fam* hair.

tige [tiʒ] *nf (de plante)* stem, stalk; *(barre)* rod; *(de botte)* leg.

tignasse [tiɲas] *nf Fam* mop (of hair).

tigre [tigr] *nm* tiger. ● **tigresse** *nf* tigress.

tigré, -ée [tigre] *a (rayé)* striped; *(tacheté)* spotted.

tilleul [tijœl] *nm* lime (tree), linden (tree); *(infusion)* lime (blossom) tea.

timbale [tɛ̃bal] *nf* **1** *(gobelet)* (metal) tumbler; **décrocher la t.** *Fam* to hit the jack-pot, have a phenomenal success. **2** *(instru-ment de musique)* kettledrum.

timbre [tɛ̃br] *nm* **1** *(tampon, vignette)* stamp; *(cachet de la poste)* postmark. **2** *(sonnette)* bell. **3** *(d'instrument, de voix)* tone (quality).

● **timbre-poste** nm (pl **timbres-poste**) (postage) stamp. ● **timbrer** vt (affranchir) to stamp (letter); (marquer) to stamp (document). ● **timbré, -ée** a 1 (voix) sonorous, resonant. 2 (fou) Fam crazy.

timide [timid] a (gêné) shy, timid; (timoré) timid. ● **timidement** adv shyly, timidly; (d'une manière timorée) timidly. ● **timidité** nf shyness, timidity; (manque d'audace) timidity.

timonier [timɔnje] nm (marin) helmsman.

timoré, -ée [timɔre] a timorous, fearful.

tintamarre [tɛ̃tamar] nm din, racket.

tinter [tɛ̃te] vi (cloche) to ring, toll; (clefs, monnaie) to jingle; (verres) to chink. ● **tintement(s)** nm(pl) (de cloche) ringing; (de clefs) jingling; (de verres) chinking.

tique [tik] nf (insecte) tick.

tiquer [tike] vi (personne) to wince.

tir [tir] nm (sport) shooting; (action) firing, shooting; (feu, rafale) fire; Football shot; (**stand de**) **t., t.** (**forain**) shooting ou rifle range; **t. à l'arc** archery; **ligne de t.** line of fire.

tirade [tirad] nf (au théâtre) & Fig Br monologue, Am monolog.

tirage [tiraʒ] nm 1 (de journal) circulation; (édition) edition; (quantité) (print) run; (action) Typ Phot printing. 2 (de loterie) draw; **t. au sort** drawing of lots. 3 (de cheminée) Br draught, Am draft.

tirailler [tiraje] 1 vt to pull (away) at; (harceler) Fig to pester, plague; **tiraillé entre** (possibilités etc) torn between. 2 vi (au fusil) to shoot wildly. ● **tiraillement** nm 1 (conflit) conflict (**entre** between). 2 (crampe) cramp.

tirant [tirã] nm **le t. d'eau** (de bateau) Br draught, Am draft.

tire [tir] nf 1 **vol à la t.** pickpocketing. 2 (voiture) Fam car.

tire-au-flanc [tiroflã] nm inv (paresseux) shirker. ● **tire-bouchon** nm corkscrew. ● **tire-d'aile** (**à**) adv swiftly. ● **tire-fesses** nm inv Fam ski tow.

tirelire [tirlir] nf Br moneybox, Am coin bank.

tirer [tire] vt to pull; (langue) to stick out; (trait, rideaux, conclusion) to draw; (balle, canon) to shoot, fire; (gibier) to shoot; (journal, épreuves de livre, photo etc) to print; **t. de** (sortir) to pull ou draw ou take out of; (obtenir) to get from; (nom, origine) to derive from; (produit) to extract from; **t. qn de** (danger, lit) to get s.o. out of; **je vous tire mon chapeau** Fig I take my hat off to you.

❙ vi to pull (**sur**, at); (faire feu) to shoot, fire (**sur** at); Football to shoot; (cheminée) to draw; **t. au sort** to draw lots; **t. à sa fin** to draw to a close; **t. sur** (couleur) to verge on; **t. à boulets rouges sur qn** (critiquer) to go for s.o. hammer and tongs.

❙ **se tirer** vpr (partir) Fam to make tracks, beat it; **se t. de** (travail, problème) to cope with; (danger, situation) to get out of; **se t. d'affaire** to get out of trouble; **s'en t.** Fam

(en réchapper) to come ou pull through; (réussir) to get along. ● **tiré, -ée** a (traits, visage) drawn; **t. par les cheveux** Fig farfetched.

tiret [tire] nm (trait) dash.

tireur [tirœr] nm gunman; **t. d'élite** marksman; **t. isolé** sniper; **un bon/mauvais t.** a good/bad shot. ● **tireuse** nf **t. de cartes** fortune-teller.

tiroir [tirwar] nm (de commode etc) drawer. ● **tiroir-caisse** nm (ₚl **tiroirs-caisses**) Br (cash) till, cash register.

tisane [tizan] nf herb(al) tea.

tison [tizɔ̃] nm (fire)brand, ember. ● **tisonner** vt (feu) to poke. ● **tisonnier** nm poker.

tisser [tise] vt to weave. ● **tissage** nm (action) weaving. ● **tisserand, -ande** nmf weaver.

tissu [tisy] nm material, cloth, fabric; Biol tissue; **du t.-éponge** Br (terry) towelling, Am toweling; **un t. de mensonges/etc** a web of lies/etc; **le t. social** the fabric of society, the social fabric.

titre [titr] nm (nom, qualité) title; (coté en Bourse) security, stock, share; (diplôme) qualification; **titres** (droits) claims (**à** to); (**gros**) **t.** (de journal) headline; **t. de propriété** title deed; **t. de transport** ticket; **t. de noblesse** title (of nobility); **à quel t.?** (pour quelle raison) on what grounds?; **à ce t.** (en cette qualité) as such; (pour cette raison) therefore; **à aucun t.** on no account; **au même t.** in the same way (**que** as); **à t. d'exemple** as an example; **à t. exceptionnel** exceptionally; **à t. privé** in a private capacity; **à t. provisoire** temporarily; **à t. indicatif** for general information; **à juste t.** rightly.

titrer [titre] vt (film) to title; (journal) to run (sth) as a headline. ● **titré, -ée** a (personne) titled.

tituber [titybe] vi to reel, stagger.

titulaire [titylɛr] a (enseignant) tenured; **professeur t. d'une chaire** professor; **être t. de** (permis etc) to be the holder of; (poste) to hold ❙ nmf (de permis, poste) holder (**de** of). ● **titulariser** vt (fonctionnaire) to give tenure to. ● **titularisation** nf (granting of) tenure.

toast [tost] nm 1 (pain grillé) piece ou slice of toast. 2 (allocution) toast; **porter un t. à** to drink (a toast) to.

toboggan [tɔbɔgã] nm 1 (de terrain de jeux etc) slide; (traîneau) toboggan. 2 (voie de circulation) Br flyover, Am overpass.

toc [tɔk] 1 int **t. t.!** knock knock! 2 nm **du t.** (camelote) trash; **bijou en t.** imitation jewel.

tocard [tɔkar] nm Fam dead loss, complete idiot.

tocsin [tɔksɛ̃] nm alarm (bell).

tohu-bohu [tɔybɔy] nm (bruit) hubbub, commotion; (confusion) hurly-burly.

toi [twa] pron 1 (après une préposition) you; **avec t.** with you. 2 (sujet) you; **t., tu peux** you may; **c'est t. qui...** it's you who.... 3 (réfléchi) **assieds-t.** sit (yourself) down; **dépêche-t.** hurry up. ● **toi-même** pron yourself.

toile [twal] *nf* **1** cloth; (*à voile, sac etc*) canvas; (*à draps*) linen; **une t.** a piece of cloth *ou* canvas *ou* linen; **t. de jute** hessian; **drap de t.** linen sheet; **t. cirée** oil cloth; **t. de fond** (*de théâtre*) & *Fig* backcloth. **2** (*tableau*) painting, canvas. **3 t. d'araignée** (spider's) web, cobweb. **4 se faire une t.** *Fam* to go and see a movie.

toilette [twalɛt] *nf* (*action*) wash(ing); (*vêtements*) clothes, outfit; **articles de t.** toiletries; **cabinet de t.** washroom; **eau/trousse/savon de t.** toilet water/bag/soap; **table de t.** dressing table; **faire sa t.** to wash (and dress); **les toilettes** (*W-C*) *Br* the toilet(s), *Am* the men's *ou* ladies' room; **aller aux toilettes** *Br* to go to the toilet, *Am* go to the men's *ou* ladies' room.

toiser [twaze] *vt* to eye scornfully.

toison [twazɔ̃] *nf* (*de mouton*) fleece.

toit [twa] *nm* roof; **t. ouvrant** (*de voiture*) sunroof. ● **toiture** *nf* roof(ing).

tôle [tol] *nf* **la t.** sheet metal; **une t.** a metal *ou* steel sheet; **t. ondulée** corrugated iron.

tolérer [tolere] *vt* (*permettre*) to tolerate, allow; (*supporter*) to tolerate, bear; (*à la douane*) to allow. ● **tolérant, -ante** *a* tolerant (*à l'égard de* of). ● **tolérable** *a* tolerable. ● **tolérance** *nf* tolerance; (*à la douane*) allowance.

tollé [tole] *nm* outcry.

tomate [tomat] *nf* tomato; **sauce t.** tomato sauce.

tombe [tɔ̃b] *nf* grave; (*avec monument*) tomb. ● **tombale** *af* **pierre t.** gravestone, tombstone. ● **tombeau, -x** *nm* tomb.

tomber [tɔ̃be] *vi* (*aux* **être**) to fall; (*température*) to drop, fall; (*vent*) to drop (off); (*cheveux, robe*) to hang down; **t. malade** to fall ill; **t. (par terre)** to fall (down); **faire t.** (*personne*) to knock over; (*gouvernement, prix*) to bring down; **laisser t.** (*objet*) to drop; (*projet, personne etc*) *Fig* to drop, give up; **tu m'as laissé t. hier** *Fig* you let me down yesterday; **se laisser t. dans un fauteuil** to drop into an armchair; **tu tombes bien/mal** *Fig* you've come at the right/wrong time; **t. de sommeil** *ou* **de fatigue** to be ready to drop; **t. un lundi** to fall on a Monday; **t. sur** (*trouver*) to come across; **t. de haut** *Fam* to be bitterly disappointed. ● **tombée** *nf* **t. de la nuit** nightfall.

tombereau, -x [tɔ̃bro] *nm* (*charrette*) tip cart.

tombola [tɔ̃bola] *nf* raffle.

tome [tom] *nm* (*livre*) volume.

tomme [tom] *nf* cow's milk cheese made in Savoie.

ton¹, ta, *pl* **tes** [tɔ̃, ta, te] (**ta** *becomes* **ton** [tɔ̃n] *before a vowel or mute h*) *a poss* your; **t. père** your father; **ta mère** your mother; **ton ami(e)** your friend.

ton² [tɔ̃] *nm* (*de voix etc*) tone; (*de couleur*) shade, tone; (*gamme*) *Mus* key; (*hauteur de son*) & *Ling* pitch; **de bon t.** (*goût*) in good

taste; **donner le t.** *Fig* to set the tone. ● **tonalité** *nf* (*timbre, impression*) tone; *Tél Br* dialling tone, *Am* dial tone.

tondre [tɔ̃dr] *vt* **1** (*mouton*) to shear; (*gazon*) to mow; (*cheveux*) to clip, crop. **2 t. qn** (*escroquer*) *Fam* to fleece s.o. ● **tondeuse** *nf* shears; (*à cheveux*) clippers; **t. (à gazon)** (lawn)mower.

tonifier [tonifje] *vt* (*muscles, peau*) to tone up; (*personne*) to invigorate. ● **tonifiant, -ante** *a* (*activité, climat etc*) invigorating.

tonique [tonik] **1** *a* (*accent*) *Ling* tonic. **2** *a* (*froid, effet*) tonic, invigorating ▮ *nm* (*médicament*) tonic; (*cosmétique*) tonic lotion.

tonitruant, -ante [tonitryɑ̃, -ɑ̃t] *a* (*voix*) *Fam* booming.

tonnage [tonaʒ] *nm* (*de navire*) tonnage.

tonne [ton] *nf* (*poids*) metric ton, tonne; **des tonnes de** (*beaucoup*) *Fam* tons of.

tonneau, -x [tono] *nm* **1** (*récipient*) barrel, cask. **2** (*acrobatie aérienne*) roll; **faire un t.** (*en voiture*) to roll over. **3** (*poids*) *Nau* ton. **4 du même t.** *Fam* of the same kind. ● **tonnelet** *nm* keg.

tonnelle [tonɛl] *nf* arbour, bower.

tonner [tone] *vi* (*canons*) to thunder; (*crier*) *Fig* to thunder, rage (**contre** against) ▮ *v imp* **il tonne** it's thundering. ● **tonnerre** *nm* thunder; **coup de t.** burst *ou* crash of thunder, thunderclap; *Fig* bombshell, thunderbolt; **du t.** (*excellent*) *Fam* terrific.

tonte [tɔ̃t] *nf* (*de moutons*) shearing; (*de gazon*) mowing.

tonton [tɔ̃tɔ̃] *nm* *Fam* uncle.

tonus [tonys] *nm* (*énergie*) energy, vitality.

top [top] *nm* (*signal sonore*) bleep, *Br* pip.

topaze [topaz] *nf* (*pierre*) topaz.

topinambour [topinɑ̃bur] *nm* Jerusalem artichoke.

topo [topo] *nm* (*exposé*) *Fam* talk, speech.

topographie [topɔgrafi] *nf* topography.

toquade [tokad] *nf* *Fam* (*pour qch*) craze (**pour** for); (*pour qn*) infatuation (**pour** with).

toque [tok] *nf* (*de fourrure*) fur hat; (*de jockey, juge*) cap; (*de cuisinier*) hat.

toquer (se) [sətoke] *vpr* **se t. de qn** *Fam* to become infatuated with s.o. ● **toqué, -ée** *a* (*fou*) *Fam* crazy.

torche [torʃ] *nf* (*flamme*) torch; **t. électrique** *Br* torch, *Am* flashlight.

torcher [torʃe] *vt* **1** (*travail*) to botch, skimp. **2** (*essuyer*) *Fam* to wipe.

torchon [torʃɔ̃] *nm* (*à vaisselle*) *Br* tea towel, *Am* dish towel; (*de ménage*) *Br* duster, cloth.

tordre [tordr] *vt* to twist; (*linge, cou*) to wring; (*barre*) to bend; **se t. la cheville/le pied/le dos** to twist *ou* sprain one's ankle/ foot/back ▮ **se tordre** *vpr* to twist; (*barre*) to bend; **se t. de douleur** to be doubled up with pain, writhe (in pain); **se t. (de rire)** to split one's sides (laughing). ● **tordant, -ante** *a* (*drôle*) *Fam* hilarious. ● **tordu, -ue** *a* twisted;

tornade

(*esprit*) warped.

tornade [tɔrnad] *nf* tornado.

torpeur [tɔrpœr] *nf* lethargy, torpor.

torpille [tɔrpij] *nf* torpedo. ● **torpiller** *vt* (*navire, Fig projet etc*) to torpedo. ● **torpilleur** *nm* torpedo boat.

torréfier [tɔrefje] *vt* (*café*) to roast. ● **torréfaction** *nf* roasting.

torrent [tɔrã] *nm* (mountain) stream, torrent; **un t. d'injures/de larmes/**etc a flood of insults/tears/etc; **il pleut à torrents** it's pouring (down). ● **torrentiel, -ielle** *a* (*pluie*) torrential.

torride [tɔrid] *a* (*chaleur etc*) torrid, scorching.

torsade [tɔrsad] *nf* (*de cheveux*) twist, coil. ● **torsader** *vt* to twist (together).

torse [tɔrs] *nm Anat* chest; (*statue*) torso; **t. nu** stripped to the waist.

torsion [tɔrsjɔ̃] *nf* twisting; *Phys Tech* torsion.

tort [tɔr] *nm* (*dommage*) wrong; (*défaut*) fault; **avoir t.** to be wrong (**de faire** to do, in doing); **tu as t. de fumer!** you shouldn't smoke!; **être dans son t.** *ou* **en t.** to be in the wrong; **donner t. à qn** (*accuser*) to blame s.o.; (*faits etc*) to prove s.o. wrong; **faire du t. à qn** to harm *ou* wrong s.o.; **à t.** wrongly; **parler à t. et à travers** to talk nonsense; **à t. ou à raison** rightly or wrongly.

torticolis [tɔrtikɔli] *nm* **avoir le t.** to have a stiff neck.

tortillard [tɔrtijar] *nm Fam Péj* slow train, local train.

tortiller [tɔrtije] *vt* to twist, twirl; (*moustache*) to twirl; (*tripoter*) to twiddle with ▮ *vi* **il n'y a pas à t.** *Fam* there's no getting around it *ou* away from it ▮ **se tortiller** *vpr* (*ver, personne*) to wriggle; (*en dansant, des hanches*) to wiggle. ● **tortillement** *nm* (*de ver etc*) wriggling; (*en dansant*) wiggling.

tortionnaire [tɔrsjɔnɛr] *nm* torturer.

tortue [tɔrty] *nf Br* tortoise; *Am* turtle; (*de mer*) turtle; **quelle t.!** *Fig* what a *Br* slowcoach *ou Am* slowpoke!

tortueux, -euse [tɔrtɥø, -øz] *a* tortuous.

torture [tɔrtyr] *nf* torture. ● **torturer** *vt* to torture; **se t. les méninges** *Fam* to rack one's brains.

tôt [to] *adv* early; **au plus t.** at the earliest; **le plus t. possible** as soon as possible; **t. ou tard** sooner or later; **je n'étais pas plus t. sorti que...** no sooner had I gone out than....

total, -e, -aux [tɔtal, -o] *a* & *nm* total; **au t.** all in all, in total; (*somme toute*) all in all. ● **totalement** *adv* totally, completely. ● **totaliser** *vt* to total. ● **totalité** *nf* entirety; **la t. de** all of; **en t.** (*détruit etc*) entirely; (*payé*) fully.

totalitaire [tɔtalitɛr] *a* (*État, régime etc*) totalitarian.

toubib [tubib] *nm* (*médecin*) *Fam* doctor.

touche [tuʃ] *nf* (*de clavier*) key; (*de télé-*

phone) (push-)button; (*de peintre*) touch; *Pêche* bite; **téléphone à touches** push-button phone; **t. de tabulation/de majuscule** (*d'ordinateur, de machine à écrire*) tab/shift key; **une t. de** (*un peu de*) a touch *ou* hint of; (*ligne de*) **t.** *Football Rugby* touchline.

touche-à-tout [tuʃatu] **1** *a* & *nmf inv* (*qui touche*) meddlesome (person). **2** *nmf inv* (*qui se disperse*) dabbler.

toucher [tuʃe] *vt* to touch; (*paie*) to draw; (*chèque*) to cash; (*cible*) to hit; (*émouvoir*) to touch, move; (*concerner*) to affect; **t. qn** (*contacter*) to get in touch with s.o., reach s.o.; **t. le fond** (**du désespoir**) to touch rock-bottom, plumb the depths (of despair) ▮ *vi* **t. à** to touch; (*sujet*) to touch on; (*but, fin*) to approach ▮ **se toucher** *vpr* (*lignes, mains etc*) to touch ▮ *nm* (*sens*) touch; **au t.** to the touch. ● **touchant, -ante** *a* (*émouvant*) moving, touching.

touffe [tuf] *nf* (*de cheveux, d'herbe*) tuft; (*de plantes*) cluster. ● **touffu, -ue** *a* (*barbe, haie*) thick, bushy; (*livre*) *Fig* heavy.

touiller [tuje] *vt* (*salade*) *Fam* to mix, toss.

toujours [tuʒur] *adv* always; (*encore*) still; **pour t.** for ever; **essaie t.!** (*quand même*) try anyhow!; **t. est-il que...** [tuʒurɛtil] the fact remains that...; **cause t., tu m'intéresses!** *Fam* you can say what you like, I don't believe a word of it!

toupet [tupɛ] *nm* (*audace*) *Fam* nerve, *Br* cheek.

toupie [tupi] *nf* (spinning) top.

tour[1] [tur] *nf* **1** (*bâtiment*) tower; (*immeuble*) *Br* tower block, high-rise. **2** *Échecs* castle, rook.

tour[2] [tur] *nm* **1** (*mouvement, ordre, tournure*) turn; (*de magie etc*) trick; (*excursion*) trip, outing; (*à pied*) stroll, walk; (*en voiture*) drive; **t. (de phrase)** turn of phrase; **t. (de piste)** (*dans une course*) lap; **faire un t. d'honneur** (*sportif*) to do a lap of honour; **t. de cartes** card trick; **t. d'horizon** survey; **t. de poitrine/**etc chest/etc measurement *ou* size; **de dix mètres de t.** ten metres round; **faire le t. de** to go round; (*question, situation*) to review; **faire un t.** (*à pied*) to go for a stroll *ou* walk; (*en voiture*) to go for a drive; (*court voyage*) to go on a trip; **jouer** *ou* **faire un t. à qn** to play a trick on s.o.; **avoir plus d'un t. dans son sac** *Fam* to have more than one trick up one's sleeve; **c'est mon t.** it's my turn; **à qui le tour?** whose turn (is it)?; **à son t.** in (one's) turn; **à t. de rôle** in turn; **t. à t.** in turn, by turns.

2 *Tech* lathe; (*de potier*) wheel.

tourbe [turb] *nf* peat. ● **tourbière** *nf* peat bog.

tourbillon [turbijɔ̃] *nm* (*de vent*) whirlwind; (*d'eau*) whirlpool; (*de neige, sable*) swirl, eddy; (*tournoiement*) *Fig* whirl, swirl. ● **tourbillonner** *vi* to whirl, swirl.

tourelle [turɛl] *nf* turret.

tourisme [turism] *nm* tourism; **faire du t.** to go sightseeing *ou* touring; **agence/office de t.**

tourist agency/office. ●**touriste** *nmf* tourist.
●**touristique** *a* guide/menu/*etc* **t.** tourist
guide/menu/*etc*; **route t.**, **circuit t.** scenic
route.

tourment [turmã] *nm* torment. ●**tourmenter**
vt to torment **I se tourmenter** *vpr* to worry
(oneself). ●**tourmenté, -ée** *a* (*mer, vie*)
turbulent, stormy; (*expression, visage*)
anguished; (*sol*) rough, uneven.

tourmente [turmãt] *nf* (*troubles*) turmoil.

tournage [turnaʒ] *nm* (*de film*) shooting,
filming.

tourne-disque [turnədisk] *nm* record player.

tournedos [turnədo] *nm* (*filet de bœuf*)
tournedos.

tournée [turne] *nf* **1** (*de livreur etc*) round;
(*de spectacle*) tour; **faire la t. de** (*magasins,
musées etc*) to make the rounds of, go to, *Br*
go round. **2** (*de boissons*) round.

tournemain (en un) [ãnœturnəmɛ̃] *adv* Litt
in an instant.

tourner [turne] *vt* to turn; (*film*) to shoot,
make; (*difficulté*) to get round; **t. en ridicule**
to ridicule; **t. le dos à qn** to turn one's back
on s.o.
I *vi* to turn; (*tête, toupie*) to spin; (*Terre*) to
revolve, turn; (*moteur*) to run, go; (*usine*) to
run; (*lait*) to go off; **t. autour de** (*objet*) to
go round; (*maison, personne*) to hang
around; (*question*) to centre on; **t. bien/mal**
(*évoluer*) to turn out well/badly; **t. au froid**
(*temps*) to turn cold; **t. à l'aigre** (*ton, conversation etc*) to turn nasty *ou* sour; **t. de
l'œil** *Fam* to faint; **t. autour du pot** *Fig* to
beat around the bush; **faire t. qn en bourrique** *Fam* to drive s.o. crazy; **ça me fait t. la
tête** (*vin etc*) it goes to my head; (*manège
etc*) it makes my head spin; **silence! on
tourne** quiet we're filming *ou* shooting!
I se tourner *vpr* to turn (*vers* to, towards).
●**tournant, -ante 1** *a* pont **t.** swing bridge. **2**
nm (*de route*) bend, turning; (*moment*) *Fig*
turning point.

tournesol [turnəsɔl] *nm* sunflower.

tourneur [turnœr] *nm* (*ouvrier*) turner.

tournevis [turnəvis] *nm* screwdriver.

tourniquet [turnikɛ] *nm* **1** (*barrière*) turnstile. **2** (*pour arroser*) sprinkler.

tournis [turni] *nm Fam* **avoir le t.** to feel
giddy; **donner le t. à qn** to make s.o. giddy.

tournoi [turnwa] *nm* (*de tennis etc*) & *Hist*
tournament.

tournoyer [turnwaje] *vi* to spin (round),
whirl.

tournure [turnyr] *nf* (*expression*) turn of
phrase; **t. d'esprit** way of thinking; **t. des
événements** turn of events; **prendre t.** (*forme*) to take shape.

tourte [turt] *nf* pie.

tourterelle [turtərɛl] *nf* turtledove.

Toussaint [tusɛ̃] *nf* All Saints' Day.

tousser [tuse] *vi* to cough.

tout, toute, *pl* **tous, toutes** [tu, tut, tu, tut] **1**
a all; **tous les livres/***etc* all the books/*etc*; **t.
l'argent/le temps/le village/***etc* all the money/

time/village/*etc*, the whole of the money/
time/village/*etc*; **toute la nuit** all night, the
whole (of the) night; **tous (les) deux** both;
tous (les) trois all three; **t. un problème** quite
a problem.
2 *a* (*chaque*) every, each; (*n'importe quel*)
any; **tous les ans/jours/***etc* every *ou* each
year/day/*etc*; **tous les deux/trois mois/***etc*
every two/three months/*etc*, every second/
third month/*etc*; **tous les cinq mètres** every
five metres; **à toute heure** at any time; **t.
homme** [tutɔm] every *ou* any man.
3 *pron pl* **tous** [tus] all; **ils sont tous là, tous
sont là** they're all there.
4 *pron m sing* **tout** everything; **dépenser t.** to
spend everything, spend it all; **t. ce qui**
everything that, all that; **t. ce que je sais**
everything that *ou* all that I know; **t. ce qui
est là** everything that *ou* all that is there; **en
t.** (*au total*) in all.
5 *adv* (*tout à fait*) quite; (*très*) very; **t. simplement** quite simply; **t. petit** very small; **t.
neuf** brand new; **t. seul** all alone; **t. droit**
straight ahead; **t. autour** all around, right
round; **t. au début** right at the beginning; **le
t. premier** the very first; **t. au plus/moins** at
the very most/least; **t. en chantant/***etc* while
singing/*etc*; **t. rusé qu'il est** however sly he
may be; **t. à coup** suddenly, all of a sudden;
t. à fait completely, quite; **t. de même** all the
same; (*indignation*) really!; **t. de suite** at
once.
6 *nm* **le t.** everything, the lot; **un t.** a whole;
le t. est (*l'important*) the main thing is (**que**
that, **de faire** to do); **pas du t.** not at all;
rien du t. nothing at all; **du t. au t.**
(*changer*) entirely, completely.

tout-à-l'égout [tutalegu] *nm inv* mains
drainage.

toutefois [tutfwa] *adv* nevertheless, however.

tout-puissant, toute-puissante [tupɥisã,
tutpɥisãt] *a* all-powerful.

tout-terrain [tuterɛ̃] *adj* **véhicule t.-terrain**
off-road *ou* all terrain vehicle; **vélo t.-terrain**
mountain bike **I** *nm* **faire du t.-terrain** to do
off-road racing.

toutou [tutu] *nm* (*chien*) *Fam* doggie.

toux [tu] *nf* cough.

toxicomane [tɔksikɔman] *nmf* drug addict.
●**toxicomanie** *nf* drug addiction.

toxine [tɔksin] *nf* toxin. ●**toxique** *a* poisonous, toxic.

trac [trak] *nm* **le t.** (*peur*) the jitters; (*de
candidat*) exam nerves; (*d'acteur*) stage
fright; **avoir le t.** to be *ou* become nervous,
have *ou* get nerves.

tracas [traka] *nm* worry. ●**tracasser** *vt*, **se
tracasser** *vpr* to worry. ●**tracasseries** *nfpl*
annoyances.

trace [tras] *nf* (*quantité, tache, vestige*) trace;
(*marque*) mark; (*de fugitif etc*) trail; **traces**
(*de bête, pneus*) tracks; **traces de pas** foot-
prints; **disparaître sans laisser de traces** to
disappear without trace; **suivre** *ou* **marcher**

sur les **traces de qn** *Fig* to follow in s.o.'s footsteps.

tracer [trase] *vt* (*dessiner*) to draw; (*écrire*) to trace; **t. une route** to mark out a route; (*frayer*) to open up a route. ● **tracé** *nm* (*plan*) layout; (*ligne*) line.

trachée [traʃe] *nf Anat* windpipe.

tract [trakt] *nm* leaflet.

tractations [traktasjɔ̃] *nfpl Péj* dealings.

tracter [trakte] *vt* (*caravane etc*) to tow. ● **tracteur** *nm* tractor.

traction [traksjɔ̃] *nf Tech* traction; *Gymnastique* pull-up; **t. arrière/avant** (*voiture*) rear-/front-wheel drive.

tradition [tradisjɔ̃] *nf* tradition. ● **traditionnel, -elle** *a* traditional.

traduire* [tradɥir] *vt* 1 to translate (**de** from, **en** into); (*exprimer*) *Fig* to express. 2 **t. qn en justice** to bring s.o. before the courts. ● **traducteur, -trice** *nmf* translator. ● **traduction** *nf* translation. ● **traduisible** *a* translatable.

trafic [trafik] *nm* 1 (*automobile, ferroviaire etc*) traffic. 2 (*de marchandises*) *Péj* traffic, trade; **faire du t.** to traffic, trade; **faire le t. de** to traffic in, trade in. ● **trafiquer 1** *vi* to traffic, trade. 2 *vt* (*produit*) *Fam* to tamper with. ● **trafiquant, -ante** *nmf* trafficker, dealer; **t. d'armes/de drogue** arms/drug trafficker *ou* dealer.

tragédie [traʒedi] *nf* (*pièce de théâtre, Fig événement etc*) tragedy. ● **tragique** *a* tragic; **prendre qch au t.** (*remarque etc*) to take sth too much to heart. ● **tragiquement** *adv* tragically.

trahir [trair] *vt* to betray; (*secret etc*) to give away, betray; (*forces*) to fail (s.o.) **I se trahir** *vpr* to give oneself away, betray oneself. ● **trahison** *nf* betrayal; (*crime*) treason.

train [trɛ̃] *nm* 1 train; **t. à grande vitesse** high-speed train; **t. couchettes** sleeper; **t. auto-couchettes** (car) sleeper; **prendre le t. en marche** *Fig* to climb aboard.
2 **en t.** (*en forme*) on form; **se mettre en t.** to get (oneself) into shape.
3 **être en t. de faire qch** to be (busy) doing sth; **mettre qch en t.** to get sth going, start sth off.
4 (*allure*) pace; **t. de vie** life style.
5 (*de pneus*) set; (*de péniches, véhicules*) string.
6 **t. d'atterrissage** (*d'un avion*) undercarriage.

traînailler [trɛnɑje] *vi Fam* = **traînasser**. ● **traînard, -arde** *nmf Br* slowcoach, *Am* slowpoke. ● **traînasser** *vi Fam* to dawdle; (*errer*) to hang around.

traîne [trɛn] *nf* 1 (*de robe*) train. 2 **à la t.** (*en arrière*) lagging behind.

traîneau, -x [trɛno] *nm* sleigh, *Br* sledge, *Am* sled.

traînée [trɛne] *nf* 1 (*de peinture, dans le ciel etc*) streak; **se répandre comme une t. de poudre** (*vite*) to spread like wildfire. 2 (*prostituée*) *Fam* tart.

traîner [trene] *vt* to drag; (*mots*) to drawl; **faire t. en longueur** (*faire durer*) to drag out.
I *vi* (*jouets, papiers etc*) to lie around; (*s'attarder*) to lag behind, dawdle; (*errer*) to hang around; (*subsister*) to linger on; **t.** (**par terre**) (*robe etc*) to trail (on the ground); **t.** (**en longueur**) (*durer*) to drag on.
I se traîner *vpr* (*avancer*) to drag oneself (along); (*par terre*) to crawl; (*durer*) to drag on. ● **traînant, -ante** *a* (*voix*) drawling.

train-train [trɛ̃trɛ̃] *nm inv* **le t.-train quotidien** *Fam* the humdrum daily routine, the daily grind.

traire* [trɛr] *vt* (*vache*) to milk.

trait [trɛ] *nm* 1 line; (*en dessinant*) stroke; (*caractéristique*) feature, trait; **traits** (*du visage*) features; **t. d'union** hyphen; (*intermédiaire*) *Fig* link; **d'un t.** (*boire*) in one gulp, in one go; **à grands traits** in outline; **t. de génie/d'esprit** flash of genius/wit; **t. de bravoure** act of bravery; **avoir t. à qch** (*se rapporter à*) to relate to sth. 2 **cheval de t.** *Br* draught *ou Am* draft horse.

traite [trɛt] *nf* 1 (*de vache*) milking. 2 (*lettre de change*) bill, draft. 3 **d'une** (**seule**) **t.** (*sans interruption*) in one go. 4 **t. des Noirs** slave trade; **t. des Blanches** white slave trade.

traité [trete] *nm* 1 *Pol* treaty; **t. de paix** peace treaty. 2 (*ouvrage*) treatise (**sur** on).

traiter [trete] *vt* (*se comporter envers, soigner*) to treat; (*problème, sujet*) to deal with; (*marché*) to negotiate; (*matériau, produit*) to treat, process; **t. qn de lâche/etc** to call s.o. a coward/etc; **t. qn de tous les noms** to call s.o. all the names under the sun.
I *vi* to negotiate, deal (**avec** with); **t. de** (*sujet*) to deal with. ● **traitant** [-ɛtɑ̃] *am* **médecin t.** regular doctor. ● **traitement** [-ɛtmɑ̃] *nm* 1 treatment; **t. de données/de texte** data/word processing; **machine à** *ou* **de t. de texte** word processor; **mauvais traitements** rough treatment. 2 (*gains*) salary.

traiteur [trɛtœr] *nm* (*fournisseur*) caterer; **chez le t.** (*magasin*) at the delicatessen.

traître [trɛtr] *nm* traitor; **en t.** treacherously **I** *a* (*dangereux*) treacherous; **être t. à une cause** to be a traitor to a cause. ● **traîtrise** *nf* treachery.

trajectoire [traʒɛktwar] *nf* (*de fusée, missile etc*) path, trajectory.

trajet [traʒɛ] *nm* trip, journey; (*distance*) distance; (*itinéraire*) route.

trame [tram] *nf* 1 (*de récit etc*) framework. 2 (*de tissu*) weft; **usé jusqu'à la t.** (completely) threadbare.

tramer [trame] *vt* (*évasion etc*) to plot; (*complot*) to hatch **I se tramer** *vpr* **il se trame quelque chose** something is brewing *ou* is afoot.

trampoline [trɑ̃pɔlin] *nm* trampoline.

tram(way) [tram(wɛ)] *nm Br* tram, *Am* streetcar.

tranche [trɑ̃ʃ] *nf* (*morceau*) slice; (*bord*) edge; (*partie*) portion; (*de salaire, impôts*) bracket; **t. d'âge** age bracket.

tranchée [trɑ̃ʃe] nf trench.

trancher [trɑ̃ʃe] 1 vt to cut. 2 vt (difficulté, question etc) to settle ‖ vi (décider) to decide. 3 vi (contraster) to contrast (avec, sur with). ● **tranchant, -ante** 1 a (couteau, voix) sharp ‖ nm (cutting) edge; **à double t.** Fig double-edged. 2 a (péremptoire) trenchant, cutting. ● **tranché, -ée** a (couleurs) distinct; (opinion) clear-cut.

tranquille [trɑ̃kil] a quiet; (mer) calm, still; (esprit) easy; (certain) Fam confident; **avoir la conscience t.** to have a clear conscience; **je suis t.** (rassuré) my mind is at rest; **laisser qch/qn t.** to leave sth/s.o. alone; **soyez t.** don't worry. ● **tranquillement** adv calmly.

tranquilliser [trɑ̃kilize] vt to reassure; **tranquillisez-vous** set your mind at rest. ● **tranquillisant** nm (médicament) tranquillizer.

tranquillité [trɑ̃kilite] nf (peace and) quiet; (d'esprit) peace of mind.

trans- [trɑ̃z, trɑ̃s] préf trans-.

transaction [trɑ̃zaksjɔ̃] nf 1 (opération commerciale) transaction. 2 (compromis) compromise.

transatlantique [trɑ̃zatlɑ̃tik] a transatlantic ‖ nm (paquebot) transatlantic liner; (chaise) deckchair. ● **transat** [trɑ̃zat] nm (chaise) deckchair ‖ nf t. **en solitaire** (course) single-handed transatlantic race.

transcender [trɑ̃sɑ̃de] vt to transcend. ● **transcendant, -ante** a transcendent.

transcrire* [trɑ̃skrir] vt to transcribe. ● **transcription** nf transcription; (document) transcript.

transe [trɑ̃s] nf **en t.** (mystique) in a trance; (excité) very exited; **entrer en t.** to go into a trance.

transférer [trɑ̃sfere] vt to transfer (à to). ● **transfert** nm transfer.

transfigurer [trɑ̃sfigyre] vt to transform, transfigure.

transformer [trɑ̃sfɔrme] vt to change, transform; (maison) to carry out alterations to; (matière première) to transform; (robe etc) to alter; (essai) Rugby to convert; **t. en** to turn into ‖ **se transformer** vpr to change, be transformed (**en** into). ● **transformateur** nm Él transformer. ● **transformation** nf change, transformation; (dans une maison) altération.

transfuge [trɑ̃sfyʒ] nm (soldat) renegade ‖ nmf Pol renegade.

transfusion [trɑ̃sfyzjɔ̃] nf t. (**sanguine**) (blood) transfusion.

transgresser [trɑ̃sgrese] vt (loi, ordre) to disobey, contravene. ● **transgression** nf (de loi) infringement, disobedience.

transi, -ie [trɑ̃zi] a (personne) numb with cold; **t. de peur** Br paralysed ou Am paralyzed by fear.

transiger [trɑ̃ziʒe] vi to compromise.

transistor [trɑ̃zistɔr] nm transistor (radio). ● **transistorisé, -ée** a (téléviseur etc) transistorized.

transit [trɑ̃zit] nm transit; **en t.** in transit; **salle de t.** (d'aéroport) transit lounge. ● **transiter** vt (faire) t. to send in transit ‖ vi to be in transit.

transitif, -ive [trɑ̃zitif, -iv] a & nm Grammaire transitive.

transition [trɑ̃zisjɔ̃] nf transition. ● **transitoire** a (qui passe) transient; (provisoire) transitional.

translucide [trɑ̃slysid] a translucent.

transmettre* [trɑ̃smɛtr] vt (message, héritage etc) to pass on (à to); Phys Tech to transmit; (à la radio, télévision) to broadcast, transmit ‖ **se transmettre** vpr (maladie, tradition etc) to be passed on. ● **transmetteur** nm (appareil) transmitter, transmitting device. ● **transmission** nf transmission; (de message etc) passing on.

transparaître* [trɑ̃sparɛtr] vi to show (through).

transparent, -ente [trɑ̃sparɑ̃, -ɑ̃t] a clear, transparent. ● **transparence** nf transparency; **voir qch par t.** to see sth showing through.

transpercer [trɑ̃spɛrse] vt to pierce, go through.

transpirer [trɑ̃spire] vi (suer) to sweat, perspire; (information) Fig to leak out. ● **transpiration** nf perspiration.

transplanter [trɑ̃splɑ̃te] vt (organe, plante etc) to transplant. ● **transplantation** nf transplantation; (greffe d'organe) transplant.

transport [trɑ̃spɔr] nm 1 (action) transport, transportation (de of); **transports** (moyens) transport; **moyen de t.** means of transport; **transports en commun** public transport; **frais de t.** transport costs. 2 (émotion) Litt rapture.

transporter [trɑ̃spɔrte] 1 vt (véhicule, train) to transport, convey; (à la main) to carry, take; **t. qn d'urgence à l'hôpital** to rush s.o. Br to hospital ou Am to the hospital ‖ **se transporter** vpr (aller) to take oneself off. 2 vt Litt to enrapture. ● **transporteur** nm t. (**routier**) Br haulier, Am trucker.

transposer [trɑ̃spoze] vt to transpose. ● **transposition** nf transposition.

transvaser [trɑ̃svaze] vt (vin etc) to decant.

transversal, -e, -aux [trɑ̃svɛrsal, -o] a rue/ etc **transversale** cross street/etc.

trapèze [trapɛz] nm (au cirque) trapeze. ● **trapéziste** nmf trapeze artist.

trappe [trap] nf (dans le plancher) trap door.

trappeur [trapœr] nm (chasseur) trapper.

trapu, -ue [trapy] a 1 (personne) stocky, thickset. 2 (problème etc) Fam tough.

traquenard [traknar] nm trap.

traquer [trake] vt to track ou hunt (down).

traumatiser [tromatize] vt to traumatize. ● **traumatisant, -ante** a traumatic. ● **traumatisme** nm (choc) trauma; **t. crânien** severe head injury.

travail, -aux [travaj, -o] nm (activité, lieu) work; (à effectuer) job, task; (emploi) job; (façonnage) working (**de** of); (ouvrage, étude) work, publication; Écon Méd labour;

travaux work; (*dans la rue*) *Br* roadworks, *Am* roadwork; (*aménagement*) alterations; **travaux pratiques** *Scol Univ* practical work; **travaux dirigés** *Scol* supervised classwork *ou* lab work; **travaux manuels** *Scol* handicrafts; **travaux ménagers** housework; **travaux forcés** hard labour; **travaux publics** public works; **t. au noir** moonlighting; **en t.** (*femme*) in labour.

travailler [travaje] **1** *vi* to work (**à qch** at *ou* on sth) ▮ *vt* (*discipline, rôle, style*) to work on; (*façonner*) to work; (*inquiéter*) *Fam* to worry; **t. la terre** to work the land. **2** *vi* (*bois*) to warp. ●**travaillé, -ée** *a* (*style*) elaborate. ●**travailleur, -euse** *a* hard-working ▮ *nmf* worker.

travailliste [travajist] *a* (*parti etc*) *Pol* Labour ▮ *nmf* *Pol* member of the Labour party.

travelling [travliŋ] *nm* (*mouvement de la caméra*) tracking; **faire un t.** to do a tracking shot.

travers [travɛr] **1** *prép & adv* **à t.** through; **en t.** (**de**) across. **2** *adv* **de t.** (*chapeau, nez etc*) crooked; **aller de t.** *Fig* to go wrong; **comprendre de t.** to misunderstand; **regarder qn de t.** (*avec suspicion*) to look askance at s.o.; **j'ai avalé de t.** it went down the wrong way. **3** *nm* (*défaut*) failing.

traverse [travɛrs] *nf* **1** (*de voie ferrée*) *Br* sleeper, *Am* tie. **2 chemin de t.** short cut.

traverser [travɛrse] *vt* to cross, go across; (*foule, période, mur*) to go through. ●**traversée** *nf* (*voyage*) crossing.

traversin [travɛrsɛ̃] *nm* bolster.

travesti [travɛsti] *nm* (*acteur*) female impersonator; (*homosexuel*) transvestite.

travestir [travɛstir] *vt* to disguise; (*pensée, vérité*) to misrepresent. ●**travestissement** *nm* disguise; (*de pensée etc*) misrepresentation.

trébucher [trebyʃe] *vi* to stumble (**sur** over); **faire t. qn** to trip s.o. (up).

trèfle [trɛfl] *nm* **1** (*plante*) clover. **2** (*couleur*) *Cartes* clubs.

treille [trɛj] *nf* climbing vine.

treillis [treji] *nm* **1** lattice(work); (*en métal*) wire mesh. **2** (*tenue militaire*) combat uniform.

treize [trɛz] *a & nm inv* thirteen. ●**treizième** *a & nmf* thirteenth.

tréma [trema] *nm Grammaire* di(a)eresis.

trembler [trɑ̃ble] *vi* to shake, tremble; (*de froid, peur*) to tremble (**de** with); (*flamme, lumière*) to flicker; (*voix*) to tremble, quaver; (*avoir peur*) to be afraid (**que** (+ *sub*) that, **de faire** to do); **t. pour qn** to fear for s.o.; **t. de tout son corps** to shake all over, tremble violently. ●**tremblement** *nm* (*action, frisson*) shaking, trembling; **t. de terre** earthquake. ●**trembloter** *vi* to quiver.

trémolo [tremolo] *nm* **avec des trémolos dans la voix** with a tremor in one's voice.

trémousser (se) [sətremuse] *vpr* to wriggle (about).

trempe [trɑ̃p] *nf* (*caractère*) stamp; **un homme de sa t.** a man of his stamp; **mettre une t. à qn** *Fam* to give s.o. a thrashing.

tremper [trɑ̃pe] **1** *vt* to soak, drench; (*plonger*) to dip (**dans in**) ▮ *vi* to soak; **faire t. qch** to soak sth ▮ **se tremper** *vpr* (*se baigner*) *Fam* to take a dip. **2** *vt* (*acier*) to temper. **3** *vi* **t. dans** (*participer*) *Péj* to be mixed up in. ●**trempette** *nf* **faire t.** (*se baigner*) *Fam* to take a dip.

tremplin [trɑ̃plɛ̃] *nm Natation & Fig* springboard.

trente [trɑ̃t] *a & nm* thirty; **un t.-trois tours** (*disque*) an LP; **se mettre sur son t. et un** to get all dressed up; **être au t. sixième dessous** *Fam* to be (feeling) really down. ●**trentaine** *nf* **une t.** (**de**) (*nombre*) (about) thirty; **avoir la t.** (*âge*) to be about thirty. ●**trentième** *a & nm* thirtieth.

trépas [trepa] *nm Litt* death; **passer de vie à t.** to pass away, depart this life.

trépidant, -ante [trepidɑ̃, -ɑ̃t] *a* (*vie etc*) hectic.

trépied [trepje] *nm* tripod.

trépigner [trepiɲe] *vi* to stamp (one's feet).

très [trɛ] *adv* ([trɛz] before vowel or mute *h*) very; **t.** **aimé/critiqué**/etc (*with past participle*) much *ou* greatly liked/criticized/etc.

trésor [trezɔr] *nm* treasure; **le T.** (**public**) (*service*) public revenue (department); (*finances*) public funds; **des trésors de tendresse/patience**/etc boundless love/patience/etc. ●**trésorerie** *nf* (*bureaux d'un club etc*) accounts department; (*gestion*) accounting; (*capitaux*) funds. ●**trésorier, -ière** *nmf* treasurer.

tressaillir* [tresajir] *vi* (*frémir*) to shake, quiver; (*de joie, peur*) to tremble (**de** with); (*sursauter*) to jump, start. ●**tressaillement** *nm* (*frémissement*) quiver; (*de joie etc*) trembling; (*de surprise*) start.

tressauter [tresote] *vi* (*sursauter*) to start, jump.

tresse [trɛs] *nf* (*cordon*) braid; (*cheveux*) *Br* plait, *Am* braid. ●**tresser** *vt* to braid; (*cheveux*) *Br* to plait, *Am* braid.

tréteau, -x [treto] *nm* trestle.

treuil [trœj] *nm* winch, windlass.

trêve [trɛv] *nf* (*de combat*) truce; (*répit*) *Fig* respite; **la T. des confiseurs** the Christmas and New Year political truce; **t. de plaisanteries!** that's enough of your joking *ou* nonsense!

tri [tri] *nm* sorting (out); **faire le t. de** to sort (out); (**centre de**) **t.** (*des postes*) sorting office. ●**triage** *nm* sorting (out).

triangle [trijɑ̃gl] *nm* triangle. ●**triangulaire** *a* triangular.

tribord [tribɔr] *nm* (*de bateau, d'avion*) starboard.

tribu [triby] *nf* tribe. ●**tribal, -e, -aux** *a* tribal.

tribulations [tribylasjɔ̃] *nfpl* tribulations.

tribunal, -aux [tribynal, -o] *nm Jur* court; (*militaire*) tribunal.

tribune [tribyn] *nf* **1** (*de salle publique etc*)

gallery; (*de stade*) (grand)stand; (*d'orateur*) rostrum. **2 t. libre** (*dans un journal*) open forum.

tribut [triby] *nm* tribute (à to).

tributaire [tribytɛr] *a* t. de *Fig* dependent on.

tricher [triʃe] *vi* to cheat. ● **tricherie** *nf* cheating, trickery; **une t.** a piece of trickery. ● **tricheur, -euse** *nmf* cheat, *Am* cheater.

tricolore [trikɔlɔr] *a* 1 (*cocarde etc*) red, white and blue; **le drapeau/l'équipe t.** the French flag/team. **2 feu t.** traffic lights.

tricot [triko] *nm* (*activité, ouvrage*) knitting; (*chandail*) sweater, *Br* jumper; **un t.** (*ouvrage*) a piece of knitting; **en t.** knitted; **t. de corps** *Br* vest, *Am* undershirt. ● **tricoter** *vti* to knit.

tricycle [trisikl] *nm* tricycle.

trier [trije] *vt* (*séparer*) to sort (out); (*choisir*) to pick *ou* sort out.

trifouiller [trifuje] *vi* *Fam* to rummage around.

trilingue [trilɛ̃g] *a* trilingual.

trilogie [trilɔʒi] *nf* trilogy.

trimbal(l)er [trɛ̃bale] *vt* *Fam* to cart about, drag around ▌ **se trimbal(l)er** *vpr* *Fam* to trail around.

trimer [trime] *vi* *Fam* to slave (away), work hard.

trimestre [trimɛstr] *nm* (*période*) *Com* quarter; *Scol* term; **premier/second/troisième t.** *Scol* *Br* autumn *ou* *Am* fall/winter/summer term. ● **trimestriel, -ielle** *a* (*revue*) quarterly; **bulletin t.** end-of-term *Br* report *ou* *Am* report card.

tringle [trɛ̃gl] *nf* rail, rod; **t. à rideaux** curtain rail *ou* rod.

Trinité [trinite] *nf* **la T.** (*fête*) Trinity; (*dogme*) the Trinity.

trinquer [trɛ̃ke] *vi* to chink glasses; **t. à la** santé/etc **de qn** to drink to s.o.'s health/*etc*.

trio [trijo] *nm* (*groupe*) & *Mus* trio.

triomphe [trijɔ̃f] *nm* triumph (**sur** over); **porter qn en t.** to carry s.o. shoulder-high. ● **triomphal, -e, -aux** *a* triumphal. ● **triompher** *vi* to triumph (**de** over); (*jubiler*) to be jubilant. ● **triomphant, -ante** *a* triumphant.

tripes [trip] *nfpl* *Culin* tripe; *Fam* guts. ● **tripier, -ière** *nmf* tripe butcher.

triple [tripl] *a* treble, triple ▌ *nm* **le t.** three times as much (**de** as). ● **tripler** *vti* to treble, triple. ● **triplés, -ées** *nmfpl* (*enfants*) triplets.

tripot [tripo] *nm* *Péj* gambling den.

tripoter [tripɔte] *vt* *Fam* *Br* to fiddle about *ou* mess about with, *Am* mess around with ▌ *vi* *Fam* *Br* to fiddle *ou* mess about, *Am* mess around.

trique [trik] *nf* cudgel, stick.

triste [trist] *a* sad; (*couleur, temps, rue*) gloomy, dreary; (*lamentable*) unfortunate, sorry. ● **tristement** [-əmã] *adv* sadly. ● **tristesse** *nf* sadness; (*du temps etc*) gloom(iness), dreariness.

triturer [trityre] *vt* (*broyer*) to grind; (*manipuler*) to manipulate.

trivial, -e, -aux [trivjal, -o] *a* coarse, vulgar.

● **trivialité** *nf* coarseness, vulgarity.

troc [trɔk] *nm* exchange, barter.

troène [trɔɛn] *nm* (*arbuste*) privet.

trognon [trɔɲɔ̃] *nm* (*de fruit*) core; (*de chou*) stump.

trois [trwa] *a* & *nm* three; **les t. quarts (de)** three-quarters (of). ● **troisième** *a* & *nmf* third; **le t. âge** (*vieillesse*) the retirement years; **personne du t. âge** senior citizen ▌ *nf* **la t.** *Scol* *Br* = fourth form, *Am* = eighth grade; (*vitesse*) *Aut* third gear. ● **troisièmement** *adv* thirdly. ● **trois-pièces** *nm inv* (*appartement*) three room(ed) *Br* flat *ou* *Am* apartment.

trolley(bus) [trɔlɛ(bys)] *nm* trolley(bus).

trombe [trɔ̃b] *nf* **trombe(s) d'eau** (*pluie*) rainstorm, downpour; **entrer/etc en t.** *Fig* to burst in *ou* rush in/*etc* like a whirlwind.

trombone [trɔ̃bɔn] *nm* 1 (*instrument de musique*) trombone. 2 (*agrafe*) paper clip.

trompe [trɔ̃p] *nf* 1 (*d'éléphant*) trunk; (*d'insecte*) proboscis. 2 (*instrument de musique*) horn.

trompe-l'œil [trɔ̃plœj] *nm inv* trompe-l'œil (painting); **en t.-l'œil** (*décor• etc*) trompe-l'œil.

tromper [trɔ̃pe] *vt* to deceive, mislead; (*escroquer*) to cheat; (*être infidèle à*) to be unfaithful to; (*échapper à*) to elude ▌ **se tromper** *vpr* to be mistaken, make a mistake; **se t. de route/de train/etc** to take the wrong road/train/*etc*; **se t. de date/de jour/etc** to get the date/day/*etc* wrong; **c'est à s'y t.** you can't tell the difference *ou* tell the two apart. ● **tromperie** *nf* deceit, deception. ● **trompeur, -euse** *a* (*apparences etc*) deceptive, misleading; (*personne*) deceitful.

trompette [trɔ̃pɛt] *nf* trumpet. ● **trompettiste** *nmf* trumpet player.

tronc [trɔ̃] *nm* 1 (*d'arbre*) & *Anat* trunk. 2 (*boîte*) collection box.

tronçon [trɔ̃sɔ̃] *nm* section. ● **tronçonner** *vt* to cut (into sections). ● **tronçonneuse** *nf* chain saw.

trône [tron] *nm* throne. ● **trôner** *vi* (*vase, personne etc*) *Fig* to occupy the place of honour.

tronquer [trɔ̃ke] *vt* to truncate; (*texte etc*) to curtail.

trop [tro] *adv* too; too much; **t. dur/loin/etc** too hard/far/*etc*; **t. fatigué pour jouer/etc** too tired to play/*etc*; **boire/lire/etc t.** to drink/read/*etc* too much; **t. de sel/etc** (*quantité*) too much salt/*etc*, **t. de gens/etc** (*nombre*) too many people/*etc*; **du fromage/etc de ou en t.** (*quantité*) too much cheese/*etc*; **des œufs/etc de ou en t.** (*nombre*) too many eggs/*etc*; **un franc/verre/etc de t.** *ou* **en t.** one franc/glass/*etc* too many; **t. souvent** too often; **t. peu** not enough; **se sentir de t.** *Fig* to feel in the way; **en faire t.** to overdo it.

trophée [trɔfe] *nm* trophy.

tropique [trɔpik] *nm* tropic; **les tropiques** the tropics; **sous les tropiques** in the tropics. ● **tropical, -e, -aux** *a* tropical.

trop-plein [trɔplɛ̃] nm (dispositif, liquide) overflow; (surabondance) Fig excess.

troquer [trɔke] vt to exchange (**contre** for).

trot [tro] nm trot; **aller au t.** to trot; **au t.** (sans traîner) Fam at the double. ● **trotter** [trɔte] vi (cheval) to trot; (personne) Fig to scurry (around ou along), trot around ou along; **une chanson qui me trotte dans la tête** a song that keeps going through my head.

trotteuse [trɔtøz] nf (de montre) second hand. ● **trotteur, -euse** nmf (cheval) trotter.

trottiner [trɔtine] vi (personne) to patter ou trot along.

trottinette [trɔtinet] nf (jouet) scooter; (voiture) Fam little car.

trottoir [trɔtwar] nm Br pavement, Am sidewalk; **t. roulant** moving walkway.

trou [tru] nm hole; (d'aiguille) eye; (village) Fam Péj dump, hole; (manque) Fig gap (**dans** in); **t. d'homme** (ouverture) manhole; **t. de (la) serrure** keyhole; **t. (de mémoire)** Fig lapse (of memory).

trouble [trubl] 1 a (liquide) cloudy; (image) blurred; (affaire) shady **I** adv **voir t.** to see things blurred. 2 nm Litt (émoi, émotion) agitation; (désarroi) distress; (désordre) confusion; **troubles** (de santé) trouble; (révolte) disturbances, troubles.

troubler [truble] vt to disturb; (vue) to blur; (liquide) to make cloudy; (esprit) to unsettle; (projet) to upset; (inquiéter) to trouble **I se troubler** vpr (liquide) to become cloudy; (candidat etc) to become flustered. ● **troublant, -ante** a (détail etc) disturbing, disquieting. ● **trouble-fête** nmf inv killjoy, spoilsport.

trouer [true] vt to make a hole ou holes in; (silence, ténèbres) to cut through. ● **trouée** nf gap; (brèche) (au combat) breach.

trouille [truj] nf **avoir la t.** Fam to have the jitters, be scared. ● **trouillard, -arde** a (poltron) Fam chicken.

troupe [trup] nf (de soldats) troop; (groupe) group; (de théâtre) company, troupe; **la t., les troupes** (armée) the troops.

troupeau, -x [trupo] nm (de vaches) & Fig Péj herd; (de moutons, d'oies) flock.

trousse [trus] nf (étui) case, kit; (d'écolier) pencil case; **t. à outils** toolkit; **t. à pharmacie** first-aid kit; **t. de toilette** Br sponge ou toilet bag, dressing case.

trousseau, -x [truso] nm 1 **t. de clefs** bunch of keys. 2 (de mariée) trousseau.

trousses [trus] nfpl **aux t. de qn** Fig on s.o.'s heels.

trouvaille [truvaj] nf (lucky) find.

trouver [truve] vt to find; **aller/venir t. qn** to go/come and see s.o.; **je trouve que** (je pense que) I think that; **comment la trouvez-vous?** what do you think of her? **I se trouver** vpr to be; (être situé) to be situated; **se t. dans une situation difficile/etc** to find oneself in a difficult situation/etc; **se t. mal** (s'évanouir) to faint; **se t. beau/petit/etc** to consider oneself attractive/small/etc, think that one is

attractive/small/etc **I** v imp **il se trouve que** it happens that.

truand [tryã] nm crook.

truander [tryãde] vi (tricher) Fam to cheat.

truc [tryk] nm 1 Fam (astuce) trick; (moyen) way; **avoir/trouver le t.** to have/get the knack (**pour faire** of doing). 2 (chose) Fam thing. ● **trucage** nm = **truquage**.

truchement [tryʃmã] nm **par le t. de qn** through (the intermediary of) s.o.

truculent, -ente [trykylã, -ãt] a (langage, personnage) colourful.

truelle [tryɛl] nf trowel.

truffe [tryf] nf 1 (champignon) truffle. 2 (de chien) nose.

truffer [tryfe] vt (remplir) to stuff (**de** with). ● **truffé, -ée** a (pâté etc) (garnished) with truffles.

truie [trɥi] nf (animal) sow.

truite [trɥit] nf trout.

truquer [tryke] vt (photo etc) to fake; (élections, match) to rig, fix. ● **truqué, -ée** a (élections, match) rigged, fixed; **photo truquée** fake photo; **scène truquée** (au cinéma) scene with special effects. ● **truquage** nm (de cinéma) (special) effect; (action) faking; (d'élections) rigging.

trust [trœst] nm Com (cartel) trust; (entreprise) corporation.

tsar [dzar] nm tsar, czar.

TSF [teɛsɛf] nf abrév (télégraphie sans fil) (poste de radio) Vieilli radio, Br wireless.

tsigane [tsigan] a (Hungarian) gipsy **I** nmf T. (Hungarian) gipsy.

TSVP [teɛsvepe] abrév (tournez s'il vous plaît) PTO.

TTC [tetese] abrév (toutes taxes comprises) inclusive of tax.

tu¹ [ty] pron you (familiar form of address).

tu² [ty] pp de **taire**.

tuant, -ante [tɥã, -ãt] a voir **tuer**.

tuba [tyba] nm 1 (instrument de musique) tuba. 2 (de plongée) snorkel.

tube [tyb] nm 1 tube; (de canalisation) pipe; **t. à essai** (de laboratoire) test tube; **marcher à pleins tubes** (stéréo etc) Fam to be going full blast; **rouler à pleins tubes** (voiture etc) Fam to be going flat out. 2 (chanson, disque) Fam hit. ● **tubulaire** a tubular.

tuberculose [tybɛrkyloz] nf TB, tuberculosis. ● **tuberculeux, -euse** a tubercular; **être t.** to have TB ou tuberculosis.

TUC [tyk] nm abrév (travail d'utilité collective) community work for the long-term unemployed. ● **tuciste** nmf worker employed under TUC scheme.

tue-mouches [tymyʃ] a inv **papier t.-mouches** flypaper.

tuer [tɥe] vt to kill; (d'un coup de feu) to shoot (dead), kill; (épuiser) Fam to wear out **I se tuer** vpr to kill oneself; (d'un coup de feu) to shoot oneself; (dans un accident) to be killed; **se t. à faire** Fig to wear oneself out doing sth. ● **tuant, -ante** a (fatigant) Fam exhausting. ● **tuerie** nf slaughter.

● **tueur, -euse** nmf killer.

tuc-tête (à) [atytɛt] adv at the top of one's voice.

tuile [tɥil] nf **1** tile. **2** (malchance) Fam (stroke of) bad luck.

tulipe [tylip] nf tulip.

tuméfié, -ée [tymefje] a swollen.

tumeur [tymœr] nf tumour, growth.

tumulte [tymylt] nm commotion; (désordre) turmoil. ● **tumultueux, -euse** a turbulent.

tunique [tynik] nf tunic.

Tunisie [tynizi] nf Tunisia. ● **tunisien, -ienne** a Tunisian ▌ nmf **T., Tunisienne** Tunisian.

tunnel [tynɛl] nm tunnel; **le t. sous la Manche** the Channel Tunnel.

turban [tyrbã] nm turban.

turbine [tyrbin] nf turbine.

turbulences [tyrbylãs] nfpl (tourbillons) turbulence.

turbulent, -ente [tyrbylã, -ãt] a (enfant) disruptive, boisterous.

turfiste [tyrfist] nmf racegoer, Br punter.

turlupiner [tyrlypine] vt **t. qn** Fam to worry s.o.

Turquie [tyrki] nf Turkey. ● **turc, turque** a Turkish ▌ nmf **T., Turque** Turk ▌ nm (langue) Turkish.

turquoise [tyrkwaz] a inv turquoise.

tuteur, -trice [tytœr, -tris] **1** nmf (d'un mineur) guardian. **2** nm (bâton) stake, prop. ● **tutelle** nf Jur guardianship; Fig protection.

tutoyer [tytwaje] vt **t. qn** to use the familiar tu form to s.o. ● **tutoiement** nm use of the familiar tu (instead of the more formal vous).

tutu [tyty] nm ballet skirt, tutu.

tuyau, -x [tɥijo] nm **1** pipe; **t. d'arrosage** hose(pipe); **t. de cheminée** flue; **t. d'échappement** (de véhicule) exhaust (pipe). **2** (renseignement) Fam tip. ● **tuyauter** vt **t. qn** (conseiller) Fam to give s.o. a tip. ● **tuyauterie** nf (tuyaux) piping.

TVA [tevea] nf abrév (taxe à la valeur ajoutée) VAT.

tympan [tɛ̃pã] nm eardrum.

type [tip] nm (modèle) type; (traits) features; (individu) Fam fellow, guy, Br bloke; **le t. même de** Fig the very model of ▌ a inv (professeur etc) typical. ● **typique** a typical (de of). ● **typiquement** adv typically.

typé, -ée [tipe] a **être (très) t.** to have all the usual distinctive features.

typhoïde [tifɔid] nf (maladie) typhoid (fever).

typhon [tifɔ̃] nm (tempête) typhoon.

typographie [typɔgrafi] nf typography, printing. ● **typographique** a typographical. ● **typographe** nmf typographer.

tyran [tirã] nm tyrant. ● **tyrannie** nf tyranny. ● **tyrannique** a tyrannical. ● **tyranniser** vt to tyrannize.

tzigane [dzigan] a (Hungarian) gipsy ▌ nmf **T.** (Hungarian) gipsy.

U

U, u [y] *nm* U, u.
Ukraine [ykrɛn] *nf* l'U. the Ukraine.
ulcère [ylsɛr] *nm* ulcer, sore.
ulcérer [ylsere] *vt* (*blesser, irriter*) to embitter.
ULM [yɛlɛm] *nm inv abrév* (*Ultra-Léger Motorisé*) (*avion*) microlight.
ultérieur, -e [ylterjœr] *a* later. ●**ultérieurement** *adv* later.
ultimatum [yltimatɔm] *nm* ultimatum; **lancer un u. à qn** to give s.o. *ou* issue s.o. with an ultimatum.
ultime [yltim] *a* final, last.
ultra- [yltra] *préf* ultra-. ●**ultra-secret, -ète** *a* (*document*) top secret.
ultramoderne [yltramɔdɛrn] *a* ultramodern.
ultrason [yltrasɔ̃] *nm* (*vibration*) *Phys* ultrasound.
ultraviolet, -ette [yltravjɔlɛ, -ɛt] *a* ultraviolet ▮ *nm* ultraviolet ray.
un, une [œ̃, yn] **1** *art indéf* a, (*devant voyelle*) an; **une page** a page; **un ange** [œ̃nãʒ] an angel.
2 *a* one; **la page un** page one; **un kilo** one kilo; **un type** (*un quelconque*) some *ou* a fellow; **un jour** one day.
3 *pron & nmf* one; **l'un** one; **les uns** some; **le numéro un** number one; **j'en ai un** I have one; **l'un d'eux, l'une d'elles** one of them; **la une** (*de journal*) page one; **j'ai eu une de ces peurs!** *Fam* I was really scared!
unanime [ynanim] *a* unanimous. ●**unanimité** *nf* unanimity; **à l'u.** unanimously.
uni, -ie [yni] *a* united; (*famille etc*) close; (*surface*) smooth; (*couleur, étoffe*) plain.
unième [ynjɛm] *a* (*after a number*) (-)first; **trente et u.** thirty-first; **cent u.** hundred and first.
unifier [ynifje] *vt* to unify. ●**unification** *nf* unification.
uniforme [ynifɔrm] **1** *nm* (*vêtement*) uniform. **2** *a* (*régulier*) uniform. ●**uniformément** *adv* uniformly. ●**uniformiser** *vt* to standardize. ●**uniformité** *nf* uniformity.
unijambiste [yniʒãbist] *a & nmf* one-legged (man *ou* woman).
unilatéral, -e, -aux [ynilateral, -o] *a* unilateral; (*stationnement*) on one side of the road *ou* street only.
union [ynjɔ̃] *nf* union; (*association*) association; (*entente*) unity; **u. libre** cohabitation (*of unmarried couple*).
unique [ynik] *a* **1** (*fille, fils*) only; (*espoir, souci etc*) only, sole; (*prix, salaire, marché*) single, one; **son seul et u. souci** his *ou* her one and only worry. **2** (*exceptionnel*) unique;

u. en son genre completely unique. ●**uniquement** *adv* only, solely.
unir [ynir] *vt* (*deux pays etc*) to unite, join (together); (*efforts*) to combine; **u. la force au courage** to combine strength with courage; **u. deux personnes** (*amitié*) to unite two people ▮ **s'unir** *vpr* (*étudiants, travailleurs etc*) to unite; (*se marier*) to be joined together; (*se joindre*) to join (together).
unisexe [ynisɛks] *a* (*vêtements etc*) unisex.
unisson (à l') [alynisɔ̃] *adv* in unison (**de** with).
unité [ynite] *nf* (*de mesure, élément, régiment*) unit; (*cohésion, harmonie*) unity; **u. de recherche** *Univ* research department; **u. de commande** *Ordinat* control unit. ●**unitaire** *a* (*prix*) per unit.
univers [yniver] *nm* universe.
universel, -elle [yniversɛl] *a* universal. ●**universellement** *adv* universally. ●**universalité** *nf* universality.
université [yniversite] *nf* university; **à l'u.** *Br* at university, *Am* in college; **professeur d'u.** university teacher. ●**universitaire** *a* **ville/restaurant/etc u.** university town/restaurant *etc* ▮ *nmf* academic.
uranium [yranjɔm] *nm* uranium.
urbain, -aine [yrbɛ̃, -ɛn] *a* urban; **population/etc urbaine** urban *ou* city population/etc. ●**urbaniser** *vt* to urbanize, build up. ●**urbanisme** *nm Br* town planning, *Am* city planning. ●**urbaniste** *nmf Br* town planner, *Am* city planner.
urgent, -ente [yrʒã, -ãt] *a* urgent, pressing. ●**urgence** *nf* (*cas*) emergency; (*de décision, tâche etc*) urgency; **mesures/etc d'u.** emergency measures/etc; **état d'u.** *Pol* state of emergency; (**service des) urgences** (*d'hôpital*) *Br* casualty (department), *Am* emergency room; **faire qch d'u.** to do sth urgently.
urine [yrin] *nf* urine. ●**uriner** *vi* to urinate. ●**urinoir** *nm* (public) urinal.
urne [yrn] *nf* **1** (*électorale*) ballot box; **aller aux urnes** to go to the polls, vote. **2** (*vase*) urn.
URSS *nf abrév* (*Union des Républiques Socialistes Soviétiques*) *Hist* USSR.
urticaire [yrtiker] *nf* nettle rash, hives.
Uruguay [yrygwɛ] *nm* Uruguay.
us [ys] *nmpl* **les us et coutumes** (*de pays etc*) the ways and customs.
usage [yzaʒ] *nm* use; (*habitude*) custom; *Ling* usage; **faire u. de** to make use of; **faire de l'u.** (*vêtement etc*) to wear well; **d'u.** (*habituel*) customary; **à l'u. de** for (the use of);

313 **vaisseau**

hors d'u. broken, not in use; **je n'en ai pas l'u.** I have no use for it. ● **usagé, -ée** a worn; (*d'occasion*) used. ● **usager** nm user.

user [yze] vt (*vêtement, personne*) to wear out; (*consommer*) to use (up); (*santé*) to ruin ▮ vi **u. de** to use ▮ **s'user** vpr (*tissu, machine*) to wear out; (*personne*) to wear oneself out. ● **usé, -ée** a (*tissu etc*) worn (out); (*sujet etc*) well-worn; (*personne*) worn out; **eaux usées** dirty ou waste water.

usine [yzin] nf factory; **u. à gaz** gasworks; **u. métallurgique** ironworks; **ouvrier d'u.** factory worker.

usiner [yzine] vt (*pièce*) Tech to machine.

usité, -ée [yzite] a in common use.

ustensile [ystãsil] nm utensil; **u. de cuisine** kitchen utensil; **u. de jardinage** garden implement.

usuel, -elle [yzɥɛl] a everyday, ordinary. ● **usuels** nmpl (*d'une bibliothèque*) reference books.

usufruit [yzyfrɥi] nm Jur beneficial ownership, usufruct.

usure [yzyr] nf (*détérioration*) wear (and tear); **avoir qn à l'u.** Fig to wear s.o. down (in the end).

usurier, -ière [yzyrje, -jɛr] nmf usurer.

usurper [yzyrpe] vt to usurp. ● **usurpateur, -trice** nmf usurper.

utérus [yterys] nm Anat womb, uterus.

utile [ytil] a useful (à to). ● **utilement** adv usefully.

utiliser [ytilize] vt to use, utilize. ● **utilisable** a usable. ● **utilisateur, -trice** nmf user. ● **utilisation** nf use. ● **utilité** nf use(fulness); **d'une grande u.** very useful; **déclaré d'u. publique** state-recognized and -approved.

utilitaire [ytilitɛr] a utilitarian; **véhicule u.** commercial vehicle.

utopie [ytɔpi] nf (*idéal*) utopia; (*projet, idée*) utopian plan ou idea. ● **utopique** a utopian.

UV [yve] nmpl abrév (*ultraviolets*) UV.

V

V, v [ve] nm V, v.
va [va] voir aller[1].

vacances [vakãs] nfpl Br holiday(s), Am vacation; **en v.** Br on holiday, Am on vacation; **prendre ses v.** to take one's Br holiday(s) ou Am vacation; **les grandes v.** the summer Br holidays ou Am vacation. ● **vacancier, -ière** nmf Br holidaymaker, Am vacationer.

vacant, -ante [vakã, -ãt] a vacant. ● **vacance** nf (*poste*) vacancy.

vacarme [vakarm] nm din, uproar.

vaccin [vaksɛ̃] nm vaccine; **faire un v. à qn** to vaccinate s.o. ● **vaccination** nf vaccination. ● **vacciner** vt to vaccinate; **se faire v.** to get vaccinated (**contre** against); **ça m'a vacciné contre...** Fam that's made me immune to....

vache [vaʃ] 1 nf cow; **v. laitière** dairy cow. 2 nf (*peau de*) v. (*personne*) Fam swine ▮ a (*méchant*) Fam nasty. ● **vachement** adv Fam (*très*) damned; (*beaucoup*) a hell of a lot. ● **vacher** nm cowherd. ● **vacherie** nf Fam (*action*) nasty trick; (*parole*) nasty remark; (*caractère*) nastiness.

vaciller [vasije] vi to sway, wobble; (*flamme, lumière*) to flicker; (*jugement, mémoire etc*) to falter, waver. ● **vacillant, -ante** a (*démarche, mémoire*) shaky; (*lumière etc*) flickering.

vadrouille [vadruj] nf en v. Fam roaming ou wandering around ou about. ● **vadrouiller** vi Fam to roam ou wander around ou about.

va-et-vient [vaevjɛ̃] nm inv (*mouvement*) movement to and fro; (*de personnes*) comings and goings.

vagabond, -onde [vagabɔ̃, -ɔ̃d] nmf (*clochard*) Br tramp, vagrant, vagabond, Am hobo ▮ a wandering. ● **vagabonder** vi to roam ou wander around ou about; (*pensée*) to wander. ● **vagabondage** nm wandering; Jur vagrancy.

vagin [vaʒɛ̃] nm vagina.

vagir [vaʒir] vi (*bébé*) to cry, wail.

vague [vag] 1 a vague; (*regard*) vacant; (*souvenir*) dim, vague ▮ nm vagueness; **regarder dans le v.** to gaze into space, gaze vacantly; **rester dans le v.** (*être évasif*) to keep it vague; **avoir du v. à l'âme** to be feeling sad in one's heart.
2 nf (*de mer*) & Fig wave; **v. de chaleur** heat wave; **v. de froid** cold spell ou snap; **v. de fond** (*dans l'opinion*) Fig tidal wave. ● **vaguement** adv vaguely.

vaillant, -ante [vajã, -ãt] a brave, valiant; (*vigoureux*) healthy. ● **vaillamment** [-amã] adv bravely, valiantly. ● **vaillance** nf bravery.

vaille que vaille [vajkəvaj] adv somehow or other.

vain, vaine [vɛ̃, vɛn] a 1 (*futile*) vain, futile; (*mots, promesse*) empty; **en v.** in vain, vainly. 2 (*vaniteux*) vain. ● **vainement** adv in vain, vainly.

vaincre* [vɛ̃kr] vt to beat, defeat; (*surmonter*) to overcome; **s'avouer vaincu** to admit defeat. ● **vaincu, -ue** nmf defeated man ou woman; (*d'un match etc*) loser. ● **vainqueur** nm victor; (*d'un match etc*) winner ▮ am victorious.

vais [vɛ] voir aller[1].

vaisseau, -x [vɛso] nm 1 Anat Bot vessel. 2

vaisselier 314

(*bateau*) ship, vessel; **v. spatial** spaceship.

vaisselier [vɛsəlje] *nm* (*meuble*) *Br* dresser, *Am* hutch.

vaisselle [vɛsɛl] *nf* crockery; (*à laver*) *Br* washing up, dirty dishes; **faire la v.** *Br* to do the washing up, wash *ou* do the dishes.

val, *pl* **vals** *ou* **vaux** [val, vo] *nm* valley.

valable [valabl] *a* (*billet, motif etc*) valid; (*remarquable, rentable*) *Fam* worthwhile.

valet [valɛ] *nm* **1** *Cartes* jack. **2 v.** (**de chambre**) valet, manservant; **v. de ferme** farmhand.

valeur [valœr] *nf* value; (*mérite*) worth; (*poids*) importance, weight; **valeurs** (*cotées en Bourse*) stocks and shares; **v. refuge** safe investment; **la v. de** (*quantité*) the equivalent of; **avoir de la v.** to be valuable; **mettre en v.** (*faire ressortir*) to highlight; **personne de v.** person of merit; **objets de v.** valuables; **prendre de la v.** to increase in value.

valide [valid] *a* **1** (*personne*) fit, able-bodied; (*population*) able-bodied. **2** (*billet etc*) valid. ● **valider** *vt* to validate. ● **validité** *nf* validity.

valise [valiz] *nf* (suit)case; **v. diplomatique** diplomatic *Br* bag *ou* *Am* pouch; **faire ses valises** to pack (one's bags).

vallée [vale] *nf* valley. ● **vallon** *nm* (small) valley. ● **vallonné, -ée** *a* (*région etc*) undulating.

valoir* [valwar] *vi* to be worth; (*s'appliquer*) to apply (**pour** to); **v. mille francs/cher/etc** to be worth a thousand francs/a lot/etc; **un vélo vaut bien une auto** a bicycle is just as good as a car; **il vaut mieux rester** it's better to stay; **il vaut mieux que j'attende** I'd better wait; **ça ne vaut rien** it's no good, it's worthless; **ça vaut la peine** *ou* *Fam* **le coup** it's worth while (**de faire** doing); **faire v.** (*faire ressortir*) to highlight, set off; (*argument*) to put forward; (*droit*) to assert; **se faire v.** to get oneself noticed, push oneself forward.
▮ *vt* **v. qch à qn** (*causer*) to bring *ou* get s.o. sth.
▮ **se valoir** *vpr* (*objets, personnes*) to be as good as each other; **ça se vaut** *Fam* it's all the same.

valse [vals] *nf* waltz. ● **valser** *vi* to waltz. ● **valseur, -euse** *nmf* waltzer.

valve [valv] *nf* (*clapet*) valve. ● **valvule** *nf* (*du cœur*) valve.

vampire [vɑ̃pir] *nm* vampire.

vandale [vɑ̃dal] *nmf* vandal. ● **vandalisme** *nm* vandalism.

vanille [vanij] *nf* vanilla; **glace/etc à la v.** vanilla ice cream/etc. ● **vanillé, -ée** *a* vanilla-flavoured; **sucre v.** vanilla sugar.

vanité [vanite] *nf* (*orgueil*) vanity; (*futilité*) *Litt* vanity, futility. ● **vaniteux, -euse** *a* vain, conceited.

vanne [van] *nf* **1** (*d'écluse*) sluice (gate), floodgate. **2** (*remarque*) *Fam* dig, jibe.

vanné, -ée [vane] *a* (*fatigué*) *Fam* knocked out, *Br* dead beat.

vannerie [vanri] *nf* (*fabrication, objets*) basketwork, basketry.

vantail, -aux [vɑ̃taj, -o] *nm* (*de porte*) leaf.

vanter [vɑ̃te] *vt* to praise ▮ **se vanter** *vpr* to boast, brag (**de** about, of); **il n'y a pas de quoi se v.** *Fam* there's nothing to brag *ou* boast about. ● **vantard, -arde** *a* boastful ▮ *nmf* bighead, boaster, braggart. ● **vantardise** *nf* boastfulness; (*propos*) boast.

va-nu-pieds [vanypje] *nmf inv* beggar, down-and-out, *Br* tramp.

vapeur [vapœr] *nf* (*brume, émanation*) vapour; **v.** (**d'eau**) steam; **cuire qch à la v.** to steam sth; **bateau à v.** steamship. ● **vaporeux, -euse** *a* hazy, misty; (*tissu*) translucent, diaphanous.

vaporiser [vaporize] *vt* to spray. ● **vaporisateur** *nm* (*appareil*) spray.

vaquer [vake] *vi* **v. à** to attend to.

varappe [varap] *nf* rock-climbing.

varech [varɛk] *nm* wrack, seaweed.

vareuse [varøz] *nf* (*d'uniforme*) tunic.

variable [varjabl] *a* variable; (*humeur, temps*) changeable. ● **variante** *nf* variant. ● **variation** *nf* variation.

varicelle [varisɛl] *nf* (*maladie*) chicken pox.

varices [varis] *nfpl* varicose veins; **bas à v.** support stockings *ou* tights.

varier [varje] *vti* to vary (**de** from). ● **varié, -ée** *a* (*diversifié*) varied; (*divers*) various.

variété [varjete] *nf* variety; **spectacle de variétés** (*chansons etc*) variety show.

variole [varjol] *nf* smallpox.

vas [va] *voir* **aller¹**.

vasculaire [vaskylɛr] *a* *Méd* vascular.

vase [vaz] **1** *nm* vase. **2** *nf* (*boue*) mud, silt.

vaseline [vazlin] *nf* Vaseline®.

vaseux, -euse [vazø, -øz] *a* **1** (*boueux*) muddy, silty. **2** (*faible, fatigué*) *Fam* under the weather, *Br* off colour. **3** (*idées etc*) *Fam* woolly, hazy.

vasistas [vazistas] *nm* (*dans une porte ou une fenêtre*) hinged panel.

vaste [vast] *a* vast, huge.

Vatican [vatikɑ̃] *nm* **le V.** the Vatican.

va-tout [vatu] *nm inv* **jouer son v.-tout** to stake one's all.

vaudeville [vodvil] *nm* *Théâtre* light comedy.

vau-l'eau (à) [avolo] *adv* **aller à v.-l'eau** to go to rack and ruin.

vaurien, -ienne [vorjɛ̃, -jɛn] *nmf* good-for-nothing.

vaut [vo] *voir* **valoir**.

vautour [votur] *nm* vulture.

vautrer (se) [savotre] *vpr* to sprawl; **se v. dans la boue/le vice** to wallow in the mud/in vice.

va-vite (à la) [alavavit] *adv* *Fam* in a hurry.

veau, -x [vo] *nm* **1** (*animal*) calf; (*viande*) veal; (*cuir*) calfskin, calf leather. **2** (*voiture*) *Fam* really slow car.

vécu, -ue [veky] *pp de* **vivre** ▮ *a* (*histoire etc*) real(-life), true.

vedette [vədɛt] *nf* **1** (*de cinéma etc*) star; **avoir la v.** (*artiste*) to head the bill; **en v.** (*personne*) in the limelight; (*objet*) in a prominent position. **2** (*bateau*) motor boat,

launch.
végétal, -e, -aux [veʒetal, -o] *a* huile/*etc* végétale vegetable oil/*etc*; règne v. vegetable kingdom ∎ *nm* plant. ●**végétarien, -ienne** *a* & *nmf* vegetarian. ●**végétation** *nf* vegetation. ●**végétations** *nfpl Méd* adenoids.

végéter [veʒete] *vi* (*personne*) *Péj* to vegetate.

véhément, -ente [veemã, -ãt] *a* vehement. ●**véhémence** *nf* vehemence.

véhicule [veikyl] *nm* vehicle; v. tout terrain *ou* tout-terrain off-road *ou* all-terrain vehicle. ●**véhiculer** *vt* to convey.

veille [vɛj] *nf* 1 la v. (de) the day before; à la v. de (*événement*) on the eve of; la v. de Noël Christmas Eve; ce n'est pas demain la v. *Fam* that's not going to happen for quite a while. 2 (*état*) wakefulness.

veillée [veje] *nf* (*soirée*) evening; (*réunion*) evening get-together; (*mortuaire*) vigil.

veiller [veje] *vi* to stay up *ou* awake; (*sentinelle etc*) to keep watch, be on watch; v. à qch to see to sth, attend to sth; v. à ce que (+ *sub*) to make sure that; v. sur qn to watch over s.o.; v. au grain to keep an eye open for trouble ∎ *vt* (*malade*) to sit with, watch over. ●**veilleur** *nm* v. de nuit night watchman. ●**veilleuse** *nf* (*de voiture*) *Br* sidelight, *Am* parking light; (*de cuisinière*) pilot light; (*lampe allumée la nuit*) night light; mets-la en v.! *Fam* put a sock in it!, shut up!

veine [vɛn] *nf* 1 *Anat Bot Géol* vein. 2 (*chance*) *Fam* luck; avoir de la v. to be lucky; une v. a piece *ou* stroke of luck. ●**veinard, -arde** *nmf Fam* lucky devil ∎ *a Fam* lucky.

vêler [vele] *vi* (*vache*) to calve.

vélin [velɛ̃] *nm* (*papier, peau*) vellum.

véliplanchiste [veliplɑ̃ʃist] *nmf* windsurfer.

velléité [veleite] *nf* vague desire.

vélo [velo] *nm* bike, bicycle; (*activité*) cycling; faire du v. to cycle, go cycling; v. tout(-)terrain mountain bike. ●**vélodrome** *nm Cyclisme* velodrome, cycle track. ●**vélomoteur** *nm* (lightweight) motorcycle.

velours [v(ə)lur] *nm* velvet; v. côtelé corduroy, cord. ●**velouté, -ée** *a* soft, velvety; (*au goût*) mellow, smooth ∎ *nm* smoothness; v. d'asperges/*etc* (*potage*) cream of asparagus/*etc* soup.

velu, -ue [vəly] *a* hairy.

venaison [vənezɔ̃] *nf* venison.

vénal, -e, -aux [venal, -o] *a* mercenary.

vendange(s) [vɑ̃dɑ̃ʒ] *nf(pl)* grape harvest, vintage. ●**vendanger** *vi* to pick the grapes. ●**vendangeur, -euse** *nmf* grape-picker.

vendetta [vɑ̃deta] *nf* vendetta.

vendre [vɑ̃dr] *vt* to sell; v. qch à qn to sell s.o. sth, sell sth to s.o.; v. qn (*trahir*) to sell s.o. out; à v. (*maison etc*) for sale ∎ se vendre *vpr* to be sold; ça se vend bien it sells well. ●**vendeur, -euse** *nmf* (*de magasin*) *Br* sales *ou* shop assistant, *Am* sales clerk; (*de voitures etc*) salesman, saleswoman; *Jur*

vendor, seller.

vendredi [vɑ̃drədi] *nm* Friday; V. saint Good Friday.

vénéneux, -euse [venenø, -øz] *a* poisonous.

vénérable [venerabl] *a* venerable. ●**vénérer** *vt* to venerate.

vénérien, -ienne [venerjɛ̃, -jɛn] *a* (*maladie*) venereal.

venger [vɑ̃ʒe] *vt* to avenge ∎ se venger *vpr* to get one's revenge, get one's own back, avenge oneself (de qn on s.o., de qch for sth). ●**vengeance** *nf* revenge, vengeance. ●**vengeur, -eresse** *a* vengeful ∎ *nmf* avenger.

venin [vənɛ̃] *nm* poison, venom; *Fig* venom. ●**venimeux, -euse** *a* poisonous, venomous; (*haineux*) *Fig* venomous.

venir* [v(ə)nir] *vi* (*aux* être) to come (de from); v. faire qch to come to do sth; viens me voir come and *ou* to see me; je viens/venais d'arriver I've/I'd just arrived; en v. à (*conclusion etc*) to come to; où veux-tu en v.? what are you getting *ou* driving at?; les jours/*etc* qui viennent the coming days/*etc*; faire v. qn to send for s.o., get s.o.; une idée m'est venue an idea occurred to me; d'où vient que...? how is it that...?; s'il venait à faire (*éventualité*) if he happened to do.

vent [vɑ̃] *nm* wind; il y a *ou* il fait du v. it's windy; coup de v. gust of wind; avoir v. de (*connaissance de*) to get wind of; dans le v. (*à la mode*) *Fam* trendy, with it.

vente [vɑ̃t] *nf* sale; v. (aux enchères) auction (sale); v. de charité bazaar, charity sale; en v. (*disponible*) on sale; point de v. sales *ou* retail outlet, point of sale; prix de v. selling price; salle des ventes auction room.

ventilateur [vɑ̃tilatœr] *nm* (*électrique, de voiture*) fan; (*dans un mur*) ventilator. ●**ventilation** *nf* ventilation. ●**ventiler** *vt* to ventilate.

ventouse [vɑ̃tuz] *nf* (*pour fixer*) suction grip; cendrier/*etc* à v. suction-grip ashtray/*etc*.

ventre [vɑ̃tr] *nm* stomach, belly; (*utérus*) womb; (*de cruche etc*) bulge; avoir/prendre du v. to have/get a paunch; avoir mal au v. to have a stomach-ache; prendre du v. to be getting a paunch; il n'a rien dans le v. *Fam* he has no guts; à plat v. flat on one's face. ●**ventru, -ue** *a* (*personne*) pot-bellied; (*objet*) bulging.

ventriloque [vɑ̃trilɔk] *nmf* ventriloquist.

venu, -ue¹ [v(ə)ny] *pp de* venir ∎ *nmf* nouveau v., nouvelle venue newcomer; le premier v. anyone ∎ *a* bien v. (*à propos*) timely; mal v. untimely; être bien/mal v. de faire to have good grounds/no grounds for doing.

venue² [v(ə)ny] *nf* (*arrivée*) coming.

vêpres [vɛpr] *nfpl Rel* vespers.

ver [vɛr] *nm* worm; (*larve*) grub; (*de fruits, fromage etc*) maggot; v. luisant glow-worm; v. de terre (earth)worm; v. à soie silkworm; v. solitaire tapeworm; tirer les vers du nez à qn *Fam* to worm it out of s.o.

véracité [verasite] *nf* truthfulness, veracity.

véranda [verɑ̃da] *nf* veranda(h); (*en verre*)

conservatory (*room attached to house*).
verbaliser [vɛrbalize] *vi* (*policiers etc*) to fine (s.o.), *Br* book (s.o.).
verbe [vɛrb] *nm* verb. ●**verbal, -e, -aux** *a* (*promesse, expression etc*) verbal.
verbeux, -euse [vɛrbø, -øz] *a Péj* verbose. ●**verbiage** *nm Péj* verbiage.
verdâtre [vɛrdɑtr] *a* greenish.
verdeur [vɛrdœr] *nf* (*de fruit, vin*) tartness; (*de vieillard*) sprightliness; (*de langage*) crudeness.
verdict [vɛrdikt] *nm* verdict.
verdir [vɛrdir] *vti* to turn green. ●**verdoyant, -ante** *a* green, verdant. ●**verdure** *nf* (*arbres etc*) greenery; **théâtre de v.** open-air theatre.
véreux, -euse [verø, -øz] *a* (*fruit etc*) wormy, maggoty; (*malhonnête*) *Fig* dubious, shady.
verge [vɛrʒ] *nf Anat* penis.
verger [vɛrʒe] *nm* orchard.
vergetures [vɛrʒətyr] *nfpl* stretchmarks.
verglas [vɛrɡlɑ] *nm Br* (black) ice, *Am* sleet. ●**verglacé, -ée** *a* (*route*) icy.
vergogne (sans) [sɑ̃vɛrɡɔɲ] *a* shameless ▮ *adv* shamelessly.
véridique [veridik] *a* truthful.
vérifier [verifje] *vt* to check, verify; (*comptes*) to audit; (*confirmer*) to confirm. ●**vérifiable** *a* verifiable. ●**vérification** *nf* checking, verification; (*de comptes*) audit(ing); (*de théorie etc*) confirmation.
vérité [verite] *nf* truth; (*de personnage, tableau etc*) trueness to life; (*sincérité*) sincerity; **en v.** in fact; **dire la v.** to tell the truth.
véritable [veritabl] *a* true, real; (*non imité*) real, genuine; (*exactement nommé*) veritable, real. ●**véritablement** [-əmɑ̃] *adv* really.
verlan [vɛrlɑ̃] *nm* back slang.
vermeil, -eille [vɛrmɛj] *a* bright red, vermilion ▮ *nm* **carte vermeil** senior citizen's rail pass.
vermicelle(s) [vɛrmisɛl] *nm(pl)* (*pâtes*) vermicelli.
vermine [vɛrmin] *nf* (*insectes, racaille*) vermin.
vermoulu, -ue [vɛrmuly] *a* worm-eaten.
vermouth [vɛrmut] *nm* vermouth.
verni, -ie [vɛrni] *a* 1 (*brillant*) (*table etc*) varnished. 2 (*chanceux*) *Fam* lucky.
vernir [vɛrnir] *vt* to varnish; (*poterie*) to glaze. ●**vernis** *nm* varnish; (*pour poterie*) glaze; (*apparence*) *Fig* veneer; **v. à ongles** nail polish *ou Br* varnish. ●**vernissage** *nm* (*d'exposition de peinture*) first day. ●**vernisser** *vt* (*poterie*) to glaze.
verra, verrait *etc* [vɛra, vɛrɛ] *voir* **voir**.
verre [vɛr] *nm* (*substance, récipient*) glass; **boire** *ou* **prendre un v.** to have a drink; **v. de bière/etc** glass of beer/etc; **v. à bière/à vin** beer/wine glass; **v. à dents** toothbrush glass; **v. de contact** contact lens; **porter des verres** to wear glasses. ●**verrerie** *nf* (*objets*) glassware. ●**verrière** *nf* (*toit*) glass roof.
verrou [vɛru] *nm* bolt; **fermer au v.** to bolt; **sous les verrous** behind bars. ●**verrouiller** *vt*

to bolt.
verrue [vɛry] *nf* wart.
vers¹ [vɛr] *prép* (*direction*) towards, toward; (*approximation*) around, about.
vers² [vɛr] *nm* (*de poème*) line; **des vers** (*poésie*) verse.
versant [vɛrsɑ̃] *nm* slope, side.
versatile [vɛrsatil] *a* fickle, volatile.
verse (à) [avɛrs] *adv* in torrents; **pleuvoir à v.** to pour (down).
versé, -ée [vɛrse] *a* **v. dans** *Litt* (well) versed in.
Verseau [vɛrso] *nm* (*signe*) Aquarius.
verser [vɛrse] **1** *vt* to pour; (*larmes, sang*) to shed. **2** *vt* (*argent*) to pay (**sur un compte** into an account). **3** *vti* (*basculer*) to overturn. ●**versement** *nm* payment. ●**verseur** *a* **bec v.** spout.
verset [vɛrsɛ] *nm Rel* verse.
version [vɛrsjɔ̃] *nf* (*de film, d'incident etc*) version; (*traduction*) *Scol* translation, *Br* unseen.
verso [vɛrso] *nm* back (of the page); **'voir au v.'** 'see overleaf'.
vert, verte [vɛr, vɛrt] *a* green; (*pas mûr*) unripe; (*vin*) young; (*vieillard*) *Fig* sprightly; **aller en classe verte** to go on a school trip to the countryside; **en dire des vertes et des pas mûres** *Fig* to say some pretty shocking things ▮ *nm* green; **se mettre au v.** to go to the country (to recuperate); **les Verts** *Pol* the Greens.
vert-de-gris [vɛrdəɡri] *nm inv* verdigris.
vertèbre [vɛrtɛbr] *nf* vertebra.
vertement [vɛrtəmɑ̃] *adv* (*réprimander etc*) sharply.
vertical, -e, -aux [vɛrtikal, -o] *a* & *nf* vertical; **à la verticale** vertically. ●**verticalement** *adv* vertically.
vertige [vɛrtiʒ] *nm* (feeling of) dizziness *ou* giddiness; (*peur de tomber dans le vide*) vertigo; **vertiges** dizzy spells; **avoir le v.** to be *ou* feel dizzy *ou* giddy; **donner le v. à qn** to make s.o. (feel) dizzy *ou* giddy. ●**vertigineux, -euse** *a* (*hauteur*) giddy, dizzy; (*très grand*) *Fig* staggering.
vertu [vɛrty] *nf* virtue; **en v. de** in accordance with. ●**vertueux, -euse** *a* virtuous.
verve [vɛrv] *nf* (*d'orateur etc*) brilliance.
verveine [vɛrvɛn] *nf* (*plante*) verbena.
vésicule [vezikyl] *nf* **v. biliaire** gall bladder.
vessie [vesi] *nf* bladder.
veste [vɛst] *nf* jacket, coat.
vestiaire [vɛstjɛr] *nm* (*de théâtre etc*) cloakroom; (*de piscine, stade etc*) changing room, *Am* locker room; (*casier*) locker.
vestibule [vɛstibyl] *nm* (entrance) hall.
vestiges [vɛstiʒ] *nmpl* (*restes, ruines*) remains; (*traces*) traces, vestiges.
vestimentaire [vɛstimɑ̃tɛr] *a* **dépense/etc v.** clothing expenditure/etc; **détail v.** dress detail, detail of dress.
veston [vɛstɔ̃] *nm* (suit) jacket.
vêtement [vɛtmɑ̃] *nm* garment, article of clothing; **vêtements** clothes; **vêtements de**

sport sportswear; **industrie**/etc **du v.** clothing industry/etc.

vétéran [veterã] nm veteran.

vétérinaire [veteriner] a veterinary ‖ nmf vet, Br veterinary surgeon, Am veterinarian.

vétille [vetij] nf trifle, triviality.

vêtir* [vetir] vt, **se vêtir** vpr to dress. ● **vêtu, -ue** a dressed (**de** in).

veto [veto] nm inv veto; **mettre** ou **opposer son v.** à to veto.

vétuste [vetyst] a dilapidated.

veuf, veuve [vœf, vœv] a widowed ‖ nm widower ‖ nf widow.

veuille(s), veuillent etc [vœj] voir **vouloir**.

veule [vøl] a feeble. ● **veulerie** nf feebleness.

veut, veux [vø] voir **vouloir**.

vexer [vɛkse] vt to upset, hurt ‖ **se vexer** vpr to be ou get upset (**de** at). ● **vexant, -ante** a upsetting, hurtful; (contrariant) annoying. ● **vexation** nf humiliation.

VF [veɛf] nf abrév (version française) **film en VF** film dubbed into French.

viable [vjabl] a (entreprise, enfant etc) viable. ● **viabilité** nf viability.

viaduc [vjadyk] nm viaduct.

viager, -ère [vjaʒe, -ɛr] a **rente viagère** life annuity ‖ nm life annuity.

viande [vjɑ̃d] nf meat.

vibrer [vibre] vi to vibrate; (être ému) to thrill (**de** with); **faire v.** (auditoire etc) to thrill. ● **vibrant, -ante** a (émouvant) emotional; (voix, son) resonant, vibrant. ● **vibration** nf vibration. ● **vibromasseur** nm (appareil) vibrator.

vicaire [viker] nm curate.

vice [vis] nm vice; (défectuosité) defect; **v. de forme** (d'un procès) (legal) flaw.

vice- [vis] préf vice-.

vice versa [vis(e)vɛrsa] adv vice versa.

vicier [visje] vt to taint, pollute. ● **vicié, -ée** a (air, atmosphère) foul, polluted.

vicieux, -euse [visjø, -øz] 1 a depraved ‖ nmf pervert. 2 a **cercle v.** vicious circle.

vicinal, -e, -aux [visinal, -o] a **chemin v.** by-road, minor road.

vicissitudes [visisityd] nfpl vicissitudes.

vicomte [vikɔ̃t] nm viscount. ● **vicomtesse** nf viscountess.

victime [viktim] nf victim; (d'un accident) casualty; **être v. de** to be the victim of.

victoire [viktwar] nf victory; (sportive) win. ● **victorieux, -euse** a victorious; (équipe) winning.

victuailles [viktɥaj] nfpl provisions.

vidange [vidãʒ] nf emptying, draining; (de véhicule) oil change; (dispositif) waste outlet. ● **vidanger** vt to empty, drain.

vide [vid] a empty ‖ nm emptiness, void; (absence d'air) vacuum; (trou, manque, espace) gap; (gouffre etc) drop; **regarder dans le v.** to stare into space; **sauter dans le v.** to jump into the void; **emballé sous v.** vacuum-packed; **à v.** empty.

vidéo [video] a inv & nf video; **jeu v.** video game. ● **vidéocassette** nf video (cassette).

● **vidéoclip** nm video (of rock group etc).

vidéodisque [videodisk] nm videodisk.

vide-ordures [vidordyr] nm inv (Br rubbish ou Am garbage) chute. ● **vide-poches** nm inv (de véhicule) glove compartment.

vider [vide] vt to empty; (lieu) to vacate; (poisson, volaille) Culin to gut; (querelle) to settle; **v. qn** Fam (chasser) to throw s.o. out; (épuiser) to tire s.o. out; **j'ai vidé mon sac** Fam I got it off my chest ‖ **se vider** vpr to empty. ● **vidé, -ée** a (fatigué) Fam exhausted. ● **videur** nm (de boîte de nuit) bouncer.

vie [vi] nf life; (durée) lifetime; **le coût de la v.** the cost of living; **gagner sa v.** to earn one's living ou livelihood; **en v.** living; **à v., pour la v.** for life; **donner la v. à** to give birth to; **avoir la v. dure** (préjugés etc) to die hard; **refaire sa v.** to start a new life; **jamais de la v.!** not on your life!, never!; **ce n'est pas une v.!** Fam that's no life!

vieil, vieille [vjɛj] voir **vieux**.

vieillard [vjejar] nm old man; **les vieillards** old people. ● **vieillerie** nf (objet) old thing; (idée) old idea. ● **vieillesse** nf old age.

vieillir [vjejir] vi to grow old; (changer) to age; (théorie, mot) to become old-fashioned ‖ vt **v. qn** (vêtement etc) to make s.o. look old(er), age s.o. ● **vieilli, -ie** a (démodé) old-fashioned. ● **vieillissant, -ante** a ageing. ● **vieillissement** nm ageing, aging.

vieillot, -otte [vjejo, -ɔt] a antiquated.

Vienne [vjɛn] nm ou f Vienna.

viens, vient [vjɛ̃] voir **venir**.

vierge [vjɛrʒ] nf virgin; **la V.** (signe) Virgo ‖ a (femme, neige etc) virgin; (feuille de papier, film) blank; **être v.** (femme, homme) to be a virgin; **forêt v.** virgin forest.

Viêt Nam [vjɛtnam] nm Vietnam. ● **vietnamien, -ienne** a Vietnamese ‖ nmf V., Vietnamienne Vietnamese.

vieux (or **vieil** before vowel or mute h), **vieille,** pl **vieux, vieilles** [vjø, vjɛj] a old; **être v. jeu** (a inv) to be old-fashioned; **v. garçon** Péj bachelor; **vieille fille** Péj old maid; **se faire v.** to get old ‖ nm old man; **les vieux** old people; **mon v.!** (mon ami) Fam Br mate!, pal! ‖ nf **vieille** old woman; **ma vieille!** (mon amie) Fam dear!

vif, vive [vif, viv] a (enfant, mouvement) lively; (alerte) quick, sharp; (intelligence, intérêt, vent) keen; (couleur, lumière) bright; (froid) biting; (pas) quick, brisk; (imagination, impression) vivid; (parole) sharp; (regret, satisfaction etc) great; (coléreux) quicktempered; **brûler/enterrer qn v.** to burn/bury s.o. alive ‖ nm **entrer dans le v. du sujet** to get to the crux ou the heart of the matter; **à v.** (plaie) open; **piqué au v.** (vexé) cut to the quick.

vigie [viʒi] nf (matelot) lookout; (poste) lookout post.

vigilant, -ante [viʒilã, -ãt] a vigilant. ● **vigilance** nf vigilance.

vigile [viʒil] nm (gardien) watchman; (de nuit) night watchman.

vigne [viɲ] nf (plante) vine; (plantation) vineyard; **pied de v.** vine (stock). ● **vigneron, -onne** nmf wine grower. ● **vignoble** nm vineyard; (région) vineyards.

vignette [viɲɛt] nf (de véhicule) road tax sticker, = Br road tax disc; (de médicament) price label (for reimbursement by Social Security).

vigueur [vigœr] nf vigour; **entrer/être en v.** (loi) to come into/be in force. ● **vigoureux, -euse** a (personne, style etc) vigorous; (bras) sturdy.

vilain, -aine [vilɛ̃, -ɛn] a (laid) ugly; (enfant) naughty; (impoli) rude; (mauvais) nasty.

villa [vila] nf (detached) house.

village [vilaʒ] nm village. ● **villageois, -oise** nmf villager.

ville [vil] nf town; (grande) city; **aller/être en v.** to go (in)to/be in town; **v. d'eaux** spa (town).

villégiature [vileʒjatyr] nf **lieu de v.** (Br holiday ou Am vacation) resort.

vin [vɛ̃] nm wine; **v. ordinaire** ou **de table** table wine; **v. d'honneur** reception (in honour of s.o.). ● **vinicole** a (région) winegrowing; **industrie/etc v.** wine industry/etc.

vinaigre [vinɛgr] nm vinegar. ● **vinaigré, -ée** a seasoned with vinegar. ● **vinaigrette** nf (sauce) vinaigrette, Br French dressing, Am Italian dressing.

vindicatif, -ive [vɛ̃dikatif, -iv] a vindictive.

vingt [vɛ̃] ([vɛ̃t] before vowel or mute h and in numbers 22–29) a & nm twenty; **v. et un** twenty-one. ● **vingtaine** nf **une v.** (de) (nombre) about twenty; **avoir la v.** (âge) to be about twenty. ● **vingtième** a & nmf twentieth.

vinyle [vinil] nm vinyl.

viol [vjɔl] nm rape; (de loi, lieu) violation. ● **violation** nf violation. ● **violenter** vt to rape. ● **violer** vt (femme) to rape; (loi, lieu) to violate. ● **violeur** nm rapist.

violent, -ente [vjɔlɑ̃, -ɑ̃t] a violent; (remède) drastic. ● **violemment** [-amɑ̃] adv violently. ● **violence** nf violence; **acte de v.** act of violence.

violet, -ette [vjɔlɛ, -ɛt] 1 a & nm (couleur) purple, violet. 2 nf **violette** (fleur) violet. ● **violacé, -ée** a purplish.

violon [vjɔlɔ̃] nm violin; **accordons nos violons** Fig let's make sure we tell the same story. ● **violoncelle** nm cello. ● **violoncelliste** nmf cellist. ● **violoniste** nmf violinist.

vipère [viper] nf adder, viper.

virage [viraʒ] nm (de route) bend; (de véhicule) turn; (revirement) Fig change of course.

virée [vire] nf Fam trip, outing.

virer [vire] 1 vi to turn, veer; (sur soi) to turn round; **v. au bleu/etc** to turn blue/etc. 2 vt (expulser) Fam to throw out. 3 vt (somme) Fin to transfer (à to). ● **virement** nm Fin (bank ou credit) transfer.

virevolter [virvɔlte] vi to spin round.

virginité [virʒinite] nf virginity.

virgule [virgyl] nf (ponctuation) comma; Math (decimal) point; **2 v. 5** 2 point 5.

viril, -e [viril] a virile, manly; (force, attribut) male. ● **virilité** nf virility, manliness.

virtuel, -elle [virtɥɛl] a potential; Phys Ordinat virtual; **réalité virtuelle** virtual reality.

virtuose [virtɥoz] nmf virtuoso. ● **virtuosité** nf virtuosity.

virulent, -ente [virylɑ̃, -ɑ̃t] a virulent. ● **virulence** nf virulence.

virus [virys] nm Méd & Ordinat virus.

vis¹ [vi] voir **vivre, voir.**

vis² [vis] nf screw.

visa [viza] nm (de passeport) visa; (timbre) stamp, stamped signature; **v. de censure** (d'un film) certificate.

visage [vizaʒ] nm face.

vis-à-vis [vizavi] prép **v.-à-vis de** opposite; (à l'égard de) with respect to; (envers) towards; (comparé à) compared to █ nm inv (personne) person opposite; (bois, maison etc) opposite view.

viscères [viser] nmpl intestines. ● **viscéral, -e, -aux** a (haine etc) Fig deeply felt.

viscosité [viskozite] nf viscosity.

viser [vize] 1 vi (à to aim at); **v. à faire qch** to aim to do sth █ vt (cible) to aim at; (concerner) to be aimed at. 2 vt (document) to stamp. ● **visées** nfpl (desseins) Fig aims; **avoir des visées sur** to have designs on. ● **viseur** nm Phot viewfinder; (d'arme) sight.

visible [vizibl] a visible. ● **visiblement** [-əmɑ̃] adv visibly. ● **visibilité** nf visibility.

visière [vizjɛr] nf (de casquette) peak; (en plastique etc) eyeshade; (de casque) visor.

vision [vizjɔ̃] nf (conception, image) vision; (sens) (eye)sight; vision; **avoir des visions** Fam to be seeing things. ● **visionnaire** a & nmf visionary. ● **visionner** vt (film) to view. ● **visionneuse** nf (pour diapositives) viewer.

visite [vizit] nf visit; (personne) visitor; (examen) inspection; **rendre v. à, faire une v. à** to visit; **v. (à domicile)** (de médecin) (house) call ou visit; **v. (médicale)** medical examination; **v. guidée** guided tour; **heures/ etc de v.** visiting hours/etc. ● **visiter** vt to visit; (examiner) to inspect. ● **visiteur, -euse** nmf visitor.

vison [vizɔ̃] nm mink.

visqueux, -euse [viskø, -øz] a viscous; (surface) sticky; (répugnant) Fig slimy.

visser [vise] vt to screw on.

visu (de) [devizy] adv Litt with one's own eyes.

visuel, -elle [vizɥɛl] a visual. ● **visualiser** vt (afficher) Ordinat to display.

vit [vi] voir **vivre, voir.**

vital, -e, -aux [vital, -o] a vital. ● **vitalité** nf vitality.

vitamine [vitamin] nf vitamin. ● **vitaminé, -ée** a (biscuits etc) vitamin-enriched.

vite [vit] adv quickly, fast; (tôt) soon; **v.!** quick(ly)! ● **vitesse** nf speed; (de véhicule) gear; **boîte de vitesses** gearbox; **changement de v.** gear change; **à toute v.** at top ou full speed; **v. de pointe** top speed; **en v.** *Fam* quickly.

viticole [vitikɔl] *a* (*région*) wine-growing; **industrie v.** wine industry. ● **viticulteur** *nm* wine grower. ● **viticulture** *nf* wine growing.

vitre [vitr] *nf* (window)pane; (*de véhicule, train*) window. ● **vitrage** *nm* (*vitres*) windows. ● **vitrail, -aux** *nm* stained-glass window. ● **vitré, -ée** *a* **porte/etc vitrée** glass *ou* glazed door/etc. ● **vitreux, -euse** *a* (*regard, yeux*) *Fig* glassy. ● **vitrier** *nm* glazier.

vitrine [vitrin] *nf* (*de magasin*) (shop) window; (*meuble*) display cabinet, showcase.

vitriol [vitrijɔl] *nm Ch & Fig* vitriol.

vivable [vivabl] *a Fam* (*personne*) easy to live with; (*endroit*) fit to live in.

vivace [vivas] *a* (*plante*) perennial; (*haine*) *Fig* inveterate.

vivacité [vivasite] *nf* liveliness; (*d'une émotion, de l'air*) keenness; (*agilité*) briskness; (*de couleur, d'impression, de style*) vividness; (*emportement*) petulance; **v. d'esprit** quick-wittedness.

vivant, -ante [vivã, -ãt] *a* (*en vie*) alive, living; (*récit, rue, enfant etc*) lively; (*être, matière, preuve*) living; **langue vivante** modern language **I** *nm* **de son v.** in one's lifetime; **bon v.** jovial fellow; **les vivants** the living.

vivats [viva] *nmpl* cheers.

vive¹ [viv] *voir* **vif**.

vive² [viv] *int* **v. le roi/etc!** long live the king/etc!; **v. les vacances!** hurray for the *Br* holidays *ou Am* vacation!

vivement [vivmã] *adv* quickly, briskly; (*répliquer*) sharply; (*regretter*) deeply; (*sentir*) keenly; **v. demain!** I can hardly wait for tomorrow!, *Br* roll on tomorrow!; **v. que** (+ *sub*) I'll be glad when.

vivier [vivje] *nm* fish pond.

vivifier [vivifje] *vt* to invigorate.

vivisection [vivisɛksjɔ̃] *nf* vivisection.

vivoter [vivɔte] *vi Fam* to jog along, get by.

vivre* [vivr] *vi* to live; **elle vit encore** she's still alive *ou* living; **faire v.** (*famille etc*) to support; **v. vieux** to live to be old; **facile/difficile à v.** easy/hard to get along *ou Br* on with; **v. de** (*fruits etc*) to live on; (*travail etc*) to live by; **avoir de quoi v.** to have enough to live on; **vivent les vacances!** hurray for the *Br* holidays *ou Am* vacation!
I *vt* (*vie*) to live; (*aventure, époque*) to live through; (*éprouver*) to experience. ● **vivres** *nmpl* food, supplies.

vlan! [vlã] *int* bang!, wham!

VO [veo] *nf abrév* (*version originale*) **film en VO** film in the original version.

vocable [vɔkabl] *nm* term, word.

vocabulaire [vɔkabylɛr] *nm* vocabulary.

vocal, -e, -aux [vɔkal, -o] *a* (*cordes, musique*) vocal. ● **vocalise** *nf* **faire des vocalises** to do one's singing exercises.

vocation [vɔkasjɔ̃] *nf* vocation, calling.

vociférer [vɔsifere] *vti* to shout angrily. ● **vocifération** *nf* angry shout.

vodka [vɔdka] *nf* vodka.

vœu, -x [vø] *nm* (*souhait*) wish; (*promesse*) vow; **faire le v. de faire qch** to (make a) vow to do sth; **tous mes vœux!** (my) best wishes!

vogue [vɔg] *nf* fashion, vogue; **en v.** in fashion, in vogue. ● **voguer** *vi Litt* to sail.

voici [vwasi] *prép* here is, this is; *pl* here are, these are; **me v.** here I am; **me v. triste** I'm sad now; **v. dix ans/etc** ten years/etc ago; **v. dix ans que** it's ten years since.

voie [vwa] *nf* (*route*) road; (*rails*) track, line; (*partie de route*) lane; (*chemin*) way; (*de gare*) platform; (*de communication*) line; (*moyen*) means, way; (*diplomatique*) channels; **en v. de** in the process of; **pays en v. de développement** developing country; **v. publique** public highway; **v. navigable** waterway; **v. sans issue** dead end, *Br* cul-de-sac; **préparer la v.** *Fig* to pave the way; **sur la bonne v.** on the right track.

voilà [vwala] *prép* there is, that is; *pl* there are, those are; **les v.** there they are; **v., j'arrive!** all right, I'm coming!; **le v. parti** he has left now; **v. dix ans/etc** ten years/etc ago; **v. dix ans que** it's ten years since; **et v.!** and that's that!

voile¹ [vwal] *nm* (*étoffe qui cache, coiffure etc*) & *Fig* veil. ● **voilage** *nm* net curtain. ● **voiler¹** *vt* (*visage, vérité etc*) to veil **I se voiler** *vpr* (*personne*) to wear a veil; (*ciel, regard*) to cloud over. ● **voilé, -ée** *a* (*femme, allusion*) veiled; (*terne*) dull; (*photo*) hazy.

voile² [vwal] *nf* (*de bateau*) sail; (*sport*) sailing; **bateau à voiles** *Br* sailing boat, *Am* sailboat; **faire de la v.** to sail, go sailing. ● **voilier** *nm* sailing ship; (*de plaisance*) *Br* sailing boat, *Am* sailboat. ● **voilure** *nf Nau* sails.

voiler² [vwale] *vt*, **se voiler** *vpr* (*roue*) to buckle.

voir* [vwar] *vti* to see; **faire** *ou* **laisser v. qch** to show sth; **fais v.** let me see, show me; **v. qn faire** to see s.o. do *ou* doing; **voyons!** (*sois raisonnable*) come on!; **y v. clair** (*comprendre*) to see clearly; **je ne peux pas la v.** (*supporter*) *Fam* I can't stand (the sight of) her; **v. venir** (*attendre*) to wait and see; **on verra bien** (*attendons*) we'll see; **ça n'a rien à v. avec** that's got nothing to do with; **elle lui en a fait v. de toutes les couleurs** *Fam* she made his life a misery.
I se voir *vpr* to see oneself; (*se fréquenter*) to see each other; (*objet, attitude etc*) to be seen; (*reprise, tache*) to show; **ça se voit** that's obvious.

voire [vwar] *adv* indeed.

voirie [vwari] *nf* (*enlèvement des ordures*) refuse collection; (*routes*) public highways.

voisin, -ine [vwazɛ̃, -in] *a* (*pays, village etc*) neighbouring; (*maison, pièce*) next (**de** to); (*idée, état etc*) similar (**de** to) **I** *nmf* neighbour. ● **voisinage** *nm* (*quartier, voisins*) neighbourhood; (*proximité*) closeness, proximity. ● **voisiner** *vi* **v. avec** to be side by side with.

voiture [vwatyr] *nf* car; (*de train*) carriage,

Br coach, *Am* car; (*charrette*) cart; **v. de course/de tourisme** racing/private car; **v. d'enfant** *Br* pram, *Am* baby carriage; **v. (à cheval)** (horse-drawn) carriage; **en v.!** (*dans le train*) all aboard!

voix [vwa] *nf* voice; (*d'électeur*) vote; **à v. basse** in a whisper; **à haute v.** aloud; **à portée de v.** within earshot; **avoir v. au chapitre** *Fig* to have a say (in the matter); **rester sans v.** to remain speechless.

vol [vɔl] *nm* **1** (*d'avion, d'oiseau*) flight; (*groupe d'oiseaux*) flock, flight; **v. libre** hang-gliding; **v. à voile** gliding; **attraper qch au v.** (*objet jeté*) to catch sth in the air. **2** (*délit*) theft; **v. à main armée** armed robbery; **v. à l'étalage** shoplifting; **c'est du v.!** (*trop cher*) it's daylight robbery!

volage [vɔlaʒ] *a* flighty, fickle.

volaille [vɔlaj] *nf* **la v.** (*oiseaux*) poultry; **une v.** (*oiseau*) a fowl. ● **volailler** *nm* poulterer.

volant, -ante [vɔlɑ̃, -ɑ̃t] *a voir* **voler.**

volatile [vɔlatil] *nm* (*oiseau domestique*) fowl.

volatiliser (se) [səvɔlatilize] *vpr* (*disparaître*) to vanish (into thin air).

vol-au-vent [vɔlovɑ̃] *nm inv Culin* vol-au-vent.

volcan [vɔlkɑ̃] *nm* volcano. ● **volcanique** *a* volcanic.

voler [vɔle] **1** *vi* (*oiseau, avion etc*) to fly; (*courir*) *Fig* to rush. **2** *vt* (*prendre*) to steal (**à** from); **v. qn** to rob s.o.; **tu ne l'as pas volé!** *Fam* it serves you right! **‖** *vi* (*prendre*) to steal. ● **volant, -ante 1** *a* (*tapis etc*) flying; **feuille volante** loose sheet. **2** *nm* (*de véhicule*) (steering) wheel; (*de badminton*) shuttlecock; (*de jupe*) flounce. ● **volée** *nf* flight; (*groupe d'oiseaux*) flock, flight; (*suite de coups*) thrashing; *Tennis* volley; **sonner à toute v.** to peal *ou* ring out; **lancer à toute v.** to throw as hard as one can.

volet [vɔlɛ] *nm* **1** (*de fenêtre*) shutter. **2** (*de programme, reportage etc*) section, part.

voleter [vɔl(ə)te] *vi* to flutter.

voleur, -euse [vɔlœr, -øz] *nmf* thief; **au v.!** stop thief! **‖** *a* thieving.

volière [vɔljer] *nf* aviary.

volley(-ball) [vɔlɛ(bɔl)] *nm* (*sport*) volleyball. ● **volleyeur, -euse** *nmf* volleyball player.

volontaire [vɔlɔ̃tɛr] *a* (*voulu*) (*geste etc*) deliberate, voluntary; (*opiniâtre*) *Br* wilful, *Am* willful **‖** *nmf* volunteer. ● **volontairement** *adv* voluntarily; (*exprès*) deliberately.

volontariat [vɔlɔ̃tarja] *nm* voluntary work.

volonté [vɔlɔ̃te] *nf* (*faculté, intention*) will; (*désir*) wish; *Phil Psy* free will; **elle a de la v.** she has willpower; **bonne v.** goodwill; **mauvaise v.** ill will; **à v.** (*quantité*) as much as desired.

volontiers [vɔlɔ̃tje] *adv* gladly, willingly; (*habituellement*) readily; **v.!** (*oui*) I'd love to!

volt [vɔlt] *nm El* volt. ● **voltage** *nm* voltage.

volte-face [vɔltəfas] *nf inv Br* about turn, *Am* about face; (*changement d'opinion etc*)

Fig U-turn; **faire v.-face** to turn round; *Fig* to do a U-turn.

voltige [vɔltiʒ] *nf* acrobatics.

voltiger [vɔltiʒe] *vi* to flutter.

volubile [vɔlybil] *a* (*bavard*) loquacious, voluble.

volume [vɔlym] *nm* (*de boîte, de son, livre*) volume. ● **volumineux, -euse** *a* bulky, voluminous.

volupté [vɔlypte] *nf* sensual pleasure. ● **voluptueux, -euse** *a* voluptuous.

vomir [vɔmir] *vt* to bring up, vomit; (*exécrer*) *Fig* to loathe **‖** *vi* to vomit, *Br* be sick. ● **vomi** *nm Fam* vomit. ● **vomissement** *nm* (*action*) vomiting. ● **vomitif, -ive** *a Fam* nauseating.

vont [vɔ̃] *voir* **aller**[1].

vorace [vɔras] *a* (*appétit, lecteur etc*) voracious.

vos [vo] *voir* **votre.**

vote [vɔt] *nm* (*action*) vote, voting; (*suffrage*) vote; (*de loi*) passing; **bureau de v.** *Br* polling station, *Am* polling place. ● **voter** *vi* to vote **‖** *vt* (*loi*) to pass; (*crédits*) to vote. ● **votant, -ante** *nmf* voter.

votre, *pl* **vos** [vɔtr, vo] *a poss* your. ● **vôtre** *pron poss* **le** *ou* **la v., les vôtres** yours; **à la v.!** (*toast*) (your) good health!, cheers! **‖** *nmpl* **les vôtres** (*votre famille*) your (own) people.

voudra, voudrait *etc* [vudra, vudrɛ] *voir* **vouloir.**

vouer [vwe] *vt* (*promettre*) to vow (**à** to); (*consacrer*) to dedicate (**à** to); (*condamner*) to doom (**à** to); **se v. à** to dedicate oneself to.

vouloir* [vulwar] *vt* to want (**faire** to do); **je veux qu'il parte** I want him to go; **v. dire** to mean (**que** that); **je voudrais rester** I'd like to stay; **je voudrais un pain** I'd like a loaf of bread; **voulez-vous me suivre** will you follow me; **si tu veux** if you like *ou* wish; **en v. à qn d'avoir fait qch** to be angry with s.o. for doing sth *ou* for having done sth; **l'usage veut que...** (+ *sub*) custom requires that...; **v. du bien à qn** to wish s.o. well; **je veux bien (attendre)** I don't mind (waiting); **que voulez-vous!** (*résignation*) what can you expect!; **sans le v.** unintentionally; **ne pas v. de qch/de qn** not to want sth/s.o.; **veuillez attendre** kindly wait; **ça ne veut pas bouger** it won't move. ● **voulu, -ue** *a* (*requis*) required; (*délibéré*) deliberate, intentional.

vous [vu] *pron* **1** (*sujet, complément direct*) you; **v. êtes** you are; **il v. connaît** he knows you. **2** (*complément indirect*) (to) you; **il v. l'a donné** he gave it to you, he gave you it. **3** (*réfléchi*) yourself, *pl* yourselves; **v. v. lavez** you wash yourself; you wash yourselves. **4** (*réciproque*) each other; **v. v. aimez** you love each other. ● **vous-même** *pron* yourself. ● **vous-mêmes** *pron pl* yourselves.

voûte [vut] *nf* (*plafond*) vault; (*porche*) arch(way). ● **voûté, -ée** *a* (*personne*) bent, stooped.

vouvoyer [vuvwaje] *vt* **v. qn** to use the formal *vous* form to s.o. ● **vouvoiement** *nm* use of the formal *vous* (*instead of the more familiar tu*).

voyage [vwajaʒ] *nm* trip, journey; (*par mer*) voyage; **aimer les voyages** to like *Br* travelling *ou Am* traveling; **faire un v.**, **partir en v.** to go on a trip; **être en v.** to be (away) travelling; **bon v.!** have a pleasant trip!; **v. de noces** honeymoon; **v. organisé** (package) tour; **compagnon de v.** *Br* travelling *ou Am* traveling companion; **agent/agence de voyages** travel agent/agency. ● **voyager** *vi* to travel. ● **voyageur, -euse** *nmf Br* traveller, *Am* traveler; (*passager*) passenger; **v. de commerce** travelling salesman, *Br* commercial traveller. ● **voyagiste** *nm* tour operator.

voyant, -ante[1] [vwajɑ̃, -ɑ̃t] **1** *a* (*couleur*) gaudy, loud. **2** *nm* (*signal*) (warning) light; (*d'appareil électrique*) pilot light.

voyant, -ante[2] [vwajɑ̃, -ɑ̃t] *nmf* clairvoyant; **les non-voyants** the blind.

voyelle [vwajɛl] *nf* vowel.

voyeur, -euse [vwajœr, -øz] *nmf* peeping Tom, voyeur.

voyou [vwaju] *nm* hooligan, hoodlum.

vrac (en) [ɑ̃vrak] *adv* (*en désordre*) in a muddle, haphazardly; (*au poids*) loose, unpackaged.

vrai [vrɛ] *a* true; (*réel*) real; (*authentique*) genuine **‖** *adv* **dire v.** to be right (in what one says) **‖** *nm* (*vérité*) truth. ● **vraiment** *adv* really.

vraisemblable [vrɛsɑ̃blabl] *a* (*probable*) likely, probable; (*plausible*) plausible. ● **vraisemblablement** *adv* probably. ● **vraisemblance** *nf* likelihood; (*plausibilité*) plausibility.

vrille [vrij] *nf* **1** (*outil*) gimlet. **2** (*acrobatie aérienne*) (tail)spin; **descendre en v.** to come down in a spin.

vrombir [vrɔ̃bir] *vi* to hum. ● **vrombissement** *nm* hum(ming).

VRP [veerpe] *nm abrév* (*voyageur représentant placier*) sales rep.

VTT [vetete] *nm inv abrév* (*vélo tout terrain*) mountain bike.

vu, -ue [vy] **1** *pp de* **voir** **‖** *a* **bien vu** well thought of; **mal vu** frowned upon. **2** *prép* in view of; **vu que** seeing that.

vue [vy] *nf* (*spectacle*) sight; (*sens*) (eye)sight; (*panorama, photo, idée*) view; **en v.** (*proche*) in sight; (*en évidence*) on view; (*personne*) *Fig* in the public eye; **avoir qch/qn en v.** to have sth/s.o. in mind; **à v.** (*tirer*) on sight; (*payable*) at sight; **à première v.** at first sight; **à v. d'œil** (*grandir etc*) rapidly, for all to see; **de v.** (*connaître*) by sight; **en v. de faire** with a view to doing.

vulgaire [vylgɛr] *a* (*grossier*) vulgar, coarse; (*ordinaire*) common. ● **vulgairement** *adv* vulgarly, coarsely; (*appeler, nommer*) commonly. ● **vulgariser** *vt* to popularize. ● **vulgarité** *nf* vulgarity, coarseness.

vulnérable [vylnerabl] *a* vulnerable. ● **vulnérabilité** *nf* vulnerability.

W

W, w [dubləve] *nm* W, w.

wagon [vagɔ̃] *nm* (*de train de voyageurs*) carriage, *Br* coach, *Am* car; (*de train de marchandises*) *Br* wag(g)on, *Br* truck, *Am* freight car. ● **wagon-lit** *nm* (*pl* **wagons-lits**) sleeping car, sleeper. ● **wagon-restaurant** *nm* (*pl* **wagons-restaurants**) dining *ou* restaurant car, diner. ● **wagonnet** *nm Br* (small) truck, *Am* (small) freight car.

wallon, -onne [walɔ̃, -ɔn] *a* Walloon **‖** *nmf* **W., Wallonne** Walloon.

walkman® [wɔkman] *nm* Walkman®, (personal) stereo.

waters [watɛr] *nmpl Br* toilet, *Am* men's *ou* ladies' room.

watt [wat] *nm Él* watt.

w-c [(dublə)vese] *nmpl Br* toilet, *Am* men's *ou* ladies' room.

week-end [wikɛnd] *nm* weekend.

western [wɛstɛrn] *nm* (*film*) western.

whisky, *pl* **-ies** [wiski] *nm Br* whisky, *Am* whiskey.

X

X, x [iks] *nm* X, x; **rayon X** X-ray; **film classé X** adult film, *Br* '18' film, *Am* X-rated film.

xénophobe [ksenɔfɔb] *a* xenophobic **‖** *nmf* xenophobe. ● **xénophobie** *nf* xenophobia.

xérès.[gzerɛs] *nm* sherry.

xylophone [ksilɔfɔn] *nm* xylophone.

Y

Y, y¹ [igrɛk] *nm* Y, y.

y² [i] **1** *adv* there; (*dedans*) in it; *pl* in them; (*dessus*) on it; *pl* on them; **elle y vivra** she'll live there; **j'y entrai** I entered (it); **allons-y** let's go; **j'y suis!** (*je comprends*) now I get it!; **je n'y suis pour rien** I have nothing to do with it, that's nothing to do with me; **il y a** there is; *pl* there are (*voir* **il**).

2 *pron* (= *à cela*) **j'y pense** I think of it; **je m'y attendais** I was expecting it; **ça y est!** that's it!

yacht [jɔt] *nm* yacht.

yaourt [jaur(t)] *nm* yog(h)urt.

Yémen [jemɛn] *nm* Yemen.

yen [jɛn] *nm* (*monnaie*) yen.

yeux [jø] *voir* œil.

yiddish [(j)idiʃ] *nm* & *a* Yiddish.

yoga [jɔga] *nm* yoga.

yog(h)ourt [jɔgur(t)] *nm* = **yaourt**.

yo-yo [jojo] *nm inv* yoyo.

Z

Z, z [zɛd] *nm* Z, z.

Zaïre [zair] *nm* Zaïre.

zapper [zape] *vi* (*téléspectateur*) *Fam* to flick channels, channel-hop. ● **zapping** *nm* **faire du z.** *Fam* = **zapper**.

zèbre [zɛbr] *nm* zebra. ● **zébré, -ée** *a* striped, streaked (**de** with). ● **zébrures** *nfpl* stripes.

zèle [zɛl] *nm* zeal; **faire du z.** to overdo it. ● **zélé, -ée** *a* zealous.

zénith [zenit] *nm* zenith.

zéro [zero] *nm* (*chiffre*) zero, *Br* nought; (*dans un numéro*) 0 [əʊ]; (*température*) zero; (*rien*) nothing; (*personne*) *Fig* nobody, nonentity; **deux buts à z.** *Football Br* two nil, *Am* two zero; **partir de z.** to start from scratch.

zeste [zɛst] *nm* **un z. de citron** (a piece of) lemon peel.

zézayer [zezeje] *vi* to lisp.

zibeline [ziblin] *nf* (*animal*) sable.

zigzag [zigzag] *nm* zigzag; **en z.** (*route etc*) zigzag(ging). ● **zigzaguer** *vi* to zigzag.

Zimbabwe [zimbabwe] *nm* Zimbabwe.

zinc [zɛ̃g] *nm* (*métal*) zinc; (*comptoir*) *Fam* bar; (*avion*) *Fam* plane.

zinzin [zɛ̃zɛ̃] *nm Fam* what's-it **1** *a inv* (*fou*) *Fam* nuts, crazy.

zizanie [zizani] *nf* discord; **semer la z.** to sow discord.

zodiaque [zɔdjak] *nm* zodiac; **signe du z.** sign of the zodiac.

zona [zona] *nm* (*maladie*) shingles.

zone [zon] *nf* zone, area; (*domaine*) *Fig* sphere; **la z.** (*faubourgs misérables*) the slum area (*around city*); **z. bleue** restricted parking zone; **z. industrielle** industrial *Br* estate *ou Am* park; **de troisième z.** (*acteur etc*) third-rate. ● **zonard** *nm Péj Fam* drifter, *Br* yob(b)o. ● **zoner** *vi Fam* to drift.

zoo [zo(o)] *nm* zoo. ● **zoologie** [zɔɔlɔʒi] *nf* zoology. ● **zoologique** *a* zoological; **jardin** *ou* **parc z.** zoo.

zoom [zum] *nm* (*objectif*) zoom lens.

zozo [zozo] *nm* (*naïf*) *Fam* drip, deadhead.

zozoter [zozote] *vi Fam* to lisp.

zut! [zyt] *int Fam* oh dear!, heck!